Directors in British and Irish Cinema

A Reference Companion

Edited by Robert Murphy

Associate Editors: Geoff Brown and Alan Burton

Publishing

For Sophie and Edward

First published in 2006 by the
BRITISH FILM INSTITUTE
21 Stephen Street, London W1T 1LN

The British Film Institute's purpose is to champion moving image culture in all its richness and diversity across the UK, for the benefit of as wide an audience as possible, and to create and encourage debate.

Supported by 

Cover design: Mark Swan
Cover image: Alfred Hitchcock on the set of *Frenzy* (1972), Universal Pictures
Stills courtesy of BFI Stills, Posters and Designs

Set by Fakenham Photosetting, Fakenham, Norfolk
Printed in the UK by The Cromwell Press, Trowbridge, Wiltshire

British Library Cataloguing-in-Publication Data
A catalogue record for this book is available from the British Library

ISBN 1–84457–126–2 (pbk)
ISBN 1–84457–125–4 (hbk)

Contents

Notes on contributors

Sergio Angelini has lectured on the films of Welles, Hitchcock, Visconti, Powell and De Palma. His most recent publications include contributions to *Dizionario dei Registi* (2005) and a translation of Virgilio Tosi's *The Origins of Scientific Cinematography* into English (2005). He is also the editor of the seventh edition of *The Researcher's Guide* (2005) and has written dozens of entries for the Screenonline database. He is the Library and Database Manager of the British Universities Film & Video Council.

Barry Anthony has written extensively about many areas of Victorian and Edwardian popular culture. He is author of *The Kinora: Motion Pictures for the Home 1896–1914* (1996) and co-author (with Richard Brown) of *A Victorian Film Enterprise: The History of the British Mutoscope and Biograph Company, 1897–1915* (1999).

Guy Barefoot is a Lecturer in Film Studies at Leicester University. He is a contributor to Screenonline and the author of *Hollywood's Gaslight Melodramas: From Victorian London to 1940s Hollywood* (2001).

Ruth Barton is O'Kane Senior Research Fellow at the Centre for Film Studies, University College Dublin. She is the author of *Jim Sheridan: Framing the Nation* (2002), *Irish National Cinema* (2004) and co-editor of *Keeping It Real: Irish Film and Television* (2004).

Dave Berry, former Research Officer for the National Screen and Sound Archive of Wales, is the author of *Wales and Cinema: The First 100 Years* (1994) and co-editor of *David Lloyd George: The Movie Mystery* (1998). He was film critic for the *South Wales Echo* (Cardiff) for sixteen years and has written essays for numerous books, including *The Lost World of Mitchell and Kenyon* (2005).

Geoff Brown writes film and music criticism for *The Times*. His studies of British cinema include *Walter Forde* (1977), *Launder and Gilliat* (1977), *The Common Touch: The Films of John Baxter* (1989) and contributions to *The British Cinema Book* (1997), *The Unknown 1930s* (1998) and *British Cinema of the 90s* (2000).

Simon Brown is a Lecturer in Film Studies at Kingston University in Surrey, as well as Senior Research Fellow for The London Project, an AHRB-funded project for the Centre of British Film and Television Studies at Birkbeck College, University of London. In addition he is currently working on his PhD on the 'Hepworth Manufacturing Company and British Cinema, 1904–1911'.

Eleanor Burke is currently a graduate film student at New York University's Tisch School of the Arts. She has directed and shot several short films in London and New York.

Alan Burton is Senior Lecturer in Film at De Montfort University, Leicester. He has co-edited books on Basil Dearden (1997) and the Boulting Brothers (2000) and is author of *The British Consumer Co-operative Movement and Film, 1890s–1960s* (2005).

Margaret Butler teaches Film and Television History at the Open University. She is the author of *Film and Community: Britain and France from* La Règle du jeu *to* Room at the Top (2004).

Sarah Cardwell is Lecturer in Film and Television Studies at the University of Kent, Canterbury. Her publications include *Adaptation Revisited: Television and the Classic Novel* (2002), *Andrew Davies* (2005) and numerous articles and chapters on film, television and adaptation.

Steve Chibnall is Professor of British Cinema at De Montfort University, Leicester. He has written numerous articles on British cinema and is author of *Law-and-Order News* (1977), *Making Mischief: The Cult Films of Pete Walker* (1998), *J. Lee Thompson* (2000), *Get Carter* (2003), *Brighton Rock* (2004) and co-editor of *British Crime Cinema* (1999) and *British Horror Cinema* (2002). He is currently writing a history of the British B-film.

Pamela Church Gibson is Reader in Cultural and Historical Studies at the London College of Fashion, within the University of the Arts, London. She has published extensively on film, fashion, fandom, heritage and history, and has co-edited three collections of essays including *The Oxford Guide to Film Studies* (1998). Her current project is a monograph on cinema, cities and consumption.

Andrew Clay is Senior Lecturer in Critical Technical Practices at De Montfort University, Leicester. He has published articles on crime and masculinity in British cinema. He is currently researching the theory and practice of online film.

Lez Cooke is researching regional British television drama at Manchester Metropolitan University. His publications include *British Television Drama: A History* (2003) and numerous articles and chapters on British film and television drama. Forthcoming publications include a book on the screenwriter Troy Kennedy Martin.

Richard Dacre is the proprietor of the Flashbacks movie poster shop and archive. He is the author of *Trouble in Store: Norman Wisdom, a Career in Comedy* (1991) and numerous articles on British cinema.

Bryony Dixon has worked at the BFI since 1992 making the collections of the National Film and Television Archive accessible to researchers, independent cinemas, film archives, universities as well as cinemathèques and film festivals all over the world. She co-founded the British Silent Cinema Festival, now in its ninth year, and has specialised in programming early British cinema, including the first-ever retrospective of 1920s' British cinema held at the National Film Theatre in 2004.

Wheeler Winston Dixon is the James Ryan Endowed Professor of Film Studies, Professor of English at the University of Nebraska, Lincoln, and, with Gwendolyn Audrey Foster, Editor-in-Chief of the *Quarterly Review of Film and Video*. His newest books are *Film and Television After 9/11* (editor, 2004), *Visions of the Apocalypse: Spectacles of Destruction in American Cinema* (2003), *Straight: Constructions of Heterosexuality in the Cinema* (2003) and *Experimental Cinema: The Film Reader* (co-edited with Gwendolyn Audrey Foster, 2002).

Sarah Easen is an archive researcher at ITN. She has published work on Kay Mander and Margaret Thomson, the role of women in the production of British newsreels, and the films made for the Festival of Britain, as well as programming accompanying film seasons at the National Film Theatre and the Imperial War Museum in London. She has also contributed to the BFI's Screenonline project and is currently working on a book about the films of women documentary film-makers of the 1940s.

Leo Enticknap is curator of the Northern Region Film and Television Archive and Senior Lecturer in Media Studies at the University of Teesside. He has published on British non-fiction film, the history of media technology and ethical issues related to archival film restoration. His book, *Moving Image Technology: From Zoetrope to Digital* (2005), is published by Wallflower Press.

Eugene Finn is a film archivist and researcher working in Ireland.

Elisabetta Girelli is currently a part-time Lecturer in Film Studies at Queen Mary, University of London. She has published various articles on the construction of identity in British cinema.

Mark Glancy is a Senior Lecturer in History at Queen Mary, University of London. His publications include *When Hollywood Loved Britain* (1999) and *The 39 Steps: A British Film Guide* (2002).

Christine Gledhill is a retired Professor of Cinema Studies, formerly at Staffordshire University, Stoke-on-Trent. She has written extensively on feminist film criticism, melodrama and British cinema. Her most recent publications include her co-edited anthology with Linda Williams, *Reinventing Film Studies* (2000), and *Reframing British Cinema 1918–1928: Between Restraint and Passion* (2003). She is currently working on the transition of British film actresses from stage to screen in the first decades of cinema.

Kevin Gough-Yates is Visiting Reader at the University of Southampton.

Stephen Griffiths lectures in television and radio studies at Staffordshire University, Stoke-on-Trent. His research interests include broadcast comedy, television drama and broadcast performance. He is researching the life and career of actor Jon Pertwee for a book and has contributed to the BFI website Screenonline.

Sheldon Hall is a Senior Lecturer in Film Studies at Sheffield Hallam University. He is the author of *Zulu: With Some Guts behind It – The Making of the Epic Film* (2005), has contributed articles on various aspects of cinema to books and journals including *Film History* and provided audio commentaries on the Paramount Home Entertainment DVDs of *Zulu* and *Once upon a Time in the West*.

Erik Hedling is Professor of Comparative Literature at Lund University, Sweden. He is the author of *Lindsay Anderson: Maverick Film-Maker* (1998), *Filmanalys* (1999) and *Brittiska fiktioner: intermediala studier i film, TV, dramatik prosa och poesi* (2001). He is the editor of *Blågult flimmer: svenska filmanalyser* (1998) and the co-editor of *Filmteori 1 and 2* (1995), *Interart Poetics: Essays on the Interrelations of the Arts and Media* (1997) and *Cultural Functions of Intermedial Exploration* (2002).

John Hill is Professor of Media at Royal Holloway, University of London. His publications include *Sex, Class and Realism: British Cinema 1956–63* (1986), *Cinema and Ireland* (co-author, 1987), *The Oxford Guide to Film Studies* (co-editor, 1998), *British Cinema in the 1980s* (1999) and *National Cinema and Beyond* (co-editor, 2004).

Martin Hunt lectures at Yeovil College, Somerset. He has an MA in Film and Television Studies from the University of Westminster, and is currently undertaking doctoral research in genre theory at Birkbeck College, London. He has previously published on the films of Terence Davies, Ealing and The Archers, and British film music.

Peter Hutchings lectures in Film at the University of Northumbria. His books include *Hammer and Beyond* (1993), *Terence Fisher* (2002), *Dracula* (2003) and *The Horror Film* (2004), and he has also written numerous articles on British cinema.

Joe Kember is a Lecturer in the School of English at the University of Exeter. He has written widely on early film and nineteenth-century visual culture and his co-authored book, *Early Cinema: From Factory Gate to Dream Factory* (2004), is an introduction to this field.

Philip Kemp is a freelance film historian based in London, a regular contributor to *Sight and Sound*, *Total Film* and *The International Film Guide*. He is the author of *Lethal Innocence: The Cinema of Alexander Mackendrick* (1991) and is currently working on a biography of Michael Balcon.

Annette Kuhn is Professor of Film Studies at Lancaster University and an editor of *Screen*. Her many publications include *Cinema, Censorship and Sexuality, 1909 to 1925* (1988); *Family Secrets: Acts of Memory and Imagination* (1995 and 2002); *An Everyday Magic: Cinema and Cultural Memory* (2002); and, as editor, *The Women's Companion to International Film* (1990); *Alien Zone* (1990); *Alien Zone II* (1999); and (with Jackie Stacey) *Screen Histories: A Screen Reader* (1998).

Marcia Landy is Distinguished Service Professor of English and Film Studies at the University of Pittsburgh. Her publications include *Fascism in Film: The Italian Commercial Cinema, 1930–1943* (1986); *British Genres: Cinema and Society, 1930–1960* (1991); *Imitations of Life: A Reader on Film and Television Melodrama* (1991); *Film, Politics, and Gramsci* (1994); *Queen Christina* (with Amy Villarejo, 1996); *Cinematic Uses of the Past* (1996); *The Folklore of Consensus: Theatricality in Italian Cinema, 1930–1943* (1998); *Italian Film* (2000); *The Historical Film: History and Memory in Media* (with Lucy Fischer, 2003); and *Monty Python's Flying Circus* (2005).

Brian McFarlane is Honorary Associate Professor in the English Department at Monash University, Melbourne. His books include *Novel to Film: An Introduction to the Theory of Adaptation* (1996), *An Autobiography of British Cinema* (1997), *Lance Comfort* (1999) and *The Encyclopedia of British Film* (2003, 2nd edn, 2005).

Luke McKernan is Head of Information at the British Universities Film & Video Council. His books include *Topical Budget* (1992), *Walking Shadows: Shakespeare in the National Film and Television Archive* (co-edited with Olwen Terris, 1994), *Who's Who of Victorian Cinema* (co-edited with Stephen Herbert, 1996) and *Yesterday's News: The British Cinema Newsreel Reader* (2002).

Martin McLoone is Professor of Media Studies at the University of Ulster and the author of *Irish Film: The Emergence of a Contemporary Cinema* (2000). He has also edited *Broadcasting in a Divided Society: 70 Years of the BBC in Northern Ireland* (1996), *Culture, Identity and Broadcasting in Ireland: Local Issues, Global Perspectives* (1991), *Big Picture, Small Screen: The Relations between Film and Television* (co-edited with John Hill, 1996) and *Border Crossing: Film in Ireland, Britain and Europe* (with John Hill and Paul Hainsworth, 1994).

Ewa Mazierska is Reader in Contemporary Cinema, Department of Humanities, University of Central Lancashire. Her publications include numerous articles in Polish and English and several books, including *Dreams and Diaries: The Cinema of Nanni Moretti* (2004) and *From Moscow to Madrid: Postmodern Cities, European Cinema* (2003) (both co-authored with Laura Rascaroli). She also co-edited *Relocating Britishness* (2004).

Janet Moat is the Keeper of the BFI Special Collections. She has published articles on the written archives and is a major contributor to Screenonline. She has also initiated, project-managed and co-authored a BFI website on the work of David Lean.

Claire Monk is Senior Lecturer in Film Studies at De Montfort University, Leicester, and a critic and writer who contributed to *Sight and Sound* for much of the 1990s. She is co-editor with Amy Sargeant of *British Historical Cinema* (2002), and has written widely on the cultural politics of film in post-1979 Britain, including the debate around heritage cinema. She is currently completing a study of British heritage-film audiences.

Robert Murphy is Professor in Film Studies at De Montfort University, Leicester, and the author of *British Cinema and the Second World War* (2000) and other books on British cinema.

Jonathan Murray is Lecturer in Film and Visual Culture at the Centre for Visual and Cultural Studies at Edinburgh College of Art. He has published or produced numerous articles and radio documentaries on Scottish cinema. He is the author of *That Thinking Feeling* (2005), a researcher's guide to Scottish film culture published in co-operation with Scottish Screen.

Lawrence Napper is a Tutor in Film and Television Studies, and Senior Researcher for the British Cinema History Research Project at the University of East Anglia. He has published on various aspects of British cinema in the inter-war period.

Kim Newman is a novelist, critic and broadcaster. He is a contributing editor to *Sight and Sound* and *Empire* magazines. His non-fiction includes *Nightmare Movies* (1988), *Millennium Movies* (1999) and BFI Classics *Cat People* (1999) and *Doctor Who* (2005); his fiction includes *The Night Mayor* (1990), *Anno Dracula* (1992) and *Life's Lottery* (1999). He is the editor of *Horror: 100 Best Books* (1988) and *The BFI Companion to Horror* (1996).

Daniel O'Brien is a freelance writer and film historian. His books include *Clint Eastwood: Film-Maker* (1996), *The Frank Sinatra Film Guide* (1998), *SF:UK – How British Science Fiction Changed the World* (2000), *The Hannibal Files* (2001), *Spooky Encounters: A Gwailo's Guide to Hong Kong Horror* (2003) and *Paul Newman* (2004).

Tim O'Sullivan is Professor and Head of the School of Media & Cultural Production at De Montfort University, Leicester. He has written widely on aspects of media and television culture and co-edited studies of Basil Dearden and Michael Relph (1997) and the Boulting Brothers (2000). He is currently completing a study of television and the British home, from 1945 to 1960.

Julian Petley is Professor of Film and Television in the School of Art at Brunel University, west London. He is the principal editor of the *Journal of British Cinema and Television*, and co-editor of *British Horror Cinema* (2002).

John Riley is a writer, lecturer, broadcaster and film programmer. His publications include *Shostakovich: A Life in Film* (2005) and he has contributed to books published by Routledge, as well as forthcoming books from Greenwood and Cambridge University Press. He works for the British Universities Film & Video Council.

James C. Robertson, a retired teacher, is the author of *The British Board of Film Censors: Film Censorship in Britain, 1896–1950* (1985), *The Hidden Cinema: British Film Censorship in Action, 1913–1972* (1989), *The Casablanca Man: The Cinema of Michael Curtiz* (1993) and (with Anthony Aldgate) *Censorship in Theatre and Cinema* (2005). He has also written a number of articles on cinema history and inter-war international affairs.

Tom Ryall is Professor of Film History at Sheffield Hallam University. His books include *Alfred Hitchcock and the British Cinema* (1986, 2nd edn, 1996), *Britain and the American Cinema* (2001) and *Anthony Asquith* (2005).

Jamie Sexton is a Lecturer in Film and New Media at the University of Wales, Aberystwyth. He is the co-editor with Laura Mulvey of *Experimental British Television* (2006), and is currently working on a book on alternative British film culture in the inter-war period.

Robert Shail is a Lecturer in Film Studies at the University of Wales, Lampeter. He has published a number of articles on film stardom and gender and is currently working on two books: a critical guide to British film directors and a study of the Welsh star Stanley Baker.

Neil Sinyard is Professor in Film Studies at Hull University. He has published over twenty books on the cinema, including studies of Richard Lester, Nicolas Roeg, Jack Clayton and 1950s' British cinema.

Andrew Spicer is Reader in Cultural History at the University of the West of England, Bristol. He is the author of *Typical Men: The Representation of Masculinity in Popular British Cinema* (2001), *Sydney Box* (2006) and numerous articles on British cinema.

Peter Todd is Information Services Manager at the BFI National Library and the director of several short films. He has curated a number of film programmes including 'Film Poems' and 'Garden Pieces', which have been screened in the UK and abroad. He is co-editor with Benjamin Cook of *Subjects and Sequences: A Margaret Tait Reader* (2004).

Paul Ward is Lecturer in Film and Television Studies at the School of Arts, Brunel University, west London. His publications include various articles on animation and documentary, and he has written the documentary volume in Wallflower Press's *Short Cuts* series of books.

Paul Wells is Director of Animation at the Animation Academy, Loughborough University. He is the author of *Art and Animation* (1997), *Understanding Animation* (1998), *Animation and America* (2002), *Animation: Genre and Authorship* (2002) and *Fundamentals of Animation* (2005). He is completing a book and a series of television programmes on British animation.

Paul Willemen is the author of *Looks and Frictions* (1994) and, with A. Rajadhyaksha, *The Encyclopaedia of Indian Cinema* (1998). He is currently Professor of Film Studies at the University of Ulster.

Linda Wood is a freelance writer and researcher whose publications include *Maurice Elvey and British Films 1927–1939* (1987); she has edited the London Film Festival Official programme, and is co-ordinating an oral history on Elstree Studios.

Acknowledgments

I am most obviously indebted to the sixty contributors to this volume, who have been diligent in their research and patient in accepting editorial intrusions. Andrew Lockett of BFI Publishing supported this project before there was any BFI involvement and rescued it from extinction when it failed to gain financial sponsorship. My thanks are also due to Sophia Contento, who kept things moving during the long interregnum before Rebecca Barden succeeded Andrew as a capable Head of Publishing. I received an AHRB 'Changing Places' Award to work with Mark Duguid, making 200 of the entries available on the website Screenonline; a British Academy Small Grant to research and write about sixty-four directors who none of the contributors had shown an interest in; and an AHRB 'Research Leave Scheme' Award, which gave me the opportunity to edit, check and update over 800 entries. I have also received considerable help and support from De Montfort University, in particular from Professor Judy Simons in preparing research proposals, Professor Tim O'Sullivan, who provided unstinting support and an invaluable supply of obituaries, and Jim Hill, who more than capably took over my scriptwriting teaching duties.

I am grateful for the help and support of: Honey Salvadori, Sylvia Baumberger, Pius Hume, Chris Goldie, David Rees, Dave Campbell, Susanne Hartley, Anne Eardley, Garth Pedler, Charlotte Brunsdon, Steve Gamble and John Mackintosh, Vivienne Robb, Stephen Burke, Helen Clay, Sarah Robotham, Cath and Glyn Jones, Ewa Mazierska, Tracey Scoffield, Bharti Mistry, April Furnival, Heinz and Charlotte Wehrli, and Tim Pulleine. Sophie and Edward Noel and Jo Mills tolerantly sat through a very mixed bag of obscure British films that they might not have chosen to watch themselves. Andrew Spicer, Richard Dacre and Sheldon Hall lent me otherwise unattainable videos and DVDs. David Simkin kindly supplied additional information on Esmé Collings (via Screenonline); Karen Alexander provided me with useful biographical information on Maureen Blackwood; Stella Bruzzi on Coky Giedroyc and Peter Webber. Some agents, producers and directors have been helpful in providing information and in some cases stills. I am indebted to Katharine Vile of PDF for ascertaining that the Peter K. Smith who directed *A Private Enterprise* is the same person as the Peter Smith who directed *No Surrender*. Pawel Pawlikowski, while providing useful corrections, disapproved of the overall tone of the entry and would have preferred to have been omitted.

I have spent a considerable amount of time in the BFI National Library over the past three years and would like to thank the staff – Anastasia Kerameos, Ayesha Khan, Christophe Dupin, Dave Reeve, David Sharp, Emma Smart, Gillian Guilmant-Smith, Ian O'Sullivan, Iratxe Gardoqui, Janice Headland, Lira Fernandes, Matt Ker, Natasha Fairbairn, Nathalie Sergent, Nicholas Potamitis, Nicola Clarke, Peter Todd, Sara Newman, Sarah Currant, Sean Delaney, Stephen Pearson, Susanna Goodson, Tony Mechele, Vivienne Jones, Victoria Crabbe, Jose De Esteban – for their unfailing support in my quest for accurate filmographic and biographical information. Special mention might be made of Sarah Currant, Sean Delaney and David Sharp, who stayed on in an eerily quiet, semi-deserted library after the London bombings of July 2005. Also to Kathleen Dickson for arranging Archive film viewings, and to Mark Duguid of Screenonline for arranging screenings, lending tapes and DVDs, and being an unfailing source of information, encouragement and advice. The first draft of this work was read by James Chapman, whose corrections, queries and comments were always erudite and useful.

I would particularly like to thank Geoff Brown, who corrected each of the entries and suggested where rewriting or further research was necessary, as well as acting as a helpful, astute editor of all the entries I wrote myself. Geoff also agreed to help clear the growing pile of additional directors, writing dozens of entries on silent, pre-war and animation directors. He checked most of the filmographies, and in the case of many silent film directors where only a sample had been requested, took on the daunting task of making them as comprehensive as possible. I am deeply grateful for his unflagging commitment to a project that at times has seemed never ending.

Finally I must thank the extraordinarily efficient NHS Direct, the reassuringly competent paramedics of the London Ambulance Service, and the nurses and doctors of the A and E and Cardiology units, and of Sam Oram Ward, King's College Hospital, London, without whose timely intervention I would have been unable to complete this book.

Introduction

Origins of the Project

Alan Burton came up with the idea for a reference guide to British film directors in 1997. With the help of Matthew Stevens of Flicks Books he compiled a list of around 600 directors and recruited Ian Christie, Julian Petley, Christine Gledhill and myself to share editorial duties. We succeeded in grading the directors and added another fifty or so names to the list, but were then stalled by the economics of publication. Alan and I sought to fund the project with a major research grant from the Arts and Humanities Research Board, but the AHRB was in the process of investing nearly £900,000 in the AHRB Centre for British Film and Television Studies and perhaps decided British cinema had already enjoyed its share of the cake. Fortunately a white knight in the form of Andrew Lockett, Head of BFI Publishing, came to the rescue. He reached agreement with Richard Paterson, the BFI's Head of Knowledge, and Mark Duguid, responsible for setting up the BFI-backed website Screenonline, that 200 of the entries would be taken by Screenonline and paid for at a rate that would allow us to give contributors a modest remuneration for their efforts. Editorial fees were insignificant but I was fortunate enough to gain research funding from the AHRB and the British Academy that covered most of my costs and (given the generous and supportive attitude of De Montfort University) released me from teaching for substantial periods.

As the bulk of the editing work had devolved onto me, the only entries I volunteered to write were those on Anna Ambrose and Carl Foreman (whom I thought in danger of being neglected); but left with a pool of unclaimed directors ill deserving exclusion, I found myself writing far more. Also, the longer I worked on the project the more missing directors I uncovered – not to mention the constant stream of new directors making their debuts during the years in which the book was being compiled. Fortunately I was able to redistribute entries from contributors who had not been able to deliver among Sheldon Hall, Ruth Barton, Sergio Angelini, Simon Brown, Brian McFarlane, Philip Kemp, Christine Gledhill, Richard Dacre, Alan Burton, Peter Hutchings and Martin Hunt; and I was able to pass on very substantial numbers of silent and pre-war directors to Geoff Brown, allowing me to concentrate on the newer directors. I finally called a halt at 1,028, fortunately discovering bright hopes Asif Kapadia and Emily Young before the gate came down.

Why Directors?

Apart from the useful, if erratic Wallflower guide to *Contemporary British and Irish Film Directors* and the valuable but brief entries in Brian McFarlane's *Encyclopedia of British Film* and *Quinlan's Film Directors*, existing dictionaries and directories include only a spattering of the more prestigious British directors. Corralling together over a thousand directors and providing identities and careers for hitherto anonymous figures does much to fill out the shadowy areas of British cinema.

Film is a collaborative art and the director does not always play the dominant role. It could certainly be argued that producers such as Michael Balcon, Alexander Korda and David Puttnam exerted a more significant impact on British cinema than the great majority of directors. Korda directed eight films in Britain, all of some merit, but it is his role as a producer that is remembered. Jack Cardiff directed fourteen films, but his reputation is based on his achievements as a cinematographer on films like *Western Approaches* (1944) and *Black Narcissus* (1947). However, the fact that Cardiff abandoned a career in which he was an acknowledged master for one in which he could claim little more than competence, or that Korda found it impossible to resist wandering onto the studio floor and interfering with the work of his directors, is testimony to the prestige of the director's role. The director, for all his dependence on producers, writers, cinematographers, actors, art directors, carpenters and prop-men, has at least the potential for acting as a focus of creativity. A compendium of all the creative contributors to British cinema would be invaluable, but to start anywhere other than with the director would be perverse.

Eligibility

The original plan was to include all directors who had made a feature film in the UK or Ireland, plus a selective sample of early silent film-makers, animators and documentary-makers. There was no agreed quality control, and by including so many obscure directors the doors were opened to many others, equally or less obscure. To take an uncontroversial example, once John Clements, a distinguished actor who co-directed one undistinguished film (*Call of the Blood*, 1948), was allowed an entry, it was difficult to make much of a case for excluding anyone. Even so, one only has to leaf through the pages of Denis Gifford's *British Film Catalogue* to find names of directors, particularly in the pre-war period, who have not made it into this volume. On the other hand, a very considerable number of interesting characters – Ivar Campbell, John Daumery, Redd Davis, Randall Faye, Reginald Fogwell, Gene Gerrard, Edwin Greenwood and Harry Hughes, to take a random sample from the 1930s – have been exposed to unfamiliar scrutiny. And although there are many omissions, most of the major figures in British silent cinema have been generously and knowledgeably treated. I have also made a concerted attempt to deal with the huge numbers of new directors who have entered the industry since 1994; fortunately, many of their films, including those that received limited exposure in cinemas, are easily and cheaply available on video or DVD via the internet.

To prevent endless expansion, I have not included new directors whose films were released in 2005 or later – my cut-off point is Saul Dibb, whose *Bullet Boy* was premiered at the 2004 London Film Festival but not given a cinema release until 2005. Films released in 2004, 2005 or due for release in 2006 have been added to existing filmographies, and where possible commented on by the contributor, Geoff Brown or myself. Given the uncertainty of film production, I have not included films that have been announced but not yet completed, except where such information marks a radical shift in a director's career (David Yates' assignment to direct *Harry Potter and the Order of the Phoenix* in 2007, for example).

Had the original planners of this project known how many indigenous directors would emerge from the undergrowth, they might have thought twice at including a 'visitor' category that has subsequently grown to 150 entries (with at least another fifty clamouring for admission). But the contribution of foreign directors – particularly of mid-European exiles in the 1930s and American directors throughout the whole period – is a substantial one, and a number of 'visitors' such as Alexander Korda and Alberto Cavalcanti played vital roles in the development of British cinema. Unfortunately, this is an endlessly expandable category; with a little more time and space I would have squeezed in John Landis for *An American Werewolf in London* (1981), David Lynch for *The Elephant Man* (1980), Lars von Trier for *Breaking the Waves* (1996) (though it is officially a Swedish/Italian/Dutch production), though I would draw the line at Steven Spielberg and George Lucas' Elstree-made Indiana Jones and *Star Wars* films. Directors who have made most of their films in Hollywood (Alan Parker and Ridley Scott, for example) are given less attention than those whose careers have been largely within British cinema. A few foreign directors who spent a substantial part of their careers in Britain, most notably Joseph Losey, Cy Endfield, Richard Lester, Terry Gilliam and Stanley Kubrick, are treated as if they were British directors in the way their filmographies are compiled; others, including Alexander Korda, Bernard Vorhaus and Cavalcanti, are treated as fully, though only the films they made in the UK are listed. Some directors who were born in Britain or Ireland but made their career abroad, notably Charlie Chaplin, are treated as visitors and only their occasional British films are dealt with here; in other cases (e.g. Eric Till and John Duigan), listing all their films seemed a useful way of showing the trajectory of their careers. British directors who have not made a British film (Sam Mendes, Rupert Wainwright and from an earlier period James Whale, for example) are not included; nor are American directors who have made films with British financial backing (such as Michael Cimino's *The Deer Hunter*, 1978, or Hal Hartley's *Trust*, 1990, and *Simple Men*, 1992).

This is a reference guide to film directors not television directors, though the line between the two is becoming increasingly narrow. Directors responsible for films made for television (or in some cases given a television screening in preference to cinema release) have been excluded, even when – as in the case of Francesca Joseph's *Tomorrow La Scala!* (2002) and Rob Rohrer's *Bumping the Odds* (1997) – those films are sharper and cleverer than many contemporary feature films. Television credits for directors who are included are also a problem. Excluding them has meant that filmographies often list insignificant early works and omit major achievements in television. The compromise has been to mention significant television credits in the text. It is particularly regrettable that two of the most talented television directors, Adrian Shergold and Dominic Savage, both made their cinema debuts (*The Last Hangman* and *Love + Hate* respectively) in 2005, too late for them to be included.

Anomalies

This is a big project that has evolved over time – I have resolved innumerable inconsistencies but left in a few others, including entries on people who should not really be here. Those with greater resources might sniff; those who work on a shoestring (most gloriously the enjoyable erratic and idiosyncratic *Film Dope*) will understand the problems; and I have not eliminated anomalies where they are harmless. Luke McKernan points out that Charles Urban was a producer, not a film director, but I would be loath to lose his entry on a technicality; similarly, with the even less eligible William Friese-Greene. Jamie Sexton rightly claims that Kenneth Macpherson 'was a novelist, photographer, artist and collector with a passionate interest in film-making', though it turns out that he made his films in Switzerland, not in Britain. Michael Grigsby has worked almost exclusively in television, to the extent that not to list his television documentaries would make his entry meaningless; he is thus an interloper, though an interesting and welcome one. Readers might puzzle over why New Zealander Martin Campbell is treated as a British director, whereas Australian Bruce Beresford is treated as a visitor; my justification would be that Campbell built his career in the British film and television industry, whereas Beresford, despite spending several years in Britain, established his reputation in Australia. Theatre director Matthew Warchus' one venture into film-making, *Simpatico* (1999), has too little British involvement to justify his presence in this work, but having mistakenly commissioned Sarah Cardwell to write his entry, it seemed a pity not to use it. Similarly Guy Jenkin, whose only theatrical feature, *The Sleeping Dictionary*, was financed by an American company, filmed in Malaysia, and only released on DVD in Britain: but a film about the love affair between a headhunter and a colonial administrator in Sarawak in the 1930s, directed by the producer and writer of *Drop the Dead Donkey*, proved too intriguing to exclude.

Nature of the Entries

Where possible, contributors have viewed and commented on a director's films, though this is impossible for the more prolific directors like Maurice Elvey and many of the silent film directors. There is also the problem of availability: despite the endeavours of the National Film and Television Archive, relatively few prints of pre-war films survive. I have discouraged contributors from making negative (or unrealistically positive) comments on films that have not been viewed. Where the contributor is writing from a fully informed position – Sheldon Hall on *A Clockwork Orange*, for example – I have not censored controversial views; though as a general rule, contributors have been asked to deal with subjects they feel some sympathy with. Many of these directors have had little written about them and a catalogue of dismissive entries would make dismal reading as well as defeating the object of a project that attempts to re-evaluate the significance of directors to British cinema. I have encouraged contributors to avoid both blandness and academic jargon – the stress is on clarity and accuracy. Inevitably in a pioneering work, there will be omissions and mistakes; I will be happy to have these pointed out to me and corrected.

Length of entries does not always reflect a director's importance or achievements. Some are shorter than they might be because of difficulty in finding out much about them; some are longer than their contribution strictly merits if the writer has been particularly diligent or enthusiastic. Where little or nothing has been previously published about a director, I have thought it worthwhile to allow a little more space, particularly when they have had a colourful or controversial career. Exact dates of birth and death are included where possible, though some directors seem reticent to divulge biographical information and others disappear into obscurity. I decided, perhaps controversially, that listings of awards and festival prizes made for dull and not necessarily useful reading, though knighthoods and Academy Award wins are generally mentioned. In jointly credited entries, contributors' names are listed alphabetically.

Sources and Bibliographies

Each entry has a brief bibliography (unless there are no sources to draw upon), but a number of reference works are so generally useful as to deserve listing separately:

Allon, Yoram, Del Cullen and Hannah Patterson (eds), *Contemporary British and Irish Film Directors* (London: Wallflower Press, 2001)

Gifford, Denis, *The British Film Catalogue: A Reference Guide. Volume 1, Fiction Film 1895–1994. Volume 2, Non-fiction Film 1888–1994* (London: Fitzroy Dearborn, 2000)

Goble, Alan (ed.), *The Complete Index to British Sound Film since 1928* (London: Bowker Saur, 1999)
Katz, Ephraim, *The Macmillan International Film Encyclopedia* (London: Macmillan, 2001)
McFarlane, Brian (ed.), *The Encyclopedia of British Film* (London: Methuen, 2003, 2nd edn, 2005)
Quinlan, David, *British Sound Films: The Studio Years 1928–1959* (London: B. T. Batsford, 1984)
Quinlan, David, *Quinlan's Film Directors* (London: B. T. Batsford, 1999)

The more sporadic but more detailed information in works such as the periodical *Film Dope*, or Brian McFarlane's *Sixty Voices* (BFI/Monash University, 1992) and *An Autobiography of British Cinema* (Methuen, 1997), along with the various collections of essays on British cinema, are included in individual bibliographies. Surveys of specific periods, studios and cinema genres are only occasionally mentioned in the individual bibliographies but provide a valuable context for the work of British film directors:

Bamford, Kenton, *Distorted Images: British National Identity and Film in the 1920s* (London: I. B. Tauris, 1999)
Barr, Charles, *Ealing Studios* (London: Studio Vista, 1977, 2nd edn, 1993)
Drazin, Charles, *The Finest Years: British Cinema of the 1940s* (London: André Deutsch, 1998)
Durgnat, Raymond, *A Mirror for England: British Cinema from Austerity to Affluence* (London: Faber and Faber, 1970)
Geraghty, Christine, *British Cinema in the Fifties: Gender, Genre and the 'New Look'* (London and New York: Routledge, 2000)
Gledhill, Christine, *Reframing British Cinema, 1918–1928: Between Restraint and Passion* (London: BFI, 2003)
Harper, Sue, *Picturing the Past: The Rise and Fall of the British Costume Film* (London: BFI, 1994)
Harper, Sue and Vincent Porter, *British Cinema of the 1950s: The Decline of Deference* (Oxford and New York: Oxford University Press, 2003)
Higson, Andrew, *English Heritage, English Cinema* (Oxford and New York: Oxford University Press, 2003)
Hill, John, *Sex, Class and Realism: British Cinema 1956–1963* (London: BFI, 1986)
Hill, John, *British Cinema in the 1980s: Issues and Themes* (Oxford and New York: Oxford University Press, 1999)
Landy, Marcia, *British Genres: Cinema and Society 1930–1960* (Princeton, NJ: Princeton University Press, 1991)
Low, Rachael, *The History of British Film* (London: George Allen & Unwin, seven volumes, 1948–85)
Murphy, Robert, *Realism and Tinsel: Cinema and Society in Britain, 1939–49* (London: Routledge, 1989)
Murphy, Robert, *Sixties British Cinema* (London: BFI Publishing, 1992)
Pym, John, *Film on Four: A Survey 1982–1991* (London: BFI, 1992)
Richards, Jeffrey, *The Age of the Dream Palace: Cinema and Society in Britain 1930–1939* (London: Routledge & Kegan Paul, 1984)
Sargeant, Amy, *British Cinema: A Critical History* (London: BFI, 2005)
Shafer, Stephen C., *British Popular Films 1929–1939: The Cinema of Reassurance* (London and New York: Routledge, 1997)
Street, Sarah, *British National Cinema* (London: Routledge, 1997)
Sweet, Matthew, *Shepperton Babylon* (London: Faber and Faber, 2005)
Walker, Alexander, *Hollywood, England: The British Film Industry in the Sixties* (London: Michael Joseph, 1974)
Walker, Alexander, *National Heroes – British Cinema in the Seventies and Eighties* (London: Harrap, 1985)
Walker, Alexander, *Icons in the Fire: The Decline and Fall of Almost Everybody in the British Film Industry* (London: Orion, 2004)
Williams, Tony, *Structures of Desire: British Cinema 1939–1955* (Albany: SUNY Press, 2000)

In the individual bibliographies, I have only put in volume numbers for journals when they seem necessary – not for journals like *Sight and Sound* and *Empire* that come out with clockwork regularity. *Time Out* is an anomaly; volume numbers are useful if not essential and are included up to the mid-1990s when the BFI Library switched from bound volumes to cuttings made available on microfiche, on which volume numbers are not included. Most newspaper references are taken from the BFI Library microfiches on the relevant films or directors, where page numbers for cuttings and documents are scant.

Internet Databases

I have included internet sites where they have been particularly useful, but information on the internet is constantly changing, and I have encouraged contributors to come up with written sources wherever possible. I have relied extensively on Film Index International, the internet version of the BFI's SIFT database, and the IMDb, an immensely useful free site that can sometimes mislead, but is impressively comprehensive. User comments range from the ineffably silly to the amazingly erudite. I am particularly indebted to regular contributor 'gavcrimson' for his detailed, perceptive analysis of films in the lower reaches of British horror and sexploitation, which made writing the entries on Kenneth Rowles, Lindsay Shonteff, Harrison Marks and the other sexploitation directors much more enjoyable than I expected. His review of Lindsay Shonteff's *How Sleep the Brave* (1981) is exemplary.

Names and Abbreviations

I have tended not to backdate the names of institutions: The London Film School in Covent Garden was earlier called the London School of Film Technique and went through a stage in the late 1970s and 80s as the London International Film School. The National Film School, set up in the early 1970s, evolved into the National School of Film and Television. Fortunately the BBFC, the British Board of Film Classification, shares the same initials as its predecessor, the British Board of Film Censorship. Organisations such as ABPC (Associated British Picture Corporation), BIP (British International Pictures), BFI (British Film Institute), GBPC (Gaumont-British Picture Corporation), LWT (London Weekend Television), NFFC (National Film Finance Corporation), NFTVA (National Film and Television Archive), RCA (Royal College of Art), RTÉ (Radio Telefís Éireann) are often displayed in full. Others such as Lew Grade's ITC are never known by their full name (Incorporated Television Company), or like MGM (Metro-Goldwyn-Mayer) are too well known to need spelling out.

Lime Grove/Shepherd's Bush is used interchangeably for the Gainsborough/Gaumont-British studio in west London; MGM-British's studio is traditionally referred to as Borehamwood, though it was as much in Elstree as the various other studios sited there. Nettlefold Studios were originally built for Cecil Hepworth at Walton-on-Thames; Warner Bros. had a small British studio at Teddington; 20th Century-Fox at Wembley. The Joe Rock studio at Elstree (not to be confused with ABPC's Elstree studio) was later taken over by British National (and eventually by the BBC).

Filmographies

Contributors writing entries on silent film directors were asked only to provide selective filmographies, though this was an instruction I failed to pass on to Dave Berry, Simon Brown and Christine Gledhill, who diligently rooted out everything they could find. Rather than discard their efforts, I accepted Geoff Brown's generous offer to attempt as full as possible filmographies for the likes of Birt Acres, Dave Aylott, James Bamforth, Ethyle Batley, Walter Booth, Esmé Collings, Alf Collins, Arthur Melbourne Cooper, Cricks and Martin, W. K.-L. Dickson, Fred and Joe Evans, Lewin Fitzhamon, Harry Furniss, Tom Green, Cecil Hepworth, Robert Paul, G. A. Smith and James Williamson. A glance at the entry for Fred and Joe Evans will indicate the mountainous scale of the task.

Dates given for films are year of release – generally taken from SIFT or from Denis Gifford's *British Film Catalogue*; where there is a significant gap between production and release dates, this has been mentioned. Industrial and training films are often included but not video pop promos – except in the case of Julien Temple, where they are too crucial to his career to exclude – and commercials. Series of shorts are not listed individually except when it seems useful to do so, as in the entry for Fred Paul, where the writer cites them as examples. Shorts and documentaries are sometimes divided from feature films, sometimes mixed in together. Forty-five minutes is the unsatisfactory dividing line between shorts and features (the alternative of having an intermediate category proved too cumbersome). In some silent film director entries, readers are left to figure out for themselves when shorts get longer and grow into features. Documentary can mean anything from *Night Mail* (1936) to *Artistry in Tureens* (1972) and includes fully fledged dramatised documentaries like "*Fires Were Started–*" (1943) and *Target for To-Night* (1941).

Directors in British and Irish Cinema

Directors marked with an asterisk are foreign-born directors treated as British/Irish in terms of their film career, and range from the undisputedly American Cy Endfield and Stanley Kubrick to the undeniably British Lindsay Anderson (born in Bangalore) and Gurinder Chadha (born in Kenya). Word-length (A=2,000, B=1,000, C=500, D=250, X=100) is approximate and does not include filmographies; V entries are of variable length. In jointly credited entries, contributors' names are listed alphabetically.

(a) = animation director

(doc.) = documentary/non-fiction director

Entries for directors marked in bold are available on <www.screenonline.org.uk>

D	KGY	ACKLAND, Rodney
B*	LMc	**ACRES**, Birt
D	RM	ADAMS, Marcus
D*	CM	ADLER, Carine
D*	RM	ADUAKA, Newton
D	RS	AGLAND, Phil
D*	AK	AKOMFRAH, John
V	RS	**ALDRICH**, Robert
C	DB	ALEXANDER, Donald
V	KGY	ALLÉGRET, Marc
D	AB	ALLEN, Kevin
V	BMc	ALLEN, Lewis
V	RD	ALTMAN, Robert
D*	AB	AMALOU, J. K.
C	MH	**AMBER** FILMS
C	RM	AMBROSE, Anna
D	LC	AMIEL, Jon
D	BMc	AMYES, Julian
C	GB	ANDERSON, David (a)
B*	BMc	**ANDERSON**, Lindsay
C	SA	**ANDERSON**, Michael
D	PH	ANDERSON, Paul
B	MB	**ANNAKIN**, Ken
C	MH	**ANSTEY**, Edgar
V	EH	ANTONIONI, Michelangelo
D	RB	APPLETON, Dudi
B	SA	**APTED**, Michael
C	GB/RM	ARDEN, Jane and Jack BOND
C	MB	ARGYLE, John
C	LN	**ARLISS**, Leslie
D	RM	ASANTE, Amma
C	RD	ASHER, Robert
A	TR	**ASQUITH**, Anthony
D	RM	ATKINSON, Jim
B	SA	ATTENBOROUGH, Richard
D	PGW	ATTWOOD, David
D	RM	AUERBACH, Shona
D	RM	AUSTIN, Michael
D	KN	AUSTIN, Ray
D	BA	AYLOTT, Dave
D	JM	BAIRD, Edward
C	PH	BAKER, Robert and Monte BERMAN
B	MB	**BAKER**, Roy Ward
C	GB	BALCH, Antony
B	JK	**BAMFORTH**, James
D	RS	BANGURA, Roberto
C*	GB	BANKS, Monty
D	AB	BARKAS, Geoffrey
C	PH	BARKER, Clive
D	RM	BARKER, Mike
B	SB	**BARKER**, William
X	GB/RM	BARR-SMITH, Albert
D	AB	BARRETT, Lezli-An
D	KN	BARRON, Steve
D	RM	BARRON, Zelda
D	RM	BASSETT, Michael J.
C	GB/SB	BATLEY, Ethyle
C	RM	BATTERSBY, Roy
B	LN	**BAXTER**, John
C	GB	BAXTER, R. K. N.
X	RM	BAXTER, Ronnie
D*	DB	BAYLY, Stephen
V	TR	BEAUDINE, William

D	DO	BEDFORD, Terry
C	AS	BENNETT, Compton
D	RB	BENNETT, Edward
C	TR	BENTLEY, Thomas
V	RD	BERESFORD, Bruce
V	GB/KGY	BERGER, Ludwig
D	JRi	BERKOFF, Steven
D	MH	BERNHARD, Chris
V	KGY	BERNHARDT, Curtis
C	AK	BERWICK STREET FILM COLLECTIVE
D	RM	BEZENCENET, Peter
D	GBa	BIERMAN, Robert
C	DO	BILLINGTON, Kevin
C	LC	**BIRD**, Antonia
D	RM	BIRD, Richard
D	RB	BIRKIN, Andrew
D	RM	BIRKINSHAW, Alan
D	MB	BIRT, Dan
D	GB	BISHOP, Terry
C	PGW	**BLACK AUDIO FILM COLLECTIVE**
C	EF	BLACK, Cathal
X	RM	BLACK, Donald Taylor (doc.)
D	RM	BLACK, George
V	BD	**BLACKTON**, Stuart
D	PGW	BLACKWOOD, Maureen
C	LC	BLAIR, Les
C	RD	**BLAKELEY**, John
V	GB/RM	BLAKEMORE, Michael
D*	RM	BOKOVA, Jana
D	RD	BOLT, Ben
D	EH	BOLT, Robert
V	LE	BOLVARY, Geza von
C	AB	**BOND**, Ralph (doc.)
B	KN	**BOORMAN**, John
D	DO	BOOTH, Harry
D	LMc	**BOOTH**, Walter (a)
B	BMc	**BOULTING**, John and Roy
C	GB	BOWER, Dallas
B	AS	**BOX**, Muriel
C	RM	BOYD, Don
D	BMc	BOYD, William
C	MH	**BOYLE**, Danny
X	RM	BRADLEY, Stephen
C	RM	BRADY, Ray
V	LW	BRAHM, Hans
D	SB	BRAMBLE, A.V.
C	SA	**BRANAGH**, Kenneth
D	RM	BRANDON, Phil
D	RB	BREATHNACH, Paddy
D	JK	BRENON, Herbert
C	DO	BRIDGES, Alan
D	GB	BRODY, Hugh
D	RM	BROMLY, Alan
D	TR	BROOK, Clive
C	EH	**BROOK**, Peter
D*	RM	BROOKFIELD, Bill
V	SA	BROOKS, Richard
B	JP	**BROOMFIELD**, Nick (doc.)
C	GB	**BROWNLOW**, Kevin and Andrew MOLLO
D	EF	BRUCE, Nicola
B	GB	**BRUNEL**, Adrian
D	RB	BRYCE, Alex
D	JMu	BRYDEN, Bill
D	AS	BUCHANAN, Jack
V	GB	BUCHOWETZKI, Dimitri
V	JR	BUCQUET, Harold S.
D	AB	BURDIS, Ray and Dominic ANCIANA
D	RD	BURGE, Stuart
C	AB	BURGER, Germain
D	SH	BURTON, Richard
D	LW	BUSHELL, Anthony
C*	SB	BUTLER, Alexander
D	AB	BUTTERWORTH, Jez
D	RM	BYE, Ed
D	LC	BYRNE, John
D	MMc	CAFFREY, David
D	MH	CALLOW, Simon
C	SA	**CAMMELL**, Donald
D*	GB	CAMPBELL, Ivar
C*	KN	CAMPBELL, Martin
C	KN	CANNON, Danny
D	RM	CAPALDI, Peter
C	SH	**CARDIFF**, Jack
D	EF	CARNEY, John and Tom HALL
C	WWD	CARRERAS, Michael
C	RD	**CARSTAIRS**, John Paddy
V	KGY	CARTIER, Rudolph
X	RM	CARTLIDGE, William
C	MB	CASS, Henry
D	GB	CATLING, Darrell
C	MH	CATON-JONES, Michael
C	SC	CATTANEO, Peter
V	AK	**CAVALCANTI**, Alberto
D	SH	CELLAN JONES, Simon

C*	MH	**CHADHA**, Gurinder
C	GB	CHAFFEY, Don
V	RD	**CHAPLIN**, Charles
C	RD	CHELSOM, Peter
X	RM	CHISNELL, Frank
X	GB/RM	CHORLTON, Michael
D	KN	CHRISTIAN, Roger
C	PGW	CINEMA ACTION
V	PK	CLAIR, René
D	RM	CLARK, Jim
C	AS	**CLARKE**, Alan
D	MH	CLARKE, Frank
V	SH	CLAVELL, James
D	RM	CLAYDON, Philip
B	PH	**CLAYTON**, Jack
D	PGW	CLAYTON, Sue
D	LC	CLEGG, Tom
D	PGW	CLEMENS, Brian
C	EG	CLEMENT, Dick
D	EG	CLEMENTS, John
V	CG	CLIFT, Dennison
D	BMc	CLOWES, St John Legh
D	SC	CLUNES, Martin
D	RM	COBHAM, David
D	RM	COE, Peter
D	MB	COHEN, Norman
D*	RM	COKLISS, Harley
D	RM	COLE, Nigel
D	PK	COLE, Sidney
C	CG	COLEBY, A. E.
C	FG	**COLLINGS**, Esmé
C	BA	COLLINS, Alfred
C	GB	COLLINS, Edwin
C	MH	**COLLINSON**, Peter
C	MMc	**COMERFORD**, Joe
C	LW	**COMFORT**, Lance
D	RM	CONNOLLY, Fintan
D	PH	CONNOR, Kevin
V	DO	CONWAY, Jack
D	RD	CONYERS, Darcy
D	LMc	COOPER, Arthur Melbourne
C	GB	COOPER, Budge (doc.)
D	GB/LN	COOPER, George A.
V	RM	COOPER, Stuart
V	SH	CORMAN, Roger
V	PK	**CORNELIUS**, Henry
D	RM	COUTTS, Don
C	MG	**COWARD**, Noël
C	LW	COX, Alex
C	WWD	CRABTREE, Arthur
C	PK	**CRAIGIE**, Jill
D	RM	CRANE, Peter
B	PK	**CRICHTON**, Charles
C	SB	**CRICKS AND MARTIN**
D	RM	CROWLEY, John
X	GB/RM	CULLIMORE, Alan
D*	RM	CURTIS, Richard
B	CG	**CUTTS**, Graham
V	GB	CZINNER, Paul
C	SC	DALDRY, Stephen
C	JR	DALRYMPLE, Ian
X	GB/RM	DANCE, Charles
V	RM	DASSIN, Jules
V	GB	DAUMERY, John
X	GB	DAVIES, Howard
C	RM	DAVIES, John and Rob SMITH
B	EM	**DAVIES**, Terence
C	MB	DAVIS, Desmond
C	MMc	DAVIS, John T.
D	GB/RM	DAVIS, Mick
D	PGW	DAVIS, Philip
D*	GB	DAVIS, Redd
C	PK	DAY, Robert
C	LN	**DEAN**, Basil
A	TO	**DEARDEN**, Basil
D	JM	DEARDEN, James
C	GB	DE COURVILLE, Albert
C	PK	DELL, Jeffrey
D	BMc	DENHAM, Reginald
X	RM	DENTON, Jack
D*	RM	DESPINS, Joseph
V	SH	DE TOTH, André
C*	PW	DE VERE, Alison (a)
D	MMc	DEVLIN, Barry
D	RM	DEXTER, John
B	GB	**DICKINSON**, Thorold
D	BMc	DICKSON, Paul
V	BA	DICKSON, W. K.-L.
V	RB	DIZDAR, Jasmin
V	MB	**DMYTRYK**, Edward
X	RM	DONALD, Simon
D	EG	DONAT, Robert
V	SH	DONEN, Stanley
B	JM	**DONNER**, Clive
V	SH	DONNER, Richard
V	GB	DONOVAN, Martin
D	RM	DONOVAN, Terence
B	GBa	**DOUGLAS**, Bill

C	SB	DOXAT-PRATT, B. E.
D	RM	DOYLE, Jim
D	RM	DOYLE, Julian
D	PGW	DRURY, David
D	GB	DRYHURST, Edward
C	NS	DUFFELL, Peter
D	EF	DUFFY, Martin
C	RM	DUIGAN, John
B	GB	**DUNBAR**, Geoff (a)
D	RM	DUNKERTON, Martin
V	GB	**DUNNING**, George (a)
V	TR	**DUPONT**, E. A.
V	GB	DUVIVIER, Julien
V	RM	DVIR, Rami
V	RM	DWANN, Alan
C*	PWi	**DWOSKIN**, Stephen
C	GB	**DYER**, Anson (a)
D	BMc	EADY, David
D	RM	EAGLES, Bill
D	RM	EDGAR, Justin
D	RD	EDMONDSON, Adrian
V	PK	EDWARDS, Blake
B	GB/BD	**EDWARDS**, Henry
C	JM	EDZARD, Christine
V	RM	EGOYAN, Atom
V	GB	EICHBERG, Richard
X	RM	ELDER, Clarence
C	GB/LE	ELDRIDGE, John
V	CM	EL HAGAR, Khaled
C	GB/LE	ELTON, Arthur (doc.)
D	RM	ELTON, Ben
C	JH	ELTRINGHAM, Billie and Simon BEAUFOY
C	LN	**ELVEY**, Maurice
C	DB	**EMLYN**, Endaf
B*	SH	**ENDFIELD**, Cy
D*	PGW	ENGEL, Andi
V	GB/KGY	ESWAY, Alexander
D	RM	EVANS, David
C	BA	**EVANS**, Joe and Fred
C	RM	EVANS, Marc
C	LC	EYRE, Richard
D	RM	EZRA, Mark
D	BMc	FAIRCHILD, William
D	MB	FAITHFUL, Geoffrey
D	RM	FARINO, Julian
D*	GB	FAYE, Randall
V	KGY	FEHER, Friedrich
V	SH	FERRER, José
V	MB	FEYDER, Jacques
C	SE	FIELD, Mary (doc.)
D	JM	FIENNES, Martha
C	GBa	**FIGGIS**, Mike
D	RM	FINBOW, Alexander
C	GB	FINBOW, Colin
D	SH	FINNEY, Albert
B	PH	**FISHER**, Terence
C	LMc	**FITZHAMON**, Lewin
V	GB	FITZPATRICK, James A.
V	AK	**FLAHERTY**, Robert (doc.)
V	SH	FLEISCHER, Richard
D	KN	FLEMYNG, Gordon
D	DO	FLETCHER, Mandie
D	GB	FOGWELL, Reginald
B	NS	**FORBES**, Bryan
V	RM	FORD, Derek
B	TR	FORD, John
V	RM	FORDE, Eugene
B	LN	**FORDE**, Walter
D	RM	FORDER, Timothy
V	RM	FOREMAN, Carl
B	MH	**FORSYTH**, Bill
D	JH	FORTE, John
C	CG	FOSS, Kenelm
D	BMc	FOSTER, Giles
C	GBa	**FRANCIS**, Freddie
C	DB	**FRANCIS**, Karl
D	BMc	FRANK, Charles H.
C	PH	FRANKEL, Cyril
B	DO	**FREARS**, Stephen
V	WWD	FREELAND, Thornton
V	SH	FREGONESE, Hugo
C	JR	FRENCH, Harold
B	MH	**FREND**, Charles
V	GB	FRENKE, Eugène
D	RM	FRESHMAN, William
C	LMc	**FRIESE-GREENE**, William
D	RM	FRY, Stephen
C	PH	FUEST, Robert
V	WWD	FURIE, Sidney J.
D	BA	FURNISS, Harry
C	RM	FURSE, John
D	RM	FYWELL, Tim
V	GB/KGY	GALLONE, Carmine
D	SC	GARNETT, Tony
C	RM	GEORGE, Terry
C	GB	GERRARD, Gene
D*	GB	GIBSON, Alan

D	WWD	GIBSON, Brian
C	WWD	**GIDAL**, Peter
D*	JRi	GIEDROYC, Coky
V	RM	GIESE, Maria
D	PCG	GILBERT, Brian
B	AC	**GILBERT**, Lewis
D	RM	GILL, Elizabeth
B*	EG	**GILLIAM**, Terry
B	GB	**GILLIAT**, Sidney
C	KN	GILLING, John
D	RB	GILSENAN, Alan
D	LE	GINEVER, Aveling
C	GB	GLADWELL, David
D	AB	GLAZER, Jonathan
C	SA	GLEN, John
C	SH	GLENVILLE, Peter
D	LW	GLYN, Elinor
V	EB	GODARD, Jean-Luc
D	MH	GODBER, John
C	SA	GODDARD, Jim
B*	PW	**GODFREY**, Bob (a)
D	MMc	GOGAN, Johnny
C	NS	**GOLD**, Jack
D	GB	GOLDBACHER, Sandra
D	RM	GOLDEN, Karl
D	CM	GOODHEW, Philip
X	RM	GORNICK, Lisa
V	CM	GORRIS, Marleen
V	GB	GOULDING, Alfred
C	RM	GOVER, Victor M.
C	PW	GRABER, Sheila (a)
D*	JS	GRAEF, Roger
D	BMc	GRAHAM SCOTT, Peter
D	GBa	GRAYSON, Godfrey
D	GB	GREAVES, Daniel (a)
C	MB	GREEN, Guy
D	RM	GREEN, Rob
D	BA	GREEN, Tom
B	ML	**GREENAWAY**, Peter
C	JP	**GREENE**, David
D*	KGY	GREENE, Max
D	LC	GREENGRASS, Paul
D	GB	GREENWOOD, Edwin
D	NS	GREGG, Colin
V	GB/BD	GRÉVILLE, Edmond
D*	RM	GREWAL, Shani
D	GB	GREY, Richard
C	LE	**GRIERSON**, John (doc.)
D	DB	GRIEVE, Andrew
V	SB	GRIFFITH, D.W.
D	DB	GRIFFITHS, Sid
C	JP	**GRIGSBY**, Michael
C	GB/PW	GROSS, Anthony and Hector HOPPIN (a)
D	RM	GROSS, Terence
D	RM	GROSSO, Nick
D	RD	GROUNDS, Tony
V	KGY	GRUNE, Karl
C	GB	GUARD, Candy (a)
B	SCh	**GUEST**, Val
C	GB	GUILLERMIN, John
D	GB	GUNDREY, V. Gareth
D	LW	GUNN, Gilbert
B	DB	**HAGGAR**, William
C	PH	HAGGARD, Piers
D	RM	HAJAIG, Hadi
B	PW	**HALAS**, John and Joy **BATCHELOR** (a)
B	GB	HALDANE, Bert
D	LN	HALE, Sonnie
C	SH	HALL, Peter
A	RM	**HAMER**, Robert
B	PH	**HAMILTON**, Guy
C	RS	HAMM, Nick
D	SA	HAMMOND, Peter
D	RM	HAMMOND, William
D	SC	HAMPTON, Christopher
D	BMc	HANBURY, Victor
V	PW	HAND, David (a)
D	RM	HAND, Harry
D	RM	HARDY, Justin
C	PH	HARDY, Robin
C	RM	HARE, David
D	MMc	HARKIN, Margo
C	MB	HARLOW, John
C	RM	HARRIS, Damien
D	GB	HART, Ben R.
C	PH	HARTFORD-DAVIS, Robert
C	JM	HARVEY, Anthony
C	EB	HATTON, Maurice
D	RM	HAY, John
D	BA	HAY, Will
C	PH	HAYERS, Sidney
C	GB	HAYES, Derek and Philip AUSTIN
D	LW	HAYMAN, David
C	GB	HAYNES, Manning
D	MB	HAYNES, Stanley
V	CM	HAYNES, Todd

C	KGY	HAZAN, Jack
X	RM	HEEL, Sue
D	JM	HEMMINGS, David
D	RM	HENDERSON, John
D	PGW	HENRIQUES, Julian
B	SB	**HEPWORTH**, Cecil
C	RM	HERBERT, Henry
X	RM	HERBERT, Leon
D★	BA	HERKOMER, Sir Hubert von
C	PW	HERMAN, Mark
C★	PH	HESSLER, Gordon
D	MH	HEWITT, Peter
C	EF	HICKEY, Kieran
C	SH	HICKOX, Douglas
C	KN	HILL, James
C	SB	HILL, Sinclair
C	LN	HISCOTT, Leslie
A	MG	**HITCHCOCK**, Alfred
B	AS	**HODGES**, Mike
D★	JMu	HOFFMAN, Michael
C	LE	HOLMES, J. B. (doc.)
C★	PK	**HOLT**, Seth
D	RS	HOOK, Harry
D	GB/RM	HOPKINS, Anthony
D★	DO	HOPKINS, Ben
D	RM	HOPKINS, Stephen
D	GB/EG	HOSKINS, Bob
D	SA	HOUGH, John
C	TR	HOWARD, Leslie
V	SA	HOWARD, William, K.
C	MH	HOWITT, Peter
C	NS	**HUDSON**, Hugh
C	GB	HUGHES, Harry
B	GB	HUGHES, Ken
D	RD	HULBERT, Jack
D	RM	HUME, Kenneth
D	RM	HUMPHRIES, Andy
D	GBa	HUNSINGER, Tom and Neill HUNTER
C	SA	HUNT, Peter
D	RM	HUNTER, Simon
V	GB	HUNTER, T. Hayes
C	BMc	HUNTINGTON, Lawrence
D	BMc	HURRAN, Nick
D	RM	HURST, Andy
C	JR	HURST, Brian Desmond
D	RM	HURST, Mike
D	RM	HÜSEYIN, Metin
C★	LW	HUSSEIN, Waris
V	PK	**HUSTON**, John
D	AS	HUTH, Harold
V	PH	HUTTON, Brian G.
C	JM	**HYTNER**, Nicholas
V	AB	INCE, Ralph
D	LW	IRVIN, John
X	RM	ISITT, Debbie
B★	SH	**IVORY**, James
B	GB/LE	**JACKSON**, Pat
D	RM	JANES, Richard
B	EH	**JARMAN**, Derek
D	JM	JARROTT, Charles
C	RS	JEAN, Vadim
D	NS	JEFFRIES, Lionel
D	RM	JENKIN, Guy
B	JP	**JENNINGS**, Humphrey (doc.)
V	KGY	JESSNER, Leopold
D	RM	JOBSON, Richard
C	LC	**JOFFE**, Roland
V	RM	JOHNSON, Lamont
D★	RM	JOHNSON, Niall
D	DO	JOLLIFFE, Geneviève
D	DO	JONES, Chris
D	SA	JONES, David
D	RB	JONES, Kirk
C	EG	**JONES**, Terry
A	ML	**JORDAN**, Neil
D	RM	JOVY, Alex
C	AK	**JULIEN**, Isaac
C	TR	KANE, David
D	KN	KANIEVSKA, Marek
D	RM	KAPADIA, Asif
V	SC	KAPUR, Shekhar
V	CM	KAURISMAKI, Aki
D	RM	KAVANAGH, Denis
D	MMc	KEATING, David
C	GB/BD	**KEILLER**, Patrick
D	RD	KELLETT, Bob
D	MB	KELLINO, Roy
C	BA	KELLINO, Will
D	RM	KEMP, Julian
D	RM	KENELM CLARKE, James
C	DO	KERRIGAN, Justin
D	AK	KIDRON, Beeban
D	RM	KILNER, Clare
C	MH	KIMMINS, Anthony
C	LN	KING, George
C	GB/AB	KNIGHT, Castleton
C	BMc	KNOWLES, Bernard

V	LW	**KORDA**, Alexander
B*	GB	**KORDA**, Zoltan
D	LC	KOSMINSKY, Peter
V	GB/WWD	KOSTER, Henry
V	BMc	KOTCHEFF, Ted
C	PK	**KOTTING**, Andrew
V	GB/KGY	KRAEMER, F. W.
D	PH	KRISH, John
D	RM	KRISHNAMMA, Suri
B*	SH	**KUBRICK**, Stanley
D	SC	KUREISHI, Hanif
C	GB/AB	KWIETNIOWSKI, Richard
D	RM	LAB KY MO
V	GB	LACHMAN, Harry
V	KGY	LAMAC, Karel
C	GB	LANE, Lupino
C*	RM	LANGLEY, Noel
C	RM	LARCHER, David
V	RM	LARRAZ, José
B	AB	**LAUNDER**, Frank
D	GB	LAW, Michael
D	BMc	LAWRENCE, Quentin
C	LW	**LEACOCK**, Philip
A	SC	**LEAN**, David
B	LW	**LEE**, Jack
C	GB	LEE, Norman
C	AK	**LEEDS ANIMATION WORKSHOP** (a)
B	LW	**LEE THOMPSON**, Jack
D	SE	LEGG, Stuart (doc.)
C	PWi	**LEGRICE**, Malcolm
A	RD	**LEIGH**, Mike
C	RM	**LELAND**, David
C*	GB	LEMONT, John
C	RM	LEONG, Po-Chih
B*	RS	**LESTER**, Richard
C*	GB/WWD	LEVY, Don
D	GB	LEWIS, Cecil
C	AS	LEWIS, Jay
D	EF	LIDDY, Kevin
C*	JM	LINDSAY-HOGG, Michael
D	PW	LINGFORD, Ruth (a)
D	RS	LITTLEWOOD, Joan
V	GB/KGY	LITVAK, Anatole
A	LC	**LOACH**, Ken
C	MH	LONCRAINE, Richard
C	RD	LONG, Stanley
A*	WWD	**LOSEY**, Joseph
D	RM	LOVE, Nick
D	MMc	LOWNEY, Declan
V	JM	LUMET, Sidney
V	GB/JS	**LYE**, Len (a)
C	GB/MG	LYNE, Adrian
D	MH	LYNN, Jonathan
D	RM	LYNN, Robert
D	RB	McADAM, Trish
C	GB	McCARTHY, Michael
C	MMc	MACARTNEY, Sydney
C	AS	MACDONALD, David
D	RM	MACDONALD, Hettie
C	JMu	MACDONALD, Kevin
D	RM	McDONAGH, John
D	EG	McDONELL, Fergus
D	RM	McGRATH, Douglas
C	RS	McGRATH, Joseph
D	RB	McGUCKIAN, Mary
C	SB	McGUIGAN, Paul
D	RM	McKAY, John
A*	AK	**MACKENDRICK**, Alexander
D	RM	MACKENZIE, David
C	SA	MACKENZIE, John
B	GB/JMu	**MacKINNON**, Gillies
C*	GB/JS	**McLAREN**, Norman (a)
C	JH	**McMULLEN**, Ken
D	RS	McMURRAY, Mary
D	DO	MacNAUGHTON, Ian
D	MMc	McPHERSON, Conor
D	JS	**MACPHERSON**, Kenneth
D	RM	McPOLIN, Owen
D	LC	MacTAGGART, James
C	MH	MADDEN, John
D	PCG	MAGUIRE, Sharon
D	GB	MAINWARING, Bernerd
V	CM	MALLE, Louis
C	SE	**MANDER**, Kay (doc.)
C	GB/JM	MANDER, Miles
V	SH	MANKIEWICZ, Joseph L.
V	SH	MANN, Anthony
D	SA	MARCEL, Terry
D	RM	MARCUS, James
D	RM	MARCUS, Shimmy
C	RM	MARKS, George Harrison
V	KN	MARQUAND, Richard
V	RM	MARSH, William
D	RM	MARSHALL, Frank
D	RM	MARSHALL, Neil
D	RM	MARSHALL, Simon
V	KGY	MARTON, Andrew

D	GB	MASON, Herbert
C	GB/BD	**MASSINGHAM**, Richard (doc.)
D	RM	MASSOT, Joe
C	CM	MATHIAS, Sean
D	RM	MATTHEWS, Paul
D	GB	MAUDE, Arthur
C	JRi	MAYBURY, John
C	GB	MAYERSBERG, Paul
C	RM	MAYLAM, Tony
V	GB	MAZZETTI, Lorenza
D	RM	MEAD, Nick
C	SH	**MEADOWS**, Shane
D*	RB	MECKLER, Nancy
C*	KN	MEDAK, Peter
D	DO	MEGAHEY, Leslie
C	RM	MEGAHY, Francis
D	RM	MELLOR, Kay
V	JR	MENDES, Lothar
C	JS	**MENGES**, Chris
V	PK	**MENZIES**, William Cameron
D*	EM	MERCHANT, Ismail
D	JMu	METZSTEIN, Saul
C*	PCG	MICHELL, Roger
D	CM	MICHELL, Scott
C	JR	MILES, Bernard
C	GB/RS	MILES, Christopher
C	RM	MILLAND, Ray
V	CG	MILLAR, Adelqui
C	RS	MILLAR, Gavin
C	GB	MILLER, Frank
C	RM	MILLER, Sam
C	RM	MILLS, John
C	RM	MILLS, Reginald
C	SC	**MINGHELLA**, Anthony
D	RB	MISKELLY, Bill
C	MB	MITCHELL, Oswald
B	GB	MITCHELL & KENYON
V	GB/KGY	MITTLER, Leo
C	DB	MONGER, Chris
C	TR	**MONTAGU**, Ivor (doc.)
D	RM	MOORE, Simon
D	JM	MORAHAN, Christopher
D	MB	MORE O'FERRALL, George
D	SB	MORGAN, Sidney
D	RS	MORRISON, Paul
B	JK	MOTTERSHAW, Frank
D	RS	MOWBRAY, Malcolm
C	PH	MOXEY, John
V	RM	MULCAHY, Russell
D	TR	MULLAN, Peter
C	PGW	MULLOY, Phil
C	EB	**MULVEY**, Laura
D	RM	MUNDEN, Marc
D	RM	MUNDEN, Maxwell
C	MMc	MURPHY, Pat
D	EF	MURPHY, Vinny
D	RM	MUSK, Cecil
C	LN	MYCROFT, Walter C.
X	RM	MYLOD, Mark
D*	RM	NALLURI, Bharat
C*	RS	NARIZZANO, Silvio
C	BA/GB	NASH, Percy
B	AS	**NEAME**, Ronald
D	RM	NEEDS, Malcolm
V	GBa	NEGULESCO, Jean
V	JR	NEILL, Roy William
D	JMu	NEILSON, Anthony
C*	PW	NEUBAUER, Vera (a)
B	CG	**NEWALL**, Guy
D	KN	NEWBROOK, Peter
D	DB	NEWBY, Chris
C	PCG	NEWELL, Mike
D	LN	NEWMAN, Widgey R.
D	RM	NIBLO, Alan
D	JS	NICHOLSON, Irene
D	SC	NOBLE, Adrian
C	SA	NOLAN, Christopher
D*	LE	NOLBANDOV, Sergei
C	MB	NORMAN, Leslie
D	RM	NOTT, Julian
D	SC	NUNN, Trevor
X	RM	O'BYRNE, Joe
D	RM	OCKRENT, Mike
D	KN	O'CONNOLLY, Jim
C	RB	O'CONNOR, Pat
C	RB	O'DONNELL, Damien
D	KN	O'HARA, Gerry
D	JS	OLDMAN, Gary
D	EF	O'LEARY, Ronan
B	GB/JR	**OLIVIER**, Laurence
D*	RM	ONWURAH, Ngozi
D	RM	ORME, Stuart
D	RB	ORMROD, Peter
D	GB	ORTON, J. O. C.
X	RM	O'SULLIVAN, Shane
C	MMc	**O'SULLIVAN**, Thaddeus
V	PGW	**OVE**, Horace
C	RD	OWEN, Cliff

D	SA	PAGE, Anthony	A	PK	**REED**, Carol
C	GB/EM	PALMER, Tony	C	TR	**REEVES**, Michael
D	GB	PALTENGHI, David	V	GB/KGY	REINIGER, Lotte (a)
B	SA	**PARK**, Nick (a)	V	KGY	REISCH, Walter
C	MH	**PARKER**, Alan	B	NS	**REISZ**, Karel
V	GB	PARKER, Albert	D	MB	RELPH, Michael
C	PCG	PARKER, Oliver	D	RM	RICHARDS, Julian
D	LMc	PARKINSON, Harry B.	C*	GB	RICHARDSON, Frank
V	GBa	PARRISH, Robert	D	RD	RICHARDSON, Peter
C	GB	PARRY, Gordon	B	SH	**RICHARDSON**, Tony
D	RM	PARRY, Richard	D	SC	RICKMAN, Alan
C*	TR	PASCAL, Gabriel	D	BA	RIDGEWELL, George
D	MB	PATRICK, Nigel	D	SC	RIDLEY, Philip
C*	GB/BD	**PAUL**, Fred	C*	AS	**RILLA**, Wolf
B	LMc	**PAUL**, Robert William	D	RM	RITCHIE, Aileen
D	RM	PAVLOU, George	C	SA	RITCHIE, Guy
C*	GBa	PAWLIKOWSKI, Pawel	V	SH	RITT, Martin
B	CG	**PEARSON**, George	D	RM	ROBERTS, John
C	RM	PECK, Ron	D	RM	ROBERTS, Steve
V	SH	PECKINPAH, Sam	D	RM	ROBINS, John
C	JH	PEDELTY, Donovan	C	MH	**ROBINSON**, Bruce
C	LW	PELISSIER, Anthony	V	GB	ROBISON, Arthur
D	AS	PENNINGTON-RICHARDS, C. M.	V	SH	ROBSON, Mark
			C	MH	RODDAM, Franc
C	GB	PEPLOE, Clare	B	NS	**ROEG**, Nicolas
D	GB	PEPLOE, Mark	C	MB	ROGERS, Maclean
C	JP	**PETIT**, Chris	C	GB	ROOKE, Arthur
V	SH	PIERSON, Frank R.	D	BMc	ROOME, Alfred
V	SB	PLAISETTY, René	D	KN	ROSE, Bernard
C	JH	PLATTS-MILLS, Barney	C	JR	ROSMER, Milton
V	JS	**POLANSKI**, Roman	D	DO	ROSS, Benjamin
C	SC	**POLIAKOFF**, Stephen	V	SH	ROSS, Herbert
D	PH	POLLOCK, George	D*	SB	ROSSO, Franco
C	RM	POPE, Angela	V	GB	ROTH, Cy
B	AK	**POTTER**, Sally	D	JS	ROTH, Tim
A	KN	**POWELL**, Michael and Emeric **PRESSBURGER**	B	SE	**ROTHA**, Paul (doc.)
			D	RM	ROTHEROE, Dom
D	RM	POWELL, Tristram	D	RM	ROWLES, Kenneth
D*	PGW	**PRASAD**, Udayan	V	DO	RUGGLES, Wesley
V	SH	PREMINGER, Otto	D	RM	RUMLEY, Simon
C*	EM	**QUAY**, Stephen and Timothy (a)	C*	GB	RUSSELL, Erica (a)
C	MMc	QUINN, Bob	B	PCG	**RUSSELL**, Ken
C	PW	QUINN, Joanna (a)	D	RM	RYAN, Terence
D*	MMc	QUINN, Paul	C	RM	ST PAUL, Stuart
C*	NS	RADFORD, Michael	D	LMc	SAMUELSON, G. B.
C*	MB	RAKOFF, Alvin	D	PH	SANGSTER, Jimmy
C	AK	**RAMSAY**, Lynne	D	PGW	SANKOFA
V	KGY	RATOFF, Gregory	D	GB	SARNE, Mike
D	BMc	RAYMOND, Jack	V	RM	SAROSSY, Paul

C*	NS	SASDY, Peter
C	BMc	SAUNDERS, Charles
C	LC	SAVILLE, Phillip
B	JR	**SAVILLE**, Victor
V	SH	SCHAFFNER, Franklin J.
V	EB	SCHEPISI, Fred
V	RM	SCHERFIG, Lone
B	EH	**SCHLESINGER**, John
V	RB	SCHUSTER, Harold
D	RM	SCHWABACH, Peter
D	RM	SCHWARTZ, Stefan
D	SA	SCOTT, Jake
C	GB	SCOTT, James
C	KN	**SCOTT**, Ridley
D	SA	SCOTT, Tony
D	GB	SEARLE, Francis
C	RS	SELLAR, Ian
C	BMc	SEWELL, Vernon
D*	PGW	SHABAZZ, Menelik
D*	DO	SHARMAN, Jim
C*	SA	SHARP, Don
D	DO	SHARP, Ian
D	PK	SHAUGHNESSY, Alfred
C	GB/RM	SHEPHERD, Horace
C	EF	**SHERIDAN**, Jim
D	RM	SHERIDAN, Kirsten
V	KN	SHERMAN, Gary
C*	RM	SHONTEFF, Lindsay
D	CG	SHUREY, Dinah
V	SH	SIDNEY, George
V	SH	SIEGEL, Don
C	GB	SIMMONS, Anthony
X	RM	SIMPSON, John
D	SA	SIMPSON, Julian
D	RS	**SINYOR**, Gary
V	LW	SIODMAK, Robert
D	RM	SKEET, Brian
V	EM	**SKOLIMOWSKI**, Jerzy
D	RM	SLOMAN, Anthony
D*	BMc	SMART, Ralph
V	SH	SMIGHT, Jack
D	RM	SMITH, Christopher
B	FG	**SMITH**, George Albert
D	AB	SMITH, Herbert
C	TR	SMITH, Mel
C	BD	**SMITH**, Percy
C	RM	SMITH, Peter
C	GB	SNOWDEN, Alison and David FINE (a)
C	PCG	SOFTLEY, Iain
C	GB/PW	SPEED, Lancelot (a)
D	CM	SPENCE, Richard
D	SG	SPIERS, Bob
C*	SA	SPOTTISWOODE, Roger
D	RM	SPURRIER, Paul
D	RM	SQUIRE, Anthony
D	RM	STAFFORD, Brendan
D	KN	STANLEY, Richard
D	EF	STAPLETON, Frank
V	MB	STEIN, Paul
D	RM	STELLMAN, Martin
D	RB	STEMBRIDGE, Gerry
X	RM	STEPHENSON, John
D	GB/RM	STERLING, William
C	MB	STEVENSON, Robert
D	DO	STEWART, David A.
D	AS	STIRNER, Brian
V	SH	STONE, Andrew L.
D	SB	STOW, Percy
V	SH	STRICK, Joseph
C	PW	**STUDDY**, G. E. (a)
V	SH	STURGES, John
C	SC	STURRIDGE, Charles
D	BMc	STYLES, Eric
D	AB	SUGARMAN, Sara
D	RM	SUGG, Stewart
D	RM	SULLIVAN, Tim
D	PH	SUMMERS, Jeremy
C	LW	**SUMMERS**, Walter
D*	PH	SYKES, Peter
D	EM	SZKOPIAK, Piotr
D	PT	TAIT, Margaret
D	GB	TAYLOR, Donald (doc.)
D	AB	TAYLOR, John (doc.)
D	RM	TEAGUE, Colin
C	JP	**TEMPLE**, Julien
C	PK	**TENNYSON**, Penrose
D	AB	TENNYSON, Walter
V	GB/KGY	THIELE, Wilhelm
D	RM	THOMAS, Edward
B	JM	**THOMAS**, Gerald
D	RM	THOMAS, Jeremy
B	BMc	**THOMAS**, Ralph
D*	SE	THOMSON, Margaret
V	SH	THORPE, Richard
D	CM	THRAVES, Jamie
D	RB	TICKELL, Paul
C	RM	TILL, Eric

D RM TOMLINSON, Lionel
V GB **TOURNEUR**, Jacques
C WWD **TOYE**, Wendy
D RM TRAVERS, Alfred
V RM TROCHE, Rose
C* GB TRONSON, Robert
V EG TRUFFAUT, François
C MB TRUMAN, Michael
D* DO TUCHNER, Michael
D* RM TUCKER, Anand
V SB TUCKER, George Loane
D RM TUCKER, Joe
D AS TULLY, Montgomery
D DB TURNER, Paul
C GB TWIST, Derek
C* LMc **URBAN**, Charles
C RM URBAN, Stuart
D EH USTINOV, Peter
V KGY VAJDA, Ladislao (Laszlo)
V GB/LE **VARNEL**, Marcel
D* BMc VARNEL, Max
V GB VARNEY-SERRAO, Arthur
C* BD **VAS**, Robert (doc.)
D RM VAUGHN, Matthew
D PW VESTER, Paul (a)
V DO VIDOR, King
V KGY VIERTEL, Berthold
D EF VILLA, Colm
V GB **VORHAUS**, Bernard
C GB WALKER, Norman
C PH WALKER, Peter
D RM WALKER, Rob
D SA **WALLACE**, Edgar
D* KN WALLER, Anthony
D RM WALLER, Tom
D GB/LN WALLS, Tom
D RM WALSH, Aisling
D RB WALSH, Kieron J.
V SH WALSH, Raoul
D SC WARCHUS, Matthew
D JRi WARNER, Deborah
D PH WARREN, Norman J.
C EH **WATKINS**, Peter
B LE **WATT**, Harry
D RM WEBBER, Peter
D PH WEEKS, Stephen
V GB/AB WEISS, Jirí (doc.)
D RM WEST, Jake
C CG WEST, Walter
D JM WHATHAM, Claude
V GB WHELAN, Tim
C GB WHITEHEAD, Peter
D KN WICKES, David
B TR **WILCOX**, Herbert
V SA WILDER, Billy
D RM WILLIAMS, Brock
D GBa WILLIAMS, Emlyn
B* PW **WILLIAMS**, Richard (a)
B FG **WILLIAMSON**, James
D EB WILLING, Nick
D RM WILLS, J. Elder
C RM WILSON, Donald B.
D BMc WILSON, Frederick
D RM WILSON, M. J.
D SA/SB WINGROVE, Nigel
C AS **WINNER**, Michael
C RM WINSOR, Terry
C RM WINTER, Donovan
B PCG/GB **WINTERBOTTOM**, Michael
V SA WISE, Robert
C EB **WOLLEN**, Peter
V DO WOOD, Sam
C LE WOODS, Arthur
C* RM WOOLCOCK, Penny
C AB WOOLFE, Bruce (doc.)
D RM WOOLLEY, Richard
D RM WORTH, Jan
D* KN WREDE, Casper
C GB/JS **WRIGHT**, Basil
D RM WRIGHT, Edgar
V SA WYLER, William
D DO WYNNE-SIMMONS, Robert
D RM YATES, David
C SH **YATES**, Peter
D RM YOUNG, Emily
C GB YOUNG, Harold
D PH YOUNG, Robert
C* RS **YOUNG**, Terence
D RM YOUNG, Tony
C* BMc ZAMPI, Mario
V EG ZEFFIRELLI, Franco
V GB/KGY ZEISLER, Alfred
V GB/KGY ZELNICK, Fred
V EH ZETTERLING, Mai
V SH ZINNEMANN, Fred

Sergio Angelini	SA
Barry Anthony	BA
Guy Barefoot	GBa
Ruth Barton	RB
Dave Berry	DB
Geoff Brown	GB
Simon Brown	SB
Eleanor Burke	EB
Alan Burton	AB
Margaret Butler	MB
Sarah Cardwell	SC
Steve Chibnall	SCh
Pamela Church Gibson	PCG
Andrew Clay	AC
Lez Cooke	LC
Richard Dacre	RD
Bryony Dixon	BD
Wheeler Winston Dixon	WWD
Sarah Easen	SE
Leo Enticknap	LE
Eugene Finn	EF
Elisabetta Girelli	EG
Mark Glancy	MG
Christine Gledhill	CG
Kevin Gough-Yates	KGY
Stephen Griffiths	SG
Sheldon Hall	SH
Erik Hedling	EH
John Hill	JH
Martin Hunt	MH
Peter Hutchings	PH
Joe Kember	JK
Philip Kemp	PK
Annette Kuhn	AK
Marcia Landy	ML
Ewa Mazierska	EM
Brian McFarlane	BMc
Luke McKernan	LMc
Martin McLoone	MMc
Janet Moat	JM
Claire Monk	CM
Robert Murphy	RM
Jonathan Murray	JMu
Lawrence Napper	LN
Kim Newman	KN
Daniel O'Brien	DO
Tim O'Sullivan	TO
Julian Petley	JP
John Riley	JRi
James C. Robertson	JR
Tom Ryall	TR
Jamie Sexton	JS
Robert Shail	RS
Neil Sinyard	NS
Andrew Spicer	AS
Peter Todd	PT
Paul Ward	PGW
Paul Wells	PW
Paul Willemen	PWi
Linda Wood	LW

ACKLAND, Rodney (1908–1991)

Rodney Ackland was born in Rochford, Essex, on 18 May 1908. He studied at the Central School for Speech Training and Dramatic Art, worked as an actor in various repertory companies and acted in three films, including an uncredited appearance in Alfred Hitchcock's *The Skin Game* (1931). By the mid-1930s he had become a successful playwright with such dramas as *Strange Orchestra* (1931) and *After October* (1936). He entered the film industry in 1930, co-writing a number of screenplays, including *Number Seventeen* (Alfred Hitchcock, 1932), *Bank Holiday* (Carol Reed, 1937), *Hatter's Castle* (Lance Comfort, 1941), *49th Parallel* (Michael Powell, 1941), *Wanted for Murder* (Lawrence Huntington, 1946) and *Temptation Harbour* (Lance Comfort, 1947). Frequently he worked with exiles from Germany such as Hans and Wolfgang Wilhelm, Emeric Pressburger and Fritz Gotfurt to help shape their dialogue. Early in the war he scripted and directed *Lady Be Kind* for the Ministry of Information, and two years later directed *Thursday's Child*, a feature film about a young actress (Sally Ann Howes) who abandons a burgeoning film career in favour of a boarding school education. It failed primarily because of Ackland's over-delicate handling of the material. A documentary for the Crown Film Unit, *The New School*, followed in 1944.

After the war, Ackland was associated with an attempt to adapt Louis Hémon's novel *Maria Chapdelaine* for Alexander Korda (the film was eventually directed by Marc Allégret); and with *The Queen of Spades*, which he wrote and expected to direct. He was removed, after only a few days, at the insistence of Dame Edith Evans; Thorold Dickinson was brought in and directed his most admired film. Subsequently Ackland found it difficult to work in the film industry. His play *The Pink Room* (1952) was condemned as a 'libel on the British people', though he was able to relaunch it in 1988 as the much admired *Absolute Hell*. He died in Richmond, Surrey, on 6 December 1991.

(Kevin Gough-Yates)

BIBLIOGRAPHY: Ackland, Rodney, 'The Bubble-Reputation', *Sight and Sound*, Summer 1943, pp. 8–11; Ackland, Rodney and Elspeth Grant, *The Celluloid Mistress or the Custard Pie of Dr Caligari* (London: Allen Wingate, 1954); 'Credits Breach: Screen Writers Given Damages', *Today's Cinema*, 23 Feb. 1950, p. 3.

FILMOGRAPHY: *Lady Be Kind* (short, 1941); *Thursday's Child* (1943); *The New School* (doc. short, 1944).

ACRES, Birt (1854–1918)

Despite increased critical attention in recent years, Birt Acres remains a comparatively neglected figure among the pioneers of British film. As a creative film-maker his contribution was negligible, but as an inventor and innovator, and simply as someone who was especially active at the start of things, his importance is undisputed.

Birt Acres was born to English parents in Richmond, Virginia, USA, on 23 July 1854, and took up the profession of photographer in London. He became the manager of a dry-plate works in Barnet, and experimented for himself with chronophotographic time-lapse studies of clouds. In December 1894, he was approached by the engineer and instrument-maker Robert Paul, who had begun to produce replicas of Edison Kinetoscopes and needed someone with photographic expertise to collaborate on the production of a camera. Together they developed a cine camera and by February 1895 made their first film experiment, showing their mutual friend Henry Short walking outside Clovelly Cottage, Acres' home in Barnet, wearing cricket whites. This untitled test film, never exhibited commercially, was the first true British film production. Acres operated the camera for this and all the succeeding Acres–Paul productions up to June 1895, made for exhibition in Paul's peepshow Kinetoscopes. They included *Oxford and Cambridge Boat Race*, *Rough Sea at Dover*, *The Arrest of a Pickpocket*, *The Carpenter's Shop*, *Boxing Kangaroo* and the film of the 1895 Derby (the last film the pair made together). Quite incompatible as personalities, Acres and Paul split acrimoniously that July, and continued to attack one another through the photographic press as each made their separate way toward projected film and the emergence of a British cinema business.

Acres travelled to Germany in June 1895, sponsored by the German chocolate company Stollwerck, and filmed several scenes, including the opening of the Kiel Canal. On his return, he turned his attention to film projection, evidently achieving success by the end of the year, for he gave the first public performance of projected film in Britain at Lyonsdown Photographic Club on 10 January 1896. Acres followed this up with a projected programme before the Royal Photographic Society on 14 January, indicating his preference for a high-minded, photographic approach. He was temperamentally unsuited for the commercial exploitation of motion pictures, but nevertheless began commercial film shows on 21 March with his Kineoptikon projector at Piccadilly Mansions, London. Acres would go on to enjoy modest success with sales of his Kineoptikon projector, though nothing to match the sales enjoyed by the financially savvy Paul, with his Theatrograph and Animatograph projectors.

Acres continued to take the elevated route, presenting a film performance at Marlborough House on 21 July 1896 by royal request, where he was assisted by Cecil Hepworth. But his position within the burgeoning British film business diminished. He turned to the production of celluloid film through his Northern Photographic Works, and in 1898 launched an ingenious miniature camera/projector, the Birtac, which employed 17.5mm film, hoping vainly to capitalise on a potential home-movie market.

Acres was involved in two intriguing controversies about what should or should not be filmed. On 27 June 1896, he filmed the visit of the Prince and Princess of Wales to the Cardiff Exhibition. Acres obtained his film by tearing a hole in the exhibition walls, reportedly by permission, though not from the royal party. His film included a brief scene where the Prince of Wales was seen to scratch his head, the sight of which caused Acres to be rebuked in some sections of the press, though the royal couple were happy enough to invite Acres to show the film at Marlborough House. More significantly, Acres was one of those who filmed the launch of HMS *Albion* on 21 June 1898, when a gantry collapsed, drowning many spectators. Paul was filming in a boat nearby, and Acres launched a furious attack upon him in the press, accusing Paul of gross insensitivity in choosing to exhibit his films (Acres had suppressed his). (In fact Paul's launch had saved a number of those who had fallen into the water.)

Acres swiftly slid from the scene, and ceased film production soon after 1900. He continued in film processing and celluloid manufacture, but was unlucky in business and was twice made bankrupt. He died in Whitechapel, London, on 27 December 1918. Acres and Paul personified the two sides of the coin offered by the invention of cinema: high-minded science versus hard-nosed commerce. While Acres hid behind science as an excuse for his business failures, Paul was able to reconcile the two disciplines and establish a leading position in moving pictures in Britain. Acres could boast some important 'firsts' in his film career, but he never built upon the head start that he gave himself as one of Britain's film pioneers.

(Luke McKernan)

BIBLIOGRAPHY: Barnes, John, *The Beginnings of the Cinema in England 1894–1901*, vols 1–5 (Exeter: University of Exeter Press, 1996–8); Brown, Richard, 'Birt Acres', in Stephen Herbert and Luke McKernan (eds), *Who's Who of Victorian Cinema: A Worldwide Survey* (London: BFI Publishing, 1996); Lange-Fuchs, Hauke, *Birt Acres: Der erste Schleswig-Holsteinische Film Pionier* (Kiel: Walter G. Muhlau, 1987); Lange-Fuchs, Hauke, *Der Kaiser, der Kanal und die Kinematographie* (Schleswig: Landesarchiv Schleswig-Holstein, 1997).

SELECTED FILMOGRAPHY: *Untitled test film*; *Oxford and Cambridge Boat Race*; *The Arrest of a Pickpocket*; *The Derby*; *Comic Shoeblack*; *Performing Bears*; *Boxing Kangaroo*; *The Carpenter's Shop*; *Rough Sea at Dover*; *The German Emperor Reviewing His Troops, Hamburg*; *Suevier Entering the Baltic Canal, Hamburg*; *The Kiel Canal* (aka *Opening of the Kiel Canal*); *Laying the First Stone on the Kaiser Wilhelm Monument*; *The Kaiser on the Bridge of the 'Hohenzollern'*; *Keystone Laying Ceremony of the Kaiser Wilhelm Canal*; *Procession Headed by the Kaiser on Horseback through the Streets of Berlin*; *Charge of Uhlan Lancers on the Tempelhof Feldt at Berlin*; *The Rialto Bridge at Venice*; *Dancing Girls* (aka *Skirt Dancers*); *Footpads*; *Studies in Animal Life at the Zoological Gardens*; *Skipping Dogs*; *Boxing Match*; *Tom Merry: Lightning Cartoonist* (series); *Steamer 'New York' in Dock*; *Steamer on Long Island Sound*; *Broadway, New York*; *Niagara Falls* (series); *Street Scene in Winter in Montreal, Canada* (1895); *London Street Scene*; *A Visit to the Zoo*; *Highgate Tunnel: Goods Train*; *Tower Bridge Working*; *Golfing Extraordinary – Five Gentlemen*; *Finsbury Park Station*; *Landing at Low Tide*; *The Derby*; *The Prince and Princess of Wales Arriving in State at the Cardiff Exhibition*; *Henley Regatta*; *Children Playing*; *Great Northern Railway: Departure of the East Coast Express*; *Ilfracombe, Capstone Parade*; *Yarmouth Fishing Boats Leaving Harbour*, *Yarmouth Sands* (aka *Children Playing, Yarmouth*); *Going for Sail*; *Steamer & Smack*; *Trip from Barnstable to Ilfracombe*; *Princess Maud's Wedding* (series); *A Surrey Garden*; *Brighton on a Bank Holiday* (series); *Military Tournament* (series); *Lancers on Horseback*; *Cycling in Hyde Park*; *A Corner of Barnet Fair*, *Pierrot and Pierrette*; *A Church Parade of Troops*; *Scrambling Urchins*; *H.R.H. The Prince of Wales*; *A Prize Fight by Jem Mace and Burke*; *The South Western Railway at Dover*, *The Lord Mayor's Show*; *Arrival of Lord Mayor at Law Courts*; *Gatwick Races* (series); *Bryant & May*; *An Unfriendly Call* (1896); *Practising for the Oxford and Cambridge University Boat Race*; *The Great Northern Mail Train Catching the Post Bags at Barnet*; *A Visit to the Northern Photographic Works, Barnet*; *Clouds*; *Queen Victoria's Diamond Jubilee Procession*; *Coaching in North Devon* (1897); *The Sheriff's Cup Football Match* (aka *Sheffield United v. Corinthians*); *Football Match, Crystal Palace*; *Launching of H.M.S. Albion*; *The Rifle Brigade at the Double*; *The Village Blacksmith* (aka *The Blacksmith's Shop*) (1898); *Charge of the 12th Lancers*; *S.S. 'New York' Leaving Southampton*; *Cockade Fight by 15th Hussars*; *Boxing Match*; *Football Match* (1899); *City Imperial Volunteers*; *The Men with the Long Knives*; *The Prince of Wales Inspecting the Honourable Artillery Company's New*

Guns; City Imperial Volunteers Embarking on the S.S. 'Pembroke Castle'; Imperial Yeomanry Shipping Their Horses on the 'Goth'; The Shipwreck; Oxford and Cambridge Boat Race; The Great Steeplechase, 1900 (aka *Steeplechasing at Sandown Park*); *Picking up the Mails at Sixty Miles an Hour; Water Polo Match; The Queen's Entry into Dublin; H.R.H. the Duke of Cambridge Bidding Farewell to His Yeomanry; Arrival of Sir George White at Portsmouth to Dine with the Naval Brigade; The Guns of the Naval Brigade being Entrained for the Royal Military Tournament; Naval Brigade Marching through Windsor; Japanese Battleship 'Asahi' Ashore off Southsea Beach; Military Medical Train Arriving at Netley Hospital; Panorama Taken in a Steam Crane* (1900).

ADAMS, Marcus

Marcus Adams studied dance with Ballet Rambert, going on to design and choreograph live shows and music videos for Meat Beat Manifesto, a group he had founded in 1986. He branched out into commercials, shorts and music promos, which led to Working Title and Universal backing his low-budget horror film *Long Time Dead*. The plot follows a well-worn path as eight young people bored with clubbing look for new excitement with a ouija board and summon up more than they bargained for. Paper-thin, disposable characters, anonymous settings and a clunky plot outweighed the occasionally deft suspense sequences, though the film proved a modest success at the UK box-office.

Adams grew more adventurous with his second feature *Octane*. Set in America but shot in Luxemburg, it charts the troubled relationship between a mother and daughter on a long night-time road journey, lurching into conspiracy and horror when the girl is sucked into a vampire cult. Though the cult's doings seem disappointingly unscary, *Octane* benefits from a sparkier cast and a less one-dimensional script than *Long Time Dead*, but proved less popular with the multiplex audience. *The Marksman*, a straight-to-video American action feature followed in 2005.

(Robert Murphy)

FILMOGRAPHY: *Android* (short); *Mr Ben* (short); *Long Time Dead* (2001); *Octane* (aka *Pulse*, UK/Lux, 2003).

ADLER, Carine (1948–)

Carine Adler was born in Rio de Janeiro, Brazil, in 1948. She came to the UK and trained at the National Film and Television School, graduating in the early 1980s. The concerns that would characterise her later work were already evident in her NFTS short film, *Jamie*, in which a schoolgirl escapes the oppressions of family through an affair with a married man. Adler has said that her next decade was largely absorbed by married life, though during this time she collaborated with Kate Saunders on an (unproduced) screenplay adapted from Saunders' novel *The Prodigal Father*, and scripted *Edward's Flying Boat* (1995), a documentary for Channel 4 about an eccentric millionaire.

In *Fever* (1994), made with backing from the BFI, Katrin Cartlidge plays a woman who compulsively seeks sexual encounters in reaction to her unresolved relationship with her mother. The same preoccupations were explored more fully in Adler's startling and internationally acclaimed 1997 debut feature, *Under the Skin*. Iris (Samantha Morton), in grief after her mother's death from cancer, embarks on a promiscuous binge that exposes her to escalating risk and degradation. Produced by the BFI and shot in Liverpool for only £655,000, *Under the Skin* stunned critics with its emotional rawness and spontaneous, poetic yet exact visual style (influenced by Wong Kar-Wai, Cindy Sherman and Nan Goldin) and Morton's extraordinary performance. While Adler's approach invites comparisons with France's Catherine Breillat, she shows scruples that Breillat does not. She conceived Iris as 'a character who was quite normal, but angry – not angry at the end, like in most women's films, but *at the beginning* . . . the connection between her anger, her grief and her sexual behaviour [had to be] clear' (Felperin, 1997, p. 16).

In March 2002, Adler married the Scottish Labour MP Dr John Reid, then Northern Ireland Secretary.

(Claire Monk)

BIBLIOGRAPHY: Andrew, Rachel, 'Under Her Skin', *Film Ireland* no. 62, Dec. 1997/Jan. 1998, pp. 16–17; Cook, Pam, 'Under the Skin', *Sight and Sound*, Dec. 1997, p. 56; Felperin, Leslie, 'Falling Angel', *Sight and Sound*, Dec. 1997, pp. 14–17.

FILMOGRAPHY: *Contrechamps* (short, 1979); *Pianists* (short); *Jamie* (short, 1980); *Touch and Go* (short, 1993); *Fever* (short, 1994); *Under the Skin* (1997).

ADUAKA, Newton (1966–)

Newton Aduaka was born in Ogidi, Eastern Nigeria, in 1966 but moved to Lagos in 1970 in the aftermath of the war in Biafra. He came to England in 1985, eventually enrolling at the London International Film School, where he made the short *Voices behind the Wall* before graduating in 1990. After leaving he worked as a sound recordist while attempting to raise finance for his feature film script about three troubled youths trying to break into the music business. In 1997 he set up Granite FilmWorks with his future wife Maria Elena L'Abbate and scored a festival success with the twenty-eight minute *On the Edge*, a harrowing drama about a man's attempt to save his girlfriend from drugs and prostitution.

Buoyed by the film's friendly reception, Aduaka and L'Abbate decided to go ahead with *Rage*, Aduaka's feature, despite inadequate funding. Production had to be halted halfway through shooting when money ran out, but enough was scraped together to finish the film. Ironically, in view of the tight schedule, a distribution deal was only struck after a substantial subplot involving a gay character (anathema to the intended hip-hop audience) was removed. Fraser Ayres' petulant rapper makes an unpromising hero, but Aduaka proves adept at dealing with the energetic delusions of youth, and his raw low-budget film-making captures something of the reality of the mean south London streets of Peckham. Though the film reached only a small audience and attracted mixed reviews, the scarcity of films about Britain's black community and the meagreness of *Rage*'s budget make its faults forgivable. Aduaka went on to direct *Funeral*, a short commissioned by the Cannes Film Festival, and his first African film, *Aïsha*.

(Robert Murphy)

BIBLIOGRAPHY: Aduaka, Newton, 'The Edge of Getting It On', *Black Film Bulletin*, Winter 1997/Spring 1998, pp. 26–7; Aduaka, Newton, 'The Cool Head behind *Rage*', *Black Filmmaker* vol. 3 no. 10, 2000, pp. 7, 29; Aduaka, Newton, 'Rage against the Machine', *Black Filmmaker* vol. 4 no. 12, July/Aug. 2001, pp. 7, 28; Charity, Tom, 'All the Rage', *Time Out*, 10 Jan. 2001, p. 66.

FILMOGRAPHY: *Voices behind the Wall* (short, 1988); *Carnival of Silence* (short, 1994); *On the Edge* (short, 1997); *Rage* (2000); *Funeral* (short, Fr/UK/Nig, 2002); *Aïsha* (short, Nig/Senegal, 2004).

AGLAND, Phil (1950–)

Phil Agland, who was born in Weymouth, Dorset, in 1950, is principally known as an award-winning maker of documentaries. He has frequently been drawn to projects that centre on cultures that fascinate Western audiences for their sense of otherness. His solitary cinema feature film brings something of this sensibility to the more familiar world of British heritage cinema.

Agland's early career was spent making wildlife films. As with his later documentaries, he usually acted as his own cameraman. His interest in the environment of the rain forest is evident in *Siarau: Life in the Mangrove Forest* (1983). Agland spent four years living with a Pygmy tribe in the Cameroon to film *Baka: The People of the Rainforest* (1987), which won him the Royal Anthropological Institute Film Prize. His broadly ethnographic approach was also brought to the subject of post-Cultural Revolution China in *China: Beyond the Clouds*, which Agland shot over five years.

His cinema version of Thomas Hardy's *The Woodlanders* might seem rather a jump from his other work, but Agland is as drawn to the unusual culture of lives lived in and around an English woodland as he is to Hardy's typically gloomy tale of repressed emotions. His sense of the strangeness of this environment, where the woodland is as strong a character as the human protagonists, gives the films a quality apart from that of other Hardy adaptations.

More recently he returned to the documentary format with two series – *Shanghai Vice* (1999) and *A French Affair* (2003) – made, like much of his other work, with the support of Channel 4.

(Robert Shail)

BIBLIOGRAPHY: Montgomery, Isobel, 'Welcome to China', *Guardian* G2 Section, 26 Feb. 1999, pp. 10–11; Rees, Jasper, 'Chopping out Hardy's Emotional Dead Wood', *Independent* Eye Section, 6 Feb. 1998, pp. 4–5.

FILMOGRAPHY: *The Woodlanders* (1997).

AKOMFRAH, John (1957–)

Born in Accra, Ghana, on 4 May 1957, John Akomfrah is one of five children of Ghanaian political activists. He was educated at local schools in west London and at Portsmouth Polytechnic, where he graduated in sociology in 1982. Akomfrah is best known for his work with the London-based media workshop the Black Audio Film Collective, which he co-founded in 1982 with the objectives of addressing issues of black British identity and developing media forms appropriate to this subject matter.

Akomfrah's work takes a deliberately questioning approach to documentary film. His debut as a director, the controversial and influential *Handsworth Songs* (1986), reworks documentary conventions to explore the history of the contemporary British black experience: the film won seven international prizes, including the prestigious John Grierson Award. *Testament* is a portrait of an African politician forced into exile after a *coup d'état*. The emergence of Black Power in Britain is the inspiration for *Who Needs a Heart?* and *Seven Songs for Malcolm X*. The BFI production *Speak Like a Child* is a psychological drama set in Northumberland and marks a departure from earlier themes.

Besides making theatrical films, Akomfrah has directed many television programmes, including one about Martin Luther King for the *Reputations* series (1997) and another on Louis Armstrong for the BBC arts programme, *Omnibus* (1999). A critic as well as a film-maker, Akomfrah has written widely about African cinema. He has been a member of the Arts Council Arts Film Committee, and is currently a BFI Governor.

(Annette Kuhn)

BIBLIOGRAPHY: Akomfrah, John, 'Wishful Filming', *Black Film Bulletin* vol. 1 no. 2, Summer 1993, p. 14; Auguiste, Reece, '*Handsworth Songs*: Some Background Notes', *Framework* no. 35, 1988, pp. 4-8; Malik, Sarita, 'Beyond the Cinema of Duty? The Pleasures of Hybridity: Black British Films of the 1980s and 1990s', in Andrew Higson (ed.), *Dissolving Views* (London: Continuum, 1996); Marks, Laura U., 'Ghosts of Stories: Black Audio Film Collective's *Who Needs A Heart?*', *CineAction!* no. 36, 1995, pp. 53–62; Petley, Julian, 'Possessed by Memory', *Monthly Film Bulletin*, Sept. 1989, pp. 260–1.

FILMOGRAPHY: *Handsworth Songs* (1986); *Testament* (1988); *Who Needs a Heart?* (1991); *Seven Songs for Malcolm X* (1993); *Speak Like a Child* (1998).

ALDRICH, Robert (1918–1983)

Robert Aldrich emerged as one of the most distinctive and forceful film-makers among the new generation who helped transform American cinema in the 1950s with their defiantly individual vision. His work was marked by a pessimistic iconoclasm, increased in intensity by an often elaborate cinematic style that sometimes verged on the melodramatic.

Born on 9 August 1918 in Cranston, Rhode Island, USA, Aldrich entered the industry in 1941 as a production clerk with RKO. Over the next ten years he undertook various roles including production manager, associate producer and assistant director to such major figures as Joseph Losey and Jean Renoir. He also worked as a writer and director in television in the early 1950s before making his feature film debut with *Big Leaguer* in 1953. Over a subsequent career spanning thirty years and virtually the same number of films, Aldrich maintained a fiercely independent approach, often working with his own production company, acting as his own producer and taking a hand in the writing of scripts.

Aldrich's films frequently centre on isolated, estranged figures whose rebellion against 'the system' leads them into violent confrontation. The belligerent, aggressive tone of the narrative is frequently matched by visual stylisation, typified by his classic film noir *Kiss Me Deadly* (US, 1955). The film has sometimes been read as an allegory of McCarthyism, and Aldrich frequently used genre subjects to construct social metaphors: there are strong Vietnam War undercurrents in his Western *Ulzana's Raid* (US, 1972), for example.

Aldrich came to Europe in 1958 to make two Second World War films: *Ten Seconds to Hell*, a co-production between Hammer and Seven Arts starring Jack Palance and Jeff Chandler; and *The Angry Hills* (1959) for the British producer Raymond Stross, an unusual film about an American journalist (Robert Mitchum) caught between the Greek Resistance and the Nazis. He returned to Britain – and the war – in 1967 for *The Dirty Dozen*, a violent action film displaying the concern with male groups and masculinity apparent in many of his films, from *Attack* (1956) to *Emperor of the North Pole* (1973). Though technically British – it was one of the last major films to come out of MGM's Borehamwood Studios – *The Dirty Dozen* has an all American cast and is less relevant to British film culture than *Too Late the Hero* (US, 1970), a fascinatingly grim study of divergent British and American values during the Second World War starring Michael Caine and Cliff Robertson.

Aldrich's only entirely British production is *The Killing of Sister George*. Adapted from the successful stage play by Frank Marcus, the film deals with the then taboo subject of lesbianism, centring on an actress (Beryl Reid) who is axed from her role as a lovable district nurse in a television soap opera and consequently loses her much younger lover (Susan George). The film was sufficiently ground-breaking in its representation of lesbian lovemaking to run into censorship difficulties, but it is probably better read as a cousin to Aldrich's gothic melodramas *Whatever Happened to Baby Jane?* (US, 1962) and *Hush . . . Hush, Sweet Charlotte* (US, 1964) or as an example of his ongoing concern for the individual at odds with an intolerant society, than as an intervention into sexual politics.

(Robert Shail)

BIBLIOGRAPHY: Combs, Richard, *Robert Aldrich* (London: BFI, 1978); Silver, Alain, *Robert Aldrich: A Guide to References and Resources* (Boston, MA: G. K. Hall, 1979); Silver, Alain and James Ursini, *Whatever Happened to Robert Aldrich?: His Life and Films* (New York: Limelight Editions, 1995).

FILMOGRAPHY (UK only): *Ten Seconds to Hell* (US/UK, 1958); *The Angry Hills* (1959); *The Dirty Dozen* (US/UK, 1967); *The Killing of Sister George* (1968).

ALEXANDER, Donald (1913–1993)

Donald Alexander was born in London on 26 October 1913, of Scottish descent. While studying at Cambridge University, he made a short film, *Rhondda* (1935), about the desperate poverty of the South Wales miners. Paul Rotha was so impressed with his footage of miners scrambling for coal on a windswept slag heap that he asked Alexander to join his company, Strand, and to shoot similar images for *Today We Live* (Ralph Bond/Ruby Grierson, 1937). He went on to make *Eastern Valley*, about a Monmouthshire agricultural collective striving to meet food and clothing needs and combat problems caused by widespread unemployment. It followed the classic Strand three-part formula, showing first an agricultural idyll in pre-Industrial Revolution days, then aspects of employment and housing problems, and lastly, a solution in which economic problems abate and the workers are given more control over their own destiny. Alexander made extensive use of brisk montage, suggesting his affinity with Russian agit-prop movies of the 1920s and 30s. He later returned to Wales to make *Life Begins Again* for Rotha and the Ministry of Education, an impressively affirmative movie about rehabilitation following traumatic wartime injuries.

For the Films of Scotland Committee Alexander directed *The Wealth of a Nation*, exploring Scotland's social and industrial recovery after the Depression. In the 1940s his democratic Socialism informed films on health, local government and education (notably in his study of a Devon school's assimilation of evacuees, *Our School*), and suggested remedies for pre-war ills. Many of them were made for DATA Film Productions, a successful directors' co-operative. He also produced *China* (1943) and *Birthday* (1945), directed by his wife, Budge Cooper, and several of the National Coal Board's Mining Review films from 1948 to 1951. He went on to manage the NCB Film Unit for a decade, making many training and educational films, before becoming Director of Audiovisual Aids at Dundee University. He retired from the post in 1979, and died in Inverness on 20 July 1993.

(David Berry)

BIBLIOGRAPHY: Berry, David, *Wales and Cinema: The First 100 Years* (Cardiff: University of Wales Press, 1994); McBain, Janet and Kevin Cowle (eds), '*With an Eye to the Future*'. *Donald Alexander and Budge Cooper – Documentary Film-makers* (Glasgow: Scottish Screen, 1997); Rotha, Paul, *Documentary Diary: An Informal History of the British Documentary Film, 1928–1939* (London: Secker and Warburg, 1973).

FILMOGRAPHY: *Rhondda* (1935); *People in the Park* (1936); *Eastern Valley; Mites and Monsters* (1937); *A Nation's Health Centre; The Wealth of a Nation* (1938); *Dundee; A Job to Be Done* (1940); *All Those in Favour, Our School; Five and Under, A Few Ounces a Day* (1941); *Life Begins Again* (1942); *Cotton Come-Back* (1946); *Here's Health* (1948); *The First Years* (1951); *Rawdon Reborn* (1955); *Workstudy Experiment at Nafodynrys Colliery* (1958; rel. 1963); *Huwood Slicer* (1958); *Powered Supports* (1960); *People Like Us* (1962); *The Four M's* (1966); *Some New Face End Methods* (1971).

ALLÉGRET, Marc (1900–1973)

Marc Allégret was born in Basle, Switzerland, on 22 December 1900. Although expected to take up a diplomatic career, he developed an early interest in cinema and made his first film, *Voyage au Congo*, in 1927 while travelling in Africa as secretary to André Gide. He entered the industry in 1930 as the set designer on Robert Florey's *L'Amour chante* and *Le Blanc et la noir*, and co-directed, with Augusto Genina, *Les Amours de minuit*. In the 1930s he became a highly successful director with films such as *Fanny* (1932), *Aventure à Paris* (1936) and *Gribouille* (1937). During the German occupation of France from 1940 to 1944, he continued to direct, but was also able to contribute to the Resistance.

In 1947 Allégret directed the first of his three films in England. *Blanche Fury*, made for Cineguild, the company set up by David Lean, Ronald Neame and Anthony Havelock-Allan, is a Victorian melodrama, with Valerie Hobson and Stewart Granger as a couple scheming to murder her husband. The idea was to replicate the success of the Gainsborough costume melodramas; but the combination of Guy Green and Geoffrey Unsworth's Technicolor photography, John Bryan's imaginative set design and Allégret's subtle direction proved to have less popular appeal and cost a great deal more than the Gainsborough films, and *Blanche Fury*'s lack of commercial success put considerable strain on Cineguild.

Blanche Fury is an ambitious and complex film; Allégret's other British efforts are much less significant. *The Naked Heart* is a disappointing version of Louis Hémon's novel, *Maria Chapdelaine*, despite or perhaps because of the odd combination of Roger Vadim and Julian Maclaren-Ross on the script. *Blackmailed* features Dirk Bogarde and Mai Zetterling, in a psychological drama that is more of a character study than a thriller, and is undermined by its restricted budget. Allégret returned to France, where he continued making films until 1970. He died in Paris on 3 November 1973.

(Kevin Gough-Yates)

BIBLIOGRAPHY: Durgnat, Raymond, 'Some Lines of Inquiry into Post-War Crimes', in Robert Murphy (ed.), *The British Cinema Book* (London: BFI, 2001); McFarlane, Brian, *An Autobiography of British Cinema* (London: Methuen, 1997); Porter, Vincent, 'Strangers in a Foreign Land', *La Lettre de la Maison Française d'Oxford* no. 11, Autumn 1999, pp. 59–74.

FILMS (UK only): *Blanche Fury* (1947); *The Naked Heart* (aka *Maria Chapdelaine*); *Blackmailed* (1950).

ALLEN, Kevin (1962–)

Kevin Allen was born in Swansea on 15 September 1962, the younger brother of comedy actor Keith Allen. He appeared in small roles in Comic Strip films including *Eat the Rich* (Peter Richardson, 1987) and *The Strike* (Peter Richardson, 1988), and played DC Kray in the sitcom *The Thin Blue Line* (1995), while pursuing a parallel career as a television documentary director. For the BBC, he made *On the March with Bobby's Army* (1991), a disturbing video diary where he accompanied football hooligans supporting the British team around Europe, and *Rotten to the Core* (1993), exploring a case of police corruption that led to two youths being wrongly jailed for murder.

Corrupt policemen and rebellious youths are at the centre of Allen's feature debut *Twin Town*. The film's executive producers had hoped to repeat the success of their black and scurrilous Scottish comedy *Trainspotting* (Danny Boyle, 1996). But *Twin Town*'s lively, anarchic celebration of vulgar Welsh low-life was dismissed by critics as nasty and sordid, and a raucous marketing campaign failed to bring in large audiences. Allen's next film was a spoof documentary, *The Big Tease*, about a gay Scottish hair stylist attending the World Freestyle Hairdressing Competition in Los Angeles. A more amiable film than *Twin Town*, it allowed Allen to draw on and parody his experience in non-fiction, poke fun at camp subculture and further explore contemporary Celtic identity. *Agent Cody Banks: Destination London*, a quickly produced sequel to *Agent Cody Banks* (Harald Zwart, 2003) with Frankie Muniz as an adolescent special agent pretending to be a musical prodigy, makes one nostalgic for the scurrilous humour of *Twin Town*.

(Alan Burton)

BIBLIOGRAPHY: Allen, Kevin, 'The Birth of *Twin Town*', *Radio Times*, 19–25 Apr. 1997, pp. 50–1; Berry, Dave, 'Feature Future', *FFOCWS*, Apr. 1997, p. 11; Wallace, Sara, 'Writer-Director Kevin Allen', *Premiere* (UK), Apr. 1997, p. 25.

FILMOGRAPHY: *Twin Town* (1997); *The Big Tease* (UK/US, 1999); *Agent Cody Banks: Destination London* (US, 2004).

ALLEN, Lewis (1905–2000)

Alfred Lewis Allen was born in Oakengates, Shropshire, on 25 December 1905. Prior to entering films with Paramount in the USA in the early 1940s, he had a stage career in Britain as actor and director for impresario Gilbert Miller. His first directorial stint was the 1942 documentary short, *Freedom Comes High*, and his reputation was made with his feature debut, the romantic and still-chilling ghost story, *The Uninvited* (1944), lushly set in a Hollywood Cornwall, and making memorable use of the (in every sense) haunted beauty of Gail Russell. He also directed Russell in an engaging version of Cornelia Otis Skinner's *Our Hearts Were Young and Gay* (1944) and another British-set thriller, *The Unseen* (1945). The latter was less striking than *The Uninvited*, but both demonstrated a talent for decorative gothic, with frightened ladies at the mercy of threats earthly and otherwise.

Allen never again had a Hollywood assignment as rewarding as his first feature, but he never made a dull film. There are spirited melodramas like *Desert Fury* (1947), with a film-stealing turn from Mary Astor as a gambling-hall proprietress, attractive romantic comedies like *The Perfect Marriage* (1946), police thrillers like *Appointment with Danger* (1949), a lively costume romp, *At Sword's Point* (1952) and several tough-guy thrillers including *A Bullet for Joey* (1955).

He made only three films in his native England, but one is a minor masterpiece. *So Evil My Love* (1948), for Paramount-British, appeared in the wake of the popular melodramas emanating from Gainsborough Pictures, but this tale of passion and betrayal, told in a marvellously decorative visual style, proved too glossy for the critics and too hard-hitting for audiences seeking escapism. In perhaps her finest role, Ann Todd plays a missionary's widow who falls in with a charming trickster (Ray Milland, who starred several times for Allen) on her way back to England, and lets her hair down, figuratively as well as literally, as she descends into treachery, blackmail and murder. Todd's chiselled blonde beauty was never put to better, more morally ambiguous use and she is genuinely moving in her final moments of revenge and contrition. Milland's bland charm, too, was brilliantly exploited as the duplicitous lover and there are superb performances from Geraldine Fitzgerald, Raymond Huntley and Martita Hunt, all seeming to know exactly the kind of enterprise in which Allen has placed them.

Sadly, his other two British films are almost unalloyed flops. *Another Time, Another Place* (1958) is a turgid romance, which makes poor use of Sean Connery as a BBC war correspondent and Lana Turner as the mistress who attempts to console his wife when he is killed. *Whirlpool* (1959), with Juliette Greco on the run from her criminal associates, abounds in gnomic utterances about the nature of love, but has no breath of life or style. Allen finished his career in US television, and died in California on 3 May 2000.

(Brian McFarlane)

BIBLIOGRAPHY: 'Lewis Allen', *Film Dope* no. 39, Mar. 1988, pp. 12–13; 'Who's Who in Hollywood', *Film Daily*, 14 Feb. 1947, p. 8.

FILMOGRAPHY (UK only): *So Evil My Love* (1948); *Another Time, Another Place* (1958); *Whirlpool* (1959).

ALTMAN, Robert (1925–)

Robert Altman was born in Kansas City on 20 February 1925. A long apprenticeship in industrial documentaries, series television and a couple of low-budget movies preceded his breakthrough with the army comedy *M.A.S.H.* in 1970. Altman, now aged forty-five, cashed in on his newly acquired A-list credentials with a string of critically acclaimed movies – *McCabe & Mrs Miller* (1971), *The Long Goodbye* (1973), *Thieves Like Us*

(1974), *California Split* (1974), *Nashville* (1975) – which established him in the pantheon of American directors. He also made *Images* (1972), a psychological thriller shot in Ireland for the British company Hemdale. Susannah York plays a children's author recuperating from a nervous breakdown at her childhood home in Ireland, where she avenges herself on phantoms of her previous lovers. Altman filmed his own script with mesmeric skill, the chilling shot of York watching her own *alter ego* enter the family home followed by the reverse shot from her double setting the edgy tone of the film. The seamless incorporation of readings from a children's book York was writing at the time is a characteristic example of Altman's improvisational openness.

By the end of the 1970s Altman's star was fading both critically and commercially. Spurned by Hollywood, he worked from New York and Paris to complete a series of low-budget stage, television, cable and film works. In Paris he shot one of the best segments for the British opera compendium *Aria* (1987), setting his performance of Jean-Philippe Rameau's 'Les Boréades' in an eighteenth-century madhouse. In 1988 the British independent, Zenith Productions, helped kick-start Altman's television masterpiece *Tanner '88* – a searing look at the Democratic primaries using a revolutionary mix of real and fictional characters shot with imaginative verve during the actual campaign. Further critical acclaim was heaped on the feature version of his British television miniseries about the life of painter Vincent Van Gogh, *Vincent & Theo* (1990), an intelligent and convincing study of the artistic process.

This hiatus in Altman's career was ended by the crowd-pleasing Hollywood satire, *The Player* (1992). He returned to Britain in 2001 for *Gosford Park*, where he makes splendid use of a constantly moving camera to capture the performances of his cast – Maggie Smith, Michael Gambon, Kristin Scott Thomas, Stephen Fry, Eileen Atkins *et al.* – in a beautifully written pastiche of the country-house murder mystery.

(Richard Dacre)

BIBLIOGRAPHY: McGilligan, Patrick, *Robert Altman: Jumping off the Cliff* (New York: St Martin's Press, 1989); Sterritt, David (ed.), *Robert Altman Interviews* (Jackson: University Press of Mississippi, 2000).

FILMOGRAPHY (UK only): *Images* (1972); *Aria* ('Les Boréades' section, 1987); *Vincent & Theo* (1990); *Gosford Park* (2001).

AMALOU, J. K.

J. K. Amalou was born in France, but came to England to study at the London International Film School and stayed on to produce short films, documentaries and pop promos. Back in France, he co-produced *La Belle Époque* (Gavin Millar, 1995), based on a script by François Truffaut, for French television, but he returned to Britain to direct *Hard Men*, the first in the late 1990s' cycle of British gangster films. A blackly comic low-budget feature film concerning a gangland hard man (Vincent Regan) who wants to retire now he has become a daddy, it was generally dismissed as too derivative of the films of Tarantino and Scorsese. The script, which Amalou wrote himself, deals superficially with its themes of honour, loyalty and betrayal, and the characters are thinly drawn. Like many of the subsequent British gangster films, flashes of visual inventiveness, designer violence and a fascination with underworld mores hardly make up for shapeless construction and glib conclusions, and Amalou's sentimental attitude towards his underworld psychopaths lacked the wit and verve of Guy Ritchie's *Lock, Stock and Two Smoking Barrels* (1998).

(Alan Burton)

BIBLIOGRAPHY: Merrill, Paul, 'Hard Men', *Empire*, Mar. 1997, p. 41; Chibnall, Steve, 'Travels in Ladland: The British Gangster Film Cycle 1998–2001', in Robert Murphy (ed.), *The British Cinema Book*, 2nd edn (London: BFI, 2001); Tse, David, 'Hard Men', *Sight and Sound*, Feb. 1997, p. 47.

FILMOGRAPHY: *Hard Men* (1996).

AMBER FILMS (1969–)

The Amber Film Collective was founded in the north-east of England in 1969 with a remit to record working-class life in the region. Many of the similar workshops set up in the late 1960s and 70s have disappeared, but Amber has continued to produce highly regarded work. Part art cinema, part documentary, Amber's work can be seen to build upon a tradition of enabling working-class self-expression that goes back to *Bugle Blast*, *Penguin New Writing* and the work of Mass Observation during the Second World War.

Amber's first film, *Maybe* (1969), had its origins as a student film by Murray Martin and Graham Denman. Having obtained financial support from Northern Arts (Amber's only continuous sponsor), they then produced *Launch* in 1973, documenting the construction and launch of a tanker at the Wallsend shipyards. Produced with a budget of only £400, *Launch* exemplifies Amber's approach to aesthetics, politics and working practices. The influence of the British documentary movement and even the newsreels is clear, but there are important differences. There is, for example, no narration, and the marginalisation of the VIPs who would conventionally be the focus of attention shifts political significance onto the representation of labour and community.

With funding from Channel 4 under the terms of the ACTT Workshop Declaration, Amber produced its first feature film, *Seacoal*, in 1985. The result of two years living and working with the region's seacoalers, the film incorporates elements of straight documentary, improvised sketches and fully dramatised reconstructions. Contrary to the charge of romanticism that is sometimes levelled against Amber, films such as *Seacoal* strive for an honest depiction of the frequently harsh realities of working-class life on the margins; a depiction that certainly pays tribute to its dignity but that is far from romantic. Furthermore, the films stand as important social documents as these different ways of life are steadily eradicated. This is not to suggest, however, that Amber's work simply follows a blend of various traditions. They consistently engage critically with the heritage of documentary and neo-realism and have not been afraid to experiment with anti-realist practices. *T. Dan Smith* (1987), for example, is a documentary that combines archive footage, interviews with Smith himself and others, and a dramatised version of the Poulson political corruption scandal that broke in 1972. All Amber's films show a respect for the audience and a political stance that is interrogative without being didactic.

Amber has survived for a period of over thirty years, in spite of the erratic financial context for independent, regional and workshop production. A commitment to accessibility, in marked contrast to the anti-narrative stance of much of the workshop movement, along with its geographical remoteness from the metropolitan media and its sometimes curious funding arrangements (including owning both a racehorse and a pub), have all played a part in ensuring Amber's survival. *In Fading Light* (1989), *Dream On* (1991), *The Writing in the Sand* (1991) and *Eden Valley* (1994), made at a time when radical film-making elsewhere in Britain was at a low ebb, were particularly significant achievements. It is unfortunate that a distribution and exhibition system increasingly aligned with mainstream commercial product has restricted opportunities for audiences to view films such as Amber's ambitious *Like Father* (2001), which interweaves the personal and the political with authenticity and emotional force, but it is still a cause for celebration that Amber continue to make original, accessible and relevant films. (Martin Hunt)

BIBLIOGRAPHY: *Amber/Side Catalogue & History of Work Since 1968* (Newcastle upon Tyne: Amber/Side, 1987) – see also <www.amber-online.com>; Dickinson, Margaret, Ann Cottringer and Julian Petley, 'Workshops: A Dossier', *Vertigo*, Spring 1993, pp. 16–20; Dickinson, Margaret (ed.), *Rogue Reels: Oppositional Film in Britain, 1945–90* (London: BFI Publishing, 1999); Fitzgerald, Theresa, 'Shoptalk', *Sight and Sound*, Summer 1988, pp. 163–9; Hattenstone, Simon, 'I Once Put Our Entire Grant on a Horse', *Guardian*, 8 June 2001; Petley, Julian and John Pym, 'Film Cities', *Sight and Sound*, Winter 1989/90, pp. 8–12; Reber, Deborah, 'Collective Insights: Four Groups that have Withstood the Test of Time', *Independent Film & Video Monthly*, Mar. 1996, pp. 22–5; Young, Neil, 'Forever Amber: An Interview with Ellin Hare and Murray Martin of the Amber Film Collective', *Critical Quarterly*, Winter 2001, pp. 61–80.

FILMOGRAPHY: *Maybe*; *A Film* (1969); *Jellyfish*; *Launch* (1973); *Mai*; *High Row* (1974); *Bowes Line* (1975); *Last Shift* (1976); *Glassworks* (1977); *That's Not Me*; *Laurie* (1978); *Quayside* (1979); *Tyne Lives* (1980); *The Filleting Machine* (1981); *Byker*; *Keeping Time*; *News from Durham*; *Where Are We Going?* (1983); *Why Support the Miners?*; *Beyond the Vote*; *Behind the Vote* (1984); *Can't Beat It Alone*; *The Sadler Story*; *Seacoal* (1985); *The Box*; *The Privatisation Series*; *Double Vision* (1986); *T. Dan Smith* (1987); *From Marks and Spencer to Marx and Engels*; *Shields Stories* (1988); *In Fading Light* (1989); *Dream On*; *The Writing in the Sand* (1991); *Eden Valley*; *Letters to Katja* (1994); *The Scar* (1997); *Like Father* (2001); *Shooting Magpies* (2005).

AMBROSE, Anna (1945–1985)

Anna Ambrose was born in London in 1945, the daughter of puppeteer and folk singer Elwyn Ambrose. She studied film at the Royal College of Art from 1971 to 1974 and won the first prize at the Knokke International Experimental Film Festival in 1975 with her short film *Noodlespinner*. She showed herself the most original of her generation of avant-garde film-makers with *Phoelix*, a forty-seven minute film made with backing from the BFI Production Board. At first the film seems to be an exploration of the way in which women have been regarded as fantasy objects, but it evolves into something much less formulaic. The female narrator, a middle-class actress working in a Soho 'posing club', fantasises a past for her elderly and eccentric neighbour, taking the film back to the 1920s and Kate Meyrick's notorious 43 Club. Back in the present, her inability to comprehend him as he rabbits on about the silk wall-coverings and fake columns that adorn his rich private world provokes her into demonstrating her striptease act and destroying the fragile relationship they have established. This development might show the sad, unbridgeable gulf between them, but it also provides a cathartic moment for two characters in danger of becoming embalmed by their own portentousness, and the film as a whole has a quirky *joie de vivre* rarely seen in the British avant-garde.

A more straightforward documentary about the Communist composer Alan Bush followed. Ambrose continued her study of idiosyncratic old men in *Honour, Profit and Pleasure*, an ambitious study of George Frederic Handel made to celebrate the tercentenary of his birth. Ambrose encourages a finely judged performance from Simon Callow as Handel, devises wonderful settings for his music and wittily employs eighteenth-century theatrical conventions in presenting his life and work.

Anna Ambrose died of cancer on 18 May 1985, five weeks before *Honour, Profit and Pleasure* was shown on Channel 4. Her husband, documentary film-maker Michael Whyte, acted as executive producer on the film.

(Robert Murphy)

BIBLIOGRAPHY: Adair, Gilbert, 'Gilbert Adair from London', *Film Comment*, Sept./Oct. 1981, pp. 6–8; Forman, Stanley, 'Obituary – Anna Ambrose', *Film and TV Technician*, July/Aug. 1985, p. 13; Petley, Julian, 'The Art of Patronage', *Listener*, 20 June 1985, p. 28.

FILMOGRAPHY: *Noodlespinner* (short, 1975); *Phoelix* (1979); *Alan Bush: A Life* (doc., 1983); *Honour, Profit and Pleasure* (1985).

AMIEL, Jon (1948–)

Jon Amiel was born in London on 20 May 1948. He studied English Literature at Cambridge University and spent most of the 1970s working in theatre before being taken on at the BBC as a script editor. He trained as a director and established his reputation with a documentary drama, *The Silent Twins* (1985). This led producer Kenith Trodd to ask him to direct Dennis Potter's drama series, *The Singing Detective* (1986). Amiel's first feature film, *Queen of Hearts* (1989), was less ambitious, a modest, likeable Anglo-Italian fable set in the East End of London, and it was the international renown of *The Singing Detective* that provided his ticket to Hollywood.

Amiel's career in America has included a bewilderingly eclectic selection of films: an adaptation of Mario Vargas Llosa's *Aunt Julia and the Scriptwriter*, with Barbara Hershey and Keanu Reeves in the title roles; *Sommersby*, a reworking of *The Return of Martin Guerre* (Daniel Vigne, 1982), with Richard Gere in the Gerard Dépardieu role; *Copycat*, a 'feminist' thriller about a serial killer with Sigourney Weaver and Holly Hunter; *The Man Who Knew Too Little*, a spoof spy film starring Bill Murray, Alfred Molina and Joanne Whalley; *Entrapment*, a big-budget caper movie with Sean Connery and Catherine Zeta-Jones; and *The Core*, a science-fiction movie about an expedition to burrow to the centre of the Earth.

Amiel's genre-roaming oeuvre highlights his versatility as a director, and though his Hollywood films indicate little of his directorial personality, he has established himself as an inventive professional, very capable of surviving in the dangerous waters of the international film industry.

(Lez Cooke)

BIBLIOGRAPHY: Murrell, Rachel, 'Direction', *Televisual*, Mar. 1995, pp. 45–6.

FILMOGRAPHY: *Queen of Hearts* (1989); *Aunt Julia and the Scriptwriter* (aka *Tune in Tomorrow*, US, 1990); *Sommersby* (US, 1993); *Copycat* (US, 1995); *The Man Who Knew Too Little* (aka *Agent Null Null Nix*, US, 1997); *Entrapment* (US, 1999); *The Core* (US, 2003).

AMYES, Julian (1917–1992)

Julian Charles Becket Amyes was born in Cambridge on 9 August 1917 and joined the Crown Film Unit after the end of the war. After playing small roles in such films as *High Treason* (Roy Boulting, 1951) and *Mandy* (Alexander Mackendrick, 1952), he became a television director. His only cinema films were *A Hill in Korea* (1956) and *Miracle in Soho* (1957). The former is a reasonably tough film about that largely forgotten war, grimly realistic in Freddie Francis' black-and-white cinematography; the latter is saccharine whimsy, despite a script by Emeric Pressburger, set in a scarcely believable Soho. Amyes made no more films for the cinema but he became a major figure in television. He joined Granada in 1961, becoming Head of Drama and then Head of Programmes. When he 'retired' in 1976 he resumed his career as a director, making an impressive series of literary adaptations for the BBC up until *Murder at the Vicarage* in 1992. He died in London on 26 April 1992, following a stroke.

(Brian McFarlane)

BIBLIOGRAPHY: 'British Feature Directors: An Index to Their Work', *Sight and Sound*, Autumn, 1958, p. 289; 'Director Who "Retired" and Found New Career' (interview), *Television Today*, 6 Dec. 1984, p. 32.

FILMOGRAPHY: *A Hill in Korea* (1956); *Miracle in Soho* (1957).

ANDERSON, David (1952–)

Among recent British animators, David Anderson's work stands out for its persistent surreal fantasy and the multiplicity of techniques used to cast a spell. Stop-motion model animation blends with orthodox cel animation; live-action footage comes unadorned, or garnished with pixillation, xerography, colourful felt-tip smears and imagery from the paintings of Ernst and Magritte. His background reflects this diversity. Born in London in 1952, David Alexander Anderson studied at the Bath Academy of Art from 1970 to 1973, spent time in Scotland on puppet theatre projects and also worked as a freelance photographer. In 1977 he enrolled at the National Film School, training as a cameraman and director; his student work climaxed in the fourteen-minute *Dream Land Express*, completed in 1982.

The most benign of Anderson's films, *Dream Land Express* takes its inspiration from a children's book of 1927 by the illustrator H. R. Millar. In the original, three boys share dream adventures aboard a fantasy train before waking safely in bed. Typically, in Anderson's version there is no return to safety: at the end, still dreaming, the boy hero faces the glinting firmament alone, frozen in existential wonder. Later work strengthened Anderson's command of his complex technical resources. *Dreamless Sleep* (1986), made for the Channel 4 series *Sweet Disaster*, spent ten wordless minutes subtly conveying a couple's fear in the face of an incoming nuclear blast. In the same year he worked alongside Aardman Animations and the Brothers Quay animating the seminal music video *Sledgehammer* (Stephen Johnson, 1986), winner of nine MTV awards.

Anderson secured his own bread-and-butter assignments when he joined the Redwing Film Company, producing successful commercials for the Royal Bank of Scotland, Mastercard and Eurostar, among other clients. The company also backed his personal projects *Deadsy* (1989) and *Door* (1990), two extraordinary and commanding films produced in conjunction with the author Russell Hoban, presented on television and video under the umbrella title *Deadtime Stories for Big Folk*. Hoban's soundtrack commentaries, written in the corrupted urban language of his futuristic novel *Riddley Walker*, inspired the boldest use yet of Anderson's dream imagery and mixed-media methods. *Deadsy*, five minutes long, fuses the lure of violence, power and sexual desire in the spectacle of the Grim Reaper acquiring additional weaponry after undergoing a sex change. The film's surface mood is jocular, but its implications are alarmingly black. The six-minute *Door*, by turns comic and scary, documents activities in a floating globe filled with doors, keys and a bickering couple whose actions appear to lead to what Hoban's narrator calls 'the end of snivvelyzashuns'.

Along with *Deadsy*, the cryptic apocalyptic warning of *Door* won numerous awards. His next film, *In the Time of Angels* (1994), a gentler fable about a woman able to undo her fate by reversing time, met with less exposure. Anderson's eminence as a stop-motion animator and latter-day Surrealist later led to a visiting professorship at Harvard University, but in the decade since *In the Time of Angels* it has not eased the business of turning projects into completed films.

(Geoff Brown)

BIBLIOGRAPHY: *Deadtime Stories for Big Folk* (TV doc., dir. David Jeffcoat, 1990, included on the Connoisseur/BFI video *David Anderson: Works on Film*).

FILMOGRAPHY: *Dream Land Express* (1982); *Dreamless Sleep* (1986); *Deadsy* (1989); *Door* (1990); *In the Time of Angels* (1994).

ANDERSON, Lindsay (1923–1994)

Born in Bangalore, India, on 17 April 1923, the younger son of a Scottish army officer, Anderson was named after the Australian poet, Adam Lindsay Gordon, who was much admired by his mother. He was educated at Cheltenham College, where he began a life-long friendship with Gavin Lambert, drawn together by their love of American films; sixty years later, Lambert would write an elegant account of Anderson's (and his own) life and work. Following Second World War service as a cryptographer with the Army's Intelligence Corps, Anderson read classics at Wadham College, Oxford. Here he co-founded with Lambert the short-lived but influential critical journal *Sequence*, in which he set down his passionately held views on John Ford and Humphrey Jennings, on Hollywood musicals and – with almost uniform severity – on contemporary British films. In *Sequence* he indulged the luxury of 'saying exactly what [he] liked', and maintained the habit, sometimes to his own cost. He was not a man who changed his mind, and the passions of those early years informed the rest of his life.

Sequence ran to fourteen polemical issues, after which Anderson continued to write for journals prepared to publish his often irascible views. He argued for a cinema that would be much more socially and morally aware than the middlebrow and middle-class British cinema of the day. In the late 1940s he began making short documentary films, consciously focusing on aspects of British life neglected by Britain's feature film industry. The most famous of these early films is *Thursday's Children*, an Academy Award-winning documentary about teaching deaf children, co-directed with Guy Brenton and photographed by Walter Lassally.

In 1956 Anderson launched 'Free Cinema' as an umbrella name for a series of film programmes he organised with Karel Reisz and Tony Richardson at the National Film Theatre. They screened their own documentaries (such as Anderson's affectionate portrait of the old Covent Garden Market, *Every Day Except Christmas*) alongside the exciting new films being made by young European directors like François Truffaut, Claude Chabrol and Roman Polanski. Its ethos of realist social concern fused with personal vision was to inform the New Wave of the early 1960s.

Anderson made his feature film debut later than Richardson and Reisz, but *This Sporting Life* (1963) is arguably the most powerful and significant of these films. Based on David Storey's novel it is an excoriating account of an emotionally inarticulate rugby player, whose aggression serves him well on the field but not in dealing with the deeply inhibited woman he loves. The film is set around Wakefield, Yorkshire, where Anderson had shot his first four documentaries, and its realism on sporting-field, in locker-room, street and pub is impeccable; but it is the rendering of the man's bruising inner life that is most remarkable.

This Sporting Life is now acknowledged as a masterpiece, but when it was released it was much less commercially successful than Reisz's *Saturday Night and Sunday Morning* (1960) and Richardson's *A Taste of Honey* (1962), and there was a five-year gap until Anderson's next feature, *if . . . .*. In between, Anderson made two curious, little-seen short films: *The White Bus*, which was one of a planned triptych of art films that never came to pass and was released alone as a short; and the Polish documentary, *The Singing Lesson/Raz, Dwa, Trzy*. *if . . . .* (1968) proved the one indisputable commercial success of Anderson's fitful screen career. Filmed at his old school, Cheltenham College, which was not made privy to the full nature of its iconoclasm, the film struck a very resonant chord in the year of student uprisings. Its image of the rebellious public schoolboy, Mick Travis (Malcolm McDowell), armed to the teeth on the chapel roof, became a treasured icon for disaffected youth. *if . . . .* railed against the debilitating class system that was Anderson's recurring *bête noire*, and, winding its exhilarating way between black-and-white and colour sequences, it exposed hypocrisy in school, church and the military. It remains Anderson's key denunciation of the ills of British society.

Anderson retained Travis/McDowell as the protagonist of two further 'state-of-the-nation' films: the picaresque Brechtian satirical fable, *O Lucky Man!* (1973), with Travis as a Candide-like coffee-salesman, and *Britannia Hospital* (1982), with Travis as a reporter and the nation now, metaphorically, an ill-run hospital, rather than a public school. Neither was much liked on release – his pessimistic socialism was out of step with the times – but hindsight may teach us to value them better.

His only other feature films were the fine, cinematically fluent 1974 adaptation of David Storey's play, *In Celebration*, which Anderson had directed at the Royal Court Theatre, and his elegiac *The Whales of August* (1987), which paid tribute to two of the screen's greatest stars, Lillian Gish and Bette Davis. Anderson never found it easy to bring his projects to screen fruition, partly because he acquired a reputation for being difficult and uncompromising, but he survived on his own terms. When producers attempted to force his artistic adventurousness into commercial channels – as in his documentary, *Wham in China: Foreign Skies* (1986) – he disowned the film.

Anderson was also a noted theatre director. He joined the English Stage Company at the Royal Court in 1957 and was responsible for several very significant productions there, including David Storey's *Home* (1970), *The Farm* (1973) and *Life Class* (1974). For television, he directed the savage Canadian miniseries, *Glory! Glory!* (1989), which dealt swingeing blows at television evangelism, and he acted in several films, including *Chariots of Fire* (1981). He wrote two valuable books about film, *The Making of a Film: The Story of 'Secret People'* (1952) and *About John Ford* (1981). He summed up his own life and work in a wry, good-natured documentary *Is That All There Is?*, made for BBC Scotland in 1992. In British cinema's history, Anderson is a lonely, curmudgeonly figure, but inspiring in his uncompromising integrity. He died in Périgueux, France, on 30 August 1994.

(Brian McFarlane)

BIBLIOGRAPHY: Aldgate, Anthony, 'Defining the Parameters of Quality Cinema for "the Permissive Society": The British Board of Film Censors and *This Sporting Life*', in Anthony Aldgate, James Chapman and Arthur Marwick (eds), *Windows on the Sixties* (London: I. B. Tauris, 2000); Hedling, Erik, *Lindsay Anderson: Maverick Film-Maker* (London: Cassell, 1998); Lambert, Gavin, *Mainly about Lindsay Anderson* (London: Faber and Faber, 2000); Richards, Jeffrey, 'The Revolt of the Young: *If . . .*', in Jeffrey Richards and Tony Aldgate, *Best of British* (Oxford: Basil Blackwell, 1983); Ryan, Paul (ed.), *Never Apologise: The Collected Writings of Lindsay Anderson* (London: Plexus, 2004); Sussex, Elizabeth, *Lindsay Anderson* (London: Studio Vista, 1969); Sutton, Paul (ed.), *The Diaries of Lindsay Anderson* (London: Methuen, 2004).

FILMOGRAPHY: Non-fiction: *Meet the Pioneers* (1948); *Idlers that Work* (1949); *Three Installations*; *Wakefield Express* (1952); *O Dreamland*; *Thursday's Children* (co-dir. Guy Brenton, 1953); *Trunk Conveyor* (1954); *Green and Pleasant Land*; *The Children Upstairs*; *Hundred Thousand Children*; *Henry*; *Foot and Mouth*; *£20 a Ton*; *Energy First* (1955); *Every Day Except Christmas* (1957); *March to Aldermaston* (co-dir. with ten other directors, 1959); *The Singing Lesson* (1967): Fiction: *This Sporting Life* (1963); *The White Bus* (1967); *if . . . .* (1968); *O Lucky Man!* (1973); *In Celebration* (1974); *Britannia Hospital* (1982); *The Whales of August* (US, 1987).

ANDERSON, Michael (1920–)

Michael Joseph Anderson was born into an acting family in London on 30 January 1920. After appearing in a few films in 1936 he joined Elstree Studios as a production runner, graduating to assistant director by 1938.

During the war, while serving with the Royal Signals Corps, he met Peter Ustinov, and after assisting him on *School for Secrets* (1946) and *Vice Versa* (1947), they co-wrote and co-directed *Private Angelo* (1949). The cinematographer was Erwin Hillier, who would go on to make ten films with Anderson before retiring in 1968. After joining the Associated British Picture Corporation and making a number of modest films, Anderson emerged from obscurity with *The Dam Busters* (1955). The performances of Richard Todd as stiff-upper-lip war hero Guy Gibson and Michael Redgrave as Barnes Wallis, the scientist convinced of the viability of his improbable bouncing bomb, made the film stand out from other war films. Anderson's handling of the action sequences – a convincing synthesis of special effects and documentary footage – is masterly, and though the film was far more successful in Britain than the USA, he was recruited by Mike Todd for the international blockbuster *Around the World in Eighty Days*.

Rather than pursuing a career in Hollywood, Anderson returned to the UK and made two more films with Richard Todd: *Yangste Incident*, another true story, this time about the capture of the British frigate HMS *Amethyst* by Chinese Communists in 1949; and *Chase a Crooked Shadow*, a psychological mystery that made the usually heroic Todd come across as convincingly sinister. Anderson's facility for handling suspense led to him being asked to take over *The Wreck of the Mary Deare* when Alfred Hitchcock pulled out; and his good working relationship with the film's star, Gary Cooper, encouraged them to work together again on *The Naked Edge*, where Cooper is shown throughout in an equivocal way, teasing audiences as to whether or not he is a psychotic killer. In collaboration with Hillier, Anderson allowed his occasionally flamboyant and aggressive visual style full reign in a film that was clearly a big influence on the Italian *giallo* films.

Anderson, Hillier and Richard Todd were reunited on *Operation Crossbow*, another wartime story that, like *The Dam Busters*, looked at the development of a new type of bomb and that made heavy use of special effects, especially in the film's fiery climax. Unlike *The Dam Busters*, the epic scale of *Operation Crossbow* overwhelms the characters, but its successor, *The Quiller Memorandum*, is quirkily original. Anderson had lived in Germany as a child and Hillier had trained at the Ufa studios in Berlin and worked on Fritz Lang's *M* (1931). They present Berlin in a uniquely knowledgeable way as the setting for this offbeat tale of espionage and Nazi resurgence.

Subsequently Anderson emigrated to Canada and has only occasionally returned to the UK, most notably for the courtroom drama *Conduct Unbecoming* and for another psychological thriller, *Dominique*. He has continued to work in the USA and Canada, in many different genres, for both television and cinema, his most recent film being the 1999 children's fantasy, *The New Adventures of Pinocchio*.

(Sergio Angelini)

BIBLIOGRAPHY: Baker, Bob, 'Michael Anderson', *Film Dope* no. 1, Dec. 1972; Bramwell, Roy C., 'Tea Boy to Top', *ABC Film Review*, Jan. 1957, p. 15; Heelas, Terence, *Michael Anderson Interviewed* (fifteen-page transcript of 1967 BBC interview, available at the BFI National Library, London); Oughton, Frederick, 'Bantam-Heavyweight Director', *Films and Filming*, Apr. 1955, p. 13; Ramsden, John, *The Dam Busters* (London: I. B. Tauris, 2002).

FILMOGRAPHY: *Private Angelo* (co-dir. Peter Ustinov, 1949); *Waterfront* (US: *Waterfront Women*, 1950); *Hell Is Sold Out*; *Night was Our Friend* (1951); *Will Any Gentleman . . .?*; *The House of the Arrow* (1953); *The Dam Busters* (1955); *Around the World in Eighty Days* (US); *1984* (1956); *Chase a Crooked Shadow*; *Yangtse Incident* (US: *Battle Hell*) (1957); *Shake Hands with the Devil*; *The Wreck of the Mary Deare* (US, 1959); *All the Fine Young Cannibals* (US, 1960); *The Naked Edge* (1961); *Flight from Ashiya* (US); *Wild and Wonderful* (US, 1964); *Operation Crossbow* (1965); *The Quiller Memorandum* (1966); *The Shoes of the Fisherman* (US, 1968): *Pope Joan* (US re-edited version: *The Devil's Imposter*, 1972); *Conduct Unbecoming*; *Doc Savage: The Man of Bronze* (US) (1975); *Logan's Run* (US, 1976); *Orca* (US, 1977); *Dominique* (1978); *Murder by Phone* (UK: *Bells*, Can, 1980); *Second Time Lucky* (NZ, 1984); *Separate Vacations* (Can, 1986); *The Jeweller's* Shop (Can, 1988); *Millennium* (1989); *Summer of the Monkeys* (Can, 1998); *The New Adventures of Pinocchio* (US, 1999).

ANDERSON, Paul (1965–)

Paul William Scott Anderson was born in Banbury, Oxfordshire, on 2 March 1965. After writing the comic detective series *El C.I.D.* (Tom Clegg) for Granada Television between 1990 and 1992, he directed a low-budget feature film, *Shopping*. Anderson stated that 'My aim has always been to make a movie that would kick some ass in this country – the sort of film you could open in Leicester Square rather than a couple of art-house cinemas' (Roddick, p. 26). Despite an aggressive marketing campaign, a topical subject (ram-raiding) and a photogenic young cast including Jude Law and Sadie Frost, *Shopping* was too stylised to appeal to audiences and took little more than £200,000 at the box office. As a calling-card film, however, it was enormously successful and Anderson was quickly snapped up by Hollywood to make the slick big-budget science-fiction horror film, *Mortal Kombat*. Surprisingly, Anderson's next film, *Event Horizon*, was made in Britain, albeit for an American company, as was his television film *The Sight* (2000). Though he returned to Hollywood to make the $75 million *Soldier*, Anderson and his production partner, Jeremy Bolt, raised $30 million in Europe for *Resident Evil* (like *Mortal Kombat* based on a best-selling computer game) without having an American distribution deal, and he remains highly unusual among British film-makers in his aspirations towards high-concept, big-budget film-making beyond Hollywood. He is credited as Paul W. S. Anderson, to avoid confusion with the American Paul Thomas Anderson.

Anderson chose to write and produce rather than direct *Resident Evil II* (Alexander Witt, 2004). He was tempted onto 20th Century-Fox science-fiction territory for *AVP: Alien vs. Predator*. The resulting film contained some striking moments – and took nearly $40 million at the American box office – but added little of substance to either the *Alien* or *Predator* series of films.

(Peter Hutchings)

BIBLIOGRAPHY: Minns, Adam, 'Close Up: Paul Anderson and Jeremy Bolt', *Screen International*, 8 Feb. 2002, p. 22; Roddick, Nick, 'Welcome to the Multiplex', *Sight and Sound*, June 1994, pp. 26–8; Salisbury, Mark, 'Never Mind the Bollocks', *Empire*, Oct. 1993, pp. 78–84.

FILMOGRAPHY: *Shopping* (1993); *Mortal Kombat* (US, 1995); *Event Horizon* (US, 1997); *Soldier* (US, 1998); *Resident Evil* (UK/Fr/Ger, 2002); *AVP: Alien vs. Predator* (UK/US/Ger/Cz, 2004).

ANNAKIN, Ken (1914–)

Ken Annakin's fifty-year career as a director generated a remarkably diverse body of work including documentaries, comedies,

Disney adventures, 'Empire' films, impressively mounted war epics and television movies. Annakin himself identified their common denominator as a 'fascination with human beings and their endless variations of behaviour in different settings' (Annakin, July 1998, p. 24). Like his fellow wartime documentary-makers Pat Jackson, Jack Lee and Philip Leacock, Annakin made a successful transition into feature film-making, retaining a concern for realism while displaying considerable technical skill. Though it would be difficult to identify a true masterpiece among his films, a number show a keen and welcome regard for humanity and the common man.

Ken Annakin was born on 10 August 1914 in Beverley, Yorkshire. He entered the civil service on leaving school, but left to travel to Australia, New Zealand and the USA. Returning home, he sold insurance, cars and advertising before joining the RAF as a flight mechanic. Invalided out in 1942 following injuries sustained in the Liverpool blitz, he worked for Sydney Box's Verity Films as a camera operator on RAF training films and documentaries for the Ministry of Information, the British Council and the army. In 1942, while working on *We Serve*, an army recruitment film for women directed by Carol Reed, he was offered the post of assistant director. His directorial debut was *London 1942*, a morale-boosting documentary about Londoners under fire. Other recruitment and information films followed until 1946 when Box, by then Head of Gainsborough Pictures, invited him to direct his first feature.

Holiday Camp (1947) introduced the Huggett family to the British public and perfectly caught the post-war mood. At a time when melodramas and 'spiv' thrillers dominated cinema screens, the *Holiday Camp* combination of down-to-earth characters and everyday dramas offered a refreshing slice of working-class life. Such was the Huggetts' popularity that the family, led by Jack Warner and Kathleen Harrison, appeared in three further films, although none were as successful as the first. Other films made for Gainsborough included *Miranda*, based on Peter Blackmore's popular play about a flirtatious mermaid, and Annakin's sensitive interpretation of 'The Colonel's Lady', one of a portmanteau of W. Somerset Maugham stories in *Quartet*. Another Maugham compendium, *Trio*, followed, for which he directed 'The Verger' and 'Mr Know-All'.

Annakin's career prospered in the 1950s. He directed *Hotel Sahara*, a comedy-drama set in North Africa during the Second World War, with Peter Ustinov as the wily proprietor who changes allegiances whenever new armies arrive, and several other comedies followed. For Disney's British operation he made four enjoyable adventure films – *Swiss Family Robinson*, *The Story of Robin Hood and His Merrie Men*, *The Sword and the Rose* and *Third Man on the Mountain*. In between came three 'Empire' films: *The Planter's Wife*, set in Malaya (though filmed mostly in Ceylon due to Malaya's political instability); *The Seekers*, set in New Zealand; and *Nor the Moon by Night*, set in South Africa. All were motivated less by a desire to explore Britain's colonial legacy than by Annakin's enjoyment of working in far-flung places – a typical British attitude to Empire in the 1950s. Annakin regards *Across the Bridge* (1957), adapted from a novel by Graham Greene, as his best film of this period. Rod Steiger gives a powerful performance as an embezzler who adopts the identity of his double only to find that the man is a wanted murderer; the film, shot in Texas and Mexico, showed that Annakin was more than capable of delivering tense, compelling drama.

Two of Annakin's most notable films of the 1960s were war epics: *The Longest Day* and *Battle of the Bulge*. In *The Longest Day*, a star-studded Anglo-American production about the Normandy landings, he was given responsibility for the British and French sequences and all the studio scenes. Producer Darryl Zanuck insisted the film be made in black and white, which helped Annakin maintain a realist ethos. Attracted by his ability to handle large-scale action, producer Milton Sperling assigned him to direct *Battle of the Bulge*, a worthy attempt to deal fairly with the German counter-attack that temporarily halted the Allied advance across Europe in the winter of 1944. The same skills were used for different ends in *Those Magnificent Men in Their Flying Machines* and *Monte Carlo or Bust!*, two comedy epics whose international casts became overshadowed by gloriously old-fashioned planes and cars.

Given his experience and international standing, Annakin's career from the 1970s onwards has been a disappointment. *Paper Tiger*, with David Niven, muddled through its mixed bag of action and sentiment; there were films for young audiences that missed their target (*The Pirate Movie*, *The New Adventures of Pippi Longstocking*) and various American television movies. The bankruptcy of its producer prevented post-production on his biggest late endeavour, *Genghis Khan*, shot in eastern Asia in the early 1990s, only packaged for release in 2004. But his earlier, purely British endeavours, *Holiday Camp* and the Maugham contributions especially, still provide well-crafted, well-observed entertainment. Annakin put his varied career in a nutshell when he declared simply, 'I make films for audiences' (*Films and Filming*, May 1962, p. 12).

(Margaret Butler)

BIBLIOGRAPHY: Annakin, Ken, *National Film Theatre Programme*, July 1998, pp. 24–7; Annakin, Ken, 'In Praise of Producers', *Sight and Sound*, Nov. 1998, p. 69; Annakin, Ken, *So You Wanna Be a Director?* (Sheffield: Tomahawk Press, 2001); Box, Muriel, *Odd Woman Out* (London: Leslie Frewin, 1974); McFarlane, Brian, *An Autobiography of British Cinema* (London: Methuen, 1992); 'Who's Who of the Critics: The Screen Answers Back', *Films and Filming*, May 1962, pp. 12–14.

FILMOGRAPHY: Non-fiction shorts: *London 1942*; *Cooks*; *The Sixteen Tasks of Maintaining Vehicles* (1942); *A Ride with Uncle Joe* (1943); *Black Diamonds*; *The New Crop*; *Combined Cadets* (1944); *A Farm in the Fens*; *Crop Rotation*; *Make Fruitful the Land*; *Pacific Thrust*; *Three Cadets*; *Know Your Enemy: The Japanese Army and How It Became What It Is Today* (1945); *We of the West Riding*; *It Began on the Clyde*; *English Criminal Justice* (1946); *Turn It Out* (1947).

Feature films: *Holiday Camp*; *Broken Journey* (1947); *Here Come the Huggetts*; *Miranda*; *Quartet* ('The Colonel's Lady' episode, 1948); *Vote for Huggett*; *Landfall*; *The Huggetts Abroad* (1949); *Trio* ('The Verger' and 'Mr Know-All' episodes); *Double Confession* (1950); *Hotel Sahara* (1951); *The Planter's Wife*; *The Story of Robin Hood and His Merrie Men* (1952); *The Sword and the Rose* (1953); *The Seekers*; *You Know What Sailors Are* (1954); *Value for Money* (1955); *Loser Takes All*; *Three Men in a Boat* (1956); *Across the Bridge* (1957); *Nor the Moon by Night* (1958); *Third Man on the Mountain* (UK/US, 1959); *Swiss Family Robinson* (UK/US, 1960); *Very Important Person*; *The Hellions* (1961); *Crooks Anonymous*; *The Fast Lady*; *The Longest Day* (co-dirs. Bernhard Wicki/Andrew Marton, US 1962); *The Informers* (1963); *Battle of the Bulge* (US); *Those Magnificent Men in Their Flying Machines* (1965); *The Long Duel* (1966); *The Biggest Bundle of Them All* (US/It, 1968); *Monte Carlo or Bust!* (US: *Those Daring Young Men in Their Jaunty Jalopies*, UK/Fr/It, 1969); *The Call of the Wild* (1972); *Paper Tiger* (1974); *The 5th Musketeer* (Aus, 1977); *Cheaper to Keep Her* (US, 1980); *The Pirate Movie* (Austral, 1982); *The New Adventures of Pippi Longstocking* (Swe/US, 1988); *Genghis Khan* (co-dir. Antonio Margheriti, It, 1992; rel. 2004).

ANSTEY, Edgar (1907–1987)

Edgar Harold MacFarlane Anstey was born on 16 February 1907 in Watford, Hertfordshire, and educated at Watford Grammar School. He joined the Empire Marketing Board Film Unit in 1931, where he edited Robert Flaherty's *Industrial Britain* (1933). In 1934 Anstey was recruited to establish the Shell Film Unit. After making a film about Croydon airport, he left and worked with Arthur Elton on his two best-known films, *Housing Problems* and *Enough to Eat?*, made for the British Commercial Gas Association and the Gas, Light and Coke Company.

Following a spell with the *March of Time* newsreel between 1936 and 1938, Anstey spent the war years directing and producing documentaries for the Ministry of Information while also acting as film critic for the *Spectator* and broadcasting on BBC Radio. In 1949 he established British Transport Films for the British Transport Commission. During his twenty-five years in charge, he produced over five hundred films, receiving the Academy Award for Best Short Subject for *Wild Wings* (1966), produced in collaboration with Sir Peter Scott's Wildfowl Trust. He finally retired in 1975.

Anstey was a mainstay of the British film establishment: he was twice Chairman of the British Film Academy, a Governor of the British Film Institute, President of the Scientific Film Association and Chairman of the Children's Film Foundation. He was awarded the OBE in 1969. He died on 26 September 1987, three weeks before the death of fellow documentary pioneer Basil Wright. At a National Film Theatre tribute, Sir Denis Forman stated 'It was largely due to the dedication of Anstey and Wright, their stamina, and above all their teaching power, that the documentary movement flourished through three decades' (Hardy, p. 8). Margaret Elton, writing of Anstey's later work as producer in the 1950s and 60s, observed that, 'At last it became clear that he could spin the gossamers as well as forge the anchors of the mind' (Elton, p. 14), a fitting tribute to a film-maker with a lifelong commitment to the service of art and science.

(Martin Hunt)

BIBLIOGRAPHY: Anstey, Edgar, 'What is a Documentary?', *Colonial Cinema*, June 1945, pp. 31–3; Anstey, Edgar, 'The New Realism in Feature Films', BBC Third Programme, 12 Oct. 1947 (transcript held in the BFI National Library, London); Anstey, Edgar, 'Television, Film and Reality', *Film Forum* vol. 8 no. 3, 1953, pp. 3–9; Anstey, Edgar, 'How We Use Films: 7 – For British Transport', *The Film User*, May 1954, pp. 213–15; Anstey, Edgar, 'How Films Serve the World's Biggest Employer', *Industrial Screen*, May/June 1959, pp. 92–4; Anstey, Edgar, 'Film and Television: Barometers of Social and Industrial Change', *Video and Film Communication*, Feb. 1975, pp. 8–12; Anstey, Edgar, 'The Grierson Influence', *Undercut*, Summer 1983, pp. 10–20; Elton, Margaret, 'Obituary: Edgar Anstey', *Independent*, 2 Oct. 1987, p. 14; Hardy, Forsyth, 'Tributes to Anstey and Wright', *Scotsman*, 7 Mar. 1988, p. 8; Macdonald, Kevin and Mark Cousins, *Imagining Reality: The Faber Book of Documentary* (London: Faber and Faber, 1996), pp. 122–5.

FILMOGRAPHY: *Uncharted Waters*; *Eskimo Village* (1933); *Airport* (1934); *Men behind the Meters*; *Housing Problems* (co-dir. Arthur Elton); *Dinner Hour*; *How Gas Is Made*; *Enough to Eat?* (co-dir. Arthur Elton) (1935); *On the Way to Work*; *Stand by for Work* (1936); *March of Time 2nd Year No. 10*; *March of Time Vol. 4 Issue 4: Alaska's Salmon War* (1937); *March of Time Vol. 4 Issue 8: Arms and the League*; *March of Time Vol. 5 Issue 1: Father's Divine Deal* (1938); *Wealth from Coal*; *Wartime Factory*; *Speed up and Welfare* (1940).

ANTONIONI, Michelangelo (1912–)

Michelangelo Antonioni was born in Ferrara, Italy, on 29 September 1912. Having made his debut as a film director in 1943, Antonioni became world famous in the early 1960s for three films – *L'avventura* (1960), *La notte* (1961) and *L'eclisse* (1962) – notable for their denial of the satisfactions of conventional narrative, their psychological subtlety and their focus on opaquely enigmatic female protagonists.

On the strengths of Antonioni's artistic reputation, Carlo Ponti and MGM signed a deal with him for three English-language films, *Blow-up* (1966), *Zabriskie Point* (1969) and *The Passenger* (1975), guaranteeing them wide international distribution. *Blow-up*, generally considered one of Antonioni's masterpieces, was inspired by Argentinian novelist Julio Cortázar's short story 'Las babas del diablo'. The film combined Antonioni's usual artistic themes – the inability of people to communicate with each other, the lack of enduring love relations and the illusions of the surface – with a 'Swinging London' setting. The film is ostensibly a murder mystery, with the photographer gradually finding incriminating details in his photo enlargements (blow-ups), but in accordance with Antonioni's usual directorial style the mystery is never solved. *Blow-up* attracted audiences well

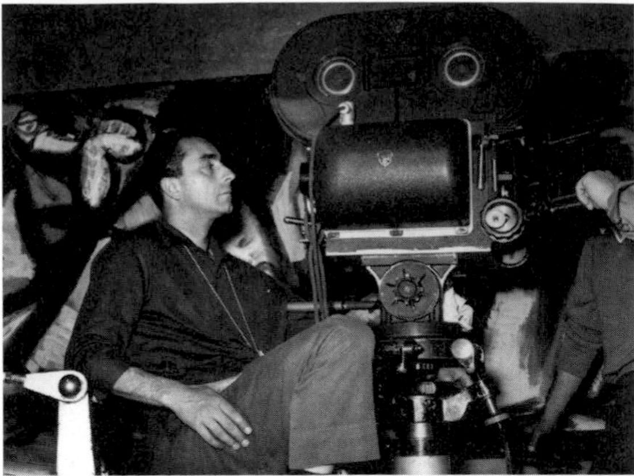

beyond those for art cinema, not least because of the film's unusually frank representation of eroticism and nudity.

The Passenger, a Franco-Italian-Spanish production scripted by Mark Peploe and Peter Wollen, was another story of psychological alienation. Jack Nicholson plays a television journalist who steals the identity of a dead man, later revealed to be an illegal arms dealer, in order to escape his emotionally empty life in London. The film uses the romantic notion of the '*doppelgänger*' to depict the essential irony of existence, and ends in an impressively long take where the protagonist is assassinated – although the audience is hardly aware of it – by people who think they are murdering his double.

Antonioni's English-language films contributed to his outstanding reputation among film historians, critics and scholars. In 1995, he received an honorary Academy Award and an honorary Fellowship from the BFI.

(Erik Hedling)

BIBLIOGRAPHY: Brunette, Peter, *The Films of Michelangelo Antonioni*, Cambridge Film Classics (Cambridge: Cambridge University Press, 1998); Chatman, Seymour, *Antonioni; or, The Surface of the World* (Berkeley, Los Angeles, and London: University of California Press, 1985); Rohdie, Sam, *Antonioni* (London: BFI, 1990).

FILMOGRAPHY (UK only): *Blow-up* (1966).

APPLETON, Dudi (1969–)

Dudi Appleton was born in Belfast on 7 May 1969. The child of Irish and Israeli parents, Appleton has always insisted on his outsider status. After graduating from Oxford, he followed an eclectic career path (manual labour, the Israeli army and acting), before teaming up with writer Jim Keeble to form Hot Film Productions. In 1995 they made the short films *A Sort of Homecoming* and *On Holy Ground*. In 1997 Appleton and Keeble scripted *Gabriela*, from the novel by Jorge Amado, and a further television film, *Game of their Lives* (1999), about the US World Cup soccer team of 1950.

In 2001 Appleton broke into theatrical features with *The Most Fertile Man in Ireland*. Written by Keeble, the film is one of a number of recent productions to view the Northern Irish troubles as material for black comedy. In this instance, the humour revolves around the discovery by nerdy Éamonn Manly (Kris Marshall) of his extraordinary fertility. Chaos enters an already surreal narrative in the figure of local Loyalist vigilante 'Mad Dog' Wilson (James Nesbitt), who 'persuades' Éamonn to offer his services to the dwindling Protestant community, thus fathering a generation of mixed-religion children.

Appleton has also acted in *Mary Shelley's Frankenstein* (Kenneth Branagh, 1994) and the television film *On Dangerous Ground* (Lawrence Gordon Clark, 1996).

(Ruth Barton)

BIBLIOGRAPHY: McCarthy, Gerry, 'Fecund Sight', *Sunday Times* Culture – Irish Edition, 22 July 2001, pp. 10–11; O'Sullivan, Tadhg, 'Most Fertile Man in Ireland', *Film West* no. 43, Spring 2001, p. 56.

FILMOGRAPHY: *A Sort of Homecoming* (short); *On Holy Ground* (short) (1995); *The Most Fertile Man in Ireland* (UK/Ir, 2001).

APTED, Michael (1941–)

Michael Apted was born in Aylesbury on 10 February 1941, the son of a building society surveyor. Through scholarships, he was able to attend the City of London School and then go on to read history and law at Cambridge, where his friends included Trevor Nunn and John Cleese. In 1963 he joined a six-month apprenticeship scheme at Granada Television in Manchester, and stayed with the company for the next seven years. During this period, Apted went from researcher to director and worked on over fifty productions, from early episodes of *Coronation Street* to dramas written by Jack Rosenthal, Alun Owen and Colin Welland.

One of Apted's first jobs after completing the training scheme was as a researcher on Granada's flagship documentary series *World in Action*, where he made his mark with a special edition entitled *Seven Up*, which charted the fortunes of a group of seven-year-old British children. Such was its success that follow-up programmes have been made every seven years since then, with Apted as director, producer and presenter. The latest in the series, *49 Up*, was shown in 2005.

In 1970 Apted decided to go freelance and spent the next two years directing plays for the BBC as well as the ITV companies. He made his cinema debut in 1972 with *The Triple Echo*, an adaptation of an H. E. Bates story set in 1942 about a young soldier who deserts and falls in love with a farmer's wife who tries to hide him by passing him off as her sister. The film was not a commercial success, but Apted was chosen by producer David Puttnam to direct *Stardust*, a sequel to Claude Whatham's *That'll Be the Day* (1973), which looked at how the character played by David Essex becomes a pop music icon in the 1960s as part of a band not too different from the Beatles.

After the success of *Stardust*, Apted, Puttnam and screenwriter Ray Connolly reunited to adapt Connolly's novel *Trick or Treat*, which began shooting in Rome with Stéphane Audran and Bianca Jagger in the lead roles. However, filming was never completed and Apted moved on to *The Squeeze*, a thriller about an alcoholic ex-detective (Stacy Keach) who has to try and rescue his ex-wife (Carol White) and her daughter from a gang of thieves. Although the film is made up of all the familiar ingredients of the private eye genre – sex, violence, a comic foil for the fallen hero (a comparatively low-key performance by Freddie Starr) – Apted's eye for detail and his interest in female characters give the film a unique resonance, as does his ability to shift dramatic gears effectively.

Agatha, Apted's next film, is a much more decorous and gentle crime film, a fictionalised embroidering of the true case of the disappearance of mystery writer Agatha Christie in 1926. Largely set in Harrogate and filmed in many of the real locations involved, such as the Old Swan Hotel and the Bath Spa, it benefits from the atmospheric cinematography of Vittorio Storaro and a first-rate performance by Vanessa Redgrave. But it proved to be a troubled production for Apted. One of the producing partners was First Artists, an actors' co-operative set up by, among others, Dustin Hoffman, whose insistence on being inserted into the film as Christie's (fictitious) love interest necessitated many rewrites.

In 1980 Apted was invited to America by Ray Stark to work on a project called *BAM* that never came to fruition. While there, however, he was offered the chance to make *Coal Miner's Daughter*, a biopic of country singer Loretta Lynn for which Sissy Spacek would win an Academy Award and which proved to be a tremendous commercial and critical success. Subsequently Apted chose to move to California, returning regularly to work in the UK and oversee the education of his children. In 1982 he made one of the first Channel 4 films to get a cinema release, *P'tang, Yang, Kipperbang*, a story about children growing up after the war that reunited him with David Puttnam and Jack Rosenthal.

Since then, Apted has continued to make films, television programmes and documentaries in the USA, but he was also responsible for two big-budget productions made in Britain: the nineteenth James Bond film *The World Is Not Enough* and an adaptation of the Robert Harris novel about the Bletchley Park code-breakers, *Enigma*. In the former, one can see Apted's hand in his imaginative use of locations (the real MI6 building and the Millennium Dome in London, the Guggenheim Museum in Bilbao) and the greater role played by women in the narrative. *Enigma* was a long time in the making, with funds eventually coming from the Netherlands, Germany, the UK and the USA. Made with Apted's consummate professionalism, the film is most notable for its intelligent assimilation of Hitchcockian motifs and situations.

Apted's varied output has consistently exhibited his interest in socially relevant themes, while his sympathetic treatment of women can be seen throughout his work: from *The Triple Echo* in 1972 to the Jennifer Lopez vehicle *Enough* thirty years later. His willingness to return to documentaries, such as *Incident at Oglala*, which explores the factual basis of his hard-hitting feature film, *Thunderheart*, displays an active, questioning intelligence rarely found among mainstream Hollywood directors.
(Sergio Angelini)

BIBLIOGRAPHY: Connolly, Ray, *Stardust Memories* (London: Pavilion, 1983); 'One on One: Michael Apted and Alan Parker', *American Film*, Sept. 1990, pp. 42–5; Petrie, Duncan (ed.), *Inside Stories: Diaries of British Film-Makers at Work* (London: BFI, 1996); Roddick, Nick, 'The Rover's Return', *Stills* no. 10, Feb./Mar. 1984, pp. 29–33; Walker, Alexander, *National Heroes* (London: Harrap, 1985).

FILMOGRAPHY: *The Triple Echo* (aka *Soldier in Skirts*, 1972); *Stardust* (1974); *The Squeeze* (1977); *Agatha* (1979); *Coal Miner's Daughter* (US, 1980); *Continental Divide* (US, 1981); *P'tang, Yang, Kipperbang* (US: *Kipperbang*, 1982); *Gorky Park* (US, 1983); *Firstborn* (US, 1984); *Bring on the Night* (doc., 1985); *Critical Condition* (US, 1987); *Gorillas in the Mist* (US, 1988); *Class Action* (US, 1991); *Thunderheart* (US); *Incident at Oglala* (doc., US) (1992); *Blink* (US); *Nell* (US); *Moving the Mountain* (doc., US) (1994), *Extreme Measures* (US, 1996); *The World Is Not Enough* (US/UK, 1999); *Enigma* (UK/US/Ger/Neth, 2001); *Enough* (US); *Lipstick* (US, short) (2002).

ARDEN, Jane (1927–1982) and Jack BOND (1937–)

Feminist avant-garde theatre and film director Jane Arden was born in Wensleydale, Yorkshire, on 29 October 1927, but brought up in Wales. She trained as an actress at RADA, and acted in television (a BBC production of *Romeo and Juliet* in 1947), and in two low-budget thrillers: Oswald Mitchell's *Black Memory* (1947) and Richard Grey's *A Gunman Has Escaped* (1948). By the mid-1950s, after a gypsy period in New York, she had turned dramatist, writing for the theatre and television, and scaling the West End peak in 1958 with her play *The Party*, directed by Charles Laughton, an exploration of adolescent problems featuring Laughton's last London stage performance and Albert Finney's first. Several television scripts (*Curtains for Harry*, 1955; *The Thug*, 1959) were directed by Philip Saville, then her husband. He also took charge of *The Logic Game* (1964), a drama about marital conflicts produced for the newly launched BBC 2; it was the first full-length BBC play to be made on film, and the first Arden script to point in a feminist direction.

'Scarlet stockings, a violet dress and lively, lucid talk are the outward marks of Jane Arden's colourful personality,' according to an ABC television publicist in 1959. She was obviously ready for the flamboyant 1960s, and became increasingly involved in feminist politics. From the middle of the decade she worked regularly with Jack Bond (born in London on 10 December 1937), colourful enough in his own right. His background lay in BBC television trailers and documentaries, but he abandoned the safety net for his first cinema venture with Arden, the experimental *Separation* (1967), set against an authentically realised 'Swinging' London background, with music by Procol Harum. Bond directed; Arden devised the story and took the main role of a middle-aged woman drifting from her husband toward an insufficiently fulfilling younger man, though the plot's precise shape was hard to spot under the fragmentary editing. In 1969 Arden cemented her reputation in the burgeoning Women's Liberation movement with the stridently feminist play *Vagina Rex and the Gas Oven*, directed by Bond: a cult hit at the Arts Lab, Drury Lane, performed with slide projections, strobe lighting and other rock concert effects. The following year saw the launch of her women's theatre company Holocaust, which shared its name with her next play. She took the directorial reins herself when adapting *The Holocaust* for the cinema as *The Other Side of the Underneath* (with Bond acting as producer). Abrasive in tone, wildly various in manner, the film explores a woman's 'madness' from the perspective of radical psychiatrist R. D. Laing, who saw schizophrenia as the result of unbearable social tensions. Its curiosity value led to occasional repertory screenings in London but wider distribution proved difficult.

In 1969 an interviewer commented that 'Jane Arden's mind works like a candy-floss machine. You put very little in and get a great deal out. But what you get out is the gut strings of a radical woman; there is no sweetness' (Gardner). Perhaps to still the machine's whirrings she spent much of the 1970s travelling, visiting ashrams in India and Morocco, turning from agit-prop feminism to a wider search for spiritual fulfilment. Bond, for his part, sailed their yacht and spent a year in America building a stone house; a more commercial asset, probably, than their next venture, *Vibration*, an exercise in meditation utilising experimental film and video techniques. Back in Britain, Bond earned money with arts documentaries for *The South Bank Show*; while Arden published a volume of prose poetry, *You Don't Know What You Want, Do You?* (1978), and shared the direction of one further film, *Anti-Clock* (1979). An unusual concoction of time-travel and mysticism shot intermittently over three years, *Anti-Clock* furthered the film/video mix of *Vibration* through a flickering narrative about a man attempting to reclaim free will in a deterministic universe. It was considered too amateurish to command much attention. In December 1982 Arden took her own life. Thereafter Bond's experimental itch declined. Music videos kept him busy, along with a feature-length offshoot, *It Couldn't Happen Here* (1988), disjointed and dismal, featuring the Pet Shop Boys in material that even Ken Russell might have left on the cutting-room floor. Ultimately Arden's is a sad career: so much energy and fury; but, with plays and films long unseen, scarcely any footprint left.

(Geoff Brown and Robert Murphy)

BIBLIOGRAPHY: Baker, Roger, 'Jane Arden', *Contemporary Dramatists*, 2nd edn (London: St James Press, 1977); Hodgson, Clive, 'Tribute to Jane Arden', *National Film Theatre Programme*, July 1983, p. 14; 'Jane Arden Talks to Raymond Gardner', *Guardian*, 26 Nov. 1969; Neustatter, Angela, 'Stale Cake', *Guardian*, 29 Aug. 1978.

FILMOGRAPHY: *Separation* (Jack Bond, 1967); *The Other Side of the Underneath* (Jane Arden, 1972); *Vibration* (Jane Arden/Jack Bond, US, 1974); *Anti-Clock* (Jane Arden/Jack Bond, 1979); *It Couldn't Happen Here* (Jack Bond, 1988).

ARGYLE, John (1911–1962)

John F. Argyle was born on 6 March 1911 in Tamworth, Staffordshire. He served his apprenticeship as an assistant cameraman at Gainsborough Pictures in the mid-1920s, and after a brief spell at British International Pictures moved into independent production in 1929. His first three productions were silent five-reel dramas and revealed an interest in fishing and mining stories. In *Flames of Fear* (Charles Barnett, 1930), which he also wrote, Argyle played Bob, a miner who proves his worth by rescuing his fiancée's brother from a fire. *The Last Tide*, his first film as director, was a romantic melodrama about fisher folk set in Devon; in *Paradise Alley*, he played another valiant miner who takes the blame for his brother's crime.

In 1932, Argyle wrote and produced two low-budget racing dramas for Equity British, both directed by Charles Barnett. *Thoroughbred*, a remake of a 1928 silent film directed by Sidney Morgan, was the story of a trainer with amnesia, and *A Game of Chance* concerned the unmasking of a dishonest bookie. *The Final Reckoning*, also for Equity British, was Argyle's last film as director until 1946. Another mining story, it told the tale of a mine-owner's son who attempts to kill a miner whom he mistakenly believes is in love with his wife. All three were made as silent films and had sound added afterwards to make them more marketable.

Argyle's companies (Argyle Talking Pictures and Argyle British) made low-budget romances throughout the 1930s – including the maudlin *My Irish Molly* (Alex Bryce, 1938), which featured an inexperienced Maureen O'Hara. He co-scripted *Old Mother Riley* (Oswald Mitchell, 1937), the first of a long-running series of comedies starring Arthur Lucan and

Kitty McShane. At the end of the decade he found his métier with the eerie *The Dark Eyes of London* (Walter Summers, 1939), which he produced and co-wrote. This above-average chiller starring Bela Lugosi was the first British film to be given an 'H' (for horror) certificate and demonstrated Argyle's flair for mysteries. During active service between 1940 and 1946, he wrote and produced a number of similarly thrilling melodramas, including *The Night Has Eyes* (Leslie Arliss, 1942), an impressively atmospheric film with James Mason giving an excellent performance as a tormented Spanish Civil War veteran.

Argyle resumed directing in 1946 with *Send for Paul Temple*, based on Francis Durbridge's popular radio series, but Anthony Hulme proved a lacklustre screen detective. Argyle retreated into musical melodrama. *The Hills of Donegal* featured Dinah Sheridan as a singer who sacrifices her career to return to Ireland with her new husband, but even the support of the Green Flag Ceilidh Band and the Gaelic Irish Dancers failed to animate this predictable romantic drama. The last three feature films Argyle produced were much better: *The Case of Charles Peace* (Norman Lee, 1949), a re-exploration of the life of the Sheffield burglar whose exploits had inspired two films in 1906; *Once a Sinner* (1950), the feature debut of Lewis Gilbert; and *The Girl Who Couldn't Quite* (Norman Lee, 1950), a strange film, starring Bill Owen as a philanthropic gardener/tramp. In the 1950s Argyle produced and directed short travelogues. He died in Salisbury (now Harare), in Southern Africa in 1962.
(Margaret Butler)

BIBLIOGRAPHY: Noble, Peter (ed.), *The British Film Yearbook, 1947–1948* (London: Skelton Robinson, 1947), p. 207.
FILMOGRAPHY: *The Last Tide*; *Paradise Alley* (1931); *The Final Reckoning* (1932); *Send for Paul Temple* (1946); *The Hills of Donegal* (1947); *Call of the Islands* (doc. short); *The Island of Sark* (doc. Short) (1955); *In Cornish Seas* (doc. short, 1956); *The Land Is Green* (doc. short, 1958).

ARLISS, Leslie (1901–1987)

Although he directed some of the biggest British box-office successes of the 1940s, Leslie Arliss' contribution to British cinema remains under celebrated. Born in London on 6 October 1901, he spent his early career as a journalist in South Africa, returning to London in the late 1920s when he entered the film industry as a scenario writer. He was a versatile screenwriter, working on a diverse range of films, including comedy vehicles, portentous historical epics and critically acclaimed realist dramas such as Ealing's *The Foreman Went to France* (Charles Frend, 1942).

Arliss was Gainsborough Pictures' resident scenario editor by 1942, when the studio announced its wartime policy of allowing members of its scriptwriting team an opportunity to direct. Among the beneficiaries were Val Guest, Frank Launder and Sidney Gilliat. Arliss had co-directed a remake of Hitchcock's silent comedy *The Farmer's Wife* (1941), and directed an impressively morbid thriller, *The Night Has Eyes* (1942), but it was *The Man in Grey* (1943) that really marked his arrival as a director. The adaptation of Lady Eleanor Smith's Regency bodice-ripper appears to have been Arliss' personal project, and its full-blooded representation of female desire and baroque visual style marked a departure both for the studio, and for British cinema in general. Although contemporary critics were appalled by a cinema so resolutely antipathetic to the respectable codes of wartime realism, the film was massively successful at the British box office, and initiated a cycle of Gainsborough melodramas. Arliss contributed two more films: *Love Story* (1944), which despite a contemporary setting shared the cycle's commitment to sexual desire as an organising principle, and *The Wicked Lady* (1945), the most famous and successful of the films.

The Gainsborough's melodramas were subject to a major reassessment in the early 1980s, when critics such as Sue Harper and Pam Cook identified within them a flamboyance and exoticism lacking elsewhere in British cinema. However, Arliss' contribution to the series was downplayed – the radicalism of the films was understood in terms of a visual style that owed much to Elizabeth Haffenden's extraordinary costume designs, John Bryan's art direction and the contribution of cinematographers Arthur Crabtree, Bernard Knowles and Jack Cox. Arliss' direction does often appear perfunctory, and his actors remembered him as a rather cold, distant figure. However, several entertaining flashes of directorial bravura are evident – the extreme close-up on Lockwood's eyes as she commits murder

in *The Wicked Lady*, the shot through the flames of the fireplace as she pretends to contemplate her own damnation, and the pull back through the window as she dies alone, all indicate a director in sympathy with the heightened mood of the design. His scripts for these films are peppered with one-liners – some of which are startlingly indecent even by today's standards – and they consistently feature heroines who unequivocally express a desire to live on their own terms.

Outside Gainsborough, Arliss failed to prosper. *A Man about the House*, made with ex-Gainsborough producer Ted Black for British Lion, offered psychological subtlety in its exploration of female desire. But Black was soon to die of cancer, and Arliss' collaboration with ex-studio boss Maurice Ostrer on *Idol of Paris* proved a disaster. Their attempt to repeat the Gainsborough costume melodrama formula with second-rate stars and a weak script deterred audiences – despite the added salaciousness of a whip fight between two women – as well as critics, and the film's box-office failure severely damaged Arliss' career. During the 1950s he was relegated to directing B-film thrillers such as *Miss Tulip Stays the Night*, and episodes of television series for Douglas Fairbanks (several of which were released as compendium films). In retirement he wrote the script for Michael Winner's 1983 remake of *The Wicked Lady* (inserting the whip fight from *Idol of Paris*). He died on 30 December 1987 on Jersey, in the Channel Islands.

(Lawrence Napper)

BIBLIOGRAPHY: Aspinal, Sue and Robert Murphy (eds), *BFI Dossier No. 18: Gainsborough Melodrama* (London: BFI, 1982); Cook, Pam, *Fashioning the Nation* (London: BFI, 1996); Harper, Sue, *Picturing the Past* (London: BFI, 1994).

FILMOGRAPHY: *The Farmer's Wife* (co-dir. Norman Lee, 1941); *The Night Has Eyes* (aka *Terror House*, 1942); *Fyffe's Film* (short); *The Man in Grey* (1943); *Love Story* (aka *A Lady Surrenders*, 1944); *The Wicked Lady* (1945); *A Man about the House* (1947); *Idol of Paris* (1948); *Saints and Sinners* (1949); *The Woman's Angle* (1952); *The Triangle* ('The Priceless Pocket' episode, 1953); *Thought to Kill* ('The Parlour Trick' episode); *Destination Milan* ('Lowland Fling' episode), *Forever My Heart* (1954); *See How They Run*; *Miss Tulip Stays the Night* (1955); *Insomnia Is Good for You* (short); *Danger List* (short); *Dearth of a Salesman* (short); *Man with a Dog* (short) (1957).

ASANTE, Amma (1969–)

Amma Asante was born 1969 in Streatham, south London, where her parents had settled after emigrating from Ghana. She attended the Barbara Speake Stage School and as a teenager acted for two years in *Grange Hill*, the BBC children's soap opera. Other acting opportunities arose, but in her late twenties Asante switched to the other side of the camera, writing and producing *Brothers and Sisters* (Blake Bedford, 1998), a television series set around a gospel church.

She made an unexpected feature debut as writer and director of *A Way of Life* (2004), a low-budget study of a group of Welsh racists led by a teenage single mother (played with startling conviction by Stephanie James). Boldly throwing out any notion of political correctness and eschewing sentimentality, Asante shows how stunted opportunities and sterile environments breed a viciousness and rage that inevitably find expression in racist violence. Though given limited exposure in UK cinemas, *A Way of Life* was well received at film festivals and seems likely to secure Asante's future as a director.

(Robert Murphy)

BIBLIOGRAPHY: Buckovics, Edith, 'Raw Power', *Factory*, 2004, pp. 60–9; Greer, Bonnie, 'From *Grange Hill* to the Valleys', *Guardian*, 8 Nov. 2004; Saner, Emine, 'My Mum and Dad Must Have Been Scared of the Racists but I Never Saw Fear on Their Faces', *Evening Standard*, 9 Feb. 2005, pp. 25–6.

FILMOGRAPHY: *A Way of Life* (2004).

ASHER, Robert (1915–1979)

Robert Asher was born in London in 1915, the older brother of cameraman Jack Asher. Robert took his first steps in the industry in 1934 as a call-boy and graduated through a number of jobs to become one of the most respected assistant directors in the industry. In this capacity he worked with the team responsible for the Rank Organisation's lucrative Norman Wisdom comedies, and on the departure of John Paddy Carstairs he was given the opportunity to take over as director. His first film, *Follow a Star*, proved one of the best in the series and Asher was retained to complete the remaining five films Wisdom was contracted to make for the studio, though he also made two non-Wisdom comedies. *Make Mine Mink*, also made for Rank, has Terry-Thomas in glorious form leading an elderly gang of eccentric female robbers. *She'll Have to Go*, co-produced by Asher and his brother Jack for Anglo-Amalgamated, is a more lacklustre affair with Alfred Marks and Bob Monkhouse playing brothers vacillating between marrying or murdering a continental cousin (disconcertingly played by Anna Karina, taking time off from starring in films made by her husband Jean-Luc Godard).

Asher's biggest success came with Wisdom's *A Stitch in Time* in 1963; but the diminutive comedian felt increasingly constrained by the formulaic constraints imposed by the Rank Organisation and he rejected the studio's 1964 offering. Asher was given the task of directing a substitute – *The Intelligence Men* – as a big screen vehicle for Eric Morecambe and Ernie Wise. Asher does his best with this 'Swinging London' spy spoof, but the comic talents of Morecambe and Wise were difficult to adapt to narrative cinema. Asher was happier reunited with Wisdom on his two final Rank films – *The Early Bird* and *Press for Time*.

Asher's main strength was his understanding of comic pacing, which he put to good use in bringing the best out of his scripts. His rapport with Norman Wisdom and his understanding of his comic persona made the films they made together particularly satisfying, especially in the space Asher allowed for long, essentially silent, single-situation physical routines (though his penchant for special-effects gags was less successful). Sadly, once Wisdom left Rank, Asher's career went into sharp decline, and after directing episodes for television series such as *The Baron* (1966), *The Prisoner* (1967) and *The Champions* (1968), poor health forced him into unhappy retirement. He died in 1979.

(Richard Dacre)

BIBLIOGRAPHY: Dacre, Richard John, *Trouble in Store: Norman Wisdom, a Career in Comedy* (Dundee: T. C. Farries, 1991); Obituary, *Screen International*, 8 Dec. 1979, p. 4.

FILMOGRAPHY: *Follow a Star* (1959); *Make Mine Mink*; *The Bulldog Breed* (1960); *She'll Have to Go* (aka *Maid for Murder*, 1961); *On the Beat* (1962); *A Stitch in Time* (1963); *The Intelligence Men* (aka *Spylarks*); *The Early Bird* (1965); *Press for Time* (1966).

ASQUITH, Anthony (1902–1968)

Anthony Asquith was born in London on 9 November in 1902. He grew up in a political household – his father was Liberal Prime Minister from 1908 to 1916 – and his mother was a noted society figure who provided him with his well-known nickname, 'Puffin'. He was educated at Winchester School and Oxford and after leaving university spent six months living in Los Angeles as a guest of Mary Pickford and Douglas Fairbanks. Here he was able to observe Hollywood working methods and meet a number of prominent directors and stars including Chaplin, Lubitsch and Lillian Gish. Back in Britain, Asquith joined the growing ranks of the university-educated young people who were drawn into the film industry in the 1920s. He went to work for Bruce Woolfe's British Instructional Films, a small innovative company that specialised in documentary reconstructions of episodes from the 1914–18 war, and naturalist films such as the *Secrets of Nature* series. Asquith was also a founder member of the Film Society and his knowledge of cinema embraced the sophisticated artistic and political cinemas of France, Germany and the Soviet Union, as well as the popular Hollywood film.

Asquith's film career began with minor duties on *Boadicea* (Sinclair Hill, 1926), including stunt-doubling for the central character as well as serving as assistant director and contributing to the script. British Instructional Films moved into feature film production in the wake of the 1927 quota legislation and Asquith was assigned to their first fictional venture, *Shooting Stars*. The film was based on a script that Asquith had written, and though the veteran A.V. Bramble is listed on the credits as director, it is now conventionally regarded as an Asquith film. It was the first of four silent films he directed in the late 1920s that established him as one of the leading directors of the day. Critics such as Paul Rotha and John Grierson were not convinced that he had harnessed technique to meaning and ideas, and Grierson complained that Asquith, like Hitchcock, was wasting his time on unimportant subjects and stories. When he did attempt the weighty subject of the Gallipoli campaign in *Tell England*, his first sound film, he was accused of trivialising it (Hardy, pp. 76–80). In retrospect, Asquith's late-1920s' films represent an inventory of silent film technique, drawing upon various influences both from popular cinema and the art film. Charles Barr argues that *Shooting Stars*, set in the world of the film industry, is an early example of meta-cinema comparable to subsequent films by Hitchcock and Powell; and according to Murray Smith, *A Cottage on Dartmoor* is equal to Hitchcock's *Blackmail* (1929) in its historical importance as a transitional film linking the silent and sound periods.

If Asquith remains one of the most important directors to emerge from the British silent cinema, his position in the 1930s is more problematic. He joined Gainsborough Pictures in 1932 and worked on a variety of projects – screenwriting, directing the English version of the multiple-language film *Unfinished Symphony*, handling second-unit work on *Forever England* – as well as directing the Clair-influenced comedy *The Lucky Number*. Asquith moved to Korda's London Films to direct *Moscow Nights*; though shooting began at the Worton Hall studio it became the first film to go on the stages at the new Denham Studios when they opened in 1936. The film prompted Graham Greene to comment, in terms reminiscent of Rotha and Grierson, that 'Mr Anthony Asquith was once a promising director, though he was always more tricky than imaginative' (Noble, p. 23). In 1937, due in part to his connections in high places, Asquith was invited to become President of the recently formed film technicians' union, the Association of Cine-Technicians – a post he held until his death in 1968.

The turning point in Asquith's career as a director came in the late 1930s. The silent films on which his artistic credentials had been established indicated a sophisticated grasp of film aesthetics; the revival of his reputation, however, was to depend upon the theatrical adaptation so often regarded by theorists as constricting for film-makers and inimical to the art of cinema. *Pygmalion* was one of three Shaw adaptations that he was to direct, and the first film on which Shaw himself worked as scriptwriter. The film was a great success both in Britain and America, earning an Academy Award nomination for Best Picture and winning Academy Awards for its adaptation and screenplay. Though Asquith shared the directing credit with the film's leading actor Leslie Howard, its success revived his flagging career. His next film, *French Without Tears*, proved equally significant to his future, becoming the first of ten collaborations with the playwright Terence Rattigan.

During the six years of the war, Asquith made feature films for Paramount's British production arm, for Filippo del Giudice's Two Cities and for Gainsborough Pictures, together with a number of short propaganda films for the Ministry of Information. Most of these were war subjects and they include one of the best films of the period, *The Way to the Stars*, designed to promote Anglo-US relationships; *The Demi-Paradise*, which aimed to do a similar job for Anglo-Soviet solidarity; and *We Dive at Dawn*, a documentary-style drama about a submarine patrol. In contrast to the sober themes of war, Asquith also made the society comedy *Quiet Wedding* and *Fanny by Gaslight*, a Gainsborough costume melodrama that was much more kindly treated by critics than those made by lesser lights like Leslie Arliss and Arthur Crabtree.

After the war, Asquith was rarely short of work, making roughly one film a year until his final picture in 1964. His collaboration with Rattigan continued: he directed adaptations of some of the playwright's most famous stage work including *The Browning Version* and *The Winslow Boy*, as well as films like *The V.I.P.s* and *The Yellow Rolls-Royce*, for which Rattigan wrote original screenplays. They also planned a film based on the life of T. E. Lawrence starring Dirk Bogarde, but the Rank Organisation cancelled the project. The theatrical strand in Asquith's work was also represented by further adaptations of Shaw – *The Doctor's Dilemma* and *The Millionairess* – together with a version of Oscar Wilde's *The Importance of Being Earnest*. Alongside such prestige material, Asquith also directed films drawn from a diversity of popular generic sources, including *The Woman in Question*, a multiple-viewpoint thriller; *The Young Lovers*, a romantic drama set against the background of the cold war; *The Net*, which crosses scientific endeavour, romance and espionage in a story about the development of the jet plane; *Orders to Kill*, about an agent sent to eliminate a suspected traitor in the French Resistance; and *Guns of Darkness*, set in the volatile world of South American politics. In addition to his feature output, Asquith made two films reflecting his passion for classical music, opera and ballet: *On Such a Night*, set at the Glyndebourne festival, and *An Evening with the Royal Ballet*.

Asquith's final films – *The V.I.P.s* and *The Yellow Rolls-Royce* – fall into the disparaged category of the 'mid-Atlantic' film, despite the director himself warning of the dangers to the British film of such international co-production in his 1963 presidential address to the ACTT conference. Both were big-budget productions with multiple-star casts including Richard Burton and Elizabeth Taylor, then the film world's most famous celebrity couple. Despite their lavish budgets, their stars and their commercial success, both films are generally regarded as an unfortunate swansong for Asquith. He fell ill while doing preparatory work on the adaptation of Morris West's best-selling novel, *The Shoes of the Fisherman*, and died in London of cancer on 20 February 1968.

At the beginning of his directorial career Asquith was seen as an emergent major talent in a British film culture dominated by American output and somewhat in awe of continental European film trends. His grasp of film technique impressed many critics and discussion of his silent films, especially *A Cottage on Dartmoor*, highlighted a director as immersed in the artistic currents of European cinema as his contemporary, Alfred Hitchcock. Indeed, many years later, *A Cottage on Dartmoor* prompted Raymond Durgnat to comment that Asquith 'out-Hitchcocks Hitchcock, before Hitchcock became Hitchcock' (Durgnat, p. 191). Yet, whereas Hitchcock went on to establish an international reputation with his 1930s' thrillers, Asquith meandered through the decade making few films until his involvement with Shaw and Leslie Howard and the international success of *Pygmalion*. The screen adaptation of middlebrow drama set a course for Asquith, and he set about modestly interpreting the work of others rather than imposing his own vision. Yet, against this, it might be argued that some of his smaller films – *The Woman in Question*, *The Young Lovers* and *Orders to Kill*, for example – display a directorial flair effectively held in check in films such as *Pygmalion*, *The Way to the Stars* and *The Importance of Being Earnest*, with their different priorities of performance, pace and timing.

(Tom Ryall)

BIBLIOGRAPHY: Barr, Charles, 'Amnesia and Schizophrenia', in Charles Barr (ed.), *All Our Yesterdays* (London: BFI, 1986); Costello, Donald P., *The Serpent's Eye* (Notre Dame, IN, and London: University of Notre Dame Press, 1965); Cowie, Peter, 'This England', *Films and Filming*, Oct. 1963, pp. 13–17; Drazin, Charles, *The Finest Years: British Cinema of the 1940s* (London: André Deutsch, 1998); Durgnat, Raymond, *A Mirror for England* (London: Faber and Faber, 1970); Hardy, Forsyth (ed.), *Grierson on Documentary* (London: Faber and Faber, 1966); Minney, R. J., *Puffin Asquith* (London: Leslie Frewin, 1973); Noble, Peter, *Anthony Asquith*, New Index Series no. 5 (London: BFI, 1951); Rotha, Paul, *The Film Till Now* (London: Spring Books, 1967); Smith, Murray, 'Technological Determination, Aesthetic Resistance and *A Cottage on Dartmoor*: Goat-Gland Talkie or Masterpiece?', *Wide Angle* vol. 12 no. 3, July, 1990, pp. 80–97.

FILMOGRAPHY: *Shooting Stars* (co-dir. A. V. Bramble, 1928); *Underground* (1928); *The Runaway Princess* (Ger: *Priscillas Fahrt ins Glück*); *A Cottage on Dartmoor* (US: *Escape from Dartmoor*, 1929); *Tell England* (US: *The Battle of Gallipoli*, co-dir. Geoffrey Barkas, 1931); *The Lucky Number*; *Dance Pretty Lady* (1932); *Unfinished Symphony* (aka *Lover Divine*, co-dir. Willy Forst, 1933); *Brown on Resolution/Forever England* (US: *Born for Glory*, 2nd unit dir. Walter Forde, 1935); *Moscow Nights* (US: *I Stand Condemned*, 1936); *Blind Dogs* (short); *Pygmalion* (co-dir. Leslie Howard) (1938); *French Without Tears* (1939); *Quiet Wedding*; *Channel Incident* (short); *Freedom Radio* (US: *A Voice in the Night*) (1940); *Cottage to Let* (US: *Bombsight Stolen*) (1941); *Uncensored* (1942); *We Dive at Dawn*; *The Demi-Paradise* (US: *Adventure for Two*) (1943); *Two Fathers* (short); *Fanny by Gaslight* (US: *Man of Evil*) (1944); *The Way to the Stars* (US: *Johnny in the Clouds*, 1945); *While the Sun Shines* (1947); *The Winslow Boy* (1948); *The Woman in Question* (US: *Five Angles on Murder*, 1950); *The Browning Version* (1951); *The Importance of Being Earnest* (1952); *The Net* (US: *Project M7*); *The Final Test* (1953); *The Young Lovers* (US: *Chance Meeting*, 1954); *On Such a Night* (short); *Carrington, V.C.*

(US: *Court Martial*) (1955); *Orders to Kill* (1958); *Libel*; *The Doctor's Dilemma* (1959); *The Millionairess* (1960); *Two Living, One Dead* (1961); *Guns of Darkness* (1962); *The V.I.Ps*; *An Evening with the Royal Ballet* (1963); *The Yellow Rolls-Royce* (1964).

ATKINSON, Jim (1934–1995)

James Horsefield Atkinson was born in Yeovilton, Somerset, on 5 August 1934, the son of an opera singer and a property dealer. He was educated at Marlborough College, and after National Service drifted through a variety of jobs before finding his niche as a sound recordist at the documentary company Stanley Schofield Productions. He switched to sound editing on feature films in the late 1960s, forming a fruitful partnership with John Boorman on *Leo the Last* (1969), *Deliverance* (1972), *Zardoz* (1973) and *The Exorcist II* (1977).

His sole venture into directing came in 1974 with *Can You Keep It Up for a Week?*, an endearingly innocent sex-comedy about an accident-prone young man (Jeremy Bulloch) whose attempts to hold down a job so that he can marry his girlfriend are continually frustrated by encounters with lascivious women. Atkinson directs with breezy good humour, and the film was a box-office success, but he preferred to return to sound, creating atmospheric electronic landscapes for Kevin Connor's fantasy-adventures *At the Earth's Core* (1976), *Warlords of Atlantis* (1978) and *Arabian Adventure* (1979). His career was cut short by a stroke in July 1979, which left him partially paralysed. He died in Streatham, south London, on 29 May 1995.

(Robert Murphy)

BIBLIOGRAPHY: Crawley, Tony, 'Jim's Winning Battle to Change Cinderella Status', *Screen International*, 12 Aug. 1978, p. 12; McGillivray, David, *Doing Rude Things: The History of the British Sex Film, 1957–81* (London: Sun Tavern Fields, 1992); Sheridan, Simon, *Keeping the British End Up: Four Decades of Saucy Cinema*, 2nd edn (London: Reynolds & Hearn, 2005); Sloman, Tony, 'Jim Atkinson', *Independent*, 29 Sept. 1995.

FILMOGRAPHY: *Can You Keep It Up for a Week?* (1974).

ATTENBOROUGH, Richard (1923–)

Richard Samuel Attenborough was born in Cambridge on 29 August 1923, one of three brothers including the BBC naturalist and presenter David Attenborough. After obtaining a scholarship to RADA, he gained his first great acting success playing Pinkie, the sinister young spiv in Graham Greene's *Brighton Rock*, first on the West End stage in 1943 and then four years later in the Boulting Brothers' film version.

Attenborough eventually became dissatisfied with the character roles he was offered. In 1959, in partnership with Bryan Forbes, he set up Beaver Films, through which he produced *The Angry Silence* (Guy Green, 1960) and *Whistle down the Wind* (Bryan Forbes, 1961). His first film as a director was *Oh! What a Lovely War* (1969), a project inherited from John Mills, who had developed the screenplay with Len Deighton from Joan Littlewood's stage production. This satiric fantasia on the First World War is largely set on Brighton Pier, but Attenborough and cinematographer Gerry Turpin successfully open out the play with a number of bravura sequences, the best remembered being the final shot that pulls back to reveal an entire hillside covered in white crosses.

Young Winston (1972), adapted by Carl Foreman from Winston Churchill's book about his early years, is seemingly a more conventional film. But its complex flashback structure is supported by a voiceover that develops into a dialectical discourse, emphasising the contrast between the letters written by the young Churchill at the turn of the century and the autobiography he wrote some fifty years later. This effect is largely lost in the truncated television version, which cuts 15 per cent from its roadshow release length of 167 minutes. Particularly regrettable is the removal of a final scene where the older Churchill dreams of a conversation between his dead father and his younger self.

Attenborough then made two films in partnership with independent producer Joseph E. Levine and screenwriter William Goldman. The first was adapted from Cornelius Ryan's book *A Bridge Too Far*, clearly an attempt to emulate the success of Darryl Zanuck's film version of Ryan's *The Longest Day* (1962). The resulting film is a sporadically effective but very episodic dramatisation of the disastrous attempt by the Allies to take possession of a series of bridges behind enemy lines in Holland. It was the last epic dealing with events from the Second World War until Steven Spielberg's *Saving Private Ryan* in 1998 and painstakingly authentic – letters to *The Times* from disgruntled generals notwithstanding. Perhaps surprisingly in view of its slow pace and downbeat ending, the film was a financial success. But instead of going on to make *Gandhi*, as he had hoped, Attenborough was persuaded to direct an adaptation of Goldman's best-selling novel *Magic*. Despite a fine performance by Anthony Hopkins as the demented ventriloquist, Attenborough never really seems comfortable with his sinister subject matter.

Gandhi eventually found financial backing from Jake Eberts' ambitious British company Goldcrest, and proved to be an enormous commercial and critical success (it won eight Academy Awards). Attenborough was faulted for his broad and untarnished presentation of his protagonist, but he shows complete mastery in his handling of both the intimate and the spectacular sequences and inspires an extraordinary performance by Ben Kingsley as Gandhi. Once again, Attenborough followed up with a subject he seemed ill suited to, an adaptation of the Broadway musical *A Chorus Line* (1985), which resolutely failed to come alive either dramatically or commercially.

Gandhi's true successor was *Cry Freedom* (1987), one of the few serious films made in the 1980s attacking apartheid in South Africa. Although the film was criticised for being too partial a view of the South African activist Steve Biko, and for giving too great an emphasis to the role played by the white journalist Donald Woods (on whose book the film is based), Attenborough's sincerity shines through. As so often with his films, *Cry Freedom* is characterised by very strong performances and concludes with a complicated stylistic flourish, in which the escape of the Woods family is intercut with flashbacks to a massacre of young black demonstrators and to scenes between Woods and Biko.

Attenborough's films of the 1990s have all been biopics that look at self-deception, showing the contrast between the private and public faces of their famous subjects while focusing on the meeting point between European and American cultures and sensibilities. Anchored by an extraordinary central performance by Robert Downey Jr, *Chaplin* (1992) is Attenborough's most underrated film. Co-written by Bryan Forbes and William Goldman (and others), structurally it extends the approach of *Young Winston*, undercutting Chaplin's self-perpetuated myths about himself and his career, most memorably in the scene showing two contrasting versions of how Chaplin came to create his famous tramp persona. *Shadowlands* (1993) is a heavily fictionalised and romanticised look at the tragic love affair between author C. S. Lewis and the American poet Joy Gresham; it was an immediate critical and commercial success. *In Love and War* (1996) is a tritely written look at the early life of Ernest Hemingway, while the little-seen *Grey Owl* (1999) tells the fascinating true story of Archibald Belaney, an Englishman who after emigrating to Canada passed himself off as an Indian guide, becoming a world-renowned environmentalist and an advocate for beavers. Despite the complex flashback structure and a memorable scene where the protagonist returns home in his new guise, the film is over earnest and humourless in performance and execution. Appropriately, it was made under the banner of Beaver Productions.

Attenborough married the actress Sheila Sim in 1945; he was knighted in 1976 and made a life peer in 1993. He was Chairman of the British Film Institute between 1981 and 1992 and continues to play a crucial role in British film culture. His ambitious and stylistically adventurous films represent a fine and often very personal body of work in genres not obviously in keeping with his manifestly liberal sensibilities. In fact his films have gained strength and individuality from his willingness to incorporate such seeming contradictions into the very fabric of his productions.

(Sergio Angelini)

BIBLIOGRAPHY: Attenborough, Richard, *In Search of Gandhi* (London: Bodley Head, 1982); Dougan, Andy, *The Actor's Director: Richard Attenborough behind the Camera* (London: Mainstream Publishing, 1994); Goldman, William, *Adventures in the Screen Trade* (New York: Warner Books, 1983); Hacker, Jonathan and David Price, *Take Ten: Contemporary British Film Directors* (Oxford: Clarendon Press, 1991); Macnab, Geoffrey, 'Eager Beaver', *Sight and Sound*, Sept. 2003, pp. 20–5.

FILMOGRAPHY: *Oh! What a Lovely War* (1969); *Young Winston* (1972); *A Bridge Too Far* (US, 1977); *Magic* (US, 1978); *Gandhi* (1982); *A Chorus Line* (US, 1985); *Cry Freedom* (US, 1987); *Chaplin* (US, 1992); *Shadowlands* (1993); *In Love and War* (UK/US, 1996); *Grey Owl* (UK/US, 1999).

ATTWOOD, David (1952–)

David Attwood was born in Sheffield on 28 August 1952. After working in television as production assistant on Alan Bleasdale's *The Black Stuff* (Jim Goddard, 1980) and *The Muscle Market* (Alan Dossor, 1981), he graduated to production manager on *The Boys from the Black Stuff* (Philip Saville, 1982). He took the BBC directors course in 1984 and quickly progressed to directing feature-length television projects. *All Together Now* (1986), like Mark Herman's *Brassed Off* ten years later, is a comedy set around a brass band; *Airbase* (1987) aroused controversy for its unflattering portrayal of life on an American airbase in Britain; and *Killing Time* (1990) is a dark tale of a killer who befriends a teenager and murders him. He also directed *The Real Eddy English* (1989), a four-part thriller series for Channel 4 about a young black man investigating his namesake uncle's mysterious death.

It was for Channel 4 that Attwood made his only cinema-released film, *Wild West* (1992), a quirky comedy-drama about a British-Asian country-and-western band. The film playfully uses the iconography of this music genre, contrasting it with the urban spaces of Southall. The clash of cultures theme and the hybridity inherent in the band act as a metaphor for ethnicity in late-twentieth-century Britain. It was well received but failed to make the sort of box-office impact of Channel 4's later Asian comedy *East Is East* (Damien O'Donnell, 1999).

Attwood returned to television to make a critically acclaimed adaptation of Daniel Defoe's *Moll Flanders* (1996) for Granada and WGBH Boston. Its success in the USA led to him making *Shot through the Heart* as a co-production between HBO and the BBC. The story of two brothers on different sides during the war in Yugoslavia, it was written by Guy Hibbert, who had written Attwood's earlier BBC film, *Saigon Baby* (1995). *Fidel* (2002), an epic biographical film about Fidel Castro for American cable television, and an adaptation of *The Hound of the Baskervilles* (2002) for the BBC confirm that Attwood's career is securely established in television if not in the cinema. *May 33rd* (2004), an uncompromising social-problem play about a woman with multiple-personality disorder, showed Attwood and his frequent collaborator Guy Hibbert refreshingly aware of the best traditions of British television drama.

(Paul Ward)

FILMOGRAPHY: *Wild West* (1992); *Shot through the Heart* (US/Can, 1998).

AUERBACH, Shona (1967–)

Shona Auerbach was born in Warwickshire in 1967, the daughter of a Polish father and a Scottish mother. After excursions into theatre and still photography she studied film in Manchester and Leeds, completing her postgraduate course in cinematography at the Polish National Film School in Lodz. Her short film *Seven* (1996), dealing with the seven stages of a woman's life, won prizes and led to a successful career directing commercials. It also led to contact with writer Andrea Gibb and a long collaboration on what would become her feature debut, *Dear Frankie*.

The story of a fearful, protective mother (Emily Mortimer) who creates a fictional father figure for her deaf son, this small-scale film made on location at the Clydeside port of Greenock skirts melodrama and avoids the tendency to represent Scotland as the repository of grim realism, Celtic whimsy or drug-fuelled fantasy. Auerbach (who acted as her own cinematographer, with her husband Graeme Dunn as camera operator) creates a vibrant setting for her fable, using a distinctive visual colour scheme and making clever use of voiceover from the otherwise silent Frankie. Though well received at the Edinburgh and Cannes film festivals and snapped up for distribution in America by Miramax, the film was only modestly successful commercially, but it generated enough enthusiasm to ensure Auerbach's permanent transfer from commercials to feature films.

(Robert Murphy)

BIBLIOGRAPHY: Curtis, Nick, 'The Unknown Brits Who Stole the Cannes Festival', *Evening Standard*, 20 May 2004, p. 27; Davies, Mike, 'Frankie Goes to Greenock' <westmidlands.ideasfactory.com/film_tv/features>; Mende, Julia, 'Interview with Shona Auerbach' <viva-berlin.de/aviva/content_Women%20+%20Work_Lead-

ing%20Ladies>; Minns, Adam, 'Miramax Deal Puts "British Kolya" under Global Spotlight', *Screen International*, 12 Dec. 2003, p. 12.
FILMOGRAPHY: *Seven* (short, UK/Pol, 1996); *Dear Frankie* (2004).

AUSTIN, Michael

Michael Austin entered the British film industry as an assistant director on *Hardcore* (James Kenelm Clarke, 1977), a misleadingly named sex-comedy starring Fiona Richmond and Anthony Steel. He then wrote three interesting scripts: *The Shout* (Jerzy Skolimowski, 1978), an adaptation of a Robert Graves story about possession and madness; the Alpine romance *Five Days One Summer* (Fred Zinnemann, 1982); and the bold if over-convoluted *Greystoke: The Legend of Tarzan, Lord of the Apes* (Hugh Hudson, 1984). Austin made his directorial debut with *Killing Dad*, a likeable Joe Orton-like black comedy set in a semi-derelict Southend boarding house. The plot wobbles into implausibility but Austin wrings funny and poignant performances from Julie Walters, Denholm Elliot and Richard E. Grant caught in a tangled net of amorous and filial relationships. He followed up, belatedly, with *Princess Caraboo*, which features Phoebe Cates, John Lithgow and Kevin Kline alongside Jim Broadbent, Wendy Hughes and Stephen Rea in a Victorian tale of identity and deception that makes a good companion piece to *The Tichborne Claimant* (David Yates, 1998). Nothing subsequently emerged to supplement this slim but interesting body of work.

(Robert Murphy)

FILMOGRAPHY: *Killing Dad* (1989); *Princess Caraboo* (1994).

AUSTIN, Ray (1932–)

Ray Austin was born in London on 5 December 1932. He worked as a stunt man in Hollywood on *North by Northwest* (Alfred Hitchcock, 1959) and, after returning to Britain, worked as an actor and stunt man on films such as *The Loneliness of the Long Distance Runner* (Tony Richardson, 1962). After arranging stunts for *The Avengers*, in 1968 he graduated to directing ('All Done with Mirrors', 'Have Guns . . . Will Haggle') and went on to direct episodes of other series in the UK (*The Saint*, *Department S*) and the US (*Hawaii 5-0*, *Barnaby Jones*).

Though the bulk of his directing work is for television, Austin's few theatrical credits are intriguingly disreputable. *Fun and Games*, also known as *1,000 Convicts and a Woman*, is grim prison exploitation drama; *Virgin Witch*, his best film, mixes sexploitation and horror as starlets Vicki and Ann Michelle are enticed into a cult run by lesbian Patricia Haines. Finally, *House of the Living Dead* is a South African-shot gothic horror film with Shirley Anne Field at the mercy of a mad scientist in a remote mansion.

Austin returned to television to direct the miniseries remake of *From Here to Eternity* (1980), and picked up the rather odd speciality of reviving cancelled series, with episodes of *The New Avengers*, *Return of the Saint* and *CI5: The New Professionals*. He was also responsible for American television movies such as *The Return of the Man from U.N.C.L.E.* (1983) and *The Return of the Six Million Dollar Man and the Bionic Woman* (1991). He is now Baron Devere-Austin of Delvin, Lord of Bradwell.

(Kim Newman)

BIBLIOGRAPHY: Noble, Peter, 'From Chauffeur to Helmsman', *Screen International*, 10 Oct. 1981, p. 57; Staff, Bryan, 'Baron Hollywood', *OnFilm*, Dec. 1993, p. 13.

FILMOGRAPHY: *The Perfumed Garden* (short); *It's the Only Way to Go* (short) (1969); *Virgin Witch* (aka *Lesbian Twins*, 1970); *Fun and Games* (aka *1,000 Convicts and a Woman*, 1971); *House of the Living Dead* (aka *Doctor Maniac*, 1973).

AYLOTT, Dave (1885–1969)

David Henry Aylott was born in Bethnal Green, London, on 7 February 1885. His film output was heavily influenced by his own theatrical and music-hall background; when he directed his first film *The Mad Dog* in 1906 he was working as an actor in melodrama at the Variety Theatre, Hoxton. More comedies for Walturdaw followed. By the spring of 1909, he had joined the pioneer James Williamson at Brighton, varying the slapstick and chases with crime dramas (*The Boy and the Convict*) and tales of war (*A Dash for Help*). Soon he settled at Cricks and Martin, generating further dramas, even a Western (*'Twixt Red Man and White*), along with *Mr Tubby's Triumph*, *Bertie's Bid for Bliss* and other outlets for tricks, tumbles and cross-dressing. He appeared in some films himself; but for comedies he mostly used stage comedians whose knockabout routines could be easily recreated for the new medium. Music-hall comics making regular appearances included Johnny Butt, Jack Lovell, Harry Paulo, Bob Reed and Ernie Westo. In 1910, he featured the future 'Pimple', Fred Evans, as a dandy character, later developed in the 'Charley Smiler' series. Other screen characters popularised included 'Muggins', 'Scroggins' and 'Mike Murphy'.

Beyond the slapstick realm, Aylott launched British and Colonial's long-running Lieutenant Daring adventure series in 1911, directing the first four instalments. Dramas continued to supplement his comedies after he had switched to J. H. Martin's independent company. Their tone darkened in line with events. Two days after the outbreak of hostilities in August 1914, Aylott began shooting *War's Grim Reality*, a one-reeler about a rape avenged, set in France. By 1916, with cinema tastes changing, he had graduated to five-reel features. *It's Never Too Late to Mend* (1917) revisited the stalwart melodrama by Charles Reade and Arthur Shirley; *The Man Who Made Good* (1917) bolstered its war story with actuality material.

Aylott at this point saw war service himself, and reviving his career after demobilisation proved difficult. He made two more features, returned briefly to shorts, but then found no more directing work until the hundred or so tiny Electrocord sound films, synchronised to gramophone records, shot in Leeds in 1929. Lean years followed, but Aylott built a new cinema career in 1935, launching himself as a make-up artist, and enrolling his sons in what became a thriving family trade. From 1941 to 1948 he was make-up artist at British National Studios. Evidence suggests Aylott was never a significant director, least of all in technical innovations; but his mixed output, and his rise and fall, tells us much about the growth of British cinema and public taste. He died in Hatfield on 31 October 1969.

(Barry Anthony and Geoff Brown)

BIBLIOGRAPHY: Aylott, Dave, *From Flicker Alley to Wardour Street* (unpublished manuscript, National Film and Television Archive).

FILMOGRAPHY: *The Mad Dog*; *The Bobby and the Bob*; *Three Halfpenny Worth of Leeks*; *Madam's Tantrums*; *The Sunday School Treat*; *The Little Conjurer*, *The Pirates of Regents Canal* (1906); *Sunday's Dinner* (c. 1907); *The Giddy Goats*; *Under the Mistletoe* (1907); *The Skirl of the Pibroch*; *The Office Boy's Dream*; *Put Me among the Girls*; *The Dog's Devotion*; *A Dash for Liberty*; *Paddy's Way of Doing It*; *Billie's Bugle*; *Dick the Kisser*, *The Pirate Ship*; *For His Child's Sake*; *Only a Dart*; *The Invisible Button*; *Wanted, a Nice Young Man*; *The Tricky Convict; or, The Magic Cap*; *My Son the Curate*; *Jessica's First Prayer* (1908); *What the Angler Caught*; *Copping the Coppers*; *Was It a Servant's Bite?*; *The Boy and the Convict*; *Scouts to the Rescue*; *Squaring the Account*; *A Dash for Help*; *Two Naughty Boys*; *The Unwelcome Chaperone*; *For Her Sake*; *Gingerbread*; *Sorry, Can't Stop!*; *Scratch as Scratch Can*; *And Then He Woke Up*; *The Wanderer's Return; or, Many Years After*, *The Young Redskins*; *Hypnotic Suggestions*; *Diver-Sions* (aka *Diver's Diversions*); *Muggins V.C.* (1909); *What Happened to Brown*; *'Twixt Red Man and White*; *Vice Versa*; *The Last of the Dandy*; *A Race for a Bride*; *From Gipsy Hands*; *The Hindoo's Treachery*; *Mr Tubby's Triumph*; *Mistaken Identity*; *A Bolt from the Blue*; *A Modern George Washington*; *The Marriage of Muggins V.C. and a Further Exploit*; *Bunker's Patient Bellows*; *A Rare Specimen*; *Erratic Power*, *Prison Reform* (co-dir. A. E. Coleby); *Comrades: or, Two Lads and a Lass*; *At the Mercy of the Tide*; *The Gamekeeper's Daughter*, *As Prescribed by the Doctor*, *The Devoted Ape*; *A Thrilling Story* (1910); 'Scroggins' (series, 1910–11); *The Poison Label*; *Well Done, Scouts!*; *Billy's Bible*; *The Pirates of 1920* (co-dir. A. E. Coleby); *The King's Pardon*; *Bertie's Bid for Bliss*; *She Would Talk*; *Run to Earth by Boy Scouts*; *That Terrible Pest*; *The Adventures of Lieutenant Daring R.N. – In a South American Port*; *Spy Fever*, *Men Were Deceivers Ever*, *A Soldier's Sweetheart*; *Auntie's Parrot*; *Good News for Jones*; *The Limit Fire Brigade*; *The Typist's Revenge*; *Lieutenant Daring R.N. and the Secret Service Agents* (aka *Lieutenant Daring R.N. Saves H.M.S. Medina*) (1911); 'Charley Smiler' series (aka 'Charlie Smiler', 1911–12); *Lieutenant Daring Avenges an Insult to the Union Jack*; *Woman's Privilege in Leap Year*, *Broken Faith*; *Sandy's New Kilt*; *Lieutenant Daring and the Ship's Mascot*; *The Mystic Ring*; *Billy Bungler the Silent Burglar*, *Honour among Thieves*; *Uncle's Present*; *Muggins V.C. – The Defence of Khuma Hospital, India*; *The Miner's Mascot*; *The Wooing of Widow Wilkins*; *The Spy Mania*; *Bagged*; *A Son of Mars*; *Captain Dandy, Bushranger*, *The Rajah's Revenge*; *A Shock-ing Complaint*; *When Father Fetched the Doctor*, *Henpeck's Double*; *What's the Joke?*; *Captain Cuff's Neighbours*; *Private Hector, Gentleman*; *Caught*; *Much Ado About – !!*; *Tootles Buys a Gun*; *Paul Sleuth Crime Investigator: The Burglary Syndicate*; *Sold, a 'Bear' Fact*; *Adhesion*; *When It Comes Off*; *Paul Sleuth: The Mystery of the Astorian Crown Prince* (1912); *The Mystic Moonstone*; *The Fairy Bottle*; *Belinda's Elopement*; *Billiken's Revolts*; *The Murder of Squire Jeffrey*; *Poor Pa Pays*; *The Mystic Mat*; *The Warty Wooing*; *Furnishing Extraordinary*; *P.C. Platt's Promotion*; *Billy's Boxing Gloves*; *A Shocking Job* (aka *Shocks and Shorts*); *For East Is East* (US: *In the Python's Den*); *Two Brown Bags*; *Uncle's Present* (aka *A Present from Uncle*); *Landladies Beware*; *The Gentleman Ranker* (aka *Raised from the Ranks/Not Guilty*); *Willie's Dream of Mick Squinter*, *Professor Hoskin's Patent Hustler*, *Willy William's Washing* (1913); 'Mike Murphy' (series, 1913–16); *To Save the King* (aka *The Enemy Within*); *The Gloves of Ptames* (aka *The Mysterious Gloves*); *Panic!*; *The Sorrows of Selina*; *An Eggs-traordinary Complaint*; *Jollyboy's Dream*; *The New Boy*; *Through the Ages*; *Lieutenant Geranium and the Stealed Orders*; *The Vengeance of the Air*, *The Daughters of Garcia, Brigand*; *Telling the Tale*; *The Ring That Wasn't*; *Shocking Bad Form*; *A Merry Night* (aka *Some Evening*); *The Strength that Failed*; *The Tricky Stick*; *Not Likely!*; *The Scout's Motto*; *Kitchener's Fighting Men*; *England's Call*; *A Box of Real Turkish*; *War's Grim Reality*; *I Should Say So!*; *The Mat that Mattered*; *Love, Poetry and Paint* (aka *Love and Bullets*); *Father's Fighting Fever*, *Held by a Child*; *Some Fish!*; *Thumbs Up!*; *The Fighting Strain of Old England*; *Biff! Bang! Wallop!!!*; *Sha(w)ly Not*; *A Joke in Jerks* (1914); *Fighting Selena*; *The Cakes of Khandipore*; *The Club of Pharos*; *Selena of the Weeklies*; *Diamond Cut Diamond*; *Maloola from Paloona*; *Jewels and Jimjams* (aka *The Defective Detective*); *The Kaiser's Present*; *A Chip off the Old Block*; *A Kweer Kuss*; *Conscription*; *Awkward Anarchists*; *Surely You'll Insure*; *When Clubs were Clubs*; *Podgy Porkins' Plot*; *Slips and Slops*; *Her Fatal Hand*; *The Second Lieutenant*; *The Charm that Charmed*; *Coppers and Cut-Ups*; *The Crimson Triangle*; *His Phantom Burglar*, *Selina-Ella*; *The Jade Heart*; *Yvonne* (1915); *Oh Auntie!*; *A Soldier and a Man*; *The Price He Paid*; *The Gay Deceivers*; *Bobbikins and the Bathing Belles*; *Bob Downe's Schooldays*; *Hitchy-Coo*; *Two Lancashire Lasses in London*; *A Shattered Idyll* (1916); *The Man Who Made Good*; *It's Never Too Late to Mend*; *When the Heart Is Young*; *The Walrus Gang*; *His Uncle's Heir* (1917); *Gambler's All* (1919); *The River of Light*; 'Parkstone Comedies' (series, 1921); *Glimpses of Golf* (series, 1925); 'Electrocord Films' (series, co-dir. E. F. Symmons); *Riverside Melodies*; *Yule*; *Popular Pieces*; *An Old Time Music Hall*; *More, Please* (1929); *The Safe* (1930).

BAIRD, Edward (1901–1975)

Edward ('Teddy') Baird was born Frederick Harold Goodman in London on 9 September 1901. He began his film career as an extra, appearing from 1917 in films made by Windsor, Gaumont and Ideal. He kept a diary of these engagements until 1921, which provides a fascinating record of this early period in British film-making. After working as a freelance journalist, Baird joined British Instructional Films, where he shared assistant directing duties with Stuart Legg on John Orton's extraordinary

Windjammer (1930). He then worked on Walter Creighton's *One Family* (1930) for the Empire Marketing Board, but the EMB plumped for Grierson and documentary rather than Creighton and allegorical fantasy, and Baird returned to BIF. He was assistant director on Anthony Asquith's *Tell England* (1931) and *Dance Pretty Lady* (1932) and acquired a reputation as 'the best assistant director in British pictures' (*Picturegoer*, p. 12) on prestige productions such as *Under the Red Robe* (Victor Sjöström, 1937), *As You Like It* (Paul Czinner, 1937) and *Pygmalion* (Anthony Asquith/Leslie Howard, 1938).

In 1946 Baird directed *Now It Can Be Told* for the RAF, in which he had served during the war. An effective dramatised documentary about British agents working with the French Resistance during the Second World War, it made good use of Harry Ree and Jacqueline Nearne, both of whom had worked undercover for the Special Operations Executive in France. A slightly shorter version, *School for Danger,* was given a theatrical release, but Baird showed no inclination to pursue a career as a director. In the 1950s he renewed his partnership with Asquith, producing *The Woman in Question* (1950), *The Browning Version* (1951), *The Importance of Being Earnest* (1952) and *Carrington, V.C.* (1955). At the end of the decade Baird's failing health led to a gradual withdrawal from professional life; he produced his last film for Asquith, *Two Living, One Dead*, in 1961.

(Janet Moat)

BIBLIOGRAPHY: A collection of ephemera relating to Baird, including his diary, is held by the BFI National Library, London; Baldwin, Oliver, 'These People Make British Pictures: Anthony Asquith, Edward Baird, David Lean', *Picturegoer*, 29 July 1939, pp. 12–13.

FILMOGRAPHY: *School for Danger/Now It Can Be Told* (1946).

BAKER, Robert S. (1916–) and Monty BERMAN (1913–)

Throughout the 1950s and early 60s Robert S. Baker and Monty Berman combined their roles as film producers (and in Berman's case cinematographer) with occasional forays into film direction.

Nestor M. Berman was born in Whitechapel in London's East End in 1913 and entered the film industry in 1932 as a camera assistant at Twickenham Studios. He rose to become a camera operator at Teddington and Ealing and was one of the three cameramen on Michael Powell's *The Edge of the World* (1937). At the outbreak of war in 1939 he joined the British Army and was posted to the Army Kinematograph Service. Robert S. Baker was born in London in 1916. He was a keen amateur film-maker and joined the film industry as an assistant director in 1937. During the war he found himself in the Army Kinematograph Service as a camera operator, meeting up with Berman in North Africa.

After the war, Baker and Berman set up Tempean Films, which from the late 1940s onwards produced a series of low-budget support features, many of them crime dramas. Such films were much in demand during the 1950s and Tempean was not the only company working in this area. But its films were often livelier and fresher than its competitors' thanks to a reliance on location shooting and the skills of directors such as John Gilling (responsible for much of Tempean's output).

Baker and Berman seem to have taken on film direction duties more for economic reasons than artistic ones and there is nothing especially distinctive about their work. In fact, their identities sometimes become interchangeable in records of their directorial activities, with one source assigning *Melody Club*, an early Tempean film, to Baker, another to Berman, and a third to Baker and Berman together. Berman acted as cinematographer on many of Tempean's productions, so it is likely that Baker did most of the directing.

When Hammer, one of Tempean's main competitors, broke into the main feature market with its horror films in the late 1950s, Baker and Berman followed suit. Of the two films they directed together, *Jack the Ripper* was a crude but effective rendition of the Ripper tale, while *The Hellfire Club* was a historical melodrama, unfortunately deficient in the vicious intensity of Hammer's *The Hound of the Baskervilles* (Terence Fisher, 1959) and *The Curse of the Werewolf* (Terence Fisher, 1961). Of Baker and Berman's other films from this period, the most interesting is *The Siege of Sidney Street*, an account of the events leading up to a real-life confrontation between anarchists and armed police in London in 1911.

In the early 1960s, Baker and Berman found new success as television producers with several highly popular series, including *The Saint* (1962–9), on which Baker directed several episodes, *Gideon's Way* (1965) and *The Baron* (1966). Berman went on to produce *The Champions* (1968), *Department S* (1969), *Randall and Hopkirk (Deceased)* (1969), *Jason King* (1971) and *The Adventurer* (1972), while Baker produced *The Persuaders!* (1971) and *The Return of the Saint* (1978).

(Peter Hutchings)

BIBLIOGRAPHY: Hutchinson, Tom, 'Tempean Films to Make Bigger Pictures', *Kinematograph Weekly*, 21 Apr. 1955, p. 37; McFarlane, Brian, 'Value for Money: Baker and Berman and Tempean Films', in Ian MacKillop and Neil Sinyard (eds), *British Cinema of the 1950s: A Celebration* (Manchester: Manchester University Press, 2003).

FILMOGRAPHY: *Melody Club* (Baker; sometimes also credited to Berman, 1949); *Blackout* (Baker, 1950); *13 East Street* (Baker, 1952); *The Steel Key* (Baker, 1953); *Passport to Treason* (Baker, 1956); *Jack the Ripper* (Baker and Berman, 1958); *The Siege of Sidney Street* (Baker and Berman); *The Hellfire Club* (Baker and Berman); *The Treasure of Monte Cristo* (Baker and Berman) (1960).

BAKER, Roy Ward (1916–)

Roy Ward Baker was born in Hornsey, north London, on 19 December 1916 and educated at the City of London School. Fascinated by wireless as a boy, he joined Gainsborough Pictures in 1934 hoping to get a job in the sound department. Starting as a 'gopher', he worked his way up to production manager, location manager and assistant director, working in that capacity on Hitchcock's *The Lady Vanishes* (1938) and three films by Carol Reed. After army service, he was recruited in 1943 to the Army Kinematograph Service as a production manager and director on training and instructional films. Eric Ambler, who also worked for the AKS, subsequently asked Baker to direct his production *The October Man* (1947), a taut thriller written by Ambler for Two Cities. With its finely observed character studies and claustrophobic, suburban atmosphere, the film provides a good showcase for Baker's directorial strengths. John Mills gives a compelling performance as the vulnerable, falsely accused central character; several other performances for Baker followed.

Baker's next two films, *The Weaker Sex*, a nicely handled version of Esther McCracken's play about a family at war, and *Paper Orchid*, a murder mystery set in the newspaper industry, both proved popular, though they were overshadowed at the box office by the larger success of *Morning Departure* (1950). Kenneth Woollard's original play, about a submarine crew trapped after the vessel hits a mine, was greatly enhanced by Baker's skill at conveying tension in a confined setting. Bizarrely, shortly after the film's completion, the entire crew of the submarine *Truculent* perished after colliding with a Dutch freighter on the Thames. Baker partly attributed the film's success to the Royal Navy approving its release as a fitting tribute to the dead, despite initial fears of its cancellation. *Morning Departure* drew international attention to Baker's talent. Darryl Zanuck at 20th Century-Fox invited him to Hollywood, where he made *Don't Bother to Knock*, still notable for Marilyn Monroe's disturbed babysitter, *Night without Sleep*, a routine film noir, and *Inferno*, a very effective suspense thriller with Robert Ryan as a businessman thirsting for revenge against his faithless wife (Rhonda Fleming).

Baker returned to Britain to make a succession of high-quality dramas for the Rank Organisation. *Passage Home* (1955) is a moody nautical melodrama with Peter Finch as a buttoned-up sea captain who becomes dangerously sulky when rejected by pretty Diane Cilento. *Tiger in the Smoke* (1955), based on a novel by Margery Allingham, is a superbly atmospheric thriller centring on a group of embittered ex-servicemen desperate to get their hands on wartime buried treasure. His next, *Jacqueline* (1956), took him to the Belfast shipyards for a surprisingly unsentimental drama about a wayward scaffolder and his young daughter. These relatively modest productions were followed by *The One That Got Away* (1957), the real-life tale of Franz von Werra, the German flyer who after several attempts successfully escaped from a British prisoner-of-war camp. It is a refreshingly generous film, allowing full credit to the bravery and endurance of its German hero, played by the likeable (and unmistakably Germanic) Hardy Kruger. International success led Rank to entrust Baker with their big-budget re-enactment of the *Titanic* disaster, *A Night to Remember* (1958). Eric Ambler's script, Baker's skilful and lively direction, and a solid British cast make it one of the period's few prestige Rank productions to stand the test of time.

The Singer Not the Song (1960), featuring a leather-clad Dirk Bogarde as a Mexican bandit and John Mills as a Catholic priest, proved a more overblown affair, though the camp quality of Bogarde's performance has won the film cult status. Baker was happier with *Flame in the Streets* (1961), adapted by Ted Willis from his television play *Hot Summer Night*. It was one of the first British films to deal with racial issues; the use of colour and CinemaScope for an essentially working-class realist subject was also unusual. Ironically, given its big budget and mainstream backing, this worthy if ponderous film performed much less well at the box office than black-and-white kitchen-sink films like *Saturday Night and Sunday Morning* (Karel Reisz, 1960), with their jazzy pace and irreverent attitudes towards sexual taboos.

An Anglo-Italian Second World War film (*The Valiant*, 1962) and a Michael Crawford comedy (*Two Left Feet*, 1963) followed, but Baker spent most of the 1960s working in television, directing episodes of *The Avengers*, *The Saint* and *The Champions*, and other series. In 1967, now deploying his middle name Ward, he made a successful return to cinema with intelligent, well-crafted films for Hammer. *Quatermass and the Pit* (1967), a workmanlike adaptation of Nigel Kneale's third and best Quatermass television serial, was followed by *The Anniversary* (1967), an entertaining black comedy featuring Bette Davis as a one-eyed malevolent matriarch, and *Moon Zero Two* (1969), an ambitious 'space Western'. *The Vampire Lovers* (1970) launched a cycle of more sexually explicit horror films; the best is *Dr Jekyll & Sister*

Hyde (1971), an inventive and chilling reworking of Robert Louis Stevenson's story.

Baker makes no claims to being an auteur and firmly rejects the idea that the audience should be aware of the director. However, his aptitude for creating claustrophobic atmospheres and a sense of isolation shows a talent beyond mere competence, and several of his films could be included among British cinema's best post-war dramas. Though he made his last feature film in 1980 he continued to work until the early 1990s on television series, including *The Irish RM* and *Minder*.

(Margaret Butler)

BIBLIOGRAPHY: Baker, Roy, 'Discovering Where the Truth Lies', *Films and Filming*, May 1961, pp. 17, 38; Baker, Roy Ward, *The Director's Cut* (London: Reynolds and Hearn, 2000); Dixon, Wheeler Winston, 'Interview with Roy Ward Baker', *Classic Images* no. 234, Dec. 1994, pp. 14–16, 18, 34; Hutchings, Peter, 'Authorship and British Cinema: The Case of Roy Ward Baker', in Justine Ashby and Andrew Higson (eds), *British Cinema: Past and Present* (London: Routledge, 2000); Mayer, Geoff, *Roy Ward Baker* (Manchester: Manchester University Press, 2005); McFarlane, Brian, *An Autobiography of British Cinema* (London: Methuen, 1997).

FILMOGRAPHY: *According to Our Records* (doc., 1943); *Techniques of Instruction in the Army* (doc., 1944); *A Letter from Home* (doc.); *What's the Next Job* (doc.); *Warner's Warnings* (series of shorts); *Read All about It* (doc.); *Think It Over* (doc.) (1945); *The October Man* (1947); *The Weaker Sex* (1948); *Paper Orchid* (1949); *Morning Departure*; *Highly Dangerous* (1950); *The House in the Square* (US: *I'll Never Forget You*, 1951); *Don't Bother to Knock* (US); *Night without Sleep* (US) (1952); *Inferno* (US, 1953); *Passage Home* (1955); *Jacqueline*; *Tiger in the Smoke* (1956); *The One That Got Away* (1957); *A Night to Remember* (1958); *The Singer Not the Song* (1960); *Flame in the Streets*; *The Valiant/L'affondamento della Valiant* (UK/It) (1961); *Two Left Feet* (1963); *Quatermass and the Pit* (US: *Five Million Years to Earth*); *The Anniversary* (1967); *Moon Zero Two* (1969); *The Vampire Lovers*; *The Scars of Dracula* (1970); *Dr Jekyll & Sister Hyde* (1971); *Asylum* (1972); *And Now the Screaming Starts*; *Vault of Horror* (1973); *The Legend of the 7 Gold Vampires* (US: *The Seven Brothers Meet Dracula*, UK/HK, 1974); *The Monster Club* (1980).

BALCH, Antony (1937–1980)

An attractive, idiosyncratic figure in an overwhelmingly conservative industry, Antony Balch liked to quote with great approval Russ Meyer's dictum, 'I'm in this business for lust and profit'. His own business for the most part was as a distributor, exhibitor and cinema manager; he was also a spirited campaigner against film censorship. Launched in London in 1963, Antony Balch Films handled a wide range of foreign exotica, artistic and otherwise, often imaginatively retitled (*Skin Skin*, *Don't Deliver Us from Evil*). Balch's more private business was as a director of avant-garde films made in collaboration with the writer William Burroughs and the artist Brion Gysin; few supporting shorts of the 1960s infuriated or transported audiences more than Balch's *The Cut Ups*.

Antony John R. Balch was born in London on 10 September 1937. He entered the British industry at the age of seventeen, progressing from production assistant to editor to director of television commercials. He made his first film (unreleased) in 1959 in Paris, where the following year he met Burroughs and Gysin, both of them eager to explore the cinema medium. The team's first completed collaboration, *Towers Open Fire* (1963), filmed in Paris, Gibraltar and London, spent eleven rampaging minutes pursuing visual echoes of Burroughs' apocalyptic and satiric fiction. Balch's editing attempted to reflect Burroughs and Gysin's 'cut-up' technique (the random scissoring and reordering of texts). More prominent ingredients included Gysin's whirring, hallucinogenic Dream Machine, Balch masturbating and Burroughs' own laconic presence. In cinemas the film supported Balch's first venture as a distributor, Tod Browning's *Freaks* (1932), banned in Britain for thirty years. With *The Cut Ups* (1966), partly drawn from *Guerilla Conditions*, an uncompleted film diary of Burroughs and Gysin's lives, Balch assumed greater control, rigorously dividing the material into shots one foot in length and constantly cutting between four locations (Paris, New York, Tangier, London). The soundtrack performed its own cut-up tricks on quotations from a Scientology manual, endlessly shuffled: 'Hello. Yes. Look at that picture. Does it seem to be persisting?' To save audiences' pain, in distribution the film was cut from nineteen minutes to twelve (Balch himself preferred the shorter version); but for any unsympathetic spectator the pictures were still persistent enough.

Uncompromising and hypnotic, Balch's *The Cut Ups* remains a milestone in British independent film-making of the 1960s, though it gives little indication of his possible success as a director of Burroughs' novel *Naked Lunch* – since the mid-1960s Balch's most cherished film project. Scripts were written by Gysin, storyboards prepared and Mick Jagger's interest stirred as leading man. To gain experience for the task, Balch decided to put avant-garde methods aside and mount several commercial features. First came *Secrets of Sex* (1970), a quirky compendium of seven tall tales about love and desire. Censorship cuts reduced Balch's absurdist black humour; the film still found critical approval, though it may not have fully satisfied the soft-core sex hunters at the Jacey, Piccadilly, the cinema that Balch adventurously programmed along with the Times Cinema, Baker Street.

Balch's next venture, *Horror Hospital* (1973), aimed jovial shots at horror film clichés. Robin Askwith plays a writer sent for recuperation to a 'health hotel' run by a crippled Michael Gough – a set-up that allowed ample room for Balch's macabre sense of fun. No further commercial films emerged, and the *Naked Lunch* project remained stalled (David Cronenberg eventually produced his own version in 1991). Balch's distributing business continued; he was diagnosed with stomach cancer in 1978, and died in London on 6 April 1980.

Material recovered after his death has been used by the performance artist Genesis P-Orridge to generate several 'new'

Balch–Burroughs films: *Ghosts at Number 9* (another raid on the material of *Guerilla Conditions*); the self-descriptive *William Buys a Parrot*; and *Transformations*, a film of Gysin painting. New exposure has also been given to *Bill and Tony*, a five-minute exercise in fusing and dislocating picture and sound, probably dating from 1968 and meant to be projected onto the faces of its two participants, Burroughs and Balch.

(Geoff Brown)

BIBLIOGRAPHY: 'Antony Balch Interview', *Cinema Rising* no.1, Apr. 1972, pp. 10–14; 'Arkadin', 'Film Clips', *Sight and Sound*, Spring 1969, p. 106; McGillivray, David, *Doing Rude Things: The History of the British Sex Film, 1957–81* (London: Sun Tavern Fields, 1992); Sargeant, Jack, *The Naked Lens: An Illustrated History of Beat Cinema* (London: Creation Cinema Collection, 2001); Wollen, Peter, 'Guerilla Conditions: The Cinema of William Seward Burroughs', *Pix* 3, 2001, pp. 86–94.

FILMOGRAPHY: *Guerilla Conditions* (short, 1961–5, unfinished); *Towers Open Fire* (short, 1963); *Ghosts at Number 9* (short, 1963–7); *The Cut Ups* (short, 1966); *William Buys a Parrot* (short, 1967); *Bill and Tony* (aka *Who's Who*, 1968), *Secrets of Sex* (US: *Tales of the Bizarre*, 1970); *Horror Hospital* (US: *Computer Killers*, 1973).

BAMFORTH, James (c. 1842–?)

James Bamforth, born in Cartworth, Yorkshire, in 1841 or 1842, is among a select group of early British film-makers, including Cecil Hepworth, George Albert Smith and Robert Paul, who played a role in the development of the story film. In two brief periods of film-making activity, 1898–1900 and 1913–15, Bamforth and Company of Holmfirth, West Yorkshire, was responsible for producing a modest but historically significant collection of films. The company had come to prominence during the 1890s with its mass production of magic lantern slides and, after 1902, for its expansion into the international market for postcards. Bamforth's excursions into cinema were relatively brief, and its business interests in other photographic forms significantly influenced many of its films.

The son of a painter and decorator, James Bamforth started in business as a studio photographer in 1870 and began the production of magic lantern slides, photographed at a studio at Station Road, Holmfirth, around 1883. At first a small-scale enterprise, Bamforth's production of photographic lantern slides was so successful that by 1898 a factory extension to the studio in Holmfirth was built, enabling production on an industrial scale. At first the company specialised in 'life-model' slide sequences, in which simple narratives, usually conveying moral, temperance and religious themes, were photographed in front of a painted backcloth; the models used were members of the Bamforth family and workforce, and other locals. By the late 1890s, Bamforth production became increasingly dominated by slides intended to accompany popular songs and hymns.

The manner in which these life-model lantern sequences were made and exhibited had a profound influence on the company's first period of film-making. Unlike other early British production companies, Bamforth already possessed a studio, painted backcloths and an available pool of local performers, not to mention years of experience in constructing visual narratives for projection on screen. Possibly in response to this expertise, Riley Brothers of Bradford, who had been involved with moving picture technology since 1896 and had already begun to make films of their own, commissioned Bamforth in 1898 to produce further films to be sold exclusively to purchasers of their equipment. Although the exact business relationship between the two firms and the production dates of the films remain unknown, the subsequent advertisement of these productions in a 1903 Hepworth catalogue as 'RAB' films acknowledges their partnership.

A large proportion of the fifteen RAB films advertised in the 1903 catalogue are comic regional subjects. Among these are several depicting mischievous local children playing schoolyard games, such as *Boys Sliding* and *Leap Frog*. Bamforth films of this period also include an unusually high proportion of fiction subjects, such as *Kiss in the Tunnel*, *Women's Rights* and *The Tramp and the Baby's Bottle*, and these are of greatest significance in terms of the early development of British narrative film. For example, *Kiss in the Tunnel* contains an early example of continuity editing in which an amorous scene from inside a darkened train is placed between shots of a train entering and departing a tunnel. The existence of another, almost identical, version, *The Kiss in the Tunnel*, produced in 1899 by the Brighton film-maker George

Albert Smith, suggests that one of these producers had 'borrowed' substantially from the other, as was common practice at the time.

Bamforth's company also adapted some of its life-model lantern material to the new medium. For example, the Bamforth film *Women's Rights*, also known as *Ladies' Skirts Nailed to a Fence*, replicates an earlier comic lantern lecture, in which 'Mr Niggle' and his son humiliate his suffragette wife and her friend. Indeed, a similar lecture may well have accompanied the film's projection. The action depicts two men nailing the women's skirts to a fence, and features the earliest known example of a continuity cut to a different perspective within the same scene. In fact, the shots, apparently taken from either side of the fence, are achieved by turning the fence and the performers through 180 degrees. Although the principle of spatial and temporal continuity implied by this cut was new to film, it had long been present in the magic lantern tradition, in which the detailed arrangement of contiguous spaces, supported by the description of a lecturer, was already fully developed.

After 1902, James Bamforth, increasingly supported by his sons, concentrated his efforts on postcard production. Sets of song and hymn illustrations remained a speciality, alongside voluminous comic subjects. Some early sets used the lantern slide negatives as source material; most required newly staged images, quasi-cinematic in their separation into three or four 'shots', one for each postcard, and the use of superimposed vignettes. A limited company after 1911, Bamforth finally returned to film production in 1913. The Holmfirth studio was enlarged, and films emerged under a named director for the first time, Cecil Birch. He concentrated on short comedies, though Birch also rose to the heights of a five-reel drama, *Paula* (1915), based on a once risqué novel. For modern viewers, the most notable among surviving Bamforth films of this period may be the bizarre comedy *Finding His Counterpart* (1913), in which a man visits a phrenologist, and then attempts to discover his ideal mate by feeling the heads of a succession of unlikely paramours. In 1914, the company engaged the music-hall comedian 'Winky' (Reginald Switz), who became the successful star of around forty of Birch's comedies, from *Winky Learns a Lesson in Honesty* through to *Winky Is the Long and Short of It*, passing through *Winky Waggles the Wicked Widow* and the especially worrying *Winky Causes a Smallpox Panic* along the way. By 1915, other comic performers such as Lily Ward, Alf Scottie and the child star Baby Langley had been signed up. Soon after, perhaps due to the impact of the war, Birch and the production team became incorporated into the newly founded Holmfirth Producing Company, which quickly moved operations to London, with Bertram Phillips as eventual managing director; the last Holmfirth film, *Meg o' the Woods* (Bertram Phillips), emerged in February 1918. Bamforth postcards ceased using models around the same time, relying instead on artists' drawings or straightforward, often garish, scenic views. Production continued until the 1990s, well into the time when Holmfirth found new renown as the location setting for the television comedy series *Last of the Summer Wine*. The Bamforth name is now chiefly remembered for its cheeky seaside postcards, drawn with crude vigour: *Kiss in the Tunnel*, perhaps, reshaped and retooled for a different era.

(Joe Kember)

BIBLIOGRAPHY: Barnes, John, *The Beginnings of the Cinema in England*, vol. 4: 1899 (Exeter: Exeter University Press, 1996); Herbert, Stephen and Luke McKernan, *Who's Who of Victorian Cinema* (London: BFI, 1996); Robinson, David, Stephen Herbert and Richard Crangle (eds), *Encyclopaedia of the Magic Lantern* (London: The Magic Lantern Society, 2001); Sutherland, Allan T., 'The Yorkshire Pioneers', *Sight and Sound*, Winter 1976/7, pp. 48–51.

SELECTED FILMOGRAPHY: *Weary Willie* (aka *An Overful Seat*); *Gardener Watering Plants* (aka *The Biter Bit/A Joke on the Gardener*, 1898); *The Nursemaid's Surprise*; *The Schoolmaster's Portrait*; *The Runaway Knock and the Suffering Milkman* (c. 1898); *The Honeymoon*; *The Would-be Conjuror*; *Chokee Bill and the Whitewash* (1899); *Catching the Milk Thief* (aka *Chokee Bill and the Milk*); *The Tramp and the Baby's Bottle* (aka *Chokee Bill and the Baby*); *Women's Rights* (aka *Ladies' Skirts Nailed to a Fence*); *Kiss in the Tunnel* (aka *Cuddling in the Dark*) (c. 1899); *Boys Sliding*; *Leap Frog*; *The Switchback*; *Fox Hounds*; *Queensbury Tunnel*; *Bolton Woods and Abbey* (c. 1900).

BANGURA, Roberto (1962–)

Roberto Bangura was born in Stepney, east London, in 1962. He studied animation at Farnham Art School in Surrey and, after various jobs on pop promos and television documentaries, won a place at the National Film and Television School. There he made three films: *Monday*, *The Long Way Home* and *Sidney's Chair*, a witty anecdote about Sidney Poitier making *To Sir, with love* (James Clavell, 1967) in London's East End. He collaborated with fellow NFTS student Jo Hodges to make *The Girl with Brains in Her Feet*, as a low-budget feature film.

The film centres on a mixed-race teenager (Joanna Ward) growing up in 1970s' Leicester, whose talent for running represents her best chance of escaping the familiar (for British cinema) trap of working-class drudgery. Though it shares elements with other British films about talented British youngsters like *Billy Elliot* (Stephen Daldry, 2000) and *Bend It Like Beckham* (Gurinder Chadha, 2002), it relies less on feelgood factors and attracted only small audiences. Bangura has expressed his admiration for the realist films of the early 1960s, particularly *A Taste of Honey* (Tony Richardson, 1963), and like them *The Girl with Brains in Her Feet* benefits from a strong sense of time and place and the evocative use of music.

Though the film was poorly distributed, it opened up a career for Bangura in television. He worked with producer Matthew Bird on the children's drama *London Bridge* (1997) and on the second series of Jimmy McGovern's *The Lakes* (1999), and has subsequently directed episodes of *Babyfather* (2001) and *Footballers' Wives* (2002). Hopefully, with this solid experience behind him, he will be able to explore more personal projects in the cinema.

(Robert Shail)

BIBLIOGRAPHY: Stimpson, Mansel, 'Profile: Roberto Bangura', *Film* [British Federation of Film Societies], vol. 4 no. 16, Sept. 1998, pp. 16–18.
FILMOGRAPHY: *Monday* (short); *The Long Way Home* (short); *Sidney's Chair* (short) (1995); *The Girl with Brains in Her Feet* (1997).

BANKS, Monty (1897–1950)

Monty Banks, born Mario Bianchi on 18 July 1897 in Cesena, Italy, acquired his new name in 1918 after settling into his first film career, acting in American two-reel comedies for Mack Sennett and others. Mountebanks, a term for itinerant players and quacks, provided the inspiration. Small and tubby, with an excitable moustachioed face, Banks played spruce young Americans anxious to succeed. He formed Monty Banks Productions in 1923, graduated to features with *Racing Luck* (Herman C. Raymaker, 1924), and developed a comedy style juxtaposing slapstick with situation humour.

'He had jumped into the melting pot and melted', wrote the American magazine journalist George Shelton in 1927. The following year Banks jumped again, to Elstree, where British International Pictures, aware of British deficiencies in comedy, had offered him a contract as actor and director. The Pat and Patachon vehicle *Cocktails* (1928) provided his directing debut; he continued directing for BIP until 1933, earning along the way a reputation for a colourful social life with or without his actress wife Gladys Frazin, and a habit of driving his yellow Hispano-Suiza car at daredevil speed. Many early films were routine assignments – in little over a year he directed seven vehicles for the homely comic Leslie Fuller. But quality improved in 1932 with *Money for Nothing*, a fast romantic comedy, and *For the Love of Mike*. *You Made Me Love You* (1933), an updated spin on *The Taming of the Shrew* with Stanley Lupino and Thelma Todd, was better still. Banks knew that comedy thrived on visual gags and speed, lessons seemingly hard for native British directors to learn.

Despite the mounting prestige of his films, Banks moved from BIP in 1933 to Warners' British studio at Teddington, where he made five modest films, three featuring Laura La Plante, wife of the studio's head Irving Asher. Much greater success followed with his films for ATP at Ealing: he steered George Formby to victory in *No Limit* and *Keep Your Seats, Please!*, and added useful touches of glamour to Gracie Fields' image in the Cinderella story *Queen of Hearts* (1936). The film's huge success cemented Banks' position, and he became Fields' regular director. *We're Going to Be Rich*, first fruit of the star's expensive contract with 20th Century-Fox, was deliberately aimed at the international market, and defeated both of them; but *Shipyard Sally* (1939), featuring Fields as saviour of the Clydeside shipyards, proved another canny popular hit.

Faced with internment as an enemy alien once Italy entered the Second World War, Banks moved with Fields to the USA in 1940, where they married. He became an American citizen, and directed one Hollywood feature, Laurel and Hardy's *Great Guns* (1941); both director and stars had seen better days. Fields, meanwhile, undertook extensive tours entertaining the troops and appeared in several Hollywood films, including *Molly and Me* (Lewis Seiler, 1945) – originally intended for Banks to direct in England. With 'Our Gracie' triumphant, Banks' own directing career faded; the war over, he abandoned cinema, returned to Italy and concentrated on domestic matters. He died of a heart attack in Arona on 7 January 1950, while travelling on a train to his birthplace.

(Geoff Brown)

BIBLIOGRAPHY: Richards, Jeffrey, *The Age of the Dream Palace: Cinema and Society in Britain 1930–1939* (London: Routledge & Kegan Paul, 1984); Shelton, George, 'He Coined His Name from Mountebanks', *Motion Picture Magazine*, Dec. 1927; Turconi, Davide, *Monty Banks* (Cesena: Centro Cinema, 1987).
FILMOGRAPHY: *Cocktails* (1928); *Amateur Night in London* (short); *Eve's Fall* (short); *The Compulsory Husband* (co-dir. Harry Lachman); *The New Waiter* (short); *The Musical Beauty Shop* (short); *Not So Quiet on the Western Front*; *The Jerry Builders* (short); *His First Car* (short); *Kiss Me Sergeant*; *Why Sailors Leave Home*; *Almost a Honeymoon*; *The Black Hand Gang* (1930); *Old Soldiers Never Die*; *What a Night*; *My Wife's Family*; *Poor Old Bill* (1931); *Tonight's the Night*; *Money for Nothing*; *L'Amour et la veine*; *For the Love of Mike* (1932); *Leave It to Me*; *Heads We Go* (US: *The Charming Deceiver*); *You Made Me Love You* (1933); *The Girl in Possession*; *The Church Mouse*; *Father and Son*; *Votre sourire* (co-dir. Pierre Caron); *Falling in Love* (US: *Trouble Ahead*) (1934); *Hello Sweetheart*; *18 Minutes*; *Man of the Moment*; *No Limit* (1935); *Queen of Hearts*; *Keep Your Seats, Please!* (1936); *We're Going to Be Rich*; *Keep Smiling* (US: *Smiling Along*, 1938); *Shipyard Sally* (1939); *Great Guns* (US, 1941).

BARKAS, Geoffrey (1896–1979)

A pioneer in the British development of actuality filming within a fictional context, Geoffrey de Gruchy Barkas was born in Richmond, Surrey, on 27 August 1896. His first job was as an insurance office clerk; after the war he farmed in Canada, then gained camera experience at Universal in Hollywood. Returning to England, he worked for G. B. Samuelson and Ideal before joining British Instructional Films in 1922, where he contributed to the acclaimed *Secrets of Nature* series, often filming aquatic topics. In 1925 BIF's distributor New Era released his series of one-reelers about the Canadian lumber industry, shot on the spot two years before using amateur actors. But these *Tall Timber Tales* proved less of a signpost to his future than the feature-length *Palaver* (1926), inspired by his visit to Nigeria while filming the Prince of Wales' Empire tour, and one of BIF's first ventures into drama. Barkas returned to Nigeria to shoot extensive location scenes for this modest drama about the daily life of a British district officer in an isolated quarter of the Empire. A decade later, Paul Rotha slighted the film in his book *Documentary Film* with a passing word, 'ingenuous'; yet for the time Barkas showed considerable originality and skill in his management of location footage.

Despite the lack of overt industry encouragement – *Palaver* was not a commercial success – Barkas pressed ahead with similar attempts to fuse actuality filming with the industry's commercial formats. Moving to New Era Productions, he began work on *The Somme* (1927), a war reconstruction venture modelled after BIF's own successes, completed with supplementary material supervised by M. E. Wetherell. He returned to the Great War in *Q-Ships* (1927), directed with Michael Barringer: a stirring account of merchant ships combating German U-boats, filmed with Admiralty co-operation, archive footage and a deliberate absence of posturing actors. The actors returned for the next Barringer collaboration, *The Infamous Lady* (1928), a crime drama with Arthur Wontner and Ruby Miller that at least tried to rise above the commercial norm. Barkas' work in this period climaxed with BIF's long-gestating Gallipoli film, based on Ernest Raymond's novel *Tell England*. Shooting began in 1928; two years later, work was still under way, with Anthony Asquith in charge of dialogue. Barkas' expertise was visible in the action footage filmed in Malta: sequences with a hard reality lacking in the surface drama of public school heroes displaying stiff upper lips.

Unveiled in March 1931, *Tell England* became a great public success, and helped set the template for future British war dramas. For Barkas its blessings were mixed: he became characterised as an expert unit director, fit for the most difficult foreign assignment, and never shaped an entire feature again. The signs were clear immediately he joined Gaumont-British in 1933, when he was sent to supervise the extensive (and expensive) filming of the Houston-Everest flights over Mount Everest, later packaged with Ivor Montagu's help into *Wings over Everest*. Subsequently he was employed garnishing the company's developing cycle of Empire adventures, shooting in Africa for *Rhodes of Africa* (Berthold Viertel, 1936) and *King Solomon's Mines* (Robert Stevenson, 1937), and in India for the aborted *Soldiers Three*. *The Great Barrier* (1937), about the building of the Canadian Pacific Railway, returned him to Canada. Initially he was to direct the entire film, but Milton Rosmer took over in the studio.

With the industry's financial crisis, Gaumont-British's foreign adventures ceased. During the Second World War, Barkas served as Director of Camouflage (Middle East Forces). Returning to cinema in 1946, ambitions lowered, he produced several children's entertainment films for Rank before settling into the industrial film sector, producing for Shell-Mex, British Petroleum and Random Film Productions. Decent enough employment though not the outcome his adventurous earlier career suggested. Geoffrey Barkas died in Esher, Surrey, on 3 September 1979.

(Geoff Brown and Alan Burton)

BIBLIOGRAPHY: Barkas, Natalie, *Behind the Camera* (London: Geoffrey Bles, 1934); Barkas, Natalie, *Thirty Thousand Miles for the Films* (London: Blackie and Son, 1937); Low, Rachael, *The History of the British Film 1918–1929* (London: George Allen & Unwin, 1971); Low, Rachael, *Films of Comment and Persuasion of the 1930s* (London: George Allen & Unwin, 1979).

FILMOGRAPHY: *Tall Timber Tales* (series of shorts, Can); *The Prince of Wales's Tour* (series of shorts, co-dir. Stanley Rodwell) (1925); *Palaver: A Romance of Northern Nigeria* (1926); *The Somme* (co-dir. M. A. Wetherell); *Q-Ships* (aka *Blockade*, co-dir. Michael Barringer); *The Infamous Lady* (co-dir. Michael Barringer) (1928); *The Third Gun* (short, 1929); *Tell England* (US: *The Battle of Gallipoli*, co-dir. Anthony Asquith, 1931); *A Symphony of the Sea* (short, 1933); *Wings over Everest* (co-dir. Ivor Montagu); *Secrets of India* (series of shorts) (1934); *Rhodes of Africa* (US: *Rhodes*, 2nd unit dir., Berthold Viertel, 1936); *The Great Barrier* (US: *Silent Barriers*, 2nd unit dir., Milton Rosmer); *King Solomon's Mines* (2nd unit dir., Robert Stevenson) (1937).

BARKER, Clive (1952–)

Clive Barker was born in Liverpool on 5 October 1952. He has written novels, short stories, plays and screenplays, is a capable graphic artist and has directed and produced films. His literary and cinematic output is often marketed as horror but this generic label does not adequately describe work that is best thought of as visionary, dark fantasy.

Barker's first involvement in cinema occurred prior to the breakthrough commercial success of his short story collection *The Books of Blood* in 1984. During the 1970s, while Barker was working mainly in theatre, he and his collaborators made several experimental shorts. Shot on Super-8 or 16mm, films such as *Salome* (1972), *Jack O Lant* (1972) and *The Forbidden* (1978) were usually screened only for friends and left uncompleted. After *The Books of Blood* made him a bankable figure, Barker wrote the screenplays for two British horror films, *Underworld* (George Pavlou, 1985) and *Rawhead Rex* (George Pavlou, 1987), both of which suffered from budgetary restrictions and difficulties in translating Barker's distinctive fiction into something conventionally horror-like. Barker's own experience of film direction would involve similar tensions between his ambitions and the commercial imperatives of the horror genre to which, with increasing frustration on his part, his work was often consigned. However, *Hellraiser* (1987), his first feature film as a director, did successfully combine Barker's vision with commercial appeal.

Hellraiser is a remarkably assured directorial debut. Its conjoining of a grim domestic realism with the fantastic realm of the 'cenobites', imaginary creatures associated with intense sadomasochistic imagery, was strikingly original and achieved with the utmost conviction. The film featured an unnerving performance from Clare Higgins as a murderous woman intent on rescuing her lover from the cenobites' tortures. It also introduced the only British-sourced horror icon of the 1980s, Pinhead, the lead cenobite (played with articulate dignity by Doug Bradley) who would go on to appear in several sequels.

Nightbreed (1990), Barker's second film as director, had a much bigger budget but was a more troubled production. Barker's original scenario – in which the monsters turn out to be the heroes while the 'normal' characters are the real monsters – proved too unconventional for the film's backers, who insisted upon extensive reshooting. The resulting film was interesting but inevitably compromised and it did not repeat the commercial success of *Hellraiser.*

In 1991 Barker relocated to California where he has continued to write, and has directed another film, *Lord of Illusions*, as well as acting as executive producer on several others, most notably *Gods and Monsters* (Bill Condon, 1998), a film about James Whale – a director who in his Britishness, his homosexuality and his reluctant association with horror bears more than a passing resemblance to Barker himself.

(Peter Hutchings)

BIBLIOGRAPHY: Bradley, Doug, *Sacred Monsters* (London: Titan, 1996); Nutman, Philip, 'The Dark Backwards', *Fangoria* no. 200, Mar. 2001, pp. 26–8, 30–2; Winter, Douglas E., *Clive Barker: The Dark Fantastic* (London: HarperCollins, 2002).

FILMOGRAPHY: *Salome* (short); *Jack O Lant* (short) (1972); *The Forbidden* (short, 1978); *Hellraiser* (1987); *Nightbreed* (US, 1990); *Lord of Illusions* (US, 1995).

BARKER, Mike (1966–)

Mike Barker entered the film industry as a clapper/loader in the 1980s, working on several films, including Derek Jarman's *Caravaggio* (1986), before becoming a director in television. After establishing his reputation with stylish episodes of the crime drama series *Silent Witness* in 1996, he was given a prestigious adaptation of Anne Brontë's *The Tenant of Wildfell Hall* to direct. An intriguing first half was followed by tedious expository flashbacks, displaying an unevenness in Barker's touch that has plagued his subsequent work.

His first feature film, *The James Gang* (1997), promised much, with its talented cast (Helen McCrory, Toni Collette, John Hannah, Jason Flemyng) and its offbeat story of a desperate mother on the run for robberies she carries out with her four little children. McCrory gives an impressive performance as the criminal supermum, and Barker's eclectically inventive style keeps the film moving, but it is let down by a pedestrian plot and the happy-clappy Polygram ethos. *Best Laid Plans*, a convoluted American film noir, was harder and slicker but it failed to establish Barker in Hollywood. He returned to Britain for another glossy BBC adaptation, R. D. Blackmore's much-filmed *Lorna Doone*.

Barker remained in the 17th century for the ambitious and expensive *To Kill a King*, an interesting attempt to make Sir Thomas Fairfax, commander of the Roundhead's New Model Army, the hero of the English Civil War. Unfortunately the film's $23 million budget was not in place when shooting started and production was twice halted while new sources of finance were sought. Concern with financial matters seems to have left little time to check whether the script bore any relationship to historical reality. Rupert Everett plays King Charles as a manipulative bitch; Tim Roth represents Cromwell as a psychopathic thug; while Dougray Scott's Fairfax – a good man in a wicked world – can find little to do beyond striding purposively around the gloomy set. Unsurprisingly, *To Kill a King* pleased neither critics nor audiences, though Barker's achievement in persuading his cast and crew to continue working when finance ran out won him respect in the industry. He went on to direct *A Good Woman* (2004), a sleek updating of Oscar Wilde's *Lady Windermere's Fan*, with Helen Hunt, Scarlet Johansson and Tom Wilkinson among the expatriates and newlyweds leading frivolous lives on the picturesque Amalfi coast in the 1930s.

(Robert Murphy)

BIBLIOGRAPHY: Hunt, Nick, 'Close Up: Mike Barker', *Screen International*, 21 Mar. 2003, p. 13; Tutt, Louise, 'In the Frame: Mike Barker', *Screen International*, June 1999, p. 27; Minns, Adam, 'UK Budgets Face the Chop', *Screen International*, 12 Apr. 2002, p. 14.

FILMOGRAPHY: *The James Gang* (1997); *Best Laid Plans* (US, 1999); *To Kill a King* (UK/Ger, 2003); *A Good Woman* (UK/Sp/It/US, 2004).

BARKER, Will (1867–1951)

William George Barker was born in London in 1867. Having dabbled with film on an amateur basis, he began his professional career in 1901 when he founded the Autoscope Company. At first he was drawn to topical films and the potential of cinema for documenting aspects of life. He undertook expeditions to Canada, Norway and Africa, and his African films were eventually released in a series called *Cape to Cairo*, premiered at the Palace Theatre in London in 1907. When Autoscope was merged with the much larger Warwick Trading Company in January 1906 Barker was left in command. He launched a daily newsreel, *London Day by Day*, but it had to be abandoned because bad weather made it impossible to film every day. He also patented a sound process, the Warwick Cinephone, which like all early sound processes suffered from a lack of controllable synchronisation and inadequate amplification. In 1909 he left Warwick to form a new company, Barker Motion Photography, with studios in the west London suburb of Ealing. That same year he travelled to America to counter the threat posed by the Motion Picture Patents Company trust, and signed a deal with the anti-trust International Projection and Producing Company to ensure the continued sale of British films in the USA. By 1911 the IPPC had failed and British film-makers like Barker had to seek other ways of restoring their fortunes.

Amid loud publicity Baker paid Sir Herbert Beerbohm Tree £1,000 for a day's work reproducing his stage role on film in *Henry VIII* (Louis N. Parker, 1911). The stage sets at His Majesty's Theatre were transported to Barker's studios and rebuilt there, and a composer, Edward German, was hired to write music especially for the film. Prints were released for hire only, at a time when showmen bought copies of films outright, and with typical flamboyance Barker announced that he would publicly burn all twenty prints after twenty-eight days, so the film would never be seen except in pristine condition. Three other extravaganzas followed: *East Lynne* (Bert Haldane, 1913), *Sixty Years a Queen* (Bert Haldane, 1913) and *Jane Shore* (Bert Haldane/F. Martin Thornton, 1915). *East Lynne*, an adaptation of a popular stage melodrama, was the first British six-reel feature. *Sixty Years a Queen*, which cost £12,000 to make, an unprecedented sum for a British feature, was a highly successful patriotic celebration of the reign of Queen Victoria. *Jane Shore*, a historical pageant centring on the life of Edward IV's charismatic mistress, condemned by Richard III as a sorceress, proved less popular, despite its lavish sets and costumes.

Barker had the bluster required to produce his mammoth epics but generally handed the directing reins to trusted comrades such as Bert Haldane. However, he did direct an astonishing early version of H. Rider Haggard's *She*. In 1915 Barker and Frenchman Horace L. Lucoque (who owned the rights to the novel and whose wife would write the screenplay) joined forces to produce *She* as a star vehicle for the French actress and singer Alice Delysia. Barker had the film designed by the artist Lancelot Speed, and festooned his sets and actors with costumes, jewellery and authentic period artefacts. The film ran one and a half hours and Barker was compared to D. W. Griffith.

Barker was a big ideas man. A wild and sometimes reckless character, he was not averse to settling disputes by beating his adversary with a whip. His trademark logo was, appropriately, a bulldog – like Barker himself, tough, pugnacious and thoroughly British. His style was simple: big stories, big actors and big battles with lots of people in them. His films contrasted markedly with the small, intimate and very British melodramas of his friend and rival Cecil Hepworth. Barker's films were closer to the epic stories coming from Italy and America, like *Cabiria* (Giovanni Pastrone, 1913) and *The Birth of a Nation* (D. W. Griffith, 1915). But sensational though they were, Barker's films were crude in their use of film language and failed to attract the international audience they needed to be economically viable.

Barker announced his retirement from the film business the day after the 1918 Armistice, but in 1920 he was coaxed by his friend William Jeapes, managing director of the Topical Film Company, to follow the Prince of Wales on his Empire tour and some of Barker's work was released as issues of Topical's newsreel, *Topical Budget*, and as a special released in 1920, *50,000 Miles with the Prince of Wales*. During the inter-war period he ran a photographic company in Wimbledon, and in 1936 gave a talk to the British Kinematograph Society about his career. He died in Wimbledon on 6 November 1951.

(Simon Brown)

BIBLIOGRAPHY: Low, Rachael, *The History of the British Film 1906–1914* (London: George Allen & Unwin, 1949); Low, Rachael, *The History of the British Film 1914–1918* (London: George Allen & Unwin, 1950).

FILMOGRAPHY: *Cape to Cairo* (1907); *She* (co-dir. H. L. Lucoque, 1916); *50,000 Miles with the Prince of Wales* (1920).

BARR-SMITH, A. (1905–?)

Albert Barr-Smith was born in Australia in 1905. By 1936 he was in England collaborating on the script of a Will Fyffe comedy, *Well Done, Henry* (Wilfred Noy). In 1938 he produced *Tea Leaves in the Wind* (Ward Wing), an atmospheric melodrama set in Ceylon, and in 1940 *Tilly of Bloomsbury* (Leslie Hiscott), an adaptation of a popular play by Ian Hay. Following the war he wrote and directed two ambitious B-films: *The Hangman Waits*, which gloomily but convincingly follows the tracking down of a murderous Eastbourne cinema organist who has chopped up an usherette; and the rather less lurid *Death in the Hand*, a suspenseful train drama relayed through flashbacks. Both films were well received, but the interesting Barr-Smith then disappears from view.

(Geoff Brown and Robert Murphy)

FILMOGRAPHY: *The Hangman Waits* (1947); *Death in the Hand* (1948).

BARRETT, Lezli-An (1957–)

Lezli-An Barrett was born in Greenford, Middlesex, on 18 April 1958. A graduate of the National Film School, she came to notice in 1982 through her short feminist film, *An Epic Poem*. Alan Fountain, a commissioning editor at Channel 4, encouraged her to develop another project, and after a protracted period managed to raise finance from the Cannon group's New Directors project for *Business as Usual*, a trenchant, committed drama of sexual harassment in the workplace, set amid the Merseyside economic recession of the 1980s. The story, derived from an actual trade union dispute, explores everyday problems of economic hardship and concentrates on the strained relations of union representative Babs Flynn (Glenda Jackson) and her husband Kieran (John Thaw), a former shop steward emasculated through redundancy. The film manages a fresh approach to gender, sexuality and workplace politics, and is sustained by excellent performances.

Barrett's early promise in features has been unfulfilled. She might be considered the victim of bad timing: attaching herself

to Cannon at the moment of its demise and producing a pro-union film at the height of Thatcherism. Speaking of her experience, she declared, 'I didn't realise that that was *it*. It felt like the beginning, but in fact it was the *pinnacle*' (Hasted, p. 44).
(Alan Burton)

BIBLIOGRAPHY: Cook, Pam, 'The Knack and How to Get It', *Monthly Film Bulletin*, Sept. 1987, pp. 262–4; Hasted, Nick, 'Where Are They Now?', *Empire*, Nov. 1992, pp. 44–5.

FILMOGRAPHY: *An Epic Poem* (short, 1982); *Business as Usual* (1987).

BARRON, Steve (1956–)

Steve Barron was born in Dublin on 4 May 1956. His mother is the producer-director Zelda Barron. He first worked in films as assistant cameraman on *Exposé* (James Kenelm Clarke, 1975) and clapper loader on Richard Attenborough's *A Bridge Too Far* (1977). In the 1980s he made his name directing pop videos for Dire Straits ('Money for Nothing'), Fun Boy Three ('It Ain't What You Do'), Human League ('Don't You Want Me'), Japan ('Visions of China'), Madonna ('Burning Up'), Michael Jackson ('Billie Jean'), Spandau Ballet ('Lifeline'), Tears for Fears ('Mad World') and many others.

His low-key debut feature, *Electric Dreams*, is a pleasant fantasy-romance, but has none of the daring of his music video work. Moving to Hollywood, he made *Teenage Mutant Ninja Turtles*. It was a timely commercial success, but Barron's next film, *Coneheads*, was a flop and diverted him from a standard Hollywood career. After directing an acceptable cinema version of *Pinocchio*, he essayed large-scale fantasy for television with the excellent miniseries *Merlin* (1998), starring Sam Neill, and the rather weaker *Arabian Nights* (2000). His odd career also takes in executive producer credits on the kids' television series *ReBoot* (1994) and the films *The Specialist* (Luis Llosa, 1994) and *While You Were Sleeping* (Jon Turteltaub, 1995).

Barron's most recent films have been smaller and more personal: the Dublin fantasy *Rat*, with Pete Postlethwaite rodentised in a weird mix of Kafka and Roddy Doyle, and the lively, ramshackle mock documentary *Mike Bassett: England Manager*.
(Kim Newman)

BIBLIOGRAPHY: Blair, Iain, 'Steve Barron's Electric Dreams', *On Location*, Sept. 1984, pp. 92–3; Maxford, Howard, 'More Turtle Action', *Starburst*, Jan. 1991, pp. 27–9.

FILMOGRAPHY: *Electric Dreams* (1984); *Teenage Mutant Ninja Turtles* (US, 1990); *Coneheads* (US, 1993); *The Adventures of Pinocchio* (US, 1996); *Rat* (Ir, 2000); *Mike Bassett: England Manager* (2001).

BARRON, Zelda

Zelda Barron worked as a production assistant on a number of important films in the 1960s, including *Morgan: A Suitable Case for Treatment* (Karel Reisz, 1966), *Our Mother's House* (Jack Clayton, 1967), *if . . . .* (Lindsay Anderson, 1968) and *Leo the Last* (John Boorman, 1969). Later she worked on several productions directed by Michael Apted, and on Warren Beatty's *Reds* (1981) and Barbra Streisand's *Yentl* (1983), two big American productions based in Britain. In the early 1980s she formed Skreba Films with Ann Skinner and Simon Relph. With financial backing from Virgin, Rank, Rediffusion and the NFFC, she made her directorial debut, *Secret Places*, a modestly enjoyable story about a German refugee in an English girls' school during the Second World War. After directing pop videos for Culture Club, she shot her second film, *Shag*, a coming-of-age dance craze film set in South Carolina in 1963, which with its promising young stars Phoebe Cates and Bridget Fonda was a modest box-office success.

At short notice, Barron stepped in as director of *Bulldance*, a film based on a legend about Cretan bull-leapers shot in Yugoslavia. In a letter complaining of production problems, she concluded that despite the difficulties, she had delivered a film that would reach a wide audience. Unfortunately it did not and Barron's career as a feature film director was snuffed out. She is the mother of director/producer Steve Barron.
(Robert Murphy)

BIBLIOGRAPHY: 'Barron: Taking the Bull by the Horns', *Screen International*, 28 Jan. 1989, p. 6; Paterson, Elaine, 'Shagged Out', *Time Out*, 10 Aug. 1988, p. 12; Vaines, Colin, 'No Risks for "Secret Places" As Barron Makes Directing Debut', *Screen International*, 15 Oct. 1983, p. 17.

FILMOGRAPHY: *Secret Places* (1984); *Shag* (aka *Shag: The Movie*, US/UK, 1987); *Bulldance* (aka *Forbidden Sun*, 1989).

BASSETT, Michael J.

Michael J. Bassett was born and brought up in rural Shropshire. After leaving school at sixteen he spent eighteen months working with a wildlife film-maker before presenting science and nature items on the children's television show *Get Fresh*. Various other television assignments followed but Bassett decided he wanted to direct films. He made a number of shorts, wrote an episode of the hi-tech television crime series *Bugs* (1998) and handled electronic press kits on *The Scarlet Tunic* (Stuart St Paul, 1996), *Waking Ned* (Kirk Jones, 1998) and a dozen other films, graduating to second-unit director on *The Abduction Club* (Stefan Schwartz, 2001).

His script for a supernatural thriller set in the French trenches during the First World War attracted interest, but Bassett's determination to use it for his directorial debut proved an obstacle. He eventually secured a $5 million budget, and *Deathwatch* was shot in the Czech Republic. Live rats and rotting corpses in abundance evoke an appropriate atmosphere for the horrors of trench warfare, but Bassett's handling of suspense and action is rudimentary, and he hampers his actors with plodding dialogue peppered with anachronisms. It remains to be seen whether his perseverance, ambition and the experience gained from this first film will be put to good use.
(Robert Murphy)

BIBLIOGRAPHY: Jones, Alan, 'In the Trenches with *Deathwatch*', *Fangoria* no. 221, Apr. 2003, pp. 56–60, 80; Macmillan, Scott, 'Case

Study: *Deathwatch*', *Screen International*, 5 July 2002, p. 14; <www.michaelbassett.com/pages/layout.htm>.

FILMOGRAPHY: *Down* (short); *The Last Waltz* (short); *The Burning* (short) (1995); *The Abduction Club* (2nd unit dir., Stefan Schwartz, 2001); *Deathwatch* (2002).

BATLEY, Ethyle (1879–1917)

A director, actress and scriptwriter, Ethyle Batley was one of the few women making films in Britain in the period before the First World War. She worked mostly alongside her husband Ernest G. Batley (1873-1955) and their daughter Dorothy (1902–1983). In 1910, Ernest began directing one-reel dramas for H. B. English Films, mostly with Dorothy as the plucky child heroine. Ethyle followed in 1912 with *Peggy Gets Rid of the Baby*, featuring Dorothy and Ernest, the first of several domestic comedies for the John Bull brand. By early 1913, the trio had established themselves at the British and Colonial Kinematograph Company, soon to expand to a large new studio in Walthamstow; from this period comes *There's Good in the Worst of Us*, one of Ethyle's few surviving films. While Ethyle concentrated on directing, Ernest took the lead roles in several adventurous B & C features directed by Charles Weston (in the four-reel *The Battle of Waterloo*, 1913, he was Napoleon). In the autumn of 1914, several Batley films emerged under the company banner of the cinematographer Frederick Burlingham, a B & C colleague; by January they had joined him officially, though they soon established a separate company, the patriotically named British Oak, operating from a studio in Ebury Street, Victoria, with their own distribution company, New Agency, in support.

In length their British Oak output was modest: Ethyle concentrated on one-reel comedies and dramas, turning out several a month, and collaborated on the script for Ernest's biggest directing venture, the four-reel *The Boys of the Old Brigade* (1916). Most of Ethyle's own productions during the war were similarly patriotic subjects: one two-reeler for Burlingham bore the brave title *War Is Hell* (1915). Very few prints have survived, but available evidence suggests that, though not spectacular, her films were finely crafted. In *Bulldog Grit* (1915) she certainly shows a mastery of crosscutting techniques, creating a truly dramatic finale, as well as drawing some excellently natural performances, especially from Dorothy. In April 1917 Ethyle died at the age of thirty-eight, following an operation; the trade journals noted her death as the sad loss of an outstanding artist. The British Oak brand soon ceased, though Ernest directed himself and Dorothy in one more film in 1919, the four-reel farm drama *The Sins of Youth*. Dorothy continued acting on stage, and married the actor-director Guy Newall; Ernest vanished into obscurity, dying in Bournemouth in 1955.

(Geoff Brown and Simon Brown)

BIBLIOGRAPHY: Low, Rachael, *The History of the British Film 1906–1914* (London: George Allen & Unwin, 1949); Low, Rachael, *The History of the British Film 1914–1918* (London: George Allen & Unwin, 1950).

FILMOGRAPHY: *Peggy Gets Rid of the Baby*; *Peggy Becomes a Boy Scout*; *Through the Flames* (1912); *Deceiving Uncle*; *Peggy as Peacemaker*; *The Little Mother* (aka *The Child Mother*); *Two Father Christmasses*; *The Artist and His Model*; *There's Good in the Worst of Us* (1913); *Three Little Orphans*; *Mary's New Blouse*; *Saved by a Dream*; *A Little Child Shall Lead Them*; *Retribution*; *Out of Evil Cometh Good*; *Peggy's New Papa*; *Uncle Maxim's Will*; *The Drawn Blind*; *The Hairpin Trail*; *The Old Old Story*; *The Girl Boy Scout*; *Answering the Call*; *A Place in the Sun*; *One Shall Be Taken* (for Burlingham Standard, like the next films); *S.O.S.*; *The Fulfilment of the Law*; *Red Cross Pluck* (1914); *Instruments of Fate*; *War Is Hell*; *Bulldog Grit*; *Deliver the Goods*; *Remember Belgium*; New Agency: *One Honest Man*; *His Mother's Sacrifice*; *The Woman Pays*; *A Justifiable Deception*; *To Save Her Life*; *Nobody's Child*; *The Lie That Became the Truth*; *The Man Who Went*; *Belinda and the Eggs*; *His Bitter Lesson*; *A Tragic Mistake*; *Falsely Accused*; *The Bargee's Daughter*; *The Ear-Ring*; *The Brothers*; *Nursery Rhymes*; *The Hatton Garden Robbery* (1915); *The Forgery of the £1 Notes*; *The Great Red War*; *Into the Light*; *Keep the Home Fires Burning*; *The Rival Captains*; *Perkin's Pheasants*; *A Higher Power*; *England's Future Safeguard*; *The Initial Brooch*; *Folks of the Fair*; *The Finger of Suspicion*; *A Little Bootblack*; *The Daylight Saving Bill* (1916).

BATTERSBY, Roy (1936–)

Roy Battersby was born in London in 1936. After scientific programmes for the BBC in the 1960s, he found backing from Ken Loach and Tony Garnett's Kestrel Films and EMI to make *The Body*, a fascinating attempt to show the workings of the human body. Tony Imi's camera explored the body's processes in graphic detail, to the accompaniment of a whimsically poetic commentary and music composed by Ron Geesin and Pink Floyd's Roger Waters. Following this bizarre first feature, Battersby built a firmer reputation as a television drama director, working with writer Colin Welland in the style of provocative social realism pioneered by Loach. *Roll on Four O'Clock* (1970) explored bullying and prejudice in a run-down Manchester school; *Leeds United* (1974) was based on a real strike by women textile workers, and was considered subversive enough to get Battersby's name included on a list of political undesirables compiled by MI5 for the BBC. When further projects dried up, Battersby, an active member of the Workers' Revolutionary Party, ran their centre for Marxist Studies in Derby and worked on the party's daily newspaper, *Newsline*.

With fellow WRP member Vanessa Redgrave he made *The Palestinian* (1977), a long documentary exploring the aftermath of the Israeli invasion of Lebanon from the Palestinian point of view. His return to television came when he was recruited by Margaret Matheson at Central to make *A Change in Time* (1982), a drama about a factory shop steward coming to terms with redundancy and terminal illness. Battersby then worked with David Puttnam on an unmade adaptation of a Marilyn French novel and two features in the *First Love* series, produced with Goldcrest and Channel 4. *Winter Flight* shows a deep humanism in its treatment of two young people given a raw deal by society but finding dignity and respect in their love for each other. *Mr Love* is a whimsical tale about a dreamy old gardener unaccountably attractive to women. Battersby's radicalism was more evident in the drama serial *King of the Ghetto* (1986), which marked his return to the BBC. Farrukh Dhondy's script explored racial tensions in London's Brick Lane area, and made some attempt to root racial tensions in the poverty and deprivation of inner-city life in the 1980s. By contrast, *Fat Chance* (1987), an 'Inspector Morse' television film, was wholesome enough to be shown at a vicar's tea party, despite its revelations of Machiavellian shenanigans in the Church of England.

Although Battersby does not appear to have reneged on his left-wing beliefs, they no longer hamper his career in television. Success with the series *Space Island One* led to *Doomwatch: Winter Angel* (1999), a ponderous but intelligent pilot intended to revive the early 1970s' BBC science-fiction series *Doomwatch*. *Red Mercury*, a feature film exploring the reality of Islamic terrorism in Britain, written by Dhondy and shot in London's East End in January and February 2005, indicates that Battersby's radical voice might yet reach the big screen.

(Robert Murphy)

BIBLIOGRAPHY: Illot, Terry, 'Battersby Enjoys Period of Optimism', *Screen International*, 27 Oct. 1984, p. 250; Shenfield, Robin, 'Out of the Ghetto', *Broadcast*, 1 Nov. 1985, p. 17.

FILMOGRAPHY: *The Body* (doc., 1970); *The Palestinian* (doc., 1977); *Winter Flight* (1984); *Mr Love* (1985); *Red Mercury* (2005).

BAXTER, John (1896–1975)

John Baxter was born in Foot's Cray, Kent, in 1896. He joined the army on the outbreak of the First World War, initially entertaining the troops in concert parties, but eventually serving at Passchendaele. After the war he continued his career in provincial music hall as a performer and later a tour manager, gaining experience that he drew on extensively in his later films. In 1932 a chance meeting with Norman Loudon brought Baxter to Sound City studios at Shepperton.

Baxter's first film as sole director at Sound City, *Doss House*, established many of the themes that were to recur throughout his directing career. Less than an hour long, and made on a minuscule budget, it was unlike anything that had emerged from a British studio before. The thin plot of a reporter spending a night in a doss house threatened with closure is merely a pretext for a series of encounters with sympathetically drawn character types, whose bad-luck stories are teased out by natural-sounding dialogue and banter. Throughout the 1930s, Baxter worked on films similar in flavour to *Doss House*, maintaining something of a repertory of loyal players and technicians and always working to the low budgets and tight schedules typical of the 'quota quickie' section of the industry. He made films for Sound City, for Julius Hagen at Twickenham Studios, and later as an independent in partnership with John Barter.

The best of these films stress the dignified humanity of ordinary working people struggling to overcome the hardships of modern life through mutual co-operation, although their realist aesthetic is undercut by an overt sentimentality and touches of melodrama. The charity benefit concert is a recurring motif, enabling the display of comic and musical acts from Baxter's beloved music hall. *Say It with Flowers* is undoubtedly the best in this mode. The long sequence introducing the various costermongers and their concerns is skilfully and unobtrusively directed, and the music-hall turns of Charles Coborn, Marie Kendall and Florrie Forde in the finale are a joy to watch – more than can be said for the variety turns that tend to dominate some of Baxter's less successful efforts. Baxter's 1930s' films were forgotten for many years, but in the late 1980s they enjoyed a revival, praised for a portrayal of working-class life deemed to be lamentably absent from mainstream British productions of the period. However, it should be noted that the films remain essentially conservative in nature – deference to authority and stolid acceptance of the status quo form a large part of their philosophy.

Sally (Deborah Kerr) isn't convinced that her elders (Mary Merrall, Marie Ault, Iris Vandelour, Marjorie Rhodes and Maire O'Neill) know best; *Love on the Dole* (John Baxter, 1941)

By the late 1930s Baxter was back at Sound City, making vehicles for Hazel Ascot, a dancing child star who was being built up as Britain's answer to Shirley Temple. At the outbreak of war, however, he made the happy move to British National, a modest studio that, like Baxter himself, appeared to hit its stride in the heightened atmosphere of wartime Britain. Here, as director and producer, he worked regularly on vehicles for Flanagan and Allen, and for Arthur Lucan as Old Mother Riley. The anarchic comedy of these performers effectively tempers Baxter's tendency towards deferential sentimentalism. Such films remained firmly in the category of modest programme material, but at British National Baxter was able to work on more personal projects as well. *The Shipbuilders*, *Let the People Sing* and *The Common Touch* (a remake of *Doss House*) all bear the stamp of his personal preoccupations, and are made on a more ambitious scale. It was with *Love on the Dole*, however, that Baxter achieved his greatest critical success, and the film remains an undoubted classic.

Walter Greenwood's 1933 novel of Depression life seems perfectly tailored to Baxter's preoccupations and to the technique of film-making that he had developed through the 1930s. The modest budget together with the essentially ensemble nature of the narrative – a portrait of the interlocking lives of characters in a community struggling against hardship – suited Baxter's directorial technique and repertory of players perfectly. The result was an adaptation that captured exactly the spirit and tone of the novel. The censors had resisted the idea of a film adaptation of *Love on the Dole* throughout the 1930s, but in 1941 the wartime context gave the film a new theme, expressed in the closing scenes – a determination that wartime hardships, unlike those of the Depression, should lead to a 'New Britain'. It is a theme that is reiterated in Baxter's later wartime films.

In 1944 Baxter left British National, making his 'John Baxter Productions' entirely independent. Such a position, however, became increasingly difficult in the harsh post-war climate. Baxter turned to producing and directing children's films intended to be shown at Rank's children's cinema clubs. In 1951 he helped set up Group 3 with John Grierson. This loose producers' co-operative was founded with the intention of attracting funds from the National Film Finance Corporation and to encourage independent and inexperienced film-makers. Baxter's role was primarily as a producer, but he did direct a final remake of *Doss House*, retitled *Judgment Deferred* and featuring a debut performance by Joan Collins. When Group 3 broke up, Baxter became an executive at Television Wales and the West (TWW), retiring in 1968.

John Baxter was remembered with immense affection by everyone who worked with him. A lifelong Christian Scientist, his sympathetic humanism shone through his work. While many of his films are undoubtedly second-feature material, some of them are remarkably affective, displaying a unique film-making talent. He died in relative obscurity in 1975.
(Lawrence Napper)

BIBLIOGRAPHY: Brown, Geoff with Tony Aldgate, *The Common Touch: The Films of John Baxter* (London: BFI, 1989); Napper, Lawrence, 'A Despicable Tradition? Quota Quickies in the 1930s', in Robert Murphy (ed.), *The British Cinema Book* (London: BFI, 1997); Richards, Jeffrey, 'A Film-Maker with the Common Touch', *Daily Telegraph*, 22 Feb. 1989, p. 16.

FILMOGRAPHY: *Reunion* (co-dir. Ivar Campbell, 1932); *Doss House*; *The Song of the Plough* (aka *County Fair*) (1933); *Say It with Flowers*; *Lest We Forget*; *Music Hall*; *Flood Tide*; *Kentucky Minstrels* (1934); *A Real Bloke*; *The Small Man*; *Jimmy Boy*; *Birds of a Feather* (1935); *Men of Yesterday*; *Hearts of Humanity* (aka *The Crypt*) (1936); *The Song of the Road*; *The Academy Decides*; *Talking Feet* (1937); *Stepping Toes* (1938); *Secret Journey* (US: *Among Human Wolves*); *What Would You Do, Chums?* (1939); *Laugh It Off*; *Old Mother Riley in Society*; *Crook's Tour*; *Old Mother Riley in Business* (1940); *Love on the Dole*; *Old Mother Riley's Ghosts*; *The Common Touch* (1941); *Let the People Sing*; *We'll Smile Again* (1942); *Theatre Royal*; *The Shipbuilders* (1943); *Dreaming* (1944); *Here Comes the Sun* (1945); *The Grand Escapade* (1946); *When You Come Home*; *Fortune Lane* (1947); *Nothing Venture*; *The Last Load* (1948); *Three Bags Full* (1949); *The Dragon of Pendragon Castle*; *The Second Mate* (1950); *Judgment Deferred* (1952); *Ramsbottom Rides Again* (1956).

BAXTER, R. K. Neilson (1909–1978)

'Brisk, enjoyable, convincing and useful,' proclaimed *Documentary News Letter* in 1941, reviewing R. K. Neilson Baxter's *New Acres*, a persuasive short about Britain's wartime field-ploughing campaign. In a career dominated by public service film-making, the phrase could almost be the director's motto. Rowan Kennedy Neilson Baxter was born in London in 1909. After studying at Exeter College, Oxford, he joined the university graduates hired by Michael Balcon at Gainsborough and Gaumont-British, and worked throughout the decade as an assistant director, production manager and location director in the commercial industry. In 1937 he directed a modestly suspenseful crime drama, *The House of Silence*, for 'quickie' producer George King. But in 1940 the needs of wartime led him decisively toward the documentary field, and the 'convincing and useful'. Initially he joined the Shell Film Unit, where his output included *New Acres* and training films for the Admiralty. Then in 1944, with his wife and frequent collaborator Kay Mander and J. B. Napier-Bell, he established Basic Films to make educational and scientific films, functioning largely as a producer. Between 1946 and 1952 he also served on the editorial staff of the *Penguin Film Review* and Penguin Books' annual survey *The Cinema* – the cultured reader's essential guides to what their editors hoped would be a brave new post-war world of socially responsible film art.

In general these hopes were dashed, especially in short film production: lacking government support, many documentary film units disbanded or shrivelled in the 1950s. But Baxter himself flourished. Leaving Basic in 1949, he quickly found work with the British Transport Commission's newly established film unit and directed *Inland Waterways*, one of the first batch of BTF films unveiled in May 1950. Ten other transport documentaries followed, among jobs for UNESCO as Visual Aids Adviser and assorted freelance work elsewhere. The films variously praise the social uses and technological glories of canals, the Transport Ferry Service, London Transport, the Hovercraft, even the unbuilt Channel Tunnel. By far the most resonant and interesting is *All That Mighty Heart* (1963), a valiant attempt to make a poetic mosaic, in the Humphrey Jennings fashion, from the travels of London's weekday workers and Saturday visitors. Red Routemaster buses, Stevenage housewives, train upholstery: all gleam equally in David Watkin's burnished photography. Linking commentary is avoided; instead we take our bearings from evocative BBC radio snippets stretching over morning, noon and night. Both in substance and documentary style, *All That Mighty Heart* vividly recalls a lost world.

No further chances for lyrical documentary poetry followed. But the films remain useful social documents and reservoirs of nostalgia – especially Baxter's swansong, *Express Link with Europe* (1972), a plea for fast rail connections to and from the Channel Tunnel. R. K. Neilson Baxter died in London on 4 July 1978.

(Geoff Brown)

BIBLIOGRAPHY: 'New Acres', *Documentary News Letter* vol. 2 no. 9, Sept. 1941, p. 167; Reed, John, *Moving Images: Commemorating 40 Years of British Transport Films* (London: Capitol Transport, 1990).

FILMOGRAPHY: *The House of Silence* (fiction feature, 1937); *Shoeing a Horse* (1940); *New Acres*; *War in the East* (1941); *Casting in Steel at Wilson's Forge* (1946); *Inland Waterways* (1950); *There Go the Boats* (1951); *Boat to Birmingham* (1953); *Under the River* (1958); *Ferry Load*; *Bridge 114* (1960); *Omnibus for All*; *All That Mighty Heart* (1963); *The Importance of being E.R.N.I.E.* (1964); *The Great Highway* (1966); *Method Study – Basic Principles* (1968); *Seaspeed across the Channel*; *Computers for Management* (1969); *Not Just for Burning* (1971); *Express Link with Europe* (1972).

BAXTER, Ronnie (1931–)

Ronnie Baxter entered the television industry in 1956; he directed popular television sitcoms from *In Loving Memory* (1969) to *A Bit of a Do* (1989). *For the Love of Ada*, which paired Wilfred Pickles and Irene Handl, and *Never Mind the Quality Feel the Width*, with John Bluthal and Joe Lynch as East End tailors, are competent spin-offs from well-characterised and gently humorous television series.

(Robert Murphy)

FILMOGRAPHY: *For the Love of Ada*; *Never Mind the Quality Feel the Width* (1972).

BAYLY, Stephen (1942–)

Stephen Bayly was born in Baltimore, Maryland, on 7 July 1942. After producing Tony Scott's *Loving Memory* (1969) he attended the National Film School between 1976 and 1979. With writer Ruth Carter and producer Linda James, he worked on *Joni Jones* (1982), a series based on R. Gerallt Jones' stories about a schoolboy's wartime experiences in rural Wales, for the fledgling S4C (Welsh Fourth Channel). Bayly and Carter also collaborated on *Aderyn Papur . . . And Pigs Might Fly* (1984), a mild but effective comedy set in a North Wales community blighted by quarry closures. They also made *Coming up Roses*, a Welsh-language feature film that drew analogies between a battle to save a South Wales local cinema and the miners' struggle against pit closures.

Bayly went on to direct a well-regarded film for the Children's Film Foundation, *Just Ask for Diamond*, and to produce Richard Loncraine's *Richard III* (1995) and Marleen Gorris' *Mrs Dalloway* (1997). He was appointed Director of the National Film and Television School in 1998 and went on to serve as Chief Executive before resigning in 2003.

(David Berry)

BIBLIOGRAPHY: Berry, David, *Wales and Cinema: The First 100 Years* (Cardiff: University of Wales Press, 1994); Bayly, Stephen, 'Sianel Pedwar Cymru – the Welsh Perspective', *Sight and Sound*, Autumn 1983, pp. 244–7; Falk, Quentin, 'Setting the Industry Standard', *Exposure*, Summer 1998, pp. 14–15.

FILMOGRAPHY: *Dream City* (short, 1976); *Smile Until I Tell You to Stop* (short, 1979); *Coming up Roses/Rhosyn a Rhith* (1986); *Just Ask for Diamond* (aka *Diamond's Edge*, 1988).

BEAUDINE, William (1892–1970)

William Beaudine was born in New York City on 15 January 1892. During his long and prolific career he directed almost 200 feature films, numerous comedy shorts and over 200 series episodes for television in the 1950s and 60s. He joined D. W. Griffith's Biograph Company in 1909, became an actor and writer with the leading comedy director of the day, Mack Sennett, and in 1915 became a director of comedy shorts for the Kalem Company. He made his first feature, *Watch Your Step*, in 1922 and worked with a number of leading stars including Mary Pickford, Clara Bow and Tom Mix in the silent era, and W. C. Fields in the early 1930s. He established a reputation for speed and efficiency and acquired the nickname William 'One Shot' Beaudine. Included in his voluminous output are a number of British films made during a brief period working in England in the 1930s. True to his reputation as a fast and prolific worker, Beaudine directed thirteen films during his three years working in Britain. A number of these were made as Warner Bros. quota pictures at their Teddington studio, but Beaudine also worked at Islington for the Gaumont-British/Gainsborough combine and at Ealing for Associated Talking Pictures.

Beaudine was one of several Hollywood directors despatched to Britain to bring American pace and glamour to British films. Along with Marcel Varnel and Monty Banks, two other foreign-born film-makers, he made a significant contribution to that most British of film genres, the music-hall-based comedy, working with some of the prominent comedians of the time. He directed four of Will Hay's pictures including *Boys Will Be Boys*, in which Hay reworked his famous stage persona of the bumbling schoolmaster for the screen, and *Windbag the Sailor*, the first film to team Hay with Moore Marriott and Graham Moffatt. Beaudine also directed films with Max Miller, Nervo and Knox before they joined the Crazy Gang, Will Fyffe and George Formby.

In 1938 Beaudine returned to Hollywood, where he specialised in low-budget films and B-picture series such as the Bowery Boys and Charlie Chan. He began directing voluminously for television in the 1950s, but his career ended with two cult classics of low-grade cinema, *Billy the Kid vs. Dracula* (1966) and *Jesse James Meets Frankenstein's Daughter* (1966). One could argue that his films with Will Hay were more memorable than his work in American cinema, where his identity tended to get lost among his tumultuous output. He died in Canoga Park, California, on 18 March 1970.

(Tom Ryall)

BIBLIOGRAPHY: Marshall, Wendy L., *William Beaudine: From Silents to Television* (Lanham, MD: Scarecrow Press, 2005); Sutton, David, *A Chorus of Raspberries: British Film Comedy 1929–1939* (Exeter: University of Exeter Press, 2000).

FILMOGRAPHY (UK only): *Dandy Dick; Two Hearts in Harmony; So, You Won't Talk?; Get off My Foot; Boys Will Be Boys* (1935); *Mr Cohen Takes a Walk; Where There's a Will; Windbag the Sailor; It's in the Bag; Educated Evans* (1936); *Take it from Me; Feather Your Nest; Said O'Reilly to McNab* (US: *Sez O'Reilly to McNab*) (1937).

BEDFORD, Terry (1943–)

Terry Bedford was born in London in 1943. After training with Ridley Scott on television commercials, he worked as a director of photography on *Monty Python and the Holy Grail* (Terry Gilliam/Terry Jones, 1974) and *Jabberwocky* (Terry Gilliam, 1977). He made his directing debut in 1983 with *Slayground*, an Anglo-American thriller backed by EMI, with Peter Coyote, Billie Whitelaw and Mel Smith. The resulting film is a disappointment despite a good pedigree – the script is by accomplished television crime writer Trevor Preston and based on a novel by 'Richard Stark' (Donald E. Westlake), whose work had previously been filmed as *Point Blank* (John Boorman, 1967) and *The Outfit* (John Flynn, 1974). A gang of small-time crooks accidentally kill a young girl during a botched robbery. Hunted down by her vengeful father, the sole survivor flees New York for England. Bedford gives the film a slick visual gloss, making atmospheric use of a funfair setting, but his direction shows little grasp of pace, tension or character. In essence, *Slayground* resembles a routine British second feature of the 1950s, complete with an imported American star.

Bedford worked as second-unit director on the Lynda La Plante television drama series *Killer Net* (Geoffrey Saxe, 1998), and directed episodes of the drama series *Harbour Lights* (1999) starring former *EastEnders* actor Nick Berry, but has made no more ventures into directing for the cinema.

(Daniel O'Brien)

FILMOGRAPHY: *Slayground* (1983).

BENNETT, Compton (1900–1974)

Robert Compton-Bennett, born in Tunbridge Wells on 15 January 1900, had a varied early career before entering the film industry as an assistant editor for London Films. He worked on documentaries during the war, directing *Find Fix and Strike* (1942), about the Fleet Air Arm, for Ealing. He worked as an editor for Sydney Box's Verity Films and directed *Men of Rochdale* (1944), celebrating the 100th anniversary of the Co-operative Movement. He moved into feature films with Box, directing the hugely popular *The Seventh Veil* (1945), a glossy, artfully plotted psychological melodrama starring Ann Todd and James Mason. Its success led to Hollywood offers, but before leaving, Bennett directed two more films for Box, *The Years Between* (1946) and *Daybreak* (1948). The former was a compelling study of the problems caused in a relationship by wartime absence, where Bennett's smooth, deft direction provides a solid framework for Valerie Hobson as a woman who has discovered her abilities during the war and finds her returning husband (Michael Redgrave) something of an encumbrance. *Daybreak*, held up by the censors for nearly two years because of its controversial stance on capital punishment, was another absorbing study of a dysfunctional relationship (Eric Portman and Ann Todd), which echoed pre-war French thrillers such as *Quai des brumes* (Marcel Carné, 1938).

In Hollywood, Bennett directed *My Own True Love* for Paramount, also about the problems of post-war relationships, and two Technicolor pictures for MGM: *That Forsyte Woman* (1949), an over-lush adaptation of Galsworthy's family saga, and *King Solomon's Mines* (1950), a spectacular version of Rider Haggard's famous tale. Bennett returned to Britain to direct *So Little Time* (1952), a Second World War tale of a tragic love affair between a German military governor and a Belgian aristocrat's daughter. He quickly followed it with *It Started in Paradise* (1952), a sub-Sirkian melodrama set in the world of *haute couture*, and *The Gift Horse* (1952), another war story, about a naval commander (Trevor Howard) blighted by an unjust accusation of negligence who redeems himself by sacrificing his ageing destroyer in a daring raid on the St Nazaire naval base. It was a film that emphasised character rather than action, as did the thriller *Desperate Moment* (1953) with Dirk Bogarde and Mai Zetterling, but neither was very successful and Bennett's career declined. The dreary thriller *That Woman Opposite* (1957) and the gruesome *Man-Eater* (1957) were low points, but *The Flying Scot* (1957) now has a deserved reputation as a tense thriller. *After the Ball* (1957), a biography of Vesta Tilley, brought a return to first features, but there was another three-year gap before *Beyond the Curtain* (1960), his last full feature, a competent, but undistinguished cold war thriller based on his own script.

Bennett is best remembered as the director of *The Seventh Veil* and his strength, even in his action films, was the ability to concentrate on tense, fraught relationships, which allowed actors

to create their characters in depth. He died in London on 13 August 1974.
(Andrew Spicer)

BIBLIOGRAPHY: 'British Feature Directors: An Index to Their Work', *Sight and Sound*, Autumn 1958, p. 291; Salmi, Markku, 'Compton Bennett', *Film Dope* no. 3, Aug. 1973, p. 25.

FILMOGRAPHY: *Fix Find and Strike* (doc., 1942); *Men of Rochdale* (doc., 1944); *The Seventh Veil* (1945); *The Years Between* (1946); *Daybreak*; *My Own True Love* (US) (1948); *That Forsyte Woman/The Forsyte Saga* (US, 1949); *King Solomon's Mines* (co-dir. Andrew Marton, US, 1950); *So Little Time*; *It Started in Paradise*; *The Gift Horse* (US: *Glory at Sea*) (1952); *Desperate Moment* (1953); *That Woman Opposite* (US: *City after Midnight*); *Man-Eater*, *The Flying Scot* (US: *Mailbag Robbery*); *After the Ball* (1957); *Beyond the Curtain* (1960); *First Left Past Aden* (doc., 1961); *How to Undress in Public without Undue Embarrassment* (short, 1965).

BENNETT, Edward (1950–)

Edward Bennett was born in Cambridge on 15 May 1950. After reading English literature at Cambridge University, he went on to study at the Royal College of Art. His films about art, funded by the Arts Council and the BFI, were followed by *Flying into the Wind* (1982), a television play written by David Leland, and *Ascendancy*, a feature film made with financial backing from the BFI. *Ascendancy* centres upon the daughter of a Belfast shipyard owner who refuses to speak and has a paralysed arm. The film suggests these are hysterical symptoms of an incestuous relationship with her brother, recently killed in the First World War. This traumatic family narrative is intertwined with the violent events surrounding the partition of Ireland. *Ascendancy* might be compared with Pat O'Connor's *Fools of Fortune* (1990) and Deborah Warner's *The Last September* (1999), which similarly explore this seismic moment in Irish history.

Ascendancy was critically well received and was joint winner of the Golden Bear Award at the 1983 Berlin Film Festival. But rather than pursuing a career in the film industry, Bennett opted for the greater security and regularity of making films and drama series for television, where he has been responsible for a number of high-quality thrillers, including one of the *Inspector Morse* films ('Last Seen Wearing', 1987), episodes of *Poirot* (1989), *Dalziel and Pascoe* (1997–8) and *Waking the Dead* (2000), and the feature-length *Second Sight II: Hide and Seek* (2000). *A Woman at War* (1991), an Anglo-French dramatisation of the wartime experiences of Hélène Moszkiewiez, a Belgian Jew who worked for the Gestapo as a cover for her Resistance activities, was screened in Britain as a television film. Production difficulties on location in Poland doubled the budget and disrupted production, but Martha Plimpton proved excellent as the perplexed but plucky heroine, and Bennett's homages to *The Third Man* (Carol Reed, 1949) and *Rear Window* (Alfred Hitchcock, 1954) bear testimony to his cine-literacy.
(Ruth Barton)

BIBLIOGRAPHY: Barton, Ruth, *Irish National Cinema* (New York and London: Routledge, 2004); Phelan, Brian, 'Logic of Horror', *The Belfast Revue*, Winter 1983, p. 4; Pym, John, 'Ulster Paralysis', *Sight and Sound*, Spring 1983, pp. 137–8; Pym, John, '*Ascendancy*: The Irish Are Coming . . .', *Monthly Film Bulletin*, May 1983, p. 144.

FILMOGRAPHY: *Hogarth* (doc. short, 1976); *The Life Story of Baal* (1977); *Four Questions about Art* (doc. 1979); *Ascendancy* (1982).

BENTLEY, Thomas (1880–1950)

Thomas Bentley was born in London in 1880 and though trained as an engineer opted instead to go on the stage as a Dickens impersonator. He embarked upon a film career shortly before the First World War as an actor with the Britannia company, appearing in *Leaves from the Books of Charles Dickens* (1912), but it was with the Hepworth company, which he joined soon after, that he established himself as a director. He spent around thirty years in the film industry working for a number of the most prominent companies of the time, directing almost sixty feature films and a great many shorts.

Unsurprisingly, his earliest films were Dickens adaptations, the most notable being *David Copperfield*, an early example of a long British film, and one hailed in the trade press as the finest British film ever made. After Hepworth he joined the newly formed British Actors Film Company, set up to bring theatrical works to the screen, and subsequently worked for some of the leading British firms of the 1920s including Ideal, Stoll, Graham-Wilcox and Welsh-Pearson. During this time he directed a number of pictures written by Eliot Stannard, best known as the screenwriter on Hitchcock's silent films. Towards the end of the decade Bentley joined British International Pictures and made one of the studio's early sound features, *The American Prisoner*, with Carl Brisson and Madeleine Carroll, and one of the first British musicals, *Harmony Heaven*, filmed partly in colour. He spent the 1930s making two or three films a year for BIP in a variety of genres together with a few titles at low-budget studios such as Twickenham and Welwyn. These include a further version of Dickens' *The Old Curiosity Shop*; an adaptation of Harold Brighouse's *Hobson's Choice*; Will Hay's first feature film, *Those Were the Days*; and *Silver Blaze*, adapted from a Sherlock Holmes story. He was also supervisory director on *Music Hath Charms*, a musical featuring the Henry Hall dance band, and *Royal Cavalcade*, BIP's epic chronicle produced to mark the Jubilee of King George V in 1935. He ended his film career in 1941 at the other end of the cultural spectrum with *Old Mother Riley's Circus* for British National Films.

Thomas Bentley had a long and prolific career in British cinema, yet his reputation remains low. Rachael Low characterised him as a 'hum-drum director' (Low, 1971, p. 238) and his work has failed to attract much attention from students of British cinema compared with his near contemporaries Hitchcock and Asquith. His identification with Dickens applies mainly to the very early part of his career, though his directorial profile, like

those of many British film-makers, is rooted in the adaptation of literature and drama. He died in 1950.

(Tom Ryall)

BIBLIOGRAPHY: 'A British Masterpiece – David Copperfield by the Hepworth Company', *The Bioscope*, 21 Aug. 1913, pp. 607–9; Burrows, Jonathan, *Legitimate Cinema* (Exeter: Exeter University Press, 2003); Low, Rachael, *The History of the British Film 1918–1929* (London: George Allen & Unwin, 1971); Low, Rachael, *Film Making in 1930s Britain* (London: George Allen & Unwin, 1985).

FILMOGRAPHY: *Oliver Twist* (1912); *David Copperfield* (1913); *The Old Curiosity Shop*; *The Chimes* (1914); *Barnaby Rudge*; *Hard Times*; *The Woman Who Dared* (US: *A Soul for Sale*) (1915); *Beau Brocade*; *Milestones* (1916); *The Labour Leader*; *Daddy*; *Les Cloches de Corneville* (1917); *Once upon a Time*; *The Divine Gift* (1918); *The Lackey and the Lady* (1919); *General Post*; *Beyond the Dreams of Avarice* (1920); *The Old Curiosity Shop*; *The Adventures of Mr Pickwick* (1921); *A Master of Craft* (1922); *Through Fire and Water*; The Jose Collins Drama Series (short films): *The Battle of Love*, *Shadow of Death*, *The Velvet Woman*, *The Courage of Despair*, *The Last Stake*, *Secret Mission* (1923); *Wanted, a Boy* (short); *Old Bill through the Ages*; *Love and Hate*; Thrilling Stories from the Strand Magazine (shorts): *The Cavern Spider*, *After Dark*; *Chappy – That's All* (1924); *Money Isn't Everything*; *A Romance of Mayfair* (1925); *The Man in the Street/Man of Mystery* (short); *White Heat* (1926); *The Silver Lining*; *The Antidote* (short) (1927); *Not Quite a Lady* (1928); *Young Woodley* (unrel.); *The American Prisoner*, *Acci-Dental Treatment* (short) (1929); *Harmony Heaven*; *Compromising Daphne* (US: *Compromised!*) (1930); *Keepers of Youth*; *Hobson's Choice* (1931); *After Office Hours*; *The Last Coupon*; *Sleepless Nights* (1932); *The Love Nest*; *Hawleys of High Street* (1933); *The Scotland Yard Mystery* (US: *The Living Dead*); *Those Were the Days*; *The Great Defender*, *The Old Curiosity Shop* (1934); *Royal Cavalcade* (US: *Regal Cavalcade*, co-dirs. Herbert Brenon/Norman Lee/Walter Summers/Will Kellino/Marcel Varnel); *Music Hath Charms* (co-dirs. Alexander Esway/Walter Summers/Arthur Woods) (1935); *She Knew What She Wanted* (1936); *The Angelus*; *Silver Blaze* (US: *Murder at the Baskervilles*); *The Last Chance* (1937); *Night Alone*; *Marigold* (1938); *Me and My Pal*; *Dead Man's Shoes*; *Lucky to Me*; *The Middle Watch* (1939); *Cavalcade of Variety*; *Three Silent Men* (1940); *Old Mother Riley's Circus* (1941).

BERESFORD, Bruce (1940–)

Bruce Beresford was born in Sydney on 16 August 1940. After a spell as a film editor in Nigeria, he found employment at the British Film Institute in London, eventually becoming the first Head of the BFI Production Board in 1966. After making a number of short films about artists, he made his breakthrough into features with *The Adventures of Barry McKenzie* (1972), based on the *Private Eye* cartoon-strip character created by Barry Humphries. The comic exploits of this rough-and-ready Australian in London proved immensely popular and led to an Australian sequel, *Barry McKenzie Holds His Own* (1974). Beresford's next British film, *Side by Side*, had Humphries co-starring with Terry-Thomas as warring nightclub owners.

The popularity of these broad comedies threatened to pigeonhole the ambitious Beresford at a time when the Australian film industry was going through a notable revival. Astutely he returned to his homeland to make a number of films – in particular *Don's Party* (1976), *The Getting of Wisdom* (1977) and *Breaker Morant* (1980) – that were successful in Australia and established Beresford as an internationally significant director. Subsequent highlights include his offbeat American films *Tender Mercies* (1983) and *Driving Miss Daisy* (1989), and the Australian/French Canadian period adventure *Black Robe* (1991). His craftsmanship, largely underestimated by critics but appreciated by producers, has taken him all round the world. Indeed, the nationality of his later films is generally academic, but those with British involvement include his staging of a sequence from Erich Wolfgang Korngold's 'Die Tote Stadt' in the opera portmanteau film *Aria*; his film about Alma Mahler, *Bride of the Wind*; and his Irish-set family melodrama, *Evelyn*.

(Richard Dacre)

BIBLIOGRAPHY: Gay, Ken, 'Dedicated Newcomers', *Films and Filming*, May 1969, pp. 32–3.

FILMOGRAPHY (UK only): *Traditional Dance* (doc. short, 1966); *Picasso the Sculptor* (doc. short); *Extravaganza* (doc. short); *Lichtenstein in London* (doc. short) (1968); *Barbara Hepworth at the Tate* (doc. short, 1969); *Cinema of Raymond Park* (doc. short, 1970); *The Adventures of Barry McKenzie* (1972); *Side by Side* (1975); *Aria* ('Die Tote Stadt' section, 1987); *Bride of the Wind* (UK/Ger/Aus, 2001); *Evelyn* (UK/US/Ger/Ir/Neth, 2002).

BERGER, Ludwig (1892–1969)

Ludwig Berger was born Ludwig Gottfried Heinrich Bamberger in Mainz, Germany, on 6 January 1892. He studied music and art at university, and launched a distinguished career as a theatre director in Mainz in 1916. In Berlin he worked for Max Reinhardt and Leopold Jessner's Prussian State Theatre, directing classic plays by Shakespeare, Strindberg and Goethe. Berger first ventured into film direction in 1920 with a Calderón adaptation, *Der Richter von Zalamea*, made for Erich Pommer. A markedly pictorial approach was apparent from the start, along with a knack for guiding players to stardom: Mady Christians, Willy Fritsch and, in the 1930s, Adolf Wohlbrück (Anton Walbrook) all benefited from his care. His major successes in the 1920s were *Der velorene Schuh/Cinderella* (1923) and *Ein Walzertraum* (1925), a widely popular adaptation of Oscar Straus' operetta. Hollywood took notice, and from 1927 to 1930 Berger directed five films for Paramount, including a stiff but visually striking early musical, *The Vagabond King* (1930), shot in Technicolor.

Berger's first connection with British cinema was tangential. Returning to Germany, in 1932 he mounted a lively contemporary musical, *Ich bei Tag und Du bei Nacht*, in three languages: for the English version, *Early to Bed*, made with Gaumont-British, Heather Angel and solid British character actors joined Fernand Gravey at Ufa's studios, but the result was not registered as a British film. Following the more traditional *Walzerkrieg* (1933) and a London stage production, *The Golden Toy*, Alexander Korda proposed he take over a ballet project; when the film never materialised, Berger directed in Holland (a version of Shaw's play *Pygmalion*, 1937) and France (the popular *Trois valses*, 1938).

In 1939 Korda brought him to Denham to direct his proposed Arabian Nights fantasy *The Thief of Bagdad*. From the beginning, Berger's approach jarred with his producer's. Berger wanted studio order, artifice and intimacy, with scenes minutely choreographed to a pre-recorded score: almost the live-action equivalent to a Lotte Reiniger silhouette. Korda's ambitions were for something looser, more colourful and extravagantly designed. In theory Berger's contract gave him complete artistic control; in practice, Korda parcelled off large chunks to others, spectacle scenes to Michael Powell, action to Tim Whelan. Berger was left primarily with intimate dialogue exchanges; even with these, Korda eventually inserted himself as co-director. Berger's prominent screen credit remained, but it is hard to see his fingerprints clearly in the released film.

For most of the war Berger stayed in Holland, where he directed *Ergens in Nederland* (1940), though he kept in semi-hiding during the German occupation. Afterwards he made *Ballerina* (1950) in France, resumed theatre productions in Germany and from 1954 until his death also worked steadily in German television, predominantly on live Shakespeare productions. Berger's retrospective feelings about his cinema career may be judged from the title he gave the relevant chapter in his memoirs, published in 1953: 'The Flea Circus'. He died on 18 May 1969 in Schlangenbad, Germany.

(Geoff Brown and Kevin Gough-Yates)

BIBLIOGRAPHY: Drazin, Charles, *Korda: Britain's Only Film Mogul* (London: Sidgwick & Jackson, 2002); Kulik, Karol, *Alexander Korda: The Man Who Could Work Miracles* (London: W. H. Allen, 1975); Powell, Michael, *A Life in Movies: An Autobiography* (London: Heinemann, 1986).

FILMOGRAPHY (UK only): *The Thief of Bagdad* (co-dirs. Michael Powell/Tim Whelan/Zoltan Korda, 1940).

BERKOFF, Steven (1937–)

Actor, writer, director Steven Berkoff was born in Stepney, London, on 3 August 1937, the son of a Russian Jewish tailor, and though he was brought up in Luton his East End roots are a constant element in his work. He studied drama at the Webber Douglas Academy in London and mime in Paris before serving three years in British repertory theatre, and from the late 1950s on played small roles in films and television dramas. In 1968 he formed the London Theatre Group to express his own ideas about theatre. His reputation as a charismatic actor led to Stanley Kubrick offering him parts in *A Clockwork Orange* (1971) and *Barry Lyndon* (1975). In the 1980s he played villainous characters in *Octopussy* (John Glen, 1983), *Beverly Hills Cop* (Martin Brest, 1984) and *Rambo: First Blood Part II* (George P. Cosmatos, 1985). He often openly vents his contempt for these ventures, explaining that they are simply a way to earn the money to support his theatre work.

Berkoff's directorial feature film career extends to just one title, *Decadence*. Adapted from his own 1983 play, it is a coruscating attack on the whole of society. The middle classes and aristocracy cynically control society while the working class conspire in their own repression by failing to fight back. Written in verse, with the same actors (Berkoff and Joan Collins) playing couples from both sides of the class divide, it reflects Berkoff's interest in Artaud's Theatre of Cruelty and Meyerhold's biomechanics. Long monologues direct to camera are livened up by self-consciously strange camera angles and speeded-up action; but Berkoff's attempt to blur the line between theatre and cinema failed to win over critics or audiences and he was unable to find backers for his plan to make a film with Robert De Niro as the escape artist Harry Houdini.

(John Riley)

BIBLIOGRAPHY: McCabe, Bob, 'Multi-Hyphenate: Steven Berkoff', *Premiere* (UK), Feb. 1994, p. 24.

FILMOGRAPHY: *Decadence* (1993).

BERNARD, Chris (1955–)

Chris Bernard was born in Liverpool on 25 October 1955 and began making films at the age of fourteen as a member of the Liverpool Youth Theatre's film club. After leaving school, he worked in local theatre and then teamed up with fellow Liverpudlian Frank Clarke to write scripts for *Brookside*. In 1985 Bernard shot to prominence as the director of Clarke's *Letter to Brezhnev*, a quirky comedy about two girls who pick up and spend a night with two Russian sailors. The Liverpool setting, the cheeky flouting of cold war orthodoxy and the sparky performances from the young cast (Alexandra Pigg, Margi Clarke, Alfred Molina, Peter Firth) turned this low-budget feature into a critical and popular success. Bernard received a number of Hollywood offers, recalling in 1992 that 'in the space of two-and-a-half years I must have turned down 20 green-lighted projects' (Hasted, p. 14).

By then he was expressing regret that he had allowed his artistic integrity to get in the way of a lucrative career as a Hollywood director; but his decision to work in television has involved him with interesting writers on innovative dramas. David Kane's *Shadow on the Earth* (1988), Barry Hines' *Shooting Stars* (1990) and Martyn Hesford's *A Little Bit of Lippy* (1992) were as idiosyncratic and original as *Letter to Brezhnev*; and the drama serials *Making Out* (1989) and *All Quiet on the Preston Front* (1994) were highly successful in deploying the theatrical writing talents of Debbie Horsfield and Tim Firth.

(Martin Hunt)

BIBLIOGRAPHY: Hasted, Nick, 'Where Are They Now?', *Empire*, Nov. 1992, p. 14.

FILMOGRAPHY: *Letter to Brezhnev* (1985).

BERNHARDT, Curtis (1899–1981)

Curtis (Kurt) Bernhardt was born on 15 April 1899 in Worms, Germany. He studied for the stage in Frankfurt am Main, and acted and directed for the Berlin stage in 1923. In 1925 he co-wrote his first film script, *Krieg im Frieden* (Karl Boese), in collaboration with Carl Zuckmayer. More writing commissions led him to directing and his *Die letzte Kompanie* (1930) was Ufa's first all-talking film. In 1931 he followed this with the German and French versions of *Der Mann, der den Mord beging*, which starred Conrad Veidt and Heinrich George. (Dimitri Buchowetzki directed the English version as *Stamboul*.) Harassed by the Nazis, he left for France in 1934 and came to England as production manager on *The Dictator* (Victor Saville, 1935). He went on to direct the French and English versions of *The Beloved Vagabond* (1936), with Maurice Chevalier, Betty Stockfield and Margaret Lockwood, a romantic comedy distinguished by Franz Planer's photography and Darius Milhaud's score. In 1937 he founded British Unity Pictures with his then brother-in-law, Eugène Tuscherer, but made only one musical farce, *The Girl in the Taxi/La Chaste Suzanne* (André Berthomieu, 1937). He left for France in 1938, where he directed *Carrefour* (1938) before moving on to Hollywood. There, he established himself as one of the most successful exiled European directors with such films as *Conflict* (1945), *A Stolen Life* (1946), *Possessed* (1947) and *Payment on Demand* (1951). He returned to Britain in 1954 to make *Beau Brummell*, a robust costume drama starring Stewart Granger that was condemned by chauvinistic British critics as bad history, bad drama and an insult to show at a Royal Film Performance. Bernhardt died on 22 February 1981 in Pacific Palisades, California.

(Kevin Gough-Yates)

BIBLIOGRAPHY: Belach, Helga, Gero Gandert and Hans Helmut Prinzler (eds), *Die Kinowelt des Curtis Bernhardt* (Munich: Verlag C. J. Bucher, 1982); Kiersch, Mary (ed.), *Curtis Bernhardt* (London: Scarecrow Press, 1986).

FILMOGRAPHY (UK only): *The Beloved Vagabond* (1936); *Beau Brummell* (1954).

BERWICK STREET FILM COLLECTIVE (1970–1978)

Co-founded by Marc Karlin and James Scott, the London-based Berwick Street Film Collective made political films – films political not only in their content but also in their radical aesthetics, and in the film-makers' collective and integrated approach to production, distribution and exhibition. Because of the commitment to collectivism – and the fact that some individuals were working with other groups (including Cinema Action, the London Women's Film Group and Lusia Films), membership of the BSFC is difficult to determine, but other names associated with the group include Mary Kelly, Richard Mordaunt, Jon Sanders and Humphrey Trevelyan. The BSFC is credited with directing three films between 1974 and 1978, made with varying levels of external funding.

The best known of its productions is *The Nightcleaners, Part 1* (1975), conceived originally as a campaign film about attempts to unionise women working at night as contract cleaners in large office blocks. The film was several years in the making, emerging eventually as a landmark work of British political cinema and of collective and feminist film-making. Influenced by Brechtian formal strategies espoused by European film-makers such as Godard, Straub and Huillet, the collective worked on the documentary footage they had shot to produce a film marked by 'an avant-garde poetics that addressed the representation of women and work' (Pollock, p. 195): they used montage, with rhythmic insertion of black spacing, asynchronous voice and image, reworked images, slow motion and silence. The objective was to address 'the fundamental contradiction between the typical cinematic means of producing a "truth" about working-class life . . . and the political aesthetics of a film that advertised its own manufacture' (Pollock, p. 205). The film's achievement was to put the subjectivity of class onto the screen. On its release, *The Nightcleaners* was praised for its boldly radical aesthetics, though there was also criticism, particularly from the women's movement, for its presumed inaccessibility to working-class audiences and its lack of relevance to the women workers' campaign for better pay and conditions.

While the originally conceived *Part 2* of *The Nightcleaners* never materialised, the BSFC, funded by the BFI Production Board, made a sequel, *'36 to '77* (1978), in which one of the cleaners in the earlier film reflects on the strike and on her life then and subsequently. Earlier, the Collective had made a film about Northern Ireland, *Ireland: Behind the Wire* (1974), also with backing from the BFI.

The work of the Berwick Street Film Collective, and above all *The Nightcleaners*, is important not only for its contribution to the aesthetics of oppositional cinema but also because of its legacy to a broader tradition of independent film-making in Britain. In its commitment to politicising all aspects of film-making, from production to distribution to exhibition, the BSFC's work was a forerunner of the integrated practice fostered by the Independent Filmmakers' Association and culminating in the ACTT's Workshop Declaration.

(Annette Kuhn)

BIBLIOGRAPHY: Dickinson, Margaret, *Rogue Reels: Oppositional Film in Britain, 1945–90* (London: BFI, 1999); Johnston, Claire, 'Re-thinking Political Cinema', *Jump Cut* nos 12/13, 1976, pp. 55–6; Johnston, Claire and Paul Willemen, 'Brecht in Britain: The Independent Political Film', *Screen* vol. 16 no. 4, Winter 1975/6, pp. 101–18; Pollock, Griselda, 'The Pathos of the Political: Documentary, Subjectivity and a Forgotten Moment of Feminist Avant-Garde Poetics in Four Films from the 1970s', in Valerie Mainz and Griselda Pollock, *Work in Modern Times: Visual Mediations and Social Processes* (Aldershot, Hants.: Ashgate, 2000).

FILMOGRAPHY: *Ireland: Behind the Wire* (1974); *The Nightcleaners, Part 1* (1975); *'36 to '77* (1978).

BEZENCENET, Peter (1914–)

Peter M. Bezencenet was born in 1914 and educated at Charterhouse and Lausanne University. He entered the film industry as an assistant editor at Alexander Korda's London Film Productions in 1935. After the war he edited Frederick Wilson's Independent Frame films *Floodtide* (1949) and *Poet's Pub* (1949) before becoming supervising editor at the Crown Film Unit from 1949 until its demise in 1952. Bezencenet moved on to Ealing, where he edited Basil Dearden's *The Square Ring* (1953), *The Rainbow Jacket* (1954) and *The Ship That Died of Shame* (1955), and Charles Crichton's *The Divided Heart* (1954). He gained experience as a second-unit director on several films, including *The Rainbow Jacket*, *That Feminine Touch* (Pat Jackson, 1956), *Dangerous Exile* (Brian Desmond Hurst, 1957) and *Floods of Fear* (Charles Crichton, 1958), as well as directing episodes of *The Pursuers* (1961) and other television series.

In 1962 Bezencenet finally took charge of his own feature, the comedy-musical *Band of Thieves* (1962), photographed by Nicolas Roeg, featuring trad jazz revivalist Acker Bilk and his band as a bunch of rascally but musically talented convicts; it now seems tediously tame and trivial. Apart from *Bomb in the High Street*, a pleasingly efficient programme-filler co-directed with Terry Bishop, Bezencenet's subsequent directorial efforts were made for cosmopolitan low-budget producer Harry Alan Towers. *High Adventure*, a short dramatised travelogue, was followed by two entries in Towers' *Secret Cities* series (*Prague* and *Berlin*), and two routine thrillers. *Twenty-Four Hours to Kill* stars Lex Barker as an airline pilot stranded with his plane in Beirut, where a gang of smugglers led by villainous Walter Slezak are intent on murdering his less-than-innocent purser (Mickey Rooney). *City of Fear*, a cold war thriller set in Budapest, has a duller cast and less to offer. Bezencenet subsequently disappeared from the film scene.

(Robert Murphy)

FILMOGRAPHY: *The Rainbow Jacket* (2nd unit dir., Basil Dearden, 1954); *That Feminine Touch* (2nd unit dir., Pat Jackson, 1956); *Dangerous Exile* (2nd unit dir., Brian Desmond Hurst); *The Secret Place* (2nd unit dir., Clive Donner) (1957); *Floods of Fear* (2nd unit dir., Charles Crichton); *Rooney* (2nd unit dir., George Pollock) (1958); *Band of Thieves*; *High Adventure* (short); *Prague* (short); *Berlin* (short) (1962); *Bomb in the High Street* (co-dir. Terry Bishop, 1963); *Twenty-Four Hours to Kill*; *City of Fear/Scharfe Küsse für Mike Foster* (UK/W. Ger) (1965).

BIERMAN, Robert (1949–)

Robert Bierman was born in London in 1949, brought up in Soho and educated in Hampstead. He started his career as an assistant fashion photographer, and became a negative cutter in a film laboratory before training as a cameraman at Thames Television. After directing a number of television commercials he made two short fiction films – *The Dumb Waiter* and *The Rocking Horse Winner*. Problems with getting British feature film projects off the ground took him to the USA in 1986, where he directed a thriller, *Apology*, for the cable company HBO, and then had a cult hit with *Vampire's Kiss*. Returning to Britain and television work, his work for the BBC included the enjoyably melodramatic eighteenth-century costume drama *Clarissa*

(1991), as well as episodes of the BAFTA-winning crime series *Between the Lines* (1992).

Bierman's small-screen success with *Clarissa* and his television adaptation of Wilkie Collins' *The Moonstone* (1996) boded well for another period adaptation, the National Lottery-funded version of George Orwell's *Keep the Aspidistra Flying*. The 1930s' setting did provide a variation on the Edwardiana of successive E. M. Forster adaptations, as did the film's combination of relatively explicit sex and satirical comedy. However, the comic tone and polished period style tended to work against Orwellian anger, and despite the appeal of Helena Bonham Carter and Richard E. Grant, the film took embarrassingly little at the box office. Bierman returned to television to make *The Blonde Bombshell* (1998), a biography of Diana Dors starring Amanda Redman, and episodes of the mountain rescue drama series *Rockface* (2002).

(Guy Barefoot)

BIBLIOGRAPHY: Ashford, Giuliana, 'With a Straight Bat', *Independent*, 15 Nov. 1990, p. 19.

FILMOGRAPHY: *The Dumb Waiter* (short, 1978); *The Rocking Horse Winner* (short, 1982); *Vampire's Kiss* (US, 1989); *Keep the Aspidistra Flying* (aka *A Merry War/Comstock and Rosemary*, 1997).

BILLINGTON, Kevin (1934–)

Kevin Billington was born on 12 June 1934 in Warrington, Lancashire. In 1959 he began a successful career in television, directing award-winning documentaries such as *All the Queen's Men* (1962) and *Madison Avenue USA* (1967). His debut feature film was the romantic drama *Interlude* (1968), a remake of a Douglas Sirk film that was itself a remake of *When Tomorrow Comes* (John M. Stahl, 1939). Third time out, the woman who falls for a married orchestra conductor (Oskar Werner) is a Mini-driving *Evening Standard* reporter (Barbara Ferris). Billington largely avoids 'Swinging London' clichés, exhibits a good eye for detail and facilitates strong performances from a cast that also includes Virginia Maskell, John Cleese and Donald Sutherland. While *Interlude* did not attract much critical acclaim, Billington seemed a promising talent.

Unfortunately his next film, *The Rise and Rise of Michael Rimmer*, a heavy-handed political satire, written by and starring Peter Cook, John Cleese and Graham Chapman, was less accomplished. Cook plays the title character, an efficiency expert who takes over an advertising agency, becomes an MP and rises to the position of Prime Minister. Billington, who also worked on the script, eschews narrative structure for a series of weakly linked sketches. Cook, an uneasy big-screen actor, is inadequate as a leading man, outshone by the likes of Ronnie Corbett and Harold Pinter. Compared to Cleese and Chapman's work on the contemporary television series *Monty Python's Flying Circus* (1969–74), *The Rise and Rise of Michael Rimmer* looked both thin and dated.

Billington's one venture into international film-making proved equally unsuccessful. Producer Alexander Salkind and Hollywood star Kirk Douglas hired him to direct *The Light at the Edge of the World*, loosely based on a Jules Verne novel about a troubled lighthouse-keeper battling pirates. Violent, tedious and poorly dubbed, the finished film has little shape or style.

Short of film offers, Billington returned to British television, directing the drama *And No One Could Save Her* (1973), a prestigious Anglo-American co-production starring Lee Remick and Milo O'Shea. His next big-screen assignment was *Voices* (1974), a ghost story starring Gayle Hunnicutt and David Hemmings as a couple haunted by their dead son. Based on a play by Richard Lortz, the film benefits from its isolated rural setting, yet the material seems badly overstretched.

Since the late 1970s, Billington has worked largely in television, on dramas such as *The Good Soldier* (1981), from a novel by Ford Madox Ford; *Reflections* (1984), one of the first films made for Channel 4; *Heartlands* (1989), a BBC Wales production with Anthony Hopkins as a Welsh farmer who kidnaps two EEC commissioners; and an adaptation of Melvyn Bragg's *A Time to Dance* (1991) for BBC Scotland.

(Daniel O'Brien)

BIBLIOGRAPHY: Badder, David, 'Kevin Billington', *Film Dope* no. 3, Aug. 1973, p. 43; Houston, Penelope, 'The Crisis We Deserve: Questions to Billington/Boorman/Brownlow/Clarke/Clement/Hall, *Sight and Sound*, Autumn 1970, pp. 174–5; Robinson, David, 'Case Histories of the Next Renascence', *Sight and Sound*, Winter 1968, pp. 36–40.

FILMOGRAPHY: *Interlude* (1968); *The Rise and Rise of Michael Rimmer* (1970); *The Light at the Edge of the World* (US/Sp/Lich, 1971); *Voices* (1974); *Reflections* (1984).

BIRD, Antonia (1959–)

Antonia Bird began her career at the Royal Court Theatre before moving to television in the mid-1980s, directing episodes of *EastEnders* and *Casualty* and drama serials *Thin Air* (1988), about the investigations of a female radio reporter, and *The Men's Room* (1991), a five-part adaptation of the novel by Ann Oakley. *Safe* (1993), a realist drama about homeless teenagers made for BBC 2's *Screenplay* series, saw her working in the social-issue tradition pioneered by Ken Loach, whose influence she has acknowledged. *Safe* won her a Best First Feature award at the Edinburgh International Television Festival and a BAFTA award for Best Single Drama. Her first cinema-released film was *Priest* (1994), written by Jimmy McGovern, a controversial study of a gay Catholic priest (Linus Roache) who faces a moral dilemma over a case of sexual abuse that the sanctity of the confessional forbids him to reveal, and has to confront his congregation's prejudices when his homosexuality is exposed.

Bird moved to Hollywood to make *Mad Love* (1995), another story of a teenage couple on the run, written by Paula Milne, and starring Drew Barrymore and Chris O'Donnell. She returned to Britain for *Face* (1997), a heist movie scripted by Ronan Bennett, with Robert Carlyle as a former left-wing activist who, disillusioned with attempts to change the world through social protest, turns to crime. The amalgam of gangland thriller and social-issue movie was a little uncomfortable but the heist narrative was skilfully handled, resulting in an entertaining gangster/social-realist hybrid.

Another genre switch came with Bird's next film, *Ravenous* (1999), which she took over from Milcho Manchevski on the recommendation of the film's star, Robert Carlyle. Directing this 'cannibal Western' proved that Bird could handle material far removed from social realism.

Bird returned to television with *Care* (2000), a fictionalised but painstakingly researched account of sexual abuse in children's homes that won a BAFTA award for Best Single Drama, and *Rehab* (2003), another hard-hitting drama about drug addiction, made as a co-production between the BBC and 4Way Pictures, a company formed by Bird with Robert Carlyle, Mark Cousins and Irvine Welsh. In 2004 she directed *Hamburg Cell*, a fascinating Channel 4 drama-documentary, written by Ronan Bennett, about the background to the attack on the World Trade Center on 11 September 2001.

(Lez Cooke)

BIBLIOGRAPHY: Ciecko, Anne T., 'Sex, God, Television, Realism, and the British Women Filmmakers Beeban Kidron and Antonia Bird', *Journal of Film and Video*, Spring 1999, pp. 22–41; McCabe, Bob, 'East End Heat', *Sight and Sound*, Oct. 1997, pp. 10–12.

FILMOGRAPHY: *Safe* (1993); *Priest* (1994); *Mad Love* (US, 1995); *Face* (1997); *Ravenous* (US/UK, 1999).

BIRD, Richard (1894–1986)

Richard Bird was born in Liverpool in 1894. After working as a shipping clerk and serving in the army during the First World War, he began acting with the Liverpool Repertory Company in 1918. By the early 1930s he was making regular appearances as a character actor in modest British films, including *The Water Gypsies* (Maurice Elvey, 1932), *White Face* (T. Hayes Hunter, 1932) and *The Warren Case* (Walter Summers, 1934). In 1937 he turned to direction, making the interesting Irish melodrama *West of Kerry*, and an adaptation of Edgar Wallace's play *The Terror*, with Linden Travers as the threatened heroine, Wilfrid Lawson as the organ-playing villain and Bernard Lee as the detective disguised as a permanently drunk silly ass. Bird lacks Bernard Vorhaus' visual inventiveness and Walter Summers' ability to create suspense, but *The Terror* remains a satisfyingly English crime film, where crooks say 'nark it' and master criminals are identifiable only by their evil laughter. Bird injects humour with some witty dialogue and scene-stealing appearances from Alastair Sim, Richard Murdoch and Kathleen Harrison, but never allows the pace to flag.

Bird played the persistent Inspector Sneed in another Wallace adaptation, *The Door with Seven Locks* (Norman Lee, 1940), but during the war there was reduced demand for lurid crime films and no further film directing opportunities arose. However, in 1952 he did produce a stage adaptation of *The Blue Lamp* (Basil Dearden, 1950), with Bonar Colleano taking over from Dirk Bogarde as the young thug who kills PC George Dixon. In the early years of commercial television, Bird shared directing credits with Maclean Rogers on the Arthur Askey comedy series *Love and Kisses* (1955). He made his final appearance in another Wallace thriller, *Return to Sender* (Gordon Hales, 1963), and his last stage appearance in 1965, after which he seems to have retired to Canada with his actress wife Joyce Barbour. Richard Bird died in Regina, Canada, on 28 September 1986.

(Robert Murphy)

BIBLIOGRAPHY: *Who's Who in the Theatre*, 15th edn (London: Pitman Publishing, 1972).

FILMOGRAPHY: *West of Kerry* (aka *Island Man/Men of Ireland*); *The Terror* (1938).

BIRKIN, Andrew (1945–)

Andrew Birkin was born in London on 9 December 1945. His mother is the actress Judy Campbell and his sister actress and singer Jane Birkin. From 1963 to 1970 he worked on a number of films as camera assistant, location manager and second-unit director before establishing himself as a screenwriter with *The Pied Piper* (Jacques Demy, 1972), *Flame* (Richard Loncraine, 1975), *The Final Conflict* (Graham Baker, 1981) and *The Name of the Rose* (Jean-Jacques Annaud, 1986). Birkin's first work as director was the short film *Sredni Vashtar*, which was nominated for an Academy Award.

A thematic link runs through his first feature film *Burning Secret*, his television screenplay *The Lost Boys* (Rodney Bennett, 1978), his book *J. M. Barrie and the Lost Boys* and his best-known work as director, *The Cement Garden*. All deal with abandoned children and a sense of youthful alienation from the adult world. *The Cement Garden* was adapted by Birkin from Ian McEwan's novel about a family of four children who retreat from the world after the death of their parents, with the older siblings developing a relationship that veers into the incestuous. The film was praised for its stylish direction and its fidelity to McEwan's strange vision of adolescent sexuality. Birkin also directed the offbeat romantic costume drama *Salt on Our Skin*, about a Victorian gentlewoman's thirty-year affair with a Scottish fisherman. Despite the critical plaudits for his direction of *The Cement Garden*, Birkin subsequently returned to working as a screenwriter, most recently on *Joan of Arc* (Luc Besson, 1999).

(Ruth Barton)

BIBLIOGRAPHY: Bergson, Philip, 'A Passion for Cinema', *What's on in London*, 12 Apr. 1989, p. 74; Francke, Lizzie, 'Child's Eye View', *Guardian* G2 Section, 14 Oct. 1993, pp. 6–7.

FILMOGRAPHY: *Sredni Vashtar* (short, 1981); *The Burning Secret* (UK/US, 1988); *Salt on Our Skin* (US: *Desire*, UK/Fr/Can, 1992); *The Cement Garden* (UK/Ger/Fr, 1993).

BIRKINSHAW, Alan (1944–)

Alan Birkinshaw was born on 15 June 1944 in Auckland, New Zealand. By the early 1960s he was working at ATV as a television cameraman. He made his first feature film *Design for Lust* (retitled *Confessions of a Sex Maniac*) in 1974. Supposedly co-written by Birkinshaw's sister Fay Weldon, the film concerns an architect who trawls Soho for a woman whose perfect breasts will serve as a blueprint for his new building. Tawdry though it was, *Design for Lust* was inoffensive in comparison with Birkinshaw's next film, *Killer's Moon*, where four drug-crazed mental patients terrorise a party of schoolgirls stranded somewhere in the Lake District.

Traditional British sexploitation had died out by the end of the 1970s, but Birkinshaw was able to continue his career beyond Britain. He made a copy of the Indiana Jones films, *Invaders of the Lost Gold*, in the Philippines, and a series of films in South Africa for the veteran producer Harry Alan Towers, including a version of Agatha Christie's *Ten Little Indians* (one of several), and sadly shoddy remakes of Roger Corman's *Fall of the House of Usher* and *The Masque of the Red Death*. After further film and television work in Germany, Birkinshaw returned to London, where *Killer's Moon* has acquired an improbable cult status. As he told an interviewer, 'One tries to put a bit of depth in these things although sometimes it doesn't really come through' (Kerekes, p. 89).

(Robert Murphy)

BIBLIOGRAPHY: Kerekes, David, 'Hungry in a Dream', in David Kerekes (ed.), *Creeping Flesh – The Horror Fantasy Film Book* (Manchester: Headpress Publishing/Critical Vision, 2003).

FILMOGRAPHY: *Confessions of a Sex Maniac* (aka *The Man Who Couldn't Get Enough*, 1974); *Killer's Moon* (1978); *Dead End* (short, 1980); *Invaders of the Lost Gold* (HK, 1982); *Agatha Christie's Ordeal by Innocence* (add. scenes: Desmond Davis); *Don't Open Till Christmas* (add. scenes: Edmund Purdom, HK) (1984); *Sweeter than Wine* (SA, 1988); *Ten Little Indians* (aka *Death on Safari*, US); *The Masque of the Red Death* (SA/US) (1989); *The House of Usher* (SA, 1990); *Punch* (Ger/Belg/Switz, 1994).

BIRT, Daniel (1907–1955)

Daniel Birt was born in Mersham, Kent, on 23 June 1907. He went to New College, Oxford, to study medicine but in 1928 joined the film industry, where eventually becoming an editor. In 1939 he set up a production company with his wife Louise, producing Adrian Brunel's *The Girl Who Forgot* (1939) and Thomas Bentley's *Three Silent Men* (1940) before the war made conditions too difficult to continue. Between 1940 and 1946 Birt made War Office training films, mainly on medical subjects. In 1948 he returned to fiction films, making his debut with *The Three Weird Sisters*, a creaky melodrama partly scripted by Dylan Thomas, enjoyable for the performances of Nancy Price, Mary Clare and Mary Merrall as three impoverished sisters plotting fratricide against their prosperous brother (Raymond Lovell). Thomas also helped to adapt Joan Temple's controversial play *No Room at the Inn* as Birt's next film, with Freda Jackson reproducing her role as the monstrous slattern whose exploitation of child evacuees made the film unacceptably sordid to contemporary critics.

During the 1950s, most of Birt's films were low-budget murder mysteries: *She Shall Have Murder* and *Three Steps in the Dark* were enlivened by feisty heroines, but *Circumstantial Evidence*, *Burnt Evidence* and *Third Party Risk* were disappointingly routine. Birt returned to controversial social issues in 1953 with *Background*, where the children of a divorcing couple – convincingly played by Janette Scott, Mandy Miller and Jeremy Spenser – succeed in reconciling their parents. In the mid-1950s Birt became seriously ill, though he rallied to direct episodes of *The Adventures of Robin Hood* for television. His last film, an Anglo-Swedish production *Laughing in the Sunshine*, was a fairy-tale romance filmed in colour. Dan Birt died from a heart attack in London on 15 May 1955.

(Margaret Butler)

BIBLIOGRAPHY: Brunel, Adrian, *Nice Work* (London: Forbes Robertson, 1949); McFarlane, Brian, *An Autobiography of British Cinema* (London: Methuen, 1997); Obituary, *Cine Technician*, 21 June 1955, p. 8; Peterman, John, *Dylan Thomas: The Complete Screenplays* (New York: Applause Books, 1995).

FILMOGRAPHY: *Silt* (doc. short, 1931); *Dai Jones* (doc. short, 1941); *Anti-Personnel Bomb* (doc. short, 1943); *Butterfly Bomb* (doc. short, 1944); *The Three Weird Sisters*; *No Room at the Inn* (1948); *The Interrupted Journey* (1949); *She Shall Have Murder* (1950); *Circumstantial Evidence* (1952); *Three Steps in the Dark*; *Background* (US: *Edge of Divorce*); *Meet Mr Malcolm* (1953); *Burnt Evidence* (1954); *Third Party Risk* (US: *The Deadly Game*); *Laughing in the Sunshine* (UK/Swe) (1955).

BISHOP, Terry (1912–1981)

Like other documentary-trained recruits in the 1950s, Terry Bishop found little scope in the mainstream industry for realistic observation. *Daybreak in Udi*, the story of modern facilities arriving in a Nigerian village, won an Academy Award in 1950 for best documentary feature; but most of his feature life was spent at the Walton-on-Thames studios, trying to locate believable moments in low-budget dramas rolled off the assembly line.

Bishop, born in Chiswick, west London, on 21 October 1912, entered the industry in 1930 and gained writing experience at Twickenham Studios. In 1940 he began directing instructional and propaganda films, mainly for Merton Park, Greenpark and the Crown Film Unit. Along with *Daybreak in Udi*, *Five Towns* (1948), about the Staffordshire Potteries, was especially praised. Like fellow documentary-makers John Eldridge and Margaret Thomson, Bishop made his feature debut at Group 3, but real life took a back seat in the whimsical comedy of *You're Only Young Twice!* (1952). Television dramas filled the gaps between subsequent films, chiefly made for Jack Parsons' Parroch Films. Well-drawn characters and atmosphere lifted several above the routine, like the rural hysteria drama *Life in Danger* (1959) and a sprightly thriller, *Cover Girl Killer* (1960).

Bishop later withdrew from British features. In Ghana in 1965 he directed *Hamile*, a student stage production of *Hamlet* filmed on location; back home, he turned to fund-raising films for medical charities. But nowhere did he again find a project worthy of the praise *Documentary News Letter* once bestowed on *Five Towns*: 'The people appear real and ordinary, their surroundings genuine, and the story simple.' He died of cancer, late in 1981, after completing *Suddenly among Strangers*, a film about cancer in children.

(Geoff Brown)

BIBLIOGRAPHY: Black, Stuart and Norman Hemsley, Obituaries, *Film and Television Technician*, Jan. 1982, p. 13; McGillivray, David, 'Now You Know', *Films and Filming*, Aug. 1982, pp. 43–4.

FILMOGRAPHY: Non-fiction: *Kill That Rat* (1941); *More Eggs from Your Hens; Western Isles; Down Our Street; Out of the Box; The Jablo Wood Blade: Its Manufacture and Repair* (1942); *The Royal Mile, Edinburgh* (1944); *A Power in the Land; Colonel Crompton, Pioneer and Prophet; Tale in a Teacup* (co-dir. Ralph Keene) (1947); *Five Towns; Thee and Me* (1948); *The Old Vic; Daybreak in Udi* (1949); *Trooping the Colour* (1950); *Journey to the Sea* (1952); *The New Age* (Ghana, 1960); *The Friendly Invasion* (co-dir. Paul Woolston-Smith, 1967); *A Small Miracle* (1970); *No Enemy but Time* (1973); *Suddenly among Strangers* (1981).

Fiction films: *You're Only Young Twice!* (1952); *West of Zanzibar* (2nd unit dir., Harry Watt, 1954); *Tim Driscoll's Donkey* (1955); *Light Fingers* (1957); *Model for Murder, Life in Danger* (1959); *Cover Girl Killer, Danger Tomorrow, The Unstoppable Man* (1960); *Hair of the Dog* (1961); *Bomb in the High Street* (co-dir. Peter Bezencenet, 1963); *Hamile* (Ghana, 1965).

BLACK AUDIO FILM COLLECTIVE (1982–1998)

The Black Audio Film Collective was formed in Hackney, London, in 1982 by John Akomfrah, Reece Auguiste, Edward George, Lina Gopaul, Avril Johnson, David Lawson and Trevor Mathison. It was one among many such collectives founded in Britain during the early to mid-1980s, including Sankofa, Ceddo and ReTake. This period was characterised on the one hand by the founding of Channel 4 and the ACCT Workshop Declaration (both 1982), which encouraged innovative independent work, and on the other hand by the increasingly free-market ideology of Thatcherism. The Collective was at the forefront of debates about the politics of representation: their work argues that 'racial identities grow out of their social and political histories; they call for a recognition that these racial differences are multiple and complex' (Jackson and Rasenberger, p. 24).

After some tape-slide experiments (*Signs of Empire; Images of Nationality*, both 1984), the Collective produced some of the most challenging and experimental documentaries in Britain in the 1980s. *Handsworth Songs* (1986) has been critically acclaimed for its political commitment and formal experimentation. The film's representation of black history refracted through the civil disturbances of the 1980s was influential because it engaged with precisely how a group can be marginalised by the practices and ideology of mainstream media. The themes of diaspora, memory and political struggle are also evident in *Testament* (1988), a film about an exiled Ghanaian politician who returns to Ghana two decades after the 1966 coup. *Twilight City* (1989) explores London as a symbolic as well as a civic space, representing ideals of affluence and the hope of a new beginning, and contrasting it with the reality of the harsh welcome afforded many black migrants.

The Collective's work in the 1990s was characterised by the same experimental interest in memory and history. *Who Needs a Heart* (1991) explores the emergence of Black Power in Britain in the 1960s and 70s. They also tackled the iconic figures of Malcolm X (*Seven Songs for Malcolm X*, 1993) and Martin Luther King (*Martin Luther King – Days of Hope*, 1997). Both these films epitomise the critical – yet celebratory – attitude that the Collective has taken towards all its subjects. According to Akomfrah, the former film attempts to look at the 'significant silences' in Malcolm X's autobiography, such as his Caribbean mother, and his ambivalent relationship to America, seeking 'to sneak a few of these ghosts into the back door' (Akomfrah 1993a, p. 3).

The Collective dissolved in 1998, though its members – most notably Akomfrah – continue to work individually.

(Paul Ward)

BIBLIOGRAPHY: Akomfrah, John, 'Sneaking Ghosts through the Back Door', *Black Film Bulletin*, Spring 1993a, p. 3; Akomfrah, John, 'Wishful Filming', *Black Film Bulletin*, Summer 1993b, p. 14; Fyle, Chenaii A., 'Black Cinema in Britain: What Way Forward?', *Artrage*, Sept. 1994, pp. 38–9; Jackson, Lynne and Jean Rasenberger, 'Young, British and Black', *Cinéaste* vol. 16 no. 4, 1988, pp. 24–5.

FILMOGRAPHY: *Handsworth Songs* (1986); *Testament* (1988); *Twilight City* (1989); *Mysteries of July; A Touch of the Tar Brush; Who Needs a Heart* (1991); *Seven Songs for Malcolm X* (1993); *Beaton but Unbowed* (1994); *Last Angel of History; The Mothership Connection* (1995); *Three Songs on Pain Light & Time* (1996); *Memory Room 451; Martin Luther King – Days of Hope* (1997).

BLACK, Cathal (1951–)

Born in Dublin in 1951, Cathal Black was prominent in the first wave of indigenous film-making that evolved in Ireland in the 1970s. Following a period working for RTÉ, the national broadcaster, Black directed *Wheels* (1974), a short, dark, rural drama, based on a story by John McGahern, which displayed his preoccupation with the tensions between Ireland's Catholic/Nationalist past and present.

Black's next film was the stark, independently produced fiction-documentary *Our Boys* (1981). An early examination of the abuse of boys in the care of the Irish Christian Brothers' industrial schools, it alternated fictional scenes of the closure of one of the schools with factual interviews with men who had been in the Brothers' care. It was banned by one of its backers, RTÉ, until 1991.

Black made his first feature, *Pigs*, in 1984. Jimmy, an unemployed gay man, is forced to squat in a run-down Dublin tenement in the economically grim 1980s. As a series of equally marginalised characters arrive, an alternative community develops, until tensions erupt between the residents and the police and social workers. The superb script and acting, sombre

Dublin setting and production design, brooding cinematography and Black's unobtrusive direction make *Pigs* a bleak masterpiece of Irish cinema.

It is an indication of the instability of support for film in Ireland that Black was not able to make his next film, *Korea*, until eleven years later. As in *Wheels*, the subject was generational conflict, but Black abandoned the realism and social concerns of *Our Boys* and *Pigs* for a more genre-oriented, melodramatic style. *Korea* is set in 1950s' Cavan on the border between Northern Ireland and the Republic. Black explores the hold of history on the present, Ireland's obsessive nationalism and notions of compromise and change in Irish society. Sumptuously mounted, with finely conceived characters and an evocative sense of place, *Korea* is Black's calm retrospective on Ireland on the cusp of modernity.

Love and Rage, produced with funding from European sources, was released, following a troubled production, in 2001. Based on a novel by James Carney, and set on Achill Island at the turn of the twentieth century, *Love and Rage* relates how a Scottish lady landowner is seduced by the sensuous, manipulative and ultimately violent Irish farmhand who destroys her freedom before embarking for America. Black's most mature and his most flawed work, *Love and Rage* adventurously blends historical melodrama and high-gothic motifs to re-examine Ireland's colonial history.

A true survivor in a country in which cinema is rarely allowed to be different, Black has persisted and delivered work of immense cinematic integrity that continually critiques the notion of Irishness itself. While his achievements (like that of the similarly stubborn Joe Comerford) have been sometimes overshadowed by the New Wave's mainstream aspirations, Black's talent and value as an Irish film-maker will not go unnoticed by future generations.

(Eugene Finn)

BIBLIOGRAPHY: Browne, Vincent, 'Interview', *Film West* no. 24, Spring 1996, pp. 18–22; Linehan, Hugh, 'In Black Country', *Irish Times*, 4 Jan. 1996, p. 11; Murphy, Michael, 'Black Stuff', *Hot Press*, 2 Nov. 1984, p. 17; Palmer, Ian, 'Paddle Your Own Canoe', *Film Base News* no. 28, Mar./Apr. 1992, pp. 16–17.

FILMOGRAPHY: *Wheels* (1974); *Our Boys* (1981; rel. 1990); *Pigs* (1984); *Korea* (1995); *Love and Rage* (1998; rel. 2001).

BLACK, Donald Taylor (1951–)

Donald Taylor Black, born in Ireland in 1951, was educated at Trinity College, Dublin. He made his mark with a documentary about the Irish film historian Liam O'Leary, and has continued to work in the non-fiction field, making films about Irish sport, theatre and institutions such as Dublin's Mountjoy prison. In 1994 he directed Gerald Barry's *The Triumph of Beauty and Deceit*, a two-act opera written for television and premiered on Channel 4; and in 1997 contributed *Irish Cinema: Ourselves Alone?* to the BFI/Channel 4 series on diverse national cinemas.

(Robert Murphy)

BIBLIOGRAPHY: Browne, Vincent, 'Donald Taylor Black Interview', *Film West* no. 21, Summer 1995, pp. 8–10.

FILMOGRAPHY: *At the Cinema Palace: Liam O'Leary* (1983); *Sam Thompson – Voice of Many Men* (1986).

BLACK, George (1911–1970)

George Black Jr was born in Sunderland, Tyneside, in 1911, the son of George Black Sr, the showman and cinema owner who ran the London Palladium as part of the Gaumont-British empire. George Jr entered the industry as assistant director on *Just My Luck* (Jack Raymond, 1933) and *Forgotten Men: The War as It Was* (Norman Lee, 1934), and helped out on Michael Powell's location shoot for *The Edge of the World* (1937). In the late 1930s he directed two low-budget comedies for John E. Blakeley's Mancunian Corporation. *The Penny Pool* (1937) has a topical plot about a factory girl who loses her winning football pools coupon, but it is Lancashire comedian Duggie Wakefield and his gang who give the film its bounce. *Calling All Crooks* (1938) also relies on Wakefield, now a comic detective whose daftness does not hinder him in unmasking a crooked businessman. Black, born and bred in the world of music hall and variety, makes no attempt to impose cinematic gloss on his performers. The films held little appeal for southern audiences, but their crude zest makes them enjoyable nevertheless and they preserve a now-lost tradition of northern slapstick humour.

During the Second World War Black organised the patriotic stage revue *Stars in Battledress*, which ran throughout the war. He also scored big successes with shows starring the Birmingham comedian Sid Field, putting him on the West End stage for the first time in *Strike a New Note* (1943) and consolidating his success with *Piccadilly Hayride* in 1946.

In the late 1940s Black returned briefly to the film business, producing in partnership with his younger brother Alfred. *Trouble in the Air* (Charles Saunders, 1948) was a cut-price production that made disappointingly little of its Ealing-like story (bell-ringing villagers are exploited by spivs but rescued by a benevolent radio commentator). *The Perfect Woman* (Bernard Knowles, 1949), ineffably silly though it is, is a much more polished production, with Patricia Roc playing a double role as an independently minded young woman and an obedient robot, modelled after her physique by her inventor uncle. The film diversion over, the Black brothers continued with successful stage production throughout the 1950s. In 1957 they joined producer Sydney Box in the consortium that set up Tyne-Tees Television. Like his father, and his uncle Edward (producer at Gainsborough Studios), George Black died at a relatively young age, on 17 November 1970, in Haywards Heath, Sussex.

(Robert Murphy)

BIBLIOGRAPHY: Obituary, *Variety*, 25 Nov. 1970.

FILMOGRAPHY: *The Penny Pool: A Musical Merry Burlesque* (1937); *Calling All Crooks* (1938).

BLACKTON, J. Stuart (1875–1941)

A pioneer animator and co-founder of the American Vitagraph Company, James Stuart Blackton was one of the most colourful personalities in early American cinema. He was born in Sheffield on 5 January 1875, but within ten years the family moved to America. By 1894 Blackton had formed an entertainment act in New York with fellow Englishmen Albert E. Smith and Ronald Reader; his own specialities included conjuring, painting and sketching. Motion pictures were added to their programmes following the success of *Edison Drawn by 'World' Cartoonist* (1896), one of three early films showing Blackton's sketches forming line by line direct from the artist's hand. At the American Vitagraph Company, Blackton and Smith further developed their cinema activities. Several films exploited the Spanish–American war, notably *The Battle of Manila Bay*, a miniature re-enactment of Admiral Dewey's naval victory, made in May 1898 only two weeks after the events. Boosted by these successes, Vitagraph widened their range to include local actualities, comic-strip spin-offs (the *Happy Hooligan* series) and adaptations of Shakespeare and Dickens. In 1905 the company established their own glassed-in studio in Brooklyn, where Blackton's 'lightning sketch' animations advanced towards the stop-frame technique deployed by Méliès and others on live-action footage; Blackton's film *Humorous Phases of Funny Faces* (1906) proved particularly successful and influential. Beyond animation, he explored new editing and camera techniques, and helped lay the foundations for the American studio system in his managerial organisation at Vitagraph and development of an acting stock company.

As Vitagraph grew, Blackton earned a considerable fortune, much of it lavished on his passion for social prestige, motorboats and yachting; his marine activities earned him the nickname 'the Commodore'. Restless for new horizons, he left Vitagraph in 1917. As an independent producer he made patriotic features and several adaptations of novels by Sir Gilbert Parker; their comparative failure encouraged him to look towards England for business.

In 1920 he planned to establish his own British studio. Though this never happened, he arrived with some fanfare the following year, armed with the improved Prizma colour process and a new belief that his salvation lay in the 'timeless' quality of period subjects. The Great Fire of London raged garishly but prettily through the otherwise stodgy *The Glorious Adventure* (1922), featuring the society beauty Lady Diana Cooper (billed as Lady Diana Manners); she also assumed the title role in *The Virgin Queen* (1923), another lavish costume drama. In between came *A Gipsy Cavalier* (1922), shot in monochrome, featuring remarkable flood scenes and, less spectacularly, the acting debut of the world's light-heavyweight boxing champion George Carpentier. The films were dramatically unsophisticated; Blackton had failed to keep pace with developments in cinema technique, though he knew the arts of showmanship

and how to hide limitations with favourable publicity. These glossy spectacles with large, glamorous casts were given society premieres in fashionable venues. British film-makers took note, especially Herbert Wilcox, who gave his own Prizma venture, *Flames of Passion* (Graham Cutts, 1922), an equally lavish baptism.

With mixed results in Britain, Blackton returned to America and Vitagraph in 1923, where he directed several more films including *Beloved Brute* (1924) starring Victor McLaglen, previously featured in *The Glorious Adventure*. After briefly surviving Vitagraph's takeover by Warner Bros. in 1926, he diversified into real estate and other business schemes. By 1931 the past millionaire had become bankrupt, but he continued spinning ideas, and compiled an ingenious history of the movies, *The Film Parade* (1934), dedicated to Edison. Blackton also delivered autobiographical lectures, one of which was titled 'My "Glorious Adventure" in England', though his biggest adventures had occurred earlier, in America. He died on 13 August 1941 following a car accident in Hollywood.

(Geoff Brown and Bryony Dixon)

BIBLIOGRAPHY: Low, Rachael, *A History of the British Film 1918–1929* (London: George Allen & Unwin, 1971); Musser, Charles, *The Emergence of Cinema: The American Screen to 1907* (New York: Charles Scribner's Sons, 1990); Trimble, Marian Blackton, *J. Stuart Blackton: A Personal Biography by His Daughter* (Metuchen, NJ: Scarecrow Press, 1985).

FILMOGRAPHY (UK only): *The Glorious Adventure*; *A Gipsy Cavalier* (1922); *The Virgin Queen* (1923).

BLACKWOOD, Maureen (1960–)

Maureen Blackwood was born in London on 30 July 1960. In 1983, while studying for a media studies degree at the Polytechnic of Central London, she formed Sankofa Film and Video Collective with Isaac Julien, Martina Attille, Nadine Marsh-Edwards and Robert Crusz, in order to address the lack of films about the contemporary black British experience.

After contributing to Sankofa projects such as *Territories* and *Looking for Langston* she co-directed *The Passion of Remembrance* (1986) with Isaac Julien. A challenging and provocative film about identity, memory and belonging, it is shot through with lyrical moments and is both poignant and celebratory, challenging the viewers to rethink their attitudes towards black cultural identity.

Blackwood's other directorial credits include *Perfect Image?* – an experimental exploration of the ways in which black women perceive themselves, made with backing from Channel 4 and the BFI – and *A Family Called Abrew*, a documentary about a black Scottish family. In 1994 she made *Home Away from Home* for Channel 4's *Short and Curlies* slot. A short film about a black single mother who builds a traditional African mud hut in her suburban garden to represent her cultural identity and roots, its theme is typical of all Blackwood's work.

(Paul Ward)

BIBLIOGRAPHY: Dixon, Wheeler Winston, 'The Practice of Theory, the Theory of Practice: The Post-Colonial Cinema of Maureen Blackwood and the Sankofa Collective', *Film Criticism* vol. 20 nos 1/2, Autumn/Winter 1995/6, pp. 131–41; 'Home from Home', *Black Film Bulletin* vol. 1 nos 3/4, Autumn/Winter 1993, p. 26.

FILMOGRAPHY: *The Passion of Remembrance* (co-dir. Isaac Julien, 1986); *Perfect Image?* (short, 1988); *A Family Called Abrew* (short, 1992); *Home Away from Home* (short, 1994).

Maureen Blackwood (second from right) directing *The Passion of Remembrance* (co-dir. Isaac Julien, 1986)

BLAIR, Les (1941–)

Les Blair was born on 23 October 1941 in Salford, Lancashire. After taking a degree in economics at Liverpool University he worked as a copywriter in a Birmingham advertising agency while involving himself in theatre work in the evenings. In 1966 Blair enrolled on a two-year course at what would become the London Film School, and in 1969 spent six months at the Prague Film School, where he made a documentary about life in Czechoslovakia after the Soviet invasion. After producing and editing Mike Leigh's *Bleak Moments* (1971) Blair was recruited to television by Tony Garnett to direct *Blooming Youth*, a 1973 BBC *Play for Today*.

From 1973 to 1983 Blair worked mainly in television, directing dramas that he often wrote or 'devised' – a term indicating a working method whereby projects would be developed through workshop improvisation. Blair's early association with Mike Leigh and Tony Garnett highlights two important formative influences on his work: from Leigh came an interest in improvisation, which Blair uses to coax naturalistic performances from his actors, while working with Garnett enabled him to pursue particular social and political concerns.

Les Blair's films, whether for television or the cinema, occupy an ideological space in British film and television drama somewhere between the heightened naturalism, bordering on caricature, of Mike Leigh, and the social realism of Garnett and Loach, where a naturalistic style is adopted to address social issues and aspects of social history. This is clearly evident in Blair's collaborations with the writer G. F. Newman: on the four-part drama *Law and Order* (1978), about the criminal justice system, and *The Nation's Health* (1983), about the health service. Blair also collaborated with Newman on his first feature film, *Number One*, about the exploitation of a snooker player (Bob Geldof) by a professional promoter.

Number One was the first of only three films directed by Blair to receive a cinema release. *Bad Behaviour*, an entertaining piece of social realism with comic undertones, considered class relations in London in the early 1990s, following the social restructuring of Thatcherism, while *Jump the Gun* was an equally perceptive and entertaining examination of life in post-apartheid South Africa. These films illustrate Blair's stylistic and thematic preoccupations: the use of improvisation and unobtrusive camerawork to achieve relaxed, naturalistic performances in the pursuit of a non-didactic critique of social reality.

The feature films, however, should not be seen apart from Blair's television films, of which there have been nine since 1985, including two – *The Accountant* (1989) and *News Hounds* (1990) – that received BAFTA awards for Best Single Drama. They range from the gentle humour of *Filipina Dreamgirls* (1991), *The Merrihill Millionaires* (1993) and *Stand and Deliver* (1998) to the bitter-sweet romance of *Leave to Remain* (1989) and *Bliss* (1995). Stylistically and otherwise Blair's films represent an impressive body of work that has not received the critical attention it deserves, probably because most of his films have been made for television. The fact that *H3*, his 2002 film about the 1981 hunger strikes by IRA prisoners in Northern Ireland, has received such little exposure is indicative of his neglect.

(Lez Cooke)

BIBLIOGRAPHY: Blair, Les, 'Northern Exposure', *Sight and Sound*, Sept. 1997, p. 61.

FILMOGRAPHY: *Number One* (1985); *Bad Behaviour* (1993); *Jump the Gun* (1997); *H3* (Ir, 2002).

BLAKELEY, John E. (1888–1958)

John E. Blakeley, more than anyone, helped to bring the northern music-hall comedian to the attention of the moviegoing public at a time when regional differences in comedy really meant something. He was born in Ardwick, Lancashire, on 1 October 1888 to an entrepreneurial father whose interests included ownership of several cinemas and a film-renting business in which his sons would eventually be employed. In 1933 John took the plunge into production and put his enthusiasm for music-hall comedy to good use by encouraging its stars to appear in front of the cameras. He produced George Formby's first two features, *Boot! Boots!* (Bert Tracey, 1934) and *Off the Dole* (Arthur Mertz, 1935), and though Formby was soon lost to Ealing Studios, a succession of other talents – Nat Jackley, Jimmy Jewel and Ben Warriss, Norman Evans, Betty Jumel, Dan Young and Harry Korris – forged film careers under Blakeley, now perched in the director's chair. His greatest star was Frank Randle, whom Blakeley directed in eight of his ten films (which in turn accounted for more than half of his own directorial output).

When Blakeley created the Mancunian Studios – Manchester's first sound film studio – in 1947, Randle's importance was underlined by his presence on the Board of Directors. Blakeley aimed to turn out his product as cheaply and quickly as possible, and Mancunian was custom-built to serve his minimalist manner of film-making. The selling point in all his films was the star comic, and any old hackneyed plot was allowed as long as space was provided for the comics to do 'bits of business' drawn from their stage acts. This lack of concern for pre-planning or any overall vision permitted inconsequential plots to ramble over sometimes inordinately long running times. If ultimately this limited the appeal of the films to a core, generally northern, working-class following, then the bonuses were also considerable. Blakeley's functional camera allows his music-hall leads to display their comedic skills unadorned.

The master was the bibulous Randle; his gloriously anarchic figure (both on and off screen) was a riot of slapstick comedic invention. Nevertheless, the lack of thought or effort put into the transfer from stage to cinema was in the end restrictive, and Blakeley's unsophisticated output lost its appeal in the affluent 1950s. The studios, in the Rusholme area of Manchester, were sold to the BBC in 1954 soon after Blakeley completed his final film, *It's a Grand Life*, with Randle and Diana Dors, a satisfying romp with one of Blakeley's favoured scenarios – resilient working-class characters thumbing their collective noses at authority. He died in Stockport on 20 February 1958 after a short illness.

(Richard Dacre)

BIBLIOGRAPHY: Gifford, Denis, 'It's a Grand Life', in *The Armchair Odeon: The Collector's Guide to the Movies* (Hemel Hempstead, Herts: Fountain Press, 1974); Williams, Philip Martin and David L. Williams, *Hooray for Jollywood: The Life of John E. Blakeley & The Mancunian Film Corporation* (Ashton-under-Lyne: History on Your Doorstep, 2001).

FILMOGRAPHY: *Dodging the Dole* (1936); *Somewhere in England* (1940); *Somewhere in Camp*; *Somewhere on Leave* (1942); *Demobbed* (1944); *Home Sweet Home*; *Under New Management* (aka *Honeymoon Hotel*) (1945); *Cup-Tie Honeymoon* (1947); *Holiday's with Pay*; *Somewhere in Politics/Full House* (1948); *What-a-Carry-On!*; *School for Randle* (1949); *Over the Garden Wall*; *Let's Have a Murder* (aka *Stick 'em Up*) (1950); *It's a Grand Life* (1953).

BLAKEMORE, Michael (1928–)

Born in Sydney on 19 June 1928, Michael Howell Blakemore trained and worked as a stage actor in Britain; after 1966 he began directing plays at the National Theatre in London and elsewhere. Each of his three films has merit. He made his debut in Australia with *A Personal History of the Australian Surf* (1981), a modest and endearing autobiographical documentary. For HandMade in the UK he adapted his Royal Shakespeare Company production of Peter Nichols' *Privates on Parade* (1982), a mood-hopping musical farce set among an army entertainment troupe during Britain's forgotten war in Malaya: less plausible on screen than on stage, but still entertaining and moving. Down under, he transported Chekhov's *Uncle Vanya* to rural Australia for his original script of *Country Life* (1994): charming, boisterous, melancholy, memorable not least for Googie Withers as the Irish cook, serving uneatable meals with remarks like 'Don't let those flies settle!'

(Geoff Brown and Robert Murphy)

BIBLIOGRAPHY: Kaufman, Tina and Peter Kemp, 'New Film on an Old Wave: Michael Blakemore Interviewed', *Film News* vol. 13 nos 8/9, Aug./Sept. 1983, pp. 16–17.

FILMOGRAPHY (UK only): *Privates on Parade* (1982).

BOKOVA, Jana (1946–)

Jana Bokova was born in Prague in 1946. She studied art history in Prague at Charles University, and at the Sorbonne, before spending two years in America, travelling and taking photographs. In 1972 she was among the first intake at the National Film School, where she directed a number of films and acted as cinematographer on Michael Radford's *Cold Night* (1974). After graduating she directed *Love Is Like a Violin*, an Arts Council documentary about a community theatre group working with the elderly. Innovative television documentaries followed: *Just One More War* (1977) for ATV and *I Look Like This*

(1979) for Granada, and several for the BBC, including *Living Room* (1977), *Quinn Running* (1980), *Dallas – The Big Store* (1981) and *Sunset People* (1984).

In 1984 she ventured into fiction with *Hotel du paradis* (1986), a slow, self-reflexive Anglo-French feature set among film-makers and theatricals marooned in a shadowy Paris hotel. In contrast to the genuine Bohemian eccentrics Bokova discovered in *Militia Battlefield* (1975), *Marevna and Marika* (1977) and *Blue Moon* (1980), her fictional characters are irritatingly contrived; despite occasional insights their interlinked stories fail to convince. Bokova continued her quest for 'the magic of captured authenticity' (Kulik, p. 203) in feature-length documentaries: *An Andalucian Journey* (1987), *Tales from Barcelona* (1989), *Havana* (1990), *An Argentinian Journey* (1992), *Bahia of All the Saints* (1994) and the honest and unpretentious *Eric Clapton and Friends* (2002). Her fascination with South America led to a sensitively handled second feature film, *Diario para un cuento* (1998), based on a story by Julio Cortázar about a novelist who translates letters for the prostitutes working in a Buenos Aires nightclub.

(Robert Murphy)

BIBLIOGRAPHY: Kulik, Karol (ed.), 'After School: Bokova/Tammes/Morrison/King', *Sight and Sound*, Autumn 1977, pp. 203–4; LeFanu, Mark, 'Jana's People', *Sight and Sound*, Summer 1984, pp. 212–16; Taylor, Paul, 'Acting Naturally: The TV Films of Jana Bokova', *Primetime* vol. 1 no. 2, Autumn 1981, pp. 9–10.

FILMOGRAPHY: *A Cette Minute* (doc. short, 1972); *Déjà Vu* (short, 1973); *Jokey* (short, 1974); *Militia Battlefield* (doc. short, 1975); *Love Is Like a Violin* (doc., 1977); *Hotel du paradis* (UK/Fr, 1986); *Diario para un cuento* (Sp/Arg, 1998); *Eric Clapton and Friends* (doc., 2002).

BOLT, Ben (1952–)

Benedict L. Bolt was born on 9 May 1952, the son of writer-director Robert Bolt. On graduation from the National Film School, Bolt found his way into television series before making his first feature for the Children's Film Foundation, *Black Island* (1979). This routine assignment about kids stranded on an island and being menaced by escaped criminals is only enlivened by Michael Elphick's over-emphatic turn as a near psychopath. Bolt's career blossomed in television, where he displayed an ability to master any television format, flitting effortlessly from the differing crime-drama demands of, for instance, *Bergerac* (1981) in Britain to *Hill Street Blues* (1985) in America. His only other feature film was *The Big Town* (1987), a lacklustre American gambling vehicle for Matt Dillon, which he took over from Harold Becker.

It is his television collaborations with writer David Pirie that give Bolt's career status. The drama serials *Never Come Back* (1990), which hypothesises a pro-Hitler plot in Britain in the early days of the war; and *Natural Lies* (1992), which presciently deals with agricultural health scares before the BSE/CJD and foot-and-mouth crises, are both taut, intelligent thrillers; but their masterpiece remains *Rainy Day Women* (1984). Bolt draws convincing performances from Charles Dance, Lindsay Duncan, Cyril Cusack, Suzanne Bertish and Ian Hogg, and his direction visually enhances the links between an English gothic tradition and this tale of sexual oppression and male violence in an isolated fen village during the Second World War. Its made-for-television status and the relative difficulty of re-viewing has prevented this intelligent and challenging reassessment of Britain's wartime experience getting the recognition it deserves. Bolt continues to work prolifically in television, latterly much with Martin Clunes.

(Richard Dacre)

BIBLIOGRAPHY: 'Trailers', *City Limits* no. 309, 3 Sept. 1987, p. 26.

FILMOGRAPHY: *Black Island* (1979); *The Big Town* (US, 1987).

BOLT, Robert (1924-1995)

Robert Oxton Bolt was born on 15 August 1924 in Sale, Cheshire. Educated at Manchester University, he became a playwright, eventually turning his writing skills to film. He became a highly successful scriptwriter, collaborating with David Lean on *Lawrence of Arabia* (1962), *Dr Zhivago* (1965) and *Ryan's Daughter* (1970), which starred his wife, Sarah Miles. He won Academy Awards for his scripts for *Dr Zhivago* and *A Man for All Seasons* (Fred Zinnemann, 1966).

Bolt's only film as a director is *Lady Caroline Lamb* (1972), based on his own script and starring Sarah Miles. The film depicts Lady Caroline's unhappy marriage to William Lamb (Jon Finch), who as Lord Melbourne would later become Prime Minister. Lady Caroline falls hopelessly in love with the poet Lord Byron (Richard Chamberlain) and causes a high-society scandal. Bolt's sympathies are with Lady Caroline, portrayed as a victim of her own naivety, of her husband's thriving ambition, of Byron's misanthropy and of moral hypocrisy. But she is not an easy figure for audiences to identify with, and despite the support of an all-star cast (Ralph Richardson, John Mills, Laurence Olivier, Pamela Brown, Margaret Leighton), the film was given a lukewarm reception. Bolt returned to scriptwriting. In 1979, during a long collaboration with David Lean on his project to retell the story of the mutiny on HMS *Bounty*, Bolt suffered a massive stroke. (His script was filmed by Roger Donaldson as *The Bounty* in 1984.) He recovered sufficiently to work with Lean on his adaptation of Joseph Conrad's *Nostromo*, but Lean's death in 1991 meant it was never filmed. Robert Bolt died on 12 February 1995 in Petersfield, Hampshire.

(Erik Hedling)

BIBLIOGRAPHY: Brownlow, Kevin, *David Lean* (London: Faber and Faber, 1997); Hayman, Ronald, *Robert Bolt* (London: Heinemann, 1969); Turner, Adrian, *Robert Bolt: Scenes from Two Lives* (London: Hutchinson, 1998).

FILMOGRAPHY: *Lady Caroline Lamb* (1972).

BOLVÁRY, Géza von (1897–1961)

Géza Maria von Bolváry-Zahn, born in Budapest on 27 December 1897, spent much of his career working in the

German film industry. His relevance to Britain stems from his involvement, between 1927 and 1930, in the so-called 'Cinema Europe' project. This was a loose alliance of producers in the UK, France and Germany (primarily Michael Balcon and Erich Pommer), formed in order to broaden the cultural appeal, increase production values and reduce the overheads of feature films produced in European studios. Clearly intended to counter the increasing dominance of the Hollywood distributors in European markets, the scheme worked essentially through a series of distribution agreements that enabled a film produced in one European country to be distributed across the continent, thus increasing its revenue base. The Cinema Europe idea eventually fell apart when the arrival of sound rendered the cost of producing multiple language versions uneconomic.

However, extensive experiments were carried out in dubbing and in producing multiple takes of a scene using different actors in different languages – experiments in which von Bolváry, along with E. A. Dupont, was at the forefront. Among his films shown widely in Britain were *The Ghost Train*, a Gainsborough/Emelka co-production and *The Gallant Hussar*, an Ivor Novello vehicle with a German supporting cast. In July 1929, von Bolváry's *The Wrecker* was the first Gainsborough sound film to be trade shown (a month after its rivals BIP had released Hitchcock's *Blackmail*). The story of a bus company owner who sabotages trains to drum up custom, it was shown with recorded music and copious synchronised sound effects of train smashes, but no dialogue (probably because the film was shot almost entirely on location and at that point the RCA Photophone system could only be used to lip-synch accurately in a studio). Shortly afterwards von Bolváry reshot scenes from his Betty Balfour melodrama *Bright Eyes* with synchronised songs. The film enjoyed considerable box-office success when released in October 1929, and it was followed by another Balfour vehicle, *The Vagabond Queen*, a lively spoof of the popular Ruritanian romances, with a spirited servant girl (Balfour) doubling for the Princess of Bolonia on the eve of her coronation and narrowly dodging a variety of ill-conceived assassination attempts.

Von Bolváry returned to Germany for good shortly afterwards and subsequently established a career in the Nazi film industry directing musicals and romantic melodramas. He died in Altenbeuern on 10 August 1961.

(Leo Enticknap)

BIBLIOGRAPHY: 'Deutsche regisseuré: Géza Maria von Bolváry, *Filmblätter*, 18 June 1954, p. 647; Dumont, Etienne, 'Geza von Bolvary: un maître de la comédie musicale allemand', *Travelling*, May/June 1974, pp. 2–30.

FILMOGRAPHY (UK only): *The Ghost Train* (aka *Der Geisterzug*, UK/Ger, 1927); *The Gallant Hussar* (aka *Der Fesche Husar*, Ger/UK, 1928); *The Wrecker* (aka *Der Wüger*, UK/Ger); *Number Seventeen* (aka *Haus Nummer 17*, UK/Ger); *Bright Eyes* (aka *Champagner*, Aus/UK); *The Vagabond Queen* (1929).

BOND, Ralph (1906–1989)

Ralph Bond was born in London on 5 December 1906 and educated at Tottenham Grammar School. After working in the insurance business, he devoted himself for the rest of his life to film and political activism. In 1929 he co-founded the London Workers' Film Society to screen progressive films to working-class audiences; he also launched the distributing company Atlas Films, which sought films deemed suitable for screening from the continent to workers throughout Britain. For the Federation of Workers' Film Societies he edited various compilation documentaries and newsreels, such as *Glimpses of Modern Russia* (1930) and at least three issues of *Workers' Topical News* (1930–1), covering May Day demonstrations, strikes and the hunger marches of the unemployed. He also took charge of *1931*, an ambitious film, now seemingly lost, promoting the Workers' Charter Campaign.

At the same time, Bond took steps to become a professional film-maker in what was fast emerging as the documentary mainstream. In 1931 he joined John Grierson's film team at the Empire Marketing Board, continuing at the GPO Film Unit, first as unit production and studio manager, later as director. Although from a very different background to many of Grierson's young recruits, Bond always retained a high regard for the social realism of his fellow documentary-makers. He wholly endorsed the aim, as he saw it, of 'putting the worker on the screen . . . as a positive and vitally important aspect of life as a whole' (Orbanz, p. 125).

Over the years Bond made films for numerous other documentary film units, including the Strand Film Company, Realist Film Unit and World Wide Pictures. With Ruby Grierson in 1937 he co-directed Strand's *Today We Live*, a film about new social services for miners, where he was able to go beyond the usual platitudes and make outspoken comment on the conditions of the unemployed. He was the natural choice to take responsibility for some of the labour movement's film commissions: for the Workers' Film Association he directed *Advance Democracy!* (1938) and for the Royal Arsenal Co-operative Society he made *People with a Purpose* (1939). In the first of these, documentary sequences shot around the London docks and the 1938 May Day parade are interspersed with dramatic scenes depicting a dockworker's rise to activism. The professionalism and ambition Bond brought to these films make them stand out from most other workers' films of the period.

During the war, Bond directed for the Ministry of Information and other official bodies. After 1945 he produced documentaries for World Wide Pictures, and devoted much of his energy to distributing and exhibiting political films. Throughout his working life Bond was a committed trade unionist: he had joined the Association of Cine Technicians in 1935, was elected to its executive committee in 1936 and served as its vice-president from 1942 to 1974. In 1953 he was a founding director of ACT Films, the production company established by the union, and served as its first production supervisor and general manager.

In the 1970s, Bond taught at the London Film School, guiding young film-makers in documentary techniques; and up to his death he continued to participate in trade union meetings. Though he lacked the cinematic brilliance of some of his colleagues, his unwavering commitment to social and economic justice, his solid professionalism and his abilities as an activist and organiser enabled Bond to make a lasting contribution to British film culture. He died in Torbay on 29 May 1989.
(Alan Burton)

BIBLIOGRAPHY: Bond, Ralph, 'One Man's Recollections', *Cinema-Technician*, May 1954, pp. 89–91; Bond, Ralph, 'Cinema in the Thirties: Documentary Film and the Labour Movement', in Jon Clark, David Margolies and Carole Snee (eds), *Culture and Crisis in Britain in the Thirties* (London: Lawrence & Wishart, 1979); Hogenkamp, Bert, *Deadly Parallels: Film and the Left in Britain 1929–1939* (London: Lawrence & Wishart, 1986); MacPherson, Don (ed.), *British Cinema: Traditions of Independence* (London: BFI, 1980); Orbanz, Eva, *Journey to a Legend and Back* (Berlin: Verlag Volker Speiss, 1977).

FILMOGRAPHY: *Glimpses of Modern Russia* (1930); *Workers' Topical News 1–3* (1930–1); *1931* (1931); *Simple Magnetism and Electricity*; *Winter* (collaborative, Film and Photo League) (1936); *Today We Live* (co-dir. Ruby Grierson, 1937); *Passport to Europe*; *Advance Democracy!*; *Paraffin Young, Pioneer of Oil* (1938); *People with a Purpose*; *Animal Geography* (1939); *Prelude to Pleasure*; *Oxford*; *The Big City*; *Neighbours under Fire* (1940); *Eating at Work*; *A1 at Lloyd's*; *Adeste Fideles* (co-dir. Ralph Keene); *Post 23* (1941); *When We Build Again*; *How to Thatch* (1942); *Keeping Rabbits for Extra Meat* (1943); *Growing Good Potatoes*; *Sport* (1944); *Unity Is Strength*; *We Who Make the Tools* (1945).

BOORMAN, John (1933–)

John Boorman was born in Shepperton, Middlesex, on 18 January 1933. After the blitzed childhood he evoked in *Hope and Glory* (1987), national service, and a spell in dry-cleaning, he progressed from journalism into television, eventually becoming Head of the BBC's Bristol-based Documentary Unit in 1962. His first feature, *Catch Us If You Can* (1965), an attempt to repeat the success of *A Hard Day's Night* (Richard Lester, 1964), is handicapped by the fact that the Dave Clark Five are infinitely less interesting, musically and as screen personalities, than the Beatles. However, within the format of the UK pop musical, the film shows traces of a distinct directorial personality. As the group make their way into the West Country, Boorman catches glimpses of unusual English landscapes: considering that he would specialise in alien or alienating worlds, it is intriguing that even at this early stage he was casting his eye around for the fantastical among the greenery. Boorman was drawn to Hollywood by the opportunity to make larger-scale cinema, and in *Point Blank* (1967), a potent distillation of a Richard Stark novel, he brought a stranger's vision to the decaying fortress of Alcatraz and the proto-hippy world of San Francisco.

After *Point Blank* Boorman teamed up again with Lee Marvin (partnered with Toshiro Mifune) for the robinsonade of *Hell in the Pacific* (1968), a war movie with a slightly too fable-like gimmick: the relationship of nations encapsulated by two representative soldiers stranded together on an island and forced to put aside war to survive. *Point Blank* is an art movie that successfully mimics genre, but *Hell in the Pacific*, like many subsequent Boorman films, does not quite manage the trick. Returning to the UK, to a London that had stopped swinging, he made *Leo the Last* (1969), which, with the presence of Marcello Mastroianni importing a Fellinian influence, won him a Best Director award at Cannes but yielded only something as interesting and half-formed as *Catch Us If You Can*. Almost the least-known of Boorman's films, *Leo the Last* was unhappily reworked as the dire *Where the Heart Is* (1990).

Boorman achieved much greater resonance with *Deliverance* (1972), adapted from another pulp novel (albeit one by a poet, James Dickey). City folks Jon Voigt, Burt Reynolds, Ronny Cox and Ned Beatty trespass into the Appalachian backwoods and discover their inner savagery as they feud with degenerate rednecks. It is another genre fable, an action movie that meditates on violence, and again finds strange corners of America, most unforgettably the porch-sitting withered child whose fast fingers play 'Feudin' Banjos'.

Though he only approached the taut perfection of *Point Blank* and *Deliverance* with *The General* (1998), a black-and-white biopic of an Irish criminal, Boorman's films are almost always ambitious and original. *Zardoz* (1973) is functionally insane as science fiction, but its bizarre production design and green Irish locations are memorable. *Excalibur* (1981) is a worthy attempt to get beyond an Arthurian *Star Wars*, with its streak of crazed humour in Nicol Williamson's Merlin and its commitment to blood, steel and magic as the dream of Camelot unrav-

els in an internecine war explicitly depicted as a multigenerational family argument.

Even at his most 'Hollywood', Boorman is committed to his own material and culture: *The Emerald Forest* (1985), a rainforest adventure, casts his actor son Charley as an eco-warrior Tarzan, and commingles commercially required elements – action and near-nudity – with anthropological detail and the gorgeous threat of the green inferno. *Beyond Rangoon* (1995) and *The Tailor of Panama* (2000) are politicised travelogues, with stars and intrigues, more interested in their gaudily corrupt settings than in editorial condemnations. *Hope and Glory*, which recreates 1940s' suburbia in the studio, is at once heritage wartime nostalgia and a spirited raspberry to the form, incarnated by Sammi Davis' joyful welcome to the bombs that destroy her stifling neighbourhood. Considering Boorman's lack of interest in being exclusively a British film-maker, it may be significant that the blitzed area of the film is Shepperton – site of a studio Boorman might have found himself confined to if he had not followed his imagination and made the world his canvas.

(Kim Newman)

BIBLIOGRAPHY: Boorman, John, *Money into Light:* The Emerald Forest: *A Diary* (London: Faber and Faber, 1985); Boorman, John, 'Bright Dreams, Hard Knocks: A Journal for 1991', in John Boorman and Walter Donohue (eds), *Projections: A Forum for Film Makers* (London: Faber and Faber, 1992); Boorman, John, *Adventures of a Suburban Boy* (London: Faber and Faber, 2003); Ciment, Michel, *John Boorman* (London: Faber and Faber, 1986); Pallenberg, Barbara, *The Making of Exorcist II: The Heretic* (New York: Warner Books, 1977).

FILMOGRAPHY: *Catch Us If You Can* (US: *Having a Wild Weekend*, 1965); *Point Blank* (US, 1967); *Hell in the Pacific* (US, 1968); *Leo the Last* (1969); *Deliverance* (US, 1972); *Zardoz* (1973); *The Exorcist II: The Heretic* (US, 1977); *Excalibur* (1981); *The Emerald Forest* (1985); *Hope and Glory* (1987); *Where the Heart Is* (US, 1990); *Beyond Rangoon* (US, 1995); *The General* (US/Ir, 1998); *The Tailor of Panama* (US, 2000); *Country of My Skull* (2004).

BOOTH, Harry

Harry Booth entered the film industry in 1941 and during the 1950s worked as an editor, producer and screenwriter on second features such as *At the Stroke of Nine* (Lance Comfort, 1957). He went on to direct and edit two feature-length documentaries, *Blitz on Britain* (1960) and *A King's Story* (1965), a sympathetic portrait of Edward VIII, Duke of Windsor, narrated by Orson Welles, which attracted favourable attention in the USA, receiving an Academy Award nomination for Best Documentary.

In the late 1960s, Booth directed and co-scripted three children's serials, *River Rivals* (1967) and two series of *The Magnificent Six and ½* (1968 and 1969) for the Children's Film Foundation. His feature film debut was *On the Buses* (1971), a spin-off from the popular television sitcom, made by Hammer as a way of diversifying out of the declining horror market. Though Booth had shown a flair for offbeat comedy – producing and scripting the Goons spin-off, *The Case of the Mukkinese Battlehorn* (Joseph Sterling, 1955) and directing Michael Bentine in *Bachelor of Arts* (1969) – *On the Buses* now seems a dreary farce, notable only for its leering sexism. Nevertheless it was a commercial success, grossing over £1 million on a £90,000 budget. Booth directed the first of two sequels, *Mutiny on the Buses,* and reunited with Reg Varney for *Go for a Take*, an equally poor comedy about two waiters on the loose in a film studio. More durable was his zany television comedy series, *The Double Deckers* (1971), about a gang of lovable cockney teenagers. He made *The Flying Sorcerer* for the CFF and a Dutch comedy *Op de Hollandse toer* in 1973, and continued to work as a director, editor and writer in television throughout the 1970s.

(Daniel O'Brien)

FILMOGRAPHY: *Blitz on Britain* (doc., 1960); *A King's Story* (doc., 1965), *River Rivals* (serial, 1967); *The Magnificent Six and ½* (serial, 1968); *Bath Time: Portrait of a Peer* (doc.); *Bachelor of Arts* (short) (1969); *On the Buses* (1971); *Mutiny on the Buses*; *Go for a Take* (1972); *The Flying Sorcerer*; *Op de Hollandse toer* (Neth) (1973).

BOOTH, Walter (1869–1938)

Walter Robert Booth, born in Worcester on 12 July 1869, was a porcelain painter and an amateur magician, who joined the magic company at the Egyptian Hall in London in the 1890s. He became a producer of trick films for Robert Paul in 1899, creating such novelties as *Upside Down; or, The Human Flies* (1899) and *A Railway Collision* (1900). *The Devil in the Studio* (1901) introduced into British cinema hand-drawing techniques that pointed the way to animated cartoons, along with a taste for the fantastical that showed the influence of Georges Méliès. The Méliès influence was further displayed in *The Adventurous Voyage of The Arctic* (1903) and *The '?' Motorist* (1906), where a motorist drives around the rings of Saturn.

In 1906 Booth moved to the Charles Urban Trading Company. He established his own studio in his garden at Isleworth, London, with Harold Bastick as his cameraman. Notable films produced there include the first British animated film, *The Hand of the Artist* (1906), *The Sorcerer's Scissors* (1907) and *When the Devil Drives* (1907). His invasion fantasies, such as *The Airship Destroyer* (1909) and *The Aerial Submarine* (1910), are entertaining proto-science-fiction fables in the Jules Verne mould.

By 1913 Booth was making shorts for UK Kinoplastikon, some featuring variety acts synchronised to gramophone records. Switching to Urban's subsidiary Kineto, he continued to generate trick films and comedies, along with numerous advertising films; his last-known release, the war comedy *Tommy's Initiation*, emerged in July 1918. Little is known of his subsequent career and he died in Birmingham in 1938. Imaginative, playful and technically adept, Booth remains one of the most underrated and neglected film-makers of early British cinema.

(Luke McKernan)

BIBLIOGRAPHY: Barnouw, Erik, *The Magician and the Cinema* (New York and Oxford: Oxford University Press, 1981); Gifford, Denis, *British Animated Films* (Jefferson, NC and London: McFarland, 1987).

FILMOGRAPHY: *The Miser's Doom; Upside Down; or, The Human Flies* (1899); *Plucked from the Burning; The Hair-Breadth Escape of Jack Sheppard; Diving for Treasure; A Railway Collision; Kruger's Dream of Empire; The Last Days of Pompeii; Hindoo Jugglers; Chinese Magic* (aka *Yellow Peril*); *Britain's Welcome to Her Sons* (1900); *The Captain's Birthday; An Over-Incubated Baby; The Devil in the Studio; The Haunted Curiosity Shop; Undressing Extraordinary; or, The Troubles of a Tired Traveller; The Cheese Mites; or, Lilliputians in a London Restaurant; The Drunkard's Conversion* (aka *The Horrors of Drink*); *'Arry on the Steamboat; Ora Pro Nobis; or, The Poor Orphan's Last Prayer; The Waif and the Wizard; or, The Home Made Happy; Britain's Tribute to Her Sons; Artistic Creation; The Famous Illusion of De Kolta; Mr Pickwick's Christmas at Wardle's; The Magic Sword; or, A Mediaeval Mystery; Scrooge; or, Marley's Ghost* (1901); *The Enchanted Cup; Father Thames' Temperance Cure; Soap versus Blacking; The Extraordinary Waiter* (aka *The Mysterious Heads*) (1902); *The Pocket Boxers; The Dice Player's Last Throw; The Adventurous Voyage of The Arctic; An Extraordinary Cab Accident* (1903); *Political Favourites* (aka *Free Trade and Protection Favourites*); *The Music Hall Manager's Dilemma; The Haunted Scene Painter; Tropical Tricks* (1904); *The Hand of the Artist; The Vacuum Cleaner Nightmare; The Magic Bottle; The '?' Motorist; Following in Father's Footsteps; Puck's Pranks on a Suburbanite; The Conjuror's Pupil* (1906); *Willie Goodchild Visits His Auntie; The Waif and the Statue; A Modern Galatea; Comedy Cartoons; The Magical Press; The £1,000 Spook; Hanky Panky Cards; The Baffled Burglar; The Haunted Bedroom; Willie's Magic Wand; Dreamland Adventures; Accidents Will Happen; A Juvenile Scientist; Catch Your Own Fish; The Sorcerer's Scissors; The Curate's Double; Sammy's Sucker; His Daughter's Voice; The Apple of Discord; When the Devil Drives; A Diabolo Nightmare* (1907); *Two Little Motorists; The Chauffeur's Dream; The Lightning Postcard Artist; Paper Tearing; Waterproof Willie; A Quick-Change Mesmerist; The Star Globe-Trotter; The Prehistoric Man; The Adventures of a Watch; The Tramp's Cycling Mania; The Guard's Alarum; Polka on the Brain; The Hands of a Wizard; Your Dog Ate My Lunch, Mum!; Following in Mother's Footsteps* (1908); *An Absorbing Tale; Why Father Grew a Beard; Saved by a Burglar; The Magic Carpet; The Wizard's Walking Stick; Why Tommy Was Late for School; Marie Lloyd's Little Joke; Professor Puddenhead's Patents: The Aerocab and Vacuum Provider; Professor Puddenhead's Patents: The Electric Enlarger; Monty Learns to Swim; From Working House to Mansion; A Bogus Motor Elopement; Animated Cotton; The Professor's Dream; The Invisible Dog; The Electric Servant; Apples; The Airship Destroyer* (aka *The Aerial Torpedo/The Battle in the Clouds*); *Bobby Wideawake; That Awful Pipe; Sooty Sketches; Up the Pole; or, How I Cook-ed Peary's Record; The Uncontrollable Bicycle* (1909); *The Hunt for a Collar; The Great Fight at All-Sereno; The Bewitching Boxing Gloves; The Freezing Mixture; The Electric Vitalizer; The Aerial Submarine; His Mother's Necklace; Seeing London in One Day; Juggling on the Brain* (1910); *Animated Putty; A Juvenile Hypnotist* (aka *Juvenile Pranks*); *The Fakir's Fan* (aka *The Magic Fan*); *The Automatic Motorist; An Aerial Elopement; Giles Has His Fortune Told; The Aerial Anarchists; The Modern Pygmalion and Galatea; Mystic Manipulations; Little Lady Lafayette; Mischievous Puck; The Hypnotist and the Convict; The Wizard and the Brigands; Simpkins' Dream of a Holiday; Uncle's Picnic; The Cap of Invisibility; Kitty in Dreamland* (1911); *The Jester's Joke* (aka *The Merry Jester*); *From behind the Flag; Animated Toys; A Modern Mystery; The Joker's Mistake* (aka *Getting His Own Back*); *An Eccentric Sportsman; Paper Cuttings; Card Manipulations; Clever Egg Conjuring; In Fairy Land; The Conjuror as a Good Samaritan; Santa Claus* (co-dirs. F. Martin Thornton, R. H. Callum); *In Gollywog Land* (US: *Gollywog's Motor Accident*, co-dir. F. Martin Thornton); *Modelling Extraordinary* (1912); *His Master's Voice: Mrs Kelly; Good Queen Bess; And Very Nice Too; Persian Dance: Eightpence a Mile; Trio: Everybody's Doing It; Little Micky the Mesmerist; Fantasie: Dresden China; A Sister to Assist 'Er; Recitation by James Welch; Sailor's Song; Artful Athletics* (1913); *The Tangram; A Little Lady Cartoonist; Love and Magic; Magical Mysteries; The Shirker's Nightmare* (1914); *The Menace of the Air; A Devil of a Honeymoon; Can You Do This?; The World's Worst Wizard; Kineto's Side-Splitters No. 1* (1915); *Too Much Sausage; The Portrait of Dolly Gray; Tanks* (aka *Tanks Cartoons*) (1916); *Tommy's Initiation* (1918).

BOULTING, John (1913–1985) and Roy BOULTING (1913–2001)

Twin brothers John Edward and Roy Alfred Clarence Boulting, born in Bray, Buckinghamshire, on 21 December 1913, constitute one of those producer-director teams responsible for so much notable British cinema. For most of their careers one produced while the other directed, but the product remained essentially a 'Boulting Brothers film'. They were socialistically inclined (John fought with the International Brigade in the Spanish Civil War), despite a somewhat patrician demeanour, and wanted film to have serious connections with social reality.

In 1937 they set up Charter Films and made several short features, including *Consider Your Verdict*, which attracted critical and commercial attention. Their first major film was *Pastor Hall* (1940), the moving account of a German preacher who refuses to kowtow to the Nazis. Its production was delayed until the Government was ready to be openly critical of Nazism, but it was well received by the critics and the public. They followed it up with *Thunder Rock*, a passionate anti-isolationist allegory distinguished by imaginative cinematography and a theatrical but highly atmospheric lighthouse setting. In 1941 Roy joined the Army Film and Photographic Section, where he was responsible for the enormously influential *Desert Victory* and *Burma Victory*; and John joined the RAF Film Unit, where he made *Journey Together*, a dramatised documentary about the training and combat experience of a bomber crew, with Richard Attenborough in the lead part.

After the war, Roy's *Fame Is the Spur*, an intelligent study of a Labour politician who loses his ideals, was coolly received in Labour-run Britain, though it is both unsentimental and very touching. John's compelling adaptation of Grahame Greene's *Brighton Rock*, with its evocation of a tawdry and violent world, was a box-office success and has proved to be an enduring classic. Roy persevered with the mission for a topical, socially relevant, cinema with *The Guinea Pig*, in which a lower-middle-class boy wins a scholarship to an English public school and has to face entrenched snobbery and class prejudice. It was followed by two films that work effectively as thrillers but are very much rooted in contemporary actuality. *Seven Days to Noon* deals with the threat of what would now be called nuclear terrorism; while *High Treason* concentrates on subversion and sabotage in the London docks. This period, between 1947 and 1951, represents the Boultings' major achievement, each of the films being trenchant, relevant and distinctive.

There was a lull in the mid-1950s when they made several films for Hollywood companies with American stars. None of these is a disgrace; nor is any of them either as socially relevant or as artistically distinctive as their 1940s' work. Roy directed *Single-Handed*, a mildly exciting remake of *Brown on Resolution* (Walter Forde, 1935), for Fox-British, and (in Hollywood) *Run for the Sun*, a remake of *The Most Dangerous Game/The Hounds of Zaroff* (Irving Pichel/Ernest B. Schoedsack, 1932), and together they directed *Seagulls over Sorrento* (a popular West End service comedy reworked with a partly American cast) for MGM-British. What is now most tenaciously associated with the Boultings is the highly successful series of institutional satires begun with *Private's Progress* in 1956. These films take sharp, but generally good-tempered swipes at such social bastions as the army, the law (*Brothers in Law*), trade unions (*I'm All Right Jack*), the Foreign Office (*Carlton-Browne of the F.O.*) and the Church of England (*Heavens Above!*). There is no Swiftian ferocity here, rather a softening of the Boultings' idealism and social purpose; but they are often very funny and hit their targets with deflating accuracy. These films benefit greatly from the collaborators with whom the brothers had surrounded themselves, including screenwriter Frank Harvey, cinematographer Max Greene, composer John Addison, editor Anthony Harvey and a brilliant repertory company of stars and character actors. Peter Sellers, Ian Carmichael and Terry-Thomas all became comedy stars under the Boultings' tutelage, and the films are studded with joyous moments of character observation from the likes of Raymond Huntley, Irene Handl and Dennis Price. These films made money, and some, especially *I'm All Right Jack*, offer acrid insights into assorted national shoddinesses, but it is hard not to feel that a certain cynicism had overtaken the brothers, even as one is laughing at their diagnoses of pomposity and moral decay.

Roy (left) and John Boulting

Apart from this popular series, several other films deserve mention. John directed the Festival of Britain film, *The Magic Box*, with a fabulous star cast, and achieved some poignancy in narrating the life of British film pioneer William Friese-Greene; Roy directed *Happy Is the Bride*, a sunny remake of *Quiet Wedding* (Anthony Asquith, 1940); the two co-directed and produced *Suspect*, an attempt at a B-film that merited respect for its treatment of politics and science, and the tenderly observed comedy-drama of marital difficulties, *The Family Way*. This latter film, based on Bill Naughton's play *All in Good Time*, tackles with sensitivity and warmth the problem of an unconsummated marriage and, even more affectingly, a long-established marriage that has shied clear of truthful understanding. Roy later married the film's star, Hayley Mills, their age gap raising considerable publicity. There was also a return to the morbid psychology of *Brighton Rock* in *Twisted Nerve*, a film that was poorly received at the time but has subsequently attained cult status for its bizarre story (by Leo Marks) and the outstanding performances of Hywel Bennett and Hayley Mills.

The Boultings were an influential force behind the scenes in British cinema. Not only were they among the most successful production teams, they also contributed to its industrial muscle as directors of British Lion, an independent distribution company that offered producers an alternative to the Rank/ABPC duopoly. John died of cancer in Sunningdale on 17 June 1985. Roy died of cancer in Oxford on 5 November 2001, without having completed the memoirs he had been working on for some years. (Brian McFarlane)

BIBLIOGRAPHY: Burton, Alan, Tim O'Sullivan and Paul Wells (eds), *The Family Way: The Boulting Brothers and British Film Culture* (Trowbridge, Wilts: Flicks Books, 2000); Conrad, Derek, 'What

Makes the English Laugh?', *Films and Filming*, Feb. 1959, pp. 7, 31; McFarlane, Brian, *An Autobiography of British Cinema* (London: Methuen, 1997).

FILMOGRAPHY: Roy Boulting: *The Landlady* (short); *Ripe Earth* (doc. short); *Seeing Stars* (short); *Consider Your Verdict* (short, 1938); *Trunk Crime*; *Inquest* (1939); *Pastor Hall* (1940); *Dawn Guard* (short) *They Serve Abroad* (doc. short); *Thunder Rock* (1942); *Desert Victory* (doc., 1943); *Tunisian Victory: An Official Record* (doc., co-dirs. Frank Capra and Hugh Stewart, 1944); *Burma Victory* (doc., 1945); *Fame Is the Spur* (1947); *The Guinea Pig* (1948); *Seven Days to Noon* (co-dir. John Boulting: 1950); *High Treason* (1951); *Single-Handed* (US: *Sailor of the King*, 1953); *Seagulls over Sorrento* (US: *Crest of the Wave*, co-dir. John Boulting, 1954); *Josephine and Men* (1955); *Run for the Sun*; *Brothers in Law* (US) (1956); *Happy Is the Bride* (1957); *Carlton-Browne of the F.O.* (co-dir. Jeffrey Dell); *A French Mistress* (1959); *Suspect* (co-dir. John Boulting, 1960); *Heavens Above!* (co-dir. John Boulting, 1963); *The Family Way* (co-dir. John Boulting, 1966); *Twisted Nerve* (1968); *There's a Girl in My Soup* (1970); *Soft Battles, Hard Beds* (1973); *The Last Word* (US, 1979).

John Boulting: *Journey Together* (1945); *Brighton Rock* (1947); *Seven Days to Noon* (co-dir. Roy Boulting, 1950); *The Magic Box* (1951); *Seagulls over Sorrento* (US: *Crest of the Wave*, co- dir. Roy Boulting, 1954); *Private's Progress* (1956); *Lucky Jim* (1957); *I'm All Right Jack* (1959); *Suspect* (co- dir. Roy Boulting, 1960); *Heavens Above!* (co-dir. Roy Boulting, 1963); *Rotten to the Core* (1965); *The Family Way* (co-dir. Roy Boulting, 1966).

BOWER, Dallas (1907–1999)

In his book *Plan for Cinema*, written in 1935, Dallas Bower foresaw a future where television would take over most of the film industry's existing functions and leave cinema to metamorphose into a new art experience – a fusion of decor and choreography projected onto a cylindrical screen. Bower's diverse cinema output never reached that lofty state, but he deserves attention nonetheless, not least for producing and originating the script for Olivier's *Henry V* (1944).

The great-great-grandson of the actress Sarah Siddons, Dallas Gordon Bower was born in London on 25 July 1907. Initially he specialised in sound recording: after experience with the Marconi and British Thomson-Houston companies, he transferred his expertise to the cinema in 1929. At Elstree he worked as sound recordist on two important early BIP talkies, *Under the Greenwood Tree* (Harry Lachman, 1929) and *Suspense* (Walter Summers, 1930), before moving on to jobs at Cricklewood. Directing experience came relatively early with a 'quota quickie', *The Path of Glory* (1934), an ambitious satirical comedy about two warring mythical countries, now seemingly a lost film.

After a period assisting the director Paul Czinner, Bower switched to television, directing the BBC's output on their first official day of transmission, 2 November 1936. His plan for television was equally lofty: he directed adaptations of ballet, opera and Shakespeare, and taught trainees the art of the camera by screening Eisenstein's *Alexander Nevsky* (1938). In 1940, Bower joined the Ministry of Information's Films Division, serving for two years as executive producer. By 1942, financially supported by Filippo Del Giudice and the Rank Organisation, he was hatching plans for a version of *Henry V* keyed to the patriotic wartime mood, based on his own television adaptation (shelved when war closed the BBC's service). Apart from his key contribution to the script, Bower navigated Whitehall on the film's behalf, supervised casting, brought in William Walton as composer, set up the Agincourt sequences in Ireland and watched closely over the daily shooting. He had hoped originally to be the film's director, but Olivier held sway; Bower was given a credit as 'associate producer'.

After *Henry V* Bower's projects included grand biographies of Talleyrand and Marlborough. But only the jumbled output of a director for hire followed. He directed the awkward but interesting live-action footage in the English edition of Lou Bunin's puppet film *Alice in Wonderland*, made largely in France. The film was completed in 1948, but unstable colour and censorship problems over the representation of Queen Victoria delayed the British release until 1981. In the 1950s, in between television work, he resurrected Pinero's play *The Second Mrs Tanqueray* as a low-budget feature, made two cold war thrillers for the American producer Gene Marcel and wrote scripts for the Children's Film Foundation. Documentary subjects, meanwhile, ranged from nuclear war to the economic benefits of a Lagos meat factory.

In a 1937 essay Bower had called cinema 'the most stupendously successful scientific machine ever brought to the services of entertaining the world's masses'; but bad luck and his own perennial back-room status conspired to make his own contributions to the machine smaller than his mind and expertise deserved. He died in Northwood, Middlesex, on 18 November 1999.

(Geoff Brown)

BIBLIOGRAPHY: Bower, Dallas, *Plan for Cinema* (London: J. M. Dent, 1936); Bower, Dallas, 'Film in the Social Scene', in *Cinema Survey* (London: Brendin Publishing, 1937); Huntley, John, 'Two Years in Production: Ansco Colour for "Alice"', *Film Industry*, 2 Dec. 1948, pp. 8–9; MacFarlane, Brian, *An Autobiography of British Cinema* (London: Methuen, 1997).

FILMOGRAPHY: *The Path of Glory* (1934); *Television Demonstration Film* (1937); *Alice in Wonderland* (1947–8, US rel. 1951; UK rel. 1981); *The Second Mrs Tanqueray* (1952); *Fire One* (US); *Doorway to Suspicion* (US) (1954); *Into the Light* (doc., 1956); *New Minds for a New World* (doc., co-dir. Seafield Head); *The Double Bond* (doc.) (1961); *Towards the High Life* (doc., 1965)

Other documentaries, undated: *Fire Planning in Nuclear War*, *All Informed*; *The Risks You Run*; *Quick Fire Plan*; *Ammunition*; *Going Places*; *Stranger in the Garden*.

BOX, Muriel (1905–1991)

Muriel Violette Baker was born in New Malden on the outskirts of London in September 1905, the third child of a family she

described as Respectable Poor. Influenced by her mother's progressive, left-wing ideas, Muriel developed a passion for writing, theatre and cinema, attempting unsuccessfully to become a professional actress and ballet dancer. She gained low-level employment in the film industry, including work as a continuity girl for British International Pictures, but the key event was her marriage to Sydney Box in 1935, which nurtured a mutual talent for playwriting. They completed nearly forty short plays before the outbreak of war in 1939. During the war, Muriel assisted her husband in running Verity Films, gaining her first experience of directing with *The English Inn* (1941), a typical Verity propaganda short produced for the British Council. The Boxes moved into features, achieving a spectacular hit with *The Seventh Veil*, the highest-grossing British film of 1945, which won them an Academy Award for Best Original Screenplay. On the strength of this success, Sydney was invited by the Rank Organisation to take over Gainsborough Pictures, where Muriel ran the scenario department. The emphasis was on volume production, but many of the Boxes' screenplays – such as *The Years Between* (Compton Bennett, 1946) or *Good Time Girl* (David Macdonald, 1948) – emphasise the problems women face in their struggle to gain recognition or independence. Muriel occasionally assisted as dialogue director, or reshot scenes that needed attention in post-production. On *The Lost People* (1949), about the plight of European refugees, she was credited as co-director for the very substantial reworking she deemed necessary.

When Sydney left Rank to set up London Independent Producers in 1951, Muriel was allowed more opportunity to direct. The majority of her films were stage adaptations: *The Happy Family* (1952), *To Dorothy a Son* (1954), *Simon and Laura* (1955), *This Other Eden* (1959), *Subway in the Sky* (1959), *Too Young to Love* (1960) and *Rattle of a Simple Man* (1964). Her directorial energies were channelled into eliciting strong performances from the actors; visually the films are competent and unfussy, with a preference for medium shots, allowing the audience to concentrate on dialogue and the telling glance or gesture. The films have a stage-bound feel, and rarely venture out on to location. The most successful, precisely because it thrives on such artifice, is *Simon and Laura*, Alan Melville's acerbic satire of early television 'soaps', where Kay Kendall and Peter Finch play an idealised couple who are actually the reverse of their real selves.

Box's films are notable for their strong, often topical and controversial themes. *This Other Eden* raises a number of complex issues about Irish politics, commemoration, hypocrisy and illegitimacy. *Too Young to Love*, which addressed the problem of teenage sex, abortion and syphilis, was sufficiently contentious to be banned by several local authorities. The semi-documentary *Street Corner* (1953), based on Muriel and Sydney's original screenplay, was a complement to *The Blue Lamp* (Basil Dearden, 1950), emphasising the courage and capabilities of women police officers. It formed part of Box's repeated attempts to foreground women's experiences, her most important subject. In her version of the famous W. Somerset Maugham tale *The Beachcomber* (1954), it is the pluck and tenacity of the missionary Martha (Glynis Johns) that dominates the film. *Simon and Laura, The Passionate Stranger* (1957), *The Truth about Women* (1958) and *Rattle of a Simple Man* were all comedies about the gulf that exists between the sexes, whose needs and aspirations are quite different, and between fantasy and reality. Box described *The Truth about Women* as 'the film personally significant to me above all others', a 'comedy with serious undertones concerning the status of women in various societies from the turn of the century until today' (Box, p. 222). She was dismayed when the distributors, British Lion, refused it a West End premiere, an indication that its subject was uncomfortable for a patriarchal industry.

Box experienced other forms of prejudice. Michael Balcon doubted her competence to direct a large-scale feature film, a modern Romeo and Juliet story that she had written in 1950, and the project was aborted. In 1952 the Boxes pretended that the direction of *The Happy Family* was a joint affair, but when word leaked out that Muriel was directing on her own, one of the principal financial backers, John Woolf, withdrew. She was particularly hurt when other women, Jean Simmons in *So Long at the Fair* (1950) and Kay Kendall in *Simon and Laura*, wished to have her replaced as a director. Simmons was powerful enough to get her way and Terence Fisher was given the director's slot. In the press her position as one of the very few women directors in the British film industry was frequently noted, but usually condescendingly. However, she was a role model for young women. Her chequered career illustrates the difficulties for a woman working in the film industry, and also its volatility, particularly in the 1950s and 60s when she and her husband struggled to retain a measure of independence and integrity. She left film-making after the tepid reception of *Rattle of a Simple Man*, but continued to write novels, and she set up a successful publishing house, Femina, which offered a more rewarding outlet for her feminism. She died in London on 18 May 1991. If Muriel Box never directed a masterpiece, her oeuvre remains the most significant achievement of a women director in the British film industry.

(Andrew Spicer)

BIBLIOGRAPHY: Aspinall, Sue and Robert Murphy (eds), *Gainsborough Melodrama* (London: BFI, 1983); Box, Muriel, *Odd Woman Out* (London: Leslie Frewin, 1974); Harper, Sue, *Women in British Cinema: Mad, Bad and Dangerous to Know* (London: Continuum, 2000); Merz, Caroline, 'The Tension of Genre: Wendy Toye and Muriel Box', in Wheeler Winston Dixon (ed.), *Re-viewing British Cinema, 1900–1992* (Albany: SUNY Press, 1994); Spicer, Andrew, *Sydney Box* (Manchester: Manchester University Press, 2006).

FILMOGRAPHY: *Action* (doc. short); *The English Inn* (doc. short) (1942); *The Lost People* (co-dir. Bernard Knowles, 1949); *The Happy Family* (1952); *Street Corner* (1953); *To Dorothy a Son*; *The Beachcomber* (1954); *Simon and Laura* (1955); *Eyewitness* (1956); *A Passionate*

Stranger (1957); *The Truth about Women* (1958); *This Other Eden*; *Subway in the Sky* (1959); *Too Young to Love* (1960); *The Piper's Tune* (1962); *Rattle of a Simple Man* (1964).

BOYD, Don (1948–)

Don Boyd was born in Nairn, Scotland, on 11 August 1948. He went to the London Film School at the end of the 1960s where he made two short films, *Daddy Says You Can Stay* and *Billiard Balls*. Despite the unfavourable climate for young film-makers in Britain in the 1970s, he managed to raise finance for a debut feature film, *Intimate Reflections*. Critics scorned its amateurish pretensions and audiences were alienated by its lack of narrative drive. His second film, *East of Elephant Rock*, set in 'A Far Eastern Colony 1948', fared little better, though in retrospect its exploration of the last days of the British Empire and enjoyable performances from John Hurt, Jeremy Kemp and Judi Bowker command some interest. Boyd then turned to production, teaming up with accountant Roy Tucker and pioneering the use of tax shelter money to produce a programme of low-budget films. Claude Whatham's *Sweet William* (1980), Matthew Chapman's *Hussy* (1980), Curtis Clark's *Blue Suede Shoes* (1980) and Chris Petit's *An Unsuitable Case for a Woman* (1982) made little impact; but Derek Jarman's *The Tempest* (1979) and Julien Temple's *The Great Rock 'n' Roll Swindle* (1979) attracted a loyal following, and Alan Clarke's *Scum* (1979) reached a much wider audience. After a brush with the mainstream as producer of EMI's sprawling and costly *Honky Tonk Freeway* (John Schlesinger, 1981), Boyd returned to more arty subjects, producing *Aria* (1987), with strikingly original contributions from Jean-Luc Godard and Robert Altman, and two films for Derek Jarman – *The Last of England* (1987) and *War Requiem* (1988).

Boyd's directorial career had suffered a severe setback with the collapse of *Gossip* (1982) after shooting had already begun, but in 1991 he directed *Twenty-One*, with Patsy Kensit as a modern young Englishwoman who shares her cynical thoughts with the camera. *Kleptomania*, with Kensit supporting Amy Irving, followed in 1995, though it had little cinema exposure. Latterly he has turned to the classics: *Lucia* weaves elements of Donizetti's opera *Lucia di Lammermoor* and its source novel by Walter Scott into a modern drama in which the characters ultimately mount a performance of the opera. The film suffers from poor visual quality (it was shot on video and transferred to 35mm) and is burdened with bad acting and bad dialogue. Much more satisfactory is *My Kingdom*, a bold transposition of *King Lear* to the Liverpool underworld in the late twentieth century; it is Boyd's best film, though it received only a limited release. Less ambitious, though possibly more appealing to audiences is *Andrew and Jeremy Get Married*, a slight but modestly engaging documentary about a gay British couple of very different backgrounds, shot with a minuscule crew as a co-production with the BBC.

(Robert Murphy)

BIBLIOGRAPHY: Falk, Quentin, 'Making the Money Go Further', *CinemaTV Today*, 4 Jan. 1975, p. 9; Hodgson, Clive, 'Don Boyd & Co', *National Film Theatre Programme*, Aug. 1982, pp. 10–13; Lynn, Francis, 'Passing through – An Interview with Don Boyd', *Cinema* no. 3, July 1982, p. 57; Murphy, Robert, 'Three Companies: Boyd's Co, HandMade and Goldcrest', in Martyn Auty and Nick Roddick (eds), *British Cinema Now* (London: BFI, 1985); NFT audiotape interview with Derek Malcolm, 19 June 1982, held in the BFI National Library, London; Summers, Sue, 'Let's "Twist" Again Says Independent Film Man Don Boyd', *Screen International*, 14 Feb. 1976, p. 16.

FILMOGRAPHY: *Daddy Says You Can Stay* (short, 1969); *Billiard Balls* (short, 1970); *Intimate Reflections* (1975); *East of Elephant Rock* (1976); *Vivaldi's Four Seasons* (short, aka *The Four Seasons*); *The Princess and the Pea* (short) (1979); *Twenty-One* (1991); *Kleptomania* (US, 1995); *Lucia* (1998); *Donald and Luba: A Family Movie* (doc., 2000); *My Kingdom* (2001); *Andrew and Jeremy Get Married* (doc., 2004).

BOYD, William (1952–)

William Boyd was born in Accra, Ghana, on 7 March 1952, and educated at Gordonstoun and the universities of Nice, Glasgow and Oxford. He won acclaim as a novelist with *A Good Man in Africa* (1982), *An Ice Cream War* (1983) and *Stars and Bars* (1988). After venturing into scriptwriting with *Good and Bad at Games* (Jack Gold, 1983), one of the early Channel 4 films, he went on to adapt *Stars and Bars* (Pat O'Connor, 1985) and *A Good Man in Africa* (Bruce Beresford, 1994) into American-financed films. He also adapted Mario Vargas Llosa's *Aunt Julia and the Scriptwriter* (Jon Amiel, 1990) and Joyce Cary's *Mister Johnson* (Bruce Beresford, 1991), and took over from Bryan Forbes on the screenplay for *Chaplin* (Richard Attenborough, 1992).

In 1999 he made his debut as director with *The Trench*, from his own screenplay covering the thirty-six hours before a squad of British soldiers go over the top on the first day of the Battle of the Somme in July 1916. Everything looks a little too clean and set-bound, but Boyd's script is satisfyingly intelligent, and he uses a team of talented actors (particularly Daniel Craig and Julian Rhind-Tutt) to bring it alive with conviction and pathos. Unfortunately, the film proved too grim and ungimmicky to enjoy much commercial success. Boyd returned to writing with *Sword of Honour* (Bill Anderson, 2001), a much-admired adaptation of Evelyn Waugh's Second World War trilogy for Channel 4.

(Brian McFarlane)

BIBLIOGRAPHY: Hofmann, Katja, 'War to End All Wars: Going over the Top with First Time Director William Boyd', *Exposure*, Spring 1999, pp. 20–1; Interview, *Creative Screenwriting*, Summer 1997, pp. 37–43.

FILMOGRAPHY: *The Trench* (UK/Fr, 1999).

BOYLE, Danny (1956–)

Danny Boyle was born on 20 October 1956 in Bury, Lancashire. After theatre work for the Joint Stock Company and Royal Court (where he was artistic director between 1982 and 1987),

Boyle moved into television, directing feature-length episodes of the popular detective series *Inspector Morse* and the well-received drama serial *Mr Wroe's Virgins* (1993). In 1993, he teamed up with producer Andrew Macdonald (grandson of screenwriter Emeric Pressburger) and doctor-turned-writer John Hodge to direct his first feature film, *Shallow Grave*.

This mordant and cynical low-budget thriller about three Edinburgh yuppies tempted into crime proved popular with audiences and most critics, though Ronan Bennett warned of 'the freezing and cruel emptiness at the film's heart.' (Bennett, p. 34). The Boyle/Macdonald/Hodge team's next venture was an adaptation of Irvine Welsh's cult novel *Trainspotting*. Visually imaginative and assured, and supported by an innovative marketing campaign, the film was an international success, and has retained a loyal following, in spite of its unsympathetic characters and their unsavoury drug habits.

The team's bigger-budget ventures proved less successful. *A Life Less Ordinary*, an updated screwball comedy about a deadbeat cleaner (Ewan McGregor) who kidnaps a sparky rich girl (Cameron Diaz) under the auspices of two indulgent guardian angels, left audiences and critics puzzled and unmoved. Their adaptation of Alex Garland's novel *The Beach* received a lukewarm critical reception; cult status and the presence of Leonardo DiCaprio in the lead brought in large audiences, but perhaps not enough to recoup the film's $50 million budget. Boyle returned to the UK to direct two boldly experimental films for BBC Television – *Vacuuming Completely Nude in Paradise* (2001) and *Strumpet* (2001) – before making *28 Days Later*, written by Alex Garland. Part-zombie horror, part-eco-thriller, and shot on digital video with Boyle's usual visual flair, this story of a rogue virus taps into contemporary concerns over the environment, genetic modification and bio-terrorism. Despite a half-hearted response to its release in Britain, the film went on to become a major success in the USA.

Encouragingly, rather than using this as a stepping stone back to American blockbusters (he reputedly turned down the opportunity of directing *Alien 4*), Boyle continued to express his faith in the future of digital video with *Millions*, an offbeat feature that incorporates many of the elements of his earlier films into the tale of a seven-year-old mystic determined to redistribute the proceeds of a train robbery in the interests of the poor. Boyle's defiance of the normal rules of success makes him an increasingly complex and interesting director.

(Martin Hunt)

BIBLIOGRAPHY: Bennett, Ronan, 'Lean, Mean and Cruel', *Sight and Sound*, Jan. 1985, pp. 34–6; Hopper, Keith, '*Trainspotting*: Interview with Danny Boyle', *Film West*, Spring 1996, pp. 12–15; Nathan, Ian, 'Interview: Danny Boyle', *The Times*, 26 Oct. 2002; Norman, Neil, 'The Boys of *Trainspotting* Go to America', *Evening Standard*, 22 Oct. 1997, p. 27; Pennington, Adrian, 'It's Such a Perfect Day', *Premiere* (UK), Mar. 1996, pp. 59–61.

FILMOGRAPHY: *Shallow Grave* (1994); *Trainspotting* (1996); *A Life Less Ordinary* (1997); *The Beach* (US, 2000); *28 Days Later*, *Alien Love Triangle* (short) (2002); *Millions* (2004); *Sunshine* (2006).

BRADLEY, Stephen

The Irish film-maker Stephen Bradley worked as a producer's assistant on Jim Sheridan's *My Left Foot* (1986) and was executive producer of Gerard Stembridge's *Guiltrip* (1995). His short black-and-white film *Reaper*, about a contract killer who spares the life of an old Hollywood actor (O. Z. Whitehead playing himself) after seeing his performance in John Ford's *The Grapes of Wrath* (1940), was followed by the feature *Sweety Barrett*. Brendan Gleeson is amiable enough as an out-of-work circus performer who becomes a popular local hero when he tackles crime and corruption in a small Irish town, but the film was too soft-centred to travel far beyond Ireland. Bradley went on to make *Boy Eats Girl*, a zombie comedy.

(Robert Murphy)

FILMOGRAPHY: *Reaper* (short, 1994); *Sweety Barrett* (aka *The Tale of Sweety Barrett*, Ir/Ice, 1998); *Boy Eats Girl* (Ir, 2005).

BRADY, Ray (1961–)

Ray Brady was born in England on 10 September 1961. After working as a plasterer he studied film at the London College of Printing in his late twenties, making the feature-length *Boy Meets Girl* (1994) for little over £10,000 while still a student. Disagreements with the lead actress in this dark tale of a man kept prisoner and tortured by the woman he had hoped to seduce led to her untimely dispatch by a shadowy accomplice, who then takes over her role as torturer. Though the unexpected exit of the sexy first torturer is disconcerting, her dowdier replacement introduces a note of convincing pathos into the proceedings. Ninety-three minutes of torture is not everybody's cup of tea, but Brady deserves credit for his constant inventiveness in handling his gruesome subject. The film attracted considerable attention – not least from the BBFC, which by blocking the video release for seven years also scuppered its chances of theatrical distribution beyond the festival circuit.

A second feature, *Kiss Kiss Bang Bang* (1997), continued Brady's fascination with morbid fantasies, though here he shows little talent for storytelling. A young writer obsessed with a woman he sees from his window hires a contract killer to murder her boyfriend and her flatmate; but having won her, he glimpses another enticing woman. Brady did better with a Channel 4 pseudo-documentary *Little England* (1997), which deploys vox-pop interviews with actors representing a wide spectrum of young people against a background of images suggesting varying kinds of Britishness.

More features followed, made on tiny budgets for Brady's Imaginary Films and promoted by his distribution company Boudicca. *Love Life* (2001) is a long-winded moral tale: boastful Scott gets modest Alison pregnant; she refuses to have an abortion, successfully completes an Oxford degree and becomes an executive for a panty corporation. Meanwhile he wastes his life on drink and football, until he has an epiphany while dancing in a gay club, does good works and persuades her to give him a second chance. Audiences should be less forgiving. *Poets* (2002) combines scenes from Brady's three previous films into a curious commentary on English society. *Day of the Sirens* (2002), Brady's most ambitious film, consists of four loosely linked stories: a man rushes his heavily pregnant wife to hospital; a hotel porter loses his job, has his cancer-ridden dog put down and is driven to suicide in his council flat; a young Spaniard picks up a girl at Piccadilly Circus, begins a romantic affair with her, but murders her and dismembers her body; a lightly pregnant police inspector hunts a gunman who is perpetrating massacres all over London. Though the stories are hardly connected, the tight crosscutting schedule saves Brady from the longueurs of his previous films.

Though Brady can count himself an auteur, often using the same actors (most notably Galit Hershkovitz and Des Backhouse-Brady) and obeying his own distinctively idiosyncratic rules, it is more debatable whether he has matured into an interesting film-maker.

(Robert Murphy)

BIBLIOGRAPHY: Blewitt, David, 'Cowardly and Self-Serving' (letter), *Sight and Sound*, June 1995, p. 64; Brady, Ray, 'Boy Censors Girl' (letter), *Sight and Sound*, May 1995, p. 64; Gallant, Chris, 'Boy Meets Girl', *Shivers* no. 95, Feb. 2002, pp. 22–6; Sampson, Sally, '"Boy Meets Girl" and the BBFC' (letter), *Sight and Sound*, June 1995, p. 64.

FILMOGRAPHY: *Boy Meets Girl* (1994); *Kiss Kiss Bang Bang* (1997; rel. 2000); *Love Life* (2001); *Poets*; *Day of the Sirens* (2002).

BRAHM, John (1893–1982)

Hans Brahm was born into a theatrical family in Hamburg on 17 August 1893. By the early 1930s he was a leading stage director, with his own theatre in Berlin, where he met his future wife, actress Dolly Haas. Brahm was Jewish and he left Germany shortly after Hitler came to power in 1933, arriving in England at the height of a film boom. Haas was offered the lead by producer Julius Hagen in a planned remake of the classic Hollywood silent film *Broken Blossoms* (D. W. Griffith, 1919), to be directed once more by Griffith. Brahm, who had spent time at the German Ufa studios, was taken on as a production supervisor but when it became clear that Griffith's alcoholism made him incapable of directing a major film, Brahm was asked to take over. Though *Broken Blossoms* was not a subject of his own choosing, he was attracted by the dark and fantastic potential of the medium, and made the most of this melodramatic story, set in London's East End, of a Chinese man who attempts to save a young woman from her brutal father. With its psychotic characters, innocence trampled underfoot and violence lurking at the edge of society, it set the pattern for Brahm's later work; but its warning about the dangers of allowing racial bigotry to go unchecked was clearly directed at the situation in Germany.

In 1937 Brahm went to Hollywood. After directing B-movies at Universal, he moved to 20th Century-Fox, where he made his two best-known films, *The Lodger* (1944) and *Hangover Square* (1945). In the 1950s he became one of the first name directors to move into television, where he worked on series such as *General Electric Theater* (1953), *Alfred Hitchcock Presents* (1955) and *The Twilight Zone* (1959). He died on 11 October 1982 in Malibu, California.

(Linda Wood)

BIBLIOGRAPHY: Badder, David, 'John Brahm', *Film Dope* no. 4, Mar. 1974, p. 44; Obituary, *Classic Images*, Dec. 1982, p. 17.

FILMOGRAPHY (UK only): *Broken Blossoms* (1936).

BRAMBLE, A. V. (1884–1963)

Albert Victor Bramble was born in Portsmouth in 1884, and started his career as a stage actor twenty years later. In 1914 he began acting in films made by the British and Colonial Kinematograph Company, and made his debut as director with the short comedy *The Boy and the Cheese* that same year, though he continued to act. After the war, Bramble went to work for the newly formed British Lion at studios in Borehamwood, and when the company was taken over by Ideal in mid-1919 he stayed on to produce some of his best work. By the end of 1923 Ideal was in decline and Bramble found work with H. Bruce Woolfe at British Instructional Films, shooting the live-action sequences for Woolfe's massive war epic, *Armageddon*. He also supervised the filming of *Shooting Stars*, the directorial debut of Anthony Asquith, for Woolfe, before making *Chick* and *The Man Who Changed His Name* for a new British Lion company formed by Edgar Wallace and his associates to exploit the quota imposed by the 1927 Cinematograph Films Act.

Bramble gave up directing after 1933, and during the Second World War he was badly injured by a land mine that left him completely deaf. Nevertheless, he was cast by Carol Reed as the tribesman Batavi in *Outcast of the Islands* (1951). He died in Friern Barnet, on the northern outskirts of London, on 17 May 1963 after a short illness.

(Simon Brown)

BIBLIOGRAPHY: Low, Rachael, *The History of the British Film 1914–1918* (London: George Allen & Unwin, 1950); Low, Rachael, *The History of the British Film 1918–1929* (London: George Allen & Unwin, 1971); Obituary, *Daily Cinema*, 20 May 1963, p. 6.

FILMOGRAPHY: *The Boy and the Cheese* (1914); *Hearts That Are Human* (1915); *Jimmy*; *The Blind Man of Verdun*; *Fatal Fingers* (1916); *When Paris Sleeps*; *The Laughing Cavalier*; *Profit and Loss* (1917); *Bonnie Mary* (1918); *A Non-Conformist Parson* (aka *Heart and Soul*); *A Smart Set*; *Her Cross*; *A Single Man* (1919); *Her Benny*; *Mr Gilfil's Love Story*; *Torn Sails*; *Wuthering Heights* (1920); *The Will*; *The Old Country*; *The Prince and the Beggarmaid*; *The Bachelor's Club*; *The Rotters* (1921); *The Card*; *The Little Mother* (1922); *Shirley* (1923); *Armageddon* (live-action sequences, H. Bruce Woolfe); *Zeebrugge* (1924); *Bodiam Castle and Eric the Slender* (Part 12 of the *Haunted Houses and Castles of Great Britain* series, 1926); *Shooting Stars* (co-dir. Anthony Asquith); *Chick* (1928); *The Man Who Changed His Name* (1929); *A Lucky Sweep* (1932); *A Veteran of Waterloo*; *Mrs Dane's Defence* (1933).

BRANAGH, Kenneth (1960–)

Born on 10 October 1960 in Belfast, Kenneth Branagh moved to Reading when he was ten years old. In 1979 he joined RADA and even before graduating was offered a place with the Royal Shakespeare Company, which he turned down, subsequently making his name in the West End production of Julian Mitchell's *Another Country*. Since then Branagh has come to be known as a protean actor/director/writer/manager/producer, equally adept on the stage, film and television.

When he set up Renaissance Films to film his adaptation of Shakespeare's *Henry V*, the comparisons with Laurence Olivier, as actor and film-maker, were inevitable. However, in his continuing attempts to find a synthesis between cinema and theatre, a comparison with Orson Welles may prove to be more apposite, for instance in Branagh's express desire to create the 'longest tracking shot in the world' for *Henry V*. With his third film, *Peter's Friends*, Branagh moved towards a style of film-making and production that he has adopted in all his subsequent films. This involves filming in a single environment where the crew is based and where most of the scenes will be filmed: a British country house in *Peter's Friends*, a Tuscan villa in *Much Ado about Nothing*, a church in *In the Bleak Midwinter* and vast adjoining sets for *Mary Shelley's Frankenstein*, *Hamlet* and *Love's Labour's Lost*. This approach is seen at its best in *Much Ado*, still his most commercially successful film, and in his 70mm, star-studded, four-hour version of *Hamlet*, in which the main chamber is completely surrounded by two-way mirrors and is full of cubbyholes and trap doors, surely a comment both on court politics and the Prince's state of mind?

In the Bleak Midwinter, which looks comically at a ramshackle attempt to stage *Hamlet* in a village church, and which Branagh both wrote and directed, is his most obviously personal film. But it is less ambitious and adventurous than *Mary Shelley's*

Frankenstein and *Love's Labour's Lost*, both of which try to collocate themselves between different cinematic traditions. Universal's approach to *Frankenstein* always favoured the monster, Hammer preferred the creator; Branagh tries to give them equal weight by stressing their interdependence. In *Love's Labour's Lost*, he radically replaced two-thirds of the text with Broadway songs. The result was a 1930s-style musical comedy filmed with 1950s' colour and CinemaScope, bringing into relief the way that the war changed cinema, audiences and history, which Branagh further emphasises by his addition of a wartime coda to the text.

Though he is sometimes accused of being indulgent and overly mannered, Branagh's energetic directorial style and his boldness in presenting radical transformations of classic texts make his films a valuable asset to the British film industry.

(Sergio Angelini)

BIBLIOGRAPHY: Branagh, Kenneth, *Beginning* (London: Chatto & Windus, 1989); Branagh, Kenneth, *Much Ado about Nothing: Screenplay, Introduction and Notes on the Making of the Film* (London: Chatto & Windus, 1993); Shuttleworth, Ian, *Ken and Em: A Biography of Kenneth Branagh and Emma Thompson* (Chatham, Kent: Headline, 1994); Weiss, Tanja, *Shakespeare on the Screen: Kenneth Branagh's Adaptations of Henry V, Much Ado about Nothing and Hamlet* (Frankfurt am Main: Peter Lang, 1999).

FILMOGRAPHY: *Henry V* (1989); *Dead Again* (US, 1991); *Peter's Friends*; *Swan Song* (short) (1992); *Much Ado about Nothing* (UK/US, 1993); *Mary Shelley's Frankenstein* (US, 1994); *In the Bleak Midwinter* (US: *A Midwinter's Tale*, 1995); *Hamlet* (UK/US, 1996); *Love's Labour's Lost* (UK/US/Fr, 1999); *As You Like It* (US/UK, 2006).

BRANDON, Phil (1898–1982)

Philip Brandon was born in London on 7 December 1898. He spent some time in Hollywood in the 1930s, working, for example, as production manager on RKO's *Woman in the Dark* (Phil Rosen, 1934). When he returned to Britain he acted as assistant director on the Gracie Fields vehicle *Keep Smiling* (Monty Banks, 1938) and on three films directed by Tim Whelan – *Smash and Grab* (1937), *The Divorce of Lady X* (1938) and *St Martin's Lane W.C.2.* (1938). During the early years of the war he worked at Ealing: as unit manager on *Saloon Bar* (Walter Forde, 1940), assistant director on *Spare a Copper* (Marcel Varnel, 1940) and production manager on *Convoy* (Pen Tennyson, 1940). After leaving to work as production manager on Brian Desmond Hurst's highly popular *Dangerous Moonlight* (1941), Brandon made his debut as director with *The Missing Million*, a routine adaptation of an Edgar Wallace thriller enlivened by the presence of Linden Travers as the heroine. Three more films followed. *We'll Meet Again* is a vehicle for Vera Lynn and *Up with the Lark* for the now forgotten comedy duo Ethel Revnell and Gracie West, but *Happidrome* is a more enduring monument. Creaky though it is, this spin-off from a popular radio show starring the large and lugubrious Harry Korris exudes a cheery 'making the best of it' spirit that encapsulates the populist culture of wartime Britain.

None of Brandon's films were distinguished by directorial flair and after the war he worked again as associate producer on films such as the big-budget musical *London Town* (Wesley Ruggles, 1946), Alexander Korda's *An Ideal Husband* (1947) and Carol Reed's *The Fallen Idol* (1948). More modest production duties followed in the 1950s, after which he faded from view. He died in August 1982.

(Robert Murphy)

FILMOGRAPHY: *The Missing Million* (1942); *We'll Meet Again*; *Happidrome*; *Up with the Lark* (1943); *Tarzan's Peril* (2nd unit dir., Byron Haskin, US, 1951).

BREATHNACH, Paddy (1964–)

Paddy Breathnach was born in Dublin on 11 April 1964. After winning the Cork Film Festival Special Prize for his short film *A Stone in the Heart*, Breathnach moved into feature film-making with *Ailsa*, a stylised treatment of a short story by Joseph O'Connor. *Ailsa* borrows from the European art-house tradition to render its tale of male fantasy and obsession as a suffocating, moody narrative. This was followed by a best-selling documentary, *The Road to America*, about the Irish football team's campaign to qualify for the 1994 World Cup; the six-part series, *WRH* (1995), a 'fly-on-the-wall' look at life in a large hospital; and the short film *The Long Way Home*. In 1997 he made the Tarantinoesque gangster comedy *I Went Down*, featuring Brendan Gleeson and Peter McDonald. A huge local hit, its quirky humour failed to make an impression on overseas audiences, where it was poorly distributed and swamped by a wave of bad British crime films. Breathnach then directed *Blow Dry*, an unsatisfactory British comedy about a hairdresser (Alan Rickman) who elects to participate in the World Hairdressing Championships in Yorkshire. His next feature, *Man about Dog*, about three Belfast chancers engaged in a greyhound racing caper, avoided the dark convolutions of *I Went Down* but had more populist appeal and proved a box-office hit in the UK and Ireland.

Breathnach has been much lauded as a new face in Irish film-making and is involved in production as well as direction through the company Treasure Films, which he established in

1992 with producer Robert Walpole. His Irish films show a desire to experiment with form and to appropriate international models of film-making to tell local stories.

(Ruth Barton)

BIBLIOGRAPHY: 'Two Went Down', *Film Ireland* no. 61, Oct./Nov. 1997, pp. 12–13.

FILMOGRAPHY: *A Stone in the Heart* (short, Ir, 1991); *Ailsa* (Fr/Ger/Ir); *The Road to America* (doc., Ir) (1994); *The Long Way Home* (short, Ir, 1995); *I Went Down* (Ir/UK/Sp, 1997); *Blow Dry* (UK/Ger/US, 2001); *Man about Dog* (Ir, 2004).

BRENON, Herbert (1880–1958)

Alexander Herbert Reginald St John Brenon was born on 13 January 1880 at Kingstown, near Dublin, into a family of poets, writers, actors and critics. He was educated at St Paul's School, London, and later emigrated with his family to America. Varied theatre work in New York from 1896 led to theatre management in Johnstown, Pennsylvania. In 1910 he was back in New York, writing one-reel scenarios for IMP. Directing assignments soon followed: the beginning of an eventful American career that reached its peak in the mid-1920s with widely popular Paramount films, including *Peter Pan* (1924) and *Beau Geste* (1926). An American citizen after 1918, he periodically worked in England; in the 1930s, with his Hollywood prestige gone, he stayed for over four years, seeking refuge at Elstree making modest quickies.

Brenon helped pioneer the Hollywood tradition of spectacular overseas shooting, and throughout his career he sold idealised images of England to both American and British audiences. His celebrated four-reel 1913 version of Walter Scott's *Ivanhoe* for IMP, filmed at Chepstow Castle and starring King Baggot, quickly proved the tactic's worth; while the action melodrama *Secrets of the Air* hit home in a different vein. By the time of his next trip to England in 1918, Brenon's fame had increased with projects both frivolous and serious, from the marine fantasy *Neptune's Daughter* (1914) to the courageous, pacifist *War Brides* (1916). In England, backed by the National War Aims Committee and a generous budget, he buckled down to *The Invasion of Britain*, lavish and earnest fictional propaganda that had to be extensively reshot after a fire destroyed the existing negative; the delay cost the film its release. The Government later ordered all material destroyed; only tiny fragments now survive. Following these labours, Brenon signed a contract with British and Colonial: a popular crime melodrama, *12.10*, featuring the American Marie Doro, emerged, but further production plans were disrupted. He departed the country under a cloud of litigation, claiming that British movies were being ruined by cheese-paring. Brenon's behaviour, sometimes grandiose and tempestuous, no doubt played a part in his fortunes: George Pearson, for one, recoiled in shock from the notice Brenon placed about his studio – 'SILENCE – As the Church is to the Devout Worshipper, so is the Studio to the Sincere Artist' (Pearson, p. 144).

With the B & C deal abandoned, Brenon proceeded to Italy, making three films designed to help boost the Italian industry's international profile. His own profile soared again once he settled in at Paramount in 1923, where he became one of America's most popular and best-paid directors. Seventeen films for the studio followed, often polished, prestige ventures: including *The Spanish Dancer*, a big success for Pola Negri; the Betty Bronson vehicles *Peter Pan* and *A Kiss for Cinderella*, delicate and imaginative; Ronald Colman in *Beau Geste*, stirringly romantic, with fine location photography (a Brenon speciality); and *The Great Gatsby*, now lost. *Sorrell and Son* (1927), for United Artists, showed a new tendency towards the slowly sentimental, but the attractive settings – filmed in England – helped make amends.

Then, suddenly, the bubble burst. He proclaimed that talkies had no future; but his own future soon depended on films clogged with dialogue, offering slim chances for visual panache. A diminishing run of RKO films in the early 1930s led to meagre work at smaller studios. And so back to England, where he won the support of Walter C. Mycroft, and between 1935 and 1939 made various modest films for British International Pictures and its successor, Associated British Picture Corporation. Most were generated from plays, squeezed into sixty or seventy minutes. Poor material sunk the comedy-thriller *Someone at the Door*, but elsewhere Brenon managed some decent and spry entertainment. A novel plot boosted the thriller *Living Dangerously*, while the proscenium arch look of *The Dominant Sex* never hindered its lively humour. Brenon's strong feeling for visual atmosphere found their best outlets in *Housemaster* (1938), based on Ian Hay's play about English boarding school life, and *Yellow Sands* (1938), a tenderly sentimental drama lovingly shot in Devon locations starring the stage veteran Marie Tempest. After *The Flying Squad*, a weak Edgar Wallace thriller shot in May 1939, Brenon retired and moved back to America. He died in Los Angeles on 21 June 1958, leaving behind a turbulent career and some films, both British and American, worth more attention than they currently receive.

(Geoff Brown and Joe Kember)

BIBLIOGRAPHY: Lodge, Jack, 'The Career of Herbert Brenon', *Griffithiana* nos 57/8, Oct. 1996, pp. 4–133; Pearson, George, 'Memories . . .', *Film Technician*, Sept./Oct. 1951, pp. 140–55; Reeves, Nicholas, *Official British Film Propaganda during the First World War* (London: Croom Helm, 1986).

FILMOGRAPHY: US unless otherwise stated: *All for Her*; *The Clown's Triumph*; *Camille*; *The Dividing Line*; *The Blind Musician*; *The Fugitives*; *Leah, the Forsaken*; *Lass o' the Light*; *The Long Strike* (1912); *Rags and Riches*; *In a Woman's Power*; *Doctor Jekyll and Mr Hyde*; *Kathleen Mavourneen*; *The Bishop's Candlesticks*; *Blood Will Tell*; *She Never Knew*; *Secret Service Sam*; *The Angel of Death*; *The Last of the Madisons*; *Robespierre*; *The Anarchist*; *The Child Stealers of Paris*; *Time Is Money*; *Mr and Mrs Innocence Abroad*; *Love or a Throne* (1913); *The Watch Dog of the Deep*; *Absinthe*; *The Price of Sacrifice*; *Neptune's Daughter*; *Love and a Lottery Ticket*; *An Old Rag Doll*; *When the World Was Silent*; *When the Heart Calls*; *Redemption*; *The Tenth Commandment* (aka *Thou Shalt Not Covet*); *In Self-Defense*; *Life's Shop Window* (co-dir. Harry Belmar); *Peg o' the Wilds* (1914); *She Was His Mother*; *The Awaited Hour*; *The Heart of Maryland*; *The Kreutzer Sonata*; *The Clemenceau Case*; *The Two Orphans*; *Sin*; *The Soul of Broadway* (1915); *A Daughter of the Gods*; *War Brides* (1916); *The Eternal Sin*; *The Lone Wolf*; *The Fall of the Romanoffs* (1917); *Empty Pockets*; *The Passing of the Third Floor Back* (1918); *A Sinless Sinner*; *Principessa Misteriosa* (It); *Il Colchio e la Rosa* (aka *Sorella contro sorella*/*Little Sister*/*Sisters*, It); *Beatrice* (US: *The Stronger Passion*, It) (1919); *The Passion Flower*; *The Sign on the Door*; *The Wonderful Thing* (1921); *Any Wife*; *A Stage Romance*; *Shackles of Gold*; *Moonshine Valley* (1922); *The Custard Cup*; *The Rustle of Silk*; *The Woman with Four Faces*; *The Spanish Dancer* (1923); *Shadows of Paris*; *The Breaking Point*; *The Side Show of Life*; *The*

Alaskan; *Peter Pan* (1924); *The Little French Girl*; *The Street of Forgotten Men*; *A Kiss for Cinderella* (1925); *The Song and Dance Man*; *Dancing Mothers*; *Beau Geste*; *The Great Gatsby*; *God Gave Me Twenty Cents* (1926); *The Telephone Girl*; *Sorrell and Son* (1927); *Laugh, Clown, Laugh* (1928); *The Rescue* (1929); *Lummox*; *The Case of Sergeant Grischa* (1930); *Beau Ideal*; *Transgression* (1931); *Girl of the Rio* (UK: *The Dove*, 1932); *Wine, Women and Song* (1933).
UK films: *Ivanhoe* (UK/US, 1913); *The Secret of the Air* (US: *Across the Atlantic*, UK/US, 1914); *The Invasion of Britain* (aka *Victory and Peace*, 1918); *12.10* (1919); *Royal Cavalcade* (US: *Regal Cavalcade*, co-dirs. Thomas Bentley/W. P. Kellino/Norman Lee/Walter Summers/Marcel Varnel); *Honours Easy* (1935); *Living Dangerously*; *Someone at the Door* (1936); *The Dominant Sex*; *Spring Handicap*; *The Live Wire* (1937); *Housemaster*, *Yellow Sands* (1938); *Black Eyes* (1939); *The Flying Squad* (1940).

BRIDGES, Alan (1927–)

Alan Bridges was born in Liverpool on 28 September 1927. He began his directing career with BBC television, working on dramas such as *Z Cars* (1963) and *Maigret* (1964), before making his film debut in 1964 with *Act of Murder*. This intelligently handled thriller, well acted by John Carson, Anthony Bate and Dandy Nicols, was one of the best of the Merton Park B-films. After making television versions of *The Brothers Karamazov* (1965) and *Miss Julie*, Bridges returned to Merton Park for *Invasion*, a low-key science-fiction thriller starring Edward Judd and Yoko Tani. The film is strong on atmosphere, slowly building up the pressure on the occupants of a country hospital trapped by a force field that steadily increases both the temperature and their sense of panic. Though kindly reviewed, *Invasion* did not lead to bigger film offers and Bridges returned to television, directing three plays by David Mercer – *Let's Murder Vivaldi* (1968), *On the Eve of Publication* (1968) and *The Cellar and the Almond Tree* (1970) – and Ingmar Bergman's *The Lie* (1970).

Seven years after *Invasion*, Bridges resumed his feature film career with *The Hireling*, a 1920s' period piece scripted by Wolf Mankowitz, from the novel by L. P. Hartley, and made for World Film Services, which had been responsible for Joseph Losey's *The Go-Between* (1971), also based on a Hartley story. As with *The Go-Between*, *The Hireling* is an indictment of England's stifling class system, with chauffeur Robert Shaw embroiled in a relationship with his employer, widowed aristocrat Sarah Miles. Despite sharing the Palme d'Or at the 1973 Cannes Film Festival (with Jerry Schatzberg's *Scarecrow*), *The Hireling* drew mixed reviews and failed at the box office.

Following a poorly received television remake of *Brief Encounter* (1974), starring Richard Burton and Sophia Loren, Bridges directed *Out of Season* with Cliff Robertson, Vanessa Redgrave and Susan George. Set against the backdrop of a wintry seaside resort, the film dwells on sexual yearnings, jealousy and implied incest. Unfortunately, the provocative material is undercut by a trite script and a needlessly obscure ending.

Four more feature films followed. *Age of Innocence*, made in Canada, explores similar concerns about romantic sensibility and sexual repression to *Brief Encounter* and *Out of Season*. *La Petite Fille en velours bleu* deals with uprooted Europeans caught on the French Riviera by the German invasion of France in 1940. *The Return of the Soldier*, set in 1916 and based on the novel by Rebecca West, examines empty lives and class boundaries, with a shell-shocked, amnesiac soldier forsaking his wife for a former lover. Despite a strong cast, including Alan Bates, Julie Christie and Glenda Jackson, the film is hampered by a slow pace, unengaging characters and an overall feeling of indifference. *The Shooting Party*, set on an English country estate in 1913, dissects class attitudes and male aggression on the eve of the First World War – an estate worker is accidentally gunned down during a pheasant shoot – and is stronger on period detail and ensemble acting than dramatic force.

Bridges has been less successful than some of his peers – such as Stephen Frears and Mike Newell – in combining a prestigious record as a television director with success in feature films. Nonetheless, the films he has made for the cinema make up a slim but by no means uninteresting body of work.

(Daniel O'Brien)

BIBLIOGRAPHY: Badder, David, 'Alan Bridges', *Film Dope* no. 5, July 1974, pp. 19–20; Falk, Quentin, 'Bridges: "Some Form of Nationalisation"', *CinemaTV Today*, 7 Dec. 1974, pp. 10–11.

FILMOGRAPHY: *Act of Murder* (1964); *Invasion* (1966); *The Hireling* (1973); *Out of Season* (US, 1975); *Age of Innocence* (UK/Can, 1977); *La Petite Fille en velours bleu* (Fr, 1978); *The Return of the Soldier* (1982); *The Shooting Party* (1984).

BRODY, Hugh (1943–)

Though a film-maker for thirty years, Hugh Brody's main passion has been anthropology. Almost all his output has consisted of television documentaries, produced as adjuncts to research and book publications on the world's native cultures, principally in North America; his one dramatic feature *Nineteen Nineteen* (1984) remains without a successor. Born in Sheffield in 1943, Brody studied at Oxford University and came to anthropology after lecturing in philosophy at the University of Belfast. In 1976 he collaborated with Michael Grigsby on a Granada Television documentary, *Eskimos of Pond Inlet – The People's Land*. Among later films, produced in Canada, *Treaty 8 County* (1982) documented a caribou hunt, while *People of the Islands* (1983) surveyed the Inuit people of the Belcher Islands, previously explored by Robert Flaherty.

Nineteen Nineteen, a beneficiary of the BFI's feature production programme, veered away from anthropology toward the landscape of the mind, and the work of memory and history in the process of personal understanding. Written by Brody and Michael Ignatieff, the film draws on one of Sigmund Freud's case histories, juggling between two patients on the couch in 1919 and their reunion in 1980s' Vienna; archive footage exploring the world beyond Freud's consulting room is interwoven between the two strands. The result, shown in competition at the 1985 Berlin Film Festival, displays admirable ambition and intelligence, not least in its acting (Maria Schell and Paul Scofield are both exceptional as the patients grown older). But Brody's talent is not strong enough to juggle the time layers with the necessary visual flair, or prevent scenes coagulating into lumps of dialogue. Modestly welcomed on release, *Nineteen Nineteen* ultimately has the talky feel of a clever television play valiantly struggling to become a film.

Given the independent market's revival in Britain in the mid-1980s, further and sturdier Brody features might have been expected. Instead, he returned to anthropological books, research and television documentaries (*On Indian Land*, 1986; *Time Immemorial*, 1991) with the occasional artist's portrait (*England's Henry Moore*, 1988; *Inside Australia*, 2003, featuring Antony Gormley) scattered in between.

(Geoff Brown)

BIBLIOGRAPHY: Brody, Hugh and Michael, Ignatieff, *Nineteen Nineteen* (London: Faber and Faber, 1985); 'In Production: *1919*', *Three-Sixty°* no. 1, Aug. 1984, pp. 10–11

FILMOGRAPHY: *Nineteen Nineteen* (1984).

BROMLY, Alan (1919–1995)

Alan James Bromly, born in Godalming, Surrey, on 13 September 1915, worked as an actor and radio commentator before directing children's television programmes in the early 1950s. *Parentcraft* (1951), a likeable comedy series offering tips to children on how to deal with parents, written by Robert Morley, proved particularly popular. Bromly was approached by producer Sidney Cole to direct *The Angel Who Pawned Her Harp* for Group 3. An innocuous tale about an angel who lands at the Angel, Islington, and pawns her harp in Camden Passage antiques market nearby in order to dispense money to Islington's poor, it is as well-meaning and whimsical as most Group 3 films. Bromly directs efficiently and captures some now interesting period detail, but his future lay with the small screen.

He established an early association with thriller writer Francis Durbridge on *Portrait of Alison* (1955). The partnership continued through *The Scarf* (1959) and *The World of Tim Frazer* (1960) to the end of the 1960s, when Bromly transplanted Durbridge's by then rather old-fashioned radio detective Paul Temple to television. He interchanged roles as producer and director on a variety of other projects, including the early episodes of Peter Ling and Hazel Adair's soap opera *Compact* (1962) and the last two seasons of the BBC's impressive science-fiction anthology *Out of the Unknown* (1969, 1971).

Bromly's second feature film *Follow That Horse!* (1960), adapted from Howard Mason's novel *Photo Finish*, provided a comfortable repository for the comic acting of British character actors (including David Tomlinson, Cecil Parker, Richard Wattis, Dora Bryan, Raymond Huntley and Sam Kydd) in a disarmingly silly story about incompetent spies competing to retrieve a roll of film swallowed by a racehorse. Doubtless it was a pleasant diversion for all concerned. He is better remembered now as director of two series of *Dr Who*. In 'The Time Warrior' (1974), a strong Robert Holmes script sends Jon Pertwee's Doctor back to the Middle Ages to prevent an alien being wreaking havoc with history; 'Nightmare of Eden' (1979), with a much sillier story about Tom Baker's Doctor dealing with intergalactic drug smuggling while also confronting the threat of the hairy Mandrels, proved a much less happy experience for Bromly, who subsequently retired. He died in Middlesex in September 1995.

(Robert Murphy)

FILMOGRAPHY: *The Angel Who Pawned Her Harp* (1953); *Follow That Horse!* (1960).

BROOK, Clive (1887–1974)

Clive Brook was born in London on 1 June 1887. He made his stage debut in 1918 after serving in the First World War. He became a popular leading man in Hollywood films such as *Shanghai Express* (Josef von Sternberg, 1933) and *Cavalcade* (Frank Lloyd, 1933), but returned to Britain in 1935 and continued his career in more modest British films like *Return to Yesterday* (Robert Stevenson, 1939) and *Freedom Radio* (Anthony Asquith, 1940).

In 1943 he directed *On Approval* – though more by accident than design. The original director, Brian Desmond Hurst, was fired soon after shooting began and Brook, together with producer Sydney Box, became co-director, as well as star of the film; Box withdrew towards the end of the production leaving Brook to complete the film and take sole directing credit.

On Approval, a comedy of manners based on a Frederick Lonsdale play from the late 1920s and filmed by Tom Walls in 1930, remains something of an oddity. Its risqué battle of the sexes and trial marriage themes, and the spirited playing by Beatrice Lillie and Googie Withers, provide it with screwball comedy qualities; yet it is a period film set in the 1890s. The unconventional documentary/montage opening (directed by Muriel Box) and protracted comic fantasy sequences led Lindsay Anderson to regard *On Approval* as a rare contribution by a feature film to a British '*avant-garde* in the widest sense'. After the film, Brook abandoned the cinema to concentrate on stage work only returning for a minor screen role in the 1960s. He died in London on 17 November 1974.

(Tom Ryall)

BIBLIOGRAPHY: Anderson, Lindsay, 'A Possible Solution', *Sequence* no. 3, Spring, 1948 pp. 7–10; Box, Muriel, *Odd Woman Out* (London: Leslie Frewin, 1974); Drazin, Charles, *The Finest Years: British Cinema of the 1940s* (London: André Deutsch, 1998).

FILMOGRAPHY: *On Approval* (1944).

BROOK, Peter (1925–)

Peter Stephen Paul Brook was born in London on 21 March 1925 and was educated at Oxford, where in 1943 he made his first film, an adaptation of Laurence Sterne's eighteenth-century travel book *A Sentimental Journey*, with Gavin Lambert. World famous for his pioneering work in the theatre, Brook has also directed some significant films in Britain and France. He made his professional debut as a director in 1953, with a lively if uncinematic adaptation of John Gay's satirical *The Beggar's Opera*, starring Laurence Olivier as the highwayman MacHeath. Six years later, he returned to cinema with a French film of moods and *longueurs*, *Moderato Cantabile*, based on Marguerite Duras' novel. Brook's next British film, *Lord of the Flies*, was an adaptation of William Golding's classic literary parable on the descent of society into primitivism. The film, produced very much *au naturel* with amateur cinematographers as well as amateur actors, deals with a group of public school children stranded on a deserted tropical island. Their initial fight for survival soon turns into a desperate power struggle between two groups: one humanist and civilised, the other savage and militarist. The film had a limited impact when first released, but has gradually achieved cult status for its striking naturalism, skilful editing and sensitive cinematic interpretation of Golding's novel.

Two of Brook's most famous theatrical productions for the Royal Shakespeare Company in the 1960s, *The Persecution and Assassination of Marat . . .* by German modernist Peter Weiss, and Shakespeare's *King Lear*, were eventually made into films. *King Lear* is arguably Brook's finest accomplishment in British cinema. His theatre production had been influenced by the epic theatre of Bertolt Brecht and the dark political vision of Polish Shakespeare scholar Jan Kott. These were now complemented by the art-cinema techniques of its discontinuous editing, unconventional camera angles and grainy black-and-white cinematography – particularly appropriate for the barren landscape of North Jutland where the film was shot. Many critics at the time found the film bleak, but it can now be seen as a brilliant investigation into the meta-cinematic, which tests the limits between the theatrical and the cinematic, most famously when Paul Scofield, as the dying Lear, literally falls out of the frame.

Brook also directed *Tell Me Lies* (1967), a collage of British anti-Vietnam War sentiment based on his London stage production *US*; and *Meetings with Remarkable Men* (1979), the story of the spiritual journey undertaken by the Asian mystic G. I. Gurdjieff, partly filmed on location in Afghanistan. Since 1979, Brook has been based mostly in France, where he has occasionally filmed versions of his later stage productions. He is married to the actress Natasha Parry.

(Erik Hedling)

BIBLIOGRAPHY: Brook, Peter, *The Shifting Point: Forty Years of Theatrical Exploration, 1916–1987* (London: Methuen, 1988); Davies, Anthony, *Filming Shakespeare's Plays: The Adaptations of Laurence Olivier, Orson Welles, Peter Brook and Akira Kurosawa* (Cambridge: Cambridge University Press, 1988); Helfer, Richard and Glenn Loney (eds), *Peter Brook: Oxford to Orghast* (Amsterdam: Harwood Academic Publishers, 1998).

FILMOGRAPHY: *A Sentimental Journey* (short, co-dir. Gavin Lambert, 1943); *The Beggar's Opera* (1953); *Moderato Cantabile* (aka *Seven Days . . . Seven Nights*, Fr, 1960); *Lord of the Flies* (1963); *The Persecution and Assassination of Jean-Paul Marat as Performed by the Inmates of the Asylum of Charenton under the Direction of the Marquis de Sade* (1966); *Tell Me Lies* (assoc. dir. Geoffrey Reeves, 1967); *King Lear* (1971); *Meetings with Remarkable Men* (US, 1979) *La Tragédie de Carmen* (Fr, 1983); *The Mahabharata* (Fr/UK/US, 1989).

BROOKFIELD, Bill

An American lawyer living in Tuscany, Bill Brookfield was recruited by Clare Peploe to adapt James Hadley Chase's *Miss Shumway Waves a Wand* for her Mexican-set *Rough Magic* (1995). Four years later he turned up as writer/director of *Milk*, Sky Television's first venture into feature films. A strong cast in a comedy set among English eccentrics no doubt raised hopes of repeating the success of *Four Weddings and a Funeral* (Mike Newell, 1994), but James Fleet, endearingly incompetent in *Four Weddings*, makes a ponderously uncharismatic leading man. Joss Ackland, Peter Jones and Phyllida Law occasionally spark their characters into life, but Brookfield's script, about a middle-aged farmer suddenly liberated by the death of his mother, is embarrassingly flat-footed. Brookfield returned to writing, helping Nick Willing in his messy but interesting adaptation of Madison Smartt Bell's novel *Doctor Sleep* (2002).

(Robert Murphy)

FILMOGRAPHY: *Milk* (UK/US, 1999).

BROOKS, Richard (1912–1992)

Richard Brooks was born in Philadelphia on 18 May 1912. After contributing to over a dozen screenplays, he made his debut as a writer-director with *Crisis* (1950), which began his ten-year association with MGM. Brooks' subsequent films, including *The Blackboard Jungle* (1955), *The Brothers Karamazov* and *Cat on a Hot Tin Roof* (both 1958), explore his characteristic preoccupation with what happens to people under extreme pressure.

Brooks spent several years trying to make *Lord Jim* (1965), Joseph Conrad's novel of cowardice and redemption through self-sacrifice. He eventually made it for Columbia British at Shepperton Studios and on location in Cambodia as a big-budget 70mm epic. Produced somewhat in the shadow of Columbia's *Lawrence of Arabia* (David Lean, 1962), it not only draws on Lean's stars, Peter O'Toole and Jack Hawkins, but also much of his crew, including cinematographer Freddie Young and costume designer Phyllis Dalton. Although never satisfying as a whole, the action scenes are excitingly staged and James Mason gives a marvellously villainous performance as Gentleman Brown.

Brooks returned to America to make his masterpiece, *In Cold Blood* (1967), a thrillingly cinematic adaptation of Truman Capote's true-crime classic, and then wrote and directed another six films, including the controversial but hugely successful *Looking for Mr Goodbar* (1977). Married for sixteen years to British actress Jean Simmons, he died in Beverly Hills on 11 March 1992.

(Sergio Angelini)

BIBLIOGRAPHY: Joyce, Paul, 'Richard Brooks and *Lord Jim*', *Film*, Winter, 1964; McGilligan, Pat, 'Richard Brooks: The Professional', in Pat McGilligan (ed.), *Backstory 2* (Berkeley: University of California Press, 1991).

FILMOGRAPHY (UK only): *Lord Jim* (US/UK, 1965).

BROOMFIELD, Nick (1948–)

Nick Broomfield was born in London in 1948. He made his first film, *Who Cares?*, with financial aid from the BFI while studying politics and law at Essex University. Its subject is a close-knit but threatened working-class community in Liverpool, and the influence of Willmott and Young's classic study *Family and Kinship in East London* is clear; but even in this early work Broomfield's characteristic sense of personal involvement is already apparent. As he himself put it: 'Everything at university was at a very conceptual, analytical level, and I felt a need to look at things in a more immediate way.'

After Essex, Broomfield joined the National Film School at Beaconsfield, where he made *Proud to Be British*, in which the town's inhabitants speak their minds on what it means to be British (or, rather, English). The already mischievous Broomfield revelled in the opportunity to record such open displays of Blimpishness, and clearly annoyed the *Buckinghamshire Advertiser*,

which disapprovingly noted that 'it was difficult to avoid the conclusion that this was a film about private schooling, the Church and the Conservative party made by a left-wing, pro-comprehensive atheist'. While there he also made the Grierson Award-winning *Behind the Rent Strike*, which features some of the people from *Who Cares?* As Broomfield points out: 'It was an answer to the views of Britain expressed in the previous film, and the two are meant to be played together.'

In 1976, Broomfield made the first of several films with the American film-maker Joan Churchill, whom he had met at the National Film School, and who had already made a name for herself in the US with documentaries such as *The American Family* (1973). Their films are less overtly confrontational than Broomfield's solo works, belonging more to the tradition of direct or observational cinema in the Frederick Wiseman mode. Of these, one of the most interesting, and certainly the most controversial, is the BFI-funded *Juvenile Liaison*, which had its roots in *Behind the Rent Strike*. The film follows two Lancashire police officers in their dealings with young people in trouble with the law. An extremely disturbing picture of harsh and oppressive police treatment of children accused of minor offences, it became a censorship *cause célèbre* when the BFI, pressured by the police, withdrew it from distribution and refused to allow it to be shown on television, thus causing its Production Board to resign *en masse*. Broomfield later revisited the subject, without the accompanying controversy, in *Juvenile Liaison 2*.

Partly because they found Britain 'such a hypocritical and repressive country in terms of media freedom', Broomfield and Churchill made a number of films in the US until their relationship, both working and personal, broke up in the mid-1980s (they were later to work together again). After this watershed, Broomfield developed a less observational, more upfront style, not so much fly on the wall as fly in the soup. As he put it:

> If you're making a film, it's more honest to make your presence felt than to hang back furtively on the other side of the room, because no-one really benefits from that. That approach really is, to use the dread word, voyeuristic. You're there with all your equipment, but pretending you're not there.

The reason why he uses a more participatory approach, he has explained, is because 'what's important is the interaction between the film-makers and those being filmed, and that the audience is aware of that interaction so they can make decisions of their own' (Wise, p. 18).

The new technique is evident – hilariously – in *Driving Me Crazy*, a film about the making of a film of a black stage musical. Broomfield moved into more dangerous territory with *The Leader, His Driver and the Driver's Wife*, his film on the South African neo-Nazi leader Eugene Terreblanche. One of his finest works, it demonstrates how effective his apparently chaotic and eccentric shooting methods can be; by concentrating on what appear to be the inessentials, approaching his subject obliquely and, apparently missing it altogether, the faux-naive Broomfield strikes to the heart of the matter – in this case regressive attitudes towards race. He used the same methods with Lady Thatcher in *Tracking Down Maggie*; needless to say, he does no such thing, and the film is thus less successful than its predecessor. Nonetheless, by repeatedly showing the remarkable extent to which Thatcher was sealed off from both the public and 'unauthorised' media by her entourage of minders, Broomfield effectively evoked the aura of unaccountability, and delusions of regal grandeur, that increasingly enveloped the lady.

In 1989 Broomfield made his first, and so far only, fictional feature film, *Diamond Skulls*. In spite of a promisingly acerbic storyline (based on the disappearance of Lord Lucan), it somehow fails to deliver the damning portrait of aristocratic sleaze, thuggery and hypocrisy that one might have expected from Broomfield. When he returned to documentary he concentrated mainly on American subjects, focusing on 'celebrities' and the media circus that surrounds and indeed constructs them. *Aileen Wuornos: The Selling of a Serial Killer* was followed by *Heidi Fleiss – Hollywood Madam*, *Kurt and Courtney* and *Biggie and Tupac*. Courtney Love proved to be an even more unco-operative subject than Lady Thatcher, and she and her lawyers make increasingly determined efforts to stop the film in its tracks. In one of the film's most characteristic moments, Broomfield interrupts an award-giving ceremony for Love hosted by the American Civil Liberties Union (which champions free speech) in order to protest at her efforts to silence him. He is rapidly evicted.

Like the work of Molly Dineen and Jon Ronson, Broomfield's later films are fascinating examples of what Stella Bruzzi calls the 'performative documentary'. By openly acknowledging that the intrusion of the film-maker into the situation being filmed inevitably affects and alters that situation, this underlines the fact that the documentary is itself a mode of representation as opposed to unmediated reality, and thus foregrounds the construction and artificiality of even the non-fiction film. This is not to imply that such documentaries are not concerned with getting at 'the truth', but, rather, that the truth emerges from the encounter between film-makers, subjects and spectators.

(Julian Petley)

Unless otherwise stated, all quotes are from Petley, 1989.

BIBLIOGRAPHY: Bruzzi, Stella, *New Documentary: A Critical Introduction* (London and New York: Routledge, 2000); Nahra, Carol, 'Anti-Celebrity Provocateur', *Dox*, Dec. 1998, pp. 10–11; Pearson, Alison, 'The Fly in the Ointment', *Independent on Sunday* Review Section, 15 May 1994, pp. 18–19; Petley, Julian, 'From Alienation . . . Nick Broomfield', *Monthly Film Bulletin*, November 1989, p. 352; Wise, Damon, 'Boom Raider', *Sight and Sound*, May 2002, pp. 16–18; Wood, Jason, 'Origins of the Agit-Fop', *Sight and Sound*, Mar. 2005, pp. 22–4.

FILMOGRAPHY: *Who Cares?* (1971); *Proud to Be British* (1973); *Behind the Rent Strike* (1974); *Juvenile Liaison* (co-dir. Joan Churchill, 1975); *Marriage Guidance* (co-dir. Joan Churchill, 1977); *Tattooed Tears* (US, co-dir. Joan Churchill, 1978); *Soldier Girls* (US, 1980); *Chicken Ranch* (1983); *Lily Tomlin – the Film behind the Show* (co-dir. Joan Churchill, 1986); *Driving Me Crazy – True Stories* (1988); *Diamond Skulls* (aka *Dark Obsession*, 1989); *Juvenile Liaison 2* (1990); *The Leader, His Driver and the Driver's Wife – True Stories* (1991); *Monster in a Box*; *Aileen Wuornos: The Selling of a Serial Killer*, *Too White for Me – True Stories* (1992); *Tracking Down Maggie – True Stories* (1994); *Heidi Fleiss: Hollywood Madam* (1995); *Fetishes* (US/UK, 1996); *Kurt and Courtney* (1998; *Biggie and Tupac* (2002); *Aileen: Life and Death of a Serial Killer* (2003); *His Big White Self* (2006).

BROWNLOW, Kevin (1938–) and Andrew MOLLO (1940–)

Kevin Brownlow's activities as a film historian and television documentary-maker have tended to erase both memory and recognition of the two extraordinary features he made in collaboration with Andrew Mollo. Both films reached the screen after considerable effort. *It Happened Here*, a 'what if' drama exploring an England under Nazi occupation, began production in 1956, concluded in 1963 and entered distribution through

United Artists in 1966. *Winstanley* found an audience more speedily in 1976, but the seventeenth-century Civil War story still took eight years to reach fruition. The films were the work of mavericks, shooting largely at weekends in between paid work as a film editor and historian (Brownlow) or a military and costume specialist (Mollo).

Kevin Brownlow was born in Crowborough, Sussex, on 2 June 1938. His passion for cinema struck early. He collected films from the age of eleven, and at the age of fourteen, with a 9.5mm camera, began making *The Capture*, an adaptation of a de Maupassant story, with its action updated from the Franco-Prussian war to 1940s' France. The fascination with the Second World War continued in the much more ambitious *It Happened Here*, based on Brownlow's own story idea. The need for authentic details in costumes brought him in contact with Andrew Mollo (born London, 15 May 1940), the son of a Russian émigré who had fought on both sides in the Russian Revolution. Serving as co-director, Mollo considerably strengthened the film's chilling realism.

During its long gestation (documented in his book *How It Happened Here*) Brownlow worked on documentaries, mostly for World Wide Pictures. *It Happened Here* emerged through its piecemeal production remarkably intact, with sharp editing, canny camera placements, evocative locations and persuasively understated performances by the largely non-professional cast. Censor cuts were enforced in one sequence showing British fascists in full vocal flight; though the suggested ease with which Britain fell under Nazi control remained disturbing enough.

With its quiet urgency and novel subject matter *It Happened Here* became a critical and public success, but within the industry Brownlow and Mollo were speedily tagged 'uncommercial'. Eventually backed by the BFI Production Board, they soldiered on with their new project, based on David Caute's novel *Comrade Jacob*, with the Civil War's Leveller and Digger movements as the background. Mollo, meanwhile, served as a film consultant on *Doctor Zhivago* (David Lean, 1965), while Brownlow edited *The Charge of the Light Brigade* (Tony Richardson, 1968) and enjoyed considerable success with his book *The Parade's Gone By . . .* (1968), an influential celebration through interviews of Hollywood's silent era. Other projects championing silent cinema followed, notably the painstaking restoration of Abel Gance's *Napoléon*, first unveiled in 1980, and the *Hollywood* series (1980) produced with David Gill for Thames Television.

Kevin Brownlow (right)

Not simply through hindsight does *Winstanley* appear as a silent film *manqué*. The film's strength lies in its images; its weakness lies in part in the earnest quantities of words, whether issuing from characters' mouths or placed in the commentary. Through editing, composition, rushing, hand-held camerawork and Prokofiev's music from *Alexander Nevsky*, the opening battle directly acknowledges Eisenstein and Gance. Other influences include Dreyer's play of faces and space, and the stark lyricism of Arthur von Gerlach's little-known classic *Zur Chronik von Grieshuus* (1925). Ernest Vincze's black-and-white camerawork creates eloquently mournful beauty from the Diggers' struggles with the land and authority: though static dialogue exchanges and elliptical plotting keep the overall dramatic impact muted.

On release in 1976, *Winstanley* demonstrated Brownlow and Mollo's estrangement from both Britain's mainstream and independent cinemas. The film did not fit the costume drama pigeonhole, nor did it pursue the Greenaway path towards elaborate games with form and content. Industry disinterest and the film's general reception pushed the film-makers decisively towards other endeavours: for Mollo, chiefly production design (most strikingly on Mike Newell's *Dance with a Stranger*, 1984); for Brownlow, silent film presentations, a David Lean biography and television portraits of Chaplin, Keaton, Griffith and other giants from the parade gone by.

(Geoff Brown)

BIBLIOGRAPHY: Brownlow, Kevin, *How It Happened Here* (London: Secker and Warburg, 1969); Brownlow, Kevin, 'Filming the Diggers', *Monthly Film Bulletin*, Apr. 1976, p. 92; Mival, Eric, *It Happened Here Again* (doc., 1976); Tibbetts, John C., 'Kevin Brownlow's Historical Films: *It Happened Here* (1965) and *Winstanley* (1975)', *Historical Journal of Film, Radio and Television* vol. 20 no. 2, 2000, pp. 227–51.

FILMOGRAPHY: *It Happened Here* (1956–63; rel. 1966); *Winstanley* (1975).

Kevin Brownlow alone: *The Capture* (short, 1952–5); *Ascot – A Race against Time* (doc., 1961); *Nine, Dalmuir West* (doc., 1962); *Abel Gance – The Charm of Dynamite* (doc.); *Millay at Steepletop* (doc., US) (1968).

BRUCE, Nicola (1953–)

Nicola Bruce was born in Kent in 1953. She made a number of animation films while a student at Middlesex Polytechnic in the 1970s and received BFI funding for her live-action short *Wings of Death* in 1986. In the 1990s she made a number of experimental arts documentaries for television, including *The Art of*

Steven Berkoff (1995) for Channel 4, and *The Human Face* (1991) and *The Monument* (1996) for the BBC. After another BFI-funded experiment, *The Loved* (1996), she directed the feature-length *I Could Read the Sky*, based on a book combining text and photos by Timothy O'Grady and Stephen Pyke. Bruce's film adheres to the book's poetic distillation of the memories experienced by an ageing Irish labourer in England as he drifts towards a lonely death in a London bedsit. Bruce replicates the textural nature of the book's verbal layering by interweaving strands of film and digital imagery and elicits an impressive performance from novelist Dermot Healy as the embittered labourer.

Now based in Hastings, Bruce continues to experiment, shooting footage as an ongoing diary to provide source material for her commissioned work. In July 2002 she received an award from NESTA (National Endowment for Science, Technology and the Arts) for a digital project looking at themes of memory and perception.

(Eugene Finn)

BIBLIOGRAPHY: Hurley, Jeanine, 'Cutting the Sky', *Film Ireland* no. 75, Apr./May 2000, pp. 36–41; Kenny, John, 'Nicola Bruce', *Film West* no. 37, July 1999, pp. 12–15; O'Sullivan, Charlotte, 'I Could Read the Sky', *Sight and Sound*, Nov. 2000, pp. 54–5; Sheedy, Francis, 'Memory's Land and Freedom', *Sight and Sound*, Nov. 2000, pp. 4–5

FILMOGRAPHY: *Excuses of How (Not) to Make an Animated Film* (short, 1975); *Breath of Air* (short, 1976); *Boolean Procedures* (short, 1980); *Clip* (short, 1983); *Wings of Death* (short, 1986); *The Loved* (short, 1996); *I Could Read the Sky* (1999).

BRUNEL, Adrian (1892–1958)

In the 1920s Adrian Brunel was one of the liveliest new directing talents working in Britain. Short comedies burlesquing cinema trends tickled insiders and sophisticates; while mainstream Gainsborough features like *Blighty* (1927) and *The Constant Nymph* (1928) achieved considerable box-office success. Talkies then removed Brunel from the limelight, along with other leading silent directors George Pearson and Graham Cutts. There were subsequently years of unemployment, and others of furious activity directing 'quota quickies'; he also worked as a film 'doctor' and helped his friend Leslie Howard on *The First of the Few* (1942), but a successful return to the director's chair eluded him.

Born in Brighton on 4 September 1892, Brunel grew up with a liberal outlook and multifarious gifts. After education at Harrow, he soon succumbed to the lure of the stage (his mother, Adey Brunel, was a respected drama teacher). He acted, wrote plays and trained as an opera singer. Cinema initially was one interest among many, but it began to dominate after local journalism in Brighton and a period in distribution with Moss Empire's Bioscope. In 1916 he formed Mirror Films with the scriptwriter Harry Fowler Mear, directing the company's sole feature, *The Cost of a Kiss*. He gained further experience during the war in the Ministry of Information's Film Department,

where he developed the concept of 'Film Tags' – short instructional films, peppered with humour, presented in the weekly newsreels. Returned to civilian life in 1919, he worked as scenario editor for the British Actors' Film Company.

The first signs of Brunel's directorial personality emerged in 1920 in *The Bump* and other short comedies, made with Leslie Howard and the writer A. A. Milne for their company Minerva Films. In 1922 Brunel raised the finance for a feature film, *The Man without Desire*, to be shot on location in Venice with studio work in Berlin; theatre idol Ivor Novello took the role of a lovelorn eighteenth-century nobleman awoken after two centuries' suspended animation. The unusual story and Brunel's atmospheric visuals distinguished the film from most British product of the time.

Brunel's visual inventiveness found a sprightlier outlet in the series of burlesque comedies beginning with *Crossing the Great Sagrada* (1924), a travel film lampoon. Some of Brunel's humour may appear unduly facetious, but the visual japes and games with film form still fascinate and entertain. These burlesques were made independently until Michael Balcon offered to produce them through Gainsborough Pictures. *The Typical Budget*, a newsreel spoof, had its first showing at the opening screening of the Film Society in October 1925.

Brunel was one of the Society's champions and served on its council; many films imported for screenings passed through his hands at his editing office. With Ivor Montagu, the Society's co-founder, who shared similar passions in cinema and politics, he turned the office into a business for hire, training new cinema recruits along the way. Until talkies curtailed business, the Brunel and Montagu company regularly prepared imported films for British distribution.

Balcon liked to attract lively minds to Gainsborough and offered Brunel the chance to direct feature films. But he was asked to withdraw from the Film Society's council for fear that it branded him a highbrow, and the feature subjects chosen for him stuck close to the popular and fashionable. *Blighty* dealt sentimentally with a family's experiences of the Great War; *The Vortex*, featuring Novello again, made polite but visually lively work of Noël Coward's sensational stage play; *The Constant Nymph,* with Novello in an Alpine setting, dealt competently if conventionally with Margaret Kennedy's story of the romance between a composer and a girl whose love he does not take seriously until it is too late.

With these films, made with the benefit of major players, eye-catching subjects and extensive promotion, Brunel reached the apex of his career. Yet after two further Gainsborough features, *A Light Woman* and *The Crooked Billet*, Brunel found little else to direct but low-budget productions or fix-up jobs.

The turbulent introduction of sound played some part in his loss of status. There were also personal matters. Following *The Crooked Billet*, Brunel was advised to instigate legal proceedings against his employers for unpaid fees. Settlement was reached, but the affair jarred the industry, and offers of work shrank. For British International Pictures in 1930, Brunel made the revue film *Elstree Calling*, but saw his editing plans ignored and Hitchcock summoned to reshoot material.

With no directing work of his own, Brunel wrote the book *Filmcraft*, first of three popular instructional guides for aspiring film-makers. By the time of publication in 1933, Brunel himself was back directing, making 'quota quickies', comedies and thrillers, mainly for Fox-British and the producer George Smith.

Some projects gave him more scope, like *Badger's Green* (1934), based on R. C. Sherriff's popular play, and *Variety* (1935), a music-hall salute. But by the end of the 1930s Brunel was functioning more as a fixer of other people's problems than a director in his own right. In 1939 he was part of a triumvirate directing Korda's rushed production of *The Lion Has Wings*; later he served as Leslie Howard's production consultant on *The First of the Few* and *The Gentle Sex* (Leslie Howard/Maurice Elvey, 1943). His own last official directing credits, in 1940, were on two Home Front propaganda shorts.

In 1949 Brunel re-emerged as the author of *Nice Work*, an entertaining account of his film experiences. Nice work or not, Brunel's career was clearly not what it might have been, and the apparent absence of surviving copies of many of his talkies makes a thorough revaluation of his work difficult. But the burlesque comedies alone give him a distinctive place in British cinema history as a satirical jester, and a key player in the film industry's uneasy war between art and commerce. He died in Gerrard's Cross on 18 February 1958.

(Geoff Brown)

BIBLIOGRAPHY: Brunel, Adrian, 'Experiments in Ultra-Cheap Cinematography', *Close Up*, Oct. 1928, pp. 43–6; Brunel, Adrian, *Filmcraft: The Art of Picture Production* (London: George Newnes, 1933); Brunel, Adrian, *Nice Work: The Story of Thirty Years in British Film Production* (London: Forbes Robertson, 1949); Sexton, Jamie, 'Parody on the Fringes: Adrian Brunel, Minority Film Culture and the Art of Deconstruction', in Alan Burton and Laraine Porter (eds), *Pimple, Pranks & Pratfalls. British Film Comedy before 1930* (Trowbridge, Wilts: Flicks Books, 2000).

FILMOGRAPHY: Shorts: *The Bump*; *Five Pounds Reward*; *Bookworms*; *Twice Two* (1920); *Too Many Cooks*; *The Temporary Lady* (1921); *Two Chinned Chow*; *The Shimmy Sheik*; *Yes, We have No – !*; *Moors and Minarets* (1923); *Sheer Trickery*; *Lovers in Arabia*; *Crossing the Great Sagrada*; *The Pathetic Gazette* (1924); *Battling Bruisers*; *So This Is Jollywood*; *Cut It Out*; *The Blunderland of Big Game*; *The Typical Budget* (1925); *Food for Thought*; *Salvage with a Smile* (1940).

Features: *The Cost of a Kiss* (1917); *The Man without Desire* (1923); *Blighty* (1927); *The Constant Nymph*; *The Vortex*; *A Light Woman* (1928); *The Crooked Billet*; *In a Monastery Garden* (1929); *Elstree Calling* (co-dir. Alfred Hitchcock, 1930); *Taxi to Paradise*; *I'm an Explosive*; *Follow the Lady*; *Little Napoleon*; *The Laughter of Fools* (1933); *Two Wives for Henry*; *Important People*; *Badger's Green*; *Sabotage* (US: *When London Sleeps*) (1934); *Variety*; *The City of Beautiful Nonsense*; *Cross Currents*; *While Parents Sleep*; *Vanity* (1935); *The Invader*; *Prison Breaker*; *Love at Sea* (1936); *The Rebel Son* (co-dirs. Alexis Granowsky/Albert de Courville); *The Girl Who Forgot*; *The Lion Has Wings* (co-dirs. Michael Powell/Brian Desmond Hurst) (1939).

BRYCE, Alex (1905–)

Alex Bryce was born on 24 March 1905 in Larbert, Scotland. He flourished during the 1930s when quota legislation ensured a steady stream of low-budget British productions. As cinematographer, Bryce worked on a series of such films, including the Gracie Fields and Jessie Matthews' vehicles *Sally in Our Alley* (Maurice Elvey, 1931) and *There Goes the Bride* (Albert de Courville, 1932). Bryce's directing career began in 1935 with *Sexton Blake and the Mademoiselle*, and his other 'quota quickies' included two films enlivened by the presence of Alastair Sim, *Wedding Group* and *The Big Noise*, and an adaptation of Dumas' *The Black Tulip*. He showed an affinity with Irish subjects with a trilogy of sentimental, quasi-musicals: *Macushla*, *The Londonderry Air* and *My Irish Molly*. All used Irish actors and the best known of the three, *My Irish Molly*, provided Maureen O'Hara with her screen debut as well as featuring the popular tenor Tom Burke, and Binkie Stuart, billed as Britain's answer to Shirley Temple. He wrote and directed *The Last Barricade*, set during the Spanish Civil War, and when world war broke out he turned his talents to directing non-fiction films for the Army Film Unit and other information bodies. Bryce ended his career working

as a second-unit director on historical adventure films and directing television series such as *Fabian of the Yard.*
(Ruth Barton)
FILMOGRAPHY: *Sexton Blake and the Mademoiselle* (1935); *Wedding Group* (co-dir. Campbell Gullan); *The End of the Road*; *The Big Noise*; *Servants All* (1936); *Macushla*; *The Black Tulip*; *Against the Tide* (1937); *My Irish Molly*; *The Londonderry Air*; *The Last Barricade* (1938); *The Answer* (doc.); *Anybody's Bugbear* (doc.); *The Owner Come Aboard* (doc.) (1940); *Two Cooks and a Cabbage* (doc.); *The Right Man* (doc.); *The Siege of Tobruk* (doc.) (1942); *The Story of Robin Hood and His Merrie Men* (2nd unit dir., Ken Annakin, 1952); *The Sword and the Rose* (2nd unit dir., Ken Annakin, 1953); *The Cockleshell Heroes* (assoc. dir., José Ferrer); *The Dark Avenger* (2nd unit dir., Henry Levin) (1955).

BRYDEN, Bill (1942–)

William Campbell Rough Bryden was born in Greenock, Scotland, on 12 April 1942. He entered the television industry in the mid-1960s as a researcher and scriptwriter before training as a director for ABC. He switched to the theatre, becoming assistant to William Gaskill at the Royal Court in London, and in 1971 was appointed Associate Director of the Royal Lyceum Theatre in Edinburgh. Among his other work, Bryden produced two of his own plays – *Willie Rough* and *Benny Lynch* (both later televised) – at the Royal Lyceum, and took up major creative and administrative positions with the National Theatre, Scottish Television, BBC Scotland, the Royal Opera House and English National Opera.

Bryden's first cinema credit, rewriting the Jesse James story as *The Long Riders* (Walter Hill, 1980), opened up a career as a Hollywood scriptwriter; as he told Colin Vaines, 'If you want to make a small film or a personal film, then you can make it for British television. But if you want to make larger films then Hollywood is where you aim.' Bryden chose to stay small and personal, writing and directing *Ill Fares the Land*, one of the first wave of Channel 4 films. A bleakly elegiac fiction depicting the lives of the last inhabitants of St Kilda before their evacuation to the mainland in 1930, it suggested that Bryden might follow in the poetically naturalist footsteps of fellow Scot Bill Douglas. Instead he moved into television, where as Head of Drama at BBC Scotland from 1985 to 1994, he played an important role in nurturing Scottish audiovisual production culture, overseeing the production of critically acclaimed projects such as John Byrne's *Tutti Frutti* (1987) and Donna Franschild's *Takin' over the Asylum* (1993) as well as directing plays, such as David Mamet's *The Shawl* (1989), and his own *The Holy City* (1986), *The Ship* (1990) and *The Big Picnic* (1996). Apart from his contribution to Don Boyd's *Aria* (1987), Bryden has remained within the world of theatre and television rather than cinema.
(Jonathan Murray)
BIBLIOGRAPHY: 'Bill Bryden New Drama Head of BBC Scotland', *Television Today*, 6 Dec. 1984, p. 33; Commo, Jo, 'Memoirs of Survivors', *City Limits*, 6 May 1983, p. 13; Murray, Jonathan, 'Contemporary Scottish Film', *Irish Review*, Winter 2001, pp. 75–88; Vaines, Colin, 'When Truth Was Legend', *Screen International*, 22 Nov. 1980, p. 23.
FILMOGRAPHY: *Ill Fares the Land* (1983); *Aria* ('I Pagliacci' section, 1987).

BUCHANAN, Jack (1890–1957)

Walter John Buchanan, born in Helensburgh, Scotland, on 2 April 1890, is best remembered as the star of a number of inter-war musical-comedies on both stage and screen, where he epitomised the elegant, urbane man about town. He was also a shrewd businessman, owning or controlling in various partnerships four theatres, Riverside Studios in Hammersmith and a television research company, Television Limited.

After a brief spell in Hollywood, he entered into a partnership with Herbert Wilcox, making a series of films tailored to his persona. *Yes, Mr Brown* (1932), which he co-directed with Wilcox, was a typical Buchanan musical comedy with a minimal plot enlivened by the song-and-dance numbers performed with his longtime partner Elsie Randolph. *That's a Good Girl* (1933), one of his best films, was a straightforward adaptation of the 1928 stage success, with Buchanan in his most typical guise of an impecunious bachelor playboy. In 1937 he set up his own production company to make more ambitious films. He brought over René Clair to direct and Maurice Chevalier to star with him in *Break the News* (1938); *The Sky's the Limit*, which tries to rival Hollywood in the lavishness of its central number 'Montreal', Buchanan directed himself.

After the war, Buchanan concentrated on stage and television work, only occasionally acting in films, though he revitalised his popularity with his brilliant performance alongside Fred Astaire and Cyd Charisse in *The Band Wagon* (Vincente Minnelli, 1952). He died in London on 20 October 1957 after suffering from spinal arthritis.
(Andrew Spicer)
BIBLIOGRAPHY: Marshall, Michael, *Top Hat and Tails: The Story of Jack Buchanan* (London: Elm Tree Books/Hamish Hamilton, 1978); Spicer, Andrew, 'Jack Buchanan: The "Man about Town" of British Musical-Comedies in the 1930s', in Ian Conrich and Estella Tincknell (eds), *Musical Moments: Film and the Performance of Song and Dance* (Edinburgh: Edinburgh University Press, 2006).
FILMOGRAPHY: *Yes, Mr Brown* (co-dir. Herbert Wilcox, 1932); *That's a Good Girl* (1933); *The Sky's the Limit* (co-dir. Lee Garmes, 1938).

BUCHOWETZKI, Dimitri (1885–1932)

Born in Russia in 1885, Buchowetzki made his name in Germany with ambitious period dramas, several featuring Emil Jannings, including *Die Brüder Karamasoff* (co-dir. Carl Froelich, 1920) and *Peter der Grosse* (1922). Pola Negri, another of his stars, requested his services in Hollywood, but the flashy trappings of *Men* (1924), *Lily of the Dust* (1924) and their successors won diminishing approval. When sound came in, Buchowetzki was reduced to making foreign-language versions, first in Hollywood, then briefly in the UK. Working for Paramount British at Elstree Studios, in the summer of 1931 he turned Kurt Bernhardt's atmospheric melodrama *Der Mann, der den Mond beging* (1931), already duplicated in French, into the overwrought *Stamboul* and the Spanish-language *El hombre que asesinó*. He died in Los Angeles in 1932.

(Geoff Brown)

FILMOGRAPHY (UK only): *Stamboul* (1931); *El hombre que asesinó* (co-dir. Fernando Gomis, UK/Sp, 1931).

BUCQUET, Harold S. (1891–1946)

Harold Spencer Bucquet was born in London on 10 April 1891, and came to America in his youth. During the 1920s he worked in Hollywood as an assistant director and in the 1930s directed shorts and several of the *Dr Kildare* series for MGM. In 1942 he was sent to Britain to direct *The Adventures of Tartu* for MGM-British. Since the late 1930s, MGM had shifted its British productions from 'quota quickies' to prestige productions that would appeal to American as well as British audiences. *The Adventures of Tartu* was a major film, starring Robert Donat, whose last film for the studio, *Goodbye, Mr Chips* (Sam Wood, 1939), had won him an Academy Award. Despite clever confusions over identity (both Donat and his co-star Valerie Hobson pretend they are pro-Nazi collaborators), the story of a bomb disposal expert (Donat) sent into Czechoslovakia as a secret agent to destroy a poison gas plant with the aid of the Czech underground resembled that of a standard Resistance drama. As a thriller it lacks suspense, but Donat's performance stands out, and the brutality of life under Nazi occupation is depicted realistically. Bucquet returned to Hollywood to co-direct *Dragon Seed* (1944) starring Katharine Hepburn, and *Without Love* (1945) with Hepburn and Spencer Tracy before his death in Los Angeles on 13 February 1946.

(James C. Robertson)

BIBLIOGRAPHY: Microfiche on *The Adventures of Tartu*, held in the BFI National Library, London.

FILMOGRAPHY (UK only): *The Adventures of Tartu* (aka *Tartu/Sabotage Agent*, 1943).

BURDIS, Ray (1958–) and Dominic ANCIANO (c. 1959–)

Raymond J. Burdis was born in London on 23 August 1958; Dominic Anciano in 1959. Together they established Fugitive Films in 1981, producing videos for pop artists, including Elton John, Queen and George Michael. They entered film production in 1988 with *The Universe of Dermot Finn*, a short film by fellow Londoner Philip Ridley, and followed it with *The Krays* (1990), scripted by Ridley and directed by Peter Medak, and two films directed by Ridley, *The Reflecting Sky* (1990) and *The Passion of Darkly Noon* (1995). They also produced three series of *Operation Good Guys* (1997–2000), a funny spoof documentary crime series, for BBC Television in 1997.

In 1998 Burdis and Anciano co-directed, wrote and produced *Final Cut*, a low-budget film about a group of friends gathered at a funeral whose iniquities are exposed in a film made by the deceased man. The improvised acting, particularly from Ray Winstone, Jude Law and Sadie Frost, is impressive, and the issues around voyeurism and trust explored boldly. They followed it with *Love, Honour and Obey*, featuring the same principal players along with other up-and-coming talents Jonny Lee Miller, Kathy Burke, Sean Pertwee, Denise Van Outen and Rhys Ifans; but the technique of getting actors to play improvised variations on some aspect of their own persona wore thin second time around. What had been welcomed as fresh and innovative in *Final Cut* was condemned as banal and indulgent in *Love, Honour and Obey*, and its treatment of lovably psychotic London gangsters had little appeal in a market already sated with British gangster films. Burdis went on to play one of the four philandering fiftysomethings in the BBC comedy *Manchild* (2002).

(Alan Burton)

BIBLIOGRAPHY: Kelly, Richard, 'Final Cut', *Sight and Sound*, Sept. 1999, p. 45; Kempster, Grant, 'Love, Honour and Obey', *Film Review*, May 2000, p. 27; Moore, Oscar, 'Tough Start, Strong Finish', *Screen International*, 12 May 1990, pp. 10–11.

FILMOGRAPHY: *Final Cut* (1998); *Love, Honour and Obey* (2000).

BURGE, Stuart (1918–2002)

Stuart Burge was born on 15 January 1918 in Brentwood, Essex. On leaving school he joined the Old Vic theatre as an actor. After the war, he turned to stage direction and in the mid-1950s branched into television, where he directed around forty 'highbrow' plays. Surprisingly, his 1960 cinema debut, *There Was a Crooked Man*, was an independent Norman Wisdom vehicle scripted by the blacklisted Canadian writer Reuben Ship. The result was one of the great British comedies, successfully meshing Wisdom's slapstick strengths with a satirically edged script. Sadly, the film did not find an audience and when Burge returned to the cinema it was with the classics, a trio of films made for Anthony Havelock-Allan and John Brabourne's BHE Productions. Each was based on a pre-existing stage production: Laurence Olivier's Chichester Festival *Uncle Vanya*, John Dexter's National Theatre *Othello* and a D'Oyly Carte Opera production of *The Mikado*. For all their virtues, these films are museum pieces fixing on celluloid something that only made sense as a live experience.

Burge returned to Shakespeare more inventively with *Julius Caesar*, an adaptation by Robert Furnival for the cinema rather than the theatre. He gets good performances from a strong cast including Charlton Heston, John Gielgud, Richard Johnson, Robert Vaughn, Richard Chamberlain, Diana Rigg, Christopher Lee and Jill Bennett. The film was a commercial success, but it was to be Burge's last cinema outing. He remained primarily a theatre director, though he continued to work regularly in television, successfully collaborating with Trevor Griffiths on *A*

Fall of Eagles (1974), *Bill Brand* (1976) and *Sons and Lovers* (1981), and Troy Kennedy Martin on his adaptation of Angus Wilson's *The Old Men at the Zoo* (1982). He died from pancreatic cancer on 24 January 2002 in Lymington, Hampshire.
(Richard Dacre)

BIBLIOGRAPHY: Lentz III, Harris, Obituary, *Classic Images* no. 321, Mar. 2002, p. 54.

FILMOGRAPHY: *There Was a Crooked Man* (1960); *Uncle Vanya* (1963); *Othello* (1965); *The Mikado* (1967); *Julius Caesar* (1970).

BURGER, Germain (1900–)

James Germain Burger, whose family was of Belgian ancestry, was born in London in 1900. After education at St Joseph's College, Norwood, he plunged into film studio work in 1916 and by 1920 had joined his brother Paul in the Stoll Film Company's camera department. Both worked frequently for Maurice Elvey; from 1920 to 1921, Burger photographed Elvey's popular Sherlock Holmes two-reelers and the feature-length *The Hound of the Baskervilles*. Later in the 1920s he gained experience in Europe with Ufa. But on his return to Britain, by accident or design, he worked entirely on the commercial industry's fringes: with the Empire Marketing Board Film Unit (*The Country Comes to Town*, Basil Wright, 1931); the independent C. H. Dand (*Men against Death*, 1933); and British Utility Films, makers of educational, advertising and industrial films.

He began directing in 1936 with a lowly comedy short, *Hard Labour*, and subsequently developed something of a speciality in Celtic subjects and canine narratives. With his own production company, Burger went to Ireland in 1937 to film *Devil's Rock*, a musical romance of poor quality featuring sheepdog driving and heroic deeds. Similar cut-price, heavily sentimental features followed in wartime, all made for Butcher's. A weepie musical, *Rose of Tralee* (1942), was followed by a similarly tearful Scottish confection with Moira Lister, *My Ain Folk* (1944). The most popular was *Sheepdog of the Hills* (1941), shot in Devon, which cast Moss, a champion sheepdog, alongside David Farrar (as a priest who goes blind); it was twice reissued in the 1940s, and *Kine Weekly* recommended it for 'particularly good characterisation, picturesque scenery and an occasional thrill'.

No further features followed *My Ain Folk*. Abandoning dogs and sentimentality, in 1946 he established Orion Picture Corporation and Burnell Productions to produce and occasionally direct sponsored industrial films and featurettes. Several commissions in the late 1940s came from the Scottish co-operative movement, an association that went back to *Two Good Fairies*, a naive attempt to promote the Beveridge Plan, which Burger had directed for the Scottish Co-operative Wholesale Society in 1944. Worthy in its approach to the 'New Jerusalem' of post-war British society, the film was judged too soft-centred by *Documentary News Letter*. Orion remained active until the late 1960s; thereafter, Burger vanishes from the records.
(Alan Burton)

BIBLIOGRAPHY: Burton, Alan, *The British Co-operative Movement Film Catalogue* (Trowbridge, Wilts: Flicks Books, 1997); 'Sheepdog of the Hills', *Kine Weekly*, 29 Jan. 1948, p. 24; 'Two Good Fairies', *Documentary News Letter* vol. 5 no. 1, 1944, p. 5.

FILMOGRAPHY: *Hard Labour* (short, 1936); *Devil's Rock* (co-dir. Richard Hayward, 1938); *Border Collie* (unfinished, 1939); *Where the Shannon Flows down to the Sea* (doc., 1940); *Sheepdog of the Hills*; *Faithful for Ever* (doc.) (1941); *Rose of Tralee* (1942); *The Tale of a Dog* (doc.); *Two Good Fairies* (short) (1943); *My Ain Folk* (1944); *Our Pals* (short, 1945); *Jungle Flight* (doc., 1946); *Counter Courtesy* (doc.); *Know Your Business* (doc.); *Your Silent Salesman* (doc.) (1947); *Achievement* (doc., 1948); *Pride and Progress* (doc., 1949); *The Swift Plan Story* (doc., 1964); *The Morris Walk Story* (doc., 1965); *The Construction of Liverpool Metropolitan Cathedral* (doc., 1966).

BURTON, Richard (1925–1984)

Richard Burton was born Richard Walter Jenkins, the twelfth of thirteen children from an impoverished working-class family, in Pontrydyfen, Wales, on 10 November 1925. He won a scholarship to Oxford, where he acted for the Oxford University Dramatic Society under the tutorship of Nevill Coghill, and following military service he established his reputation on the stage. Having made his screen debut in Emlyn Williams' *The Last Days of Dolwyn* (1949), he went to Hollywood in 1952 with a contract at 20th Century-Fox, but few of his films there gained him any distinction. On returning to Europe he was effectively cast in *Bitter Victory* (Nicholas Ray, 1957) and *Look Back in Anger* (Tony Richardson, 1959), but it was playing opposite Elizabeth Taylor in *Cleopatra* (Joseph L. Mankiewicz, 1963) that turned Burton into a superstar. They went on to marry and co-star in a further nine films over the ensuing decade.

In 1966 Burton and Taylor honoured a promise to Nevill Coghill to appear in an OUDS production of Christopher Marlowe's version of the Faust legend, *Doctor Faustus*, to raise money for a student theatre. The same year, Burton and Coghill co-directed a screen version at Dino De Laurentiis' studios in Rome, with Burton again playing Faustus, Taylor in a wordless role as his vision of Helen of Troy and an otherwise all-student cast. The film was financed by Burton himself at a cost of $1 million (at a time when he and Taylor could each command a similar sum, they took no acting fees) and was bought by Columbia for distribution as a roadshow.

The film is earnest but rather turgid, larded with overly self-conscious attempts at 'cinematic' visual effects, and was not well received by either critics or the public. Its failure was generally regarded as an early sign that the presence of Burton and Taylor in a movie was no longer an automatic guarantee of commercial interest. Having divorced Taylor and remarried several times (including once more to her), Burton died of a cerebral haemorrhage in Geneva, Switzerland, on 5 August 1984.
(Sheldon Hall)

BIBLIOGRAPHY: Cottrell, John and Fergus Cashin, *Richard Burton* (London: Arthur Barker, 1971); 'Dr *Faustus*', *Films and Filming*, Jan. 1967, pp. 53–5.

FILMOGRAPHY: *Doctor Faustus* (co-dir. Nevill Coghill, UK/It, 1967).

BUSHELL, Anthony (1904–1997)

Anthony Bushell was born on 19 May 1904 in Westerham, Kent. Tall, fair and handsome, he played the quintessential upper-class Englishman in innumerable films, maturing from dashing juvenile lead in thrillers such as *The Ghoul* (T. Hayes Hunter, 1933) and *Dark Journey* (Victor Saville, 1937) to the crustily ill-tempered Colonel Breen in Rudolph Cartier and Nigel Kneale's television serial *Quatermass and the Pit* (1958).

After spending the Second World War in the Guards he returned to acting but moved behind the camera when his friend Laurence Olivier made him associate producer on *Hamlet* (1948). In 1949 Alexander Korda gave Bushell an opportunity to direct *The Angel with the Trumpet*, a poignant story of a Jewish family in pre-Nazi Austria. This was followed by *The Long Dark Hall*, a well-made courtroom drama starring Rex Harrison. Bushell showed himself to be a competent director, adept at coping with the pressures of the studio floor, and he was asked to take on second-unit and associate directing duties on a variety of big-budget films, including Olivier's *Richard III* (1955) and *The Prince and the Showgirl* (1957).

Bushell made another feature film in 1961, *The Terror of the Tongs*, a Hammer film with Christopher Lee adding to his repertoire of villains as the master of a secret society terrorising Hong Kong. Bushell also ventured into television, directing episodes for several series including *Sir Francis Drake*, *Danger Man* and *The Saint*. He died in Oxford on 2 April 1997.

(Linda Wood)

BIBLIOGRAPHY: Vallance, Tom, Obituary, *Independent*, 17 Apr. 1997

FILMOGRAPHY: *The Angel with the Trumpet* (1950); *The Long Dark Hall* (co-dir. Reginald Beck, 1951); *The Red Beret* (US: *Paratrooper*, location dir., Terence Young); *Hell below Zero* (Antarctica sequence dir., Mark Robson, 1953); *Richard III* (assoc. dir., Laurence Olivier, 1955), *Bhowani Junction* (2nd unit dir., George Cukor, 1956); *The Prince and the Showgirl* (assoc. dir., Laurence Olivier, 1957); *The Terror of the Tongs* (aka *Terror of the Hatchet Men*, 1961); *A Woman's Privilege* ('Scales of Justice' short, 1962).

BUTLER, Alexander

Alexander Butler was born Alexandre Beaulieu in Ontario, Canada. He moved to England and began directing for Barker Motion Photography before the First World War. When the war ended, he went to work for the Samuelson Film Company at their studios at Worton Hall in Isleworth, alongside directors like Dave Aylott and Maurice Elvey. Bertie Samuelson produced all Butler's films, first under the Samuelson name, and then under Napoleon Films (1923–4) and Reciprocity Films (1924–5). Butler acted in some of his films, using the name Andre Beaulieu.

Butler's particular interest was melodrama, and he became the first specialist director of British horror feature films. He hit his stride in 1917 with *The Sorrows of Satan*, an adaptation of the best-selling Victorian novel by Marie Corelli, featuring Gladys Cooper as the young lady whose princely lover (Cecil Humphreys) turns out to be Satan; the story was framed at either end with scenes set in hell. Butler followed this up two years later with an adaptation of Richard Marsh's 1897 gothic novel *The Beetle*. It is probable that he also directed the 1916 adaptation of Conan Doyle's Holmes story *The Valley of Fear*, which had been serialised in the *Strand* magazine at the end of 1914 (though some sources attribute the film to Fred Paul).

Though Butler was one of Samuelson's principal directors, in reviews his name is rarely mentioned and little is known about him. Early in 1920 he travelled to the USA with Samuelson, making four films at Universal City, including *The Night Riders*, a romantic drama set on a Canadian ranch, and *David and Jonathan*, based on E. Temple Thurston's novel of love and rivalry among shipwrecked friends. He courted controversy in 1919 with *Damaged Goods*, a drama about an engaged man who catches a venereal disease, and again in 1923 with a drama loosely based upon Dr Marie Stopes' book *Married Love*. The film dealt with the politically volatile subject of birth control's place in married life, and ran into predictable problems with the

BBFC. They ordered a title change, from *Married Love* to *Maisie's Marriage*, and demanded the removal of Stopes' name from publicity. Butler's last recorded films as director were three series of short films produced by Samuelson and released at the end of 1925.

(Simon Brown)

BIBLIOGRAPHY: Low, Rachael, *The History of the British Film 1914–1918* (London: George Allen & Unwin, 1950); Low, Rachael, *The History of the British Film 1918–1929* (London: George Allen & Unwin, 1971).

FILMOGRAPHY: *A Little Child Shall Lead Them*; *In the Toils of the Blackmailer*, *In London's Toils*; *O.H.M.S*; *For £50,000*; *The Passions of Men*; *The Anarchist's Doom*; *The Great Bullion Robbery*; *London by Night*; *Greater Love Hath No Man*; *In the Hands of the London Crooks* (1913); *A Pair of Spectacles*; *The Valley of Fear*, *Just a Girl*; *Nursie! Nursie!*; *The Girl Who Loves a Soldier*, *A Fair Impostor* (1916); *In Another Girl's Shoes*; *The Sorrows of Satan*; *Little Women*; *My Lady's Dress* (1917); *Jo the Crossing Sweeper*, *On Leave* (1918); *The Odds against Her*, *The Beetle*; *The Thundercloud*; *The Disappearance of the Judge*; *The Life of a London Actress*; *Lamp of Destiny*; *Damaged Goods* (1919); *Love in the Wilderness* (UK/US); *Her Story* (UK/US); *David and Jonathan* (UK/US); *The Night Riders* (UK/US); *The Ugly Ducking* (1920); *For Her Father's Sake* (1921); *A Royal Divorce*; *The Knockout*; *Should a Doctor Tell?*; *Married Love* (aka *Maisie's Marriage*) (1923); *Twisted Tales* (series); *Proverbs* (series); *Milestone Melodies* (series) (1925).

BUTTERWORTH, Jez (1969–)

Jeremy Butterworth was born in Southwark, London, on 4 March 1969 and brought up in St Albans. He studied English at Cambridge, after which he worked in advertising and acted in the television series *The Bill* and *Chandler and Co*. He then spent a year writing *Mojo*, a play about pop stars and gangsters in late 1950s' Soho, which was produced at the Royal Court theatre to great acclaim. Butterworth agreed to adapt it for BBC Films on condition he was allowed to direct. A fragmentary style, and a fast flow of witty, if archly anachronistic, dialogue, was no doubt appealing to a stage audience; but crudely transposed to film, Butterworth's play becomes irritating and virtually meaningless. The clever conceit of having Harold Pinter appear as an enigmatically threatening character from one of his own plays leads nowhere, and the ethos of the film is captured in the image of Aidan Gillen riding a bicycle round the confines of a flat roof before childishly throwing it down to the street below. Not surprisingly, the film's theatrical release in the UK brought in less than £27,000.

Birthday Girl, a more expensive co-production between Miramax and Channel 4, is less embarrassingly bad, saved by a mesmerising performance from Nicole Kidman as a Russian internet bride. She speaks only a few words in English during the first hour of the film, and Butterworth relies clumsily on voiceover. But once she finds her voice the film livens up, and the quirky conceit of having a Russian femme fatale and an English bank clerk on the run in snooty rural Berkshire compensates for an otherwise predictable plot. Nonetheless, quota quickie production values hardly justify a $13 million budget, and it remains to be seen whether Butterworth's expensive apprenticeship will eventually yield rewarding results.

(Alan Burton)

BIBLIOGRAPHY: O'Sullivan, Charlotte, 'Birthday Girl', *Sight and Sound*, July 2002, pp. 40–1; Santini, Derek, 'Mojo Working', *Daily Telegraph* Weekend Magazine, 13 June 1998, pp. 52–3; Wolf, Matt, '"Mojo" Rising', *Variety*, 9 Dec. 1996, p. 8.

FILMOGRAPHY: *Mojo* (1997); *Birthday Girl* (UK/US, 2001).

BYE, Ed (1955–)

Edward Richard Morison Bye was born in London in 1955. After training at Ravensbourne College he joined the BBC. He worked as production manager on *The Young Ones* (1982), but went freelance to seize the opportunity of directing *Girls on Top*, starring Dawn French, Jennifer Saunders, Joan Greenwood and Ruby Wax (whom he later married). He consolidated his reputation as a competent director of comedy shows, with series such as *The Full Wax* (1991), *The Detectives* (1993) and *Red Dwarf* (1988–98).

Bye broke into feature films with the clumsy but profitable *Kevin & Perry Go Large*, a spin-off from one of the regular sketches in the Harry Enfield television comedy shows. Unfortunately his next film, *Fat Slags*, based on cartoon characters from *Viz* magazine, was a badly conceived project where the absence of a coherent script left the witless characters little to do beyond testing the audience's patience.

(Robert Murphy)

BIBLIOGRAPHY: Killick, Jane, 'Back in the Red', *StarBurst* no. 248, Apr. 1999, pp. 30–3; Matthias, Fiona, 'You Have to Laugh . . .', *Television Today*, 3 Mar. 1994, p. 25; Webster, Howard, 'Hero of Comedy', *Broadcast*, B+ Supplement, 13 June 2003, p. 8.

FILMOGRAPHY: *The Secret Policeman's Third Ball* (2nd unit dir., Ken O'Neill, 1987); *Kevin & Perry Go Large* (2000); *Fat Slags* (2004).

BYRNE, John (1940–)

Artist, set designer, playwright, screenwriter and director, John Byrne was born in Paisley, Scotland, on 6 January 1940. After studying at both the Glasgow and Edinburgh Schools of Art Byrne worked for a while as a 'slab boy' in a carpet factory, mixing paints on stone slabs for the designers, an occupation that he was to draw on for his 1978 stage play *The Slab Boys*, which was eventually made into a feature film in 1997. Byrne worked as a set designer with the 7:84 Theatre Company before establishing himself as a playwright in the late 1970s and a writer of tragi-comic musical dramas for television with the award-winning six-part serial *Tutti Frutti* (1987), the comedy-drama *Normal Service* (1988) and the six-part country-and-western serial *Your Cheatin' Heart* (1990). Each of these television dramas was resolutely Scottish in temperament and dialect, perplexingly so to some reviewers south of the border. The same was true of

Byrne's 1993 television drama *Boswell and Johnson's Tour of the Western Islands* and the feature film version of *The Slab Boys*, filmed entirely in an old Glasgow warehouse on lovingly constructed 1950s' sets, designed with meticulous attention to period detail and featuring talented young Scottish actors in the central roles. The resulting film was a witty, stylised evocation of 1950s' working-class culture, expressing Byrne's musical and thematic preoccupations as well as his unique visual style. It reached only disappointingly small audiences.

(Lez Cooke)

BIBLIOGRAPHY: Kennedy, A. L., 'Edging Close to the Bone', *Sight and Sound*, Dec. 1996, pp. 23–5.

FILMOGRAPHY: *The Slab Boys* (1997).

C

CAFFREY, David (1969–)

David Caffrey was born in Greystones, Co. Wicklow, in 1969, and studied film at West Surrey College of Art and Design in Farnham, England. He returned to Ireland in the early 1990s, just as new government schemes to promote indigenous film production were beginning to have an impact, and took advantage of these arrangements to gain film-making experience. He worked for a short time in Roger Corman's Connemara studio and went on to make a number of highly regarded short films, including *Bolt*, which he both wrote and directed.

His feature film debut was *Divorcing Jack*, scripted by Colin Bateman from his own blackly comic novel. The film attempted to catch the prevailing *Zeitgeist* of British cinema, epitomised by scabrously irreverent films such as *Trainspotting* (Danny Boyle, 1996) and *Human Traffic* (Justin Kerrigan, 1999). The humour is drawn from satirising the pretensions and incompetent but bloody antics of paramilitaries as they manoeuvre for political influence in an independent Northern Ireland about to elect its own prime minister. The film won the Critic's Prize at Cannes in 1998 and was modestly successful at the box office.

Caffrey then directed the four-part miniseries *Aristocrats* (1999) for the BBC and showed himself to be a competent and stylish television director. He returned to feature film production with two more comedies, both in the same zany vein as *Divorcing Jack*. *On the Nose*, despite the presence of Robbie Coltrane and Dan Ackroyd, was considered too Irish for widespread distribution. *Grand Theft Parsons*, a hippy saga about doing the right thing with the body of dead country rock singer Gram Parsons, bypassed the mainstream audience but found a substantial cult following.

(Martin McLoone)

BIBLIOGRAPHY: Lennon, Elaine, 'How to Be a Film Director in Three Easy Lessons', *Film Ireland* no. 67, Oct./Nov. 1998, pp. 14–16; McLoone, Martin, *Irish Film: The Emergence of a Contemporary Cinema* (London: BFI, 2000); Pettitt, Lance, *Screening Ireland* (Manchester: Manchester University Press, 2000).

FILMOGRAPHY: *The Connivers* (short, Ir, 1994); *Bantams* (short, 1996); *Bolt* (short, Ir, 1997); *Divorcing Jack* (1998); *On the Nose* (Can/Ir, 2001); *Grand Theft Parsons* (UK/US, 2003).

CALLOW, Simon (1949–)

Simon Phillip Hugh Callow was born on 15 June 1949 in London and was educated at the London Oratory, Queen's University, Belfast, and the London Drama Centre. Following a series of acclaimed stage performances, he made his film debut in 1984 as Emanuel Schikaneder in Milos Forman's *Amadeus*. In 1986, Callow enjoyed the first of many collaborations with Merchant–Ivory, playing the Reverend Mr Beebe in *A Room with a View* (1985). Arguably his most notable role, however, came as the ebullient, openly gay Gareth in *Four Weddings and a Funeral* (Mike Newell, 1994).

Callow's long-standing working relationship with Ismail Merchant led to his only directorial assignment to date, a 1991 screen adaptation of Carson McCullers' novella *The Ballad of the Sad Café*. This dark and disturbing love story set in the rural American South starred Vanessa Redgrave and Keith Carradine. It was always going to be a challenge to translate McCullers' poetic complexities to the screen and the film was generally poorly received, many reviewers regarding it as mannered and theatrical. Subsequently, Callow was to enjoy more success in the opposite direction with a 1996 stage adaptation of Carné's screen masterpiece *Les Enfants du paradis*. Given this and his continued success on screen, in the theatre and as an author of biographies of Charles Laughton and Orson Welles, the 'interesting failure' (Hirschhorn, p. 46) of *The Ballad of the Sad Café* is perhaps not too much of a disappointment.

(Martin Hunt)

BIBLIOGRAPHY: Hirschhorn, Clive, 'Deep-Fried Southern Losers', *Sunday Express*, 5 May 1991, p. 46.

FILMOGRAPHY: *The Ballad of the Sad Café* (US/UK, 1991).

CAMMELL, Donald (1934–1996)

Donald Seton Cammell was born in Edinburgh on 17 January 1934 into a formerly wealthy family that had lost its considerable fortune in the crash of 1929. A precocious boy, he obtained a scholarship to the Royal Academy and after further studies in Florence successfully set himself up as a portrait artist in London in the early 1950s.

By the mid-1960s he had given up painting to concentrate on film-making. His first two scripts, *The Touchables* (Robert Freeman, 1968) and *Duffy* (Robert Parrish, 1968), combine crime and hippies to unremarkable effect (*The Touchables* was rewritten by Ian La Frenais). Cammell decided to try the same formula again in his next script, but to preserve his work insisted on directing as well. His agent, the aspiring producer Sandy Lieberson, paired him with cinematographer Nicolas Roeg as co-directors of *Performance*. The film brilliantly melds the narcissistic glamour of London's East End gangsters and the late 1960s rock star phenomenon, but its mixture of homo-eroticism, violence and rock music so alarmed its backers that it sat on the shelf for over a year before its release in 1970. The final version, completed without Roeg in Los Angeles by Cammell and editor Frank Mazzola, is a rich, sophisticated and stimulating work, elliptically shot and magnificently 'performed' by its stars James Fox and Mick Jagger. The themes of masculinity in crisis, sexuality, death and rebirth, transformation and extreme violence would reappear throughout the rest of the films Cammell directed, all of which were made in America.

After a number of false starts, Cammell accepted an offer from MGM to direct *Demon Seed*, a science-fiction horror story (from a novel by Dean Koontz) about a super-computer that imprisons the wife of its creator inside their home in order to make her bear its child. The film was eventually taken out of his hands but it remains notable, despite its lurid premise, for a strong performance from Julie Christie and a kinetic finale with an emotional ambiguity reminiscent of the ending of Roman Polanski's *Rosemary's Baby* (1968). Cammell subsequently wrote a number of scripts, spending a long and fruitless period collaborating with Marlon Brando on 'Jericho', a project that was never made. The only one of his films over which he maintained complete control was *White of the Eye*, co-written with his wife China Kong, a sympathetic look at a homicidal psychopath featuring an uncompromising performance by David Keith as the misogynist killer.

Wild Side, Cammell's last film, was first released in a version heavily re-edited by its production company, but was eventually returned to an approximation of his original intentions by Kong and Mazzola and re-released as *Donald Cammell's Wild Side*. With its original non-linear structure restored, this version closely resembles *Performance* in its fragmentary editing style – full of flashbacks and flash-forwards – and in its candid and exhilarating sex scenes. A true visionary, Cammell sadly only completed four films as a director before committing suicide at his home in Los Angeles on 26 April 1996.

(Sergio Angelini)

BIBLIOGRAPHY: Chang, Chris, 'Cinema, Sex, Magick: The Films of Donald Cammell', *Film Comment*, July/Aug. 1996, pp. 14–19, 83; MacCabe, Colin, *Performance* (London: BFI, 1998); Savage, Jon, '*Performance*: Interview with Donald Cammell', in Steve Chibnall and Robert Murphy (eds), *British Crime Cinema* (London: Routledge, 1999).

FILMOGRAPHY: *Performance* (co-dir. Nicolas Roeg, 1968; rel. 1970); *Demon Seed* (US, 1977); *U2: Unforgettable Fire* (doc., co-dirs. Meivert Avis/Barry Devlin, 1984); *White of the Eye* (US, 1987); *Wild Side* (under pseudonym 'Franklin Brauner', US, 1995; re-rel. as *Donald Cammell's Wild Side*, 2000); *The Argument* (short, 1998).

CAMPBELL, Ivar (1904–)

Ivar Campbell was prominent among the cinema novices and gentlemen amateurs who gathered round Norman Loudon's new film studio Sound City, established at Littleton Park, Shepperton, in 1932. Born in Otaki, New Zealand, in 1904, Campbell's immediate background was impeccably British: a public school education at Charterhouse, followed by employment on the stock exchange. At Littleton Park he was hired as production supervisor, but after two months' experience producing Sound City's first features he began to direct as well, working at first with John Baxter on *Reunion* (1932), the sentimental tale of an impoverished major attending his regiment's reunion dinner. Subsequently he served as producer on Baxter's ground-breaking portrait of London down-and-outs, *Doss House* (1933), and his rural drama *The Song of the Plough* (1933). Campbell's own films never shared Baxter's social-evangelical goals; instead he pursued straight entertainment in a mixed portfolio of what Loudon preferred to call 'modest second features' (rather than 'quota quickies').

Campbell's nickname among some Sound City workers was 'Midnight', prompted by his habit of shooting into the early hours. Night or day, there was no time for directorial subtleties, though some relief from the bald visual approach of *Reunion* was offered in *Side Streets*, whose 'fistic action, naïve romance, and hearty villainy' impressed the reviewer of *The Cinema*, and the romantic comedy-drama of *The Golden Cage*. After the comedy-musical *Radio Pirates* Campbell moved to Elstree and second features for Paramount-British, achieving modestly pleasing results in the improbable comedy *The Mad Hatters* (1935), and ensuring respectable acting in the tangled thriller *Expert's Opinion* (1935). Thereafter he decamped to Worton Hall studios, Isleworth, trying his luck with Liberty Films. He found success with *Captain's Orders* (1937), a breezy drama with music featuring Henry Edwards, but luck failed to strike twice with the crook melodrama *Too Many Husbands*. In 1938 Liberty's feature production imploded, along with much of the British film industry; thereafter, the midnight hour strikes and Ivar Campbell disappears from history.

(Geoff Brown)

BIBLIOGRAPHY: Brown, Geoff with Tony Aldgate, *The Common Touch: The Films of John Baxter* (London: BFI, 1989); Robinson, Martha, *Continuity Girl* (London: Robert Hale, 1937); Threadgall, Derek, *Shepperton Studios: An Independent View* (London: BFI, 1994).

FILMOGRAPHY: *Reunion* (assoc. dir., John Baxter, 1932); *Side Streets*; *The Golden Cage*; *Eyes of Fate* (1933); *Designing Women* (aka *House of Cards*, 1934); *Radio Pirates* (aka *Big Ben Calling*); *The Mad Hatters*; *Expert's Opinion* (1935); *Talking Hands* (short, aka *Hands in Harmony*); *Grand Finale*; *The Belles of St Clement's* (1936); *Captain's Orders* (1937); *Too Many Husbands* (1938).

CAMPBELL, Martin (1943–)

Martin Campbell was born in New Zealand in 1943, the son of a sheep farmer. Though now deemed a Hollywood director of international action movies, Campbell began on the fringes of British cinema and made his reputation with UK television work. He came to England in 1965 and joined ATV as a cameraman the following year. He worked as assistant director on *The Love Box* (Billy and Teddy White, 1972), an unremarkable British sex film, and quickly progressed to directing *The Sex Thief* and the unusually self-reflexive comedy *Eskimo Nell*, which benefits from a spirited performance by Roy Kinnear as sleazy British producer Benny U. Murdoch of BUM Productions.

Campbell moved on to produce Anthony Simmons' Brixton musical *Black Joy* (1977) and act as associate producer on Alan Clarke's *Scum* (1978), but returned to television in 1980 to direct episodes of British crime series (*The Professionals*, *Shoestring*, *Minder*, *Bergerac*). He progressed to more prestigious projects – *Muck and Brass* (1982) and *Reilly: Ace of Spies* (1983) – and made his breakthrough with the BBC serial *Edge of Darkness* (1985), an eco-thriller scripted by Troy Kennedy Martin, with satiric, supernatural overtones, which remains Campbell's masterpiece. Moving to America, he rose from solid minor thrillers (*Criminal Law*, *Defenseless*) to action franchises, though his most intriguing American work has been for television: *Cast a Deadly Spell* (1991), a cable television movie with Fred Ward as a private eye in a 1940s' Los Angeles overrun by demons and monsters, and the outstanding 'Three Men and Adena' episode of *Homicide: Life on the Street* (1993). He finally made the A-list through his sure handling of the British-based Bond film, *GoldenEye* (1995), following up with two films resurrecting the silent cinema swashbuckler Zorro, and a second Bond film *Casino Royale* (2006).
(Kim Newman)

BIBLIOGRAPHY: Clarke, Steve, 'Campbell's Scoop', *Broadcast*, 21 May 1986, p. 17; Fuller, Graham, 'The Trouble with Gary', *Listener*, 17 Dec. 1987, p. 63; McGillivray, David, *Doing Rude Things: The History of the British Sex Film, 1957–81* (London: Sun Tavern Fields, 1992); Mitchell, Wendy, 'Campbell Trades Masks for Martinis', *Screen International*, 28 Oct. 2005, p. 18; 'Out of the Edge of Darkness', *Film and TV Technician*, Apr. 1986, p. 7.

FILMOGRAPHY: *The Sex Thief* (1973); *Three for All* (US: *My Little Darling*, 1974); *Eskimo Nell* (1975); *Her Family Jewels* (1976); *Criminal Law* (US, 1990); *Defenseless* (US, 1991); *No Escape* (US, 1994); *GoldenEye* (US, 1995); *The Mask of Zorro* (US, 1998); *Vertical Limit* (US, 2000); *Beyond Borders* (US, 2004); *The Legend of Zorro* (US, 2005); *Casino Royale* (UK/US, 2006).

CANNON, Danny (1968–)

Danny Cannon was born in London in 1968. He won the BBC's Young Film-Maker of the Year award with his forty-minute film *Sometimes* in 1987 and went on to write and direct *Strangers*, an almost feature-length (sixty-seven-minute) thriller set in Los Angeles. He enjoyed a degree of commercial success with *The Young Americans*, a British gangster film with Harvey Keitel mingling among British supporting players in a tale of drug-dealing and criminal empire-carving in London. Flashy and

obvious, but with genre-fuelled verve and an interesting performance by Thandie Newton to recommend it, the film landed Cannon a dream project whose failure derailed his career for some time.

Judge Dredd is based on the comic strip from *2000AD* that presents a British satirical take on a post-holocaust America, but Cannon hammers it into a dispiritedly average vehicle for Sylvester Stallone. A vastly expensive film that did badly at the box office and failed to ignite a *Dredd* franchise, it left Cannon in a position where the only offers to come his way were a direct-to-video thriller (*Phoenix*, US, 1998) and a sequel to a horror film he had been offered and turned down. He acted as executive producer on coming-of-age-in-Stevenage drama *Boston Kickout* (Paul Hills, 1996), but career redemption and credibility only came in 2000 when he directed the pilot and several subsequent episodes for Jerry Bruckheimer's television series *C.S.I.: Crime Scene Investigation*. He returned to the cinema with the crowd-pleasing football drama *Goal!*.
(Kim Newman)

BIBLIOGRAPHY: Fuller, Graham, 'Brit Movies Get Big, Brash and American', *Interview*, Apr. 1994, p. 74; Thompson, Ben, 'Listen to Britain', *Sight and Sound*, Oct. 1993, pp. 16–17.

FILMOGRAPHY: *Strangers* (1991); *The Young Americans* (1993); *Judge Dredd* (US, 1995); *I Still Know What You Did Last Summer* (US, 1998); *Goal!* (US, 2005).

CAPALDI, Peter (1958–)

Peter Capaldi was born in Glasgow in 1958. While studying at the Glasgow School of Art he was offered a major role in Bill Forsythe's *Local Hero* (1983). A successful acting career in film and television followed. In 1992 he provided the screenplay for the low-budget road movie *Soft Top Hard Shoulder* (Stefan Schwartz, 1992), and in 1993 directed *Franz Kafka's It's a Wonderful Life*, a witty fantasy about Kafka (Richard E. Grant) struggling to create his short story *Metamorphosis*, which won an Academy Award for Best Short Film in 1995. He made his feature debut, *Strictly Sinatra*, for Andrew Macdonald and Duncan Kenworthy's DNA Films in 2001. Ian Hart plays a Sinatra-obsessed Glasgow pub singer who gets comically entangled with local gangsters. Capaldi's sad little story occasionally captures moments of poignancy, but the audience is left hopelessly at sea as to whether or not Hart's singer is supposed to have hidden talents, and the cartoonish unreality of the plot craves too much indulgence. As the bottom half of a 1950s' double bill *Strictly Sinatra* might have been acceptable; but Capaldi's direction is disappointingly uninventive after the promise shown by his Kafka short.

(Robert Murphy)

BIBLIOGRAPHY: Lawrenson, Edward, 'Strictly Sinatra', *Sight and Sound*, Dec. 2001, p. 58; Marsh, James, 'Peter Capaldi: Flirting with Glory', *Rushes*, Apr./May 1995, pp. 11–12.

FILMOGRAPHY: *Franz Kafka's It's a Wonderful Life* (short, 1993); *Strictly Sinatra* (2001).

CARDIFF, Jack (1914–)

Born on 18 September 1914 in Great Yarmouth, Jack Cardiff worked both in front of and behind the camera from the age of four. In the 1930s, he acquired a reputation as a proficient camera operator and worked with Ray Rennahan on the first British Technicolor film, *Wings of the Morning* (Harold Schuster, 1937). As director of photography he worked almost exclusively in colour, using the cumbersome Technicolor camera with extraordinary dexterity in Pat Jackson's dramatised documentary *Western Approaches* (1944), and winning an Academy Award for his beautifully atmospheric cinematography on Powell and Pressburger's *Black Narcissus* (1947).

He made an abortive directorial debut with *William Tell*, an independently financed vehicle for Errol Flynn that ran out of money before completion. Twentieth Century-Fox then gave him a five-year contract to direct, beginning with *Intent to Kill*. It was followed by two independent productions: *Beyond This Place*, an incoherent, overwrought mystery melodrama adapted from an A. J. Cronin novel; and *Scent of Mystery*, which, despite being shot in 70mm and initially presented in Smell-O-Vision, performed disastrously in the US and was not released in Britain until 1966. The abridged and deodorised version, retitled *Holiday in Spain*, is pure 'cinema of attractions', with a delightfully dry impersonation of the stereotypical Englishman abroad from Denholm Elliott.

Cardiff's most respectable projects were *Sons and Lovers*, which won an Academy Award for Freddie Francis' mono-

chrome CinemaScope photography and nominations for Best Director and Best Picture; and *Young Cassidy*, based on Sean O'Casey's autobiography, which Cardiff took over from John Ford when Ford fell ill after three weeks' shooting. The former, though regarded by Cardiff as his best film, suffers from an overly schematic adaptation of Lawrence's novel, which the plain, literal direction abets. *Young Cassidy*, while uneven, feels less like a condensed book and is full of good scenes and performances, which surely owe at least as much to Cardiff as to Ford.

Notable among his more exotic assignments are *The Long Ships*, an engagingly tongue-in-cheek Norse epic, and *The Mercenaries*, a Wilbur Smith African adventure whose gloating brutality impressed Martin Scorsese. *The Girl on a Motorcycle*, which Cardiff also photographed, has acquired a cult reputation but is nonetheless a grotesquely silly pop artefact, its attempts at visual style merely vulgar.

After directing two low-budget genre pot-boilers – *Penny Gold*, an old-fashioned policier, and *The Mutations*, a perfunctory mating of *Freaks* and *The Island of Dr Moreau* – Cardiff resumed his former role of director of photography, albeit on a string of considerably less distinguished films than he had been responsible for in the 1940s and 50s. He was made an OBE, and given an honorary Academy Award for his contributions to cinematography, in 2000.
(Sheldon Hall)

BIBLIOGRAPHY: Archer, Steve, 'Out on a Limb with Errol Flynn', *Movie Collector* vol. 1 no. 8, Nov./Dec. 1994, pp. 31–3; Bowyer, Justin, *Conversations with Jack Cardiff: Art, Light and Direction in Cinema* (London: Batsford, 2003); Cardiff, Jack, *Magic Hour* (London: Faber and Faber, 1996); Earnshaw, Tony (ed.), *Painter with Light: A Tribute to Jack Cardiff* (Bradford: National Museum of Photography, Film and Television, 2000); Petrie, Duncan, *The British Cinematographer* (London: BFI, 1996); Scorsese, Martin, 'Martin Scorsese's Guilty Pleasures', *Film Comment*, Sept./Oct. 1978, pp. 63–6.

FILMOGRAPHY: *Montmartre* (doc., 1950); *Montmartre Nocturne* (doc., 1951); *William Tell* (unfinished, 1953); *Intent to Kill* (1958); *Beyond This Place* (US: *Web of Evidence*, 1959); *Scent of Mystery* (US, 1960; re-edited version: *Holiday in Spain*, 1962), *Sons and Lovers* (1960); *My Geisha* (US), *The Devil Never Sleeps* (US: *Satan Never Sleeps*, uncredited dir. additional scenes only, Leo McCarey), *The Lion* (1962); *The Long Ships* (UK/Yug, 1963); *Young Cassidy* (co-dir. John Ford, 1965); *The Liquidator* (1966); *The Mercenaries* (US: *The Dark of the Sun*), *The Girl on a Motorcycle* (US re-edited version: *Naked under Leather*, UK/Fr) (1968); *Penny Gold* (1973); *The Mutations* (1974); *Delius* (doc., 1989); *Vivaldi's Four Seasons* (doc., 1991).

CARNEY, John (1972–) and Tom HALL (1975–)

The work of directors John Carney and Tom Hall is characterised by a freewheeling style of shooting and editing, naturalistic acting and a use of jazz and pop soundtracks. Their concentration on relationship dramas marks them off from other Irish New Wave film-makers obsessed with notions of Irishness and identity.

Carney, a former member of cult Dublin band the Frames, made short films and music videos before collaborating with Hall on a black-and-white video feature film, *November Afternoon*, a Cassavetes-inspired examination of the interaction between two couples who spend a weekend in Dublin haunted by sexual anxieties. The film was well received on the festival circuit and led to further collaboration on the hour-long *Just in Time*, the tale of a middle-aged academic who leaves his lover in London to spend a week in the company of his wife, a painter, at a rural retreat in Ireland. This incisive satire on the new Irish middle class was followed by *Park* (1999), a drama about a schoolgirl's abuse at the hands of a paedophile park attendant in Dublin. While directed with flair, and commendable for its guts in tackling such sensitive subject matter, *Park* lacked the spontaneous character dissections of Carney and Hall's earlier works.

Carney went on to make the bigger-budgeted *On the Edge* (2001), a black comedy about a recklessly suicidal teenager (Cillian Murphy) that demonstrated his talent as a solo director, though he enjoyed more commercial success with Hall, and his brother Kieran Carney, as writer/director of the television comedy series *Bachelors Walk* (2001). The trio's space comedy *Zonad*, despite favourable reports, appears not to have been released.
(Eugene Finn)

BIBLIOGRAPHY: Mulrooney, Deirdre, 'Love in the Afternoon', *Film Ireland*, no. 56, Dec. 1996/Jan. 1997, pp. 18–19; O'Connor, Derek, 'Life on the Edge', *Film West* no. 45, Autumn 2001, p. 14; Shields, Paula, 'The Carney', *Film Ireland*, no. 82, Aug./Sept. 2001, pp. 12–15.

FILMOGRAPHY: John Carney: *Shining Star* (short, Ir, 1995); *Hotel* (short, Ir, 1995); *On the Edge* (Ir, 2001).
John Carney and Tom Hall: *November Afternoon* (Ir, 1996); *Just in Time* (Ir, 1998); *Park* (Ir, 1999).

CARRERAS, Michael (1927–1994)

Michael Carreras, born on 21 December 1927 in London, is better known as a producer than a director. The son of Hammer co-founder Sir James Carreras, he moved into the family business where, after thorough training at the distribution company Exclusive Films, he acted as producer or executive producer on many of Hammer's best-known films. Under the pseudonym Henry Younger, he occasionally contributed screenplays, none of them of any particular merit. As a director, Carreras' output is surprisingly varied. *The Steel Bayonet* is a Second World War film where realistic violence (several of the likeably mundane soldiers come to grisly ends) seems at odds with the unconvincing settings. *Curse of the Mummy's Tomb* makes a dull follow-up to Terence Fisher's *The Mummy* (1959), hampered as it is by a second-rate cast. *Blood from the Mummy's Tomb* is much more interesting, but this should be credited to its chief director Seth Holt, who died of a heart attack during post-production; Carreras' additional footage works against the disturbingly claustrophobic air Holt had strived for.

He seemed much more at home with contemporary horror. *Maniac*, a convoluted story of a drifter who becomes entangled with a mad incestuous family, is psychologically convincing and scarily atmospheric. Carreras himself was particularly proud of *What a Crazy World*, an adaptation of a Joan Littlewood theatrical production featuring Joe Brown and Marty Wilde, two of the more talented pre-Beatles rock and rollers. It is a useful reminder that Hammer had a life beyond horror, one that Carreras was keen to foster. His other 1960s' films include the primitive epic *Slave Girls* and the Jules Verne-like sea fantasy, *The Lost Continent*, both of which have gained a cult following for their extravagant absurdity. Michael Carreras died of cancer in London on 19 April 1994.

(Wheeler Winston Dixon)

BIBLIOGRAPHY: Interview, *Little Shoppe of Horrors*, Apr. 1978, pp. 30–6; 'Michael Carreras', *The House That Hammer Built*, Oct. 1998, pp. 70–4, 113–16; Younger, E. Van, 'Michael Carreras 1927–1994', *Dark Terrors*, Nov. 1994, pp. 42–4.

FILMOGRAPHY: *Cyril Stapleton and the Show Band* (short); *The Eric Winstone Show* (short) (1955); *Just for You* (short); *Eric Winstone's Stagecoach* (short); *Parade of the Bands* (short); *Copenhagen* (short) (1956); *The Edmundo Ross Half Hour* (short); *The Steel Bayonet* (1957); *Visa to Canton* (US: *Passport to China*, 1960); *The Savage Guns* (US/Sp, 1962); *Maniac*; *What a Crazy World* (1963); *Curse of the Mummy's Tomb* (1964); *Slave Girls* (US: *Prehistoric Women*, 1966); *The Lost Continent* (1968); *Blood from the Mummy's Tomb* (co-dir. Seth Holt, 1971); *Shatter* (1974).

CARSTAIRS, John Paddy (1910–1970)

John Paddy Carstairs was born in London in 1910, the son of comedian Nelson Keys. All the Keys brothers (Anthony Nelson, Basil and Roderick) were to make their mark in the film industry, but in John's case only after changing his name by deed poll to avoid charges that he was cashing in on his father's name – Carstairs was his mother's maiden name. He made an amateur film, *The Hero of St Jim's*, in 1927 while still a pupil at Repton public school, which helped to get him his first job in the industry as a camera assistant with Herbert Wilcox. It was the start of an intense, wide-ranging apprenticeship both here and in the US, leading eventually to his professional debut as director with the thriller *Paris Plane* in 1933. Thereafter he averaged over a film a year until his last, *A Weekend with Lulu*, in 1962.

Carstairs was the perfect producer's director, reliably turning out well-crafted films, usually thrillers or comedies, on time and on budget. His best thrillers include *The Saint in London* (1939), *Dancing with Crime* (1947) and *Sleeping Car to Trieste* (1948), where he proved adept in conjuring up forbidding atmosphere on a low budget. Indeed, up to this time the majority of Carstairs' films had been thrillers, notwithstanding his notable George Formby Ealing comedy *Spare a Copper* (1940). The emphasis changed in 1948, after which he made a straight run of eighteen comedies before completing his final thriller in 1961.

This was the excellent *The Devil's Agent*, a hard-edged cold war drama that Carstairs directed with a sure hand.

However, it is for the comedies that Carstairs will be remembered. He had the much underrated skill, both as a writer and a director, of transferring stage-honed comic personas to the big screen in sustained feature-length outings. This, coupled with his personal rapport with comics, gave him a string of successes with Charlie Drake, Jimmy Edwards and Frankie Howerd. But the five films he made for the Rank Organisation with Norman Wisdom constitute his greatest legacy. Carstairs guided the comic through his starring debut, *Trouble in Store* (1953), shielding him from a background of pessimism within Rank. The resulting film triumphed resoundingly at the box office, guaranteeing Wisdom's position as Britain's top post-war film comedian.

Outside his film career, Carstairs directed for stage and television. He was also an exhibited painter and wrote over thirty books between 1937 and 1966, several dealing with the film-making milieu. He died in London on 12 December 1970 after a period of ill health.

(Richard Dacre)

BIBLIOGRAPHY: Carstairs, John Paddy, *Honest Injun!* (London: Hurst & Blackett, 1943); Carstairs, John Paddy, *Hadn't We the Gaiety?* (London: Hurst & Blackett, 1945); Carstairs, John Paddy, *Kaleidoscope and a Jaundiced Eye* (London: Hurst & Blackett, 1946); Dacre, Richard John, *Trouble in Store: Norman Wisdom, a Career in Comedy* (Dundee: T. C. Farries, 1991).

FILMOGRAPHY: *Paris Plane* (1933); *Night Ride*; *Missing, Believed Married*; *Holiday* (doc. short); *Incident in Shanghai*; *Holiday's End*; *Double Exposures* (1937); *Lassie from Lancashire* (1938); *The Saint in London*; *Meet Maxwell Archer* (US: *Maxwell Archer, Detective*) (1939); *Spare a Copper*; *The Second Mr Bush*; *All Hands* (short); *Dangerous Comment* (short); *Now You're Talking* (short) (1940); *Telefootlers* (short); *He Found a Star* (1941); *Dancing with Crime* (1947); *Sleeping Car to Trieste* (1948); *Fools Rush In*; *The Chiltern Hundreds* (US: *The Amazing Mr Beecham*) (1949); *Tony Draws a Horse* (1950); *Talk of a Million* (US: *You Can't Beat the Irish*, 1951); *Treasure Hunt*; *Made in Heaven* (1952); *Trouble in Store*; *Top of the Form* (1953); *Up to His Neck*; *One Good Turn* (1954); *Man of the Moment*; *Jumping for Joy* (1955); *Up in the World* (1956); *The Big Money* (1956; rel. 1958); *Just My Luck* (1957); *The Square Peg* (1958); *Tommy the Toreador* (1959); *Sands of the Desert* (1960); *The Devil's Agent/In Namen des Teufels* (UK/Ir/Ger); *A Weekend with Lulu* (1962); *Top Chef* (doc. short, 1968).

CARTIER, Rudolph (1904–1994)

Rudolph Cartier was born Rudolf Katscher in Vienna on 17 April 1904, the son of a Hungarian silk merchant. He trained as an architect at the Maltura School of Art and from 1925 contributed feature articles, primarily on mountaineering, to *Neues Tagblatt*. After winning a film script competition he went to Berlin where between 1929 and 1933 he worked for Alfred Zeisler at Ufa, collaborating with Egon Eis on scripts for such films as *Der Greifer/Night Birds* (Richard Eichberg, 1930) *Der Schuss in Tonfilmatelier* (Alfred Zeisler, 1930), *Das Gelbe Haus des King-Fu/La Maison jaune de Rio* (Karl Grune, 1931), *Salto Mortale* (E. A. Dupont, 1931) and *Teilnehmer antwortet nicht* (1932), which he co-directed with Marc Sorkin.

Cartier left for Vienna in 1933, where he directed *Unsichtbare Gegner* (1933) for Sam Spiegel, who brought him to London via Paris in 1935 for a project on the opera singer Dame Nellie Melba that did not materialise. He had great difficulty establishing himself in Britain, working uncredited on scripts for Anatole de Grunewald, working on another with Emeric Pressburger that aroused little interest and adapting novels for BIP that went unmade. After internment as an enemy alien from 1940 to 1942, he changed his name from Katscher to Cartier and worked at the Ministry of Information as a script consultant to Ivor Montagu. In 1945 he formed Apollo Films to produce the bizarre melodrama *Corridor of Mirrors* (Terence Young, 1948), but his career only took off when he joined the BBC as a producer and director in 1952. Although he is best known for his adaptation of George Orwell's *1984* (1954), he was also responsible for *The Quatermass Experiment* (1953), *Quatermass II* (1955) and notable dramas such as *It Is Midnight Dr Schweitzer* (1953), *Wuthering Heights* (with Yvonne Mitchell and Richard Todd, 1953), *Liebelei* (1954) and *The Saint of Bleecker Street* (1956). After 1956, he produced another fourteen television dramas for Austrian and German television.

Cartier returned to Britain to direct *Passionate Summer*, an adaptation of Richard Mason's novel *The Shadow and the Peak*, which Robert Hamer had wanted to make at Ealing. As directed by Cartier for Rank it emerges as a plodding colonial saga featuring big Bill Travers as a saintly schoolmaster brought low by three lovesick females: a sexually frustrated headmaster's wife (Yvonne Mitchell), a freckled, destructive adolescent (Ellen Barrie) and a flighty air stewardess (Virginia McKenna). It is an enjoyable farrago but not one that displays any directorial flair. Cartier returned to the BBC, where he remained a prolific director until the mid-1970s, directing *Quatermass and the Pit* (1958), *Mother Courage* (1959), *The Aspern Papers* (1962), another version of *Wuthering Heights* (with Claire Bloom and Keith Michell, 1962), along with episodes of *Maigret* (1961–3), *Z Cars* (1963), several 'Thirty Minute Theatre' dramas and prestigious plays of the month. He died in London on 7 June 1994.

(Kevin Gough-Yates)

BIBLIOGRAPHY: Cartier, Rudolph, BECTU History Project interview, 1991, tape held in the BFI National Library, London; Cartier, Rudolph, 'A Foot in Both Camps', *Films and Filming*, Sept. 1958, pp. 10, 31; Fraser-Cavassoni, Natasha, *Sam Spiegel: The Biography of a Hollywood Legend* (New York: Little, Brown, 2003); Myles, Lynda and Julian Petley, 'Rudolph Cartier', *Sight and Sound*, Spring 1990, pp. 126–9; Myles, Lynda and Michael Poole, 'Rudolph Cartier', *The Late Show*, BBC Television, 1 July 1994; Jacobs, Jason, J. <www.museum.tv/archives/etv/C/htmlC/cartierrudo/cartierrudo.htm>, 23 July 2003.

FILMOGRAPHY (UK only): *Passionate Summer* (aka *Storm over Jamaica*, 1958).

CARTLIDGE, William P. (1942–)

William P. Cartlidge was born in Buckinghamshire in 1942. He rose from second assistant director on *The Young Ones* (Sidney J. Furie, 1961) to associate producer on *The Spy Who Loved Me* (Lewis Gilbert, 1977) and *Moonraker* (Lewis Gilbert, 1979) and executive producer on *The Scarlet Tunic* (Stuart St Paul, 1997). His one venture into directing, an updated adaptation of Oscar Wilde's *An Ideal Husband*, fared badly against Oliver Parker's more lively version.

(Robert Murphy)

FILMOGRAPHY: *An Ideal Husband* (1998).

CASS, Henry (1902–1989)

Henry Cass was born in London on 24 June 1902. He began his career as a stage actor in the 1920s and in 1931 moved into theatre production, becoming Artistic Director of the Old Vic in 1934. His first film was *Lancashire Luck* (1937), in which Wendy Hiller made her debut as the daughter of a carpenter who wins a small fortune on the football pools but objects to her falling for a local aristocrat. Hiller remembered it as a 'very friendly, cosy affair' (McFarlane, p. 295). Between 1941 and 1945, Cass made shorts for Sydney Box's documentary company Verity, including *H.M.S. Minelayer* (1941), *Ask the CAB* (1942) and *Danger Area* (1943). *Jigsaw* (1944), a cautionary tale about 'careless talk' as seen through the eyes of a bereaved woman, was typical ofVerity's story documentary style.

Cass directed Box's independent feature *29, Acacia Avenue* (1945), a risqué comedy by Mabel and Denis Constanduros, which he had previously produced on stage. The film attracted the disapproval of Methodist J. Arthur Rank, but the story of a brother and sister who flirt with, then shy away from, the idea of extramarital sex when their parents go on holiday is mild and enjoyably naive. Cass' next film, *The Glass Mountain* (1949), a lush romance about a married composer who falls in love with an Italian girl after being shot down during the Second World War, was more squarely aimed at the mainstream market. Exotic location photography and a memorable score by Nino Rota helped make it a huge box-office success. Another tear-jerker, *No Place for Jennifer* (1949), scripted by J. Lee Thompson, was notable for the performance of Janette Scott as a nine-year-old who becomes seriously disturbed following her parents' divorce.

In 1950 Cass directed *Last Holiday*, a wry comedy written specifically for the screen by J. B. Priestley, with Alec Guinness as an unassuming salesman who is told he is terminally ill and decides to spend his last weeks in a seaside hotel. The new perspective offered by encroaching death encourages him to act in a radically outspoken way. He transforms the lives of the guests and staff, banishing snobbery and isolation and creating an atmosphere of harmony and co-operation. More conventional comedies followed: *Young Wives' Tale* (1951), about the antics of two married couples who share a house; *Castle in the Air* (1952), with Margaret Rutherford as a genealogist striving to prove the royal ancestry of an impoverished Scottish earl; and *Father's Doing Fine* (1952), a jolly romp about a titled widow with four capricious daughters.

Cass continued to direct until the end of the 1960s – but on diminishingly prestigious pictures. The most interesting are a whodunit, *The High Terrace* (1956), where he makes good use of the theatre setting he obviously knew so well; *Blood of the Vampire* (1958), a grim horror film featuring a charismatic performance from Donald Wolfit; and *Boyd's Shop* (1960), a whimsical Irish tale featuring the Dublin-based Abbey Players. Cass' last three films, *Give a Dog a Bone*, *Mr Brown Comes down the Hill* and *Happy Deathday*, were produced by the Moral Rearmament Association, which he had long supported. His first wife was actress Nancy Hornsby; his second actress Joan Hopkins. He died in Sussex in March 1989.

(Margaret Butler)

BIBLIOGRAPHY: McFarlane, Brian, *An Autobiography of British Cinema* (London: Methuen, 1997); Noble, Peter (ed.), *The British Film Yearbook, 1947-1948* (London: Skelton Robinson, 1947).

FILMOGRAPHY: *Lancashire Luck* (1937); *H.M.S. Minelayer* (doc. short, 1941); *Ask the CAB* (doc. short), *Free House* (doc. short); *The Sword of the Spirit* (doc. short) (1942); *Common Cause* (doc. short), *Danger Area* (doc. short) (1943); *Jigsaw* (doc. short), *Catholics in Britain* (doc. short); *Other Men's Lives* (doc. short) (1944); *The Great Game* (doc. short); 'Famous Scenes from Shakespeare': *Julius Caesar*, *Macbeth* (shorts); *29, Acacia Avenue* (US: *The Facts of Love*) (1945); *The Glass Mountain*; *No Place for Jennifer* (1949); *Last Holiday* (1950); *Young Wives' Tale* (1951); *Castle in the Air*; *Father's Doing Fine* (1952); *The Reluctant Bride* (US: *Two Grooms for a Bride*); *Windfall*; *No Smoking* (1953); *Bond of Fear*, *Breakaway*; *The High Terrace* (1956); *The Crooked Sky*; *Booby Trap*; *Professor Tim* (1957); *Blood of the Vampire* (1958); *The Hand*; *The Man Who Couldn't Walk*; *Boyd's Shop* (1960); *Give a Dog a Bone* (1965); *Mr Brown Comes down the Hill* (1966); *Happy Deathday* (1968).

CATLING, Darrell (1909–1991)

Darrell Charles Catling was born in London on 10 January 1909. He entered the industry in 1931 as an assistant director, and in 1935 began directing short documentaries for Gaumont-British Instructional. His range widened in the 1940s, beginning with *Tom's Ride* (1944), a one-reel comedy with a moral, and Rank's first production for children. Other children's films followed: *Trouble at Townsend* (1946) featured Petula Clark; the serial *Dusty Bates* (1948), particularly successful, made good use of Anthony Newley; while *Under the Frozen Falls* (1948) played its part in history by ushering in David Rawnsley's Independent Frame technique. Catling continued directing documentaries and occasional children's films into the 1960s. He died in Hertfordshire in July 1991.

(Geoff Brown)

BIBLIOGRAPHY: Cardiff, Jack, 'Darrel Catling' (obituary), *FTT & BETA News*, Sept. 1991, p. 24; Field, Mary, *Good Company: The Story of the Children's Entertainment Film Movement in Great Britain 1943–1950* (London: Longmans Green, 1952).

SELECTED FILMOGRAPHY: *Energy* (doc., 1935); *Colour Craft* (doc., 1936); *Into the Blue* (doc., 1940); *Colour in Clay* (doc., 1942); *Bits of Our Aircraft Are Missing* (doc.); *An English Village* (doc.) (1943); *Tom's Ride* (short, 1944); *Trouble at Townsend* (short, 1946); *Under the Frozen Falls*; *Dusty Bates* (five-part serial, US: *The Adventures of Dusty Bates*); *Material Evidence* (short); *The First Year* (doc.) (1948); *The Magic Marble* (short); *The Marble Returns* (short) (1951); *The Case of the Old Rope Man* (short, 1952); *Isle of Bays* (doc., 1955); *Bloodstock* (doc., 1956); *The Cat Gang* (1958); *Learning to Read* (doc., 1967).

CATON-JONES, Michael (1958–)

Michael Caton-Jones was born in Broxburn, near Edinburgh, in 1958. He acquired an early love of the cinema, obtaining free tickets for delivering posters to local shops, and developing an admiration for directors such as Hawks, Ford and Sturges. He left school at fifteen and worked at a variety of jobs before moving to London in 1976. After directing a short film about unemployment, Caton-Jones entered the National Film School. The success of his student films, *Liebe Mutter* and *The Riveter*, brought a commission from Channel 4 to direct *Brond* (1987), an odd political thriller starring Stratford Johns. Caton Jones' flashy directorial style appealed to Steve Woolley of Palace Pictures, who approached him to direct *Scandal*, a retelling of the 1963 Profumo scandal (in which the Minister of War was forced to resign following an affair with a woman who was also closely associated with a Russian diplomat). The film was a box-office and critical success.

Caton-Jones then teamed up with David Puttnam to make *Memphis Belle*, which follows the fortunes of a young US bomber crew on a tour of duty over Germany during the Second World War. Its genre qualities, the link to William Wyler's 1944 documentary of the same name and the male group in adversity theme all demonstrated Caton-Jones' respect for the golden age of Hollywood film-making, and he claimed to draw inspiration from Hawks' *Air Force* (1943).

The success of these two films provided Caton-Jones with his passport to Hollywood. He left armed with an attitude likely to endear him to the studio bosses: 'The bottom line is that you have to make films that make money to keep making films' (Docherty, p. 13). His first American project, the Capra-esque comedy *Doc Hollywood*, did well both critically and commercially. This was followed by the coming-of-age drama *This Boy's Life* and the period action-adventure tale *Rob Roy*. Though an American-financed film, which recaptured the energy and entertainment of early Hollywood epics such as Michael Curtiz's *The Adventures of Robin Hood* (1938), *Rob Roy* drew effectively on British (and Irish) talent, with Liam Neeson as a convincing Scottish hero and Tim Roth as his villainous English adversary.

Caton-Jones' subsequent Hollywood films – *The Jackal*, a loose remake of Fred Zinnemann's *The Day of the Jackal* (1973), and the crime drama *City by the Sea* – have been less impressive; but his *Shooting Dogs*, made for BBC Films, is a worthwhile, realistic treatment of the genocide in Rwanda in 1994, written and produced by David Belton, a BBC journalist who himself witnessed the horrific events. In 2005 Caton-Jones took over the much-delayed *Basic Instinct 2*, relocating the action to London and substituting the solidly reliable David Morrissey for the roster of Hollywood stars cast as adversaries against Sharon Stone. As he admitted: 'I'm very old-fashioned in many ways because all my influences are old-fashioned films that are not necessarily hip or trendy now. I'm a career director just like John Ford; set them up, knock them off' (Hunter, p. 23).

(Martin Hunt)

BIBLIOGRAPHY: Andrew, Geoff, 'Flying Scotsman', *Time Out*, 15 Aug. 1990, pp. 14–16; Docherty, Cameron, 'Non-Local Boy Makes Good', *Scotsman*, 19 Oct. 1991, p. 13; Hunter, Allan, 'Scandal! This is the Affair that was', *Films and Filming*, Mar. 1989, pp. 21–3.

FILMOGRAPHY: *Liebe Mutter* (short, 1986); *The Riveter* (short, 1987); *Scandal* (1989); *Memphis Belle* (UK/Jap/US, 1990); *Doc Hollywood* (US, 1991); *This Boy's Life* (US, 1993); *Rob Roy* (US, 1995); *The Jackal* (US/UK/Jap/Ger/Fr, 1997); *City by the Sea* (US, 2002); *Shooting Dogs* (UK/Ger, 2005); *Basic Instinct 2* (US, 2006).

CATTANEO, Peter (1965–)

Peter Cattaneo was born in London in 1965, the son of animator Tony Cattaneo. After three years studying film at Leeds Polytechnic, he returned to London for the postgraduate film course at the Royal College of Art. His graduation film *Spotters*, about a boy learning to accept his father's obsession with trainspotting, won him the Young Film-maker of the Year award at the 1990 Edinburgh Film Festival.

In 1991 Cattaneo was nominated for an Academy Award and a BAFTA for his short film *Dear Rosie*, about a struggling writer catapulted to fame when her agent publishes a collection of her slimming tips under the title 'The Armchair Slimmer'. Cattaneo moved into television, where he directed a six-part series, *Teenage Health Freak* (1993), for Channel 4 and episodes of *The Bill* (1993–4) before making *Loved Up* (1995), a sympathetic account of a teenage girl's drift into the rave culture of the 1990s, for the BBC.

Loved Up was well received at the Sundance Film Festival and Cattaneo was approached to direct *The Full Monty*, Simon Beaufoy's offbeat tale about unemployed Sheffield steel workers shedding their inhibitions to make a living as male strippers. Although made on a budget of little more than £2 million, and with a star, Robert Carlyle, barely known outside Britain, it proved to be a huge international success. Surprisingly, Cattaneo failed to take advantage of his new-found fame. It was not until 2001 that he directed another film, *Lucky Break*; it proved to be an amiable but poorly structured prison comedy that never looked like emulating the success of *The Full Monty*.

(Sarah Cardwell)

BIBLIOGRAPHY: Hasted, Nick, 'Asset Stripper', *Independent* Tabloid Section, 28 Aug. 1997, pp. 4–5; Marriott, John, 'The Making of the Full Monty: A Magnificent Body of Work', *Guardian*, 13 Dec. 1997, p. 6; Vincent, Sally, 'Winning Streak', *Guardian*, 4 Aug. 2001, p. 32.

FILMOGRAPHY: *Spotters* (short, 1990); *Dear Rosie* (short, 1992); *The Full Monty* (UK/US, 1997); *Lucky Break* (2001); *Opal Dream* (aka *Pobby and Dingan*, Austral/UK, 2006).

CAVALCANTI, Alberto (1897–1982)

In a film-making career spanning half a century and at least half a dozen countries, Brazilian-born Alberto Cavalcanti spent some fifteen years in Britain during the 1930s and 40s, bringing a cosmopolitan outlook and a talent for the poetry of sound and image to both documentary and fiction cinema.

Alberto de Almeida Cavalcanti was born in Rio de Janeiro on 6 February 1897, the son of a noted mathematician. He left Brazil at the age of fifteen to study architecture and interior design at the School of Fine Arts in Geneva, after which he moved to Paris and eventually found work as a set designer with Marcel l'Herbier's Cinégraphic Films. As one of a group of young avant-garde artists surrounding l'Herbier and Louis Delluc, Cavalcanti soon began producing and directing films on his own account, among them the 'city symphony' *Rien que les heures* (1926), which reputedly inspired Dziga Vertov's more celebrated *Man with a Movie Camera* (1929).

In 1934, at the invitation of John Grierson, Cavalcanti left Paris for London to join the GPO Film Unit. There he worked on numerous films in a variety of creative capacities, including producer, director, sound supervisor, editor, scriptwriter and art director. In *Pett and Pott* (1934) – a satirical tale of shopping, the telephone and two suburban families – Cavalcanti established a blend of poetry, realism and fiction that pushed to the limit Grierson's definition of documentary as 'the creative interpretation of actuality'. In *Coal Face* (1935) he offers an audacious visual and aural tone poem celebrating the lives and work of Britain's coal miners. Other documentary-makers argued for a plain, unadorned style more appropriate for a mass audience, but Cavalcanti's commitment to artistic adventurousness attracted young artists like Benjamin Britten and W. H. Auden to the documentary movement. When Grierson left for Canada in 1937 it was Cavalcanti who took over as Head of the Unit.

When war broke out in 1939 Cavalcanti mobilised the Unit to make *The First Days* (Harry Watt/Humphrey Jennings, 1939), which was to set the quietly muted tone of British documentary-making during the war. But it was deemed inappropriate that a Brazilian should be running one of the Government's most important outlets for propaganda, and Cavalcanti went to work for Michael Balcon at Ealing. Here his distinctive aesthetic contribution to British cinema – a melding of actuality and the commonplace with a non-naturalistic, even surreal, approach to fiction – was deployed in feature as well as in documentary films. After producing key Ealing films such as *The Foreman Went to France* (Charles Frend, 1942), he directed the uniquely disturbing *Went the Day Well?* (1942). An army detachment, supposedly Royal Engineers on an exercise, appears in a quiet English village; but it gradually dawns on the villagers that they are Germans who have been parachuted in by night. By the time the traitorous squire has been shot by the vicar's daughter, the village's placid surface has been torn aside to reveal unexpected violence and brutality. The same quality of surrealist unpredictability permeates Cavalcanti's contributions to the portmanteau film *Dead of Night* (1945), particularly in the episode where a ventriloquist, possessed by his dummy, is led into degradation, murder and madness. Two more features followed at Ealing – *Champagne Charlie* and *Nicholas Nickleby* – both outwardly more sunny and undisturbing, but both with edgy undercurrents.

In 1947 Cavalcanti parted company with the studio; the three features he went on to direct – *They Made Me a Fugitive* (Alliance), *The First Gentleman* (Columbia-British) and *For Them That Trespass* (Associated British) – all lie outside the tradition of realism espoused by the documentary movement and by Ealing. By far the most significant of these is *They Made Me a Fugitive*, a grim tale of a discontented RAF ex-officer (Trevor Howard) who seeks excitement in crime. Atmospheric, thrilling and full of fine performances, the film is now regarded as a genuine British film noir; but at the time critics condemned it as

sordid and unsavoury. *The First Gentleman*, based on a West End play and part of a vogue for historical romances that engulfed Britain in the 1940s, is stolidly entertaining, but much less visually adventurous than Basil Dearden and Michael Relph's contemporaneous Ealing film *Saraband for Dead Lovers* (1948). *For Them That Trespass*, the story of a novelist who lets someone else take the blame for a murder he has accidentally committed and then betrays himself by using the murder in a radio play, is more ambitious. But the tale, more loosely told than *They Made Me a Fugitive*, suffers from wooden performances by Stephen Murray and Richard Todd.

Early in 1950 Cavalcanti returned to Brazil to take up a post as Head of Production at the Companhia Cinematografica Vera Cruz. Shortly afterwards, at the height of the cold war and under suspicion of Communist activity, he returned to Europe, where he continued making films until the late 1970s, working in East Germany, France, Israel and elsewhere. During this period he made a brief return to Britain to direct *The Monster of Highgate Ponds*, an hour-long children's film produced by Joy Batchelor and John Halas. He died in Paris on 23 August 1982.

Cavalcanti's British work, defying clear-cut distinctions between art and entertainment, is arguably his best: it is certainly his most consistent. He was an outsider at both the GPO and Ealing, but clearly an inspiring mentor to younger colleagues. The sheer variety of his work in Britain and the problems of categorising his films – documentary or fiction? realism or fantasy?

– make him a fascinating maverick whose valuable contribution to British cinema is too easily overlooked.
(Annette Kuhn)

BIBLIOGRAPHY: Aitken, Ian (ed.), *The Documentary Film Movement: An Anthology* (Edinburgh: Edinburgh University Press, 1998), pp. 179–214; Aitken, Ian, *Alberto Cavalcanti: Realism, Surrealism and National Cinemas* (Trowbridge, Wilts: Flicks Books, 2000); Cavalcanti, Alberto, *Filme e realidade* (Rio de Janeiro: Editora Artenova, 1977); Hillier, Jim, Alan Lovell and Sam Rohdie, 'Interview with Alberto Cavalcanti', *Screen* vol. 13 no. 2, 1972, pp. 36–53; Monegal, Emir Rodriguez, 'Alberto Cavalcanti', *The Quarterly Review of Film, Radio and Television* vol. 9 no. 4, 1955, pp. 341–58.

FILMOGRAPHY (UK only): Documentary: *The Glorious Sixth of June: New Rates*; *Pett and Pott* (1934); *Coal Face* (uncredited, 1935); *Line to Tschierva Hut*; *Men of the Alps*; *Message from Geneva*; *Who Writes to Switzerland?*; *We Live in Two Worlds*; *Four Barriers* (1937); *The Chiltern Country* (1938); *A Midsummer Day's Work* (1939); *Alice in Switzerland*; *La Cause Commune* (1940); *Yellow Caesar* (uncredited, 1941); *Film and Reality* (compilation film, 1942); *Watertight* (1943). Fiction: *Went the Day Well?* (1942); *Champagne Charlie* (1944); *Dead of Night* (co-dirs. Robert Hamer/Basil Dearden/Charles Crichton, 1945); *The Life and Adventures of Nicholas Nickleby*; *They Made Me a Fugitive* (US: *I Became a Criminal*) (1947); *The First Gentleman* (US: *Affairs of a Rogue*); *For Them That Trespass* (1948); *The Monster of Highgate Ponds* (1961).

CELLAN JONES, Simon

Simon Cellan Jones began his career working in lowly capacities on films such as *Ninety Eighty-Four* (Mike Radford, 1984) and television series such as *Edge of Darkness* (Martin Campbell, 1985). He gained directing experience on several single dramas on film for the BBC, including *Bitter Harvest* (1992), *In Your Dreams* (1997) and *Storm Damage* (1999), and the 'One Day a Lemming Will Fly' episode of *Cracker* (1993), but he made his reputation with the highly acclaimed serial *Our Friends in the North* (1996), written by Peter Flannery and set in Newcastle.

In Cellan Jones' first theatrical feature, the FilmFour production *Some Voices*, Daniel Craig, who had been one of the three male leads in *Our Friends in the North*, plays a recovering psychiatric patient released into the care of his brother (David Morrissey), a small-time restaurateur. Although adapted by Joe Penhall from his stage play (performed at the Royal Court), the film is wholly cinematic in style and approach, finding expressive and inventive yet economical visual imagery to convey recurrent mental disturbance. Cellan Jones and Peter Flannery were then reunited in Newcastle for *The One and Only*, a remake of a Danish romantic comedy. Despite some obtrusive plot contrivances and generally unimaginative use of the city's now overfamiliar locations, it is nonetheless very funny and beautifully acted by Justine Waddell and the Australian Richard Roxburgh (achieving the near impossible for an outsider, an immaculate Geordie accent).

Cellan Jones returned to television for *Eroica* (2003), a BBC dramatisation of the first performance of Beethoven's Third Symphony. Though Nick Dear's screenplay tends to be obvious and over explicit in explaining the music's significance for the benefit of classical neophytes, the director is eloquent in his use of the camera to capture the reactions of the recital's listeners. His revisionist *Sherlock Holmes and the Case of the Silk Stocking* (2004), with Rupert Everett as Holmes, Ian Hart as Watson and Helen McCrory as his pushy American fiancée, is visually stylish if not entirely convincing.
(Sheldon Hall)

BIBLIOGRAPHY: Minns, Adam, 'Simon Cellan Jones', *Screen International*, 5 May 2000, p. 34; Van Dijk, Maria, 'Case Study: *The One and Only*', *Screen International*, 26 Apr. 2002, p. 17.

FILMOGRAPHY: *Some Voices* (2000); *The One and Only* (UK/Fr, 2002).

CHADHA, Gurinder (1960–)

Gurinder Chadha was born in Kenya in 1960 and came to Britain with her parents in 1961. She grew up in Southall, London, and studied at the University of East Anglia in the early 1980s. After working as a broadcast journalist, her first directorial venture was *I'm British but . . .*, a documentary made for Channel 4 and the BFI in 1989. The film uses the phenomenon of bhangra music to explore issues of identity and belonging among young British-born Asians.

In 1990 Chadha made her first dramatic short film, *Nice Arrangement*, concerning a British-Asian family on the morning of their daughter's wedding. This was followed by another documentary, *Acting Our Age* (1991), in which elderly Asians living in Southall recount their experiences of living in Britain. In 1993 these various concerns came together in Chadha's first feature film, the comedy-drama *Bhaji on the Beach*, which centres on the experiences of a group of Asian women from three generations on a day trip to Blackpool. As Chadha has said, in the

film 'You have tradition on the one side and modernity on the other, Indianness on the one side, Englishness on the other, cultural specificity and universality – but in fact there is a scale between each of these polarities and the film moves freely between them' (Bhattacharyya and Gabriel, pp. 60–1).

After a two-part drama for the BBC, *Rich Deceiver* (1995), and a number of television documentaries, Chadha went to Los Angeles to make her next feature film, *What's Cooking?*, a series of overlapping stories involving four families (Hispanic, Vietnamese, African-American and Jewish), all preparing for Thanksgiving dinner. Once again the film stresses diversity over difference through an increasingly adept mix of drama and comedy.

Chadha's next film, *Bend It Like Beckham*, is her most accomplished. Set in Southall where Chadha grew up, it tells the story of a young Asian woman trying to pursue her ambitions as a footballer while accommodating the demands of family and tradition. Chadha presents a subtly nuanced picture of a very specific community and the film makes the point that British-Asian experiences are as diverse as those of any cultural or ethnic group. Rewardingly, it proved to be an international success – popular with audiences from Italy to India as well as in Britain and the USA.

Rather than taking up invitations to Hollywood, Chadha chose to go to India to make *Bride and Prejudice*, a cross-cultural musical adaptation of Jane Austen's *Pride and Prejudice*. Critics were generally unimpressed, but the transfer of this quintessentially English eighteenth-century tale to twenty-first-century India works surprisingly well and the film has attracted wide audiences.

(Martin Hunt)

BIBLIOGRAPHY: Bhattacharyya, Gargi and John Gabriel, 'Gurinder Chadha and the *Apna* Generation', *Third Text*, Summer 1994, pp. 55–63; Korte, Barbara and Claudia Sternberg, *Bidding for the Mainstream? Black and Asian British Film since the 1990s* (Amsterdam and New York: Rodopi, 2004); Wambu, Onyekachi and Kevin Arnold, *A Fuller Picture: The Commercial Impact of Six British Films with Black Themes in the 1990s* (London: BFI, 1999).

FILMOGRAPHY: *Nice Arrangement* (short, 1992); *Bhaji on the Beach* (1993); *What's Cooking?* (US, 2000); *Bend It Like Beckham* (2002); *Bride and Prejudice* (2004).

CHAFFEY, Don (1917–1990)

In a cinema career stretching over thirty years, Don Chaffey directed stories featuring Raquel Welch and a fur bikini; prostitutes; Lassie; a crazed Lana Turner; Edinburgh's favourite terrier, Greyfriars Bobby; artificial insemination; Jason, the Argonauts and the Golden Fleece; and Bob Monkhouse as a dental student. The quality of his direction was fitful, sometimes veering between the mannered and lumbering in the same film, but you could rarely claim to be bored.

Donald G. Chaffey was born in Hastings on 5 August 1917. After attending Hastings Grammar School he worked in the Lime Grove studios' art department. By 1947 he was designing sets for Lewis Gilbert's *The Little Ballerina* and other Gaumont-British Instructional children's films. Apart from two early factual shorts, Chaffey's own first directorial jobs were also for the juvenile market; his first 'adult' feature was a routine thriller, *Time Is My Enemy*. Audiences took much more notice of the lurid vice-ring exposé *The Flesh Is Weak* (1957), one of two exploitation dramas made for the producer Raymond Stross; the second, *A Question of Adultery*, trapped Anthony Steel and Julie London in an unsavoury film that trampled clumsily over its subject matter, the problems of infertility. Chaffey's skills in heightened drama were much better displayed in *The Man Upstairs* (1958), made for A.C.T. Films, a taut drama about social tensions, with Richard Attenborough as a rooming-house resident running amok; and *Danger Within*, a clever and grim tale of betrayal in an Italian prisoner-of-war camp.

In 1960 *Dentist in the Chair*, the first of two frantic comedies for producer Bertram Ostrer, suggested that this was not Chaffey's forte, an impression only partially dispelled by the later black comedy *A Jolly Bad Fellow*. *Greyfriars Bobby* (1961), slow, sentimental and entirely amiable, inaugurated a clutch of other fondly received Disney entertainments, most notably *The Horse without a Head* (1963) and *The Three Lives of Thomasina* (1964). As the 1960s advanced, fantasy steadily became Chaffey's preferred mode. In Charles Schneer's production *Jason and the Argonauts* (1963) and Hammer's tomfoolery *One Million Years B.C.* (1966), Chaffey's direction was hard-pressed to compete with Ray Harryhausen's special effects or Raquel Welch's anatomy. But he stirred the films' plots merrily, something he was unable to achieve later with *The Viking Queen* or *Creatures the World Forgot*.

Chaffey's gift for attracting bizarre assignments led him in 1974 to *Persecution*, a tawdry psycho-drama featuring Lana Turner; another Hollywood veteran, Lassie, had only slightly better luck in *The Magic of Lassie*. Prospects once more improved with Disney: if *Pete's Dragon* (Pete was orphaned, the dragon animated) never quite gelled, *Ride a Wild Pony*, shot in Australia, handled its own outdoor adventure with robustness and charm.

Since the mid-1950s, Chaffey's bulging portfolio had included British television work – he contributed, among other series, to *The Adventures of Robin Hood*, *The Four Just Men* and *The Avengers*. With *Charlie's Angels* in 1976 he continued business in America, including stints on *Fantasy Island* and the late 1980s' revival of *Mission: Impossible* – entirely suitable series for a director who in a long career never turned down any fantasy, however impossible. Don Chaffey died of heart disease on Kawau Island, New Zealand, on 13 November 1990.

(Geoff Brown)

BIBLIOGRAPHY: Kaminsky, Stuart M., 'Don Chaffey', *Film Reader* no. 1, 1975, p. 78; Maltin, Leonard, *The Disney Films*, 3rd edn (New York: Hyperion, 1995).

FILMOGRAPHY: *Cape Cargoes* (short); *Cathedral City* (short) (1949); *The Mysterious Poacher* (1950); *The Case of the Missing Scene* (1951); *Skid Kids*; *Bouncer Breaks Up* (short); *A Good Pull-Up* (short); *Watch Out!* (short); *The Mask* (short); *Strange Stories* (co-dir. John

Guillermin) (1953); *Time Is My Enemy* (1954); *Dead on Time* (short, 1955); *The Secret Tent* (1956); *The Girl in the Picture*; *The Flesh Is Weak* (1957); *The Man Upstairs* (1958); *A Question of Adultery*; *Danger Within* (US: *Breakout*) (1959); *Lies My Father Told Me*; *Dentist in the Chair* (1960); *Nearly a Nasty Accident*; *Greyfriars Bobby*; *A Matter of WHO* (1961); *The Webster Boy* (1962); *The Horse without a Head*; *Jason and the Argonauts*; *The Three Lives of Thomasina* (1963); *A Jolly Bad Fellow* (US: *They All Died Laughing*); *The Crooked Road* (1964); *One Million Years B.C.* (1966); *The Viking Queen* (1967); *A Twist of Sand* (1968); *Creatures the World Forgot* (1971); *Clinic Xclusive* (US: *With These Hands*, 1972); *Charley-One-Eye* (1972; rel. 1974); *Persecution* (1974); *Ride a Wild Pony* (US, 1975); *The Fourth Wish* (Austral, 1976); *Born to Run* (US), *Pete's Dragon* (US) (1977); *The Magic of Lassie* (US, 1978); *C.H.O.M.P.S.* (US, 1979).

CHAPLIN, Charles (1889–1977)

Charles Spencer Chaplin was born in Kennington, south London, on 16 April 1889 to music-hall parents, though his alcoholic father was soon to disappear and his mother would increasingly suffer from debilitating mental problems. At the age of five Chaplin took to the stage and within two years enjoyed sufficient success to catch the eye of comedy impresario Fred Karno. While touring America for Karno in 1912, Chaplin was poached by Mack Sennett and began appearing in films. His apprenticeship with Sennett rapidly turned him into a major comic star and when he left in 1915 Chaplin was already well on the path to cinematic immortality.

Chaplin's impoverished Victorian working-class roots colour all his Hollywood work and are perfectly encapsulated in his comic persona of the little tramp, a true icon of world cinema. But by the 1950s his resentment at the creeping hostility from his host nation over his perceived Communist values began to distort his clarity of vision. With his first British feature *A King in New York* he turned ferociously on his tormentors, mocking their hypocritical views on freedom. Bitterness is to the fore and the crudeness of his argument is not leavened by enough comic moments. But at least Chaplin retains the balletic grace of the true slapstick clown that his directorial style – proscenium framing of complete routines to emphasise body movement – is designed to showcase.

Unfortunately, in his second British comedy, *A Countess from Hong Kong*, he allows himself only a cameo role and his heavyweight leads (Marlon Brando, Sophia Loren) are ill served by such a rigid

style and overcompensate by mugging and frenetic action. The film marked a dispiriting end to Chaplin's career, but it confirms that it was as the custodian of his own undisputed genius that his talents as a director were best employed. Chaplin was knighted in 1975. He died in Vevey, Switzerland, on 25 December 1977.

(Richard Dacre)

BIBLIOGRAPHY: Chaplin, Charles, *My Autobiography* (London: Bodley Head, 1964); Huff, Theodore, *Charlie Chaplin* (New York: Henry Schuman, 1951); Robinson, David, *Chaplin: His Life and Art* (London: William Collins, 1988).

FILMOGRAPHY (UK only): *A King in New York* (1957); *A Countess from Hong Kong* (1966).

CHELSOM, Peter (1956–)

Peter Chelsom was born in Blackpool on 20 April 1956. His first steps in the entertainment business were as an actor, making regular appearances on stage and television, in Alan Bennett's *An Englishman Abroad* (John Schlesinger, 1983), for example. His short film *Treacle*, which reflected his fascination with end-of-the-pier showbusiness, comic traditions and his Blackpool roots, was followed by a feature, *Hear My Song*, loosely based on real events in the life of tax-fugitive Irish tenor Josef Locke. A desperate impresario wants to get the great man to do a concert in Liverpool despite the attentions of a police officer bent on vengeance. Chelsom's sympathy with actors manifests itself in a string of fine performances, and his ability to get the best out of visual gags without disrupting the narrative marked him out as a director to watch.

The masterful Blackpool-set *Funny Bones* was even more impressive. Chelsom and his co-scriptwriter Peter Flannery take on serious issues about comedy: originality versus tradition, verbal versus physical, the relationship between comedy and cruelty, the relationship between comedy and tragedy. The son of a great American comic struggles to follow in his father's footsteps and comes to Blackpool in search of a routine he can purchase to revive his fortunes. Instead he discovers the roots and traditions that nurtured his father's career and also comes into contact with his own stepbrother (Lee Evans), the naturally gifted visual comic he can never be. Jerry Lewis is the father, here largely eschewing physical comedy in an effortless demonstration of verbal comic delivery. Chelsom gives space for fabulous performances by a string of great comic players – including rare film appearances from clowns George Carl and Freddie Davis – but nothing in the film is gratuitous.

Since *Funny Bones* Chelsom has been based in America. He apparently clashed in an unequal battle with star Warren Beatty during the troubled shoot of his Hollywood debut *Town & Country*. Before the reworked film emerged to general disdain, Chelsom had released *The Mighty*, a welcome return to a more intimate style. *Serendipity*, his first commercial success since *Hear My Song*, followed in 2001. An American man (John Cusack) and an Englishwoman (Kate Beckinsale) clash over a pair of gloves in Bloomingdale's department store one Christmas; they fall in love, but leave it to chance whether they will meet again. Several years later both are on the verge of marrying someone else but make a last desperate attempt to seek each other out. The unique zaniness of *Funny Bones* is much watered down, but the charm and the visual flair remain. Chelsom's remake of Masayuki Suo's *Shall we dansu?* (1996), with Richard Gere and Jennifer Lopez, confirmed his movement into the mainstream.

(Richard Dacre)

BIBLIOGRAPHY: Medhurst, Andy, 'Unhinged Invention', *Sight and Sound*, Oct. 1995, pp. 6–10.

Freddie Davis, Lee Evans and George Carl in *Funny Bones* (Peter Chelsom, 1995)

FILMOGRAPHY: *Treacle* (short, 1987); *Hear My Song* (1991); *Funny Bones* (UK/US, 1995); *The Mighty* (US, 1998); *Town & Country* (US); *Serendipity* (US) (2001); *Shall We Dance* (US/Can, 2004).

CHISNELL, Frank (1898–?)

Frank Chisnell was born in Chelsea, London, on 16 September 1898. After sixteen years working in newsreels, he formed his own production company in 1946, making three-reel shorts and B-features, none of them distinguished.

(Robert Murphy)

FILMOGRAPHY: *Tom Tom Topia* (short, 1946); *Jim the Penman* (1947); *It Happened in Soho* (1948); *Rover and Me*; *Slick Tartan* (short) (1949).

CHORLTON, Michael C. (1913–)

Born in Disley, Cheshire, on 27 December 1913, Michael Chorlton was a respected film editor in the 1940s, working most notably on *Love on the Dole* (John Baxter, 1941), *Dear Octopus* (Harold French, 1943) and *The Silver Fleet* (Gordon Wellesley/Vernon Sewell, 1943). He also edited some naughtiness out of *The Wicked Lady* (Leslie Arliss, 1945) to fit the film for American release. Chorlton directed occasional documentaries and location sequences (including the motorbike shots in the Powell/Pressburger *A Matter of Life and Death*, 1946), but managed only one fiction feature, the low-budget *Late at Night*, a weakly handled underworld thriller.

(Geoff Brown and Robert Murphy)

FILMOGRAPHY: *Salute the Soldier* (doc., 1944); *Late at Night* (1946).

CHRISTIAN, Roger (1944–)

Roger Christian was born in London on 25 February1944. He gained experience as associate art director on Ken Russell's *Mahler* (1974) before making his reputation as a brilliant set decorator on *Star Wars* (George Lucas, 1977) and art director on *Alien* (Ridley Scott, 1979). He then took the unusual step of training to be a director at the National Film School, and his first short film, *Black Angel*, was released as support for *The Empire Strikes Back* (Irvin Kershner, 1979). This medievalised reworking of Ambrose Bierce's *An Occurrence at Owl Creek Bridge* was followed by another short, *The Dollar Bottom*, and his first feature film, *The Sender*, a psychic thriller distinguished by genuinely terrifying moments and powerful performances from Zeljko Ivanek and Shirley Jones.

Christian's subsequent career as a director has been erratic. He followed *The Sender* with an inept Australian space opera, *Lorca and the Outlaws*, and *Nostradamus*, an ambitious Euro-pudding that failed to cash in on millennial interest in the sixteenth-century seer. He moved to America to make *The Final Cut* (1995), *Underworld* (1996) and *Masterminds* (1997), small, semi-eccentric, direct-to-video thrillers; and George Lucas had sufficient faith in Christian's visual flair to employ him as second-unit director on *Star Wars Episode 1. The Phantom Menace* (1999). John Travolta then chose him to direct his pet project, *Battlefield Earth: A Saga of the Year 3000*, an adaptation of the science-fiction novel written by Scientology founder L. Ron Hubbard. The resulting epic proved a critical and commercial disaster, but Christian soldiered on with *Bandido*, a Mexican spy thriller, and *American Daylight*, a romantic thriller, written by Farrukh Dhondy, starring Nick Moran as an unhappy American millionaire who falls for a telephonist before realising that she is based in a call centre in India. If Christian's career has yet to yield a masterpiece, at least he can never be accused of being dull and predictable.

(Kim Newman)

BIBLIOGRAPHY: Bancroft, Shelley, 'School Report: Class of '78', *AIP and Co*, Nov. 1985, p. 22; Jones, Alan, '*2084*: Interview with Roger Christian', *Starburst*, May 1984, pp. 34–7; Persons, Dan, '*Battlefield Earth*: Roger Christian', *Cinefantastique*, June 2000, pp. 22–4.

FILMOGRAPHY: *Black Angel* (short, 1980); *Dollar Bottom* (short, 1981); *The Sender* (1982); *Lorca and the Outlaws* (1985); *Nostradamus* (UK/Ger, 1994); *The Final Cut* (US, 1995); *Underworld* (US/Can, 1996); *Masterminds* (US, 1997); *Star Wars Episode 1: The Phantom Menace* (2nd unit dir., George Lucas, 1999); *Battlefield Earth: A Saga of the Year 3000* (US, 2000); *Bandido* (Mex/US/Ger, 2001; rel. 2004); *American Daylight* (Ind, 2004).

CINEMA ACTION (1968–)

The Cinema Action Collective was founded in London in 1968. It was the first of a range of similar collectives, such as Amber (1969), Berwick Street Film Collective (1970) and the London Women's Film Group (1972). Their work was characterised by a determination to aid the direct action of working-class people, acting to defend their rights.

Cinema Action films were broadly speaking 'campaign' films, outlining a specific cause and calling for support. For instance, *Not a Penny on the Rents*, made in 1968, depicted the London rent strikes of that year, and the various tenants' meetings that were called to protest at the Greater London Council's attempts to increase council rents. *London Transport* (1969) showed the tube strikers and their fight for decent wages and acceptable safety standards. *People of Ireland* (1973) examined the fight for civil rights in Northern Ireland by looking at the causes and effects of the 1969 Battle of the Bogside. The common thread running through the films is the recognition that these struggles are interconnected and that solidarity between different groups is essential to the fight for a fairer society.

To Cinema Action, film-making was part of a social process. They regarded their films as evolving projects, and encouraged the audience to participate in their creation through dialogue. To this end, discussions after screenings were vital, a tradition that can be traced back to the workers' film societies of the 1930s. A key example is *The Miners' Film*, initially concerned with the 1974 miners' strike. First produced during 1974–5, it eschewed voiceover narration, preferring to allow the miners and their families to speak for themselves; it made connections to previous struggles in the same communities, and it showed the links to other parts of the labour movement. During the miners' strike of 1984, this film was updated by framing a screening of the 1975 film with current strikers talking about their experiences.

The feature-length *So That You Can Live* (1981) broke new ground, focusing on the life of a single individual, Cardiff union convenor Shirley Butts, and her struggle to survive in a climate increasingly hostile to union activity. Cinema Action's last two films, *Rocinante* (1986) and *Bearskin: An Urban Fairytale* (1989), both directed by Eduardo and Ann Guedes for Channel 4, are allegorical and avant-garde and seem to defy the group's commitment to relevance and accessibility.

(Paul Ward)

BIBLIOGRAPHY: 'Cinema Action', in Margaret Dickinson (ed.), *Rogue Reels: Oppositional Film in Britain 1945–90* (London: BFI, 1999), pp. 263–88; Glyn, David and Paul Marris, 'Seven Years of Cinema Action', *Afterimage* no. 6, 1976, pp. 64–85.

FILMOGRAPHY: *White Paper*; *Not a Penny on the Rents* (1968); *London Transport* (1969); *Squatters*; *GEC I*; *Vauxhalls*; *Us All*; *Fighting the Bill* (1970); *The U.C.S. Struggle* (1971); *Hands off Student Unions* (1972); *People of Ireland*; *Arise Ye Workers* (1973); *The Miners' Film* (1975; updated version, 1984); *Viva Portugal* (1975); *Class Struggle: Film from the Clyde* (1977); *So That You Can Live* (1981); *Rocking the Boat* (1983); *Rocinante* (1986); *Bearskin: An Urban Fairytale* (UK/Port, 1989).

CLAIR, René (1898–1981)

Clair was born René Lucien Chomette in Paris on 11 November 1898, the son of a soap merchant. At the age of seven he was given a puppet theatre and began to mount productions using his own scripts. With his parents' active encouragement he resolved to become a writer and in 1919, after war service in the ambulance corps, launched his career as a journalist. His involvement in cinema began almost casually – to amuse himself he took roles as an extra – but the medium soon captured his interest and he directed his first film, *Paris qui dort*, in 1923. Clair's greatest success of the silent era was *Un Chapeau de paille d'Italie* (1927), a scintillating adaptation of the famous Labiche stage farce. His international reputation was secured by his first four sound movies: *Sous les toits de Paris* (1930), *Le Million* (1931), *À Nous la liberté* (1932) and *Quatorze juillet* (1932) – light, effervescent and widely influential comedies that made witty and creative use of the new technology of sound.

His attempt at a more pointed political satire, *Le Dernier milliardaire* (1934), was poorly received in France and Clair, disillusioned by the experience, accepted an offer from Alexander Korda to work in Britain. *The Ghost Goes West* is a whimsical story about a brash American millionaire (Eugene Pallette) who buys a haunted Scottish castle and ships it to Florida. Robert Donat gives a likeable performance in the double role of the castle ghost and his present-day descendant, but the film lacks the technical audacity and dancing lightness of Clair's earlier films, falling back on conventional national stereotypes for most of its laughs. Even so, it scored a commercial success, and Clair went on to direct another film in Britain. *Break the News*, with Maurice Chevalier and Jack Buchanan (uneasily paired as a song-and-dance team) embroiled in a far-fetched plot about Chevalier faking Buchanan's death for publicity purposes. The director's heart evidently was not in it, and the film is flat and drably shot.

Back in France Clair embarked on an unexpected project, a semi-documentary called *Air pur* about poor city children being taken to the country, but it was aborted on the outbreak of war. He spent the war years in America, making four films – *The Flame of New Orleans* (1941), *I Married a Witch* (1942), *It Happened Tomorrow* (1944) and *And Then There Were None* (1945) – before returning to France in 1946. His later films, not surprisingly, rarely recaptured the light-hearted nature of his pre-war French movies, but gained in maturity and emotional depth. In the late 1950s he came under attack from the *nouvelle vague* school as a representative of the ossified *cinéma de papa* that they loathed. His last films were critically dismissed, and his reputation is still at a lower standing than it deserves. He died in Neuilly on 15 March 1981.

(Philip Kemp)

BIBLIOGRAPHY: Dale, R. C., *The Films of René Clair* (Metuchen, NJ: Scarecrow Press, 1986); McGear, Celia, *René Clair* (Boston, MA: Twayne, 1980).

FILMOGRAPHY (UK only): *The Ghost Goes West* (1935); *Break the News* (1938).

CLARK, Jim (1931–)

James Clark was born in Boston, Lincolnshire, in 1931. His interest in films was sparked at the age of ten by his father's gift of a 9.5mm projector. He began his career in his family's printing business, but established links with other aspiring film-makers through the film society movement. In 1952 he was taken on as a cutting-room assistant at Ealing Studios. By the 1960s he had established himself as an accomplished and innovative editor, working with Jack Clayton on his two most ambitious and complex films: *The Innocents* (1961) and *The Pumpkin Eater* (1964). He also edited John Schlesinger's *Darling* and struck up a productive partnership with the director, continued over several films, including *Midnight Cowboy* (1969), *The Day of the Locusts* (1975), *Marathon Man* (1976) and *Yanks* (1979).

Clark's early film-making efforts included an adventurous short film, *Summer Daydream*, in 1956, and a documentary about the 1913 Senghenydd mining disaster in 1964 (two years before tragedy engulfed the nearby village of Aberfan). A children's film, *The Christmas Tree*, followed in 1969, but the feature films he subsequently directed were sub-standard. *Every Home Should Have One* is one of a clutch of relentlessly zany comedies that have given British cinema of the 1960s a bad name; while *Rentadick*, a lame comedy, and *Madhouse*, a formulaic horror film, exemplify all the shoddiness of the succeeding decade. For

Clark, these were not very important diversions from an increasingly prestigious editing career, which culminated in 1985 in his Best Editor Academy Award for *The Killing Fields* (Roland Joffé). In 1986–7 he served as Senior Vice-President in charge of production during David Puttnam's ill-fated reign at Columbia Pictures. He remains a well-respected and liked figure, as willing to work on interesting low-budget films, such as Mike Leigh's *Vera Drake* (2004), as on Hollywood blockbusters.

(Robert Murphy)

BIBLIOGRAPHY: 'Cutter's Way' (interview), *Stills* no. 11, Apr./May 1984, pp. 64–5; 'Marty Feldman's First Film is a "Verbal Treat"', *Today's Cinema*, 22 Sept. 1969, p. 5; Perkins, Roy and Martin Stollery, *British Film Editors: 'The Heart of the Movie'* (London: BFI, 2004); 'The Crisis We Deserve: Questions to Billington/Boorman/Brownlow/Clark/Clement/Hall', *Sight and Sound*, Autumn 1970, pp. 172–8.

FILMOGRAPHY: *Summer Daydream* (short, 1956); *Senghenydd* (doc. short, 1964); *The Christmas Tree*; *Soldier 67* (doc. short) (1966); *Every Home Should Have One*; *Day of Rest* (short) (1970); *Rentadick* (1972); *Madhouse* (1974); *Honky Tonk Freeway* (2nd unit dir., John Schlesinger, 1981).

CLARKE, Alan (1935–1990)

Alan Clarke was born in Birkenhead, Cheshire, on 28 October 1935, the son of an insurance salesman. He directed only three films specifically for cinema release; the bulk of his prolific output being made for television. A radical, uncompromising and innovative director, his best work concerned the exposure of injustice towards the most despised and neglected groups in society.

After leaving grammar school and completing National Service, he turned his back on a steady job as an insurance clerk and emigrated to Canada, working as a gold miner before enrolling in a course in Radio and Television Arts in Toronto between 1958 and 1961. He returned to England after graduating to work in television, moving to the BBC in 1969 where he began to develop his directorial style in *The Wednesday Play* and *Play for Today*. Clarke's three best-regarded works dealt with the violence of young males. He achieved notoriety with *Scum* (1978), a brutal exposé of conditions in Borstal starring Phil Daniels and Ray Winstone. A timorous BBC banned the film before it could be shown, but it was remade as a feature, released in 1979. *Made in Britain* (1983), written by David Leland, starred Tim Roth as Trevor, an incandescently violent, racist skinhead. For the first time Clarke used the Steadicam to shoot the characters in long, continuous takes to give the impression of ceaseless motion and neurotic energy, a technique he used extensively in later films. The final film of this 'trilogy', *The Firm* (1988), starred Gary Oldman as 'Bex' Bissell, a wisecracking estate agent, addicted to football violence. No solution is offered to the problems of their protagonists, and their violence is not explained by social deprivation, but as an atavistic force released by a Thatcherite morality that emphasised individuality at the expense of society.

Clarke's 1980s' films made for the cinema are very different. *Billy the Kid and the Green Baize Vampire* is a Brechtian musical about snooker that attracted little critical or box-office attention at the time; but Trevor Preston's witty script and fine performances from Alun Armstrong, Phil Daniels and Bruce Payne have subsequently brought it a loyal cult following. *Rita, Sue and Bob Too*, based on a play by the young Bradford writer Andrea Dunbar, was more immediately successful, demonstrating Clarke's talent for comedy. A raunchy tale about a *ménage à trois* between two working-class teenagers and a married middle-aged man, set around a run-down Bradford council estate, its humour does not dilute the bleakness of the girls' lives.

Before Clarke's premature death from cancer on 24 July 1990 in London he was experimenting with a minimalist style. *Elephant* (1988) is the most extreme example, a 16mm colour film of eighteen killings in Northern Ireland. Critical appreciation has been hampered by an unjust tendency to dismiss Clarke as an ultra-realist, lacking in art and artifice, but there is an increasing recognition that his films represent a trenchant and original contribution to British cinema.

(Andrew Spicer)

BIBLIOGRAPHY: *Director Alan Clarke* (Corin Campbell-Hill, 12 July 1991); Kelly, Richard (ed.), *Alan Clarke* (London: Faber and Faber, 1998); Thomson, David, 'Walkers in the World: Alan Clarke', *Film Comment*, May/June 1993, pp. 78–83.

FILMOGRAPHY: *Scum* (1979); *Billy the Kid and the Green Baize Vampire* (1985); *Rita, Sue and Bob Too* (1986).

CLARKE, Frank (1956–)

Frank Clarke was born in 1956 in Kirkby, Liverpool. He left school with no qualifications, but drifted into theatre work after meeting Chris Bernard. Turning to writing he worked on the Channel 4 soap opera *Brookside*, and scripted *Letter to Brezhnev*, which was funded as a low-budget feature film by Channel 4 and Palace Pictures. This sharp-edged romantic comedy-drama about two working-class Liverpool girls and two

Russian sailors they meet on shore leave, boisterously directed by Bernard and making lively use of its talented young cast (Alfred Molina, Peter Firth, Alexandra Pigg and Clarke's sister Margi), was a surprise hit with audiences and critics alike.

Clarke followed the success of *Letter to Brezhnev* by scripting the gay drama *The Fruit Machine* (Philip Saville, 1988) for Granada Television. It was less well received, with a number of reviewers commenting on the film's uneven blend of realism and fantasy. Clarke felt that veteran director Saville was not fully attuned to his script, and directed his next film himself with backing from the independent distributor, Blue Dolphin. *Blonde Fist* is a comedy-drama starring Margi Clarke as a woman who has inherited the boxing skills of her bare-knuckle fighter father. Although the premise, and the setting in New York and Liverpool, seemed promising, Clarke's direction was generally perceived as inadequate and the film received hostile reviews and took little at the box office. Clarke has subsequently run a casting agency in Liverpool.

(Martin Hunt)

BIBLIOGRAPHY: McCoid, Bill, 'Big Mouth, Big Script, Big Hopes of Hitting the Jackpot', *Television Today*, 10 Dec. 1987, p. 20; Newman, Kim, 'Review: *Blonde Fist*', *Empire,* Dec. 1991, p. 36; Salewicz, Chris, 'Moscow on the Mersey', *Time Out*, 7 Nov. 1985.

FILMOGRAPHY: *Blonde Fist* (1991).

CLAVELL, James (1924–1994)

James Clavell was born Charles Edmund Du Maresq de Claville in Sydney, Australia, on 10 October 1924. He spent much of the Second World War in a Japanese prisoner-of-war camp, an experience that formed the basis for his first novel, *King Rat* (1962). After emigrating to America in 1953 he entered the film industry, first as a screenwriter with *The Fly* (Kurt Neumann, 1958), then as producer-director with *Five Gates to Hell* (1959).

His greatest success in the cinema came with *To Sir, with love*, which he adapted from the novel by E. R. Braithwaite about a West Indian teacher (Sidney Poitier) in a tough East End school. Filmed in London for $640,000, it grossed $19 million in the US, but beneath its swinging, streetwise surface it is a glib, sentimental film that makes gratingly repetitious use of Lulu's title song.

Clavell's final two films were expensive period dramas that achieve both vivid historical authenticity and a strikingly lyrical, poetic quality. *Where's Jack?*, set in eighteenth-century London and filmed at Dublin's Ardmore Studios, features a rare serious performance from Tommy Steele as Jack Sheppard and a charismatic one from producer-star Stanley Baker as his nemesis Jonathan Wild. *The Last Valley*, a magnificent, cerebral epic set during the Thirty Years War, is full of gory detail yet pervaded by an air of enchantment that lifts it into the realm of allegory. Filmed in the Tyrol at a cost of $8 million, it was the last film to be shot in 70mm Todd-AO for over two decades, and benefits from one of Michael Caine's finest screen performances as the German mercenary captain.

Neither of these films was well received and Clavell returned to writing novels, notably the best-selling *Shôgun* (1975), though he occasionally served as producer for their television and film adaptations. He died in Vevey, Switzerland, on 7 September 1994.

(Sheldon Hall)

BIBLIOGRAPHY: Clarke, Sue, 'My Position Is One of Control – James Clavell', *Today's Cinema*, 28 July 1969, p. 6; '"No Deal on *To Sir* if Poitier and I Took Salaries": Clavell', *Hollywood Reporter*, 31 July 1967, p. 4.

FILMOGRAPHY (UK only): *To Sir, with Love* (1967); *Where's Jack?* (1969); *The Last Valley* (1971).

CLAYDON, Phil (1976–)

Philip James Claydon was born in Bury St Edmunds, Suffolk, on 9 January 1976. When he was fifteen, with backing from the Prince's Trust, he made *Legion*, a short film set in a future where drug gangs terrorise rural areas. More shorts followed during his four years at Newport Film School. Claydon's constructive criticism of a horror film treatment from Welsh production company CSI led to an offer to direct the film himself. Unfortunately this turned out to be a case of too much too soon. *Alone* is packed with kinetic energy but the unseen, sexually indeterminate serial killer is a depressingly derivative creation, while John Shrapnel's world-weary detective is saddled with an unbelievable female assistant and embarrassing dialogue. Claydon's sympathetic treatment of the first three female victims, lonely young women surprised at being singled out for murder, suggests hope for his future, but *Alone* was not considered enticing enough to horror film aficionados to merit cinema release and slipped straight to the video/DVD market.

(Robert Murphy)

BIBLIOGRAPHY: Falk, Quentin, 'Through the Lens Darkly', *Exposure*, Spring 2001, pp. 28–9

FILMOGRAPHY: *Legion* (short, 1992); *Skipping without Rope* (short, 2000); *Championship* (short); *Alone* (2002).

CLAYTON, Jack (1921–1995)

Jack Clayton's work as a film director is difficult to categorise. Since all his feature films were adapted from novels, he could be regarded as one of the most literary of British film-makers; yet he was also deeply committed to making imaginative use of cinema's resources. His films are always carefully crafted, but they also contain raw and spontaneous moments. The craftsmanship earned him the respect of fellow film-makers, but – with the notable exception of *Room at the Top*, in many ways his least typical film – he rarely enjoyed substantial commercial success. Though a director of remarkable talent, Clayton's uncompromising independence led not just to a relatively small output (only eight features in his entire career); the films he actually made often seemed out of step with what the market, and sometimes the critics, wanted.

Jack Clayton was born in Brighton on 1 March 1921. He began working in the film industry at the age of fourteen at Denham Studios as a third assistant director for Alexander Korda's London Films. His first experience as a director himself was on *Naples Is a Battlefield* (1944), a short wartime documentary for the RAF Film Unit. During the late 1940s and early 50s, he worked on a range of features as assistant director, production manager, second-unit director, associate producer and, from 1956 onwards, producer. In 1955 he received his first official directorial credit for the short *The Bespoke Overcoat*, an adaptation of a ghost story by Gogol. Although the film was a considerable success, winning both an American and a British Academy Award, Clayton returned to producing for several years before John and James Woolf, backers of *The Bespoke Overcoat*, gave him the chance to return to direction with the feature adaptation of John Braine's novel *Room at the Top*.

The release of *Room at the Top* in 1959 inaugurated a cycle of realist films notable for what then seemed an unusually frank treatment of sexual mores. With its focus on a sexually predatory working-class male seeking the good life in a northern town, *Room at the Top* signalled a new maturity in British cinema. As the British New Wave developed, Laurence Harvey's Joe Lampton came to be seen as an inadequately convincing working-class hero compared to Albert Finney in *Saturday Night and Sunday Morning* (Karel Reisz, 1960) and Tom Courtenay in *The Loneliness of the Long Distance Runner* (Tony Richardson, 1962), but Simone Signoret's powerful performance as Lampton's doomed lover Alice Aisgill resonates through the film. It was the first of several distinguished performances by women in Clayton's films, including Deborah Kerr (*The Innocents*), Anne Bancroft (*The Pumpkin Eater*) and Maggie Smith (*The Lonely Passion of Judith Hearne*).

Confirming his distance from the New Wave ethos, Clayton's next film was a chillingly eerie adaptation of Henry James' celebrated ghost story 'The Turn of the Screw', masterfully photographed in black and white by Freddie Francis, and one of a developing series of precise psychological studies. In *The Bespoke Overcoat* Clayton had already explored a haunting's psychological dimension, with the film's ghost as a potential externalisation of the tailor's guilt. *The Innocents* develops the theme, strengthened and enlarged by Deborah Kerr's sensitive performance as the increasingly troubled governess Miss Giddens, and a compelling exploration of the emotional world of children. Clayton's almost claustrophobically tight control of visual details was also apparent in his next film, *The Pumpkin Eater* (1964), crisply adapted by Harold Pinter from a short novel by Penelope Mortimer, with Anne Bancroft very much centre stage as another disturbed heroine, haunted by fears of a mental breakdown. The offbeat drama *Our Mother's House* (1967), more haphazard in effect, continued the line with its tale of children who conceal the fact that their mother has died. As in *The Innocents*, Clayton proves particularly adept at showing children struggling to make sense of an adult world from their own limited perspective.

Clayton's next two films were made in America. *The Great Gatsby* (1974), a long, slow, respectful adaptation of F. Scott Fitzgerald's novel, failed to please the critics but has stood the test of time. *Something Wicked This Way Comes* (1983), adapted from Ray Bradbury's story and made after Clayton had recovered from a stroke suffered in the mid-1970s, fitted more closely with ideas explored earlier in his career, especially in its focus on children's exposure to evil. But the end result was compromised by Disney's insistence on a more 'commercial' product than Clayton had envisaged.

He returned to Britain for his final two films, *The Lonely Passion of Judith Hearne* (1987), based on Brian Moore's novel, set in Dublin but filmed largely in England, and the BBC's Muriel Spark adaptation *Memento Mori* (1992) – both quietly moving meditations on disappointment and ageing. Mournful but never depressing, and made with Clayton's characteristic sharp eye, they provide a fitting conclusion to a working life that had its own disappointments, but at best demonstrated a governing intelligence lacking in many more productive careers. He died on 25 February 1995 in Slough, Berkshire.

(Peter Hutchings)

BIBLIOGRAPHY: Gow, Gordon, 'The Way Things Are: An Interview with Jack Clayton', *Films and Filming*, Apr. 1974, pp. 10–14; Higson, Andrew, 'Gothic Fantasy as Art Cinema: The Secret of Female Desire in *The Innocents*', in Allan Lloyd-Smith and Victor Sage (eds), *Gothick Origins and Innovations* (Amsterdam: Rodopi, 1994); McFarlane, Brian, *An Autobiography of British Cinema* (London: Methuen, 1997); Palmer, R. Barton, 'What Was New in the British New Wave? Reviewing *Room at the Top*', *Journal of Popular Film and Television* no. 3, 1986, pp. 125–35; Sinyard, Neil, *Jack Clayton* (Manchester: Manchester University Press, 2000).

FILMOGRAPHY: *Naples Is a Battlefield* (doc. short, uncredited, 1944); *The Bespoke Overcoat* (short, 1955); *Room at the Top* (1959); *The Innocents* (UK/US, 1961); *The Pumpkin Eater* (1964); *Our Mother's House* (UK/US, 1967); *The Great Gatsby* (US, 1974); *Something Wicked This Way Comes* (US, 1983); *The Lonely Passion of Judith Hearne* (1987).

CLAYTON, Sue (1955–)

Sue Clayton was born in Newcastle-upon-Tyne on 28 July 1955. After reading English at Cambridge, she went to the Royal College of Art to study photography. Her early work is characterised by a politicised sense of history and the need for the role and place of women to be recognised. *The Song of the Shirt*, made over several years in the latter half of the 1970s, examined the legacy of the Industrial Revolution through the interweaving stories of women workers in the sewing trade. For Channel 4 in 1983 she made a series of introductory short films to contextualise their *Women on Film* season of screenings. *The Commodities Series* (1983–6) explored how the production of various different commodities – tea, coffee, sugar, oil, opium and gold – has shaped the history of the modern world.

Clayton made a number of probing television documentaries, including *Theme Park Britons* (1989), *Japan Dreaming* (1991) and *Dracula: The Undiscovered Country* (1993). She ventured into fiction with *The Last Crop*, a sixty-minute adaptation of an Australian short story about a cleaner who lets her friends loose on the homes of the rich; and *Heart Songs*, an atmospheric short about a romantic encounter in the Canadian backwoods. Her first full-length feature film, *The Disappearance of Finbar*, is a European road movie about the quest of a Dublin youth (Luke Griffin) for a friend (Jonathan Rhys-Meyers) who has transplanted himself to the wilds of Sweden. Though the film took little at the box office it has acquired a cult reputation on video/DVD.

(Paul Ward)

BIBLIOGRAPHY: 'The Song of the Shirt: An Interview with Susan Clayton', *Wide Angle* vol. 6 no. 3, 1984, pp. 68–75; Wayne, Mike, *The Politics of Contemporary European Cinema: Histories, Borders, Diasporas* (Bristol: Intellect, 2002).

FILMOGRAPHY: *Women and the Welfare State* (doc. short, co-dir. Jonathan Curling, 1977); *The Song of the Shirt* (co-dir. Jonathan Curling, 1979); *The Last Crop* (1990); *Heart Songs* (short, 1992); *The Disappearance of Finbar* (Ir/Swe/UK, 1996).

CLEGG, Tom

Tom Clegg's long career in film and television spans six decades. Beginning as a cameraman and then staff director at ABC Television, Clegg has directed dozens of television dramas, from *Special Branch* in 1969 to *My Uncle Silas* in 2003; his functional, efficient style was put to good use on the fourteen feature-length episodes of *Sharpe* (1993–7), starring Sean Bean as Bernard Cornwell's early nineteenth-century soldier hero. He also directed ten television films, including *Regan* (1974), the *Armchair Cinema* film that led to *The Sweeney*; *Bravo Two Zero* (1999), an adaptation by Troy Kennedy Martin of Andy McNabb's Gulf War best-seller; and the Agatha Christie mystery *Poirot: Murder in Mesopotamia* (2001).

Clegg has also directed six feature films, beginning with *Love Is a Splendid Illusion* (1969), a tepid love story set in Italy. Unsurprisingly it failed to launch him into a cinema career, and it was nearly ten years before he made a second feature film. *Sweeney 2*, spun off from the television series (fourteen episodes of which Clegg had directed), was much more his *métier;* Clegg knew exactly how to handle Troy Kennedy Martin's script about a well-organised gang robbing banks to fund their sun-soaked crime-free Maltese commune. Modest success led on to *McVicar*, starring Roger Daltrey as criminal-turned-sociologist John McVicar, a taut, authentic-looking film with excellent performances from Daltrey, Adam Faith and Steven Berkoff. Clegg quickly followed up with his enjoyably offbeat *World Cup: A Captain's Tale*, about the 1909 football World Cup. But his career was settling comfortably back into television, from which his two subsequent features – *The Inside Man*, a Swedish cold war thriller featuring Dennis Hopper as a CIA agent, and *Any Man's Death*, a more routine South African-set drama – are minor diversions.

The only (intermittently) consistent theme in Clegg's eclectic career seems to be a facility for action, with crime, war, espionage and historical action films featuring prominently in his oeuvre. Yet with television films such as the science-fiction *Destination Moonbase Alpha* (1976) and the modern Cinderella story *Stroke of Midnight* (1990), starring Jennifer Grey and Rob Lowe, also to his credit, plus bit-part acting roles in miscellaneous films from *The Flanagan Boy* (1953) to *Carry on Loving* (1970), one can conclude that Tom Clegg has an eclectic and durable talent.

(Lez Cooke)

FILMOGRAPHY: *Love Is a Splendid Illusion* (1969); *Sweeney 2* (1978); *McVicar* (1980); *The World Cup: A Captain's Tale* (1982); *G'olé!* (doc., 1982); *The Inside Man/Slagskämpen* (Swe, 1984); *Any Man's Death* (SA/US, 1988; rel. 1990).

CLEMENS, Brian (1931–)

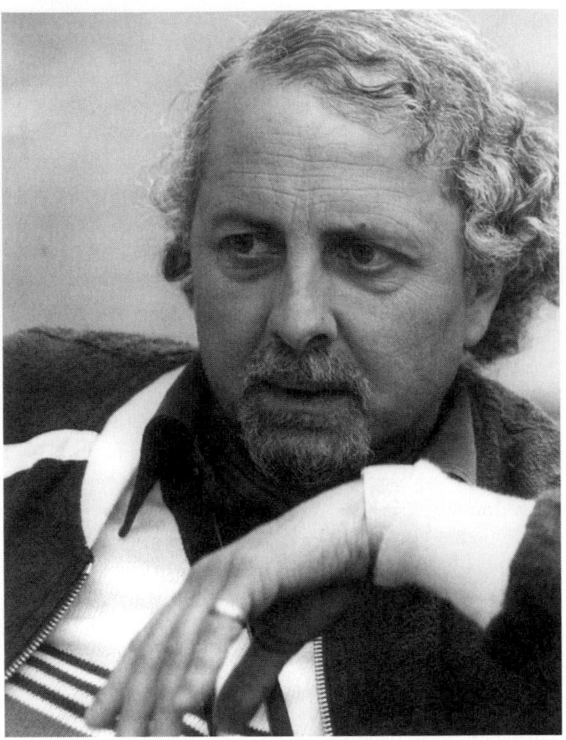

Brian Clemens was born in Croydon, Surrey, in 1931. He entered the film business in 1953 and by 1956 he was working as a screenwriter for the Danziger brothers, who specialised in making B-movies with minor American stars. Writing scripts for eighty-minute films in ten to twelve days proved good training for working in television. In 1961, Clemens found an outlet for his talents in *The Avengers*. He became the dominant writer and gained production experience handling second-unit direction.

In the 1970s Clemens combined his television work with cinema projects, scripting films such as *Dr Jekyll & Sister Hyde* (Roy Baker, 1971) and *The Golden Voyage of Sinbad* (Gordon Hessler, 1973). In 1974 he produced and directed *Captain Kronos: Vampire Hunter* for Hammer. Clemens drew inspiration from Kurosawa, Sergio Leone and Bergman's *The Seventh Seal* (1957) to make a likeable and original addition to Hammer's gothic horror cycle; but the film's crisp black and white photography and gentle sensationalism failed to appeal to audiences yearning for more blood and sex. Clemens returned to television, repeating the success of *The Avengers* with *The Professionals* (1978–82). He continues to write prolifically, most recently creating *Bugs* (1995–9), an espionage thriller series, and revamping *The Professionals* as *CI5: The New Professionals* (1998).

(Paul Ward)

BIBLIOGRAPHY: Dixon, Wheeler Winston, 'The Man Who Created *The Avengers*: An Interview with Brian Clemens', *Classic Images* no. 287, May 1999, pp. C18–20, C33–5; Fleming, John, Interview with Brian Clemens, *Starburst* no. 29, 1980, pp. 38–42 (Part 1); *Starburst* no. 30, 1981, pp. 38–42 (Part 2).

FILMOGRAPHY: *Captain Kronos: Vampire Hunter* (1974).

CLEMENT, Dick (1937–)

Dick Clement was born in Westcliff-on-Sea, Essex, on 5 September 1937. After working for five years in BBC radio, he enrolled in a scriptwriting course. He met Ian La Frenais, and the pair wrote a pilot sketch, which eventually resulted in the BBC series *The Likely Lads* (1964–6). Other successful sitcoms followed, including *Whatever Happened to the Likely Lads?* (1973–4) and *Porridge* (1974–7). Their brand of humour follows in a British tradition of verbal wit, sympathy for the underdog and mistrust of authority, poking gentle fun at national institutions.

Clement made his first foray into cinema with *Otley* (1968), a witty parody of the spy film cycle and the clichés of 'Swinging London', set around Notting Hill. La Frenais produced and co-wrote the script, a practice he continued on most of Clement's films, though not *A Severed Head*, adapted by Iris Murdoch from her own novel and showing little of the cinematic flair displayed in *Otley*. La Frenais did collaborate on *Catch Me a Spy*, but overburdened by a big budget and an international cast ranging from Kirk Douglas to Bernadette Lafont, it too failed to capture the freshness of *Otley*.

In 1974 Clement and La Frenais moved to the USA, though they continue to contribute to British cinema and television. Their biggest cinema box-office success proved to be *Porridge*, a spin-off of the popular television series, starring Ronnie Barker as Fletcher, a seasoned convict described by Clement as 'a survivor, in the tradition of Falstaff or *The Good Soldier Schweik*' (Webber, p. 10). *Bullshot*, a caricature of inter-war fictional hero Bulldog Drummond, and *Water*, an anti-colonialist farce starring Michael Caine, both made for George Harrison's HandMade films, fared less well with critics and audiences.

In recent years, Clement and La Frenais have carved out a successful career as 'script doctors', while continuing to write popular sitcoms for British television, notably *Auf Wiedersehen, Pet* (1983–4, 1986, 2002). Busy with lucrative writing assignments like *Pearl Harbor* (Michael Bay, 2001), Clement now seems to have abandoned his directing activities.

(Elisabetta Girelli)

BIBLIOGRAPHY: Ogle, Tina, 'Still the Likely Lads', *Observer*, 28 Apr. 2002; Webber, Richard (ed.), *Porridge: The Scripts* (London: Headline, 2002).

FILMOGRAPHY: *Otley* (1968); *A Severed Head* (1970); *Catch Me a Spy* (US: *To Catch a Spy*, UK/Fr/US, 1971); *Porridge* (1979); *Bullshot* (US: *Bullshot Crummond*, 1983); *Water* (1985).

CLEMENTS, Sir John (1910–1988)

John Clements was born in London on 25 April 1910. Educated at Cambridge, he was soon drawn to the theatre, where he made his first appearance in 1930. It was the start of a long and distinguished stage career, which saw him achieve fame as an actor, director and producer.

A versatile and prolific artist, Clements also worked in cinema and television, mainly as an actor and producer, although he never managed to parallel his stage reputation; his best film roles are from the 1940s, especially in wartime productions, though he is chiefly remembered for his part as the 'cowardly' Lieutenant Faversham in the pre-war version of *The Four Feathers* (Zoltan Korda, 1939).

Clements' only foray into film direction was *Call of the Blood*, which he co-directed with Ladislao Vajda; he also acted in the film, as well as co-scripting and producing it. Clement's second wife, the actress Kay Hammond, played the lead female role. Set at the turn of the twentieth century, the plot follows a newly married English couple on their journey to Sicily, the land of the husband's ancestors. Aided by the scheming of an English expatriate (Clements), the husband falls prey to local superstition and immorality, forsaking English civilisation to heed the call of his Sicilian blood. Despite its talented cast, the film was condemned as turgid and clichéd. John Clements was knighted in 1968 in recognition of his theatrical achievements. He died in Brighton, on 6 April 1988.

(Elisabetta Girelli)

FILMOGRAPHY: *Call of the Blood* (co-dir. Ladislao Vajda, UK/It, 1948).

CLIFT, Denison (1892–1961)

Denison Halley Clift was born on 2 May 1892 in San Francisco. He was educated at Stanford University and worked in advertising while writing a novel and short stories. He was then employed as a scenario writer for Cecil B. DeMille and Thomas Ince, and in 1919 became production editor at the Fox Film Corporation and was given the opportunity to direct three films.

In September 1920 Clift came to England and joined the Ideal Film Company, where he was perceived as an inspiring new director, and aroused hopes for British cinema's rejuvenation. Clift was sympathetic to the cultural context of British film-making, but took the industry to task for neglecting scenario construction and failing to invest in modern production methods. Writing in *The Motion Picture Studio*, he argued that the American market was open to technically competent films that were distinctively different, and that British literature was a storehouse of richly imaginative stories, which, if filmed in their regional and architectural settings, could be internationally successful.

Between 1921 and 1923 Clift made eleven largely successful films, mostly reworkings of classic authors, including Guy de Maupassant (*The Diamond Necklace*), George Gissing (*Demos*), Oscar Wilde (*A Woman of No Importance*), Arnold Bennett (*The Old Wives' Tale*) and George Meredith (*Diana of the Crossways*). His films were praised for their sensitivity to everyday English life and atmospheric use of locations, their understated emotions, pictorial values and generally well-crafted narration. In the war-damaged hero of *Sonia*, Clive Brook found his first film role offering depth of characterisation, alerting him to the expressive potential of cinema.

In December 1921 Clift set up Denison Clift Art Productions to make more ambitious films. *The Loves of Mary Queen of*

Scots, starring Fay Compton, took nearly twelve months to make. It was followed by a thrill-packed melodrama, *Out to Win*, with Clive Brook playing doubled roles; and *This Freedom*, a melodrama about the calamity befalling the family of a modern career woman (Compton again), which led to Clift being invited back to America to direct films for Fox.

Nostalgic for the teamwork at Ideal, Clift wished to return to Britain, but by the time he did, in 1928, the company had ceased production. He found work at the new BIP studios at Elstree, and was praised for his direction of Betty Balfour in *Paradise*. Two part-talking films for Gainsborough followed: *The City of Play*, involving high jinks on the Eiffel Tower with Chili Bouchier and Pat Aherne, and *Taxi for Two* with Mabel Poulton and John Stuart. Despite his experience with dialogue, Clift found fewer directing opportunities in the new era following the coming of sound. But before he returned to America in the late 1930s, he made an atmospheric version of *The Mystery of the Marie Celeste* for Hammer, starring Bela Lugosi; and he wrote the script for Roy Kellino's unusual tale of Grimsby trawlermen, *The Last Adventurers* (1937). He died in Hollywood following a heart attack on 17 December 1961.

(Christine Gledhill)

BIBLIOGRAPHY: Clift, Denison, 'Britain's Film Opportunities', *The Motion Picture Studio*, 11 June 1921, p. 9; Clift, Denison, 'According to Clift: The Difference between English and American Films', *The Motion Picture Studio*, 28 Jan. 1922, p. 8; Clive Brook Special Collection, BFI National Library, London; Low, Rachael, *The History of the British Film 1918–1929* (London: George Allen & Unwin, 1971).

FILMOGRAPHY (UK only): *The Diamond Necklace*; *Demos*; *A Woman of No Importance*; *Sonia*; *The Old Wives' Tale* (1921); *Princess Mary's Wedding Presents* (doc. short); *Bentley's Conscience*; *Diana of the Crossways*; *A Bill of Divorcement* (1922); *This Freedom*; *Out to Win*; *The Loves of Mary Queen of Scots* (aka *Marie, Queen of Scots*) (1923); *Paradise* (1928); *The City of Play*; *Taxi for Two* (co-dir. Alexander Esway) (1929); *High Seas* (1930); *The Mystery of the Marie Celeste* (US: *Phantom Ship*, 1935).

CLOWES, St John Legh (1907–?)

St John Legh Clowes is now remembered chiefly as author of the sexy stage thriller *Dear Murderer* and, especially, as writer and director of the notorious *No Orchids for Miss Blandish* (1948). Born in 1907 and educated at the Royal Naval College, Dartmouth, he served briefly in the Royal Navy before entering the film industry as a writer at BIP in 1927. He quickly moved on to British Screen Productions where he co-directed two features, *Northwards* and *Frozen Fate*, along with a variety of short films. He made several 'quota quickies' in the 1930s, including *Dora* (1933), a forty-five-minute comedy that he wrote and directed, and *Grand Prix* (1934), a racing melodrama that he wrote, directed and produced. During the war he was assistant producer on Anthony Asquith's *Welcome to Britain* (1943); he wrote *Battle for Music* (Donald Taylor, 1943), a history of the London Philharmonic Orchestra; and co-wrote the semi-documentary *Soldier, Sailor* (Alexander Shaw, 1944), which mixes real-life servicemen with actors like George Carney, Rosamund John and Jean Kent.

Dear Murderer was adapted by Sydney and Muriel Box and Peter Rogers, and stylishly filmed by Arthur Crabtree in 1947 at Gainsborough's Islington studio. Clowes wrote the sub-Aldwych farce *Things Happen at Night* (Francis Searle, 1948) before returning to directing with *No Orchids for Miss Blandish*. Few films have been more reviled in their time. Perhaps it was the ersatz American quality that angered realist-minded critics; perhaps it was the spectacle of a beautiful woman (Linden Travers amply fulfilling the job description) falling for the thug who kidnaps her; or, possibly, it was some of Clowes' dialogue (e.g. 'I wanna get a gander at that baby'). According to Travers, Clowes became ill halfway through filming, and associate producer Oswald Mitchell took over direction. Where it was allowed to be shown in Britain, the film was a massive box-office success, but critical outrage seems to have put an end to Clowes' directing career.

(Brian McFarlane)

BIBLIOGRAPHY: McFarlane, Brian, 'Outrage: *No Orchids for Miss Blandish*', in Steve Chibnall and Robert Murphy (eds), *British Crime Cinema* (London and New York: Routledge, 1999).

FILMOGRAPHY: *Santa Claus* (short, co-dir. Ben R. Hart); *Yachting Thrills* (short, co-dir. Ben R. Hart) (1927); *Land of My Fathers* (series of shorts, co-dir. Ben R. Hart); *Homes of Our King* (short, co-dir. Ben R. Hart); *Northwards* (co-dir. Ben R. Hart) (1928); *Frozen Fate* (co-dir. Ben R. Hart, 1929); *Dora* (1933); *Grand Prix* (1934); *No Orchids for Miss Blandish* (uncredited co-dir. Oswald Mitchell, 1948).

CLUNES, Martin (1961–)

Martin Clunes was born in Wimbledon, south London, on 28 November 1961, the son of actor Alec Clunes. He is married to the producer Philippa Braithwaite. Clunes is best known for his role in the popular sitcom *Men Behaving Badly* (1992–8), though he has also undertaken serious roles on film, television and the stage, for example as the acid-bath murderer John George Haigh in Yorkshire Television's *A Is for Acid* (Harry Bradbeer, 2002).

He has made two ventures into directing. In 1994 he directed the feature film *Staggered*, a comedy about a toy demonstrator, Neil Price (Clunes), whose jealous friend arranges for him to be drugged and abandoned, penniless and naked, on a remote Scottish island on his stag night. Neil then has to find a way to return in time for his wedding. Clunes invents ingenious plot twists and an array of eccentric characters who help or hinder his progress – notably Virginia McKenna's resourceful old boat lady, Griff Rhys Jones' bondage-loving sales rep and Anna Chancellor's morbidly enthusiastic medical researcher. Though made on a tiny budget, the film's robust humour, leavened by moments of pathos and bleakness, made it an unexpected success at the British box office.

In 1999 Clunes directed *Hunting Venus*, a comedy film for television where he plays a retired petty criminal who is persuaded to re-form the band he used to play with. With able support from Neil Morrissey and Jane Horrocks, and guest appearances from Simon Le Bon, Gary Numan and Jools Holland, he succeeds admirably in parodying the excesses of 1980s' New Romanticism.

(Sarah Cardwell)

BIBLIOGRAPHY: Berens, Jessica, 'Funny Face', *Independent* Magazine, 18 June 1994, pp. 34, 36; Saynor, James, 'Staggered at the Thought of It All', *Observer* Review Section, 3 July 1994, p. 8.

FILMOGRAPHY: *Staggered* (1994).

COBHAM, David

David Cobham was born in Yorkshire in the 1930s. After studying at Cambridge he made a short film about falconry (*Bells on Her Toes*) and joined the BBC, where he specialised in wildlife documentaries. *The Vanishing Hedgerows* brought him in contact with Henry Williamson, who eventually entrusted him with the film rights to his classic 1927 novel *Tarka the Otter*. With the backing of Sir John Terry of the National Film Finance Corporation, Cobham made the film as part of the Rank Organisation's final production programme over a two-year period in the late 1970s, shooting over 250,000 feet of film, entirely on location. Cobham avoids the trap of whimsical sentimentality by focusing on the savage beauty of the otter's world, leaving the huntsmen, farmers and fishermen stiff and unsympathetic intruders. Superb wildlife photography and an unfussy narration (written by Cobham and Gerald Durrell and delivered by Peter Ustinov) sustain interest; though the film's respectful distance from its subject makes for limited emotional involvement and impaired its popularity at the box office.

Cobham returned to television: he was responsible for a fine series based on Jack London's *Tales of the Klondike* (1982), using Orson Welles as his narrator, but more typically concentrated on programmes involving children and animals like *Seal Morning* (1986) and *Woof!* (1988). His second wife is the actress Liza Goddard.

(Robert Murphy)

BIBLIOGRAPHY: 'Cobham Ventures Afar', *Screen International*, 25 Apr. 1981, p. 26; McAsh, Iain F., 'First Takes', *Films Illustrated*, Dec. 1978, p. 124.

FILMOGRAPHY: *Bells on Her Toes* (short, 1956); *Tarka the Otter* (1978).

COE, Peter (1929–1987)

Peter Leonard Coe was born in London on 18 April 1929. He became a successful stage producer, most notably of Lionel Bart's musical *Oliver!* in the early 1960s. In 1969, he branched out into film with *Lock up Your Daughters!*, a bawdy eighteenth-century romp that Coe had directed at the Mermaid Theatre as a musical put together by Bart, Bernard Miles and composer Laurie Johnson from Henry Fielding's *Rape upon Rape* and Sir John Vanbrugh's *The Relapse*. Perhaps hoping to emulate the success of *Tom Jones* (Tony Richardson, 1963) and avoid competition with the film version of *Oliver!* (Carol Reed, 1968), Johnson and Bart's songs were jettisoned; but this non-musical musical, uncertainly poised between *Carry On* vulgarity and Restoration comedy sophistication, left audiences dissatisfied and bemused. Coe resumed his stage career, eventually co-directing a television version of his stage hit *Barnum!* (1986), notable for the virtuoso performance of Michael Crawford. Peter Coe was killed in a traffic accident in London on 1 June 1987.

(Robert Murphy)

FILMOGRAPHY: *Lock up Your Daughters!* (1969).

COHEN, Norman (1936–1983)

Norman Cohen was born in Dublin to Jewish parents on 11 June 1936. His membership of the Irish Film Society fuelled his ambition to be a director, and in 1955 he entered the film industry as an editor. In the mid-1960s he directed *Down Boy*, a short comedy about dogs, and two critically praised documentaries: *Brendan Behan's Dublin*, a vivid evocation of the city from the hard-drinking Behan's perspective, and *The London Nobody Knows*, an insightful look at London, enhanced by a moody but humorous narration by James Mason. Its gently offbeat view of London – a sharp contrast to the fashionable image of 'Swinging London' – made it a popular programme-filler in West End cinemas for several years.

Cohen's first feature films were spin-offs from the television series *Till Death Us Do Part* (1969) and *Dad's Army* (1971), both successful at the box office, and *Adolf Hitler – My Part in His Downfall* (1972), based on Spike Milligan's hilarious memoirs. They were succeeded by three sex-comedies in the 'Confessions' series and *Stand up Virgin Soldiers* (1977), which all proved very popular, but seemed to betray the promise of Cohen's early career. *Burning Rubber* (1981), a German-made film about dragster racing starring the Bay City Rollers, and the South African melodrama, *The Lion's Share* (1984), did little to redeem his reputation. However, at the time of his death from a heart attack on 26 October 1983 he was in Hollywood to sign contracts for two films with serious themes, and in his obituary Terence Maher wrote that Cohen's 'integrity and patient attitude to his craft gained him great affection and respect'.

(Margaret Butler)

BIBLIOGRAPHY: Falk, Quentin, 'To Hell with All the Brickbats! Nothing Succeeds Like Sexcess', *CinemaTV Today*, 22 Feb. 1975, pp. 8–9; Maher, Terence, Obituary, *Film and TV Technician*, Jan. 1984, p. 12.

FILMOGRAPHY: *Down Boy* (short, 1964); *Brendan Behan's Dublin* (doc. short, 1966); *The London Nobody Knows* (doc. short, 1967); *There Ought to Be a Law* (doc. short, 1968); *Till Death Us Do Part* (1969); *Dad's Army* (1971); *Adolf Hitler – My Part in His Downfall* (1972); *The Importance of Being Dublin* (doc. short, 1974); *Boxcar Willie 'Glad to be Back among Friends'* (short); *Confessions of a Pop Performer* (1975); *Confessions of a Driving Instructor* (1976); *Stand up Virgin Soldiers*; *Confessions from a Holiday Camp* (1977); *Burning Rubber* (Ger, 1981) *Lion's Share* (SA, 1984).

COKLISS, Harley (1945–)

Harley Cokliss was born in San Diego, California, on 11 February 1945, and brought up in Chicago. He studied at the University of Illinois before moving to England to learn film-making at the London Film School. After graduating, he worked in the London story departments of Warner Bros. and Paramount, served as assistant director on Barry Salt's experimental *Six Reels of Film to be Shown in Any Order* (1971) and made the documentary *Chicago Blues*. He went on to direct several television documentaries and two inventive and enjoyable children's films – *The Battle of Billy's Pond* and *The Glitterball* – for the Children's Film Foundation. After the mildly realistic coming-of-age-on-holiday-in-Torquay drama *That Summer!*, he was taken on as second-unit director for *The Empire Strikes Back* (Irvin Kershner, 1980); this in turn led to the apocalyptic New Zealand fantasy *Battletruck*. Two disappointingly routine Hollywood action films followed: *Black Moon Rising* fails to make much sense despite a John Carpenter script and a solidly competent performance from Tommy Lee Jones; while *Malone* dissipates its noirish premise in routine action and facile conspiracies.

Cokliss returned to Britain to direct Chris Wicking's ingenious, if often annoying, *Dream Demon*. He subsequently found a niche directing television fantasy-adventures including *Hercules: The Legendary Journey* and *Xena: Warrior Princess*, where his lack of subtlety proved more an asset than a liability. In 1999 he made *Pilgrim*, a straight-to-video thriller, with Ray Liotta as an amnesiac with a dangerously unhealthy past; then with typical unpredictability Cokliss returned to the world of childhood with the pleasingly old-fashioned *An Angel for May*, for the renamed Children's Film and Television Foundation. No one has claimed Cokliss as an exceptionally talented director, but his career outside the safe confines of television is an interesting one.

(Robert Murphy)

BIBLIOGRAPHY: Castell, David, 'Getting Started', *Films Illustrated*, Nov. 1978, p. 85; Clarke, Jeremy, 'Directing Demons', *Films and Filming*, Oct. 1988, pp. 21–3; McGillivray, David, 'Now You Know: Harley Cokliss', *Films and Filming*, Jan. 1986, p. 18; Newman, Kim, 'The Russians Are Coming!', *City Limits* no. 246, 19 June 1986, p. 17; Vaines, Colin, 'In the Good Young Summertime', *Screen International*, 6 Jan. 1979, p. 15

FILMOGRAPHY: *The Battle of Billy's Pond* (1976); *The Glitterball* (1977); *That Summer!* (1979); *The Empire Strikes Back* (2nd unit dir., Irvin Kershner, US, 1980); *Battletruck* (aka *Warlords of the 21st Century*, NZ, 1982); *Black Moon Rising* (US, 1986); *Malone* (US, 1987); *Dream Demon* (1988); *Pilgrim* (UK/Can/Mex, 1999); *An Angel for May* (2002).

COLE, Henry

Cole drew on his experience as a rich ex-heroin addict for his debut feature, *Mad Dogs and Englishmen*. He told a reporter: 'In this film, this young beautiful socialite becomes an unpleasant horrible bitch, and that mood change is brought about by addiction' (Dunkley, p. 16). Cole's insider view of the corrupt upper echelons of British society might have been fascinating, but he finds it impossible to locate a viable moral standpoint and the convoluted story becomes increasingly implausible. Elizabeth Hurley plays the 'unpleasant horrible bitch' with gusto, but other distinguished members of the cast (Joss Ackland, Claire Bloom, Jeremy Brett) are unable to bring their cardboard characters to life. Unsurprisingly the film failed to win over critics or attract an audience.

(Robert Murphy)

BIBLIOGRAPHY: Dunkley, Cathy, 'Drug Tale Hooks Duo', *Moving Pictures International*, 30 June 1994, p. 16; Monk, Claire, 'Mad Dogs and Englishmen', *Sight and Sound*, June 1995, p. 49.

FILMOGRAPHY: *Mad Dogs and Englishmen* (1994).

COLE, Nigel

Nigel Cole began his career in television, establishing his reputation with enjoyable celebrity wildlife documentaries – *Orang Utans with Julia Roberts* (1998), *Horsemen of Mongolia with Julia Roberts* (2000), *White Elephants with Meg Ryan* (2001) – which he interspersed with episodes of *Peak Practice* (1997–8) and *Cold Feet* (1998). In 2000 he broke into feature films with the chaotically amusing *Saving Grace*, starring Brenda Blethyn as a Cornish widow who pays off her husband's debts by farming marijuana. The film was made for Rupert Murdoch's satellite broadcasting company BSkyB, and promoted in cinemas by sister company 20th Century-Fox. Plot weaknesses were more than made up for by a likeable and exuberant cast, and *Saving Grace* was a surprise box-office success in the US as well as in Britain.

Another comedy about feisty middle-aged women doing daring and unconventional things followed. *Calendar Girls* was based on the real story of the women of the Rylstone and District Women's Institute, who raised funds for leukaemia by allowing themselves to be photographed in discreetly provocative poses for a calendar. Despite a weak second half once the calendar battle has been won, warm performances, pretty settings and the topical theme of older women rediscovering their sexuality made the film a huge commercial success. Cole went to Hollywood to direct *A Lot Like Love*, a pleasing if inconsequential American romantic comedy, though his desire to work with small-scale units on projects of his choice will probably gravitate him back to the UK industry.

(Robert Murphy)

BIBLIOGRAPHY: Kemp, Stuart, 'The Snow and the Fury', *Screen International*, 14 Jan. 2000, p. 24.

FILMOGRAPHY: *Saving Grace* (2000); *Calendar Girls* (2003); *A Lot Like Love* (US, 2005).

COLE, Sidney (1908–1998)

Sidney Cole was born in Kennington, south London, on 31 October 1908 and educated at Westminster City School. He won a scholarship to the London School of Economics, where he imbibed his staunch left-wing principles. After graduating,

Cole, a keen moviegoer since childhood, fired off letters to numerous people in the film industry asking for a job. Two of the recipients were Anthony Asquith and Thorold Dickinson, who became his lifelong friends.

In 1930, Cole started work as a script reader at the Stoll studios at Cricklewood. He moved on to the editing department and, on Dickinson's recommendation, was loaned to Ealing to edit Carol Reed's directorial debut, *Midshipman Easy* (1934). Around this time Dickinson and Asquith were actively organising the Association of Cine-Technicians into an effective professional union, and Cole became closely involved. In 1937 he accompanied Dickinson to Spain, and helped him direct two documentary shorts supporting the Republican cause, *Behind Spanish Lines* and *Spanish ABC*.

Back in Britain, Cole directed a documentary short, *Roads across Britain*, before joining Ealing in 1941. He edited *Went the Day Well?* (Alberto Cavalcanti, 1942) and *San Demetrio London* (Charles Frend, 1943), as well as the co-operatively made propaganda short *Our Film* (Harold French, 1942), before turning associate producer (at Ealing, effectively producer) on such productions as the multi-directed ghost film *Dead of Night* (Cavalcanti/Hamer/Dearden/Crichton, 1945), *Scott of the Antarctic* (Charles Frend, 1948), *The Man in the White Suit* (Alexander Mackendrick, 1951) and *Secret People* (Thorold Dickinson, 1952). His only directorial assignment at Ealing was one segment of the portmanteau film *Train of Events*, accomplished in workmanlike style if with no special flair.

After leaving Ealing Cole concentrated mainly on television, producing such popular series as *The Adventures of Robin Hood* (1955) and *The Adventures of Black Beauty* (1972–4). He also ran the editing department at the London Film School in the early 1970s and was elected President of the ACTT (as it had then become) in 1973. He died in Ealing on 25 January 1998.

(Philip Kemp)

BIBLIOGRAPHY: Bond, Ralph, 'Close Ups, No. 23: Sid Cole', *Cine-Technician* vol. 10 nos 46/7, Jan./Apr. 1944, pp. 18–20; Cole, Sidney, 'Our Film', *Film and TV Technician*, July 1990, pp. 26–7; Dunbar, Robert, 'Sidney Cole', *Stage Screen and Radio*, Mar. 1998, p. 18; BECTU History Project interview, tape held in BFI National Library, London; Obituary, *Classic Images* no. 276, June 1998, pp. 49–50.

Sidney Cole (left)

FILMOGRAPHY: *Behind Spanish Lines* (doc. short, co-dir. Thorold Dickinson); *Spanish ABC* (doc. short, co-dir. Thorold Dickinson) (1938); *Roads across Britain* (doc. short, co-dir. Paul Rotha, 1939); *Train of Events* ('The Engine Driver' episode, co-dirs. Charles Crichton/Basil Dearden, 1949).

COLEBY, A. E. (1876–1930)

A. E. Coleby was born in London in 1876. A genial, larger-than-life figure, he tried a number of occupations – bookseller, fish salesman's assistant, engineering apprentice, professional cyclist, racing bookie and stage actor – before turning to film-acting in 1905 for Cricks and Sharp. From 1907 he began to direct as well as act in numerous short comedies and chase films, remaining with the new partnership of Cricks and Martin, which in 1910 moved to a modernised studio in Croydon. As films lengthened, the devices of earlier trick films were used to serve sensational melodramas such as Coleby's *The Pirates of 1920*, the first British film of 'feature rank', which boasted a spectacular battle between an airship and a liner.

Following the dissolution of Cricks and Martin, Coleby worked for Pathé in 1912, where he directed one of George Pearson's early scenarios, *Peg Woffington*. In 1914 he began working for I. B. Davidson, who operated from a converted tram shed in Leyton, north-east London. Here his output alternated between fighting and boxing films, such as *Kent, the Fighting Man* or *The Great Game*, starring boxer (and later striker of the Rank gong) Bombardier Billy Wells, and romances adapted from middlebrow novelists, such as Marie Corelli's *Thelma*, and Eden Phillpotts's *The Secret Woman*.

Ever the showman, Coleby frequently invented his own scenarios, combining fisticuffs and sentiment in picaresque adventures in which he played leading or supporting roles himself. Typical is *The Call of the Road* (1920), with Victor McLaglen, whom Coleby 'discovered' at the National Sporting Club, as its scapegrace hero. The well-regarded *Fifth Form at St Dominic's* and *Froggy's Little Brother* followed, but I. B. Davidson was now in trouble and Coleby moved to Stoll. Here he embarked on his most ambitious project, adapting at length Sir Hall Caine's *The Prodigal Son*, with Stewart Rome and Henry Victor as brothers tragically divided through their courtship of the same girl. The film was made on location in Iceland, Paris and Italy, and when completed ran for nearly five hours and was initially released in two parts. Although it deals in momentous emotions among epic landscapes, the film suffered from insensitive editing and ill-placed subtitles.

Undaunted, Coleby went on to direct the Dr Fu-Manchu series, with Agar Lyons making the most of the Chinese villain who constantly threatens to overthrow Western civilisation. Two Sessue Hayakawa films made on the Riviera followed, sandwiched between two George Robey productions. With the industry in recession, Coleby left Stoll to form his own F. H. C. (Faith, Hope and Charity) Company; but apart from the likeable Inspector Drew shorts, his career floundered.

Coleby was respected for his experienced showmanship, and warmly liked for his charm, good-humoured patience on the set, and liking for rumbustious, often irreverent, low-life subjects. His absence from film-making was regretted and in 1929 *Film Weekly* dramatised his life story to herald his comeback with *Unto Each Other*. The film was released in January 1930, but Coleby died six months later on 15 July.

(Christine Gledhill)

BIBLIOGRAPHY: 'Filming Novels in Full: What Coleby's Dictum Would Really Mean', *The Motion Picture Studio*, 17 Feb. 1923, p. 6; Low, Rachael, *The History of the British Film 1906–1914* (London: George Allen & Unwin, 1948); Low, Rachael, *The History of the British Film 1914–1918* (London: George Allen & Unwin, 1950); Low, Rachael, *The History of the British Film 1918–1929* (London: George Allen & Unwin, 1971); 'Man Who Found McLaglen: Veteran Director "Comes Back"', *Film Weekly*, 18 Mar. 1929, p. 5.

FILMOGRAPHY: *Day Duty*; *Don't Go to Law*; *A Drink Cure*; *Even a Worm Will Turn*; *Fun in the Studio*; *His Only Pair of Trousers*; *May and December*; *Only a Limerick*; *Saved from the Burning Wreck*; *Serving a Summons* (1907); *Billy Borntired*; *Brave Children; Or, The Young Thief Catchers*; *The Devil's Bargain*; *Diabolo Mad*; *Father Buys a Picture*; *A Fight for Honour*; *The Flies* (aka *Those Flies*); *For Baby's Sake*; *Freddy's Little Love Affair*; *The Freebooters*; *Grandfather's Birthday; Or, The Last Roll-Call*; *The Guardian of the Bank*; *High Game*; *His Wedding Morn*; *How Jones Got a New Suit*; *How the Artful Dodger Secured a Meal*; *An Ingenious Revenge*; *The Interrupted Bath*; *Lord Algy's Beauty Show*; *Love's Strategy*; *March Winds*; *The Mission of a Flower*; *The Phantom Ship*; *Polly's Excursion*; *Professor Bounder's Pills*; *She Would be Wed; Or, Leap Year Proposals*; *The Somnambulist's Crime*; *Tommy and the Sticktite*; *A Traitor to His King*; *'Twixt Love and Duty; Or, A Woman's Heroism*; *The Village Blacksmith* (1908); *Adopting a Baby*; *Bertie Buys a Bulldog*; *The Biter Bit*; *Boxing Fever*; *The Butcher's Boy and the Penny Dreadful*; *Cold and Its Consequences*; *The Convict's Dream*; *Dancing Tabloids*; *Father Hold My Wool*; *Getting Father's Consent*; *How Potts Backed a Winner*; *Little Jim*; *A Man Housemaid*; *A Motherless Waif*; *My Word, If I Catch You Smoking!*; *Nat's Conversion*; *The Receiver's Doom*; *The Robber's Ruse; Or, Foiled by Fido*; *Salome Mad*; *Saved by Carlo*; *A Seaside Episode*; *The Secretary's Crime*; *The Unfortunate Canvasser*; *When Jack Comes Home*; *When Jack Got His Pay*; *A Youthful Hero*; (1909); *Accompanied on the Tom-Tom*; *Billy's Bulldog*; *Bumpkin's Patent Synopticon*; *A Clown's Crime*; *Compromised by a Key*; *A Costly Gift*; *The Five Pound Note*; *Married for Love*; *A Modern Paul Pry*; *A Noble Outcast*; *Prison Reform*; *Professor Piecan's Discovery*; *A Rake's Romance*; *Scroggins Puts up for Blankshire*; *The Sculptor's Dream*; *Sleepy Sam's Awakening*; *The Squire's Romance*; *The Stolen Heir*; *Temptation and Forgiveness*; *The Terror and the Terrier*; *Too Many Admirers*; *Wanted, a Mummy* (1910); *The Advantages of Hypnotism*; *The Adventures of PC Sharpe*; *The Stolen Child*; *Aunt Tabitha's Visit*; *A Bag of Monkey Nuts* (aka *The Mad Monkey*); *The Brigand's Revenge*; *Brown Bewitched*; *A Case for Sherlock Holmes*; *Charlie Smiler Is Stage Struck* (aka *Smiler Has Stage Fever*); *Constable Smith's Dream of Promotion*; *The Courtship of Miss Twiggles*; *Dusty Dick's Awakening* (aka *Dusty Gets a Shock*); *Fate and the Woman*; *Father's Saturday Afternoon*; *Fool's Fancy* (aka *Scroggins Wins the Fiddle Faddle Prize*); *Have It Out*

My Boy, Have It Out; *How Puny Peter Became Strong*; *The Hunchback*; *Left in Trust* (aka *Saved by a Child*); *Little Red Riding Hood*; *Love and War*; *Mephisto's Plight* (aka *Dippy's Plight*); *The Mighty Atom*; *Our Village Heroes*; *A Pair of Antique Vases*; *Pirates of 1920*; *Polly the Girl Scout*; *The Portrait* (aka *Zillah, A Gipsy Romance*); *The Resourceful Scout* (aka *A Scout's Strategy*); *Royal England, A Story of an Empire's Throne*; *A Ruined Life*; *Scroggins Goes in for Chemistry and Discovers a Marvellous Powder*; *Scroggins Has His Fortune Told* (aka *Scroggins Visits a Palmist*); *Scroggins Plays Golf*; *She Dreamt of Onions*; *Signor Potti's Love Affair*; *Tatters; a Tale of the Slums*; *Topsy's Dream of Toyland*; *A Woman in the Case* (1911); *Battling Kelly*; *Big Ben's Dream of Greatness*; *The Bloomsbury Burglars*; *Bob, the Coster's Pony*; *Bobby's Letter*; *A Brute's Revenge*; *Compulsory Insurance*; *Constable Smith in Trouble Again*; *Coster Bill*; *Doctor Russell's Lie*; *From Country to Town*; *Her Sister's Silence*; *His Burglar Brother*; *His Secret Sin*; *His Wife's Brother*; *The Little Mother*; *The Lonely Inn*; *The Mummy*; *The Old Colonel's Gratitude*; *The Orphan*; *Out of His Element*; *A Pair of Trousers*; *Peggie and the Roundheads*; *Peg Woffington*; *Soppy Green Loses a Legacy*; *A Telephone Tangle*; *To Their Mutual Benefit*; *The Vapour Bath*; *What Happened to Mary*; *While the Cook Slept*; *The Widow's Legacy* (1912); *A Case of Arson*; *A Dream of Glory*; *The False Clue*; *The Fate of a King*; *The Grip*; *Mary the Flower Girl*; *A Master of Men*; *The Opal Stealers* (1913); *The Gurkha's Revenge* (1914); *And Then He Woke Up*; *The Cobbler* (aka *The Fighting Cobbler*); *The Lure of Drink*; *Mysteries of London*; *Satan's Amazon*; *The Under-Secretary's Honour* (1915); *The Blackmailers*; *Chains of Bondage*; *Kent, the Fighting Man*; *The Wheel of Death* (1916); *A Just Deception*; *A Pit Boy's Romance* (co-dir. Arthur Rooke); *The Third Witness*; *The Treasure of Heaven*; *The Village Blacksmith* (co-dir. Arthur Rooke); Holy Orders (co-dir. Arthur Rooke); *The Will of the People* (aka *A Strong Man's Weakness*) (1917); *For All Eternity*; *The Great Game* (aka *The Straight Game*); *Matt*; *The Secret Woman*; *Thelma* (co-dir. Arthur Rooke); *World Power or Downfall* (1918); *I Hear You Calling Me*; *The Silver Lining* (1919); *The Hour of Trial*; *The Pride of the North*; *Way of the World*; *The Call of the Road* (1920); *The Right to Live*; *Froggy's Little Brother* (aka *Children of Courage*); *The Fifth Form at St Dominic's* (1921); *The Peacemaker*; *Long Odds* (1922); *The Prodigal Son*; *The Return of the Prodigal*; *The Mystery of Dr Fu-Manchu* (series); *The Rest Cure* (1923); *The Prehistoric Man*; *The Great Prince Shan*; *Sen Yan's Devotion* (1924); *The Flying Fifty-Five* (1924; rel. 1928); *The Inscrutable Drew* (series of twelve shorts, 1924–6); *Spiritualism Exposed* (aka *Fake Spiritualism Exposed*, 1926); *The Prodigal Son* (re-edited and shortened version); *Unto Each Other*; *Over the Sticks* (co-dir. G. B. Samuelson) (1929).

COLLINGS, Esmé (1859–1936)

Arthur Albert Collings, born the son of a prosperous bootmaker in Weston-super-Mare in 1859, was a commercial photographer who became one of Britain's first film-makers. Initially he followed his father into the bootmaking trade; but his artistic ambitions were encouraged by his future wife Ketura Beedle, and by 1888 he had formed a partnership with William Friese-Greene, setting up photographic studios in London and Brighton. Collings adopted the middle name of Esmé, and in the 1891 census he is described as an 'Artist/Photographer'. By this time he had quarrelled with Friese-Greene and in 1892 he set up his own portrait studio in Hove.

In October 1896 his first public exhibition of the films he had made in Brighton opened to great acclaim at the Empire Theatre of Varieties. Only two films from his Brighton series (from a possible total of nineteen) have survived: *Boys Scrambling for Pennies under the West Pier, Brighton* and *Children Paddling*. They both feature strong compositions and are engaging demonstrations of how animated photography could be used. The iconography of *Children Paddling* is of particular interest because of its similarity to Constable's painting *Chain Pier, Brighton* (1826–7). In addition to these actualities, Collings also made a film featuring the actor/cellist Auguste van Biene in a scene from the play *The Broken Melody*.

Collings and the Vitagraph returned to the Empire for a week in early 1897. After this date there is no further evidence of him being active in moving pictures. His photographic business continued to thrive up to 1914, though Collings appears to have been increasingly interested in painting miniature portraits. He died in Eastbourne, Sussex, in 1936.
(Frank Gray)

BIBLIOGRAPHY: Barnes, John, *The Beginnings of the Cinema in England 1894–1901, Volumes 1 & 2* (Exeter: University of Exeter Press, 1996–8); Low, Rachael and Roger Manvell, *The History of the British Film, 1896–1906* (London: George Allen & Unwin, 1948); Pepper, Terence, *High Society: Photographs 1897–1914* (London: National Portrait Gallery, 1998).

FILMOGRAPHY: *Boys Scrambling for Pennies under the West Pier, Brighton* (aka *Children on the Beach*); *Children Paddling* (aka *Children Playing in the Sea*); *A Street in Brighton*; *A Street in Portsmouth*; *Ocean Waves in a Storm*; *Bathers on the Beach at Brighton*; *Crowds at Brighton*; *Donkey Rider*; *The Promenade at Brighton*; *Portsmouth: The Ferry*; *Sailors of an English Warship*; *Soldiers in Portsmouth*; *Workmen Leaving Portsmouth Dockyard*; *Railway Scene*; *Bicycle Rider*; *Street Scene*; *English Cavalry in Aldershot*; *Military Scene*; *Runners at Gatwick*; *The Broken Melody*; *Street Traffic in London*; *Crowded Streets in London*; *Westminster Bridge*; *The Lord Mayor's Show* (1896); *A Victorian Lady in Her Boudoir* (aka *Woman Undressing*, 1897).

COLLINS, Alf (1867–1951)

As one of the originators of the chase movie, Alf Collins added the realism of filming in urban locations to the stereotyped characters and situations of popular theatre. Although emanating from a stage background he developed innovative cinematic devices such as interpolated close-ups, panning shots and subjective views. Born in 1867, probably in Newington, south London, Collins became an actor at the age of eighteen, appearing in melodrama and pantomime at the Surrey Theatre, Southwark. Throughout the 1880s and 90s he appeared in minor roles, supporting many of the Victorian stage's greatest actors. Having gained film-making experience with R. W. Paul and the British Mutoscope and Biograph Company, Collins joined Gaumont in 1902.

Almost immediately, he began to employ the lessons of the pantomime harlequinade in a series of chase films, which rivalled the popularity of the productions of Frank Mottershaw and William Haggar. *Welshed – A Derby Day Incident* (1903) opened with a panning shot of bookmakers at the Epsom racecourse, fixing suddenly on an individual booth. A bookmaker's view of the race through binoculars was followed by a multi-shot chase. The final scene, to become typical of many early chases, depicted the villain moving towards and past the camera. Collins' next chase continued to mix dramatic action with comedy, showing the same incident as perceived by pursuer and pursued. *The Runaway Match; or, Marriage by Motor* (1903), with its views from two speeding cars, was popular in Britain and the United States. A third film, *The Pickpocket; or, A Chase through London* (1903), developed the comic-dramatic theme to construct a complex twelve-shot chase with a violent conclusion rivalling Mottershaw's *A Daring Daylight Robbery* (1903).

Collins, ably assisted by his wife Maude, directed about two hundred and twenty films before the First World War, alternating comedies with dramas that often reflected his stage background. Appearing at music halls with the Coster comedienne Kate Carney throughout his film-making career, Collins showed close affinity with working-class life. His films were almost certainly influenced by music-hall songs written by his brother Charles Collins, author of cockney classics like 'Are We to Part Like This?' and 'Don't Dilly Dally'. When not working at Gaumont's open-air studio at Champion Hill, Collins took to the streets of south-east London, filming against a background of everyday life. The crowds required for Collins' elaborate chase sequences were often recruited – and rewarded – at local pubs. Collins, his wife and son frequently appeared as actors, while even Gaumont's managing director, A. C. Bromhead, was sometimes induced to join the chase. As a director, Collins employed a static, conventional approach to dramas like *Rip Van Winkle* and *The Blacksmith's Daughter*, whereas his handling of comedy subjects showed fluidity and an interest in varying camera angles. Having played a crucial role in developing the chase movie, Collins bowed out of film-making in the early 1910s to pursue an unremarkable career in live theatre.

(Barry Anthony)

BIBLIOGRAPHY: Anthony, Barry, 'Alfred Collins: Britain's Forgotten Film-Maker', in Alan Burton and Laraine Porter (eds), *Pimples, Pranks and Pratfalls: British Film Comedy before 1930* (Trowbridge, Wilts: Flicks Books, 2000).

FILMOGRAPHY: *The Professor and the Butterfly*; *The Tramp's Surprise*; *The Dead Cat*; *A Policeman's Dream*; *Trained Dogs*; *Serpentine Dancer*; *Boudoir Secrets*; *A Resourceful Dentist*; *American Knockabouts*; *Baker and Boy*; *Clown, Pantaloon and Bobby* (1902); *The Marvellous Syringe*; *The Effects of Too Much Scotch*; *A Photographic Episode*; *Papa's Bath*; *King of Coins*; *Welshed – A Derby Day Incident*; *Mind the Wet Paint*; *The Rivals*; *A Lover's Troubles*; *Notice to Quit*; *The Mysterious Mechanical Toy* (aka *Phroso the Mysterious Mechanical Doll*); *Little Nell and the Burglar*; *Rip Van Winkle*; *Our New Cook*; *A Row in a Laundry*; *A Pleasant Breakfast*; *A Substantial Ghost*; *The Inspector's Birthday*; *That Naughty Girl*; *The Double-Bedded Room*; *Tommy Atkins's Dream*; *Two Little Vagabonds; or, The Pugilistic Parson*; *Murphy's Wake*; *A Practical Discussion*; *Dotheboys Hall; or, Nicholas Nickleby*; *The Sportive Navvies*; *The Christmas Waits; or, High Life below Stairs*; *Such Is Life; or, Mind Your Own Business*; *The Somnambulist* (aka *The Sleepwalker*); *The Runaway Match; or, Marriage by Motor*; *The Pickpocket; or, A Chase through London* (1903); *No Room for Father*; *That Busy Bee*; *The Silver Tenor; or, The Song That Failed*; *Father's Birthday Party*; *Jack's Rival*; *The Apple Woman*; *All through the Page Boy*; *The Coster's Wedding*; *Cook's Lovers*; *Military Tactics*; *A Smart Capture*; *Two Deceived Old Maids*; *Dr Cut'emup*; *The Office Boy's Revenge*; *The Eviction*; *The Jealous Wife*; *Chased by Dogs*; *The Electric Shock*; *The Lost Shuttlecock*; *The Fatal Wig*; *Behind the Scenes; or, Algy's Mishap*; *Mr Mosenstein*; *The Masher's Dilemma*; *The Sweep*; *Artist and Musician*; *An Affair of Honour*; *Night Duty*; *Fixing the Swing*; *Stewed Missionary*; *Revenge!*; *The Tramp's Toilet*; *Brown's Pudding* (aka *When Father Makes a Pudding*); *The Amorous Militiaman*; *Future Hackenschmidts*; *Bill Bailey's Return*; *The Fruits of Matrimony*; *Bed and Breakfast Two Shillings*; *My Mother-in-Law*; *Rejected by Pa*; *The Haunted Houseboat*; *The Blacksmith's Daughter*; *Mixed Bathing*; *Lovers on the Sands; or, A Stroll on the Sands*; *On Brighton Pier*; *A Day at Brighton*; *Hands Up!; or, Captured by Highwaymen*; *Raid on a Coiner's Den* (1904); *The Scent Spray*; *As Sparrows See Us*; *The Alien Question*; *The Three Tramps*; *A Motor Masquerade*; *The Electric Goose*; *Auntie's Cycling Lesson*; *Wigs and Buttons*; *Nobbler's Card Party*; *Eyes Right*; *A Macaroni Feast*; *A Raid on a Canteen*; *Darling Puggy*; *A Motorbike Adventure*; *The Birthday Umbrella* (aka *The Unlucky Umbrella*); *The Coster's Christening*; *The Gardener's Nap*; *The Ups and Downs of Murphy*; *That Awful Baby*; *The Tale of a Coat*; *Married Bliss*; *Keiro's Cat* (aka *Pussy's Breakfast*); *The Henpecked Hindoo*; *The Burglar Lover*; *Father in the Kitchen*; *The Young Ladies' Dormitory*; *Stump Speech*; *Jack's Return*; *Greedy Billy*; *W. Weary and T. Tired*; *The Bobby's Nightmare*; *The Awkward Horseman*; *The Gentleman Beggar*; *Who's That A-Calling?*; *A Day with the Fresh Air Fiend*; *When Extremes Meet*; *How the Poor Help the Poor*; *The New Woman*; *The Record Sneeze*; *Grandpa and the Butterfly*; *The Milkmaid*; *A False Alarm; or, The Masher's Ducking*; *How Brown Brought Home the Goose*; *Why the Lodger Left*; *The Peashooter; or, A New Weapon for the Army*; *An Artful Dodge*; *The Gipsy Fortune Teller*; *The Burglar; or, The Hue and Cry*; *The Motor Competition*; *Mixed Bathing at Home*; *Robbery with Violence*; *Tommy's Experiments in Photography*; *Santa Claus' Mistake*; *Father Makes Love to the Pump*; *The Blind Man's Child* (1905); *The Missing Legacy; or, The Story of a Brown Hat*; *The Henpecked Husband*; *This Side Up*; *It's a Have*; *Dinner Hour*; *In Our Alley*; *Hot Pie*; *Lost! A Leg of Mutton* (US: *The Lost Leg of Mutton*); *Saved by a Pillar Box*; *All's Well That Ends Well*; *My Wife's a Teetotaler*; *Uncle George's Trip to London*; *Nosey Parker*; *Not Detained at the Office*; *The Catch of the Season*; *The Undergraduates*; *The Two Orphans*; *Willie and Tim Get a Surprise*; *Dolly Varden*; *Wanted – A Husband*; *A Lodging House Comedy*; *Flypaper*; *Jane on the Warpath*; *The Convict's Daughter*; *The Puzzle Maniac*; *The Postman's Christmas Box*; *The Four Hooligans*; *A Sailor's Courtship*; *When Cripples Meet*; *Her Morning Dip*; *Rescued by Lifeboat*; *Jam Now in Season*; *Curfew Shall Not Ring Tonight*; *The Two Tomboys* (1906); *Catch the Kid*; *The Drunken

Motorcyclist; A Shilling Short of His Wages; Ju-Jitsu; The Ice-Cream Jack; All for Nothing; Short-Sighted Jane; The Bachelor's Piece of Wedding Cake; Oh That Cat!; Cheap Beer, Father Buys a Lawn Roller, Remember Remember the Fifth of November, Tommy the Tinpot Hero; The Adventures of a Roll of Lino (aka *Father Buys Some Linoleum*) (1907); *A Race for a Rose; Honours Even; Only a Penny a Box; The Woman Who Wasn't; Napoleon and the English Sailor, Tommy and the Policeman's Whistle; Mechanical Legs; Moving In; Harry Lauder in a Hurry; A Stitch in Time; Washing Day; The Burglar's Joke with the Automatic Doll; The Dancing Girl; The Drunkard's Dream; The Convict and the Dove; Put Pa amongst the Girls; Sweet Liberty; The Sloshton Quartette; A Christmas Raffle* (aka *Father Wins a Turkey*) (1908); *How Percy Won the Beauty Competition; The Martyrdom of Adolph Beck; The Four Tomboys; The Boxing Waiter, From Servant Girl to Duchess; Quicksilver Pudding* (1909); *The Travelling Stiltwalkers; Algy Tries for Physical Culture; The Coster's Phantom Fortune; Wait and See; Father Minds the Baby; The Sleep Breakers; Winning a Widow; Algy Goes on Stage* (1910); *A Maid of the Alps; Algie's Expensive Stick* (1912).

COLLINS, Edwin J. (1875–1937)

Edwin Joseph Collins was born in Cheltenham, Gloucestershire, in 1875, and was working as a stage actor by 1901, when he was counted for that year's census in Birkenhead. By 1910, he had begun appearing in Cricks and Martin films; his first directorial work for the company emerged in March 1912. He continued in the business for a little over ten years.

Viewing one of his last films, a 1923 two-reel adaptation of *The Taming of the Shrew*, the American scholar Robert Hamilton Ball concluded that 'except for the cross-cutting, there is hardly a trace of recognition of the true nature of the motion picture medium' (Ball, p. 286). The few surviving prints, *Shrew* included, certainly suggest a comparative primitive at work, pursuing the kind of stage blocking, camera rigidity and comic tropes that other countries had long moved beyond. Yet this was seen in Britain as no great burden, and did not bar quite ambitious assignments, like Ideal's six-reel *Tom Jones* of 1917 – 'received with cordial approval', announced the *Bioscope*, despite a December fog invading the trade show's auditorium (27 December 1917, p. 45).

Collins began with one-reel shorts. The few surviving Cricks and Martin titles include plain comedies laden with crude make-up, basic camera tricks and out-of-date gags (*Express Delivery, Here We Are Again*). Despite extensive semaphore acting, the surviving dramas remain more persuasive. *A Man's Shadow* (1912), the compact story of a criminal past rebounding, offers attractive lighting and an enjoyably melodramatic death; the two-reel *The Scapegrace* (1913), featuring a wastrel's redemption in a pluckily imagined Yukon, crowns its action with a collapsing bridge and the heroine hoisted up a rock cliff. By June 1914, with his adaptation of Bulwer Lytton's novel *Eugene Aram*, Collins had reached four reels and a steady, if low, level of competence; later films for Ideal and Harry Parkinson's Master Films bedded down with other Victorian novels by Charles Reade (*Foul Play, Hard Cash*), Mrs Henry Wood (*The Channings*) and H. Rider Haggard (*Stella*). Fielding's voluminous *Tom Jones* had been bashed into scenario shape by the prolific Eliot Stannard, who stressed the dramatic rather than the comic. Collins' more ambitious features often received trade praise for their detailed, realistic atmosphere: but with no prints surviving, it is hard now to check.

Collins joined Parkinson in December 1919 and followed his company's fortunes in the early 1920s, making subjects heavy with popular sentiment and, when the funding for features shrank, several series of short subjects. *The Taming of the Shrew*, well meaning but marred by Lyceum Theatre veteran Lauderdale Maitland's pudgy Petruchio, was one of the *Gems of Literature*. His last feature, *A Gamble with Hearts*, a fanciful crime drama, emerged in 1923. No further activity is known, beyond the recreations listed in his entries in issues of the *Kinematograph Year Book*: walking and watercolour sketching. He died in Richmond, Surrey, on 14 January 1937.

(Geoff Brown)

BIBLIOGRAPHY: Ball, Robert Hamilton, *Shakespeare on Silent Film: A Strange Eventful History* (London: George Allen & Unwin, 1968); Low, Rachael, *The History of the British Film 1914–1918* (London: George Allen & Unwin, 1950); 'Tom Jones', *The Bioscope*, 27 Dec. 1917, p. 45.

FILMOGRAPHY: Shorts: *The Stolen Violin; Not Such a Fool; Jones' Mistake; Pursued by Priscilla; Turning the Tables; The Harvest of Sin; Constable Smith and the Magic Baton; Out of the Past; Cold Steel; Constable Smith in Command; The Farmer's Daughter, The Patched Coat; A Country Lass; Constable Smith on the Warpath; The Sixth Commandment; The Vengeance of Daniel Whidden; A Man's Shadow, The Masked Smuggler, The Hearts of Men; Oh What a Peach!; The Dancing Girl; Brown's Day Off; Economical Peter, Against the Tide; Peter's Rival; Blackmail; The Bandit's Daughter, Nan in Fairyland; Caught in His Own Net; Her Brother's Tutor, What Matter the Price; The Thief* (1912); *Oh! My Aunt; From the Depths; Won by a Child; A Broken Life; The Sport of Fate; All's Well That Ends Well; Social Aspirations; A Sporting Chance; The Diamond Star, Wooing Auntie; The Smuggler's Daughter, The Postman; Daydreams; The Jailbird; Hitchy-Koo; The Scapegrace; The Adventures of a Bad Shilling; The Headman's Vengeance; Will He Do It?; An Island Romance; The Whirligig of Time; Algy and the Pierrette; Express Delivery; Revenge Is Sweet; A Fishy Story; A Brigand's Wooing; Money for Nothing; When Father Learnt to Bike; The Heart of a Gipsy Maid; Time Flies; A Fishergirl's Love; Nabbem Joins the Force; Land and Sea; PC Nabbem and the Anarchists; A Newsboy's Christmas Dream; How Cecil Played the Game; His Wonderful Lamp; Here We Are Again* (aka *The Harlequinade*); *In the Smuggler's Grip; Good for the Gout; For Her Mother's Sake* (aka *A Typist's Love Affair*); *A Tale of Two Tables; PC Nabbem's Smart Capture; He Attended the Meeting* (1913); *Meddlesome Mike; PC Nabbem and the Coiners; Selina's Flight for Freedom; Bertie Buys a Caretaker, Percy Attends a Masquerade; A Double Exposure; The Electric Doll; They All Want a Girl; Non-Suited; No Cure Like Father's; When the Ink Ran Out; Asking for Trouble; Snuffy Stuff, Snuff; A Kiss, Nearly; Sniffkins Detective and the Missing Cigarette Cards; A Hair-Raising Episode in One Splash; Whose Baby?; Auntie's Dilemma; A Novel Wooing; Swanker Meets His*

Girl; Swanker and the Witch's Curse; The Pursuit of Venus; One Winter's Night (aka *One Christmas Eve*); *For the Honour of Belgium; Aubrey's Birthday; Constable Coppem and the Spy Peril; Ah! Ahh!! Tishoo!!* (aka *Some Snuff*); *The New Dentist* (1914); *Odd Man Out; John Pawkson's Brutality; A Fluke in the 'Fluence; P'raps, P'raps Not; Discord in Three Flats; The Devil to Pay; Nabbed!; Spoof for Oof; Bosh!; Watch Your Watch; Dowell's Duels; Left in the Lurch; Going! Going!! Gone!!!; Well I'm –; Love and Spanish Onions; Boots? Not 'Arf!; Young Nick at the Picnic; Nobbling the Bridge; Which Is Witch?; Tough Nuts and Roughs; Puss and Boots; Dream Bad, Luck Ditto; The Silence of Jasper Holt; Mad Mokes and Motors; Fickle Flo's Flirtation; Two of a Suit* (1915); *Many Happy Returns; A Deuce of a Girl; Rays That Erase; On the Carpet; Boots from Bootle; £66.13.9 ¾ for Every Man, Woman and Child; Blood Tells; or, The Anti-Frivolity League* (1916); *Doing His Bit; The Blind Boy* (1917); *Rations* (1918); *Jane Shore, The Lady of the Camelias, Esmeralda* (aka *The Hunchback of Notre Dame*) (episodes from the series *Tense Moments from Great Plays*); *Il Trovatore, Samson and Delilah, Don Juan* (episodes from the series *Tense Moments from Operas*); *Ticket o' Leave, The Lights o' London, The Parson's Fight, Sal Grogan's Face* (episodes from the series *Famous Poems by George R. Sims ('Dagonet')*); *Won by Warr, Pluck v. Plot, Quitter Grant* (episodes from the series *The Sporting Twelve*) (1922); *The Mistletoe Bough, The Taming of the Shrew, Curfew Must Not Ring Tonight* (episodes from the series *Gems of Literature*, 1923).
Features: *A Daughter of Satan; Eugene Aram; The Grip of the Past* (1914); *Tom Jones* (1917); *God and the Man* (1918); *In the Gloaming; The Starting Point* (1919); *Calvary; Foul Play; The Channings* (1920); *Hard Cash; Stella; Miss Charity; Single Life; The God in the Garden* (1921); *The Green Caravan* (1922); *A Gamble with Hearts* (1923).

COLLINSON, Peter (1936–1980)

Peter Collinson was born into a theatrical family on 1 April 1936 in Cleethorpes, Lincolnshire. After his parents divorced, he lived briefly with his grandmother before being sent to the Actors' Orphanage in Chertsey, Surrey. There he appeared in a number of plays, coming to the notice of the Orphanage's president, Noël Coward, who watched over the young Collinson's career, arranging an audition at RADA and his first job as a stagehand at the New Cross Empire.

Following National Service in Malaya, Collinson went to work in independent television as a trainee director at ATV. He then moved to the new Ulster Television channel in Northern Ireland, where he became Senior Drama Director and won a number of awards before returning to ATV. His break into features came in 1967 with *The Penthouse*, a menacing thriller about an estate agent and his lover terrorised by psychopaths who pretend they have come to read the gas meter. Collinson desperately tries to make what was a stage play (*The Meter Man* by Scott Forbes) cinematic by the use of shock cuts and strange angles, but he was accused of merely dressing up a derivative and exploitative mix of sex and violence. His next project was a cinema version of Nell Dunn's *Up the Junction*, which had been filmed for television by Ken Loach in 1965. It was equally poorly received by the critics, but Collinson's strategy of downplaying social criticism in favour of the romance between middle-class Polly (Suzy Kendall) and working-class Peter (Dennis Waterman), and the enjoyably vulgar performances of Maureen Lipman, Adrienne Posta and Liz Frazer, made the film popular with audiences. Despite its crudities it remains one of the more interesting London films of the late 1960s.

Collinson continued to follow the *Zeitgeist* with his next project, the anti-war drama *The Long Day's Dying*, a brave attempt to explore the tensions between hostility to the idea of war and exhilaration at the experience of combat. The film benefits hugely from the fine performances of David Hemmings, Tony Beckley, Tom Bell and Alan Dobie as the scared but enterprising soldiers, but it was too violent to appeal to critics and too downbeat to attract audiences. Much more acceptable was *The Italian Job*, Collinson's best-known and most popular film. With an excellent script from Troy Kennedy Martin and a strong cast headed by Michael Caine and Noël Coward, this crime caper has remained an audience favourite. It was remade in Hollywood by F. Gary Gray in 2003.

Collinson was prolific in the 1970s, though the general decline of British cinema during the decade meant he had to be ingenious in his funding arrangements. The comedy-adventure *You Can't Win 'Em All*, starring Tony Curtis and Charles Bronson as American mercenaries in 1920s' Turkey, was backed by Columbia. With *Fright* and *Straight on Till Morning* Collinson returned to the exploitation market where *The Penthouse* had been nurtured. After making the interestingly downbeat spy film *Innocent Bystanders*, he turned to Europe, making *The Man Called Noon*, a Western, and *Open Season*, another innocents terrorised by oddballs scenario, in Spain. *Ten Little Indians*, a remake of the old Agatha Christie whodunit filmed by René Clair in 1945 as *And Then There Were None*, is a more typical Europudding, with a cast ranging from Elke Sommer and Gert Frobe to Oliver Reed and Richard Attenborough, and finance from Italy, France, Spain, Germany and Britain. Though the film did not enjoy the success of EMI's more mainstream *Murder on the Orient Express* (Sidney Lumet, 1974) its eclectic cast and unusual setting (a grand Iranian hotel) at least make for interesting viewing. Collinson's remake of Robert Siodmak's *The Spiral Staircase*, on the other hand, is vastly inferior to the original. Subtlety was never Collinson's strong point and what had been a frighteningly atmospheric thriller is reduced to a dull story punctuated by too-obvious shocks.

Ever enterprising, Collinson went to Israel to make *The Sell-Out*, South Africa to make *Tigers Don't Cry*, Canada to make *Tomorrow Never Comes*, and finally Australia, where he made his last film, *The Earthling*. He died from cancer on 16 December 1980 in Los Angeles, aged only forty-four. In 2003, a poll of British moviegoers voted Charlie Croker's (Michael Caine) exclamation in *The Italian Job*, 'You were only supposed to blow the bloody doors off', the greatest one-liner in cinema – a fitting epitaph, perhaps, for Collinson's career.
(Martin Hunt)

BIBLIOGRAPHY: Carr-Smith, Rodney, 'Peter Collinson', *Photoplay*, Dec. 1968, pp. 55, 61; Murphy, Robert, *Sixties British Cinema* (London: BFI, 1992); Walker, Alexander, *Hollywood, England: The British Film Industry in the Sixties* (London: Michael Joseph, 1974), pp. 395–6.

FILMOGRAPHY: *The Penthouse*; *Up the Junction* (1967); *The Long Day's Dying* (1968); *The Italian Job* (1969); *You Can't Win 'Em All* (1970); *Fright* (1971); *Straight on Till Morning*; *Innocent Bystanders* (1972); *The Man Called Noon/Un hombre llamado Noon* (Sp/It/UK, 1973); *Open Season/Los cazadores* (Sp/Switz); *Ten Little Indians* (UK/Ger/It/Sp/Fr) (1974); *The Sell-Out* (UK/It); *The Spiral Staircase* (1975); *Tigers Don't Cry* (1976); *Tomorrow Never Comes* (UK/Can, 1977); *The Earthling* (US/Austral, 1980).

COMERFORD, Joe (1949–)

Joe Comerford was born in Dublin in 1949 and became involved in film-making while studying at the National College of Art and Design in the 1960s. In the early 1970s he worked for RTÉ (Ireland's national broadcaster), where he trained as a camera operator as well as in general studio production. Comerford later admitted, however, that he found it difficult to work within the institutional constraints of RTÉ. He left in 1972 to begin a long and distinguished career as an independent film-maker whose own film practice was to challenge the conventions of popular studio production.

In the 1970s little in the way of funding existed for independent production in Ireland so Comerford was drawn inevitably into a political role as well. He was a founding member of the Association of Independent Producers (AIP) with fellow independent film-makers like Bob Quinn, Cathal Black, Pat Murphy and Thaddeus O'Sullivan, all of whom worked on each others' films in these formative years. Throughout the late 1970s, the AIP lobbied government on behalf of the fledgling independent sector and was finally vindicated in 1981 when the Government established the first Irish Film Board.

Comerford's own films illustrate well his commitment to a form of politically engaged and aesthetically challenging cinema that was impossible within the constraints of television. His early short films – *Swan Alley* (1969), *Emtigon* (1972), *Withdrawal* (1974, later re-edited and reworked in 1982) and *Down the Corner* (1978) – demonstrate this predilection for an experimental, avant-garde practice. All his films are elliptical, with complex narratives, challenging the audience to make sense of seemingly unmotivated plot turns. Over the years, however, he has applied this essentially avant-garde sensibility to a relentless exploration of social and political issues, giving his experimental forms the unadorned flatness of naturalist film-making.

Comerford has also been particularly concerned with the political situation in Northern Ireland, and the conflict there has been a theme in most of his films. His three feature films – *Traveller* (1982), *Reefer and the Model* (1988) and *High Boot Benny* (1993) – share a general concern with those on the margins of an increasingly affluent Irish society, but Comerford is particularly concerned in these films to explore the political and cultural implications of violence in Northern Ireland. In his most critically successful film, *Reefer and the Model* (winner of the Europa Prize for Best Film in 1988), his marginal characters – a prostitute, a gay man, a Republican on the run and a disenchanted criminal – form an alternative 'family' to that of the official nation. This attempt to reimagine Ireland in radical ways has been a feature of Comerford's film-making throughout his career, and in the commercial climate of the 1990s and beyond, his challenging vision has been largely out of favour. Thus, despite a long and distinguished contribution to film-making in Ireland, he has been able to make relatively few films and, as the Europa Prize testifies, he has found critical favour more often abroad than in Ireland itself.

(Martin McLoone)

BIBLIOGRAPHY: Finn, Eugene, 'Peripheral Visions', *Film Base News* no. 23, May/June 1991, pp. 8–12; Finn, Eugene, 'From the Ex-Country', *Film Ireland* no. 100, Sept./Oct. 2004, pp. 22–4; Mac Reamoinn, Laoise, 'Crossing the Border', *Film Ireland* no. 43, Oct./Nov. 1994, pp. 10–11; McLoone, Martin, *Irish Film: The Emergence of a Contemporary Cinema* (London: BFI, 2000); Pettitt, Lance, *Screening Ireland* (Manchester: Manchester University Press, 2000); Rockett, Kevin, John Hill and Luke Gibbons, *Cinema and Ireland* (London: Routledge, 1988).

FILMOGRAPHY: *Swan Alley* (short, Ir, 1969); *Emtigon* (short, Ir, 1972); *Withdrawal* (shorts, Ir, 1974/82); *Down the Corner* (short, Ir, 1978); *Traveller* (Ir, 1982); *Waterbag* (Ir, 1984); *Reefer and the Model* (Ir, 1988); *High Boot Benny* (Ir/Ger, 1993).

COMFORT, Lance (1908–1966)

Over a twenty-five-year period Lance Comfort was one of the most prolific directors working in Britain, but despite the initial impression of a successful career, he received scant critical attention during his lifetime and worked mostly at the margins of the industry.

Born in Harrow in 1908, he entered the film industry around 1926 as an animator and cameraman on medical films. After several years in the camera department, he became a sound recordist at Stoll studios in 1932. Then in 1934 he joined producer/director John Baxter's UK Films as a technical supervisor; over the next few years Baxter was to be a formative influence on Comfort and did much to foster his career.

After directing documentaries and children's films, Comfort took the opportunity to direct his first feature, a piece of wartime propaganda, *Penn of Pennsylvania* (1941). Unfortunately, this was not the kind of subject Comfort warmed to and the result was a rather leaden biopic. By contrast, his next film, *Hatter's Castle* (1941), the darkly melodramatic story of a megalomaniac businessman who terrorises his family, provided him with exactly the kind of material he responded to. The dramatic focus is a group of self-interested individuals who are prepared to (and indeed relish) betraying and destroying anyone who gets in their way; while they meet the obligatory sticky end, the power of these characters is such that the nominal hero and heroine appear insipid in comparison.

Through the 1940s Comfort directed a series of quality dramas such as *Great Day* (1945), *Bedelia* (1946), *Temptation Harbour* (1947) and *Daughter of Darkness* (1948) with similarly amoral or tortured protagonists at their centre. When the box-office failure of *Portrait of Clare* (1950) coincided with a contraction of the UK film industry, work dried up, and Comfort was reduced to directing supporting features and episodes of television series such as *Douglas Fairbanks Presents*. Subsequently he never managed to shake off the B-film label and climb back into the first division, despite the obvious quality of films such as *Bang! You're Dead* (1954) and *Tomorrow at Ten* (1962). Nevertheless this quality – a consequence of his all-round technical competence, excellent organisation skills and an innate feel for film-making – ensured he remained busy almost up to his death in Worthing on 25 August 1966.

Perhaps what kept Lance Comfort outside the mainstream industry was not a lack of ability but the bleakness of his own personal vision, which is most clearly expressed in the melodramas and thrillers. His villains tend to be more psychotic, and his subsidiary characters more likely to be murdered, than in most films. Unlike his mentor John Baxter his films steer clear of social messages; they are more concerned with the individual than with society, and they present a picture of mankind in which evil is not simply an occasional aberration but an integral part.

(Linda Wood)

BIBLIOGRAPHY: McFarlane, Brian, 'Lance Comfort: Melodrama and an Honourable Career', *Journal of Popular British Cinema* no. 1, 1998; McFarlane, Brian, *Lance Comfort* (Manchester: Manchester University Press, 2002).

FILMOGRAPHY: *Sandy Steps Out* (short, 1938); *Laddie's Day Out* (short); *Judy Buys a Horse* (short); *Toddlers and a Pup* (short); *Thoroughbreds* (short) (1939); *Penn of Pennsylvania* (US: *The Courageous Mr Penn*); *Hatter's Castle* (1941); *Squadron Leader X*; *Those Kids from Town* (1942); *Old Mother Riley Detective*; *When We Are Married*; *Escape to Danger* (co-dir. Max Greene) (1943); *Hotel Reserve* (co-dirs. Max Greene, Victor Hanbury, 1944); *Great Day* (1945); *Bedelia* (1946); *Temptation Harbour* (1947); *Daughter of Darkness*; *Silent Dust* (1948); *Portrait of Clare* (1950); *The Girl on the Pier*; *The Genie* (co-dir. Lawrence Huntington); *The Triangle* (co-dirs. Leslie Arliss/Bernard Knowles); *Bang! You're Dead* (US: *Game of Danger*) (1953); *Eight O'Clock Walk*; *The Last Moment* (1954); *The Man in the Road*; *Atom at Spithead* (1956); *At the Stroke of Nine*; *Face in the Night* (US: *Menace in the Night*); *The Man from Tangier* (US: *Thunder over Tangier*) (1957); *Make Mine a Million* (US: *Look Before You Laugh*); *The Ugly Duckling* (1959); *Pit of Darkness*; *Rag Doll* (US: *Young, Willing and Eager*); *The Breaking Point* (US: *The Great Armoured Car Swindle*); *Touch of Death*; *The Break*; *Tomorrow at Ten*; *The Painted Smile* (1961); *Live It Up* (US: *Sing and Swing*); *Blind Corner* (US: *Man in the Dark*) (1963); *Devils of Darkness* (1964); *Be My Guest* (1965).

CONNOLLY, Fintan

After making *Angel on the Rocks*, a short film about a teenage girl coping with obstreperous boys and nagging parents, film-maker Fintan Connolly directed television documentaries on unemployment and emigration (*No Comment*, 1988), the eviction of elderly tenants (*Notice to Quit*, 1992), women and abortion (*50,000 Secret Journeys*, 1994) and asylum seekers (*Out of Nowhere*, 2000). He branched into documentary-influenced fiction with *Flick*, a low-budget feature about a middle-class Dublin cannabis dealer who gets out of his depth and finally seeks redemption by escaping from the city. Though well received at festivals the film has been poorly distributed. His second feature, *Trouble with Sex*, a romantic drama exploring the relationship between a pushy career woman (Renee Weldon) and a sleepy Dublin pub landlord (Aidan Gillen), was released in Ireland in May 2005.

(Robert Murphy)

BIBLIOGRAPHY: Ging, Debbie, 'Partners in Crime', *Film West* no. 41, Autumn 2000, pp. 26–8; McLoone, Martin, *Irish Film: The Emergence of a Contemporary Cinema* (London: BFI, 2000)

FILMOGRAPHY: *Angel on the Rocks* (short, Ir, 1985); *Flick* (Ir, 2000); *Trouble with Sex* (Ir, 2005).

CONNOR, Kevin (1937–)

Kevin Connor was born in London in 1937 and entered the film industry in the mid-1950s as assistant editor on Val Guest's *They Can't Hang Me* (1955). By the late 1960s he was editing films such as *Oh! What a Lovely War* (Richard Attenborough, 1969), *The Magic Christian* (Joseph McGrath, 1969) and *Hitler: The Last Ten Days* (Ennio De Concini, 1973). His debut as a director came with *From beyond the Grave*, a portmanteau horror film for the British company Amicus. With the aid of an excellent cast and a superior screenplay, Connor came up with one of the best of Amicus' horror films. Surprisingly for an ex-editor, his camerawork was highly mobile and his compositions bold and precise, most notably in the Pinteresque Donald Pleasence–Ian Bannen episode upon which the film's subsequent reputation largely rests.

Connor then directed a series of fantasy films in collaboration with producer John Dark. *The Land That Time Forgot* and *At the Earth's Core* were lively and stylish adaptations of Edgar Rice Burroughs' stories that made atmospheric use of their period settings and contained just enough humour to offset some of the limitations of the low-tech special effects. The remaining films in the cycle – *The People That Time Forgot*, *Warlords of Atlantis* and *Arabian Adventure* – were more formulaic and consequently less effective.

In the US, Connor has made *Motel Hell*, a strikingly effective cannibal-horror film, *The House Where Evil Dwells*, a ghost story set in Japan, and a murder mystery, *Sunset Grill*, along with several films and series for American television. He returned to Britain for an Anglo-American television adaptation of *Great Expectations* (1989), with Anthony Hopkins as Magwitch, and Jean Simmons (Estella in the 1946 David Lean version) as Miss Havisham; and for *Diana: Her True Story* (1993), with Serena Scott Thomas as Princess Diana and Mancunian David Threlfall unexpectedly cast as Prince Charles.

(Peter Hutchings)

BIBLIOGRAPHY: *Arabian Adventure*, director biography, July 1979, microfiche held in the BFI National Library, London; Pirie, David, 'Entretien: Kevin Connor', *Écran fantastique* no. 4, 1978, pp. 10–13.

FILMOGRAPHY: *From beyond the Grave* (1973); *The Land That Time Forgot* (1975); *Trial by Combat*; *At the Earth's Core* (1976); *The People That Time Forgot* (1977); *Warlords of Atlantis* (1978); *Arabian Adventure* (1979); *Motel Hell* (US, 1980); *The House Where Evil Dwells* (US, 1982); *Sunset Grill* (US, 1992).

CONWAY, Jack (1887–1952)

Jack Conway was born in Graceville, Minnesota, on 17 July 1887. A former stage actor with the West Coast Belasco stock company, Conway moved to California in 1909, where he played lead roles for the Nestor studio. Switching to behind-the-camera duties, he worked as an assistant to D. W. Griffith, before making his own directorial debut in 1915. A technically adroit craftsman with a flair for action, Conway found gainful employment at MGM, where he worked for most of his career. When MGM embarked on a series of British co-productions in the late 1930s, Conway was assigned to direct the first, *A Yank at Oxford*. Produced by Michael Balcon, the film was a vehicle for rising MGM star Robert Taylor, cast as a brash American student who clashes with the reserved Oxford University establishment, both sides eventually realising that they can learn something from the other. A major success at the time, *A Yank at Oxford* has the standard MGM production gloss and a high-calibre supporting cast that includes Vivien Leigh, Maureen O'Sullivan and Lionel Barrymore. Decades later, the film was remade with Rob Lowe as *Oxford Blues* (Robert Boris, 1984). Conway retired from films in 1948 and died in Pacific Palisades, California, on 11 October 1952.

(Daniel O'Brien)

BIBLIOGRAPHY: Obituary, *Motion Picture Herald*, 18 Oct. 1952, p. 26; Salmi, Markku, 'Jack Conway', *Film Dope* no. 8, Oct. 1975, pp. 2–4.

FILMOGRAPHY (UK only): *A Yank at Oxford* (1937).

CONYERS, Darcy (1919–1972)

Darcy Conyers, often credited as D'Arcy, was born on 19 July 1919 in Tanganyika. His first steps into the industry after arriving in England were as an actor. By 1950 he had moved into production, teaming up with Don Sharp to produce the low-budget *Ha'penny Breeze* (Frank Worth). In 1955 he wrote and directed his first feature, *The Secrets of the Forest*. This was the first of three energetic, if predictable, Children's Film Foundation films. Conyers then moved into comedy, teaming up with Brian Rix, with whom he formed a business partnership that lasted for three films and several television outings. Rix's undoubted brilliance as a stage farceur did not translate happily to the screen, where the exquisiteness of his timing counted for nothing, but they nevertheless proved successful at the box office. The partnership eventually split up over budgetary arguments when transferring a series of Rix's farces to television. Conyers' last film, *In the Doghouse* (1961) is by far his most satisfactory, with a fine cast – including Leslie Phillips, James Booth, Esma Cannon, Dick Bentley, Fenella Fielding, Joan Hickson and Hattie Jacques – making the most of a witty Michael Pertwee script. Between 1958 and 1960, Conyers was a regular director of the popular African safari television adventure *White Hunter*. He died in November 1972.

(Richard Dacre)

FILMOGRAPHY: *The Secrets of the Forest* (1955); *The Devil's Pass*; *Soapbox Derby* (1957); *Gateway to Adventure* (short, 1958); *The Night We Dropped the Clanger* (aka *Make Mine a Double*, 1959); *The Night We Got the Bird* (1960); *Nothing Barred*; *In the Doghouse* (aka *Vet in the Doghouse*) (1961).

COOPER, Arthur Melbourne (1874–1961)

Arthur Melbourne Cooper, born in St Albans on 15 April 1874, was a minor figure in the early years of British film, whose posthumous reputation became wildly over-inflated through the insistence of family and supporters who came to relish the idea that Cooper's reputation was being thwarted by some institutional conspiracy. The plain facts are these. Cooper appears to have worked for Birt Acres, before establishing the Alpha Trading Company in St Albans in 1901. He made some low comedies and trick films, but his true innovation came in animated film. *Dreams of Toyland* (1908), with toys chaotically disporting themselves across a village set, and the similar *The Tale of the Ark* (1909), are delightful surviving examples.

Cooper directed films for William Jeapes' Graphic Cinematograph Company, opened a cinema in St Albans in 1908 and made industrial films. He was not a pioneer of film form, he did not make films credited to G. A. Smith, and many films attributed to him are patently the films of others, being only 'his' in so far as he retained copies of some films shown in his cinema. The arguments behind Cooper's supposed direction of films like *Grandma's Reading Glass* have opened up some intriguing debates about the nature of authorship and the identification of early films, but enough is enough. One day, a measured tale of a modest pioneer of the animation film may be told. He died at Coton, Cambridgeshire, in 1961.

(Luke McKernan)

BIBLIOGRAPHY: Frank Gray, 'Smith versus Melbourne-Cooper', *Film History* vol. 11, Autumn 1999, pp. 246–61.

FILMOGRAPHY: *Blind Man's Bluff*; *Bill Sykes up to Date* (1903); *Car Ride* (c. 1903); *The Enchanted Toymaker* (aka *The Old Toymaker's Dream*); *The Smallest Railway in the World* (1904); *Ducks on Sale or Return* (c. 1904); *The Death of the Iron Horse*; *The Motor Highwayman*; *His Washing Day*; *In the Good Old Times* (aka *Poor Old Mr and Mrs Brown in the Stocks*); *The Ducking Stool*; *Who's to Blame?* (aka *Why the Typist Got the Sack*); *McNab's Visit to London*; *What Is It Master Likes So Much?* (1905); *Grandfather's Tormentors* (c. 1905); *The Motor Valet* (aka *The New Motor Valet*); *The Happy Man*; *The Guinea Entertainer*; *When the Cat's Away*; *The Policeman's Love Affair*; *Held to Ransom*; *A Catching Story*; *Target Practice*; *A Slippery Visitor*; *A Visit to a Spiritualist*; *The Modern Pirates* (aka *The Raid on the Armoured Motor*); *The Fairy Godmother* (aka *Noah's Ark*) (1906); *Youth Regained*; *Robbing H.M. Mails* (c. 1906); *Oh That Molar!*; *The Poet's Bid for Fame*; *Our New Pillar Box* (aka *The Animated Pillar Box*); *Lottie's Pancakes* (aka *Her First Pancake/Lottie's First Attempt*); *The Luck of Life*; *Seen at the Chiropodist's*; *When the Mistress Took Her Holiday*; *In Quest of Health*; *The Wily Fiddler*; *The Adventures of a Performing Flea*; *The 5-30 Collection*; *The Lodger Had the Haddock*; *The Lovers' Charm*; *The Tricky Twins*; *The Showman's Treasure*; *The Smoker's Joke*; *A Sacrifice for Work*; *His Sweetheart When a Boy* (1907); *Soapy Soup*; *The Woes of a Married Man*; *The Bad Sixpence* (US: *The Bad Shilling*); *The Boys' Half Holiday* (aka *Those Boys Again*); *Between One and Two A.M.* (c. 1907); *The Hypnotist's Joke*; *Dreams of Toyland*; *In the Land of Nod* (aka *Grandpa's Forty Winks*); *Animated Matches*; *Oh Those Boys!*; *A Little Stranger*; *Green's Goose*; *It's Just My Luck*; *Grandpa's Pension Day*; *The Curate's Honeymoon*; *Tommy on a Visit to His Aunt*; *Harlequinade*; *What Farmer Jones Saw at the Picture Show* (1908); *The Tale of the Ark* (1909); *The Toymaker's Dream*; *An Empire's Money Maker* (doc.) (1910); *Road Hogs in Toyland* (1911); *The Wooden Athletes*; *Father's Forty Winks*; *The Cats' Cup Final*; *Old Mother Hubbard*; *Cinderella*; *Ten Little Nigger Boys* (1912); *The Old Toymaker's Dream*; *Larks in Toyland* (1913).

COOPER, Budge (1913–1983)

Budge Cooper was born Brigid Cooper in Putney, London, on 2 September 1913. She entered the film industry with British International Pictures in 1934, initially as a shorthand typist and secretary. Subsequently she worked as a script-girl at Elstree; from 1940 she performed a similar function at the GPO (later Crown) Film Unit, especially on Humphrey Jennings' films. Her promotion to director came when she joined Paul Rotha Productions in 1941; a segment in the magazine series *Workers and Warfront* led to her first complete film, *Rat Destruction* (1942), a ten-minute information short on the work of local rodent officers in exterminating one of the Second World War's less appreciated menaces.

Cooper came into her own as a film-maker with *Children of the City* (1944), produced by Donald Alexander (the pair married the following year). Like other projects of Rotha's unit, this thirty-minute film eschewed the war's frontline battles for a report on the nation's social health. The topic was juvenile delinquency, investigated through the dramatised story of three children caught stealing from a pawnbroker's till. Cooper's persuasive handling of her non-professional actors and the eloquent realism of Wolfgang Suschitzky's photography added considerably to the film's impact.

In 1944, partly irked by Rotha's domineering ways, Cooper joined Alexander and other documentary talents in a new co-operative venture, the Documentary Technicians Alliance (DATA). Cooper's feeling for ordinary people emerged again in her first DATA production *Birth-day* (1946), dealing with maternity welfare facilities. The topic's treatment showed signs of battles behind the scenes over how the Government's heath policy should be presented; something even more marked in Alexander's National Health Service film *Here's Health* (1948), the pair's most prized post-war project, which she scripted through two years of bureaucratic wrangling.

In 1950 Alexander left DATA to go freelance, while Cooper concentrated on family matters. After returning to cinema in 1957, she made health and safety training films for the National Coal Board. Her entry into the mining industry's masculine environment was not without problems: to enable her to complete *Burns from a Colliery Explosion* in 1959, the technicians' union ACTT sponsored a legal challenge to an Act of Parliament forbidding women from venturing underground at coal mines. With *Labour of Love* (1961), made for the Bristol Public Health Department, she returned to the subject of childbirth.

Budge Cooper died in 1983 after a career marginalised by family duties and British documentary's decline. Yet in the 1940s she was a major talent in embryo, praised by *Documentary News Letter* in 1946 as 'one of the best directors of ordinary people that documentary has produced'.

(Geoff Brown)

BIBLIOGRAPHY: '*Children of the City*', *Documentary News Letter* vol. 5 no. 3, 1944, p. 28; 'Films of 1945', *Documentary News Letter* vol. 6 no. 51, 1946, pp. 8–9; McBain, Janet and Kevin Cowle (eds), *'With an Eye to the Future'. Donald Alexander and Budge Cooper – Documentary Film Makers* (Glasgow: Scottish Screen, 1997).

FILMOGRAPHY: *Rat Destruction*; *The Magician* (1942); *China* (1943); *Children of the City* (1944); *Birth-day* (1946); *Wounds and Bleeding* (1957); *Asphyxia and Artificial Respiration* (1958); *Burns from a Colliery Explosion* (1959); *Labour of Love* (1961); *Resuscitation by Mouth to Mouth Breathing and External Pressure on the Heart* (1963).

COOPER, George (1896–1947)

George A. Cooper was born on 29 April 1896. After initial experience as a journalist, playwright and film editor for Unione Cinematografica Italia, he came to prominence in the British film industry during the early 1920s with a series of two-reel 'Quality Plays'. Produced by Cooper, with direction shared between Cooper and Leslie Hiscott, the films were critically well enough received for him to be taken on by Gaumont as a feature director. A highwayman drama *Claude Duval* (1924) was followed by an adaptation of Ian Hay's family melodrama *The Happy Ending* (1925), which was praised by critics for its scenic beauty and finely modulated performances.

Cooper gained early experience of sound by making shorts for DeForest Phonofilm from 1926, but his progress in a changing industry was not helped by the poor reception given his silent melodrama *Master and Man* (1929), one of the products of the ill-fated British Screen Productions. Cooper re-emerged in 1932 as a director of low-budget quota product for Julius Hagen at Twickenham. Films such as *The Shadow* (1933) and *Tangled Evidence* (1934) show him at home in the rather playfully self-conscious country-house mystery genre that became a Twickenham staple. Despite their low production values, these films display wit and sophistication, particularly at the level of script and performance.

Cooper continued in quota production for Hagen and others throughout the 1930s. Often involved in the scripting and editing of his own films, he increasingly focused on his writing during the 1940s, contributing script work to features and wartime documentary shorts. His last film as director, *London Terminus* (1944), was a sixteen-minute documentary about the patriotic efforts of London railway workers. George Cooper died in August 1947.

(Lawrence Napper and Geoff Brown)

BIBLIOGRAPHY: Low, Rachael, *The History of British Film 1918–1929* (London: George Allen & Unwin, 1971); Napper, Lawrence, 'A Despicable Tradition? Quota Quickies in the 1930s', in Robert Murphy (ed.), *The British Cinema Book* (London: BFI, 1997); Pearson, George, 'George Cooper: An Appreciation', *Kinematograph Weekly*, 4 Sept. 1947, p. 12; 'Obituary. George Cooper: Film Pioneer', *Kinematograph Weekly*, 28 Aug. 1947, p. 8.

FILMOGRAPHY: *The Thief* (short); *The White Rat* (short); *A Question of Principle* (short); *Fallen Leaves* (short); *Geraldine's First Year* (short); *The Big Strong Man* (short); *Poetic License* (short); *The Cunninghames Economise* (short); *Keeping Man Interested* (short); *The Letters* (short); *Her Dancing Partner* (short); *Pearl for Pearl* (short); *His Wife's Husband* (short) (1922); *Three to One Against* (short); *The Reverse of the Medal* (short); *The Man Who Liked Lemons* (short); *Finished* (short); *Darkness* (short); *Constant Hot Water* (short) (1923); *Claude Duval*; *The Eleventh Commandment* (1924); *Somebody's Darling*; *Settled out of Court*; *The Happy Ending* (1925); *If Youth but Knew*; *Julius Caesar* (short); *Santa Clause* (short) (1926); *Topsey Turvey* (short); *His Rest Day* (short); *Nan Wild* (short); *Olly Oakley* (short) (1927); *The Coffee Stall* (short); *The Clue of the Second Goblet* (short); *Blake the Lawbreaker* (short) (1928); *Master and Man* (1929); *The World, the Flesh and the Devil* (1932); *The Shadow* (1933); *His Grace Gives Notice*; *The Roof*; *Puppets of Fate* (US: *Wolves of the Underworld*); *The Man Outside*; *Home Sweet Home*; *Mannequin* (1933); *Tangled Evidence*; *The Case for the Crown*; *The Black Abbot*; *Anything Might Happen* (1934); *Sexton Blake and the Bearded Doctor* (1935); *Royal Eagle* (1936); *Down Our Alley* (1939); *London Terminus* (doc. short, 1944).

COOPER, Stuart (1942–)

Stuart Cooper was born in Hoboken, New Jersey, but moved to Newport Beach, California, when he was six. In 1960 he came to London to study at RADA; he was to spend the next twenty years in Britain, initially as an actor, later as a director. After a handful of appearances in television plays he landed roles in Michael Winner's *I'll Never Forget What's 'is Name* (1967) and Robert Aldrich's *The Dirty Dozen* (1967). However, his interest was already shifting from acting to directing. In 1970 he gained financial backing from Universal's London office to make *A Test of Violence*, a seventeen-minute documentary about the work of Spanish painter Juan Genovese; it won prizes at festivals and brought Cooper the opportunity to make a longer documentary on Sidney Nolan's paintings of the Australian outback for the BBC arts programme *Omnibus*. More surprisingly, it prompted George Harrison's financial support for a low-budget adaptation of David Halliwell's satire on student radicalism, *Little Malcolm and His Struggle against the Eunuchs*. Cooper's film is massively uneven, but teems with rowdy life.

Cooper had disagreed with Aldrich's gung-ho attitude to war in *The Dirty Dozen* and began working on a very different account of the Second World War, sifting through thousands of hours of documentary and newsreel footage at the Imperial War Museum for material to supplement a fictional war story from the perspective of an ordinary young soldier. *Overlord* finally emerged in 1975. Made on a tiny budget of £100,000 with an inexperienced cast, the film has its *longueurs*, but Cooper impressively integrates the wartime footage with his own material (shot in black and white with old lenses to eliminate any hint of inauthenticity). Poignantly, the shy, unremarkable young man we have watched adjust to army life (finding a good mate, meeting a nice girl when on leave) dies on the first day he finally sees action. But the use of actuality footage (particularly covering the preparations for the D-Day landings) puts his death in a context that avoids both mawkish heroics and anti-war rhetoric.

Though hardly shown beyond the London art-house cinema where it opened, *Overlord*'s originality and professionalism won Cooper credit with critics and fellow film-makers. Nonetheless, he found it difficult to raise the $2 million budget for his next film, *The Disappearance*. American distributors objected to the murky morality of Paul Mayersberg's script, and wanted to legitimise the contract killer hero by giving him a CIA- or MI6-approved licence to kill. Fortunately the National Film Finance Corporation and the Canadian Film Development Corporation were more understanding, and the film was made as an Anglo-Canadian co-production. Many years before Luc Besson's *Léon* (1994) and Jim Jarmusch's *Ghost Dog* (1999), Donald Sutherland plays a sympathetic contract killer, though one with none of his successors' cuddly tendencies. By structuring the film around Sutherland's obsession with his wife, an enigmatic devil-woman (played by his actual wife, Francine Racette), Cooper makes the film more melodrama than thriller, but he resists Mayersberg's tendency to meander and keeps the film taut and psychologically convincing. Too little bloodshed, multiple flashbacks and a delicate Ravel-based score left distributors nonplussed and kept audiences at bay; though *The Disappearance* displayed Cooper's talents as a mature and sophisticated director, it was only when the film was shown on American cable television in 1982 that its virtues were recognised.

After a long period in the wilderness of aborted projects, Cooper was recruited by Italian producer Vincenzo Labella to make *A.D.* (1985), a ten-hour miniseries charting the early years of Christianity. A starry cast playing emperors and saints proved irresistible to the international audience and the series relaunched Cooper's career in American television films. It is a field where compromise is inevitable, but Cooper has generally managed to bring a degree of originality and integrity to his projects.

(Robert Murphy)

BIBLIOGRAPHY: 'Business File: John Williams Meets Stuart Cooper, Director of *Overlord*', *Films Illustrated*, Nov. 1975, p. 91; Falk, Quentin, 'Stuart Cooper: From *The Dirty Dozen* to *A.D.*', *Sight and Sound*, Autumn 1985, pp. 236–7; Krueger, Ron, 'Director Cooper's "*AD*" Set to Air on NBC', *Screen International*, 9 Mar. 1985, p. 205; Woodman, Sue, 'Doing Things in Style', *Screen International*, 23 Apr. 1977, p. 8.

FILMOGRAPHY (UK only): *A Test of Violence – the Paintings of Juan Genovese* (doc., 1970); *Kelly Country* (doc., 1973); *Little Malcolm and His Struggle against the Eunuchs* (1974); *Overlord* (1975); *The Disappearance* (UK/Can, 1977).

CORMAN, Roger (1926–)

Born in Detroit, Michigan, on 5 April 1926, Roger Corman studied engineering at Stanford University and modern English literature at Oxford. He found a job as a messenger boy at 20th Century-Fox, eventually becoming a story analyst before setting up as an independent producer of low-budget exploitation movies. He has subsequently directed some fifty films, beginning with *Five Guns West* (1955), and produced more than three hundred.

Taking advantage of the Eady Levy, Corman came to Britain to make the last two, and arguably finest, of the eight-film series of Edgar Allan Poe adaptations initiated by *The House of Usher*/*The Fall of the House of Usher* in 1960. *The Masque of the Red Death* was filmed at Shepperton, partly on re-dressed sets left over from *Becket* (Peter Glenville, 1964), and gained additional production value from the ingenious colour experiments of cinematographer Nicolas Roeg. *The Tomb of Ligeia*, written by Robert Towne, is unique among the Poe cycle for its extensive use of exterior locations (in Norfolk). Poetic and dreamlike, it provides Vincent Price with his most romantic role as the tormented Verden Fell.

The comparatively big-budget *Von Richthofen and Brown* – a weakly written, woodenly acted but exhilaratingly shot First World War flying drama about the death of chivalry – was made in Ireland for United Artists. Corman has since directed only *Frankenstein Unbound* (1990), but he continues to produce cheap straight-to-video films and to profit from leasing remake rights to his vast back catalogue. He returned to Ireland in 1995 to open a film studio in Connemara.

(Sheldon Hall)

BIBLIOGRAPHY: Corman, Roger and Jim Jerome, *How I Made a Hundred Movies in Hollywood and Never Lost a Dime* (New York: Random House, 1990); Strick, Philip, 'Ma Barker to Von Richthofen', *Sight and Sound*, Autumn 1970, pp. 179–83; Willemen, Paul and David Pirie (eds), *Roger Corman: The Millenic Vision* (Edinburgh: Edinburgh Film Festival/Cinema Magazine, 1970).

FILMOGRAPHY (UK only): *The Masque of the Red Death*; *The Tomb of Ligeia* (1964); *Von Richthofen and Brown* (UK: *The Red Baron*, US/UK, 1971).

CORNELIUS, Henry (1913–1958)

Henry Cornelius was born in Cape Town, into a South African German-Jewish family, on 18 August 1913. While he was still young his family moved back to Berlin, where at the age of eighteen he was accepted to study acting and theatrical production with Max Reinhardt. Before he was twenty he was producing plays at Berlin's Schiller Theatre, but he left Germany with the advent of the Nazis and moved to Paris. He worked as a journalist and made his entry into the film industry as an assistant editor at the Studios de Montrouge. From there he moved on to London, where René Clair was about to start work on *The Ghost Goes West* for Alexander Korda. Clair wanted a French-speaking assistant editor, 'inexperienced enough to take instead of giving advice' (de la Roche, p. 11); Cornelius fitted the bill perfectly.

Cornelius remained with Korda for the next four years. He was promoted to editor on *Men Are Not Gods* (Walter Reisch, 1936), and also worked on *Forget Me Not* (Zoltán Korda, 1936), *The Drum* (Zoltán Korda, 1938), *The Four Feathers* (Zoltán Korda, 1939) and *The Lion Has Wings* (Michael Powell/Adrian Brunel/Brian Desmond Hurst, 1939). In 1939 he briefly joined Alberto Cavalcanti at the GPO Film Unit, then went back to his native country to become Deputy Director of the Film Section of the South African government's Propaganda Unit. In this capacity he wrote, produced, directed and edited some fifteen propaganda shorts. He returned to Britain in 1943 and at Cavalcanti's suggestion joined Ealing Studios as an associate producer (producer, in effect, at this studio).

Cornelius' first assignment was the drama-documentary *Painted Boats* (1945), directed by Charles Crichton. He went on to produce two key Ealing movies: *Hue and Cry* (1946), again for Crichton, the first of the true 'Ealing comedies', and Robert Hamer's poetic-realism-influenced East End drama *It Always Rains on Sunday* (1947). The success of these persuaded Michael Balcon to let Cornelius try his hand at directing a feature. *Passport to Pimlico* (1949), in which the London district of Pimlico declares independence from Britain and shrugs off post-war controls, has become one of the most fondly remembered of the Ealing comedies, a classic example of Balcon's 'mild revolution' (Barr, p. 9). But to Balcon's dismay the shoot went seriously over schedule and over budget, not wholly through Cornelius' fault; the action, set during the summer of 1947, one of the driest on record, was shot during the summer of 1948, one of the wettest.

Still, *Passport to Pimlico* easily recouped its cost, giving Ealing one of its biggest box-office hits. On the strength of it Cornelius demanded a raise, never a wise tactic with the frugal Balcon; he was turned down flat, and promptly quit the studio. Together with another Ealing alumnus, the publicist-turned-producer Monja Danischewsky, he formed a production company, Sirius. Their first film, *The Galloping Major* (1951), was a sub-Ealing comedy about an ex-army officer who bands together with friends and neighbours to buy a racehorse. Returns were unimpressive, and Danischewsky quit the company to return to Ealing. Cornelius, thinking to follow his example, offered his next project to Balcon; but the manner of his departure still rankled, and Balcon declined the offer. As a result, 'the most Ealing film not made by Ealing' was produced by the Rank Organisation.

Genevieve (1953), a comedy about two rival males – and their long-suffering female companions – taking part in the London to Brighton Veteran Cars rally, was scripted by William Rose, an American-born writer with a wry eye for British foibles. He went on to script, *inter alia*, Alexander Mackendrick's *The Maggie* (1954) and *The Ladykillers* (1955), and Basil Dearden's *The Smallest Show on Earth* (1957). Initial omens for the film were not promising: it was shot with a disgruntled cast under conditions of some discomfort, and once finished was loathed by John Davis, Rank's autocratic Chief Executive, who pronounced it too bad to distribute and wanted it shelved. Only Cornelius' persistence rescued it from limbo. When finally released, *Genevieve* met with overwhelming enthusiasm from critics and public, and went on to become one of the Rank Organisation's most profitable films. The second leads, Kenneth More and Kay Kendall, stole the picture from its stars, John Gregson and Dinah Sheridan, and Larry Adler's perky harmonica score stole it from all of them.

On the strength of this triumph, Cornelius seemed poised to become one of the foremost British directors working in the commercial mainstream. But ill-health was hampering his career, and he directed only two more films. *I Am a Camera* was a double adaptation, taken from the Broadway play by John Van Druten, itself adapted from Christopher Isherwood's Berlin novels, *Mr Norris Changes Trains* and *Goodbye to Berlin*. The material – later the basis for Kander and Ebb's smash-hit musical *Cabaret* – was heavily bowdlerised thanks to the British Board of Film Censors, and the film showed scant sense of period style. It was further encumbered by Laurence Harvey, disastrously miscast as Herr Issyvoo. Isherwood himself described it as 'a truly shocking and disgraceful mess', and the US critic Walter Kerr dismissed it with the famous crack, 'Me no Leica'.

Cornelius' last film, which he wrote himself from a short story by Paul Gallico, was *Next to No Time* (1958), a flaccidly whimsical comedy about a mild-mannered engineer (played by Kenneth More) on a transatlantic liner. Learning that each day on board gains a 'lost hour' to compensate for the change in time zones, he is emboldened to change his life and achieve his ambitions. By the time the film was released Cornelius had succumbed to his illness. He died in London on 2 May 1958.

(Philip Kemp)

BIBLIOGRAPHY: Barr, Charles, *Ealing Studios* (London and Newton Abbot, Devon: Cameron & Tayleur/David & Charles, 1977); de la Roche, Catherine, 'The Independent', *Films and Filming*, Feb. 1955, pp. 11, 30.

FILMOGRAPHY (UK only): *Passport to Pimlico* (1949); *The Galloping Major* (1951); *Genevieve* (1953); *I Am a Camera* (1955); *Next to No Time* (1958).

COUTTS, Don (1950–)

Donald Coutts was born in Scotland on 14 January 1950. He joined the film industry when he was nineteen, working at Columbia's British distribution branch. Work in a film laboratory and as an assistant editor followed; he then switched to television, initially as an editor, later as a director on programmes such as Channel 4's *After Dark*. Coutts teamed up with Scots-Italian journalist Sergio Casci to make an award-winning short, *Dead Sea Reels*, and two television dramas for BBC Scotland, *Rose* (1997) and *St Anthony's Day Off* (1998), before embarking on a low-budget feature shot on 16mm Fujicolour. *American Cousins* is a far-fetched tale about lovable Mafia gangsters hiding out with their long-lost cousin, the owner of a Glasgow fish-and-chip shop and ice-cream parlour. Good performances from Gerald Lepakowski as the cousin and Dan Hedaya and Danny Nucci as the gangsters help carry the hoary old plot, and Shirley Henderson's perky waitress injects a refreshing dose of realism. But in a market glutted with gangster comedies *American Cousins* passed by virtually unnoticed.

(Robert Murphy)

FILMOGRAPHY: *Dead Sea Reels* (short, 1996); *American Cousins* (2003).

COWARD, Noël (1899–1973)

Noël Pierce Coward was born in Teddington, Middlesex, on 16 December 1899. By the mid-1920s he had become one of Britain's leading playwrights, songwriters and stage actors. Several of his comedies and musicals were adapted by others for the screen in the 1920s and 30s, but Coward himself scorned the majority of these productions. Until the Second World War, he had little interest in film-making and only the most limited regard for cinema generally. In 1941, however, he was inspired by the story of the sinking of HMS *Kelly* in the Battle of Crete, related to him by his friend Lord Mountbatten, to write *In Which We Serve*. This classic wartime film brought Coward together with David Lean as co-director, Ronald Neame as cinematographer and Anthony Havelock-Allan as producer. Lean, Neame and Havelock-Allan would go on to make *This Happy Breed* (1944), *Blithe Spirit* (1945) and *Brief Encounter* (1945), based on Coward's plays, with Lean taking over as sole director.

In Which We Serve was an unlikely film for Coward. He had previously written sentimental and patriotic plays (most notably *Cavalcade* in 1931), but for the most part he was known for drawing-room comedies that were distinguished by their flippant dialogue and irreverent wit. Moreover, his public image was balanced somewhere between the effete decadence of a dandy and the stilted manners of an upper-class gentleman. He was thus an unlikely figure to write, direct and star in a film that paid tribute to the Royal Navy in wartime. He also had little knowledge of film-making, and his initial treatment was said to be lengthy enough for a film of eight or nine hours. The inspiration that helped to overcome these problems was Orson Welles' *Citizen Kane* (1941); its flashback structure and 'lightning mixes' offered a model for condensing a wide-ranging story and moving swiftly between different characters and locales, enabling Coward to dramatise the stories of officers on the upper decks and sailors on the lower decks. *In Which We Serve* interweaves the storylines of characters from a variety of class backgrounds and gives the impression that the nation itself is unified by its class structure; a significant achievement in wartime. It was also a stunning cinematic debut and, as Coward himself admitted, one assisted in large part by Lean's inventive direction and the impressive performances of the actors, particularly John Mills, Celia Johnson, Bernard Miles and Richard Attenborough. Coward died on 26 March 1973 in Blue Harbour, Jamaica.

(Mark Glancy)

BIBLIOGRAPHY: Aldgate, Anthony and Jeffrey Richards, *Britain Can Take It* (Oxford: Basil Blackwell, 1986); Coward, Noël, *Autobiography* (London: Methuen, 1986).

FILMOGRAPHY: *In Which We Serve* (co-dir. David Lean, 1942).

COX, Alex (1954–)

Alex Cox was born in Liverpool on 12 December 1954 and studied law at Oxford and film at Bristol before attending UCLA's film school. He worked as a screenwriter and in 1984 persuaded two ex-film school friends to produce *Repo Man,* a black and anarchic science-fiction comedy, with a punk score, partly based on his own experiences helping out a neighbour who worked as a car repossessor. Its anti-corporate and anti-nuclear stance placed the film outside the Hollywood mainstream, but word of mouth turned it into a cult hit.

Cox's interest in the punk movement led to *Sid and Nancy*, a sympathetic portrayal of two unsympathetic people who find in each other a temporary respite from the demons that possess them. Cox's reputation as an exciting new film-maker, however, was dented by *Straight to Hell*, a parody spaghetti Western, which showed his ability to incorporate natural landscapes into the mood of the story, but displayed an indulgence that also marred his next film. *Walker* was released in 1987 in the wake of the Iran/Contras scandal, and told the highly relevant (and true) story of a nineteenth-century American adventurer who became President of Nicaragua. But Cox's jarring use of anachronisms – such as the appearance of helicopters – overstressed contemporary parallels and alienated audiences.

In the 1990s, two of his projects – *Richard III* (Richard Loncraine, 1995) and *Fear and Loathing in Las Vegas* (Terry Gilliam, 1998) – were handed to other directors, but despite his reputation as a difficult and unpredictable director, Cox was able to continue along his highly idiosyncratic path. He was able to get American and Mexican backing for *Highway Patrolman*, which charted an idealistic policeman's journey of discovery, and showed an impressive psychological maturity and depth of characterisation. *The Winner* (1996), a very unglamorous view of Las Vegas, was followed by *Death and the Compass* (which Cox had made as a short film for the BBC in 1992), based on Jorge Luis

Alex Cox directs his actors in *Sid and Nancy* (1986)

Borges' surreal murder mystery. Ever unpredictable, the director's next two films were *Three Businessmen*, an amiable, low-key comedy about two art dealers in search of a meal, and *Revengers Tragedy*, a futuristic version of Thomas Middleton's Jacobean play exploring the corrupting nature of power. The only factor linking them was that both films were set in Liverpool.

Despite their minuscule budgets Cox's films are often remarkable for their inventive use of the medium. Few directors integrate their musical scores as well as Cox, and for each film he carefully works out a distinctive visual style (beginning with Robby Muller on *Repo Man*, he has been fortunate in finding exceptional cameramen capable of realising his visions). Though sometimes flawed by imperfect takes and rushed post-production work, Cox's films reflect his own integrity, intelligence, humour and commitment, and are always challenging, both visually and intellectually. Immensely knowledgeable about cinema – his 'Moviedrome' screenings of (often neglected) classics on BBC Television throughout the 1990s were always stimulating – he might be considered the quintessential maverick independent film-maker.

(Linda Wood)

BIBLIOGRAPHY: <alexcox.com>; Davies, Steven Paul, *Alex Cox: Film Anarchist* (London: B. T. Batsford, 2000); Davies, Steven Paul, 'Mad Alex beyond Moviedrome', *StarBurst* no. 270, Feb. 2001 pp. 50–3; Hunt, Nick, 'Close Up: Alex Cox', *Screen International*, 29 Mar. 2002, p. 13; Leigh, Danny, 'Gross and Disgusting', *Sight and Sound*, Mar. 2001, p. 65.

FILMOGRAPHY: *Edge City* (aka *Sleep is for Sissies*, short, US, 1980); *Repo Man* (US, 1984); *Sid and Nancy*; *Straight to Hell* (1986); *Walker* (US/Mex/Sp, 1987); *Highway Patrolman/El patrullero* (US/Mex, 1992); *The Winner* (US/Austral, 1996); *Death and the Compass/La muerte y la brújula* (US/Mex/Jap, 1997); *Three Businessmen* (US/UK/Neth, 1998); *Revengers Tragedy* (2002).

CRABTREE, Arthur (1900–1975)

Born on 29 October 1900 in Chorlton, Lancashire, but brought up in Shipley, Yorkshire, Arthur Crabtree entered the film industry as a clapper-loader for British International Pictures at Elstree in 1928. In 1932 he switched to Gaumont-British where he worked as camera operator for the American cinematographer Glen MacWilliams on films such as the Jessie Matthews musical *Evergreen* (Victor Saville, 1934). He shared photographic duties with Ernest Palmer on a number of films and was solely responsible for the cinematography on Michael Powell's visually inventive 'quota quickies' *Lazybones* (1935) and *The Love Test* (1935). Numerous other assignments as a cinematographer followed, including *Oh, Mr Porter!* (Marcel Varnel, 1937) and *Bank Holiday* (Carol Reed, 1938).

During the Second World War Crabtree photographed Carol Reed's Victorian comedy *Kipps* (1941), Gainsborough melodramas such as *The Man in Grey* (Leslie Arliss, 1943) and *Fanny by Gaslight* (Anthony Asquith, 1944), and Sidney Gilliat's *Waterloo Road* (1945), a superb wartime drama with Stewart Granger, John Mills and Alastair Sim. In 1944 he made his debut as a director with another exotic melodrama, *Madonna of the Seven Moons*. Though the film was more distinguished by its visual flair than its rambling narrative, it was a great popular success and established Crabtree as a director. Two other melodramas followed, the downbeat, contemporary *They Were Sisters* and the splendidly flamboyant *Caravan*. But in 1946 management of the Gainsborough studio passed from Maurice Ostrer to Sydney Box; and after directing *Dear Murderer*, an atmospheric thriller made at Gainsborough's second-string Islington studio, Crabtree was relegated to routine assignments.

In the 1950s, he directed B-films such as *Morning Call* and *Death over My Shoulder* and worked in television, directing numerous episodes of *Colonel March of Scotland Yard* (1954), featuring Boris Karloff as the Head of the 'Department of Queer Complaints', and *Ivanhoe* (1958), starring Roger Moore as the trusty knight. He also delved successfully into the horror genre with *Fiend without a Face* and *Horrors of the Black Museum*. *Fiend without a Face*, shot in moody black and white, is an effective science-fiction thriller in which rogue scientist Professor Walgate (Kynaston Reeves) accidentally creates a group of monsters, in the form of disembodied human brains attached to spinal columns, that strangle their victims at will. In *Horrors of the Black Museum*, made for American producer Herman J. Cohen at Anglo-Amalgamated, a crime writer (Michael Gough) commits a series of hideous murders merely to furnish material for his best-selling books. In the opening scene, a young woman has her eyes put out with a pair of spring-loaded 'spike' binoculars; in another sequence an innocent victim is beheaded in her bed. Shot in lurid colour and CinemaScope, the film was an instant success, but like Michael Powell with his own Anglo-Amalgamated shocker *Peeping Tom* (1959), the film's notoriety harmed Crabtree's reputation and he never directed again. He retired to Worthing, Sussex, where he died in March 1975.

(Wheeler Winston Dixon)

BIBLIOGRAPHY: Petrie, Duncan, 'Innovation and Economy: The Contribution of the Gainsborough Cinematographer', in Pam Cook (ed.), *Gainsborough Pictures* (London: Cassell, 1997); Sainsbury, Frank, 'Close-Ups: No. 14 – Arthur Crabtree', *Cine-Technician*, Nov./Jan. 1941–2.

FILMOGRAPHY: *Madonna of the Seven Moons*; *They Were Sisters* (1945); *Caravan* (1946); *Dear Murderer* (1947); *Quartet* ('The Kite' episode); *The Calendar* (1948); *Don't Ever Leave Me* (1949); *Lilli Marlene* (1950); *Hindle Wakes* (US: *Holiday Week*, 1951); *The Wedding of Lilli Marlene* (1953); *West of Suez* (US: *Fighting Wildcats*); *Morning Call* (1957); *Death over My Shoulder*, *Fiend without a Face* (1958); *Horrors of the Black Museum* (1959).

CRAIGIE, Jill (1911–1999)

Jill Craigie was born in Fulham, London, of Scots-Russian parentage, on 7 March 1911. She had, by her own account, a 'terrible' upbringing, with divorced parents who spent much of their time abroad, packing her off to various boarding schools where she 'never learned anything . . . I turned to writing because I was lonely' (*Daily Telegraph*, p. 23). Her first job after school was on a teenage magazine, *Betty's Paper*, from where she moved to the London office of Hearst Newspapers. Her first contact with the film industry came when she married Claude Begbie-Clench,

an assistant studio manager. After this marriage had collapsed she married the playwright and screenwriter Jeffrey Dell, having taken a small role in a film he had written, *Make-Up* (Alfred Zeisler, 1937). They collaborated on a play, *The Judge*, and also on the script of his first film as a director, *The Flemish Farm* (1943).

The experience convinced Craigie that she too could direct. 'I developed a great urge to make a documentary for myself. I did decide, quite deliberately, why shouldn't a woman make a film? It was a male-dominated industry from top to bottom' (Vallance, p. 7). Her first film, *Out of Chaos* (1944), a short documentary about wartime art, featuring among others Henry Moore, Graham Sutherland, Paul Nash and Stanley Spencer, was released through Filippo Del Giudice's Two Cities company. It was well received, and with Del Giudice's encouragement Craigie embarked on a feature-length documentary.

Strongly left-wing in her views (her third husband was the influential Labour MP Michael Foot), Craigie decided to show how the post-war town planning programme of the Labour government could affect, and be affected by, ordinary people. *The Way We Live* (1946), set in the war-shattered city of Plymouth, shows how planning should be integrated into everyday life, with the *vox populi* opinions Craigie gleaned while filming being incorporated in the city authorities' final plan – a rare British example within the mainstream industry of film-making as political activism. Despite the hostility of John Davis, Managing

Director of the Rank Organisation, which now controlled Two Cities, the film was released to widespread acclaim.

After *Children of the Ruins* (1948), a short documentary about the work of UNESCO, Craigie and the producer William MacQuitty formed a production company, Outlook, to make her first fiction feature, *Blue Scar* (1949), set in the mining valleys of South Wales. It mixed professional actors with local non-professionals to tell a rather novelettish story of a young woman enticed away from her mining-family background by the bright lights of London. The performances betrayed Craigie's inexperience in directing actors, and she later dismissed the film as 'amateurish', but the underlying social passion was unmistakable. Outlook had to struggle to get the film a release, and Craigie, discouraged, quit directing after making one more documentary short, *To Be a Woman* (1951), a plea for equal pay for women. She scripted two comedies for Rank, both directed by Ronald Neame, *The Million Pound Note* (1953) and *Windom's Way* (1957), and resumed her journalism. In 1992 she returned once more to directing, making a television documentary, *Two Hours from London* (screened in 1994), denouncing Serbian aggression in the former Yugoslavia. She died in London on 13 December 1999.

(Philip Kemp)

BIBLIOGRAPHY: Lennon, Peter, 'Labour of Love', *Guardian*, 17 July 1997, pp. 4–5; Medhurst, Andy, '*Blue Scar*/Valley of Song', in David Lusted (ed.), *Raymond Williams: Film TV Culture* (London: NFT/BFI Education, 1989), pp. 31–3; Obituary, *Daily Telegraph*, 15 Dec. 1999, p. 23; Rollyson, Carl, *To Be a Woman: The Life of Jill Craigie* (London: Aurum Press, 2004); Vallance, Tom, 'Jill Craigie', *Independent*, 15 Dec. 1999, p. 7.

FILMOGRAPHY: *Out of Chaos* (doc. short, 1944); *The Way We Live* (doc., 1946); *Children of the Ruins* (doc. short, 1948); *Blue Scar* (1949); *To Be a Woman* (doc. short, 1951).

CRANE, Peter

Peter Crane was born in London. He made his film debut with *Hunted*, a featurette starring Edward Woodward as a misanthropic gunman intent on his own destruction. Two feature films followed. *Moments*, with Keith Michell as a suicidal accountant come to out-of-season Eastbourne to die, was considered too gloomy by distributors and put out as a supporting feature to Robert Parrish's *The Marseille Contract* (1974). *Assassin*, with Ian Hendry as a doom-laden contract killer, was action-packed enough to gain a proper cinema release, though reviewers like Tom Milne made predictable objections to Crane's reliance on zooms and distorted camera angles. During the mid-1970s' slump in British film production, Crane went to the US, where he re-emerged as a successful television director on series such as *Knight Rider* (1982) and *Murder She Wrote* (1984). More recently he has turned to production on Showtime's *The Passion of Ayn Rand* (Christopher Menaul, 1999) and *One Eyed King* (Robert Moresco, 2001), a drama about tough kids growing up in New York.

(Robert Murphy)

BIBLIOGRAPHY: Elley, Derek, 'Moments', *Films and Filming*, Feb. 1985, pp. 37–8; Milne, Tom, 'Assassin', *Monthly Film Bulletin*, Jan. 1974, p. 3.

FILMOGRAPHY: *Hunted* (short, 1971); *Moments; Assassin* (1973).

CRICHTON, Charles (1910–1999)

Charles Ainslie Crichton was born on 6 August 1910 in Wallasey, Cheshire, and educated at Oundle public school. His father worked in the shipping industry, and was unconventional enough to wear a beret to work instead of the statutory bowler hat. While studying history at Oxford, Crichton met Zoltan Korda, who offered him a job at London Films as an assistant editor.

Crichton joined London Films in 1932 and stayed there for eight years, graduating from assistant editor to editor in 1935. The films he worked on included several of the studio's prestige productions: *The Private Life of Henry VIII* (Alexander Korda, 1933), *Sanders of the River* (Zoltan Korda, 1935), *Things to Come* (William Cameron Menzies, 1935), *Elephant Boy* (Robert Flaherty/Zoltan Korda, 1937) and *The Thief of Bagdad* (Ludwig Berger/Michael Powell/Tim Whelan, 1940). Among the things Crichton learned there, he later recalled, was the valuable lesson that 'a script is not the bible, it is not a blueprint that must be followed precisely, word for word' (Vallance, p. 6).

In 1940 Crichton joined Alberto Cavalcanti at the Crown Film Unit and moved with him to Ealing Studios, where he edited documentary-influenced war movies such as *The Big Blockade* (Charles Frend, 1942) and *Nine Men* (Harry Watt, 1943). He was now recognised as one of the finest editors in the business, skilled at letting a scene tell its story with terse economy but no loss of lucidity. Appreciative of Crichton's talents in the cutting room, Ealing boss Michael Balcon eventually let him direct *For Those in Peril* (1944) and *Painted Boats* (1945). They were in much the same drama-documentary mould as those films he had been editing, but his comic contribution to the ghost-story anthology *Dead of Night* (1945) pointed the way his career would soon go.

Though he made as many dramas as comedies, it is as a comedy director that Crichton is best remembered. *Hue and Cry* (1946) was a precursor to the great cycle of post-war comedies with which the name of Ealing became associated. Scripted, like many of its successors, by ex-special policeman T. E. B. ('Tibby') Clarke, it set the template for the Ealing comedy style – realistic, everyday settings against which were played out events pushed just over the edge of absurdity, and a tone of mildly populist insubordination. The plot was Boys' Own Adventure stuff – a group of schoolboys foil a gang of crooks who are passing coded messages through the boys' favourite magazine – but Crichton handled it with a light, dancing brio that kept it fresh and diverting.

Crichton's next four films were less successful. For its period, *Against the Wind* (1948) was an unconventional war movie that took a downbeat, disenchanted view of Allied undercover work in occupied Belgium. It now looks impressively authentic, but audiences were not yet ready for such an unheroic take on the recent conflict. *Another Shore* (1948), a flaccid, Irish-set comedy, was followed by an episode of another anthology film, *Train of Events* (1949), and *Dance Hall* (1950), which offers a surprisingly vivid snapshot of its era, tracing the loves and dreams of four London factory girls in and around their local *palais de danse*. Crichton's best, and best-loved, Ealing film is *The Lavender Hill Mob* (1951), a crime comedy that gave Alec Guinness, as the meek Bank of England clerk who plots to rob his employers, one of his classic roles. Guinness and Stanley Holloway, as his partner-in-crime, play off each other in masterly style, and Crichton paces the comedy impeccably, keeping the rhythm crisp and alert while relishing the wealth of quirky detail. Tibby Clarke's screenplay, gleefully spoofing heist-movie conventions, was awarded an Academy Award.

Crichton worked with independent producer Julian Wintle on *Hunted* (1952), a taut killer-and-a-child thriller featuring Dirk Bogarde and Jon Whiteley, made with backing from Rank and the NFFC. When he returned to Ealing to make *The Titfield Thunderbolt* (1953), again scripted by Tibby Clarke, the studio's comic impulse was declining into cosiness, and the film lacked the sharp social insights of Crichton's earlier comedies. His last Ealing comedy, *The Love Lottery* (1954), was even feebler. *The Divided Heart* (1954), by contrast, was Ealing in its worthy, conscience-wracked mode, dealing with the post-war problem of displaced children and disputed parentage. Well received at the time, it now looks sententious and over-contrived.

When the studio folded, Crichton, like most of his Ealing colleagues, had trouble keeping his career on the rails. He revisited his documentary influences to bring realism to the melodramatic *Floods of Fear* (1958), but *The Battle of the Sexes* (1959), which offered ideal black-comedy material (James Thurber's classic short story 'The Catbird Seat'), was softened and sentimentalised. Invited to Hollywood to make *Birdman of Alcatraz* (1962) for Hecht-Hill-Lancaster, Crichton clashed with Burt Lancaster and was replaced by John Frankenheimer. After two interesting thrillers – *The Third Secret* (1964) and *He Who Rides a Tiger* (1965) – marred by clumsy scripting, he cut his losses and retreated into television.

Crichton's career as a feature director seemed over, especially when he moved from television work to directing corporate videos. But the company involved was John Cleese's Video Arts, and it was at Cleese's invitation that Crichton made his return to the cinema, after twenty-three years, with the heist comedy *A Fish Called Wanda* (1988). Pacy, crisply edited and mining a vein of ruthless black humour that recalls *The Ladykillers* (Alexander Mackendrick, 1955), *Wanda* looks like what Ealing comedy might have become by the 1980s had the studio survived. The film scored a major international hit, and Crichton was nominated for an Academy Award. Rumours

that he might direct a sequel came to nothing, but the success of *Wanda*, and Cleese's generosity in sharing the profits, allowed Crichton to live out his final years in unprecedented comfort. He died in South Kensington, London, on 14 September 1999. (Philip Kemp)

BIBLIOGRAPHY: Barr, Charles, *Ealing Studios* (London and Newton Abbot, Devon: Cameron & Tayleur/David & Charles, 1977); BECTU History Project interview, held on CD and cassette in the BFI National Library, London; LeFanu, Mark, 'Entretien avec Charles Crichton', *Positif*, Feb. 1989, pp. 31–7; Palin, Michael, 'Farewell to the Admirable Charlie', *The Times*, 1 Oct. 1999, p. 48; Perry, George, *Forever Ealing* (London: Michael Joseph/Pavilion Books, 1981); 'The Old Man and the Fish', *Independent*, 18 Mar. 1989, p. 18; Vallance, Tom, 'Charles Crichton' (obituary), *Independent* Review Section, 16 Sept. 1999, p. 6.

FILMOGRAPHY: *For Those in Peril* (1944); *Painted Boats* (US: *The Girl of the Canal*); *Dead of Night* (co-dirs. Cavalcanti/Robert Hamer/Basil Dearden) (1945); *Hue and Cry* (1946); *Against the Wind*; *Another Shore* (1947); *Train of Events* (co-dirs. Sidney Cole/Basil Dearden, 1949); *Dance Hall* (1950); *The Lavender Hill Mob* (1951); *Hunted* (US: *The Stranger in Between*, 1952); *The Titfield Thunderbolt* (1953); *The Love Lottery*; *The Divided Heart* (1954); *The Man in the Sky* (US: *Decision Against Time*, 1957); *Floods of Fear*; *Law and Disorder* (uncredited, co-dir. Henry Cornelius) (1958); *The Battle of the Sexes* (1959); *The Boy Who Stole a Million* (1961); *Birdman of Alcatraz* (uncredited, co-dir. John Frankenheimer, US, 1962); *The Third Secret* (1964); *He Who Rides a Tiger* (1965); *Tomorrow's Island* (doc. short, 1968); *A Fish Called Wanda* (1988).

CRICKS, G. H. (1861–1936) and J. H. MARTIN

George Howard Cricks and John Howard Martin first met when they both worked for Robert Paul around 1900 at his Animatographe Depot in High Holborn, London. Cricks, born in Woodford, Essex, in 1861, managed the sale of films and equipment; Martin, whose dates are unknown, was in charge of the darkroom. In 1904, along with Henry Martin Sharp, Cricks formed his own company, Cricks and Sharp, with studios in Mitcham in Surrey; when J. H. Martin replaced Sharp as partner in 1908, the company became Cricks and Martin. In 1910 they moved to bigger studio premises at Waddon New Road in Croydon.

A keen amateur photographer, Cricks made his first known films at the end of the 1890s when employed by the London stationery and photographic firm George Harrison and Co. Using the premises' roof as his studio, he staged several miniature editions of popular melodramas, including *Maria Marten* and *East Lynne*. Martin was directing by 1905, taking charge of numerous Paul trick films, dramas and comedies, featuring the customary repertoire of the time: explosions, conjuring tricks, policemen and crooks, and in *The Curate's Dilemma* a curate sitting on an anthill. At Cricks and Sharp, Cricks handled the early productions himself – mostly simple one-scene comedies, with occasional lengthier dramas like the six-scene *A Day in the Life of a Thames Fireman* (1904). But he soon began employing others to direct: from 1905, Tom Green; from 1907, the prolific A. E. Coleby; and in the 1910s, Edwin J. Collins, Charles Calvert and Will Kellino. Martin never seemingly directed again after his time with Paul.

As producers, Cricks and Martin were tireless self-promoters, as well as promoters of quality British film production in general. They boasted in the trade press that their Lion's Head brand generated more successful films than any other British concern, and that a Lion's Head Film was clean, moral and above all British. Along with many other British manufacturers, their output consisted of short comedies, melodramas and industrial subjects. The comedies were routine, although *The Biter Bit* (A. E. Coleby, 1909) exhibited some invention within the chase format by showing an escalating chase on foot, by bicycle and finally by car. Plots were not especially original, and frequently drew on other companies' product, as in *Saved by Carlo* (A. E. Coleby, 1909), an imitation of Cecil Hepworth's animal films. Although derivative, the films' narrative construction, framing and pictorial quality maintained a very high standard. Cricks and Martin particularly excelled at industrial subjects. They produced a great number of well-executed subjects chronicling aspects of British industries, including *A Day in a Pottery Works* (1909), *The Birth of a Big Gun* (1908) and *Making Christmas Crackers* (1910), all directed by Coleby. In *Cliff Climbing: The Egg Harvest of Flamborough Head* (1908) they secured amazing views of a professional egg collector dangling from a cliff face at Flamborough Head in Yorkshire.

On the fiction side, by 1911 Cricks and Martin were developing series with recurring comic characters like Charley Smiler, played by Fred Evans (later to find fame with the Clarendon Film Co. as the character Pimple). But the company's ambitions were growing. In February 1911 they released their most elaborate film yet, the 945-feet *The Pirates of 1920* (A. E. Coleby and Dave Aylott), a fantasy-adventure featuring airship pirates, a ship carrying bullion, a kidnapped girl and integrated trick effects. In October the company announced an ambitious programme of expansion, promising longer films with better plots, better acting and better production: by the end of the year they had the largest staff of any British manufacturer. The expansion left the company financially vulnerable, and with a disunited management. Unhappy with Cricks' plan to move away from short comic production, Martin left in 1913 to set up his own studio at Merton Park. By 1915 Cricks had worked up to three- and four-reel dramas, including an unusually lavish Bulwer-Lytton adaptation *Eugene Aram* (Edwin J. Collins, 1914). But feature production proved a serious strain on the small company's resources; in 1916 other film-makers moved into the Croydon studio, and Cricks, increasingly disillusioned, soon retired from active production. Martin ran into equal difficulties at Merton Park, and abandoned production in 1917. Cricks died in Surrey in 1936.

(Geoff Brown and Simon Brown)

BIBLIOGRAPHY: Low, Rachael, *The History of the British Film 1914–1918* (London: George Allen & Unwin, 1950); Low, Rachael, *The History of the British Film 1906–1914* (London: George Allen & Unwin, 1973).

FILMOGRAPHY: Cricks (selected): *Maria Marten; or, The Mystery of the Red Barn*; *East Lynne* (late 1890s); *The Giddy Girl and the Butterfly*; *Jap the Giant Killer*; *A Day in the Life of a Thames Fireman*; *Saving the Dispatches*; *A Wife's Revenge; or, The Gambler's End* (1904); *The Burglar's Dilemma*; *She Would Sing*; *The Pilfered Porker*; *Father's Picnic on the Sands* (1905).

Martin: *The Fatal Necklace*; *A Race for Bed*; *Trouble below Stairs*; *The King of Clubs*; *While the Household Sleeps*; *He Learned Jiu-Jitsu – So Did the Missus*; *The Adventures of a £100 Banknote*; *The Pierrot and the Devil's Dice* (aka *The Conjuring Clown*); *The Dancer's Dream*; *When the Wife's Away*; *Short-Sighted Sammy*; *The Visions of an Opium Smoker*; *The Misguided Bobby*; *A Christmas Card; or, The Story of Three Homes*; *A Shave by Instalments on the Uneasy System*; *The Freak Barber* (1905); *The Doctored Beer*; *Mistaken Identity*; *He Cannot Get a Word in Edgeways*; *The Old Lie and the New*; *The Fakir and the Footpads*; *A Lively Quarter Day*; *The Madman's Fate*; *Seaside Lodgings*; *Brown's Fishing (?) Excursion*; *The Curate's Dilemma*; *Home without Mother*; *House to Let*; *The Medium Exposed*; *Just a Little Piece of Cloth*; *The World's Wizard*; *Various Popular Liquors Illustrated*; *Spooning*; *Woman Supreme*; *Introductions Extraordinary*; *How to Make Time Fly*; *Jim the Signalman*; *The Lover's Predicament* (1906); *The Cook's Dream*; *A Tragedy of the Ice*; *The Chef's Revenge*; *Saved by a Sailor* (US: *The Sailor's Return*); *A Mother's Sin*; *A Knight Errant*; *His First Top Hat*; *The Fatal Hand*; *The Bothered Bathers*; *Adventures of a Broker's Man*; *The Bookmaker*; *The Burglar's Surprise*; *How a Burglar Feels*; *An Inhuman Father*; *My Lady's Revenge*; *The Fidgety Fly*; *The Tale of a Mouse*; *The Cheater's Cheated*; *Pity the Poor*

Blind; *The Amateur Paper Hanger* (1907); *The Phantom Ship* (co-dir. A. E. Coleby, 1908).

CROWLEY, John

John Crowley studied at University College, Cork, before pursuing a successful career as a theatre director. He contributed *Come and Go* to the 'Beckett on Film' project and made a lively feature debut with *Intermission* for Neil Jordan and Steve Woolley's Company of Wolves. Crowley manoeuvres his bright young cast (headed by Colin Farrell, Kelly Macdonald and Cillian Murphy) through a complex set of coincidences and contrivances involving a myriad of minor characters, each with their story to tell. Brisk pacing and engaging acting fail to prevent a slow slide into sentimental mushiness.

(Robert Murphy)

BIBLIOGRAPHY: Marlow, Jane, 'Directors and Scripts', *Scriptwriter* no. 22, May 2003, pp. 40–4.

FILMOGRAPHY: *Come and Go* (short, Ir, 2001); *Intermission* (Ir/UK/US, 2003).

CULLIMORE, Alan (1922–)

Alan Brian Cullimore was born in Burnham, Buckinghamshire, on 10 March 1922. At first a child actor, he worked as a camera assistant and operator before forming an independent company with Ben Arbeid in 1947. His first stabs at directing were the low-budget thriller *Vengeance Is Mine* and a bottom-drawer comedy, *The Clouded Crystal*. These were followed by *Let's Go Crazy*, a half-hour revue film headed by Peter Sellers and Spike Milligan, which emerged in 1951 alongside their radio programme *Crazy People*, prototype of *The Goon Show*. Cullimore also produced a more muted comedy, *Penny Points to Paradise*, with Sellers, Milligan and Harry Secombe (Tony Young, 1951).

(Geoff Brown and Robert Murphy)

FILMOGRAPHY: *Vengeance Is Mine*; *The Clouded Crystal* (1948); *Let's Go Crazy* (short, 1951).

CURTIS, Richard (1956–)

Richard Whalley Anthony Curtis was born on 8 November 1956 in New Zealand, but educated at Harrow and Oxford, where he began his long collaboration with Rowan Atkinson in the Oxford University Dramatic Society. His career as a television comedy writer (*Not the Nine O'Clock News*, *Mr Bean*, *Blackadder*) was followed by big-screen success with *Four Weddings and a Funeral* (Mike Newell, 1994) and *Notting Hill* (Roger Michell, 1999). He made his directorial debut with *Love Actually*, an ambitious interweaving of eight separate romantic stories. None of them add up to much, and though there are cursory crossovers – in this idyllic world everyone from the Prime Minister to his lowly tea-lady send their children to the same school – there is little interaction. Curtis proves competent enough as a director, wisely refraining from ostentatious stylistic effects and relying on good performances from his talented if overfamiliar cast. What makes the film attractive – it was a huge box-office hit in the UK, US and elsewhere – is Curtis' vision of a world where love is the answer, and one available to the damaged, the misfits and the nondescript low-achievers, not just the well-heeled denizens of Notting Hill.

(Robert Murphy)

BIBLIOGRAPHY: Norman, Barry, 'Richard Curtis: *Love Actually*', *Radio Times*, 19 June 2004, p. 45; Sarler, Carol, 'The Funniest Man Not on TV', *Radio Times*, 5 Nov. 1994, pp. 37–8.

FILMOGRAPHY: *Love Actually* (2003).

CUTTS, Graham (1885–1958)

John Henry Graham Cutts was born in 1885 in Brighton and trained as a marine engineer. Attracted by the cinema, he entered exhibition in Newcastle and Birmingham before joining the Wilcox brothers to form Graham-Wilcox Productions in 1922. Cutts had already directed *Cocaine* (1922), a sensationalist drama retitled *While London Sleeps* in response to censorship problems. His first film for Graham-Wilcox, the pictorialist and poetically conceived *The Wonderful Story* – a rural psycho-drama about a man crippled on the eve of his wedding – received a rapturous critical response for its 'truth, realism and perfect acting' but failed at the box office (*Kinematograph Weekly*, 1 June 1922, p. 56). Its successor, *Flames of Passion* (1922), concocted by Herbert Wilcox and his wife, deployed more sensationalist melodrama: an American star, Mae Marsh, playing a carefree schoolgirl seduced into tragedy by the drunken family chauffer. The film was commercially successful – it was the first post-war British film to be sold in America – and admired for its technical skill and authentic Old Bailey sets; but the story, involving seduction, illegitimacy and baby murder, offended critical taste.

Following the well-received *Paddy-the-Next-Best-Thing* (1923), and armed with an option on Michael Morton's stage hit *Woman to Woman*, Cutts joined the newly formed Balcon-Saville-Freedman company, soon to become Gainsborough Pictures. The film, made at the well-equipped Islington studio, was a runaway critical and commercial success. An ecstatic Morton declared: 'The emotion projected from the screen amazed me, America has her Griffith; we have our Graham Cutts' ('Woman to Woman', p. 72).

Contributing to Cutts' script meetings was the young Alfred Hitchcock, employed at Islington as title designer and general factotum while assiduously learning about film-making. He not only offered to design the sets but acted as assistant director and his career became increasingly entangled with that of Cutts. *The Passionate Adventure* (1924), like *Woman to Woman*, features Clive Brook as a neurasthenic upper-class husband, torn between his frigid wife and a loving working-class girl. *The Blackguard* (1925), made at Ufa, and *The Prude's Fall* (1925) fell prey to turbulence in Cutts' private life, and Hitchcock was often left in charge.

Nevertheless, until the late 1920s Cutts was considered the saviour of the British film industry, 'a sure-fire maker of box-office attractions' and courted by American studios ('Gainsborough's Progress', 1925). To defuse Cutts' growing dislike of Hitchcock, Balcon separated them, giving Cutts *The Rat* (1925), starring its co-author Ivor Novello, in a romantic role as a class-boundary-crossing Parisian Apache. Cutts' direction was noted for its audacious tracking shots and dramatic camera angles, which made full use of N. G. Arnold's complex, multi-level set for the 'White Coffin' nightclub. *The Rat* and its sequel, *The Triumph of the Rat* (1926), raised hopes that with better material Cutts would become a world-class director. He returned to Germany to make *The Queen Was in the Parlour* (1927), Noël Coward's Ruritanian romance, now sexually energised by Cutts' increasingly sadistic camera, travelling with the movement of the drunken Prince's whiplash into a cowering Lili Damita's ear. After making the technically inventive *Confetti* (1927) for First National, Cutts returned to Gainsborough for *The Return of the Rat*. It showed Cutts at the height of his visual powers, but the film was overtaken by the switch to sound.

In the early 1930s Cutts made four films for Basil Dean, including Gracie Fields' second film, the popular *Looking on the Bright Side* (1932). According to Dean, Cutts resented 'talking pictures' (Dean, p. 165). However, a sound version of *The Return of the Rat* with dialogue scenes added had been enthusiastically greeted, and in the 1930s Cutts directed a number of well-photographed, breezy comedies and musicals, including a freely adapted *Three Men in a Boat* (1933). However, he was never able to recapture his earlier success. After directing a number of 'quota quickies' and a couple of films for Balcon, he found a niche at BIP, where he made his last feature films, mostly comedies and musicals, including *Over She Goes* (1937) with Stanley Lupino, and a popular adaptation of *Just William* (1939). In 1940 Cutts joined World Wide, making wartime documentaries and shorts until 1947. He died on 7 September 1958, in London, leaving a daughter, the actress Patricia Cutts.

Hitchcock's authorial pre-eminence has effaced the reputation of his mentor; but Cutts' 1920s' films were notable for their spectacular production values, experimental virtuosity of camerawork and lighting, and the intense performances and attractive characterisations of his actors, several of whom rose to stardom under his direction. Cutts refused to subject his showman's instincts to the discipline of narrative development, and his melodramatic and romantic scenarios sometimes disappointed his admirers by their improbability, 'jumpy continuity' and dubious moral tone. But Cutts argued that spectacle and topical controversy could be used as a conduit to his audience's underlying instincts and passions (Cutts, 14 February 1924, pp. 50–1). He used unexpected camera angles and movements, often combined with glass filters and framing devices, to traverse between depth and surface and he recognised the voyeuristic potential of the camera to explore subjectivity and sexuality, a domain that Hitchcock would later claim as his own.

(Christine Gledhill)

BIBLIOGRAPHY: Balcon, Michael, *Michael Balcon Presents . . . A Lifetime of Films* (London: Hutchinson, 1969); Barry, Iris, 'A British Director', *Daily Mail*, 18 Aug. 1926, in Sydney Carroll's scrapbooks, BFI Special Collection, BFI National Library, London; Cutts, Graham, 'What Does the Public Want? A Consideration of Collective Demands', *Kinematograph Weekly*, 14 Feb. 1924, pp. 50–1; Cutts, Graham, 'Secrets of a Film Director', *Picturegoer*, Oct. 1926, pp. 8–9; Dean, Basil, *Mind's Eye: An Autobiography 1927–1972* (London: Hutchinson, 1973); 'Gainsborough's Progress', *Kinematograph Weekly*, 22 Oct. 1925, p. 44; Gledhill, Christine, *Reframing British Cinema, 1918–1928: Between Restraint and Passion* (London: BFI Publishing, 2003); 'Low and High, No. 1 – With Cutts at Islington', *Motion Picture Studio*, 20 July 1922, pp. 10–11; Low, Rachael, *The History of the British Film 1918–1929* (London: George Allen & Unwin, 1971); Low, Rachael, *The History of the British Film 1929–1939: Film Making in 1930s Britain* (London: George Allen & Unwin, 1985); Wilcox, Herbert, *Twenty-Five Thousand Sunsets: The Autobiography of Herbert Wilcox* (London: Bodley Head, 1967); 'Woman to Woman' (trade show review), *The Bioscope*, 1 Nov. 1923, pp. 71–2.

FILMOGRAPHY: *Cocaine* (aka *While London Sleeps*); *The Wonderful Story*; *Flames of Passion* (aka *Tides of Passion/A Woman's Secret*) (1922); *Paddy-the-Next-Best-Thing*; *Woman to Woman*; *The White Shadow* (US: *White Shadows*) (1923); *The Passionate Adventure*; *The Blackguard*; *The Prude's Fall/Seine zweite Frau* (US: *Dangerous Virtue*) (1924); *The Rat* (1925); *The Sea Urchin*; *The Triumph of the Rat* (1926); *The Queen Was in the Parlour/Die letzte Nacht* (US: *Forbidden Love*); *The Rolling Road*; *Chance the Idol*; *Confetti* (1927); *God's Clay*; *Eileen of the Trees* (aka *Glorious Youth*) (1928); *The Return of the Rat* (1929); *The Temperance Fete*; *The Sign of Four*; *Love on the Spot*; *The Impassive Footman*; *Looking on the Bright Side* (1932); *As Good as New*; *Three Men in a Boat* (1933); *Oh, Daddy!* (co-dir. Austin Melford); *Car of Dreams* (co-dir. Austin Melford) (1935); *Aren't Men Beasts?*; *Let's Make a Night of It*; *Over She Goes* (1937); *Just William*; *She Couldn't Say No* (1939); *Miss Knowall* (short, aka *The Scaremongers*, 1940); *Rationing in Britain* (doc. short, 1944); *Air Transport Support* (doc. short, co-dir. Clifford Dyment, 1945); *Combined Operations* (doc. short); *Food Manufacture* (doc. short); *Our Daily Bread* (doc. short) (1946); *The 9.2 Inch Gun* (doc. short, 1947).

CZINNER, Paul (1890–1972)

Paul Czinner was born in Budapest on 30 May 1890. He worked initially in journalism and the theatre, and made his first film, *Der Unmensch*, in Austria in 1919. By the time he moved to England in 1932 with his star performer, Elisabeth Bergner, Czinner enjoyed a distinguished reputation, first established with Bergner in *Nju* (1924), an intimate triangular drama in the German *Kammerspielfilm* tradition. Czinner's earlier films and his Viennese theatre work had been coloured by Expressionism; but Bergner's subtle and mercurial skills drew him steadily towards a quasi-realist cinema of psychological moods, with the actress very much at the centre (until the 1940s she worked with no other film director).

Czinner's first venture in Britain, *The Woman He Scorned* (1929), featuring Pola Negri and a Cornish lighthouse, offered few opportunities for grace notes. But after two multilingual ventures in Europe, *Ariane* (1931) and *Mélo* (1932), he returned with Bergner and the promise of a Korda contract. In January 1933 the couple married (they became British citizens five years later), and by September were at work on the lavish costume drama *Catherine the Great* (1934). Conflict with Korda, who insisted on directing some scenes himself, stopped subsequent collaborations. Four British films for other producers followed: *Escape Me Never*, a wearing romantic drama adapted from Bergner's first British stage success; *As You Like It*, with live animals, a leaping Laurence Olivier and enough gnarled trees to stock a German fairy tale; the novelettish *Dreaming Lips*, an inferior remake of *Mélo*; and *Stolen Life*, a twin-sister melodrama preposterous enough to be remade as a Bette Davis vehicle in Hollywood.

In these films Bergner's gamine prancings and emotional volatility enormously impressed contemporary audiences. Her

husband was accorded parallel respect; publicity referred to him as Dr Czinner (he was a Doctor of Philosophy and Literature), and critics followed suit. Czinner's *Kammerspiel* training undoubtedly ensured some mastery of atmosphere and moods, but by the end of the 1930s his leisured pace and European finesse proved increasingly limiting. When the couple retreated to America during the Second World War, he produced Bergner's theatre productions in New York, but her one Hollywood film, *Paris Calling* (1941), was directed by an MGM contract director, Edwin L. Marin.

Sensing changed times, after returning to Europe in 1949 Czinner abandoned fiction films with Bergner for cinema transcriptions of ballet and opera. With technical help from Alfred Travers, he devised a multi-camera system allowing existing stage spectacles to be filmed in performance, some at the Salzburg Festival, others in London theatres. His last film, *Romeo and Juliet* (1966), a useful document of Kenneth MacMillan's Royal Ballet production with Rudolf Nureyev and Margot Fonteyn, was chiefly recreated at Pinewood Studios, though the end results still paid obeisance to the stage. Czinner died in London on 22 June 1972.

(Geoff Brown)

BIBLIOGRAPHY: Czinner, Paul, 'Bergner as I Know Her', *Film Weekly*, 5 Apr. 1935, p. 19; Schöning, Jürg, 'Paul Czinner', *CineGraph: Lexicon zum deutschsprachigen Film* (Munich: edition text+kritik, 1985, supplement 3).

FILMOGRAPHY (UK only): *The Woman He Scorned* (aka *The Way of Lost Souls*, 1929); *Catherine the Great/The Rise of Catherine the Great*

(1934); *Escape Me Never* (1935); *As You Like It* (1936); *Dreaming Lips* (co-dir. Lee Garmes, 1937); *Stolen Life* (1939); *Don Giovanni* (1955); *The Bolshoi Ballet* (1957); *The Royal Ballet* (1960); *Der Rosenkavalier* (1962); *Romeo and Juliet* (1966).

D

DALDRY, Stephen (1960–)

Born in Bridport, Dorset, on 2 May 1960, Stephen Daldry studied English at university and then spent a year travelling through Italy as a clown's apprentice. He returned to work in the theatre; his inventive production of J. B. Priestley's *An Inspector Calls* at the National Theatre in 1992 was widely acclaimed, and he went on to become Artistic Director at the Royal Court. Daldry made his film debut with the BAFTA-nominated short film *Eight*. Based on a script by Tim Clague, it explores a day in the life of a young boy, uprooted from his home town and anxious to hide his obsession with Liverpool Football Club from his mother, who still grieves for her husband, killed in the disaster at Hillsborough when ninety-five football fans were crushed to death at an FA Cup semi-final between Liverpool and Nottingham Forest.

Three years later, Daldry released his first feature film, *Billy Elliot*, scripted by Lee Hall, who had made his mark with the startlingly unique radio play *Spoonface Steinberg*. Though it is set in a Durham pit village during the 1984 miners' strike, the main concern of the film is with dance as a vocation. From the opening shot in which Billy jumps exuberantly on his bed (an image echoed in the film's final, striking image of the dancer Adam Cooper in mid-flight in *Swan Lake*), to the poignant and inspiring way in which Billy describes at his Royal Ballet School audition how he feels when he dances, the film explores the way in which a vocation opens up new possibilities for expression, growth and fulfilment.

Daldry's next film was an adaptation by David Hare of Michael Cunningham's novel *The Hours*. It explores the connections between three women in different eras: Clarissa Vaughan (Meryl Streep), a sophisticated woman living in present-day Manhattan, Laura Brown (Julianne Moore), a 1950s' housewife, and Virginia Woolf (Nicole Kidman). The link between them is Woolf's novel *Mrs Dalloway*, in which the titular protagonist is undertaking preparations for a party – just as Clarissa and Laura are doing. Woolf is notoriously difficult to film, but Daldry manages to convey something of her personality and the extensive influence of her work. The film's differences from *Billy Elliot* reveal Daldry to be an adaptable and versatile director.

Daldry was appointed the 2002 Cameron Mackintosh Visiting Professor of Contemporary Theatre at Oxford University and he retains an active interest in the stage, claiming that his biggest achievement has been the £16.3 million Lottery funding that he helped to secure for the rebuilding of the Royal Court Theatre. His stage musical version of *Billy Elliot* in 2005 proved a critical and popular success.

(Sarah Cardwell)

BIBLIOGRAPHY: Goodridge, Mike, 'Time Traveller', *Screen International*, 29 Nov. 2002, p. 17; Johnston, Sheila, 'A Day in the Life', *Sight and Sound*, Feb. 2003, pp. 24–7; Lawrenson, Edward, 'Profile: Cosmic Dancer', *Sight and Sound*, Oct. 2000, pp. 12–13.

FILMOGRAPHY: *Eight* (short, 1999); *Billy Elliot* (2000); *The Hours* (US/UK, 2002).

DALRYMPLE, Ian (1903–1989)

The son of a Scottish entrepreneur, Ian Murray Dalrymple was born in Johannesburg, Transvaal, on 26 August 1903. After education at Rugby School and Trinity College, Cambridge, he entered the film industry in the mid-1920s. He quickly established himself as an editor, building strong links with Michael Balcon at Gainsborough-Gaumont-British; in 1932 he became the studio's supervisory editor, taking charge among others of Walter Forde's *Rome Express* (1932), and Victor Saville's *Sunshine Susie* (1931) and *Evergreen* (1934). He also worked occasionally as a scriptwriter, achieving most success in the late 1930s with his adaptations of Winifred Holtby's *South Riding* (Victor Saville, 1938) and A. J. Cronin's *The Citadel* (King Vidor, 1938).

Dalrymple's work as a director is slim but not undistinguished. After co-directing a short documentary about the fate of refugee Basque children with Basil Wright, he shared credits with Victor Saville on *Storm in a Teacup*, a refreshingly lively comedy about a young reporter (Rex Harrison) challenging an overbearing Scottish provost (Cecil Parker) over his callousness towards a dog. Vivien Leigh, a wonderful supporting cast and exciting canine action help make it one of the best British films of the late 1930s. However, it is arguable how much this was due to Dalrymple and how much to Saville – then at the height of his powers. Certainly Dalrymple's next film, *Old Bill and Son*, is a much less impressive affair. John Mills plays the spivvish son of First World War veteran Old Bill (Morland Graham) who heeds the call to arms and serves with the British Expeditionary Force in France. Plotting and production values are rudimentary, and the film is mainly interesting for its representation of the BEF – though the sort of trench-raiding warfare shown is misleadingly reminiscent of the First World War – and the attitudes expressed by its characters. 'You don't have to be a toff to be an officer nowadays', Young Bill brightly points out; but his mother is more sceptical of propaganda, and fiercely resists pressure to evacuate: 'I hate the nasty little farmers. I hate the countryside and everything concerned with it – pigs, cows, chickens, all the smelly lot.'

In August 1940 Dalrymple accepted the post of Head of the GPO Film Unit (subsequently renamed the Crown Film Unit).

During his three years there he was responsible for the groundbreaking drama-documentaries *Target for To-night* (Harry Watt, 1941), *"Fires Were Started –"* (Humphrey Jennings, 1943), *Close Quarters* (Jack Lee, 1943) and *Western Approaches* (Pat Jackson, 1944), as well as numerous shorter documentaries. A two-year stint with Alexander Korda, for whom Dalrymple had produced *The Lion Has Wings* (Brian Desmond Hurst/Michael Powell/Adrian Brunel, 1939), followed, and in 1945 he established Wessex Films as an autonomous unit within the Rank Organisation.

Dalrymple again ventured into directing with *Esther Waters*, an adaptation of George Moore's controversial novel about a serving maid who bears an illegitimate child. Peter Proud is credited as co-director and co-producer, but his role was largely confined to co-ordinating the nineteenth-century sets and costumes. Upon its delayed release, the film was unfairly dismissed as a plodding Victorian melodrama and failed at the box office, a reverse that damaged Dalrymple so severely he never directed a feature film again. More than fifty years later it compares favourably with other immediate post-war British period films and displays at times a gritty social realism rare for the genre. Dark though the film is, there is a refreshing lack of sentimentality in the way the servant girl rejects salvation among evangelical Christians in favour of the disreputable but tolerant world of the Victorian racing fraternity. Dirk Bogarde, cast by Dalrymple in his first starring role as the raffish servant who makes good as a bookmaker and marries Esther, thought he was too shy and gentle to be a director: 'He simply loved everything you did. He was so astonished to see it happening before his very eyes. There was a sense of enormous innate gentleness and of being out of his depth' (quoted in Drazin, p. 169).

In 1949 Dalrymple and Rank parted company, just before Wessex enjoyed its biggest box-office success with the prisoner-of-war-camp drama *The Wooden Horse* (Jack Lee, 1950). Dalrymple and his company continued into the 1960s making documentaries and children's films. He died in London on 28 April 1989.

(James C. Robertson)

BIBLIOGRAPHY: Barr, Charles, 'War Record', *Sight and Sound*, Autumn 1989, pp. 260–5; Bogarde, Dirk, 'Obituary – Ian Dalrymple', *Independent*, 1 May 1989, p. 4; Drazin, Charles, 'Ian Dalrymple', in *The Finest Years: British Cinema of the 1940s* (London: André Deutsch, 1998); Press book on *Esther Waters* held in BFI National Library, London.

FILMOGRAPHY: *Modern Orphans of the Storm* (doc. short, co-dir. Basil Wright); *Storm in a Teacup* (co-dir. Victor Saville) (1937); *Old Bill and Son*; *Sea Fort* (doc. short) (1940); *Esther Waters* (co-dir. Peter Proud, 1947); *The Bank of England* (doc. short, 1960).

DANCE, Charles (1946–)

A prolific and talented actor, Charles Dance was born in Redditch, Worcestershire, on 10 October 1946. His directorial debut, *Ladies in Lavender*, gives meaty roles to Judi Dench and Maggie Smith as sisters whose tranquil twilight years are disrupted when they rescue a young Polish sailor. The film defied groans about predictability and theatricality to become a surprising box-office success.

(Geoff Brown and Robert Murphy)

FILMOGRAPHY: *Ladies in Lavender* (2004).

DASSIN, Jules (1911–)

Jules Dassin was born in Middletown, Connecticut, on 18 December 1911, the son of Russian immigrants. He travelled around Europe after leaving school, returning in 1936 to join the New York Yiddish Theatre. In 1940 he was offered a contract by RKO, though his debut came with a twenty-minute adaptation of Edgar Allan Poe's *The Tell Tale Heart* for MGM in 1941. Modest propaganda features (*Nazi Agent*, *Reunion in France*) and light comedies (*The Affairs of Martha*, *Young Ideas*) followed in the next couple of years, but it was with the hard-hitting realist films *Brute Force* (1947) and *The Naked City* (1948), made for producer Mark Hellinger at Universal, that Dassin established his reputation. After Hellinger's death Dassin moved to 20th Century-Fox, where he directed the equally effective *Thieves Highway* (1949) and his one British film *Night and the City*.

Based on a sprawling picaresque novel by Gerald Kersh, *Night and the City* attempts to graft contemporary American film noir style onto a Dickensian London full of eccentric small-time crooks. Dassin captures something of Kersh's vision of the English underworld as a phantasmagoria where innocence and goodness are remorselessly crushed, and the film still resonates as a remarkable portrait of the dingy underside of Britain after the war. But by Americanising the central character, Harry Fabian (played with whiny conviction by Richard Widmark), and giving him a beautiful and respectable girlfriend (Gene Tierney), Dassin allows a sentimentality to creep in that is absent from his best American work.

Named as a member of the Communist Party by Edward Dmytryk at the HUAC hearings in 1952, Dassin found himself blacklisted. After fruitlessly attempting to clear his name he returned to Europe. His huge success with the French heist movie *Du Rififi chez les hommes* (1955) restored him to favour, but rather than return to Hollywood he settled in Greece with the actress Melina Mercouri, whom he married in 1966. He made three films in Greece – *Celui qui doit mourir* (1957), based on Nikos Kasantzakis' novel *Christ Re-crucified*; *Never on Sunday* (1960), with Dassin playing the American lead; and *Phaedra* (1960), a modern adaptation of the Greek myth – plus the Istanbul-set caper film *Topkapi* (1964), but was forced into exile once again when the Greek government was toppled by a right-wing army coup. Ironically, Dassin's film *The Rehearsal* (1974), a reconstruction of the massacre of protesting students at the Athens Polytechnic School, was overtaken by events when the Junta fell in 1974. Mercouri eventually became Minister of Culture after democracy was restored.

Dassin, who continued making films until 1980, often expressed his preference for European over Hollywood methods of film production. It is arguable whether he achieved more than Edward Dmytryk and Elia Kazan, who abandoned their principles and made their peace with Hollywood and the HUAC, but his life as an exile has proved a long and happy one.

(Robert Murphy)

BIBLIOGRAPHY: Baker, Bob, 'Jules Dassin', *Film Dope* no. 9, Apr. 1976, pp. 35–6; Horton, Andrew, 'Jules Dassin: A Multi-National Filmmaker Considered', *Film Criticism* vol. 8 no. 3, Spring 1984, pp. 21–35.

FILMOGRAPHY (UK only): *Night and the City* (1950).

DAUMERY, John (1898–1934)

Jean Daumery was born in Brussels in 1898 to a French and Belgian family; his father was a musician, his mother a stage actress who later worked in American films as Carrie Daumery. Mother and son arrived in America in straitened circumstances after hard times in the First World War (Daumery himself suffered from the effects of poison gas). From the early 1920s, Carrie secured small Hollywood roles as dowagers and banquet guests; in 1927 Jean became John, and found work as an assistant director. He spent a period in France as production manager at Rex Ingram's Nice studios, where he failed to impress the young Michael Powell; then a directing position at Warner Bros. took him back to Los Angeles. After shouting 'Action!' at Rin-Tin-Tin in the canine showcase *Rough Waters* (1930), he spent a whirlwind twelve months directing six French-language versions of Warners' early talkies, much appreciated on release in France.

Given his colourful CV, the next Warners' assignment may have seemed tedious. When Irving Asher became production chief of Warners' new London offshoot at Teddington Studios in 1931, Daumery was shipped over to help him. In two years he directed eleven 'quota quickies', their casts the usual mix of theatre stars (Irene Vanbrugh), film regulars (John Stuart) and passing fancies (the Danish import Winna Winifried). *Mr Quincy of Monte Carlo* (1933), featuring Stuart as a cautious bank clerk who receives a windfall, proved more felicitous than most; though contemporary reports suggest Daumery's best results were achieved in *Meet My Sister* (1933), a vehicle for Clifford Mollison's light comedy skills, made with larger resources at BIP. Daumery's last films, for BIP and British Lion, were shot late the same year. On 10 May 1934, the *Kinematograph Weekly* reported his death in Lausanne after a 'fatal illness, borne with quiet fortitude'.

To estimate properly Daumery's output today requires considerable imagination: most of his British films appear lost, along with all his French-language ventures. In his autobiography, Powell recalled his chagrin at finding Daumery a business manager and organiser, rather than an artist or technician. But managers also served, especially in the early 1930s, when the industry's demand for product far exceeded any need for artistic expression.

(Geoff Brown)

BIBLIOGRAPHY: 'John Daumery Passes: Tragedy of Director', *Kinematograph Weekly*, 10 May 1934, p. 39; Powell, Michael, *A Lifetime in Movies* (London: William Heinemann, 1986).

FILMOGRAPHY (UK only): *Postal Orders* (short); *A Letter of Warning* (short); *Help Yourself*; *The Blind Spot* (1932); *Naughty Cinderella*; *Mr Quincy of Monte Carlo*; *Little Miss Nobody*; *The Thirteenth Candle*; *Call Me Mame*; *Head of the Family*; *Meet My Sister*, *This Acting Business* (1933); *Over the Garden Wall*; *Without You* (1934).

DAVIES, Howard

Howard Davies is a respected theatre director. His one venture into cinema is a well-acted, cramped and word-laden treatment of David Hare's family melodrama *The Secret Rapture*, which he had previously directed at the National Theatre. He has also directed versions of his stage productions for television, including Michael Frayn's *Copenhagen* (2002) and Joe Penhall's *Blue/Orange* (2005).

(Geoff Brown)

FILMOGRAPHY: *The Secret Rapture* (1993).

DAVIES, John and Robert SMITH (1949–)

John Davies and Robert Smith (born in Leicester in 1949) studied film at the Royal College of Art between 1976 and 1979, where they collaborated on *My Favourite from the South*, adapted from Leopold von Sacher-Masoch's *Venus in Furs*. More typical of their future output was *City Farm* (1979), a slab of mumbling realism built around a family reunion in Leicester. Smith and Davies waste no time explaining the relationship between their characters and allow them to pursue unremarkable activities and ramble on about their uneventful lives. But with the camera always ready to observe from an interesting angle, a magical reality slowly unfurls.

Their activities took a more political turn with *Maeve* (1982), backed by the BFI Production Board and Radio Telefís Éireann, which Davies co-directed with Pat Murphy. The film's viewpoint of an expatriate Catholic woman returning to strife-torn Belfast is Murphy's, but Smith and Davies supply radical aesthetic strategies that challenge any simple identification with the heroine. After setting up Front Room Productions under the ACTT workshop agreement with Channel 4, they returned to Northern Ireland for *Acceptable Levels* (1984), a wry look at the moral dilemmas facing well-meaning film-makers in a war zone. Despite the controversial subject matter – a human-interest documentary team almost witness the killing of a Belfast teenager by a British Army patrol – the film is more black comedy than tragedy, as much about the insular life on location and the back-biting and compromise involved in bringing a film to the screen as it is about the Irish problem.

Back in England Davies directed *Ursula and Glenys* and Smith *Intimate Strangers* (each acting as the other's cinematographer), both hour-long films released together in 1985. *Ursula and Glenys* is ostensibly more dramatic, a series of revelations about incest and other dark family secrets; *Intimate Strangers* is less consequential but more pleasing, a hesitant exploration of the relationship between a mother and her teenage son living in a Brixton squat, with Smith allowing the film to meander creatively and Davies' cinematography constantly stimulating in its odd compositions and adventurous reliance on natural light.

The Love Child, Front Room's most ambitious production, followed in 1987. Well-known actors (Sheila Hancock, Peter Capaldi) boosted the film's commercial prospects, but its story about a young man deflected from his desire for ordered normality by his roots (he is the child of a dead cult rock star) lacks narrative drive and lapses into whimsy. Smith was more successful with the sparser script (by playwright Sharman Macdonald) of

Wild Flowers, made for Channel 4 in 1989. A lustily heterosexual Edinburgh girl (Beatie Edney) goes home to a Scottish island to meet her boyfriend's family only to form a passionate attachment to his mother, a secret lesbian with a youthful *joie de vivre* that has survived her own mother's cruel repression and the hard compromises of married life. The characters and setting are consistently intriguing, and Smith's evocation of a community where rigid conformity is the price paid for tight-knit warmth is startling.

Wild Flowers attracted scant attention and had no progeny. Davies proved no more prolific, directing only an interesting documentary about visually impaired artists, *Behind the Eye* (1992), with Smith as producer and cinematographer. Though Smith and Davies achieved little of the fame accorded Peter Greenaway and Derek Jarman, their low-key experiments yielded a significant body of work, which deserves more attention than it has so far received.

(Robert Murphy)

BIBLIOGRAPHY: Gray, Laurie, 'Other Stories', *City Limits* no. 315, 15 Oct. 1987, p. 22.

FILMOGRAPHY: John Davies: *My Favourite from the South* (short, 1977); *City Farm* (co-dir. Robert Smith, 1979); *Maeve* (co-dir. Pat Murphy, 1982); *Acceptable Levels* (1983); *Ursula and Glenys* (1985); *Behind the Eye* (doc., 1992).

Robert Smith: *City Farm* (co-dir. John Davies, 1979); *Intimate Strangers* (1985); *The Love Child* (1987); *Wild Flowers* (1989).

DAVIES, Terence (1945–)

Terence Davies was born in Liverpool on 10 November 1945, the youngest child in a large working-class family. After working for ten years as a clerk in a shipping office and a book-keeper in an accountancy firm, he entered Coventry School of Drama in 1971. There he wrote the script for *Children*, which he directed after he left with backing from the BFI Production Board. He then went to the National Film School, where he completed *Madonna and Child* as his graduation film in 1980. Three years later, thanks to funding from the Greater London Arts Association and the BFI, he made *Death and Transfiguration*. These three short to medium-length films comprise *The Terence Davies Trilogy*, which put him on the cinematic map as one of the most original British film-makers of the late twentieth century.

In the *Trilogy* and the two films that followed, *Distant Voices, Still Lives* (1988) and *The Long Day Closes* (1992), Davies reconstructs his childhood and youth in a working-class district of Liverpool in the 1940s and 50s. His *alter ego*, called Robert Tucker in the later films, is shy and introverted; his teachers and peers treat this as testimony to his mental slowness and as an excuse to bully him. His family life is traumatised by his violent and unpredictable father, who regularly harasses his sisters and his mother, the most important person in his life. Another cause of unhappiness is his homosexuality. The pain of being different is exacerbated by his Catholic upbringing, which makes him believe that homosexuality is the gravest sin possible. Yet Davies regards the past with nostalgia as well as resentment. All the films are imbued with tender memories of the communality of working-class life and the old forms of entertainment, such as listening to the wireless, visiting the cinema and singing together.

The uniqueness of Davies' representation of the past lies in the way he uses cinematic means to convey the fragmented nature of memory and the partial knowledge of his young protagonist. Instead of using a smooth narrative, we receive a succession of loosely connected episodes, with no dominant storyline. A moving image is sometimes replaced by a discoloured photograph to convey the impression of time frozen by memory and to emphasise the gap between the real and a recollected past. Thanks to the subjective camera, objects lose their hard, material existence, becoming only shadows on the wall or floor. Such a technique also suggests that children – his viewpoint characters in all his films except *The House of Mirth* – tend to over-interpret facts and mix truth with fiction. He also makes extensive use of songs, which play as important a role as dialogue in revealing his characters' feelings.

In 1984 Davies published a novel, *Hallelujah Now*, based on his memories of life in Liverpool; he turned to someone else's autobiographical novel for his next film. *The Neon Bible*, written in secret by John Kennedy Toole when he was sixteen, is set in Georgia in the American South, but it shares thematic, stylistic and ideological similarities with Davies' earlier work, such as the constricting influence of religion, the special bond between a boy and older women, male violence (at one point the father takes his sensitive son to a Ku Klux Klan lynching) and the distorted nature of memory. The novel is set during and shortly after the Second World War, a period Davies had already explored in *Distant Voices, Still Lives* and *The Long Day Closes*. As

in those films, his adaptation of *The Neon Bible* leaves the viewer with a bitter-sweet mixture of pain and nostalgia.

The House of Mirth (2000) marks Davies' furthest departure from his childhood obsessions. Based, like Scorsese's *The Age of Innocence* (1993), on a novel by Edith Wharton set in America at the beginning of the twentieth century, the main theme explores the struggle of an individual with a culture. In *The Neon Bible* Davies seemed to have difficulty connecting with the feelings of his characters, but here he offers penetrating insights into an emerging American industrial society defined by greed, narcissism and hypocrisy. The fight ends in the defeat of the heroine (Gillian Anderson), confirming Davies' view that against the backdrop of history an individual human being is only a particle of dust.

Davies' carefully composed tableaux and highly stylised narratives have led to him being grouped with Peter Greenaway and Derek Jarman. But Davies is no post-modernist: his use of popular songs and constant allusions to Hollywood musicals reflect a sincere affection for popular culture. Davies' intensely emotional cinema makes him unique among contemporary British film-makers.

(Ewa Mazierska)

BIBLIOGRAPHY: Coe, Jonathan, 'Jolly and Grim', *Sight and Sound*, Oct. 1995, pp. 12–14; Davies, Terence, *A Modest Pageant* (London: Faber and Faber, 1992); Eley, Geoff, '*Distant Voices, Still Lives*: The Family Is a Dangerous Place: Memory, Gender and the Image of the Working Class', in Robert A. Rosenstone (ed.), *Revisioning History: The Construction of a New Past* (Princeton, NJ: Princeton University Press, 1995); Horne, Philip, 'Beauty's Slow Fade', *Sight and Sound*, Oct. 2000, pp. 14–18; Hunt, Martin, 'The Poetry of the Ordinary: Terence Davies and the Social Art Cinema', *Screen*, Spring 1999, pp. 1–16; Powrie, Phil, 'On the Threshold between Past and Present', in Justine Ashby and Andrew Higson (eds), *British Cinema, Past and Present* (London: Routledge, 2000); Williams, Tony, 'The Masochist Fix: Gender Oppression in the Films of Terence Davies', in Lester Friedman (ed.), *British Cinema and Thatcherism* (London: UCL Press, 1993).

FILMOGRAPHY: *The Terence Davies Trilogy: Children* (1974–6); *Madonna and Child* (1980); *Death and Transfiguration* (1983) (rel. together in 1984); *Distant Voices, Still Lives* (1988); *The Long Day Closes* (1992); *The Neon Bible* (1995); *The House of Mirth* (2000).

DAVIS, Desmond (1928–)

Desmond Davis was born in London on 24 May 1926. He began work as a camera assistant on Herbert Mason's Gert and Daisy farce *It's in the Bag* in 1943, graduating to camera operator in 1954. Unusually, he became a director rather than a cinematographer. After working on three films directed by Tony Richardson – *A Taste of Honey* (1961), *The Loneliness of the Long Distance Runner* (1962) and *Tom Jones* (1963) – he made his debut as director with *Girl with Green Eyes* (1963), made for Richardson's Woodfall company. Davis captures the poignancy and delicacy of Edna O'Brien's novel about a young Irish girl and her love affair with an older man, and elicits fine performances from Rita Tushingham, Peter Finch and Lynn Redgrave. His next film, *The Uncle*, which he and Margaret Abrams adapted from her novel, was about a seven-year-old boy who finds that his nephew is his own age. It was a more personal project and its reflexive style alienated distributors, who allowed it only a limited release.

I Was Happy Here (1965), a tender story written by Edna O'Brien, returned to the Irish theme of *Girl with Green Eyes* but failed to repeat its success. The much grosser *Smashing Time* (1966), which effectively mocked the idea of Swinging London, proved to be Davis' most commercially successful film. Tushingham and Redgrave play naive girls from the North who come seeking glamour and excitement in the capital. Though its slapstick sequences were condemned by some critics, the film successfully evokes the zany atmosphere, colourful characters and cultural dynamism of London in the mid-60s. In *A Nice Girl Like Me* (1969), Davis reverted to comic lyricism in a quiet, pastel-shaded London very different from that of *Smashing Time*. The adventures of a sheltered young woman (Barbara Ferris), whose desire to see life is thwarted by her continual pregnancies, are wispily lightweight, but Davis directs with patient charm and is rewarded with excellent performances from Ferris, Harry Andrews as the unlikely romantic interest and a gallery of British eccentrics.

Davis entered television in the 1970s to work on subjects as diverse as *The New Avengers* (1976) and Shakespeare's *Measure for Measure* (1979). In 1981 he returned to the cinema as director of *Clash of the Titans*, a mythological extravaganza with appropriately prestigious actors (Laurence Olivier, Claire Bloom, Maggie Smith, Burgess Meredith) cast as gods and goddesses, Flora Robson and Freda Jackson as Stygian witches and Ursula Andress and her then-partner Harry Hamlin as Aphrodite and Perseus. Unfortunately the actors turned out to be far less lively than the monsters created by Ray Harryhausen. Davis returned to more familiar territory with *The Country Girls* (1983), based on Edna O'Brien's novel set in Ireland in the 1950s. Made on a low budget as one of the first Channel 4 films, it recaptures some of the charm of *Girl with Green Eyes*, but received only limited theatrical release. It was followed by *Ordeal by Innocence* (1984), a star-studded but lacklustre Agatha Christie adaptation. Davis continued to work in television in the 1990s, most notably on the ramshackle but enjoyable *Doggin' Around* (1994), Alan Plater's tale of an old American jazzman (Elliott Gould) 'doggin' around' the North of England.

(Margaret Butler)

BIBLIOGRAPHY: Davis, Desmond, 'Reflections', *Films and Filming*, Sept. 1973, pp. 20–3; Luckett, Moya, 'Travel and Mobility: Femininity and National Identity in Swinging London Films', in Justine Ashby and Andrew Higson (eds), *British Cinema, Past and Present* (London and New York: Routledge, 2000); Murphy, Robert, *Sixties British Cinema* (London: BFI, 1992); Salmi, Markku, 'Desmond Davis', *Film Dope* no. 9, Apr. 1976, pp. 41–2.

FILMOGRAPHY: *Girl with Green Eyes* (1963); *The Uncle* (1964); *I Was Happy Here* (1965); *Smashing Time* (1967); *A Nice Girl Like Me* (1969); *Clash of the Titans* (1981); *The Country Girls* (1983); *Ordeal by Innocence* (1984).

DAVIS, John T. (1947–)

John T. Davis was born in Belfast on 7 March 1947 and studied painting at Belfast School of Art in the early 1970s. When he inherited an 8mm camera in 1974 (an episode explored in his 1996 documentary, *The Uncle Jack*) he taught himself the rudiments of cinematography and began making films. His central obsession has been to explore and celebrate popular music in its socio-cultural context and he is specifically concerned with the cultural impact of American popular music and imagery on the collective subconscious of Northern Ireland.

Davis' style and musical obsessions are in evidence in embryo form in *Shellshock Rock*, which chronicles the punk music scene in Northern Ireland during the winter of 1978–9. The constantly moving, hand-held cameras catch the immediacy and vitality of the music scene of the time, and despite being barred from the Cork Film Festival, it proved a great success. Davis was invited to the United States, where he made *Route 66*, an influential two-hour documentary on the significance of the road myth and its music. He returned to the subject in 1991 in *Hobo*, his study of itinerant life in America.

In two memorable films, *Power in the Blood* and *Dust on the Bible*, Davis explored the similarities – in fundamentalist religion and country music – between the American bible belt and Northern Ireland's Protestant communities. Recently he has returned to his other interests to make a documentary on photography (*Traveller*) and on painting (*A House Divided*), both of which say as much about the political and cultural mood of contemporary Ireland as they do about the artists' work they chronicle.

An accomplished stylist and cinematographer, Davis has also played an influential role in the development of film-making in Ireland more generally, as director of photography on dozens of short fiction and documentary films.

(Martin McLoone)

BIBLIOGRAPHY: McCracken, Kathleen, 'Poetic Documentary: The Films of John T. Davis', in James MacKillop (ed.), *Contemporary Irish Cinema* (Syracuse, NY: Syracuse University Press, 1999); McLoone, Martin, *Irish Film: The Emergence of a Contemporary Cinema* (London: BFI, 2000); Pettitt, Lance, *Screening Ireland* (Manchester: Manchester University Press, 2000); Rockett, Kevin, John Hill and Luke Gibbons, *Cinema and Ireland* (London: Routledge, 1988).

FILMOGRAPHY: *What Colour Is the Bird?* (short, UK/Ir, 1978); *Shellshock Rock* (doc., UK/Ir, 1979); *Protex Hurrah* (short, UK/Ir, 1980); *Self Conscious Over You* (short, UK/Ir, 1981); *Route 66* (doc., 1985); *Power in the Blood* (doc., UK/Ir, 1989); *Dust on the Bible* (doc., UK/Ir); *Heart on the Line* (doc.) (1990); *Hobo* (doc., 1992); *Atlantic* (doc., 1993); *The Uncle Jack* (short, Ir, 1996); *Traveller* (doc., co-dir. Alen MacWeeney, Ir, 2000); *A House Divided* (doc., Ir, 2003).

DAVIS, Mick

Scriptwriter-director Mick Davis was born in the Gorbals, Glasgow. In Los Angeles he worked as a fitness trainer and football coach while writing and pitching scripts. *Love in Paris* (Anne Goursand, 1997), a needless sequel to Adrian Lyne's *Nine ½ Weeks* (1986), was one result; his directing debut, *The Match*, a rose-tinted, well-packaged comedy about an underdog Scottish football team, was another. The more ambitious *Modigliani*, centred on the artistic rivalry between Modigliani and Picasso, followed in 2004: uncertainly set in its time and place (Paris, after the First World War), and too earnest for its own good. Davis also collaborated on the script for *Wake of Death* (Philippe Martinez, 2004).

(Geoff Brown and Robert Murphy)

FILMOGRAPHY: *The Match* (UK/US/Ir, 1999); *Modigliani* (UK/Fr/Ger/It/Rom, 2004).

DAVIS, Philip (1953–)

Philip Davis was born in Grays, Essex, on 30 July 1953. Best known as an actor, he has appeared in key roles in *Quadrophenia* (Franc Roddam, 1979), *The Firm* (Alan Clarke, 1988), *High Hopes* (Mike Leigh, 1988), *Face* (Antonia Bird, 1997) and *Vera Drake* (Mike Leigh, 2004), as well as many other smaller but highly memorable roles. He now divides his time between acting, writing and directing.

His first directing credit was for the BBC television film *Skulduggery*, which he had written and produced for the stage two years earlier. The story of three young dropouts and their relationship with an older man (David Thewlis) seemingly stuck in adolescence, it showed the influence of Mike Leigh and Alan Clarke. *ID*, a co-production between the BBC and Parallax Pictures, the company responsible for Ken Loach's films, confirmed Davis as a hard-hitting realist director. Set in the dangerous world of football hooligans – a milieu Davis was familiar with from his work on Alan Clarke's *The Firm* – it tells the tale of a police officer (Reece Dinsdale) who goes undercover in order to infiltrate a gang and whose life falls apart as he begins to enjoy the violent aspects of his assignment.

Hold Back the Night, made for Parallax and the Lottery-backed Film Consortium, is a much more quirky project, with Sheila Hancock as a terminally ill woman, on her way to the Orkneys to die, helping an abused girl and an eco-activist on the run from the police. Disappointingly, it failed to find an audience. On television Davis has demonstrated his ability to direct popular drama with *Prime Suspect 5 – Errors of Judgement* (1996) and the *Real Women* series (1998), starring a female ensemble cast including Pauline Quirke, Michelle Collins, Lesley Manville and Frances Barber.

(Paul Ward)

BIBLIOGRAPHY: Drinkwater, Rob, 'Yobs for the Boys', *The Times*, 4 May 1995, p. 35; Matheou, Demetrious, 'Tough Talk', *Guardian G2* Section, 17 Dec. 1999, p. 9.

FILMOGRAPHY: *Skulduggery* (1989); *ID* (1995); *Hold Back the Night* (1998).

DAVIS, Redd (1897–?)

In one respect, Redd Davis would have been the perfect director for Claude Autant-Lara's sole British film, *The Mysterious Mr Davis* (1936). Little is known about his life beyond a few facts and assumptions: he was of Canadian origin, born in 1897, with experience in America as an actor for Edison and, in the 1920s, as a director – both activities now hard to trace. He arrived in Britain in 1928 with Monty Banks and other American film personnel lured by the increase in local production following the 1927 Cinematograph Films Act. From the beginning Davis belonged to the 'cheap and cheerful' school of British film-making. Under his real name, Herbert Davis, he directed comedian Tubby Phillips in a silent two-reeler and one feature, *The Bells of St Mary's*. But his career became properly launched with sound in 1932; now armed with the nickname Redd, he made twenty-four films in ten years, weaving between studios and companies from Julius Hagen's Real Art and Fox-British's Wembley 'quickie' factory to smaller fry like the City Film Corporation and Alexander Film Productions, early victims of the industry's financial upheavals in the mid-1930s. A few of the films earned decent money, like the comedy *King of the Castle*, with Billy Milton and June Clyde.

Davis' chief distinction as a director was as the promoter of new cinema entertainers, though he was never summoned to direct them again if their careers flourished. Among comedians, he directed Flanagan and Allen's second feature showcase (the lively *Underneath the Arches*) and Sid Field's first (*That's the Ticket*). Betty Fields, sister of Gracie, was tried out for stardom as the mill-girl heroine of *On Top of the World*; the attempt was not repeated. In *Excuse My Glove* Davis' hopeful was the boxer Len Harvey; while in June 1939 a jumble of amateurs squeezed onto Highbury studios' tiny stages for *Discoveries*, inspired by Carroll Levis' amateur talent radio programme, and a film most notable now for its patriotic finale featuring Glyn Davies marching through massed Empire troops, singing 'There'll Always Be an England'. By November 1939, after the film's release, the song was the country's biggest sheet-music seller.

Two war-flavoured films followed: Warner Bros.' spy comedy *That's the Ticket*, unsuccessful as a showcase for Field, though kindly received by some critics at the time; and the modest comedy *The Balloon Goes Up*, featuring variety artists Ethel Revnell and Gracie West. According to Billy Milton's autobiography, Davis subsequently lost his money gambling in Monte Carlo and returned to Canada, where he worked as a chef on the Canadian Pacific Railway.

(Geoff Brown)

BIBLIOGRAPHY: Milton, Billy, *Milton's Paradise Mislaid* (London: Jupiter Books, 1976).

FILMOGRAPHY: *The Bells of St. Mary's* (1928); *Bunkered* (short, 1929); *The Spare Room* (short); *The Umbrella*; *Here's George* (1932); *The Medicine Man*; *Excess Baggage*; *Send 'em Back Half Dead*; *Ask Beccles* (1933); *Seeing Is Believing*; *The Girl in the Flat*; *Easy Money* (1934); *Say It with Diamonds*; *Handle with Care* (1935); *King of the Castle*; *Excuse My Glove*; *On Top of the World* (1936); *Underneath the Arches*; *Sing as You Swing*; *Calling All Ma's* (aka *The Biter Bit*); *Variety Hour* (1937); *Special Edition*; *Anything to Declare?* (1938); *Discoveries* (1939); *That's the Ticket* (1940); *The Balloon Goes Up* (1942).

DAY, Robert (1922–)

Robert Day was born in Sheen, on the south-western edge of London, on 9 November 1922. He was fascinated by movies from an early age: 'Even at ten or eleven I was determined that, when the time came, I would get into the business' (Weaver, p. 92). In 1938, straight out of school, he joined Warner Bros. – initially on the distribution side, then moving to the camera department at the company's Teddington Studios. He worked his way up from clapper-boy to camera operator on an eclectic series of movies that took in everything from edgy British noir – *Noose* (Edmond T. Gréville, 1948), *Obsession* (Edward Dmytryk, 1949), *Home at Seven* (Ralph Richardson, 1952) – to the overblown post-imperialist pomp of *Storm over the Nile* (Zoltán Korda/Terence Young, 1955), and two films for Carol Reed: *The Man Between* (1953) and *A Kid for Two Farthings* (1955).

Day moved on to direct episodes of the television adventure series, *The Buccaneers* (1956), and was given his first chance to direct a feature film by Sidney Gilliat, who offered him *The Green Man* (1956), a breezy black comedy with Alastair Sim on top form as a professional assassin. After this promising start *Strangers' Meeting*, a rickety murder mystery, was a letdown but two horror movies with Boris Karloff, *Grip of the Strangler* and *Corridors of Blood*, showed a certain knack for the genre. They were both made for John Croydon's pinchpenny Producers' Associates, as was *First Man into Space*, a shameless Quatermass rip-off, but in all three films Day overcame budgetary limitations with craft and narrative gusto. 'So often, directors make their best movies when they don't have that much money,' he later observed. 'They have to use their imaginations instead' (Weaver, p. 88).

Life in Emergency Ward 10 was a lacklustre spin-off from the popular television hospital series, and Day could do little with the flaccid whimsy of *Bobbikins*, about a baby that gives stock-market tips. But *Two-Way Stretch*, a lively heist comedy, gave Peter Sellers one of his best roles as a criminal mastermind, with vigorous support from Lionel Jeffries as an apoplectic prison warder. That same year, *The Rebel* captured at least something of the lugubrious genius of Tony Hancock, with the comedian playing an artist whose aspirations far outstrip his abilities. In between them came *Tarzan the Magnificent*, the first of five later-day Tarzan movies that Day would direct for Sy Weintraub.

In 1962 Day made *Operation Snatch*, a spasmodically amusing wartime comedy, with Terry-Thomas as a harassed officer tackling ape problems in Gibraltar, but the call of the jungle took him to Thailand to make *Tarzan's Three Challenges*. After returning to Britain to direct an unexciting remake of H. Rider Haggard's grandiose Victorian-African fantasy, *She*, he decamped permanently to the USA. Further Tarzan films followed but Day's future career was in American television. He had directed several episodes of the cult series *The Avengers* (1961) in Britain and he proved equally proficient on *The Streets of San Francisco* (1972), *Kojak* (1973) and *Dallas* (1978) before progressing to American television movies in the 1980s.

(Philip Kemp)

BIBLIOGRAPHY: Weaver, Tom, *Attack of the Monster Movie Makers: Interviews with Twenty Genre Giants* (Jefferson, NC and London: McFarland, 1994), pp. 85–98.

FILMOGRAPHY: *The Green Man* (1956); *Strangers' Meeting* (1957); *Grip of the Strangler*; *Corridors of Blood*; *First Man into Space*; *Life in Emergency Ward 10* (1958); *Bobbikins* (1959); *Two-Way Stretch*; *Tarzan the Magnificent*; *The Rebel* (1960); *Operation Snatch* (1962); *Tarzan's Three Challenges* (US, 1963); *She*; *Tarzan and the Valley of Gold* (US) (1965); *Tarzan and the Great River* (US, 1967); *Tarzan and the Jungle Boy* (1968); *The Big Game* (SA/It, 1972).

DEAN, Basil (1888–1978)

Basil Dean is a paradoxical figure in British cinema. He represented a theatrical approach to film-making much despised by modern critics, but is responsible as producer for some of the most domestically successful films of the 1930s, and for establishing British cinema's two biggest stars of the period, George Formby and Gracie Fields. He was born on 27 September 1888 in Croydon. Always primarily a man of the theatre, he joined Annie Horniman's famous Manchester repertory company in 1907. He became the first director of Liverpool Repertory Theatre in 1911, and in 1918 was awarded an MBE for his services to national entertainment during the First World War. In the next ten years he rose to be one of the most influential theatrical producers and directors in the country, responsible for London and New York productions of new plays by John Galsworthy, W. Somerset Maugham, Noël Coward, Dodie Smith, Clemence Dane and J. B. Priestley.

In 1926 his adaptation of Margaret Kennedy's best-selling novel *The Constant Nymph* was a major success and Dean produced the screen version, directed by Adrian Brunel for Gainsborough. Dean's real involvement in the screen, however, came with the introduction of sound, which he saw as an opportunity to bring his style of theatrical drama to a wider audience. He founded Associated Talking Pictures in 1929 with the intention of producing cinematic adaptations of serious modern plays. Brunel remembered Dean as a director with little understanding of the film medium, while Rachael Low suggests that the cinematic touches in many of his films are attributable to other members of the production personnel, Thorold Dickinson, Carol Reed and David Lean, working as uncredited co-directors.

Whatever his failings as a film director, there is little doubt that Dean was a film producer of considerable talent and drive. ATP's studios at Ealing were the first in Britain built for sound production and he was able to attract highly talented production personnel to his company. His serious adaptations failed to achieve the success he hoped for, but the fine casts and unusual reliance on location photography in *Escape*, *Autumn Crocus* and *Lorna Doone* have ensured their durability. Dean's commercial success came from his perspicacity in recognising the potential of Fields and Formby, bringing them to the screen in vehicles that enhanced their peculiarly local appeal. After directing *Looking on the Bright Side*, *Sing as We Go!* and *Look up and Laugh*, Dean handed over the direction to others – Monty Banks for Fields, Anthony Kimmins for Formby – but he ensured that they had well-crafted scripts (from the likes of J. B. Priestley and Walter Greenwood) and the films deserved their box-office success. These films can be understood as belonging to a wider studio tradition of the modest representation of ordinary British life that Dean encouraged – the best example of which is perhaps Carol Reed's *Penny Paradise* (1938).

During the late 1930s Dean directed less, and began to return to his theatrical commitments. Eventually he was succeeded at Ealing by Michael Balcon, whose stress on teamwork owed much to the tradition that Dean established at ATP. During the Second World War, Dean founded and ran the Entertainments National Service Association (ENSA), remaining an influential figure in the theatre until shortly before his death from a heart attack in London on 22 April 1978.

(Lawrence Napper)

BIBLIOGRAPHY: Brunel, Adrian, *Nice Work: The Story of Thirty Years in British Film Production* (London: Forbes Robertson, 1949); Dean, Basil, *Mind's Eye: An Autobiography 1927–1972* (London: Hutchinson, 1973); Low, Rachael, *Film Making in 1930s Britain* (London: George Allen & Unwin, 1985).

FILMOGRAPHY: *The Return of Sherlock Holmes* (US, 1929); *Escape*; *Birds of Prey* (US: *The Perfect Alibi*) (1930); *Nine Till Six*; *Looking on the Bright Side* (co dir. Graham Cutts); *The Impassive Footman* (US: *Woman in Bondage*) (1932); *Loyalties* (1933); *The Constant Nymph*; *Sing as We Go!*; *Autumn Crocus* (1934); *Lorna Doone*; *Look up and Laugh* (1935); *Whom the Gods Love* (US: *Mozart*, 1936); *The Show Goes On* (1937); *21 Days* (US: *21 Days Together*, 1937; rel. 1940).

DEARDEN, Basil (1911–1971)

Basil Dearden was born Basil Dear in Westcliff-on-Sea, Essex, on 1 January 1911. He left school early to work as an office boy in a London underwriting and insurance company. Experience in amateur dramatics led to work with the Ben Greet Company and to his appointment as assistant stage manager at the Grand Theatre, Fulham. In 1931 he became a general stage manager for the theatrical enterprises of the impresario Basil Dean. By the mid-1930s, Dearden had shifted from theatre to film, working at the Ealing studios of Associated Talking Pictures, where

Dean was Head of Production, as writer, script editor, dialogue director and assistant director. In an attempt to avoid the confusions that resulted from the similarity between their names, Dear changed his surname to Dearden.

When Dean was superseded by Michael Balcon, Dearden stayed on at Ealing, progressing to associate producer on three George Formby films, and co-directing three films with the studio's other top comedy star, Will Hay. He made his solo directorial debut with *The Bells Go Down* (1943), which – like Humphrey Jennings' *"Fires Were Started –"* (1943) – celebrates the heroism of those who worked in the Auxiliary Fire Service during the Blitz. The art director on the film was Michael Relph, who was to form a fruitful creative partnership with Dearden that was to last nearly thirty years. Relph shared a background in the theatre, but in set and production design. By the end of the war, with Dearden directing and Relph as associate producer, script collaborator and sometimes production designer, they had completed *The Halfway House* (1944) and *They Came to a City* (1944) and were preparing to make the prisoner-of-war-camp drama *The Captive Heart* (1946).

Dearden and Relph became Ealing's most prolific film-makers and, unlike most of their contemporaries at the studio, seemed to thrive on a rapid turnover of production projects requiring flexibility and planning, which they delivered to budget and on schedule. Their films made a distinctive contribution to Ealing's search for a new direction as it sought to negotiate and adjust to the changed realities of post-war Britain. In particular, they carried forward and extended the mix of social purpose, fictional realism and preoccupation with a nation of united communities and public service that had become the wartime hallmark of Ealing. But they also began to probe into the issues that now confronted social stability and the establishment of the promised peacetime consensus. Dearden and Relph made several social-problem films that confronted audiences with ethical and moral dilemmas relating to the interplay between communities and institutions adjusting to changing social circumstances. Sometimes condemned for their middle-class, liberal point of view with its touching faith in national institutions and public service, the films often seek to link, within the conventions of the crime/melodrama genre, private problems with public issues.

Their first social-problem film, *Frieda* (1947), explores issues of prejudice and reconciliation in the aftermath of the war as a young German woman marries into the heart of an English community. *The Blue Lamp* (1950), *I Believe in You* (1952) and *Violent Playground* (1958) all deal with problems associated with youth, criminality and delinquency. In a similar fashion, *Sapphire* (1959) takes a timely look at Britain's black community and confronts racism, while *Victim* (1961), made in the wake of the Wolfenden Report, focuses on the persecution of homosexuals.

These six feature films constitute the core of Dearden's explicit and self-conscious engagement with the social-problem film. More tangential but also deserving serious consideration are *The Gentle Gunman* (1952), dealing with Irish nationalism; *Life for Ruth* (1962), which explores the conflict between modern medicine and fundamentalist religious belief; *The Mind Benders* (1963), with its themes of brainwashing and scientific responsibility; and the youth drama, *A Place to Go* (1963). Outside this area, Dearden and Relph's films include melodramas, thrillers, comedies and the gloomy costume drama *Saraband for Dead Lovers* (1948), Ealing's first Technicolor film. *Cage of Gold* (1950), *Pool of London* (1951), *The Square Ring* (1953) and *The Rainbow Jacket* (1954) are varied in tone and theme but they all deal with damaged, unsettled and insecure characters. Like a number of their films from the mid-1950s onwards, they also focus on themes of masculine adjustment – in particular, how the experience and memories of wartime action resonate within the post-war present. In *Out of the Clouds* (1955), a former RAF pilot has to come to terms with a peacetime ground job. *The Ship That Died of Shame* (1955) unravels and juxtaposes the past and present of three sailors who have had a 'good' war but slip into sordid illegality in their attempt to recapture wartime thrills. *The League of Gentlemen* (1960), made after Dearden and Relph left Ealing, is more light hearted in its treatment of a group of disillusioned ex-servicemen who reunite for a robbery, but here too the contrast between the excitement of war and the dull disillusions of peace dominate.

Dearden returned to comedy to direct Benny Hill in *Who Done It?* (1956), the last comedy made at Ealing before the studio was sold to the BBC. It was much less memorable than his first independent feature, *The Smallest Show on Earth* (1957), which takes in familiar Ealing themes as bright young couple Bill Travers and Virginia McKenna mobilise aged eccentrics Peter Sellers, Bernard Miles and Margaret Rutherford in their battle to preserve a pre-war flea-pit against the might of a shiny, modern corporate cinema. Dearden also acted as producer on the three comedies directed by Michael Relph: *Davy* (1957), *Rockets Galore!* (1958) and *Desert Mice* (1959). In 1959 Dearden and Relph joined Richard Attenborough, Bryan Forbes, Jack Hawkins and Guy Green to form Allied Film Makers, a production consortium with financial and distribution links with the Rank Organisation, under whose aegis they made *The League of Gentlemen* and *Man in the Moon* (1960), which were box-office successes, and the bold, location-shot *Life for Ruth*, which was not.

From the mid-1960s, Dearden and Relph worked on a number of large-scale international productions: *Woman of Straw* (1964), *Masquerade* (1965), *Khartoum* (1966), all for United Artists, *Only When I Larf* (1968) for Columbia, and *The Assassination Bureau* (1969) for Paramount. *The Man Who Haunted Himself* (1970), Dearden's final film, was a return to tragic melodrama with its story of a quiet family man (played by Roger Moore) who dies in a car crash, only to unleash his charismatic alter ego. By a bizarre coincidence, Dearden himself died as a result of injuries sustained in a car accident on the M4, while returning home from Pinewood Studios on 23 March 1971. He was sixty years old and was survived by his wife, the actress Melissa Stribling, who had appeared in a number of his films, and their two children, Torquil and (the director) James Dearden.

Critical assessments of Dearden's work have generally been less than positive. The breadth, volume and variability of his work have counted against him and while some critics have grudgingly acknowledged his technical professionalism, he has rarely been singled out for critical praise in stylistic, aesthetic or political terms. The critical agenda regarding his work was set in the early 1960s by writers for whom Dearden and Relph's films epitomised the stiltedness of British cinema. More recently, their achievements have been reassessed, their contribution to the Ealing ethos recognised and their social-problem films – particularly *Victim* and *Sapphire* – valued more highly. As film studies gropes beyond auteurism towards a greater recognition of the importance of collaboration and versatility, the contribution of Basil Dearden and his collaborator Michael Relph might be more generously acknowledged.

(Tim O'Sullivan)

BIBLIOGRAPHY: Barr, Charles, *Ealing Studios*, 2nd edn (London: Studio Vista, 1993); Burton, Alan, Tim O'Sullivan and Paul Wells (eds), *Liberal Directions: Basil Dearden and Postwar British Film Culture* (Trowbridge, Wilts: Flicks Books, 1997); Durgnat, Raymond, 'Dearden and Relph: Two on a Tandem', *Films and Filming*, July 1966, pp. 26–33; Durgnat, Raymond, *A Mirror for England* (London: Faber and Faber, 1970); Hill, John, *Sex, Class and Realism: British Cinema 1956–1963* (London: BFI, 1986); Landy, Marcia, *British Genres: Cinema and Society, 1930–1960* (Princeton, NJ: Princeton University Press, 1991); McFarlane, Brian, *An Autobiography of British Cinema* (London: Methuen, 1997).

FILMOGRAPHY: *The Black Sheep of Whitehall* (co-dir. Will Hay, 1941); *The Goose Steps Out* (co-dir. Will Hay, 1942); *The Bells Go Down*; *My Learned Friend* (co-dir. Will Hay) (1943); *The Halfway House*; *They Came to a City* (1944); *Dead of Night* ('The Hearse Driver' episode and the linking story, co-dirs. Alberto Cavalcanti/Charles Crichton/Robert Hamer, 1945); *The Captive Heart* (1946); *Frieda* (1947); *Saraband for Dead Lovers* (1948); *Train of Events* ('The Prisoner of War' and 'The Actor' episodes, co-dirs. Sidney Cole/Charles Crichton, 1949); *The Blue Lamp*; *Cage of Gold* (1950); *Pool of London* (1951); *I Believe in You* (co-dir. Michael Relph); *The Gentle Gunman* (1952); *The Square Ring* (1953); *The Rainbow Jacket* (1954); *Out of the Clouds*; *The Ship That Died of Shame* (1955); *Who Done It?* (1956); *The Smallest Show on Earth* (1957); *Violent Playground* (1958); *Sapphire* (1959); *The League of Gentlemen*; *Man in the Moon* (1960); *The Secret Partner*; *Victim* (1961); *All Night Long*; *Life for Ruth* (1962); *The Mind Benders*; *A Place to Go* (1963); *Woman of Straw* (1964); *Masquerade* (1965); *Khartoum* (1966); *Only When I Larf*; *The Assassination Bureau* (1968); *The Man Who Haunted Himself* (1970).

DEARDEN, James (1949–)

James Dearden was born in London on 14 September 1949 into a distinguished film family. His father was respected director Basil Dearden and his mother actress Melissa Stribling. After education at Eton and Oxford he spent a year as a cutting-room trainee before progressing to film editor. He was a production assistant on his father's film *The Assassination Bureau* (1968) and then worked for five years on commercials and documentaries. His first film as director was an eight-minute short, *The Contraption* (1977), which he also scripted and produced. It won the Silver Bear Award at the 1978 Berlin Film Festival. The gothic overtones of much of Dearden's later work were already apparent in this dark tale. He followed it with *Panic*, a horror story in which a girl unwittingly gives a werewolf a lift in her car, and a ghost story set in Germany, *The Cold Room*, made with backing from American cable company HBO. In 1980, Dearden scripted and directed *Diversion*, a forty-two-minute cautionary tale about the consequences of casual adultery, which was later to form the basis of his script for *Fatal Attraction* (Adrian Lyne, 1987). He argued that controversy over the film was misplaced and that it should be seen as a gothic fairy tale rather than a backlash against feminism.

Dearden' s first feature film was *Pascali's Island* (1988), which he adapted from a novel by Barry Unsworth. The story, about betrayal in the years leading up to the First World War, echoes some of Dearden's earlier preoccupations, and the film, photographed by Roger Deakins, is ambitious and visually rich, despite its modest budget. *Rogue Trader* (1999), with Ewan

McGregor as Nick Leeson, the man who brought down Barings Bank, marked a change in direction for Dearden, though it consolidated his reputation as a director interested in telling complex stories full of moral ambiguities.

(Janet Moat)

BIBLIOGRAPHY: Kennedy, Harlan, 'Dearden's Island', *Film Comment*, July/Aug. 1988, pp. 17–18, 20–2.

FILMOGRAPHY: *The Contraption* (short, 1977); *Panic* (short, 1978); *Diversion* (short, 1980); *The Cold Room* (US/UK/E. Ger, 1984); *Pascali's Island* (1988); *Rogue Trader* (1999).

DE COURVILLE, Albert (1887–1960)

By the time Albert de Courville entered the film industry in 1929 he had already acquired a formidable reputation as the producer of spectacular stage revues. Throughout the years of the First World War and the 1920s the London Hippodrome was rarely without a de Courville production. During his ten active years in the British film industry he never achieved similar status; though he successfully positioned Jessie Matthews as a screen star in *There Goes the Bride* (1932) and serviced other Gaumont-British performers with a bullish conviction in his own merits.

Born to wealthy French parents in London on 26 March 1887, Albert Pierre de Courville initially found work as a journalist. In the theatre he began by assisting Sir Edward Moss, founder of Moss Empires, at the London Hippodrome. By 1912 he was producing his own shows, importing American music fashions for *Hullo, Ragtime!*; subsequent productions were equally topical and lavish. The invitation to work in talkies came from British and Dominion's producer Herbert Wilcox, eager to exploit stage talent; but de Courville's first film, *Wolves*, a melodrama of the frozen North featuring Charles Laughton and Dorothy Gish, proved less of a pointer to his future than *There Goes the Bride*.

Matthews' appeal in stage musicals had not yet been mirrored in films; against advice, de Courville insisted she took the role of the runaway bride in Paris in this remake of a German film. Fluid direction, her engaging personality and some muted naughtiness ensured a modest success. De Courville had been vindicated, though his quixotic manner and strong-arm tactics led to stormy relations with Gaumont's production chief Michael Balcon and the company's top players.

De Courville subsequently showcased Gaumont's new star in *The Midshipmaid*. After that Matthews declined his further services, and he moved on to any attraction the company offered: Gordon Harker and Binnie Hale in *This Is the Life*; Cicely Courtneidge in *Things Are Looking Up*; even Mick the Miller, a star greyhound, in *Wild Boy*. With a strong theatrical performer like Courtneidge, de Courville's camera did nothing but sit and watch. With a detective comedy-thriller like *Seven Sinners* (1936) he mingled more with the material, muffling some gags in Launder and Gilliat's fast-talking script, doing no harm to others, damaging still others with overemphasis (a regular de Courville trait).

During the industry recession of the late 1930s, de Courville's film projects were less prestigious, and overall less successful. *Crackerjack* (1938), a burglar comedy featuring Tom Walls and Lilli Palmer, maintained a breezy charm, but fun slipped through everyone's fingers in *The Lambeth Walk* (1939), a version of the stage hit *Me and My Girl*.

With the onset of war de Courville went to America. He engaged himself peripherally in Hollywood (for *The Shanghai Gesture* he was associate producer) but concentrated primarily on Broadway theatre productions. He returned to Britain in 1948, but by then his glory days, in either field, were over. He died, bankrupt, in March 1960.

(Geoff Brown)

BIBLIOGRAPHY: De Courville, Albert, *I Tell You* (London: Chapman and Hall, 1928).

FILMOGRAPHY: *Wolves* (US: *Wanted Men*, 1930); *77 Park Lane*; *Night Shadows/A Night in Marseilles* (1931); *There Goes the Bride*; *The Midshipmaid* (US: *Midshipmaid Gob*) (1932); *This Is the Life* (1933); *Wild Boy* (1934); *Things Are Looking Up*; *The Case of Gabriel Perry*; *Charing Cross Road* (1935); *Seven Sinners* (US: *Doomed Cargo*); *Strangers on Honeymoon* (1936); *Clothes and the Woman* (1937); *Oh Boy!*; *Star of the Circus* (US: *The Hidden Menace*); *Crackerjack* (US: *The Man with 100 Faces*) (1938); *The Lambeth Walk*; *The Rebel Son* (co-dirs. Alexis Granowsky/Adrian Brunel); *An Englishman's Home* (US: *Madmen of Europe*) (1939).

DELL, Jeffrey (1899–1985)

John Edward Flowers Dell was born in Shoreham-by-Sea, Sussex, on 7 May 1899, the son of a solicitor. He was educated at Berkhampsted School (where a fellow pupil was Graham Greene) and, after a short period at Brighton College of Art, he joined his father's firm and qualified as a solicitor, though without much enthusiasm. Taking up writing in his spare time, he scored his first success in 1931 with a dramatisation of C. S. Forester's *Payment Deferred*, which gave Charles Laughton one of his best early stage roles and allowed Dell to abandon the law for good.

Payment Deferred was soon filmed (directed by Lothar Mendes in 1932 for MGM), as was another of Dell's stage adaptations, *The Firebird* (William Dieterle, 1934). This brought him to the notice of Alexander Korda, for whom he co-scripted *Sanders of the River* (Zoltán Korda, 1935). After Korda's grandiose empire at Denham collapsed in 1937, Dell turned the experience to good account in his first novel, *Nobody Ordered Wolves* (1938), a wittily satirical account of the British film industry with Korda trenchantly, though affectionately, lampooned as Napoleon Bott.

Dell continued to write scripts as well as stage plays; among the films he co-scripted were the flag-wavers *Freedom Radio* (Anthony Asquith, 1941) and *Thunder Rock* (Roy Boulting, 1942), Dell's first association with the Boulting Brothers. He made his directorial debut in the same patriotic vein with *The Flemish Farm* (1943), a Resistance movie co-scripted with his first wife, the future film-maker Jill Craigie. Graced with a rousing score by Ralph Vaughan Williams, it was successful enough for Dell to go on to *Don't Take It to Heart!* (1944), a whimsical comedy set in a crumbling old stately home stuffed with stock characters; it anticipated something of the gentle anarchy of Ealing and gave him his greatest hit as a director.

Dell directed two more films from his own scripts: *It's Hard to Be Good* (1948), a comedy about demobbed servicemen with mild social overtones, and *The Dark Man* (1951), a thriller let down by weak plotting. He published two further novels, *News for Heaven* and *The Hoffman Episode*, and renewed his association with the Boulting Brothers when he co-scripted the second of their series of satirical comedies, *Brothers in Law* (Roy Boulting, 1957). He went on to collaborate on several more Boulting films, including *Lucky Jim* (1957), *Happy Is the Bride* (1957) and *Suspect* (1960). He also took co-directing credit with Roy Boulting on *Carlton-Browne of the F.O.* (1959), with Terry-Thomas in the title role as an upper-class-twit diplomat. Dell's last script credit was on *Rotten to the Core* (John Boulting, 1965), though he is said to have helped with uncredited dialogue on the screen adaptation of Bill Naughton's *The Family Way* (Roy Boulting, 1966). He died in Sussex on 24 February 1985.

(Philip Kemp)

BIBLIOGRAPHY: Boulting, Roy, Obituary, *Film and TV Technician*, May 1985, p. 6; Obituary, *Screen International*, 16 Mar. 1985, p. 41.

FILMOGRAPHY: *The Flemish Farm* (1943); *Don't Take It to Heart!* (1944); *Call Up* (doc.); *It's Hard to Be Good* (1948); *The Dark Man* (1951); *Carlton-Browne of the F.O.* (co-dir. Roy Boulting, 1959).

DENHAM, Reginald (1894–1983)

Born in London on 10 January 1894, Reginald Denham is best known as co-author, with Edward Percy, of the splendid stage melodrama *Ladies in Retirement* (1939), filmed in Hollywood by Charles Vidor in 1941, and, as *The Mad Room*, by Bernard Girard in 1969. Educated at the City of London School and the Guildhall School of Music, he made his debut as actor in 1913. He acted, produced and wrote plays and film and television scripts throughout his career. His films as director are essentially formulaic exercises in such characteristic 1930s' genres as the crime thriller and romantic comedy. The two most notable are *Death at Broadcasting House* (1934), which benefits from its swag of radio guest stars, with Donald Wolfit as murder victim; and *The Silent Passenger* (1935), adapted from Dorothy L. Sayers, with Wolfit as murderer, and Peter Haddon as languid detective Lord Peter Wimsey. In both films the narrative moves swiftly and effectively; *Death at Broadcasting House* is also interesting for its radio studio setting, and *The Silent Passenger* has a well-shot fight set in a railway yard. As 1930s' genre films go, his attracted popular stars (such as Jack Hulbert in *Kate Plus Ten*) and more than fulfilled their ephemeral purpose. His last film was *Anna di Brooklyn* (1958), a Franco-Italian production starring Gina Lollobrigida. He died of apoplexy in Englewood, New Jersey, on 4 February 1983.

(Brian McFarlane)

BIBLIOGRAPHY: Denham, Reginald, *Stars in My Hair* (London: T. Werner Laurie, 1958); Obituary, *Classic Images* no. 94, April 1983, p. 8.

FILMOGRAPHY: *The Jewel*; *Called Back* (1933); *The Primrose Path*; *Lucky Loser*; *Death at Broadcasting House*; *Brides to Be*; *Borrow a Million* (1934); *The Village Squire*; *The Silent Passenger*; *The Price of Wisdom*; *Lucky Days*; *Lieutenant Daring RN* (1935); *The House of the Spaniard*; *Dreams Come True*; *The Crimson Circle*; *Calling the Tune* (1936); *Kate Plus Ten*; *Flying Fifty-Five* (1938); *Blind Folly* (1939); *Anna di Brooklyn/Fast and Sexy* (co-dir. Carlo Lastricati, supervisory dir. Vittoria De Sica, It/Fr 1958).

DENTON, Jack

Jack Denton was born in Ashby-de-la-Zouche, Leicestershire. He began acting in Hepworth films from 1909, continuing into the 1920s with many character and comedy parts, notably in *Old Bill Through the Ages* (Thomas Bentley, 1924). He began directing at Neptune in 1914, and made eight features between 1919 and 1921, chiefly for Ideal and Union Photoplays. The most notable is his lively, fast-moving version of the much-filmed Victorian novel, *Lady Audley's Secret*, from a scenario by Eliot Stannard.

(Robert Murphy)

FILMOGRAPHY: *The Yule Log* (short, 1914); *The Airman's Children* (short, 1915); *The Heart of a Rose*; *The Call of the Sea*; *A Lass o' the Looms*; *Barnaby* (1919); *The Twelve Pound Look*; *Lady Audley's Secret*; *Ernest Maltravers* (1920); *Sybil*; *Our Aggie* (short, 1921); *The Doddington Diamonds* (short, 1922).

DESPINS, Joseph

Canadian-born Joseph (Chuck) Despins moved to Britain in 1963, worked as an editor on documentaries and BBC features, and took an active part in the London avant-garde film-making scene in the 1960s and 70s. He first attracted attention with the very low-budget black-and-white feature *Duffer* (1971), a bold and funny though fatally undisciplined exploration of a sado-masochistic relationship between two young men in London's run-down bedsitter-land. After helping to produce *Brown Ale with Gertie* (Alan Brown, 1974) and *A Private Enterprise* (Peter K. Smith, 1974) for the BFI Production Board, Despins was rewarded with BFI backing for *The Moon over the Alley*, an attempt at a Brecht/Weill musical set in then-seedy Notting Hill. Despins' ambition to combine social comment with artistic experimentation is admirable, but, blighted by a skinflint budget, dingy lighting and wild lurches in tone, this tale of injustice, doom and lurking dangers in the lower depths scores higher on uniqueness than achievement.

Despins then taught at the National Film School and worked as a production manager, but his feature career lay dormant until 1981, when he was rediscovered by Channel 4, eager to promote adventurous film-makers for the first wave of *Film on Four*. *The Disappearance of Harry*, which traced textile worker Annette Crosbie's quest to find her husband in Nottingham, gave him a more generous budget to work with but also a near-incomprehensible script, which his own elliptical style proceeded to further obscure. A single television transmission and screenings at the Edinburgh and London Film Festivals did little to promote Despins' future as a director.

(Robert Murphy)

BIBLIOGRAPHY: 'Directory of UK Independent Film-Makers: Joseph Despins & William Dumaresq', *Cinema Rising* no. 1, Apr. 1972, p. 7; Ellis, John (ed.), *1951–1976 British Film Institute Production* (London: BFI, 1977).

FILMOGRAPHY: *Duffer* (co-dir. William Dumaresq, 1971); *The Moon over the Alley* (1975); *The Disappearance of Harry* (1982).

DE TOTH, André (1910–2002)

Sásvrái Farkasfawi Tóthfalusi Tóth Endre Antai Mihaly was born in Mako, Hungary, on 15 May 1910. He studied law in Budapest but chose to enter the theatre, subsequently joining the film industry as actor, writer and assistant director. He made his directorial debut as Tóth Endre with *Wedding in Toprin* (1939) and completed four more films in Hungary that year. From 1937 de Toth had worked as a production assistant and second-unit director for fellow Hungarian Alexander Korda in Britain, and when Korda went to Hollywood in 1940 de Toth went with him. From 1943 he directed modestly budgeted thrillers, melodramas and Westerns with economy and flair. Though missing an eye, he nonetheless scored his biggest hit with the 3-D *House of Wax* (1953).

The Two-Headed Spy is a taut wartime thriller, filmed in Britain and West Germany, with Jack Hawkins as a double agent among the top echelon of Nazi generals. Allegedly based on fact, it works up a fine level of tension and is characteristically grim and tough-minded. Michael Caine, who plays an uncred-

ited bit part, starred in de Toth's last film as director a decade later. *Play Dirty* proved to be one of his best: a thoroughly anti-heroic war adventure, set in a world ruled by Machiavellian ambition and cynical self-preservation, about a doomed mission to blow up a German fuel dump in North Africa. Dismissed at the time as a 'Dirty Dozen in the Desert', it delivers on action and excitement while continually undercutting audience expectations.

De Toth also worked uncredited on *Lawrence of Arabia* (David Lean, 1962), *Superman* (Richard Donner, 1978) and other films, and produced *Billion Dollar Brain* (Ken Russell, 1967) and *El Condor* (John Guillermin, 1970). In later life he enjoyed critical rediscovery, before he died of an aneurism in Burbank, California, on 27 October 2002.

(Sheldon Hall)

BIBLIOGRAPHY: Cousins, Mark and Kevin MacDonald (eds), *André de Toth: The Director* (London: Guardian, 1994); de Toth, André, *Fragments: Stories from the Inside* (London: Faber and Faber, 1994); Slide, Anthony, *De Toth on de Toth: Putting the Drama in Front of the Camera* (London: Faber and Faber, 1996).

FILMOGRAPHY (UK only): *The Two-Headed Spy* (1958); *Play Dirty* (1969).

DE VERE, Alison (1927–2001)

Alison de Vere was born on 16 September 1927 in Khanspoor, India (now Pakistan), where her father was a company sergeant-major in the Royal Tank Corps. She returned to England when she was three, and endured a number of moves from camp to camp as her father changed ranks. Eventually she studied fine art in Brighton, and at the Royal Academy in London, though she gave up her course and in 1948 married the painter Karl Weschke, a former German prisoner of war. Her experience in the late 1940s as a painter and tracer on Paul Grimault's cel-animated film *La Bergère et le ramoneur* (eventually released in 1953) inspired her to work in animation full time.

De Vere's fame rests on her personal films of the 1970s and 80s: films marked by their pursuit of the characters' interior lives, the interweaving of dream, reality and myth, and the general avoidance of dialogue. She began at the Halas and Batchelor studio in 1951, working as a background designer for technical and promotional shorts, along with advertisements for the burgeoning commercial market. *False Friends*, a ten-minute diatribe against opium addiction, made for the World Health Organisation, emerged in 1967. But frustrated by the lack of creative opportunities, de Vere had begun to express ideas in stories and published poems. Several became the springboard for her first personal project, *Two Faces* (1968), comparatively simple in technique, but typical in its interior viewpoint: the four-minute film features two heads, subjectively describing a meeting and a parting.

Like many animation professionals, de Vere joined the creative team working in London on George Dunning's *Yellow Submarine* (1968). She proved highly successful in using designer Heinz Edelmann's psychedelic artwork as an animation background, and made a cameo appearance in the 'Eleanor Rigby' sequence as one of the 'lonely people' – a woman taking a snapshot in a doorway. With her industry reputation boosted, de Vere joined the Wyatt Cattaneo studio, specialising in innovative commercial work, but was encouraged to pursue personal films in her spare time. *Café Bar*, an insightful exploration of the male/female relationship, emerged in 1975. The six-minute film, directly inspired by a Soho café, projects the thoughts of a man and woman having coffee, brilliantly mixing the everyday environment with myth, symbol and cartoon gags. De Vere also drew on authentic London settings for the tender but unsentimental *Mr Pascal* (1979), dealing with the effect of a crucifix sculpture on the life of a widowed shoemaker. Both films won Grand Prix awards at the Annecy Animation Festival. By the 1980s de Vere had moved to Cornwall to work independently from her own studio. Channel 4, newly established, gave her several half-hour commissions, beginning with an adaptation of George Eliot's novel *Silas Marner* (1984). De Vere's personal life – indeed her own dreams – then took centre stage in *The Black Dog* (1987), her most elaborate animation, widely regarded as her masterpiece. Dream, reality and primal archetypes fluctuate in a masterful stream-of-consciousness flow as the film charts a woman's journey from naivety and innocence to fulfilment. The title character, a variation on the Egyptian God Anubis, serves throughout as conscience and guide. Less ambitious projects followed, including children's series. But the mythic archetypes returned in *Psyche and Eros* (1994), a lyrical meditation on physical and material experience based on the Greek legend. Alison de Vere continued working on children's animation until her death in St Just, Cornwall, on 2 January 2001.

(Geoff Brown and Paul Wells)

BIBLIOGRAPHY: Codelli, Lorenzo, 'Alison de Vere: An Interview', in Jayne Pilling (ed.), *Women and Animation: A Compendium* (London: BFI Exhibition & Distribution Division, 1992); Law, Sandra, 'Putting Themselves in the Pictures: Images of Women in the Work of Joanna Quinn, Candy Guard and Alison de Vere', in Jayne Pilling (ed.), *A Reader in Animation Studies* (Sydney: John Libbey, 1997).

FILMOGRAPHY: *False Friends* (1967); *Two Faces* (1968); *Café Bar* (1975); *Mr Pascal* (1979); *Silas Marner* (1984); *Black Dog* (1987); *The Angel and the Soldier Boy* (1989); *Psyche and Eros* (1994).

DEVLIN, Barry (1948–)

Barry Devlin was born on 27 November 1948 in Ardboe, Co. Tyrone, and began his professional career as an advertising writer in Dublin in the early 1970s. Dissatisfied with corporate life, he formed the highly influential and innovative Irish folk/rock band Horslips, which enjoyed a considerable degree of success in Ireland and the US. When the band broke up in 1980 Devlin forged a new career in pop videos and rock documentaries. He made videos for Clannad, Hothouse Flowers and Gerry Rafferty, among others, but made his reputation with U2's 'Unforgettable Fire'.

In 1988 he wrote and directed his first film for RTÉ, *Lapsed Catholics*, a humorous look at a reformed rock band that drew heavily on his knowledge of the Irish rock scene and that also established his characteristic style of drama based on gentle humour and sentiment. Subsequently, he wrote for a number of Irish and British television series, including *The Darling Buds of May*, *Perfect Scoundrels* and *Ballykissangel*, as well as contributing a number of original scripts for television, including *Runway One* (David Drury, 1995) and *Soul Survivors* (Sandy Johnson, 1995) for the BBC. He also wrote the screenplays for the films *A Man of No Importance* (Suri Krishnamma, 1995), *Spaghetti Slow* (Valerio Sebastiano Ialongo, 1996) and *Not Afraid, Not Afraid* (Annette Carducci, 2001) and wrote and directed his second feature, *All Things Bright and Beautiful* (1994), set in a pastoral 1950s' Northern Ireland. His directing career, however, remains secondary to his writing.

(Martin McLoone)

BIBLIOGRAPHY: Clarke, Jocelyn, 'Bright Spark', *Film Ireland* no. 40, Apr./May 1994, pp. 8–9; McLoone, Martin, *Irish Film: The Emergence of a Contemporary Cinema* (London: BFI, 2000); Murrell, Rachel, 'Bright and Beautiful – It's Barry's Third Career', *Television Today*, 10 Mar. 1994, p. 23; Pettitt, Lance, *Screening Ireland* (Manchester: Manchester University Press, 2000).

FILMOGRAPHY: *All Things Bright and Beautiful* (UK/Ir, 1994).

DEXTER, John (1925–1990)

John Dexter was born in Derby on 2 August 1925. He left school at fourteen and joined the army during the Second World War. He gained some experience with army entertainment troupes and after the war worked as an actor, eventually becoming an associate director at the Royal Court Theatre in Chelsea. In the 1960s Dexter also worked at the Chichester Festival Theatre and the National Theatre, where his powerful production of *Othello*, starring Laurence Olivier, was filmed by Stuart Burge in 1965. He made his own screen debut with an adaptation of Leslie Thomas' *Virgin Soldiers*, a black comedy about British Army conscripts based in Malaya during the insurgency of the early 1950s. It was successful enough for Dexter to attempt an American film, *The Sidelong Glances of a Pigeon Kicker*, a post-hippy comedy that proved too unexcitingly derivative to attract an audience.

Dexter's final film venture, *I Want What I Want*, was a typical Raymond Stross production: a *mélange* of exploitation and social daring, with Stross' wife Anne Heywood playing a moody young man who only finds contentment when he transforms himself into a woman. Dexter treats what could have been a bad-taste farrago with unsensational seriousness; though no artistic masterpiece, the film offers fascinating insights into blinkered attitudes to sexuality at the height of the supposedly permissive society.

While the British film industry shrunk during the 1970s, Dexter found plenty of creative challenges in the theatre, directing Peter Shaffer's *Equus* in London and on Broadway, and producing operas at the Metropolitan Opera, New York. Diabetes began to restrict his career in the 1980s; he died of heart failure in London on 23 March 1990.

(Robert Murphy)

FILMOGRAPHY: *The Virgin Soldiers* (1969); *The Sidelong Glances of a Pigeon Kicker* (US: *Pigeons*, US, 1971); *I Want What I Want* (1972).

DICKINSON, Thorold (1903–1984)

Thorold Dickinson remains a paradoxical figure among Britain's major film directors. Taken overall, his nine features display a degree of visual refinement and intellectual ambition unusual in a director attached to the mainstream British film industry. Yet the projects into which he put most effort and personal commitment, like *Secret People* and *Men of Two Worlds*, proved less artistically successful than his hastier, more commercial assignments, notably *Gaslight* and *The Queen of Spades*. During the undulations of his career he assumed various key official positions – co-ordinator of the Army Kinematograph Service's film unit, Chief of Film Services at UNESCO, Professor of Film at the Slade School of Fine Art – but whether beyond or behind the film camera Dickinson remained the eternal outsider, never comfortable in an Establishment niche.

Thorold Barron Dickinson was born in Bristol on 16 November 1903, the son of the city's Archdeacon, with claimed ancestral links to Lady Godiva and the dwarf Thorold, featured in the Bayeux tapestry. He read history at Keble College, Oxford, but was expelled in his final year for neglecting study in favour of theatre and film. Like other 1920s' undergraduates he had caught the passion for film as art, and found fruitful work in the industry as an odd-jobbing assistant to George Pearson, one of the few established British silent directors with a visionary approach to the medium. He co-wrote the fanciful scenario for Pearson's *The Little People* (1926) and launched his early career as an editor on two other Pearson features, the more conventional *Love's Option* (1928) and *Auld Lang Syne* (1929). At Cricklewood and Ealing during the 1930s, he built a reputation as a skilful and imaginative cutter with clear knowledge of European and Soviet practices; his montages and second-unit effects gave a particular lift to Basil Dean's *Loyalties* (1933) and *Sing As We Go!* (1934). Dickinson's international grasp widened through his long association with the Film Society, where he supervised technical operations from 1930 until its last programme in April 1939; he also served on the Society's council.

In 1934 Dickinson completed ATP's *Java Head* after its American director, J. Walter Ruben, fell ill. His official directing debut occurred two years later, when he plunged into independent production, forming Fanfare Pictures with the screenwriter Gordon Wellesley. *The High Command* (1936) remained constricted by its novelettish story of murder, blackmail and family secrets, but the verve of Dickinson's direction still shone through. Fanfare's first blast proved its last: with work scarce in British studios, Dickinson went to Spain early in 1938, collaborating on *Spanish A.B.C.* and *Behind the Spanish Lines*, two Civil War reports for Ivor Montagu's Progressive Film Institute.

After a second-unit stint on *The Mikado* (Victor Schertzinger, 1939), he was given his own directing assignment for G and S Films. The result was *The Arsenal Stadium Mystery* (1939): circuit fodder, but given genuine freshness and distinction by Dickinson's tongue-in-cheek approach, Leslie Banks' sprightly antics as the Scotland Yard inspector and the authentic presence of Arsenal Football Club. With *Gaslight* (1940), his next job, undertaken for British National at three weeks' notice, he cemented his status as one of Britain's liveliest directors. Out of Patrick Hamilton's stage play Dickinson created a harrowing and claustrophobic film of domestic fear and trembling, with a darkly insidious Anton Walbrook, and Diana Wynyard, fragile and tortured as the wife whose sanity is under siege. The success of *Gaslight* on stage and film encouraged MGM to buy the remake rights, with a clause insisting that all existing prints of Dickinson's version be destroyed. New prints were secretly made, but unlike George Cukor's Hollywood film of 1944 Dickinson's *Gaslight* was forced to lead a shadowy existence for decades.

The continuing war brought other opportunities. Miscasting, cramped sets and a turgid script helped to sink *The Prime Minister* (1941), a biography of Benjamin Disraeli made for Warner Bros., featuring John Gielgud. But Dickinson quickly mastered the wartime information short with *Yesterday Is over Your Shoulder* (1940), a spunky call for white-collar workers to retrain, which broke through the British Censor's language barrier when Robertson Hare's character cried 'Bugger the neighbours!' The feature-length *The Next of Kin* marked a far more important milestone. Made at Ealing in 1941 on request from the War Office, the film combines the narrative drive of a realistic thriller with the special needs of an army instruction manual on the perils of careless talk (the project's starting point). Service chiefs attempted to delay the film's general release in 1942; a tribute in part to Dickinson's chillingly understated manner, thrown off only in the powerfully edited final raid, when information from spies helps the Germans inflict heavy losses on a British unit's expedition in France.

Significantly, Dickinson never joined the Ealing 'family'. For a year he worked setting up and co-ordinating the Army Kinematograph Service film unit, based at Wembley Studios, but at the end of 1942 he returned to the commercial sector, working for Two Cities on a venture to advertise the foreign goals and partnership projects of the Colonial Office. Dickinson poured much of his hopes for education and social improvement into the Technicolor feature film *Men of Two Worlds* (1946), but its overly worthy air, artificial studio settings and awkward central character (a European-trained composer returning to face African tribal superstitions) considerably weakened the film's potential.

By 1947 Dickinson was a freelance again, going where the work took him. At three days' notice he took over *The Queen of Spades* (1949) from its inexperienced director Rodney Ackland, whisking the Pushkin story into a stylistic *tour de force*, convincingly foreign in mood and setting. Mobile camerawork and disorienting compositions brought eerie life to William Kellner and Oliver Messel's baroque sets, powerfully suggesting the web of fate enveloping Anton Walbrook's St Petersburg officer, determined to steal an aged countess's recipe for winning at cards. Edith Evans made a striking screen debut as the decrepit countess. After plans fell through for a prestigious Hardy adaptation, *The Mayor of Casterbridge*, timed for the 1951 Festival of Britain celebrations, Dickinson managed to place his long-cherished *Secret People* project at Ealing. Aware of the need for a guide to help aspiring film-makers, he arranged for Lindsay Anderson to document its production in the book *Making a Film* (1952). Valentina Cortesa and Audrey Hepburn play two exiled sisters in Britain in the late 1930s, sucked into political violence against the tyrants controlling their unnamed country. Through foreign casting, atmosphere and avoidance of frills, Dickinson attempted to make *Secret People* an art film to match the productions of France and Italy; but the strain showed, and neither critics nor audiences proved receptive. Reviews were bleak, and Dickinson never made another British feature.

For a while he moved into the international sphere. He made a propaganda short for the Israeli Army, *The Red Ground*, followed by an Israeli feature in English, *Hill 24 Doesn't Answer*

(1955); it is best in urgent, realistic fight scenes, where the bland dialogue and characterisations matter least. He then worked for UNESCO (1956–60) as Chief of Film Services, supervising many projects including the episode film *Power among Men* (1958). Thereafter he gave up active film-making for teaching, establishing a pioneering film studies department in 1960 at the Slade School of Fine Art in London, where his first students were Don Levy and Raymond Durgnat; the School appointed him Britain's first Professor of Film in 1967. He retired from the post in 1971, just as structuralism, semiotics and other French imports began their invasion of film studies, a development he felt no sympathy for. But he remained a much respected figure, both as a teacher and as a director whose scattered films and curtailed career give eloquent evidence of the unequal battle in British cinema between idealism and commercial necessity, imagination and servitude. Thorold Dickinson died in Oxford on 14 April 1984.

(Geoff Brown)

BIBLIOGRAPHY: Anderson, Lindsay, *Making a Film: The Story of 'Secret People'* (London: George Allen & Unwin, 1952); Badder, David and Bob Baker, 'Thorold Dickinson', *Film Dope* no. 11, Jan. 1977, pp. 1–21, 38–9; Dickinson, Thorold, *A Discovery of Cinema* (Oxford: Oxford University Press, 1971); Richards, Jeffrey, *Thorold Dickinson and the British Cinema* (Lanham, MD and London: Scarecrow Press, 1997) (first published as *Thorold Dickinson: The Man and His Films*; London: Croom Helm, 1986); Scorsese, Martin and Philip Horne, '"Moving at the Speed of Emotion": Martin Scorsese on Thorold Dickinson', *Sight and Sound*, Nov. 2003, pp. 24–6.

FILMOGRAPHY: *Java Head* (uncredited, J. Walter Ruben, 1934); *The High Command* (1936); *Spanish A.B.C.* (doc. short, co-dir. Sidney Cole); *Behind the Spanish Lines* (doc. short, co-dir. Sidney Cole) (1938); *The Mikado* (2nd unit dir., Victor Schertzinger); *The Arsenal Stadium Mystery* (1939); *Gaslight* (US: *Angel Street*); *Westward Ho! – 1940* (doc. short); *Yesterday Is over Your Shoulder* (doc. short) (1940); *The Prime Minister* (1941); *The Next of Kin* (1942); *Men of Two Worlds* (US: *Kisenga: Man of Africa*, 1946); *The Queen of Spades* (1949); *Secret People* (1952); *Hakarka ha a dom/The Red Ground* (doc. short, Isr, 1953); *Hill 24 Doesn't Answer* (Isr, 1955).

DICKSON, Paul (1920–)

Paul Dickson was born in Cardiff on 18 January 1920, and educated at Ellesmere College, Shropshire. After army service during the Second World War, he entered the film industry as a maker of documentaries and established his reputation with *The Undefeated* (1950), which he co-wrote with Ted Willis. A sympathetic account of a glider pilot who overcomes the loss of his legs and the power of speech during the war to become a useful member of the community, it won a British Academy Award for Best Documentary. Dickson followed it with *David*, made for the Festival of Britain, recalling the life story of a Welsh school caretaker. It was warmly reviewed by Gavin Lambert in *Sight and Sound* as 'one of the few authentic regional films made here'. Lambert and his colleagues on the short-lived but influential journal *Sequence* had already noted Dickson as a fresh and original talent, and the way in which his films celebrate ordinary lives anticipates the work of the Free Cinema directors of the late 1950s.

Turning to fiction, Dickson was caught up with the budget-conscious Danziger brothers. His features include the moderately entertaining three-part thriller *Gilbert Harding Speaking of Murder* (1953); and *Star of My Night* (1954), a lugubrious romantic melodrama about a sculptor (Griffith Jones) going blind and the selfless ballerina who loves him enough to penetrate his cynical disguise. Less preposterous were the three half-hour films he made for Anglo-Amalgamated's *Scotland Yard* series under the name 'Paul Gherzo' – *Fatal Journey*, *The Mysterious Bullet* and *The Stateless Man* – all of them effectively atmospheric little thrillers. He also directed B-films – most notably *The Count of Twelve* (1955) – as 'Paul Gerrard' for the Danziger brothers. In the 1960s Dickson turned to television, a medium in which he continued to work until the early 1970s.

(Brian McFarlane)

BIBLIOGRAPHY: 'British Feature Directors: An Index to Their Work', *Sight and Sound*, Autumn 1958, p. 293; Lambert, Gavin, '*David*', *Sight and Sound*, June 1951, pp. 45, 47.

FILMOGRAPHY: *Country Homes* (doc.); *Shipshape* (doc.) (1947); *Personal Hygiene* (doc., 1948); *The Craftsman* (doc., 1949); *Chick's Day* (doc.); *The Undefeated* (doc.) (1950); *David* (doc., 1951); *A Story of Achievement* (doc., 1952); *Gilbert Harding Speaking of Murder*; *The Javanese Dagger*; *The Sable Scarf* (1953); *Star of My Night*; *A Tale of Three Women*; *Fatal Journey* (short, as Paul Gherzo) (1954); *The Mysterious Bullet* (short, as Paul Gherzo); *The Stateless Man* (short, as Paul Gherzo); *The Count of Twelve* (as Paul Gerrard); *The Man Who Stayed Alive* (1955); *Satellite in the Sky* (1956); *Look This Way* (short); *A Dill Pickle* (short); *The Depraved*; *The Film That Never Was* (1957); *An Enquiry into General Practice* (doc., 1959); *Triple Blackmail* (as Paul Gerrard, 1963).

DICKSON, W. K. L. (1860–1935)

William Kennedy Laurie Dickson was a seminal figure in the development of cinema, both as an inventor and as the first person to direct fiction and actuality films. He was born on 3 August 1860 in Minihic-sur-Rance, France, to English and Scottish parents, and lived in Germany and Britain before moving to the United States in 1879. From 1883 he was associated with Thomas Edison, heading a research team, which by October 1892 had developed the world's first practicable motion picture camera. In a studio of his own design, Dickson made many short films of variety performers, athletes and comedy subjects for use in the Kinetoscope, an electrically powered peepshow device introduced in 1894. Following a dispute, Dickson left Edison in 1895, concentrating on the development of the Mutograph, a large-gauge movie camera, and on the Mutoscope viewer and Biograph projector. Although Dickson was not part of the senior management of the American Mutoscope

Company, he played a major role in its success by supplying a succession of innovative film subjects during 1896 and 1897. Even at this early date, he preferred to direct his films, leaving the operation of the camera to his assistant 'Billy' Bitzer, later to achieve fame with D. W. Griffith. In 1897 Dickson returned to England to help establish the Mutoscope and Biograph Syndicate, later British Biograph. For the next five years he and his cameraman toured Britain and Europe, filming major news events and choreographing 'animated portraits' of statesmen, religious leaders and royalty.

A dandy in appearance, Dickson was also a fastidious film-maker. As the son of an artist and himself an accomplished photographer, he took great care in framing his subjects, often employing a distinctive scenic layering effect, which imbued his work with a feeling of depth and volume. To this skill in pictorial composition, Dickson added a remarkable efficiency in imposing narrative movement upon films, which seldom reached one minute in length. A curiosity of Dickson's directorial style was his frequent appearance, supervising operations, before the camera. Although he directed many short comedies and performances by actors of the status of Joseph Jefferson and Sir Herbert Beerbohm Tree, his most striking achievements were in filming actuality subjects. The distinction between fiction and actuality was often blurred, however, for he frequently stage-managed reality by initiating such exciting events as lifeboat rescues and cavalry charges. Dickson's greatest challenge as a film-maker occurred in 1899–1900, when he endured harsh and dangerous conditions covering hostilities in the Anglo-Boer War. By 1903 he had set up his own experimental laboratory, working on a diversity of largely uncommercial inventions. A flamboyant character, Dickson actively promoted himself in a number of periodical articles and in his book *The Biograph in Battle* (1901). With his sister Antonia, he was also author of the first book on the cinema, *History of the Kinetograph, Kinetoscope and Kineto-Phonograph* (1895). He died in Twickenham, Middlesex, on 28 September 1935.

(Barry Anthony)

BIBLIOGRAPHY: Spehr, Paul C., 'Throwing Pictures on a Screen: The Work of W. K. L. Dickson, Film Maker', *Griffithiana* vols 66/70, 1999/2000, pp. 10–65.

SELECTED FILMOGRAPHY: *Blacksmithing Scene* (1893); *Sandow*; *The Corbett–Courtney Fight*; *Fire Rescue Scene* (1894); *Rip Van Winkle*; *A Stable on Fire* (1896); *A Terrible Spill – Aldershot*; *Panoramic View of Conway on the L. & N. W. Railway*; *Pope Leo XIII* (1898); *Launch of the 'Oceanic'*; *A Scene – 'King John', Now Playing at Her Majesty's Theatre*; *Battle of Colenso* (1899).

DIZDAR, Jasmin (1961–)

Jasmin Dizdar was born in Zenica, Bosnia, on 8 June 1961. He attended the FAMU film school in Prague and his graduation films, *After Silence* (1987), about a Czech man who acquires a hearing aid after being deaf since the 1960s, and *Our Sweet Homeland* (1988), won awards at student film festivals. He moved to London in the late 1980s, where he wrote a book on the Czech director Milos Forman (*Audition for a Director*, 1990) and had a screenplay, *Horseman*, commissioned by the BBC. His first feature film was *Beautiful People*, an ambitious attempt to mesh together narratives drawn from immigrant Serb, Croat and native London lives set against the background of the 1994 World Cup. A number of disparate characters are brought together in a London hospital; while in another strand an English soccer hooligan finds redemption after he is accidentally parachuted into the Bosnian conflict. *Beautiful People* is chaotic and intensely emotional, mixing realism and surrealism; it won the 'Un Certain Regard' Prize at the 1999 Cannes Film Festival, though its insistence that all people are indeed beautiful leaves Dizdar's film prey to accusations of naivety.

(Ruth Barton)

BIBLIOGRAPHY: Dizdar, Jasmin, 'A Film-Maker's Diary', *Sight and Sound*, July 1999, p. 23; Verhaagen, Annelotte, 'Jasmin Dizdar: Humor is de penicilline van de wereld', *Skrien*, Apr. 2000, pp. 32–3.

FILMOGRAPHY (UK only): *Beautiful People* (1999).

DMYTRYK, Edward (1908–1999)

Edward Dmytryk was born in Grand Forks, British Columbia, on 4 September 1908. He grew up in California and at fourteen began work at Paramount Studios. He had become an editor by 1930 and directed his first film *The Hawk* in 1935. In 1942 he joined RKO Radio, where notable successes included *Murder My Sweet/Farewell My Lovely* (1944) and *Crossfire* (1947); one of his assignments, *So Well Remembered*, was a collaboration with Rank's Alliance Productions, made at Denham in 1946. Dmytryk's career subsequently became overshadowed by his dealings with the House Committee on Un-American Activities, which summoned him in September 1947 to answer questions about Communist infiltration in Hollywood. After pleading the Fifth Amendment, he was promptly fired by RKO. Pending appeals, he spent three years in England where he made *Obsession* and *Give Us This Day*. On his return to the USA in 1951, he was jailed for six months, but in order to salvage his career he rescinded his original testimony before the second HUAC hearing. Though his career revived through a four-picture deal with Stanley Kramer and films like *The Young Lions* (1958), Dmytryk was never completely forgiven for his volte-face by his former left-wing friends.

So Well Remembered starred John Mills as a mill-town mayor who recalls how he abandoned a parliamentary seat to devote himself to improving social conditions. Dmytryk found the experience exasperating due to what he felt was the intransigence of industry unions, but the film itself displays a compassion nicely in tune with post-war Britain. *Obsession*, a psychological thriller made in 1949, is a far darker subject. It centres on the painstaking efforts by a psychiatrist, played by Robert Newton, to murder his wife's lover by imprisoning him in a bombed-out

building's basement and disposing of the body in a bath that he gradually fills with acid. Dmytryk achieves an anxious intensity in the dynamics between Newton and his hapless prisoner in this highly original, very English thriller. *Give Us This Day* was Dmytryk's favourite film. Set in Brooklyn during the Depression, it is a grim tale of poverty and tragedy that befalls an Italian immigrant – a curious subject for a British studio. The film was little seen in the USA because of the HUAC debacle, but received tremendous reviews for its realist style and deeply moving story.

In 1954 Dmytryk returned to Britain to direct an adaptation of Graham Greene's *The End of the Affair*, notable for Deborah Kerr's passionate and sincere performance as the tragic Sarah and its accomplished recreation of wartime London. Two further British ventures followed. The storyline of *Shalako*, a British Western shot in Spain, has potential: a group of European aristocrats go hunting in Apache country and find that their wealth and privileges count for nothing in this unfamiliar and dangerous world. But the film only skims the plot's surface, and Dmytryk – perhaps hampered by a starry cast that includes Sean Connery and Bridget Bardot – never manages to bring the story to life. *The 'Human' Factor*, a sloppily directed revenge thriller with George Kennedy as an American NATO expert in Italy out to avenge his murdered family, is interesting only as a reminder that there was a time when 'terrorists' were vaguely anonymous and easily disposed of.

From 1976 until the late 1990s, Edward Dmytryk taught film at the University of Texas in Austin and at the University of Southern California. He also wrote a number of books on film-making. He died in Encino, California, on 1 July 1999.

(Margaret Butler)

BIBLIOGRAPHY: Dmytryk, Edward, *It's a Hell of a Life but Not a Bad Living* (New York: Times Books, 1978); Friedman, Lester D., 'A Very Narrow Path: The Politics of Edward Dmytryk', *Film/Literature Quarterly* vol. 12 no. 4, 1984, pp. 214–24; Neilsen, Ray, 'Edward Dmytryk and *Crossfire*', *Classic Images* no. 89, Nov. 1982, pp. 30–1; 'The Films of Edward Dmytryk', *Films Illustrated*, Dec. 1971, pp. 14–18.

FILMOGRAPHY (UK only): *So Well Remembered* (1947); *Obsession* (US: *The Hidden Room*); *Give Us This Day* (US: *Salt to the Devil*) (1949); *The End of the Affair* (1954); *Shalako* (1968); *The 'Human' Factor* (1975).

DONALD, Simon

A promising Scottish playwright misguidedly allowed to direct the film version of his successful stage play *The Life of Stuff*, set in a Glasgow dance hall. His scripts for *My Life So Far* (Hugh Hudson, 1999) and *Beautiful Creatures* (Bill Eagles, 2000) are less stage-bound but irritatingly erratic.

(Robert Murphy)

FILMOGRAPHY: *The Life of Stuff* (1997).

DONAT, Robert (1905–1958)

Robert Donat was born in Withington, Manchester, on 18 March 1905, the son of a Polish clerk. Since childhood he was burdened by severe asthma, as well as by a bad stammer; the latter, however, led to his taking elocution lessons, helping him develop a remarkable speaking voice. Donat went on to forge a brilliant acting career on stage and screen, becoming one of the most prominent stars of pre-war British cinema.

Making his theatre debut at the age of sixteen, Donat spent the next decade working his way up to the West End, where he was noticed and offered a film contract by Alexander Korda. Cast as Catherine Howard's lover, Thomas Culpepper, in *The Private Life of Henry VIII* (Alexander Korda, 1933), he achieved international fame, and subsequently starred in hugely successful films including *The 39 Steps* (Alfred Hitchcock, 1935) and *Goodbye, Mr Chips* (Sam Wood, 1939), which earned him an Academy Award.

Though courted by Hollywood, Donat had little interest in stardom, rarely appearing in films after the war. In 1950 he directed, produced and starred in *The Cure for Love*, a romantic comedy set in Lancashire: Donat played Jack, a war hero, who avoids marrying his fiancée because he is in love with another woman. The film received only lukewarm reviews. Robert Donat's health continued to deteriorate through a worsening of his asthmatic condition, and he died on 9 June 1958, in Los Angeles, before the release of the last film he appeared in, *The Inn of the Sixth Happiness* (Mark Robson, 1958).

(Elisabetta Girelli)

BIBLIOGRAPHY: Barrow, Kenneth, *Mr Chips: The Life of Robert Donat* (London: Methuen, 1985); Trewin, J. C., *Robert Donat: A Biography* (London: Heinemann, 1968).
FILMOGRAPHY: *The Cure for Love* (1950).

DONEN, Stanley (1924–)

Stanley Donen was born on 13 April 1924 in Columbia, South Carolina. As a boy he sang and danced in local theatre, and aged sixteen he joined the Broadway chorus of *Pal Joey*. Its star, Gene Kelly, employed Donen as his assistant choreographer on other shows and on a number of films before inviting him to co-direct *On the Town* (1949). He made his solo directorial debut with *Love Is Better Than Ever* (1950; rel. 1952), but *Royal Wedding* (UK: *Wedding Bells*, 1951) was released first. A lesser Fred Astaire vehicle set in London at the time of Princess Elizabeth's marriage, it was all too obviously filmed entirely at MGM's Culver City studio save for a few stock shots bought in from Gaumont-British. After eleven more films, including two further musical collaborations with Kelly, *Singin' in the Rain* (1952) and *It's Always Fair Weather* (1955), Donen left both the genre and Hollywood behind.

Now based in London, he made two films with Cary Grant – *Indiscreet* and *The Grass Is Greener* – for their joint company, Grandon, and two with Yul Brynner – *Once More, with Feeling!* and *Surprise Package* – for his own Stanley Donen Productions. *Indiscreet* is Donen's finest non-musical, a delightful, mildly risqué romantic comedy with Grant and Ingrid Bergman, set amid a theatrical English high society no more plausible than *Royal Wedding*'s but a good deal more stylish. A final picture with Grant, *Charade* (1963), co-starred Audrey Hepburn in an elegantly empty Hitchcockian concoction that skilfully juggles thrills, romance and laughter. This was Donen's biggest box-office hit, and he followed it with *Arabesque*, a strained spy caper apparently more influenced by Sidney J. Furie than by Hitchcock. Like Donen's remaining films of the decade, it is afflicted by all the most distracting 1960s' tics: distorted angles, obtrusive zooms, hazy telephoto images and a marked preference for shooting through glass. *Two for the Road*, the serio-comic story of a marital crisis unfolded in multiple flashbacks during a drive across southern France, won praise for Frederic Raphael's tart, glib screenplay, but it too is more New Look than New Wave.

Bedazzled is a broad but very funny Faust burlesque, written by and starring Peter Cook and Dudley Moore. Thereafter, however, the quality of Donen's work suffered a complete collapse. *Staircase* (1969), set in London's East End but filmed in Paris for tax purposes, is an excruciatingly overwritten theatre piece with Richard Burton and Rex Harrison grotesquely miscast as a bitchy gay couple. After that career nadir Donen took five years to set up *The Little Prince*, a decidedly unmagical musical adaptation of Antoine de Saint-Exupéry's classic fantasy, saddled with an inferior Lerner and Loewe score and a child actor unable to act.

Donen then returned to Los Angeles, though he subsequently took over direction of the muddled British-based science-fiction thriller *Saturn 3* from production designer John Barry when the latter fell ill. Of his later work only the nostalgic double-bill pastiche *Movie Movie* (1978) recaptures any of the director's old pizzazz. Donen's last theatrical film to date is the vulgar sex-comedy *Blame It on Rio* (1984), though he has since directed a misguidedly opened-out, over-literal adaptation of A. R. Gurney's stage two-hander *Love Letters* (1999) for American television.

(Sheldon Hall)

BIBLIOGRAPHY: Casper, Joseph Andrew, *Stanley Donen* (Metuchen, NJ: Scarecrow Press, 1995); Harvey, Stephen, 'Stanley Donen', *Film Comment*, July/Aug. 1973, pp. 4–9; Hillier, Jim, 'Interview with Stanley Donen', *Movie* no. 24, Spring 1977, pp. 26–35; Silverman, Stephen M., *Dancing on the Ceiling: Stanley Donen and His Movies* (New York: Alfred A. Knopf, 1996).
FILMOGRAPHY (UK only): *Indiscreet* (1958); *Once More, with Feeling!*; *Surprise Package*; *The Grass Is Greener* (1960); *Arabesque* (1966); *Two for the Road*; *Bedazzled* (1967); *The Little Prince* (1974); *Saturn 3* (1980).

DONNER, Clive (1926–)

Clive Donner shone brightly as one of the most inventive and stylish directors of the 1960s. Although he faded from view as the decade ended, he continued to work creatively, though mainly for television, where he subsumed personal interests to direct adaptations and remakes. He was born in West Hampstead, London, on 21 January 1926. His father was a concert violinist and his mother ran a dress shop. After attending Kilburn Grammar School he worked as an office clerk until an encounter with Michael Powell inspired him to find employment in the cutting rooms at Denham Studios. He worked on *The Way Ahead* (Carol Reed, 1944) and *On Approval* (Clive Brook, 1944), but was then conscripted into the army. He served from 1944 to 1947, ending in the Education Corps where he was responsible for training new recruits. Working with young people would be a recurring theme in his later career.

After leaving the army Donner went to Pinewood as first assistant editor and continued his apprenticeship under David Lean. From 1951 he began making a name for himself as an editor on films such as *Scrooge* (Brian Desmond Hurst, 1951), *The Card* (Ronald Neame, 1952) and *Genevieve* (Henry Cornelius, 1953). By 1956 he had become a Rank contract director. His first film, *The Secret Place*, was a crime thriller about a policeman's son who thwarts a pair of small-time East End crooks. Donner drew a convincing performance from Michael Brooke as the boy, and took pains to choose appropriate East End locations, especially for the concluding chase over the scaffolding of a vast building site. Donner's next film, *Heart of a Child*, was a more routine affair; once again a child is the central character, this time with an abusive father (Donald Pleasence) who threatens to kill his beloved St Bernard dog.

Donner then moved into television, directing documentaries and episodes of the series *Danger Man* (1960) and *Sir Francis Drake* (1962). By 1961 he was making television commercials for J. Walter Thompson and was voted Best TV Commercials Director of that year. He returned to the film industry to direct two tightly effective films in the Merton Park Edgar Wallace B-film series – *Marriage of Convenience* and *The Sinister Man*. His next film, *Some People*, designed to promote the Duke of Edinburgh's award scheme, was a surprise box office hit. Donner makes good use of the Bristol locations and the film is unpatronisingly sympathetic to the potential teenage delinquents (Ray Brooks and David Hemmings) who are persuaded to join the scheme. Despite this success Donner had to rely on private finance (from Elizabeth Taylor, Richard Burton, Noël Coward and Peter Sellers among others) for his next venture, an adaptation of Harold Pinter's play *The Caretaker*, for which Alan Bates and Donald Pleasence repeated their stage roles. Donner's imaginative direction used close-ups and two-shots to unsettling and menacing effect on the claustrophobic set, photographed by Nicolas Roeg in atmospheric black and white. The film won the Silver Bear Award at the Berlin Film Festival.

Nothing but the Best, a black comedy of greed and heartlessness written by Frederic Raphael, again starred Alan Bates, as an opportunistic young man who will stop at nothing, even murder, to achieve success. The film ran counter to the hippy ethos of the 1960s but proved eerily prescient of the Thatcher years and remains an effectively humorous critique of British social values. Donner established his international reputation with the stylish farce *What's New, Pussycat?*, written by Woody Allen and starring Peter O'Toole as a serial womaniser and Peter Sellers as the wacky psychoanalyst who attempts to cure him. Seen by Hollywood as a 'with-it' director, Donner was asked to film the Broadway comedy *Luv*, starring Jack Lemmon; but the play transferred poorly to film and Donner returned to England to make the more congenial comedy *Here We Go Round the Mulberry Bush*. It is an annoyingly gauche film with an irritatingly smug hero (Barry Evans), but Donner has a fine eye for detail, and his representation of young people coming of age in the new town of Stevenage in the post-permissive 1960s – a huge contrast to the Bristol teenagers of *Some People* only five years earlier – is illuminating.

The success of *Here We Go Round the Mulberry Bush* allowed Donner the opportunity to make the ambitiously unorthodox epic *Alfred the Great*. It was a surprising change of pace and genre for Donner and proved a step too far for critics and audiences. There is an uneasy mix between ninth-century concerns over blood lust and carnal desire with late 1960s' anxieties around masculinity and the morality of war, and in the struggle for authenticity narrative momentum wavers. David Hemmings plays King Alfred as modishly neurotic and Michael York is too effete as the savage Dane Guthrum, but Donner deserves credit for attempting to strip the historical epic of its stuffiness and make the distant past relevant and exciting.

Donner returned to making television commercials, not directing another feature until the Dracula spoof *Vampira* in 1974. He proved that his talent was undiminished with the television film *Rogue Male* (1976), the first in a BBC trilogy based on famous adventure stories. John Buchan's *The Three Hostages* (1977) and Dornford Yates' *She Fell among Thieves* (1978) followed. For the next decade Donner alternated between Britain and Hollywood, directing television remakes of *The Thief of Baghdad* (1978), *The Scarlet Pimpernel* (1982), *Oliver Twist* (1982) and *A Christmas Carol* (1984) and other American television films, including *Merlin and the Sword* (1982), *To Catch a King* (1984), *Agatha Christie's Dead Man's Folly* (1986) and *Babes in Toyland*. *The Thief of Baghdad* and *A Christmas Carol* (with its vivid performance by George C. Scott as Scrooge) were both given limited theatrical distribution.

At the height of his fame, in the 1960s, Donner was spoken of as Britain's answer to Vincente Minnelli. In later years this elegant film-maker never enjoyed the big-screen success that might have enabled him to take on more personal projects, though the lively approach to historical characters in *Alfred the Great* found at least a distant echo in *Stealing Heaven*, his last cinema film, a glossy drama about the doomed twelfth-century lovers Abelard and Héloïse.

Clive Donner has deposited his papers at the BFI.

(Janet Moat)

BIBLIOGRAPHY: Baker, Bob, 'Clive Donner', *Film Dope* no. 12, June 1977, pp. 36–7; Cameron, Ian and Mark Shivas, '*What's New, Pussycat?* Directed by Clive Donner', *Movie* no. 14, Autumn 1965, pp. 12–16; Cavander, Kenneth, 'Harold Pinter and Clive Donner', in Joseph F. McCrindle (ed.), *Behind the Scenes: Theatre and Film Interviews from the Transatlantic Review* (London: Pitman Publishing, 1971); Gow, Gordon, 'The Urge of Some People', *Films and Filming*, July 1969, pp. 4–11.

FILMOGRAPHY: *The Secret Place* (1957); *Heart of a Child* (1958); *Marriage of Convenience* (1960); *The Sinister Man* (1961); *Some People* (1962); *The Caretaker* (1963); *Nothing but the Best* (1964); *What's New, Pussycat?* (US/Fr, 1965); *Luv* (US); *Here We Go Round the Mulberry Bush* (1967); *Alfred the Great* (1969); *Fly Me to the Bank* (doc. short, 1973); *Vampira* (US: *Old Dracula*, 1974); *Johnny's Diary* (doc. short, 1975); *Spectre* (US, 1977); *The Thief of Baghdad* (1978); *The Nude Bomb* (US); *Charlie Chan and the Curse of the Dragon Queen* (US) (1980); *Oliver Twist* (1982); *A Christmas Carol* (1984); *Stealing Heaven* (UK/Yug, 1988).

DONNER, Richard (1930–)

Richard Donald Schwartzberg, born on 24 April 1930 in New York City, started out as a bit-part actor before assisting Martin Ritt on television productions. He began directing commercials, documentaries and industrial films and, after moving to California in 1958, graduated to television drama with episodes for *Wanted: Dead or Alive*, *The Rifleman*, *The Twilight Zone* and many others. His first big-screen feature, *X-15* (1961), had no follow-up until 1968's *Salt & Pepper*, a dire vehicle for two members of the 'Rat Pack', Sammy Davis Jr and Peter Lawford, shot in the remnants of Swinging London (mostly recreated at Shepperton Studios). Donner's next picture was *Twinky*, a crude *Lolita*-ish comedy for the Rank Organisation, with Charles Bronson as a middle-aged writer and Susan George as his schoolgirl bride. Set in London and New York, the film was beset with nudge-nudge crosscutting; its truncated US release version was pointlessly retitled *Lola* by American International.

After that Donner went back to television, directing the pilot episode of *Kojak* and a half-dozen made-for-television features, before making his breakthrough movie, *The Omen*. A showmanlike supernatural thriller made on a modest budget, it was enhanced by the presence of Gregory Peck and Lee Remick and the production skills of a largely British crew. *The Omen* achieved notoriety for its spectacular set-piece death scenes (superbly edited by the director's regular collaborator, Stuart Baird), and its enormous box-office popularity led to three sequels. So too did Donner's next and biggest assignment: *Superman*, produced in Britain by Alexander and Ilya Salkind on a budget of $55 million. Donner took over the project from Guy Hamilton, creating in the process the first superhero blockbuster. The film's success derives in large part from the director's determination to take the comic-book mythology seriously, and the air of gravitas he brought to it contrasts markedly with the broadly comic approach of his replacement on *Superman II* and *Superman III* (1983), Richard Lester. (Donner had shot some material for the first sequel concurrently with the original film, and much of his footage survives in *Superman II*.)

After more action-adventures, comedies and four *Lethal Weapon* escapades, Donner made a further Anglo-American co-production, *Timeline*. An ill-conceived and poorly executed time-travel adventure, with a cast including Anna Friel and Billy Connolly, came nowhere near recouping its $80 million budget, but Donner bounced back with *16 Blocks* (US, 2006), a modestly enjoyable New York cop story starring Bruce Willis and hip-hopper Mos Def.

(Sheldon Hall)

BIBLIOGRAPHY: Castell, David, 'Richard Donner & *The Omen*', *Films Illustrated* no. 63, Nov. 1976, pp. 102–3; Donner, Richard, 'Dialogue on Film', *American Film*, May 1981, pp. 57–63; <www.supermancinema.net/superman2>; Samuelson, David, 'Directing the filming of an American Superhero', *American Cinematographer* vol. 60 no. 1, Jan. 1979, pp. 36–9, 68–9, 96–9.

FILMOGRAPHY (UK only): *Salt & Pepper* (1968); *Twinky* (US: *Lola*, 1970); *The Omen* (1976); *Superman* (1978); *Superman II* (co-dir., uncredited, Richard Lester, 1980); *Timeline* (US/UK, 2003).

DONOVAN, Martin (1952–)

The mystery of Martin Donovan begins with his name. He was born Carlos Enrique Varela y Peralta-Ramos on 21 January 1952, in Buenos Aires. Abandoning his middle-class upbringing at the age of fourteen, he found his way to Italy, where he worked as an actor and personal assistant to Luchino Visconti, whose opulent visuals became a strong influence; his pseudonym pays homage to friends who helped him survive in tough times. In 1975 he made an experimental film, *Souls and Shadows*. Eight years later, after several failed attempts, Donovan managed his first feature, *State of Wonder*, a naive, fey fable about peace, war and human understanding, prettily shot in rural Ireland. At the 1984 Berlin Film Festival, audiences emerged more perplexed than entertained, and no commercial release followed. Donovan's international reputation was established instead by *Apartment Zero* (1988), his only other British-based feature, shot in his native Argentina. Emotional, sexual and political repression is the theme, played out between a priggish film buff (Colin Firth) and the handsome, mysterious man who becomes his lodger (Hart Bochner). Lethargic pacing lessened the material's resonance, though the film marked Donovan as an interesting talent in development.

The rest of Donovan's disappointing career has unfolded in America. His most visible credit has been his script work on *Death Becomes Her* (Robert Zemeckis, 1992). As a director, he has handled chiefly television dramas and video fodder, veering toward horror and the supernatural. The werewolf diversion *Mad about the Moon* (1992) at least renewed Donovan's credentials for crafting atmospheric oddities; but the psychological drama *Somebody Is Waiting* (1996), a more personal project about a boy's relationship with his father, never surmounted the hurdle of his own shaky script. The Donovan mystery remains.

(Geoff Brown)

BIBLIOGRAPHY: Vaines, Colin, 'Donovan Debuts with "Wonder"', *Screen International*, 28 Jan. 1984, p. 11.
FILMOGRAPHY (UK only): *State of Wonder* (1983); *Apartment Zero* (1988).

DONOVAN, Terence (1936–1996)

Terence Daniel Donovan was born in Ealing, west London, on 14 September 1936. He worked as assistant to the fashion photographer John French before becoming a highly successful fashion photographer himself in the 1960s. He founded his own company to make film and television commercials, and in 1973 directed *Yellow Dog*, financed mainly from his own resources after Hemdale withdrew their support. With a script by respected Japanese screenwriter Shinobu Hashimoto – the writer of Kurosawa's *Rashômon* (1950) and *The Seven Samurai* (1954) – and a Japanese actor (Jiro Tamiya) in the main role, this eccentric espionage thriller was always going to have problems reaching the mainstream audience. Its potential as a popular cult film – with an inscrutable Japanese secret agent up against even more inscrutable British civil servants – was scuppered by Donovan's inability to build interesting sequences into a coherent whole.

Donovan returned to his successful career as a photographer. He made a promotional film for the Conservative Party during the 1979 General Election campaign but no more feature films followed. He committed suicide in Ealing on 22 November 1996.

(Robert Murphy)

BIBLIOGRAPHY: Castell, David, 'The Cool Nerve of Terence Donovan', *Films Illustrated*, Nov. 1973, p. 176; Watkin, David, 'Obituary: Terence Donovan', and Kevin Kavanagh, biographical sketch reprinted from *GBCT News*, Mar. 1979, *Eyepiece*, Feb./Mar. 1997, p. 29.
FILMOGRAPHY: *Yellow Dog* (1973).

DOUGLAS, Bill (1937–1991)

Bill Douglas' reputation as a film director rests largely on three films he made in the 1970s, the total running length of which is only just over three hours. *My Childhood*, *My Ain Folk* and *My Way Home* provide a painfully intense picture of a harsh upbringing marked by poverty, isolation and the complex family background of a boy who only gradually discovers that his father is the man who lives down the road and that his mother is in an asylum. All three films were closely modelled on the director's own experiences and memories. They were largely filmed in Newcraighall, the mining village on the outskirts of Edinburgh where Douglas was born on 17 April 1937, and where he spent his childhood.

Fiercely unsentimental, often bleak, with sparse use of dialogue and camera movement, the films also include moments of exhilaration. One such moment occurs at the beginning of *My Ain Folk*, when a visit to the cinema allows a brief splash of Technicolor, differing sharply from the otherwise dominant grainy black and white. Here also Douglas was drawing upon his own childhood memories. He later described the cinema as 'my real home', writing (in 'Palace of Dreams') of the magical contrast it offered to the outside world where 'whether in the village or the city, whether I was seven or seventeen, it always seemed to be raining or grey'.

In 1955, while doing his National Service in Egypt, Douglas met a fellow film enthusiast, Peter Jewell, who was to remain a friend and key support for the rest of his life. After a period of work as an actor for Joan Littlewood's Theatre Workshop and as one of the cast of Granada Television's *Younger Generation* series (1961), Douglas enrolled at the London Film School in 1969. The short films he made as a student included *Come Dancing*, which was screened at the National Film Theatre in 1970.

His script for what would eventually become *My Childhood* was rejected by Films of Scotland on the grounds that it failed to project Scotland as a forward-looking nation, but the project was taken up by Mamoun Hassan, recently appointed Head of Production at the BFI Production Board. *My Childhood* was shot on 16mm, with a cast of non-professionals and a budget of £3,500. Set at the end of the Second World War, it takes the story of Jamie (Stephen Archibald, who was to play the character in all three films) up to the death of his maternal grandmother. While firmly based in the locality, it was not a film that fitted neatly into a Scottish or British tradition of film-making. Key inspirations were Soviet montage, silent cinema and the European art film. On its release in 1972 it was greeted with some local dismay, but went on to gather high critical praise and a series of awards at festivals from Venice to Tehran. The following year the story was continued in *My Ain Folk*, after which there was a longer gap before the appearance of *My Way Home*, which took Jamie from a welfare institution in Edinburgh to National Service in Egypt.

The second and third films in the trilogy were slightly longer than the forty-eight-minute *My Childhood*, and made with larger, though still very small budgets (little more than £12,000 and £33,000 respectively). All three films were made in trying circumstances. By all accounts (including his own) Douglas' perfectionism meant he could be a difficult person to work with and his relationship with the BFI grew increasingly fraught. Despite the critical success gained by the films, by the 1980s he found himself out of step with the turn towards formal experimentation that the BFI Production Board was taking. Difficulties in raising finance for a further project led him to teaching, first at the National Film and Television School, then at Strathclyde University.

Eventually he managed to find backing from Skreba Films, the National Film Finance Corporation, Channel 4 and Curzon Film Distributors for a film about the Dorset farm labourers who in 1834 were deported for forming a trade union. This marked a break from his previous work in several respects. Shot in colour, in both England and Australia, with a cast that included established actors such as Robert Stephens and Vanessa Redgrave, the three-hour film was a move away from the intimate, autobiographical concerns of the Trilogy, and a shift in its concern with collective action rather than individual isolation. Going under the full title of *Comrades: A Lanternist's Account of the Tolpuddle Martyrs and What Became of Them*, the film allowed Douglas to use his fascination with early optical entertainments to highlight the role of images and illusion in the telling of history. Eight years after the project had been initiated, *Comrades* was eventually released in 1987, receiving generally sympathetic reviews, but only limited distribution.

Douglas continued to work on other projects, including a film based on the life of cinema pioneer Eadweard Muybridge and a version of James Hogg's *Confessions of a Justified Sinner*, but *Comrades* was to be his final film. He died of cancer on 18 June 1991, aged fifty-four. He left behind his collection of cinematic and pre-cinematic artefacts (now held at the Bill Douglas Centre for the History of Cinema and Popular Culture at Exeter University) and a body of work that was hardly extensive, but contains moments as intense and lyrical as any in British film history.

(Guy Barefoot)

BIBLIOGRAPHY: Caughie, John, 'The Way Home', *Sight and Sound*, Nov. 1991, pp. 26–7; Dick, Eddie, Andrew Noble and Duncan Petrie (eds), *Bill Douglas: A Lanternist's Account* (London: BFI, 1993); Douglas, Bill, 'Palace of Dreams: The Making of a Film-Maker' <www.ex.ac.uk/bill.douglas/palace.html> (1978); Ellis, John (ed.), *1951–1976 British Film Institute Production* (London: BFI, 1977); Hassan, Mamoun, 'His Ain Man', *Sight and Sound*, Nov. 1991, pp. 22–4, 26; Noble, Andrew, 'Bill Douglas's Trilogy', in Eddie Dick (ed.), *From Limelight to Satellite: A Scottish Film Book* (London: BFI, 1990).

FILMOGRAPHY: *Charlie Chaplin's London* (short); *Striptease* (short) (1969); *Globe* (short); *Come Dancing* (short) (1970); *My Childhood* (1972); *My Ain Folk* (1973); *My Way Home* (1978); *Comrades* (1987).

DOXAT-PRATT, B. E. (1886–)

Bernard Edwin Doxat-Pratt was born in Annerley, south London, in 1886 and worked as an architect before entering the film business. He worked behind the scenes for Samuelson and Ideal before becoming an art director for Barker Motion Photography after the war. In 1919 he was hired as a director for the Anglo-Dutch concern Anglo-Hollandia. Based in Haarlem, Holland, but seeking a wider market, Anglo-Hollandia set out, under managing director Maurits Binger, to produce films of particularly British character using British directors. Doxat-Pratt made several films under the Anglo-Hollandia banner, the first being *The Hidden Life*, released in the UK by Urban.

Doxat-Pratt's adaptation of John Galsworthy's stage play *The Skin Game* (1921) compares well with Hitchcock's 1931 sound version. Fine ensemble acting from the well-rehearsed stage cast, evocative location shooting and a strong narrative drive result in a sophisticated film, revealing sharp class tensions beneath the placid surface of Edwardian England. His two collaborations with the actor/writer/director Adelqui Millar – *Laughter and Tears* and *Circus Jim* – are cruder, but enjoyable for the performances of the truculent Millar and spirited Evelyn Brent, and the glimpses they afford into the lives of ex-patriate Bohemians in Venice and the rough thrills of circus life. Binger's company folded when he died of cancer in 1923, and though Doxat-Pratt continued to work as a screenwriter, he directed only one more film, *My Lord the Chauffeur*, in 1927, and his career faded with the coming of sound.

(Simon Brown)

BIBLIOGRAPHY: Bishoff, Ruud, *Hollands Hollywood: de geschiedenis van de Filmfabriek Hollandia 1912–1923* (Amsterdam: Thoth, 1988); Donaldson, Geoffrey, *Of Joy and Sorrow: A Filmography of Dutch Silent Fiction* (Amsterdam: Nederlands Filmmuseum, 1997); Low, Rachael, *The History of the British Film 1918–1929* (London: George Allen & Unwin, 1971).

FILMOGRAPHY: *The Hidden Life/Het Verborgen leven* (co-dir. Maurits Binger, UK/Neth); *Joy/Zonnetje* (co-dir. Maurits Binger UK/Neth); *Sister Brown/Zuster Brown* (co-dir. Maurits Binger, UK/Neth); *The Little Hour of Peter Wells* (co-dir. Maurits Binger); *Fate's Plaything/Wat eeuwig blijft* (co-dir. Maurits Binger UK/Neth); *As God Made Her/Zooals ik ben* (co-dir. Maurits Binger, UK/Neth); *John Heriot's Wife* (co-dir. Maurits Binger) (1920); *The Skin Game*; *The Other Person*; *Laughter and Tears*; *Circus Jim* (co-dir. Adelqui Millar) (1921); *De Jantjes* (co-dir. Maurits Binger, Neth, 1922); *My Lord the Chauffeur* (1927).

DOYLE, Jim

Jim Doyle was born in Liverpool. He studied fine art at Nottingham College of Art and film at the Royal College of Art in London; his short *Wendy* (1990) won a Fuji Scholarship Award. After working as a writer and director in television, most notably as one of the directors of the comedy series *The World of Lee Evans* (1995), he teamed up with producer Ian Brady, writer Neil Fitzmaurice and cinematographer Damian Bromley to make *Going off Big Time*. A modest, well-paced film noir, it is reminiscent of the best 1950s' British crime films. The prison sequences are less resonant than Joseph Losey's *The Criminal* (1960), and the slide towards nemesis lacks the desperate inevitability of Seth Holt's *Nowhere to Go* (1958); but Fitzmaurice is convincing in the Stanley Baker role as a bright Liverpudlian plummeted into a life of crime, Doyle directs with ungimmicky directness, and the clever plot twist and uncompromising ending avoid the sentimentality afflicting most contemporary British crime films.

Doyle and Brady went on to make *Re-inventing Eddie*, an Anglo-Irish production about a father whose libertarian approach to parenting leads to accusations of sexual abuse. John Lynch is effective as the fun-loving father, and Bromley's location cinematography around the grim industrial hinterland of Liverpool adds visual interest; but Doyle and Brady's screenplay, based on a one-man play by Dennis Lumborg, lacks the tautness of *Going off Big Time*, and the father's fecklessness is too tediously indulged.

(Robert Murphy)

BIBLIOGRAPHY: 'First Frames', *Screen International*, 5 June 1992, pp. 10–12; 'Jim Doyle – Director', studio publicity for *Going off Big Time* held on microfiche in BFI National Library, London; Soutar, Ian, 'North by Northwest', *Exposure*, Summer 2001, pp. 8–9.

FILMOGRAPHY: *Wendy* (short, 1990); *Going off Big Time* (2000); *Re-inventing Eddie* (UK/Ir, 2002); *Lost Dogs* (2005); *Flirting with Flamenco* (2006).

DOYLE, Julian

Julian Doyle studied at the London Film School in the late 1960s, where he made *Chippingham House*, an interesting documentary about a London artists' community. On leaving he went into partnership with fellow LFS student Mark Forstater to make industrial and sponsored films. Their big break came when they teamed up with the Monty Python team, who had been disappointed by the unambitious scope of their first film . . . *And Now for Something Completely Different* (Ian MacNaughton, 1971). At considerable personal financial risk, Doyle and Forstater raised the £2 million budget for *Monty Python and the Holy Grail* (Terry Gilliam/Terry Jones, 1975). A modest success at the time, the film has gone on to win huge cult popularity. Doyle formed a partnership with Terry Gilliam, producing his *Jabberwocky* (1977), editing and acting as second-unit director on *Time Bandits* (1981) and *Brazil* (1985). He continued to work with the other Pythons, as editor on *Life of Brian* (Terry Jones, 1979) and second-unit director on *Erik the Viking* and *The Wind in the Willows*. Doyle's own efforts as a director are more modest; his only feature is *Shock Treatment* (1987), a witty sex/horror comedy, co-written with Mark Ezra, set in a clinic for celebrity drug addicts.

(Robert Murphy)

BIBLIOGRAPHY: Shackleton, Liz, 'Monty Python Veteran Conceives New Messiah', *Screen International*, 15 Sept. 2000, p. 21.

FILMOGRAPHY: *Time Bandits* (2nd unit dir., Terry Gilliam, 1981); *Brazil* (2nd unit dir., Terry Gilliam, 1985); *Shock Treatment* (aka *Love Potion*, 1987); *Erik the Viking* (2nd unit dir., Terry Jones, 1989); *The Wind in the Willows* (2nd unit dir., Terry Jones, 1996).

DRURY, David

David Drury was born in Leeds. He trained as a painter, but moved on to work as a film editor. He formed his own company to make documentaries and produced *City* (Peter Carr, 1980), a revealing examination of Manchester City Football Club, for Granada Television. He followed it with *Minter* (1981), a sympathetic study of the boxer Alan Minter, and made his feature film debut with *Forever Young*, written by Ray Connolly for David Puttnam's series of 'First Love' films for Channel 4. It is a likeable drama about friendship and betrayal, but it showed little of the magnetism of Drury's next film, *Defence of the Realm*, a taut political thriller written by Martin Stellman and starring Gabriel Byrne as a cynical journalist who stumbles onto a cover-up. The film was successful enough to take Drury to America, where he made a television film, *Intrigue* (1988), and the theatrically released *Split Decisions*, with Gene Hackman as the father of two aspirant boxers. It performed moderately at the box office and Drury returned to Britain to make films for television.

Drury's television record is impressively idiosyncratic. His rapport with actors, aided by his preference for wide-angle lenses and the Steadicam to encourage fluid and natural performances, make his television dramas distinctive and memorable. His choice of material ranges from the BBC drama series *Children of the North* (1991), based on the trilogy of novels by M. S. Power exploring political intrigue in Northern Ireland, to *Bad Company* (1993), a dramatisation of events surrounding the murder of thirteen-year-old newspaper delivery boy Carl Bridgwater, to *Rhodes* (1996), the story of Cecil Rhodes and his plans for the annexation of Southern Africa. Of his television films, the most impressive is *Hostile Waters* (1997), a co-production between HBO and the BBC, based on an incident when Soviet and American nuclear submarines collided in the Bermuda triangle. Written by Troy Kennedy Martin, with extensive use made of the two vessels' logs, it boasts an impressive international cast headed by Martin Sheen, Rutger Hauer and Max von Sydow.

Drury has proved adept at surviving in the star-driven climate of twenty-first-century television drama: making good use of Ray Winstone and Adrian Dunbar in the police thriller, *Tough Love* (2000), Sarah Lancashire as a woman who becomes con-

vinced that a friend is abusing her own child in *The Cry* (2002), and Martin Kemp in the crime drama series *The Family* (2003).
(Paul Ward)

BIBLIOGRAPHY: Frampton, Diana, 'Master of the Art of Film Economics', *Broadcast*, 4 Apr. 1986, p. 17; Webster, Howard, 'In Your Face', *Broadcast*, B+ Supplement, 7 Feb. 2003, p. 8.

FILMOGRAPHY: *Maritime Managers* (doc. short, 1978); *Minter* (doc. short, co-dir. Peter Carr, 1981); *Forever Young*; *Defence of the Realm* (1985); *Split Decisions* (US, 1988).

DRYHURST, Edward (1908–1989)

Edward Dryhurst was primarily a screenwriter and film producer, but he also worked as a director, chiefly in the hectic aftermath of the 1927 Cinematograph Films Act and the advent of talkies. Born Edward Dryhurst Roberts in Desborough, Berkshire, on 28 December 1908, he quickly developed a passion for cinema, abandoning school in St Albans for office work at Ideal Films based in Borehamwood. In 1922 he tried his hand at production, shooting three two-reel comedies, among them the quaintly titled *Hims Ancient and Modern*. In 1924 Dryhurst set sail for America and spent the next three years flitting between studios, learning and doing odd jobs.

Hollywood production, however, bore little resemblance to the constraints and chaos of British 'quota quickies', to which he returned. Teamed with Edward G. Whiting, a St Albans friend, Dryhurst delivered four cheap comedies and melodramas to distributors. *The Dizzy Limits* and *The Woman from China* were shot silent in the winter of 1929–30; two talkies, *Dangerous Seas* and *Commissionaire*, followed. Dryhurst did his best with the materials to hand, including the sultry actress Julie Suedo (then Whiting's girlfriend) and, in *Commissionaire*, a typically patriotic and sentimental script by Herbert Ayres; but these were not the films on which to base a successful directing career.

Instead, Dryhurst concentrated on writing, showing a special penchant for the more lurid crime thriller, before acquiring greater eminence in the immediate post-war period as an independent producer. *Noose* (1948) and *The Romantic Age* (1949) benefited from the quirky eye of their director, Edmond T. Gréville. *While I Live*, featuring three key ingredients of the period's melodramas – amnesia, classical music, a seaside cliff – had the more prosaic John Harlow at the helm, but Charles Williams' soundtrack concerto 'The Dream of Olwen' helped to ensure a hit. Credits tapered off in the 1950s, but Dryhurst kept busy writing: *Gilt off the Gingerbread*, a lively autobiography marred by an astonishing litany of sexual adventures, emerged in 1987. He died in London on 7 March 1989.
(Geoff Brown)

BIBLIOGRAPHY: Dryhurst, Edward, *Gilt off the Gingerbread* (London: Bachman & Turner, 1987); 'Edward Dryhurst', *Cinema and Theatre* vol. 15 no. 6, May 1948, pp. 19–21.

FILMOGRAPHY: *The Cause of All the Trouble* (short, as Edward D. Roberts, 1922; rel. 1923); *Fatty's Overtime* (short, as Edward D. Roberts); *Hims Ancient and Modern* (short, as Edward D. Roberts) (1922); *The Dizzy Limit* (sound version: *Kidnapped*); *The Woman from China* (1930); *Dangerous Sea* (1931); *Commissionaire* (1933).

DUFFELL, Peter (1924–)

More self-effacing craftsman than self-indulgent auteur, Peter Duffell entered the industry after studying at Oxford University. Early directing experience was acquired on commercials, documentaries, television series like *The Avengers*, and the fondly remembered *Scotland Yard* shorts, so ponderously introduced by criminologist Edgar Lustgarten. *The House That Dripped Blood* (1970) marked his proper screen debut, one of the portmanteau horror features from Amicus Films whose lurid title masked a work of some style, wit and intelligence. The film presented stories by Robert Bloch (author of *Psycho*) and contained an outstanding performance from Denholm Elliott as a haunted writer.

Duffell's following feature, *England Made Me*, remains one of the most successful attempts at filming a Graham Greene novel. By shifting the setting from 1930s' Sweden to Nazi Germany, Duffell gave extra resonance to the situation of Greene's effete Englishman (Michael York), whose public school morality and mild criminality are seen as hopelessly and prophetically ineffectual among new Europe's brutalities. The changes to the novel are subtle and well judged; the performances uniformly excellent; and even Greene, famously dismissive of film versions of his work, pronounced himself 'pleased enough'. He also approved Duffell's fine adaptation of another novel, *The Honorary Consul*, but the rights fell into other hands, and the film was eventually made in 1983, with John Mackenzie directing from a script by Christopher Hampton.

Thereafter, Duffell's film career spluttered rather than developed. His direction added a touch of class to otherwise modest material in the heist movie *Inside Out* (1975), starring Telly Savalas and James Mason; *Letters to an Unknown Lover* (1985), a Boileau-Narcejac thriller made in France; and *King of the Wind* (1989), a seventeenth-century adventure about an Arab groom and his horse made for Welsh television but with American financial backing; colourful action and a starry cast (headed by Glenda Jackson and Richard Harris) helped it gain a sporadic cinema release. Other projects included second-unit work on *Superman* (1978); a popular television miniseries based on M. M. Kaye's *The Far Pavilions* (1984); and a notably offbeat *Inspector Morse* episode, 'Last Bus to Woodstock' (1987), where the surprise twist was that no crime had actually been committed.

Apart from *England Made Me*, Duffell's best work has been seen in two exceptional television films of the early 1980s. The BBC's award-winning *Caught on a Train* (1980) with Peggy Ashcroft and Michael Kitchen, based on one of Stephen Poliakoff's finest screenplays, offered a powerful and probing reflection on the condition of modern Europe. Channel 4's *Experience Preferred – But Not Essential* (released with some success in American cinemas) delicately dramatised the first love of a student while working over the summer as a hotel maid. Duffell's

Peter Duffell on the set of *England Made Me* (1973) with Peter Finch

filmography is frustratingly brief, but his name on the credits offers the promise of civilised, rewarding entertainment.
(Neil Sinyard)

BIBLIOGRAPHY: Falk, Quentin, 'Making a Spectacle of the Small Screen', *Screen International*, 29 Nov. 1980, p. 11; Falk, Quentin, *Travels in Greeneland: The Complete Guide to the Cinema of Graham Greene* (London: Reynolds & Hearn, 2000); Mercorio, Giuliana, 'Return of the King', *Films and Filming*, Mar. 1990, pp. 23–5.

FILMOGRAPHY: *The Silent Weapon* (short); *The Grand Junction Case* (short); *The Never Never Murder* (short); *Partners in Crime* (1961); *Company of Fools* (short, 1966); *Payment in Kind* (short, 1967); *The House That Dripped Blood* (1970); *England Made Me* (UK/Yug, 1972); *Inside Out* (1975); *Superman* (2nd unit dir., Richard Donner, 1978); *Experience Preferred – But Not Essential* (1983); *Letters to an Unknown Lover* (UK/Fr, 1985); *King of the Wind* (US, 1989).

DUFFY, Martin (1952–)

Martin Duffy was born in Dublin in 1952, and began his career as a film editor. In 1988 he directed *Splice of Life*, a short comedy about the hardships of a film editor, and in 1990 collaborated on *The Cure*, a film about a group of teenage cancer sufferers. In 1996 he wrote and directed *The Boy from Mercury*, a charming childhood fantasy drawing on memories of his upbringing in 1950s' Dublin, and a playful homage to the *Flash Gordon* serials of the 1930s.

Duffy directed his next feature, *The Bumblebee Flies Anyway*, in 1998; a subdued, sensitive portrayal of a child's attempt to overcome amnesia, it never saw a theatrical release. He returned to the theme of childhood once again with *The Testimony of Taliesin Jones* (2000), the story of a Welsh boy who compensates for his mother's absence through contact with the supernatural and the spiritual.

Duffy occupies an anomalous position in the context of New Irish Cinema – he belongs neither to the first wave of indigenous film-making in the 1970s nor the youth cinema that took hold in the 1990s. A talented, visionary director whose work deserves closer critical scrutiny both at home and abroad, Duffy has developed a visual style and a theme – the child's wonder at a seemingly incomprehensible world – recognisable across his body of films. (Eugene Finn)

BIBLIOGRAPHY: Duffy, Martin, 'Mercury Rising', *Film Ireland* no. 56, Dec. 1996/Jan. 1997, pp. 5–6; Duffy, Martin, 'Someone Else's Dreams. . .Will Get You Nowhere', *Film West* no. 39, Feb. 2000, pp. 26–8.

FILMOGRAPHY: *The Boy from Mercury* (Ir, 1996); *The Bumblebee Flies Anyway* (Ir, 1998); *The Testimony of Taliesin Jones* (UK/US, 2000).

DUIGAN, John (1949–)

John Lawless Duigan was born in Hartley Wintney, Hampshire, on 19 June 1949 but emigrated to Australia in 1961 when his Australian father, who had served with the RAF during the war, decided to return home. In Melbourne he worked extensively in experimental theatre and contributed as scriptwriter and actor to various low-budget 16mm films, most prominently *Bonjour Balwyn* (Nigel Buesst, 1971). He also wrote a novel, *Badge* (1975). Duigan's debut as a director came with *The Firm Man* (1975), an ambitious if disorganised social fantasy about business drudgery and middle-aged discontent. Later films like *Mouth to Mouth* (1978), *Winter of Our Dreams* (1981), *The Year My Voice Broke* (1987) and *Flirting* (1991) established Duigan as one of the key directors of the New Australian Cinema, able to offer sympathetic insights into the underside of Australian society and the growing pains of adolescence. Following a luridly over-stuffed adaptation of Jean Rhys' *Wide Sargasso Sea* (1993) he restored his balance with the British-backed *Sirens* (1994), his first international success. Duigan's feeling for the sensuous irradiates this warmly humorous film, built round an encounter in the 1930s between the Australian painter Norman Lindsay (Sam Neill) and a fictional English clergyman (Hugh Grant), whose liberal tendencies become severely tested by Lindsay's erotic relations with a broad-minded wife and three voluptuous models.

All Duigan's subsequent films have been made in the UK or North America. He came to Britain to make *The Leading Man* (1996), an acidly adult drama, written by his sister Virginia Duigan, about a Hollywood actor rehearsing for a West End play who volunteers to seduce the author's wife to make it easier for her to accept him leaving her for his younger mistress. The plot works only too well, though Duigan leaves us to wonder whether the wife (Anna Galiena) is a naive fool taken in by the actor's manipulative charm, or whether the actor (Jon Bon Jovi) is wise as well as clever and genuinely appreciates the love of a good and beautiful woman. *Lawn Dogs* (1997) is a less complex but more emotionally nourishing fairy tale centring on the relationship between an annoyingly precocious ten-year-old girl and a laconic outsider employed to mow the lawns of a gated Kentucky community rife with bigotry and prejudice. The film was too critical of American society to do well at the box office, but its extraordinary mixture of magic realism and sharp social comment ensured a vigorous afterlife on video/DVD. *Molly* (1999), a sympathetic study of an autistic American woman, and *Paranoid* (2000), a too-pretentious British thriller, also fared badly in cinemas.

Duigan reunited with *Lawn Dogs* producer Duncan Kenworthy to make *The Parole Officer* (2001), a vehicle for television comedian Steve Coogan, for the Lottery-funded franchise DNA. Coogan's fans ensured modest box-office success in Britain, but cardboard characters and a flimsy plot meant there were few takers outside the UK. Duigan's erratic career continued with *The Engagement* (2001), a low-budget experiment shot on digital video, about a Serb refugee in London, and *Head in the Clouds* (2004), an Anglo-Canadian epic starring Stuart Townsend as an English working-class boy who becomes involved with French beauty Charlize Theron in 1930s' Paris. Duigan's brother-in-law is the director Bruce Beresford. (Robert Murphy)

BIBLIOGRAPHY: Bloom, Philipa, 'John Duigan: Writer/Director, *Empire*, Dec. 1991, p. 49; Parker, Donna, 'Duigan Having Some Fun with Sex, Religion', *Hollywood Reporter*, 28 Jan. 1994, p. 24; Willmott, Nigel, 'From Hand to Mouth . . .', *Film and TV Technician*, Jan. 1981, p. 11.

FILMOGRAPHY: *The Firm Man* (Austral, 1975); *The Trespassers* (Austral, 1976); *Mouth to Mouth* (Austral, 1978); *Dimboola* (Austral, 1979); *Winter of Our Dreams* (Austral, 1981); *Far East* (Austral, 1982); *One Night Stand* (Austral, 1984); *The Year My Voice Broke* (Austral, 1987); *Romero* (US, 1989); *Flirting* (Austral, 1991); *Wide Sargasso Sea* (Austral, 1993); *Sirens* (Austral/UK, 1994); *The Journey of August King* (US, 1995); *The Leading Man* (1996); *Lawn Dogs* (UK/US, 1997); *Molly* (US, 1999); *Paranoid* (2000); *The Parole Officer* (2001); *The Engagement* (2001); *Head in the Clouds* (UK/Can, 2004).

DUNBAR, Geoff (1944–)

Geoff Dunbar established his reputation in animation with *Lautrec* and *Ubu*, two films that dazzled, surprised and even alarmed audiences used to conventional styles and subjects. The intoxicating six-minute *Lautrec*, completed in 1974, paraded before the spectator figures derived from Toulouse-Lautrec's drawings of can-can dancers, circus clowns, mice, ducks and the music-hall singer Yvette Guilbert. Four years later the far more confrontational *Ubu* arrived with ink splashes, smudges, guttural sounds and lewd violence: an arsensal entirely fit for adapting Alfred Jarry's late-nineteenth-century theatrical fusillade. The design of the monstrous, foul-mouthed Pa Ubu, usurper of King Wenceslas' crown, drew on Jarry's own woodcut illustrations. Both films won major festival prizes, *Lautrec* at Cannes, the twenty-minute *Ubu* at Berlin, firmly cementing Dunbar's position as a lively and adventurous talent.

Born in Abingdon on 25 March 1944, Dunbar received no formal art training. After leaving school at fifteen he passed from one odd job to another before joining Larkins studios at the age

of twenty-one, learning the rudiments, painting and tracing cels on productions made for the Film Producers Guild. After three years he graduated to Halas and Batchelor's animation company, where he began directing (*This Love Thing*, *The Condition of Man*) and supervising a new commercials division. In 1973 he joined Oscar Grillo at Dragon Productions, co-financiers of *Lautrec* with the Arts Council of Great Britain.

Seeking more freedom, after three years Dunbar formed his own company, Grand Slamm Animation (later Grand Slamm Partnership). At Grand Slamm Dunbar led the artistically schizophrenic life typical of animation directors, juggling personal projects with the necessary bread-and-butter jobs (including commercials for Guinness, McEwan's Lager and Dulux paints). Half of the finance for *Ubu* came from Dunbar's commercials work; but since the 1980s, market forces have reduced the chances for ambitious, adventurous projects and designs. Even Dunbar's bigger ventures have necessitated a more traditional animation style, in keeping with family audiences.

In interviews Dunbar has stood up strongly for maturity and a wide expressive range in animation. 'Single stick-figures can be just as exciting as 500 flopsy bunnies,' he proclaimed during an interview in *Broadcast* (1985, p. 17). Yet by that time work had already taken him from the shrieks and splodges of *Ubu* to *Rupert and the Frog Song* (1984). This thirteen-minute short was mounted with Paul McCartney's MPL Communications as a pilot for a proposed feature starring the veteran comic-strip bear from the *Daily Express*. An animation and Rupert fan, McCartney had first planned a Rupert feature in the late 1970s with Oscar Grillo as director. This second attempt also foundered, though the pilot, lightly charming, won a BAFTA Best Animated Short award, and McCartney's 'frog song', 'We All Stand Together', reached number three in the British singles chart. In time the flopsy bunnies themselves arrived, along with their creator Beatrix Potter: for television in the 1980s Dunbar directed three episodes of the popular TVC London series *The World of Peter Rabbit and Friends*.

Dunbar's partnership with McCartney continued in the fifteen-minute *Daumier's Law* (1992), a partial return to the drive and imagination that had generated *Lautrec*. Honoré Daumier's drawings provided the visual seed for the pair's storyline about an ordinary citizen buffeted by the system. The film won another BAFTA award. *Tuesday* followed in 2000, a faithful and beguiling thirteen-minute adaptation of David Wiesner's picture book for children, describing a nocturnal flying visit by frogs, floating on lily pads through the houses and gardens of American suburbia. As with *Daumier's Law*, McCartney supplied the soundtrack's music.

Despite the technical brilliance of these later films, one still misses the dash and almost jugular bite that made Dunbar's earlier work so distinctive. With his current company, High Eagle Productions, Dunbar has now made his biggest project to date, *The Cunning Little Vixen* (2003), a fifty-eight-minute television encapsulation for the BBC and Opus Arte of Janácek's opera (itself based on cartoon drawings from a newspaper comic strip). The images and action come greatly strengthened by the director's gifts for characterisation and comedy, and his genuine feeling for the countryside; though if Dunbar's Pa Ubu saw the film, let alone *Rupert* or *Peter Rabbit*, he would probably let loose with rude noises and an expletive.

(Geoff Brown)

BIBLIOGRAPHY: Griffin, Sue, 'Dunbar: Still Drawing Notice', *Broadcast*, 11 Oct. 1985, p. 17; Lockey, Nicola, 'From Commercials to Features and Back', *Broadcast*, 19 Mar. 1979, p. 16.

FILMOGRAPHY: *This Love Thing* (1970); *The Condition of Man* (series, 1971); *Lautrec* (1974); *Ubu* (1978); *Rupert and the Frog Song* (1984); *Daumier's Law* (1992); *Tropic Island Hum* (1997); *Tuesday* (2000).

DUNKERTON, Martin (c. 1963–)

Martin Dunkerton made a couple of interesting shorts – *Fire and Steel*, about a soldier traumatised by his experiences during the Falklands War, and *From a Sheltered Flame*, about homelessness in London – before he blew his chances with *Brothers*. This lads-on-holiday feature fell uncomfortably between the authentic representation of youth culture in Justin Kerrigan's *Human Traffic* (1999) and the tongue-in-cheek mockery of *Kevin & Perry Go Large* (Ed Bye, 2000). The production's amateurism seems to have scared off the private investors who had financed *Brothers* from backing his next project, *More Than a Woman*, where Dunkerton had proposed extending his examination of philosophy, friendship and bodily functions to women.

(Robert Murphy)

BIBLIOGRAPHY: Brett, Anwar, 'Greek Odyssey', *Exposure*, Winter/Feb. 1999, pp. 2–23; 'Martin Dunkerton: Photographer and Film-Maker, 28', *Sunday Times* Magazine, 29 Sept. 1991, p. 49.

FILMOGRAPHY: *Fire and Steel* (short, 1989); *From a Sheltered Flame* (short, 1998); *Brothers* (2000).

DUNNING, George (1920–1979)

George Dunning's name became known to the wider world in 1968 with the release of the wildly popular and influential Beatles' animation extravaganza *Yellow Submarine*, produced by Dunning's company TVC London. He served as the overall director, supervising the army of over two hundred artists entrusted with realising the film in the frighteningly brief period of eleven months. He also conceived and took personal charge of the 'Lucy in the Sky with Diamonds' sequence. Photographs and behind-the-scenes footage suggest that throughout production Dunning was the only animator on the staff who wore a suit.

The title of Paul Madden's television portrait of Dunning, made for Channel 4 in 1994, encapsulates his posthumous reputation: he was 'The Man Who Moved the Beatles'. But animation connoisseurs knew of Dunning's achievements long before *Yellow Submarine* premiered in London. Born in Toronto on 17 November 1920, George Garnett Dunning first made his mark at the National Film Board of Canada among the animators grouped around Norman McLaren. He had joined the Board in 1943 after study at the Ontario School of Art and freelance work as an illustrator, and directed his first film the same year, *Auprès de ma blonde*, one in a series of 'Chants populaires'. But it was *Cadet Rouselle* in 1947 that pronounced the arrival of a distinctive talent, especially keen to develop new techniques. Instead of conventional animation, the film used flat metal figures, treated almost as puppets, their position altered frame by frame. Further experimentation followed in 1948 during a year spent working for UNESCO in Paris; he painted designs onto glass (a favourite technique), and absorbed advice from the Czech-born animator of *L'Idée* (1932), Berthold Bartosch.

Returning to Canada in 1949, Dunning secured a grant from the NFB to continue his experiments with painting on glass. To cement his livelihood, he formed the company Graphic Associates with another former NFB artist, Jim McKay, and began to generate the commercials and industrial spots that provided his life's bread and butter. After working on UPA's *Gerald McBoing Boing* television show in New York, he arrived in Britain in 1956 with the job of managing UPA's new London office. This London offshoot collapsed after seven months, but from the nucleus of UPA staff Dunning set up TV Cartoons (after 1961, TVC London), one of several animation companies formed to satisfy the new demand for television advertising. Talents working with Dunning included Richard Williams and Teru Murakami. Among the mountain of commissioned work – commercials for Mother's Pride bread, Start-Rite shoes, even Mentholatum Deep-Heat Rub – Dunning slowly began to generate his own personal short films, beginning in 1958 with *The Wardrobe*.

In these films Dunning's style is in marked contrast to the Pop Art and psychedelic abandon of *Yellow Submarine*. Initially Dunning favoured lean lines and spare backgrounds: the need for financial economy played a part, but it was style entirely suited to the absurdist comedy of Stan Hayward's scripts. *The Wardrobe*, set against a white background, features the comings and goings of two men, a wardrobe and two pairs of shoes. *The Apple* (1962), winner of a British Film Academy award, concludes a man's Herculean efforts at snatching an apple from a tree with the droll revelation of a secret attic containing an arrow, a small boy and dozens of split apples on the floor. The hero's design is typical: the head and body fused in a potato-shaped whole, with a bow-tie perched halfway down, and nose, eyes and hair clumped together on top. He could easily have stepped out of a magazine cartoon.

In *The Flying Man* (1962) Dunning revisited his experimental impulses, delineating characters and props – a man who can fly, a man who cannot, a coat, a dog – through loose watercolour brushstrokes floating in space without any defining lines. Witty and technically innovative, the film won the Grand Prix at Annecy's International Animation Festival. *The Ladder* (1967) further developed the brushstroke technique in a story with the 'eternal triangle' theme. These films established Dunning alongside Richard Williams and Bob Godfrey as a major new voice in British animation.

In between these personal shorts, TVC London ploughed ahead with the daily grind, producing about a hundred commercials a year in the 1960s, along with eight films for the National Coal Board's work safety campaign, featuring the characters Thud and Blunder. Producing *Canada Is My Piano*, a triple-screen film for the Montreal 1967 Expo, provided Dunning with a greater challenge. His managerial skills were also tested with *The Beatles* and *Cool McCool*, two animation series aimed at American television.

The Beatles episodes featured animated Beatles figures in brief domestic comedy scenes usually pegged to a particular Beatles song. The challenge for *Yellow Submarine*, commissioned by King Features in America, was to find a storyline and a visual approach capacious enough to sustain a feature and embrace a dozen Beatles songs. Dunning decided to go for variety, rotating the graphic style with each song, consciously using the film to showcase the wealth of visual techniques available in the late 1960s. Throughout, Dunning worked closely with his art director Heinz Edelmann, the German poster artist whose boldly coloured, 'trippy' designs generated much of the film's power and cult following. Other key contributions were made by Charles Jenkins, responsible for specific technical effects; animation directors Robert Balser and Jack Stokes; Erich Segal, who shaped much of the final script; Alison de Vere, the chief background supervisor; and, as line producer, John Coates, Dunning's partner at TVC since the beginning.

For 'Lucy in the Sky', annoyingly brief in its finished form, Dunning returned to the brushstroke technique of *The Flying Man* and *The Ladder*. The paint is overlaid on rotoscoped images derived from live-action footage featuring carousel girls from MGM's musical *Dancing Lady* and Fred Astaire dancing 'Cheek to Cheek' with Ginger Rogers – the whorls and splotches continuously changing colour and shape as the song progresses.

Dunning's carnival of new techniques in *Yellow Submarine* and his other films greatly influenced other talents, and extended the horizons of British animation. But the success of *Submarine* brought no direct financial reward: TVC London made the film for a fixed fee, soon exceeded when the production went over budget. Back at the grindstone, Dunning directed more safety films for the National Coal Board. Greater satisfaction resulted from the 'say no to drugs' animation *The Maggot* (another Annecy prize-winner) and his powerful treatment of Andrew Marvell's pastoral poem, *Damon the Mower*. The film proceeds through numbered graphite sketches, the rostrum camera deliberately positioned to capture both the mechanics and the magic of the animation process.

After *Damon*, Dunning began to lay plans for a feature based on Shakespeare's *The Tempest*. Dunning had been unwell throughout the production of *Yellow Submarine*, and poor health continued to dog him. When he died in London on 15 February 1979, *The Tempest* remained sadly unfinished. The collated surviving material – black-and-white pencil tests, pose sketches, a few full-colour animation sequences – hints at a bold expansion of past techniques, with figures, landscapes, even the Shakespeare text, in perpetual flux.
(Geoff Brown)

BIBLIOGRAPHY: Baker, Bob, 'George Dunning', *Film Dope* no. 13, Jan. 1978, pp. 38–40; Canemaker, John, 'The Dunning Touch', in *Sightlines* vol. 20 no. 2, Winter 1986/7, pp. 26–8; *The Man Who Moved the Beatles* (Paul Madden, Channel 4, 1994).

FILMOGRAPHY (UK only): Shorts: *The Wardrobe* (1958); *Visible Manifestations* (1961); *The Ever-Changing Motor Car* (co-dir. Alan Ball); *The Apple*; *The Flying Man*; *The Redemption of a Retailer* (1962); *The First Adventure of Thud and Blunder*; *Knock Off Time*; *Haulage Hazards* (1964); *The Loco*; *Charley* (1965); *Safety Boots*; *The Helmet*; *The Roof*; *Materials Handling* (1966); *The Ladder* (1967); *Lazy River* (1968); *Hands, Knees and Boomps-a-Daisy*; *Memory* (1969); *Moon Rock* (1970); *Damon the Mower* (1972); *Horses of Death* (co-dir. Jim Duffy); *How Not to Lose Your Head While Shot Firing* (co-dir. Jim Duffy); *The Maggot* (1973); *Teamwork* (co-dir. Jim Duffy, 1977).
Feature: *Yellow Submarine* (1968).

DUPONT, E. A. (1891–1956)

Born in Zeitz, Saxony, on 25 December 1891, Ewald André Dupont was the most prominent of several distinguished Europeans who came to Britain in the late 1920s to work in a production industry embarking upon expansion stimulated by government legislation. Following journalism and script work he had begun directing in 1918, becoming a prominent talent at Gloria-Film in Berlin, a satellite of the great Ufa company; he established a substantial worldwide reputation after the international success of *Varieté* (UK: *Vaudeville*, 1925), a film marked stylistically by the boldness and fluidity of its camera movements and the use of the subjective camera. He arrived in England in December 1926 after a brief and unsuccessful period in Hollywood and joined the newly formed British National Pictures as supervisor of production. British National was soon absorbed by British International Pictures and Dupont became BIP's leading foreign director, making films aimed at the international market.

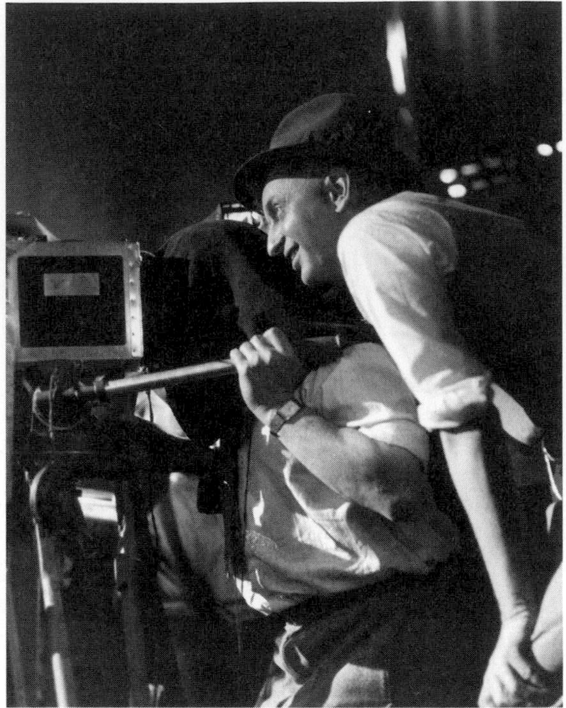

Moulin Rouge, his first film for BIP, was a markedly cosmopolitan product. The famous Paris theatre, with its surrounding streets and nightlife, provided the setting; Russian actress Olga Tschechowa took the lead role as a self-sacrificing dancer; while Dupont was supported by other key German technicians, cinematographer Werner Brandes and art director Alfred Jünge. The film shared the bravura qualities of Dupont's previous work, though it relied less on the elaborate camera movements of *Varieté*, and pushed its characters toward blatant melodrama in the hurtling climax involving a car with damaged brakes. Dupont's next production was *Piccadilly*, set in London's West End and the dockland Chinatown area of Limehouse. In novelist Arnold Bennett's well-constructed scenario, a nightclub owner (Jameson Thomas) abandons his mistress (Gilda Gray) for a Chinese scullery maid (Anna May Wong), who revives the club's fortunes with her dancing talents but stirs up passionate and deadly jealousies. Werner Brandes' glittering cinematography and Anna May Wong's startlingly erotic performance add to the film's glossy sophistication; Dupont's direction is inventive if sometimes laborious. But talkies were already taking over. The heavyweight subjects of Dupont's BIP sound films reflected his prestigious status, though, less beneficially, they also encouraged his tendency towards a slow, portentous pace. *Atlantic*, BIP's first attempt at a big-budget talkie, recreated the sinking of the *Titanic*; Dupont handles the tragedy with dignity, but the dialogue sequences are painfully stilted. He was also responsible for a German version (*Atlantik*, 1929); a French version (*Atlantis*, 1930) was directed along the same lines by Jean Kemm.

Dupont made two further multilinguals for BIP – *Two Worlds/Zwei Welten/Les Deux Mondes* and *Cape Forlorn/Menschen im Käfig/Le Cap Perdu* – with separate casts performing on common sets, a practice soon discontinued in favour of dubbing into different languages. *Cape Forlorn*, a tale of melodramatic infidelities in a lighthouse, and *Two Worlds*, a First World War romance between a Jewish woman and an Austrian officer, are both strong on atmosphere but slow moving and stiffly acted.

Dupont returned to Germany late in 1930. When the Nazis came to power in 1933 he was in Los Angeles completing exterior shooting on *Der Laüfer von Marathon*, set against the 1932 Olympics. Going home was not an option. Adjusting to the Hollywood studio system after the artistic freedom he enjoyed in Europe proved difficult, and Dupont found it demeaning working on B-movies like the Philo Vance detective thriller *Night of Mystery* (1937). After being fired in 1939 from the Dead End Kids picture *Hell's Kitchen*, he worked as a Hollywood journalist and press agent. In 1950 he modestly returned to production with several pot-boiling dramas. He died of cancer in Los Angeles on 12 December 1956.
(Tom Ryall)

BIBLIOGRAPHY: Baker, Bob, 'E. A. Dupont', *Film Dope* no. 13, Jan. 1978 pp. 40–2; Elsaesser, Thomas, *Weimar Cinema and After* (London and New York: Routledge, 2000); Higson, Andrew, 'Polyglot Films for an International Market', in Andrew Higson and Richard Maltby (eds), *'Film Europe' and 'Film America'. Cinema, Commerce and Cultural Exchange 1920–1939* (Exeter: University of Exeter Press, 1999); Luft, Herbert G., 'E. A. Dupont, 1891–1956', *Films in Review*, June/July 1977, pp. 342–58; Vincendeau, Ginette, 'Hollywood Babel', *Screen*, Spring 1988, pp. 24–39 (reprinted in Higson and Maltby, *'Film Europe'*).

FILMOGRAPHY (UK only): *Moulin Rouge* (1928); *Piccadilly*; *Atlantic* (1929); *Two Worlds* (1930); *Cape Forlorn* (US: *The Love Storm*, 1931).

DUVIVIER, Julien (1896–1967)

Born in Lille on 8 October 1896, Julien Duvivier's long and diverse career as a director, chiefly in France, spanned seventy films, from 1919 to the year of his death, from the time of Feuillade's serials to the fractured experiments of the French *nouvelle vague*. His contribution to British cinema consists essentially of one film, *Anna Karenina* (1948), though his links with its producer Alexander Korda stretched over a decade. Korda first contacted him in 1938, when Duvivier's reputation was at its peak following a series of observant, atmospheric, strongly acted, often bitter-sweet films, crowned in 1937 by *Pépé-le-Moko* and *Un Carnet de bal*. Korda was hatching plans to host several French productions at Denham, and proposed that Duvivier direct a French colonial property, *Raz el Guea*. Nothing emerged, but their association was renewed in Hollywood, when Korda suggested *Un Carnet de bal* as a vehicle for Merle Oberon. Rights problems made a straight remake impossible, though the film that emerged, *Lydia* (1941), shared the same

departure point – an old woman revisiting past amours. Director of photography Lee Garmes and other gifted technicians supplied a glossy artificial surface, but performances were plain and the film's heart distant. Duvivier's wartime successes in America came elsewhere, with *Tales of Manhattan* (1942) and *Flesh and Fantasy* (1943).

Still contracted to Korda, Duvivier pursued plans for joint ventures in Britain, initially with MGM-British. For London Films he wanted to make Mary Webb's novel *Gone to Earth* with Vivien Leigh; she preferred Tolstoy and *Anna Karenina*. Duvivier felt little enthusiasm. The job was made harder by interpretative differences (Leigh wanted the heroine hard-lined, not romantic) and the unavailability of Laurence Olivier, a natural choice for her lover, Vronsky. From their first fateful glance through a train window, Leigh and Kieron Moore (Olivier's stolid substitute) keep passion at bay; so much so that sympathies turn to Ralph Richardson – lively, subtle and touching as Anna's wronged husband. The central relationship's lack of fire prompted poor box-office returns, particularly damaging for a film that cost £430,000. The ponderousness of the visual trappings, a further cavil at the time, is now less apparent. Duvivier's visual choreography, the light and shade of Henri Alékan's photography and Cecil Beaton's elaborate costumes combine to conjure a brooding, effective poetic atmosphere, despite too much artificial snow.

After the ordeal of *Anna Karenina*, Duvivier actively considered further Korda collaborations, but none reached production. Back in France, he enjoyed a big popular success in 1952 with the Fernandel comedy *Le Petit Monde de Don Camillo*, after which he increasingly faced sniping from the new critics and film-makers determined to distinguish themselves from what was dubbed '*le cinéma de Papa*'. On 29 October 1967 in Paris, a month after finishing shooting the thriller *Diaboliquement vôtre*, Duvivier died following a heart attack at the wheel of his grey Jaguar.

(Geoff Brown)

BIBLIOGRAPHY: Bonnefille, Eric, *Julien Duvivier: Le mal aimant du cinéma français* (Paris: L'Harmattan, 2002); Kulik, Karol, *Alexander Korda: The Man Who Could Work Miracles* (London: W. H. Allen, 1975).

FILMOGRAPHY (UK only): *Anna Karenina* (1948).

DVIR, Rami

Rami Dvir was born in Israel, where he studied philosophy, theatre and art. After serving with the Israeli Air Force he pursued a career in theatre and television in Israel and the UK. A shared interest in flying led to partnership with writer Nigel Horne on a one-act play, *Broken Skies*, performed at the Bristol QEH Theatre, and a low-budget feature, *The Wedding Tackle*, set during the stag night of a reluctant bridegroom (James Purefoy) whose fiancée (Susan Vidler) is also having second thoughts. Dvir's inexperience shows in a number of poorly executed sequences, Horne's script is too loosely written and an irrelevant 1960s' pop song soundtrack distances the action from any contemporary reality. The central couple are surprisingly thinly drawn and allowed little opportunity to interact; but the scheming, interfering friends, played with relish by Adrian Dunbar, Tony Slattery and Victoria Smurfit, are far more vivid, and the flow of incidents they generate makes the film more enjoyable than one might expect from the hostile reviews and small audiences it attracted. A comedy short followed in 2004, but after his inauspicious feature debut Dvir's future as a director cannot be certain.

(Robert Murphy)

FILMOGRAPHY: *The Wedding Tackle* (2000); *Italian Breakfast* (short, 2004).

DWAN, Allan (1885–1981)

Joseph Aloysius Dwan was born in Toronto on 3 April 1885. After studying engineering at Notre Dame University, Indiana, he worked for a company developing mercury-vapour arc lights, which led him into the film industry in 1909. Within two years he had moved from technical adviser to scenario editor to director, building a reputation for efficiency and ingenuity. In 1915 he joined D. W. Griffith at Triangle, where he directed, supervised and helped the cameraman Billy Bitzer shoot the gigantic Babylon set constructed for *Intolerance* by devising a flexible, raised platform to run along railway tracks with the camera positioned on top. Dwan established his own

reputation as one of Hollywood's pre-eminent silent film directors with a series of films starring Douglas Fairbanks, most notably *The Half-Breed* (1916) and the massively lavish spectacle *Robin Hood* (1923); later in the 1920s he successfully showcased Gloria Swanson's talents in romantic dramas and vigorous comedies, including *Manhandled* (1924) and *Stage Struck* (1925).

Always a technical innovator, Dwan easily adapted himself to the talkies. He added sound effects and dialogue sequences to *The Iron Mask* (1929), the last of his Fairbanks pictures, and showed his affinity for the new medium in the speedy melodrama of *While Paris Sleeps* (1932). Passing through London in 1932, he was offered a film to direct, *Her First Affaire*; two other assignments swiftly followed. 'I enjoyed the chance of working in England, not the pictures themselves,' he said years later (Bogdanovich, p. 97). A better script would have strengthened his hand in *Her First Affaire*, a typical West End stage adaptation, but Dwan's smooth direction and a good cast – including a young Ida Lupino in her first role – still make it pleasant viewing. *Counsel's Opinion* is also burdened by trifling stage material, but Dwan makes the most of the pairing between sharp, sassy Binnie Barnes and bumbling Henry Kendall, and producer Alexander Korda ensured high production values. The least of the trio is the increasingly tiresome *I Spy*, with Ben Lyon and Sally Eilers, made at the more pinchpenny BIP studios from a strenuously comic Ruritanian plot cobbled together by Dwan and Arthur Woods.

Dwan returned to Hollywood to a less than rapturous welcome. Initially he was offered only B-films, but his solid professionalism eventually brought him a couple of Shirley Temple vehicles – *Heidi* (1937) and *Rebecca of Sunnybrook Farm* (1938) – and *Suez* (1938), a prestigious if fanciful biography of the Suez canal's architect, Ferdinand de Lesseps. Comedies and Westerns followed, but his biggest success came with the tough Second World War melodrama *Sands of Iwo Jima* (1949). Dwan continued to direct throughout the 1950s, most happily on Westerns like *Cattle Queen of Montana* (1954) and the flamboyant Technicolor film noir *Slightly Scarlett* (1955). As he told Kevin Brownlow, 'Directing movies – I'd do it for free, I like it that well' (Brownlow, p. 120). Allan Dwan died in Woodland Hills, California, on 21 December 1981, aged ninety-six.

(Robert Murphy)

BIBLIOGRAPHY: 'Allan Dwan', *Film Dope* no. 14, Mar. 1978, pp. 4–9, and Kevin Brownlow, 'Allan Dwan – The Silent Era', p. 9; Bogdanovich, Peter, *Allan Dwan: The Last Pioneer* (London: Studio Vista, 1971); Brownlow, Kevin, *The Parade's Gone By . . .* (London: Abacus, 1973); McGillivray, David, Obituary, *Films and Filming*, Mar. 1982, pp. 6–7.

FILMOGRAPHY (UK only): *Her First Affaire* (1932); *Counsel's Opinion*; *I Spy* (1933).

DWOSKIN, Stephen (1939–)

Stephen Dwoskin, born in New York on 15 January 1939, is one of the most visually rich and emotionally intense film-makers in British cinema. After working as a graphic designer and art director for CBS and Epic Records, he made two short films, *Asleep* and *American Dream*, in 1961, and became part of the bohemian world of New York 'underground' film-makers. In 1964 he moved to London on a Fulbright Fellowship to research British design, and in 1966 set up the London Film Makers Co-op with two other New Yorkers, Andy Meyer and Simon Hartog.

Working as a painter, designer and photographer, Dwoskin established his reputation as a film-maker with a series of short films that won him the Solvay Prize at the Knokke Experimental Film Festival in 1967–8. His films were characterised by an obsessively intense scrutiny of the (mostly female) figures in front of his static or slowly moving camera, and an attention to image textures, printing processes and hypnotic soundtracks. Whereas most of his contemporaries in the world of avant-garde cinema espoused a modernist aesthetic focusing on the properties of the medium, Dwoskin explored the relations of desire that can be woven between the camera's way of looking, the subject's wish to be seen, the film-maker's irrevocable 'separation' from what he wants to see and show, and the viewer's relation to this intricate network of imbricated desires. In films such as *Moment*, *Chinese Checkers* and *Alone*, he allows shadowy narratives to be surmised by the viewer as s/he is gradually caught in the workings of a cinematic apparatus conceived not so much as a technological device than as a way of activating and playing with the desire to look. With these films, and others such as the emotionally overwhelming features *Times For*, *Dyn Amo* and *Behindert*, he drew as much attention to the viewer's desire to become captivated by the filmed image as he did to the performer's fascination in being captivated within the camera's field of vision. The films often extend their engagement with performance to letting the actors improvise and 'stage' their own images, as in *Central Bazaar*, or to near-dramatic narratives, as in *Silent Cry* and *Tod und Teufel* (an adaptation of a Wedekind play).

From the 1990s onwards, Dwoskin embarked on a series of autobiographical films turning the camera on himself and the spaces and people around him. *Trying to Kiss the Moon*, an autobiographical film-poem, contains poignant home-movie footage of his life in the US prior to the childhood polio attack that forced him to rely on crutches and eventually confined him to a wheelchair. It was followed by personal (*Behindert*) and historical (*Face of Our Fear*, *Pain Is?*) explorations of disability, made in the context of trying to secure full human rights for disabled people. After suffering bouts of severe illness, he made three profoundly moving video-films, *Intoxicated by My Illness*, *Some Friends* and *Another Time*, all pervaded by an unsettling sense of death's proximity that imbues each image and sound with an almost painful intensity.

In London, Dwoskin taught new generations of film-makers at the Royal College of Art (1973–83) and at the London College of Printing (1983–7). He has been active in various cultural institutions throughout his career, and published a personal account of the American and British avant-garde film worlds, *Film Is*, in 1975, and a book of his surreal and witty photomontages *Ha Ha! (La solution imaginaire)* in 1993.

(Paul Willemen)

BIBLIOGRAPHY: Curtis, David, *Experimental Cinema* (New York: Universe, 1971); Dwoskin, Stephen, *Film Is . . .* (London: Peter Owen, 1975).

FILMOGRAPHY: *Asleep* (US); *American Dream* (US) (1961); *Alone* (US, 1963); *Naissant*; *Chinese Checkers*; *Soliloquy* (1964); *Dirty* (1965); *Me Myself and I* (1967); *Take Me*; *Moment* (1968); *Trixi* (1969); *C-Film*; *To Tea* (1970); *Times For* (1971); *Jesus Blood*; *Dyn Amo*

(1972); *Tod und Teufel* (1973); *Behindert/Hindered* (1974); *Laboured Party*; *Just Waiting*; *Girl* (1975); *Central Bazaar*, *Kleiner Vogel* (1976); *Silent Cry* (1977); *Outside In* (1981); *Shadows from Light* (1983); *Ballet Black* (1986); *Further and Particular* (1988); *L'Esprit de Brendan Behan*; *Face Anthea* (1990); *Video Letters* (with Robert Kramer, 1991–2000); *Face of Our Fear* (1992); *Trying to Kiss the Moon* (1994); *Pain Is?* (1997); *Intoxicated by My Illness Pt 1 & 2* (2000–1); *Some Friends*; *Another Time* (2002).

DYER, Anson (1876–1962)

For all the current lack of critical attention, Anson Dyer was a major figure in British animation for over thirty years, from the First World War to the aftermath of the Second. Stylistically he remained unadventurous, avoiding the playful mixed-media games of Sid Griffiths' Jerry the Tyke cartoons of the 1920s, let alone the speed and wilder anthropomorphic habits of Hollywood studio animation. Yet he was promoted for a time as Britain's equivalent of Walt Disney, with a prolific and popular output of children's cartoons and advertisements; and only producer Archibald Nettlefold's caution prevented him from being credited with Britain's first animated feature, *The Story of the Flag* (1927), released to cinemas as a series of six shorts.

Ernest John Anson Dyer was born on 18 July 1876 in Brighton. After studying at Brighton School of Art, specialising in industrial design, he worked on church commissions in C. E. Kempe's stained-glass studio, using the surname Anson-Dyer. With the onset of war such work dwindled. Rejected for army service, Dyer applied for work in films as an actor. His excessive height told against him, but his design skills earned him employment at the British Colonial and Kinematograph Company; three of his *Dicky Dee* cartoons emerged in 1915. Dyer soon specialised in topical wartime cartoons, finally switching to children's material with Kine Komedy Kartoons' *Uncle Remus* series in 1919. He joined Hepworth's company at Walton that same year, supplying a series of Shakespeare parodies and developing his own cartoon character, Bobby the Scout. After Hepworth's bankruptcy, Dyer continued at the Walton studio, working for its new owner Archibald Nettlefold, and ultimately securing backing from him for his own animation studio, which opened in 1935. *The Story of the Flag*, a bracingly patriotic survey of changes in the Union Jack's design, aimed more for respectability than popular success; but Dyer returned triumphantly to favour with sound, colour and his highly successful cartoons featuring the Sam character from Stanley Holloway's comic monologues. *Sam and his Musket* (1935) became the first of six. Advertisements for Bush radios like *All the Fun of the 'Air* equally enlivened British cinemas' supporting programmes.

Responding once more to changing times, Dyer formed Analysis Films in 1939, supplying material for the Ministry of Information and other propaganda outlets. With peacetime he returned to his forte, children's entertainment, at his studio in Stroud, Gloucestershire, providing cartoons for Rank's subsidiary Children's Entertainment Films, including an animated serial, *Squirrel War* (1947). At his peak, Dyer was notable enough to be featured in two films showing his studio in action: *You're Telling Me* (1939) and *Cartoonland* (1949), but changes in taste and his own iron-clad style contributed to his later neglect. Dyer died in Cheltenham on 22 February 1962, long forgotten by the industry. (Geoff Brown)

BIBLIOGRAPHY: Dyer, Anson, *Technique of Film Cartoons* (London: British Kinematograph Society, 1936); Gifford, Denis, 'Anson Dyer', in Maurice Horn (ed.), *The World Encyclopaedia of Cartoons* (New York: Chelsea House, 1980); Gifford, Denis, *British Animated Films, 1895–1985: A Filmography* (Jefferson, NC: McFarland, 1987).

FILMOGRAPHY: *Dicky Dee's Cartoon No. 1*; *Dicky Dee's Cartoon No. 2*; *Dicky Dee's Cartoon No. 3*; *John Bull's Animated Sketchbook No. 8* (1915); *Before the Beak*; *The Early Bird*; *John Bull's Animated Sketchbook No. 15*; *John Bull's Animated Sketchbook No. 16*; *John Bull's Animated Sketchbook No. 18*; *John Bull's Animated Sketchbook No. 20*; *John Bull's Animated Sketchbook No. 22* (1916); *Food for Reflection*; *The Kaiser's Record*; *Peter's Picture Poems*; *Old King Coal*; *Agitated Adverts* (1917); *More Agitated Adverts*; *The British through German Eyes*; *A Child's Dream of Peace*; *A 'Plane Tale*; *Foch the Man* (1918); *Uncle Remus No. 1*; *Uncle Remus No. 2*; *Uncle Remus No. 3*; *The Merchant of Venice*; *Romeo and Juliet*; *'Amlet*; *Ophelia* (1919); *Othello*; *The Taming of the Shrew* (1920); *Bobby the Scout No. 1*; *Bobby the Scout No. 2*; *Bobby the Scout No. 3*; *Dollars in Surrey* (live action, co-dir. George Dewhurst) (1921); *Little Red Riding Hood*; *The Three Little Pigs* (1922); *The Story of the Flag* (series, 1927); *A Day in Liverpool* (1929); *The Story of the Port of London* (1932); *Sam and His Musket* (1935); *Carmen*; *'Alt! 'Oo Goes There?*; *Beat the Retreat*; *Sam's Medal* (1936); *The Lion and Albert*; *Drummed Out*; *Three Ha'Pence a Foot*; *Gunner Sam*; *All the Fun of the 'Air*, *The King with the Terrible Temper* (1937); *The King with the Terrible Hiccups*; *This Button Business* (1938); *Red, White and Blue*; *The Queen Was in the Parlour*, *You're Telling Me* (co-dir. A. G. Jackson) (1939); *I'm Forever Blowing Bubbles* (1940); *Behind the Clock* (1943); *Robbie Finds a Gun* (1945); *Bee Wise!* (1946); *The Farmyard Rising*; *Squirrel War* (serial); *Dashing Away with the Smoothing Iron*; *Who Robbed the Robins?* (1947); *Timber!*; *Jump to It* (1948); *Going Up*; *No Fishing*; *Cherry the Boots* (1949); *Very Good Sergeant*; *Fowl Play* (co-dir. Len Kirley) (1950).

EADY, David (1924–)

Born in Hampstead, London, in 1924, David L. Eady was the son of Sir Wilfred Eady, the civil servant who originated the Eady Levy, which subsidised British film production between 1949 and

1985. He began his career as assistant cutter on *The Third Man* (Carol Reed, 1949) for London Films, where he subsequently edited Zoltán Korda's *Cry, the Beloved Country* (1952) and wrote and directed several shorts. He was one of three directors involved in *Three Cases of Murder*, and three of his 1950s' B-films reveal a likeable, slightly off-centre talent. *The Heart Within* is a thoughtful little film, a combination of thriller and racial problem drama, with West Indian characters in a dockside setting; the action turns on a junk-dealer's thirteen-year-old grandson (David Hemmings) who helps an unjustly accused docker (Earl Cameron) and exposes the real villain (Clifford Evans). In *Zoo Baby* a small boy, sent 'home' to school from South Africa, steals a coati-mundi bear from Chessington Zoo. There is a perfunctory romance, but the awkward relationship between the boy and his aunt (Angela Baddeley) is handled with unusual care. *The Man Who Liked Funerals* is persistently fresh and funny as it chronicles the attempts of a printer (Leslie Phillips) to get the money needed to renew the lease on a boys' club premises by blackmailing the bereaved with the threat of publishing scandal about the deceased.

Eady's sympathetic treatment of child characters led him to a satisfying career as the director of numerous films in the 1960s and 70s that were made for, as well as about, children. From the late 1970s onwards he made a series of instructional films about horse riding, and several guides to financial management.

(Brian McFarlane)

BIBLIOGRAPHY: BECTU History Project interview, tape held in the BFI National Library, London.

FILMOGRAPHY: Shorts and documentaries: *Bridge of Time* (co-dir. Geoffrey Boothby, 1950); *Edinburgh*; *The Road to Canterbury*; *Persona Non Grata*; *Why Not Uncle Willy?* (1952); *Handling Frozen Fish* (1960); *Cranwell, The R.A.F. College*; *Winter Building* (1966); *Throwaway Society*; *In the Dark* (1968); *Betcher* (1972); *Someone, Somewhere* (1974); *The Hands of Fate* (1975); *Play Safe* (1978); *Dressage Movements* (1979); *23* (1979); *The Prepared Mind*; *Finance for Managers: The Micawber Equation* (1980); *Training the Young Horse* (1982); *The Perils of Easy Credit* (1986).

Features: *Malaga* (2nd unit dir., Richard Sale); *Beautiful Stranger* (2nd unit dir., David Miller) (1954); *Three Cases of Murder* (co-dirs. Wendy Toye/George More O'Ferrall, 1955); *Seven Waves Away* (2nd unit dir., Richard Sale, 1956); *The Heart Within* (1957); *Zoo Baby* (1957; rel. 1960); *The Man Who Liked Funerals* (1958); *The Crowning Touch*; *In the Wake of a Stranger* (1959); *Faces in the Dark* (1960); *The Verdict* (1964); *Operation Third Form*; *The Brides of Fu Manchu* (2nd unit dir., Don Sharp) (1966); *Scramble* (1970); *Hide and Seek*; *Anoop and the Elephant* (1972); *The Laughing Girl Murder* (1973); *Where's Johnny?* (1974); *The Hostages* (1975); *Echo of the Badlands* (co-dir. Tim King); *Night Ferry* (1976); *The Hand of Fate* (aka *Crime Casebook*, short, 1977); *Deep Waters* (1978); *Danger on Dartmoor* (1980).

EAGLES, Bill

Bill Eagles started out in television with oddball projects such as *Weird Shit Happens* (1994) and *Bring Me Sunshine: The Heart and Soul of Eric Morecambe* (1998), made for the BBC arts programme *Omnibus*. He moved into the mainstream to direct episodes of the noirish police drama serial *Touching Evil* (1999). DNA, least prolific of the three Lottery-funded franchise consortia, noted Eagles' penchant for the macabre and appointed him to direct *Beautiful Creatures*, a tale of two women struggling to survive amid violent and predatory Glasgow men. The film was released during a storm of criticism around the Lottery-funding system and given a harsh reception. Perhaps greater generosity might have been extended to the performances of Susan Lynch and Rachel Weisz, convincing as good women trapped in relationships with violent men; but Simon Donald's script is patchy and trivial, and Eagles is unable to establish any connection to a world beyond jejune pulp fiction imaginings.

Eagles went back to television, directing episodes of the ill-fated soap opera *Night & Day* (2001), and a too-predictable Anthony Horowitz thriller, *Menace* (2002). He found his feet with a more meaty television film: *Daddy's Girl* (2002), featuring Martin Kemp as a father who indulges in an incestuous relationship with his daughter. Similarly dark dramas – *The Book of Ruth* (2004) and *The Riverman* (2004) – made for American television followed.

(Robert Murphy)

BIBLIOGRAPHY: Monk, Claire, 'Beautiful Creatures', *Sight and Sound*, Feb. 2001, p. 35.

FILMOGRAPHY:

Beautiful Creatures (2000).

EDGAR, Justin (1971–)

Justin Edgar was born in Handsworth, Birmingham, on 18 August 1971, and brought up in nearby Sutton Coldfield. He studied film at Portsmouth University, graduating in 1996; afterwards he made two well-received shorts, *Largin It* (1997) and *Dirty Phonecalls* (1998). Seen as a promising young film-maker with more interest than most in making films for the teenage market, he was encouraged to develop a feature script and won backing from Channel 4 and the Lottery-funded Film Consortium to make *Large* (2001) as his feature debut.

The rudimentary plot – a rock star's son will only inherit his wealth if he fulfils stringent conditions for steadiness and responsibility – is brought alive with frenetic energy, garish sets and zany slapstick action; though for a script that supposedly went through twenty drafts, a little more finesse in rounding out one-dimensional characters might have been expected. The film's fast pace makes suspension of disbelief easy, and there are funny moments, but its insubstantial story and anonymous cast made it difficult to market to its intended teenage audience. Edgar returned to shorts with *Round* (2003) and a series of television documentaries dealing with disability.

(Robert Murphy)

BIBLIOGRAPHY: Wistreich, Nic, Interview with Justin Edgar, <www.netribution.co.uk/features/interviews/2000/justin_edgar/2html>.

FILMOGRAPHY: *Largin It* (short, 1997); *Dirty Phonecalls* (short, 1998); *Large* (2001); *Round* (short); *All Aboard* (short, 2003); *Special People* (short, co-dirs The Kielder Kids, 2005).

EDMONDSON, Adrian (1957–)

Adrian Edmondson was born in Bradford on 24 January 1957. While studying at Manchester University he met Rik Mayall; together they formed a comedy double-act that proved a success at the Comedy Store and the Comic Strip in London's Soho. Moving into television, they reached a national audience with the seminal 1980s' sitcom, *The Young Ones* (1982–4). In 1982 a Comic Strip team was formed to produce a series of one-off comedies for television, with Edmondson directing *Private Enterprise* (1986) and *More Bad News* (1988), both of which centred on the pop music industry. The popularity of *More Bad News* ensured it a limited theatrical outing, and Edmondson went on to direct his wife, Jennifer Saunders, and her partner Dawn French in an efficient video recording of their splendid early 1990s' stage act. His one directorial effort intended for the big screen, *Guest House Paradiso*, is a tired variation on his double-act with Mayall, traceable on video through other incarnations such as *The Dangerous Brothers* and *Bottom*.

(Richard Dacre)

BIBLIOGRAPHY: Harrigan, Brian, 'British Film Comedy Comes back Blacker', *Video Business*, 18 Aug. 1988, p. 46; Wilmut, Roger and Peter Rosengard, *Didn't You Kill My Mother-in-Law?* (London: Methuen, 1989).

FILMOGRAPHY: *More Bad News* (1988); *Guest House Paradiso* (1999).

EDWARDS, Blake (1922–)

Blake Edwards was born into a showbiz family in Tulsa, Oklahoma, on 26 July 1922; his grandfather was J. Gordon Edwards, a director of the silent era, and his father was a production manager. When he was three his family moved to Los Angeles. Edwards gravitated to Hollywood as soon as he left high school, starting out as an actor and then, after war service in the US Coast Guards, turning his hand to scriptwriting for cinema, television and radio. He began directing B-movies in 1955, graduating to the A-list with the navy comedy *Operation Petticoat* (1959) and achieving international success with the romantic comedy *Breakfast at Tiffany's* (1961). Extending his range, he directed a taut thriller, *Experiment in Terror* (1962) and a harrowing study of alcoholism, *Days of Wine and Roses* (1962), before scoring another major hit with the crime-comedy *The Pink Panther* (1963), which introduced one of the classic comic characters of cinema, the bumbling French detective Inspector Clouseau, played by Peter Sellers.

Edwards promptly followed up with another Clouseau film, *A Shot in the Dark* (1964), which did equally well. But after this his career started to hit trouble with several overambitious projects such as the unwieldy slapstick marathon, *The Great Race* (1965), *Darling Lili* (1970), a period romance showcasing Edwards' wife Julie Andrews, and a Western, *Wild Rovers* (1971). Feeling unappreciated in Hollywood, Edwards moved to Britain to make *The Tamarind Seed* (1974), a lushly exotic romance. He was then persuaded (reluctantly, as Sellers was becoming increasingly difficult to work with) to resume the Pink Panther series. Three more Clouseau films, *Return of the Pink Panther* (1974), *The Pink Panther Strikes Again* (1976) and *Revenge of the Pink Panther* (1978), did well at the box office, but the joke was wearing steadily thinner with each repetition.

His reputation partially restored, Edwards returned to the USA where he made the sex-comedy *10* (1979), which was well received, and a splenetic satire on Hollywood, *S.O.B.* (1981), which was not. Once again he retreated to Britain to direct *Victor/Victoria* (1982), a handsomely mounted period comedy about sex roles, with Julie Andrews as a showgirl who disguises herself as a (male) female impersonator. Based on a German film of 1933 (which had been previously remade by Victor Saville as *First a Girl* with Jessie Matthews in 1935), Edwards' film was let down by smug, anachronistic dialogue and some heavy-handed slapstick. It was a masterpiece, though, beside his next two films. Peter Sellers had died in 1980, but *Trail of the Pink Panther* (1982) dragged him from his grave, splicing together a feeble story from assorted out-takes, while *Curse of the Pink Panther* (1983) was equally dire, with Clouseau's incompetent successor sent to find the missing Inspector.

Since then Edwards has worked mainly in the USA, where his career has continued its downward spiral. He even made one more desperate attempt to scrape the Pink Panther barrel, with Roberto Benigni as *Son of the Pink Panther* (1993). More recently he has concentrated on theatre work.

(Philip Kemp)

BIBLIOGRAPHY: Lehman, Peter and William Luhr, *Blake Edwards* (Athens: Ohio University Press, 1981); Luhr, William and Peter Lehman, *Returning to the Scene: Blake Edwards, Volume 2* (Athens: Ohio University Press, 1989).

FILMOGRAPHY (UK only): *A Shot in the Dark* (US/UK, 1964); *The Tamarind Seed*; *Return of the Pink Panther* (1974); *The Pink Panther Strikes Again* (1976); *Revenge of the Pink Panther* (1978); *Victor/Victoria*; *Trail of the Pink Panther* (1982); *Curse of the Pink Panther* (1983).

EDWARDS, Henry (1883–1952)

To his many cinema fans in the silent period, Henry Edwards' main claim to his considerable fame was as an actor: the tall, tousled, sensitive man who beat off tribulations to win the hand of Chrissie White in pictorially splendid Hepworth dramas, or proved himself noble and self-sacrificing in stout-hearted adventures like *The Flag Lieutenant* (Maurice Elvey, 1926). But the acting career and his star aura developed hand in hand with pioneering and innovative work as a director, producer and writer. In the 1910s and 20s Edwards proved himself one of the industry's most enlightened and important film-makers, helping to advance British cinema beyond its early concentration on

physical action towards the subtleties of characterisation, feeling and visual design required for the mature feature film. Edwards could sometimes produce imaginative work even when working under the severe constraints of low-budget film-making in the 1930s.

Arthur Harold Ethelbert Edwards was born in Weston-super-Mare, Somerset, on 18 September 1883. Lured to the stage, he trod the boards for fifteen years as an actor, producer and playwright. He began in 1900 in provincial theatres, graduated to London's West End in 1911, and in 1913 played opposite Ethel Barrymore in New York. In films, he played a small role for Harold Shaw in *Clancarty* (1914), but his cinema career only began in earnest when he repeated his stage role in Cecil Hepworth's version of the spy drama *The Man Who Stayed at Home* (1915). The Americans Larry Trimble and Florence Turner, based at Hepworth's Walton studios, quickly hired his services, initially as an actor and writer; his directing debut came with *A Welsh Singer* (1915), adapted from a popular romantic novel. After Edwards' *East Is East* (1916), Turner and Trimble returned to the USA; Edwards then formally joined the Walton studio, generating much of its product along with Hepworth at a time when war service had thinned the company's ranks. The series of films Edwards made co-starring the blonde and lissom Chrissie White flourished until financial woes brought down Hepworth's enterprise in 1924.

From the beginning, Edwards explored new territory in British cinema, particularly in films based on his own original scenarios. The outlines of the mature Edwards hero were already clear in *East Is East*, where Edwards' charmingly boyish East End garage worker kept faith with his love for Florence Turner's cockney heroine through every twist and turn of fate. Other typical early parts included the newsboy in love with an heiress (*Merely Mrs Stubbs*, 1917), a hunchback with a brusque exterior but gentleness within (*Towards the Light*, 1918) and an insane husband accused of murder (*Broken Threads*, 1917): roles requiring Edwards to direct the audience's attention away from melodramatics towards tender interior feelings. As a director he showed a surprising sophistication in his methods of visual storytelling and the use of three-dimensional space, particularly evident in *East Is East*. He became famous for what *The Bioscope*, reviewing *The City of Beautiful Nonsense*, termed 'poetic embellishments' and 'symbolistic touches' (11 November 1919 p. 62): the subjective flashes of dreams or allegory, or other spotlit visual incidents designed to express hopes, fears or particular character traits. In 1923 Edwards' experiments with cinema narrative led him to mount an entire feature without using intertitles: the result, *Lily of the Alley*, now seemingly a lost film, broke new ground in Britain, though contemporary comment suggests a brave attempt rather than a stylistic triumph.

For the bulk of British audiences, the stylistic advances in Edwards' films mattered far less than the allure of their leading players. The films may have been unexportably English in tone – charming, quietly intelligent, rather like the man himself – but at home they raised Edwards and White to a degree of stardom rare in British silent cinema; their marriage in January 1924 created considerable public tumult. With the collapse of the Hepworth company, White withdrew from silent cinema. But Edwards continued working, directing less ambitious films, chiefly at Stoll, before he found renewed acting success with Astra-National as the manly and jovial Dick Lascelles in Elvey's lively account of *The Flag Lieutenant* (1926), a stalwart naval drama.

The film's success, coupled with new prospects offered by government legislation and the new sound technology, encouraged Edwards to join Astra-National's ambitious general manager Julius Hagen in independent production. In 1927 they co-founded the W.P. Film Company to produce films at Twickenham; in 1929 he took over the studio with Hagen and Leslie Hiscott, and personally spearheaded its conversion to sound. 1931 saw his third managerial venture, when he and E. G. Norman purchased, rebuilt and re-equipped Teddington Studios, previously damaged in a fire. Seeking a base for their British product, Warner Bros. promptly negotiated a lease for the property, though not before Edwards shot a lowly production of his own, *Stranglehold* (1931).

Once Edwards' managerial burden lessened, his own output as director increased. Between 1932 and 1933 he made eight low-budget films at Elstree for British and Dominions, beginning with a remake of *The Flag Lieutenant*; afterwards came sixteen for Hagen at Twickenham. None shared the personal imprint of his best silent work; assembly-line production schedules scarcely encouraged the lingering camera details or atmospheric locations previously evoked by his regular cameraman Charles Bryce. Yet Edwards still managed several minor successes. *Squibs* (1935) made a fair attempt at reviving Betty Balfour's cockney charmer, with songs and dances heroically squeezed into Twickenham's cramped spaces. *Scrooge* (1935), featuring the veteran theatre actor Seymour Hicks, rolled along pleasantly in an unusually convincing Victorian setting, while in *Vintage Wine* (1935), another Hicks vehicle, Edwards' determination to avoid a canned play generated camera set-ups and compositions almost as exuberant as the film's star.

Industry recession and the 1938 Films Act cut the demand for 'quota quickies', and Edwards' directing career came to a halt after making *The Vicar of Bray* and *Song of the Forge*, two vehicles for Stanley Holloway, in 1937. But 'Tedwards', as he was genially known, continued to act, playing modest roles as authority figures (police inspectors, majors, judges), and retaining enough of the star aura to worry about whether the cameramen were capturing his best profile. His last appearance was in Robert Hamer's *The Long Memory* (1952). He died suddenly from a heart attack at his home in Chobham, Surrey, on 2 November 1952. Chrissie White lived in retirement until 1987; their daughter, Henryetta Edwards, appeared in several films in the 1950s.

(Geoff Brown and Bryony Dixon)

BIBLIOGRAPHY: Edwards, Henry, 'The Language of Action', *The Bioscope*, 1 July 1920 (supplement), p. iv; Gledhill, Christine, *Reframing British Cinema 1918–1928: Between Restraint and Passion* (London: BFI, 2003); Low, Rachael, *The History of the British Film 1914–1918* (London: George Allen & Unwin, 1950); Low, Rachael, *The History of the British Film 1918–1929* (London: George Allen & Unwin, 1971); Roffe, Edward, 'O! Henry!', *Picturegoer*, Feb. 1924, pp. 38–9; 'So This Is Henry Edwards', *Picturegoer*, Feb. 1921, pp. 12–13.

FILMOGRAPHY: *A Welsh Singer* (1915); *Doorsteps*; *East Is East* (1916); *Merely Mrs Stubbs*; *The Failure* (aka *Dick Carson Wins Through*); *Broken Threads* (1917); *The Hanging Judge*; 'Film Tags' (shorts series: *The Message*); *Against the Grain*; *Old Mother Hubbard*; *Anna*; *Her Savings Saved*; *The Poet's Windfall*; *The Inevitable*; *What's the Use of Grumblin'?*; *The Secret*; *Towards the Light*; *His Dearest Possession*; *The Kinsman*; *Aylwin*; *The Amazing Quest of Mr Ernest Bliss* (serial); *Possession*; *The City of Beautiful Nonsense*; *John Forrest Finds Himself* (1919); *A Temporary Vagabond* (1920); *The Lunatic at Large*; *The Bargain* (1921); *Simple Simon*; *Tit for Tat* (1922); *Lily of the Alley*; *Boden's Boy*; *The Naked Man* (1923); *The World of Wonderful Reality*; *Owd Bob* (1924); *King of the Castle*; *A Girl of London* (1925); *The Island of Despair*; *One Colombo Night* (1926); *The Girl in the Night*; *Stranglehold* (1931); *Brother Alfred*; *The Flag Lieutenant*; *The Barton Mystery* (1932); *Discord*; *Lord of the Manor*; *Purse Strings*; *Anne One Hundred*; *General John Regan*; *One Precious Year* (1933); *Lord Edgware Dies*; *Are You a Mason?*; *The Lash*; *The Man Who Changed His Name* (1934); *D'ye Ken John Peel?* (US: *Captain Moonlight*); *The Lad*; *The Private Secretary*; *Squibs*; *Vintage Wine*; *Scrooge*; *The Rocks of Valpré* (US: *High Treason*) (1935); *In the Soup*; *Juggernaut*; *Eliza Comes to Stay* (1936); *Beauty and the Barge*; *The Vicar of Bray*; *Song of the Forge* (1937).

EDZARD, Christine (1945–)

Christine Edzard was born in Paris on 15 February 1945 to a German father and Polish mother, both artists. After studying economics, her first job was as an assistant to theatre designer Lila di Nobili, and she went on to work in theatre and opera design. While working on an Italian stage production of *Romeo and Juliet* by Franco Zeffirelli, she met and married producer Richard Goodwin, with whom she subsequently formed Sands Films. Her first film credit is as set decorator on Zeffirelli's film version of *Romeo and Juliet* (1968). She worked for two years on the designs for the ballet film *The Tales of Beatrix Potter* (Reginald Mills, 1971), and wrote the script with Richard Goodwin.

In 1975, Edzard and Goodwin took over two disused warehouses in Rotherhithe, London, where they built and equipped a small film studio. Working with the same group of collaborators, Edzard scripted and directed three short films based on stories by Hans Christian Andersen that were released under the

Christine Edzard on the set of *Little Dorrit* (1987)

title *Stories from a Flying Trunk* (1979). Her first feature film, *Biddy* (1983), told how a Victorian nanny, after a lifetime of devotion to one family, is left alone and neglected in old age.

Sands Films' next project was its most ambitious, a six-hour two-part film adaptation of Charles Dickens' *Little Dorrit* (1987). For the huge cast, the company gathered together the cream of the British acting profession from Alec Guinness and Derek Jacobi to music-hall survivor Max Wall, and built a slab of Victorian London in their Rotherhithe studio. As well as adapting the novel with regular collaborator Oliver Stockman and directing the films, Edzard supervised the making of the meticulously accurate handmade costumes. When the film opened, many critics and industry figures were bemused, but it brought Guinness an Academy Award nomination, and attracted enthusiastic audiences.

Edzard followed this with *The Fool* (1990), based on Henry Mayhew's tract *London Labour and the London Poor*, in which Derek Jacobi played a man leading a double life, one poor and one rich. It was a perfect film with which to sign off the 'Thatcher' years of greed and self-interest, though box-office returns were disappointing. She then returned to Shakespeare, adapting *As You Like It* for the screen in 1992, setting the Court in the City of London and the Forest of Arden in an urban wasteland, complete with graffiti. Again, the film had a mixed critical reception and audiences proved elusive. Undaunted, Edzard filmed another Shakespearean adaptation, *The Children's Midsummer Night's Dream* (2001), performed entirely by south London schoolchildren from culturally diverse backgrounds.

Christine Edzard is a unique figure in British cinema, making idiosyncratic films that reflect her personal preoccupations; inevitably this has limited her opportunities for making commercial feature films, though she has been able to retain a degree of independence by a profitable sideline in supplying high quality nineteenth-century costumes for films, musicals and television productions.

(Janet Moat)

BIBLIOGRAPHY: Bergson, Phillip, 'Arden-Fast', *What's on in London*, 7 Oct. 1992, p. 11; Johnston, Sheila, 'Inner-City Fairies Make Magic', *Sunday Telegraph* Review, 10 June 2001, p. 5; Malcolm, Derek, 'The Victorian Virtuoso', *Guardian*, 17 Jan. 1991, p. 22.

FILMOGRAPHY: *Stories from a Flying Trunk* (1979); *The Nightingale* (short, 1981); *Biddy* (1983); *Little Dorrit* (1987); *The Fool* (1990); *As You Like It* (1992); *Amahl and the Night Visitors* (1996); *The IMAX Nutcracker* (short, 1997); *The Children's Midsummer Night's Dream* (2001).

EGOYAN, Atom (1960–)

Atom Egoyan was born in Cairo on 19 July 1960 to Armenian parents, but was brought up in Canada. He began making short films while studying international relations and music at the University of Toronto in the late 1970s, and made his feature debut with *Next of Kin* in 1984. Several more highly acclaimed features followed, most notably *Calendar* (1993), *The Sweet Hereafter* (1997) and *Ararat* (2002). In 1999 he came to Britain to film his adaptation of William Trevor's novel *Felicia's Journey*, the gruesome tale of a pregnant Irish girl preyed upon by a deeply disturbed and grossly overweight catering manager. Egoyan lightens and softens everything, with Bob Hoskins a dapper and saner Mr Hilditch and Elaine Cassidy a prettier and less put-upon Felicia. The use of video to bring alive Hilditch's previous victims (filmed voyeuristically before their deaths) and the character of his monstrous mother (rewritten as a television celebrity chef) are not entirely convincing. The voyeuristic filming is almost forgotten as far as Felicia is concerned, and the sulky pudding of a boy glimpsed on his mother's shows never seems likely to grow into the neat and compact Hoskins. But helped by Paul Sarossy's cinematography, which succeeds in making the Midlands industrial landscape look exotic, and a mesmerising performance from Hoskins, Egoyan captures the aura of the lost and the lonely that pervades Trevor's novel.

Felicia's Journey's Irish connection led to an invitation to make *Krapp's Last Tape* for the 'Beckett on Film' project. His big-budget, Anglo-Canadian-financed *Where the Truth Lies*, featuring Kevin Bacon and Colin Firth as a 1950s' showbiz double-act seedily implicated in sex and murder, thrilled film festival audiences but faced a more mixed reception beyond.

(Robert Murphy)

BIBLIOGRAPHY: Dillon, Mark, 'A Dramatic Quest', *American Cinematographer*, Dec. 1999, pp. 24–31; Porton, Richard, 'The Politics of Denial: An Interview with Atom Egoyan', *Cinéaste* vol. 25 no. 1, Dec. 1999, pp. 39–41; Romney, Jonathan, 'This Green Unpleasant Land', *Sight and Sound*, Oct. 1999, pp. 34–5; Romney, Jonathan, *Atom Egoyan* (London: BFI, 2003); Seguin, Dennis, 'Splitting the Atom', *Screen International*, 3 June 2005, p. 9; Tracy, Tony, 'Atom Egoyan's Journey', *Film West* no. 38, Oct. 1999, pp. 12–17.

FILMOGRAPHY (UK only): *Felicia's Journey* (UK/Can, 1999); *Krapp's Last Tape* (UK/Ir, 2000); *Where the Truth Lies* (UK/Can, 2005)

EICHBERG, Richard (1888–1953)

When Richard Eichberg signed his first contract with British International Pictures early in 1928 he was firmly established as one of Germany's most prolific and popular film-makers, skilled at satisfying audience taste with thrills, the exotic and laughter. Born in Berlin on 27 October 1888, he began as a theatre actor, appearing in films from 1912. His first film as a director, *Strohfeur*, emerged in March 1915; from the beginning he served as his own producer, with his own production company. Crime melodramas were an early speciality, but he was malleable enough to score with other genres, from the historical spectacular (*Monna Vanna*, 1922) to frothy sex-comedies like *Die keusche Susanne* (1926) with Lilian Harvey – one of numerous performers he led to stardom.

Perceived as one of the more 'American' of European directors, Eichberg was an obvious hiring choice when in 1928 British International Pictures in 1928 joined other companies to fight strong American competition through European production alliances. A German distribution outlet, Südfilm, was acquired, and a deal struck for a series of German-language Eichberg-BIP films, with production based in Berlin; six emerged within thirteen months, with Eichberg himself directing four. *Song* (UK: *Show Life*, US: *Wasted Love*), an increasingly melodramatic vehicle for Anna May Wong, was the first to roll in May 1928. The Chinese-American performer also inspired *Grossstadtschmetterling* (UK: *Pavement Butterfly*, 1929), thinner as drama, but equally in thrall to a stereotyped scenario of mixed-race relationships (death or loneliness was always Wong's fate) and the star's oriental beauty. English locations – London, Southampton harbour – were sometimes visited, but perhaps the chief English influence on these German films was the cautious treatment of sex and race. 'Eroticism without sex-appeal, exoticism without miscegenation', snorted *Film-Kurier*, reviewing the later *Hai-Tang* (quoted in Bergfelder, p. 313) – a film typical in the plot's opposition of a fragile innocent woman and a brutal male, and the preponderance of isolating, often tearful, close-ups.

By 1930 Eichberg was launched on his second BIP contract, requiring production at Elstree. Sound production was now firmly established; each film was to be executed in three versions, in English, German and French, using changing casts and Eichberg's regular cameraman (Heinrich Gärtner) and art director (Willi A. Herrmann). Tawdry in plot, halting in execution, unlikely in setting, *Hai-Tang*, produced in English as *The Flame of Love*, placed Wong's passive Chinese dancer in pre-Revolutionary Russia, at imminent risk from a Grand Duke's attentions. Following production problems and poor box-office takings, Eichberg's French partner Jacques Haïk then abandoned ship. Subsequent multilingual projects sought material closer to England. *Der Greifer*, the German version of the second subject, a crime drama, *Night Birds*, proved popular abroad, and encouraged Hans Albers, cast as its Scotland Yard detective, to pursue similar action parts; the English version featuring Jameson Thomas found much less favour. The third and last of these BIP multilinguals, the musical comedy *Let's Love and Laugh* (in German, *Die Bräutigamswitwe*), dallied briefly with sophistication but increasingly settled for broad comedy, lightened by two attractive songs and Gene Gerrard's endearing turn as the bridegroom who wakes from a boozy celebration to discover he's married a chorus girl.

By 1931 BIP's expansionist, international phase was drawing to a close. Eichberg returned to Germany, where he cultivated more stars, pursued more film 'sensations' and mounted further multi-language ventures. The wide success in 1938 of *Der Tiger von Eschnapur* and *Das indische Grabmal* – exotic adventure stories first filmed by Joe May in 1921 – finally emboldened Eichberg to try his fortune in America. He took American citizenship and signed with Paul Kohner, faithful agent to German-speaking émigrés who considered Hollywood the Promised Land. Yet ironically for this 'American' director, America gave him few opportunities. No known film work resulted, though he did help mount a revival season of operettas at Carnegie Hall in 1942.

Eichberg returned to Germany in 1949, a decade of his career essentially lost. He directed again (*Die Reise nach Marrakesch*) and launched another film company, which enjoyed neither clout nor success. He died in Munich on 8 May 1953 – a German pioneer, and one of the people who briefly made BIP 'international', but a figure who had outlived his time.

(Geoff Brown)

BIBLIOGRAPHY: Bergfelder, Tim, 'Negotiating Exoticism: Hollywood, Film Europe and the Cultural Reception of Anna May Wong', in Andrew Higson and Richard Maltby (eds), *'Film Europe' and 'Film America': Cinema, Commerce and Cultural Exchange, 1920–1939* (Exeter: University of Exeter Press, 1999); Wedel, Michael and Ingrun Spazier, 'Richard Eichberg', *CineGraph: Lexicon zum deutschsprachigen Film* (Munich: edition text+kritik, 1984, supplement 33).

FILMOGRAPHY (UK only): *The Flame of Love*; *Night Birds* (1930); *Let's Love and Laugh* (US: *Bridegroom for Two*, 1931).

ELDER, Clarence

Clarence Elder was born in Glasgow. He worked in British films as an art director from 1929 onwards, supervising the art department at Elstree for British International Pictures and its successor, Associated British. His most ambitious designs, devised with John Mead, appeared in Karl Grune's expensive epic *Abdul the Damned* (1935). After supervising a camouflage unit during the war, Elder briefly joined Grune in production, shepherding actor Clifford Evans through *The Silver Darlings*, a worthy if romanticised history of the Scottish herring fleet. Elder's documentary *The Little Singer* dealt with Glasgow housing problems.

(Robert Murphy)

FILMOGRAPHY: *The Silver Darlings* (co-dir. Clifford Evans, 1947); *The Little Singer* (doc. short, 1956).

ELDRIDGE, John (1917–1962)

John Stuart Eldridge was born in Folkestone, Kent, on 26 July 1917 and educated at Haileybury School. After working for Herbert Wilcox as an assistant editor between 1936 and 1939, Eldridge formed an independent company with the cinematographer Martin Curtis to make short documentaries. This venture did not last long, and he spent the bulk of the war as a director for Strand Films, where the team included the poet Dylan Thomas. Eldridge worked with Thomas on *New Towns for Old*, a seven-minute film publicising plans to rebuild Britain's blitzed inner cities, which anticipated many of the better-known feature documentaries dealing with post-war reconstruction, such as Paul Rotha's *Land of Promise* (1946) and Jill Craigie's *The Way We Live* (1946). Both director and writer found more room to manoeuvre in the forty-five-minute *Our Country*, an impressionistic and poetic survey of British life seen through the eyes of a merchant seaman returning after two years at sea. The film lacks the imaginative leaps and juxtaposi-

tions of Humphrey Jennings' *A Diary for Timothy* (1945), but its lyrical style and ambition secured Eldridge's position as a major new talent in the field.

After the war, Eldridge moved to Greenpark Productions, one of the many documentary production companies that had sprung up during the war under the Ministry of Information sponsorship. Here he built on the foundations of *Our Country* with two impressive documentaries, both photographed by Martin Curtis: the half-hour *Waverley Steps*, another impressionistic portrait, followed a day in the life of an Edinburgh train driver and his family; the sixty-one-minute *Three Dawns to Sydney*, commissioned by BOAC, ingeniously saluted the company's new passenger service to Australia by focusing on incidents from daily lives in the countries flown over *en route*. After leaving Greenpark, Eldridge worked briefly at Ealing, where he put his documentary background to profitable use on the screenplay for *Pool of London* (Basil Dearden, 1951).

Eldridge's own move into fiction direction followed shortly afterwards under the auspices of Group 3, a production outfit funded by the National Film Finance Corporation, which offered opportunities to various new talents. Eldridge's *Brandy for the Parson* (1952) was among the first products to emerge. Benign, lyrically photographed, but dramatically lackadaisical, this comedy about a young yachting couple who become mixed up with brandy smuggling established the timidly whimsical, sub-Ealing style of Group 3 comedies. Eldridge's next film, *Laxdale Hall*, which featured Hebridean villagers battling Whitehall bureaucracy, took Group 3 further into Ealing territory, with equally pleasant if mild results. *Conflict of Wings*, Eldridge's only film in colour, strengthened its hand by using community conflict for drama rather than comedy, though the pastoral appeal of its story about Norfolk villagers fighting to prevent a bird sanctuary becoming an RAF rocket-firing range was not the kind to inflame wide audiences.

Eldridge's Group 3 films remained among the company's most watchable product, yet they scarcely fulfilled the distinctive talent shown in his documentaries of the 1940s. Worsening health (he contracted tuberculosis in the early 1950s) restricted further opportunities. *Out of the Clouds* (1955), which he was to direct for Ealing, had to be reassigned to Relph and Dearden; but he continued in work chiefly as a valued screenwriter for features and documentaries, notably on Clive Donner's fresh, nuanced youth drama *Some People* (1962). He also directed commercials for J. Walter Thompson. Eldridge died of tuberculosis in Brompton Hospital, London, on 14 June 1962.

(Geoff Brown and Leo Enticknap)

BIBLIOGRAPHY: Ackerman, John (ed.), *Dylan Thomas: The Complete Screenplays* (New York: Applause Books, 1995); Richard Dyer, 'Subsidy for the Screen: Grierson and Group Three, 1951–55', *Sight and Sound*, Summer 1977, pp. 168–73; 'Two Views on *Our Country*', *Documentary News Letter* vol. 5 no. 4, 1944, p. 46.

FILMOGRAPHY: Documentaries: *Sea Lights* (co-dir. Martin Curtis, 1939); *The Story of Michael Flaherty*; *The Village School*; *Ashley Green Goes to School*; *S.O.S.* (1940); *War Front*; *Tank Patrol*; *Architects of England* (1941); *Young Farmers*; *New Towns for Old*; *Trinity House*; *Wales – Green Mountain Black Mountain* (1942); *Fuel for Battle*; *Our Country*; *Conquest of a Germ* (1944); *A City Reborn*; *Time and Tide*; *A Soldier Comes Home* (1945); *Civil Engineering: Post-War Jobs*; *North East Corner*; *Park Here* (1947); *Waverley Steps*; *Three Dawns to Sydney* (1948); *A Penny for Your Thoughts* (1960).

Features: *Brandy for the Parson* (1952); *Laxdale Hall* (US: *Scotch on the Rocks*, 1953); *Conflict of Wings* (US: *Fuss over Feathers*, assoc. dir. Don Sharp, 1954).

EL HAGAR, Khaled (also Khalid Al Hagar, Khalid Al Haggar) (1963–)

Khaled El Hagar was born in Egypt in 1963. After graduating in law from Cairo University, he entered the Egyptian film industry in 1985, working as a casting and assistant director on local and foreign productions. During this period he served a three-year apprenticeship with the great Egyptian director Youssef Chahine. El Hagar's first short film, *You Are My Life* (1989), made him £15,000 via television sales, enabling him to enrol at the UK's National Film and Television School where he made a further short, *Doody's Dream*. He then took leave from the course to direct his first feature, *Little Dreams* (*Ahlam Saghira*, 1993) – set in Suez during the 1967 Six-Day War against Israel – in Egypt.

However, Egyptian official reaction to El Hagar's forty-minute 1994 NFTS graduation film, *A Gulf between Us*, set in

London during the 1991 Gulf War, made it near impossible for him to direct in Egypt again. El Hagar had thought his film – about family opposition to the romance between an Arab (played by El Hagar) and his young Jewish landlady – told a 'very simple human story', but in Egypt it was banned as 'unpatriotic and supportive of Israel' and he was dropped even by the liberal Chahine.

Room to Rent, so far El Hagar's only British feature, expanded on the theme of the search for love and acceptance amid the London melting pot of cultures and personalities, but played it as fast-moving, cartoonish farce. Saïd Taghmaoui plays a young Egyptian would-be screenwriter in search of a free room and a British visa whose looks provide the passport to an atypical illegal-immigrant experience as a belly-dancing teacher and gay photographer's model, while the eccentricities of his various landlords provide a mind-broadening education.

Co-produced by the Film Consortium, FilmFour and France's Canal+, *Room to Rent* exuded considerable visual style and comic energy. But its sexual frankness and social liberalism brought another Egyptian ban and its UK reception was dismissive. The blend of comedy, illegal immigration and public subsidy incensed some British critics; many more were perplexed by the film's denouement involving reincarnation and a marriage of convenience to a blind septuagenarian (Anna Massey). It was better liked abroad, winning a 2001 prize at the pan-African film festival FESPACO and the 2000 Audience Award at Turin. Subsequently, El Hagar has directed *Hob el banat* (2004), a lightweight Egyptian romantic comedy.

(Claire Monk)

BIBLIOGRAPHY: Kemp, Philip, '*Room to Rent*', *Sight and Sound*, July 2001, pp. 52–3; Malcolm, Derek, 'Banned Again', *Guardian* G2 Section, 19 June 2001; '*Room to Rent*', *44th London Film Festival* catalogue, 2000, p. 45.

FILMOGRAPHY (UK only): *Doody's Dream* (short, 1992); *A Gulf between Us* (short, 1994); *Room to Rent* (2000).

ELTON, Arthur (1906–1973)

Sir Arthur Hallam Rice Elton was a key figure in the documentary movement of the 1930s. He first won acclaim for exquisitely photographed instructional films showing the stylistic influences of silent Russian cinema, and pioneered the use of location photography and sound recording – a fearsome technical challenge when the equipment needed to record sound on location occupied a lorry. Born in London on 10 February 1906, the son of the ninth Baron Elton, he attended Marlborough School and studied English and psychology at Jesus College, Cambridge. After leaving university he worked briefly in the scenario department at Gainsborough before joining John Grierson at the Empire Marketing Board Film Unit in 1931. His younger brother Ralph (1914–1968) also worked in documentaries as a director and assistant.

Grierson was anxious to establish other sources of funding for documentaries besides the taxpayer, and he encouraged Elton to develop links with industry in producing commercially sponsored films. He had an early success with *Voice of the World* (1932), about the manufacture of radios, sponsored by His Master's Voice. Elton's sophisticated tastes in montage and visual composition found their best outlet in *Aero Engine* (1933), a meticulous six-reel documentation of the construction of aeroplane engines. With its coverage of unemployed men speaking directly to camera, *Workers and Jobs* (1935), made for the Ministry of Labour, marked a change in direction, further pursued in *Housing Problems* and *Enough to Eat?*, devised with Edgar Anstey for the British Commercial Gas Association and the Gas Light and Coke Company. In *Housing Problems* (1935) Elton and Anstey turned their back on aesthetic experiments to concentrate on showing the appalling conditions in slum tenements and – uniquely – allowing the inhabitants to talk about their problems. *Housing Problems* (jointly directed with Anstey) and *Enough to Eat?* (1936, credited to Anstey alone) proved highly influential with politicians and town planners as well as other documentary film-makers.

Arthur Elton (left)

Elton's last work as a director was on two gas promotion films featuring the London chef Marcel Boulestin; from the late 1930s onwards he became increasingly involved in the organisation of film production in Britain and abroad. In 1938 he co-founded the documentary co-ordinating body Film Centre. During the war, he worked as a producer for the Ministry of Information, and later advised the Danish government and the Allied authorities running the film industry in post-war occupied Germany. An adviser and producer with the Shell Film Unit since 1936, he cemented his association in 1957 by becoming the Unit's Head of Production, further strengthening its position among British documentary companies at a time of modest revival in the non-fiction movement's fortunes. He assumed the Elton baronetcy in 1951, and complemented his later film activities with community projects in Somerset, where the family home, Clevedon Court, was handed to the National Trust in 1960. He died in London on 1 January 1973.

(Geoff Brown and Leo Enticknap)

BIBLIOGRAPHY: Rotha, Paul, *Documentary Film*, 3rd edn (London: Faber and Faber, 1952); 'Sir Arthur Elton', *Film Dope* no. 21, Oct. 1980, pp. 29–30; Sussex, Elizabeth, *The Rise and Fall of British Documentary* (Berkeley: University of California Press, 1975).

FILMOGRAPHY: *Shadow on the Mountain/An Experiment in the Welsh Hills*; *Upstream* (shortened version, *Salmon Leap*, 1931); *Voice of the World* (1932); *Aero Engine* (1933); *John Atkins Saves Up* (1934); *Housing Problems* (co-dir. Edgar Anstey); *Men behind the Meters; Workers and Jobs* (1935); *A Scratch Meal* (1936); *Party Dish by X. Marcel Boulestin* (1937).

ELTON, Ben (1958–)

Ben Elton was born in London on 3 May 1958. His family, originally surnamed Ehrenberg, were Jewish émigrés from Nazi Germany; his uncle was the formidable Tudor historian Geoffrey Elton, his grandfather the classical scholar Victor Ehrenberg. After studying at Manchester University, Elton established himself as one of the pioneers of alternative comedy. He performed regularly at the Comedy Store in Soho, and broke into television in 1982, writing *The Young Ones* with Rik Mayall and Lise Mayer, going on to compere *Saturday Live*, help Richard Curtis on the various *Blackadder* series and write *The Thin Blue Line* as an alternative vehicle for Rowan Atkinson.

Elton also wrote half a dozen best-selling novels, among them *Inconceivable*, simultaneously written as a screenplay with the more catchy title of *Maybe Baby*. He insisted on directing the film himself, telling an interviewer: 'It's a romantic comedy and it's about people. And I felt I understood it best. I didn't want to be sitting on the sidelines, white-knuckled with frustration while some gag got mistimed' (Martinez, p. 18). Anxious to avoid the results being labelled 'a comedy about infertility', Elton steered away from any head-on treatment of the pain and anxiety that failure to conceive can bring, and directed the film as a farce. Unfortunately, he handles the silly plot (husband uses wife's secret diary about attempts to overcome infertility to resurrect his flagging writing career) with little sense of pace, and the leaps from vulgarity to sentimentality, from pathos to caricature, stretch audience sympathy for Hugh Laurie and Joely Richardson's smug couple. Well-known television faces in the cast proved enough to bring respectable UK box-office returns, but foreign audiences were more discerning.

Elton went on to write *We Will Rock You*, a successful West End musical showcasing the hit songs of the glam-rock band Queen. His venture into film directing looks like a one-off digression rather than a serious career move.

(Robert Murphy)

BIBLIOGRAPHY: Martinez, José, 'Maybe Baby – An Interview with Ben Elton', *Creative Screenwriting* vol. 8 no. 4, July/Aug. 2001, p. 18; Medhurst, Andy, 'Funny Games', *Sight and Sound*, Nov. 2000, pp. 28–31; Wise, Damon, 'Ben Elton', *Total Film*, July 2000, p. 34.

FILMOGRAPHY: *Maybe Baby* (UK/Fr, 2000).

ELTRINGHAM, Bille and Simon BEAUFOY (1967–)

Bille Eltringham worked in the theatre before attending the Bournemouth Film School, where she directed the short film *Lune* (1992), a success on the lesbian and gay festival circuit. Following graduation, she teamed up with fellow students Simon Beaufoy and Mark Blaney to form Footprint Films. Various shorts followed, including two co-directed with Simon Beaufoy: *Physics for Fish* (1993) for the BBC shorts slot '10 x 10' and *Yellow* (1996) for Channel 4. In 1998 Eltringham and Beaufoy collaborated on their first full-length movie, *The Darkest Light*. Beaufoy had by this time enjoyed enormous success with his script for the working-class comedy *The Full Monty* (Peter Cattaneo, 1997), but *The Darkest Light* is a much bleaker affair. Set in Yorkshire during an outbreak of foot-and-mouth disease, the film deals with the response of a young girl's family and community to her apparent religious vision. Sympathetically observed and shot in a clear, unfussy style, the film is quietly effective in a way that successfully combines Ken Loach's social observation with an unforced sense of the supernatural; it is also notable for anticipating the ravages that befell the countryside in the wake of Britain's BSE crisis. Although well received critically, the film's lack of commercial elements led only to limited distribution. Eltringham then worked on *Kid in the*

Corner (1999), a three-part series for Channel 4 written by Tony Marchant.

Beaufoy and Eltringham were reunited on *This Is Not a Love Song* (2002). A cat-and-mouse thriller, concerning the pursuit of two fugitives by vigilante farmers following an accidental shooting, the film was shot entirely on digital video over twelve days. Although shown in cinemas, *This Is Not a Love Song* was also officially premiered on the net, prompting the website to crash when it initially went 'live'. Deliberately committed to a DV rather than a film aesthetic, *Love Song* is notable for its experimental approach to camerawork and point of view, contrasting sharply with the observational style of *The Darkest Light* and the careful reconstruction of the recent past in her telling television adaptation of Jake Arnott's collection of tales around a 1960s gangster, *The Long Firm* (2004).

(John Hill)

BIBLIOGRAPHY: James, Nick, 'Digital Deluge', *Sight and Sound*, Oct. 2001, pp. 20–4; Soutar, Ian, 'Keeping Faith with a Vision' (interview with Simon Beaufoy), *Exposure*, Autumn 1998 pp. 26–7.

FILMOGRAPHY: *Lune* (short, 1992); *Physics for Fish* (short, co-dir. Simon Beaufoy, 1993); *Linger* (short, 1994); *Yellow* (short, co-dir. Simon Beaufoy, 1996); *The Trick is to Keep Breathing* (short, co-dir. Simon Beaufoy, 1997); *The Darkest Light* (co-dir. Simon Beaufoy, 1998); *This Is Not a Love Song* (2002).

ELVEY, Maurice (1887–1967)

Maurice Elvey was born William Seward Folkard on 11 November 1887 in Stockton-on-Tees. He left home while still a child, seeking his fortune in London, where he worked variously as a kitchen hand and hotel pageboy, and later as an actor and stagehand. Ambitious and hard-working, Elvey rose quickly to directing and producing plays, establishing his own theatrical company before switching to films in 1912. He directed an array of comedies and dramas for the Motograph company and British and Colonial, most of them starring Elizabeth Risdon and Fred Groves, including the melodrama *Maria Marten; Or, The Murder in the Red Barn* (1913), an adaptation of Robert Louis Stevenson's *The Suicide Club* (1914), and a version of Shakespeare's *As You Like It*, more plainly titled *Love in a Wood* (1915).

By the end of the First World War, Elvey was making popular features in a variety of genres. Best known are his biographical films, of Florence Nightingale, Nelson and Lloyd George. These reveal a Janus-faced director, working firmly in a tradition of Victorian hagiography, but clearly searching for contemporary relevance. They show some startlingly modern touches of associative editing and a facility for location and crowd scenes. Indeed it has been argued that if his *Life Story of David Lloyd George* (1918) had not been suppressed for political reasons, British cinema may have taken a different direction (Berry and Horrocks). The rediscovery of this remarkable film has forced a reappraisal both of British cinema in this period generally, and of Elvey's (largely lost) output in particular.

By the early 1920s Elvey had become the chief director at Stoll, a studio that gained a reputation for swift, unimaginative literary adaptations, but was one of the first to model itself as a major producer with a distinctively national output. In 1924 he went to America, where he made five films for the Fox Film Corporation. He returned in 1925, putting his experience to especially good use on the psychologically sophisticated Anglo-German melodrama *Human Law/Tragödie Einer Ehe* (1926) and *Hindle Wakes* (1927), *Roses of Picardy* (1927), *Palais de Danse* (1928) and *High Treason* (1929): films that display an awareness of visual storytelling and spectacle often lacking in his later work. *Hindle Wakes* is a particularly successful example of Elvey's blend of realism, melodrama and sense of location.

During the 1930s Elvey's tireless energy led him to work across the spectrum of British production, on 'quota quickies' as well as on ambitious productions such as *The Tunnel* for Gaumont-British. At Ealing he made Gracie Fields' first film, *Sally in Our Alley* (1931) – notably more realistic and downbeat in tone than her later vehicles – and subsequently *This Week of Grace* and *Love, Life and Laughter*. During the Second World War he worked with Leslie Howard on the critically praised *The Gentle Sex* (1943) and took over direction on *The Lamp Still Burns* (1943) after Howard's death. *Medal for the General*, his wartime production for British National, and his big-budget post-war melodrama *Beware of Pity* are also worthy of consideration. Elvey continued to direct a wide variety of dramas and comedies until failing eyesight forced his retirement in 1957.

With such a massive output, and working at such speed, it is inevitable that many of Elvey's films have a perfunctory flavour. But the best of his work, particularly from the silent period, reveals a sympathetic and imaginative craftsman whose role in shaping British cinema has been unjustly neglected in favour of more flashy and less experienced contemporaries. He died in Brighton on 28 August 1967.

(Lawrence Napper)

BIBLIOGRAPHY: Berry, David and Simon Horrocks (eds), *David Lloyd George: The Movie Mystery* (Cardiff: University of Wales Press, 1998); Wood, Linda, *The Commercial Imperative in the British Industry: Maurice Elvey, a Case Study* (London: BFI, 1987).

FILMOGRAPHY: *The Fallen Idol* (short); *Bridegrooms Beware* (short); *The Great Gold Robbery* (short); *Maria Marten; Or, The Murder in the Red Barn*; *Popsy Wopsy* (short) (1913); *The Cup Final Mystery* (short); *Inquisitive Ike* (short); *Black-Eyed Susan* (aka *The Battling British/In the Days of Trafalgar*); *The Suicide Club*; *The Loss of the Birkenhead*; *Beautiful Jim* (US: *The Price of Justice*); *Lest We Forget* (short); *The Bells of Rheims* (short); *The White Feather* (short); *It's a Long, Long Way to Tipperary*; *Her Luck in London*; *The Sound of Her Voice* (short); *The Idol of Paris* (1914); *There's Good in Everyone* (short); *A Honeymoon for Three*; *Gilbert Gets Tiger-itis* (short); *Gilbert Dying to Die* (short); *Midshipman Easy*; *London's Yellow Peril* (short); *Florence Nightingale*; *From Shopgirl to Duchess*; *Her Nameless Child*; *Grip*; *Home*; *A Will of Her Own*; *Charity Ann*; *Fine Feathers*; *Love in a Wood* (1915); *Meg the Lady*; *Esther*; *Driven* (US: *Desperation*); *Money for Nothing*; *Vice Versa*; *Mother Love*; *When Knights Were Bold*; *Trouble for Nothing* (short); *The Princess of Happy Chance*; *The King's Daughter* (1916); *Smith*; *The Grit of a Jew*; *The Woman Who Was Nothing*; *Justice*; The *Gay Lord Quex*; *Flames*; *Dombey and Son*; *Mary Girl* (1917); *Nelson: The Story of England's Immortal Hero*; *The Greatest Wish in the World*; *Hindle Wakes*; *Goodbye*; *Adam Bede*; *The Life Story of David Lloyd George* (1918); *Comradeship*; *Keeper of the Door*; *The Rocks of Valpre*; *God's Good Man*; *Mister Wu*; *The Swindler*; *The Elusive Pimpernel*; *Bleak House* (1919); *The Victory Leaders* (short); *The Amateur Gentleman*; *At the Villa Rose*; *The Hundredth Chance*; *Question of Trust*; *The Tavern Knight* (1920); *Innocent*; *The Tragedy of a Comic Song* (short); *A Gentleman of France*; *The Adventures of Sherlock Holmes* (series); *The Hound of the Baskervilles*; *The Fruitful Vine*; *A Romance of Westdale* (1921); *The Passionate Friends*; *Man and His Kingdom*; *Dick Turpin's Ride to York*; *Running Water*; *A Debt of Honour* (1922); *The Sign of Four*; *The Wandering Jew*; *Guy Fawkes*; *The Royal Oak*; *Don Quixote*; *Sally Bishop* (1923); *Henry, King of Navarre*; *Slaves of Destiny*; *The Love Story of Aliette Brunton*; *My Husband's Wives* (US); *The Folly of Vanity* (US); *Curleytop* (US) (1924); *She Wolves* (US); *Every Man's Wife* (US) (1925); *Haunted Houses and Castles of Britain* (series of shorts); *The Woman Tempted*; *Human Law/Tragödie Einer Ehe* (UK/Ger); *The Flag Lieutenant*; *Mademoiselle from Armentières* (1926); *Hindle Wakes* (US: *Fanny Hawthorne*); *Roses of Picardy*; *The Glad Eye*; *The Flight Commander*; *Quinneys* (1927); *Mademoiselle Parley-Voo*; *Palais de Danse*; *You Know What Sailors Are*; *Balaclava* (US: *Jaws of Hell*, co-dir. Milton Rosmer) (1928); *High Treason* (1929); *The School for Scandal*; *Potiphar's Wife* (US: *Her Strange Desire*) (1930); *Sally in Our Alley*; *A Honeymoon Adventure* (US: *Footsteps in the Night*); *Water Gipsies*; *Frail Women* (1931); *In a Monastery Garden*; *The Marriage Bond*; *The Lodger* (US: *The Phantom Fiend*); *Diamond Cut Diamond* (US: *Blame the Woman*, co-dir. Fred Niblo); *Soldiers of the King* (US: *The Woman in Command*) (1932); *The Lost Chord*; *I Lived with You*; *This Week of Grace*; *The Wandering Jew*; *Lily of Killarney* (US: *The Bride of the Lake*); *Princess Charming* (1933); *Love, Life and Laughter*; *My Song for You*; *Road House*; *Heat Wave* (1934); *The Clairvoyant* (US: *The Evil Mind*); *The Tunnel* (US: *Transatlantic Tunnel*) (1935); *Spy of Napoleon*; *The Man in the Mirror*; *A Romance in Flanders* (US: *Lost on the Western Front*) (1936); *Change for a Sovereign*; *Who Killed John Savage?*; *Melody and Romance* (1937); *Who Goes Next*; *Lightning Conductor*; *The Return of the Frog* (1938); *Sword of Honour*; *Sons of the Sea*; *The Spider* (1939); *For Freedom* (co-dir. *Castleton Knight*); *Room for Two*; *Under Your Hat*; *Goofer Trouble* (short) (1940); *Salute John Citizen* (1942); *The Gentle Sex* (co-dir. Leslie Howard); *The Lamp Still Burns* (1943); *Medal for the General* (US: *The Gay Intruders*, 1944); *Strawberry Roan* (1945); *Beware of Pity* (1946); *The Third Visitor*; *The Late Edwina Black* (US: *The Obsessed*) (1951); *My Wife's Lodger*; *The Great Game*; *Is Your Honeymoon Really Necessary?*; *House of Blackmail* (1953); *The Gay Dog*; *The Happiness of Three Women* (US: *Wishing Well*); *What Every Woman Wants*; *The Harassed Hero* (1954); *You Lucky People*; *Room in the House* (1955); *Fun at St Fanny's*; *Dry Rot*; *Stars in Your Eyes* (1956); *Second Fiddle* (1957).

EMLYN, Endaf (1944–)

Endaf Emlyn was born near Bangor, North Wales, on 31 July 1944 and grew up in Pwllheli. He worked as a musician and presenter with HTV and a television comedy scriptwriter before directing S4C youth programmes. His pop group documentary *Shampw* won the 1983 Spirit of the Festival award at the Celtic Film and Television Festival. Later in the 1980s he made a quirky, television quasi-Western set in Patagonia, *Gaucho* (S4C, 1985), which became the name of his production company. His next drama, *Stormydd Awst/Storms of August*, dealing with television's arrival in a North Wales community, was marred by laboured caricature and seemed regressive – but it was the first Welsh-language feature to be distributed on 35mm in cinemas. His next two films, *Un Nos Ola Leuad/One Full Moon* and *Gadael Lenin/Leaving Lenin*, established him as the most important director in Wales to work in his indigenous language.

Un Nos Ola Leuad, an overtly downbeat but strangely affirmative chamber piece of great beauty and maturity, drew on a 1961 novel by Caradog Prichard and certain of Prichard's other autobiographical works. It centres on a morose man (played by Dyfan Roberts) who finds absolution in suicide. Scenes showing his inexorable moves towards oblivion are intercut with flashbacks of the incidents in his youth that created his overwhelming sense of guilt – especially his role in his mother's incarceration and treatment for insanity. The film, which made fine use of Welsh rural locations, won acclaim in Japan and Australia but failed to travel beyond art houses in Britain.

Leaving Lenin/Gadael Lenin, which won the audience award for the most popular British feature at the 1993 London Film Festival, was shot in Leningrad, and uses the comic misadventures around a secondary school trip to Russia to explore marital and homosexual relationships, culture clashes at a time of great political upheaval and, through one character's observations on Soviet iconographic painting, the responsibilities and conflicting loyalties of the artist.

Emlyn's *Mapiwr/The Making of Maps* (1995) made impressive use of bucolic characters and pastoral backdrops for an absorbing, tactile rites-of-passage film that carried interesting echoes of Andrew Birkin's adaptation of Ian McEwan's *The Cement Garden* (1993). Emlyn later directed one series of S4C's BAFTA Cymru award-winning contemporary serial *Tair Chwaer/Three Sisters* (1997–9), centring on the lives of modern working-class women. In 1999 he made his English-language drama debut with HTV's three-part *In the Company of Strangers*, revolving around murder, corruption and the then newly formed Welsh Assembly, but set in 2001.

(David Berry)

BIBLIOGRAPHY: Berry, David, *Wales and the Cinema: The First 100 Years* (Cardiff: University of Wales Press, 1994); Dobson, Patricia, 'Profile: Endaf Emlyn', *Screen International Supplement, LFF*, 8 Nov. 1993, p. 5.

FILMOGRAPHY: *Stormydd Awst/Storms of August* (1988); *Un Nos Ola Leuad/One Full Moon* (1991); *Gadael Lenin/Leaving Lenin* (1993); *Mapiwr/The Making of Maps* (1995).

ENDFIELD, Cy (1914–1995)

Cyril Raker Endfield was born in Scranton, Pennsylvania, on 10 November 1914. He attended Yale University, where he became briefly involved with the Young Communist League. He also developed an interest in magic and card tricks, forming the basis for a later reputation as one of the world's leading magicians.

After working with progressive theatre groups in New York, touring the Catskills mountain resorts with his own satirical revue troupe and running an amateur theatre in Montreal, Endfield moved to Los Angeles, where his card skills so impressed Orson Welles that he was taken on as an apprentice in Welles' production company, Mercury. He made his own debut film with *Inflation* (1942), a witty propaganda short for MGM warning the wartime public against the dangers of excessive materialism. It was condemned as anti-capitalist by the US Chamber of Commerce and shelved, not being publicly shown until nearly fifty years later.

Military service and seven other short films followed before Endfield was able to make his debut feature in 1946. His seven American features are all low-budget affairs, including three Poverty Row B-films, an RKO Tarzan adventure and *The Argyle Secrets*, a mystery based on his own radio show. Most notable were two striking and powerful independent productions of 1950. *The Sound of Fury* is perhaps Endfield's most highly regarded work: despite a tendency to preach, its story of an ordinary man drawn into crime and ultimately becoming the victim of a lynch mob offers little in the way of easy comfort or optimism. Less celebrated but just as extraordinary is *The Underworld Story*, a comprehensively subversive film noir with Dan Duryea as possibly the least sympathetic protagonist in the genre's history.

In 1951 Endfield was identified as a Communist by the HUAC, and rather than name names or submit to blacklisting he opted to leave Hollywood for Britain. Like Joseph Losey and others, he found work directing filmed series for television. Three episodes of *Colonel March of Scotland Yard*, starring Boris Karloff, were edited together as *Colonel March Investigates* (1953), his first British feature. Four other B-thrillers followed, all with second-rank American leads, and directed and written pseudonymously to avoid distribution problems in the USA. A friend, Charles de Lautour, lent his name as a 'front' for two of these films and as co-director on a third, *Child in the House*. This sentimental drama was also Endfield's first film with the Welsh actor Stanley Baker, who became his most frequent collaborator, though its bourgeois setting seems uncongenial for both star and director.

By contrast, *Hell Drivers* is a proletarian action melodrama grounded in authentically grubby settings and with a remarkable cast of rugged character actors (Baker, Patrick McGoohan, Sean Connery) as fiercely competitive road haulage workers. Its brawling, brute vigour bears out Endfield's conviction that 'there is plenty of natural drama in the everyday jobs of men with physical contact with reality . . . with the survival jobs, the basic

jobs, the contact with reality is reduced to simple, basic terms. And that is essentially cinematic' (quoted in Peters, p. 27). *Sea Fury*, with Baker, Victor McLaglen and Robert Shaw as tugboat seamen in action off the Spanish coast, is structurally and thematically similar but otherwise inferior, being disproportionately dominated by romantic interest until an excitingly staged climax in a storm.

Endfield's next few films were more conventional assignments. *Jet Storm* is a routine 'group jeopardy' suspenser of a kind common in the 1950s. *Mysterious Island* is a Jules Verne fantasy with several sub-standard Ray Harryhausen monsters. The poorly received *Hide and Seek*, a cold war comedy-drama starring Ian Carmichael, sat on the shelf for nearly two years before being released. Throughout this period Endfield worked extensively in television commercials and also returned to the stage, directing Bob Monkhouse and Michael Crawford in a long West End run of Neil Simon's *Come Blow Your Horn*.

His greatest success, however, came with *Zulu*, the epic story of the defence of Rorke's Drift, which he co-produced with Baker. Endfield evidently responded to the opportunity to work on a large scale, and the film vividly displays his penchant for lateral tracking shots and composition in depth. A smash hit in Britain and in most world territories, it is one of the cinema's finest portrayals of close-quarters military combat, of masculine grace under pressure and of heroism without triumphalism.

A sixth and final film with Baker, *Sands of the Kalahari*, was hit by various problems, including the withdrawal of original casting choices Richard Burton, Elizabeth Taylor and George Peppard. Nonetheless, the struggle for survival and supremacy between plane crash victims in the African desert makes for an impressively stark adventure, with the ostensible all-American hero (Stuart Whitman) gradually revealed as a fascistic psychopath. *De Sade*, an attempt by American International Pictures to make a 'prestige' movie, was another troubled production. Screenwriter Richard Matheson disliked the restructuring of his deliberately fragmentary narrative into a more orthodox, but still confusing, chronological biography, while Endfield fell seriously ill on location in Germany and had to be replaced, without credit, by Roger Corman.

Endfield's last and most overtly 'political' film, *Universal Soldier*, stars George Lazenby as a mercenary seduced by the peace movement. Loosely structured and semi-improvised in style, it is, frankly, an incoherent mess, though the director himself appears in a small role with some tellingly autobiographical dialogue. Apart from co-writing the screenplay and publishing a novelisation of *Zulu Dawn* (Douglas Hickox, 1979), a belated prequel to *Zulu*, Endfield subsequently pursued a variety of other interests, including designing a gold-and-silver chess set and inventing a computerised pocket note-taker, the Microwriter. He remained resident in Britain until his death, from cerebral vascular disease, on 16 April 1995.

(Sheldon Hall)

BIBLIOGRAPHY: Hall, Sheldon, *Zulu: With Some Guts behind It – The Making of the Epic Film* (Sheffield: Tomahawk Press, 2005); Neve, Brian, *Film and Politics in America: A Social Tradition* (London and New York: Routledge, 1992); Peters, Andrew, 'Natural Drama Is Just Waiting to Be Found', *Films and Filming*, May 1958, p. 27; Rosenbaum, Jonathan, 'Pages from the Endfield File', in *Movies as Politics* (Berkeley, Los Angeles, and London: University of California Press, 1997).

FILMOGRAPHY: In US, as Cyril Endfield (feature films only): *Gentleman Joe Palooka* (1946); *Stork Bites Man* (1947); *The Argyle Secrets* (1948); *Joe Palooka in the Big City* (1949); *The Underworld Story*; *The Sound of Fury* (aka *Try and Get Me!*) (1950); *Tarzan's Savage Fury* (1952).

In UK: *Colonel March Investigates* (as Cyril Endfield); *The Limping Man* (credited dir. Charles de Lautour) (1953); *The Master Plan* (as Hugh Raker, 1954); *Impulse* (credited dir. Charles de Lautour); *The Secret* (as C. Raker Endfield) (1955); *Child in the House* (credited co-dir. Charles de Lautour, 1956); *Hell Drivers* (as C. Raker Endfield, 1957); *Sea Fury* (as C. Raker Endfield, 1958); *Jet Storm* (as C. Raker Endfield, 1959); *Mysterious Island* (1961); *Hide and Seek* (1962; rel. 1964); *Zulu* (1964); *Sands of the Kalahari* (1965); *De Sade* (uncredited co-dir. Roger Corman, US/Ger, 1969); *Universal Soldier* (1971; rel. 1972).

ENGEL, Andi (1942–)

Andi Engel was born in Berlin in 1942. Since the late 1960s he has been a key figure in the independent film sector in Britain. After programming a season of Cuban films at the National Film Theatre in 1969, he and his wife Pam went on to found

Politkino to distribute and organise screenings of the avant-garde films of Jean-Luc Godard and Jean-Marie Straub/Danièle Huillet. In 1973 Politkino, which had been subsidised by Engel's earnings as the London representative of Polygram Films, merged with The Other Cinema. In 1976 Engel founded Artificial Eye, a more commercially viable distribution company, handling a wide range of art films and owning a number of London cinemas (beginning with the old Camden Plaza) in which to show them.

Artificial Eye was involved in the production of Peter Greenaway's *A Zed and Two Noughts* (1986) and a Portuguese adaptation of Dickens' *Hard Times* (*Tempos Dificeis*, João Botelho, 1988) and in 1989 Engel wrote and directed *Melancholia*. Based partly on his own experience as an ageing radical who has prospered in the society he once sought to subvert, it tells the story of a London-based German art critic (played by Jeroen Krabbé) who is blackmailed by an associate from his radical student past into carrying out the assassination of a visiting Chilean doctor. Made for less than £1 million provided by Channel 4, the BFI and a number of German companies, *Melancholia* makes effective use of a number of European locations and was well received critically. As Engel himself predicted, however, the fortysomething audience the film would most appeal to was too small to make it a commercial success. Engel returned to running Artificial Eye, which now owns two of the remaining London art-house cinemas, the Chelsea and the Renoir.

(Paul Ward)

BIBLIOGRAPHY: Bergson, Phillip, 'Auspicious Debut', *What's on in London*, 18 Oct. 1989; Johnston, Sheila, 'A Different Engel', *Independent*, 20 Oct. 1989, p. 28.

FILMOGRAPHY: *Melancholia* (UK/Ger, 1989).

ESWAY, Alexander (1898–1947)

In the 1930s the American *International Motion Picture Almanac* listed Alexander Esway's hobby as 'collecting old porcelain': not an activity commensurate with an adventurous life that saw him on the move working in films in four countries, fighting in both world wars, escaping from a German prison camp and generally pouncing on every chance for success. He was born on 20 January 1898 in Debreczin, Hungary, and fought in the Wilhelm Hussars in the First World War; afterwards he joined the Hungarian diplomatic service, wrote for the stage and found assorted work in the German film industry. His directorial break came in 1927 with Reinhold Schünzel's production *Herkules Maier*, an engaging light drama easily dominated by Schünzel's dryly comic performance in the main role.

At the beginning of 1929 Esway began what turned into a seven-year siege of the British film industry. He started at Gainsborough, directing the silent version of a romantic comedy, *Taxi for Two*, featuring John Stuart as an aristocrat's son who poses as a chauffeur to win the hand of Mabel Poulton (sound sequences for a separate part-talkie version were directed by Denison Clift). Then he moved to BIP. On the bilingual *Children of Chance* (1930), a light melodrama with Elissa Landi cast in the lookalike roles of a virtuous chorus girl and a notorious actress, Esway just about managed to keep the unconvincing material afloat (he also handled the German version, *Kinder des Glücks*). A second assignment, the laboured thriller *Shadows*, proved more intractable.

Esway's relative inexperience sparked studio gossip that he had touted for work in Germany and England with letters of recommendation from Lubitsch and Emil Jannings that failed to make clear that both had employed him only as their chauffeur. But he pressed ahead as a director, moving to Paris to make *Le Jugement de minuit* (1932) – a version of the Edgar Wallace thriller *The Ringer* (Walter Forde, 1931), featuring Fernandel in Gordon Harker's role – and *Mauvaise graine* (1933), a lively drama about Parisian car thieves, co-directed by another ambitious émigré, Billy Wilder. In 1934 he found work at London Films, but his assignments were either menial (promotional films about electricity) or in the nature of a poisoned chalice: with Zoltan Korda he directed early sequences of *The Conquest of the Air*, the aviation documentary that defeated all efforts to bring it to heel. He also renewed contact with BIP, making a minor amusement with Gene Gerrard, *It's a Bet*, and contributing to *Music Hath Charms*, a zany showcase for Henry Hall and the BBC Dance Orchestra. Anxious for bigger assignments, he borrowed City money to found Atlantic Film Productions in 1935 and mounted *Thunder in the City*, a whimsical satire pitting British decorum against American ballyhoo, clearly designed to catch Hollywood's eye. The star (Edward G. Robinson), the director (Marion Gering) and the story material were all imported from America; but the film proved less popular than hoped on either side of the ocean.

With his production venture's collapse, Esway retreated to France and began to build a settled and modestly fruitful career, making decent comedies with Fernandel, Raimú and others. But the Second World War brought immediate disruption: a naturalised French citizen, he volunteered for the French Air Force, was swiftly captured and spent two years in a prisoner-of-war camp. Escaping, he made his way to America, where he found Hollywood work co-writing MGM's prisoner-of-war film *The Cross of Lorraine* (Tay Garnett, 1943); he also directed a crime-comedy, *Steppin' in Society* (1945), at Republic. Back in France after the war, where he remained an admired director, Esway finally achieved the splash he had yearned for with *Le Bataillon du ciel* (1946), a lavish two-part production saluting the 400 Free French paratroopers and their part in the Normandy invasion. But his success proved short-lived: five months after the film's release he died in St Tropez, on 23 August 1947, and his last film, *L'Idole* (1947), a boxing drama featuring Yves Montand, was released posthumously.

(Geoff Brown and Kevin Gough-Yates)

BIBLIOGRAPHY: Ackland, Rodney and Elspeth Grant, *The Celluloid Mistress; or The Custard Pie of Dr Caligari* (London: Allen Wingate, 1954).

FILMOGRAPHY (UK only): *Taxi for Two* (silent version; sound version co-dir. Denison Clift, 1929); *Children of Chance* (1930); *Shadows* (1931); *Well I Never!* (short); *The Wizard in the Wall* (short); *Plenty of Time for Play* (short) (1934); *It's a Bet* (1935); *Music Hath Charms* (co-dirs. Thomas Bentley/Walter Summers/Arthur Woods, 1936); *The Conquest of the Air* (co-dirs. Zoltan Korda/William Cameron Menzies/John Monk Saunders/Alexander Shaw/Donald Taylor, 1936; rel. 1940).

EVANS, David

David Evans cut his teeth directing *Common as Muck*, William Ivory's fine television series about a team of North of England dustbin-men, before breaking into features with a Channel 4 adaptation of Nick Hornby's autobiographical *Fever Pitch*. Turning Hornby's unique study of his obsession with Arsenal Football Club into a feelgood comedy was perhaps the only way to make it cinematically viable – and it was Hornby who wrote the screenplay – but much is trivialised in the process. A likeable cast headed by Colin Firth, Ruth Gemmell and Mark Strong, and location shooting in Haringey and Highbury, hardly lift the film beyond the commonplace; understandably it has been more popular for home viewing on video/DVD than it was in the cinema. Evans' *Our Boy* (1998), a dark revenge tragedy written by Tony Grounds, was much more trenchant, though it was never allowed beyond the confines of BBC Television.

Settling back into the bosom of television drama, Evans displayed his versatility directing instalments of P. D. James' thriller *An Unsuitable Job for a Woman* (1997); *Manchild* (2002), Nick Fisher's comedy about still lascivious fiftysomethings; and Paul Abbot's wickedly funny study of underclass life, *Shameless* (2003). He renewed his acquaintance with *Fever Pitch* as an executive producer on the American remake starring Jimmy Fallon (as a fanatical Boston Red Sox fan) and Drew Barrymore, directed by the Farrelly brothers in 2005.

(Robert Murphy)

BIBLIOGRAPHY: Interview with Colin Firth, Nick Hornby and David Evans, *Guardian* 1996, <hem.passagen.se/lmw/guardian.html>; Power, Paul, 'Team Spirit' (interview with Nick Hornby), *Film Ireland* no. 58, Apr./May 1997, pp. 31–2.

FILMOGRAPHY: *Fever Pitch* (1997).

EVANS, Fred (1889–1951) and EVANS, Joe (1891–1967)

Fred Evans was a talented comedian whose two hundred or so films were immensely popular before and during the First World War. He relied less on observational comedy than his childhood friend Charles Chaplin, but drew more heavily on theatrical burlesque. His films abounded with punning intertitles, written by his brother Joe, and the relentless substitution of ludicrous for dramatic themes. As the anarchic 'Pimple', Fred rivalled Chaplin's early popularity in Britain, but changing circumstances led both Evans brothers to less exalted careers.

Fred and Joe Evans came from a family of popular entertainers. Their grandfather was a well-loved clown; their uncle Will Evans was a leading comedian and founder of the Sunny South film company. Following a circus apprenticeship Fred and Joe performed with their parents in a pantomime act, the Florador Quartet. Fred joined Cricks and Martin in 1910 where his early screen appearances were as 'Charley Smiler', a disaster-prone 'dude', introduced in *The Last of the Dandy* (Dave Aylott, 1910). By 1912, Joe had joined him on the screen. The same year, when their uncles Seth and Albert Jee, both music-hall performers, combined with Will Kellino to launch the company Ec-Ko, Fred began to appear for them as 'Pimple', a clown-like character with tight clothes and lank strands of hair framing a whitened face. Shortly afterwards, Fred and Joe launched their own brand, Folly Films, producing at studios on Eel Pie Island, Twickenham, and sharing the directing themselves on all future 'Pimple' productions, issued almost weekly.

Separately, both also directed comedies with other slapstick characters: the more prolific Joe's included the Terrible Two, Joey and Mr and Mrs Piecan. The 'Pimple' knockabout comedies soon began to be replaced by 'Pimple' send-ups of films, plays and novels. The humour derived from theatrical burlesque and music-hall satire. The more sensational the original production, the more their powers of ridicule were engaged. *Pimple's Battle of Waterloo* (1913) set the pattern for many farcical pastiches, mercilessly satirising an early film epic, *The Battle of Waterloo* (Charles Weston, 1913). In *Pimple in The Whip* (1917), a famous melodrama inspired them to re-enact its thrilling race scene with pantomime horses; while a series of Lieutenant Pimple films poked fun at the screen exploits of the swashbuckling Lieutenant Daring (1911–14). In keeping with such broad caricature, Pimple was liable to extreme character changes, appearing both as a criminal and a law-enforcer; occasionally, he would even appear as a woman or a child.

In private life Fred resembled Pimple, skilfully evading a succession of creditors until bankruptcy caught up with him in 1920. The brothers' film productions, already thinning out, finally ceased after one last burlesque, *Pimple's Three Musketeers*, released in September 1922. Fred and Joe returned to the music-hall stage: Joe toured the United States, while Fred appeared in revues with his wife and two daughters. The brothers reunited during the Second World War to present a puppet show; after Fred died working in a London circus in 1951, Joe continued to appear in a concert party. He died in Brighton in 1967.

(Barry Anthony)

BIBLIOGRAPHY: Hammond, Michael, 'Cultivating Pimple': Performance Traditions and the Film Comedy of Fred and Joe Evans', in Alan Burton and Laraine Porter (eds), *Pimple, Pranks & Pratfalls: British Film Comedy before 1930* (Trowbridge, Wilts: Flicks Books, 2000); Interview with Joe Evans (1966), Denis Gifford Audiotape Collection, BFI National Library, London; Low, Rachael, *The History of the British Film 1906–1914* (London: George Allen & Unwin, 1949).

FILMOGRAPHY: Fred Evans: *Stop the Fight* (1911); *The Little General*; *Fifty Years After*; *A Novel Burglary* (1912); *The Story of Hyam*

Touched; Pimple's Battle of Waterloo (1913); *The Smugglers; For Her Brothers' Sake; Driven by Hunger, Some Fun* (co-dir. Will Evans); *A Study in Skarlit* (co-dir. Will Evans) (1915).

Joe Evans: *Who Will Marry Martha?; The Passing of Black Pete; Stolen Honours; Pearls of Death; The Terrible Two* (series); *Archibald's Egg Diet; Archibald in a Tangle* (1914); *Mr and Mrs Piecan – The Giddy Husband; Piecan's Tonic; Poor Old Piecan; When the Germans Came; In the Clutches of the Hun; The Lady Detective; The Kidnapped King; Liza's Legacy; Liza on the Stage; Shells, More Shells; When Women Rule* (1915); *Joey* (series, 1915–16); *Silas at the Seaside; Taming Liza; A Boarding House Scandal* (1916).

Fred and Joe Evans: *Pimple Gets a Quid; Pimple Wins a Bet; Pimple's Fire Brigade; Pimple Becomes an Acrobat; Pimple's Eggs-traordinary Story; Pimple as a Cinema Actor, Pimple as a Ballet Dancer, Pimple as a Rent Collector* (1912); *Pimple's Motor Bike; Pimple Goes A-Busking; Pimple, Detective; Pimple Writes a Cinema Plot; Pimple and the Gorilla; Miss Pimple, Suffragette; Pimple Meets Captain Scuttle; Pimple's Complaint; Two to One on Pimple; Pimple's Motor Trap; Pimple's Sporting Chance; Pimple Takes a Picture; Pimple Gets the Sack; Pimple's Wonderful Gramophone; Pimple's Rest Cure; Pimple Joins the Army; A Bathroom Problem; A Tragedy in Pimple's Life; Dick Turpin's Ride to York; Pimple Does the Hat Trick; Pimple's Wife; Pimple's Inferno; Pimple Goes Fishing; Pimple the Sport; Pimple Gets the Jumps; Pimple's Ivanhoe; Once Upon a Time; Slippery Pimple; Lieutenant Pimple on Secret Service; How Pimple Saved Kissing Cup; Pimple's Great Bull Fight; Pimple's Midnight Ramble; Pimple's New Job* (1913); *The Adventures of Pimple* (series); *When Pimple Was Young* (series); *What Happened to Pimple* (series) (1913–1914); *Pimple's Humanity; Lieutenant Pimple and the Stolen Submarine; Pimple Elopes; Lieutenant Pimple's Dash for Freedom; Pimple and Galatea; Pimple in the Grip of the Law; The House of Distemperley; Young Pimple and His Little Sister, Pimple Goes to Paris; The Battle of Gettysownback; Lieutenant Pimple's Sealed Orders; The Whitewashers; How Pimple Won the Derby; Pimple's Burglar Scare; Lieutenant Pimple Goes to Mexico; Pimple 'Midst the Raging Beasts; Pimple in Society; Pimple's Advice; Pimple's Trousers; Big Chief Little Pimple; Pimple Turns Honest; Pimple, Anarchist; Broncho Pimple; Pimple, Counter Jumper, Pimple's Vengeance; Pimple Pinched; Pimple's Last Resource; Pimple Beats Jack Johnson; Pimple's Escape from Portland; Lieutenant Pimple, Gun Runner, Pimple, M.P.; Pimple's Proposal; Pimple's Charge of the Light Brigade; Lieutenant Pimple and the Stolen Invention; Pimple Enlists; Pimple's Great Fire; Pimple, Special Constable; Pimple's Prison; Lieutenant Pimple, King of the Cannibal Islands; Pimple's Leap to Fortune; The Clowns of Europe; Inspector Pimple; How Lieutenant Pimple Captured the Kaiser, Pimple and the Stolen Plans; Pimple on Football; Young Pimple's Frolics* (1914); *Mrs Raffles nee Pimple; Pimple in the Kilties; Judge Pimple; Sexton Pimple; Flash Pimple the Master Crook; Pimple's Storyette; Pimple's Dream of Victory; Pimple, the Bad Girl of the Family; Pimple, Child Stealer, Pimple Copped; Pimple's Art of Mystery; Pimple's Rival; Pimple's Dilemma; Pimple's Holiday; Tally Ho! Pimple; Pimple's Scrap of Paper, The Kaiser Captures Pimple; Pimple's Boy Scout; Mademoiselle Pimple; Pimple's Burlesque of the Still Alarm; Pimple Has One; Pimple's Good Turn; Ragtime Cowboy Pimple; Pimple's Willit-Wasit-Isit; Pimple's Some Burglar, Pimple's Motor Tour, Pimple's Three O'clock Race; Pimple up the Pole; Pimple's Three; Pimple's Road to Ruin; Pimple Explains; Aladdin; Was Pimple W(right)?; Pimple's Uncle; Pimple Sees Ghosts; Pimple Acts; Pimple Will Treat; Pimple's Artful Dodge; Pimple Gets the Hump* (1915); *Pimple's Great Adventure; Pimple's Crime; Pimple's Part; Pimple Ends It; Pimple's Zeppelin Scare; Pimple's Double; Pimple's Pink Forms; Pimple Splits the Difference; Pimple's Arm of the Law; Pimple – Himself and Others; Pimple's Midsummer Night's Dream; Pimple Poor but Dishonest; Pimple as Hamlet; Pimple's A Woman in the Case; Diamond Cut Diamond; Pimple's Tenth Commandment; Pimple's Silver Lagoon; Pimple's Monkey Business; Pimple's Clutching Hand; Pimple's Merry Wives; Pimple's Nautical Story; Pimple Strafing the Kaiser* (1916); *Pimple in The Whip* (aka *Pimple's The Whip*); *Pimple's Senseless Censoring; Pimple's Mystery of the Closed Door, Some Dancer, Saving Raffles; Pimple's Tableaux Vivants; Oliver Twisted; Pimple – His Voluntary Corps; Pimple's Romance; Pimple's Pitter-Patter, Pimple's Lady Godiva; Pimple's The Woman Who Did* (1917); *Pimple's Better 'Ole; Ins and Outs* (1918); *Pimple's Topical Gazette* (1920); *Pimple's Three Musketeers* (1922).

EVANS, Marc (1959–)

Marc Evans was born in Cardiff in 1959. He was a member of the National Youth Theatre of Wales and studied at Churchill College, Cambridge, before enrolling on the postgraduate course in film-making at Bristol University. His likeable short film *Johnny Be Good* – an exploration of rock and roll's impact in rural Wales following the introduction of the first jukebox to Cardiganshire – led to a career in television. His work included Welsh-language dramas for S4C and the BBC, including the feature-length science-fiction comedy *Ymadawiad Arthur/Arthur's Departure* (1995). He also made pop videos for Welsh bands Super Furry Animals and Catatonia.

Silent Village, a documentary made with Edward Thomas about the South Wales mining village of Cwmgiedd (used by Humphrey Jennings in his homage to the massacred Czech villagers of Lidice in 1943), led to *House of America*, an adaptation of Thomas' play about a Welsh family undermined by dark secrets. This grim tale of incest, guilt, deprivation and fantasy, set in a deprived South Wales community where the landscape is being torn apart by open-cast mining, was hardly likely to appeal to any audiences attuned to Celtic whimsicality; equally, the film was too abstruse and intellectual to attract the Tarantino generation. Nonetheless it displayed Evans' confident talent, and he found no difficulties setting up a second feature.

Resurrection Man (1998) was based on Eoin McNamee's fictionalised account of the exploits of a band of psychopathic Protestant hoodlums, the so-called Shankhill Butchers. Evans' willingness to show the cruel and pointless torture of ordinary people is cathartically shocking; but, like the burnt-out killer played by John Hannah, he becomes increasingly unfocused and disorientated, scurrying away from the evil protagonist (convincingly played by Stuart Townsend) into trivial subplots around James Nesbitt's barely relevant journalist and Geraldine O'Rawe's decorative floozy. The film's idiosyncratic style and firm roots in the grim reality of 1970s' Northern Ireland

confirmed Evans' originality, though the mix did little for its commercial prospects.

Box-office success finally came with *My Little Eye*, an equally bleak but more fantastic study of a reality television show that becomes a forum for gruesome murder. Evans' confident manipulation of expectations and witty pastiche of hidden camera techniques won over young audiences in the UK, though American distributors thought the film too strange and disturbing to have much multiplex appeal. He returned to horror in *Trauma*, which features Colin Firth as a disturbed car crash victim who believes he has caused the death of his wife and might also be guilty of murdering a popular celebrity. Evans creates a wonderfully eerie atmosphere – part spooky interiors, part run-down and hostile London streets – and there is a dream sequence worthy of Hideo Nakata, but the film's downbeat ending comes as an unwelcome surprise and alienated audiences. Nevertheless, Evans seems set to emulate Michael Winterbottom in his ability to make a steady stream of films that are stimulating and unique even when flawed.

(Robert Murphy)

BIBLIOGRAPHY: Clarke, Jim, 'Sectarian Psycho', *Film Ireland* no. 62, Dec. 1997/Jan. 1998, pp. 21–2; Evans, Marc, 'Trauma', *Empire*, Sept. 2004, p. 69; Floyd, Nigel, 'With "My Little Eye"', *Fangoria* no. 218, Nov. 2002, pp. 30–3; McLoone, Martin, *Irish Film: The Emergence of a Contemporary Cinema* (London: BFI, 2000); Newman, Kim, 'Endurance', *Sight and Sound*, Oct. 2002, pp. 26–8.

FILMOGRAPHY: *Johnny Be Good* (short, 1984); *Silent Village* (doc., 1993); *House of America* (1997); *Resurrection Man* (1998); *Beautiful Mistake* (doc.); *Giuseppe Tornatore, A Dream Dreamt in Sicily* (doc.) (2000); *My Little Eye* (2002); *Otherworld/Y Mabinogi* (live-action sequences, Derek Hayes, 2003); *Trauma* (UK/Ir/US, 2004); *Snowcake* (UK/Can, 2006).

EYRE, Richard (1943–)

Born in Barnstaple, Devon, on 28 March 1943, Richard Eyre went to Cambridge University in the early 1960s, where he was part of a lively drama scene that included Trevor Nunn, Stephen Frears and Michael Apted. Throughout his career Eyre has moved between theatre, television and cinema, making significant contributions to each. He was director of the Nottingham Playhouse in the 1970s before joining the BBC later in the decade. He directed several films in the *Play for Today* slot, including Ian McEwan's *The Imitation Game* (1980), and two plays by Trevor Griffiths: *Comedians* (1979), which Eyre had previously directed at Nottingham Playhouse, and *Country* (1981), which examined the impact on the ruling class of Labour's post-war election victory, at a time when the post-war dream of a socialist society was being swept away by Thatcherism. *The Ploughman's Lunch*, with an incisive script by McEwan, was similarly political, drawing comparisons between the Suez Affair of 1956 and the recently fought Falklands War, and exploring the developing 'culture of lies', through the activities of a self-serving journalist (Jonathan Pryce). Eyre's direction is functional and anonymous, respectful of McEwan's script, but allowing little emotional involvement. The film, made for Channel 4 but given a theatrical release, received considerable critical attention but was too coldly analytical to have much appeal at the box office.

Eyre followed up with *Loose Connections*, a comic road movie with a feminist (Lindsay Duncan) and a football fan (Stephen Rea) sharing an eventful car journey from London to Munich. *Laughterhouse*, again made for Channel 4, is spikier, though it is not easy to maintain interest in the long trek farmer Ian Holm and his flock of geese make from Norfolk to Smithfield Market in London. Suspending the struggle to break into mainstream commercial cinema, Eyre returned to television where his more interesting ventures included Alan Bennett's Kafkaesque *The Insurance Man* (1986) and Charles Wood's hard-hitting Falklands drama *Tumbledown* (1988).

In 1988 Eyre was appointed director of the National Theatre, a post he held until 1997, when he was awarded a knighthood. In 2001 he returned to the cinema with *Iris*, a biopic of the novelist Iris Murdoch, with Kate Winslet and Judi Dench as her younger and older selves. Critically acclaimed, *Iris* was a modest commercial success, unlike Eyre's next film, *Stage Beauty* (2004), about the moment in seventeenth-century British theatre when Charles II allowed women to tread the boards for the first time, bringing to an end the tradition of male actors like Edward 'Ned' Kynaston (Billy Crudup) who specialised in playing women's roles. *Stage Beauty* attempted to capitalise on the success of films like *Shakespeare in Love* (John Madden, 1998) but failed to live up to its extensive pre-release publicity. Eyre had more success with his West End stage production of *Mary Poppins*.

(Lez Cooke)

BIBLIOGRAPHY: Lennon, Peter, 'Richard Eyre – National Heir Presumptive', *Listener*, Jan. 1987, pp. 10–11; Wyver, John, 'Cruel Alliance (or the Englishness of England)', *Stills* no. 7, July/Aug. 1983, pp. 64–7.

FILMOGRAPHY: *The Ploughman's Lunch*; *Loose Connections* (1983); *Laughterhouse* (aka *Singleton's Pluck*, 1984); *Iris* (UK/US, 2001); *Stage Beauty* (UK/Ger/US, 2004); *Scandal* (2006).

EZRA, Mark (1950–)

Mark Ezra was born in Brighton on 30 August 1950. He studied film and photography at the Polytechnic of Central London, where he directed a number of short films. Subsequently he co-directed *April Fool's Day* (1985), a gory slasher movie with an English cast masquerading as American high-school students. Writing assignments followed, including the sentimental South African drama *Hold My Hand, I'm Dying* (Terence Ryan, 1989) and *Living Doll* (1990), another exploitation horror film directed by his collaborators Peter Mackenzie-Litten and George Dugdale. *Savage Hearts*, which he wrote and directed, was a more personal project, interesting as the first British film to try out Quentin Tarantino's blend of violent action and sassy dialogue. A dying woman (Maryam D'Abo) steals £2 million from a wicked old robber baron (Richard Harris); she is impersonated by an American hustler (Miriam Cyr), who teams up with a longhaired wide-boy (Jamie Harris). By exploitation film standards this was an acceptable package (Harris father and son more or less balance each other out, and the two tough women make up for a simpering Jerry Hall), but *Savage Hearts* was aimed at a more mainstream audience and distributors turned up their noses at Ezra's sloppy production values. It was not until January 1997 that the film was allowed even a video release.

Since that misfortune, Ezra has served as one of the associate producers on the unexpectedly successful comedy *Waking Ned* (Kirk Jones, 1998); collaborated with Terry Marcel on *Darkest Knight* (2000), an attempt to build a television series around Sir Walter Scott's medieval hero Ivanhoe; and written *Riders* (Gérard Pirès, 2002), a slick Anglo-French-Canadian heist movie. He is obviously a survivor.

(Robert Murphy)

FILMOGRAPHY: *Miss Jennifer Jones* (short); *Hitler Couldn't Have Bombed Us Out* (short, 1971); *April Fool's Day* (US: *Slaughter High*, co-dirs. George Dugdale/Peter Litten, UK/US, 1985); *Savage Hearts* (1993).

FAIRCHILD, William (1918–2000)

William Edward Cranston Fairchild was born in Boscastle, Cornwall, on 1 June 1918. Educated at Dartmouth Naval College from age thirteen, he served in the Spanish Civil War as a midshipman, and rose to be a lieutenant-commander in the Second World War. After the war he established a reputation as a playwright, notably of *The Sound of Murder* (filmed by Gordon Hessler in 1970 as *The Last Shot You Hear*). He began screenwriting at Rank's Highbury Studios on second features such as *Song for Tomorrow* (Terence Fisher, 1948) and the remake of *Badger's Green* (John Irwin, 1949), and won acclaim for his screenplays for the submarine drama *Morning Departure* (Roy Baker, 1950) and Carol Reed's undervalued Conrad adaptation, *Outcast of the Islands* (1951).

The films he directed (as well as wrote) are more modestly rewarding. *John and Julie* (1955), made for Group 3, won an award at the Venice Biennale; it is an attractive account of the adventures of two small children who decide to run away to attend the Queen's coronation. *The Extra Day* (1956), made for his own production company, is an enjoyable if overcrowded comedy-drama, about rounding up the extras to reshoot a missing reel of film; and *The Silent Enemy* (1958) is a lively, good-humoured retelling of the real-life exploits of Lieutenant 'Buster' Crabb in saving the Allied invasion fleet from Italian submariners. His second of three wives was actress Isabel Dean. He died of natural causes in London on 9 May 2000.

(Brian McFarlane)

BIBLIOGRAPHY: Lentz III, Harris, Obituary, *Classic Images* no. 303, Sept. 2000, p. 56; Obituary, *The Times*, 8 June 2000, p. 25.

FILMOGRAPHY: *John and Julie* (1955); *The Extra Day* (1956); *The Silent Enemy* (1958); *The Horsemasters* (1961, originally a two-part Disney television programme).

FAITHFULL, Geoffrey (1893–1979)

Geoffrey Faithfull was born on 26 January 1893 in Walton-on-Thames, Surrey. In 1907 he began work at Cecil Hepworth's Walton Studios and by 1912 he had become a cameraman. His picturesque photography on Hepworth's celebrated pastoral drama *Comin thro' the Rye* (1923) was greatly admired by the critics. When Hepworth went bankrupt in 1925, Faithfull remained at the Walton Studios (renamed Nettlefold), where he worked on films made by the main tenant company, Butchers, as well as 'quota quickies' for a number of directors including Michael Powell, Maclean Rogers and Oswald Mitchell.

During the war, Faithfull worked on regional comedies and farces and the occasional crime drama. In the mid-1940s Butchers gave him the opportunity to direct two pleasingly sentimental films about young people adjusting to post-war society. *For You Alone* has vicar's daughter Lesley Brook torn between childhood sweetheart John Bradshaw and blind war veteran Manning Whiley. *Picturegoer* commented on its 'simple sentiment' and 'pleasant English countryside settings' (26 May 1945). *I'll Turn to You* (1946) has heroic but impoverished flyer Don Stannard unable to adjust to peacetime life with young wife Terry Randall. With their musical interludes and stilted dialogue, both films seem to move slowly, but they have a period charm.

After this brief venture into directing, Faithfull continued his prolific career as a cinematographer until the early 1970s. He died in Bledlow, Buckinghamshire, on 1 December 1979 after over sixty years working in the film industry.

(Margaret Butler)

BIBLIOGRAPHY: Collier, Lionel, 'For You Alone', *Picturegoer*, 26 May 1945, p. 12; *Focus on Film*, Special: 'Great Cameramen' no. 13, 1973, p. 27; Noble, Peter (ed.), *The British Film Yearbook, 1947–1948* (London: Skelton Robinson, 1947), p. 251.
FILMOGRAPHY: *For You Alone* (1945); *I'll Turn to You* (1946).

FARINO, Julian (1961–)

Julian Farino worked as the sports editor for the *Guinness Book of Records*, which enabled him to break into television in 1985 as one of the presenters on the BBC's *Record Breakers*. He went on to direct episodes of *Coronation Street* and the police drama series *Out of the Blue* (1995), and made his name with an engrossing adaptation of Charles Dickens' *Our Mutual Friend* (1998).

The break into feature films came with *The Last Yellow* for Nik Powell's Scala Productions. Mark Addy plays a fat, unemployed chef who passes himself off as an ex-SAS paratrooper prepared to carry out a contract killing for £500. In the first half Farino makes the most of his comically inadequate characters and the seedy Leicester settings, but once the action moves south he resorts to sloppy clichés – fooling around at London Zoo, riding on open-top tourist buses – to pad out Paul Tucker's stage play. The long wait for the victim to return from shopping – unconscionably long even in film time – is enlivened by Samantha Morton's mesmerising performance as his atavistic girlfriend; but Farino struggles to maintain narrative momentum without the solid structure of a classic serial or a genre format.

The Last Yellow was unkindly treated by critics and neglected by audiences, and a follow-up project for Scala, *Eggshell Blue*, was abandoned. Farino returned to television, where he showed his competence and versatility with the surprisingly unromantic drama serial *Byron* (2003). He also consolidated his reputation in the American television industry, where he had directed an episode of *Sex and the City* in 1998, with several episodes of HBO's series about actors and agents, *Entourage* (2004).
(Robert Murphy)

BIBLIOGRAPHY: Craven, John, 'Julian Goes on Record', *Radio Times*, 26 Oct. 1985, p. 102; Tutt, Louise, 'Scala to Make Follow-Up Mellor, Farino Projects', *Screen International*, 12 Nov. 1999, p. 18.
FILMOGRAPHY: *The Last Yellow* (UK/Ger, 1999).

FAYE, Randall (1892–1948)

As with several other Americans, Randall H. Faye's British career in the 1930s was generated and sustained by the low-budget production boom brought about by the 1927 Cinematograph Films Act. Born in America on 26 July 1892, Faye entered the industry as a scriptwriter; by 1926 he was busy at Fox, chiefly writing comedies. His first contact with the British industry came in 1929, when he co-wrote two musicals for British International Pictures, though he only buckled down in earnest when he joined Warners' quota factory at Teddington in 1932. The first scripts he worked on, *High Society* and *Lucky Ladies*, were elaborated from material sent from California and directed by John Rawlins, a Hollywood journeyman. Faye's directorial debut, *Hyde Park* (1934), with its creaky plot about a butcher's daughter in love with an aristocrat, could not have been more English. He tapped into another British tradition, the lurid stage melodrama, with *Maria Marten; or, The Murder in the Red Barn* (Milton Rosmer, 1935), one of eleven collaborations with the successful quota merchant George King, and the screen debut of the barnstorming stage actor Tod Slaughter.

Emboldened perhaps by King's success in the quota field, Faye established his own company, producing and directing five films in 1935–6, chiefly at the Nettlefold Studios in Walton-on-Thames. Faye's plot for *The Vandergilt Diamond Mystery* (1936) was almost worthy of P. G. Wodehouse; not so the jokes. Greater success came with *Born That Way* (1936), a domestic comedy kindly received for its human touches, and *Luck of the Turf* (1936), another modest, observant comedy, about a shopkeeper's entanglements with race-track betting. The satirical tone of *Mr Stringfellow Says 'No'* (1937) struck a different note; as did the unabashed sentiment of *Scruffy* (1938), featuring a tearful child, attractive riverside scenes and Scruffy himself, briefly Britain's best-loved animal.

The industry's financial problems and changes in quota requirements in the 1938 Cinematograph Films Act helped to end Faye's directing career. Initially he moved up-budget with King, writing the script for another roaring Slaughter vehicle, *The Face at the Window* (George King, 1939), praised by Graham Greene for its 'fine firm traditional dialogue'. But Britain in wartime held little appeal, and by 1943 he had resumed work as a Hollywood writer, mostly of Westerns for Republic. He returned to England only in his imagination for *Scotland Yard Investigator* (George Blair, 1945), the tall tale of Sir C. Aubrey Smith and Erich von Stroheim battling over the *Mona Lisa*, supposedly sent for safekeeping during the war to London's National Gallery. Randall Faye died on 5 December 1948 in Orange County, California.
(Geoff Brown)

BIBLIOGRAPHY: Richards, Jeffrey, 'Tod Slaughter and the Cinema of Excess', in Jeffrey Richards (ed.), *The Unknown 1930s: An Alternative History of the British Cinema 1929–1939* (London: I. B. Tauris, 1998).
FILMOGRAPHY: *Hyde Park* (1934); *The Vandergilt Diamond Mystery* (1936); *This Green Hell*; *If I Were Rich*; *Born That Way*; *Luck of the Turf*; *Such Is Life* (1936); *Mr Stringfellow Says 'No'* (1937); *Scruffy* (1938).

FEHER, Friedrich (1895–1950)

Friedrich Feher was born Friedrich Weiss in Vienna on 16 March 1895. After training at the Vienna Konservatorium, he acted at the Deutschestheater, Berlin, and at theatres in Vienna, Prague and Hamburg. He appeared in at least twelve films before 1920, most notably as Francis in *Das Cabinet des Dr Caligari* (Robert Wiene, 1919). He then concentrated on directing, working in both theatre and cinema, with figures such as Leopold Jessner, Fritz Kortner and Werner Krauss. He fre-

quently included his wife, the singer Magda Sonja, and their son Hans in the cast of his films. In his sound films, which include *Sensations-prozess* (1928), *Hotel Geheimnisse* (1929), *Kdyz struny Lkaji/Ihr Junge* (1931) and *Gehetzte Menschen* (1932), he experimented with musical structure, finally attempting to edit to a predetermined soundtrack. His experiments culminated in the elaborately mounted and influential *The Robber Symphony* (1936). British and French versions were made of this first 'pre-scored film', but without distributor involvement it was a financial disaster. Feher's London-based company, Concordia, had envisaged a number of similar films, including a version of *Caligari* with Robert Wiene co-directing, but their plans came to nothing. In 1939 Feher left for Hollywood, where he established a production company, Symphony Films, and worked on musical shorts for Paramount. He returned to Germany after the war and died in Frankfurt am Main on 30 September 1950.
(Kevin Gough-Yates)

BIBLIOGRAPHY: Cocchi, John, 'Additions & Corrections', *Films in Review*, Nov. 1961, p. 567; Steen, T. M. F., 'The Sound Track', *Films in Review*, Oct. 1961, pp. 491–4.

FILMOGRAPHY (UK only): *The Robber Symphony* (1936).

FERRER, José (1909–1992)

José Vicente Ferrer de Otero y Cintrón was born on 8 January 1909 in Santurce, Puerto Rico, and grew up in the USA. He was educated at Princeton, and acted and directed on Broadway from 1935; he made his screen debut as the Dauphin in *Joan of Arc* (Victor Fleming, 1948). Acclaimed for his versatility, he won the Best Actor Academy Award for *Cyrano de Bergerac* (Michael Gordon, 1950) and was nominated again for his portrayal of Henri de Toulouse-Lautrec in the British-produced biopic *Moulin Rouge* (John Huston, 1953). The first of his seven films as actor-director was adapted from another stage success, *The Shrike* (1955).

Ferrer was lured to Britain by Warwick Film Productions to direct and star in *The Cockleshell Heroes*, in which a team of commandos in two-man canoes sabotages a fleet of German battleships. Although Ferrer's own performance is muted and the climactic raid poorly staged (it was reportedly reshot following the premiere when the Duke of Edinburgh pointed out historical errors), the film is still lively, and achieved great popular success in the UK.

I Accuse!, a dramatisation of the Dreyfus Affair, has an intelligent screenplay by Gore Vidal, elegant black-and-white CinemaScope photography by Freddie Young and fine performances from an all-star cast, including Ferrer himself as Dreyfus and Emlyn Williams as Émile Zola. However, it waited a year after its UK premiere before going out on general release as support to *Party Girl* (Nicholas Ray, 1958) and in France it was banned. After the failure of *State Fair* (1962), his remake of the Rodgers and Hammerstein musical, Ferrer returned exclusively to acting, but the quality of his roles dropped off precipitously after he played the sadistic Turkish Bey in *Lawrence of Arabia* (David Lean, 1962). He nonetheless worked prolifically until his death from colonic cancer in Coral Gables, Florida, on 26 January 1992.
(Sheldon Hall)

BIBLIOGRAPHY: Buckley, Michael, 'José Ferrer', *Films in Review*, Feb. 1987, pp. 67–75; Mar. 1987, pp. 131–45; Ferrer, José, 'Cyrano and Others', *Films and Filming*, July 1962, pp. 13–14, 45; London, Julie, 'The Two Faces of Ferrer', *Films and Filming*, June 1958, p. 12.

FILMOGRAPHY (UK only): *The Cockleshell Heroes* (1955); *I Accuse!* (1958).

FEYDER, Jacques (1885–1948)

Jacques Feyder was born Jacques Frédérix in Ixelles, Belgium, on 21 July 1885. He attended military school but decided to go to France and become an actor. In 1911 he entered the film industry and in 1915 began directing shorts. His first feature, *Tête de femmes, femme de tête* (1916), featured his future wife Françoise Rosay in a supporting role. Success came with the extravagant fantasy *L'Atlantide* (1921), the first of several strikingly original silent films. In 1928 censorship problems with *Les Nouveaux messieurs* prompted Feyder to accept MGM's invitation to go to Hollywood. Assignments included *The Kiss* (1929) starring Greta Garbo, and German and Swedish versions of her first 'talkie', *Anna Christie* (Clarence Brown, 1930).

Returning to France in 1932, Feyder directed (and co-wrote with Charles Spaak) *Le Grand jeu* (1934), *Pension Mimosas* (1935) and his most famous film, *La Kermesse héroïque* (1935), set in a seventeenth-century Flemish town occupied by the Spanish. Alexander Korda invited him to England to make *Knight without Armour*, a sumptuous, romantic adventure starring Marlene Dietrich and Robert Donat, at his new Denham Studios. Despite being set during the Russian Revolution, Feyder's film manages to avoid politics, though with Dietrich as a Russian countess there was little danger of it being accused of pro-Communist sympathies.

Feyder and Rosay spent most of the German occupation in Switzerland, where he made *Une Femme disparait* (1941), and North Africa, where they worked in radio. They returned to France in 1944, but Feyder was already in bad health during his last film, *Macadam* (1946). He died in Paris on 25 May 1948. (Margaret Butler)

BIBLIOGRAPHY: Bachy, Victor, *Jacques Feyder: Artisan du cinéma* (Louvain: Librarie Universitaire, 1969); Badder, David, 'Jacques Feyder', *Film Dope* no. 15, Sept. 1978, pp. 43–5; Feyder, Jacques and Françoise Rosay, *Le Cinéma, notre métier* (Geneva: Skira, 1944).

FILMOGRAPHY (UK only): *Knight without Armour* (1937).

FIELD, Mary (1896–1968)

Agnes Mary Field was born in Wimbledon in 1896. Latterly best known for producing children's entertainment films during the 1950s as executive officer of the Children's Film Foundation, she established her reputation in the late 1920s and 30s with her cogent, often witty nature films in the *Secrets of Nature* and *Secrets of Life* series. Field started her career as a history and English teacher, but after acting as a historical adviser on educational films she was invited by Bruce Woolfe to join his British Instructional company in 1925 as education manager. Within a year she transferred to production, working on educational, documentary and feature films. By 1927 she was directing for their pioneering wildlife series *Secrets of Nature* with Percy Smith, an expert in time-lapse and micro-photography. Their equipment was cumbersome and noisy compared with the sophisticated technology of today, but much of the footage produced was remarkable. In 1929 Field became the *Secrets of Nature* series editor and directed over fifty of the films during the next four years. She occasionally handled fiction: editing Anthony Asquith's First World War film *Tell England* (1931), contrasting the courtship behaviour of humans, animals and plants in *The Mystery of Marriage* (1931) and co-directing a minor comedy, *Strictly Business* (1932), with the actress Jacqueline Logan, using extensive London locations.

When British Instructional was taken over in 1933, Field moved to Gaumont-British Instructional, where Woolfe later joined her to make a new series of nature films under the title

Secrets of Life. Invited onto the board of Gaumont-British Instructional, Field became active in promoting the pedagogical use of film in a wider context and sat on various education committees; she also continued to direct many educational films of her own.

Throughout the Second World War, along with other documentary and educational film-makers, Field made government films for the war effort. In *Wisdom of the Wild* (1940) and *Winged Messengers* (1941), she humorously adapted the wildlife genre for home-front and military use, demonstrating the clarity of thought and assured direction that had become her hallmark.

In 1944, J. Arthur Rank established the Children's Entertainment Films Division to produce films for children's cinema clubs and appointed Field as its head. In its six years of existence nearly two hundred films emerged, beginning with *Tom's Ride* (Darrel Catling, 1944). Initial attempts at blending entertainment with moral uplift were poorly received by the industry and critics. But she continued her efforts, and in 1951 became Head of the industry-funded Children's Film Foundation. Before retiring in 1963, she worked as a consultant for children's television and founded the International Centre of Films for Children. Mary Field died in Worthing, Sussex, on 23 December 1968.

(Sarah Easen)

BIBLIOGRAPHY: Field, Mary, *Good Company: The Story of the Children's Entertainment Film Movement in Great Britain, 1943–1950* (London: Longmans Green, 1952); Field, Mary and Percy Smith, *Secrets of Nature* (London: Faber and Faber, 1934); Hardy, Forsyth (ed.), *Grierson on Documentary*, rev. edn (London: Faber and Faber, 1966); Low, Rachael, *Documentary and Educational Films of the 1930s* (London: George Allen & Unwin, 1979); Macnab, Geoffrey, *J. Arthur Rank and the British Film Industry* (London and New York: Routledge, 1993).

SELECTED FILMOGRAPHY: *Secrets of Nature* (series ed. and dir., 1926–33); *Roman Britain* (1927); *Naval Warfare in Nelson's Time* (1928); *Deferred Payment* (1929); *The Mystery of Marriage* (revised version: *The Changing Year*, 1931); *Strictly Business* (co-dir. Jacqueline Logan, 1932); *The King's English*; *The Flag* (1933); *Farming in Suffolk* (series); *Wheatlands of East Anglia*; *Fruitlands of Kent*; *The French 'U'*; *La Gare* (1934); *Farming in East Anglia* (series, 1934–9); *This Was England*; *Washing Time at the Zoo*; *The Farm Factory* (1935); *Secrets of Life* (series) (1935–45); *Physical Training: Carriage*; *The Quiet of the Countryside* (series) (1936); *London Visitors* (1936); *Devon Beef Cattle Farming*; *Hereford Pedigree Cattle*; *Somersetshire Dairy Farming*; *Hoplands of Kent* (1937); *See How They Run*; *Kings in Exile* (1938); *Voice of the Vintage*; *They Made the Land* (1939); *Fitness Wins* (series); *The Medieval Village*; *Wisdom of the Wild*; *Thrift*; *Handicraft Happiness*; *Miss T*; *Civilian Front*; *Atlantic*; *Quilting*; *Rugmaking* (1940); *Indian Ocean*; *Winged Messengers* (longer version: *Carrier Pigeons*); *Mrs T and Her Cabbage Patch* (1941); *Market Town*; *The Development of the Rabbit*; *The Development of the English Town*; *Water*; *The Life Cycle of Maize*; *The Life Cycle of the Pin Mould*; *The Life Cycle of the Newt*; *The Life Cycle of the Onion* (1942); *The History of the English Language*; *Double Thread* (1943); *Two Thousand Years Ago* (series, 1946); *Czechoslovakia* (1947).

FIENNES, Martha (1964–)

Martha Fiennes is one of six children from an unusually artistic and creative family. Her brothers include the actors Ralph and Joseph Fiennes, and her mother was the author Jennifer Lash. She studied film at Harrow College, London where she directed *Migrants* (1988), a film about the strained relationship between a mother and son while on holiday in Suffolk. Her professional career began with a number of award-winning music videos and commercials. *Onegin*, her first feature film, stars Ralph Fiennes as the rakish hero of Aleksandr Pushkin's epic poem who realises too late that the passionate young woman who pledges her heart to him is his true love. The visual sumptuousness of Remi Adefarasin's cinematography is impressive, and Fiennes evokes good performances from her brother and Liv Tyler, but the script (by Peter Ettedgui and Michael Ignatieff) makes Onegin's fate trite rather than tragic. The film attracted only lukewarm critical support and audience indifference.

Fiennes returned to commercials until finally finding backing for her second feature film, *Chromophobia*, from Tunisian financier Tarak Ben Ammar. A distinguished cast (Ralph Fiennes, Penélope Cruz, Kristin Scott Thomas) play unlikeable characters in an increasingly dark ensemble comedy purporting to represent contemporary life in London. Fiennes deserves credit for her lack of sentimentality, but as in *Onegin* she fails to maintain audience interest in her characters' fates,

(Janet Moat)

BIBLIOGRAPHY: Connelly, Cressida, 'A Family Affair', *Daily Telegraph* Weekend Magazine, 13 Nov. 1999, pp. 32, 34, 36–7; Crewe, Candida, 'Labour of Love', *The Times* Magazine, 13 Nov. 1999, pp. 30–1, 33–4, 36; Macnab, Geoffrey, 'Fiennes Nails Her Colours to the Mast', *Screen International*, 3 June 2005, p. 7.

FILMOGRAPHY: *Migrants* (short, 1988); *Onegin* (1999); *Chromophobia* (2005).

FIGGIS, Mike (1948–)

Born in Carlisle, Cumberland, on 28 February 1948, Michael Lawrence Dundus Figgis was brought up in Nairobi until the age of eight, when his family's return to England took him to Newcastle. He did not start directing for the cinema until he was in his late thirties, coming to film-making after working as a musician and in the theatre. He played alongside Bryan Ferry in an R & B band, Gas Board, moved to London to study music, then became involved in the fringe theatre group the People Show, before forming his own company, the Mike Figgis Group, in 1980. As a film director he has continued to draw upon his musical and theatrical background: writing the scores for almost all his films; adapting August Strindberg's *Miss Julie* and Terence Rattigan's *The Browning Version*; and filming *The Loss of Sexual Innocence*, a work originally conceived as a theatre performance piece.

Figgis started using film in multimedia theatre productions such as *Slow Fade* (1982), where live music and performance were supplemented by the use of film and slides. That production provided the basis for *The House* (1984), a television film commissioned by Channel 4. Despite encouraging reviews, it did not immediately lead to further screen work, though FilmFour eventually provided some of the finance for Figgis' cinema debut, *Stormy Monday*. The strength of this story of inner-city romance, crime and corruption, set in Newcastle during 'America Week', lay in the use of music and evocation of mood. Music, cast (which included Melanie Griffith and Tommy Lee Jones), storyline and Edward Hopper-influenced *mise en scène* clearly signalled Figgis as a director looking across the Atlantic. But his viewpoint – epitomised by the scene in which the 'Krakow Jazz Ensemble' play a free jazz version of 'Star Spangled Banner', to the evident bemusement of Tommy Lee Jones' businessman/gangster – is a complex and by no means uncritical one. His next film, *Internal Affairs*, an exploration of corruption in the LAPD, was made in the USA.

Figgis' American work has included significant critical and commercial successes, particularly *Internal Affairs* and the relatively low-budget *Leaving Las Vegas*. The dark, convoluted melodrama *Liebestraum*, and *Mr Jones*, transformed by the studio from a sombre psycho-drama into something more feel-good, were commercially less successful. While attracted by Hollywood, his experience has clearly also led him to treat the place with suspicion, a perspective made apparent in the series of interviews with actors and others working in the industry that Figgis gave to the periodical *Projections*. His films have revealed an increasing desire to escape from conventional narrative structure and to exploit the potential that technological developments offer for smaller-scale productions. He used Super-16 to shoot *Leaving Las Vegas* – a film made for far less than was spent on promoting it – while his most notable experiment came in the use of digital cameras for *Timecode*, his satire on the movie business, which abandoned editing and split the screen into four quarters.

Maintaining a certain distance from Hollywood has also led Figgis to work as a documentary film-maker, continuing his relationship with Channel 4 with films on the fashion designer Vivienne Westwood (*On Liberty*, 1994); the avant-garde ballet choreographer William Forsythe (*Just Dancing Around*, 1995), his dramatic reconstruction *The Battle of Orgreave* (2002), set during the 1984–5 miners' strike; and 'Red, White and Blues', his well-informed contribution to Martin Scorsese's *The Blues* (2003).

Figgis has continued to make occasional feature films in Britain. *The Browning Version*, based on a play by Terence Rattigan (filmed by Anthony Asquith in 1951), seemed a surprisingly conservative choice for Figgis. He handles the sad story of a public school classics teacher facing enforced retirement and the break-up of his marriage with unfussy seriousness, updating the play only to the extent that he encourages Albert Finney to give a more openly emotional performance than Asquith had allowed Michael Redgrave in the part of the cruelly repressed Crocker-Harris. *The Loss of Sexual Innocence* is an example of the director's more experimental side. Filmed in England, Italy and Africa, after Figgis had completed the $25 million *One Night Stand* in New York, it represented a move away from both big budgets and conventional narrative form. Intercutting an interracial retelling of the story of Adam and Eve with a series of autobiographical fragments, the film is centred around the character of Nic (Figgis regular Julian Sands), at the beginning seen as a voyeuristic five-year-old in Kenya, at the close as a documentary film-maker looking for locations in Tunisia, whose brief liaison with the girlfriend of his sound-recordist leads to a tragic finale.

Figgis' concern with exploring the tensions within sexual relationships was evident also in *Miss Julie*. But where *The Loss of Sexual Innocence* moved freely across time and countries, *Miss Julie* – set in late nineteenth-century Sweden but filmed at Pinewood – remained positively claustrophobic in the way it restricted the action to a single set. The use of hand-held cameras and occasional split-screen framings also revealed a director experimenting with the limitations and potentials of film and intent on a Dogme-like return to film-making at its most raw.

Having explored these limitations and potentials more systematically in *Timecode*, Figgis continued his experimentation with digital cinematography and dividing the frame in *Hotel*, a British-Italian co-production set in a Venetian hotel whose residents include assorted vampires, a film crew making a Dogme version of *The Duchess of Malfi* and a television crew making a film about the Dogme film. Lacking the tight, real-time structure of *Timecode*, *Hotel* was a sign of how uneven Figgis' work can be (as is his disappointingly routine *Cold Creek Manor*, a big-budget 'Yuppies-in-peril thriller'). Yet his strength can be found in this variable quality. Not a director who has been content to restrict himself to home ground, nor one fitting neatly into that group of British directors who have made Hollywood their home, Mike Figgis has continued to experiment and to extend the language of film.

(Guy Barefoot)

BIBLIOGRAPHY: Dargis, Manohla, 'Hard and Fast', *Sight and Sound*, Mar. 1995, pp. 24–7; Figgis, Mike (ed.), *Projections 10:*

Hollywood Film-Makers on Film-Making (London: Faber and Faber, 1999); Figgis, Mike, '*Stormy Monday*', in Stephen Lowenstein (ed.), *My First Movie* (London: Faber and Faber, 2000); Macnab, Geoffrey, 'Wilful Amateur', *Sight and Sound*, May 1999, pp. 24–6.

FILMOGRAPHY: *Stormy Monday* (1988); *Internal Affairs* (US, 1990); *Liebestraum* (US, 1991); *Mr Jones* (US, 1993); *The Browning Version* (1994); *Leaving Las Vegas* (US, 1995); *One Night Stand* (US, 1997); *The Loss of Sexual Innocence* (UK/US); *Miss Julie* (UK/US) (1999); *Timecode* (US, 2000); *Hotel* (UK/It, 2001); *Ten Minutes Older. The Cello* ('About Time 2' episode, UK/Ger/US, 2002); *Cold Creek Manor* (US/Can, 2003); *Co-Ma* (doc., co-dir. Jovan Arsenic and 18 others, Slovenia, 2004).

FINBOW, Alexander

Alexander Finbow directed a short thriller, *Killing Time*, in 1997 before making his debut feature, *24 Hours in London*. The latter was released to derisive reviews and meagre audiences in July 2000, shortly before the death from cancer of Gary Olsen, who plays the film's flamboyant villain. Olsen's London gang boss, like Harold Shand in *The Long Good Friday* (John Mackenzie, 1979), is engaged in sealing his authority over rival gangsters and establishing an alliance with an American mob. But comparisons between the two films are hardly appropriate. Whereas Mackenzie makes Harold's empire-building a metaphor for the amoral materialism coming to dominate British society, Finbow, by setting his film ten years in the future, excuses himself from any connection with reality and presents a child's world of cardboard characters and impossible gun battles. At the Cannes Film Festival in 1999, Finbow proffered the sadly prophetic advice, 'If you're going to have a screening, don't let any journalists in.'

(Robert Murphy)

BIBLIOGRAPHY: 'Independents' Day: *24 Hours in London*', *Total Film*, Sept. 1999, pp. 126–7.

FILMOGRAPHY: *Killing Time* (short, 1997); *24 Hours in London* (2000).

FINBOW, Colin (1940–)

With some twenty feature films bearing his name between 1976 and 1996, Colin Finbow may well be the period's most prolific British director. He is certainly one of the most distinctive: a director operating outside the professional industry, devoted entirely to making films with children behind the camera as well as in front. Born in Ipswich in 1940, Finbow made amateur films as a teenager before studying at Ipswich College of Art and Goldsmiths College, London. In the 1960s he worked as a freelance writer for television and radio, then switched to teaching, serving as Head of English at the Forest Hill Comprehensive School in south London. By 1969 the Forest Hill Film Unit had been formed, producing many films under his supervision, ranging from documentaries to feature-length fiction. A season mounted in 1980 by ICA Children's Cinema brought the Unit's work to wider audiences, notably the evacuee drama *The Custard Boys*, adapted from the John Rae novel that Philip Leacock had filmed as *Reach for Glory* in 1962. Its warm reception encouraged Finbow to leave teaching and establish a new organisation, the Children's Film Unit.

The CFU's first production *Captain Stirrick*, based on a stage musical and crawling with nineteenth-century ragamuffins, proved a stylistic misstep; thereafter Finbow and his young colleagues avoided distant history and produced a wide variety of films, many of high technical quality. The atmospheric *A Swarm in May* (1983), based on the first of William Mayne's choir school novels, was the last drawn from existing material. Successors sprang from group discussions; the plots explored themes of the outcast child, courage, self-fulfilment and problem adults, viewed through the prisms of various film genres and social issues. *Dark Enemy* dealt with post-nuclear fears; *How's Business* and *Willie's War* returned to the 1940s' evacuee experience. *Hard Road* took the road movie for a ride, while *Doombeach* reflected concern for the environment. After its launch in 1982 Channel 4 became the Unit's sponsor and production partner; CFU films appeared at film festivals, but increasingly bypassed theatrical distribution for television screenings. Since 1998, production activities have waned, but the Unit, housed at Leavesden Studios, still mounts workshops and technical courses.

Interviewed for *Making Better Pictures* in 1986, Finbow said 'I like to use the "documentary" technique where we're just capturing whatever the actors are giving us'; Truffaut's cinema work with youngsters seems an obvious inspiration. Yet even in the early features Finbow's direction included artfully arranged camera compositions; and various elements – from the nostalgia for childhood's supposed innocence to the recurring topic of the wartime evacuee – prompt one to ask how much of the children's creative input has been filtered and controlled by an adult mind. But there is no questioning the freshness, novelty and polish of many CFU productions; the fact that the Unit seems to claim no famous film alumni among past members probably

says more about the parlous British industry than it does about the skills developed under Finbow's guidance.
(Geoff Brown)

BIBLIOGRAPHY: Hawkins, Rosalind, 'Movie Brats', *Times Educational Supplement*, 14 Mar. 1980; Herbert, Stephen, 'A Career in Films: Colin Finbow, Director', *Making Better Movies* vol. 2 no. 6, June 1980, pp. 324–6; Heron, Liz, 'Swashbuckling Feature', *Times Educational Supplement*, 4 June 1982, p. 31; Peachment, Chris, 'Blackboard Jungle?', *Time Out* no. 517, 14 Mar. 1980, p. 36.

FILMOGRAPHY (Shorts selected, features complete): *Dream* (short, 1969); *A View to a Death* (short, 1970); *Crows* (short); *Young Acton* (short) (1972); *Waves* (short, 1973); *Homecoming* (short, 1974); *Sequence* (short); *24 Frames* (short) (1975); *Summer of the Fox* (short, 1976); *Sons of Satan* (short, 1977); *Something Wicked This Way Comes* (1978); *Stockholm Suite* (short, 1979); *The Custard Boys* (1980); *Captain Stirrick* (1982); *A Swarm in May* (1983); *Dark Enemy*; *Mister Skeeter* (1985); *Daemon*; *School for Vandals* (1986); *Time to Talk* (short); *Take Cover* (1987); *Infantile Disorders*; *Under the Bed* (1988); *Hard Road* (1989); *Doombeach*; *Survivors* (1990); *How's Business* (1992); *Emily's Ghost* (1993); *The Higher Mortals* (1994); *Willie's War* (1995); *Nightshade*; *The Gingerbread House* (1996); *Awayday* (short, 1997); *A Beginner's Guide to Love* (short, 1998).

FINNEY, Albert (1936–)

Albert Finney was born in Salford, Lancashire, on 9 May 1936 and trained at the Royal Academy of Dramatic Art. After stage experience with Birmingham Rep and the Old Vic, including the title role in Keith Waterhouse and Willis Hall's *Billy Liar*, he made his film debut with a small role as Laurence Olivier's son in *The Entertainer* (Tony Richardson, 1960). His next two films, *Saturday Night and Sunday Morning* (Karel Reisz, 1960) and *Tom Jones* (Tony Richardson, 1963), brought him critical acclaim and international stardom, but Finney remained selective about his movie appearances, often choosing to go back to the theatre.

With fellow actor Michael Medwin he formed a production company, Memorial Enterprises, to make *Charlie Bubbles*. Based on an original screenplay by Shelagh Delaney, it concerns a wealthy writer (Finney), bored with his success, who returns to northern England to visit his ex-wife (Billie Whitelaw) and young son. The theme of affluent ennui was common in European art cinema, and the film borders on the precious in some of its more introspective moments. But Finney's treatment of the material is unusually disciplined and controlled for a first-time director (and for the period), and it is one of the few British films of the 1960s to suggest what an authentic, personal New Wave cinema might have looked like had one been allowed to develop in the UK.

Despite critical acclaim, *Charlie Bubbles* was not a commercial success and Finney complained publicly about Rank's mishandling of its much-delayed UK distribution. He returned exclusively to acting, aside from a television movie, *The Biko Inquest* (1984), co-directed with Graham Evans. Memorial did, however, go on to produce a number of other key British films, including *Privilege* (Peter Watkins, 1967), *if. . . .* (Lindsay Anderson, 1968), *Bleak Moments* (Mike Leigh, 1971), *Gumshoe* (Stephen Frears, 1971) and *O Lucky Man!* (Lindsay Anderson, 1973).
(Sheldon Hall)

BIBLIOGRAPHY: Falk, Quentin, *Albert Finney in Character* (London: Robson Books, 1993); Finney, Albert (letter), *Today's Cinema*, 27 June 1969, p. 2; *The South Bank Show: The Nowness* (London Weekend Television, 28 April 1996).

FILMOGRAPHY: *Charlie Bubbles* (1968).

FISHER, Terence (1904–1980)

Terence Fisher's critical reputation rests almost entirely on the horror films he directed for Hammer in the 1950s and 60s, but he was a more versatile film-maker than his horror output suggests. Born in London on 23 February 1904, he served in the merchant navy before entering the film industry in 1933. From 1936 to 1947 he worked as a film editor for a variety of production companies: the Gainsborough melodrama *The Wicked Lady* (Leslie Arliss, 1945) is probably his best-known project. His first three films as director – *Colonel Bogey*, *To the Public Danger* and *Song for Tomorrow* – were short dramas produced at Highbury Studios, which was being used by the Rank Organisation to develop new talent. *To the Public Danger* (1948), an impressively staged adaptation of a Patrick Hamilton radio play, was the best of these, and some critics have retrospectively seen it as anticipating Fisher's later horror work. In a further sign of things to come, future Hammer star Christopher Lee made a brief appearance in *Song for Tomorrow*. After Highbury, Fisher moved to Gainsborough where he directed (or co-directed with Antony Darnborough) four feature films. The nineteenth-century mystery drama *So Long at the Fair* (1950) is an interesting horror precursor, but Fisher's other Gainsborough films show him adept at a range of subjects: the plight of post-war refugees in *Portrait from Life*, tragic romance in the Noël Coward vehicle *The Astonished Heart* and light comedy in the portmanteau drama *Marry Me!*

When Gainsborough closed in the early 1950s, Fisher became a prolific specialist in the low-budget support feature that was beginning to be an increasingly important aspect of British film production. None of these films, nineteen in total, were strikingly original but some of them – notably the melodrama *Stolen Face* and the science-fiction drama *Four-Sided Triangle* – contained flashes of talent and ambition. Eleven of these films were made for Hammer, an up-and-coming independent production company with which Fisher's future career would become inextricably linked. When Hammer decided in the mid-1950s to concentrate on horror, Fisher became its main director. He was part of the team that produced all the classic Hammer horrors – including *The Curse of Frankenstein*, *Dracula*, *The Mummy*, *The Hound of the Baskervilles* and *The Curse of the Werewolf* – and his measured and stately style was a key aspect of the Hammer formula. Given the low budgets involved and the breakneck production schedules, the quality of these films

was inevitably uneven, but some of them, especially *Dracula*, were remarkable achievements, thought not generally feted by critics at the time. After the box-office failure of *The Phantom of the Opera*, Fisher worked less often for Hammer, although his later Hammer films arguably comprise his best work, reflecting both a technical maturity and a willingness to innovate. Although Fisher is regularly accused of representing a conservative moralistic force within British horror, films like *Frankenstein Created Woman* and *The Devil Rides Out* show a tentative and questioning attitude to social authority and morality. Fisher's other films from the 1960s – the science-fiction invasion fantasies *The Earth Dies Screaming*, *Island of Terror* and *Night of the Big Heat*, and a German-produced Sherlock Holmes story – are less successful, though interesting nevertheless. Fisher's final film, the Hammer production *Frankenstein and the Monster from Hell*, was completed in 1972 (although not released until 1974).

Fisher received very little critical attention throughout his career. Ironically, as that career ended, the publication of *A Heritage of Horror*, David Pirie's book-length study of the British horror film, led to a reappraisal of his work. Since then, Fisher has come to be seen as a major British film director, especially for his contribution to a popular British genre cinema. It is still the case, however, that Fisher's pre-horror work has not received the critical attention it merits. Terence Fisher died in London on 18 June 1980.

(Peter Hutchings)

BIBLIOGRAPHY: Dixon, Wheeler Winston, *The Charm of Evil: The Life and Films of Terence Fisher* (London and Metuchen, NJ: Scarecrow Press, 1991); Fisher, Terence, 'Horror Is My Business', *Films and Filming*, July 1964, p. 8; Hutchings, Peter, *Terence Fisher* (Manchester: Manchester University Press, 2001); Meikle, Dennis, *A History of Horrors: The Rise and Fall of the House of Hammer* (London and Metuchen, NJ: Scarecrow Press, 1996); Pirie, David, *A Heritage of Horror* (London: Gordon Fraser, 1973).

FILMOGRAPHY: *Colonel Bogey* (1947); *To the Public Danger*; *Song for Tomorrow*; *Portrait from Life* (US: *The Girl in the Painting*) (1948); *Marry Me!*; *The Astonished Heart* (co-dir. Antony Darnborough) (1949); *So Long at the Fair* (co-dir. Antony Darnborough, 1950); *Home to Danger* (1951); *The Last Page* (US: *Manbait*); *Wings of Danger* (US: *Dead on Course*); *Stolen Face*; *Distant Trumpet* (1952); *Four-Sided Triangle*; *Mantrap* (US: *Woman in Hiding*); *Spaceways*; *Blood Orange*; *Three's Company* (co-dir. Charles Saunders) (1953); *Face the Music* (US: *The Black Glove*); *The Stranger Came Home*; *Mask of Dust* (US: *Race for Life*); *Final Appointment*; *Children Galore* (1954); *Murder by Proxy*; *The Flaw*; *Stolen Assignment* (1955); *The Last Man to Hang?* (1956); *Kill Me Tomorrow*; *The Curse of Frankenstein* (1957); *Dracula* (US: *Horror of Dracula*); *The Revenge of Frankenstein* (1958); *The Hound of the Baskervilles*; *The Man Who Could Cheat Death*; *The Mummy*; *The Stranglers of Bombay* (1959); *The Two Faces of Dr Jekyll*; *The Brides of Dracula*; *The Sword of Sherwood Forest* (1960); *The Curse of the Werewolf* (1961); *The Phantom of the Opera*; *Sherlock Holmes und das Halsband des Todes* (aka *Sherlock Holmes and the Deadly Necklace*) (1962); *The Horror of It All*; *The Gorgon*; *The Earth Dies Screaming* (1964); *Dracula – Prince of Darkness*; *Island of Terror* (1966); *Frankenstein Created Woman*; *Night of the Big Heat* (1967); *The Devil Rides Out* (US: *The Devil's Bride*, 1968); *Frankenstein Must Be Destroyed* (1969); *Frankenstein and the Monster from Hell* (1974).

FITZHAMON, Lewin (1869–1961)

Lewin Fitzhamon was born at Aldingham, Cumbria, on 5 June 1869. He became a music-hall performer and first worked in film for Robert Paul in 1900, acting in some titles, directing others, including *Briton vs Boer* (1900). In 1904 he left the theatre world to joined Cecil Hepworth as 'stage manager', replacing Percy Stow, who went on to form the Clarendon Film Company. 'Fitz' stayed with Hepworth for eight years, during which time he wrote, directed and frequently acted in two films per week. Hepworth later remembered him as 'a rattling good sort – one of the very best' (Hepworth, p. 67). All told, he directed around five hundred films.

Fitzhamon made his mark early on with the hugely popular *Rescued by Rover*, made for Hepworth in 1905; the most enduring and familiar of his films, it relied upon a classic cinematic narrative: stolen baby, pursuit of miscreant gypsy (by Rover, the dog), joyful reunion of baby and parents. Fitzhamon proved himself accomplished across a wide range of narrative forms suitable for the emerging cinema business. He produced comic trick films (*That Fatal Sneeze*), nightmarish fantasies (*The Man and His Bottle*), social comedies (*What the Curate Really Did*), Westerns (*The

Squatter's Daughter), melodramas (*Falsely Accused*) and chase films (*A New Hat for Nothing*), alongside actualities and topicals. He developed comic series for Hepworth, including 'the Poorlucks', and the anarchic 'Tilly' series with the young Chrissie White and Alma Taylor; in 1905–6 he also pioneered political films in Britain, with the Pictorial Politics Association, also formed with Hepworth. Fitzhamon particularly loved working with animals, which he portrayed in a heroic light. Rover (real name Blair) subsequently featured in titles like *The Dog Outwits the Kidnappers*, in which he rescues a kidnapped child by driving a car. Fitzhamon continued to show animals to be man's best friend in *Dumb Sagacity* and *Father's Lesson*, and he always considered the best actor he ever worked with to be his horse Tariff.

Fitzhamon left Hepworth in 1912 and formed his own company, Fitz Films, operating from Walthamstow. This enjoyed little success, and he briefly worked for other producers before leaving the film business in 1914. He was also the author of two novels, *The Rival Millionaires* (1904) and *The Vixen* (1915), and wrote comic pieces for popular magazines. His was a simple gift, to tell stories that, as he put it, 'could be told by a few words thrown upon the screen' (Gifford, p. 317). He died in London on 10 October 1961.

(Luke McKernan)

BIBLIOGRAPHY: Gifford, Denis, 'Fitz: The Old Man of the Screen', in Charles Barr (ed.), *All Our Yesterdays* (London: BFI, 1986); Hepworth, Cecil M., *Came the Dawn: Memories of a Film Pioneer* (London: Phoenix House, 1951).

FILMOGRAPHY: *Briton vs Boer*; *His Mother's Portrait*; or, *The Soldier's Vision* (1900); *Two Leap Year Proposals*; *The Stolen Puppy*; *The Coster's Wedding*; *After the 'Oliday*; *The Parson's Cookery Lesson*; *The Haunted Oak*; *A Rough Time for the Broker*, *The Great Servant Question*; *The Slavey's Dream*; *The Honeymoon: First, Second and Third Class*; *When the Sleeper Wakes*; *The Press Illustrated*; *The Spoilt Child*; *A Cheap Boot Store*; *The Lover's Crime*; *The Jonah Man*; or, *The Traveller Bewitched* (US: *The Bewitched Traveller*, co-dir. Cecil Hepworth); *The Nigger Boy's Revenge*; *The Confidence Trick*; *Lady Plumpton's Motor*, *A Trip to Paris* (US: *An Englishman's Trip to Paris from London*); *Don't Interfere with a Coalheaver*, *A Den of Thieves*; *His Superior Officer*; *Won by Strategy*; *A Race for a Kiss*; *The Story of Two Christmasses*; *For the Hand of a Princess* (1904); *Bathers Will Be Prosecuted*; *The Other Side of the Hedge* (US: *Over the Hedge*); Lost, *Stolen or Strayed*; *The Two Imps*; *An Interrupted Honeymoon*; *Poison or Whisky* (US: *The Lover's Ruse*); *The Amateur Architect*; The *Rival Sportsmen*; *Paint and Perfidy*; *Charity Covers a Multitude of Sins*; *Only Her Brother*; *Table Turning*; *Falsely Accused*; *A Terrible Flirt*; *The Duel*; *A Battle of Cauliflowers*; *Rehearsing a Play*; *False Money*; *The Reluctant Bridegroom*; *The Inquisitive Boots*; *The Annual Trip of the Mothers' Meeting*; *Children v. Earthquakes – Earthquakes Preferred*; *Two Sentimental Tommies*; *Rescued by Rover*, *Prehistoric Peeps*; *The Death of Nelson*; *How the Tramps Tricked the Motorist*; *Rover Takes a Call*; *What the Curate Really Did*; *The Stolen Guy*; *The Butterfly Chase*; *Lodgings to Let*; *The Aliens' Invasion*; *International Exchange*; *The Babes in the Wood*; *The Villain's Wooing*; *The Burglar's Boy* (1905); *The Voter's Curse*; *The Tramp's Dream*; *The Rivals*; *The Best Little Girl in the World*; *A Tragedy of the Sawmills*; *A Cure for Lumbago*; *The Peasant Girl's Revenge*; *Cupid and the Widow*, *A Poet and His Babies*; *Dick Turpin's Ride to York*; *In the Summer Time*; *The Kidnapper and the Child*; *An Episode of the Derby*; *When Father Eloped with Cook*; *The Pirate Ship*; *The Valet Who Stole the Tobacco*; *The Burglar and the Cat*; *His Daughter and His Gold*; *The Pill Maker's Mistake*; *The Squatter's Daughter*, *Black Beauty*; *When Jenkins Washed Up*; *Our New Policeman*; *The Burglar and the Judge*; *The Fatal Leap*; *The Lucky Necklace*; *Just in Time*; *The Brigands*; *After the Matinee*; *A Grandchild's Devotion*; *Harlequinade*; *The Doll Maker's Daughter*, *Little Meg and the Wonderful Lamp*; *The Jerry-Built House*; *The Magic Ring* (1906); *Burglars at the Ball*; *The Busy Man*; *The Green Dragon*; *Pillage by Pillar Box*; *The Nun*; *The Doll's Revenge*; *A Smart Capture*; *A Feather in His Cap*; *Not Such a Fool as He Looks*; *The Artist's Model*; *A Father's Vengeance*; The *Fraudulent Solicitor*, *Kidnapped*; *A Lovers' Quarrel*; *Young Scamps*; *Hair Restorer*, *The Boaster*, *Sister Mary Jane's Top Note*; *The Man Who Could Not Commit Suicide*; *The Milkman's Wedding*; *The New Dress*; *That Fatal Sneeze*; *Never Complain to Your Laundress*; *The Absent Minded Man*; *The Madman's Bride*; *A Modern Don Juan*; *The Tramp's Revenge*; *The Ghosts' Holiday*; *A Too Devoted Wife*; *Drink*; *Mischievous Girls*; *A Soldier's Jealousy*; *A Sailor's Lass*; *Simpkin's Saturday Off*, *A Seaside Girl*; *A Tramp's Dream of Wealth*; *Dumb Sagacity*; *The Sticky Bicycle*; *A Letter in the Sand*; *Rebellious Schoolgirls*; *The Artful Lovers*; *Dying of Thirst*; *The Heavenly Twins*; *Preserving Edwin*; *Johnny's Gun*; *Cinderella*; *The Stolen Bridle*; *Serving the Writ*; *A Painless Extraction* (1907); *The Faithless Friend*; *The Curate's Courtship*; *The Stubborn Moke*; *The Greedy Girl*; *The Doctor's Dodge*; *The Tell-Tale Kinematograph*; *The Man and His Bottle*; *Catching a Burglar*, *The Tramps and the Purse*; *Father's Lesson*; *The Burglar and the Clock*; *The Artful Dodger*, *The Electric Torch*; *Our Cousin from Abroad*; *Bicycles Repaired*; *The Hidden Hoard*; *The Dog Outwits the Kidnappers*; *The Thief at the Casino*; *My Little Lady Bountiful*; *Hi! Stop Those Barrels*; *Catching a Tartar*, *The Troubles of a House Agent*; *The Motherly Pram*; *The Love Token*; *The Man Who Learned to Fly*; *The Gentleman Gypsy* (aka *The Trials of a Gypsy Gentleman*; *When Women Rule*; *The Harmless Lunatic's Escape*; *The Serpent's Tooth*; *Weary Willie Steals a Fish*; *An Attractive Catch*; *Baby's Playmate*; *The Ne'er-Do-Well and the Baby*; *Jack in the Letterbox*; *Don Quixote's Dream*; *A Free Pardon*; *Snatched from a Terrible Death*; *Cabby's Sweetheart*; *A Heartless Mother*, *A Convict's Dash for Liberty*; *The Man and the Latchkey*; *A Ticket for Two*; *Marrying under Difficulties*; *The Photographer's Flirtation*; *A Thoughtless Beauty* (aka *Forced to Consent*); *The Pets' Tea Party*; *The Unlucky Thief*, *A Fascinating Game*; *An Unfortunate Bathe*; *The Deserter*, *The Lucky Pie*; *Tomkins Buys a Donkey*; *The Amorous Nurse*; *The Safety Suit for Skaters*; *John Gilpin's Ride*; *The Organ Grinder's Luck*; *The Schoolboy's Revolt*; *The Nursemaid's Dream*; *A Country Girl*; *For the Little Lady's Sake*; *The Dishonest Barber*, *The Professor's Antigravitational Fluid*; *The Hottentot and the Gramophone*; *The Wrong Medicine*; *The Devil and the Cornet*; *The Beauty Competition*; *The Dog Thief*, *An Enemy in the Camp*; *The Fickle Husband and the Boy*; *The Unlucky Bridegroom*; *The Detective's Ruse*; *The Fairy's Sword*; *The Runaway Kids*; *Unemployed and Unemployable* (1908); *A Friend in Need*; *A Present for Her Husband*; *In the Service of the King*; *A Plucky Little Girl*; *No More Hats Wanted*; *The Dog Came Back*; *Last Year's Timetable*; *All's*

Fair in Love and War; The Rival Mesmerists; The Spoilt Child; Mother-in-Law Has All the Luck; The Lost Memory; Why Father Learned to Ride; The Cat Came Back; The Shepherd's Dog; That Marvellous Gramophone; The Cabman's Good Fairy; That Never-to-Be-Forgotten Day; The Dentist's Daughter; The Gipsy Child; The Miser and the Child; A Pair of Truants; The Villain's Downfall; The Fancy Dress Ball; The Curate at the Races; His Only Friend; Too Much Lobster, Invisibility (co-dir. Cecil Hepworth); *The Race for the Farmer's Cup; The Story of a Picture; The Rivals; Baiting the Bobby; The Boy and His Kite; A Man and His Bees; A Cheap Removal; The Spy; The Ranch Owner's Daughter* (aka *The Redskin's Offer*); *Saved by the Telegraph; Necessity Is the Mother of Invention; The Meanest Man on Earth; The Jewel Thieves; The Little Milliner and the Thief; The Penalty of Beauty; The Wrong Cab; The Sorrows of a Chaperone; The Gypsy Lover, A Drunkard's Son; The Fatal Appetiser, The Gypsy's Baby; A Pair of Desperadoes; A Gamin's Gratitude; A Street Arab; A Brutal Master, Saved from the Sea; The Faithful Clock; Cupid's Loaf; The Girl Who Joined the Bushrangers; Mr Poorluck Gets Married; The Little Flower Girl's Christmas; An Attempt to Smash a Bank; The Lazy Boy* (1909); *Tempered with Mercy; Love's Strategy; Hot Pickles; Saved by His Sweetheart; Are You John Brown?; A Fickle Girl; Unlucky Bill; The Little Housekeeper, Who's Got My Hat?; The Burglar and Little Phyllis; Black Beauty; Mary the Coster, The Scaramouches; The Sharp-witted Thief; The Little Blue Cap; Invigorating Electricity; Persuading Papa; A Baby's Powder, Dave Craggs, Detective; Mr Poorluck's Lucky Horseshoe; Married in Haste; Fits and Misfits; The Stowaway; A Present for His Wife; The Telephone Call; The New Reporter, The Fakir's Flute; Seven, Seventeen, and Seventy; The Farmer's Daughter, A Night in Armour, A New Hat for Nothing; The Merry Beggars; Extracting a Cheque from Uncle; The Poorlucks' First Tiff; A Chanticleer Hat; Without Her Father's Consent; His New Mama; The Detective's Dog; Never Send a Man to Match a Ribbon; The Poorlucks Take Part in a Pageant; The Mechanical Mary Anne; Tilly the Tomboy Plays Truant; In the Good Old Days; Mr Poorluck's Dream; The Short-Sighted Errand Boy; The Cardsharpers; A Difficult Courtship; Over the Garden Wall; Tilly the Tomboy Goes Boating; All's Fair in Love; A Modern Love Potion; The Adventures of a £5 Note; Tilly the Tomboy Visits the Poor, Mr Poorluck Buys Some Furniture; Uncle Joe; The Widow's Wooers; He Eloped with Her Father, Josephine and her Lovers; A Sailor's Lass; Love Me Love My Dog; Dumb Comrades; The Black Kitten; Tilly the Tomboy Buys Linoleum; A Woman Scorned; The Sheriff's Daughter, The Moneylender's Mistake; Heart of Oak; A Spoilt Child of Fortune; The Conquering Cask; Tilly at the Election; The Detective in Peril; In Pursuit of Fashion; Father Buys a Screen; The Heart of a Fishergirl* (1910); *The Three Lovers; College Chums; The Double Elopement; The Dog's Devotion; N Stands for Nelly; The Parson's Wife; The Detective and the Jewel; M. Poorluck Buys Some China; Tilly's Unsympathetic Uncle; The Bailiff's Little Weakness; Now I Have to Call Him Father, Poorluck's Excursion Tickets; The Lawyer's Message; Children Mustn't Smoke; The Course of True Love; Evicted; Exceeding His Duty; When Tilly's Uncle Flirted; Harry the Footballer, Tilly's Party; The New Cook; Mother's Boy; A Sprained Ankle; Toodles, Scout; The Amateur Burglar, The Subaltern's Joke; Tilly at the Seaside; A Happy Event in the Poorluck Family; P.C. Hawkeye's Busy Day; A Double Deception; Till Death Do Us Part; The Little Black Pom; Rover the Peacemaker, P.C. Hawkeye Leaves the Force; Mr and Mrs Poorluck Separate; Tilly – Matchmaker, Twin Roses; Gipsy Nan; The Early Worm; The Wisdom of Brother Ambrose; Tracked by Tiger, Tilly and the Mormon Missionary; An Absorbing Game; A Horse and Mrs Grundy; P.C. Hawkeye Turns Detective; A Fight with Fire; Janet's Flirtation; Tilly and the Fire Engines; Jim of the Mounted Police; My Dear Love; Love and a Sewing-Machine; Hawkeye Learns to Punt; The Smuggler's Step-Daughter, A Wilful Maid; The Gay Lord Ducie; A Seaside Introduction; The Fireman's Daughter, Many a Slip; A Halfbreed's Gratitude; The Greatest of These; Envy, Hatred and Malice; In Jest and Earnest; Rachel's Sin; Tilly and the Smugglers; Tiger the 'Tec; All's Right with the World; The Stolen Letters; Not Guilty; For a Baby's Sake* (1911); *The Burglar's Daughter, An Indian Vendetta; Her Only Pal; A Curate's Love Story; The Mermaid; The Lost Will; The Editor and the Millionaire; A Fisherman's Love Story; The Blind Man's Dog; Never Again, Never!; A Gipsy Girl's Honour, Hubby's Letter, A Mother and Sons of 1776; A Case of Explosives* (aka *Munition Workers*); *Children of the Forest; The Broken Melody; A Day in the Country; Saving the Royal Mail; The Flapper's Elopement; Amorous Arthur, Repaying the Debt; Unlucky Ann; Jemima and the Editor, The Wrong Envelopes; The Unjust Steward; The Flapper and the Curates; Flo the Flapper, The Pony Who Paid the Rent; A Day in London; A Village Scandal; The Copper's Revenge* (1912); *Freddy's Dumb Playmates; The First Steeplechase; With Human Instinct; He Was So Fond of Animals; A Race for Love; The Picnic on the Island; Little Willie's Apprenticeship; Three Little Vagabonds* (aka *Home for the Holidays*); *Her Pony's Love; Beauty and the Boat; The Flapper and the Colonel; A Terrible Plant; Love in a Boarding House; The Flappers and the Nuts; Algy's Tormentor, Daddy's Darlings; Gipsy Hate; While Shepherds Watched; The Lass of Gloucester, A Day on Rollers; When the Hurricanes Visited the Doughnuts; A Bore of a Boy; The Girl Next Door* (1913); *When the Hurricanes Bought the Lino; When the Hurricanes Took up Farming; A Hateful Bondage; A Footballer's Honour, The Whirlwind Kids; The Loosened Plank; Her Faithful Companions; Two Little Angels; When the Hurricanes Visited the Sawmills; The Scallawag; Men Will Deceive* (1914).

FITZPATRICK, James (1895–1980)

James A. FitzPatrick was the American maker of bland but beautiful travelogue shorts, famous in the popular memory for the concluding lines of his soundtrack narrations ('And we most reluctantly say farewell to . . .'). His role in British cinema production was small – he made the first of his two features here, *The Lady of the Lake* (1928), and returned in the 1930s for 'quota quickies' – though his travelogues formed a regular part of the 'full supporting programmes' enjoyed (or suffered) by local audiences on their way to the main attraction.

Born in Shelton, Connecticut, on 26 February 1895, FitzPatrick studied at Yale and entered films in 1916, writing and directing short comedies for children, made in New York. In the 1920s several series of biographical shorts emerged, squeezing into nutshells the lives of great composers and authors. In 1928 he struck a production deal with Gainsborough Pictures to make a dramatised version of Sir Walter Scott's poem *The Lady of the Lake*, featuring Percy Marmont and Benita Hume. Ready by the end of the year, the film was relaunched in 1931, still lacking dialogue, but with an elaborate synchronised score by the American musician Nathaniel Shilkret. By this time the production must have seemed even more antique than it did three years before. Shots of lakes and mountains are pretty, but FitzPatrick shows no aptitude for handling actors: the drama quickly expires in a welter of bad beards, oppressive brick interiors and intertitles (often in rhyme) displayed against tartan backgrounds.

In America FitzPatrick finally found his industry niche in 1931 with his 'Traveltalk' one-reelers produced by MGM. The series burst into Technicolor in 1936, perfect for capturing *Chile, Land of Charm* (1937) or *Picturesque South Africa* (1937). Back in black-and-white Britain, he toiled for a year at Shepperton on MGM quota productions of fragmentary structure, modest demeanour and decreasing length. The run began with *David Livingstone* (1936), featuring Marmont as the English missionary, and concluded with a half-hour trio devoted to Bizet, Chopin and Liszt. Higher-quality results emerged from his production of Marmont's sole directorial effort, *The Captain's Table* (1936), a lively crime thriller.

In 1944 FitzPatrick tried features again with *Song of Mexico*, a comedy-drama travelogue with music, made for Republic. There were no successors, and he returned to one-reelers, saying reluctant farewell over the years to *A Wee Bit of Scotland* (one of a batch filmed in Britain in 1945), *Beautiful Bavaria* (1953) and many other wonders in a world shortly to change for ever with the tourist stampede. Even when supporting programmes faded he still kept working, only relinquishing the company reins in 1973. James FitzPatrick died following a stroke in Palm Springs, California, on 12 June 1980.

(Geoff Brown)

BIBLIOGRAPHY: Fisher, Bob, '"Voice of the Globe" Tradition Revived on Tapes', *American Cinematographer* vol. 69 no. 6, June 1988, pp. 81–2, 84, 86.

FILMOGRAPHY (UK only): *The Lady of the Lake* (1928; sound version 1931); *David Livingstone* (1936); *Auld Lang Syne*; *The Last Rose of Summer*; *The Bells of St Mary's* (short) (1937); *A Dream of Love* (short); *Georges Bizet, Composer of Carmen* (short); *The Life of Chopin* (short) (1938).

FLAHERTY, Robert (1884–1951)

Robert Flaherty, widely regarded as the inventor of documentary cinema, approached film-making with an ethnographer's eye. Generating ideas 'in the field', he would shoot a vast amount of footage from which he would distil ideas and material. Flaherty is credited with eight films, all distinguished by an instinct for finding lyrical images. Three of them were made during his eight-year stay in Britain during the 1930s.

The eldest of seven children, Robert Joseph Flaherty was born in Iron Mountain, Michigan, on 16 February 1884. He received little formal schooling, though he briefly attended Upper Canada College, Toronto, and the Michigan School of Mines (where he met his wife and collaborator, Frances Hubbard). He spent the years between 1910 and 1920 prospecting for iron ore

in north Canada, and shooting material for what was to be his first film, *Nanook of the North* (1922).

In 1931 Flaherty came to Britain at John Grierson's behest to make a documentary for the Empire Marketing Board: this was to be a study of craftsmanship in Britain's major industries. After some weeks travelling around the country and shooting a great deal of 'test' footage, the EMB's limited film stock and funds ran out and Flaherty was taken off the film, which was completed by EMB personnel. A sound version of *Industrial Britain*, incorporating much of Flaherty's footage, was distributed to commercial cinemas in 1933.

For his next assignment, *Man of Aran*, Flaherty and his crew spent over a year on the island of Aran off Ireland's Galway coast, shooting the film and absorbing Irish life. The production, financed by Gaumont-British, overran its budget again and the shoot was closed down: this time, however, Flaherty took part in editing the film, which was enthusiastically received, despite charges of inauthenticity (the islanders had re-enacted long-abandoned fishing practices for the camera). *Man of Aran* won several awards, including Best Film of 1934 at the Venice Film Festival.

In 1935 Flaherty was commissioned by Alexander Korda to film *Elephant Boy* in India. This was a big-budget production by comparison with Flaherty's earlier work, but once again he was unable to complete it: after two years of shooting, the film was finished at Denham Studios by Korda's brother Zoltan. A 'wretched piece of cinema by all standards', was Paul Rotha's verdict, 'but it does contain some fine examples of Flaherty's work' (Rotha, p. 177).

When Flaherty returned to London, no further projects were forthcoming, and in 1939 he and Frances returned to the USA, where he made two more seminal documentaries – *The Land* (1942) and *Louisiana Story* (1948) – and collaborated on a third, *Titan: The True Story of Michaelangelo* (co-dirs. Richard Lyford/Curt Oertel, 1950), before his death from cerebral thrombosis in Dummerston, Vermont, on 23 July 1951. His work continues to be commemorated at the annual Flaherty Seminar, inaugurated by his widow in 1954.

The single-minded, imaginative Flaherty's sojourn in Britain delivered a stimulating culture shock to the staid men dominating the British film scene. More significantly, the scenes Flaherty shot for his British-made films remain among the most beautiful in the history of documentary cinema.

(Annette Kuhn)

BIBLIOGRAPHY: Murphy, William T., *Robert J. Flaherty: A Guide to References and Resources* (Boston, MA: G. K. Hall & Co., 1978); Rotha, Paul, *Robert J. Flaherty: A Biography*, edited by Jay Ruby (Philadelphia: University of Pennsylvania Press, 1983); Ruby, Jay, 'A Re-examination of the Early Career of Robert J. Flaherty', *Quarterly Review of Film Studies* vol. 5 no. 4, 1980, pp. 431–57.

FILMOGRAPHY (UK only): *Industrial Britain* (1931; rel. 1933); *Man of Aran* (1934); *Elephant Boy* (co-dir. Zoltán Korda, 1937).

FLEISCHER, Richard (1916–)

Richard Fleischer was born in Brooklyn on 8 December 1916, the son of animator Max Fleischer. He studied psychology at Brown University and began directing at Yale Drama School. This led to a contract at RKO, where he worked on newsreels, documentaries and shorts before making his feature debut with *Child of Divorce* (1946). Following the success of *The Narrow Margin* (1952), Fleischer broke out of B-movies to direct international films of every conceivable genre, among them *20,000 Leagues under the Sea* (1954), *The Vikings* (1958), *Compulsion* (1959) and *Doctor Dolittle* (1967). The last, a lavish but flaccid musical adaptation of Hugh Lofting's stories, was shot partly on location in Castle Combe, Wiltshire, where local residents including Sir Ranulph Fiennes tried to sabotage the production (though inclement weather inflicted far greater damage).

Fleischer returned to Britain for the last of his four recreations of true-life crimes. *10 Rillington Place* is a coldly matter-of-fact dramatisation of the Christie murders, centred on a chilling performance from Richard Attenborough. With its sallow lighting, drab colour scheme and dank, cramped sets it has a palpably fetid sense of place. Fleischer keeps in check the potential for gothic melodrama he subsequently allowed uninhibited expression in his next British film, *Blind Terror*, an unsubtle, brazenly manipulative and highly suspenseful blind-woman-in-peril thriller written by Brian Clemens.

At his best an exceptionally skilled *metteur en scène* – 'I'm not interested in doing a picture about what I think', he once told Brendan Behan – Fleischer began an irreversible decline with *The Incredible Sarah*, a stilted biopic of Sarah Bernhardt financed by *Reader's Digest*, and a stolid all-star version of Mark Twain's *The Prince and the Pauper* (US: *Crossed Swords*, 1977) with an unfortunate choice – the teenage Mark Lester – for the title roles. This was produced by Ilya Salkind and filmed in Britain and Hungary but copyrighted to Panama. Fleischer's last film to date is the large-format Showscan featurette *Call from Space* (1989).

(Sheldon Hall)

BIBLIOGRAPHY: Fleischer, Richard, *Just Tell Me When to Cry: A Memoir* (London: Souvenir Press, 1994); Gow, Gordon, 'Don't Throw Them Away', *Films and Filming*, Dec. 1970, pp. 20–5; Pulleine, Tim, 'Richard Fleischer', *Films and Filming*, Nov. 1984, pp. 29–31; Roberts, John, 'Richard Fleischer: Filmmaking Is in His Genes', *Classic Images*, Sept. 1992, pp. 34–6.

FILMOGRAPHY (UK only): *10 Rillington Place*; *Blind Terror* (US: *See No Evil*) (1971); *The Incredible Sarah* (US/UK, 1976).

FLEMYNG, Gordon (1934–1995)

Gordon Flemyng was born in Glasgow on 7 March 1934. He began his career in television, directing episodes of Granada's showcase for young writers and actors, *The Younger Generation* (1961). His first cinema films, *Soho for Sparrow* and *Five to One*, were lively contributions to *Edgar Wallace Presents . . .*, the Merton Park B-films series. Writer-producer Milton Subotsky hired Flemyng for the cheerfully makeshift pop musical *Just for Fun!* (1963) and kept him on to make colourful features starring BBC television's popular time traveller, Doctor Who. The films recast the Doctor (played by Peter Cushing) as an inventor/scientist who has created a time machine rather than the mysterious alien of the television series. If Cushing's gently eccentric Doctor fails to match William Hartnell's crotchety ambiguity, the films remain engaging for their bright look, campy costumes (the heroic Thals of the first film all look like Julian Clary) and the memorably rasping robotic villains ('Ex-ter-min-ate!'). The second film, with its Wellsian conquered and ruined Earth, is a spirited mix of comedy knockabout and war-torn science-fiction thrills.

Flemyng's international films are less known, but all unusual: *Great Catherine* is a quirkily cast (Peter O'Toole, Zero Mostel, Jeanne Moreau, Jack Hawkins) adaptation of George Bernard Shaw's play; his Hollywood film, *The Split*, is a Donald Westlake caper with pre-blaxploitation leads (Jim Brown, Diahann Carroll) and solid character support (Ernest Borgnine, Warren Oates, Gene Hackman); and *The Last Grenade* is a downbeat military drama with Stanley Baker, Honor Blackman and Richard Attenborough. After his theatrical career petered out, Flemyng returned to television to make the effective drama reconstruction *Philby, Burgess and Maclean* (1977), the British agents in Nazi-occupied France series *Wish Me Luck* (1988) and episodes of *Lovejoy* and *Minder* (notably 'The Immaculate Con-

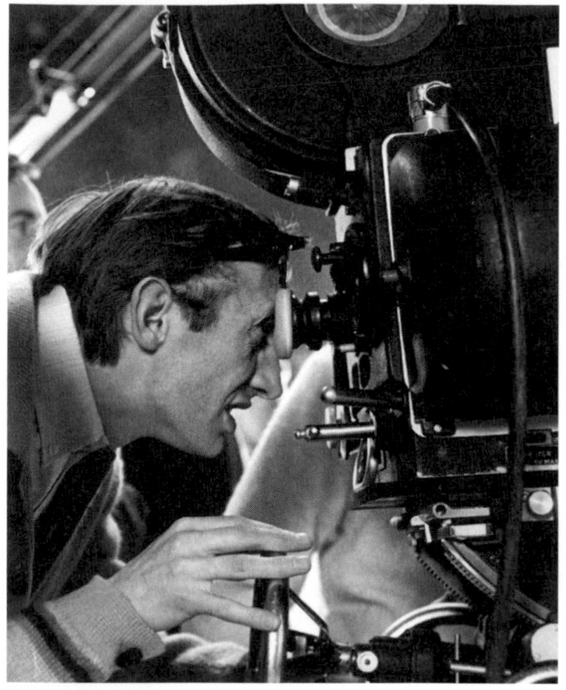

traption', 1994). He died in London on 12 July 1995. His son is the actor Jason Flemyng.
(Kim Newman)

BIBLIOGRAPHY: Obituary, *Classic Images* no. 246, Dec. 1995. p. 57; Obituary, *The Stage*, 10 Aug. 1995.

FILMOGRAPHY: *Solo for Sparrow* (1962); *Just for Fun!* (1963); *Five to One* (1964); *Dr Who and the Daleks* (1965); *Daleks' Invasion Earth 2150 A.D.* (1966); *Great Catherine*; *The Split* (US) (1968); *The Last Grenade* (1970).

FLETCHER, Mandie (1954–)

Mandie Fletcher was born on 27 December 1954. She began her career in British television, working on such popular sitcoms as *Only Fools and Horses* (1981), *Blackadder II* (1985), *Brush Strokes* (1986), *Blackadder the Third* (1987) and *Desmond's* (1989). She subsequently directed the television play *Shalom Joan Collins* (1989) and the television film *Born Kicking* (1992). Fletcher's only feature film to date is *Deadly Advice*, a black comedy set in Hay-on-Wye. Jane Horrocks stars as Jodie, a depressed young woman treated as a servant by her overbearing mother (Brenda Fricker), who is inspired by fantasy visits from 1920s' poisoner Major Herbert Armstrong (Edward Woodward) – along with several other famous murderers – to consider deadly solutions to her problems. Having established its outlandish premise, *Deadly Advice* has nowhere much to go. For all Fletcher's success with the dark, literary humour of *Blackadder*, her flat, perfunctory direction seems ill suited to the feature film format, and she returned to television to direct *Hamish Macbeth* (1996–7).
(Daniel O'Brien)

BIBLIOGRAPHY: Fletcher, Mandie, 'Killingly Funny', *Sight and Sound* Comedy Supplement, Mar. 1994, p. 12.

FILMOGRAPHY: *Deadly Advice* (1994).

FOGWELL, Reginald (18?–1957)

In the early 1930s, distributors and audiences were regularly invited to sample the output of Reginald Fogwell Productions. At various times Fogwell directed, produced and contributed to the screenplays. Several films bore serious, impressive titles – *Guilt*, *The Written Law*, *Betrayal* – though contemporary reviews indicate that Fogwell's ambitions generally loomed larger than any entertainment on offer. None of his output appears to have survived.

Reginald Gilbert Fogwell was born in Dartmouth, Devon, the son of an engraver, and initially worked as a bank clerk. A later job in advertising led to the film industry. After working in London as the Fox Film Corporation's director of publicity, he spent several years in Hollywood writing scenarios, returning to Britain in 1926. He co-wrote scenarios for Graham Cutts' *The Triumph of the Rat* (1926) and Sinclair Hill's *The Guns of Loos* (1928) and made his debut as director with *The Warning* (1928), a drama about a wronged wife's revenge, made for the producer A. E. Bundy. It was exhibited both as a silent and a talkie, but there was little novelty in either version. Fogwell pressed on to mount his own productions, beginning in 1930 with *Guilt*, another infidelity melodrama. His next film, *Madame Guillotine*, aimed for a bigger

splash. Madeleine Carroll and Brian Aherne, stars of Victor Saville's *The 'W' Plan* (1930), were secured; period trappings were summoned to conjure up the French Revolution. Audiences were attracted, but critics failed to find a vital spark.

Carroll subsequently signed a contract with Fogwell for what his publicity suggested was a 'record figure', but their association only produced one further film, *The Unwritten Law*, yet another melodrama of infidelity. Perhaps now reading the signs, Fogwell diversified: alongside further domestic dramas he served as the producer of comedian George Robey's talkie debut, *The Temperance Fete* (Graham Cutts, 1932), and two musical vehicles for Danish star Carl Brisson. Fogwell's last film as a director was *Murder at the Cabaret* (1936), a musical whodunit trounced by the *Monthly Film Bulletin* for failures in every department. He died on 8 June 1957.

Fogwell's brother Roy, born in 1901, worked in the industry as a cameraman until the 1950s.

(Geoff Brown)

BIBLIOGRAPHY: Reed, Langford and Hetty Spiers (eds), 'Reginald Fogwell', *Who's Who in Filmland*, 3rd edn (London: Chapman & Hall, 1931).

FILMOGRAPHY: *The Warning* (1928; sound version, *Cross Roads*, 1930); *Dick Turpin* (serial, co-dir. Leslie Eveleigh, 1929); *Guilt* (1930); *The Written Law*; *Madame Guillotine* (1931); *The Wonderful Story*; *Betrayal* (1932); *Murder at the Cabaret* (1936).

FORBES, Bryan (1926–)

Bryan Forbes was born John Theobald Clarke on 22 July 1926 in Stratford, London. From an early age he had set his heart on an acting career; he entered the Royal Academy of Dramatic Arts when he was seventeen, but did not complete his studies. During the war he served in the Intelligence Corps and later the Combined Forces Entertainment Unit. After changing his professional name to Bryan Forbes, he made his screen-acting debut in 1948 and over the next decade became a familiar and dependable supporting player in several notable British films, including *The Small Back Room* (Michael Powell/Emeric Pressburger, 1949), *An Inspector Calls* (Guy Hamilton, 1954) and *The Colditz Story* (Guy Hamilton, 1955).

However, acting began to take second place to screenwriting and then directing. He made significant contributions to the scripts of exciting war dramas such as *The Cockleshell Heroes* (José Ferrer, 1955) and *I Was Monty's Double* (John Guillermin, 1958), before receiving great acclaim for his screenplay for Basil Dearden's *The League of Gentlemen* (1960), in which a group of ex-servicemen on the social scrap heap revive their former skills to plan a daring robbery. A similar astringency enlivens his script for Sidney Gilliat's *Only Two Can Play* (1962), a frisky version of a Kingsley Amis novel about thwarted adultery; and *Station Six Sahara* (Seth Holt, 1962), a scorching drama about men in the desert on heat over a woman. His most ambitious and controversial screenplay was for Guy Green's *The Angry Silence* (1960), in which Richard Attenborough is 'sent to Coventry' by his workmates after refusing to join an unofficial strike. Left-wing critics were outraged by the film's portrayal of the unions and its caricatured Communists, but Forbes (who politically has always leaned to the right) maintained that he achieved a fair balance by portraying the management as equally crass.

Forbes began his directing career in 1961 with *Whistle down the Wind*, a tender portrayal of innocence in rural Lancashire in which three children believe the criminal they are hiding in their barn is a reincarnation of Christ. Tenderness was also the hallmark of his next film, *The L-Shaped Room*, in which a pregnant, unmarried Frenchwoman shares a house with motley characters including a writer (Tom Bell) with whom she falls in love. Leslie Caron was nominated for an Academy Award for her leading performance, as were two other actresses in Forbes' films later in the decade: Kim Stanley as the psychic in *Seance on a Wet Afternoon* who instigates a bizarre kidnapping plot in order to draw attention to her powers; and Edith Evans in *The Whisperers*, a poignant study of loneliness and old age in which Evans gave her finest screen performance. (Forbes was later to be her official biographer.) Other films during the 1960s, including the black comedy *The Wrong Box* and *Deadfall*, a ponderous but intriguingly pretentious thriller where a robbery is elaborately cross-cut with a performance of a John Barry guitar concerto, were less successful but not without interest. By the end of the decade he had established himself as an important figure in the national industry. 'I may not have come up the hard way,' he would say, 'but I have come up the whole way.'

In 1969 Forbes was appointed Chief of Production and Managing Director of Associated British Productions (subsequently EMI Film Productions). It was the greatest challenge of his career and was to prove his biggest disappointment. Most of the projects dear to his heart foundered through lack of managerial support and finance; some films that were made were frankly disappointing; and, frustrated and thwarted, Forbes resigned in 1971. The venture is now remembered essentially for having produced two charming films for children, *The Railway Children* (Lionel Jeffries, 1970) and *The Tales of Beatrix Potter* (Reginald Mills, 1971), which became respectable money-makers; and for facilitating one masterpiece, Joseph Losey's *The Go-Between*, which won the Golden Palm at Cannes in 1971 and proved a substantial critical and commercial success. Forbes' own contribution, *The Raging Moon*, which daringly cast his wife Nanette Newman and Malcolm McDowell as paraplegics who fall in love and have to confront the practical problems involved in having a sexual relationship, was ahead of its time; its humour and sincerity make it one of his best films.

Forbes' subsequent film career never recovered the impetus of the 1960s. He had made a successful film in Hollywood in 1965, *King Rat*, a sharp study of opportunism and survival in a prisoner-of-war camp, and ten years later he returned to America and did a similarly capable and well-received job with the thriller *The Stepford Wives*, an ironic take on the new feminism, based on the novel by Ira Levin. After the EMI debacle, Forbes'

only British films were *The Slipper and the Rose* (1976), a long musical version of the Cinderella story, and the MGM-backed *International Velvet* (1978) – a not entirely successful updating of Clarence Brown's *National Velvet* (1944) with Nanette Newman as the now grown-up Velvet Brown. He has also written several novels, two highly entertaining volumes of autobiography and collaborated on several screenplays, most notably Richard Attenborough's *Chaplin* (1992).

Forbes was always good with actors; had an eye for the unusual aspects of love; could write an argument scene as well as the best of them; and was a prodigious craftsman with words (it is typical of his literary finesse that the kidnappers in *Seance* even quibble about the exact wording and punctuation of a ransom note). If there is an element of disappointment about his career, it is simply that a distinctive voice, with a personal and political edge, has not been heard as loudly and as often as one would ideally have liked.

(Neil Sinyard)

BIBLIOGRAPHY: BECTU History Project, tape no. 331, held in the BFI National Library, London; Forbes, Bryan, *Notes for a Life* (London: Collins, 1974); Forbes, Bryan, *A Divided Life* (London: Heinemann, 1992); Walker, Alexander, *Hollywood England* (London: Michael Joseph, 1974).

FILMOGRAPHY: *Whistle down the Wind* (1961); *The L-Shaped Room* (1962); *Seance on a Wet Afternoon* (1964); *King Rat* (US, 1965); *The Wrong Box*; *The Whisperers* (1966); *Deadfall* (1968); *The Madwoman of Chaillot* (UK/US, 1969); *The Raging Moon* (US: *Long Ago, Tomorrow*, 1970); *The Stepford Wives* (US, 1975); *The Slipper and the Rose* (1976); *International Velvet* (UK/US, 1978); *Sunday Lovers* ('An Englishman's Home' episode, co-dirs. Edouard Molinaro/Dino Risi/Gene Wilder, Fr/It/UK/US, 1980); *Better Late than Never* (Can/HK, 1983); *The Naked Face* (US, 1984).

FORD, Derek (1932–1995)

Derek Ford was born near Tilbury in Essex on 6 September 1932. In 1948 he wrote a play with his elder brother Donald for BBC Radio's *Children's Hour*, but his writing career was disrupted by national service in Germany. After being demobbed he joined Morton Lewis' television commercials company but walked out in frustration five years later. He was asked to salvage a Swedish sex-comedy – *Svenska flickor i Paris* (Barbro Boman, 1961) – which subsequently ran successfully in London as *Paris Playgirls*; his directing debut – *Los tres que robbaran una banco* (made in Ibiza in 1962) – was less successful, and Ford returned to the writing partnership with his brother. Together they wrote a series of effective exploitation films for Tony Tensor's Compton companies, including *A Study in Terror* (James Hill, 1965) and four directed by Robert Hartford-Davis: *The Yellow Teddybears* (1963), *Saturday Night Out* (1964) *The Black Torment* (1964), and *Corruption* (1967).

Ford returned to directing in 1969 with *A Promise of Bed* (1969), quickly followed by *Groupie Girl*, *The Wife Swappers* and *Suburban Wives*. Tongue-in-cheek but glum exposés of suburban sexuality and the permissive society's excesses, they proved successful enough to ensure Ford's survival in the choppy waters of 1970s' film production. As he told an interviewer, 'It's all very nice having awards for films and showing to the National Film Theatre but unfortunately this doesn't help earning a living' (*Premiere*, p. 25).

In the unsubsidised world of the 1970s this was true enough, but it meant a constant search for the lowest common denominator. After *Secret Rites*, a documentary dwelling on rituals performed by self-styled King of the Witches, Alex Sanders, Ford returned to the *Wife Swappers* format with *Commuter Husbands* and a routine sex comedy *Keep It Up, Jack*. The next two films departed more interestingly from the usual formula. *Sexplorer*, with German actress Monika Ringwald appropriately cast as a woman from Venus, is witty enough to make the bad acting forgivable; and *Sex Express* (at least in the expanded form released outside the UK as *Diversions*) has an erotic charge rarely evident in British sexploitation films. Decline set in rapidly with *What's Up Nurse!* and *What's Up Superdoc!*, which have neither the cheery vulgarity of the *Carry On* films nor the youthful panache of the 'Confessions' series. They ended Ford's attempts at sex comedy, and the mediocre slasher movies that followed have little to recommend them, though Edmund Purdom's *Don't Open 'Til Christmas* (1984), on which he co-wrote the script, stands out as a bad-taste landmark. Ford was more fruitfully employed on two novels about the seamier side of the film business, *Panic on Sunset* (1989) and *Casting Couch* (1990).

According to Stanley Long, who collaborated with Ford as producer and cinematographer on his early output, 'he was a sensitive man with a keen sense of humour' – which may explain why some of the films transcend their trite, exploitative material. He died from a heart attack in Bromley, Kent, on 19 May 1995.

(Robert Murphy)

BIBLIOGRAPHY: Long, Stanley, Obituary, *Stage, Screen & Radio*, July/Aug. 1995, p. 36; 'Low Budget High Jinks', *Screen International*, 27 May 1978, p. 12; McGillivray, David, *Doing Rude Things: The History of the British Sex Film, 1957–81* (London: Sun Tavern Fields, 1992); Obituary, *Classic Images* no. 243, Sept. 1995, p. 57; 'The Guys behind the Groupies: Or How Long & Ford Beat the Majors to the Youth-Theme of the Day', *Premiere* [UK] no. 3, July 1970, pp. 24–8.

FILMOGRAPHY: *Los tres que robbaran una banco* (Sp, 1962); *A Promise of Bed* (US: *This, That and the Other!*, 1969); *Groupie-Girl*; *The Wife Swappers* (1970); *Secret Rites* (doc.); *Suburban Wives* (1971); *Commuter Husbands* (1972); *Keep It Up, Jack* (1973); *Sexplorer* (*Diary of a Space Virgin*); *Sex Express* (released with extra footage as *Diversions*) (1975); *What's Up Nurse!* (1977); *What's Up Superdoc!*; *Erotic Fantasies/Proibito erotico* (co-dir., Luigi Batzella, HK (1978); *La casa delle orchidee/The House of Orchids* (It, 1983); *For Members Only*; *Blood Tracks* (uncredited, Mats Helge, as Mike Jackson, Swe/US) (1985); *Urge to Kill* (unrel. in UK, 1989).

FORD, John (1894–1973)

John Ford was born Sean Aloysius O'Feeney on 1 February 1894, in Cape Elizabeth, Maine, USA, the child of an Irish immigrant couple. He directed few films outside America (one in England, two in Ireland), but a number of his Hollywood films reflect his transatlantic roots. These include the historical film *Mary of Scotland* (1936), the British Army films *The Black Watch* (1929), *Wee Willie Winkie* (1937) and *Four Men and a Prayer* (1938), set in India, and *The Lost Patrol* (1934), set in the deserts of Mesopotamia during the First World War. There were also adaptations of British novels such as Richard Llewellyn's *How Green Was My Valley* (1941) and Graham Greene's *The Power and the Glory* (filmed as *The Fugitive* in 1947). His best-known film made outside Hollywood is *The Quiet Man* (1952), filmed extensively on the west coast of Ireland, and one of a number of Ford films – *The Informer* (1936), *The Plough and the Stars* (1936) and *The Rising of the Moon* (1957) – set in the country of his parents' birth. His Irish ancestry was also evident in the colourfully stereotyped character Sergeant Quincannon played by Victor McLaglen in the Westerns *She Wore a Yellow Ribbon* (1949) and *Rio Grande* (1950), and in thoughtful character studies such as Tyrone Power's army cadet, Martin Maher, in *The Long Gray Line* (1954), and Spencer Tracy's Boston-Irish politician, Frank Skeffington, in *The Last Hurrah (*1958).

Gideon's Day, the one film Ford made in England, was a 'runaway' production for Columbia-British. It was not particularly successful either in Britain or America, where it was released in a cut-down version, in black and white rather than the Technicolor of the original, on the lower half of a double bill, and on the 'art-house' circuits (Anderson, p. 164; Gallagher, p. 358). Though a police film with a payroll snatch, a hit-and-run killing, a sex murder and police corruption, its tone is comic; it was, in fact, scripted by Ealing writer T. E. B. Clarke, who had written *The Blue Lamp* (Basil Dearden, 1950) some years earlier. Though the film has some Fordian elements – the domesticity versus professional life theme, the occasional bouts of cinematic expressionism – the most fruitful critical approach may well be in terms of its relationship to other British crime/police films such as *The Long Arm* (Charles Frend, 1956) and *Hell Is a City* (Val Guest, 1960). Indeed, American critic Andrew Sarris noted that Ford 'seems to be mocking not only the English but also the nouveau-Scotland Yard genre of which *Gideon's Day* . . . was a typical example' (Sarris, p. 141).

In 1965 Ford returned to Ireland to film *Young Cassidy*, but after directing a few scenes he fell ill and was replaced as director by Jack Cardiff. He died from stomach cancer in Palm Desert, California, on 31 August 1973.

(Tom Ryall)

BIBLIOGRAPHY: Anderson, Lindsay, *About John Ford* (London: Plexus, 1981); Gallagher, Tag, *John Ford: The Man and His Films* (Berkeley and London: University of California Press, 1986); Sarris, Andrew, *The John Ford Movie Mystery* (London: Secker and Warburg, 1976).

FILMOGRAPHY (UK only): *Gideon's Day* (US: *Gideon of Scotland Yard*, 1959); *Young Cassidy* (co-dir. Jack Cardiff, 1965).

FORDE, Eugene (1898–1986)

Eugene Francis Forde was born in Providence, Rhode Island, on 8 November 1898. He was a stage and film actor before taking his chance to direct short comedies in 1926. He became a 20th Century-Fox contract director, handling several *Charlie Chan* films and comedies such as *Step Lively, Jeeves!* (1937). In 1938 he was despatched to England to direct the enjoyable radio adaptation *Inspector Hornleigh*. The teaming of Gordon Harker as the Inspector and Alastair Sim as his assistant Sergeant Bingham was successful enough to justify two successors, both directed by Walter Forde. Eugene Forde returned to Hollywood, where he directed routine films throughout the 1940s, and early television shows such as *Mark Saber* in the 1950s. He died in Port Hueneme, California, on 27 February 1986.

(Robert Murphy)

FILMOGRAPHY (UK only): *Inspector Hornleigh* (1939).

FORDE, Walter (1898–1984)

A prolific and versatile director of the 1930s and 40s, Walter Forde is a good example of a film-maker who thrived in the collaborative atmosphere of the British studio system. While for a short time in the early 1930s he was discussed as a director of international stature, Forde appears to have been content to make a variety of quality star vehicles primarily for a British market.

He was born Thomas Seymour Woolford, in Lambeth, south London, on 21 April 1898, the son of Tom Seymour, a music-hall performer and comedian. Most of his early life was spent touring in stage melodramas and music-hall comedy acts, where he played the piano, juggled and performed impersonations. From 1920, often in collaboration with his father, Forde wrote and directed various short film comedies featuring himself as 'Walter' – a hapless innocent, sporting a boater and Oxford bags, always landing in a series of gentle scrapes. They were essentially visual in appeal, filled with slapstick, and popular with audiences. In 1923 he spent a short period working for

Universal in America, but unlike his father, who remained in Hollywood as a gag-writer for Laurel and Hardy, Forde failed to achieve success and soon returned to Britain. He resumed the 'Walter' series, this time in collaboration with James B. Sloan, and by the late 1920s had become recognised as one of British cinema's major comic talents, the director and star of successful feature-length comedies. In *Wait and See* (1928), *What Next?* (1928), *Would You Believe It!* (1929) and *You'd Be Surprised!* (1930), all made for Archibald Nettlefold at Walton-on-Thames, the 'Walter' characterisation remained unaltered; otherwise, Forde's ambitions expanded with the footage. Instead of relying on simple slapstick, he began to conceive gag sequences cinematically, building in prowling camerawork and incisive editing, concluding the films with elaborate trick and physical effects that in intention if not precision recalled the rousing finales of Buster Keaton and Harold Lloyd.

These feature comedies – all silent, though the last two carried musical soundtracks – proved a milestone in British visual comedy. But his 'Walter' persona failed to make the transition to talkies, and from 1930 onwards Forde stayed behind the screen, concentrating solely on directing. He joined producer Michael Balcon at Gainsborough, and quickly established himself as one of the company's most reliable and versatile directors, increasing his generic range to include thrillers (*The Ghost Train* and *The Ringer*, both 1931), musical spectaculars (*Chu-Chin-Chow*, 1934) and prestige productions like *Rome Express* (1932).

Rome Express is a measure of the esteem in which Forde was then held as a director. The first film to be made at the refurbished Shepherd's Bush studios and released under the Gaumont-British name, it was conceived and executed on an international scale. Forde's skill shows in his confident handling of Sidney Gilliat's complex scenario, weaving together several plotlines about passengers on board a trans-Europe express train, in a satisfying mix of crime, romance and comedy. Forde's technical handling is equally adroit: the train's constant motion is conveyed through sophisticated use of back projection, while striking visual and aural hooks carry the viewer from one story thread to the next. *Rome Express* became a critical and commercial success, winning particular praise for its cinematic quality, technical skill and the direction of its international cast.

While *Rome Express* remains Forde's most durable achievement, *The Ghost Train* (1931) is more typical of the kind of film he successfully directed during Balcon's regime. Arnold Ridley's stage thriller was rewritten (again by Gilliat) to suit the comic talents of the popular revue comedian Jack Hulbert. Forde returned to the light comedy-thriller genre in the vigorously directed *Bulldog Jack* (1934) – easily the best of his three other Hulbert films, with playful echoes of Fritz Lang's spy films as well as the intended comic target, the 'Bulldog Drummond' stories of Sapper. Less flamboyantly, Forde revived the formula for his two Inspector Hornleigh films, spun off from a radio series, starring Gordon Harker and Alastair Sim. A fast-paced adaptation of Edgar Wallace's novel *The Four Just Men* (1939), made at Ealing, placed the emphasis on thrills and relished the topical overtones of foreigners plotting against Britain. Comedy returned in the remake of *The Ghost Train* (1941), updated to suit the Second World War and its new leading players, radio comedians Arthur Askey and Richard Murdoch.

Walter Forde maintained in interviews that directing comedy was more difficult than directing straight drama. But it was a genre he was consistently drawn to, and he worked with many leading comics of the 1930s and 40s, from Hulbert to Tommy Handley, striving to strike a balance between the anarchic improvisational pull of the performer and the illusion of narrative order. In this he undoubtedly drew on his early career, but he was also lucky enough to work chiefly for a studio with an experienced scenario department specialising in this brand of comedy. Sidney Gilliat, J. O. C. Orton, Val Guest and Marcel Varnel were among Forde's influential collaborators. With straight dramatic material, success often depended on the strength or weakness of Forde's material: the penal camp melodrama *King of the Damned* was doomed to fail, but *Forever England* (1935) carved stirring scenes out of *Brown on Resolution*, C. S. Forester's novel of naval heroism and courage.

In the wake of reorganisation and cutbacks in 1936, both Balcon and Forde left Gaumont-British. After two fluent musicals made for independent outfits, he joined forces with Balcon to form a new company, CAPAD, to make modestly budgeted films at Ealing, beginning with *The Gaunt Stranger*, an effective remake of *The Ringer*. More significant for Ealing's future direction under Balcon were *Cheer Boys Cheer* (1939) and *Saloon Bar* (1940), two films with ensemble casts and a conscious community spirit that helped set the parameters of the studio's later output. With its battle between two breweries, the charmingly traditional Greenleaf and the aggressively modern Ironside, *Cheer Boys Cheer* clearly pointed the way towards Ealing's post-war comedies; but Forde himself took no part in the genre's flowering. No longer allied to a single studio, his prolific output faltered during the 1940s and he went where the assignments took him: to Gainsborough for comedies with Tommy Handley, to Warner Bros. at Teddington for wartime flagwavers, back to Nettlefold for an archetypal 'trouble at t'mill' family saga, *Master of Bankdam* (1947). He began to find it more difficult to get projects off the ground; and his own enthusiasm for the business waned after *Cardboard Cavalier* (1949), a lumpy and misconceived period farce starring Sid Field. It became his last film, and in 1954 he retired permanently to California.

Forde was often described in profiles as a painfully shy but likeable man, who brought his dog Chum to the studio and played the piano on the floor in between set-ups. But both piano and dog paled into insignificance beside his wife, Adeline Culley, an editor and former 'continuity girl'. Culley Forde, as she became known, never received a screen credit for direction (indeed, she went into print with the opinion that women were unequipped emotionally to direct), but she was a formidable and permanent presence on the set, and it is clear the Fordes worked as a single creative team. An article in *Picturegoer* in 1934 pointedly described them as 'One director who is two'. Walter Forde died in Los Angeles on 7 January 1984. (Lawrence Napper)

BIBLIOGRAPHY: Brown, Geoff, *Walter Forde* (London: BFI, 1977); Gilliat, Sidney, 'From Comedian to Director', *Film and TV Technician*, Mar. 1984, p. 12; Hollis, Gwen, 'Walter Forde Has Scored 49 Not Out', *Picturegoer*, 26 Apr. 1947, p. 9; Low, Rachael, *The History of British Film 1918–1929* (London: George Allen & Unwin, 1971); 'One Director Who Is Two', *Picturegoer*, 14 July 1934, p. 13.

FILMOGRAPHY: *The Wanderer* (short, 1919); *Never Say Die* (short); *The Handy Man* (short); *Fishing for Trouble* (short) (1920); *Walter Wins a Wager* (short, co-dir. Tom Seymour); *Walter Wants Work* (short, co-dir. Tom Seymour); *Walter's Trying Frolic* (short, co-dir. Tom Seymour); *Walter Makes a Movie* (short, co-dir. Tom Seymour) (1922); *Wait and See*; *What Next?* (1928); *The Silent House*; *Would You Believe It!* (1929); *Red Pearls*; *You'd be Surprised!*; *The Last Hour*; *Lord Richard in the Pantry*; *Bed and Breakfast* (1930); *Third Time Lucky*; *The Ringer*, *The Ghost Train*; *Splinters in the Navy* (1931); *Condemned to Death*; *Lord Babs*; *Jack's the Boy*; *Rome Express* (1932); *Orders Is Orders* (1933); *Jack Ahoy!*; *Chu-Chin-Chow*; *Bulldog Jack* (1934); *Forever England/Brown on Resolution* (US: *Born for Glory*, 1935); *King of the Damned*; *Land Without Music* (US: *Forbidden Music*, 1936); *Kicking the Moon Around* (US: *The Playboy*); *The Gaunt Stranger* (US: *The Phantom Strikes*) (1938); *Let's Be Famous*; *The Four Just Men* (US: *The Secret Four*); *Cheer Boys Cheer*, *Happy Families* (short); *Inspector Hornleigh on Holiday* (1939); *Charley's (Big Hearted) Aunt*; *Saloon Bar*, *Sailors Three* (US: *Three Cockeyed Sailors*) (1940); *Inspector Hornleigh Goes to It*; *The Ghost Train*; *Atlantic Ferry* (US: *Sons of the Sea*) (1941); *Go to Blazes* (short); *Flying Fortress*; *The Peterville Diamond* (1942); *It's That Man Again* (1943); *Time Flies*; *One Exciting Night* (US: *You Can't Do without Love*) (1944); *Master of Bankdam* (1947); *Cardboard Cavalier* (1949).

FORDER, Timothy

After *Indian Summer*, a low-budget infidelity drama centring on a film director making a film in India, Timothy Forder worked with the animator Dave Thwaites on a version of *Beauty and the Beast*. His most ambitious project is *The Mystery of Edwin Drood*, an adaptation of Charles Dickens' last novel that makes less satisfying sense of the doom-laden enigmas of Dickens' unfinished tale of murder and deception than Stuart Walker's 1935 version. Despite a Royal Premiere it failed to attract audiences and properly launch Forder's career, though subsequently it has become a collector's item, doubtless for the gutsy performances of Robert Powell and Freddie Jones. Forder continues to work in animation, including adaptations of Rudyard Kipling's *Just So Stories* and a collection of children's fairy tales brought together under the title *Tell Me a Story*, both released on DVD in 2001. (Robert Murphy)

FILMOGRAPHY: *Indian Summer* (1987); *Beauty and the Beast* (co-dir. Dave Thwaites, 1992); *The Mystery of Edwin Drood* (1993).

FOREMAN, Carl (1914–1984)

Carl Foreman was born in Chicago, the son of Russian immigrants, on 23 July 1914. He left law school to work as a newspaper reporter, eventually gravitating towards the theatre and subsequently Hollywood. After experience as a story analyst, a laboratory assistant at Technicolor and a reluctant radio gag-writer, he broke into pictures as co-writer of *Spooks Run Wild* (1941), a Monogram B-movie that ingeniously brought together the 'Bowery Boys' and Bela Lugosi. More work followed for Republic and MGM before Foreman joined the American Infantry during the Second World War. He was transferred to the Signal Corps, where he worked under Frank Capra making documentary and propaganda films.

The experience of working as a team on projects he could passionately believe in persuaded Foreman not to return to MGM once the war was over; instead, with similarly committed producer Stanley Kramer, he set up an independent production company to make films that espoused a desire for social justice in America. *Home of the Brave* (Mark Robson, 1949) *Champion* (Mark Robson, 1949), and *The Men* (Fred Zinnemann, 1950) established his reputation; but his refusal to testify before the House Un-American Activities Committee in 1951 destroyed his Hollywood career at the moment of his greatest triumph, the unusual Western *High Noon* (Fred Zinnemann, 1952). Effectively blacklisted, he found refuge in Britain. A deal with Rank was annulled due to American pressure, but Alexander Korda proved less supine and employed Foreman as a production adviser. Soon after, he set up his own production company, Open Road.

Foreman worked with David Lean on the script for *The Bridge on the River Kwai* (1957), but differences over the film's ethos led to a parting of the ways, and he received no credit for his work. But it was an open secret how much he had contributed to the film and Columbia decided to ignore political considerations and back Foreman's future projects. As writer/producer he exercised considerable influence over *The Key* (Carol Reed, 1958) and *The Guns of Navarone* (J. Lee Thompson, 1961), but in both cases he was dissatisfied with the end result. In 1963 he finally fulfilled his ambition to direct with *The Victors*, a film that he hoped would finally express the anti-war message that *The Bridge on the River Kwai* had muffled and *The Guns of Navarone* contradicted.

The lack of visually spectacular action sequences, and the grim fate meted out to so many of the American platoon whose progress we follow from their first battle experience in Italy through to the post-war occupation of Berlin, conceded little to audience expectations, and *The Victors* was not a box-office success. But Foreman achieves a remarkable authenticity, and the film teems with memorable scenes capturing the callousness, casual horrors and unexpected moments of kindness thrown up by war. As an unglamourised account of American soldiers fighting on the Western Front the film remains unequalled, even by Steven Spielberg's television series *Band of Brothers* (2001).

Carl Foreman (left) on location for *The Guns of Navarone* (J. Lee Thompson, 1961)

Despite frequently expressing the desire to do so, Foreman never directed again, and his subsequent record as a producer is unexcitingly respectable. Open Road was successful with the hugely popular wildlife films *Born Free* (James Hill, 1966) and *Living Free* (Jack Couffer, 1972), more moderately so with Dick Clement and Ian La Frenais' witty spy comedy *Otley* (1968) and the adaptation of Leslie Thomas' *The Virgin Soldiers* (John Dexter, 1969). Foreman was more personally involved with Richard Attenborough's *Young Winston* (1972). The nomination of his screenplay for an Academy Award marked his rehabilitation in Hollywood and he returned to America in 1975. What should have been an honourable retirement was disrupted by *Force 10 from Navarone* (Guy Hamilton, 1978), a shambolic sequel that cast no credit on anyone involved. Carl Foreman died of a brain tumour in Beverly Hills, on 26 June 1984. His contribution to British cinema as writer and producer is well known, but his one film as director remains unfairly neglected.
(Robert Murphy)

BIBLIOGRAPHY: Baker, Bob, 'Carl Foreman', *Film Dope* no. 17, Apr. 1979, pp. 17–19; Brownlow, Kevin, *David Lean* (London: Faber and Faber, 1997); Cavander, Kenneth and Penelope Houston, 'Interview with Carl Foreman', *Sight and Sound*, Summer 1958, pp. 220–3, 265; Chibnall, Steve, *J. Lee Thompson* (Manchester: Manchester University Press, 2000); Foreman, Carl, 'The Road to *The Victors*', *Films and Filming*, Sept. 1963, pp. 11–12; Gow, Gordon, 'Interrogation', *Films and Filming*, Aug. 1972, pp. 14–17; Medjuck, Joe, 'Carl Foreman' (interview), *Take One* vol. 3 no. 9, Jan./Feb. 1972, pp. 21–4.

FILMOGRAPHY: *The Victors* (1963).

FORSYTH, Bill (1946–)

William David Forsyth was born in Glasgow on 29 July 1946 and educated at Knightswood School. On leaving school, aged seventeen, he answered an advertisement for a 'Lad required for film company' and spent the next eight years making short documentary films. Leaving documentary production in 1977, Forsyth wrote the scripts for *Gregory's Girl* and *That Sinking Feeling* in the hope of breaking into feature films. Obtaining finance, however, proved frustrating and problematic. The BFI Production Board rejected *Gregory's Girl* three times. Forsyth later observed, 'I remember one torment of a meeting when I tried to explain that *Gregory's Girl* was really a structuralist comedy . . . I suspect my script was too conventional although nobody actually told me as much' (Forsyth, p. 243). *That Sinking Feeling* was eventually made in 1979 with amateur actors from the Glasgow Youth Theatre, including John Gordon Sinclair (who later took the lead in *Gregory's Girl*), its tiny budget raised from a variety of sources. Forsyth's distinctive voice as writer-director is already apparent in this tale of a robbery of stainless-steel sinks by a gang of unemployed Glasgow teenagers – intensely humanistic and humorous yet with an underlying seriousness of purpose. This ability to create a self-contained yet believable world with a keen sense of the absurd and bizarre in the everyday is perhaps only rivalled by the work of British television writer Alan Plater. The film opened to great popular and critical success at the Edinburgh and London Film Festivals but was unable to secure more widespread distribution.

Gregory's Girl (1981) was Forsyth's breakthrough film. This acutely observed story of adolescence and first love set in Cumbernauld, a Scottish new town, was rapturously received by both critics and public alike. Forsyth's reputation seemed to be secured by the success of his next venture, *Local Hero* (1983), a first collaboration with producer David Puttnam. The film has been compared to the great comedies of Ealing Studios, to Forsyth's sometime irritation. He has complained of being labelled as 'whimsical' by a film establishment that fails to see the more serious aspects of his work. However, it is perhaps fair to say that there remains an affinity between Forsyth's early work and that of certain Ealing directors, notably Alexander Mackendrick and Robert Hamer, whose comedies also had their darker side. Forsyth's next film, *Comfort and Joy* (1984) was indeed an altogether more sombre work, detailing the trials and tribulations of a local radio DJ whose long-term partner leaves him and who becomes embroiled in the Glasgow 'ice-cream wars' between competing families of ice-cream vendors.

Forsyth's first American film, shot in Canada and produced by Puttnam during his brief tenure as Head of Columbia Pictures, was *Housekeeping* (1987), a faithful and affectionate adaptation of Marilynne Robinson's acclaimed first novel. Although well received by the critics, it was not a huge success at the box office. Difficulties in production, with Diane Keaton withdrawing from the film closely followed by financiers Cannon, were a foretaste of things to come. *Breaking In* (1989) was blighted by arguments over tone and casting, with the consequence that for Forsyth the film was 'a bastard child. The saddest thing is that it's now a film that none of us wanted' (Green, 1990, p. 23). His experiences of his third American film, *Being Human* (1993), were even worse. Production was dogged by arguments between director and producers and the film was a major flop at the box office. Forsyth's attitude, that 'The only ambitions I have for the films I make is that they're appreciated as poetical works' (Hunter, p. 27), was hardly likely to have endeared him to Hollywood.

Forsyth returned to Britain when the producers of *Gregory's Girl* approached him with the idea of making a television series based around the character of Gregory. The series never materialised, but Forsyth reworked the material into the long-awaited sequel to his first hit. However, with typical Forsythian perversity, *Gregory's Two Girls* (1999) is more of a deliberate non-sequel. Of the original cast and characters, only John Gordon Sinclair remains, the thirty-five-year-old Gregory still single, still in Cumbernauld, and working as a teacher at his old school. Nevertheless, the film adeptly blends humour, drama and close observation of character in a way that shows that Forsyth, despite his American experiences, has lost none of his earlier humanism or skill.

The difficulties in obtaining finance, the problems in securing distribution and the ill-fated encounter with the American film industry are unfortunately all too typical of the experience of a number of British film-makers in recent years. That a director of Forsyth's originality has been restricted to eight feature films in twenty-three years is indicative of the structural defects relating to production, distribution and exhibition that have hampered British film-makers since the 1960s.

(Martin Hunt)

BIBLIOGRAPHY: Flynn, Bob, 'Local Hero in Hollywood', *Guardian* Weekend Section, 13 Aug. 1994, pp. 8–9; Forsyth, Bill, 'Bill Forsyth: Director', *Sight and Sound*, Autumn 1981, p. 243; Green, William, '*Housekeeping*', *Sunday Telegraph* Magazine, 6 Dec. 1987, pp. 16–18; Green, William, 'The Forsyth Saga', *Sunday Telegraph* 7 Days Magazine, 24 July 1990, pp. 21–3; Hacker, Jonathan and David Price, *Take Ten: Contemporary British Film Directors* (Oxford: Clarendon Press, 1991), pp. 107–45; Hunter, Allan, 'Being Human', *Sight and Sound*, Aug. 1994, pp. 24–7; Malcomson, Scott L., 'Modernism Comes to the Cabbage Patch: Bill Forsyth and the "Scottish Cin-

ema"', *Film Quarterly*, Spring 1985, pp. 16–21; Sinyard, Neil, 'The Forsyth Saga', *Films Illustrated*, Aug. 1981, pp. 424–7; Vaines, Colin, 'Interview with Bill Forsyth', *Screen International*, 12 Mar. 1983, p. 16.
FILMOGRAPHY: *Islands of the West* (short, 1972); *Shapes in the Water* (short, 1974); *Robert Adam – Architect* (short, 1975); *Tree Country* (short, 1976); *That Sinking Feeling* (1979); *Gregory's Girl* (1981); *Local Hero* (1983); *Comfort and Joy* (1984); *Housekeeping* (US, 1987); *Breaking In* (US, 1989); *Being Human* (US, 1993); *Gregory's Two Girls* (1999).

FORTE, John

A native of Belfast, John Forte studied at Bristol University and the National Film and Television School. Following graduation he wrote the screenplay for BBC Northern Ireland's *Henri* (Simon Shore, 1994), a witty comedy about a ten-year-old Protestant girl from the country who travels to Belfast to take part in a music festival and ends up staying with a Catholic family. As part of the Northern Lights short films scheme, funded by the BBC and the Northern Ireland Film Council, he went on to direct his own script in *Skin Tight* (1994), a gentle send-up of an Orangeman's preparations for the Twelfth of July celebrations. Since then Forte has largely worked as a television writer, providing the BBC with scripts for the successful series *Ballykissangel*. He also wrote the screenplay for Michael Winterbottom's *With or Without You* (1999), and directed his own *Mad about Mambo* (2000), both romantic comedies aimed firmly at the mainstream. Though it lacks the witty social observation characteristic of Forte's early writing, *Mad about Mambo* retains a feel for the absurdities and anachronisms of Northern Irish society. Telling the story of a young Catholic boy who seeks to improve his chances of playing the 'British imperialist' game of soccer by taking classes in Latin dance, the film successfully deflates several ethnic and gender stereotypes and enjoyably pursues the utopian dream of Belfast uniting to the beat of the samba.

(John Hill)

BIBLIOGRAPHY: Power, Paul, 'The Irish Are Rising Again', *Cinéaste* vol. 24 nos 2/3, Mar. 1999, p. 74.

FILMOGRAPHY: *Skin Tight* (short, 1994); *Mad about Mambo* (Ir/UK, 2000).

FOSS, Kenelm (1885–1963)

Kenelm Foss was born on 13 December 1885. After attending art school, he joined the Vedrenne-Barker company in 1902 as an actor, subsequently producing a repertoire of new drama in Glasgow and London, including plays by Anton Chekhov, George Bernard Shaw, G. K. Chesterton and Thomas Hardy. Meanwhile, he wrote light comedies for the theatre and published poems and stories.

In 1915 he joined the London Film Company as actor and scenario-writer and soon became a prolific and sought-after writer of original and adapted screenplays, as well as a versatile actor. In 1918 he took up direction 'through discontent at the frequent mutilation of his scripts by strangers', adapting his novel *Till Our Ship Comes In* (1919) for Kew Films (Foss, c. 1919, p. 4). He subsequently scripted three and directed two of Guy Newall's Lucky Cat comedies, including the popular *I Will*, whose aristocratic hero courts a socialist girlfriend.

Better at generating schemes than fulfilling them, Foss briefly embarked on independent production, making *The Joyous Adventures of Aristide Pujol* (Frank Miller, 1920), according to *Kinematograph Weekly* an essentially 'joyous film' in which he played an 'irresponsible and cheerful French adventurer' (1 April 1920, p. 94). At the same time he attempted to buy the Catford studios, ultimately ending up in court for non-payment. Following this escapade, Foss worked for the hard-nosed H. W. Thompson company, directing and scripting twelve films, beginning with Sir John Martin-Harvey's stage success, *The Breed of the Treshams*. Of the others, *The Wonderful Year* was appreciated for capturing the whimsicality of W. J. Locke's novel, as a young man and woman bicycle round France 'in the unconventional modern manner' (*Bioscope*, 22 Sept. 1921, p. 50). *All Roads Lead to Calvary* – a Jerome K. Jerome adaptation – and *No. 5 John Street*, both dealt with the 'labour question', the former more convincing to critics than the latter; while *House of Peril* brought a 'new woman' (Fay Compton) to near grief in a tale mixing continental gambling and duplicitous seances.

The crossover in Foss' career between serious contemporary drama and popular storytelling shared the predilection, typical of the period, for mixing fey fantasy with topical issues, knowing comedy with melodramatic incident. Such combinations form an often uneasy amalgam in Foss' work. While his exploitation in *The House of Peril* of the subjective moving camera and cut-ins to visual clues successfully creates anxiety and suspense, the over-complicated *A Romance of Old Baghdad* (1922) makes little sense of the story and poor use of the acting talent of Matheson Lang and Barbara Everest. Convinced that acting was an art of 'typage', Foss's unfulfilled ambition was to work with non-actors. Always ambivalent about the role of commerce in film-making, Foss left for France, to work on Mousjoukine's *Kean ou Désorde et génie* (1923). In 1931 *Who's Who in Filmland* reported that, since acquiring a string of 'popular theatrical "quick-time" lunch restaurants', Foss did little film work. He continued to write novels into the 1950s as well as editing editions of Swinburne's poems and Aubrey Beardsley drawings. He died in London on 28 November 1963.

(Christine Gledhill)

BIBLIOGRAPHY: Foss, Kenelm, *The Work of the Film Producer* – Lesson 3 of *Cinema: A Practical Course in Ten Lessons* (London: Standard Art Book Company, c. 1919); Foss, Kenelm, 'Actors and Amateurs', *The Motion Picture Studio*, 22 Oct. 1921, p. 7; Foss (Kenelm) Papers, 1908–1953, University of Rochester (fifty-nine letters written to Foss by theatrical people); Gledhill, Christine, *Reframing British Cinema: 1918–1928* (London: BFI, 2003); Low, Rachael, *The History of the British Film 1914–1918* (London: George Allen & Unwin, 1950); Low, Rachael, *The History of the British Film 1918–1929* (London: George Allen & Unwin, 1971); Reed, Langford and Hetty Spiers (eds), *Who's Who in Filmland* (London: Chapman and Hall, 1931).

FILMOGRAPHY: *A Peep behind the Scenes* (co-dir. Geoffrey Malins, 1918); *Eena, Deena, Dinah, Do/Till Our Ship Comes In* (series); *A Little Bit of Fluff*; *I Will* (co-dir. Hubert Herrick); *Fancy Dress* (1919); *The Glad Eye*; *The Breed of the Treshams*; *A Batchelor Husband* (1920); *The Headmaster*, *The Double Event*; *Street of Adventure*; *Cherry Ripe*; *The Wonderful Year*, *No. 5 John Street*; *All Roads Lead to Calvary* (1921); *The House of Peril*; *Dicky Monteith*; *A Romance of Old Baghdad* (1922).

FOSTER, Giles (1948–)

Born in Somerset in 1948, Giles Foster is better known as a director of films for television than cinema. Much of his television work displays a strong literary bent – such as his delicately witty version of Anita Brookner's Booker Prize-winning novel *Hotel du Lac* (1986), directed with a sensitive regard for the heroine's fragile romanticism. He was also responsible for television adaptations of George Eliot's *Silas Marner* (1985) and *Adam Bede* (1991); and Rex Warner's allegorical *The Aerodrome* (1983), which, like its source novel, is long on ideas and short on characterisation. More personal projects include his collaborations with Alan Bennett, most notably *All Day on the Sands* (1979) and *A Woman of No Importance* (1982).

After boarding school in Bath, Foster studied at York University and the Royal College of Art's School of Film and Television. His fifty-five-minute *Devices and Desires* (1976), a sensitive portrait of an eccentric Anglican cleric, won the 1976 Grierson Award and led to his first film for television, *The Obelisk* (1977), an adaptation of a short story by E. M. Forster. It was not until 1988 that he made his mainstream cinema debut with *Consuming Passions*, a comedy set in a chocolate factory based on a play by Terry Jones and Michael Palin. It failed to attract much attention. Foster's other theatrical feature, an adaptation of Ruth Rendell's novel *Tree of Hands*, is essentially a television film, boosted by the performance of Lauren Bacall. Foster continues to direct prestigious television drama, including the interesting Second World War detective series *Foyle's War* (2002).

(Brian McFarlane)

BIBLIOGRAPHY: Felstein, Roma, 'Foster's Laager of Independence', *Broadcast*, 28 Feb. 1986, p. 16; Preston, John, 'Hard-Work Hotel', *Time Out*, 27 Feb. 1986, p. 85.

FILMOGRAPHY: *Devices and Desires* (1976); *Consuming Passions* (UK/US, 1988); *Tree of Hands* (US: *Innocent Victims*, 1989).

FRANCIS, Freddie (1917–)

Unusually, Freddie Francis combined a career as one of the world's top cameramen with a second substantial career as a director, during which he made significant contributions to the British horror film. Born in Islington, London, on 22 December 1917, he served as an apprentice stills photographer before joining Gaumont-British as a clapper-loader in 1936. After serving in the Army Kinematograph Service during the Second

World War, he became a camera operator at British Lion Studios. Graduating to director of photography with *A Hill in Korea* (Julian Amyes, 1956), he soon became one of the major British cinematographers, working on films such as *Room at the Top* (Jack Clayton, 1959) and *Saturday Night and Sunday Morning* (Karel Reisz, 1960), and winning an Academy Award for *Sons and Lovers* (Jack Cardiff, 1960).

As a director Francis quickly became associated with the horror genre (though his debut was a romantic comedy, *Two and Two Make Six*). His first box-office success, *Paranoiac*, began an association with Hammer Films, for whom he made two further psychological thrillers (*Nightmare* and *Hysteria*) and contributions to the studio's Frankenstein and Dracula series. His prolific output also included television episodes of *The Saint* and *Man in a Suitcase*, and cinema assignments in Germany. In the 1960s he was also involved with Hammer's rival Amicus Pictures, where he launched a series of story anthologies with *Dr Terror's House of Horrors*, and made other films ranging from the imaginative (*The Skull*) to the dire (*They Came from beyond Space*).

In the 1970s Francis made *The Ghoul* and *Legend of the Werewolf* for Tyburn Films, the company set up by his son, Kevin. He returned to cinematography and critical prestige in the 1980s, working with Martin Scorsese and David Lynch on several occasions, and winning a second Academy Award for *Glory* (Edward Zwick, 1989). Periodic returns to directing, which included filming the Dylan Thomas screenplay *The Doctor and the Devils*, failed to win him the praise given to his cinematography.

In interviews, Francis expressed his unhappiness at being typed as a horror film director and insisted that he had no particular affinity for the genre. Some critics would agree: David Pirie, for example, condemns *The Evil of Frankenstein* as 'a thoroughly pedestrian and cardboard thriller' and compares him unfavourably with fellow Hammer director Terence Fisher (Pirie, p. 75). Yet among an uneven output *The Creeping Flesh* stands as an intriguing essay in late Victorian gothic, and *Nightmare*, an eerily effective thriller, makes a worthy companion piece to Seth Holt's *Taste of Fear* (1961). His cinematographer's eye gives his better work for Hammer and Amicus an undeniable visual power. *Dracula Has Risen from the Grave*, for example, is full of striking images and uses colour in a boldly expressive way. His willingness to challenge genre conventions, as in his combination of horror and humour in the strange and perverse black comedy *Mumsy, Nanny, Sonny and Girly*, suggests that the originality and adventurousness of his cinematography might, in a different context, have found greater expression in his directorial assignments.

(Guy Barefoot)

BIBLIOGRAPHY: Buscombe, Ed, *Making 'Legend of the Werewolf'* (London: BFI, 1976); Dixon, Wheeler Winston, *The Films of Freddie Francis* (Metuchen, NJ and London: Scarecrow Press, 1991); Jackson, Kevin, 'Gothic Shadows', *Sight and Sound*, Nov. 1992, pp. 16–19; Pirie, David, *A Heritage of Horror* (London: Gordon Fraser, 1975).

FILMOGRAPHY: *Two and Two Make Six*; *Vengeance/Ein Toter sucht seinen Mörder* (US: *The Brain*, UK/Ger); *Paranoiac* (1962); *Nightmare* (1963); *The Evil of Frankenstein*; *Hysteria*; *Traitor's Gate/Das Verrätertor* (UK/Ger) (1964); *The Skull*; *Dr Terror's House of Horrors*; *The Psychopath* (1965); *The Deadly Bees* (1966); *They Came from beyond Space*; *Torture Garden* (1967); *Dracula Has Risen from the Grave* (1968); *The Intrepid Mr Twigg*; *Mumsy, Nanny, Sonny and Girly* (US: *Girly*) (1969); *Trog* (1970); *Gebissen wird nur Nachts – Happening der Vampire/The Vampire Happening* (Ger, 1971); *Tales from the Crypt*; *The Creeping Flesh* (1972); *Tales That Witness Madness*; *Craze* (1973); *Son of Dracula* (1974); *Legend of the Werewolf*; *The Ghoul* (1975); *Golden Rendezvous* (co-dir. Ashley Lazarus, 1977); *The Doctor and the Devils* (1985); *Dark Tower* (as Ken Barnett, 1989).

FRANCIS, Karl (1942–)

Throughout his career, writer-director Karl Francis, born in Bedwas, Wales, on 1 April 1942, has tended to make partisan films seeking to illuminate aspects of proletarian life and achieve social and political change. His works have generally been set in the South Wales mining communities, and for more than two decades he has been the most significant English-language film-maker in Wales. Francis' features and drama-documentaries are sometimes too promiscuous, trying to stress too many social ills at the expense of establishing inner dramatic and psychological cohesion, but his best work has raw emotional power.

A former television documentary and current affairs director, Francis made an impressive feature debut in 1977 with *Above Us the Earth*, which used amateur and professional actors to explore the community impact of a Rhymney Valley pit closure. Francis teases out the forces creating a schism in the community, explores the fractious interactions between politicians and union leaders and makes cogent criticisms of the National Coal Board and the trade unions.

He drew on his media experiences to make *Giro City* (1982), one of the first crop of films made for Channel 4. Glenda Jackson and Jon Finch star as television reporters compellingly enmeshed in Northern Ireland political intrigue and South Wales local government corruption. Francis' mining concerns surfaced again in *Ms Rhymney Valley 1985* (BBC Wales, 1985), which humorously observed sexual politics during the 1984 miners' strike.

Francis attracted both praise and opprobrium for *Boy Soldier* (1986), an S4C Welsh-language film with English subtitles, which secured a London West End cinema premiere. An unemployed South Wales valleys youth, made a scapegoat through political machinations after a tragic incident on army patrol in Northern Ireland, discovers more affinities with the Irish than with his English superiors. Overheated scenes of military prison violence attracted criticism, but the film is a fascinating examination of national identity and class warfare.

The Angry Earth (S4C, 1989), which charts the coalfield history of South Wales through the life of a fictional 110-year-old woman, proved schematic and simplistic, but Francis hit his stride again with *Streetlife* (BBC, 1994). Despite being well received at the Edinburgh Film Festival, it gained only a limited and belated cinema release. Centred on a jilted single mum on a drug-ridden council housing estate, the drama, strident and unconvincing at times, contained effective scenes and a superb central performance from Helen McCrory.

Francis endured an unsatisfactory two years as the Head of BBC Drama, Wales, but later made the cinema biopic *One of the Hollywood 10* (2000), a tribute to US director Herbert Biberman, blacklisted with his Academy Award-winning actress wife Gale Sondergaard in the anti-Communist Hollywood purges of the 1940s and 50s. Francis' feature, yet to obtain US or British cinema release, contained graphic recreations of FBI-inspired arson and thuggery on the location of *Salt of the Earth* (1953), Biberman's celebrated film of a strike by Mexican-American zinc miners.

(Dave Berry)

BIBLIOGRAPHY: Berry, David, *Wales and Cinema: The First 100 Years* (Cardiff: University of Wales Press, 1994); Freer, Steve, *Karl Francis: A Sense of Direction* (Cardiff: HTV booklet, 1990).

FILMOGRAPHY: *Above Us the Earth* (1977); *The Mouse and the Woman* (1980); *Giro City* (1982); *Milwr Bychan/Boy Soldier* (1986); *Rebecca's Daughters* (1991); *Streetlife* (1994); *One of the Hollywood 10* (2000).

FRANK, Charles (1910–)

Charles Frank was born in Belgium on 23 January 1910, and, after experience in dubbing European films into English and such British films as *Fanny by Gaslight* (Anthony Asquith, 1944) into French, made one memorable film in Britain. This was the adaptation of Sheridan Le Fanu's *Uncle Silas*, a wild and whirling melodrama that in a cinema less addicted to sober realism might have launched a remarkable career. The orchestration of excess seemed his forte: excess of flamboyant incident and image (dead birds hanging in the courtyard of a manor house fallen into desuetude), of editing (archetypal montage sequences, such as one in which the heroine, Jean Simmons, is whisked away by baleful abductors), of cinematography and production design (courtesy of Laurence Irving and Robert Krasker) and a cast of willing players (Katina Paxinou, Derrick De Marney and Manning Whiley, as threats to Simmons).

There are no doubt some ludicrous moments in *Uncle Silas*, but it exhibits a sort of *folie de grandeur*. What was British cinema to do with this talent? The answer is: almost nothing. He co-authored the screenplay for *The Late Edwina Black* (1951), continued to adapt French and German films for English-speaking screens, directed *Malachi's Cove* (1950) for US television and directed, translated and adapted Jean Cocteau's *Les Parents terribles*, first to the stage and then to the screen as the ill-fated *Intimate Relations* (1953). The very title should have alerted him to its improbability as a survivor in 1950s' British cinema. His only other film is a Belgian comedy, *De Ordonnans*, which he co-scripted with the actor Trevor Peacock.

(Brian McFarlane)

FILMOGRAPHY: *Uncle Silas* (1947); *Intimate Relations* (1953); *De Ordonnans* (Belg, 1962).

FRANKEL, Cyril (1921–)

Cyril Frankel was born in Stoke Newington, north London, in 1921 and studied at Oxford University before joining the Crown Film Unit in 1947. *Man of Africa*, his first major film project, displayed the influence of documentary, but Frankel's subsequent films showed him to be an adept genre specialist who rarely adopted a straightforwardly realist approach. After two films for Group 3, *Devil on Horseback* and *Make Me an Offer*, Frankel made *It's Great to Be Young!*, an attempt to locate an American-style musical within an English school, and *No Time for Tears*, an expertly mounted tear-jerker set in a children's hospital. *She Didn't Say No!* and *Alive and Kicking* are lively Irish comedies that, while overly reliant on stereotypes, display an energy in pacing and performance that makes them seem more distinctive than they actually are. (*Alive and Kicking* also marked the screen debut of Richard Harris.)

An association with Hammer in the 1960s took Frankel even further from his documentary roots. *Never Take Sweets from a Stranger* is one of Hammer's most untypical films. A sombre story of a child abuser being protected by the community in which he lives, it is a powerful work that is rarely seen today (and was a commercial flop at the time of its release). *The Witches* is more flamboyant, although in comparison with Terence Fisher's *The Devil Rides Out* (1968) and Robin Hardy's *The Wicker Man* (1973), its presentation of pagan worship seems rather decorous. Nevertheless, Nigel Kneale's intelligent script, an intense performance from Kay Walsh as the chief witch and Frankel's unfussy but precise direction combine to produce an unsettling drama. The briefest of glimpses that Frankel affords us of the paraphernalia required for the climactic sacrifice makes it clear that when Kay Walsh announces that she wants 'a skin for dancing in', she is not talking metaphorically.

Frankel's other 1960s' work is uneven. *On the Fiddle* is a service comedy with pre-Bond Sean Connery as the not-too-bright sidekick of slick cockney shyster Alfred Lynch; *Don't Bother to Knock*, a mildly risqué sex-comedy featuring Richard Todd and Elke Sommer; *The Very Edge*, one of the offbeat dramas Raymond Stross created for his ex-beauty queen wife Ann Heywood; and *The Trygon Factor*, a stylish but silly comedy-thriller based loosely on an Edgar Wallace novel. From the late 1960s, Frankel worked mainly for television, principally on fantasy-based series such as *The Champions*, *Randall and Hopkirk (Deceased)* and *UFO*, though he made a belated return to feature films in 1990 with the German comedy *Eine Frau namens Harry*.

(Peter Hutchings)

BIBLIOGRAPHY: 'Cyril Frankel', *Film Dope* no. 21, Oct. 1980, p. 30; Kruger, Rolf, 'Return from the Dead' (letter), *Screen International*, 10 Apr. 1982, p. 10; Spark, David, 'Man of Africa', *Sight and Sound*, Spring 1987, pp. 80–1.

FILMOGRAPHY: *Eagles of the Fleet* (doc. short); *Explorers of the Depths* (doc. short) (1950); *Wing to Wing* (doc. short, 1951); *The Nut-Cracker* (short); *Man of Africa* (aka *Kigusi Story*) (1953); *Devil on Horseback*; *Make Me an Offer* (1954); *It's Great to Be Young!* (1956); *No Time for Tears* (1957); *She Didn't Say No!*; *Alive and Kicking* (1958); *Never Take Sweets from a Stranger* (US: *Never Take Candy from a Stranger*); *Scheidungsgrund: Liebe* (Ger) (1960) *On the Fiddle* (US: *Operation Snafu*); *Don't Bother to Knock* (US: *Why Bother to Knock*) (1961); *The Very Edge* (1962); *The Witches* (aka *The Devil's Own*); *The Trygon Factor* (1966); *Permission to Kill* (1975); *Eine Frau namens Harry* (Ger, 1990).

FREARS, Stephen (1941–)

After a tentative start in films, Stephen Frears rose to prominence on British television in the 1980s with a series of well-observed state-of-the-nation dramas. More concerned with character and narrative than visual flourishes, Frears gives due credit to writers, and has enjoyed fruitful collaborations with Hanif Kureishi, Alan Bennett and Christopher Hampton. His most notable films deal with outsiders on the margins of society and exhibit insight and compassion rather than easy sentiment. Since the American-financed *Dangerous Liaisons* (1988), Frears has alternated personal projects, usually shot in Britain, with a bewildering variety of bigger-budget American assignments.

Stephen Frears was born on 20 June 1941 in Leicester. Educated at Gresham's School, Norfolk, he studied law at Trinity College, Cambridge, between 1960 and 1963. In 1964 he joined the Royal Court Theatre, where he worked with directors Lindsay Anderson and Karel Reisz and actor Albert Finney. Reisz employed Frears as an assistant director on *Morgan: A Suitable Case for Treatment* (1966), as did Finney on *Charlie Bubbles* (1968) and Anderson on *if. . . .* (1968). Finney's production company, Memorial Enterprises, part-financed Frears' directorial debut, *The Burning* (1967), a short political fable filmed in Morocco. Frears also worked regularly in British television, directing *St Ann's* (1969), a documentary about a slum district of Nottingham (the birthplace of Alma Reville), and episodes of *Parkin's Patch* (1969) and *Tom Grattan's War* (1970).

Frears made his feature film debut in 1971 with *Gumshoe*, a Memorial production starring Albert Finney as a Liverpool bingo caller who dreams of being a Bogart-style private eye. The film was more of a critical than a popular success, and Frears returned to television, working on the BBC's *Play for Today* and *Play of the Week* slots, collaborating with Alan Bennett on several plays, including *A Day Out* (1972) and *Me! I'm Afraid of Virginia Woolf* (1978). At the start of the 1980s, Frears directed three bigger-budgeted television films: *Bloody Kids* (1980), a spirited attack on Thatcher's Britain, co-written by Stephen Poliakoff, its juvenile leads caught up in adult incompetence and social breakdown; *Walter* (1982), the first *Film on Four*, and its sequel *Walter & June* (combined into *Loving Walter* for release in the US), two unsentimental accounts of the life of a mentally handicapped man; and *Saigon: Year of the Cat* (1983), David Hare's drama set during the American evacuation of Saigon.

Frears returned to feature films in 1984 with *The Hit*, an off-beat thriller with a script by Peter Prince, who had previously collaborated with Frears on four television plays. The film centres on a supergrass (Terence Stamp), exiled to Spain, who accepts his inevitable 'execution' with apparent good grace. The story is thin, though laced with black humour; Frears sustains tension and inspires fine performances from Stamp, and John Hurt and Tim Roth as the hired killers. Although it was favourably reviewed, *The Hit* made little impact at the box office and looked like a one-off return to the cinema for its director.

Frears achieved his career breakthrough the following year with Hanif Kureishi's *My Beautiful Laundrette*, a Channel 4 film shot on 16mm for £600,000 (around half the cost of *The Hit*). Though it was made for television, the provocative and entertaining fashion in which Frears and Kureishi tackle racism, sexuality and the ethos of Thatcherism made it an international theatrical success. Now in demand, Frears reunited with Alan Bennett for *Prick up Your Ears*, a long-standing personal project to tell the story of Leicester playwright Joe Orton. Strong performances from Gary Oldman and Alfred Molina, and a candid depiction of Britain's gay subculture in the 1950s and 60s brought a modest success. Frears reunited with Kureishi for *Sammy and Rosie Get Laid*, which was as boldly outspoken about riot-torn, divided

Britain as *My Beautiful Laundrette*; but the film's examination of social and sexual mores lacks clarity and conviction, and Frears and Kureishi fail to evoke much sympathy for the mismatched Rosie (Frances Barber) and Sammy (Ayub Khan-Din).

Frears made his Hollywood debut with *Dangerous Liaisons*, adapted from Christopher Hampton's stage success, which was followed by the impressively downbeat dramatisation of Jim Thompson's *The Grifters*. Though commercially less successful than *Dangerous Liaisons*, *The Grifters* earned Frears an Academy Award nomination for Best Director, and is a film much admired by other film-makers. Following the disappointing *Hero/Accidental Hero*, Frears returned to Britain to make *The Snapper* (1993), the second in Roddy Doyle's Barrytown trilogy, for BBC Television. The film offers a convincing, whimsy-free portrait of working-class life in Ireland, with a gutsy performance from Tina Kellegher as a pregnant teenager. It received limited theatrical distribution in Britain but proved popular in the USA, encouraging Frears to film the final part of Doyle's trilogy, *The Van*, for BBC Films. Second time out, Frears seemed over-anxious to maintain the feel-good factor in a tale of unemployment, fast food and World Cup fever.

Mary Reilly, a big-budget adaptation of Valerie Martin's retelling of the Jekyll and Hyde story, starring Julia Roberts and John Malkovich is hampered by an odd mixture of accents, and proved too slow and too dark to attract much of an audience. But visually the film is a treat, and Frears and writer Christopher Hampton make psychological sense of the hoary old tale. His rambling Western *The Hi-Lo Country* was received without enthusiasm, but Frears restored his Hollywood reputation with *High Fidelity*, a surprisingly effective transposition of Nick Hornby's North London novel to Chicago. *Liam*, a British-Italian-German co-production written by Jimmy McGovern, dealt with poverty, racism and religious bigotry in Depression-era Liverpool, with mixed results. But *Dirty Pretty Things*, another modestly budgeted film backed by BBC Films, proved a revealing exploration into the underside of London society where asylum-seekers and illegal immigrants live exploited lives. Frears had dealt with the plight of political refugees in the television play *Cold Harbour* (1978), scripted by Peter Prince, but in *Dirty Pretty Things* he uses the wider scope offered by a feature film to mount a damning critique of an affluent but increasingly unequal society.

Frears' commitment to British cinema is evident from his intelligent and informative television documentary *Typically British: A Personal History of British Cinema by Stephen Frears*, made for the BFI and Channel 4 in 1997. His continuing interest in the British political scene is evident in his dramatic reconstruction of the negotiations between Tony Blair and Gordon Brown over who should lead the Labour Party – and become Prime Minister – in Granada Television's *The Deal* (2003). Fortunately for the British film industry, Frears shows no signs of wanting to migrate to Hollywood.

(Daniel O'Brien)

BIBLIOGRAPHY: Bergen, Ronald, 'Dangerous Director', *Films and Filming*, Mar. 1989, pp. 18–20; Goodridge, Michael, 'Profile: Stephen Frears', *Screen International*, 17 Oct. 2003, p. 19; Hacker, Jonathan and David Price, *Take 10: Contemporary British Film Directors* (Oxford: Oxford University Press, 1991); Kureishi, Hanif, *Sammy and Rosie Get Laid* (London: Penguin, 1988); McCloy, Sean, 'Focus on Stephen Frears', *Film West* no. 23, Winter 1995, pp. 26–8; Minns, Adam, 'Frears Bares All', *Screen International*, 11 June 2004, p. 9; O'Neill, Eithne, *Stephen Frears* (Paris: Editions Payot & Rivages, 1994); Saynor, James, 'Accidental Auteur', *Sight and Sound*, Apr. 1993, pp. 4–8; *Typically British: A Personal History of British Cinema by Stephen Frears* (television documentary, co-dirs. Mike Dibb/Stephen Frears) Channel 4, 1995.

FILMOGRAPHY: *The Burning* (short, 1967); *Gumshoe* (1971); *Bloody Kids* (1980, limited theatrical rel. 1983); *The Hit* (1984); *My Beautiful Laundrette* (1985); *Prick up Your Ears*; *Mr Jolly Lives Next Door*, *Sammy and Rosie Get Laid* (1987); *Dangerous Liaisons* (US, 1988); *The Grifters* (US, 1990); *Accidental Hero* (US: *Hero*, US, 1992); *The Snapper* (1993); *The Van*; *Mary Reilly* (US, 1996); *The Hi-Lo Country* (US, 1998); *High Fidelity* (US); *Liam* (UK/Ger/It) (2000); *Dirty Pretty Things* (2002); *Miss Henderson Presents* (2005).

FREELAND, Thornton (1898–1987)

Born in Hope, North Dakota, on 10 February 1898, Thornton Freeland began working as a child actor in vaudeville, then joined Vitagraph in 1918 as an assistant cameraman. He rose through the ranks as a cutter, assistant director and production manager, working in various capacities for D. W. Griffith, Roland West, Frank Lloyd and Ernst Lubitsch. He made his directorial debut in 1929 with the lightweight comedy *Three Live Ghosts*. Several other films followed before he made his mark with *Flying Down to Rio* (1933), the first Fred Astaire and Ginger Rogers musical.

In 1935 Freeland came to England to make the first sound version of *Brewster's Millions* with Jack Buchanan and Lili Damita. In 1937 he directed the Paul Robeson vehicle *Jericho* and in 1939 *The Gang's All Here*, a serviceable comedy starring Jack Buchanan, Edward Everett Horton and Googie Withers. After taking over from William K. Howard on the Merle Oberon vehicle *Over the Moon* in 1939, Freeland returned to America for the duration of the war. He came back to Britain in 1946 where he made his last three films – *Meet Me at Dawn*, a costume comedy, *The Brass Monkey*, a thriller starring radio comedian Carroll Levis and the ill-fated American actress Carole Landis, and a comedy romance, *Dear Mr Prohack* (1949), which starred Cecil Parker, Glynis Johns, Hermione Baddeley and a young Dirk Bogarde. After *Dear Mr Prohack* was released to indifferent reviews, Freeland retired and returned to the US. He died in Fort Lauderdale, Florida, on 22 May 1987.

Most of Freeland's films run for about seventy to eighty minutes and are marked by an economy of footage and camera set-ups that works well with comedians and dancers, who are usually best on the first take. He had a knack for discovering

Thornton Freeland with June Clyde

young artists on their way up (such as Terry-Thomas, who played a bit-part in *The Brass Monkey*), and his skills as a dependable genre craftsman are undeniable.

(Wheeler Winston Dixon)

BIBLIOGRAPHY: Freeland, Thornton, 'Elstree Tunes in to Hollywood', *Film Weekly*, 16 Nov. 1934, pp. 8–9; Low, Rachael, *Film Making in 1930s Britain* (London: George Allen & Unwin, 1985).

FILMOGRAPHY (UK only): *Brewster's Millions* (1935); *Accused*; *The Amateur Gentleman*; *Skylarks* (1936); *Jericho* (US: *Dark Sands*); *Paradise for Two* (US: *Gaiety Girls*) (1937); *Hold My Hand* (1938); *The Gang's All Here* (US: *The Amazing Mr Forrest*); *So This Is London*; *Over the Moon* (uncredited co-dir. William K. Howard) (1939); *Meet Me at Dawn* (aka *The Gay Duellist*, 1947); *The Brass Monkey* (aka *Lucky Mascot*, 1948); *Dear Mr Prohack* (1949).

FREGONESE, Hugo (1908–1987)

Hugo Fregonese was born in Mendoza, Argentina, on 8 April 1908. After studying in New York and a brief interlude in Hollywood as a technical adviser, he entered his native film industry in 1939, and co-directed his first film (with Lucas Demare), *Donde mueren las palabras*, in 1944. In 1950 he moved back to Hollywood, where he made ten films in the space of five years, notably *Apache Drums* (1951), a taut B-Western produced by Val Lewton, *Blowing Wild* (1953), a rip-roaring romantic adventure, and *The Raid* (1954), an excellent Civil War drama. Thereafter he became a truly international figure, working in Britain, Spain, Italy, France, Germany and Yugoslavia before again returning to Argentina, where he made his last film in 1975. His three British features were all shot partly on foreign locations: *Decameron Nights* in Spain, *Seven Thunders* in France and *Harry Black* in India.

Fregonese was well enough regarded by the iconoclastic critics writing for *Movie* in the early 1960s to be ranked second only to Joseph Losey among the 'British' directors listed in their 'talent histogram'. At this distance it is difficult to see why. *Decameron Nights* is a coy period sex-comedy, and though the multi-character narrative of *Seven Thunders* is skilfully handled, its reconstruction of occupied Marseilles suffers from poor back projection, artificial sets and stolid romantic interest. Despite similarly wobbly production values, *Harry Black* is a white hunter yarn with an uncommonly complex, troubled hero (Stewart Granger) whose feline quarry represents his own inner demons. Fregonese died of a heart attack in Buenos Aires on 17 January 1987.

(Sheldon Hall)

BIBLIOGRAPHY: Salmi, Markku, 'Hugo Fregonese', *Film Dope* no. 17, Apr. 1979, pp. 51–2; 'The Talent Histogram', *Movie* no. 1, June 1962, pp. 8–9.

FILMOGRAPHY (UK only): *Decameron Nights* (1953); *Seven Thunders* (US: *The Beasts of Marseilles*, 1957); *Harry Black* (US: *Harry Black and the Tiger*, 1958).

FRENCH, Harold (1900–1997)

Born in Wimbledon of Irish parents on 23 April 1900, Harold Arthur George French began his career at the age of twelve as a stage actor. He continued acting until 1933, and directed plays from 1932, gaining a striking success in 1936 with Terence Rattigan's *French without Tears*. He also acted in films during the 1920s and early 30s before becoming a dialogue director for Criterion Films in 1936 and then a full director for other studios from 1937. His autobiographies, which only cover the period up to 1936, reveal that his film career was always secondary to his passion for theatre, to which he devoted all his attention after 1955; he continued directing stage plays into the 1970s.

French's early crime films lack sufficient suspense to lift them above the routine; his most notable features were made during the Second World War. The agreeable romantic comedy *Jeannie* was followed by *Unpublished Story*, an ambitious Fleet Street thriller about fifth columnists masquerading as pacifists, and two films dealing with European resistance to the Nazis: *The Day Will Dawn*, set in Norway, and *Secret Mission*, set in France. Both films benefit from Hugh Williams' excellent performances as a suave representation of English decency who wins over a local girl (Deborah Kerr, Carla Lehmann) to the cause of anti-Nazi resistance. They are less distinguished, however, than *Mr Emmanuel*, the story of an elderly British Jew (Felix Aylmer) who visits Nazi Germany prior to the outbreak of war and winds up in a Gestapo prison; it is the only British film of the war years to take Nazi anti-Semitism as its central theme.

Harold French (centre)

French also directed two enjoyable upper-middle-class comedies during the war. *Dear Octopus*, adapted by Patrick Kirwan and Esther McCracken from Dodie Smith's stage play, is his most accomplished film. Its stage origins are masked by the visual sumptuousness of John Bryan's production design and Arthur Crabtree's glossy cinematography; and French draws impressive performances from Celia Johnson, Margaret Lockwood, Michael Wilding and an array of fine British character actors. The evocation of an idealised English way of life is more scrappy and irreverent in *English Without Tears*, scripted by his friend Terence Rattigan, where the war wreaks havoc on class and national barriers, but there is the same affection and respect for upper-middle-class English eccentricity.

French enjoyed his biggest commercial success in 1946 with *My Brother Jonathan*, a weepie starring Michael Denison and Dulcie Gray. Subsequent assignments were often disappointing. His most prestigious 1950s' film was *Rob Roy the Highland Rogue*, made for Disney; the most enjoyable is *Isn't Life Wonderful?*, a gently whimsical comedy in which a habitually inebriated bicycle shop owner (Donald Wolfit) reconciles an estranged loving couple.

Almost all French's films are derived from novels or plays, and he was happy to remain within a theatrical tradition, relying more on dialogue and character than on action, movement or visual design. Nevertheless, he was highly regarded within the film industry as an efficient and competent craftsman. In 1942 he had been elected by his colleagues to direct the co-operatively made propaganda short *Our Film*, which compared the conditions of British and Russian workers and stands as a fascinating landmark to warm Anglo-Soviet relations in the middle years of the war. His own forte was light comedy, but his versatility, and his ability to draw exemplary performances from his actors, enabled him to make a significant contribution to British cinema. Harold French died in London on 19 October 1997.
(James C. Robertson)

BIBLIOGRAPHY: French, Harold, *I Swore I Never Would* (London: Secker and Warburg, 1970); French, Harold, *I Thought I Never Could* (London: Secker and Warburg, 1973); McFarlane, Brian, *An Autobiography of British Cinema* (London: Methuen, 1997); Shorter, Eric, 'Harold French', *Guardian*, 24 Oct. 1997, p. 20.

FILMOGRAPHY: *The Cavalier of the Streets* (1937); *Dead Men Are Dangerous* (1939); *The House of the Arrow* (1940); *Major Barbara* (co-dirs. Gabriel Pascal/David Lean); *Jeannie* (1941): *Unpublished Story*; *The Day Will Dawn*; *Our Film* (short); *Secret Mission*; *Talk about Jacqueline* (1942); *Dear Octopus*; *English Without Tears* (1943); *Mr Emmanuel* (1944); *Quiet Weekend*; *My Brother Jonathan* (1946); *White Cradle Inn*; *The Blind Goddess* (1947); *Quartet* ('The Alien Corn' episode, co-dirs. Ken Annakin/Arthur Crabtree/Ralph Smart, 1948); *Adam and Evelyne* (1949); *The Dancing Years*; *Trio* ('Sanatorium' episode, co-dir. Ken Annakin) (1950); *Encore* ('The Ant and the Grasshopper' episode, co-dirs. Pat Jackson/Anthony Pélissier, 1951); *The Hour of 13*; *The Man Who Watched Trains Go By*; *Isn't Life Wonderful?* (1952); *Rob Roy the Highland Rogue* (1953); *Forbidden Cargo* (1954); *The Man Who Loved Redheads* (1955).

FREND, Charles (1909–1977)

Charles Herbert Frend was born in Pulborough, Sussex, on 21 November 1909. He was educated at the Kings School, Canterbury, and Oxford University, where he was film critic for the university magazine *Isis*. He began his career in the cutting rooms of British International Pictures in 1931. Two years later, after editing Alfred Hitchcock's *Waltzes from Vienna* (1934), he moved to Gaumont-British Pictures, where he edited several notable films, including Hitchcock's *Secret Agent* (1936), *Sabotage* (1936) and *Young and Innocent* (1937). He also began his long collaboration with Michael Balcon, moving with him to MGM-British, where he edited *A Yank at Oxford* (Jack Conway, 1938), *The Citadel* (King Vidor, 1938) and *Goodbye, Mr Chips* (Sam Wood, 1939), and, in 1941, to Ealing Studios, where he made his directorial debut with a competent propaganda piece, *The Big Blockade*. Between 1942 and 1957 he directed a further eleven films for Ealing, becoming one of the studio's most prolific and perhaps most characteristic directors. According to Balcon, Frend, 'a man with his roots firmly planted in the soil of this country, was . . . the ideal man to deal with any subject concerning the traditional English values' (Balcon, 1969, p.138).

Frend's first major film as a director was *The Foreman Went to France* in 1942. Working closely with producer Alberto Cavalcanti, Frend employed elements of a true story to create a film that combines humour and drama, and remains a landmark in the development of the documentary-influenced feature film. Furthermore, sequences such as that of the attack on the refugee caravan demonstrate Frend's control of the camera and his cutting-room expertise. This was followed by the equally accomplished story-documentary film, *San Demetrio London*, which stands as a lasting tribute to the courage and determination of the men of the British merchant navy. This was also the first of Frend's films to concern itself with the representation of a certain type of quiet masculine courage – a theme to which he was to return repeatedly throughout his career. His other two films of the war years were *The Return of the Vikings*, a propaganda piece made for the Norwegian government-in-exile, and *Johnny Frenchman*, a film emphasising the need for Anglo-French co-operation. Both Frend and Balcon were subsequently honoured for their wartime service to the Norwegian cause with the award of the Knighthood First Class of the Order of St Olav in 1953.

In 1945 Frend gave a lecture to a BFI summer school that provides a valuable insight not only into his view of the director's role, but also into the Ealing approach to film-making. 'The Director', Frend states,

> is, in fact, an interpreter. He translates the written word into moving pictures, and this process is not confined to the actual shooting of the film on the studio floor. The method of translation is preconceived in the script and is carried out in the editing just as much as in shooting. It follows that the Director, the man responsible for the interpretation, should be present at all stages of production. (Frend, 1945a, p. 3)

However, this statement is promoted at least as much by pragmatic as authorial interests. Efficiency and economy, just as much as artistry, were Frend's and Ealing's concerns.

Frend's first post-war film, *The Loves of Joanna Godden*, was a romantic melodrama set on Romney Marsh. Frend's sympathy for the pastoral English countryside was perfectly matched by Vaughan Williams' magnificent score. A year later, Frend was to collaborate again with Vaughan Williams on *Scott of the Antarctic*. In this film, together with *The Cruel Sea*, Frend created an image of British masculinity that defined a generation through the screen personas of, respectively, John Mills and Jack Hawkins. Both are films of male comradeship where women play only peripheral roles. If *Scott of the Antarctic* panders a little too indulgently to the British fondness for honourable failures, *The Cruel Sea*, with its gritty adherence to the realist ethos, is Frend's finest hour.

Frend also directed three moderately successful comedies, *A Run for Your Money*, *The Magnet* and *Barnacle Bill*, in the 1950s, along with the more poignant *Lease of Life* and the stolid police thriller *The Long Arm*. After the break-up of Ealing he directed two films for Michael Balcon's Bryanston consortium in 1961. *Cone of Silence* was an airline drama again concerned with issues of integrity and quiet heroism, while *Girl on Approval* was a typical social drama of the period. Despite his honourable record, Frend found it difficult to sustain his career in the film industry and from the 1960s onwards he worked mainly in television, notably on *Danger Man* and *Man in a Suitcase*. His final film was *The Sky Bike*, made for the Children's Film Foundation, although he ended his long and quietly distinguished career as second-unit director on Disney's *Guns in the Heather* and David Lean's *Ryan's Daughter*. It is appropriate to leave the last word to his career-long friend and collaborator, Michael Balcon. Writing shortly after Frend's death, Balcon observed that 'this broad-minded, liberal man without any trace of chauvinism in his outlook nevertheless had a proper pride in Britain and the British people and it is this characteristic which emerges so strongly in all his work' (Balcon, 1977).

(Martin Hunt)

BIBLIOGRAPHY: Balcon, Michael, *Michael Balcon Presents . . . A Lifetime of Films* (London: Hutchinson, 1969); Balcon, Michael, 'Mr Charles Frend', *The Times*, 24 Jan. 1977; Barr, Charles, *Ealing Studios*, 3rd edn (Moffat, Dumfries & Galloway: Cameron & Hollis, 1998); Frend, Charles, *The Film Director* (London: BFI, 1945a); Frend, Charles, 'Cutting Room Practice', *The Journal of the British Kinematograph Society*, July/Sept. 1945b, pp. 56–64; Frend, Charles, 'Realism in British Films', *The Living Cinema*, Winter 1956, pp. 21–9; Hawkins, Jack, *Anything for a Quiet Life: The Autobiography of Jack Hawkins* (London: Elm Tree Books, 1973); Richards, Jeffrey, *Films and British National Identity: From Dickens to 'Dad's Army'* (Manchester: Manchester University Press, 1997).

FILMOGRAPHY: *The Big Blockade*; *The Foreman Went to France* (1942); *San Demetrio London*; *The Return of the Vikings* (doc.) (1943); *Johnny Frenchman* (1945); *The Loves of Joanna Godden* (1947); *Scott of the Antarctic* (1948); *A Run for Your Money* (1949); *The Magnet* (1950); *The Cruel Sea* (1952); *Lease of Life* (1954); *The Long Arm* (US: *The Third Key*, 1956); *Barnacle Bill* (US: *All at Sea*, 1957); *Cone of Silence* (US: *Trouble in the Sky*, 1960); *Girl on Approval* (1961); *Finché dura la tempesta/ Torpedo Bay* (co-dir. Bruno Vailati, It/Fr, 1963); *The Sky Bike* (1967); *Guns in the Heather* (2nd unit dir., Robert Butler, 1968); *Ryan's Daughter* (2nd unit dir., David Lean, 1970).

FRENKE, Eugène (1907–?)

Born in Russia on 1 January 1907, Eugène Frenke found no success with his first directorial venture in America, *Girl in the Case* (1934), a comedy banned from exhibition in New York State for supposed indecency. For his second, *Life Returns*, Universal held up release for four years, deservedly wary of any drama that climaxed in authentic laboratory footage of a scientist, Dr Robert E. Cornish, reviving a dead dog. Frenke was the second husband of the Russian actress Anna Sten, who had been imported by Samuel Goldwyn with much fanfare but to little public approval. After Goldwyn terminated her contract, the couple came to England in 1935, where Frenke directed her in *A Woman Alone*, an elaborately packaged melodrama featuring Sten as a Russian peasant pursued by army officer Henry Wilcoxon. 'Tone of picture is mopey. Everybody broods,' reported *Variety* (16 June 1937). The characters may have had more life if censorship requirements had not gutted the story. Back in America, Frenke turned producer on three minor films featuring his wife. But he found greater success closer to the mainstream, working in the 1950s and beyond with John Huston and Robert Aldrich. He returned to Britain as the producer of Irving Lerner's film of Peter Shaffer's *The Royal Hunt of the Sun* (1969).

(Geoff Brown)

FILMOGRAPHY (UK only): *A Woman Alone* (US: *Two Who Dared*, 1936).

FRESHMAN, William (1902–1980)

William A. Freshman was born in Sydney, New South Wales, in 1902 but was brought to Britain as a child. His good looks led to a profitable acting career in British films, peaking at the end of the 1920s with romantic roles in *Eileen of the Trees* (Graham Cutts, 1928) and *A Broken Romance* (J. Steven Edwards, 1929). His wife was the leading silent scenarist Lydia Hayward; he wrote scripts himself from the mid-1930s, as well as producing for Associated British. Early in 1939 the couple left for Australia, where Freshman wrote and directed Cinesound's low-budget comedy-musical *Come up Smiling*, but he returned to Britain after the outbreak of war to join the armed forces and work in the Army Kinematograph service. Demobilisation brought a job in Rome co-directing *Teheran*, an unlikely cut-price thriller with Derek Farr as a British war correspondent and Marta Labarr as the Russian ballerina who join forces to foil a plot to assassinate President Roosevelt. Only a jokey documentary about a pleasure cruise along the Rhine followed, though Freshman made a successful move into television as one of the directors on Associated-Rediffusion's spy series *Destination Downing Street* (1957), and went on to direct six episodes of *The Telegoons* (1963) for the BBC. He died in London in 1980.

(Geoff Brown and Robert Murphy)

BIBLIOGRAPHY: Pike, Andrew and Ross Cooper, *Australian Film 1900–1977: A Guide to Feature Film Production* (Melbourne: Oxford University Press, 1980).

FILMOGRAPHY: *Come up Smiling* (aka *Ants in His Pants*, Austral, 1939); *Teheran* (US: *The Plot to Kill Roosevelt*, co-dir. Giacomo Gentilomo, UK/It, 1946); *Rhineland Serenade* (co-dir. Peter Hamilton doc., 1952).

FRIESE-GREENE, William (1855–1921)

William Friese-Greene is the most maddening figure in early British film history. He was maddening at the time, and he has continued to create confusion and division ever since. In simple terms, he was an inventor who experimented with putative moving-image devices at the dawn of cinema, but whose practical results did not match the claims that he made for them. Others took on those claims after his death, which resulted in Ray Allister's romanticised biography and the still more romanticised and inaccurate feature film *The Magic Box* (John Boulting, 1951). Friese-Greene was then subjected to critical burial, but in recent years there has been a tentative revival of interest from historians.

William Greene was born in Bristol on 7 September 1855, the son of a metal worker. He added to his surname when he married Helena Friese in 1874. He was apprenticed to a photographer, and soon established his own business in Bath. There, around 1880, he met John Rudge, who was experimenting with magic lanterns to create an illusion of movement. Friese-Greene adopted such ideas with enthusiasm, and began experimenting with Rudge and on his own. In 1885, he opened two photographic shops in London with Esmé Collings, who would go on to be one of the pioneers of British film-making in the Brighton area. In 1889–90 Friese-Greene worked with engineers Mortimer Evans and Frederick Varley on cameras that could take up to four or five pictures per second, but they were not successful in practice, and had far too low a frequency rate for a successful illusion of motion.

Friese-Greene obsessively patented insufficiently thought-out devices. However, the true advances in taking and projecting motion picture films were being made elsewhere. He began experimenting with colour cinematography in 1898, and became the rival of G. A. Smith, the developer of Kinemacolor, who lived in the Brighton area, to which Friese-Greene had moved in 1905. A court decided against Kinemacolor in favour of Friese-Greene's Biocolour system in 1913, but Friese-Greene was unable to capitalise on his victory.

Beset by financial troubles (including a spell in prison for borrowing money while an undischarged bankrupt), Friese-Greene remained an incorrigible optimist. He died on 5 May 1921 while giving an incoherent speech to a meeting considering the parlous state of the British film industry. His claims to have been the 'inventor of kinematography' were then taken up by the uncritical film historian Will Day. The burgeoning myth was eventually punctured by a series of articles written by Brian Coe in the 1960s. Having been damned for claiming to invent what he did not invent, recent commentators have sought to view in a more sympathetic light someone who was undoubtedly one of the very first to work on the concept of moving images. As a founding father of British film, Friese-Green has his place, but more as a dreamer than as an inventor.

(Luke McKernan)

BIBLIOGRAPHY: Allister, Ray, *Friese-Greene: Close-Up of an Inventor* (London: Marsland, 1948); Chanan, Michael, *The Dream That Kicks* (London: Routledge & Kegan Paul, 1980); Coe, Brian, 'William Friese-Greene and the Origins of Cinematography', *Screen* vol. 10 nos 2–4, 1969.

FRY, Stephen (1957–)

Big, genial and eccentric, Stephen Fry seems to fit the stereotype of the traditional English toff, though behind the actor's mask lies a more troubled and complex character. Stephen John Fry was born in Hampstead, north London, on 26 August 1957, and grew up in Norfolk. 'I was very bright, arrogant, and felt that rules didn't apply to me' (Gerrie, p. 12). Consequently he was expelled from schools and given a three-month jail sentence for credit-card fraud. He found more creative outlets for his energies once he studied English at Queens College, Cambridge, and joined the Cambridge Footlights, where he formed a fruitful writing partnership with Hugh Laurie. Leaving university, he earned unexpected riches updating the book for Noel Gay's

1930s' musical *Me and My Girl*, and came to public attention through television appearances in the various *Blackadder* series (1986–9), *A Bit of Fry and Laurie* (1986–95) and most memorably in *Jeeves and Wooster* (1990–3). Roles in British films inevitably followed: Peter Morton, patiently coping with his friends' petty problems while facing a tragic personal crisis in *Peter's Friends*; a not quite waspish enough Oscar Wilde in Brian Gilbert's *Wilde* (1997).

After many travails over finance (FilmFour, the original backer, found itself in no position to provide an $11.5 million budget), Fry made his directing debut with *Bright Young Things* (2003), an adaptation of Evelyn Waugh's *Vile Bodies*. Though the film is packed with cameos by Fry's famous friends, he keeps them firmly in check and gives the main roles to the then hardly known Stephen Campbell-Moore and Emily Mortimer. Avoiding the seductions of costumes and period detail, he keeps his eye on his characters, encouraging us to view them as young and vulnerable rather than rich and stupid, eliciting sympathy where there might have been contempt. Demand for Fry's services as an actor might deflect him from further directing ventures, but his achievement here is far from negligible.

(Robert Murphy)

BIBLIOGRAPHY: Dickson, E. Jane, 'Middle-Age Dread', *Radio Times*, 13 Sept. 2003, pp. 24–7; 'First Person: Bright Young Things', *Empire*, Nov. 2003, p. 29; Gerrie, Anthea, 'No Sex Please, I'm Working', *TV Times*, 5 Nov. 1994, p. 12; Jays, David, '24 Hour Party People', *Sight and Sound*, Oct. 2003, pp. 20–1; Minns, Adam, 'Looking on the Bright Side', *Screen International*, 22 Nov. 2002, p. 18.

FILMOGRAPHY: *Bright Young Things* (2003).

FUEST, Robert (1927–)

Robert Fuest was born in London in 1927. Before becoming a film director he worked as a production designer and, from the late 1960s onwards, as a television director, notably on *The Avengers* (1961–9). However, his first three cinema films as director display little of the visual style or surreal humour associated with that series. *Just Like a Woman* is a conventional comedy featuring Wendy Craig and Francis Matthews, stars best known for their television appearances. *Wuthering Heights* (with Timothy Dalton as Heathcliff), the first of three films Fuest made in Britain for American International Pictures, replaces the gothic stylisation of William Wyler's 1939 version of the tale with a more dour and downbeat approach. The thriller *And Soon the Darkness*, which Fuest made for Associated British in 1970, reunited him with *Avengers* collaborators, producer Albert Fennell and writer Brian Clemens, but the film itself could not have been more different from their earlier work together. This

simple story about an English tourist investigating the disappearance of her friend takes place in one small part of the French countryside during the course of one day and is heavily reliant on Fuest's ability to create a foreboding atmosphere. The opening scenes, in which the two tourists, oblivious to the danger they might be in, bicker their way across France is particularly effective, although the ruthlessly linear narrative becomes predictable towards the end.

Fuest's other three British films are more stylised. Two horror films for AIP, *The Abominable Dr Phibes* and *Dr Phibes Rises Again* (the latter co-written by Fuest), make extensive use of 1930s' design and feature an *Avengers*-like playfulness in the depiction of the nasty retribution meted out by Dr Phibes (played by Vincent Price) to his enemies. For example, a sight gag from *Dr Phibes Rises Again* that might have come directly from *The Avengers* involves a desert storm suddenly and bathetically revealed as the product of a large electric fan operated by Phibes. Fuest's final British film was *The Final Programme*, an adaptation of a Michael Moorcock novel, which combined some impressive science-fiction sets – designed by Fuest himself – with heavy-handed social satire.

After *The Devil's Rain*, an American horror film, Fuest has worked mainly in television, making American television movies such as *Return of the Stepford Wives* (1980) and *The Golden Bug* (1981) and episodes of British television series, including *The Optimists* (1984–5) and *C.A.T.S. Eyes* (1985–6).

(Peter Hutchings)

BIBLIOGRAPHY: Koetting, Christopher, 'Mr Fuest Rises Again', *Fangoria* no. 177, Oct. 1998, pp. 12–17; Koetting, Christopher, 'On Beyond Phibes', *Fangoria* no. 178, Nov. 1998, pp. 15–20.

FILMOGRAPHY: *Just Like a Woman* (1966); *Wuthering Heights*; *And Soon the Darkness* (1970); *The Abominable Dr Phibes* (1971); *Dr Phibes Rises Again* (1972); *The Final Programme* (1973); *The Devil's Rain* (US, 1975); *The Road to Mandalay* (doc., 1977); *Aphrodite* (Fr/UK/Ger/Switz, 1982); *Family of Strangers* (short, US, 1983).

FURIE, Sidney J. (1933–)

Sidney J. Furie was born in Toronto, Canada, on 28 February 1933. He broke into the film industry with an ambitious low-budget Canadian feature *A Dangerous Age* (1958), which he wrote and directed. He followed this with another low-budget thriller, *A Cool Sound from Hell* (1959), and then directed episodes of the Canadian television series *Hudson's Bay* (1959). Furie moved to England in 1961, where he directed the low-budget horror films *Dr Blood's Coffin* and *The Snake Woman*, and the immensely successful Cliff Richard musical *The Young Ones*. He followed up with two more serious films about teenagers. *The Boys* is a courtroom drama enlivened by the presence of Robert Morley, Dudley Sutton, the now-forgotten pop idol Jess Conrad and a young Tony Garnett. *The Leather Boys*, a superb film about teenage bike gangs, was temporarily shelved by exhibitors who objected to its controversially frank treatment of a homosexual relationship between a young mar-

ried biker (Colin Campbell) who finds he has more in common with his mate (a free spirit played by Dudley Sutton) than he does with his feckless wife (Rita Tushingham). Shot on location at run-down transport cafés and on bike runs, *The Leather Boys* can now be recognised as a masterpiece of early 1960s' British realism.

Another Cliff Richard film, *Wonderful Life*, was followed by Furie's first international success, *The Ipcress File*, produced by Harry Saltzman as the first in a series of adaptations of the espionage novels of Len Deighton, which presented a much less glamorous view of the world of spies and secret agents than that peddled by the James Bond films. Furie's use of disorientating camera angles, Peter Hunt's sharp editing, John Barry's memorable score, Caine's definitive performance and a supporting cast that included such reliable character actors as Nigel Green, Guy Doleman and Gordon Jackson made *The Ipcress File* a worldwide hit. Furie immediately succumbed to an offer from Hollywood to direct the problematic but not uninteresting Western *The Appaloosa* (1966), starring Marlon Brando. Unfortunately, his directorial style did not mesh well with the Hollywood machine, and his films became progressively less interesting.

In an interview he gave in 1970, Furie claimed that

> My first successes, *The Leather Boys* and *The Ipcress File*, were instinctive, but I'd never analysed how they work. It took my last two failures [*The Appaloosa* and *The Naked Runner*] to learn for myself you need a beginning, middle and end, a

central character you can root for, in a conflict you can understand and care about. (Geist, p. 5)

Despite this insight, Furie's early films show a vitality and originality lacking in his later work. He remains a prolific director of low-budget American action and science-fiction films.
(Wheeler Winston Dixon)

BIBLIOGRAPHY: Baker, Bob, 'Sidney Furie', *Film Dope* no. 18, Sept. 1979, p. 18; Geist, Kenneth, 'Interview', *Interview* vol. 1 no. 6, 1970, pp. 5, 12; Haigh, Peter S., 'The Young Furies', *ABC Film Review*, Apr. 1962, pp. 6, 32.

FILMOGRAPHY (UK only): *Dr Blood's Coffin*; *During One Night* (1961); *The Snake Woman*; *Three on a Spree*; *The Young Ones* (1961); *The Boys* (1962); *The Leather Boys* (1963); *Wonderful Life* (1964); *The Ipcress File* (1965); *The Naked Runner* (1967).

FURNISS, Harry (1854–1925)

Born in Wexford on 26 March 1854 to English and Scottish parents, Harry Furniss came to London in 1873 to pursue a vigorous career in pictorial journalism and caricature. In this he was outstandingly successful, becoming a regular contributor to *The Illustrated London News* and, from 1880, *Punch*, for which he supplied some 2,600 cartoons over fourteen years. He was equally prolific as a book illustrator. A bumptious figure, fond of controversy and the public eye, Furniss' torrent of illustrations and cartoons of political figures and social events were supplemented by other remarkable enterprises. In 1887 he hired the Gainsborough Gallery, London, to mount his 'artistic joke', a collection of works painted in parody of a typical Royal Academy exhibition: one contribution to a long and loud feud with the august body. Between 1889 and 1902, he presented a series of humorous lectures that combined his own histrionic talents with lantern slides of his work.

Having moved to the United States his career took yet another turn in 1911 when he began working for the Edison Film Company, writing and acting in comic shorts, often with 'artistic' themes (*The Artist and the Brain Specialist*, *The Artist's Joke*). Returning with an Edison contingent the next year to begin production in England, he generated scripts for several dramas, and acted his favourite role – 'The Artist' – in the first of them, *The Foundling* (Ashley Miller, 1912). But Furniss was meant to be his own boss; he soon left Edison's outfit, and formed his own company, Furniss Films, with a studio at East Cliff House, Hastings. The first film to emerge was *Peace and War: Pencillings by Harry Furniss*, a series of topical lightning sketches featuring Furniss' pencil in action, premiered at the London Coliseum in August 1914. Three other war-related 'pencillings' followed, along with two live-action comedies: *Mrs Scrubbs' Discovery*, a domestic spat featuring Mary Brough, and *Rival Reflections*, another jest about an artist's travails. There were also travelogues, one on Hastings' fishing industry, another on *Winchelsea and Its Environs* (again featuring his magic pencil). None of his films appear to have survived.

Although he directed few films, Furniss still made a significant contribution to the British film industry. His public profile and distinguished artistic career brought reflected lustre to the trade of film-making. He also boosted the developing medium with the perceptive commentary and criticism in his book *Our Lady Cinema* (1914), where he championed the importance of visual storytelling. He died in Hastings, East Sussex, on 14 January 1925.
(Barry Anthony)

BIBLIOGRAPHY: Gifford, Denis, *British Animated Films, 1895–1985: A Filmography* (Jefferson, NC: McFarland, 1987); Low, Rachael, *The History of the British Film 1906–1914* (London: George Allen & Unwin, 1949); Robinson, David, 'Harry Furniss – Lantern Showman', *The New Magic Lantern Journal* vol. 6 no. 3, Jan. 1992, pp. 1–4.

FILMOGRAPHY: *Peace and War. Pencillings by Harry Furniss*; *War Cartoons*; *Winchelsea and Its Environs*; *Fourth Harry Furniss Cartoon*; *Mrs Scrubbs' Discovery*; *Rival Reflections* (1914); *The Fishing Net Industry* (1915).

FURSE, John

John Furse is a respected documentary producer/director. After working as one of several production assistants on Maurice Hatton's witty low-budget feature *Long Shot* (1978), he took on the task of production manager on Karl Francis' *The Mouse and the Woman* (1980) and produced Michael Grigsby's acclaimed documentary *Living on the Edge* (1987).

In 1990, shortly after Brian Keenan had been released by his Islamic kidnappers from over four years in captivity in Lebanon, Furse approached him with the idea of making a film based on his experiences. Though they agreed on an approach that would eschew sensationalism and avoid demonising Keenan's jailers, Furse failed to secure a deal with a succession of interested directors (including Danny Boyle, Kenneth Branagh, John Boorman and Nicolas Roeg). Ten years later, with his own reputation enhanced by two fascinating television documentaries – *Looks That Kill* (2000), which deals with Perceived Ugliness/Elephant Man Syndrome (which Furse himself had suffered from); and *Helen Bamber: On the Trail of Torture* (2002), a study of the founder of the Medical Foundation for the Care of Victims of Torture, presented by Keenan's fellow hostage John McCarthy – Furse decided to direct the Keenan (and McCarthy) story himself.

The worthiness of the story enabled producer Sally Hibbin to secure backing from the Irish Film Board, Scottish Screen, the UK Film Council, the Northern Ireland Film and Television Commission and the German broadcaster ZDF. *Blind Flight* has been well received at festivals and attracted favourable reviews, though wider distribution has been a problem. Furse shows commendable sensitivity in his dramatisation of the story of two very different men (brilliantly represented by Ian Hart as Keenan and Linus Roache as McCarthy) kept in a succession of dark, cramped cells, in constant danger of being murdered by their captors. Without softening the horror of the men's situation, their sojourn becomes a voyage of self-discovery, with the deep friendship they forge proving the means of their salvation. We see little more than they do of the world outside, or learn of the motivations of their captors (whose arbitrary switches between kindness and cruelty reflect their own wretched plight in a war-shattered society). Furse's 'cinematic' touches hardly disguise the fact that this intimate drama might have been equally effective – and reached a far larger audience – on television; but one can still welcome *Blind Flight* as a refreshingly adult film on a very topical subject.

(Robert Murphy)

BIBLIOGRAPHY: Keenan, Brian, 'Cry Freedom', *Guardian* Review Section, 20 Mar. 2004, p. 18; Phillips, Richard, 'An Interview with John Furse, Writer and Director of *Blind Flight*', 13 July 2004, World Socialist website, <www.wsws.org/articles/2004/jul2004/sff3-j13.shtml>; Publicity material for *Blind Flight* held on microfiche in the BFI National Library, London.

FILMOGRAPHY: *Blind Flight* (UK/Ger/Ir, 2003).

FYWELL, Tim

Tim Fywell was born in London. After studying English at Cambridge University he directed plays in London's fringe theatres in the 1970s, eventually graduating to the National Theatre and the West End. In the late 1980s he switched to television, taking the BBC directors course and working for a year on Channel 4's *Brookside* before progressing to more prestigious assignments, including adaptations of Ruth Rendell's *A Fatal Inversion* (1992) and *A Dark Adapted Eye* (1994), and the memorable 'To Be a Somebody' episode of *Cracker* (1994). He showed his ability to handle costume material with David Pirie's adventurous adaptation of Wilkie Collins' *The Woman in White* (1997) and was chosen by BBC Films to direct an $8 million adaptation of Dodie Smith's novel *I Capture the Castle*.

Fywell armed himself with an attractive cast and picturesque 1930s' decor, but both he and his writer Heidi Thomas nervously flinched before the problems of Smith's rickety narrative, whose plot pales in interest beside the uniquely eccentric world summoned up by seventeen-year-old narrator, Cassandra Mortmain. Romola Garai makes a splendid Cassandra, but her story is poorly served by syrupy music, gooey flashbacks and sugary fantasy sequences. The life of the Mortmains in their derelict castle is presented well, but the prominence given to the romantic entanglements between Cassandra, her headstrong sister Rose and two cardboard Americans pushes the film towards bathos.

Fywell stayed more happily in the past to direct *Cambridge Spies* (2003), a well-balanced four-part BBC serial about Guy Burgess, Donald Maclean, Anthony Blunt and Kim Philby, Communist sympathisers who undermined British Intelligence from the 1930s to the 1950s. He then went to Hollywood, where he appeared surprisingly at home with the simple-minded pleasures of *Ice Princess*, a modern Disney fairy tale about an awkward teenager who blossoms as she learns to express her physicality through ice-skating.

(Robert Murphy)

BIBLIOGRAPHY: Carpenter, Louise, 'Dogged Determination', *Daily Telegraph* Weekend Magazine, 19 Apr. 2003, pp. 33–6.

FILMOGRAPHY: *I Capture the Castle* (UK/SA, 2003); *Ice Princess* (US/Can, 2005).

G

GALLONE, Carmine (1886–1973)

Carmine Gallone was born in Taggia, Imperia, in Italy on 18 September 1886 and quickly established himself as a prolific leading Italian director of romantic melodramas and costume epics with films such as *La marcia nuziale* (1915), *Il bacio di Cirano* (1919) and *Gli ultimi giorni di Pompei* (1926). By the late 1920s he had spread his wings abroad, working in France and Germany. He first worked in England at Wembley Studios in 1930, directing the operetta singer Jan Kiepura in the German-financed bilingual film *City of Song*, which continually ran into technical problems, not least with its Tobis-Klangfilm sound

equipment. The end product proved mildly tuneful, but dramatically sluggish. Six other British films followed, of a similarly light musical nature: *King of the Ritz*, a Stanley Lupino vehicle enlivened by sparky performances from Henry Kendall, Gina Malo, Hugh Wakefield and Betty Stockfield; *Going Gay*, featuring Naunton Wayne and Arthur Riscoe as English bachelors competing for the affections of Viennese songstress Magda Schneider; *For Love of You*, with Wayne and Riscoe involved in similar amorous exploits in Venice; *Two Hearts in Waltz Time*, a highly Viennese musical produced by Reginald Fogwell at the Nettlefold Studios, Walton-on-Thames; *My Heart Is Calling*, another Kiepura musical made in French, German and English; and *The Divine Spark*, an English version of Gallone's *Casta diva*, an Italian biopic of the composer Bellini.

With the darkening of Europe's political climate, Gallone's European rovings came to an end. *Casta diva* won the Mussolini Cup for Best Italian Film at the Venice Film Festival in 1935; he was subsequently summoned to direct the expensive, pro-fascist *Scipione l'africano* (1937). More frivolous entertainments followed, including further musicals, and vacuous 'white telephone' films like *Amami, Alfredo!* (1940). Switching hats after the war, he made the anti-fascist *Avanti a lui tremava tutta Roma* (1946) with Anna Magnani and Tito Gobbi; but the musical films continued, with numerous versions of Italian operas. He also made two of the popular *Don Camillo* comedies. Gallone continued directing until 1962, and died in Frascati on 11 March 1973.

(Geoff Brown and Kevin Gough-Yates)

BIBLIOGRAPHY: Bondanella, Peter, *Italian Cinema* (New York: Continuum, 2001); Dalle Vache, Angela, *The Body in the Mirror* (Princeton, NJ: Princeton University Press, 1992).

FILMOGRAPHY (UK only): *City of Song* (US: *Farewell to Love*, 1931); *King of the Ritz*; *Going Gay* (US: *Kiss Me Goodbye*); *For Love of You* (1933); *Two Hearts in Waltz Time*; *My Heart Is Calling/Mein Herz ruft nach dir/Mon coeur t'appelle* (UK/Fr/Ger) (1934); *Casta diva/The Divine Spark* (UK/It, 1935).

GARNETT, Tony (1936–)

Tony Garnett was born in Birmingham on 3 April 1936. After studying psychology at the University of London, he worked briefly as an actor, and in 1963 was hired as script editor for the BBC's *Wednesday Play*. By 1965 he had become a producer, and he began his fruitful collaboration with Ken Loach on two grittily realist dramas, *Up the Junction* (1965) and *Cathy Come Home* (1966), and the bleak study of madness *In Two Minds* (1967). In 1969 the pair founded Kestrel Films to make Loach's second feature film *Kes*, from Barry Hines' novel *A Kestrel for a Knave*. It was a popular and critical success, but its successor, *Family Life* (Ken Loach, 1971), a reworking of *In Two Minds*, proved too grim to attract audiences and Loach and Garnett retreated to television. In the 1970s Garnett produced seminal television dramas by Mike Leigh (*Hard Labour* in 1973) and Roland Joffé (*The Spongers* in 1978), as well as Loach's *Rank and File* (1971) and his ambitious four-part series *Days of Hope* (1975).

Garnett's first film as director, *Prostitute* (1980), proffers a sympathetic portrait of protagonist Sandra (Eleanor Forsythe), a prostitute working in Birmingham, and her friendship with a well-intentioned welfare officer, Louise (Kate Crutchley). *Handgun*, released three years later, is a rape-revenge film, in which a naive but well-intentioned teacher (Karen Young) is raped by local lothario (Clayton Day). However, the film is more accomplished than its B-movie storyline suggests, and raises some interesting and troubling questions about the American constitutional right to own and use a gun.

Garnett produced a number of other films in the 1980s, some of them – such as the *Sesame Street* spin-off, *Follow that Bird* (Ken Kwapis, 1985) and the space comedy *Earth Girls Are Easy* (Julien Temple, 1988) – lively diversions from the realist aesthetic that characterises most of his work. In the 1990s Garnett returned to television, where he was responsible for groundbreaking series such as *Between the Lines* (1992–4), *Cardiac Arrest* (1994), *This Life* (1996) and *The Cops* (1998).

(Sarah Cardwell)

BIBLIOGRAPHY: Brooks, Richard, 'Tony Garnett, TV's Secret Godfather', *Observer* Review Section, 11 Oct. 1990, p. 18; Brown, Maggie, 'Meet the Producer', *Guardian* G2 Section, 28 Oct. 2002, p. 2.

FILMOGRAPHY: *Prostitute* (1980); Handgun (aka *Deep in the Heart*, US, 1983).

GEORGE, Terry (1952–)

Terry George was born in Belfast on 20 December 1952. A Catholic brought up in a Protestant area, he was interned in 1972 on false information and later spent three years in Long Kesh Prison. On his release he studied at Queen's University, and then moved to New York in 1981. After three years working as a journalist he found success with his play *The Tunnel*. Director Jim Sheridan then worked with him on the script for *In the Name of the Father* (Jim Sheridan, 1993), an account of the wrongful arrest, trial and imprisonment of Gerry Conlon and others for the Guildford pub bombing of 1974. The film's box-office success in America made it easier to raise finance from the Irish Film Board and the American Castle Rock company for George's directorial debut. *Some Mother's Son* (1996), produced and co-written by Jim Sheridan, examines the controversial 1981 IRA prisoners' hunger strike in a relatively non-partisan way by viewing it through the eyes of two women (Helen Mirren, Annie Higgins) with very different attitudes towards the sacrifices their sons seem prepared to make. George's refusal to view issues in simple black-and-white terms limited the film's box-office appeal but won him respect for his integrity. He then wrote *The Boxer* (1997) for Sheridan: its story about an IRA gunman who renounces political violence for community action on his release from prison reflects the move towards reconciliation that later found expression in the Good Friday Agreement of 1998.

After *The Boxer* George turned away from Irish subjects: directing a creditable adaptation of Neil Sheehan's Vietnam novel *A Bright Shining Lie* (1998) for HBO, shot in Thailand on a budget of $13.5 million; creating the Washington DC-set police series *The District* (2000); and writing the screenplay for *Hart's War* (Gregory Hoblit, 2002). In 2004 he drew once more on his experience of living in a violently divided community for *Hotel Rwanda*, a study of the Rwanda genocide based on the true story of Paul Ruseabagina, a Kigali hotel manager who turned the Mille Collines hotel into a sanctuary for over a thousand Tutsi and moderate Hutu refugees. Perceptive, unsentimental and searingly honest, the film finally established George as a major director.

(Robert Murphy)

BIBLIOGRAPHY: Crowdus, Gary and O'Mara Leary, 'The "Troubles" He's Seen in Northern Ireland: An Interview with Terry George', *Cinéaste* vol. 23 no.1, July 1997, pp. 24–9; George, Terry, 'Look Back in Anger', *Premiere*, Dec. 2004, pp. 46–50; 'Home and Away' (interview), *Film Ireland* no. 66, Aug./Sept. 1998, p. 20; McLoone, Martin, *Irish Film: The Emergence of a Contemporary Cinema* (London: BFI, 2000); McSwiney, Seamás, 'From Hollywood Barracks to Hollywood Boulevard', *Film West* no. 25, Summer 1996, pp. 10–17 (also on <www.iol.ie/~galfilm/filmwest/25terry.htm>.

FILMOGRAPHY: *In the Name of the Father* (2nd unit dir., Jim Sheridan, Ir/UK, 1993); *Some Mother's Son* (Ir/US, 1996); *Hotel Rwanda* (UK/It/SA, 2004).

GERRARD, Gene (1892–1971)

Gene Gerrard, born Eugene Maurice O'Sullivan in Clapham, south London, on 31 August 1892, was among various stage entertainers who through ambition, ego or studio convenience moved behind the camera to direct or produce in the industry's expansive years in the 1930s. Fellow crossover talents included Tom Walls, Sonnie Hale, Jack Buchanan and Jack Hulbert, and on paper Gerrard looked the least likely of the quintet to succeed. The son of a tailor, he began his stage career in 1910 as sidekick to the character comedian George Mozart; he made his film debut in 1913 in several of Mozart's Hepworth shorts. By the mid-1920s he was winning light comedy roles in musical comedies in London, achieving particular success in *Katja, the Dancer* (1924–5), though he never became the talk of the town.

Between 1931 and 1935 Gerrard concentrated primarily on cinema, acting and directing for British International Pictures. BIP took care to cushion their new acquisition. Jack-of-all-trades J. O. C. Orton supervised Gerrard's directorial debut, *Out of the Blue* (1931), while he shared his credit on the next films with the comedy writer and shorts director Frank Miller. The material remained unambitious and escapist (*Out of the Blue* and *Lucky Girl* were derived from his stage musicals); but these tales of Biarritz love tangles, flirtatious husbands and stolen jewels well suited Gerrard's nonchalant clowning and debonair air. Though *Out of the Blue* left unresolved the problem of photographing Jessie Matthews sympathetically, other technical hurdles were successfully overcome; Gerrard's films proved neither as slow nor as egocentric as those of some of his stage colleagues.

After 1935 Gerrard left BIP to freelance, returning to the stage for the pantomime seasons; his last film as director was a Warner quickie, *It's in the Blood*, an unpretentious vehicle for silly-ass comic Claude Hulbert. Wartime cinema found little use for Gerrard's overtly 'West End' personality, and he concentrated on stage work, predominantly pantomime. In 1948 he retired to Sidmouth, Devon, much to the regret, said his *Times* obituary, of those who appreciated his avoidance of laughter obtained 'by doubtful methods'. Gerrard died in Sidmouth on 1 August 1971.

(Geoff Brown)

BIBLIOGRAPHY: 'Here's Gene Gerrard. The Story of Britain's New Star', *Film Weekly*, 12 Mar. 1932, pp. 8, 26; 'Mr Gene Gerrard', Obituary, *The Times*, 3 June 1971, p. 17; Parker, John (ed.), *Who's Who in the Theatre*, 11th edn (London: Sir Isaac Pitman, 1952).

FILMOGRAPHY: *Out of the Blue* (1931); *Lucky Girl* (co-dir. Frank Miller); *Let Me Explain, Dear* (co-dir. Frank Miller) (1932); *Wake up Famous* (1937); *It's in the Blood* (1938).

GIBSON, Alan (1938–1987)

Blood, fangs and the decadent swirl of 'Swinging London' occupied most of Alan Gibson's brief film career, though he began his work in more rarefied fields. Born in London, Ontario, on 28 April 1938, Gibson arrived in England in 1961 to study at the Bristol Old Vic School of Drama. Two years later he joined BBC Television as a director; from 1965 he directed quality dramas for BBC 2, including play scripts by Arthur Miller, Samuel Beckett and Tom Stoppard. Then in 1968 Hammer called. After directing three episodes in their supernatural television series *Journey into the Unknown*, he progressed to the big screen with *Crescendo* (1970), a ridiculous but enjoyable psychodrama originally intended for the director Michael Reeves. At the heart of the tale lay twin brothers, one crippled, one mad; *Goodbye Gemini*, made for Josef Shaftel, found Gibson applying surface gloss to an even more heated sibling drama, featuring incest, blackmail and murder in London's fashionable Chelsea.

Two years later, Gibson returned to Hammer for *Dracula A.D. 1972*, followed by *The Satanic Rites of Dracula*. Both transplanted Christopher Lee's Count and Peter Cushing's adversary Van Helsing to modern-day London. Weak scripts and Gibson's flashy but shallow style left the possibilities of modern vampirism glimpsed rather than explored. Crashing cars filled much of the footage in his America debut *Checkered Flag or Crash* (1977), made in the Philippines. Television continued to give him better chances. For the BBC, he directed and co-wrote *The Flipside of Dominick Hide* (1980), a comic time-travelling fantasy conceived in the early 1970s, and popular enough to warrant a sequel. For American producers he provided respectable television movies, most prominently *A Woman Called Golda* (1982), for which Ingrid Bergman won a posthumous Emmy award for her portrayal of Israeli politician Golda Meir. Cinema itself only had one more film to offer, *Martin's Day* (1985), a bland family film made in Canada. Gibson died of cancer in London on 5 July 1987.

(Geoff Brown)

BIBLIOGRAPHY: Gibson, Alan and Jeremy Paul, 'The Flipside of Dominick Hide', in Michael Church (ed.), *Intensive Care: Four TV Plays* (Harlow: Longman Imprint Books, 1989); Kinsey, Wayne, 'Dracula A.D. 1972' and 'The Satanic Rites of Dracula', *The House That Hammer Built* no. 8, Apr./May 1998, pp. 431–4, 449–56.

FILMOGRAPHY: *Crescendo*; *Goodbye Gemini* (1970); *Dracula A.D. 1972* (1972); *The Satanic Rites of Dracula* (US: *Count Dracula and His Vampire Bride*, 1974); *Checkered Flag or Crash* (aka *Crash*, US, 1977); *Martin's Day* (Can, 1985).

GIBSON, Brian (1944–2004)

Brian Gibson was born on 22 September 1944 in Southend-on-Sea, Essex. He began his career making dramatised documentaries such as *Hospital 1922* (1972) and *Joey* (1974) before moving on to more prestigious projects, including Dennis Potter's *Where Adam Stood* (1976) and *Blue Remembered Hills* (1979) and Leon Griffith's *Dinner at the Sporting Club* (1978). He made his cinema debut with *Breaking Glass*, a punk rock drama starring Hazel O'Connor, Jon Finch, Phil Daniels and Jonathan Pryce. Though the film was not kindly reviewed by British critics, it remains an indelible marker of the 1970s' UK punk scene.

Gibson then moved to America where he made a workmanlike sequel: *Poltergeist II: The Other Side* and intelligent, sympathetic biopics of female artists: *The Josephine Baker Story* (HBO, 1991) and the hugely successful *What's Love Got to Do with It*, with Angela Bassett as Tina Turner. After making a $44 million thriller, *The Juror*, Gibson returned to Britain to make *Still Crazy*, an astute comedy about the revival of a 1970s' rock band whose members (Stephen Rea, Jimmy Nail, Bill Nighy, Billy Connolly and Timothy Spall) have sadly gone to seed. It was his last film as director. He acted as executive producer on *Frida* (2002), Julie Taymor's bold biography of the Mexican painter Frida Kahlo, before he died of bone cancer on 4 January 2004.

(Wheeler Winston Dixon)

BIBLIOGRAPHY: Bardach, Ann-Louise, 'Obituary: Brian Gibson', *Guardian*, 7 Jan. 2004; Roberts, Hilary, 'Frustrating Years Are behind Gibson', *Screen International*, 17 Aug. 1985, p. 31; Wyver, John, 'The Nature of Gossip', *Time Out*, 27 July 1979, p. 17.

FILMOGRAPHY: *Breaking Glass* (1980); *Poltergeist II: The Other Side* (US, 1986); *What's Love Got to Do with It* (US, 1993); *The Juror* (US, 1996); *Still Crazy* (UK/US, 1998).

GIDAL, Peter (1946–)

Peter Gidal was born in 1946 and grew up in Switzerland. After studying psychology and German literature at Brandeis University and the University of Munich, he enrolled at the Royal College of Art in London and began his career as an experimental film-maker. In the 1960s his films were shown at such 'underground' London venues as the New Arts Lab in Drury Lane and the London Film-Maker's Co-op (which he helped to establish) in Chalk Farm. An admirer of structuralist film-makers such as Michael Snow and Hollis Frampton, Gidal's own works are also interrogations into the formalist aspect of film, with an emphasis on grain, duration, tempo and editing structures. This is accompanied by an almost wilful insistence on the film-maker as the ultimate arbiter of the construction of any work. As he puts it:

> The question of making things difficult for the spectator in my films is absolutely crucial and historically so, because that is where the break always comes. In the cinema, more than any other art form, the question of difficulty is always raised. With other things there are conventions: for example, it's okay to spend until two o'clock in the morning checking a difficult footnote in a book; difficult paintings are okay because you can walk past them in seconds. But film has an authoritarian structure built into its mechanism in terms of time, being held there for a period of time, which is why most film goes out of its way to avoid precisely that as an issue, whereas my work goes out of its way to raise it as one. (O'Pray, 1996, p. 64)

Gidal's films invite audiences to consider various aspects of the mediation between the real and the reel. In his most famous work, *Room Film 1973*, for example, the artist's camera restlessly investigates a room in minute detail.

Along with Malcolm LeGrice, Peter Gidal is the foremost exponent of British structural cinema. He taught at the RCA from 1971 to 1983 and he remains active as ever as a film-maker and theorist, as evidenced by a gorgeously hallucinogenic website: <www.scs.khm.de/semclips/petergidal.html>. His films were given a retrospective at the Pompidou Centre, Paris, in 1996 and at the Lux, London, in 1998.

(Wheeler Winston Dixon)

BIBLIOGRAPHY: Auty, Chris, 'State of Siege', *Time Out*, 18–24 Jan. 1980, pp. 14–15; Dusinberre, Deke, 'Consistent Oxymoron: Peter Gidal's Theoretical Strategy', *Screen*, Summer 1977, pp. 79–88; Gidal, Peter (ed.), *Structural Film Anthology* (London: BFI, 1974); Gidal, Peter, 'Flashbacks: Peter Gidal', *Filmwaves* no. 7, Spring 1999, pp. 16–20; O'Pray, Mike, 'Action at a Distance', *Monthly Film Bulletin*, Mar. 1986, p. 64; O'Pray, Mike, *The British Avant-Garde Film 1926–1995* (Luton: University of Luton Press/Arts Council of England, 1996).

FILMOGRAPHY: *Room (Double Take)*; *Lovelight* (destroyed) (1967); *George Segal Sculptor* (destroyed); *Key*; *Hall* (1968); *Clouds*; *Heads* (1969); *Loop*; *Concept-Hall*; *Half (Concept)*; *Secret* (destroyed); *Neck* (destroyed); *Takes* (destroyed) (1970); *Focus*; *Clockwise*; *Bedroom*; *View*; *Post-card Film*; *8mm Film Notes on 16mm* (1971); *Movie No. 1*; *Upside Down Feature* (1972); *Photo/Graph/Film*; *Room Film 1973*; *Still Andy* (1973); *Film Print*; *C/O/N/S/T/R/U/C/T* (1974); *Condition of Illusion* (1975); *Kopenhagen/1930*; *Silent Partner* (1977); *Fourth Wall*; *Epilogue* (1978); *Untitled* (1979); *Action at a Distance* (1980); *Close Up* (1983); *Denials* (1986); *Guilt* (1988); *Flare Out* (1992); *Assumption* (1997); *No Night, No Day* (1998). Undated films include: *Boots Trilogy*, *Ten Film Pieces*, *Movie No. 2*, *Portrait – Subject – Object* and *Exit*.

GIEDROYC, Coky (1963–)

Coky Giedroyc (sister of comedienne Mel) was born in Kowloon, Hong Kong, on 6 February 1963. She studied film at Bristol University, where she made *House Party* about the contemporary rave scene. In 1989 she began working in television, where she directed extracts from literary classics such as Angela Carter's *Wise Children* (1993) and James Joyce's *Ulysses* (1993), and a documentary series, *Letters from the Homeless* (1993), which proved effective research for her first feature, *Stella Does Tricks*. Giedroyc offsets the Loachian social realism of her tale of a young prostitute and her relationship with her paternal but sadistic pimp with flashbacks and fantasy sequences exploring Stella's dreams. Kelly Macdonald gives a compelling performance as Stella, and the usually genial James Bolam is effectively sinister as her pimp. Unsurprisingly the subject matter generated publicity, and though the film's shortcomings did not go unnoticed, it was moderately successful.

Giedroyc's next film, the misleadingly entitled *Women Talking Dirty*, was made for Elton John's Rocket Pictures and starred Helena Bonham Carter and Gina McKee as close friends who help each other through their disastrous relationships with men. Intended as a more overtly commercial venture than *Stella Does Tricks*, it failed to profit from the fashion for chick-flicks, and though made in 1999 was only released in 2001. Giedroyc subsequently returned to television, securing her career with *Carrie's War* (2004), a pleasantly cosy adaptation of Nina Bawden's novel about Second World War evacuees, episodes of Peter Bowker's idiosyncratic comedy/musical/drama serial *Blackpool* (2004) and the prestige BBC drama *The Virgin Queen* (2006).

(John Riley)

BIBLIOGRAPHY: Spencer, Liese, 'Personal Services', *Independent* Weekend Section, 31 Jan. 1998.

FILMOGRAPHY: *House Party* (short, 1988); *Stella Does Tricks* (1996); *Women Talking Dirty* (1999; rel. 2001).

GIESE, Maria

Born in Cape Cod, Massachusetts, and educated at Wellesley College and UCLA's Film School, Maria Giese might seem an unlikely candidate to direct a British working-class realist film set in Sheffield. Abetted by her then-husband, producer James Daly, who had once aspired to a football career, she set up *When Saturday Comes*, the story of a talented footballer whose career with Sheffield United is blighted by his heavy drinking. Sean Bean, despite being far too old for the part, returned to his home town to play the lead role with characteristic energy and commitment. The film is curiously old-fashioned, with Sheffield still a city of miners and steelworkers (a view that would be wittily debunked by Peter Cattaneo and Simon Beaufoy's *The Full Monty* two years later); and it is easy to deride the creaking melodrama of Giese's plot. But her undoubted sincerity and integrity, and the skewed vision an American woman brings to this quintessentially British subject, makes the film a likeable contribution to Anglo-American cinema.

Giese went on to make *Hunger* (2001), an adaptation of the novel by Knut Hamsun, shot on digital video, updating the action from Oslo in 1890 to Los Angeles in 2000.

(Robert Murphy)

FILMOGRAPHY (UK only): *When Saturday Comes* (1995).

GILBERT, Brian (1960–)

Brian Gilbert was born in England in 1960 but lived in Australia until he was fourteen. He read English at Oxford, where he began to direct and write for the stage; after graduating, he acted professionally. He gained film experience by working on a documentary about crime fiction in California, and enrolled at the National Film and Television School in 1979. His graduation film, *The Devotee*, impressed David Puttnam, who offered him the opportunity to direct *Sharma and Beyond* (1984) as part of his 'First Love' series of low-budget films for Channel 4. Though it was not given a theatrical release, the performances of Robert Urquhart, Suzanne Burden and Michael Maloney and the cinematography of Ernest Vincze gave the film a pleasing competence, and Puttnam offered Gilbert *The Frog Prince*, Posy Simmonds' autobiographical story of her amorous adventures in Paris in the 1960s. The resulting film was too low key to make much impact, but its charm and integrity consolidated Gilbert's reputation and he was able to make two films in America. *Vice Versa* was an updated version of F. Anstey's Victorian comic novel comedy about a child and an adult changing places, filmed by Peter Ustinov in 1947; *Not without My Daughter* featured Sally Field as an American woman forced to fight for her rights against a husband who has whisked her back to his oppressive homeland in Iran.

Back in England, Gilbert directed *Tom & Viv*, which charts the relationship between T. S. Eliot (Willem Dafoe) and his first wife Vivienne Haigh-Wood (Miranda Richardson). Despite the picturesque period settings, there is a sharp critique of the medical establishment that failed to understand or correctly diagnose the troubled heroine. Three years later, he again recreated the past to attack its institutions in *Wilde*, which concentrates on the playwright's trial and imprisonment. Stephen Fry gives a charismatic performance as Wilde and Jude Law is a suitably self-absorbed Bosie, though the film is much more soft-centred than Ken Hughes' *The Trials of Oscar Wilde* (1960). He followed this with *The Gathering*, an ambitious supernatural thriller scripted by the prolific television writer Anthony Horowitz, with Christina Ricci and Kerry Fox; it has not been widely distributed.

(Pamela Church Gibson)

BIBLIOGRAPHY: Hodges, Adrian, 'Writer/Director Gilbert Captures the "Extra Dimension" in "Sharma"', *Screen International*, 3 Dec. 1983, p. 11; Murphy, Robert, 'Sharma and the Shooting Party', *Stills* no. 10, Feb./Mar. 1984, pp. 57–8; '*The Gathering*: A Shivers Interview', *Shivers* no. 95, Feb./Mar. 2002, pp. 10–13.

FILMOGRAPHY: *The Devotee* (short, 1982); *The Frog Prince* (1985); *Vice Versa* (US, 1988); *Not without My Daughter* (US, 1991); *Tom & Viv* (UK/US, 1994); *Wilde* (UK/US/Jap/Ger, 1997); *The Gathering* (UK/US, 2002); *Allegiance* (2005).

GILBERT, Lewis (1920–)

Lewis Gilbert's career as a writer, producer and director of varied films spans the entire post-war history of British cinema, a contribution acknowledged by the award of a BFI Fellowship in 2001. In the 1950s Gilbert was particularly associated with the war film; three James Bond films followed in the late 1960s and 1970s. A more personal touch emerged in smaller films adapted from stage plays, such as Willy Russell's *Educating Rita* (1983) and *Shirley Valentine* (1989).

Lewis Gilbert was born in Hackney, London, on 6 March 1920. He was raised among a family of music-hall performers, and his early stage experience allowed him to continue as a child actor in films, including *Dick Turpin* (Victor Hanbury/John Stafford, 1933). Alexander Korda offered to send him to RADA, but Gilbert chose to study direction instead, notably as an assistant on Hitchcock's *Jamaica Inn* (1939). During the war, he joined the RAF and directed several documentaries on attachment to the US Air Corps Film Unit. After the war, he continued to write and direct documentary shorts for Gaumont-British, before entering low-budget feature film production with companies like Butchers and Group 3.

His breakthrough film was *Emergency Call* (1952), a multiple-character hospital melodrama, elevated to first-feature status on the Rank circuit. This was the first time that Gilbert collaborated with Vernon Harris, a writer who contributed to most of his films over the next forty years. Subsequently, he was offered more expensive productions, mostly produced by Daniel Angel. The hoodlum drama *Cosh Boy* (1953) was one of the earliest films to receive an 'X' certificate, though war films like *Albert R.N.* (1953), *Reach for the Sky* (1956) and *Carve Her Name with Pride* (1958) proved more typical of their partnership.

In the 1960s other Second World War subjects followed, but with more varied generic treatments. *Sink the Bismarck!* (1960) is a large-scale dramatisation of a real sea battle, whereas *Light up the Sky!* (1960) is a parochial comedy about an army searchlight unit. Other films at this time range from the romantic whimsy of *The Greengage Summer* (1961) to the historical adventure of *H.M.S. Defiant* (1962). *Alfie* was the first of a number of stage play adaptations that brought Gilbert commercial and critical success in the latter part of his career. The film received multiple Academy Award nominations, most notably for Michael Caine, consolidating the presence he had established in Sidney J. Furie's *The Ipcress File* (1965). Later, this achievement was repeated with Julie Walters in *Educating Rita* and Pauline Collins in *Shirley Valentine*. The success of *Alfie*, however, also had its downsides. Contractual obligations to Paramount, who had financed the film, tied Gilbert to a poorly received American production of Harold Robbins' *The Adventurers* (1970). Gilbert had been preparing *Oliver!* (1968) with Vernon Harris, but had to abandon the project, which was passed to Carol Reed.

In between *Alfie* and *The Adventurers*, Gilbert directed the first of his three Bond films, *You Only Live Twice* (1967). When he returned to the series in the late 1970s, he recognised that many of the Bond conventions had become anachronistic because of changing attitudes to gender identity that challenged Bond's male chauvinism. For *The Spy Who Loved Me* (1977), he suggested that women's roles be 'just as virile as Bond himself' (Summers, p. 6). He also showed himself adept at handling action sequences effectively on the massive sets characteristic of the Bond films.

Gilbert's career has ranged from low-budget programmers to international co-productions and big-budget action films. He is admired for his efficient professionalism and knowledge of the business and craft of film-making. But critics have struggled to fathom Gilbert as an 'author-personality' in a body of work that ranges from explorations of various forms of machismo (in *Cosh Boy*, *Reach for the Sky*, *Alfie* and the Bond films, for example) to celebrations of female resilience in *Educating Rita* and *Shirley Valentine*. Yet clearly his films do have recurring themes, such as his interest in the lives of children and their entry into adulthood, evident in *The Little Ballerina*, *Cosh Boy*, *Johnny on the Run*, *A Cry from the Streets*, *The Greengage Summer*, *Friends* and *Paul and Michelle*. More generally, one could claim that Gilbert's films cover the personal lives of everyday people experiencing problems, or undergoing change, or people who become extraordinary through their involvement in momentous historical events. Gilbert continued to work on personal projects into his eighties, though *Before You Go*, an adaptation of a stage play by Shelagh Stephenson about three women (Julie Walters, Joanne Whalley and Victoria Hamilton) coming to terms with their mother's death, attracted little attention.
(Andrew Clay)

BIBLIOGRAPHY: Baker, Bob, 'Lewis Gilbert', *Film Dope* no. 19, Dec. 1979, p. 29; Chapman, James, *Licence to Thrill* (London: I. B. Taurus, 1999); McFarlane, Brian, *An Autobiography of British Cinema* (London: Methuen, 1997); Summers, Sue, 'The Man Who's Ensured 007 Has Kept up with the Times', *Screen International*, 26 Feb. 1977, pp. 6–7.

FILMOGRAPHY: *The Ten Year Plan* (doc. short); *Sailors Do Care* (doc. short) (1944); *Arctic Harvest* (doc., 1946); *Fishing Grounds of the World* (doc. short, 1947); *Under One Roof* (doc. short); *The Little Ballerina* (1949); *Once a Sinner* (1950); *It's a Small World* (doc. short); *There Is Another Sun* (US: *Wall of Death*); *Scarlet Thread* (1951); *Time Gentlemen Please!*; *Emergency Call* (US: *The Hundred Hour Hunt*) (1952); *Cosh Boy* (US: *The Slasher*); *Johnny on the Run*; *Albert R.N.* (US: *Break to Freedom*) (1953); *Harmony Lane* (as Byron Gill, short); *The Sea Shall Not Have Them*; *The Good Die Young* (1954); *Cast a Dark Shadow* (1955); *Reach for the Sky* (1956); *The Admirable Crichton* (US: *Paradise Lagoon*, 1957); *Carve Her Name with Pride*; *A Cry from the Streets* (1958); *Ferry to Hong Kong* (1959); *Sink the Bismarck!*; *Light up the Sky!* (1960); *The Greengage Summer* (US: *Loss of Innocence*, 1961); *H.M.S. Defiant* (US: *Damn the Defiant!*, 1962); *The 7th Dawn* (1964); *Alfie* (1966); *You Only Live Twice* (1967); *The Adventurers* (US, 1970); *Friends* (1971); *Paul and Michelle* (UK/Fr, 1974); *Operation Daybreak* (US, 1975); *Seven Nights in Japan* (1976); *The Spy Who Loved Me* (1977); *Moonraker* (UK/Fr, 1979); *Educating Rita* (1983); *Not Quite Jerusalem* (US: *Not Quite Paradise*, 1984); *Shirley Valentine* (1989); *Stepping Out* (Can/US, 1991); *Haunted* (1995); *Before You Go* (2002).

GILL, Liz

Elizabeth Gill worked as assistant director on a number of Irish productions including *Ordinary Decent Criminal* (Thaddeus O'Sullivan, 2000) and *Disco Pigs* (Kirsten Sheridan, 2001). She had made her own directorial debut in 1996 with *Gold in the Streets*, a low-budget adaptation of a stage play about contemporary Irish immigrants in New York. The film received little distribution, and it was not until 2002 that Gill attempted a second bite at the cherry. *Goldfish Memory* is a glossier affair, despite being shot on digital video, and concerns a more upmarket group of well-heeled Dubliners in a tangle of romantic relationships. Initially targeted at gay and lesbian audiences, the film was later promoted in the UK as '*Love Actually* – Irish-style', though the similarities are superficial. Working from her own script, Gill creates ten characters of varied sexual orientations, interweaving their lives with some panache and plausibility; and her use of eccentric versions of Antonio Carlos Jobim songs contrasts favourably with the predictably middlebrow soundtrack of Richard Curtis' film. Attractive though they are, without the allure of stars, the numerous characters of *Goldfish Memory* were never likely to attract a mass audience. Gill went on to direct episodes of *The Big Bow Wow* (2004), an Irish television series about young people sharing a Dublin apartment block.
(Robert Murphy)

BIBLIOGRAPHY: Duggan, Seamus, 'Digital Goldfish', *Film Ireland* no. 81, June/July 2001, p. 47; Griffin, Joe, 'The Golden Bowl', *Film Ireland* no. 94, Sept./Oct. 2003, pp. 30–1; Phelan, James, 'Gold in the Streets', *Film West* no. 28, May 1997, p. 58.

FILMOGRAPHY: *Gold in the Streets* (UK/Ir, 1996); *Goldfish Memory* (2003).

GILLIAM, Terry (1940–)

Terence Vance Gilliam was born in Minneapolis, Minnesota, on 22 November 1940. His family lived on the city's rural outskirts until 1951, when they moved to California, settling near Los Angeles. The proximity of Hollywood reinforced Gilliam's early fascination with cinema, which had been fuelled by science-fiction and animated films; radio, however, was his most creative influence, together with comic books and magazines. His student years saw him as the editor of *Fang*, Occidental College's satirical journal. After majoring in physics in 1962, Gilliam left LA for New York, securing a job as assistant editor on Harvey Kurtzman's magazine *Help*. A stint in advertising and as a freelance illustrator followed, but the turning point came in 1967, when Gilliam moved to London and was introduced to television producers.

After collaborating on sketches and animation pieces for a number of comedy shows, in 1969 he joined *Monty Python's Flying Circus*, the ground-breaking BBC series characterised by subversive and surreal humour. Gilliam's ambitious, fantasy-led work was ideally suited to the Python ethos, providing the bizarre animated sequences that greatly contributed to the show's cult appeal.

The next breakthrough came as Python made the leap to the big screen, with *Monty Python and the Holy Grail* affording Gilliam his first directing role, which he shared with fellow Python Terry Jones. An irreverent take on the Arthurian legend, the film combined narrative and visual surrealism with a realistic approach to medieval *mise en scène*, a style maintained by Gilliam in his solo directorial debut, *Jabberwocky*. This film bore little resemblance to its original inspiration, Lewis Carroll's poem, but allowed the director to explore further his vision of the Middle Ages as a Western-like world filled with clear archetypes (McCabe, p. 69). Protagonist Dennis Cooper, forced to abandon his dreams by society's powers that be, epitomised Gilliam's key preoccupation, the crushing of the individual by a soulless system; *Jabberwocky* bears Gilliam's signature on its script and special effects, as do all his subsequent films. *Time Bandits* continued the theme of embattled individuality: the film's hero, Kevin, lives a fantasy life in opposition to his parents' conformist, materialistic values. The victory of fantasy over reality, another favourite subject of Gilliam's, is expounded in Kevin's alliance with six time-travelling dwarfs, relentlessly pursued by the Supreme Being, the heartless creator of a bureaucracy-driven universe. Gilliam's next film was *The Crimson Permanent Assurance*, a short film that served as a disassociated prologue to *Monty Python's The Meaning of Life*. It features a group of elderly, exploited accountants, and charts their rebellion against corporate power, as they transform themselves into a gang of pirates who spread terror through the world of finance.

Farcical elements are still present in *Brazil*, a dystopian odyssey set in the future, but they are used by Gilliam to highlight his vision of a society dominated by censorship and bureaucracy: pervasive propaganda posters, designed in the idealised, happy-family style of 1950s' American adverts, urge citizens to spy on their neighbours. The result is a highly disturbing film, where protagonist Sam Lowry (Jonathan Pryce) vainly tries to escape the clutches of totalitarianism, machinery and conformity. Gilliam struggled successfully to maintain an unhappy ending, against the producers' wish; together with the dense narrative, dream-world imagery and gloriously monstrous visuals, it gained *Brazil* its reputation as the quintessential Gilliam film. Critical recognition matched the film's popular success, with awards from the Los Angeles Film Critics Association for Best Picture, Best Director and Best Screenplay in 1985, as well as two Academy Award nominations. Gilliam's next and last British film, *The Adventures of Baron Munchausen*, acquired a different distinction, as this time the director's grandiose imagination was outstripped by production costs. A lavish, large-scale rendition of the classic

tale, including a whole Turkish army and a journey to the moon, *Munchausen* rapidly ran into huge debts; although critically praised and nominated for four Academy Awards, it was given a limited release and lost money.

Gilliam's next three films – *The Fisher King*, *12 Monkeys* and *Fear and Loathing in Las Vegas* – were made in America but he returned to Europe for *The Man Who Killed Don Quixote*. The film collapsed after its leading actor fell ill and although a documentary (*Lost in La Mancha*, Keith Fulton and Lou Pepe, 2002) has been made outlining Gilliam's ideas, he has not been able to relaunch the project. Instead he concentrated on two other ambitious ventures, both of which finally came to fruition at the end of 2005. *The Brothers Grimm*, an $80 million extravaganza set in eighteenth-century Germany, proved a suitable vehicle for Gilliam's view of the past as a nightmarish mix of wonders, horrors and uncomfortable grubbiness. *Tideland*, made on a much smaller budget in the wilds of Saskatchewan, centres on the lurid fantasies of its eight-year-old heroine (Jodelle Ferland) while she is stuck in an isolated farmhouse with her junky father. Unsurprisingly it upset some critics and audiences, though it demonstrates Gilliam's continuing refusal to be bound by polite conventions.

Gilliam's status as auteur has been assured by his strikingly idiosyncratic style, recurrent themes and insistence on control of all stages of film-making. An open hostility towards the studio system has complemented his criticism of mainstream American culture, pragmatically sealed by a thirty-five-year residence in Britain. While he has had to turn to his native country to finance his most recent films, he has continued to denounce Hollywood as an accessory to the 'lie' lived by American society; accordingly, he has declined the direction of many a US box-office hit. In Britain as elsewhere, Gilliam's directing skills have been at times overshadowed by the stunning impact of his visual creations: he remains best known as a visionary maker of fantastic worlds, monsters and machines. Likewise, critics and audiences have tended to overlook the outstanding performances given by his actors: Jonathan Pryce and Robert De Niro in *Brazil*, John Neville and Robin Williams in *Munchausen*, to name but a few.
(Elisabetta Girelli)

BIBLIOGRAPHY: Ashbrook, John, *Terry Gilliam* (Harpenden, Herts: Pocket Essentials, 2000); Christie, Ian (ed.), *Gilliam on Gilliam* (London: Faber and Faber, 1999); Johnson, Kim 'Howard', *The First 280 Years of Monty Python* (New York: St Martin's Griffin, 1999); Mathews, Jack, *The Battle of Brazil* (New York: Crown Publishers, 1987); McCabe, Bob, *Dark Knights & Holy Fools* (London: Orion, 1999); Rushdie, Salman, 'The Location of Brazil', in *Imaginary Homelands* (London: Granta, 1991); Yule, Andrew, *Losing the Light: Terry Gilliam and the Munchausen Saga* (New York: Applause Books, 1991).

FILMOGRAPHY: *Story Time* (short, 1970); *The Miracle of Flight* (short); *Monty Python and the Holy Grail* (co-dir. Terry Jones, 1974); *Jabberwocky* (1977); *Time Bandits* (1981); *The Crimson Permanent Assurance* (as part of *Monty Python's The Meaning of Life*, Terry Jones, 1983); *Brazil* (1985); *The Adventures of Baron Munchausen* (1988); *The Fisher King* (US, 1991); *12 Monkeys* (US, 1995); *Fear and Loathing in Las Vegas* (US, 1998); *The Brothers Grimm* (US/Ger); *Tideland* (UK/Can) (2005).

GILLIAT, Sidney (1908–1994)

From the 1940s to the mid-60s, Sidney Gilliat and his film-making partner Frank Launder carved a distinctive niche in British cinema, offering middlebrow entertainments stamped with intelligence, an impish wit and a close regard for the quirks of British life. They initially joined forces in the mid-1930s as scriptwriters, specialising in comedy-thrillers; then the upheavals of the Second World War gave them their chance to direct their own scripts, beginning with *Millions Like Us* (1943). Many projects were developed jointly, yet each had their own preferences. Gilliat's forte was dry social comedy with a pessimistic streak, an ideal platform for his caustic sense of humour; Launder was happiest with lighter, farcical comedy, or subjects with a Celtic flavour. Neither matched their ingenious scripts with a particularly developed visual style, though the flourishes of European silent cinema – an early passion – found distant echoes in some of Gilliat's scripts, and both knew much about comic timing.

Gilliat was born in Stockport, on 15 February 1908. His father was a journalist and newspaper editor, and Gilliat entered films in 1928 in tandem with Walter C. Mycroft, formerly the film critic on his father's paper, the London *Evening Standard*. For ten months he performed dogsbody chores in Mycroft's scenario department at British International Pictures at Elstree, but learned more about film-making assisting the comedian and

director Walter Forde at the more modest Nettlefold Studios. In 1931 he joined Gaumont-British as a junior writer, and won his industry breakthrough writing the lion's share of Forde's fast-moving thriller *Rome Express*, a prestige product for the company. He cemented his success writing comedy-thrillers with Launder that were consciously modelled along Hollywood lines but had English eccentricities writ large. In their script for *The Lady Vanishes* (1938), written before Alfred Hitchcock was assigned to direct, they established the characters of Charters and Caldicott, two imperturbable Englishmen abroad who proved popular enough to be resurrected in a number of other films.

Edward Black at Gainsborough Pictures gave the team their first chance to direct. They jointly wrote and directed *Millions Like Us*, an unusually lively and vivid portrait of Home Front life. Gilliat's first solo project as writer-director, *Waterloo Road* (1945), displayed the same beady eye for ordinary wartime lives, compromised slightly by the demands of melodrama. But in *The Rake's Progress* (1945), made through the team's own company Individual Pictures, Gilliat shook off popular conventions to write and direct his most distinctive film: a sharp, sometimes touching social comedy about the escapades of an upper-class cad who finally finds a niche fighting in the Second World War. The role was perfectly pitched to the acting style of Rex Harrison, its lead performer. *Green for Danger* (1946), adapted from Christianna Brand's thriller about murder stalking a wartime hospital, was a less personal project, but Gilliat's handprints stayed visible in the sardonic tone, the expert blending of laughter and fear, and the proud parade of Alastair Sim's eccentricities as the fallible Inspector Cockrill.

With Powell–Pressburger's The Archers, David Lean, Ronald Neame and Anthony Havelock-Allan's Cineguild, Individual Pictures formed part of Independent Artists, a high-profile group sheltering inside the Rank Organisation. When relations with Rank soured, Launder and Gilliat joined the exodus towards Alexander Korda's London Films. Gilliat's first film for Korda, the crisply paced chase thriller *State Secret* (1950), was based on another strong original script; his passion for detail helped enormously in creating the setting, an imaginary Central European country. There was less opportunity to put a personal mark on *The Story of Gilbert and Sullivan* (1953), a lavish musical biography that had its incidental pleasures but never came to heel.

During the 1950s, inside and outside Korda's domain, Launder and Gilliat enjoyed box-office success with the St Trinian's farces, beginning with *The Belles of St Trinian's*. But these high-spirited romps were Launder's chief concern; Gilliat himself experienced less success finding outlets for his larger ambitions. *The Constant Husband* (1955) reunited him with Rex Harrison for a sophisticated comedy about an amnesiac sufferer who discovers he has six wives; but compared to *The Rake's Progress*, the film's social observations remained on the surface. The thriller *Fortune Is a Woman* (1957) and the political comedy *Left, Right and Centre* (1959) offered further polished, but relatively mild, entertainment.

Once Launder and Gilliat ascended into management with the Boulting Brothers on the board of the British Lion Film Corporation in 1958, chances to practice film-making themselves began to shrink. However, Gilliat achieved substantial critical and popular success with *Only Two Can Play* (1962), adapted by Bryan Forbes from Kingsley Amis' novel *That Certain Feeling*. Gilliat charted the progress of Peter Sellers' philandering Welsh librarian with mordant wit, fine timing and an appropriate regard for the sordid side of domesticity. As the 1960s advanced, upheavals in the industry increasingly kept Gilliat chained to a desk at British Lion, but he emerged to direct scenes in *The Great St Trinian's Train Robbery* (1965). Other planned productions fell by the wayside – one was *Modesty Blaise*, subsequently filmed by Joseph Losey; but in 1971 he managed to direct *Endless Night*, an elegant version of an Agatha Christie thriller, unfairly mauled by the contemporary press.

Launder and Gilliat resigned from British Lion in 1972, and no other film project stirred Gilliat sufficiently to emerge from retirement; his chief participation in Launder's *The Wildcats of St Trinian's* was in offering the advice that it should not be made. Much of his time was spent writing a meticulously researched comic novel, *Catch Me Who Can*, set against the railway frauds of the 19th century; it was almost finished at his death on 31 May 1994.

(Geoff Brown)

BIBLIOGRAPHY: Babington, Bruce, *Launder and Gilliat* (Manchester: Manchester University Press, 2002); Brown, Geoff, *Launder and Gilliat* (London: BFI, 1977); Gilliat, Sidney, interviewed by Kevin Macdonald, 'The Early Life of a Screenwriter II', in John Boorman and Walter Donohue (eds), *Projections 2. A Forum for Film-Makers* (London: Faber and Faber, 1993).

FILMOGRAPHY: *Partners in Crime* (short, co-dir. Frank Launder, 1942); *Millions Like Us* (co-dir. Frank Launder, 1943); *Waterloo Road*; *The Rake's Progress* (1945); *Green for Danger* (1946); *London Belongs to Me* (1948); *State Secret* (1950); *The Story of Gilbert and Sullivan* (1953); *The Constant Husband* (1955); *Fortune Is a Woman* (1957); *Left, Right and Centre* (1959); *Only Two Can Play* (1962); *The Great St Trinian's Train Robbery* (co-dir. Frank Launder, 1966); *Endless Night* (1972).

GILLING, John (1912–1984)

John Gilling was born in London on 29 May 1912. He entered the industry in 1935 as an assistant director, served in the navy during the Second World War and returned to cinema as a screenwriter in the late 1940s, first directing in 1949. Gilling remained prolific as a director and writer until the late 1960s.

Though he turned out brisk, efficient crime movies and colourful low-budget adventures, Gilling is most associated with horror. He could do little with the bizarre but dull Bela Lugosi–Arthur Lucan vehicle *Mother Riley Meets the Vampire* (1952), and uncomfortably replaced Robert Aldrich on the Ruritanian cold war science-fiction film *The Gamma People* (1956). His first notable film is *The Flesh and the Fiends* (1959), a

Burke and Hare story adapted from the script he wrote for the Tod Slaughter vehicle *The Greed of William Hart* (Oswald Mitchell, 1948). This takes a widescreen monochrome fire-and-brimstone approach to historical horror, distant in style from contemporary Hammer Eastmancolor efforts, and features excellent performances from Peter Cushing, Donald Pleasence and Billie Whitelaw.

Hammer employed Gilling as a writer (on Terence Fisher's *The Gorgon*, 1964, for example), but preferred Fisher as director for most of their gothic horror films. Gilling directed the black-and-white, Val Lewton-influenced *Shadow of the Cat* (1961) for Hammer, but he seemed to find his niche with the company directing three swashbucklers – *The Pirates of Blood River*, *The Scarlet Blade* and *The Brigand of Kandahar*. He left Hammer to make *Panic*, a routine melodrama, and *The Night Caller*, a much more inventive black-and-white science-fiction thriller in which an alien seeks to recruit women for the planet Ganymede by advertising in British glamour magazines. Then he returned to make his two best films. *The Reptile* and *The Plague of the Zombies* were made back-to-back on location in Cornwall, where Gilling had set his pre-Hammer swashbuckler *Fury at Smuggler's Bay*. Tales of exotic curses, invoked in far-flung Borneo and Haiti but worked out in Victorian Cornwall, both films are tightly constructed and boast fine performances from Jacqueline Pearce (especially as the snake-girl of *The Reptile*), Noel Willman, André Morell and John Carson. Gilling constructs terrific action and horror sequences illustrating the return of the repressed: Pearce hypnotised into moving like a snake by Eastern music in *The Reptile*; red-coated huntsmen disrupting a funeral; and the rotting dead clawing through their graves in *The Plague of the Zombies*. Unfortunately, *The Mummy's Shroud*, the last Hammer film made at Bray, lacked the intensity and originality of Gilling's Cornish films. André Morell soon comes to a grisly end, and the father–son conflict between John Philips and David Buck generates little interest. Greatest enjoyment comes from the performances of Michael Ripper – given far more to do than usual in a Hammer film – and Catherine Lacey, exultantly watching the rampaging Mummy in her crystal ball.

After falling out with Hammer chief Sir James Carreras, Gilling turned to television, directing episodes of series such as *The Saint*, *The Champions* and *Department S*. His last film, *La cruz del diablo*, made in Spain, looks like a routine assignment undertaken to pay for the holiday villa. He died in Spain on 22 November 1984.

(Kim Newman)

BIBLIOGRAPHY: Humphreys, Fred and Mike Murphy, 'The Reptile', *Dark Terrors*, Nov./Dec. 1992, pp. 24–30; Meikle, Denis, *A History of Horrors: The Rise and Fall of the House of Hammer* (Lanham, MD and London: Scarecrow Press, 1996); Pirie, David, *A Heritage of Horror* (London: Gordon Fraser, 1973).

FILMOGRAPHY: *Escape from Broadmoor* (short, 1948); *A Matter of Murder* (1949); *The Quiet Woman*; *No Trace* (1950); *The Voice of Merrill*; *Mother Riley Meets the Vampire*; *The Frightened Man* (1952); *Recoil*; *Escape by Night*; *Deadly Nightshade* (1953); *3 Steps to the Gallows*; *The Embezzler*; *Double Exposure*; *Destination Milan* (1954); *The Gilded Cage*; *Tiger by the Tail* (1955); *Odongo*; *High Flight*; *The Gamma People* (1956); *Land of Laughter* (short); *Interpol* (1957); *The Man Inside* (1958); *The Bandit of Zhobe*; *Idle on Parade*; *The Flesh and the Fiends* (1959); *The Challenge*; *Fury at Smuggler's Bay* (1960); *Shadow of the Cat*; *The Pirates of Blood River* (1961); *The Scarlet Blade* (1963); *The Brigand of Kandahar*, *Panic* (1965); *The Night Caller* (1965; rel. 1968); *The Plague of the Zombies*; *The Reptile*; *Where the Bullets Fly* (1966); *The Mummy's Shroud* (1967); *La cruz del diablo/The Devil's Cross* (Sp, 1974).

GILSENAN, Alan (1962–)

Alan Gilsenan was born in County Meath, Ireland on 2 August 1962. After making *Eh Joe* from a screenplay by Samuel Beckett, Gilsenan made his name with *The Road to God Knows Where*, a series of interviews with young people that summed up a general sense of disenchantment with Irish society. He followed this with a number of controversial television documentaries: *Stolen from Silence* (1987), where he interviewed AIDS patients; *Prophet Songs* (1990), about priests who had lost their vocation; *Between Heaven and Woolworths* (1992), a study of the storytelling tradition; and six programmes on American writers, *God Bless America* (1994). Between 1996 and 1998 Gilsenan made *Home Movie Nights*, a collage of amateur and historical footage.

In 1997 Gilsenan moved into fiction with *All Souls Day*, shot on a mixture of Super-8, VHS and Super-16 and blown up to 35mm. The film divided critics – some admiring its technical virtuosity, others critical of its regressive gender politics. Gilsenan returned to documentary with *The Green Fields of France* (1998), a poetic memorial to the Irish who died in the First World War; and *The Ghost of Roger Casement* (2001), a reassessment of the Irish diplomat executed as a traitor by the British government after the 1916 Easter Rising. In 2001 he made a fictional short, *Zulu 9* about stowaway refugees, and in 2004 made a feature film, *Timbuktu*, set in North Africa.

(Ruth Barton)

BIBLIOGRAPHY: O'Brien, Harvey, *The Real Ireland* (Manchester and New York: Manchester University Press, 2004); Shields, Paula, 'On the Road', *Film Ireland*, July/Aug. 2002, pp. 16–18.

FILMOGRAPHY: *Eh Joe* (short, Ir, 1986); *The Road to God Knows Where* (doc., UK/Ir, 1989); *All Souls Day* (Ir, 1997); *Zulu 9* (short, Ir, 2001); *Timbuktu* (Ir, 2004).

GINEVER, Aveling (1896–1960)

Thomas F. Aveling Ginever was born in Islington, London, and worked as a journalist and advertising executive before entering films in 1928, directing sponsored and religious shorts. He is chiefly remembered today as the director who introduced the flour magnate and Methodist Joseph Arthur Rank to the film industry in 1934. Ginever's *In Our Time*, reputedly the first religious sound film made in Britain, impressed Rank, though Rachael Low dismisses it as an unremarkable production 'which uses every cliché possible' (Low, p. 145). Rank subsequently commissioned Ginever to direct *Mastership* (1934) at Merton Park Studios, a modest success when screened in churches and schools. Ginever and Rank parted company soon afterwards, due to theological differences over how Christianity should be promoted through film.

Ginever continued working in both non-fiction and low-budget 'quota quickie' features during the 1930s and 40s and established his own production company, Gee Films, for sponsored shorts. During the war he directed a number of films for the services including *Enemy Interrogation of Prisoners* for the RAF and *Meeting the U-boat Menace* for the Admiralty. After the war he continued as Managing Director of Gee Films, directing some of its films. He died at Chertsey, Surrey, on 3 April 1960.

(Leo Enticknap)

BIBLIOGRAPHY: Low, Rachael, *Films of Comment and Persuasion of the 1930s* (London: George Allen & Unwin, 1979); Macnab, Geoffrey, *J. Arthur Rank and the British Film Industry* (London: Routledge, 1993).

FILMOGRAPHY: *In Our Time* (short); *Men and Machines* (doc. short) (1933); *Mastership* (short); *This Progress* (doc. short); *A Dickensian Fantasy* (short) (1934); *Twenty-Five Years a King* (doc.); *Triumph* (short) (1935); *Knights for a Day* (co-dir. Norman Lee, 1937); *Cross Beams* (short); *Enemy Interrogation of Prisoners* (doc. short) (1940); *Meeting the U-boat Menace* (doc. short, 1943); *Walking on Air* (1946); *Pathways to the Sky* (doc. short, 1947); *Driving Instructor* (doc. short, 1960).

GLADWELL, David (1935–)

David Gladwell, born in Gloucester on 2 April 1935, came to prominence in 1975 with his BFI production *Requiem for a Village*, an eloquent and imaginative memorial to old ways of country living disappearing under modern development. Gladwell had developed his themes and techniques in short films from an early age: he began making fiction fantasies at school, using his father's home-movie equipment. The sixteen-minute *Miss Thomson Goes Shopping* (1958), completed in London following study at Gloucester Art College, displayed the influence of Lorenza Mazzetti's Free Cinema film *Together* (1956), particularly in its mix of music and natural sound; the Free Cinema group's favourite cameraman, Walter Lassally, worked on both of Gladwell's later features. Switching careers from teaching to film, Gladwell worked in the British Transport Films cutting rooms, then settled into a long association with Derrick Knight & Partners, in the 1960s prolific makers of documentaries with a social conscience. His editing skills were given a bigger profile in two features for Lindsay Anderson: Gladwell cut *if . . . .* (1968) and *O Lucky Man!* (1973). On his own time he pursued personal experiments with film form: the nine-minute *An Untitled Film* (1964) used slow-motion to convey a child's experience of witnessing a chicken slaughtered. Along with montage, slow-motion became a key device in *Requiem for a Village* for suggesting the cyclical nature of time, with past and present fluctuating and finally commingling.

Emerging into Britain's alternative cinema scene as experimental and structuralist concerns were taking hold, the lyrical and humane *Requiem for a Village* represented a way of film-making as much under threat as Gladwell's rural utopia. With this sixty-eight-minute film as his calling card, Gladwell eventually mounted an ambitious narrative feature, *Memoirs of a Survivor* (1981), based on Doris Lessing's novel, featuring Julie Christie as the disturbed woman in a decayed city who starts to believe in an alternative world lying beyond her flat's living room. The clinching finance, almost half the budget, came from EMI Films, half-heartedly diverting resources to home-grown projects from its obsessive concern with the American market; Anderson's *Britannia Hospital* (1982) was another beneficiary. After lengthy gestation Gladwell's film was pushed into production with indecent haste and an insufficient budget. Lessing's material allowed Gladwell to further explore themes of unfriendly urban life and the past co-existing with the present, but the reduced budget and the Christie character's passivity presented dramatic and visual problems beyond his capacity to solve. Little noticed by critics or audiences, the film proved a box-office disaster.

'His case could be used as the perfect indictment of a system too dominated by the industrial aspect', Walter Lassally, the film's director of photography, wrote in his autobiography *Itinerant Cameraman* (p. 171). Bruised by the experience, Gladwell found no further directing assignments, not even in the 1980s' revival of independent film-making spearheaded by Channel 4. He returned to the cutting room and obscurity, editing *Nineteen Nineteen* (Hugh Brody, 1984) and *Lost Angels* (Hugh Hudson, 1989) and several television documentaries.

(Geoff Brown)

BIBLIOGRAPHY: Ellis, John (ed.), *1951–1976: British Film Institute Productions* (London: BFI, 1977); Gladwell, David, 'The Path of a Film Director' (interview), microfiche held in the BFI National Library, London; Hodges, Adrian, 'Anatomy of a 'Survivor', *Screen International*, 24 Jan. 1981, p. 25; Lassally, Walter, *Itinerant Cameraman* (London: John Murray, 1987); Perkins, Roy and Martin Stollery, *British Film Editors: 'The Heart of the Movie'* (London: BFI, 2004); Sussex, Elizabeth, *'Requiem for a Village'*, *Sight and Sound*, Winter 1975/6, pp. 60–1.

FILMOGRAPHY: *A Young Man's Fancy* (short, 1951); *A Summer Discord* (short, 1955); *Miss Thomson Goes Shopping* (short, 1958); *The Great Steam Fair* (doc. short, co-dir. Derrick Knight); *An Untitled Film* (short) (1964); *28b Camden Street* (doc. short, 1965); *Port Health* (doc. short); *Dance* (doc. short) (1967); *New Ways at Northgate* (doc. short, 1969); *Demolition* (short); *Aberdeen by Seaside and Deeside* (doc. short, 1970); *Requiem for a Village* (1975); *Memoirs of a Survivor* (1981).

GLAZER, Jonathan (1965–)

Jonathan Glazer was born in March 1965 and raised in north London. He studied theatre design and direction at Nottingham Trent Polytechnic and directed stage plays, film trailers, and television before joing the production company Academy in

1993. His commercials – particularly for Guinness and Stella Artois, and his highly inventive pop videos – particulary of Jamiroquai's *Virtual Insanity* and U.N.K.L.E's *Rabbit in Your Headlights* (1998), marked him out as an outstanding director who would inevitably move on to feature films. Glazer collaborated with Louis Mellis and David Scinto on a screenplay based on their play *Gangster No. 1*, but disagreements with the producer led the trio to abandon the project and work on a script about a British gangster forced out of happy retirement in Spain for a last big job. Ironically, *Sexy Beast* proved to be a much more commercially attractive proposition than *Gangster No. 1*; a witty script, impressive performances (particularly from Ben Kingsley as the psychopath who comes to bring Ray Winstone's genial ex-crook home), and Glazer's acute, stylish, direction made it one of the very few British gangster films to attract American as well as British audiences. Glazer, now a partner at Academy, was able to draw in American financial support for *Birth*, a metaphysical thriller he had written with Jean-Claude Carrière and Milo Addica. The resulting film, set among well-to-do New Yorkers, is as convoluted and intriguing as Hitchcock's *Vertigo* (1958) and Brian De Palma's *Obsession* (1976). Glazer is softer on his characters' self-deceptions, and visual flamboyance sometimes comes at the expense of character development, but he is unique among British directors who made their debut during the crime cycle in following up with a film of enduring international significance.

(Alan Burton and Robert Murphy)

BIBLIOGRAPHY: Clarke, Roger, 'Grief Encounter', *Sight and Sound*, Nov. 2004, pp. 22–4; James, Nick, 'Thieves on the verge of a nervous breakdown', *Sight and Sound*, Jan. 2001, pp. 19–20; Olsen, Mark, 'Discovery. Jonathan Glazer', *Film Comment*, March/April 2001, pp. 16–17.

FILMOGRAPHY: *Sexy Beast* (UK/Spain/US, 2000); *Birth* (US, 2004).

GLEN, John (1932–)

Born in Sunbury-on-Thames on 15 May 1932, John Glen began working in films while still in his teens. Starting as a messenger boy in the Shepperton Studios sound department, he became an editor in the 1960s, working on various television series made by ITC including *The Avengers* and *Danger Man*, and made his directorial debut in 1967 with an episode of *Man in a Suitcase*.

Glen's association with the James Bond series began with *On Her Majesty's Secret Service* (1969), on which he served as both editor and second-unit director. He acted in both capacities throughout the 1970s, making many films for producer Euan Lloyd before rejoining the Bond unit on *The Spy Who Loved Me* (Lewis Gilbert, 1977). For the latter, Glen edited and directed the definitive Bond pre-credit sequence, an elaborate ski chase capped by Rick Sylvester's ski jump off Asgard Peak with a Union Jack parachute. Glen was promoted to full director for the twelfth Bond adventure *For Your Eyes Only* (1981), the film that signalled a more sober approach after the campy and flamboyant films made by Guy Hamilton and Lewis Gilbert in the 1970s. Glen went on to direct all five of the Bond films made in the 1980s and after testing James Brolin, Sam Neill and Pierce Brosnan, oversaw the introduction of Timothy Dalton in the main role after Roger Moore's departure in 1985. Their first film together, *The Living Daylights* (1987), begins splendidly with two parachute jumps and with Dalton's 007 only revealed after two lookalike secret agents have been assassinated. The film also includes a suspenseful defection scene and an extended sequence set on the same Viennese Ferris wheel featured in *The Third Man* (Carol Reed, 1949), one of the first films on which Glen worked.

Licence to Kill (1989), the most violent and 'adult' film of the series, was Glen's last Bond film. Largely derived from Ian Fleming's novel *Live and Let Die* and designed to reinvigorate the formula, the action was brought even further down to earth with Colombian drug lords becoming the new villains. Glen managed to fulfil a long-term ambition by designing the spectacular Kenwood Truck climax, spread across as many as three concurrent planes of action. Glen and Dalton left the franchise when a series of legal disputes kept the series on hold for several years. They were initially due to shoot *Christopher Columbus: The Discovery* together, but Dalton eventually left to be replaced by French actor Georges Corraface. The film, while a pleasantly old-fashioned swashbuckler, pales when compared with Ridley Scott's sumptuous rival production *1492: Conquest of Paradise* (1992) and was a financial disappointment. Glen returned to British television to direct eight episodes of Gerry Anderson's big-budget science-fiction series *Space Precinct* (1994–5). Glen's most recent film, *The Point Men*, an efficient spy thriller starring Christopher Lambert, was edited by his son Matthew and photographed by Alec Mills, both of whom have worked with Glen for decades.

(Sergio Angelini)

BIBLIOGRAPHY: Bilbow, Marjorie, 'Director Glen Attributes "View" Success to Teamwork', *Screen International* no. 509, 10 Aug. 1985, p. 21. Feinleib, Kenneth R., 'Directing Bond', *Cinefantastique* vol. 19 no. 5, July 1989, pp. 24–5, 61; Glen, John, *For My Eyes Only* (London: B.T. Batsford, 2001); Lee, Nora, 'John Glen Has Long Bond History', *American Cinematographer* vol. 68 no. 7, July 1987, pp. 67–8, 70, 72; 'Something Historic in Glen's Scrapbook', *Screen International* no. 606, 27 June 1987, pp. 18, 20.

FILMOGRAPHY: *On Her Majesty's Secret Service* (2nd unit dir., Peter Hunt, 1969); *Catlow* (2nd unit dir., Sam Wanamaker, UK/US/Sp, 1971); *Gold* (2nd unit dir., Peter Hunt, 1974); *Conduct Unbecoming* (2nd unit dir., Michael Anderson, 1975); *Shout at the Devil* (2nd unit dir., Peter Hunt, 1976); *The Spy Who Loved Me* (2nd unit dir., Lewis Gilbert, 1977); *The Wild Geese*, (2nd unit dir., Andrew V. McLaglen, UK/Switz); *Superman* (2nd unit dir., Richard Donner) (1978); *Moonraker* (2nd unit dir., Lewis Gilbert, UK/Fr, 1979); *For Your Eyes Only* (UK/US, 1981); *Octopussy* (UK/US, 1983); *A View to a Kill* (UK/US, 1985); *The Living Daylights* (UK/US, 1987); *Licence to Kill* (UK/US, 1989); *Christopher Columbus: The Discovery* (UK/US); *Aces: Iron Eagle III* (US) (1992); *The Point Men* (UK/Fr/Lux, 2001).

GLENVILLE, Peter (1913–1996)

Peter Glenville was born into a theatrical family in Hampstead, London, on 28 October 1913. Both his parents were actors and he began performing while studying law at Oxford, dropping out to turn professional. He appeared in the West End and in a few British films, including *Good Time Girl* (David Macdonald, 1948), where he plays a vicious small-time spiv, and from 1944 he directed in both London and New York. Glenville was primarily a man of the theatre, and all of his seven films are adaptations of plays – four of which he had also directed for the stage – or novels.

He made his debut with *The Prisoner*, Bridget Boland's drama of the interrogation of a dissident cardinal in an unnamed Communist state. Though necessarily static and verbose, the film is sustained by the strong performances of Alec Guinness and Jack Hawkins, and there are blessedly few attempts at 'cinematic' flourishes. Glenville's next two films were made in America. *Me and the Colonel*, set in wartime France, provides a rare straight role for Danny Kaye and a regrettably comic one for Curt Jürgens, and is unable to survive the archness of the material. *Summer and Smoke* is a Southern melodrama adapted from one of Tennessee Williams' more ludicrous confections, but given the full Paramount production works and gorgeously photographed by Charles Lang Jr.

Term of Trial, which Glenville also wrote and produced from James Barlow's novel, may be the crucial film in assessing his career, and the conclusions are not favourable. Flaunted locations, contrived scene transitions, hackneyed punctuation devices (an attempted seduction is underscored by passing trains *and* a thunderstorm), meretricious social comment, thumpingly obvious irony – it's all here. Laurence Olivier and Sarah Miles, as an idealistic schoolteacher and his infatuated nymphet pupil, escaped with good notices, but the film goes out of its way to neuter possible frissons between them by denying its noble hero any sexual instincts at all.

Becket, adapted by Edward Anhalt from Jean Anouilh's play, is Glenville's best film – witty, handsome and absorbing. While credit may be due as much to its American producer, Hal B. Wallis, Glenville can at least be congratulated for drawing a decently restrained performance from Richard Burton as the sainted archbishop (though restraint does not trouble Peter O'Toole's flamboyantly loud king). Glenville then went to France to make *Hotel Paradiso*, an elegantly appointed but unfunny Feydeau farce in which the director appeared on screen as the playwright as well as adapting the script. A box-office flop in the US, it was shelved in Britain until 1971.

The studio interiors for Glenville's last film, *The Comedians*, were also shot in France, with locations in Africa. It is an expensive, overlong adaptation by Graham Greene of his own novel, set in Haiti under the oppressive Duvalier regime, in which virtually every scene of dramatic action takes place off screen while the camera is preoccupied with the conversations of clichéd, self-absorbed characters. The first of the Burton/Taylor combinations to fail commercially, it seems to have prevented Glenville from directing again for the cinema, though he was reportedly fired from *Man of La Mancha* (Arthur Hiller, 1972) before shooting started. He died in New York on 3 June 1996.

(Sheldon Hall)

BIBLIOGRAPHY: *Becket* Supplement, *The Daily Cinema*, 10 April 1964, pp. 4–20; Glenville, Peter, 'Reflections of *Becket*', *Films and Filming*, Apr. 1964, pp. 7–8; 'Peter Glenville', *Films and Filming*, May 1962, p. 5.

FILMOGRAPHY: *The Prisoner* (1955); *Me and the Colonel* (US, 1958); *Summer and Smoke* (US, 1961); *Term of Trial* (1962); *Becket* (1964); *Hotel Paradiso* (UK/Fr, 1966); *The Comedians* (US/Bermuda/Fr, 1967).

GLYN, Elinor (1864–1943)

Elinor Sutherland was born on 17 October 1864 in Jersey, the Channel Islands. She was a compulsive writer from an early age and turned her hobby into a means of supporting her family and a lavish lifestyle when her husband, Clayton Glyn, ran up massive debts. From 1890 to her death, she turned out one romantic novel after another and while their florid style now makes them difficult to read, during her lifetime they sold in their millions. Glyn revelled in celebrity and worked hard at creating a glamorous persona, which her readers were encouraged to buy into, but her books also gave voice to the changing attitudes of women at that time. No simpering Victorian misses with smelling salts for her; Glyn shaped her own destiny, and so did her heroines.

In the 1920s Glyn enjoyed a successful stint in Hollywood, where she was feted, paid vast sums of money for her stories and coined the term 'it' as a euphemism for sexual allure. When she returned to the UK in 1929 she expected to continue her film career, but her announcement that she would direct (and finance) *Knowing Men* was greeted with hostility in the male-

dominated industry. Despite a good cast (Elissa Landi and Carl Brisson) and a top Hollywood cameraman (Charles Rosher), the film was savaged by the critics and sank without trace. Undaunted, she attempted to recoup her losses with *The Price of Things* (1930), a variation on *The Prisoner of Zenda*, but this was also cold-shouldered by the industry. The broke but ever-resilient Glyn waved goodbye to her film career and set about repairing her fortunes by returning to writing. She died on 23 September 1943 in London.

(Linda Wood)

BIBLIOGRAPHY: Glyn, Anthony, *Elinor Glyn, a Biography* (London: Hutchinson, 1955); Etherington-Smith, Meredith and Jeremy Pilcher, *The 'It' Girls: Lucy, Lady Duff Gordon, the Couturiere 'Lucile' and Elinor Glyn, Romantic Novelist* (Hollywood, CA: Hamish Hamilton, 1988); Hardwick, Joan, *Addicted to Romance: The Life and Adventures of Elinor Glyn* (London: Trafalgar Square, 1995); McCreadie, Marsha, 'Pioneers', *Films in Review*, Jan./Feb. 1995, pp. 22–32.

FILMOGRAPHY: *Knowing Men* (1929; rel. 1930); *The Price of Things* (1930).

GODARD, Jean-Luc (1930–)

Jean-Luc Godard was born in Paris on 3 December 1930, the son of affluent Swiss parents. With the outbreak of war he was sent to Switzerland, returning to Paris in the late 1940s to prepare for the Sorbonne. It was the *cinéphile* culture of the Left Bank that really engaged him and in 1952 Godard started writing for *Cahiers du cinéma* along with other future film-makers François Truffaut, Jacques Rivette and Eric Rohmer. Godard developed an extraordinary critical voice, edging quotation-riddled articles with semiotics and proselytising with dramatic fervour. After making several shorts, he embarked on his feature debut, *À bout de souffle* (1959), which established his reputation as a bold and inventive director. Godard worked prolifically throughout the 1960s producing stylised, formally experimental works, imbued with cinematic passion, including *Vivre sa vie* (1962), *Le Mépris* (1963) and *Masculin/Féminin* (1966). Always aesthetically challenging, after 1968 Godard's films became increasingly politically radical.

It was a militant Godard who came to London in 1968 to make *One Plus One*. Combining documentary images of the Rolling Stones rehearsing and staged sequences exploring aesthetics and politics, notably Black Power, Godard aimed to overturn cinema's 'bourgeois' foundations. It now seems a naive and overbearingly didactic document of the era. *British Sounds* (1969), co-directed by Godard with Jean-Henri Roger for the Maoist-Marxist Dziga-Vertov Group, proved too avant-garde for London Weekend Television, which had commissioned it but refused to show it. Its emphatic soundtrack, long sequence shots (including a ten-minute track through Ford's car assembly line at Dagenham) and images of fists punching through the British flag made for disquieting, propagandistic cinema. As with most of the director's work for the Dziga-Vertov Group, circulation was limited.

After the Dziga-Vertov Group disbanded, Godard experimented with a more narrative-based cinema in *Tout va bien* (1972), with Yves Montand and Jane Fonda. But fascinated by the possibilities of video, he and his partner, film-maker Anne-Marie Miéville, set up the SonImage company to pioneer video production throughout the 1970s. At the end of the decade he made *Sauve qui peut (la vie)* (1979), which was followed by a string of critically acclaimed films including *Passion* (1982), *Prénom: Carmen* (1983), *Détective* (1985) and *Je vous salue, Marie* (1985).

In 1987 he made a third contribution to British cinema as one of the ten directors – including Robert Altman, Ken Russell, Nicolas Roeg and Derek Jarman – invited by producer Don Boyd to direct a section of *Aria*. Eschewing the more obvious operas of Verdi, Puccini and Wagner some of his colleagues plumped for, Godard chose Jean-Baptiste Lully's eerily beautiful *Armide* and, with typical irreverent originality, used it as a backcloth against which two world-weary women clean and bodybuilders exercise in a dilapidated Parisian gym.

(Eleanor Burke)

BIBLIOGRAPHY: MacCabe, Colin, *Godard: Images, Sounds, Politics* (London: Macmillan, 1980); Temple, Michael and James S. Williams, *The Cinema Alone* (Amsterdam: Amsterdam University Press, 2000).

FILMOGRAPHY (UK only): *One Plus One* (aka *Sympathy for the Devil*, 1968); *British Sounds* (aka *See You at Mao*, co-dir. Jean-Henri Roger, 1969); *Aria* ('Armide' section, 1987).

GODBER, John (1956–)

John Godber was born on 15 May 1956 in Upton, Yorkshire, into a working-class mining family. In 1978 he qualified as a drama teacher at Bretton Hall College and gained an MA in theatre at Leeds University. As Head of Drama at Minsthorpe High School, Godber wrote and directed a series of plays, winning awards at the National Student Drama Festival. In 1981 he started writing for television, contributing episodes to *Crown Court*, *Grange Hill* and *Brookside*. He has subsequently written drama series such as *The Ritz* (1987), *The Continental* (1987) – which grew out of his play *Bouncers* – and *My Kingdom for a Horse* (1991).

In 1984 Godber became Artistic Director of the Hull Truck Theatre Company and he has remained there, writing and producing several successful plays, including *Up 'n Under*, which won the Laurence Olivier Comedy of the Year Award in 1984. Godber was cast in the role of Dave for *The Full Monty* (Peter Cattaneo, 1997) but withdrew to devote full attention to his debut as a film director, a screen version of *Up 'n Under*, starring Gary Olsen, Neil Morrisey, Samantha Janus and, in his last screen role, Brian Glover. Little had changed in the world of amateur rugby since Godber wrote the play and the film was a modest success, but it stubbornly remains a regional comedy, never likely to replicate the box-office phenomenon of *The Full Monty*.

(Martin Hunt)

BIBLIOGRAPHY: Austin, Jeremy, 'Outside Looking In', *Stage*, 28 June 2000, p. 11; The Official John Godber Website, <www.johngodber.co.uk>.

FILMOGRAPHY: *Up 'n Under* (1998).

GODDARD, Jim (1936–)

James Goddard was born in Battersea, south London, on 2 February 1936, the son of a dockyard worker. He trained as an apprentice printer before going on to study as a painter at the Slade School of Art. While still a student he got the chance to work at the Royal Opera House, designing sets for Luchino Visconti and Franco Zeffirelli. He joined the independent television company ABC in 1958 and worked as an art director on series such as *The Avengers* and *Out of this World*. He started to direct in 1964, emerging in the 1970s as one of the most reliable members of the stable of directors employed by Thames Television. Quickly labelled as an action specialist, Goddard worked on most of ITV's flagship dramas, including *Public Eye*, *Callan*, *The Sweeney* and *Van Der Valk*. Most eye-catching though were the two crime drama series written by Trevor Preston – *Out* (1978) and *Fox* (1980) – which broke new ground in their realistic depiction of the criminal underworld and their perception of police corruption.

In the 1980s Goddard showed considerable versatility, working on a diverse range of high-profile projects. After directing Alan Bleasdale's *The Black Stuff* (1980), he directed most of the episodes of *Reilly: Ace of Spies* (1983), Troy Kennedy Martin's impressive dramatisation of real-life espionage events between the wars. He directed the marvellous nine-hour television version of David Edgar's theatrical triumph, *The Life and Adventures of Nicholas Nickleby* (1982); and he made the 1983 political biopic *Kennedy* (almost entirely shot in the UK, although set in the US).

Goddard made his cinema debut in 1984 with *Parker*, a dark thriller from a script by Trevor Preston. Goddard was able to demonstrate his interest in colour and design by shooting the story of an unexplained kidnapping in an elliptical and visually imaginative style. Goddard himself called the film 'a study of the bourgeois mind under pressure', and it is on this level that it works best. The last-minute explanations and the villain's come-uppance provide only the merest hint of commercially required closure to an otherwise powerfully nightmarish tale, set in a universe in which irrationality and violence always seem to have the upper hand. *Hitler's SS: Portrait in Evil* (1985) received a limited theatrical release in the UK, but was actually a miniseries shot by Goddard for NBC television.

Shanghai Surprise, set in 1930s' China (but shot in Hong Kong), was an unlikely vehicle for the (then) husband and wife team of Sean Penn and Madonna. While handsomely mounted and attractively shot by Ernest Vincze, this comedy-adventure was a critical and commercial disaster, crumbling under the weight of banal dialogue ('Guns cause pain, opium eases pain'), an unconvincing plot and its two seriously miscast leads. Since then Goddard has returned to television, handling episodes of *Inspector Morse* ('The Secret of 5B', 1983) as well as such one-off dramas as *The Free Frenchman* (1989) and *The House of Angelo* (1997), a swash-buckler that reunited him with *Callan* star Edward Woodward. This independently made feature, which also starred Woodward's three children, Peter, Sarah and Tim, was originally intended for a cinema release but premiered on television instead. More recently Goddard has handled episodes of such popular television series as *The Bill* and *Holby City*, giving ample evidence of his sure hand with actors and vigorous handling of action.

(Sergio Angelini)

BIBLIOGRAPHY: Auty, Martin, 'The Man Who Shot Kennedy', *Stills* no. 9, Nov./Dec. 1983, pp. 37–40; Petley, Julian, 'Travel and Rest: Jim Goddard, from Theatre to TV to Cinema', *Monthly Film Bulletin*, May 1985, pp. 143–4.

FILMOGRAPHY: *Parker* (US: *Bones*, 1984); *Shanghai Surprise* (1986); *The House of Angelo* (1997).

GODFREY, Bob (1921–)

Bob Godfrey was born in West Maitland, Australia, on 27 January 1921, but was educated in Ilford, and later at Leyton Art School. He started his career as a graphic artist for Lever Brothers in the 1930s, advertising soap and sausages for Lintas; then he gained work for the Rank-financed G-B animation unit, based at Cookham, and worked in London on ancillary products related to the Disney-styled *Animaland* series, featuring 'Ginger Nutt'. In 1950 he joined the W. M. Larkins studio, which sought to draw upon modern art sources and comic-strip idioms in the creation of sophisticated promotional and technical films. Godfrey initially resented the 'animation' in front of his backgrounds, but he became a member of the semi-professional Grasshopper group and in 1952 made his first animated cartoon, *The Big Parade*. In the mid-1950s, Godfrey joined up with Jeff Hale and Keith Learner, and later Nancy Hanna and Vera Linnecar, to form Biographic Films, making some of the first commercials for ITV.

Polygamous Polonius (1958) and *Do It Yourself Cartoon Kit* (1959), two of Godfrey's earliest personal films, display the range of influences and preoccupations that characterise his work – music-hall routines, avant-garde comedy in the spirit of the Goons, political satire and concerns with British attitudes to sex and social conduct. *Do It Yourself Cartoon Kit* sends up the myth of the lone animator who spends hundreds of hours on a brief sequence, only to see it cut from the final film – an indication of Godfrey's anti-Disney stance and his distance from the aspirational modernism of the Halas and Batchelor studio. Crude but energetic, the film sets the tone for the ways in which Godfrey was seeking to reinvent the cartoon outside the American tradition, and at the same time poke fun at orthodoxy and establishment thinking.

He left Biographic in 1964 to form Bob Godfrey Films and more fully engage with his own vision – best epitomised in his mock-erotic exploitation films (co-written with Stan Hayward), *Henry 9 'til 5* (1970), *Kama Sutra Rides Again* (1971), *Dream Doll* (1979), *Instant Sex* (Graeme Jackson, 1980) and *Bio-Woman* (1981). These films work as a surreal satire on the social identity of the 'small' man and the inhibitions of British masculinity. The juxtaposition of the passionless and restrained British male in the face of seemingly outlandish and extreme sexual practices comically exposes the essential repression and hypocrisy at the heart of British culture.

In his Academy Award-winning biography of Isambard Kingdom Brunel, *GREAT* (1975), Godfrey concentrates less on feats of engineering and more on satirising Victorian attitudes, invoking a degree of pathos for Brunel's failures as well as his achievements, and hinting at the slow demise of Britain as a world power. In 1994 Godfrey received his fourth Academy Award nomination for *Small Talk*; the following year he was asked by John Halas to make the British contribution to the *Know Your Europeans* series. A *tour-de-force* engagement with all things British from Disraeli to Arthur Daley, the film enjoys the diversity of British culture but ultimately finds enigma at its heart. Similarly, *Millennium – the Musical* (2000) amusingly condenses the whole of British history into a manageable half-hour. Somewhat bizarrely, given his sustained criticism of British government, Godfrey was awarded an MBE in 1986. Much of Godfrey's work has been predicated on satirising the foibles and minutiae of what it means to be 'British', but he has also been responsible for a number of cartoon characters – in *Roobarb and Custard* (1975), *Skylark* (1978), *Henry's Cat* (1983) and most recently *Kevin Saves the World* (2002) – popular on children's television in the US as well as in Britain.

(Paul Wells)

BIBLIOGRAPHY: Baker, Bob, 'Bob Godfrey', *Film Dope* no. 20, Apr. 1980, pp. 7–9; Bendazzi, Giannalberto, *Cartoons: One Hundred Years of Cinema Animation* (London: John Libbey, 1994); Halas, John, *Master of Animation* (London: BBC Books, 1987); Wells, Paul, *Understanding Animation* (London and New York: Routledge, 1998).

FILMOGRAPHY: *The Big Parade* (co-dir. Keith Learner); *Formation* (co-dir. Keith Learner) (1952); *Watch the Birdie* (co-dirs. Vera Linnecar/Keith Learner, Dick Taylor, 1954); *Polygamous Polonius* (1958; rel. 1960); *Do It Yourself Cartoon Kit* (co-dirs. Keith Learner/Vera Linnecar/Nancy Hanna, 1959; rel. 1961); *The Battle of New Orleans* (1960); *That Noise*; *What Kind of Fool Am I?* (1961); *Plain Man's Guide to Advertising* (1962); *Morse Code Melody*; *A Productivity Primer* (1963); *The Rise and Fall of Emily Sprod*; *Alf, Bill & Fred* (1964); *One Man Band*; *L'Art pour l'art* (1965); *Rope-trick*; *Bang!*; *What Ever Happened to Uncle Fred?* (1967); *Two Off the Cuff* (1968); *Henry 9 'til 5*; *Ways and Means*; *The Electron's Tale* (co-dir. Peter Green) (1970); *Kama Sutra Rides Again* (1971); *GREAT* (1975); *The Hand*; *The Trap*; *The Line*; *The Shadow*; *The Key* (1976); *Dear Margery Boobs* (1977); *Dream Doll/Lutka snova* (co-dir. Zlatko Grgic, UK/Yug., 1979); *Bio-Woman* (1981); *Polygamous Polonius Revisited* (1984); *Small Talk* (1994); *Know Your Europeans* (1995); *Millennium – The Musical* (2000).

GOGAN, Johnny (1963–)

The career of Johnny Gogan represents something of a bridge between the politically charged work of Ireland's first wave independent directors of the 1970s and 80s and the more commercial film-makers who emerged in the economic boom of the 1990s. Born in Sussex, England, on 18 June 1963 the family moved back to Ireland when he was very young. He studied politics at University College, Dublin, and began his career writing occasional journalism in the mid-1980s.

Gogan and his sister Jane (now commissioning editor of independent production for Ireland's commercial channel TV3) were founding members of FilmBase, a resource and lobbying body for independent film production in Ireland. Gogan was the editor for three years of *FilmBase News* (now *Film Ireland*, the country's leading film journal) before making his debut in 1990 as a writer/director with the short film *Stephen*.

Using the euphoria surrounding the Tour de France victory in 1987 of Dublin cyclist Stephen Roach as a point of contrast, the film depicts the more sombre prospects of another Stephen, an unemployed Dubliner. Gogan's next film, *The Bargain Shop* (1992) – made for Irish and German television – similarly contrasts the commercial glamour and glitzy promise of inner-city redevelopment with the realities of traditional Dublin life, a timely and prescient consideration of consumer culture on the cusp of the Celtic Tiger phenomenon. Gogan's first feature film, *The Last Bus Home*, uses the false radicalism of a punk band, and the ambiguous status of its gay drummer, to pose more politically pointed questions at the economic success of post-1980s' Ireland. He followed it with *The Mapmaker*, a low-key film exploring the nature of Irish provincial life and the unresolved sectarian tensions along its borders with Northern Ireland.

A determinedly independent writer/director, Gogan has sought out Irish and European funding to allow him to make the low-budget but politically engaged cinema that he prefers.

(Martin McLoone)

BIBLIOGRAPHY: Gogan, Johnny *et al.* 'Irish Cinema at the Crossroads: A Filmmakers' Symposium', *Cinéaste* vol. 24 nos 2–3, 1999, p. 71; McLoone, Martin, *Irish Film: The Emergence of a Contemporary Cinema* (London: BFI, 2000); Pettitt, Lance, 'A Construction Site Queered: Gay Images in New Irish Cinema', *Cinéaste* vol. 24 nos 2–3, 1999, pp. 61–3; Pettitt, Lance, *Screening Ireland* (Manchester: Manchester University Press, 2000).

FILMOGRAPHY: *Stephen* (short, Ir, 1990); *The Last Bus Home* (Ir/Ger, 1997); *The Mapmaker* (Ir/UK/Ger, 2002).

GOLD, Jack (1930–)

Jack Gold was born in London on 28 June 1930. After completing degrees in law and economics at London Polytechnic and University College, London, he joined the BBC, and worked as an editor on the *Tonight* news programme with the reporters Alan Whicker and Fyfe Robertson. His humanistic concerns surfaced in his anti-fox-hunting film for the BBC, *Death in the Morning* (1964), while his left-wing perspective was clearly evident in his direction of Jim Allen's television play *The Lump* (1967), which harshly criticised the building industry.

In 1959 Gold made a thirty-five-minute domestic drama, *The Visit*, clearly influenced by Italian neo-realism, for the BFI's Experimental Film Fund. But his cinema career only began in earnest with *The Bofors Gun* (1968), adapted by John McGrath from his own play: an observant, well-acted account of the

conflict that flares between a young officer (David Warner) and an embittered, unstable private (Nicol Williamson) in a peacetime army unit. McGrath and Williamson collaborated again on Gold's second feature, *The Reckoning* (1969), a more strenuous concoction featuring another of the actor's violent anti-heroes – a businessman brutal in love and work, who returns to his Liverpool roots to avenge his father's murder. Gold's films of the 1970s were generally well received, particularly *The National Health*, set in a men's terminal ward, faithfully duplicating the comedy and criticism in Peter Nichols' play. Also of interest were *Man Friday*, with Peter O'Toole and Richard Roundtree acting out a Robinson Crusoe variation that subverts Defoe's colonialist theme; and *Aces High*, an aerial version of R. C. Sheriff's classic anti-war play *Journey's End*.

At this stage, Gold was commonly considered a competent but cautious cineaste, perhaps a little too reverential towards his scripts. Greater flair, and a sturdier budget, would certainly have helped *Who?* (1974), an intriguing blend of spy thriller and science fiction that took four years to reach Britain. But all expectations were defied with his most stylistically exuberant film, *The Medusa Touch* (1978), a horror thriller with an unnerving vision of social apocalypse, featuring one of Richard Burton's most riveting performances as an intellectual anarchist with the telekinetic power to cause disasters. *The Sailor's Return*, for Euston Films, proved much less ambitious, but there is fascination in its novel treatment of racial issues in nineteenth-century Dorset.

During the 1970s, Gold alternated freely between film and television, but since then, apart from a genial comedy about moving house, *The Chain*, television has taken over. On the small screen he has proved a self-effacing but sensitive director, much admired by actors for his attention to a character's inner motives and the emotional truth of a situation. The results have sometimes been quite exceptional, in particular *The Naked Civil Servant* (1975), a poignant and funny portrait of Quentin Crisp, superbly acted by John Hurt, and *Goodnight Mister Tom* (1998), a sensitive adaptation of Michele Magorian's wartime novel about a grumpy old countryman (Gold regular John Thaw) who forms a mutually beneficent bond with a maltreated urban evacuee.

(Neil Sinyard)

BIBLIOGRAPHY: BECTU History Project, tape no. 128, held in the BFI National Library, London; Madden, Paul and David Wilson, 'Getting in Close: An Interview with Jack Gold', *Sight and Sound*, Summer 1974, pp. 134–7; Whitaker, Sheila, 'Jack Gold', *Framework*, Winter 1978/9, pp. 38–42.

FILMOGRAPHY: *The Visit* (short, 1959); *Living Jazz* (1960); *The Bofors Gun* (1968); *The Reckoning* (1969); *The National Health* (1973); *Who?* (1974); *Man Friday* (1975); *Aces High* (1976); *The Medusa Touch* (UK/Fr); *The Sailor's Return* (1978); *The Chain* (1984).

GOLDBACHER, Sandra (1960–)

Sandra Goldbacher was born in London in 1960 to a Jewish father and a Catholic mother who converted one year after Goldbacher's birth; the tussle between conflicting traditions became a major theme in her first completed feature, *The Governess* (1998). After reading French at Sussex University she changed direction and in 1983 embarked on a one-year practical course at Middlesex Polytechnic, studying film and video. Two student films, *Polka Dots and Moonbeams* and *Night of a Thousand Eyes*, explored the images sold by Hollywood and television. Clearer signposts to Goldbacher's future emerged in the human dramas of *Seventeen* (1994) and *Piccadilly Circus by Night* (1995), short personal films made alongside a profusion of television documentaries and commercials.

At the same time, Goldbacher began writing what became *Me without You*, but *The Governess* reached the screen first. Minnie Driver played Goldbacher's surrogate – a Jewish girl passing herself off as Gentile to work as governess on the Isle of Skye. Goldbacher's visual eye was immediately apparent, though underneath the sumptuous surface lay a muddled, overcrowded script. Where *The Governess* never escaped from its art-house cocoon, with *Me Without You* Goldbacher successfully aimed at a broader audience. This light-fingered but psychologically acute comedy presented a portrait of two childhood friends, one volcanic (Anna Friel), the other a plodder (Michelle Williams), growing into adulthood through punk rock, boyfriends, drugs and college in the 1970s and 80s. The friends' bonds grow strained and snarled, but the players' skills and Goldbacher's sympathetic treatment make most of the twists believable.

(Geoff Brown)

BIBLIOGRAPHY: Gibson, Janine, 'Direction: Sandra Goldbacher', *Televisual*, Apr. 1996, pp. 47–8; James, Nick, 'Medium Cool – Interviews with Up and Coming Film-Makers, *Sight and Sound*, Aug. 1998, pp. 12–15.

FILMOGRAPHY: *Polka Dots and Moonbeams* (short, 1983); *Night of a Thousand Eyes* (short, 1984); *Seventeen* (short, 1994); *Piccadilly Circus by Night* (short, 1995); *The Governess* (1998); *Me Without You* (2001).

GOLDEN, Karl (1974–)

Born in Dublin in 1974, Karl Golden made a number of short films before directing *The Honeymooners*, a romantic comedy shot on digital video. Golden turns the film's tiny budget and tight shooting schedule to his advantage. Unfamiliar actors (Jonathan Byrne as a rich, surly jilted bridegroom and Alex Reid as a jaded, slightly shop-soiled waitress) give committed, heartfelt performances; while the hand-held camerawork encourages a delicate intimacy that lays bare complex emotions. There are occasional *longueurs* and the plot sometimes threatens to lurch off course, but this is a small price to pay for a romantic comedy that avoids zany silliness and complacent sentimentality.

(Robert Murphy)

BIBLIOGRAPHY: Farren, Paul, 'Something Borrowed, Something New', *Film Ireland* no. 97, Mar./Apr. 2004, pp. 12–14.

FILMOGRAPHY: *Love and Death on Rapid Transit* (short, Ir, 1997); *Dogsbody* (short, Ir, 1999); *Still Rain* (short, Ir, 2000); *Beached* (short, Ir, 2001); *The Honeymooners* (Ir/UK, 2003).

GOODHEW, Philip (1960–)

Philip Goodhew was born in Aldershot, Hampshire, on 28 October 1960. After graduating in drama from Manchester University, he made his professional acting debut at Manchester's Royal Exchange Theatre. London stage appearances followed as did television roles: for two years in the mid-1980s, Goodhew was *Crossroads* villain Daniel Freeman. After a stint working for industrial film producers Milestone Pictures, Goodhew enrolled at the New York Film Academy in 1994, where he directed several shorts; in 1995 he formed Boxer Films with Angela and Lisa Hope to write, produce and direct his own work.

Goodhew's first feature, *Intimate Relations*, was adopted by HandMade Films – newly acquired by Canada's Paragon Entertainment – as its relaunch production after a six-year gap, and taken up for distribution by Fox Searchlight. A cruel, analytic and verbally explicit black comedy of sexual hypocrisy, blackmail and murder in 1950s' suburbia, it was based on a little-known real-life case in which a mother and her teenage daughter were killed by their lodger, a young sailor who had become sexually embroiled with both of them. Julie Walters excelled in a rare unsympathetic starring role; Rupert Graves was voted Best Actor at the 1996 Montreal Film Festival for his performance as the lodger; and fourteen-year-old Laura Sadler (who was to die in 2003 after falling from the window of her boyfriend's flat) was impressive as the sexually unsettled daughter.

Goodhew's follow-up feature, *Another Life*, was based on the better-known adultery/murder case of Edith Thompson, who was hanged in 1923 for conspiring with her lover to murder her husband, although supporters protested her innocence. It starred voguish names – Natasha Little, Ioan Gruffudd and Nick Moran – but was less precise in its intent, execution or performances than its predecessor and was less generously received.

(Claire Monk)

BIBLIOGRAPHY: Bradshaw, Nick, 'A Family Affair', *Time Out*, 18–25 June 1997, p. 77; '*Intimate Relations*', 40th London Film Festival catalogue, 1996, p. 48; Monk, Claire, '*Intimate Relations*', *Sight and Sound*, July 1997, pp. 42–3; Turner, Jenny, '*Another Life*', *Sight and Sound*, May 2001, pp. 40, 42.

FILMOGRAPHY: *Requiem* (short); *Frogs* (short); *Strange Dreams* (short) (1994); *Intimate Relations* (1996); *Another Life* (2000).

GORNICK, Lisa

Gornick expanded her short film *Do I Love You?* into a feature film exploring lesbian relationships in the Hackney area of north London. A low-budget film shot on digital video, it was well received on the festival circuit and released on DVD.

(Robert Murphy)

FILMOGRAPHY: *Do I Love You?* (2003).

GORRIS, Marleen (1948–)

Maria Madeleine (Marleen) Gorris was born on 9 December 1948 in Roermond, Limburg, in the Netherlands and studied drama at the University of Amsterdam and the University of Birmingham in the UK. Her film-directing career developed in the Netherlands, where she has produced her most distinctive work. Since 1990 she has also directed English-language features in the US and UK and drama for Dutch television.

Gorris' early features were uncompromising but accessible products of 1980s' radical feminism. Few films have divided audiences as sharply by gender as her debut, *A Question of Silence* (*Der Stilte Rond Christine M*, 1982), an investigative thriller in which a female psychiatrist must establish whether three women who have murdered a male boutique manager on impulse are mad or sane. Its 1984 successor, *Broken Mirrors* (*Gebroken Spiegels*), juxtaposing life in a brothel with the activities of a businessman who incarcerates and slowly kills women, proved less controversial.

After a further Dutch feature, *Lost Island* (1990), Gorris achieved unexpected international success as writer-director of *Antonia's Line* (*Antonia*), which won the Best Foreign Language Film Academy Award in 1995. A utopian celebration of the titular Dutch matriarch and her female descendants through five generations, it combined robust feminism with a winning warmth and humour. This led to Gorris being invited to direct *Mrs Dalloway*, an adaptation of Virginia Woolf's modernist 1925 multi-strand novel, set on a single day in a London haunted by echoes of the First World War. Veteran British actress Eileen Atkins – renowned for her own self-scripted stage performances as Woolf – had already written the script for Vanessa Redgrave before Gorris was approached, and the film can be viewed as theirs as much as the director's. In contrast with Sally Potter's 1993 film of Woolf's *Orlando*, Gorris left few authorial traces, filming a radically experimental – and supposedly 'unfilmable' – novel in an attractive but conventional art-cinema style. Yet her film captured the tough, atheistic vision of the novel, and its strong performances and lucid treatment of the narrative's shifts across time and space were warmly received in both the US and UK.

Gorris subsequently directed *The Luzhin Defence* (2000), an impressively intelligent adaptation of Vladimir Nabokov's 1930 modernist novel, starring John Turturro as a chess master and Emily Watson as an independent woman who releases his tightly repressed emotions. Its modest success led her to Hollywood, where she made *Carolina* (2003), a romantic comedy starring Julia Stiles.

(Claire Monk)

BIBLIOGRAPHY: Allen, Carol, 'Losing My Fear of Virginia Woolf', *Independent* Eye Section, 6 Mar. 1998, pp. 2–3; Gritten, David, 'I'm Allowed to Be Thrilled', *Daily Telegraph*, 6 Mar. 1988, p. 21; Monk, Claire, '*Mrs Dalloway*', *Sight and Sound*, Mar. 1998, pp. 53–4.

FILMOGRAPHY (UK only): *Mrs Dalloway* (UK/US/Neth, 1997); *The Luzhin Defence* (UK/Fr/It/Hung/US, 2000).

GOULDING, Alfred (1896–1972)

Recalling the director who took charge of many of his early shorts, Harold Lloyd wrote in his 1928 volume of autobiography, *An American Comedy*, 'Goulding proved to be innocent of any camera knowledge; but, an old vaudevillian, he could pull gags out of the air, and thin air at that.' Born in Katoomba, Australia, on 26 January 1896, Goulding had arrived in the United States as a member of Pollard's Lilliputian Opera Company, a vaudeville act. By 1916 he was directing comedy shorts for Fox; the following year he began a four-year association with Lloyd. He continued directing shorts up to the mid-1930s, working chiefly for Mack Sennett, Vitaphone and RKO; the farce *Excuse Me*, for Metro-Goldwyn, marked his feature debut in 1925.

Armed with a contract with the expatriate American producer Joe Rock, Goulding began his work in England in 1936. His cinema sense remained rudimentary; luckily the personality vehicles assigned to him, all comedies or musicals, required little finesse. *Everything Is Rhythm* (1936) breezed along on the strengths of ten musical numbers and the band-leader Harry Roy. *The Gang Show* (1937), derived from Ralph Reader's Boy Scout stage shows, slapped another popular property onto the screen.

With the British film industry shrivelling, Goulding returned to America and directed Laurel and Hardy in *A Chump at Oxford* (1939); later (uncredited) he was hired to patch up *Atoll K* (Leo Joannon, 1952), the team's last film, shot in the south of France. The war years were spent in Australia. Returning to Britain Goulding found slim pickings, all at the market's bottom end. The most saleable commodity was Hammer's *Dick Barton – Special Agent* (1948), a cheap and cheerful spin-off from the popular BBC radio series, and a schoolboy's delight. His last film, *The Devil's Jest* (1954), was a stale wartime drama. Goulding died in Hollywood of pneumonia on 25 April 1972.

(Geoff Brown)

BIBLIOGRAPHY: Lloyd, Harold and Wesley W. Stout, *An American Comedy* (New York: Dover Publications, 1928/1971).

FILMOGRAPHY (UK only): *One Good Turn*; *Everything Is Rhythm* (US: *A Royal Romance*); *Olympic Honeymoon/Honeymoon Merry-Go-Round* (1936); *Splinters in the Air*; *The Gang Show*; *Sam Small Leaves Town* (1937); *There Is No Escape* (1947); *Dick Barton – Special Agent*; *The Dark Road* (1948); *An International Affair* (short, 1950); *At the Pirate's Head* (short, 1951); *The Devil's Jest* (1954).

GOVER, Victor (1908–1970)

Victor M. Gover was born on 22 February 1908. He was trained as an accountant but entered the industry through the cutting rooms in 1928. Alongside his work as an editor, in 1935 he established the Crown Theatre, a small Wardour Street cinema used mainly for press screenings and previews. During the Second World War he directed documentaries and worked as chief editor at the Colonial Film Unit headed by George Pearson. When the unit was disbanded Gover set up his own company to provide services to developing Commonwealth countries. He was also associated with Ambassador Films, an independent production company based at the tiny Bushey Studios on London's northern outskirts. It was here that Gover first attempted fiction, directing Tod Slaughter, the last great villain of stage melodrama, in *The Curse of the Wraydons* (1946), an adaptation of the Victorian favourite *Spring-Heeled Jack; or, The Terror of London*. The taste for old-fashioned blood and thunder had probably evaporated with the war, but Gover's ponderous handling of the story (the film ran to ninety-four minutes, considerably longer than Slaughter's earlier vehicles) guaranteed a critical drubbing and audience indifference.

Gover returned to documentaries, instructionals and travelogues, enjoying some success with *How to Play Cricket* and *It's a Great Game* (showcases for Billy Edrich and Denis Compton). In the early 1950s he teamed up again with Slaughter, casting him as master criminal Terence Reilly, locked in eternal combat with Patrick Barr's Inspector Morley of Scotland Yard in a series of half-hour films aimed at film and television markets in Britain and the USA. They proved less successful than was hoped and episodes were combined to make the feature-length *King of the Underworld* and *Murder at Scotland Yard*. In *A Ghost for Sale* the ingenious Gover cast Slaughter as a lugubrious butler who proceeds to narrate large chunks of *The Curse of the Wraydons* as a warning to Patrick Barr and Tucker McGuire's house-hunting couple.

Gover never abandoned his interest in the British colonies, now struggling towards independence. He worked with the Nigerian Film Unit to cover a royal visit in *Nigeria Greets Her Queen* (Lionel Snazelle, 1956), and the Malayan Film Unit on an enterprising attempt to reveal some aspects of the country's identity through its postage stamps (*Our Story in Stamps*, 1958). A well-liked figure at home and in the new nations that had emerged from the Empire, Victor Gover died in St Thomas' Hospital, London, on 21 June 1970.

(Robert Murphy)

BIBLIOGRAPHY: Obituary, *Film and TV Technician*, June 1971, p. 13.

FILMOGRAPHY: *Jungle Fury* (doc.); *Rainbow round the Corner* (doc.) (1944); *Land of the Springbok* (doc. short, 1945); *Dancing Thru* (doc. short); *Land of the Kangaroo* (doc. short); *The Curse of the Wraydons* (1946); *How to Play Cricket* (doc. short, 1947); *It's a Great*

Game (doc. short, 1948); *Billy Mayerl Entertains No. 1* (short); *Billy Mayerl Entertains No. 2* (short) (1951); *Dark Passage* (short, 1952); *False Alibi* (short); *Murder in the Strand* (short); *Red Flame* (short); *Reilly at Bay* (short); *Rough Justice* (short); *The Showdown* (short); *Silent Witness* (short); *Murder at the Grange* (short); *A Ghost for Sale* (short); *King of the Underworld*; *Murder at Scotland Yard* (1952); *Bunty Wins a Pup* (short, 1953); *All Living Things* (short, 1955); *Our Story in Stamps* (doc. short, 1958); *Butterfly People* (doc. short, 1965).

GRABER, Sheila (1940–)

Sheila Graber, who was born in South Shields, Tyne and Wear, in 1940, has been an extremely influential figure in the promotion and execution of art and animation in community and educational contexts. She studied fine art at Sunderland Art College and trained to be a teacher. On becoming Head of Creative Studies at King George Comprehensive School, South Shields, she introduced animation into the curriculum and helped win its acceptance as an examination subject by the Schools Council. A prolific amateur film-maker, her experiments in Super-8 enabled her to perfect a simple and direct approach to animated movement, a 'primitive' technique used in films like *Michelangelo*, *Four Views of Landscape* and *Mondrian*. *William Blake* (1978) accompanied a Tate Gallery exhibition and was followed by *Henry Moore*. All these films were made with the purpose of making art accessible to people who might not otherwise encounter it.

In 1980 French producer Nicole Jouve commissioned Graber to make a series based on Rudyard Kipling's 'Just So Stories', including *The Cat That Walked by Himself*, *How the Leopard Got His Spots* and *How the Camel Got His Hump*. This enabled her to become a full-time film-maker and make more personal films such as *Face to Face* (1980), a simple but effective example of the use of metamorphosis, showing a human face moving through life from babyhood to old age and death. Further art-based educational films included *Expressionism*, *The Face in Art* and *Leonardo da Vinci*. *Heidi's Horse* (1987), like *Face to Face*, uses metamorphosis to reveal a child's development in drawing horses: as the young girl matures the spontaneity and immediacy of youthful expression is replaced by an imitative style, moving increasingly towards impersonal realism. In 1991, having embraced computer animation – for Graber, a much longed-for reconciliation between art and science – she was invited to contribute to a touring exhibition of Turner's paintings by the Tate Gallery, and to conduct multimedia projects with local artists. Her recent work has used digital art and animation to explore the processes and methodologies of communication between patients and health-care professionals. *Westall's War*, made in collaboration with Tyne and Wear Archives Service, uses animation as part of an interactive guide to the North-East's experiences during the Second World War.

Graber's continuing passion for animation is evident in her development of 'Club Hype', a scheme for young animators at the University of Teesside, and the completion of *Lifelines* (2002), a personal and evocative film, drawing upon many aspects of her career. Graber's greatest achievement is her unrelenting enthusiasm for animation and its use in furthering involvement and investment in community welfare and the arts.

(Paul Wells)

BIBLIOGRAPHY: Graber, Sheila, *Animation Is Fun* (Newcastle: Tyneside Cinema Publications, 1984); Johnson, Nerys A. (ed.), *The Animated World of Sheila Graber* (Durham: DLI Museum & Arts Centre, 1985); Pilling, Jayne (ed.), *Women and Animation: A Compendium* (London: BFI Exhibition & Distribution Division, 1992); Wells, Paul (ed.), *Art and Animation* (London: Academy Group/John Wiley, 1997).

SELECTED FILMOGRAPHY: *Boy & Microscope* (1972); *Michelangelo* (1975); *Four Views of Landscape* (1976); *Inside Look North* (1977); *William Blake*; *Mondrian* (1978); *Evolution* (1979); *Face to Face*; Expressionism (1980); *How the Rhinoceros Got His Skin* (1981); Henry *Moore* (1982); *Art Horses* (1985); *Heidi's Horse* (1987); *Toys Will Be Toys* (1989); *Lifelines* (2002).

GRAEF, Roger (1936–)

Roger Graef was born in New York on 18 April 1936. After gaining experience at CBS in America, he came to Britain, where he worked on *The Challenge* (1963), Maurice Hatton's film about the 1963 Labour Party conference, and directed *One of Them Is Named Brett* (1965), a documentary dealing sympathetically with Thalidomide children. He made his name with a series of pioneering cinéma vérité-inflected television documentaries, notably *Police* (1982), a series of eleven studies of the Thames Valley Constabulary. Many of these documentaries have focused on the internal workings of institutions, ranging from British Steel to the Communist Party of Great Britain, exposing detailed minutiae hitherto hidden from view.

In the 1980s he directed three films documenting comic charity benefits for Amnesty International: *The Secret Policeman's Ball* (1979), *The Secret Policeman's Other Ball* (1982) and *The Secret Policeman's Private Parts* (1984), the latter two in collaboration with Julien Temple. In 1988 he tried his hand at dramatic direction with *Closing Ranks*, a television film about a tough London policeman who begins to indulge in domestic violence when transferred to a dull rural beat. He has also directed stage plays and operas in the UK and North America, but his most distinctive achievement is in television documentary.

(Jamie Sexton)

BIBLIOGRAPHY: Hogenkamp, Bert, *Film, Television and the Left, 1950–1970* (London: Lawrence and Wishart, 2000); Wilson, David, 'The Space between Film-Makers', *Sight and Sound*, Autumn 1972, pp. 190–1; Wyver, John, *Nothing but the Truth: Cinéma Vérité and the Films of the Roger Graef Team* (London: BFI/ICA, 1982).

FILMOGRAPHY: *One of Them Is Named Brett* (doc. short, 1965); *The Secret Policeman's Ball* (1979); *The Secret Policeman's Other Ball* (co-dir. Julien Temple, 1982); *The Secret Policeman's Private Parts* (co-dir. Julien Temple, 1984).

GRAHAM SCOTT, Peter (1923–)

Peter Graham Scott was born in East Sheen, London, on 27 October 1923. He trained at the Italia Conti School and entered films as a child actor. After wartime documentary experience he became an editor, notably cutting *Brighton Rock* (John Boulting, 1947) and a half-dozen other films, while tentatively launching into a career as a director. He began inauspiciously with *Panic at Madame Tussaud's* (1948), which he later dismissed as 'a load of rubbish'. He never became a major film director, though he enjoyed considerable success in television, with such shows as *The Four Seasons of Rosie Carr* (1964) and *The Onedin Line* (1974–8). Nevertheless, some of his B-movies are exemplary: *Devil's Bait* is a neat thriller about cyanide-contaminated loaves in a family bakery, acted with unpretentious conviction by Jane Hylton and Geoffrey Keen; and *The Big Day* is a sharply scripted account of the strategies used by a company boss to select a new board member, also acted and directed with intelligently observed detail for ordinary lives. Not all of his B-films are as good as these, but they all move swiftly, making the best of meagre resources. His modest main features include *Captain Clegg*, a vigorous reworking of Russell Thorndike's novel about eighteenth-century Kentish smugglers, *Dr Syn* (filmed by Roy William Neill in 1937); *Bitter Harvest*, a sympathetic cautionary tale about a girl from the provinces who is led to despair in London; and two excruciating comedies – *The Cracksman* and *Mister Ten Per Cent* – starring diminutive comedian Charlie Drake.

(Brian McFarlane)

BIBLIOGRAPHY: Graham Scott, Peter, *British Television: An Insider's History* (Jefferson, NC: McFarland, 2000); McFarlane, Brian, *An Autobiography of British Cinema* (London: Methuen, 1997).

FILMOGRAPHY: *CEMA* (doc., co-dirs. Charles de la Tour/Alan Osbiston/Dylan Thomas/Desmond Dickinson, 1942); *Vegetable Seed Growing* (doc. short, 1943); *Potato Turn Up* (doc. short, 1945); *Sudan Dispute* (doc. short, 1947); *Panic at Madame Tussaud's* (1948); *Sing Along with Me*; *Escape Route* (co-dir. Seymour Friedman) (1952); *Hideout* (1956); *Account Rendered*; *The Big Chance* (1957); *Breakout*; *The Headless Ghost*; *Devil's Bait* (1959); *Let's Get Married*; *The Big Day* (1960); *Captain Clegg* (US: *Night Creatures*); *The Pot Carriers* (1962); *Bitter Harvest*; *The Cracksman*; *Father Came Too* (1963); *Mister Ten Per Cent* (1967); *Subterfuge* (1968).

GRAYSON, Godfrey (1913–1998)

Godfrey Ramsey H. Grayson was born in Birkenhead on 2 August 1913, the twin brother of Ambrose Grayson (who later scripted some of the films Godfrey directed). After making *She Couldn't Say No* for Associated British in 1939, he worked for Exclusive Films, and then for Hammer, the production company Exclusive set up in 1948. He directed (and occasionally shared writing credits on) a number of Hammer's earliest productions, specialising in crime thrillers. He continued in this vein when he went to work for Harry Lee and Edward J. Danziger, directing episodes of television series including *Mark Saber* (1957–60) and *The Cheaters* (1960–2), as well as many second features.

Considering the number of films Grayson directed, he remains a surprisingly obscure figure. He worked with limited budgets (around £15,000 a film when employed by the Danzigers), and when he strayed from the crime genre in later films such as *She Always Gets Their Man* the results could be unfortunate. However, his career includes interesting curiosities such as *An Honourable Murder*, in which Shakespeare's *Julius Caesar* is transplanted to the office boardroom. Of his work at Hammer, the Dick Barton films are enjoyable ripping yarns, and while *Room to Let* is minor period melodrama framed by laboured modern sequences, its Jack the Ripper narrative offered an intriguing foretaste of the horror films for which the studio was to become famous. Grayson died in Kingston-on-Thames, Surrey, in June 1998.

(Guy Barefoot)

FILMOGRAPHY: *She Couldn't Say No* (1939); *Dr Morelle: The Case of the Missing Heiress*; *The Case of the Guardian Angel*; *Dick Barton Strikes Back* (1949); *Room to Let*; *Dick Barton at Bay*; *What the Butler Saw*; The *Lady Craved Excitement*; *Meet Simon Cherry*; *To Have and to Hold* (1950); *The Fake* (1953); *Innocent Meeting*; *High Jump*; *Black Ice* (1958); *Woman's Temptation*; *Date at Midnight* (1959); *The Spider's Web*; *An Honourable Murder*, *Escort for Hire* (1960); *So Evil, So Young*; *The Pursuers* (1961); *She Always Gets Their Man*; *The Lamp in Assassin Mews*; *The Durant Affair*, *Design for Loving*; *The Battleaxe* (1962).

GREAVES, Daniel (1959–)

Daniel Greaves, born in Woburn, Bedfordshire, on 1 October 1959, studied animation at the West Surrey College of Art and Design; his graduation film was *Alarm Call* (1980), an atmospheric parody of the 'Old Dark House' genre. After freelancing as an animator with various London studios he founded Tandem Films in 1986 with Nigel Pay, fitting in personal projects between commercials and other assignments. Greaves' playfulness and experimental bent burst out spectacularly in the seven-minute *Manipulation*, winner of the 1992 Academy Award for the Best Animated Short. Using gag humour and mixed techniques (pencil-drawn animation, 3-D modelling, pixillated live action), the film delights in teasing with animation's rules and methods. Poised above sheets of paper, a gloved live-action hand flicks, squeezes, smudges and crumples a roughly drawn figure, who keeps fighting back with kicks and scowls. In a mock-serious note for its London Film Festival debut, Greaves pointed to the theme of repression in society; but the true worth of *Manipulation* lies in its brilliantly timed visual gags, persuasively matched to exaggerated noises from the animator's instruments of torture – pencil, paper and a little spilled paint.

Despite Greaves' Academy Award success, five years passed before another substantial film emerged. Luxuriating in a budget partly funded by the BBC, Greaves developed *Flatworld* (1997) into a thirty-minute extravaganza. Three flat cut-out figures – a road-mender, his pet cat and fish – are pitched from their drab reality into the colourful, 3-D world of television programming through the whims of a remote-control button. The stylistic mixture is only partly successful and the crowded screen chokes some of the comedy's potential. The eleven-minute *Little Friends*, a compendium of life's annoyances, completed in 2004, echoes the tormenting games of *Manipulation*, but turns up the volume with a degree of violence and abruptness that again eats into the humour. On the other hand, the minuscule *Rabbit Rabbit*, with its procreating rabbit patterns steadily filling the screen, is a witty exercise in technique; while the gentler comedy of the four-minute *Rockin' and Rollin'*, written and devised by co-director Richard Jack, successfully imparts personality to a most unlikely object – the billiard ball. An inventive and imaginative animator, Greaves still has a lot to offer.

(Geoff Brown)

BIBLIOGRAPHY: Carter, Meg, 'It May Be Flat, but It Sure Isn't Boring', *Independent* Eye Section, 23 Dec. 1997, p. 1.

FILMOGRAPHY: *Alarm Call* (1980); *Family Tree* (1988); *Manipulation* (1991); *Rabbit Rabbit* (1995); *Flatworld* (1997); *Rockin' and Rollin'* (co-dir. Richard Jack, 2001); *Little Things*; *Beginning, Middle and End* (2004).

GREEN, Guy (1913–2005)

Guy Green was born in Frome, Somerset, on 5 November 1913. After leaving school he joined the Commercial Maritime Film Service as an assistant projectionist, showing films aboard ocean liners. Returning to England, he opened a photographic studio in Soho before entering the film business proper. For Sound City studios he worked as a clapper-boy; at Elstree he pulled focus and operated the cameras. At Denham, as camera operator on *One of Our Aircraft Is Missing* (Michael Powell and Emeric Pressburger, 1942), he became friendly with David Lean, its editor. Lean later employed him in the same capacity on his first films as a director, *In Which We Serve* (1942) and *This Happy Breed* (1944).

Green's breakthrough as a lighting cameraman came with the realistic surfaces of Carol Reed's *The Way Ahead* (1944). His gifts for painting with light and shadow found grander, more imagin-

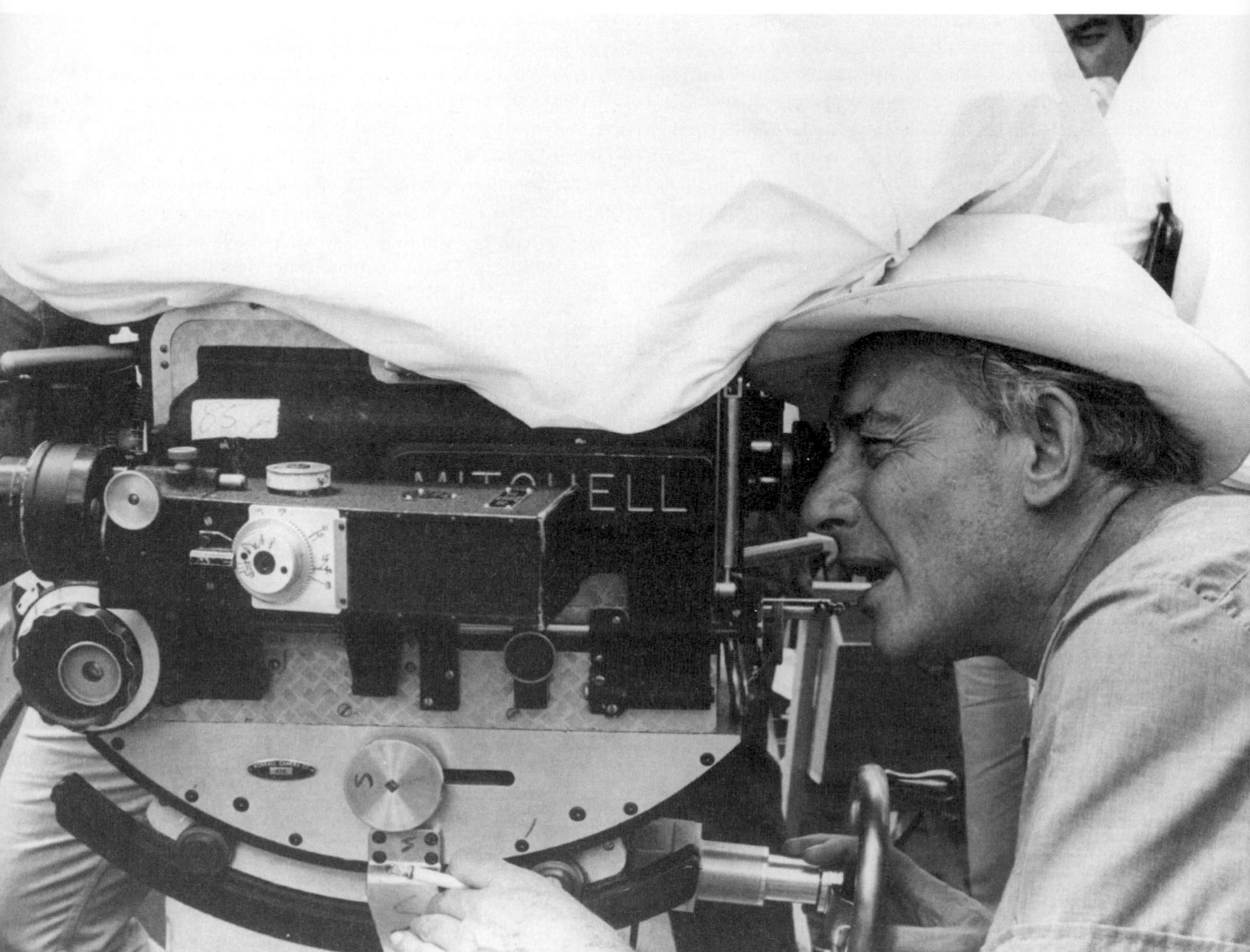

ative outlets when he resumed his collaboration with Lean. As cinematographer on *Great Expectations* (1946), *Oliver Twist* (1948), *The Passionate Friends* (1948) and *Madeleine* (1950), his fastidious, atmospheric images played a key part in the films' impact. The sumptuous melodrama *Blanche Fury* (Marc Allégret, 1947) proved his ability to work in colour; he also photographed American-backed Technicolor costume pictures, including *Captain Horatio Hornblower R.N.* (Raoul Walsh, 1951) and *Rob Roy the Highland Rogue* (Harold French, 1953).

Green began directing in 1953. The first two films were nicely paced thrillers, *River Beat* (1954) and *Portrait of Alison* (1955). *Lost* (1955), from a story by Janet Green about a kidnapped child, was more ambitious – a compelling drama with some unusual insights on career mothers. After two more thrillers, *House of Secrets* (1956) and *The Snorkel* (1958), Green made *Sea of Sand* (1958). A Second World War drama shot in Libya, it is the last and best of Green's routine pictures, successfully capturing the group dynamics of its well-rounded characters. During the long desert nights Green and two of his cast – Michael Craig and Richard Attenborough – devised something more ambitious. *The Angry Silence* (1960), made as the debut production of Attenborough and Bryan Forbes' Beaver Films, concerns a factory hand ostracised by his co-workers when he refuses to go on strike, and provoked attacks on its supposed anti-union bias (the union is seen to be manipulated by a shadowy Communist agitator). Green's vigorous handling leaves the cruder aspects of Forbes' script exposed; but there is plenty to rivet attention in Attenborough's heartfelt central performance, the equally committed acting of Pier Angeli as his Italian wife and Michael Craig's vacillating lodger and workmate. Green followed up with another controversial film for Raymond Stross, *The Mark* (1961). This did less well at the box office, though Stuart Whitman's performance as the sex offender trying to reintegrate himself into society was nominated for an Academy Award.

Green had established an international reputation and his next three films were big-budget American social issue films. In *Light in the Piazza* (1962) Olivia De Havilland ponders the ethics of marrying off her beautiful but brain-damaged daughter (Yvette Mimieux) to a rich Italian; Green treads a fine line here between the offensive, the intriguing and the unintentionally hilarious. The serious and the melodramatic also collided in *Diamond Head* (1963), in which racist pineapple-grower Charlton Heston tries to thwart his sister (Mimieux again) in her determination to marry a Hawaiian. *A Patch of Blue* (1965) is the best of the three: a contrived but bold and sometimes moving drama about a sophisticated black man (Sidney Poitier) and his friendship with a downtrodden blind white girl (Elizabeth Hartman) who only belatedly discovers her benefactor's colour.

Rather than staying in Hollywood, where he might have directed Poitier in the films that made him an international star, Green chose to make *Pretty Polly* (1967) on location in the Far East. Sumptuous location photography and a sparky performance from Hayley Mills hardly make up for a hopelessly quaint script, based on a short story by Noël Coward. Unsurprisingly the film recouped little of its budget at the box office. Green moved on to Greece for *The Magus* (1968), an adaptation of a modish and very long novel by John Fowles, with Michael Caine as an English schoolteacher out of his depth among esoteric Greek rituals. Even in 1968 the film was considered pretentious and obscure, and the slack, meandering narrative suggested that Green had lost his way in the maze. His subsequent films did little to restore his reputation, and after the experience of directing the unashamedly silly *Jacqueline Susann's Once Is Not Enough* and a prosaic German production *Des Teufels Advokat*, based on Morris West's novel, he turned to the safety of American television films. Green's interestingly eclectic career as a director can hardly be deemed a failure, but different choices might have served his talents better. He died at his home in Beverly Hills on 15 September 2005.

(Margaret Butler)

BIBLIOGRAPHY: Bergen, Ronald, 'Obituary: Guy Green', *Guardian*, 17 Sept. 2005, p. 33; Brownlow, Kevin, *David Lean* (London: Faber and Faber, 1997); McFarlane, Brian, *An Autobiography of British Cinema* (London: Methuen, 1997); Most, Madelyn, 'The Most Report: Guy Green', *Eyepiece*, Oct./Nov. 1997, pp. 23–34; Murphy, Robert, *Sixties British Cinema* (London: BFI, 1992).

FILMOGRAPHY: *River Beat* (1954); *Portrait of Alison* (US: *Postmark for Danger*); *Lost* (US: *Tears for Simon*) (1955); *House of Secrets* (US: *Triple Deception*, 1956); *The Snorkel*; *Sea of Sand* (US: *Desert Patrol*) (1958); *S.O.S. Pacific* (1959); *The Angry Silence* (1960); *The Mark* (1961); *Light in the Piazza* (US, 1962); *Diamond Head* (US); *55 Days at Peking* (uncredited, Nicholas Ray, US, 1963); *A Patch of Blue* (1965); *Pretty Polly* (US: *A Matter of Innocence*, 1967); *The Magus* (1968); *Walk in the Spring Rain* (US, 1969); *Luther* (UK/Can/US, 1973); *Jacqueline Susann's Once Is Not Enough* (US, 1974); *Des Teufels Advokat/The Devil's Advocate* (Ger, 1977).

GREEN, Rob

Rob Green entered the film industry as a trainee assistant editor, progressing to work as assistant to Eric Boyd-Perkins, Stu Linder and Lou Lombardo. He directed a series of inventive short films and *Valentine* (1996), a pilot for a comedy-drama series, before linking up with enterprising producer Daniel Figuero – who had backed Edgar Wright's *A Fistful of Fingers* (1995), Stuart St Paul's *The Scarlet Tunic* (1997) and Colm Villa's *Sunset Heights* (1998) – for his feature debut *The Bunker*. This spooky film about a platoon of German soldiers torn apart by paranoia and guilt in the last months of the Second World War proved difficult to finance, but Figuero managed to raise a small budget of $1.5 million from private investors. Despite his limited experience, Green directs like a man who actually knows what he is doing. Consistently interesting compositions, well-paced scenes and effective suspense supplement Clive Dawson's solidly constructed script, John Pardue's inventive cinematography and Richard Campling's cheap but effective sets. Without any big names to aid promotion, *The Bunker* was allowed little space in the multiplexes, but its low-budget ingenuity – reminiscent of both the Val Lewton horror films of the 1940s and early Ealing war films like Harry Watt's *Nine Men* (1943) – ensured it an afterlife on DVD that bodes well for Green's future.

(Robert Murphy)

BIBLIOGRAPHY: Floyd, Nigel, '*The Bunker*: Deadly Tunnel Vision', *Fangoria* no. 221, Apr. 2003, pp. 62–5.

FILMOGRAPHY: *The Black Cat* (short, 1994); *Shopping with the Enemy* (short, 1995); *The Trick* (short, 1997); *The Bunker* (2001).

GREEN, Tom (1852–?)

Wright Thomas Green, born on 17 September 1852, in Spalding, Lincolnshire, directed a number of films during the 1900s and was familiar to filmgoers as the grimacing bon viveur in the comedies of G. A. Smith. After performing in stage comedy, Green first appeared on film in 1897 when he played the sexually rampant master of the house in Smith's *Hanging out the Clothes*. His influence on the content and appearance of Smith's films was considerable. Surviving account books show that he constructed much of the scenery, while the plots of the films, in which he frequently appeared with Smith's actress wife Laura Bayley, were often derived from the sort of Victorian stage farces Green would have known well. Between 1897 and 1902, Green performed in the highly successful series of 'Two Old Sports' comedies, alongside stage comedian John Danby Hunter. Unlike other film-makers of the time, Smith credited both performers, conferring upon them celebrity status.

By 1905 Green had begun to direct and act in films for both the Urban Trading Company and Cricks and Sharp. Operating from a studio at 106 Fairholme Road, Croydon, Green recreated many of the facial close-up films that he had originally made for Smith, but also began to work on longer narrative productions. The extant *The Horse Stealer; or, A Casual Acquaintance* (1905) has a relatively complex plot and contains a number of attractively framed scenes.

(Barry Anthony)

BIBLIOGRAPHY: Gray, Frank, 'George Albert Smith's Comedies of 1897', in Alan Burton and Laraine Porter (eds), *Pimple, Pranks & Pratfalls: British Film Comedy before 1930* (Trowbridge, Wilts: Flicks, 2000).

FILMOGRAPHY: *A Difficult Shave; Reversing a Shave; Natural Laws Reversed; Jovial Expressions; Attempted Nobbling of the Derby Favourite; Drink and Repentance; A Quarter Day Episode; Beware of the Raffled Turkey; The Coster Burglar and His Dog; Inquisitive Visitors at the Dye Works; The Disappointed Suitor's Strategy and Reward; The Advent of the Mother-in-Law; Mistaken for a Burglar in His Own House; The Old Homestead; or, Saved from the Workhouse; Carving the Christmas Turkey; The Adventures of an Insurance Man; The Horse Stealer; or, A Casual Acquaintance; Peeping Tom; Shamus O'Brien; or, Saved from the Scaffold; The Same Old Tale* (1905); *A Comic Duel; Portraits for Nothing; Night Duty; or, A Policeman's Experiences; Down by the Old Bull and Bush; The Return of the Missus; A Bather's Difficulties; The Master's Razor; The Tell-Tale Telephone; The Attack on the Agent; Slippery Jim the Burglar; The Animated Dress Stand; Father's Derby Trip* (aka *Father and the Bookmaker*); *Poor Pa; or, Mother's Day Out; Foiled by a Woman; or, Falsely Accused; Sweet Suffragettes; Seaside Views; The Humours of a River Picnic; A Woman's Sacrifice; The New Apprentice; or, Fun in a Bakehouse; Punch and Judy* (1906); *Their First Cigar; The Wrong Chimney; Bertie's Love Letter; Schoolboys' Pranks* (1907).

GREENAWAY, Peter (1942–)

Peter Greenaway was born in Newport, Wales, on 5 April 1942. He studied at Forest Hills public school, and then at Walthamstow College of Art. An artist who is a believer in the subversive power of the image, his critical relation to visualisation is expressed in paintings, films, television and multimedia formats that have earned him international acclaim as well as charges of mannerism, elitism, obscurantism, intellectual exhibitionism, even misogyny. Greenaway has come to be recognised as a philosopher of cinema, since the style and substance of his work address the changing status of the image in the contemporary world. His films draw self-consciously on various arts – painting, literature, calligraphy, theatre, architecture and music – however, they are not merely formal exercises in style. Though they are obsessed with the nature and importance of form, they address profound questions of the historical role of art in culture.

Greenaway's work is critical of Hollywood methods of film-making that he sees as mere illustration of nineteenth-century novels. For him, cinema must resist appropriating existing novels and plays. His early films are 'not illustrations of already existing texts, or vehicles for actors, or slaves to a plot, or an excuse to provide emotional catharsis' (Woods, p. 18). The non-feature films and videos that he made from the 1960s into the 80s can be described rather as 'theoretical deliberations' (Gras and Gras, p. 52). They are encyclopaedic in scope, visualising aspects of modern life; for example, transportation, funeral architecture, telephone boxes, domestic and public landscapes, dress designers, composers, lakes, water towers, roads, conspiracies, riots and demonstrations, etc. However, these films are not conventional documentaries; instead they demonstrate Greenaway's mode of subverting realism, of highlighting the theatricality and artifice of the visual image so as to enable an understanding of the 'vast amount of data that's pushed at us all the time' (Pally, p. 6).

The Draughtsman's Contract (1982), Greenaway's first mainstream feature film, is set in the 17th century, a time of social and economic transformation. The film portrays the draughtsman's encounters with the moneyed upper classes as he seeks to fulfil his commission. Though the film involves intrigue, even murder, it is not a conventional crime narrative. It is a whodunit that is also a complex exploration of the production of the visual image and its relation to sound, particularly music (thanks to Greenaway's collaboration with Michael Nyman). It examines perspective through the visual and verbal references to painting – the focus on framing of the drawings and of the film itself, on

conversations that are as stylised as the images of architecture and formal gardens. In effect, the film uses all of these strategies to invite the spectator to consider different ways of visualising history, contemplating language, storytelling and, above all, cinema.

A Zed and Two Noughts captures similar images of nature and artifice to those Greenaway created in his short documentaries. The film involves twins, Oliver and Oswald, but the narrative is not a story; it is a compendium of animals as in the zoo of the title. But Greenaway's zoo is the world, and, more specifically, the world of cinema. The cinematic and philosophical focus is on the world as reflected, on issues of sameness (as in the case of identical twins), emerging from the dualities of cinema and reality, art and nature, forgery and authenticity. Greenaway also introduces a motif from his other films – mortality seen through the lens of the cinema that both captures death and is itself doomed to decay and death.

According to Greenaway, *The Belly of an Architect*, his third feature film, 'tried to explore all the different means whereby art has produced the human form' (Gras and Gras, p. 49). The film reprises Greenaway's ubiquitous and complex motif of doubling with two architects, one an eighteenth-century historical personage, Étienne-Louis Boullée, the other a contemporary American, Stourley Krackley, who has come to Rome to set up a Boullée exhibit. Greenaway seeks further doubling in the film's conjunction of past and present, particularly in the linking of Boullée's buildings to Fascist architecture and by linking architects to film-makers in relation to the dilemmas they face in being dependent on patrons while attempting to express their own personal and cultural vision.

Drowning by Numbers, Greenaway's next film, is generally regarded as more accessible to spectators than his other narratives. The film involves three women dissatisfied with their husbands and determined to do something with their disaffection – through death by drowning. By this act, the women develop 'a deeper form of kinship' and 'a primordial affinity with water' (Lawrence, p. 100). As the film's title suggests, the film relies on the elemental nature of water. The numbers alluded to in the title involve the doubling and tripling of characters, the four elements, the visual presence of ciphers and the frequent allusions to counting. In Greenaway's films numbers often play a prominent role, signifying complex modes of ordering the world.

The Cook, the Thief, His Wife, and Her Lover, made during the last years of Thatcherism, was commercially his most successfu1film and revealed Greenaway's penchant for allegory and his ability to combine political with cultural critique. The film draws on popular images of crime and violence, food and fashion, and links them to Thatcher's England. The focus on consuming is not only a critique of contemporary capitalism as gangsterism, but of the violence of history as conveyed through the fictions by which it is consumed.

Prospero's Books (1991) carries Greenaway's investigation of representation to greater complexity. The film engages with Shakespeare's *The Tempest*, not as theatre transposed to film but rather – through the overarching figure of Prospero (Sir John Gielgud) – with issues of art and science, human intelligence, the powers of reason and unreason. The most striking aspect of the film has to do with the role of 'books', the archive of human knowledge, covering the natural sciences, history, magic, painting and calligraphy. *Prospero's Books* typifies Greenaway's encyclopaedic strivings. The 'books' are the artist's archive and are also indicative of the potential of cinema to capture the multiplicity of life and thought. Utilising allegory, the film draws on visual images, dialogue and music to invoke theatre, masque, opera, high and low comedy and create a complex vision of authorship, cinematic narration and the clash between words and images.

The Baby of Mâcon draws on a play performed in Italy in 1659 and focuses on the slippery relation between theatrical illusion and 'reality' within the performance of a play, exploring the complex role of ritual (and cinema), in Greenaway's terms, as both 'paradoxical and dangerous' (Wiloquet-Maricondi and Alemany-Galway, p. 245), an opportunity for critical reflection or an instrument of deceit and manipulation. In creating *The Pillow Book* (1995) Greenaway follows another trajectory, pursuing connections between writing and the body: the body of thought, the body of writing and the body as writing. Working with a thousand-year-old diary, *The Pillow Book of Sei Shonagan*, he reshapes the text to address his primary aesthetic and philosophical concerns. As both this allegory and *Prospero's Books* suggest, Greenaway is wrestling with relations between word and image: Japanese calligraphy provides him, as it did earlier for Sergei Eisenstein, with a rethinking of the separation of the body and the text. The film is a cornucopia of images and allusions; Greenaway explores within the film and in the form of the film the creation of new languages, generating different visual effects with framing, multiple screen images, letter-boxing, overlaid texts, writing superimposed on visual images as well as writings on the bodies of the actors.

Greenaway's later films – *8½ Women, Rosa, Death of a Composer, The Man in the Bath* and *The Tulse Luper Suitcases* – rely on new media, particular CD-ROMs and DVDs, breaking him free of the confines of cinema. In his investigations of media and language Greenaway continues to expand his exploration of the various arts, their changes and interconnections and their implications for understanding the relationship between expression and power. (Marcia Landy)

BIBLIOGRAPHY: Bencivenni, Alessandro and Anna Samueli, *Peter Greenaway: Il cinema delle Idea* (Genoa: Le Mani, 1996); Elliott, Bridget and Anthony Purdy, *Peter Greenaway: Architecture and Allegory* (Chichester, W. Sussex: Academy Editions, 1997); Gras, Vernon and Marguerite Gras (eds), *Peter Greenaway Interviews* (Jackson, MS: University of Mississippi, 2000); Greenaway, Peter, 'Body Talk,' *Sight and Sound*, Nov. 1996, pp. 14–17; Greenaway, Peter, 'Avez-vous en fait déjà vu un film', *Positif*, Jan. 1997, pp. 95–103; Lawrence, Amy, *The Films of Peter Greenaway* (Cambridge: Cambridge University Press, 1997); Pally, Marcia, 'Cinema as the Total Art Form: An Interview with Peter Greenaway', *Cinéaste* vol. 18 no. 3, 1991, pp. 6–11, 45; Perlmutter, Ruth, 'Peter Greenaway: An Inter-Review', *Post Script*, Winter 1989, pp. 56–64; Wiloquet-Maricondi, Paula and Mary Alemany-Galway, *Peter Greenaway's Postmodern/Postructuralist Cinema* (Lanham, MD: Scarecrow Press, 2001); Woods, Alan, *Being Naked Playing Dead: The Art of Peter Greenaway* (Manchester: Manchester University Press, 1996).

FILMOGRAPHY: Shorts: *Death of a Sentiment* (1959–62); *Train*; *Tree* (1966); *Revolution*; *Five Postcards from Capital Cities* (1967); *Intervals* (1969); *Erosion* (1971); *H Is for House* (1973–8); *Windows*; *Water*; *Water Wrackets* (1975); *The Falls* (1980); *Goole by Numbers* (1976); *Dear Phone* (1977); *1–100*; *A Walk through H*; *Vertical Features Remake* (1978); *Act of God*; *Zandra Rhodes* (1981); *Four American Composers* (1983); *A TV Dante – Canto 5* (1984); *Inside Rooms – The Bathroom* (1985); *Visions of Europe* ('The European Showerbath' episode, twenty-four other dirs. Den/Ger, 2004).

Feature-length films: *The Draughtsman's Contract* (1982); *A Zed and Two Noughts* (aka *A Zoo*, 1985); *The Belly of an Architect* (1986); *Drowning by Numbers* (1988); *The Cook, the Thief, His Wife, and Her Lover* (1989); *Prospero's Books* (1991); *The Baby of Mâcon* (1993); *The Pillow Book* (1995); *8½ Women*; *Rosa, Death of a Composer* (1999); *The Man in the Bath* (2001); *The Tulse Luper Suitcases, Part 1: The Moab Story* (2003); *The Tulse Luper Suitcases, Part 2: Vaux to the Sea*; *The Tulse Luper Suitcases, Part 3: From Sark to Finish* (UK/Neth) (2004); *A Life in Suitcases* (UK/Sp/Lux/Hung/It/Ger, 2005).

GREENE, David (1921–2003)

Born in Manchester on 22 February 1921 to a Russian father and Irish mother, David Greene's first professional contact with the arts came in 1941 when, invalided out of the merchant navy, he became publicity manager for London's Everyman Theatre. Bitten by the stage bug, he studied at RADA and went on to act in repertory, and in films such as *The Small Voice*

Unswinging London: *The Strange Affair* (David Greene, 1968)

(Fergus McDonell, 1948) and *The Wooden Horse* (Jack Lee, 1950).

While touring the USA in the Olivier/Leigh production of *Antony and Cleopatra* in 1951–2, he decided to stay in North America, and was offered a job as director in the television department of the Canadian Broadcasting Company. In 1956 he moved to the USA; working on numerous television series, he was to become by the end of the decade the highest-paid director in the medium. At this point, in search of new challenges, he went to the UK and began a stint in television series there, before making his first feature, *The Shuttered Room* (1966), which marked the beginning of a short but productive period of work in British cinema.

The most striking aspect of Greene's British features is their feeling for locale: the island landscape dominated by pylons in *The Shuttered Room* (an early entry in the H. P. Lovecraft cinematic canon), the London cityscapes of *Sebastian* (1967) and *The Strange Affair* (1968), and the bleak New Town environment (in fact, Bracknell) of *I Start Counting* (1969). Of these, *Sebastian* and *The Strange Affair* are the most interesting; like Antonioni in *Blow-up* (1967), Greene casts an outsider's eye over the superficial paraphernalia of 'Swinging London' and paints a disturbing vision of a city and nation in transition. *Sebastian* (based on a story by Leo Marks and produced by Michael Powell) is nominally a spy film in the cynical Le Carré mould, but what strikes one most forcibly is its chilly vision of the new glass and concrete London then being constructed, and its perceptive take on late-1960s' Britain, its exuberant permissiveness already tainted.

Greene's outsider's view allowed him to present a picture of unmitigated police corruption in *The Strange Affair*. A detective's obsession with purity causes him to trample on the law in his relentless pursuit of a Kray-like family, and the young constable Strange (Michael York) who is caught in his machinations is used by corrupt senior officers to thwart him. *The Strange Affair* exudes the same corrupt, rancid odour as American films noirs like *The Big Combo* (Joseph H. Lewis, 1955) and *On Dangerous Ground* (Nicholas Ray, 1952), and it shares their sense of heightened, sadistic violence.

In the mid-1970s Greene returned to America where he continued his career as a prolific director of films for television, and occasionally cinema, until his death from pancreatic cancer on 7 April 2003 in Ojai, California.

(Julian Petley)

BIBLIOGRAPHY: Castell, David, 'Why Not?', *Films Illustrated*, Aug. 1971, pp. 24–7; 'David Greene', *Film Dope* no. 21, Oct. 1980, pp. 6–7; Murphy, Robert, *Sixties British Cinema* (London: BFI, 1992); Robinson, David, 'Case Histories of the Next Renascence', *Sight and Sound*, Winter 1968–9, pp. 36–40.

FILMOGRAPHY: *The Shuttered Room* (1966); *Sebastian* (1967); *The Strange Affair* (1968); *I Start Counting* (1969); *The People Next Door* (US, 1970); *Madame Sin* (1972); *Godspell* (US, 1973); *London Conspiracy* (co-dir. James Hill, 1976); *Gray Lady Down* (US, 1978); *Hard Country* (US, 1981).

GREENE, Max (1896–1968)

Max Greene was born Mutz Greenbaum on 3 February 1896 in New York. He grew up in Berlin and in 1914 joined his father's company, (Julius) Greenbaum Films. He quickly became a well-regarded cine-cameraman and photographed his first film, *Der Fakir im Frack* (Max Mack), in 1916. He came to Britain as chief photographer for Gaumont-British and worked on two films directed by Victor Saville, *Sunshine Susie* (1931), which starred Renate Müller, repeating her role from the German original, *Die Privatsekretärin* (Wilhelm Thiele, 1931); and *Hindle Wakes* (1931), with Belle Chrystall as the spunky mill worker who turns down the opportunity to marry the factory owner's son after their holiday affair. Numerous films followed, including Saville's *Evensong* (1934), Robert Stevenson's *Tudor Rose* (1936) and Carol Reed's *The Stars Look Down* (1939).

During the Second World War, Greenbaum changed his name to Greene, and formed a partnership with producer Victor Hanbury and director Lance Comfort. On *Hotel Reserve* they shared credits, though there is little evidence that Comfort concerned himself with photography or Greene and Hanbury interfered too much with directing. Greene did go on to direct one film himself, *The Man from Morocco*, which, although discursive and scrappy, is notable for its subject matter – the treatment of Spanish Republican refugees by the Vichy government – and the passionate performances of Anton Walbrook, Margaretta Scott and Mary Morris.

Greene returned to cinematography after this not wholly successful venture, working on films as diverse as *Maytime in Mayfair* (Herbert Wilcox, 1949) and *Night and the City* (Jules Dassin, 1950). Towards the end of the 1950s he began working with the Boulting Brothers, lighting most of their films between *Brothers in Law* (1957) and *Heavens Above!* (1963). He died in London in July 1968.

(Kevin Gough-Yates)

BIBLIOGRAPHY: McFarlane, Brian, *Lance Comfort* (Manchester: Manchester University Press, 1999); Noble, Peter (ed.), *The British Film Yearbook, 1947–1948* (London: Skelton Robinson, 1947), p. 264.

FILMOGRAPHY: *Hotel Reserve* (aka *Epitaph for a Spy*, co-dirs. Lance Comfort/Victor Hanbury, 1944); *The Man from Morocco* (1945).

GREENGRASS, Paul (1955–)

Paul Greengrass was born in Cheam, Surrey, on 13 August 1955. His work on current affairs television programmes such as Granada's *World in Action* in the 1980s has clearly been an important influence on his subsequent career as a director. Nearly all of his films have been based on real-life subject matter, and he has acquired a reputation as one of Britain's leading directors of drama-documentaries. His first feature, *Resurrected* (1989), took the subject of the Falklands War as the basis for an anti-war polemic in which a young soldier (David Thewlis), thought killed in the war and honoured in a memorial service, suddenly returns home suffering memory loss, to be greeted as less than a national hero.

Most of Greengrass' subsequent films have been made for television, including *Open Fire* (1994), the story behind the police shooting of Stephen Waldorf, a film editor who was mistaken for the cross-dressing armed robber David Martin; *The One That Got Away* (1996), about the SAS 'Bravo Two Zero' patrol in the 1991 Gulf War; and *The Fix* (1997), a dramatisation of a football bribery scandal in the early 1960s. Greengrass' second feature, *The Theory of Flight* (1998), a BBC film about a woman with motor neuron disease determined to lose her virginity before she is claimed by death, starring Kenneth Branagh and Helena Bonham Carter, failed to fulfil its potential. Greengrass was more successful when he returned to drama-documentary with two BAFTA award-winning television films: *The Murder of Stephen Lawrence* (1999) and *Bloody Sunday* (2002), the latter also winning the Golden Bear award at the Berlin Film Festival and gaining a limited cinema release.

In 2004 Greengrass co-wrote and co-produced *Omagh* (directed by Pete Travis), a convincing recreation of the Omagh bomb outrage of August 1998, for Channel 4. He also directed his first big-budget Hollywood film, *The Bourne Supremacy*, an intelligent action movie given added gravitas by Greengrass, whose drama-documentary background served him well in the realisation of some gripping action sequences. He went on to make *United 93*, the first mainstrream commercial film to deal with the 9-11 hijackings.

(Lez Cooke)

BIBLIOGRAPHY: Hattenstone, Simon, '"A Lot of Factual Drama Is Crap"', *Guardian*, 20 May 2004, pp. 8–9; Keighron, Peter, 'ITV's Risk Taker', *Broadcast*, 15 Feb. 2002, p. 19.

FILMOGRAPHY: *Resurrected* (1989); *The Theory of Flight* (1998); *Bloody Sunday* (2002); *The Bourne Supremacy* (US, 2004); *United 93* (UK/US, 2006).

GREENWOOD, Edwin (1895–1939)

When he died aged forty-six, Edwin Greenwood was fondly recalled by Pat Mannock as 'a cultivated scholar and an extremely likeable personality' (*Kinematograph Weekly*, 1939). His activities were numerous: in twenty years in the industry he worked as a set designer, director, scriptwriter and actor; he also wrote crime novels, marked by an amused air and a liking for amorality in cosy places. One, *Old Goat*, was dedicated to Hitchcock ('Good Maker of Good Pictures, Good Judge of Good Things, Good Friend'), for whom Greenwood co-wrote *The Man Who Knew Too Much* (1934) and *Young and Innocent* (1937).

His directorial career proceeded by fits and starts. Younger brother of the film composer John Greenwood, Theodore Edwin Greenwood was born in Fulham, London, in 1895, and after education at St Paul's School and the Sorbonne worked in the theatre as a director and actor, chiefly with the Liverpool Repertory Company. He entered films in 1919 as the art director on Ideal productions. Three years later he began directing shorts for the revived British and Colonial company, including nutshell versions of English history and *Wonder Women of the World* (ranging from demure Lady Jane Grey to wicked Lucrezia Borgia). The features that followed from 1923 were initially well received. Jack Buchanan's light touch helped the comedy in *The Audacious Mr Squire*, while *Heartstrings*, a variant on the 'Enoch Arden' motif of the presumed-dead lover returning home, benefited from location scenes of docks and mills. His Scott adaptation *The Fair Maid of Perth*, however, stayed on the shelf for several years. Greenwood's next features emerged at Gaumont. Signs of talent flickered again in the crime drama *The Woman in Pawn*, but even the presence of Madeleine Carroll failed to justify his adaptation of the Lyceum Theatre melodrama *What Money Can Buy*.

In 1929 Greenwood hit the talkies with New Era's *The Co-optimists* and Tiffany's *To What Red Hell*. Both have survived, but neither proves a good advertisement. *The Co-optimists* transferred a popular stage revue to the screen with a static camera staring from the middle distance. 'Monotony beyond conception', moaned Ralph Bond in *Close Up*; 'it isn't even dead, because it was never alive' (Bond, p. 86). The sordid drama of *To What Red Hell*, made just before, was far more ambitious. Initially shot silent, the film was awkwardly reconvened as a talkie, with music by Greenwood's brother. Dialogue crawls with painful deliberation, though sound is used occasionally for good dramatic effect. The material, based on Percy Robinson's play about an epileptic's murder of a prostitute and an innocent faced with execution, brought its own problems, stirring the Censor, and prompting further reshooting. Sybil Thorndike, as the innocent man's mother, acts with dignity; but John Hamilton as the epileptic, though praised at the time, gives one of British cinema's great bad performances, constantly twitching and clutching his chest like a shivering rat.

In a scathing *Close Up* review, Hugh Castle wrote that Greenwood showed 'no reason why he should ever make another picture' (Castle, p. 331). And barring the stillborn *Co-optimists* he did not. He worked instead on his books and on film scripts, first at BIP, then after 1934 chiefly at Gaumont. Greenwood's love of black humour, apparent in the novels, must have cemented his friendship with Hitchcock, who cast him as the tattooed boat wrecker Dandy in his last British film, *Jamaica Inn* (1939). Greenwood's precarious health can hardly have been helped by the buffeting of studio wind and water, and he died on 17 September 1939 – mourned, said *Kinematograph Weekly*, by 'countless friends of the British studio world'.

(Geoff Brown)

BIBLIOGRAPHY: Bond, Ralph, ['The Co-optimists'], *Close Up* vol. 6 no. 1, Jan. 1930, pp. 85–6; 'British Studios To-day', *The Bioscope* 18 Sept. 1929, p. 26; Castle, Hugh, 'What a Red Hell', *Close Up* vol. 5 no. 4, Oct. 1929, pp. 331–2; Low, Rachael, *The History of the British Film 1918–1929* (London: George Allen & Unwin, 1971); Mannock, Pat L., 'Actor-Producer Dead: Tribute to Work of Edwin Greenwood', *Kinematograph Weekly*, 19 Oct. 1939, p. 22; 'To What Red Hell', *The Bioscope*, 23 Oct. 1929, pp. 37–8.

FILMOGRAPHY: Features: *The Audacious Mr Squire* (1923); *Heartstrings* (1923); *The Fair Maid of Perth* (1923); *A Woman in Pawn* (1927); *What Money Can Buy* (1928); *To What Red Hell*; *The Co-optimists* (1929).

Shorts: *Mary Queen of Scots*, *An Affair of Honour*, *The Threefold Tragedy*, *The Unwanted Bride*, *The Queen's Secret*, *Seadogs of Good Queen Bess* (episodes from the series *The Romance of British History*, 1922); *Wonder Women of the World* (series); *The Dreams of Eugene Aram*, *Scrooge*, *The Bells*, *The School for Scandal*, *She Stoops to Conquer*, *The Test*, *The Sins of the Father*, *Falstaff the Tavern Knight*, *Love in an Attic* (episodes from the series *Gems of Literature*) (1923); *The Art of Love* (series of shorts, co-dir. W. P. Kellino, 1925); *The Escape*, *Miss Bracegirdle Does Her Duty*, *Back to the Trees*, *Whispering Gables*, *Fear* (aka *Fangs of Death*) (episodes from the series *Screen Playlets*, 1926–7).

GREGG, Colin (1947–)

Colin Gregg was born on 10 January 1947 in Cheltenham, Gloucestershire, and trained as a teacher. Early experiences with a cine camera in childhood led to quasi-documentary shorts and an atmospheric short fiction film funded by the BFI Production Board, *The Flying Man* (1972). He launched his professional career in 1975. Commissioned films supplied his bread and butter; the first prominent sign of his directing talent was the impressive if overstretched fifty-minute drama *Begging the Ring* (1979), exploring the impact of First World War conscription on a small Cornish village. The threat of war also lay at the centre of his ambitious first feature, *Remembrance*, shot in Portsmouth, following the fortunes of a group of young sailors on the eve of their departure for a NATO tour of duty. Written by Hugh Stoddart, a regular Gregg collaborator, the film was one of Channel 4's earliest cinema ventures; its release as the Falklands War erupted softened hearts toward some awkward moments in the acting and script.

Since then, Gregg's cinema work has become more intermittent, but stronger in impact and assurance. For television he has directed episodes for serials like *Inspector Morse* and *Kavanagh QC*, starring John Thaw. Gregg and Stoddart have also proved gifted adapters of literature, making well-crafted television versions of D. H. Lawrence's little-known novel *The Trespasser* (1981) and Virginia Woolf's *To the Lighthouse* (1983): fine examples of imaginative fidelity, each finding a visual style that does justice to the books' complexities. A similar sense and sensibility emerged in their cinema film of J. R. Ackerley's *We Think the World of You* (1988), the wryly comic semi-autobiographical story of a literary editor's entanglements with his working-class boyfriend, his boyfriend's family and Alsatian dog. Perhaps the set dressers went overboard simulating East London and the drab 1950s, but as the central odd couple Alan Bates and Gary Oldman were alert to the script's every nuance and suggestive silence.

Gregg's most memorable achievement is *Lamb* (1986), another Channel 4 venture, adapted from Bernard MacLaverty's novel. Here the dramatic spine appears firmer and straighter than in any other Gregg film. Most of the weight is carried by Liam Neeson, excellent as the priest whose attempt to free a sick boy (Hugh O'Conor) from a strict remand home brings disastrous consequences. Like much of Gregg's best work, *Lamb* is distinguished by atmospheric location shooting, strong performances and a quirky, touching observation of the tragic as well as happy consequences of love. Gregg has continued working for television series, including *Peak Practice* and *Thief Taker*, but the sense remains of a talent not being sufficiently exerted by the opportunities available.

(Geoff Brown and Neil Sinyard)

BIBLIOGRAPHY: Pym, John, 'Before and After School – Colin Gregg', *Monthly Film Bulletin*, June 1986, p. 192.

FILMOGRAPHY: *The Flying Man* (short); *One Man Band* (short) (1972); *Peter and Ruby* (short, 1973); *Begging the Ring* (1979); *Remembrance* (1982); *Lamb* (1986); *We Think the World of You* (1988).

GRÉVILLE, Edmond T. (1906–1966)

Edmond Thonger Gréville was born in Nice on 20 June 1906, the son of Anglo-French parents, a schoolteacher and a Protestant evangelist. Initially he worked in France as a film journalist and critic. His first studio experience came in England in 1928 when he worked as an assistant on *Piccadilly* for E. A. Dupont, whose methods of visual storytelling he much admired. Gréville's first feature as a director was *Le Train des suicides* (1931), a fanciful drama featuring his actress wife, Vanda Gréville. But the milestone film was *Remous* (1934), a provocative drama of desire and frustration, tardily released in France after its success in Britain. *Remous* firmly established Gréville's baroque visual style, marked by mobile camerawork, surprising transitions and much play with reflections in mirrors and puddles; it also demonstrated his fascination with sexual anguish.

Building on the British attention given to *Remous*, Gréville established his own London company in June 1935. *Gypsy Melody*, a hoary melodrama starring Lupe Velez and the gypsy orchestra leader Alfred Rode, was its sole feature, and the company never lived up to its chosen name, British Artistic Films. Gréville's susceptibilities found much better outlets in subsequent British films. His knack for exploring complex, sometimes erotic relationships bore particular fruit in Phoenix Films' *Brief Ecstasy*, a tale of passion raging outside marriage, featuring Linden Travers, Paul Lukas and Hugh Williams, strongly praised in a review by Graham Greene for its camera sense and atmosphere of 'starved sexuality'. Phoenix's *Secret Lives*, a visually resplendent anti-war film wrapped up in a spy story, and the more ponderous *Mademoiselle Docteur*, made for Max Schach's Grafton Films, dealt with ambiguous allegiances and treasonable love.

Edward Rigby's Slush the Forger caught red-handed in *Noose* (Edmond T. Greville, 1948)

Gréville was happy working in Britain, but an ambitious film project about Shakespeare failed to make headway with financiers, and he returned to Europe in 1938. French successes included *Menaces* (1939), an evocative portrait of war clouds gathering, set in a Paris hotel, and a powerful Zola adaptation, *Pour une nuit d'amour* (1946). In his visual language and attitudes to sex he stayed defiantly continental, although several post-war British ventures led him further into British society than any of his 1930s' films. Soho prostitutes and vice racketeers peopled *Noose* (1948), a vigorous, slyly comic spiv drama adapted from Richard Llewellyn's play; over a decade later, *Beat Girl* (1960) deployed Adam Faith, Shirley Ann Field and other signs of the times in a lurid tale of Soho strip clubs and murder.

As Gréville's output continued, his artistic urge became increasingly dwarfed by commercial needs: his last British venture was *The Hands of Orlac* (1960), a disappointingly routine horror film (he also directed its French version). But in the late 1950s and 60s his best work found new vocal champions among French critics, including the film-maker Bertrand Tavernier. Gréville died in Nice on 26 May 1966.

(Geoff Brown and Bryony Dixon)

BIBLIOGRAPHY: 'Edmond T. Gréville', *Film Dope* no. 21, Oct. 1980, pp. 12–14; Gréville, Edmond T., *Trente-cinq ans dans la jungle du cinéma* (Lyon: Institut Lumière/Actes Sud, 1995); Gréville, Edmond T., 'The Lady Spy and the Legless Man', *Film Comment*, Jan./Feb. 1998, pp. 57–6; Porter, Vincent, 'Strangers in a Foreign Land', *La Lettre de la*

Maison Française d'Oxford no. 11, Autumn 1999, pp. 59–74; Tavernier, Bertrand, 'Edmond T. Gréville', *Film Comment*, Jan./Feb. 1998, pp. 54–6, 61–2.

FILMOGRAPHY (UK only): *Gypsy Melody* (1936); *Secret Lives* (US: *I Married a Spy*); *Brief Ecstasy*; *Mademoiselle Docteur* (1937); *What a Man!* (1938); *Noose* (US: *The Silk Noose*); *But Not in Vain* (1948); *The Romantic Age* (US: *Naughty Arlette*, 1949); *Captain Horatio Hornblower R.N.* (2nd unit dir., Raoul Walsh, 1951); *Guilty?* (1956); *Beat Girl* (US: *Wild for Kicks*); *The Hands of Orlac* (US: *Hands of the Strangler*) (1960).

GREWAL, Shani (1958–)

Shani S. Grewal was born on 16 August 1958 in the Punjab, but educated in Britain. After making a number of short films, he gained backing from Channel 4 to make *After Midnight* (1990), a feature-length Anglo-Irish production set during a night in a Dublin hotel. Despite a cast that included Ian Dury, Saeed Jaffrey, Hayley Mills and Vladek Sheybal, results were unprepossessing and the film was not given a theatrical release. Two low-budget features followed. In *Double X*, Grewal showed enterprise in using the Business Expansion Scheme to provide a meagre budget, dragging Norman Wisdom out of comfortable retirement and inducing a performance of eye-rolling villainy from Bernard Hill, but this unconvincing gangster film sunk under its implausible plot and banal dialogue.

Grewal was on less shaky ground with *Guru in Seven*, another micro-budget affair about a young Indian cajoled into attempting to have sex with seven different women on seven consecutive nights. With its succession of set-piece seductions, *Guru in Seven* harks back to the sexploitation films of the 1970s, and Nitin Chandra Ganatra shares some of the puppy-like charm of Robin Askwith. Grewal's device of having his hero talk to the audience directly is sometimes very effective, but it emphasises the impression that one is watching a home movie; insights into multicultural metropolitan society tend to be lost amid careless plotting and underdeveloped characters. Grewal moved on to television, directing episodes of *Holby City* and *Casualty*.

(Robert Murphy)

FILMOGRAPHY: *Pincher Martin* (short, 1983); *Vengeance* (short, 1984); *After Midnight* (Ir/UK, 1990); *Double X* (aka *Double X: The Name of the Game*, 1992); *Guru in Seven* (1998).

GREY, Richard (1916–)

Born in London on 19 November 1916, Richard Michael Grey was educated at Eton and entered the industry as a scriptwriter at the Joe Rock studio in 1936. Two years later he left to join the International Brigade in Spain. During the Second World War he served with the Royal Navy; and after being demobbed in 1945 he formed Condor Film Productions, one of the numerous short-lived independent firms that sprouted in the late 1940s. The company used the small and inflexible Carlton Hill studio in Maida Vale; interest items about fashion and film-making were interspersed with two modest features exploiting the post-war scene. Nothing proved very believable about the atomic scientist kidnapped by a Nazi war criminal in *Eyes That Kill*, but the spivs-on-the-run drama *A Gunman Has Escaped* at least filled the screen with blood and bullets. Grey's last known film, made for Vandyke, is a three-reel Sherlock Holmes story, *The Man with the Twisted Lip*, featuring John Longden and Campbell Singer.

(Geoff Brown)

FILMOGRAPHY: *Birth of a Film* (short); *Eyes That Kill*; *Spotlight on Glamour* (short) (1947); *A Gunman Has Escaped* (1948); *The Man with the Twisted Lip* (short, 1951).

GRIERSON, John (1898–1972)

John Grierson was born on 26 April 1898 at Deanston, Perthshire, Scotland. After serving on minesweepers during the First World War, he studied at Glasgow University. Awarded a Rockefeller fellowship in 1924, he pursued research into public opinion and mass communications at the University of Chicago, travelled widely and spent some time in Hollywood. After returning to Britain in 1927 he became Assistant Films Officer at the Empire Marketing Board and was commissioned to make *Drifters*, a documentary about the North Sea herring fleet. When the Board was closed down in 1933, Grierson became Films Officer at the General Post Office, where his team formed the basis of the GPO Film Unit.

Grierson's specific achievement as a director is not easy to assess, as the documentary movement took a collaborative

approach to production. Though there is strong evidence to attach his name to several other films, including *Granton Trawler* and the puppet burlesque *Our Dumb Friend*, Grierson is only credited as director on *Drifters*. But he exerted a significant influence on the talented team of young film-makers he attracted around him. *Drifters* contains many of the traits that would later characterise the documentary movement's output, notably an emphasis on the social interaction and everyday routine of the fishermen at sea, and on the economic importance of the fishing industry, as well as technical innovations such as the 'underwater' shots achieved at the Plymouth Marine Biological Research Station. The new montage style of Soviet cinema and the poetical style of Robert Flaherty were clear influences on Grierson; the term 'documentary' was first used in Grierson's review for the *New York Sun* of Flaherty's film *Moana* (1926).

In June 1937 Grierson resigned from the GPO and formed Film Centre, an advisory and co-ordinating body for the documentary film movement. It was this kind of supervisory capacity that characterised Grierson's role and influence on factual film; he also served throughout the war as Film Commissioner at the National Film Board of Canada.

After a brief and fairly fruitless period in New York, Grierson returned to the UK in 1946. In February 1948 he was appointed to the Films Division of the Central Office of Information. Over the next two years he attempted to re-establish a major programme of government documentary production, but he was repeatedly frustrated by political opposition, some of it related to his work in Britain before the war, some to the belief that his agenda was less suited to the post-war political and cultural climate. From 1950 to 1952 Grierson acted as executive producer of Group 3, set up with backing from the National Film Finance Corporation to allow young film-makers the opportunity to make low-budget feature films; and in 1957 began presenting *This Wonderful World*, a weekly television programme that continued until 1968. He finished his career teaching at McGill University, Montreal.

Grierson's supporters claim that he single-handedly established the principle of public service film-making; his detractors maintain that Grierson's documentaries reached limited audiences and that their cultural impact has been exaggerated. *Drifters* shows him to have been a talented director, but he was always more interested in encouraging others to make films than in pursuing his own career as a director. He died in Bath on 19 February 1972. His sisters Ruby Grierson (1904–1940) and Marion Grierson (1907–1999) also directed documentaries, mostly for Strand, Crown and the Realist Film Unit.

(Leo Enticknap)

BIBLIOGRAPHY: Aitken, Ian, *Film and Reform* (London: Routledge, 1990); Ellis, Jack C., *John Grierson: A Guide to References and Resources* (Boston, MA: G. K. Hall, 1986); Hardy, H. Forsyth (ed.), *John Grierson: A Documentary Biography* (London: Faber and Faber, 1979); 'John Grierson', *Film Dope* no. 21, Oct. 1980, pp. 17-33; Pronay, Nicholas (ed.), 'John Grierson: A Critical Retrospective', *Historical Journal of Film, Radio and Television* vol. 9 no. 3, 1989.

FILMOGRAPHY: *Our Dumb Friend* (short); *Drifters* (1929); *Port of London* (unfinished, 1930); *Granton Trawler* (short, 1933).

GRIEVE, Andrew (1939–)

Andrew Grieve was born in Cardiff on 28 November 1939 and brought up in West Wales (after evacuation during the Blitz) and in Blackwood, Gwent. He became an assistant floor manager with the BBC in 1962, but also worked as an assistant director on feature films such as Ken Loach's *Poor Cow* (1967) and Tony Richardson's *Ned Kelly* (1970). After making a short television film, *Notice to Quit* (1976), and acting as second unit director on *Young Sherlock Holmes* for Barry Levinson, he was given the opportunity to direct an Anglo-American television remake of Hitchcock's *Suspicion* (1987), on which Levinson was co-producer.

His first cinema feature, *On the Black Hill*, financed by Channel 4 and the BFI, followed soon after. Based on Bruce Chatwin's extraordinarily rich novel tracing a symbiotic relationship between twin brothers spanning eighty years, it enabled Grieve to make use of his knowledge of the landscape of Breconshire and the Welsh borders. Grieve treated the book with admirable fidelity, and the film benefited from Thaddeus O'Sullivan's photography and fine performances from brothers Robert and Mike Gwilym, and Gemma Jones as their genteel mother.

On the Black Hill was critically well received but it was not a commercial success. Grieve returned to television where he directed the highly popular *Poirot* television detective series (1990–5), and eight films featuring C. S. Forester's naval hero, Captain Horatio Hornblower, between 1998 and 2003, which have been equally successful with American and British audiences.

(David Berry)

BIBLIOGRAPHY: Berry, David, *Wales and Cinema: The First 100 Years* (Cardiff: University of Wales Press, 1994).

FILMOGRAPHY: *Young Sherlock Holmes* (2nd unit dir, Barry Levinson, 1985); *On the Black Hill* (1987).

GRIFFITH, D. W. (1875–1948)

David Wark Griffith, born in Crestwood, Kentucky, on 22 January, 1875, twice crossed paths with British cinema, in very different circumstances. Over the winter of 1916–17, Lord Beaverbrook, Head of the newly formed British War Office Cinematograph Committee, encouraged Griffith, then the world's most celebrated film-maker, to come to London to make a film with War Office co-operation, promoting the Allied cause. He arrived in March 1917, in time for the London premiere of *Intolerance* (1916), whose disappointing American response he was probably glad to escape. Griffith's regular players and technicians joined him in Europe to make *Hearts of the World*, the story of a small French village suffering under German occupation, with a love story between the son and daughter of

American expatriates entwined within. For finance, Griffith called upon Famous Players-Lasky, his new production partner in America; Beaverbrook arranged for unprecedented access to the front line (much exploited in publicity to advertise the film's authenticity), along with the use of thousands of troops for re-enactments on Salisbury Plain. For all the material taken (in comparative safety) in France, two-thirds of the released film was shot after Griffith's return to California in October. Some German actuality footage was also included.

Despite the jumble of its production, *Hearts of the World* lived up to much of its publicity. Though artifice dogged the personal stories of Robert Harron and Lillian Gish, battlefield scenes always looked authentic: experiencing the front line inspired Griffith to produce one of his most honest films, showing warfare without romance or adventure. Issued in different versions in England, America and France, with further changes made after the Armistice, *Hearts of the World* was especially successful in America, where the marketing campaign suggested that to miss it would be unpatriotic; ultimately the film is of more interest to Britain for its origins than its content.

When Griffith brushed against British cinema again, in 1935, his fortunes were low. Cinema tastes and technology had left him behind; a reputation for grandiosity and alcohol had further weakened his position. An offer of work came from Julius Hagen at Twickenham Studios. Four years after his last film, *The Struggle*, Griffith arrived in May 1935 to direct a sound remake of his 1919 melodrama *Broken Blossoms*, but was fired after several weeks' work on the script. The official reason was a dispute over the choice of actress to play the heroine, the Limehouse waif tormented by her vicious father; a more likely reason was Griffith's deteriorated condition. Émigré studio supervisor Hans Brahm (John Brahm in his later Hollywood work) took over the job of direction; the result, featuring Brahm's wife Dolly Haas, and weighed down with fake studio atmosphere, was not a success. Griffith returned to America, rightly honoured for his past, but with only more professional disappointments ahead; he died in Los Angeles on 23 July 1948.

(Geoff Brown and Simon Brown)

BIBLIOGRAPHY: Brownlow, Kevin, *The War, the West and the Wilderness* (London: Secker and Warburg, 1978); Merritt, Russell, 'D. W. Griffith Directs the Great War: The Making of *Hearts of the World*', *Quarterly Review of Film Studies*, Winter 1981, pp. 45–65; Schickel, Richard, *D. W. Griffith* (London: Pavilion Books, 1984).

FILMOGRAPHY (UK only): *Hearts of the World* (1918).

GRIFFITHS, Sid (c. 1899–1967)

Sid Griffiths, born in Wales in 1898, started in the industry as a projectionist in a Cardiff cinema. He collaborated with fellow projectionist Bert Bilby in creating a cartoon dog, 'Jerry the Troublesome Tyke'. This greedy, rebellious canine appeared in about forty short episodes shown fortnightly in Pathé Pictorial screen magazines from mid-1925 to 1927. The Jerry series was much influenced in style and content by Paramount's successful *Felix the Cat*, though Griffiths' and Bilby's blend of live action and animation, and the ingenious (often fractious) interaction between Griffiths and the pooch, also recalled the fusion of actuality film and drawn animation in the Fleischer brothers' *Out of the Inkwell* series. No other British cartoon creature survived as many adventures and episodes as Jerry.

In the 1930s Griffiths established Comedy Cartoon Sound Films and Raycol with the animator Brian White, for which they made *Colonel Capers* and *On the Farm*, based on the cartoon drawings of H. M. Bateman. Griffiths was supervisor on Anson Dyer's pioneering colour films of the 1930s, notably *Sam and His Musket* (1935), *Carmen* (1936) and *The Lion and Albert* (1937), featuring droll monologues by Stanley Holloway; and he was one of the four photographers on the first British animation feature, Halas and Batchelor's *Animal Farm* (1954). He died in Newton Abbot, Devon on 11 November 1967, too soon to enjoy the Jerry cartoons' successful revival in the early 21st century.

(David Berry)

BIBLIOGRAPHY: Berry, David, 'Jerry the Tyke – Felix's Canine Cousin', in Alan Burton and Laraine Porter (eds), *Crossing the Pond: Anglo-American Film Relations before 1930* (Trowbridge, Wilts: Flicks Books, 2002); Gifford, Denis, *British Animated Films, 1895–1985* (Jefferson, NC, and London: McFarland, 1987); White, Brian, 'Obituary: Sid Griffiths, *Film and Television Technician*, March, 1968.

FILMOGRAPHY: *Jerry the Troublesome Tyke* (series, co-dir. Bert Bilby, 1925–7); *Tropical Breezes* (co-dir. Bert Bilby, 1930); *Colonel Capers*; *On the Farm* (co-dir. Brian White) (1933); *You're Telling Me* (1939).

GRIGSBY, Michael (1936–)

Michael Grigsby was born in Reading, Berkshire, in 1936. His first job in television was as a Granada cameraman, but while there he bought his own movie camera and formed the independent film-making group Unit Five Seven. Encouraged by Karel Reisz and Lindsay Anderson and part-funded by the BFI Experimental Film Fund, he made two films with the group, *Enginemen* and *Tomorrow's Saturday*, the former being shown in the last of the Free Cinema's programmes at the National Film Theatre.

Even in these early films the quality that so distinguishes Grigsby's later works is already apparent, namely a concern for the lives of ordinary people. As he himself has put it: 'My driving force for the last 20 or so years has been trying to find a way, through films, to give voice to the voiceless' (Grigsby and McLintock, p. 6). Thus, whether he is filming trawler-men (*Deckie Learner*, *A Life Apart*), farm workers (*Working the Land*), Eskimos (*The People's Land*), the survivors on both sides of the Vietnam War (*I Was a Soldier*, *The Search*, *Thoi Noi*), Indian railwaymen (*Before the Monsoon*), the inhabitants of rural Northern Ireland (*Too Long a Sacrifice*) or the generally dispossessed (*Living on the Edge*), Grigsby does his utmost to let people speak for themselves. 'People are perfectly capable of talking in their

own terms and we should allow them to do so' (Petley, 1981, p. 12).

This concern for both his subjects and his audience helps to explain the distinctive look of Grigsby's films. The camera often lingers on people after they have finished speaking, and the action often pauses for long landscape shots that, though often remarkable in themselves, seem to play no obvious narrative role – most strikingly in *Before the Monsoon*, *Too Long a Sacrifice*, *Hidden Voices* and *Lockerbie: A Night Remembered*. But as Grigsby explains:

> what I try to do is to find the frame which will allow one just to watch and absorb what is going on in front of one without us having to interfere with the people, with the subject one is making the film about. I think it is very important to see the context in which people live and work, because without a context how can you understand how people function? (Petley, 1981, p. 12)

If the calmness of the resulting gaze puts one in mind of Flaherty, the other obvious influence on Grigsby is Jennings. This is clear in his intense feeling for landscape, both urban and rural, but it is also evident in the remarkable way in which he uses sound and image, often in highly effective counterpoint, in two of his finest works, *Living on the Edge* and *The Time of Our Lives*. Impossible here not to think of *Listen to Britain* (Humphrey Jennings, 1942), but impossible, too, not to watch these images of the desolation and fragmentation of Thatcherised Britain and wonder if more apt titles might not have been borrowed from Jennings, such as *The Dim Little Island* or *A Defeated People*.

(Julian Petley)

BIBLIOGRAPHY: Corner, John, *The Art of Record* (Manchester: Manchester University Press, 1996); Grigsby, Mike and Nicolas McLintock, 'The State We're In', *Dox*, Summer 1995, pp. 6–10; Petley, Julian, 'Mike Grigsby', *Primetime*, Autumn 1981, pp. 11–12; Petley, Julian, 'Out of the Perpetual Present' and 'After Free Cinema – Mike Grigsby', *Monthly Film Bulletin*, June 1987, pp. 168–9, 192.

FILMOGRAPHY (apart from *Enginemen* – all television): *Enginemen* (1959); *Tomorrow's Saturday* (1962); *Unmarried Mothers* (1963); *Take It or Leave It; Men in Prison, Young Offenders, Women in Prison – Inside* (1965); *The Pommies – This England; A World Inside – This England* (1966); *Death by Misadventure: S.S. Lusitania* (1967); *If the Village Dies; Deep South; Stones in the Park* (contributing dir.) (1969); *I Was a Soldier* (1970); *A Well Kept Secret; Working the Land* (1972); *A Life Apart: Anxieties in a Trawling Community* (1973); *A Life Underground* (1974); *The Eskimos of Pond Inlet: The People's Land – Disappearing World* (1976); *The Roots of Violence, State of Emergency, The Seeds of Democracy – Before the Monsoon* (1979); *For My Working Life* (1981); *Too Long a Sacrifice* (1985); *Living on the Edge – Viewpoint '87* (1987); *Dear Mr Gorbachev; The Silent War – True Stories* (1990); *The Search* (1991); *Thoi Noi* (1992); *The Time of Our Lives – Fine Cut* (1993); *Pictures on a Piano – Sound on Film* (1994); *Hidden Voices – Fine Cut* (1995); *Living with the Enemy – Witness* (1996); *The Score; Lockerbie: A Night Remembered* (1998); *Billion Dollar Secret; The Voice Box – Sound on Film* (1999); *Solway Harvester: Lost at Sea – Everyman* (2001); *Rehearsals* (2005).

GROSS, Anthony (1905–1984) and Hector HOPPIN

Anthony Gross, born in Dulwich, south London, on 19 March 1905, was one of England's foremost twentieth-century painters and engravers. His paintings and etchings reflect his love of European and North African vistas; and his stylistic diversity ranges from line drawing to Rembrandt-influenced landscapes and neo-abstract prints. Studies at the Central School of Art and Design and the Slade School of Fine Art in London were followed by periods at the Académie Julian, Paris, and the Academia de San Fernando, Madrid. In 1930 he set-

tled in Paris and began exhibiting. Animation work began in 1931 when he joined forces with another Julian student, the wealthy American expatriate Courtland 'Hector' Hoppin. The pair established an animation studio, 'Animat', and started work on *Une Journée en Afrique*, seemingly unreleased on completion in 1933. Production also began on *Les Funerailles* (1932–4) and their most famous work, *La Joie de vivre*, completed in 1934 and the only early film to survive. Aside from financial backing, Hoppin provided photographic and compositional skills, but despite its shared directorial credit *La Joie de vivre*, like the later films, is plainly dominated by Gross' graphic flare and distinctive linear style. Hungarian Tibor Harsanyí composed an attractive score, enhancing the film's visual ballet, where nature imagery is juxtaposed with pylons, train lines and other manifestations of industrialisation, and its playful narrative of a boy pursuing two girls with one of the girls' lost shoes.

The success of *La Joie de vivre* led to Gross and Hoppin moving to London to establish an animation outfit at Alexander Korda's London Films. The immediate result was *Fox Hunt* (1936), less visually inventive but attractive in Technicolor and lightly satirical; the fox leads the hunt onto London's new arterial route, the Great West Road. Contracted to assist in general design matters at London Films, Gross became unhappy with his assignments and returned to Paris in 1937; no further Korda cartoons emerged. Gross quickly began work on an ambitious scheme for a feature-length colour adaptation of Jules Verne's *Around the World in Eighty Days*. In 1938 gouaches from the film were exhibited at the City of Paris Petit Palais exhibition, but further production was curtailed by the outbreak of war. Returning to Britain, Gross was appointed an Official War Artist, travelling with army forces in the Middle East, India and France. Subsequent attempts to complete *Eighty Days* were blocked by Korda's ambition to make his own live-action version; with financial help from the BFI, the finished sequences, flamboyantly stylised to reflect the adventures' geographic locations, were finally assembled in 1955 into an eighteen-minute version entitled *Indian Fantasy*, with a narration by Donald Pleasence. In later life Gross remained productive with prints, engravings, paintings and book illustrations of literary classics. He served as President of the Film Jury at Annecy in 1973, and died on 8 September 1984 in Le Boulvé, France, acknowledged as an innovative force in British animation.

(Geoff Brown and Paul Wells)

BIBLIOGRAPHY: Bendazzi, Giannalberto, *Cartoons* (London and Paris: John Libbey, 1994); Gross, Mary and Peter (eds), *Anthony Gross* (London: Scolar Press, 1992).

FILMOGRAPHY (all films co-directed by Gross and Hoppin): *Une Journée en Afrique* (Fr, 1931–3); *Les Funerailles* (Fr, 1932–4); *La Joie de vivre* (Fr, 1932–4); *Fox Hunt* (1936); *Around the World in Eighty Days* (unfinished, 1937–9; short version, *Indian Fantasy*, completed in 1955).

GROSS, Terence (1958–)

Terence Gross was born in London on 14 February 1958. He established himself as a director of commercials, music promos and instructional films, some on video, including a seven-part series on *Elements of Acting*. In 1997 he wrote and directed *The Sin Eater*, a witty little film about sin, sex, food and death in an isolated rural setting. The same elements creep into the erratically surreal *Hotel Splendide* (2000), in which the vigorous Kath (Toni Colette) returns to disrupt a family still dominated by their dead health-fetishist mother. Inconsistencies, ramshackle plotting and a weak end drain enjoyment from Gross' rich visuals and the eccentric performances of Daniel Craig, Stephen Tompkinson, Helen McCrory, Peter Vaughan and Katrin Cartlidge, but the film still marked an impressive feature debut.

In 2001 Gross was invited to Hollywood to direct a modestly budgeted remake of Roger Corman's *The Day the World Ended* for HBO. He seems uncertain how seriously to take the dated B-movie plot, but delivers watchable entertainment, helped by a non-computer-generated monster and likeable performances from Nastassja Kinski and Randy Quaid. Gross stayed on in America to make a documentary about the Dutch landscape painter Luc Leestemaker.

(Robert Murphy)

FILMOGRAPHY: *Streetsense* (doc. short, 1988); *Elements of Acting* (series, 1990); *The Sin Eater* (short, 1997); *Hotel Splendide* (UK/Fr, 2000); *Leestemaker: Portrait of an Artist* (doc. short, US, 2003).

GROSSO, Nick (c. 1970–)

Born in London to Argentinian parents, Nick Grosso joined the writing group at the Royal Court Young People's Theatre in his early twenties, while also making short amateur films on 8mm. His first play, *Peaches*, charting laddish behaviour in London, was a success when staged in 1994, and was belatedly filmed in 2000 with backing from the Irish Film Board. This could have been a sharp little parable about missed opportunities, but the result is painful to watch apart from a few scattered scenes with Kelly Reilly, Sophie Okonedo and Eddie Marsan – the only convincing characters. Matthew Rhys, struggling with a mock-cockney accent, fails to make the central figure – an ex-student who wastes a summer before going back to his studies – more than fleetingly interesting; and his two mates are gruesome clichés. Dialogue that might have seemed witty on the stage grinds on interminably and there is little in the way of visual interest to compensate. Disparaging critical comment and poor box-office returns opened few doors for Grosso as a director, though he continues to flourish as a playwright.

(Robert Murphy)

FILMOGRAPHY: *Peaches* (Ir, 2000).

GROUNDS, Tony (1957–)

Tony Grounds was born in Ilford, Essex, on 17 November 1957. He found some success in writing for the theatre and adapted one of his plays, *Made in Spain*, for television in 1989. He made his mark as a television writer with episodes of *The Bill* (1989) and *EastEnders* (1990) before moving on to comedy series such as *Gone to the Dogs* (1991) and *Gone to Seed* (1991). In 1997 he wrote a darkly convoluted drama, *Our Boy* (David Evans), about an East End family derailed by the death of their son in a hit-and-run accident. Grounds continued to explore East End life in the miniseries *Births, Marriages and Deaths* (Adrian Shergold, 1999), featuring regular collaborator Ray Winstone alongside Mark Strong and Philip Davis as self-made men whose past sins come back to haunt them.

Tiger Aspect, the successful independent television company responsible for *Births, Marriages and Deaths*, also backed *The Martins*, a feature film written and directed by Grounds. The Martins are the archetypal next-door neighbours from hell – workshy, squalid, noisy and with a pregnant unmarried teenage daughter – but Grounds, consciously reacting against exploitative 'reality' television, switches perspective to tell the story from their point of view. The Martin family turn out to be surprisingly likeable and Grounds elicits thoughtful and refreshingly unclichéd performances from his cast. Dad (Lee Evans) might be a childish loser who waves a gun around too freely, and mother-in-law is played by Linda Bassett in the formidable Peggy Mount tradition; but the teenage children are amiable and obedient, and Mum (Kathy Burke) is an angel in the house and 'sex on legs' to her devoted husband. However, audiences were disappointed in being denied the slapstick romp that the casting and the film's misleading marketing campaign promised and the film attracted only hostile reviews and small audiences.

(Richard Dacre)

BIBLIOGRAPHY: Mulholland, Garry, '"Funlovin" Criminal', *Time Out*, 10 Feb. 1999, pp. 15–16.

FILMOGRAPHY: *The Martins* (2001).

GRUNE, Karl (1890–1962)

Karl Grune was born a Czechoslovakian citizen in Vienna on 22 January 1890. After training as an actor, he toured the Austrian provincial theatres and joined the Volksbühne, before moving to Max Reinhardt's Deutsches Theater in Berlin. In 1918 he met the Austro-Hungarian Max Schach and together they worked as a producer/director team on a number of films including *Die Strasse* (1923), an influential melodrama exploring ordinary lives in the lower reaches of German society. In 1931 they resigned from Emelka studios and together left for Paris and London. In England they made three ambitious films that, had they been successful, would have made Grune and Schach as influential as Alexander Korda within the British film industry.

Abdul the Damned, which features Fritz Kortner as the tyrannical Sultan Abdul Hamid, and explores intrigue and murder in the Ottoman Empire, drew unmistakable parallels with the situation in Nazi Germany. It was critically well received but had insufficient box-office appeal to recoup its lavish budget. *The Marriage of Corbal*, a drama set during the French Revolution, and *Pagliacci*, an adaptation of Ruggero Leoncavallo's popular opera starring the tenor Richard Tauber, shot partly in 'British Chemicolor', were weaker. Their poor commercial returns brought about the collapse of Schach's companies and provoked a major crisis in British film production. Grune's reputation never recovered, though in 1947 he was able to produce *The Silver Darlings* (Clarence Elder and Clifford Evans), a worthy realist drama about the Scottish herring industry. He died in Bournemouth, Dorset, on 2 November 1962.

(Kevin Gough-Yates)

BIBLIOGRAPHY: Breen, Max, 'Send Directors to School', Interview with Karl Grune, *Picturegoer Weekly*, 12 Oct. 1935, p. 10; Eisner, Lotte H., *The Haunted Screen* (London: Thames and Hudson, 1969). Grune, Karl, 'All Films Are Documentary Says Karl Grune', *Picturegoer Weekly*, 23 May 1936, pp. 10–11.

FILMOGRAPHY (UK only): *Abdul the Damned* (1935); *The Marriage of Corbal* (US: *Prisoner of Corbal*); *Pagliacci* (US: *A Clown Must Laugh*) (1936).

GUARD, Candy (1961–)

The animation director Candy Guard told one of her interviewers, 'I'm not interested in animation; it's very boring. What's interesting is telling the story' (Pariser, p. 88). Guard's unique style of animation in her short comic films follows directly from this remark. Echoing the technique of the simplest cartoon drawings, human figures defined by wobbly black outlines strut their stuff with the minimum of props against white backgrounds. In place of visual fireworks, the viewers' attention is focused exactly where Guard wants it, on the biting comic dialogue, and the stories of domestic jealousies, obsessions and fears, always told from a female perspective. Her films owe little to animation traditions: acknowledged influences instead include Mike Leigh, comic papers from her childhood like *The Beano* and the television comedy of French and Saunders.

Born in Ealing in 1961, Candida Guard studied fine art at Newcastle-upon-Tyne Polytechnic, and at St Martin's School of Art and Design in London. Live-action filming was her first goal and remains an aspiration; she shot several films in Super-8, and at Newcastle made the live-action short *And All Those Hours in the Paddy Fields . . .* (1985), which established her fascination with life's trivial round. But animation proved a more practical option, and in 1988 she found her forte in a series of three-and-a-half-minute cartoon squibs, screened on Channel 4. In *Alternative Fringe*, drawn on paper, Guard's hapless, beak-faced protagonist Betty goes in search of a hair make-over, but suffers brutal treatment from the salon apprentice. In *A Little Something*, less tentative in style, Guard's heroine is a teenage girl whose response to life's challenges is to place a paper bag over her head. Weight and dieting are the focus of *Fatty Issues*, while *Wishful Thinking*, particularly sharp in its social comedy, observes Betty and her friend Rose getting their high hopes briskly squashed at a London party. Throughout, jokes are chiefly conveyed by rapid-fire dialogue, mordantly written and delivered, though modest visual enchantment is supplied by the line drawings' low-cost nonchalance, and the patches of pulsating colour placed on clothes, sofas, phones and pictures.

Guard's position as a refreshing, painfully honest commentator on female insecurities was cemented in 1996 with her Channel 4 animation series, *Pond Life*; a second series emerged in 2000. Twenty eleven-minute episodes were produced documenting the attempts of the heroine Dolly Pond – frustrated, single, in big glasses and spotty shorts – to escape her life's cul-de-sac. The production format necessitated working for the first time with a large team of assistants. The process straightened a few kinks in Guard's visual style; but the humour's distinctive quality remained as Dolly faced her challenges, clearly set out in episode titles like *Driving Test*, *Fat* and *Good-Looking Boyfriend*. Guard has also taught animation scriptwriting, and devised newspaper comic strips.

(Geoff Brown)

BIBLIOGRAPHY: Law, Sandra, 'Putting Themselves in the Pictures: Images of Women in the Work of Joanna Quinn, Candy Guard and Alison de Vere', in Jayne Pilling (ed.), *A Reader in Animation Studies* (Sydney: John Libbey, 1997); Pariser, Linda, 'Candy Guard', in Jayne Pilling (ed.), *Women and Animation: A Compendium* (London: BFI Exhibition & Distribution Division, 1992).

FILMOGRAPHY: *And All Those Hours in the Paddy Fields . . .* (1985); *Alternative Fringe*; *Wishful Thinking*; *Fatty Issues*; *A Little Something* (1988); *Untitled*; *What about Me?*; *Moanologue* (1990); *Fantastic Person* (1991); *Ladies* (1997).

GUEST, Val (1911–2006)

Val Guest is a uniquely versatile craftsman with a career in British cinema that stretches over fifty years. After beginning as an actor on stage and screen in the early days of sound pictures, he went on to distinguish himself in the fields of journalism, scriptwriting, songwriting and film production, directing nearly fifty feature films. Although Guest made his name as a writer and director of quick-witted, often bizarre comedies, his serious dramas – which brought a refreshing realist aesthetic to the science-fiction, war and crime genres – may prove the more memorable.

Valmond Guest, born in Maida Vale, London on 11 December 1911, the son of a jute broker, spent his early life in India and London and was educated at Seaford College, Sussex. In the 1930s he single-handedly ran the British office of *The Hollywood Reporter*, and came to the attention of director Marcel Varnel who, in 1935, invited him to join Gainsborough Studios as a writer. Here he worked with Frank Launder, Sidney Gilliat and Alfred Hitchcock, and impressed Varnel so much that he was signed to an exclusive partnership. Guest showed a genuine flair for comedy writing, contributing to scripts for Will Hay classics including *Oh, Mr Porter!* (1937) and *Convict 99* (1938), and pumping out a stream of gags for Arthur Askey and the Crazy Gang.

Guest moved with Gainsborough to Lime Grove studios at the outbreak of the Second World War, and continued to write hit comedies while also serving as an auxiliary fireman. His first directorial commission came from the Ministry of Information, which agreed to him writing and directing *The Nose Has It!* (1942), an Askey short warning of the dangers of coughs and sneezes. On the strength of its success, Gainsborough asked Guest to direct two feature-length scripts for Askey, the racy musical comedies *Miss London Ltd.* and *Bees in Paradise*. However, the fledgling director's most original film of the war years was the quirky *Give Us the Moon* (1944), an absurdist comedy about post-war idlers trying to run a hotel, featuring the teenage Jean Simmons in her first major part. The serious political undertones that Guest gave to the comedy pointed the way to the issue-based cinema he would develop a decade later.

In the post-war years, Guest further developed his reputation for sharp and fast-paced comedies, working with various producers, notably Daniel M. Angel. Increasingly, his films featured the vivacious American actress Yolande Donlan, who became Guest's second wife in 1953. Having written Donlan into one of his *William* films (based on the children's books of Richmal Crompton), Guest went on to create five vehicles for her. Three were comic fantasies, mild in content, brash in execution, written along Ealing lines: *Miss Pilgrim's Progress*,

where Donlan saves a British village from the ravages of town planning; *Mr Drake's Duck*, satirising cold war paranoia and military inefficiency; and *Penny Princess*, where a young American inherits a pocket European republic that manufactures alcoholic cheese.

When Hammer hired Guest to direct his friends Ben Lyon and Bebe Daniels in two spin-offs from their successful radio series *Life with the Lyons*, it seemed he was firmly typecast in comedy. But Hammer surprisingly offered him the chance to explore different genres. Guest pointed the company in a new direction with the taut and eerily atmospheric *The Quatermass Xperiment* (1955), an adaptation of Nigel Kneale's ground-breaking teleplay, and one of the high points of British science-fiction/horror cinema. The same team generated *Quatermass II* (from Kneale's television sequel) and *The Abominable Snowman*, two thoughtful and intelligent films that similarly tapped into widespread fears about government secrecy and nuclear proliferation.

Although Guest did not abandon comedy – his adaptation of the stage musical *Expresso Bongo*, for instance, was a memorable satire on Tin Pan Alley – his new trajectory would lead him to write, produce and direct British cinema's definitive expression of post-war anxiety and ambivalence about scientific progress, *The Day the Earth Caught Fire* (1961). The film won the British Film Academy Award for Best Screenplay, though its strengths lie mainly in the total package of words and images, bonded together with techniques usually associated with social-realist cinema: overlapping dialogue, location filming, hand-held camera, all designed to keep the narrative credible. The same techniques, pictorial sensibilities, pace and conviction are evident in Guest's crime and war films, made at the peak of his powers in the late 1950s and early 60s. *Yesterday's Enemy* and *The Camp on Blood Island* do not flinch from showing the horrors of the war in East Asia, or the amorality encouraged by the struggle for survival. In *Hell Is a City* and *Jigsaw*, Guest enlisted the aid of local police forces to facilitate location shooting and bring a new level of authenticity to the crime melodrama. His fondness for a documentary approach to drama and his increasingly accomplished use of Arthur Grant's shimmering widescreen cinematography are exemplified in *80,000 Suspects* (1963), Guest's homage to one of the key influences on his film-making, Elia Kazan's *Panic in the Streets* (US, 1951).

As the 1960s began to swing, Guest's cinema also became more decadent and flippant, eventually returning to its roots in

comedy via the shenanigans of the James Bond spoof *Casino Royale* and the salaciousness of *Confessions of a Window Cleaner*. Later he worked more in television than cinema, and made his last films in the early 1980s. He usefully revived his Ealing style in *The Shillingbury Blowers*, but the magic of vintage formulae failed to work in *The Boys in Blue*, a slipshod retread of his script for *Ask a Policeman*, with television comedians Cannon and Ball. A career stamped with such energy, tenacity and alertness to the prevailing mood deserved a better swansong. Val Guest died in Palm Springs, California, on 10 May 2006.
(Steve Chibnall)

BIBLIOGRAPHY: BECTU History Project, tape no. 48, held in the BFI National Library, London; Brunas, Michael, Richard Scrivani and Tom Weaver, 'Guest Shots', *Scarlet Street* no.15, 1994, pp. 25–33; Guest, Val, *So You Want to Be in Pictures?* (London: Reynolds and Hearn, 2001); Hunter, I. Q. (ed.), *British Science-Fiction Cinema* (London: Routledge, 1999); Jezard, Adam, 'Reel Life', *Hammer Horror* no. 7, 1995, pp. 8–13; Kinsey, Wayne, 'Val Guest', *The House That Hammer Built* no. 11, 1999, pp. 117–21.

FILMOGRAPHY: *The Nose Has It!* (short, 1942); *Miss London Ltd.* (1943); *Give Us the Moon*; *Bees in Paradise* (1944); *I'll Be Your Sweetheart* (1945); *Just William's Luck* (1947); *William Comes to Town* (1948); *Miss Pilgrim's Progress*; *Murder at the Windmill* (US: *Mystery at the Burlesque*) (1949); *The Body Said No!*; *Mr Drake's Duck* (1950); *Penny Princess* (1952); *The Runaway Bus* (1953); *Life with the Lyons* (US: *Family Affair*); *Dance Little Lady*; *The Lyons in Paris*; *Men of Sherwood Forest* (1954); *Break in the Circle*; *The Quatermass Xperiment* (US: *The Creeping Unknown*); *They Can't Hang Me* (1955); *It's a Wonderful World*; *The Weapon*; *Quatermass II* (US: *Enemy from Space*) (1956); *The Abominable Snowman* (US: *The Abominable Snowman of the Himalayas*); *Carry on, Admiral* (US: *The Ship Was Loaded*); *Up the Creek* (1957); *Further up the Creek*; *Life Is a Circus* (1958); *The Camp on Blood Island*; *Expresso Bongo*; *Yesterday's Enemy* (1959); *Hell Is a City*; *The Full Treatment* (US: *Stop Me before I Kill!*) (1960); *The Day the Earth Caught Fire* (1961); *Jigsaw* (1962); *80,000 Suspects* (1963); *The Beauty Jungle* (US: *Contest Girl*, 1964); *Where the Spies Are* (1966); *Assignment K*; *Casino Royale* (co-dirs. John Huston/Ken Hughes/Robert Parrish/Joe McGrath, 1967); *When Dinosaurs Ruled the Earth*; *Toomorrow* (1970); *Au Pair Girls* (1972); *Confessions of a Window Cleaner* (1974); *The Diamond Mercenaries* (US: *Killer Force*, 1975); *The Shillingbury Blowers* (US: *And the Band Played On*, 1979); *The Boys in Blue* (1983).

GUILLERMIN, John (1925–)

John Guillermin was born to French parents in London on 11 November 1925. Following Cambridge and war service with the RAF, he worked as an assistant on French documentaries. He entered the British film industry in humble circumstances, writing scripts for Robert Jordan Hill's low-budget films featuring the forgotten, rubber-necked comic Ben Wrigley. A suspense thriller, *Torment* (1949), gave him his first directing experience; other minor films followed. A French critic, writing much later, called Guillermin 'the Paganini of *mise en scène*' (quoted in Durgnat, p. 218). But even in his early films he showed a penchant for oddly angled shots, mobile camerawork and other tricks meant to galvanise his scripts into life.

Guillermin finally established himself with the Group 3 comedy *Miss Robin Hood* (1952), featuring Richard Hearne and Margaret Rutherford. The mode was eccentric, Ealing-esque comedy; Guillermin pushed the style hard – not to the film's advantage. A quieter, more disciplined manner appeared in a well-received children's film *Adventure in the Hopfields* (1954); the adult drama *Thunderstorm*, set in a Spanish fishing village, also adopted a simpler style. But Guillermin's way forward lay with energetic thrillers and dramas, often caustically reflecting contemporary British life. *Town on Trial* (1957) set the template with its story of a CID superintendent (John Mills, unusually bullish) solving an unpleasant murder in a cosy country town. *I Was Monty's Double* (1958) usefully matched Guillermin's jaunty manner with the tall but true story of the actor M. E. Clifton-James' wartime impersonation of General Montgomery. *The Day They Robbed the Bank of England* (1960) offered an equally skilful mix of suspense and humour, while *Never Let Go* (1960) startled many with its violent surface and decidedly non-comic turn by Peter Sellers as a car theft gang's sadistic boss. The visual cut and thrust of these films set Guillermin apart from many British directors of his generation, and by the early 1960s he looked like one of Britain's liveliest and most versatile younger directors. *Waltz of the Toreadors* (1962), a boisterous stab at Gallic sauciness adapted from Jean Anouilh's play, was followed by *Tarzan Goes to India* (1962), the second of two modernised Tarzan adventures made on location, and the interesting end of Empire film, *Guns at Batasi* (1964).

Guillermin's genre work impressed Hollywood, though his first non-British film of the 1960s, the American-French production *Rapture* (1965), a mannered account of a retarded girl and a man on the run, too obviously aimed for art. Thereafter, box-office concerns became paramount. The First World War epic *The Blue Max* (1966), filmed in Ireland, established the new

Guillermin norm with length, width and spectacular action (aerial dogfights were the work of a second unit directed by Anthony Squire). *Guns at Batasi*, *Rapture* and *The Blue Max* were all made for 20th Century-Fox and henceforth Guillermin pursued his career in Hollywood. His American productions reached a climax with *The Towering Inferno* (1974) – rampant all-star silliness with splendid pyrotechnics but little spark of imagination – and *King Kong* (1976), an enjoyable, teasing pastiche unfairly mauled by critics.

Guillermin's British swansong was the lavish Agatha Christie thriller, *Death on the Nile* (1978), handsomely shot on Egyptian locations, good for star-spotting, but a film with the pace of a tortoise. By this point Guillermin had become a Paganini with no tunes left to play. His output in America slithered downhill with the weak comic-strip nonsense of *Sheena* and *King Kong Lives*, and a final television Western, *The Tracker* (1988), featuring Kris Kristofferson.

(Geoff Brown)

BIBLIOGRAPHY: Durgnat, Raymond, *A Mirror for England* (London: Faber and Faber, 1970); Guérif, François, 'John Guillermin, l'homme à toute faire', *Positif*, Nov. 1968, pp. 35–8.

FILMOGRAPHY: *Torment* (US: *Paper Gallows*, 1949); *Smart Alec*; *Two on the Tiles*; *Four Days* (1951); *Song of Paris* (US: *Bachelor of Paris*); *Miss Robin Hood* (1952); *Strange Stories* (co-dir. Don Chaffey); *Operation Diplomat* (1953); *Adventure in the Hopfields*; *The Crowded Day* (1954); *Thunderstorm* (aka *Tormenta*); *Dust and Gold*; *Double Jeopardy* (1955); *Town on Trial* (1957); *The Whole Truth*; *I Was Monty's Double* (1958); *Tarzan's Greatest Adventure* (1959); *The Day They Robbed the Bank of England*; *Never Let Go* (1960); *Waltz of the Toreadors*; *Tarzan Goes to India* (1962); *Guns at Batasi* (1964); *The Blue Max* (1966); *New Face in Hell* (aka *P.J.*, US); *House of Cards* (US, 1968); *The Bridge at Remagen* (US, 1969); *El Condor* (US, 1970); *Skyjacked* (aka *Sky Terror*, US, 1972); *Shaft in Africa* (US, 1973); *The Towering Inferno* (co-dir. Irwin Allen, US, 1974); *King Kong* (US, 1976); *Death on the Nile* (aka *Agatha Christie's Death on the Nile*, 1978); *Mr Patman* (aka *Crossover*, Can, 1980); *Sheena* (US, 1984); *King Kong Lives* (US, 1986).

GUNDREY, V. Gareth (1893–1965)

Victor Gareth Gundrey was born in London in 1893, seemingly under an unlucky star. After four years serving with honours in the First World War, he was shot in the leg shortly before the Armistice; for the rest of his life he wore an aluminium artificial leg, or used crutches. In 1923 he joined Gaumont as scenario editor and later became their production manager, collaborating with Victor Saville and Maurice Elvey on a string of successful films, including *Hindle Wakes* (Maurice Elvey, 1927) and *Roses of Picardy* (Maurice Elvey, 1927). Relations between them were not always cordial; and after directing a silent drama, *The Devil's Maze* (1929), he left the company.

Gainsborough's Michael Balcon now commissioned Gundrey to prepare a script for the film of *Journey's End* to be shot in America, and proposed him as the film's director. But James Whale, director of the original play, had fiercer champions, and once appointed he abandoned Gundrey's script. Gundrey continued working for Balcon, directing four talkies at Gainsborough. Surviving evidence reveals a director with the flimsiest visual sense, but a sturdy concern for good box-office properties. He showcased Ivor Novello's suffering blind composer in *A Symphony in Two Flats* (1930), and squeezed Dartmoor locations into the static set-ups of *The Hound of the Baskervilles* (1931). *The Stronger Sex* (1931), a triangular drama with a colliery background, equally benefited from exterior shooting.

Gundrey then withdrew from film-making. He joined the Film Rights agency, ran a second-hand bookshop, worked for the RAF in the Second World War and subsequently sought what employment he could. By the time he died, on 22 July 1965, his role in Britain's burgeoning film industry had long been forgotten.

(Geoff Brown)

BIBLIOGRAPHY: Aldgate, Tony, 'Loose Ends, Hidden Gems and the Moment of "Melodramatic Emotionality"', in Jeffrey Richards (ed.), *The Unknown 1930s: An Alternative History of the British Cinema 1929–1939* (London: I. B. Tauris, 1998).

FILMOGRAPHY: *The Devil's Maze* (1929); *Just for a Song*; *A Symphony in Two Flats* (1930); *The Stronger Sex*; *The Hound of the Baskervilles* (1931).

GUNN, Gilbert (1905–1967)

Gilbert Gunn was born in Glasgow in 1905. After gaining experience as a playwright, composer and theatrical producer, he joined Associated British in 1937 as a scriptwriter. During the Second World War he directed propaganda and instructional films for the Ministry of Information and the armed services, and continued making documentaries until the late 1940s.

Gunn returned to Associated British to script the Ken Annakin film *Landfall* (1949), a satisfying story of love across the class barriers that epitomises the ethos of post-war welfare state Britain. He was then asked to organise *The Elstree Story*, a compilation film to celebrate the studio's twenty-fifth anniversary. Its success led to him being given two second features to direct, *The Good Beginning* and *Valley of Song*. Gunn made the most of the opportunity and *Valley of Song* in particular, a gentle comedy about the rivalry between two choirs, with a good script and an excellent Welsh cast, revealed him to be a talented feature director. *The Strange World of Planet X*, a science-fiction film shot on a shoestring, whose special effects – produced by magnifying insects – still induce a shudder, demonstrated his versatility, but he returned to comedy with the jolly *Girls at Sea* and its successor, *Operation Bullshine*.

Gunn seemed poised to move on to more prestigious projects, but like many directors of his generation, he was left behind by the cultural revolution of the 1960s. He made *What a Whopper!*, a family film starring Adam Faith, a host of comedians and the Loch Ness monster, and *Wings of Mystery* and *The Young Detectives* for the Children's Film Foundation. But by 1965

he was reduced to making a series of short instructional films about golf, *Golf for All*. He died on 6 December 1967 in Finchley, north London.
(Linda Wood)

BIBLIOGRAPHY: 'Character behind the Camera, No. 1. Director Gilbert Gunn', *ABC Film Review*, Oct. 1956, p. 15; Obituary, *The Daily Cinema*, 8 Dec. 1967, p. 7.

FILMOGRAPHY: Non-fiction: *Royal Observer Corps* (1941); *Is Your Journey Really Necessary*; *The Owner Goes Aloft*; *Be Prepared*; *Birth of a Tank*; *Women Away from Home* (1942); *Doing Without*; *Firewatch Dog*; *The Sacred Flame*; *Canteen Command*; *Catering*; *Order of Lenin* (1943); *Tyneside Story*; *Outworking*; *Careless Talk*; *Men from the Sea*; *Burning Results* (1944); *The Star and the Sand*; *Housing in Scotland* (1945); *Routine Job*; *Country Policeman* (1946); *Return to Action* (1947); *Centuries Between* (1948); *Beethoven or Boogies* (1949); *Golf for All* (series, 1965).
Fiction: *Elstree Story*; *The Good Beginning* (1952); *Valley of Song* (aka *Men Are Children Twice*, 1953); *My Wife's Family* (1956); *The Strange World of Planet X* (aka *The Cosmic Monster*/*The Crawling Horror*/*The Crawling Terror*); *Girls at Sea* (1958); *Operation Bullshine* (1959); *What a Whopper!* (1961); *Wings of Mystery*; *The Young Detectives* (serial) (1963).

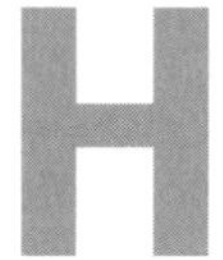

HAGGAR, William (1851–1925)

No other early British screen director shared William Haggar's range of experience in cinema, fairground and the theatre, but the Welsh-based pioneer is chiefly known for his film-making, and particularly for his advanced use of editing and depth of staging in his robust melodramas and crime films. Of more than thirty documented films made between 1901 and 1908, only four shorts are known to survive in their entirety. Yet two of Haggar's extant films, *A Desperate Poaching Affray* (1903) and *The Life of Charles Peace* (1905), a potted biopic of a murderer hanged in 1879, are among the most important British films of the twentieth century's first decade.

Arthur William Haggar was born in Dedham, Essex, in March 1851. He became a peripatetic musician, then a stage carpenter before joining a travelling theatre company and later forming his own troupe as an actor-singer and manager, performing with his wife, Sarah, often in Shakespeare. After acquiring a Wrench projector in 1898, he ran a travelling cinema (Bioscope), appearing regularly at fairgrounds in the west of England and the South Wales coalfields.

Haggar made his own films from around 1902, most of which were distributed by Gaumont, Charles Urban or the Warwick Trading Company. The film-maker's 'stock company' was his own family (eight of his eleven children appeared in his films, with son Walter as lead in the *Charles Peace* film, for example). Haggar drew on his rural background and early experiences of impoverishment to make several poaching films. One, *The Salmon Poachers*, sold more copies in pre-rental days than any other Gaumont film made in Britain up to that time. His screen melodramas included truncated versions of stage plays (sometimes derived from his company's own performances) such as *Duel Scene from The Two Orphans* (1902), *The Sign of the Cross* (1904), *The Dumb Man of Manchester* (1908) and the repertory staple *The Red Barn Crime, or Maria Marten* (1908).

Haggar's films included comedies, burlesques, crime thrillers and trick movies. His *A Desperate Poaching Affray*, including Haggar's earliest extant panning shot, is one of two or three British films that influenced early narrative drama in the United States, particularly the development of the chase film. It featured several shootings during the prolonged pursuit of the poachers. Haggar, steeped in the tastes of his proletarian fairground and theatre melodrama audiences, was never averse to using violence in his films, even though his film-making middle period (1903–5) coincided with the rise of puritan religious Nonconformism in Wales.

Mirthful Mary – A Case for the Blacklist (1903) was the first of a humorous trilogy featuring a violent fat woman at odds with the law; and his surviving 1904 film, *The Bathers' Revenge*, is a

perfectly constructed, one-minute park-bench comedy, with son Walter Haggar canoodling in drag as one half of a courting couple. The *Charles Peace* movie – long mistaken for the now-missing 1905 version by Frank Mottershaw of the Sheffield Photo Company – flaunted William Haggar's love of theatre. He employed overt stage sets in the film's first half, and the killer is in heavy stage make-up throughout. The later location scenes are choreographed with typical energy and brio and include a rooftop chase and a hanging scene. The film, interestingly, also has content and stylistic similarities to Mottershaw's *A Daring Daylight Burglary* (1903). Haggar displays fine use of *mis en scène* and makes intelligent use of depth of staging and the frame edges, with characters often running towards the camera before exiting to right or left; re-entering the frame after a cut, moving away from camera. This gave the film immediacy, and injected pace. *Charles Peace* also displays Haggar's empathy with the humours of his predominantly working-class fairground audiences, often cowed at work, chapel and leisure by intolerant authority figures. He even invites the audience's complicity with Sheffield ex-steelworker Peace in a tantalising close-up of the criminal disguised as a churchman. He sends the police off in the wrong direction, then advances to the camera and thumbs his nose, or 'cocks a snook', at the retreating officers – a familiar gesture in early British films.

The Sheepstealer (distributed by Walter Tyler in 1908) was discovered in the 1970s in the extensive collection of the early film educator Abbé Joseph Joye in Switzerland, and identified in the 1990s after restoration by the BFI. The film includes oval portraits of Haggar over its two intertitles, the earliest known UK film identifying a film-maker in this way.

Following the death of his wife, Haggar ceased operating travelling shows and opened a cinema chain in Wales, with members of the family as managers. He died in Aberdare in February 1925. His son William (1871–1935) and his wife Jenny played the leads in Will Jr's only known film as director, *The Maid of Cefn Ydfa – The Love Story of Ann Thomas* (1914) – a surviving version of a lost film made by his father in 1908. It featured, in his film debut as comic relief, Will Fyffe, who would become a leading British screen comedian in the 1930s. Haggar's daughter Lily May Richards' unpublished brief biography traces the main strands of his career and conveys the atmosphere of early Bioscope shows. (David Berry)

BIBLIOGRAPHY: *A Penny for Your Dreams* (television drama-documentary, Ken Howard, S4C/BBC Wales, 1987); Berry, David, *Wales and Cinema: The First 100 Years* (Cardiff: University of Wales Press, 1994); Burch, Noël, *Life to Those Shadows* (London: BFI, 1990); Burch, Noël, *In and out of Synch* (Aldershot, Hants: Scolar Press, 1991); Jenkins, John, 'A Penny for Your Dreams', *Film and TV Technician*, Nov. 1987, pp. 8–9; Richards, Lily May, unpublished biography of William Haggar held in the BFI National Library, London.

FILMOGRAPHY: *The Maniac's Guillotine*; *Duel Scene from The Two Orphans*; *The Wild Man of Borneo*; *True as Steel* (1902); *Mirthful Mary – A Case for the Blacklist*; *Weary Willie and Tired Tim Turn Barbers*; *The Tramp and the Washerwoman*; *The Tramp and the Baby's Bottle*; *A Dash for Liberty, or the Convict's Escape and Capture*; *A Desperate Poaching Affray* (1903); *Whitewashing the Policeman*; *Mirthful Mary in the Dock*; *The Sign of the Cross*; *The Bathers' Revenge*; *Brutality Rewarded*; *The Meddling Policeman*; *Flynn's Birthday Celebrations*; *The Biter Bitten*; *Snowballing* (1904); *The Rival Painters*; *The Squire's Daughter*; *Charles Peace* (aka *The Life of Charles Peace*); *DT's, or the Effects of Drink*; *Fun at the Waxworks*; *Bathing Not Allowed*; *A Boating Incident*; *Two's Company, Three's None*; *The Salmon Poachers – A Midnight Melee*; *Mary Is Dry*; *A Message from the Sea* (1905); *Desperate Footpads* (1907); *The Red Barn Crime, or Maria Marten*; *The Dumb Man of Manchester*; *The Maid of Cefn Ydfa*; *The Sheepstealer* (1908).

HAGGARD, Piers (1939–)

Piers Haggard, a distant relation of the writer H. Rider Haggard, was born in London on 18 March 1939. During the 1960s he worked at both the Royal Court Theatre and the National Theatre, as well as being one of Michelangelo Antonioni's assistants on *Blow-up* (1966). *I Can't . . . I Can't*, his first feature film, was a downbeat drama about marital difficulties and sexual repression. By contrast, *Blood on Satan's Claw*, his second feature, was an impressive tale of demonic possession in seventeenth-century rural England. It shared with other British horror films from the late 1960s and early 70s an anti-authoritarian attitude and a sympathetic portrayal of the younger generation, but Haggard's unflinchingly realistic approach to the story made it one of the more disturbing films of its type.

Haggard's subsequent cinematic career has been uneven. *The Fiendish Plot of Dr Fu Manchu*, which turned out to be Peter Sellers' final film, was an embarrassingly weak comedy (with sections directed by Sellers himself rather than by Haggard). *Venom* was an enjoyable but silly thriller featuring scene-stealing performances from Sterling Hayden, Klaus Kinski and Oliver Reed, while *A Summer Story* was a well-crafted adaptation of a John Galsworthy story.

Haggard has also been active as a television director since the mid-1960s. His early credits include several television plays as well as a contribution to the television series *Callan*. In 1978 he directed both Dennis Potter's ground-breaking *Pennies from Heaven*, and *Quatermass*, a highly effective revival of the 1950s' television science-fiction series, written by the original author Nigel Kneale, and featuring John Mills as Professor Quatermass. A shortened version was released in some markets under the title *The Quatermass Conclusion*. He was also responsible for *Centrepoint* (1990), a Channel 4 drama serial written by Nigel Williams, with Murray Head as a ravaged 1960s' radical returning from the dead to trouble his now-affluent family. Haggard turned back to witchcraft with the musical *Which Witch* in 1992; though popular with witches and Norwegians, it failed to attract a broad enough audience to survive in the West End. Haggard continues to work regularly in television, latterly on comedy-drama series such as *Big Bad World* (1999); his last feature film was an unassuming romantic comedy, *Conquest*, set in a tiny rural community in Saskatchewan.

(Peter Hutchings)

BIBLIOGRAPHY: Christy, George, 'The Great Life', *Hollywood Reporter*, 29 July 1988, p. 47; Haggard, Piers, 'The Importance of Being Honest', *Screen International*, 25 Oct. 1975, p. 21; Vaines, Colin, 'Jumping in at the Deep End', *Screen International*, 13 Mar. 1982, p. 20.

FILMOGRAPHY: *I Can't . . . I Can't* (1969); *Blood on Satan's Claw* (aka *Satan's Skin*, 1970); *The Fiendish Plot of Dr Fu Manchu* (1980); *Venom* (1981); *A Summer Story* (1987); *Conquest* (UK/Can, 1998).

HALAS, John (1912–1995) and Joy BATCHELOR (1914–1991)

John Halas was born in Budapest on 16 April 1912; Joy Batchelor in Watford, Hertfordshire, on 22 May 1914. The couple initially worked as a graphic design partnership in the pre-war period and married in 1940, when they also founded the Halas and Batchelor studio to make animated advertisements for clients of the J. Walter Thompson agency, such as Kelloggs and Lux. Their work was immediately identifiable by its combination of Disney-style characters and Eastern European aesthetics (largely a product of Halas' training under former Bauhaus tutors, Alexander Bortnyik and Laszlo Moholy-Nagy). The Ministry of Information, recognising the capacity of animated films to entertain as well as educate, invited the couple to make wartime public information and propaganda shorts. *Dustbin Parade* (1941), about recycling materials for munitions, and *Filling the Gap* (1941), concerning the effective deployment of garden space for growing vegetables and other foodstuffs, are two examples of the seventy artful but highly engaging cartoon films made by the studio addressing domestic, government and military needs.

Promotional and instructional films made by the studio, including the Admiralty-sponsored *Handling Ships* (1944–5), and *Water for Fire Fighting* (1948), a 3-D model animation made for firefighter recruitment purposes, led to an acceptance of animation as a mode of expression that could engage with mature subjects and serious themes. The studio was commissioned by Chancellor of the Exchequer Sir Stafford Cripps to make a series of cartoons featuring the sourpuss 'Charley', a vociferous opponent of the proposed welfare state reforms – and self-evidently in the wrong. Similarly, *The Shoemaker and the Hatter* (1949) and *Think for the Future* (1949) were commissioned by the US government to promote Marshall Aid and post-war European co-operation.

Halas and Batchelor also used animation in the service of high art, making the *Poet and Painter* series for the 1951 Festival of Britain and such experiments as *The Owl and the Pussycat* (1952), a 3-D stereoscopic short based on Edward Lear's nonsense poem; *The Figurehead* (1953), a puppet animation with a progressive score by Matyas Seiber, a student of Bartok; and *Ruddigore* (1964), a cartoon adaptation of the Gilbert and Sullivan opera. They are best known, however, for their adaptation of George Orwell's *Animal Farm* (1954). Rumours persist that the film was funded by a CIA covert operation, but Halas insisted that it was humanist and anti-totalitarian rather than anti-Communist, and the film is a considerable achievement: a feature-length work of poignancy and affect that revises our expectations of animal characters as comic or sentimental figures. The sombre satire of Orwell's novel is muted by a controversially upbeat ending in which the animals once again mobilise in resistance to authoritarian leadership, but the film's highly politicised viewpoint still seems a bold and unusual one, particularly within the context of the British film industry of the 1950s.

Further innovation occurred through Halas and Batchelor's animated bridging sequences in *Cinerama Holiday*, designed for a three-screen 'half-cylinder' projection; their 'Foo Foo' cartoons (1960) for ABC-Television, featuring an Emile Cohlesque matchstick character with echoes of Otto Mesmer's early Felix the Cat cartoons; and the part BBC-funded *Tales of Hoffnung* series (1964–7), animating Gerard Hoffnung caricatures. The studio was sold to Tyne-Tees Television in the early 1970s, resulting in Halas and Batchelor making popular Saturday-morning cartoons like *The Jackson Five* (1972) and *The Osmonds* (1973). Later in the decade they broke free to engage in further experimental film-making in the area of computer animation, and international co-productions. Halas published *Masters of Animation* in 1987 and served as President of the International Animated Film Association (ASIFA). Joy Batchelor kept a lower profile but she was undoubtedly a brilliant and influential designer and animator. She died in 1991, followed four years later by her husband. They leave a legacy in the hands of their daughter Vivien, and an extraordinary archive of work that defines some of the greatest achievements in British animation.

(Paul Wells)

BIBLIOGRAPHY: Halas, John, *Master of Animation* (London: BBC Books, 1987); Manvell, Roger, *The Animated Film* (London: Sylvan

Press, 1954); Manvell, Roger, *Art and Animation: The Story of Halas & Batchelor Animation Studio 1940–1980* (Keynsham, Avon: Clive Farrow, 1980).

SELECTED FILMOGRAPHY: *Train Trouble* (1940); *Digging for Victory* (1942); *Charley's March of Time* (1947); *Magic Canvas* (1948); *Moving Spirit* (1951); *The Owl and the Pussycat* (1952); *The Figurehead* (1953); *Animal Farm* (1954); *History of the Cinema* (1957); *Hamilton the Musical Elephant* (1961); *Automania 2000* (1963); *Ruddigore* (1964); *The Tales of Hoffnung* (series, 1964–7); *Flurina* (1970); *Autobahn* (1979); A *Memory of Moholy-Nagy* (1990); *Know Your Europeans* (1995).

HAJAIG, Hadi

Hadi Hajaig graduated from the London College of Printing in 1994 and spent several years setting up his debut feature *The Late Twentieth*, eventually completing it in 2002. A thriller about a man who wreaks vengeance on London's low-life criminals after seeing his girlfriend gunned down in a supermarket robbery, it was kindly received by some film critics, but proved too amateurish to get much exposure in cinemas. Hajaig attracted enough attention to raise a £2 million budget for his second film, *Puritan*, a melodrama about a fake medium (Nick Moran) confronted by the reality of the supernatural.

(Robert Murphy)

FILMOGRAPHY: *The Late Twentieth* (2002); *Puritan* (2005).

HALDANE, Bert

For a director who worked on three of the British industry's most prestigious features of the mid-1910s – *East Lynne*, *Sixty Years a Queen* and *Jane Shore* – Bert Haldane remains an unusually shadowy figure. His birth and death dates are unknown, and even at the peak of his career his name received scant mention in the trade press. Attention instead was focused on the films' showman of a producer, Will Barker. It was Barker who addressed critics at the *Jane Shore* trade show, puffing up chests with talk of his ambitions to make British films match the best product from America and the continent (*Bioscope*, 25 March 1915); Haldane and his American-born co-director F. Martin Thornton must have been seen, if seen at all, only as Barker's handymen. Since then, the spotty print survival of Haldane's films has not encouraged any sustained reassessment.

Haldane worked as a stage manager with Fred Karno before he began his known cinema career directing for Cecil Hepworth. Between 1910 and 1912, from *A Village Love Story* to *Bill's Reformation*, Haldane handled over sixty shorts: moralistic, sentimental tales of tramps, convicts, orphans, policemen, burglars, the blind, the drunk, family members lost or disowned, with Flora Morris the regular heroine. During 1912, Warwick Buckland took over much of the output; Haldane advanced to Barker Motion Picture Photography, single-handedly directing all product until Alexander Butler joined the outfit in 1913. Short films were the initial burden, but Barker's taste for the spectacular soon generated the six-reel *East Lynne* (1913), briefly Britain's longest film, adapted from Mrs Henry Wood's popular novel of elopement, murder and disguise. Photographed with a largely static camera, the complex plot unravels slowly, and the acting remains expostulatory, with much outstretching of hands; yet in both editing and camera positions there are glimpses of cautious creative progress in narrative technique.

Later in the year, national pride prompted a rapturous welcome for *Sixty Years a Queen*, a seven-reel, seemingly jumbled arrangement of reconstructed incidents from Queen Victoria's reign, with Blanche Forsythe, Barker's regular heroine, among the three actresses impersonating the monarch at different ages. The *Bioscope*, quick to hoist the Union Jack, declared it 'one of the finest films ever made' ('A Memorable Triumph', p. 537); no known print survives. In humbler films, Haldane continued to show signs of modest cinematic intelligence. *The Road to Ruin* (1913), independently produced with the stage actor George Gray, decorates its rollicking sermon about the evils of gambling and drink with occasionally deft juggling of foreground and background action. The juggling occurs more pointedly during the Palace Garden scene in Haldane's next history epic, the War of the Roses drama *Jane Shore* (1915), where the drama sparking between the foreground characters is piquantly positioned between a circle of carefree dancers seen in the camera's far distance. With its opening battle of Mortimer's Cross, massed crowds and the pride taken in picturesque locations, *Jane Shore* does indeed make surface headway toward Barker's dream of British super-productions. But the predominant tableau-style staging, the lack of powerful close-ups and an uninviting central performance from the hard-worked Blanche Forsythe combine to produce a film that now seems easier to respect than enjoy.

Among Haldane's other feature work for Barker, *Five Nights* (1915) won extra publicity when the chief constable of Preston announced the naked arm and shoulder of an artist's model (Eve Balfour) as too much to bear, and banned further screenings; the matter ignited industry debate about local administration of censorship. Dignified fare returned in the rousingly patriotic *Jack Tar* (1915), and the handsomely accoutred *Brigadier Gerard* (1915), from Conan Doyle's novel, with the stage actor Lewis Waller making his belated screen debut as the dashing Hussar captain.

During 1915 Haldane left Barker's employment, though in 1918 he returned to an outfit of now reduced ambitions for a version of the Victorian melodrama *The Ticket-of-Leave Man*. Elsewhere, he made assorted fare for Trans-Atlantic and the Birmingham Film Producing Company before settling in to a run of features from 1919 with the newly founded Famous Pictures, using studios at Whetstone. *The Romance of Lady Hamilton* (1919), with Malvina Longfellow, built upon the success of Maurice Elvey's *Nelson* (1918), also with Longfellow, issued three months earlier. Other releases equally relied on the tried, tested and popular, with another revived Victorian melodrama, *The Grip of Iron*, and confections of equal colour. Whatever the films' appeal to audiences, their unoriginal subject matter suggests that, for all his earlier flickers of cinematic sensibility, Haldane was perhaps not best equipped in the 1920s to advance British cinema much further. After the short comedy *Gipsy Blood* (1922), Haldane disappears from view.

(Geoff Brown)

BIBLIOGRAPHY: 'A Memorable Triumph: The First Exhibition of *Sixty Years a Queen*', *The Bioscope*, 6 Nov. 1913, pp. 535, 537; '*Jane Shore*: A Spectacular Triumph', *The Bioscope*, 25 Mar. 1913, p. 1117; Low, Rachael, *The History of the British Film 1906–1914* (London: George Allen & Unwin, 1949); Low, Rachael, *The History of the British Film 1914–1918* (London: George Allen & Unwin, 1950); Williams, David R., 'The *Five Nights* Affair', *Journal of Popular British Cinema* no. 3, 2000, pp. 20–30.

FILMOGRAPHY: Shorts: *A Village Love Story*; *Tried and Found True*; *Coals of Fire*; *Cast Thy Bread upon the Waters*; *Behind the Scenes*; *The Thieves' Decoy*; *The Queen of the May*; *Her Debt of Honour*; *The Miser's Lesson*; *All Is Not Gold That Glitters*; *Dora*; *Circumstantial Evidence*; *Hunger's Curse*; *A Flowergirl's Romance*; *Lust for Gold*; *A Chum's Treachery*; *A Plucky Kiddie*; *The Farmer's Two Sons*; *Woman v. Woman* (1910); *A Fool and His Money*; *A Girl's Love-Letter*; *Right Is Might*; *The Faith Healer*; *The Man Who Kept Silent*; *The Road to Ruin*; *Lottery Ticket No. 66*; *A Touch of Nature*; *A Struggling Author*; *A Nephew's Artifice*; *The Silver Lining*; *Hilda's Lovers*; *The Baby and the Bomb*; *Kiddie*; *The Convict's Sister*; *Elsie the Gamekeeper's Daughter*; *For Better or Worse*; *Jack's Sister*; *The Trail of Sand*; *Proud Clarissa*; *An' Good in the Worst of Us*; *The Torn Letter*; *A Burglar for One Night*; *His Son*; *Wealthy Brother John* (US: *Our Wealthy Nephew John*); *The Foreign Spy*; *A Bid for Fortune*; *The Impediment*; *The Reclamation of Snarky*; *The Broad Arrow* (1911); *The Girl at the Lodge*; *Bill's Temptation*; *A Night of Peril*; *Her Sacrifice*; *The Lieutenant's Bride*; *A Girl Alone*; *Our Bessie*; *The Child Detective*; *Phoebe of the Inn*; *The Deception*; *His Actress Daughter*; *The Blind Heroine*; *Bill's Reformation*; *The Birthday That Mattered*; *A Dumb Matchmaker*; *When Gold Is Dross*; *Ethel's Danger*; *Was He Justified?*; *The Disinherited Nephew*; *Her Better Self*; *Peter Pickles' Wedding*; *Pippin up to His Pranks*; *The Poacher's Fight for Liberty*; *Only an Outcast*; *The Irony of Fate*; *The Little Poacher*; *The Reward of Perseverance*; *His Honour at Stake*; *The Eccentric Uncle's Will*; *The Poacher's Reform*; *The Trail of the Fatal Ruby*; *The Prodigal Wife*; *Won by a Snapshot*; *Muriel's Double*; *A Brother's Sacrifice*; *A Fight for Life*; *The Tell-Tale Umbrella*; *Neighbours*; *How Vandyke Won His Wife*; *For Baby's Sake*; *The Stab of Disgrace*;

Robert's Lost Supper, *Jeff's Downfall*; *How Molly and Polly Got Pa's Consent*; *The Draughtsman's Revenge* (1912); *Mary of Briarwood Dell*; *The Interrupted Honeymoon*; *Suspicious Mr Brown*; *The Price of Deception*; *Alfred Harding's Wooing*; *That Awful Pipe*; *Was He a Coward?*; *Allan Field's Warning*; *A Village Scandal*; *The Debt of Gambling*; *Just Like a Mother*, *Peter Tries Suicide*; *Polly the Girl Scout and Grandpa's Medals*; *The Test*; *A Double Life*; *Binks' Wife's Uncle*; *Uncle as Cupid*; *Never Forget the Ring*; *Now She Lets Him Go Out*; *Polly the Girl Scout and the Jewel Thieves*; *Peter Pens Poetry*; *When Paths Diverge*; *Luggage in Advance*; *Zaza the Dancer*, *Polly the Girl Scout's Timely End*; *A Lucky Escape for Dad*; *Peter's Peril*; *Little Elsie*; *In the Shadow of Darkness*; *Molly's Burglar*, *Fisherman's Luck* (1913); *A Brother's Atonement*; *The Last Encampment*; *Jim the Fireman*; *By His Father's Orders*; *The German Spy Peril*; *Your Country Needs You* (1914); *Beneath the Mask*; *The Barnstormers* (1915); *The Lady Slavey* (aka *The Slavey's Legacy*); *Some Detectives* (1916); *A Boy Scout's Dream; or, How Billie Captured the Kaiser*, *A Birmingham Girl's Last Hope* (aka *The Last Hope*); *Men Were Deceivers Ever*, *The Child and the Fiddler* (1917); *The Affected Detective*; *Auntie's Wedding Present*; *Eliza's Romeo*; *Gipsy Blood* (1922).

Features: *The Fighting Parson* (1912); *East Lynne; Humanity; or, Only a Jew* (co-dir. John Lawson, 1913); *Younita – From Gutter to Footlights*; *Sixty Years a Queen*; *The Road to Ruin* (co-dir. George Gray) (1913); *The Last Encampment*; *The Lure of London*; *The Lights o' London*; *The Last Round*; *As a Man Sows; or, An Angel of the Slums* (1914); *Tommy Atkins*; *Jane Shore* (US: *The Strife Eternal*, co-dir. F. Martin Thornton); *Darkest London; or, The Dancer's Romance*; *The Rogues of London*; *Five Nights*; *Do Unto Others*; *By the Shortest of Heads*; *Brigadier Gerard*; *Jack Tar* (1915); *Truth and Justice* (1916); *The Ticket-of-Leave Man* (1918); *The Romance of Lady Hamilton* (1919); *The Grip of Iron*; *Mary Latimer, Nun*; *The Winding Road* (co-dir. Frank Wilson); *The Woman and Officer 26* (co-dir. Harry Lorraine) (1920).

HALE, Sonnie (1902–1959)

Sonnie Hale's directing career looks curious by any standards. He only has three films to his credit, but these films – all starring his then-wife Jessie Matthews – are key titles in the ambitious production strategy of Gaumont-British studios in the mid-1930s.

John Robert Hale-Monro was born in London on 1 May 1902, the son of actor Robert Hale, and brother of the charming light comedienne Binnie Hale. He made his stage debut aged nineteen and worked extensively in theatre and revue as a comedian. Quick-witted and engaging, but rather weak-looking, he was ideally suited to play the comic sidekick – a characterisation he successfully transferred into several film roles. While appearing on stage in Cochran's revue *One Damn Thing after Another* he met Jessie Matthews with whom he began an affair, which involved them both in messy divorces but eventually resulted in their marriage. Matthews became central to the attempt by Gaumont-British to break into the American market, starring in a series of lavish musicals (in which Hale also appeared) directed by Victor Saville.

Matthews, however, was a difficult figure to work with and when, after the third of these films, Saville left the studio, Hale was

deemed the only other person able to coax a performance out of her. His Matthews musicals are less well regarded than Saville's *Evergreen* (1934) and *First a Girl* (1935), but they are still highly pleasurable, often wittily self-conscious and well paced, despite the inexperience of their director. This may have a lot to do with the strength and continuity of the production team working on the films, and when Gaumont-British collapsed Hale gave up directing. He appeared in two more films – Harry Watt's *Fiddlers Three* (1944) and the ill-fated musical *London Town* (Wesley Ruggles, 1946) – after which he concentrated on his stage work. Sonnie Hale died of myelofibrosis in London on 9 June 1959.
(Lawrence Napper)

BIBLIOGRAPHY: Thornton, Michael, *Jessie Matthews* (London: Granada Publishing, 1975).

FILMOGRAPHY: *Head over Heels*; *Gangway* (1937); *Sailing Along* (1938).

HALL, Peter (1930–)

Peter Hall was born the son of a railwayman in Bury St Edmunds on 22 December 1930. He directed plays while studying at Cambridge and began his professional career working for a variety of repertory companies. While still in his early twenties he was appointed director of London's Arts Theatre, where he scored an early success with the first English-language production of *Waiting for Godot*. In 1960 Hall co-founded the Royal Shakespeare Company and managed it until 1968, by which time he had also moved into film-making.

Work Is a Four Letter Word and *Three Into Two Won't Go* were both part of Jay Kanter's ill-fated UK production programme at Universal. The former, a would-be satirical comic fantasy starring David Warner and Cilla Black, is just the kind of determinedly zany self-indulgence that put nails in the coffin of the British film industry. The latter is an intelligent, incisive study of the *ménage-à-trois* between a frustrated middle-aged businessman (Rod Steiger), his barren wife (Claire Bloom) and a teenage hitch-hiker (Judy Geeson). Adapted by Edna O'Brien from an Andrea Newman novel, its brand of adult domestic drama is usually seen to better advantage on television; in fact, a minor scandal erupted when Universal filmed new scenes for its US television broadcast, without the director's input or approval.

Between these two films Hall made a cinema version of *A Midsummer Night's Dream* under the aegis of the RSC, with a cast including Judi Dench, Helen Mirren, Diana Rigg, Ian Holm and Ian Richardson. Filmed entirely on location using hand-held cameras, it is a ragbag of bright ideas gone awry, with uneven performances, consistently ill-chosen camera angles and ham-fisted editing. After *Perfect Friday*, a lightweight, modish but likeable bank robbery caper with Stanley Baker and Ursula Andress, and a tightly controlled transfer of his RSC production of Harold Pinter's *The Homecoming* for the American Film Theatre series, Hall's involvement in cinema was more sporadic. He became director of the National Theatre and was knighted for services to theatre.

Akenfield, a long-planned dramatised documentary based on Ronald Eyre's book about life in a rural village, won Hall wide critical acclaim. Co-financed by London Weekend Television, it was premiered simultaneously on the ITV network and in cinemas, the first ever such tie-up in the UK. *She's Been Away*, an overwritten Stephen Poliakoff drama made for the BBC, won festival plaudits for the performances of Peggy Ashcroft and Geraldine James but was not widely released. Hall also made television adaptations of his Glyndebourne production of Benjamin Britten's opera *Albert Herring* (1985) and Tennessee Williams' *Orpheus Descending* (US, 1990), as well as a two-part episode, *Jacob* (It/Ger/UK/US, 1994), of a series of biblical stories for international television. After a risible mainstream erotic thriller, *Never Talk to Strangers*, starring Rebecca De Mornay and Antonio Banderas, and *The Final Passage* (1996), a television film about West Indian immigrants scripted by Caryl Philips, Hall returned to the stage.

(Sheldon Hall)

BIBLIOGRAPHY: Gillett, John, 'Film into Detergent', *Sight and Sound*, Winter 1970–1, p. 22; Gow, Gordon, 'In Search of a Revolution', *Films and Filming*, Sept. 1969, pp. 40–6; Houston, Penelope, 'Scripts Unlimited', *Sight and Sound*, Spring 1972, p. 70; Jones, Gareth, '*Akenfield*', *Sight and Sound*, Autumn 1973, pp. 192–3; Whitman, Mark, 'Country Matters', *Films Illustrated*, Nov. 1974, pp. 108–9.

FILMOGRAPHY: *Work Is a Four Letter Word* (1968); *A Midsummer Night's Dream*; *Three Into Two Won't Go* (1969); *Perfect Friday* (1970); *The Homecoming* (US/UK, 1973); *Akenfield* (1974); *Landscape* (short, 1976); *She's Been Away* (1989); *Never Talk to Strangers* (Can/US, 1995).

HAMER, Robert (1911–1963)

Robert James Hamer was born on 31 March 1911 in Kidderminster, Worcestershire. After being sent down from Cambridge, he began his career in films as a cutting-room assistant for Gaumont-British studios in 1934. A year later he joined London Films at Denham, where Alexander Korda had attracted a number of European film-makers to England including Erich Pommer, the producer of German films such as *The Cabinet of Dr Caligari* (Robert Wiene, 1920) and *Metropolis* (Fritz Lang, 1927). When Pommer formed a production company with Charles Laughton, Mayflower Pictures, he asked Hamer to join him and gave him the opportunity to edit *Vessel of Wrath* (Erich Pommer, 1938) and *Jamaica Inn* (Alfred Hitchcock, 1939).

As war approached, Pommer and Laughton left for Hollywood and Mayflower's operations were suspended. Hamer joined the GPO Film Unit under Alberto Cavalcanti, and when Cavalcanti moved to Ealing Studios he recruited Hamer to edit the George Formby vehicle *Turned Out Nice Again* (Marcel Varnel, 1941) and the war films *Ships with Wings* (Sergei Nolbandov, 1941) and *The Foreman Went to France* (Charles Frend, 1942). Hamer was then promoted to associate producer (in effect producer, though this was a credit that studio head Michael Balcon reserved for himself) on *My Learned Friend* (Basil Dearden/Will Hay, 1943), *San Demetrio London* (Charles Frend, 1943) and *Fiddlers Three* (Harry Watt, 1944). He also gained some experience directing, shooting sequences of *San Demetrio London* when Charles Frend fell ill, and reshooting some of the musical parts of *Fiddlers Three*. Cavalcanti then gave him the chance to direct one of the episodes of the omnibus horror film *Dead of Night* (1945). His contribution, 'The Haunted Mirror', has come to be seen as a clever allegory of sexual repression, and the disturbing presence of mirrors was to become a recurring motif in Hamer's films. The allure of a glamorous, sexually charged other world that seduces the hitherto bland and respectable hero of 'The Haunted Mirror' was also apparent in *Pink String and Sealing Wax* (1946), Hamer's first feature film. It was based on a play by Roland Pertwee and is comparable to Gainsborough costume films like *The Man in* Grey (Leslie Arliss, 1943) and *Fanny by Gaslight* (Anthony Asquith, 1944); but in the Gainsborough films passionate love is allowed full rein. In *Pink String and Sealing Wax* young David Sutton (Gordon Jackson) is dazzled by a sexy unscrupulous barmaid, but retrieved for respectable domesticity when she is driven to murder and suicide.

Hamer used Googie Withers, who had played the main female roles in 'The Haunted Mirror' and *Pink String and Sealing Wax*, as the protagonist in his next film, *It Always Rains on Sunday* (1947). Although adapted from a picaresque low-life novel by Arthur La Bern, and set in the East End community of

Robert Hamer (right)

Bethnal Green, the film shows Hamer's admiration for the French poetic realist films of the 1930s. The proliferation of cheery subplots distract too much from the central story of a woman stuck in a dull marriage whose sharp, flashy lover from the past reappears as an escaped convict desperate for food and shelter, but the film is nonetheless a major achievement and was a critical and popular success.

Kind Hearts and Coronets (1949), an ironic comedy based on an obscure novel with an unacceptable title (*Israel Rank* by Roy Horniman), with Alec Guinness playing all the members of an aristocratic family who have to be eliminated by the dispossessed hero (Dennis Price) if he is to succeed to a dukedom, was a less than obvious follow-up. Its reputation as a masterpiece of British cinema only began to coalesce after its ecstatic reception in the United States and France, and Hamer was never to benefit properly from its success. The wit and sophistication, innovatory use of voiceover and refreshingly frank attitudes towards sex and murder have kept *Kind Hearts and Coronets* fresh and popular, but it has tended to overshadow Hamer's career. He had expected to return to the demi-monde of petty crime to make a film set in Soho written by a reformed burglar, Mark Benney, but a critical outcry against films dealing with spivs and the sordid underbelly of British society led to it being shelved. Another project to make a film about the Thompson–Bywaters case, with Margaret Lockwood playing Edith Thompson, who had been hanged in 1923, was considered too daring. Hamer was also enthusiastic about adapting Richard Mason's novel *The Shadow and the Peak*, and shooting it on location in the West Indies, but Balcon was wary of anything so expensive and erotic. He agreed to release Hamer to make a film for his old company, Mayflower, now run by Aubrey Baring and Maxwell Setton.

The Spider and the Fly (1949), set in France in the period leading up to the First World War, is the bleakest of all Hamer's films, a powerful melodrama exploring the triangular relationship between a policeman (Eric Portman), a master thief (Guy Rolfe) and the woman they both love (Nadia Gray). Hamer makes no concessions to the optimism with which most Ealing films end and he found it difficult to adjust to the ethos of the studio when he returned to make *His Excellency* (1951), featuring Eric Portman as a working-class trade union leader appointed Governor of a British colony. It was a task for which he had little interest and the film is unconvincing and carelessly plotted. After it was finished he failed to reach agreement with Balcon on a mutually acceptable project and left Ealing for good.

Hamer's first film on leaving Ealing was *The Long Memory* (1952), produced by Hugh Stewart who had worked with him co-editing *St Martin's Lane W.C.2* (Tim Whelan, 1938). Critics compared it to Marcel Carné's *Quai des brumes* (1938) and there is a similar mood of haunted pessimism. John Mills plays a convict released after serving twelve years in prison for a murder he did not commit and determined on vengeance against those responsible. Visually it is an extraordinary film, which makes exciting use of the desolate landscape around the Thames estuary and ends with the wounded hero chased from Tower Bridge to the mudflats around Gravesend by the man he is supposed to have murdered. The ending is less gloomy than that of *The Spider and the Fly* – the embittered man is redeemed by the love of a wartime refugee whose experience of injustice is even greater than his – but the film is equally uncompromising in its treatment of human suffering and injustice.

Hamer's next film, *Father Brown* (1954), made with backing from the American company Columbia, and starring Alec Guinness as G. K. Chesterton's detective-priest, was well received by critics and public alike. But he squandered his restored reputation on *To Paris with Love* (1955), a frivolous Technicolor comedy of the type that has given British cinema of the 1950s a bad name. Hamer makes the most of a turning point when Alec Guinness' ageing widower realises that he is too old to start a new life with the vivacious young French woman (Odile Versois) whose attentions he has been so flattered by; but there is precious little else to recommend the film. As if to comment on the silliness of the projects offered him by the film industry, Hamer directed an adaptation of Turgenev's *A Month in the Country* (1955) for the television company Rediffusion. An intimate drama where bored, unhappy people yearn for but are never able to achieve happiness in love, it seemed to mirror Hamer's own outlook on life and he evokes superb performances from Margaret Leighton, Michael Gough, Laurence Harvey and Geoffrey Keen.

Hamer's own life seems to have taken a turn for the worse around this time. In the mid-1930s he had married the actress Joan Holt (whose brother Seth Holt worked as an editor and director at Ealing). After the marriage broke up in the 1950s, he began a relationship with Pamela Wilcox, daughter of producer/director Herbert Wilcox, living with her until six weeks before his death. Her autobiography, *Between Hell and Charing Cross*, offers a fascinating insight into Hamer's lifestyle – and his alcoholism, into which she was eventually drawn. Hamer's close friend, the Ealing scriptwriter Diana Morgan, thought that 'probably he would have been happier to live as a homosexual' (quoted in Drazin, 1998, p. 73).

It was not until 1958 that Hamer returned to the cinema. Despite their disagreements at Ealing, Balcon and Hamer maintained amicable relations and it was at Balcon's suggestion that he was taken on to direct an adaptation of Daphne du Maurier's *The Scapegoat*. This was a big-budget production backed by MGM and its story of a bored Englishman tricked into assuming the life of his aristocratic French doppelgänger (with Guinness in both parts) seemed ideal for Hamer. Unfortunately there were disagreements over the script between Guinness, du Maurier, Hamer and Gore Vidal, and the resulting film is a disappointment. Though it begins well it becomes increasingly haphazard and disjointed and Hamer seems not to know what to do with his three leading actresses: Bette Davis, Irene Worth and Pamela Brown. However, he stuck to his vow not to drink while directing, and his own cut of the film, which was jettisoned by MGM, might well have been more interesting than the version released.

Hamer's frustration at the mangling of a film that would have restored his reputation seems to have destroyed any desire he had to reform his life. On his next and last film, *School for Scoundrels* (1960), based on the humorous books by Stephen Potter, drink got the better of him and he was replaced by Cyril Frankel after collapsing on the set. It would be unfair to attribute only the good sequences to Hamer, but it is appropriate that the first half of the film, where the hero played by Ian Carmichael is an incompetent failure at life, is much more satisfying and convincing than the second half, where, with the help of a course in 'lifemanship', he learns how to manipulate the world to his advantage. This was something Hamer himself conspicuously failed to do. He was declared bankrupt in November 1961 and although he completed and sold a script (an adaptation of C. E. Vulliamy's novel *Don among the Dead Men*, made as *A Jolly Bad Fellow* by Don Chaffey in 1963) and worked for a few weeks rewriting David Niven's dialogue for *55 Days at Peking* (Nicholas Ray, 1963), he was unable to overcome his addiction to alcohol and he died of pneumonia on 4 December 1963 at St Thomas' Hospital in London.

Hamer's contribution to British cinema is a significant one, most obviously for the wit and charm of *Kind Hearts and Coronets* and *Father Brown*, but equally for the impressive poetic realism of *It Always Rains on Sunday* and *The Long Memory* – films that showed he had the emotional range, the humanity and the visual imagination to have been one of the world's great film-makers. (Robert Murphy)

BIBLIOGRAPHY: Balcon, Michael, *Michael Balcon Presents . . . A Lifetime in Films* (London: Hutchinson, 1969); Barr, Charles, *Ealing Studios* (London and Newton Abbot, Devon: Cameron & Tayleur/ David & Charles, 1977); Benney, Mark (Henry Ernest Degras), *Almost a Gentleman* (London: Peter Davies, 1966); 'Biography of Robert Hamer', Ealing Studios publicity statement, Dec. 1947, held on microfiche in the BFI National Library, London; Bruce Lockhart, Freda, 'Interview with Hamer', *Sight and Sound*, Oct./Dec. 1951, pp. 74–5; Drazin, Charles, 'Robert Hamer', *London Magazine*, June/July 1995, pp. 87–100; Drazin, Charles, *The Finest Years: British Cinema of the 1940s* (London: André Deutsch, 1998); Kemp, Philip, 'The Long Shadow: Robert Hamer after Ealing', *Film Comment*, May/June 1995, pp. 71–8. Revised and reprinted in Ian MacKillop and Neil Sinyard (eds), *British Cinema of the 1950s: A Celebration* (Manchester: Manchester University Press, 2003); Robert Hamer Special Collection held in the BFI National Library, London; Vincent, John, 'Hamer's Potted Lifemanship', *Films and Filming*, July 1959, p. 27; Wilcox, Pamela, *Between Hell and Charing* Cross (London: George Allen & Unwin, 1977).

FILMOGRAPHY: *Dead of Night* ('Haunted Mirror' episode, 1945); *Pink String and Sealing Wax* (1946); *It Always Rains on Sunday* (1947); *Kind Hearts and Coronets*; *The Spider and the Fly* (1949); *His Excellency* (1951); *The Long Memory* (1952); *Father Brown* (1954); *To Paris with Love*; *Rowlandson's England* (doc. short) (1955); *Bernard Shaw* (doc. short, 1957); *The Scapegoat* (1959); *School for Scoundrels* (co-dir. Cyril Frankel, 1960).

HAMILTON, Guy (1922–)

Though not a director with a distinctively personal vision, Guy Hamilton has been a skilful film-maker, with a particular knack for staging large-scale action sequences. As with John Guillermin and J. Lee Thompson, this talent led him from slick genre films in the 1950s to big-budget international productions in the 1960s.

Born in Paris on 16 September 1922, Hamilton spent his early childhood in France. He obtained his first film job at the Victorine Studios in Nice in 1938, where his duties included acting as clapper-boy for the distinguished French director Julien Duvivier. On the outbreak of war he returned to London, where he worked briefly in the Paramount News film library before joining the Royal Navy. After the war, Hamilton became an assistant director, most importantly on two films directed by Carol Reed, *The Fallen Idol* (1948) and *The Third Man* (1949), where he also doubled for Orson Welles in several long shots. Reed, whom Hamilton later dubbed his cinematic father (McFarlane, p. 273), gave his young assistant more freedom than usual in the industry, and was instrumental in getting him his first job as director, an adaptation of Edgar Wallace's *The Ringer* (1952).

Other modestly budgeted genre films followed. Hamilton seemed most comfortable with scenarios centred on male characters, especially those within a military context. *The Intruder* (1953), his second film, dealt very effectively with soldiers' difficulties adjusting to post-war civilian life; while for all its Boy's Own Paper heroics, the prisoner-of-war drama *The Colditz Story* (1955), his most commercially successful film of the period, offered a nuanced presentation of the intricacies of male camaraderie. Other 1950s' films were more imperfectly realised. Alastair Sim's absorbing performance apart, *An Inspector Calls* (1954) remained a timidly workmanlike version of

J. B. Priestley's play; while craftsmanship could do little to lift Leslie Bricusse's sickly musical vehicle for Max Bygraves, *Charley Moon* (1956). *Manuela* (1957), an unusually torrid melodrama, with Trevor Howard matching his performance in Reed's *Outcast of the Islands* (1952) as a middle-aged man risking all for an exotic charmer, is much more interesting, though it was frowned on by strait-laced British critics.

Hamilton moved to bigger budgets at the end of the 1950s, first with Hill-Hecht-Lancaster's gripping Shaw adaptation *The Devil's Disciple* (1959), where he replaced Alexander Mackendrick, and then, more spectacularly, with the lively war comedy *The Best of Enemies* (1961), an Italian co-production mounted with Dino De Laurentiis. Here he proved himself particularly adept at set-piece action sequences, notably one in which soldiers are trapped by a huge forest fire. Turning down the opportunity to direct *Dr No* (Terence Young, 1962), he took on *The Party's Over*, a low-budget excursion into the world of the Chelsea Set – reckless, arty young people who shocked convention with their irreverent attitude to sex and work. He ran into censorship difficulties and when a cut version of the film was finally released in 1965 he removed his name from the credits in protest.

By this time his career had taken a more conventionally commercial turn. *Goldfinger* (1964), the third James Bond film and the first of four directed by Hamilton, marked the crystallisation of the distinctive Bond mix of action, sex and humour. In no small part this was due to Hamilton's ability to present the film's outrageous and absurd elements – including an Aston Martin equipped with an ejector seat – in a no-nonsense manner that commanded if not belief then at least pleasurable acceptance. Before returning to Bond, he made two more films for Bond producer Harry Saltzman, the dour spy drama *Funeral in Berlin* (1966) and *Battle of Britain* (1969), a war epic that confirmed Hamilton as a director more interested in action highlights than the perfunctorily presented personal stories of his characters. From this perspective, he was the ideal director for the increasingly gadget-dependent Bond films of the 1970s: the chases in cars and speedboats in *Diamonds Are Forever*, *Live and Let Die* and *The Man with the Golden Gun* remain their most memorable sequences.

Hamilton's last few films were uneven. *Force 10 from Navarone* failed to revive the glories of *The Guns of Navarone* (J. Lee Thompson, 1961), and the Agatha Christie mystery *The Mirror Crack'd* became overwhelmed by the presence of so many American stars. By contrast, his second Christie adaptation, *Evil Under the Sun*, proved delightfully witty, revealing a lightness of touch not seen in his work since the 1950s. He retired from the industry after two further films – the hit-and-miss action-adventure *Remo Williams* and the scarcely seen *Try This One for Size*, a flat mélange of Bond ingredients adapted from a James Hadley Chase novel. Hard-working and enterprising, Hamilton's bonhomie and technical skills made him a valued director for big-budget adventures; though his commercial success with glossy thrills was achieved at the expense of earlier and subtler skills in taut story-telling and the celebration of male camaraderie.

(Peter Hutchings)

BIBLIOGRAPHY: Edelman, Rob, 'Guy Hamilton and *The Mirror Crack'd*', *Films in Review*, Feb. 1988, pp. 105–7; Gow, Gordon, 'Get Your Own Way', *Films and Filming*, July 1973, pp. 12–17; McFarlane, Brian, *An Autobiography of British Cinema* (London: Methuen, 1997); Macnab, Geoffrey, 'The Escape Artist', *Sight and Sound*, Sept. 2002, p. 86; Turner, Adrian, *Goldfinger* (London: Bloomsbury, 1998).

FILMOGRAPHY: *The Ringer* (1952); *The Intruder* (1953); *An Inspector Calls* (1954); *The Colditz Story* (1955); *Charley Moon* (1956); *Manuela* (1957); *The Devil's Disciple*; *A Touch of Larceny* (1959); *The Best of Enemies/I due nemici* (UK/It, 1961); *The Party's Over* (1963; rel. 1965); *Man in the Middle* (1963); *Goldfinger* (1964); *Funeral in Berlin* (1966); *Battle of Britain* (1969); *Diamonds are Forever* (1971); *Live and Let Die* (1973); *The Man with the Golden Gun* (1974); *Force 10 from Navarone* (1978); *The Mirror Crack'd* (1980); *Evil Under the Sun* (1981); *Remo Williams: The Adventure Begins . . .* (US, 1985); *Try This One for Size* (*La Grande fauche*, Fr, 1989).

HAMM, Nick

Nick Hamm was born in Belfast, Northern Ireland and first came to prominence as a director in residence at the Royal Shakespeare Company (1983–8). After making a dramatised documentary, *Unmasking Aids* (1989), for the International Planned Parenthood Federation, he moved into television, where he directed episodes of *The Bill* (1990), *Soldier, Soldier* (1992) and three one-hour comedy-dramas for the *Rik Mayall Presents* (1993) slot. He also made a one-off drama for the BBC, *Out of the Blue* (1991), with a cast including Colin Firth, Catherine Zeta-Jones, Cathy Tyson and John Lynch. His half-hour adaptation of a story by Anton Chekhov, *The Harmfulness of Tobacco* (1991), featuring Edward Fox and Celia Imrie, won the BAFTA award for Best Short Film and opened the door to feature production.

Hamm's first project, an adaptation of Guy Burt's 1993 novel *After the Hole*, was stalled by problems with the script and he made his debut in 1994 with *Talk of Angels*, a lush romance set against the backdrop of the Spanish Civil War. However, Miramax delayed the film's release until November 1998, six months after the release of Hamm's second film, the Channel 4-funded romantic comedy *Martha – Meet Frank, Daniel and Laurence*. Joseph Fiennes, Rufus Sewell and Tom Hollander star as three friends competing for the affections of a penniless American (Monica Potter) and the film taps into the same vein of light farce as *Four Weddings and a Funeral* (Mike Newell, 1994), though without comparable commercial success.

The Hole, as finally scripted by NFTVS graduates Ben Court and Caroline Ip, is considerably more interesting. A genuinely disturbing psychological thriller, it chillingly recounts the story of four school friends trapped in a Second World War bunker where they have hidden to avoid a school trip. The film is as much a study of the sexual tensions between the four characters as it is a conventional suspense narrative and the enclosed setting adds to the sense of claustrophobia. *The Hole* was the first film released under the aegis of the newly formed UK Film Council with £1.5 million in Lottery money supporting its production and proved popular with British audiences. Hamm's *Godsend* (2004) is a much bigger-budgeted American film, with Robert De Niro as a genetic engineer who agrees to clone a young boy who has been killed in an accident.

(Robert Shail)

BIBLIOGRAPHY: Brealey, Louise, 'Spotlight: Nick Hamm', *Premiere*, May 1998, p. 4; Kaye, Don, 'Godsend: Attack of the Clone', *Fangoria* no. 232, May 2004, pp. 42–5; Publicity material for *The Hole*, held on microfiche in the BFI National Library, London.

FILMOGRAPHY: *Talk of Angels* (US, 1994; rel. 1998); *Martha – Meet Frank, Daniel and Laurence* (US: *The Very Thought of You*, 1998); *The Hole* (2001); *Godsend* (US, 2004).

HAMMOND, Peter (1923–)

Peter Hammond was born Peter C. H. Hill in London on 15 November 1923. He spent over a decade working as an actor, first coming to prominence after the war in the series of films centring on the Huggett family. His first chance to direct came in 1956, with an episode of the television series *The Buccaneers*, in which he was playing Lieutenant Beamish. Subsequently he abandoned acting, and became a prolific television director. Notable achievements include the atmospheric BBC drama serials *The Count of Monte Cristo* (1964), *Hereward the Wake* (1965) and *The Three Musketeers* (1966); a perceptive adaptation (by the Irish poet Derek Mahon) of Elizabeth Bowen's *The Death of the Heart* (1985); and several episodes of *The Return of Sherlock Holmes* (1986–7) and its successor *The Memoirs of Sherlock Holmes* (1994), where Hammond's dense, highly textured images, crowded with reflections and refracted light, complement Jeremy Brett's febrile and neurotic interpretation of Holmes.

Hammond's only excursion into feature film-making, an adaptation of Bill Naughton's working-class comedy *Spring and Port Wine* (1970), is stylistically less flamboyant. Made on location in Bolton, with interiors filmed at Lee International Studios in London, Hammond opens out the play without sacrificing its essential sense of claustrophobia. James Mason dominates as Rafe Crompton, a stern and overbearing cotton-mill worker who, after coming into serious conflict with his four children, finally relents and allows them to lead their own lives. It makes an interesting companion piece to Roy Boulting's *The Family Way* (1966), also based on a Naughton stage play. Hammond is married to the actress Maureen Glynne.

(Sergio Angelini)

FILMOGRAPHY: *Spring and Port Wine* (1970).

HAMMOND, William C. (1890–?)

William Charles Hammond was born in London on 28 January 1890. Working with producer Mary Field, he directed two enjoyable and popular children's adventures, *Jean's Plan* and *The Secret Tunnel*, at the small Merton Park Studios: key early films in Rank's post-war programme for children's entertainment. Merton Park also housed his brave, if very low-budget, adaptation of Stephen Spender's comic novel of post-war adjustment, *The Fool and the Princess*, his only adult feature. Back with children, he scaled the Austrian alps in *The Lone Climber* and saw off foreign agents in the spirited adventure *The Flying Eye*, one of several made for the Rank scheme's successor, the Children's Film Foundation. Hammond eked out his career with training films – including two for the Conservative Party – but he was at his best with the innocent thrills of the post-war children's film.

(Robert Murphy)

BIBLIOGRAPHY: Field, Mary, *Good Company: The Story of the Children's Entertainment Film Movement in Great Britain 1943–1950* (London: Longmans Green, 1952).

FILMOGRAPHY: *Jean's Plan* (short, 1946); *The Secret Tunnel* (1947); *The Fool and the Princess* (1948); *Hey Presto!* (doc. short, 1949); *The Lone Climber*, *Club Together* (doc. short); *The Personal Touch* (doc. short) (1950); *This Way to Holidays* (short); *Looking for Trouble* (1951); *Juno Helps Out* (short, 1953); *The Flying Eye* (1955); *Transatlantic Town* (doc. short, 1957); *The Carringford School Mystery* (eight-part serial, 1958); *Rockets in the Dunes* (1960).

HAMPTON, Christopher (1946–)

Christopher Hampton was born to British parents on 26 November 1946 on the island of Fayal in the Azores. He studied at Oxford University and then worked as resident writer at the Royal Court Theatre in London from 1968 to 1970. His plays *The Philanthropist* (1970) and *Savages* (1974) were given successful West End runs and he wrote scripts – often adaptations of novels – for stage and television throughout the 1970s and 80s. In 1988 he won an Academy Award and a BAFTA for his screenplay for *Dangerous Liaisons* (Stephen Frears, 1988), an adaptation of his own highly successful stageplay *Les Liaisons Dangereuses* (which was in turn adapted from the novel by Choderlos de Laclos).

Hampton's first venture into film directing was *Carrington*, based on the real-life relationship between artist Dora Carrington and writer Lytton Strachey. Although there is an emotional emptiness at the heart of the film, it nevertheless captures something of the complex and tangled relationships within the Bloomsbury group. His second film, *The Secret Agent*, adapted from Joseph Conrad's novel (and filmed in 1936 by Alfred Hitchcock as *Sabotage*), effectively conveys the shifting tensions of the book. As in *Carrington*, Hampton uses a restlessly moving camera to observe objects and characters with detached curiosity.

Hampton has also adapted the Jekyll and Hyde story, *Mary Reilly* (1996) for Stephen Frears, and Graham Greene's *The Quiet American* (2002) for Philip Noyce. His third film, as director, *Imagining Argentina*, a drama set during the dark days of the 1980s, when opponents of the Argentinian military rulers were ruthlessly eliminated, provoked hostile reactions for its use of magic realism when it was screened at the Venice Film Festival in 2003. Subsequent critical reaction was more favourable and the performances of Antonio Banderas and Emma Thompson praised.
(Sarah Cardwell)

BIBLIOGRAPHY: Newman, Charles, 'Hampton – Luck and Talent in a Brutal Business', *AIP + Co* no. 50, Jan. 1984, pp. 22–5; Philips, Gene D., 'To Sup on Horrors: Christopher Hampton's Film Version of Joseph Conrad's *The Secret Agent*, *Literature/Film Quarterly* vol. 27 no. 3, 1999, pp. 173–7.

FILMOGRAPHY: *Carrington* (1995); *The Secret Agent* (1996); *Imagining Argentina* (US/Arg/Sp, 2004).

HANBURY, Victor (1897–1954)

The Hanbury brothers (left to right): Jack, Victor and Ralph

Born in London in 1897, Victor Hanbury is probably best known for a film he did not direct: his name is on the blacklisted Joseph Losey's first British film, *The Sleeping Tiger* (1954). But he had been involved with British films since the early 1930s, making a dozen features, as contract director for producer John Stafford's company, sometimes in collaboration with RKO. Most of these films are long forgotten, but *No Funny Business*, a comedy about divorce correspondents, starring Laurence Olivier and his then-wife Jill Esmond, is brightly played, though dialogue and situation reek of the stage. The rest are in characteristic 1930s' genres: operetta (*The Beggar Student*), crime thrillers (*Return of a Stranger*) and two Second World War melodramas (*The Crouching Beast* and *Second Bureau*).

The other name with which he is associated is Lance Comfort, sound recordist on *Dick Turpin* (1933), which Hanbury co-directed. Hanbury went on to produce several notable films for Comfort in the 1940s, including *Squadron Leader X* (1942), *Escape to Danger* (1943), *Hotel Reserve* (1944) and *Daughter of Darkness* (1947). On *Hotel Reserve* he is co-credited as director-producer, but contemporary sources make clear that Comfort was the director. Hanbury was never very ambitious as a director himself and worked better as a producer; thus it must have come as something of a surprise to movie buffs to see him credited as director of Losey's flawed but nonetheless stylish *The Sleeping Tiger*, a film Hanbury produced shortly before his death on 14 December 1954.
(Brian McFarlane)

BIBLIOGRAPHY: Ciment, Michel, *Conversations with Joseph Losey* (London: Methuen, 1985); McFarlane, Brian, *Lance Comfort* (Manchester: Manchester University Press, 1999); Obituary, *Motion Picture Herald*, 1 Jan. 1955, p. 34.

FILMOGRAPHY: *The Beggar Student* (co-dir. John Stafford, 1931); *Where Is This Lady?* (co-dir. Ladislao Vajda, 1932); *Dick Turpin* (co-dir. John Stafford); *No Funny Business* (co-dir. John Stafford) (1933); *There Goes Susie* (co-dir. John Stafford); *Spring in the Air* (co-dir. Norman Lee) (1934); *Admirals All*; *The Crouching Beast* (1935); *Ball at Savoy* (co-dir. John Stafford); *The Avenging Hand* (co-dir. Frankland Richardson); *Beloved Impostor*, *Second Bureau* (1936); *Return of a Stranger* (1937).

HAND, David (1900–1986)

David Hand was born in Plainfield, New Jersey, on 23 January 1900, and educated at the Academy of Fine Arts in Chicago. He worked on 'Andy Gump' cartoons in 1919, and joined the staff at the John Bray studios before becoming a director at the Fleischer and then the Disney studio. He became Disney's principal right-hand man, teamed with Bert Lewis as one of the three director/composer teams Disney set up and was instrumental in creating classic 'Silly Symphonies', like *Who Killed Cock Robin?* (1935) and *Pluto's Judgement Day* (1935). He went on to become supervising director of *Snow White and the Seven Dwarfs* (1937) and *Bambi* (1941) and his expertise won him an invitation to head J. Arthur Rank's GB Animation unit at Cookham in 1947.

The influence of the Disney aesthetic is clear in Cookham's *Animaland* cartoons, featuring Ginger Nutt and his forest friends in, for example, *Bee Bother, Forest Dragon, The Cuckoo* and *Christmas Circus* (all 1947); but the cartoons were unfunny and suffered from the fact that they were similar but inferior to their Disney templates. British audiences had grown used to the more frenetic and streetwise Warner Bros. cartoons and the *Animaland* output seemed old-fashioned. The studio had more success with the more indigenous preoccupations of the *Musical Paintbox* series, which looked at national and regional landmarks and eccentricities. Hand recognised that these films needed to be made on a more cost-effective budget, and introduced the Disney technique of using storyboarded stills shown in quick succession to tell the story, with minimal animation in limited action sequences. Successful Cookham films embraced this technique: *Yorkshire Ditty* (1948), for example, even used the conceit of a magic lantern show to privilege stills legitimately as part of the narrative. Rapid montage sequences were used with limited animation, but the most successful aspect of the films, which included *Wales* (1948), *Cornwall, Devon Whey* and *Sketches of Scotland* (all 1949), was a return to indigenous design principles that chimed with the neo-romantic art movement in post-war Britain. The use of popular folk tales and songs was also appealing, speaking to some enduring traditions in the redefinition of national identity in the late 1940s. With the closure of the studio in 1949, Hand returned to the United States. He died in San Luis Obispo, California, after suffering a stroke, on 11 October 1986.

(Paul Wells)

BIBLIOGRAPHY: Barrier, Michael, *Hollywood Cartoons: American Animation in Its Golden Age* (New York and Oxford: Oxford University Press, 1999); Clark, K., 'GBA – A Great British Achievement', *Animator* no. 19, Apr./June 1987 pp. 25–7; Hand, David, *Memoirs* (Cambria, CA: Lighthouse Litho, 1986); Hand, D. Hale, 'My Father, David Dodd Hand', *Animation*, Winter 1989, pp. 32–3; Macnab, Geoffrey, *J. Arthur Rank and the British Film Industry* (London and New York: Routledge, 1993).

SELECTED FILMOGRAPHY (UK only, as director/producer): *Bee Bother, Forest Dragon; The Cuckoo; Christmas Circus* (1947); *Wales* (1948); *Cornwall; Devon Whey; Sketches of Scotland* (1949).

HAND, Harry (1902–?)

Harry E. H. Hand, popularly known as Slim Hand, was born in London on 13 December 1902, and entered the industry in 1920. He worked as sound recordist on many British films in the early 1930s, including Robert Flaherty's *Man of Aran* (1934). Later he became an assistant director, sorting order from the chaos of William Cameron Menzies and William K. Howard's *The Green Cockatoo* (1937), enjoying a smoother ride on Victor Saville's ambitious *South Riding* (1938). He joined Michael Balcon at Ealing as production manager, but spent the war years on active service. In 1947 he was tempted to direct a low-budget detective thriller, *Penny and the Pownall Case*, one of the Rank Organisation's 'curtain raisers' made at the tiny Highbury Studios. Peggy Evans plays a model and amateur detective who discovers her own boss (Christopher Lee) is a traitor and Nazi sympathiser while investigating the murder of a British secret service agent. Diana Dors and future director Philip Saville from Rank's 'Company of Youth' make fleeting appearances; Hand directs with a verve partially deflected by a voyeuristic concern for Penny's curves. The directing experiment was not repeated and Hand went back to Ealing to serve as production manager on Charles Crichton's *Another Shore* (1948), *Dance Hall* (1950) and *The Lavender Hill Mob* (1951).

(Robert Murphy)

FILMOGRAPHY: *Penny and the Pownall Case* (1948).

HARDY, Justin (1964–)

The son of film director Robin Hardy, Justin Hardy was born in London on 30 October 1964. He was educated at Oxford and directed short films before teaming up with aspiring producer Yoshi Nishio to make *A Feast at Midnight* (1994). The need to reduce the budget by shooting in a single location with a cast made up chiefly of non-actors helped to generate a story anticipating the fashion for quirky boarding school stories set off by Harry Potter. Newcomer Magnus (Freddie Findlay), bullied and bad at sports, teams up with other school misfits to form the 'Scoffers Club', whose midnight feasts subvert long-established school routines and hierarchies. Unfortunately, the stakes are too low and the drama lacks bite: Robert Hardy and Christopher Lee's spoilsport teachers turn out to be toothless old tigers, and the school bully is disappointingly unthreatening. But Lisa Faulkner, as the shy, bespectacled under-matron whom the Scoffers adopt as their guest of honour, brings the film to life with pantomime magic as she transforms herself into a swan-like beauty and every boy's ideal big sister.

Gauche but endearing, the film was well enough received to launch Hardy on a career in television, initially on drama series (*London Bridge, Harbour Lights*); latterly on more prestigious dramatised documentaries, *Fire, Plague, War and Treason* (2001), *The Peterloo Massacre* (2003), *Medici: Godfathers of the Renaissance* (2004); and fact-based dramas, *Princes in the Tower* and *Trafalgar Battle Surgeon* (both 2005).

(Robert Murphy)

BIBLIOGRAPHY: Barnes, Alan, 'A Feast at Midnight', *Hammer Horror* no. 3, May 1995, pp. 8–11.

FILMOGRAPHY: *A Feast at Midnight* (1994).

HARDY, Robin (1929–)

Robin Hardy was born in Surrey on 10 October 1929. He trained as an artist in Paris before forming his own film company. Throughout the 1960s, Hardy directed commercials, documentaries, training films and television programmes mainly in Canada and the United States. *The Wicker Man*, his first and most famous feature film, resulted from a collaboration with the writer Anthony Shaffer, Hardy's partner in their production company Hardy Shaffer & Associates. Employing the much-used device of a stranger entering a community that is mysteriously threatening, Hardy and Shaffer invest their film with such atmospheric intensity that it becomes a memorably grim experience. While earlier British films had touched fleetingly on the subject of paganism, *The Wicker Man*'s treatment of pagan practices as an alternative belief system was unprecedentedly sustained and serious. The film also benefited from impressive performances from Edward Woodward as the unwitting sacrificial victim and Christopher Lee as Lord Summerisle, the charismatic leader of the pagans.

The Wicker Man was made during the last days of British Lion; after the company was taken over by EMI, their senior executives told producer Peter Snell that it was 'the worst film ever made' (Billson, p. 32), and it was released, heavily cut, on the lower half of a double bill with Nicolas Roeg's *Don't Look Now* (1973). Since then, *The Wicker Man* has acquired a formidable cult reputation. In 2001 a director's cut of the film restored the previously excised material, most of which involved atmospheric details of the life of the pagan community.

Thirteen years passed before Hardy's second feature emerged. *The Fantasist*, which he adapted, without the help of Shaffer, from a novel by Patrick McGinley, was a less successful attempt to transform another stock genre situation – a serial killer stalking the streets of Dublin – into a study of character and fantasy. Hardy also supplied the story and original script for the pagan-themed *Bulldance* (Zelda Barron, 1989). His son is the director Justin Hardy.

(Peter Hutchings)

The animals celebrate a human sacrifice: *The Wicker Man* (Robin Hardy, 1973)

BIBLIOGRAPHY: Billson, Anne, 'Fantasy Ireland', *Time Out*, 25 Feb. 1987, p. 32; Brown, Allan, *Inside 'The Wicker Man'* (London: Sidgwick & Jackson, 2000); Ramsay, Gary, 'Killing Joke', in David Kerekes (ed.), *Creeping Flesh – The Horror Fantasy Film Book* (Manchester: Headpress Publishing/Critical Vision, 2003).

FILMOGRAPHY: *The Wicker Man* (1973); *The Fantasist* (1986).

HARE, David (1947–)

David Hare was born in St Leonards, Sussex, on 5 June 1947 and brought up in nearby Bexhill-on-Sea. After studying at Lancing College and Cambridge he founded the Portable Theatre Company with Tony Bicât to tour the country presenting radical experimental drama. His first play *Slag* (1970) attracted attention and he was soon being hailed as one of Britain's leading new playwrights. Other plays, notably *Plenty*, produced at the National Theatre in 1978, consolidated his reputation.

He directed his own play for television, *Licking Hitler*, in 1977: a sparse and elliptical study of a British black propaganda unit that cuts cleanly and efficiently to the heart of Second World War mythology. *Dreams of Leaving* (1980) and his cinema debut *Wetherby* (1985) were equally innovative but less successful in pulling together Hare's attempts to examine the legacy of the past on contemporary reality. Fred Schepisi did rather better with his 1985 adaptation of *Plenty*, helped by Meryl Streep's luminous performance as the British agent who finds that nothing in post-war Britain can match the excitement of her experience working with the French Resistance against the Nazis.

Channel 4 gave Hare the opportunity to direct two low-budget features almost back to back. *Paris by Night* (1988) is a slow, stylish film about a British member of the European Parliament (Charlotte Rampling) who looks set for a dazzling political career just at the moment that her husband (Michael Gambon) drifts into alcoholic failure. An unwelcome voice on the telephone, a man from the past seeking compensation for past wrongs, an affair with a younger man and an accidental murder all combine intriguingly with Machiavellian political scheming to produce a coldly effective contemporary film noir.

David Hare (left) directing *Paris By Night* (1988)

Strapless (1988) is brighter and more erratic, with Blair Brown as a warm, sensible American doctor settled in England, the exact opposite of Rampling's cold exponent of Thatcherite greed. By the end of the film she has agreed to lead a campaign against the cuts that are decimating her NHS hospital, but this political commitment stems from the clarity she gains from her encounter with an enigmatic entrepreneur (Bruno Ganz). He wins her with unexpectedly generous gifts, marries her and runs off leaving bills unpaid; but untypically for Hare this is a beneficent romance, with both characters healed and renewed rather than saddened and destroyed by their brush with all-consuming passion.

For the next ten years Hare concentrated on his theatrical career, though the startling melodrama *Damage* (1992), which he adapted for Louis Malle, bears comparison with *Paris by Night* in its study of a politician deflected by passion from the pursuit of power. As if to compensate for this flirtation with a more mainstream cinema, Hare's next film as director, *The Designated Mourner* (1997), is a defiantly uncommercial adaptation of a play by Wallace Shawn. Jack (Mike Nichols), an unambitious writer, gives an anecdotal account of his relationship with his wife and her father, a famous radical poet, which becomes a lament for the intelligentsia wiped out by an increasingly repressive regime in some unnamed but presumably South American country. Miranda Richardson and David de Keyser, as the daughter and father, make their own interventions from the grave, but this is essentially a dramatic monologue, all the more convincing and moving for being delivered by a character whose regret is tempered by relief at the passing of an elite he secretly despised.

Hare returned to the stage with renewed political vigour for his one-man show *Via Dolorosa* (2002), a sharp analysis of the Arab/Israeli conflict; and *Stuff Happens* (2004), an indictment of New Labour's fuzzy politics in the months before the Iraq War. Hare is too closely wedded to the stage to pursue a full-time career in cinema, but his interventions are always radical and original. He is married to the fashion designer Nicole Farhi and was knighted in 1998. (Robert Murphy)

BIBLIOGRAPHY: Kerr, Paul, 'David Hare and Saigon: Leaping out of the Cage', *Stills* no. 9, Nov./Dec. 1983, pp. 64–7; Lawson, Steve, 'Hare Apparent', *Film Comment*, Sept./Oct. 1985, pp. 18–22; Lustig, Vera, 'Paris by Night', *Films and Filming*, June 1989, pp. 24–6; Murray, Scott, 'Paris by Night', *Cinema Papers* no. 76, Nov. 1989, pp. 64–5; NFT audiotape interview (jointly with Juliet Stevenson) held in the BFI National Library, London; Roberts, Alison, 'The IoS profile: David Hare', *Independent on Sunday*, 15 Sept. 2004, p. 23; Sweet, Matthew, 'Hare's Breadth', *Independent on Sunday* Review Section, 8 June 1997, pp. 14–15; Tynan, Kathleen, 'Dramatically Speaking', *Interview* vol. 19 no. 4, Apr. 1989, pp. 80, 128, 130.

FILMOGRAPHY: *Wetherby* (1985); *Paris by Night*; *Strapless* (1988); *The Designated Mourner* (1997).

HARKIN, Margo (1951–)

Margo Harkin was born in Derry in 1951 and studied art and design at Belfast Art College. In the early 1980s she worked on theatre design with the influential Field Day Company in Derry. In 1984 she helped found Derry Film and Video, a Channel 4-franchised workshop, where she produced Ann Crilly's documentary *Mother Ireland* (1988), which was banned under new censorship regulations brought in by the Thatcher government. She co-wrote, and directed, the feature film *Hush-a-Bye Baby* in 1989 for Channel 4 and RTÉ. This was an enormously popular film on television in Britain and Ireland; it also enjoyed international critical acclaim and proved a box-office attraction in various European countries. At a time of great uncertainty in Irish film, its success demonstrated the relevance of an indigenous cinema and provided ammunition for the campaign to re-establish government funding for film production. The film's concerns – an exploration of the pressures that are exerted on a pregnant teenager (Emer McCourt) in the Catholic community of Derry – also proved prescient and anticipated many of the scandals that befell the Church in the 1990s.

After the workshop disbanded in 1990, Harkin formed her own company, Besom Productions, and has worked mostly as a producer of art and educational documentaries for both British and Irish television. In 1997 she directed a highly acclaimed documentary for Channel 4, *12 Days in July*, about the contentious Orange parade at Drumcree.

(Martin McLoone)

BIBLIOGRAPHY: Butler Cullingford, Elizabeth, 'Seamus and Sinéad: From "Limbo" to *Saturday Night Live* by Way of *Hush-a-Bye Baby*', in *Ireland's Others: Gender and Ethnicity in Irish Literature and Popular Culture* (Cork: Cork University Press, 2001); Kirkland, Richard, 'Gender, Nation, Excess: Reading *Hush-a-Bye Baby*', in Scott Brewster, Virginia Crossman, Fiona Beckett and David Alderson (eds), *Ireland in Proximity: History, Gender, Space* (London: Routledge, 1999); McLoone, Martin, *Irish Film: The Emergence of a Contemporary Cinema* (London: BFI, 2000); Pettitt, Lance, *Screening Ireland* (Manchester: Manchester University Press, 2000).

FILMOGRAPHY: *Hush-a-Bye Baby* (Ir/UK, 1989).

HARLOW, John (1896–?)

John Harlow was born on 19 August 1896 in Ross-on-Wye, Herefordshire, and was educated at Kingswood College, Bath. Following active service in the First World War, he performed in concert parties, music hall and the theatre. He began his film career in the mid-1920s as a scriptwriter at Elstree and in 1929 was assistant director to the German director E. A. Dupont on *Atlantic* (1929), a prestigious early talkie about the sinking of the *Titanic*. In 1933 he wrote and co-directed *My Lucky Star*, featuring comedienne Florence Desmond, and followed it with *Master and Man*, written by Wallace Lupino, with Wallace and brother Barry playing two tramps mistaken for 'toffs'. However, for most of the 1930s he worked behind the scenes in various production roles.

Harlow made a promising return to direction in 1940 with *Spellbound*, an absorbing drama about a young man (Derek Farr) possessed by an evil reincarnation of his dead fiancée, who is rescued from near-insanity by the prayers of a childhood friend. After a wartime espionage thriller, *This Was Paris*, Harlow found a niche directing enjoyably convoluted melodramas. *The Dark Tower* makes good use of its circus background and features a blood-curdlingly villainous performance from Herbert Lom; *Headline* revolves around a reporter (David Farrar) who finds himself in a tricky position when his boss's wife is implicated in a murder; and Farrar features again as the intrepid detective Sexton Blake in *Meet Sexton Blake* and *The Echo Murders*. *Candles at Nine*, an attempt to revive the career of Jessie Matthews by casting her as the heroine of an Agatha Christie-like murder mystery, was less successful.

Harlow made a contribution to the debate about what sort of society should emerge from the war with *The Agitator*, in which William Hartnell plays an embittered mechanic who learns tolerance when he is given a chance to run the factory where he works. It proved less popular than *Appointment with Crime*, an above-average crime drama with Hartnell seeking revenge on the gang who abandoned him during a bungled robbery. Harlow's direction was praised in the *Monthly Film Bulletin* and *Kinematograph Weekly* (which described him as 'an excellent purveyor of red meat'), but he failed to make the breakthrough into major features. *While I Live* is a slow-moving thriller that was popular at the time for Charles Williams' popular piano score, 'The Dream of Olwen'; *Green Fingers* is a more engrossing romantic melodrama, with an interesting slant on osteopathy. Harlow managed to squeeze some humour out of *Old Mother Riley's New Venture*, but not from its successor, *Old Mother Riley Headmistress*. In the 1950s he returned to thrillers, the best of which is *The Blue Parrot*, with John Le Mesurier as a murderous Soho club-owner.

(Margaret Butler)

BIBLIOGRAPHY: 'Appointment with Crime', *Monthly Film Bulletin*, May 1946, pp. 60–1; Billings, Josh, 'Appointment with Crime', *Kinematograph Weekly*, 23 May 1946, p. 26; Hartnell, William, 'I Thought I Was a Star!', *Picturegoer*, 23 Nov. 1946, p. 8; Noble, Peter (ed.), *The British Film Yearbook, 1947–1948* (London: Skelton Robinson, 1947), pp. 269–70.

FILMOGRAPHY: *Photophone Reels* (shorts, co-dir. James Sloane, 1929); *My Lucky Star* (co-dir. Louis Blattner, 1933); *Master and Man* (aka *Songbirds*); *Bagged* (short) (1934); *Spellbound* (US: *Ghost Story/Passing Clouds/The Spell of Amy Nugent*, 1940); *This Was Paris* (1941); *One Company* (short, 1942); *The Dark Tower*, *Headline* (1943); *Meet Sexton Blake*; *Candles at Nine* (1944); *The Agitator*; *The Echo Murders* (1945); *Appointment with Crime* (1946); *While I Live* (aka *The Dream of Olwen*); *Green Fingers* (1947); *Old Mother Riley's New Venture* (1949); *Old Mother Riley Headmistress* (1950); *Those People Next Door* (1952); *The Blue Parrot* (1953); *Dangerous Cargo*; *Delayed Action* (1954); *Beyond the Curtain* (2nd unit dir., Compton Bennett, 1960).

HARRIS, Damian (1958–)

Damian Harris was born in London on 2 August 1958, the son of Sir Richard Harris and Elizabeth Rees. He put in a brief appearance as a chicken-pox-afflicted schoolboy in Dick Clement's *Otley* (1968); drew on his own experience to make a short film showing drunkenness and homosexuality at a public school; worked as an assistant on the South African thriller *Golden Rendezvous* (Ashley Lazarus, 1977), in which his father was starring; and returned to study at the London International Film School in Covent Garden. After completing the course he went to America, where he shot background footage for HBO concert films and made two shorts, *Greasy Lake* and *Killing Time*, which won him influential friends who helped him make his feature debut, an adaptation of Martin Amis' first novel *The Rachel Papers*. Dexter Fletcher's teenage Casanova is an irritating hero, but Harris places him in situations where we are forced to take his side, and he surrounds him with vivid characters who fling open the windows of his self-obsessed world, not least the object of his desire (played with conviction and subtlety by Ione Syke).

Poor marketing and snooty reviews restricted the film's box-office returns, but Amis approved and American producers were impressed by the slickness of Harris' direction. He was invited to take over from Alan J. Pakula (who had himself taken over from Mark Rydell) on *The Mrs*, a convoluted thriller starring Goldie Hawn subsequently retitled *Deceived* (1991). Harris does his best with a script that is too laborious in setting up its uninvolving story of false identity and fraud. Bright colours, tight direction and a persuasive performance from Hawn made it a box-office success in America, though it failed to reach cinemas in Britain. Darker projects followed. Along with episodes of off-beat television drama series *Strangers* (1996) and *Sins of the City* (1998), Harris made two impressively slick features. In *Bad Company*, a conspiracy thriller set in Seattle (though shot in Vancouver), Laurence Fishburne plays an ex-CIA agent whose task of bribing a Supreme Court judge is complicated by the scheming of Ellen Barkin's oozingly evil femme fatale. In *Mercy* (2000) Barkin is more sympathetic as a tough Toronto detective delving into a netherworld of murder, incest and sado-masochism; but in both films the view of North American society as riddled with corruption is a bleak one. Though hardly known in Britain, Harris is unusual as a British director capable of maintaining an individual profile in the jungle of American genre film-making.

(Robert Murphy)

BIBLIOGRAPHY: 'People in the Picture', *Screen International*, 6 May 1978, p. 14; Seguin, Denis, 'Director Damian Harris', *Premiere*, Oct. 1991, p. 41.

FILMOGRAPHY: *The Friend* (short, 197?); *All Good Clean Fun* (short, 197?); *Greasy Lake* (short, US); *Killing Time* (short, US) (c. 1987); *The Rachel Papers* (1989); *Deceived* (US, 1991); *Bad Company* (US, 1995); *Mercy* (US, 2000).

HART, Ben R. (1904–1968)

Born in London in 1904, Ben Hart entered the industry as assistant to Harry Parkinson in 1926, earning his directing spurs with British Screen Productions' Lapland melodrama *Frozen Fate* (1929) and an impoverished early talkie, *Birds of a Feather*. Turning to cinematography, Hart spent fourteen years as a Paramount newsreel cameraman, where assignments included the Spanish Civil War. Following wartime photography work for the navy, he joined Hal Wilson, another industry veteran, at Knightsbridge Films, directing unambitious documentaries and features. *Old Father Thames* idled along with pretty scenery, while *Crime Reporter* and *River Patrol* tried to feed off the post-war malaise, with nylon gang smugglers and Soho's black market. No doubt they offered more rewarding work than photographing two of Mancunian's Frank Randle vehicles, *Holidays with Pay* and *Somewhere in Politics* (both John E. Blakeley, 1948). Another strictly modest crime film, *Dangerous Assignment*, followed in 1950. Hart later concentrated on television documentaries and information films.

(Robert Murphy)

FILMOGRAPHY: *Frozen Fate* (co-dir. St John Legh Clowes, 1929); *Birds of a Feather* (1931); *Once upon a Horse* (doc. short); *Footlight School* (doc. short) (1945); *Old Father Thames* (doc. short, co-dir. Hal Wilson, 1946); *Airport International* (doc. short); *Crime Reporter* (short); *River Patrol* (1947); *Dangerous Assignment* (1950).

HARTFORD-DAVIS, Robert (1923–1977)

Robert Hartford-Davis was born in Ramsgate, Kent, on 23 July 1923. He spent most of his film-making career in the low-budget exploitation sector that he helped to establish in Britain during the 1960s. Beginning as a technician working at Teddington Studios, he directed four short films from the mid-1950s onwards, and *Crosstrap*, an hour-long support feature. His first full-length feature, *The Yellow Teddybears*, which he co-produced with fellow exploitation specialist Michael Klinger, took as its topical subject a newspaper article about schoolgirls losing their virginity. The film combined a prurient, voyeuristic treatment with a moralistic message designed to appease the censors. *Saturday Night Out*, another collaboration with Klinger, was less sensational but still risqué in its depiction of the sexual and romantic antics of merchant seamen on shore leave in London. As with *The Yellow Teddybears*, the film's fascination with new sexual freedoms was accompanied by an emphasis on the need to be decent and true.

Hartford-Davis spent the next few years attempting to cash in on box-office trends, although his films were often highly idiosyncratic. *The Black Torment*, a third and final collaboration with Klinger, is a gothic horror in the Hammer style; *Gonks Go Beat* is a teenage pop musical involving an alien (Kenneth Connor) sent to Earth to pacify the warring tribes of Ballad Isle and Beatland; *Corruption* is a gory surgical-horror film of a type more associated with continental European horror; and *The Smashing Bird I*

Used to Know is a salacious tale of female delinquency in which the main character is traumatised through witnessing her father die in a bizarre merry-go-round accident. According to Derek Ford, who wrote the scripts for several Hartford-Davis films, 'He lived at fever pitch. Somebody screaming, somebody dying, a throat slit – that was a great picture to him' (quoted in McGillivray, 1992, p. 12).

In the midst of this outré activity, Hartford-Davis also made *The Sandwich Man*, a comedy in which the hero (Michael Bentine) travels across London while awaiting news of his beloved homing pigeon. Though poorly received at the time of its release, its genial good humour contrasts markedly with the glum sensationalism that characterises most of Hartford-Davis' films. In the 1970s he directed two more horror films. *The Fiend* was a powerful and grim study of religious repression. *Incense for the Damned*, based on Simon Raven's novel *Doctors Wear Scarlet*, was meant to be a serious exploration of the sexual pathology of vampirism. However, the film was extensively re-edited by its backers and Hartford-Davis removed his own name from the credits and was billed instead as Michael Burrowes. He then moved to the United States where he directed two blaxploitation films, *Black Gunn* and *The Take*, before dying of a heart attack in Beverly Hills on 12 June 1977.

(Peter Hutchings)

BIBLIOGRAPHY: Clarke, Sue, 'Hollywood? It's Just Another Place to Make a Movie', *CinemaTV Today*, 6 May 1972, p. 26; Falk, Quentin, Obituary, *Screen International*, 15 June 1977, p. 110; McGillivray, David, *Doing Rude Things: The History of the British Sex Film, 1957–81* (London: Sun Tavern Fields, 1992); McGillivray, David, 'High Blood Pressure', *Shivers* no. 10, Jan. 1994, pp. 12–15.

FILMOGRAPHY: *The Man on the Cliff* (short, 1955); *City of Contrasts* (unfinished, 1959); *A Christmas Carol* (short, 1960); *Stranger in the City* (doc.); *Crosstrap* (1961); *The Yellow Teddybears* (aka *Gutter Girls*) (1963); *Saturday Night Out* (1964); *The Black Torment*; *Gonks Go Beat* (1965); *The Sandwich Man* (1966); *Corruption* (1967); *The Smashing Bird I Used to Know* (aka *Hell House Girls/House of Unclaimed Women*, 1969); *Nobody Ordered Love*; *The Fiend* (US: *Beware My Brethren*) (1971); *Incense for the Damned* (as Michael Burrowes, aka *Doctors Wear Scarlet/Bloodsuckers*); *Black Gunn* (US) (1972); *The Take* (US, 1974).

HARVEY, Anthony (1931–)

Anthony Harvey was born in London on 3 June 1931 and became the adopted son of British actor Morris Harvey. He attended Highgate School and won a scholarship to RADA, but left after three months, following Morris' death. Despite appearing as the boy Ptolemy in *Caesar and Cleopatra* (Gabriel Pascal, 1945), Harvey decided to quit acting altogether. He then sought work behind the camera, joining Douglas Fairbanks Jr Productions at Merton Park as second assistant editor in 1952. By 1955 he was editor on such films as *Brothers in Law* (Roy Boulting, 1956), *I'm All Right Jack* (John Boulting, 1959) and *The L-Shaped Room* (Bryan Forbes, 1962). He also edited Stanley Kubrick's *Lolita* (1961) and *Dr Strangelove* (1963).

Harvey's first film as a director was *Dutchman* (1966), a fifty-five-minute black-and-white film about a stormy encounter between a white woman and a black man on the New York subway. It won the Golden Lion Award at Venice and ran in London for six months. Harvey followed this success with a much more lavish one: *The Lion in Winter*, an adaptation of James Goldman's hit stage play detailing the troubled family life of Henry II (Peter O'Toole) and his queen, Eleanor (Katharine Hepburn). The anachronistic dialogue and over-the-top performances appealed to contemporary audiences and Harvey's editorial expertise resulted in a taut and visually rhythmic film. It won Academy Award nominations in all the major categories, including Hepburn as Best Actress. Harvey went to America to make *They Might Be Giants*, based on another Goldman play, and a television version of Tennessee Williams' *The Glass Menagerie* (1973) with Katharine Hepburn and Sam Waterston. He returned to Britain to film another historical subject, *The Abdication*, the story of Queen Kristina (Liv Ullman) and her love for Cardinal Azzolino (Peter Finch).

Harvey's most extraordinary project was *Eagle's Wing* (1978), a beautiful and enigmatic film in which Sam Waterston's Kiowa Indian, 'White Bull', competes with Martin Sheen's young American soldier for possession of a white stallion. With virtually no dialogue, the film is intense and conjures up an elemental world. Harvey was never to reach such heights again. *Richard's Things*, based on a novel by Frederic Raphael exploring the relationship between a dead man's wife (Liv Ullman) and his mistress (Amanda Redman), was his last British film, though he has continued to direct for cinema and television in America.

Like another editor-turned-director, Clive Donner, Harvey was often unable to raise the finance for the films he wanted to make – though he turned down the chance of directing both *Cabaret* (Bob Fosse, 1972) and *The Godfather* (Francis Ford Coppola, 1972). Like the most famous editor-turned-director, David Lean, he is a romantic and his best films deal honestly and sensitively with emotional problems.

(Janet Moat)

BIBLIOGRAPHY: Combs, Richard and Tom Milne, 'The Romantic Englishman', *Sight and Sound*, Autumn 1979, pp. 210–14; Gallagher, John, 'Anthony Harvey', *Films in Review*, May 1983, pp. 261–71; Malcolm, Derek, 'The Magic Ingredient Is Love', *Guardian*, 28 July 1979.

FILMOGRAPHY: *Dutchman* (1966); *The Lion in Winter* (1968); *They Might Be Giants* (US, 1971); *The Abdication* (1974); *Eagle's Wing* (1978); *Players* (US, 1979); *Richard's Things* (1980); *The Ultimate Solution of Grace Quigley* (aka *Grace Quigley*, US, 1984).

HATTON, Maurice (1938–1997)

Maurice Hatton was born in Manchester on 22 May 1938. He left school without qualifications and went on to study photography at college before becoming a photographers' assistant and then a freelance photo-journalist. In the early 1960s he formed Mithras Films with Richard De La Mare and John

Voting for revolution: *Praise Marx and Pass the Ammunition* (Maurice Hatton, 1969)

Irvin. Hatton produced, photographed and directed a series of political documentaries, beginning with *The Challenge*, a humorous depiction of the 1963 Labour Party conference. The high-octane *Scene Nun, Take One*, a short film distributed by Columbia Pictures and starring Susannah York, showed him to be similarly adept at handling fiction. *One in Every Hundred* was a stark documentary comparing treatment of the mentally disabled under the Canadian private system and the British state system, which Hatton claimed was the most strenuous but most rewarding film he ever made.

Hatton's continued concern with the political was manifest in his first feature film, *Praise Marx and Pass the Ammunition*, a depiction of the political activities and sexual conquests of a Marxist-Leninist activist (John Thaw) eager for revolution in 1968. A landmark film, it couples left-wing fervour with a distinguishing edgy wit. Hatton's characteristic humour was displayed once more in *The Bouncing Boy* (1972), a BBC *Play for Today*. His political sympathies also found expression in the television documentary *Bitter Harvest* (1973), an account of César Chávez's struggle to unionise Californian migrant workers, and *Women and Crime* (1975), a searching feminist review of how the social perception of women influences their treatment in legal spheres.

Having managed to procure free black-and-white film stock and to raise modest funds for another feature film, Hatton started shooting *Long Shot* at the 1977 Edinburgh Festival. Partially scripted and partially improvised, the film is essentially an in-joke from this most idiosyncratic of British directors, commenting with a sense of the absurd on the lack of investment in British film and the difficulty of retaining independence within the industry. The following year he made a full-length documentary, *Exiles in London*, with the financial backing of the BFI Production Board.

Hatton was funded by Channel 4 to make *Nelly's Version*, a convoluted psychological thriller based on a novel by Eva Figes, with Eileen Atkins as an amnesiac struggling with claims on her identity. Michael Nyman's powerful score heightens the tension at every turn. He went on to make *American Roulette*, the story of a South American poet who is made president in exile in London and pursued by a death squad, with the KGB, the CIA and MI5 all sticking their oars in. It did well on the festival circuit but, even with Andy Garcia as the poet-president, its plot implausibilities made it a disappointing commercial prospect. Hatton's final film, *Satan at His Best* (1995), made for television, was drawn from a series of interviews with British servicemen who had been imprisoned at the Auschwitz concentration camp. He died of a heart attack in London on 25 October 1997.

(Eleanor Burke)

BIBLIOGRAPHY: MacPherson, Don, 'Shooting in the Dark', *Time Out* no. 531, 20 June 1980, p. 31; Ward, John, 'Professionals of Wardour Street', *Film Making*, Jan. 1971, pp. 49–52.

FILMOGRAPHY: *The Challenge* (short, 1963); *Scene Nun, Take One* (short, 1964); *What about the Workers* (short, 1965); *One in Every Hundred* (doc., 1966); *Okavango* (doc. short, 1968); *Praise Marx and Pass the Ammunition* (1969); *Exiles in London* (doc., 1976); *Long Shot* (1978); *Nelly's Version* (1983); *American Roulette* (1988).

HAY, John

John Hay studied film at the University of Reading before working in television, where he directed radical documentaries for Channel 4, such as *We're Not Mad . . . We're Angry* (1986) and *Not What the Doctor Ordered* (1989). Successful dramatisations of Heathcote Williams' *Falling for a Dolphin* (1990) and *Autogeddon* (1991) and the documentary *Every Time I Cross the Tamar I Get into Trouble* (1993) led to Williams playing the lead in Hay's *The Steal* (1995), a zany comedy about computer hacking and globalisation that squanders its good intentions in careless plotting and indulgent performances. Better results followed from Hay's second feature *There's Only One Jimmy Grimble* (2000), a predictable but likeable fairy tale about a fifteen-year-old Manchester City supporter who overcomes the handicaps of small stature, disruptive home life and low self-esteem to achieve footballing glory. Hay's direction lacks finesse, and he burdens the film with too many slow-motion clichés on the football pitch, but he enthusiastically handles the essential ingredients: big nasty bully, pixie-like female admirer, coach with a secret past, fairy godmother with a pair of magic boots. *Jimmy Grimble* lacked the crossover appeal of *Kes* (Ken Loach, 1969) and *Billy Elliot* (Stephen Daldry, 2000), but was warmly received at film festivals and performed modestly well at the box office.

Hay returned to television to direct a BBC serialisation of Clive King's popular children's story *Stig of the Dump* (2002) before making *The Truth about Love* (2006), a wobbly romantic comedy with American Jennifer Love Hewitt cast as an English housewife who foolishly sends her husband an anonymous Valentine's Day card to test his fidelity.

(Robert Murphy)

BIBLIOGRAPHY: Biographical information, John Hay, <www.mcguffin.dircon.co.uk/comp.htm>.

FILMOGRAPHY: *The Steal* (1995); *There's Only One Jimmy Grimble* (UK/Fr, 2000); *The Truth about Love* (2006).

HAY, Will (1888–1949)

William Thompson Hay, born in Stockton-on-Tees on 6 December 1888, was apprenticed as an engineer before making his music-hall debut in 1908. Later he appeared with Dares' Minstrel Troupe and with Fred Karno. By the early 1920s he had extended a schoolmaster song into a sketch in which he played a bumbling, unprincipled teacher presiding over a class that included an eccentric old man and a plump, cheeky boy. Hay's first feature film, *Those Were the Days* (Thomas Bentley, 1934), was a version of Pinero's *The Magistrate*, but it was with *Boys Will Be Boys* (William Beaudine, 1935), *Windbag the Sailor* (William Beaudine, 1936) and *Good Morning, Boys!* (Marcel Varnel, 1937) that Hay established his screen persona of an authoritarian figure gone to seed. With his frequent co-stars Moore Marriott and Graham Moffatt, Hay achieved his greatest screen success with *Oh, Mr Porter!* (Marcel Varnel, 1937), a tale of dark doings at a disused railway station. Hay's short directorial career commenced when he moved to Ealing Studios. In collaboration with Basil Dearden, he directed *The Black Sheep of Whitehall* (1941) and *The Goose Steps Out* (1942), films that deployed comedy for the war effort, and *My Learned Friend* (1943), a black comedy that rivalled the best of his previous films. Hay starred in all three films. Beyond the world of popular entertainment, Hay was a famous amateur astronomer, an expert linguist and a pilot. He died in London on 18 April 1949.

(Barry Anthony)

BIBLIOGRAPHY: Seaton, Ray and Roy Martin, *Good Morning Boys: Will Hay, Master of Comedy* (London: Barrie and Jenkins, 1978).

FILMOGRAPHY: *The Black Sheep of Whitehall* (co-dir. Basil Dearden, 1941); *The Goose Steps Out* (co-dir. Basil Dearden, 1942); *My Learned Friend* (co-dir. Basil Dearden, 1944).

HAYERS, Sidney (1921–2000)

Sidney Hayers was born in Edinburgh on 24 August 1921. A prolific director, his films never cohered into a distinctive body of work but he nevertheless showed intermittent flair and originality. Hayers worked as an editor from the late 1940s, winning respect for his work on such films as *White Corridors* (Pat Jackson, 1951), *A Town Like Alice* (Jack Lee, 1956) and *Tiger Bay* (J. Lee Thompson, 1959). After second-unit work on *A Night to Remember* (Roy Baker, 1958), he made his directorial debut with the supporting feature *Violent Moment*. More notable, however, was his 1960 horror film *Circus of Horrors*, part of what David Pirie later dubbed Anglo-Amalgamated's Sadian trilogy (the other two being Arthur Crabtree's *Horrors of the Black Museum* in 1959 and Michael Powell's *Peeping Tom* in 1960). Hayers' enthusiastic direction suited *Circus of Horror*'s lurid and vulgar stock-horror scenario about a mad cosmetic surgeon wreaking havoc among the misfits and mavericks of a circus.

Subsequent films were often engaging but also bewilderingly varied in subject matter, style and tone. *Payroll* was a downbeat crime drama set and largely filmed in Newcastle-on-Tyne; *Night of the Eagle* a fine supernatural drama whose subtleties were a world away from the grosser charms of *Circus of Horrors*;

This Is My Street a low-life melodrama linking the kitchen-sink dramas to later realist films like Ken Loach's *Poor Cow* (1967); and *Three Hats for Lisa* a stylish teen musical set around London's docklands. He also directed several episodes of television series including *The Human Jungle* (1961-2) and *The Avengers* (1963-4).

In the late 1960s Hayers moved into international co-production with the Anglo-Canadian *The Trap* and the Anglo-French *The Southern Star*. In the 1970s he made a series of British films (*Assault*, *Revenge*, *All Coppers Are . . .*, and the tamer *Deadly Strangers* and *Diagnosis: Murder*) that sought to benefit from a relaxation in film censorship by inserting controversial and exploitative scenes of sexual violence within their traditional whodunit narratives. Hayers also directed episodes of *The Professionals* (1977) and *The New Avengers* (1977–8) and acted as a second-unit director on Richard Attenborough's war epic *A Bridge Too Far*, before beginning a second career as a prolific director of American television series from *Galactica 1980* (1980) to *Space Precinct* (1994). He died of cancer on 8 February 2000 in Altea, Spain.

(Peter Hutchings)

BIBLIOGRAPHY: Baker, Bob, 'Sidney Hayers', *Film Dope* no. 23, Sept. 1981, pp. 45–6; Maxford, Howard, 'Sidney Hayers: Sawdust and Sorcery', *Shivers* no. 61, Jan. 1999, pp. 30–3; Pirie, David, *A Heritage of Horror* (London: Gordon Fraser, 1973); Weaver, Tom, 'Dread and Circuses', *Fangoria* no. 161, Apr. 1997, pp. 12–17.

FILMOGRAPHY: *Violent Moment* (1958); *Operation Amsterdam* (2nd unit dir., Michael McCarthy); *The White Trap* (1959); *Circus of Horrors*; *The Malpas Mystery*; *Echo of Barbara* (1960); *Payroll* (1961); *Night of the Eagle* (US: *Burn, Witch, Burn!*, 1962); *This Is My Street* (1963); *Three Hats for Lisa* (1965); *The Trap* (UK/Can); *Finders Keepers* (1966); *The Southern Star/L'Étoile du sud* (UK/Fr, 1968); *Mister Jerico* (1969); *The Firechasers*; *Assault* (US: *In the Devil's Garden*) (1970); *Revenge* (US: *Inn of the Frightened People*); *All Coppers Are . . .* (1971); *Deadly Strangers*; *What Changed Charley Farthing?* (US: *The Banana Boat*); *Diagnosis: Murder* (1974); *One Away* (US, 1976); *A Bridge Too Far* (2nd unit dir., Richard Attenborough, 1977); *Conquest of the Earth* (co-dirs. Sig Neufeld/Barry Crane, US 1980).

HAYES, Derek (1952–) and Philip AUSTIN (1951–1990)

In the 1970s Derek Hayes and Philip Austin established themselves as British animators blessed with admirable exuberance and cheek. Austin was born in Liss, Hampshire, on 18 November 1951; Hayes in Standish, Wigan, on 8 June 1952. They met in 1971 at Sheffield Polytechnic's School of Art and Design, emerging with first-class degrees in sculpture, though more time had been spent on animation. The principal result was *Custard* (1974), the brief tale of a victimised custard-factory worker who takes avenging himself to a yellow and viscid extreme. The film that made their names was *Max Beeza and the City in the Sky*: twenty-two minutes of futuristic nonsense produced during their time at the National Film School (1974–7). The towering city contains the UK population, crammed together following poison gas contamination on land, and now subject to attacks from alien spaceships. The film's tottering story matters much less than the animation's gusto, the intricate detail in the backgrounds and the battery of in-jokes (at one point conman Max Beeza disappears up a scratch mark).

An ideal calling card, *Max Beeza* led to animation inserts in Julien Temple's Sex Pistols affray *The Great Rock 'n' Roll Swindle* (1979) and the formation of Hayes and Austin's company, Animation City. Personal projects were put to one side for pop videos, commercials and television title designs, though the team revealed their spurs again in three shorts for Channel 4: the airborne fantasy *Skywhales*; *The Victor*, dealing with drugs, the military and violence; and the music-hall themed *Binky and Boo*.

On 24 January 1990 Austin died from AIDS complications in London. Hayes has continued in business, working since 1993 as a freelance, though changes in markets and television operations have necessitated a change in direction. The well-received *Prince Cinders* aside, the wild imaginings and carnivals of jokes have largely been replaced by the solid skills of a master craftsman, assigned to interpret biblical matters and folk myths for family audiences. *Elijah*, a half-hour contribution to BBC Wales' *Testament: The Bible in Animation*, was followed by the feature-length *The Miracle Maker* (2000), co-produced with Russia, a safe portrayal of Christ's life, with a strong voice cast led by Ralph Fiennes. Happily, Hayes had greater room for manoeuvre in his second feature, *Otherworlds/Y Mabinogi* (2003), using 2-D animation, computer effects, models and live action to bring alive fantastical Celtic sights from the Welsh folk tales of the Mabinogian.

(Geoff Brown)

BIBLIOGRAPHY: *Otherworld* site <www.s4c.co.uk/otherworld>.

FILMOGRAPHY: Hayes and Austin (shorts): *Custard* (1974); *Max Beeza and the City in the Sky* (1977); *Arcade Attack* (1981); *Skywhales* (1983); *The Victor* (1985); *Binky and Boo* (1987)

Hayes alone: *Albion* (short, 1978); *Prince Cinders* (short, 1993); *Elijah* (short, 1996); *The Miracle Maker* (UK/Russ, co-dir. Stanislav Sokolov, 2000); *Otherworld/Y Mabinogi* (live-action dir. Marc Evans, 2003); *Summer Sunday 1960* (short, 2004).

HAYMAN, David (1950–)

David Hayman was born in Bridgeton, Glasgow, in 1950. He left school at the age of fifteen to work in the same steelworks as his father, but decided he wanted to be an actor and enrolled at the Royal Scottish Academy of Music and Drama. After drama school, he spent ten years with the Citizens' Theatre company before reaching a wider audience with his portrayal of reformed Glasgow gangster Jimmy Boyle in *A Sense of Freedom* (John Mackenzie, 1981). A powerful actor, he has worked consistently in theatre, television and films such as *Hope and Glory* (John Boorman, 1987) and *Regeneration* (Gillies MacKinnon, 1997).

In the 1980s Hayman began directing in the theatre and on highly acclaimed television films such as *You've Never Slept in Mine* (1985), *Govan Ghost Story* (1989) and *Black and Blue* (1992), as well as David Kane's Newcastle gangster family saga *Finney* (1994), and the offbeat medical drama series, *Cardiac Arrest*

(1994). Hayman seems particularly attracted to realistic crime dramas that function effectively at the narrative level but also show crime as a manifestation of a wider malaise in society. His 1990 feature film debut, *Silent Scream*, based on the true story of convicted murderer Larry Winters, argued the need for prisons to provide the opportunity for redemption as well as exacting retribution. His next film, *The Hawk*, is a taut thriller about a woman (Helen Mirren) who suspects that her husband is a serial killer. *The Near Room* uses the story of a journalist's search for a missing girl to examine the link between individual morality and public corruption.

Since 1997 Hayman has been playing anti-hero detective Michael Walker in the successful television series *Trial and Retribution*. This has restricted his opportunities for doing other work, but he remains an interestingly idiosyncratic director.
(Linda Wood)

BIBLIOGRAPHY: Dobson, Patricia, 'Profile: David Hayman', *Screen International*, LFF Supplement, 17 Nov. 1993, p. 5; Edwardes, Jane, 'Making Hayman', *Time Out*, 10 June 1987, p. 39; Rix, Juliet, 'Change in Direction for Versatile Hayman', *Television Weekly*, 9 Mar. 1984, p. 8.

FILMOGRAPHY: *Silent Scream* (1990); *The Hawk* (1993); *The Near Room* (1995).

HAYNES, Manning (1888–1957)

Few British film-makers' reputations can have suffered the vagaries of fate as sharply as that of the actor and director Manning Haynes. For a few years in the later 1920s, the time of Hitchcock's and Asquith's ascendance, his work in features won him popular prestige and glowing trade reviews. Fresh from watching *Passion Island*, the *Bioscope* labelled him 'our most imaginative and versatile director' (18 June 1927); even *Close Up*, notoriously grudging about home-grown talent, admitted that he had 'potentialities' (March 1929, p. 16). But by the early 1930s, Haynes' star was already eclipsed: ahead in his career lay mostly factory pap and 'quota quickies'. By now, few prints survive to judge properly the glory of what once was, or was supposed to have been.

Born in Lyminster, West Sussex, in 1888, Manning Haynes began his career in the theatre in 1906, working variously as a touring manager, scenic artist, musician and actor, particularly associated with Sir Herbert Beerbohm Tree. Cinema beckoned in 1914: he took roles in several Clarendon productions and portrayed the heroine's aristocratic husband in the melodrama *Lady Audley's Secret* (Jack Denton, 1920). He first ventured into direction with Artistic Films, collaborating with Challis Sanderson on *Monty Works the Wires* (1921), a comedy vehicle for the dog featured earlier with Haynes in *Three Men and a Boat* (Challis Sanderson, 1920). In 1922 he began a popular series of shorts adapted by scenarist Lydia Hayward from W. W. Jacobs' stories. Among surviving examples, *The Boatswain's Mate* (1924) stands out for its sustained light-comedy atmosphere.

With Artistic in liquidation, Haynes moved elsewhere, initially to Gaumont. *London Love* (1926), with Fay Compton, John Stuart and Miles Mander, picked up kindly comments for the director's attempts to freshen an otherwise antique tale of rags, riches and murder. But it was another lost film, Pathé's *Passion Island*, with Moore Marriott and Lillian Oldland, that set the superlatives spinning, especially over Haynes' favoured technical trick of superimposing a close-up over a long shot, used to enliven a fight scene. The *Bioscope* claimed this as 'an amazingly effective device which to-morrow will be adopted by the world' (2 June 1927, p. 21), though it was essentially only a subtle variation on the long-established dissolve. Production was based at Rex Ingram's Nice studios: crucial for realistically duplicating the Corsican settings of W. W. Jacobs' tale of murder, revenge and blackmail.

Haynes' third major production of the period, *The Ware Case* (1928), has survived. The close-up trick, beautiful open-air camerawork, one telling tracking shot and some carefully considered compositions all suggest a relatively sophisticated cinematic mind, though one limited in its manoeuvres by the material chosen. George Pleydell Bancroft's doughty play about a country-house murder, circumstantial evidence and an aristocrat's guilt generates high drama sequence by sequence; but inattention to the characters' inner turmoils ultimately renders Stewart Rome's switch from solid brick to crazed cad hectic and unconvincing.

With the onset of talkies, Haynes' small but genuine visual niceties seem to have crumpled before the demands of dialogue and the expanded industry's factory requirements; once again, few prints survive. Certainly his status as a gifted director faded. At British Lion, he dutifully made the required Edgar Wallace properties, including *Should a Doctor Tell?* (strenuous drama) and *To Oblige a Lady* (comedy with music-hall star Maisie Gray). *Love's Old Sweet Song* (1933), for producer John Argyle, presented its sentimental romantic drama with mild success; but Haynes stayed stuck in low-budget fare, settling in at Fox-British in 1934 for five comedies and thrillers, modest in results and ambition. After a domestic comedy for producer George Smith, *Coming of Age* (1938), his only other known credit is on a 1947 documentary about the history of the trolley bus: not an assignment the *Bioscope* had in mind when it called Haynes 'an artist in celluloid'. Forgotten by most of the industry, Manning Haynes died in Surrey in 1957 after a long illness.
(Geoff Brown).

BIBLIOGRAPHY: Castle, Hugh, 'The Battle for Wardour Street', *Close Up*, Mar. 1929, pp. 10–17; Collier, Lionel, 'Trade Shows Surveyed', *Kinematograph Weekly*, 29 July 1926, p. 31; H.T., 'British Directors To-day', *The Bioscope*, British Film Number, 18 June 1927, p. 99; 'Passion Island', *The Bioscope*, 2 June 1927, p. 30; 'To Manning Haynes, a Great British Film Director', *The Bioscope*, 2 June 1927, p. 21.

FILMOGRAPHY: *Monty Works the Wires* (co-dir. Challis Sanderson, 1921); *A Will and a Way*; *Sam's Boy*; *The Head of the Family*; *The Skipper's Wooing* (1922); *An Odd Freak* (short); *The Monkey's Paw*; *The*

Convert (short); *The Constable's Move* (short) (1923); *Lawyer Quince* (short); *Dixon's Return* (short); *The Boatswain's Mate* (short) (1924); *London Love* (1926); *Passion Island* (1927); *The Ware Case* (1928); *Those Who Love* (1929); *Should a Doctor Tell?* (1930); *To Oblige a Lady*; *The Officer's Mess*; *The Old Man* (1931); *Love's Old Sweet Song* (aka *The Missing Witness*, 1933); *The Perfect Flaw* (1934); *Smith's Wives* (1935); *Tomorrow We Live*; *Highland Fling* (1936); *Pearls Bring Tears*; *East of Ludgate Hill* (1937); *The Claydon Treasure Mystery*; *Coming of Age* (1938); *Heart of the Trolley Bus* (doc., 1947).

HAYNES, Stanley (1906–1955)

Stanley Haynes was born in Birmingham on 14 November 1906 to Catholic parents. An extremely bright pupil, Haynes won a scholarship to study for the priesthood and later read classics at Oxford. His career in film began as a screenwriter in 1936 on *The Man behind the Mask* (Michael Powell). He then worked for Victor Saville as associate producer on *Storm in a Teacup* (1937) and *South Riding* (1938). During the war, he was associate producer on some notable films including *The Way Ahead* (Carol Reed, 1944), on which, in Reed's absence, he supervised the North African sequence (McFarlane, p. 233).

Stanley Haynes fulfilled his long-standing ambition to direct in 1946. *Carnival* was based on Compton Mackenzie's novel about a ballet dancer who chooses security over passion with fatal consequences (filmed in 1932 by Anthony Asquith as *Dance Pretty Lady*). The film's period costumes, Guy Green's photography and Sally Gray's gutsy performance should have guaranteed success, but Haynes' lack of experience and a crudely written script resulted in an unprofessional finish. 'The film's appeal', wrote *Kinematograph Weekly* ungenerously, '. . . is limited to the unwary and unsophisticated.'

Stanley Haynes suffered from personal difficulties. Two divorces, numerous failed love affairs and years of psychoanalysis, compounded by a falling-out with close friend and collaborator David Lean, adversely affected his professional career. He continued to write and produce into the 1950s, but after the prestige films he had worked on earlier, it was something of a comedown to produce John Harlow's B-crime films, *The Blue Parrot* (1953) and *Dangerous Cargo* (1954). Repeated frustration over his attempts to get a CinemaScope version of *A Tale of Two Cities* off the ground drove him to commit suicide in 1955.

(Margaret Butler)

BIBLIOGRAPHY: Billings, Josh, 'Carnival', *Kinematograph Weekly*, 17 Oct. 1946, p. 23; Brownlow, Kevin, *David Lean* (London: Faber and Faber, 1997); McFarlane, Brian, *An Autobiography of British Cinema* (London: Methuen, 1997).

FILMOGRAPHY: *Carnival* (1946).

HAYNES, Todd (1961–)

Todd Haynes was born in Encino, California, on 2 January 1961. He had begun to make amateur movies as a child, and after graduating from Brown University, where he majored in art and semiotics, he moved to New York City. His first film as an adult was the short *Superstar: The Karen Carpenter Story* (1987), a post-modern commentary on the life of the late singer and her battle with anorexia enacted by Barbie dolls. It attracted instant attention – at film festivals, and from Richard Carpenter, who all but suppressed it with a lawsuit over music rights. Haynes' first feature, *Poison* (1991), inspired by Jean Genet – won the Grand Jury Prize at the Sundance Film Festival and was hailed as a founding film of the New Queer Cinema.

Velvet Goldmine, Haynes' third feature fits oddly between his US features – *Safe* (1995) and the meticulously stylish *Far from Heaven* (2002). In a narrative structurally modelled on *Citizen Kane* (Orson Welles, 1941), Arthur (Christian Bale), a British reporter based in the US, investigates the faked on-stage assassination ten years earlier of his former glam-rock idol and object of furtive desire, the Bowie-esque Brian Slade (Jonathan Rhys Meyers). An indisputably queer film, it frustrated expectations of nostalgia and chafed against British cultural memories of glam and its era, attracting some critical resistance and derision. Nonetheless, Haynes' reading of glam as a fleeting (pre-HIV and pre-1980s) utopian moment of polymorphous sexual exploration is rigorously researched and conceptualised; *Velvet Goldmine* also captures the greyness of 1970s' Britain, the transformative power of glam, and the disappointment of its aftermath.

(Claire Monk)

BIBLIOGRAPHY: James, Nick, 'American Voyeur', *Sight and Sound*, Sept. 1998, pp. 8–10; Sargeant, Amy, 'The Content and the Form: Invoking "Pastness" in Three Recent Retro Films', in Amy Sargeant and Claire Monk (eds), *British Historical Cinema* (London and New York: Routledge, 2002); Sinker, Mark, 'Here's Looking at You Kid', *Sight and Sound*, Sept. 1998, pp. 11–13; Vachon, Christine, *Shooting to Kill: The Making of* Velvet Goldmine (London: Bloomsbury, 1998).

FILMOGRAPHY (UK only): *Velvet Goldmine* (1998).

HAZAN, Jack (1939–)

Jack Hazan was born in Manchester on 31 March 1939 and studied motion picture arts at the University of California. After freelance work in America, he joined the BBC as an assistant cameraman, but in 1967 he reverted to being freelance and set up Solus Enterprises, a camera rental, editing and post-production facility. Throughout his career he has worked as lighting cameraman on other directors' projects, from Maurice Hatton's *Okovango* (1968) to Pierre Lasry's *Shylock* (1999), and directed car commercials for Ford, Lincoln Mercury, Mitsubishi and Fiat.

Hazan's first short film, *Especially at My Time of Life*, on the relocation of an artists' colony in Camden Town, points to the direction of his later work: it was filmed over a long period of time and the story emerges from his observational camera. With his Solus partner, the film editor David Mingay, he made *A Bigger Splash*, which centres on David Hockney and friends, Peter Schlesinger, Ossie Clark and Celia Birtwell. The cinéma vérité approach, the patient assembling of footage and the search for a narrative within the material leads to a slightly off-balanced, but fascinating portrait of the London scene of the time. Hazan and Mingay continued in the same vein with *Rude Boy*, which integrates the punk rock group the Clash into the social context of Thatcherism. Here, 'Rude Boy' Ray Gange gradually becomes disillusioned with the group, as he discovers that, instead of being revolutionary, even radical, they are part of the commercial music scene. When the Clash realised that the film was less flattering than they had hoped, they disowned it. After eighteen years Hazan returned to the London scene with *Comic Act*, from an idea by David Mingay, but the vitality of his earlier work is missing.

(Kevin Gough-Yates)

BIBLIOGRAPHY: Richmond, Len, 'Breaking up Is Hard to Do', *Time Out*, 14 Mar. 1975, p. 7.

FILMOGRAPHY: *Especially at My Time of Life* (short, 1968); *Grant North* (short, 1972); *The Films of Robert Bolt* (short, 1973); *A Bigger Splash* (1974); *Rude Boy* (co-dir. David Mingay, 1980); *Cinema, Cinema* 'Letter from London' (short, 1982); *This Is What She's Like/Knowledge of Beauty* (short, 1985); *Comic Act* (1998).

HEEL, Sue

Sue Heel made her debut with the low-budget regional comedy *School for Seduction*, about a mysterious Italian beauty (Kelly Brook) who promises to transform the lives of Newcastle housewives by making them sexy. Lacking the amusingly subversive commentary on northern masculinity of *The Full Monty* (Peter Cattaneo, 1997) and the ribald undermining of respectable femininity of *Calendar Girls*, it failed to fizzle at the box office.

(Robert Murphy)

FILMOGRAPHY: *School for Seduction* (UK/Ger, 2004).

HEMMINGS, David (1941–2003)

David Hemmings was born on 18 November 1941 in Guildford, Surrey. He had his first professional engagement at the age of eleven, as a boy soprano in Benjamin Britten's opera, *The Turn of the Screw*. He acted in Basil Dearden's *The Rainbow Jacket* (1954) aged twelve, left home at fourteen and had his first painting exhibition at fifteen. In the late 1950s and early 60s he appeared in a string of youth movies including Clive Donner's *Some People* (1962) and Michael Winner's *Play It Cool* (1962) and *The System* (1964). It was still a surprise, however, when Michelangelo Antonioni cast him (rather than Terence Stamp) as Thomas, the David Bailey-like photographer in *Blow-up* (1966). It made Hemmings one of the iconic faces of the 1960s.

Other interesting roles followed – notably as the complex, angst-ridden Anglo-Saxon hero of Clive Donner's *Alfred the Great* (1969), and the trickster who seduces a crippled Samantha Eggar in *The Walking Stick* (Eric Till, 1970). But Hemmings was always too restless and driven to confine his creative energies to acting. He began his own company, Hemdale, with his business manager John Daly, in 1967, and directed his first feature in 1972, *Running Scared*, a stylish effort in which Robert Powell plays a Cambridge student who watches his friend commit suicide without intervening. *The 14* was another unusual story unsentimentally told, concerning fourteen disadvantaged siblings who fight to stay together following their mother's death.

Hemmings spent three years restoring *Just a Gigolo/Schöner Gigolo, armer Gigolo*, in which he appears alongside David Bowie and Kim Novak, after a fire destroyed much of the footage. He then relocated to Australia and New Zealand, where he made *The Survivor* with Robert Powell, and set the trend for exciting adventure films with *Race for the Yankee Zephyr*. He returned to Hollywood in 1984 and spent the rest of the decade directing episodes of American television series like *The A-Team* and *Quantum Leap*. Hemmings continued to combine notable film performances – in Fred Schepisi's *Last Orders* (2001) and Martin Scorsese's *Gangs of New York* (2002), for example – with modest but effective directing credits, such as his Welsh–American adaptation of a classic children's story, *A Christmas Reunion* (1993), until his death in Bucharest, Romania, from a heart attack on 3 December 2003. Between 1968 and 1974 he was married to the actress Gayle Hunnicutt.

(Janet Moat)

BIBLIOGRAPHY: Gow, Gordon, 'The Extended Arm', *Films and Filming*, May 1973, pp. 13–20; Obituary, *The Times*, 5 Dec. 2003, p. 45.

FILMOGRAPHY: *Running Scared* (1972); *The 14* (aka *The Wild Little Bunch*, 1973); *Just a Gigolo/Schöner Gigolo, armer Gigolo* (Ger, 1979); *The Survivor* (Austral); *Race for the Yankee Zephyr* (Austral/NZ, 1981); *Dark Horse* (US, 1992).

HENDERSON, John (c. 1949–)

John Henderson studied law at Liverpool University but made his career in advertising, branching into television in the early 1980s as one of the writers on the comedy series *Not the Nine O'Clock News* (1979). Along with innumerable commercials and video promos, Henderson went on to direct series of *Spitting Image* (1987–9) and *Sticky Moments with Julian Clary* (1989), graduating to an adaptation of Mary Norton's children's classic *The Borrowers* in 1992. His first feature film *Loch Ness* (1996) is best seen as another children's film, with its too-easily unravelled romantic entanglements and sentimental plot made excusable by strong messages about trust, integrity and respect for nature.

After *The Return of the Borrowers*, made for television in 1996, Henderson directed *Bring Me the Head of Mavis Davis* (1998), a laborious Rik Mayall comedy about a record producer who hires an incompetent hitman to kill off the Madonna-like star who ungratefully threatens to leave him. Much better were *The Last Englishman* (1995), a sixty-minute television play based on the life of the absurdly eccentric Colonel Alfred Wintle (played with conviction by Jim Broadbent); and *How Do You Want Me?* (1998–9), a witty, original BBC comedy series with a superb cast headed by Dylan Moran and Charlotte Coleman.

Henderson returned to the cinema for *Two Men Went to War* (2002), which like *The Last Englishman* features an over-patriotic soldier who pursues his own military campaign against the enemy. However, Kenneth Cranham's Sergeant King and his helpmate Private Cuthbertson are more humble characters: Henderson puffs out their petty exploits with scenes from the life of the busy prime minister (who saves them from court martial), but the film's small-scale virtues seem more suited to television than the cinema. Henderson moved on to *The Water Giant*, a long-nurtured monster-in-a-lake project relocated to New Zealand when British Columbia became too cluttered with holiday homes. No reports have yet filtered through of how successfully this utilises the talents of this erratically energetic director.

(Robert Murphy)

BIBLIOGRAPHY: Davies, Nina, 'A Real Live Wire', *Televisual*, Dec. 1987, pp. 24–5.

FILMOGRAPHY: *Loch Ness* (1996); *Bring Me the Head of Mavis Davis* (1998); *Two Men Went to War* (2002); *The Water Giant* (aka *Mee-Shee: The Water Giant*, UK/Can, 2002: rel. 2005).

HENRIQUES, Julian (1955–)

Julian Henriques was born in Yorkshire in 1955. After studying psychology, he worked as a lecturer and journalist before becoming a television researcher. He subsequently combined television work – mainly as a documentary director – with teaching scriptwriting at Goldsmiths College, London.

After making *Exit No Exit* (1988) for the *Dance on Four* series, Henriques made three substantial documentaries for *Made in Latin America* (Channel 4, 1989): *Dictating Terms*, *States of Exile* and *City Limits*, and *Derek Walcott* (1993), a profile of the Caribbean poet for the BBC arts programme *Arena*. In 1992 Henriques made a short fiction film, *We the Ragamuffin*, depicting the dance-hall subculture of black British youth in Peckham, south London. His feature film *Babymother*, which tells the story of a young black woman (Anjela Lauren Smith) who defies her errant boyfriend to succeed as a charismatic dance-hall performer, returns to the same cultural milieu, though in Harlesden, in north-west London. Lively, colourful and loud, *Babymothers* showed the positive side of London's Black community; vibrant energy and resilience overcoming the problems of sexism and poverty.

Henriques returned to television to make *Ding Dong Merrily on High* (2000), a comic monologue with Marcus Powell as an ageing Jamaican stand-up comedian, in the ITV *Single Voices* series.

(Paul Ward)

BIBLIOGRAPHY: Goldberg, Marcy, 'Julian Henriques' *Babymother*', *CineAction!* no. 49, June 1999, pp. 66–8; Hall, Stuart,

Babymother (Julien Henriques, 1998)

'A Rage in Harlesden', *Sight and Sound*, Sept. 1998, pp. 25–6; Korte, Barbara and Claudia Sternberg, *Bidding for the Mainstream? Black and Asian British Film since the 1990s* (Amsterdam and New York: Rodopi, 2004); Shabazz, Menelik, 'Interview with Julian Henriques', *Black Filmmaker*, Feb./Mar. 1998, pp. 7–9, 12.

FILMOGRAPHY: *We the Ragamuffin* (short, 1992); *Babymother* (1998).

HEPWORTH, Cecil (1874–1953)

A producer, director, writer and scenic photographer, Cecil Hepworth survived in the film business longer than any other British pioneer film-maker. In the course of his career, Hepworth became one of the most respected, if never the most dynamic, figures in British cinema. He established his own film company in 1899, when he converted a small house in Walton-on-Thames into a studio. Twenty-five years later it would be the overambitious expansion of the studio that would drive him out of business.

Cecil Milton Hepworth was born on 19 March 1874 in Lambeth, south London, the son of celebrated magic lantern showman T. C. Hepworth. In the early days of cinema he worked on the industry's periphery, assisting Birt Acres in a Royal Command cinematograph performance, and writing the first British book on cinema, *Animated Photography, The ABC of the Cinematograph*, in 1897. The following year, as cameraman for the Maguire and Baucus agency, remodelled by Charles Urban into the Warwick Trading Company, Hepworth shot numerous actualities, from the 1898 Oxford and Cambridge boat race and Gladstone's funeral to naval scenes and the popular 'phantom rides'. After being sacked by Urban, Hepworth and his cousin Monty Wicks set up their own outfit, Hepworth and Co., with their trade logo Hepwix. From May 1899 a steady stream of scenic films and actualities emerged, beginning with three trains steaming through a railway cutting (*Express Train*); the filming of Queen Victoria's funeral in 1901 gave the company their first big success. There were also simple comedies and effects films. *The Explosion of a Motor Car* (1900) proved particularly popular; three years later Hepworth co-directed with Percy Stow the sixteen-scene *Alice in Wonderland*, at 800ft the longest film yet produced in Britain. In 1904 the company was renamed the Hepworth Manufacturing Company; Hepworth stopped directing for a time, handing over the reins to Lewin Fitzhamon, Frank Wilson, Bert Haldane and others. A house style developed, based on simple stories told with high photographic quality. The company produced on average three films a week, straddling the range from melodramas and slapstick comedies to scenics and travel films. In 1905 Hepworth presented the public with their first British movie star: a collie with the character name of Rover. *Rescued by Rover* (Lewin Fitzhamon, 1905) was an enormous popular success and was remade several times to meet popular demand. The following year in *Black Beauty* (Lewin Fitzhamon, 1906) a new star was offered – a horse, subsequently teamed with Rover in *Dumb Sagacity* (Lewin Fitzhamon, 1907). By 1910 Hepworth furthered the cinema's growing cult of personality with two series featuring recurring comic characters: Mr Poorluck, played by Harry Buss, and Tilly the Tomboy, featuring Alma Taylor and Chrissie White.

Rescued by Rover is notable for its efficient narrative style, with the action clarified by consistency of direction from one shot to the next. Yet Hepworth himself showed little interest in the development of film language; indeed in later years he spoke out against the narrative system of classical Hollywood films. His heart remained in simple scenic photography, and he brought a notably pictorial style to bear upon his own fiction films, often at the expense of their drama. In 1911, after sales in the UK had dwindled and the formation of the Motion Picture Patents Corporation had closed the US to British films, the company began adapting famous novels and plays, using famous actors in an attempt to revitalise its product. Dickens adaptations included *Oliver Twist* (Thomas Bentley, 1912); there was also a prestige edition of *Hamlet* (Hay Plumb, 1913), starring Sir Johnston Forbes-Robertson, greeted with superlatives by the critics. In his own films particularly, Hepworth still promoted the film language that he had fostered before 1910: frontal staging with action played out in pantomimic gestures in a single long-shot tableau. Rarely was a space broken down in a Hepworth shot. Ultimately as the classical narrative system took over, the Hepworth films began to look more and more old-fashioned. They were, however, championed in the film press, and popular enough to turn both Chrissie White and Alma Taylor into major British stars.

Hepworth Picture Plays, as the company became, continued making modestly successful films into the 1920s. His film subjects at this time were still mostly melodramas, although a foray into comedy with *Alf's Button* (1920) proved massively popular, even in America; in Britain the film was revived several times. Buoyed by this financial success, Hepworth planned to build a large studio complex; he also bought a local country house with large grounds, Oatlands Lodge Estate, to use for filming purposes. To fund this expansion he released a share prospectus; it was badly undersubscribed, and Hepworth found himself unable to raise the capital required to pay off what he already owed. For a while the company limped on, and he was able to complete the remake of his *Comin' thro' the Rye*, filmed earlier in 1916, based on Helen Mathers' novel of rural love and jealousy. The 1923 version proved quaintly pretty, doused with his trademark 'vignette' shots and abundant intertitles; Hepworth regarded it as his finest achievement. Unfortunately audiences did not share his opinion, and it failed to revive his fortunes. On 17 June 1924 a receiver was appointed who sold off Hepworth's company for a fraction of its worth. All his original negatives were melted down to reclaim the silver. After an unsuccessful mystery melodrama *The House of Marney*, produced at his old studio, now owned by Archibald Nettlefold, Hepworth retreated from frontline filming. But he retained an industry foothold for twenty years, making trailers in the 1930s,

'Food Flashes' for the Ministry of Information during the war and – back to his old love – scenic films of the countryside for the National Screen Service.

Hepworth was a film-maker with a unique visual style but one that barely changed from the early melodramas to his features of the 1920s. He was justifiably proud of his place in cinema history, and toured in later life with a lecture programme telling the story of the birth of cinema. As *Variety* wrote on 19 May 1922, he was apt to allow the artist in his nature to conquer the commercialism of the showman. But in the process he gave a rough-and-tumble industry respectability, poise and many films of picturesque beauty. He died on 9 February 1953 in Greenford, Middlesex.

(Simon Brown)

BIBLIOGRAPHY: Hepworth, Cecil M., *Came the Dawn* (London: Phoenix House, 1951); Higson, Andrew, *Waving the Flag* (Oxford: Oxford University Press, 1995); Low, Rachael, *The History of the British Film 1918–1929* (London: George Allen & Unwin, 1971); Low, Rachael, *The History of the British Film 1906–1914* (London: George Allen & Unwin, 1973); Low, Rachael and Roger Manvell, *The History of the British Film 1896-1906* (London: George Allen & Unwin, 1948).

SELECTED FILMOGRAPHY: *Oxford and Cambridge Boat Race*; *Gladstone's Funeral* (series); *An Interrupted Picnic*; *Exchange Is No Robbery*; *The Immature Punter*; *The Quarrelsome Anglers* (aka *The Stolen Drink*); *Two Fools in a Canoe* (aka *Two Cockneys in a Canoe*) (1898); *Express Trains* (1899); *Wiping Something off the Slate*; *The Conjuror and the Boer*; *The Queen's Visit to Dublin, Entering the City Gates*; *The Punter's Mishap*; *The Gunpowder Plot*; *The Explosion of a Motor Car* (US: *The Delights of Automobiling*); *The Egg-Laying Man*; *Clown and Policeman*; *Leapfrog as Seen by the Frog*; *How It Feels to Be Run Over*; *The Solar Eclipse* (series); *The Eccentric Dancer*; *The Bathers*; *The Sluggard's Surprise*; *The Electricity Cure*; *The Beggar's Deceit*; *The Burning Stable*; *Topsy-Turvy Villa* (1900); *Funeral of Queen Victoria* (series); *The Comic Grimacer* (1901); *The Call to Arms*; *Peace with Honour* (co-dir. Percy Stow) (1902); *Alice in Wonderland* (co-dir. Percy Stow); *Firemen to the Rescue* (1903); *The Jonah Man; or, The Traveller Bewitched* (co-dir. Lewin Fitzhamon, 1904); *Invisibility* (co-dir. Lewin Fitzhamon, 1909); *The Funeral of King Edward VII* (1910); *Speech by Mr Bonar Law, MP* (1911); *Blind Fate*; *Unfit; or, The Strength of the Weak*; *The Hills Are Calling*; *The Basilisk*; *The Call* (aka *His Country's Bidding*); *The Quarry Mystery*; *Time the Great Healer*; *Morphia the Death Drug*; *Oh My Aunt!* (1914); *Be Sure Your Sins* (aka *The Canker of Jealousy*); *A Moment of Darkness*; *Traitor* (aka *Court-Martialled*); *The Passing of a Soul*; *The Bottle*; *The Baby on the Barge*; *The Man Who Stayed at Home*; *Sweet Lavender*; *The Golden Pavement*; *The Outrage*; *Iris* (1915); *Trelawney of the 'Wells'*; *Cabinet Interviews* (aka *Cinema Interviews*, series); *A Fallen Star*; *Sowing the Wind*; *Annie Laurie*; *The Marriage of William Ashe*; *Comin' thro' the Rye*; *Molly Bawn* (1916); *The Cobweb*; *The American Heiress*; *Nearer My God to Thee* (1917); *The Touch of a Child*; *A New Version*; *The W.L.A. Girl*; *The Leopard's Spots*; *The Refuge*; *Tares*; *Boundary House* (1918); *Broken in the Wars*; *The Nature of the Beast*; *Sunken Rocks*; *Sheba*; *The Forest on the Hill* (1919); *Anna the Adventuress*; *Alf's Button*; *Helen of the Four Gates*; *Mrs Erricker's Reputation* (1920); *The Tinted Venus*; *Narrow Valley*; *Wild Heather*, *Tansy* (1921); *Through Three Reigns* (1922); *The Pipes of Pan*; *Mist in the Valley*; *Strangling Threads*; *Comin' thro' the Rye* (1923); *Celebrities at Home* (series, 1925); *The House of Marney* (1926).

HERBERT, Henry (1939–2003)

Henry George Charles Alexander Herbert, 17th Earl of Pembroke and 14th Earl of Montgomery, was born on 19 May 1939 in Pembroke, Wales. He entered the film industry as an assistant on *The Heroes of Telemark* (Anthony Mann, 1965) and then turned towards documentaries. He made a film about the opening of the Playboy club in London in 1966; two short films about a school for blind children followed in 1972, which were later shown in the BBC's *Man Alive* slot. In 1973, financed by Canadian tax shelter money, Herbert made his first feature film, *The Seaweed Children*, which he adapted himself from a story about Cornish seaweed gatherers by Anthony Trollope; its release was delayed until 1977. His next film *Emily* was aimed at a different audience: a soft-core sex drama featuring the briefly famous Koo Stark as a well-brought-up young woman anxious to lose her virginity in 1928 Britain. It failed to emulate the success of the similarly themed *Emmanuelle* (Just Jaeckin, 1974) and Herbert turned to television. He established himself as a proficient and adaptable craftsman, directing episodes of *Danger UXB* (1979), *Shoestring* (1980), *Bergerac* (1981), *Q.E.D.* (1982) and *King & Castle* (1986). In the 1990s he returned to the film industry, co-producing *The Girl with Brains in Her Feet* (Roberto Bangura, 1997), a low-budget realist film set in the 1970s, and acting as executive producer on Don Boyd's *Lucia* (1998). Boyd returned the favour by producing Herbert's *Crossmaheart*, an unexpectedly gritty film about Northern Ireland based on Colin Bateman's novel *Cycle of Violence*. A (Southern) Irish correspondent welcomed its refusal to sentimentalise its setting: 'It's a piss-smelling hell-hole whose inhabitants' squalid hatreds are only matched by their hypocrisy. Billy Boys, Provos, rapists and venal journalists all get their fair measure of bile . . .' (Linehan, 1998). However, lacking the zany humour of an earlier Bateman adaptation, *Divorcing Jack* (David Caffrey, 1998), *Crossmaheart* suffered the usual fate of films about Northern Ireland and failed to reach an audience. Latterly Herbert spent much time supervising the restoration of the family seat, Wilton House. He died of cancer on 7 October 2003, in Wiltshire.

(Robert Murphy)

BIBLIOGRAPHY: Falk, Quentin, 'More Sex Please, We're British', *Screen International*, 1 May 1976, pp. 8-9; Linehan, Hugh, 'Crossmaheart', *Film West* no. 32, May 1998, p. 60; McGillivray, David, *Doing Rude Things: The History of the British Sex Film, 1957–81* (London: Sun Tavern Fields, 1992); Obituary, *Classic Images* no. 341, Nov. 2003, p. 55.

FILMOGRAPHY: *Playboy Comes to London* (doc. short, 1966); *What Colour Is the Wind?* (doc. short); *What Is the Sky?* (doc. short) (1972);

The Seaweed Children (aka *Malachi's Cove*, 1973); *Emily* (1976); *Crossmaheart* (1998).

HERBERT, Leon

Leon Herbert, a black British actor, spent four years trying to set up his feature debut *Emotional Backgammon*. The premise that restless thirtysomethings unwilling to commit themselves to mundane family life risk damaging themselves with emotional game-playing is intriguing; but its appeal fades as we lose interest in the film's selfish, mean-spirited characters.

(Robert Murphy)

BIBLIOGRAPHY: Harvey, Mae, 'Emotional Backgammon . . . Hits the States', *Black Filmmaker* vol. 6 no. 24, May/June 2004, pp. 16–17; *Movie Virgins* (four-part documentary about Leon Herbert and Alex Jovy's attempts to get their debut features off the ground, Channel 4, 2000).

FILMOGRAPHY: *Emotional Backgammon* (2003).

HERKOMER, Sir Hubert von (1849–1914)

Hubert Herkomer was born in Waal, Bavaria, in 1849 but brought to England as a child by his father, a distinguished woodcarver. After art school in Southampton and South Kensington, he found fame in 1875 with a large narrative painting, 'The Last Muster' depicting a group of Chelsea pensioners. Sharply realistic subjects showing Victorian poverty such as 'Hard Times' (1885) and 'On Strike' (1891) alternated with society portraits which brought him a lucrative income and a knighthood. His approach to art was both practical and aesthetic. During the 1880s he built a small theatre in the gardens of his home 'Lululaund', at Bushey, Hertfordshire, where he designed and produced his own musical plays. In 1913 he turned his attention towards film-making, converting the garden theatre into a studio. Although the five films produced by Herkomer and his son Siegfried were not particularly successful, they provided a link between high art and popular culture. Herkomer expressed a visionary commitment to the cinema, likening films to 'the old masters' and foreseeing a future in which screenless, coloured sound productions would be possible. The actor A. E. Matthews recalled that Herkomer's last production, *A Highwayman's Honour*, was filmed over the leisurely schedule of ten months, without recourse to a script. Herkomer both appeared in and directed his films, and his mission to legitimise cinema was maintained after his death when Matthews, on behalf of the British Actors' Film Company, acquired the Bushey studio.

(Barry Anthony)

BIBLIOGRAPHY: MacCormick Edwards, Lee, *Hubert von Herkomer: A Victorian Artist* (Aldershot, Hants: Ashgate Publishing, 1999); Pitt, Peter, 'The Oldest Studio', *Films and Filming*, Mar. 1983, pp. 29–31; Pritchard, Michael, *Sir Hubert von Herkomer and his Film-Making in Bushey 1912–1914* (Bushey, Herts: Bushey Museum Trust, 1987).

FILMOGRAPHY: *The Old Woodcarver*; *Love in a Teashop*; *The White Witch*; *His Choice* (1913); *A Highwayman's Honour* (1914).

HERMAN, Mark (1954–)

Mark Herman was born in Bridlington, in the East Riding of Yorkshire, in 1954. He attended the National Film and Television School in the mid-1980s as a prospective animator, but intimidated by the work of fellow student Nick Park, he chose to specialise more in scriptwriting and live action. His final-year film, *See You at Wembley, Frankie Walsh*, won the Student Academy Award for Best Foreign Film in 1987. He also wrote lyrics for pop group the Christians, penning the chart success, 'Ideal World'.

Herman worked for two years at the BBC before his script for a comedy of mistaken identity set in Venice, *Blame It on the Bellboy*, attracted American financial backing. Though it failed to equal the success of the more polished Anglo-American comedy *A Fish Called Wanda* (Charles Crichton, 1988), Herman's feature debut – which cleverly deployed Dudley Moore, Bryan Brown and a host of British character actors – was successful enough for him to raise finance for his more personal and parochial film about a Yorkshire colliery brass band, *Brassed Off*. Ironically, it turned out to be a major international success. The performances of Pete Postlethwaite, Tara Fitzgerald and Ewan McGregor, and Herman's intelligent treatment of the fate of a mining community decimated by the drastic contraction of coal mining in Britain, aroused sympathy and understanding far beyond those with direct experience of these problems.

Herman's next film, an adaptation of Jim Cartwright's play *The Rise and Fall of Little Voice*, had been directed on stage by Sam Mendes and planned as a film by Beeban Kidron for Channel 4. Herman's version, made for Miramax and Steve Woolley's Scala Productions, benefits hugely from Jane Horrocks reprising her stage performance as the reticent, bullied girl who finds identity and purpose through her impersonations of Judy Garland, Marilyn Monroe and Shirley Bassey. But Herman also makes a valuable contribution, shooting the film on location in Scarborough but in a stylised way that suggests a dark fairy tale about young people breaking free of the selfishly materialistic concerns of their elders. Secure in her fantasy world and the love of a shy electrician (Ewan McGregor), LV survives the machinations of her bad mother (Brenda Blethyn) and a sleazy has-been agent (Michael Caine) to find her own identity.

Purely Belter, an adaptation of Jim Tulloch's novel, *The Season Ticket*, followed. It portrays the antics of two young Newcastle United supporters in pursuit of season tickets. Though well liked by those who saw it, Herman's film was overshadowed by *Billy Elliot* (Stephen Daldry, 2000) and failed to reach a wide audience. Similarly, Herman's romantic comedy, *Hope Springs*, illustrates his ability to avoid sentiment while creating touching and affecting relationships (in this case between Colin Firth, torn between fetching Heather Graham and demanding Minnie Driver), but it was not a box-office success. Herman has attracted little critical attention but his preoccupation with the underdog and personal and social injustice makes him a pertinent commentator

on the decline of the English working class and its strategies for survival.
(Paul Wells)

BIBLIOGRAPHY: 'Headliners', *Empire*, Dec. 2000, p. 20; Miller, John, 'Pure Gold', *Film Review*, Dec. 2000, pp. 50–1; Morrison, Alan, 'Interview: Mark Herman', *Total Film*, Dec. 2000, p. 147.

FILMOGRAPHY: *Unusual Ground Floor Conversion* (short); *See You at Wembley, Frankie Walsh* (short) (1987); *Blame It on the Bellboy* (1992); *Brassed Off* (UK/US, 1997); *Little Voice* (1998); *Purely Belter* (2000); *Hope Springs* (UK/US, 2002).

HESSLER, Gordon (1925–)

Gordon Hessler was born in Berlin on 12 December 1925 and educated in England, but his first significant credit was on American television as a director and producer on the *Alfred Hitchcock Presents* series in 1961, and his first feature film, the British thriller *Catacombs*, was based on a story originally turned down for the Hitchcock series. While some of Hessler's later British films were also thrillers – namely *The Last Shot You Hear* and *Embassy* – his most distinctive work was in British horror of the late 1960s. This was a time when young and ambitious film-makers in both Britain and America were turning to the horror genre as a legitimate form of cultural expression. Hessler took over from Michael Reeves (who died of a drugs overdose shortly after) on American International Pictures' *The Oblong Box*. Although Hessler lacked the auteurist ambitions of Reeves and *The Oblong Box* is conventional in terms of its narrative, Hessler's style is strikingly modern, with an extensive use of subjective camerawork and distorting lenses.

Hessler's next two films for AIP, the science-fiction horror *Scream and Scream Again* (a co-production with the British company Amicus) and the gothic horror *Cry of the Banshee* reunited him with key collaborators from *The Oblong Box*, screenwriter Christopher Wicking, cinematographer John Coquillon and star Vincent Price. *Scream and Scream Again*, a deliriously fragmented tale of superstrong humanoids and serial killers, is Hessler's most stylish film and has become a cult favourite. *Cry of the Banshee* more closely resembles *The Oblong Box*, although its focus on tensions between an authoritarian, and implicitly masculine, Christianity, and a vaguely counter-cultural, and implicitly feminine, paganism, is an unusual one in British gothic horror. After another film for AIP, *Murders in the Rue Morgue*, and *The Golden Voyage of Sinbad*, one of the best of the Ray Harryhausen special-effects extravaganzas, Hessler returned to the United States where he has pursued a successful career directing series and television films.
(Peter Hutchings)

BIBLIOGRAPHY: Pirie, David, 'New Blood', *Sight and Sound*, Spring 1971, pp. 73–5; Pirie, David, *A Heritage of Horror* (London: Gordon Fraser, 1973).

FILMOGRAPHY: *St John's Story* (doc., US, 1954); *Catacombs* (aka *The Woman Who Wouldn't Die*, 1964); *The Last Shot You Hear* (1968); *The Oblong Box*; *Scream and Scream Again* (1969); *Cry of the Banshee* (1970); *Murders in the Rue Morgue* (UK/US, 1971); *Embassy* (1972); *The Golden Voyage of Sinbad*; *Medusa* (aka *The Rhodes Incident*/*Twisted*, Gr) (1973); *Attracto en la jungla* (aka *Dynamite and Blue Jeans*, Sp/Venez, 1975); *Escape from El Diablo* (US, 1982); *Pray for Death* (US, 1985); *Rage of Honor* (US); *Wheels of Terror* (aka *The Misfit Brigade*, US, 1987); *The Girl in a Swing* (UK/US, 1988); *Out on Bail* (US, 1989); *Shogun Mayeda* (aka *Journey of Honor*, US/Jap, 1992).

HEWITT, Peter (1962–)

Peter W. H. Hewitt was born in 1962 in Brighton, Sussex. He studied film-making at the London College of Printing, and the National Film School, where his graduation film, *The Candy Show*, won a BAFTA award for Best Short Film. This brought Hewitt to the attention of Hollywood, and after making an episode of HBO's *Tales from the Crypt* (1989) he was hired to direct *Bill and Ted's Bogus Journey*, a successful sequel to the hit comedy *Bill and Ted's Excellent Adventure* (Stephen Herek, 1989). Declining offers to direct other sequels, Hewitt then made two episodes of Oliver Stone's science-fiction miniseries, *Wild Palms* (1993).

After this excursion into the bizarre, Hewitt moved into the mainstream with the Disney family adventure *Tom and Huck*, an adaptation of Mark Twain's *The Adventures of Tom Sawyer*. Hewitt decided his future lay in family-oriented movies and he returned to Britain for *The Borrowers*, Working Title's adaptation of Mary Norton's popular series of children's novels. It was an international box-office success, but Hewitt's next film, *Whatever Happened to Harold Smith?*, a quirky comedy starring Tom Courtenay, failed to catch on with the multiplex audience and quickly disappeared, though it has subsequently acquired a cult reputation. After *Princess of Thieves* (2001), an Anglo-American television movie with Keira Knightley as Robin Hood's daughter and Malcolm McDowell as the Sheriff of Nottingham, Hewitt returned to the cinema with *Thunderpants* (2002), a comedy centred on the adventures of a flatulent schoolboy. Although the film offended some older reviewers and lacked the crossover appeal of the Harry Potter films, it proved highly popular with the children's audience at which it was aimed. Hewitt, who seems to combine commercial acumen with a genuinely cinematic intelligence, moved on to direct the live-action/computer-animated *Garfield: The Movie*, based on the popular comic strip, with Bill Murray voicing the eponymous feline. The film's $75 million American box-office takings should be sufficient to guarantee Hewitt a secure future.
(Martin Hunt)

BIBLIOGRAPHY: Berry, Joanna, 'Peter Hewitt: Director', *Empire*, Feb. 1992, p. 39; Jones, Alan, 'Peter Hewitt: The Director Wants to Do Family Fare', *Cinefantastique*, Mar. 1998, p. 57.

FILMOGRAPHY: *The Candy Show* (short, 1989); *Bill and Ted's Bogus Journey* (US, 1991); *Tom and Huck* (US, 1995); *The Borrowers* (1997); *Whatever Happened to Harold Smith?* (1999); *Thunderpants* (2002); *Garfield: The Movie* (US, 2004).

HICKEY, Kieran (1936–1993)

Kieran Hickey was born in Dublin on 29 September 1936. After studying at the London Film School, he returned to Ireland and established his production company, BAC Films, where he produced sophisticated cultural and literary documentaries, including the moving *Faithful Departed* (1967). In 1978 Hickey made his first foray into fiction with *A Child's Voice*, a ghost story influenced by the horror films of Val Lewton. In the same year he made *Exposure*, from a script by Philip Davison, a brilliant dissection of Irish masculinity. Staying at a guesthouse in the west of Ireland, three male land surveyors become distracted by the presence of a confident French woman photographer. The two more emotionally crippled men react primitively when their younger colleague starts an affair with the woman. Hickey's climactic scene, when the men drunkenly ransack the woman's room and her belongings, remains one of the more shocking in Irish cinema. Equally probing and controversial was *Criminal Conversation* (1980), again scripted by Davison. Hickey sets out again to expose male–female relationships, this time by focusing on the hypocrisy and lies of a pair of middle-class married couples who meet up for a Christmas Eve house party. Drunkenness leads to some nasty revelations. 'Criminal Conversation' is an Irish legal term for adultery.

While his previous two films had focused on troubled relations between men and women, *Attracta* (1983), based on a story by William Trevor, examines the descent into madness of an elderly Protestant schoolteacher, haunted by memories of the Irish Struggle and the Troubles in the North. Hickey's engagement with Irish history continued in his final film, *The Rockingham Shoot*, based on an original script by John McGahern and produced by BBC Northern Ireland. Again focusing on the North, the film presented a stirring character study of another schoolteacher, a rabid Nationalist, played by Bosco Hogan, who bullies his classroom with lessons in Gaelic. When some of his students skip class to find work assisting in the pheasant shoot at aristocratic Rockingham Castle, Hogan exacts his revenge on the oppressor by punishing the students. A portrait of blind allegiance to 'the cause', *The Rockingham Shoot* is a stunningly mounted piece dealing with a favourite Hickey theme, the repressiveness of the Irish male.

Kieran Hickey died on 14 July 1993, but he left behind an enduring cinematic legacy: provocative, intelligent and deeply critical of what was then still a deeply conservative society.

(Eugene Finn)

BIBLIOGRAPHY: Hickey, Kieran, 'The Cinema and Ireland – A Short History', *Green on the Screen Festival Programme*, 1984; McIlroy, Brian, *Irish Cinema* (Dublin: Anna Livia Press, 1988), pp. 48–50; O'Connor, John, 'Ground Breaker', *Film Ireland* no. 37, Oct./Nov. 1993, pp. 20–3.

FILMOGRAPHY (fiction complete; documentary selective): *Faithful Departed* (doc.); *Jonathan Swift* (doc.) (1967); *The Light of Other Days* (doc., 1972); *Portrait of a Library* (doc., 1976); *A Child's Voice*; *Exposure* (1978); *Criminal Conversation* (1980); *Attracta*; *On Our Own Doorstep* (doc.) (1983); *Short Story – Irish Cinema 1945–1958* (doc., 1986); *The Rockingham Shoot* (1987).

HICKOX, Douglas (1929–1988)

Douglas Hickox was born in London on 10 January 1929, and entered the film industry in 1946 as an office boy at Pinewood. By 1950 he had risen to assistant director, mostly on B-movies and television series such as *William Tell*. He cut his directorial teeth making *Behemoth, the Sea Monster* (with Eugène Lourié), one of the most inept and ridiculous of the period's atomic creature features, thirty-two musical shorts and three supporting features showcasing various jazz and pop performers.

In 1966 Hickox formed Illustra Films to make commercials, winning more than seventy advertising awards over the next five years. For this company he also directed a more ambitious musical short, *Les Bicyclettes de Belsize*, influenced by Jacques Demy's *Les Parapluies de Cherbourg* (1964). Modish and twee, it was nonetheless well enough received to allow Hickox to make his first, and best, major feature, Joe Orton's kinky black comedy *Entertaining Mr Sloane*. The director's vulgar visual style is, for once, properly attuned to the grotesquerie of his material: Hickox was of the generation for whom the zoom lens was a way of life, and much of his work is marked by the extremes of wide-angle and telephoto.

His subsequent films at best demonstrate proficient opportunism but no discernible personality. *Sitting Target* is a nasty, flashy crime thriller with a couple of well-staged action sequences. *Theatre of Blood* is crude, witless *Grand Guignol*, squandering a good idea – a ham actor (Vincent Price) murders his critics in a series of Shakespearean charades – in a slew of illogicalities. *Brannigan* is a shoddily scripted but rather genial vehicle for John Wayne as a Chicago cop at large in tourist London. *Sky Riders* is a preposterous adventure yarn with an exciting climax in which James Coburn leads a team of hang-gliders to rescue kidnap victims from their mountain-top prison.

Hickox's biggest assignment was *Zulu Dawn*, the $8.5 million prequel to *Zulu* (1964), with a screenplay by the original film's director, Cy Endfield. Though a worthy attempt to reconstruct the events leading up to the massacre of 1,300 British soldiers at Isandhlwana in 1879, the profusion of dates and characters makes for tedium and muddle rather than the intended epic sweep. Despite a starry cast (Burt Lancaster, Peter O'Toole) and thousands of extras for the sprawling battle scenes, it was a commercial disaster.

Most of Hickox's subsequent career was spent directing films and miniseries for television. A superior remake of *The Hound of the Baskervilles*, starring Ian Richardson as a dashing Holmes, was shown out of competition at Cannes but did not receive a theatrical release. Hickox died following heart surgery on 25 July 1988. His first wife was the distinguished editor Anne V. Coates; the director Anthony Hickox is their son.

(Sheldon Hall)

BIBLIOGRAPHY: Lukk, Tiiu, 'Filming *Zulu Dawn* on Location in South Africa', *American Cinematographer*, Feb. 1979, pp. 148–51, 178–9, 184; McAsh, Ian F., 'Sitting Target', *Films Illustrated* no. 7, Jan. 1972, pp. 20–3.

FILMOGRAPHY: *Behemoth, the Sea Monster* (US: *The Giant Behemoth*, co-dir. Eugène Lourié, 1959); *Four Hits and a Mister* (short, 1963); *It's All Over Town*; *Just for You* (1964); *Discotheque Holiday* (US: *Disk-o-Tek Holiday*, co-dir. Vincent Scarza, 1966); *Les Bicyclettes de Belsize* (short, 1968); *Entertaining Mr Sloane* (1970); *Sitting Target* (1972); *Talk of the Devil* (doc. short); *Theatre of Blood* (1973); *A Whole New World of Colour* (doc. short); *Brannigan* (1975); *Sky Riders* (US, 1976); *Zulu Dawn* (US/Neth, 1979); *The Hound of the Baskervilles* (1983).

HILL, James (1919–1994)

James Hill was born in Eldwick, Yorkshire, on 9 July 1919. He began his career with the GPO Film Unit, and directed several documentaries in the 1940s and 50s, winning an Academy Award in 1960 for *Giuseppina*. By this time he had already directed four hour-long juvenile thrillers including *The Stolen Plans* (1952), the first production of the Children's Film Foundation. He followed up with three theatrical adaptations, *Lunch Hour* and *The Dock Brief* from John Mortimer, and *The Kitchen* from Arnold Wesker. Of these, *The Dock Brief*, with duffer solicitor Peter Sellers attempting to defend phlegmatic murder suspect Richard Attenborough, is the strongest, even though the direction is stubbornly indoorsy and stage-bound. He unbent a little with *Every Day's a Holiday*, a breezy seaside-set teen movie with John Leyton, Mike Sarne, Freddie and the Dreamers, Ron Moody, Danny La Rue, Michael Ripper, Nicholas Parsons and Liz Fraser.

Born Free, a true-life adventure adapted from Joy Adamson's autobiography, shot on African locations with Virginia McKenna and a pride of lions (and a hit song), secured Hill a modest place in mainstream cinema, but his most interesting film is the fog-bound *A Study in Terror*. First of several attempts to pit Sherlock Holmes (an excellent John Neville) against Jack the Ripper, the film is blessed with an intricate, literate script from Donald and Derek Ford, sterling character work from Robert Morley (as Mycroft Holmes), Anthony Quayle and Frank Finlay and an array of sexy cockney tarts played by Edina Ronay, Barbara Windsor, Judi Dench, Georgia Brown and Adrienne Corri.

The call of the wild accounts for *An Elephant Called Slowly*, *Black Beauty* and *The Belstone Fox*, but Hill pursued stranger interests in *Captain Nemo and the Underwater City*, a colourfully bogus Jules Verne sequel with Robert Ryan's Nemo pitted against a disappointingly unscary fish monster; *Die Hölle von Macao*, a caper with Robert Stack and Elke Sommer mixed up in torture and intrigue in the Far East; and *Man from O.R.G.Y.*, a sexy spy spoof. Aside from *London Conspiracy*, a compilation of episodes from *The Persuaders*, and a children's ghost story, *The Man from Nowhere*, Hill's cinema career evaporated in the 1970s and the man who had run with the lions settled for directing the television series *Worzel Gummidge* (1979–80). The American television movie *The Wild and the Free* (1980), with chimps instead of lions, marked a return to old turf, but he ventured into new territory with a television drama series celebrating the exploits of *Owain Glyndwr, Prince of Wales* (1983), before returning to Jon Pertwee's scarecrow for eighteen episodes of *Worzel Gummidge Down Under* (1986). He died in London on 7 October 1994.

(Kim Newman)

BIBLIOGRAPHY: Hill, James, 'Not a Sniff of the %age Due', *Film and TV Technician*, June 1977, p. 9; Obituary, *The Times*, 10 Oct. 1994, p. 21; Obituary, *Classic Images* no. 234, Dec. 1994, p. 57.

FILMOGRAPHY: *Paperchain* (doc. short); *Britain Can Make It No. 7* (doc. short, 1946); *Journey for Jeremy* (short, 1947); *Behind the Flame* (doc. short, 1948); *Friend of the Family* (doc. short, 1949); *The Marshall Plan at Work* (doc. series, 1950); *Britain's Comet* (doc. short); *Tips* (doc. short); *District Nurse* (doc. short); *The Stolen Plans* (1952); *Big Enough to Care* (doc. short, US); *The Clue of the Missing Ape* (1953); *The New Explorers* (doc.); *Gasmanship* (doc. series); *Reach for the Sky* (2nd unit dir.); *Peril for the Guy* (1956); *Cold Comfort* (doc. short, 1957); *Skyhook* (doc. short, 1958); *Mystery in the Mine* (serial); *A Walk in the Forest* (doc. short) (1959); *Giuseppina* (doc. short, 1960); *David and Golightly* (doc. short); *The Kitchen* (1961); *Lunch Hour*, *The Dock Brief* (US: *Trial and Error*) (1962); *The Home-Made Car* (short, 1963); *A Study in Terror*, *Every Day's a Holiday* (US: *Seaside Swingers*) (1965); *The Specialist* (short); *Born Free* (1966); *Die Hölle von Macao* (aka *Hell to Macao*, Ger/It/Fr, 1967); *Journey into Darkness* (co-dir. Peter Sasdy, 1968); *Captain Nemo and the Underwater City*; *An Elephant Called Slowly* (1969); *Man from O.R.G.Y.* (aka *The Real Gone Girls*, 1970); *Black Beauty* (1971); *The Belstone Fox* (1973); *The Lion at World's End* (US: *Christian the Lion*, co-dir. Bill Travers, 1974); *The Man from Nowhere*; *Death Trap* (doc., co-dirs. Hugh Falkus/Bill Travers, 1975); *London Conspiracy* (co-dir. David Greene, 1976); *Focus on Sight* (doc. short); *The Pru* (doc. short); *The Great Pram Race* (doc. short); *The Queen's Garden* (doc.) (1977); *The Young Visiters* (1984).

HILL, Sinclair (1894–1945)

Gerald Sinclair-Hill was born in Surbiton, Surrey, on 10 June 1894. He became interested in the film business while still at school; at the age of sixteen he began working as an office boy and then as a projectionist for the Tyler Film Company, an import company and agent for Italian and French films. He learned to speak Italian and was sent to Turin, where he became English adviser to the Taviola Film Company. After war broke out, he returned to London, where he briefly managed New Agency Films for Ethyle and Ernest Batley before joining up and serving in the Middlesex Regiment. Despite being gassed in France, Hill joined the Royal Flying Corps and rose to the rank of major. He was awarded the OBE for his services.

When the war was over Hill returned to Turin, but after producing a couple of films he came back to Britain, where he worked for a while as an actor before being taken on as a writer by Stoll Picture Productions in January 1920. He became Head of the scenario department at the Stoll studios in Cricklewood and made his debut as a director with *The Tidal Wave*, from his own script, the same year. By 1922 he was directing regularly, and when Maurice Elvey, Stoll's star director, left the company in 1924, Hill was entrusted with larger productions such as *Sahara Love* and *Boadicea*. In 1927, by which time he was Stoll's managing director, he made the First World War epic *The Guns of Loos*, which he test-screened on the wartime Prime Minister Lloyd George, who was highly impressed. The film contains some stunning recreations of battle, though they have to be offset against an unconvincing love story.

After leaving Stoll, Hill was hired by Michael Balcon to make films for Gainsborough such as *The Man from Toronto*, with Jessie Matthews, and *My Old Dutch*, with Betty Balfour. In 1935 he formed Grosvenor Sound Films with producer Harcourt Templeton. Unfortunately, Grosvenor's films emerged as the industry entered a slump and by 1937 the company had closed down. The last film Hill directed was *Follow Your Star*, again for Templeton, this time under the banner of Belgrave Films. During the war he served as a wing commander in the RAF; he was killed in a plane crash on 13 March 1945.

(Simon Brown)

BIBLIOGRAPHY: Breen, Max, 'A Silver Jubilee of the Silver Screen', *Picturegoer*, 7 Aug. 1937, p. 21; Low, Rachael, *The History of the British Film 1918–1929* (London: George Allen & Unwin, 1971); Low, Rachael, *Film Making in 1930s Britain* (London: George Allen & Unwin, 1985); 'Sinclair Hill Dies in Plane Accident', *Kinematograph Weekly*, 15 Mar. 1945, p. 8.

FILMOGRAPHY: *The Tidal Wave* (1920); *The Place of Honour*; *The Mystery of Mr Bernard Brown*; *One Week to Hire* (short) (1921); *The Lonely Lady of Grosvenor Square*; *Half a Truth*; *The Nonentity*; *The Truants*; *The Experiment*; *Expiation*; *Open Country* (1922); *The Indian Love Lyrics*; *One Arabian Night* (aka *Widow Twan-Kee*) (1923); *The Conspirators*; *Thrilling Stories from The Strand Magazine* (series of shorts); *White Slippers* (1924); *The Honourable Member for Outside Left* (short); *The Presumption of Stanley Hay MP*; *The Squire of Long Hadley*; *The Secret Kingdom*; *The Qualified Adventurer* (1925); *Sahara Love*; *The Chinese Bungalow*; *Boadicea* (1926); *A Woman Redeemed*; *The King's Highway* (1927); *The Guns of Loos*; *The Price of Divorce* (1928); *Dark Red Roses*; *Mr Smith Wakes Up* (short); *Unwritten Law*; *Peace and Quiet* (short) (1929); *Greek Street* (US: *Latin Love*); *Such Is the Law* (1930); *Other People's Sins* (1931); *The Great Gay Road*; *A Gentleman of Paris* (1931); *The First Mrs Fraser* (1932); *The Man from Toronto*; *Britannia of Billingsgate* (1933); *My Old Dutch* (1934); *Hyde Park Corner* (1935); *The Cardinal*; *Gay Adventure* (1936); *Take a Chance*; *Midnight Menace* (US: *Bombs over London*); *Command Performance* (1937); *Follow Your Star* (1938).

HISCOTT, Leslie (1894–1968)

Leslie Stephenson Hiscott was born on 25 July 1894 in London. He started his career in the film industry as an actor, assistant director, production manager and writer, contributing to the scripts of the highly successful 'Squibs' films of the early 1920s starring Betty Balfour. In 1925 he directed several short comedies for George A. Cooper.

After the passing of the 1927 Cinematograph Films Act Hiscott joined Julius Hagen in his new company Twickenham Film Studios, set up in 1929 to acquire the long-established studios at St Margaret's, Twickenham. Throughout the 1930s the studio was one of the most prolific generators of cheap feature films for American distributors legally obliged to offer a percentage of British films alongside their Hollywood product. Twickenham worked round the clock, making full use of a permanent studio staff of writers and technicians. Such conditions and speed of production would lead one to assume a lack of quality, but it is clear from the films that survive that producers played to their strengths. Hagen's studio developed a house style that emphasised murder-mystery plots in dark and sinister settings. Hiscott's atmospheric pieces, *When London Sleeps* (1932) and *Death on the Set* (1935), are good examples. Among his Twickenham films are several Agatha Christie adaptations, and a series of films featuring Arthur Wontner as Sherlock Holmes. Hiscott also directed several comic stars; his *A Fire Has Been Arranged* (1935) features an extended comic routine by Flanagan and Allen that is one of their best on film.

Hiscott worked for other 'quota quickie' producers throughout the 1930s, particularly for Herbert Smith at British Lion. There he developed a working relationship with the writer Michael Barringer that he maintained during the war when he began making films on his own account at the British National studios, with his wife Elizabeth Hiscott acting as producer. These films were more favourably received than much of his 1930s' work, particularly *Lady from Lisbon*, an effective comedy-thriller featuring Francis L. Sullivan as a South American racketeer who competes with other dubious characters to extract the *Mona Lisa* from the Nazis. After the war Hiscott made only two comedies, both vehicles for Richard Hearne's character 'Mr Pastry'. Returning to writing, he published two thrillers in the 1960s. He died on 2 May 1968.

(Lawrence Napper)

FILMOGRAPHY: *Mrs May Comedies* (series of shorts, 1925); *This Marriage Business* (1927); *S.O.S.*; *The Passing of Mr Quin* (1928); *Ringing the Changes*; *The Feather* (1929); *At the Villa Rose*; *The House of the Arrow*; *The Call of the Sea* (1930); *The Sleeping Cardinal*; *A Night in Montmartre*; *Brown Sugar*; *Black Coffee*; *Alibi* (1931); *The Missing Rembrandt*; *When London Sleeps*; *A Tight Corner*; *A Safe Proposition*; *Once Bitten*; *Murder at Covent Garden*; *The Face at the Window*; *Double Dealing*; *The Crooked Lady* (1932); *Yes, Madam*; *That's My Wife*; *Strike It Rich*; *The Stolen Necklace*; *Out of the Past*; *The Melody Maker*; *Marooned*; *The Iron Stair*; *I'll Stick to You*; *Great Stuff*; *Cleaning Up* (1933); *Flat No. 3*; *Keep It Quiet*; *Gay Love*; *Passing Shadows*; *The Man I Want*; *Crazy People* (1934); *The Triumph of Sherlock Holmes*; *Three Witnesses*; *She Shall Have Music*; *Inside the Room*; *A Fire Has Been Arranged*; *Department Store*; *Death on the Set*; *The Big Splash*; *Annie, Leave the Room!* (1935); *The Interrupted Honeymoon*; *Fame*; *Millions* (1936); *Ship's Concert*; *Fine Feathers* (1937); *Take Cover* (short, 1938); *Tilly of Bloomsbury* (1940); *The Seventh Survivor* (1941); *Sabotage at Sea*; *Lady from Lisbon* (1942); *The Butler's Dilemma* (1943); *Welcome Mr*

Washington (1944); *The Time of His Life* (1955); *Tons of Trouble* (1956).

HITCHCOCK, Alfred (1899–1980)

In the early part of his career, Alfred Hitchcock was widely considered to be Britain's best film director. Silent films such as *The Lodger*, *The Ring* and *The Farmer's Wife* were greeted with great enthusiasm by critics, and, at a time of expansion and increasing optimism for the British film industry, they were heralded as evidence that British films had reached an international standard of artistry. In 1929, *Blackmail* was hailed by British critics as a film that used sound and dialogue with more flair and imagination than any Hollywood or European film of the time. And in the mid-1930s, Hitchcock's *The 39 Steps* and *The Lady Vanishes* reinvigorated the thriller genre with their fast pace and distinctively British sense of wit and irony.

Hitchcock was thus an admired and prominent figure in British film culture, so much so that a newspaper report on the premiere of *The 39 Steps* in 1935 could affectionately refer to him as 'the Buddha of British films'. In the wake of his departure for Hollywood in 1939, however, his centrality within British film culture quickly waned. After the outbreak of the Second World War he was one of those accused in the British press as having 'gone with the wind up' to Hollywood. Throughout the 1940s and 50s, British critics favoured realism above all else, and they looked with disdain upon the Hollywood glamour and opulence that characterises much of Hitchcock's work during this time. In the 1960s and 70s, when auteurist critics celebrated Hitchcock's films, it was mainly the Hollywood Hitchcock that they admired, and these (largely American and French) critics had little interest in his British films. Of course, Hitchcock's public persona in his later years was still very closely associated with his English background, as his appearances on the *Alfred Hitchcock Presents* television programmes demonstrate. But his dark suits, careful formality, deadpan irony and macabre humour seemed to be the contrivances of a longtime expatriate.

Hitchcock commanded considerable esteem in Britain during his first dozen years as a director. When *The Lodger* was first shown in 1926, it was declared to be a masterpiece and its director was proclaimed as a youthful genius. Hitchcock was already twenty-seven years old at the time, but his rise does seem to have been remarkable. Alfred Joseph Hitchcock had been born on the north-eastern edge of London, in Leytonstone, Essex, on 13 August 1899, and his family lived above their greengrocer's shop on Leytonstone High Road and later in the East End neighbourhoods of Poplar and Stepney. He left school at the age of fourteen, and worked as a clerk at the Henley Telegraph Company and took evening lessons in draughtsmanship and drawing at the University of London. In 1919 these skills enabled him to get a job as a title-card designer with the American production company Famous Players-Lasky when it began making films in a converted power station in Islington. The Americans did not stay long in Islington, but Hitchcock's ascent quickened when the studio was taken over by Michael Balcon's Gainsborough Pictures in 1924. Balcon allowed Hitchcock to work at an array of jobs for Gainsborough: as a set designer, scenario writer, editor and as the assistant director to Graham Cutts, who was then Gainsborough's top director. In 1925 Hitchcock was given his own directorial assignments with *The Pleasure Garden* and *The Mountain Eagle*, both of which were filmed in Munich's Emelka studios as part of a co-production deal between Gainsborough and the German producer Erich Pommer. Neither film garnered much attention, and it was not until the release of his third film, *The Lodger*, that both the critics and the public took notice of Hitchcock. *The Lodger*'s artistic pretensions aroused the hostility of the influential distributor C. M. Woolf, but when it was finally released it was enthusiastically received by critics and audiences. With filmic techniques informed by the international art cinema of the 1920s, an Oedipal narrative format borrowed from Hollywood and subject matter that was distinctly English (a Jack the Ripper story with authentic London settings), it remains a remarkable hybrid and a stunning example of late silent cinema. *The Lodger* also introduced several of Hitchcock's most enduring story elements: a protagonist whose innocence is in doubt, a romance filled with suspicion and mistrust, wry humour and a murderous fascination with blondes, to name but a few, that would endure for many years.

His reputation as the 'master of suspense' was far in the future, however, and during these early years Hitchcock was known primarily for the visual creativity of his films. The German director F. W. Murnau was a strong influence in this regard. While filming in Germany in 1924, Hitchcock visited the set of *Der Letzte Mann/The Last Laugh* (1924) and observed Murnau at work. It was a key moment in his development as a film-maker. Murnau's interest in an 'unchained' camera and his pursuit of 'pure cinema' (telling the story in visual terms alone) would be lifelong interests of Hitchcock's too. He was also a member of the Film Society and its screenings of French, German and Soviet art films, as well as early and pioneering American films, provided a unique forum for the consideration of film form and technique, and one that influenced Hitchcock and many other aspiring British film-makers of the time.

One can point further to Hitchcock's interest in drawing and draughtsmanship as factors that enriched and informed the visual dynamic of his films. In his silent films, this was so striking that critics regularly cited 'the Hitchcock touch', referring to the visually dramatic sequences that distinguished his work. Such moments might convey an amusing, sinister or romantic story point, or they might dramatise a thematic element of the story, but they always demonstrated the director's ability to tell the story without recourse to intertitles for dialogue or explanation. Perhaps the most striking example is the use of a glass ceiling in *The Lodger*, enabling the cinema audience to see what the characters 'hear': their lodger pacing back and forth in

the room above them. In *Downhill* there is a recurrent visual motif of descent; in *The Ring* a boxer's career progress is demonstrated through his improved billing on a succession of posters and billboards; and in *Easy Virtue* the audience is able to 'listen' to a marriage proposal over the telephone by watching the facial expressions of an eavesdropping switchboard operator. These techniques were particularly useful and even liberating narrative devices, given that in these years most of Hitchcock's stories were adaptations of stage plays and the witty dialogue of West End favourites such as Noël Coward could not be transferred directly to the silent screen.

In 1927 Hitchcock left Gainsborough for the larger British International Pictures (BIP), and his new contract made him the highest-paid director in Britain. After making three impressive silent films – *The Ring*, *The Farmer's Wife* and *The Manxman* – all with bigger budgets than had been allowed at Gainsborough, Hitchcock surreptitiously shot enough sound footage to be able to release *Blackmail* as what is generally regarded as Britain's first fully-fledged talking picture. At the time, many cinephiles thought that 'talkies' would reduce cinema to being only 'pictures of people talking' but Hitchcock's inventive and expressionist use of sound demonstrated that the new technology actually opened a new realm of possibilities. However, Hitchcock's subsequent BIP films proved disappointing. Adaptations of high-profile West End plays (*Juno and the Paycock*, *The Skin Game*) confined his inventiveness; two thrillers (*Murder!*, *Number Seventeen*), interesting though they are, failed to emulate *The Lodger* and *Blackmail*. *Rich and Strange*, an intriguingly odd marital drama that did seem to open up new directions, failed to attract popular or critical support. After producing Benn Levy's *Lord Camber's Ladies* (1932) and leaving BIP to direct the musical operetta *Waltzes from Vienna*, Hitchcock's career seemed in serious decline. Fortunately a remarkable reversal of fortune was achieved when Hitchcock's old mentor, Michael Balcon, invited him to join Gaumont-British in 1934.

Balcon was now the executive producer at this ambitious company, and he gave Hitchcock his choice of film projects, the freedom to develop his films without interference and his choice of collaborators. Hitchcock chose to return to the thriller genre, and to work with Charles Bennett (the writer of *Blackmail*) on an original screenplay that became *The Man Who Knew Too Much*. This proved to be the first of several witty, suspense-filled and highly popular thrillers that continued with *The 39 Steps*, *The Secret Agent*, *Sabotage*, *Young and Innocent* and *The Lady Vanishes*. Like *Blackmail*, these 1930s' thrillers often progress from the depiction of private, hidden and repressed impulses to much more public displays of unleashed fear and violence in very public and well-known venues (such as the Royal Albert

Hall and the London Palladium). By contrast with *Blackmail*, though, the 1930s' thrillers seem more politically aware and attuned to their times. All except *Young and Innocent* are centred on espionage, and they convey a strong sense of political complacency, instability and an impending threat from abroad. In reviving this genre, Hitchcock had also found the means of circumventing Britain's strict system of censorship, which insisted that films should be escapist entertainment and not engage with topical or controversial issues.

Many have said that Hitchcock found his true calling with the 1930s' thrillers, while for others this concentration on one genre represents a limiting of Hitchcock's talent and interests. Either way, their popularity ensured that he was invited to Hollywood, and in 1939 he took up a contract with the producer David O. Selznick. This opportunity must have been an irresistible one. In the late 1930s the British film industry had become mired in a financial crisis, and its difficulties would only intensify with the outbreak of war. It must have been all the more galling, for those eager to criticise him, that he was able to go to Hollywood and yet continue to work on British stories and with largely British casts in films such as *Rebecca* (1940), *Foreign Correspondent* (1940) and *Suspicion* (1941). Yet it is evident that Hitchcock was eager to maintain ties with Britain. He returned in wartime to make two short films for the Ministry of Information, *Bon Voyage* and *Aventure Malgache*. In the immediate post-war period he and the Granada cinema-chain owner Sidney Bernstein formed a production company, Transatlantic Pictures, that was designed to enable him to make films in Britain, and to free him from the interference of Hollywood producers such as Selznick. Of the company's two films, *Rope* (1948) and *Under Capricorn* (1949), only the latter was filmed in Britain, and although both are remembered for the bold experimentation with long takes and deep focus, neither was a popular success. Transatlantic soon folded, and Hitchcock subsequently worked with a range of Hollywood studios.

He made only two further films in Britain. The first, *Stage Fright* (1950), was a thriller set in the West End theatre world that had enthralled him in his youth, but the film's sense of time and place is weakened by its international cast and its curiously limited use of location shooting. The second, *Frenzy* (1972), seems to hit much closer to home and can be seen to represent a remake or an updating of *The Lodger*. The story is centred on a man wrongly accused of being a sadistic serial killer of women, and it was filmed with a largely British cast and in a London setting that benefits from extensive location shooting around the un-modernised Covent Garden market. *Frenzy* was not Hitchcock's last film, but it can be seen as a revisiting of his career's dramatic beginnings in Britain and as a homecoming for a director who found his greatest success and celebrity abroad. He died in Los Angeles on 29 April 1980.

(Mark Glancy)

BIBLIOGRAPHY: Barr, Charles, *English Hitchcock* (Moffat, Dumfries & Galloway: Cameron and Hollis, 1999); Durgnat, Raymond, *The Strange Case of Alfred Hitchcock* (London: Faber and Faber, 1974); Glancy, Mark, The 39 Steps: *A British Film Guide* (London: I. B. Tauris, 2002); Hutchings, Peter, '*Frenzy*: A Return to Britain', in Charles Barr (ed.), *All Our Yesterdays*, (London: BFI, 1986); McArthur, Colin, 'The Critics Who Knew Too Much: Hitchcock and the Absent Class Paradigm', *Film Studies* no. 2, 2000, pp. 15–28; Ryall, Tom, *Alfred Hitchcock and the British Cinema* (London: Croom Helm, 1987); Ryall, Tom, *Blackmail* (London: BFI, 1993); Spoto, Donald, *The Dark Side of Genius: The Life of Alfred Hitchcock* (New York: Little, Brown, 1983); Taylor, John Russell, *Hitch: The Life and Work of Alfred Hitchcock* (London: Faber and Faber, 1978); Truffaut, François, with Helen G. Scott, *Hitchcock* (London: Secker and Warburg, 1968); Yacower, Maurice, *Hitchcock's British Films* (Hamden, CT: Archon, 1977).

FILMOGRAPHY: *The Pleasure Garden* (1925); *The Mountain Eagle* (US: *Fear o' God*); *The Lodger: A Story of the London Fog* (US: *The Case of Jonathan Drew*) (1926); *Downhill* (US: *When Boys Leave Home*); *Easy Virtue*; *The Ring* (1927); *The Farmer's Wife*; *Champagne*; *The Manxman* (1928); *Blackmail*; *Juno and the Paycock* (US: *The Shame of Mary Boyle*) (1929); *An Elastic Affair* (short); *Elstree Calling* (co-dir. Adrian Brunel); *Murder!*; *Mary* (German-language version of *Murder!*) (1930); *The Skin Game*; *Rich and Strange* (US: *East of Shanghai*) (1931); *Number Seventeen* (1932); *Waltzes from Vienna* (US: *Strauss' Great Waltz*); *The Man Who Knew Too Much* (1934); *The 39 Steps* (1935); *The Secret Agent*; *Sabotage* (US: *A Woman Alone*) (1936); *Young and Innocent* (US: *The Girl Was Young*, 1937); *The Lady Vanishes* (1938); *Jamaica Inn* (1939); *Rebecca* (US); *Foreign Correspondent* (US) (1940); *Mr & Mrs Smith* (US); *Suspicion* (US) (1941); *Saboteur* (US, 1942); *Shadow of a Doubt* (US, 1943); *Lifeboat* (US); *Bon Voyage* (short); *Aventure Malgache*/*The Malgache Adventure* (short) (1944); *Spellbound* (US, 1945); *Notorious* (US, 1946); *The Paradine Case* (US, 1947); *Rope* (US, 1948); *Under Capricorn* (1949); *Stage Fright* (1950); *Strangers on a Train* (US, 1951); *I Confess* (US, 1953); *Dial M for Murder* (US); *Rear Window* (1954); *To Catch a Thief* (US); *The Trouble with Harry* (US) (1955); *The Man Who Knew Too Much* (US); *The Wrong Man* (US) (1956); *Vertigo* (US, 1958); *North by Northwest* (US, 1959); *Psycho* (US, 1960); *The Birds* (US, 1963); *Marnie* (US, 1964); *Torn Curtain* (US, 1966); *Topaz* (US, 1969); *Frenzy* (1972); *Family Plot* (US, 1976).

HODGES, Mike (1932–)

Mike Hodges' spasmodic career as a director illustrates many of the besetting problems of the British film industry. Born in Bristol on 29 July 1932, Hodges had a comfortable middle-class upbringing, qualifying as a chartered accountant. But two years of national service prompted a desire for a more creative occupation. In the 1960s he worked in television, producing and directing hard-hitting documentaries for *World in Action*, then making profiles of European directors for the arts series *Tempo*. The combination of gritty, combative realism and European modernism informs his crime thrillers, where Hodges felt could delve 'deep into the underbelly of society. Done well they can be like an autopsy of society' (Adams, p. 14).

Hodges wrote and directed two innovative television thrillers, *Suspect* (1969) and *Rumour* (1970), before gaining the

opportunity to direct his first feature, *Get Carter* (1971). The story of London gangster Jack Carter's return to his native Newcastle to investigate his brother's sudden death, which Hodges adapted from a novel by Ted Lewis, is told in a detached, analytical style, matched by Michael Caine's frightening yet compelling performance. The film evokes a society in the throes of profound change, capturing a mood of disillusionment that signalled the replacement of 1960s' idealism by the rampant materialism of the 1970s. Carter is an ambivalent figure, a seemingly emotionless killer who weeps at the sexual exploitation of his brother's daughter, and whose death symbolises the end of an era. *Get Carter* has now acquired cult status, regarded as one of the finest and most influential British crime thrillers, but at the time of its release it was considered soulless and too violent, and was poorly distributed.

Hodges' next film, *Pulp* (1972), was based on his original story of a sleazy pulp-fiction writer (Michael Caine), caught up in a real-life murder mystery. An intermittently successful comedy-thriller, *Pulp* was also poorly handled by its distributors, who found it hard to market. Although the film had little impact, Hodges' reputation was sufficiently well established for Warner Bros. to invite him to direct *The Terminal Man* (1974). Hodges' adaptation of Michael Crichton's science-fiction thriller about a computer scientist (George Segal) who becomes psychotic after a brain implant, proved too tough and uncompromising to be a commercial success. Now judged a box-office risk, Hodges' career floundered with scripts unmade and a disagreement with 20th Century-Fox that caused him to withdraw from the direction of *Damien – Omen II* (Don Taylor, 1978) after three weeks. The decade ended on a higher note with *Flash Gordon* (1980), a modern version of the 1920s' comic-strip character. Hodges found the production chaotic but nonetheless managed to make a lavish and enjoyable science-fiction romp.

The 1980s showed Hodges' versatility, but he suffered further problems with financing and distribution. *Morons from Outer Space* (1985) was another science-fiction spoof, written and starring Mel Smith and Griff Rhys Jones. Hodges embraced the idea of aliens being stupid and unco-operative as refreshingly 'anti-Spielbergian', but he was unable to prevent the film sinking beneath its lame script. *A Prayer for the Dying* (1987) was another grim thriller about the impossibility of an IRA hit man (Mickey Rourke) renouncing violence. The film is difficult to judge as it suffered drastic re-editing and the substitution of what Hodges deemed to be a crassly inappropriate musical score. Hodges disowned the film and had a public row with the producers. He was given full control of *Black Rainbow* (1989), which he wrote and directed, a hybrid psycho-supernatural thriller shot on location in North Carolina about a stage medium (Rosanna Arquette) who may indeed have terrifying powers of prophecy. Once again, despite excellent reviews, the impact of this perceptive film was undermined by severe distribution problems in both America and Britain.

This apparent failure meant that Hodges did not direct another feature film for nearly a decade, returning with *Croupier* (1998), a European co-production financed by Channel 4 and a variety of French and German companies, based on an original screenplay by Paul Mayersberg. An ironic, existentialist fable about greed and the corrupting power of money, *Croupier* draws on both film noir and European modernism. The archetypal anti-hero Jack Manfred, superbly realised by Clive Owen, is a struggling author-cum-croupier who gradually turns into his dark self, Jake, whose one desire is to 'fuck the world over'. It was Hodges' best film since *Get Carter*, his fluid camerawork and tautly economical direction creating a stylised world where the tawdry casino with its mirror walls becomes a modern limbo in which the gamblers play for their souls. Although *Croupier* also suffered from a very limited release in Britain, its substantial success in America led to its re-release in Britain in summer 2001, where it was received warmly by both critics and audiences.

Hodges has argued that films should try to express often difficult truths about the human condition and contribute to the formation of a meaningful national identity in the face of the onslaught of American money and culture (Hodges, pp. xv–xvii). The vicissitudes of his career have exemplified that struggle, and he has remained true to that purpose. The success of *Croupier* and the status of *Get Carter* as a modern classic have led to a renewed interest in his work and to further projects: a documentary about the representation of serial killers, *Murder by Numbers* (2001), and an existentialist thriller, *I'll Sleep When I'm Dead*, written by Trevor Preston and starring Clive Owen. Parallels with *Get Carter* afforded it considerable publicity and boosted its commercial prospects though its subtle plot and bleak outlook made it less popular than *Croupier* with American audiences. Hodges is now seen as one of the most significant voices in post-1960s' British cinema.

(Andrew Spicer)

BIBLIOGRAPHY: Adams, Mark, *Mike Hodges* (Harpenden, Herts: Pocket Essentials, 2001); Chibnall, Steve Get Carter, *A British Film*

Guide 6 (London: I. B. Tauris, 2004); Davies, Steven, *'Get Carter' and Beyond: The Cinema of Mike Hodges* (London: B. T. Batsford, 2002); Hodges, Mike, 'Introduction: Can a Film have a Soul?', in Yoram Allon, Del Cullen and Hannah Patterson (eds), *Contemporary British and Irish Film Directors* (London: Wallflower Press, 2001); Murphy, Robert, 'A Revenger's Tragedy – *Get Carter*', and 'Mike Hodges Discusses *Get Carter* with the NFT Audience, 23 September 1997', in Steve Chibnall and Robert Murphy (eds), *British Crime Cinema* (London and New York: Routledge, 1999); Spicer, Andrew, *Film Noir* (Harlow: Longman, 2002).

FILMOGRAPHY: *Get Carter* (1971); *Pulp* (1972); *The Terminal Man* (US, 1974); *Flash Gordon* (US, 1980); *Morons from Outer Space* (1985); *A Prayer for the Dying* (1987); *Black Rainbow* (US, 1989); *Croupier* (1998); *I'll Sleep When I'm Dead* (UK/US, 2003).

HOFFMAN, Michael (1957–)

Michael Hoffman was born in Honolulu in 1957 and came to Oxford University as a Rhodes scholar in 1979. Having already made a documentary about the plight of German families under Nazi rule, he was able to establish the Oxford Film Company with Richard Stevenson and Peter Schwabach. Their first film, *Privileged* (1982), a low-budget feature about upper-class undergraduate life, benefited from the performances of a cast that included the young Hugh Grant, James Wilby and Imogen Stubbs. Hoffman and Stevenson also inaugurated a national screenwriting competition; the winning script, by Scottish teenager Ninian Dunnett, was directed by Hoffman and produced by Stevenson as the offbeat comedy *Restless Natives* (1985).

From this enterprising starting point, Hoffman went on to become an extremely prolific and versatile director. Initially working from a British base, he subsequently graduated to a series of Hollywood and international co-production projects. Hoffman's international career straddles a variety of mainstream genres, from the seventeenth-century English period drama *Restoration* (1995) to the contemporary New York romantic comedy *One Fine Day* (1996) and the Shakespeare adaptation *A Midsummer Night's Dream* (1999). It is perhaps a combination of Hoffman's chameleon quality and mainstream orientation that has prevented his work from receiving sustained critical attention.

(Jonathan Murray)

BIBLIOGRAPHY: McCarthy, Tara, 'Michael Hoffman: A Midsummer Night's Dreamer', *Written By* vol. 3 no. 5, May 1999, pp. 32–5; Tunney, Tom, 'A Great Notion', *City Limits*, 28 Apr. 1988, p. 21.

FILMOGRAPHY: *Regentroffen* (doc., Ger, 1981); *Privileged* (1982); *Restless Natives* (1985); *Promised Land* (US, 1988); *Some Girls* (UK: *Sisters*, US, 1989); *Soapdish* (US, 1991); *Restoration* (US/UK, 1995); *One Fine Day* (US, 1996); *William Shakespeare's A Midsummer Night's Dream* (US, 1999); *The Emperor's Club* (US, 2002); *Game 6* (US, 2005).

HOLMES, J. B. (1901–1968)

John Bruce Holmes was born in Bickley, Kent. Along with Harry Watt and Pat Jackson he was a key figure in the development of the wartime 'story documentary'. Holmes began his career at Gaumont-British Instructional, where he established a directorial style notable for its technical proficiency and ability to convey complex information simply and clearly. *The Cathode Ray Oscillograph*, which describes the operation of specialised electrical testing equipment, and *The Mine*, claimed by some to be the first British film shot underground in a colliery, are typical of his work from this period. More aesthetic concerns surfaced in his 1936 Strand film *The Way to the Sea*, featuring music and words by Benjamin Britten and W. H. Auden.

At the end of 1937 Holmes left Strand for the GPO Film Unit under its new leader Alberto Cavalcanti, and stayed there during the war when it became the Crown Film Unit headed by Ian Dalrymple. After two popular wartime documentaries, *Merchant Seamen* and *Ordinary People* (co-directed with Jack Lee), Holmes was given the opportunity to direct *Coastal Command*, a feature-length story documentary describing the work of flying-boat patrols in protecting the North Atlantic merchant convoys. Though now less celebrated than Harry Watt's *Target for To-night* (1941), Humphrey Jennings' *"Fires Were Started –"* (1943) and Pat Jackson's *Western Approaches* (1944), Holmes' film is nonetheless fascinating in its depiction of a little-known aspect of the war.

When Dalrymple resigned in May 1943, Holmes took charge of the Unit for the closing period of the war. In the late 1940s he worked as a consultant to the Indian government before returning to the UK, where he was instrumental in founding British Transport Films (BTF). He directed several of the early films on which BTF's reputation mainly rests today, notably *Berth 24* and *Ocean Terminal*, which examine the economic and social role of the merchant marine in Britain's post-war reconstruction, and *This Is York*, a two-reel impressionistic 'day in the life' of a major railway station. This film is still shown regularly in York to enthusiastic audiences.

From 1954 to 1959, Holmes worked for the Shell Film Unit in Egypt and then established its South-East Asian Film Unit. He returned to Britain in 1961 and continued to work as a freelance producer for the Central Office of Information. He produced two landmark government publicity films, *Traffic in Towns* (1963) and *The Smoking Machine* (1965) – the first government-backed anti-smoking film – before his sudden death in 1968.

(Leo Enticknap)

BIBLIOGRAPHY: Holmes, Winifred, 'What's Wrong with Documentary', *Sight and Sound*, Spring 1948, pp. 44–5; Obituary, *Film and TV Technician*, Oct. 1968, p. 27; Rotha, Paul, *Documentary Film*, 3rd edn (London: Faber and Faber, 1952).

FILMOGRAPHY: *Humber-Hillman*; *Where the Road Begins* (1933); *The Cathode Ray Oscillograph*; *Shakespeare: Backgrounds to Literature* (1934); *Physical Education – Children Aged 4 to 6 Years*; *Feeding Time at the Zoo*; *Physical Education – Children Aged 7 Years*; *Mediaeval Village*; *Progressive Training in Ball Handling Games* (1935); *The Way to the Sea*; *Wake Up – and Feed*; *The Mine*; *Analysis of Agility Exercises*; *Boys' Summer Playing Field Activities*; *Children Aged Seven*; *Keyboard Talks No. 1* (1936); *How to Cook*; *Pots and Plans*; *Daisy Bell Comes to Town*; *How *to Plan a Kitchen* (1937); *Ordinary People* (co-dir. Jack Lee, 1941); *Merchant Seamen* (1941); *Coastal Command* (1942); *The Centre*; *The Story of Peckham Health Centre* (1947); *The People at No. 19*; *Probation Officer* (1949); *Berth 24* (1950); *This Year – London* (1951); *Ocean Terminal* (1952); *This Is York* (1953); *Kent Oil Refinery* (1954); *Looking at Gold and Silver* (1963); *Shell Moulding – Fault Recognition* (1968).

HOLT, Seth (1924–1971)

Seth Holt was born in Palestine to British parents, and educated at Blackheath School in south London. He spent a term at RADA in 1940 before acting with repertory companies in Liverpool and Bideford, Devon. In 1942 he joined a documentary film company, Strand, as assistant editor and then, at the invitation of his brother-in-law Robert Hamer, moved to Ealing. 'In some ways features were a step back,' he later commented. 'One was much nearer the movie makers in documentary but in features you might be the fifth assistant cutter's nark' (Gough-Yates, p. 5).

Over the next fifteen years Holt moved steadily up the Ealing hierarchy. Among the films he worked on as assistant editor were *Champagne Charlie* (Alberto Cavalcanti, 1944), *Scott of the Antarctic* (Charles Frend, 1948) – where he also featured as 'the voice of the Blizzard' on the soundtrack – and *Passport to Pimlico* (Henry Cornelius, 1949). Graduating to editor, he cut (among others) *The Lavender Hill Mob* (Charles Crichton, 1951) and *Mandy* (Alexander Mackendrick, 1952), before becoming associate producer on Mackendrick's *The Ladykillers* (1955).

Seth Holt (right) directs Ronald Lewis and Susan Strasberg in *Taste of Fear* (Seth Holt, 1961)

At last Holt was poised to realise his ambition and direct. But Ealing was now in its dying days, camped in a corner of the MGM studios at Borehamwood, and Holt directed only one film for the company before it folded. *Nowhere to Go* (1958), which he intended as 'the least "Ealing" Ealing film ever made', was also the only Ealing film scripted by Kenneth Tynan during his brief, uneasy stint as the company's script editor (Gough-Yates, p. 9). A coolly downbeat crime thriller, it aimed – according to Holt – 'for a certain kind of stylishness in the dialogue which doesn't quite come off' (Cameron, p. 1). It also suffered from having fifteen minutes excised by MGM to fit it into a double bill. But it showed that Holt could bring a flavour and style of his own to genre material.

The same was true of *Taste of Fear* (1961), a psychological thriller made for Hammer with more than a nod to *Les Diaboliques*. *Station Six Sahara* (1962), which involved five men at an isolated desert outpost panting after Carroll Baker, Holt regarded as 'a sort of dirty film really but (with) something in it that was quite interesting' (Gough-Yates, p. 13). Back at Hammer, *The Nanny* (1965) was a taut piece of *Grand Guignol* starring Bette Davis as the ambivalent domestic; Davis paid tribute to Holt as 'the most ruthless director I've ever worked with outside of William Wyler' (Hutchinson).

Holt was by now recognised – by *Movie* magazine at least – as one of the finest talents working in the British film industry, but it was clear that none of his films so far had fully displayed his talents. Holt set up his own company, Holtmallinson Productions, to develop more ambitious material. But none of his projects – a film about Bakunin, an adaptation of David Garnett's 1922 novel *Lady into Fox*, a modern reworking of Middleton's play *Women Beware Women* – came to fruition. *Monsieur Lecoq*, a comedy *policier* starring Zero Mostel, was shut down by Columbia midway through production.

Holt's last completed feature was *Danger Route* (1967), a sub-Bondian spy thriller. Good performances from Richard Johnson and Diana Dors make it more watchable than one might expect from Holt's dismissal of it as 'dreadful . . . I needed the bread' (Gough-Yates, p. 13). But the film's non-sequitors and underdeveloped subplots indicate that he had little control over it. He was slated to direct *if . . . .* (1968), which he had helped develop; but illness and heavy drinking had weakened his morale and he handed over to Lindsay Anderson. He returned to Hammer to direct *Blood from the Mummy's Tomb* (1971), an inventive adaptation of Bram Stoker's *The Jewel of the Seven Stars*; but he died a week from the end of shooting, on 13 February 1971, and the picture was completed by Michael Carreras.

(Philip Kemp)

BIBLIOGRAPHY: Cameron, Ian and Paul Mayersberg, V. F. Perkins and Mark Shivas, 'Interview with Seth Holt', *Film Dope* no. 25, Nov.

1982, pp. 1–5; Gough-Yates, Kevin, 'Interview with Seth Holt', *Screen* vol. 10 no. 6, Nov./Dec. 1969, pp. 4–23; Hutchinson, Tom, 'Daddy of the Mummy Scene, *Guardian*, 18 Jan. 1971; Pirie, David, *A Heritage of Horror: The English Gothic Cinema 1946–1972* (London: Gordon Fraser, 1973); Waymark, Peter, 'A Master that Might have been', *The Times*, 8 Dec. 1984.

FILMOGRAPHY: *Nowhere to Go* (1958); *Taste of Fear* (US: *Scream of Fear*, 1961); *Station Six Sahara* (1962); *The Nanny* (1965); *Danger Route* (1967); *Monsieur Lecoq* (unfinished, 1968); *Blood from the Mummy's Tomb* (completed by Michael Carreras, 1971).

HOOK, Harry (1959–)

Harry Hook was born in England in 1959 but from the age of four he was brought up in Kenya, an experience that has some bearing on his subsequent film career. He trained at the London College of Printing and the National Film and Television School, and a preoccupation with notions of national identity in the context of colonialism is already apparent in his short films *The Unknown Region* (1980) and *Sins of the Father* (1982). These concerns are also apparent in *The Kitchen Toto*, a feature film he was asked to write by producer Anne Skinner of Skeba Films. Set against the backdrop of the Mau Mau rebellion against British rule in Kenya in the 1950s, the film observes the escalating violence through the innocent eyes of a kitchen servant (Edwin Mahinda) working in the home of a colonial police officer (Bob Peck). The sensitively handled drama focuses more on the interplay of character than on political struggle, opting for understated humanism over radical commentary.

Hook's adaptation of William Golding's *Lord of the Flies* has the same concern for innocence and experience, as well as a similarly low-key style, though it fails to eclipse Peter Brook's earlier version. Following the film's disappointing reception, Hook has pursued a successful career in television. His interest in the conflict between nature and civilisation is further explored in *The Last of His Tribe* (1992) made for HBO in America, but his British television assignments are more mixed and less personal. His 'Buried Lies' episode of *Silent Witness* (1996), scripted by Kevin Hood, investigates the suspicious death of a child; *All for Love* is based on a romantic adventure story by Robert Louis Stevenson; *Pure Wickedness* (1999), a four-part series written by Lucy Gannon, is a domestic melodrama centred on adultery; and *The Many Lives of Albert Walker* is a police investigation mystery.

(Robert Shail)

BIBLIOGRAPHY: Green, William, 'Call of the Wild', *Sunday Telegraph* 7 Days Magazine, 10 June 1990; Johnston, Sheila, 'Two African Childhoods', *Independent*, 27 Nov. 1987, p. 28.

FILMOGRAPHY: *A Conversation between Art and Madness* (short); *The Unknown Region* (short) (1980); *Sins of the Father* (short, 1982); *Before I Die Forever* (short, 1986); *The Kitchen Toto* (1987); *Lord of the Flies* (1990); *All for Love* (aka *St Ives*, Ir/Fr/Ger/UK, 1997); *The Many Lives of Albert Walker* (US: *Albert Walker*, UK/Can, 2002).

HOPKINS, Anthony (1937–)

The illustrious actor Anthony Hopkins, now best known for his portrayal of psychopath Hannibal Lecter, was born in Margam, near Port Talbot, Wales, on 31 December 1937. He was knighted in 1993. His one venture into directing is *August*, an awkward adaptation of Chekhov's *Uncle Vanya*, transposed to a Welsh country house in the 1890s. A lack of dramatic rhythm, and Hopkins' rampaging central performance hinder progress, but fortunately he encourages the rest of the cast, especially Leslie Phillips and Kate Burton, to bring out their finer points. It is interesting to compare the film with Louis Malle's enjoyably eccentric *Vanya on 42nd Street* and Michael Blakemore's Australian version, *Country Life*, both made in 1994.

(Geoff Brown and Robert Murphy)

BIBLIOGRAPHY: Samuelson, Sydney, 'The Wales of August (Interview with Anthony Hopkins)', *Framework* no. 2, Apr. 1995, pp. 4–5.

FILMOGRAPHY: *August* (prod. 1994; rel. 1996).

HOPKINS, Ben (1969–)

Ben Hopkins was born in Hong Kong on 2 May 1969 but was brought up in north London. After studying at Oxford and the Royal College of Art, he made a short black-and-white film, *National Achievement Day*, and co-wrote the script for Clare Kilner's *Janice Beard: 45 Words per Minute* (1999). He made his feature film debut as writer and director of *Simon Magus*, an offbeat allegorical tale about a nineteenth-century Jewish outcast, distrusted and feared for his supposed magical powers. An ersatz folk tale, shot through with 'magic realism', the film blends religious fervour, economic collapse, anti-Semitism and spiritual redemption into its narrative. Hopkins handles the material with confidence and imagination, securing strong performances from his cast and bringing much-needed humour to the film's dark universe. His next film, *The Nine Lives of Tomas Katz*, is a modestly budgeted apocalyptic fantasy, set in London during a solar eclipse. The style ranges from German Expressionism to Monty Pythonesque absurdity. Most of the film's scenes were heavily improvised, often on the day of shooting. Documentaries on the menace of unexploded mines (footprints) and the travails of Kirkhiz nomads in an age of globalisation (*37 Uses for a Dead Sheep*) followed.

(Daniel O'Brien)

BIBLIOGRAPHY: Frater, Patrick, 'In the Frame: Ben Hopkins', *Screen International*, 12 Feb. 1999, p. 12.

FILMOGRAPHY: *National Achievement Day* (short, 1995); *Simon Magus* (UK/Ger/Fr/It, 1999); *The Nine Lives of Tomas Katz* (UK/Ger, 2000); *Footprints* (doc., 2002); *37 Uses for a Dead Sheep* (co-dir. Ekber Kutlu, doc. 2006).

HOPKINS, Stephen (1958–)

Stephen Hopkins was born in Kingston, Jamaica, in 1958, and moved to Britain when he was twelve. He studied at the

London College of Printing, but dropped out and was homeless in London for nine months. Work on punk rock videos brought him in touch with Russell Mulcahy, who employed him as a graphic designer and subsequently invited him to act as second-unit director on *Highlander* (1986). Hopkins followed Mulcahy's example in making his debut with an Australian horror film. *Dangerous Game*, set mainly in a shopping mall, is a very different kettle of nastiness to the Outback terrors of Mulcahy's *Razorback* (1984) and did less well at the box office. But it displayed Hopkins' talent for suspense and led to a career in Hollywood directing efficient sequels, including the fifth *Nightmare on Elm Street* and the second *Predator*.

He moved on to direct the crude but exciting *Blown Away*, with Jeff Bridges as a poacher-turned-gamekeeper who is tracked down by an old enemy (Tommy Lee Jones) with whom he shares a history in Irish terrorism. After co-directing the classy Puerto Rican-set thriller *Under Suspicion* with Morgan Freeman, Hopkins made a canny move sideways with the cultish American television series *24* (2001) and *Traffic* (2004). He returned to Britain to make *The Life and Death of Peter Sellers* for HBO and BBC Films, a small-minded interpretation of Sellers as a pathetic fantasist. Geoffrey Rush plays Sellers as a podgy English version of Woody Allen, forever whining and complaining – an irritating screen presence, and one impossible to take much interest in. There are moments when the film comes brilliantly to life, particularly when Rush immerses himself in recreating Inspector Clouseau and Dr Strangelove, but as with the worst Sellers films they are outweighed by mounds of tedious gimmickry. Hopkins is likely to find other outlets for his talents, but they will more probably be in Hollywood than in the British film industry.

(Robert Murphy)

BIBLIOGRAPHY: Jones, Alan, 'Predator 2 & Stephen Hopkins', part 1, *StarBurst* no. 154, June 1991, pp. 32–5; part 2, *Starburst* no. 155, July 1991, pp. 22–5; Thompson, Malissa, 'Cameo: Director Stephen Hopkins', *Premiere*, July 1994, p. 25.

FILMOGRAPHY: *Highlander* (2nd unit dir., Russell Mulcahy, UK/US, 1986); *Dangerous Game* (co-dir. David Lewis, Austral, 1988); *A Nightmare on Elm Street: The Dream Child* (US, 1989); *Predator 2* (US, 1990); *Judgment Night* (US, 1993); *Blown Away* (US, 1994); *The Ghost and the Darkness* (US, 1996); *Lost in Space* (co-dir. Friedrich Karl Praetorius, US, 1998); *Under Suspicion* (co-dir. Morgan Freeman, Fr/US, 2000); *The Life and Death of Peter Sellers* (UK/US, 2004).

HOSKINS, Bob (1942–)

One of British cinema's strongest acting personalities, Bob Hoskins' intermittent work as a film director includes the gypsy drama *The Raggedy Rawney* (1989) and the children's fantasy *Rainbow* (1995): both explore an unusual vein of didactical whimsy. Born Robert William Hoskins in Bury St Edmunds, Suffolk, on 26 October 1942, Hoskins fell into stage acting by chance after leaving school at fifteen. Small cinema parts followed. His breakthrough came as the song-sheet salesman hero of Dennis Potter's pioneering television series *Pennies from Heaven* (Piers Haggard, 1978). In cinema he won wide recognition as the East End gang leader Harold Shand in John Mackenzie's *The Long Good Friday* (1979) and George, the more innocent small-time gangster of *Mona Lisa* (Neil Jordan, 1986). Forgoing his trademark cockney accent, Hoskins played a convincing American in *Who Framed Roger Rabbit* (Robert Zemeckis, 1988), firmly establishing his credentials for international stardom.

Hoskins has varied roles in big-budget Hollywood films with smaller, more adventurous fare, including Shane Meadows' *TwentyFourSeven* (1997), Atom Egoyan's *Felicia's Journey* (1999), Fred Schepisi's *Last Orders* (2001) and his own films as a director. Based on stories told by his grandmother, *The Raggedy Rawney*, filmed in Czechoslovakia in 1987, offers a downbeat ramble through Romany life and lore. Hoskins' mixture of gypsy atmosphere, romantic archetypes and anti-war sentiment – the plot hinges on a shell-shocked army deserter (Dexter Fletcher) hiding out with gypsies – won a muted response from critics and audiences.

Rainbow is an uneven fantasy with an ecological twist, filmed in Canada. Poor pacing and adult overacting mar the scenes when four children, echoing *The Wizard of Oz*, travel over the rainbow to Kansas. But Freddie Francis' digital high-definition video camerawork gives a genuinely eerie feel to the later presentation of a world turning pale and sick after a raid on the rainbow's gold nuggets. The film received scant distribution. Hoskins has since contributed a simple and affecting episode to the anthology film *Tube Tales* (1999), set in and around the London Underground; but it seems likely that he will remain best known for his lively, unpredictable performances.

(Geoff Brown and Elisabetta Girelli)

BIBLIOGRAPHY: 'Bob's New Directions', *Screen International*, 17 Feb. 1995, pp. 16–28; Moline, Karen, *Bob Hoskins: An Unlikely Hero* (London: Sidgwick & Jackson, 1988).

FILMOGRAPHY: *The Raggedy Rawney* (1989); *Rainbow* (UK/Can, 1995); *Tube Tales* ('My Father the Liar' episode, 1999).

HOUGH, John (1941–)

Born in London on 21 November 1941, John Hough started working in television at the age of twenty as a second-unit director on *The Avengers* series. After directing several episodes, he made his cinema debut in 1969 with *Wolfshead*, a sober telling of the Robin Hood story, originally intended as a television pilot. He followed up with *Eyewitness* (1970), a neat variation on the boy who cried wolf story starring Mark Lester.

His first horror film, *Twins of Evil* (1971), the penultimate entry in Hammer's lesbian vampire cycle, gives ample evidence of the baroque tendencies of Hough's style. *The Legend of Hell House* (1973), his best film, showcases his economy and visual panache and his facility for generating fear and suspense. Hough subsequently made many genre films in the US, as well as Disney's tentative attempt at a horror movie, *The Watcher in the Woods* (1980), which was filmed in the UK. This sporadically effective chiller, which makes good use of a creepy Bette Davis, was withdrawn and shelved for a year before being re-released with twenty minutes removed and a new ending added by Disney stalwart Vincent McEveety.

Apart from the calamitous *Biggles* (1986), a misguided attempt to update Captain W. E. John's First World War hero with time travel and an American dimension, Hough has spent the last two decades making feature-length television films for Hammer and Lew Grade, and low-budget American horror sequels. In 1998 he directed Lew Grade's last production, *Something to Believe In* (1998), which he also co-wrote and co-produced. A stodgy gallimaufry of classical music, disease of the week, European locations, road movie and religiosity, it nonetheless serves as a testament to the professionalism and versatility that have characterised Hough's long and varied career. He returned to America and horror for *Bad Karma* (2002).

(Sergio Angelini)

BIBLIOGRAPHY: Koetting, Christopher, 'The Legend of Hough House', *Fangoria*, June 1999, pp. 18–23, 78; 'Letter', *Screen International*, 26 Mar. 1993, p. 314.

FILMOGRAPHY: *Wolfshead* (aka *Wolfshead: The Legend of Robin Hood*, 1969); *Eyewitness* (US: *Sudden Terror*, 1970); *Twins of Evil* (1971); *Treasure Island* (UK/Fr/Sp/Ger, 1972); *The Legend of Hell House* (1973); *Dirty Mary Crazy Larry* (US, 1974); *Escape to Witch Mountain* (US, 1975); *Return from Witch Mountain* (US); *Brass Target* (US) (1978); *The Watcher in the Woods* (UK/US, 1980); *The Incubus* (US, 1981); *Triumphs of a Man Called Horse* (Sp/US/Can, 1982); *Biggles* (US: *Biggles: Adventures in Time*, 1986); *Howling IV: The Original Nightmare* (SA/US); *American Gothic* (aka *Hide and Shriek*, US) (1988); *Something to Believe In* (1998); *Bad Karma* (aka *Hell's Gate*, US, 2002).

HOWARD, Leslie (1893–1943)

Leslie Howard was born Lesley Howard Steiner on 3 April 1893 in Forest Hill, south London, to a Hungarian father and an English mother. He spent much of his early childhood in Vienna, but when the family returned to England he was educated in traditional English fashion at Dulwich College. He began his screen acting career in Britain in 1914 but it was in America that his career really took off. He established a substantial reputation as a stage actor on Broadway, then became a major Hollywood film star in the 1930s. His screen persona as a cultivated Englishman was cleverly exploited by Alexander Korda in his British production *The Scarlet Pimpernell* (Harold Young, 1934) where Howard's Sir Percy Blakeney masks his boring deeds as the Pimpernell by pretending to be an effete fop. In Hollywood Howard enhanced his reputation by his performances in *The Petrified Forest* (Archie Mayo, 1935), *Romeo and Juliet* (George Cukor, 1936) and most notably *Gone With the Wind* (Victor Flemyng, 1939), where his 'Southern gentleman' Ashley Wilkes acts as a foil to Clark Gable's more overtly masculine Rhett Butler.

Howard had set up a film production company, Minerva Films, with Adrian Brunel in 1920 and been involved in the production of a number of short films. His directorial career began in 1938 when he worked with Anthony Asquith co-directing *Pygmalion*, in which he also starred as Professor Henry Higgins. Howard went back to Hollywood for *Gone with the Wind*, but he soon returned to Britain and threw himself energetically into the war effort, producing, directing and acting in a range of films and becoming a member of the Ministry of Information Films Division's Joint Planning Committee (informally labelled the 'ideas committee'). He also worked as a BBC broadcaster, delivering talks and appearing on the intellectual radio forum *The Brains Trust*. His gentle cultivated voice became as familiar to audiences both in Britain and abroad as those of Winston Churchill and J. B. Priestley, and it has been suggested that he was 'almost as important for his wartime broadcasting as he was for his films' (Aldgate and Richards, p. 66). He directed three wartime films. *'Pimpernel' Smith* was criticised by the documentarists for its somewhat romantic view of the conflict, but it nevertheless attracted and entertained audiences during the early years of the war; *The First of the Few*, a biographical film about R. J. Mitchell, inventor of the Spitfire, set mainly in the inter-war years, was framed by footage of RAF action, and became the most successful British picture of 1942. *The Gentle Sex*, his final film, despite incorporating a somewhat awkward and patronising voiceover by Howard himself, publicised the important role that women played in the fighting services, and displayed a concern with the contribution of ordinary people to the war effort in marked contrast to the focus on extraordinary figures (which he had played himself) in the two previous films.

Leslie Howard died in 1943, a victim of the war, when a plane carrying him back to Britain after a lecture tour of Spain and Portugal was shot down by the Germans.

(Tom Ryall)

BIBLIOGRAPHY: Aldgate, Anthony and Jeffrey Richards, *Britain Can Take It* (Edinburgh: Edinburgh University Press, 1994); Lant, Antonia, *Blackout* (Princeton, NJ: Princeton University Press, 1991); Richards, Jeffrey, 'Leslie Howard: The Thinking Man as Hero', *Focus on Film* no. 25, Summer/Autumn 1976, pp. 37–50.

FILMOGRAPHY: *Pygmalion* (co-dir. Anthony Asquith, 1938); *'Pimpernel' Smith* (US: *Mister V*, 1941); *The First of the Few* (US: *Spitfire*, 1942); *The Gentle Sex* (co-dir. Maurice Elvey, 1943).

HOWARD, William K. (1899–1954)

Born in St Mary's, Ohio, on 16 June 1899, William Kerrigan Howard got his start in movies working in film exhibition for Vitagraph before making his directorial debut with *Get Your Man* in 1921. After a number of stylish and popular films, Howard began a profitable collaboration with the great cinematographer James Wong Howe, climaxing with *The Power and the Glory* (1933), a stylistically and structurally impressive precursor of *Citizen Kane* (1941).

In the mid-1930s, like several other Hollywood denizens, Howard decamped to the UK to make films for Alexander Korda. Howard and Howe had an instant hit with *Fires over England* (1937), a patriotic swashbuckler starring Flora Robson as

Elizabeth I that made many allusions to the worsening situation in Europe. He then produced a neat little gangland thriller, scripted by Graham Greene, *The Green Cockatoo* (William Cameron Menzies, 1937), to which he also made an uncredited directorial contribution. Helped by the production design of Vincent Korda and the glossy cinematography of Georges Périnal, Howard made a stylish remake of Edgar Wallace's *The Squeaker*, which Wallace himself had directed in 1930. He was also briefly linked to *Revolt in the Desert*, a T. E. Lawrence biography that was subsequently abandoned, and *Jamaica Inn*, which was eventually made by Alfred Hitchcock. He was removed from the Merle Oberon vehicle *Over the Moon* (unreleased until 1940) after falling from favour with Korda. Returning to Hollywood, Howard's career, apparently blighted by alcohol, never really recovered. His last film (*A Guy Could Change*) was released in 1946; he died in Los Angeles on 21 February 1954.
(Sergio Angelini)

BIBLIOGRAPHY: Richards, Jeffrey, *The Age of the Dream Palace* (London: Routledge & Kegan Paul, 1984); Williams, R. Ewart, 'Forget Britain's Past – Remember the Present', *Film Pictorial*, 27 Nov. 1937, p. 15.

FILMOGRAPHY (UK only): *Fires over England*; *The Squeaker* (US: *Murder on Diamond Row*) (1937); *Over the Moon* (uncredited; co-dir. Thornton Freeland, 1940).

HOWITT, Peter (1957–)

Peter Howitt was born in Manchester on 5 May 1957. After acting on both stage and screen, most notably in the role of Joey Boswell in Carla Lane's long-running BBC sitcom *Bread* (1986–91), Howitt made his debut as writer-director with *Sliding Doors* in 1998. As Howitt subsequently observed, 'I got bored with acting. Dressing up pretending to be someone else seemed like a really silly thing to do. But I did like telling stories, so I thought I would have a go at doing it from the other side of the camera' (Smith, 2003).

Sliding Doors, starring Gwyneth Paltrow, John Hannah and John Lynch, cleverly interweaves two narratives featuring the same characters, exploring alternative futures depending upon whether Paltrow's Helen catches or misses a train on the London Underground. Having been turned down by Channel 4, the BBC, Granada and British Screen, the project was rescued by American producer-director Sydney Pollack, who had been shown the script by John Hannah. Howitt gratefully acknowledged Pollack's contribution, both in getting the film off the ground and in guiding it through to successful completion.

Following the success of *Sliding Doors*, Howitt went to Hollywood to direct the internet thriller *AntiTrust*, starring Ryan Phillippe, Rachael Leigh Cook, and Tim Robbins as the villainous computer boss. Although the film was not particularly well received, a number of reviewers commented favourably on Howitt's crisp direction and his valiant efforts to overcome a weak and formulaic script. For his next film, Howitt returned to the UK to direct Rowan Atkinson in the James Bond spoof *Johnny English*. Although poorly received by the critics, the film was an international box-office success, appealing particularly to younger audiences. Immediately after completing *Johnny English*, Howitt was signed up to replace Michael Caton-Jones on *Laws of Attraction*, a return to romantic comedy with Pierce Brosnan and Julianne Moore as two New York divorce lawyers who fall in love. Though less adventurous than *Sliding Doors*, star appeal and Howitt's competent direction ensured big enough international audiences to recoup its $28 million budget.
(Martin Hunt)

BIBLIOGRAPHY: Mueller, Matt, 'Spotlight: Peter Howitt', *Premiere*, May 1998, UK Film Section, p. 3; Smith, Anne, 'Interview with Peter Howitt', 7 Apr. 2003 <www.bbc.co.uk/films/2003/04/07/peter_howitt_johnny_english_interview.shtml>

FILMOGRAPHY: *Sliding Doors* (1998); *AntiTrust* (US, 2001); *Johnny English* (2003); *Laws of Attraction* (US, 2004).

HUDSON, Hugh (1936–)

Hugh Hudson's directing debut could hardly have been more auspicious: a critically acclaimed work that was not only a huge international hit but won the Academy Award as the year's best film. Yet within five years, Hudson's film career was floundering, amid accusations of being a perfectionist who had squandered his opportunities.

Born in London on 25 August 1936, Hudson was educated at Eton, an association he has since, like one of his literary heroes George Orwell, strenuously attempted to live down. He worked at a London advertising agency, before making documentaries and award-winning television commercials that brought him to the attention of the producer David Puttnam, ever eager to give new young directors a chance. The result in Hudson's case was *Chariots of Fire*, the true story of two British athletes from widely different backgrounds (played by Ben Cross and Ian Charleson) who overcome various forms of social and religious prejudice to triumph at the 1924 Olympics. Undeniably impressive in its emotional sweep, the film became one of the decade's most controversial British films, regarded by its left-leaning makers (Puttnam, Hudson and the writer Colin Welland) as a radical indictment of Establishment snobbery and privilege, but appropriated by others as a conservative paean to Thatcherite values of individualism and enterprise.

Hudson's next film was *Greystoke: The Legend of Tarzan, Lord of the Apes*, an ambitious but not wholly successful attempt to use the familiar tale as a springboard for an exploration of the outsider's view of the English class system and for a contrast between Victorian and Darwinian man. Nemesis came with *Revolution*, an epic about the American War of Independence that was controversially cast, went hugely over budget and was torn to shreds by the critics. However, a loyal few saw in it a visually stirring film that courageously attempted an ambivalent, even nightmarish evocation of America's historical struggle for identity at a time when the national mood of patriotic fervour was embodied by Reagan, Rocky and Rambo. Despite the presence

of Al Pacino, Donald Sutherland and Nastassja Kinski, the film was a commercial disaster. Hudson's following film, *Lost Angels* (1989), made in America and starring Donald Sutherland, also failed. Since then, Hudson's biggest film success has been a much-imitated party political broadcast on behalf of Neil Kinnock's Labour Party. His next feature, *My Life So Far*, based on the childhood memoir of Sir Denis Forman, attracted only modest attention, although a strong cast (Colin Firth, Rosemary Harris, Irène Jacob, among others) and an intense father/son theme that obsessively underpins much of his work make it an honourable enough addition to his slim body of work. Little fuss was also made about his American production *I Dreamed of Africa*, an uncertainly paced romantic drama starring Kim Basinger. With this intriguing collection of films, Hudson could be seen as one of British cinema's most talented underachievers.

(Neil Sinyard)

BIBLIOGRAPHY: Eberts, Jake and Terry Ilott, *My Indecision Is Final: The Rise and Fall of Goldcrest Films* (London: Faber and Faber, 1990); Friedman, Lester (ed.), *British Cinema and Thatcherism* (London: UCL Press, 1993); National Film Theatre audiotape interview, 1985, held in the BFI National Library, London.

FILMOGRAPHY: *A . . . Is for Apple* (doc. short, 1963); *The Tortoise and the Hare* (co-dir. Donald Cammell, 1967); *Fangio* (doc., 1971); *12 Squadron-Buccaneers* (doc. short, 1979); *Chariots of Fire* (1981); *Greystoke: The Legend of Tarzan, Lord of the Apes* (UK/US, 1984); *Revolution* (UK/Nor, 1985); *Lost Angels* (US, 1989); *Marathon, The Flames of Peace* (co-dir. Carlos Saura, Sp, 1994); *Lumière et compagnie* (fifty-two-second episode, Fr/Sp/Swe, 1995); *My Life So Far* (US/UK, 1999); *I Dreamed of Africa* (US/Ger, 2000).

HUGHES, Harry

Reviewing the trade show of Harry Hughes' *The Hell Cat* on 22 March 1928, *The Bioscope* categorised the film as 'excellent British product'; one year later, Hugh Castle in the April 1929 *Close Up* memorably called it 'one of the world's worst'. Hughes was never the critics' darling, but for ten years in the 1920s and 30s, chiefly at Nettlefold and BIP, he supplied enough useful commercial product to be steadily employed as a director in the feature industry. Born in Leyton, north-east London (the year is unknown), he entered the business in 1907 as a ledger clerk with the distributors Pathé Frères, and gained experience in selling, renting and publicity before settling into scenario writing and editing following service in the First World War.

Hughes made his directing debut with *Unnatural Life Studies* and *Adam's Film Review*, two short comedy burlesques made alongside Adrian Brunel's similar squibs in 1922. In 1926 he re-edited *The House of Marney*, Cecil Hepworth's last unsuccessful feature, made after Archibald Nettlefold had purchased his Walton studio; for several years afterwards Nettlefold's feature output was shared between Hughes and Walter Forde. Forde's inventive comedies won most respect and the biggest audiences; but after a rocky start with *A Daughter in Revolt* (1927), Hughes' more artificial confections earned a modest place on cinema bills through their spirited female star, Mabel Poulton. In *The Hell Cat*, though weighed down with clichés, she features strongly as a slum girl adopted by a scientist; her vivacity proved equally crucial in *Troublesome Wives*, an unlikely stew of comedy and spy melodrama.

In 1930 Hughes arrived at British International Pictures; at first progress was slow, but with *The Man at Six* in 1931 he achieved a modestly exciting mystery thriller, with action and suspense neatly balanced, and a plausible heroine in Anne Grey's lady detective. In 1933 Hughes reached his peak in the industry with a popular and bouncy Stanley Lupino comedy, *Facing the Music*. The budget increased for his next property, the operetta *A Southern Maid*, a stage sequel to *The Maid of the Mountains*, but studio politics and a dishevelled script left the material more unconvincing than necessary. One of its writers, Frank Launder, determined to leave BIP and go freelance as a result; the same thinking may have led Hughes to try his fortunes as a low-budget independent producer in 1934. His City Film Corporation, formed with Basil Humphreys, collapsed after two years, and his own output of comedies made a muted impact, with the happy exception of the last, *The Improper Duchess* (1936), a play adaptation with Yvonne Arnaud in sparkling form as a Ruritanian duchess in New York. Continuing elsewhere, Hughes managed to breathe fresh life into the cornfields of the musical *Mountains o' Mourne* (1938), but further opportunities shrank and the Second World War found him outside features, working occasionally on information films. His last known credits were on children's films for Rank in 1946–7. After that, Hughes disappears from the record, perhaps in the company of his old brier pipe –

once referred to in trade paper chatter as 'his inseparable friend in leisure moments'. His death date is unknown.

(Geoff Brown)

BIBLIOGRAPHY: Hughes, Harry, 'A Few Cutting Remarks', *The Bioscope*, British Film Number, 18 June 1927, p. 154; Hughes, Harry, 'How It's Done: A British Director Tells Everything', *Film Weekly*, 26 May 1933, pp. 26–7, 64; Low, Rachael, *The History of the British Film 1918–1929* (London: George Allen & Unwin, 1971); 'Who's Who of British Film Directors', *The Bioscope*, British Film Number, 18 June 1927, p. 101.

FILMOGRAPHY: *Unnatural Life Studies* (short); *Adam's Film Review* (short) (1924); *A Wet Night* (short, 1926); *A Daughter in Revolt* (1927); *The Hell Cat*; *Virginia's Husband*; *Troublesome Wives* (1928); *Little Miss London* (1929); *We Take off Our Hats* (short); *Star Impersonations* (short) (1930); *Glamour* (co-dir. Seymour Hicks); *The Man at Six* (US: *The Gables Mystery*) (1931); *Bachelor's Baby*; *His Wife's Mother* (1932); *Their Night Out*; *Facing the Music*; *A Southern Maid* (1933); *Song at Eventide*; *The Broken Rosary* (US: *Her Song of Love*); *Womanhood* (1934); *Barnacle Bill*; *Joy Ride*; *Play up the Band* (1935); *Tropical Trouble*; *The Improper Duchess* (1936); *The Gables Mystery*; *Mountains o' Mourne* (1938); *In the Drink* (doc. short); *Guy Fawkes* (doc. short); *A Matter of Interest* (doc. short) (1943); *The Voyage of Peter Joe* (series, 1946); *Stage Frights* (short, 1947).

HUGHES, Ken (1922–2001)

Ken Hughes experienced one of the more fluctuating careers among post-war British film-makers. For most of the 1950s he was clearly marked as a director of promise, a reliable crafter of slick, lively crime thrillers in the American mould, often wrapped around imported American players. By the early 1960s the solid virtues of *The Trials of Oscar Wilde* (1960) and the friskier habits of *The Small World of Sammy Lee* (1963) finally made him a director of substance. Major-league film-making appeared to beckon, and in terms of budgets it did so. The children's film *Chitty Chitty Bang Bang* (1968) proved popular with audiences, though Hughes himself took little pride in its success. His personal commitment rested instead with his historical epic *Cromwell*, a long-standing project, released in 1970 to mixed reviews and small audiences. The film's box-office failure cast a dark shadow over the rest of Hughes' career.

Kenneth Graham Hughes was born in Liverpool on 19 January 1922. He set out with high hopes and a burning passion for the cinema medium, gaining early recognition at the age of fourteen with a prize-winning entry to *Amateur Cine World* magazine's annual film competition. Henceforth he learned on the job; as a cinema projectionist, a BBC sound engineer and, during the Second World War, as a unit member making army and navy training films. A privately made documentary, *Soho* (1943), led to directing assignments with World Wide Pictures; between 1945 and 1947 he made films on topics including fuel conservation and customer relations. After another period with the BBC, he finally emerged as a fiction director with *Wide Boy* in 1952, working for Anglo-Amalgamated and other low-budget specialists in crime thrillers. He made perky contributions to Anglo-Amalgamated's generally dolorous Scotland Yard series; and for Hammer turned his own novel *High Wray* into *The House Across the Lake* (1954), an atmospheric and well-constructed melodrama.

'My cars used to go faster than anybody else's,' Hughes recalled later (Eyles, p. 45). 'Police cars never drew up – they pulled up, usually on the pavement.' Speed indeed was of the essence, though even in the liveliest features like *The Brain Machine* (1955) and *Timeslip* (1955), Hughes' technical acumen faced battles with script deficiencies and uneven casts. *Joe Macbeth* (1955) displayed increased ambition – the script by the American Philip Yordan transposed *Macbeth* to a nominally American gangland setting – though in this instance the marriage of artistic pretensions and B-movie pulp proved uneasy.

Hughes' reputation became firmly established with *The Trials of Oscar Wilde* – his first period film, and his first in colour, handsomely mounted, though hurriedly produced in tandem with a rival project, *Oscar Wilde* (Gregory Ratoff, 1960). The film sometimes veered toward the obvious in its dramatic effects, but Hughes' script provided a firm foundation, centring conflicts squarely on the characters' competing personalities: Peter Finch's Wilde, dignified and touching for all the flamboyance; John Fraser's young peacock Lord Alfred Douglas; and Lionel Jeffries' fiercely repressed Marquis of Queensberry. Sexual details were of necessity discreet or non-existent, despite the film's X certificate.

The Small World of Sammy Lee, though less successful artistically, marked another step in Hughes' progress. Based on Hughes' 1957 television play, a monologue for Anthony Newley, the film returned to the Soho setting of his early documentary. Newley repeated his role as the strip-show compère struggling to pay off a gambling debt; the widened focus weakened the material dramatically, but Wolfgang Suschitzky's European-style, off-the-cuff photography took the film into stylistic realms quite separate from Hughes' early thrillers.

Frustratingly, he then marked time. Replacing Henry Hathaway on *Of Human Bondage*, shot in Ireland, Hughes supplied an attractive visual surface but could do nothing to shake the dust from W. Somerset Maugham's plot or turn Kim Novak into a convincing cockney waitress. *Drop Dead, Darling* offered modest black comedy frivolity. Having turned down an offer to direct *Dr No* (Terence Young, 1962), Hughes then became embroiled in two other spin-offs from Ian Fleming's pen: the messy Bond spoof *Casino Royale* (he directed the Berlin sequences), and the enormously expensive *Chitty Chitty Bang Bang*, overtly modelled after Disney's *Mary Poppins* (US, Robert Stevenson, 1964). Lackadaisical construction, bad special effects and an overdose of saccharine severely reduced adult appeal, but children took the film to their hearts.

With *Cromwell* audiences proved harder to find. Hughes first prepared a script on the subject in 1960; mounted ten years later, the two-and-a-half-hour film bore all the marks of an unhappy compromise between popular appeal (elaborate battles, fabricated incidents) and the serious retelling of history. Alec Guinness sup-

plied an agreeably nuanced Charles I, but Richard Harris' Cromwell gave the film a fatally cold centre.

Before the release of *Cromwell*, Hughes' future projects had been large and ambitious. Thereafter, his prospects shrank. Financial problems played their part: in the year of *Alfie Darling* (1975), a coarsely trivial sequel to Lewis Gilbert's *Alfie* (1966), Hughes declared himself bankrupt and claimed to have lived for a year on baked beans on toast. A spy thriller, *The Internecine Project* (1974), passed the time moderately well, but no good came of *Sextette*, an unwise vehicle for Mae West's ego, or *Night School* (1981), the lowly and lurid American thriller that brought his career full circle. On 28 April 2001 Hughes died in Panorama City, California, of complications from Alzheimer's disease.

(Geoff Brown)

BIBLIOGRAPHY: Eyles, Allen, 'A Passion for Cinema: Ken Hughes', *Focus on Film* no. 6, Spring 1971, pp. 42–51; Hughes, Ken, 'Those Nutty Intellectuals', *Films and Filming*, Jan. 1963, pp. 9–10.

FILMOGRAPHY: Documentaries and shorts: *Soho* (1943); *War on Wheels* (1944); *The Burning Question*; *A Day in the Life of a D.R.* (1945); *Beach Recovery*; *Those Nuisances*; *Radar 262* (1946); *If the Cap Fits*; *The Mystery of the White Handkerchief*; *The Man on the Flying Trapeze* (1947); *The Drayton Case*; *The Missing Man*; *The Candlelight Murder* (1953); *The Blazing Caravan*; *The Dark Stairway*; *The Strange Case of Blondie*; *Passenger to Tokyo* (1954); *Night Plane to Amsterdam*; *Murder Anonymous* (1955).

Features: *Wide Boy* (1952); *The House Across the Lake* (US: *Heat Wave*); *Black Thirteen* (1954); *The Brain Machine*; *Little Red Monkey* (US: *The Case of the Red Monkey*); *Confession* (US: *The Deadliest Sin*); *Timeslip* (US: *The Atomic Man*); *Joe Macbeth* (1955); *Wicked as They Come* (1956); *The Long Haul* (1957); *Jazzboat*; *In the Nick*; *The Trials of Oscar Wilde* (US: *The Man with the Green Carnation*, 1960); *The Small World of Sammy Lee* (1963); *Of Human Bondage* (add. scenes, Henry Hathaway, 1964); *Drop Dead, Darling* (US: *Arrivederci, Baby!*, 1966); *Casino Royale* (co-dirs. John Huston/Robert Parrish/Joe McGrath/Val Guest, 1967); *Chitty Chitty Bang Bang* (1968); *Cromwell* (1970); *The Internecine Project* (1974); *Alfie Darling* (1975); *Sextette* (US, 1978); *Night School* (aka *Terror Eyes*, US, 1981).

HULBERT, Jack (1892–1978)

John Norman Hulbert was born on 24 April 1892 in Ely, Cambridgeshire, the son of a doctor and the elder brother of comedian Claude Hulbert. He studied law at Cambridge University but spent much of his time with the Footlights Dramatic Club devising and writing revues. Success took him to the London stage, and by 1930 Hulbert was a national institution through the impeccably staged musical comedies that showcased his jaunty personality. He entered the film industry in order to stave off bankruptcy after a brush with a crooked accountant, and his self-directed debut – a segment in *Elstree Calling* (1930) – showed only static camera front-cloth action. But Hulbert was a perfectionist, and once committed to the medium he went about it with dedicated professionalism, adapting his work to ensure maximum impact on the big screen. He should have taken co-directing credit on all his pre-war starring vehicles, but did so only on two – *Falling for You* and *Jack of All Trades* – both of which superbly display his talents as comic and dancer. His use of the tracking shot to monitor his dance routines has seldom been bettered in the genre. After the war, though his film-starring days were over, he appeared regularly on stage, television and film until his death in Mayfair on 25 March 1978, aged eighty-six. His lifelong marriage to comedienne and frequent collaborator Cicely Courtneidge began in 1916.

(Richard Dacre)

BIBLIOGRAPHY: Courtneidge, Cicely, *Cicely* (London: Hutchinson, 1953); Hulbert, Jack, *The Little Woman's Always Right* (London: W. H. Allen, 1975).

FILMOGRAPHY: *Elstree Calling* (section, 1930); *Falling for You* (co-dir., Robert Stevenson, 1933); *Jack of All Trades* (US: *The Two of Us*, co-dir. Robert Stevenson, 1936).

HUME, Kenneth (c. 1926–1967)

Kenneth Hume was assistant editor on Carol Reed's *The Way Ahead* (1944), and editor on Maurice Wilson's *The Turners of Prospect Road* (1947) and Jill Craigie's *Blue Scar* (1949) before making his directing debut. *Cheer the Brave* (1951) is an amusing B-film about a man who is suddenly liberated from a loveless marriage by the unexpected reappearance of his wife's rascally first husband, which Hume also wrote and produced. Other modest films followed, including *Bullet from the Past* (1957), one of the better episodes of Merton Park's 'Scotland Yard' series, and the Mediterranean-set *Sail into Danger* (1957). Occasional television work failed to sustain a viable career, and Hume's venture into youth musical territory in the 1960s failed to yield dividends. *Mods and Rockers* (1964), despite its topical title and contribution from the Beatles, consists of a brace of modern ballets without much audience appeal. *I've Gotta Horse* (1965), a combination of backstage musical and lovable animal story, is more conventionally commercial, but its star, the likeable balladeer Billy Fury, had been eclipsed by the raucous rock bands of the mid-1960s and the film failed to relaunch Hume's career. His troubles exacerbated by a lawsuit against an American distributor who had combined *Mods and Rockers* with two other musical shorts to release as the feature-length *U.K. Swings Again* (aka *Go-Go Bigbeat*, 1965), Hume committed suicide in London on 25 June 1967.

(Robert Murphy)

BIBLIOGRAPHY: Clark, L. H., 'One Man's Job', *Cinema Studio* vol. 6 no. 117, Jan. 1951, pp. 20–1; Clark, L. H., Obituary, *Daily Cinema*, 28 June 1967, p. 6.

FILMOGRAPHY: *Cheer the Brave* (1951); *Hot Ice* (1952); *Bullet from the Past* (short); *Sail into Danger* (1957); *Mods and Rockers*; *This Is Gulf* (doc. short, US/UK) (1964); *I've Gotta Horse* (aka *Wonderful Day*, 1965).

HUMPHRIES, Andy

Andy Humphries' debut film as writer and director, *Sex Lives of the Potato Men*, aroused controversy as an unfit receptacle for Film Council funding. Its exploration of the sex lives of unattractive, low-achieving characters upset critics, though seaside postcard vulgarity about nose pickings and the sexual use of strawberry jam hardly merited media hysteria. Johnny Vegas is a one-trick pony but his pairing with the skeletal and surprisingly subtle Mackenzie Crook works well and their buffoonish characters become almost endearing. A widespread release and the oxygen of free publicity meant that box-office returns were sufficient to recoup the modest budget.

(Robert Murphy)

BIBLIOGRAPHY: Demetriou, Danielle, 'The Critics Agree: Johnny's "Sex Life" Is a Disaster. So How Did It Ever Get Made?', *Independent*, 21 Feb. 2004; Humphries, Andy, 'If It's Too Smutty, You're Too Snooty', *Guardian* Friday Review Section, 27 Feb. 2004.

FILMOGRAPHY: *Sex Lives of the Potato Men* (2004).

HUNSINGER, Tom (1952–) and Neil HUNTER (1963–)

Writer/director team Tom Hunsinger and Neil Hunter have worked together since the early 1990s. Born in Texas, on 21 December 1952, Hunsinger trained as an actor, made occasional screen appearances and worked extensively in British theatre as a writer, director and teacher. Answering an advertisement for performers for a short film about a group of gay, lesbian and bisexual student journalists, he landed the job of producer. The film, *Tell Me No Lies*, was directed by Neil Hunter, who was born on 27 December 1963 near Maldon, Essex (later the setting for *The Lawless Heart*). After teaching in India, Nepal and London, he had taken a Working Men's College course in film-making before directing *Tell Me No Lies*.

Hunsinger and Hunter's next project was feature-length, though still made on a minimal budget. *Boyfriends*, in which a weekend in the country sees three gay couples break up or make up, won Best Feature at the 1996 Turin Lesbian and Gay Film Festival. Wider recognition, and considerable acclaim, came with their more complex *The Lawless Heart*, a film that retraced the same timespan from different perspectives, unearthing divergent responses to the sudden death of a gay restaurateur.

Distinctively but never flashily contemporary, the approach adopted by Hunsinger and Hunter involves careful preparation, building up narrative and characterisation through improvisation work. This prevents them from being prolific film-makers, but has resulted in subtle and sympathetic examinations of gay and straight relationships.

(Guy Barefoot)

BIBLIOGRAPHY: Kemp, Philip, 'Parallel Lives', *Sight and Sound*, July 2002, pp. 10–11.

FILMOGRAPHY: *Tell Me No Lies* (short, Hunsinger prod. only, 1993); *Boyfriends* (1996); *The Lawless Heart* (2001).

HUNT, Peter (1928–2002)

Peter Roger Hunt was born in east London on 11 March 1928 and entered the film industry in 1947, quickly gaining a reputation as a creative and resourceful editor. He edited the first five Bond films, developing an ultra-fast-paced style known variously as 'crash' or 'sharp' cutting – a highly influential technique that largely dispensed with bridging and establishing shots. Having taken on increasing production responsibilities with each successive Bond, Hunt was promoted to overall director with the sixth in the series, *On Her Majesty's Secret Service*. Its unusually strong love story, mellow tone and tragic ending distinguish it from the rest of the series, while its climactic series of five consecutive set-pieces, making up the last third of the movie, remains an extraordinary feat in action films.

Unfortunately the substitution of George Lazenby for Sean Connery as James Bond proved unpopular and the film was less commercially successful than its predecessors. Though he never made another Bond film, Hunt worked with Roger Moore on his television series *The Persuaders* (1971–2), and on two adaptations of novels by Wilbur Smith: *Gold*, which is set in a South African gold mine and has a thrilling action climax; and *Shout at the Devil*, an unsatisfactory mixture of humour and thrills set in Zanzibar during the First World War.

After making a musical version of *Gulliver's Travels* (with Richard Harris as Gulliver), Hunt moved to America, where he made *Death Hunt*, an above-average outdoor adventure film with Charles Bronson and Lee Marvin. He returned to Europe to remake *The Last Days of Pompeii* (1984), an Anglo-Italian television miniseries; two episodes for LWT's *Marlowe – Private Eye* series (1984); and *Wild Geese II*, a sequel that lost its *raison d'être* when Richard Burton, set to reprise his role from the first film, died a few days before shooting was due to begin. Hunt then settled permanently in the US, making *Hyper Sapien*, a feeble science-fiction adventure, which he took on at short notice; and *Assassination*, a vehicle for Charles Bronson and his wife Jill Ireland.

Peter Hunt died of heart failure in Santa Monica, California, on 14 August 2002. He should not be confused with the American television director often billed as 'Peter H. Hunt'.

(Sergio Angelini)

BIBLIOGRAPHY: Bergan, Ronald, 'The Man Who Cut Down 007', *Guardian*, 16 Aug. 2002; Lightman, Herb, 'Directing the New 007', *American Cinematographer*, Mar. 1970, pp. 218-21.

FILMOGRAPHY: *You Only Live Twice* (2nd unit dir., Lewis Gilbert, 1967); *On Her Majesty's Secret Service* (1969); *Gold* (1974); *Shout at the Devil* (1976); *Gulliver's Travels* (UK/Belg, 1977); *Death Hunt* (US, 1981); *The Jigsaw Man* (2nd unit dir., Terence Young, 1983); *Wild Geese II* (1985); *Hyper Sapien: People from Another Star* (US, 1986); *Assassination* (US, 1987).

HUNTER, Simon (1969–)

Simon Hunter was born in England on 26 May 1969 but brought up in Dumfriesshire, Scotland. He made several Super-

8 home movies, including an ambitious documentary about a river-boat in Zaire, before studying film for three years at West Surrey College of Art and Design. British Screen showed an interest in Hunter's idea for a suspense film set on a lighthouse, and financed a short thriller, *Wired*, to test his abilities. The results proved satisfactory enough and a budget of £1.5 million was raised to make *Lighthouse*. When a suitably accessible lighthouse proved hard to find, Hunter shot the film on sets built at the Three Mills Island Studios in London's East End. Despite meticulous preparation, ingenious low-budget special effects and a dramatic script about a criminal psychopath killing his way through shipwreck survivors, the results were considered too routine to gain more than a DVD release in the US (as *Dead of Night*), and a brief theatrical window in London (four years after the film's completion). Nonetheless Hunter had been given the chance to show competence and efficiency; he has subsequently made commercials, and plans future feature films.

(Robert Murphy)

BIBLIOGRAPHY: Clare, 'Merger Most Foul', *Creation*, Sept. 1998, pp. 8–10; Falk, Quentin, 'Making Waves in London', *Exposure*, Autumn 1998, pp. 22–3; <www.simonhunter.net/>.

FILMOGRAPHY: *Wired* (short, 1997); *Lighthouse* (1998; rel. 2002).

HUNTER, T. Hayes (1882–1944)

An American trade advertisement rashly prophesied that audiences would proclaim T. Hayes Hunter 'the greatest director of his time' after seeing his 1920 Goldwyn production *Earthbound*. This drama about an adulterer's spirit seeking repose remained Hunter's biggest success in his American years (1914–25); but the bulk of his output was less ambitious, marked by a theatrical quality possibly retained from his days as an actor and stage manager with David Belasco.

Thomas Hayes Hunter was born in Philadelphia on 1 December 1882, and in the late 1920s joined other American and European talents trying their fortunes in Britain. He directed four silents, beginning at Gainsborough in 1927 with *One of the Best*, and concluding with *The Silver King*, a Victorian play misguidedly made into a major production by Welsh-Pearson-Elder. He modestly came into his own with sound, in a run of Edgar Wallace properties made by Gainsborough and British Lion: *The Calendar*, *The Frightened Lady* and *White Face*. An amiable disposition – his nickname was 'Happy' – made him popular with cast, crew and the front-office.

His best-known film now is *The Ghoul* (1933), a Boris Karloff vehicle about an Egyptologist's bid for immortality, and Britain's first real horror film. Hunter's staging remains basic, but Gunther Krampf's camerawork and Alfred Junge's sets display an impressive command of horror atmospherics, with no daylight visible.

In 1934, after two further thrillers, Hunter was demoted to the low-brow antics of *Josser on the Farm*. He left film-making, and established a successful agency, Film Rights, where clients included Flora Robson, Robert Morley and Sabu. He died of heart disease in London on 14 December 1944. His son is the scriptwriter John Hunter.

(Geoff Brown)

BIBLIOGRAPHY: Balcon, Michael, *Michael Balcon Presents . . . A Lifetime of Films* (London: Hutchinson, 1969).

FILMOGRAPHY (UK only): *One of the Best* (1927); *A South Sea Bubble*; *The Triumph of the Scarlet Pimpernel* (US: *The Scarlet Daredevil*) (1928); *The Silver King* (1929); *The Man They Couldn't Arrest*; *The Calendar* (US: *Bachelor's Folly*) (1931); *The Frightened Lady* (US: *Criminal at Large*); *White Face*; *Sally Bishop* (1932); *The Ghoul* (1933); *Warn London*; *The Green Pack*; *Josser on the Farm* (1934).

HUNTINGTON, Lawrence (1900–1968)

Born in London in 1900, Lawrence Huntington is one of the neglected directors of British cinema. He started his career in long-forgotten late silent films, directed equally obscure 1930s' genre pieces and finished on some flavourless adventures and thrillers, along with television playlets, in the 1950s and 60s; but in between he revealed an attractive flair for melodrama. Originally a writer (short stories and, later, a few screenplays), he was also briefly a dance-band musician in the 1920s before turning to movies. The 1930s' films are mainly formulaic crime stories, with rare exceptions such as the musical *Romance in Rhythm* (1934), featuring Carroll Gibbons' orchestra, and the romantic comedy *Café Mascot* (1936), starring Geraldine Fitzgerald.

Huntington hit his stride in the 1940s. After the over-hectic plotting of *Tower of Terror* (1941), he turned out some highly enjoyable thrillers, starting with *Night Boat to Dublin* (1946), a hearty, swift-moving spy tale. The plot centres on a Swedish scientist whose services are sought by British and German agents; British Intelligence officer Robert Newton (in an unusually straightforward hero's role) unmasks a German spy ring, thrashes Nazi swine Raymond Lovell and ends up with the scientist's daughter, Muriel Pavlow. This was good 'thick-ear' fun, but in his next film, *Wanted for Murder* (1946), Huntington offered more. In one of his striking 1940s' studies in twisted psychology, Eric Portman played Victor Colebrooke, a wealthy businessman descended from a hangman, who has a penchant for killing pretty girls. There is good, conventional cat-and-mouse tension as Inspector Conway (Roland Culver) marshals his suspicions of Victor, but the relationship between Victor and the loyal mother (Barbara Everest) he lives with is handled with particular subtlety and complexity.

The Upturned Glass (1947), a Sydney Box project with James Mason, which grew out of their successful collaboration on *The Seventh Veil* (Compton Bennett, 1945), is an atmospherically effective British film noir, though Mason's troubled protagonist seeking revenge for the death of the woman he loved (on a character played by his own wife Pamela Kellino/Mason) is difficult to identify with. *When the Bough Breaks* (1947), made for Betty Box at the small Gainsborough Islington studios, is a more conventional social-problem film focusing bravely, if without much flair, on an unmarried mother's struggle to win back the child she gave up for adoption.

Another mother–son relationship dominates Huntington's finest film, *Mr Perrin and Mr Traill* (1948), from Hugh Walpole's novel of conflicts in a boys' boarding school. Perrin (Marius Goring) lives with his mother, like Mrs Colebrooke kindly and non-possessive, and as in *Wanted for Murder*, Huntington avoids potentially clichéd possibilities. Rivalry flares when dashing ex-war hero Traill (David Farrar) is appointed and attracts the attention of the (improbably) glamorous school matron (Greta Gynt). There is a finely melodramatic, literally cliffhanging climax, but the film's real strength is in the interplay of tensions, sexual and otherwise, caught by Huntington in a series of tightly composed confrontations, skilfully lit by cinematographer Max Greene.

James Mason and upturned wife Pamela in *The Upturned Glass* (Lawrence Huntington, 1947)

Man on the Run (1949), with Derek Farr as an army deserter implicated in a robbery, is little more than a B-film, but it sympathetically deals with a topical issue, and Joan Hopkins' prim, unhappy widow, prepared to flirt with danger, makes an unusual heroine. It was followed by two minor but pleasing entertainments starring Michael Denison and Dulcie Gray: *The Franchise Affair* (1950), adapted from Josephine Tey's mystery novel, and the comedy-thriller *There Was a Young Lady* (1953), which effectively exploited Gray's flair for comedy. Huntington's subsequent films became progressively less interesting: *Death Drums along the River* (1963), for example, is a hopelessly outmoded retelling of *Sanders of the River*. He died in 1968 after working on the script of what was intended to be Michael Reeves' follow-up to *Witchfinder General* (1968), *The Oblong Box* (Gordon Hessler, 1969).

(Brian McFarlane)

BIBLIOGRAPHY: McFarlane, Brian, 'Lance Comfort, Lawrence Huntington, and the British Program Feature Film', in Wheeler Winston Dixon (ed.), *Re-viewing British Cinema, 1900–1992* (Albany: SUNY Press, 1994).

FILMOGRAPHY: *After Many Years* (1930); *Romance in Rhythm* (1934); *Two on a Doorstep*; *Strange Cargo*; *Full Speed Ahead*; *Café Mascot*; *The Bank Messenger Mystery* (1936); *Twin Faces*; *Passenger to*

London (1937); *Bad Boy* (1938); *This Man Is Dangerous* (aka *The Patient Vanishes*); *Tower of Terror* (1941); *Women Aren't Angels*; *Suspected Person*; *Warn That Man* (1942); *Night Boat to Dublin*; *Wanted for Murder* (1946); *When the Bough Breaks*; *The Upturned Glass* (1947); *Mr Perrin and Mr Traill* (1948); *Man on the Run* (1949); *The Franchise Affair* (1950); *There Was a Young Lady*; *Thought to Kill* (co-dirs. Leslie Arliss/Bernard Knowles); *The Genie* (co-dir., Lance Comfort) (1953); *The Red Dress*; *Destination Milan* (co-dirs. Leslie Arliss/John Gilling) (1954); *Contraband Spain* (1955); *Deadly Record* (1958); *Stranglehold*; *The Fur Collar* (1962); *Death Drums along the River* (UK/US/Zanz, 1963); *The Vulture* (UK/Can/US, 1966).

HURRAN, Nick (1959–)

Born in London in 1959, Nick Hurran entered the television industry in the mid-1980s and after working as a floor manager quickly rose to directing light-entertainment shows (*Telly Addicts*, 1988), sitcoms (*Never the Twain*, 1989) and comedy-drama (*Boon*, 1992). He came to filmgoers' notice in the later 1990s with *Girls' Night*, a touching story of friendship between two women who go for a last-fling trip to Las Vegas, after one of them develops cancer. Brenda Blethyn as the cancer victim and Julie Walters as the dominant friend are encouraged to play for maximum emotional effect, their character contrasts underscored by intelligent camera placements and skilful variations on their familiar personas. Blethyn, who shares with Hurran a capacity for mining the everyday for quiet humour and pathos, also starred in his little-seen debut feature, *Remember Me?* (1997), centred on a suburban family upset by the arrival of the wife's old flame.

Hurran moved on to *Virtual Sexuality* (1999), an attractive British teen movie given some depth by its insights into the nature of love and its connection with narcissism. He returned to television for *Happy Birthday Shakespeare* (2000), which makes good use of Neil Morrisey's blokey affability under strain; and *Take a Girl Like You* (2000), a stylish dramatisation of Kingsley Amis' sourly witty novel, with Sienna Guillory ideally cast as the not-as-innocent-as-she-seems heroine. Hurran's next feature, *Plotz with a View*, an Ealing-like comedy about rival Welsh funeral directors was hardly distributed in Britain, despite its fine cast (Christopher Walken, Brenda Blethyn, Alfred Molina, Robert Pugh, Lee Evans). Nevertheless, Hurran was snapped up by Hollywood for *Little Black Book*, a big-budget but too predictable romantic comedy starring Brittany Murphy, Holly Hunter and Kathy Bates. On returning to Britain he made *Walk Away and I Stumble* (2005), a characteristic ITV feature-length drama, with Mark Strong as a strangely affluent security advisor who abandons his loving wife and children for Tamzin Outhwaite, only to find that she is terminally ill. Hurran is married to television producer Michele Buck.

(Brian McFarlane)

FILMOGRAPHY: *Remember Me?* (1997); *Girls' Night* (1998); *Virtual Sexuality* (1999); *Plotz with a View* (aka *Plots with a View/Undertaking Betty*, UK/US, 2002); *Little Black Book* (US, 2004).

HURST, Andy

After co-directing *Project: Assassin* (1997), a low-budget thriller, Andy Hurst won American and German financial support to make *You're Dead . . .* (1999), a convoluted heist comedy set in London but shot in Germany. What had seemed to be the main thread, the bank robbery set up by decadent gangster's son Rhys Ifans, is pushed aside as the film centres on the relationship between a veteran safe-breaker and his policewoman daughter. Despite sentimental clichés, John Hurt and Claire Skinner struggle successfully to bring this to life, and Hurst's fragmentary flashback structure camouflages some of the plot's gaping holes. The film was still too sloppy to do much business at the box office, but its inventive energy showed promise.

Hurst also served as second-unit director on two films directed by his brother Michael Hurst (*New Blood* and *The Baby Juice Express*) and has undertaken various writing assignments, including Tibor Takacs' disaster movie *Earthquake* (1994) and the German fairy tale *The Nutcracker and the Mouse King* (Tatjana Ilyina/Michael G. Johnson, 2004).

(Robert Murphy)

FILMOGRAPHY: *Project: Assassin* (co-dir. Robin Hill, 1997); *New Blood* (2nd unit dir., Michael Hurst, 1999); *You're Dead . . .* (US/Ger) (1999); *The Baby Juice Express* (2nd unit dir., Michael Hurst, 2002).

HURST, Brian Desmond (1895–1986)

The son of a blacksmith, Brian Desmond Hurst was born as Hans Moore Hawthorn Hurst in Belfast on 12 February 1895. After First World War army service, where he took part in the Gallipoli campaign, he studied art in Toronto and Paris before making his way to Hollywood, where by chance he became John Ford's production assistant. Upon returning to Britain in 1932 he was unable to find work in British films until he made *The Tell-Tale Heart* independently with private finance. He later explained that he selected this Edgar Allan Poe story because it was sensational film material that would attract attention to himself (Hurst, pp. 95–6).

After the modest success of *The Tell-Tale Heart*, Hurst went on to direct another eight films before the Second World War. One of these, the Irish drama *Ourselves Alone*, was banned in Northern Ireland, though the claim by the Minster of Home Affairs that it was 'purely Sinn Fein propaganda' is belied (despite the title) by the sympathetic treatment of the Royal Irish Constabulary in their struggle against the IRA. More favourable attention was directed at Hurst's sombre thriller *On the Night of the Fire*, praised by the critics for its realism and the performance of Ralph Richardson as a barber driven to murder by the needs of his materialistic wife. Hurst's most striking commercial success came in 1941 with *Dangerous Moonlight*, a muddled melodrama that owed much of its popularity to Richard Addinsell's *Warsaw Concerto* and Anton Walbrook's dashingly romantic performance.

Irishman Derrick de Marney and Pole Anton Walbrook join the RAF to fight in the Battle of Britain (*Dangerous Moonlight*, Brian Desmond Hurst, 1941)

After the war, Hurst made *Theirs Is the Glory*, an impressive reconstruction of the 1944 Arnhem disaster using real rank-and-file participants in the battle, which compares favourably with Richard Attenborough's *A Bridge Too Far* (1977). Subsequent achievements were patchy but not inconsiderable. *Trottie True*, a starring vehicle for Jean Kent, possesses period charm, and *Scrooge* is an outstanding adaptation of Charles Dickens' *A Christmas Carol*. *The Malta Story* is an offbeat Second World War story that eschews empty heroics and benefits from the sympathetic performances of Alec Guinness as an archaeologist-turned-reconnaissance flyer and Muriel Pavlow as the Maltese operations-room plotter he falls in love with. *Tom Brown's Schooldays*, which Hurst claimed to have largely directed as well as produced, *Simba*, a contemporary look at the Mau-Mau rebellion in Kenya, and *Behind the Mask*, dealing with British medical politics, all display solid cinematic virtues. In the early 1960s Hurst became active in efforts to revive the ailing Irish film industry, but after an adaptation of J. M. Synge's *Playboy of the Western World* in 1962, he drifted into retirement. He died in London on 26 September 1986.

Hurst's films cover many genres, although crime and period productions are most prominent. Ireland provides the setting for five of his feature films, and *Dangerous Moonlight*, unusually for a film about the war, shows an Irishman (Derrick de Marney) serving valiantly with the RAF and dying in battle. Hurst's disposition towards unusual themes presumably derived from his Irish birth (he had nationalist sympathies after the partition of Ireland in 1921 despite his Protestant upbringing) and his open homosexuality (when this was a British criminal offence). Although his output is uneven, *On the Night of the Fire*, *Theirs Is the Glory* and *Scrooge* in particular show considerable talent.
(James C. Robertson)

BIBLIOGRAPHY: Hill, John, ' "Purely Sinn Fein Propaganda": The Banning of *Ourselves Alone* (1936)', *Historical Journal of Film, Radio and Television* vol. 20 no. 3, 2000, pp. 317–33; Hurst, Brian Desmond, unpublished autobiography in BFI National Library, London; undated but no earlier than 1977; McIlroy, Brian, 'British Filmmaking in the 1930s and 1940s: The Example of Brian Desmond Hurst', in Wheeler Winston Dixon (ed.), *Re-viewing British Cinema, 1900–1992* (Albany: SUNY Press, 1994); Robbins, Christopher, *The Empress of Ireland* (London: Scribner's Sons, 2004).

FILMOGRAPHY: *The Tell-Tale Heart*; *Irish Hearts* (US: *Norah O'Neale*, UK/Ir, 1934); *Riders to the Sea* (UK/Ir, 1935); *Ourselves Alone* (co-dir. Walter Summers); *The Tenth Man*; *Sensation* (1936); *Glamorous Night* (1937); *Prison without Bars* (co-dir. Maxwell Wray, 1938); *On the Night of the Fire* (US: *The Fugitive*); *The Lion Has Wings* (co-dirs.

Michael Powell/Adrian Brunel) (1939); *The Call for Arms* (short); *Miss Grant Goes to the Door* (short) (1940); *Dangerous Moonlight* (US: *Suicide Squadron*, 1941); *A Letter from Ulster* (doc. short); *Alibi* (1942); *The Hundred Pound Window* (1943); *Caesar and Cleopatra* (co-dir. some scenes, uncredited, Gabriel Pascal, 1945); *Theirs Is the Glory* (1946); *Hungry Hill* (1947); *The Mark of Cain* (1948); *Trottie True* (US: *The Gay Lady*, 1949); *Scrooge* (US: *A Christmas Carol*); *Tom Brown's Schooldays* (co-dir. uncredited, Gordon Parry) (1951); *The Malta Story* (1953); *Simba* (1955); *The Black Tent* (1956); *Dangerous Exile* (1957); *Behind the Mask* (1958); *His and Hers* (1961); *Playboy of the Western World* (Ir, 1962).

HURST, Michael (1973–)

Michael Hurst was born in Shoreham, West Sussex, on 3 March 1973. He worked as second-unit director on *You're Dead . . .*, directed by his brother Andy Hurst (1999), and made his own debut with *New Blood*, a crime thriller set in Canada. Credibility is strained by a confused plot and the ability of Nick Moran to function normally when pumped full of bullets. But there are enjoyable moments and Hurst, who also wrote the script, introduces original elements with the would-be gangsters who act like scared rabbits in a gunfight; and a son so bitter at his father's neglect that he deliberately uses him as a fall guy guaranteed a violent death.

Hurst and Moran collaborated again on *The Baby Juice Express*, a likeable crime-comedy set in the sedate seaside town of Bognor Regis (though Southend-on-Sea proved a more convenient location). A loose script and patchy acting (Hurst boldly if not wisely cast boxer Joe Bugner and comedian Julian Clary among his villains) ruled out any theatrical release. But much of the film is funny and clever, with Moran as a middle-class policeman's son seduced by the mythology of the underworld but brow-beaten by a fiery girlfriend (Lisa Faulkner) impatient of male fantasies, effectively mocking his character in *Lock, Stock and Two Smoking Barrels* (Guy Ritchie, 1998). Jokey inventiveness might not have impressed distributors, but Hurst has at least shown himself to be versatile and competent.

(Robert Murphy)

FILMOGRAPHY: *You're Dead . . .* (2nd unit dir. Andy Hurst, US/Ger, 1999); *New Blood* (UK/Can, 1999); *The Baby Juice Express* (2002; rel. 2004).

HÜSEYIN, Metin

Metin Hüseyin attended the National Film and Television School in the late 1980s. His short film *Tight Trousers* (1989) was nominated for a BAFTA award and led to a successful career as a television director, initially on television comedy-drama series like *Teenage Health Freak* (1991) and *Common as Muck* (1994), and later on the prestigious costume drama *The History of Tom Jones, a Foundling* (1997). He broke into features with a low-budget crime-comedy, *It Was an Accident* (2000), about a genial but accident-prone black ex-convict continually frustrated in his desire to go straight and marry a policeman's daughter. His involvement with an embittered old-timer (James Bolam) 'who used to drive for the Krays' and wants to turn the clock back to the days when criminals helped old ladies with their shopping raises issues of racism, nostalgia and the centrality of crime to poor communities; but they are elbowed aside by absurdly stereotyped gangsters and a sentimental romance that even Thandie Newton cannot bring to life.

Hüseyin scored greater success with *Anita and Me* (2002), a gentle comedy based on a semi-autobiographical novel by Meera Syal. In contrast to the nebulous north London of *It Was an Accident*, there is a real sense of place and time here; what begins in indulgent nostalgia gradually acquires authenticity and significance as its twelve-year-old heroine (Chandeep Uppal) comes to terms with her proud, ambitious Indian family, and the poor, culturally deprived, casually racist West Midlands community in which she grows up. Hüseyin continues to work in television, directing, for example, *The Legend of the Tamworth Two* (2004), a fictionalised account of the escape of two pigs from a Midlands abattoir, which had captured the public's imagination in 1998.

(Robert Murphy)

BIBLIOGRAPHY: Tutt, Louise, 'In the Frame: Metin Hüseyin', *Screen International*, 3 Dec. 1999, p. 23.

FILMOGRAPHY: *Tight Trousers* (short, 1989); *It Was an Accident* (2000); *Anita and Me* (2002).

HUSSEIN, Waris (1938–)

Waris Hussein was born in Lucknow, India, on 9 December 1938. His family moved to Britain in 1947 and he read English at Queen's College, Cambridge, where he directed a number of student productions. He went on to study stage design at the Slade School of Art, and in 1962 became the first Indian to be taken onto the BBC's programme for trainee television directors. He worked on *Dr Who* and a soap opera, *The Newcomers*, and quickly established himself as one of television's top drama directors with productions such as *A Passage to India* (1965).

In 1969 he directed his first film, *A Touch of Love*, adapted from Margaret Drabble's novel *The Millstone*, about a young middle-class woman intent on a successful academic career who finds herself pregnant after a casual sexual encounter. Sandy Dennis successfully conveys her initial resentment towards an obstacle to her long-cherished goal giving way to the realisation of how emotionally arid her life had been up to then. Hussein stayed with whimsical realism for his next two films, though they were increasingly quirky. *S.W.A.L.K.* (retitled *Melody* for those unable to decipher 'sealed with a loving kiss') was based on a script by Alan Parker about two eleven-year-olds who decide to marry. Hussein directs with a delicacy that makes the children seem like complex individuals rather than the usual one-dimensional screen moppets. *Quackser Fortune Has a Cousin in the Bronx* is a bitter-sweet romantic comedy, with Gene Wilder happily making a living collecting horse dung from the streets of Dublin until he comes up against the modern world in the form of a city council ban on horses and a pretty, bright American student.

Hussein then went to America to direct *The Possession of Joel Delaney*, an effective demonic thriller treading the same sort of territory as *Rosemary's Baby* (Roman Polanski, 1968) and *The Exorcist* (William Friedkin, 1973). A powerful and disturbing film, it would have been sufficient to establish Hussein in Hollywood, but he preferred the calmer waters of British television. He returned to Britain to make *Henry VIII and His Six Wives*, a well-thought-out spin-off from the BBC's highly successful six-part drama serial, with Keith Michell repeating his portrayal of Henry, though with a different selection of wives. Hussein then settled down to direct several award-winning series, including *Shoulder to Shoulder* (1974), *The Glittering Prizes* (1976) and *Edward and Mrs Simpson* (1978). In the 1980s he went back to America, where he enjoyed equal success directing glossy television films and miniseries, several of them – such as *Little Gloria – Happy at Last* (1982) and *Onassis* (1988) – set among the rich and famous.

In 1992 Hussein returned to Britain to make *Clothes in the Wardrobe*, a star-studded BBC television film that was given a limited theatrical release. He maintains a fine balance between the comedy revolving around a group of characters coming together for a wedding, and the story's mystical undertones, represented by dreamlike flashbacks to a life-changing experience in Egypt that the bride is attempting to block out. In 1998 he directed the Lynda La Plante thriller *Supply and Demand* and a feature film *The Sixth Happiness*, an adaptation of Ferdaus Kanga's moving semi-autobiographical novel about an Indian boy confined to a wheelchair by brittle bone disease. It is handled by Hussein with sensitivity and dark humour and steadfastly refuses to indulge in self-pity. Like much of Hussein's cinema work it shows a journey through which the character develops and acquires self-knowledge. While not ignoring the cruelties fate offers, Hussein's vision is basically humanist and his characters find happiness when they face their destiny and follow their own path rather than the one designated by society. (Linda Wood)

BIBLIOGRAPHY: Gronvall, Andrea, 'Essays on Selected Directors: Waris Hussein', *Film Reader* no. 1, 1975, pp. 85–6; Mathur, Rakesh, 'A Sense of Belonging: Waris Hussein', *Cinemaya* no. 9, Autumn 1990, pp. 52–3; Salmi, Markku, 'Waris Hussein', *Film Dope* no. 26, Jan. 1983, pp. 18–19.

FILMOGRAPHY: *A Touch of Love* (aka *The Millstone/Thank You All Very Much*, 1969); *Quackser Fortune Has a Cousin in the Bronx* (aka *Fun Loving*, US/Ir); *S.W.A.L.K.* (aka *Melody*) (1970); *The Possession of Joel Delaney* (US); *Henry VIII and His Sixth Wives* (1972); *The Clothes in the Wardrobe* (aka *The Summer House*, 1993); *The Sixth Happiness* (1997).

HUSTON, John (1906–1987)

John Huston was born in Nevada, Missouri, on 5 August 1906, the son of actor Walter Huston and journalist Rhea Gore. He enjoyed a colourful and peripatetic upbringing, shuttling between his divorced parents. After trying his hand at acting, journalism and riding with the Mexican cavalry, he joined his father in Hollywood and in 1931 began working as a screenwriter. After a few hiccups – and a brief period working for Gaumont-British in London – his career took off, and by 1941 he was successful enough as a writer to be allowed to direct his first film, *The Maltese Falcon*. Its immediate success launched him as a major director.

Huston was always a wildly uneven director, but enough of his films scored critical and commercial hits to sustain his reputation. After his wartime service, he enjoyed another triumph with *The Treasure of the Sierra Madre* (1948) and a solid success with the archetypal heist movie, *The Asphalt Jungle* (1950). But, disgusted by the political climate of McCarthyite America and its repercussions in the film industry, he distanced himself from Hollywood, increasingly preferring to make movies elsewhere. *The African Queen* (1951), made for the UK-based Romulus company, was the first of these, an adventure-romance set in First World War Africa that rapidly became a much-loved classic, not least for the sparky chemistry between Humphrey Bogart as a disreputable river-boat captain and Katharine Hepburn as a strait-laced missionary. Huston made two more films for Romulus: *Moulin Rouge* (1952), a lavishly staged, flatly scripted biopic of Toulouse-Lautrec; and the absurdist adventure-movie spoof *Beat the Devil* (1953), whose zany plot and private jokes baffled audiences at the time, though it has since become a minor cult classic.

Huston's valiant attempt at filming Melville's classic novel *Moby Dick* (1956) foundered on a patently phoney whale and a wooden performance from a miscast Gregory Peck as Captain Ahab. *Heaven Knows, Mr Allison* (1957), set on a Pacific island

during the Second World War, and starring Robert Mitchum and Deborah Kerr, tried to recreate the vital chemistry of *The African Queen* but suffered by the comparison. In 1952 Huston had settled in Ireland, where he took up citizenship in 1964. In the 1960s his British work consisted only of a segment of the woefully unfunny James Bond spoof *Casino Royale* (1967); and *Sinful Davey* (1968), a *Tom Jones*-style period film, with John Hurt in his first lead role, as a Scottish highwayman.

Huston's strike rate improved in the 1970s with such films as *Fat City* (1972), *The Man Who Would Be King* (1975) and *Wise Blood* (1979). His only British film of the decade, though, was the glumly downbeat spy movie *The Mackintosh Man* (1973). Illness slowed him down in the 1980s, though he scored a notable success with *Prizzi's Honor* (1985). In the final stages of emphysema he summoned up the energy to make his last film, *The Dead* (1987), a British-German-American co-production based on James Joyce's elegiac short story. Restrained, poignant, impeccably judged, it rounded off Huston's variable film-making career with a valediction of sheer mastery. He died in Newport, Rhode Island, on 28 August 1987.

(Philip Kemp)

BIBLIOGRAPHY: Brill, Lesley, *John Huston's Filmmaking* (Cambridge: Cambridge University Press, 1997); Grobel, Lawrence, *The Hustons* (New York: Scribner's, 1989); Long, Robert Emmett (ed.), *John Huston Interviews* (Jackson: University Press of Mississippi, 2001); McCarthy, John, *The Films of John Huston* (Secaucus, NJ: Citadel Press, 1987); Pratley, Gerald, *The Cinema of John Huston* (South Brunswick, NY and London: Barnes/Tantivy, 1977).

FILMOGRAPHY (UK only): *The African Queen* (1951); *Moulin Rouge* (1953); *Beat the Devil* (UK/US); *Moby Dick* (1956); *Heaven Knows, Mr Allison* (UK/US, 1957); *Casino Royale* (co-dirs. Ken Hughes/Val Guest/Robert Parrish/Joe McGrath, 1967); *Sinful Davey* (1968); *The Mackintosh Man* (1973); *The Dead* (UK/Ger/US, 1987).

HUTH, Harold (1892–1967)

Harold Huth, born in Huddersfield on 20 January 1892 to theatrical parents, became a well-known actor in 1930s' films before ill-health forced his retirement. He remained in the film industry as casting director for MGM-British before becoming a producer and director in the 1940s and 50s. He directed three modest thrillers for ABPC: *Hell's Cargo* (1939), starring Robert Newton as a British commander pursuing a

tanker loaded with poison gas; *East of Piccadilly* (1940), where a crime-fiction writer (Sebastian Shaw) and an intrepid reporter (Judy Campbell) collaborate to discover the identity of the Soho Strangler; and *Bulldog Sees It Through* (1940), in which Jack Buchanan unmasks an armaments saboteur. They were followed by *Breach of Promise*, an enjoyable courtroom comedy starring Clive Brook. Huth went on to act as a successful producer at Gainsborough Pictures, where his credits include *Love Story* (Leslie Arliss, 1944) and *Caravan* (Arthur Crabtree, 1946).

In 1948 Huth produced and directed *Night Beat*, a topical crime thriller about post-war unrest, and formed Burnham Productions with John Corfield, where he co-produced and directed *My Sister and I*, a rather convoluted crime thriller, and *Look before You Love*, a lumbering romance about a gambler (Griffith Jones) who tries to blackmail a millionaire who is in love with his wife (Margaret Lockwood). In the 1950s he worked for Douglas Fairbanks Jr, producing many television programmes for export and one film, *The Hostage*, a far-fetched adventure-thriller in which an American pilot saves a president's daughter from revolutionaries. He joined Irving Allen and Cubby Broccoli's Warwick Films in 1957, producing, among other films, *The Trials of Oscar Wilde* (Ken Hughes, 1960). Huth died in London on 26 October 1967.

(Andrew Spicer)

FILMOGRAPHY: *Hell's Cargo* (US: *Dangerous Cargo*, 1939); *East of Piccadilly* (US: *The Strangler*); *Bulldog Sees It Through* (1940); *Breach of Promise* (US: *Adventure in Blackmail*, 1941); *Night Beat*; *My Sister and I*; *Look before You Love* (1948); *The Hostage* (1955).

HUTTON, Brian G. (1935–)

Brian Geoffrey Hutton was born in North Harlem, New York, in 1935. After working as an actor he began making American television films before making the transition to cinema with an effective romance, *Wild Seed* (1965). He came to England to direct the MGM production *Where Eagles Dare*, an Alistair Maclean-scripted war film in which traditional 'Boy's Own' heroics are combined with James Bond-like ruthless violence in a flamboyant, amoral and highly entertaining manner. As critics noted at the time of the film's release, Richard Burton did most of the talking while American co-star Clint Eastwood did most of the killing. He followed up with another successful action-adventure, *Kelly's Heroes* (US/Yug, 1970) scripted by Troy Kennedy Martin. Hutton made two further British films: *Zee and Co*, a melodrama starring Elizabeth Taylor, Michael Caine and Susannah York, scripted by Edna O'Brien; and *Night Watch*, a thriller adapted from a play by Lucille Fletcher, again starring Elizabeth Taylor. Hutton returned to America and, after a long hiatus, made *The First Deadly Sin* (1980), with Frank Sinatra in his last starring role as a New York detective, and *High Road to China* (1983), another action-adventure film, which failed to repeat the success of *Where Eagles Dare* and *Kelly's Heroes*.

(Peter Hutchings)

BIBLIOGRAPHY: Hutton, Brian G., 'Nothing Was Going to Stand in My Way . . .', *Today's Cinema*, 23 June 1969, p. 10; Salmi, Markku, 'Brian G. Hutton', *Film Dope* no. 26, Jan. 1983, pp. 27–8.

FILMOGRAPHY (UK only): *Where Eagles Dare* (1968); *Zee and Co* (1972); *Night Watch* (1973).

HYTNER, Nicholas (1956–)

Nicholas Hytner was born in Didsbury, a smart suburb of Manchester, on 7 May 1956, to parents of East European Jewish extraction. After attending Manchester Grammar School, where he played Toad in *Toad of Toad Hall* and thought of becoming an actor, he read English at Cambridge University. While still a student, he co-scripted and performed in a televised production of the 1977 Cambridge Footlights Revue and directed Brecht and Weill's *Rise and Fall of the City of Mahagonny*. On leaving Cambridge he became assistant to Colin Graham at the English National Opera. Distinguished work followed, at the Royal Exchange in Manchester, the Royal Shakespeare Company and the Royal National Theatre, as well as more opera work with Kent Opera and the ENO. Hytner's witty production of Handel's *Xerxes* for the ENO in 1985 was a huge popular success. He went on to direct a number of stage musicals, including *Miss Saigon* (which made him rich) and *Carousel*. In 1986 his Kent Opera production of *King Priam* was televised.

In 1992 Hytner directed Alan Bennett's play *The Madness of George III* at the National Theatre, and in 1994 he was invited by Hollywood to direct an Anglo-American film version retitled *The Madness of King George*. Hytner insisted that Nigel Hawthorne rather than a more famous cinema name was engaged to repeat his acclaimed performance as the King. Hytner's visual flair, technical daring and experience of working with large forces enabled him to make the transition to film-making with comparative ease; in a 1997 interview he claimed that with 'a good script, actors and technicians, Mickey Mouse could direct a movie' (*Daily Telegraph*, 24 February 1997). Bennett's play was opened up to embrace suitably royal-looking locations; and Hytner made good use of camera movement to suggest the King's mental instability, and close-ups to add extra poignancy to such scenes as the moment when the King 'recovers his wits'.

The Madness of King George was a critical and commercial success. Hytner's next film, *The Crucible*, an adaptation by Arthur Miller of his play about the Salem witch trials, was well received by some critics but did poorly at the box office. Two more Hollywood films followed, but Hytner maintained his involvement with the English stage. He was thwarted in his desire to film the musical *Chicago* but in April 2003 succeeded Trevor Nunn as Artistic Director of the National Theatre. He filmed an adaptation of his production of Bennett's *The History Boys* in the autumn of 2005.

(Janet Moat)

BIBLIOGRAPHY: Christiansen, Rupert, 'How Hytner Became a Contender', *Daily Telegraph*, 24 Feb. 1997, p. 17; Forde, Leon, 'Back

to School', *Screen International*, 7 Oct. 2005, p. 18; Gritten, David, 'Hytner Goes to Hollywood', *Daily Telegraph*, 22 Mar. 1995, p. 2; Teeman, Tim, 'Leading Man', *The Times*, 12–18 May 2001, p. 27; Wolf, Matt, 'No Thorns in Hytner's Hollywood', *The Times*, 21 Jan. 1997, p. 34.
FILMOGRAPHY: *The Madness of King George* (US/UK, 1994); *The Crucible* (US, 1996); *The Object of My Affection* (US, 1998); *Center Stage* (US, 2000); *The History Boys* (2006).

I

INCE, Ralph (1887–1937)

Ralph Waldo Ince, born in Boston, Massachusetts, on 16 January 1887, was the youngest of three film-making brothers. Both Ralph and the eldest brother, John, were actors and directors, but they lived in the shadow of middle brother, Thomas, a major figure as producer and director in the emergent Hollywood of the 1910s.

Ralph was a prolific actor and director in the silent American cinema, which he had entered as a prop boy in 1907. He worked as a director in Britain from 1934, regularly turning out second features at the Teddington studios of Warner Bros. The company had installed itself there in 1931 to produce quota pictures relying on a combination of veteran American film-makers and cheap young British talent. At Teddington, Ince made several crime and comedy second features and appeared in four of them himself. *Murder at Monte Carlo* (1935) introduced a promising male lead, Errol Flynn, and his thriller *Twelve Good Men* (1936) was the first script collaboration of Frank Launder and Sidney Gilliat to make it to the screen. Only two of Ince's British films survive (*Crime Unlimited* and *The Perfect Crime*), but according to Barry Salt, 'they are solidly made, very good-looking productions, appreciably better than the usual idea of British "quota quickies".' He was killed on 11 April 1937, when his car hit a traffic island outside the Albert Hall, London.
(Alan Burton)

BIBLIOGRAPHY: Low, Rachael, *Film Making in 1930s Britain* (London: George Allen & Unwin, 1985); Salt, Barry, 'The Unknown Ince', *Sight and Sound*, Autumn 1988, pp. 268–72.
FILMOGRAPHY (UK only): *A Glimpse of Paradise*; *No Escape*; *What's in a Name* (1934); *Black Mask*; *Blue Smoke*; *Crime Unlimited*; *Mr What's-His-Name*; *Murder at Monte Carlo*; *Rolling Home* (1935); *Fair Exchange*; *Gaol Break*; *Hail and Farewell*; *It's You I Want*; *Jury's Evidence*; *Twelve Good Men* (1936); *It's Not Cricket*; *The Man Who Made Diamonds*; *The Perfect Crime*; *Side Street Angel*; *The Vulture* (1937).

IRVIN, John (1940–)

John Irvin was born in Newcastle-upon-Tyne on 7 May 1940. He studied at the London School of Film Technique and went on to work as an editor for documentary companies such as Rank Special Features Division and British Movietone News before founding Mithras Films with Maurice Hatton and others in the early 1960s. In 1963 he made *Gala Day*, a film about the Durham miners, with financial backing from the BFI Production Board. The film established Irvin's credentials as a documentary director and he spent the rest of the decade working in the world's trouble spots directing award-winning documentaries such as *Mafia No!* (1967). In the mid-1970s he turned to television drama and found success with a gritty adaptation of Charles Dickens' *Hard Times* (1977); and the universally acclaimed *Tinker, Tailor, Soldier, Spy* (1979), starring Alec Guinness as John Le Carré's master spy George Smiley.

Irvin's first cinema feature was *The Dogs of War*, based on Frederick Forsyth's novel about a group of mercenaries but lifted above the usual Boy's Own adventure by Irvin's use of documentary techniques and strong characterisation. After going to the US to direct the moderately successful *Ghost Story* in 1981, he returned to make two likeable British films. In *Champions* John Hurt gives a good impersonation of jockey Bob Champion, who, despite being diagnosed with cancer, rode the steeplechaser Aldaniti to victory in the 1981 Grand National. A genuinely popular crowd pleaser, it could not have been more different from *Turtle Diary*, an adaptation by Harold Pinter of a novel by Russell Hoban, with Glenda Jackson and Ben Kingsley plotting to liberate a giant tortoise from a zoo. Henceforth Irvin became an international director with a talent for infusing fast-moving action films with a wry sense of humour.

Irvin has shown himself as a multifaceted talent and one not easily pigeonholed. His mainstream action movies such as *Raw Deal*, with Arnold Schwarzenegger, and *Next of Kin*, with Patrick Swayze, have to be balanced against films such as *Hamburger Hill*, a searing indictment of the Vietnam War made with a cast of unknowns; *Widow's Peak* (1993), a delicious comedy of manners set in 1920s' Ireland; and *Shiner*, with Michael Caine giving a *tour-de-force* performance as a dodgy boxing promoter. What all his films tend to have in common is their stress on individuals doing what is necessary to survive and occasionally beating the system.
(Linda Wood)

BIBLIOGRAPHY: Baker, Bob, 'John Irvin', *Film Dope* no. 27, July 1983, pp. 16–17; Tanner, Louise, 'John Irvin: An Interview', *Films in Review*, June/July 1986, pp. 343–5.
FILMOGRAPHY: Documentaries/shorts: *Inheritance*; *Gala Day* (1963); *The Malakeen* (1964); *Carousella*; *Exile*; *Pedro Cays* (1965); *Mafia No!*; *Bedtime* (1967); *Days of Our Youth* (1968); *Bismarck*; *Germany from Blood and Iron* (1975).
Features: *The Dogs Of War* (1980); *Ghost Story* (US, 1981); *Champions* (1983); *Turtle Diary* (1985); *Raw Deal* (US, 1986); *Hamburger Hill* (US, 1987); *Next of Kin* (US, 1989); *Eminent Domain* (Can/Isr/Fr, 1990); *Robin Hood* (aka *Adventures of Robin Hood*, US, 1991); *Widow's Peak* (UK/US); *Freefall* (US/UK/Venez) (1993); *A Month by the Lake* (UK/US, 1995); *City of Industry* (US, 1997); *Shiner* (2000); *The Fourth*

Angel (UK/Can, 2001); *The Boys from County Clare* (UK/Ir/Ger, 2003); *The Fine Art of Love – Mine Ha-Ha* (UK/Cz/It, 2005).

ISITT, Debbie

A prolific theatre director, best known for popular black comedies such as *The Woman Who Cooked Her Husband* and *Matilda Liar!*, Debbie Isitt branched into film with the BFI-backed *Wasps* and a number of other shorts for television. Her feature debut was an adaptation of her stage success *Nasty Neighbours*, notable mainly for the performances of Ricky Tomlinson and Marion Bailey as the suburban couple whose failure to make their mark is shown up when flashy new neighbours move in next door. The film was well received at the Venice Film Festival in 1997 but proved too small-scale to appeal to cinema audiences. Isitt had more success with her BAFTA award-winning adaptation of Jacqueline Wilson's *The Illustrated Mum* (Cilla Ware) for Granada Television.

(Robert Murphy)

FILMOGRAPHY: *Wasps* (short, 1997); *Nasty Neighbours* (1999); *Confetti* (2006).

IVORY, James (1928–)

James Francis Ivory was born in Berkeley, California, on 7 June 1928. In 1933 his family moved to Oregon, where his father had bought a lumber mill, but Ivory later returned to California to join the USC film school. His first film, a history of Venice through its art, was made as part of his MA thesis. Its successor, a short documentary about miniature Indian paintings, brought him into contact with the Indian producer Ismail Merchant when the latter attended a screening in New York. The two formed a production company, Merchant Ivory Productions, to make English-language films in India.

Filming on Ivory's third documentary was interrupted by the opportunity to make his first feature with Merchant. They persuaded Ruth Prawer Jhabvala, a German-born, English-educated writer of Polish-Jewish extraction, then resident in India, to adapt her novel *The Householder*. She became their most frequent collaborator, writing or co-writing twenty of Ivory's twenty-five features to date. The partnership and close working relationship between Merchant, Ivory and Jhabvala has lasted for over four decades, making it more than usually difficult to isolate the director's contribution to each project.

The Householder is rather an uncertain debut, awkwardly staged and stiffly acted, but it was picked up for distribution by Columbia, earning the company enough to finance its second film. *Shakespeare-Wallah*, inspired by and starring an Anglo-Indian theatre repertory troupe (Geoffrey Kendal, his wife Laura Liddell and their daughters Felicity and Jennifer Kendal), is a far more assured work. It introduced a recurrent Ivory/Jhabvala theme: the mutual fascination and incomprehension between people of different cultures. The low-key, intimate-realist style of these films suggests the influence of Satyajit Ray, and indeed Ray helped edit the first and composed the music for the second (Ivory also used Ray's regular cinematographer, Subrata Mitra, for his first four features). Their warm critical reception and modest commercial success established Merchant Ivory's international reputation.

Ivory next made two films about the then-fashionable search for spiritual enlightenment by European visitors to India. *The Guru*, backed by 20th Century-Fox, cost more than ten times the budget of *Shakespeare-Wallah*, but suffers from the miscasting of Rita Tushingham and of Michael York as a cockney pop star. *Bombay Talkie* is part tragic melodrama, part satire of the popular Hindi film industry. Neither was successful, critically or commercially, and Ivory's next three full-length features were made in America. *Savages* is a stylised allegory of the rise and fall of civilisation, which Ivory described as 'a kind of Hudson River *Last Year at Marienbad*' (Long, 1997, p. 65). *The Wild Party*, based on a narrative poem about a silent film comedian's fall from grace with the arrival of sound, was much re-edited by its distributor on first release, and only later became available in a 'director's cut'. *Roseland* is a gently melancholic portmanteau, telling three short stories set in the eponymous New York ballroom.

Since 1971, Merchant Ivory has made a number of films for British television, several of which have been shown theatrically. *Autobiography of a Princess* incorporates documentary footage of a vanished India into a wistful chamber drama, less than an hour long, featuring James Mason and Madhur Jaffrey. London Weekend Television provided backing for two arts-themed films that premiered on ITV's *The South Bank Show*. *Hullabaloo over Georgie and Bonnie's Pictures* echoes Ivory's first Indian documentary in its wry comedy about attempts to acquire a set of miniature paintings from a Maharaja; while *Jane Austen in Manhattan* was inspired by a fragment of an unproduced opera by Austen. It was not until 1982 that the company established a permanent London production office, in preparation for *Heat and Dust*, Ivory's last, most complex and sophisticated Indian-set project. However, it remains based in New York, where Ivory, though resides.

The Europeans, adapted from Henry James' novel and made in New England with wholly British funding and a largely British crew, marked something of a watershed in Ivory's career. Before it, all his films besides *The Householder* and *The Wild Party* had been made from original screenplays. Afterwards, all except *Jane Austen in Manhattan* and *Jefferson in Paris* were taken from books. Its success also marked the beginning of Ivory's identification with period subjects. His subsequent literary adaptations, all among his best and most popular work, include two more from James (*The Bostonians*, *The Golden Bowl*) and three from E. M. Forster (*A Room with a View*, *Maurice*, *Howards End*). These films are also more professionally finished than Ivory's often engagingly rough earlier work.

Perhaps as a consequence, Merchant Ivory now tends to be regarded as the cinematic equivalent of Fortnum and Mason: a provider of tasteful, exquisitely crafted, upmarket fare, but slightly dull and very definitely bourgeois. This is more than a little unjust. It is easy to assume that Ivory's reticent, classically self-effacing style – camera generally kept at a discreet medium distance; priority given to performances and dialogue; a detailed but not florid *mise en scène*; a refusal to manipulate the audience's emotions – is merely decorative, dry or inert. But given sympathetic attention, the films are rich in nuance and suggestion; they are best seen on a large screen, not just because of their splendid fixtures and fittings but to draw the viewer in to their intimate observation of manners and unspoken desires.

Eroticism is not absent from Ivory's films, but tends to be depicted coolly, dispassionately. His characters may occasionally lose their sense of decorum; his direction never does. A careful restraint is placed upon excess, and he seems uncomfortable with the bohemian worlds of Picasso, Jean Rhys' *Quartet*, or Tama Janowitz's *Slaves of New York*. This last, Ivory's only film since 1980 with a contemporary setting until the lightweight romantic comedy *Le Divorce*, is perhaps his worst. His masterpieces are *Mr & Mrs Bridge* and *The Remains of the Day*, both ironic yet characteristically compassionate and non-judgmental studies of emotional repression.

(Sheldon Hall)

BIBLIOGRAPHY: Gillett, John, 'Merchant Ivory', *Sight and Sound*, Spring 1973, pp. 95–7; Long, Robert Emmet, *The Films of Merchant Ivory* (New York: Harry N. Abrams, 1991); Pym, John, *The Wandering Company: Twenty-One Years of Merchant Ivory Films* (London and New York: BFI/Museum of Modern Art, 1983); Pym, John, *Merchant Ivory's English Landscapes* (New York: Abrams, 1994); <www.merchantivory.com>.

FILMOGRAPHY: *Venice: Themes and Variations* (doc. short, US, 1957); *The Sword and the Flute* (doc. short, US, 1959); *The Householder* (Ind, 1963); *The Delhi Way* (doc. short, US, 1964); *Shakespeare-Wallah* (Ind, 1965); *The Guru* (US/Ind, 1969); *Bombay Talkie* (Ind, 1970); *Savages* (US, 1972); *The Wild Party* (US, 1975; re-edited version, 1982); *Autobiography of a Princess* (1975); *Roseland* (US, 1977); *Hullabaloo over Georgie and Bonnie's Pictures* (Ind/UK, 1978); *The Europeans* (1979); *Jane Austen in Manhattan* (UK/US, 1980); *Quartet* (UK/Fr, 1981); *Heat and Dust* (1983); *The Bostonians* (1984); *A Room with a View* (1986); *Maurice* (1987); *Slaves of New York* (US, 1989); *Mr & Mrs Bridge* (US, 1990); *Howards End* (1992); *The Remains of the Day* (US/UK, 1993); *Jefferson in Paris* (US), *Lumière et compagnie* (one segment only, Fr/Sp/Swe) (1995); *Surviving Picasso* (US/UK, 1996); *A Soldier's Daughter Never Cries* (US/Fr, 1998); *The Golden Bowl* (US/UK, 2000); *Le Divorce* (US/Fr, 2003); *The White Countess* (UK/US/Ger/Cn, 2006).

JACKSON, Pat (1916–)

Pat Jackson, born in Eltham, south London, in 1916, was instrumental, along with J. B. Holmes and Harry Watt, in developing the 'story documentary' during the Second World War, and subsequently worked to promote realist narratives in commercial fiction cinema. On his seventeenth birthday in March 1933 Jackson joined the GPO Film Unit as an assistant, working in this capacity on several key productions, including *Night Mail* (Basil Wright and Harry Watt, 1936). His first directing assignment was *The Horsey Mail*, a one-reel informational film about the postal service in a remote Suffolk village. Though clearly an apprentice piece, this film provides some important pointers towards his future directing style and technique, notably the prominence given to the local postman's role in the life of his community.

Jackson's most celebrated documentaries were produced during the war years. *The First Days*, co-directed with Harry Watt and Humphrey Jennings, contrasted everyday routine with the political and social upheaval of the 'phoney war' period of autumn 1939, and was the first significant wartime documentary. After more shorts, including films on public health and the work of ferry pilots, Jackson made *Western Approaches*, the film for which he is now best remembered.

Western Approaches remains remarkable for its technical proficiency, narrative drive and the performances of its non-professional cast. A merchant ship in one of the Atlantic convoys is torpedoed by a German submarine while attempting to rescue survivors from an earlier attack. The submarine is sunk in a subsequent battle and the sailors are eventually rescued. Apart from one scene, the film was produced entirely at sea; six gruelling months were spent on the lifeboat scenes alone. Shooting in Technicolor generated extra difficulties, with the camera and studio lighting rigs placed in the lifeboat and on board merchant ships. Also remarkable were the fresh, uncontrived performances of the merchant navy crew who formed the cast. The technique of using improvisation to develop scenes in which individuals depict their professional roles within a fictional framework had been used by Harry Watt, Humphrey Jennings and others in their story documentaries; but the ambition and scope of *Western Approaches* set the film apart from its predecessors.

After the war, Jackson went to Hollywood under a contract with MGM brokered by Alexander Korda. His experience was not a happy one, and after *Shadow on the Wall*, a B-movie thriller about a child who accidentally witnesses the murder of his stepmother, Jackson returned to the UK. Here he directed his best commercial feature, *White Corridors* (1951), an adaptation of a wartime novel by Helen Ashton about the work of a provincial hospital. The script updated the material, placing Yeoman's Hospital in the Midlands within the new National Health Service, for which the film served as subtle propaganda. But the chief focus rests on the human drama found in the hospital's daily round, much of it triggered by a boy seriously ill with blood poisoning. Drawing upon all his story documentary skills, Jackson blends the diverse storylines, emotional dramas and moments of comic relief with a remarkably sure hand, smoothly integrating the realist aesthetic with the commercial feature's narrative needs. Performances are excellent, particularly those by Googie Withers and James Donald, the conscientious young doctors.

Though *White Corridors* was a popular and critical success, Jackson received little encouragement to further the semi-documentary approach in features. *The Feminine Touch* (1956), made for Ealing, revisited hospitals and nursing, but allowed soap suds to dominate. *The Birthday Present* (1957) pursued the consequences of a white-collar crime with appealing sobriety, but remains, like most of Jackson's later films, modest both in execution and intent. He worked increasingly in commercial television, directing several episodes of popular dramas in the 1960s and 70s, including *Danger Man*, *The Prisoner* and *The Professionals*; cinema work became mainly confined to independent producers and second features. A little of the documentary spirit surfaces in *Virgin Island*, a benign tale of love and romantic hardship on the Virgin Islands, and a concern for eerie atmosphere strengthens the thriller *Don't Talk to Strange Men*. Jackson enjoyed his biggest commercial success with *What a Carve Up!* (1961), a lively 'old dark house' comedy-thriller that strikes a fine balance between laughs and thrills, but it is not a film that ever suggests the brilliant young innovator of *Western Approaches*.

(Geoff Brown and Leo Enticknap)

BIBLIOGRAPHY: Aldgate, Anthony, 'The War the Documentarists Won: *Western Approaches*', in Anthony Aldgate and Jeffrey Richards, *Britain Can Take It* (Oxford: Blackwell, 1986); Baker, Bob and Markku Salmi, 'Pat Jackson', *Film Dope* no. 27, July 1983, pp. 1–9, 28–30; Barr, Charles, 'The National Health: Pat Jackson's *White Corridors*', in Ian MacKillop and Neil Sinyard (eds), *British Cinema of the 1950s: A Celebration* (Manchester: Manchester University Press, 2003); BECTU History Project, tape no. 185, held in the BFI National Library, London; Drazin, Charles, *The Finest Years: British Cinema of the 1940s* (London: André Deutsch, 1998); Jackson, Pat, *A Retake Please! Night Mail to Western Approaches* (Liverpool: Liverpool University Press/Royal Naval Museum Publications, 1999); Sussex, Elizabeth, *The Rise and Fall of British Documentary* (Berkeley: University of California Press, 1975).

FILMOGRAPHY: *The Horsey Mail* (doc.); *Big Money* (doc., co-dir. Harry Watt) (1937); *Men in Danger* (doc., 1938); *The First Days* (doc., co-dir. Harry Watt and Humphrey Jennings, 1939); *Health in War* (doc., 1940); *Ferry Pilot* (doc., 1941); *The Builders* (doc., 1942); *Western Approaches* (US: *The Raider*, 1944); *Plastic Surgery* (doc.); *Patent ductus arteriosus* (doc.) (1946); *Shadow on the Wall* (US, 1949); *White Corridors*; *Encore* ('The Ant and the Grasshopper' sequence, co-dirs. Anthony Pelissier/Harold French) (1951); *Something Money Can't Buy* (1952); *The Feminine Touch* (US: *The Gentle Touch*, 1956); *The Birthday Present* (1957); *Virgin Island* (US: *Our Virgin Island*, 1958); *Snowball* (1960); *What a Carve Up!* (US: *No Place Like Homicide*, 1961); *Seven Keys*; *Don't Talk to Strange Men* (1962); *Seventy Deadly Pills* (1963); *Dead End Creek* (serial, 1965); *The Stable Door* (short, 1966); *On the Run* (1969); *Beajamar* (doc., 1970).

JANES, Richard (1978–)

Richard Janes was born in Sussex in 1978. He acted in the children's television series *Mike & Angelo* and *The Demon Headmaster* from the age of fourteen, later moving behind the camera to direct the anarchic short *Representative Radio* (2001). In 2004 he made *Fakers*, a likeable feature about a shady wide boy (Matthew Rhys) who has four days to pay off a £50,000 debt and persuades a depressed artist (Tom Chambers) to make copies of a rare drawing to sell to gullible Bond Street art dealers. Janes makes enterprising use of locations, and writer Paul Gerstenberger tries to avoid narrative clichés by constantly shifting between genres. But the plot is irritatingly underdeveloped, and the relationship between the conman, the artist and his sister (Kate Ashfield cast ambivalently as a femme fatale with a heart of gold) obstinately refuses to come to life.

Unsurprisingly, the film failed to attract much of an audience, though its stylish enthusiasm might lead to future projects for Janes.

(Robert Murphy)

FILMOGRAPHY: *Representative Radio* (short, 2001); *Fakers* (2004).

JARMAN, Derek (1942–1994)

Derek Jarman was the maverick radical of British cinema during the last quarter of the twentieth century. His highly idiosyncratic form of avant-garde art cinema managed to sustain itself through his personal reputation as an auteur, as an *enfant terrible* and his more or less public private life. Jarman was an artist of many dimensions: an author of autobiographical journals, a poet, a painter, a scriptwriter, a film director, a cinematographer and a set designer. Jarman was a modernist but one who attempted to live as a Renaissance artist. Scathing attacks on British politics, challenging use of aesthetic forms and images from popular culture were all combined with a neo-romantic fascination for – and a subversion of – traditional English high art. Jarman was also famous for his outspoken homosexuality, his constant public fight for gay rights and his subsequent personal struggle with AIDS.

Michael Derek Elworthy Jarman was born in Northwood, Middlesex, on 31 January 1942; he died in London on 19 February 1994. He was educated at the University of London and at the Slade School of Art. His first work in the cinema was as a set designer on Ken Russell's *The Devils* (1970) and *Savage Messiah* (1972); at the same time he began making his own experimental films with a Super-8 camera. Jarman's first feature film was the low-budget *Sebastiane*, a story about the martyrdom of St Sebastian, which created a stir on the art-cinema market because of its overt depiction of homosexual desire and its use of Latin dialogue. Jarman's next venture, *Jubilee*, was fiercely anti-Establishment in its post-punk vision of a social wasteland, depicting Queen Elizabeth II's twenty-fifth year on the throne, partly through the eyes of Elizabeth I and her astrologer magician John Dee. His use of the anachronism was further employed in a bold adaptation of Shakespeare's *The Tempest*.

Jarman continued throughout his career to make films on Super-8, films that were later cut together and blown up into cinema formats; this was his major form of artistic practice in the early 1980s. The best-known example from this period is *The Angelic Conversation*, where the imagery is accompanied by a voice reciting Shakespeare's sonnets, obviously chosen for their openness towards a homoerotic re-reading. With the advent of Channel 4 funding in the mid-1980s and the ensuing wave of internationally distributed low-budget British art cinema, Jarman was able to enhance his status as a major European auteur, a position clinched with *Caravaggio*, a pastiche period biopic based on the life of Italian seventeenth-century painter Michelangelo da Caravaggio, funded by the BFI and produced by film theorist Colin MacCabe. The overt depiction of homosexual love, the narrative ambiguity, the superb visuals, particularly the live representations of Caravaggio's most famous paintings, gave full expression to Jarman's aesthetic concerns. Again he deploys anachronisms to disrupt the realist illusion – notably when Caravaggio's angriest critic writes his condemnations on a typewriter in his bath – an image alluding to both David's painting of the murdered Marat in his tub and to Waldo Lydecker typing vigorously in his bath in Otto Preminger's film noir *Laura* (1944).

The Last of England, another collage of Super-8 films, offered a harsh judgment on the Thatcherite politics of the late 1980s; the title ingeniously reinterpreted Ford Madox Brown's famous painting of emigrants leaving the English shores for a life in the New World. The film has been compared to Humphrey Jennings' documentary *Listen to Britain* (1942), which constitutes its very antithesis. Where *Listen to Britain* invokes the idyllic, *The Last of England* tries to expose the decay.

In the 1980s Jarman was diagnosed as HIV-positive and became a major public spokesman against what he perceived to be anti-gay politics. He published some well-received monographs and moved to a cottage in Dungeness, on a bleak stretch of the Kent coast, where he cultivated a much-publicised garden. He directed *War Requiem*, a film version of Benjamin Britten's musical interleaving of Wilfred Owen's war poetry with a Latin Requiem Mass; subsequently *Edward II*, a visually magnificent adaptation of Christopher Marlowe's Elizabethan drama, blending theatricalised staging, poetic dialogue, pop video aesthetics, overt homoeroticism and covert misogyny. *Edward II* à la Jarman emphasised the tragedy of martyrdom, political violence and sexual oppression against the homosexual king and his followers. This return to more narrative forms continued in Jarman's next film, *Wittgenstein*, a brilliantly surrealistic and provocative biography of homosexual philosopher Ludwig Wittgenstein.

Jarman's last film, apart from the posthumously released Super-8 collage *Glitterbug*, is *Blue*. Visually the film consists of a blue frame, a monochrome surface inspired by French painter Yves Klein, and deployed as a metaphorical reflection of the blindness brought on by his disease. The image is accompanied by Simon Fisher Turner's synthesised music and quotations from Jarman's writings spoken by Jarman with Nigel Terry, John Quentin and Tilda Swinton (three of his favourite actors). *Blue*, first shown at the Venice Biennial in 1993 and later as an installation at modern art museums around the world, was a considerable artistic achievement in a commercial medium – one much in line with the high spirits and aesthetic extravagance of Jarman's approach to film-making.

(Erik Hedling)

BIBLIOGRAPHY: Lippard, Chris (ed.), *By Angels Driven: The Films of Derek Jarman* (Trowbridge, Wilts: Flicks Books, 1996); O'Pray, Michael, *Derek Jarman: Dreams of England* (London: BFI Publishing, 1996); Peake, Tony, *Derek Jarman: A Biography* (Woodstock, NY: Overlook Press, 2000).

FILMOGRAPHY: Selected shorts and experimental videos: *Studio Bankside* (1970); *A Journey to Avebury*; *Electric Fairy* (1971); *Miss Gaby*; *Andrew Logan Kisses the Glitterati*; *Garden of Luxor*; *Tarot* (1972); *Art of Mirrors*; *A Walk on Møn*; *Sulphur*; *Art of Mirrors*; *Stolen*

Apples for Karen Blixen (1973); *Ula's Fete*; *Fire Island*; *Duggie Fields*; *The Devils at the Elgin* (1974); *Sebastiane Wrap*; *Picnic at Ray's* (1975); *Sea of Storms*; *Houston Texas*; *Gerald's Film*; *Art and the Pose* (1976); *Jordan's Dance*; *Every Woman for Herself and All for Art* (1977); *The Pantheon* (1978); *Broken English: Three Songs by Marianne Faithfull* (1979); *Film Diary Vol. 8*; *In the Shadow of the Sun* (1980); *T. G.: Psychic Rally in Heaven*; *Sloane Square: A Room of One's Own*; *Jordan's Wedding* (1981); *Pontormo and Punks at Santa Croce*; *Ken's First Film* (1982); *Waiting for Waiting for Godot*; *B2 Tape*; *Pirate Tape* (W. S. Burroughs Film) (1983); *Imagining October*, *Catalan* (1984); *The Smiths: The Queen Is Dead* (co dirs. John Maybury/Richard Heslop/Christopher Hughes/Sally Yeadon, 1986); *L'Ispirazione* (1988); *Pet Shop Boys: Videography* (1991); *The Next Life* (1993); *Glitterbug* (1994).

Features: *Sebastiane* (1976); *Jubilee* (1977); *The Tempest* (1979); *The Angelic Conversation* (1985); *Caravaggio* (1986); *Aria* ('Depuis le jour' episode); *The Last of England* (1987); *War Requiem* (1989); *The Garden* (1990); *Edward II* (1991); *Wittgenstein*; *Blue* (1993).

JARROTT, Charles (1927–)

Charles Jarrott was born in London on 16 June 1927. His mother was an artiste at London's Gaiety Theatre, and after the war Jarrott sought a career as an actor and director. In 1953, while touring in Canada, he met and married the actress Katharine Blake, and began directing drama for television in Toronto. This led to a meeting with the producer Sydney Newman, Head of Drama at CBC, who offered him a permanent contract. Directing a half-hour play live on television every week for the next eight months honed his skills, both as a technician and a director of actors.

When Newman moved to London to produce *Armchair Theatre* for ABC Television, Jarrott went too, working on the show on and off from 1959 to 1970. His television production of *The Young Elizabeth* in 1964 led to film producer Hal B. Wallis engaging him to direct *Anne of the Thousand Days*, a major film starring Richard Burton and Geneviève Bujold. Its success led to another historical epic, *Mary, Queen of Scots*, with Vanessa Redgrave and Glenda Jackson. Both films were box-office hits and were nominated for several American Academy Awards.

Jarrott's remake of *Lost Horizon* proved less successful, though like *Anne of the Thousand Days* and *Mary, Queen of Scots* it was chosen for the Royal Film Performance. He switched to more modest subjects with *The Dove* (based on a true story of a sixteen-year-old boy sailing his yacht around the world), and *Escape from the Dark*, a children's story about pit ponies in the Yorkshire coal mines. He returned to commercial favour with the long and gushing melodrama *The Other Side of Midnight*, and made a series of family films and an outstanding Anglo-American television film, *A Married Man* (1983), starring Anthony Hopkins and Ciaran Madden. Latterly he has become a director of mainstream American television films and miniseries.

(Janet Moat)

FILMOGRAPHY: *Anne of the Thousand Days* (1969); *Mary, Queen of Scots* (1971); *Lost Horizon* (US, 1973); *The Dove* (US, 1974); *Escape from the Dark* (US: *The Littlest Horse Thieves*, 1976); *The Other Side of Midnight* (US, 1977); *The Last Flight of Noah's Ark* (US, 1980); *Condorman* (US); *The Amateur* (US, 1981); *The Boy in Blue* (Can, 1986); *Turn of Faith* (US, 2001).

JEAN, Vadim (1963–)

Vadim Jean was born in Bristol on 9 December 1963. After studying at Warwick University, he began his film career as a runner on *Stormy Monday* (Mike Figgis, 1988). He then set up a production company, making a wide range of work from corporate videos to sports programmes for the BBC. Then in 1992 he made a notable feature debut with the infectious, high-spirited low-budget comedy *Leon the Pig Farmer*, co-directed with Gary Sinyor. Vaguely in the tradition of Ealing comedy, the film tells the increasingly unlikely story of a Jewish estate agent (Mark Frankel) who discovers his natural father is actually a Yorkshire pig farmer. Exuberantly directed, neatly balancing low farce and social satire, *Leon* proved a modest precursor of later hits like *The Full Monty* (Peter Cattaneo, 1997).

After scoring with comedy, Jean and his regular producer Paul Brooks plunged into far different territory in *Beyond Bedlam*, a vigorous shocker for the multiplex market, gruesome enough to be initially denied a video release. Jean sprays the viewer with gothic sights as Elizabeth Hurley, everyone's favourite neurological scientist, tries to help Craig Fairbrass' detective by meddling with a serial killer's brain; it is a pity so much energy had to be spent bolstering foolish material. Gears shifted again for *Clockwork Mice*, a drama about a sensitive teacher (Ian Hart) at a special-needs school and his misunderstood attempts to encourage a pupil's cross-country running. Though fluently made, the film looks shallow next to ancestors like *Kes* (Ken Loach, 1969) or *The Loneliness of the Long Distance Runner* (Tony Richardson, 1962). Neither of these genre pieces made much impression on their different audiences. Jean next moved toward the international arena, working as a second-unit director on Paul Anderson's big-budget *Event Horizon* (1997); the same year, with Canadian funds and locations, he directed *The Real Howard Spitz*, a family comedy starring Kelsey Grammer as a world-weary writer – too mild a film to make a mark, though stamped with the mix of the fantastic and the everyday, something of a Jean trademark. Back home for *One More Kiss* (1999), Jean's artistic horizons finally widened: he gave this melancholy romance about the last days of a thirty-year-old woman dying of cancer a visual widescreen sweep and an emotional punch no previous project either needed or summoned.

The audience response was small, and for a while Jean marked time. Alongside television commercials and pop promos, he made the engaging short comedy *Just Desserts* (2000) for HTV, and acted as producer on *The Virgin of Liverpool* (Lee Donaldson, 2003). Avoiding the seriousness of *One More Kiss*, his uneven career has since continued in North America with *Jiminy Glick in Lalawood*, a broad, helter-skelter vehicle for Martin Short's obnoxious television talk show character. Swings and roundabouts have so far marked Jean's progress, but at least he seems to have established a small place in the international industry.

(Robert Shail)

BIBLIOGRAPHY: Salisbury, Mark, 'Never Mind the Bollocks', *Empire*, Oct. 1993, pp. 78–84; Tutt, Louise, 'One-Man Show', *Screen International*, 28 Aug. 1998, p. 14; Wrathall, John, 'Director: Vadim Jean', *Premiere*, May 1994, pp. 34–5.

FILMOGRAPHY: *Leon the Pig Farmer* (co-dir. Gary Sinyor, 1992); *Beyond Bedlam* (1993); *Clockwork Mice* (1995); *The Real Howard Spitz* (UK/Can, 1998); *One More Kiss* (1999); *Jiminy Glick in Lalawood* (Can/US, 2004).

JEFFRIES, Lionel (1926–)

Lionel Jeffries, born in Forest Hill, south London, on 10 June 1926, was educated at the Royal Academy of Dramatic Arts, and is best known to filmgoers as a resourceful character actor, with a distinctive bald dome and rasping voice. During the 1970s, he became one of British cinema's most promising, if short-lived, popular directors.

Jeffries was given the opportunity to direct by his friend Bryan Forbes, who was production chief at Elstree at the end of the 1960s. Jeffries directed a much-loved version of E. Nesbitt's *The Railway Children* (1970), smoothing out the novel's social conflicts, and conjuring up a picture of childhood that alternated between affection, anxiety and adventure. The world of children was the common thread that united his subsequent films. *The Amazing Mr Blunden* was an excitingly executed ghost story in which two children are transported into the past to prevent an earlier tragedy. His most emotionally subtle film, *Baxter!*, concerned a young American (Scott Jacoby) in London, whose precarious world falls apart due to his ineffectual mother (Lynn Carlin) and the death of a beloved friend. However, the delicacy of his touch deserted him on *Wombling Free*, an ill-conceived elaboration of the children's television series; he was equally at sea with *The Water Babies*, diluting Charles Kingsley's hard-hitting Victorian classic with primitive animation and poor songs. Jeffries then returned to acting, leaving an uneven body of work that at its best displayed real skill with actors, gripping storytelling and sensitive renderings of childhood experience.

(Neil Sinyard)

BIBLIOGRAPHY: Baker, Bob, 'Lionel Jeffries', *Film Dope* no. 28, December 1983, pp. 7–8.

FILMOGRAPHY: *The Railway Children* (1970); *The Amazing Mr Blunden*; *Baxter!* (1972); *Wombling Free* (1977); *The Water Babies* (UK/Pol, 1978).

JENKIN, Guy

Guy Jenkin began his career as a television comedy writer, often in collaboration with Andy Hamilton, with whom he created the successful television newsroom comedy series *Drop the Dead Donkey* (1990). He went on to direct as well as write a number of television films, including the clever political satires *Lord of Misrule* (1996) and *Crossing the Floor* (1996), and the more outlandish comedy *Jeffrey Archer: The Truth* (2000).

Jenkin branched out into new territory with *The Sleeping Dictionary*, a likeable colonial tale set in Sarawak in 1936. A young English gentleman (Hugh Dancy) is deflected from his plans to educate the local headhunters by a passionate affair with his 'sleeping dictionary' (Jessica Alba), an attractive woman assigned to him for sexual gratification while teaching him the language of the people he is supposed to govern. Glamorous American beauty Alba makes an improbable (if irresistible) headhunter, and Emily Mortimer and Noah Taylor struggle with thankless roles as the inadequate English wife and the embittered rival who might have made her a good husband, but thanks to a large cast of authentic locals, a cheerily malevolent Brenda Blethyn, a Kiplingesque Bob Hoskins and the exotic locations, the film comes across as enjoyably charming.

Unfortunately Alba's star was no longer rising when the film was completed and its American backers slipped it out on video/DVD rather than risk the expense of a cinema release.

Jenkin returned to television, writing *The Private Life of Samuel Pepys* (Oliver Parker, 2003), an hour-long drama that makes good use of comedian Steve Coogan as Pepys.
(Robert Murphy)
BIBLIOGRAPHY: Ellis, Geoff, 'Donkey Put out to Grass', *Radio Times*, 24 Oct. 1998, p. 7.
FILMOGRAPHY: *The Sleeping Dictionary* (US, 2003).

JENNINGS, Humphrey (1907–1950)

Frank Humphrey Sinkler Jennings was born in Walberswick, Suffolk, on 19 August 1907 and became not only a film-maker but a photographer, literary scholar, theatrical designer, poet, painter and theorist of modern art. While studying English at Cambridge, he designed the first British productions of Stravinsky's *The Soldier's Tale* and Honegger's *King David*, and founded and edited the literary magazine *Experiment* with William Empson and Jacob Bronowski. By 1936 he had become a leading Modernist and with Herbert Read, Roland Penrose and André Breton organised the International Surrealist Exhibition in London.

Jennings joined the GPO Film Unit in 1934. His early films, like those of Alberto Cavalcanti (with whom he often collaborated), were criticised by the documentary movement's realists for their experimental qualities, and one could argue that Jennings' work is better situated in the context of experimental film and the European avant-garde than within the documentary movement.

In 1937 Jennings became involved in another kind of documentary project: the Mass Observation movement, founded with the anthropologist Tom Harrison and the poet Charles Madge. This early attempt at representing popular subjectivity had its own Surrealist tinge, as witnessed by its interest in 'shouts and gestures of motorists; the aspidistra cult; anthropology of football pools; bathroom behaviour; beards, armpits, eyebrows' and other unlikely topics. (Mary-Lou Jennings, p. 17). Jennings worked on only one major project, *May the Twelfth*, a published collection of observers' reports of Coronation Day 1937, although he himself continued to write regular reports as an observer.

Jennings' own films, like those of European documentarists Joris Ivens, Henri Storck and Jean Rouch, discover the surreal in the everyday as opposed to the artistically contrived. As he put it: 'To the real poet the front of the Bank of England may be as excellent a site for the appearance of poetry as the depths of the sea' (Jackson, 1993, p. 220). Like André Breton, he agreed that Surrealism had replaced the 'apparition' with the 'coincidence'; and for Jennings, coincidences 'have the infinite freedom of appearing anywhere, anytime, to anyone . . . probably least to petty seekers after mystery and poetry on deserted sea-shores and in misty junk-shops' (Jackson, 1993, p. 220).

Jennings employed his Surrealist imagination and his Mass Observation interest in working-class leisure pursuits in *Spare Time* (1939). With its intermittent, minimalist commentary, a music track that often bears little obvious relationship to the images and a perfunctory, snapshot-like *mise en scène*, the film is a far cry from the realism of a documentary such as *Housing Problems* (Arthur Elton/Edgar Anstey, 1935) and was disliked by the movement's traditionalists, who mistook its refusal to ennoble its working-class subjects as an attempt to satirise them.

For Jennings, the sights and sounds of wartime Britain were especially rich in 'coincidences' as the landscape itself had undergone radical metamorphosis, and his finest wartime works present us with a Britain both strange and familiar. But he was by no means simply a recorder of striking images; with the help of his regular editor, Stewart McAllister (who received co-directorial credit on *Listen to Britain*), he was able to assemble those images with remarkable imaginative power. As he put it in *Pandaemonium*, a vast, Walter Benjamin-esque collage of quotations from literature and documents charting the lure of the machine and the arrival of the Industrial Revolution: 'Just as the usual history does not consist of isolated events, occurrences – so this "imaginative history" does not consist of isolated images, but each is in a particular place in an unrolling film' (Humphrey Jennings, p. xxxv). *Pandaemonium* also includes a passage from the physicist Michael Faraday describing the sight of a balloon rising in which he remarks how the beauty of the scene derives from 'the combination of many effects, each utterly insensible alone, into one sum of fine effect' (Humphrey Jennings, p. 249). In a similar way, it is the combination of sounds and images in Jennings' wartime films that makes them so powerful.

The most famous example of the power of his associative montage is provided by the commentary-less *Listen to Britain*, an extraordinarily poetic evocation of daily life in Britain at war; but also very striking is *Words for Battle*, in which images of wartime Britain are imaginatively counterpointed on the soundtrack by passages from Milton, Blake, Browning, Kipling and others. His feature-length dramatised documentary *"Fires Were Started –"* is equally resonant but also broke new ground for Jennings in its use of a fictional narrative. In addition it is a remarkably authentic recreation of London during the Blitz and depicts its working-class characters in a notably unpatronising and naturalistic fashion; as does the sombre *The Silent Village*, in which Jennings transposes the Nazis' destruction of the Czech village of Lidice onto a mining community in Wales.

Watching Jennings' films, it is hard not to be reminded of E. M. Forster's dictum: 'Only connect'. Significantly, it was Forster who wrote the commentary for *A Diary for Timothy*, the last of Jennings' major works. Again, much of the meaning of the film is carried by its structure, although in a way that never draws attention to itself. Jennings paints a highly complex picture of life in Britain during the final year of the war in Europe, focusing on the personal lives of various representative characters and on the wider wartime context, utilising the form of a diary covering a

Humphrey Jennings directing Welsh miners in *The Silent Village* (1943)

baby's first year of life. Especially striking is the way in which he uses commentary not as the omniscient, explicatory 'voice of truth' but in a ruminative, questioning way; the images do not so much illustrate the commentary as engage with it in dialogue.

The end of the war and the Labour election victory of 1945 promised a new era of enlightenment that Jennings' gifts in theory seemed ideally suited to celebrate. But the modest socialist revolution proved less inspirational than the threats posed by the war. Jennings' role as public poet of the new order became increasingly difficult to sustain. Though the films he made between 1945 and 1950 – *A Defeated People, The Cumberland Story, The Dim Little Island, Family Portrait* – remained innovatory and stimulating, their optimistic tone became increasingly strained.

For all his involvement with Modernism, Jennings was much preoccupied with the national identity of a country that was socially and culturally conservative. He believed that the task of the documentary film-maker was to capture the distinctive 'legacy of feeling' of the nation. In trying to capture and communicate this legacy, Jennings made considerable, and highly distinctive, use of images familiarly associated with England and Englishness, 'public' images whose power is essentially cultural and social, the result of centuries of accretion of significance. There are distinct parallels here with Blake's attempt to discover and activate the collective symbols of England. His concern with the nature of Englishness also brings him close to George Orwell, and both share a vision of England that is essentially inclusive, focusing on unity in diversity: industry and art, country and city, middle and working class, high and popular culture, science and religion. Indeed, Orwell's famous montage of the sights and sounds of Britain can be seen as the prose equivalent of a Jennings film:

> The clatter of clogs in the Lancashire mill towns, the to-and-fro of lorries on the Great North Road, the queues outside the Labour Exchanges, the rattle of pin-tables in Soho pubs, the old maids biking to Holy Communion through the mists of the autumn morning – all these are not only fragments, but characteristic fragments, of the English scene. How can one make a pattern out of this muddle? (Orwell, pp. 75–6)

Jennings' films provide one answer to this question. It is particular to its time and has nothing of the bleak social critique of a later documentarist like Mike Grigsby; but it is no less powerful and moving, and the question itself remains as pressing today as when it was first posed.

Humphrey Jennings died on 24 September 1950 in an accident in Greece, while preparing *The Good Life*, part of a documentary series on European post-war life, made for the European Economic Commission.

(Julian Petley)

BIBLIOGRAPHY: Aldgate, Anthony and Jeffrey Richards, *Britain Can Take It* (Edinburgh: Edinburgh University Press, 1994); Anderson, Lindsay, 'Only Connect: Some Aspects of the Work of Humphrey Jennings', *Sight and Sound*, Apr./June 1954, pp. 181–6; Hodgkinson, Anthony W. and Rodney E. Sheratsky, *Humphrey Jennings: More than a Maker of Films* (Hanover, N.H.: University Press of New England, 1982); Jackson, Kevin (ed.), *The Humphrey Jennings Film Reader* (Manchester: Carcanet Press, 1993); Jackson, Kevin, *Humphrey Jennings* (London: Picador, 2004); Jennings, Humphrey (compiler), *Pandaemonium, 1660–1886: The Coming of the Machine as Seen by Contemporary Observers*, edited by Mary-Lou Jennings and Charles Madge (London: Picador, 1987); Jennings, Mary-Lou (ed.), *Humphrey Jennings: Film-Maker/Painter/Poet* (London: BFI, 1982); Lovell, Alan and Jim Hillier, *Studies in Documentary* (London: Secker and Warburg/BFI, 1972); Nowell-Smith, Geoffrey, 'Humphrey Jennings: Surrealist Observer', in Charles Barr (ed.), *All Our Yesterdays* (London: BFI, 1986); Orwell, George, 'The Lion and the Unicorn', in Sonia Orwell (ed.), *Collected Essays, Journalism and Letters of George Orwell. Volume 2* (Harmondsworth: Penguin Books, 1970).

FILMOGRAPHY: *The Story of the Wheel*; *Post Haste*; *Locomotives* (1934); *Farewell Topsails* (1937); *Making Fashion* (shorter version, *Design for Spring*); *The Farm* (shorter version, *English Harvest*); *Penny Journey*; *Speaking from America* (1938); *Spare Time*; *S.S. Ionian/Her Last Trip* (shorter version, *Cargoes*); *The First Days/A City Prepares* (co-dirs. Harry Watt/Pat Jackson) (1939); *Spring Offensive/An Unrecorded Victory*; *Welfare of the Workers* (co-dir. Pat Jackson); *London Can Take It* (shorter version, *Britain Can Take It*, co-dir. Harry Watt) (1940); *The Heart of Britain* (US: *This Is England*); *Words for Battle* (1941); *Listen to Britain* (co-dir. Stewart McAllister, 1942); *"Fires Were Started –"*; *I Was a Fireman*; *The Silent Village* (1943); *The True Story of Lili Marlene*; *The Eighty Days*; *V1* (1944); *A Diary for Timothy*; *Myra Hess* (1945); *A Defeated People* (1946); *The Cumberland Story* (1947); *The Dim Little Island* (1949); *Family Portrait*; *The Good Life* (completed by Graham Wallace) (1950).

JESSNER, Leopold (1878–1945)

Leopold Jessner was born on 3 March 1879 in Königsberg, Germany. An important figure in German theatre, his Expressionist convictions are evident in films such as *Die Hintertreppe* (co-dir. Paul Leni, 1921), *Erdgeist* (1923) and *Maria Stuart* (co-dir. Friedrich Feher, 1927). In 1933 he left Germany for Palestine, where he produced theatre in Tel Aviv, and then came to Britain to direct a thinly disguised film of exile, *Children of the Fog* (1935), in which a young couple escape the boy's brutal father and London's East End slums for Australia. Shortly afterwards he left for Hollywood, where he acted as adviser on MGM's *The Great Waltz* (Julien Duvivier, 1938), and produced Schiller's *William Tell* for the stage. He died in Hollywood, in humble circumstances, on 13 October 1945.

(Kevin Gough-Yates)

BIBLIOGRAPHY: Patterson, Michael, *The Revolution in German Theatre 1900–1933* (London: Routledge & Kegan Paul, 1981).

FILMOGRAPHY (UK only): *Children of the Fog* (co-dir. John Quin, 1935).

JOBSON, Richard (1960–)

Richard Jobson was born in Fife, Scotland, on 6 April 1960. His punk band the Skids enjoyed considerable success, though Jobson left after two years, pursuing a career as a male model and later as a film critic and television presenter. After producing *Tube Tales* (1999), a collection of nine short films set on the London Underground, and co-writing and producing Damien O'Donnell's *Heartlands* (2002), he was encouraged by the Chinese director Wong Kar-Wai to turn his semi-autobiographical story *16 Years of Alcohol* into a feature film. The modest budget of £400,000, and an evocatively poetic voiceover, might lead to expectation of a glorified home movie, but with the help of digital video technology, a clear vision and an outstanding cast, Jobson's debut is visually exciting, emotionally convincing and

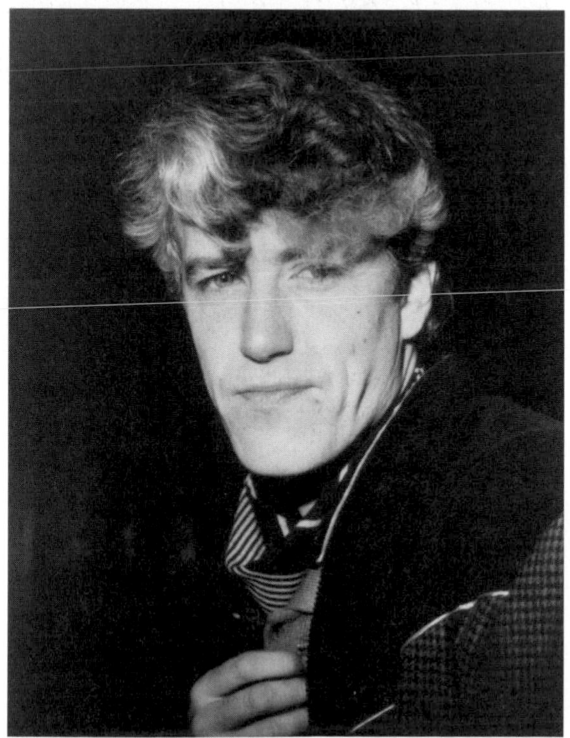

painfully revealing about the pleasures and costs of a life fuelled by alcohol.

Critical acclaim enabled Jobson to continue his film-making efforts, directing *The Purifiers*, a stylish if superficial martial arts film that makes good uses of its Glasgow locales; and *A Woman in Winter*, a philosophical science-fiction film set in Edinburgh. His success in making three innovative low-budget films in three years makes him impatient with other film-makers who spend more time raising budgets than they do making films – 'they're like bloody farmers, dependent on subsidies, they should go out there and get on with it' (Macnab, 2004, p. 28). Though this is not a view likely to endear him to the funding councils, it expresses a vigorous independence that bodes well for his future as a prolific and provocative film-maker.

(Robert Murphy)

BIBLIOGRAPHY: Dunnigan, Brian, 'Hard Stuff', *Sight and Sound*, Aug. 2004, pp. 26–8; Earle, Harriet, 'Case Study: 16 Years of Alcohol/Close Up: Richard Jobson', *Screen International*, 28 Mar. 2003, p. 15; Hunter, Allan, 'The Fast and the Flexible', *Screen International*, 11 Feb. 2005, p. 10; Macnab, Geoffrey, 'Lyrical Lads', *Sight and Sound*, Aug. 2004, pp. 27–8; Macnab, Geoffrey, 'Jobson on a Roll', *Screen International*, 14 Oct. 2005, p. 18.

FILMOGRAPHY: *16 Years of Alcohol* (2003); *The Purifiers* (2004); *A Woman in Winter* (2005).

JOFFÉ, Roland (1945–)

Roland Joffé was born in London on 17 November 1945, the grandson of sculptor Jacob Epstein. He directed for the theatre and television before making his impressive feature film debut, the Academy Award-winning *The Killing Fields* (1984). Ten years earlier Joffé had been directing episodes of *Coronation Street* and his journey from there to big-budget film production, directing stars such as Robert De Niro, Paul Newman and Demi Moore, has been both remarkable and, ultimately, disappointing.

In his ten years of directing for television Joffé developed a reputation for handling radical drama, such as Trevor Griffiths' serial about a Labour politician, *Bill Brand* (1976), and controversial plays such as *The Spongers* (1978), *The Legion Hall Bombing* (1978) and *United Kingdom* (1981). It was on such dramas that Joffé's humanist socialism was first in evidence, for it was ultimately the effect that politics had on individuals that interested him, rather than the larger issues that the plays raised; it is this concern with the fate of individuals subject to forces beyond their control that has characterised Joffé's feature films.

In *The Killing Fields* it is the fate of a *New York Times* reporter and his Cambodian translator, caught up in the escalating war in Cambodia, that forms the emotional core of the film, and it is this human drama that is foregrounded, rather than the politics of the war in Cambodia. Similarly, *The Mission* (1986), a big-budget Goldcrest production about a Jesuit mission in South America in the mid-18th century, is concerned with the idealistic missionary played by Jeremy Irons, and the Christian community he has formed among the Guarani tribespeople with the help of Robert De Niro's slave-trader, rather than with the broader historical and political context. Joffé was unequivocal about his interest in the film: 'What I liked about it was that there was a mythical element to the story – which was more than political, which was also to do with redemption and love' (Saynor, 1986, p. 97).

In *Fat Man and Little Boy* (1989), about the Los Alamos project to develop the atomic bombs that were dropped on Hiroshima and Nagasaki, Joffé's interest was once again in the scientific challenge and moral dilemmas facing the scientists rather than the global consequences of their invention. Though the film was made for an American studio (Paramount) and featured an American star (Paul Newman), the involvement of Tony Garnett as producer led the film towards having a more restrained, almost documentary, quality, in contrast to the extravagant spectacle of *The Mission*.

Fat Man and Little Boy was perhaps too serious a subject, and too undramatic in its realisation, to be a box-office success. Joffé's subsequent films – the Anglo-French co-production *City of Joy*, and the Hollywood features *The Scarlet Letter* and *Goodbye*

Lover – were both box-office and critical failures. *Vatel*, set in the court of Louis XIV and starring Gérard Depardieu and Uma Thurman, was received poorly at Cannes in 2000 and with limited distribution it failed to recoup much of its $36 million budget. Hopefully luck will change for this idiosyncratic and talented director.

(Lez Cooke)

BIBLIOGRAPHY: Saynor, James, 'The Road to Cambodia', *Stills*, Dec. 1984/Jan. 1985, pp. 20–3; Saynor, James, 'Columbia Picture', *Stills*, May/June 1986, pp. 92–101.

FILMOGRAPHY: *The Killing Fields* (1984); *The Mission* (1986); *Shadow Makers* (UK: *Fat Man and Little Boy*, US, 1989); *City of Joy* (UK/Fr, 1992); *The Scarlet Letter* (US, 1995); *Goodbye Lover* (US, 1999); *Vatel* (UK/Fr, 2000).

JOHNSON, Lamont (1922–)

Ernest Lamont Johnson Jr was born in Stockton, California, on 30 September 1922. He studied drama at the University of California, but left in 1943 and pursued a successful career as an actor in radio and television. From the mid-1950s he began directing for *Matinee Theater*, and established a reputation for inventive competence on long-running television series such as *The Twilight Zone*, *The Defenders* and *Dr Kildare*. He made his feature debut with the noirish thriller *A Covenant with Death* (1967) and came to Britain in 1970 to direct *The McKenzie Break*, a boldly different Second World War film dealing with Germans incarcerated in a British prisoner-of-war camp. Like his hero, a disgraced Irish army captain (Brian Keith) somewhat implausibly drafted into British Military Intelligence, Johnson rides roughshod over conventions: British officers are shown as stiff-necked incompetents, anti-Nazi prisoners are murdered, most of the German escapees get away and their leader, a fanatical Nazi U-boat commander (Helmut Griem), is afforded considerable respect.

Interestingly offbeat Hollywood films followed in the 1970s, notably *The Last American Hero* (1973) and *Lipstick* (1976), though subsequently Johnson returned to television, where he was able to continue making the sort of films that interested him – 'small, well-crafted, absorbing movies that don't cost a lot of money and don't have big stars' (Orner, p. 16) – into the 1990s.

(Robert Murphy)

BIBLIOGRAPHY: 'Award Winner: Lamont Johnson', *Action* vol. 6 no. 3, May/June 1971, pp. 21–2; Castell, David, 'Johnson's Polish', *Films Illustrated*, Sept. 1977, pp. 28–9; Orner, Eric, 'A- Lamont Johnson Interviewed', *Film Comment*, Sept./Oct. 1977, pp. 16–22; Vahimagi, Tise, 'Lamont Johnson', *Film Dope* no. 28, Dec. 1983, pp. 14–16.

FILMOGRAPHY (UK only): *The McKenzie Break* (aka *Wolfpack*, 1970).

JOHNSON, Niall (1965–)

After studying film at the University of Bristol and making a number of short films, Niall Johnson managed to raise a modest budget for a Bristol-based feature, *The Big Swap*. Five couples spending a drunken evening together decide, unwisely, to swap partners. Johnson puts his characters through an impressive range of suffering – jealousy, envy, frustration, rejection, embarrassment, humiliation, disappointment – until his misguidedly mushy ending tries to win back affection for people already revealed as short-sighted and selfish. Good performances from a cast of unknowns and a refusal to succumb to romantic comedy clichés make the film far gutsier than one might expect.

Johnson's next film, *The Ghost of Greville Lodge*, could not be more different: a slow and sentimental fairy tale about a modern adolescent haunted by Second World War ghosts who need to set the record straight and free his Great Uncle James (George Cole) from guilt over the death of a wartime evacuee. Johnson unexpectedly hit the big time with his script for *White Noise* (Geoffrey Sax, 2005), a scarier, modern ghost story about malign spirits disrupting the airwaves, which appealed to North American audiences. He went on to direct *Keeping Mum*, a comedy starring Rowan Atkinson, Kristin Scott Thomas, Maggie Smith and Patrick Swayze.

(Robert Murphy)

BIBLIOGRAPHY: 'Let's Talk about Sex', *Preview* no. 27, May 1997, pp. 40–3.

FILMOGRAPHY: *The Big Swap* (1998); *The Ghost of Greville Lodge* (2000); *Keeping Mum* (2006).

JOLLIFFE, Geneviève (1970–)

Geneviève Jolliffe works in partnership with fellow producer-writer-director Chris Jones, whom she met while they were students at Bournemouth Film School. She produced and co-wrote *Survival Island* (aka *The Runner*) (Chris Jones, 1992) and *White Angel* (Chris Jones, 1993) and made her own directing debut in 1998 with *Urban Ghost Story*. A low-budget horror film produced and co-written by Jones, it centres around a twelve-year-old girl traumatised by a car crash that kills her best friend. The film makes good use of its bleak Glasgow locations, and balances carefully built scares with social commentary; the imaginative use of sound suggests the existence of a poltergeist-style spirit without resorting to heavy-duty special effects. Though previewed at the Edinburgh Film Festival in 1998, *Urban Ghost Story* was not given a theatrical release in Britain until 2001 and its scarcity of shocks and special effects gave it little to attract the multiplex audience. Jolliffe and Jones drew upon their own experiences to write a useful guide to low-budget film-making, *The Guerrilla Film Makers Handbook*.

(Daniel O'Brien)

BIBLIOGRAPHY: Fewins, Clive, 'The Road to Fame', *Financial Times Weekend*, 23 Oct. 1993; Floyd, Nigel, 'Urban Ghost Story', *Fangoria* no. 198, Nov. 2000, pp. 71–3; Jolliffe, Geneviève and Chris Jones, *The Guerrilla Film Makers Handbook* (London and New York: Continuum, 1996).

FILMOGRAPHY: *Urban Ghost Story* (1998).

JONES, Chris (1968–)

Chris Jones was born in Wales in 1968, and enrolled at the Bournemouth Film School, where he met Geneviève Jolliffe. After six months they abandoned the course to found Living Spirit Pictures and make *Survival Island* (1992), a very low-budget thriller set on a remote island, where a television news crew discover that a survival course has a sinister hidden purpose. The film received only limited theatrical release, but Jones and Jolliffe were able to follow up with *White Angel*, shot for under £11,000. Peter Firth plays Leslie, a cross-dressing dentist with a habit of murdering women who wear white. Moving to north London, he lodges with Ellen (Harriet Robinson), an expatriate American writer who specialises in lurid crime fiction (and also turns out to be a killer). Restricting much of the action to Ellen's house seems more a reflection of the film's low budget than an evocation of the characters' growing claustrophobia, and Jones' repeated use of tight angles and 'intense' close-ups wears thin. *White Angel* was premiered at the London Film Festival, though it subsequently failed to gain widespread distribution.

Jones and Jolliffe switched roles for their next film, *Urban Ghost Story*, a more ambitious and accomplished film, made on the comparatively generous budget of $300,000. Their manual *The Guerrilla Film Makers Handbook*, which details ruses and devices for making films on restricted budgets, has become an essential guide for aspiring film-makers.

(Daniel O'Brien)

BIBLIOGRAPHY: Anwar, Brett, 'The Spirit of Independence', *Exposure*, Summer 1998, pp. 12–13; Jolliffe, Geneviève and Chris Jones, *The Guerrilla Film Makers Handbook* (London and New York: Continuum, 1996); Jones, Chris, 'Spirit Levels', *Guardian*, 11 July 2001.

FILMOGRAPHY: *Survival Island* (aka *The Runner*, 1992); *White Angel* (1993); *Darklands* (2nd unit dir., Julian Richards, 1997); *Urban Ghost Story* (2nd unit dir., Geneviève Jolliffe, 1998).

JONES, David (1934–)

Born in Poole, Dorset, on 19 February 1934, David Hugh Jones was first drawn to the theatre and then worked as a producer and presenter on the BBC's ground-breaking *Monitor* series from 1958 to 1964. Jones began directing television plays in the 1970s and made his film debut with *Betrayal* (1983), adapted from Harold Pinter's drama of marital infidelity. As in the play, scenes occur in reverse chronological order – a device employed later in Christopher Nolan's *Memento* (2001) and Gaspar Noé's *Irreversible* (2002). Jones' film is essentially a three-hander, and features a particularly fine performance from Ben Kingsley as the cuckolded husband. Jones went on to direct *84 Charing Cross Road* (1984), based on Helene Hanff's memoir of her twenty-year transatlantic correspondence with the London bookshop Marks & Co., which had already been adapted for the stage and for television. Jones' film version, which is full of Brechtian asides to the audience, benefits from strong performances by Anne Bancroft and Anthony Hopkins as the long-term correspondents who never actually meet.

Jones collaborated with both Hopkins and Pinter on *The Trial* (1993), an adaptation of Kafka's existential masterpiece for BBC Films. Made on location in Prague, its neutrality and restraint contrasts with the poetry and neurotic flair of Orson Welles' 1963 version. Since then Jones has continued to work prolifically in both British and American television.

(Sergio Angelini)

BIBLIOGRAPHY: Hodges, Adrian, 'All-Rounder Jones Makes Transition for *Betrayal*', *Screen International*, 29 Oct. 1983, p. 269; Sweeney, Kevin, 'Constructivism in Cognitive Film Theory', *Film and Philosophy*, no. 2, 1995, pp. 33–44.

FILMOGRAPHY: *Betrayal* (1983); *84 Charing Cross Road* (1984); *Jacknife* (US/Can, 1989); *The Trial* (1993); *The Confession* (US, 1999).

JONES, Kirk (1964–)

Kirk Jones was born in Bristol on 31 October 1964. After attending film school he worked as an assistant editor before making a name for himself as a successful director of commercials. His first feature film was *Waking Ned*, an Ealing-esque comedy set in a small Irish village but shot on the Isle of Man. The Irish input comes from gleeful performances by David Kelly, Fionnula Flanagan, Susan Lynch, James Nesbitt and an ensemble of actors playing the inhabitants of a village community desperate to conceal the fact that the owner of a winning lottery ticket has died from shock on realising his good fortune.

Irish critics greeted the film with derision, deploring its 'oirishry' and anachronistic depiction of local life. It was feared that as the film had done well in America, it would encourage similar regressive productions (a fear confirmed by Aileen Ritchie's *The Closer You Get* the following year). An alternative view might propose that the film's pleasures reside in its self-conscious play on the conventional signifiers of stage Irish representations. Certainly, Irish audiences displayed few ideological reservations about the film, making it one of the highest local earners of the year. *Waking Ned* also performed strongly in the UK and even better in America, where it grossed $25 million.

Jones, who spent five years fine-tuning the script of *Waking Ned*, took seven years to produce a follow-up, working with Emma Thompson on the solidly well-crafted *Nanny McPhee*, an eccentric children's film about a singularly brusque and unglamorous nanny who sorts out the life of a disorganised widower and his brood of unruly children.

(Ruth Barton)

BIBLIOGRAPHY: Barton, Ruth, *Irish National Cinema* (New York and London: Routledge, 2004); Dwyer, Michael 'Wake up and Smell the Blarney', *The Irish Times* Weekend Section, 5 Dec. 1998, p. 6; Gretten, David, 'Turning Whimsy into Dollars', *Daily Telegraph*, 16 Mar. 1999, p. 23; Power, Paul, 'Waking Ned Devine', *Film West* no. 36, May 1999, p. 61.

FILMOGRAPHY: *Waking Ned* (aka *Waking Ned Devine*, UK/Fr/US, 1998); *Nanny McPhee* (UK/Fr/US, 2005).

JONES, Terry (1942–)

Terence Jones was born in Colwyn Bay, North Wales, on 1 February 1942. In 1961 he enrolled at St Edmund's Hall, Oxford, to read history, and soon became involved in the university theatre scene, performing at the Edinburgh Festival and in London. While at Oxford he met Michael Palin, who after graduating joined him in working for the BBC Light Entertainment Script Department. The pair wrote sketches for various comedy shows, combining forces with Eric Idle and Terry Gilliam in 1967 to create a popular children's programme, *Do Not Adjust Your Set*, which acquired a cult following among adults. In 1969 the group, now including John Cleese and Graham Chapman, launched *Monty Python's Flying Circus*, a television series, amply consolidated by three feature films, whose fame was to become legendary. While following in a British comic tradition of nonsense, word-play and cross-dressing, Python broke established comedy rules, eliminating punch lines and narrative causality, relying instead on subversion and surrealism; its sheer originality led to the inclusion of the adjective 'Pythonesque' in *The Oxford English Dictionary*.

Monty Python and the Holy Grail, co-directed by Jones and Gilliam, was an absurdist revision of the Arthurian legend; shot on a small budget, it combined surrealism with a painstaking recreation of medieval squalor. Jones' obsessive perfectionism clashed with Gilliam's own strong views on direction, and Jones directed the next two Python films alone. *Monty Python's Life of Brian* charted the misadventures of the hapless protagonist,

born at the same time as Jesus Christ and mistaken for the Messiah; the film was ferociously attacked as blasphemous by the Church, although controversy merely enhanced its popularity. *Monty Python's The Meaning of Life* was a series of loosely linked sketches, a hint of the impending dissolution of the Python group; however, it contained some of their finest material, including the quintessentially Pythonesque musical-style sequence 'Every Sperm Is Sacred' and Jones' own portrayal of the exploding eater, Mr Creosote.

Jones' directing career has been overshadowed by Python's collective formula, yet he was largely responsible for the stylistic presentation of the group's work. After Python split up, he won critical praise for his next directing effort, *Personal Services*, a fictional biography inspired by real-life English madam Cynthia Payne. *Erik the Viking*, based on his children's book *The Saga of Erik the Viking*, was negatively received by critics and audiences, who expected a Pythonesque farce rather than a fairy tale aimed at children. Undeterred, Jones scripted and directed *The Wind in the Willows*: a fast-moving, adventurous version of the classic children's story, with fine performances from former Pythons Idle, Palin and Cleese, as well as from Steve Coogan and Stephen Fry. Jones himself excelled in the role of Toad and the film was released to general acclaim.

(Elisabetta Girelli)

BIBLIOGRAPHY: Johnson, Kim 'Howard', *The First 280 Years of Monty Python* (New York: St Martin's Griffin, 1999); Morgan, David, *Monty Python Speaks!* (London: Fourth Estate, 1999).

FILMOGRAPHY: *Monty Python and the Holy Grail* (co-dir. Terry Gilliam, 1974); *Monty Python's Life of Brian* (1979); *Monty Python's The Meaning of Life* (1983); *Personal Services* (1987); *Erik the Viking* (UK/Swe, 1989); *The Wind in the Willows* (1996).

JORDAN, Neil (1950–)

Neil Jordan was born on 25 February 1950 in County Sligo, Ireland, and educated at University College, Dublin, where he studied Irish history and English and founded the Irish Writers' Co-operative. He published a volume of short stories, *Night in Tunisia*, which won the *Guardian* Fiction Prize in 1976, and has since published three novels: *The Past* (1979), *The Dream of a Beast* (1983) and *Sunrise with Sea Monster* (1994). After working as script consultant on John Boorman's *Excalibur* (1981), Jordan made his feature debut with *Angel*, which dramatises the experiences of an Irish saxophonist (Stephen Rea, in the first of many roles for Jordan) who witnesses the murder of his band manager and a young woman, and determines to wreak revenge. Though made as a low-budget film for television, its surreal style, oneiric use of colour and lighting, and poetic use of dialogue persuaded Channel 4 to distribute *Angel* theatrically. The film established Jordan's reputation as a director and led to a fruitful collaboration with distributor-turned-producer Stephen Woolley. Their first venture, *The Company of Wolves*, reveals an important component of Jordan's imaginative vision, the world of dream and fantasy. As in many subsequent films, he addresses history and politics through images of horror, the gothic, the supernatural and the macabre.

Mona Lisa, Jordan's next film, starring Bob Hoskins, Cathy Tyson and Michael Caine, is reminiscent of Pier Paolo Pasolini's *Accatone* (1961) and *Mamma Roma* (1962) in its focus on a world of pimps and prostitutes, where the protagonist is the city and where politics emerge through images portraying the economic and social relations of underworld life. A modern film noir, *Mona Lisa* shows the complex ways in which Jordan's films draw on existing genres and transform them to suit contemporary contexts and issues.

Mona Lisa's commercial success led Jordan to Hollywood, where he made two comedies, *High Spirits* and *We're No Angels*. But both films were box-office flops and he returned to Ireland, where he wrote and directed *The Miracle*, starring Beverly D'Angelo and Donal McCann. The film dramatises the coming of age of a young boy, Jimmy, who is tied to an alcoholic father (another saxophonist), but the conflict between the two is more than an Oedipal conflict between father and son. It is a clash of past and present and testifies to Jordan's unrelenting engagement with Irish culture and society and changing attitudes toward gender, sexuality and the family. Despite its consummate weaving of characters, images and sound into its multifaceted motifs, *The Miracle* attracted little attention from critics or audiences. Thus the international success of *The Crying Game*, a modestly budgeted film echoing many of the themes and concerns of *Angel*, came as a surprise. Like many of Jordan's films it involves romance, but here there is a twist on the normative heterosexual scenario. The oddness of the relationship between reluctant IRA gunman Fergus (Stephen Rea) and Dil (Jaye Davidson), the black girl/boyfriend of a British soldier whose death he is indirectly responsible for, fascinated audiences and critics and overshadowed Jordan's other concerns with Irish nationalism and the role of the IRA.

If *The Crying Game* marked a return to the Irish subject matter of *Angel*, *Interview with the Vampire*, based on Anne Rice's best-selling novel and drawing on the talents of Tom Cruise, Christian Slater, Brad Pitt, Antonio Banderas, Kirsten Dunst and Jordan's *alter ego*, Stephen Rea, returns to the horror and fantasy of *The Company of Wolves*. It grossed $220 million in the international market, and demonstrated Jordan's ability to explore serious philosophical issues within popular cinematic forms.

With *Michael Collins*, centred around the 1916 Easter Rising that sparked the bitter and bloody war of Irish independence, Jordan came in for harsh criticism, not only from a predictably hostile English right-wing press but from Irish sources too. Alan Rickman's portrayal of Éamon de Valéra, Ireland's first president, was considered particularly provocative and Jordan was accused by many critics of bending events to suit his political agenda. De Valéra's defiance of Collins in the Dáil, his petulance and his 'nervous breakdown' shortly before the ambush where Collins is killed contribute to the film's discrediting of his masculinity (as does his escape from Lincoln Prison in women's clothes). But this is part of Jordan's wider strategy of combating inherited cinematic images of Irish masculinity. Collins, 'the Big Fella' (Liam Neeson), is portrayed as neither gratuitously violent nor sexually puritanical. Reinventing and inverting images of Irishness, Jordan associates him with intelligence, cleverness and wit. Furthermore, he stresses purposeful action rather than indiscriminate violence on the part of the IRA. The scenes in Marsh's Library and in Dublin Castle with Broy (Stephen Rea) and

Collins highlight the role that information and intelligence play in Collins' strategy to defeat the British, and present the men as more than vicious gunmen. Julia Roberts' characterisation of Kitty Kiernan serves to highlight Collins' ambivalence over the use of violence, but even more to accentuate the melodramatic sense of mourning and loss that permeates the film.

In *The Butcher Boy* (based on a novel by Patrick McCabe), Jordan uses a young boy as the focal point, circumventing conventional moral distinctions to create a compassionate – even humorous – view of a child murderer who chops a woman to pieces like a slab of meat, and casts the spectator adrift from clichés of childhood innocence. The increasingly unfamiliar character of the world seen through the child's eyes frustrates and confounds judgment. The spectator is treated to images of everyday life where everything is metamorphosed through recollection, dream and fantasy. As he experiences loss after loss – his mother, his uncle, his father and his friend Joe – Francie, the butcher boy, retreats to an inner and feminised world where he assumes his mother's domestic chores and wears women's clothes. In this fantasy world, he conjures up his own image of the Virgin Mary (played by Sinéad O'Connor, notorious for tearing up a picture of the Pope on television). Jordan's treatment of this most sacred icon of the Catholic Church signals an attack on its debilitating effects on Irish culture.

The Butcher Boy is particularly self-conscious about the role of the media in representing Ireland, incorporating television, films and radio into the fabric of the film as evidence of the modernisation begun long before Ireland's new-found economic prosperity. The television segments play a key role in undermining historical images of Irish social and family life, introducing controversial subjects, particularly the threat of nuclear war. Everything in this world erupts and becomes hallucinatory – images of landscape, family, childhood, sexuality, Catholicism, small-town life, conceptions of sanity and conceptions of cinematic realism and their debt to melodramatic representation. In this context, the film has no 'resolution', shifting its burden of uncertainty onto the audience.

In 1999, Jordan released two films, *In Dreams*, a psychological thriller starring Annette Bening, Stephen Rea, Aidan Quinn and Robert Downey, Jr, and *The End of the Affair*, based on Graham Greene's novel about a passionate wartime affair. The obsession with nightmares and pernicious fantasies that dominates *In Dreams* might indicate that this was the more personal project, but *The End of the Affair*'s exploration of marriage, extramarital sexual passion and self-denial seems to have engaged Jordan more fruitfully.

Jordan then made *The Good Thief*, a reworking of Jean-Pierre Melville's 1956 thriller, *Bob le flambeur*, with Nick Nolte taking the part of Bob Montaganet, gambler and drug addict. Fast-paced, with brilliantly photographed shots of the Riviera, Jordan's version focuses on images of the international underworld and the intricacies of survival in this milieu of robbery, romance and male bonding. Like so many of his films, it is both a reflection on the genre form and an allegory of contemporary global politics. The 'good thief' is, as Bob tells his antagonist, Roger the policeman, 'the man hanging on the cross next to Jesus who repented just before his death'. *Breakfast on Pluto* (2005), renewed Jordan's collaboration with Patrick McCabe, and benefits from a hypnotic performance from Cillian Murphy as the transvestite erratically searching for his mother; but the lurches between outrageous comedy and stark drama never settle into the richly textured complexity of *The Butcher Boy*.

Jordan's diverse work to date as a director has brought new conceptions of Irish culture to international audiences and helped to create close ties between British and Irish film-making. His movement between Britain, Europe, Ireland and the USA demonstrates the increasingly international nature of contemporary cinema.

(Marcia Landy)

BIBLIOGRAPHY: Byrne, Terry, *Power in the Eye: An Introduction to Contemporary Irish Film* (Lanham, MD: Scarecrow Press, 1997); Coles, Robert, '1922 and All That: The Inner War in Features of Independence', *Historical Journal of Film, Radio and Television* vol. 20 no. 3, Aug. 2000, pp. 445–52; Crowdus, Gary, 'The Screenwriting of Irish History: Neil Jordan's *Michael Collins', Cinéaste* vol. 22 no. 1, Mar. 1997, pp. 14–20; Jordan, Neil, 'Neil Jordan's Guilty Pleasures', *Film Comment*, Nov./Dec. 1992, pp. 36–9; MacSwiney, Seamus, 'Trying to Take the Gun out of Irish Politics: An Interview with Neil Jordan', *Cinéaste* vol. 32 no. 4, 1997, pp. 14–24; McLoone, Martin, *Irish Film: The Emergence of a Contemporary Cinema* (London: BFI, 2000); NFT interview, 4 Feb. 2000 <www.filmguardian.co.uk>; Pettit, Lance, *Screening Ireland: Film and Television Representation* (Manchester: Manchester University Press, 1988); Schulze, Laurie, 'Performativity in Disguise: Ideology and the Denaturalisation of Identity in Theory and *The Crying Game*', *The Velvet Light Trap*, Spring 1999, pp. 51–63.

FILMOGRAPHY: *Angel* (US: *Danny Boy*, 1982); *The Company of Wolves* (1984); *Mona Lisa* (1986); *High Spirits* (US, 1988); *We're No Angels* (US, 1989); *The Miracle* (1991); *The Crying Game* (1992); *Interview with the Vampire* (US, 1994); *Michael Collins* (US, 1996); *The Butcher Boy* (US, 1997); *In Dreams* (US); *The End of the Affair* (US/Ger, 1999); *Not I* (short, 2000); *The Good Thief* (UK/Fr/Ir, 2002); *Breakfast on Pluto* (UK/Ir, 2005).

JOVY, Alex (1971–)

Alexander Jovy was born in Germany on 27 January 1971. After studying at the University of Buckingham he became a club DJ and produced the Academy Award-winning short, *Holiday Romance* (J. J. Keith, 1998). He made his own debut in 2000 with *Sorted*, a glossy and occasionally convincing thriller set around London's rave club scene. Clever references to *Get Carter* (Mike Hodges, 1971) are spoiled by the misconception that Scunthorpe is in Yorkshire, and Jovy's slapdash approach to his already undernourished plot almost proves fatal. The film is saved by its fast pace, which eases attention from the sentimental clichés, and the attractive performances – particularly from Jason Donovan, whose transvestite DJ doubles as a close-cropped Customs Officer, and Tim Curry, whose oily villain speaks in Shakespearean verse that has to be explained to his bemused victims by his long-suffering girlfriend. Cynical reviewers gave the film a hard time and box-office returns proved disappointing, but many worse debuts were being made around the same time. Jovy has since directed two shorts – *White Bits* and *Two's Company* – while attempting to raise the £50 million budget for an epic about the Persian emperor Cyrus.

(Robert Murphy)

BIBLIOGRAPHY: 'Headliners: Alexander Jovy', *Empire*, Nov. 2000, p. 32; *Movie Virgins* (four-part documentary about Alex Jovy and Leon Herbert's attempts to get their debut features off the ground, Channel 4, 2000).

FILMOGRAPHY: *Sorted* (2000); *White Bits* (short, 2002); *Two's Company* (short, 2005).

JULIEN, Isaac (1960–)

A key figure in the film and video workshop movement of the early 1980s, Isaac Julien is now a leading international film and video artist, producing work for cinema, television and art galleries. He was born in London's East End on 21 February 1960, one of five children of parents who migrated to Britain from St Lucia: his mother was a nurse, his father a welder. He attended local schools, and in his teens was involved with Four Corners Films, the Newsreel Collective and the London Youth Dance Theatre. In 1983, while studying fine art and film at St Martin's School of Art, he co-founded Sankofa, a film and video collective dedicated to developing an independent black film culture in the areas of production, exhibition and audience.

Julien co-directed Sankofa's highest-profile production, *The Passion of Remembrance*, a film inspired by the idea of reconstructing a black political history that recognises the difficulty of reclaiming a past based upon unproblematic notions of identity. At this point, he was already stressing the importance of addressing questions of sexuality and gender in tandem with issues of race and class; and in his next film, *Looking for Langston*, a meditation on the Harlem Renaissance poet Langston Hughes, he explores black masculinity alongside questions of pleasure and sexuality.

Julien has said that music is the only space for a discourse that simultaneously addresses black sexuality, desire and pleasure; and the BFI-funded feature *Young Soul Rebels* both explores the tensions between politics and pleasure for his generation of British-born blacks and celebrates that generation's contribution to an interracial youth culture, and the centrality of soul music to that moment.

In the early 1990s Julien worked mainly in television and music video: productions from this period include a four-part series for US television, *The Question of Equality* (1995), and a music video for Des'ree, *Feel So High* (1991). More recently he has moved into gallery and museum-based work, with installation pieces including *Trussed* (1996), *The Conservator's Dream* (1999), *Vagabondia* (2000) and the triple-screen version of *The Long Road to Mazatlan* (1999), which was shortlisted for the 2001 Turner Prize. Alongside his work as a film-maker, he holds visiting professor and research posts at Harvard University and Goldsmiths College, London.

Running through all Isaac Julien's work is a commitment to examining the politics of sexuality, masculinity and blackness through the distinctive pleasures of the moving image. Informed as it is by a complex multi-layering of ideas, his work is always aesthetically pleasing as well as intellectually and emotionally challenging.

(Annette Kuhn)

BIBLIOGRAPHY: Julien, Isaac and Colin MacCabe (eds), *Diary of a Young Soul Rebel* (London: BFI, 1991); Korte, Barbara and Claudia Sternberg, *Bidding for the Mainstream? Black and Asian British Film since the 1990s* (Amsterdam and New York: Rodopi, 2004); Mercer, Kobena and Chris Darke, *Isaac Julien* (London: Ellipsis, 2001); Orgeron, Devin Anthony and Marsha Gabrielle Orgeron, 'Interventions: An Interview with Isaac Julien', *Coil* nos 9/10, 2000, pp. 110–19.

FILMOGRAPHY: *Who Killed Colin Roach?* (1983); *Territories* (1984); *The Passion of Remembrance* (co-dirs. Martina Attille/Robert Crusz/Nadine Marsh-Edwards, 1986); *This Is Not an AIDS Ad*

(1987); *Looking for Langston* (1989); *Young Soul Rebels* (1991); *The Attendant* (1993); *The Darker Side of Black* (1994); *Frantz Fanon: Black Skin, White Mask* (co-dir. Mark Nash, 1997); *Three*; *The Long Road to Mazatlan* (1999).

K

KANE, David

David Kane was born in West Lothian, Scotland. After establishing himself in the theatre, he wrote two interesting television films: *Shadow on the Earth* (Chris Bernard, 1988) and *Dream Baby* (Angela Pope, 1989); and two fine serials: *Jute City* (Stuart Orme, 1991), exploring the dark underside of Dundee, and *Finney* (David Hayman, 1994), set among feuding Newcastle criminal families and inspired by Mike Figgis' *Stormy Monday* (1988). Kane's directorial debut *Ruffian Hearts* (1995), a Glasgow-set comedy drama made for BBC Scotland, displayed an ensemble acting pattern that was to characterise his two subsequent feature films.

This Year's Love is set in London's Camden Town, though three of the leading players – Douglas Henshall, Catherine McCormack and Dougray Scott – are Scots and the film was funded partly by the Scottish Arts Council National Lottery Fund. The ensemble is made up by Kathy Burke, Ian Hart and Jennifer Ehle, and the film skilfully interweaves the six characters in a series of romantic relationships with each other over a three-year period. *Born Romantic* also focuses on six characters, though the emphasis is on the sustaining or the rebuilding of relationships. The film is also set in London and reuses Ian Hart and Catherine McCormack along with the Glasgow comedian Craig Ferguson and the star of *Finney*, David Morrison. If *This Year's Love* has something of a desperate feel to it, despite its apparent happy ending, *Born Romantic* is a shade more

Dougray Scott and Catherine McCormack in *This Year's Love* (David Kane, 1999)

optimistic, tracing the ways in which the substantial obstacles to its three relationships are overcome. The film ends with a joyful dancing sequence in the Brixton salsa club where much of the film is based.

Kane's two films sit interestingly in the context of one of British cinema's most successful genres of the late 1990s, the romantic comedy, providing a grittier alternative to the fairy-tale world of *Four Weddings and a Funeral* (Mike Newell, 1994) and *Notting Hill* (Roger Michell, 1999), injecting a bleak quality into the subject matter of heterosexual relationships. *This Year's Love*, the film that contrasts most sharply with the softer feel of other romantic comedies, was more successful at the box office than its lighter and more cheerful successor. In 2004 Kane returned to writing, creating the BBC series *Sea of Souls*, an ambitious – if not always convincing – venture into the paranormal, and writing the screenplay for Nick Willing's *The River King* (2005).

(Tom Ryall)

BIBLIOGRAPHY: Floyd, Nigel, 'Romantic Comedian', *Time Out*, 17–24 Feb. 1999, p. 75; Hunter, Allan, 'Close Up on David Kane', *Screen International*, 24 Nov. 2000, p. 21; Kemp, Philip, 'This Year's Love', *Sight and Sound*, Mar. 1999, p. 55; Murphy, Robert, 'Citylife: Urban Fairy-tales in Late 90s British Cinema', in Robert Murphy (ed.), *The British Cinema Book*, 2nd edn (London: BFI, 2001); Petrie, Duncan, *Screening Scotland* (London: BFI, 2000).

FILMOGRAPHY: *This Year's Love* (1999); *Born Romantic* (2000).

KANIEVSKA, Marek (1952–)

Marek Kanievska was born in Battersea, London, in 1952, the son of Polish refugees who had come to England after the Second World War. He was educated at Wandsworth Comprehensive School but left at fifteen to work as a stagehand. By the late 1970s he was directing episodes of television series *Hazell* (1978) and *Shoestring* (1978) and in 1982 made his breakthrough with the drama serial *Muck and Brass*. Producer Alan Marshall asked him to direct an adaptation of Julian Mitchell's play *Another Country*, an account of the public school experiences of future traitors Guy Burgess and Donald MacLean. It introduced the pouting prettiness of Rupert Everett and Colin Firth in the lead roles, and gained Kanievska his passage to Hollywood.

Pigeonholed (despite his own humble origins) as a specialist in upper-class homosexual decadence, he was given *Less Than Zero*, an adaptation of Bret Easton Ellis' novel about a rich American youth's slide into degradation. Despite a prophetic performance from Robert Downey Jr and an occasionally interesting tendency to gaze at male suffering, the film was a flop and Kanievska fell from favour.

A long hiatus, during which he worked mainly in television commercials, was ended in 2000 with the mildly engaging Paul Newman–Linda Fiorentino caper, *Where the Money Is*. In 2003 he returned to the world of *Another Country* for *A Different Loyalty*, with Rupert Everett cast as a double agent clearly based upon Kim Philby.

(Kim Newman)

BIBLIOGRAPHY: Goodman, Joan, 'Digging down to an Emotional Tangle', *The Times*, 6 June 1984, p. 9; Robbins, Harriet, 'Mixed Heritage Aids Director in Making *Another Country*', *Argonaut*, 16 Aug. 1984, p. 17.

FILMOGRAPHY: *Another Country* (1984); *Less Than Zero* (US, 1987); *Where the Money Is* (UK/Ger/US, 2000); *A Different Loyalty* (US, 2004).

KAPADIA, Asif (1972–)

Asif Kapadia was born in Hackney, east London, in 1972, the youngest son of parents who emigrated from Gujurat in the 1960s. He gained experience working in various capacities on films and television programmes before studying at Newport Film School, the University of Westminster and the Royal College of Art. The money won with his prize-winning entry for the Kodak Student Film Commercial Award in 1996 helped fund his ambitious RCA graduation film *The Sheep Thief* (1997), shot in Hindi on location in Rajasthan. A career directing commercials beckoned, but Kapadia stuck out for a feature. Raising money for *The Warrior* was made more difficult by his insistence that the film should be in Hindi rather than English; but the capacity for visual storytelling displayed in *The Sheep Thief* convinced French producer Bernard Faivre that he was worth the risk. FilmFour and British Screen, along with German and Indian investors, also agreed to contribute to the £2.5 million budget.

Kapadia shot the film on location in the deserts of Rajasthan and the Himalayan mountains of Manikaran, relying where possible on local people rather than extras to populate the crowd scenes. Irfan Khan is entirely convincing as the warrior Lafcardia, who tires of killing but finds he has to pay a heavy price to become a man of peace; and Kapadia's bold decision to cast non-actors in the other major roles helps ground his hero's mystical quest in a mundane and brutal reality. Despite superstitious villagers, unpredictable weather and problems with footsteps in the desert sand, Kapadia succeeds in creating an intelligent and unusual epic. The film's universal theme and visual appeal made it much easier to sell in the international market than most British films.

(Robert Murphy)

BIBLIOGRAPHY: 'How We Met: Terry Gilliam & Asif Kapadia', *Independent on Sunday* Review Section, 12 May 2002, pp. 5–6; James, Nick, 'Hired Hand', *Sight and Sound*, May 2002, pp. 22–4; Johnston, Trevor, 'Out of India', *Time Out*, 24 Mar. 2002, p. 69; Kapadia, Asif, 'Bollywood and Beyond', *Guardian* G2 Section, 19 Apr. 2002, pp. 12–13; Minns, Adam, 'Close Up: Asif Kapadia', *Screen International*, 12 Oct. 2001, p. 15; Rainford, Paul, 'Go East!', *Creation*, Mar. 1997, p. 54.

FILMOGRAPHY: *Indian Tales* (short, 1994); *The Waiting Room* (short); *Wild West* (short, 1996); *The Sheep Thief* (short, 1997); *The Warrior* (UK/Fr/Ger/Ind, 2001); *The Return* (US, 2006).

KAPUR, Shekhar (1945–)

Shekhar Kapur was born in Lahore in December 1945. After establishing his reputation as an actor and director in Indian cinema, he reached an international audience with *Bandit Queen* (1994) and *Elizabeth* (1998). Both films focus on strong and eventually powerful women who are forced to fight against patriarchal conventions and prejudice. The respective central performances of Seema Biswas as Phoolan Devi and Cate Blanchett as Queen Elizabeth I are outstanding. Kapur uses the camera to establish and utilise an extraordinary sense of space – as in the deep-focus shots of Indian landscape, rich in colour and texture, in *Bandit Queen*. In *Elizabeth* the overhead shots that open the film give the audience a god's-eye view of the protagonists in this historical drama, and later shots taken from dark corners, around pillars, between curtains, create an ominous sense of forces gathering against the heroine. Kapur's rich visual style, the subtlety of his characterisations and the care with which the machinations of plot are constructed enrich his remake of the old imperial epic *The Four Feathers*, turning what might have been considered irredeemably old-fashioned into something refreshing and relevant.

(Sarah Cardwell)

BIBLIOGRAPHY: Karney, Robyn, 'Making History', *Interview*, Dec./Jan. 1999, p. 16; Tanner, Louise, 'Accents and Umlauts: *Bandit Queen*', *Films in Review*, Sept./Oct. 1995, pp. 38–9; Wise, Damon, 'The Battle over The Four Feathers', *Empire*, Dec. 2002, pp. 106–11.

FILMOGRAPHY (UK only): *Bandit Queen* (Ind/UK, 1994); *Elizabeth* (1998); *The Four Feathers* (US/UK, 2002).

KAURISMÄKI, Aki (1957–)

Aki Olavi Kaurismäki was born in Orimattila, Finland, on 4 April 1957. After studying journalism at the University of Tampere and getting involved in film clubs and criticism, he worked as an editor and in 1981 co-directed the rock documentary *The Salmaa Gesture* (*Salmaa-limiö*) with his older brother Mika. Aki's solo directorial debut came in 1983 with *Crime and Punishment*

(*Rikos ja rangaistus*), which set Dostoyevsky's novel in contemporary Helsinki.

By the 1990s the Kaurismäkis were Finland's most prolific producers, directors and scriptwriters. In Britain, Aki acquired cult status with *Leningrad Cowboys Go America* (1989) – the escapades of the absurdly quiffed 'worst rock band in the world'. He employed his deadpan, miserablist style effectively in his only British film, *I Hired a Contract Killer*. Jean-Pierre Léaud stars as a suicidal French clerk adrift in the armpits of east and north London. He fails to hang himself, takes out a contract on his own life, falls in love and changes his mind. But in a classic Kaurismäki hard-luck twist, the killer (Kenneth Colley), himself terminally ill, is determined to fulfil the contract for his own existential reasons. Both Léaud and London proved peculiarly well suited to Kaurismäki's sensibilities. Standard British critical opinion was that the film's decrepit version of the capital was unrecognisably alien; but to those who know London, its spare, stylised, selectively colour-saturated observation of place – from Whitechapel to Abney Park Cemetery – is central to its fascination. Kaurismäki has continued to direct in Finland, and in 2002 won the Grand Jury Prize at Cannes for *The Man without a Past*.

(Claire Monk)

BIBLIOGRAPHY: Kaurismäki, Aki, *I Hired a Contract Killer* (Helsinki: Love Kirjat, 1990) (screenplay: in English with Finnish translation); Malik, Rachel, 'On Location with *I Hired a Contract Killer*', *Producer*, Autumn 1990, p. 28; Romney, Jonathan, 'The Kaurismäki Effect', *Sight and Sound*, June 1997, pp. 11–14.

FILMOGRAPHY (UK only): *I Hired a Contract Killer* (1990).

KAVANAGH, Denis (1906–1984)

The supporting programmes of Britain's circuit cinemas would have been lost without Denis Kavanagh. For over twenty years he supplied interest shorts about scenic wonders, women in sports and Hyde Park from dawn to night, alongside lowly features that never scraped over sixty minutes. At times, almost by a fluke, his cameras caught something of interest. *Rock You Sinners* (1957) became the first British feature to feed off rock and roll, while his last identified travelogue, *Beyond the Riviera* (1960), rounded up Lena Horne and Jean Cocteau. But while the output was lowly, it served a purpose.

Born in County Carlow, Ireland, on 6 May 1906, Kavanagh began in cinema in 1926 as an assistant director, first in Hollywood, after 1931 in Britain. In 1937 he switched to Gaumont-British documentaries and shorts, and began directing. A stint assisting The Archers followed war service with the RAF, but in 1943 he was back in business with the variety film *Starlight Serenade*. The 1950s saw his most useful feature work. *Flight from Vienna*, one of numerous assignments for E. J. Fancey, created modest tension from its cold war story; *Return to the Desert* revived potent wartime footage inside a fictional frame; while *Rock You Sinners*, if a print survives, would offer culture historians period flotsam, like Rory Blackwell and the Blackjacks or Don Sollash and his Rockin' Horses. Denis Kavanagh died after a heart attack on 14 June 1984 in Moreton-in-Marsh, in the Cotswolds.

(Geoff Brown)

FILMOGRAPHY: Shorts: *On Top of the Underworld* (series, co-dir. Mickey Delamar, 1938); *Spotlight on Dogs* (doc., 1945); *Glamour Girl* (doc.); *Women and Sport* (doc.); *The Dover Road* (doc.); *Hyde Park* (doc.) (1946); *Plenty Questions* (doc.); *Signed, Sealed and Delivered* (doc.) (1947); *Information Please* (doc., 1948); *Women in Sport* (doc., 1953); *Dollars for Sale* (1955); *Sicilian Memories*; *A Date with Gulienne* (1958); *Beyond the Riviera* (1960).

Features: *Starlight Serenade* (1943); *Night Comes Too Soon* (US: *The Ghost of Rashmon Hall*, 1947); *Flight from Vienna*; *Return to the Desert* (doc.) (1955); *Fighting Mad*; *They Never Learn* (1956); *Rock You Sinners* (1957).

KEATING, David (1960–)

David Keating was born in Dublin on 30 May 1960. He studied drama at the École de Mimodrame in Paris and then worked on films as an editor at the Ardmore Studios in Wicklow and as assistant director to the likes of Tony Scott, Michael Radford and John Boorman. In 1995 he made *Where Do I Begin*, a documentary film in which his father, the politician and television presenter Justin Keating, discusses the life and work of his own father, the celebrated Irish landscape painter, Sean Keating. It was well received and Keating went on to make his first feature film, *Last of the High Kings*, based on a novel by Ferdia McAnna. Through the humorous story of a boy's coming-of-age problems in a ramshackle family in suburban Dublin, the film explores the momentous economic and social changes occurring in Ireland in the 1970s. The film was a critical and commercial success in Ireland and Keating received a nomination for 'Best Newcomer' at the 1997 London *Evening Standard* Film Awards. Keating also directs for the stage.

(Martin McLoone)

BIBLIOGRAPHY: McLoone, Martin, *Irish Film: The Emergence of a Contemporary Cinema* (London: BFI, 2000); Pettitt, Lance, *Screening Ireland* (Manchester: Manchester University Press, 2000).

FILMOGRAPHY: *Where Do I Begin* (aka *Sean Keating: The Pilgrim Soul*, doc., 1995); *Last of the High Kings* (aka *Summer Fling*, Ir, 1996).

KEILLER, Patrick (1950–)

One of the most distinctive voices to emerge in British cinema since Peter Greenaway, Patrick Keiller was born in Blackpool in 1950. He studied at the Bartlett School of Architecture, University College London, and initially practised as an architect. Chris Marker's film *La Jetée* (1962) left a deep impression, but he only made practical steps towards cinema in 1979, when he joined the Royal College of Art's Department of Environmental Media as a postgraduate student. Slide-tape presentations blending architectural photography with fictional narratives pointed the way towards his first acknowledged film, *Stonebridge Park* (1981), visually inspired by a railway bridge in an outer London suburb. Images from a hand-held camera are accompanied by a voiceover

commentary presenting the thoughts of a petty criminal panicked by the consequences of robbing his former employer. *Norwood* (1983) continued the 'story', and the technique, in another London suburb. Short films of increasing technical sophistication climaxed in 1989 with *The Clouds*, a further topographical exploration combining another anxious fictional commentary with imagery derived from a journey across the north of England from Jodrell Bank to Whitby.

None of these films stretched beyond twenty minutes. But any doubts about the limits of Keiller's idiosyncratic approach were obliterated by the feature-length *London*, an electrifying, slyly witty portrait of a city in decay, shot in 1992, and successfully premiered at the 1994 Berlin Film Festival. The essay format and audiovisual mix may superficially recall early Greenaway films, but the polemical punch and artistic strategies remain Keiller's own. Its success generated a sequel, *Robinson in Space* (1997), so similar in technique and spirit that for all the differences in emphasis and geography it seems as though we are watching the same film.

Stylistically, these features extend the habits developed in Keiller's shorts. The visual material consists of static camera shots: images of urban decay and other socio-economic signifiers, road sign clutter, glowering skies – a landscape sharing some territory with the poetic realism of Humphrey Jennings and the Free Cinema film-makers, but framed and cut with a sharper, more avant-garde edge. Narrative input is chiefly found in the commentaries, spoken with quiet irony by Paul Scofield as an unseen friend of the equally unseen Robinson, a reclusive academic who undertakes research journeys into the 'problem' of London and England. Matters of architecture, French literature, fine art, Surrealism, photography, geography, history, sociology and economics all mingle in Robinson's analyses – aptly described in the *London* narration as 'exercises in psychic landscaping, drifting, and free association'. Both films explore and criticise Britain in the aftermath of Thatcherism, but *Robinson in Space* pursues points more rigorously, advancing the contrast between prosperous new development and trade exports and the de-industrialised landscapes created by Thatcherite economics.

Keiller returned to architecture as the subject for his third and most cogent feature, *The Dilapidated Dwelling* (2000), made for television but never broadcast, with Tilda Swinton as the voice of another researcher, surveying the dilapidated state of England's housing stock after a twenty-year absence. Conventional documentary elements are featured (archive footage, talking heads), but Keiller continues to press home his points with the kind of intellectual fibre, wit and precision rarely given a chance to bloom in British cinema. In between film work, Keiller teaches, writes, undertakes his research and works on gallery installations.

(Geoff Brown and Bryony Dixon)

BIBLIOGRAPHY: Barwell, Claire, 'Interview with Patrick Keiller', *Pix* no. 2 Jan. 1997, pp. 160–5; Dave, Paul, 'Representations of Capitalism, History and Nation in the Work of Patrick Keiller', in Justine Ashby and Andrew Higson (eds), *British Cinema, Past and Present* (London: Routledge, 2000); Keiller, Patrick, 'The Visible Surface', *Sight and Sound*, Nov. 1994, p. 35; Keiller, Patrick, *Robinson in Space/and an Interview with Patrick Wright* (London: Reaktion Books, 1999); Keiller, Patrick, 'Architectural Cinematography', in Kester Rattenbury (ed.), *This Is Not Architecture* (London and New York: Routledge, 2002); Martin-Jones, David, 'Patrick Keiller', *Journal of Popular British Cinema* no. 5, 2002, pp. 123–32; Sinclair, Iain, 'London: Necropolis of Fretful Ghosts', *Sight and Sound*, June 1994, pp. 12–15.

FILMOGRAPHY: *Stonebridge Park* (short, 1981); *Norwood* (short, 1983); *The End* (short, 1986); *Valtos* (short, 1987); *The Clouds* (short, 1989); *London* (1994); *Robinson in Space* (1997); *The Dilapidated Dwelling* (2000).

KELLETT, Bob (1927–)

Robert Kellett was born in Lancaster on 25 December 1927. As a child he lived in various parts of the world, including Ceylon, where his father ran a tea plantation. After completing his national service in the army, he studied medicine but gave it up to become an assistant stage manager at Bedford Repertory Company. He entered the film industry as a writer for Ian Dalrymple's Wessex Films before writing, producing and directing for television. He found a niche in the feature film industry producing short comedies that dispensed with dialogue and relied on sound effects and mime. *A Home of Your Own* (Jay Lewis, 1964) and *San Ferry Ann* (Jeremy Summers, 1966), featuring Ronnie Barker, Richard Briers, Wilfrid Brambell, Warren Mitchell and a host of other British comedy actors, all proved popular programme fillers. Ronnie Barker, enthused by this anachronistic format, wrote the longer *Futtocks End*, which Kellett directed in 1970. The following year Kellett moved into mainstream comedy, directing a cinema spin-off from Frankie Howerd's television comedy, *Up Pompeii!*. Its success led to two enjoyable sequels that balance a contemporary visual explicitness with classic British sauciness. Kellett's confidence with broad humour at the limits of taste (preferably indulging a spot of cross-dressing) was apparent throughout most of his films, though his forays into that most uncinematic of forms, the bedroom farce (*Don't Just Lie There . . .*, *All I Want Is You . . .*), were less satisfying. His last two television sitcom spin-offs were also disappointing, relying on the tired standbys of going back in history (*The Alf Garnett Saga*) and relocating overseas (*Are You Being Served?*) to justify their bigger budgets.

In 1982 Kellett unexpectedly directed a thriller for the Children's Film Foundation, *Tightrope to Terror*. This tense, well-told children's mountain adventure story is filmed by Kellett with panache and is arguably the best of the later CFF films. He continues to work in various capacities in the industry: in 1995 he co-wrote the screenplay and completed second-unit direction for Lewis Gilbert's *Haunted*; in 2002 he acted as line producer on Gilbert's *Before You Go*.

(Richard Dacre)

BIBLIOGRAPHY: 'Bob Kellett – the Director', publicity material for *Our Miss Fred*, held on microfiche at the BFI National Library, London; Gow, Gordon, 'Bob Kellett', *Photoplay*, Apr. 1974, pp. 11, 50.

FILMOGRAPHY: *Futtocks End* (1970); *Up Pompeii!*; *Up the Chastity Belt*; *Girl Stroke Boy* (1971); *Up the Front*; *Our Miss Fred*; *The Alf Garnett Saga* (1972); *Don't Just Lie There, Say Something!* (1973); *All I Want Is You . . . and You . . . and You . . .!* (1974); *Spanish Fly* (aka *La mosca hispánica*, UK/Sp/Can, 1975); *Are You Being Served?* (1977); *Tightrope to Terror* (1982).

KELLINO, Roy (1912–1956)

Roy Kellino was born Philip Roy Gislingham in London on 22 April 1912, the son of W. P. Kellino (Gislingham), a former circus performer who had founded the Ec-Ko Film Company in 1912. Roy Kellino acted in films from 1915 and in 1926 joined Gainsborough as an assistant cameraman, graduating to become cinematographer on such films as Michael Powell's *The Phantom Light* (1935) and the Ben Travers farce *Foreign Affaires* (Tom Walls, 1935). While photographing *Jew Süss* (Lothar Mendes, 1934), he met and married Pamela Ostrer, the precocious daughter of Gaumont-British Chairman Isidore Ostrer. The family did not approve, and Kellino moved to Fox-British, where his directorial career began in 1937 with *Concerning Mr Martin*, a clever thriller, and *The Last Adventurers*, a finely photographed story of Grimsby trawlermen. Less interesting was a

diamond smuggling tale, *Catch as Catch Can*. The lead, James Mason, went on to collaborate with the Kellinos on *I Met a Murderer*, an independent production largely shot on location. By the time filming was complete, Pamela and Mason, who were playing the main roles, had fallen in love. Kellino gracefully agreed to a divorce and retained his friendship with both of them.

During the war, Kellino worked at Ealing as a cameraman and special-effects designer on films such as *The Proud Valley* (Pen Tennyson, 1940), *Ships with Wings* (Sergei Nolbandov, 1941) and *Nine Men* (Harry Watt, 1943). He returned to directing in 1950 with *Guilt Is My Shadow*, a crime drama, but left for Hollywood to take over the direction of *Lady Possessed*, produced, written by and starring James and Pamela Mason. He stayed on to direct another of the Masons' projects, *Charade*, and several episodes of *Four Star Playhouse* for American television. Back in England, his last assignment was *The Silken Affair*, a disappointing comedy starring David Niven. He died of a heart attack in Los Angeles on 18 November 1956, his career as a director never fully realised.

(Margaret Butler)

BIBLIOGRAPHY: Mason, James, *Before I Forget* (London: Hamish Hamilton, 1981).

FILMOGRAPHY: *Concerning Mr Martin*; *The Last Adventurers* (aka *Down to the Sea in Ships*); *Catch as Catch Can* (aka *Atlantic Episode*) (1937); *Father O'Nine* (1938); *I Met a Murderer* (1939); *Guilt Is My Shadow* (1950); *Lady Possessed* (co-dir. William Spier, US, 1951); *Charade* (US, 1953); *The Silken Affair* (1956).

KELLINO, Will (1873–1957)

Professionally known as Will Kellino, William Philip Gislingham left the music-hall stage to become a leading figure in the infant cinema industry. In a career extending over three decades he became one of the country's most prolific film directors. Born in London in 1873, from childhood he was one of the Famous Kellinos, a tumbling act whose frantic athleticism is presented in their film *A Fête in Venice* (1909). Kellino retained strong links with the world of music hall, marrying the performer Blanche Bella in 1904 and numbering many stars as his close friends. On the break-up of the family act in 1912, he founded the Ec-Ko Film Company with a group of well-known entertainers. Supplying the 'K' in the company's title, Kellino joined Seth and Albert Egbert, Fred Russell, Will Poluski and several other performers in an enterprise that paralleled professional convivial societies such as the Water Rats.

Kellino directed many short films around the rural byways of Teddington, Middlesex, and at a makeshift studio in St Alban's Yard, many of them comedies featuring Fred Evans, who appeared as 'Pimple', and Sam T. Poluski, who portrayed 'Nobby'. (He is often credited as W. P. Kellino.) After directing for Cricks, Kellino combined with several of his Ec-Ko colleagues to launch the Homeland Productions Syndicate in 1915. The largest shareholder in the new company was also its major star – the variety and revue comedian Billy Merson, who was heralded as a rival to Chaplin when he appeared in nine two- and three-reel comedies directed by Kellino. Another popular Homeland comedian was the young Lupino Lane.

After the First World War Kellino directed films for Gaumont, including a series of 'Will O'Wisp' comedies (1920) and the historical adventure *Rob Roy* (1922), and another Scottish epic, *Young Lochinvar* (1923) for Stoll. In 1926 he moved to the United States, where he worked with Lupino Lane in a non-directorial capacity. By 1927, he had returned to England, filming *Further Adventures of the Flag Lieutenant*, an adventure in which he found room for his old friends the Egberts. Kellino's first sound film, *Alf's Carpet* (1929), was followed by *Alf's Button* (1930), a comedy based on the Aladdin theme starring the variety favourites Nervo and Knox. A series of short comedies made for Gainsborough also featured Kellino's music-hall colleagues, and he was entrusted with a sequence for *Royal Cavalcade* (1935), a prestige production recreating the events of George V's reign. But Kellino's directing credits grew less frequent as the 1930s progressed.

While Kellino was a workmanlike director of romantic dramas, crime stories and historical epics, his main contribution to films was in the field of comedy. It was appropriate that one of his last films, *Hot News*, starred Lupino Lane, a comedian whose film career he helped launch some twenty years earlier. He was joined in the profession by his son Roy Kellino. Will died in Edgware, Middlesex, on 31 December 1957.

(Barry Anthony)

BIBLIOGRAPHY: Honri, Baynham, 'The Kellinos – The Influence of a Music Hall Family in Film Production', *The Call Boy* vol. 8 no. 1, Mar. 1971, pp. 12–14.

FILMOGRAPHY: *Pimple Does the Turkey Trot*; *The Taming of Big Ben*; *Pimple and the Snake*; *The Whistling Bet*; *Grand Harlequinade*; *The Coster's Honeymoon*; *Yiddle on My Fiddle* (1912); *Everybody's Doing It*; *A Knife to Grind*; *Bumbles' Walk to Brighton*; *Mrs LeTare Lets Apartments*; *The Flight of Wealth*; *He Did It for the Best*; *The Jovial Fluid*; *Juggling Mad*; *Bumbles' Diminisher*, *Oh That Woollen Undervest!*; *On the Hop*; *Parcels or the Baby*; *Bumbles' Goose*; *Bumbles' Radium Minstrels*; *How Willy Joined Barnum Bill*; *Bumbles Photographer*, *Bumbles Becomes a Crook*; *Nosey Parker*, *The Rival Musicians*; *Nobby the New Waiter*, *Bumbles and the Bass*; *Bumbles' Holiday*; *Nobby and the Pearl Mystery*; *Money Making Coats*; *Baby's Photograph*; *The Happy Dustmen*; *The Dustmen's Holiday*; *Stoggles' Christmas Dinner*, *Bumbles' Electric Belt* (1913); *The Domestic Game Hunt*; *The Student's Night Out*; *Nobby the Knut*; *Bumbles Goes Butterflying*; *Betty's Birthday*; *The White Stocking*; *Nobby Wins the Cup*; *Nobby's Tango Teas*; *After the Ball Was Over*, *The Postman's Dilemma*; *Nobby's Stud*; *Snooks as a Fireman*; *You're Wanted on the Phone, Sir*, *Love and a Tub*; *Picture Palace Piecans*; *Happy Dustmen Play Golf*; *How Spotted Duff Saved the Squire*; *Bertie's Baby*; *The Mystery of the Landlady's Cat*; *Conspicuous Bravery*; *Dr Dosem's Deputy*; *Nobby's Ju-Jitsu Experiments*; *Fidgett's Superstitions*; *The Gypsy's Curse*; *Chums*; *Who Was to Blame?*; *Ginger Seeks a Situation*; *Spy Catchers*; *The Trombone's Strong Note*; *The Happy Dustmen's Christmas*; *Grand Christmas Harlequinade*; *The Pet Hen*; *Potted Pantomimes* (1914); *Some Actors*; *Extravagant Molly*; *Pote's Poem*; *The Wrong House*; *His Father's Sin*; *The Order of the Bath*; *Playing the Deuce*; *Bill's Monicker*, *Fighting Billy*; *Spoof!*; *He Would Act*; *Who Kissed Her?*; *What a Bounder*, *Hamlet by the M.U.D.S.*; *The Dustman's Nightmare*; *Eggs!*; *Oh That Face!*; *A Fight for Life*; *Caught in a Kilt*; *Inventing Trouble*; *Paying Him Out*; *Romeo and Juliet by the M.U.D.S.*; *None but the Brave*; *Billy's Spanish Love Spasm*; *The Man in Possession*; *The Only Man* (1915); *The Terrible 'Tec*; *Patriotic Mrs Brown*; *The Tale of a Shirt*; *The Dustman's Wedding*; *The Perils of Pork Pie*; *A Wife in a Hurry*; *Billy's Stormy Courtship*; *Parker's Weekend*; *The Dummy*; *The Dustmen's Outing*; *Screen Struck* (1916); *Economy*; *Billy the Truthful*; *Hullo! Who's Your Lady Friend?*; *The Missing Link*; *How's Your Poor Wife?*; *Billy Strikes Oil*; *Splash Me Nicely* (1917); *The Exploits of Parker* (1918); *The Green Terror*, *Angel Esquire* (1919); *The Fall of a Saint*; *Will O'Wisp Comedies* (series of shorts: *Sweep*, *On the Reserve*, *Cupid's Carnival*, *Run! Run!*, *A Broken Contract*, *Cousin Ebenezer*, *Souvenirs*, *The Lightning Liver Cure*); *The Fordington Twins*; *Saved from the Sea* (1920); *The Fortune of Christina McNab* ; *The Autumn of Pride*; *Class and No Class* (1921); *A Soul's Awakening*; *Rob Roy* (1922); *Young Lochinvar* (1923); *The Colleen Bawn* (aka *The Loves of Colleen Bawn*; *His Grace Gives Notice*; *The Mating of Marcus*; *Not for Sale* (1924); *We Women*; *Confessions*; *The Gold Cure*; *The Art of Love* (series of shorts, co-dir. Edwin Greenwood: *The Lady in Silk Stockings* [aka *The Weakness of Men*], *The Painted Lady* [aka *Red Lips*], *The Lady in Furs* [aka *Sables of Death*], *The Lady in Lace* [aka *Caught in the Web*], *The Lady in Jewels* [aka *Hearts Trump Diamonds*], *The Lady in High Heels* [aka *Heel Taps*], *The Only Man* [aka *The Leading Man*]) (1925); *Further Adventures of the Flag Lieutenant* (1927); *Sailors Don't Care*; *Smashing Through* (1928); *Alf's Carpet* (1929); *Alf's Button*

(1930); *Hot Heir, Bull Rushes; Who Killed Doc Robin?; Aroma of the South Seas; My Old China* (1931); *Sometimes Good; Wishes; The Poisoned Diamond* (1934); *Royal Cavalcade* (co-dirs. Herbert Brenon/Thomas Bentley/Marcel Varnel/Norman Lee/Walter Summers); *Lend Me Your Wife* (1935); *Hot News; Paybox Adventure* (1936).

KEMP, Julian

After working as an actor (as Julian Aubrey), Julian Kemp began directing children's television shows, including Tim Firth's weird and funny *Roger and the Rottentrolls* (1996). An amusing black-and-white short, *Suckers*, about the hard lives of vacuum cleaner salesmen, was followed in 2000 by his low-budget feature debut, *House!*. Kemp's affection for Ealing comedy is apparent in this genial tale about a magnificent old opera house -cum-cinema struggling to survive as a bingo hall against a bigger, plusher competitor. The visual gimmickry intended to inject pizzazz into a plot based around bingo mostly misfires, though the masque-like playing out of events from the past is genuinely clever and Kemp's relentless inventiveness bodes well for his future. Reviewers were generally kind in their comments – being nasty about such an innocuous film is like kicking a kitten – but there was too little bite to make any impression on cinema audiences. Afterwards Kemp returned to television, writing and directing *Dangerville* (2003), a fantasy drama series set around Nottingham, featuring enterprising teenagers teaming up to cope with escaped lions, runaway buses and shattering meteorites. (Robert Murphy)

BIBLIOGRAPHY: Clarke, Natacha, 'In the Frame: Julian Kemp', *Screen International*, 24 Sept. 1999, p. 19.

FILMOGRAPHY: *Suckers* (short, 1995); *House!* (2000).

KENELM CLARKE, James (1941–)

James Kenelm Clarke was born in Gloucestershire in 1941. A noted documentary film-maker, he was diverted into more lurid fields after making a *Man Alive* exposé of the British sex film industry for the BBC. He set up his own company, Norfolk International Pictures, and made his fiction debut in 1974 with *Got It Made*, an erotic drama about a young woman (Lalla Ward) who tentatively attempts to widen her sexual horizons before settling down to conventional upper-class marriage.

Got It Made appeared stodgily demure compared to the sensational French success *Emmanuelle* (Just Jaeckin, 1974), but in *Exposé* Kenelm Clarke cast caution to the winds, combining an abundance of sex scenes featuring Linda Hayden and Fiona Richmond with a grisly tale of madness and violence. Retribution came when the film was listed as one of the 'video nasties' deemed responsible for undermining moral standards, but Kenelm Clarke had already turned to less contentious subjects: *Hardcore* a risibly softcore biography of sex queen Richmond; and the more stylish *Let's Get Laid*, a sex-comedy set during the Second World War that incorporates a film within a film, an affectionate parody of the fluffy musicals of Herbert Wilcox and Anna Neagle.

With the end of the sexploitation boom, Kenelm Clarke turned to crime-comedies: *Funny Money* proved a relatively pleasing caper film; but *Going Undercover*, a spoof on hard-boiled detective thrillers, continually misses its mark and had problems finding a distributor. Kenelm Clarke has also composed film scores, most effectively for José Larraz's *Vampyrs* (1974). (Robert Murphy)

BIBLIOGRAPHY: Harrigan, Brian, 'Time for Video to Put Some Oomph back into Film Industry', *Video Business* vol. 3 no. 29, 12 Sept. 1983, pp. 48–9; Hodges, Adrian, 'Taking a Gamble with "Funny Money" ', *Screen International*, 20 Feb. 1982, p. 18; McGillivray, David, *Doing Rude Things: The History of the British Sex Film, 1957–81* (London: Sun Tavern Fields, 1992); Sheridan, Simon, *Keeping the British End Up: Four Decades of Saucy Cinema*, 2nd edn (London: Reynolds & Hearn, 2005); Vaines, Colin, 'On Doing the Unexpected', *Screen International*, 14 May 1977, p. 8.

FILMOGRAPHY: *Got It Made* (aka *Sweet Virgin*, 1974); *Exposé* (1975); *Hardcore* (US: *Fiona*); *Let's Get Laid* (aka *Love Trap*) (1977); *Funny Money* (1982); *Going Undercover* (aka *Yellow Pages*, 1984; rel. 1988).

KERRIGAN, Justin (1974–)

Justin Kerrigan was born in Cardiff in 1974. After attending film school in Newport, Gwent, he wrote and directed *Human Traffic*, with his film school tutor Allan Niblo acting as co-producer. Kerrigan's visual flair and technical skill gave the film a polished look that belied its minuscule £340,000 budget, and it was praised as an authentic depiction of the 1990s' club scene. Drawing on his own experience of Cardiff's rave culture, and using hallucinatory visuals, bizarre humour and fantasy sequences, Kerrigan follows five teenage friends over a long weekend, as they temporarily forget their dead-end jobs and ride a wave of dance music and Ecstasy. The cast, led by John Simm and Lorraine Pilkington, engage the viewer's sympathy, despite their one-dimensional characters and the lack of narrative structure. Defiantly non-judgmental in tone, *Human Traffic* eschews the standard anti-drugs message, the characters suffering nothing worse than a hangover. While this might be interpreted as a radical stance, Kerrigan's preoccupation with surface details undermines any sense of serious propaganda.

Marketed as the next *Trainspotting* (Danny Boyle, 1996), *Human Traffic* made a respectable £2.2 million at the UK box office and was picked up for distribution in the US by Miramax's Harvey Weinstein. The film was re-edited (with Kerrigan's consent) to make it more accessible for US audiences but still flopped badly, grossing barely $100,000. While *Human Traffic* picked up numerous international awards, critical acclaim was not matched by large profits and many of the cast and crew (including Kerrigan) felt they had not been adequately rewarded for their efforts. Niblo, who owned the rights to the film, claimed that its modest domestic success did not cover its marketing costs. (Daniel O'Brien)

BIBLIOGRAPHY: Brooks, Xan, 'The Party's Over', *Guardian*, 18 Oct. 2002, p. 13; Morris, Mark, 'Something Fine for the Weekend', *Observer*, 16 May 1999; Rider, Dan, 'Club Nation', *Total Film*, June 1999, pp. 82-4.
FILMOGRAPHY: *Human Traffic* (1999).

KIDRON, Beeban (1961–)

Beeban Kidron was born in London on 2 May 1961, one of three children of socialist publishers Michael and Nina Kidron. Having taken up photography at the age of eleven, she was offered a job by Magnum photographer Eve Arnold on the strength of pictures taken in Portugal during the country's 1974 revolution. She left Camden School for Girls at sixteen and worked as Arnold's assistant for eighteen months before setting off to travel the world. On returning to Britain in the early 1980s she enrolled at the National Film School, initially specialising in cinematography and later moving to directing. During her time there she made the award-winning political documentary *Carry Greenham Home* (1983).

Although her early ambition had been to make documentaries, Kidron soon turned to fictional subjects. Her first feature, *Vroom* (1988), was backed by Channel 4 and British Screen; and in 1990 she made a one-off drama, *Antonia and Jane*, for BBC Television. Her reputation was secured, however, by her work on the 1990 BAFTA award-winning television adaptation of Jeanette Winterson's novel *Oranges Are Not the Only Fruit*.

Kidron's US-made features, *Used People* (1992) and *To Wong Foo, Thanks for Everything! Julie Newmar* (1995), are generally regarded as less successful; and though intended for theatrical release, her BBC film *Great Moments in Aviation* (1994) was only shown on television. Her lavish adaptation of a Joseph Conrad story, *Amy Foster* (1997), was also poorly distributed, and Kidron returned to television to make an updated *Cinderella* (2000), a four-part drama serial, *Murder* (2002), and a programme about Eve Arnold for the BBC's *Omnibus* series. She then made the leap to big-budget production as director of *Bridget Jones: The Edge of Reason*, a jolly but vacuous sequel to *Bridget Jones's Diary* (Sharon Maguire, 2001), which was less favourably received than the original. If Kidron's direction is unsubtle, her concentration on the simple story of a less than beautiful, socially inept woman proving irresistible to suave, handsome – if slightly long-in-the-tooth – men paid off at the box office. It will be interesting to see what effect this film has on Kidron's unpredictable career.

(Annette Kuhn)

BIBLIOGRAPHY: Ciecko, Anne, 'Sex, God, Television, Realism and the British Women Filmmakers Beeban Kidron and Antonia Bird', *Journal of Film and Video*, vol. 51 no. 1, Spring 1999, pp. 22–41; Gritten, David, 'Beeban Kidron, Director', *Empire*, May 1993, p. 48.
FILMOGRAPHY: *Carry Greenham Home* (1983); *Vroom* (1988); *Alex* (short, 1990); *Used People* (US, 1992); *Hookers Hustlers Pimps and Their Johns* (doc., US, 1993); *Great Moments in Aviation* (1994); *To Wong Foo, Thanks for Everything! Julie Newmar* (US, 1995); *Amy Foster* (aka *Swept from the Sea*, UK/US/Fr, 1997); *Bridget Jones: The Edge of Reason* (2004).

KILNER, Clare

After making *Daphne & Apollo*, a short film about a statue, Kilner was given National Lottery and Channel 4 financial backing to make *Janice Beard: 45 Words Per Minute*, a bizarre office comedy. Kilner's direction is irritatingly gimmicky, but her gawky Scottish heroine, like Kilner bursting with incoherent ambition, is refreshingly unusual. The film was hardly seen in UK cinemas, though its odd charms made it more popular on video/DVD. Kilner redeemed herself in Canada with *How to Deal*, an acute and perceptive medium-budget teen movie based on two novels by Sarah Dessen; but *The Wedding Date* (2005), an American romantic comedy set in London, starring Debra Messing as an unlucky-in-love woman who hires a handsome male escort to show off at her sister's wedding, seemed yawningly derivative of *Four Weddings and Funeral* (Mike Newell. 1994).

(Robert Murphy)

FILMOGRAPHY: *Daphne & Apollo* (short, 1997); *Janice Beard: 45 Words Per Minute* (1999); *How to Deal* (US, 2003); *The Wedding Date* (US, 2005).

KIMMINS, Anthony (1901–1964)

Anthony Martin Kimmins was born in Harrow-on-the-Hill, Middlesex, on 10 November 1901. After serving in the Royal Navy, where he rose to become a lieutenant-commander, Kimmins discovered a talent for comedy. His plays *While Parents Sleep* and *The Night Club Queen* brought him to the attention of the film industry, and in January 1934 he directed *By-Pass to Happiness*, his first 'quota quickie'. Within thirteen months he had completed four others, most notably an engaging musical, *How's Chances?*, and an unusual fantasy drama, *Once in a New Moon*. Throughout his career he wrote or co-wrote most of his films, and occasionally performed screenwriting duties on other films, among them Carol Reed's 1935 naval adventure *Midshipman Easy* and the Gracie Fields vehicle *Queen of Hearts* (Monty Banks, 1936).

Following *All at Sea*, a slim shipboard romance enlivened by the presence of Rex Harrison and Googie Withers, Kimmins was teamed with producer Jack Kitchin by Basil Dean to make films with the comedian George Formby at Ealing Studios. Between 1937 and 1939, Kimmins wrote and directed five Formby comedies: *Keep Fit, It's in the Air, I See Ice, Trouble Brewing* and *Come on George!* With the outbreak of war Kimmins returned to naval service, and reported on the war at sea for the BBC. According to Michael Balcon, with whom he had worked at Ealing, Kimmins' 'fine, unmistakable voice brought home to a vast listening public a graphic on-the-spot picture of the operations he was reporting' (Balcon, p. 122). Kimmins was awarded the OBE in 1946 for his contribution to the war effort.

Returning to civilian life, Kimmins was offered the opportunity to work as writer-producer-director by Alexander Korda on a broader range of projects than his pre-war efforts. His first post-war film was *Mine Own Executioner* (1947), a psychological thriller based on Nigel Balchin's novel about an ex-serviceman traumatised by his experience in a Japanese prisoner-of-war camp. It was highly praised by the critics, though the two costume dramas that followed, *Bonnie Prince Charlie*, with an improbably cast David Niven as the Jacobite Pretender, and *Flesh and Blood*, were less well received. After a popular thriller, *Mr Denning Drives North*, Kimmins returned to comedy with *Who Goes There!*, *The Captain's Paradise* and *Aunt Clara*. *The Captain's Paradise* (1953), featuring Alec Guinness as a ship's captain leading a happily bigamous life with homely Celia Johnston in Gibraltar and exotic Yvonne de Carlo in North Africa, was particularly amusing and commercially very successful.

In the final phase of his long career, Kimmins made two Australian-set children's adventure films, *Smiley* and *Smiley Gets a Gun*, and a last comedy, *The Amorous Prawn* (1962), adapted from his own long-running play. Following a long illness, Kimmins died on 19 May 1964 at Hurstpierpoint, Sussex.

(Martin Hunt)

BIBLIOGRAPHY: Balcon, Michael, *Michael Balcon Presents . . . A Lifetime of Films* (London: Hutchinson, 1969); Kimmins, Anthony, *Half-Time* (London: Heinemann, 1947); Richards, Jeffrey, *The Age of the Dream Palace: Cinema and Society in Britain 1930–1939* (London: Routledge & Kegan Paul, 1984).

FILMOGRAPHY: *By-Pass to Happiness*; *How's Chances?* (1934); *Once in a New Moon*; *His Majesty and Co.*; *All at Sea* (1935); *Keep Fit* (1937); *It's in the Air* (US: *George Takes the Air*); *I See Ice* (1938); *Trouble Brewing*; *Come on George!* (1939); *Mine Own Executioner* (1947); *Bonnie Prince Charlie* (1948); *Flesh and Blood* (1951); *Mr Denning Drives North*; *Who Goes There!* (1952); *The Captain's Paradise* (1953); *Aunt Clara* (1954); *Smiley* (1956); *Smiley Gets a Gun* (1959); *The Amorous Prawn* (1962).

KING, George (1900–1966)

It is typical of George King's bravado that his entry in *Picturegoer's* 'Who's Who' of 1933 boasts that he 'made his first picture, *Too Many Crooks*, in three nights for Fox, and produced a new star in Laurence Olivier'. While the latter claim is touched by showman's hyperbole, it is certainly the case that King was proud to be one of the fastest and cheapest director/producers of the 1930s.

George William King was born in West Ham, east London, in 1900. He entered the film industry in 1922, working throughout the 1920s in a variety of roles, as agent, title-card composer and scenario writer. King's first works as director were a series of shortish dramas made for 20th Century-Fox. These films were typical of American distributors' early response to the Cinematograph Films Act of 1927, which had been intended to boost investment in British production by requiring distributors to offer a certain percentage of British-made films on their list,

but created a sub-industry churning out very cheap films. It was in the production of these 'quota quickies' that King specialised, earning a reputation as the 'quota King'. Throughout the 1930s he worked as a director and producer, initially at Warners' studio at Teddington, although later independently, hiring studio space as necessary. Good-looking and charismatic, his extreme efficiency enabled him to direct and produce numerous comedies and dramas on the very lowest budgets for various American distributors, while still maintaining a narrow margin of profit.

In 1935 King formed an alliance with Tod Slaughter, an actor-manager who had made a theatrical reputation by reviving several famous Victorian melodramas in a self-consciously 'barnstorming' mode. It was the perfect union of two consummate showmen, working together in a sector of the industry that was ideally suited to their dramatic oeuvre. The resulting seven films, beginning with *Maria Marten; or, the Murder in the Red Barn* (Milton Rosmer, 1935), all revel in overt theatricality, schematic character and plot situations, and Slaughter's extraordinary performances. Jeffrey Richards has identified them as forerunners to the 'cinema of excess' celebrated in the later productions of the Gainsborough and Hammer studios. Much loved by horror fans, these films triumphantly reverse the conventional criticisms of 'quota quickies', making a virtue of their low budgets, cramped staging and sensational themes. They are not, however, simply records of elderly plays. Richards points out that while King's budget does not allow him the extent of scene dissection one would usually expect (the films are typically constructed through mid-shots and long takes), moments of dramatic tension are heightened with well-chosen close-ups and reaction shots. Moreover the plays are carefully adapted to heighten Slaughter's star presence in the villainous central role, and to mediate between the modern audience and the morality of the age they purport to represent.

King's experience in the 1930s prepared him well for the difficulties and shortages of wartime production – a theme he often alluded to in his wartime statements in the trade press. Paradoxically, these conditions enabled him to make more ambitious films. With Leslie Howard, he helped form British Aviation Pictures, co-producing Howard's *The First of the Few* (1942) and his own *Tomorrow We Live* (1943), a film celebrating the achievements of the Gaullist Free French Resistance, and *Candlelight in Algeria* (1944), an espionage thriller about a British agent foiling Nazi attempts to discover the plans for the Allied invasion of North Africa. They were critically well received, and clearly on a different level from his earlier work, as were his post-war thrillers – *The Shop at Sly Corner* and *Forbidden* – and his period musical, *Gaiety George*. However, despite this late respectability, it is probably for his collaborations with Slaughter that he will be best remembered. In the 1950s King moved into television, producing the series *The Gay Cavalier* for Associated-Rediffusion in 1957. He died of bronchial pneumonia on 26 June 1966, in Poplar, a few miles from where he was born.

(Lawrence Napper)

BIBLIOGRAPHY: Botting, Josephine, 'The Archive Presents . . . George King', *National Film Theatre Programme*, May 2000, pp. 24–5; Napper, Lawrence, 'A Despicable Tradition? Quota Quickies in the 1930s', in Robert Murphy (ed.), *The British Cinema Book* (London: BFI, 1997); Richards, Jeffrey, 'Tod Slaughter and the Cinema of Excess', in Jeffrey Richards (ed.), *The Unknown 1930s* (London: I. B. Tauris, 1998).

FILMOGRAPHY: *Too Many Crooks* (short); *Leave It to Me* (short) (1930); *Number Please* (short); *The Professional Guest* (short); *Two Way Street* (short); *Midnight* (short); *Deadlock* (1931); *Self Made Lady*; *Men of Steel* (1932); *Too Many Wives*; *To Brighton with Gladys*; *Smithy*; *Mayfair Girl*; *Matinee Idol*; *I Adore You*; *High Finance*; *Her Imaginary Lover*, *Enemy of the Police*; *Beware of Women* (1933); *To Be a Lady*; *The Silver Spoon*; *Oh No Doctor!*; *The Office Wife*; *Nine Forty-Five*; *Murder at the Inn*; *Little Stranger*, *Guest of Honour*, *Get Your Man*; *The Blue Squadron*; *Adventure Limited* (1934); *Windfall* (co-dir. Frederick Hayward); *The Man Without a Face*; *Gay Old Dog*; *Full Circle* (1935); *Sweeny Todd: The Demon Barber of Fleet Street*; *Reasonable Doubt*; *The Crimes of Stephen Hawke* (1936); *Wanted*; *Under a Cloud*; *The Ticket of Leave Man*; *Merry Comes to Town* (1937); *Silver Top*; *Sexton Blake and the Hooded Terror*, *John Halifax, Gentleman* (1938); *The Face at the Window* (1939); *Crimes at the Dark House*; *The Chinese Bungalow* (US: *The Chinese Den*); *The Case of the Frightened Lady* (US: *The Scarf Murder Mystery*); *Two for Danger*, *George and Margaret* (1940); *Tomorrow We Live* (US: *At Dawn We Die*, 1943); *Candlelight in Algeria* (1944); *Gaiety George* (US: *Showtime*, 1946); *The Shop at Sly Corner* (US: *Code of Scotland Yard*, 1947); *Forbidden* (1948).

KNIGHT, Castleton (1894–1970)

Leonard Castleton Knight was born on 9 August 1894 in Bromley, Kent, and joined the industry in 1913 as an office boy. A buccaneering figure, he ventured into film-making during a colourful career in cinema management, directing himself in *Prelude*, a brief but adventurous adaptation of Poe's story *The Premature Burial* considered interesting enough to be shown at the Film Society in 1927. The following year Knight's lively mind led him to British International Pictures, where he took charge of three silent features, eventually released with added sound effects and dialogue. With its authentic train footage, sounds of steam and shovel, and the handsome presence of Ray Milland, the sound version of *The Flying Scotsman* (1929) made the biggest impact, though its story remained childishly simple.

After a brief period at Butcher's, Knight arrived at Gaumont-British in 1931. After managing the Kit-Kat Club, one of the corporation's peripheral ventures, in 1934 he moved into the mainstream as producer and editor at Gaumont-British News. Knight's mastery of creative chicanery was proved during the England–Australia Test matches of 1934: having secured joint rights to the cricket series with Movietone News, he beat off pirate cameramen by blocking their rooftop views with air balloons, smoke screens and searchlights. During the Second World War he co-directed *For Freedom*, with Maurice Elvey. Knight devised the story, and sketched a semi-portrait of himself in Will Fyffe's newsreel chief, urgently shouting across the studio, 'Get it printed and developed at once!'. The film ingeniously blended fiction, newsreel compilations and reconstruction: a mixture never attempted later, though his showmanship as a producer helped make *Theirs Is the Glory* (Brian Desmond Hurst, 1946) a convincing reconstruction of the Battle of Arnhem.

Knight left his position as Gaumont-British News producer to tackle his biggest post-war assignment, the official film of the 1948 Olympic Games held in London. Shot in variable Technicolor and compiled in three weeks, *XVth Olympiad – The Glory of Sport* offered a piquant British contrast to Leni Riefenstahl's pretentious and monumental film of the 1936 Berlin Olympics. Further independent ventures followed, all distributed by Rank, mostly documenting the Royal Family. Chances for mischief were nil here; instead, armed with Rank's contract with Technicolor, Knight helped to build Britain's heritage industry with accounts of Princess Elizabeth and Prince Philip's wedding, the 1953 Coronation and the subsequent Commonwealth tours. The most valuable film is *A Queen Is Crowned* (1953), a fascinating document of its time, complete with Christopher Fry's purple-phrased script and Technicolor's heroic attempts to prettify bad weather. Knight's efforts brought him an OBE, but the future for news reporting lay with television: over twenty million people had watched the Coronation on newly acquired sets. In 1955 a short cinema tribute to Churchill emerged; then in 1958 Knight retired. He died in Battle, Sussex, on 3 April 1970.

(Geoff Brown and Alan Burton)

BIBLIOGRAPHY: 'A Film Based on Rachmaninov's Prelude in C Sharp Minor', in *The Film Society Programmes 1925–1939* (New York: Arno Press, 1972), p. 50; British Universities Newsreel Database, <www.bufvc.ac.uk/databases/newsreels>; Chapman, James, 'Cinema, Monarchy and the Making of Heritage: *A Queen Is Crowned* (1953)', in Claire Monk and Amy Sargeant (eds), *British Historical Cinema* (London: Routledge, 2002); Norman, Philip, 'The Newsreel Boys', in Luke McKernan (ed.), *Yesterday's News: The British Cinema Newsreel Reader* (London: British University Film & Video Council, 2002).

FILMOGRAPHY: Non-fiction: *Sons of the Air*; *The Second Battle of London* (1944); *The Victory Parade* (1946); *Royal Wedding* (1947); *The Royal Wedding Presents*; *XVth Olympiad – The Glory of Sport* (1948); *The Carlsen Story* (1952); *Gentlemen – The Queen*; *Focus on Ethiopia*; *Focus on the Nile*; *Focus on Leisure*; *A Queen Is Crowned* (1953); *Royal Symphony* (1954); *Churchill, Man of the Century* (1955). [From 1953 onwards, except for the Churchill film, the films carry no director credit; CK is credited as producer only.]
Fiction: *Prelude* (short, 1927); *The Plaything*; *The Flying Scotsman* (1929); *The Lady from the Sea* (1929); *The Cockney Spirit in the War* (aka *Cockney War Stories*, series of shorts); *Kissing Cup's Race* (1930); *For Freedom* (co-dir. Maurice Elvey, 1940).

KNOWLES, Bernard (1900–1975)

Born in Manchester on 20 February 1900, Bernard Joseph Knowles had two separate careers in films. After a stint as a reporter with the *Detroit News*, he returned to Britain in 1922, and during the 1930s and early 40s became one of British cinema's most celebrated cinematographers. During this period, he worked for several major directors, including Victor Saville (*The Good Companions*, 1933), Anthony Asquith (*Quiet Wedding*, 1940), Thorold Dickinson (*Gaslight*, 1940) and Alfred Hitchcock (*The 39 Steps*, 1935; *The Secret Agent*, 1936; *Sabotage*, 1936; *Young and Innocent*, 1937). Arguably, nothing in his directing career approached the excellence of the black-and-white sheen he conferred on these varied works.

He ushered in his second career in 1944 by directing *A Place of One's Own*, a ghost story unusually alert to class nuances, starring James Mason, Margaret Lockwood and Barbara Mullen. Knowles creates a pervasive sense that there is more going on in the world than is susceptible to rational explanation – an aura of mystery the more effective for being understated and made without recourse to creaky 'old dark house' phenomena. He was unlucky enough to be stuck with one of the weaker Gainsborough melodramas as his follow-up: *The Magic Bow*, a farrago based on the life of Paganini, with Stewart Granger smouldering and fiddling to little avail apart from the satisfaction of rich box-office returns. He had more luck with the studio's first two Technicolor films. *The Man Within*, based on an early Graham Greene novel, is extraordinary in its suggestion of homoerotic feeling between the characters played by Michael Redgrave and Richard Attenborough, and the romantic melodrama of smuggling and seduction is underpinned with an Oedipal motif of unusual explicitness. *Jassy*, like *The Man Within* impressively photographed by Geoffrey Unsworth, is a tale of inheritance and passion, with Margaret Lockwood as an honest gypsy righting wrongs. It is overloaded with characters and machinations, but Knowles directs with a feeling for its perfervid melodrama.

The rest of Knowles' career is pretty much downhill. There is some value in the displaced persons drama *The Lost People*, but producer Muriel Box was so dissatisfied with Knowles' direction that she reshot large sections of the film herself. *The Reluctant Widow* offers flashes of Regency fun and games, but compared to contemporaries like Lance Comfort, who did excellent work in B-movies, Knowles lacked the flair to transmute modest material. From the mid-1950s he worked in television, producing thirty half-hour episodes of *The Adventures of Sir Lancelot* (1956–7) and directing episodes of many others, including *The Buccaneers* (1956) and *Ivanhoe* (1958). Episodes he directed for *Douglas Fairbanks Jr. Presents* were packaged for cinema release as parts of *The Triangle* and *Thought to Kill*. His brother, Cyril Knowles, was a camera operator and sometimes second-unit cinematographer. Bernard Knowles died in Taplow, Buckinghamshire, on 12 February 1975.

(Brian McFarlane)

BIBLIOGRAPHY: Obituary, *Film and TV Technician*, July/Aug. 1975, p. 11; Petrie, Duncan, *The British Cinematographer* (London: BFI, 1996).

FILMOGRAPHY: *A Place of One's Own* (1944); *The Magic Bow* (1946); *The Man Within* (US: *The Smugglers*); *Jassy*; *The White Unicorn* (US: *Bad Sister*) (1947); *Easy Money* (1948); *The Perfect Woman*; *The Lost People* (co-dir. Muriel Box) (1949); *The Reluctant Widow* (1950); *The Triangle* (co-dirs. Leslie Arliss/Lance Comfort); *Thought to Kill* (co-dirs. Lawrence Huntington/Leslie Arliss); *Park Plaza 605* (US: *Norman Conquest*) (1953); *Barbados Quest* (US: *Murder on Approval*); *Handcuffs, London* (1955); *Frozen Alive/Der Fall X701* (UK/Ger, 1964); *Spaceflight IC-1* (1965); *Hell Is Empty* (co-dir. John Ainsworth, UK/Cz, 1967; rel. 1970).

KORDA, Alexander (1893–1956)

Alexander Korda remains an elusive figure and might be considered both a charlatan and a visionary. In British cinema his principal achievement is as an ambitious and far-seeing producer, though it was as the director of *The Private Life of Henry VIII* (1933) that he first found fame in Britain, and he had already established a considerable reputation as a director in various European countries as well as in Hollywood.

Korda was born Sándor László Kellner on 16 September 1893 in Puszta Turpásztó, an isolated village in Hungary. His family was plunged into poverty on the death of his father, an overseer on a large estate. In 1909 Sándor moved to Budapest, where he worked in journalism before getting a job as an assistant with a film company. He changed his name from Kellner to Korda, and by 1918 had become Hungary's most prominent director. Political instability and anti-Semitism following the end of the First World War forced him to flee Hungary, but, with his actress wife Maria Corda, he was able to resume his career with great success, first in Vienna and then in Berlin. Hollywood, where he and Maria divorced, proved less congenial, though it taught Korda that real power lay with the producer not the director. He arrived in Britain in 1931 just as the newly burgeoning film industry opened a door of opportunity, and founded London Film Productions in February the following year.

Korda's first two British films – *Service for Ladies* (1932), made for Paramount-British, and *Wedding Rehearsal* (1932), his own company's inaugural film – were undemanding comedies, the kind of stories then routinely produced in most British studios. But these fledgling efforts differed from their counterparts in their polished production values. Established with his own company, Korda combined the roles of director and producer and thought in terms of marketing his product internationally. For *The Girl from Maxim's*, a bilingual version of a Feydeau farce, filmed in Paris in December 1932, he gathered around him a team of gifted collaborators, including his brother, art director Vincent Korda, script supervisor Lájos Biro and cinematographer Georges Périnal. But the film that definitively proved their worth was *The Private Life of Henry VIII*: a huge critical and financial success, it became the first British film to break into the American market. *Henry VIII* is a highly enjoyable romp, with a witty script, inventive production design and an impressive array of supporting players, but its most notable ingredient remains the Academy Award-winning performance of Charles Laughton, who manages to make the unappetising Henry both human and sympathetic. *The Private Life of Don Juan*, which followed in 1934, was a flawed attempt to reproduce a winning formula and is principally of interest for the last film appearance of the great silent star Douglas Fairbanks.

Rembrandt (1936) is remarkable for another *tour-de-force* performance from Laughton, for Vincent Korda's sets and for

Georges Périnal's lighting, which wonderfully recreates the play of light and shade in Rembrandt's paintings. It was Korda's own favourite among his films, but the downbeat story of an artist at odds with society proved uncommercial. With two flops in a row and large new studios at Denham to run, Korda now concentrated on his responsibilities as a producer. He eventually returned to the studio floor in the Second World War to direct *That Hamilton Woman* (1941) – in Hollywood, where he had decamped with Churchill's blessing to make pro-British movies. He was knighted in June 1942 (for his contribution to the war effort).

Korda's first post-war film as director was the charming *Perfect Strangers* (1945) starring Robert Donat and Deborah Kerr. Its topical story concerned a drab but deeply devoted couple who get separated by the war, blossom, decide that they have outgrown their former partner and face reunion with trepidation – a common concern at the time. It proved more popular than *An Ideal Husband* (1948), a faithful and sophisticated adaptation of Oscar Wilde's witty play about upper-class society, which received only a lukewarm welcome in the egalitarian Britain of the late 1940s. Officially this was Korda's last film as a director, though his insistence on controlling events on the studio floor later led to him directing much of Anthony Kimmins' *Who Goes There!* (1952) and Ralph Richardson's *Home at Seven* (1952).

Korda is strongly associated with gung-ho imperialist epics such as *The Drum* (Zoltán Korda, 1938) and *The Four Feathers* (Zoltán Korda, 1939), and he has been criticised for being culturally and politically conservative. Ironically, most of these films were directed by his much more left-wing brother, Zoltán. The films Alexander directed himself are a more accurate reflection of his own personality – that of an intelligent, urbane, cultured man with a detached cynical eye. While Korda had little interest in social movements, his films deal with the struggle to pursue an individual destiny within the context of a particular society.

As a director, Korda is inventive in transforming scripts into images, though there are times when his films display an uncertain touch; perhaps his understanding of the complexities of film-making induced occasional paralysis. His charisma and charm were integral to his success, but as both producer and director he showed resilience, talent, dedication and a love of films that enabled him to inspire a generation of film-makers. He died of a heart attack in London on 23 January 1956.

(Linda Wood)

BIBLIOGRAPHY: Drazin, Charles, *Korda: Britain's Only Movie Mogul* (London: Sidgwick & Jackson, 2002); Korda, Michael, *Charmed Lives: A Family Romance* (New York: Random House, 1979); Kulik, Karol, *Alexander Korda: The Man Who Could Work Miracles* (London: W. H. Allen, 1975); Stockham, Martin, *Alexander Korda Film Classics* (London: Boxtree, 2002); Tabori, Paul, *Alexander Korda* (London: Oldbourne, 1959).

FILMOGRAPHY (UK only): *Service for Ladies* (US: *Reserved for Ladies*); *Wedding Rehearsal* (1932); *The Private Life of Henry VIII* (1933); *The Private Life of Don Juan* (1934); *Rembrandt* (1936); *Perfect Strangers* (1945); *An Ideal Husband* (1947).

KORDA, Zoltán (1895–1961)

Zoltán Korda, middle sibling of Alexander and Vincent Korda, was born Zoltán Kellner in Túrkeve, Hungary, on 3 May 1895. Much of his career was spent following the path of his eldest brother Sandór (Alex) from one company and country to the next. After odd jobs and active service in the First World War, he worked as an editor at Alex's first major production base, the new Corvin studios in Budapest, and co-directed his first feature, *Károly-bakák*, later in 1918. When Alex moved to Vienna in 1920, Zoltán was close behind, gaining experience in photography. When Alex tried his luck in Hollywood, Zoltán packed his bags again, and stayed by his side on the return to Europe in 1930. This may suggest a pliant character, but both brothers shared a volatile temperament; most of the features Zoltán directed for Alex only emerged after furious arguments conducted in Hungarian, punctuated by slammed doors and screams.

At the heart of these battles lay a crucial difference in aspirations. Alex, the instigator and hands-on producer, wanted his major films shaped as colourful entertainments, fit for international audiences, though with a patriotic British stamp. Zoltán – once past thankless duties on Leontine Sagan's *Men of Tomorrow* and the frivolous quota comedy *Cash* – yearned to direct exotic but realistic adventures, focusing on social justice and the lives of native people, particularly in Africa. The conflict in goals is clearly visible in London Films' increasingly ambitious series of British Empire subjects, launched with Edgar Wallace's African story, *Sanders of the River*, begun in the summer of 1933. *Sanders* is a film not so much directed as assembled, with the studio scenes centred on Leslie Banks' sympathetic commissioner regularly interrupted by vocal opportunities for Paul Robeson and Zoltán's respectful footage of tribal life and scenery. *Elephant Boy* (1937), inspired by Kipling, never achieved fusion either. Elephants and scenery lyrically and expansively filmed in India by Robert Flaherty, Zoltán and others were forced to rub shoulders in the editing with makeshift sets and animals from Whipsnade Zoo, corralled into patchy narrative scenes filmed at Denham.

But one saving grace emerged from *Elephant Boy*: Sabu, the stable-hand chosen for the role of the boy who earns enough British approval to become a mahout, an elephant driver. Sabu's youthful charm and popularity encouraged Alex to build his future Empire films with a more careful regard for character and a stronger dramatic spine. In *The Drum*, from a story written to showcase Sabu by the novelist A. E. W. Mason, Zoltán struggled to bring to life the indifferently written interior scenes. But the entire film punched out its breezy tale with a new degree of narrative and visual cohesion, even though production economies showed and the 'Indian' scenery was mostly Welsh. Much of the melding was provided by the dazzling Technicolor photography (Georges Périnal and Osmond Borradaile), and the set designs of the third Korda brother, Vincent – a key contributor to Alex's films throughout the 1930s and 40s.

Zoltan Korda with Rene Ray

The quality gap between interiors and exteriors was significantly shortened in *The Four Feathers* (1939), fluidly and incisively directed by Zoltán, and the best of all film accounts of Mason's early adventure novel about a guardsman's cowardice redeemed in Egypt. Open talk of 'fuzzy wuzzies', the loud trumpeting of patriotic and family duty, and the subservient role of women combine to make the film a monument of the politically incorrect. Yet it remains genuinely exciting and moving, powered as much by the strongly defined character conflicts as the visual panoply of bright red tunics, sand, rock and massed local extras. The extensive location footage shot in the Sudan was later raided by other directors (chunks surface in the 1955 *Storm Over the Nile*, Zoltán's last production for Alex). But only the 1939 *Four Feathers* presents Harry Faversham's agonies of conscience with an even hand, or enjoys the benefit of John Clements and Ralph Richardson, who make the tussles and desert adventures so believable and gripping.

Subsequently Zoltán joined the army working on *The Thief of Bagdad* and moved with Alex to America to direct another Sabu vehicle derived from Kipling, *Jungle Book* (1942). Artistically this marked a backward step: Alex's desire for colourful fantasy, controlled in the studio, won over Zoltán's itch for realism, though the public liked the mix and the wild animals. Zoltán's expertise with adventure films and deserts no doubt helped him land an outside job for Columbia, directing Humphrey Bogart in *Sahara* (1943). The taut war drama's success led to an independent American career. The Hemingway adaptation *The Macomber Affair* (1947) offered further African wildlife and an intelligent exploration of the human jungle; while the polished melodrama *A Woman's Vengeance* (1948), set in England, made juicy work of Aldous Huxley's story 'The Giaconda Smile'.

Zoltán returned to the family firm for two more productions. With *Cry, the Beloved Country* (1952), based on Alan Paton's novel about relations in South Africa between the races, he was finally able to make an African film of his own choosing, without the burden of glamour and surface entertainment. Filmed extensively in and around Johannesburg, the long-gestating project met with many hurdles, but Zoltán stuck to his guns and let the anti-apartheid message emerge naturally through the entwined fates of Canada Lee's simple black minister and Charles Carson's bigoted landowner. Though the acting shone only in patches, the film's sincerity never wavered; and the public's muted response was balanced by critical respect.

Zoltán had other ambitions – he was keen to film Pierre Boulle's novel *The Bridge on the River Kwai* when Alex briefly held the rights – but increasing ill-health made further work difficult. On the mildly enjoyable *Storm Over the Nile* he functioned chiefly as the producer: it was Terence Young's task to direct Anthony Steel and company in new material, fitted around Zoltán's location footage, now stretched to fit the newly fashionable CinemaScope frame. Alex's death in 1956 closed the door on further collaborations. Zoltán went into semi-retirement, and died in Beverly Hills, California on 13 October 1961. He was married to the actress Joan Gardner, featured in his untypical *Forget Me Not*: a film strong on operatic singing, but with none of the dash and exotic colour that makes his best work so exhilarating. (Geoff Brown)

BIBLIOGRAPHY: Zoltán Korda, *Film Dope* no. 31, Jan. 1985 p. 30; Korda, Zoltan, 'Filming in Africa', *Film Weekly* no. 338, Apr. 1935, p. 52; Kulik, Karol, *Alexander Korda: The Man Who Could Work Miracles* (London: W. H. Allen, 1975); Patar, Benoit, 'Zoltán Korda, prince oublié', *24 Images* no.12, Apr. 1982, pp. 47–52.

FILMOGRAPHY: *Károly-bakák* (Hun, co-dir. Miklós M. Pásztory, 1918); *A csodagverek* (Hun, 1924); *Die elf Teufel* (Ger, 1927); *Men of Tomorrow* (co-dir. Leontine Sagan, 1932); *Cash* (US: *For Love or Money*, 1933); *Pa Puts His Foot Down* (short, 1934); *Sanders of the River* (US: *Bosambo*, 1935); *Forget Me Not* (US: *Forever Yours*, 1936); *Elephant Boy* (co-dir. Robert Flaherty, 1937); *The Drum* (1938); *The Four Feathers* (1939); *The Conquest of the Air* (co-dirs. Alexandre Esway/Donald Taylor/Alexander Shaw/John Monk Saunders/William Cameron Menzies); *The Thief of Bagdad* (co-dirs. Michael Powell/Tim Whelan/Ludwig Berger) (1940); *Jungle Book* (US, 1942); *Sahara* (US, 1943); *Counter-Attack* (UK: *One Against Seven*, US, 1945); *The Macomber Affair* (US, 1947); *A Woman's Vengeance* (US, 1948); *Cry, the Beloved Country* (US: *African Fury*, 1952); *Storm Over the Nile* (co-dir. Terence Young, 1955).

KOSMINSKY, Peter (c. 1956–)

After studying chemistry at Oxford University in the late 1970s Peter Kosminsky worked as a trainee at the BBC in the early 1980s, getting his first opportunity to direct on current affairs programmes. In 1985 he joined Yorkshire Television, directing documentaries including *The Falklands War: The Untold Story* (1987) before making *Shoot to Kill* (1990), a two-part drama-documentary about Northern Ireland written by Michael Eaton, which was also the subject of Ken Loach's *Hidden Agenda* (1990). Kosminsky's first feature film, the Paramount-financed *Wuthering Heights*, with Juliette Binoche and Ralph Fiennes, was a clear departure from his previous work and its lack of commercial success and mixed critical response prompted a return to television. Kosminsky won BAFTA awards for *No Child of Mine* (1997), his drama about the sexual abuse of a young girl, and for *Warriors* (1999), a convincing three-hour exploration of the dilemmas faced by a group of British soldiers attempting to serve as peacekeepers in Bosnia. Kosminsky continued his collaboration with Leigh Jackson, who had written *Warriors*, on *The Project* (2002), an intelligent fictional investigation of the group of political activists who would dominate New Labour, a rare recent outing for political drama on British television.

Kosminsky's second feature film, *White Oleander*, a coming-of-age drama adapted from the novel by Janet Fitch, featuring Michelle Pfeiffer and Renee Zellweger, was another incongruous project given his television oeuvre; it received mixed reviews following its delayed UK release. He returned to what he does best with *The Government Inspector* (2005), an impressively well-researched documentary-drama, made for Channel 4, about the events leading to the suicide of British government scientific adviser Dr David Kelly. While maintaining an absolute seriousness in his treatment of the fallible but immensely sympathetic Kelly, Kosminsky provides light relief by showing press secretary Alastair Campbell as a petulant bully and Prime Minister Tony Blair as more concerned with guitar riffs than intricate plotting. With such an acute and original talent for political drama, Kosminsky would seem to be wasting his time with the fripperies of feature film romance.

(Lez Cooke)

BIBLIOGRAPHY: Kosminsky, Peter, 'Goodbye to All That', *Sight and Sound*, Dec. 1999, p. 32; Owen, John, 'Direction', *Televisual*, May 1994, pp. 33–4.

FILMOGRAPHY: *Wuthering Heights* (US/UK, 1992); *White Oleander* (US/Ger, 2003).

KOSTER, Henry (1905–1988)

Born Hermann Kosterlitz in Berlin on 1 May 1905, Henry Koster contributed most to cinema history in his domestic musical comedies, made in Europe and Hollywood with producer Joe Pasternak and writer Felix Joachimson (later Jackson). His sole brush with British cinema was *No Highway* (1951), produced by 20th Century-Fox in England.

Fascinated by movies from an early age, Kosterlitz began writing scripts in Germany in 1924, and was soon specialising in light-hearted comedies. Work on Pasternak's *Fünf von der Jazzband* (Erich Engel, 1932) quickly led to his directing debut under Pasternak's aegis. With Hitler's rise to power, Kosterlitz – Jewish and fervently anti-Nazi – continued with Pasternak and Joachimson in Austria and Hungary, directing among others *Frühlingsparade* (1934) and *Kleine Mutti* (1935), pleasing vehicles for the innocent charms of Franziska Gaal. Arriving in Hollywood in 1936, Kosterlitz became Koster, but the winning formula continued. Universal's *Three Smart Girls* (1936) became the first of Koster's six musical-comedies featuring the teenage singer Deanna Durbin. The films' popularity helped to stabilise the company's economic fortunes.

Later Koster widened his range, particularly after he became a Fox contract director late in 1947. In 1951, the company's schedule took him to London, where he took charge of *No Highway*, a craftsmanlike, suspenseful and commercially successful adaptation of Neville Shute's best-selling scientific thriller. Chiefly set on a transatlantic airliner, the film features James Stewart in whimsical vein as an absent-minded aeronautical researcher, convinced that the plane will become damaged by metal fatigue. Marlene Dietrich (Koster's own casting) enjoys herself as the glamorous film star passenger across the aisle, dressed to kill in Christian Dior.

Leaving the shooting schedule's final shots in the hands of George More O'Ferrall, the film's dialogue coach, Koster hurried back to Hollywood for his next Fox assignment. Over the years, whatever they wanted he supplied: CinemaScope spectacle in *The Robe* (1953), the widescreen process's first feature; lavish war drama in *D-Day the Sixth of June* (1956); family comedy with *Mr Hobbs Takes a Vacation* (1962). Handling a difficult Debbie Reynolds in *The Singing Nun* (1965), however, proved an assignment too far, and in 1966 he retired. Koster died on 21 September 1988 in Camarillo, California.

(Geoff Brown and Wheeler Winston Dixon)

BIBLIOGRAPHY: Asper, Helmut G. and Jan-Christopher Horak, 'Three Smart Guys: How a Few Penniless German émigrés Saved Universal Studios', *Film History* vol. 11 no. 2, 1999, pp. 134–53; Koster, Henry and Irene Kahn Atkins, *Henry Koster* (Metuchen, NJ and London: Directors Guild of America/Scarecrow Press, 1987); Steinbacher, John, 'Henry Koster – The Human Touch', *Films of the Golden Age*, Summer 2000, pp. 38-49.

FILMOGRAPHY (UK only): *No Highway* (US: *No Highway in the Sky*, 1951).

KOTCHEFF, Ted (1931–)

William Theodore Kotcheff was born in Toronto on 7 April 1931. Educated at the University of Toronto, he became drama director of the Canadian Broadcasting Corporation in 1955. On moving to England in 1957, he joined another Canadian, Sydney Newman, at ABC Television's *Armchair Theatre*, where he directed such celebrated productions as Alun Owen's *No Trams to Lime Street* (1959) and *Lena, O My Lena* (1960), and Clive Exton's *Where I Live* (1960). He made his feature debut in 1962 with the mildly diverting social comedy *Tiara Tahiti*, which, like Ronald Neame's *Tunes of Glory* (1960), cast John Mills as a pompous military martinet. Here Mills is persistently undermined by the perfect manners and calculated insolence of his Captain (James Mason), inferior in rank but effortlessly superior in class. There is some nicely observed satire at the expense of contrasting styles and the British abroad, but the film draws back from the real ferocity the situation could have used.

Kotcheff's skill in orchestrating character confrontations was put to better use in his next film, *Life at the Top*, a rare example of a sequel worthy of its predecessor. *Room at the Top* (Jack Clayton, 1959) is a landmark in British film history, with its tale of the rise and rise of Joe Lampton, who gets the boss's daughter pregnant, marries her reluctantly and, as the sequel (based on John Braine's follow-up novel) makes clear, lives none-too-happily ever after. In *Life at the Top*, Joe, again played by Laurence Harvey, succumbs to an affair (with Honor Blackman), flirts with almost-swinging London, but is eventually brought to heel. Kotcheff is unsentimental about the consequences of Joe's selling out and the film simplifies issues canvassed more subtly in the earlier film. But it benefits from a witty screenplay (by friend and fellow-Canadian Mordecai Richler) and some well-directed rancorous exchanges between Joe and his wife – now a formidable character, with Jean Simmons acting the part.

In *Two Gentlemen Sharing* (1969), an affable contribution to the British cinema's treatment of race relations, a white advertising man comes to terms with his own prejudices when he shares his Knightsbridge flat with a 'hopelessly' black solicitor. Kotcheff adeptly handles the culture clash; the dialogue crackles intermittently; and, as always, his supporting cast is effective (particularly Philip Stone and Elspeth March as the very upper- middle-class parents). Unfortunately the film was caught up in the American withdrawal from the British film industry at the end of the 1960s and was poorly distributed. Kotcheff went to Australia to make possibly his finest film, *Outback* (aka *Wake in Fright*, 1971), a penetrating study of a young English schoolteacher who suffers a descent into a moral hell in an isolated outback town.

In the same year, Kotcheff returned to television to direct Jeremy Sandford's *Edna the Inebriate Woman* for the BBC. After *Billy Two Hats*, an Anglo-American Western shot in Israel, his cinema career finally took off in 1974 with *The Apprenticeship of Duddy Kravitz*, a successful Canadian adaptation of Mordecai Richler's novel about a bumptious Jewish kid in Montreal in the 1940s, first filmed by Kotcheff in 1960 as a television play for *Armchair Theatre*. His later films include *Fun with Dick and Jane* (US, 1977), a counter-cultural caper film with George Segal and Jane Fonda; *North Dallas Forty* (US, 1979), a realistic study of American football with a highly convincing performance from Nick Nolte; *First Blood* (US, 1982), the film that launched the Rambo cycle; and another Richler tale of Jewish experience in Canada, *Joshua Then and Now* (Can, 1985).

(Brian McFarlane)

BIBLIOGRAPHY: Castell, David, 'The Apprenticeship of Ted Kotcheff', *Films Illustrated*, Feb. 1975 pp. 230–1; Peachment, Chris, 'Teds's Tracks', *Time Out* vol. 711, 5 Apr. 1984, p. 43.

FILMOGRAPHY (UK only): *Tiara Tahiti* (1962); *Life at the Top* (1965); *Two Gentlemen Sharing* (1969); *Billy Two Hats* (1973).

KÖTTING, Andrew (1958–)

Andrew Kötting was born on 16 December 1958, one of five children of a middle-class family, in Farnborough, Kent. His father, like his German-born grandfather, sold belts and buckles. As a child he 'spent hours off ground in trees or tending rhubarb' (Kötting, p. 10). He studied art at the Slade School of Art, where he used an old 16mm camera to capture his outdoor performance pieces. One of his first attempts at film-making 'involved inserting iron filings in the shape of religious icons into his penis and then drawing them out again' (Matheou, p. 13). For his degree film, a short called *Klipperty Klop* (1986), Kötting ran round and round a Gloucestershire field pretending to ride a horse.

Over the next ten years Kötting directed a number of experimental shorts, often produced via the London Film-Makers Co-op. The best received were *Hoi Polloi* (1990), and *Smart Alek* (1993) – the latter being 'an attempt to rework some of my darker childhood memories' (Kötting, p. 10). He used these shorts to experiment with format, texture and sound to 'transport an audience to a place cinematically where possibly they've never been before' (Calhoun, October 2000, p. 8). 'I like to sculpt with the sound in the same way I like to sculpt with the picture and the ideas,' he explained. 'The story may change just to accommodate a sound' (Calhoun, 8 December 2000, p. 2).

Kötting's first feature-length movie was *Gallivant* (1996). A highly idiosyncratic documentary, it records a journey the director took clockwise around the coast of Britain accompanied by his eighty-five-year-old grandmother, Gladys, and his seven-year-old daughter, Eden, who suffers from an incurable condition that impedes her speech. The growing closeness between these two and the sense of impending mortality give the film its emotional underpinning, so that Kötting's celebration of sheer human daffiness never descends into whimsy. In the course of his trip he meets, and blithely indulges, a fine gallery of amiable eccentrics – himself not least. The flavour is rather as though a film by Humphrey Jennings had been remade by Richard Lester, with occasional input from John Betjeman

and Spike Milligan. *Gallivant* was premiered to great acclaim at the Edinburgh Film Festival, where it won the Channel 4 Best New Director prize.

The harsher, grittier side of Kötting's work emerged in his second feature, *This Filthy Earth* (2001). Loosely adapted from Zola's novel *La Terre*, the film is set in a rural community somewhere and some time in the north of England. The melodramatic plot matters far less than the brutal, phantasmagoric atmosphere, a timeless nightmare vision of blood and shit and all-engulfing mud. Kötting summed up his aim as 'trying to show the landscape in its full beauty and brutality' (Calhoun, October 2000, p. 8). Critical reaction was generally respectful but stunned. Since then he has completed *Mapping Perception* (2002), a short 'science, film and art project' inspired by his daughter Eden. Kötting still sees himself as essentially a performance artist. 'Even to this day,' he says, 'I wouldn't think of myself as a feature film-maker. I'm just making longer pieces of work' (Calhoun, October 2000, p. 8).

(Philip Kemp)

BIBLIOGRAPHY: Calhoun, David, 'Britain as You've Never Seen It Before', *Observer* Review Section, 14 Oct. 2000, pp. 8–9; Calhoun, Dave, 'Up to His Neck in Mud and Blood', *Independent on Sunday* Culture Section, 8 Dec. 2000, p. 2; Kötting, Andrew, 'It's a Dirty Job', *Guardian* G2 Section, 2 Nov. 2001, pp. 10–11; Matheou, Demetrios, 'Profile, Andrew Kötting', *Premiere*, Oct. 1997, p. 13.

FILMOGRAPHY: *Klipperty Klop* (short, 1986); *Self Heal* (short, 1987); *Hub-bub in the Baobabs* (short, 1989); *Hoi Polloi* (short, 1990); *Acumen* (short, 1991); *Diddykoi* (short, 1992); *Smart Alek* (short, 1993); *Là Bas* (short, 1994); *Jaunt* (short, 1995); *Gallivant* (1996); *Kingdom Protista* (short, 2000); *This Filthy Earth* (2001); *Mapping Perception* (short, 2002).

KRAEMER, F. W.

Friedrich Wilhelm Kraemer, co-director of BIP's *Dreyfus* (1931), was a brief beneficiary of British cinema's continental ambitions in the early days of sound. Born in Germany or Austria (the date is also uncertain), he was fully established in Berlin as a producer by the end of the 1920s, with credits on the Sherlock Holmes film *Der Hund von Baskerville* (Richard Oswald, 1929) and an Anny Ondra musical, *Die vom Rummelplatz* (Karel Lamac, 1930). Later in 1930 he came to Britain as co-director and production supervisor for *Dreyfus*, the last of British International Pictures' multilingual output, based on Hans Rehfisch and Wilhelm Herzog's famous play *Die Affäre Dreyfus*. Dialogue scenes were probably handled by Kraemer's directing partner, the actor Milton Rosmer. In his cinema debut, Cedric Hardwicke gave a quietly impressive performance as the French army officer tried for treason and vigorously defended by Zola (George Merritt). Among BIP's multilingual ventures, *Dreyfus* featured greater movement, atmosphere and intelligence than most, though the company's shrinking artistic horizons denied Kraemer any further prestige assignments. In October 1931 he was directing BIP's potboiling South Seas melodrama, *Tin Gods*; the following year he made an Edgar Wallace thriller, *The Flying Squad*, for British Lion, lending a slow Germanic pace even to the fight sequences. Forming his own company, FWK Productions, he was able to generate only one feature, *Daughters of Today*, an unconvincing drama about two provincial girls, daughters of a puritanical farmer, seeking fortunes in London. A return to BIP proved equally unrewarding: he was assigned to direct boxer Jack Doyle in *McGlusky the Sea Rover* (1935), but the project passed to Walter Summers. By the time the film was released, Kraemer had moved on to Czechoslovakia, where he picked up the reins on a sentimental drama about a returning soldier . . . *A Život jde dál . . . (And Life Goes On)*, begun by Carl Junghans in 1933. Kraemer's later whereabouts and career remain unknown.

(Geoff Brown and Kevin Gough-Yates)

BIBLIOGRAPHY: Low, Rachael, *Film Making in 1930s Britain* (London: George Allen & Unwin, 1985); Winchester, Clarence, *The World Film Encyclopaedia* (London: Amalgamated Press, 1933).

FILMOGRAPHY (UK only)**:** *Dreyfus* (US: *The Dreyfus Case*, co-dir. Milton Rosmer, 1931); *Tin Gods*; *The Flying Squad* (1932); *Daughters of Today* (1933).

KRISH, John (1923–)

John Jeffery Krish was born in London on 4 December 1923. He began his career with the Crown Film Unit in 1940, working on Harry Watt's *Target for To-night* (1941) and Humphrey Jennings' *Listen to Britain* (1942) before editing wartime newsreels. In the 1950s and early 60s he directed documentaries on apartheid (*Let My People Go*), the educational system (*Mr Marsh Comes to School*, *Our School*) and the plight of refugees (*Return to Life*). While these films – sponsored by the likes of the Central Office of Information and the National Union of Teachers – have an instructional purpose, they are also creative and compassionate. Fellow film-maker Kevin Brownlow thought Krish's best-known documentary, *The Elephant Will Never Forget*, an elegiac study of the London tram, 'as skilful an evocation of nostalgia as I've ever seen' (Brownlow, p. 8).

During the early 1950s, Krish also directed several short crime films as part of the 'Stryker of the Yard' series, and in the early 1960s he switched more emphatically to fiction. *The Wild Affair* was an uneven comedy, but *Unearthly Stranger*, in which the hero (John Neville) discovers that his new wife (Gabriella Licudi) is part of an alien invasion force, is one of British cinema's most sustained exercises in male paranoia, and benefits immeasurably from Krish's restrained and realistic treatment of the narrative's increasingly fantastic events. Krish's next two feature films – *Decline and Fall* and *The Man Who Had Power over Women* – were ambitious but lacked the deftness of touch apparent in his earlier work. In the 1970s Krish returned to making documentaries and commercials, though he was also responsible for two well-regarded films for the Children's Film Foundation, *Friend or Foe* and *Out of the Darkness*, and co-directed the much-shown *Jesus* with Peter Sykes.

(Peter Hutchings)

BIBLIOGRAPHY: BECTU History Project interview with John Krish, tape held in the BFI National Library, London; Brownlow, Kevin, 'John Krish', *Film Dope* no. 32, Mar. 1985, pp 7–8; Krish, John, 'A Backward Glance at a Retrospective', *Vertigo* vol. 2 no. 5, Summer 2003, pp. 18–19; Lennon, Peter, 'All Quiet on Set', *Guardian* Society Section, 7 May 2003, p. 5.

FILMOGRAPHY: Documentaries: *Jet-Propelled Germs*; *What's in a Number*; *Health in Our Time*; *Pattern for Progress*; *What a Life*; *Every Drop to Drink* (1948); *One Day in Perfect Health* (1950); *This Year – London* (1951); *Away for the Day* (1952); *The Elephant Will Never Forget*; *They Had an Idea* (1953); *Counterpoint* (1957); *I Want to Go to School*; *Captured* (1959); *Return to Life* (1960); *Let My People Go*; *Mr Marsh Comes to School*; *They Took Us to the Sea* (1961); *Our School*; *Consider Your Verdict* (1962); *I Think They Call Him John* (1964); *Maths with Everything* (1971); *Communications with a Group* (1972); *What Are They Doing at College*; *Observer – Sex* (1973); *Red Cross – That's Us*; *Searching – Keep Matches away from Children*; *Snatch of the Day* (1974); *Drive Carefully, Darling*; *I Stopped, I Looked and I Listened*; *Make Sure the under Fives Stay Inside*; *London Fire Brigade – Night Smoke* (1975); *HMP* (1976); *The Finishing Line* (1977). Fiction: *Stryker of the Yard* (shorts): 'The Case of the Bogus Count' (1953); 'The Case of the Black Falcon'; 'The Case of Diamond Annie'; 'The Case of the Two Brothers'; 'The Case of the Pearl Payroll'; 'The Case of the Second Shot'; 'The Case of Canary Jones'; 'Companions in Crime' (1954); *The Salvage Gang* (1958); *The Wild Affair*, *Unearthly Stranger* (aka *Beyond the Stars*) (1963); *Decline and Fall* (aka *Decline and Fall . . . of a Birdwatcher*, 1968); *The Man Who Had Power over Women* (1970); *Jesus* (US, co-dir. Peter Sykes, 1979); *Friend or Foe* (1981); *Out of the Darkness* (1985).

KRISHNAMMA, Suri (1961–)

Suri Krishnamma was born in London in 1961. He studied film and photography at Bournemouth College of Art between 1983 and 1986, where his two ambitious shorts, *Departure* and *Mohammed's Daughter*, won him a place at the National School of Film and Television. *Comrades and Friends*, a witty documentary co-directed by Nick Godwin about Tony Benn's challenge for the leadership of the Labour Party in 1988, and the prize-winning drama *Water's Edge* opened up a career in television even before he completed the course. Episodes of *South of the Border*, *The Curry Connection*, *The Bill*, *Soldier, Soldier* and *Spender* were followed in 1994 by *The Turnaround*, one of the feature-length Nick Sharman private-eye thrillers, and *O Mary This London*, a harrowing a BBC television film about dispossessed Irish teenagers in London. The Irish connection led to his first feature film, *A Man of No Importance*, an arch if vigorously directed feature set in Dublin in 1963, starring Albert Finney as an artistically inclined gay bus conductor.

Krishnamma returned to television, directing a number of interesting assignments, including *The Place of the Dead* (1996), an unusual fact-based drama about a platoon of British soldiers lost in the Malayan jungle, written by Jeff Pope; and *A Respectable Trade* (1998), an impressive four-hour serial about eighteenth-century Bristol slave traders. Television was a field Krishnamma was happy to work in: 'I don't share the snobbery that draws distinctions between working in film and working in television . . . frankly I'd rather make high quality British television than a low-quality international movie just because it's a movie' (Hunter, p. 22). Thus it was not until 2001 that he made his second cinema feature, *New Year's Day*, a small-scale drama that starts intriguingly with two teenage survivors of an avalanche postponing suicide until they have done all the outrageous things teenagers think they should do before dying. Unfortunately, the lurches of tone between comedy, tragedy and sentimentality, grim realism and flimsy fantasy, while occasionally appropriate to the film's combustible subject matter, make for irritatingly uneven viewing. Krishnamma wandered into more treacherous teenage minefields with an MTV-financed adaptation of *Wuthering Heights* (2003); Heathcliff transformed into a blond Ameri-

can rock musician proved a leap too far even for American teenagers. His 'Empty Promise' episode of David Kane's paranormal television series *Sea of Souls* (2004) was more substantial, with strong performances and a far-fetched but convincingly told story showing the director at his best.
(Robert Murphy)

BIBLIOGRAPHY: Hunter, Allan, 'The Snow and the Fury: New Year's Day', *Screen International*, 14 Jan. 2000, p. 22; Matthias, Fiona, 'Direction: Suri Krishnamma', *Televisual*, Apr. 1994, pp. 31–2.

FILMOGRAPHY: *Departure* (short, 1985); *Mohammed's Daughter* (short, 1986); *Comrades and Friends* (doc., co-dir. Nick Godwin); *Water's Edge* (short) (1988); *A Man of No Importance* (UK/Ir, 1994); *New Year's Day* (UK/Fr, 2001).

KUBRICK, Stanley (1928–1999)

Stanley Kubrick was born in New York City on 26 July 1928 and grew up in the Bronx. A precociously intellectual child, he inherited from his father, a doctor, an interest in still photography and became a staff photographer on *Look* magazine at the age of seventeen. Turning to motion pictures, in the space of five years Kubrick directed three short documentaries and three low-budget independent features – *Fear and Desire*, *Killer's Kiss* and *The Killing* – which he also wrote and/or photographed. These gained sufficient notice for him to attract Kirk Douglas to star in his first major Hollywood picture, *Paths of Glory*. The actor later returned the favour by hiring Kubrick at a weekend's notice to take over his massive production of *Spartacus* after Douglas had dismissed its original director, Anthony Mann.

Spartacus was the only film over which Kubrick did not have full control. Henceforth, despite dealing exclusively with the major studios, he exercised autonomy over every aspect of his films' conception, execution and release. This creative independence was no doubt assisted by Kubrick's decision in the early 1960s to work and reside permanently in Britain, which lent a certain distance from the seats of executive power in Hollywood. Once a project had been approved he was generally left alone to complete it to his own satisfaction, at his own pace and under his own guidance. His titanic international reputation, especially among his fellow film-makers, no doubt derives in part from this rare privileged position, shared by few other directors since Chaplin and Griffith.

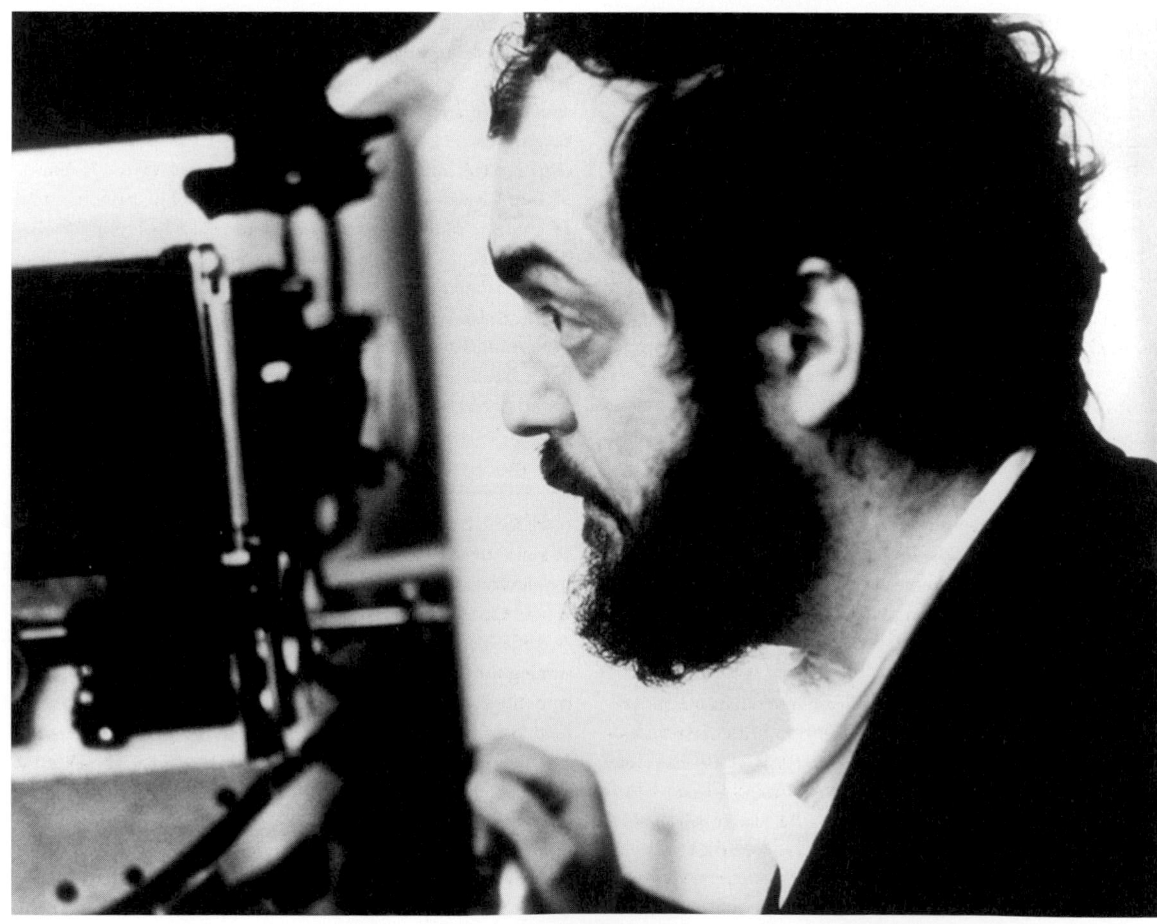

Kubrick's adaptation of Vladimir Nabokov's scandalous novel *Lolita* was made in Britain partly for reasons of economy, but also to escape the censorious moral climate in America. Though he compromised the book's most intractable elements by casting the fourteen-year-old Sue Lyon as the twelve-year-old nymphet and by avoiding physical eroticism, he nonetheless fashioned from it a brilliant black comedy of manners. The first half in particular is exemplary for its witty *mise en scène* and the superb performances of James Mason, Shelley Winters and, as the chameleon-like Clare Quilty, Peter Sellers. Kubrick again turned controversial subject matter into the stuff of high comedy when Peter George's novel *Red Alert*, a straight thriller about an accidental American nuclear attack on the USSR, became a cold war satire with Sellers performing three different roles, including the mad scientist Dr Strangelove. Dazzlingly designed by Ken Adam and photographed by Gilbert Taylor, it is one of the few film comedies where an extremely stylised visual surface does not detract from the hilarity of the characters, dialogue and situations.

Strangelove's critical and commercial success helped persuade MGM to shell out $10.5 million for a science-fiction epic to be shot in 70mm and exhibited in Cinerama theatres as a prestige roadshow. *2001: A Space Odyssey*, as the film was eventually known after four years of planning and production, is unquestionably the most abstract, avant-garde blockbuster ever made, as well as one of the biggest box-office hits of the 1960s. Justly regarded as Kubrick's masterpiece, it largely eschews the gleeful humour of his preceding two films in favour of the glacial detachment that came to dominate his work, sometimes to its detriment. *2001* is nonetheless a breathtakingly immersive experience as well as a compelling cerebral puzzle: technically audacious, richly patterned and even, in the demise of HAL-2000 and the birth of the Star Child, surprisingly moving.

A recession in the industry led MGM to cancel Kubrick's planned biopic of Napoleon and he turned instead to adapting Anthony Burgess' satirical fantasy *A Clockwork Orange*. The resultant film embodies all his worst tendencies: it is glib, vulgar, schematic, misanthropic, over-designed and evades confronting the full implications of its subject – the necessity of free choice between good and evil – by dealing in grotesque cartoon caricatures rather than human beings. The film's cult reputation was enhanced in Britain by the director's ban on its UK exhibition from 1973 until a posthumous reissue in 2000. The willingness of Warner Bros. – financier and distributor of this and all his subsequent projects – to indulge him speaks volumes about Kubrick's unique status.

A Clockwork Orange was conceived as a modern picaresque tale, and Kubrick returned to that narrative form with a lavish adaptation of William Thackeray's novel *Barry Lyndon*. An exquisite, painterly series of eighteenth-century tableaux, filmed in Ireland and lasting over three hours, it remains the most rarefied of all Kubrick's films and something of a test case for his admirers. Its disappointing reception set the pattern for his later work: initial bafflement and dismissal followed some time later by favourable re-evaluation. *The Shining*, adapted from Stephen King's horror best-seller, was widely derided for Jack Nicholson's leering performance, but it is both a genuinely frightening ghost story and one of the screen's most intensely evocative portraits of madness. The first third of *Full Metal Jacket*, set in a Marines' training camp, is its companion piece in theme and style: in both films, incarceration in a gleaming human rat-trap leads to psychosis and murder. Subsequent scenes in Vietnam reveal that Kubrick's main concern is with the brutal rituals, language and sexual repression of the military ethos rather than the war's political issues.

Both these films combine elements of Surrealism and Expressionism with the precisely calculated camera movements and wide-angle, deep-space images characteristic of all Kubrick's work, including his last film, *Eyes Wide Shut*. An erotic melodrama with the narrative logic of a dream and a slow, hypnotic rhythm that alienated most critics as much as the public, it is surely now due for rediscovery. Kubrick died suddenly on 7 March 1999 soon after delivering its final cut. A long-planned collaboration with Steven Spielberg subsequently emerged as *A.I. Artificial Intelligence* (2001), predictably displaying more of Spielberg's authorship than Kubrick's.

(Sheldon Hall)

BIBLIOGRAPHY: Baxter, John, *Stanley Kubrick: A Biography* (London: HarperCollins, 1997); Kagan, Norman, *The Cinema of Stanley Kubrick* (New York: Continuum, 1994); LoBrutto, Vincent, *Stanley Kubrick: A Biography* (London: Faber and Faber, 1998); Phillips, Gene D. (ed.), *Stanley Kubrick: Interviews* (Jackson: University Press of Mississippi, 2001); *Sight and Sound*, Sept. 1999 (special issue on Kubrick); Walker, Alexander, Sybil Taylor and Ulrich Ruchti, *Stanley Kubrick, Director: A Visual Analysis* (London: Weidenfeld & Nicolson, 1999).

FILMOGRAPHY: In the US: *Day of the Fight* (doc. short); *Flying Padre* (doc. short) (1951); *The Seafarers* (doc. short); *Fear and Desire* (1953); *Killer's Kiss* (1955); *The Killing* (1956); *Paths of Glory* (1957); *Spartacus* (1960).

In the UK: *Lolita* (1961); *Dr Strangelove or: How I Learned to Stop Worrying and Love the Bomb* (1963); *2001: A Space Odyssey* (1968); *A Clockwork Orange* (1971); *Barry Lyndon* (1975); *The Shining* (1980); *Full Metal Jacket* (1987); *Eyes Wide Shut* (1999).

KUREISHI, Hanif (1954–)

Hanif Kureishi was born on 5 December 1954 in Bromley, on the outskirts of London. His first play was produced at the Royal Court Theatre Upstairs in 1976 and he went on to become the Royal Court's writer-in-residence. He began writing for film in 1985 with the acclaimed *My Beautiful Laundrette* (Stephen Frears, 1985), followed by *Sammy and Rosie Get Laid* (Stephen Frears, 1987), *London Kills Me* (1991), *My Son the Fanatic* (Udayan Prasad, 1997), *Mauvaise Passe/The Escort* (Michel Blanc, 1999) and *The Mother* (Roger Michell, 2003). He adapted his novel *The Buddha of Suburbia* for a BBC television series (directed by Roger Michell) in 1993; *Intimacy* (Patrice Chereau, 2000) was based on a novel by Kureishi, although he did not write the screenplay.

Kureishi's only foray into directing is *London Kills Me*, where Clint (Justin Chadwick), a young drug dealer tries to leave dealing behind in search of a more useful life. Unlike much of Kureishi's work, the film does not foreground questions of racial identity, though Clint, like Parvez and Farid in *My Son the Fanatic*, and Karim in *The Buddha of Suburbia*, is trying to 'grow up', and work out who he is and what his place in society might be. Kureishi dwells interestingly on run-down houses, backstreets, wastelands and markets, which are presented as warmer and more human than the cold, glassed-in environment of the restaurant in which Clint works to achieve respectability, but his handling of pace and character is uncertain.

Critical opinion of *London Kills Me* was generally low, pointing out that bored and disillusioned drug addicts are not inherently interesting protagonists and that the film 'fails because it has precious little to say about characters who have precious little to say' (Romney, p. 31). Certainly it is a much less original and stimulating debut than *My Beautiful Laundrette*. Kureishi's continuing success as a writer makes it unlikely that he will repeat the experiment of directing his own work rather than seeking the collaboration of his friends Stephen Frears and Roger Michell.

(Sarah Cardwell)

BIBLIOGRAPHY: Dodd, Philip, 'Requiem for a Rave', *Sight and Sound*, Sept. 1991, pp. 9–13; Moore-Gilbert, Bart, *Hanif Kureishi* (Manchester: Manchester University Press, 2001); Romney, Jonathan, 'The Sound of Silence', *New Statesman and Society*, 13 Dec. 1991, pp. 30–1.

FILMOGRAPHY: *London Kills Me* (1991).

KWIETNIOWSKI, Richard (1957–)

Richard Kwietniowski, the son of a Polish violinist, was born in London on 17 March 1957, and studied at the universities of Kent (at Canterbury) and California (at Berkeley). He received no formal training in film-making, but learned on the job in numerous shorts and contributions to Channel 4's *Out* series in the late 1980s and early 90s, all reflecting his own experience of being homosexual and feeling an outsider. *Next Week's Rent* (1986), a training project made for the Bristol Film and Video Workshop, was about growing up gay in Bristol; *Alfalfa* (1987) spelled out a gay alphabet, while *Girls in Boy Bars* (1989), one of his television contributions, visited a Newcastle drag bar. Greater fame and visual advances were achieved in quirky interpretations of gay classics and icons. In *The Ballad of Reading Gaol* (1988), Quentin Crisp narrated Oscar Wilde's poem to a parade of homoerotic images; *Proust's Favourite Fantasy* (1991) spent two curious minutes with a hotel room, a gendarme and a chicken. But it was the wordless, eighteen-minute *Flames of Passion* (1989), inspired by Noël Coward and David Lean's *Brief Encounter* (1945), that put Kwietniowski on the map. Stylish homage is paid to the original film's externals: the high-contrast black-and-white photography; the station setting; the plangent classical music. But the participants in this updated variation are male, and the erotic appeal of repressed feelings is pushed far further than Coward's period and temperament allowed.

Kwietniowski pursued related themes in his debut feature, the Anglo-Canadian *Love and Death on Long Island*, an entertaining, fastidiously handled journey through repression and self-knowledge, based on Gilbert Adair's novel. As in Thomas Mann's novella *Death in Venice*, infatuation reaches across huge differences in age and culture. A reclusive British author untainted by the twentieth century chances upon an American teen movie, falls hopelessly in love with its male hunk and strikes out for Long Island to make his new dream come true. Former television heart-throb Jason Priestley gives creditable support to John Hurt's beguiling performance as the bemused back number suddenly enchanted by popular culture. Narrative power lessens as the action advances in America, and the space allowed for showing real feelings is limited; but its gentle playfulness won the film numerous friends, along with a belated 'Most Promising Newcomer' award for Kwietniowski at the British Academy Awards.

Problems in financing projects restricted further progress until another Canadian co-production *Owning Mahowny* (2003), the true story of a mild-mannered bank manager addicted to gambling who defrauds his employer of over $10 million. The film confirmed Kwietniowski's interest in transcendence, 'secret outsiders' and narratives propelling private individuals into the glare of public scrutiny, though its distant demeanour and clinical visual surface helped it find only a limited audience.

(Geoff Brown and Alan Burton)

BIBLIOGRAPHY: Bruzzi, Stella, 'Two Sisters, the Fogey, the Priest and His Lover: Sexual Plurality in 1990s British Cinema', in Robert Murphy (ed.), *British Cinema of the 90s* (London: BFI, 2000); Chaw, Walter, 'Love, Death & Gambling', <www.filmfreakcentral.net/notes/rkwietniowskiinterview.htm> (2003); Kemp, Philip, 'Love and Death on Long Island', *Sight and Sound*, July 1998, pp. 45–6.

FILMOGRAPHY: *Next Week's Rent* (1986); *Alfalfa* (short, 1987); *The Ballad of Reading Gaol* (short, 1988); *Girls in Boy Bars* (short); *Flames of Passion* (short) (1989); *Proust's Favourite Fantasy* (short); *The Cost of Love* (short) (1991); *Actions Speak Louder than Words* (short, 1992); *Love and Death on Long Island* (UK/Can, 1997); *Owning Mahowny* (Can/UK, 2003).

LAB KY MO (1970–)

Lab Ky Mo was born into a Chinese family in Ireland. After studying fine art at St Martin's School of Art in London he won a screenwriting fellowship to California State University Film School in Long Beach, where he made the short *Pablo's Ironing Board*. Other shorts followed, including *Three Miles from China*, shot in Hong Kong. He worked as an assistant director on Frances-Anne Solomon's *Peggy Su!* (1997), a television film set among the Chinese community in Liverpool, and made his own feature debut with the scurrilous black comedy *9 Dead Gay Guys*. Two young Irishmen – Glen Mulhern and Brendan Mackey – explore a heavily caricatured gay scene in London, gaining riches, but only after involvement in a plethora of murders. Though regarded by some critics as crude and offensive, the film has been well received at gay and lesbian film festivals, and its exuberant grotesquerie seems likely to ensure cult status. Lab Ky Mo has subsequently been kept busy making commercials.

(Robert Murphy)

BIBLIOGRAPHY: Richardson, Jay, 'Interview with Lab Ky Mo', <www.futuremovies.co.uk>.

FILMOGRAPHY: *9 Dead Gay Guys* (2003).

LACHMAN, Harry (1886–1975)

Among the new film-making intake hired by British International Pictures in 1927, the American Harry Lachman had a unique bohemian background. Born in La Salle, Illinois, on 29 June 1886, he concentrated initially on painting, attending the Chicago Art Institute and taking lessons from Charles Collet in Paris, where he lived from 1911. His landscape canvases in Post-Impressionist style were exhibited and acquired by museums; he also worked as a portrait photographer, under the name Havrah. Cinema beckoned in 1922, when he began working as an assistant and set designer for the director Rex Ingram at the Nice studios. He designed the faun dance in Ingram's *The Magician* (1925), and helped inspire Michael Powell, a younger Ingram employee, with a taste for flamboyant visual cinema. In Paris, Matisse introduced Lachman to a Chinese opera singer, Jue Quon Tai, who became his wife.

BIP hired Lachman as a technical supervisor on the basis of his *Travelaughs*, a series of larkish two-reel comedies made in Nice after he parted from Ingram. After directing a farce, *Weekend Wives*, he was given a prestige project, an adaptation of Thomas Hardy's *Under the Greenwood Tree*. Begun in the autumn of 1928 as a silent, the production was relaunched as a talkie the following summer. Lachman shouldered the task well, keeping the camera as mobile as possible, making the most of sound effects and the rustic characters' music-making. To Hugh Castle in *Close Up*, a magazine usually fiercely critical of home-grown product, the film showed 'perhaps the best direction yet produced from a British studio' (Castle, p. 288).

In his autobiography, *A Life in Movies*, Powell pitched Lachman's qualities even higher: 'If he had stayed in Europe, Harry would have become one of the Masters. His individuality was stamped on every composition in his films. He followed no-one. He blazed his own trail' (Powell, pp. 156–7). But as BIP's ambitions withered, any trail that Lachman blazed was confined to play adaptations and other entertainment fodder. They were often well received by the trade – *The Outsider*, a darker-toned drama about an unqualified osteopath and a surgeon's paralysed daughter, proved particularly popular – but few prints of Lachman's British films have survived. In 1931 he spread his wings in Paris, working mostly for Films Paramount, where he formed a fruitful collaboration with the cameraman Rudolph Maté; *Mistigri* (1931) and *La Couturière de Luneville* (1932), both featuring Madeleine Renaud, were big local successes.

By now Lachman's ability to squeeze the best from assignments had attracted Hollywood's attention. After returning to Britain to direct three quota productions for Paramount British, he was summoned by Fox to California in the summer of 1932. He became one of their contract directors; even Shirley Temple passed through his hands (*Baby Take a Bow*, 1934), though greater opportunities arose with the Spencer Tracy vehicle *Dante's Inferno* (1935). In the course of a prosaic modern morality tale, Lachman and Maté created a ten-minute *tour de force* with a boiling presentation of Hell's torments (shaped by designer Ben Carré with an obvious eye to Gustave Doré's illustrations). In no other film could Lachman orchestrate similar wonders; least of all in Laurel and Hardy's *Our Relations*, or in his final British film, *They Came by Night*, a slight but amusing thriller starring Will Fyffe and Phyllis Calvert, made in the summer of 1939.

Eventually Lachman's relationship with Fox soured, and he left the studio in 1942 after making the horror film *Dr Renaud's Secret*. He withdrew from cinema, leaving behind a gaudy reputation and more promise than achievement. Afterwards he worked in the antiques business and returned to his first love, painting. He died in Los Angeles on 20 March 1975.

(Geoff Brown)

BIBLIOGRAPHY: Castle, Hugh, 'Lachman and Others', *Close Up*, Oct. 1929, pp. 285–93; Powell, Michael, *A Life in Movies* (London: Heinemann, 1986).

FILMOGRAPHY (UK only): *Weekend Wives* (1928); *Under the Greenwood Tree* (US: *The Greenwood Tree*, 1929); *The Compulsory Husband* (co-dir. Monty Banks); *Song of Soho*; *The Yellow Mask* (1930); *The Love Habit*; *The Outsider* (1931); *Aren't We All?*; *Down Our Street*; *Insult* (1932); *They Came by Night* (1940).

LAMAC, Karel (1897–1952)

Karel Lamac was born in Prague on 27 January 1897. He studied chemistry but entered the film industry, shooting reportage from the front for newsreel companies during the First World War. In 1918 he turned to acting; the following year he directed himself in a melodrama made with Jan S. Kolár, *Akord smrti*, launching a career that eventually encompassed over a hundred films, made throughout Europe. In some films he was teamed with the actress Anny Ondráková (later Ondra); the couple subsequently married, and formed a production partnership with the cine-photographer Otto Heller; together they made a string of routine films, before Lamac turned to musicals starring the singers Martha Eggerth and Jan Kiepura. He worked in Russia, France, Germany and Czechoslovakia until 1938, when the political crisis brought him to England where he served as a captain in the Czech Air Force.

Lamac directed three films in Britain. *Schweik's New Adventures* was a low-budget attempt to revive Jaroslav Hasek's comic hero Schweik as an anti-Nazi saboteur; Lloyd Pearson makes a good stab at Schweik, and there is an early appearance by Richard Attenborough as a patriotic railway worker, but the film is let down by a weak script and poor production values. *They Met in the Dark*, produced with backing from J. Arthur Rank, is a much more ambitious affair. It is hampered by an over-convoluted plot and the misguided attempt to push sweet but shallow Joyce Howard into a starring role, but the cast headed by James Mason is otherwise strong – Tom Walls and Karel Stepanek make splendid villains – and Otto Heller's lighting is superbly atmospheric. *It Happened One Sunday* is a blandly pleasant film based on a play by Frank Harvey. After the war, Lamac directed films in France and Germany. He died in Hamburg after a heart attack on 2 August 1952.

(Kevin Gough-Yates)

BIBLIOGRAPHY: Dewey, Langdon, 'Czechoslovakia: Silence into Sound', *Film* [British Federation of Film Societies] no. 60, 1970, pp. 4–7; Hrbas, Jiri, 'Karel Lamac', *Film a Doba* vol. 19 no. 12, Dec. 1973, pp. 626-39.

FILMOGRAPHY (UK only): *They Met in the Dark*; *Schweik's New Adventures* (US: *It Started at Midnight*) (1943); *It Happened One Sunday* (1944).

LANE, Lupino (1892–1959)

Lupino Lane – born Henry William George Lupino in London on 16 June 1892 – worked in Hollywood and directed a stream of British features in the early 1930s. Yet he remained tied to the family tradition of popular live entertainment. His father's family, originally Luppino, was of Italian origin, first recorded in London in 1642 performing at St Bartholomew's Fair; his mother came from another long-established theatrical family, the Lanes. In his practical handbook *How to Become a Comedian* Lane listed the training given by one family generation to another; skills included acrobatics, dancing, acting, boxing, juggling, mime and all aspects of theatrical production. Lane himself acted in pantomime and variety from the age of four, becoming renowned for his precision timing and extraordinarily flexible body.

By 1915 he was appearing on Britain's cinema screens in short comedies. W. P. Kellino is the only recorded director's name, but Lane might well have taken control of some films himself. In the 'Kinekature Komedies' of 1918, his gag repertoire expanded with photographic effects and the use of distorting mirrors – an interest further developed in his American shorts of the 1920s. The two-reelers were crammed with physical antics, camera tricks and movie parodies, but lacked a strong comic personality at their centre. He began to direct the films themselves in 1928, devising a pseudonym, Henry W. George, from his own birth name.

The talkie revolution curtailed Lane's career in shorts, but he found roles in early Hollywood musicals, notably in Lubitsch's *The Love Parade* (1929). Early in 1930 he returned to England for the stage musical *Silver Wings*. One month after the run closed in July, Lane began shooting his first British feature, *No Lady*. Eleven others followed within five years, produced chiefly for British International Pictures. Five featured himself in the starring role; two featured his cousin Stanley Lupino. Lane's brother Wallace Lupino regularly assumed the roles of stooge and villain.

Lane's Hollywood experience was widely heralded in the industry, not least by Lane himself. Yet the nature of his films was far more determined by his years on the English stage. In 1915, reviewing *His Cooling Courtship*, one of his earliest recorded shorts, the *Kinematograph Monthly Film Record* noted the pile-up of physical antics, the plot's scantiness and the unhelpful positioning of the camera (quoted in Low, 1950, p. 163). Similar comments could be made about his 1930s' features, slackly edited, the camera assuming the head-on position of a spectator in the theatre stalls. West End audiences paid little mind to the films. But provincial cinemas lapped them up, and in 1932 BIP thought sufficiently of Lane's abilities to assign him to *The Maid of the Mountains*, a popular stage musical given a budget to match. Cinematically ponderous, the film still satisfied general audiences.

Unhappy with BIP's developing tendency to ape American fashions, and missing the theatre's live audiences, Lane left the company in 1933 with the unfulfilled hopes of making the cinema equivalent of an English pantomime. He found no takers elsewhere. When he returned to film-making the following year, shrouded under his directing pseudonym, the films were unambitious, shoddy and ill-advised. But on the stage he flourished. The musical *Me and My Girl* (1937), featuring Lane as Bill Snibson, the cockney who finds himself a duke, sparked a dance craze (the Lambeth Walk) and kept him busy for 1,646 performances. In 1939 he appeared in Albert de Courville's limp film version; thereafter he left cinema behind. Lupino Lane died in London on 10 November 1959.

(Geoff Brown)

BIBLIOGRAPHY: Kerr, Walter, *The Silent Clowns* (New York: Alfred A. Knopf, 1975); Lane, Lupino, *How to Become a Comedian* (London: Frederick Muller, 1945); Low, Rachael, *The History of the British Film 1914–1918* (London: George Allen & Unwin, 1950); Low, Rachael, *Film Making in 1930s Britain* (London: George Allen & Unwin, 1985); Roberts, Richard M., 'Lupino Lane: Music Hall Comedian', *Classic Images* no. 256, Oct. 1996, pp. 22–5; White, James Dillon, *Born to Star: The Lupino Lane Story* (London: Heinemann, 1957).

FILMOGRAPHY: Shorts, as Henry W. George: *Fandango* (US); *Hectic Days* (US); *Roaming Romeo* (US); *Pirates Beware* (US); *Fisticuffs* (US); *Be My King* (US) (1928); *Only Me* (US); *Summer Saps* (US); *Ship Mates* (US); *Good-Night Nurse* (US); *Battling Sisters* (US); *Buying a Gun* (US); *Joyland* (US); *Purely Circumstantial* (US) (1929). Features: *No Lady*; *Never Trouble Trouble*; *Love Lies*; *The Love Race* (co-dir. Pat Morton) (1931); *The Innocents of Chicago* (US: *Why Saps Leave Home*); *Old Spanish Customers*; *The Maid of the Mountains* (1932); *Letting in the Sunshine*; *Oh, What a Duchess!* (aka *My Old Duchess*) (1933); *Who's Your Father?* (as Henry W. George); *The Deputy Drummer* (as Henry W. George); *Trust the Navy* (as Henry W. George) (1935).

LANGLEY, Noel (1911–1980)

Noel Langley, a talented scriptwriter most famous for his work adapting L. Frank Baum's *The Wizard of Oz*, was born in Durban, South Africa, on 25 December 1911. In the early 1930s he came to England, where he enjoyed some success as a playwright and contributed to the scripts of Walter Forde's melodrama *King of the Damned* (1936) and Andrew Marton's *The Secret of Stamboul* (1936). In 1938 one of his plays, *Queer Cargo* (Harold D. Schuster), was adapted for the screen, but by this time Langley was in Hollywood. His rewrite of the rejected script for the Jeanette Macdonald/Nelson Eddy musical *Maytime* (Robert Z. Leonard, 1937) won approval, and he was retained by MGM to work on *The Wizard of Oz* (Victor Fleming, 1939).

After the war Langley returned to Britain, where he had a huge stage success with *Edward, My Son*, a play written in collaboration with Robert Morley (it was filmed by George Cukor for MGM in 1949). Langley also re-established himself as a leading screenwriter, creatively adapting Jackson Budd's slim novel *A Convict Has Escaped* into the mordantly witty film noir *They Made Me a Fugitive* (Alberto Cavalcanti, 1947). Other interesting script assignments included W. Lee Wilder's *The Vicious Circle* (US, 1948), *Cardboard Cavalier* (1949), swansong for both director Water Forde and star Sid Field, and two Anglo-Italian co-productions: *Quel bandito sono io!/Her Favourite Husband* (Mario Soldati, 1950) and *Due mogli sono troppe/Honeymoon Deferred* (Mario Camerini, 1951).

In the early 1950s Langley teamed up with producer George Minter on two literary adaptations: *Tom Brown's Schooldays* (Gordon Parry, 1951) and *Scrooge* (Brian Desmond Hurst, 1951); both were successful and Langley was tempted to direct *The Pickwick Papers* (1952) himself. The resulting film lacks dramatic tension but its geniality and the presence of familiar, likeable faces as well-known Dickensian characters served it well. Langley's inadequacies as a director were much more apparent in *Our Girl Friday*, a tedious and contrived romantic comedy packed with cardboard characters (most embarrassingly Kenneth More's stage Irishman and Joan Collins' spoiled rich girl). *Svengali*, Langley's last British film, proved more satisfying: a gripping, if stolidly stage-bound, story with a barnstorming performance from Donald Wolfit as the evil maestro.

By 1955 Langley had had enough of Britain. Complaining that he was 'assessed as an alien influence not welcome in the theatre or British Broadcasting Corporation and not considered essential to film production' (Wiseman), he sold his cottage in Cornwall, removed his five children from their English schools and moved to Hollywood. His new start began promisingly with *The Search for Bridey Murphy* (1956), a strange and ambitious film that continued Langley's exploration of the issues around hypnosis in a more modern setting than *Svengali*; but it was not a commercial success. After a handful of scriptwriting assignments, including the bizarre *Snow White and the Three Stooges* (Walter Lang, 1961), Langley turned to novel writing, most successfully with *The Loner* (1967). He died at his home in Desert Hot Springs, California, on 4 November 1980.

(Robert Murphy)

BIBLIOGRAPHY: Harper, Sue and Vincent Porter, *British Cinema of the 1950s: The Decline of Deference* (Oxford: Oxford University Press, 2003); Obituary, *Hollywood Reporter*, 12 Nov. 1980, p. 21; Obituary, *The Times*, 15 Nov. 1980; Wiseman, Thomas, 'Langley Going to Live in America', *Evening Standard*, 24 Feb. 1955.

FILMOGRAPHY (UK only): *The Pickwick Papers* (1952); *Our Girl Friday* (US: *The Adventures of Sadie*); *Svengali* (1954).

LARCHER, David (1942–)

David Larcher was born in London in 1942. He showed an early propensity for the avant-garde, acting as stills photographer on Peter Whitehead's *Wholly Communion* (1965) and Conrad Rooks' *Chappaqua* (1966), and was closely involved with the London Film-maker's Co-op, where he was able to experiment with optical effects in the Co-op's processing laboratory. Shorts were followed by an ambitious two-and-three-quarter-hour feature, *Mare's Tale* (1970), described by fellow avant-garde film-maker Steve Dwoskin as 'an epic film flight into an inner space . . . There is a face, your face, his face, a face that looks and slits into forms that form new forms, which we can discover once again as tiny monolithic monuments' (Dwoskin, p. 41). Five years later Larcher presented *The Monkey's Birthday*, a six-hour film based on his wanderings through Europe. Hendrik Henderson describes it as 'at once a diary of that voyage, a romanticisation of the quest implicit in the conceit of the wandering protagonist, and a universalisation of the quest beyond the individual protagonist' (Hendrikson). But with only traces of a narrative to hold it together, *The Monkey's Birthday* demanded too much from all but the most dedicated audiences; Larcher's suggestion that the film be divided and shown simultaneously on two projectors hardly made it easier to assimilate.

In the 1980s Larcher was involved in various projects for Channel 4, including *Spirit of Albion* (Richard Philpott, 1987), a sympathetic account of the Peace Convoy, a community of New

Age travellers who pursued an alternative nomadic lifestyle despite continual harassment. He also directed *E Etc.* (1988), a magical kaleidoscope exploring his concern with the fleeting traces of what has passed and the ways in which images can be captured. During the film, 'photographs, movie footage and mattes are churned into an electronic flux of grain, colour, distortion and vestigial images. The representation of processes seen earlier in the work are themselves processed and incorporated into ever more complex collages' (Hamlyn, p. 44). *E Etc.* was partly shot on video, and marked Larcher's transition to this cheaper and more malleable medium in which he continues to work.

Though hardly fashionable in the twenty-first-century world of slick deals and commercial art, Larcher's relentlessly experimental juxtaposition and manipulation of images represents a tradition of visual, non-narrative film-making too valuable to be allowed to wither away.
(Robert Murphy)

BIBLIOGRAPHY: 'Directory of UK Independent Film-Makers: David Larcher', *Cinema Rising* no.1, Apr. 1972, p. 7; Dwoskin, Steve, 'Mare's Tail', *Afterimage* no. 2, Autumn 1970, pp. 41–3; Hamlyn, Nicky, 'Film, Video, TV (1)', *Coil* nos 9/10, 2000, pp. 38–49; Hendrikson, Hendrik, 'Perspectives on British Avant-Garde Film', Hayward Gallery Exhibition Notes, Apr. 1977.

SELECTED FILMOGRAPHY: *Mare's Tail* (1970); *The Monkey's Birthday* (1975); *E Etc.* (1988); *Ich Tank* (1999).

LARRAZ, José R. (1929–)

José Ramón Larraz was born in Barcelona in 1929. He pursued a career as a fashion photographer until 1969 when he switched to film, producing and directing the low-budget Danish sex-thriller *Whirlpool*. Other Danish and Spanish-Italian productions followed. In 1971 he came to Britain to make *Deviation*, an unstable amalgam of sex, horror and violence that failed to find a British distributor. But Larraz enjoyed the experience of working in Britain – 'I am neurotic, like any good Latin and for me England is a big pill of Valium' – and he returned to make three interesting horror films. *Scream ... and Die!* suffers from a disjunction between Larraz's stylish visual effects and the ineffectually shallow characters of Derek Ford's tale about a model stalked by a murderer seeking help from the wrong man. *Symptoms*, which Larraz co-scripted himself, is more sophisticated and complex. Angela Pleasence may be a mad lesbian, but her mental disintegration is sympathetically observed and her murders chillingly effective.

Symptoms borrows themes and atmosphere from Polanski's *Repulsion* (1965); *Vampyres*, with its caravanning couple, lecherous businessman and sultry femmes fatales, seems more closely modelled on *Carry On Screaming* (Gerald Thomas, 1966). But Larraz takes his horror seriously and what begins in cliché becomes shocking and disturbing as opportunities for a safe escape to normality dwindle, and victims find that scepticism, sensitivity and manly virility afford no protection against the atavistic lesbian vampires. Loose ends and non-sequiturs bear witness to a pinched budget, but Larraz coaxes likeable performances from his anonymous cast and uses Harry Waxman's cinematography and James Kenelm Clarke's stark music to create a genuine sense of enchantment.

Unfortunately, *The Golden Lady*, a weak James Bond spoof, had none of the virtues of Larraz's British horrors, and his later films, such as the English-set *Los Ritos sexuales del diablo/Black Candles* (1980), blatantly tip over into exploitation.
(Robert Murphy)

BIBLIOGRAPHY: Falk, Quentin, 'Cutting the Costs for a Profitable Love Affair with Celluloid', *CinemaTV Today*, 20 Apr. 1974, p. 12.

FILMOGRAPHY (UK only): *Deviation* (1971); *Scream . . . and Die!* (aka *Psycho Sex Fiend/The House That Vanished*, 1973); *Symptoms* (aka *The Blood Virgin*, UK/Belg, 1974); *Vampyres* (1975); *The Golden Lady* (UK/HK, 1979).

LAUNDER, Frank (1906–1997)

Frank Launder and Sidney Gilliat formed one of the great partnerships of British cinema. As writers, directors and producers they provided intelligent commercial entertainment, and were especially successful with their thrillers and comedies. While sustaining a long and close working relationship, they each demonstrated personal preferences, although it would be wrong to attribute to them, collectively or singularly, any strong authorial identity. These were versatile film-makers with a pronounced common touch, who generally conceived films together, collaborated on scripts and handed over direction to the one most suited to the subject. Writing was a consistent part of Launder's career and he wrote for the stage and radio as well as for cinema. In 1937 the pair had helped to found the Screenwriters' Association and Launder became its President in 1946.

Frank Sydney Launder was born in Hitchin, Hertfordshire, on 28 January 1906. He was educated in Brighton, began employment in the office of the Official Receiver of Bankruptcy and acted with the Brighton Repertory Company. A play he wrote for the company was well enough received to gain him entry to the scenario department of British International Pictures at Elstree in 1928. Throughout the 1930s Launder fulfilled a variety of writing jobs at British studios and on more than one occasion his path crossed with Gilliat's. Their script for Hitchcock's *The Lady Vanishes* (1938), their third together, established the partnership as a top writing team and their reputation was consolidated with two films written for Carol Reed: *Night Train to Munich* (1940) and *The Young Mr Pitt* (1942). The wartime propaganda short *Partners in Crime* (1942) provided them with the opportunity to co-direct, and was followed in 1943 by their first feature, *Millions Like Us*. The film stood out as a home-front war film detailing the conscription of women into an armaments factory, and was a considerable commercial and critical success. However, the film-makers determined not to co-direct again as they felt that having two directors on the set impeded and confused the actors.

After making his first solo feature, *Two Thousand Women* (1944), set in France in an internment camp for women, Laun-

der reunited with Gilliat to set up Individual Pictures, one of a number of production concerns that made films under the Independent Producers umbrella for J. Arthur Rank. Individual was the first of a succession of production companies established by the team to give themselves control over their films. The late 1940s proved a fruitful period: Launder's *The Blue Lagoon* (1948), with its Technicolor photography, exotic Pacific island locations and good-looking young stars Jean Simmons and Donald Houston, was particularly popular in austerity-racked Britain.

Launder's films tended to focus on female characters. After the factory workers of *Millions Like Us* and the cross-section of types in *Two Thousand Women*, he provided an intriguing role for Deborah Kerr as an Irish spy in *I See a Dark Stranger* (1946), and a quintessentially English eccentric for Margaret Rutherford to play in *The Happiest Days of Your Life* (1950). Throughout the 1950s he shepherded the rampaging schoolgirls of the *St Trinian's* films, contrasting their burgeoning sexuality with the various repressions, inhibitions and oddities of their teachers and Joyce Grenfell's policewoman Ruby Gates. Launder also showed a penchant for Celtic subjects such as *Captain Boycott* (1947), which dealt with the mid-nineteenth-century Irish land question, and the two Scottish comedies *Geordie* (1955) and *The Bridal Path* (1959). His comedies provided defining roles for some of Britain's leading character performers: Rutherford, Grenfell, and particularly Alastair Sim, whose dour eccentricity was employed effectively in *The Happiest Days of Your Life*, *Folly to Be Wise* and the next two *St Trinian's* films.

Between 1958 and 1972 Launder and Gilliat devoted much of their energy to executive duties at British Lion Films. This resulted in a reduced output of personal productions and a decline in the quality of those films they did direct. The formula of the *St Trinian's* comedies wore increasingly thin, and with the anachronistic service comedy *Joey Boy* (1965) Launder showed himself to be out of touch with the new trends in British cinema. He shared direction with Gilliat on the mediocre but commercially successful *The Great St Trinian's Train Robbery* in 1966, but moved to France in the 1970s, only returning to direct *The Wildcats of St Trinian's* in 1980. It was a depressingly limp addendum to the series and performed poorly at the box office. More useful and entertaining were the brief introductions Launder and Gilliat made for a retrospective of their films on Channel 4 in 1984. Frank Launder died in Monte Carlo on 23 February 1997.

(Alan Burton)

BIBLIOGRAPHY: Babington, Bruce, *Launder and Gilliat* (Manchester: Manchester University Press, 2002); Brown, Geoff, *Launder and Gilliat* (London: BFI, 1977); Brown, Geoff, *National Film Theatre Booklet*, Nov./Dec. 1977; Durgnat, Raymond, *A Mirror for England* (London: Faber and Faber, 1970); 'Frank Launder' *Film Dope* no. 33, Nov. 1985, pp. 26–7; Landy, Marcia, *British Genres* (Princeton, NJ: Princeton University Press, 1991).

FILMOGRAPHY: *Partners in Crime* (short, co-dir. Sidney Gilliat, 1942); *Millions Like Us* (co-dir. Sidney Gilliat, 1943); *Two Thousand Women* (1944); *I See a Dark Stranger* (1946); *Captain Boycott* (1947); *The Blue Lagoon* (1948); *The Happiest Days of Your Life* (1950); *Lady Godiva Rides Again* (1951); *Folly to Be Wise* (1952); *The Belles of St Trinian's* (1954); *Geordie* (1955); *Blue Murder at St Trinian's* (1957); *The Bridal Path* (1959); *The Pure Hell of St Trinian's* (1960); *Joey Boy* (1965); *The Great St Trinian's Train Robbery* (co-dir. Sidney Gilliat, 1966); *The Wildcats of St Trinian's* (1980).

LAW, Michael (1917–2001)

Michael Law's obituarist in the *Daily Telegraph* bluntly declared, 'He was an accomplished film-maker, but, by common consent, his chief interest was women.' His bohemian activities in 1950s' Soho, well documented in autobiographies, belie his family background: Michael Evelyn Murray Law, born on 11 October 1917 in Salisbury, was the son of a cathedral clergyman. Trained in painting at Chelsea Polytechnic, he began working in documentary and publicity films in the late 1930s. After navy service and a period with the Admiralty Film Unit, he joined Richard Massingham's Public Relationship Films in 1944 and became his employer's most trusted director. The slate included comic information trailers like *Pedestrian Crossing*; the overly whimsical gas publicity film *Facts and Fancies*; and the starkly dramatic warning *Playing with Fire*. There were also two idiosyncratic comedies: *The Cure*, a boisterous joke at the expense of Massingham's former profession, medicine; and the deliciously mordant *What a Life!*, a parody of post-war gloom. The one feature Law directed, the crime drama *The Six Men* (1951), offered few chances for quirks, though there were far worse supporting

features. Thereafter, in between pubs and clubs, Law worked in television and documentaries, finding particular success with commercials. He died in London on 2 December 2001.
(Geoff Brown)

BIBLIOGRAPHY: 'Michael Law: Film-Maker and Denizen of Soho Whose Chief Interest Was Women', *Daily Telegraph*, 20 Dec. 2001, p. 23.

FILMOGRAPHY: Selected shorts: *Letter from Home*; *Typing Technique* (1945); *Greensleeves*; *Playing in the Road*; *'An Englishman's Home . . .'* (1946); *Playing with Fire*; *How to Use the Telephone* (1947); *Thirty Miles an Hour*, *Pedestrian Crossing*; *Women in Industry*; *What a Life!* (1948); *The Cure* (co-dir. Richard Massingham) (1950); *Facts and Fancies* (1951); *Fire-Fighting at Naval Air Stations* (1952); *The Michael Holliday Show* (1956); *The Tyrex Story* (1962).
Feature: *The Six Men* (1951).

LAWRENCE, Quentin (1920–1979)

Nathaniel Quentin Lawrence was born in Gravesend, Kent, on 6 November 1920. He entered the film industry in 1946 and moved into television in the mid-1950s, where his directorial assignments ranged from *Small Pox*, a BBC drama-documentary about the 1953 smallpox outbreak, to the ATV science-fiction serials *The Strange World of Planet X* (1956) and *The Trollenberg Terror* (1956). Gilbert Gunn was assigned the task of bringing *The Strange World of Planet X* to the big screen, but Lawrence was allowed to make a modestly effective cinema debut with *The Trollenberg Terror* for Baker and Berman's Tempean Films.

Much more impressive was his next cinema venture, *Cash on Demand*, an atypical Hammer film based on *The Gold Inside*, a television play by Jacques Gillies, which Lawrence had directed for ATV in 1960. It is set almost entirely inside a provincial bank, presided over by a thin-lipped martinet (Peter Cushing at his subtlest) who is subjected to a day of terror at the hands of a suave criminal (André Morell) and emerges a changed and shaken man. The ending is contrived, but the rest is a model of economical film-making, transcending its meagre budget and endowing the story's everyday ambience with a reality uncommon in second features.

Unfortunately Lawrence blew his chances of major-league directing with *The Man Who Finally Died*, a lugubrious, snail-paced melodrama that even an exceptionally strong cast – Stanley Baker, Mai Zetterling, Eric Portman, Nigel Green – could not animate. Its failure meant that Lawrence was reduced to directing two unexceptional Edgar Wallace supporting features – *Playback* and *We Shall See* – and *The Secret of Blood Island*, a weak and belated sequel to Val Guest's grim *The Camp on Blood Island* (1958). With British actors playing Japanese officers and Barbara Shelley as a 'secret agent' passed off as a man, it makes an unconvincing prisoner-of-war camp drama.

Lawrence returned to television, where he directed episodes of serials including *The Baron* (1966) and *Doomwatch* (1970). He spent most of the 1970s working for Granada on their long-running series *Coronation Street* and *Crown Court*. His last assignment, an adaptation of Turgenev's *A Month in the Country* for American television, only saw the light of day in 1986, seven years after his death in Halifax, Yorkshire, on 9 March 1979.
(Brian McFarlane)

BIBLIOGRAPHY: Obituary, *Film and TV Technician*, June 1979, p. 19; Obituary, *International Film Collector*, 26 June 1979, p. 15; Obituary, *Screen International*, 24 Mar. 1979, p. 22.

FILMOGRAPHY: *The Trollenberg Terror* (US: *The Crawling Eye*, 1958); *Cash on Demand* (1961); *The Man Who Finally Died*; *Playback* (1962); *We Shall See* (1964); *The Secret of Blood Island* (1964).

LEACOCK, Philip (1917–1990)

Philip David Charles Leacock was born in London on 8 October 1917, and like his younger brother, the future documentary film-maker Richard Leacock, spent his childhood in the Canary Islands and at the progressive English boarding school, Bedales (where he was encouraged to take an interest in photography). At seventeen, he worked briefly as an assistant to his brother-in-law, Harold Lowenstein, on his documentary *Out to Play* (1936), before going to Spain to help Thorold Dickinson on his pro-Republican *Behind the Spanish Lines* and *Spanish ABC* (both 1938).

Leacock spent most of the Second World War with the Army Kinematograph Service and joined the Crown Film Unit after being demobbed. Story documentaries such as *Life in Her Hands*, which makes good use of Kathleen Byron and Bernadette O'Farrell, and *Out of True*, with Jane Hylton and Muriel Pavlow, opened the way to feature films. In 1952 John Grierson asked Leacock to direct a film about a Scottish coal-mining disaster for the NFFC-backed company, Group 3. Leacock instilled a strong documentary quality into *The Brave Don't Cry*, despite the fact that it was filmed largely in a studio, but he also showed a talent for dramatic storytelling and the film appealed to both audiences and critics.

The success of *The Brave Don't Cry* led to a contract with the Rank Organisation at Pinewood, where Leacock's first film was *Appointment in London*, with Dirk Bogarde as a war-weary wing commander struggling to maintain morale amid the heavy losses of the Second World War bombing campaign. Though the action moves along stiffly, Leacock cleverly integrates documentary footage of a large-scale night bombing raid to build to an exciting climax. In his next film, *The Kidnappers*, a beautifully shot and deeply moving story of two orphans living in turn-of-the-century Nova Scotia who, starved of affection, 'adopt' a baby, Leacock revealed his talent for getting superb performances from children. There followed a series of films that feature children but also explore complex social and moral issues – *Escapade*, in which the children of an anti-war campaigner decide to make their own anti-war protest; *The Spanish Gardener*, which follows a father's realisation that he has been taking his thwarted ambitions out on his son; and *Innocent Sinners*, about the resilience of a neglected child who manages to find beauty in the bleakest of environments.

Leacock was then lured to America, where he made a handful of interesting films such as *Take a Giant Step*, which had a largely black cast and tackled racism. The audience for such socially committed films was a limited one, however, and Leacock returned to Britain to make *Reach for Glory*, his most disturbing film about children – this time not so innocent in their mirroring of the jingoism of their elders; *The War Lover*, with Steve McQueen as a psychopathic variant on the bomber commander played by Dirk Bogarde in *Appointment in London*; and *Tamahine*, a comedy with Nancy Kwan as an exotic South Sea Islander disrupting the placid environment of an English public school. None of the films were big box-office successes, and Leacock, perhaps feeling out of tune with Britain's burgeoning youth culture, went back to America where, as a talented and reliable director, he was able to work regularly in American television on series ranging from *Gunsmoke* to *The Waltons* to *Dynasty*; and on television films as different as the thriller *Key West* (1973), the comedy *The Wild Women of Chastity Gulch* (1982) and the acclaimed drama based on the Salem witchcraft trials, *Three Sovereigns for Sarah* (1985). He died of a collapsed lung on 14 July 1990 while on holiday in London.

Philip Leacock was an intelligent film-maker whose documentary training strongly influenced his approach to features – he felt it was always important to make the basis of what is going on as real as possible. But unlike many ex-documentary directors he was a sensitive director of actors. His concern with human relationships and values lent itself to small-scale drama, and made him an excellent television director. He brought an integrity and a sense of decency to his work, and his films, because they explore universal themes, remain as topical today as they were when they were made.

(Linda Wood)

BIBLIOGRAPHY: BECTU History Project, Stephen Peet, interview with Philip Leacock, tape held in the BFI National Library, London; Cole, Sidney and John Taylor, 'Philip Leacock: A Gentle Man', *Film and TV Technician*, Oct. 1990, p. 31; Salmi, Markku, 'Philip Leacock', *Film Dope* no. 33. Nov. 1985, pp. 39–41.

FILMOGRAPHY: Documentaries: *Kew Garden* (1937); *The Story of Wool*; *Letter from Aldershot* (co-dir. John Taylor); *Island People* (co-dir. John Taylor) (1940); *Rehabilitation*; *A Day in the Line* (1943); *Back to Service* (1944); *Pillar to Post*; *Deadly Lampshade*; *Sorting It Out* (1948); *Health* (co-dir. Richard Warren); *Television* (1950); *Life in Her Hands*; *Out of True*; *The Glassmakers*; *Festival in London* (1951); *Local Newspaper* (co-dir. Richard Warren, 1952).

Features: *Riders of the New Forest* (serial, 1946); *Mr Perrin and Mr Traill* (2nd unit dir., Lawrence Huntington, 1948); *The Brave Don't Cry* (1952); *Appointment in London*; *The Kidnappers* (aka *The Little Kidnappers*) (1953); *Escapade* (1955); *The Spanish Gardener* (1956); *High Tide at Noon* (1957); *Innocent Sinners*; *The Rabbit Trap* (US) (1958); *Take a Giant Step* (US, 1959); *Let No Man Write My Epitaph* (US); *Hand in Hand* (US); *Reach for Glory* (1961); *13 West Street* (US); *The War Lover* (1962); *Tamahine* (1963); *Adam's Woman* (US/Austral, 1969).

LEAN, David (1908–1991)

David Lean was born in the first decade of the twentieth century (25 March 1908, in Croydon, Surrey) and died in the last (16 April 1991, in London). With their focus on the lives of 'ordinary people', his earlier films reflect more of the sensibility of their times than did the dramatic landscapes, unorthodox heroes and extravagant *mise en scène* of the later epics. It is the epics, however, that made him an internationally significant film-maker.

Lean has often been called a great craftsman, and his films are notable for their meticulous attention to detail, shown in the careful composition of each frame, the precise and eloquent use of sound and music, and the nuanced performances drawn from each member of the cast. However, Lean's *mise en scène* moves beyond craftsmanship: the themes and concerns of each film are variously articulated through dialogue and plot, sound, colour, editing, music and lighting. If there seems to be too much eclecticism in Lean's oeuvre for the director to imprint a 'signature style', it is because his films are concerned with the integration of style and theme, with the expression of character, emotion, mood and the particularities of place and period. In this sense his most successful films attain a level of stylistic sophistication that guarantees their integrity as artworks.

Lean started his career in film in the late 1920s, as a clapper-boy, but soon found his *métier* in the cutting rooms. He edited his first film, *The Night Porter* (Sewell Collins), in 1930 and by the middle of the decade had moved up from low-budget 'quota quickies' to prestigious productions including *As You Like It* (Paul Czinner, 1936) and *Pygmalion* (Anthony Asquith/Leslie Howard, 1938). In the early 1940s, when he cut Michael Powell's *49th Parallel* (1941) and *One of Our Aircraft Is Missing* (1942), he was regarded as the industry's top editor, poised to make the leap into the director's chair. After gaining experience directing sections of *Major Barbara* (Gabriel Pascal, 1941), he agreed to collaborate with Noël Coward on *In Which We Serve* (1942) – provided he was given equal billing as co-director. In fact he largely directed it single-handed. The film follows the crew of a destroyer who reminisce (in flashback) about their loved ones at home as they cling to a raft and wait for rescue. It captures the intricate hierarchy that exists between crew members and, beyond the particular, between classes, and upholds values of duty, loyalty and responsibility over the pursuit of personal happiness and gain.

This Happy Breed (1944), the first of three further collaborations with Coward, continued this theme. The film is set almost entirely in the house inhabited by the lower-middle-class Gibbons family in the period between the two world wars. The use of delimited and confined space prioritises the everyday events of the household (births, weddings, deaths, children growing up, family conflicts and reunions) over larger historical events and developments. Through these daily conflicts and negotiations between parents and children, siblings and spouses, broader concerns with politics and class are explored.

Lean's next Coward adaptation was the strange, dark comedy *Blithe Spirit* (1945) – a stagy four-hander in which the ghost of Charles Condomine's former wife returns to the marital home and attempts to retrieve her husband from the bosom of his second wife. Lean was far less stage-bound with *Brief Encounter* (1945). Laura (Celia Johnson) and Alec (Trevor Howard), the two leading characters, meet at a train station and fall in love, despite being married to others. The film charts their progress from poignant rendezvous to the eventual demise of their doomed affair. The performances, dialogue and presentation of the story reflect the restraint of the two characters – a restraint both internally and externally created, for the film is much less interested in society's strictures than the rules and restrictions applied by the lovers themselves. The exploration of morality is central: values of fidelity, trust, loyalty and history are weighed against those of spontaneity, romance, truthfulness and freedom. This co-existence of vital passions alongside admirable restraint is a recurring motif in Lean's films.

While literary adaptations are frequently criticised in comparison to their source novels, Lean managed to impress critics with *Great Expectations* (1946), despite some ruthless editing of Dickens' narrative. John Bryan's production design and Guy Green's cinematography play a major part in the film's sophisticated and complex visual style; lighting, staging and sound summon a world that is always one stage removed from reality. *Oliver Twist* (1948), also made with Bryan and Green, was slightly less well received; in Britain Lean was accused of repeating himself, and in America the supposed anti-Semitism of Alec Guinness' portrayal of Fagin caused the film to become caught up in Jewish protests against British government policy in Palestine.

Between 1949 and 1952 Lean directed three films starring his third wife, Ann Todd. *The Passionate Friends* (1949), based on a novel by H. G. Wells, bore resemblances to *Brief Encounter* in its study of a married woman with romantic feelings for another man (again played by Trevor Howard). However, although carefully crafted and performed, *The Passionate Friends* lacks the earlier film's emotional intensity. In 1950 Lean directed *Madeleine*, a stark melodrama based on the murder case of Madeleine Smith, who was charged in the 1850s with poisoning her spurned lover. Todd, who had played the role in a play based on the same events, makes a superbly enigmatic heroine, concealing violent passions beneath her demure exterior. In *The Sound Barrier* (1952), Lean's first production for Alexander Korda, Todd's role is more conventional and less interesting, but expansive sky shots, impressive flight sequences and the topical subject of advances in aviation made the film commercially very successful.

One of Korda's best attributes was his gift for forging creative partnerships out of disparate talents. It was his idea that Lean direct an adaptation of Harold Brighouse's popular stage comedy *Hobson's Choice*, with Charles Laughton (by this time a well-established Hollywood star) as the overbearing boot-maker whose daughter rebels and marries one of his downtrodden employees. The collaboration worked well; Lean extracts from Laughton an ebullient and larger-than-life performance that avoids caricature and self-parody. Equally satisfying are the performances of Brenda de Banzie and John Mills as the disgruntled underlings whose faith in each other gives them the strength to take on the tyrannical boot-maker. Lean conjures up a style of 'comic expressionism', most obviously in the sequence where we see the world through the eyes of the drunken Hobson as he staggers home.

Summer Madness (1955), based on Arthur Laurents' play *The Time of the Cuckoo*, marked a change in Lean's work. One of Korda's last productions, it was shot in colour entirely on location in Venice, with backing from the American Lopert company. Katharine Hepburn was imported for the role of Jane Hudson, the American spinster who discovers new romance, friendship and greater self-confidence on her European holiday. Though more conventionally melodramatic than Lean's earlier work, the film remains visually impressive: the Venice locations prove integral rather than decorative, and Lean uses Jack Hildyard's expressive colour photography to reflect Jane's changing feelings and perceptions. Exotic settings, opulent colour and international casts were to characterise all Lean's subsequent films.

The Bridge on the River Kwai (1957) won Lean enormous commercial and critical success, along with his first Academy Award. The film concerns prisoners of war held in a Japanese camp, forced to build a bridge for the Burma railway. Beyond its scale and splendid photography, it is also impressive for its depiction of the relationship between the British officer Colonel Nicholson (Alec Guinness) and his Japanese counterpart, Colonel Saito (Sessue Hayakawa), both of them proud, stubborn men blindly obedient to their own rigid codes of honour.

The success of *The Bridge on the River Kwai* allowed Lean to plan the even more ambitious *Lawrence of Arabia* as his next venture. Earlier attempts had been made to film the life of First World War hero T. E. Lawrence, but they had foundered on opposition from the Lawrence family to anything that might tarnish his reputation. Michael Wilson and Robert Bolt's script managed to win approval, and Lean succeeds in presenting Lawrence (charismatically played by Peter O'Toole) as a morally ambiguous but definitively heroic character. *Lawrence of Arabia* brought Lean together with cinematographer Freddie Young, production designer John Box and writer Robert Bolt; they were to be his key collaborators in this last and most ambitious phase of his career.

Lawrence of Arabia won Academy Awards, was hugely admired and attracted big enough audiences to justify its extravagant budget. But Lean's greatest popular success came with *Doctor Zhivago* (1965), an adaptation of Boris Pasternak's epic novel set around the Russian Revolution of 1917. Though well regarded, Pasternak's novel was less than obvious material for a major blockbuster, and Lean increased the risk factor by casting Omar Sharif and Julie Christie, then little known internationally, in the lead parts. Beautifully photographed, intricately structured and carefully paced, the film presents Zhivago's story within the context of the turbulent events of the Russian Revolution and the subsequent civil war. The emotional import of events is captured and sustained through stylised understatement, as in the moment when a long shot from the point of view of massed peaceful marchers reveals the sabres of armed Tsarist guards glittering in the dark, and we hear the muffled sound of hooves in the snow as the ranks surge towards us. The sequence is typical of the way the film positions us with characters who come to realise the terrible truth of a situation or the inevitable drift towards dreadful events. Lean's boldness paid off; the film's critical reception was mixed, but it became a major box-office success.

In 1970 Lean made *Ryan's Daughter*, a melodrama set in Ireland and very loosely based on the plot of *Madame Bovary*. Audiences were unenthusiastic, while many critics were openly hostile. Lean's deliberately overblown style, representing the romantic viewpoint of its heroine Rosy, was misunderstood and condemned as grandiose and extravagant. Disappointed and hurt – and rich enough from the profits of *Doctor Zhivago* not to have to work again – Lean did not make another feature film for fourteen years, though during that time he fought hard to make a two-part epic telling the true story of the mutiny on the *Bounty*. His final film, *A Passage to India* (1984), was generally well received and proved a box-office success, although some critics complained that the more radical, anti-colonial aspects of E. M. Forster's novel had been lost in the adaptation. Lean was knighted in June 1984.

One can regret, as with Michael Powell, the unproductiveness of Lean's later years, but it is difficult to imagine him either successfully transplanted to Hollywood or working fruitfully within the restricted horizons of the British film industry of the 1970s and 80s. His body of work, from *In Which We Serve* to *A Passage to India*, remains uniquely impressive. David Lean died of pneumonia on 16 April 1991 while making preparations to begin filming his adaptation of Joseph Conrad's *Nostromo*.
(Sarah Cardwell)

BIBLIOGRAPHY: Brownlow, Kevin, *David Lean* (London: Faber and Faber, 1997); London Weekend Television, *The South Bank Show*, 'David Lean: A Life in Film', 1986; McFarlane, Brian, 'David Lean', in *An Autobiography of British Cinema* (London: Methuen, 1997) pp. 354–5; Moraitis, Catherine, *The Art of David Lean: A Textual Analysis of Audio-Visual Structure* (Bloomington, IN: 1st Books Library, 2002); Pratley, Gerald, *The Cinema of David Lean* (South Brunswick, NJ and New York: A. S. Barnes/London: Tantivy Press, 1974); Silver, Alain and James Ursini, *David Lean and His Films* (London: Leslie Frewin, 1974).

FILMOGRAPHY: *In Which We Serve* (co-dir. Noël Coward, 1942); *This Happy Breed* (1944); *Blithe Spirit*; *Brief Encounter* (1945); *Great Expectations* (1946); *Oliver Twist* (1948); *The Passionate Friends* (1948); *Madeleine* (1950); *The Sound Barrier* (US: *Breaking the Sound Barrier*, 1952); *Hobson's Choice* (1954); *Summer Madness* (US: *Summertime*, UK/US, 1955); *The Bridge on the River Kwai* (UK/US, 1957); *Lawrence of Arabia* (1962); *The Greatest Story Ever Told* (uncredited, some scenes only, US, George Stevens); *Doctor Zhivago* (UK/US) (1965); *Ryan's Daughter* (1970); *A Passage to India* (1984).

LEE, Jack (1913–2002)

Wilfred John Raymond Lee was born on 27 January 1913 in Stroud, Gloucestershire. His childhood and upbringing in near poverty is well covered in his brother Laurie's classic book *Cider with Rosie*. After studying photography at the Regent Street Polytechnic in London, Lee was taken on by Alberto Cavalcanti in 1938 as an assistant at the GPO Film Unit. Working in the unstructured world of documentary allowed him the opportunity to do a bit of everything: camerawork, editing, even directing the occasional second-unit sequence. The need to produce large numbers of documentaries during the Second World War gave Lee the chance to direct. He proved himself with two short films – *The Pilot Is Safe* and *Ordinary People* – before Ian Dalrymple, the Head of the Crown Film Unit, put him in charge of *Close Quarters* (1943), a feature-length drama-documentary about life aboard a Royal Navy submarine.

When the war ended Lee made *Children on Trial* (1946), a sympathetic account of the treatment of young offenders, and then joined Dalrymple's new production company, Wessex, where he made his first three feature films. *The Woman in the Hall* (1947), a studio-bound melodrama about a mother who uses her children to extort money, may seem atypical of Lee's later films, but the struggles of an individual to achieve a goal and through that struggle develop into a better person became a recurrent theme. In *Once a Jolly Swagman* (1948), set against the background of speedway racing, Lee still needed to refine his dramatic skills but used his documentary experience to deliver some stunning racing sequences. *The Wooden Horse*, a reconstruction of the escape from Stalag Luft III during the Second World War, showed that Lee had reached maturity as a film-maker. Well paced, unsentimental and exciting, *The Wooden Horse* convincingly represents the boredom and frustrations of camp life and the hazards involved in an escape attempt. It

MOY
LONDON

was a box-office success and set the parameters in the 1950s and beyond for an entire genre of British prisoner-of-war camp films.

After *South of Algiers* (1952), a robust adventure yarn set in North Africa, and *Turn the Key Softly* (1953), a small-scale drama about three women released from prison, Lee offered a deeper, darker exploration of the prisoner-of-war theme in *A Town Like Alice* (1956). His ability to handle an ensemble cast and create an atmosphere of outdoor realism helped make it a critical and popular success. Though using little more than half the Neville Shute novel it is based on, Lee's film subtly integrates the framing love story with the odyssey of a group of women stranded by the Japanese capture of Singapore. Virginia McKenna convinces as the secretary who leads the motley band of women and children as they trek through the jungle, desperately trying to cope with a perilous environment that their colonial lifestyle has ill-prepared them to survive. But it is Lee's attention to detail in the meticulously developed plot and the acting of even the minor characters that make the film outstanding.

Lee's last three features were *Robbery under Arms* (1957), a worthwhile but commercially unsuccessful Australian Western, *The Captain's Table* (1958), an amiable comedy, and *Circle of Deception* (1960), a dark wartime tale of cynicism and betrayal. The latter centres upon an idealistic young man sent into occupied France by British Intelligence, where he is tortured by the Nazis to reveal the false information with which he has been entrusted. It proved too grim to do well at the box office and Lee found himself being passed over when it came to projects that interested him, such as *Saturday Night and Sunday Morning*. Disillusioned, he emigrated to Australia, where he made commercials before becoming Chairman of the South Australian Film Board during the Australian film industry's formative years. He helped to foster the careers of several young directors, but showed no inclination to revive his own directing activities.

With *The Wooden Horse* and *A Town Like Alice*, Lee made two of the finest British films of the 1950s; but there is a transparency to his work that almost invites his dismissal as a competent but conventional director. A taciturn man who felt his films should speak for themselves, he nevertheless had a strong belief in the need for realism in characterisation, story and setting – something that grew from his experience in the documentary movement and the radical commitment to improve society provoked by the war. His films succeed in telling clear stories but they also explore ideas. His heroes are ordinary people (epitomised by the characters played by Virginia McKenna and Peter Finch in *A Town Like Alice*, and Bradford Dillman and Suzy Parker in *Circle of Deception*), fallible human beings who show themselves capable of extraordinary behaviour when put to the test, and acquire self-knowledge as they battle with adversity.

Though the New Wave directors of the 1960s were credited with bringing realism to British cinema, the important groundwork had been done for them by Lee and his ex-documentary colleagues Philip Leacock, Pat Jackson and Harry Watt, who all pushed for location filming at a time when British cinema was studio-bound. This added an extra dimension to the quality of their films, and certainly in Lee's case was never achieved at the expense of the script or characters. Largely unacknowledged in the UK, his influence has still been considerable. He died in Sydney on 15 October 2002.

(Linda Wood)

BIBLIOGRAPHY: Bergen, Ronald, Obituary, *Guardian*, 21 Oct. 2002, p. 20; Lee, Laurie, *Cider with Rosie* (London: Hogarth Press, 1959); Lee, Jack, 'A Free Hand', *Sight and Sound*, Spring 1959, p. 63.

FILMOGRAPHY: *The Pilot Is Safe* (doc. short, 1941); *Ordinary People* (doc. short, 1942); *Close Quarters* (shorter version *Up Periscope!*, 1943); *By Sea and Land* (doc. short, 1944); *The Eighth Plague* (doc. short, 1945); *Children on Trial* (1946); *The Woman in the Hall* (1947); *Once a Jolly Swagman* (US: *Maniacs on Wheels*, 1948); *The Wooden Horse* (1950); *South of Algiers* (US: *The Golden Mask*, 1952); *Turn the Key Softly* (1953); *A Town Like Alice* (1956); *Robbery under Arms* (1957); *The Captain's Table* (1958); *Circle of Deception* (1960); *From the Tropics to the Snow* (doc. short, co-dir. Richard Mason, Austral, 1964).

LEE, Norman (1898–1964)

Norman Harold Lee was born in Sutton, Surrey, on 10 October 1898. Between 1918 and 1921 he assisted the South African Film Production Company on adventure films. Returning to Britain, he moved into theatre management, bringing the American serial queen Pearl White to London for his production *The London Revue* (1925).

Lee's first berth in the British film industry was with the producer Harry B. Parkinson in 1928. To *The Streets of London* he brought an eye for local colour; to *The City of Shadows*, a nose for the sensational subject. Shot in 1928 as *The Night Patrol*, the film featured the social worker Elizabeth Baxter, moving among London's down-and-outs; the plot's inclusion of a girl victim of the white slave trade led to censorship trouble and the championship of George Bernard Shaw. Release was delayed until 1931.

Most of Lee's other films steered clear of controversy. From 1931 he supplied artless vehicles for British International Pictures' contract comedians Ernie Lotinga and Leslie Fuller. Later his range and budgets increased; he directed thrillers (*Bulldog Drummond at Bay*), musical farces (*Yes, Madam?*), and showcases for new comic talent (*Save a Little Sunshine*). The films had spit, but little polish. Among the circuit fodder, two non-fiction ventures stand out. In 1934, BIP's production chief Walter Mycroft inaugurated *Forgotten Men: The War as It Was*, a strong attack on the waste and horror of war, compiled from soldiers' interviews and First World War footage. Six years later Lee directed *Mein Kampf – My Crimes*, the English edition of a French semi-documentary. The film clumsily presented Hitler's life and atrocities for censure, but easily found appreciative audiences.

During the early years of the war, Lee made an exotic thriller, *The Door with Seven Locks*, with Leslie Banks and Lilli Palmer well cast as villain and heroine, and co-directed two mildly amusing comedies, *The Farmer's Wife* and *Spring Meeting*. After serving in the merchant navy, he returned to the industry to help script *Idol of Paris* (1948), his friend Leslie Arliss' disastrous attempt to repeat the Gainsborough melodrama formula, and to remake two melodramatic chestnuts. Lee's conscientious attention to detail makes *The Monkey's Paw* less risible than one might expect; while *The Case of Charles Peace*, with fine performances from old-stagers Michael Martin-Harvey and Chili Bouchier, and an ambitious flashback-within-flashback structure, is a fine example of what can be done with a low-budget genre film. *The Girl Who Couldn't Quite*, a very odd film about a tramp (Bill Owen) who cures a sheltered and disturbed middle-class girl of her inability to smile, followed in 1950. But by this time Lee was settled into a new profession. Fifty crime thrillers, numerous juvenile stories, memoirs and other books clattered from his typewriter, some under pseudonyms (chiefly Mark Corrigan), until his death in Surbiton, Surrey, on 3 June 1964.

(Geoff Brown)

BIBLIOGRAPHY: Lee, Norman, *My Personal Log* (London: Quality Press, 1947); Lee, Norman, *Log of a Film Director* (London: Quality Press, 1949); Low, Rachael, *Films of Comment and Persuasion of the 1930s* (London: George Allen & Unwin, 1979).

FILMOGRAPHY: *The Streets of London*; *The Night* Patrol/*The City of Shadows* (rel. 1931); *Lure of the Atlantic* (1929); *Dr Josser K.C.* (1931); *The Strangler*, *Josser Joins the Navy*; *Strip! Strip! Hooray!!!*; *Josser on the River*, *Josser in the Army*; *Money Talks* (1932); *The Pride of the Forces* (1933); *A Political Party*; *The Outcast*; *Doctor's Orders*; *Spring in the Air* (co-dir. Victor Hanbury); *Forgotten Men: The War as It Was* (doc.) (1934); *Royal Cavalcade* (US: *Regal Cavalcade*, co-dirs. Thomas Bentley/Herbert Brenon/Marcel Varnel/Will Kellino/Walter Summers, 1935); *Don't Rush Me!*; *Happy Days Are Here Again*; *No Escape* (1936); *Kathleen Mavourneen* (US: *Kathleen*); *Knights for a Day* (co. dir. Aveling Ginever); *Bulldog Drummond at Bay*; *French Leave*; *Saturday Night Revue*; *Dangerous Fingers* (US: *Wanted by Scotland Yard*) (1937); *Mr Reeder in Room 13* (US: *Mystery of Room 13*); *Almost a Honeymoon*; *Save a Little Sunshine*; *Luck of the Navy* (US: *North Sea Patrol*); *Yes, Madam?* (1938); *Murder in Soho* (US: *Murder in the Night*, 1939); *Mein Kampf – My Crimes* (doc., US: *After Mein Kampf?*); *The Door with Seven Locks* (US: *Chamber of Horrors*, 1940); *The Farmer's Wife* (co-dir. Leslie Arliss); *Spring Meeting* (assoc. dir., Walter C. Mycroft); *The Team* (short) (1941); *How a Bicycle Is Made* (short, 1945); *The Monkey's Paw* (1948); *The Case of Charles Peace* (1949); *The Girl Who Couldn't Quite* (1950).

LEEDS ANIMATION WORKSHOP (1978–)

Founded in 1978 to produce animated films on social issues, the Leeds Animation Workshop (LAW) was one of the first groups to be franchised under the ACTT's Workshop Declaration, and has produced around thirty short films as well as several title sequences and inserts for television programmes. The Yorkshire-based group was set up as a women's collective, and maintains its commitment to feminist and collectivist principles and to an 'integrated practice' of film production.

Together, LAW's five members (Jane Bradshaw, Terry Wragg, Stephanie Munro, Janis Goodman and Milena Dragic) combine skills in artistic, educational, administrative, media and cultural work and deal with every aspect of the making and dissemination of their films, from initial ideas and research through shooting to promotion and distribution. In addition, the Workshop has organised international festivals of films by female and ethnic minority film-makers, and runs regular workshops in basic animation techniques for community groups.

Their first production, *Who Needs Nurseries? We Do!* (1978), an eight-minute film promoting day-care provision for the under-fives, remains in use today. Later films deal with health and safety at work, violence against women, women and homelessness, environmental pollution, energy conservation, stress at work, racism, harassment and bullying at work and school, and child sexual abuse. LAW's films have been screened in a variety of contexts: government agencies, housing associations, universities, colleges, training centres, trade unions, hospitals, banks and schools. Many have been broadcast on television; and a number translated into other languages. All the films are accompanied by substantial discussion notes; and their brevity (running times range from eight to fifteen minutes) makes them convenient for use in classroom and training settings.

LAW is a hardy survivor of the vicissitudes that have brought about the virtual demise of the independent film workshop sector since the early 1990s. Its early objectives intact, LAW flourishes because it has succeeded in securing support from bodies other than the media and arts organisations that were the mainstay of the broader workshop movement, and it continues to attract funding by virtue of remaining focused about the purposes of every production. Over the years, LAW has kept in constant touch with its constituencies, building a solid base of expertise in producing and distributing films that are accessible, engaged and provocative.

(Annette Kuhn)

BIBLIOGRAPHY: Lant, Antonia, 'Women's Independent Cinema: The Case of Leeds Animation Workshop', in Lester Friedman (ed.), *British Cinema and Thatcherism: Fires Were Started* (London: UCL Press, 1993).

FILMOGRAPHY: *Who Needs Nurseries? We Do!* (1978); *Risky Business* (1980); *Pretend You'll Survive* (1981); *Give Us a Smile* (1983); *Council Matters* (1984); *Crops and Robbers* (1986); *Home and Dry?* (1987); *Out to Lunch* (1989); *A Matter of Interest* (1990); *Alice in Wasteland* (1991); *All Stressed Up* (1993); *Through the Glass Ceiling*; *Who Runs the World?* (1994); *In Sickness and in Health* (1995); *No Offence*; *Waste Watchers* (1996); *A World of Difference* (1997); *Did I Say Hairdressing? I Meant Astrophysics* (1998); *Working with Care*; *Home Truths* (1999); *Tell It Like It Is* (2000); *Bridging the Gap* (2001); *Grief in the Family*; *Believe Me* (2002); *Joined-Up Families*; *Beyond Belief* (2003); *Good to Be Home*; *Dads Inside and Out* (2004); *Minding the Baby* (2005).

LEE THOMPSON, J. (1914–2002)

Lee Thompson's career falls clearly into two parts. For ten years he made modestly effective British films, including *Yield to the Night* (1956), *Woman in a Dressing Gown* (1957), *Ice Cold in Alex* (1958) and *Tiger Bay* (1959): films that in retrospect look increasingly impressive. Between 1959 and 1989, as a prolific international director, he failed to fulfil the potential displayed in his early years, but within an uneven body of work achieved some films of considerable merit, notably *Cape Fear* (1962), *Mackenna's Gold* (1968) and *The Reincarnation of Peter Proud* (1974).

John Lee Thompson was born into a theatrical family in Bristol on 1 August 1914. After leaving Dover College he briefly went on the stage, writing crime plays in his spare time. One of these, *Double Error*, secured a West End run, which led to a job at Elstree as a scriptwriter for British International Pictures. In 1938 he worked as dialogue coach on Alfred Hitchcock's *Jamaica Inn* (1939) and was struck by the way Hitchcock 'had everything plotted down to the last detail and . . . knew exactly what he wanted' (Chibnall, p. 18). It was a system Lee Thompson was to adopt himself.

After serving in the Second World War as a tail-gunner and wireless operator in the RAF, Lee Thompson returned to Elstree as a scriptwriter. In 1950 he was given the opportunity to direct his first film, *Murder without Crime*. Largely unnoticed at the time, this well-structured melodrama about a man who thinks he has committed murder deployed many of the themes that were to characterise Lee Thompson's work: a good person's struggle with his or her conscience, an external force of evil and an out-of-character moment of violence that brings long-term consequences.

The Yellow Balloon (1952), the story of a boy stricken with guilt over the death of a friend, blackmailed into a spiral of criminal acts, attracted more attention. It was followed by *The Weak and the Wicked* (1954), a sympathetic portrayal of a group of women in prison. After making three amiable comedies – *For Better, for Worse* (1954), *As Long as They're Happy* (1955) and *An Alligator Named Daisy* (1955) – he returned to women in prison with *Yield to the Night*, a film combining a strong human story about a woman driven to murder with a passionate argument against capital punishment. Diana Dors, boldly cast in a serious role, gives a moving and understated performance, and Lee Thompson effectively captures the prison's trapped, oppressive atmosphere. *Woman in a Dressing Gown* was also impressive as a domestic drama that treats with equal sympathy the harassed, no longer glamorous housewife, the adulterous husband and the young woman who seems to offer an attractive alternative. Following an uninspired remake of *The Good Companions* (1957), Lee Thompson directed *Ice Cold in Alex* a Second World War film that salutes the heroism of four fallible people whose growing understanding and mutual respect (despite the discovery that one of them is an enemy soldier) enable them to survive their trek across the Libyan desert. He returned to domestic melodrama in *No Trees in the Street* (1959) and *Tiger Bay*, a skilfully made film about a lonely child who resists betraying a sailor wanted for murder.

Several of these films confront social issues, but they are not political in the sense that they espouse a particular set of political principles. Rather, they demonstrate a wariness of the established order, whether right or left. The Second World War taught Lee Thompson the importance of mutual responsibility within society and offered an object lesson in the consequences of prejudice and intolerance. But his own experience of a rootless and insecure way of life made him sensitive to life's complexities. The best of his British films argue the case for those whom society disapproves of or fails, such as the mistreated and misunderstood women and children of *Yield to the Night* and *Tiger Bay*, and explore how people respond to, and can be shaped by, their environment. He questions commonly held attitudes by presenting issues in terms of human dilemmas. Characters, trapped by circumstances, are forced to actions that normally they would never contemplate – the husband in an arid marriage desperately seeking solace in *Woman in a Dressing Gown*, the boy from a loving home stealing in *The Yellow Balloon* – or the audience condone. Lee Thompson shows the world as a complex place, where people are often confronted with difficult choices and the innocent get hurt. Often his characters have to choose between doing what the law requires and what they feel is right. The young girl decides that the sailor in *Tiger Bay* does not deserve to be hanged for murder, the survivors in *Ice Cold in Alex* allow the 'South African' to evade his fate as a spy despite a clear duty to turn him in. Lee Thompson empowers his protagonists, and by extension the audience, to make their own decisions according to their consciences, not according to the rules of society.

The presence of ordinary people in ordinary environments may reinforce the image of Lee Thompson as a realist film-maker. However, from the first his films contained instances of heightened theatricality (the dramatic pre-credits sequence of *Yield to the Night*, for example, in powerful contrast with the low-key nature of the rest of the film). Attracted to stories with characters battling for survival, emotionally and physically, he required an acting style that could mirror the extreme reactions prompted by moments of extreme stress. In his subsequent career it is these personal crises rather than the more general social concerns of his early films that predominate.

North West Frontier (1959), set in India at the turn of the twentieth century, marked the beginning of Lee Thompson's career as an international director. A fast-paced adventure with well-rounded portrayals from a strong cast (Lauren Bacall, Kenneth More, Herbert Lom), it was one of the few Rank films to become a success on both sides of the Atlantic. Having shown his aplomb in handling outdoor adventures, he was drafted in to take over the direction of *The Guns of Navarone* (1961), Alistair MacLean's Second World War story of betrayal and derring-do set on a Greek island. Lee Thompson maintained pace and tension through the film's 156 minutes, and confirmed his reputation as a director who could be trusted with star casts in big-budget films.

Moving to Hollywood, he made an impressive American debut with *Cape Fear*. A smaller-scale film than his previous two epics, it illustrates Lee Thompson's ability to handle suspense, and he musters fine performances from Robert Mitchum as the vengeful Max Cady and Gregory Peck as the lawyer forced to confront his own moral culpability. Subsequent American efforts were less impressive and the films he made in Britain in the late 1960s – *Return from the Ashes* (1966), *Eye of the Devil* (1967), *Before Winter Comes* (1969) and *Country Dance* (1970) – did little to enhance his reputation, though in retrospect they might be seen as interestingly idiosyncratic. *Return from the Ashes* is a darkly ironic story of a woman surviving the evil of a concentration camp only to encounter evil on her return home; *Eye of the Devil* is an occult parable showing savage forces lurking beneath the rational veneer of modern society. *Before Winter Comes*, set in a displaced persons' camp after the Second World War, may progress scrappily, but there are moments of real interest in the relationships between its oddly cast characters (David Niven, Anna Karina, Topol and John Hurt); while *Country Dance* (based on James Kennaway's *Household Ghosts*) is a flawed but beautifully shot tragi-comedy about the moral disintegration of a Scottish aristocrat (an extravagant Peter O'Toole). On his return to Hollywood Lee Thompson found renewed commercial success with two of the sequels to *Planet of the Apes* (Franklin J. Schaffner, 1968), but few of his subsequent films rise above the routine, apart from the exciting outdoor adventure *Mackenna's Gold* and the highly original thriller *The Reincarnation of Peter Proud*. Of his final British credits, *The Greek Tycoon* (1978) proved a creditable attempt at fictionalising the life of Aristotle Onassis, with a finely judged performance from Anthony Quinn, but *The Passage* (1979) is a sadly clumsy Second World War adventure with gross caricatures for characters and a dull plot. J. Lee Thompson died in Sooke, Vancouver Island, Canada, on 30 August 2002.

(Linda Wood)

BIBLIOGRAPHY: Chibnall, Steve, *J. Lee Thompson* (Manchester: Manchester University Press, 2000); Durgnat, Raymond, *A Mirror for England* (London: Faber and Faber, 1970); 'J. Lee Thompson', *Film Dope* no. 34, Mar. 1986, pp. 19–20; Lee Thompson, J., 'The Still Small Voice of Truth', *Films and Filming*, Apr. 1963, p. 5.

FILMOGRAPHY: *Murder without Crime* (1950); *The Yellow Balloon* (1952); *The Weak and the Wicked*; *For Better, for Worse* (US: *Cocktails in the Kitchen*) (1954); *As Long as They're Happy*; *An Alligator Named Daisy* (1955); *Yield to the Night* (US: *Blonde Sinner*, 1956); *Woman in a Dressing Gown*; *The Good Companions* (1957); *Ice Cold in Alex* (US: *Desert Attack*, 1958); *No Trees in the Street*; *Tiger Bay*; *North West Frontier* (US: *Flame over India*) (1959); *I Aim at the Stars* (US/Ger, 1960); *The Guns of Navarone* (1961); *Cape Fear* (US, 1962); *Taras Bulba* (US); *Kings of the Sun* (US) (1963); *What a Way to Go!* (US, 1964); *John Goldfarb Please Come Home* (US, 1965); *Return from the Ashes* (1966); *Eye of the Devil* (UK/US, 1967); *Mackenna's Gold* (US, 1968); *Before Winter Comes*; *The Chairman* (UK: *The Most Dangerous Man in the World*, US) (1969); *Country Dance* (US: *Brotherly Love*, 1970); *Conquest of the Planet of the Apes* (US, 1972); *Battle for the Planet of the Apes* (US, 1973); *Huckleberry Finn* (US); *The Reincarnation of Peter Proud* (US) (1974); *St Ives* (US, 1976); *The White Buffalo* (US, 1977); *The Greek Tycoon* (US, 1978); *The Passage* (1979); *Caboblanco* (US, 1980); *Happy Birthday to Me* (Can, 1981); *Ten to Midnight* (US, 1983); *The Evil That Men Do* (US); *The Ambassador* (US, 1984); *King Solomon's Mines* (US, 1985); *Murphy's Law* (US, 1986); *Firewalker* (US, 1987); *Deathwish 4: The Crackdown* (US); *Messenger of Death* (US) (1988); *Kinjite: Forbidden Subjects* (US, 1989).

LEGG, Stuart (1910–1988)

Francis Stuart Legg, born in London in 1910, was a key member of John Grierson's British documentary film movement as an editor, producer and director as well as writing scripts, recording sound and narrating films. He joined Grierson's Empire Marketing Board film unit in 1932 after graduating from Cambridge, transferring with Grierson to the GPO Film Unit in 1934. Here he produced, scripted, directed and edited *BBC – The Voice of Britain* (1935), one of the earliest documentaries to use synchronised sound. He provided the narration for *Night Mail* (Basil Wright/Harry Watt, 1936) and collaborated on many other GPO films including *Pett and Pott* (Alberto Cavalcanti, 1934) and *Coal Face* (Alberto Cavalcanti, 1935). He was also responsible, along with F. D. Klingender, for the influential pamphlet *Money behind the Screen* (1936), which exposed the dubious financial operations that had fuelled the expansion in British film production.

In 1938 Legg, Grierson, Basil Wright and others interested in the idea of sponsorship and film-making for social purposes established the Film Centre as an advisory body to liaise between

documentary units and government and industrial sponsors. In 1939 Legg became Grierson's chief producer at the National Film Board of Canada compiling and editing a news-film series, *Canada Carries On*, later renamed *World in Action* and distributed across North America from 1942 to 1945. Although he turned more to production during the war, his NFB film about the Battle of Britain, *Churchill's Island* (1941), won the Academy Award that year for Best Short Documentary. On his return to London in 1948 he joined the Crown Film Unit as a producer and in 1950 left to produce films through Film Centre International, predominantly for the Shell Film Unit. Legg retired from the industry in 1964 to concentrate on writing naval and military histories. He died in Wiltshire on 23 July 1988.
(Sarah Easen)

BIBLIOGRAPHY: Low, Rachael, *Documentary and Educational Films of the 1930s* (London: George Allen & Unwin, 1979); Sussex, Elizabeth, *The Rise and Fall of British Documentary* (London and Los Angeles: University of California Press, 1975); Swann, Paul, *The British Documentary Film Movement 1926–1946* (Cambridge: Cambridge University Press, 1989).

FILMOGRAPHY: *Varsity* (1930); *The New Generation*, Part 1; *Cambridge* (co-dir. G. F. Noxon); *The New Generation*, Part 2 (1931); *Cable Ship*; *Telephone Workers*; *The Coming of the Dial* (1933); *The New Operator*, *Savings Bank* (1934); *Introducing the Dial*; *BBC – The Voice of Britain* (1935); *Roadways*; *The League at Work* (1937); *Free to Roam* (1938); *Youth Is Tomorrow*, *Wing over Empire* (1939); *War Clouds in the Pacific* (Can); *Churchill's Island* (Can) (1941); *World in Action* (series Can., 1942–5); *Inside France* (Can, 1944); *Wonder Jet* (1950); *Food or Famine* (1962).

LEGRICE, Malcolm (1940–)

Born in Plymouth on 15 May 1940, Malcolm LeGrice is probably the most influential Modernist film-maker in British cinema. His work has explored the complex relationships between the film-making, projecting and viewing processes that constitute cinema as a medium; as well as showing an intense interest in what can be done with optical printers, and by the combination of different types and gauges of film stock. He started out as a painter in London in the early 1960s and turned to film-making in the middle of the decade with the Super-8 film *China Tea*, which he followed with *Castle 1* and *Little Dog for Roger*, made mostly from reworked found footage. *Castle 1* can be seen as prophetic: for screenings of the film in 1968 LeGrice hung a light bulb next to the screen, flashing on and off at regular intervals, and, when on, obliterating the screen image – a practice used in Martin Creed's Turner-Prize-winning installation some thirty-five years later.

In the 1960s his work was informed by the radical politics around opposition to the Vietnam War and US cultural imperialism, and extended to a deep hostility towards the 'illusionism' of Hollywood and other commercial cinemas. This tendency was particularly manifest in *Spot the Microdot or How to Screw the CIA*, which includes found footage of GIs in battle. But LeGrice's approach to cinema was also animated by a Modernist impulse to put the central focus on the properties of the medium itself, turning them into the 'content' of the work. For instance, in *White Field Duration*, a white screen marked only by a scratch running across clear celluloid activates an intense perception of projection time. This film was also performed as a two-screen event and LeGrice's installations at times extended to four or even six screens. From the late 1960s onwards, his multiple screen work was often accompanied by live performances interacting with the projection event (*Horror Film 1 and 2*).

LeGrice's best and most complex work was done in the 1970s when, in the face of an intense hostility towards narrative cinema manifested by some of his avant-garde colleagues, he made a trilogy – *Blackbird Descending*, *Emily* and *Finnegan's Chin* – which elaborated a critical kind of storytelling in which both the formal aspects of cinema and the very structures of narrative are explored in relation to each other. The films are set in the film-maker's own domestic environment and achieve a combination of intellectual and aesthetic intensity rarely seen in any kind of British cinema. LeGrice also engaged with art history (*After Manet*, *After Leonardo*) and with the pioneers of cinema (*After Lumière* and *Berlin Horse* – in which he incorporated a re-filmed Hepworth film of 1900, *The Burning Barn*).

In addition to being a prolific film-maker, LeGrice played an influential role in the critical and institutional promotion of avant-garde cinema in Britain. He was a prominent activist in the Drury Lane Arts Lab, where he formed Filmaktion with William Raban, Annabel Nicolson, Gill Eatherley, Mike Dunford and David Crosswaite, and organised mixed-media shows. He was also a pioneer in the educational domain, initiating the trend towards establishing film-making sections in art colleges, a policy that bore fruit in the 1980s as new generations of film-makers emerged from these courses. He is also an inveterate polemicist: his book *Abstract Film and Beyond* (1977) provides both a historical and a philosophical context for the British and European avant-garde cinemas, and he has contributed regularly to the journal *Studio International*.

LeGrice carried out the first experiments with computer-based film-making in Britain (*Your Lips 1*), and though it was a preoccupation that he laid aside after 1971, it came to dominate his media practice (along with research into digital art) from the 1980s onwards. Since 1997 he has headed the media research programme at Central St Martin's art college in London, accompanying his activities with critical-historical reflections.
(Paul Willemen)

BIBLIOGRAPHY: Dawson, Jan and Claire Johnston, 'More British Sounds', *Sight and Sound*, Summer 1970, pp. 144–7; Kiernan, Joanna, 'Two Films by Malcolm LeGrice', *Millennium Film Journal*, Winter/Spring 1979, pp. 62–71; LeGrice, Malcolm, *Abstract Film and Beyond* (London: Studio Vista, 1977); LeGrice, Malcolm, 'Towards Temporal Economy', *Screen*, Winter 1979/80, pp. 58–79; LeGrice, Malcolm, 'Problematising the Spectator Placement in Film', *Undercut*, Spring 1981, pp. 13–18; LeGrice, Malcolm, 'The Cronos Project', *Vertigo*, Autumn/Winter 1995, pp. 21–5; LeGrice, Malcolm, 'Mapping

in Multi-Space – Expanded Cinema to Virtuality', in *Cube/Black Box – Skulpturensammlung* (Vienna: E. A. Generali Foundation, 1996).
FILMOGRAPHY: *China Tea* (1965); *Castle 1* (aka *The Light Bulb Film*, 1966); *Little Dog for Roger*; *Yes, No, Maybe, Maybe Not*; *Castle 2* (1967); *Talla*; *Blind-White-Duration*; *Drama in a Wide Media Environment*; *Grass*; *Wharf* (1968); *Spot the Microdot or How to Screw the CIA* (1969); *Your Lips 1*; *Lucky Pigs*; *Reign of the Vampire*; *Berlin Horse* (1970); *Love Story 1*; *Love Story 2*; *Horror Film 1*; *1919*; *Your Lips 3*; *Whitchurch Down* (1971); *Love Story 3*; *Horror Film 2*; *Newport*; *Threshold*; *Blue Field Duration*; *White Field Duration* (1972); *Pre-Production*; *Matrix*; *Joseph's Coat*; *Four-Wall Duration*; *Gross Fog*; *After Leonardo*; *Don't Say*; *Principles of Cinematography: After Leslie J. Wheeler* (1973); *Screen-Entrance-Exit*; *After Lumière: L'arroseur arrosé*; *After Manet, After Giorgione: Le Déjeuner sur l'herbe or Fête Champêtre* (1974); *Art Works 1: Academic Still Life (Cézanne)*; *Art Works 2: Time and Motion Study* (1976); *Blackbird Descending (Tense Alignment)* (1977); *Emily: Third Party Speculation* (1978); *Finnegan's Chin: Temporal Economy* (1981); *Heads I Win – Tails You Lose* (1985); *Sketches for a Sensual Philosophy*; *Digital Still Life* (1988); *Et in Arcadia Ego*; *Like a Fox*; *Veritas* (1988); *Prelude*; *Wier* (1993); *Balcony Water Colour*; *Cidre Bouche*; *Seeing the Future*; *Warsaw Windows* (1994); *Chronos Fragmented*; *Out of the Crypt*; *Joseph's New Coat* (1995); *Joseph's Newer Coat*; *Even a Cyclops Pays the Ferryman* (1998); *Still Life and Letter from Toronto* (2000); *Jazzy Jazzy Jazzy* (2001); *Neither Here Nor Here*; *Unforgettable – That's What You Are* (2002).

LEIGH, Mike (1943–)

Mike Leigh completed his second feature film seventeen years after his stunning debut with *Bleak Moments* in 1971. In those intervening years he solidified his reputation with innovatory theatre and television productions, but his ambition to be a film-maker looked in danger of being unfulfilled. Other directors, including Stephen Frears, retreated into television during this period, but Leigh was additionally hampered by his method of evolving a script through improvisational workshops – too uncertain a process for most film financiers.

Mike Leigh was born in Salford on 20 February 1943, the son of a doctor, and was educated at Salford Grammar School before gaining a scholarship to RADA in 1960. This was followed by spells at the Camberwell School of Arts and Crafts, the Central School of Art and Design and the London Film School. In 1965 he started to devise and direct his own plays, completing nine before the production of *Bleak Moments* at the Open Space Theatre in 1970. *Bleak Moments* became the basis for Leigh's first film, a seemingly simple tale about a woman (Anne Raitt) who looks after her mentally disabled sister in suburban south London. Struggling towards meaningful social contact, she has a desultory friendship with another woman from work and embarks on a fumbling relationship with an emotionally stunted teacher (Eric Allan). But audience expectations are constantly undercut, and the portrayal of individuals adrift among social forces they are ill equipped to handle, an aspect that came to characterise Leigh's work, is edgy and uncomfortable.

In the years between *Bleak Moments* and *High Hopes* (1988), his next fully fledged cinema film, Leigh made nine feature-length television plays (one of which, *Meantime*, was given a limited theatrical release), as well as shorts and theatrical productions. Leigh encouraged actors to go beyond the naturalistic in their characterisations; desperate situations, masked by humour, are caught unflinchingly by dramatic lighting and an often static, but precisely positioned camera. The best known of these television plays is *Abigail's Party* (1977), a quickly taped studio reconstruction of one of Leigh's most successful stage works. Despite the fact that it was conceived for the stage rather than television, it became a comedic *tour de force* that impinged on the English national psyche. Beverly, the woman played by Leigh's then-wife Alison Steadman, is a kind of character who recurs in various guises throughout Leigh's work – a person who adopts the trappings of what they regard as a sophisticated lifestyle with an overconfidence and lack of taste that serve to emphasise their empty existence. It takes them into a cultural vacuum that both mirrors and masks a personal despair.

In 1988 FilmFour and British Screen agreed to back Leigh in a second theatrical feature. The resulting film, *High Hopes*, centres on a disjointed working-class family. Cyril is in a loving relationship with his long-time girlfriend Shirley in a run-down flat in King's Cross. His sister has followed the upwardly mobile path to unhappiness, emptiness and appalling taste with her aggressive entrepreneurial husband. Their mother lives in a council house marooned among gentrifying neighbours. Within this framework Leigh explores many interconnecting themes, not least the possibility of having children, an issue that threatens to divide many of Leigh's couples. Through Cyril's frustrations at the futility of his socialist beliefs and his struggle to keep bitterness at bay, Leigh comments sharply on the changes in British society and re-endorses the importance of humanist over materialist values.

Much of the family drama was familiar to people from Leigh's television work; but a renewed visual confidence appeared in scenes like the explosive family argument at the elderly mother's surprise birthday party where the camera focuses hard on Edna Doré's expressive face as voices are raised in anger around her. The film's critical acclaim and relative commercial success, plus the support of producer Simon Channing-Williams, joint founder of Thin Man Films in 1989, established Leigh as a major British film director. International renown steadily increased with his three subsequent films – *Life Is Sweet* (1990), *Naked* (1993) and *Secrets & Lies* (1996), all made with backing from Channel 4.

Although Leigh has been accused of patronising his characters and encouraging the audience to look down and snigger at their antics, most of them, despite their eccentricities, are ordinary individuals courageously struggling with limited resources to confront life's problems. Brenda Blethyn's Cynthia in *Secrets & Lies* – an unmarried woman who endures a boring factory job, lives unhappily with a daughter who regards her with sullen resentment and is dependent for survival on her more successful brother – faces life's injustices with enterprise and

humanity. It is one of Leigh's greatest strengths that his films recognise and celebrate the heroism of seemingly insignificant characters as they try to overcome their limitations, express themselves and do the right thing.

The character quirks of speech, gesture and appearance encouraged in his actors – what Leigh terms a 'running condition' – sometimes inspire acting that plays too close to the surface and distracts the viewer from the film's action, as with Jane Horrocks in *Life Is Sweet* and Katrin Cartlidge in the flashback sequences of *Career Girls*. But these characters remain flesh and blood, and are never merely caricatures, monsters or victims. Leigh's films demand second (or more) viewing, after which things usually fall into place and what initially appeared irritating can subsequently seem extraordinary. *Career Girls*, especially, is a film that grows in stature as time passes. The flashbacks, acting more as the essence of memory rather than accurate depiction of the past, yield a contrast that helps define the characters and plot changes in the social realities between the two eras.

In *Naked*, David Thewlis' performance was regarded as controversial less for its stylistic quirks than the character's unrelenting misogyny. We first see him attacking a woman at night in Manchester, and then follow him to London on a journey that becomes a picaresque cruise through other peoples' vulnerabilities. Thewlis makes his character, Johnny, an articulate misanthropist. He acts with a breathtaking disregard for people's feelings, but the fact that he remains unshakeably committed to his own view of the world allows even this despicable character a sort of heroism.

If *Naked* revealed Leigh as bold enough to disregard political correctness and allow his characters unfettered freedom of expression, *Topsy-Turvy*, his study of Gilbert and Sullivan, showed him flexible enough to adapt his usual method of working to create a unique costume drama built around well-known historical personages. Leigh takes his time – a leisurely 160 minutes – and breaks all the rules about character arcs and plot structure. Gilbert's eccentric father, sisters and mother appear unannounced and disappear as unexpectedly; long sequences of rehearsal and performance break up the narrative. But this enhances rather than diminishes the film. Leigh's fascination with the process of artistic creation, and his willingness to give his supporting cast the space to develop as rounded characters, moves the film beyond a conventional film biography. Jim Broadbent's Gilbert and Alan Corduner's Sullivan are charismatically convincing, but Leigh's real achievement is in setting their lives and work among a vividly depicted array of performers, lovers, servants, wives and the paraphernalia of backstage life. Gilbert, Sullivan and their collaborators were the epitome of Victorian optimism, but like most of the characters in most of Leigh's films, they are shown to be troubled, flawed and deeply human, the dying fall of the film's ending capturing the melancholy as well as the exuberance of artistic performance.

All or Nothing – set like all his cinema films in London – marked a return to small-scale family drama. Over time Leigh has built up a pool of actors, constantly refreshed, on which he can draw with confidence. In *All or Nothing*, regulars Timothy Spall, Lesley Manville, Ruth Sheen and Marion Bailey join talented newcomers Alison Garland and James Corden as struggling working-class people facing huge emotional crises. The depth of characterisation achieved is typical of Leigh's deeply compassionate and thoughtful films, and is equally evident in *Vera Drake*, which is set in 1950 and focuses on a cheery working-class housewife who helps women rid themselves of unwanted pregnancies at a time when abortion was illegal. Despite its low budget, clever casting (Vera is played with uncanny conviction by Imelda Staunton, but as in *Topsy-Turvy* all the characters surrounding her come dramatically to life) and an unerring sense of the grim austerity of post-war Britain make it one of Leigh's most satisfying films, confirming his status as a major film-maker.
(Richard Dacre)

BIBLIOGRAPHY: Carney, Ray and Leonard Quart, *The Films of Mike Leigh – Embracing the World* (Cambridge: Cambridge University Press, 2000); Clements, Paul, *The Improvised Play* (London: Methuen, 1983); Coveney, Michael, *The World According to Mike Leigh* (London: HarperCollins, 1996); Movshovitz, Howie (ed.), *Mike Leigh Interviews* (Jackson, MI: University Press of Mississippi, 2000).

FILMOGRAPHY: *Bleak Moments* (1971); *Meantime* (1983); *High Hopes* (1988); *Life Is Sweet* (1990); *Naked* (1993); *Secrets & Lies* (UK/Fr, 1996); *Career Girls* (UK/Fr, 1997); *Topsy-Turvy* (1999); *All or Nothing* (UK/Fr, 2002); *Vera Drake* (UK/Fr/NZ, 2004).

LELAND, David (1947–)

David Leland was born in Cambridge on 20 April 1947. He trained at the Central School of Speech and Drama and enjoyed some success as an actor on stage and screen. After graduating to theatre management and direction, he launched out as a scriptwriter, earning respect and attention with a trilogy of plays for Central Television. *Made in Britain* (Alan Clarke, 1982), *Flying into the Wind* (Edward Bennett, 1983) and *RHINO* (Jane Howells, 1983) offer a remarkable critique of British society at the time and marked Leland out as a highly talented writer.

Popular success in the cinema came with *Mona Lisa* (1986), which Leland co-scripted with director Neil Jordan. It is difficult to disentangle their contributions, but several of the film's characteristics – relationships across the divides of class or race, sexual frankness, romantic aspirations and their exploitation within a fallen world – reappear in Leland's subsequent films. *Personal Services* (Terry Jones, 1987), a thinly disguised biography of the notorious suburban madam Cynthia Payne, handled such themes more lightly; as did his script for *Wish You Were Here* (1987), Leland's directorial debut. Set in an English seaside resort in the 1950s, the film charts the progress of a sexually precocious girl through a drab, repressed, hypocritical world. She is protected by her wit and exuberance, delightfully conveyed by Emily Lloyd, and the film ends in hard-won optimism.

Unlike the pungent and popular *Wish You Were Here*, Leland's next two films were out of tune with contemporary audiences. *Checking Out* (1987), an American-set comedy written by Joe Eszterhas, but made for George Harrison's HandMade Films, missed the mark completely, and flopped on both sides of the Atlantic. *The Big Man* (1990), adapted from a Scottish novel by William McIlvanney and featuring Liam Neeson as a bare-knuckle fighter, was certainly more gritty, but its exploration of troubled masculinity seemed overburdened by gangster melodrama and anti-Thatcher rhetoric. Severe re-cutting by American backers Miramax failed to win over audiences in the USA; dismal returns helped to bankrupt its main sponsor, Palace Pictures.

For six years Leland returned to writing, crafting a series of scripts that failed to reach production. After directing a succession of rock videos, he finally found backing from Channel 4 and others for *The Land Girls* (1998), his adaptation of Angela Huth's novel about young women drafted into farm work during the Second World War. Leland is less assured than in *Wish You Were Here*, occasionally lapsing into heritage clichés and melodramatic sentimentality. But the relationship between Tom Georgeson's old farmer and Catherine McCormack's land girl, who like an earlier land girl in Powell and Pressburger's *A Canterbury Tale* has a feeling for the mystical beauty of the English landscape, is evocative and moving.

The Land Girls was a modest commercial and critical success and resurrected Leland's career as a director. He was chosen by Steven Spielberg to direct the 'Bastogne' episode of *Band of Brothers* (2001), and repaid his friendship with George Harrison in *Concert for George* (2003), a film record of the concert held at the Royal Albert Hall a year after the ex-Beatle's death.

(Robert Murphy)

BIBLIOGRAPHY: Bhegani, Belkis, 'The Man Who Is Cynthia', *Broadcast*, 9 May 1986, p. 14; Finney, Angus, *The Egos Have Landed* (London: Heinemann, 1996); Hunter, Allan, 'Intolerance', *Films and Filming*, Nov. 1987, p. 22; Nathan, Ian, 'Where Are They Now? David Leland', *Empire*, July 1996, p. 46.

FILMOGRAPHY: *Wish You Were Here*; *Checking Out* (1987); *The Big Man* (US: *Crossing the Line*, 1990); *The Land Girls* (1998); *Concert for George* (doc., UK/Austral/US, 2003).

LEMONT, John (1914–)

For a short while at the beginning of the 1960s, John Lemont and his writing partner Leigh Vance worked to bring to British low-budget films something of the visual briskness and exploitative material of the hard-boiled American programmer. *The Shakedown* (1959), a story of blackmail, nude photography and prostitution, emerged in the wake of the Wolfenden Report on the legislation of sexual practices in Britain. *And Women Shall Weep* (1960) focused on juvenile delinquency; while *The Frightened City* (1961), Lemont's best film, toughened up the period's

normally placid crime film for a story about the protection racket. Lemont also put an overgrown chimpanzee through its paces in Herman Cohen's monster movie *Konga* (1961), an American-backed co-production.

Born in 1914 in Toronto, Lemont worked in lowly capacities in the British film industry before the Second World War. He began to direct during three years making training films for the Army Kinematograph Service (1943–6). Commercial shorts and documentaries and work for Associated British Pathé followed, but he found most employment in the 1950s in the newly expanding field of television. As executive producer for Associated-Rediffusion he produced British television's first daily serial, *Sixpenny Corner* (1955–6); he also directed episodes for *Errol Flynn Theatre*, *Ivanhoe* and other series, along with commercials.

None of Lemont's cinema features followed the constraints of family viewing. His first feature, *The Green Buddha* (1954), made by Republic Pictures, presented the boisterous tale of a hunt for international thieves, climaxing at Battersea fun fair. But Lemont's cinema career only took off with his collaborations with Leigh Vance, a former journalist, on thrillers and plots ripped from newspaper headlines. With *And Women Shall Weep* and the X-certificate *The Shakedown*, both made for Norman Williams' company, Ethiro, melodrama and the rush to shock won over genuine thrills and authentic atmosphere.

In *The Frightened City*, produced by Lemont and Vance for their own company, Zodiac Film Productions, style and content successfully fused. The basic storyline – thieves falling out after a plan to amalgamate protection gangs – offered little new. But script and direction pursued the matter with rapier speed, dry wit and enough concern for authenticity to justify using a former detective-inspector of Scotland Yard's Flying Squad as a technical adviser. Travelling through the plot, Desmond Dickinson's camera closed in on newspaper headlines that declared 'Chicago Comes to London' and 'Gunfight at the Soho Corral'. Lively characterisations and the thuggery's gusto made the comparisons halfway plausible.

With its giant chimpanzee on the rampage in London, *Konga* enjoyed the most inflammatory plot material of any Lemont feature; but the director functioned only as a traffic policeman, trying to avoid accidents as Michael Gough and company navigated poor special effects and dialogue. After the lowbrow popcorn of *Konga* and the taut thrills of *The Frightened City*, Lemont's cinema career could legitimately have flourished in several directions. But Zodiac Film Productions made no further films; from that point on, Lemont's career disappears into television, anonymity and silence. In the late 1970s he re-emerged as the producer of two films for the Children's Film Foundation.

(Geoff Brown)

BIBLIOGRAPHY: Conrich, Ian, 'Trashing London', in I. Q. Hunter (ed.), *British Science-Fiction Cinema* (London: Routledge, 1999).

FILMOGRAPHY: *The Mirror and Markheim*; *People's Playground*; *The Green Buddha* (1954); *The Shakedown* (1959); *And Women Shall Weep* (1960); *Konga*; *The Frightened City* (1961).

LEONG, Po-Chih (1939–)

Po-Chih Leong was born in Northampton on 31 December 1939, the son of a Chinese seaman who set up one of the first Chinese restaurants in London's West End. He studied at the London School of Film Technique and Exeter University before being taken on as a trainee at BBC Television in 1963. In 1966, at the height of 'Swinging London', he made his film debut with a half-hour documentary about life around the King's Road, Chelsea, *Count Me Down*. The following year he moved to Hong Kong, where he worked in television and on commercials before making a break into feature films with *Jumping Ash* (1976), an action-packed thriller about drug-running that proved a big popular success. Another nine films in various genres followed, establishing Po-Chih Leong as a dynamic and versatile director during the short-lived golden age of the Hong Kong film industry.

In 1986 he returned to Britain to make *Ping Pong*, which along with Ian McEwan's adaptation of Timothy Mo's *Soursweet* (Mike Newell, 1988) treated London's Chinese community as a subject for something more than sinister villainy. The death of a wealthy Chinese businessman leads to an exploration of the mixed Chinese and English identities of his beneficiaries and descendants, which Po-Chih Leong handles with visual flair and deft humour. He continued his career with further Hong Kong genre films and a four-part documentary series, *Riding the Tiger: The Hong Kong Handover Years*, written, produced and directed for Channel 4 between 1997 and 1998.

His second British feature film, *The Wisdom of Crocodiles* (1998), is an intelligent modern vampire tale boosted by the charismatic presence of Jude Law as a thoughtful, considerate vampire, an unusually restrained Timothy Spall as the police inspector on his trail, and Elina Löwensohn as the enigmatic woman who makes him long to be ordinarily human. A slow pace, pretentious dialogue and the avoidance of the usual vampire clichés made for restricted distribution, but discerning horror fans appreciated the film's boldness and originality. Po-Chih Leong was able to relocate to Los Angeles and establish a niche as the director of made-for-television horror thrillers, most successfully with *Cabin by the Lake* (2000), *Walking Shadow* (2001) and episodes of the nine-part series *Wolf Lake* (2001–2). (Robert Murphy)

BIBLIOGRAPHY: Crawford, Travis, 'The Wisdom of Crocodiles: A Different Kind of Bite', *Fangoria* no. 192, May 2000, pp. 50–3; Glaessner, Verina, 'Beyond Banana Cop – Po Chih Leong', *Monthly Film Bulletin*, Sept. 1987, p. 287; Jones, Alan, 'The Wisdom of Crocodiles', *Cinefantastique* vol. 30 no. 12, Jan. 1999, pp. 58–60.

FILMOGRAPHY: *Count Me Down* (doc. short, 1966); *Handshakes Like These* (doc. short, HK, 1971); *Ready to Wear Festival* (doc. short, HK, 1974); *Tiaohui/Jumping Ash* (co-dirs. Josephine Siao/Siu Fong Pong, HK, 1976); *Woo fook/Foxbat* (co-dir. Terence Young, HK, 1977); *Shen tou miao tan shou duo duo/Itchy Fingers* (HK, 1979); *You ni mei ni/No Big Deal* (HK, 1980); *Long gan wei/Super Fool* (HK, 1981); *Ye jing hun/He Lives by Night* (HK, 1982); *Deng dai liming/Hong Kong 1941* (HK, 1983); *Ying lun pipa/Banana Cop* (HK, 1984); *Shengsi Xian/The Island* (HK); *Bu huo ying xiong/Welcome* (HK) (1985); *Ping Pong* (1986); *Sha zhi lian/Fatal Love* (HK); *Jixu taiowu/Continue Dancing* (HK) (1988); *Shang Hai yi jiu er ling/Once upon a Time in Shanghai/Shanghai 1920* (HK, 1991); *Heonggong ya fungkwong/Crazy Hong Kong* (HK, 1993); *The Wisdom of Crocodiles* (1998).

LESTER, Richard (1932–)

If any single director can encapsulate the popular image of Britain in the Swinging 60s, then it is probably Richard Lester. With his use of flamboyant cinematic devices and liking for zany humour, he captured the vitality, and sometimes the triviality, of the period more vividly than any other director. This has been somewhat to the detriment of his later work, which, while more conventional in style, has its own admirable qualities.

Lester was born in Philadelphia on 19 January 1932. After graduating in clinical psychology from the University of Pennsylvania, he began his career in American television as a stagehand, rising to become a director at the age of twenty. He left for Europe in 1954, settling in Britain in 1956. His sympathy for anarchic comedy made him an ideal director for the television series *A Show Called Fred* (1956), where he worked with Peter Sellers and Spike Milligan. He teamed up with them again for the eleven-minute short, *The Running, Jumping and Standing*

Still Film (1960). Shot in under two days for a mere £70, the film captures the playful surrealism of the two performers in a way few of their other screen appearances managed.

An affinity with Britain's emerging youth culture is already apparent in his debut feature, *It's Trad, Dad!*, which is moderately successful in capturing the buoyant mood of the British jazz revival. The whimsical *The Mouse on the Moon* was an inconsequential commercial chore, but *A Hard Day's Night* (1964) made Lester's name. With its combination of semi-documentary observation and brash fantasy sequences, this first film vehicle for the Beatles manages to connect the grittiness of the New Wave to the frivolity of the emergent Swinging London scene. The film does justice to the group's youthful energy and conveys a gently anti-Establishment insolence; it also provided a stylistic model for many later pop videos.

Lester's second Beatles vehicle, *Help!*, featuring rapid-fire gags, inventive visuals and colourful designs, builds on skills developed in his television commercials. However, without the grounding in reality that gave *A Hard Day's Night* its insight into the band's lifestyle, the film is little more than a loosely connected sequence of music promos. Accusations of superficiality appeared again with the release of *The Knack ... and How to Get It*, which obscures its rather conventional romantic plot behind a barrage of tricks and cinematic devices, from silent movie captions to a Greek chorus of disapproving adults. There are certainly patches of considerable visual flair, and the film conveys the innocent exuberance of the moment, but its experimentation with form is never more than decorative.

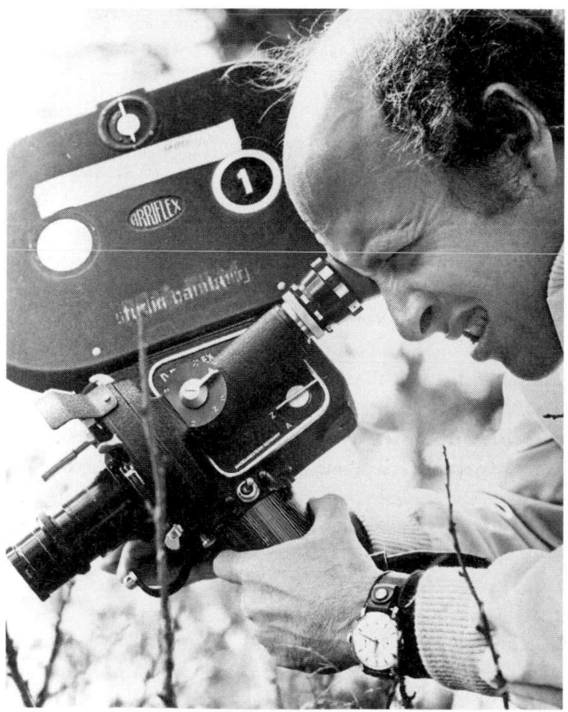

Lester next applied his style to Stephen Sondheim's stage musical *A Funny Thing Happened on the Way to the Forum*, playing it as broad farce and pushing the action along at a typically frenetic pace. A strong cast, including Buster Keaton and Phil Silvers, often struggle to register above the noise.

A darker, satirical tone begins to emerge in Lester's work with *How I Won the War* (1967). The generalised irreverence of his earlier films has hardened into a focused attack on the equal absurdities of war and the British class system. His desire to make more personal critical statements is taken even further in *The Bed Sitting Room*, adapted from a play by Spike Milligan and John Antrobus. This apocalyptic vision of a future world devastated by nuclear war, where the survivors transmute into items of household furniture, gets close to the bleak, surreal heart of Milligan's humour, where absurdist comedy reflects a pessimistic vision of human failure. Between these films Lester made his American debut with *Petulia*, a critique of 1960s' values that confirmed his increasingly misanthropic viewpoint.

The commercial failure of *The Bed Sitting Room*, combined with the crisis in British film production following the withdrawal of American funding in the late 1960s, pushed Lester away from experimentation and social comment into more mainstream commercial productions (he even returned to directing television commercials for a period). He brings a genuine zest, and irreverence, to his adaptation of Alexandre Dumas' classic in *The Three Musketeers* (1973) and *The Four Musketeers* (1974), originally shot as one film, but released as two. The amiable cast, including Oliver Reed and Richard Chamberlain, play along with the air of pastiche; David Watkin's cinematography is stylish, and Lester's direction inventive and fast-paced. He returned to the formula again with *The Return of the Musketeers*, a rather tired reprise marred by the accidental death during production of Roy Kinnear; and *Royal Flash*, based on George Macdonald Fraser's Flashman novels. Lester's ability to bring an appropriately light touch to genre subjects was confirmed by *Juggernaut*, an effective addition to the disaster movie genre of the 1970s set aboard a transatlantic liner, and by the commercial success of the big-budget *Superman II* and *Superman III*.

A vein of nostalgia is apparent in the best of his later films, the elegiac *Robin and Marian* (1976), with Sean Connery and Audrey Hepburn giving fine performances as the legendary figures, now in their autumn years. Despite its sentimentality, the film conveys a genuine longing for a time when real heroes bestrode the land. Something of the same mood underlies his American films *Cuba* (which again profits from the performance of Sean Connery) and *Butch and Sundance: The Early Days*; echoes of the past also prove the strongest feature of his last film, *Get Back*, a modest record of a Paul McCartney tour. Perhaps, for Lester, there really is no way to recapture that 1960s' heyday when he was so attuned to the *Zeitgeist*.

(Robert Shail)

BIBLIOGRAPHY: Armes, Roy, *A Critical History of British Cinema* (London: Secker and Warburg, 1978); Murphy, Robert, *Sixties*

British Cinema (London: BFI, 1992); Rosenfeldt, Diane, *Richard Lester: A Guide to References and Resources* (Boston, MA: G. K. Hall, 1978); Sinyard, Neil, *The Films of Richard Lester* (London: Croom Helm, 1985); Walker, Alexander, *Hollywood, England* (London: Michael Joseph, 1974).

FILMOGRAPHY: *The Running, Jumping and Standing Still Film* (short, 1960); *It's Trad, Dad!* (1962); *The Mouse on the Moon* (1963); *A Hard Day's Night* (1964); *The World Is Your Oyster* (short); *Help!*; *The Knack . . . and How to Get It* (1965); *A Funny Thing Happened on the Way to the Forum* (1966); *How I Won the War*; *Mondo Teeno/Teenage Rebellion* (co-dirs. Jörn Donner/Eriprando Visconti/Jean Herman/George Lefferts/Walter J. Sheldon, US) (1967); *Petulia* (UK/US, 1968); *The Bed Sitting Room* (1969); *The Three Musketeers* (1973); *The Four Musketeers*; *Juggernaut* (1974); *Royal Flash* (1975); *Robin and Marian* (US); *The Ritz* (1976); *Cuba* (US); *Butch and Sundance: The Early Days* (US) (1979); *Superman II* (1980); *Superman III* (1983); *Finders Keepers* (US, 1984); *The Return of the Musketeers* (UK/Fr/Sp, 1989); *Get Back* (1991).

LEVY, Don (1932–)

Don Levy was born in Bathurst, New South Wales, in 1932. After studying science at Sydney University he came to England for postgraduate work in theoretical physics at Cambridge and in 1960 made his first film, *Ten Thousand Talents*, for the Cambridge Film Society. Subsequently he became one of the first students of Thorold Dickinson at the newly established Film Department of the Slade School of Fine Art in London. Documentary work for the Nuffield Foundation's Unit for the History of Ideas followed; the thirty-minute *Time Is* (1964) won particular acclaim for its exploration of a difficult concept through a dazzling torrent of images, both horrifying and lyrical. Alongside his Nuffield documentaries, Levy experimented with sound and vision in *Five Short Films*, pursued plans for his wildly ambitious fiction project, *Herostratus*, directed a three-screen film for Expo '67, *Sources of Power*, and made a tumultuous celebration of contemporary British culture, *Opus* (1967) – his only film to reach wide audiences.

First conceived in 1962, *Herostratus* was finally completed in 1967. The running time was 142 minutes: a daunting length for a fragmentary narrative erratically propelled by staccato imagery, stylised colour and some unsuccessful improvisatory acting. Inspired by the fame-seeking, self-destructive Greek hero, Levy invented a modern parallel in the story of Max (Michael Gothard), a nihilistic poet who agrees to let an advertising agency turn his suicide into a publicity stunt. A night with Gabriella Licudi makes him regret his Faustian pact and he becomes the agent of another's death rather than his own. Unveiled in art cinemas in 1968 accompanied by a viewing guide from the director, the film's avant-garde fireworks drew a mixture of critical dismissal, bafflement and pockets of praise. A cult following gathered and in time dispersed.

The noisy release of *Herostratus* stirred industry interest in Levy: in a 1969 interview in the Cambridge magazine *Cinema* he claimed to have turned down four commercial features. One year later the figure had become nine; he told the Australian *Cinema Papers*, 'You can't talk about film as an art if the director hasn't got total control. A film has to be the personal expression of one person' (Bowman, p. 6). Levy's commitment to an extremely personal cinema seriously curtailed his creative output, but it has also made him a stimulating teacher. Moving to America, he became Associate Dean of the California Institute of Arts film school in the 1970s. He has also taught at the Carpenter Center for Visual Arts, Harvard, where he experimented with holography and multi-screen films.

(Geoff Brown and Wheeler Winston Dixon)

BIBLIOGRAPHY: Beresford, Bruce, 'Don Levy', *Cinema* no. 2, Mar. 1969, pp. 14–17; Bowman, Anna, 'Interview with Don Levy', *Cinema Papers*, 13 Apr. 1970, pp. 6–7; 'Interview: Don Levy', *Cantrills Filmnotes*, Aug. 1973, pp. 18–21.

FILMOGRAPHY: *Ten Thousand Talents* (short, 1960); *Garret Hostel Bridge* (doc. short, 1961); *Time Is* (doc. short); *The Perfection of Matter* (doc short, co-dir. June Goodfield); *Strictly for Kids* (short, 1964); *Crafts of Fez* (doc. short, 1966); *Five Films* (short); *Opus*; *Sources of Power* (doc. short, 1967); *Herostratus*; *Techniques of Contraception* (doc. short, 1968); *IT* (short, US, 1982).

LEWIS, Cecil (1898–1997)

During a long life, Cecil Arthur Lewis, born in Birkenhead on 29 March 1898, served as a First World War fighter pilot; programme manager for the BBC's fledgling radio service (1922–6); a film director (1930–2); a writer of travel books, fiction and memoirs; a disciple of the mystic teachings of Gurdjieff; a sheep farmer in South Africa; a midwife at the birth of the independent television company Associated-Rediffusion; and a journalist on the *Daily Mail* (1956–66).

Cinema proved one of his lesser adventures. 'As much like a movie as a cow is like a pianola,' Lewis wrote, a little harshly, about his Shaw adaptation *How He Lied to Her Husband* (1931). There were reasons for this first film's static nature: Shaw decreed that his play had to be followed word by word. *Arms and the Man* (1932), operating under a similar edict, was further troubled by location dialogue scenes suggesting an open-air pageant. For Lewis' employers, British International Pictures, the Shaw films served as connoisseur items at a time when economics were tipping company policy towards mass entertainment comedies. Lewis' other films, the *Carmen* adaptation *Gipsy Blood*, and *Indiscretions of Eve*, a musical attempting the René Clair manner, had equally sophisticated intentions, if not always results. After *Arms and the Man*, the meagre box-office receipts of Lewis' films became a luxury BIP could no longer afford.

Briefly he pursued other cinema endeavours. He wrote screenplays, notably for *Pygmalion* (Anthony Asquith/Leslie Howard, 1938), and in Hollywood developed a script about aviation. Forty years later, his 1936 book *Sagittarius Rising*, a popular memoir of his war experiences, became source material for *Aces High* (Jack Gold, 1976). He died in London on 27 January 1997.

(Geoff Brown)

BIBLIOGRAPHY: Costello, Donald P., *The Serpent's Eye: Shaw and the Cinema* (Notre Dame, IN: University of Notre Dame Press, 1965); Lewis, Cecil, *Never Look Back* (London: Hutchinson, 1974).
FILMOGRAPHY: *How He Lied to Her Husband* (1931); *Gipsy Blood* (US: *Carmen*, 1931); *Indiscretions of Eve* (1932); *Arms and the Man* (1932).

LEWIS, Jay (1911–1969)

James Gardner Lewis was born in King's Norton, Warwickshire, on 12 September 1911. After two years in the theatre as an actor, stage director and producer, he joined British International Pictures in 1933. He worked as an assistant director and production manager before moving to the Strand Film Company as writer and editor, and directing advertising films including *Grime Doesn't Pay* (1935) for Lifebuoy soap. In 1940 he set up Verity Films with Sydney Box, initially to make further advertising films (such as *Little White Lies* for Solidox toothpaste). But he found a more insistent demand for government propaganda, most notably with a series of *Cookery Hints* offering advice on how to handle 'Steaming', 'Potatoes', 'Casserole Cooking', 'Herrings' and 'Oatmeal Porridge'. Two years later Lewis was recruited into the Army Kinematograph Service's new production unit. On demobilisation in 1945 he formed Concord Productions, producing a range of documentary, educational and specialist films for various sponsors, and directing a modest first feature film, *A Man's Affair* (1949).

For his new company, Jay Lewis Productions, he produced *Morning Departure* (Roy Baker, 1950), the dramatic story of a stranded submarine, and *Front Page Story* (Gordon Parry, 1953), a lively newspaper drama, which he also co-scripted: these films firmly established his industry reputation. He returned to directing with *The Baby and the Battleship* (1956), one of the funnier of the post-war service comedies, with John Mills and Richard Attenborough sparking havoc on duty in the Mediterranean as the reluctant chaperones of a baby. Though the film became a major box-office success, it took another five years before Lewis directed his next feature, *Invasion Quartet* (1961), a Second World War comedy that makes disappointingly poor use of its zany cast (Spike Milligan, John Le Mesurier, Thorley Walters, Millicent Martin, Eric Sykes *et al.*).

Lewis' most interesting film is *Live Now – Pay Later* (1962), a critique of the new consumerism, with Ian Hendry at his best as a seedy and relentlessly self-serving door-to-door salesman. His final film, *A Home of Your Own* (1964) with Ronnie Barker as the leader of a gang of builders, was the strongest of the silent slapstick farces that enjoyed a small vogue in the mid-1960s. Lewis is a minor talent, but his films are refreshing for the fun they poke at the dominant values of post-war Britain. He died in London on 4 June 1969.

(Andrew Spicer)

BIBLIOGRAPHY: Durgnat, Raymond, *A Mirror for England* (London: Faber and Faber, 1970).
FILMOGRAPHY: Non-fiction: *Grime Doesn't Pay* (1935); *Bringing It Home*; *Little White Lies*; *Cookery Hints* (series) (1940); *Mobile Canteen* (aka *Canteen on Wheels/YMCA on Wheels*); *Queen's Messengers*; *Curds and Ways*; *Sea Cadets*; *Roots of Victory* (1941); *Knights of St John* (1942); *Hurry West* (1964).
Fiction: *A Man's Affair* (1949); *The Baby and the Battleship* (1956); *Invasion Quartet* (1961); *Live Now – Pay Later* (1962); *A Home of Your Own* (1964).

LIDDY, Kevin (1962–)

Kevin Liddy was born in 1962 into small-town rural Limerick, where, he once claimed, 'expressing yourself or having an interest in the finer things of life like music or art would have been viewed with suspicion' (Lineham). At sixteen Liddy joined the Focus Theatre in Dublin before studying film production at Dublin Institute of Technology. While teaching film at Rathmines College, Liddy directed *Horse* (1992), his first short. Deeply influenced by the director's childhood milieu, the film is a bleak account of a boy's development against the narrow parochialism of Irish rural life in the 1960s. Liddy's second short, *A Soldier's Song*, again examined social mores in rural Ireland and reinforced the director's poetic style and preoccupation with the development of the individual. *Country*, Liddy's first feature, is a résumé of his existentialist concerns. Set in an undefined place sometime in the 1960s or 70s, it is a lavishly mounted rural drama wherein an adolescent boy witnesses the aggressive hold of the past on his widowed father, disgruntled older brother and Republican grandfather – and the escalation of familial and communal violence brought about by the arrival home of a migrant aunt. *Country* earned critical accolades at home and abroad, though Liddy's subsequent work, as one of the directors of the popular television drama series, *On Home Ground* (2001), has been less personal.

(Eugene Finn)

BIBLIOGRAPHY: Fennell, Nicky, 'The Run of the Country', *Film West* no. 41, Autumn 2000, pp. 12–16; Friemann, Gretchen, 'The Country Boys', *Film Ireland* no. 78, Oct./Nov. 2000, pp. 22–3; Lineham, Hugh, 'The Moment When Life Changes', *Irish Times Weekend*, 14 Oct. 2000, p. 14.
FILMOGRAPHY: *Horse* (short, Ir, 1992); *A Soldier's Song* (short, Ir, 1996); *Country* (Ir, 2000).

LINDSAY-HOGG, Michael (1940–)

Michael Lindsay-Hogg was born in New York City on 5 May 1940. His mother is the actress Geraldine Fitzgerald. He earned early acting experience at the Shakespeare Festival in Stratford, Connecticut, and then came to England, becoming a trainee floor manager at Granada Television before briefly attending Oxford University. Returning to New York, he established an upstate summer theatre company with friends, including Peter Bogdanovich. This was followed by three years' work in Irish theatre and television, before moving to London to work for producer Elkan Allan at Associated-Rediffusion on *Ready, Steady, Go!* (1963–6).

Lindsay-Hogg directed numerous short films to promote pop singles (the forerunner to the music video), culminating in

1970 with his first full-length film, *Let It Be*, which documented in a cinéma-vérité style the Beatles' impending break-up. He went on to direct episodes of television drama series and several BBC plays, notably Trevor Griffiths' *All Good Men* (1974) and Tom Stoppard's *Professional Foul* (1977). He also directed Griffiths' political drama series *Bill Brand* (1976), and began work on Granada's prestige adaptation of Evelyn Waugh's *Brideshead Revisited* (1981) before handing over to Charles Sturridge.

Lindsay-Hogg's second feature film was *Nasty Habits*, a heavy-handed satire on the Watergate scandal, set in a nunnery in Philadelphia, and based on Muriel Spark's novel *The Abbess of Crewe*; he was not at his best with its star-studded cast and rambling story. Television continued to offer better opportunities, both in Britain and America, particularly in films featuring musicians (Neil Young, Paul Simon, Randy Newman, Pete Townshend, Wynton Marsalis), though he was also entrusted with starry dramas like *Dr Fischer of Geneva* (1985), adapted from Graham Greene's last novel. *The Beate Klarsfield Story*, about the tracking down of Klaus Barbie, head of the Gestapo in Lyons during the Second World War, was released theatrically in Europe.

Lindsay-Hogg returned to comedy with his cinema film *The Object of Beauty*, less successful than *A Fish Called Wanda* (Charles Crichton, 1998) and *Four Weddings and a Funeral* (Mike Newell, 1994) in its use of quirky American actors (John Malkovich, Andie McDowell) in an attempt to sell London as an appropriate setting for screwball comedy. *Frankie Starlight*, a rambling tale about a Franco-Irish-American dwarf, was more ambitious. But Lindsay-Hogg seems more comfortable working on a smaller canvas, as in *Guy*, an intriguing documentary-style feature about a young woman film-maker (Hope Davis) relentlessly pursuing a man with her camera. *Two of Us* (2000), a plausible fictional account for American television of the last meeting between John Lennon and Paul McCartney, is also fascinating, with highly convincing performances from Jared Harris (as Lennon) and Aidan Quinn (as McCartney).

(Janet Moat)

BIBLIOGRAPHY: Morley, Sheridan, 'Michael Lindsay-Hogg', *The Times*, 12 July 1976.

FILMOGRAPHY: *Let It Be* (1970); *Nasty Habits* (1977); *The Beate Klarsfield Story* (1986); *The Object of Beauty* (UK/US, 1991); *Frankie Starlight* (US/UK/Ir/Fr, 1995); *The Rolling Stones Rock and Roll Circus* (US); *Guy* (UK/Ger/US) (1996); *Waiting for Godot* (Ir, 2001).

LINGFORD, Ruth (1953–)

Ruth Lingford has become a highly distinctive animator in her ground-breaking work using an Amiga computer to make experimental narrative films. Her resistance to the now-established Pixar or Dreamworks SKG 'aesthetic' in the deployment of computer-generated imagery is welcome, and has served to make her films visually innovative and stylistically provocative. Born in 1953, she first worked as an occupational therapist before taking a degree in fine art and history at Middlesex Polytechnic. There she made *Whole Lotta Love* (1989), using the Led Zeppelin song as the ironic backdrop to an AIDS-related narrative; and *Sea in the Blood* (1990), about the contradictory feelings inherent in being a mother. She studied animation at the Royal College of Art, making *Baggage* (1992), about fertility, and *Crumble* (1992), using shots of an old people's home and recalling her time as a therapist. She gained an Arts Council 'Animate!' grant to make *What She Wants* (1993), exploring the relationship between sexual identity, representation and consumerist exploitation; and later won a three-month residency at the Museum of the Moving Image.

Lingford's work is highly transgressive in its treatment of extreme feelings from desire to grief to anger. *Death and the Mother* (1995), based on a story by Hans Christian Andersen, plays out the anxieties of motherhood in the face of the needs of a sick child; *Pleasures of War* (1999), created with writer Sara Maitland, explores the deep-rooted eroticism and pleasure in acts of violence; and *The Old Fools* (2002), her most recent film, combines Philip Larkin's poem (read by Bob Geldof) with digitally manipulated footage of her father.

(Paul Wells)

BIBLIOGRAPHY: Andrew, Geoff (ed.), *Film: The Critics Choice* (London: Aurum Press, 2001); Pilling, Jayne (ed.), *Women and Animation: A Compendium* (London: BFI Exhibition & Distribution Division, 1992).

SELECTED FILMOGRAPHY: *Whole Lotta Love* (1989); *Sea in the Blood* (1990); *Baggage*; *Crumble* (1992); *Death and the Mother* (1995); *Pleasures of War* (1998); *The Old Fools*; *An Eye for an Eye* (co-dir. Shynola, 2002).

LITTLEWOOD, Joan (1914–2002)

Joan Maude Littlewood was born in Stockwell, south London, on 6 October 1914. Her belief in the importance of community and political commitment, made her one of the most influential and radical figures in post-war British theatre. She set up Theatre Workshop in 1945 and in 1953 found a home for her company at the Theatre Royal in Stratford, east London. Her productions of Shelagh Delaney's *A Taste of Honey*, Brendan Behan's *The Quare Fellow* and Charles Chilton's *Oh! What a Lovely War* (filmed by Richard Attenborough in 1969) went beyond realism, incorporating experimentation that acknowledged the essential artifice of the stage.

In 1962 she planned to film Behan's *The Hostage*, but her deal with the American Seven Arts company fell through. She was more successful with *Sparrows Can't Sing*, a jolly celebration of working-class life based on one of her own popular stage productions. In this tale of chirpy cockneys the tendency to slip into class caricature is offset by the warmly individual performances of James Booth, Roy Kinnear, Barbara Ferris and, especially, Barbara Windsor, as well as the genuine sense of authenticity of place and character. Littlewood made no further ventures into film. She died in London on 20 September 2002.

(Robert Shail)

BIBLIOGRAPHY: Lentz III, Harris, Obituary, *Classic Images* no. 331, Jan. 2003, p. 59; Littlewood, Joan, *Joan's Book* (London: Minerva, 1995).
FILMOGRAPHY: *Sparrows Can't Sing* (1963).

LITVAK, Anatol (1902–1974)

Mikhail Anatol Litvak was born on 10 May 1902 in Kiev. After studying philosophy at the University of St Petersburg, he took to acting and directing in the theatre. By 1924 he was working as an assistant director and set designer at the Nordkino studio. In 1925 he went to Germany, where he directed a number of films, including the successful Cine-Allianz musical *Das Lied einer Nacht* (1932), made in Berlin alongside French and British versions (*La Chanson d'une nuit/Tell Me Tonight*) which he also directed. By January 1933 he was working for Gaumont-British at Shepherd's Bush on *Sleeping Car*, a featherweight romantic comedy starring Ivor Novello and Madeleine Carroll. He then settled briefly in France, finally achieving international success with *Mayerling* (1936), a plush and affecting historical romance starring Charles Boyer as the Habsburg Crown Prince who loves a commoner (Danielle Darrieux): it proved his passport to Hollywood. During the Second World War, Litvak joined the US Army Special Services Film Unit, making propaganda films such as *The Battle of Russia* (1944) and *War Comes to America* (1945).

Both in Europe and America Litvak showed a particular aptitude for characters placed in extreme circumstances. Several films are notable for *tour-de-force* performances from actresses – Darrieux in *Mayerling*, Bette Davis in *The Sisters* (1938) and *This above All* (1942), Barbara Stanwyck in *Sorry, Wrong Number* (1948) and Olivia de Havilland in *The Snakepit* (1948). Results in his British films were generally less successful. *Sleeping Car* is determinedly trivial, while Vivien Leigh disappoints in Litvak's later adaptation of *The Deep Blue Sea* (1955); the film as a whole fails to reproduce the bitter passion of Terence Rattigan's play. In contrast, *The Night of the Generals* (1967), his penultimate film, is a splendidly flamboyant melodrama exploring intrigue and sexual deviance among the German high command. Litvak died on 15 December 1974 in Neuilly-sur-Seine, France.
(Geoff Brown and Kevin Gough-Yates)

BIBLIOGRAPHY: Nolan, Jack Edmund, 'Anatole Litvak', *Films in Review*, Nov. 1967, pp. 548–65; Walker, Michael, 'Anatole Litvak', *Film Dope* no. 35, Sept. 1986, pp. 34–7.
FILMOGRAPHY (UK only): *Sleeping Car* (1933); *The Deep Blue Sea* (1955); *The Night of the Generals* (UK/Fr, 1967).

LOACH, Ken (1936–)

Ken Loach has proved an unlikely but very successful survivor. None of his fellow directors who began their careers in Britain in the 1960s has continued to work so prolifically and inventively throughout the 1990s and into the 21st century. This is all the more remarkable because Loach has remained a doggedly left-wing film-maker in a society that has shifted politically towards the right. Since 1995 Loach's films, which with few exceptions deal with indigenous and unfashionable aspects of British life, have been funded by a consortium of European countries.

Kenneth Loach was born on 17 June 1936 in Nuneaton, Warwickshire. The son of an electrician, he attended grammar school in Nuneaton and after two years of National Service studied law at Oxford University, where he was president of the Dramatic Society. After university he briefly pursued an acting career before turning to directing, joining Northampton Repertory Theatre as an assistant director in 1961 and then moving to the BBC as a trainee television director in 1963.

Loach's first directorial assignment was a thirty-minute drama written by Roger Smith (who worked as story editor on Loach's early *Wednesday Plays* and was still collaborating with him over thirty years later). In 1964 he also directed episodes of *Z Cars*, which taught Loach the difficulties of directing live television drama, and *Diary of a Young Man*, a series about two young northerners arriving in London, where he saw the possibilities film afforded of getting out of the studio onto the streets. *Diary of a Young Man* also used non-naturalistic elements, including stills sequences cut to music and a voiceover commentary, in its attempt to forge a new kind of narrative drama; Loach was to incorporate some of these innovations into his early *Wednesday Plays*.

Of the six *Wednesday Plays* Loach directed in 1965, *Up the Junction* was the most innovatory for its elliptical style and its inclusion of a controversial abortion sequence. He continued his stylistic experiments in *The End of Arthur's Marriage*, an uncharacteristic musical drama from a script by Christopher Logue; but in 1966 *Cathy Come Home*, written by Jeremy Sandford, consolidated the documentary-drama approach of *Up the Junction* and established Loach's reputation for social-issue drama. *Cathy Come Home*'s exposure of homelessness as a social problem, at a time when the media was preoccupied with the hedonistic fantasy of Swinging London, aroused national concern and gave a boost to the homelessness charity Shelter – coincidentally launched a few days after the play's transmission.

Loach's next *Wednesday Play*, *In Two Minds* (1967), written by David Mercer, explored the issue of schizophrenia and the ideas of the radical psychiatrist R. D. Laing, but for his first feature film, *Poor Cow* (1967), he returned to the world of *Up the Junction* and *Cathy Come Home*. Co-written by Nell Dunn (author of *Up the Junction*), and starring Carol White as a more feckless version of her Cathy character, it emerged as a transitional film, retaining some of the stylistic innovations and non-diegetic music of *Up the Junction* and *Cathy Come Home* while striving towards the naturalistic style that became Loach's trademark.

Poor Cow was produced by Joseph Janni – who had been responsible for John Schlesinger's *A Kind of Loving* (1962), *Billy Liar!* (1963) and *Darling* (1965) – but Loach's most important production partner was Tony Garnett, who had worked as story editor for the *Wednesday Plays*. Together they established Kestrel Films and embarked on Loach's second feature, *Kes*, adapted by Barry Hines from his novel. The film

tells the story of Billy Caspar, a Barnsley working-class lad alienated from school and the prospect of a coal miner's life, who finds a sense of personal achievement in learning to train and fly a kestrel. The cinematographer Chris Menges collaborated with Loach on developing a more observational style that allowed for improvisation and the use of untrained actors, like David Bradley (cast as Billy). *Kes* proved a commercial and critical success, but Loach's next film, *Family Life*, a reworking of *In Two Minds*, held little appeal for mainstream cinema audiences. In the face of a declining British film industry, Loach and Garnett returned to television for most of the 1970s, making a series of extraordinarily radical political dramas. The cycle had begun in 1969 with *The Big Flame*, an ambitious dramatisation of a fictional strike at the Liverpool docks that threatens to escalate into a working-class revolution, written by the Trotskyite Jim Allen. *The Rank and File* (1971), a further collaboration with Allen, was less daring but more realistic, directly based on the real strike of the Pilkington glass factory workers. These gritty contemporary dramas were succeeded by *Days of Hope* (1975), four feature-length period dramas shot in colour, showing the politicisation of a working-class family in the period from the First World War to the 1926 General Strike; historical events were recounted from an explicitly Trotskyite point of view. After a return to contemporary politics with the two-part drama *The Price of Coal* (1977), Loach was able to make his fourth feature film *Black Jack* (1979), a children's adventure film set in the 18th century, based on a novel by Leon Garfield. The film scored high on authenticity but clumsy plotting and poorly delivered dialogue hampered its popular appeal.

Loach began the 1980s with two dramas written by Barry Hines, *The Gamekeeper* (1980), made for ATV, and *Looks and Smiles*, made for Central Television but given a limited theatrical release. But Garnett had left (temporarily) for America, and Loach found it difficult to raise money for cinema films in the Thatcher era's hostile political climate. Even with television documentaries Loach ran into political censorship. *Questions of Leadership*, the four-part series about trade unions commissioned by Channel 4, was never shown; a film about the miners' strike for *The South Bank Show* was withheld by LWT, to be screened eventually on Channel 4; and Jim Allen's stage play about Zionism, *Perdition*, which Loach was going to direct, was withdrawn at the last minute by the Royal Court Theatre.

Loach's only other feature film of the 1980s was *Fatherland* (1986), written by Trevor Griffiths and funded by Channel 4 with French and German co-production money. Compared to many of Loach's previous films, it is more European in subject matter and less social realist in manner. Loach and Griffiths shared a similar political outlook, but Griffiths' script, more literary and abstract than the broader and simpler writing of Jim Allen, was less suited to Loach's naturalistic style. It remains one of his least loved films.

Hidden Agenda (1990), a political thriller about the British Army's 'shoot-to-kill' policy in Northern Ireland, regained the polemical edge of Loach's best earlier work. But it was not until *Riff-Raff* (1991), the first of several films produced by Sally Hibbin's Parallax Pictures and photographed by Barry Ackroyd, that Loach's career revived. In addition to Jim Allen, who wrote *Hidden Agenda* and would go on to write *Raining Stones* and *Land and Freedom*, Loach renewed his sense of purpose by drawing on a new generation of left-wing writers, including Bill Jesse (*Riff-Raff*), Rona Munro (*Ladybird, Ladybird*), Rob Dawber (*The Navigators*), and Paul Laverty (*Carla's Song, My Name Is Joe, Bread and Roses, Sweet Sixteen* and *Ae Fond Kiss . . .*).

In this latter phase of Loach's career, naturalism veers productively into melodrama in *Raining Stones, Ladybird, Ladybird* and *My Name Is Joe*; while elements of humour temper his earnest didacticism, particularly in *Riff-Raff* and *Ae Fond Kiss . . .*; he has even been tempted to look beyond British shores in *Land and Freedom* (the Spanish Civil War), *Carla's Song* (Nicaragua) and *Bread and Roses* (Mexican migrant workers in Los Angeles). *My Name Is Joe, Sweet Sixteen* and *Ae Fond Kiss . . .*, all written by Paul Laverty, produced by Rebecca O'Brien and set in Glasgow, form an impressive trilogy on modern British life and might be usefully compared to the much rosier view of Britain presented in three Richard Curtis films: *Four Weddings and a Funeral* (Mike Newell, 1994), *Notting Hill* (Roger Michell, 1999) and *Love Actually* (Richard Curtis, 2003). The cross-cultural comedy of *Ae Fond Kiss . . .* balances out the utter bleakness of *Sweet Sixteen*, and is more characteristic of later Loach in finding a degree of humour in potentially tragic events.

One can only admire Loach for relentlessly championing the underdog, revealing the hardships and struggles of those at the bottom of the social hierarchy. It is no accident that his best work has been produced at times of supposed affluence, in the mid-1960s and the 1990s, when he has often been a lone voice, bravely and resolutely standing up for the disadvantaged and the downtrodden. In a career spanning five decades, few directors have been as consistent as Loach in their themes and their filmic style, or as principled in their politics.

(Lez Cooke)

BIBLIOGRAPHY: Fuller, Graham (ed.), *Loach on Loach* (London: Faber and Faber, 1998); Hayward, Anthony, *Which Side Are You On? Ken Loach and His Films* (London: Bloomsbury, 2004); Hill, John, 'Every Fuckin' Choice Stinks', *Sight and Sound*, Nov. 1998, pp. 18–21; Kerr, Paul, 'The Complete Ken Loach', *Stills*, May/June 1986, pp. 144–8; Leigh, Jacob, *The Cinema of Ken Loach* (London: Wallflower Press, 2002); McKnight, George (ed.), *Agent of Challenge and Defiance: The Films of Ken Loach* (Trowbridge, Wilts: Flicks Books, 1997).

FILMOGRAPHY: *Poor Cow* (1967); *Kes* (1969); *Family Life* (1971); *Black Jack* (1979); *Looks and Smiles* (1981); *Fatherland* (UK/Ger/Fr, 1986); *Hidden Agenda* (1990); *Riff-Raff* (1991); *Raining Stones* (1993); *Ladybird, Ladybird* (1994); *Land and Freedom* (UK/Ger/Sp, 1995); *Carla's Song* (UK/Ger/Sp, 1996); *My Name Is Joe* (UK/Ger/Fr/It/Sp, 1998); *Bread and Roses* (UK/Ger/Fr/It/Sp/Switz, 2000); *The Navigators* (UK/Ger/Fr/It/Sp, 2001); *Sweet Sixteen* (UK/Ger/Fr/It/Sp); *11′09″01* (segment, Fr/Egypt/US/UK/Mex) (2002); *Ae Fond Kiss. . .* (UK/Ger/Fr/It/Sp, 2004); *Tickets* (co-dirs. Ermanno Olmi/Abbas Kiarostami, UK/It/Iran, 2005); *The Wind That Shakes the Barley* (Ir/Fr/UK, 2006).

LONCRAINE, Richard (1946–)

Richard Loncraine was born on 20 October 1946 in Cheltenham, Gloucestershire, and educated at Wellington College. Leaving school at sixteen, he studied sculpture and painting at Cheltenham College of Art, the Central School of Art and the Royal College of Art. At twenty-two, Loncraine directed a documentary, *The Most Beautiful Hotel in the World* (1968), for Yorkshire Television, before joining the BBC to direct items for the science programme *Tomorrow's World*. He then honed his directorial skills making television commercials, for which he won three major awards.

Loncraine was reputedly the model for Murray Head's character in John Schlesinger's *Sunday Bloody Sunday* (1971) – for which he created the sculptures and played a small role – and he also worked as second-unit director on Jim Clark's private-eye comedy, *Rentadick* (1972). After directing *Radio Wonderful*, a short film about BBC Radio 1 shown with *That'll Be the Day* (Claude Whatham, 1973), he made his feature debut with *Flame*, a lively rock movie featuring Birmingham chart-toppers Slade. Following work on the abortive Harry Saltzman project *The Micronauts*, Loncraine directed *Full Circle*, a mystery thriller starring Mia Farrow. The film was poorly received and he returned to work in television, where he re-established his reputation with a number of highly acclaimed plays, including *Oy Vay Maria* (1977), *Vanishing Army* (1978), *Secret Orchards* (1980) and Dennis Potter's spy drama *Blade on the Feather* (1980), for which Loncraine received a BAFTA nomination.

Loncraine's return to feature films came in 1981 with the popular Michael Palin comedy *The Missionary*, but his film version of Dennis Potter's *Brimstone and Treacle*, starring Sting, Denholm Elliott and Joan Plowright, and the crime drama *Bellman and True*, were less successful, and he was replaced by Wolfgang Petersen on the Hollywood science-fiction film *Enemy Mine* (1985). An effective and moving television drama, *Wide-Eyed and Legless* (1993), starring Julie Walters and Jim Broadbent, and a highly praised adaptation of *Richard III* (1995) with a cast that included Ian McKellen, Annette Bening, Jim Broadbent, Robert Downey Jr, Nigel Hawthorne, Kristin Scott Thomas and Maggie Smith, was followed by a period of what Loncraine termed 'development hell' (Falk, p. 23). He then directed three projects for the American cable television company, HBO: the D-Day episode for Steven Spielberg's *Band of Brothers* (2001); *The Gath-*

ering Storm (2002), a BBC Films-initiated biography that charts the changing political fortunes of Winston Churchill (Albert Finney) in the lead-up to war; and *My House in Umbria* (2003), an adaptation of a novel by William Trevor. *The Gathering Storm* put Loncraine's career firmly back on track, and he moved into the limelight with Working Title's *Wimbledon*, a romantic comedy set around the English tennis championships, with Kirsten Dunst well cast as the brattish American star who discovers a surprising affinity with fading Brit Paul Bettany. *My House in Umbria* was given a belated UK cinema release late in 2004 to a lukewarm critical reception. But *Firewall*, an action film starring Bettany and Harrison Ford, scored high at the American box office.
(Martin Hunt)

BIBLIOGRAPHY: Bygrave, Mike, 'Heaven and Hell', *Time Out* no. 629, 10 Sept. 1982, p. 20; Falk, Quentin, 'Out of the Wilderness: How *The Gathering Storm* Propelled Churchill Back into the Fray', *Exposure*, Spring 2002, pp. 22–3; Loncraine, Richard, *BBC Learning Zone: Masterclass* <www.bbc.co.uk/education/lzone/master/richard.shtml>.

FILMOGRAPHY: *Rentadick* (2nd unit dir., Jim Clark, 1972); *Radio Wonderful* (short, 1973); *Flame* (1974); *Full Circle* (US: *The Haunting of Julia*, Can/UK, 1976); *The Missionary* (1981); *Brimstone and Treacle* (1982); *Bellman and True* (1987); *Richard III* (1995); *My House in Umbria* (2003); *Wimbledon* (UK/Fr/US, 2004); *Firewall* (US, 2006).

LONG, Stanley (1933–)

Stanley Long was one of the key players in the close-knit world of British soft-core sex movies of the 1960s and 70s. Starting as a glamour photographer, he teamed up with Arnold L. Miller to market self-made 8mm striptease films via mail order before graduating to feature-length nudist films and pseudo-documentaries, which Long photographed. He took co-directorial credit on a travelogue shot in Circlorama, an obscure Russian 360-degree screen system, before making *Bread*, a sex-comedy set around a pop festival. Far better were his intermittently amusing pseudo-sex-documentaries *Naughty!*, *On the Game* and *It Could Happen to You*. In 1975 Long produced Martin Campbell's *Eskimo Nell*, a splendid satire on the British sex industry to which he contributed uncredited direction. The same year he directed the box-office smash sex-comedy *Adventures of a Taxi Driver*; its success spawned a series.

Long is also a talented cameraman and has worked in that capacity with directors as diverse as David Bailey (*G.G. Passion*, 1966); Michael Reeves (*The Sorcerers*, 1967); and Vernon Sewell (*The Blood Beast Terror*, 1967). He also shot, uncredited, a third of Roman Polanski's *Repulsion* (1965) after cameraman Gil Taylor was forced to leave to fulfil other commitments when shooting fell behind schedule. Long gave up film-making in 1978, profitably turning his hand to film distribution. He now runs Salon, one of the largest post-production facilities houses in Europe.
(Richard Dacre)

BIBLIOGRAPHY: McGillivray, David, *Doing Rude Things: The History of the British Sex Film 1957–1981* (London: Sun Tavern Fields, 1992); 'The Guys behind the Groupies: Or How Long & Ford Beat the Majors to the Youth-Theme of the Day', *Premiere* [UK] no. 3, July 1970, pp. 24–8.

FILMOGRAPHY: *Nudist Memories* (co-dir. Arnold L. Miller, 1961); *Circlorama Cavalcade* (co-dir. Arnold L. Miller, 1964); *Bread*; *Naughty!* (1971); *Sex and the Other Woman* (1972); *On the Game* (1973); *It Could Happen to You*/*Intimate Teenage Secrets*; *Adventures of a Taxi Driver* (1975); *Adventures of a Private Eye* (1977); *Adventures of a Plumber's Mate* (1978) *Dreamhouse*/*Screamhouse* (short, co-dir. Michael Armstrong, 1981); *That's the Way to Do It*/*Killer Punch* (short, 1982); *Do You Believe in Fairies?*/*Garden of Blood*/*Virgin Mutant Fairies* (short, 1983); *Screamtime* (co-dir. Michael Armstrong – jointly credited as Al Beresford; compilation of *Dreamhouse*, *That's the Way to Do It* and *Do You Believe in Fairies*, 1985).

LOSEY, Joseph (1909–1984)

Joseph Losey was born on 14 January 1909 in La Crosse, Wisconsin. After high school he studied at Dartmouth and Harvard, majoring in medicine and English, but soon drifted to New York City, where he became involved in the theatre and began making short films. He caught the attention of MGM and was asked to make *A Gun in His Hand* (1945), a two-reel short in the 'Crime Does Not Pay' series. Losey was unhappy during his tenure at MGM, and left in 1947 for RKO, where he directed his first feature, *The Boy with Green Hair* (1948). Other films followed that established him as an inventive, individualistic director. But in 1951 his links with left-wing theatre groups (in 1947 he had collaborated with Bertolt Brecht on a production of *Galileo*) and the concern for social justice in several of his films attracted the attention of the House of Representatives Un-American Activities Committee (HUAC) and led to him being blacklisted.

In 1952 he arrived in England and began rebuilding his career. He directed his first British feature film, *The Sleeping Tiger*, in 1954, though the credit went to the producer Victor Hanbury. The stage-bound plot makes it the least interesting of Losey's early British films, but it marked his first collaboration with Dirk Bogarde, whose career was to become inextricably linked with Losey's.

In 1955 Losey directed the twenty-nine-minute colour film *A Man on the Beach* for Hammer, with a cast including Donald Wolfit, Michael Medwin and Michael Ripper. Immaculately photographed by Wilkie Cooper, this peculiar and atmospheric caper film centring on a casino robbery, scripted by Jimmy Sangster, offers an interesting hint to Losey's future direction in British cinema. His next feature was a thriller, *The Intimate Stranger* (1956). Rising film studio executive Reggie Wilson (Richard Basehart) is almost forced out of the profession when he becomes the target of a vicious campaign of innuendo engineered by studio production chief Ernest Chapple (Mervyn Johns). The parallels with Losey's own plight are obvious, and *The Intimate Stranger* succeeds admirably despite its modest budget. It was followed by *Time without Pity* (1957), featuring Michael Redgrave, Ann Todd, Leo McKern and Alec McCowen in an adroit suspense film in which a young man (McCowen) is convicted of killing his girlfriend and sentenced to death. His estranged father (Redgrave), an alcoholic writer, becomes convinced of his son's innocence and tries desperately to clear him in the twenty-four hours before his date with the hangman. Superbly photographed by Freddie Francis, *Time Without Pity* was the first British film officially to carry Losey's name. *The Gypsy and the Gentleman* (1958) showed Losey had little aptitude for costume drama, but *Blind Date* (1959) confirmed the promise of *Time Without Pity*, showing Losey capable of turning a routine genre film into an incisive comment on the human condition.

Now well established in the UK, Losey began to look for more adventurous projects. *The Criminal* (1960), rewritten by Alun Owen from a script by Jimmy Sangster, told the story of criminal Johnny Bannion as he tries to come to terms with the world he has made. Half the film is set in the precincts of a dank and dreary prison, with highly theatrical sets and lighting, the remainder in brashly affluent modern Britain. Impeccable performances from Stanley Baker as Bannion and Sam Wanamaker as his oily, smooth-talking nemesis, help give the film an aura of authenticity. John Dankworth's compelling score, marking the beginning of a long collaboration between the composer and the director, adds intensity and depth to Losey's striking pictorial compositions.

After *The Criminal*, doors that had been closed to Losey finally began to swing open. Hammer offered him the chance to direct *The Damned*, one of the most underrated of his films. At a seaside resort, teenage gang leader King (Oliver Reed) and his mates terrorise the locals. Nearby, in an underground cave complex, government officials contrive to keep a group of radioactive children alive in order to study them. A vicious psychopath at the film's outset, King is gradually humanised, and attempts to help the children escape. Momentarily liberated, but spreading contamination, the children are rounded up by government workers in radiation suits and returned to their underground prison. Losey's collaboration with Hammer was predictably stormy; using a script by Evan Jones that he substituted at the last minute, Losey delivered a bleak and uncompromising film, far from the conventional science-fiction thriller Hammer had wanted. After heavy cuts, the film was released by Hammer in August of 1962; it was not until July 1965 that it reached US cinemas as the bottom half of a double bill.

Undaunted, Losey pressed ahead with *Eve*, an examination of sexual obsession, in which Welsh writer Tyvian (Stanley Baker) falls for femme fatale Eve (Jeanne Moreau). The film was not well received, but once again Losey suffered interference from his producers (the Hakim brothers), who cut some sixteen minutes

from the film before its release and jettisoned Losey's Billie Holiday song soundtrack.

Losey's next film, *The Servant* (1963), his first collaboration with Harold Pinter, was a critical and commercial success. Dirk Bogarde appeared as Hugo, a valet who gradually manipulates his employer, Tony (James Fox), into a position of hopeless subservience. The result is a nightmarishly claustrophobic film: an attack on the class system and the weakness of the English aristocracy. Bogarde's contribution was not limited to the disturbing performance, which helped him make the transfer from matinée idol to art-cinema actor. When Losey fell ill with pneumonia during filming, Bogarde filled in for several days as the director. He also starred in *King & Country* (1964), a low-budget black-and-white First World War drama; *Modesty Blaise* (1966), a Pop Art spy spoof that appears in danger of falling apart as it moves from one opulent location to the next; and *Accident* (1967), the film that finally brought Losey international acclaim.

Accident focuses on Stephen (Bogarde), a weak and insecure Oxford don whose life is thrown into turmoil when he falls in love with one of his students, Anna (Jacqueline Sassard). She also commands the affections of William (Michael York), a rich upper-class student, and Charley (Stanley Baker), a media don who despite his surface assurance is undergoing his own mid-life crisis. Harold Pinter's adaptation of Nicholas Mosley's novel is spare and epigrammatic: for all its visual splendour, *Accident* is a film about interior states of being, and the impossibility of knowing how other people think and feel. With John Dankworth's cool jazz score, Pinter's crisp dialogue and Gerry Fisher's atmospheric colour cinematography, simultaneously invoking the indolence and privilege of academe, *Accident* combines the discipline of his early films with a mature artistic ambition.

Subsequent films, however, were too often a disappointment. *Boom* (1968) is an embarrassingly indulgent Richard Burton/Elizabeth Taylor vehicle from a Tennessee Williams script. *Secret Ceremony* (1968), a more intriguing misfire starring Robert Mitchum, Elizabeth Taylor and Mia Farrow, was marred by an unfinished script, production problems and executive interference. *Figures in a Landscape* (1970) and *The Assassination of Trotsky* (1972) – featuring Richard Burton as Trotsky and Alain Delon as his murderer – lack the passion and energy of Losey's early films. Only *The Go-Between* (1970), an adaptation of an L. P. Hartley novel by Harold Pinter, featuring confident performances from Julie Christie, Alan Bates, Margaret Leighton and Michael Redgrave, recaptured some of the director's old assurance; it might be seen as the final statement of a man who had run out of energy and resources.

An air of exhaustion certainly marks Losey's subsequent output – *A Doll's House* (1973), *The Romantic Englishwoman* (1975), *Galileo* (1975), *Monsieur Klein* (1976), *Les Routes du sud* (1978), *Don Giovanni* (1979), *Boris Godunov* (1980), *La Truite* (1982) and *Steaming* (1985). Even the best regarded of the films, *Don Giovanni* and *La Truite*, appear unambitious compared with his earlier work's vitality and originality. Losey's health, never robust, failed during the production of *Steaming* and he died in London on 22 June 1984.

Losey's greatest works were those created out of a desperate need to make his vision whole on the screen; his exile from America sharpened that vision, forcing him to identify ever more closely with the outsiders depicted in his most successful films. Despite the disappointment of his later career, Joseph Losey remains a major figure in the history of cinema.

(Wheeler Winston Dixon)

BIBLIOGRAPHY: Caute, David, *Joseph Losey: A Revenge on Life* (London: Faber and Faber, 1994); Ciment, Michel, *Conversations with Losey* (London and New York: Methuen, 1985); de Rahm, Edith, *Joseph Losey* (London: André Deutsch, 1991); Hirsch, Foster, *Joseph Losey* (Boston, MA: Twayne, 1980); Leahy, James, *The Cinema of Joseph Losey* (New York and London: A. S. Barnes/Zwemmer, 1967); Milne, Tom, *Losey on Losey* (London: Secker and Warburg, 1967); Palmer, James and Michael Riley, *The Films of Joseph Losey* (Cambridge: Cambridge University Press, 1993).

FILMOGRAPHY: USA: *Pete Roleum and His Cousins* (short, 1939); *Youth Gets a Break* (doc. short); *A Child Went Forth* (doc. short) (1941); *A Gun in His Hand* (short, 1945); *The Boy with Green Hair* (1948); *The Lawless* (UK: *The Dividing Line*); *The Prowler* (1950); *M*; *The Big Night* (1951); *Stranger on the Prowl/Imbarco a mezzanotte* (UK: *Encounter*, uncredited, Andrea Forzano, 1952).

UK and Europe: *The Sleeping Tiger* (uncredited, Victor Hanbury, 1954); *A Man on the Beach* (short, 1955); *The Intimate Stranger* (as Joseph Walton, US: *Finger of Guilt*, 1956); *Time Without Pity* (US: *No Time for Pity*, 1957); *The Gypsy and the Gentleman* (1958); *Blind Date* (US: *Chance Meeting*, 1959); *First on the Road* (short); *The Criminal* (US: *The Concrete Jungle*) (1960); *The Damned* (US: *These Are the Damned*); *Eve* (US: *Eva*, Fr/It) (1962); *The Servant* (1963); *King & Country* (1964); *Modesty Blaise* (1966); *Accident* (1967); *Boom*; *Secret Ceremony* (1968); *Figures in a Landscape* (1970); *The Go-Between* (1971); *The Assassination of Trotsky* (It/Fr, 1972); *A Doll's House* (UK/Fr, 1973); *Galileo* (UK/Can, 1975); *The Romantic Englishwoman* (UK/Fr, 1975); *Monsieur Klein* (Fr/It, 1976); *Les Routes du sud* (Fr/Sp, 1978); *Don Giovanni* (It/Fr/Ger, 1979); *La Truite/The Trout* (Fr, 1982); *Steaming* (1985).

LOVE, Nick (c. 1969–)

Londoner Nick Love pursued a successful career as a model and actor before turning to writing and directing in the late 1990s. He made his debut with the uncomfortable short *Love Story* (1999), a fragment of a tale about a drug-addicted couple (Jamie Forman and Love's then-wife Patsy Palmer) bringing a baby into their grotesquely sordid world. The feature film that followed, *Goodbye Charlie Bright* (2001), is a little more cheerful, a tragi-comedy set on a Bermondsey council estate (though shot in safer Kingston upon Thames). Paul Nicholls plays Charlie Bright, the floppily handsome leader of a group of lads who zigzag towards their predetermined futures (the army, crime, death, escape) in a tough, claustrophobic working-class world.

Half-developed subplots impair the film's dramatic impact but its energy and authenticity make the faults forgivable.

The Football Factory (2004), made with backing from producer Alan Niblo and based on a popular novel by John King about the perils and pleasures of football hooliganism, attracted much more attention. Love uses many of the cast from *Charlie Bright*, but he is helped by a clearer structure and a strong central performance from Danny Dyer as the genial office worker whose personality is disintegrating under the strain of his addiction to violence. Love cleverly uses Dudley Sutton – who in his youth tended to play disreputable outsiders himself – as the voice of solid working-class virtue, but he refuses to condemn his protagonist and set him on the road to reform. It is Love's willingness to show the world from the viewpoint of characters generally regarded as beyond the pale that makes his films both disturbing and interesting.

The Business, a crime film set among British gangsters in the 1980s' Costa del Crime, with Dyer escaping from council-estate limbo to the fresh air and violent fun of southern Spain, followed in 2005.

(Robert Murphy)

FILMOGRAPHY: *Love Story* (short, 1999); *Goodbye Charlie Bright* (2001); *The Football Factory* (2004); *The Business* (2005).

LOWNEY, Declan (1960–)

Declan Lowney was born in Dublin on 23 April 1960 and in 1978 began his career as a trainee film editor. His first film was *Wavelength*, a short film about a chaotic pirate radio station; it was voted Best Irish Film at the 1980 Cork Film Festival. This success helped him land a trainee producer/director place at RTÉ where he specialised in music and entertainment programming (winning an Irish Jacobs Award for his direction of the 1988 Eurovision Song Contest).

Lowney's background in live-event and multi-camera television made him a much sought-after director when he moved to London in 1988 to work for pop-promo outfit MGMM. Since then his music direction credits include live specials and concerts with a host of rock, pop and opera stars including U2 and Pavarotti. His feature documentary about Bob Marley, *Time Will Tell*, won an award at the New York Film Festival. Since 1995 Lowney has concentrated on television comedy, directing specials with several British television comedians, and directing popular comedy-drama shows like *Cold Feet*. In 1996 he won a BAFTA Award for his direction of the cult Channel 4 sitcom *Father Ted*.

His first fiction feature film was the romantic comedy *Wild About Harry*, a film that, through comedy and gentle parody, introduced to the screen a new image of 'post-Troubles' Belfast, and more generally ushered in a new engagement with Northern Ireland. Though it was well received, Lowney remains more committed to British television, working productively with Paul Whitehouse on his innovative comedy drama series *Happiness* (2001–3) and *Help* (2005).

(Martin McLoone)

BIBLIOGRAPHY: McLoone, Martin, *Irish Film: The Emergence of a Contemporary Cinema* (London: BFI, 2000); McLoone, Martin, 'Internal Decolonisation? British Cinema in the Celtic Fringe', in Robert Murphy (ed.), *The British Cinema Book*, 2nd edn (London: BFI, 2001); Pettitt, Lance, *Screening Ireland* (Manchester: Manchester University Press, 2000).

FILMOGRAPHY: *Wavelength* (Ir, short, 1980); *Time Will Tell* (doc., 1992); *Wild About Harry* (UK/Ir/Ger, 2000).

LUMET, Sidney (1924–)

Sidney Lumet was born in Philadelphia, Pennsylvania, on 25 June 1924, the son of a dancer and the Yiddish actor Baruch Lumet. At the age of four he made his acting debut with his father in New York City; his Broadway debut followed in 1935. After military service in the Second World War, Lumet formed an off-Broadway stage group; then in 1950 he joined CBS, one of the three major American television companies, as an assistant director. He was soon directing live drama, and made his cinema debut in 1957 with a version of Reginald Rose's television play *12 Angry Men*; it immediately marked him out as a major new talent.

Although predominantly a New York film-maker, Lumet has made six British films, all imaginative and visually exciting despite their reliance on literary or theatrical sources. The best are the first three. *The Hill* (1965), set in a North African prison camp during the Second World War, explores the thin line between discipline and sadism in a powerful, brilliantly acted study of male behaviour under extreme pressure. *The Deadly Affair* (1966) is a gripping spy thriller adapted from John le Carré's first novel, *Call for the Dead*, set in a world choked by a miasma of treachery: its gloomy, rainy, nocturnal London, a city that shows no sign of swinging, is as unwelcoming as the bright desert glare in *The Hill*. Lumet inspires his actors to create likeable characters in sympathetic dilemmas, making these films cathartic rather than depressing. In *The Deadly Affair* Mason's secret agent Charles Dobbs, a prototype for George Smiley, is cuckolded, tricked and betrayed, but his odd alliance with Harry Andrews' pensioned-off policeman – a man whose only remaining emotional investment is in his pet rabbits – gradually brings redemption.

His next British film abandoned le Carré's dark world for the sunset glow of Chekhov. *The Sea Gull* (1968) emerged as a straightforward adaptation, eschewing showy visual effects, with fine performances by Mason, Andrews and the other mainstay of *The Deadly Affair*, Simone Signoret, though the trio are upstaged by Vanessa Redgrave's startlingly emotional Nina.

Lumet returned to Britain in the early 1970s for *The Offence* (1972), a relentless and disturbing study of a policeman's breakdown and his subsequent killing of a suspected child molester. The impassioned performances of Sean Connery (as the policeman) and Ian Bannen (as the suspect) more than compensate for the restricted plot and settings. *Murder on the Orient Express* (1974) could not have been more different: a visually sumptuous adaptation of a famous Agatha Christie novel, with Albert Finney as

the eccentric Belgian detective Hercule Poirot, investigating the murderer lurking within the film's international all-star cast. Gears changed again with *Equus* (1977), a powerful if imperfect adaptation of Peter Shaffer's highly stylised stage play. Lumet's probing camera centred proceedings squarely on the character of the psychiatrist Dysart, played by Richard Burton; but despite some austere lighting effects the film inevitably missed much of the sense of mythic spectacle apparent in the theatre.

Lumet's British-made films share the variety of his American work, where prestigious stage plays (*Long Day's Journey into Night*, 1962) rub shoulders with serious social dramas (*The Pawnbroker*, 1965), realistic thrillers (*Dog Day Afternoon*, 1975) and the odd commercial miscalculation (*The Wiz*, 1979). Nonetheless themes recur, on both sides of the Atlantic. Several films deal with police corruption; weary, white middle-aged men facing professional and emotional crises are another common feature. In his visual handling of his material Lumet may give little sign of the influences he has claimed from Carl Dreyer and Robert Bresson, but, like Chekhov himself, he has told his stories with an attractive compassion for human frailty.

(Janet Moat)

BIBLIOGRAPHY: Bogdanovich, Peter, *Who the Devil Made It? Conversations with Legendary Film Directors* (New York: Alfred A. Knopf, 1997); Boyer, Jay, *Sidney Lumet* (New York: Twayne, 1993); Cunningham, Frank R., *Sidney Lumet: Film and Literary Vision* (Lexington, KY: University Press of Kentucky, 1991).

FILMOGRAPHY (UK only): *The Hill* (1965); *The Deadly Affair* (1966); *The Sea Gull* (1968); *The Offence* (1972); *Murder on the Orient Express* (1974); *Equus* (1977).

LYE, Len (1901–1980)

Len Lye's brilliantly inventive and technically accomplished films made him one of the few film-makers working in inter-war Britain to establish an international reputation in the experimental field.

Born Leonard Charles Huia Lye in Christchurch, New Zealand, on 5 July 1901, he took courses in commercial art but drew far more sustenance from European modernism and aboriginal art, a 'pre-rational' tradition central to his evolving quest to portray kinetic energy in artworks. He moved to London in 1926, and soon joined the Seven and Five Society, a modernist group of British artists; Lye exhibited paintings and sculptures before devoting increasing attention to his first experiment with animated film.

Between 1926 and 1929, Lye made around four thousand drawings for what would eventually become *Tusalava* (1929), a striking attempt at a creation myth, visually inspired by biological cell structures as well as aboriginal art. The powerful and disturbing nine-minute film consists of a host of shifting shapes – dots, circles, blobs – that wriggle, twist around and attack a recurring totem figure. Premiered at the Film Society, *Tusalava* only secured limited screenings. Lye struggled to attract sponsors for further animations, though in 1934 Sidney Bernstein, the progressive owner of the Granada cinema chain, funded the filming of a three-minute puppet exercise, commonly known as *Experimental Animation*, set to the popular tune 'Peanut Vendor'. *Full Fathom Five* (1935), now lost, was Lye's first effort at painting directly onto celluloid, then a relatively unexplored technique; the film gained him entry into the GPO Film Unit. In *A Colour Box* (1935), he had to incorporate a message about cheaper parcel rates, but placed at the end it scarcely interfered with Lye's abstract objectives. Painting celluloid proved not only cheaper and less time-consuming than conventional animation; it also allowed Lye greater expressive freedom. *Tusalava* performs a comparatively slow ritualistic dance, but *A Colour Box*, shot in Dufaycolor, pulsates with complex and jumbled movements and creates a greater sense of off-screen space, as if the patterns are streaming in and out of the frame. Furthermore, imaginative synchronisation by Lye's sound editor, Jack Ellitt – a key partner in the early films – makes the dynamic shapes dance in step with the popular Cuban music on the soundtrack. Five minutes long, *A Colour Box* was popular with audiences and gained significant critical acclaim.

Lye increasingly incorporated more 'concrete' symbols within his films, but continued to experiment formally with music, colour and movement, using puppets and live-action footage. After working with Humphrey Jennings on an elaborate puppet film advertising Shell Oil, *The Birth of the Robot* (1936), he experimented with the Gasparcolor process in his next GPO film, *Rainbow Dance* (1936). A silhouetted figure (portrayed by dancer Rupert Doone) threads through scenes of a city dweller enjoying leisure pursuits; using stencil patterns and de-registration effects, Lye transforms the surrounding *mise en scène* into a constantly changing landscape – a mid-1930s' Britain given the dazzling colours, shapes and rhythms never available in real life.

Lye continued to incorporate live-action material in his next film, *Trade Tattoo* (1937), featuring stock GPO documentary footage, overlaid this time with more sophisticated colour abstractions, using the Technicolor process. His last film for the GPO was *N or NW* (1937). A simple live-action story about lovers at cross-purposes eventually reunited is used to convey a message about the importance of addressing letters correctly. The mundane theme is wonderfully enlivened by the creative verve of Lye's unconventional edits, extreme close-ups, trick shots and superimposed animation.

Lye returned to fully abstract film-making in *Colour Flight* (1939), used as an advertisement for Imperial Airways, and the musical short *Swinging the Lambeth Walk* (1939). During the Second World War available avenues for Lye's experimentation narrowed; but even in live-action propaganda he remained relentlessly adventurous. In *When the Pie Was Opened*, one of seven films made for the Realist Film Unit, a simple recipe for vegetable pie becomes a peg for playful games with images, words and surreal sound effects. All humour vanishes, though, in the powerful *Kill or Be Killed* – at eighteen minutes Lye's longest film, largely shot with a hand-held camera but rigorously controlled, showing in graphic detail how a British soldier hunts down a German sniper.

Following *Cameramen at War*, a compilation of footage taken by newsreel teams, Lye moved to New York City to take up a permanent assignment with *The March of Time*, editing and sometimes generating footage on social and political topics. After the newsreel closed in 1951, picking up the reins as an experimental artist proved difficult, and no American sponsor behaved as benevolently as the GPO. Declaring himself on strike as a film-maker, Lye turned increasingly to kinetic sculptures, easier to finance, though not before revealing his old fire and stature as a major non-representative artist in the films *Free Radicals* (1959) and *Particles in Space* (1961–80). Lye died in Warwick, New York State, on 15 May 1980.

(Geoff Brown and Jamie Sexton)

BIBLIOGRAPHY: Christie, Ian, 'Colour, Music, Dance, Motion. Len Lye in England, 1927–44', in Jean-Michel Bouhours and Roger Horrocks (eds), *Len Lye* (Paris: Éditions du Centre Pompidou, 2000); Curnow, Wystan, 'Len Lye & *Tusalava*', *Cantrills Filmnotes* nos. 29/30, Feb. 1979, pp. 38–42; Curnow, Wystan and Roger Horrocks (ed.), *Len Lye, Figures of Motion: Selected Writings* (Auckland: Auckland University Press, 1984); Dusinberre, Deke, 'The Avant-Garde Attitude in the Thirties', in Don Macpherson (ed.), *Traditions of Independence: British Cinema in the Thirties* (London: BFI Publishing, 1980); Horrocks, Roger, *Len Lye: A Biography* (Auckland: Auckland University Press, 2001); Low, Rachael, *The History of the British Film: Documentary and Educational Films of the 1930s* (London: George Allen & Unwin, 1979); Nash, Paul, 'The Colour Film', in Charles Davy (ed.), *Footnotes to the Film* (London: Lovat Dickson, 1937).

FILMOGRAPHY (UK only): *Tusalava* (1929); *Experimental Animation* (aka *The Peanut Vendor*, 1934); *Full Fathom Five*; *A Colour Box*; *Kaleidoscope* (1935); *The Birth of the Robot* (co-dir. Humphrey Jennings); *Rainbow Dance* (1936); *Trade Tattoo*; *N or NW* (1937); *Colour Flight*; *Swinging the Lambeth Walk* (1939); *Musical Poster No. 1* (1940); *When the Pie Was Opened* (1941); *Newspaper Train*; *Work Party*; *Collapsible Metal Tubes* (1942); *Kill or Be Killed*; *Planned Crops*; *Cameramen at War* (1943).

LYNE, Adrian (1941–)

Adrian Lyne was born in Peterborough, Cambridgeshire, on 4 March 1941. He worked in advertising during the 1960s and 70s and, along with fellow British directors Ridley Scott, Tony Scott, Hugh Hudson and Alan Parker, was credited with revolutionising British television advertising through the adventurous use of visual imagery, cheeky dramatics and parody. In 1970 he turned producer for Michael Hayes' *The Table*, a fiction short presenting a table's view of a young couple's breakfast quarrel. Four years later, he made his own narrative debut with the thirty-eight minute *Mr Smith*, introduced at the London Film Festival (some distribution followed in 1976). The film concerns a middle-aged man in London (Peter Barkworth) so fed up with life's petty annoyances that he shoots himself. Hindsight reveals some obvious links to the American films that followed. There is the same dependence on flashy editing, lighting and compositions (a clear result of Lyne's advertising work) and a similar fondness for extravagant nihilism and shallow sociology; though the film's witty observational humour, its most attractive aspect, never found a place in the director's armoury.

No British feature debut followed. Hollywood beckoned instead, and with David Puttnam as producer he directed *Foxes* (1980), a coming-of-age teen saga set in the San Fernando Valley. Critics noted the visible clashes between honest intentions and melodramatic excess – another sign of things to come – but the film was successful enough for Lyne to begin building a secure position inside the Hollywood mainstream. *Flashdance* (1983), *Fatal Attraction* (1987) and *Indecent Proposal* (1993) proved enormously successful box-office hits, demonstrating Lyne's ability to tap into the *Zeitgeist* and generate films prompting quick and easy sociological analysis. (*Fatal Attraction*, for example, was labelled as a 'post-feminist' thriller and one that fed into anxieties about AIDS). The films have been dismissed by many critics for their formulaic plots and simplistic characters, and for emphasising glamour, style and slick imagery above all else. *Unfaithful* (2002), however, shows more ambition and maturity. With its references to Hitchcock, *Don't Look Now* (Nicolas Roeg, 1973) and what Lyne has declared to be his favourite film, *Brief Encounter* (David Lean, 1945), this domestic suspense drama also provides a rare demonstration of the director's British lineage, almost thirty years after his own British cinema career started and finished.

(Geoff Brown and Mark Glancy)

BIBLIOGRAPHY: Bloom, Phillipa, 'Profiles: Adrian Lyne, Director', *Empire*, Oct. 1991, p. 48; Interview, 'Dialogue on Film: Adrian Lyne', *American Film*, Sept. 1988, pp. 16–20; Lyne, Adrian, 'Personal Pick: Brief Encounter', *Premiere*, Mar. 1992, p. 94.

FILMOGRAPHY: *Mr Smith* (short, 1974; rel. 1976); *Foxes* (US, 1980); *Flashdance* (US, 1983); *Nine ½ Weeks* (US, 1986); *Fatal Attraction* (1987); *Jacob's Ladder* (aka *Dante's Inferno*, US, 1990); *Indecent Proposal* (US, 1993); *Lolita* (Fr/US, 1997); *Unfaithful* (US, 2002).

LYNN, Jonathan (1943–)

Jonathan Lynn was born on 3 April 1943 in Bath, Somerset, and educated at Cambridge University, where he joined the Footlights Revue. He made his stage debut on Broadway in the 1964 Footlights production, *Cambridge Circus*, and returned to England to build a successful acting career on both stage and television. Lynn also established himself as a talented and prolific television comedy writer, having his greatest success with the hugely popular and critically acclaimed series *Yes Minister* (1980–2) and *Yes Prime Minister* (1986–7), which he co-wrote with Antony Jay.

Lynn made his debut as a film director in America with *Clue*, based on the 'Cluedo' board game. It was followed by *Nuns on the Run*, a crude but popular British comedy starring Eric Idle and Robbie Coltrane. Lynn's next film, *My Cousin Vinny*, where he elicits excellent performances from Joe Pesci and Marisa Tomei, was considerably more sophisticated and might be judged his most accomplished film. *The Distinguished Gentleman*, a political comedy starring Eddie Murphy, and *Greedy*, with Kirk Douglas and Michael J. Fox in a comedy of family in-fighting, were disappointing in comparison. With *Sgt Bilko*, *Trial and Error*, *The Whole Nine Yards* and *The Fighting Temptations*, Lynn, who now lives in Los Angeles, established himself as a mainstream Hollywood comedy director.

(Martin Hunt)

BIBLIOGRAPHY: McGregor, Alexander, 'Nun the Wiser', *Time Out*, 2 May 1990, p. 23; The Official Jonathan Lynn website, <www.jonathanlynn.com>.

FILMOGRAPHY: *Clue* (US, 1985); *Nuns on the Run* (1990); *My Cousin Vinny* (US); *The Distinguished Gentleman* (US, 1992); *Greedy* (US, 1994); *Sgt Bilko* (US, 1996); *Trial and Error* (US, 1997); *The Whole Nine Yards* (US, 2000); *The Fighting Temptations* (US, 2003).

LYNN, Robert (1917–1982)

Robert Bryce Lynn was born in London on 9 June 1917, the son of the famous farceur Ralph Lynn. He entered the film industry as a camera assistant, and after the Second World War worked as an assistant director on films ranging from Powell and Pressburger's *Black Narcissus* (1947) to Terence Fisher's *Dracula* (1958). After directing episodes of television series, including *Interpol Calling* (1959), *Ghost Squad* (1961) and *The Saint* (1962), he made his cinema debut with the low-budget Merton Park thriller *Invitation to Murder*. Other Edgar Wallace second features followed before Lynn moved slightly up-market for *Dr Crippen*. Helped by Leigh Vance's well-structured script, the atmospheric cinematography of Nicolas Roeg and a strong cast (Donald Pleasence, Coral Browne, Samantha Eggar), Lynn renders the story of a middle-aged man who murders his wife and runs off with an attractive young woman both convincing and moving. But with attention fixed on New Wave realism, the film made little impact, and Lynn's career failed to flourish.

Take Me Over, a weak stab at the youth market, and a wartime supporting feature *Blaze of Glory* led only to three tacky Harry Alan Towers adventures – *Victim Five*, *Coast of Skeletons* and *Mozambique* – before a return to Merton Park for one of the last (and best) Wallace films, *Change Partners*. Though he lacked prestige as a director, Lynn's reputation as a competent and amiable craftsman enabled him to continue working throughout the 1960s. Towers, before lurching into sexploitation, offered him an unpromising children's film, *Sandy the Seal*. Lynn's own family production, an adaptation of *The Railway Children* (1970) directed by Lionel Jeffries, was much more successful.

In the 1970s, as film production contracted, Lynn returned to the role of assistant director, ensuring that shooting proceeded as smoothly as possible on the chaotic *Dracula A.D. 1972* (Alan Gibson, 1972) and the routine but very popular *Can You Keep It up for a Week?* (Jim Atkinson, 1974). He was more creatively employed as second-unit director on the first two *Superman* films. Lynn died in London on 15 January 1982.

(Robert Murphy)

BIBLIOGRAPHY: Obituary, *Screen International*, 23 Jan. 1982, p. 4.

FILMOGRAPHY: *Invitation to Murder* (1959); *Information Received*; *Postman's Knock* (1961); *Two Letter Alibi* (US: *Death and the Sky Above*; *Dr Crippen* (1962); *Take Me Over*; *Blaze of Glory* (1963); *Victim Five*; *Coast of Skeletons*; *Mozambique* (1964); *Change Partners* (1965); *Gern hab' ich die Frau'n gekillt* (aka *Le Carnaval des barbouzes/Killer's Carnival/Spy against the World*, co-dirs. Sheldon Reynolds/Alberto Cardone, Aus/It/Fr, 1966); *The Face of Eve* (co-dir. Jeremy Summers, UK/Sp, 1968); *Sandy the Seal* (1969); *Superman* (2nd unit dir., Richard Donner, 1978); *Superman II* (2nd unit dir., Richard Lester, 1980).

MCADAM, Trish (1952–)

Trish McAdam was born in Dublin on 17 June 1952. She became interested in film-making after working in New York with photographer Nan Golden and Super-8 film-maker Vivienne Dick. Her early short films, *The Drip*, *The Big Time* and *Berlin*, are influenced by fine art practices and are formally experimental. McAdam made her first feature film, *Snakes and Ladders*, in 1996. A comedy about two generations of women, set in the newly hip Temple Bar area of Dublin, the film provoked wildly divergent critical responses. It remains one of the few films directed by women about contemporary Irish women's lives, although its lengthy production period left it appearing slightly anachronistic on release.

Snakes and Ladders was followed by the three-part documentary series, *Hoodwinked*, made in 1997 for RTÉ television. McAdam traces the position of Irish women since independence, arguing that they have been sidelined by a paternalistic combination of Church and state. Although visually unchallenging, the series is an important contribution to Irish women's history.

McAdam's next feature project, *The Crock of Gold*, adapted from the novel by James Stephens, has been delayed by the usual difficulties in raising funding faced by women directors in Ireland.

(Ruth Barton)

BIBLIOGRAPHY: Power, Paul, 'Snake Charmer', *Film Ireland* no. 48, Aug/Sept. 1995, pp. 10–12.

FILMOGRAPHY: *The Drip* (short, Ir, 1984); *The Big Time* (short, Ir, 1985); *Berlin* (short, Ir, 1991); *Snakes and Ladders* (Ir/Ger/UK, 1996).

McCARTHY, Michael (1917–1959)

Early in 1959, after twelve years directing documentaries and features, Michael McCarthy's career reached its peak with the release of his Second World War thriller *Operation Amsterdam*, his biggest and best-received venture to date. It had no successor; he died shortly afterwards, aged forty-two.

McCarthy was born in Birmingham on 27 February 1917. Educated in Manchester, he began in the film industry in 1934, working chiefly at Twickenham Studios as an assistant and second-unit director. Later he performed similar chores at the Crown Film Unit and Ealing. He also collaborated on the script for Ealing's drama of canal life, *Painted Boats* (Charles Crichton, 1945). From 1946, McCarthy began writing and directing at the Film Producers' Guild and its associate company Verity Films. Most projects were instructional films made for the Army Kinematograph Service: topics included the duties of the Military Police, the Tank corps and road safety.

McCarthy moved into features with *Assassin for Hire* in 1950, working initially for his Guild colleague Julian Wintle at Merton Park. Army instructions were swept aside; now his subject matter included Soho killers, murder suspects on the run and other staples of the low-budget thriller. In 1954 television drama episodes began to engage him; that year he directed Buster Keaton in *The Awakening*, an adaptation of Gogol's story *The Overcoat*, for the anthology series *Douglas Fairbanks Presents . . .* None of this work earned him much attention.

McCarthy's fortunes in the industry began to rise with his return to the big screen in 1955. *Shadow of a Man*, made for the producer and distributor E. J. Fancey, included conventional thriller thuggery, but the lively direction and seaside locations injected some fresh air. *It's Never Too Late* (1956) found him moving closer to the industry mainstream with a popular stage comedy, garishly filmed in Eastman Colour. Phyllis Calvert starred as the housewife-authoress whisked to Hollywood who gives up the lonely bright lights for crowded English domesticity. But comedy was not McCarthy's forte. *The Traitor* (1957), his next film for Fancey, concerned the search for a traitor among a former Resistance group. Despite his own loquacious script and the theatrical excesses of its star, Donald Wolfit, tension still flickered here and there.

With *Operation Amsterdam*, financed by Rank, script and direction fought another battle. The plot, concerning British agents and Dutch patriots endeavouring to rescue industrial diamonds from the hands of the advancing Germans in 1940, allowed McCarthy's old documentary instincts to flourish. Shooting on location, he vividly illustrated the turmoil of war in Amsterdam: the sudden bombings, the café drinkers soldiering on despite snipers' fire, the planes peppering escaping refugees. But the script, adapted by McCarthy and John Eldridge from David E. Walker's novel, settled increasingly for artifice, and left characterisations underdeveloped. The film's pace, atmospheric visuals and credible performances from Tony Britton, Peter Finch, Malcolm Keen, Eva Bartok and Alexander Knox all helped to blanket deficiencies.

Other mainstream Rank assignments would probably have followed *Operation Amsterdam*. But McCarthy's death on 7 May 1959, in Eversfield Chest Hospital, St Leonard's, cut short his career, and his promise.

(Geoff Brown)

BIBLIOGRAPHY: 'Associated British Sign up Director Michael McCarthy', held on microfiche in the BFI National Library, London; Obituary, *Daily Cinema*, 11 May 1959, p. 8.

FILMOGRAPHY: *Films in the Making* (doc.); *Road Surface Dressing* (doc.) (1947); *Town Patrol* (doc., co-dir. Geoffrey Busby); *Dangerous Journey* (doc.); *Men in Armour* (doc.) (1948); *Look Mum, Soldiers!* (doc., 1949); *Road Sense* (doc., co-dir. Dick Tambling); *Assassin for Hire*; *Mystery Junction* (1951); *John of the Fair*, *Crow Hollow* (1952); *Shadow of a Man* (1955); *It's Never Too Late* (1956); *The Traitor* (US: *The Accused*, 1957); *Operation Amsterdam* (1959).

MACARTNEY, Sydney (1954–)

Sydney Macartney was born on 24 July 1954 in Ballymena, County Antrim. He was educated at the University of Ulster and at the National Film and Television School where he trained as a lighting cameraman. He gained extensive experience as a camera operator and on graduation continued, throughout the early 1980s, to hone his skills making music videos. He graduated to feature films as director of photography on *Party Party* (Terry Winsor, George Pavlou, 1983) and *Underworld* (1985). In the late 1980s he set up his own production company specialising in commercials and in 1989 moved into television as director of Yorkshire Television's *Yellowthread Street*. His credits include a special two-hour episode of *The Young Indiana Jones Chronicles* (1992), episodes of the BBC series *The Ambassador* (1998) and *Linda Green* (2001), and the television films *The Whipping Boy* (1994) and *The Canterville Ghost* (1996).

Macartney's feature film debut was *The Bridge* – based on Maggie Hemmingway's novel about English Impressionist painter Paul Wilson Steer – and his accomplished eye for cinematic composition is evident in the film's recreation of the rural Suffolk of the 1860s. The film reveals the suffocating conformity of privileged English society, but there is also a sense in which Macartney glorifies in the genteel Englishness of the world he has created. This is in stark contrast to his second film, *A Love Divided*, a powerful evocation of rural Ireland in the 1950s and real events that took place in the small Wexford town of Fethard-on-Sea. Sheila Cloney was a Protestant woman married to a local Catholic, and as a condition of such a mixed marriage being blessed by the Catholic Church, the couple agreed to bring their children up as Catholics. When Sheila defied the Church and took her children away, the Catholic priest organised a boycott of the local Protestant community accusing them of helping Sheila to 'kidnap' the children for Protestantism. The situation quickly deteriorated into the kind of bitter sectarian division more commonly associated with Northern Ireland. Macartney pursues his themes visually as well as through dialogue and performance, but his rural Ireland is a landscape replete with menace, violence and irrational behaviour, far removed from nostalgia and the 'heritage' tradition evident in *The Bridge*.

(Martin McLoone)

BIBLIOGRAPHY: McLoone, Martin, *Irish Film: The Emergence of a Contemporary Cinema* (London: BFI, 2000); Pettitt, Lance, *Screening Ireland* (Manchester: Manchester University Press, 2000).

FILMOGRAPHY: *The Bridge* (1992); *A Love Divided* (UK/Ir, 1999).

MACDONALD, David (1904–1983)

David Macdonald was born in Helensburgh, Scotland, on 9 May 1904 into an upper-middle-class family. He worked in Hollywood for three years as an assistant director to Cecil B.

DeMille before returning to Britain, where he directed several 'quota quickies' beginning with *Double Alibi* (1937). These low-budget crime thrillers and comedies offered limited opportunities, though *It's Never Too Late to Mend* is one of the best of the Tod Slaughter melodramas, and *Dead Men Tell No Tales*, with a thrilling performance from Emlyn Williams, is well above average. Macdonald's most accomplished pre-war film was *This Man Is News*, a lively, fast-paced and entertaining comedy-thriller, inspired by the American 'Thin Man' series, and starring Barry K. Barnes and Valerie Hobson. It led to a sequel, *This Man in Paris*, and the similarly cast *Law and Disorder*.

Men of the Lightship (1940) showed Macdonald's abilities as a documentary director and led to a distinguished period as Head of the No. 1 Army Film and Photographic Section in North Africa. He showed inventiveness, courage and great organisational ability, producing the highly regarded feature-documentaries *Desert Victory* (1943) and *Burma Victory* (1945), both directed by Roy Boulting. He was made a lieutenant-colonel and was awarded an OBE in 1944.

After demobilisation, Macdonald joined Sydney Box at Gainsborough. *The Brothers* (1947), which he directed and co-adapted with the novel's author L. A. G. Strong, was his finest film. Shooting on location on the Isle of Skye, Macdonald evokes the harsh, violent world of this remote community in 1900, a world of clan and fraternal rivalry, of thwarted sexual passion and brooding revenge. He followed *The Brothers* with *Snowbound*, a rather ham-fisted adaptation of a Hammond Innes thriller, and the social-comment drama *Good Time Girl*, one of the better films about delinquency and institutional life. Macdonald was entrusted with Box's two flagship productions, *The Bad Lord Byron* and *Christopher Columbus*, but the scripts and the execution failed to match their ambition. *Diamond City*, *Cairo Road* and *The Adventurers* were undistinguished adventure stories set in Africa, which further damaged Macdonald's career, and he descended into B-features, making a number of forgettable low-budget crime thrillers – though *The Lost Hours* (1952) is well handled and the science-fiction film *Devil Girl from Mars* (1954) has attained cult status. The success of *The Moonraker* (1957), a swashbuckling adventure story set during the English Civil War, did not relaunch Macdonald's career, and he returned to second features and television, except for the Charlie Drake comedy *Petticoat Pirates* (1961).

Macdonald was characterised as 'quick-thinking, dynamic and decisive in action, a fast worker who knows exactly what he wants and gets it in the shortest possible time' (Wallace, p. 5). These qualities served him well as a documentary-maker, but he was less successful with occasionally temperamental stars. At their best – as in *The Brothers* – Macdonald's films display a bold, vigorous and uncompromising style, but he only occasionally managed to impose this on often intractable material. He died in London on 22 June 1983.

(Andrew Spicer)

BIBLIOGRAPHY: Obituary, *The Times*, 28 June 1983, p. 12; Wallace, Leonard, 'Backroom Boys at the Bush', *Picturegoer*, 14 Feb. 1948.

FILMOGRAPHY: *Double Alibi*; *When the Poppies Bloom Again*; *The Last Curtain*; *It's Never Too Late to Mend*; *Death Croons the Blues* (1937); *Meet Mr Penny*; *A Spot of Bother*; *This Man Is News*; *Make It Three*; *Dead Men Tell No Tales* (1938); *Riding High*; *This Man in Paris* (1939); *Spies of the Air*; *The Midas Touch*; *Men of the Lightship* (doc. short); *Law and Disorder* (1940); *This England* (aka *Our Heritage*, 1941); *Left of the Line* (doc. short, 1944); *The Brothers* (1947); *Snowbound*; *Good Time Girl* (1948); *The Bad Lord Byron*; *Christopher Columbus*; *Diamond City* (1949); *Cairo Road* (1950); *The Adventurers* (US: *The Great Adventure*, 1951); *Tread Softly*; *The Lost Hours* (1952); *The Yellow Robe*; *Operation Malaya* (doc.) (1953); *One Just Man*; *Devil Girl from Mars*; *The Gamblers* (short); *The Diamond Expert*; *Lucky Man* (short) (1954); *Three Cornered Fate*; *Man in Demand*; *Final Column*; *The Weekend Guest* (short); *Death Walks by Night* (short); *Murder of a 'Ham'* (short); *The Very Silent Traveller* (short); *Diplomatic Error* (short); *Double Pay-Off* (short); *The Eighth Window* (short); *Fame and the Fury* (short); *The Homing Chinaman* (short); *The Imperfect Gentleman* (short); *Ring of Greed* (short); *The Schemer* (short): *The Secret Place* (short); *The Cruel Test* (short); *The Better Chance* (short); *The Man in Demand* (short); *Triple Blackmail*; *The Price of Greed* (1955); *Alias John Preston* (1956); *Small Hotel*; *The Moonraker* (1957); *A Lady Mislaid* (1958); *The Festival of Baalbeck 1960* (doc. short, 1960); *Petticoat Pirates*; *The Golden Rabbit* (1961).

MACDONALD, Hettie (1962–)

Henrietta Macdonald was born in London in 1962. She studied English at Bristol University, joining the Royal Court Theatre under the Regional Theatre Trainee Director Scheme in 1985. Her West End production of Larry Kramer's *The Normal Heart* in 1986 led to a successful theatrical career in London and elsewhere. In 1993 she directed Jonathan Harvey's *Beautiful Thing*, a play about two working-class teenage boys exploring the implications of their homosexuality, at the Bush Theatre, Shepherd's Bush, and was asked to direct a film version, adapted by Harvey, for Tony Garnett's World Productions and Channel 4. She shot the film on a Thamesmead council estate, rough enough to be convincing, airy and sunny enough to allow Harvey's optimism to shine through. Characters and dialogue remain theatrical, but Macdonald gets enthusiastic and convincing performances from her players. The novelty of a film that deals realistically with working-class life without reducing it to comic caricature or irredeemable misery makes occasional lapses into sentimentality forgivable.

She showed similar panache directing the opening episodes of the ambitious BBC saga *In a Land of Plenty* (2001), but her next feature film, *Lily and the Secret Planting*, was derailed when Winona Ryder dropped out four days into production. Macdonald returned to television, directing half the episodes of Lucy Gannon's Victorian below-stairs series *Servants* (2003). The enduring popularity of *Beautiful Thing* should ensure that doors are held open for her should she choose to return to the cinema.

(Robert Murphy)

BIBLIOGRAPHY: 'Biography – Hettie Macdonald', World Productions publicity material for *Beautiful Thing* held on microfiche in the BFI National Library, London.

FILMOGRAPHY: *Beautiful Thing* (1996).

MACDONALD, Kevin (1967–)

Kevin Macdonald was born in Glasgow on 28 October 1967. His film-making career began when he and his brother Andrew set up the independent production company Figment Films in 1991 in order to co-produce a short film, *Dr Reizer's Fragment*. Andrew went on to produce *Shallow Grave* (Danny Boyle, 1995) and *Trainspotting* (Danny Boyle, 1996); Kevin became a documentary film-maker. After writing a superb biography of his grandfather, the Hungarian screenwriter Emeric Pressburger, he directed *The Making of an Englishman* (1995) a Channel 4 documentary charting Pressburger's European career prior to coming to Britain and beginning his film-making collaboration with Michael Powell. Other impressive television documentaries were to follow, notably *Humphrey Jennings: The Man Who Listened to Britain* (2000). But Macdonald is unusual in managing to secure a cinema release – however limited – for his documentaries: *Chaplin's Goliath* (1996) narrated the life of actor Eric Campbell, an important presence in many of Charlie Chaplin's films. *Donald Cammell: The Ultimate Performance* (1998) provided insight into and new knowledge about a neglected film-maker. *One Day in September*, a 'documentary thriller' that examines the massacre of eleven Israeli athletes by Palestinian terrorists at the 1972 Munich Olympic Games, won the Academy Award for Best Documentary Feature in 2000. Like Michael Moore's *Bowling for Columbine* (2001), which won the following year, Macdonald's film is a key reference point for those aiming to produce politically engaged documentary features with a prospect of international distribution. *Touching the Void*, a dramatised account of Joe Simpson's feat of endurance in crawling over the Andes to safety after a near-fatal climbing accident, superbly captures the hazardous attractions of mountaineering and becomes a moving tribute to the human spirit.

(Jonathan Murray)

BIBLIOGRAPHY: Collins, David, 'What's Up Doc?', *Creation*, Nov. 2000, pp. 10–12; 'Director Q & A', *The Face*, June 2000, p. 244; Hughes, Penny, 'Peak Viewing', *Broadcast*, 12 July 2002, p. 12.

FILMOGRAPHY: *Chaplin's Goliath* (1996); *Donald Cammell: The Ultimate Performance* (1998); *One Day in September* (2000); *Touching the Void* (2003); *The Last King of Scotland* (2006).

McDONAGH, John (?–1961)

John McDonagh was born in Cloughjordan, Tipperary. He worked as an actor and producer in English and American theatre, and wrote the scenario for D. W. Griffith's *The Fugitive* (1910) before returning to Ireland. He continued to write and produce for the stage but he was also involved in the struggle for independence; his brother Thomas was executed as one of the leaders of the 1916 Easter Rising. After making a number of short films he directed *Willy Reilly and His Colleen Bawn* for the nationalist Film Company of Ireland. Though based on a mid-Victorian novel and set a century earlier, the story of a gentlemanly Catholic farmer who suffers prejudice and discrimination when he seeks the hand of his Protestant sweetheart struck a chord with Irish audiences. Subsequent films – *Paying the Rent*, *The Casey Millions*, *Wicklow Gold* and *Cruiskeen Lawn* – were less ambitious comedies about racehorses and lovable tricksters.

Irish film production contracted after independence and McDonagh returned to the theatre. His play *The Irish Jew* enjoyed considerable success. Between 1938 and 1947 he was productions director at Radio Éireann. He died in Dublin in July 1961.

(Robert Murphy)

BIBLIOGRAPHY: Rocket, Kevin, John Hill and Luke Gibbons, *Cinema and Ireland* (New York: Syracuse University Press, 1987).

FILMOGRAPHY: *Blarney* (short); *The Upstart* (short); *The Byeways of Fate* (short); *The Irish Girl* (short) (1917); *A Girl of Glenbeigh* (short, 1918); *Willy Reilly and His Colleen Bawn*; *Paying the Rent* (1920); *The Casey Millions* (Ir); *Wicklow Gold* (Ir); *Cruiskeen Lawn* (Ir) (1922).

McDONELL, Fergus (1910–1984)

Fergus McDonell was born in Tunbridge Wells on 6 October 1910. He began to work as a film editor in the late 1930s, and

came to prominence with his work on Carol Reed's *The Way Ahead* (1944) and *Odd Man Out* (1946), and Anthony Asquith's *The Way to the Stars* (1945). Although chiefly remembered as an editor, McDonell directed three feature films. *The Small Voice* (1948) is the most impressive: a noirish crime drama, where a maladjusted couple (James Donald and Valerie Hobson) have their lives further disrupted when they are held hostage in their country house by two escaped convicts (Howard Keel and the future director David Greene).

Prelude to Fame (1950) was a more syrupy production: based on a story by Aldous Huxley, it focused on Guido (Jeremy Spenser), an Italian peasant boy and musical genius. Guido becomes a rich and famous child-conductor, but misses the simple life he has left behind; he is eventually rescued by Englishman abroad John Morell (Guy Rolfe), and returned to his world of blissful rural poverty. *Private Information* (1952), McDonell's last feature film, dealt with the theme of government corruption from a citizen's point of view; its unusual slant on society might be attributed to the fact that it was produced by the company set up by the film-workers' union, the Association of Cinema Technicians.

In the mid-1950s McDonell went to Canada, where he directed fifteen short documentaries for the National Film Board. On returning to Britain, he worked as an editor rather than a director, generally on projects of his own choosing. He edited most of the films directed by Clive Donner, along with interestingly offbeat projects such as Anthony Simmons' *Four in the Morning* (1965) and Albert Finney's *Charlie Bubbles* (1967). He died in Norwich on 3 January 1984.

(Elisabetta Girelli)

BIBLIOGRAPHY: Obituary, *Film and Television Technician*, Feb. 1984, p. 12.

FILMOGRAPHY: Documentaries (Canada): *The Yellow Leaf*; *The Nativity Cycle*; *Morning Incident*; *Methods of Instruction/Méthodes d'instruction*; *Longer Trail*; *Crash Rescue and Fire Fighting*; *The Cage*; *Back into the Sun* (1956); *Test Pilot*; *The Street*; *None but the Lonely*; *The Harvest*; *The Happy Fugitive*; *Double Verdict*; *Capital City* (1957).
Features: *The Small Voice* (US: *Hideout*, 1948); *Prelude to Fame* (1950); *Private Information* (1952).

McGRATH, Douglas (1958–)

A Hollywood actor equally at home in the tough guy atmosphere of Clint Eastwood films and the sophisticated New York comedies of Woody Allen, Douglas McGrath unexpectedly launched himself on a new career as the director of likeable adaptations of English classic novels. His *Emma* is gently unobtrusive, occasionally to the point of dullness, but the crucial relationship between Emma (a convincingly English Gwyneth Paltrow) and Mr Knightley (an unshowy Jeremy Northam) is convincingly handled and builds to a moving emotional climax.

Company Man, in which McGrath took the starring role as an American schoolteacher caught up in comic attempts at spying in Cuba at the time of the Bay of Pigs disaster, was much less successful, despite a supporting cast featuring Sigourney Weaver, John Turturro and Woody Allen. He returned to Dickens with a *Nicholas Nickleby* very different from Cavalcanti's 1947 Ealing version and the famous eight-and-a half-hour RSC production filmed for Channel 4 in 1982 by Colin Callendar and Jim Goddard. Though McGrath retains period trappings this is very much Dickens for the 21st century, with the cruelty and grotesquerie played down and Nicholas (an emotional Charlie Hunnam) and his sister Kate wafted along the path to happiness by lovable eccentrics. One might disapprove of this brightening up of Dickens' dark side, but the enthusiastic performances McGrath inspires from his cast – outstanding in the case of Juliet Stevenson's Mrs Squeers and Romola Garai's unusually spirited Kate – make it difficult to resist his sunny vision of a beneficent Victorian universe.

(Robert Murphy)

BIBLIOGRAPHY: McGrath, Douglas, 'Raising Jane', *Premiere*, Sept. 1996, pp. 74–7, 117.

FILMOGRAPHY: *Emma* (UK/US, 1996); *Company Man* (UK/US/Fr, 2000); *Nicholas Nickleby* (UK/US, 2002).

McGRATH, Joseph (1930–)

Joe McGrath was born in Glasgow on 28 March 1930, the son of a stand-up comedian. After performing and producing with a Combined Services Entertainment Unit while on National Service in Malaya, McGrath spent four years at art school before joining Associated-Rediffusion as a set designer. He moved to ABC Television to direct *Candid Camera* (1961) and the arts programme *Tempo* (1961), and finally found his niche directing Michael Bentine's zany comedy show *It's a Square World* (1963) for the BBC. This was followed by the ground-breaking *Not Only . . . But Also* (1965) series starring Peter Cook and Dudley Moore. Its phenomenal success led to a feature film, *30 Is a Dangerous Age, Cynthia*, which McGrath scripted with Moore and John Wells. Intended as a vehicle for Moore, it parodies 1960s' attitudes while employing a barrage of cinematic tricks ranging from wipes to jump-cuts.

McGrath was one of five directors named in the credits for *Casino Royale*, a James Bond parody that is the quintessential example of late 1960s' excess, with its roster of stars in cameo roles and deliberately inconsequential playfulness. Something of the same frenetic style is apparent in *The Bliss of Mrs Blossom*, where Shirley MacLaine leads a double life, one of prosaic domesticity with her bra-manufacturer husband (Richard Attenborough), the other of exotic fantasy with her sewing-machine mechanic lover (James Booth), who she keeps hidden in the attic.

McGrath's most ambitious film is *The Magic Christian*. Written by McGrath with Terry Southern and Peter Sellers, the film combines the episodic, revue-style structure that typifies much of McGrath's work with a more directly satirical stance, and features an eclectic cast including Peter Sellers, Spike Milligan, Ringo Starr, Raquel Welch and Roman Polanski.

McGrath's association with Milligan dated from the televised broadcast of the last *Goon Show*, which he directed. They worked together again on the amiable children's film *Digby, the Biggest Dog in the World* and on *The Great McGonagall*. Both films capture something of the chaotic quality of Milligan's imagination as well as his irreverent humour and surreal inventiveness.

The remainder of McGrath's work is less original and belongs within formulaic British film traditions. *Girls Come First* and *I'm Not Feeling Myself Tonight* are typical 1970s' sex-farces (on the former McGrath is credited as Croisette Meubles), while *The Strange Case of the End of Civilisation as We Know It* features John Cleese as the grandson of Sherlock Holmes. *Rising Damp*, which reunited McGrath with Leonard Rossiter, whom he had directed in *Justin Thyme* (1964) and *The Loser* (1978), was better than most television spin-offs and captures the pathos as well as the humour of the original series. McGrath's last project was the television film *Night Train to Murder* (1985), starring Eric Morecambe and Ernie Wise.

(Robert Shail)

BIBLIOGRAPHY: McGillivray, David, *Doing Rude Things: The History of the British Sex Film, 1957–81* (London: Sun Tavern Fields, 1992); Murphy, Robert, *Sixties British Cinema* (London: BFI, 1992); Walker, Alexander, *Hollywood, England* (London: Harrap, 1986); Wicking, Chris, 'The Other Side of the Screen No. 2: Joseph McGrath', *Primetime* vol. 1 no. 2, Autumn 1981, pp. 19–22.

FILMOGRAPHY: *Casino Royale* (co-dirs. John Huston/Ken Hughes/Val Guest/Robert Parrish, 1967); *30 Is a Dangerous Age, Cynthia*; *The Bliss of Mrs Blossom* (1968); *The Magic Christian* (1970); *Digby, the Biggest Dog in the World* (1973); *The Great McGonagall* (1974); *Girls Come First* (as Croisette Meubles); *I'm Not Feeling Myself Tonight* (1975); *Escape to Entebbe* (short, co-dir. David Grant, 1976); *The Strange Case of the End of Civilisation as We Know It* (1977); *Rising Damp* (1980).

McGUCKIAN, Mary (1963–)

Mary McGuckian was born in Northern Ireland on 27 March 1963. After an early career with the Abbey Theatre, McGuckian gained experience on Jim Sheridan's *The Field* (1990) and moved into feature film-making as writer/director of *Words upon the Window Pane*. An adaptation of a one-act play by W. B. Yeats, the film is a whimsical reconstruction of the relationship between Jonathan Swift and his two lovers juxtaposed with a parallel narrative set in Dublin in the 1920s concerning the medium who has facilitated this access to the past and her assistant.

McGuckian's next film, *This Is the Sea*, is a 'love-across-the-divide' narrative set around two families in contemporary Northern Ireland, with Samantha Morton and Ross McDade as the lovers. This was followed by the biopic *Best*, featuring John Lynch as Northern Ireland's most famous footballer. Critically panned, the film suffers from miscasting and a failure to reproduce George Best's extraordinary footballing ability. She went on to film *The Bridge of San Luis Rey*, an adaptation of Thornton Wilder's 1927 novel (filmed twice before, in 1929 and 1944) set in eighteenth-century Peru, starring Robert De Niro, Harvey Keitel and Gabriel Byrne. Box-office returns were disappointing, and McGuckian's *Rag Tale* (2005) is a much less grand project, a frenetic, semi-improvised comedy set on the editorial floor of a tabloid newspaper.

McGuckian has attracted many of Ireland's leading actors to her films (*This Is the Sea* includes a charismatic performance from Richard Harris). She writes her own screenplays and was producer on *Best*. Her familiarity with the film industry has helped her retain control over her work, which, except for *The Bridge of San Luis Rey*, has tended to be small in scale and eclectic in content.

(Ruth Barton)

BIBLIOGRAPHY: Collins, Pat, 'Interview: Mary McGuckian', *Film West* no. 20, Spring 1995, pp. 18–20; Power, Paul, 'McGuckian's Travels', *Film Ireland* no. 45, Feb./Mar. 1995, pp. 10–12.

FILMOGRAPHY: *Words upon the Window Pane* (1994); *This is the Sea* (Ir/UK/US, 1998); *Best* (2000); *The Bridge of San Luis Rey* (Fr/Sp/UK, 2004); *Rag Tale* (2005).

McGUIGAN, Paul (1963–)

Paul McGuigan was born in Bellshill, Scotland, on 19 September 1963. After working on controversial documentary subjects for Channel 4 such as *Playing Nintendo with God*, he adapted *The Granton Star Cause* (1997), a short story by Irvine Welsh. McGuigan approached his subject with unflinching visuals and a bravura style that perfectly captured Welsh's urban fable of a down-on-his-luck amateur footballer who, at a point when it seems his life cannot get any worse, meets God in a pub and is changed into a fly. When Welsh's popularity was boosted by the success of *Trainspotting* (Danny Boyle, 1996), McGuigan was offered the opportunity to adapt two more Welsh tales into a triptych for theatrical release as *The Acid House*. Stylish though they were, audiences failed to flock to three shorts masquerading as a feature film.

McGuigan's next project, *Gangster No. 1*, was based on a play by Louis Mellis and David Scinto, but did much less well than Mellis and Scinto's *Sexy Beast* (Jonathan Glazer, 2000), which is shallower but far wittier. A psychotic epic that owes more to Kubrick's *A Clockwork Orange* (1971) than to the contemporary wave of British crime films, *Gangster No. 1*'s disturbing scenes of violence proved less acceptable to audiences than the ersatz gangsters of Guy Ritchie's *Lock, Stock and Two Smoking Barrels* (1998).

McGuigan's follow-up film, *The Reckoning*, brought together Paul Bettany from *Gangster No. 1* and Ewen Bremner from *The Acid House* with Brian Cox, Gina McKee and the American Willem Dafoe for a medieval mystery tale based on a novel by Barry Unsworth. The film had a respectable budget of £8 million and involved the building of an entire medieval village in southern Spain, but distributors showed little interest and the film failed to reach the screen until 2004.

By then McGuigan had directed *Wicker Park*, a remake of Gilles Mimouni's romantic thriller *L'Appartement* (1996), with the action transposed from Paris to New York and Vincent Cassel (who had played a cameo role in *The Reckoning*) replaced by Josh Hartnett. An obviously talented director, McGuigan seems yet to have found his place in the industry though he enjoyed some success with his American crime comedy *Lucky Number Slevin* (US, 2006).

(Simon Brown)

BIBLIOGRAPHY: 'New Flag for UK Film', *Televisual*, May 2000, pp. 26–8; 'Not-So-Merrie Englande', *Sight and Sound*, Apr. 2001, pp. 4–5; Silberg, Jon, '. . . Blood Brothers', *American Cinematographer*, June 2002, pp. 30–3.

FILMOGRAPHY: *The Acid House* (1998); *Gangster No. 1* (2000); *The Reckoning* (UK/Sp, 2001; rel. 2004); *Wicker Park* (aka *The Apartment*, US, 2003) *Lucky Number Slevin* (2006).

McKAY, John (1965–)

John McKay was born in Scotland in 1965. His two inventive short films, *Point Taken* and *Wet and Dry*, led to his admission to the National Film and Television School. On leaving he was able to win backing from FilmFour and the Film Council for his feature debut *Crush*. The idea of recasting Andie McDowell and Anna Chancellor in ironic variations on their roles in *Four Weddings and a Funeral* (Mike Newell, 1994) is weak enough, but proves less annoying than a messy script that kills off the only interesting character. Better guidance from the nine lackadaisical producers might have induced McKay to dovetail more carefully his sad tale of *amour fou* between McDowell's Chipping Camden headmistress and one of her lustier ex-pupils (Kenny Doughty) into the film's flimsy framework of female camaraderie. McKay redeemed himself with 'The Miller's Tale' (2003), the best of BBC Television's updated stories taken from Chaucer's *The Canterbury Tales*. Helped by a good script from Peter Bowker and a fine cast, McKay handles this broader comedy with considerable panache. *Piccadilly Jim*, a £9 million adaptation of P. G. Wodehouse's 1918 novel about an American adventurer in London, first filmed by Robert Z. Leonard in 1936, emerged in 2005.

(Robert Murphy)

BIBLIOGRAPHY: Falk, Quentin, 'Free, Three, and Easy', *Exposure*, Spring 2002, pp. 26–7.

FILMOGRAPHY: *Point Taken* (short); *Wet and Dry* (short, 1996); *Doom and Gloom* (short); *Favourite* (short) (1997); *Crush* (UK/Ger, 2001); *Piccadilly Jim* (2005).

MACKENDRICK, Alexander (1912–1993)

Alexander Mackendrick, the youngest and most idiosyncratic of the directors who forged their careers at Ealing Studios, is best known for his comedies *Whisky Galore!* (1949), *The Man in the White Suit* (1951) and *The Ladykillers* (1955). But he also made three impressive films about children – *Mandy* (1952), *Sammy Going South* (1963) and *A High Wind in Jamaica* (1965) – and enjoyed an influential second career as Dean of the Film School at the California Institute of Arts.

He was born in Boston, Massachusetts, on 8 September 1912, the only child of a shipbuilding draughtsman and civil engineer, Francis Robert Mackendrick, and his wife Martha, who had migrated to the USA from their native Glasgow the previous year. When Alexander was six years old, his father died in the post-First World War influenza epidemic; his mother, attempting to pursue a career as a dress designer, gave the boy over to his grandfather, who took him back to Glasgow in 1919. He was never reunited with his mother, and later in life realised that his childhood had been lonely and rather unhappy. After attending Hillhead High School between 1919 and 1926, Mackendrick enrolled for three years at the Glasgow School of Art before moving to London to take up a job at the advertising agency J. Walter Thompson (JWT). Quickly promoted from layout artist to art director, he remained at JWT throughout the 1930s. During this period he co-wrote a feature script with his cousin Roger MacDougall, which was filmed by Associated British and released as *Midnight Menace* (Sinclair Hill, 1937). Between 1936 and 1938 he also scripted and storyboarded five cinema commercials for Horlicks, shot in Technicolor by the stop-motion puppet animator George Pal.

During the early years of the Second World War, Mackendrick scripted and storyboarded wartime propaganda films for a new animation unit at JWT headed by John Halas and Joy

Batchelor. In 1942 he and MacDougall set up their own production company; Mackendrick cut his directorial teeth on three ninety-second instructional films to be inserted into the *Pathé Gazette* newsreel. The following year, he travelled to Algiers and Italy with the Army Psychological Warfare Branch (PWB), drawing cartoons for Allied propaganda leaflets. After the fall of Rome he directed two documentaries with the art director Peter Proud, *I granai del popolo* (a propaganda piece aimed at persuading Italian farmers to make surplus grain available for general distribution) and *Le fosse Ardeatine* (about the aftermath of the Nazis' massacre of partisans at the Fosse Ardeatine in Rome).

After the war, Mackendrick established Merlin Productions with MacDougall, making documentaries for the Ministry of Information. When the company ran into financial difficulties Mackendrick sought work at Ealing Studios, and in 1946 was taken on as scriptwriter and production designer on Basil Dearden's *Saraband for Dead Lovers* (1948). This was the start of a new phase in his career: he stayed at Ealing for nine years, directing five films, establishing himself as a key figure in Britain's post-war film industry and acquiring a considerable international reputation.

Mackendrick's first Ealing film, *Whisky Galore!*, ranks high among the comedy classics of British cinema. Based on Compton Mackenzie's novel, the film focuses on disagreements between inhabitants of the Hebridean island of Todday and officialdom (represented by the Englishman in charge of the island's Home Guard) over the fate of a cargo of whisky crates shipwrecked off the island. In a variant of a theme that surfaces repeatedly in Mackendrick's work, the Englishman represents innocence, the islanders experience. But in Mackendrick's world, oppositions are rarely clear cut and humour is always double edged: in *Whisky Galore!* innocence is potentially dangerous, experience devious and exploitative.

The Man in the White Suit, Mackendrick's next assignment, was based on a play by MacDougall about the invention of an indestructible cloth by a scientist working for a textile mill: in the film the scientist, Sidney Stratton (Alec Guinness), is an idealist who regards his invention as potentially revolutionary. One of Mackendrick's dangerous innocents, Stratton fails to take account of the less positive aspects of his brainchild; and it is his lack of awareness that provides the comedy's theme. *The Man in the White Suit* is stamped with its director's mordant humour and displays degrees of irony and ambiguity exceptional even for Mackendrick.

Mandy, the only non-comedy in Mackendrick's Ealing output, concerns a deaf-mute child's struggle to learn to speak in the face of her parents' obtuseness as well as of her own disability. The extraordinary performance Mackendrick elicited from child actress Mandy Miller in the title role helped *Mandy* become a popular and critical success, but Mackendrick makes no attempt to milk the audience's sympathy. A collision between awareness and unawareness is inscribed in the film's organisation of spaces: walls, windows and doors figure as markers of isolation and of freedom. This powerful and moving film, which remains underrated, indicate that Mackendrick's talent was not confined to comedy.

The Maggie, co-scripted and directed by Mackendrick, is generally considered the least satisfactory of his Ealing films. 'Maggie', an ancient steamboat working off the west coast of Scotland, is chartered to carry household equipment for a rich American. The skipper and his client have totally different notions of time, and the American is repeatedly frustrated by the endless delays to the delivery of his cargo. Notwithstanding similarities in plot and setting to *Whisky Galore!*, *The Maggie* offers no easy points of identification, and is even more morally ambiguous than the earlier films. Its humour, in consequence, is often uncomfortable, though by the same token it avoids Ealing's increasing tendency towards cosiness.

By the mid-1950s Ealing was in decline, and Mackendrick's *The Ladykillers* is widely regarded as the last of the great Ealing comedies. Five gangsters fall under the spell of a little old lady (Katy Johnson) whose innocuous exterior belies a steely core. Like Mackendrick's earlier films, *The Ladykillers* stands apart from Ealing's other comedy output: it is a 'problem comedy', a film of cruelty and cunning as well as charm, ending ambiguously and denying any comfortable audience identification. The film – and especially the character of the old lady – deliberately stretches the studio's most cherished conventions to the limit, but the irony of its approach, not fully appreciated at the time, proved no handicap to its winning two British Film Academy awards.

Mackendrick's Ealing films are distinguished by their visual flair and mastery of narrative technique, and represent the most distinctive and stimulating body of work of any of the studio's directors. In different modes and genres, all five films develop variations on the themes of unawareness and misperception, innocence as a destructive force, and the outsider versus the community.

Mackendrick was now ready to tackle more challenging projects than a declining Ealing Studios could offer, and by 1955 had left Britain for Hollywood. For the remainder of his directorial career he moved between Hollywood and London, completing just four further films, including the acridly brilliant Hecht-Hill-Lancaster production *Sweet Smell of Success* (1957). Its making was a fraught affair: Mackendrick's perfectionism brought him into conflict with his producers, and disagreements dogged him on his return to England to make *The Devil's Disciple* for the same company. He was dismissed a month after shooting began – a severe blow to Mackendrick's confidence, and to his future career.

During this difficult period, Mackendrick returned to advertising, directing eight forty-five second television commercials for Horlicks; and made a brief excursion into stage directing. He also worked for a short time on *The Guns of Navarone*, but differences with his producer Carl Foreman proved insurmountable and he was replaced by J. Lee Thompson. His directorial career was put back on track by his old Ealing boss, Michael Balcon, now an independent producer, who asked him to direct *Sammy Going South*, an ambitious film about a ten-year-old boy (Fergus McClelland) who undertakes an odyssey through Africa following the death of his parents in a British air raid on Port Said during the conflict over the Suez Canal. The film was made on location and has an epic sweep that led to its selection for the 1963 Royal Film Performance. Once again Mackendrick shows himself an acute director of children, avoiding sentimentality, and uses the child's perspective to offer an unclichéd, unpatronising view of Africa. Despite its solid story and visual splendour, and a likeable performance from Edward G. Robinson as the most sympathetic of the adults Sammy meets on his journey, *Sammy Going South* received lukewarm reviews and made too little at the box office to recoup its large budget.

Two years passed before Mackendrick made his next film, *A High Wind in Jamaica*. He had proposed an adaptation of Richard Hughes' classic novel at Ealing, but the rights were owned by 20th Century-Fox, who refused to relinquish them. After many vicissitudes, Mackendrick found himself directing the film for Fox, who expected a Disney-like tale of plucky children and lovable pirates rather than the disturbing account of lethal innocence and misjudged experience that had attracted Mackendrick. With the front office showing little confidence in the project and the director unhappy with the compromises forced on him, the shoot was tense, and Mackendrick was taken off the picture at post-production stage. Nonetheless, *High Wind* offers well-observed portraits of children as it explores the dangerous interface between child and adult perceptions of the world. The film met with a good deal of critical praise, but Mackendrick remained dissatisfied. Increasingly, he was finding that the frustrations of film directing outweighed the satisfactions. His next picture was to be his last.

Don't Make Waves (1967), a satire on south Californian mores in the mid-1960s, was later condemned by Mackendrick as a film 'of such silliness that it is a humiliation even to have to talk about it' (Kemp, p. 218). Subsequent critics have been less unkind, but it is certainly the least known and the least accomplished of his films. The experience of making it put him off Hollywood for good, and he returned to London to foster another long-cherished project, *Mary, Queen of Scots*, for Universal. But as work on the film was about to start, the studio fell victim to the late-1960s recession and Universal closed its London office, cancelling all productions. (The project was successfully resuscitated in 1971, with Charles Jarrott directing and Vanessa Redgrave as the Queen).

In late 1969, faced with the prospect of having to return to Hollywood if he wanted to continue directing films, Mackendrick accepted an offer to become Dean of the Film School at the newly established California Institute for the Arts. This proved a highly successful career change; he remained in his post as Dean until 1978, and after stepping down continued to teach as a Fellow of the Institute. In the summer of 1979 he returned to Britain to teach a course at the National Film School, but further return visits were precluded by poor health: a lifelong asthma sufferer, he now had emphysema. He died of pneumonia on 23 December 1993.

Alexander Mackendrick never looked back after he stopped directing films. A perfectionist in an industry devoted to profit, his film-making career faltered after he left Ealing and set up as a freelance director on the open market. It was both his luck and his misfortune to have served apprenticeships in large organisations (JWT, the army, Ealing Studios), where he was insulated from the hard-edged, deal-making side of the creative industries: 'I've always been happiest in these big organisations,' he once said, 'where I'm free to make mischief from within – where I get all the centralised support, but I've got enough skill to exploit it for my own benefit' (Kemp, p. 236). But if the overall sense of Mackendrick's career is of great potential unfulfilled, his output, though small, is distinctive and rewarding. A visually acute director, he thought in images and movement while always remaining in control of cinematic storytelling. The tone of his films is equally distinctive: a complex and ambiguous mix of pessimism, callousness, mordant humour and startling empathy with the innocent and brutal world of the child.

(Annette Kuhn)

BIBLIOGRAPHY: Barr, Charles, '"Projecting Britain and the British Character": Ealing Studios, Part II', *Screen* vol. 15 no. 2, 1974, pp. 126–63; Cronin, Paul (ed.), *Alexander Mackendrick on Film-Making: An Introduction to the Craft of the Director* (London: Faber and Faber, 2004); Kemp, Philip, *Lethal Innocence: The Cinema of Alexander Mackendrick* (London: Methuen, 1991); Sinyard, Neil, 'Ealing Studios and Alexander Mackendrick', in Boris Ford (ed.), *The Cambridge Guide to the Arts in Britain, Volume 9: Since the Second World War* (Cambridge: Cambridge University Press, 1988).

FILMOGRAPHY: *Save Your Bacon (Kitchen Waste for Pigs)* (doc., co-dir. Roger MacDougall, 1942); *Contraries* (doc., co-dir. Roger MacDougall); *Nero* (doc., co-dir. Roger MacDougall) (1943); *I granai del popolo/ Grain for the People* (doc., co-dir. Peter Proud, 1944); *Le fosse Ardeatine/ Massacre of the Fosse Ardeatine* (doc., co-dir. Peter Proud, 1945); *Whisky Galore!* (US: *Tight Little Island*, 1949); *The Man in the White Suit* (1951); *Mandy* (US: *Crash of Silence*, 1952); *The Maggie* (US: *High and Dry*, 1954); *The Ladykillers* (1955); *Sweet Smell of Success* (US, 1957); *The Devil's Disciple* (co-dir., uncredited, Guy Hamilton, 1959); *The Guns of Navarone* (co-dir., uncredited, J. Lee Thompson, 1961); *Sammy Going South* (US: *A Boy Ten Feet Tall*, 1963); *A High Wind in Jamaica* (1965); *Don't Make Waves* (US, 1967).

MACKENZIE, David (1966–)

David Mackenzie was born in Corbridge, Scotland, on 10 May 1966. He made a number of promising shorts, most notably *Marcie's Dowry*, a fifteen-minute black comedy with Edward Woodward and Sheila Donald as wily Scottish crofters who survive a brush with violent criminals during efforts to fund their daughter's wedding. It led to a low-budget digital feature, *The Last*

Great Wilderness, about two men (Jonny Phillips and the director's brother Alastair Mackenzie) who journey up to Scotland and become trapped among the strange inhabitants of an old dark house. Though there are deliberate echoes of *Psycho* (Alfred Hitchcock, 1960) and *The Wicker Man* (Robin Hardy, 1973), Mackenzie's film is refreshingly original, emulating the Dogme films of Lars von Trier and Thomas Vinterberg in its cinematic ingenuity and adherence to humanist values.

Young Adam, a strikingly bleak evocation of life around the Glasgow canals of the 1950s, based on a novel by Alexander Trocchi, followed in 2003. Giles Nuttgens' washed-out colour photography and David Byrne's atmospheric score help Mackenzie create a genuinely innovative film that captures the louche amorality of Trocchi's novel, reassessing rather than nostalgically indulging its bohemian modernism. Despite the film's eroticism and the starring role of Ewan McGregor, *Young Adam* was too gloomy to become a major box-office success, but it consolidated Mackenzie's credentials as a creative and idiosyncratic director.

Asylum, Mackenzie's third film, has more mainstream aspirations, with Natasha Richardson shining as the reluctant wife of a psychiatrist, who starts a passionate affair with a patient when her husband become deputy director of an asylum for the criminally insane. Mackenzie continues to explore the issues around passion, manipulation and obsession that haunted his first two films; but dull period detail and a portentous script (adapted by Patrick Marber from a novel by Patrick McGrath) shoulder him out onto well-trodden territory about *amour fou* and the hypocrisy and sexual repression of Britain in the 1950s. Grown-up film-making no doubt, but less original, less resonant and less exciting than his more experimental efforts.

(Robert Murphy)

BIBLIOGRAPHY: Gilbey, Ryan, 'Written on the Body', *Sight and Sound*, Sept. 2003, pp. 16–19; James, Nick, 'Digital Deluge', *Sight and Sound*, Oct. 2001, pp. 20–4; Mackenzie, David, 'Confessions from Cannes', *Roughcuts*, July 2000, p. 11.

FILMOGRAPHY: *Wanting and Getting* (short, 1996); *California Sunshine* (short); *Two Fingers* (doc. short, 1997); *Marcie's Dowry* (short); *Somersault* (short, 1999); *The Last Great Wilderness* (UK/Den, 2002); *Young Adam* (UK/Fr, 2003); *Asylum* (2004).

MACKENZIE, John (1932–)

John Mackenzie was born in Edinburgh in 1932. He studied history at Edinburgh University and worked as a teacher before joining the city's Gateway Theatre. In the early 1960s Mackenzie moved to London, where he worked at the BBC as an assistant floor manager. He was one of a group of young, socially conscious and generally left-wing men working at the Corporation including Ken Loach, Jim Allen, James MacTaggart, Kenith Trodd and Tony Garnett. Mackenzie worked as an assistant to Loach on *Up the Junction* (1965) and *Cathy Come Home* (1966) before making his directorial debut in 1967 with *Voices in the Park*, a *Wednesday Play* produced by Tony Garnett.

Subsequently Mackenzie went freelance, making various one-off dramas for the BBC and ITV before embarking on his first cinema film, *One Brief Summer*, one of many 1960s films to explore a relationship between a middle-aged man and a young woman. More distinctive was his remake of Giles Cooper's sinister 1965 BBC play *Unman, Wittering and Zigo*, a finely wrought psychological suspense drama with David Hemmings as a public school teacher menaced by three murderous pupils. After directing Carol White and the singer-songwriter Roy Harper in *Made*, an interesting companion piece to Ken Loach's *Poor Cow* (1967), Mackenzie went back to television. His *Plays for Today*, such as Dennis Potter's excoriating *Double Dare* (1975), Alan Garner's *Red Shift* (1978) and Peter McDougall's Scottish trilogy – *Just Another Saturday* (1975), *The Elephant's Graveyard* (1979) and *Just a Boy's Game* (1979) – represent some of the best television drama of the 1970s.

Mackenzie made a triumphant return to the cinema with *The Long Good Friday*, which combines East End gangsters, the American Mafia and the IRA in a revenge tragedy that brilliantly prefigured the *Zeitgeist* of Thatcher's new enterprise culture. Another impressive television film, *A Sense of Freedom* (1981), again written by Peter McDougall, was followed by an intermittently successful adaptation by Christopher Hampton of Graham Greene's *The Honorary Consul*. Richard Gere is miscast as the young doctor caught in a struggle between Latin American revolutionaries and the state, but Michael Caine gives a fine performance in the title role. Mackenzie returned to make *The Innocent*, set in the Yorkshire Dales in the 1930s, and since then has alternated regularly between film and television productions in the UK and the US. Caine also starred in an adaptation of Frederick Forsyth's *The Fourth Protocol*, reportedly an unhappy experience for Mackenzie; it emerged as little more than an efficient reworking of Forsyth's *The Day of the Jackal* (filmed by Fred Zinnemann in 1973).

In the 1990s Mackenzie made a number of modest American films, including a solid cop drama, *The Last of the Finest*, and a biopic of Jack Ruby, the man who shot Lee Harvey Oswald. For the BBC he made *The Deadly Voyage* (1996), based on a grisly true story of African migrants stowing away on a Ukrainian ship; and the series *Looking After Jo Jo* (1998), set in 1980s' Edinburgh and featuring a blistering performance by Robert Carlyle as a small-time drug-dealer. More recently Mackenzie demonstrated his energy, seriousness and vigour with *When the Sky Falls*, a biography of the murdered Irish journalist Veronica Guerin.

(Sergio Angelini)

BIBLIOGRAPHY: Berry, Jo, 'Profiles', *Empire*, July 1992, pp. 41–2; Grundy, Gareth, 'East End Boys', *Neon*, July 1998, pp. 108–13; Hill, John, 'Allegorising the Nation: British Gangster Films of the 1980s', in Steve Chibnall and Robert Murphy (eds), *British Crime Cinema* (London: Routledge, 2001).

FILMOGRAPHY: *One Brief Summer* (1969); *Unman, Wittering and Zigo* (1971); *A Pretty Good Management* (doc. short); *Made* (1972); *The Long Good Friday* (1979); *The Honorary Consul* (US: *Beyond the Limit*, UK/US, 1983); *The Innocent* (1985); *The Fourth Protocol* (1987); *The Last of the Finest* (US, 1990); *Ruby* (US/Jap, 1992); *When the Sky Falls* (UK/Ir/US, 2000); *Quicksand* (UK/Fr, 2001).

MacKINNON, Gillies (1948–)

Gillies MacKinnon was one of the most prolific and versatile British directors of the 1990s. The subject matter of his films is notably cosmopolitan, exploring aspects of disparate societies past and present in Scotland, Ireland, Morocco and elsewhere.

MacKinnon was born in Glasgow on 8 January 1948. After studying mural painting at Glasgow School of Art, he became an art teacher and professional cartoonist, though he also spent six months travelling with a nomadic tribe in the Sahara. Anxious to consolidate his interest in film, he studied at Middlesex Polytechnic in the 1970s and the National Film and Television School in the early 1980s. His graduation short *Passing Glory*, an austere recreation of the Glasgow of his youth, was premiered at the 1986 Edinburgh International Film Festival, where it won the first Scottish Film Prize. MacKinnon's early preference for bleak realist content married with *tableau vivant* visuals is evident in his feature debut *Conquest of the South Pole* (1989), which imaginatively transferred Manfred Karge's German play about heroism and urban hopelessness to the docks of Leith. MacKinnon cemented his critical reputation with two remarkable television films: *Needle* (1990), a salutary exploration of the lure of heroin, brilliantly scripted by Jimmy McGovern; and the equally powerful *The Grass Arena* (1991), adapted from the autobiography of John Healy, a boxer-turned-alcoholic-turned-chess master portrayed by Mark Rylance. The film won several prizes, including the Edinburgh Film Festival's Michael Powell Award for Best British Film.

MacKinnon's first three features make much use of angled shots, high-impact editing and a restless camera. A more commercially accessible variant of the style emerged in *The Playboys*, a popular Irish comedy set in the 1950s, made with American finance and American leads, who are easily swamped by Albert Finney's turn as a lovelorn policeman. The tragic-comic plot about love and jealousy offered little that was new, but the film's American success brought MacKinnon results, including an episode of the television series *The Young Indiana Jones Chronicles*, and *A Simple Twist of Fate*, a sentimental update of George Eliot's *Silas Marner*, with Steve Martin as the miser redeemed by a child's love.

Better and more personal films resulted once he returned to Britain. *Small Faces* (1996), a convincing snapshot of Glasgow gang and art-school subcultures in 1968, co-scripted with his brother Billy and relying on a cast chosen largely from Glasgow teenagers, shines with authenticity and emotional truth. *Trojan Eddie* (1996), written by Billy Roche, switched to contemporary Ireland for a rumbustious, unsentimental tale of a small-time market peddler (Stephen Rea) dreaming of the big time. MacKinnon engaged with more sombre matters in his powerful and poignant *Regeneration* (1997), based on the first of Pat Barker's trilogy of First World War novels. Set in the Craiglockhart Military Hospital in 1917, the film cleverly approaches Dr William Rivers' treatment of Wilfred Owen and Siegfried Sassoon and other shell-shocked soldiers through a narrative maze that blurs the distinctions between doctors and patients. The brilliantly staged opening offers one of cinema's most vivid recreations of wartime trenches; but nowhere does MacKinnon push for his effects. MacKinnon's hectic output of the 1990s concluded with *Hideous Kinky* (1998), an adaptation of Esther Freud's autobiographical novel about a young hippy mum in the 1970s seeking fulfilment in Morocco. MacKinnon neither sneers at nor venerates his irritating heroine (Kate Winslet), and John de Borman's flamboyant cinematography allows us to share her fascination with the sun-drenched exoticism of Morocco; but the film's viewpoint finally settles with her two pushy, precocious and irredeemably English daughters, who just want to go home.

The Playboys excepted, MacKinnon's chosen path towards thoughtful, idiosyncratic films made without much consideration of market viability has never led to large audiences, and much of his recent work has been for British television. Following *The Escapist*, a routine revenge thriller, *Pure* (2002) marked a powerful return to the world of heroin addiction, but this critically acclaimed film proved too grim to succeed at the cinema box

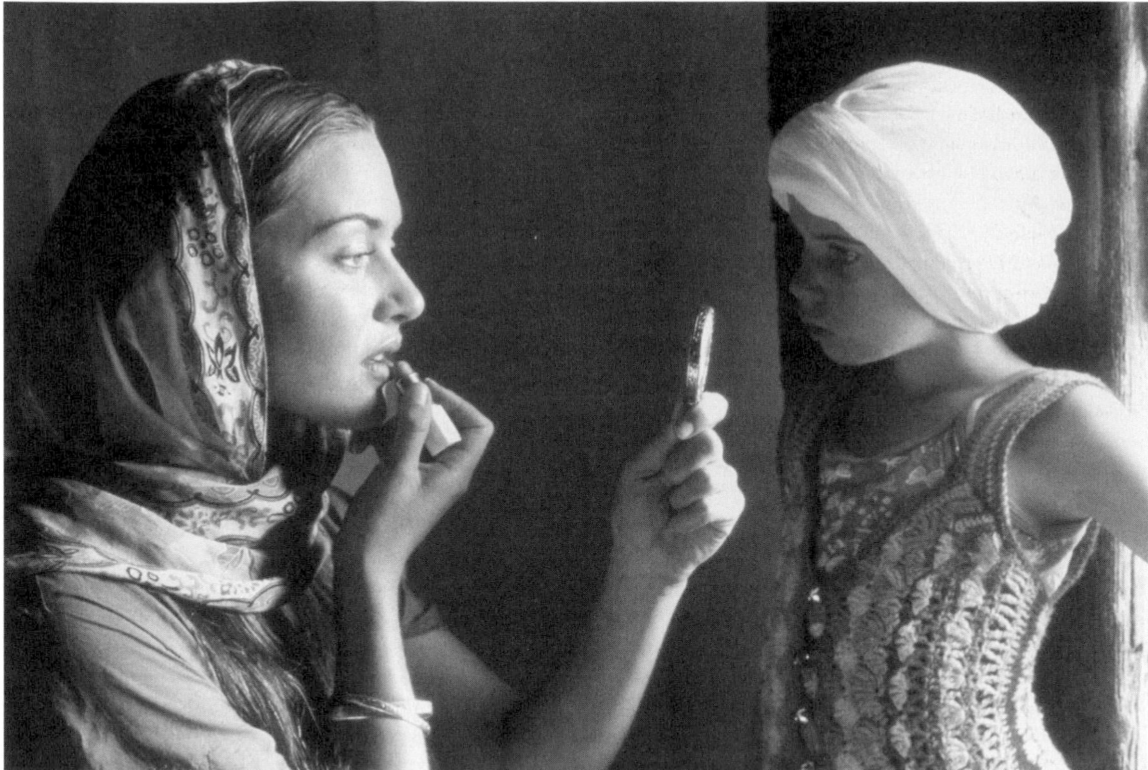

Hideous Kinky (Gillies MacKinnon, 1998)

office. Wider success greeted *The Last of the Blonde Bombshells* (2000), a deservedly popular and witty small-screen drama about the reunion of an all-girl swing band, written by Alan Plater. MacKinnon reunited with Jimmy McGovern for *'Gunpowder, Treason and Plot'* (2004), a bloodthirsty BBC miniseries tracing the turbulent reign of Mary Queen of Scots and the Guy Fawkes plot that would have blown her son James I and the English Parliament to kingdom come. Bold casting and atmospheric direction in the treatment of Mary's story are followed by an oddly contrived representation of the Gunpowder Plot, marred by weak writing and overwrought stylistic devices.

Consistently adventurous in form and theme, the best of MacKinnon's films exemplify that most elusive of creatures: an inventive, entertaining British art cinema – though without a notable box-office success, it remains uncertain how long the creature will be able to stay alive.

(Geoff Brown and Jonathan Murray)

BIBLIOGRAPHY: Kermode, Mark, 'The American Connection', *Sight and Sound*, June 1992, p. 29; MacKinnon, Gillies, 'Small Faces', in Duncan Petrie (ed.), *Inside Stories: Diaries of British Film-Makers at Work* (London: BFI, 1996); McKibbin, Tony, 'Gillies MacKinnon: recurring themes', *Film West*, no. 31, Jan. 1998, pp. 36–7; Petrie, Duncan, *Screening Scotland* (London: BFI, 2000).

FILMOGRAPHY: *Rota* (short, 1976); *Kids and the Law* (short, 1977); *Where He Comes* (short, 1985); *Passing Glory* (short, 1986); *Somebody's Wee Nobody* (short, 1987); *Close Shave* (short, 1988); *Conquest of the South Pole* (1989); *The Playboys* (UK/US/Ir, 1992); *A Simple Twist of Fate* (US, 1994); *Small Faces* (1996); *Trojan Eddie* (1996); *Regeneration* (UK/Can, 1997); *Hideous Kinky* (UK/Fr, 1998); *The Escapist* (2001); *Pure* (2002).

McLAREN, Norman (1914–1987)

Norman McLaren's high reputation in the field of animation rests securely on his work at the National Film Board of Canada, though the seeds of his typical themes and techniques were laid during his early work in Britain. Born on 11 April 1914 in Stirling, Scotland, he entered the Glasgow School of Art in 1932, where he became interested in cinema's possibilities and helped form the School's Kinecraft Society. His earliest extant film, the live-action *7 Till 5* (1933), documented a day's activities at the art school through discontinuous cutting and multiple-angled shots: formalist practices clearly showing the influence of Eisenstein.

McLaren's next film, *Camera Makes Whoopee* (1935), undertook more elaborate if inchoate variations on the visual themes of *7 Till 5* – variations inspired by the art school's Carnival Ball and the acquisition of a cine-Kodak camera enabling him to shoot single frames and execute trick shots. Using superimpositions, animation, and pixillation effects, McLaren both displayed the event's settings and endeavoured to conjure the aesthetic sensations the Ball supposedly generated. McLaren made two further abstract films in 1935: *Colour Cocktail* (now lost) and *Polychrome Fantasy*, interweaving dancing with colour abstractions.

The following year McLaren's political commitment came to the fore; at one stage he was a member of the Communist Party of Great Britain. He planned a series of films on social and political problems; though the only known result is the stridently anti-war *Hell Unltd* (1936), a complex mixture of found footage, animation and graphics, co-directed with a fellow Glasgow student, the sculptress Helen Biggar. Later in the year he went to Spain and acted as a cameraman on Ivor Montagu's *Defence of Madrid* (1936), documenting the Republican resistance in the Spanish Civil War.

John Grierson's interest in McLaren, stimulated at the third Scottish Amateur Film Festival when he awarded a prize to *Colour Cocktail*, led to McLaren joining the GPO Film Unit in October 1936. Believing that McLaren's talents needed discipline, Grierson put him to work with Cavalcanti as producer on live-action instructional films: *Book Bargain* (1937), about the London telephone directory, became the first McLaren film with a soundtrack. Privately, McLaren continued his animation experiments and began to explore synthetic sound. In public, pixillation techniques were briefly explored in his sequence in *Mony a Pickle* (1938), (co-dir. Richard Massingham). But his biggest chance came in *Love on the Wing* (1938), a Dufaycolor short promoting the Post Office's new airmail service. Following Len Lye in drawing directly onto celluloid, McLaren suggested romance between two airmail correspondents by a series of mutating shapes – envelopes, hearts, kissing mouths, a horse – outlined in white against pastel-coloured, multi-plane backgrounds to the sprightly music of Ibert's *Divertissement*.

McLaren moved to New York in 1939. Two years later he teamed up again with Grierson at the National Film Board of Canada, where he developed the animation unit and built on the promise of *Love on the Wing* in films like *Hen Hop* (1942), the *Chants Populaires* series (1944) and *Begone Dull Care* (1949), inventively matching animation to existing or improvised music. In 1950 McLaren developed two experimental 3-D shorts for the Festival of Britain, *Around Is Around* and *Now Is the Time*, made with a mixture of cut-out shapes, direct drawing and cathode-ray oscilloscope patterns – both of them more like exercises than artistically complete films.

McLaren remained based in Canada, where he worked prolifically and successfully for the Board until his retirement in 1984, producing prettified abstract and ballet films and whimsical, pixillated satires. His experimental instincts and left-wing slant may have been softened by Board bureaucracy and routine, but he still explored widely in numerous styles and techniques: from the scratched animal shapes of *Blinkety Blank* (1954) and the ballet dancers rippling suavely through an optical printer's multiple exposures in *Pas de deux* (1968) to the pixillated domestic warfare of a gentler anti-war film, *Neighbours*, winner of the Academy Award for Best Documentary Short in 1952. One of the world's outstanding visual artists, McLaren died in Montreal on 27 January 1987.

(Geoff Brown and Jamie Sexton)

BIBLIOGRAPHY: Beveridge, James, *John Grierson: Film Master* (New York: Macmillan, 1978); Collins, Maynard, *Norman McLaren* (Ottawa: Canadian Film Institute, 1976); McWilliams, Don, *Creative Process: Norman McLaren* (doc., 1990); Moritz, William, 'Norman McLaren and Jules Engel: Post-Modernists', in Jayne Pilling (ed.), *A Reader in Animation Studies* (Sydney: John Libbey, 1997); Richard, Valliere T., *Norman McLaren: Manipulator of Movement* (East Brunswick, NJ: Associated University Presses, 1982); Scottish Arts Council, *Norman McLaren* (Edinburgh: Scottish Arts Council, 1977).

FILMOGRAPHY (UK): *Untitled Hand-Painted Abstraction* (co-dir. Stewart McAllister); *7 Till 5* (1933); *Camera Makes Whoopee*; *Colour Cocktail*; *Polychrome Fantasy* (1935); *Hell Unltd* (co-dir. Helen Biggar, 1936); *Book Bargain* (1937); *News for the Navy*; *Mony a Pickle* (co-dir. Richard Massingham); *Love on the Wing* (1938); *The Obedient Flame* (1939); US: *NBC Valentine Greeting*; *Allegro*; *Stars and Stripes* (aka *Étoiles et bandes*, 1939); *Dots* (aka *Scherzo* and *Points*); *Loops* (aka *Boucles*); *Rumba* (unfinished); *Boogie Doodle* (1940).

CANADA: *Mail Early* (aka *Mail Early Christmas*); *V for Victory* (1941); *Five for Four*, *Hen Hop* (1942); *Dollar Dance* (1943); *Alouette* (co-dir. René Jodoin); *C'est l'aviron*; *Keep Your Mouth Shut* (1944); *Là-haut sur ces montagnes* (1945); *A Little Phantasy on a 19th century Painting*; *Hoppity Pop* (1946); *Fiddle-de-dee*; *La poulette grise* (1947); *Begone Dull Care* (aka Caprice *en couleurs*, 1949); *Pen Point Percussion* (aka *À la pointe de la plume*); *Around is Around* (UK/Can); *Now is the Time (To Put On your Glasses)* (UK/Can) (1951); *A Phantasy*; *Neighbours* (aka *Voisins*); *Two Bagatelles* (co-dir. Grant Munro) (1952); *Blinkity Blank* (1954); *Rhythmetic* (co-dir. Evelyn Lambart, 1956); *A Chairy Tale* (aka *Il était une chaise*, co-dir. Claude Jutra, 1957); *Le Merle* (aka *The Blackbird*, 1958); *Short and Suite*; *Serenal*; *Mail Early for Christmans* (1959); *Lines: Vertical* (aka *Lignes verticals*, co-dir. Evelyn Lambart); *Opening Speech: McLaren* (aka *Discours de bienvenue de Norman McLaren*)

(1960); *New York Lightboard; New York Lightboard Record* (1961); *Lines: Horizontal* (aka *Lignes horizontales*, co-dir. Evelyn Lambart, 1962); *Canon* (co-dir. Gramt Munro) (1963); *Mosaic* (aka *Mosaïque*, co-dir. Evelyn Lambert, 1965); *Pas de deux* (aka *Duo*, 1968); *Spheres* (aka *Sphères*, co-dir. René Jodoin, 1969); *Striations* (1970); *Synchromy* (aka *Synchromie*, 1971); *Ballet Adagio* (1972); *Pinscreen* (1973); *Animated Motion #1* (co-dir. Grant Munro, 1976); *Animated Motion #2*; *Animated Motion #3*; *Animated Motion #4* (co-dir. Grant Munro, 1977); *Animated Motion #5* (co-dir. Grant Munro, 1978); *Narcissus* (aka *Narcisse*, 1983).

McMULLEN, Ken (1948–)

Born in Manchester on 31 August 1948, Ken McMullen has been responsible for a series of unusual films mixing philosophical meditations and politically radical ideas with a formally self-conscious and theatrical approach to cinema. He initially went to the Slade School of Fine Art to train as a painter but became increasingly interested in cinema, partly as a result of regular film screenings organised by Thorold Dickinson. International in outlook and experimental in attitude, McMullen's early work involved collaboration with several major art figures, including the German artist Joseph Beuys, with whom he made *The Discussion* (1972), and the Polish theatre director Tadeusz Kantor, whose work is explored in *Lovelies and Dowdies* (1974). Kantor's approach to theatre also influenced McMullen's first feature, *Resistance* (1975), a complex amalgam of archive material, original music (by Brian Eno) and improvised re-enactments by performance artist Stuart Brisley and others, of group therapy sessions with former Resistance fighters in 1948. The film, funded by the BFI, explores the psychic consequences of the French Resistance for the survivors as well as the resistance of the conscious mind to repressed memories. In doing so, it also reflects upon the status of the film medium itself and its own capacity to represent the past.

McMullen continued his collaboration with Stuart Brisley in *Being and Doing* (1984), a series of performance-art pieces recorded over five years, as well as his second feature, *Ghost Dance* (1983), made for Channel 4. *Ghost Dance* follows the escapades of two women in Paris and London as they explore the historical and psychic ghosts haunting contemporary post-industrial society. Influenced by Jacques Rivette's *Céline et Julie vont en bateau* (1974), the film provides a playful and visually arresting mix of philosophical speculation and cinematic experiment: including appearances by the philosopher Jacques Derrida ('playing himself'), encounters at the site where survivors of the Paris Commune were executed, re-enactments of cargo cult rituals and Robbie Coltrane dancing 'like a snake'.

McMullen's next project was *Zina* (1985), an imaginative realisation of the relationship between the exiled Trotsky and his troubled daughter Zina, who is undergoing psychoanalytic treatment in Berlin at a time when the Nazis are in the ascendant. Partly modelled on the classical myth of Antigone, the film employs archive footage, dramatised reconstructions of actual events and elements of fantasy to explore the links between private trauma and public history.

Historical events also provide the basis of *Partition* (1987) and *1871* (1990). *Partition*, loosely adapted by McMullen and Tariq Ali from a novel by the Urdu writer Saadat Hasan Manto, deals with the damage wrought by the division of India. The films focuses on plans to despatch Hindi and Sikh inmates of Pakistan's mental asylums to India and Muslim lunatics in India to Pakistan, and seeks to demonstrate the 'insanity' of partition by showing how even those who are 'mad' reject it. McMullen maintains a studied formality, shooting in colour and black and white and using long takes (a recurring feature of his work), to move through time and space and evoke a dreamlike state.

1871, dealing with events surrounding the Paris Commune, was filmed in Portugal in three different languages. McMullen boldly rejects surface realism in favour of a historically anachronistic, overtly theatrical account that emphasises ideas as much as atmosphere and incident. This approach involves the use of theatrical settings and elaborate camera movements, 'Brechtian' interruptions and musical interludes, as well as non-naturalistic performances and casting (including the appearance of the Mauritanian director Med Hondo as Karl Marx).

With the decreasing availability of film funding in the UK for 'art cinema', McMullen has moved away from feature production towards art documentaries and gallery installations. His documentaries have included essays on Manet's *Execution of Emperor Maximilian, 1867* (1990) and the biblical paintings of Rembrandt, *R: The Dutchman* (1992), as well as portraits of the British film-makers Derek Jarman, *There We Are John . . .* (1993), and Lindsay Anderson, *Lucky Man* (1995). Better appreciated abroad than at home, Ken McMullen has produced a substantial body of innovative film work that successfully combines serious, often subversive, ideas with formal complexity and visual invention.

(John Hill)

BIBLIOGRAPHY: Henderson, Elaina, 'Behind Our Ken', *Stills* no. 22, Nov. 1985, p. 13; Leahy, James, 'Taking Objective Shape on the Streets' (interview with Ken McMullen), *Monthly Film Bulletin* no. 628, May 1986, pp. 138–40; Tournès, Andrée, 'Rencontre avec Ken McMullen', *Jeune Cinema* no. 243, May/June 1997, pp. 12–15.

FILMOGRAPHY: *Pieces* (short); *Room to Move* (short) (1971); *The Discussion* (doc., 1972); *Lovelies and Dowdies* (doc., 1974); *Resistance* (1975); *Ghost Dance* (1983); *Being and Doing* (1984); *Zina* (1985); *Partition* (1987); *1871*; *Execution of Emperor Maximilian, 1867* (doc. short) (1990); *R: The Dutchman* (doc. short, 1992); *There We Are John . . .* (doc. short, 1993); *Lucky Man* (doc. short, 1995).

McMURRAY, Mary (1949–)

Mary McMurray was born in Manchester on 31 March 1949. She gained some experience of television while a student at Sussex University between 1967 and 1971, producing a daily live news show for the university campus. After graduating she joined Radio Manchester, then moved on to Granada Television as a researcher. She worked with documentary-maker Denis Mitchell before becoming a director, first of documentaries, then of fiction, with *Coronation Street* and the Catherine Cookson serial *The Mallens* (1978). Her dramatisation of the true story of two old ladies who lived in the same house all their lives, *A Pattern of Life* (1982), led her to her first (and only) feature film, *The Assam Garden*. A widow (Deborah Kerr) returns from India and forges a friendship with an Indian woman (Madhur Jaffrey), long settled in England, who helps her to create the garden her late husband had always dreamed of. The film skilfully unpicks the tensions in their differing experiences of the British in India and offers hope of reconciliation and understanding. The sensitive handling of the central relationship and the strong pictorial qualities of the film make it regrettable that McMurray has not made further ventures into cinema.

After completing *The Assam Garden*, McMurray confessed, 'I always thought of films as something that other people did. I am ambitious, but as I get older my ambition is to do really good work, rather than being successful on the big screen' (Henry, 1985). Her subsequent career has been confined to television where she has directed vehicles for Jimmy Nail (*Spender*, 1991), Michael Elphick (*Harry*, 1993) and Martin Shaw (*Judge John Deed*, 2001), episodes of *Taggart* (1992), *Cadfael* (1998) and several series of *Ruth Rendell Mysteries*.

(Robert Shail)

BIBLIOGRAPHY: Considine, Pippa, 'Direction', *Televisual*, Oct. 1993, pp. 37–8; Henry, Georgina, 'Mary McMurray', *Televisual*, July 1985, p. 90.

FILMOGRAPHY: *The Assam Garden* (1985).

MacNAUGHTON, Ian (1925–2002)

Edward Ian MacNaughton was born in Glasgow on 30 December 1925. Beginning as an actor, MacNaughton played small roles in films such as *X the Unknown* (Leslie Norman, 1956), *The Silent Enemy* (William Fairchild, 1958) and *Lawrence of Arabia* (David Lean, 1962). At the BBC, he directed Spike Milligan's *Q5* (1969) and forty-one of the forty-five episodes of *Monty Python's Flying Circus* (1969–72) and *Monty Python* (1974). In 1971 he directed the first Python feature film, *And Now for Something Completely Different*, financed by *Playboy* executive Victor Lownes. Intended to launch *Monty Python* on the American market, the film restaged the best-known sketches from the first two television series, notably 'Lumberjack Song', 'The Upper-Class Twit of the Year Race', 'Dead Parrot' and 'The World's Deadliest Joke'. It was shot in five weeks for £80,000, and most of the interiors were filmed in a converted milk depot. Python team members Terry Gilliam and Terry Jones felt that MacNaughton's direction lacked visual sense and frequently questioned his choice of camera set-ups. Certainly, MacNaughton's perfunctory staging does little to enhance the material. Ironically, *And Now for Something Completely Different* proved a hit in England, where the sketches were familiar to audiences, but flopped in the USA. MacNaughton continued to work on the television series but when the Python team decided to make a second film, *Monty Python and the Holy Grail* (1974), Gilliam and Jones took over the direction. His direction of the comedy-drama series *Rising Damp*, starring Leonard Rossiter, led to a delightfully odd spin-off: *Le Petomane*, a half-hour biography of the 'anal entertainer' Joseph Pujol, with Rossiter in the main part. MacNaughton worked on Handmade's *Monty Python Live at the Hollywood Bowl* in 1982 but then moved to Germany with his second wife Ike Ott. He died in Munich on 10 December 2002 from injuries sustained in a car crash.

(Daniel O'Brien)

BIBLIOGRAPHY: Obituary, *Broadcasting and Cable*, 13 Jan. 2003, p. 55; MacNaughton, Ian, 'Craft Classics', *Broadcast*, B+ Supplement, 6 July 2001, pp. 4–5.

FILMOGRAPHY: *And Now for Something Completely Different* (1971); *Le Petomane* (short, 1979); *Monty Python Live at the Hollywood Bowl* (co-dir. Terry Hughes, 1982).

McPHERSON, Conor (1971–)

Conor McPherson was born in Dublin in August 1971. He studied moral philosophy at University College, Dublin, and found early success as a playwright with a series of witty and irreverent monologue pieces. He achieved international recognition with his stage plays *This Lime Tree Bower* (1995) and *The Weir* (1996), and by the end of the decade he was as celebrated in New York and London as he was in Dublin. McPherson turned to film in the late 1990s, writing Paddy Breathnach's *I Went Down* (1997), a film that gently plays with the thriller/road-movie formats and makes witty and irreverent references to the Coen brothers' work and the films of Quentin Tarantino. The film's stylishness and irreverent comedy made it a box-office success in Ireland and it played to generally positive reviews elsewhere.

McPherson's first film as director was *Saltwater*, a version of his play *This Lime Tree Bower*, and although the film was typically witty and playful in its genre borrowings, it did not open out well enough to work fully for the screen. In 2001 he directed *Endgame* for the 'Beckett on Film' project, and in 2003 released his second feature, *The Actors*, a much more commercial venture starring Dylan Moran, Michael Caine and Michael Gambon, which attracted a good deal of attention but disappointing box-office returns.

(Martin McLoone)

BIBLIOGRAPHY: McLoone, Martin, *Irish Film: The Emergence of a Contemporary Cinema* (London: BFI Publishing, 2000); Pettitt, Lance, *Screening Ireland* (Manchester: Manchester University Press, 2000); Wood, Gerald C., *Conor McPherson: Imagining Mischief* (Dublin: The Liffey Press, 2003).

FILMOGRAPHY: *Saltwater* (2000); *Endgame* (2001); *The Actors* (2003).

MACPHERSON, Kenneth (1903–1971)

Born in Scotland in 1903, Kenneth Macpherson was a novelist, photographer, artist and collector with a passionate interest in film-making. In Switzerland in the 1920s, he became a key member of the POOL collective, developed with Bryher (Annie Winifred Ellerman), the heiress to a shipping fortune, whom he married in 1927. Using Bryher's resources, POOL produced experimental films, published fiction and non-fiction books, and in July 1927 launched the influential film journal *Close Up* (1927–33), aimed at an international readership, with Macpherson as editor.

Alongside his work on the journal, Macpherson began to make his own small-scale avant-garde films in Switzerland under the POOL umbrella. The first issue of *Close Up* contained stills from his first film, *Wing Beat* (1927), an investigation of telepathy featuring himself and the Imagist poet H. D. (Hilda Doolittle), another POOL member. The film now exists only in fragments; according to Anne Friedberg, it used techniques such as triple superimpositions in order to represent thought processes. His other two shorts – *Foothills* (1928), concerning a city woman visiting the countryside, and *Monkey's Moon* (1929), about Macpherson's pet monkeys – are entirely lost.

Borderline (1930) is Macpherson's only surviving film and his sole feature. A dissection of race and gender relations, it is centred on a love triangle – an adulterous relationship between a black woman (Eslanda Robeson) and a white man (Gavin Arthur), though Paul Robeson and H. D. have the more flamboyant parts as the wronged spouses. Macpherson attempts to delve into the mental states of his characters, but his elliptical narrative, ambiguous images and hectic montage sequences confused and bewildered contemporary critics. Deeply upset by the film's hostile reception, Macpherson withdrew from directing to focus on writing, photography and nurturing his art collection; *Close Up* itself ceased publication in December 1933. He only once returned to film-making, acting as associate producer on Hans Richter's avant-garde compendium film *Dreams That Money Can Buy* (USA, 1947). Macpherson died in Cetona, Italy, on 14 June 1971.

(Jamie Sexton)

BIBLIOGRAPHY: Donald, James, Anne Friedberg and Laura Marcus (eds), *Close Up 1927–1933: Cinema and Modernism* (London: Cassell, 1998); Friedberg, Anne, 'Approaching *Borderline*', *Millennium Film Journal* nos 7/9, Autumn/Winter, 1980–1, pp. 130–9.

FILMOGRAPHY: *Wing Beat* (short, UK/Switz, 1927); *Foothills* (short, UK/Switz, 1928); *Monkey's Moon* (short, UK/Switz, 1929); *Borderline* (UK/Switz, 1930).

McPOLIN, Owen (1969–)

Owen McPolin was born in County Kerry, Ireland, in 1969. After studying film-making at West Surrey College of Art he raised a tiny budget from private investors to make *Drinking Crude* (1997), a brave little film that followed the fortunes of an Irish school-leaver who seeks his fortune in London but ends up cleaning oil storage tanks back in Ireland. No further features followed but McPolin has established himself as a cinematographer with a fine eye for the Irish landscape in a number of low-budget Irish films, including Nicola Bruce's *I Could Read the Sky* (1998), Fintan O'Connolly's *Flick* (2000) and *Trouble with Sex* (2005), Jonny Gogan's *The Mapmaker* (2001) and Shimmy Marcus's *Headrush* (2004).

(Robert Murphy)

BIBLIOGRAPHY: McLoone, Martin, *Irish Film: The Emergence of a Contemporary Cinema* (London: BFI, 2000); McPolin, Owen, 'The Making of *Drinking Crude*', *Film West* no. 28, May 1997, pp. 18–19.

FILMOGRAPHY: *Drinking Crude* (Ir, 1997).

MacTAGGART, James (1928–1974)

James MacTaggart was born in Glasgow in 1928. After National Service and a spell as an actor he joined BBC Scotland in 1956. MacTaggart's production of the innovative television drama *Three Ring Circus* in 1961 brought his creativity in the television studio to wider notice and led to him moving to London where he became a central figure in developments in television drama at the BBC. As the producer on the first season of *The Wednesday Play* in 1965, MacTaggart was responsible for many of the plays that earned the series its controversial reputation.

In 1966 he switched from producing to directing with *The Boneyard*, and went on to direct eleven more plays for *The Wednesday Play/Play for Today* between 1966 and 1972. These contemporary dramas were interspersed with a number of classic adaptations for *Play of the Month*, including an innovative version ofVoltaire's *Candide* (1973). In 1969 MacTaggart was a co-founder of Kestrel Films with Tony Garnett, Ken Loach and Kenith Trodd and he directed two plays for Kestrel, both screened on London Weekend Television: *Pig in a Poke* and Dennis Potter's *Moonlight on the Highway*. His only feature film was *All the Way Up*, based on David Turner's stage play *Semi-Detached*, a relentlessly cynical comedy about social climbing and sexual blackmail, featuring Warren Mitchell as a lower-middle-class family man abetted by his grubbily ambitious children in his attempt to climb the greasy pole.

MacTaggart was a pioneer in the creative use of the electronic television studio and it was in recognition of this that he was awarded the Desmond Davis Award for Outstanding Contribution to Television Drama in 1974. Following his early death, in London on 29 May 1974, the MacTaggart Lecture was founded in his name at the 1976 Edinburgh Television Festival.

(Lez Cooke)

BIBLIOGRAPHY: Cooke, Lez, *British Television Drama: A History* (London: BFI, 2003).

FILMOGRAPHY: *All the Way Up* (1970).

MADDEN, John (1949–)

John Madden was born on 8 April 1949 in Portsmouth, Hampshire, and educated at Cambridge University, where, together with Jon Amiel, he ran the Oxford and Cambridge Shakespeare Company. After a brief spell working as a director on

BBC Radio, Madden was seconded in 1975 to work for National Public Radio in the United States. His first assignment, directing Arthur Kopit's play *Wings*, won the Prix Italia, and Madden was invited to direct the stage version, first on Broadway and then at the National Theatre in London. Madden also taught on the acting and scriptwriting programme at Yale University while continuing to direct stage productions, but in the early 1980s he returned to England to work in television, where he directed the BBC television film *Poppyland* (1985) and episodes of *The Return of Sherlock Holmes* (1986) and *Inspector Morse*.

Madden's break into movies came when, following the withdrawal of Trevor Nunn, he was invited to direct the film adaptation of the Edith Wharton novel *Ethan Frome* (1993) as a co-production for American Playhouse and the BBC. Although well received critically, the film received only a short run at the National Film Theatre in London before being broadcast. His next film for American Playhouse, the romantic drama *Golden Gate* (1994), fared less well and without waiting, as Madden put it, to 'hang around in the chill wind of American disfavour', he returned to television work in the UK (Sloman, p. 11).

Two very different television films for the BBC's *Screen One* slot – *Meat* (1994), set among prostitutes and young offenders, and *Truth or Dare* (1996), a yuppie thriller – were followed by *Mrs Brown* (1997). Shot on Super-16 and originally intended for television, this romantic drama concerning the friendship between Queen Victoria and her Scottish servant John Brown was a hit with both critics and audiences and brought Madden into the mainstream. *Shakespeare in Love* (1998), backed by Miramax and Universal, was a much bigger-budgeted project, which received several Academy Award nominations and won Madden a BAFTA Best Director award. Madden's fluid camera style provided an apt complement to Tom Stoppard's agile and witty script and created a vivid sense of bustling Elizabethan theatre life.

The upward trajectory of Madden's career was hampered by the disappointing reception given his adaptation of Louis de Bernières *Captain Corelli's Mandolin* (2001), a project he came to late in its development when the original director, Roger Michell, fell ill. With his visual flair and ability to handle complex narratives, however, Madden's future seems assured. His return to the theatre to direct David Auburn's prize-winning play *Proof* at the Donmar Warehouse in London led to him directing the $20 million film adaptation, with Gwyneth Paltrow reprising her role as the daughter of a brilliant but erratic mathematician who fears that if she has inherited his gifts she may also have inherited his madness.

(Martin Hunt)

BIBLIOGRAPHY: Higgs, Andrew, 'Madden in Love with Directing', *Direct*, Summer 1999, pp. 12–15; Malcolm, Derek, 'John Madden at the NFT', *Guardian*, 8 May 2001 <film.guardian.co.uk/interview/interviewpages/0,6737,487587,00.html>; Sloman, Tony, 'Interview with John Madden: Shakespeare and Mrs Brown', *British Film & TV Facilities Journal*, Summer 1998, pp. 9–12.

Renée Zellweger in *Bridget Jones's Diary* (Sharon Maguire, 2001)

FILMOGRAPHY: *Ethan Frome* (US, 1993); *Golden Gate* (US, 1994); *Mrs Brown* (1997); *Shakespeare in Love* (US/UK, 1998); *Captain Corelli's Mandolin* (UK/Fr/US, 2001); *Proof* (US, 2005).

MAGUIRE, Sharon

Sharon Maguire was born in the late 1960s in Coventry, where her father managed a shoe shop. She originally wanted to act, and attended speech and drama classes from the age of four. However, after graduating from Aberystwyth University she took a teacher-training course and then moved to London, where she worked in the publicity department at Penguin Books. A postgraduate course in journalism at City University led to a job in television as a researcher on *The Media Show*. In 1991 she joined the BBC and directed items for *The Late Show* and documentaries for *Omnibus* and *Bookmark*. She had begun to make a name for herself directing commercials when her friend Helen Fielding suggested her as the director for Working Title's adaptation of Fielding's best-seller, *Bridget Jones's Diary*.

Maguire was the model for Fielding's character 'Shazzer' (played by Sally Phillips in the film) but seemed otherwise under qualified to direct a big-budget feature film. However, it was only after Maguire's involvement that its budget was expanded from $5 to $26 million, and she proved competent enough to bring it in on time and under budget. *Bridget Jones's Diary* subsequently became one of the most successful British comedies ever made.

(Pamela Church Gibson)

BIBLIOGRAPHY: Hunt, Nick, 'Close Up – Sharon Maguire', *Screen International*, 20 Apr. 2001, p. 15; Quinn, Anthony, 'She Wasn't Bossy but in Control. Sort of Erich von Stroheim Dressed in a Skirt', *Evening Standard*, 23 Apr. 2000, pp. 38–9.

FILMOGRAPHY: *Bridget Jones's Diary* (UK/US/Fr, 2001).

MAINWARING, Bernerd (1899–1963)

Born in Stoke-on-Trent in 1899, the eccentrically spelled Bernerd Wilfrid Mainwaring entered the industry in 1920 after whirlwind experience as a clerk, acrobat, librarian and band-leader. He started out as an editor and scenario writer, and in 1924 began writing scripts in New York. Directing work in England arrived with the talkies, but assignments never moved beyond the humble. Two-reel comedies for BIP led to quota features chiefly for American outfits. MGM issued Hammer's *The Public Life of Henry the Ninth*, a vehicle for comedian Leonard Henry, but with no ambitions as a Korda spoof; two others were made for Paramount-British, and four for Fox-British. Dramas and crime thrillers predominated. Prints are now elusive, but reviews suggest moderate success in *Jennifer Hale* (1937), featuring René Ray as a chorus girl suspected of murder, and a decent showing by Evelyn Ankers (a future Universal scream queen) in *The Villiers Diamond* (1938).

Service with the RAF in the Second World War led to straightforward training and information films, and the formation of his own company, B. M. Productions. The cadet school drama *High Flight* (John Gilling, 1957) briefly returned him to features as a second-unit director. Towards the end of his life he found his last niche as Britain's answer to James FitzPatrick with travelogues of the usual rosy disposition. He began in 1959 with *Wonders of Gibraltar*, passed through wonderful Africa and Israel, and finally reached *The South Pacific* and *Bali Is a Happening* in 1973. His material was apparently durable enough to allow for packaging and distribution some years after his death, which occurred on 27 July 1963 in Ealing, west London.

(Geoff Brown)

FILMOGRAPHY: Shorts: *Realities*; *O.K. Chief* (1930); *Cupboard Love*; *The Lame Duck* (1931); *Local Government* (1944); *Wonders of Gibraltar* (1959); *Wings to the Sun* (1960); *Wonderful Greece*; *Wonderful Switzerland No. 1*; *Wonderful Israel* (1961); *Wonderful Africa*; *Wonderful Beaulieu* (1962); *Wonderful Switzerland No. 2*; *Looking in on the Royal Navy*; *Wonderful Sardinia* (1963); *Wings to the Sun* (1964); *Wonderful Sicily* (1966); *A Choice of Castles*; *Romanian Rendezvous* (1972); *The South Pacific*; *Europe*; *The Islander*; *The Orient*; *Bali Is a Happening* (1973).

Features: *The New Hotel* (1932); *The Crimson Candle* (1934); *The Public Life of Henry the Ninth*; *Old Roses*; *Line Engaged* (1935); *Show Flat* (1936); *Cross My Heart* (aka *Loaded Dice*); *Member of the Jury*; *Jennifer Hale* (1937); *The Villiers Diamond* (1938); *High Flight* (2nd unit dir. with Max Varnel and Anthony Squire, John Gilling, 1957)

MALLE, Louis (1932–1995)

Louis Malle was born on 30 October 1932 in Thumeries, northern France, where a sugar refinery owned by his mother's family was the main local employer. He studied at the Institut d'Études Politiques at the Sorbonne, then at the Institut des Hautes Études Cinématographiques, but after one year at the latter he joined the pioneer oceanographer Jacques Cousteau as his co-director on *Le Monde du silence* (*The World of Silence*, 1956), the documentary record of Cousteau's explorations. After working briefly as assistant to Robert Bresson, Malle directed his first feature, *Ascenseur pour l'échafaud/Lift to the Scaffold* (1957), and in 1958 bought the Parisian production company Nouvelles Éditions de Films, which would co-produce most of his subsequent twenty features and ten documentaries.

Although Malle was a contemporary of the French *nouvelle vague* directors, his films lacked the showy iconoclasm of a Godard or the restless experimentation of Resnais and Rivette. They became known instead for their spare directorial style, subtle but then-startling eroticism (beginning with *Ascenseur pour l'échafaud* and 1959's *Les Amants/The Lovers*, both starring Jeanne Moreau) and sometimes taboo-breaking sexual subjects – incest in the part-autobiographical *Le Souffle au coeur* (1971), child prostitution in *Pretty Baby* (1978).

While two of Malle's French films, *Black Moon* (1975) and *Milou en mai* (1990), feature British actresses – respectively, Cathryn Harrison and Harriet Walter – he made only one British film, *Damage*, adapted from the much-hyped 1991 debut novel by London theatre producer Josephine Hart (wife of advertising millionaire Maurice Saatchi). *Damage*'s subject matter – a British Conservative minister's erotic obsession and violent affair with the 'damaged' fiancée of his son leads to the son's death and the destruction of the family – had obvious affinities with Malle's earlier work. Yet his attraction to the project was morbid, coloured by the beginnings of terminal illness and a long-held belief that he would not live past sixty. Rushed to hospital during work on the script – which was taken over by playwright and director David Hare – he insisted on deferring urgent surgery until filming was complete. A £13 million co-production between Malle's company and Simon Relph's Skreba Films, *Damage* displayed every signifier of cultural and financial prestige, but Hare's cold script, and Malle's over-identification with Jeremy Irons' protagonist and over-investment in Juliette Binoche's erotic allure blunted narrative and psychological tension, and the film's reception in Britain was generally poor. After making the low-key but immensely likeable *Vanya on 42nd Street* (US, 1994), Malle died from lymphoma in Beverly Hills, California, on 23 November 1995.

(Claire Monk)

BIBLIOGRAPHY: Camber Porter, Melinda, 'Damage Due to His Self-Sacrifice', *The Times*, 29 Jan. 1993, p. 29; Lloyd Parry, Roger, 'Damaged but Unbowed', *Daily Telegraph*, 27 Jan. 1993, p. 14; Spike, Paul, 'Love Hurts', *GQ* [UK], Feb. 1993, pp. 62–7, 124–5.

FILMOGRAPHY (UK only): *Damage/Fatale* (UK/Fr, 1992).

MANDER, Kay (1915–)

Kay Mander was born in Hull on 29 September 1915. After working for the 1935 Berlin International Film Congress, she returned to Britain where she found work at Alexander Korda's London Films. She spent several years in publicity, continuity and as an interpreter at several feature studios, and became one of the first women members of the ACT (Association of Cinematograph Technicians). Through contact with people in the burgeoning documentary movement, she met Arthur Elton, and in 1940 he offered her a job as a production assistant at the Shell Film Unit. A year later she directed her first film, an instructional short, and by the time she left to join Paul Rotha Productions in 1943 had directed a further four films for the civilian home-front propaganda campaign. These instructional films are characterised by their clarity and humanity – a difficult task considering the frequently dry subject matter.

In 1945 Mander and her husband, the documentary producer R. K. Neilson Baxter, established their own company, Basic Films. One of the first commissions they received was from the Labour Party for their 1945 election campaign. The film, *Homes for the People* (1945), presents the Labour Party's post-war reconstruction policies from a woman's perspective and is a remarkable social document. Mander followed the example of Ruby Grierson on *Housing Problems* (Arthur Elton/Edgar Anstey, 1935) – who found that women were more comfortable talking to another woman about their lives – and prompted her interviewees with questions rather than scripting their responses. The women talk as they go about their domestic work, resulting in a remarkably honest portrayal of the 'ordinary' woman in 1940s' Britain.

Basic Films continued to make educational and promotional films for government and industrial sponsors. In 1948 and 1949, Mander made a series of French-language films for the Ministry of Education, including *La Famille Martin* (1949), which won a British Film Academy Award in 1949. At the end of the 1940s, Neilson Baxter went to Indonesia to help set up a film unit and in the early 1950s Mander joined him there. Here, she wrote and directed two short films: *Mardi and the Monkey* (1953) and *The New Boat* (1955). On her return to Britain, she proved her ability to direct entertaining fiction with a feature for the Children's Film Foundation, *The Kid from Canada* (1957). But reluctant to be pigeonholed as a director of children's or 'women's' films and frustrated by the lack of other directorial opportunities, she returned to continuity, working on many films including *The Four Horsemen of the Apocalypse* (Vincente Minelli, 1961), *The Heroes of Telemark* (Anthony Mann, 1965), *Fahrenheit 451* (François Truffaut, 1966) *Tommy* (Ken Russell, 1975) and *Straight to Hell* (Alex Cox, 1986) until the late 1990s.

(Sarah Easen)

BIBLIOGRAPHY: Haggith, Toby, *Castles in the Air: British Films and the Reconstruction of the Built Environment 1939–1951* (London: I. B. Tauris, 2004).

FILMOGRAPHY: *How to File* (1941); *Fruit Spraying*; *Model Procedure for Water Relaying*; *NFS Mobilising Procedure* (1942); *Debris Tunnelling*; *Highland Doctor* (1943); *New Builders*; items for *Worker and Warfront* cinemagazine (1944); *Penicillin*; *Homes for the People* (1945); *Near Home*; *Cine Panorama* (1946); *Take Thou*; *Twenty-Four Square Miles* (1947); *A Plan to Work On*; *How, What and Why?* (series) (1948); *La Famille Martin*; *Histoire de poissons*; *Départ des grandes vacances*; *A Quiet Morning* (1949); *Working in a Store* (1950); *Clearing the Lines* (1952); *Mardi and the Monkey* (1953); *The New Boat* (1955); *The Kid from Canada* (1957).

MANDER, Miles (1888–1946)

Miles Mander was born Lionel Mander at Wightwick Manor in Wolverhampton on 14 May 1888. His wealthy family included two brothers, one of whom, Geoffrey Mander, became the Liberal MP for Wolverhampton East and an outspoken champion of the British film industry in Parliament. Miles was educated at Harrow and McGill University, Montreal, before embarking on a varied early career that included aviation, big-game hunting, motor racing and sheep farming in New Zealand. He entered the film business in 1913 as a film exhibitor and distributor, but then turned to acting, making his debut under the name of Luther Miles in *Once Upon a Time* (Thomas Bentley, 1918). More substantial roles followed in Adrian Brunel's *The Temporary Lady* (1920), Graham Cutts' *The Prude's Fall* (1924) and Alfred Hitchcock's *The Pleasure Garden* (1925), where his role as the bigamous villain Levett helped to establish Mander's screen image of the moustachioed cad.

Mander himself directed a number of short sound films for De Forest Phonofilms in 1926–7, and gained further experience assisting Gustaf Molander on his suggestive comedy *Parisiskor* (1928). Mander's sophisticated understanding of the cinema medium found a greater outlet in his first British feature, *The First Born* (1928), adapted from his play *Those Common People*, produced independently at Gainsborough. Mander played the unsympathetic male lead, with Madeleine Carroll as his sorely put-upon wife. Trade disinterest and unsympathetic editing by the distributors limited its impact, though the film's underground reputation was sealed in 1930 when Paul Rotha, usually no friend of British features, singled out Mander's work for praise in his influential book *The Film Till Now*.

Mander's subsequent talkies as a director showed occasional glimpses of the *First Born* stylist in their editing conceits and camerawork, both influenced by continental practices; they also proved the difficulty of combining visual ambitions with commercial constraints. Least ambitious was *Fascination*, starring Carroll in a barnacled tale of adultery taken from the stage. *The Woman Between*, adapted by Mander from a play by Miles Malleson, deployed its artistic effects on the love of an earl's daughter for a Labour political candidate. Class divisions were equally a concern of *Youthful Folly* and a version of W. J. Locke's novel *The Morals of Marcus*, the last enlivened by Lupe Velez's turn as the half-caste woman who falls under a bachelor archaeologist's wing. His last directing credit was on the outdoors adventure *The Flying Doctor* (1936), an Australian-British endeavour featuring Hollywood's Charles Farrell, and only reluctantly distributed in the UK.

Mander stood as a Labour candidate in the 1935 General Election, but the result was a landslide victory for the Tory-dominated national government. From 1936, he pursued his acting career in Hollywood, where he was popular, successful and not always the dapper cad: memorable roles also included Cardinal Richelieu in Allan Dwan's *The Three Musketeers* (1939) and Aramis in James Whale's *The Man in the Iron Mask* (1939). He also played a leading role in promoting British propaganda during the Second World War. Mander died in Hollywood from a stroke on 8 February 1946, and was still fondly enough

recalled to summon tributes over twenty years later; in a letter to *Sight and Sound*, Rotha returned to *The First Born* again, praising 'a man of great wit, immense charm and a filmic skill unrecognised in England' (Rotha, 1969).
(Geoff Brown and Janet Moat)

BIBLIOGRAPHY: Aldgate, Tony, 'Loose Ends, Hidden Gems and the Moment of "Melodramatic Emotionality"', in Jeffrey Richards (ed.), *The Unknown 1930s: An Alternative History of the British Cinema 1929–39* (London: I. B. Tauris, 1998); Catling, Darrel, 'Miles Mander', *Sight and Sound*, Winter 1968/9, p. 54; Mander, Miles, 'Sidelights on the Talkie Situation', *Theatre World*, Sept. 1930, pp. 66–7; Rotha, Paul, *The Film Till Now* (London: Jonathan Cape, 1930; revised edn., Spring Books, 1967); Rotha, Paul, 'Miles Mander', *Sight and Sound*, Spring 1969, p. 108.

FILMOGRAPHY: *The Fair Maid of Perth* (short); *The Whistler* (short); *The Sheik of Araby* (short); *Knee Deep in Daisies* (short); *Castles in the Air* (short) (1926); *As We Lie* (short); *The Sentence of Death* (aka *The Great Moment*, short); *Packing Up* (short); *False Colours* (short) (1927); *The First Born* (1928); *Fascination*; *The Woman Between* (US: *The Woman Decides*) (1931); *Youthful Folly* (1934); *The Morals of Marcus* (1935); *The Flying Doctor* (Austral/UK, 1936).

MANKIEWICZ, Joseph L. (1909–1993)

Joseph Leo Mankiewicz was born on 11 February 1909 in Wilkes-Barr, Pennsylvania, the youngest of three children of German-Jewish immigrants. After working as a journalist in Berlin, where he also translated intertitles for the German company Ufa, he went to Hollywood in 1929 to join his screenwriter brother Herman. Joseph was a title-writer and screenwriter at Paramount and a producer at MGM before graduating to writer-director at 20th Century-Fox, where he directed his first film, *Dragonwyck* (1946). He became known as a purveyor of sophisticated literary and theatrical entertainments, and won both writing and directing Academy Awards two years in succession, for *A Letter to Three Wives* (1949) and *All about Eve* (1950).

Atypically, he neither wrote nor produced any of his three British films. *Escape*, starring Rex Harrison as a gentleman convict on the run, was adapted by Philip Dunne from a John Galsworthy play first filmed by Basil Dean in 1930; *Suddenly, Last Summer* was bowdlerised from Tennessee Williams' one-act play by Williams and Gore Vidal; and *Sleuth* was adapted by Anthony Shaffer from his own long-running stage play. The elaborately cluttered interior sets designed by Oliver Messel for *Suddenly, Last Summer* and Ken Adam for *Sleuth* provide appropriately baroque settings for Mankiewicz's consciously theatrical *mise en scène*, and for the finely wrought performances of Elizabeth Taylor and Katharine Hepburn in the former and Laurence Olivier and Michael Caine in the latter. *Sleuth* proved to be Mankiewicz's final film. He died of heart failure in Bedford Hills, New York, on 5 February 1993.
(Sheldon Hall)

BIBLIOGRAPHY: Conrad, Derek, 'Joseph Mankiewicz – Putting on the Style', *Films and Filming*, Jan. 1960, pp. 9, 33; Geist, Kenneth L., *Pictures Will Talk: The Life and Films of Joseph L. Mankiewicz* (New York: Scribner's, 1978).

FILMOGRAPHY (UK only): *Escape* (1948); *Suddenly, Last Summer* (1959); *Sleuth* (1972).

MANN, Anthony (1906–1967)

Anthony Mann was born Emile Anton Bundesmann in San Diego on 30 June 1906. When he was ten his school-teacher parents moved to New York, where Mann entered the theatre as an actor and in various production capacities. After directing plays on Broadway he was recruited by David O. Selznick as a movie talent scout, casting director and maker of screen tests, and in 1942 he directed his first feature, *Dr Broadway*, at Paramount. Though he subsequently worked in most genres and for most studios, he specialised first in film noir (such as *T-Men*, 1947), then Westerns (*Winchester '73*, 1950; *The Man from Laramie*, 1955) and big-budget epics shot in Europe (*El Cid*, 1961; *The Fall of the Roman Empire*, 1964).

Mann's last two films were based in Britain, though they involved extensive overseas locations. *The Heroes of Telemark*, the true story of a wartime mission to destroy Nazi heavy-water plants in Norway, seems an ideal Mann subject, but despite a few good action scenes and superb snowscapes photographed by Robert Krasker, it is slackly narrated, cliché-ridden and displays some alarmingly poor day-for-night work. While shooting in Berlin for *A Dandy in Aspic*, a typically convoluted spy saga, Mann suffered a heart attack and died on 29 April 1967. Its star, Laurence Harvey, completed directing the film in England, his footage – seemingly distinguishable from Mann's by its obtrusively modish style, all zooms, canted angles and echo-chamber sound effects – comprising perhaps one-third of the final cut.
(Sheldon Hall)

BIBLIOGRAPHY: Basinger, Janine, *Anthony Mann* (Boston, MA: Twayne, 1979); Fenwick, J. H., and Jonathan Green-Armytage, 'Landscape and Anthony Mann', *Sight and Sound*, Autumn 1965, pp. 186–9; Pattison, Barrie and Christopher Wicking, 'Interviews with Anthony Mann', *Screen*, July/Oct. 1969, pp. 32–54; 'The Heroes of Telemark', Supplement to *Kinematograph Weekly*, 2 Sept. 1965.

FILMOGRAPHY (UK only): *The Heroes of Telemark* (UK/US, 1965); *A Dandy in Aspic* (1968).

MARCEL, Terry (1942–)

Terry Marcel was born in Oxford on 10 June 1942 and began working at Pinewood Studios as a teenager. He eventually became one of the busiest assistant directors in the business, working with Sam Peckinpah on *Straw Dogs* (1972) and Ridley Scott on *The Duellists* (1977), as well as forging long-term relationships with such directors as Richard Fleischer and Blake Edwards.

After co-writing and producing *Prey* (aka *Alien Prey*, Norman J. Warren, 1978), Marcel made his directorial debut in the late

1970s with two Ray Cooney farces, *Why Not Stay for Breakfast?* and *There Goes the Bride*, on which he met composer Harry Robertson. The two set up their own company and made *Hawk the Slayer*, a cheap and cheerful production shot in six weeks on a budget of less than £1million, and one of the first films to jump on the sword-and-sorcery bandwagon after the success of *Star Wars* (George Lucas, 1977). They next collaborated on a television movie, *Prisoners of the Lost Universe* (1983), and then on *Jane and the Lost City*, based on the wartime comic strip, and featuring Jasper Carrott as a crudely comic Nazi villain.

Subsequently Marcel has worked predominantly for television on such series as *The Bill*, *Bergerac*, *Trainer* and *Heartbeat*. More recently he collaborated with *Fast Show* writer Dave Cummings on the incongruously titled *The Last Seduction II* (1998), a disappointing sequel to John Dahl's superior 1994 neo-noir, relocated to Barcelona. Marcel returned to episodic television and fantasy with *Dark Knight* (2000–2), a retelling of the Ivanhoe story.

(Sergio Angelini)

BIBLIOGRAPHY: McAsh, Iain, 'Special Delivery', *Films Illustrated Monthly*, Jan. 1979, p. 169; Vaines, Colin, 'Unveiling the New "Bond", a Swordsman', *Screen International*, 19 Apr. 1980, p. 45.

FILMOGRAPHY: *Why Not Stay for Breakfast?* (1979); *There Goes the Bride*; *Hawk the Slayer* (1980); *The Wall* (2nd unit dir., Alan Parker); *Trail of the Pink Panther* (2nd unit dir., Blake Edwards) (1982); *Curse of the Pink Panther* (2nd unit dir., Blake Edwards, 1983); *Sky Bandits* (2nd unit dir., Zoran Persic, 1986); *Jane and the Lost City* (1987); *The Last Seduction II* (US/UK/Sp, 1998).

MARCUS, James (1942–)

James Marcus was born in 1942. He became an apprentice printer, then at the age of twenty-four enrolled at the East 15 Drama School in Essex. After playing one of Alex's Droogs in *A Clockwork Orange* (Stanley Kubrick, 1971) he appeared in various films and television dramas ranging from *Let's Get Laid* (James Kenelm Clarke, 1977) to *London's Burning* (1986–90), where he played the likeable station officer Sidney Tate. He made his debut as director with the accurately titled *No Grass in Lewisham* (1979), a fifty-minute black-and-white film, made with a local youth drama group and centred on a West Indian girl arrested for shoplifting. His one feature film, *Tank Malling* (1988), made on a tight budget of £750,000, is a crude but vigorous conspiracy thriller with Ray Winstone as a hard-bitten investigative reporter who milks high-class whore Amanda Donohoe for juicy information on a corrupt moral rearmament campaigner (a smarmily convincing Peter Wyngarde). 'I have been sorely tested and found wanting', Marcus confessed when the shooting schedule overran by a week. No further features followed, though he subsequently wrote and produced the stage play *Family Tree* (1993), and continues to act in television series such as *Heartbeat* and *The Bill*.

(Robert Murphy)

BIBLIOGRAPHY: 'Shooting Tank', *Producer* no. 6, Winter 1988, p. 3; 'Sidney Tate', <www.londons-burning.co.uk/sidneytate.htm>.

FILMOGRAPHY: *No Grass in Lewisham* (aka *What Jacky Did Next*, 1979); *Tank Malling* (1988).

MARCUS, Shimmy

The son of Irish film-maker Louis Marcus, Shimmy Marcus established his reputation with two short films, *7th Heaven* and *Ivor the Insomniac*, and *Aidan Walsh: Master of the Universe*, a spoof documentary ridiculing the Irish rock music scene. He found it difficult to secure backing for *Headrush*, a crime-comedy set in Dublin, and had to make drastic script changes when the similarly offbeat *Lock, Stock and Two Smoking Barrels* (Guy Ritchie, 1998) burst onto the scene. Marcus' film was eventually made in 2002 on high-definition digital video, and after positive festival screenings released in Ireland in 2004. By this time, however, zany and dope-smoking criminals appeared too familiar to cause much excitement.

(Robert Murphy)

BIBLIOGRAPHY: Kemp, Rebecca, 'High Time', *Film Ireland* no. 98, May/June 2004, pp. 22–3.

FILMOGRAPHY: *7th Heaven* (short, Ir, 1999); *Aidan Walsh: Master of the Universe* (Ir, 2000); *Ivor the Insomniac* (short, Ir, 2001); *Headrush* (Ir/UK/Neth, 2002; rel. 2004).

MARKS, George Harrison (1926–1997)

George Harrison Marks was born in Tottenham, north London, on 6 August 1926. His father, a debt-collector invalided by gas poisoning during the First World War, died when he was six. In the 1940s Harrison Marks was part of a music-hall cross-talk act, but he saw little future among the decaying Palaces, Empires and Hippodromes, and switched to photography, initially of actors, more profitably of nudes. His partnership with ex-art school student and model Pamela Green (whom he married) flourished and led to his first film, *Naked – as Nature Intended* (1961). Ostensibly a serious account of the British Naturist movement, the film in reality was a playful romp, with Green and others running, laughing, waving and throwing beach balls in as revealing postures as the censors would allow. More of the same followed in *The Naked World of Harrison Marks* (1965).

Pattern of Evil, a darker film, presided over by the fierce Monique Devereaux, followed in 1967, by which time Green and Harrison Marks had parted company. Two years later he played his own leading man in *The Nine Ages of Nakedness*, seeking advice from a psychiatrist about why he gets into so much trouble with women. After casting him back into the past (where Marks imagines himself in similar difficulties whether he is a prehistoric cave painter or a Victorian showman), the psychiatrist, played by Marks' second wife, Toni, advises him to stay away from beautiful women. Though acting and directing is crude, the film is redeemed by a strangely innocent ineptness.

In 1971 Harrison Marks was found guilty of dealing in pornography, a harsh judgment in view of the comic ethos of

most of his work. It took some time for him to get his career back on track, though he did so remarkably successfully with *Come Play with Me* (1977), a sex-comedy backed by David Sullivan (later to launch his newspaper empire with the *Sunday Sport*) featuring Sullivan's protégée Mary Millington among a cast of comedy stalwarts. The film ran for nearly four years in London's West End, despite the declining cinema demand for sex films. Harrison Marks spent his final years making spanking films with comical titles such as *Kane Assignment* (1991), *Stinging Tails* (1992) and *Rawhide* (1994), all for the home video market. He died of cancer in London on 27 June 1997.
(Robert Murphy)

BIBLIOGRAPHY: Ezard, John and David McGillivray, 'Naked Ambitions' (obituaries), *Guardian*, 1 July 1997, p. 15; McGillivray, David, *Doing Rude Things: The History of the British Sex Film, 1957–81* (London: Sun Tavern Fields, 1992); Sheridan, Simon, *Keeping the British End Up: Four Decades of Saucy Cinema*, 2nd edn (London: Reynolds & Hearn, 2005).

FILMOGRAPHY: *Naked – as Nature Intended* (US: *As Nature Intended*, 1961); *The Naked World of Harrison Marks* (US: *The Dream World of Harrison Marks*, 1965); *Pattern of Evil* (US: *Fornicon*, 1967); *The Nine Ages of Nakedness* (1969); *Come Play with Me* (1977).

MARQUAND, Richard (1938–1987)

Richard Marquand was born in Cardiff on 17 April 1938. Though he has a permanent place in the box-office pantheon as the director of *Return of the Jedi*, the *Star Wars* film with the annoying teddybear-like Ewoks, it is by a long stretch the worst of the series and Marquand does little to usurp George Lucas' position as creator of the film.

After a career in television concentrating mainly on documentaries such as *Nixon's Secret Legacy* (1975) and *Ernest Hemingway: Rough Diamond* (1977), Marquand made his cinema debut with an unremarkable country-house thriller, *The Legacy*. His next film, *The Birth of the Beatles*, though made in 1979, was not released until 1982 after the relative success of his adaptation of Ken Follett's Second World War woman-in-peril-in-a-lighthouse thriller, *Eye of the Needle*.

After directing *Jedi*, Marquand had the clout to get a personal project made, the Parisian romance *Until September*, but he showed a much surer hand with the Joe Eszterhas-scripted thriller *Jagged Edge*, by far his best film. His strongest suit seems to have been working with underrated actresses: Katharine Ross in *The Legacy*, Kate Nelligan in *Eye of the Needle*, Karen Allen in *Until September*, Glenn Close in *Jagged Edge*; he even managed to make Carrie Fisher's Princess Leia seem sexy. Sadly, his final film was the wretched Bob Dylan–Rupert Everett pop music movie *Hearts of Fire*, which he also produced. He died after suffering a stroke in London on 4 September 1987.
(Kim Newman)

BIBLIOGRAPHY: Obituary, *Films and Filming*, Nov. 1987, p. 13; Obituary, *Screen International*, 12 Sept. 1987, p. 4; Pirie, David, 'Leading Edge', *Time Out*, 26 Mar. 1986, p. 25.

FILMOGRAPHY: *The Iron Village* (doc. short); *Men, Men, Men* (doc. short); *Between the Anvil and the Hammer* (doc. short) (1973); *Martin Luther King* (doc. short, 1977); *The Legacy* (1978); *The Birth of the Beatles* (1979; rel. 1982); *Eye of the Needle* (1981); *Return of the Jedi* (US, 1983); *Until September* (US, 1984); *Jagged Edge* (US, 1985); *Hearts of Fire* (US, 1987).

MARSH, William

William Marsh was born in Minneapolis. He arrived in London in the 1980s, working as an actor and director in fringe theatre, though a more lucrative income came from film appearances, including *Saving Private Ryan* (Steven Spielberg, 1998). He spent nine years trying to realise his pet project of adapting Martin Amis' 1975 novel, *Dead Babies*, eventually convincing Richard Holmes and Neil Peplow, producers of *Shooting Fish* (Stefan Schwartz, 1997) and *Waking Ned* (Kirk Jones, 1998), that this tale of sex, drugs and violence during an English stately home weekend would appeal to young cinema audiences. Marsh directs crudely but energetically, injecting sufficient pace to make bad acting and inconsequential sequences forgettable. The plot, based on a haphazard updating of Agatha Christie's *Ten Little Indians*, with a nihilist internet terrorist group masking the threat from within, has the virtue of meting out nemesis to the most unlikeable characters (including Marsh himself as a smug American drugs guru). Critics and the tiny audiences who saw the film in its fleeting UK cinema release were not impressed; cannier handling might have attracted an internet/DVD cult audience. As it is, *Dead Babies* seems unlikely to secure Marsh's shift from actor to director.
(Robert Murphy)

BIBLIOGRAPHY: 'Dead Funny', *Creation*, Aug. 2000, pp. 22–5.

FILMOGRAPHY: *Hotel* (short, 1997); *Dead Babies* (US: *Mood Swingers*, 2000).

MARSHALL, Frank

Frank Marshall made five B-films in the early 1960s. The best is the first, *Identity Unknown* (1960), where the Brian Clemens script gives him plenty to do juggling the stories of ten people involved in an airline crash. Marshall's other three films for the Danziger brothers' company are disappointingly routine: though cut-price budgets and cramped, outdated studio facilities hardly encouraged creativity. He failed to inject life into *Feet of Clay* (1960), even with likeable Australian Vincent Ball as a crime-busting solicitor. Similarly, Terence Alexander as a shy office worker with an undeserved reputation as a tough guy and Angela Douglas, struggling to conceal her assets as the office ugly duckling, are unable to prevent boredom striking in *The Gentle Terror* (1962). *Gang War* (1962) shows indigenous cockney criminals getting the better of their American counterparts, but one suspects that the high body count rather than patriotic sentiment accounted for any audience appeal. *A Guy Called Caesar* (1962), made along the same lines for independent producer Bill Luckwell, showed little improvement. After 1962 Marshall

disappeared into the undergrowth and has proved impossible to trace.
(Robert Murphy)
FILMOGRAPHY: *Identity Unknown*; *Feet of Clay* (1960); *The Gentle Terror*; *Gang War*; *A Guy Called Caesar* (1962).

MARSHALL, Neil (1970–)

Neil Marshall was born in Newcastle upon Tyne on 25 May 1970. He co-wrote *Killing Time* (Bharat Nalluri, 1998), a convoluted crime melodrama released on video/DVD, and formed Northmen Productions with producer Keith Bell. After making *Combat*, an eight-minute short accompanying events in a rowdy pub with a soundtrack of jet planes and explosions, the pair gained financial backing for a horror feature film. *Dog Soldiers*, written and directed by Marshall, is a pleasingly outrageous tale of a band of squaddies besieged by Scottish werewolves. Occasionally pedestrian dialogue and a hoary old plot hardly deflected audience appreciation of the film's thrills.

A bigger budget allowed him to spend more time getting things right on his next film, *The Descent*. Marshall shows a real flair for suspense, and he is able to sustain the intense, claustrophobic atmosphere of his underground settings, where six women out for an adventure holiday find they have more to contend with than darkness, bats and blocked tunnels. His female cavers lack the raw vitality of *Dog Soldiers'* squaddies, but Marshall is careful to avoid stereotypes among this unsisterly band, and they fit neatly into the plausible and well-worked-out plot. Good notices and box-office success should ensure him a bright future.
(Robert Murphy)
BIBLIOGRAPHY: Greenway, Tony, 'Independent's Day: Combat', *Total Film* no. 36, Jan. 2000, p. 143; Jones, Alan, 'Going to the Dogs', *Shivers* no. 92, Sept./Oct. 2001, pp. 14–17; Jones, Alan, 'The Bark of *Dog Soldiers*', *Fangoria* no. 212, May 2002, pp. 40–4.
FILMOGRAPHY: *Combat* (short, 1999); *Dog Soldiers* (UK/Lux, 2002); *The Descent* (2005).

MARSHALL, Simon

Simon Marshall Darwell-Taylor grew up in South Norwood, London, and won a scholarship to Dulwich College. He turned to film-making only after the murder of a working-class friend, making *Out of Depth* (1999) to tell his story and counteract the image of cosy London gangsters propagated by films like *Lock, Stock and Two Smoking Barrels* (Guy Ritchie, 1998). The film opens with images borrowed from *Get Carter* (Mike Hodges, 1971), intimating the revenge tragedy that will ensue; but Paul (Sean Maguire), the happily upwardly mobile designer whose life unravels when he tries to avenge an insult to his mum, proves an irritatingly ineffective hero. Ironically, the film only comes alive with the introduction of Pussy Cat Lenny (Nicholas Ball),

New British horror: *Dog Soldiers* (Neil Marshall, 2002)

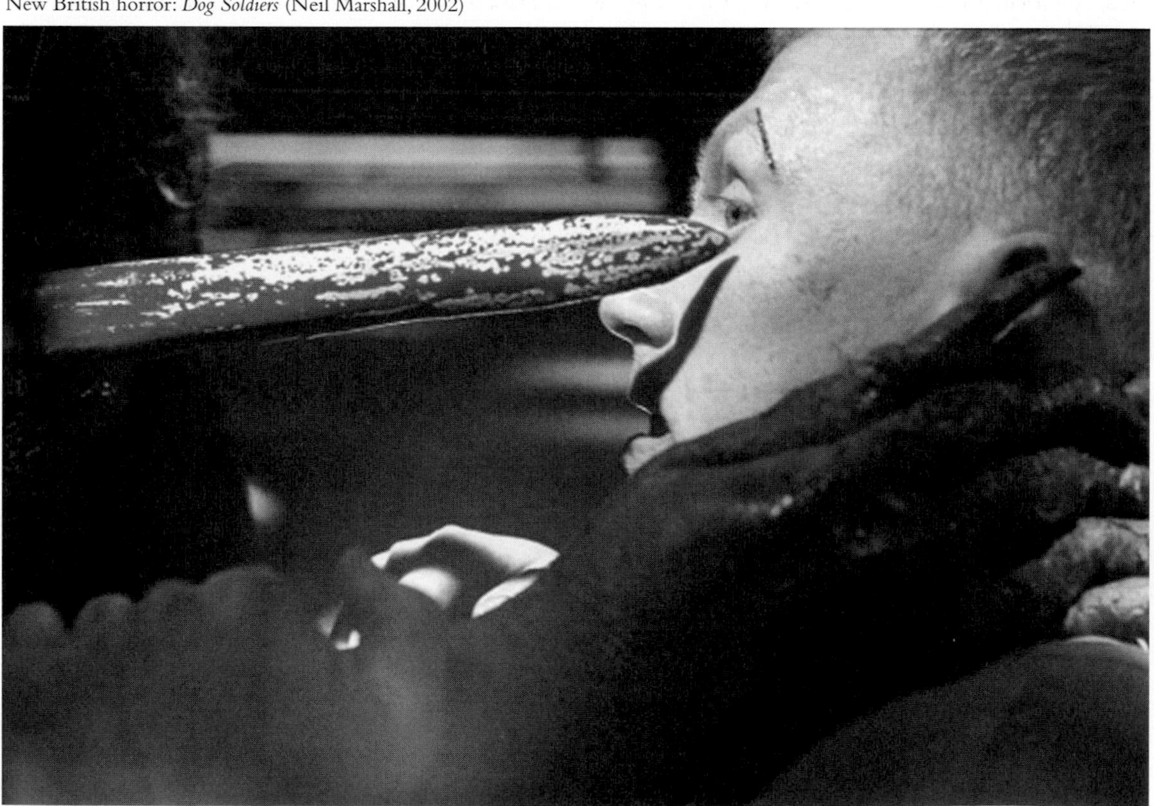

an endearingly psychotic hitman whose propensity to microwave cats and throw teapots at the wall shifts the film back to the gangland clichés it set out to avoid.

An excellent score by Barry Adamson, strong performances from the older actors (including Rita Tushingham, Leigh Lawson and Clive Russell) and Marshall's obvious sincerity make *Out of Depth* one of the more honourable British gangster films; but it proved too flat to generate much excitement among audiences.
(Robert Murphy)

BIBLIOGRAPHY: Edge, Simon, Interview 16 June 2001 <www.seanmaguire.co.uk/expressarticle.htmThe Express>; Hattenstone, Simon, 'Rule One for All Budding Film-Makers: Get Yourself a Business Plan', *Guardian* G2 Section, 27 Nov. 1998, pp. 14–15.
FILMOGRAPHY: *Out of Depth* (1999).

MARTON, Andrew (1904–1991)

Endre Marton was born in Budapest on 26 January 1904. He entered the film industry in Vienna in 1922 as an editor for Max Linder and the following year went with Ernst Lubitsch to Hollywood, where he edited two of his films and directed one of his own, *Two O'Clock in the Morning* (1929), a thriller with Noah Beery. Back in Europe, he became chief editor at the Tobis studios in Germany, where he edited, among others, *Der Rebell* (Curt Bernhardt and Luis Trenker, 1932) and *S.O.S. Eisberg* (Arnold Fank, 1933) and directed less prestigious films himself. He left Germany in 1933, working his way through Switzerland and Hungary before arriving in England in 1936.

Marton directed three British films before returning to Hollywood in 1940. *Wolf's Clothing*, based on Evadne Price and Brock Williams' play *The Emancipation of Ambrose*, is a typical Claude Hulbert silly-ass comedy, but has the benefit of a strong supporting cast – Gordon Harker, Helen Haye and, in an early film appearance, Lilli Palmer. *The Secret of Stamboul* is a fascinating but unfathomable adaptation of a Dennis Wheatley thriller, with James Mason, Frank Vosper and Valerie Hobson. *School for Husbands* is a clever farce with Rex Harrison out to seduce the wives of stuffy husbands Henry Kendall and Romney Brent.

In Hollywood Marton acquired a good reputation as a second-unit director and after the Second World War he was associated with a number of lavish Hollywood productions, including *Ben-Hur* (William Wyler, 1957), where he was responsible for the sea battle sequence, *The Longest Day* (Ken Annakin, 1962), *Cleopatra* (Joseph L. Mankiewicz, 1963) and *The Fall of the Roman Empire* (Anthony Mann, 1964). He died on 7 January 1991 in Santa Monica, California.
(Kevin Gough-Yates)

BIBLIOGRAPHY: Obituary, *Screen International*, 7 Feb. 1992, p. 8.
FILMOGRAPHY: (UK only): *Wolf's Clothing*; *The Secret of Stamboul* (1936); *School for Husbands* (1937).

MASON, Herbert (1891–1960)

Herbert Mason, born in Moseley, Birmingham, in 1891, began his entertainment career in 1908 as a stage performer; the actor Edward Terry was an uncle. During the First World War he served in the Machine Gun Corps, and was awarded the MC in 1916. Demobilised, he moved into theatre production, mounting a series of revues in the 1920s for the producer André Charlot. His initial contact with cinema came in 1928, when he began producing stage presentations featured in the larger cinemas on the Gaumont-British circuit.

In 1931, after the fashion for 'cine-variety' faded, Mason moved into film production, working as assistant director for Michael Balcon at the Shepherd's Bush studios of Gaumont-British. He finally graduated to the director's chair in 1935, and for a while, through luck or judgment, worked on some of the period's more interesting star vehicles. He caught George Arliss at his liveliest in *East Meets West* (1936); coaxed a relatively subtle performance from Tom Walls in the spy thriller *Strange Boarders* (1938); and did equally well by Jack Hulbert and Cicely Courtneidge in the musical comedy *Take My Tip* (1937). Several other films had French connections. His directing debut, *First Offence* (1936), about car thieves, was a remake of *Mauvaise graine* (Billy Wilder, 1934); while *A Window in London* (1939) drew on *Métropolitain* (Maurice Cam, 1938) for its story about a man (Michael Redgrave) sucked into an infatuation after he believes he sees a murder from a train. This is easily Mason's strongest film, strikingly shot by Glen MacWilliams, with plentiful locations and a European feeling of urban unease.

During the 1940s Mason worked prolifically for the British offshoots of Warner Bros. and 20th Century-Fox. The films' subject matter was less ambitious, the pedigree lower and the successes fewer, though the Arthur Askey comedy *Back-Room Boy* (1942) tried hard to please. Mason's profile faded further after the war when he moved into production; among others he worked on Korda's *Anna Karenina* (1948) and the Group 3 films designed to promote new talent. He died in London on 20 May 1960.
(Geoff Brown)

BIBLIOGRAPHY: Obituary, *Daily Cinema*, 25 May 1960, p. 18.
FILMOGRAPHY: *First Offence*; *East Meets West*; *His Lordship* (US: *Man of Affairs*, co-dir. Maude Howell) (1936); *Take My Tip* (1937); *Strange Boarders* (1938); *The Silent Battle* (US: *Continental Express*); *A Window in London* (US: *Lady in Distress*) (1939); *Dr O'Dowd*; *The Briggs Family*; *Fingers* (1940); *Mr Proudfoot Shows a Light* (short); *Once a Crook* (1941); *A Yank in the RAF* (dir. of RAF flying sequences, Henry King); *Back-Room Boy* (1942); *The Night Invader*, *It's in the Bag* (1943); *Flight from Folly* (1944).

MASSINGHAM, Richard (1898–1953)

Richard Massingham was born on 31 January 1898 in Sleaford, Lincolnshire, the son of a distinguished newspaper editor. He trained in medicine, and reached the position of Senior Medical Officer at the London Fever Hospital. Passionate about cinema and sophisticated in his tastes, he began making amateur films in his spare time; his first known foray, in 1933, was about the hospital where he worked. The following year he completed a short about a traumatic visit to the dentist, *Tell Me if It Hurts*, made with experimental trimmings and great assurance; critical acclaim followed its distribution in 1935. *And So to Work* (1936), a comic account of a lodger's miseries preparing for the day, offered the same leading player, Russell Waters, in another wry variation on the same basic theme, further capturing the essence of mundane existence in Britain in the 1930s. Champions in the industry helped Massingham secure a part-time berth at the GPO Film Unit, though his output there proved less successful. Awkward whimsy, indebted to French cinema, particularly afflicted *The Daily Round*; the black humour of his independently made *Come for a Stroll* survives the years better.

Professionally insecure and a hypochondriac, Massingham finally made the difficult decision to leave medicine for full-time professional film-making. He registered his own company, Public Relationship Films, in 1938, though it took the Second World War to make the outfit active, producing short films for the Ministry of Information and other government departments, along with numerous advertisements. As well as directing, Massingham began to loom large on screen, appearing as an avuncular figure exhorting audiences in trailer-length films to save fuel, sneeze into a handkerchief or bathe in the war's recommended limit of five inches of water. As an actor he possessed an amazingly expressive face and a childlike charm that made for easy identification across all classes; by casting himself as the absent-minded 'everyman', always a little denser than the audience, he allowed them to feel amused and superior, though with the film's message firmly dinned into their heads. Longer post-war films like *They Travel by Air* and *Pool of Contentment*, made for private training purposes, adopted a similar strategy, constructing hypothetical scenarios of good behaviour and bad to lighten the business of becoming an expert secretary in a government typing pool or an air steward for BOAC.

In his earliest films Massingham used relatively sophisticated contemporary film-making techniques, borrowed particularly from Russian and European art cinema: *Tell Me if It Hurts* especially contains obvious twinges of German Expressionism and the 'city symphony' films. Wartime needs required a more simplified approach, though his delight in abrupt cutting and surreal juxtapositions, and an aversion to dialogue, remained. After 1945, when the company output expanded, Massingham often relegated the director's duties to young recruits on his staff, most notably Michael Law, but he remained in charge as producer, deviser and on-screen presence. The black humour of *What a Life!* (Michael Law, 1948), inspired by contemporary moans about post-war Britain, could only have come from Massingham; while *The Cure* (1950), a satire on the medical profession and his own hypochondria, is a home movie writ large. In the early 1950s the sponsored film market began to shrink in ambition. Massingham moved sideways with a lightly charming short for children, *To the Rescue* (1952), co-directed with Jacques Brunius; the film won a prize at the Venice Film Festival, though it gives no clinching proof that Massingham's skills were fitted for fiction.

As a director, actor, producer and original creative talent who worked outside the feature format, Massingham is easily overlooked by film history. But within the ninety or so films he made – many only a few minutes long – there is enough British eccentricity and cinematic wit to earn him a special place alongside the other individualists of the British short film, Humphrey Jennings and Len Lye. Massingham died at his home in Biddenden, Kent, on 1 April 1953, during production of *The Blakes Slept Here*, a lavish and curious Technicolor amalgam of gas advertisement and historical cavalcade.

(Geoff Brown and Bryony Dixon)

BIBLIOGRAPHY: Baker, Bob, 'Richard Massingham', *Film Dope* no. 41, Mar. 1989, pp. 1–3; Brown, Geoff, 'Richard Massingham: The Great English Cineaste?', *Cinegraphie* no. 15, 2000, pp. 351–61 (earlier version: 'Richard Massingham: The Five-Inch Film-Maker', *Sight and Sound*, Summer 1976, pp. 156–9); Langlois, Henri *et al.*, *Richard Massingham: A Tribute by His Friends and a Record of His Films* (London: BFI, 1955).

FILMOGRAPHY: *London Fever Hospital* (1933); *Tell Me if It Hurts* (1934); *And So to Work* (1936); *The Daily Round* (co-dir. Karl Urbahn, 1937); *Mony a Pickle* (co-dir. Norman McLaren, 1938); *At the Third Stroke*; *Come for a Stroll* (1939); *Fear and Peter Brown* (1940); *Dangers in the Dark* (co-dir. Lewis Grant Wallace, 1941); *Young and Healthy* (co-dir. Alex Strasser); *Who'll Buy a Warship?*; *We Speak to India*; *The Five Inch Bather*; *Salvage*; *Rhapsody in White* (1942); *Believe It or Not*; *Random Harvest* (1943); *Piccadilly Roundabout*; *In Which We Live*; *Cambridge*; *Some Like It Rough*; *Elopement in France*; *First Aid in Action* (1944); *Down at the Local*; *Coughs and Sneezes*; *Post Haste* (1945); *Family Doctor*, *Influenza*; *Come Back Alive*; *Women after the War*, *The Long, Long Trail*; *The Mirror Can Lie*; *Oil on Troubled Waters*; *Agricultural Holiday Camps*; *Pool of Contentment* (shortened version, *Take a Letter Please*) (1946); *Arthur Askey on Going to the Dentist* (series); *Harvest Camp*; *They Travel by Air* (aka *Flight of Fancy*); *Pedal Cyclists*; *Women Must Work*; *Professional Sport* (unfinished) (1947); *Lilliput*; *The Greedy Boy's Dream*; *X-100* (1948); *Moving House* (1949); *The Cure* (co-dir. Michael Law, 1950); *British Adventure* (co-dir. Martin Wilson); *He Won't Bite You*; *Introducing the New Worker* (1951); *To the Rescue* (co-dir. Jacques Brunius, 1952); *The Blakes Slept Here* (shortened version, *Family Album*; co-dir. Jacques Brunius, 1953).

MASSOT, Joe

Joseph Massot began his film-making career in Cuba, where he made documentaries and newsreel items. He came to England in 1962 and worked for BBC Television, directing short items and working as an assistant to Ken Russell and Philip Saville. His *Reflections on Love* (1965), a short poetic love story set in gently Swinging London, was well enough considered to be nominated for the Best Short Film at Cannes, and he went on to direct *Wonderwall*, a feature-length psychedelic fantasy about an eccentric professor who knocks a hole in his wall to spy on the fabulous life of the beautiful young model next door. Though the film's genesis is uncertain, it looks very much like a Polanski project: based on a story by his regular collaborator Gérard Brach and relying on two of his favourite actors, Jack MacGowran, who plays the professor, and Iain Quarrier, the model's boyfriend. The professor's obsession threatens to spiral into the sort of reclusive madness suffered by Catherine Deneuve in Polanski's *Repulsion* (1965), but Massot busily brushes away the dark shadows. Lifted by George Harrison's sweet Indian music and lulled by Assheton Gorton's soft, gorgeous settings, Professor Collins' obsession proves entirely benevolent, making *Wonderwall* a fitting offering for the 'Summer of Love', though even then it was considered dreamily inconsequential.

Massot scripted the hippy musical Western *Zachariah* (George Englund, 1971) and Cy Endfield's African mercenary saga *Universal Soldier* (1971) before moving away from fiction to chart musical landmarks. *The Song Remains the Same* (1976), with Led Zeppelin at the height of their fame performing at Madison Square Gardens, casts nostalgic glances back to 1960s' psychedelia and echoes the overblown bombast and fey mythologising that ultimately spelled the end for progressive rock. *Dance Craze* (1981) uses a parody of the Rank Organisation's screen-filler 'Look at Life' for a tongue-in-cheek exposé of the ska/bluebeat revival of the late 1970s. After *Space Riders* (1983), an odd, lightly fictionalised account of world championship motorcycle racing, starring Barry Sheene, Ron Harris and Japanese rival Toshiya Ito, he disappeared from view; but the success of Noel Gallagher's song 'Wonderwall' in 1995 led Massot to revive the film that had inspired it, eventually reissuing a lengthened 'director's cut' in 2000.

(Robert Murphy)

BIBLIOGRAPHY: 'Diccionario Filmografico de Cineasts Cubanos: Joe Massot, *Cinema 2002* no. 46, Dec. 1978, p. 75; Massot, Joe, *Wonderwall The Film* (London: Pilar, 2000).

FILMOGRAPHY: *Carnaval* (co-dir. Fausto Canal, Cuba, 1960); *Parasitismo* (doc. short, Cuba, 1961); *Reflections on Love* (short, 1965); *Wonderwall* (1968); *The Song Remains the Same* (doc., 1976); *Dance Craze* (doc., 1981); *Space Riders* (1983).

MATHIAS, Sean (1956–)

Shaun G. (later Sean) Mathias was born in Swansea, Wales, on 14 March 1956. He began his stage and screen career as an actor, initially in fringe theatre, then with small film roles in *A Bridge Too Far* (Richard Attenborough, 1977), *Priest of Love* (Christopher Miles, 1980) and *White Mischief* (Michael Radford, 1987). In 1978 Mathias met Ian McKellen, already among Britain's most lauded stage actors and seventeen years his senior, and the pair began a ten-year relationship.

From the early 1980s Mathias began to find acclaim as a playwright, then as a theatre director. His directing debut came in 1985 when his third play, *A Prayer for Wings*, moved to the Bush Theatre in west London after winning the Fringe First Award at Edinburgh. In 1988 he published a novel, *Manhattan Mourning*, and reached a wider audience as screenwriter of BBC Television's *The Lost Language of Cranes* (Nigel Finch, 1991), adapted from David Leavitt's novel in which a gay son's openness about his sexuality throws his secretly gay father into turmoil. His one film as director, *Bent* (1997), a screen version of Martin Sherman's harrowing play about the treatment of homosexuals under the Third Reich, is best understood as an offshoot of this career rather than a change in direction. Premiered at London's Royal Court Theatre in 1979, where it was directed by Robert Chetwyn with McKellen in the starring role, *Bent* became a theatrical phenomenon and a landmark of gay theatre, produced on Broadway with Richard Gere and performed in more than thirty-five countries. Mathias directed the London stage revival in 1989–90, again starring McKellen.

There had been proposals to film *Bent* ever since the play's premiere – Fassbinder and Costa-Gavras were among the directors who had shown an interest – but they had been stalled by the difficulty of finding bankable stars willing to take on the explicitly gay lead roles. Mathias' film did not wholly overcome this hurdle, casting star names (McKellen, Mick Jagger, Rupert Graves, Jude Law, Rachel Weisz) – many of them collaborators from his stage productions – in small roles alongside Clive Owen, Lothaire Bluteau and the little-known Brian Webber as leads. Aware of the minefield of attempting realist representation of the Nazi camps and the Holocaust, Mathias instead created a stylised world, invoking the decadent Berlin gay scene in old industrial buildings and using a cement factory as Dachau. Under-reviewed, *Bent* was seen by only a limited audience. While its claustrophobic theatricality was seen as a defect by mainstream critics, it suited Sherman's text and the almost unbearable subject matter.

Mathias has continued to direct high-profile productions in the theatre, including Bernard Pomerance's *The Elephant Man* on Broadway in 2002 and the pantomime *Aladdin*, with McKellen as Widow Twankey, at the Old Vic for Christmas 2004.

(Claire Monk)

BIBLIOGRAPHY: Kimberly, Nick, '*Bent*', *Sight and Sound*, Mar. 1998, pp. 39–40; Wolf, Matt, 'Bent on More Lights and Camera Action', *The Times*, 5 Mar. 1998, p. 36.

FILMOGRAPHY: *Bent* (1997).

MATTHEWS, Paul

Welsh film-maker and former concrete moulder, Paul Matthews has been responsible for a number of fantasy films, with his sister Elizabeth Matthews as producer. They began unpromisingly with *Grim* (1995), the dire tale of a group of witless Americans who encounter a head-crushing monster while venturing underground to investigate the old mine workings they fear are undermining their suburban homes. More of the same followed in *Deadly Instincts*, though with added nudity and the Isle of Man rather than Gloucestershire standing in for America. Two children's films, *The Unicorn* and *The Fairy King of Ar*, failed to show any significant improvement, even with the presence of once-good actors David Warner and Malcolm McDowell. Continuing to confuse audiences with the settings of his films, Matthews transposes a South African forest and gold mine to the Isle of Man for *The Fairy King of Ar*, though there could be no mistake about *Africa* (1999), where a miniskirted model loses herself in the South African veldt and encounters elephants, monkeys and lions in her journey of self-discovery.

South Africa – cheap, versatile and sunny – proved the ideal location for Matthews. In 1998 his company Peakviewing established a studio complex near Johannesburg and all his subsequent films have been made there. *Merlin: The Return*, an occasionally scary children's story, benefits from good special effects and an international cast that for once fit their parts. Rik Mayall plays Merlin with a pleasing lack of bombast and Patrick Bergin's King Arthur, grumpily baffled by bananas, oil tankers and other accoutrements of the modern age, is finely poised on the right side of parody. *Berserker: Hell's Warrior*, which reuses several of the *Merlin* team but without Mayall and without humour, is less successful. *Hooded Angels* (2001), Matthews' most accomplished film, takes a vital South African issue – the conflict between the need to right past wrongs and the indiscriminate cruelty of revenge – and explores it in the context of the American West, where a group of women who have lost everything in the Civil War take to robbery and murder. Former Miss South Africa Chantelle Stander makes an unlikely gang leader (though her sidekick Amanda Donohoe is impressively iconic), and the mechanics of the plot need oiling, but the handling of action and performance is light years in advance of the risible *Grim*.

Matthews and his sister (and other family members involved in their productions) deserve credit for finding ways to make films without subsidy and without studio or television backing, but attention to better scripts and more careful casting would pay dividends.

(Robert Murphy)

BIBLIOGRAPHY: Thomas, Ceri, 'Dream Factory UK', *Exposure*, Apr. 1999, pp. 8–9; 'UK Co Shoots 10th Film in SA', *Screen Africa*, Nov. 2000, p. 4; Worsdale, Andrew, 'Two Big Budget Foreign Films Wrap in South Africa, *Africa Film and TV* no. 24, Feb./Apr. 2000, pp. 17–18.

FILMOGRAPHY: *Grim* (1995); *The Proposition* (2nd unit dir., Strathford Hamilton); *Deadly Instincts* (aka *Breeders*) (1997); *The Unicorn* (aka *The Little Unicorn*, 1998); *The Fairy King of Ar* (aka *Beings*, co-dir. Christopher Atkins); *Africa* (1999); *Merlin: The Return* (2000); *Hooded Angels* (aka *Glory Glory*); *Berserker: Hell's Warrior* (2001).

MAUDE, Arthur (1881–?)

Born in Pontefract, Yorkshire, in 1881, Arthur Maude pursued a fitful career as a film director in both England and America. He began as a stage actor, working among others with the actor-manager Sir John Martin-Harvey. In 1913, while performing in the USA, he found film acting jobs on the East Coast; by the following year, Maude had joined forces with a British colleague, Constance Crawley, mounting and starring in American features of a historical or romantic bent, including *That Fatal Night* (1914), about the St Bartholomew's Day Massacre, and *Thais* (1914), set in ancient Greece. In 1917 Maude's war service and Crawley's poor health curtailed their partnership; when Maude resumed cinema work he acted for others, Harry Houdini included, before returning to direction in 1925 with a series of shorts, mostly showcases for the Technicolor process.

Maude's career details impressed the newly formed British International Pictures, who hired him in 1927. When his fellow Elstree recruit Hitchcock began shooting *The Ring* on 20 June, Maude started directing the flimsier *Poppies of Flanders*, a sentimental war story. *Toni*, comic fluff featuring Jack Buchanan, followed in November; unimpressed with Maude's handling, BIP then released him from further service. Ambitious plans to produce colour features at Elstree led nowhere; instead, Maude found a berth at Beaconsfield in 1928, directing three of the British Lion Film Corporation's Edgar Wallace properties. Sticking closely to the plays' scripts, he fared reasonably well with the thrills of *The Ringer* and *The Flying Squad*, but *The Clue of the New Pin* (1929) suffered technical difficulties: mounted as the country's first talkie using British Photophone's sound-on-disc system, the film was only released as a silent.

No further big chances came Maude's way. A Twickenham quickie, *The Lyons Mail* (1931), with Sir John Martin-Harvey, bottled some of the spirit of one of his former employee's favourite stage vehicles; but none of the subsequent films for Sound City or his own Maude Productions were of a kind to lead to better things. Following *Live Again* (1936), a creaky musical vehicle for John Garrick, Maude picked up occasional acting roles, plus a short children's film in 1951, before fading into obscurity. His death date is unknown.

(Geoff Brown)

BIBLIOGRAPHY: Reed, Langford and Hetty Spiers (eds), *Who's Who in Filmland*, 3rd edn. (London: Chapman & Hall, 1931).

FILMOGRAPHY: *That Fatal Night* (US, co-dir. Constance Crawley); *Thais* (US, co-dir. Constance Crawley); *The Volunteer Parson* (US, co-dir. Constance Crawley); *The Virgin of the Rocks* (US, co-dir. Constance Crawley) (1914); *The Alternative* (US); *The Blood of Our Brothers* (US); *The Wraith of Haddon Towers* (US) (1915); *Lord Loveland Discovers America* (US); *Powder* (aka *The Final Argument*, US); *Embers* (US); *Revelations* (US); *The Courtesan* (US) (1916); *Peggy's Reward* (short, US); *The Vision* (short, US); *The Blue Boy* (short, US); *The Mona Lisa* (short, US) (1926); *The Flag* (short, US); *Poppies of Flanders* (1927); *Toni* (1927; rel. 1929); *The Ringer* (1928); *The Flying Squad*; *The Clue of the New Pin* (1929); *The Lyons Mail* (1931); *Watch Beverley* (1932); *The Lure*; *She Was Only a Village Maiden*; *The Wishbone* (1933); *Borrowed Clothes*; *Boomerang* (1934); *Live Again* (1936); *One Good Turn* (short, 1951).

MAYBURY, John (1958–)

John Maybury was born in London on 25 March 1958 and attended North East London Polytechnic, before going on to work with Derek Jarman on *Jubilee* (1978), *The Last of England* (1987) and *War Requiem* (1989). His experimental Super-8 films such as *Pantomime Incubus* and *Tortures That Laugh* share Jarman's queer sensibility, often referencing pop culture and containing recyclings of his own work. They led to a successful spell directing music videos, climaxing with the award-winning and chastely languorous *Nothing Compares 2U* (1990) for Sinead O'Connor. His longer video works, made with backing from Channel 4, include *Remembrance of Things Fast* and his adaptation of Manfred Karge's one-woman play *Man to Man*, both making good use of Tilda Swinton.

Maybury's first feature film, *Love Is the Devil* (1998), is about the relationship between the painter Francis Bacon and his lover George Dyer. The film-makers were refused permission to use Bacon's paintings, but the film's fragmentary structure reflects Bacon's triptychs, and visually the film seems to view the world through the bottom of a glass. To recreate the ambience of Bacon's bohemian haunt, the Colony Room, Maybury peoples the film with Bacon's friends such as Daniel Farson, and anachronistically supplements them with young British artists like Sarah Lucas and Gary Hume and fashion designers Paul Smith and Stella McCartney.

After the success of *Love Is the Devil*, Maybury was linked to various projects, including a biopic of the playwright Christopher Marlowe; his second feature, *The Jacket*, an ambitious experimental psychological thriller, starring Adrien Brody and Keira Knightley, was presented to considerable critical acclaim at the Sundance Film Festival in 2005, though cinema audiences in America and the UK were less enthusiastic.

(John Riley)

BIBLIOGRAPHY: Kirby, Tim, 'Pride and Prejudice', *Sight and Sound*, July 1991, pp. 20–3; Macnab, Geoffrey, 'Bohemian Rhapsody', *Sight and Sound*, July 1997, pp. 18–20.

FILMOGRAPHY: Shorts and video work: *The Court of Miracles* (1982); *Pantomime Incubus*; *The Dream Machine*; *Circus Logic I-IV* (1983); *Pagan Idolatry*; *Glistening with Energy*; *Big Love: An Invitation to Disaster* (1984); *Tortures That Laugh* (1986); *Union Jack Up* (1987); *Absurd* (1989); *You Do Something to Me* (1990); *Tunnel of Love* (1991); *Premonition of Absurd Perversion in Sexual Personae, Part I*; *Man to Man* (1992); *Remembrance of Things Fast: True Stories Visual Lies* (1994); *Genetron* (1996).

Features: *Love Is the Devil: Study for a Portrait of Francis Bacon* (aka *Love Is the Devil*, UK/Fr/Jap, 1998); *The Jacket* (UK/US, 2005).

MAYERSBERG, Paul (1941–)

Of part Hungarian parentage, Paul Mayersberg was born in Royston, Hertfordshire, on 18 June 1941. He developed a passion for cinema so strong that he turned down a place at Cambridge University for the life of a freelance film critic. But he soon itched for practical film experience, and secured work with French director Jean-Pierre Melville (an abiding influence) as production assistant on *Le Doulos* (1962). Similar assignments with Joseph Losey and Roger Corman followed, alongside editorial work on Ian Cameron's *Movie* magazine, and film criticism for *New Society*. Interviews with *Movie*-approved directors like Richard Brooks, Robert Aldrich and Nicholas Ray formed the basis of his entertaining book *Hollywood, the Haunted House* (1967), which reached the conclusion that Hollywood film-makers would abandon contemporary America for productions filmed in history-laden Europe, a part of the world 'packed with houses just begging to be haunted' (Mayersberg, p. 181).

Mayersberg's notion has been proved wrong, though for his own career the Old World has certainly offered better prospects than the New. For the Hollywood machine he wrote the screenplay for the quite unnecessary *Return from the River Kwai* (Andrew V. McLaglen, 1988); but for European producers he prepared the scripts for two of Nicolas Roeg's most multi-layered conundrums, *The Man Who Fell to Earth* (1976) and *Eureka* (1982), and worked fruitfully with Nagisa Oshima on the Japanese prisoner-of-war-camp drama *Merry Christmas, Mr Lawrence* (1983). He also, less helpfully, filled Stuart Cooper's contract killer melodrama *The Disappearance* (1977) with oblique twists and flashbacks. When Mayersberg finally directed his own script with the French co-production *Captive* in 1985, the influences were entirely European, with camera explorations and cryptic plotting worthy of Roeg, powerful, encompassing settings by the production designer Voytek and a carefully cultivated atmosphere of the *insolite* overtly inspired by Melville's 1949 Cocteau adaptation, *Les Enfants terribles*.

The film's subject matter drew parallels with Patty Hearst's kidnapping; Mayersberg's story tells of a fictional rich man's daughter (Irina Brook, daughter of Peter Brook) who finds emancipation in adopting her kidnappers' anarchic lifestyle. Voytek's designs and Mike Southon's camerawork added their own subtleties to the screenplay's smoke and mirrors; but not all the acting equalled Oliver Reed's powerful turn as the heroine's father, and the film's success lay principally with critics rather than audiences.

None of Mayersberg's subsequent directing ventures has allowed for any advances beyond the promise of *Captive*. *Nightfall* (1988), originally planned in 1977, frittered away a classic Isaac Asimov science-fiction story in a jittery low-budget production for Roger Corman; while in *The Last Samurai* (1990), a safari kidnap drama with pretentious twinges filmed in South Africa, Mayersberg had to settle for Lance Henriksen's muscles, action movie clichés and an almost unnoticed video release. Back home, his script for Mike Hodges' *Croupier* (1998) needed sharper treatment from the director (and indeed Mayersberg himself), but this low-powered psychological drama about a croupier seduced by opportunities for crime has gradually acquired champions. Meanwhile, Mayersberg's directing career remains in limbo.

(Geoff Brown)

BIBLIOGRAPHY: Aziz, Christine, 'Dream Lover', *Stills* no. 25, Mar. 1986, p. 11; Mayersberg, Paul, *Hollywood, the Haunted House* (London: Allen Lane/Penguin Press, 1967); Milne, Tom, 'Captive', *Monthly Film Bulletin*, Sept. 1986, pp. 259–60.

FILMOGRAPHY: *Captive* (UK/Fr, 1986); *Nightfall* (US, 1988); *The Last Samurai* (US, 1990).

MAYLAM, Tony (1943–)

Tony Maylam was born in London in 1943. His first films were sporting documentaries – mostly on football and motor-racing – and a record of Genesis in concert in 1976. As his feature debut he directed *The Riddle of the Sands* (1978), a low-key but persuasive adaptation of Erskine Childers' 1903 novel about two young yachtsmen who uncover a dastardly plot for the German invasion of England in the slow build-up to the First World War. Made as part of the Rank Organisation's ill-fated last production programme, the film failed to open up the sort of opportunities Maylam might have expected. He turned to America, teaming up with the Weinstein brothers to make a summer camp slasher movie, *The Burning* (1980), which caused controversy for its blood-curdling violence but put the Weinsteins' Miramax company on the road to success. In contrast to the gentlemanly thrills of *The Riddle*, *The Burning* is scarily visceral; but Maylam is surprisingly sensitive towards his American teenagers, subjecting them only to teasing shocks for the first half of the film, allowing audiences to become interested in their fates when nemesis strikes in the second.

After *The Sins of Dorian Gray* (1983), made for American television, a too-gimmicky update of Oscar Wilde's parable, with a Hollywood starlet (Belinda Bauer) replacing Wilde's vain artist, Maylam returned to Britain to make a series of sporting documentaries for television and *Hero: The Official Film of the 1986 FIFA World Cup*, where he is helped enormously by having Diego Maradona, an outstanding sporting hero, as his focus. He then made *Across the Lake* (1988), a fine BBC dramatisation of Donald Campbell's fatal attempt to break the world water-speed record on Coniston Water in January 1967, with Anthony Hopkins well cast as the reckless Campbell. *Split Second* (1992) was less reputable but more ambitious: a futuristic horror film shot in London at a time when most British film-making was confined to cheap comedies and television spin-offs.

Maylam's film of the 1998 World Cup failed to materialise, and *Phoenix Blue* (2001), a convoluted thriller about a journalist's quest to trace the whereabouts of a reclusive pop star implicated in a violent robbery, proved too much of a hotch-potch to secure a cinema release. But his eclectic filmography deserves a little more consideration than it has attracted so far.
(Robert Murphy)

BIBLIOGRAPHY: Brett, Anwar, 'Netting the World Cup Winner', *Exposure*, Summer 1998, pp. 32–3.

FILMOGRAPHY: *Cup Glory* (doc.); *Grand Prix School* (doc. short); *Andretti & Friends* (doc. short) (1971); *Just to Prove It* (US, 1972); *Racers* (doc. short, 1973); *Go West* (doc. short); *Entertainment for Millions* (doc. short) (1974); *An Introduction to Dressage* (doc. short, 1975); *White Rock* (doc., UK/US); *Prince Charles and Canterbury Cathedral* (doc. short); *Genesis – A Band in Concert* (doc.) (1976); *Olympic Harmony* (doc. short); *Bobby Deerfield* (add. racing footage, Sydney Pollack) (1977); *The Riddle of the Sands* (1978); *The Burning* (US, 1980); *Hero: The Official Film of the 1986 FIFA World Cup* (1987); *Split Second* (uncredited co-dir. Ian Sharp, 1992); *Phoenix Blue* (2001).

MAZZETTI, Lorenza (1928–)

Born in Florence in 1928, Lorenza Mazzetti attended film classes at Centro Sperimentale, Rome, and arrived in England in 1952 as a painting student at the Slade School of Fine Art. Two shorts emerged during her time at the Slade, both of them inspired by Kafka's stories. When attempts to make films in Italy failed, she returned to England and found funding from the BFI to create a drama with Denis Horne, based on his story about the lives of two deaf-mute dock workers tormented by East End children. The result, after editorial help and extra shooting by Lindsay Anderson, Walter Lassally and John Fletcher, was the idiosyncratic and poignant *Together*, fifty minutes long, included in the National Film Theatre's first Free Cinema programme in February 1956. Another foreign perspective was later offered with Claude Goretta and Alain Tanner's *Nice Time* (1957), a candid-camera impression of Piccadilly Circus.

For Mazzetti, *Together* provided a way to explore her feelings of alienation and the disturbances of her own childhood in Italy during the war. The restructuring by Anderson's team – Lassally later called it a 'transformation' – emphasised the poetic qualities of the film's two enclosed souls in London's docklands, running the gauntlet of an uncaring world in precisely framed images of grey, flat spaces. Unhurried takes and editing contributed to the hypnotic spell, further strengthened by touching performances from the sculptor Eduardo Paolozzi and the painter Michael Andrews, and the evocative music by Danièle Paris, ambitiously blended with natural sounds. No other Free Cinema product attempted Mazzetti's dangerous, tremulous, slow-motion balance between poetic imagery, the magnified small detail and a slender, almost internal narrative; though the film was much admired.

Personal turmoil aborted plans for a successor about London teddy boys, and Mazzetti returned to Italy. In the late 1950s and 60s she worked on television documentaries and series with one of her chief influences, the neo-realist screenwriter and theoretician Cesare Zavattini; she also wrote novels, revisiting her anguished childhood in *Il cielo cade* (1961). More recently she has run a puppet theatre in Rome. Though brief, Mazzetti's career in England was significant, for in the poetic narrative of *Together* we see, tantalisingly, one of the roads Britain's revitalised cinema of the 1950s and 60s never finally took.
(Geoff Brown)

BIBLIOGRAPHY: Lambert, Gavin, 'Free Cinema', *Sight and Sound*, Spring 1956, pp. 173–7; Lassally, Walter, *Itinerant Cameraman* (London: John Murray, 1987); Lovell, Alan and Jim Hillier, *Studies in Documentary* (London: Secker and Warburg, 1972); Mazzetti, Lorenza, Christophe Dupin and Bryony Dixon, 'Soup Dreams', *Sight and Sound*, Mar. 2001, pp. 28–30.

FILMOGRAPHY (UK only): *Metamorphosis* (short); *The Country Doctor* (short, 1952); *Together* (1956).

MEAD, Nick

After directing music videos Nick Mead attracted attention with a well-received Channel 4 documentary, *Black Leather Jacket* (1989), narrated by Dennis Hopper. He worked on the script for Michael Winner's *Bullseye!* (1990), and then went to Los Angeles, where he wrote and directed *Bank Robber*, a wry low-budget comedy about a wanted man sponged on by everyone he meets. It failed to attract the cult audience aimed for, and Mead returned to the UK to share writing credits with Jimmy Nail on the television series *Crocodile Shoes II* (1996) and rejoin Winner on *Parting Shots* (1998).

He raised American backing for *Swing*, a zany comedy co-written and produced by his wife, Su Lim, about an ex-convict (Hugo Speer) who redeems himself by starting a swing band and winning back his girlfriend (Lisa Stansfield) from the jealous policeman she is now married to. Speer's ex-con does not have a dishonest bone in his body, and why his cellmate, the wise and lovable Clarence Clemens, is banged up is even more difficult to fathom. But despite the ramshackle script and Mead's annoying visual ticks, the infectious gaiety of the music and Stansfield's gutsy heroine make the film irresistibly pleasurable. Mead moved on to a different kind of performance in *Dice Life* (2004), a television meditation on chance voiced by Luke Rhinehart and danced by Laila Diallo and Leo Lerus.

(Robert Murphy)

FILMOGRAPHY: *Bank Robber* (US, 1993); *Swing* (UK/US, 1999).

MEADOWS, Shane (1972–)

Shane Meadows was born on 26 December 1972 in Uttoxeter, Staffordshire, and grew up in Nottingham. That city's estates and suburbs have provided the locations and settings for all his work to date. While on the dole, Meadows completed some twenty-five short films shot on a borrowed video camcorder. One of these, *Where's the Money Ronnie!*, won a short film competition sponsored by Channel One and the National Film Theatre. With funding from the BFI he was then able to complete *Smalltime*, an hour-long comedy-drama about inept petty criminals, with himself as the bewigged, boorish 'Jumbo'. These two apprentice works, which were transferred to 35mm for a limited theatrical release, clearly revealed his flair for larger-than-life characters in (mostly) ordinary situations and his ability to extract accomplished, semi-improvised performances from talented non-professionals.

Meadows' first full-length professional feature, *TwentyFourSeven* stars Bob Hoskins in a tragi-comic tale of the rise and fall of a boxing club for unemployed and delinquent youths. Beautifully lit in black and white by Ashley Rowe and favouring medium-distance long takes rather than the tight close-ups and quick cuts preferred by most directors of his generation, it is as much poetic as naturalistic, suggesting that for Meadows social realism is an artistic means rather than a political end. *TwentyFourSeven* was co-written, like its successors, with Paul Fraser, Meadows' close friend since childhood. *A Room for Romeo Brass* is partly based on their own experiences and relationship, and follows the involvement of two young boys with Morell, an eccentric loner. Initially a figure of fun, he is gradually revealed as a dangerous sociopath. With its audacious shifts of tone and the extraordinary central performance of Paddy Considine (another friend, making an astonishing acting debut), *Romeo Brass* is Meadows' richest, most impressive work to date.

Shane Meadows (right) on location for *A Room for Romeo Brass* (1999)

His two subsequent films have been somewhat uneven attempts at offbeat genre movies. *Once Upon a Time in the Midlands* is a disappointingly thin and flaccid contemporary English 'Western' that fails to come off as anything other than a quirky conceit. Its cast of stars (Rhys Ifans, Robert Carlyle, Kathy Burke, Ricky Tomlinson), none of whom is readily associated with the Midlands, is the first sign that Meadows might be willing to compromise his regional loyalties in order to reach the mainstream, though he has yet to achieve a major popular success. The more satisfying revenge thriller *Dead Man's Shoes* reunited him with the always excellent Considine and marked a partial return to form. Yet, powerful though it is, and distinguished by Meadows' commendable inability to regard even the worst villains as other than human beings, the film's intentions remain somewhat unclear and its central character unresolved.

Unlike the work of Ken Loach and Mike Leigh, the film-makers with whom he is most often compared, Meadows' observations of lower-class losers and misfits are made from the perspective of a native insider rather than a sympathetic visitor. Their occasional rawness and lack of polish are manifested in a rather desultory approach to narrative – situations tend to peter out or get diverted into musical montages rather than be fully developed and resolved – but also in an invigorating playfulness that is rarely permitted to coarsen into parody or caricature. Above all, Meadows always appears to like his characters, even the grotesques like Jumbo and Morell.

(Sheldon Hall)

BIBLIOGRAPHY: Macnab, Geoffrey, 'The Natural', *Sight and Sound*, Mar. 1998, pp. 14–16.

FILMOGRAPHY: *Where's the Money Ronnie!* (short, 1995); *Small-time* (1996); *TwentyFourSeven* (1997); *A Room for Romeo Brass* (UK/Can, 1999); *Once Upon a Time in the Midlands* (UK/Ger, 2002); *Dead Man's Shoes* (2004); *This Is England* (2006).

MECKLER, Nancy (1941–)

Nancy Meckler was born on 26 April 1941 on Long Island, USA. She started her career in theatre, and has run the Shared Experience theatre company, based in London, since 1987. She is married to the producer David Aukin and has made two feature films that explore lesbian and gay themes.

Sister My Sister was adapted by Wendy Kesselman from her play *My Sister in This House* (which Meckler had directed on stage), and draws on the real-life murders of two French women by their servants in Le Mans in 1933. The story had already been rendered as a stage play, *Les Bonnes*, by Jean Genet, which had been filmed in 1974 by Christopher Miles as *The Maids*. In Meckler and Kesselman's version the two servants – sisters played by Joely Richardson and Jodhi May – form an incestuous relationship, which they fear will be broken up when the daughter of the house marries and leaves. Resentment and misunderstanding lead to a melodramatic climax where their mistress (Julie Walters) and her daughter (Sophie Thursfield) are brutally murdered. Rather than opening out the play, Meckler keeps almost all of the action within the claustrophobic bourgeois home of Madame Danzard, making the bloody finale all the more shocking.

Meckler's second feature film, *Alive and Kicking*, centres around a gay dancer, Tonio (Jason Flemying), whose company has suffered a series of deaths because of AIDS. Tonio has himself been pronounced HIV-positive but he embarks on a new relationship that becomes threatened by his dedication to his work. Meckler found herself challenged to break away from her training in theatre, and the film, despite its structured motif of dance, often seems unaware of the possibilities of cinematic movement.

(Ruth Barton)

BIBLIOGRAPHY: Bruzzi, Stella, 'Two Sisters, the Fogey, the Priest and His Lover: Sexual Plurality in 1990s British Cinema', in Robert Murphy (ed.), *British Cinema of the 90s* (London: BFI, 2000); Shireen, Jilla, 'Women on the Verge', *Premiere*, Dec. 1994, pp. 41–6.

FILMOGRAPHY: *Sister My Sister* (1994); *Alive and Kicking* (aka *Indian Summer*, 1996).

MEDAK, Peter (1937–)

Peter Medak was born in Budapest on 23 December 1937. He fled Hungary after the crushing of the 1956 uprising and became a trainee in London at Associated British-Pathé. He then worked in television in America as an associate producer (*Wagon Train*, *Alfred Hitchcock Presents*) and director (*Court Martial*), and in British-based international features as an associate producer and second-unit director.

His first feature was the arty *Negatives*, with Peter McEnery and Glenda Jackson as a couple whose sex play is based on the crimes of Dr Crippen (though an obsession with Baron von Richthofen eventually takes over). It led to a pair of theatrical adaptations also rooted in game-playing as a way of avoiding unbearable realities. *The Ruling Class*, based on a play by Peter Barnes, is a black comic fantasy, with Peter O'Toole as an English milord eventually cured of his belief that he is Jesus Christ and fitting far more easily into society in his new persona as Jack the Ripper; *A Day in the Death of Joe Egg*, adapted from his play by Peter Nichols, features Alan Bates and Janet Suzman as the free-associating parents of a brain-dead child.

Like many directors in Britain in the 1970s, Medak had to retreat to television to eke out his career. In the UK he made episodes of *The Persuaders*, *Space 1999*, *The Professionals* and *The Return of the Saint*; and in the US, *Hart to Hart*, *Magnum PI*, *Remington Steele* and *The Twilight Zone*. His other 1970s' features were offbeat comedies: *Ghost in the Noonday Sun* (with Peter Sellers and Spike Milligan) and *The Odd Job* (with Graham Chapman). He also took over *The Changeling* from Donald Cammell and delivered perhaps his best film, a solid mix of suspense, scares, mystery and character. George C. Scott's muted grief at the death of his wife and daughter, for instance, is far more moving than the endless wound-scratching of *Joe Egg*.

Aside from a limp comedy, *Zorro, the Gay Blade*, with George Hamilton and the talky drama *The Men's Club*, Medak spent the 1980s directing American television films (*Mistress of Paradise*, 1981; *Cry for the Strangers*, 1982) and episodes of everything from *Faerie Tale Theater* to *Tales from the Crypt*, none of which was as interesting as his first American television film, *The Third Girl from the Left* (1973), scripted by Dory Previn, and featuring Kim Novak as an ageing chorus girl. An unexpected return to the limelight came in 1990 with *The Krays*, a powerful and daring gangster biopic scripted by Philip Ridley, with Gary and Martin Kemp well cast as the criminal twins. It led him to other interesting crime projects: *Let Him Have It* (which he took over from Alex Cox), a sensitive recreation of the events leading up to the hanging of nineteen-year-old Derek Bentley in January 1953; *Romeo Is Bleeding*, a convincing New York film noir; and finely directed episodes of *Homicide: Life on the Street*. He remains a difficult director to classify, his occasional feature films reflecting eagerly seized opportunities rather than deeply cherished personal projects.

(Kim Newman)

BIBLIOGRAPHY: Julius, Marshall, 'Blood Ties', *What's on in London*, 27 Apr. 1994, p. 30; Malcolm, Derek, 'A Director's Reversal of Fortune', *Guardian*, 3 Oct. 1991, p. 27.

FILMOGRAPHY: *Kaleidoscope* (2nd unit dir., Jack Smight); *Funeral in Berlin* (2nd unit dir., Guy Hamilton) (1966); *Fathom* (2nd unit dir., Leslie Martinson, 1967); *Negatives* (1968); *The Ruling Class*; *A Day in the Death of Joe Egg* (1972); *Ghost in the Noonday Sun* (1973); *The*

Odd Job (1978); *The Changeling* (Can, 1980); *Zorro, the Gay Blade* (US, 1981); *The Men's Club* (US, 1986); *The Krays* (1990); *Let Him Have It* (1991); *Romeo Is Bleeding* (US, 1993); *Pontiac Moon* (US, 1994); *Species II* (US, 1998).

MEGAHEY, Leslie (1944–)

Born in Belfast in 1944, Leslie Megahey established himself as a director for the BBC arts programme *Omnibus*, for which, along with several documentaries, he made *Schalken the Painter* (1979), a supernatural tale based on a story by J. Sheridan Le Fanu. After a television film, *Cariani and the Courtesans* (1987), about a sixteenth-century painter's obsession with a mysterious woman, Megahey made his feature film debut with *The Hour of the Pig*. Set in medieval France, the film chronicles the exploits of Parisian lawyer Richard Courtois (Colin Firth) as he sets up shop in a backward rural district and defends a pig against a charge of murder, pitting his enlightened attitudes against ecclesiastical dogma, superstition, corruption and anti-Semitism. Working with cameraman John Hooper and production designer Bruce Macadie, Megahey conjures a plausible medieval world that recalls the work of both Pier Paolo Pasolini and Terry Gilliam. The fine cast – which includes Nicol Williamson, Amina Annabi, Donald Pleasence, Michael Gough, Ian Holm, Harriet Walter, Jim Carter and Elizabeth Spriggs – and the blending of elements of courtroom drama, comedy and dark thriller, make *The Hour of the Pig* a lively and original film, marking out Megahey as a talented director. Unfortunately he has found few subsequent opportunities to display his talents, though he adapted Julio Cortázar's Latin American mystery tale *Diario para un cuento* for Jana Bokova in 1998.

(Daniel O'Brien)

BIBLIOGRAPHY: Dobson, Patricia, 'Profile: Leslie Megahey', *Screen International*, LFF Supplement, 15 Nov. 1993, p. 5; Megahey, Leslie, 'The Wonderful Face', *Sight and Sound*, July 1993, p. 5.

FILMOGRAPHY: *The Hour of the Pig* (UK/Fr, 1993).

MEGAHY, Francis (1937–)

Francis Megahy was born in Manchester in 1937. After producing, writing and directing *Just One More Time* (1962), an eye-catching short about a young Bayswater spiv, and *None but the Tortoise* (1963), a short satire on Britain's traffic problems, he worked in television making documentaries, including a series on *China Now* (1964), and *No Worse Heresy* (1967), a study of how people are affected by power. He also wrote the Jacques Demy pastiche, *Les Bicyclettes de Belsize* (Douglas Hickox, 1968), and episodes of ITC's *Man in a Suitcase* (1967).

Megahy's return to the cinema with a low-budget sex-film, *Nymphs a Go-Go* (1970), was not a success, though he was able to recycle some of it for the blue cinema club opening of his first proper feature film, *Freelance* (1970). Megahy's story of an upwardly mobile contact man (Ian McShane) whose rise towards respectability is disrupted when he unwisely intervenes in a gangland killing promises much but delivers disappointingly little beyond resonant London locations and a likeably unpredictable hero. The late lamented Alan Lake makes a frighteningly realistic villain, pursuing McShane's sleazy charmer like a vengeful goblin, but he is too easily disposed of, and the plot reverts to B-film crime clichés.

Megahy survived the 1970s directing episodes of London Weekend's *The Professionals* and the BBC's controversially violent police series *Target*, and two further features. *One Take Two* (1978) is a better- than-average international hotchpotch starring Gayle Hunnicutt as a resourceful reporter in the midst of a violent African rebellion. *Dirty Money* (aka *The Great Riviera Bank Robbery*, 1979), made for ITC but shown only on television, is a well-plotted heist film, with McShane convincing as a right-wing French idealist determined to rob a Nice bank to fund his political dreams.

The legacy of *Freelance* continued to haunt Megahy through the 1980s, when he directed several episodes of *Minder*, where George Cole plays an older and funnier variation on McShane's spiv character; and *Lovejoy*, a showcase for McShane as a lovably roguish antique dealer. Megahy was also responsible for the feature-length *Minder on the Orient Express* (1985). For cinema, he directed *Real Life* (1983), an unpersuasive romantic comedy, and *Taffin* (1987), another crime film about a small-timer (pre-Bond Pierce Brosnan) taking on bigger and nastier crooks; the mild historical interest aroused by its provincial Irish setting and its later-to-be-famous cast has to be set against plodding dialogue and a predictable plot. In 1992 *Freelance* was released on video, retitled *Con Man* in some markets. Megahy moved on to new fields with *Red Sun Rising*, an enjoyable if routine Japanese martial arts vehicle for Don 'the Dragon' Wilson; *The Disappearance of Kevin Johnson*, a spoof documentary slyly exposing Hollywood smugness; and *The Trouble with Ross*, another stab at romantic comedy.

The number of times Megahy has worked with the same actors, the same writers (particularly Bernie Cooper) and the same production companies testifies to his competent professionalism, though his overexposure to the shallow waters of popular television has perhaps blunted the edge necessary to make strongly dramatic cinema films.

(Robert Murphy)

BIBLIOGRAPHY: 'In Focus: Francis Megahy', *Premiere*, 3 July 1970, pp. 59–61.

FILMOGRAPHY: *Just One More Time* (short, 1962); *None but the Tortoise* (doc. short, 1963); *Nymphs a Go-Go* (short); *Freelance* (1970); *One Take Two* (aka *Flashpoint Africa*, SA/Ger, 1978); *Mirella: Portrait of a Photographer* (doc., 1981); *Real Life* (1983); *Taffin* (UK/US, 1987); *Red Sun Rising* (US, 1994); *The Disappearance of Kevin Johnson* (UK/US, 1997); *The Trouble with Ross* (2006).

MELLOR, Kay (1952–)

Kay Mellor was born in Leeds in 1952. She married and had children young; aged twenty-eight, she went to Bretton Hall College near Wakefield to study drama. After graduating she set up the Yorkshire Theatre Company in Leeds before working as an actor and subsequently a writer on Granada's short-lived soap opera *Albion Market* (1985). Mellor moved on to *Coronation Street* where she met Paul Abbott, later collaborating with him to create the series *Children's Ward* (1989). A projected Anglo-Australian soap, *Families*, failed to materialise, and Mellor's breakthrough was postponed until 1995, when Granada backed *Band of Gold*, her gritty and acutely observed drama serial about prostitution in the Leeds/Bradford area. Two sequels followed, as well as the equally successful but much lighter series *Playing the Field*, a semi-comic ensemble drama centred on a women's football team.

Mellor collaborated on the script for the Robert Young version of *Jane Eyre* (1997), and wrote her first film script, *Girls' Night* (Nick Hurran, 1998), about two women on the run from terminal disease in Las Vegas. Though made for television, the film was considered good enough for a cinema release. Mellor was tempted into directing her next script, *Fanny & Elvis*, herself. Results were disappointing. A romantic comedy set in the hilly Yorkshire town of Hebden Bridge might have seemed a pleasing alternative to the London locations of *Four Weddings and a Funeral* (Mike Newell, 1994) and its successors, but Mellor's crude plot devices and misplaced lurches into fantasy make the sugary romance between Ray Winstone's second-hand car dealer and Kerry Fox's fey novelist irritating rather than charming, and the film failed to attract much of a cinema audience. Mellor returned to television, writing the successful comedy-drama series *Fat Friends* (2000) and two television films, *A Good Thief* (2002) and *Gifted* (2003), both directed by Douglas Mackinnon.
(Robert Murphy)

BIBLIOGRAPHY: Irwin, Ken, 'Creating Family Ties to Break an Ocean's Divide', *Television Today*, 19 Apr. 1990, p. 18; Lockyer, Daphne, 'Behind the Scenes: The Vicar Got It Wrong', *TV Times*, 9 Mar. 1996, pp. 8–9; Tutt, Louise, 'Scala to Make Follow-up Mellor, Farino Projects', *Screen International*, 12 Nov. 1999, p. 18.
FILMOGRAPHY: *Fanny & Elvis* (1999).

MENDES, Lothar (1894–1974)

Born in Berlin on 19 May 1894, Lothar Mendes briefly acted in the Vienna theatre before directing Austrian and German films from 1920. Between 1926 and 1934, and again from the late 1930s to 1946, he directed in Hollywood before finally settling in Britain.

Mendes directed three 1930s' British features. The first, a big-budget adaptation of Lion Feuchtwanger's novel *Jew Süss*, for Gaumont-British, dealt with eighteenth-century German anti-Semitism and the horrifying execution of an overambitious Jew (Conrad Veidt). Mendes' direction might be pedestrian, but the film is infinitely more humane than the Nazi version, directed by Veit Harlan in 1940; despite its historical setting, it is obviously intended as a condemnation of Nazi anti-Semitism. Mendes' third British film, *Moonlight Sonata*, is also historically important, though for different reasons: it contains rare footage of eminent Polish classical pianist Ignace Jan Paderewski, then over seventy. Mendes' treatment is competent rather than striking and as a film *Moonlight Sonata* is much duller than *The Man Who Could Work Miracles*, an adaptation of a short story by H. G. Wells made for Alexander Korda as a follow-up to his spectacular *Things to Come* (William Cameron Menzies, 1936). Mendes' film, his first comedy, is considerably less portentous and traces the antics of a humble man who acquires supernatural powers. With a strong central performance from Roland Young and solid support from Ralph Richardson and Ernest Thesiger, it is arguably his most enjoyable contribution to British cinema. He died in London on 25 February 1974.
(James C. Robertson)

BIBLIOGRAPHY: Danvers Williams, J. (interview with Lothar Mendes), 'Common-Sense about the Cinema', *Film Weekly*, 12 Jan. 1934, p. 11; Witt, Peter, 'Lothar Mendes and Berthold Viertel Talk about Their Latest Films', *Picturegoer* no. 150, 7 Apr. 1934, pp. 14–15.
FILMOGRAPHY (UK only): *Jew Süss* (US: *Power*, 1934); *The Man Who Could Work Miracles* (1936); *Moonlight Sonata* (1937).

MENGES, Chris (1940–)

Chris Menges established his reputation as a cinematographer, working in television on documentaries and dramas, where he developed a unique style, a contradictory mixture of the spontaneous and picturesque, before winning Academy Awards for his work on Roland Joffé's *The Killing Fields* (1984) and *The Mission* (1986). His work as a director has been less successful, but is of considerable interest.

Christopher J. Menges was born in Kingston, Herefordshire, on 15 September 1940 and began his career as a production assistant on the Campaign for Nuclear Disarmament documentary *March to Aldermaston* (Lindsay Anderson and others, 1959). Television work followed, including the current

affairs series *World in Action* and the anthropological documentaries of Adrian Cowell. In 1967 he began a long and fruitful collaboration with Ken Loach as camera operator on *Poor Cow* (1967), progressing to become cinematographer on *Kes* (1969), *Black Jack* (1979), *Looks and Smiles* (1981) and *Fatherland* (1986).

In 1982 Menges made his directorial debut with a feature-length documentary about life in New York's Spanish Harlem, *East 103rd Street*, but six years passed before his first fiction film, *A World Apart*. The coming-of-age story is based on Shawn Slovo's experiences in South Africa in the 1960s as a white middle-class girl growing up with parents involved in the anti-apartheid struggle. By presenting events from the perspective of a lonely teenage girl, too young to involve herself in politics, separated from her parents and unable to share the privileges of her peers, Menges exposes the iniquities of the apartheid regime without making easy appeals to the emotions. The film was well received and it seemed that Menges had made a successful transition to director, but his next two films proved a disappointment. *CrissCross*, another tale of growing up in the 1960s, is a likeable if unfocused story about a twelve-year-old boy (David Arnott) in Florida's Key West; like the young heroine in *A World Apart* he finds little support from his parents. *Second Best* follows the slow, stuttering relationship that develops between William Hurt's lonely English postmaster and the son he adopts. These low-key dramas failed to make much of a splash and Menges found it difficult to get other projects off the ground. In the mid-1990s he worked as cinematographer on Neil Jordan's *Michael Collins* (1996) and Jim Sheridan's *The Boxer* (1997), but returned to direction after securing Anglo-French backing for *The Lost Son* (1999), a crime-thriller featuring Daniel Auteuil as a disgraced French cop, marooned in London. Auteuil's character undertakes an assignment to find the missing son of a rich family and uncovers an international paedophile ring. A glossier film with a much darker view of the perils of childhood than *Second Best*, *The Lost Son* benefits from a splendid cast (including Katrin Cartlidge and Nastassja Kinski), and Barry Ackroyd's impressively atmospheric photography. But its plot is too predictable and, like most Euro-thrillers, it failed to find an audience. Menges has since returned again to his successful career as a cinematographer, imbuing Stephen Frears' *Dirty Pretty Things* (2002) and Neil Jordan's *The Good Thief* (2002) with a distinct visual look, adding immeasurably to their appeal.

(Jamie Sexton)

BIBLIOGRAPHY: Falk, Quentin, 'All the Glittering Prizes', *Exposure*, Autumn 2001, pp. 4–7; Hunter, Allan, 'Torn Feelings' (interview), *Films and Filming*, Aug. 1988, pp. 12–13; White, Armond, 'The Camera and I' (interview), *Film Comment*, Mar./Apr. 1988, pp. 48–50.

FILMOGRAPHY: *East 103rd Street* (doc., US/UK, 1982); *A World Apart* (UK/Zimbabwe, 1988); *CrissCross* (US, 1992); *Second Best* (US/UK, 1994); *The Lost Son* (US/UK/Fr, 1999).

MENZIES, William Cameron (1896–1957)

William Cameron Menzies was born in New Haven, Connecticut, on 29 July 1896 to Scots immigrant parents. He studied at Yale and the University of Edinburgh before serving in the US Army during the First World War. After the war he attended the Art Students League in New York, then joined Famous Players-Lasky (later to evolve into Paramount) working in special effects and design. He went independent in 1923 to work with prominent directors of the period such as Allan Dwan, Raoul Walsh and Fred Niblo, and soon made a name for himself as one of the most individual and gifted of cinematic designers. His status was confirmed at the first Academy Awards ceremony, when he won the Best Art Direction award for *The Dove* (Roland West, 1927) and *Tempest* (Sam Taylor, 1928).

In 1931 Menzies took up direction, and made half a dozen pictures – but always as co-director. The art director Lyle Wheeler, who worked with him later at Fox, felt that Menzies was 'no damn good as a director. . . . He wanted to photograph ceilings and didn't give a damn what the actors were saying' (Frayling, p. 30). His first solo directing commission came in 1935, when Alexander Korda invited him to Denham to direct the massively ambitious science-fiction project *Things to Come* (1936).

The script was adapted from H. G. Wells' book *The Shape of Things to Come*, and Korda had ill-advisedly given Wells control over the script and every phase of the film's production. Korda hoped that Menzies would make up for Wells' lack of visual imagination, but he found himself hamstrung and out of his depth. Wells took against him, describing him as 'an incompetent director . . . his mind ran on loud machinery and crowd effects and he had no grasp of my ideas' (Frayling, p. 31). Lacking experience with actors, Menzies could do little to help his cast with Wells' stiff, didactic dialogue, and the film is constantly toppled into pomposity by its script. Its strengths are almost entirely visual, for which Menzies can surely claim some input, although the shimmering Bauhaus-influenced sets were partly the work of the uncredited Lászlo Moholy-Nagy, and Korda's brother Vincent took final credit for set design.

Apart from *Things to Come*, Korda also put Menzies to work with Zoltan Korda and Alexander Esway directing material for his ill-fated dramatised history of flight, *The Conquest of the Air*. Menzies directed one more film in Britain: *The Green Cockatoo*, a low-budget thriller, with John Mills as a tap-dancing nightclub owner, made for a 20th Century-Fox subsidiary in 1937. It featured some striking visual images, and Graham Greene's story, set against a background of racetrack racketeers, offers intriguing pre-echoes of *Brighton Rock* (published in 1938). But the producers were unhappy about Menzies' direction of the dialogue sequences and brought in another expatriate American director, William K. Howard, to reshoot scenes and supervise the re-editing.

Back in the USA, Menzies won an Academy Award for Art Direction on *Gone with the Wind* (1939) and directed a few more films, of which the best was the cold war science-fiction allegory *Invaders from Mars* (1953). He died in Beverly Hills on 5 March 1957.
(Philip Kemp)

BIBLIOGRAPHY: Albrecht, Donald, *Designing Dreams: Modern Architecture in the Movies* (London: Thames and Hudson, 1987); Frayling, Christopher, *Things to Come* (London: BFI, 1995); Neumann, Dietrich (ed.), *Film Architecture: Set Designs from Metropolis to Blade Runner* (Munich and New York: Prestel Verlag, 1996); Stephens, Michael L., *Art Directors in Cinema: A Worldwide Biographical Dictionary* (Jefferson, NC: McFarland, 1998).

FILMOGRAPHY (UK only): *Things to Come* (1936); *The Conquest of the Air* (co-dirs. Zoltan Korda/Alexander Esway, and others, 1936; rel. 1940); *The Green Cockatoo* (aka *Four Dark Hours/Race Gang*, 1937; rel. 1940).

MERCHANT, Ismail (1936–2005)

Ismail Noormohamed Abdul Rehman, better known as Ismail Merchant, was born in Bombay on 25 December 1936, the only son of an affluent Muslim family. He studied business in Bombay and New York in order to take over the family firm, but dreamed about moving into the world of cinema. This dream was fulfilled largely thanks to meeting James Ivory, with whom Merchant formed Merchant Ivory Productions in 1961. In this partnership he acted as producer while Ivory directed, with Ruth Prawer Jhabvala writing most of the scripts. Together Merchant and Ivory have made over thirty films: most of the earlier ones set in India, most of the later ones adaptations of classic English and American novels.

Merchant has made far fewer films as a director and all of them have Indian settings and subjects. He directed the acclaimed shorts *The Creation of a Woman* (1960) and *Mahatma and the Mad Boy* (1974) and the television documentary *The Courtesans of Bombay* (1983), before making his first feature, *In Custody*, in 1993. Based on a novel by Anita Desai, it focuses nostalgically on a once revered Urdu poet, who like the whole literary tradition that he represents has fallen into neglect. *Cotton Mary* (1999) is the story of a rich English family in India, whose prematurely born baby is rescued by an Anglo-Indian wet nurse; it might be read as a metaphor for the importance of India to English identity and well-being. *The Mystic Masseur* (2001), scripted by Caryl Phillips from the novel by V. S. Naipaul, is a sporadically amusing comedy following the career of a very fallible Indian writer, healer and politician in 1940s' Trinidad. Like Merchant's other feature films it seems more worthy in its intentions than its execution. He died in London on 25 May 2005.
(Ewa Mazierska)

BIBLIOGRAPHY: Falk, Quentin, 'Island in the Sun', *Exposure*, Summer 2001, pp. 25–7; Long, Robert Emmet, *The Films of Merchant Ivory* (London: Viking, 1992); Pym, John, *The Wandering Company: Twenty-One Years of Merchant Ivory Films* (London: BFI, 1983).

FILMOGRAPHY: *The Creation of a Woman* (short, 1960); *Mahatma and the Mad Boy* (short, 1974); *In Custody* (aka *Hifazaat*, UK/Ind, 1993); *The Proprietor* (UK/Fr, 1996); *Cotton Mary* (co-dir. Madhur Jaffrey, 1999); *The Mystic Masseur* (UK/Ind, 2001).

METZSTEIN, Saul (1970–)

Saul Metzstein was born in Glasgow on 30 December 1970. After studying architecture he began his film-making career as a runner on *Shallow Grave* (Danny Boyle, 1994). His shorts *Magic Moments* and *Santa/Claws* (1997), and the television documentary *The Name of This Film Is Dogme95* (2000), established his credentials, and he was able to raise a budget of £1.5 million for his own Dogme-inspired debut feature, *Late Night Shopping* (2001). Like *Santa Claus*, the film was written by Jack Lothian, and draws on Lothian's experience working in low-paid, unskilled jobs at night. Three young men and a woman, all doing dull night-time jobs, meet in a café during their breaks to commiserate with each other over their unsatisfactory lives. Though the story is flimsy, the characters take on a life of their own and Metzstein makes good use of Brian Tufano's cinematography to capture the out-of-kilter, ennui-laden world of the night-worker.

Late Night Shopping attracted critical plaudits and awards, though it failed to attract the sizeable audiences who had flocked to *Shallow Grave* and *Trainspotting* (Danny Boyle, 1996). It took four years for Metzstein to set up his next feature, *Guy X* (2005), a European/Canadian co-production set on an American Army base in Greenland in the aftermath of the Vietnam War. Comedy and serious issues meld less well than in *Late Night Shopping*, but once again he succeeds in evoking a strange, isolated world where fantasy constantly seeps into everyday life.
(Jonathan Murray)

BIBLIOGRAPHY: <www.netribution.co.uk/features/interviews/2001/saul_metzstein/2.html>; Metzstein, Saul, 'Grit and Polish', *Sight and Sound*, May 2001, pp. 12–13; Murray, Jonathan, 'Sundance in Scotland?', *Vertigo*, Spring 2002, pp. 18–19.

FILMOGRAPHY: *The Piper* (short, 1995); *Café Rendezvous* (short, 1996); *Magic Moments* (short); *Santa/Claws* (short) (1997); *The*

Name of This Film Is Dogme95 (doc., 2000); *Late Night Shopping* (2001); *Guy X* (UK/Can/Ice, 2005).

MICHELL, Roger (1956–)

Roger Michell was born in Pretoria, South Africa, in 1956. The son of a diplomat who was later posted to Syria and Czechoslovakia, he went from public school to read English at Cambridge, where he developed an interest in theatre. After graduation, he worked as an assistant director at the Royal Court and in 1985 moved to the Royal Shakespeare Company, directing plays in London and New York. In 1990 he enrolled on the BBC drama director's course and found success with Hanif Kureishi's serialisation of his semi-autobiographical novel *The Buddha of Suburbia* (1993). This was followed in 1995 by Jane Austen's *Persuasion*, a BBC Television film that was critically lauded in Britain and successfully screened in cinemas across the United States.

After another television adaptation – Kevin Elyot's gay tragicomedy *My Night with Reg* (1996), which he had directed on stage – Michell made his first feature, *Titanic Town*. The film was adapted by Anne Devlin from Mary Costello's novel about the women's peace movement of the early 1970s, and starred Julie Walters as a new resident in West Belfast who becomes unwittingly involved in religious feuding and tries to do something to halt it. As with most films tackling the difficult subject of Northern Ireland, *Titanic Town* faced mixed critical reviews and audience indifference.

By contrast, Michell's next project was the long-awaited successor to *Four Weddings and a Funeral* (Mike Newell, 1994), *Notting Hill*. Richard Curtis' script successfully reworks the formula of the earlier film, with Hugh Grant playing a charming but indecisive Englishman who thinks he might be in love with an elusive and enigmatic American beauty. Michell contributes by presenting Curtis' circle of friends as genuinely quirky rather than a set of spoiled English eccentrics; making good use of the big budget in the idealised recreation of Portobello Road market; and in coaxing a performance from Julia Roberts that makes us believe she is susceptible to Grant's diffident charm.

The last shot in *Notting Hill* shows Hugh Grant reading *Captain Corelli's Mandolin*, the best-selling novel that Michell intended to make as his next film. But a heart attack meant that he had to hand over to John Madden. When he recovered he turned instead to *Changing Lanes*, a mainstream, big-budget American drama, with Samuel L. Jackson and Ben Affleck as New Yorkers from opposite ends of the social spectrum whose lives become unwillingly intertwined after a minor traffic accident.

Both *Notting Hill* and *Changing Lanes* were made with budgets of around $45 million, but like the denizens of *Notting Hill*, Michell seems unlikely to be seduced away to Hollywood. With Hanif Kureishi he went on to make *The Mother*, a film made for less than $3 million about a sixty-eight-year-old woman's affair with her daughter's boyfriend. Though it failed to repeat the commercial success of Michell's previous two films, *The Mother* attracted favourable critical interest. *Enduring Love*, a powerfully claustrophobic adaptation of Ian McEwan's novel about lives and relationships threatened by the aftermath of a fatal ballooning accident, confirms Michell's reputation as a thoughtful and perceptive director, increasingly discerning in his choice of films.

(Pamela Church Gibson)

BIBLIOGRAPHY: Blair, Iain, 'Director Roger Michell's Blithe Spirit', *Film and Video* vol. 16 no. 6, June 1999, pp. 89–92; Fleming, Michael, 'King of the Hill', *Movieline* vol. 10 no. 10, July 1999, pp. 64–7; Minns, Adam, 'Roger Michell Set to String Working Title's Mandolin', *Screen International*, Oct. 1997, p. 8.

FILMOGRAPHY: *Persuasion* (1995); *Titanic Town* (UK/Ger/Fr/Ir, 1998); *Notting Hill* (UK/US, 1999); *Changing Lanes* (US, 2000); *The Mother* (2003); *Enduring Love* (2004).

MICHELL, Scott (1967–)

Scott Michell was born in England in 1967. After studying at Southampton University, he worked his way into the industry via a job at the First Film Foundation, a charity supporting young film-makers. Richard Holmes, an FFF contact, employed Michell as assistant director on his own first feature as producer, the Scottish road movie *Soft Top, Hard Shoulder* (Stefan Schwartz, 1992). In the same year, with funding from his father, Michell made a dystopian 35mm science-fiction short, *Seeds*, of curiosity value for a cameo appearance by the screenwriter David McGillivray. After Michell had gained further experience as third assistant director on Metrodome's *Beyond Bedlam* (Vadim Jean, 1993) and on corporate videos and commercials, he used family money to develop and direct his first feature, *The Innocent Sleep*.

Encouraged by producer Matthew Vaughan, Michell aspired to make a film that would be commercial in spite of its low budget. *The Innocent Sleep* casts Rupert Graves as a vagrant who witnesses a murder very like that of Robert Calvi, the Papal banker found hanged under Blackfriars Bridge in 1982. The film touches on intriguing themes, including the machinations of the modern media and the real vulnerability of the powerless: Graves' dosser is the ultimate dispensable witness. The treatment given his relationship with an American investigative journalist played by Annabella Sciorra is also notable – an unusually spiky take on male–female relations that resists any suggestion of romance.

Critics praised the film's low-budget achievements, particularly its strikingly shot widescreen London and the credible performances of the two stars. But despite *Screen International*'s prediction that 'Michell should no longer have to turn to private backers for future projects' (Moore, 1995), Scott Michell has yet to make another film.

(Claire Monk)

BIBLIOGRAPHY: Brooks, Xan, 'Homeless in the Movies', *The Big Issue*, 29 Jan./4 Feb. 1996, pp. 18–19; Cameron Wilson, James, '*The Innocent Sleep*', *Film Review*, Feb. 1996, p. 23; Moore, Oscar, '*The Innocent Sleep*', *Screen International*, 17 Nov. 1995, p. 39.

FILMOGRAPHY: *Seeds* (short, 1992); *The Innocent Sleep* (1995).

MILES, Bernard (1907–1991)

Born in Uxbridge, Middlesex, on 27 September 1907, Bernard James Miles was the son of a farm labourer who became a successful market gardener. Miles' father paid for his son's education at Pembroke College, Oxford, after which he briefly became a teacher before making his stage acting debut in 1930 and his film debut in 1932. In 1951 he and his actress wife, Josephine Wilson, founded the Mermaid Theatre, which eight years later found a permanent home at Blackfriars in London. He was created a CBE in 1953, a knight in 1969 and a peer in 1979. Under the pressures of theatre management, he abandoned his screen career during the 1960s.

Throughout his life Miles was an avowed socialist, and the Mermaid project, which survived under his leadership until 1984, was intended to rid the theatre world of snobbery and class distinction. His film acting, initially undertaken for financial reasons, was sporadic, but in the early 1940s he also turned to scriptwriting to bring his political philosophy to the screen. After the acclaim given his performance in Two Cities' *In Which We Serve* (David Lean/Noël Coward, 1942), the company allowed him to co-direct *Tawny Pipit*, a modest comedy in which a village unites to protect a pair of rare birds and their eggs from a variety of predators. Miles (who also appears as Colonel Barton-Barrington, the local squire) gently satirises rural eccentricities, but he amusingly links the hospitality offered the pipits with that extended to foreign allies in the war – particularly the Russians. The quintessential Englishness of the film – almost every scene is shot outdoors – has given it an enduring popularity among audiences and critics as a precursor of the later Ealing comedies.

By the time Miles came to direct his second film, *Chance of a Lifetime*, the war was over and Labour had been in office for over four years. The film concerns a group of factory workers who come to control the factory, only to discover that to do so successfully they need the business expertise of their conservative boss (Basil Radford). This plea for greater class co-operation, a probable moderation of Miles' pre-1945 views, aroused the hostility of the distributors and the film was only given a circuit release after government intervention. Though it now seems an amiable and amusing film, it was poorly promoted and failed to reach a wide audience.

These two films were essentially Miles' own, for he co-wrote, produced and co-directed both. They are primarily memorable for their offbeat content, but they also demonstrate that as a director he possessed a flair for comedy, treated in a cinematic rather than a theatrical fashion despite his stage leanings. He died in Knaresborough, North Yorkshire, on 14 June 1991.

(James C. Robertson)

BIBLIOGRAPHY: 'Bernard Miles: A "Versatile" of the Film Industry', Two Cities Films' publicity material, held on microfiche in the BFI National Library, London; Cleeve, Maureen, 'The Mermaid Man', *Observer* Magazine, 28 June 1981.

FILMOGRAPHY: *Tawny Pipit* (co-dir. Charles Saunders, 1944); *Chance of a Lifetime* (co-dir. Alan Osbiston, 1950).

MILES, Christopher (1939–)

Christopher Miles, elder brother of actress Sarah Miles, was born in London on 19 April 1939. His early short film *The Six-Sided Triangle* (1963) gave him a reputation as a visual prankster, but the most typical later films rest firmly within the literary tradition of British cinema, and are characterised by their eye for minor details and sensitive if detached approach to potentially melodramatic material.

Miles took his first steps in cinema in childhood in 1951, when he directed his sister in a fictional short, *All That Sparkles Is Not Champagne*, set in the 1920s. Serious study and film-making began at the Institut des Hautes Études Cinématographiques in Paris in the early 1960s. *À Vol d'oiseau*, a fantasy about a lost umbrella, attracted the Boulting Brothers' interest and led to British Lion supporting *The Six-Sided Triangle*, a half-hour spoof of different national film styles. Miles' visual gags and pastiches appeared less impressive in his feature debut, *Up Jumped a Swagman* (1965), a whimsical pop fantasy featuring the Australian singer Frank Ifield. A more sober approach to film-making surfaced five years later in *The Virgin and the Gypsy* (1970), adapted from D. H. Lawrence's novella. With a brooding Franco Nero as the gypsy and Joanna Shimkus as the clergyman's daughter, some of the original's sexual tensions were captured, though Miles' heavily pictorial surface left the story's inner depths little disturbed.

The director's French connections showed in his next two assignments. The uneven *Time for Loving*, written by Jean Anouilh and produced by Dimitri de Grunwald, offered three bitter-sweet tales of love, built round differing occupants of a flat in a tourist's version of Paris, while his adaptation of *The Maids* for the American Film Theatre waded heavy-handedly into Jean Genet's play of sexual intrigue. After another de Grunwald trifle, the inconsequential romantic comedy *That Lucky Touch*, Miles returned to more familiar ground with *Priest of Love* (1981), a portrait of D. H. Lawrence's declining years. Despite Ian McKellen's strong central performance, the film's overt tastefulness drained the drama of much of its potential intensity, a flaw hardly touched in the re-edited version Miles issued in 1985.

A busy provider of television commercials in the 1960s, Miles returned to the small screen in 1979 with episodes for *Roald Dahl's Tales of the Unexpected*. Much of his subsequent product has been for television: *Lord Elgin and Some Stones of No Value* (1985), based on Elgin's letters, remains the most notable and elaborate. His boisterous cinema feature *The Clandestine Marriage* (1999), based on an eighteenth-century comedy, marked a return to literary cinema, period settings and class relationships, though financial problems limited its visual sheen and technical polish.

(Geoff Brown and Robert Shail)

BIBLIOGRAPHY: BECTU History Project tape no. 351, held in the BFI National Library, London; Gontarski, S. E., 'Christopher Miles on His Making of *The Virgin and the Gypsy*', *Literature/Film Quarterly* vol. 11 no. 4, 1983, pp. 249–56; Hodge, Adrian, 'A Love Affair with Lawrence', *Screen International*, 16 Aug. 1980, p. 11; Telotte, J. P., 'Christopher Miles: An Interview', *Post Script*, Winter 1986, pp. 2–18; Williams, John, 'All That Sparkles Is Not Champagne', *Films Illustrated* vol. 1 no. 6, Dec. 1971, pp. 30–1.

FILMOGRAPHY: *All That Sparkles Is Not Champagne* (short, 1951); *China Today* (doc. short, 1960); *À Vol d'oiseau* (short, Fr); *L'Ami d'Ionesco* (doc. short, Fr) (1961); *Stockgrove* (doc. short, 1962); *The Six-Sided Triangle* (short, 1963); *Rhythm 'n' Greens* (short, 1964); *Up Jumped a Swagman* (1965); *The Rue Lepic Slow Race* (short, 1968); *The Virgin and the Gypsy* (1970); *Time for Loving* (US: *A Time for Loving*, 1972); *The Maids* (UK/Can, 1974; rel. 1976); *That Lucky Touch* (1975); *Priest of Love* (1980); *Daley's Decathlon* (doc., 1982); *The Clandestine Marriage* (1999).

MILLAND, Ray (1907–1986)

Reginald Alfred John Truscott-Jones was born in Neath, Glamorgan, on 3 January 1907. He studied at King's College, London, and served in a Guards regiment for three years before entering the British film industry in 1929, when he adopted the name Raymond (later Ray) Milland. He made a mark in Castleton Knight's thriller *The Flying Scotsman* (1929). But by 1931 he was in Hollywood, where he gradually established his reputation as a suave, charming, reliable leading man. Fame came with his performance in *Beau Geste* (William A. Wellman, 1939); respect for his acting abilities followed with his unexpectedly convincing portrayal of an alcoholic writer in *The Lost Weekend* (Billy Wilder, 1945), for which he won an Academy Award for Best Actor.

Milland played strong roles in John Farrow's marvellously eccentric film noirs *The Big Clock* (1947) and *Alias Nick Beal* (1948), and in Lewis Allen's British-based *So Evil My Love* (1948), but these were exceptions to generally banal studio fare. In 1950 he told *Picturegoer* that he looked forward to switching from acting to directing, though the interviewer expressed scepticism over whether his studio (Paramount) would let him: 'It takes the line – with apparently sound reasoning – that Ray is a far better property as a tried and tested hero than as an untried director' (Forrest, p. 13). He had first ventured into the field in 1948, directing an episode of *The Ford Television Theatre*, but it was not until 1955, after he had left Paramount, that he directed *A Man Alone*, a modest but pleasingly intelligent Western, for Republic. It was enough of a success to lead to *Lisbon*, a good-looking crime thriller shot on location in Portugal in colour and 'Naturama', Republic's version of CinemaScope. Milland had proved his competence, but Republic's days were numbered. His next opportunity to direct came from John R. Sloan and David E. Rose in England, who had earlier produced Jacques Tourneur's *Circle of Danger* (1950), featuring Milland as a character up against a conspiracy of silence from disgruntled British war veterans. *The Safecracker* (1957), based on the true story of a career criminal offered the chance to annul his long jail sentence by safe-breaking in Nazi-occupied Belgium, was a more cheerful affair, with Milland's cracksman proving that even Britain's crooks were brave patriots at heart.

Once again Milland showed himself a talented director, but *The Safecracker* was too parochial to make any splash in Hollywood and insufficient offers arrived for him to reroute his career away from acting. He made an enjoyable and effective apocalyptic B-movie for AIP, *Panic in Year Zero!* (1962), but AIP had hordes of enthusiastic young directors at their command, and as at Paramount Milland was valued more for his acting skills. His final directorial effort was an adaptation of his successful Broadway production *Hostile Witness*, shot in Britain with little sign of his previous efforts' energy and ingenuity. He continued to act to the end, winning plaudits for his performance as Ryan O'Neal's patrician father in *Love Story* (Arthur Hiller, 1970), though he often had to content himself with less respectable fare. In *La serpiente de mar* (Amando de Ossorio, 1985), his last film, he played an oceanographer battling against a Spanish sea monster aroused from the deep by a nuclear explosion. Ray Milland died of lung cancer on 10 March 1986 in Torrance, California.

(Robert Murphy)

BIBLIOGRAPHY: Doyle, Neil, 'Ray Milland: Against Type', *Films of the Golden Age* no. 29, Summer 2002, pp. 56–69; 'Ray Milland', *Film Dope* no. 43, Jan. 1990, pp. 16–19; Forrest, Elizabeth, 'Ray Milland: The Reluctant Hero', *Picturegoer*, 11 Nov. 1950, p. 13; Milland, Ray, *Wide-Eyed in Babylon: An Autobiography* (London: Hodder & Stoughton, 1977).

FILMOGRAPHY: *A Man Alone* (US, 1955); *Lisbon* (US, 1956); *The Safecracker* (1957); *Panic in Year Zero!* (US, 1962); *Hostile Witness* (1968).

MILLAR, Adelqui (1891–1956)

Adelqui Migliar Icardi was born on 5 August 1891 in Concepción, Chile, to a Chilean father and an Italian mother; he later changed his surname to Millar. After a childhood spent on a Chilean farm, he was educated in Italy and France and graduated from theatre to film-making. He acted in a number of Dutch films and came to Britain in 1920 while working for Maurits Binger's Anglo-Hollandia company. After acting in several films for B. E. Doxat-Pratt, he wrote the screenplay for his imaginative *Laughter and Tears* (1921), and co-directed *Circus Jim* with him. Both films explore themes of life and art through the motifs of carnival and circus. Millar then produced, directed and starred in two independent productions: *Pages of Life* and *The Apache*.

Seeking to benefit from the 1927 Quota Act, Millar formed Whitehall Films, with its own small studio at Elstree. Whitehall's two films – *Life* (which Millar shot in Spain) and *The Inseparables* – were released when the market for silent films was being eroded by the talkies and the company lurched into bankruptcy. Millar's acting career failed to survive the transition to sound, but he continued directing in Europe, initially making French and Spanish versions of American films. In 1939 he moved to Argentina, where he directed films until 1954. He died in Santiago, Chile, on 6 August 1956.

A romantic, cosmopolitan adventurer, at home with multilingual casts and scripts, Millar gravitated towards melodrama and exotica, opening up the liminal spaces between theatre, life and death, happiness and loss.

(Christine Gledhill)

BIBLIOGRAPHY: Cohen, Elsie, 'Adelqui Migliar – Star of the Netherlands: Interviewed by Elsie Cohen', Anglo-Hollandia Publicity Department, 1920, held on microfiche at the BFI National Library, London; Cohen, Elsie, 'Adelqui Millar – Interview', *Picture Show*, 17 July 1920, pp. 57–8; Donaldson, Geoffrey 'In de Nedeerlandsse film tot 1930: Wie is wie: Adelqui Migliar, Adelqui Millar', *Skrien* no. 138, Nov./Dec. 1984, pp. 47–53; Low, Rachael, *The History of the British Film 1918-1929* (London: George Allen & Unwin, 1971).

FILMOGRAPHY (UK only): *Circus Jim* (co-dir. B. E. Doxat-Pratt); *Pages of Life* (1922); *The Apache* (1925); *The Blind Ship* (UK/Fr, co-dir. Joseph Guarino-Glavany, 1928); *Life*; *The Inseparables* (co-dir. John Stafford) (1929).

MILLAR, Gavin (1938–)

Gavin Millar was born in Clydebank, Scotland, on 11 January 1938. After studying at Oxford, he joined the BBC in the early 1960s, working on the arts programme *Monitor*, where he assisted Ken Russell on *Elgar* (1962) and *Always on Sunday* (1965). He learned to direct on the topical news programme *Tonight* and showed his talent with *The Eye Hears, The Ear Sees* (1970), an effective documentary on the Scottish-born animator Norman McLaren. For the next thirteen years he worked extensively for the BBC, establishing his reputation as a director with Dennis Potter's *Cream in My Coffee* (1980). He made his feature film debut with *Secrets* (1983), one of the *First Love* films produced by David Puttnam for Channel 4. His next film, his most ambitious, was *Dreamchild*, written by Dennis Potter. Through carefully structured flashbacks it tells the story of Lewis Carroll's muse, Alice Hargreaves. The nature of her complex relationship with Carroll is subtly unfolded as the film develops into a typical Potter meditation on the nature of childhood and the power of nostalgia.

Apart from *Danny, the Champion of the World* (1989), made for television in Britain but successfully released theatrically, Millar's only other cinema feature is *Complicity*, an adaptation of an Iain Banks' novel. This depiction of a journalist on the trail of a serial killer was less successful than his television serialisation of

Banks' *The Crow Road* (1996) and was released direct to video in the UK. Millar's work for television is of a bewildering variety, from studies of film-makers such as Michael Powell, Gene Kelly, Jean Renoir and Norman McLaren, to serious drama and adaptations of literary classics (Rosamond Lehmann's *The Weather in the Streets* in 1983; Evelyn Waugh's *Scoop* in 1987), to the American children's serial *The Young Indiana Jones Chronicles* (1992) and vehicles for Dawn French (*Sex and Chocolate*, 1997) and Sarah Lancashire (*My Fragile Heart*, 2000).

Millar was co-author with Karel Reisz of the revised edition of *The Technique of Film Editing* (1968), film critic of *The Listener* between 1970 and 1984 and presenter of the BBC's *Arena Cinema* (1976-80) and *Talking Pictures* (1980). His prolific film-making career has been largely confined to television.

(Robert Shail)

BIBLIOGRAPHY: Blake, J. C., 'Gavin Millar, *Film Dope* no. 43, Jan. 1990, p. 19; Millar, Gavin, 'British Cinema: Life before Death on Television', *Sight and Sound*, Spring 1984, p. 120; Millar, Gavin, Biographical letter, *Film Dope* no. 44, Mar. 1990, pp. 20c–20d.

FILMOGRAPHY: *The Eye Hears, The Ear Sees* (doc., UK/Can, 1970); *Secrets* (1983); *Dreamchild* (1985); *Complicity* (2000).

MILLER, Frank (1891–c. 1950)

Coming across Frank Miller at British Screen Productions in the late 1920s, the scriptwriter Edward Dryhurst was not impressed. 'A man in his forties who dressed and looked like a farmer', he wrote later (Dryhurst, p. 158); a man, moreover, whose standard of work made Dryhurst keen to avoid collaboration. Colourful autobiographies are not the best historical evidence, though with all Miller's feature work seemingly lost, evidence of any kind is in short supply.

Born in London in 1891, Miller entered films as a youthful actor in early comedies: in Cricks and Martin's *The Terror and the Terrier* (A. E. Coleby, 1910) he was the Terror. As a director, he initially kept distinguished company, first at the high-quality London Film Company, where he made four short comedies in 1916 adapted from W. W. Jacobs stories. Later, after LFC's eclipse, he worked with Kenelm Foss and Guy Newall, two of the period's more promising film-makers. His first feature, *The March Hare* (1919), the third of Newall's Lucky Cat productions, pleased critics with its whimsical comedy and New Forest settings, though the ultimate key to its charms was Newall's appealing screen personality. With Foss he collaborated on a droll domestic comedy series *Till Our Ship Comes In*, and a second feature, *The Joyous Adventures of Aristide Pujol* (1920), shot partly in Paris: a film fractured as a narrative (inevitable with W. J. Locke's episodic novel as its source), but suitable as a showcase for Foss' versatility as an actor.

Miller also kept busy scriptwriting, writing by his own estimation some two hundred silent films, long and short. Some were distinguished, like Harold Shaw's lively *Kipps* (1920); but by 1922 he had yoked himself to Harry B. Parkinson, a master opportunist rather than an artist. The more respectable results include co-direction of the *Wonderful London* shorts (1924), invaluable now as a record of past sights; there were also scripts for lurid exercises like Parkinson's *Trapped by the Mormons* (1922). Miller's later features with British Screen Classics and its quota-filling successor British Screen Productions failed to enhance his industry status: *Houp-la!*, an absurd circus story, frittered away its best potential by neglecting to include any Big Top action, while *Cupid in Clover* dawdled through its rural drama with only pleasing settings for company. Once BSP crumpled, Miller found steady if lowly work in the scriptwriting team at British International Pictures. Occasionally he supplied technical assistance. With the actor Gene Gerrard he co-directed rumbustious farces *Lucky Girl* and *Let Me Explain, Dear*, most of his script work was also in a light vein, including two adaptations of Arthur Pinero plays for Will Hay and various films with the Lupino family. In the 1940s he kept in employment writing commentaries for travelogue and wildlife shorts. Miller's exact death date is unknown.

(Geoff Brown)

BIBLIOGRAPHY: Dryhurst, Edward, *Gilt off the Gingerbread* (London: Bachman & Turner, 1987).

FILMOGRAPHY: Shorts: *Odd Charges*; *The Skipper of the Osprey*; *A Marked Man*; *The Persecution of Bob Pretty* (1916); *Till Our Ship Comes In* (series, 1919); *Stop Press Comedies* (series, 1920); *Treasure Trove* (1922); *Wonderful London* (two series, co-dir. Harry B. Parkinson, 1924); *The Happy Rascals* (series, 1926); *When We Were Very Young* (series, 1928).

Features: *The March Hare* (1919); *The Joyous Adventures of Aristide Pujol* (1920); *Mr Nobody* (1927); *Houp-la!* (aka *The Lion Tamer*, 1928); *Cupid in Clover* (1929); *Verdict of the Sea* (co-dir. Sydney Northcote); *Lucky Girl* (co-dir. Gene Gerrard); *Let Me Explain, Dear* (co-dir. Gene Gerrard) (1932).

MILLER, Sam (1962–)

Sam Miller was born in Saxmundham, Suffolk, on 28 September 1962. He began his career as an actor, but after making two short films, *Love's Lost Hour* and *Fluke*, he was hired by Tony Garnett as one of the directors on the television hospital series *Cardiac Arrest*. Its relentless, fast-moving, hand-held style was carried over to Garnett's next venture, *This Life*, a drama series about a group of young London lawyers, which captured the spirit of irreverent optimism that flowered briefly in the late 1990s. Miller directed the first three episodes and struck up a good working relationship with writer Amy Jenkins, encouraging her to write the feature film script that would eventually emerge as *Elephant Juice*.

After directing *King Girl* (1996), a hard-hitting television drama about brutal rivalries among troubled teenage girls, Miller made his feature debut with *Among Giants*, a comedy-drama by Simon Beaufoy about a group of unemployed men and a female Australian hitchhiker, recruited to paint a line of electricity pylons stretching across the Peak District between Sheffield and Manchester. Despite attractive performances from

Daniel LaPaine and Emmanuelle Béart in *Elephant Juice* (Sam Miller, 1999)

Pete Postlethwaite and Rachel Griffith, the film never looked like emulating the success of *The Full Monty* (Peter Cattaneo, 1997), but its small-scale virtues pleased some people and upset nobody.

Elephant Juice, which followed in 1999, is a more glossy affair, though Jenkins and Miller seemed blithely unaware that their concerns about commitment, fidelity and the prospect of parenthood were by this time common currency in cinema and television, and they would need something more than a gimmicky title and a glamorous cast to attract an audience. The charismatic Emmanuelle Béart and the solidly reliable Mark Strong give good performances; but too many elements meant to indicate signs of the times end up as tired clichés, and the attempt to escape from a conventional narrative with a flashback structure and a fragmented plot looked dilettantish beside the more adventurous strategies of David Kane's *This Year's Love* (1999) and Michael Winterbottom's *Wonderland* (1999).

Elephant Juice's lack of critical and commercial success checked Miller's career in the cinema. He returned to television to direct episodes of the spy drama *Spooks* (2002) and the detective thriller *Murder City* (2004); along with two excellent television films: *Quite Ugly One Morning* (2004), featuring James Nesbitt as a Scottish investigative journalist, and an inventive remake of *The Quatermass Experiment* (2005), with Jason Flemyng as the intrepid professor.
(Robert Murphy)

BIBLIOGRAPHY: Burrows, Kerry Anne, 'Among Lunatics', *Eyepiece* vol. 18 no. 4, Aug./Sept. 1997, pp. 13–15; Kemp, Philip, 'Among Giants', *Sight and Sound*, June 1999, pp. 34–5; Stok, Witold, 'Filming Giants Striding the Ridings of Yorkshire', *In Camera*, Winter 1997, pp. 14–15.

FILMOGRAPHY: *Love's Lost Hour* (short); *Fluke* (short, 1993); *Among Giants* (1998); *Elephant Juice* (1999).

MILLS, John (1908–2005)

Lewis Ernest Watts Mills was born on 22 February 1908, at Watts Naval Training College, North Elmham, Norfolk, where his father was a teacher. Experience with amateur dramatics led him to escape life as a corn merchant's clerk and a travelling salesman of toilet rolls and make his debut in the chorus line of *The 5 O'Clock Girl* at the London Hippodrome in 1929. Success on the stage was paralleled by a film career beginning at Gaumont-British with *The Midshipmaid* (Albert de Courville, 1932). Major roles followed in *Forever England* (Walter Forde, 1935) and *Tudor Rose* (Robert Stevenson, 1936), but it was not until his appearance as Ordinary Seaman 'Shorty' Blake in David Lean and Noël Coward's *In Which We Serve* (1942) that he achieved real distinction. Several equally powerful performances followed, particularly in war films, though it was his role as Pip in *Great Expectations* (David Lean, 1946) that brought him international renown.

In the late 1940s he directed a short charity film for the Royal National Institute for the Blind, and produced *The History of Mr Polly* (1948) and *The Rocking Horse Winner* (1949), both directed by his friend Anthony Pélissier. They provided Mills with strong and unusual roles, but neither was as successful at the box office as they deserved and there were no further ventures behind the camera until he directed *Sky West and Crooked* in 1966.

Wisely, Mills resisted playing a role himself and concentrated his attention on encouraging a convincing performance from his daughter Hayley as a possibly brain-damaged teenager and injecting a degree of plausibility into his wife Mary Hayley Bell's whimsical story (originally titled *Bats with Baby Faces*). He shows little interest in the main plot – about the aftermath of some dreadful accident in the past – but the romance between Hayley's smarter-than-she-looks Bridie and Roibin the gypsy (a convincingly cast Ian McShane) is sensitively handled. Even better is the subplot concerning the village children's plan to give animals a decent burial in the churchyard. The kindly vicar tries to ignore the small memorials to beloved moles and hamsters, but things get out of hand when plucked pheasants and snared rabbits are brought in, and even Bridie baulks at burying joints of meat: 'We want whole dead'uns, not bits,' she tells the small offender. Critics were not impressed and audiences stayed away, but forty years on this strange vision of rural life, populated exclusively by oddballs and eccentrics, makes compelling entertainment.

Mills was knighted in 1976, and continued his career in films, television and on the stage until his death on 23 April 2005, in Denham, Buckinghamshire.
(Robert Murphy)

BIBLIOGRAPHY: Dacre, Richard, 'John Mills', *Film Dope* no. 43, Jan. 1990, pp. 31–4; Mills, John, *Up in the Clouds Gentlemen Please* (London: Orion, 2001); Tanitch, Robert, *John Mills* (London: Collins & Brown, 1993).

FILMOGRAPHY: *Three Days* (doc. short, 1948); *Sky West and Crooked* (US: *Gypsy Girl*, 1966).

MILLS, Reginald (1912–1990)

Reginald Cuthbert Mills was born on 15 July 1912. After completing his Cambridge degree he entered the film industry as an assistant editor, working with David Lean on Paul Czinner's glossily packaged *As You Like It* (1936) and *Dreaming Lips* (1937). As an editor he started small on advertising and publicity films at Merton Park Studios, later serving in the Army Kinematograph Unit during the Second World War. On demobilisation he joined Michael Powell and Emeric Pressburger's Archers company, editing their films for ten years, from *A Matter of Life and Death* (1946) to *The Battle of the River Plate* (1956). Powell recalled that 'he always used to remind me of a brown owl. He would sit at his cutting table and look at me with his round eyes, with his round face, with his round spectacles, blinking amiably and cutting ruthlessly' (Powell, p. 534). His other notable partnership was with Joseph Losey, for whom he edited *The Sleeping Tiger* (1954), *Blind Date* (1959), *The Criminal* (1960), *The Damned* (1963), *The Servant* (1963) and *King & Country* (1964).

Mills had directed various commercials, but it was not until 1971 that Bryan Forbes, during his brief period as Head of Production at Elstree Studios, gave him the opportunity to direct a feature film. *Tales of Beatrix Potter* is an original ballet (danced by the Royal Ballet), based on five of Potter's stories about Squirrel Nutkin, Hunca Munca and their friends. The Powell influence is unmistakable – there is even an echo of *Peeping Tom* (Michael Powell, 1960) in Fox's voyeuristic spying on Jemima Puddleduck – but this is a much more placid affair than *The Tales of Hoffmann* (Michael Powell/Emeric Pressburger, 1951) and its successors. Christine Edzard's costumes, Frederick Ashton's choreography and Rostislav Doboujinsky's animal masks are pleasing enough (the Royal Ballet adapted the film for live performance at Covent Garden in 1992), and Mills occasionally uses startling compositions, but any hint of drama and danger is smothered by tasteful discretion. Delightful but unengaging, the film failed to make much of an impact, though it remains an enjoyably eccentric anomaly. Mills went on to direct a documentary about the making of Franco Zeffirelli's *Brother Sun, Sister Moon* (1972), which he had worked on as supervisory editor, and returned to Italy to edit Zeffirelli's six-hour miniseries *Jesus of Nazareth* (1977). He died in London in July 1990.
(Robert Murphy)

BIBLIOGRAPHY: Obituary, Reggie Mills, *Film and TV Technician*, Aug./Sept. 1990, p. 32; Perkins, Roy and Martin Stollery, *British Film Editors: 'The Heart of the Movie'* (London: BFI, 2004); Powell, Michael, *A Life in Movies* (London: Heinemann, 1986).

FILMOGRAPHY: *Tales of Beatrix Potter* (US: *Peter Rabbit and Tales of Beatrix Potter*, 1971); *Franco Zeffirelli: A Florentine Artist* (doc., 1973).

MINGHELLA, Anthony (1954–)

Anthony Minghella was born in Ryde on the Isle of Wight on 6 January 1954. After leaving the University of Hull, he worked as a script editor and writer for television series including *EastEnders* and *Boon*. He rose to prominence after winning the 1986 London Theatre Critics' Award for his play *Made in Bangkok* and went on to write three of the *Inspector Morse* television films and to collaborate with Jim Henson on the prestigious television series *The Storyteller* (1988).

Minghella's debut as a writer-director was the elegiac and darkly comic *Truly, Madly, Deeply*, made for BBC Television but released as a feature film. His experience of writing for television melodramas is evident in the film's preoccupation with its protagonists' inner lives, but Minghella's vision is individual and highly imaginative. At the centre is Juliet Stevenson's heroine, torn between joy at the return of her lover (Alan Rickman) and a growing desire for her own independence: a dilemma whose emotional truth is complicated and enriched by the fact that Rickman is dead and returns as a demanding and increasingly inconvenient ghost.

Truly, Madly, Deeply won critical and popular acclaim. Minghella went to Hollywood to direct the pleasing if slight *Mr Wonderful*, a romantic comedy about an electrician (Matt Dillon) oppressed by alimony payments who is determined to find a suitable husband for his ex-wife (Annabella Sciorra). His next offering, an adaptation of Michael Ondaatje's novel *The English Patient*, was far more personal and ambitious. Set at the end of the Second World War, the film presents the memories and past experiences of a seriously wounded soldier, Laszlo de Almásy (Ralph Fiennes), stranded in a ruined house in Italy. Minghella keeps his focus on human relationships rather than violent action, but the war provides an epic dimension, and the contrast between the immobilised state of the 'narrator' and his vividly depicted adventures and passions in the North African desert is dramatically effective. One can debate whether so much sand had to be so lovingly photographed; nonetheless critics and audiences greeted the film warmly. It won nine Academy Awards.

Gleaming visual surfaces returned in Minghella's fourth feature, *The Talented Mr Ripley*, adapted from Patricia Highsmith's novel of murder and identity-swapping. The seductions are manifold: a ritzy production, persuasive acting, the sun-drenched setting of Italy in the 1950s, where Matt Damon's Ripley worms his way into the affections of a rich wastrel, then traps himself in violence and deceit. Minghella's new tendency to inflate robs the material of some of its potential, but it remains a haunting film.

After directing *Play* (2000), a television adaptation of Beckett's miniscule stage play, Minghella acted as producer on Richard Eyre's *Iris* (2001), Tom Tykwer's *Heaven* (2002) and Phillip Noyce's *The Quiet American* (2002). He was awarded a CBE in 2001 and became Chairman of the BFI in 2003. He returned to the theme of enduring romantic love in his $83 million adaptation of Charles Frazer's American Civil War novel, *Cold Mountain*. Romanian locations were used, but the result was still a convincing American epic, celebrating individuality, resilience and endurance. Though more conventional than *The English Patient* and *The Talented Mr Ripley*, it is a satisfyingly well-told tale. With his vulnerable hero (Jude Law) and fierce, independent women (Nicole Kidman and Renée Zellweger), Minghella avoids macho posturing, concentrating less on the glories of war than on war's opportunities for cruelty, bullying and exploitation. Gratifyingly, it was as favourably received in the US as in Britain.
(Sarah Cardwell)

BIBLIOGRAPHY: Argent, Daniel, 'The Talented Mister: An Interview with Anthony Minghella', *Creative Screenwriting*, Jan./Feb. 2000, pp. 63–7; Bignell, Darren, 'The Sunshine Girls', *Empire*, Apr. 1997, pp. 60–4; Clarke, Natacha, 'Minghella Poised to Climb Next Mountain', *Screen International*, 3 Mar. 2000, p. 18; Griffin, Nancy, 'Making Love & War', *Premiere*, Dec. 2003, pp. 102–8; James, Nick, 'My Bloody Valentine', *Sight and Sound*, Feb. 2000, pp. 14–17; Stilwell, Robynn, 'Symbol, Narrative and the Musics of *Truly, Madly, Deeply*', *Screen*, Spring 1997, pp. 60–75.

FILMOGRAPHY: *Truly, Madly, Deeply* (1990); *Mr Wonderful* (US, 1993); *The English Patient* (US, 1996); *The Talented Mr Ripley* (US, 1999); *Cold Mountain* (US, 2003).

MISKELLY, Bill (1940–1991)

Bill Miskelly was born in Belfast in 1940. He enjoyed a lengthy career with BBC Northern Ireland, progressing from editor to director and winning many plaudits for his dramas, including *Phonefun Limited* (1982), written by Bernard MacLaverty, and documentaries – among them *When Genesis Begins* (on poet Patrick Kavanagh) and *Hidden Ground: Maurice Leitch*. After being dismissed by the BBC for making the film *The Schooner* (1983) while on holiday but still on contract, Miskelly formed his own production company, Aisling Films, in 1983 with a former colleague, Marie Jackson.

The Schooner, a one-hour television film, dramatised the relationship between a lonely older woman, Annie (Lucy Jameson), whose husband has disappeared at sea, and her young grandnephew, Terry (Michael Gormley). The two are brought together when Michael finds a model schooner (handmade by Miskelly) and this allows Annie to work through her memories of her life with her husband.

Jackson and Miskelly followed this with the children's film *The End of the World Man*, scripted by both of them and directed by Miskelly. They were determined to create a drama that would foreground young female characters and that would take place in Belfast without revolving around the Troubles. The result was an ecological parable about reclaiming a wasteland from development. It was much praised for the performances of its child actors, Leanne O'Malley and Claire Weir, and won numerous awards. Jackson and Miskelly were preparing their next script when Miskelly died unexpectedly in December 1991.
(Ruth Barton)

BIBLIOGRAPHY: Harkin, Margo, 'Bill Miskelly', *Film Base News*, Mar./Apr. 1992, p. 6.

FILMOGRAPHY: *The End of the World Man* (Ir, 1985).

MITCHELL, Oswald (1890–1949)

Oswald Mitchell was born in London in 1890 and began his film career as a producer at Stoll studios. His first directorial venture was *Danny Boy* (1934), a sentimental musical that he also wrote and produced. One of his bigger successes was *Old Mother Riley* (1937), starring husband-and-wife team Arthur Lucan and Kitty McShane who had made their film debut in Mitchell's *Stars on Parade* in 1935. The first of Mitchell's five *Old Mother Riley* films, it reveals Lucan's boisterous energy and gift for verbal comedy. Mitchell stayed with farces and musical revues that often starred established variety performers, the best of which include *Almost a Gentleman* (1938), an amusing story about mistaken identity, *Music Hall Parade* (1939) and *Jailbirds* (1939), a jolly farce with variety star Albert Burdon.

During the war Mitchell made topical comedies. *Sailors Don't Care* concerned two new recruits to the River Patrol who are caught up in a spy ring; *Pack up Your Troubles* followed the exploits of two captured 'Tommies' outwitting the Germans in France; and *Bob's Your Uncle* charted the rise of a lowly porter to stalwart of the Home Guard. In 1941 Mitchell remade *Danny Boy*, with Ann Todd as a singer who returns from America during the Blitz to search for her missing husband. He saw out the war with a zany comedy *Asking for Trouble*, starring Max Miller; a thriller *The Dummy Talks*, set in a variety theatre, with more music than thrills; and two more *Old Mother Riley* films.

Mitchell attempted a change of direction with *Loyal Heart*, a sheepdog story set in the Cumberland Fells. He told *Picturegoer* readers that it was his response to requests for more films showing the English countryside and pointed out that, along with his cast and crew he had spent five arduous months on location during the summer of 1944, often huddling for hours under canvas waiting for a break in the weather. Although *Loyal Heart* was favourably reviewed in the trade press, Mitchell obviously decided audiences required more red-blooded subjects. *The Mysterious Mr Nicholson* (1947) was followed by *Black Memory* (1947), a gripping crime drama with Michael Medwin as a baby-faced but vicious 'spiv', and *The Greed of William Hart* (1948), a 'blood-and-thunder' version of the Burke and Hare story starring the famous melodrama villain Tod Slaughter. Mitchell's last three films were more sophisticated psychological thrillers, the most successful of which, *House of Darkness* (1948), is eerily effective, with Laurence Harvey in his first starring role as an embittered young man who murders his wealthy stepbrother. Oswald Mitchell died in London on 27 April 1949.

(Margaret Butler)

BIBLIOGRAPHY: Mitchell, Oswald, 'Putting England on the Screen', *Picturegoer*, 23 Dec. 1944, p. 7.

FILMOGRAPHY: *Danny Boy* (1934); *Cock o' the North*; *Stars on Parade* (1935); *Variety Parade*; *Shipmates o' Mine*; *King of Hearts* (1936); *Old Mother Riley*; *Rose of Tralee*; *Lily of Laguna* (1937); *Old Mother Riley in Paris*; *Night Journey*; *Almost a Gentleman* (1938); *Old Mother Riley MP*; *Music Hall Parade*; *Jailbirds* (1939); *Sailors Don't Care*; *Pack up Your Troubles* (1940); *Danny Boy*; *Bob's Your Uncle* (1941); *Asking for Trouble* (1942); *Old Mother Riley Overseas*; *The Dummy Talks* (1943); *Old Mother Riley at Home* (1945); *Loyal Heart* (1946); *The Mysterious Mr Nicholson*; *Black Memory* (1947); *The Greed of William Hart*; *House of Darkness* (1948); *The Temptress*; *The Man from Yesterday* (1949).

MITCHELL, Sagar (1866–1952) and James KENYON (1850–1925)

Writing in the first volume of *The History of British Film*, published in 1948, Rachael Low characterised the Lancashire firm of Mitchell and Kenyon thus: 'typical of the small but hardy companies which sprang up early in England and continued to flourish until swamped by the American companies of the early twenties . . . This company, however, has left little trace' (Low and Manvell, pp. 22–3). The trace remained small until the discovery in 1994 of 780 original nitrate negatives, mostly between fifty and a hundred feet in length, stored in sealed barrels in Blackburn shop premises previously owned by the company's co-proprietor, Sagar Mitchell. The Cinema Museum in London subsequently acquired and restored some fiction titles; in 2000, the entire collection was then donated to the National Film and Television Archive. Aided by the television series and DVD *The Lost World of Mitchell & Kenyon* (2004), their research and restoration programme, undertaken with the National Fairground Archive, has now raised Mitchell and Kenyon's output to a public perception unusual for early British film-makers. In terms of the films' restricted techniques and absence of cinematic ambition, the prominence may seem unwarranted. But general audiences, as well as scholars, have been rightly entranced by the films as human documents and social history, reflecting the daily toil, pleasures and living conditions of a working-class generation previously unseen in surviving films in such bulk or such crisp black-and-white beauty.

Sagar Jones Mitchell, born in Blackburn on 28 October 1866, founded a photographic business with his father in 1887. James Kenyon, born in Blackburn on 26 May 1850, inherited a furniture business in 1880; by the late 1890s he also handled penny-in-the-slot machines. In November 1897 the pair joined forces to acquire a projector, and shot their first documented film, *Blackburn Market on a Saturday Morning*. Before the 1994 rediscovery, M & K's small reputation as film-makers was centred on their vigorous re-enactments of combat scenes and enemy atrocities from the Boer War and the Boxer Rebellion, among them *Hands off the Flag* (1901) and *Attack on a Mission Station* (1900). Such films were popular and shown nationwide, which helped the prints to survive. The 1994 haul, however, represents an output largely regional in subject and intent, with genuine actualities outnumbering the 'fakes' and outright dramas by a ratio of ten to one. Following Blackburn's Saturday market in 1897, M & K and their operatives gradually spread out over the north-east of England and occasionally North Wales and Ireland, training their cameras on local fairs and processions, workers leaving factory gates, football matches, street scenes, panoramic views, visiting royals and military heroes of the Boer War. *Tram Ride into Halifax*; *Lord Roberts' Visit to Manchester*, *Pendlebury Colliery*; *Burnley v. Manchester United*: the titles, indicated only by the scratched markings put onto the reels to aid projectionists, are bluntly explanatory. For some ten years from 1898, much of the company's output was commissioned by fairground showmen for exhibition later on the day of shooting. The advertising slogan used by the showman George Green encapsulates the films' original appeal: 'See yourself as others see you'. To label Mitchell and Kenyon as directors is probably to stretch the term beyond its limit, but no film was shot without some kind of guiding hand. In some cases Kenyon can be seen 'directing', signalling movements to the crowds; at other times, crowd management was performed by the showmen themselves, or M & K employees. By aiming and turning their cameras, the camera operators, *ipso facto*, became 'directors' too; beside the proprietors, the known names include Louis de Clerq (1871–1966), active for M & K in Ireland in 1902; the Welsh film-maker Arthur Cheetham (1864–1936), based in Rhyl; and Albert Wilkinson (also an exhibitor). By 1908, M & K's output had lessened following Kenyon's retirement from the furnishing business, and became mostly restricted to the Lancashire area; but films continued to be made until 1913. The partnership was finally wound up in 1922, three years before Kenyon's death on 6 February 1925 in Blackburn; Mitchell died in Houghton on 2 October 1952.

Low's conclusion, based on the evidence available in 1948, was that M & K exerted no influence on the development of cinema technique. The abundant evidence suddenly available has not radically changed matters. Films shot with equipment positioned on trams glided with the movement of the popular 'phantom rides', but the M & K norm was a static camera, varied with just a few pans. The first films unfolded mostly in continuous shots, only broken by the 'jump-cuts' prompted when the camera cranking stopped and restarted. But *The Arrest of Goudie*, made late in 1901, an elaborate account of the arrest of a Liverpool bank clerk who had written forged cheques worth £170,000, proved the power of a narrative-driven assemblage, and might be cinema's first crime reconstruction. Cinematically, the most exceptional and 'modern' films in the corpus are those documenting football matches. The need to follow the moving ball liberated the camera from its fixed positions; close-up shots were used more frequently. Despite historical differences – the length of football shorts, the Edwardian players' often bulky physiques – the activities of M & K's footballers also seem far closer to twenty-first-century life than the factory gate films' shawls and clogs or the festivities of *Buxton Well Dressing*.

Mitchell and Kenyon were businessmen: their films were simply products for sale, like Kenyon's furniture. There is no sign that they saw artistic possibilities in the new medium or chafed at the technical limitations that ensured they never moved beyond being observers and gentle manipulators of the passing scene. But therein lies their value. In M & K's films, as now restored, dust is shaken from history, and the dead brought to life; everyone captured by their cameras has in effect become our contemporary.

(Geoff Brown)

BIBLIOGRAPHY: Low, Rachael and Roger Manvell, *The History of the British Film 1896–1906* (London: George Allen & Unwin, 1948); *The Lost World of Mitchell & Kenyon* (BBC Television/BFI, produced by Annabel Hobley, 2004); Toulmin, Vanessa, Simon Popple and Patrick Russell, *The Lost World of Mitchell and Kenyon: Edwardian Britain on Film* (London: BFI, 2004).

SELECTED FILMOGRAPHY: *Blackburn Market on a Saturday Morning* (1897); *The Tramp's Surprise*; *The Tramps and the Artist*; *Kidnapping by Indians* (1899); *The Dispatch Bearers*; *Winning the VC*; *White Flag Treachery*; *Shelling the Red Cross*; *Washing Boer Prisoners* (aka *Washing a Boer Prisoner in Camp*; *Attack on a China Mission* (aka *Attack on a Mission Station*); *Attempted Capture of an English Nurse and Children*; *The Assassination of a British Sentry*; *The Clever Correspondent*; *The Nurse's Brother*; *Cresswell and Longworth Miners*; *Preston Egg Rollers*; *The 'Hands' Leaving Work at North Street Mills*; *Pilkington Glass Works*; *Messrs. Lumb and Co. Leaving the Works*; *20,000 Employees Entering Lord Armstrong's Elswick Works*; *Ropener & Co., Shipworks*; *Haslam's Ltd. Colne*; *Ormerod's Mill, Great Moor Street, Bolton* (1900); *Pay, Factory Gate* (c. 1900); *The Lost Scout on the Veldt*; *Blowing up the Powder Magazine*; *Poisoning the Well*; *Hands off the Flag*; *Tommy's Revenge*; *Tommy's Last Shot*; *Saved by a Woman*; *The Fight for the Gun*; *A Tight Corner*, *A Sneaky Boer*, *The Surprise of a Boer Camp*; *Chasing de Wet*; *Private Ward, VC, Leeds Hero*; *The Newcastle Fire Brigade*; *Employees Leaving the North Eastern Engine Works in Gateshead*; *The Arrest of Goudie*; *Sedgwick's Bioscope Shopfront and Stage Show*, *Employees Leaving Alexandra Dock*; *Manchester and Salford Harriers' Procession*; *Manchester Band of Hope Procession*; *Pendlebury Spinning Co.*; *Pendlebury Colliery*; *Alfred Butterworth and Sons, Glebe Mills*; *Mister Moon*; *Morecambe Church Lads' Brigade at Drill*; *University Procession on Degree Day*; *Panoramic View of the Morecambe Sea Front*; *Parade on Morecambe West End Pier*, *Tynemouth Swimming Gala in the Haven*; *Torpedo Flotilla Visit to Manchester*, *Parkgate Ironworks*; *Workers Leaving Brooks and Doxey, West Gorton Works*; *North Sea Fisheries*; *Jamaica Street, Glasgow*, *Ride on the Tramcar through Belfast*; *Manchester Street Scene*; *General Buller's Visit to Manchester and the Thousands of Spectators*; *Lord Roberts' Visit to Manchester*, *Captain Payne at Darwen*; *Lord Dunham at Sunderland*; *Salford v. Batley* (1901); *Cunard Vessel at Liverpool* (c. 1901); *Ambush II*; *West Bromwich – Comic Pictures in the High Street*; *Albert Quay*; *Wexford Bull Ring*; *Wexford Railway Station*; *Boat Race Cork Exhibition*; *Cork Fire Brigade Turning Out*; *Train Drive from Blarney*; *Lieutenant Clive Wilson and the Tranby Croft Party*; *Visit of the Duke of Connaught CIC Forces in Ireland and Prince Henry of Prussia*; *Coronation Festivities at Accrington*; *Hull Fair*, *Living Wigan*; *Tram Ride through the City of Sheffield*; *Mayor Entering His Carriage near the Town Hall, Halifax*; *Cool Proceedings*; *A Slippery Job*; *Who Stole the Bike?*; *The Rival Snow Shovellers*; *No Bathing Allowed*; *Warrington Walking Day*; *Tram Rides through Nottingham*; *A Trip to North Wales on the St Elvies*; *The King's Ride in the Isle of Man*; *Leeds Athletic and Cycling Club Carnival*; *Dewsbury v. Manningham*; *The Great Local Derby: Accrington v. Church Cricket Match*; *Burnley v. Manchester United*; *Hull FC v. Hull Kingston Rovers*; *Panorama of College Green*; *Tram Ride through Halifax*; *Street Scenes in Halifax*; *His Worship the Mayor Leaving the Town Hall*; *The Champion Athletes at Birmingham*; *Story's Moor Lane Mill, Lancaster*, *Lady Godiva Procession*; *Hollow Drift Children's Procession*; *Congregation Leaving St Mary's Dominican Church*; *Congregation Leaving St Patrick's Roman Catholic Church*; *Congregations Leaving St Hilda's Church*; *Congregations Leaving the Centenary Chapel*; *The Fleet in the Tyne*; *Visit of Earl Roberts and Viscount Kitchener to Receive the Freedom of the City*; *Rough Sea in Sunderland* (aka *Waves at Sunderland*) (1902); *Bootle May Day Demonstration*; *Bradford City v. Gainsborough Trinity*; *Blackpool North Pier*, *Blackpool North Pier Steamboat*; *A Tragic Elopement; or, Her Terrible Mistake*; *Diving Lucy*; *Royal Visit to Barrow and Launch of H.M.S. Dominion*; *Lytham Trams and the Views along the Route* (1903); *A Train Ride through Sunderland*; *Weary Willie in Search of Hidden Trea-*

sure; Driven from Home; The Miser and His Daughter; Manchester Catholic Whitsuntide Procession; Buxton Well Dressing; Opening of the Drill Hall in Accrington by General Baden-Powell; Blackpool Victoria Pier; Black Diamonds; or, The Collier's Daily Life (1904); *Leyland May Festival; Special March Past of St Joseph's Scholars and Special Parade of St Matthew's Pupils; England v. Ireland at Manchester ; Visit of H.R.H. Princess Louise* (1905); *Whitsuntide Fair at Preston; Who's Taken My Parcel?; The Interrupted Picnic* (1906); *Sunderland v. Leicester Fosse; Blackburn Rovers v. West Bromwich Albion; Blackburn Rovers v. Sheffield United; Crewe Hospital Procession; Opening of Accrington Electric Trams* (1907); *Miners' Demonstration at Wakefield* (1908); *East Lancashire Territorials* (1909); *Chorley Coronation Procession* (1911); *Accrington Catholic Procession* (1912); *Clitheroe Whitsuntide Processions* (1913).

MITTLER, Leo (1893–1958)

Leo Mittler was born in Vienna on 18 December 1893. His early career as a stage director in Germany took him to Breslau, Dresden, Frankfurt and finally Berlin, where he worked for Max Reinhardt in the late 1920s. He began a versatile career directing films in 1926 with Reinhold Schünzel's production *In der Heimat . . . da gibt's ein Wiedersehn!* At first comedies predominated; then in 1930 a French-German venture, *Le Roi de Paris/Der König von Paris*, filmed in both languages, led to concentrated work at the Joinville Studios in Paris making German-language versions of Paramount's Hollywood productions. Work in France continued with the murder drama *Voix sans visage* (1933) and *La Dernière valse*, a Ruritanian romance based on the operetta by Oscar Straus, filmed in French and English versions in 1934 with Jarmila Novotna and Gerald Barry. The English edition, *The Last Waltz*, co-directed by Barry, proved dull and unwanted on release in 1936. Mittler experienced better fortunes at the ATP studios, Ealing, in 1935, where he directed two lively independent productions mounted by Stanley Lupino after the comedian's break with BIP. First on the floor was *Cheer Up!*, a zany musical farce hinging on the worries of putting on a show; Mittler maintained a breezy tempo and glided happily through the musical numbers, even when Lupino and Hughes sang 'Steak and Kidney Pudding, I Adore You'. Lupino's resolutely British humour also proved no obstruction in *Honeymoon for Three*, another high-spirited frolic with Lupino cast as a playboy facing marital difficulties on board a transatlantic liner.

Despite Mittler's successful handling of British material, no other local opportunities followed. Returning to France, he collaborated with Victor Trivas on a First World War screenplay, *Les Otages* (Raymond Bernard, 1938); the following year he left for America, where the pair worked on the story for MGM's elaborate propaganda film *Song of Russia* (Gregory Ratoff, 1944). For Mittler, scriptwriting was the only Hollywood employment on offer – he also wrote the story for Lewton's psychological horror film *The Ghost Ship* (Mark Robson, 1943), subject of an opportunistic plagiarism suit. Later he directed in the theatre and in 1952 returned to Germany, where he introduced German theatre audiences to *The Teahouse of the August Moon* and *The Diary of Anne Frank*. He also directed for German television. Mittler died in Berlin on 16 May 1958.

(Geoff Brown and Kevin Gough-Yates)

BIBLIOGRAPHY: Goergen, Jeanpaul, 'Mittler zwischen Europa und Amerika', *Filmexil* no. 6, July 1995, pp. 40–52

FILMOGRAPHY (UK only): *The Last Waltz* (co-dir. Gerald Barry, 1934; rel. 1936); *Honeymoon for Three; Cheer Up!* (1935).

MONGER, Christopher (1950–)

Christopher Monger was born in 1950 in Taffs Well, Glamorgan, and attended Cardiff College of Art and the Slade School of Art in London. In the 1970s he played a key role in the development of the Chapter Film Workshop in Cardiff. His initial features as writer-director signalled his fine art background and taste for avant-garde cinema.

Monger embraced a wider public with his feature *Repeater*, a promisingly unconventional thriller shown at the Edinburgh Film Festival. His follow-up feature, *Voice Over*, was made for £11,700 from the Welsh Arts Council. It is a harrowing study of the emotional disintegration of a local radio presenter (the lugubrious Fats Bannerman, played unforgettably by Ian McNeice). A novel Fats reads on radio, redolent of Jane Austen, becomes the improbable catalyst for violence against the woman he rescues and idealises. This violence provoked protests at the Edinburgh and London film festivals and accusations of misogyny, which Monger (and film censor James Ferman) vigorously refuted.

Monger moved to Los Angeles, where he managed to gain the support of Shirley MacLaine for *Waiting for the Light*, a genial comedy with MacLaine gently sending herself up as a spry, fake spiritualist arousing misguided religious fervour in the Midwest, against a backdrop of the Cuban missile crisis. Monger returned to Britain to direct the offbeat comedy *Just Like a Woman*, which delved into the relationship between a rich young transvestite (Adrian Pasdar) and his sympathetic landlady (Julie Walters); and *The Englishman Who Went up a Hill but Came Down a Mountain*, an Ealing-like comedy about two English cartographers (Hugh Grant and Ian McNeice) who are fooled and cajoled by a Welsh village community into certifying a local hill as a mountain. Though it was considered regressive and condescending in some quarters, this affable comedy was a box-office success in America and the UK. Since then, Monger has directed episodes of the American comedy-drama series *That's Life* (2000), and *That Girl from Rio*, a light comedy with Hugh Laurie as a London bank clerk who unexpectedly gets to live out his fantasy of escaping to South America and meeting a passionate, beautiful and loving woman (Vanessa Nunes).

(David Berry)

BIBLIOGRAPHY: Berry, David, *Wales and Cinema: The First 100 Years* (Cardiff: University of Wales Press, 1994); Chapter Film Workshop, 'Letter to Workshops'; South Wales Women's Co-op, 'Voice Over'; Christopher Monger, 'Closer to Home', *Undercut* no. 6, Winter 1982–3, pp. 44–8.

FILMOGRAPHY: *Narcissus* (short, 1973); *Story from a Corner* (short, 1975); *Cold Mountain* (short); *Aesthete's Foot* (short) (1976); *Enough Cuts for a Murder* (short, 1978); *Repeater* (1980); *Voice Over* (1981); *Waiting for the Light* (US, 1990); *Just Like a Woman* (1991); *The Englishman Who Went up a Hill but Came Down A Mountain* (1995); *That Girl from Rio* (aka *Chica de Rio*, UK/Sp, 2002); *Special Thanks to Roy London* (doc., US, 2005).

MONTAGU, Ivor (1904–1984)

Ivor Goldsmid Samuel Montagu was born on 23 April 1904 in London. His father owned the bank Samuel Montagu and Company, but his family's wealthy background only encouraged Montagu to lean further to the left; in 1931 he joined the Communist Party of Great Britain, and never relinquished membership. Cinema took its place among many other interests: zoology, the promotion of table tennis, Mongolia, above all the class struggle and the redistribution of wealth. Even within cinema itself Montagu's activities were protean: directing comedy shorts and agit-prop documentaries; producing and writing commercial features; promoting foreign, especially Soviet, films through film societies and 16mm distribution; translating the key writings of Eisenstein and Pudovkin; writing his own criticism and polemics; and active involvement in the ACT, the film technicians' union. In her obituary reminiscence in *Sight and Sound* Penelope Houston used the phrase 'an inspired odd-job man', though that perhaps underplays his importance to the development in Britain of a vibrant intellectual and oppositional film culture during the inter-war years.

At Cambridge, Montagu studied zoology, graduating in 1924. The following year he helped form the Film Society in London, serving as Chairman until it closed fifteen years later. Throughout, he acted as an important conduit in getting foreign films onto British screens, often battling the censors in the process. In 1926 he formed an editing company, Brunel and Montagu, with Adrian Brunel, regularly servicing the Society's films and other imports; he also pitched in as editor on Brunel's comedy burlesques. Editing and titling work at Gainsborough on Hitchcock's *The Lodger* (1926) led to further commercial work for Michael Balcon's company. After directing a short film about table tennis, Montagu made his own independent bid for glory in 1928 with the comedy shorts *Blue Bottles*, *The Tonic* (now lost) and *Day-dreams*, based on story ideas provided by H. G. Wells, and produced with Frank Wells, the author's son. Elsa Lanchester featured in all three as a lowly maidservant caught up in adventures, real or imagined; the humour style mixed popular elements with industry in-jokes and mild satire, typified by the cartoon images of massed policemen and striped-shirted burglars slugging it out in *Blue Bottles*. Though praised by some for echoes of Chaplin, the films met with little public success in Britain. Montagu's growing impatience with the industry deepened during three years in Hollywood (1929–31), when he worked alongside Eisenstein and Grigori Alexandrov, trying to mount projects at Paramount. After returning to Britain in 1931, Montagu maintained a schizophrenic life within and outside the mainstream. In 1933 he began a stint at Gaumont-British, working as associate producer on Hitchcock's run of classic thrillers from *The Man Who Knew Too Much* (1934) to *Sabotage* (1936); he also struggled to shape something sensible from footage shot for the luxurious expedition film *Wings over Everest* (1934). At the same time, much energy was directed elsewhere at low-budget, independent political film-making. To further the agit-prop cause he established the Progressive Film Institute in 1935, and after leaving Gaumont-British made two trips to Spain, documenting the Civil War with Norman McLaren, Thorold Dickinson, Sidney Cole and others in cinematically modest films, beginning with *In Defence of Madrid*. Far greater verve was displayed in *Peace and Plenty* (1939), made for the Communist Party of Great Britain. Here Montagu found an abrasive new use for the larkish humour of his silent shorts, vigorously mixing stock footage with graphics, titles, still photographs, puppetry and animation in a savage polemic against Chamberlain's National Government.

None of Montagu's subsequent film work showed the sting and energy of *Peace and Plenty*. *Man – One Family*, a short for the Ministry of Information, aiming to demolish Nazi race theories, endured a difficult path towards its eventual distribution in 1946. Other time was spent with Balcon advising on Ealing wartime productions and working as associate producer, primarily on *Scott of the Antarctic* (Charles Frend, 1948). He also co-wrote the film's script, buttressing its portrait of Scott as an explorer let down by his commitment to the code of the English gentleman. His last association with the British industry was as adviser and scriptwriter on several modest features produced by the ACT in the 1950s. Small beer perhaps for one who once walked with Eisenstein; but Montagu's reputation and significance rest securely on his multiple endeavours between the wars as Britain's chief polymorphic cinephile, vaulting between the popular, the artistic and the political, a Hitchcock budget sheet in one hand, a Communist manifesto in the other. He died in Watford on 5 November, 1984.

(Geoff Brown and Tom Ryall)

BIBLIOGRAPHY: Brown, Geoff, 'Table Tennis over Everest', *Sight and Sound*, Spring 1984, pp. 98–9; Higson, Andrew (ed.), *Young and Innocent? The Cinema in Britain 1896–1930* (Exeter: University of Exeter Press, 2002); Houston, Penelope, 'In Memoriam', *Sight and Sound*, Winter 1984/5, p. 6; 'Interview: Ivor Montagu', *Screen* vol. 13 no. 2, Autumn 1972, pp. 71–113; 'Ivor Montagu', *Film Dope* no. 44, Mar. 1990, pp. 31–4; Low, Rachael, *The History of the British Film 1918–1929* (London: George Allen & Unwin, 1971); Low, Rachael, *Films of Comment and Persuasion of the 1930s* (London: George Allen & Unwin, 1979); Marris, Paul, 'Politics and "Independent" Film in the Decade of Defeat', in Don Macpherson (ed.), *British Cinema: Traditions of Independence* (London: BFI, 1980); Montagu, Ivor, *With Eisenstein in Hollywood* (New York: International Publishers, 1969); Montagu, Ivor, *The Youngest Son* (London: Lawrence & Wishart, 1970).

FILMOGRAPHY: *Table Tennis Today*; *The Tonic*; *Day-dreams*; *Blue Bottles* (1928); *Wings over Everest* (co-dir. Geoffrey Barkas, 1934); *In Defence of Madrid* (1936); *The XVth Congress Film*; *Britain Expects*; *Testimony of Non-Intervention* (1938); *Peace and Plenty* (1939); *Man – One Family* (1944; rel. 1946); *Wild Camel* (Mongolia, 1956).

MOORE, Simon (1958–)

Simon Moore directed two short films – *Coasters* and *Sleepwalking* – while a student at the National Film School, and went on to achieve considerable success as the writer of Channel 4's hard-hitting crime serial *Traffik* (Alastair Reed, 1989), remade as a Hollywood feature film by Steven Soderbergh in 2000. Moore made his own feature debut with *Under Suspicion* (1991), an intelligent English film noir set in Brighton at the end of the 1950s, with Liam Neeson as a seedy private eye suspected of the murder of his wife and a rich old painter. Moore makes good use of Neeson's sneaky charm to subvert expectations as we are led through a convoluted plot, but his chameleon-like character means the film lacks a focus.

Moore's proficiency with thriller conventions might have led to a career in Hollywood. Instead he made *Up on the Roof* (1997), based on his semi-musical co-written with Jane Prowse. The first act, with a group of ill-matched students (one dressed as a Womble) regaling a late-1970s' university campus with a cappella versions of 10cc and Queen songs, is gruesomely embarrassing. Fortunately when we meet them again in 1986 and 1994 the five students have grown into interesting characters with troubled lives, though the soothing balm of the human voice singing in harmony still seems more for their benefit than for ours. Moore reached a much wider public as the writer of *The 10th Kingdom* (2000), a ten-hour fantasy serial mingling fairy-tale characters with contemporary New Yorkers, funded by BSkyB and the American NBC television network.

(Robert Murphy)

BIBLIOGRAPHY: 'Simon Moore Interview: The 10th Kingdom', *TV Zone* no. 125, Apr. 2000, pp. 50–4.

FILMOGRAPHY: *Coasters* (short, 1980); *Sleepwalking* (short, 1980); *Under Suspicion* (1991); *Up on the Roof* (1997).

MORAHAN, Christopher (1929–)

Christopher Morahan was born in London on 9 July 1929. His father, art director Tom Morahan, worked on early Alfred Hitchcock and Ealing films. After acting and directing in the theatre, he turned to television and directed episodes of *Emergency – Ward Ten* and *Z Cars*. In the 1960s he handled more prestigious projects such as the ground-breaking four-part drama *Talking to a Stranger* (1966), by John Hopkins, and adaptations of George Orwell's *Nineteen Eighty-Four* (1965) and Robert Tressell's *The Ragged Trousered Philanthropists* (1967). Later he was to co-direct (with Jim O'Brien) Granada's prestigious adaptation of Paul Scott's novels about the last days of the British Raj in India, *The Jewel in the Crown* (1984).

Morahan made his feature film debut in 1968 with *Diamonds for Breakfast*, a frothy comedy-thriller starring Marcello Mastroianni. He followed it with *All Neat in Black Stockings*, a 'Swinging London' piece about the rewards and dangers of sexual permissiveness that transcended the usual limitations of the genre with witty dialogue, unfussy direction and lively performances from Susan George, Victor Henry and Jack Shepherd. Throughout the 1970s Morahan confined his activities to television and the theatre, finally making a third feature film in 1985, the John Cleese comedy *Clockwise*. It was modestly successful but it was another five years before Morahan made another, the solidly effective thriller *Paper Mask*, in which a hospital porter (Paul McGann) passes himself off as a doctor.

Morahan's career has primarily been in theatre and television – he served four years at the National Theatre and four years as Head of Plays at the BBC. His feature films, though always competent and enjoyable, make up a relatively minor part of his work.

(Janet Moat)

BIBLIOGRAPHY: Dix, Carol, 'Christopher Morahan', *Guardian*, 8 Mar. 1972; Fiddick, Peter, 'Christopher Morahan', *Guardian*, 12 Apr. 1976; Morley, Sheridan, 'Stage to Studio and Back', *The Times*, 18 July 1984, p. 7.

FILMOGRAPHY: *Diamonds for Breakfast* (1968); *All Neat in Black Stockings* (1969); *Clockwise* (1985); *Paper Mask* (1990).

MORE O' FERRALL, George (1907–1982)

George More O' Ferrall was born in Bristol on 4 July 1907. He studied directing at the Central School of Speech and Drama in London and began his career in television, producing and directing drama for the BBC from 1936. After war service he worked in a similar capacity until 1950.

More O'Ferrall made his feature film debut in 1952 with *The Holly and the Ivy*, an engaging Christmas comedy set in a vicarage, starring Ralph Richardson and Celia Johnson. He followed it with *Angels One Five*, with John Gregson as a pompous young pilot who is gradually assimilated into a squadron of battle-hardened flyers. This proved to be one of the most interesting and commercially successful of 1950s' war films, notable for its fine performances and aura of authenticity. *The Heart of the Matter*, from Graham Greene's novel about a Catholic Deputy Commissioner in Sierra Leone, torn between husbandly duty and unexpected passion, was equally intelligent; Greene praised it as 'one of the better films made out of my books' (Knight, p. 82). But it was not a commercial success and the ending imposed by the censor, making Scobie's death murder rather than suicide, was widely criticised.

More O'Ferrall's remaining films before returning to television in 1957 included 'Lord Mountdrago' (with Orson Welles), one of the *Three Cases of Murder* he shared with David Eady and Wendy Toye; *The Green Scarf*, a thrilling courtroom drama with a deaf mute as the accused; *The Woman for Joe*, which had a well-designed fairground setting; and *The March Hare*, a piece of Irish whimsy filmed in CinemaScope. He retired to Spain in the 1970s, where he died on 18 March 1982.

(Margaret Butler)

BIBLIOGRAPHY: Knight, Vivienne, *Trevor Howard: A Gentleman and a Player* (London: Sphere Books, 1988).

FILMOGRAPHY: *The Holly and the Ivy*; *Angels One Five* (1952); *The Heart of the Matter* (1953); *The Green Scarf*; *Three Cases of Murder* (co-dirs. David Eady/Wendy Toye) (1954); *The Woman for Joe* (1955); *The March Hare* (1956).

MORGAN, Sidney (1874–1946)

Sidney Morgan was born in Bermondsey, south London, on 2 August 1874. He entered the film business by winning a scenario competition and worked for a string of short-lived companies, including Theatre and General, P & M Films, Kearton Films and Renaissance Films. In 1917 he was among the first members of the industry to propose the idea of a quota system, suggesting cinemas should be made to show a percentage of British films.

After the war, Morgan set to work in a small film studio in Shoreham, West Sussex, which had been founded in 1913 by the comedian Will Evans, and had the distinction of being the only remaining studio in Britain to rely entirely on sunlight. His films were low budget and often featured his young daughter, Joan Morgan. Given the necessity of daylight, most of them were made between April and September, with Morgan editing the films himself in a small cutting room attached to the studios, screening rushes in the local cinema. The studio burned down in 1922.

Morgan adapted his own scenarios, basing the majority on classic novels such as Dickens' *Little Dorrit*, an impressive version of which he shot on location in London; Thomas Hardy's *The Mayor of Casterbridge*; and his most famous surviving film, *A Lowland Cinderella*, from the novel by S. R. Crockett. Morgan was a good director but a poor businessman, often agreeing to waive a fee to get a film made, relying on its success to make his fortune. British films suffered from the competition of bigger-budgeted Hollywood films in the 1920s, and Morgan was keenly aware of the consequences of this for himself and the industry. As Secretary of the British Association of Film Directors, he lobbied for his resurrected plan for a film quota, and succeeded in making it a key aspect of the Cinematograph Act of 1927. Ironically, Morgan ended his career making 'quota quickies', many of them written by his daughter, for American companies wanting to fulfil their legal obligations under the Act as cheaply as possible. He died on 11 June 1946 in Boscombe, Hampshire.

(Simon Brown)

BIBLIOGRAPHY: Low, Rachael, *The History of the British Film 1918–1929* (London: George Allen & Unwin, 1971); Low, Rachael, *Film Making in 1930s Britain* (London: George Allen & Unwin, 1985).

FILMOGRAPHY: *The Brass Bottle*; *The Great Spy Raid*; *Huns of the North Sea*; *Dr Paxton's Last Crime* (1914); *Our Boys*; *The World's Desire*; *Iron Justice*; *Esther Redeemed*; *Light* (1915); *Temptation's Hour*; *The Charlatan*; *The Stolen Sacrifice* (1916); *Auld Lang Syne*; *Derelicts*; *A Bid for Fortune* (1917); *Drink*; *Because*; *Democracy* (1918); *After Many Days*; *All Men Are Liars*; *Sweet and Twenty* (1919); *Lady Noggs – Peeress*; *The Black Sheep*; *The Scarlet Wooing*; *Little Dorrit*; *The Woman of the Iron Bracelets*; *Two Little Wooden Shoes*; *The Children of Gibeon*; *By Berwen Banks*; *A Man's Shadow* (1920); *Moth and Rust*; *The Mayor of Casterbridge*; *A Lowland Cinderella* (1921); *The Lilac Sunbonnet*; *Fires of Innocence* (1922); *The Woman Who Obeyed* (1923); *Miriam Rozella*; *The Shadow of Egypt* (1924); *Bulldog Drummond's Third Round* (1925); *A Window in Piccadilly*; *Thoroughbred* (1928); *Contraband Love*; *Her Reputation* (1931); *Mixed Doubles*; *Chelsea Life* (1933); *Faces* (1934); *The Minstrel Boy* (1937).

MORRISON, Paul (1944–)

Paul Morrison was born in London on 6 December 1944. Over a distinguished career in documentary films, and in his first two feature films, he has demonstrated a continuing concern with those marginalised by society.

Morrison began his career making socially committed documentaries for the arts collective Inter-Action. *Like Other People* (1972), a film about sexuality and disability, won the Grierson Award and for the next twenty-five years he pursued a successful career in television, making documentaries such as *From Bitter Earth – Artists of the Holocaust* (1988) for the BBC's arts programme *Omnibus*, and *Degas and Pissarro Fall Out* (1994) for Channel 4's *Without Walls*. He had worked as assistant director on Ken Loach's *Looks and Smiles* (1981) and Jan Worth's *Doll's Eye* (1982), and after making three satirical shorts for Channel 4 as part of their series *The Night Show* (1993–4), Morrison made his feature film debut, *Solomon and Gaenor*, with backing from Channel 4 and S4C. Set in the early years of the twentieth century, it centres upon the forbidden love affair between a Jewish man and the daughter of a working-class Christian family in the South Wales valleys. The film was critically well received and demonstrates Morrison's empathy with those ostracised by their own community, as well as his sensitivity with actors and strong eye for landscape.

Wondrous Oblivion, an enjoyable tale of a cricket-mad boy's friendship with his Jamaican neighbours in 1960s' Britain, reinforced Morrison's reputation as a sensitive director, capable of handling a story well and inspiring good performances from his actors, but it proved too low key to attract the multiplex audience.

(Robert Shail)

BIBLIOGRAPHY: Forde, Leon, 'Close up on Paul Morrison', *Screen International*, 31 Jan. 2003, p. 26.

FILMOGRAPHY: *Solomon and Gaenor* (1999); *Wondrous Oblivion* (2003).

MOTTERSHAW, Frank (1850–1932)

Frank Mottershaw was the founder and manager of the Sheffield Photo Company (SPC), one of the most influential of the early British film production companies. The SPC – an inventively run family business, best known locally as a photographic dealer and developer – was involved in the film industry occurred mainly from the years 1903 to 1909, when under the guidance of Mottershaw's son, Frank Storm (1882–1930), the company was responsible for producing a series of celebrated story films.

Frank Mottershaw was born in Sheffield in 1850, and left school at fourteen to work for the Sheffield Coal Company. He set up in the coal business for himself in the early 1880s, but soon afterwards his interest in photography led him to open a portrait studio; after abandoning the coal business altogether, he opened a dealership in photographic equipment. From 1889 to 1896 he operated a dealership, studio and photographic development service from larger premises in Sheffield's principal shopping district, and employed his three eldest children, Frank Storm, John Arthur and Edith Marion, when they left school.

The two elder brothers became interested in the moving picture craze well before the celebrated story-film productions of the SPC, soon buying a camera and projector, and cultivating the local market with films of football matches and topical events. They shot these local films in front of large crowds, then rapidly developed them for exhibition the same evening; audiences would often visit an entertainment in order to see events they had attended, with their friends and relatives represented on screen.

In 1904 the SPC acquired sole rights to photograph Edward VII's visit to Sheffield and Manchester, using at least three moving picture cameras. These films were rapidly processed and delivered to local music halls, and then presented to the Royal party under the expert guidance of the famous early film showman A. D. Thomas. In the same year, Frank Storm filmed the coronation of King Peter of Serbia, producing several films thought to be the first taken in that country.

John Arthur proved an adept showman and was the driving force behind the earliest SPC exhibitions. By 1904 the SPC offered its own programme of films for local social events. For a little over £2, a programme of ninety minutes, comprising short comedies, locals and actualities, was available for rent. For a little more, the services of a ventriloquist, a Punch and Judy man, or a choirboy (to accompany illustrated songs) could also be obtained. After John Arthur's death in 1905, Frank Storm continued presenting occasional film shows, often including many of his own productions.

After 1902, Frank Storm assumed primary responsibility for film production at the SPC. Following a year's apprenticeship in London with film pioneer Robert W. Paul, he returned to new premises in Hanover Street, Sheffield, equipped with an open-air stage, alongside rooms for developing and printing cinematograph films. Here, and in a variety of exterior locations in the Sheffield area, he produced the multi-shot story films for which the SPC is best remembered. In his first, *A Daring Daylight Burglary* (1903), a burglar escapes from the police by jumping aboard a train, but with the aid of a telegraph message is arrested at the next station. Reputedly, Charles Urban of the Warwick Trading Company bought the film for £50 – an unprecedented sum for Frank Storm that was gratefully, if rather naively, accepted. Urban sold the picture to Edison in America, where it was released under the title *Daylight Robbery*, and became a major influence on *The Great Train Robbery* (Edwin S. Porter, 1903), a seminal early film in the history of narrative filmmaking.

The crime and punishment scenario of *A Daring Daylight Burglary* proved so popular that Frank Storm repeated it in two more chase films of 1903: *Robbery of the Mail Coach* and *The Convict's Escape from Prison*. Most famously, Mottershaw's twelve-scene 1905 production, *The Life of Charles Peace the Notorious Burglar*, depicted a series of significant events in the Sheffield criminal's career and capture. Catalogue descriptions took some pains to emphasise that filming had taken place at authentic locations, though the execution itself was deemed 'too ghastly and repulsive' to warrant reproduction.

The SPC catalogue included an unusually large proportion of relatively long multi-shot films, including many comedies and chase films that were distributed, according to Frank Storm, as far afield as Paris, New York and South Africa. However, as

American narrative film-making grew in scale and ambition, the levels of investment required for the SPC to remain in the international marketplace became untenable. The production of story films soon ceased, though the SPC continued to produce actualities into the 1920s. Although these films were seldom marketed nationally, from 1902 until at least 1926 the SPC's popular annual films of the St Leger horse race at Doncaster were exhibited on the same night as the event at music halls across the country.

In the mid-1920s, as a private limited company now called Sheffield Photo-Finishers, the Mottershaws also began to specialise in industrial film-making. Following Frank Storm's death in 1930, and that of his father in 1932, other members of the family inherited the long-standing contacts with local industry. Alongside their photographic processing businesses, the Mottershaw group was still producing successful commercial films for local firms as late as the 1960s. The company, still managed by the Mottershaw family, finally collapsed – alongside Sheffield's heavy industries – in the 1980s.

(Joe Kember)

BIBLIOGRAPHY: Clay, Andrew, 'True Crime? Charles Peace and the British Crime Film, 1895–1905', in Linda Fitzsimons and Sarah Street (eds), *Moving Performance: British Stage and Screen, 1890s–1920s* (Trowbridge, Wilts: Flicks Books, 2000), pp. 123–36; Sutherland, Allan T., 'The Yorkshire Pioneers', *Sight and Sound*, Winter 1976/77, pp. 48–51.

SELECTED FILMOGRAPHY: *A Daring Daylight Burglary* (US: *Daylight Robbery*); *Robbery of the Mail Coach* (US: *Jack Sheppard*); *The Convict's Escape from Prison* (1903); *A Dash with the Dispatches*; *Attack on a Japanese Convoy*; *The Tramp's Duck Hunt*; *Boys Will Be Boys*; *The Market Woman's Mishap*; *A Cycle Teacher's Experiences*; *The Coiners*; *The Bobby's Downfall*; *Late for Work*; *Fly Catchers*; *A Trip to the Pyramids*; *Bertie's Courtship*; *The Tramps and the Washerwoman*; *A Picnic Disturbed*; *That Dreadful Donkey*; *A Soldier's Romance*; *The King's Visit to Sheffield*; *A Ride on the Kinver Light Railway* (1904); *An Eccentric Burglary*; *Two Young Scamps*; *Lazy Workmen*; *The Masher and the Nursemaid*; *When Father Laid the Carpet on the Stairs*; *A Fireman's Story*; *The Scarecrow*; *The Shoplifter*, *A Man Although a Thief*; *The Demon Motorist*; *Mixed Babies*; *The Life of Charles Peace the Notorious Burglar* (1905); *Lost in the Snow*; *Our Boyhood Days*; *The Lucky Horseshoe*; *The Eccentric Thief*; *His First Silk Hat*; *Our Seaside Holiday*; *That Terrible Dog*; *The Impossible Lovers*; *After the Club*; *The Troubles of the Twins* (1906); *Sold Again*; *Johnny's Rim*; *The Romany's Revenge*; *Willie's Dream*; *His Cheap Watch*; *The Blackmailer*, *My Word If You're Not Off*; *The Dodgers Dodged*; *Oh That Limerick!* (aka *The Limerick Craze*) (1907); *Banana Skins*; *That Nasty Sticky Stuff*; *Father's First Baby*; *When Boys Are Forbidden to Smoke*; *The Fighting Curate* (aka *The Little Flower Girl*); *The Stolen Duck*; *The Artful Tramps*; *An Indian's Romance*; *What Willie Did* (1908); *The Mad Musicians* (1909).

MOWBRAY, Malcolm (1949–)

Malcolm Mowbray was born in Knebworth, Hertfordshire, in 1949. He made films while at Ravensbourne Art College and was among the first intake of students at the National Film School in 1972. He worked with the writer Barry Keefe on a television film for the BBC, *Hanging Around* (1978), and wrote and directed *Days at the Beach* (1981). A collaboration with Alan Bennett on a television play, *Our Winnie* (1982), led to Mowbray's feature debut, *A Private Function*, which Bennett scripted from Mowbray's research into the austerity ridden period after the Second World War. Set in 1947, the film centres upon the comic exploits of a small-town community rearing a black-market pig intended to be slaughtered in celebration of Princess Elizabeth's wedding. In typical Bennett fashion, the film is a mixture of sharp observation, particularly of class snobberies and social climbing, combined with broad physical humour. With its popular cast (Michael Palin, Maggie Smith) and nostalgic setting, the film was a success and took Mowbray to Hollywood.

Unfortunately neither of his American films – *Out Cold* (1989), a dark comedy-thriller, and *Don't Tell Her It's Me*, a romantic farce – impressed critics or audiences. He returned to Britain to work on television assignments such as *Crocodile Shoes* (1994), a comedy-drama serial with Jimmy Nail as an aspiring singer/songwriter, the medieval monk detective series *Cadfael* (1994); and *Monsignor Renard* (1999), a Second World War drama serial starring John Thaw. His second British feature film, backed by BBC Films and money from the National Lottery Fund, was *The Revengers' Comedies*, a potentially comic riposte to Hitchcock's *Strangers on a Train* (1951), adapted from two plays by Alan Ayckbourn about an upper-class woman (Helena Bonham Carter) and a failed businessman (Sam Neill) who frustrate each others' suicide attempts and team up to plot revenge on those who have made their lives a misery. The strong cast and witty dialogue make the film enjoyable, though it never quite transcends its theatrical origins.

(Robert Shail)

BIBLIOGRAPHY: Bilbow, Marjorie, 'Illicit Pig-Raising to the Fore in "Private Function"', *Screen International*, 24 Nov. 1984, pp. 9, 26; Flaherty, Richard, 'Directorial Debut . . . Make or Break', *Films*, Oct. 1984, pp. 8–11.

FILMOGRAPHY: *Path of the Weft* (doc. short, 1970); *Beach of Information* (short, 1971); *Trombone* (short, 1974); *Capital City – A Portrait of London* (doc. short, 1980); *A Private Function* (1984); *Out Cold* (US, 1989); *Don't Tell Her It's Me* (aka *The Boyfriend School*, US, 1990); *The Revengers' Comedies* (US: *Sweet Revenge*, UK/Fr, 1998).

MOXEY, John (1920–)

John Llewellyn Moxey was born in Burlingham, Norfolk, in 1920. After being wounded in the Second World War, he entered the film industry in the cutting rooms of Walton-on-Thames studios in 1945. Ambitious to direct, Moxey worked as an actor and assistant director before moving into television to direct drama. His army training film *They Escaped* attracted the attention of producer Donald Taylor and he was asked to direct a wartime espionage drama, *Foxhole in Cairo*. A routine plot is enlivened by unexpected casting – including Michael Caine as a German wireless operator and Fenella Fielding as a Jewish secret agent – but the film is visually undistinguished. *The City of the Dead*, a black-and-white horror film made on an elaborate set at Shepperton, allowed Moxey more creative leeway. His imaginative camera angles and expressive use of shadows and fog have more in common with the Italian horror films of Mario Bava than with contemporary Hammer films.

The City of the Dead has subsequently become a cult classic, but at the time critics were more likely to comment on the incongruous presence of popular British crooner Denis Lotis in a tale about American witchcraft. Moxey was subsequently relegated to minor-league work, alternating Merton Park supporting features with episodes of television series including *The Avengers* (1961-6), *The Saint* (1962–7) and *The Baron* (1965–6). His contributions to Anglo-Amalgamated's Edgar Wallace series – *Death Trap*, *Ricochet*, *The £20,000 Kiss*, *Face of a Stranger*, *Downfall* and *Strangler's Web* – are exemplary B-films: taut, atmospheric and economical. *Circus of Fear*, by contrast, from the German cycle of Wallace films, is disappointingly flaccid, despite the presence of both Klaus Kinski and Christopher Lee in the cast (a German version was directed on the same sets by Werner Jacobs).

In 1967 Moxey directed an Anglo-American television film, *Dial M for Murder*, and was invited to work in the United States by producer David Susskind. He fell out with Lee Bouvier (Jacqueline Kennedy's sister), his star for a television remake of *Laura* (1968), and removed his name from the film, but went on to become a successful and prolific director on American television series ranging from *Mission: Impossible* to *Murder, She Wrote*. He has also made over forty television movies, the best of which is *The Night Stalker* (1972), a modern-day vampire story that attracted record-breaking audience figures and was an acknowledged influence on the cult series *The X Files*. On his American films he is credited as John Llewellyn Moxey.

(Peter Hutchings)

BIBLIOGRAPHY: 'Films on TV', *Films in Review*, May 1971, pp. 299–303; Lindsay, Michael, 'Interview with John Moxey', *Cinema* [US] vol. 4 no. 4, Dec. 1968, pp. 8–10; Weaver, Tom, 'Fright Stalker', *Fangoria* no. 16, Oct. 1997, pp. 68–73, 82.

FILMOGRAPHY: *They Escaped* (short, 1958); *Foxhole in Cairo*; *The City of the Dead* (US: *Horror Hotel*) (1960); *Death Trap* (1962); *Ricochet*; *The £20,000 Kiss*; *Downfall* (1963); *Face of a Stranger* (1964); *Strangler's Web* (1965); *Circus of Fear* (US: *Psycho-Circus*, UK/Ger, 1966).

MULCAHY, Russell (1953–)

Russell Mulcahy was born in Melbourne on 23 June 1953. After experience in Australian television, two prize-winning shorts and several pop music video promos, he came to the UK in 1979, making his debut with Peter Cook and Dudley Moore's scurrilously vitriolic *Derek and Clive Get the Horn*, but building his reputation on video promos for the likes of Ultravox and Duran Duran. He returned to Australia for *Razorback* (1984), a ferociously thrilling horror film where the giant wild boar on the loose is less scary than the mad kangaroo-killing locals. Mulcahy's big break came with *Highlander*, an Anglo-American fantasy starring Christopher Lambert as a sixteenth-century Scottish swordsman doomed to continue fighting across the centuries. It spawned several sequels, but after *Highlander II: The Quickening* (1999), Mulcahy turned his attention to other superheroes (*The Shadow*, 1994), supernatural entities (*Talos the Mummy*, 1998) and the more prosaically heroic Australian swimmer Tony Fingleton (*Swimming Upstream*, 2003).

Too much of a maverick to fit happily within the Hollywood studio system (he was sacked as director of *Rambo III* for daring to suggest that Sylvester Stallone might broaden his range and vary the formula), Mulcahy has maintained his interesting profile with low-budget thrillers such as *Blue Ice*, a downbeat spy film with Michael Caine mockingly reprising his persona from the Harry Palmer films of the 1960s; and *Silent Trigger*, improbably pairing Swedish action man Dolph Lundgren with Gina Bellman, star of Dennis Potter's *Black Eyes* (1989). He has also ventured into television drama, directing several episodes of *Queer as Folk* (2000), Channel 4's controversial series built around the Manchester gay scene.

(Robert Murphy)

BIBLIOGRAPHY: Davies, Nina, 'Highland Hurdy Gurdy', *City Limits* no. 256, 28 Aug. 1986, pp. 16–17; Jones, Alan, 'Highlander: Starbust Interview', *StarBurst* no. 96, Aug. 1986, pp. 26–9, and no. 97, Sept. 1986, pp. 34–7; Jones, Alan, 'Coming Soon, Highlander 2', *StarBurst* no. 127, Mar. 1989, pp. 20–1; McGillivray, David, 'Now You Know: Russell Mulcahy', *Films and Filming*, Jan. 1990, p. 25.

FILMOGRAPHY (UK only): *Derek and Clive Get the Horn* (1979); *Highlander* (UK/US, 1986); *Blue Ice* (UK/US, 1992); *The Real McCoy* (US, 1993); *Silent Trigger/Franc-tireur en péril* (UK/Can, 1996).

MULLAN, Peter (1959–)

Glasgow-born Peter Mullan started his career in the theatre before establishing a distinctive profile as a film actor. He appeared in a variety of films including the international blockbuster *Braveheart* (Mel Gibson, 1995) and the youth-orientated *Trainspotting* (Danny Boyle, 1996); he won the Best Actor prize at Cannes for his role in Ken Loach's *My Name Is Joe* (1998), and played the central character in *The Claim* (Michael Winterbottom, 2000). He made his first short film in 1994, directed episodes of the television series *Cardiac Arrest* in 1996 and made his first feature, *Orphans*, in 1997. A Glaswegian black comedy with little of the fashionable appeal of *Trainspotting*, *Orphans* unsurprisingly encountered distribution difficulties, yet the story of four young adults coming to terms with the death of their mother is funny and original, and Mullan's direction lively and inventive.

His second feature, *The Magdalene Sisters*, was more restrained and realist, as befits its subject – an examination of the repressive and cruel Magdalene homes for 'fallen' young women in

1960s' Ireland. Mullan brings a Loachian passion to his presentation of the plight of these women, and audiences and critics responded positively. Despite Catholic complaints of the unfairness of Mullan's polemic, *The Magdalene Sisters* won the Golden Lion at Venice in 2002, consolidating Mullan's reputation as an idiosyncratic and talented new director.

(Tom Ryall)

BIBLIOGRAPHY: James, Nick, 'Keeping It Clean', *Sight and Sound*, Mar. 2003, pp. 16–17; Petrie, Duncan, *Screening Scotland* (London: BFI, 2000); Petrie, Duncan, 'Devolving British Cinema. The New Scottish Cinema and the European Art Film', *Cinéaste*, Autumn, 2001, pp. 55–7.

FILMOGRAPHY: *Close* (short, 1994); *Good Day for the Bad Guys* (short, 1995); *Fridge* (short, 1996); *Orphans* (1997); *The Magdalene Sisters* (2002).

MULLOY, Phil (1948–)

Phil Mulloy was born in Wallasey, Cheshire, in 1948. He studied painting at Ravensbourne College before going to the Royal College of Art in the late 1960s. He started working in live-action film-making but has since become more famous for his animated work.

Mulloy's early films exhibit an overt concern for theory and political engagement. John Wyver described his first film, *A History and the City* (1977), as 'theory on celluloid, concerned with memory, politics and, obliquely, Northern Ireland'. *In the Forest* (1978) is an experimental foray into British history, using a troupe of travelling players to tell stories that shed a different light on the past. *Mark Gertler – Fragments of a Biography* (1981) and *Give Us This Day* (1982), a biographical account of the life of Robert Tressell interspersed with extracts from his novel *The Ragged Trousered Philanthropists*, take as their subject two artists who have been largely ignored in orthodox histories.

Since 1988, Mulloy has concentrated on making animated films and is now celebrated as one of Britain's foremost purveyors of scabrous animated satire. His trademark roughly drawn, cut-out figures, often speaking in grunts, groans and shrieks, make a Mulloy film instantly recognisable. The main recurring themes of his films are mendacity and hypocrisy, the way that social institutions have a stunting effect on human expression, and the debilitating constraints of masculinity. His *Cowboys* sextet (1991), for instance, shows a world peopled by ludicrously macho males: *'That's Nothin"* has them boasting about sexual exploits in a frenzy of one-upmanship that concludes with a predictably Mulloy-esque violent mêlée. *The Discovery of Language* (1994), part of his ongoing *The History of the World* series, features a parallel narrative of men and women discovering stone letters buried in the ground. As soon as the women have the letters V – A – G – I – N – A, they become self-conscious of their genitals: mayhem ensues. Meanwhile, the men have P – E – N – I spelled out, but the man carrying the letter S trips and it shatters on the ground, leaving the men blissfully ignorant of their sexuality's potential destructiveness.

Mulloy's work is characterised by a surreal, yet politically informed, sense of the world around him. While his films are grotesque and distorted, they say more about human relations and the institutions that inform them than any number of more apparently realistic films. His three *Intolerance* films (2000, 2001 and 2004) explore with brilliant simplicity the ways in which different cultures can become hostile towards one another. A documentary showing the lifestyle of the Zogs, alien life-forms that resemble humans in every way except that their heads and genitalia are transposed, so outrages the inhabitants of Earth that they launch into space to annihilate the Zogs. Meanwhile, the Zogs, equally outraged, have set off to destroy Earth. It is Mulloy's use of a very simple conceit (inversion) that shows apparently innocent things like kissing and shaking hands to be cultural constructs; as ever, his scathing satire is the vehicle for an underlying humanity.

(Paul Ward)

BIBLIOGRAPHY: <www.philmulloy.com/filmog.html>; Wells, Paul, 'The Films of Phil Mulloy', BFI online essay <www.bfi.org.uk/videocat/more/philmulloy/article.html>; Wyver, John, 'An Unknown Land', *The Listener*, 17 May 1984, p. 34.

FILMOGRAPHY: *A History and the City* (1977); *In the Forest* (1978); *Mark Gertler – Fragments of a Biography* (1981); *Give Us This Day* (1982); *Through an Unknown Land* (1983); *The Return* (1988); *Eye of the Storm* (1989); *Tinfish*; *Possession* (1990); *Cowboys* (*Slim Pickin's*, *'That's Nothin"*, *Murder!*, *The Conformist*, *High Noon*, *Outrage!*) (1991); *Ding Dong Bell* (1992); *The Sound of Music*; *Laughing Moon Films* (1993); *The History of the World* (*The Invention of Writing*, *The Discovery of Language*); *Laughing Moon 2* (1994); *The Ten Commandments* (1994–6); *Great Moments in Film* (1995); *The Wind of Changes* (1996); *The Chain*; *I Still Love You* (1997); *The Sexlife of a Chair* (1998); *Season's Greetings* (1999); *Intolerance* (2000); *Flik Flak* (co-dir. Paul Bush); *Intolerance II: The Invasion*; *The Henries*; *The Two Magicians* (2001); *Love Is Strange* (2002); *Intolerance III: The Final Solution* (2004).

MULVEY, Laura (1941–)

Laura Mulvey was born in Oxford on 15 August 1941. After studying history at St Hilda's College, Oxford, she came to prominence in the early 1970s as a film theorist, writing for periodicals such as *Spare Rib* and *Seven Days*. Much of her early critical work investigated questions of spectator identification and its relationship to the male gaze, and her writings, particularly the 1975 essay 'Visual Pleasure and Narrative Cinema', helped establish feminist film theory as a legitimate field of study.

Between 1974 and 1982 Mulvey co-wrote and co-directed six projects with her husband Peter Wollen: theoretical films, dealing in the discourse of feminist theory, semiotics, psychoanalysis and leftist politics. The first of these, *Penthesilea: Queen of the Amazons* (1974), explored concerns central to Mulvey's writings: the position of women in relation to patriarchal myth, symbolic language and male fantasy. *Penthesilea* represents an experimental British venture into territory pioneered by the likes of Jean-Luc Godard. With its counter-cinema style and relentlessly didactic approach, however, its appeal was inevitably limited to a restricted audience.

Riddles of the Sphinx (1977), the most influential of Mulvey and Wollen's collaborative ventures, presented avant-garde film as a space in which female experience could be expressed. Formal innovation, notably 360-degree pans, informs the film's content, describing the mother's loss of and search for identity. The result is a challenging, forceful and intelligent film.

Amy! (1980), a tribute to the aviator Amy Johnson, is a more accessible reworking of themes previously covered by Mulvey and Wollen, but it is too ponderous. Johnson is used as a symbolic figure, her journey exemplifying the transitions between female and male worlds required by women struggling towards achievement in the public sphere.

Crystal Gazing (1982) represented a departure from the emphatic formalism of Mulvey and Wollen's earlier films. It demonstrated more spontaneity than previous works, both in performances and in the storyline, elements of which were left undecided until the moment of filming. Bleak, but with playful touches, this representation of London during the Thatcher recession was generally well received, despite criticism of Mulvey for the lack of a feminist underpinning to the film. She admitted she had been reluctant to incorporate feminist polemics, fearing they would unbalance the film.

Frida Kahlo & Tina Modotti (1982) and *The Bad Sister* (1982) followed, revisiting feminist film issues. After these, Mulvey did not return to film-making until 1991 when she began production on *Disgraced Monuments*, an examination of the fate of revolutionary monuments in the Soviet Union after the fall of Communism.

Laura Mulvey is Professor of Film and Media Studies at Birkbeck College, University of London.

(Eleanor Burke)

BIBLIOGRAPHY: Danino, Nina and Lucy Moy-Thomas, 'Interview with Laura Mulvey', *Undercut* no. 6, 1982/3, pp. 11–16; Mulvey, Laura and Peter Wollen, 'Written Discussion', *Afterimage*, July 1976, pp. 31–9; Silverman, Kaja, *The Acoustic Mirror: The Female Voice in Psychoanalysis and Cinema* (Bloomington, IN: Indiana University Press, 1988).

FILMOGRAPHY: *Penthesilea: Queen of the Amazons* (co-dir. Peter Wollen, 1974); *Riddles of the Sphinx* (co-dir. Peter Wollen, 1977); *Amy!* (short, co-dir. Peter Wollen, 1980); *Crystal Gazing* (co-dir. Peter Wollen); *Frida Kahlo & Tina Modotti* (short, co-dir. Peter Wollen); *The Bad Sister* (co-dir. Peter Wollen) (1982); *Disgraced Monuments* (co-dir. Mark Lewis, 1994).

MUNDEN, Marc (1959–)

Marc Munden was born in London on 26 July 1959, the son of director Max Munden. He studied philosophy and maths at London University, and after a variety of jobs worked as a runner on Michael Winner's remake of *The Wicked Lady* (1983), subsequently graduating to assistant director on Terence Davies' *Distant Voices Still Lives* (1988), Mike Leigh's *High Hopes* (1988) and Derek Jarman's *War Requiem* (1989), and production manager on Karl Francis' *Angry Earth* (1989). Over a two-year period he worked with future cinematographer John Mathieson on *Beverly Hills Is Bournemouth with Sunshine* (1989), a thirty-eight minute-documentary about Munden's brother-in-law's uncle, a poker-player in the casinos of Bournemouth. BBC executives were impressed with the film's juxtaposition of the mundane and the surreal and Munden began a career in television. He directed *Bermondsey Boy* (1991), about a south London debt collector, and several more acclaimed documentaries before moving into drama, directing episodes of the crime series *Touching Evil* (1997) and establishing his reputation with Andrew Davies' stylish adaptation of *Vanity Fair* (1998).

FilmFour backed Munden's feature *Miranda* (2002), a noirish thriller that slowly settles into comedy as John Simm's Scarborough librarian wins the love and trust of Christina Ricci's tough American conwoman, along the way transforming her from enigmatic femme fatale to lovably girlish doll. With a sharper script, prepared to draw bolder parallels between the infatuated Simm and Kyle MacLachlan's dangerously perverted millionaire, also obsessed with the gawky Ricci, this could have been an intriguing film. Instead Munden opts for easy comedy and a smug happy ending celebrating the virtues of small-

town provincial life – something that particularly enraged metropolitan critics. Munden returned to television, redeeming himself with Tony Marchant's adaptation of 'The Knight's Tale' for the BBC's clever modernisation of Chaucer's *The Canterbury Tales* (2003), and episodes of the grim police drama serial *Conviction* (2004).

(Robert Murphy)

BIBLIOGRAPHY: Hunt, Nick, 'Case Study: *Miranda*', *Screen International*, 11 Jan. 2002, p. 26; Stringer, Robin, 'Lights, Hot Water Bottle, Action!', *Evening Standard*, 21 Mar. 2001, p. 9.

FILMOGRAPHY: *Beverly Hills Is Bournemouth with Sunshine* (doc. short, 1989); *Miranda* (UK/Ger, 2002).

MUNDEN, Maxwell (1912–1973)

Maxwell Munden was born in London on 5 November 1912. He worked as a journalist and short-story writer for most of the 1930s, taking up screenwriting at Merton Park Studios in 1937. During the war Sydney Box, whose Verity Films operated from Merton Park, employed him as scenario editor and encouraged him to produce, write and direct some of the company's prolific output of documentary and information films, among them *Shunter Black's Night Off* (1941), the excitingly atmospheric tale of an off-duty railway worker who shunts a burning explosives truck to where it can be doused with water. After 1944 Munden formed the Horizon Film Unit within the Film Producers' Guild, concentrating mostly on documentary and sponsored films such as *Song of the People* (1945), a survey of the influence of the common people on British history from the Peasant's Revolt to the General Strike, made for the Co-operative Wholesale Society. With Dennis Shand he established his own independent company, Film Workshop, in 1947.

During the 1950s Munden continued in non-fiction production, occasionally for television, for which he also made commercials; but at the end of the decade he ventured into the fiction market with two B-films. *The Bank Raiders* (1958), despite the presence of perennial favourites Sydney Tafler and Sandra Dorne, is a singularly unconvincing depiction of life in the English underworld. Munden was on much more solid ground with *The House in the Woods* (1959), a psychological thriller centred on a middle-class writer (Michael Gough) in a rural hideaway who gradually realises that his wife is in danger from the sinister landlord (Ronald Howard). Munden was more at home with these sorts of characters than with low-life criminals and he responds with sensitive, well-paced direction. Frustratingly, after this display of talent Munden returned to less exciting matters like *Fishing in Scotland*. He died of cancer after a two-year struggle on 5 June 1973; his son is the director Marc Munden.

(Robert Murphy)

FILMOGRAPHY: Selected shorts: *A-Tish-Oo*; *Shunter Black's Night Off* (1941); *Off Duty* (1943); *Song of the People*; *Post-War Road Safety*; *Resettlement Advice Service*; *How a Car Engine Works* (1945); *University of Flying*; *One Man's Story* (co-dir. Dennis Shand) (1948); *The Long Wait* (1960); *The Security Men* (1966); *Fishing in Scotland* (1970). Features: *The Bank Raiders* (1958); *The House in the Woods* (1959).

MURPHY, Pat (1951–)

Pat Murphy was born in Dublin on 31 December 1951 and attended art college in Belfast, London and New York during the 1970s, when avant-garde theory and practice dominated teaching. Since then she has retained an interest in feminist art and radical and politically engaged film-making. During a career that has included teaching, lecturing, curating and lobbying, Murphy has established herself as Ireland's leading feminist film-maker and her work continues to have a relevance in the more commercial climate of contemporary Ireland. Both her gallery-based installation work and her films are imbued with the formal and political concerns of the political avant-garde and her two films from the 1980s – *Maeve* and *Anne Devlin* – represent a high point for radical film-making in Ireland.

Murphy's first experimental short film, *Rituals of Memory* (1977), explores women's memories through a montage of photographs and postcards and readings from diaries. She establishes here a main theme for her film work – the secret or hidden life of women, so often ignored or downplayed in dominant male culture. Her first feature film, *Maeve* (co-directed with John Davies), explores these themes in the context of an embattled Republican community in Belfast. The film is concerned with the disregarded and disguised voice of women who have to fight to be heard in a world dominated by the radical but nonetheless male voice of Irish Republicanism. The film mixes an authentic naturalism (it was the first film for nearly fifty years to be shot on location in Belfast) with a complex narrative structure and a range of anti-narrative strategies that challenge this surface naturalism. *Maeve* is unusually complex and intellectually challenging, a visual exploration of its themes rather than a statement.

The 'counter-cinema' style of *Maeve* was a considerable challenge for audiences used to orthodox narrative cinema, and in her next film, *Anne Devlin*, Murphy adopted a more conventional style, although the film's use of long takes and a tableau style of cinematography was nonetheless adventurous. Again, Murphy's concern was with a woman 'hidden from history' – Anne Devlin, who played a small but significant role in Robert Emmet's failed rebellion against the British in 1803. The film was critically acclaimed both in Ireland and internationally, and its six-week run in a city-centre Dublin cinema seemed to demonstrate that politically radical films could connect with an indigenous audience.

During the 1990s, Murphy concentrated on curating and organising political and public art events and did not direct another feature film until *Nora* in 1999. By this time the prevailing film culture demanded easily accessible narratives with star appeal. Nevertheless, the film shares similarities with her other films in its exploration of a woman whose own radical sensibilities have been hidden behind the achievements of her male partner: in this case an exploration of Nora Barnacle's relationship to James Joyce. Since then, Murphy has directed a short film, *What Miro Saw*.

(Martin McLoone)

BIBLIOGRAPHY: Farley, Fidelma, *Anne Devlin* (Trowbridge, Wilts: Flicks Books, 2000); Gibbons, Luke, *Transformations in Irish Culture* (Cork: Cork University Press, 1996); McLoone, Martin, *Irish Film: The Emergence of a Contemporary Cinema* (London: BFI, 2000); Petley, Julian, 'State of the Union', *Monthly Film Bulletin*, Jan. 1986, p. 32; Pettitt, Lance, *Screening Ireland* (Manchester: Manchester University Press, 2000).

FILMOGRAPHY: *Rituals of Memory* (short, 1977); *Maeve* (co-dir. John Davies, 1981); *Anne Devlin* (Ir, 1984); *Nora* (Ir/UK/It/Ger, 1999); *What Miro Saw* (short, Ir, 2002).

MURPHY, Vinny (1961–)

Actor, writer, musician and director, Vincent Murphy was born in Dublin in 1961. Since 1982 he has been closely associated with the Jobstown Screen Acting Workshop for working-class people in Dublin. His first incursion into film-making was a short film, *Late*, produced in London in 1987. With the Jobstown Workshop he produced a trio of shorts, *Trouble*, *Hairspray* and *Football*, in the mid-1990s. In 1992 he produced an ambitious feature-length video adaptation of Shakespeare, *H Is for Hamlet*, whose modern setting and use of young working-class actors foreshadowed his debut feature, *Accelerator*.

Accelerator reworked the road-movie genre to explore joyriding, working-class youth culture and the divide between Northern and southern Ireland. The film centres on a pair of joyriding gangs, one from the North and one from the Republic, who settle a dispute by holding a car race from Belfast to Dublin. Like Larry Clark in *Kids* (1995) and *Bully* (2001), Murphy refrains from moral comment on the action and behaviour of his teenage protagonists and shows them as victims of a barren modern Ireland, peopled by dispossessed, insensitive adults. Not since Joe Comerford's *Traveller* (1981) has Irish youth been portrayed with such raw energy – or has Ireland been shown in such an unflattering light.

(Eugene Finn)

BIBLIOGRAPHY: Sheehy, Ted, 'Drive, He Said', *Film Ireland* no. 75, Apr./May 2000, pp. 16–17, 19.

FILMOGRAPHY: *Accelerator* (UK/Ir, 2000).

MUSK, Cecil

Edward Cecil Musk was born in London. He was educated at Dulwich College and began work at the Riverside Studios, Hammersmith, in 1933. In the mid-1930s he visited Hollywood (the origins perhaps of his nickname 'Cecil B. De Musk') but returned to direct and produce documentaries at Merton Park Studios. After the war he branched out briefly into fiction with two children's films for Rank. *Circus Boy* (1947), widely popular at the time, is a pleasant if insipid tale of a boy (James Kenney) who overcomes his crisis of confidence by immersing himself in the thrills and spills of the circus. *Trapped by the Terror* (1949), Rank's first children's film with a period setting (the French Revolution), promises more; but Merton Park's cramped stages were not built for spectacle, and Musk shows little ingenuity in getting round the restrictions of a tight budget and a hackneyed story.

After a decade of non-fiction production, Musk directed another feature, *Blow Your Own Trumpet* (1958), for the Children's Film Foundation. The story is simple: a working-class boy wants to join the local colliery's brass band but his richer rival hides his cornet. But Musk (helped by energetic performances from Peter Butterworth and a young Michael Crawford) conveys his material with no-nonsense efficiency and a tangible feeling for the atmosphere of a northern working-class town. He remained active as a producer of industrial and children's films into the 1970s.

(Robert Murphy)

FILMOGRAPHY: Selected shorts: *Time off My Hands*; *It's about Time* (1933); *The Man Who Made up His Mind* (1937); *Fulfilment* (1939); *Furnaces of Industry* (1940); *Queen Cotton* (1941); *We Were There* (1942); *Looking through Glass*; *Savings Cavalcade*; *Born in Britain*; *Twelve Days* (1943); *Tom Johnstone's Appeal* (1944); *Progress*; *Can We Be Rich?*; *Flying with Prudence* (1946); *Endurance: Fantasy of Le Mans* (1950); *All the World Over* (1952); *Public Service* (1953); *How to Sell Your Husband a Washing Machine* (1956); *A Taste of the Sun* (1960).

Features: *Circus Boy* (1947); *Trapped by the Terror* (1949); *Blow Your Own Trumpet* (1958).

MYCROFT, Walter (1890–1959)

Walter Charles Mycroft was born in Peckham, south London, in 1890, the son of a sporting journalist. Despite physical disability, he drove army lorries during the First World War, after which he became a sub-editor on the London *Evening Standard*, becoming their film critic in 1923. Mycroft was a key figure in the development of serious journalistic film criticism in Britain: he was involved in the Film Society and championed European art cinema during this period.

Mycroft entered production in January 1928 after an invitation from John Maxwell to become the Head of the scenario department at British International Pictures. Later he became Head of Production, a role he would retain until Maxwell's death in 1940. Ironically, Mycroft was to preside over the most ruthlessly commercial major studio in Britain. In the 1930s it was run along strict factory lines, with noticeably few prestige productions or opportunities to explore film-making as an art. His rigorous parsimony made Mycroft one of the most disliked men in British cinema, and he is the butt of numerous scurrilous industry stories revolving around his meanness, his incompetence, his extreme right-wing views and his spinal deformity.

After Maxwell's death in 1940 Mycroft turned briefly to directing, making three light comedies – *Spring Meeting*, *My Wife's*

Family and *Banana Ridge* – which are enjoyable for the performances of Margaret Rutherford, Leslie Fuller and Robertson Hare but show little of the directorial flair displayed by Anthony Asquith and Harold French on similar subjects. They made little box-office impact, and as ABPC turned to low-budget shockers, Mycroft found himself without a job. His post-war *Comin' thro' the Rye* was not a remake of the Cecil Hepworth favourite but a musical biography of Robbie Burns, with Terence Alexander, later best known for playing English toffs, as the Scottish poet.

During the 1950s Mycroft returned to ABPC under Robert Clarke, giving uncredited scenario advice on many films. However, he never managed to regain the powerful producing position he had held in the 1930s. He died in Hampstead, London, on 14 June 1959.

(Lawrence Napper)

BIBLIOGRAPHY: Baldwin, Oliver, 'These People Make British Pictures, No. 1: Walter Mycroft', *Picturegoer*, 17 June 1939, p. 10; Porter, Vincent, 'The Construction of an Anti-Hollywood Film Aesthetic: The Film Criticism of Walter Mycroft in the 1920s', in Alan Burton and Larraine Porter (eds), *Crossing the Pond: Anglo-American Film Relations before 1930* (Trowbridge, Wilts: Flicks Books, 2002).

FILMOGRAPHY: *Spring Meeting* (US: *Three Wise Brides*); *My Wife's Family*; *Banana Ridge* (1941); *Comin' thro the Rye* (1947).

MYLOD, Mark

Mark Mylod made his name directing comedy and comedy-drama (*The Fast Show*, *The Royle Family*, *Cold Feet*, *Shameless*). He enjoyed box-office success with his debut feature, *Ali G Indahouse*, a monument to adolescent bad taste built around Sacha Baron Cohen's outrageously silly television character. Mylod brings in a couple of heavyweight actors – Michael Gambon and Charles Dance – and sends Ali G to Parliament, but he wisely makes no attempt to raise the tone of irreverent vulgarity. It did good enough business to secure Mylod an American comedy, *The Big White*, starring Robin Williams.

(Robert Murphy)

FILMOGRAPHY: *Ali G Indahouse* (UK/Ger, 2002); *The Big White* (US, 2005).

NALLURI, Bharat (1965–)

Bharat Nalluri was born on 22 February 1965 in Guntur, India, but emigrated to England when he was six and was brought up in Newcastle. In 1993 he co-founded the production company Pilgrim Films to make Newcastle-based commercials, corporate videos and local television programmes, such as the short crime comedy *Driven* (1994). His first feature film, *Killing Time* (1995), a gangster film set in Newcastle, differentiated itself from *Get Carter* (Mike Hodges, 1971) by having a female Italian killer (Kendra Torgan) ruthlessly scything her way through the underworld. The film failed to attract a distributor and was only finally released on video in 1998, but Nik Powell and Steve Woolley of Scala Productions were sufficiently impressed with Nalluri's direction to offer backing for his next film, *Downtime*, a social-realist thriller set on a run-down Newcastle housing estate.

Ironically, though the film received financial support from the Arts Council of England and Channel 4, the Newcastle city authorities objected to the negative light it shone on the city and it was eventually shot in Liverpool with backing from the Merseyside Film Production Fund. The confusion of setting unfortunately spread to the poorly developed plot, which digresses from a cross-cultural romance between wimpish social worker Paul McGann and desperate working-class housewife Susan Lynch into clumsy suspense, when feral teenagers sabotage the lift in a high-rise housing block. Though *Downtime* was poorly received and patchily distributed, Nalluri was considered to have shown a potential talent for action-adventures and he was invited to Hollywood to direct a $25 million entry in the *Crow* cycle.

He returned to Britain to handle more modest assignments: 'Cyclops' (2001), an intriguing drama about the dangers of surveillance cameras for Channel 4's *Shockers* series, and episodes of the BBC's *Spooks* (2002), *Hustle* (2004) and *Life on Mars* (2006). But he was able to put his Hollywood action-film experience to good use as second-unit director on his school-friend Paul Anderson's *Resident Evil Genesis* (2002) and *AVP Alien vs. Predator* (2004).

(Robert Murphy)

BIBLIOGRAPHY: 'Band of Gold: Bharat Nalluri', *Creation*, Apr. 1998, p. 11.

FILMOGRAPHY: *Killing Time* (prod. 1995; rel. 1998); *Downtime* (UK/Fr, 1997); *The Crow: Salvation* (aka *The Crow 3*, US, 2000); *Resident Evil Genesis* (2nd unit dir., Ger/UK/Fr, Paul Anderson, 2002); *AVP Alien vs. Predator* (2nd unit dir., UK/US/Cz/Can/Ger, Paul Anderson, 2004).

NARIZZANO, Silvio (1924–)

Silvio Narizzano, who was born in Montreal on 8 February 1924, has had a long and varied career in film, television and theatre. After attending Bishop's University in Quebec, he began his career as an actor and director in the Canadian theatre. Moving into television in the late 1950s, he worked on single dramas and series in Canada, the USA and Britain.

Narizzano made his feature film debut as co-director of the American-Italian co-production *Under Ten Flags* (1960), a war adventure starring Van Heflin. His first British feature was *Fanatic*, one of a series of psychological thrillers made by Ham-

mer in an attempt to cash in on the commercial success of Alfred Hitchcock's *Psycho* (1960). He handles the *Grand Guignol* with efficiency and a touch of humour, giving full rein to the melodramatic potential of Tallulah Bankhead as the deranged mother-in-law. His next film, *Georgy Girl*, is his best known and most critically acclaimed. Although labelled as a 'Swinging London' film, its depiction of the sensible Georgy (Lynn Redgrave), who is contrasted favourably with her glamorous but amoral flatmate Meredith (Charlotte Rampling), has rather more in common with the sober pessimism of the New Wave than might be expected. Narizzano's next film, *Blue*, was made in America, but this enigmatic Western has something of the mood of 1960s' Britain about it, confirmed by the casting of Terence Stamp as its Mexican bandit hero. The film developed cult status for its existential ambiguities, as well as its cinematography, which is as entranced by Stamp's physical beauty as by that of its desert landscapes. Narizzano returned to Britain to film Ray Galton and Alan Simpson's adaptation of Joe Orton's *Loot*, a frenetic black comedy with strong performances from Milo O'Shea, Richard Attenborough, Lee Remick and Hywel Bennett.

As the British film industry went into decline, Narizzano made two forays into international co-production: the brutal British-Italian kidnap drama *Senza ragione/Redneck*, featuring Telly Savalas and Franco Nero, and the equally lurid *El cielo se cae/Bloodbath*, which brought together Dennis Hopper, Richard Todd and Carroll Baker in a tale of drug abuse and witchcraft in rural Spain. Retreating to more reputable territory, Narizzano then made two realist films about the difficulties of teachers confronted by troublesome pupils. *Why Shoot the Teacher?* was shot in Canada and is upbeat in tone, whereas the British-made *The Class of Miss MacMichael*, with Glenda Jackson and Oliver Reed in the central roles, adopts a more stylised and humorous approach. They were followed by *Choices*, a low-budget American teen drama of modest ambitions, and *Blood Relations*, a retelling of the Lizzie Borden murder story, made in Canada. He also worked on the Russian-set political drama *The Final Assignment*, but was replaced by Paul Almond. Occasional television assignments have followed but Narizzano's career has hardly fulfilled the potential he showed as a talented director in the 1960s.

(Robert Shail)

BIBLIOGRAPHY: Maxford, Howard, 'Georgy Girl', *Film Review*, Oct. 1996, pp. 44–7; McGillivray, David, 'Q & A', *Films and Filming*, July 1975, p. 8.

FILMOGRAPHY: *Under Ten Flags/Sotto dieci bandiere* (co-dir. Duilio Coletti, It/US, 1960); *Fanatic* (US: *Die! Die! My Darling*, 1965); *Georgy Girl* (1966); *Blue* (US, 1968); *Loot* (1970); *Senza ragione* (aka *Redneck*, UK/It, 1973); *El cielo se cae* (aka *The Sky Is Falling/Bloodbath/Las flores del vicio*, Sp, 1975); *Why Shoot the Teacher?* (Can, 1976); *The Class of Miss MacMichael* (1978); *Final Assignment* (co-dir. Paul Almond, Can, 1980); *Choices* (US, 1981); *Blood Relations* (Can, 1983).

NASH, Percy (1869–1958)

Percy Nash, born in Kensington, London, in 1869, first established himself in the theatre, working as a stage manager for Sir Henry Irving and Sir Herbert Beerbohm Tree. He entered cinema in his mid-forties, after a period on Selfridge's advertising staff; the newly founded London Film Company appointed him resident producer in 1913. He also directed a number of their films before leaving to found his own outfit, the Neptune Film Company, established in 1914 at a new studio at Boreham Wood, the first to be built on the site. Nash's stage background informed two early films directed for Neptune in 1915, versions of George R. Sims' stirring melodramas *The Trumpet Call* and *Master and Man*. Not content with staid replicas of stage productions, Nash revelled in special lighting effects and location work, filming above and below ground at a Stoke-on-Trent colliery for *The Coal King* (1915) and on the Cornish seashore for *Enoch Arden* (1914). His wife, Joan Ritz, played leading roles in several films.

Ambitious, with a bumptious personality to match, Nash abruptly left Neptune in 1915 in search of fresh challenges. After directing some early films of the American-owned Trans-Atlantic Company, he moved briefly to Rome, where he directed and occasionally acted for Tiber, a company keen to increase British sales by using British material and talent. Back in Britain, Nash launched another company, N. B. Films, with a six-reel special of Louis N. Parker's play *Disraeli* (1916), with actor-manager Dennis Eadie repeating his stage performance. Humbler output followed at Trans-Atlantic, where his casts ranged from the famous male impersonator Ella Shields in the one-reeler *Herself* to Sir Robert Baden-Powell in *Boys of the Otter Patrol*. But his ambitions returned in prestige dramas: for Will Barker he filmed a version of the popular play *The Flag Lieutenant* (1919), for Master Films, *Hobson's Choice* (1920) and *Rodney Stone* (1920), based on Conan Doyle's historical novel. In 1922 Nash urged the establishment of the British Association of Film Directors and became its first president, though ironically his own career as a leading director was now over: following *How Kitchener Was Betrayed* (1921), criticised for its old-fashioned melodramatics, he shrank to the production of shorts for the Federation of British Industries. In 1927 Nash was appointed production manager for the British Lion Film Corporation, which had been set up to exploit the works of the writer Edgar Wallace. He retired from the industry in the 1930s, his eyesight badly affected by experiments with film lighting, and died in Brighton in 1958.

(Barry Anthony and Geoff Brown)

BIBLIOGRAPHY: East, John M., *'Neath the Mask* (London: George Allen & Unwin, 1967).

FILMOGRAPHY: *David Garrick*; *Jack Sheppard* (1912); *In the Shadow of the Rope*; *The Golden Chance*; *Monty's Proposal*; *Black-Eyed Susan*; *The Burglar's Child* (1913); *Almost Human*; *The Harbour Lights*; *Enoch Arden*; *In the Ranks*; *The Little Match Girl*; *The Steeple-jacks*; *Bill's Rise in the World*; *Over the Garden Wall* (1914); *A Strong Argument*; *The Waifs*; *The Love of Their Lives*; *The Mesmerist*; *Chicken Hearted*; *Sisters*; *Did He, the Brute!*; *Bunting's Blink*; *Taking a Film*; *Her First Husband*; *Just in Time*; *The Little Minister*; *Rosy Rapture*; *The Romany Rye*; *The Motorist's Dream*; *A Touch of Nature*; *The Trumpet Call*; *Master and Man*; *Flying from Justice*; *Married for Money*; *The Coal King*; *Royal Love*; *The Devil's Bondsman* (US: *The Scorpion's Sting*); *A Rogue's Wife* (1915); *Sul trapezio* (It.); *I briganti* (It.); *L'isola della rose* (It.); *Il potere sovrano* (UK: *Temporal Powers*, co-dir. Baldassarre Negroni, It.); *Nella jungla nera* (It.); *Disraeli* (co-dir. Charles Calvert) (1916); *A King of the People*; *Motherhood*; *Boy Scouts Be Prepared* (US: *Boy Scouts to the Rescue*) (1917); *Herself*; *Boys of the Otter Patrol*; *The Elder Miss Blossom* (US: *Wanted a Wife*) (1918); *Women Who Win*; *Her Lonely Soldier*; *The Flag Lieutenant*; *Westward Ho!*; *Darby and Joan* (1919); *The Story of the Rosary*; *Hobson's Choice*; *Won by a Head*; *Rodney Stone*; *The Old Arm Chair* (1920); *The Likeness of the Night*; *The Croxley Master*; *His Other Wife*; *Ships That Pass in the Night*; *How Kitchener Was Betrayed* (1921); *Our National Industries* (series, 1924); *British Industries* (series, 1925); *History of Electricity* (1932).

NEAME, Ronald (1911–)

Ronald Neame was born in London on 23 April 1911, the son of the celebrated portrait photographer and director Elwin Neame and the actress Ivy Close. Financial problems caused by his father's death in 1923 forced Neame to leave public school and he gained employment in 1928 at British International Pictures' newly opened Elstree Studios. He was a clapper-boy on Hitchcock's *Blackmail* (1929) before becoming an assistant cameraman to Jack Cox, and subsequently Claude Friese-Greene. After photographing many 'quota quickies' he graduated to slightly more prestigious films at Ealing, including several George Formby comedies.

The turning point came on *Major Barbara* (Gabriel Pascal, 1941) when Neame met David Lean. Both men were consummate professionals and there was an instant rapport between them. After working together on *In Which We Serve* (Noël Coward/David Lean, 1942), they joined producer Anthony Havelock-Allan to form Cineguild, an independent unit within the Rank Organisation. Their first three films were adapted from Noël Coward plays: *This Happy Breed* (David Lean, 1944), where Neame's muted Technicolor photography was much praised; *Blithe Spirit* (David Lean, 1945), for which he won an

Academy Award nomination for his special-effects photography; and *Brief Encounter* (David Lean, 1946), where he acted as co-producer and co-screenwriter. Neame also produced Lean's two Dickens adaptations, *Great Expectations* (1946) and *Oliver Twist* (1948), but when Lean replaced Neame as director on *The Passionate Friends* (1949) their relationship soured and Cineguild collapsed soon after.

Neame's first feature as director was the noirish thriller *Take My Life* (1947), a modest film by Cineguild's standard, but full of atmospheric touches and inventive plot twists. After the debacle over *The Passionate Friends*, he made *The Golden Salamander* (1949), a more conventional thriller set in North Africa, for the Rank Organisation. Unlike many cinematographers, Neame was not tempted back to his earlier profession, and established himself properly as a director with *The Card* (1952), a vibrant comedy that confirmed his ability to elicit accomplished performances from his cast, notably Alec Guinness as the upwardly mobile anti-hero. *The Card*'s success led to *The Million Pound Note* (1953), a breezy Technicolor comedy starring Gregory Peck, and a sombre true story about a wartime deception, *The Man Who Never Was* (1956), featuring Clifton Webb, Gloria Grahame and Stephen Boyd. Neame worked in Hollywood on MGM's *The Seventh Sin* (1957), but it proved an unhappy experience, ending with his replacement by Vincente Minnelli. He returned to Britain to direct *Windom's Way* (1957), an ambitious if fudged colonial film about a liberal doctor (Peter Finch) caught between two warring factions in Malaya. He left Rank in December 1957, complaining that its business ethos stifled creativity.

Together with the art director John Bryan, who had produced two of his films, Neame formed Knightsbridge Films and, with financial backing from United Artists, directed two slightly offbeat films that are now acknowledged as his finest, *The Horse's Mouth* (1958) and *Tunes of Glory* (1960). *The Horse's Mouth* captures the combative iconoclasm of Joyce Cary's celebrated novel through Alec Guinness' compelling performance as the irascible artist Gulley Jimson. In *Tunes of Glory*, armed with another excellent screenplay (by James Kennaway from his own novel), Neame encouraged outstanding performances from Alec Guinness and John Mills, representing two antithetical forms of militarism, engaged in bitter and tragic rivalry.

Neame started the 1960s with the lame thriller *Escape from Zahrain* (1962), and like many directors of his generation seemed to lose his way for most of the decade. With their clumsy scripts and ponderous performances, *I Could Go on Singing* (1963), *The Chalk Garden* (1964), *Mister Moses* (1965), *Gambit* (1966) and *Prudence and the Pill* (1968) did Neame little credit; but he redeemed his reputation with his splendid adaptation of Muriel Spark's *The Prime of Miss Jean Brodie* (1969) and his lively musical *Scrooge* (1970).

In the 1970s opportunities in Britain dwindled and Neame decamped to Hollywood to make *The Poseidon Adventure* (1972). Its action-packed story of ten passengers trying to escape from an ocean liner overturned by a freak wave inaugurated a new subgenre of disaster films. Hugely profitable, the film made Neame financially secure for the rest of his life. He returned to Europe to make *The Odessa File* (1974), adapted from Frederick Forsyth's novel about a secret Nazi organisation. An ingenious if convoluted plot, good performances and Neame's unflashy, confident direction helped make it an international box-office success. He was less fortunate with the Hollywood blockbuster *Meteor* (1979); Neame was so unhappy with the poor special effects that he tried to remove his name from the credits and henceforth steered clear of big studio projects. His next two films, *Hopscotch* (1980) and *First Monday in October* (1981) – engaging comedy-thrillers starring Walter Matthau – had the same likeable virtues as Neame's best 1950s' films. His final efforts were *Foreign Body* (1986), a lame sex-comedy about a poor Indian (Victor Banerjee) passing himself off in British society as a doctor; and *The Magic Balloon* (1990), a promotional film for Douglas Trumbull's ShowScan process, which few cinemas were able to show.

Neame regarded directing as an interpretative rather than a truly creative act and never aspired to be an innovative auteur imposing his vision on the material. Though capable of handling big-budget action assignments, he preferred films like *The Horse's Mouth*, *Tunes of Glory* and *The Pride of Miss Jean Brodie*, 'art house pictures – good stories with interesting characters' (Neame, p. 271). One of the most successful examples of a cinematographer turned director, Neame's unflappable competence won him the confidence of actors and the respect of producers and financiers.

(Andrew Spicer)

BIBLIOGRAPHY: Frumkes, Roy, 'Icons: Ronald Neame', *Films in Review*, May/June 1996, pp. 13–22; Neame, Ronald, *Straight from the Horse's Mouth* (Lanham, MD and Oxford: Scarecrow Press, 2003); Pulleine, Tim, 'Practically Born in a Film Studio', *Films and Filming*, Apr. 1987, pp. 24–7; Robinson, David, 'Neame the Film-Maker', *Financial Times*, 24 March 1971.

FILMOGRAPHY: *Take My Life* (1947); *The Golden Salamander* (1949); *The Card* (1952); *The Million Pound Note* (US: *Man with a Million*, 1953); *The Man Who Never Was* (1956); *The Seventh Sin*; *Windom's Way* (1957); *The Horse's Mouth* (1958); *Tunes of Glory* (1960); *Escape from Zahrain* (1962); *I Could Go on Singing* (1963); *The Chalk Garden* (1964); *Mister Moses* (UK/US, 1965); *A Man Could Get Killed* (co-dir. Cliff Owen, US); *Gambit* (US) (1966); *Prudence and the Pill* (co-dir. uncredited, Fielder Cook, 1968); *The Prime of Miss Jean Brodie* (1969); *Scrooge* (1970); *The Poseidon Adventure* (US, 1972); *The Odessa File* (UK/Ger, 1974); *Meteor* (US, 1979); *Hopscotch* (US, 1980); *First Monday in October* (US, 1981); *Foreign Body* (1986); *The Magic Balloon* (US, 1990).

NEEDS, Malcolm

Malcolm Needs has written and directed two feature films. *Shoreditch* (2003), into which lead actor Shane Ritchie sunk half a million pounds to ensure its completion, is a muddled production switching between an East End jazz club, where Ritchie's brilliantined Lothario falls for Joely Richardson's singing femme fatale as the country prepares for war in 1939, and present-day London when young descendants unmask dark secrets after inheriting the long-bricked up club.

Charlie is nastier but less risible, charting the true-life rise and fall of south London gang boss Charlie Richardson. Ex-pop star Luke Goss is charismatic if one-dimensional as Richardson, and the witnesses at his trial look seedily authentic and squeal convincingly in the flashbacks when their teeth are pulled out and their toes broken. But the film founders on the difficulty of setting out the case for its articulate, incorrigible and unrepentant protagonist – who makes a fleeting appearance in the film – without displaying a prurient delight in his ruthless violence. There are always problems in telling the tales of criminals who think they are hard done by, but Needs is especially weasly in showing Richardson's misdeeds in graphic detail but asserting that the trial was a set-up, the witnesses lied and Richardson would not hurt a fly never mind shrivel a man's private parts with an electric fire. Though less dismissively reviewed than *Shoreditch*, *Charlie*'s modest box-office returns would be unlikely to have endeared Needs to his investors and ensured his future as a film-maker.

(Robert Murphy)

BIBLIOGRAPHY: Van Schalkwyk, Karen, 'That Was Business – This Is Personal', *Screen Africa*, Nov. 2002, p. 18.

FILMOGRAPHY: *Shoreditch* (2001; rel. 2003); *Charlie* (2004).

NEGULESCO, Jean (1900–1993)

Jean (Ion) Negulesco was born on 29 February 1900, in Craiova, Romania, the son of a hotelier. He studied painting at the Académie Julian in Paris in the 1920s, and moved to the United States in 1927, where his portraits of Hollywood stars like Dolores Del Rio led to involvement in film production. He worked in various capacities for different Hollywood studios before becoming a director at Warner Bros., where he made melodramas such as *Singapore Woman* (1941), *The Mask of Dimitrios* (1944) and *Humoresque* (1946). He then moved to 20th Century-Fox, and was sent to England to make two films set in Victorian Britain – *Britannia Mews* and *The Mudlark*.

Britannia Mews effectively combines Hollywood stars Dana Andrews and Maureen O'Hara with the sharply etched character acting of Dame Sybil Thorndike, and is enlivened by some scenes of Dickensian squalor. *The Mudlark*, in which Queen Victoria is persuaded to come out of mourning by a cockney urchin (Andrew Ray), has the benefit of Alec Guinness' impersonation of Disraeli (though contemporary British reviewers were less enthusiastic about the Queen being played by the American Irene Dunne). Returning to America, Negulesco switched to the CinemaScope glamour of films such as *How to Marry a Millionaire* (1953). He continued directing up till 1969, published a not entirely reliable autobiography in 1984 and died in Marbella, Spain, on 18 July 1993.

(Guy Barefoot)

BIBLIOGRAPHY: Negulesco, Jean, *Things I Did . . . and Things I Think I Did* (New York: Simon & Schuster, 1984); Owen, Derek, 'Jean Negulesco' *Film Dope* no. 47, Dec. 1991, pp. 4–6.

FILMOGRAPHY (UK only): *Britannia Mews* (US: *The Forbidden Street*, 1949); *The Mudlark* (1950).

NEILL, Roy William (1887–1946)

Born Roland de Gostrie at sea off Ireland on 4 September 1887, Roy William Neill had a varied career before finally becoming a Hollywood director in 1917. He was a prolific director of silent films and low-budget sound features, some of the latter being well above average; Neill was particularly strong in handling horror themes and creating a gothic atmosphere.

Between 1937 and 1939 he also directed twelve British films: *Dr Syn* for Gaumont-British and the other eleven for Warner Bros. *Dr Syn*, a lively eighteenth-century pirate yarn, is more suited to Neill's natural directorial style than all but one of the Warners' films that followed. The exception was the ingenious thriller *Murder Will Out*, which Neill also co-wrote. The other ten included four Max Miller and three Claude Hulbert farces, only two of which seem to be extant. To judge from contemporary reviews, the two comedians display their best theatre form only intermittently, although one of the surviving films, *Hoots Mon!*, captures a (cleaned-up) version of Miller's sexual innuendo-based stage act. He was to have returned to Gaumont-British to direct Launder and Gilliatt's *The Lady Vanishes*

(Alfred Hitchcock, 1938), but went back to Hollywood, where he directed a number of stylish Sherlock Holmes films with Basil Rathbone as Holmes and Nigel Bruce as Watson.

In 1937 Neill told an interviewer that he preferred England to Hollywood: 'There's nothing stimulating about the place. You feel you want a keen wind to whip up your mind and set it working at full speed' (Masters). After the war he returned to Britain, but before he could make any further British films, he died from a heart attack in London on 14 December 1946.

(James C. Robertson)

BIBLIOGRAPHY: Masters, Leslie, 'Star-Spotting Is His Hobby', *Film Weekly*, 15 July, p. 37; Press books on *Dr Syn* and *The Good Old Days* held in the BFI National Library, London.

FILMOGRAPHY (UK only): *Dr Syn* (co-dir. Maude Howell); *Gypsy* (1937); *Thank Evans*; *The Viper*; *Simply Terrific*; *Double or Quits*; *Quiet Please*; *Everything Happens to Me*; *Many Tanks Mr Atkins* (1938); *The Good Old Days*; *Murder Will Out*; *Hoots Mon!*; *A Gentleman's Gentleman* (1939).

NEILSON, Anthony (1967–)

Anthony Neilson was born in Edinburgh in 1967. One of Scotland's best-known and most controversial modern playwrights, author of *The Penetrator* (1993), *The Censor* (1997) and *Stitching* (2002), he made his feature film debut with *The Debt Collector* in 1999.

Neilson was able to draw on funds from the Scottish National Lottery Panel, which tended to support applications for literary adaptations or from established literary figures. Arguing that 'our stories can be as big as anyone else's' and expressing his desire to make a 'Scottish Western' (Spencer), he based *The Debt Collector* on fictionalised events around the life of Glasgow criminal Jimmy Boyle. The film might be seen almost as a sequel to John Mackenzie's *A Sense of Freedom* (1981), which was based on Boyle's autobiography. In Neilson's film the reformed gangster (Billy Connolly) has his affluent middle-class lifestyle disrupted by a vengeful policeman (Ken Stott). Unfortunately Neilson's mixture of violence, melodrama and sentimentality is much less involving than Mackenzie's harrowing study of human resilience, and *The Debt Collector* attracted little in the way of critical or commercial success. Like other visitors from the theatre, it is uncertain whether Neilson will further pursue a film-making career.

(Jonathan Murray)

BIBLIOGRAPHY: Spencer, Liese, 'Small Country, Big Ideas', *Independent*, 29 April 1999, p. 11.

FILMOGRAPHY: *Deeper Still* (short, 1993); *The Debt Collector* (1999).

NEUBAUER, Vera (1948–)

Although she has often refuted the claim that she is a feminist film-maker, Vera Neubauer is clearly a highly politicised and sometimes polemical animator, predicating her work on the revelation and interrogation of intensely personal feelings and

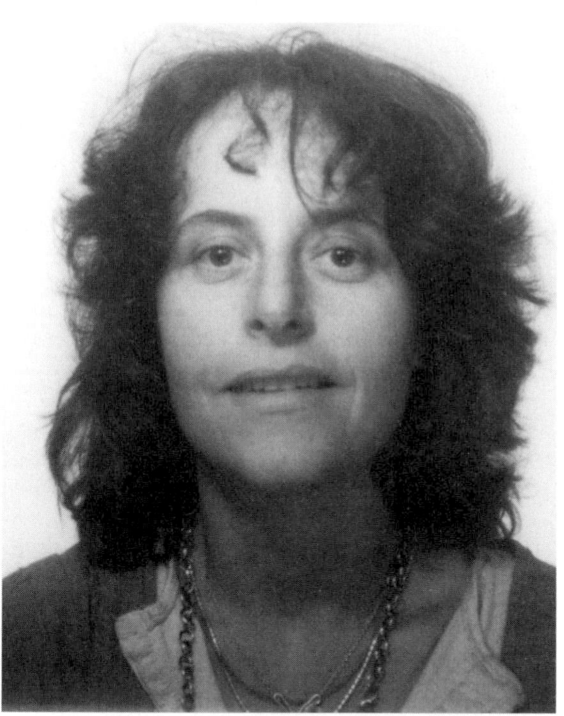

preoccupations. Her diverse approaches to both live action and animation make her a genuinely innovative and experimental artist, eager to provoke rather than provide the easy pleasures of cartoon humour. Born in Prague in 1948, she worked in Stuttgart and Dusseldorf before arriving in London, where she studied print-making at the Royal Academy of Art, before converting to film-making. The often fragmented but autobiographical narratives of her films create a stream of consciousness that deconstructs 'masculine' modes of film-making practice. *Animation for Live Action*, for example, is a deliberately primitivist take on the interfaces of live action and animation as it was played out in the Fleischers' 'Out of the Inkwell' series, revealing the way identity is constructed and multiple points of view denied in conventional cinema. *The Decision* further engages with these preoccupations, re-working fairy tale conventions to privilege the brutal ambiguities of romantic expectation, pointing up the rhetorics of domestic contentment for women only to see them confounded by the mundaneness and drudgery of lived experience. In *Mid-Air* a bored housewife studies witchcraft in order to challenge her husband's domestic dominance, and eventually discovers how to make men menstruate. In *The Wheel of Life* she explores the implications of 'original sin', effectively exposing the lie of ideological or historically determined 'control' in the face of the chaos of nature and material change. *The Lady of the Lake* returns to more familiar themes: a fairy tale about a mermaid who may live with her chosen partner on land as long as he does not hit her three times. The BAFTA Award-winning *Woolly Wolf* revisits the Red Riding Hood story in a similar vein, and plays out unfashionable resistance to masculine norms embodied in the wolf.

Neubauer's work engages with the physical and conceptual materials of the storytelling process and radicalises their presence and effect; for example, in converting the 'comfort' of a knitted artefact into a living, challenging character. *Hooked* takes her concerns into a South American context, and literally plays out the Laingian 'knots' of relationships through knitted and crocheted figures. Overlooked in the wider context of British cinema, but internationally rewarded and appreciated within the animation community, Neubauer is one of the most progressive artists working in the experimental animation field.

(Paul Wells)

BIBLIOGRAPHY: Barwell, Claire, 'Interview with Vera Neubauer', *Undercut* no. 6, Winter 1982/3, pp. 34–40; Pilling, Jayne (ed.), *Women and Animation: A Compendium* (London: BFI Exhibition & Distribution Division, 1992).

FILMOGRAPHY: *Animation Allegation* (1971); *Aligator* (1972); *Pip and Bessie* (six shorts, 1973–5); *Animation for Live Action* (1975); *Loop* (1976); *The Decision* (1981); *The World of Children* (1984); *Mid-Air* (1986); *The Mummy's Curse* (1988); *Passing On* (1989); *Don't Be Afraid* (1990); *Live TV* (1993); *The Wheel of Life* (1994); *The Lady of the Lake* (1995); *The Dragon and the Fly* (1997); *Woolly Wolf*; *Hooked* (2001).

NEWALL, Guy (1885–1937)

Guy P. Newall was born on 25 May 1885 on the Isle of Wight. After gaining his first experience of the stage in a travelling pantomime, he drifted into the London and provincial theatre, specialising in comic dude roles and writing one-act plays and music-hall sketches. He entered the film industry playing small roles and writing scenarios for the London Film Company. When war broke out, he was on tour with Marie Tempest in America, but after appearing in a string of films by Maurice Elvey and assisting George Loane Tucker on *The Manxman* (1916), he joined the Royal Garrison Artillery. There he met George Clark – a self-styled expert in photography – and after the war ended they set up Lucky Cat Films with Clark as business manager and Newall in artistic control as well as acting as lead player. Realising the significance of American competition but convinced of 'the superior talent of British players', Lucky Cat set out to 'vindicate to the world the possibility of all-British pictures' (*Bioscope*, 1919). Important for these ambitions was the pictorial camerawork of Bert Ford and Joe Rosenthal Jr, tasteful set designs by Charles Dalmon and the talented directing of Kenelm Foss and Arthur Rooke. Crucial too was Newall's partnership with Ivy Duke, a musical-comedy actress whom he met during the war, persuaded to join Lucky Cat as his leading lady, and married in 1922.

Three months after successfully trade-showing four comedies, the company, working from cramped studios in Ebury Street, announced expansion under the name George Clark Productions; six months later, construction of a modern studio at Beaconsfield was under way. The accompanying stream of production saw Newall come into his own as writer and director. He scripted and starred in *The Garden of Resurrection* (Arthur Rooke, 1919), *The Lure of Crooning Water* (Arthur Rooke, 1920) and *Duke's Son* (Franklin Dyall, 1920), but forwent acting in his fine directorial debut, *Testimony* (1920). While Beaconsfield was still under construction, he took the company to Nice to direct *The Bigamist* (1921) and *The Persistent Lovers* (1922); and went down to the New Forest and Salisbury Plain to make the racing drama *Boy Woodburn* (1922) and the Hardy-esque *Fox Farm* (1922). Beaconsfield opened in May 1922, and in November his Cornish drama *The Maid of the Silver Sea* was trade-shown.

During this hectic programme, Newall not only provided George Clark Productions with artistic inspiration but – as he later joked – performed all roles from general manager to scenario writer, leading man and director to office cleaner (*Pictures*). In these films Newall developed a pathos-laden, if whimsically ironic, protagonist defined by social marginalisation and personal isolation. Unloved, misunderstood and wryly self-deprecating oddballs, these wounded men, so frequent in 1920s' films, attempt to draw those around them into the fatalistic, melodramatic life of their imagining. With Ivy Duke as foil, Newall wove from this material a series of stylish fantasies, laced with wry humour, in which his outsider heroes confront the materialistic corruption of a dying aristocracy and the changing class and gender relations of post-war modernity.

Although regretting the loss of Newall's charming dude performances of the Lucky Cat comedies, British review press and audiences responded positively to this new direction. Feted as 'Britain's finest actor', Newall's new style of minimalist but psychologically revealing performance projected the ordinariness of inarticulate characters whose yearning for the extraordinary was realisable only in fantasy. Appreciation of Newall's sincerity, restraint and naturalness was supported by pictorial camerawork displaying skilfully contrived framing and lighting, and by powerfully restorative images of the English countryside, which set his self-centred protagonists within a broader context of rural hardships and timeless landscapes.

After 1922, the film industry's downturn refocused Newall's career. He handed over the scripting of *Mirage* (1923) to Duke and direction to Arthur Rooke and after making *The Starlit Garden* (1924) retreated to his Norfolk Broads home to concentrate on his novel and play *Husband Love*. Between 1924 and 1927 Newall was absent from the cinema, though, like Ivy Duke, he appeared regularly on the stage. When he returned, in Geza von Bolvary's 1927 version of *The Ghost Train*, it was in a silly-ass role that can be seen as a satirical undermining of the soulful protagonists of his George Clark films.

Newall was divorced by Ivy Duke in 1929, and returned to directing, making a series of low-budget films, most of them starring Elizabeth Allan, for Julius Hagen at Twickenham. Competent and amusing though they are, they share little with the artistically adventurous films Newall had made in the 1920s. His health deteriorated in the mid-1930s and he died suddenly on 25 February 1937 at his home in Hampstead, leaving a four-year-old daughter by his third wife, actress Dorothy Batley.

(Christine Gledhill)

BIBLIOGRAPHY: 'Down on the Farm: A Visit to the George Clark Film', *Pictures: The Screen Magazine*, Mar. 1922; 'Film Favourites on the British Screen: no. 26: Guy Newall', *Picture Show*, 25 Aug. 1923, p. 18; 'George Clark Productions', Supplement to *The Bioscope*, 1 July 1920, p. xxiv; entry on Guy Newall, p. xliv; Gledhill, Christine, *Reframing British Cinema 1919–1928: Between Restraint and Passion* (London: BFI, 2003); 'Guy Newall and Ivy Duke: All British Stars', *Stoll's Editorial News*, 15 Apr. 1920, pp. 5–6; Low, Rachael, *The History of British Film 1918–1929* (London: George Allen & Unwin, 1971); 'More British Pictures: George Clark's Plans', *The Bioscope*, 2 Oct. 1919, p. 31; Newall, Guy, *Husband Love* (London: Constable, 1924); 'The Importance of Being Ernest', Interview with Newall and Ivy Duke, *Picturegoer*, Mar. 1922, pp. 43–6, 58; 'The New George Clark Studios', *Kinematograph Weekly*, 8 Apr., 1920, pp. 88–9.

FILMOGRAPHY: *Testimony* (1920); *The Bigamist* (1921); *Beauty and the Beast*, *The Persistent Lovers*; *Boy Woodburn*; *Fox Farm*; *The Maid of the Silver Sea* (1922); *The Starlit Garden* (1924); *Rodney Steps In* (short); *The Rosary*; *Chin Chin Chinaman* (US: *Boat from Shanghai*); *The Other Mrs Phipps* (short) (1931); *The Chinese Puzzle* (1932); *The Admiral's Secret* (1934).

NEWBROOK, Peter (1920–)

Peter Newbrook was born in Chester in 1920 and entered the film industry in 1934, working in the front office of the Warner Bros. studio at Teddington. He moved to Ealing in 1940, and enlisted in the Army Kinematograph Service in 1942. After the war he rejoined Ealing as a camera operator. In the 1950s he worked as David Lean's operator on *Hobson's Choice* (1954), *Summer Madness* (1955) and *The Bridge on the River Kwai* (1957), and handled second-unit cinematography for *Lawrence of Arabia* (1962). In parallel, he was cinematographer for less-exalted directors: Gordon Parry (*Third Time Lucky*, 1949), Monty Berman (*Melody Club*, 1949) and George More O'Ferrall (*The March Hare*, 1956).

In 1964 he formed his own production company, Tigon International, with Robert Hartford-Davis, and made films such as *The Yellow Teddybears* (1963), *The Black Torment* (1964), *Gonks Go Beat* (1965), *The Sandwich Man* (1966), *Corruption* (1967) and *The Smashing Bird I Used to Know* (1969) with Hartford-Davis as director and Newbrook as cinematographer and producer. His one film as a director, *The Asphyx* (1973), features Robert Stephens as a Victorian doctor who discovers that death is caused by a phantom that can be captured to ensure immortality. *The Asphyx* is more odd than good but it has a distinctive demented solemnity. In 1975 Newbrook became Lighting Director for Anglia Television, where he was responsible for the cinematography on series such as *Tales of the Unexpected*. In 1986 he was elected President of the British Society of Cinematographers.

(Kim Newman)

BIBLIOGRAPHY: Brownlow, Kevin, *David Lean* (London: Faber and Faber, 1996); 'Interview: Peter Newbrook', *The Perfect Vision* vol. 6 no. 21, Spring 1994, pp. 61–3.

FILMOGRAPHY: *The Asphyx* (aka *Spirit of the Dead*, 1973).

NEWBY, Chris (1957–)

Christopher Newby was born in Leeds in 1957 and educated at Leeds Polytechnic and the Royal College of Art, where he made his first film, *Black Nectar*, in 1980. He continued to make shorts for more than a decade, including *Kiss* (1991), financed by Channel 4, and *Relax* (1992), backed by the BFI.

Newby made his feature debut with the stylish – and stylised – *Anchoress*, a sombre film centred on a fourteenth-century peasant girl who gives up worldly temptation and seeks spiritual comfort by allowing herself to be walled up. An overbearing sense of a small community's anguish and repression faced with zealotry is conveyed through the spare but telling script by Christine Watkins and Judith Stanley Smith, Michael Baudour's black-and-white chiaroscuro camerawork and Newby's intimate directorial style.

Newby's next film was *Madagascar Skin*, a leisurely exploration of a slow-burning homosexual relationship between two very different men; one a mercurial kleptomaniac (Bernard Hill), the other introverted and hitherto isolated by a physical disfigurement (John Hannah). The film, shot in Pembrokeshire, depended heavily on atmosphere.

(David Berry)

BIBLIOGRAPHY: Murphy, Kathleen, 'Nativity Scenes', *Film Comment*, Jan./Feb. 1995, pp. 12–16.

FILMOGRAPHY: *Black Nectar* (short, 1980); *Elegy* (short, 1981); *Feast* (1983); *Hoy* (short, 1984); *The Old Man of the Sea* (short) (1990); *Kiss* (short, 1991); *Relax* (short, 1992); *Anchoress* (1993); *Madagascar Skin* (1995); *Stromboli* (short, 1998).

NEWELL, Mike (1942–)

Michael Newell was born on 28 March 1942 in St Albans. While reading English at Cambridge he began directing student theatrical productions. After graduating in 1963 he joined Granada as a trainee director, moving from news and documentaries via serials to plays. By the mid-1970s he had established a solid reputation, directing episodes of the violent crime serial *Big Breadwinner Hog* (1968), the witty Adam Faith series *Budgie* (1971), and several well-received plays. His Anglo-American television film *The Man in the Iron Mask* (1977) received a limited theatrical release, but Newell's move away from television was gradual.

In 1980 he directed *The Awakening*, a horror film based on Bram Stoker's *The Jewel of the Seven Stars*, backed by EMI and Orion. It was followed by the grim New Zealand-set *Bad Blood*, made for a short-lived subsidiary of Southern Television, TVS, and five films – *Dance with a Stranger* (1985), *The Good Father* (1987), *Soursweet* (1988), *Into the West* (1992) and *Four Weddings and a Funeral* (1994), partly financed by Channel 4. *Dance with a Stranger*, scripted by Shelagh Delaney, is the story of Ruth Ellis (Miranda Richardson), the last woman to be hanged in Britain. Newell cleverly deploys his limited resources to evoke Britain in the 1950s; and Miranda Richardson and Rupert Everett give fine performances as victims of a society riven by class prejudice and moral hypocrisy. *The Good Father*, set in contemporary London, with Anthony Hopkins and Jim Broadbent as disgruntled fathers seemingly outsmarted by their newly independent ex-wives, is less flamboyantly cinematic, but it draws an uncomfortably accurate portrait of the selfish, divisive society of the 1980s. *Soursweet*, from a script by Ian McEwan, and *Into the West*, scripted by Jim Sheridan, explore ethnic identity and employ elements of magic realism. Taken together, these films constitute a modestly impressive body of work and showed Newell to be a sensitive and versatile director.

In 1992 Newell directed *Enchanted April* for BBC Television, but released theatrically in the USA, its whimsical Englishness proved highly popular. *Four Weddings and a Funeral* was even more

Squabbling lovers Rupert Everett (left) and Miranda Richardson in *Dance With a Stranger* (Mike Newell, 1985)

of a success, breaking box-office records in Britain after its warm reception in America and going on to reap huge financial rewards internationally. Though it raised the profile and revived the fortunes of British film production, Newell made no attempt to confine himself to its formula of feel-good romantic comedy. His next film was the sourly realist *An Awfully Big Adventure* (1995) – with Hugh Grant defying his enveloping stereotype of ineffable niceness, and a drab, provincial 1950s' setting worlds away from the sumptuous churches and stately homes of *Four Weddings*.

Newell then seized the opportunity to make a big-budget American film, but his chosen subject, *Donnie Brasco* (1997), was a downbeat Mafia film rather than a jaunty comedy. Dramatically strong and utterly unsentimental, with a virtuoso performance from Al Pacino, it recalls *Dance with a Stranger* in its measured sympathy for those who fall foul of society's conventions and find their lives sucked into a downward spiral. He returned to comedy with *Pushing Tin*, starring John Cusack and Billy Bob Thornton as rival air-traffic controllers in New York; but *Mona Lisa Smile*, starring Julia Roberts as a radical art teacher in a conservative American girls' college, once again returned him to women in the 1950s. He acted as executive producer on BBC Films' *I Capture the Castle* (Tim Fywell, 2003), but suspicion that his directorial ambitions now extend far beyond small-scale films for television was confirmed by his assignment as director of the $130 million *Harry Potter and the Goblet of Fire*.

(Pamela Church Gibson)

BIBLIOGRAPHY: Baker, Bob, 'Mike Newell', *Film Dope* no. 47, Dec. 1991, p. 17; McNab, Geoffrey, 'The Infiltrator', *Sight and Sound*, May 1997, pp. 6–9; Shackleton, Liz, 'Playing the English Joker', *Screen International*, 19 Aug. 1994, p. 16.

FILMOGRAPHY: *The Man in the Iron Mask* (1976); *The Awakening* (1980); *Bad Blood* (1981); *Dance with a Stranger* (1985); *The Good Father*; *Amazing Grace and Chuck* (US) (1987); *Soursweet* (1988); *Enchanted April*; *Into the West* (Ir/UK) (1992); *Four Weddings and a Funeral* (1994); *An Awfully Big Adventure* (1995); *Donnie Brasco* (US, 1997); *Pushing Tin* (US/Ger, 1999); *Mona Lisa Smile* (US, 2003); *Harry Potter and the Goblet of Fire* (US, 2005).

NEWMAN, Widgey (1900–1944)

It is hard not to feel a certain affection for Widgey Newman, who continued tirelessly to make numerous short films, travelogues and comics at the lowest end of the market, apparently undiscouraged by lack of recognition or the opportunity for greater things.

Born 30 September 1900 in Bedford, Widgey Raphael Newman entered the film industry as a publicist in the early 1920s. After gaining experience as an editor, he joined DeForest Phonofilms around 1926. There he specialised in making early sound shorts capturing performances of comics like John Henry (featured in a series about the pleasures of the wireless) and music-hall singers, along with more serious acts (one film is devoted to Edith Sitwell reading her own poetry). In 1929 Newman set up the first of many production companies and for the next ten years directed a wide variety of short films as well as some feature-length quota films. His two horror films *Castle Sinister* (1932) and *The Unholy Quest* (1934), appear to had been low-budget attempts to appeal to audiences who have flocked to Universal's *Frankenstein* (James Whale, 1931) and *Dracula* (Todd Browning, 1931), though judging from contemporary reviews with little success.

During 1932 Newman produced a series of more culturally ambitious shorts, introducing the music of famous classical composers in the series *Musical Memories*. In 1935 he ventured back to Elizabethan England with *Immortal Gentleman*, a cut-price attempt to popularise Shakespeare, which *Today's Cinema* assured its readers was 'no mere quota quickie', rather 'a sincere and courageous attempt to present the more beloved passages of the immortal bard in a fashion thus far foreign to them' (*Today's Cinema*, 23 March 1935). Newman appears to have been more comfortable producing travelogues, and films featuring animals as principal characters. These genres were combined in his curious series of 'Parrot' films, where the viewer is guided through a series of tourist locations by a chatty bird. This sort of programme material was given increasingly kindly reviews by the trade press as the nation entered the war, with the good quality of the photography often mentioned. Newman's wife, Joan, also worked as a director, filming shorts for the production company Ariston Films, which they were running jointly by the time of his early death in Hill Ends Hospital, St Albans, on 29 July 1944.

(Lawrence Napper)

BIBLIOGRAPHY: Low, Rachael, *Films of Comment and Persuasion of the 1930s* (London: George Allen & Unwin, 1979).

FILMOGRAPHY: (Shorts) *Off the Beaten Track*; *The Romance of Broadcasting* (1925); *John Henry Calling* (series, co-dir. Challis Sanderson); *Nervo and Knox* (1926); *Edith Sitwel*; *Saint Joan*; *Madalon*; *Daily Jesters* (series); *The Merchant of Venice*; *A Few Melodious Moments from Lawrence Wright's Sensations of 1927*; *A Reckless Gamble*; *Hot Water and*

Vegetabuel; *Clonk!* (1928); *Inns and Outs*; *Musical Memories* (series); *The Merry Men of Sherwood*; *Derby Secrets* (series, 1932–9); *What the Stars Foretell* (series); *Gordon Richards* (1933); *Faces of Destiny* (series); *Thoroughbred*; *For Ladies Only*; *The Unknown Warrior*, *Here Comes the Zoo*; *Lucky Dogs* (1934); *This Fishy Business*; *How to Pass the Driving Test*; *Miniature Thoroughbreds*; *This Riding Business*; *What the Parrot Saw*; *His Apologies* (1935); *What the Puppy Said* ; *Pal O'Mine*; *Apron Fools*; *This Motoring* (1936); *Our Royal Heritage* (series, co-dir. Roy Boulting); *Songs of the Organ* (series); *The Inspector* (1937); *What the Heavens Reveal* (series); *Horse Sense*; *Land of the Clans*; *Ghost Tales Retold* (series); *From Pigskin to Park Lane*; *Romances of the Turf* (series) (1938); *The Compleat Angler*, *The King's Favourites*; *Under Dogs*; *Pandamonium*; *Zoo in Spring* (1939); *Animal Moments* (series, 1939–43); *The Right to Live*; *Zooland Shoulder Arms*; *Waterways of the Sky*; *This Island Called Britain*; *London's Got Grit* (1940); *Pet's Corner* (co-dir. Joan Newman); *Live Stock Taking*; *Britain Beats the Blitz*; *Racing Odds*; *Alive Alive-o* (1941); *The Centre of England*; *Atlantic Interlude*; *Let's Go Scilly*; *South of the Border* (1942); *In the Sound of Big Ben*; *Next Stop New York*; *Liquid History*; *Devon by the Sea*; *The Spirit o' Burns*; *Watling Street*; *Zoo's Who*; *Climbing the Peaks*; *Up from Somerset*; *Reflections*; *Yorkshire Relish*; *Dick Turpin's Trail*; *Jock*; *Tre, Pol and Pen*; *Your Dog's Tale*; *The Parrot Goes to Sea*; *The Parrot Remembers*; *Strange to Relate* (1943); *Chartered Waters*; *Shirts and Tails*; *Sugar and Sluice*; *This Our Land*; *The Peke Speaks*; *The Four Seasons*; *Road to Yesterday*; *Jock: Man's Best Friend*; *Land of My Fathers*; *River Folk* (1944). Features: *Heroes of the Mine*; *The Little Waitress*; *Castle Sinister* (1932); *The Lucky Blaze* (1933); *The Unholy Quest* (1934); *Immortal Gentleman* (1935); *A Sister to Assist 'Er* (co-dir. George Dewhurst); *On Velvet* (1938); *Men Without Honour* (1939); *Henry Steps Out*; *Two Smart Men* (1940).

NIBLO, Allan (c. 1964–)

After graduating from the National Film and Television School in 1993 Allan Niblo directed a number of short films before breaking into features with *Loop*, a bizarre comedy written by fellow NFTS graduate Tim Pears. The passionate feuds of family life that would characterise the adaptation of Pears' novel *In a Land of Plenty* (Hettie MacDonald/Dave Moore, 2001) are explored here in lighter form, with Andy Serkis' psychopathic stockbroker played for laughs and Pears' philosophical aphorisms plonked disconcertingly between bouts of slapstick comedy. Liveliness and originality weighed insufficiently against amateurism, and the film failed to reach an audience. Niblo found more success during a spell teaching at Newport Film School: he encouraged one of his students, Justin Kerrigan, to develop *Human Traffic* (1999), a fresh, unpretentious film about the rave scene in Cardiff, produced by Niblo and McCourt.

Despite falling out with Kerrigan over a re-cut version for the American market, Niblo has been able to attract the projects of other young and ambitious directors. Richard Parry's *South West Nine* (2001) dissolved into an unsatisfactory mishmash, but Nick Love, with *The Football Factory* (2004) and *The Business* (2005), and Michael Dowse, with *It's All Gone Pete Tong* (2004), proved sturdier production partners. In 2002 Niblo established the production/distribution company Vertigo Films with other producers, directors and distributors.

(Robert Murphy)

FILMOGRAPHY: *Bernie and Holly* (short, 1993); *Touch* (short, 1994); *Boom Boom* (short, 1994); *Loop* (1997).

NICHOLSON, Irene

Irene Nicholson was one of the few women to be involved in experimental film-making in inter-war Britain. From 1933 she co-edited the journal *Film Art* with B. Vivian Braun; the following year she ventured into practical film-making with *Ephemeral* (now lost), an abstract impression of the passing of the seasons. She and Braun then made *Beyond This Open Road*, a ten-minute poetic documentary showing city dwellers visiting the countryside at the weekend. Elaborate montage sequences, rapid camera movements, unusual visual composition and the contrast between leisure and mechanisation express the modernist concerns Nicholson and Braun explored in *Film Art*, and the film survives as a fascinating contribution to Britain's fragmented art-cinema tradition. A dispute between the two aspiring film artists put paid to further collaborations, and Braun resigned from *Film Art* in 1935, two years before the magazine ceased publication. Nicholson made only one final film, a sponsored documentary on Trinidadian life, *Callaloo*, co-directed with Brian Moore in 1936.

(Jamie Sexton)

BIBLIOGRAPHY: Braun, B. Vivian, review of *Ephemeral*, *Film Art*, Winter 1934, p. 42; Dusinberre, Deke, 'The Avant-Garde Attitude in the Thirties', in Don Macpherson (ed.), *Traditions of Independence: British Cinema in the Thirties* (London: BFI, 1980).

FILMOGRAPHY: *Ephemeral*; *Beyond This Open Road* (co-dir. B. Vivian Braun) (1934); *Callaloo* (co-dir. Brian Moore, 1936).

NOBLE, Adrian (1950–)

Adrian Noble was born in Chichester on 19 July 1950. After studying English at Bristol University and theatre directing at the Drama Centre in London, he worked at the Trinity Arts Centre in Birmingham and the Bristol Old Vic. In 1980 he became an Associate Director at the Royal Shakespeare Company and later assumed overall responsibility for the company as Artistic Director. Noble has attracted critical acclaim for his stagings of Chekhov, Eliot and Stoppard, as well as Shakespearean and Jacobean drama. His theatrical work for children includes productions of *The Secret Garden*, *The Lion, the Witch and the Wardrobe*, and the West End musical *Chitty Chitty Bang Bang*.

This eclectic background is evident in Noble's film adaptation of *A Midsummer Night's Dream*. Presenting the story through the eyes of a young boy, the film appears to be half-dream, half-play, with the boy moving between being an awestruck observer and an active instigator of events (he manipulates miniature versions of the characters within his toy theatre, and they respond accordingly). In this, the film crystallises Noble's view that theatre should inspire wonder and active participation in child and adult alike.

(Sarah Cardwell)

BIBLIOGRAPHY: Brown, Georgina, 'Thanks to Tarantino, It's Suddenly Ok for Characters on Stage to Deliver Lengthy Pieces', *Independent* Weekend Section, 20 Apr. 1996, p. 7; Sinker, Mark, '*A Midsummer Night's Dream*', *Sight and Sound*, Jan. 1997, p. 41; Van Sale, Jonat, 'It Was Our Little Eden', *Independent* Education Section, 8 Mar. 2001, p. 6.

FILMOGRAPHY: *A Midsummer Night's Dream* (1996).

NOLAN, Christopher (1970–)

Born in London on 30 July 1970, Christopher Nolan studied English at University College London, where he made a number of films including the surreal, three-minute *Doodlebug*, featuring Jeremy Theobald. Nolan also used Theobald in *Following*, his debut feature about a struggling writer who attaches himself to a seductive burglar. A seventy-two minute, micro-budget black-and-white thriller, it was filmed on 16mm over a period of several months at weekends, using only available light and real locations. Making a virtue of these limitations, Nolan's script is episodic and fragmentary, telling its Patricia Highsmith-like story in an elliptical non-linear fashion, and delivering a finale with a neat Darwinian sting in the tale.

In 1997 Nolan and his wife, American producer Emma Thomas, relocated to the United States, the setting for *Memento*, a convoluted homage to film noir that employs a reverse chronological structure with dazzling skill. This stylistic approach had been used before in Harold Pinter's play *Betrayal* (filmed by David Jones in 1983) and Martin Amis' novel *Time's Arrow*, and might be traced back to J. B. Priestley's time plays from the 1930s. Nolan's ingenuity lies in his successful integration of this gimmick into the narrative framework, using it as an objective correlative for the protagonist's medical condition, a form of amnesia that makes it impossible for him to retain new memories for longer than fifteen minutes. This is effectively contrasted with the chronologically straightforward and forward-moving subplot, shot in black and white, which in the end reveals that even the protagonist's 'real' and safe memories, from before his illness, are in fact unreliable. Nolan's discontinuous narratives use the cinematic properties of authorial omniscience to provide stylistic counterpoint to his stories, where weak or compromised individuals abrogate personal responsibility, inviting others to manipulate their lives for them, usually with deadly results.

Nolan went on to direct *Insomnia*, a big-budget thriller starring Al Pacino, Hilary Swank and Robin Williams. Although more conventional than the 1997 Norwegian film by Erik Skjoldbjærg on which it is based, and more linear than Nolan's previous work, it has a number of fine set-pieces, and was a big hit at the box office. As with his two preceding features, the film's opening shot is a close-up of a pair of hands at work, which in *Insomnia* is used as a recurring motif until its incriminating context is revealed at the film's end. In all Nolan's films, the narrative dexterity and sheer delight in telling stories, reminiscent of authors like Jorge Luis Borges and Paul Auster, is strongly felt. He is one of the few new British directors to combine commercial acumen with artistic ambition. He proved adept at handling the starry cast and $135 million budget of *Batman Begins*, securing both critical acclaim and substantial box-office success.

(Sergio Angelini)

BIBLIOGRAPHY: Mottram, James, *The Making of Memento* (London: Faber and Faber, 2002); Neff, Renfreu, 'Interview with Christopher Nolan', *Creative Screenwriting*, Mar./Apr. 2001, pp. 47–56; Pavlus, John, 'Sleepless in Alaska', *American Cinematographer*, May 2002, pp 34–45.

FILMOGRAPHY: *Tarantella* (short, 1989); *Larceny* (short, 1996); *Doodlebug* (short, 1997); *Following* (1998); *Memento* (US, 2000); *Insomnia* (US, 2002).

NOLBANDOV, Sergei (1895–1971)

Sergei Nolbandov was born in Moscow on 12 September 1895, studied law at the University of Odessa and emigrated to London in the early 1920s, where he worked as a film editor for Ivor Montagu and Adrian Brunel, among others. In the late 1930s he was hired by Michael Balcon at Ealing, where he worked closely with director Pen Tennyson as writer and producer. His own directorial debut was the wartime flag-waver *Ships with Wings* (1941), a melodramatic naval drama starring John Clements as a reckless pilot who redeems himself with a supreme act of heroism. The film was popular with audiences but drew the hostility of critics who were beginning to favour documentary realism. He followed this with the resistance drama *Undercover* (1943), also starring Clements, and showed once again that he was impervious to the realist strain of film-making at Ealing. It was the only film to deal with the partisan war in Yugoslavia and proved something of a minor embarrassment through celebrating the discredited Chetniks of General Mihailovic rather than the more effective Partisans led by General Tito.

After leaving Ealing in 1943 Nolbandov worked at the Ministry of Information until 1946, when he was appointed Head of a Rank Organisation unit responsible for producing *This Modern Age* (*TMA*), a documentary/newsreel series modelled on *The March of Time*. *TMA* produced forty-one twenty-minute films during its four-year existence, each addressing a specific aspect of domestic politics, international affairs or cultural life. Although there are obvious structural similarities with its better-known American counterpart – such as the length and format of each issue and the technique of combining high-quality location footage with voiceover commentary – *TMA* adopted a more discursive and less dogmatic approach to the subjects under discussion. The series was cut in 1950, a victim of the Rank Organisation's financial retrenchment. Nolbandov returned to producing feature films, most successfully with Philip Leacock's *The Kidnappers* (1953). He died in Lewes, Sussex, in August 1971.

(Leo Enticknap)

BIBLIOGRAPHY: Enticknap, Leo, 'This Modern Age and the British Non-Fiction Film', in Justine Ashby and Andrew Higson (eds), *British Cinema, Past and Present* (London and New York: Routledge, 2000); Richards, Jeffrey, 'Wartime Cinema Audiences and the Class System: The Case of *Ship with Wings* (1941)', *Historical Journal of Film, Radio and Television* vol. 7 no. 2, 1987, pp. 129–41.
FILMOGRAPHY: *Ships with Wings* (1941); *Undercover* (1943).

NORMAN, Leslie (1911–1993)

Leslie Norman was born in London on 23 February 1911, and entered the film industry at the age of sixteen. In 1930 he joined British International Pictures and edited *The Man from Chicago* (Walter Summers). He worked as an editor throughout the 1930s and co-directed a low-budget thriller, *Too Dangerous to Live*, in 1939. After serving as a major in the sonic-warfare unit in Burma during the war he joined Ealing Studios, where his first assignment was as supervising editor on the Australian production *The Overlanders* (Harry Watt, 1946). He edited *The Life and Adventures of Nicholas Nickleby* (Alberto Cavalcanti, 1947) and *Frieda* (Basil Dearden, 1947), and teamed up again with Harry Watt to produce more overseas adventures in *Eureka Stockade* (1949), *Bitter Springs* (1950) and *Where No Vultures Fly* (1951). He also produced Ealing's two best non-comedies – *Mandy* (Alexander Mackendrick, 1952) and *The Cruel Sea* (Charles Frend, 1952) – before competently directing *The Night My Number Came Up* (1955), a thriller revolving around a nightmare about a plane crash. It was critically and commercially successful, and Norman was borrowed by Hammer to replace the blacklisted Joseph Losey on *X the Unknown*.

After directing *The Shiralee*, a drama starring Peter Finch in the Australian outback, Norman returned home to make his best-known film, *Dunkirk*, a large-scale project made as an Ealing Studios production for MGM. It was one of the last of such epics to be made in black and white and failed to justify its heavy costs, but its honesty and lack of grandiloquence has allowed it to age gracefully. When Ealing closed down, Norman returned to Australia to make *Summer of the Seventeenth Doll* and worked with Michael Balcon on another Second World War story, *The Long and the Short and the Tall*, a stage success that its director, Lindsay Anderson, had hoped to bring to the screen himself. Norman was considered a safer pair of hands and the producers played even safer by insisting that the film be shot at Elstree rather than in the jungles of Burma.

Like most of Ealing's directors, Norman found it difficult to acquire projects in the different climate of the 1960s. *Spare the Rod*, starring Max Bygraves, is a lively precursor of the huge commercial success *To Sir with Love* (James Clavell, 1967), but *Mix Me a Person*, starring Adam Faith, shows Norman uncomfortable and wary of the emerging youth culture. Apart from his uncredited co-direction of *The Lost Continent* (1968), Norman's subsequent career was confined to television, where he directed episodes of *The Avengers*, *The Champions* and *The Persuaders*. Having survived cancer of the larynx, he died, aged eighty-one, after suffering a seizure while driving near his home in Knebworth, Hertfordshire, on 18 February 1993. His son is the television film critic Barry Norman.

(Margaret Butler)

BIBLIOGRAPHY: Bergan, Ronald, 'Leslie Norman', *Guardian*, 23 Feb. 1993, p. 10; McFarlane, Brian, *An Autobiography of British Cinema* (London: Methuen, 1992); Norman, Leslie, 'Those Were the Days', *Film and TV Technician*, Nov. 1990, pp.18–19.
FILMOGRAPHY: *Too Dangerous to Live* (co-dir. Anthony Hankey, 1939); *The Night My Number Came Up* (1955); *X the Unknown* (1956); *The Shiralee* (1957); *Dunkirk* (1958); *Summer of the Seventeenth Doll* (UK/US/Austral, 1959); *The Long and the Short and the Tall* (1960); *Spare the Rod*; *Mix Me a Person* (1962); *The Lost Continent* (uncredited co-dir., Michael Carreras, 1968).

NOTT, Julian

Julian Nott studied music at Oxford, but pursued a career as a management consultant and a writer for *The Economist* before entering the National Film and Television School in the mid-1980s. As one of the few students enrolled as a composer he was kept very busy scoring films made by his fellow students, including Peter Hewitt, Suri Krishnamma and Nick Park. *A Grand Day Out* (1989), Park's successful graduation film, eventually led to further collaborations on two more lavish Wallace & Gromit adventures, *The Wrong Trousers* (1993) and *A Close Shave* (1995). Along with other composing assignments, notably for Krishnamma's *A Man of No Importance* (1994) and *New Year's Day* (2000), and the television crime series *The Vice* (1999), Nott directed documentaries for Channel 4's science series *Equinox*.

Nott's only feature is *Weak at Denise* (2001), a comedy about a shy middle-aged man who marries his childhood sweetheart, only to find that she plans to murder him for his money. Denise and all the other characters are irredeemably selfish: her boyfriend plans to dump her once he has got his hands on her money and marry a younger woman, who in turn intends to murder him and run off with Denise's lesbian daughter. Colin, the dupe for all these parasites, survives because his adoration of Denise masks a myopic commitment to his own comfort and convenience. Unfortunately, what might have been a compelling black comedy is so flatly presented that all trace of dramatic tension is squeezed out. Though a genuinely eccentric film, and almost odd enough to be likeable, it proved too dull to attract favourable comment or significant audiences.

Fortunately, Nott, who had been displaced in favour of a more blowsy Hollywood score for *Chicken Run* (2000), was restored by Park for *Wallace & Gromit: The Curse of the Were-Rabbit* (2005) and is likely to continue his career as a talented and perceptive film composer rather than a director.

(Robert Murphy)

BIBLIOGRAPHY: Larson, Randall D., 'Nott's Nice Music: Julian Nott Interviewed', *Soundtrack: The Collector's Quarterly*, Winter 2001, pp. 8–10.
FILMOGRAPHY: *Weak at Denise* (2001).

NUNN, Trevor (1940–)

Trevor Nunn was born in Ipswich, Suffolk, on 14 January 1940 and studied at Cambridge University before beginning his career in the theatre. In 1965 he was made a resident director at the Royal Shakespeare Company and was appointed their youngest-ever Artistic Director and Chief Executive in 1968. In 1975 he directed his first feature film, *Hedda*, an adaptation of Ibsen's *Hedda Gabler*. This was a spin-off from his theatrical activities rather than an attempt to reroute his career, and it was not until 1985 that he directed another film, *Lady Jane*, with Helena Bonham Carter as the nine-day queen, Lady Jane Grey. The following year he resigned from the RSC and pursued his interests in the commercial theatre.

Nunn's third and best film is an adaptation of Shakespeare's *Twelfth Night*. He captures the emotional breadth of the play: its sharp humour, playfulness and wit, balanced by pathos and humanity. No character is simply an object of derision or mockery: compassion is afforded Nigel Hawthorne's Malvolio; the rowdy Toby Belch (Mel Smith) barely conceals a steely selfishness; the otherwise silly Aguecheek (Richard E. Grant) conveys an occasional, endearing wistfulness; Ben Kingsley's Feste is the perfect 'wise fool': mischievous, malicious and extremely perceptive.

Twelfth Night was generally well received, but Nunn showed no inclination to abandon the stage for the vicissitudes of the film industry. From 1997 to 2003 he had a controversial reign as Artistic Director of the National Theatre; in 2002 he was awarded a knighthood.

(Sarah Cardwell)

BIBLIOGRAPHY: Bilbow, Marjorie, 'Nunn Makes Directorial Debut with *Lady Jane*', *Screen International*, 15 Dec. 1984, p. 24; Crowdus, Gary, 'Adapting Shakespeare for the Cinema', *Shakespeare Bulletin* vol. 17 no. 3, Summer 1999, pp. 37–40; Vincent, Sally, 'As We Like It', *Guardian*, 12 Oct. 1996, p. 24.

FILMOGRAPHY: *Hedda* (1975); *Lady Jane* (1985); *Twelfth Night* (1996).

O'BYRNE, Joe (1958–)

Joe O'Byrne was born in Ireland on 25 January 1958. His stage production *Frank Pig Says Hello*, an adaptation by Pat McCabe of his novel *The Butcher Boy* (filmed by Neil Jordan in 1997), was a popular and critical success in Dublin and New York and allowed him the opportunity to direct a feature film – *Pete's Meteor* – based on his own script about a troubled adolescent, a kindly scientist and a well-intentioned drug-dealer. The presence of Brenda Fricker, Alfred Molina and Mike Myers failed to compensate for the erratic plot and haphazard direction.

(Robert Murphy)

BIBLIOGRAPHY: Campbell, Triona, 'Winter Shooting on the Set of *Meteor*', *Film West* no. 31, Jan. 1998, pp. 56–7.

FILMOGRAPHY: *Pete's Meteor* (1998).

OCKRENT, Mike (1946–1999)

Michael Robert Ockrent was born in London on 18 June 1946. He became a stage producer, enjoying particular success with Willy Russell's *Educating Rita* and the revival of Noel Gay's *Me and My Girl*. His first film, *Dancin' thru the Dark* (1991), based on Russell's play *Stags & Hens*, was made as a co-production between Palace Pictures, British Screen and the BBC. Critical reception was favourable, but the film, set mainly in the ladies and gents lavatories of a Liverpool dance hall, remained stubbornly stage-bound; it received only minimal cinema release before being shown on television. After another stage success with the musical *Crazy for You* (an updated version of George and Ira Gershwin's *Girl Crazy*) Ockrent directed the television film *Money for Nothing* (1993), a sentimental story of a schoolboy who bamboozles his way into the world of high finance but is steered away from disaster by a loyal friend and a loving woman. Tim Firth's dialogue and Ockrent's unfussy direction make it unexpectedly enjoyable. Ockrent's promising career was cut short by his early death from acute leukaemia in New York on 2 December 1999.

(Robert Murphy)

BIBLIOGRAPHY: Amiel, Vincent and Lorenzo Codelli, 'Mike Ockrent', *Positif* no. 361, Mar. 1991, pp. 13–20; Lentz III, Harris, 'Obituaries: Mike Ockrent', *Classic Images* no. 295, Jan. 2000, pp. 63–4; Pym, John, 'Film Cities: Liverpool & Foremost', *Sight and Sound*, Winter 1989/90, pp. 11–12.

FILMOGRAPHY: *Dancin' thru the Dark* (1991).

O'CONNOLLY, Jim (1926–1987)

Jim O'Connolly was born in Birmingham in 1926. After working as assistant director on Ealing films such as *The Man in the White Suit* (Alexander Mackendrick, 1951), *The Lavender Hill Mob* (Charles Crichton, 1951) and *Mandy* (Alexander Mackendrick, 1952), he switched to the exploitation side of the industry, with credits as production manager on *Horrors of the Black Museum* (Arthur Crabtree, 1959), associate producer on *Konga* (John Lemont, 1961) and screenwriter of *The Night Caller* (John Gilling, 1965).

The first films he directed were hour-long *policiers*, with jazzy scores and distinctive locales. *The Hijackers* is one of a select group of British lorry-driving/transport caff thrillers; while *Smokescreen* is notable for a fine cast (headed by Peter Vaughan and John Carson), a tight plot and some well-observed locations. Unfortunately, by the mid-1960s this sort of B-film had been banished from British cinema screens. O'Connolly entered the still buoyant horror market with *Berserk!*, a circus slasher with Joan Crawford in tights as a domineering ringmistress, and *Tower of Evil*, a murky psycho-on-an-island melodrama with lashings of gore and nudity. This pair of demented horror films is considerably more fun than his biggest picture, *The Valley of Gwangi*, a cowboys-versus-dinosaur fantasy from the Ray Harryhausen stable, and the comedy-thriller *Crooks and Coronets*.

His last feature, *Mistress Pamela* – which he wrote, produced and directed – is based on Samuel Richardson's eighteenth-century novel *Pamela*, and features 1970s' starlet Ann Michelle as the heroine who refuses to surrender her virtue until properly wed. It was not a notable success. O'Connolly died in Hythe, Kent, in 1987.

(Kim Newman)

BIBLIOGRAPHY: Obituary, *Film and TV Technician*, Sept. 1987, p. 11; Press release for *Mistress Pamela*, Jim O'Connolly microfiche held at the BFI National Library, London.

FILMOGRAPHY: *The Hijackers* (1963); *Smokescreen* (1964); *The Little Ones* (1965); *Berserk!* (1967); *The Valley of Gwangi* (US, 1968); *Crooks and Coronets* (1969); *Tower of Evil* (US: *Horror on Snape Island*, 1972); *Mistress Pamela* (1973).

O'CONNOR, Pat (1944–)

Pat O'Connor was born in Ardmore, County Waterford, on 17 June 1944. After studying film at UCLA and the Ryerson Institute, Toronto, and working in television as a director of serials and stand-alone dramas, he made his critical breakthrough in 1982 with the BBC/Radio Telefís Éireann co-production *The Ballroom of Romance*, adapted from a short story by William Trevor. O'Connor's film perceptively captures Trevor's unsentimental scrutiny of life in rural Ireland in the late 1950s, wiping away nostalgia in its exposure of the sad consequences of poverty and sexual repression.

O'Connor's reputation was cemented by two films for Channel 4, both of which were given a limited theatrical release. *Cal* (1984) was adapted from a short story by Bernard MacLaverty about a young Republican (John Lynch) not entirely convincingly involved in a sexual relationship with the widow (Helen Mirren) of a Protestant policeman he has (unwillingly) helped to murder. *A Month in the Country* (1987) follows two traumatised veterans (played by Colin Firth and Kenneth Branagh) as they return to England after the First World War. Both films won critical approval and O'Connor moved to Hollywood, where he directed two comedies: *Stars and Bars*, with Daniel Day-Lewis and Harry Dean Stanton, and *The January Man*, with Kevin Kline, Harvey Keitel and Alan Rickman. Neither were well received. O'Connor returned to Ireland to make another William Trevor adaptation, *Fools of Fortune*, notable for its gothic look and intense, often hysterical performances.

Pat O'Connor (left)

In 1995 O'Connor made *Circle of Friends*, an adaptation of a 'coming-of-age' tale by the popular novelist Maeve Binchy. This bore the now-established trademarks of an O'Connor film – the foregrounding of new acting talent (in this case Minnie Driver and Chris O'Donnell), a period setting and a leisurely pace broken up by moments of kinetic activity. It was a commercial success, though some critics objected to its pastoral view of the Irish countryside and accused O'Connor of pandering to American audiences.

After *Inventing the Abbotts*, a small-town American romance starring Liv Tyler and Joaquin Phoenix, O'Connor directed a big-budget adaptation of Brian Friel's *Dancing at Lughnasa*, with Meryl Streep playing one of five Donegal sisters living a life not dissimilar to that of the leading characters of *The Ballroom of Romance*. The film was criticised for its somewhat inert style, and has remained overshadowed by the original stage play. O'Connor moved back to Hollywood for *Sweet November*, an overly sentimental romantic comedy starring Keanu Reeves and Charlize Theron as an ill-matched couple spending a month together.

O'Connor's Irish works remain his most interesting; his American films have been hampered by a disengaged, languid quality and an emphasis on performance to the detriment of narrative. He has said that he is fascinated by outsiders and remains himself something of an outsider in Irish cinema; one could argue that he has yet to fulfil the promise shown in his early films.

(Ruth Barton)

BIBLIOGRAPHY: Barton, Ruth, *Irish National Cinema* (New York and London: Routledge, 2004); Lennon, Elaine, 'Inventing the Director', *Film Ireland* no. 58, Apr./May 1997, pp. 12–17.

FILMOGRAPHY: *Cal* (1984); *A Month in the Country* (1987); *Stars and Bars* (US, 1988); *January Man* (US, 1989); *Fools of Fortune* (1990); *Circle of Friends* (Ir/UK/US, 1995); *Inventing the Abbotts* (US, 1997); *Dancing at Lughnasa* (Ir/UK/US, 1998); *Sweet November* (US, 2001).

O'DONNELL, Damien (1964–)

Damien O'Donnell was born in Dublin on 11 April 1964. He gained his early experience directing commercials and pop promos before moving into fiction film-making with the

acclaimed short film *Thirty Five Aside.* The story of a young boy who finds himself a misfit at his new school, the film established many of O'Donnell's thematic and stylistic traits, notably the sense of an off-kilter world that his somewhat innocent central male character must learn to negotiate. This was followed by two more short comedies: *Danger Doyle's Doo* (1996) about pigeon racing, made for BBC Scotland; and *Chrono-Perambulator* (1999), a time-travel adventure set principally in Ireland, starring Charles Dance and Bill Paterson.

In 1999 O'Donnell broke through into feature film-making with *East Is East*, adapted by Ayub Khan-Din from his stage play about an Asian fish-and-chip shop owner (Om Puri) whose family rebel against his tyrannical insistence on traditional Muslim ways. O'Donnell's convincing recreation of the ambience of life in a north of England town in the 1970s, well-judged performances and a witty script made the film hugely popular; it won the BAFTA for Best British Film in 2000 and was the last major film success for Channel 4's film production subsidiary.

O'Donnell returned to Ireland to make *What Where* for the 'Beckett on Film' project before directing his second feature film, *Heartlands* (2003), about a darts fanatic (Michael Sheen) who loses his wife to the local policeman and journeys across the Pennines to win her back during the finals of a darts competition in Blackpool. Sheen's likeable performance and a surprisingly unsoppy ending make up for the inconsequentiality of the story, though audiences (and financial backer Miramax) lacked the patience to stay with this very gentle comedy. O'Donnell heeded the lesson, and made *Inside I'm Dancing* (2004), a much more pacy affair, carefully calculated to tug the audience's heartstrings in its tale of two disabled young men (one suffering from muscular dystrophy, the other from cerebral palsy) who discharge themselves from a care home and try to make a life for themselves in Dublin. Cleverly, he uses romance (with the sassy helper they depend upon) as a means of curbing the drift towards 'everything is possible if you believe in it' clichés, introducing a note of sardonic realism where one hopes for fairy-tale transformation.

Though neither *Heartland* nor *Inside I'm Dancing* replicated the success of *East Is East*, they confirm O'Donnell's status as a promising director determined to make idiosyncratic and original films with some relevance to contemporary society.

(Ruth Barton)

BIBLIOGRAPHY: 'East Is East' (interview with Damien O'Donnell), *Film Ireland* no. 73, Oct./Nov. 1999, pp. 14–16; Mac Cárthaigh, Lir, 'One Flew over My Left Foot', *Film Ireland* no. 100, Sept./Oct. 2004, pp. 14–16.

FILMOGRAPHY: *Thirty Five Aside* (short, UK/Ir, 1995); *Danger Doyle's Doo* (short, 1996); *Chrono-Perambulator* (short, 1999); *East Is East* (1999); *What Where* (short, UK/Ir, 2000); *Heartlands* (UK/US, 2003); *Inside I'm Dancing* (2004).

O'HARA, Gerry (1924–)

Gerry O'Hara was born in Boston, Lincolnshire, in 1924. After a long apprenticeship as an assistant director on films such as *So Long at the Fair* (Anthony Darnborough/Terence Fisher, 1950), *The Clouded Yellow* (Ralph Thomas, 1950), *Richard III* (Laurence Olivier, 1955), *Our Man in Havana* (Carol Reed, 1959) and *Tom Jones* (Tony Richardson, 1963), he worked as a writer-director in the livelier fringes of British film and television. His credits include the Merton Park B-crime thriller *Game for Three Losers*, mainstream soft-porn films like *Fanny Hill* and *The Bitch*, several films for the Children's Film Foundation, including *Professor Popper's Problems*, a serial featuring the diminutive comedian Charlie Drake and episodes of television series ranging from *The Avengers* in the 1960s to *The Professionals* in the 1980s.

O'Hara's best films are distinctive contemporary dramas. *The Pleasure Girls* (1965), ostensibly a sexploitation item, has a melancholy streak, interesting performers (Francesca Annis, Carol Cleveland, Suzanna Leigh, Klaus Kinski and Mark Eden) and an unfussy realism. *Amsterdam Affair* (1968) is a well-told Euro-thriller that makes good dramatic use of its setting among Amsterdam's canals. *All the Right Noises* (1969), scripted from his own novel, is knowledgeably set around backstage life, with Tom Bell as an adulterous stage electrician and Judy Carne as his bit-player wife. *The Brute* (1976), despite it exploitation framework, offers some insight into British traditions of violent misogyny.

When *Sight and Sound* reviewed O'Hara's most recent film, *The Mummy Lives*, a Golan-Globus effort with Tony Curtis as a Brooklynese mummy, and reported that the director had passed away, he wrote in to prove otherwise.

(Kim Newman)

BIBLIOGRAPHY: Baker, Bob, 'Gerry O'Hara', *Film Dope* no. 49, June 1993, pp. 7–8; Summers, Sue, 'Harlequin Hopes to Carve a Niche', *Screen International*, 12 Mar. 1997, p. 6.

FILMOGRAPHY: *That Kind of Girl* (1963); *Game for Three Losers*; *The Pleasure Girls* (1965); *Maroc 7* (1966); *Amsterdam Affair* (1968); *All the Right Noises* (1969); *The Chairman's Wife* (short); *The Spy's Wife* (short) (1971); *Paganini Strikes Again*; *And Now for Some Good News* (doc. short) (1973); *Professor Popper's Problems* (1974); *Feelings* (1975); *The Brute* (1976); *Blind Man's Bluff*; *Leopard in the Snow* (1977); *The Bitch* (1979); *Fanny Hill* (1983); *The Mummy Lives* (US, 1993).

OLDMAN, Gary (1958–)

Leonard Gary Oldman was born in New Cross, south-east London, on 21 March 1958. After training as an actor at Rose

Bruford College, he made a name for himself in the theatre, and in television films, notably Mike Leigh's *Meantime* (1984) and Les Blair's *Honest, Decent & True* (1985). Cinema roles followed: Sid Vicious in *Sid and Nancy* (Alex Cox, 1986), Joe Orton in *Prick up Your Ears* (Stephen Frears, 1987), Rosencrantz in *Rosencrantz and Guildenstern are Dead* (Tom Stoppard, 1990) – films where he was often paired with contemporaries Tim Roth and Alfred Molina. He moved into the international arena playing Lee Harvey Oswald in Oliver Stone's *JFK* (1991) and an attractively eccentric Count Dracula in *Bram Stoker's Dracula* (Francis Ford Coppola, 1992), before scaling new heights of villainy as Sirius Black in *Harry Potter and the Prisoner of Azkaban* (Alfonso Cuarón, 2004) and *Harry Potter and the Goblet of Fire* (Mike Newell, 2005).

In 1997 Oldman made his debut as director with *Nil by Mouth*, based on his own script and his own experience of a rough working-class upbringing. Oldman acknowledged the influence of Alan Clarke, who had given him one of his best acting parts as Bex Bissell, the leader of a football hooligan gang in *The Firm* (1988); *Nil by Mouth* consciously adopts Clarke's mixture of social realism (documentary-style camera movements, downtrodden locations) with a stylised aesthetic that makes the representation of violence seem authentic without being gratuitous. The film centres upon the violent, hard-drinking Ray (Ray Winstone), and Oldman ruthlessly exposes the misogyny, cruelty and pettiness of the London hard-man culture (so indulgently celebrated in the late-1990s' wave of British gangster films). Despite its unrelentingly grim picture of British society, *Nil by Mouth* attracted considerable interest and respect, though its success is unlikely to deflect Oldman from his high-profile career as an actor.
(Jamie Sexton)

BIBLIOGRAPHY: James, Nick, 'Being There', *Sight and Sound*, Oct. 1997, pp. 6–9; Matheou, Demetrios, 'Gary New-Man', *Premiere* [UK], Oct. 1997, pp. 68–71; Monk, Claire, 'Men in the 90s', in Robert Murphy (ed.), *British Cinema of the 90s* (London: BFI, 1999).

FILMOGRAPHY: *Nil by Mouth* (1997).

O'LEARY, Ronan (1959–)

Ronan O'Leary was born in Dublin in 1959 and moved to Los Angeles in the 1980s where he worked for PBS. His early films, *Riders to the Sea* (1987) and *Diary of a Madman* (1990), were literary adaptations that deftly blended cinema and theatre, resolutely low budget but ambitious in their literary content and their endeavour to cross-fertilise cinematic and theatrical traditions. His first feature, *Fragments of Isabella* (1989), was an imaginative adaptation of Isabella Leitner's book about the experiences of sisters held in the Auschwitz concentration camp during the Second World War. *Hello Stranger*, an adaptation of a short story by Truman Capote, was produced for television in 1992.

O'Leary's first contemporary narrative film, *Driftwood* (1997), featured James Spader as a man mysteriously washed ashore on an isolated Irish beach and Anne Brochet as the French artist who accommodates and then obsessively entraps him. Like *Fragments of Isabella* and *Diary of a Madman*, the film is distinguished by Walter Lassally's cinematography, but production difficulties (O'Leary was removed during post-production, and subsequently disowned the film) hampered its pace and narrative development. Hopefully future projects will allow O'Leary to explore and develop further his visual flair and talent for offbeat literary adaptation.
(Eugene Finn)

BIBLIOGRAPHY: Kavanagh, Linda, *RTE Guide*, 6 Apr. 1990, pp. 4–5; Kehoe, Paddy, 'Fragments of Ronan O'Leary', *Irish Stage and Screen*, Dec. 1989, p. 6.

FILMOGRAPHY: *Riders to the Sea* (Ir, 1987); *Fragments of Isabella* (Ir, 1989); *Diary of a Madman* (Ir, 1990); *Hello Stranger* (Ir, 1992); *Driftwood* (UK/Ir, 1997).

OLIVIER, Laurence (1907–1989)

The most commanding and incisive British stage actor of his generation, Laurence Olivier showed similar energy and sense of purpose in his best work as a cinema director, particularly his first two Shakespeare productions, *Henry V* (1944) and *Hamlet* (1948), among the most striking British films of the decade. Laurence Kerr Olivier was born in Dorking, Surrey, on 22 May 1907, the son of a clergyman. Precociously talented, he made his stage debut at the age of fifteen. Four years later in 1926, he joined the Birmingham Repertory Company, beginning a fifty-year stage career that took him from young romantic parts through the major Shakespeare roles to important management positions at the Old Vic, St James' Theatre and finally the National Theatre. He started acting in films in 1930, looking awkward and callow; portraying Orlando in Paul Czinner's over-decorative *As You Like It* (1936) only intensified his initial suspicion of cinema as a vehicle for Shakespeare.

By the time Two Cities' *Henry V* project was put before him by the Ministry of Information's Films Division in 1942 as a suitable wartime spirit booster, Olivier's views had mellowed. He had now acted with success in Hollywood, and he initially hoped that William Wyler, his congenial director from *Wuthering Heights* (1939), would hold the reins on *Henry V*. In the event he became his own director, with the editor Reginald Beck and the actor Anthony Bushell standing by, in Beck's words, as 'a kind of insurance against technical defect' (Cross, p. 15); similar arrangements occurred on later films. Other team members played key creative roles in *Henry V*, including the production designer Roger Furse; William Walton, composer of the stirring music; and the associate producer Dallas Bower, the project's instigator. But Olivier alone shaped and inspired, and conceived two of the film's most adventurous elements: the framing scenes featuring Shakespeare's Chorus, opening and closing a bustling performance at the original Globe Theatre; and the filtering of the designs through the influence of the fifteenth-century illuminated miniatures of *Les Très riches heures du duc de Berry*

– ideal material for Robert Krasker's colour photography, filmed with the only Technicolor camera in England. Olivier's performance as the warrior king matches the visuals in panache and daring. Through the elaborate and exhilarating Agincourt battle filmed in Eire, cosmetic surgery of speeches and the general patriotic clamour, *Henry V* presents itself clearly as a Second World War film in historical guise.

Critics and audiences were enraptured. Further emboldened, Olivier mounted his next Shakespeare venture, *Hamlet*, with a heavily cut and rejigged text and a determinedly sombre stylistic approach. Inspired by Gregg Toland's deep-focus camerawork in America, Olivier played intricate spatial games with his characters, slowly progressing with Desmond Dickinson's tracking camera through the rooms, corridors and stairways of Roger Furse's austerely oppressive Elsinore. Freudian theories gave Olivier insights into ways of playing his blond, tortured Prince of Denmark; with its stark black-and-white imagery, swirling smoke, visions, flashbacks, obsessions and jealousies, this *Hamlet* equally displays signs of 1940s' film noir. Though the sets' weight and size flatten some of the drama, the largely excellent cast and brooding atmosphere, Walton's music and Olivier's visual adventures ('To be or not to be' begins with a dissolve into the back of Hamlet's head) help give the film lasting stature.

Olivier's third and last Shakespeare production, *Richard III* (1955), in Technicolor and VistaVision, was mounted by Korda's London Films. Furse, Bushell, Walton and the skilled art director Carmen Dillon all returned as collaborators. Cinema's possibilities are still acknowledged: Richard's soliloquies, knowing winks and malevolent shadow always catch the camera's eye, while roving camerawork and extreme angles periodically enliven Furse's composite grey set. But the theatre here has visibly reclaimed ground. The Bosworth battle, shot in Spain, is half-hearted compared to Agincourt; and in a cast emblazoned with theatrical knights (Richardson, Gielgud, along with Sir Cedric Hardwicke) Olivier's psychologically shallow if mesmerising hunchback, scheming to secure England's throne, overwhelmingly occupies centre stage. The spectacle was sufficient to make the film hugely successful, commercially and critically.

Whereas the Shakespeare films were allied to Olivier's high theatrical endeavours at the Old Vic, his next venture, *The Prince and the Showgirl* (1957), reflected the more commercial plays mounted in the West End at St James' Theatre and elsewhere. In 1953 Olivier had starred with his second wife, Vivien Leigh, in *The Sleeping Prince*, a flimsy if popular Terence Rattigan comedy about an American showgirl in London, stirring the sleeping heart of a Balkan Grand Duke. Marilyn Monroe bought the film rights with a view to Olivier as her co-star and director. Her view prevailed. Vestiges of Olivier's favoured directorial devices can be found – the camera choreography, the deep-focus games inside Furse's plush sets. But the undemanding material is better suited to Monroe's loose acting style than Olivier's manicured manner; and the luscious Technicolor photography and costumes only go so far in easing the 117-minute running time.

Once Olivier became Director of the National Theatre in 1963, chances for his own cinema projects diminished. In 1965 his overpowering portrayal of Othello in John Dexter's stage production was captured on film, but only in a straight transcription, directed by Stuart Burge. Four years later, when his own production of Chekhov's *Three Sisters* went before the cameras, featuring his third wife, Joan Plowright, he assumed directorial control himself, inserting himself into the stage cast as the retired doctor Chebutikin, one among the family and friends idling and dreaming in a Russian provincial town. William Walton again provided music, but apart from one fantasy and one flash forward, the script simply telescoped the play's action, looking somewhat marooned by the camera among Josef Svoboda's spare sets. The film is worthy, but dull.

Considering the fireworks of *Henry V*, this unambitious *Three Sisters* may seem a particularly tame conclusion to Olivier's work as a film director. But Chekhov's preoccupations with Tsarist upper-class frustrations transfer with difficulty onto film; and if the arc of Olivier's career proves anything, it is that theatre always and deservedly took the best of his energies and talents. His two films of the 1940s derived their cinematic impact partly from their alliance with the needs and spirit of the times: in *Henry V*, with patriotic trumpeting and the desire to present Britain's theatrical tradition in battle dress; in *Hamlet*, post-war anguish and introspection. Without a firm base in the national mood, *Richard III* emerged as more of a theatrical pageant, a vehicle for an exuberant stage turn; while *The Prince and the Showgirl* could offer nothing beyond upholstered nostalgia and two mismatched stars, pickled in Technicolor aspic. Nonetheless, Olivier's cinema career matters. His three Shakespeare films did more to popularise Shakespeare and bridge the gap between stage and screen than any previous productions; and his visionary conception of *Henry V* alone gives him a place high among British film directors. Laurence Olivier died at Steyning, West Sussex, on 11 July 1989.

(Geoff Brown and James C. Robertson)

BIBLIOGRAPHY: Brown, Constance A., 'Olivier's *Richard III* – A Re-evaluation', *Film Quarterly* vol. 20 no. 4, Summer 1967, pp. 23–32; Cottrell, John, *Laurence Olivier* (London: Weidenfeld & Nicolson, 1975); Cross, Brenda (ed.), *The Film Hamlet: A Record of Its Production* (London: The Saturn Press, 1948); Geduld, Harry M., *Film Guide to Henry V* (Bloomington: Indiana University Press, 1973); Olivier, Laurence, *Confessions of an Actor* (London: Weidenfeld & Nicolson, 1982); Silviria, Dale, *Laurence Olivier and the Art of Film Making* (Rutherford, NJ: Fairleigh Dickinson University Press, 1985).

FILMOGRAPHY (as director only): *Henry V* (1944); *Hamlet* (1948); *Richard III* (assoc. dir. Anthony Bushell, 1955); *The Prince and the Showgirl* (assoc. dir. Anthony Bushell, 1957); *Three Sisters* (1970).

ONWURAH, Ngozi (c. 1967–)

Ngozi Onwurah was born in Nigeria but returned to Britain with her Scottish mother when she was ten. After working as a model she studied film and made a number of refreshingly original documentaries exploring the lives of black women and children in Britain and Nigeria, including the semi-autobiographical *Coffee Coloured Children* (1988) and *The Body Beautiful* (1991). In 1994 she contributed 'White Men Are Cracking Up' to *Siren Spirits*, a BFI/BBC four-part feature exploring various aspects of family and race relations from the perspective of black and Asian women.

In 1995 Onwurah received Channel 4 backing for *Welcome II the Terrordome* (1995), a futuristic feature that aroused considerable controversy for its dystopian vision, unforgiving attitude towards the slavery of black people and seeming assertion of black superiority. Onwurah's rage over her black heritage led her to bludgeon the audience with clumsy, sometimes cruelly prolonged images, leaving little room for nuanced thought. After this debacle she ventured briefly into mainstream television drama, directing episodes of *Heartbeat*, but chose to return to more political forms of film-making with the non-fiction short *The Desired Number* (1995), and *Hang Time* (2001), an ironic tale of a Nigerian boy who turns to crime in a desperate bid to achieve his sporting ambitions. Onwurah is married to the German cinematographer Alwin Küchler, her cameraman on *Welcome II the Terrordome* and subsequent films.

(Robert Murphy)

BIBLIOGRAPHY: Ellerson, Beti, *Sisters of the Screen: Women of Africa on Film, Video and Television* (Trenton, NJ: Africa World Press, 2000); Foster, Gwendolyn Audrey, *Women Film Directors: An International Bio-Critical Dictionary* (Westport, CT: Greenwood, 1995); Foster, Gwendolyn Audrey, *Women Filmmakers of the African and Asian Diaspora: Decolonizing the Gaze, Locating Subjectivity* (Carbondale: Southern Illinois University Press, 1997); Woodford, Elizabeth, 'Film-Maker Onwurah in Residence at Humanities Institute' <www.umich.edu/~urecord/9798/Mar11_98/onwurah.htm>.

FILMOGRAPHY: *Coffee Colored Children* (short, 1988); *The Body Beautiful* (short, 1991); *And Still I Rise* (short, US); *Flight of the Swan* (short); *Monday's Girls* (doc., UK/Nig) (1993); *Siren Spirits* ('White Men are Cracking Up' episode, co-dirs. Pratibha Parmar/Frances-Anne Solomon/Dani Williamson, 1994); *Welcome II the Terrordome*; *The Desired Number* (doc. short, Nig) (1995); *Hang Time* (short, UK/Nig, 2001); *Making Mischief* (2006).

ORME, Stuart (1954–)

Stuart Orme was born in Derby in 1954. After studying at drama school he joined Thames Television in 1970, eventually moving on to Granada and freelancing as a director of music promos. Television offered more opportunities than cinema: achievements range from a solid Euston Films crime serial, *The Fear* (1988); David Kane's Dundee-set thriller *Jute City* (1990); a remake of *Goodbye Mr Chips* (2002); and an adaptation of Raymond Briggs' *Fungus the Bogeyman* (2004). His two films that have received a theatrical release are both adaptations of popular novels. *The Wolves of Willoughby Chase*, shot on location in a snow-covered, wolf-ridden Czechoslovakia, is based on Joan Aitken's ripping yarn about two smart Victorian girls thwarting the plans of their evil governess (Stephanie Beacham). It was followed six years later by a Hollywood adaptation of Robert A. Heinlein's *The Puppet Masters*, in which Donald Sutherland and Julie Warner are plagued by slug-like aliens. An atypical adult production for the Disney Corporation, it was allotted the relatively modest budget of $15 million and not heavily promoted as a cinema film. Orme remains a prolific director of television drama.

(Robert Murphy)

BIBLIOGRAPHY: Beeler, Michael, 'The Puppet Masters', *Cinefantastique*, Dec./Jan. 1994/5, pp. 40–3; Griffin, Sue, 'Genesis Leads to Exodus from Mainstream TV', *Broadcast*, 24 Jan. 1986, p. 17; Jones, Alan, 'Preview: *The Wolves of Willoughby Chase*', *StarBurst* no. 128, Apr. 1989, pp. 20–1.

FILMOGRAPHY: *The Wolves of Willoughby Chase* (1988); *The Puppet Masters* (US, 1994).

ORMROD, Peter (1950–)

Peter Ormrod was born in 1950 in England, the son of an army major and a Cretan resistance fighter. After making amateur films he worked as a runner for a Greek film company, as a film librarian at the BBC and as a boom operator and clapper/loader on feature films. He then spent three years at the Royal College of Art, where, with additional funding from the Gulbenkian Foundation and the Southern Arts Association, he made *Rachel and the Beelzebub Bombardiers*, a feature-length film, about a girl caught up in the struggle between the rival Salvation and Skeleton Armies over the perils and delights of strong drink in late-nineteenth-century Berkshire.

Ormrod was recruited by John Kelleher, Controller of Programmes at Radio Telefís Éireann, to direct television magazine items. He moved on to make the highly regarded four-part series *Caught in a Free State* (1984), about German agents in Ireland during the Second World War, as a co-production between RTÉ and Channel 4. With Kelleher and producer David Collins he set up Strongbow Films, which raised around £1 million on the Irish Stock Exchange to make *Eat the Peach*, a subject based on a news item Ormrod had filmed about a man who constructed a Wall of Death after seeing Elvis Presley in *Roustabout* (John Rich, 1964). A further £500,000 was contributed by Channel 4. The completed film had much charm, with strong performances by Stephen Brennan, Eamon Morrissey and Niall Toibin. Ormrod makes creative use of the flat, boggy Irish Midlands as a setting, a welcome move from international cinema's fixation with the west coast of Ireland as the locale for escapist, romantic dramas. *Eat the Peach* was well received in Ireland but poor distribution arrangements meant that, apart from its Channel 4 screening, it remained virtually unseen in the UK, and Strongbow Films became insolvent. In 1987 Ormrod made *Sage Stuck*, written by Barry Simner, for the Channel 4 series *Tandoori Nights*, but he subsequently disappeared from the film and television industry.

(Ruth Barton)

BIBLIOGRAPHY: Banner, Simon, 'Refusing to Be Too Sensible', *The Times*, 4 Dec. 1986, p. 12; Barton, Ruth, 'Kitsch as Authenticity', *Irish Studies Review* vol. 9 no. 2, 2001, pp. 193–202; Peachment, Chris, 'Flight of Fancy', *Time Out* no. 851, 10 Dec. 1986, p. 34; Publicity material for *Eat the Peach*, 'Peter Ormrod – Director', Dec. 1986, held on microfiche in the BFI National Library, London.

FILMOGRAPHY: *Rachel and the Beelzebub Bombardiers* (1977); *Eat the Peach* (UK/Ir, 1986).

ORTON, John (1889–1962)

J. O. C. Orton is a regular name among the scriptwriters on Will Hay films and other Gainsborough comedies. But in the turbulent years of transition between silents and talkies Orton lived another existence as John Orton, a director and editor at large. Born in London in 1889, he spent fifteen years in the army before entering the film industry via Adrian Brunel's cutting rooms in 1923. After working in Sweden as an editor for Gustaf Molander, he returned home to perform various duties for British Instructional Films, co-writing Asquith's breakthrough feature *Shooting Stars* (A.V. Bramble/Anthony Asquith, 1928).

In October 1928 Orton moved into the director's chair for *The Celestial City*, an escapist drama set in Russia. His next feature assignment was as director of studio interiors for *Windjammer*, a semi-documentary constructed around footage shot by two Australian journalists during the long voyage to Britain of one of the last commercial sailing ships. Artifice clashed with reality, but Orton's scenes had the merit of Michael Hogan's impressive performance as a hard-bitten seaman.

His eclectic career continued at British International Pictures, with *Creeping Shadows*, a raging melodrama, and *Bill and Coo*, an eccentric vehicle for the music-hall comic Billy Merson. After directing Jessie Matthews' screen test he supplied cinematic grace notes to her feature debut, *Out of the Blue*, nominally directed by its star, Gene Gerrard. But nothing substantial followed. From 1932 until the mid-1950s Orton concentrated on comedy writing, being valued more for ideas than dialogue. 'I might have made a good cutter, but not – repeat not – a writer,' he declared in 1960. By that time even Orton seemed to have forgotten his directing career. He died in London on 23 May 1962.
(Geoff Brown)

BIBLIOGRAPHY: Orton, John, 'Notes on Direction', in Adrian Brunel, *Filmcraft* (London, George Newnes, 1933).

FILMOGRAPHY: *The Celestial City*; *R.A.D.A. Film Class* (doc.) (1929); *Windjammer* (1930); *Creeping Shadows* (US: *The Limping Man*); *Bill and Coo*; *Out of the Blue* (Gene Gerrard, supervised by Orton) (1931); *The Bad Companions* (1932).

O'SULLIVAN, Shane (c. 1969–)

Irish-born Shane O'Sullivan taught English in Japan before settling in London. After failing to raise industry finance for his script set among the multicultural community in London's East End, he persuaded private investors to put up a tiny budget of £25,000 and shot *Second Generation* on digital video. Though the concept of seeing London through the eyes of a naive Chinese girl on the run from an arranged marriage could have been interesting, the film is let down by ponderous dialogue and amateurish acting.
(Robert Murphy)

FILMOGRAPHY: *Second Generation* (2000); *Lemon Crush* (short, 2002).

O'SULLIVAN, Thaddeus (1947–)

The trajectory of Thaddeus O'Sullivan's career mirrors that of film production in Ireland more generally – from experimental and avant-garde beginnings in the 1970s to more mainstream commercial cinema and television from the 1990s onwards. O'Sullivan played a key role in the early development of Irish cinema and, with fellow independent film-makers Bob Quinn, Pat Murphy, Joe Comerford and Cathal Black, was an early lobbyist on behalf of an indigenous Irish cinema.

O'Sullivan was born in Dublin on 2 May 1947 but moved to London in 1966, where he received his early film training at the Ealing School of Art and the Royal College of Art. As with some of his Irish contemporaries, his earlier films were influenced by avant-garde theories and experimental film-making (especially those of Stephen Dwoskin, a tutor at the RCA). In the late 1970s he made two influential experimental films about the life of the Irish immigrant in London: the short film *A Pint of Plain* and the feature-length *On a Paving Stone Mounted*. Using a combination of documentary footage and fictional recreation, both films explore the place of the exile in culture – never really belonging in the adopted country and yet drifting further from the home left behind. These films encapsulate O'Sullivan's own position as a film-maker caught between the two cultures of Britain and Ireland, and his best work has explored personal identities caught in complex cultural interplay.

During the 1980s, O'Sullivan developed into a highly regarded lighting cameraman, working on important Irish independent films, including Comerford's *Traveller* (1981), Black's *Pigs* (1984) and Murphy's *Anne Devlin* (1984), for which he provided the atmospheric and highly effective long takes and tableau shots that characterise the film. His international breakthrough came as cinematographer on Andrew Grieve's *On the Black Hill* (1987), which was critically acclaimed for its beautiful and evocative landscapes.

He continued to direct his own films during this period – a documentary on the painter Jack B. Yeats in 1981 and a critically acclaimed short fiction film, *The Woman Who Married Clark Gable*, which received a BAFTA nomination and presaged his move into more conventional narrative cinema. His first fiction feature as director was *December Bride* (1990), an adaptation of Sam Hanna Bell's Northern Irish novel about a scandalous *ménage à trois* set in a rural Presbyterian community in Ulster. It was an important film in the development of contemporary Irish cinema, notable for its exploration of an aspect of Irish rural life far removed from the romantic whimsy of Hollywood.

O'Sullivan subsequently tackled contemporary urban Ireland in two contrasting films. He became the first director to explore Loyalist paramilitaries in Northern Ireland in his stylish but sombre political thriller *Nothing Personal*, and he revisited the Dublin gangster world of John Boorman's *The General* (1998) in his own more light-hearted version of the Michael Cahill story, *Ordinary Decent Criminal*. *The Heart of Me* (2002) marked a break: a costume film set in the 1930s about an upper-middle-class English love triangle (based on Rosamund Lehmann's novel *The Echoing Grove*). A slight, sad story and a dearth of exotic locations gave the film little chance of repeating the box-office success of James Ivory's more weighty *Howards End* (1992) or Iain Softley's flamboyant *The Wings of the Dove* (1997); but O'Sullivan's patient, low-key exploration of sibling rivalry and doomed love gives *The Heart of Me* a genuine poignancy. Directing the opening episodes of Granada's *Island at War* (2004) was a more routine period assignment; though dealing with a plethora of stories and characters no doubt proved useful in extending his range.

(Martin McLoone)

BIBLIOGRAPHY: McLoone, Martin, 'A Landscape Peopled Differently: *December Bride*', in James MacKillop (ed.), *Contemporary Irish Cinema* (New York: Syracuse University Press, 1999); McLoone, Martin, *Irish Film: The Emergence of a Contemporary Cinema* (London: BFI, 2000); Pettitt, Lance, *Screening Ireland* (Manchester: Manchester University Press, 2000); Pettitt, Lance, *December Bride* (Cork: Cork University Press, 2001).

FILMOGRAPHY: *A Pint of Plain* (short, 1977); *On a Paving Stone Mounted* (1978); *Jack B. Yeats: Assembled Memories 1871–1957* (doc. short, 1981); *The Woman Who Married Clark Gable* (short, Ir, 1985); *December Bride* (UK/Ir, 1990); *Nothing Personal* (UK/Ir, 1995); *Ordinary Decent Criminal* (US/Ir/Ger, 2000); *The Heart of Me* (UK/Fr, 2002).

OVÉ, Horace (1939–)

Horace Ové was born in Belmont, Trinidad and Tobago, in 1939. He came to Britain in 1960 to study painting, photography and interior design. After working as a film extra in Rome, he returned to London to study at the London School of Film Technique. He began work on *Man Out*, a surreal film about a West Indian novelist who has a mental breakdown. The project was never completed, but in 1966 Ové directed *The Art of the Needle*, a short film for the Acupuncture Association. This was followed by another short, *Baldwin's Nigger*, in which novelist James Baldwin discusses black experience and identity in Britain and America.

Ové's next film, *Reggae*, was a documentary examining what was then an underground music genre. It was the first feature-length film financed by black people in Britain (funded by Junior Lincoln, a record producer), and was successful in cinemas and shown by the BBC. *Reggae*'s success helped open some hitherto closed doors for Ové. Films made for the BBC's *World about Us* series, such as *King Carnival* (1973) and *Skateboard Kings*

(1978), showed Ové's interest in representing multi- and subcultural lifestyles. Similarly, work for Channel 4 such as *Music Fusion* (1982) and *Street Arts* (1983) documented the hybridity and vitality of black British life. *Playing Away* (1986), a feature film made for Channel 4, written by Caryl Phillips, explored the plight of a team of black cricketers from Brixton invited to play against a white English team as part of a village's 'Third World Week' celebrations. The film demonstrates Ové's ability to balance comedy with more serious issues, skilfully bringing out the race and class tensions underlying the cricket match.

Ové has often looked to combine the form and style of documentary with more conventional drama. *Pressure* (1975) – the first feature-length fiction film by a black director in Britain – and *A Hole in Babylon*, made in 1979 as a BBC *Play for Today*, explore the problems facing young British blacks, using the conventions of drama-documentary with gritty, naturalistic performances. Both films caused controversy: *Pressure* was shelved for almost three years by its funders, the BFI, ostensibly because it contained scenes showing police brutality; *A Hole in Babylon*, an account of the 1975 Spaghetti House siege, was criticised for its sympathetic portrayal of the main characters, who were vilified in the press as a 'bunch of black hooligans'. As Ové says, he wanted to show 'that black people were fighting for their rights under a very racist situation and . . . were finding ways and means of demonstrating their feelings' (Pines, p. 126). His importance as a film-maker therefore lies not just in his being the 'first' black director to break into the mainstream of television, but also in the committed political voice he retained once he had got there. Ové now lives in the Caribbean, working there and in the US.

(Paul Ward)

BIBLIOGRAPHY: Ellis, John (ed.), *1951–1976 British Film Institute Production* (London: BFI, 1977); Givanni, June, 'Horace Ové – Reflection on a Thirty-Year Experience', *Black Film Bulletin*, Summer 1996, pp. 16–21; Jaafar, Ali, 'Interview', 'Black World', *Sight and Sound* supplement, July 2005, p. 6; Korta, Barbara and Claudia Sternberg, *Bidding for the Mainstream? Black and Asian British Film Since the 1990s* (Amsterdam and New York: Rodophi, 2004); Pines, Jim (ed.), *Black and White in Colour: Black People in British Television since 1936* (London: BFI, 1992).

FILMOGRAPHY (UK only): *The Art of the Needle* (short, 1966); *Baldwin's Nigger* (short, 1969); *Reggae* (1970); *Coleherne Jazz and Keskidee Blues* (short, 1972); *Pressure* (1975); *Stretch Hunter* (short, 1980); *Who Shall We Tell?* (short, 1985); *Playing Away* (1986).

OWEN, Cliff (1919–1993)

Cliff Owen was born in London on 22 April 1919. He entered the film industry in 1937, working his way through various jobs before reaching the position of first assistant director on a variety of films including *The Magic Box* (John Boulting, 1951) and *The Yellow Balloon* (J. Lee Thompson, 1953). In 1955 he moved to television as a director – both for one-off dramas such as Arthur Miller's *All My Sons* (1958) and Terence Rattigan's *The Browning Version* (1958), and on drama series, notably *The Third Man* (1959). His first two feature films were effective crime thrillers: *Offbeat*, starring William Sylvester as an unconventional law officer who ultimately foils a gang of jewel thieves; and *A Prize of Arms*, with Stanley Baker leading a raid on an army payroll office. Both deal with the subject of loyalty and trust within the criminal underworld; *Offbeat* is particularly impressive, with the shifting allegiances of the undercover officer inspired more by admiration for the gang's ethics than thoughts of financial reward. For his third film, *The Wrong Arm of the Law*, Owen takes the same themes but skews them for comic effect, with gangster Peter Sellers calling a truce with the authorities to thwart an interpolating gang of confidence tricksters.

Sadly, Owen was never again able to scale the heights of his first three films, and his deft touch seemed to have forsaken him when he returned to the cinema after four years working in television comedy. In *Offbeat* small visual flourishes compensated for the occasional weakness in dialogue, but in the later films everything is submerged under the weight of poor scripts. Most of these films showcased small-screen stars in unambitious comedies – Eric Morecambe and Ernie Wise in *That Riviera Touch* and *The Magnificent Two* (1967); Harry H. Corbett and Wilfrid Brambell in *Steptoe & Son*; Dick Emery in *Ooh . . . You Are Awful*; and Ronnie Corbett and Arthur Lowe in *No Sex Please – We're British*. The pleasures to be had from the performances of these seasoned comedy specialists pale next to those of their best television work.

Owen fared no better on other projects. He shot the exteriors for *A Man Could Get Killed*, largely consisting of dispiriting slapstick violence in a convoluted comedy-thriller held together only by James Garner's presence; and he supplied Hammer with a lamentable fantasy, *The Vengeance of She*. His final film was *The Bawdy Adventures of Tom Jones* – a musical version of Henry Fielding's classic that had been filmed so successfully by Tony Richardson in 1963 – with Nicky Henson replacing Albert Finney in the title role. The latter years of his career were confined to directing informational shorts. He died in Banbury in 1993.

(Richard Dacre)

BIBLIOGRAPHY: Interview, *CinemaTV Today*, 26 Apr. 1975, p. 11; Withall, Keith, 'Cliff Owen', *Film Dope* no. 49, June 1993, p. 42.

FILMOGRAPHY: *Offbeat* (1960); *A Prize of Arms* (1961); *The Wrong Arm of the Law* (1962); *That Riviera Touch* (1966); *A Man Could Get Killed* (co-dir. Ronald Neame, US, 1966); *The Magnificent Two* (aka *What Happened at Campo Grande?*); *The Vengeance of She* (1967); *Steptoe & Son*; *Ooh . . . You Are Awful* (US: *Get Charlie Tully*) (1972); *No Sex Please – We're British* (1973); *The Bawdy Adventures of Tom Jones* (1975); *Health Education Council 'Walkies'* (short, 1977); *Health Education Council 'Ageing Man'* (short, 1978); *Sweetex Lumps* (short, 1980).

PAGE, Anthony (1935–)

Anthony Page, born to a military family in Bangalore, India, on 21 September 1935, read English at Oxford before obtaining a grant to study acting at the Neighbourhood Playhouse in New York under Sanford Meisner. In 1958 he joined Tony Richardson's company at the Royal Court, becoming an Artistic Director in 1964, by which time he had already directed episodes of the television series *Z Cars*. He had a long association with the playwright John Osborne, and in 1968 directed the film of their greatest triumph, *Inadmissible Evidence*, starring Nicol Williamson. Page perhaps unwisely uses flashbacks to 'open out' the play, but the film remains a mesmerising portrait of a mid-life crisis.

After leaving the Royal Court in 1973, Page concentrated on directing television movies in America, though he made two films in Britain in the late 1970s. *Absolution*, written by Anthony Shaffer, bears comparison with Sidney Lumet's *Child Play* (1972) and is notable for Page's restrained handling and for a haunted performance by Richard Burton as a priest manipulated into murder by an evil student. *The Lady Vanishes* cheekily uses American stars Elliot Gould and Cybill Shepherd in an enjoyable if inconsequential remake of the Hitchcock classic. Critics were not amused, though it fared moderately well at the box office.

Since returning to the UK in the 1990s Page has worked mainly for the stage, though in 1991 he directed an impressive adaptation of Rodney Ackland's *Absolute Hell* and in 1994 directed the hugely successful BBC dramatisation of George Eliot's *Middlemarch*.

(Sergio Angelini)

BIBLIOGRAPHY: Christopher, James, 'Page Keeps Theatre Turning', *Evening Standard*, 2 June 2000.

FILMOGRAPHY: *Inadmissible Evidence* (1968); *Alpha Beta* (1973; rel. 1976); *I Never Promised You a Rose Garden* (US, 1977); *Absolution* (1978); *The Lady Vanishes* (1979); *Forbidden* (Ger/UK, 1983).

PALMER, Tony (1941–)

Anthony Palmer was born in London on 29 August 1941. He joined the BBC after graduating from Cambridge in 1964, progressing from assistant jobs with Ken Russell and Jonathan Miller to directing and producing his own films. He was best known originally for flamboyant pop music projects, including *All My Loving* (1968), a portrait of the Beatles for the BBC, and the ambitious LWT series *All You Need Is Love* (1977), covering popular music's history throughout the twentieth century. The work spilled over into cinema with rock concert films, a flashy portrait of Leonard Cohen on tour (*Bird on a Wire*) and the wildly incoherent *200 Motels* (1971), an intermittently amusing attempt to capture the bizarre musical humour of Frank Zappa and the Mothers of Invention. But the emergence in the early 1980s of two prize-winning, sensitive television biographies of Benjamin Britten (*A Time There Was . . .*) and William Walton (*At the Haunted End of the Day*) changed both critical perceptions and Palmer's career. From henceforth, with a few exceptions, he concentrated on classical music biographies, with subjects ranging from Wagner and Chopin, Menuhin and Callas, to Shostakovich, Stravinsky and Malcolm Arnold.

Palmer's preferred genre and his stylistic ebullience invite parallels with Ken Russell, but there are clear distinctions between their work. Typically, Russell portrays his artists as madmen, detached from the outside world, with excessive libido or sexual problems. Palmer represents musicians' lives against a closely observed cultural and political background. The dramatic focus is usually located in the subjects' struggles to fit into society and fulfil their artistry – recurring themes central to the lengthy *Testimony* (1987), structured around Shostakovich's ambivalent relationship with Stalin. *Testimony* and the more ponderous, five-hour *Wagner* (1983; nine hours in its television edition) represent Palmer's most ambitious attempts to explore musical lives, moving far beyond documentary into full-scale dramatic reconstructions laced with fiction, meticulously researched, with costumes and interiors carefully designed, and major players (Richard Burton as Wagner, Ben Kingsley as Shostakovich) shouldering the principal roles.

On the basis of *Testimony*, Channel 4 commissioned Palmer to direct *The Children* (1990), his sole purely fictional venture, a period drama of awkward love and entanglements, adapted from Edith Wharton's novel. A slow pace, overindulged Steadicam photography, and an ill-suited cast lowered the chances of success. No mighty cinema endeavour has followed *Wagner*, but small-screen ventures like his Malcolm Arnold portrait *Toward the Unknown Region* (2004) continue to demonstrate Palmer's technical flair and vivid ability to present the human cost of artistic creativity.

(Geoff Brown and Ewa Mazierska)

BIBLIOGRAPHY: Elley, Derek, 'The Palmer Touch', *Guardian*, 28 June 1989, pp. 23–5; Tibbetts, John C., 'Shostakovich's Fool to Stalin's Czar: Tony Palmer's *Testimony* (1987)', *Historical Journal of Film, Radio and Television* vol. 22 no. 2, June 2002, pp. 173–96; <www.tonypalmer.org>.

FILMOGRAPHY: *Cream's Farewell Concert* (1968; rel. 1970); *Colosseum and Juicy Lucy* (short, 1970); *Fairport Convention and Matthews Southern Comfort* (short, 1970; rel. 1972); *200 Motels* (co-dir. Frank Zappa, 1971); *Bird on a Wire* (1972; rel. 1974); *The Space Movie* (1980); *Wagner* (UK/Hung/Aus, 1983); *Testimony* (1987); *The Children* (UK/Ger, 1990).

PALTENGHI, David (1919–1961)

David Paltenghi, born in Bournemouth on 20 July 1919, was among the new directing talent brought into feature films in the 1950s by the government-funded Group 3 company. In 1954 he was assigned to two comedies: *Orders Are Orders*, the nonsensical tale of a film unit invading an army barracks, notable for appearances by Tony Hancock and Peter Sellers; and *The Love Match*, an old-style northern farce starring Arthur Askey.

Of Swiss nationality, Paltenghi came to cinema from the ballet. He joined Sadler's Wells Ballet in 1941 and became one of its principal male dancers. Anxious to spread his wings, he left in 1947 to explore other media and choreograph his own ballets. He choreographed sequences in *Hamlet* (Laurence Olivier, 1948), *The Queen of Spades* (Thorold Dickinson, 1949), *The Black Knight* (Tay Garnett, 1954) and other films; in 1952 he danced the role of the husband in the 'Ring around the Posy' segment of Gene Kelly's *Invitation to the Dance* (1956).

Paltenghi's comedies scarcely required balletic grace, though a sense of movement and timing peeps through the broad tomfoolery in *Orders Are Orders*. *The Love Match* found greater public success, but only earned Paltenghi the dubious privilege of directing the lowbrow comic Ronald Shiner in *Keep It Clean*. Subsequent work was scarce: a short each for Hammer and Merton Park, a travelogue, commercials, a little television (*Armchair Theatre*), plus bizarre dream sequences for Montgomery Tully's *Escapement* (1958). It was not the career he left ballet for. He died in Windsor on 4 February 1961.

(Geoff Brown)

BIBLIOGRAPHY: Davidson, Gladys, *Ballet Biographies* (London: Werner Laurie, 1952).

FILMOGRAPHY: *Orders Are Orders* (1954); *The Love Match*; *Keep It Clean* (1955); *Dick Turpin – Highwayman* (1956); *The Tyburn Case*; *By Lochabar I Will Go* (1957); *Escapement* (US: *The Electronic Monster*, co-dir. Montgomery Tully, 1958).

PARK, Nick (1958–)

Over the last twenty years Nick Park and Aardman Animations have become synonymous with 3-D stop-motion animation in the UK, successfully straddling advertising, music videos, television series, internet animations, Academy Award-winning shorts and big-budget feature films.

Nicholas Wulstan Park was born in Preston, Lancashire, on 6 December 1958 and started making amateur films in his teens, going on to gain a degree in Communications Arts at Sheffield City Polytechnic before being accepted at the National Film and Television School. During his time there, Park arranged for Peter Lord and Dave Sproxton of Aardman to speak to the students, and after graduating was invited to join the studio

Aardman was established in Bristol by Sproxton and Lord in 1972, in their own student days. Its name came from the nerdish superhero created by Peter Lord for a 2-D cel animation, the first of their work to be bought by the BBC for its children's programme *Vision On*. Over the next few years they continued to work part time for the series, going full time in 1976 when they were asked to devise a regular character for Tony Hart's follow-up series, *Take Hart*. The result was 'Morph', a happy-go-lucky Plasticine creation that proved hugely popular, effectively putting Aardman Animations on the map. In 1981 the character starred in a series of twenty-six five-minute episodes, *The Adventures of Morph*.

Having already made several unsuccessful animations aimed at an older audience in the 1970s, Aardman found a new outlet with the arrival of Channel 4 in 1982. The series *Conversation Pieces* (1983) and *Lip Sync* (1989) followed, featuring animated characters mouthing words recorded during interviews with members of the public. The standout episode was Nick Park's *Creature Comforts*, with its memorable range of animals musing about their captivity in a zoo; the jaguar with the voice of a Brazilian student complaining about his accommodation is perhaps the most notable. The short went on to win many awards, including Aardman's first Academy Award, and inspired the celebrated advertising campaign for Heat Electric (often misremembered as being for British Gas). Aardman has subsequently worked on numerous advertisements, the most distinctive of which are probably the Lurpak spots featuring Douglas, a character made of butter.

Arriving at Aardman in the mid-1980s, Park worked on David Hopkins' anti-war short *Babylon* (1986); he also contributed the dancing chicken sequence to the ground-breaking video made to accompany Peter Gabriel's *Sledgehammer* (Stephen Johnson, 1986). Aardman's later music videos include Nina Simone's *My Baby Just Cares for Me* (Peter Lord, 1987) and the Spice Girls' *Viva Forever* (Steve Box, 1996). When Park moved to Bristol he had made a deal with the NFTS that they would continue to finance his unfinished graduation film, with Aardman providing the facilities. Thus he was able to complete *A Grand Day Out* (1991), the first Wallace & Gromit adventure and Park's first film to be shot on 35mm. In it Wallace, the enthusiastic Lancastrian inventor (based on Park's father), and Gromit, his faithful and forbearing canine sidekick, travel to the moon to replenish his stock of cheese. Later episodes toned down the whimsy and fantasy, but Park's subsequent trademarks – gentle wit, unforced jollity and charm, and a love of improbable Heath Robinson-type machines – are already in evidence here. The film was a great success when shown on the BBC and the Corporation commissioned two further adventures, *The Wrong Trousers* (1993) and *A Close Shave* (1995), both of which later won Academy Awards. These increasingly elaborate productions became glossier and more assured with each new edition, with Park's love of film lore very much in evidence. The train climax in *The Wrong Trousers* may well be Park's finest single sequence to date, although the extended *Thunderbirds* homage that opens *A Close Shave*, along with its bungee-jumping window-cleaning gags and aeroplane climax, comes very close.

Armed with their Academy Awards, Aardman decided to move into features, making a multi-picture deal with the Hollywood studio DreamWorks. *Chicken Run* is set in Park's usual 1950s-style Britain, but takes as its template John Sturges' *The Great Escape* (1963), substituting a battery farm for the German prisoner-of-war camp. Voices for the romantic leads were capably provided by Julia Sawalha and Mel Gibson, though they are upstaged by a pair of cheerful rodents voiced by Timothy Spall and Phil Daniels. The finished film was a resounding critical and commercial success and Aardman soon announced that its next DreamWorks project would be *Tortoise vs. Hare*, a version of the celebrated fable to be directed by Aardman mainstay Richard Goleszowski. In the summer of 2001, after eighteen months in pre-production, the decision was made to postpone it; reasons cited were script problems and an over-hasty pre-production schedule. Instead, Park and Aardman decided to bring their most famous characters to the big screen in *Wallace & Gromit in The Curse of the Were-Rabbit*, a horror pastiche co-directed by Park and Steve Box.

(Sergio Angelini)

BIBLIOGRAPHY: Lyons, Mike, 'Aardman Animations', *Cinefantastique*, Feb. 1999, pp. 50–5; Macdonald, Kevin, 'A Lot Can Happen in a Second', in *Projections* 5 (London: Faber and Faber, 1996), pp. 60–93; Oliver, James (compiler), *Insideaard* (Southwold: Suffolk: ScreenPress Books, 2000); Quigley, Marian, 'Globalisation versus Globalization: The Work of Nick Park and Peter Lord', *Animation Journal* vol. 10, 2002, pp. 85–94; Sibley, Brian, *Cracking Animation: The Aardman Book of 3-D Animation* (London: Thames and Hudson, 1998).

FILMOGRAPHY: *Creature Comforts* (short, 1989); *A Grand Day Out* (short, 1991); *The Wrong Trousers* (short, 1993); *A Close Shave* (short, 1995); *Chicken Run* (co-dir. Peter Lord, UK/US, 2000); *Wallace & Gromit in The Curse of the Were-Rabbit* (co-dir. Steve Box, 2005).

PARKER, Alan (1944–)

Alan William Parker was born on 14 February 1944 in Islington, north London. He left school in 1962 and joined the advertising agency Collett Dickenson Pearce as a copywriter, where he worked alongside David Puttnam, Charles Saatchi and Alan Marshall, among others. His screenplay for a schoolboy romance, *S.W.A.L.K.* ('sealed with a loving kiss'), was produced by David Puttnam, directed by Waris Hussein and released as *Melody* in 1970, in which year he and Marshall went freelance, forming the Alan Parker Film Company. They made a string of

highly successful and well-regarded commercials, including the Cinzano series with Leonard Rossiter and Joan Collins. Parker then wrote and directed two short films, *Our Cissy* (1973) and *Footsteps* (1973), and a television play set in wartime London, *No Hard Feelings* (BBC 2, 1976). His first major success came with *The Evacuees* (1975), a television play written by Jack Rosenthal about the experiences of two Jewish boys evacuated from London during the Blitz, for which Parker won the BAFTA television award for Best Director.

Despite this success, Parker found the transition to features difficult. He failed to attract financing for a number of screenplays, which he described as 'about things that were very close to me . . . very English, very London, very angry working class' (Roddick, p. 42). They were considered too parochial; thus it was as a purely pragmatic exercise that he wrote *Bugsy Malone* (1976), a children's musical set in 1920s' Chicago, as a pastiche of the conventions of the American gangster movie. Though the subject matter was chosen with the aim of attracting American finance, the film was mainly funded by the National Film Finance Corporation and Rank.

Nevertheless, the success of *Bugsy Malone* led to the call from Hollywood, and Parker, frustrated with both the commercial and state-sponsored industry in Britain, has rarely worked here since. His first US venture was the critically acclaimed story of a young American's harrowing experiences of the Turkish prison system, *Midnight Express* (1978). This was followed by the hugely successful musical *Fame* (1980), set in the New York City High School for the Performing Arts, and, in quick succession, the domestic drama *Shoot the Moon* (1982), a film version of the Pink Floyd concept album *The Wall* (1982), and the post-Vietnam drama *Birdy* (1984).

Parker expressed his views on the state of the British film industry in his vitriolic television documentary, *A Turnip-Head's Guide to the British Cinema* (1986). He continued to live in England, but all his subsequent films have been made with American backing. He has maintained a constant output, with thrillers such as *Angel Heart* (1987) and *The Life of David Gale* (2003); dramas like *Mississippi Burning* (1988), *Come See the Paradise* (1990) and *Angela's Ashes* (1999); two very different musicals, *The Commitments* (1991) and *Evita* (1996); and a comedy, *The Road to Wellville* (1994). Surprisingly, given his well-known views on British film culture, Parker accepted the chairmanship of the BFI in 1998, moving on to become the first Chairman of the UK Film Council in 1999.

Parker is a deeply paradoxical figure: a film-maker committed to popular, mainstream, narrative cinema, yet whose work is often challenging in theme and distinctive in look; a persistent critic of the British film establishment, yet a man who chaired two of the establishment's major institutions; a working-class 'turnip-head' who was awarded the CBE in 1995 and a knighthood in 2002. Nevertheless, he has consistently pursued his own particular vision of film and film-making, and has always been prepared to put his reputation on the line, never taking refuge in whinging from the sidelines. A profile in *The Face* acutely defined him as 'an outsider with a superiority complex'. (Martin Hunt)

BIBLIOGRAPHY: 'Dialogue on Film: Alan Parker', *American Film*, Jan./Feb. 1988, pp. 12–15; Floyd, Nigel, 'Alan Parker', *Direction*, Oct. 1991, pp. 13–16; Hacker, Jonathan and David Price, *Take Ten: Contemporary British Film Directors* (Oxford: Clarendon Press, 1991); Roddick, Nick, 'Alan Parker: From *Bugsy* to *Birdy*', *Cinema Papers*, July 1985, pp. 40–3; 'The Film Brat', *The Face*, July 1985, pp. 46–51.

FILMOGRAPHY: *Our Cissy* (short); *Footsteps* (short) (1973); *Bugsy Malone* (1976); *Midnight Express* (US/UK, 1978); *Fame* (US, 1980); *Shoot the Moon* (US); *Pink Floyd – The Wall* (1982); *Birdy* (US, 1984); *Angel Heart* (US/Can/UK, 1987); *Mississippi Burning* (US, 1988); *Come See the Paradise* (US, 1990); *The Commitments* (UK/Ir/US, 1991); *The Road to Wellville* (US, 1994); *Evita* (US, 1996); *Angela's Ashes* (US, 1999); *The Life of David Gale* (US, 2003).

PARKER, Albert (1885–1974)

Interviewed by Kevin Brownlow, Albert Parker declared, 'When talkies arrived we were making fine pictures . . . Then we went into reverse gear' (Brownlow). Parker knew what he was talking about. In the 1920s he moved with the Hollywood elite, directing star vehicles for John Barrymore, Douglas Fairbanks and Gloria Swanson. But for most of the 1930s he was based at Fox's outpost in Wembley, making dialogue-heavy 'quota quickies' to fulfil a legal requirement.

Born in Brooklyn on 11 May 1885, Albert Edwin William Parker initially worked in the theatre, both as actor and producer. He made his cinema acting debut in 1916 and turned director in the spring of 1917 with *Her Excellency, the Governor*. He reached his peak in 1926, confidently handling Douglas Fairbanks in the expensive but highly popular *The Black Pirate*, Hollywood's first two-colour Technicolor feature. The following year he directed

Gloria Swanson in the pictorially lavish *The Love of Sunya*, a remake of an earlier success, *Eyes of Youth* (1919). The arrival of talkies and shifting studio politics then knocked him off his perch. He found work as a dialogue director, and in 1931 joined the Fox Film Corporation as a talent scout and director of screen tests. In July 1932 the Fox-British company was registered in Britain for the production of quota product; Parker became a key component, making the outfit's first feature, the comedy *After Dark*, joining the company's board and directing thirteen other short features before new quota regulations led to Fox's retreat from Wembley in 1938.

Parker's British films, few of which appear to survive, were mostly dramas. Though a colourful presence on the set, bullying and ranting, chafing at unenthusiastic technicians, not all of his energy produced results. As with most Fox-British product, trade critics often complained about the large numbers of words said, the slow pace and the over-complicated plots, usually involving crooks, dead bodies and scientists with a formula to steal. But evidence suggests that *The Right to Live* (1933) and *The Riverside Murder* (1935) assembled their ingredients with speed and efficiency. Some American pep also benefited *Late Extra* (1935), featuring James Mason, Parker's chief British discovery, making his debut as a cub reporter on a crime case. The casts would probably now be the films' chief point of interest: Mason apart, they included Basil Sydney, Donald Wolfit, Chaplin's *City Lights* heroine Virginia Cherrill, Alastair Sim and Jessica Tandy.

When Fox's quota production in Britain ceased, Parker established a more successful career as an agent. Mason became the first client of Al Parker Ltd; many other stage and film performers followed, from Robert Newton and Trevor Howard to Helen Mirren. After 1965, the business was run by Parker's second wife, the actress Margaret Johnston. 'There's no romance today,' Parker told Brownlow. 'It's just a business . . . But when you start reflecting on the past, you're in the old poop class.' He died in London on 10 August 1974.

(Geoff Brown)

BIBLIOGRAPHY: Brownlow, Kevin, 'Directors of the Golden Age', *Amateur Cine World*, 22 June 1961, pp. 958–9; Low, Rachael, *Film Making in 1930s Britain* (London: George Allen & Unwin, 1985); Mason, James, *Before I Forget* (London: Hamish Hamilton, 1981); Monaghan, Jno. P., *James Mason* (London: World Film Publications, 1947); Parker, Al, 'Agent', in Oswell Blakeston (ed.), *Working for the Films* (London: Focal Press, 1947); Powell, Michael, *A Life in Movies: An Autobiography* (London: Heinemann, 1986).

FILMOGRAPHY (UK only): *After Dark* (1932); *The Right to Live* (1933); *Rolling in Money*; *The Third Clue* (1934); *The Riverside Murder*, *White Lilac*, *Late Extra* (1935); *Troubled Waters*; *Blind Man's Bluff* (1936); *Strange Experiment*; *The £5 Man*; *There Was a Young Man* (1937); *Murder in the Family*; *Second Thoughts* (1938).

PARKER, Oliver (1960–)

Oliver Parker was born on 6 September 1960 in Kensington, London, the son of the former Chairman of British Rail, Sir Peter Parker. He left Cambridge University after a few weeks to work as an actor with a fringe theatre company, moved on to repertory companies, made several West End appearances and played bit-parts in films such as Clive Barker's *Hellraiser* (1987) and *Nightbreed* (1990). He also played one of the regular characters, Mark Calder, in the BBC's medical soap opera *Casualty* (1993–4).

In 1994 he made a short film, *Unsigned*, and won the backing of Lord Attenborough and Kenneth Branagh for a film version of *Othello* featuring Laurence Fishburne as the Moor, Branagh as Iago, Irène Jacob as Desdemona and Parker's brother Nathaniel as Cassio. Interpreting the play as an erotic thriller, Parker cut three-quarters of the dialogue and made liberal use of music, dance and the spectacle offered by his Venetian locations. He found a wider audience with his next film, an adaptation of Oscar Wilde's *An Ideal Husband*. An accomplished cast – Cate Blanchett, Julianne Moore, Minnie Driver, Rupert Everett, Jeremy Northam – and the perennially topical story of a successful politician threatened with scandal over a past indiscretion made it a box-office success on both sides of the Atlantic. Parker followed up with *The Importance of Being Earnest*. But whereas *An Ideal Husband* had only to compete with Alexander Korda's virtually forgotten 1947 version, Anthony Asquith's *The Importance of Being Earnest* (1952) – with Dame Edith Evans' definitive Lady Bracknell – remains a celebrated classic, and Parker's updated version was compared less favourably.

Parker has made clever use of the conventions of 'heritage cinema' – sumptuous costumes and decor, the evocation of the past as a rich and spectacular backcloth for eccentric characters and quaint stories. He proved he could work on a more modest canvas with *The Private Life of Samuel Pepys* (2003), a witty television film made for the BBC, with Steve Coogan giving an impressively restrained performance as Pepys.

(Pamela Church Gibson)

BIBLIOGRAPHY: Jilla, Shirley, 'Oliver Parker', *Premiere*, Mar. 1996, p. 23; 'Shakespeare in the Cinema: A Film Directors' Symposium', *Cinéaste* vol. 24 no. 1, Dec. 1998, pp. 48–55; Starks, Lisa S., 'An Interview with Michael Maloney', *Post Script* vol. 17 no. 1, Autumn 1997, pp. 79–87.

FILMOGRAPHY: *Unsigned* (short, 1994); *Othello* (UK/US, 1995); *A Little Loving* (short); *The Short Cut* (short) (1996); *An Ideal Husband* (UK/US, 1999); *The Importance of Being Earnest* (UK/US, 2002); *Fade to Black* (2006).

PARKINSON, Harry B. (1884–1970)

Harry Broughton Parkinson, born in Blackburn on 29 September 1884, was typical of the wheeler-dealers who thrived in the lower reaches of the British film industry in the 1920s. Parkinson entered the business in 1908 as a renter and exhibitor, and turned to production and direction in 1920, when he was general manager of Master Films, a company whose output often strove for the lowest common denominator. Short series became a Master speciality in the early 1920s; Parkinson took the lead with releases including *Tense Moments with Great Authors* (1922) and *Film Song Album* (1921–2), an extended series illustrating popular songs. Once Master went out of business, he continued the format in his own productions, including *Romances of the Prize Ring* (1926) and *Bindle* (1926), a comic series based on the character created by Herbert Jenkins. In print, Parkinson claimed that public taste actually preferred the short dramas of earlier days to unnecessarily elongated features (Low, p. 139), though it is now hard to estimate audiences' reaction to the cinemas' burgeoning supporting programmes.

Alongside his shorts, Parkinson produced and occasionally directed features. His taste for the controversial was well displayed in the tastelessly sensational *Trapped by the Mormons* (1922) and *Married to a Mormon* (1922), both featuring American actress Evelyn Brent wriggling in the Mormons' clutches. Another film, *The Life Story of Charles Chaplin* (1926), attempted to present what was essentially a travelogue of London as the star's biography, with Chick Wango impersonating Chaplin revisiting his old haunts; Chaplin's lawyers, unimpressed, managed to prevent its release. Stripped of pretensions, the travelogue form proved to be Parkinson's forte – the two *Wonderful London* series of 1924 provide a strikingly varied and evocative record of London locations and merit further investigation. In 1929, with talkies ascending, bad timing left him with five silent feature productions to distribute. After producing one sound feature, *A Sister to Assist 'Er* (George Dewhurst, 1930), Parkinson withdrew from the mainstream industry, and eventually ran a hotel. He died in Wallasey on 19 August 1970.

(Geoff Brown and Luke McKernan)

BIBLIOGRAPHY: Low, Rachael, *The History of the British Film 1918–1929* (London: George Allen and Unwin, 1971).

FILMOGRAPHY: *The Law Divine* (co-dir. Challis Sanderson, 1920); *Film Song Album* [first edition] (series); *Leaves from My Life* (series) (1921); *Tense Moments with Great Authors* (series); *Master Song Scenas* (aka *Capitol Song Cycle*, series); *Film Song Album* [second edition] (series); *Trapped by the Mormons* (aka *The Mormon Peril*); *Married to a Mormon*; *Crushing the Drug Traffic* (short); *Tense Moments from Great Plays* (series); *Famous Poems by George R. Sims* (series); *The Sporting Twelve* (series) (1922); *Wonderful London* (series, 1924); *London's Famous Cabarets* (series); *London after Dark* (series); *The Only Man* (aka *The Leading Man*, short) (1925); *Bindle* (series); *Horsey* (series); *Romances of the Prize Ring* (series); *The Life Story of Charles Chaplin*, unrel.); *Across the Footlights* (series); *Wonderful Britain* (series) (1926); *Cameo Operas* (series); *On with the Dance* (series) (1927); *Building the Body Beautiful* (series); *Laughter and Tears* (short); *Sacred Dramas* (series) (1928); *Romantic England* (series, 1929).

PARRISH, Robert (1916–1995)

Robert Parrish was born on 4 January 1916, in Columbus, Georgia. A child actor in Hollywood (where his mother also acted, along with his three siblings), he appeared in several films directed by John Ford, and later worked with him as an editor during the Second World War. He won an Academy Award (with Francis Lyon) for editing *Body and Soul* (Robert Rossen, 1947), and continued his Hollywood career into the early 1950s as the director of a handful of efficient, low-budget thrillers. Parrish first came to Britain to make *Rough Shoot* (1953), a moderate thriller scripted by Eric Ambler from Geoffrey Household's novel. He eventually set up base in London; following the powerfully brooding Western *The Wonderful Country* (1959), all his features were made in Europe. His next British film, *The Purple Plain*, adapted by Ambler from a novel by H. E. Bates, is one of his best: an intelligent examination of heroism and endurance, with a refreshingly adult treatment of the underplayed redemptive romance between the angst-ridden Canadian flyer (Gregory Peck) and a young Burmese teacher (Win Min Than). On that evidence, Parrish had the ability to bring an American tautness to British cinema, but its successor, *Fire Down Below* (1957), failed to fulfil the melodramatic potential of its sultry love triangle between Rita Hayworth, Jack Lemmon and Robert Mitchum.

The rest of his career proved erratic. He was among the host of directors employed on the chaotic *Casino Royale*, and then worked unhappily on *The Bobo*, a weak vehicle for Peter Sellers and Britt Ekland. *Duffy*, a caper film written by Donald Cammell, offered more opportunities with its Tangier setting and charismatic if ill-assorted cast (James Mason, James Fox, James Coburn and Susannah York).

Doppelgänger, an intelligent science-fiction drama written by Gerry and Sylvia Anderson, and the offbeat Spanish Western *A Town Called Bastard*, also displayed Parrish's irregular knack for making highly improbable stories involving and intriguing. The bigger-budgeted Euro-thriller *The Marseille Contract* proved a disappointment despite the presence of Anthony Quinn, Michael Caine and James Mason. With no further projects forthcoming, Parrish turned author, writing a vivid memoir of his early years, *Growing up in Hollywood*, gleaming with a personal charm that never properly appeared in his films until the very end when he collaborated with Bertrand Tavernier on the engaging documentary *Mississippi Blues* (Fr/US, 1983). Settled into retirement, Parrish wrote *Hollywood Doesn't Live Here Anymore*, charting later developments in an industry where he was either too unlucky or simply too modest to extract the best from his talents. He died in Southampton, Long Island on 4 December 1995.

(Guy Barefoot)

BIBLIOGRAPHY: Courdoson, Jean-Pierre and Bertrand Tavernier, *50 Ans de cinéma Américain* (Paris: Éditions Nathan, 1995); Lentz III, Harris, Obituary, *Classic Images* no. 247, Nov. 1995, p. 58; Parrish, Robert, *Growing up in Hollywood* (London: Bodley Head, 1976); Parrish, Robert, *Hollywood Doesn't Live Here Anymore* (New York: Little, Brown, 1988); Parrish, Robert, 'The Paper Chase', *American Film*, Mar. 1988, pp. 53–4.

FILMOGRAPHY (UK only): *Rough Shoot* (1953); *The Purple Plain* (1954); *Fire Down Below* (1957); *Casino Royale* (co-dirs. John Huston/Ken Hughes/Val Guest/Joe McGrath, UK/US); *The Bobo* (1967); *Duffy* (1968); *Doppelgänger* (US: *Journey to the Far Side of the Sun*, 1969); *A Town Called Bastard* (US: *A Town Called Hell*, UK/Sp, 1971); *The Marseille Contract* (US: *The Destructors*, UK/Fr, 1974).

PARRY, Gordon (1908–1981)

Near the end of Parry's *Front Page Story* (1954), Jack Hawkins, news editor of the *Daily World*, reproaches Michael Goodliffe's idealistic reporter by praising Fleet Street's regular army, people without 'any grand ideas about themselves, just honest hacks who trod the middle way'. Hawkins could almost have been talking about his director. Gordon Parry directed Britain's first X-certificate film, *Women of Twilight* (1953), a melodramatic portrait of the plight of unmarried mothers; he brought to the screen both anointed classics (*Tom Brown's Schooldays*, 1951) and popular stage farces (*Sailor Beware*, 1956). He handled anything placed before him efficiently and anonymously, never quite hitting the high ground, nor scraping the low.

Born in Aintree on 24 July 1908, Parry studied electro-engineering and acted on stage before entering the film industry in 1933 as an assistant director at Gaumont-British. During the war he worked as unit manager on Ealing's propaganda shorts, then settled in at Two Cities, directing the second unit for *In Which We Serve* and assisting the producer Anatole de Grunwald on Anthony Asquith's *The Demi-Paradise* (1943) and *The Way to the Stars* (1945). The association continued when Parry became a fully fledged director with *Bond Street* (1948), the first of four features produced by de Grunwald. All offered tapestries of stories and characters in various settings: Bond Street in London's West End, prison (*Now Barabbas Was a Robber . . .*), the British tourist's Paris (*Innocents in Paris*) or the dreaming minds of male passengers on the Golden Arrow express (*Three Men and a Girl*).

Although it now seems an innocuous entertainment, *Three Men and a Girl* was not released until 1953, four years after it was made. With other films, Parry made an immediate impact. *Tom Brown's Schooldays*, a handsome production, overplayed some incidents but enjoyed the benefits of shooting at the authentic location, Rugby School. The strident *Women of Twilight* stirred some critical disdain ('Not a film to be proud of in Coronation year,' declared the *People*); the film's spikes and shrieks still make for unsettling viewing. *Front Page Story* had its clichés, but they unravelled in realistic settings, and the concern for journalists' moralities was unusual.

Given these dramas' muscle, Parry's later concentration on comedy is surprising. In *Sailor Beware*, the apotheosis of the mother-in-law joke, Parry produced one of the decade's key comedies, a bridge between stage farce traditions and kitchen-sink realism, presided over by Peggy Mount's battle-axe Ma Hornett. With the inanities of *A Yank in Ermine* and *A Touch of the Sun* he also produced two of the decade's weakest.

Diana Dors and *Tread Softly Stranger* briefly brought Parry back to lurid drama. Then the honest hack trod into obscurity via a weak radio spin-off (*The Navy Lark*), television work (*The Adventures of Robin Hood*) and a 1967 promotional short for Brighton town council. Parry retired to Rambouillet in France, where he died on 6 May 1981. His daughter is the actress Natasha Parry.

(Geoff Brown)

BIBLIOGRAPHY: Aldgate, Anthony, '*Women of Twilight*, *Cosh Boy*, and the Advent of the "X" Certificate', *Journal of Popular British Cinema* no. 3, 2000, pp. 59–68.

FILMOGRAPHY: *In Which We Serve* (2nd unit dir., Noël Coward/David Lean, 1942); *Bond Street* (1948); *Third Time Lucky*; *Now Barabbas Was a Robber . . .* (1949); *Three Men and a Girl/Golden Arrow* (US: *The Gay Adventure*, 1949; rel. 1953); *Midnight Episode* (1950); *Tom Brown's Schooldays* (1951); *Women of Twilight* (US: *Twilight Women*, 1952); *Innocents in Paris*; *Front Page Story* (1953); *Fast and Loose* (1954); *A Yank in Ermine* (1955); *Sailor Beware* (US: *Panic in the Parlor*); *A Touch of the Sun* (1956); *The Surgeon's Knife* (1957); *Tread Softly Stranger* (1958); *The Navy Lark*; *Friends and Neighbours* (1959); *Brighton – A Town for All Seasons* (short, 1966).

PARRY RICHARD (1967–)

Richard Parry was born in Kenya in 1967. After experimenting with amateur films he spent five years in Croatia and the Nagorno-Karabakh region of Azerbaijan filming war crimes. Given this harrowing experience, his first feature film, *South West Nine*, is surprisingly fuzzy in its realism. Ugly hand-held camerawork shows the best-known bits of Brixton (much of it in SW2 rather than SW9), but the characters are cardboard cut-outs mouthing rag-bags of clichés. Producer Alan Niblo had hoped to duplicate his success with *Human Traffic* (Justin Kerrigan, 1999); but Parry's more ambitious project – taking in the anarchist anti-capitalist movement as well as the Brixton drug scene – probably required more than the £1.6 million budget provided and a less contrived 'all-happening in twenty-four hours' plot. Flashes of wit and originality indicate that Parry might have done better had he been surrounded by more professional collaborators.

(Robert Murphy)

BIBLIOGRAPHY: Espensen, Sam, 'SW9 Stories', *Televisual*, Nov. 2000, pp. 55–6; Leo, Paul André, 'In Production: SW9', *Black Filmmaker* vol. 3 no. 10, 2000, p. 6.

FILMOGRAPHY: *The Exorcist of Wood Green* (short, 199?); *Through the K Hole* (short, 199?); *South West Nine* (UK/Ir, 2001).

PASCAL, Gabriel (1894–1954)

Gabriel Pascal was the other Hungarian to make a significant impact on the British cinema, and though his career was less prolific than that of his countryman Alexander Korda, his association with playwright George Bernard Shaw, whom he first met in the 1920s, has earned him a lasting place in the history of the British film.

Pascal was born in Arad, Austria-Hungary (now Romania), on 4 June 1894; and, after an itinerant career including spells in the theatre and the film industry in Germany and Italy, arrived in England in 1935. His first British films – two quota pictures, *Cafe Mascot* and *Reasonable Doubt* – gave little indication of either the extravagance or the cultural respectability that was to characterise his subsequent films; but once he had renewed his acquaintance with Shaw, he devoted his career entirely to the adaptation of the playwright's work for the screen. Although numerous titles were planned, only four films were actually made: *Pygmalion* (Anthony Asquith/Leslie Howard, 1938), *Major Barbara* (1941) and *Caesar and Cleopatra* (1945), both directed by Pascal, and *Androcles and the Lion* (Chester Erskine, 1952).

Shaw himself wrote the screenplays for *Major Barbara* and *Caesar and Cleopatra* and was closely involved in their production. *Major Barbara*'s credits include two 'assistants to the director', Harold French and David Lean, both of whom spent more time on the studio floor than did Pascal. The film benefits from strong performances by Rex Harrison, Wendy Hiller, Robert Newton and Donald Calthrop (who died just before shooting was completed), and fascinating location footage shot in a Sheffield steel factory by Ronald Neame and David Lean, but it failed to match *Pygmalion*'s success either in critical or commercial terms. *Caesar and Cleopatra* cost more than double its original budget of around half a million pounds and was more than a year in production. It enjoyed some success in America, where the performances of Vivien Leigh and Claude Rains and its prestigious literary origins afforded it some box-office cachet; but British critics disapproved of the film's ponderous extravagance and Pascal was censured by the technicians' union for flouting wartime economy measures. Though the film has considerable merit, Pascal had proved himself painfully inefficient as a director, and he was not to be given another chance. He produced one further Shaw film in Hollywood before his death from cancer in New York on 6 July 1954. Among the projects he was working on up to his death were a musical version of *Pygmalion* (which would eventually become *My Fair Lady*) and a film on the life of Gandhi.

(Tom Ryall)

BIBLIOGRAPHY: Brownlow, Kevin, *David Lean* (London: Faber and Faber, 1997); Costello, Donald P., *The Serpent's Eye: Shaw and the Cinema* (Notre Dame, IN and London: University of Notre Dame Press, 1965); Drazin, Charles, *The Finest Years: British Cinema of the 1940s* (London: André Deutsch, 1998); Macnab, Geoffrey, *J. Arthur Rank and the British Film Industry* (London: Routledge, 1993); Pascal, Valerie, *The Disciple and His Devil* (London: Michael Joseph, 1971).

FILMOGRAPHY: *Major Barbara* (1941); *Caesar and Cleopatra* (1945).

PATRICK, Nigel (1913–1981)

Nigel Patrick was born Nigel Dennis Wemyss-German on 2 May 1913 in Wandsworth, London, the son of actress Dorothy Turner. His career began on stage in 1932 and he made his screen debut in 1939. Patrick endowed all his characters – villains, policemen and army officers alike – with his unique brand of charm.

Having directed in the theatre, Patrick turned to film directing in 1957. *How to Murder a Rich Uncle* was based on Didier Daix's black comedy, in which an impoverished aristocrat (Patrick) attempts to murder his wealthy relative. Despite a talented cast, the film suffered from Patrick's uncertain direction and the pace flags. Wendy Hiller remarked that she had expected it to be 'rather larkish', but Patrick 'was not as happy a director as he was an actor' (McFarlane, p. 297).

Undeterred, Patrick attempted another film in 1960. *Johnny Nobody* was a strange tale with an Irish setting about the trial of Johnny Nobody (Aldo Ray), who claims he was commanded by God to shoot an unpopular, blasphemous drunk (William Bendix). A bizarre but original plot was let down by Patrick's uneven handling of the action and his own miscasting as a conscience-stricken priest.

Nigel Patrick continued as a successful actor well into his sixties. He died in London on 21 September 1981, a year after the death of his wife, actress Beatrice Campbell, whom he married in 1951.

(Margaret Butler)

BIBLIOGRAPHY: 'How to Murder a Rich Uncle', *Monthly Film Bulletin*, July 1957, pp. 87–8; McFarlane, Brian, *An Autobiography of British Cinema* (London: Methuen, 1997).

FILMOGRAPHY: *How to Murder a Rich Uncle* (1957); *Johnny Nobody* (1960).

PAUL, Fred (1880–1967)

Born Frederick Paul Luard was born in Lausanne, Switzerland, in 1880, but came to England in his teens. After varied work as a theatrical actor, stage manager and producer, he began acting in comedies for Cricks and Martin's film company in 1907. He played villains in British and Colonial's Lieutenant Daring films; but Paul's handsome features brought him to public attention as the male lead, Archibald Carlyle, in Will Barker's production of the popular society melodrama *East Lynne* (Bert Haldane, 1913). In 1914 he joined the Samuelson Film Company at their new studio at Worton Hall; the following year he began supplementing acting with directing.

As a director Paul hit his stride in 1916 with a series of prestige adaptations of popular novels and plays for the Ideal Film Company. *Lady Windermere's Fan* (1916), *The Vicar of Wakefield* (1916), *The Second Mrs Tanqueray* (1916) and *Masks and Faces* (1917) featured many leading players from the London stage; *Masks and Faces* was specifically mounted to boost the funds of the Royal Academy of Dramatic Art. The theatre's thumb prints were also apparent in Paul's visual technique. A largely static camera kept to the middle distance; inter-scene cutting or dissolving was rare, except for 'memory' shots encircled in black or inserted close-ups of documents or props like Lady Windermere's fan. Despite the hurdle of the camera's distance, players often managed expressive performances, particularly in *Masks and Faces*.

In 1917 Paul left Ideal to serve in the Royal Flying Corps. Returning to the industry after the war, he remained a busy and competent director, though one with none of the artistic ambitions of leading figures like George Pearson or Henry Edwards. Instead of prestige adaptations, Paul now concentrated on making and sometimes starring in adventure stories and melodramas. Explaining the philosophy behind his *Grand Guignol* series of short films, he claimed that

> I attempt to show life as it really is, its sordidness and cruelty; the diabolical humour of the destiny we call fate, which plays with us as it will, raises us to high places or drags us to the gutter; allows one man to rob the widows and orphans of their all and makes a criminal of the starving wretch who in his misery has stolen a mouthful of bread. (Paul, 1921)

These films were strong on atmosphere and often had interesting storylines and settings. *The Gentle Doctor*, for example, centres on a murder in the Russian émigré community in London's East End; *The Last Appeal* takes the ironic situation of a judge failing to recognise the man he has sentenced to death for murder as his own son.

Paul then made *The Further Mysteries of Fu Manchu* for Stoll, based on Sax Rohmer's stories, with Harry Agar Lyons as the sinister Oriental and Paul as his adversary, Nayland Smith; and *The*

Mysterious Dr Sin Fang, a similar series where, as Lieutenant John Byrne, Paul confronts another Eastern threat, again in the form of Harry Agar Lyons. Paul's career, both as actor and director, barely survived the coming of sound, and in the 1930s he was only able to make a few low-budget musicals. By the time he died, in 1967, his role in the industry's early decades had been long forgotten. (Geoff Brown and Bryony Dixon)

BIBLIOGRAPHY: 'Early Days', *News Review*, 13 Feb. 1936, p. 26; Kemp, Philip, *Lady Windermere's Fan* (sleeve notes for the BFI video release, 2001); Low, Rachael, *The History of the British Film 1906–1914* (London: George Allen & Unwin, 1949); Low, Rachael, *The History of the British Film 1914–1918* (London: George Allen & Unwin, 1950); Low, Rachael, *The History of the British Film 1918–1929* (London: George Allen & Unwin, 1971); Paul, Fred, 'Concentrated Production', *Kinematograph Weekly*, 24 Mar. 1921, p. 53.

FILMOGRAPHY: *The Angel of Mons* (co-dir. L. C. MacBean); *The Face at the Telephone* (co-dir. L. C. MacBean); *Infelice* (co-dir. L. C. MacBean); *The Adventures of Deadwood Dick* (series of shorts, co-dir. L. C. MacBean); *The Dop Doctor* (US: *The Love Trail*, co-dir. L. C. MacBean) (1915); *Whoso Is without Sin*; *Still Waters Run Deep*; *The Second Mrs Tanqueray*; *The New Clown*; *Lady Windermere's Fan*; *Her Greatest Performance*; *The Vicar of Wakefield*; *Dr Wake's Patient*; *The Lyons Mail* (1916); *Masks and Faces* (1917); *The Duchess of Seven Dials*; *Lady Tetley's Decree*; *The Little Welsh Girl*; *The English Rose*; *The House on the Marsh*; *The Lights of Home*; *Uncle Dick's Darling*; *The Money Moon* (1920); *Grand Guignol* (series of shorts: *The Oath*, *The Flat*, *The Last Appeal*,

The Woman Upstairs, The Gentle Doctor, Delilah, A Voice from the Dead, The Guardian of Honour, The Happy Pair, The Return, The Sting of Death, The Nurse, Polly, The Secret of the Safe, The Jest, A Bit of Black Stuff, Six and Half a Dozen, Her Romance, That Love Might Last, Letters of Credit, The Upper Hand, A Game for Two, The Flirtations of Phyllis, Mary's Work, The Curse of Westacott, A Woman Misunderstood, The Joke That Failed, Barbara Elopes (all co-dir. Jack Raymond, 1921); *The Faithful Heart; Brown Sugar; If Four Walls Told* (1922); *Castles in the Air/Let's Pretend* (1922; rel. 1937); *The Right to Strike; The Hotel Mouse* (1923); *The Further Mysteries of Fu Manchu* (series of shorts: *The Midnight Summons, The Coughing Horror, Cragmire Tower, The Green Mist, The Café L'Egypte, The Golden Pomegranates, Karamaneh, Greywater Park*, 1924); *The Last Witness; A Madonna of the Cells* (short); *Ragan in Ruins* (short) (1925); *Safety First; Thou Fool; Guy of Warwick* (short) (1926); *The Luck of the Navy* (1927); *The Mysterious Dr Sin Fang* (series of shorts: *The Scarred Face, The Zone of Death, The Light on the Wall, The Living Death, The Torture Cage, Under the Tide*, 1928); *The Broken Melody* (1929); *Morita* (short); *Romany Love; In a Lotus Garden* (1931).

PAUL, Robert (1869–1943)

Robert William Paul was the leading pioneer of British film, and made the successful transfer from inventor to entrepreneur to remain a major figure in the industry for its first ten years. He was primarily an electrical engineer, and it was to engineering that he successfully returned when he decided to bow out of film.

Paul was born in Highbury, north London, on 3 October 1869 and educated at the City and Guilds Technical College, Finsbury. He ran his electrical engineering business at 44 Hatton Gardens from 1891. He stumbled into film in 1894 when asked to produce replica Kinetoscopes by two Greek businessmen who were exploiting the fact that Edison had neglected to patent his invention in Europe. Paul produced his own Kinetoscopes and, finding Edison's films barred to him, went into film production himself, employing Birt Acres, a photographer, to assist him. Together they constructed a camera, and shot a private test film featuring Henry Short, a mutual acquaintance, outside Acres' home in Barnet in February 1895. Films made for public exhibition followed, including *Oxford and Cambridge University Boat Race, Rough Sea at Dover* and *The Derby*, before the two men split acrimoniously in July 1895.

Paul now worked on the logical next step, projecting motion pictures on a screen. He first exhibited the results on 21 February 1896 at Finsbury Technical College, the same day that the Lumière Cinématographe opened to the London public at the Polytechnic. Paul's first film show was riddled with technical problems, but these were resolved by the time that his Theatrograph projector made its public debut at the Egyptian Hall, Piccadilly. Two days later, he exhibited the projector at Olympia, London's premier exhibition centre. He began to find a rapidly growing market for his projectors, and to keep up supply started producing films once more in April.

Paul's first films were actualities, but he produced what was arguably the first British story film, *The Soldier's Courtship* (Alfred Moul, 1896), featuring Fred Storey, Julie Seale and Paul's wife, Ellen. However, his most successful film of 1896 was his coverage of the Derby. Paul was fortunate in filming one of the most celebrated of all Derby wins, that of Persimmon (owned by the Prince of Wales). His feat of being able to show the film of the race's finish at two London music halls the day after the race caused a sensation, and firmly established Paul at the forefront of British cinema.

Paul's business flourished over the next ten years, built as much upon his reliable film machinery as the films he actually made. Marked by a distinctive black edging to the prints, Paul's film output was distinguished particularly by trick films and news films. For the trick films, Paul turned to a former magician, Walter Booth, who in films like *The '?' Motorist* (1906) produced some ingenious effects in the Méliès mould. His most notable actualities came from the films of the Boer War taken for him by Colonel Walter Beevor and Sydney Melsom, such as *Cronje's Surrender to Lord Roberts* (1900). Paul only served as his own film-maker for a relatively short period, but a playful ingenuity is readily in evidence among those films that survive, among them *The Twins' Tea Party* (1896); *Two A.M.; or, The Husband's Return* (1896); *Come Along, Do!* (1898), and *A Chess Dispute* (1903). Paul also produced proto-propaganda films in the form of the series *Army Life; or, How Soldiers Are Made* (1900). He gathered round him a talented group, several of whom would go on to play significant parts in early British film: G. H. Cricks, J. H. Martin, Frank Mottershaw Jr and Jack Smith among them. His Animatograph projector was exported all over the world, and he played a significant part in encouraging the spread of motion pictures worldwide, as well as establishing the foundations of a film industry at home.

During his years of film production Paul maintained his electrical business: he opened factories in London and New York, and in 1903 introduced the innovative Unipivot galvanometer. He retired from the film business in 1910 and returned to engineering until 1920, when he amalgamated his business with the Cambridge Instrument Company. On his death in Wandsworth, London, on 28 March 1943, he left £100,000 in shares to provide instruments of an unusual nature to aid physical research. Paul's career seems to have been blissfully free from crisis; he simply did everything right, and left the film business at exactly the right time. For all the brevity of his own film-making career, his creative and industrial influence was immense. (Luke McKernan)

BIBLIOGRAPHY: Barnes, John, *The Beginnings of the Cinema in England 1894–1901* vols 1–5, (Exeter: Exeter University Press, 1996–8); Barnes, John, 'Robert William Paul', in Stephen Herbert and Luke McKernan (eds), *Who's Who of Victorian Cinema: A Worldwide Survey* (London: BFI, 1996); Coe, Brian and Gordon Woodward, 'Paul, Robert William', in Lance Day and Ian McNeil (eds), *Biographical Dictionary of the History of Technology* (London: Routledge, 1996); Low, Rachael and Roger Manvell, *The History of the British Film 1896–1906* (London: George Allen & Unwin, 1948); Paul, Robert W., 'Before 1910: Kinematograph Experiences', *Proceedings of the British Kinematograph Society*, no. 38 (London: BKS, 1936); Rossell, Deac, *Living Pictures: The Origins of the Movies* (Albany: SUNY Press, 1998).

SELECTED FILMOGRAPHY: *Rough Sea at Ramsgate* (series); *The Derby*; *A Comic Costume Race*; *Princess Maud's Wedding*; *Up the River* (aka *Rescue of a Drowning Child*); *On Westminster Bridge*; *Children at Play* (series); *The Tea Party*; *The Engineer's Shop at Nelson* (aka *Smith and Machinery at Work*); *Henley Regatta*; *Blackfriars' Bridge*; *The Gordon Highlanders*; *The Arrest of a Bookmaker*; *The Twins' Tea Party*; *Two A.M.; or, The Husband's Return*; *Gardener Watering Plants*; *New Westminster* (aka *Traffic Outside St Thomas's Hospital*); *Children in the Nursery*; *Feeding Pelicans at the Zoo*; *The Lord Mayor's Show*; *You Dirty Boy* (1896); *The Geisha* (series); *The Miller and the Sweep*; *The Derby*; *Queen Victoria's Diamond Jubilee Procession*; *Sweden* (series); *The Young Rivals*; *Robbery*; *Jealousy*; *The Village Blacksmith* (1897); *Fregoli the Protean Artiste*; *Come Along, Do!*; *A Favourite Domestic Scene*; *When the Cat's Away*; *A Switchback Railway*; *The Derby*; *Gladstone's Funeral*; *Launch of H.M.S. Albion*; *The Blackwall Disaster*; *S.S. Carisbrooke* (series); *The Servant Difficulty*; *Mistress and Maid*; *High Life below Stairs*; *Fun on the Clothesline*; *A Rescue from Drowning*; *The Stockbroker*; *Birdsnesting*; *Difficulties of an Animated Photographer*; *The Sailor's Departure*; *The Sailor's Return*; *The Monks*; *The Jovial Monks in the Rectory*; *Mr Bumble's Courtship* (aka *Mr Bumble the Beadle*); *Old Time Scene in the Village Stocks*; *The Little Breadwinner*; *Tommy Atkins in the Park*; *The Lodger*; *In the Queen's Name: The Arrest of a Deserter*; *Our New General Servant*; *The Rival Bill-Stickers*; *A Lively Dispute*; *Theft*; *Tramps*; *Spree*; *Goat*; *Quarrelsome Neighbours*; *The Twins' Tea Party* (second version); *Repose*; *The Gamblers*; *Cupid and the Wash-Tub*; *Santa Claus and the Children* (1898); *Photographic Convention, Gloucester*; *Bertie's Bike; or, The Merry Madcaps*; *The Country Waiter; or, The Tale of a Crushed Hat*; *Two Tipsy Pals and the Tailor's Dummy*; *A Gretna Green Wedding*; *The Bricklayer and His Mate; or, A Jealous Man's Crime*; *Thrilling Fight on a Scaffold* ; *On a Runaway Motor Car through Piccadilly Circus*; *An Unexpected Visit; or, Our Flat*; *Caught Flirting* (1899); *Snowballing Oom Paul*; *The Brutal Burglar*; *A Morning at Bow Street*; *The Worried German*; *A Naughty Story*; *The 1900 Derby*; *Punished*; *Army Life; or, How Soldiers Are Made* (series); *A Wet Day at the Seaside*; *The Drenched Lover* (1900); *Scenes During Regatta Week* (series); *The Derby*; *Five Years' Derbies*; *The Deonzo Brothers*; *Garters versus Braces; or, Algy in a Fix*; *The Artist and the Flower* (1901); *The Automatic Machine; or, Oh What a Surprise*; *Handy and the Clumsy Servant*; *His Brave Defender*; *An Interrupted Rehearsal; or, Murder Will Out*; *The Muddled Bill-Poster*; *William Tell*; *The Tramp at the Spinster's Picnic*; *The Countryman and the Cinematographer*; *Punch and Judy*; *Hair Soup; or, A Disgruntled Diner*; *The Tramp and the Turpentine Bottle; or, Greediness Punished*; *The Gambler's Fate; or, The Road to Ruin* (1901); *State Opening of Parliament*; *Race for the Grand National*; *Oxford and Cambridge Boat Race*; *Their Majesties at Chelsea Hospital*; *The King's Birthday and Trooping of the Colour*; *A Convict's Darling*; *Love's Ardour Suddenly Cooled*; *Little Willie's Coronation Celebrations*; *The Hotel Mystery*; *The Troublesome Collar*, *His Only Pair*, *The Swells*; *A B-Oysterous Dispute*; *New Zealand Maori Dancers*; *London's Reception of Lord Kitchener*, *Coronation of King Edward VII* (series); *Boer Generals Arrive at Southampton*; *Royal Procession*; *The Arrest of a Deserter* (1902); *Opening of Parliament*; *Weary Willie's Wiles*; *The Old Love and the New*; *The Washerwoman and the Sweep*; *Race for the Grand National*; *Bloodhounds Tracking a Convict* (US: *Trailed by Bloodhounds*); *The Swell's Interrupted Nap*; *A Chess Dispute*; *High Diving at Highgate*; *Marionette Performance*; *Nigger Courtship*; *The Fine Fisherman*; *A Good Catch* (1903); *The Adventures of a Window Cleaner*, *An Artful Young Truant*; *An Affair of Outposts*; *Jap versus Russian*; *Funeral of the Duke of Cambridge*; *All for the Love of a Geisha*; *A Russian Surprise*; *That Terrible Sneeze*; *The Capture and Execution as Spies of Two Japanese Officers*; *The Snapshot Fiend*; *The Chappie at the Well*; *The Talking Head*; *Drat That Boy!*; *Funny Faces*; *All the Fun of the Fair*, *Buy Your Own Cherries*; *The Student, the Soot and the Smoke*; *That Terrible Barber's Boy*; *The Ploughboy's Dream*; *Looking for Trouble*; *How Coal Is Secured* (aka *Down a Coal Mine*); *The Spiteful Umbrella Maker*, *Mr Pecksniff Fetches the Doctor* (aka *Oh, What a Surprise!*); *The Sculptor's Jealous Model*; *Love Laughs at Locksmiths*; *Why Marriage Is a Failure* (1904); *Papa Helps the Painters*; *Auntie's First Attempt at Cycling*; *A Victim of Misfortune*; *The Motor Hooligans*; *Goaded to Anarchy* (1905); *Domesticated Elephants* (1909).

PAVLOU, George (1953–)

George Pavlou was born on 5 November 1953. He studied at the London International Film School in Covent Garden in the late 1970s, then helped out on Michael Papas' *Avrianos Polemistis* (1981), a Cypriot film about the Turkish invasion of the island in 1974, and served as associate producer of Anwar Kawadri's *Nutcracker* (1982). On the strength of his short films *Bad Company* and *The Antagonist* he persuaded Clive Barker to collaborate on a screenplay for what would become *Underworld* (1985). Barker's fertile imagination conjured up a fantastic world of mutant heroes and sharp-dressing baddies, but Pavlou's direction made little sense of it and the film found few outlets.

Despite this disappointment, a second collaboration ensued. *Rawhead Rex* (1987), based on a Barker short story about an age-old demon unintentionally released to ravage the Irish countryside, is tighter and simpler. An Ireland populated by credulous peasants, dubious priests and feckless tinkers can hardly have pleased the Irish Tourist Board, but the bleak atmosphere fits Barker's theme of communities forever struggling to keep dark forces at bay. Unfortunately, Pavlou's direction is primitive and his demon Rex is a comically amateurish creation whose decisions to spare someone or rip them apart seem determined by whether they have any further use in the plot. Unsurprisingly, Barker then decided he could do a better job himself, directing *Hellraiser* (1987) to great acclaim.

Pavlou's third feature, *Little Devils: The Birth* (1992), made without the advantage of a Barker script, proved an odd mix of thrills and comedy, which even the wry performance of Russ Tamblyn and the lively antics of the pint-sized demons failed to pull together.

(Robert Murphy)

BIBLIOGRAPHY: Bhose, Indra, 'Entretien avec George Pavlou', *Écran Fantastique* no. 71, Aug. 1986, pp. 46–9; Henry, Georgina, 'George Pavlou', *Televisual*, May 1985, p. 94.

FILMOGRAPHY: *Bad Company* (short, 1980); *The Antagonist* (short, 1982); *Underworld* (US: *Transmutations*, 1985); *Rawhead Rex* (1987); *Little Devils: The Birth* (US, 1992).

PAWLIKOWSKI, Pawel (1957–)

Pawel Pawlikowski was born in Warsaw in 1957. Brought to England by his mother when he was fifteen, he subsequently lived in Germany and Italy. He returned to England in the late 1970s, found work at the Community Programme Unit of the BBC. From the late 1980s he made documentaries, often for the BBC's *Bookmark* programme, which presented distinctive, often surreal, takes on Eastern Europe's past and present. He attracted particular notice with *From Moscow to Pietushki* (1991), *Serbian Epics* (1992), *Dostoevsky's Travels* (1991), and *Tripping with Zhirinovsky* (1995), which won the Grierson Award for Best British Documentary.

Finding himself increasingly limited by television's devotion to 'reality shows', Pawlikowski took the opportunity to move into drama with *The Stringer*, a troubled production backed by the BBC along with British Screen and Pepper Pictures. His characteristically off-centred take on post-perestroika Russia received a Directors' Fortnight screening at Cannes and was well-received in Russia but received minimal distribution elsewhere. He returned to the small screen with the improvised drama *Twockers* (1999).

Pawlikowski's next film, *Last Resort*, was also initially intended for television, though after attracting critical acclaim and winning a string of prizes it was shown in cinemas in Britain and abroad. It centres upon Tanya (Dina Korzon), a Russian woman who arrives in Britain with her son and while seeking political asylum forms an uncertain relationship with Alfie (Paddy Considine), a bingo caller and amusement-arcade worker. In this vaguely futuristic world, where the seaside town of Margate has become a grim citadel of bureaucratic oppression, it is impossible to predict what will happen – we are never sure whether Alfie is a psychopath or a genuinely kind person – and Pawlikowski's vision of Britain is thrillingly original compared with that of most of his British contemporaries.

Following the success of *Last Resort*, Pawlikowski began work on a film about the poet Sylvia Plath but left long before the film came to fruition (as *Sylvia*, starring Gwyneth Paltrow and directed by Christine Jeffs). Instead he loosely adapted *My Summer of Love*, a novel by Helen Cross about the relationship between two young women in rural Yorkshire. Pawlikowski draws vivid performances from the two girls (Nathalie Press and Emily Blunt) but a rather haphazard story leaves the most interesting and complex character – Paddy Considine's hardman-turned-Christian evangelist – disappointingly sidelined. The film's economy, intensity and originality attracted good reviews and festival prizes but it failed to become the art-house hit one might have expected.

Pawlikowski's career has not been a smooth one, but, like earlier Polish directors Roman Polanski and Jerzy Skolimowski, his outsider's perspective has helped him make a highly distinctive contribution to British film and television.

(Guy Barefoot)

BIBLIOGRAPHY: Pulver, Andrew, 'An Interview with Pawel Pawlikowski', in John Boorman, Fraser MacDonald and Walter Donohue (eds), *Projections 12: Film-Makers on Film Schools* (London: Faber and Faber, 2002); Sinclair, Iain, 'The Cruel Seaside', *Sight and Sound*, Mar. 2001, pp. 16–18.

FILMOGRAPHY: *The Stringer* (1997); *Last Resort* (2000); *My Summer of Love* (2004).

PEARSON, George William (1875–1973)

George Pearson was born on 19 March 1875 in Kennington, London. His father was a craftsman in the silk industry. A happy home and stimulating schooldays led him in 1893 to Culham College, Oxfordshire, where he gained his Teacher's Certificate, followed by senior teaching posts and headships. However, he rejected the rigid discipline and curriculum of School Board education and yearned to realise undefined desires for artistic expression. Around 1911, a travelling film show suggested to him the power of cinema as a medium for mass enlightenment through entertainment. By now he was married with three children, his fourth born in 1919.

In January 1913, at the age of thirty-seven, Pearson abandoned his respectable career as headmaster and entered the then-disreputable film industry as film producer in charge of Pathé's tiny London studio. The following year he joined George Samuelson at Worton Hall, moving in 1915 to Gaumont's new Lime Grove studios. From realising popular paintings and poems on film, and recreating topical wartime events as fictitious newsreels, Pearson would forge radical ways of reconciling

British pictorialism to the moving cinematic image. Working in a range of popular genres, he helped film actors communicate emotion, while trying to make cinema the 'lingua franca of the human eye' (Pearson, 1957, p. 28). Responding to Gaumont's demand for a British hero to match the French 'Fantômas', Pearson invented 'Ultus', an avenger of injustice whose police-foiling adventures fuelled four stylish and highly popular films between 1915 and 1917.

In 1918 Pearson joined Thomas Welsh to establish Welsh-Pearson in new studios at Craven Park and forge his own position as a leading voice in 1920s' British film-making. *The Better 'Ole* (1918), based on Bruce Bairnsfather's popular soldier character Old Bill, was followed by four 'Squibs' films (1921–3), that ensured the company's financial stability, established Pearson's reputation as a successful director and took Betty Balfour (their ebullient cockney heroine) to stardom. The 'Squibs' films' popularity was based on the down-to-earth humour of their working-class characters, combined with a touch of pathos acknowledging life's misfortunes. But Pearson's authorial stature was recognised in the human emotions he drew from traditional types, the charismatic performances of his actors and the inventive use he made of visual and symbolic effects.

The 'Squibs' films ran in tandem with a series of more personal productions, for which Pearson wrote original scenarios that disregarded the constraints of plot and continuity – 'that shibboleth' imported from America (as Pearson phrased it in his notebooks). Rather, believing 'cinema should be a lawless medium, as free as the vision of the human eye', he sought glimpses of life caught in the gestures of his actors and symbolic images rooted in popular culture and everyday experience (Pearson, 1957, p. 140). *Nothing Else Matters* (1920), *Love, Life and Laughter* (1923), *Reveille* (1924) and *The Little People* (1926) were intensely personal films centring on figures who, yearning to communicate the ineffable like Pearson himself, seek to exceed life's limitations only to encounter disillusion and eventually reconcile to its terms. Pearson's ambition – expressed in his notebooks, discussions with his production teams, press books, articles and public lectures – was to build his films 'emotion by emotion', capturing in moving images (and later sounds) moments of human pain and hope (Pearson, 1957, p. 185). The result was often a roller-coaster of clashing moods, of laughter and tears, as in *Squibs Wins the Calcutta Sweep*, which bookends its uproarious social comedy with a murder and a suicide.

Though held in great respect and frequently hailed a 'genius' – a Dickens or Barrie of the screen, Britain's D. W. Griffith – Pearson's practice increasingly departed from the industry norms established by Hollywood, and retained an idealism and commitment to popular visual culture out of kilter with the modernist avant-garde. While *Reveille*, a meditation on the injustices of peacetime and ordinary people's spirit of survival, was premiered in front of the Prince of Wales in 1924, two years later *The Little People* was withdrawn for re-editing and retitling by another hand. Pearson never experienced the same creative

freedom again. With the economic downturn of 1926, Craven Park was sold and Welsh-Pearson forced to seek American deals.

However, Pearson remained an indefatigable defender of film art in broadcasts and lectures, becoming a founding member of the Film Society, and as President of the Association of British Film Directors led a deputation to the Board of Trade to oppose the Quota Act's threat to quality. After a visit to America, he perceived the inevitable onset of sound cinema, but he argued in vain with his struggling company about the necessity of conversion. Eventually, after supervising the successful film version of *Journey's End* (James Whale, 1930) in a Hollywood sound studio, Pearson returned to find Welsh-Pearson in liquidation and his films sold for their celluloid.

In 1934, after piecemeal production, Pearson parted from Welsh, finding work on 'quota quickies' with Julius Hagen at Twickenham. With the outbreak of war, he joined Cavalcanti, his former designer for *The Little People*, at the GPO Film Unit. From there he became Director-in-Chief of the Colonial Film Unit, returning to his starting point, film in education, and finally running film schools for budding Commonwealth film-makers. In 1948 the Royal Photographic Society made him an Honorary Fellow, as did the British Film Academy in 1951, when he also received the OBE for his services to the film industry.

At eighty he retired, publishing his autobiography in 1957. He died on 6 February 1973 in a Malvern nursing home, having touched a succeeding generation of film-makers with his generosity and advocacy for film art. If in the 21st century we return

to his few surviving films and his writings, it is perhaps to rediscover in his visionary populism a cinematic language of emotion rejected by modernism.
(Christine Gledhill)

BIBLIOGRAPHY: Bamford, Kenton, *Distorted Images: British National Identity and Film in the 1920s* (London: I. B. Tauris, 1999); Denis Gifford Audiotape Collection, BFI National Library, London; Gledhill, Christine, *Reframing British Cinema: 1918–1928* (London: BFI, 2003); Low, Rachael, *The History of the British Film 1914–1918* (London: George Allen & Unwin, 1950); Low, Rachael, *The History of the British Film 1918–1929* (London: George Allen & Unwin, 1971); Low, Rachael, *The History of the British Film 1929–1939 – Film Making in 1930s Britain* (London: George Allen & Unwin, 1985); Pearson, George, 'Memories . . .', *Film Technician*, Sept./Oct. 1951, pp. 140–55; Pearson, George, *Flashback: The Autobiography of a British Film-Maker* (London: George Allen & Unwin, 1957); Pearson, George, Notebooks, Scrapbooks and Press books, BFI Special Collections, BFI National Library, London; Peet, Stephen, 'George Pearson 1875–1973', *Sight and Sound*, Spring 1973, p. 88; *The Silent Picture* no. 2, Spring 1969, special issue on George Pearson.

FILMOGRAPHY: *The Fool*; *A Lighter Burden*; *Mr Henpeck's Dilemma*; *The Sentence of Death*; *Through Fair Wessex*; *In Dickens Land* (aka *Through Dickens Land*); *Rambles through Hopland*; *Where History Has Been Written*; *A Day at the Boy Scouts' Farm*; *The Isle of Wight*; *In the Garden of England*; *Some Kentish Industries*; *Fair Sussex*; *Lynmouth and Its Beauty Spots*; *Heroes of the Mine* (1913); *Wonderful Nights with Peter Kinema* (series); *The Live Wire*; *A Fisher Girl's Folly*; *A Study in Scarlet*; *The Great European War*, Part 1: *The Cause of the Great European War*, Part 2: *Incidents of the Great European War*, *A Son of France*; *Christmas Day in the Workhouse*; *The Man of Mystery* (uncompleted); *The Life of Lord Roberts, VC* (1914); *A Cinema Girl's Romance*; *The True Story of the Lyons Mail*; *Buttons*; *John Halifax, Gentleman*; *Ultus, the Man from the Dead* (1915); *For the Empire*; *Ultus and the Grey Lady*; *Ultus and the Secret of the Night*; *Glorious Devon*; *Derbyshire*; *Edge of Dartmoor*, *Lynton and Lynmouth*; *Sally Bishop* (1916); *Ultus and the Three Button Mystery*; *Vignettes of the Great War* (series) (1917); *The Better 'Ole; Or, The Romance of Old Bill* (US: *Carry On*); *The Kiddies in the Ruins* (1918); *Hughie at the Victory Derby* (1919); *Garryowen*; *Nothing Else Matters* (1920); *Mary Find the Gold*; *Squibs* (1921); *Mord Em'ly*; *The Wee MacGregor's Sweetheart*; *Squibs Wins the Calcutta Sweep* (1922); *Love, Life and Laughter*, *Squibs, MP*; *Squibs' Honeymoon* (1923); *Reveille* (1924); *Satan's Sister*, *Mr Preedy and the Countess* (unrel.) (1925); *The Little People*; *Blinkeyes* (1926); *Huntingtower* (1927); *Love's Option* (1928); *Auld Lang Syne* (1929); *Harry Lauder Songs* (series); *East Lynne on the Western Front* (1931); *The Third String* (1932); *A Shot in the Dark*; *The Pointing Finger* (1933); *The River Wolves*; *The Four Masked Men*; *Whispering Tongues*; *Open All Night* (1934); *The Ace of Spades*; *That's My Uncle*; *Gentleman's Agreement*; *Jubilee Window*; *Once a Thief*; *Checkmate* (1935); *The Secret Voice*; *Wednesday's Luck*; *Midnight at Madame Tussaud's* (US: *Midnight at the Wax Museum*); *Murder by Rope* (1936); *The Fatal Hour* (1937); *Mother of Men*; *Souvenirs*; *Old Soldiers* (1938). Non-fiction (several of the early silent films in the list are also non-fiction): *When Day Is Done* (aka *End of the Day*, 1939); *The Chiltern Country*; *Seed Time to Harvest*; *British Made*; *A British Family in Peace and War*, *Land of Water*, *Rural School*; *'Take Cover'*; *Special Constables*; *A.R.P. Wardens* (1940); *The British Army*; *English and African Life*; *The Story of Cotton*; *Searchlights* (1940?); *An African in London*; *British Youth* (1941)

Pearson lists the following Colonial Film Unit films, which he dates from between 1940 and 1955: *Barrage Balloons*; *Paratroops*; *Tanks and Bren Guns*; *Anti-Aircraft Guns*: *London Firemen*; *Self-Help in Food*; *Comforts from Uganda*; *Feeding the Army*; *Blind People*; *Pilot Officer*, *Peter Thomas*; *Colonial Centre*; *Nurse Ademola*; *Your People in Britain*; *Margarine*; *A Secondary Modern School*; *A Village School*; *Young Farmers' Clubs*; *Deck Chair*, *Better Hides and Skins*; *African Timber*, *An African in England*; *Learie Constantine*; *African Village Cinema*; *Springtime in England*.

PECK, Ron (1948–)

Ronald L. Peck was born in London in 1948. He studied at Sussex University and the London Film School in the early 1970s, and in 1973 formed the Four Corners film workshop in Bethnal Green, east London, with fellow LFS students Joanna Davis, Mary Pat Leece and Wilfried Thust. Peck collaborated on several short films while working as a schoolteacher, and used his experience of leading a double life as a conventional teacher by day and a gay man cruising bars by night as the basis for *Nighthawks* (1978), a low-budget feature co-directed with writer Paul Hallam. *Nighthawks* used innovatory improvisational techniques, but what attracted attention was its depiction of a gay lifestyle, still hardly visible in British films even ten years after the Sexual Offences Act of 1967 had decriminalised homosexuality.

Nighthawks caused quite a splash, but apart from a brief stint as an assistant director on James Ivory's *The Bostonians* (1984), Peck stayed at Four Corners, making a perceptive documentary about Edward Hopper for the Arts Council, and two short dramas about artists, actors and models. *Empire State* (1987), his next feature, began as a low-budget experiment funded by Channel 4's avant-garde *Eleventh Hour* strand but grew into something more mainstream, a glossy gangster film inhabiting the same world as John Mackenzie's *The Long Good Friday* (1979). Peck's London Dockland swarms with self-seeking yuppies and casually brutal gangsters, a sharp indictment of Thatcherite prosperity; but too many plot strands and a fatal lack of focus prompt a collapse into implausible melodrama. *Strip Jack Naked* (1991), a semi-documentary made for the BFI and Channel 4, returned Peck to the world of *Nighthawks*, charting his own experience growing up gay in Britain.

Smaller projects followed for Team Pictures, the company Peck established with producer Mark Ayres: *Fighters* (1992), a documentary exploring the lives of young East End boxers, led to *Real Money* (1996), an improvised drama that Peck devised with the help of the boxers he had come to know. He also set up the Team Project, a film production and education facility equipped with digital technology, and in 2002 was awarded a NESTA fellowship to pursue his own digital experiments. The

talent displayed in his feature films might have led Peck to a conventional career in film and television; his choice to remain within a more community-based area of film-making no doubt offers different satisfactions.
(Robert Murphy)

BIBLIOGRAPHY: 'Entretien avec Ron Peck et Paul Hallam', *Cahiers du cinéma*, Oct. 1979, pp. 67–70; Hodgson, Clive, '"Nighthawks" – An Interview with Ron Peck and Paul Hallam', *Film* [British Federation of Film Societies] vol. 2 no. 67, Nov. 1978, pp. 6–7; Meek, Scott and Mandy Merck, 'The Cause without a Rebel', *Time Out* no. 464, 9 Mar. 1979, pp. 14–15.

FILMOGRAPHY: *His Ugly Head* (short, co-dirs. Joanna Davis/Wilfried Thust, 1974); *On Allotments* (doc. short, co-dirs. Joanna Davis/Mary Pat Leece/Wilfried Thust, 1976); *Nighthawks* (co-dir. Paul Hallam, 1978); *Actors* (short, 1980); *Edward Hopper* (doc. short, 1981); *What Can I Do with a Male Nude?* (short, 1985); *Empire State* (1987); *Strip Jack Naked* (aka *Strip Jack Naked: Nighthawks II*, doc., 1991); *Fighters* (doc. short, 1992); *Real Money* (1996).

PECKINPAH, Sam (1925–1984)

David Samuel Peckinpah was born on 21 February 1925 in Fresno, California, the son of a lawyer descended from pioneer stock. After completing military service and an MA in theatre studies at the University of California, he entered the film industry as an assistant to the director Don Siegel. He gained experience writing and directing for television before making his feature debut with *The Deadly Companions* (1961). Several subsequent Westerns, including *The Wild Bunch* (1969), secured his dual reputation as the genre's major latter-day director and as a film-maker obsessed with violence.

Neither image was contradicted by *Straw Dogs*, one of the most controversial British films of the 1970s and one of the finest. A magnificent gothic melodrama about man's innate savagery, it reaches an extraordinary pitch of intensity only partly attributable to its graphic physical action and notorious rape sequence. The performances of Dustin Hoffman and, especially, Susan George, create a powerful study of marital breakdown, as domesticity is destroyed in the course of its defence.

Peckinpah subsequently completed his war film *Cross of Iron* in Britain when its German financier ran out of money and EMI came to the rescue. EMI then co-financed, with United Artists, the trucking Western *Convoy*, which though often reckoned the director's worst film – he was incapacitated by drugs and alcohol throughout much of the shoot, and was fired from the editing – still retains traces of his talent. He died following a massive stroke in Inglewood, California, on 28 December 1984.
(Sheldon Hall)

BIBLIOGRAPHY: Kael, Pauline and Charlie Sotelo, 'A Glorious High', in Charlie Sotelo (ed.), *Peckinpah* (Austin, TX: Austin Film Society, 1999); '*Playboy* Interview: Sam Peckinpah', *Playboy*, Aug. 1972, pp. 65–78, 192; Weddle, David, 'They Want to See Brains Flying Out?'; and Williams, Linda Ruth, 'Women Can Only Misbehave', *Sight and Sound*, Feb. 1995, pp. 20–7.

FILMOGRAPHY (UK only): *Straw Dogs* (UK/US, 1971); *Cross of Iron* (UK/Ger, 1977); *Convoy* (US/UK, 1978).

PEDELTY, Donovan

Of Irish descent, Donovan Pedelty (whose birth and death dates are unknown) was born in England and initially pursued a career on the family farm. Tiring of this, he moved to London and became a film publicist before leaving for Hollywood, where he worked as a film journalist. On his return to England he joined Paramount as a talent scout, organising among other things their 'Search for Beauty' competition. After writing scripts for Paramount's production partner British and Dominions in the early 1930s, Pedelty teamed up with Victor Greene to form Crusade Films, with the aim of making their own quota films for Paramount.

Paramount had attempted to avoid the stigma attached to 'quota quickies' by commissioning more ambitious British films such as Alexander Korda's *Service for Ladies* (1932), and the Pedelty-scripted *That's a Good Girl* (Jack Buchanan, 1933) and *The Little Damozel* (Herbert Wilcox, 1933). Pedelty made his debut as a director with *School for Stars* (1935), a romantic comedy set in a drama college. This was followed by *Flame in the Heather* (1935), a historical drama set during the Jacobite rebellion of 1745 partly shot on location in Scotland. Irish locations were also used in a series of musical comedies involving the Northern Ireland singer and actor Richard Hayward and other members of the Belfast Repertory Players: *The Luck of the Irish* (1935), *The Early Bird* (1936) and *Irish and Proud of It* (1936). Although regarded as examples of Irish whimsy in Britain, these films proved immensely popular with audiences in Belfast where they ran as first features. *Irish and Proud of It* was also notable for the screen debut of fifteen-year old Dinah Sheridan in the guise, as one review put it, of a 'bonny colleen' (*Daily Film Renter*, October 1936). Pedelty worked with his 'discovery' on a further two features: the theatrical comedy *Behind Your Back* (1937) and *Landslide* (1937), a murder mystery set in a Welsh village, where the dramatic highlight consists of a theatre being engulfed by a landslide.

Crusade appears to have been a victim of the 1938 Cinematograph Films Act, which reduced the demand for low-budget quota films. Pedelty's career as a director more or less ended in 1938, though after the Second World War he reunited with Richard Hayward to direct *Back Home in Ireland*, a documentary-cum-travelogue dealing with the historical ties between the USA and Northern Ireland. In the 1950s Pedelty became editor of the popular film fan magazine *Picturegoer*.
(John Hill)

BIBLIOGRAPHY: Hill, John, *Cinema and Northern Ireland* (London: BFI, 2006).

FILMOGRAPHY: *School for Stars*; *Flame in the Heather*; *The Luck of the Irish* (1935); *The Early Bird*; *Irish and Proud of It* (1936); *Landslide*; *Behind Your Back*; *First Night*; *False Evidence* (1937); *Murder Tomorrow*; *Bedtime Story* (1938); *Back Home in Ireland* (doc. short, 1946).

PÉLISSIER, Anthony (1912–1988)

Harry Anthony Compton Pélissier was born in 1912 in Finchley, north London, the son of actress Fay Compton and composer and entertainer H. G. Pélissier. He was educated at Charterhouse but left at seventeen to go on the stage, and quickly became a West End regular. Around the mid-1930s he started writing plays and revues, which led to work polishing film scripts. After serving in the army during the Second World War, he worked as an assistant producer on films such as *Lisbon Story* (Paul Stein, 1946), but his breakthrough as a director came in the theatre with the success of *Duet for Two Hands* (1945). The play's leading performer, John Mills, became a lifelong friend and produced and starred in Pélissier's debut feature, an adaptation of H. G. Wells' *The History of Mr Polly*. A period film with a contemporary message – 'if you don't like your life you can change it' – it reflected disillusion with the values of an increasingly materialistic urban society and showed happiness to be found in a more simple country life.

Mr Polly is essentially good humoured and optimistic. Mills and Pélissier's next film, *The Rocking Horse Winner*, from a short story by D. H. Lawrence, is a scathing indictment of pre-war society. The story centres upon a young boy who appears to be able to predict the outcome of real horse races by riding on his rocking horse. Mills, using his native Suffolk accent, plays a sympathetic groom, but the boy's aristocratic family is portrayed as selfish and shallow, willing to exploit and in the end destroy a loving child in order to maintain a life of hedonistic pleasure. Both films were well received but Pélissier seemed unable to consolidate his reputation as a major director. After an atmospheric but slow-moving thriller, *Night Without Stars*, he was given the weakest of the three N. Somerset Maugham stories that make up *Encore*, a trilogy of dated Noël Coward playlets for *Meet Me Tonight* and a clumsy Ealing satire on television, *Meet Mr Lucifer*, which the studio's regular directors had wisely turned down. However, his final feature, *Personal Affair*, reaffirmed that, with the right material, Pélissier was a powerful and talented director. A dark and taut psychological drama about a village schoolteacher suspected of sexually abusing one of his pupils, it proved too controversial to be commercially successful at a time when the industry was concentrating on frothy comedies and Second World War adventures.

Pélissier returned to the theatre and also became involved in television production. In 1959 he headed up an experimental drama unit at the BBC, where his adaptations of works by Ivan Turgenev and Thomas Mann pioneered the kind of serious drama for which the BBC has since become famous. He then turned his hand to directing documentaries, and won the Screenwriters Guild Award for Outstanding British Documentary with *Suspects All* in 1964.

It is possible to view Pélissier as a bit of a dilettante – somewhat ruefully he described himself as a jack-of-all-trades and a master of none. But while a famous mother helped him get a foot in the door, he quickly became known as a hard-working and conscientious professional. Though Pélissier came from the theatre, he fully appreciated the difference between the two mediums and he worked with cinematographer Desmond Dickinson to give his films a satisfyingly glossy look. Most of his films have a quintessentially English feel about them, but there is little sympathy for the class-bound society of the past and Pélissier insists on probing beneath the surface to uncover disturbing undercurrents. He died on 2 April 1988 in Seaford, East Sussex.

(Linda Wood)

BIBLIOGRAPHY: Mills, John, *Up in the Clouds, Gentlemen Please* (London: Orion, 2001).

FILMOGRAPHY: *The History of Mr Polly* (1948); *The Rocking Horse Winner* (1949); *Night Without Stars*; *Encore* ('Winter Cruise' episode, co-dirs. Harold French/Pat Jackson) (1951); *Meet Me Tonight* (aka *Fumed Oak/ Tonight at 8.30*, 1952); *Meet Mr Lucifer*, *Personal Affair* (1953); *Risk Taker* (doc., 1960); *Suspects All* (doc., 1964); *Voyage North* (doc., 1965); *All in a Day's Work* (doc.); *Diamonds* (doc.) (1967); *Talkback* (doc., 1969); *Portrait of a People – Impressions of Britain* (doc., 1970); *Problem Solving – Some Basic Principles* (doc.); *Managing in Action* (doc.); *Listening* (doc.) (1971); *A Matter of Confidence* (doc., 1973).

PENNINGTON-RICHARDS, C. M. (1911–2005)

Born in South Norwood, London, on 17 December 1911, Cyril Pennington-Richards started his film career in 1932 working on advertising shorts before moving into documentaries as camera assistant, camera operator and, by the late 1930s, lighting cameraman. In 1940 he joined the Crown Film Unit, serving as cinematographer on several productions, including Humphrey Jennings' "*Fires Were Started –*" (1943). He continued in this capacity, and as an occasional screenwriter, through to the early 1960s, working for a number of British and American companies. He was given his first opportunity to direct in 1953 with *The Oracle*, a typically whimsical Group 3 comedy. He directed two B-feature crime thrillers for Tempean in 1957, *Stormy Crossing* and *Hour of Decision*, and episodes of television series such as *The Buccaneers* (1956), *Ivanhoe* (1958) and *The Invisible Man* (1958).

In the 1960s he directed a series of popular comedies: *Inn for Trouble*, a spin-off from *The Larkins* television series, starring Peggy Mount and David Kossoff; *Double Bunk*, which he also wrote, about honeymooners (Jeanette Scott and Ian Carmichael) on a houseboat who become involved in a race to Calais; *Dentist on the Job*, a mildly amusing satire of advertising with Bob Monkhouse; and *Ladies Who Do* (1963) featuring the redoubtable Peggy Mount as the leader of a gang of charladies who use tips from a dealer's waste-paper basket to move into property speculation.

Pennington-Richards was at his best with light comedy, but as a versatile, competent director with a cameraman's eye for composition, he was more than competent to handle other genres, as he demonstrated with his undeservedly forgotten Second World War film *Mystery Submarine*, and his lively action-adventure *A Challenge for Robin Hood*. By the late 1960s he had

fallen out of fashion, though the Children's Film Foundation provided a last refuge for his unflashy professionalism, as it did for others of his generation of directors. He lived in retirement in Bognor Regis and died on 2 January 2005.
(Andrew Spicer)

BIBLIOGRAPHY: BECTU History Project interview, tape no. 122, held in the BFI National Library, London.

FILMOGRAPHY: *The Oracle* (US: *The Horse's Mouth*, 1953); *Stormy Crossing* (US: *Black Tide*); *Hour of Decision* (1957); *Inn for Trouble* (1960); *Double Bunk*; *Dentist on the Job* (1961); *Mystery Submarine* (US: *Decoy*); *Ladies Who Do* (1963); *A Challenge for Robin Hood*; *Danny the Dragon* (serial) (1967); *Sky Pirates* (1977).

PEPLOE, Clare (1942–)

Clare Peploe's directorial output has been shaped by her bohemian upbringing and her strong ties with European art cinema. Born in Tanganyika in 1942, she grew up in Kenya, England and Italy. Her paternal grandfather was the painter S. J. Peploe, one of the Scottish Colourists; while the family tree of her mother, Clothilde, a painter herself, includes the German sculptor Adolf von Hildebrand. Peploe's passion for cinema was fanned by friendship with aspiring film-makers Peter Wollen and Laura Mulvey.

Peploe's first major credit was as a co-writer of Michelangelo Antonioni's *Zabriskie Point* (1970); her brother Mark later collaborated regularly with the director. Peploe's career developed further with Bernardo Bertolucci, whom she married in 1979; among other Bertolucci films, she assisted generally on *La luna* (1979), and co-wrote and co-produced *Besieged* (1998). She began directing with the half-hour short *Couples & Robbers* (1981), a droll, neatly patterned tale of burglary and middle-class desire, laced with criticisms of the Thatcher era's materialist ethic. The layers in her first feature, *High Season* (1987), written with Mark Peploe, proved more complicated. On the surface lay Chris Menges' dazzling images of Greek islands, and a flimsy tale featuring a photographer, obnoxious tourists and a Russian spy. Further down lay serious but playfully expressed thoughts about colonialism, history, culture and myth. The interesting mixture never quite gelled.

Peploe's next two films were thriller adaptations. 'Sauce for the Goose' (1990), an hour-long episode in the television series *Mistress of Suspense*, pursued a straight line through Patricia Highsmith's story. But *Rough Magic* (1995), set in Mexico, took James Hadley Chase's novel *Miss Shumway Waves a Wand* for a particularly wild ride, whisking Bridget Fonda, Russell Crowe and the viewer from magical realism to lowbrow humour and film noir pastiche. There were awkward moments, but at best Peploe created a liberated and enchanted space for her parade of human follies.

Both cinema features suffered limited exposure and left wider audiences bemused. In theory Peploe's next film, an adaptation of Marivaux's eighteenth-century play *The Triumph of Love* (2001), should have conquered the art houses with its vim, fresh air and Mira Sorvino's seductive performance as the princess ready to don male attire to win a reluctant heart. But this film too has been little seen: Peploe's work seems doomed to get mislaid in that difficult zone between commercial entertainment and high art.
(Geoff Brown)

BIBLIOGRAPHY: Demme, Jonathan, 'Clare Peploe', *Interview*, May 1988, p. 44; Peploe, Clare, 'On the Road', *Sight and Sound*, May 1996, pp. 14–15.

FILMOGRAPHY: *Couples & Robbers* (short, 1981); *High Season* (1987); *Rough Magic* (1995); *The Triumph of Love* (2001; rel. UK, 2004).

PEPLOE, Mark (1943–)

Born in Kenya, to bohemian parents, in 1943, Mark Peploe enjoyed the same unconventional, international upbringing as his sister Clare Peploe. Both their film careers have roughly followed the same trajectory: script work with Antonioni and Bertolucci; a directing debut with a British short; and sporadic, flawed features thereafter.

In the mid-1960s Mark Peploe worked in documentary television with the Canadian film-maker Allan King. The script of Jacques Demy's *The Pied Piper*, produced by David Puttnam and Sandy Lieberson in 1971, provided a notable early cinema credit. But the film that established Peploe's reputation was Antonioni's *The Passenger* (1975); he devised the story and collaborated with Peter Wollen on the script. The use of philosophical filigree to decorate an enigmatic thriller narrative became a Peploe characteristic; the identity crisis of Jack Nicholson's television reporter also found later echoes. The identity topic appeared straightforwardly in Peploe's directing debut, *Samson and Delilah* (1984), a twenty-four-minute short adapted from a D. H. Lawrence story. Bertolucci's *The Last Emperor* (1987) supplied an elaborate visual framework for a real-life identity crisis; Peploe's work on the script won him an Academy Award. A further script for Antonioni, *The Crew*, was left unrealised in 1988.

By this time Peploe had his own feature projects. *Out of the Blue*, an ecological thriller, failed to find a buyer; but with Bertolucci's support he mounted *Afraid of the Dark* in 1991 as an Anglo-French co-production. Peploe's script about a sensitive child with a blind mother and a policeman father allowed room for homages to Antonioni and Michael Powell. Disagreeable violence and dull acting marred the film's chances of success, though the first half managed an eerie evocation of London's unlovely suburbs.

Peploe continued his script collaboration with Bertolucci on *The Sheltering Sky* (1990) and *Little Buddha* (1993), and renewed his association with Antonioni in 1996 on another unfulfilled project, *Just to Be Together*. In 1997 his own film of Joseph Conrad's novel *Victory*, shot in 1994, finally emerged. Conrad's story about a European misfit's fortunes in the Dutch East Indies allowed for handsome trappings and lush locations, but Peploe's stodgy handling did little to bring the material to cinematic life. On the evidence so far, Peploe produces his best work when he writes but does not direct.

(Geoff Brown)

BIBLIOGRAPHY: Bloom, Phillippa, 'Mark Peploe', *Empire*, Mar. 1992, p. 40; Halberstadt, Ilona, 'Interview with Mark Peploe', *Pix* no. 1, Winter 1993/4, pp. 140–7.

FILMOGRAPHY: *Samson and Delilah* (short, 1984); *Afraid of the Dark* (1992); *Victory* (1994; rel. 1997).

PETIT, Chris (1949–)

While working as editor of the film section of the London listings magazine *Time Out* in the mid-1970s, Chris Petit interested Wim Wenders in backing his first feature, *Radio On* (1979). In spite – or perhaps because – of having no previous film-making experience, Petit pulled off an extraordinary debut, a highly 'European' road movie that, greatly aided by the cinematography of Wenders regular Martin Schäfer, presented the British landscape, both rural and urban, in a manner unparalleled before or since. Moody and angst-ridden, it announced a singular talent – but also one that was clearly not destined to find a niche easily. Nevertheless, Petit managed to make three more impressive features: a dark, stylised adaptation of P. D. James' *An Unsuitable Job for a Woman* (1981), and, in Germany, the thrillers *Flight to Berlin* (1983) and *Chinese Boxes* (1984), which displayed Petit's increasing desire to experiment with narrative forms and marked his effective break with mainstream cinema.

It was while looking for novels about Soho as research for a non-fiction book on the area that Petit met the bookseller, psycho-geographer, poet and novelist Iain Sinclair, and the two began work on the first part of what would become a loose trilogy for Channel 4 about marginalised cultural figures. This was *The Cardinal and the Corpse* (1992), which, like Petit's other programmes at the time (with the exception of *Miss Marple* episode), had begun to push at the limits of the aesthetically acceptable on British television.

More recently, this trend has become even more pronounced. According to Petit, the second film in the trilogy, *The Falconer* (1997), 'never really aspired to be a film, more to a state of mutation or hybrid. It was an essay or graphic novel as much as it was a film, an exercise in vertical layering rather than linear unfolding' (Petit, 2001). Clearly influenced by Chris Marker and Jean-Luc Godard, Petit has become increasingly fascinated by the textural possibilities of the new digital technologies, both at the shooting and the editing stage. Going beyond the camera-stylo to the camcorder-stylo, then constantly refilming and manipulating his images, he creates a 'heavily textured, multilayered tapestry of formats' (Darke).

That these explorations of visual forms can become solipsistic is illustrated by *Asylum* (2000), which carries the ominous subtitle *The Last Commission*. On the other hand, Petit's film about the veteran film critic Manny Farber, *Negative Space* (1999), is a fascinating interrogation of the image – and demonstrates just how bland and conventional are most of the images that we watch on television today. Despite not having made a film specifically for the cinema since 1984, Petit remains an inventive and wholly original British film-maker.

(Julian Petley)

BIBLIOGRAPHY: Darke, Chris, 'TV Afterlife', *Film Comment*, July/Aug. 2000, pp. 37–8; Jackson, Kevin, 'Lunatics on the Pitch', *Sight and Sound*, June 2000, pp. 26–8; Mulvey, Laura, 'Detail, Digression, Death', *Afterall* no. 5, 2002, pp. 98–105; Nowell-Smith, Geoffrey, 'Radio On', *Screen*, Winter 1979–80, pp. 29–39; Petit, Chris, 'ICA

Biennial', *Vertigo*, Autumn/Winter 1995, pp. 5–8; Petit, Chris, 'Pictures by Numbers', *Film Comment*, Mar./Apr. 2001, pp. 38–43; Serafino, Murri, 'Anatomies of the Image', *Afterall* no. 5, 2002, pp. 86–92; Sinclair, Iain, *Lights Out for the Territory* (London: Granta, 1997).
FILMOGRAPHY: *Radio On* (UK/Ger, 1979); *An Unsuitable Job for a Woman* (1981); *Fluchtpunkt Berlin/Flight to Berlin* (UK/Ger, 1983); *Chinese Boxes* (UK/Ger, 1984); *More Than Meets the Eye* (short, 1989).

PIERSON, Frank R. (1925–)

Frank Pierson was born on 12 May 1925 in Chappaqua, New York, and educated at Harvard. Following a spell in magazine journalism he went into television as a writer, producer and director, notably on the Western series *Have Gun, Will Travel* (1957–63). He established his screenwriting credentials with *Cat Ballou* (Elliot Silverstein, 1965) and *Cool Hand Luke* (Stuart Rosenberg, 1967). He was nominated for an Academy Award for both films, and parlayed this success into his first writer-director assignment.

The Looking Glass War, the third British adaptation of a John Le Carré novel, was filmed at Shepperton Studios and on location in Spain. It adds a topical generational conflict to the jaded view of cold war espionage as guilty of manipulating, exploiting and wilfully sacrificing the innocent. A young Polish refugee (Christopher Jones) is sent on a misguided mission to East Germany that goes tragically awry from the start. Unfortunately, all the film's dramatic interest resides with the older characters, while narrative drive is frittered away on a doomed romance and a surfeit of moralistic attitudinising.

Pierson has since directed only two other cinema films, the Streisand–Kristofferson remake of *A Star Is Born* (1976) and *King of the Gypsies* (1978). Most of his work has been in writing screenplays – he won an Academy Award for *Dog Day Afternoon* (Sidney Lumet, 1975) – and directing movies for television, notably *Conspiracy* (2001), with Kenneth Branagh as Reinhard Heydrich, architect of Hitler's Final Solution. Since 2001 Pierson has been President of the Academy of Motion Picture Arts and Sciences.
(Sheldon Hall)
BIBLIOGRAPHY: Bean, Robin, 'Through the Looking Glass', *Films and Filming*, Sept. 1969, pp. 29–31; Murphy, Robert, *Sixties British Cinema* (London: BFI, 1992).
FILMOGRAPHY (UK only): *The Looking Glass War* (1970).

PLAISETTY, René (1889–1955)

Born in Chicago in 1889, René Plaisetty moved to France and set up his own company in 1914 exclusively for making detective films. He returned to America later in the war to direct films for Metro Pictures and Lubin, and moved to England to work for the Stoll Film Company in 1920. His first feature was an adaptation of Sax Rohmer's novel *The Yellow Claw*, which was released as part of Stoll's Eminent British Authors Series. An extravagant adventure film, shot at Cricklewood, then the largest studio in England, it climaxed with a motorboat chase on the Thames, and established Plaisetty's reputation as a director who could present exciting subject matter on a big scale. He was asked to film A. E. W. Mason's novel *The Four Feathers* and took his cast and crew to France and the deserts of Algeria. On the same trip he also filmed *The Broken Road*, another story by Mason, using mostly the same cast. The films were extremely expensive to produce given the extensive location work and the large numbers of extras, and despite the commercial success of *The Four Feathers* Stoll refused to sanction further exotic location shooting. Plaisetty's last film for the company, *The Woman with the Fan*, was a more modest production. He returned to France where he directed further features, including *L'Île sans nom* (1922) and *Chair ardente* (1932). He died in New York in 1955.
(Simon Brown)
BIBLIOGRAPHY: Low, Rachael, *The History of the British Film 1918–1929* (London: George Allen & Unwin, 1971).
FILMOGRAPHY: *The Yellow Claw* (1920); *The Broken Road*; *The Four Feathers*; *The Knave of Diamonds*; *The Woman with the Fan* (1921).

PLATTS-MILLS, Barney (1945–)

Barney Platts-Mills was born in London in 1945, the son of John Platts-Mills, a barrister and former Labour MP who was expelled from the party for Communist sympathies. He left school at fifteen and trained as a film editor at Shepperton and Pinewood before moving into television, where he worked as an editor on *Survival* and *World in Action*. He subsequently joined John and Marlene Fletcher, veterans of the Free Cinema movement, in the making of a short drama involving boys from a Paddington youth club. In 1966 he set up Maya Films with James Scott and Nicholas Gormanston, and went on to direct *St Christopher*, a short film about the Rudolf Steiner organisation made with students from the Bath Academy of Arts. Through the Fletchers he met Joan Littlewood, and with support from the National Film Finance Corporation made *Everybody's an Actor, Shakespeare Said* (1968), a documentary record of her use of improvisation with East End youngsters at her Theatre Workshop.

Inspired by the idea of 'accessible, free, working class Cinema', Platts-Mills then embarked on his first feature, *Bronco Bullfrog* (1969), a bitter-sweet tale of youthful romance struggling in the face of parental hostility and economic disadvantage. Shot in and around east London on a budget of less than £20,000 the film self-consciously departs from the conventions of mainstream commercial cinema. The plot is loose and episodic, many of the scenes (involving youngsters from the Theatre Workshop) have been improvised and the shooting style draws heavily on documentary technique. The film's aura of conviction, and seeming closeness to its subject, not only attracted favourable critical comment but also ensured the film's cult status as an index of changes in working-class youth culture.

While Platts-Mills was often compared to Ken Loach, his interest was less in class than generational conflict. This is particularly evident in his next feature, *Private Road* (1971), dealing with a group of middle-class drifters torn between the demands of social conformity and personal rebellion. Despite a bigger budget and the use of professional actors (Susan Penhaligon, Bruce Robinson, Robert Brown, Kathleen Byron) the film was less kindly received than its predecessor. Critics were impatient with the film's apparent shapelessness and audiences failed to empathise with the predicaments of the film's middle-class drop-outs – though Robinson drew fruitfully on his experience for his own directorial debut, *Withnail and I* (1986). The film itself received very limited distribution and Platts-Mills became embroiled in a long-running dispute with British Lion over their handling of the film's release. Increasingly disillusioned with the state of the British film industry, Platts-Mills attempted to set up community video projects in London and Glasgow, and in 1973 moved to the west coast of Scotland to take up farming on a Scottish estate. He did not re-emerge until 1982, when the new Channel 4 funded *Hero*, an eccentric historical drama based on Scottish folklore and legend. Shot in the Scottish countryside, and performed in Gaelic by working-class kids from Glasgow, the film lacked the connection between experience and performance that had been a feature of Platts-Mills' earlier work and failed to find an audience. Although Platts-Mills vowed his next film would be 'very much more controlled' ('Home from the Hills'), there have been no features since. In 1989, however, he did contribute a prescient documentary (*The Ultimate Blasphemy*) to Channel 4's series *Dispatches*. (John Hill)

BIBLIOGRAPHY: Elsaesser, Thomas, 'Interview – Barney Platts-Mills', *Monogram* no. 3, 1972, pp. 39–42; 'Home from the Hills', *Monthly Film Bulletin*, Dec. 1982, pp. 287–8; Platts-Mills, Barney, *Three Screenplays* (London: platts-mills.com, 2004); Robinson, David, 'Around Angel Lane', *Sight and Sound*, Summer 1970, pp. 132–3; <www.barneyplatts-mills.com/biog.html>.

FILMOGRAPHY: *St Christopher* (doc. short, 1966); *Everybody's an Actor, Shakespeare Said* (doc. short, 1968); *Bronco Bullfrog* (1969); *Private Road* (1971); *Hero* (1982).

POLANSKI, Roman (1933–)

Roman Polanski has enjoyed a successful if controversial career in the cinema for almost forty years, directing in various countries including Poland, Britain, America, France and Italy. While highly diverse, his films are usually set in restricted spaces and involve small groups of characters, often alienated from modern society. The world he evokes is unstable, marked by sudden and shocking tendencies towards violence.

Polanski was born Roman Liebling in Paris on 18 August 1933. Two years before the outbreak of the Second World War, the family returned to Poland. His mother died in the Auschwitz concentration camp; Roman and his father survived and were reunited in 1945. Adopting the surname Polanski, he acted in Polish films, most notably as one of the youths organising resistance to the Nazis in *Pokolenie/A Generation* (Andrzej Wajda, 1955), before studying at the Lodz Film School. Numerous short films, including *Dwaj ludzie z szafa/Two Men and a Wardrobe* (1958), were followed by a taut, minimalist thriller, *Nóz w wodzie/Knife in the Water* (1962), which gained an Academy Award nomination for Best Foreign Film, but was denounced by the Communist regime for its negative portrayal of Polish life.

Polanski departed for France, where he teamed up with the writer Gérard Brach. The Polish producer Eugene Gutowski, who had established himself in London, invited them to work with him at the adventurous exploitation film company Compton Film Productions. Brach's script for *Cul-de-Sac* was initially considered too uncommercial, and *Repulsion* was quickly written as an alternative. A tense psycho-drama about a woman both attracted and repulsed by sexuality, *Repulsion* achieved the perfect art/exploitation balance – scary effects, graphic violence, a claustrophobic air of soured sexuality, placed within a moving and psychologically convincing story. Barely handicapped by his limited grasp of the English language – the film's dialogue is regularly subsumed under action and atmosphere – Polanski secures a *tour-de-force* performance from Catherine Deneuve as the young woman who retreats into defensive, psychotic madness.

The film's success encouraged Compton to go ahead with *Cul-de-Sac*, a Pinteresque drama that offered few of the thrills that had attracted audiences to *Repulsion*. The action takes place in an isolated castle where two criminals (Lionel Stander and Jack MacGowran) hold an eccentric husband (Donald Pleasence) and his young wife (Françoise Dorléac) hostage. The interplay between the characters, the shifting power balance and the threat of violence mixed with absurd comedy make the film unique. *Dance of the Vampires*, Polanski's third British film was ostensibly more conventional, a comedy-horror film made in colour for MGM-British, but this was partly because MGM insisted on re-cutting and shortening the film. Enough of Polanski's macabre vision survives to make it at least an interesting curiosity.

Polanski then moved to Hollywood, where he was able to retain much tighter control over *Rosemary's Baby* (1968), an adaptation of Ira Levin's novel about demonic possession. The film was a huge success and would have secured Polanski's career as a coveted Hollywood director. But in 1969 his wife Sharon Tate,

eight months pregnant, was brutally murdered by Charles Manson and his acolytes. Polanski came back to Britain to make *Macbeth* (1971), a violent, bloody version of Shakespeare's play that many critics read as reflecting Polanski's personal life.

After a sojourn in Europe, Polanski returned to Hollywood to direct *Chinatown* (1974), a stylish film noir that repeated the critical and box-office success of *Rosemary's Baby*. However, his career was disrupted once again when he was accused of having sex with a thirteen-year-old girl. He fled America and pursued an erratic career in Europe. Most of the best films he made subsequently have had some British involvement. *Tess*, his adaptation of Thomas Hardy's *Tess of the D'Urbervilles*, treats Hardy's story with respect and makes superb use of the English landscape; *Bitter Moon*, for all its threatened lurches into the ridiculous, presents an intriguing study of the Englishman's fascination with esoteric sexuality; *Death and the Maiden* offers a convincing and powerful version of Ariel Dorfman's play about the relationship between a torturer and his victim. *The Pianist* (which reunited Polanski with Gutowski) is an unflinchingly brave study of a man's will to survive among the horrors of Nazi-occupied Warsaw; the film won the Academy Award for Best Director in 2002. *Oliver Twist*, filmed in Prague, but notable for the detailed grime and decrepitude of its settings, connects Oliver's deprived childhood and the brutality of the workhouse with Polanski's own grim past and dour outlook on life. Though there have been times when Polanski's career seemed in terminal decline, he has proved himself across the decades as the consummate survivor and a major international director.

(Jamie Sexton)

BIBLIOGRAPHY: Butler, Ivan, *The Cinema of Roman Polanski* (New York and London: A. S. Barnes/A. Zwemmer, 1970); Goulding, Daniel J. (ed.), *Five Filmmakers: Tarkovsky, Forman, Polanski, Szabo, Makavejev* (Bloomington: Indiana University Press, 1994); Leaming, Barbara, *Polanski: His Life and His Films* (London: Hamish Hamilton, 1982); Parker, John, *Roman Polanski* (London: Victor Gollancz, 1993); Polanski, Roman, *Roman* (London: Heinemann, 1984).

FILMOGRAPHY (UK only): *Repulsion* (1965); *Cul-de-Sac* (1966); *Dance of the Vampires* (US: *The Fearless Vampire Killers*, 1967); *Macbeth* (1971); *Tess* (UK/Fr, 1980); *Lune de fiel/Bitter Moon* (Fr/UK, 1992); *Death and the Maiden* (UK/US/Fr, 1995); *The Pianist* (UK/Fr/Ger/Pol/Neth, 2002); *Oliver Twist* (Fr/UK/Cz, 2005).

POLIAKOFF, Stephen (1952–)

Stephen Poliakoff was born in London on 1 December 1952, to a Russian-Jewish father and an Anglo-Jewish mother. After abandoning his undergraduate degree at Cambridge, he established a reputation in the theatre in the mid-1970s with plays such as *Hitting Town* and *City Sugar*. Success as a television playwright followed: *Stronger than the Sun* (Michael Apted, 1977), *Bloody Kids* (Stephen Frears, 1979) and *Caught on a Train* (Peter Duffell, 1980) showed Poliakoff to be a versatile and original new voice. In 1987 he wrote and directed his first feature film, *Hidden City*, financed by Channel 4 and premiered at the

Venice Film Festival. In it one can perceive structural, thematic and stylistic traits that were to be explored and developed in Poliakoff's later work. Historian James Richards (Charles Dance) is approached by Sharon Newton (Cassie Stuart), a picture researcher in a film archive who has found a short black-and-white film that she believes, reveals an abduction. She needs James' help to find the next vital piece of evidence: a second film reel. Reluctantly at first, he agrees to help her, and their investigation leads them into a dangerous world of defence secrets and government cover-ups. Although there is narrative resolution at the end of the film, the plot is loosely structured and the genre of the film is uncertain. Foregrounded instead are Poliakoff's recurring thematic preoccupations: the thrill of discovering concealed histories and secrets; the secret aspects of places and family; and the potential power of documents (especially photographs and film images) to help us retrieve the past and its undisclosed stories.

After writing *She's Been Away* (Peter Hall, 1989), Poliakoff wrote and directed *Close My Eyes*, which focuses on hidden secrets within families, and tackles the taboo of incest. Despite its subject matter, the film is unsentimental and avoids the conventions of melodrama, some of the most intense scenes being quietly underplayed and restrained. Similarly *Century*, Poliakoff's next film, refuses the generic confines of historical drama and employs a 'costume drama' setting to explore the abiding question of potential conflict between scientific progress and common humanity. *The Tribe*, made in 1996 but denied a cinema release, was broken into episodes and slipped out on television in 1998. The Channel 4 film *Food of Love*, about a group of friends revisiting their student past, was shown in cinemas but attracted small audiences and hostile reviews.

Subsequently Poliakoff has concentrated on writing and directing drama serials for television. Quirkiness and eccentricity have always been present in his work; in the films this tends to result in laboured characterisations and portentous dialogue; in his later television work – *Shooting the Past* (1999), *Perfect Strangers* (2001) and *The Lost Prince* – it is more fruitfully integrated. Poliakoff's penchant for elaborate montage sequences, odd juxtapositions of sound and image, and discursive narratives fit more comfortably within the extended length of a three- or four-hour serial. (By contrast his two 2005 television films *Friends and Crocodiles* and *Gideon's Daughter* appear disappointingly one-dimensional.) Though his maverick talent excludes him from mainstream cinema, Poliakoff remains one of the most inventive and intriguing of writer-directors in Britain today. (Sarah Cardwell)

BIBLIOGRAPHY: Benedict, David, 'The Race against Time', *Independent*, 9 Jan. 1999, p. 12; Dobson, Patricia, 'Stephen Poliakoff: Profile', *Screen International Supplement, LFF*, 9 Nov. 1993, p. 5; Kemp, Philip, 'English Manners', *Sight and Sound*, Autumn 1987, pp. 288–9.

FILMOGRAPHY: *Hidden City* (1987); *Close My Eyes* (1990); *Century* (1993); *Food of Love* (1997).

POLLOCK, George (1907–)

George Pollock was born in Leicester in 1907 and entered the film industry in the 1930s. As an assistant director during the 1940s and 50s, he worked with major film-makers including Anthony Asquith, Thorold Dickinson, Leslie Howard and David Lean. However, this experience does not appear to have had much influence on Pollock's own work as a director, which has tended to be efficient but anonymous. He started out as a specialist in comedies and thrillers and in the early 1960s successfully combined the two genres with a series of comedy-thrillers for MGM-British based on the novels of Agatha Christie, featuring Margaret Rutherford as the amateur detective Miss Marple. *Murder She Said*, *Murder at the Gallop*, *Murder Most Foul* and *Murder Ahoy* conjured up a cosy world of English eccentricity, embodied most of all by Rutherford herself, who was accompanied in all the films by her assistant (and real-life partner) Stringer Davis and a long-suffering police officer played by Charles Tingwell. Pollock mounts the occasional moment of shock – notably the murder scene in *Murder She Said* and Finlay Currie's death in *Murder at the Gallop* – but generally he adopts a self-effacing approach to the material. Pollock's final film was another Christie adaptation, *Ten Little Indians*. An efficient but forgettable rendition, it lacked a strong central performance to match that of Rutherford and offered instead the 'whodunit break', a silly gimmick involving the narrative being stopped while the audience is invited to guess the identity of the killer. (Peter Hutchings)

BIBLIOGRAPHY: Noble, Peter (ed.), *The British Film Yearbook, 1947–1948* (London: Skelton Robinson, 1947), p. 332.

FILMOGRAPHY: *Stranger in Town* (1957); *Rooney*; *Sally's Irish Rogue*; *Broth of a Boy* (1958); *Don't Panic Chaps!*; *And the Same to You* (1959); *Murder She Said*; *Village of Daughters* (1961); *Kill or Cure* (1962); *Murder at the Gallop* (1963); *Murder Most Foul*; *Murder Ahoy* (1964); *Ten Little Indians* (aka *And Then There Was None*, 1965).

POPE, Angela (1945–)

Angela Pope was born in Surrey in 1945. She established herself with the accomplished television documentary *Yesterday's Men* (1971), following the fate of Labour Party politicians defeated in the 1970 general election. Other documentaries followed, including her perceptive four-part series *A Childhood* (1984), before she turned to fiction with Jack Rosenthal's *Shift Work* (1986), a witty television play about a woman taxi-driver having a bad night. Over the next ten years Pope directed a succession of moving, relevant and original dramas for the BBC. William Nicholson's *Sweet as You Are* (1987) intelligently explores issues around AIDS, with Liam Neeson's one-night stand destroying the harmony of his happy family life; David Kane's *Dream Baby* (1989) treats life on a run-down Edinburgh housing estate with surprising good humour; Trevor Preston's adaptation of Verity Bargate's disturbing study of a woman's disintegration, *Children Crossing* (1990), is uneven but compelling. Pope changes her style to suit her writers, but all these films are characterised by sharp observation and a strong sympathy for the characters.

Ronan Bennett's *A Man You Don't Meet Every Day* and Frank Deasy's *Captives*, both made in 1994, are companion pieces featuring well-off middle-class women pursuing affairs with unsuitable men who conceal dark secrets. The former is modest and funny, jollied along by a raucous soundtrack from Shane MacGowan and the Pogues; the latter, a bigger-budget affair given a limited cinema release, is richer and more flamboyant. The affair between preposterously glamorous prison dentist Julia Ormond and wife-murderer Tim Roth seems an improbable fantasy; but the hothouse atmosphere Pope conjures up with cameraman Remi Adefarasin, and her insistence on viewing events from the woman's point of view, make it easy to suspend disbelief. Complex psychological difficulties are washed away in a tide of melodrama, but as with much of Pope's work disturbing resonances linger.

Ironically, *Hollow Reed*, her only feature made directly for the cinema, turned out to be visually dull and thematically shallow, its well-meaning attempt to show that being a Gay Dad does not mean being a Bad Dad hardly making up for a predictable story and cardboard characters. Pope made a successful return to documentary with *Kosovo: Road to Nowhere* (1999), an in-depth account of the wretched lives endured by Kosovan refugees. (Robert Murphy)

BIBLIOGRAPHY: Seecoomar, Robin, 'Non-Conformist Pope', *Time Out* no. 728, 2 Aug. 1984, p. 13.

FILMOGRAPHY: *Captives* (UK/SA, 1994); *Hollow Reed* (UK/Ger/Sp, 1996).

POTTER, Sally (1949–)

Sally Potter has made successful commercial features and experimental films in a career that also encompasses dance, choreography, music and performance art – elements interwoven in all her films, which confront issues of performance, gender and genre.

Charlotte Sally Potter was born in London on 19 September 1949 into an artistic family: her father was a designer and poet, her mother a musician. Both her grandmothers had been actresses and one of them, 'Hunny' Quennell, was to become a key influence in her life. Potter attended schools in north London, and had already determined to be a film director before leaving school at the age of sixteen. During a one-year foundation course at St Martin's School of Art she learned draughtsmanship and composition, and between 1971 and 1974 studied dance and choreography at the London School of Contemporary Dance. Potter's apprenticeship as a film-maker was at the London Film-makers' Co-op, which she joined in the late 1960s.

Between 1969 and 1971 she made several short experimental films exploring cinematic time and space. Most of these early films are multi-screen pieces: *Black and White* is an eight-minute, two-screen piece; and the fifteen-minute *Play* uses a double-screen format to 'play' with cinematic space in a film about children playing in a street. *Daily* and *Combines* are experiments in expanded cinema, combining live performances of music and dance with multi-screen film projections.

During the 1970s, Potter trod the boards, touring as a dancer, choreographer, musician and performance artist: with Richard Alston's dance company Strider; with the Limited Dance Company, which she co-founded with Jacky Lansley; with performance artist Rose English; and with fellow musicians in the Feminist Improvisation Group (FIG).

In 1979 Potter's career entered a new phase with the launch of her 16mm short film *Thriller*, produced, scripted, directed and edited by Potter herself and funded by the Arts Council of Great Britain. Its deconstruction of the heroine's role in Puccini's opera *La Bohème* was very much in tune with contemporary thinking in feminist film criticism, and Potter's wit and a lightness of touch made her film highly watchable.

Thriller's success brought Potter the opportunity to direct her first 35mm feature film, *The Gold Diggers*, funded by the BFI and Channel 4. Like *Thriller*, which draws a distinction between the romantic bohemian poverty of Rodolfo, hero of Puccini's opera, and the less glamorous poverty of seamstresses like Mimi, *The Gold Diggers* explores the relationship between economics and money on the one hand and women as icons and exchange objects on the other. The film, much of which was made on location in Iceland, involved an all-female crew and cast, including Julie Christie as the iconic woman, the star. Stunningly shot in black and white by Babette Mangolte, it includes numerous references to the history of cinema, from D. W. Griffith to David Lean via the Hollywood musical. Unfortunately the film was poorly received, a fact Potter attributes to its lack of a proper script, her own struggles with storytelling on film and a failure to communicate with the audience. It was to be nearly a decade before Potter returned to feature film production.

After the disappointment of *The Gold Diggers*, Potter completed *London Story*, a fifteen-minute spoof spy thriller, in 1986. During the remainder of the 1980s, while trying to put together another feature production, she made *Tears, Laughter, Fear and Rage* (1986), a series about emotions; and *I Am an Ox, I Am a Horse, I Am a Man, I Am a Woman* (1990), on Soviet cinema, both for Channel 4.

It took eight years of international deal-making to set up Potter's first venture into mainstream art cinema; based on Virginia Woolf's *Orlando*, a playful homage to the androgynous Vita Sackville-West, with a narrative stretching over four centuries and a protagonist who changes sex halfway through the story, it was a less than obvious literary adaptation. Potter's willingness to experiment and her experience with unconventional narratives enabled her to handle this complex project with panache. Assisted by a masterly performance from Tilda Swinton – equally convincing as both man and woman – *Orlando* proved a critical and commercial success.

In her next feature, *The Tango Lesson*, a cosmopolitan co-production, Potter returned to her interest in dance with a story about a film director (played by Potter herself) who becomes distracted from writing a Hollywood script by a fascination with the Argentinian tango, which she decides she must learn. The film deals with the attraction between Latin American and Anglo-Saxon cultures and between male and female, exploring the imbalance of power between men and women on the one hand and between the mainstream film industry and the film director on the other. Potter returned to complex and lavish historical drama in *The Man Who Cried*, starring Cate Blanchett, Johnny Depp and Christina Ricci. With an operatic theme and sensibility, this sensual, colourful melodrama set in various European cities in the inter-war years centres on the story of a displaced young

Jewish woman and her relationships with a Romany horse wrangler, a Russian dancer and an Italian opera singer.

The Tango Lesson and *The Man Who Cried* were less warmly received than *Orlando*, but Potter represents a British strand of artistically ambitious film-making that is inherently risky and commercially uncertain. *Yes* (2004) certainly shows no dampening of Potter's adventurousness, using rhyming dialogue and freewheeling camerawork to convey the liberating love affair between a British politician's Irish-American wife (Joan Allen) and a Lebanese waiter (Simon Abkarian). Potter's audacious and visually sumptuous films, with their challenging, bending and transcending of genders and genres and their complex interweaving of image, performance and music, is something to be celebrated in an increasingly commercialised world cinema.

(Annette Kuhn)

BIBLIOGRAPHY: Ciecko, Anne, 'Sally Potter: The Making of a British Woman Filmmaker', in Yvonne Tasker (ed.), *Fifty Contemporary Filmmakers* (London: Routledge, 2002); Fischer, Lucy, '"Dancing through the Minefields": Passion, Pedagogy, Politics and Production in *The Tango Lesson*', *Cinema Journal* vol. 43 no. 3, Spring 2004, pp 42–58; Florence, Penny, 'A Conversation with Sally Potter', *Screen*, vol. 34 no. 3, 1993, pp. 275–84; MacDonald, Scott, *A Critical Cinema: Interviews with Independent Filmmakers* (Berkeley: University of California Press, 1998), pp. 397–427; Potter, Sally, *Orlando, Based on the Book by Virginia Woolf* (London: Faber and Faber, 1994); Potter, Sally, *The Tango Lesson* (London: Faber and Faber, 1997); Potter, Sally, *The Man Who Cried* (London: Faber and Faber, 2000).

FILMOGRAPHY: *Jerk* (short); *Black and White* (short, 1969); *The Building* (short, 1970); *Hors d'oeuvres* (short); *Play* (short) (1971); *Combines* (short); *Daily* (short) (1972); *Thriller* (short, 1979); *The Gold Diggers* (1983); *The London Story* (short, 1986); *Orlando* (UK/Fr/Neth/Arg/Jap/Ger, 1992); *The Tango Lesson* (UK/Jap/Ger, 1997); *The Man Who Cried* (UK/Fr/US, 2000); *Yes* (UK/US, 2004).

POWELL, Michael (1905–1990) and Emeric PRESSBURGER (1902–1988)

Emeric (Imre) Pressburger was born in Miskolc, Hungary, on 5 December 1902. He worked as a journalist, translator and short-story writer in Weimar Republic Berlin, before turning screenwriter for directors Robert Siodmak (*Abschied*, 1930) and Max Ophüls (*Dann schon lieber Lebertran*, 1931). He left Germany for England in 1935, and settled into a film industry especially congenial to Hungarian émigrés, scripting Alexander Korda's attempt to co-opt the German mountain movie genre, *The Challenge* (Milton Rosmer, 1938). Korda assigned Pressburger to rewrites on *The Spy in Black*, directed by Michael Powell. The two hit it off; Pressburger became Powell's favoured screenwriter, and got his first producer credit on . . . *One of our aircraft is missing* (1942). Thirteen major films made between 1943 and 1955 bear the credit 'Produced, written and directed by Michael

Powell and Emeric Pressburger', and though Powell continually expressed his debt to Pressburger's creative input, no suggestion has ever been made that Pressburger co-directed these films. Without Powell, he directed only the undistinguished *Twice upon a Time*. He died in Aspall, Suffolk, on 5 February 1988.

Michael Powell was born in Bekesbourne, near Canterbury, Kent, on 30 September 1905. He left Dulwich College to work (briefly) in a bank before his father, a hotelier on the French Riviera, secured him an introduction to the Hollywood-Irish director Rex Ingram, who was working at the Victorine Studios in Nice. Powell worked for Ingram as a bit-player (*The Magician*, 1926) and general assistant, then entered the nascent British film industry as story analyst and stills photographer. He formed a partnership with American producer Jerry Jackson to make 'quota quickies', hour-long films needed to satisfy a legal requirement that cinemas screen a certain quota of British movies. Between 1931 and 1936, Powell directed twenty-three films, some ordinary, some very sprightly: *The Phantom Light*, for example, is an enjoyable comedy-thriller set in a purportedly haunted Welsh lighthouse.

Even before meeting Pressburger, Powell showed ambitions beyond studio-made films with their shuffle of stock characters, West End players and tidy resolutions. In 1937 he ventured to Foula, an island in the Hebrides, to film a drama inspired by the 1930 evacuation of St Kilda. Compared at the time to Robert Flaherty's documentary *Man of Aran* (1934), *The Edge of the World*, for all its real locations and semi-authentic accents, signals that Powell works at the opposite end of the filmic spectrum from Flaherty; it is at once a properly told dramatic story a mainstream audience can follow, and a mystical contemplation of British landscape. *The Spy in Black* might seem a retreat to commercialism after the artistic venture of *The Edge of the World*, with a dashing Conrad Veidt in black leathers tooling a motorbike around John Buchanland, but it is another Scots-set film, and quite apart from the addition of Pressburger's influence marks Powell's style in transition. The first real Powell–Pressburger project was the follow-up Veidt thriller, *Contraband*, which takes full advantage of the atmospheric opportunities offered by blacked-out wartime London.

Powell worked on Korda's rapidly assembled flag waver, *The Lion Has Wings*, and directed parts of *The Thief of Bagdad* before Korda transferred the production to Hollywood. He then formed an alliance with Pressburger that yielded a string of important films. At first, their great subject was the war, but this gradually came to encompass intense, strange discussions of national character and consequent flights of fancy. *49th Parallel* and *One of our aircraft is missing* are companion pieces, one about stranded Nazi submariners making their way across Canada, the other about downed RAF fliers assisted by the Dutch underground. Boldly, in view of the political climate, Powell and Pressburger insisted on stressing the difference between being German and being a Nazi, a crucial theme in *49th Parallel* and subsequently in *The Life and Death of Colonel Blimp*.

Invited by J. Arthur Rank to make films for his expanding organisation, Powell and Pressburger set up their own production company, The Archers, to make films under the Rank umbrella. After producing *The Silver Fleet* (Vernon Sewell/Gordon Wellesley, 1943), they made *The Life and Death of Colonel Blimp*, an altogether more complex and ambitious film that aroused the hostility of Winston Churchill, who did everything in his power to prevent it being made, and when it was made, prevent it being shown. Shot in Technicolor, it is an English epic, following a representative army officer, Clive Wynne-Candy (Roger Livesey), from youthful turn-of-the-century hothead to crusty Home Guard conservative. Much more than a state-of-the-nation address, the film covers Blimp's bitter-sweet adoration of an eternal feminine (represented by Deborah Kerr in several characters) and his lifelong relationship with a Prussian officer, Theo Kretschmar-Schuldorff (Anton Walbrook), whose joys and sufferings are even more intense than his own.

After *Blimp*, The Archers made *A Canterbury Tale*, which was criticised and misunderstood when it was first released but now seems even stronger and stranger entering the Kentish world of Powell's childhood and discovering a strain of the magical too often ignored in the English landscape and character. The film explicitly evokes Chaucer, with a dazzling jump-cut from a medieval falconer to an ARP lookout, but is also informed by Shakespeare and Blake. Its peculiar, often-ridiculed, plot (magistrate Eric Portman pours glue in local girls' hair to deter them from distracting soldiers from attending his lectures on history and culture) spins off into personal miracles, bizarre comedy charades and an ultimately moving hymn to the endurance of a Blitzed people. Other wartime films contemplate bomb-torn ruins; this one celebrates an unspoiled English countryside and ends in Canterbury, where neat signs promise the re-opening of temporarily bombed-out businesses, and the cathedral hosts a service for troops destined for the second front and long-awaited victory.

'I Know Where I'm Going!' returns to Scots isles and a romance that prompts Wendy Hiller to choose mysticism over modernity. The war is a background presence, related to the social (though not the literal) whirlpool that throws the characters together and has modified even the traditionalists in the community. *A Matter of Life and Death*, The Archers' first peacetime film, is set during the last days of the war and again discusses national conflicts, though the emphasis of this fantasy is on the troubled relationship between Britain and the rest of the world, most especially America. The strain of magic in earlier films, incarnated by characters like Pamela Brown's kelpie-like Catriona in *'I Know Where I'm Going!'*, blossoms in this tale of a pilot (David Niven) who misses the heavenly messenger (Marius Goring) supposed to convey him to the afterlife. With a serene, black-and-white heaven and a bursting, gorgeous Technicolor living world, *A Matter of Life and Death* is a glorious mingling of too many styles, themes and ideas, pulled together by the honest emotion flowing between RAF officer Niven and the American radio operator (Kim Hunter) with whom he falls in love.

Black Narcissus, from Rumer Godden's novel, is another exotic extravaganza, with five British nuns plagued by erotic impulses in a studio-created Himalayan brothel-turned-nunnery. Powell was the only Englishman working in Britain who would tackle such material, and this is one of the few British movies that could match the delirium of Josef von Sternberg or Vincente Minnelli. Deborah Kerr and Kathleen Byron give astonishing performances, white-faced and doll-like in their nuns' habits, but revealed bare-headed as wild beauties – Kerr in a flashback to her Irish girlhood, Byron succumbing to madness when she dons a red dress and lipstick and stalks vampire-like through the forest.

Powell and Pressburger's next film, *The Red Shoes*, is a dazzling twist on the showbiz star-is-born story. Winsome ballerina Moira Shearer falls under the spell of Diaghilev-like impresario Anton Walbrook, neglects her private life in favour of a passionate devotion to art and comes to a choreographed tragic end. With a sinister edge that perfectly catches the ambiguity of traditional as opposed to Disney's de-gutted fairy tales, this luminous masterpiece represented the peak of The Archers' acceptance as great popular artists.

For five years Rank had allowed The Archers unfettered artistic freedom, but disagreement over the handling of *The Red Shoes* (ironically their most commercially successful film) and the financial crisis faced by the Rank Organisation in the late 1940s led them to rejoin Korda. Their first film for him, *The Small Back Room*, from Nigel Balchin's wartime novel, marked a return to lower-budget black-and-white movie-making. David Farrar, one of the few English actors capable of playing sexy, neurotic, noirish heroes, is a war-damaged bomb-disposal expert, struggling with his own dream demons in alcoholic fantasy sequences, but most memorably and quietly pitted against a fiendish new strain of explosive device. It is Powell's most purely suspenseful film, and is still the benchmark for red-wire-or-blue-wire bomb-disposal scenes. But it came out when the public were fed up with reminders of the war and not yet ready for 'finest hour' nostalgia, and it remains under-appreciated.

Korda's yen for international success pushed The Archers into projects where their artistic daring was hampered and compromised. *Gone to Earth*, a partnership with David O. Selznick, starring his wife Jennifer Jones, suffered badly from the producer's interference. For its American release (as *The Wild Heart*), it was heavily cut and partially reshot by Rouben Mamoulian. *The Elusive Pimpernel* was a Technicolor remake of one of Korda's previous successes, *The Scarlet Pimpernel* (Harold Young, 1936), but despite fine casting (David Niven's charm versus Cyril Cusack's glower), too much compromise between the conflicting visions of Powell and Pressburger and Korda make it the only Archers film to seem chocolate-boxy and staid.

The Tales of Hoffman returns to the artistic fantastic world of *The Red Shoes* (with Moira Shearer as an enchanting but scary automaton). Wonderful though it now seems, it was a step too far for critics and audiences, and its successors, *Oh . . . Rosalinda!!*, a modernised *Fledermaus*, and the post-Archers *Luna di miel* and *Bluebeard's Castle* suggest filmed operetta was a dead end. Before The Archers split, they tried to fit in with the 1950s' trend for Second World War stories, returning to Rank for the naval drama *The Battle of the River Plate* (remarkable for its use of real ships rather than models) and the Cretan guerrilla-fighting *Ill Met by Moonlight* (notable for a poetic, weird Dirk Bogarde bandit performance). Both films maintain Powell and Pressburger's unfashionable sympathy for the enemy (Peter Finch's valiant naval commander, Marius Goring's canny, dignified general), but they lack the flair and originality of the wartime films.

Without Pressburger (but with Leo Marks), Powell made a late masterpiece, *Peeping Tom*, at once a lurid horror film and a profound meditation on the unhealthiness of cinema. Powell's personal investment is obvious from his own appearance as murderer Carl Boehm's blameworthy father, and casting that includes a star he had made (Shearer), the daughter of another old comrade (Anna Massey) and, in a crucial role, his own son Columba. Though it attracted a torrent of critical abuse, the film probably did less harm to its director's subsequent career than his conservatively patriotic *The Queen's Guards*, which seemed to fly in the face of the radical *Zeitgeist* of the 1960s. Powell reunited with Pressburger for an Australian odyssey (*They're a Weird Mob*) and for a children's fantasy (*The Boy Who Turned Yellow*). Neither film did anything to restore Powell's reputation, and his final film, *Age of Consent* – also made in Australia, with James Mason and a young, often nude Helen Mirren – was misunderstood and critically maligned.

In his last twenty years, Powell was recognised by disciples and critics as a major film-maker, to the point where this once-despised figure now seems too comfortably swallowed by the accepted canon. But no one greenlit the many projects he would like to have made, from *The Tempest* to *The Fall of the House of Usher*. Powell married Thelma Schoonmaker (the editor of his American champion Martin Scorsese's films) in 1984, and completed two fine volumes of autobiography. He died in Avening, Gloucestershire, on 19 February 1990.

(Kim Newman)

BIBLIOGRAPHY: Christie, Ian (ed.), *Powell, Pressburger and Others* (London: BFI, 1978); Christie, Ian, *Arrows of Desire: The Films of Michael Powell and Emeric Pressburger* (London: Waterstone, 1985); Christie, Ian, *A Matter of Life and Death* (London: BFI, 2000); Cook, Pam, *I Know Where I'm Going!* (London: BFI, 2002); Gough-Yates, Kevin (ed.), *Michael Powell in Collaboration with Emeric Pressburger* (London: BFI, 1971); Kennedy, A. L., *The Life and Death of Colonel Blimp* (London: BFI, 1997); Macdonald, Kevin, *Emeric Pressburger: The Life and Death of a Screenwriter* (London: Faber and Faber, 1994); Powell, Michael, *A Life in Movies: An Autobiography* (London: Heinemann, 1986); Powell, Michael, *Edge of the World* (London: Heinemann, 1990); Powell, Michael, *Million Dollar Movie* (London: Heinemann, 1992).

FILMOGRAPHY: Directed by Michael Powell: *Two Crowded Hours*; *My Friend the King*; *Rynox*; *The Rasp*; *The Star Reporter* (1931); *Hotel Splendide*; *C.O.D.*; *His Lordship*; *Born Lucky* (1932); *The*

Fire Raisers (1933); *The Night of the Party*; *Red Ensign*; *Something Always Happens*; *The Girl in the Crowd* (1934); *Lazybones*; *The Love Test*; *The Phantom Light*; *The Price of a Song*; *Someday* (1935); *The Man behind the Mask*; *Crown Versus Stevens*; *Her Last Affair*; *The Brown Wallet* (1936); *The Edge of the World* (1937); *Smith* (short); *The Lion Has Wings* (co-dirs. Brian Desmond Hurst/Adrian Brunel); *The Spy in Black* (US: *U-Boat 29*) (1939); *Contraband* (US: *Blackout*); *The Thief of Bagdad* (co-dirs. Ludwig Berger/Tim Whelan) (1940); *An Airman's Letter to His Mother* (short); *49th Parallel* (US: *The Invaders*) (1941); . . . *One of our aircraft is missing* (1942); *The Sorcerer's Apprentice* (short, 1955); *Luna de miel/Honeymoon* (UK/Sp, 1956); *Peeping Tom* (1960); *The Queen's Guards* (1961); *Bluebeard's Castle/Herzog Blaubarts Burg* (Ger, 1964); *They're a Weird Mob* (Austral, 1966); *Age of Consent* (Austral, 1969); *The Boy Who Turned Yellow* (1972).

Directed by Emeric Pressburger: *Twice upon a Time* (1953).

'Produced, written and directed' by Michael Powell and Emeric Pressburger: *The Life and Death of Colonel Blimp* (1943); *The Volunteer* (short); *A Canterbury Tale* (1944); *'I Know Where I'm Going!'* (1945); *A Matter of Life and Death* (US: *Stairway to Heaven*, 1946); *Black Narcissus* (1947); *The Red Shoes* (1948); *The Small Back Room* (1949); *Gone to Earth* (US: *The Wild Heart*); *The Elusive Pimpernel* (US: *The Fighting Pimpernel*) (1950); *The Tales of Hoffmann* (1951); *Oh . . . Rosalinda!!* (1955); *The Battle of the River Plate* (US: *Pursuit of the Graf Spee*, 1956); *Ill Met by Moonlight* (US: *Night Ambush*, 1957).

POWELL, Tristram (1940–)

Tristram Powell was born in Oxford in May 1940. His career in television was launched by a series of Arts Council-sponsored documentaries about artists. *I Build My Time* (1975) looks back on the time the German Dadaist artist Kurt Schwitters spent in the Lake District as a refugee from Nazi Germany during the Second World War. *Mucha* (1975) examines the life and work of Czech Art Nouveau artist Alphonse Mucha; *Landscape from a Dream* (1978) traces the development of the visionary landscapes of Paul Nash. Several interesting television films followed, including two odd ventures into the past: *The Kremlin Farewell* (1990), written by Nigel Williams, takes a wry look at Stalin's Russia; *The Count of Solar* (1991), written by David Nokes, investigates the case of a deaf-mute boy in pre-Revolutionary France. Powell also directed John McGrath's *The Long Roads* (1993), a moving account of an old couple's journey round Britain to say goodbye to their scattered children before they die.

His most notable collaborations have been with Michael Palin, directing his scripts for *East of Ipswich* (1987) and *Number 17* (1988), and sharing the writing of *American Friends*, Powell's only cinema film. Though inspired by true events, *American Friends* represents a throwback to the popular Alpine romances of the inter-war years like Margaret Kennedy's *The Constant Nymph* and Dodie Smith's *Autumn Crocus*. It tells an amiable tale, with Palin as a crusty Oxford Fellow poised to achieve his lifetime's ambition but distracted by the siren call of love. An unexpected twist and the performances of Palin and a beautifully poised Connie Booth help to make up for the slow pace.

(Robert Murphy)

FILMOGRAPHY: *I Build My Time* (doc. short); *Mucha* (doc. short) (1975); *Landscape from a Dream* (doc. short, 1978); *American Friends* (1991).

PRASAD, Udayan (1953–)

Udayan Prasad was born in Sevagram, India, on 4 February 1953, but emigrated to Britain with his family in 1962. He studied at the National Film and Television School and then moved into television, where he directed a number of documentaries, including *A Corner of a Foreign Field* (1986) and *Indian or British or Both?* (1986). He then directed a series of television films for the BBC: *Here Is the News* (1989), a conspiracy-theory thriller written by G. F. Newman; *102 Boulevard Haussmann* (1991), an Alan Bennett-scripted account of the relationship between Marcel Proust and his maid Celeste; and three comedies – *They Never Slept* (1991), *Running Late* (1992) and *Femme Fatale* (1993) – written by Simon Gray.

Prasad moved into feature films with *Brothers in Trouble* (1995) and *My Son the Fanatic* (1997), both of which show British society from a radically different perspective. *Brothers in Trouble*, a likeably modest film based on a novella by Abdullah Hussein, is set in the 1960s; it centres on a group of Pakistani illegal immigrants marooned in a grim north of England industrial town and finding barriers to integration difficult to surmount. *My Son the Fanatic*, scripted by Hanif Kureishi from his own short story, is more sharply focused. The conflict between Om Puri's easy-going taxi-driver, who drinks and has a relationship with a prostitute, and his fundamentalist son is both topical and funny, neatly inverting the expectation that 'Westernised' youths will rebel against their traditionalist parents. As with most of Kureishi's work there is acute observation of the social setting of the drama; and Prasad directs with sensitivity, avoiding clichés and allowing his characters to become individuals rather than types. Unfortunately, the film seemed to fall between art-house and multiplex audiences and was more widely seen in Europe than in the UK. His fourth feature *Opa!*, a sunny romantic comedy set on a Greek island, was premiered at the 2005 Toronto Film Festival.

(Paul Ward)

BIBLIOGRAPHY: Korte, Barbara and Claudia Sternberg, *Bidding for the Mainstream? Black and Asian British Film since the 1990s* (Amsterdam and New York: Rodopi, 2004); Qureshi, Irtiza, 'Fundamental Truths', *Black Film Bulletin* vol. 5 nos 2/3, 1997, pp 32–3.

FILMOGRAPHY: *Just a Walk in the Dark* (short, 1983); *Brothers in Trouble* (1995); *My Son the Fanatic* (1997); *Gabriel and Me* (2001); *Opa!* (2005).

PREMINGER, Otto (1906–1986)

Otto Ludwig Preminger was born in Vienna on 5 December 1906. The son of a prominent Jewish lawyer, Preminger gained a law degree at the age of twenty but had already become involved in the theatre as both actor and director. He directed his first film, *Die Große Liebe*, in 1931 and two years later took over Max Reinhardt's theatre company. Receiving offers of work both on Broadway and in Hollywood, he emigrated to America in 1935, directing two minor films at 20th Century-Fox before returning to the stage. Preminger was lured back to Fox with a long-term contract in 1942, and made his name with *Laura* (1944), his fifth American film. He became an independent producer-director with *The Moon Is Blue* (1953), and throughout his subsequent career he exercised control over every aspect of his work, from scripting to publicity.

Preminger's first film in Britain was an adaptation by Graham Greene of George Bernard Shaw's play about Joan of Arc, *Saint Joan*. Made largely on studio sets at Shepperton, the film preserves the original's theatricality and suffers from the miscasting of Richard Widmark as the Dauphin, but Preminger's teenage discovery Jean Seberg is better in the title role than most contemporary critics allowed. He also cast her in his next film, one of his masterpieces, an adaptation of Françoise Sagan's novel *Bonjour tristesse*. Filmed on location in the South of France, it is both technically audacious – Preminger makes exquisite use of CinemaScope and long takes, and it is one of the few films to alternate colour and black-and-white stock successfully – and dramatically eloquent: David Niven's performance as the ageing roué Raymond far surpasses his Academy Award-winning role the same year in Delbert Mann's *Separate Tables*.

After major successes with *Anatomy of a Murder* (1959), *Exodus* (1960), *Advise and Consent* (1962) and *The Cardinal* (1963), Preminger returned to Britain to make *Bunny Lake Is Missing*, a deliciously baroque, blackly comic mystery-thriller that draws an uncharacteristically disciplined performance from Laurence Olivier as a weary police inspector and a marvellously piquant one from Noël Coward as a pickled red herring. Most of Preminger's remaining six films were poorly received and his career steadily declined, but he made a partial return to form with his last film, on which he was reunited with Graham Greene (albeit as source material rather than collaborator). Scripted by Tom Stoppard, *The Human Factor* sketches several sharp character vignettes and is remarkable for its avoidance of the glib platitudes that usually typify the espionage genre. Suffering from both cancer and Alzheimer's disease, Preminger died in New York on 23 April 1986.

(Sheldon Hall)

BIBLIOGRAPHY: Crawley, Tony, 'Vot You Mean: Ogre?', *Films Illustrated* no. 101, Jan. 1980, pp. 196–202; Frischauer, Willi, *Behind the Scenes of Otto Preminger* (London: Michael Joseph, 1973); *Movie* no. 2, Sept. 1962 (special issue on Preminger); Peters, Andrew, 'Preminger Goes to War with St Joan', *Films and Filming*, Mar. 1957, p. 27; Pratley, Gerald, *The Cinema of Otto Preminger* (New York: Castle/London: Tantivy, 1971); Preminger, Otto, *Preminger: An Autobiography* (New York: Doubleday, 1977).

FILMOGRAPHY (UK only): *Saint Joan* (UK/US, 1957); *Bonjour tristesse* (1958); *Bunny Lake Is Missing* (1965); *The Human Factor* (UK/US, 1979).

QUAY, Stephen and Timothy (1947–)

Stephen and Timothy Quay, identical twins, were born in Norristown, near Philadelphia, in 1947. After graduating in 1969 from the Philadelphia College of Art, where they studied illustration and graphics, they won a scholarship to the Royal College of Art, London. At the RCA's School of Film and Television they made their first short films (mostly lost), and met fellow student Keith Griffiths, who first collaborated with them on *Nocturna Artificialia* (1979), funded by the BFI Production Board. Working together as Koninck Studios, with Griffiths producing, the Quays have maintained a steady output of surreal and fastidious puppet animation films, supplemented by design work for opera, theatre and ballet. To help finance their avant-garde projects they have also worked on television commercials, channel identification footage and numerous music videos, including the *Stille Nacht* series, and, less characteristically, Peter Gabriel's *Sledgehammer*.

The Quays are renowned for their craftsmanlike methods and their unusual sources of inspiration. Apart from their puppets, which typically look like old dolls abused by many generations of children, they construct their own sets, arrange the lighting and operate the cameras. The films draw heavily on twentieth-century European visual and literary culture, especially the Surrealist and Expressionist traditions represented by the Polish writer Bruno Schulz, the painter Max Ernst and their fellow director of puppet films, the Czech Jan Svankmajer. As with Svankmajer, the Quays' cinema is short on conventional narrative but long on enigmatic visuals; music usually plays a major part in creating a bizarre, sinister atmosphere.

The world invented by the Quays appears frozen in time, covered with dust and cobwebs, full of mirrors and strange machinery – a world stored in a locked room or glass cabinet that nobody has accessed for decades. The colour scheme often suggests the hues of old photographs: sepias, browns and dirty yellows predominate. *Nocturna Artificialia*, describing the cataleptic hero's adventures when he leaves his room for the city, immediately established their individual technique and propensity for dream narratives. Subsequent films in the early 1980s, made for the Arts Council or Channel 4, paid specific homage to the team's European influences, including the Punch and Judy tradition, the artistic vortex of 1920s' Paris, Svankmajer, the Czech composer Janáček and, in *Ein Brudermord*, the claustrophobic imagination of Franz Kafka.

The twenty-minute *Street of Crocodiles* (1986), their first film shot in 35mm, decisively lifted the Quays beyond the quasi-documentary orbit. The film is a homage to Bruno Schulz, one

of whose novels bears the same title. The setting is a mythical land, somewhere in pre-Second World War provincial Poland, which operates like a living organism (Schulz in his work often compared a city to a living body). The population consists of half-dead people, with empty heads, who move in a circular, mechanical way, oblivious to anyone else's movements. The Quays suggest that this degraded land is stored in a deserted museum and activated by an old Kinetoscope machine – something that could be interpreted as a sign of their faith in the creative powers of cinema.

Further impressive film puzzles followed, among them *The Comb*, a sexually suggestive dream of damaged dolls, ladders, passageways and a live-action woman (perhaps the dreamer), and *De Artificiali Perspectiva*, a quirky analysis of the optical distortions of anamorphosis. Then in 1995 the Quays mounted their first live-action feature, *Institute Benjamenta*, inspired by the writings of the Swiss novelist Robert Walser. Like the *Street of Crocodiles*, the Benjamenta Institute for the training of domestic servants presents a sinister microcosm, with its inhabitants leading a half-life of repetitive, largely pointless activities. Typically, the presence of actors prompted no change in the brothers' stylistic approach: Mark Rylance, Alice Krige and Gottfried John became willingly used as quasi-objects, scrupulously positioned alongside forks, stag horns and dripping water in a fascinating if static symphony of light and shade constructed on the prevailing Quay themes of death, decay and nothingness.

Recent collaborations with the choreographer William Tuckett and their small insert in Julie Taymor's *Frida* (2002) have introduced wider audiences to the Quays; while *The Piano Tuner of Earthquakes* (2005), a live-action fairy tale, where a piano tuner attempts to rescue an opera singer from the clutches of a mad doctor in the Carpathian Mountains, is so bizarrely beautiful in its foggy, artificial, de-colourised way that it is sure to attract new admirers. But the Quays remain director-animators for the cognoscenti – happy to live, like their films' characters and objects, in a remote, hermetic maze.

(Ewa Mazierska)

BIBLIOGRAPHY: Buchan, Suzanne H., 'The Quay Brothers: Choreographed Chiaroscuro, Enigmatic and Sublime', *Film Quarterly* vol. 51 no. 3, Spring 1998, pp. 2–15; Greenaway, Peter, 'Street of Crocodiles', *Sight and Sound*, Summer 1986, pp. 182–3; Hammond, Paul, 'In Quay Animation', *Afterimage* no. 13, Autumn 1987, pp. 54–67; Quay, Stephen and Timothy, 'Picked-Up Pieces', *Monthly Film Bulletin*, June 1986, pp. 164–5; Romney, Jonathan, 'The Same Dark Drift', *Sight and Sound*, Mar. 1992, pp. 24–7; Romney, Jonathan, 'Life's a Dream', *Sight and Sound*, Aug. 1995, pp. 12–15; Tomlinson, Lynne, 'Launching the Quays', *Animation Journal* vol. 9, 2001, pp. 5–19.

FILMOGRAPHY: *Der Loop der Loop*; *Palais en flammes*; *Il duetto* (c. 1971); *Nocturna Artificialia (Those Who Desire without End*, 1979); *Punch and Judy: Tragical Comedy or Comical Tragedy* (co-dirs. Keith Griffiths/Larry Sider, 1980); *Ein Brudermord*; *The Eternal Day of Michel De Ghelderode 1898–1962* (1981); *Igor – The Paris Years Chez Pleyel* (co-dir. Keith Griffiths); *Leos Janáček: Intimate Excursions* (co-dir. Keith Griffiths) (1983); *The Cabinet of Jan Svankmajer – Prague's Alchemist of Film* (co-dir. Keith Griffiths, 1984); *Little Songs of the Chief Officer of Hunar Louse, or This Unnameable Little Broom (Being a Largely Disguised Reduction of the Epic of Gilgamesh) Tableau II* (co-dir. Keith Griffiths, 1985); *Street of Crocodiles* (1986); *Rehearsals for Extinct Anatomies* (1987); *Dramolet* (*Stille Nacht I*, 1988); *The Pond* (1989); *The Comb (From the Museums of Sleep*, 1990); *De Artificiali Perspectiva, or Anamorphosis* (UK/US); *The Calligrapher* (1991); *Are We Still Married? (Stille Nacht II)*; *Long Way Down/Look What the Cat Drug In* (1992); *Tales from Vienna Woods* (*Stille Nacht III*); *Can't Go Wrong without You (Stille Nacht IV)* (1993); *Institute Benjamenta, or This Dream People Call Human Life* (1995); *Duet – Variations for the Convalescence of 'A'* (1999); *The Sandman* (co-dir. William Tuckett); *In Absentia* (2000); *Frida* (hospital puppet sequence, Julie Taymor, US, 2002); *The Phantom Museum: Random Forays into the Vaults of Sir Henry Wellcome's Medical Collection* (2003); *The Piano Tuner of Earthquakes* (Ger/Fr/UK, 2005).

QUINN, Bob (1935–)

Bob Quinn was born in Dublin in 1935 and went to work in Ireland's embryonic national television service (now RTÉ) in 1961. With a number of other radically minded producers, Quinn resigned from RTÉ in 1969, in protest over the commercialised nature of the station's programming and the negative impact on Irish culture of the emerging consumer society that this commercialism promoted. In 1969 he co-authored *Sit Down and Be Counted*, a famously controversial book on his RTÉ experience, which articulates the challenging and acerbic radicalism that was to characterise Quinn's subsequent career as an independent film-maker. In the early 1970s he moved to Connemara, the Irish-speaking area of County Galway, and set up his own film and video company, Cinegael, through which he has produced, for nearly three decades, an influential body of documentary and robustly challenging fiction films.

His 1975 short *Caoineadh Airt Ui Laoire/Lament for Art O'Leary* is now recognised as one of the most influential films ever made in Ireland. The first fiction film to be produced in the Irish language, it demonstrated the viability of indigenous film-making and, in its mixture of formal experiment and radical content, it became a template for the kind of avant-garde film-making that emerged from Ireland in the 1970s and early 80s. Thus Quinn became something of a father figure for a whole generation of emerging independent film-makers, including Joe Comerford and Cathal Black, and he played an influential role in the campaign to establish state support for film-making in Ireland. The film itself reflected Quinn's cantankerous radicalism – critiquing traditional romantic historical narratives but at the same time chastising the historical amnesia that came as an adjunct to Ireland's economic development.

Quinn's film-making has continued to probe the contradictions of contemporary Ireland. *Poitin* was a harsh rural narrative that did much to challenge the romantic whimsy of Hollywood's vision of the west of Ireland, while at the same time undermining sedimented romantic notions from within Ireland itself. In his celebrated three-part television series *Atlantean* (1984) Quinn explored, with a mixture of irreverence and mischief, the relationship between the Arab and Gaelic worlds and again attempted to complicate the received narrative of Irish cultural identity. His next fiction film was *Budawanny*, the story of a Catholic priest who has an affair, and a child, with his housekeeper. He later expanded and completed this as *The Bishop's Story*. Both films anticipate and comment on the real-life controversies surrounding celibacy in the Catholic priesthood and in a typically adventurous cinematic form, Quinn probes the relationship between contemporary organised religion and a more primitive, more instinctual form of belief.

Quinn has continued to rail against the commercial values that underpin contemporary Irish film-making: 'Ireland has become a backlot to Hollywood', he has famously declared (Quinn *et al.*). His own films can be seen to exist in an uneasy relationship to both the tradition of Irish nationalism and the modernity of global culture and explains why in Ireland he is regarded as something of a cultural maverick.

(Martin McLoone)

BIBLIOGRAPHY: Doolan, Leila, Jack Dowling and Bob Quinn, *Sit Down and Be Counted: The Evolution of a Television Station* (Dublin: Wellington Press, 1969); Gibbons, Luke, *Transformations in Irish Culture* (Cork: Cork University Press, 1996); McLoone, Martin, *Irish Film: The Emergence of a Contemporary Cinema* (London: BFI, 2000); Pettitt, Lance, *Screening Ireland* (Manchester: Manchester University Press, 2000); Quinn, Bob *et al.*, 'Irish Cinema at the Crossroads: A Filmmakers' Symposium', *Cinéaste* vol. 24 nos 2/3, 1999 (Contemporary Irish Cinema Supplement), p. 73; Quinn, Bob, 'Degeneration Gap', *Film Ireland* no. 100, Sept./Oct. 2004, pp. 18–20.

FILMOGRAPHY: *Caoineadh Airt Ui Laoire/Lament for Art O'Leary* (short, Ir, 1975); *Self Portrait with a Red Car* (short, Ir, 1977); *Poitin* (Ir, 1978); *Budawanny* (Ir, 1987); *The Bishop's Story* (Ir, 1994).

QUINN, Joanna (1962–)

Joanna Quinn was born in Birmingham in 1962 and educated at Middlesex Polytechnic; her graduation film, *Girls' Night Out* (1987) – one of the first Channel 4-funded animation shorts – enjoyed both public acclaim and positive critical reception. A hugely entertaining tale about Beryl, a rotund middle-aged housewife, who goes out with her factory colleagues to a male strip show at a local pub, the film works as both a feminist critique of the oppressive domesticity that characterises many women's lives, and a deconstruction of the ways in which live-action cinema has represented women. By simply turning the tables, Quinn uses Beryl to point up the macho posturing and impossible physical dexterity of the male stripper, while also reducing the idea of phallic potency to the unimpressive reality of a small penis and an embarrassed demeanour.

During the next four years Quinn made television title sequences and films with the Chapter Film and Animation Workshop in Cardiff; but Beryl returned again in *Body Beautiful* (1990) once more to engage with masculine bravura in the shape of Vince, muscular chauvinist and factory Lothario. Beryl, constantly preoccupied by her size and her childhood memories of being the school 'fat girl', endures Vince's patronising mockery, but secretly trains with the local rugby team to compete in the factory's 'Body Beautiful' contest. In a *tour-de-force* finale, Beryl's body – a vehicle as much to demonstrate the flexibility of the animation vocabulary in representing physical impossibility as of the qualities of womanhood and femininity – gains her victory. Quinn's preoccupation with the energy and presence of the female body, as well as the self-conscious vitality of animation as a form, is evidenced again in the can-can dancers in *Elles* (1992), and in one of her most impressive films, *Britannia* (1993). A scathing critique of British imperialism, *Britannia* draws upon the tradition of satire and caricature in the political cartoon from Gilray to Low, reconfiguring the mythic quality of the British bulldog, reducing the patriarchal 'hound' to the parochial 'pup'.

Quinn embraced the mainstream in 1996 with an adaptation of Posy Simmonds' *Famous Fred* cartoon strip, and her distinctive commercials for Whiskas and Charmin. But she continued with her more personal work in her 1998 adaptation of Chaucer's *The Wife of Bath's Tale*, in which she once again engages with the battle of the sexes.

(Paul Wells)

BIBLIOGRAPHY: Pilling, Jayne (ed.), *Women and Animation: A Compendium* (London: BFI Exhibition & Distribution Division, 1992); Wells, Paul, *Understanding Animation* (London and New York: Routledge, 1998); Wells, Paul, *Animation: Genre and Authorship* (London: Wallflower Press, 2002).

SELECTED FILMOGRAPHY: *Superdog* (1983); *Girls' Night Out* (1987); *Body Beautiful* (1990); *Elles* (1992); *Britannia* (1993); *Famous Fred* (1996); *The Wife of Bath's Tale* (1998).

QUINN, Paul (1960–)

Paul Quinn was born in Chicago in 1960, the younger brother of actor Aidan and cinematographer Declan Quinn. He spent some time in Ireland in the 1980s before returning to the USA to become a teacher, an actor and a director in local theatre. In the early 1990s he played small roles in films by Barry Levinson, Mike Figgis and Tim Robbins.

Quinn's experiences in Ireland and his family's situation of living in and between two cultures is the theme of his debut as writer and director, *This Is My Father*. The film contrasts the Ireland of the 1930s with contemporary affluent Ireland, and in a complicated narrative explores the emotional and cultural links between Ireland and America across the generations. The personal nature of the project is emphasised by the fact that the main part is played by Aidan Quinn (with a small part for their sister Marian), with Declan acting as cinematographer. It is a film of some complexity and emotional power, the best of a number of late-1990s' films that explored Irish-American cultural identity.

Quinn's second film, *Never Get Outta the Boat* (2002), is a gritty realist portrait of drug abuse in Chicago, suggesting that his career will follow the strongly independent route of those directors he worked for in his younger days.

(Martin McLoone)

BIBLIOGRAPHY: Collins, Pat, 'Paul Quinn', *Film West* no. 33, July 1998, pp. 16–18; McLoone, Martin, *Irish Film: The Emergence of a Contemporary Cinema* (London: BFI, 2000); Pettitt, Lance, *Screening Ireland* (Manchester: Manchester University Press, 2000).

FILMOGRAPHY: *This Is My Father* (Can/Ir, 1998); *Never Get Outta the Boat* (US, 2002).

RADFORD, Michael (1946–)

Michael Radford was born to a British father and an Austrian mother in New Delhi on 24 February 1946. After studying at Oxford University, he enrolled at the National Film School, where his work included a short film, *Cold Night* (1974), based on a story by Jorge Luis Borges. A contract with BBC Scotland and several documentaries, some on Celtic and Italian subjects, followed, along with a feature-length drama, *The White Bird Passes* (1980), based on a semi-autobiographical novel by the Scottish writer Jessie Kesson. Its successful reception led to Radford's cinema feature debut, *Another Time, Another Place* (1983), inspired by Kesson's memory of encounters in Scotland with Italian prisoners-of-war during the Second World War. The poetic, well-observed films of Ermanno Olmi were an acknowledged influence for this adroit examination of the culture clash between the emotionally volatile Italians and the rigidly reserved Scots. Radford draws a magnificent performance from Phyllis Logan as the housewife, imprisoned herself in a passionless marriage, who begins an affair with one of the Italians.

A different kind of prison was evoked in Radford's next film, *Nineteen Eighty-Four* (1984), a compelling adaptation of George Orwell's prophetic novel in which the hero Winston Smith (John Hurt) struggles to free himself from a totalitarian oppression of body and mind. The film kept to the ration-book, Kafkaesque world of the original, but at the same time seemed a deliberately topical comment on state power in the year of the bitter dispute between Britain's coal miners and Margaret Thatcher's militantly anti-union government. With these two films, Radford staked a claim as one of the most promising directors of his generation, though his progress faltered with his next film, *White Mischief* (1987), inspired by the notorious true-life case of the shooting of a British aristocrat, Lord Erroll, in Kenya. Radford uses the case as the basis for a stinging attack on British colonialism, but apart from Sarah Miles, mesmerising as the decadent Alice de Janze, his cast seem bored and adrift in their over-privileged enclave, and the film remains emotionally uninvolving.

A long and unproductive gap followed before Radford secured French and Italian backing for *Il postino* (1994), an elegant and touching romance about the friendship that develops between the exiled Chilean poet Pablo Neruda and the Italian fisherman's son who discovers new horizons in life when he delivers the writer's post. The director's Italian influences – Olmi, the sentimental neo-realism of Vittorio De Sica – proved beneficent, and the film became a significant international success. In 1996 Radford was nominated for Academy Awards as writer and director, though a good deal of the film's emotional power rested in the central performance of Massimo Troisi, who also collaborated on the direction. Subsequent ventures proved less appealing. *B. Monkey*, an adaptation of an improbable Andrew Davies novel about the romance between a frustrated schoolteacher and a glamorous bank robber, fell disappointingly flat and received only limited distribution; *Dancing at the Blue Iguana*, a downbeat drama about nightclub strippers, fared little better.

Radford's attempts to move beyond the gentle lyricism of *Another Time, Another Place* and *Il postino* – the latest is a sumptuous, painterly adaptation of *The Merchant of Venice* with Al Pacino and Jeremy Irons – have met with patchy success, but his search for offbeat, unconventional stories at least makes him refreshingly unpredictable. In 1977, caught in the limbo between his film school years and a cinema career, he declared: 'I want more than anything else to make films in this country, about this country', adding prophetically that should this not prove possible, 'the only realistic thing to do is to emigrate, thus proving that this country is a wonderful training ground for skills to use abroad' (Kulik, p. 203).

(Neil Sinyard)

BIBLIOGRAPHY: Kulik, Karol (ed.), 'After School: Michael Radford', *Sight and Sound*, Autumn 1977, p. 203; Park, James, *Learning to Dream: The New British Cinema* (London: Faber and Faber, 1984); Taylor, Paul, 'Outcast of the Islands', *Monthly Film Bulletin*, Aug. 1983, p. 228.

FILMOGRAPHY: *Concerning the Surface* (short, 1973); *Cold Night* (short, 1974); *Attitudes* (short); *Sugar* (doc.) (1976); *Another Time, Another Place* (1983); *Nineteen Eighty-Four* (1984); *White Mischief* (1987); *Il postino* (co-dir. Massimo Troisi, It/Fr, 1994); *B. Monkey* (1996; rel. 1998); *Dancing at the Blue Iguana* (UK/US, 2000); *Ten Minutes Older – The Cello* ('Addicted to the Stars' episode, UK/Ger/US, 2002); *William Shakespeare's The Merchant of Venice* (UK/US/It/Lux, 2004).

RAKOFF, Alvin (1927–)

Alvin Rakoff was born on 6 February 1927 in Toronto, where he attended university and worked as a journalist. He came to London in the early 1950s, joined the BBC in 1953 as a writer and began directing original dramas and adaptations ranging from the prestigious (Eugene O'Neill's *The Emperor Jones*) to the conventional (Francis Durbridge's thriller *The Teckman Biography*, subsequently filmed by Wendy Toye). His film debut, *Passport to Shame* (1959), tackled a risqué subject: prostitution. Innocent Odile Versois is lured from France under false pretences by the madam of a London brothel (Brenda de Banzie) and undergoes a marriage of convenience to taxi-driver Eddie Constantine in order to obtain a passport. Meanwhile, sultry Diana Dors spends much of the film shimmering in doorways, displaying her curvaceous body to its best advantage. According to the introductory words spoken by Inspector Fabian of Scotland Yard, the film dealt 'frankly, dramatically and accurately' with this 'awful social evil', but the film's serious premise was enjoyably eroded by flamboyant characters and an improbably melodramatic story.

Rakoff's second film with Constantine, *The Treasure of San Teresa* (1959), was a lively action-thriller about an American agent who discovers stolen Nazi treasure in a convent in Czechoslovakia. A European co-production, *On Friday at Eleven*, based on a thriller by James Hadley Chase, followed, but it was *The Comedy Man* (1963), a bitter comedy combining gritty realism with the zest of his earlier films that marked him out as a talented director. Rakoff's evocation of the seedy underside of the showbiz world is both touching and convincing, and the film mocks society's lurch towards materialism. Kenneth More, whose own career had been disrupted by a dispute with John Davis of the Rank Organisation, gives a superb performance as 'Chick' Byrd, the failing actor who becomes a celebrity by appearing in television ads for breath sweeteners.

The Comedy Man was well received by the critics, but Rakoff's subsequent cinema career proved disappointing. After being replaced by Roy Ward Baker on Hammer's Bette Davis vehicle *The Anniversary* (1967), he made *Crossplot*, a spy story starring Roger Moore, marred by an unconvincing plot and meagre budget. *Hoffman*, an adaptation of Ernest Gebler's television play exploring the favoured 1960s' theme of a middle-aged man obsessed with a young woman, is much more worthy. Rakoff secures grippingly convincing performances from Peter Sellers and Sinéad Cusack, but Sellers fans were not interested in watching him play a serious part as a seedy middle-aged businessman and the film failed to attract an audience. *Say Hello to Yesterday* is less glum in exploring the relationship between a middle-aged woman (Jean Simmons) and a young man (Leonard Whiting), but fatally inconsequential.

In the mid-1970s Rakoff returned to Canada, where he made four cheap and cheerful genre pieces – a version of H. Rider Haggard's *King Solomon's Mines*, featuring Britt Ekland as Queen Nyleptha, a disaster film (*City on Fire*), a supernatural thriller (*Death Ship*) and a secret-agent comedy (*Dirty Tricks*). With the unpredictability that characterises Rakoff's career, he then made a successful transition back to British television, directing quality dramas and miniseries including *A Voyage Round My Father* (1982), *Paradise Postponed* (1986) and *A Dance to the Music of Time* (1997).

(Margaret Butler)

BIBLIOGRAPHY: Laikan, Jean, 'An Interview with Alvin Rakoff: Forewarned Is Forearmed', *Cinema Canada* no. 60, Dec. 1979/Jan. 1980, pp. 8–11.

FILMOGRAPHY: *Passport to Shame* (US: *Room 13*); *The Treasure of San Teresa* (1959); *On Friday at Eleven* (Ger/ Fr/It, 1960); *The Comedy Man* (1963); *Money-Go-Round* (doc. short, 1967); *Crossplot* (1969); *Hoffman* (1970); *Say Hello to Yesterday* (1971); *King's Solomon's Treasure* (Can, 1977); *City on Fire* (Can/US, 1979); *Death Ship* (UK/Can, 1980); *Dirty Tricks* (Can, 1981).

RAMSAY, Lynne (1969–)

Born in Glasgow on 5 December 1969, Lynne Ramsay was educated at Napier College in Edinburgh, where she studied photography. From there she went to the National Film and Television School, specialising in cinematography and direction. Her graduation film, *Small Deaths*, won the Prix du Jury at Cannes in 1996, and her other short films, *Kill the Day* and *Gasman*, also attracted numerous awards. Hailed as one of the brightest new talents of British cinema, in a short directorial career Ramsay has already produced a promising and distinctive body of work.

Ramsay's acclaimed debut feature, *Ratcatcher* (1999), is a darkly redemptive film set in 1970s strike-bound Glasgow, piled high with bags of rotting refuse. A boy is pushed into a polluted canal, and the rest of the film follows his accidental killer, twelve-year-old James. Its grim setting notwithstanding, *Ratcatcher* is more Dovzhenko than Loach, and ultimately James finds a world of hope and redemption at the end of a bus line. *Ratcatcher* opened the Edinburgh Film Festival in 1999 and won its director the 2000 BAFTA Carl Foreman Award for a newcomer in British film.

Reduced to its storyline, *Morvern Callar*, Ramsay's next film – adapted from Alan Warner's cult novel – sounds grim, too: a

young supermarket worker in the west of Scotland discovers that her boyfriend has committed suicide, claims authorship of the novel manuscript he has left behind and goes on a spree in Spain with her best friend. But the plot is hardly the point: *Morvern Callar* is as emotionally open as it is narratively spare, allowing the silent, and strangely innocent, world of its heroine to unfold in a succession of haunting images.

Relentlessly experimental, Ramsay brings a photographer's eye to the cinematic image: through silence and space within the frame her films unfold in expanded time, showing rather than telling. Everything is on the surface; there are no hidden depths. Against this visual canvas, sound assumes a special importance, carrying weight and resonance in its own right. 'Sound is the other picture,' Ramsay has said; and this is certainly true of *Morvern Callar*'s sophisticated use of the music on Morvern's compilation tape (a posthumous gift from her boyfriend), which works at every level from (apparent) underscoring to expression of Morvern's near-autistic relationship with her surroundings.

Lynne Ramsay acknowledges the influence of the work of US avant-garde film-maker Maya Deren, with its trance-like meditation on detail; and of Robert Bresson's *Notes on the Cinematographer* ('If the eye is entirely won, give nothing or almost nothing to the ear'). Other film-makers whose work has been likened to Ramsay's include Bill Douglas and Terence Davies – both influences that probably have less to do with cinematic style than with a shared openness to the silent, brutal and magical world of the child and the innocent.

(Annette Kuhn)

BIBLIOGRAPHY: Kennedy, Harlan, '*Ratcatcher*', *Film Comment*, Jan./Feb. 2000, pp. 6–9; Ramsay, Lynne, *Ratcatcher* (London: Faber and Faber, 1999); Williams, Linda Ruth, 'Escape Artist', *Sight and Sound*, Oct. 2002, pp. 22–5.

FILMOGRAPHY: *Small Deaths* (short, 1996); *Kill the Day* (short); *Gasman* (short) (1997); *Ratcatcher* (1999); *Morvern Callar* (2002).

RATOFF, Gregory (1897–1960)

Gregory Ratoff was born on 20 April 1897 in Samara, Russia. After a period in the army, he joined the Moscow Art Theatre as an actor and then left for the USA, where he acted in Yiddish theatre productions and Hollywood films such as *Symphony of Six Million* (Gregory La Cava, 1932) and *What Price Hollywood?* (George Cukor, 1932). He came to England in 1934 and appeared in three Monty Banks films, *Falling in Love* (1934), *Hello Sweetheart* and *18 Minutes* (both 1935), a deftly crafted drama with Ratoff playing a lion-tamer who marries his adopted daughter against her will. Back in America he began directing, making his name with his 1939 remake of Goster Stevens' *Intermezzo*, with Ingrid Bergman repeating her role as the young piano teacher tragically caught in a love triangle.

After the Second World War, Ratoff returned to Britain to direct and produce an adaptation of the Margaret Kennedy play *That Dangerous Age* (1949), with Myrna Loy married to Roger Livesey and tempted to infidelity by Richard Greene before he realises he is better off with her daughter, Peggy Cummins. Ratoff went on to make *My Daughter Joy* with Cummins and Greene, and Edward G. Robinson brought in to enhance the US box-office potential. Ratoff himself took the lead in the Technicolor melodrama *Abdullah the Great*, lusting fruitlessly after English rose Kay Kendall. His last – and perhaps best – British film is *Oscar Wilde*, an adaptation of Leslie Stokes' play, with Robert Morley in the part he created on the Dublin stage in 1936. Over twenty years on, Morley, charismatic though he is, comes across as a fruity old gentleman rather than the wickedly amoral Wilde, and Ratoff's film was outclassed by Ken Hughes' *The Trials of Oscar Wilde*, released at the same time, with Peter Finch as an anguished and convincingly gay Wilde. However, Ratoff does extract from Ralph Richardson the definitive performance as Edward Carson, the implacably bigoted prosecution counsellor whose lack of a sense of humour gave him immunity to Wilde's sharp wit. This was Ratoff's last film. He died of leukaemia on 14 December 1960 in Solothurn, Switzerland.

(Kevin Gough-Yates)

BIBLIOGRAPHY: Meehan, Jeannette, 'Quadruple-Threat Man of the Movies', *Picturegoer*, 18 Dec. 1937, p. 15; Obituary, *Hollywood Reporter*, 15 Dec. 1960, p. 4.

FILMOGRAPHY (UK only): *That Dangerous Age* (1949); *My Daughter Joy* (1950); *Abdullah the Great* (1954); *Oscar Wilde* (1960).

RAYMOND, Jack (1886–1953)

Born John Caines in Wimborne, Dorset, in 1886, Jack Raymond worked as a silent screen actor with Cecil Hepworth before beginning to direct in the 1920s. After several silent melodramas, including *Second to None* and *The Greater War*, both starring Moore Marriott, he made two dozen popular thrillers, musicals, farces and romantic melodramas in the 1930s. The comedies frequently starred the grandiose and eccentric Sydney Howard and some were adapted from Aldwych farces, using Aldwych regulars including Ralph Lynn and Winifred Shotter; there were lively thrillers, including two with Will Fyffe as a Bank of England detective, *The Mind of Mr Reeder* and *The Missing People*. American actress Ruth Chatterton starred in two melodramas, *The Rat* and *A Royal Divorce*; and he made two musicals starring Jack Buchanan, *Come Out of the Pantry* and *When Knights Were Bold*. Several of these films were made for Herbert Wilcox's British and Dominions company, which aimed at producing films above the level of the routine 'quota quickies'; Raymond's record suggests his output might repay further exploration.

During the war, Raymond made shorts for the War Office and the Ministry of Information; from the mid- to late 1940s he was involved in the dubbing of French films into English. After drifting into semi-retirement, he made a triumphant return with three rough-edged comedies – a remake of *Up for the Cup*, starring northern comic Albert Modley, which he had first made in 1931, and two National Service comedies, *Worm's Eye View* and *Reluctant Heroes*, with the cockney Ronald Shiner – all highly successful at the box office despite their low budgets. He died of heart failure in London on 20 March 1953. (Brian McFarlane)

BIBLIOGRAPHY: Obituary, *Today's Cinema*, 23 Mar. 1953, p. 4; Breen, Max, 'Since Films Were Young', *Picturegoer*, 23 Oct. 1937, p. 13.

FILMOGRAPHY: *Barbara Elopes* (1921); *The Greater War* (short); *Second to None* (1926); *Somehow Good* (1927); *Zero* (1928); *Splinters*; *A Peep behind the Scenes* (1929); *The Great Game*; *French Leave* (1930); *Up for the Cup*; *Tilly of Bloomsbury*; *The Speckled Band*; *Mischief*; *Almost a Divorce* (1931); *Say It with Music*; *Life Goes On* (1932); *Up to the Neck*; *Night of the Garter*; *Just My Luck*; *Sorrell and Son* (1933); *The King of Paris*; *Girls Please!* (1934); *Where's George?* (aka *The Hope of His Side*); *Come out of the Pantry* (1935); *When Knights Were Bold* (1936); *The Frog*; *The Rat* (1937); *A Royal Divorce*; *No Parking*; *Blondes for Danger* (1938); *The Mind of Mr Reeder* (US: *The Mysterious Mr Reeder*); *The Missing People* (1939); *You Will Remember* (1941); *Paper Chase* (short); *Scottish National Savings* (short); *Bicycle Made for Two* (short); *Censorship of Prisoners' Mail* (short) (1943); *Up for the Cup* (1950); *Worm's Eye View*; *Take Me to Paris*; *Reluctant Heroes* (1951); *Little Big Shot* (1952).

REED, Carol (1906–1976)

Carol Reed was born in Putney, south London, on 30 December 1906, one of six children of the actor-manager Sir Herbert Beerbohm Tree and his mistress, Beatrice Mae Pinney. Tree, who was respectably married, supported his second household substantially. Reed grew up in solid middle-class comfort, and was sent to a traditional public school, King's School, Canterbury, which he loathed. He planned to follow his father and become an actor, but in 1922 his mother, hoping to deflect this ambition, sent him to Massachusetts to join his elder brother on a chicken farm. Having neither taste nor aptitude for farming, Reed was back in England within six months. His mother gave way, and he joined a company headed by Dame Sybil Thorndike, making his stage debut in 1924.

Edgar Wallace, the alarmingly prolific thriller writer, had formed a troupe to put on stage adaptations of his novels. Reed joined him and appeared in three Wallace productions, doubling as assistant stage manager. When Wallace accepted the chairmanship of the newly formed British Lion Film Corporation in 1927, Reed became his personal assistant, helping to supervise filmed adaptations of Wallace's thrillers during the day while still acting and stage-managing in the evenings. This hectic double life continued until Wallace died of pneumonia in 1932. Abandoning the stage for good, Reed moved to Ealing Studios as dialogue director for Associated Talking Pictures, then being run by Basil Dean.

At Ealing Reed swiftly worked his way up from dialogue director to assistant director. His first experience of directing was on *It Happened in Paris* (1935), a comedy directed by Robert Wyler (William Wyler's elder brother) to which Reed contributed additional footage. The following year he directed his first solo film, *Midshipman Easy*, adapted from Captain Marryat's Victorian adventure novel. Graham Greene, writing in *The Spectator*, felt that Reed showed 'more sense of the cinema than most veteran British directors' (Greene, p. 61). Greene was even more taken by Reed's next film, *Laburnum Grove* (1936), adapted from a stage comedy by J. B. Priestley. 'Here at last is an English film one can unreservedly praise,' he wrote with an almost audible sigh of relief; both films, he went on, were 'thoroughly workmanlike and unpretentious, with just the hint of a personal manner which makes one believe that Mr Reed, when he gets the right script, will prove far more than efficient' (Greene, pp. 124–5).

The right script took a while to arrive. Reed's next half-dozen pictures were an assortment of modest features, mostly compromised by the jaunty parochialism that beset so many British films of the period. The use of location shooting – uncommon at this time in British cinema – lends *Bank Holiday* (1938) a touch of documentary realism, but the portrayal of its working-class characters now looks stilted and patronising. The most individual film of this batch, in its bizarre way, is *Climbing High* (1939), a screwball comedy starring Jessie Matthews and Michael Redgrave, but Reed's unhappiness with this kind of fluffy material is palpable.

The documentary influence, fitfully evident in *Bank Holiday*, makes itself felt to more purpose in Reed's first major film, *The Stars Look Down* (1939). Adapted from a novel by the popular middlebrow author A. J. Cronin, the film charts the rise of an ambitious, idealistic young man (Michael Redgrave), a miner's son, to a seat in Parliament, diluting its political message – urging public ownership of the mines – with a novelettish romantic subplot. But there is a grim authenticity to the pithead scenes, notably a mining disaster that invites comparison with Pabst's *Kameradschaft*. By contrast, Reed's next film openly emulates Hitchcock. *Night Train to Munich* (1940), a comedy-thriller with Rex Harrison enjoying himself as a British agent impersonating a Nazi officer, might be seen as an unofficial sequel to *The Lady Vanishes* – the same screenwriters (Frank Launder and Sidney Gilliat), the same train-bound high jinks and, with Basil Radford and Naunton Wayne reprising their cricket-mad buffoons Charters and Caldicott, even two of the same characters. But given its acknowledgment of Nazi horrors – the systematic extermination of Czech intellectuals, the glimpses into concentration camp life – *Night Train*'s comic elements inevitably seem less amusing.

With *The Stars Look Down* and *Night Train to Munich* well received in both Britain and America, Reed's second-feature years were behind him. But though he could now command better material, he seemed to be uncertain about what kind of film suited him best. *The Girl in the News* (1941) is a routine thriller; *Kipps* (1941), adapted from H. G. Wells' semi-autobiographical novel, with Michael Redgrave uneasy in the title role, feels stiff and old-fashioned; while *The Young Mr Pitt* (1942), a propaganda piece masquerading as a biopic (Napoleon = Hitler, Pitt = Churchill), proved that costume drama was not Reed's forte. Still, his technical skill was by now evident, as was his sympathetic handling of actors. Redgrave recalled him as 'the gentlest of directors . . . able, with infinite pains and care, to bestow on his actors the feeling that everything was up to them and that all he was doing was to make sure that they were seen to their best advantage' (Drazin, 2000, p. 59).

Reed's next assignment, *The New Lot* (1943), was a forty-two-minute dramatised documentary commissioned by the Army Kinematograph Service to show civilians about to join up what they could expect from life in the army: the film demonstrates how new recruits from various social backgrounds become moulded into a cohesive fighting unit. Reed's handling of the subject was so well received that the authorities asked him to expand it to fit a full-length feature for public showing. The result was *The Way Ahead* (1944). Eric Ambler and Peter Ustinov's script explores the confusion, bewilderment and resentment experienced by many conscripts, and Reed captures the sparse discomfort of service life. The stress on tradition and hierarchy recalls Noël Coward and David Lean's *In Which We Serve* (1942); but with David Niven as an up-from-the-ranks officer and William Hartnell as the sergeant-major whose bark is worse than his bite, this is very much an everyman's army where ordinary men can become modest heroes.

From the documentary-tinged *The Way Ahead* Reed moved on to *The True Glory* (1945), a compilation of combat footage shot by dozens of Allied cameramen, tracing the last year of the war in Europe from the D-Day invasion to the fall of Berlin. Since this was an Anglo-American venture, Reed was teamed as co-director and deviser with the American film-maker Garson Kanin. Though saddled with a stilted, would-be poetic voiceover commentary, the film tells its story with power and lucidity, and is most eloquent when the combatants and civilians involved are allowed to speak for themselves. Hailed in America as one of the finest cinematic accounts of the war, *The True Glory* received an Academy Award for Best Documentary in 1946.

Now considered the foremost British director, able to choose any subject he liked, Reed was lucky enough to hit on three good scripts in succession. *Odd Man Out* (1947), adapted from a novel by the Ulster Protestant writer F. L. Green, is Reed's first truly personal film and has 'major work of art' written all over it, maybe a touch too plainly (the influence of Carné and Prévert's pre-war poetic realism, and the contemporaneous American noir cycle, is obvious). But Reed's sense of place – he preferred to shoot on location whenever possible – and his openness to his actors prevent the film being merely an academic exercise in style. James Mason brings an impressive sensitivity to his portrayal of Johnny McQueen, the wounded IRA man on the run in a snowy, nocturnal Belfast, struggling towards his personal Calvary through the gathering shadows of Robert Krasker's moody cinematography. Reed and his screenwriter R. C. Sherriff, co-scripting with Green, erased the novel's Protestant bias; Reed was no political film-maker, and the film takes no sides.

Odd Man Out was made for the Rank Organisation, but with the creative climate at Rank hardening, Reed moved over to Alexander Korda's London Films. And it was Korda, with his flair for such linkages, who teamed Reed with the writer who had spotted his talent a decade earlier, Graham Greene. Reed, Greene later wrote, was 'the only director I know with that particular warmth of human sympathy, the extraordinary feeling for the right face in the right part, the exactitude of cutting, and not least important the power of sympathising with an author's worries and an ability to guide him' (Greene, pp. 435–6).

Their first film together, *The Fallen Idol* (1948), was adapted from Greene's short story 'The Basement Room', in which a lonely, sensitive boy in London, son of an ambassador, becomes devoted to the embassy's butler and unwittingly betrays him to the police. Under Reed's direction the eight-year-old Bobby Henrey, making his screen debut, gives a performance of exceptional subtlety and emotional impact, while the use of wide-angle lenses heightens the chilly, formal spaces of the embassy that enclose him. But, accomplished and deftly controlled as it is, *The Fallen Idol* feels like a chamber piece beside the two baroque, expressionistic works made on either side.

The film that followed, *The Third Man* (1949), is widely reckoned his masterpiece. If Reed's limitation as a director was that he was only ever as good as his collaborators, here he benefited from the best. Apart from Greene and Orson Welles (on screen for barely fifteen minutes as Harry Lime, yet dominating the whole film with his unseen presence), there was Krasker again with his skewed, tilted framings and melodramatic lighting, and the wheedling, insinuating zither score of Anton Karas; and, far from least, the shattered occupied city of Vienna, its professional charm turned sour and corrupt, visibly embodying the intolerable burden of post-war guilt. In *The Third Man* Reed's feeling for location and his flair for casting and direction of actors reach their apogee; every role, down to the smallest, is impeccably cast, and the film's disenchanted, haunted romanticism still exerts considerable power.

The Third Man scored a huge international success, and in some quarters Reed was now being touted as the world's greatest living director (though never by Reed himself, a modest and self-effacing man). But from this high point his career went into

abrupt decline. *Outcast of the Islands* (1952), adapted from a novel by Joseph Conrad, should in theory have provided ideal material, with its powerful sense of place and its theme of a proudly self-sufficient outsider who contrives his own doom. But the film is seriously weakened by its script, and neither plot nor characters ever come fully into focus. Poor scripting also affected *The Man Between* (1953), a cold war thriller set in Berlin with James Mason playing a charming Harry Lime-style crook; inevitably, it felt like a tired retread of *The Third Man*.

Even more disappointing were Reed's first two ventures into colour. *A Kid for Two Farthings* (1955) is indigestible whimsy with a sentimentalised East End setting. *Trapeze* (1956), despite its widescreen circus thrills, is a stodgy love triangle wasting the teaming of Burt Lancaster and Tony Curtis that would prove so rivetingly lethal a year later in Mackendrick's *Sweet Smell of Success*. *The Key* (1958), a long black-and-white Second World War film that explores the morbid connections between romance, superstition and death, was more ambitious, but it is let down by the ponderous improbabilities of Carl Foreman's script.

Our Man in Havana (1960), based on Greene's novel about a vacuum-cleaner salesman in Cuba struggling to pass himself off as a British spy, marked something of a return to form. The film revealed a lighter, more sardonic side to both men's work; shrewd use was made of Alec Guinness (the salesman) and Noël Coward (his spy chief), while American comic Ernie Kovacs enjoyed the finest role of his brief film career as the local police chief. Reed next took on the remake of *Mutiny on the Bounty* (1962) but proved unable to cope with Marlon Brando's ego and resigned from the film, handing over to Lewis Milestone. After *The Running Man* (1963), a drably routine thriller, and the commercial disaster of the Michelangelo epic *The Agony and the Ecstasy* (1965), Reed seemed to have hit rock bottom barely fifteen years after his greatest triumph. But he had one final unexpected success to come: his first and only musical. *Oliver!* (1968), adapted from *Oliver Twist* with music by Lionel Bart, considerably softened the brutalities of Dickens' novel, but got by on the brio of its song-and-dance numbers and a fair helping of Dickensian gusto. The film picked up a stack of Academy Awards, including Reed's only Oscar as Best Director.

Given this revival in his fortunes, Reed should have been able to round off his career with some worthwhile assignments, but his judgment seemed to have deserted him. He directed only two more films, *The Last Warrior* and *Follow Me*, both of them miscast and leadenly scripted. They received minimal distribution and passed almost unnoticed.

Michael Powell observed of Reed that 'Carol could put a film together like a watchmaker puts together a watch' (Thomson, p. 14). The watchmaker in him is visible in his early films, the films of a complete professional able to make something presentable out of virtually any kind of material, though rarely imposing any personal signature. Then, three times in rapid succession, he directed films that seemed to reveal something deeper and darker in his personality – a fatalism, a sense of the tragic ironies of life. After *Odd Man Out*, *The Fallen Idol* and *The Third Man* he appeared to lose his professional assurance, as if this moment of self-revelation had disturbed his equilibrium. Most of the later films are a sad disappointment. But for that brief time in the late 1940s Carol Reed was perhaps what some earlier critics had claimed him to be: the greatest director in the world.
(Philip Kemp)

BIBLIOGRAPHY: Davies, Brenda (ed.), *Carol Reed* (London: BFI, 1978); Drazin, Charles, *The Finest Years: British Cinema of the 1940s* (London: André Deutsch, 1998); Drazin, Charles, *In Search of the Third Man* (London: Limelight Editions, 2000); Greene, Graham and Carol Reed, *The Third Man: A Film* (London: Lorrimer, 1984); Greene, Graham, *The Graham Greene Film Reader: Mornings in the Dark*, edited by David Parkinson (Manchester: Carcanet, 1993); Moss, Robert F., *The Films of Carol Reed* (London: Macmillan, 1987); Thomson, David, 'Reeds and Trees', *Film Comment*, July/Aug. 1994, pp. 14–23; Vaughan, Dai, *Odd Man Out* (London: BFI, 1994); Voigt, Michael, 'Pictures of Innocence', *Focus on Film*, Spring 1974, pp. 17–38; Wapshott, Nicholas, The Man Between: *A Biography of Carol Reed* (London: Chatto & Windus, 1990); White, Rob, *The Third Man* (London: BFI, 2003).

FILMOGRAPHY: *It Happened in Paris* (uncredited, co-dir. Robert Wyler); *Midshipman Easy* (US: *Men of the Sea*, 1935); *Laburnum Grove* (1936); *Talk of the Devil*; *Who's Your Lady Friend?* (1937); *Bank Holiday* (US: *Three on a Weekend*); *Penny Paradise* (1938) *Climbing High*; *The Stars Look Down* (1939); *Night Train to Munich* (aka *Gestapo*, US: *Night Train*, 1940); *The Girl in the News*; *Kipps* (1941); *The Young Mr Pitt*; *We Serve* (short); *A Letter from Home* (short) (1942); *The New Lot* (short, 1943); *The Way Ahead* (1944); *The True Glory* (co-dir. Garson Kanin, 1945); *Odd Man Out* (1947); *The Fallen Idol* (1948); *The Third Man* (1949); *Outcast of the Islands* (1951); *The Man Between* (1953); *A Kid for Two Farthings* (1955); *Trapeze* (1956); *The Key* (1958); *Our Man in Havana* (1959); *Mutiny on the Bounty* (uncredited co-dir., Lewis Milestone, 1962); *The Running Man* (1963); *The Agony and the Ecstasy* (1965); *Oliver!* (1968); *Flap* (UK: *The Last Warrior*, US, 1970); *Follow Me* (1972).

REEVES, Michael (1944–1969)

On the evidence of his best-known film, *Witchfinder General*, the early death of Michael Reeves at the age of twenty-five robbed the cinema of a potential major talent. He was born in London in 1944 and after an English public school education worked in various minor capacities, first for Don Siegel, then on American-backed European films such as *The Long Ships* (Jack Cardiff, 1963) and *Genghis Khan* (Henry Levin, 1965). His break came when he went to work in Italy for producer Paul Maslansky, first on *Il castello dei morti vivi* (1964), then as director and co-writer of *La sorella di Satana*. Though hampered by budgetary constraints, *La sorella di Satana* does contain some notable moments, such as the witch-hunt at the beginning that looks like a sketch for the opening of *Witchfinder General*. His second feature, *The Sorcerers*, was made back in Britain for Tigon, a small exploitation films company. Despite its low budget, Reeves was able to draw on fine performances from Boris Karloff and Catherine Lacey as old people who become obsessed with the violent sexual possibilities created by the permissive society, and Ian Ogilvy as the young man who becomes their unwitting tool. Its theme of controlling subjects at a distance and vicariously experiencing their sensations can be seen as a reflexive commentary on the cinema experience.

Witchfinder General, though set during the English Civil War, ignores conflicts between Cavaliers and Roundheads to dwell on the seedy lawlessness sown by the war. Matthew Hopkins (Vincent Price), the so-called Witchfinder General, arrives in an idyllic English village and proceeds to spread terror and degradation. Reeves coaxes a chillingly subtle performance from Vincent Price, and the rest of the cast (Ian Ogilvy, Hilary Dwyer, Rupert Davies, even Robert Russell and Nicky Henson) play their parts with an inspired conviction they fail to evince elsewhere. John Coquillon's cinematography, Paul Ferris' score and the veteran Jim Morahan's art direction combine to create an atmosphere of terror, all the more disturbing for being set against the tranquil beauty of the English countryside, but it is Reeves who holds things together.

Reeves' next film was to be a Victorian melodrama, *The Oblong Box*, for American International Pictures (which had part-funded *Witchfinder General*). However, during pre-production he died of a barbiturate overdose on 11 February 1969; Gordon Hessler took over as director. Reeves left a tantalising cinematic legacy and much speculation about the impact he would have had on British cinema had he lived.
(Tom Ryall)

BIBLIOGRAPHY: Fischer, Dennis, *Horror Film Directors, 1931–1990* (Jefferson NC, and London: McFarland, 1991); Halligan, Benjamin, *Michael Reeves* (Manchester: Manchester University Press, 2003); Hutchings, Peter, *Hammer and Beyond: The British Horror Film* (Manchester: Manchester University Press, 1993); Murray, John B., *The Remarkable Michael Reeves: His Short and Tragic Life* (London: Cinematics Publishing, 2002); Pirie, David, *A Heritage of Horror* (London: Gordon Fraser, 1973); Rigby, Jonathan, *English Gothic* (London: Reynolds and Hearn, 2000); Wood, Robin, 'In Memoriam Michael Reeves', *Movie* no. 17, Winter 1969/70, pp. 2–6.

FILMOGRAPHY: *Carrion* (short, c. 1958); *Down* (short, c. 1958–9); *Intrusion* (short, 1961); *Il castello dei morti vivi/Castle of the Living Dead* (uncredited co-dirs. Luciano Ricci/Lorenzo Sabatini, It, 1964); *La sorella di Satana/Revenge of the Blood Beast* (UK/It/Yug, 1966); *The Sorcerers* (1967); *Witchfinder General* (US: *The Conqueror Worm*, 1968).

REINIGER, Lotte (1899–1981)

Charlotte Eleanor Elizabeth Reiniger, cinema's pre-eminent maker of silhouette films, was born on 21 June 1899 in Berlin. While studying to be an actress at Max Reinhardt's theatre school during 1916–17, she met the actor-director Paul Wegener, who offered her small parts in several of his films and occasionally used her silhouette vignettes in intertitles. He introduced her to the Institut für Kulturforschung, a group of young people headed by Hans Cürlis, bent on producing scientific and experimental films. Beginning with *Das Ornament des verliebten Herzens* (1919), she began to design and direct short silhouette films for them; she also made commercials advertising ink, chocolate and talcum powder for the producer Julius Pinschewer. An undoubted cinema pioneer and innovator, Reiniger's adventurousness remained circumscribed by an unwavering allegiance to traditional tastes in popular storytelling and the decorative arts. She drew repeatedly on fairy tales and legends, bringing the fantastic to life with a baroque intricacy and precision, and, once sound arrived, an exquisite musical sensibility. With *Die Geschichte des Prinzen Achmed/Die Abenteuer des Prinzen Achmed* (1923–6), mounted with her husband, the art historian Carl Koch, she made cinema's first full-length animated feature, based on tales from *The Arabian Nights*. Finance was provided by the Berlin banker Louis Hagen; his son Louis Hagen Jr. supported her work in England after the Second World War.

Though widely popular with audiences and critics, *Achmed* had no direct successor, and apart from the feature-length *Die Jagd nach dem Glück* (co-dirs. Carl Koch/Rochus Gliese, 1930), an ambitious but unsuccessful mixture of animation and live action, Reiniger's remaining films were all shorts. She moved to England in 1936. In her first British film, the independently made *The King's Breakfast*, her ornate silhouette style clashed with the whimsical simplicity of A. A. Milne's poem. Greater artistic success came with two films of fragile charm made for the GPO Film Unit, *The Tocher* and *The H.P.O.*, the latter her first film in colour. Both drew on folk tales and fantasy to advertise Post Office services. In 1939 Reiniger joined her husband in Rome, where he was working with Jean Renoir, a close friend, on a film of *La Tosca*, one of several unfinished ventures at the time. Reiniger and Koch became trapped in Italy by the war, and were ultimately obliged to return to Germany, where she made another silhouette film in Berlin, *Die goldene Gans* (1944), and helped found a shadow play theatre. In 1948 the couple returned to London and took British citizenship. Promotional films made through the Crown Film Unit followed; but the lure of the fairy tale proved irresistible. In 1953 she founded Primrose Productions with Koch and Hagen Jr, and began another cycle of tales, made for television, including *The Magic Horse* (1953), *The Gallant Little Tailor* (1954) and *Thumbelina* (1955). She later discovered another niche making silent silhouette films for use in Christmas pantomimes. Following Koch's death in 1963 she temporarily withdrew from production, but with support from the National Film Board of Canada returned to make the prize-winning *Aucassin and Nicolette* (1975) and several others, her eyes still sharp and her fingers nimble. Reiniger's influence on animation in Britain and beyond has proved negligible, but her skill in her chosen field was unrivalled. She died on 19 July 1981, in Dettenhausen, Germany. (Geoff Brown and Kevin Gough-Yates)

BIBLIOGRAPHY: Pilling, Jayne (ed.), *Women and Animation: A Compendium* (London: BFI Exhibition & Distribution Division, 1992); Reiniger, Lotte, *Shadow Theatres and Shadow Films* (London: Batsford, 1970); Reiniger, Lotte, 'The Adventures of Prince Achmed, or What May Happen to Somebody Trying to Make a Full Length Cartoon in 1926', *The Silent Picture* no. 8, Autumn 1970, pp. 2–4; Strobel, Christel and Hans, *Lotte Reiniger* (Duisburg: Atlas Film, 1988).

FILMOGRAPHY (UK only): *The King's Breakfast* (1937); *The Tocher, The H.P.O.* (1938); *Dream Circus* (unfinished, 1939); *Greetings Telegrams*; *Post Early for Christmas*; *Radio Licenses* (1949); *The Happy Prince*; *The Wise Jackal* (1950); *Christmas Is Coming*; *Mary's Birthday* (1951); *Helene la belle* (aka *La Belle Helene*, 1957); *The Seraglio* (aka *A Night in a Harem*, 1958); *The Pied Piper of Hamelin* (1960); *The Frog Prince* (1961); *Wee Sandy* (1962); *Cinderella* (1963).

REISCH, Walter (1903–1983)

Walter Reisch was born in Vienna on 23 May 1903. He entered films in Vienna as an assistant to Alexander Korda in 1920 and wrote his first scripts in 1921. By 1927 he had moved to Berlin, where he established a reputation as one of Europe's top screenwriters, especially skilled at light domestic dramas and musicals. Major successes included *Zwei Herzen im Dreiviertel-Takt* (Geza von Bolvary, 1930), and various multilingual ventures, including the Lilian Harvey vehicle *Ein blonder Traum* (Paul Martin, 1932, written with Billy Wilder) and the futuristic adventure *F.P. 1 antwortet nicht* (Karl Hartl, 1932).

Reisch left Germany quickly on Hitler's accession to power, working in Austria with Willi Forst on the highly popular *Leise flehen meine Lieder/Unfinished Symphony* (Willi Forst/Anthony Asquith, 1933), a fanciful musical romance about Schubert, and turning director himself for his romantic dramas *Episode* (1935) and *Silhouetten* (1936). He arrived in England in 1936 with a contract with Korda's London Films; by August he was directing Miriam Hopkins, Gertrude Lawrence, Sebastian Shaw and Rex Harrison in *Men Are Not Gods*, a comedy-drama with a strong feminine angle, featuring Hopkins as a London drama critic's secretary who falls in love with a married stage actor currently starring in *Othello*. Reisch's instincts were to play the material for light comedy, best achieved in the early scenes; but the novelettish melodrama of G. B. Stern and Iris Wright's scenario, climaxing in Othello's on-stage efforts to kill his Desdemona for real, became a burden he could not ignore. Critics sniffed at this handsome film's improbabilities, but it still became a popular hit.

Reisch then moved to America, working first for MGM and later, in the 1950s, for 20th Century-Fox, where he was often teamed with Charles Brackett. He rejoined his old men-

tor for one more assignment in America, co-writing *That Hamilton Woman* (Alexander Korda, 1941). At MGM Reisch specialised in tailoring material for the studio's female stars, including Garbo in *Ninotchka* (Ernst Lubitsch, 1939) and Ingrid Bergman in *Gaslight* (George Cukor, 1944). At Fox his range broadened: popular successes included *Titanic* (Jean Negulesco, 1953) and the Jules Verne adventure *Journey to the Centre of the Earth* (Henry Levin, 1959), his last credited film. Further opportunities to direct were few. For Universal he directed his script for *Song of Scheherazade* (1947), colourful twaddle inspired by Rimsky-Korsakov's life and music; he also made two films in post-war Germany, *Die Mücke* (1954), a comedy about a lady spy, and *Der Cornet – Die Weise von Liebe und Tod* (1955), from the novel by Rainer Maria Rilke. But his home remained in the USA, where in his later years he doctored scripts and wrote for television; he died on 28 March 1983 in Los Angeles.
(Kevin Gough-Yates)

BIBLIOGRAPHY: Elsaesser, Thomas, 'Walter Reisch: Vienna – Berlin – London – Hollywood', *Pix* no. 3, 2001, pp. 43–67; Greenberg, Joe, 'Walter Reisch: The Tailor', in Patrick McGilligan (ed.), *Backstory 2: Interviews with Screenwriters of the 1940s and 1950s* (Berkeley, University of California Press, 1991); Obituary, *Screen International*, 23 Apr. 1983, p. 10; Reisner, Ingeborg, 'Nur der nationale Film hat Chancen', *Kino-Information* vol. 7 no. 12, 12 June 1980, pp. 4–5.

FILMOGRAPHY (UK only): *Men Are Not Gods* (1936).

REISZ, Karel (1926-2002)

In terms of themes if not in style, Karel Reisz was the most consistent of the young directors most closely associated with the British New Wave of the late 1950s and early 60s. Though his output was disappointingly small and some of his films performed poorly at the box office, Reisz regularly commanded critical respect and esteem as a film-maker, critic and educator. His later work as a stage director of uncommon insight also brought him acclaim.

Reisz was born on 21 July 1926 in Ostrava, Czechoslovakia. At the insistence of his parents, he came to England when he was twelve, just before the Nazis invaded his country (his parents stayed behind and perished in a concentration camp). Reisz attended Leighton Park, a Quaker school in Reading, where David Lean had been educated a few years earlier. Towards the end of the Second World War he served as a fighter-pilot in one of the RAF's Czech squadrons. Afterwards he studied chemistry at Emmanuel College, Cambridge, before teaching for two years at a London grammar school.

His association with cinema began with film criticism written for the magazine *Sequence*; he co-edited the last issue in 1952 with Lindsay Anderson. He then wrote *The Technique of Film Editing* – less of a textbook than an aesthetic appreciation of the expressive possibilities of montage, containing illuminating analyses of sequences from Thorold Dickinson's *The Queen of Spades* (1948), Lean's *The Passionate Friends* (1949) and other British classics. The book has rarely been out of print since its publication in 1953. After working as a programme planner at the National Film Theatre, Reisz became a driving force behind the Free Cinema movement, which aimed to provide an alternative to a national cinema considered tepid, uncommitted and class-bound. Under the Free Cinema umbrella he co-directed *Momma Don't Allow* (1956) with Tony Richardson, a short, vivid social portrait shot in a north London jazz club; co-produced Lindsay Anderson's film about Covent Garden market, *Every Day Except Christmas* (1957); and directed the fifty-two-minute *We Are the Lambeth Boys* (1959), an ambitious, often poetic survey of life in and around a south London youth club.

Reisz's debut as a fiction feature director took place the following year. *Saturday Night and Sunday Morning* (1960), an adaptation of Alan Sillitoe's controversial novel of working-class life, though made with limited resources and no established stars, proved a critical and popular success. Albert Finney's Arthur Seaton, the hero who compensates for his job's monotonous grind with regular boozing and an affair with a married woman, represented something entirely new in British cinema. Subsequently Reisz produced Lindsay Anderson's equally powerful *This Sporting Life* (1963), but this was essentially the last gasp of the New Wave. For his next film, he turned to an updated adaptation of Emlyn Williams' 1930s' melodrama *Night Must Fall*. Finney gives a virtuoso performance as the psychopath happy to keep a previous victim's head in a hatbox; but the film's emotional coldness makes it less satisfying than Richard Thorpe's American version (1937), where the psychopath (Robert Montgomery) is matched against a plucky and resourceful woman (Rosalind Russell).

Reisz was far less detached in *Morgan: A Suitable Case for Treatment* (1966), based on a television play by David Mercer. The director – at this time – shared Mercer's attitudes towards madness and Marxism, and he shows uncharacteristic warmth and humour in his treatment of David Warner's gangling, anarchic working-class artist, hostile to the stuffy conformism of bourgeois society but unable to believe in the comforting platitudes of his old Mum's Communism. Morgan is very different from Finney's Arthur Seaton, but both men can be seen as representatives of rebellious youth, unwilling to accept their allotted roles in life or the assumption that their elders are their betters.

With *Isadora* Reisz focused on an earlier rebel, the early twentieth-century dancer and free spirit Isadora Duncan, who flirted with Russian revolutionaries and shook up European audiences with her sensual, uninhibited performances. But in contrast to the exuberant fun of *Morgan*, *Isadora* seems fatally afflicted by vapidity, as though over two hours of pretentious dancing had drained even the stoic Reisz of energy. He revived himself – after a six-year gap – with two vigorous American films, *The Gambler* (1974) and *Who'll Stop the Rain* (1978), both featuring tough heroes struggling to survive in a sleaze-ridden, dystopian society. James Caan in *The Gambler* is a university professor (a thinly veiled portrait of screenwriter James

Toback) whose gambling addiction leads him into the violent lower depths of inner-city life. Nick Nolte, in *Who'll Stop the Rain* (based on Robert Stone's novel *Dog Soldiers* – the title retained for the film's UK release), is a Vietnam veteran who returns to an America, where the 1960s' counter-cultural revolution has been degraded by drugs and pornography. The bleak vision of America presented in these films attracted critical interest but not a mass audience.

Ironically, Reisz's biggest commercial success came with his adaptation of a novel set in nineteenth-century Dorset. John Fowles' *The French Lieutenant's Woman* (1981) centres upon a new woman at odds with rigid Victorian morality – precisely the kind of outsider sympathetically explored in the director's earlier films. Reisz and his screenwriter Harold Pinter turned this supposedly unfilmable text into a boldly imaginative screen adaptation, juggling between past and present in a film-within-a-film structure that effectively replicates the book's modern perspective on the Victorian novel. If audiences felt confused, they still stayed the course, soothed by visual finery and the passionate entanglements of Meryl Streep and Jeremy Irons.

By contrast, Reisz's next film, *Sweet Dreams*, pursued an overly rigid narrative line. The plot of this biopic about the American country singer Patsy Cline offered nothing unfamiliar, though gutsy music and heartfelt performances give emotional satisfaction. For Reisz, this was another story of a character trapped in an uncaring society, seeking personal fulfilment. *Everybody Wins* (1990) a private-eye thriller written by Arthur Miller, with Nick Nolte as a tough but honest man in a corrupt world, failed to generate the same excitement; as the title implies, Reisz and Miller hedge their bets too cautiously, wryly shrugging off the bitter critique they seem to offer of American society. The film was greeted with critical and commercial indifference. Aside from a minuscule Beckett adaptation, Reisz turned his back on cinema and spent his last years working in the theatre, where his productions of Ibsen, Rattigan and Pinter met with greater acclaim.

Two qualities stand out from Reisz's film work: its intelligence, and its fastidiousness. Both became double-edged swords. He brought to the screen some of the best work of major actors, British and American, from Albert Finney to Jessica Lange, and he collaborated fruitfully with writers from Alan Sillitoe to Arthur Miller. At times his precision in detail, in framing and editing, could cool the films' temperatures, and obscure another of Reisz's strengths: the warm sympathy with ordinary people he displayed in his pioneering Free Cinema films and his contributions to the British New Wave. Reisz is undeniably a significant figure in British film culture – though, like Alexander Mackendrick, Thorold Dickinson and Robert Hamer, one impossible to contemplate without pondering what more might have been achieved. Reisz's second marriage was to the American actress Betsy Blair. He died in London of a blood disorder on 25 November 2002.

(Neil Sinyard)

BIBLIOGRAPHY: BECTU History Project, tape no. 193, held in the BFI National Library, London; Gaston, Georg, *Karel Reisz* (Boston, MA: Twayne, 1980); Hill, John, *Sex, Class and Realism: British Cinema and Society, 1956–1963* (London: BFI, 1986); Kennedy, Harlan, 'The Czech Director's Woman', *Film Comment*, Sept./Oct. 1981, pp. 26–31; Reisz, Karel, *The Technique of Film Editing* (London: Focal Press, 1953); Török, Jean-Paul, 'To Stand Outside and to Risk', *Positif* no. 212, Nov. 1978, pp. 2–3; 'Entretien avec Karel Reisz', pp. 6–11; and Michel Ciment, 'Bio-biblio filmographie de Karel Reisz, and 'Nouvel entretien avec Karel Reisz', pp. 12–21.

FILMOGRAPHY: *Momma Don't Allow* (doc. short, co-dir. Tony Richardson, 1955); *Three Graces* (short, 1956); *We Are the Lambeth Boys* (doc., 1959); *Time Off* (doc. short); *Saturday Night and Sunday Morning* (1960); *Night Must Fall* (1964); *Morgan: A Suitable Case for Treatment* (US: *Morgan!*, 1966); *Isadora* (1968); *The Gambler* (US, 1974); *Who'll Stop the Rain* (UK: *Dog Soldiers*, US, 1978); *The French Lieutenant's Woman* (1981); *Sweet Dreams* (US, 1985); *Everybody Wins* (1990); *Act Without Words I* (short, Ir, 2000).

RELPH, Michael (1915–2004)

Michael Leighton George Relph was born on 16 February 1915 in Broadstone, Dorset, the son of actor George Relph. Family friend Michael Balcon gave him a start at Gaumont-British in 1932. He prospered under the tutelage of the great German art director Alfred Junge, and from 1934 was sufficiently well qualified to design for the stage. In 1936 he moved to the Warner Bros. British studio at Teddington, where he worked on over thirty films, most notably as art director on Arthur Woods' atmospheric thriller *They Drive by Night* (1939). In 1942 Relph rejoined Balcon as chief art director at Ealing, where his first assignment was *The Bells Go Down* (1943), directed by Basil Dearden. He designed sets on Dearden's films until 1948, and from 1946 also began acting as associate producer. In this role he was responsible for Robert Hamer's comic masterpiece *Kind Hearts and Coronets* (1949), but his most fruitful partnership was with Dearden. Between 1946 and 1970 Relph produced all but two of Dearden's films and was credited as co-director with Dearden on *I Believe in You*.

Relph made his directorial debut proper in 1957 with *Davy*, made for Ealing after the studio had been sold to the BBC and the company was enduring an unsatisfactory afterlife on a couple of stages at MGM-Borehamwood. Not surprisingly, the film has a hangdog feel to it, with opera-aspiring Harry Secombe trapped within a family of third-rate music-hall entertainers headed by George Relph. *Rockets Galore!*, a belated sequel to *Whisky Galore!* (Alexander Mackendrick, 1949), also has a backwards-looking, old-fashioned air to it. Relph's final effort, *Desert Mice* (1959), a farce about a wartime ENSA troupe, is the least ambitious of his three films but the most fun, with a strong ensemble cast, witty dialogue and a no-nonsense plot.

Dearden and Relph survived the demise of Ealing, and made an impressive trilogy of social-problem films – *Sapphire* (1959), *Victim* (1961) and *Life for Ruth* (1962) – before beginning a slow decline. Relph wrote the screenplays for several of their later films – *Woman of Straw* (1964), *Masquerade* (1965), *The Assassination Bureau* (1968) and *The Man Who Haunted Himself* (1970). These were big-budget films aimed at the international market; but as Chairman of the Film Producers Association between 1971 and 1976 Relph fought to maintain an artistically distinct indigenous film industry in a world dominated by Hollywood. In 1979 he joined Don Boyd in producing a slate of low-budget films, including Alan Clarke's *Scum* (1979) and Chris Petit's *An Unsuitable Job for a Woman* (1981).

Relph's substantial contribution to British cinema has been as a brilliant art director and an efficient and supportive producer rather than a director. He died on 30 September 2004 in Selsey, West Sussex. His son is the producer Simon Relph.

(Margaret Butler)

BIBLIOGRAPHY: Adams, Mark, 'Michael Relph: A Birthday Tribute', *National Film Theatre Programme*, Feb. 1995; Burton, Alan, Tim O'Sullivan and Paul Wells (eds), *Liberal Directions: Basil Dearden and Postwar British Film Culture* (Trowbridge, Wilts: Flicks Books, 1997); Durgnat, Raymond, 'Two on a Tandem', *Films and Filming*, July 1966, pp. 26–33; McFarlane, Brian, *An Autobiography of British Cinema* (London: Methuen, 1997).

FILMOGRAPHY: *I Believe in You* (co-dir. Basil Dearden, 1952); *Davy* (1957); *Rockets Galore!* (1958); *Desert Mice* (1959).

RICHARDS, Julian (1968–)

Julian Richards was born in Newport, South Wales, on 31 July 1968. He studied at the Bournemouth Film School, where he made two of his 'Tales from Wales', *Pirates* and *Queen Sacrifice*. The third, *Bad Company*, followed in 1992 when he was a student at the National School of Film and Television, where he also directed *In with the Rent* (1990), a television play for BBC Wales. On graduating he moved into television to direct episodes of Channel 4's *Brookside*, but he was impatient to break into features. In 1997 he made his debut with the wildly overambitious occult thriller *Darklands*, shot on location, and clearly following in the footsteps of Robin Hardy and Peter Shaffer's *The Wicker Man* (1973) with its mixture of Celtic mysticism, conspiracy and human sacrifice. A host of characters, a complex story and lavish set-piece action sequences stretched the £500,000 budget beyond breaking point. *Darklands* is unconvincing and often ludicrous, but Richards' bravado in getting the project made won him credit.

Silent Cry, with a simpler story and a budget five times that of *Darklands*, was more polished. Douglas Henshall and Emily Woof (as in Stewart Sugg's 1998 film *Fast Food*) make engaging leads, and the film, at least initially, presents a frightening vision of a society where ordinary people's lives are thrown into nightmarish confusion by the arbitrary, omniscient forces of the state. Unfortunately, the plot's final goal – the discovery of the precise fate of Woof's newborn baby – is irredeemably banal. Richards returned to ultra-low-budget production with *The Last Horror Movie*, a less than original reworking of the serial-killer-who-likes-to-film-his-murders theme; it proved popular on the horror festival circuit and was granted a brief cinema release in London in 2005. His production company, Prolific Films, looks set to live up to its name.

(Robert Murphy)

BIBLIOGRAPHY: Williams, David E., 'Aura of Evil', *American Cinematographer*, Mar. 1997, pp. 70–6; Dunkley, Cathy, 'Close-Up: Julian Richards', *Moving Pictures International*, 12 May 1994, p. 8.

FILMOGRAPHY: *The Girl That Cried Wolf* (short, 1985); *Pirates* (short); *Queen Sacrifice* (short, 1988); *Bad Company* (short, 1992); *Will the Real Richard III* (short, 1995); *Darklands* (1997); *Silent Cry* (2001); *The Last Horror Movie* (2003; rel. 2005).

RICHARDSON, Frank (1893–1975)

Frankland Attwood Richardson was born in New York City on 28 November 1893, but most of his curious directing career unfolded in Britain. In the early 1920s he brushed against mild artistic aspirations in the Dutch-British co-productions of Mauritz Binger and the London renters Granger's Exclusives; but commercial necessities soon won over art, and by the 1930s he was directing 'quota quickies', never to rise again. 'No more exciting than Monday's hash,' complained *Kinematograph Weekly* about *Money Mad* (7 March 1934), though that was mild compared to the criticisms his last productions endured.

He arrived in Europe in 1920 after American experience as an assistant director, chiefly with Donald Crisp at Famous Players-Lasky. His own assignments came quickly: two comedies for Joseph Bamberger's Zodiac with Mary Glynne, both poorly received, then four Dutch co-productions of larger ambitions but no great fire, filmed at Binger's Haarlem studio with extensive location forays. The second of these, *Kitty Tailleur* (1921), featuring Marjorie Hume, Lewis Dayton and Richardson's Canadian-born wife, Nora Hayden, pitch-forked a commonplace social drama into the luscious scenery of the Italian Riviera. The third, *The Black Tulip* (1921), a print of which has survived, placed the plot of Alexandre Dumas' historical novel among seventeenth-century period bustle and several authentic locations, including Haarlem's town hall. The polite *Bioscope* reviewer considered the film 'careful and dignified' (15 September 1921). But without any vivid characterisations or signs of a shaping directorial hand, that dignity now appears deadly dull. There are passing attractions in Feiko Boersma's interior photography as Gerald McCarthy and Zoe Palmer, hero and heroine, pursue their romance, chiefly on either side of a prison door's grille.

The Binger adventure over, Richardson returned to America, where he assisted Crisp on the Fairbanks vehicle *Don Q, Son of Zorro* (1925) and directed two exercises in thrills and spills: *King of the Pack*, starring Peter the Great (a bottom-budget Rin-Tin-Tin), and a horse-racing drama, *Racing Blood*. The quota fodder he generated in Britain after 1931 suffered similar financial restraints, but lacked those films' narrative cheek. From Twickenham, Walton-on-Thames and Teddington emerged ten footling tales of crooks, marital tiffs, a pawned necklace and a bogus millionaire; all films are seemingly lost. *Flat No. 9* (1932), a marital comedy with Jane Baxter and Reginald Gardiner, mildly amused *Picturegoer*, others left trade critics complaining of feeble material left to fester (*Oh, What a Night!*) or interesting material ruined by clumsy handling (*Money Mad*). The quota market's collapse at the end of the 1930s left Richardson scrapping for work; but he re-emerged after the war with advertising shorts, three impoverished variety films and, finally, *I Was a Dancer* and *Bait*, two shoddy dramas featuring Richard Tauber's wife, Diana Napier, then recently widowed. It was all a long way from pretty Dutch interiors, or indeed Donald Crisp. Richardson died on 18 July 1975 in Chelsea, London.

(Geoff Brown)

BIBLIOGRAPHY: Cohen, Elsie, 'Filming on the Italian Riviera', *Kinematograph Weekly*, 17 Feb. 1921, p. 73; Donaldson, Geoffrey, *Of Joy and Sorrow: A Filmography of Dutch Silent Fiction* (Amsterdam: Nederlands Filmmuseum, 1997).

FILMOGRAPHY: *In the Night/In den nacht* (UK/Neth, 1920); *The White Hen*; *Candytuft, I Mean Veronica*; *Kitty Tailleur/In de macht van het noodlot* (UK/Neth); *The Black Tulip/De zwarte tulp* (UK/Neth); *Sheer Bluff/Zaken zijn zaken* (UK/Neth)(1921); *Racing Blood* (US); *King of the Pack* (US, 1926); *We Dine at Seven*; *Peace and Quiet* (1931); *Above Rubies*; *Flat No. 9*; *The River House Ghost*; *Don't Be a Dummy* (1932); *Double Wedding* (1933); *Oh, What a Night!* (1933; rel. 1935); *Money Mad* (1934); *The Avenging Hand* (co-dir. Victor Hanbury); *The Howard Case* (1936); *Sweethearts Forever* (short); *Cabaret* (short) (1945); *Amateur Night* (short, 1946); *I Was a Dance*; *Bait* (1949).

RICHARDSON, Peter (1953–)

Peter Richardson was born in Newton Abbot, Devon, in October 1953. At the age of seventeen he moved to London to pursue a career as an actor. A mutual interest in music and comedy brought him into contact with another hopeful, Nigel Planer, and together they found success at the Soho clubs the Comedy Store and the Comic Strip. In 1982 Richardson led a group of performers from the Comic Strip into television, co-writing (with Pete Richens) the majority of the first two series of *The Comic Strip Presents. . . .* His first cinema film, *The Supergrass*, showed Richardson to be a talented director, but its successor, *Eat the Rich*, was a weak satire suffering from too many targets and lacking a strong central performance. *The Strike*, made for television but given a limited theatrical showing, is a masterly outlandish comedy with Richardson masquerading as Al Pacino, who agrees to play the loquacious South Yorkshire trade union leader Arthur Scargill in a Hollywood dramatisation of the 1984 coal miners' strike.

The Pope Must Die (pusillanimously retitled *The Pope Must Diet* for the American market) is less daring, but benefits from a terrific performance by Robbie Coltrane as the priest mistakenly elected Pope. Richardson returned to television with *Stella Street*, a clever satire on the rich and famous with Phil Cornwell and John Sessions impersonating a variety of celebrities, including Michael Caine, Jack Nicholson, Joe Pesci, David Bowie, Mick Jagger and Keith Richards, who find themselves living next door to each other in a leafy suburban street. Surreal juxtapositions and outrageous appropriations of star mannerisms made it a cult success. A feature-length version emerged in 2004, though its modest comedy makes it better suited to the small-screen market. *Churchill: The Hollywood Years* is a similarly ramshackle endeavour, though its outrageous concept – a Hollywood rewrite of the Second World War with Winston Churchill as a dashing young American – is irresistible.

(Richard Dacre)

BIBLIOGRAPHY: Perretta, Don, 'Laughing Matter', *Time Out*, 17 Feb. 1988, pp. 22–4; Wilmut, Roger and Peter Rosengard, *Didn't You Kill My Mother-in-Law?* (London: Methuen, 1989).

FILMOGRAPHY: *The Supergrass* (1985); *The Strike*; *Eat the Rich* (1987); *The Pope Must Die* (US: *The Pope Must Diet*, 1991); *Stella Street* (UK/US, 2003); *Churchill: The Hollywood Years* (UK/Ir, 2004).

RICHARDSON, Tony (1928–1991)

Cecil Antonio Richardson was born on 5 June 1928 in Shipley, Yorkshire, where his family owned a chemist's shop. He was educated at Wadham College, Oxford, and his imaginative staging of student plays led to the offer of a place on a BBC training course.

While gaining experience directing television and live theatre, Richardson became friendly with the critics writing for *Sequence* magazine, including Lindsay Anderson and Karel Reisz, with whom he was to spearhead the British New Wave. From 1954 to 1956 he published film criticism in *Sight and Sound*, including an article on 'The metteur en scène' (Oct./Dec. 1954). This he defined as a film-maker who, neither true creator nor faithful interpreter, is preoccupied with superficial style over dramatic content: a description later critics would apply to Richardson himself. Rarely can any director's reputation have been so much at variance between his peers – to whom Richardson was brilliant, passionate, mercurial – and his reviewers, for whom his films rarely cohered as unified wholes.

Richardson's first film credit was *Momma Don't Allow* (1956), a short documentary co-directed with Karel Reisz, vividly capturing the energy of the Wood Green Jazz Club in north London. The same year, with George Devine and others, he founded the English Stage Company, based at Chelsea's Royal Court Theatre. The company had a commitment to new writing, and after a slow start the third production of its first season, John Osborne's *Look Back in Anger*, proved a sensational success. Richardson continued to direct regularly at the Royal Court until 1964, and with Osborne and the Canadian producer Harry Saltzman was also able to set up a film production company, Woodfall, to make adaptations of his and Osborne's most notable stage successes.

The films of *Look Back in Anger* and Osborne's *The Entertainer* display a disconcerting clash of styles: naturalist location shooting for the exteriors, theatrical mannerism for the indoor scenes. The experience led Richardson to resolve never to shoot in a studio again. His next two British films benefited from a greater control over performances, but reveal the strengths and weaknesses of his attachment to location filming. *A Taste of Honey*, a reworking of Shelagh Delaney's play, which Richardson had directed on Broadway, is artistically as well as commercially his most successful early film, despite its over-literal attempts at cinematic lyricism. *The Loneliness of the Long Distance Runner*, adapted by Alan Sillitoe from his own short story about a working-class rebel, is more radical, but forces its realist observation too heavily into a rhetorical mould.

For his next project, *Tom Jones*, based on Fielding's picaresque comic novel, Richardson sought backing from United Artists when Michael Balcon's Bryanston balked at the cost of a period costume film to be shot in colour. The film took over $17 million at the US box office and UA financed all Woodfall's subsequent productions throughout the 1960s. Richardson's uninhibited gusto, the exuberant acting of young British stars Albert Finney and Susannah York, and the brash mixture of realism and stylisation combine to make *Tom Jones* Richardson's most enjoyable film.

After his experiences with 20th Century-Fox on the William Faulkner adaptation *Sanctuary* (1961), Richardson was reluctant to direct another Hollywood studio project. But he relented when MGM promised him creative autonomy on an updated version of Evelyn Waugh's *The Loved One*, written by Terry Southern and Christopher Isherwood. The film is a mess, distinguished only by Haskell Wexler's high-contrast cinematography and some bizarre celebrity cameos, especially by Liberace.

The next few years saw a variety of troubled international projects. Two of them starred Jeanne Moreau: *Mademoiselle*, filmed simultaneously in French and English from an original screenplay by Jean Genet, and *The Sailor from Gibraltar*, adapted from a Marguerite Duras novel. *Red and Blue*, a musical featurette, was originally intended to form a portmanteau film with Lindsay Anderson's *The White Bus* and Peter Brook's *Ride of the Valkyrie* (both 1967). *Laughter in the Dark* was an adaptation of Vladimir Nabokov's novel, and *Ned Kelly* an Australian Western starring a miscast Mick Jagger. Richardson's career was severely damaged by the films' hostile reception. But *Mademoiselle* at least is a curiosity worth discovering: an unabashedly overripe art movie, replete with fevered erotic imagery and a soundtrack of amplified natural sounds suggesting its anti-heroine's repressed and perverted sexual drives.

In the middle of this uneven period came Richardson's most lavish and ambitious project, a revisionist account of *The Charge of the Light Brigade*. Charles Wood's script, which uses a stylised form of period dialogue, offers a waspish satire of the Victorian military Establishment. Richard Williams' witty animated interludes provide their own parallel entertainment, but flaws creep in through the reliance on buffoonish caricatures, and the intrusive romantic subplot involving Vanessa Redgrave, then Richardson's wife.

Richardson continued to alternate stage and film work, and in 1969 he adapted his production of *Hamlet*, starring Nicol Williamson, Anthony Hopkins and Marianne Faithfull, for the screen. Filmed largely in tight close-up on the bare sets at London's Roundhouse Theatre, it shows Richardson at his most disciplined. By contrast *A Delicate Balance*, is a flat transcription of Edward Albee's stage play, despite its dazzling cast.

Richardson's last two British films were a flaccid Dick Francis thriller, *Dead Cert*, and a second Fielding adaptation, *Joseph Andrews*, which at times is barely distinguishable from a soft-core period sex romp. Wisely, he decamped to America. Although he was driven to resign from Berry Gordy's Diana Ross vehicle *Mahogany*, he made three more theatrical features – *The Border*, *The Hotel New Hampshire* and *Blue Sky* – which despite their faults show a return to the restless creativity of his early years. Richardson died from AIDS-related causes in Los Angeles on 14 November 1991. The manuscript of his entertaining and illuminating, if unreliable, autobiography was discovered by his actress daughters, Natasha and Joely, on the day of his death, and published posthumously.

(Sheldon Hall)

BIBLIOGRAPHY: Durgnat, Raymond, 'Loved One', *Films and Filming*, Feb. 1966, pp. 19–23; Mar. 1966, pp. 37–40; Lellis, George, 'Recent Richardson: Cashing the Blank Cheque', *Sight and Sound*, Summer 1969, pp. 130–3; Richardson, Tony, *Long Distance Runner: A Memoir* (London: Faber and Faber, 1993); Welsh, James M. and John C. Tibbetts (eds), *The Cinema of Tony Richardson: Essays and Interviews* (Albany: SUNY Press, 1999).

FILMOGRAPHY: *Momma Don't Allow* (doc. short, co. dir. Karel Reisz, 1956); *Look Back in Anger* (1959); *The Entertainer* (1960); *Sanctuary* (US); *A Taste of Honey* (1961); *The Loneliness of the Long Distance Runner* (1962); *Tom Jones* (1963; re-edited version, 1989); *The Loved One* (US, 1965); *Mademoiselle* (UK/Fr, 1966); *The Sailor from Gibraltar*; *Red and Blue* (short) (1967); *The Charge of the Light Brigade* (1968); *Laughter in the Dark* (UK/Fr); *Hamlet* (1969); *Ned Kelly* (1970); *A Delicate Balance* (US/UK, 1973); *Dead Cert* (1974); *Mahogany* (US; uncredited dir. some scenes only, 1975); *Joseph Andrews* (1977); *The Border* (US, 1982); *The Hotel New Hampshire* (US, 1984); *Blue Sky* (US, 1991; rel. 1994).

RICKMAN, Alan (1946–)

Alan Sydney Patrick Rickman was born on 12 February 1946 in Acton, west London. After attending Chelsea College of Art and Design and RADA, he acted in several television productions, most notably as Obadiah Slope in *The Barchester Chronicles* (David Giles, 1982). He made his name, however, in the RSC production of *Les Liaisons dangereuses* in 1985. Passed over in favour of John Malkovich in *Dangerous Liaisons* (1988), Stephen Frears' film version of the play, Rickman found himself propelled to stardom as the villainous terrorist Hans Gruber in *Die Hard* (John McTiernan, 1988), Juliet Stevenson's dead lover in *Truly, Madly, Deeply* (Anthony Minghella, 1990) and the Sheriff of Nottingham in *Robin Hood Prince of Thieves* (Kevin Reynolds, 1991).

Rickman's one film as director is *The Winter Guest*, an adaptation of a play by Sharman Macdonald that he had staged in 1995. The film is set in a remote town in Scotland in the depths of winter; snow blankets the entire landscape and it is so cold that the sea has begun to freeze. While this offers a credible realistic setting, it also creates a stark and desolate background – a blank slate that reflects the way in which the film's characters must face harsh realities and begin their lives again. The film explores what it is to be alone and to face death (the winter guest), yet it is thoughtful and accepting rather than morbid. *The Winter Guest* was critically well received, though Rickman's acting career (most recently as the obnoxious Severus Snape in the *Harry Potter* films) has left little time for further directorial ventures.

(Sarah Cardwell)

BIBLIOGRAPHY: Grant, Steve, 'A Winter's Tale', *Time Out*, 7–14 Jan. 1998, pp. 16–18; Mackenzie, Suzie, 'Angel with Horns', *Guardian* Weekend Section, 3 Jan. 1998, pp. 10, 13–16.

FILMOGRAPHY: *The Winter Guest* (US/UK, 1997).

RIDGWELL, George (1867–1935)

George Ridgwell, sometimes credited as George Ridgewell, was born in Woolwich, south-east London, in 1867, and followed his father into the Coldstream Guards, where he performed bandsman duties. Leaving the army after twelve years, he went directly onto the musical comedy stage; in 1898 he mounted, starred in and co-wrote the book of a popular musical comedy, *The Skirt Dancer*. Between 1899 and 1900 he sang baritone roles in the D'Oyly Carte Opera Company, appearing at the Savoy Theatre, London, and on provincial tours. After establishing himself as a favourite at London's Palace Theatre of Varieties, Ridgwell provided the vocal accompaniment to a series of filmed 'Biograph Dramatised Songs' when they were shown at the music hall in 1902. By 1910 he was in America, working for Vitagraph's scenario department; within four years he had begun directing, mostly shorts. Films for other companies followed, including Edison, Sunbeam and Triangle. Returning to England, he began directing crime dramas, often cut by himself to a quick tempo, beginning with British and Colonial's *The Sword of Damocles* (1920). In 1921 he transferred to Stoll and until 1924 maintained a busy production schedule, including the well-received *The Amazing Partnership* (1921), adapted from an E. Phillips Oppenheim novel, and *The Further Adventures of Sherlock Holmes* (1922) and *The Last Adventures of Sherlock Holmes* (1923), the final two in a trio of two-reel series featuring Ellie Norwood as the great detective. In an entirely different vein, Ridgwell earned considerable respect for a sensitive, soundly performed and pictorially impressive version of Tennyson's historical drama *Becket* (1923), featuring the great Shakespearian actor Sir Frank Benson; *Kinematograph Weekly* considered it one of the best films of its type in the world ('Becket'). In the same year, convinced of the need to protect British film production from the might of the American industry he had himself toiled in, Ridgwell began agitating for a set quota for British film production, joining Percy Nash and Sidney Morgan in a campaign that led to the Cinematograph Films Act of 1927. Ironically, the quota's

arrival failed to stimulate his own career. In September 1928 he shot a pleasant enough updated version of Dion Boucicault's Irish play *Lily of Killarney* for BIP. But nothing more followed apart from acting bits and a minor position with Gaumont-British Sound News: 'Pioneers always get it in the neck', he told a trade journalist philosophically in 1933. Ridgwell died of a heart attack in Hampstead, London, in April 1935.
(Barry Anthony and Geoff Brown)

BIBLIOGRAPHY: 'Becket', *Kinematograph Weekly*, 15 Nov. 1923, pp. 45–6; 'George Ridgwell Dead: Director Who Initiated Quota Agitation', *Kinematograph Weekly*, 11 Apr. 1935, p. 14; George Ridgwell microfiche, BFI National Library, London.

FILMOGRAPHY: *Mr Santa Claus* (US, 1914); *The Lady of the Lighthouse* (US); *Old Good-for-Nuthin'* (US); *Brown's Summer Boarders* (US); *The Butler* (US); *Sis* (US); *The Mystery of Room 13* (US); *Life's Pitfalls* (US) (1915); *Helen of the Chorus* (US); *The Matchmakers* (US); *Behind the Secret Panel* (US); *The Heart Wrecker* (US); *Peggy and the Law* (US); *The Intruder* (US); *The Clever Mrs Carter* (US); *Her Mother's Sweetheart* (US); *Somewhere in Georgia* (US) (1916); *Captain Bobby of the Home Defenders* (aka *Bobby and the Home Defence*, US); *Bobby and Company* (US); *Bobby to the Rescue* (US); *Bobby's Country Adventure* (US); *Bobby's Fairy* (US); *Bobby Takes a Wife* (US); *Bobby, the Magician* (US); *Whistling Dick's Christmas Stocking* (US) (1917); *The Thing's the Play* (US); *The Trimmed Lamp* (US); *The Rathskeller and the Rose* (US); *The Song and the Sergeant* (US); *The Brief Debut of Tildy* (US) (1918); *The Water Lily* (US); *Fruits of Passion* (US); *The Root of Evil* (US) (1919); *His Pal's Gal* (US); *The Hobo of Pizen City* (US); *The Hold Up Man* (US); *The Law of the Border* (US); *Tex of the Timberlands* (US); *The Sword of Damocles*; *A Gamble in Lives* (1920); *The Four Just Men*; *Greatheart*; *The Amazing Partnership* (1921); *The Knight Errant*; *The Further Adventures of Sherlock Holmes* (series of fifteen shorts); *The Pointing Finger*, *A Lost Leader*, *The Crimson Circle*; *The Romance of British History* (series of shorts: *The Flight of the King*, *The Great Terror*, *The Last Crusade*, *A Story of Nell Gwynne*, *The Last King of Wales*, *The Story of Amy Robsart*) (episodes from the shorts series *The Romance of British History*); *Don't Blame Your Children*; *The Eleventh Hour*, *The Missioner*, *Petticoat Loose* (1922); *The Last Adventures of Sherlock Holmes* (series of fifteen shorts); *Becket* (1923); *The Notorious Mrs Carrick* (1924); *Lily of Killarney* (1929).

RIDLEY, Philip (1960–)

Philip Ridley was born in London in 1960. He studied painting at St Martin's School of Art, and his artistic background is evident in the careful framing and unusual use of colour and shade in his films. Ridley is also a playwright (for radio and theatre), novelist and an author of children's books. He directed two short films, *Visiting Mr Beak* and *The Universe of Dermot Finn*, before writing the screenplay for *The Krays* (Peter Medak, 1990). He has won awards for his work across all these fields.

Ridley's feature debut, *The Reflecting Skin*, is a dark film set in 1950s' Midwest America, and follows the childhood experiences of its unsympathetic yet suffering protagonist, Seth Dove (Jeremy Cooper), simultaneously exploring the underside of a remote community and exposing its hidden secrets. The visual style of the film is arresting – especially in terms of the exaggerated, intense colours – but the tone of the film denies us any sense of nostalgia or warmth. This sense of excess is mirrored in Nick Bicât's impressive and unnerving score.

Ridley's second film, *The Passion of Darkly Noon*, is more openly melodramatic: the repressed son of religious fanatics (Brendan Fraser) finds shelter with a beautiful woman (Ashley Judd) in a cottage in the woods. When her husband (Viggo Mortensen), a semi-autistic woodcutter returns, Darkly's sexual jealousy provokes a bloody, fiery climax. The American theme of a clash between Puritan fundamentalism and Southern sensuality is filtered through Ridley's very European sensibility – stylised composition, the interpolation of surreal imagery (a giant silver shoe floats down the river), flamboyant use of colour – making for a compellingly memorable film. Mixed reviews and poor box-office returns made it difficult for Ridley to continue along his idiosyncratic path, and he has preferred to express his vision through other forms rather than compromise them to fit the confines of commercial cinema.
(Sarah Cardwell)

BIBLIOGRAPHY: Franke, Lizzie, 'Filming thru the Dark', *Producer* no. 12, Summer 1990, p. 18; McLeish, Jamie, 'Darkness Visible', *Sight and Sound*, June 1996, pp. 16–17.

FILMOGRAPHY: *Visiting Mr Beak* (short, 1987); *The Universe of Dermot Finn* (short, 1988); *The Reflecting Skin* (UK/Can, 1990); *The Passion of Darkly Noon* (UK/Ger/Belg, 1995).

RILLA, Wolf (1920–2005)

Wolf Peter Rilla was born in Berlin on 16 March 1920, the son of the actor-producer Walter Rilla. The family left Germany and settled in England in 1934. After graduating from Cambridge, Rilla joined the BBC, producing plays for radio and television. He entered the film industry in 1953, directing four features that year: the gentle domestic comedy *Glad Tidings*, which he adapted from R. F. Delderfield's play, and three crime thrillers, *Noose for a Lady*, *Marilyn* and *The Large Rope*. Though B-films, at best they demonstrate an eye for dynamic composition and the creative use of space. Using bold chiaroscuro lighting, *Marilyn* looks like an attempt at an English *The Postman Always Rings Twice*, with Leslie Dwyer, Sandra Dorne and Maxwell Reed forming a satisfyingly parochial wife-husband-lover triangle. American models were also Anglicised in two subsequent thrillers, the lively newspaper story *The Black Rider* and *Stock Car*, a tale of corruption and romance set in the seedy world of stock-car racing.

Rilla made more socially responsible films for Group 3, though without sacrificing the pace and economy of his thrillers. *The End of the Road*, a sensitive study in the problems of old age, is moving rather than maudlin; and the colour A-feature *The Blue Peter*, which recommended outward-bound training to counter juvenile delinquency, never patronises its young subjects. But Rilla's later films of the 1950s – *Pacific Destiny*, a sentimental tale of a novice district officer based on Sir Arthur Grimble's *A Pattern of Islands*; *The Scamp*, a gentle flirtation with social realism;

and *Bachelor of Hearts*, a lightweight romantic comedy about a German student at Cambridge – seemed to epitomise an industry gripped by timidity.

Rilla's talent proved undiminished in *Village of the Damned*, his adaptation of John Wyndham's novel *The Midwich Cuckoos*. He sustains a tense ambivalence between adult paranoias and the frighteningly amoral power of the twelve 'alien' children born simultaneously in a sleepy English village. Unexpectedly evocative, convincingly acted, and resolved with a chilling climax, the film is justifiably regarded now as a science-fiction classic; at the time, however, MGM showed Rilla scant gratitude, bringing in veteran American television director Anton Leader to direct the sequel, *Children of the Damned* (1963).

After two crime films, *Piccadilly Third Stop* and *Cairo*, both compelling studies in corruption and betrayal, Rilla wrote and directed *The World Ten Times Over* (1963). This tale of two nightclub hostesses (played by Sylvia Syms and June Ritchie) unfolds in a deracinated Britain where moral certainties are being eroded by affluence. Neither New Wave realist drama nor exploitation (despite its strip joints, nightclubs and hints of lesbianism), the film puzzled and irritated critics. But Rilla's visual and thematic boldness is refreshing: it is the first film to portray London as a 'swinging' city, and there is no easy condemnation of the new permissive climate: instead the film ends with the two women rejecting men and determining to bring up a baby together.

Rilla's attempt to make an outspoken, modernist film seems to have scuppered his career, though he subsequently wrote scripts for television serials. He did not direct again for a decade, only returning for two sexploitation films in the 1970s: *Secrets of a Door-to-Door Salesman* (1973), which he took over from Jonathan Demme; and *Bedtime with Rosie* (1975), a better-than-average entry with likeable performances from Diana Dors and Una Stubbs. Further attempts to direct came to nothing, but Rilla continued to write crime fiction and guides to film-making (he was an occasional course director at the London Film School), and helped launch the Directors' Guild of Great Britain in 1985 before retiring to run a hotel in France. He died on 19 October 2005. Rilla's best films – powerful, claustrophobic studies in the destructiveness of relationships and the paranoias of small communities – make him a figurer worth reassessing.

(Andrew Spicer)

BIBLIOGRAPHY: 'British Feature Directors: An Index to Their Work', *Sight and Sound*, Autumn 1958, pp. 289–304; Purser Philip, 'Wolf Rilla', *Guardian*, 25 Oct. 2005; Rilla, Wolf, *A–Z of Movie Making* (New York: Viking Press, 1970); Rilla, Wolf, *The Writer and the Screen* (London: W. H. Allen, 1973); Stratton, David, 'Checkout Time', *Variety*, 6–12 June 1994, p. 8.

FILMOGRAPHY: *Noose for a Lady*; *Glad Tidings*; *Marilyn* (aka *Roadhouse Girl*); *The Large Rope* (1953); *The End of the Road*; *The Black Rider* (1954); *Stock Car*; *The Blue Peter* (US: *Navy Heroes*) (1955); *Pacific Destiny* (1956); *The Scamp*; *Bachelor of Hearts* (1957); *Witness in the Dark* (1959); *Die zornigen jungen Männer/ The Angry Young Men* (Ger); *Village of the Damned*; *Jessy* (short); *Piccadilly Third Stop* (1960); *Watch It Sailor!* (1961); *Cairo*; *The World Ten Times Over* (1963); *Symphony in Gold* (doc. short, 1967); *Secrets of a Door-to-Door Salesman* (1973); *Bedtime with Rosie* (1975).

RITCHIE, Aileen

After studying at Glasgow University Aileen Ritchie wrote a number of plays, including *Can Ye Sew Cushions?*, *Shang-a-Lang* and *Asking for It* , before becoming Artistic Director of Clyde Unity Theatre in 1990. She transferred her talents to film after taking a scriptwriting course at the National School of Film and Television. Her directorial debut with the short *Double Nougat* attracted the attention of Uberto Pasolini, producer of *The Full Monty* (Peter Cattaneo, 1997), who asked her to direct *The Closer You Get* with backing from Fox Searchlight.

Bored men in a Donegal village seemingly untouched by the rapid modernisation elsewhere in Ireland attempt to broaden their romantic horizons by inviting glamorous American women to the local festival. Their womenfolk, unsurprisingly, take umbrage and retaliate by flirting with Spanish sailors. One suspects there must have been more originally to William Ivory's script, but only vestiges of his characteristic adventurousness remain – as in the unexpected sexual activity between the glumly virginal tractor driver and the prudish post-mistress. Ritchie's fuzzy direction fluffs any opportunity for poignancy, significance or humour, though she is hardly helped by Rachel Portman's predictable score and the disastrous miscasting of

Liverpudlian Ian Hart in the main part. *The Closer You Get* received short shrift from Irish critics; it was also given the cold shoulder by the British and American audiences who had lapped up the smartly presented Oirish clichés of *Waking Ned* (Kirk Jones, 1998).
(Robert Murphy)

BIBLIOGRAPHY: Power, Paul, 'The Closer You Get', *Film West* no. 40, May 2000, p. 61.

FILMOGRAPHY: *Double Nougat* (short, 1996); *The Closer You Get* (UK/Ir/US, 2000).

RITCHIE, Guy (1968–)

Guy Stuart Ritchie was born in Hatfield, Hertfordshire, on 10 September 1968 and brought up in London. Beginning as a film runner in Wardour Street, Ritchie eventually moved on to make music videos and commercials before writing and directing a short film, *The Hard Case*, which he used to set up financing for his debut feature, *Lock, Stock and Two Smoking Barrels*. Juggling seven separate storylines with great confidence and verve, Ritchie displays a magpie talent, taking inspiration from Peter Collinson's *The Italian Job* (1969) and the ITV series *Minder* (1979–94) to tell a fast-moving tale of East End gangsters and gamblers. The film's delight in gangland slang and its sharp eye for fashion and London locations made it an unexpected box-office success. Ritchie served as executive producer on *Lock, Stock . . .* (2000), a spin-off series of dramas for Channel 4.

Ritchie's follow-up film, *Snatch*, is more of the same on a bigger budget, but it is let down by a super-abundance of plot and big stars it does not know how to handle: Brad Pitt and Benicio Del Toro are often barely recognisable and frequently unintelligible. Although the style is more assured, tedium soon envelops the film's stodgy gallimaufry of a story involving double- and triple-crosses among jewel thieves, gypsies, bare-knuckle fighters and Ritchie's usual coterie of comic gangland figures.

After his marriage to Madonna in 2000, Ritchie worked with his new wife on a remake of *Swept Away* (1974), Lina Wertmüller's tart tale of Marxist and sexual politics. Madonna takes on Mariangela Melato's role of a rich and spoiled woman, on a boating trip, stranded on a Mediterranean island with a deck hand (Andrea Giannini: his father Giancarlo had played the role in the original). Ritchie's version, while faithful in terms of plot and character, strips away Wertmüller's irony and trivialises her dark vision with a musical dream sequence to showcase Madonna's talents. It was withdrawn from release in America after a fortnight and went straight to video in the UK.

Lock, Stock and Two Smoking Barrels was one of the most distinctive and energetic British films of the 1990s; Ritchie's return to the genre with *Revolver* has the virtue of setting off the gangster film on a different tangent, though not one likely to be eagerly embraced by audiences, critics or other film-makers.
(Sergio Angelini)

BIBLIOGRAPHY: Chibnall, Steve, 'Travels in Ladland: The British Gangster Film Cycle, 1998–2001', in Robert Murphy (ed.), *The British Cinema Book*, 2nd edn. (London: BFI, 2001); Dinning, Mark, 'Diamond Geezers', *Empire*, Oct. 2000, pp. 82–91; Fortnum, Ian, 'We Are the Boys', *Neon*, Jan. 1999, pp. 43–52.

FILMOGRAPHY: *The Hard Case* (short, 1995); *Lock, Stock and Two Smoking Barrels* (1998); *Snatch* (2000); *The Hire: Star* (short, US, 2001); *Swept Away* (US, 2002); *Revolver* (UK/Fr, 2005)

RITT, Martin (1914–1990)

Martin Ritt was born on 2 March 1914 in New York City, the son of first-generation Jewish immigrants of Russian and Polish origin. He was educated in North Carolina and briefly studied law in New York before becoming an actor and subsequently a director with the left-wing Theatre of Action and the Group Theatre. Following wartime military service, Ritt directed plays on Broadway and then began directing and acting for live television, a career development cut short by his unofficial blacklisting by the HUAC for his Communist associations. He returned temporarily to the theatre, but after making his first film, *Edge of the City* (UK: *A Man Is Ten Feet Tall*, 1957), he worked exclusively in the cinema.

Ritt's sole British film, an adaptation of John le Carré's *The Spy Who Came in from the Cold*, was made by Salem, the production company he had founded with Paul Newman for *Hud* (1963), for release through Paramount. Filmed largely in Ireland, from a screenplay co-written by the critic Paul Dehn, it is one of the best of the anti-Bond espionage thrillers of the late 1960s. Its plague-on-both-their-houses view of the cold war takes a back seat to a fine study in self-destructive disillusionment by Richard Burton, enhanced by the bleak, wide-angle cinematography of Oswald Morris. The two-and-a-half-minute opening shot estab-

lishing Berlin's Checkpoint Charlie seems deliberately to evoke *Touch of Evil* (Orson Welles, 1958). Ritt died of heart disease in hospital in Santa Monica on 8 December 1990, shortly after completing his final film, *Stanley & Iris* (1990).
(Sheldon Hall)

BIBLIOGRAPHY: Godfrey, Lionel, 'Tall When They're Small', *Films and Filming*, Aug. 1968, pp. 42–8; Jackson, Carlton, *Picking up the Tab: The Life and Movies of Martin Ritt* (Bowling Green, OH: Bowling Green State University Popular Press, 1994); Whitaker, Sheila, *The Films of Martin Ritt* (London: BFI, 1972).

FILMOGRAPHY (UK only): *The Spy Who Came in from the Cold* (1965).

ROBERTS, John

John Roberts made the short film *So What* (1987) before enrolling at the National School of Film and Television, where he directed two shorts, *The Soulful Shack* (1988) and *Say Good-bye* (1989), and gained Channel 4 support for his fifty-minute graduation film *This Boy's Story* (1992), about two brothers who make a pilgrimage to Liverpool to seek out their idol, footballer George Best. David Puttnam entrusted him with Colin Welland's adaptation of Louis Pergaud's French children's novel *War of the Buttons*, transposed to Ireland in the 1970s. The film proved disappointingly uncommercial and Robert's career drifted into the doldrums. But his work as second-unit director on fellow NSFTV student Peter Hewitt's successful adaptation of *The Borrowers* (1997) led to a Hollywood commission to direct *Paulie* (1998), a big-budget DreamWorks comedy about a highly articulate parrot. Though he returned to Britain to direct *Station Jim* (2001), a BBC children's film featuring Queen Victoria (Prunella Scales), a kindly stationmaster (George Cole), steam trains, plucky children and a circus dog, Roberts' future probably lies in Hollywood.
(Robert Murphy)

BIBLIOGRAPHY: Collins, Pat, 'This Boy's Story', *Film West* no. 19, Winter 1994, pp. 22–4; 'First Frames', *Screen International*, 5 June 1992, pp. 10–12.

FILMOGRAPHY: *So What* (short, 1987); *The Soulful Shack* (short, 1988); *Say Good-bye* (short, 1989); *This Boy's Story* (1992); *War of the Buttons* (aka *La Guerre des boutons, ça recommence* UK/Fr, 1994); *The Borrowers* (2nd unit dir., Peter Hewitt, 1997); *Paulie* (US, 1998).

ROBERTS, Steve

Steve Roberts was born in Bishop Auckland, County Durham, on 23 June, probably in the early 1950s. He worked as a director and producer for BBC Television before making his cinema debut with *Sir Henry at Rawlinson End*, a spin-off from Vivian Stanshall's bizarre radio stories and album, financed by record company Charisma. The humour remains primarily verbal, but Trevor Howard gives a grumpily effective last performance as the perpetually drunk Sir Henry ('If I had all the money I've spent on drink, I'd spend it on drink'), and Stanshall is even better as his brother Hubert, whose de-trousered ghost topples the film into a world beyond absurdity. Sequences such as Hubert fishing for submerged barbers in the quiet lake, and the night-time retrousering ritual, have their visual charm, and Roberts works hard to forge an appropriate style.

Subsequently he co-directed *Pumping Up*, a facetious documentary about bodybuilders, but otherwise concentrated on writing. He was one of the creators of Channel 4's *Max Headroom* (1985), and transplanted himself to America, where the show was recreated as a cyberpunk television drama series. Writing assignments on Disney's *The Return of Jafar* (1994) and *Hercules: The Legendary Journeys* (1995) led to him adapting Brian Jacques' *Redwall* series of books about heroic mice and villainous rats into a long-running animated television series. Experience with Stanshall's surreal dialogue no doubt made it easy to tune in to Jacques' Molespeak and Sparra.
(Robert Murphy)

BIBLIOGRAPHY: 'An Interview with Steve Roberts' <members.aol.com/m3may/rwtv/roberts.html>; Randall, Lucian and Chris Welch, *Ginger Geezer* (London: Fourth Estate, 2001).

FILMOGRAPHY: *Sir Henry at Rawlinson End* (1980); *Pumping Up* (doc., co-dir. Mike Adams, 1982).

ROBINS, John (1934–)

John Robins, born in London in 1934, entered the television industry in 1953 and developed into a busy producer, responsible for a BBC adaptation of *Swallows and Amazons* (1963) and the detective series *Thorndyke* (1964). He soon gravitated towards comedy, directing and producing the first nine outings of *The Benny Hill Show* between 1969 and 1972, after which he was recruited by Hammer to make a successful series of television sitcom spin-offs. In *That's Your Funeral* the jokes about rival undertakers are given a topical twist with the introduction of cannabis-filled coffins. *Nearest and Dearest* allows old troupers Jimmy Jewel and Hylda Baker to have fun when they inherit a pickle factory. *Love Thy Neighbour* introduces mother-in-law jokes into this already ideologically dubious attempt at multicultural comedy. *Man About the House* surprisingly fails to take the opportunity to spice up its disarmingly innocent sex-comedy, set among young people in Earl's Court's bedsit land.

Robins then struck out for more adventurous fields, writing the script for Alvin Rakoff's spooky Canadian thriller *Devil Ship* (1980) and directing a teenage sex-comedy in the West Indies, before reversing the spin-off process by directing episodes of the American sitcom *9 to 5* (1986).
(Robert Murphy)

BIBLIOGRAPHY: Falk, Quentin, 'John Robins . . . Spinning off to Better Things', *CinemaTV Today*, 6 Apr. 1974, pp. 12–13.

FILMOGRAPHY: *That's Your Funeral*; *Nearest and Dearest* (1972); *Love Thy Neighbour* (1973); *Man About the House* (1974); *Hot Resort* (US, 1984).

ROBINSON, Bruce (1946–)

Bruce Robinson was born on 2 May 1946 in Broadstairs, Kent. He acted while at school, and trained formally at the Cen-

tral School of Speech and Drama in London. In his third year, he was cast as Benvolio in Franco Zeffirelli's *Romeo and Juliet* (1968). For the next few years he continued his acting career, appearing most notably in Barney Platts-Mills' *Private Road* (1971) and François Truffaut's *L'Histoire d'Adèle H* (1975).

By this time, however, Robinson had developed stronger ambitions as a writer, and after appearing in Carlo Lizzani's *The Kleinhoff Hotel* (1977) largely abandoned acting. His debut as a screenwriter was for Roland Joffé's *The Killing Fields* (1984). This harrowing tale of life in Cambodia under the Khmer Rouge earned Robinson both the BAFTA for Best Adapted Screenplay and an Academy Award nomination. He then wrote and directed *Withnail and I* (1986), a picaresque comedy set at the tail-end of the 1960s, following the misadventures of two out-of-work actors (Richard E. Grant and Paul McGann), who forsake their squalid Camden Town flat for a weekend in the country at a farmhouse owned by Withnail's Uncle Monty (Richard Griffiths). Well received on its release, the film subsequently acquired a strong cult following, particularly among those who shared its irreverently un-nostalgic view of the 1960s.

Robinson's next venture was as writer-director of the vitriolic satirical comedy *How to Get Ahead in Advertising* (1989), again starring Richard E. Grant. Its wholesale attack on 1980s' consumer culture frequently toppled over from satire into rant and the film did less well than the good-humoured *Withnail and I*. Robinson collaborated with Roland Joffé on the script for *Fat Man and Little Boy* (1989), Joffé's film about the creation of the atom bomb, before writing and directing *Jennifer 8* (1992). With Lance Henriksen and Andy Garcia as cops on the trail of a serial killer, Uma Thurman as the blind woman they expect to be the next victim and striking cinematography from veteran cameraman Conrad L. Hall, this might be seen as Robinson's most mainstream film. Nonetheless, it was considered a disappointment by its distributor, Paramount, and released straight-to-video in the UK. Robinson has subsequently written screenplays for Joseph Ruben's *Return to Paradise* (1998) and Neil Jordan's *In Dreams* (1999), but as a director he has yet to recapture the prestige of his debut film.

(Martin Hunt)

BIBLIOGRAPHY: 'Bruce Robinson: *Withnail* Director and Dipso's Delight', *Empire*, Sept. 1995, p. 48; 'Bruce Robinson: Writer/Director', *Empire*, Sept. 1993, pp. 57–8.

FILMOGRAPHY: *Withnail and I* (1986); *How to Get Ahead in Advertising* (1989); *Jennifer 8* (US, 1992).

ROBISON, Arthur (1888–1935)

Arthur Robison's first connection with the British film business came in November 1924, when his 1923 film *Schatten* was released in London at the Tivoli cinema under the title *Warning Shadows*. With its Expressionist lighting and design, lack of subtitles and unity of time and place, *Schatten* startled audiences and critics, establishing Robison's strong but short-lived reputation as a leading light in Germany's art cinema.

Born in Chicago on 25 June 1888 to German parents of Jewish descent, Robison originally trained in medicine. By 1914, after stage experience in Germany and America, he began writing for films in Berlin; his first known film as director, *Nächte des Grauens*, dates from 1916. In *Schatten* Robison fused two separate German traditions – the unified, intimate *Kammerspiel film* and the shadow-driven Expressionist drama – to illuminate a story of raging jealousy. The script had been developed from an idea by his set and costume designer, Albin Grau; throughout Robison's career, designers and photographers exerted a major influence over the visual look of his films. Paul Leni's designs, in particular, contributed much to the texture of the costume drama *Manon Lescaut* (1926).

Robison came to London in 1928 to shoot locations for his Ufa production *Looping the Loop*, a circus drama. He was recruited by British International Pictures, eager to advance its standing by hiring directors of international allure, and assigned Liam O'Flaherty's novel of love and betrayal during the Irish Troubles, *The Informer* (subsequently filmed by John Ford in America). Camerawork by Werner Brandes and Theodor Sparkuhl and sets based on sketches and models by Robert Herlth and Walter Röhrig ensured a claustrophobic, Germanic look. The triangular drama was played out by Lars Hanson, Warwick Ward and Lya de Putti (heroine of *Manon Lescaut*). Robison shot *The Informer* from February to April 1929 as a silent film, but by July he had bowed to the march of time and added talkie sequences, requiring cumbersome dubbed voices for the Hungarian de Putti and the Swedish Hanson. On the talkie version's release in October critics complained, not without reason, that an authentic Irish atmosphere proved elusive. But in both versions, silent and sound, Robison amply maintained the story's suspense, and the film's visual power obviously struck home with John Ford, whose 1935 version bears its clear influence.

The Informer was Robison's only British film. Writing in *The Film Till Now* in 1930, Paul Rotha succinctly expressed the aesthetic problems of BIP's foreign directors: 'They were unable to understand our idea of picture-sense and we were at a loss to interpret their filmic outlook' (p. 317). Yet Robison's filmic outlook experienced equally hard times outside England. Following BIP, he moved to Hollywood and MGM, but was only allowed to direct German- and French-language versions of existing popular dramas like *The Trial of Mary Dugan* (Bayard Veiller, 1929). In 1932, when that work petered out, he returned to work in Germany, winning some commercial success with the romantic drama *Fürst Woronzeff*. He died in Berlin on 20 October 1935, a few weeks after completing a talkie version of *Der Student von Prag*.

(Geoff Brown)

BIBLIOGRAPHY: Bock, Hans-Michael and Werner Sudendorf, 'Arthur Robison', *CineGraph: Lexicon zum deutschsprachigen Film* (Munich: edition text+kritik, 1993, supplement 21); Pedler, Garth, 'Lars Hanson in *The Informer* (1929)', *Classic Images* no. 134, Aug. 1986, pp. c11–13; Rotha, Paul, *The Film Till Now* (London: Spring Books, 1967).

FILMOGRAPHY (UK only): *The Informer* (1929).

ROBSON, Mark (1913–1978)

Mark Robson, the son of a wealthy banker, was born on 4 December 1913 in Montreal and educated in California. He started in the film industry as a property boy, progressed to assistant set dresser at 20th Century-Fox and subsequently became a film librarian at RKO. He assisted Robert Wise in editing Orson Welles' *Citizen Kane* (1941) and *The Magnificent Ambersons* (1942) and as a core member of Val Lewton's production unit edited several films, including *Cat People* (Jacques Tourneur, 1942), before making his directorial debut with *The Seventh Victim* (1943). After four more B-movies with Lewton and several years working for Stanley Kramer and Samuel Goldwyn, Robson began producing his own films, alternating slick entertainments (*Von Ryan's Express*, 1965) with trashy pabulum (*Valley of the Dolls*, 1967).

His first films in Britain were *Hell Below Zero* and *A Prize of Gold*, competent but undistinguished thick-ear thrillers for Warwick Film Productions, and *The Little Hut*, a studio-bound bowdlerisation of a risqué West End drawing-room comedy set on a desert island. *The Inn of the Sixth Happiness*, based on Gladys Aylward's life as a missionary in China but shot partly in Wales, became a huge popular success despite some bizarre casting choices – not least that of tall Swede Ingrid Bergman as the small Englishwoman – and Robson's own pedestrian treatment. *Nine Hours to Rama*, a slow-moving fictionalised account of events leading to the assassination of Mahatma Gandhi, filmed and subsequently banned in India, was less well received.

Robson's last film, *Avalanche Express*, an absurd cold war actioner scripted by Abraham Polonsky, proved ill-fated. Robson suffered a heart attack while on location in Italy and died in a London hospital on 20 June 1978. Two months later its star, Robert Shaw, succumbed to a similar fate. Shooting was completed by cinematographer Jack Cardiff, Shaw's voice was dubbed by Robert Rietty and the film salvaged – though not redeemed – by post-production doctors Monte Hellman and Gene Corman.

(Sheldon Hall)

BIBLIOGRAPHY: 'Mark Robson: Right Place', *Films and Filming*, Mar. 1958, p. 5; Higham, Charles and Joel Greenberg, *The Celluloid Muse: Hollywood Directors Speak* (London: Angus and Robertson, 1969); Peary, Danny, 'Mark Robson Remembers RKO, Welles, & Val Lewton', *The Velvet Light Trap* no. 10, Autumn 1973, pp. 32–7; Robson, Mark, 'Nine Hours of My Life', *Films and Filming*, Nov. 1962, p. 47.

FILMOGRAPHY (UK only): *Hell Below Zero* (1953); *A Prize of Gold* (1955); *The Little Hut* (1957); *The Inn of the Sixth Happiness* (1958); *Nine Hours to Rama* (UK/US, 1963); *Avalanche Express* (Ir/US, 1979).

RODDAM, Franc (1946–)

Franc George Roddam was born on 29 April 1946 in Norton, near Stockton-on-Tees, County Durham. After graduating from the London Film School, he spent two years as an advertising copywriter and producer with the Ogilvy Benson Mather agency before joining the BBC in the early 1970s. He made over twenty films there, most notably *The Family* (1974), a landmark 'fly-on-the-wall' series co-directed with Paul Watson; and *Dummy* (1977) a drama-documentary about a deaf girl drifting into prostitution.

Roddam broke through into feature films with *Quadrophenia* in 1979, directing his own screenplay based on the concept album by rock band The Who, set around the clashes between 'mods' and 'rockers' in mid-1960s' Britain. The film was a major box-office hit, and an important early success in the careers of a generation of English actors, including Phil Daniels, Ray Winstone and Phil Davies; it also launched the screen career of the singer Sting.

The success of *Quadrophenia* brought Roddam Hollywood backing for his next film, *The Lords of Discipline*, a drama of racism in a military academy in the American Deep South of the 1960s, though it was made in England on location at Wellington College, Berkshire. Similarly, *The Bride* (1985), a remake of *The Bride of Frankenstein* (James Whale, 1935), was financed by Columbia but made at Shepperton. Jennifer Beals plays the woman created by Dr Frankenstein (Sting) as a mate for his lonely monster (Clancy Brown), but audiences and critics were confounded by the film's uneven blend of fantasy, horror, romance and feminism. *The Bride* is most enjoyable now for Roddam's casting of an array of eccentrics – David Rappaport, Alexei Sayle, Ken Campbell, Phil Daniels, Quentin Crisp, Veruschka, Timothy Spall – who bring a genuinely bizarre aura to the film.

Roddam contributed a section ('Liebestod') to Don Boyd's portmanteau opera film *Aria* (1987) and finally went to America to make *War Party* (1988), a sympathetic analysis of continuing prejudice against Native Americans that failed to find an audience. He was more successful with his television enterprises. Eschewing directing to act as executive producer, he has been responsible for a number of innovative drama series, including Debbie Horsfield's *Making Out* (1989), Gavin Millar's adaptation of Iain Banks' *The Crow Road* (1996) and a clever contemporary reworking of *The Canterbury Tales* (2003), as well as Stuart Urban's impressive Falklands War film, *An Ungentlemanly Act* (1992). He also gave Dick Clement and Ian La Frenais the idea for *Auf Wiedersehen, Pet* (1983–6), a comedy-drama series about the misadventures of a group of Geordie builders working in Germany, and acted as executive producer on the series' successful revival in 2002.

Roddam's later directing assignments have been more routine. *K2* (1991), a mountain adventure film, was followed by the American television movie *Moby Dick* (1998), and a miniseries, *Cleopatra* (1999), all of which received only a lukewarm response. (Martin Hunt)

BIBLIOGRAPHY: Campbell, Duncan, 'A Rover's Return: Guten Abend, Franc', *Broadcast*, 23 May 1983, pp. 14–15; Gallagher, John, 'Franc Roddam: An Interview', *Films in Review*, May 1983, pp. 297–300; McVicar, John, 'A Geordie in Hollywood', *Time Out* no. 681, 8 Sept. 1983, p. 17.

FILMOGRAPHY: *Birthday* (short, 1969); *Quadrophenia* (1979); *The Lords of Discipline* (US, 1983); *The Bride* (US/UK, 1985); *Aria* ('Liebestod' segment, 1987); *War Party* (US, 1988); *K2* (US/Jap, 1991).

ROEG, Nicolas (1928–)

Nicolas Roeg's films deal in raw emotion, and shake our preconceptions about civilisation and cinema. At the peak of his form he is one of Britain's most adventurous directors. The medium's expressive potential is stretched through a masterly montage of time and space; the films' characters are equally tested, forced into journeys of self-exploration, cut adrift from their usual moral and physical surroundings. None of his best films conform to the normal rules of commercial entertainment; they operate more like experimental visual machines, bent on puncturing human complacency. He has filmed Joseph Conrad's classic novella *Heart of Darkness* (for cable television in 1994) and it was Conrad who uttered what could be Roeg's credo: 'A man who believes he has no illusions has at least that one.'

Roeg was born in London on 15 August 1928. After National Service he joined the film industry as tea-maker and clapper-boy at Marylebone studios, working his way up to camera operator on Ken Hughes' *The Trials of Oscar Wilde* (1960), Fred Zinnemann's *The Sundowners* (1960) and other films; he also contributed to scripts for Cliff Owen (*A Prize of Arms*, 1961) and Lawrence Huntington (*Death Drums along the River*, 1963). However, it was as an inventive cinematographer that Roeg first attracted critical attention, especially on Roger Corman's *The Masque of the Red Death* (1964), François Truffaut's *Fahrenheit 451* (1966) and Richard Lester's *Petulia* (1968). Intriguingly, each of these assignments anticipated aspects of his own feature films. *Petulia* foreshadows the complex time leaps and splintered narratives of Roeg's mature work; while its depiction of 1960s' permissiveness disintegrating into despair and violence finds resonant echoes in *Performance*. *The Masque of the Red Death* features a 'Red Death' figure that re-materialises in a different, even more sinister guise in *Don't Look Now*. The cold, futuristic surface of *Fahrenheit 451* re-emerges in *The Man Who Fell to Earth*, with its penetrating, alien vision of the emptiness of modern life.

Roeg moved into direction in 1968, paired with the painter and writer Donald Cammell on *Performance*, an ambitious film centring on the confrontation between a gangster on the run (James Fox) and a pop idol in retreat (Mick Jagger). Cockney accents, graphic violence, a sympathetic view of London's hallucinatory drug culture and a complex narrative concerned with identity and power proved too heady a brew for Warner Bros. executives and the film's release was delayed for two years. By that time Roeg was in Australia directing and photographing *Walkabout*, his solo debut, a rite-of-passage drama built round the relationship between a teenage Aborigine (David Gulpilil) and two white children (Jenny Agutter and Luc Roeg), who become lost in the Australian desert after their suicidal father tries to kill them. Playwright Edward Bond supplied sinewy dialogue, but nothing could compete with Roeg's startling images of fierce orange suns, lizards and insects, and savage terrain. The film's unique resonance attracted both audiences and critics.

Roeg's biggest success, however, came with *Don't Look Now* (1973), a bizarre supernatural tale, based on a Daphne du Maurier short story. A glamorous, fashionable couple (Julie Christie and Donald Sutherland) are haunted by the accidental drowning of their little daughter. In Venice, where Sutherland's John Baxter is restoring the church of San Nicolo' dei Mendicoli, they attempt to come to terms with their grief: she through faith in two eccentric English mediums, he through the pursuit of an elusive red-hooded figure that seems to resembles his dead daughter. Mystery, tragedy, sensuality and the evocative depiction of decaying Venice as a city of death helped give the film both genuine profundity and popular appeal.

Roeg's subsequent films have been uneven. *The Man Who Fell to Earth* (1976) makes clever use of David Bowie's otherworldly weirdness by casting him as a benign but unhappy alien; but the character's drift into exhaustion and confusion gives the film an unsatisfactory dying fall. *Bad Timing* (1980) is sharper and much more vicious, with convincing performances by Theresa Russell (subsequently Roeg's second wife) as a sensual, sexually liberated young woman and Art Garfunkel as the inhibited psychoanalyst who becomes destructively obsessed with her. Shot in Vienna and Marrakesh, the film is visually remarkable, but the disturbingly frank depiction of cruelty and sexual perversion upset the Rank Organisation, which preferred to lose their substantial investment rather than show the film in their cinemas.

A similar fate awaited *Eureka* (1982), a big-budget film backed by MGM, based on the real-life story of the successful gold prospector Sir Harry Oakes, murdered (most probably by the American Mafia) in 1943. An enthralling beginning in the frostbitten goldfields of the Yukon gives way to languid decadence after Gene Hackman's miner strikes it rich and discovers that fabulous wealth brings disappointment and tragedy. Though Roeg's imagery is fascinating, the visual attractions cannot prevent the story's collapse into an ill-resolved murder mystery.

MGM complained that Roeg had not delivered the film he had promised, and avoided giving it the expected wide release; one can understand their point of view.

Roeg restored his commercial credibility with the more modest *Insignificance* (1985), which imaginatively fantasised an encounter between four post-war American icons, Marilyn Monroe, Albert Einstein, Joe DiMaggio and Joseph McCarthy. It was considered audacious enough to win a Cannes Festival prize, but the originality lay in Terry Johnson's play rather than Roeg's direction, and the film creaks under the weight of philosophical dialogue. *Castaway* (1986), with Oliver Reed and Amanda Donohoe marooned on a desert island, left no such shackles on Roeg's visual exuberance, though pretty settings and excellent performances did little to disguise the thinness of the material. Roeg's last mainstream movie was an adaptation of Roald Dahl's children's story *The Witches* (1989): black, cruel and entertaining enough, but far removed in style and intent from the subtlety and imaginative flair of his other venture into the world of children, *Walkabout*.

Elsewhere, Roeg appeared to drive himself into a cul-de-sac, making films of little public appeal. The unrewardingly eccentric comedy-drama *Track 29* (1988), from a Dennis Potter script originally earmarked for Joseph Losey, was followed by a disappointing adaptation of Brian Moore's novel *Cold Heaven* (1992), unusually dour and dry in its treatment of guilt and paranoia. *Two Deaths* (1995), an oppressive, talky chamber piece about romantic obsession, set in Bucharest as the Ceauşescu government falls, was equally disappointing.

Subsequent features were made for cable television. Roeg's later decline is regrettable; but it has done nothing to dent the potency of his best work, or lessen the inspiration his career has given to younger film-makers like Michael Winterbottom and all cineastes who view cinema as a provocation not a palliative, the ideal medium for shedding light into our own dark places. (Neil Sinyard)

BIBLIOGRAPHY: Hacker, Jonathan and David Price, *Take Ten: Contemporary British Film Directors* (Oxford: Oxford University Press, 1991); Izod, John, *The Films of Nicolas Roeg* (Basingstoke, Hants.: Macmillan, 1992); Salwolke, Scott, *Nicolas Roeg Film by Film* (Jefferson, NC: McFarland, 1993); Sinyard, Neil, *The Films of Nicolas Roeg* (London: Letts, 1991).

FILMOGRAPHY: *Performance* (co-dir. Donald Cammell, 1968; rel. 1970); *Walkabout* (Austral, 1971); *Don't Look Now* (UK/It, 1973); *The Man Who Fell to Earth* (1976); *Bad Timing* (1980); *Eureka* (UK/US,

1982); *Insignificance* (1985); *Castaway* (1986); *Aria* ('Un ballo in maschera' sequence, 1987); *Track 29* (US/UK, 1988); *The Witches* (1989); *Cold Heaven* (US, 1992); *Two Deaths* (1995); *Hotel Paradise* (episode in 'Exotic Tales II', others dir. by Cinzia Torrini and Janusz Majewski, Ger/UK, 1996).

ROGERS, Maclean (1899–1962)

Maclean Rogers was born in Croydon, Surrey, on 13 July 1899. After fighting in the First World War, he used his demob gratuity to go to Hollywood. By the mid-1920s he was back in England, working in the film rental field. In 1929 he began directing for Herbert Wilcox. His first film, a crime drama, *The Third Eye* (1929), which he co-wrote, was followed by three films starring the comedian Sydney Howard, including *The Mayor's Nest* (1932). He also edited early sound films for Wilcox, such as the Aldwych farce *Rookery Nook* (Tom Walls, 1930), and Leslie Henson's first talkie, *A Warm Corner* (Victor Saville, 1930). Some routine thrillers followed but also the occasional sparkling comedy, such as *Summer Lightning* (1933), a well-made adaptation of a P. G. Wodehouse novel. Over the next few years Rogers proved himself to be a very efficient director of B-pictures, several of which he also wrote. By 1939 he had made over forty comedies, dramas and thrillers for Wilcox and the independent producer George Smith.

During the war Rogers concentrated on comedies and farces. *Old Mother Riley Joins Up* (1939) was followed by *Garrison Follies* (1940), and two delightfully boisterous comedies featuring the popular duo Elsie and Doris Waters, *Gert and Daisy Clean Up* and *Gert and Daisy's Weekend* (both 1942). From 1944 Rogers was under contract with British National and directed a variety of dramas and comedies, such as *The Trojan Brothers* (1946), with David Farrar and Bobby Howes as the two ends of a pantomime horse, and the remake of Michael Balcon and Victor Saville's first film, *Woman to Woman* (1947). He also made a series of films with Dinah Sheridan including *Dark Secret* (1949), a remake of his *The Crime at Blossoms* (1933), *The Story of Shirley Yorke* (1948) and *Calling Paul Temple* (1948), the first of three films where she plays Steve, the tough, sensible wife of private detective Paul Temple. John Bentley, who played Temple, returned as 'The Toff', the society sleuth created by John Creasey, in two enjoyable comedy-thrillers, *Salute the Toff* (1952) and *Hammer the Toff* (1952).

Rogers continued to direct until 1960. Most of the films were efficient comedies and thrillers, though he occasionally took on idiosyncratic projects like *Down Among the Z Men* (1952), starring Harry Secombe, Peter Sellers, Spike Milligan and Michael Bentine of the Goons, and a live-action version of *Noddy in Toyland* (1957). Apart from being extremely industrious, Maclean Rogers was fondly remembered by those who knew him. He was a director who would strive to find a part even for a day or two for an actor who had been out of work. 'Few men in his position', wrote E. S. Laurie in his obituary for Rogers, 'could have left behind so many friends and so few enemies.' He died in Harefield, Middlesex, on 4 January 1962.

(Margaret Butler)

BIBLIOGRAPHY: 'British Film Directors: An Index to Their Work', *Sight and Sound*, Autumn 1958, p. 301; Laurie, E. S., Obituary, *Film and TV Technician*, Oct. 1962, p. 174.

FILMOGRAPHY: *The Third Eye* (1929); *The Mayor's Nest* (1932); *Trouble*; *Summer Lightning*; *Up for the Derby*; *The Crime at Blossoms* (1933); *A Wife or Two*; *Virginia's Husband*; *The Scoop*; *It's a Cop*; *The Feathered Serpent* (1934); *The Right Age to Marry*; *Old Faithful*; *Marry the Girl*; *A Little Bit of Bluff* (1935); *Twice Branded*; *A Touch of the Moon*; *To Catch a Thief*; *The Shadow of Mike Emerald*; *Not So Dusty*; *Nothing Like Publicity*; *The Happy Family* (1936); *When the Devil Was Well*; *The Strange Adventures of Mr Smith*; *The Heirloom Mystery*; *Fifty-Shilling Boxer*; *Father Steps Out*; *Farewell to Cinderella*; *Busman's Holiday*; *All That Glitters* (1937); *Why Pick on Me?*; *Romance à la carte*; *Racing Romance*; *Miracles Do Happen*; *Merely Mr Hawkins*; *Paid in Error*; *If I Were Boss*; *His Lordship Regrets*; *Easy Riches*; *Darts Are Trumps*; *Weddings Are Wonderful* (1938); *Shadowed Eyes*; *Old Mother Riley Joins Up*; *His Lordship Goes to Press* (1939); *Garrison Follies* (1940); *Name Rank and Number*; *Gert and Daisy's Weekend*; *Facing the Music* (1941); *Variety Jubilee*; *Gert and Daisy Clean Up*; *Front Line Kids* (1942); *Somewhere in Civvies*; *I'll Walk beside You*; *Heaven Is Round the Corner* (1943); *Give Me the Stars*; *Don Chicago* (1944); *The Trojan Brothers* (1946); *Woman to Woman* (1947); *The Story of Shirley Yorke*; *Calling Paul Temple* (1948); *Dark Secret* (1949); *Paul Temple's Triumph*; *Something in the City* (1950); *Old Mother Riley's Jungle Treasure* (US: *Jungle Treasure*); *Madame Louise* (US: *The Madame Gambles*) (1951); *Paul Temple Returns* (US: *Bombay Waterfront*); *Salute the Toff* (US: *Brighthaven Express*); *Hammer the Toff*; *Flannelfoot*; *Down Among the Z Men*; *Behind the Headlines*

(1952); *Johnny on the Spot*; *Forces' Sweetheart*; *Alf's Baby* (1953); *Not So Dusty*; *Assignment Redhead* (US: *Million Dollar Manhunt*) (1956); *You Pay Your Money*; *Not Wanted on Voyage*; *Noddy in Toyland* (1957); *Mark of the Phoenix* (1958); *Not a Hope in Hell*; *Just Joe* (1960).

ROOKE, Arthur (1876–?)

Around the years 1919–20, Arthur Rooke was a director of ambition and some achievement. Films bore the proud legend 'Produced under the sole direction of Arthur H. Rooke'; he worked regularly with Kenelm Foss and Guy Newall, the period's most sensitive and discerning actor-writer-directors; while critics wrote of his promising individual style, even his 'master hand'. But his reputation was in decline some time before he made his last film in 1928. Only recently, with revivals of one of his Newall features, *The Lure of Crooning Water*, has it started to climb even slightly above zero.

Born in Islington, London, in 1876, Arthur Henry Rooke began his career as a stage actor. He made his name as Wilfred Denver, the man convinced he is a murderer in the Victorian melodrama *The Silver King*, regularly staged around the provinces. By 1915 he was acting in the romances and action-dramas churned out by A. E. Coleby at I. B. Davidson's Leyton studios; in two of them he was featured as John Drew, upstanding detective, facing fire and torture. With *A Pit-Boy's Romance* in 1917 he began directing himself, sharing credit at first with Coleby. The Davidson product came in two shades, the sentimental and the action-packed, and Rooke only varied the formula when he moved on to work with Newall, Foss and producer George Clark on their relatively sophisticated 'Lucky Cat' releases. His first surviving film of merit is *The Garden of Resurrection* (1919), from an E. Temple Thurston novel: tenuous and ridiculous in its plot, but displaying a good feeling for whimsical humour, English scenic beauties, niceties of framing and, in photographer Joe Rosenthal Jr's hands, the emotional possibilities of chiaroscuro. Guy Newall's character of a supposedly ugly misfit seeking love, mostly forlornly, with a discreetly half-caste Ivy Duke found a subtler echo in the team's next film, *The Lure of Crooning Water* (1920). A strong narrative drive was again lacking, but the episodic treatment of the flickering love between Newall's plain farmer and Duke's actress, sent to the country to sedate frazzled nerves, allowed ample room for delicate characterisations, flexible camerawork and an unforced rural atmosphere of genuine charm.

Following Coleby's departure from Davidson in 1921, Rooke returned to his first home, lowered his ambitions and settled in to a run of less elegant features aimed at popular audiences, primarily outside London. The old formulas returned. Three films featured Coleby's acting discovery Victor McLaglen – untypically dressed in top hat and evening wear in Rooke's *The Sport of Kings* (1921), but a master of his fists in the convincing boxing scenes. The *Bioscope* predicted the film would 'be popular in any country where the love of manly sport obtains' (19 January 1922); since it was quickly followed by *A Sporting Double* and *The Sporting Instinct*, this prediction must have come true. Different tones were struck with the pleasing warm comedy of *A Bachelor's Baby* (1922), the Regency period *M'Lord of the White Road* (1923), featuring McLaglen in a dual role, and the fiercely morbid *Eugene Aram* (1924), based on Bulwer Lytton's novel. When a declining market prompted Davidson's company collapse in 1924, Rooke's career collapsed in tandem. He returned to the industry, just at the wrong time, in 1928, directing British Filmcraft's interesting but bad *The Blue Peter*: a film limply visualised, imprisoned in dated attitudes toward race and gender, with a rock-hard Matheson Lang as the mining engineer who comes to regret leaving thrills and spills with African natives for the dullness of a good British marriage. *The Blue Peter* soon became lost in the advances of sound, as did Rooke himself: we hear no more of him, and his death is so far untraced. His 'master hand' may not in the long run have been that strong, but there is enough evidence to suggest a place for him among those directors, post-1918, who tried, however timidly, to penetrate their characters, tell stories visually and push British cinema forward.

(Geoff Brown)

BIBLIOGRAPHY: Gledhill, Christine: *Reframing British Cinema, 1918–1928: Between Restraint and Passion* (London: BFI, 2003); Low, Rachael, *The History of the British Film 1918–1929* (London: George Allen & Unwin, 1971); 'The Garden of Resurrection', *The Bioscope*, 11 Dec. 1919, p. 96; 'The Lure of Crooning Water', National Film Theatre programme notes 2004.

FILMOGRAPHY: *A Pit-Boy's Romance* (co-dir. A. E. Coleby); *The Village Blacksmith* (co-dir. A. E. Coleby); *Holy Orders* (co-dir. A. E. Coleby); *For All Eternity* (co-dir. A. E. Coleby) (1917); *Thelma* (co-dir. A. E. Coleby); *Consequences* (short); *The Rugged Path* (1918); *More Than He Bargained For* (short); *Exceeding the Limit* (short); *Horace Earns a Halo* (short); *Horace's Triumph* (short); *The Double Life of Mr Alfred Burton*; *God's Clay*; *The Garden of Resurrection* (1919); *The Lure of Crooning Water*, *The Mirage*; *Brenda of the Barge* (1920); *The Education of Nicky*; *The Sport of Kings* (1921); *A Bachelor's Baby*; *A Sporting Double*; *The Sporting Instinct*; *Weavers of Fortune* (1922); *The Scandal*; *M'Lord of the White Road* (1923); *Eugene Aram*; *The Wine of Life*; *The Gay Corinthian*; *Nets of Destiny*; *The Diamond Man* (1924); *The Blue Peter* (1928).

ROOME, Alfred (1908–1997)

Born in London on 22 December 1908, the son of the *Daily Mirror*'s managing director, Alfred Wallace Roome began his career in Elstree's property department in 1927. He then moved on to the cutting room, though he also served as assistant camera operator on the first British talkie, *Blackmail* (Alfred Hitchcock, 1929). He made his debut as editor on Tom Walls' screen version of the Aldwych farce *Thark* (1933) and edited several more for the intransigently theatrical Walls. He cut Hitchcock's *The Lady Vanishes* (1938) under R. E. Dearing's supervision, worked on Will Hay's pre-war comedies, edited propaganda shorts during the war, and after the war edited several 'Doctor' comedies and all the 'Carry On' films from 1967 until his retirement in 1975. His editor's filmography is a microcosm of popular British film history.

By comparison, his directing career is meagre – but not negligible. Claiming in 1992 to be 'really a back-room boy by nature', he nevertheless directed two films (assisted by 'dialogue director' Roy Rich) that hold up surprisingly well. *My Brother's Keeper* (1948) charts the fugitive adventures of an old lag (Jack Warner) and a first offender (George Cole) handcuffed together. The world they traverse evinces a strong whiff of post-war tiredness, and Roome elicits sharply observed, unusual vignettes from Jane Hylton and Beatrice Varley as Warner's mistress and wife. His other film is the often wildly funny chase comedy *It's Not Cricket* (1949), starring Maurice Denham as a mad Nazi pursuing a diamond-bearing cricket ball. He married actress Janice Adair, who retired on their marriage. He died in Gerrard's Cross on 19 November 1997.
(Brian McFarlane)

BIBLIOGRAPHY: McFarlane, Brian, *An Autobiography of British Cinema* (London: Methuen, 1997); Murphy, Robert, *Realism and Tinsel: Cinema and Society in Britain 1939–49* (London: Routledge, 1989); Perkins, Roy and Martin Stollery, *British Film Editors: 'The Heart of the Movie'* (London: BFI, 2004).

FILMOGRAPHY: *My Brother's Keeper* (1948); *It's Not Cricket* (1949).

ROSE, Bernard (1960–)

Bernard Rose was born in London in 1960. After graduating from the National Film and Television School in 1983, he directed important early pop videos, including UB40's 'Red Red Wine', Frankie Goes to Hollywood's 'Relax' and Bronski Beat's 'Smalltown Boy'. Though he has two minor features and episodes of the television series *Prospects* (1986) on his CV, he tends to list *Paperhouse* as his debut. Based on Catherine Storr's novel *Marianna Dreams*, this is a powerful horror film for children, with Charlotte Burke as a sulky mid-teen dreaming her way into a landscape that resembles her scrawled drawings.

Rose's career has see-sawed alarmingly, though this perhaps signifies ambitions that take in a willingness to fail. *Chicago Joe and the Showgirl*, a British Second World War couple-on-the-run crime film with Emily Lloyd and Kiefer Sutherland, entirely fails to live up to the potential of its true-life subject, the so-called 'Cleft-Chin' murder; and *Anna Karenina* (which was taken away from the director during post-production) is a stuffy literary adaptation. Far more achieved is the horror film *Candyman*, a Chicago-set take on Clive Barker's Liverpudlian legend 'The Forbidden', which manages the trick of being frightening, psychologically apt and socially relevant without seeming strained. *Immortal Beloved*, a Beethoven biopic with Gary Oldman throwing furniture out of hotel rooms like a rock star, sprawls but has inspired moments. Rose's best work to date is *ivansxtc.*, a DV-shot Hollywood insider take on Tolstoy's story 'The Death of Ivan Illych' starring Danny Huston as a dying agent at sea among Californian sharks.
(Kim Newman)

BIBLIOGRAPHY: Jones, Alan, '*Paperhouse*: British Fantasy is a Thinking Man's Nightmare', *Cinefantastique*, Mar. 1989, pp. 13, 57; MacCabe, Colin, 'More Things in Heaven and Earth', *Sight and Sound*, Mar. 1993, pp. 22–4.

FILMOGRAPHY: *Smart Money* (1986); *Body Contact* (1987); *Paperhouse* (1988); *Chicago Joe and the Showgirl* (1990); *Candyman* (US); *Immortal Beloved* (US) (1992); *Anna Karenina* (US, 1997); *ivansxtc.* (aka *To Live and Die in Hollywood*) (US, 2000); *Snuff* (aka *Snuff-Movie*, UK/Romania, 2005).

ROSMER, Milton (1881–1971)

A notable stage and screen actor, Milton Rosmer was born Arthur Milton Lunt to theatrical parents in Southport, Lancashire, on 4 November 1881. Educated at Manchester Grammar School, he made his stage debut in 1899 and his screen debut in 1913, when he also commenced stage direction. Distinguished screen roles included Lord Windermere in *Lady Windermere's Fan* (Fred Paul, 1916) and Heathcliff in Ideal's *Wuthering Heights* (A. V. Bramble, 1920). By the time talkies arrived, he was settling into character parts and, increasingly, directing: between 1928 and 1937 he directed, or co-directed, fifteen features, chiefly for Gaumont-British or British International Pictures.

Rosmer's primary concern was the stage and his forte was working with actors. But among his varied output – there are historical films, comedies and melodramas – his willingness to share the task of directing sometimes resulted in very satisfying films. German director F. W. Kraemer and his fellow technicians probably provided the filmic imagination in *Dreyfus* (1931), but Rosmer is more likely to have coaxed Sir Cedric Hardwicke to give his fine performance (his first for cinema) as the wronged French officer. *The Great Barrier* (1937), about the building of the Canadian-Pacific railway, co-directed with Geoffrey Barkas, and *The Challenge* (1938), about the conquest of the Matterhorn, co-directed with Luis Trenker, boast less impressive performances, but in the pinched context of late-1930s' British cinema they remain refreshingly ambitious films.

On his own Rosmer happily relied on stage traditions in *P.C. Josser*, one of the period's numerous vehicles for Sunderland comedian Ernie Lotinger. In the blood-curdling melodrama *Maria Marten; or, The Murder in the Red Barn*, the first of Tod Slaughter's cinema excursions, the actors are pointedly introduced to the audience from a theatre stage, and Slaughter is given every encouragement to display his villainy to the gallery. But elsewhere Rosmer shows himself by no means stage-bound. In *The Guv'nor* (1935) he sets George Arliss' more restrained performance against a background of outdoor realism; while *Channel Crossing* (1933), a tale of murder and intrigue on a cross-Channel ferry, creates a frighteningly atmospheric environment. *After the Ball* (1932), a diverting remake of *Opernredoute* (Max Neufeld, 1931), showed him equally at home adapting German musical comedy.

The slump in film production in the late 1930s brought Rosmer's directorial career to an end, but he continued to act in films, television and on the stage into the 1950s. The man who was Heathcliff now played judges, magistrates and other authority figures – most memorably as Professor Mair, the bumbling head of the research unit in *The Small Back Room* (Powell and Pressburger, 1949). Rosmer's career as a film director may have been only an interlude in his long working life as an actor, but it is an interesting one. He was married to the stage and film actress Irene Rooke, and died in Chesham, Buckinghamshire, on 7 December 1971.

(James C. Robertson)

BIBLIOGRAPHY: 'Milton Rosmer', in Freda Gaye (ed.), *Who's Who in the Theatre*, 14th edn. (London: Pitman Publishing, 1967); Obituary, *Daily Telegraph*, 7 Dec. 1971.

FILMOGRAPHY: *Cash on Delivery* (short); *The Woman Juror* (short) (1926); *Balaclava* (co-dir. Maurice Elvey, 1928); *P. C. Josser*; *Dreyfus* (co-dir. F. W. Kraemer); *The Perfect Lady* (co-dir. Frederick Jackson); *Many Waters* (1931); *After the Ball* (1932); *Channel Crossing* (1933); *The Secret of the Loch*; *What Happened to Harkness* (1934); *Emil and the Detectives*; *Maria Marten; or, The Murder in the Red Barn*; *The Guv'nor* (US: *Mister Hobo*) (1935); *Everything Is Thunder* (1936); *The Great Barrier* (US: *Silent Barriers*, co-dir. Geoffrey Barkas, 1937); *The Challenge* (co-dir. Luis Trenker, 1938).

ROSS, Benjamin (1964–)

Benjamin Ross was born in north London in 1964 and after leaving St Catherine's College, Oxford, won a scholarship to Columbia University's film school in New York, where he studied under Emir Kusturica. On returning to England, he made a short film for Channel 4, *My Little Eye* (1992), before making his feature debut with *The Young Poisoner's Handbook*, a black comedy about a teenage psychopath based on the real-life case of Graham Young, 'The St Albans Poisoner'. Relocated to Neasden in the seedy suburbs of north-west London, the film recreates a pre-Swinging London, and presents its homicidal protagonist with a degree of sympathy. Hugh O'Conor gives an unsettling, blank-faced performance as Young, an outsider alienated both at home and at school, whose lack of empathy with those around him renders his relatives and friends mere research material. Though sympathetically reviewed, *The Young Poisoner's Handbook* made little impact at the box office, but its amoral wit has helped it to acquire a cult following subsequently.

Ross subsequently directed *RKO 281* (1999), an American television film about the making of *Citizen Kane* (Orson Welles, 1941), but his career in Britain seems jinxed. *Simon Magus* (1999), which Ross was slated to direct, was passed over to Ben Hopkins; *Jack Sheppard and Jonathan Wilde* was abandoned on the eve of shooting when its financial support collapsed; and *Deathwatch* (2003), a supernatural tale set in the First World War trenches, was switched from Ross to the writer of the screenplay, Michael J. Bassett. He returned with *Torte Bluma*, a short film about the relationship between the commandant of the Treblinka concentration camp and his Jewish cook.

(Daniel O'Brien)

BIBLIOGRAPHY: Collis, Clark, 'The Young Director's Handbook', *Empire*, Oct. 1995, pp. 72–3; Salisbury, Mark, 'Raising Kane', *American Cinematography*, Oct. 1999, pp. 82–90.

FILMOGRAPHY: *My Little Eye* (short, 1992); *The Battle of Barmouth Bay* (short, 1993); *The Young Poisoner's Handbook* (1994); *Torte Bluma* (short, UK/US, 2005).

ROSS, Herbert (1927–2001)

Herbert David Ross, the son of a postal worker, was born in Brooklyn on 13 May 1927 and grew up in Miami. After playing Shakespeare in small-town repertory he became a dancer, choreographer and director on Broadway for the American Ballet Theatre and on television. For the cinema he choreographed Otto Preminger's *Carmen Jones* (1954) and, in Britain, *The Young Ones* (Sidney J. Furie, 1961), *Summer Holiday* (Peter Yates, 1963) and *Doctor Dolittle* (Richard Fleischer, 1967). His direction of the musical sequences in *Funny Girl* (William Wyler, 1968) was followed by his first full directorial assignment, MGM's remake of James Hilton's *Goodbye, Mr Chips*, scripted by Terence Rattigan. Perhaps the most cruelly underrated of all the late-1960s big-budget musical roadshows, it was a critical and commercial disaster, but arguably improves on Sam Wood's more celebrated 1939 version. The performances of Peter O'Toole and Petula Clark achieve great warmth and tenderness and it remains one of Ross' best films, despite having only one traditional production number: most of Leslie Bricusse's original score is sung in voiceover.

The bulk of Ross' subsequent work is blandly glossy light entertainment, often with a theatrical basis. His clumsily handled adaptation of Nicholas Meyer's Conan Doyle pastiche *The Seven-Per-Cent Solution*, which brings together Sherlock Holmes and Sigmund Freud to purely gimmicky effect, suffers some of the worst miscasting in Holmesian history, with Nicol Williamson as a gibbering, neurotic sleuth and a marble-mouthed Robert Duvall as Dr Watson. *Nijinsky* is a stolid biopic, more concerned with Alan Bates' Diaghilev than its dancer subject (George De La Peña) and with backstage politicking than ballet. Ross' last completed film was *Boys on the Side* (1995). He died of heart failure in New York on 9 October 2001.

(Sheldon Hall)

BIBLIOGRAPHY: Gelatt, Roland, 'At Long Last, *Nijinsky*', *American Film*, Dec. 1979, pp. 18–23; Laffel, Jeff, 'Forgotten Beauties', *Films in Review*, Nov./Dec. 1992, pp. 362–7; Ross, Herbert, 'Choreographers Make Good Film Directors', *Films and Filming*, Sept. 1969, p. 52; Zito, Stephen, 'The Rise of Herbert Ross', *American Film*, Nov. 1978, pp. 35–9.

FILMOGRAPHY (UK only): *Goodbye, Mr Chips* (1969); *The Seven-Per-Cent Solution* (US/UK, 1976); *Nijinsky* (US/UK, 1980).

ROSSO, Franco (1941–)

Franco Rosso was born in Turin in 1941 and came to live in London at the age of nine. He entered the Camberwell School of Art before going on to study film at the Royal College of Art

in the late 1960s. He was editor on Horace Ové's documentary *Reggae* (1970), and in 1973 directed *The Mangrove Nine*, a defence of the nine black youths blamed for the Notting Hill riots of 1970. He then made *Dread, Beat an' Blood*, a forty-five-minute documentary about the Jamaican poet Linton Kwesi Johnson, who had become an important cultural figure among London's black community. This led to Rosso's first feature film, *Babylon*, the story of a disaffected black youth who dreams of winning a contest as a reggae disc jockey. The film, which was shot in Deptford, south-east London, cost £300,000, funded mainly by the National Film Finance Corporation and the Chrysalis music company. It was well received, but like most British political film-makers in the 1980s, Rosso found few opportunities to build on his success. He turned to television, where he was able to pursue racial themes in the BBC children's drama *The Bride* (1983) and musical ones in *Ian Dury* (aka *Spasticus or Autisticus*, 1983).

In 1985 Rosso won backing from Channel 4 and the BFI Production Board for *Sixty-Four Day Hero: A Boxer's Tale*, a feature-length documentary about the black British boxer Randolph Turpin, who became a popular hero after he defeated the World Middleweight Champion Sugar Ray Robinson in July 1951, but committed suicide in 1966. Three years later Rosso made a second feature film, *The Nature of the Beast*, which combined a political story of mill closures and poverty with a boy's obsession about a rampaging beast out on the moors. It lacked the poignancy and intensity of *Kes* (Ken Loach, 1969) – which Rosso had worked on as an assistant editor – and failed to find a market. Rosso explored radical political themes more successfully as producer of the Channel 4 serial *Centrepoint* (Piers Haggard, 1990), which juxtaposes the materialistic world of the late 1980s with a mystery set during the seismic events in Paris in May 1968.
(Simon Brown)

BIBLIOGRAPHY: Korte, Barbara and Claudia Sternberg. *Bidding for the Mainstream? Black and Asian British Film since the 1990s* (Amsterdam and New York: Rodopi, 2004); Wrathall, John, 'Francly Speaking', *City Limits*, 24 Nov. 1988, p. 29.

FILMOGRAPHY: *Rainbows Are Insured against Old Age* (short, 1967); *Dream Weaver* (short, 1968); *The Mangrove Nine* (doc. short, 1973); *Dread, Beat an' Blood* (doc., 1978); *Babylon* (1980); *Sixty-Four Day Hero: A Boxer's Tale* (doc., 1985); *The Nature of the Beast* (1988).

ROTH, Cy (1912–)

Cy Roth was born Seymour Roth in Chicago on 16 March 1912. A writer, producer and director with abundant experience in action and thick-ear B-movies and television, he came to Britain in 1956 to propagate the bottom-of-the-barrel science-fiction fantasy *Fire Maidens from Outer Space*. Roth's film, set on Jupiter's thirteenth moon, lacks the lunatic charm of America's Edward D. Wood Jr at his best, or worst. But a cult movie reputation has still developed, spearheaded no doubt by the sixteen fire maidens undulating before their sacred fires, and amplified by Borodin's *Polovtsian Dances*, which dominates Roth's soundtrack. Harry Fowler and Sydney Tafler, among the suitably awed Earthmen, seem a long way from cockney London; so does Susan Shaw, sadly on her way down from stardom as fire maiden number one. Following production, Roth quickly returned to America.
(Geoff Brown)

FILMOGRAPHY (UK only): *Fire Maidens from Outer Space* (1956).

ROTH, Tim (1961–)

Tim Roth was born in London on 14 May 1961. Best known as an actor, he came to prominence in two key films: Alan Clarke's *Made in Britain* (1983), in which he gives an extraordinary performance as the violent neo-fascist skinhead Trevor, and Mike Leigh's *Meantime* (1983), where he plays the socially awkward Colin. In the 1990s Roth moved to Hollywood, where he made an impact as the fatally wounded undercover agent in Quentin Tarantino's *Reservoir Dogs* (1992) and the luckless Pumpkin in *Pulp Fiction* (1994). Roth utilised his high profile within mainstream Hollywood to make *The War Zone* (1999), a highly personal film, which draws more on European art-house conventions than on commercial American cinema.

A bleak drama set in an isolated, rain-drenched part of Devon, *The War Zone* concerns a family who live in fear of the father who verbally and physically mistreats them, and who is revealed to be having an incestuous relationship with his daughter. Like his friend Gary Oldman in his debut feature *Nil by Mouth* (1997), Roth casts Ray Winstone as the abusive father, though Winstone's working-class inadequate in *Nil by Mouth* is very different from his sinister middle-class counterpart in *The War Zone*. Roth moves away from the British social-realist tradition Oldman's film had embraced, and *The War Zone*, carefully composed and imbued with stillness, puzzled British critics and audiences. Nevertheless, with its unsettlingly lush visuals and aura of stifled corruption, Roth's directorial debut is a valuable contribution to British cinema.
(Jamie Sexton)

BIBLIOGRAPHY: Danielson, Shane, 'Welcome to My Nightmare', *Sight and Sound*, Aug. 1999, pp. 8–10; Pride, Ray, 'My Generation', *Filmmaker*, Autumn 1999, pp. 62–8.

FILMOGRAPHY: *The War Zone* (UK/It, 1999).

ROTHA, Paul (1907–1984)

Paul Rotha, one of the most fiery of Britain's documentary talents, was born in London on 3 June 1907. In 1924, aged seventeen, he entered the Slade School of Fine Art to study design and graphics and a year later won an award for costume design at the Paris International Theatre Exhibition. Told by his professor that he would never succeed with his birth name, Paul Thompson, he changed his name to Paul Rotha.

In 1928, keen to get into the film business, Rotha took his portfolio of set designs to British International Pictures at Elstree Studios. He was offered work in the props department and rose to become an assistant art director before being fired for writing an article in *Film Weekly* bemoaning the lack of creative set design in British films. Within a few months of leaving BIP he was commissioned to write *The Film Till Now*, published in 1930; the first English-language history of silent and sound cinema, the book firmly established Rotha's reputation as a film intellectual. The following year he met John Grierson and Basil Wright and began making promotional films for the Empire Marketing Board Film Unit. However, Rotha's maverick and uncompromising nature, which was to characterise his role in the documentary movement, led to conflicts with Grierson and he was again dismissed.

Rotha returned briefly to the feature industry to work as an art director; he also wrote several scripts with Miles Mander, including Maurice Elvey's remake of *The Lodger* (1932). He went back to documentary in 1932 when Jack Beddington, Head of Publicity at Shell-Mex and BP, secured him a commission for his first major film, *Contact* (1933), made at British Instructional for Imperial Airways on the theme of air travel opening up the world. The abbreviated released version offers a chilly but rhythmically brisk assemblage of titles and shots illustrating the planning of an air route, the construction of an aeroplane and the resulting flights across the world. For all the practical difficulties encountered, Rotha's talent for didactic image-making shone clearly enough. *Contact* was praised for its clarity of exposition and lyrical editing, and pointed the way for others in the fledgling documentary movement to make sponsored films. Rotha's next significant project was *Shipyard* (1935), a powerful two-reeler that deftly blends the nuts and bolts of building a liner at Barrow-in-Furness with an acute awareness of the ship's impact on the depressed local economy. One of the first documentaries to display a strong social conscience, *Shipyard* clearly demonstrated the difference between Grierson's realist documentary tradition and Rotha's more socio-political concerns; a division equally apparent in his next film, *The Face of Britain* (1935), sponsored by the Central Electricity Board, where the clean glories of an electrified Britain pale in impact beside the smoke and slag of the Industrial Revolution and the appalling living and working conditions of the working class.

In 1935 Rotha joined the Strand Film Unit, a new independent documentary company, as Director of Productions. His socialist beliefs are reflected in many of the films he produced there, including *Today We Live* (Ralph Bond/Ruby Grierson, 1937), *Here is the Land* (Stanley Hawes, 1937) and the collaborative *Peace of Britain* (1936). For this three-minute compilation short, Rotha edited together library footage, stills and interviews advocating international peace and opposing public expenditure on rearmament; the British Board of Film Censorship continually delayed granting a certificate, but the film, distributed for free, was still widely shown. In 1938 Rotha returned to directing at the Realist Film Unit, winning a commission through Grierson's Film Centre, a liaison body between the documentary units and potential sponsors. The unexpected result was *New Worlds for Old* (1938), made for the Gas Council, a laboriously impish comedy about the pros and cons of gas and electricity. Rather more skill and feeling was expended on *The Fourth Estate*, an elaborate portrait of *The Times* newspaper (not Rotha's natural reading matter), finally completed in January 1940, but relegated to the vaults by its sponsor for unclear reasons. The film only emerged in the public eye in 1970.

For all the brilliance of individual sequences, Rotha's documentaries to date bore scars of the running battles between his own film-making ambitions and the restrictions imposed by both sponsors and subject matter. But working conditions improved in the Second World War and its aftermath. Rotha advised the Ministry of Information on the use of propaganda films, and in 1941 formed Paul Rotha Productions, producing the cinemagazine *Worker and Warfront* as well as numerous films for the civilian war effort and Britain's post-war reconstruction. Two of his most famous films were made in this period: *World of Plenty* (1943) and *Land of Promise* (1945), both illustrating Rotha's didactic aims with cinematic dexterity. Packed with Isotype diagrams, facts, library material and talking heads, *World of Plenty* investigated the problem of world hunger, contrasting the situation before and during the war and advocating the need for a post-war World Food Plan. The seventy-minute *Land of Promise*, made by Rotha's new production company, Films of Fact, stirred the same ingredients with greater urgency and passion as it surveyed pre-war slum housing and the prospect of post-war reconstruction improving the lives of the poor with a planned economy. *The World Is Rich* (1947), offered another but more congested plea for a global solution to the problem of world hunger. *World Without End* (1953), filmed with units in Mexico and Thailand and co-directed with Basil Wright, broke with the compilation style, but maintained the same thematic concerns, highlighting the work of the United Nations in underdeveloped nations.

Between 1953 and 1955, Rotha was Head of the BBC's documentary department, where he furthered his socio-economic explorations, commissioning a series on world problems, *The World Is Ours*, before BBC bureaucracy intervened. He also intermittently returned to fiction film-making, directing three features, each in their own way idiosyncratic. *No Resting Place* (1951) was made on a limited budget but benefits hugely from a rumbustious Irish cast including Noel Purcell, Jack MacGowran and Maureen O'Sullivan, among whom Michael Gough acquits himself well enough as a tinker on the run for murder. The unusual realism of the film, shot almost entirely on location by Wolfgang Suschitsky, makes it something of a landmark in British cinema. *Cat and Mouse* (1958), a thriller about an American deserter (Lee Patterson) caught up in blackmail and murder, is more conventional, but shows Rotha handling genre material with more ease than most documentary directors. The most ambitious, and the closest to Rotha's documentary background, is *De Overval/The Silent Raid* (1962), a Dutch film about a raid on a Nazi prison in Leeuwarden that liberated fifty Dutch prisoners. Rotha skilfully recreates the oppressive atmosphere of occupied Holland and, helped by surviving members of the Resistance, reconstructs the raid itself with startling authenticity.

By the mid-1960s Rotha's practical film-making career was at an end. But his energies remained, and he returned to writing, stirring old controversies with *Documentary Diary* (1973), a personal memoir of the documentary movement in the 1930s. A biography of Robert Flaherty, long-planned, emerged ten years later, shortly before his death in Wallingford, Oxfordshire, on 7 March 1984. Always a combative figure, Rotha's ambition and talent may have been only intermittently fulfilled in his own films, but through his cinema work and writing he still exerted a powerful influence on the documentary movement and British film culture.

(Sarah Easen)

BIBLIOGRAPHY: Aitken, Ian (ed.), *The Documentary Film Movement: An Anthology* (Edinburgh: Edinburgh University Press, 1998); Haggith, Toby, *Castles in the Air: British Films and the Reconstruction of the Built Environment 1939–1951* (London: I. B. Tauris, 2004); Low, Rachael, *Documentary and Educational Films of the 1930s* (London: George Allen & Unwin, 1979); Marris, Paul (ed.), *Paul Rotha* (London: BFI, 1982); Petrie, Duncan and Robert Kruger (eds), *A Paul Rotha Reader* (Exeter: University of Exeter Press, 1999); Rotha, Paul, *Documentary Film*, 3rd edn (London: Faber and Faber, 1952); Rotha, Paul, *Rotha on the Film: A Selection of Writings about the Cinema* (London: Faber and Faber, 1958); Rotha, Paul, *The Film Till Now*, revised edn (London: Spring Books, 1967); Rotha, Paul, *Documentary Diary: An Informal History of the British Documentary Film, 1928–1939* (London: Secker and Warburg, 1973); Sussex, Elizabeth, *The Rise and Fall of British Documentary* (Berkeley and London: University of California Press, 1975); Swann, Paul, *The British Documentary Film Movement, 1926–1946* (New York: Cambridge University Press, 1989).

FILMOGRAPHY: Documentaries: *Contact*; *Roadwards* (1933); *Rising Tide*; *Steel* (1934); *Shipyard*; *The Face of Britain* (1935); *Death on the Road*; *Peace of Britain* (aka *The Peace Film*); *Power in the Highlands* (1936); *New Worlds for Old* (assoc. dir. Frank Sainsbury, 1938); *The Fourth Estate*; *Mr Borland Thinks Again* (1940); *They Speak for Themselves* (1942); *Total War in Britain* (1945); *World of Plenty* (assoc. dir. Yvonne Fletcher, 1943); *Land of Promise* (assoc. dir. Francis Gysin, 1946); *A City Speaks*; *The World Is Rich* (assoc. dir. Michael Orrom) (1947); *World Without End* (co-dir. Basil Wright, 1953); *Cradle of Genius* (1959); *Das Leben von Adolf Hitler/The Life of Adolf Hitler* (Ger, 1961).

Features: *No Resting Place* (1951); *Cat and Mouse* (aka *The Desperate Men*, 1958); *De Overval/The Silent Raid* (Neth, 1962).

ROTHEROE, Dom (1964–)

Dom Rotheroe was born on 24 April 1964. After studying photography, film and video at the Harrow campus of the University of Westminster he set up W.O.W. Productions with Carl Schönfeld and took a Hi 8 camera to Bosnia, where he shot *A Sarajevo Diary* (1993) with a budget of £1,000. Channel 4 bought the film and sent him back to make *Sarajevo – from Bad to Worse* (1993). More television documentaries in dangerous places followed, including *Blockade* (1996), a sympathetic portrait of the freedom fighters of East Timor, and *The Coconut Revolution* (2000), about the struggle for independence in Bougainville, the largest of the Solomon Islands.

His first feature, *My Brother Tom* (2001), was developed over a six-year period with fellow Harrow student Alison Beeton-Hilder, and shot on digital video by Robby Müller. Rotheroe's improvisational style fits the exploration of the tentative but eventually obsessive love affair between a kindly middle-class girl and a feral, sexually abused boy; though he is less assured in providing a convincing social framework for their story. Made on a small budget, the film had little exposure in cinemas but was well received at festivals, and marks a bold and original debut. (Robert Murphy)

BIBLIOGRAPHY: Calhoun, David, 'Britain as You've Never Seen It Before', *Observer* Review Section, 14 Sept. 2000, pp. 8–9; Freedman, Andrew, 'Interview with Dom Rotheroe', <www.netribution.co.uk/features/interviews/2001/dom_rotheroe/1.html>.

FILMOGRAPHY: *Gents* (short, 1990); *A Sarajevo Diary* (doc., 1993); *Trip – A Mythology* (short, 1995); *The Stick Up* (short, 1999); *My Brother Tom* (UK/Ger, 2001).

ROWLES, Kenneth F. (1945–)

Kenneth F. Rowles was born in Chesham, Buckinghamshire, in 1945, and entered the film industry as a runner at Merton Park Studios when he was sixteen. He trained as an editor and progressed from sponsored films such as *Calf Conservation* (Simon Campbell-Jones, 1966) and *Spot Heating* (Chris Rowley, 1967) to Jean-Luc Godard's *One Plus One/Sympathy for the Devil* (1968). In the late 1960s he went on location in Europe, producing and co-directing *Go Girl*, a television pilot centred on an adventurous go-go dancer in Spain; and producing Peter Sykes' *Venom* (1971), an odd concoction involving Nazis, nerve gas, spiders and a spider woman, written by Chris Wicking and Derek and Donald Ford, and filmed in Bavaria.

The Ups and Downs of a Handyman (John Sealey, 1975), which Rowles produced, was a more straightforward sex-comedy, but weirdness crept back in his own *Take an Easy Ride*, a forty-four-minute pseudo-documentary packed with stories about the perils of hitch-hiking. An innocuous short, *The Perils of Mandy*, followed in 1981, but respectability descended with *Tribute to Her Majesty* (1986), made to celebrate Queen Elizabeth's sixtieth birthday, and *Creature Comforts* (1991), a documentary about James Herriot. A French thriller – *Torment* – announced in the early 1990s failed to materialise. Rowles is vice-chairman of the producer and directors' section of the trade union BECTU.

(Robert Murphy)

BIBLIOGRAPHY: McGillivray, David, *Doing Rude Things: The History of the British Sex Film, 1957–81* (London: Sun Tavern Fields, 1992); Sheridan, Simon, *Keeping the British End Up: Four Decades of Saucy Cinema*, 2nd edn (London: Reynolds & Hearn, 2005).

FILMOGRAPHY: *Go Girl* (short, co-dir. Steven Collins, 1970); *Take an Easy Ride* (1976); *The Perils of Mandy* (short, 1981); *Tribute to Her Majesty* (doc., 1986); *Creature Comforts* (doc., 1991).

RUGGLES, Wesley (1889–1972)

Wesley Ruggles was born in Los Angeles on 11 June 1889, the younger brother of comic actor Charles Ruggles. Ruggles himself started out on the stage, and made his film debut in 1914 as one of the Keystone Kops; he acted in Chaplin's Essanay shorts, and turned director in 1917. Hollywood respectability was won with his epic drama of frontier life, *Cimarron*, chosen as Best Picture at the 1931 Academy Awards; in a different vein, he also directed the lubricious and definitive Mae West vehicle *I'm No Angel* (1933). By the early 1940s Ruggles was profitably directing Clark Gable and Lana Turner at MGM, and came to Britain in 1943 to work on the studio's British ventures with Korda, including *Perfect Strangers*. Once filming started, disagreements spread, and Korda himself took over direction. J. Arthur Rank then offered Ruggles a poisoned chalice: a chance to direct a British anomaly, a Technicolor musical pumped up with American consumption in mind, designed as a showcase for music-hall comedian Sid Field, who had recently become a major West End star. Though inexperienced at musicals, Ruggles was given wide control over *London Town* (1946), writing the story as well as producing; up to a million pounds was spent endeavouring to make the film work, a feat of extravagance rivalling Rank's support for Gabriel Pascal's *Caesar and Cleopatra*. Running over two hours, *London Town* suffers from a clichéd script about hard-won showbiz success, handled by Ruggles with little flair. On the plus side, the film preserves five of Field's best-known routines; relative newcomers Petula Clark and Kay Kendall also enjoyed useful exposure. On both sides of the Atlantic Ruggles' musical proved a critical and commercial flop; America only saw it in 1953, seriously shortened, and retitled *My Heart Goes Crazy*. Ruggles returned to Hollywood, but he had lost his footing in the industry, and never made another film. He died in Santa Monica on 9 January 1972.

(Geoff Brown and Daniel O'Brien)

BIBLIOGRAPHY: Huntley, John, *British Film Music* (London: Skelton Robinson, 1947); Macnab, Geoffrey, *J. Arthur Rank and the British Film Industry* (London: Routledge, 1993); 'Obituary: Wesley Ruggles', *The Times*, 11 Jan. 1972; 'Wesley Ruggles, Director, Dead; His *Cimarron* Won Oscar in '31', *Classic Film Collector*, Spring 1972, p. x-2; Winnington, Richard, *Drawn and Quartered* (London: The Saturn Press, 1948).

FILMOGRAPHY (UK only): *London Town* (1946).

RUMLEY, Simon (c. 1969–)

Simon Rumley was born in Tunbridge Wells around 1969. After completing a law degree he worked as a runner for a Soho post-production house while writing scripts and making short films. His first feature, *Strong Language* (1998), was made on a budget raised from friends when the finance for his film about the early 1990s' clubbing scene, *Club Le Monde*, fell through. Sixteen people in their twenties talk about sex, clubbing, debt, politics and the Brit-Pop phenomenon, while a more shadowy figure tells a tragic story about love, rape, suicide and murder that finally involves all the other characters. Witty, enlightening and unusual, the film was acquired for distribution by the BFI and showcased at the National Film Theatre.

After failing to win Arts Council backing for *Club Le Monde*, Rumley teamed up with Lottery assessor and producer Piers

Jackson to make *The Truth Game* (2001). Three couples, each with their problems, meet for a dinner party that disastrously veers off course as hostility, secrets and deceptions spill out. Rumley is no Chekhov, and his characters can seem irritatingly trivial; but he is adept at capturing their uncomfortable interaction through body language and gesture, camera movement and framing as much as dialogue, and the film is full of humorous and perceptive moments.

Club Le Monde, now the third part of the trilogy, was shot on Super-16 for around £500,000, and emerged in 2002, though it is set at the height of the clubbing scene in 1993. Without the macabre undertones of *Strong Language* and *The Truth Game*, the film is curiously sweet and soft-centred. Frothy working-class girls, naive public schoolboys, comical eccentrics, star-crossed young lovers: both characters and ethos have hardly changed from the well-meaning social-realist films of the 1950s; even the cynical club-owner turns out to be a lovable rogue. *Club Le Monde* is less innovative than its companions, but Rumley shows considerable aplomb in juggling between his thirty-two characters. These three unique films have all reached big enough audiences to allow them to retrieve their tiny budgets: a praiseworthy achievement.

(Robert Murphy)

BIBLIOGRAPHY: Dawson, Tom, 'The Truth Game', *Total Film*, Apr. 2000, p. 131; Hammond, Wally, 'Mouthing Off', *Time Out*, 26 Feb. 2000, p. 70; NFT audiotape interview with Nigel Floyd, 28 Jan. 2000, held at the BFI National Library, London; 'Simon Rumley', *Close Up Film* <www.close-upfilm.com/features/Kent/simon-rumley.htm>.

FILMOGRAPHY: *Laughter* (short, 1995); *Thon* (short, 1996); *Strong Language* (1998); *The Truth Game* (2001); *Club Le Monde* (2002).

RUSSELL, Erica (1951–)

Erica Russell's animations proclaim the pleasures of sinuous, sensuous human bodies moving in time to African-influenced melodies and rhythms in an explosion of kinaesthetic delight scarcely seen in British cinema since Len Lye's abstract films of the 1930s. Like Lye himself, Russell was born in New Zealand (Auckland, in 1951); like Lye, any formal art training took second place to the experience and stimulus of tribal art. Where Lye drew on Asian and Polynesian influences, Russell found inspiration at first hand in folk traditions absorbed in South Africa, where her childhood was spent after 1953. In 1971 at the age of twenty she arrived in London, where she claimed she saw her first television set. Avoiding art school, she eventually joined Richard Williams' animation studio, where she assisted the Disney veteran Art Babbitt; assignments on projects with Gerald Scarfe and Paul Vester followed. Her own animation style began to crystallise at Rocky Morton's Cucumber Studios, where she worked with Morton and Annabel Jankel on pop videos and television material before launching her first personal venture, *Feet of Song* (1988), completed with funds from Channel 4.

This four-minute animation, synchronised to music by Charlie Hart, firmly established the material and core style for subsequent films. The stylised bodies, with warm earth colours and thrusting thighs predominant, suggest a fusion of African tribal art and Russian Constructivist design. Russell's visual/aural ballet is gentler, less abstract, than Lye's creations, though the imagery's sexual exuberance is clear: the director's reward perhaps for a childhood spent in a repressive society. In 1992 she formed her own company, Gingco: two further dance animations have since emerged between commercial work. The eight-minute *Triangle* (1994) extends the celebration of body movement with a wider kaleidoscope of rhythm and design, and a greater dramatic thrust. A man and a woman's dance relationship becomes disturbed by the introduction of a third character, identified by Russell as a shamaness, but in the final seconds a new harmony is reached, with shapes and genders fused. *Soma* (2001) completes the trilogy, and widens the visual component further with elements of graffiti art. The simple joy of Russell's films clearly distinguishes her work from much contemporary British animation, a joy reflecting her unfettered delight in human movement and the act of creation. Though her own work is clearly fired by African heat, when asked in 1995 by the *Mail on Sunday* why Britain excelled at animation Russell pointed, only partly in jest, to the English weather: 'Animation is a good medium for a cold climate. It gives you an excuse to sit in a warm, cosy room and simply draw away.'

(Geoff Brown)

BIBLIOGRAPHY: Beard, Steve, 'Erica Russell's Cartoon Capers', *Mail on Sunday* You Magazine, 18 Feb. 1996, p. 13; Faber, Liz and Helen Walters, *Animation Unlimited: Innovative Short Films since 1940* (London: Laurence King Publishing, 2004); Kotlarz, Irene, '*Feet of Song*', *Sight and Sound*, Nov. 1992, p. 57; Pilling, Jayne (ed.), *Women and Animation: A Compendium* (London: BFI Exhibition & Distribution Division, 1992).

FILMOGRAPHY: *Feet of Song* (1988); *Triangle* (1994); *Soma* (2001).

RUSSELL, Ken (1927–)

Ken Russell was born in Southampton on 3 July 1927. After serving in the merchant navy and the RAF, he worked as an actor and dancer and in the 1950s became a successful freelance photographer. His short films *Peepshow* (1956) and *Amelia and the Angel* (1957) won him admission to the BBC, where he made several documentaries for the arts programme *Monitor*. His *Elgar* (1962) brought him national attention and the chance to direct his first feature film, *French Dressing* (1963), a seaside farce starring James Booth and Roy Kinnear. It proved insufficiently popular to sustain Russell's cinema career and he went back to television to make an economical adaptation of *The Diary of a Nobody* (1964) and a series of highly original dramatised documentaries – *Bartok* (1964), *The Debussy Film* (1965) *Always on Sunday* (1965), and *Isadora* (1966).

Russell returned to the cinema to make *Billion Dollar Brain* (1967), the third of the Len Deighton spy films for Harry Saltzman starring Michael Caine as Harry Palmer. Cinema audiences were unprepared for Russell's stylish excess – his recreation of the Battle on the Ice from Eisenstein's *Alexander Nevsky* (1938), for example – and *Billion Dollar Brain* was less successful than its predecessors. Russell went back once again to the BBC and made two of his best dramatised documentaries, *Dante's Inferno* (1967) and *Song of Summer* (1968), before finally establishing himself as a cinema director with *Women in Love* (1969). Russell's rough vitality fits well with D. H. Lawrence's exploration of sexuality and there is more than 1960s' modishness in the way in which Jennie Linden, Alan Bates and even more Glenda Jackson and Oliver Reed recreate Lawrence's driven young people.

There was more controversy over Russell's next film, *The Music Lovers* (1970), which dwelt as much upon the troubled sex life of Tchaikovsky (Richard Chamberlain) and his wife (Glenda Jackson) as it did upon his music-making. Odd casting (Chamberlain was still best known for playing the pleasantly bland Dr Kildare) and a meandering storyline made it less satisfying than *Women in Love*, but Russell's boldness and visual inventiveness remained undiminished. His next film, *The Devils* (1971), took that boldness to extremes and, along with Peckinpah's *Straw Dogs* (1971) and Kubrick's *A Clockwork Orange* (1971), was taken as a sign that permissiveness had gone too far. The sensationalist combination of sexual activity and religious iconography that Russell had pioneered in *Dante's Inferno* was deemed too offensive to be allowed to be seen uncensored. But the film is a plea for tolerance and freedom, both personal and political, and marks the high point of Russell's cinema career.

In the same year, Russell completed a very different film, *The Boy Friend*, an extravagant adaptation of Sandy Wilson's musical in the style of the Busby Berkeley musicals of the 1930s. *Savage Messiah* (1972) a life of the artist Gaudier-Brzeska, and *Mahler* (1974) seemed to return Russell to the sort of subject he had made his name with in television, and hardly seemed to break new ground. His appetite for excess found a suitable outlet in his highly successful film of Pete Townshend's rock opera *Tommy* (1975), but since then Russell has found it difficult to recapture his former creativity. *Lisztomania* (1975) and *Valentino* (1977) seem like parodies of his earlier artist films. His two American films, *Altered States* (1980) and *Crimes of Passion* (1984), show a broadening of his concerns, but he returned to baroque excess with *Gothic* (1986) and *The Lair of the White Worm* (1988), and much later *The Fall of the House of Usher* (2001). His adaptations of D. H. Lawrence's *The Rainbow* (1988) and *Lady Chatterley's Lover* (1993) are competent rather than inspired, though he acts the part of Lady Chatterley's raffish father with great panache.

Russell's career is disappointing in the sense that he failed to continue the creative momentum of his earlier years, but the revival of some of his BBC films on DVD has displayed what a remarkable talent he possessed and what an impressive body of work he produced.

(Pamela Church Gibson)

BIBLIOGRAPHY: Atkins, Thomas R., *Ken Russell* (New York: Monarch Press, 1976); Baxter, John, *Ken Russell – An Appalling Talent* (London: Michael Joseph, 1973); Grant, Barry Keith, 'The Body Politic: Ken Russell in the Eighties', in Lester Friedman (ed.), *Fires Were Started: British Cinema and Thatcherism* (Minneapolis: University of Minnesota Press, 1993); Hake, Ken, *Ken Russell's Films* (Metuchen, NJ and London: Scarecrow Press, 1980); Phillips, Gene D., *Ken Russell* (New Jersey and London: ASU Presses, 1999); Russell, Ken, *Altered States* (New York: Bantam, 1991); Russell, Ken, *The Lion Roars* (London: Faber and Faber, 1994); Wilson, Colin, *Ken Russell: A Director in Search of a Hero* (London: Intergroup, 1979).

FILMOGRAPHY: *Peepshow* (short, 1956); *Amelia and the Angel* (short, 1957); *French Dressing* (1963); *Billion Dollar Brain* (1967); *Women in Love* (1969); *The Music Lovers* (1970); *The Devils*; *The Boy Friend* (1971); *Savage Messiah* (1972); *Mahler* (1974); *Tommy*; *Lisztomania* (1975); *Valentino* (1977); *Altered States* (US, 1980); *Crimes of Passion* (US, 1984); *Gothic* (1986); *Aria* ('Nessun dorma' episode, 1987); *The Lair of the White Worm*; *Salome's Last Dance*; *The Rainbow* (1988); *Whore* (1991); *Tales of Erotica* ('The Insatiable Mrs Kirsch' episode, 1996); *Lion's Mouth* (short, 2000); *The Fall of the House of Usher* (2001).

RYAN, Terence (1948–)

Terence Ryan was born in London on 2 March 1948. After studying at the London Film School he made sponsored films for the Salvation Army and the Cheshire Homes Society, progressed to health and sports documentaries, and in the early 1980s moved into television to direct Jasper Carrott comedy shows. He made his feature debut with the Canadian-financed *Going Home* (1987), a well-researched, factually based story about Canadian soldiers impatiently waiting for demobilisation long after the First World War is over. It appears not to have received theatrical distribution in the UK; *Hold My Hand, I'm Dying*, a South African feature starring Christopher Cazenove and Oliver Reed, which followed in 1989, also eluded British audiences.

Ryan produced Eric Sykes' forty-five-minute silent comedy *The Big Freeze* (1994) and *Superstars of Soccer* for BskyB while writing his feature *The Brylcreem Boys*, the fascinating story of German and British servicemen held in a prisoner-of-war camp in neutral Ireland during the Second World War. Unfortunately, the interesting conflicts set up between the various nationalities degenerate into a glutinous triangular romance between the Canadian hero (Bill Campbell), a spirited, flame-haired colleen (Jean Butler) and an aristocratic Messerschmitt pilot (Angus Macfadyen). Painstakingly accurate details about uniforms, songs and passbooks fail to compensate for the woodenly modern acting of Campbell and Butler, and Ryan lets his story meander far too freely to generate any dramatic excitement.

Another Irish film, *Puckoon*, based on Spike Milligan's 1963 comic novel, followed in 2002. Ryan assembles an impressively talented cast, and directs with economy and restraint. But it proved impossible to make what seemed hilarious on the page even mildly funny on the screen, where the story – about a village divided down the middle by the boundary commission that set the border between Northern Ireland and the Irish Free State – seems silly rather than sharply satirical. No doubt Milligan's enduring popularity encouraged the financial participation of the Northern Irish Film Commission, the Arts Council of Northern Ireland and the Irish Film Board, but no one seems to have considered whether there was any overlap between easily pleased Milligan fans and the cinema audience. Ryan sought shelter from hostile critical reaction directing episodes of *Crossroads* for television.

(Robert Murphy)

FILMOGRAPHY: *Date* (short, co-dirs. Peter Browne/Carlos Castellanos/Pierre Gaudry/Norman Mackay/Kevin Marsland/Paul Turtle, 1970); *Achill Island* (doc. short); *A Need to be Loved* (doc. short) (1972) *Total Economy Drive* (doc. short); *A Place Called Home* (doc. short) (1975); *Focus on Football* (doc. series, 1978); *Immunisation* (doc. series, 1980); *Focus on Rugby* (doc. series, 1983); *To the North of Katmandu* (short, 1986); *Going Home* (aka *Soldats en transit*, Can, 1987); *Hold My Hand, I'm Dying* (aka *Blind Justice*, SA, 1989); *The Brylcreem Boys* (1996; rel. 1998); *Puckoon* (Ir/UK/Ger, 2002).

ST PAUL, Stuart (1954–)

Stuart St Paul was born in Walthamstow, north-east London, in 1954. After spending a year at Sussex University he left to work as a radio presenter. By the late 1970s he had moved on to become a stuntman, initially in television (where he organised the air crash that facilitated a wholesale cast change in *Emmerdale*), later on big-budget films such as *Aliens* (James Cameron, 1986) and *Batman* (Tim Burton, 1989). His organisational skills and general competence brought him additional responsibilities as a popular second-unit director.

St Paul's first film as director, *The Usual Children* (1996), won prizes at festivals but appears not to have been shown in Britain. In 1998 he directed *The Scarlet Tunic*, a low-budget adaptation of a Thomas Hardy story. Making a virtue of necessity he shot the film entirely on location, much of it outdoors and at night, allowing firelight and moonlight to contribute an atmospheric moodiness in place of the brightly lit interiors of more traditional costume dramas. His second-unit experience ensures that even the minor characters get due attention; and the central performances of Jean-Marc Barr as the melancholy German hussar, caught in the clutches of the British Army though the war he joined up for is over, and Emma Fielding as a country landowner's daughter torn between the passion of romantic love and the satisfactions of a prosperous marriage, are particularly effective. St Paul never quite gets the measure of his heroine, and the tragic climax brought about by her vacillation lurches into melodrama; but the film remains likeably out-of-the-ordinary.

St Paul attracted sympathetic publicity for his attempt to bypass the usual channels and distribute the film himself, holding the premiere in Dorchester. Beyond Dorset, audiences were harder to come by, indifferent to a film without major stars and an expensive marketing campaign. He tried again with *Devil's Gate* (2003), a Shetlands-set triangular romance pursued under the disapproving gaze of crotchety old crofter Tom Bell, before returning to second-unit work.

(Robert Murphy)

BIBLIOGRAPHY: Brett, Anwar, 'Stunts to Scarlet', *Exposure*, Spring 1998, p. 24; Falk, Quentin, 'Trusting Your Instinct: An Interview with Malcolm McLean', *Exposure*, Spring 2002, pp. 2–3; 'St Paul Converted', *Time Out*, 10 June 1998, p. 74.

FILMOGRAPHY: *The Krays* (2nd unit dir., Peter Medak, 1990); *De Johnsons* (2nd unit dir., Rudolf van den Berg, Neth); *Shadowchaser* (2nd unit dir., John Eyres, US) (1992); *The Usual Children* (1996); *Passion in the Desert* (2nd unit dir., uncredited, Lavinia Currier, US); *An American Werewolf in Paris* (2nd unit dir., Anthony Waller, US/UK/Lux/Neth/Fr); *The Scarlet Tunic* (1997); *Devil's Gate* (2003); *Spirit Trap* (2nd unit dir., David Smith, 2004); *On a Clear Day* (2nd unit dir., Gaby Dellal, 2005).

SAMUELSON, G. B. (1889–1947)

George Berthold (Bertie) Samuelson was born on 6 July 1889 in Southport, Lancashire. After some success in exhibition and distribution he entered production with a feature film of the life of Queen Victoria. *Sixty Years a Queen* (1913), produced by Will Barker and distributed by Samuelson, was a considerable success and led him to open a studio at Worton Hall, Isleworth, in 1914. The first production was the Sherlock Holmes drama *A Study in Scarlet*, directed by George Pearson, and it was followed by four years of modest hits for the Samuelson Film Company. Samuelson's directors after Pearson included Alexander Butler and Fred Paul; he directed few titles himself until late in his career.

An ebullient, optimistic figure, Samuelson's response to the wretched state of the British post-war film business was to take a company to Hollywood and make six features, though the shoddy results let down the boldness of the initiative. His fearlessness led to controversial British productions on venereal disease in *Damaged Goods* (Alexander Butler, 1919) and birth control in *Married Love* (aka *Maisie's Marriage*, Alexander Butler, 1923). Samuelson's film career was set back with the disastrous production of *She* (Leander de Cordover, 1925), and he was made personally bankrupt. He resurfaced to direct several 'quota quickies' in the early 1930s, but died in obscurity in Staffordshire on 24 April 1947. His sons, however, and their offspring after them, have ensured that the Samuelson name has remained an important one in British film-making to this day.

(Luke McKernan)

BIBLIOGRAPHY: Dunham, Harold and David Samuelson, *Bertie: The Life and Times of G. B. Samuelson* (unpublished biography, 1989–96) held in the BFI National Library, London.

FILMOGRAPHY: *Little Women*; *In Another Girl's Shoes* (1917); *The Way of an Eagle*; *The Admirable Crichton* (1918); *Convict 99*; *The Bridal Chair* (1919); *At the Mercy of Tiberius*; *The Winning Goal*; *Her Story* (1920); *The Game of Life*; *The Faithful Heart* (1922); *I Pagliacci*; *Afterglow* (1923); *Motherland*; *Two Little Drummer Boys* (1927); *The Forger*, *For Valour* (1928); *Over the Sticks*; *La canción del día/Song of the Day* (co-dir. J. Samuelson, Sp); *Spanish Eyes*; *Souls in Pawn*; *The Valley of Ghosts* (1930); *Inquest*; *Jealousy*; *The Other Woman*; *The Wickham Mystery* (1931); *The Callbox Mystery*; *Collision*; *Threads* (1932); *The Ace of Trouble*; *An Affair of the Heart*; *The Crucifix*; *The Delusion*; *The End of the Act*; *The Greatest of These*; *The Green Leather Note Case*; *Husbands Are So Jealous*; *Jade*; *Lipsky's Christmas Dinner*, *Off the Scent*; *Spoils*; *Spotting*; *A Touching Story* (1934).

SANGSTER, Jimmy (1924–)

Jimmy Sangster was born in London on 2 December 1924. He entered the film industry in the late 1940s as an assistant director for Hammer Films. After working his way up to production management, he moved into screenwriting with *X the Unknown* (Leslie Norman, 1956). Sangster went on to write most of the classic Hammer horrors of the late 1950s and early 60s for director Terence Fisher, including *The Curse of Frankenstein* (1957), *Dracula* (1958) and *The Mummy* (1959). As a writer-producer, he also initiated Hammer's cycle of psychological thrillers with *Taste of Fear* (Seth Holt, 1961).

Although Sangster's main contribution to British cinema is as a writer, he did direct three films in the 1970s. *The Horror of Frankenstein*, Hammer's attempt to update the Frankenstein cycle, is a plodding affair enlivened only by Ralph Bates' performance as Frankenstein. *Fear in the Night* is an effective psychological thriller of the type that Sangster himself had helped to create but does not add much to the formula. Best of the three is *Lust for a Vampire*, a follow-up to the lesbian vampire film *The Vampire Lovers* (Roy Ward Baker, 1971); the project had been intended for Terence Fisher but illness forced him to withdraw. Though the film was much maligned by critics, Sangster's direction successfully conjures up an atmosphere of sensual decadence, notably in the scene where Ralph Bates abases himself before the vampiric Yutte Stensgaard.

Since the early 1970s Sangster has worked mainly in the United States, although he did contribute to the screenplay for the British horror film *The Legacy* (Richard Marquand, 1978).

(Peter Hutchings)

BIBLIOGRAPHY: Sangster, Jimmy, *Do You Want It Good or Tuesday? From Hammer Films to Hollywood* (Baltimore, MD: Midnight Marquee

Press, 1997); Sangster, Jimmy, *Inside Hammer* (Richmond, Surrey: Reynolds & Hearn, 2003).

FILMOGRAPHY: *The Horror of Frankenstein* (1970); *Lust for a Vampire* (1971); *Fear in the Night* (1972).

SANKOFA

The Sankofa Film and Video Collective was formed in 1983 by Martina Attille, Maureen Blackwood, Robert Crusz, Isaac Julien and Nadine Marsh-Edwards, who met while studying media and visual arts at colleges in London. Under the aegis of the ACTT Workshop Declaration, Sankofa was funded by, among others, the Greater London Council and the British Film Institute. The term Sankofa refers to looking back to the past in order to understand who one is in the present. (The West African phrase, literally translated, is 'it is not taboo to go back and fetch what you forgot'.) As such it calls to mind the themes of remembrance, cultural identity and belonging that resonate throughout all of Sankofa's films. They are particularly evident in the experimental and allusive style of their radical documentary *Territories* and their feature-length *The Passion of Remembrance*, a densely woven tapestry interweaving a narrative drama about a young black woman with archive footage and stylised, didactic speakers in a barren landscape. The intention, as Attille puts it, is to 'make people remember things that we choose to forget. . . putting the different footage together forces people to make the connections' (Jackson and Rasenberger).

(Paul Ward)

BIBLIOGRAPHY: Jackson, Lynne and Jean Rasenberger, '*The Passion of Remembrance*: An Interview with Martina Attille and Isaac Julien', *Cinéaste* vol. 16 no. 4, 1988, p. 23; Pines, Jim, '*Territories*: An Interview with Isaac Julien', *Framework* nos 26/7, 1985, pp. 2–9.

FILMOGRAPHY: *Who Killed Colin Roach?* (1983); *Territories* (1985); *The Passion of Remembrance* (1986); *This Is Not an AIDS Advert* (1987); *Looking for Langston*; *Dreaming Rivers*; *Perfect Image?* (1988); *Young Soul Rebels* (1991); *A Family Called Abrew* (1992); *Home Away from Home* (1994).

(*Looking for Langston* and *Young Soul Rebels* are discussed in the entry on Isaac Julien; *The Passion of Remembrance* and *Dreaming Rivers* in the entry for Maureen Blackwood.)

SARNE, Mike (1939–)

In the interview book *Talking Pictures* the director of *Myra Breckinridge* reveals an unlikely mentor in film-making: Basil Dearden. Michael Sarne, born 6 August 1939 in London, began in films as an actor, though he found greater fame singing pop songs: in 1962 his first single, 'Come Outside', topped the British charts. Dearden, who cast him in *A Place to Go* (1963) as a Bethnal Green lad in trouble, encouraged Sarne to explore film-making techniques. After limbering up with still photography and commercials, he launched himself as a director in 1965 with *Road to Saint Tropez*, a thirty-minute short billed as 'the first ever Anti-Travelogue'.

Christian Doermer and Genvieve Waite enjoy party life in Swinging London: *Joanna* (Mike Sarne, 1968)

From the beginning Sarne's subject was youth, and in the 1960s he tackled it with a directness and fury generally unmatched by older directors. In *Saint Tropez*, Sarne's stylistic japes had only the slimmest plot to decorate; but with *Joanna* (1968), vividly photographed by Walter Lassally, Swinging London and the fortunes of a Chelsea art student provided the perfect background for Sarne's freewheeling flourishes and social insights.

Keen to champion young film-makers, 20th Century-Fox's new President Richard Zanuck brought Sarne to Hollywood to direct *Myra Breckinridge* (1970), based on Gore Vidal's outrageous novel about an American transsexual on an avenging rampage. 'Everything you've heard about *Myra Breckinridge* is true', the advertisements proclaimed. Most reports were negative, fuelled by the film's dishevelled manner, though Mae West's comeback role as a lecherous agent deservedly received approval.

After the *Myra* controversy Sarne picked up work as an actor, and his directing career entered a long eclipse. *The Punk*, released as *The Punk and the Princess* in 1994, showed him briefly back in full control, hurtling a hand-held camera around Notting Hill in a spirited, even touching, variation on *Romeo and Juliet*. Sarne deliberately picked the bulk of his technical crew from young film school graduates, and later collaborated with three of them on their own debut feature, *Glastonbury the Movie*. Sarne has since returned to acting, and a life on the industry's fringes.

(Geoff Brown)

BIBLIOGRAPHY: Jones, Graham, 'Mike Sarne', in Lucy Johnson (ed.), *Talking Pictures: Interviews with Contemporary British Film-*

Makers (London: BFI, 1997); Sarne, Mike, 'For Love of Myra', *Films and Filming*, Feb. 1971, pp. 26–7.

FILMOGRAPHY: *Road to Saint Tropez* (short, 1966); *Joanna* (1968); *Myra Breckinridge* (1970); *Intimidade/Intimacy* (co. dir. Perry Salles, 1975); *From Stags to Stardust* (add. sequences, James C. Katz, 1977); *The Punk/The Punk and the Princess* (1994); *Roland: A Knight in the Big Apple* (1995); *Glastonbury the Movie* (add. sequences, co-dirs. Robin Mahoney/Matthew Salkeld/William Beaton/Lisa Lake, 1996).

SAROSSY, Paul (1963–)

Paul Sarossy was born in Barrie, Ontario, on 24 April 1963. After acting as cinematographer on a number of distinguished films, notably Denys Arcand's *Love and Human Remains* (1993) and Atom Egoyan's *The Sweet Hereafter* (1997) and *Felicia's Journey* (1999), he directed a metaphysical drama, *Mr In-Between*, about an unhappy contract killer whose accidental meeting with an old school friend makes him realise how much he yearns for a mundane, non-violent life. Stylish direction, an original plot and fine acting – particularly from the scarily convincing Andrew Howard as the killer and David Calder as his tattooed mentor – make this an interesting debut. But the violence is more compelling than the metaphysics, and the horribly bleak ending offers little in the way of enlightenment, let alone enjoyment. *Mr In-Between* did well at film festivals but suffered a delayed and limited cinema release. Sarossy returned to cinematography on John Duigan's *Head in the Clouds* (2004), Egoyan's *Where the Truth Lies* (2005) and Sam Millar's *The River King* (2005). He is married to the actress Geraldine O'Rawe, who played the diminutive but enticing heroine in *Mr In-Between*.

(Robert Murphy)

BIBLIOGRAPHY: Probst, Chris, 'Big Moments on the Small Screen: Paul Sarossy', *American Cinematographer*, May 1996, pp. 70–86.

FILMOGRAPHY: *Mr In-Between* (2001; rel. 2003).

SASDY, Peter (1933–)

Peter Sasdy was born in Budapest, Hungary, on 27 May 1933. He left his homeland following the 1956 uprising and began his career in British television in the early 1960s, where he became closely associated with the fantasy series *Out of the Unknown* (1965–71). He was then recruited by Hammer in their search for new directors to replace the ageing Terence Fisher. Much was promised by his stylish debut feature, *Taste the Blood of Dracula*, a tale of the vampiric violence and sexual havoc provoked by a degenerate aristocrat who unwisely arouses the bloodthirsty Count from his unquiet grave. Sasdy's subsequent two films gave further evidence of his ability to revive the genre. *Countess Dracula* harnessed its horror imagery (the Countess bathing in the blood of murdered virgins) to a powerful idea (the fear of ageing and the yearning for eternal youth and beauty), and built to an extraordinary finale in which a wedding ceremony goes hideously wrong. As the Countess, Ingrid Pitt gave arguably her finest screen performance. No less remarkable was *Hands of the Ripper*, in which a Freudian psychologist (Eric Porter)

uncovers but also unleashes the violent urges of Jack the Ripper's daughter (Angharad Rees). As with *Countess Dracula*, the gory generic ingredients were meaningfully transformed to support a thoughtful, powerfully acted and even poignant tale about a doomed main character leading a tormented double life and inadvertently bringing destruction on the man she loves. The finale is again striking, uniting hero and heroine in a redemptive double death scene, played out against the setting of the Whispering Gallery of St Paul's Cathedral, with part of Verdi's Requiem as soundtrack accompaniment.

Despite these signs of new growth, British horror seemed set towards irreversible decline. Sasdy resisted the trend with *Nothing but the Night*, an eerie thriller predating *The Exorcist* (William Friedkin, 1973) and *The Omen* (Richard Donner, 1976) in its concern with demonically possessed children; and *Doomwatch*, a prescient ecological disaster film, based on a successful television series. But his last horror film, *I Don't Want to Be Born*, featuring Joan Collins as a pampered wife whose past life as a stripper returns to haunt her in the form of a murderous, immensely strong baby, proved too ludicrous even for Sasdy to make exciting. His later films, the science-fiction Western *Welcome to Blood City* (1977) and *The Lonely Lady* (1982), based on a novel by Harold Robbins, look like poorly conceived afterthoughts.

Fortunately Sasdy was able to pursue a more fruitful career in television. *The Stone Tape* (1972) a convincingly scary ghost story written by Nigel Kneale, is his most impressive achievement, but he also showed undiminished flair in his dashing contributions to the *Hammer House of Mystery and Suspense* series, and the television film *Sherlock Holmes and the Leading Lady* (1991), featuring Christopher Lee as Holmes and Patrick Macnee as Watson. Away from fiction, he took a refreshingly personal approach to fellow Hungarian Alexander Korda in a two-part documentary *'I Don't Grow on Trees'* (1993). Sasdy's sheer versatility in the medium – his television subjects range from King Arthur to Adrian Mole – makes it easy to overlook his unique and original talent.

(Neil Sinyard)

BIBLIOGRAPHY: Cumbow, Robert C., 'Pictures on the Walls of the House of Hammer', *Film Comment*, May/June 1992, pp. 51–3; Kinsey, Wayne, 'Hammer – The Directors: Peter Sasdy', *The House That Hammer Built* no. 11, Mar. 1999, p. 125; Murphy, Mike, 'The Team behind the Screams', *Dark Terrors*, Oct./Dec. 1993, pp. 9–19; Pirie, David, 'New Blood', *Sight and Sound*, Spring 1971, pp. 73–5.

FILMOGRAPHY: *Taste the Blood of Dracula*; *Countess Dracula* (1970); *Hands of the Ripper* (1971); *Nothing But the Night*; *Doomwatch* (1972); *I Don't Want to Be Born* (1975); *Welcome to Blood City* (Can/UK, 1977); *The Lonely Lady* (US, 1982).

SAUNDERS, Charles (1904–1997)

Born in Paddington, London, on 8 April 1904, Charles Joel Saunders had a long and prolific film career. Educated at the progressive school Bedales, he joined Ideal Films in 1927 and became assistant director on the weekly *Ideal Cinemagazine*. Saunders worked as assistant director and editor throughout the 1930s, having stints as editor at Gaumont-British (1935–7, 1940–2) and Ealing (1938–40), cutting such films as *The Guv'nor* (Milton Rosmer, 1935) and *Young Man's Fancy* (Robert Stevenson, 1939). In 1942 he became editor at Two Cities where he cut Leslie Howard's propaganda piece *The Gentle Sex* (1943) and with Bernard Miles co-wrote and co-directed the charming rural comedy *Tawny Pipit*. Decades later Miles gave Saunders major credit for its success.

Saunders then ceased editing and directed nearly forty B-movies, some of them more than routinely entertaining. In 1930 he had directed (and produced and written) a long-forgotten comedy, *No Exit*, for Warners; but his director's career really began at Rank's Highbury Studios in the late 1940s, where he was entrusted with the daft comedy *Trouble in the Air*, in which a sleepy village is invaded by radio people, and the good-humoured family comedy-drama *Fly Away Peter*. *One Wild Oat* (1951), a hectic farce derived from the stage, was his only near-brush with A-features, and it is now only remembered for Audrey Hepburn's first film appearance.

In the 1950s he collaborated with producer Guido Coen on fast-moving thrillers, using competent second-string actors and making economical use of settings, whether in studios or conveniently available locations. In *Black Orchid* a sexual triangle is complicated by murder, marriage laws and a Mrs Danvers-like housekeeper. *One Jump Ahead* and *Behind the Headlines* are smartly paced comedy-thrillers, both starring Canadian Paul Carpenter, swapping quips with police, other reporters and smart women (Diane Hart and Adrienne Corri respectively). In *There's Always a Thursday*, experienced players such as Charles Victor and Marjorie Rhodes, and some nice visual touches, like the identically dressed businessmen emerging from their gateways at the same time each morning (a metonym for an about-to-be-disrupted routine), make it one of Saunders' most attractive films. *Naked Fury* takes more than usual care to motivate its characters and action and shows a feel for the brutalities of criminal life; and *Jungle Street* creates a convincing sense of a squalid underworld of strip clubs and of drab urban working-class life. Saunders was responsible for some irredeemable junk (such as *The Hornet's Nest*) but most of his films show what can be done with modest means if the director cares enough. He died in Buckinghamshire in April 1997.

(Brian McFarlane)

BIBLIOGRAPHY: 'British Feature Directors: An Index to Their Work', *Sight and Sound*, Autumn 1958, p. 302; Clay, Andrew, 'Men, Women and Money', in Steve Chibnall and Robert Murphy (eds), *British Crime Cinema* (London and New York: Routledge, 1999).

FILMOGRAPHY: *No Exit* (1930); *Tawny Pipit* (co-dir. Bernard Miles, 1944); *The Way to the Stars* (2nd unit dir., Anthony Asquith, 1945); *Trouble in the Air*; *Fly Away Peter* (1948); *Dark Interval* (1950); *One Wild Oat*; *Chelsea Story*; *Death of an Angel* (1951); *Black Orchid*; *Come Back Peter*; *Blind Man's Buff* (1952); *Love in Pawn*; *The Accused*; *Three's Company* (1953); *The Scarlet Web*; *The Red Dress*; *Meet Mr Callaghan*; *The Golden Link* (1954); *A Time to Kill*; *One Jump Ahead*; *The Hornet's Nest* (1955); *The Narrowing Circle*; *Find the Lady*; *Behind the Headlines* (1956); *Womaneater*; *There's Always Thursday*; *The Man Without a Body*; *Kill Her Gently*; *A Date with Disaster*; *Murder Reported*; *The End of the Line* (1957); *Nudist Paradise* (1958); *Strictly Confidential*; *Naked Fury*; *Operation Cupid* (1959); *The Gentle Trap* (1960); *Jungle Street*; *Dangerous Afternoon*; *Danger by My Side* (1961).

SAVILLE, Philip (1930–)

Philip Saville's long career in film and television has spanned more than six decades. Born in London on 28 October 1930 to a family of Russian descent, he initially worked as an actor before entering television as a producer/director in 1955. Between 1956 and 1964 he directed more than forty *Armchair Theatre* plays for ABC Television and became known as a proficient and inventive craftsman – a reputation later consolidated with his startlingly bleak treatment of Harold Pinter's play *A Night Out* (1960), and *The Machine Stops* (1966), an impressive adaptation of E. M. Forster's story.

Saville's cinema career began in the mid-1960s with an ill-conceived attempt to film the successful Anthony Newley/Leslie Bricusse musical *Stop the World I Want to Get Off* without the charismatic Newley. He was more fortunate in the casting of *Oedipus the King*, with its fine performances by Christopher Plummer, Orson Welles, Richard Johnson and Lilli Palmer, though Saville's adaptation is much less audacious than Pasolini's contemporary *Oedipus Rex* (1967). *The Best House in London*, a vacuous Victorian comedy, did little to boost his cinema prospects. With the tedious *Secrets* (1971), cheaply mounted on Super-16 Saville made his pitch for an economically viable British independent cinema, but aside from increased sexual content this dialogue-driven exploration of marital discontent stuck close to the habits of television drama.

Working within television, Saville continued to find the discipline and focus often lacking in his cinema projects. Later television ventures ranged from the ground-breaking Birmingham crime series *Gangsters* (1975) and Alan Bleasdale's Liverpudlian critique of Britain in the 1980s, *Boys from the Blackstuff* (1982), to a popular adaptation of Fay Weldon's *The Life and Loves of a She-Devil* (1986).

With the advent of Channel 4's film productions, his television work began to spill over into the cinemas. *Those Glory, Glory Days* (1983), a sweet-toothed evocation of schoolgirl football fandom in the 1960s, and *Shadey* (1985), an elaborately strange and unwieldy fantasy by playwright Snoo Wilson, were both given limited theatrical releases. *The Fruit Machine* (1988), Frank Clarke's undisciplined comedy-drama about two gay teenagers who witness a murder, was financed by Granada but aimed at cinema audiences; like the European-funded *Metroland* (1997), a surprising hymn to suburban contentment given some credibility by the luminous performance of Emily Watson, it failed to attract much attention. The most interesting and artistically successful of Saville's cinema/television mutants is *Fellow Traveller* (1989), co-produced by the BBC, HBO and the BFI, and written by Michael Eaton: an ambitious, imaginative and fluidly handled semi-fictional treatment of a Hollywood blacklist victim in the 1950s who starts a new life in Britain writing *Robin Hood* scripts for television but is haunted by the betrayals and injustices of the McCarthy witch-hunts. The unpredictable Saville's most recent film is *The Gospel of St John* (2003), produced for Visual Bible International: guaranteed a larger audience than many of his ventures, though not one that congregates in multiplexes.

(Lez Cooke)

BIBLIOGRAPHY: Cooke, Lez, *British Television Drama: A History* (London: BFI, 2003); Cormack, Bill, 'A Man for All Seasons', *Stills*, July/Aug. 1983, pp. 32–5; Farrah, Leila, 'The Art of Philip Saville', *Broadcast*, 11 May 1984, p. 25; Fiddy, Dick and Veronica Taylor, 'British TV of the '70s and '80s: Philip Saville', 'National Film Theatre Programme', June 2001, pp. 17–18; Aug. 2001, pp. 24–5; Summers, Sue, 'Looking at the Ceiling with Loner Saville', *Screen International*, 13 Sept. 1975, p. 22.

FILMOGRAPHY: *Stop the World I Want to Get Off* (1966); *Oedipus the King* (1967); *The Best House in London* (1968); *Secrets* (1971); *Those Glory, Glory Days* (1983); *Shadey* (1985); *The Fruit Machine* (1988); *Fellow Traveller* (UK/US, 1989); *Metroland* (UK/Fr/Sp, 1997); *The Gospel of St John* (UK/Can, 2003).

SAVILLE, Victor (1897–1979)

Victor Saville, born Victor Myer Salberg, was born in Birmingham on 5 September 1897, the second son of an art dealer. He entered the film industry as a film salesman in 1916 after wounds sustained at the battle of Loos had brought about his army discharge. In 1919 he moved into film distribution with Michael Balcon, a boyhood friend from Birmingham. Advertising films about oil marked their first venture into production; then in 1923 they took flight with a successful feature, *Woman to Woman* (Graham Cutts), a wartime romance based on a West End play, featuring the American star Betty Compson. The following year Balcon formed his own company, Gainsborough; Saville, meanwhile, went into partnership at Gaumont with the director Maurice Elvey, producing five films, including *Mademoiselle from Armentières* (1926) and *Hindle Wakes* (1927). Their success together was not matched by Saville's own feature debut as a director, *The Arcadians*, a slapdash, updated version of the Edwardian musical comedy. But greater strides were taken in films directed at BIP through his own independent outfit, Burlington: first, *Tesha* (1928), polished in its visuals, delicate in its treatment of a triangular affair; then *Kitty* (1929), a halting but touching war melodrama from a novel by Warwick Deeping. Prepared as a silent, the film was later released with talking scenes shot in New York. While he was in America, Saville teamed up with Balcon and Compson for a talkie remake of *Woman to Woman*, but the results were disappointing.

Saville's first full British talkie was *The 'W' Plan* (1930), a spirited if unlikely spy drama with Madeleine Carroll and Brian Aherne, which fared extremely well at the box office. He then rejoined Balcon at Gainsborough, serving up a strong talkie version of *Hindle Wakes*, Stanley Hoguhton's play about a mill girl who thwarts convention by rejecting the marriage proposal of her boss's son; finding truth in the emotional dramas *The Faith-*

ful Heart and *Michael and Mary*; and crafting a delightful musical for Jack Hulbert in *Love on Wheels.* Once Balcon was appointed production head at Gainsborough's parent body, Gaumont-British, Saville's range and importance widened: between 1931 and 1935 Saville became the company's most prolific director and also, until Alfred Hitchcock's arrival in 1934, the most valued. He proved equally adept at comedies, musicals and serious dramas, establishing Jessie Matthews as a star in *The Good Companions*, *Evergreen* and *First a Girl*, launching Jack Hulbert onto a successful screen career with *Sunshine Susie* and *Love on Wheels*, and opening doors in Hollywood for Madeleine Carroll with her roles in *The 'W' Plan* and the gutsy and realistic *I Was a Spy*.

After the lively Jessie Matthews musical *It's Love Again* (1936), Saville left Gaumont-British to work independently, setting up Victor Saville Productions with the editor and scriptwriter Ian Dalrymple to make films for Alexander Korda at Denham. Despite the industry's deepening financial crisis, Saville and Dalrymple managed to make three fine films – the vivid spy thriller *Dark Journey*, the droll comedy *Storm in a Teacup* and *South Riding* (1938), a remarkably moving and far-sighted adaptation of Winifred Holtby's novel of Yorkshire life. Nevertheless, Saville subsequently turned back to production. As he explained to the trade journal *Film Weekly*:

> I have never considered myself highly as a director. I know I haven't the brilliance of Hitchcock, Lubitsch or Capra – nor have I the application to settle down like them and perfect, with years of labour, one particular style of direction. I have made scores of films during my career. I have also written scenarios and turned a camera – but my own ambition has always been to produce. (Quoted in National Film Archive, p. 7)

Saville had bought the rights to A. J. Cronin's novel *The Citadel*, which, like *South Riding*, was highly critical of social conditions in contemporary Britain. Louis B. Mayer persuaded him to sell them to MGM in return for the opportunity to produce a big-budget adaptation. Made in Britain but with an American director, King Vidor, *The Citadel* (1938) proved highly popular on both sides of the Atlantic; Saville's next production, *Goodbye, Mr Chips* (Sam Wood, 1939), was even more successful.

Thereafter, Saville's output lurched in quality; the craftsman became more of a factory employee. In Hollywood when war broke out in September 1939, he was advised that he could best serve his country by producing American films with a pro-British slant. He obliged with *The Mortal Storm* (Frank Borzage, 1940), an anti-Nazi film that provoked Goebbels into banning all MGM pictures in German-controlled territories and brought Saville before a Senate committee that demanded his expulsion (he was saved by the attack on Pearl Harbour). Tiring of uncongenial assignments after producing a further eight films for MGM, he moved to Columbia to direct a musical romance inspired by London's Windmill Theatre, *Tonight and Every Night* (1944), starring Rita Hayworth. Returning to MGM, he continued to direct, making adaptations of popular novels; aside from the Errol Flynn vehicle *Kim* (1950) they displayed little energy. Sporadic visits to Britain generated *Conspirator* (1949), a disappointing cold war thriller, the bearable *Calling Bulldog Drummond* (1951), with Walter Pidgeon as Sapper's hero, and the slow-moving melodrama *24 Hours of a Woman's Life* (1952). In 1960, after a stolid biblical drama *The Silver Chalice*, and an unlikely period masterminding versions of Mickey Spillane thrillers, Saville moved back to Britain, where he produced his last two films, *The Greengage Summer* (Lewis Gilbert, 1961) and *Mix Me a Person* (Leslie Norman, 1962). He died in London on 8 May 1979.

At his peak in Britain Saville was a splendidly versatile and competent director who inspired strong performances, particularly from female players (Estelle Brody, Belle Chrystall, Edna Best, Madeleine Carroll, Jessie Matthews, Vivien Leigh), and he was well liked on both sides of the camera. Surprisingly, in view of the period's strict censorship and Saville's career at MGM (the most conservative of Hollywood majors), many of his films come across as radical and progressive, particularly in their treatment of women. *Woman to Woman*, *Hindle Wakes* and *The Faithful Heart* all centre upon unmarried liaisons and invite sympathy and support for their female protagonists. The beautiful spies of *Dark Journey* and *I Was a Spy* are brave, principled, independently minded women rather than femmes fatales. *The Good Companions*, *Storm in a Teacup* and, much more directly, *South Riding* and *The Citadel* address the issue of British class divisions in a society where economic depression had ruined the lives of many working people, a situation most British film-makers preferred to ignore. *Dark Journey* implicitly speaks out against the threat from Germany when appeasement was the British government's favoured strategy for dealing with Hitler. Though Saville's status as an Englishman with a successful career as a Hollywood producer and director is unique (at one time he was thought of as Mayer's likely successor at MGM), it is for the British films he directed in the 1930s – particularly *South Riding* – that he will be best remembered.

(James C. Robertson)

BIBLIOGRAPHY: Balcon, Michael, *Michael Balcon Presents . . . A Lifetime in Films* (London: Hutchinson, 1969); Moseley, Roy and Victor Saville, *Evergreen: Victor Saville in His Own Words* (Carbondale: Southern Illinois University Press, 2000); National Film Archive, *Victor Saville* (London: BFI, 1972); Saville, Victor, 'A Life with Films', *BFI News* no.3, Jan. 1973, p. 4.

FILMOGRAPHY: *The Arcadians* (1927); *Tesha* (US: *A Woman in the Night*, 1928); *Kitty*; *Woman to Woman*; *Me and the Boys* (short) (1929); *The 'W' Plan* (1930); *A Warm Corner*, *The Sport of Kings*; *Hindle Wakes*; *Michael and Mary*; *Sunshine Susie* (1931); *The Faithful Heart* (US: *Faithful Hearts*); *Love on Wheels* (1932); *The Good Companions*; *I Was a Spy*;

Friday the Thirteenth (1933); *Evergreen*; *Evensong* (1934); *The Iron Duke*; *The Dictator* (co-dir. Alfred Santell); *First a Girl*; *Me and Marlborough* (1935); *It's Love Again* (1936); *Dark Journey*; *Storm in a Teacup* (co-dir. Ian Dalrymple) (1937); *South Riding* (1938); *Forever and a Day* (co-dirs. René Clair/Edmund Goulding/Cedric Hardwicke/Frank Lloyd/Robert Stevenson/Herbert Wilcox, US, 1943); *Tonight and Every Night* (US, 1944); *The Green Years* (US, 1946); *Green Dolphin Street* (US); *If Winter Comes* (US) (1947); *Conspirator* (1949); *Kim* (US, 1950); *Calling Bulldog Drummond* (1951); *24 Hours of a Woman's Life* (US: *Affair in Monte Carlo*, 1952); *The Long Wait* (US, 1954); *The Silver Chalice* (US, 1955).

SCHAFFNER, Franklin J. (1920–1989)

Franklin James Schaffner was born in Tokyo on 30 May 1920 and moved to Lancaster, Pennsylvania, following the death of his father, a Protestant missionary. He went into summer stock after graduating in law from Columbia, saw active wartime service and then worked on *The March of Time* newsreel and television current affairs programmes. He moved into live television drama before making his big-screen debut with *The Stripper* (UK: *Woman of Summer*, 1963).

The Double Man, a potboiling thriller in which callous CIA agent Yul Brynner is duplicated with the aid of plastic surgery and back projection, was constructed around footage shot for an aborted Peter Yates picture, *Legacy of a Spy* (1961). The least interesting of Schaffner's early films, it was followed by two enormous hits, *Planet of the Apes* (1968) and the multi-Academy Award-winning *Patton* (1970). Schaffner was then given the prestigious task of making *Nicholas and Alexandra* in Spain for Sam Spiegel, after three other directors had quit. An $11 million epic charting the fall of the Romanoffs, it is handsome, literate and historically scrupulous but dramatically plodding and was poorly received.

Schaffner's last viable project was an adaptation of Ira Levin's *The Boys from Brazil* for Lew Grade's ITC. Despite the cunning off-casting of Gregory Peck as Nazi fugitive Josef Mengele, its paranoid fantasy is curiously lethargic and lacking in suspense. Thereafter, Schaffner's acumen seemed to desert him: *Sphinx* (1981) and *Lionheart* (1987), made in Egypt and Hungary with largely British casts and crews, are flat, lifeless adventures, without a trace of his former talent. Schaffner died of cancer in Santa Monica on 2 July 1989, shortly after completing his last film, *Welcome Home* (1989).

(Sheldon Hall)

BIBLIOGRAPHY: Appelbaum, Ralph, 'Master Plans', *Films and Filming*, Feb. 1979, pp. 12–18; Geist, Kenneth, 'Chronicler of Power', *Film Comment*, Sept./Oct. 1972, pp. 29–36; Kim, Erwin, *Franklin J. Schaffner* (Metuchen, NJ: Scarecrow Press, 1986); 'TV to Film: A History, a Map and a Family Tree', *Monthly Film Bulletin*, Feb. 1983, pp. 34–6; Wilson, David, 'Franklin Schaffner', *Sight and Sound*, Spring 1966, pp. 73–5.

FILMOGRAPHY (UK only): *The Double Man* (1967); *Nicholas and Alexandra* (1971); *The Boys from Brazil* (UK/US, 1978).

SCHEPISI, Fred (1939–)

Fred Schepisi was born in Melbourne, Australia, on 26 December 1939, the son of a used-car salesman. Educated at Catholic boarding school, he persuaded his parents to let him enter a seminary. He left at fifteen, finding employment as an advertising agency dispatch boy. By 1964 Schepisi was manager of Cinesound Productions, and two years later he formed his own production company, the Film House, where he scripted, produced and directed commercials, documentaries and public relations films.

In 1973 Schepisi contributed *The Priest* as one of the four episodes of *Libido* (David Baker/Tim Burstall/John B. Murray/Fred Schepisi). During the following two years he raised funds for his first full-length feature, *The Devil's Playground* (1976). This semi-autobiographical story of a teenager's troubled life in a Catholic seminary won several Australian Film Institute awards. He followed it with an adaptation of Thomas Keneally's novel *The Chant of Jimmie Blacksmith* (1978). A powerful, vivid film depicting the revenge of a mixed-race Aborigine, cast out and driven to murder, it affronted Australian audiences with its disquieting representation of their culture, but was well received by critics in the USA, where Schepisi went to direct *Barbarosa* (1982) and *Iceman* (1984).

Schepisi's first British film, the American-funded *Plenty* (1985), a compelling exploration of identity and Englishness, was remarkably faithful to David Hare's play about a woman who finds it impossible to adapt to the dreary conformity of post-war English society after the excitement and danger of fighting with the French Resistance. He draws a restrained, convincing performance from Meryl Streep as the troubled Englishwoman Susan Traherne, a role Hare had created for Kate Nelligan.

Schepisi continued his career with an eclectic series of films ranging from *Roxanne* (1987), a modern version of *Cyrano de Bergerac* starring Steve Martin, to an adaptation of John Le Carré's *The Russia House* (1990). He returned to Britain in 1997 to take over direction of *Fierce Creatures*, the moderately successful follow-up to Charles Crichton's *A Fish Called Wanda* (1988); and again in 2001 to film Graham Swift's 1996 Booker Prize-winning novel, *Last Orders*. Through intricately layered flashbacks, Schepisi builds his depiction of friendship between a group of ageing Bermondsey drinking buddies (played by Bob Hoskins, David Hemmings, Tom Courtenay and Ray Winstone) who journey to Margate to scatter their friend's ashes. The difficulty of classifying Schepisi's diverse works has told against his reputation, but *Plenty* and *Last Orders* show him as a sensitive director with the confidence to deal with complex narrative structures and push against the boundaries of mainstream cinema.

(Eleanor Burke)

BIBLIOGRAPHY: Gilbey, Ryan, 'Unmade Freds', *Sight and Sound*, Jan. 2002, pp. 12–13; Matthews, Sue, *35mm Dreams* (Ringwood, Australia: Penguin, 1984); *Myth & Meaning* (Sydney, Australia: Currency Press, 2001).

FILMOGRAPHY (UK only): *Plenty* (US/UK, 1985); *Fierce Creatures* (US/UK, co-dir. Robert Young, 1997); *Last Orders* (UK/Ger, 2001).

SCHERFIG, Lone (1959–)

Lone Wrede Scherfig was born in Copenhagen on 2 May 1959. She studied at the Danish Film Academy and went on to make two low-budget features, *Kaj's fødselsdag/ The Birthday Trip* (1990) and *Når mor kommer hjem/ On Our Own* (1998), along with several shorts and episodes of television drama series. Her breakthrough came in 2000 with *Italiensk for begyndere/ Italian for Beginners*, a comedy about six bored characters in a small Danish town who find romance when they join an Italian-language class. Its droll humour proved universally appealing: the film won the Silver Bear at the Berlin Film Festival and brought in $20 million at the box office.

Scherfig had intended to use the same cast for her next film, but disputes over fees led her to relocate *Wilbur Wants to Kill Himself* to Scotland. A gentle tale about two brothers, one with a compulsion to attempt suicide, the other unexpectedly stricken with terminal cancer, the film is an odd combination of tearjerker, black comedy and fairy tale. Scherfig gains winsome performances from her cast, particularly Jamie Sives and Adrian Rawlins as the brothers, and Shirley Henderson as Alice, the Snow White figure who brings love and order to their lives. She sidesteps bathos and whimsy, but a concentration on the narrow world of her characters – seemingly confined to the brothers' bookshop and the hospital where Alice works and Wilbur and Harbour receive treatment – brings a constricting aura of unreality. *Wilbur Wants to Kill Himself* failed to replicate the success of *Italian for Beginners*, though harmonious relations between Danes and Scots seem likely to encourage further co-productions.

(Robert Murphy)

BIBLIOGRAPHY: Hunter, Allan and Jacob Neiiendam 'Case Study: Wilbur Wants to Kill Himself', *Screen International*, 6 Jan. 2003, p. 27; Macnab, Geoffrey, 'Killing Me Softly' and 'Lone Scherfig: Suicide for Beginners', *Sight and Sound*, Dec. 2003, pp. 24–5; Neiiendam, Jacob, 'Close Up: Lone Scherfig', *Screen International*, 6 Jan. 2003, p. 27.

FILMOGRAPHY (UK only): *Wilbur Wants to Kill Himself/ Wilbur begår selvmord* (UK/Den/Nor/Fr, 2002).

SCHLESINGER, John (1926–2003)

John Schlesinger was one of the brightest directorial hopes of early 1960s' British cinema, when he was responsible for two of the classic kitchen-sink films, *A Kind of Loving* and *Billy Liar*. Later he would become a strong exponent of the realist film renaissance in the USA of the late 1960s and 70s. In all, he has been one of the most versatile of prominent British film directors.

John Richard Schlesinger was born in London on 16 February 1926 and educated at Oxford. He took a keen interest in amateur film-making, acted in repertory theatres and played small roles in various films, including *The Divided Heart* (Charles Crichton, 1954) and *The Battle of the River Plate* (Powell and Pressburger, 1956). He was eventually hired by the BBC, where he directed several episodes of the arts programme *Monitor*, including studies of Benjamin Britten (1958) and Georges Simenon (1959). Following *Terminus* (1961), a highly praised drama-documentary for British Transport Films about a day in the life of London's Waterloo Station, producer Joseph Janni asked Schlesinger to direct an adaptation of Stan Barstow's novel *A Kind of Loving*. Though less gritty and less sensational than Karel Reisz's *Saturday Night and Sunday Morning* (1960) and Lindsay Anderson's *This Sporting Life* (1963), Schlesinger's film has its own low-key virtues, and Alan Bates' Vic Brown served as a likeable representative for a generation of young men eager to escape the grinding conformity of working-class life. Critically as well as commercially, *A Kind of Loving* proved to be one of the most successful British films of the early 1960s and was awarded the Golden Bear at the Berlin Film Festival in 1962.

Schlesinger and Janni followed this success with *Billy Liar*, an adaptation of a popular play by Willis Hall and Keith Waterhouse, with Tom Courtenay as a more anarchically discontented young man who slips into fantasy whenever his desire for a more exciting life is frustrated. His relationships with women, particularly with the footloose character played by Julie Christie who almost succeeds in taking him with her to London, signposted the film's stylistic transition away from northern realism. With *Darling*, Schlesinger entered 'Swinging London' territory wholeheartedly, depicting the life of a woman (Julie Christie) whose sexual life gradually turns her into a commodity. Though the film explores the affluence and promiscuity of the 1960s, Schlesinger and his scriptwriter Frederic Raphael remain cautiously critical, stressing the unhappiness and emptiness of this new permissive society.

The success of Schlesinger's films enabled him to secure financial backing from MGM for a lavish adaptation of Thomas Hardy's *Far from the Madding Crowd*, featuring Christie as the wilful Bathsheba Everdene and Terence Stamp, Peter Finch and Alan Bates as her three suitors. With its breathtaking location photography (by Nicolas Roeg), the film is now generally regarded as a classic; but at the time its slow pace and convoluted story proved too demanding for American audiences and it failed to recover its $2.75 million costs.

It was in the USA, nevertheless, that Schlesinger reached the height of his directorial fame with the hugely successful *Midnight Cowboy* (1969), for which he won an Academy Award for best direction. Returning to London to work with Joseph Janni, Schlesinger directed the unsettling drama *Sunday Bloody Sunday* (1971) dealing with the theme of confused sexual identity in London at the end of the 1960s. The film's emphasis on the cost exacted in loneliness and unhappiness by the 'permissive society' makes it a bleak complement to the more exuberant *Darling*.

The 1970s saw Schlesinger complete his contribution to a great period in American cinema with the Hollywood-on-Hollywood drama *The Day of the Locust* (1975), after Nathanael

West's novel, and the thriller *Marathon Man* (1976), from a novel by William Goldman. *Yanks*, a co-production between Janni and United Artists, with a script by Colin Welland, explored with rather too much reserve the impact of the American GI invasion of Britain in the latter days of the Second World War. At the beginning of the 1980s, Schlesinger was teamed with maverick producer Don Boyd to make an American blockbuster with a Florida setting and American actors for the British company EMI Films. An expensive proposition with its $24 million budget, *Honky Tonk Freeway* proved a total disaster at the box office.

This failure was followed by modest but more rewarding projects. *An Englishman Abroad* (1983), written by Alan Bennett from a real-life encounter in Moscow between the actress Coral Browne and the notorious British spy Guy Burgess, was only a sixty-minute television production but it demonstrated that Schlesinger had not lost the ability to direct intimate drama. His adaptation of Terence Rattigan's *Separate Tables* (1983) for the American cable company HBO is similarly enjoyable for the acting of Alan Bates, Julie Christie, Claire Bloom and Irene Worth. Between the espionage thriller *The Falcon and the Snowman* (1985) and the yuppie paranoia film *Pacific Heights* (1990), by far the biggest box-office success of Schlesinger's later films, he returned to London to make *Madame Sousatzka* (1988), quaintly old-fashioned confectionery manufactured from Bernice Rubens' novel with a showy performance from Shirley MacLaine as a fiery and eccentric piano teacher in a house of lost souls and eccentrics. Schlesinger also directed operas and stage plays and though plagued by illness remained an active film-maker up to 2000, when he made a sugary and predictable Madonna vehicle, *The Next Best Thing*. Shortly after its release Schlesinger suffered a stroke from which he never fully recovered. He died in Palm Springs, California, on 25 July 2003.

Schlesinger's disparate output has attracted only limited appreciation. But there is a pleasing scepticism about many of his films: in *A Kind of Loving*, *Billy Liar*, *Darling* and *Sunday Bloody Sunday*, Vic Brown, Billy Fisher, Robert Gold and Daniel Hirsh are all wary of the affluent society of the 1960s; and *Midnight Cowboy* and *The Day of the Locust* are scathing indictments of the American Dream. Jewish and openly gay, Schlesinger knew something about being an outsider even while finding acceptance in the highest social and artistic circles. While none of the British New Wave directors – Richardson, Clayton, Anderson, Reisz – can be said to have fully fulfilled their potential, Schlesinger's survival against the odds is something to be celebrated.

(Erik Hedling)

BIBLIOGRAPHY: Brooker-Bowers, Nancy, *John Schlesinger: A Guide to References and Resources* (Boston, MA: G. K. Hall, 1978); Hill, John, *Sex, Class and Realism: British Cinema 1956–1963* (London: BFI, 1986); Mann, William J., *Edge of Midnight: The Life of*

John Schlesinger (London: Hutchinson, 2004); Murphy, Robert, *Sixties British Cinema* (London: BFI, 1992); Phillips, Gene D., *John Schlesinger* (Boston, MA: Twayne, 1981); Walker, Alexander, *National Heroes* (London: Harrap, 1985); Walker, Alexander, *Hollywood, England* (London: Harrap, 1986).

FILMOGRAPHY: *Black Legend* (doc., 1948); *The Starfish* (short, co-dir. Alan Cooke, 1952); *Sunday in the Park: The Face of London* (doc. short) (1956); *Terminus* (short, 1961); *A Kind of Loving* (1962); *Billy Liar* (1963); *Darling* (1965); *Israeli* (doc. short, co-dirs. Harry Saltzman/Wolf Mankowitz); *Far from the Madding Crowd* (1967); *Midnight Cowboy* (US, 1969); *Sunday Bloody Sunday* (1971); *Visions of Eight* ('The Longest' episode, US, 1973); *The Day of the Locust* (US, 1975); *Marathon Man* (US, 1976); *Yanks* (1979); *Honky Tonk Freeway* (1981); *The Falcon and the Snowman* (US, 1985); *The Believers* (US, 1987); *Madame Sousatzka* (1988); *Pacific Heights* (US, 1990); *The Innocent* (UK/Ger, 1993); *Cold Comfort Farm*; *Eye for an Eye* (US) (1995); *The Next Best Thing* (US, 2000).

SCHUSTER, Harold D. (1902–1986)

Harold Schuster was born in Cherokee, Iowa, on 1 August 1902. He worked as an actor and assistant cameraman before establishing his reputation as editor on F. W. Murnau's *Sunrise* (1927). He came to Britain to edit *Wings of the Morning*, the first Technicolor film to be shot in Britain or Ireland. When the director, Glenn Tryon, fell ill, Schuster took over, and his rapport with French star Annabella persuaded 20th Century-Fox to allow him to complete the film. An unlikely tale set around gypsies and the aristocracy, its Killarney landscapes and colourful representation of Epsom on Derby Day, the romance between Henry Fonda and the cross-dressing Annabella, and the appearance of popular Irish tenor Count John McCormack, made the film a huge commercial success. *Wings of the Morning* established Schuster as a director and after making *Dinner at the Ritz* with Annabella and David Niven set on an ocean liner bound for America, and *Queer Cargo*, set among pirates and smugglers in the China Seas, he returned to Hollywood to make films such as *My Friend Flicka* (1943), *So Dear to My Heart* (1947) and *The Tender Years* (1948). In the 1950s Schuster moved into television, working on series ranging from *Lassie* to *The Twilight Zone*. He died on 19 July 1986 in Westlake Village, California.
(Ruth Barton)

BIBLIOGRAPHY: Williams, J. Danvers, 'Success for Two', *Film Weekly*, 18 Sept. 1937, pp. 16–17.

FILMOGRAPHY (UK only): *Wings of the Morning*; *Dinner at the Ritz* (1937); *Queer Cargo* (1938).

SCHWABACH, Peter

Peter Schwabach studied at Oxford in the late 1970s, where he helped Michael Hoffman and Richard Stevenson set up the Oxford Film Company; he played a small role and served as art director on their low-budget feature *Privileged* (Michael Hoffman, 1982). A long interval elapsed before he directed *Attenborough*, a short thriller widely shown as support to *Things to Do in Denver When You're Dead* (Gary Fleder, 1995). Schwabach then won backing from HandMade Films and various funding bodies to make *The Secret Laughter of Women*, a feature-length romantic comedy, with Colin Firth as a comic-book writer uncertainly committed to an independently minded West African woman (Nia Long) in the South of France. HandMade's financial collapse put the project in jeopardy and delayed release, though the film was eventually premiered to an enthusiastic audience at the 1999 London Film Festival. Bright colours, general good humour and a Nigerian heroine (albeit played by an American) more or less compensate for uncertain direction and soft-centred whimsy, but the film failed to break out of the festival circuit and secure a proper cinema release.
(Robert Murphy)

BIBLIOGRAPHY: 'Against the Odds', *Time Out*, 24 Nov. 1999, p. 95.

FILMOGRAPHY: *Attenborough* (short, 1995); *The Secret Laughter of Women* (UK/Can, 1999).

SCHWARTZ, Stefan (1963–)

Stefan Schwartz was born in 1963. After acting in several television plays he began directing and proselytising on behalf of the ideal of a commercially orientated, internationally ambitious British film industry. He made two short films in conjunction with the producer Richard Holmes, and worked with him on his feature debut, *Soft Top, Hard Shoulder* (1993), a low-budget road movie following a book illustrator's thwarted attempts to drive from London to Glasgow to attend a family birthday party. Though it made little financial impact, the film established Schwartz sufficiently for him to go on to make the amusingly prescient television film *Giving Tongue* (1996), about the political storms blown up when a Labour MP (Claire Holman) introduces a bill to ban fox-hunting. Enjoyable supporting performances from Peter Capaldi, Charlotte Coleman and a host of British character actors make up for a ramshackle story.

Schwartz had his breakthrough with *Shooting Fish*, a romantic comedy-caper movie that attracted funding from the National Lottery. Two orphans (Dan Futterman and Stuart Townsend) share an obsession to own an English stately home, which involves them in various scams but also brings them into contact with an heiress (Kate Beckinsale), whom they save from being disinherited. Erratic direction and lackadaisical plot were overlooked by the British youth audience, who enjoyed its zany comedy and made it one of the few late 1990s Lottery-funded films to make a profit. Schwartz's subsequent film, *The Abduction Club* (2002), a period comedy set in eighteenth-century Ireland, proved disappointingly tame and lacked the cult appeal of *Shooting Fish*.

Schwartz belongs to a generation of young British directors who emerged in the early 1990s and took mainstream Hollywood, 'where film is thought of as a serious industry, with serious money making potential', as their creative and industrial benchmark (Schwartz, p. 44). Yet as his career illustrates, British cinema achieves these goals at best infrequently and on a comparatively modest financial scale.

(Jonathan Murray)

BIBLIOGRAPHY: 'First Frames', *Screen International*, 5 June 1992, pp. 10–12; 'Honest Entertainer Gets the People's Vote', *The Times*, 24 Nov. 1992, p. 11; Schwartz, Stefan, 'The Director', in Lucy Johnson (ed.), *Talking Pictures: Interviews with Contemporary British Film-Makers* (London: BFI, 1997).

FILMOGRAPHY: *Bonded* (short, 1989); *The Lake* (short, 1992); *Soft Top, Hard Shoulder* (1993); *Shooting Fish* (1997); *The Abduction Club* (UK/Ger/Fr/Ir, 2002).

SCOTT, Jake (1965–)

Jake Scott was born in 1965, the son of director Ridley Scott. He studied at the London College of Printing and then moved to Los Angeles, where he worked as an art director and set designer for commercials and promos. The commercial he directed for Blaupunkt was well received and led to music videos for prestigious bands such as Oasis, U2 and the Rolling Stones. His video for REM's 'Everybody Hurts' won many awards, including the 1994 MTV Best Director trophy.

Scott's success led to the offer of a feature film, *Plunkett & Macleane*, starring Robert Carlyle and Jonny Lee Miller as eighteenth-century highwaymen. The film is a blood-and-thunder romp with a deliberately anachronistic contemporary soundtrack, and wears its influences – from *Butch Cassidy and the Sundance Kid* (George Roy Hill, 1969) to Baz Luhrmann's *William Shakespeare's Romeo + Juliet* (1996) – on its sleeve. It was released to a mixed critical reception, but enjoyed enough commercial success to augur well for Scott's future.

(Martin Hunt)

BIBLIOGRAPHY: Brown, Glyn, 'Scott of the Arch Antics', *Independent* Review Section, 1 Apr. 1999, p. 12; 'Jake Scott: Director', *Total Film*, Apr. 1999, pp. 56–7; Moggach, Lottie, 'Trendspotting', *The Times* Metro Section, 3 Apr. 1999, p. 15.

FILMOGRAPHY: *Plunkett & Macleane* (1999).

SCOTT, James (1941–)

The son of the painter William Scott, James Scott was born in Wells, Somerset, on 9 July 1941. From 1960 to 1962 he studied painting and sculpture at the Slade School of Fine Art, London, where his contemporaries included Don Levy and Peter Whitehead. In 1962, on the strength of *The Rocking Horse*, a twenty-five-minute psychological drama made for the BFI Experimental Film Fund, Tony Richardson at Woodfall put up the money for an entire feature, *The Sea*. An explosive argument halfway through terminated production: an indication of future travails and conflicts in the career of one of the most independent of Britain's independent film-makers.

His second BFI short, *In Separation*, pursued experiments with narrative and film form. In 1966, working through Maya Films, founded with Barney Platts-Mills, Scott began filtering similar concerns through the conservative medium of the art documentary. In a series of increasingly ambitious films for distribution by the Arts Council of Great Britain, Scott rejected the film-maker's usual supine position before the appointed topic. Disruptive, questioning stylistic procedures, influenced by Godard and Brecht, were brought into play with subjects ranging from Pop Artists David Hockney and Claes Oldenberg to gangster-turned-artist Jimmy Boyle. With *Richard Hamilton* (1969), made in close collaboration with the artist, Scott achieved a major success, brilliantly twisting film form to mirror the habits of Hamilton's Pop Art creations. Later Arts Council films grew more unwieldy and fractured, climaxing in the self-reflexive jungle of *Chance, History, Art . . .* (1979).

In the 1970s Scott's endeavours beyond his Arts Council films followed two different paths. Political and social interests became reflected in his work with the Berwick Street Collective on *Night Cleaners Part 1* and its successor, *'36 to '77*. Elsewhere, Scott broke through the fiction feature barrier with two obdurate exercises in narrative form. The intriguing *Adult Fun* (1972) jettisoned dramatic cohesion for a fragmented portrait of urban and industrial malaise, its modes shifting perilously between thriller, fantasy and the documentary interview. *Coilin and Platonida* (1976) pitched a nineteenth-century Russian story into the scenery of Ireland's west coast, using amateur actors, grainy images and (one song apart) silence. Neither film, especially *Coilin*, was the work of someone who entertained commercial concessions. Yet during the 1980s, economics and independent cinema's cul-de-sac nature drove Scott into commerce's arms. Initially he found success. *A Shocking Accident*, seen across Britain supporting *Tootsie* (Sydney Pollack, 1982), offered a pleasingly cryptic treatment of Graham Greene's story about an absurd social embarrassment, earning Scott and his new company, Flamingo Pictures, an Academy Award for Best Live Action Short. And in his modest feature *Every Picture Tells a Story* (1984), recreating scenes from his father's early days, subject matter and Scott's characteristically quizzical editing and imagery became admirably fused in a far more personal story of chance, history and art. Scott's tendency to court creative problems that others would make efforts to avoid led him next to Miramax and an American co-production, *Loser Takes All*, from Greene's novella. This finally peeped out in 1990, with no chemistry apparent between its stars (Robert Lindsay, Molly Ringwald), but every sign of a director ill at ease. The experience was decisive; Scott abandoned cinema, relocated to Los Angeles and successfully resumed painting. One of his 1991 canvases used Harvey and Bob Weinstein, the Miramax brothers, as inspiration for a cold, garish composition featuring two naked men with phone and briefcase standing beside a deserted road at night, a wine bottle and a chesty naked woman glowering on a distant billboard. As the film title says, every picture tells a story.

(Geoff Brown)

BIBLIOGRAPHY: Hodgson, Clive, 'From Artists to Cleaners: an Interview with James Scott', *Film* [British Federation of Film Societies] series 2, no. 4, July 1973, pp. 6–7; Scott, James, 'Independent Cinema', *Stills* vol.1 no. 4, Winter 1982, pp. 40–2; <www.james-scott.com> [official website].

FILMOGRAPHY: *The Rocking Horse* (short, 1962); *In Separation* (short, 1963; rel. 1965); *Love's Presentation* (aka *Twelve Poems by C. P. Cafavy Chosen and Illustrated by David Hockney*, short, 1966); *R. B. Kitaj* (short, 1967); *Richard Hamilton* (short, assoc dir. Richard Hamilton); *Ejectoret* (short) (1969); *The Great Ice-Cream Robbery* (short, 1971); *England's Historic Churches* (short); *Adult Fun* (1972); *Night Cleaners Part 1* (Berwick Street Film Collective, 1974); *Coilin & Platonida* (UK/W. Ger, 1976); *'36 to '77* (Berwick Street Film Collective, 1978); *Chance, History, Art . . .* (1979); *A Shocking Accident* (short, 1982); *Film No. 1* (short); *Every Picture Tells a Story* (1984); *Loser Takes All* (US: *Strike It Rich*, UK/US, 1990).

SCOTT, Ridley (1937–)

Ridley Scott was born in South Shields, Northumberland, on 30 November 1937. While studying at the Royal College of Art in London, he directed a short film, *Boy and Bicycle* (1961), featuring his brother Tony (also to become a director). He later obtained funding from the BFI to complete post-production, including a snippet of score from John Barry, demonstrating his ambitions for technical perfection even at this early stage. While working as an art director for BBC Television, he began freelancing as a director of commercials, a sideline he has always kept up.

He directed a half-hour version of *Paths of Glory* (1963) as classwork at a BBC directors' course and then handled episodes of drama series ranging from *Softly, Softly* to *Adam Adamant Lives!* Rather than pursuing a career as a television director, in 1965 he set up his own company, Ridley Scott Associates, to make commercials. It was not until 1977 that he made his feature debut with the Joseph Conrad adaptation *The Duellists* (1977). From the first, Scott intended to be an international director, and *The Duellists* is as scrambled in national identity as Conrad himself: a British producer (David Puttnam), a Polish-English literary source, a French historical setting, American stars (Keith Carradine, Harvey Keitel) and a British supporting cast. The film attracted enough notice, especially for its visual qualities, to land Scott *Alien* (1979), an American science-fiction horror film made in Britain, with an interesting clash of American and British character actors aboard a haunted ship in deep space. The film's phenomenal success turned Scott into a major Hollywood director and he seized the opportunity to make the radical, futuristic *Blade Runner* (1982).

Scott has become a classic outsider-in-America director, drawn to stories of people voyaging in worlds not their own: a Replicant on Earth in *Blade Runner*, an American cop in Japan in *Black Rain*, Christopher Columbus discovering the New World in *1492: Conquest of Paradise*, women breaking free in the American West in *Thelma & Louise*, a Spaniard in Ancient Rome in *Gladiator*, a woman coping with the macho ethos of the US Army in *G.I. Jane*, Hannibal Lecter in Florence, US marines in Mogadishu, a French blacksmith in Jerusalem. Scott has combined reputations as a visionary and a crowd-pleaser, surviving major flops to re-establish his A-list status with the box-office and Academy Awards hit *Gladiator*. None of his films have a British setting, with the possible exception of the fairy tale *Legend*, which imports Tom Cruise into a Tolkien-like imagined European world.

Nevertheless, Scott has contributed two key images of national self-image to the British consciousness: in his ads for Strongbow cider, a first experiment with the romantic medieval look of *Legend*, and for Hovis bread, with a gravely nostalgic Yorkshire voiceover and sweetly mournful Dvořják music as a child struggles up a cobbled hill in some pre-war Arcadia of long shorts and flat caps. He and his brother Tony were part of a consortium that bought Shepperton Studios in 1995. He was knighted in January 2003.

(Kim Newman)

BIBLIOGRAPHY: Johnston, Sheila, 'The Visualist', *Films and Filming*, Nov. 1985, pp. 6–8; McGillivray, David, 'Ridley Scott', *Films and Filming*, June 1984, p. 45; Robb, Brian J., *The Pocket Essential Ridley Scott* (London: Pocket Essentials, 2001); Thomson, David, 'The Riddler Has Had His Day', *Sight and Sound*, Apr. 2001, pp. 18–21.

FILMOGRAPHY: *Boy and Bicycle* (short, 1961); *The Duellists* (1977); *Alien* (US, 1979); *Blade Runner* (US, 1982); *Legend* (1985); *Someone to Watch over Me* (US, 1987); *Black Rain* (US, 1989); *Thelma & Louise* (US, 1991); *1492: Conquest of Paradise* (US, 1992); *White Squall* (US, 1996); *G.I. Jane* (US, 1997); *Gladiator* (US, 2000); *Hannibal* (US); *Black Hawk Down* (US) (2001); *Matchstick Men* (US, 2003); *Kingdom of Heaven* (US/UK/Sp, 2005); *All the Invisible Children* (*Jonathan* episode, co-dir. Jordan Scott, Fr/It, 2005).

SCOTT, Tony (1944–)

Tony Scott was born in Stockton-on-Tees on 21 July 1944. After studying at the Royal College of Art, he gained backing from the BFI to make three medium-length, black-and-white productions. The most distinctive of these is *Loving Memory*, a fifty-minute drama scripted by Scott, about two siblings living on a remote farm in Yorkshire, sensitively photographed by Chris

Menges. He then followed his brother Ridley Scott into advertising, directing hundreds of television commercials before making his feature film debut with the underrated vampire tale, *The Hunger*, set in New York but partly made in the UK. Its vampires (Catherine Deneuve, David Bowie) are well cast, but Scott privileges visual texture over plot coherence and audiences were left baffled.

Scott hit the Hollywood big time with the jingoistic flag-waver *Top Gun*, the first of many such films he has made with producer Jerry Bruckheimer. Of the flashy, handsomely mounted, big-budget thrillers that followed, the most interesting are his two collaborations with Quentin Tarantino: *True Romance*, a pop culture road movie reminiscent of Terrence Malik's *Badlands* (1973); and *Crimson Tide* (for which Tarantino supplied uncredited rewrites), which forcefully depicts the racial tensions leading to mutiny aboard a nuclear submarine in a Third World War scenario.

In 2001 Scott made *Spy Game* in the UK at Shepperton Studios, which Tony and Ridley Scott's company, Scott Free Productions, bought as part of a consortium in 1995.

(Sergio Angelini)

BIBLIOGRAPHY: Dawson, Jeff, 'Natural Born Killers', *Empire*, Nov. 1993, pp. 96–109; Figgis, Mike, 'Interview', in *Projections 10* (London: Faber and Faber, 1999), pp. 127–33.

FILMOGRAPHY: *Loving Memory* (short); *Early One Morning* (short) (1969); *One of the Missing* (short, 1971); *The Hunger* (US/UK, 1983); *Top Gun* (US, 1986); *Beverly Hills Cop II* (US, 1987); *Revenge* (US); *Days of Thunder* (US) (1990); *The Last Boy Scout* (US, 1991); *True Romance* (US, 1993); *Crimson Tide* (US, 1995); *The Fan* (US, 1996); *Enemy of the State* (US, 1998); *Spy Game* (US/UK, 2001); *The Hire: Beat the Devil* (short, US, 2002); *Man on Fire* (US, 2004); *Domino* (US/Fr, 2005).

SEARLE, Francis (1909–2002)

Born in Putney, London, on 14 March 1909, the son of a dentist, Francis Alan Searle worked as a dance-band drummer and in advertising and the theatre before settling at Gaumont-British Screen Services to make instructional films and commercials. *The War Without End* (1938), a portrait of a modern hospital, brought him early prominence in the field. His last documentary short before his jump to features was the glossily packaged *Student Nurse*: 'Extremely good for the unthinking,' proclaimed *Documentary News Letter* in 1945, assessing its propaganda value. On the strength of *Student Nurse* Sydney Box recruited Searle in 1946 to direct his production of *A Girl in a Million*, a pleasant lightweight comedy that gave Joan Greenwood her first starring role. It remained Searle's only top-of-the-bill feature: otherwise he worked in the depths with low-budget thrillers and comedies that rarely received any critic's admiration.

Between 1949 and 1951 he made eight films for Hammer, four based on radio series; the liveliest included *The Man in Black* and *A Case for P.C. 49*. Larger ambitions were visible in *Cloudburst* (1951), a taut revenge-thriller featuring Robert Preston, made with an eye to the American market. Ill-suited to Hammer's subsequent speciality, horror, Searle concentrated on crime thrillers for Butcher's, Renown and similar suppliers, reaching his peak in 1962 with *Emergency*, *Gaolbreak* and *Dead Man's Evidence* – routine material, but crisply presented. When British B-movies were squeezed out of distribution patterns, Searle returned to shorts, ending his career with seven thirty-minute colour comedies, not of the freshest inspiration. He died in Wimbledon, London, on 31 July 2002.

(Geoff Brown)

BIBLIOGRAPHY: BECTU History Project interview, May 1988, tape held in BFI National Library, London; MacFarlane, Brian, *An Autobiography of British Cinema* (London: Methuen, 1997); Murphy, Mike, 'An Interview with Francis Searle', *Dark Terrors*, Nov. 1994, pp. 36–9.

FILMOGRAPHY: Shorts: *Fares Fair*; *Little Known England*; *An Ocean Tempest*; *Scenes in Harmony*; *A Cornish Idyll* (1936); *Ace Cinemagazine* (series, co-dir. Andrew Buchanan, 1937); *The War Without End* (1938); *English Oil Wells* (1939); *Citizen's Advice Bureau*; *Hospital Nurse*; *Airwoman*; *Cool Front*; *Sam Pepys Joins the Navy* (1941); *They Keep the Wheels Turning*; *An English Oilfield* (1942); *First Aid on the Spot* (1943); *Student Nurse* (1945); *Day of Grace* (1957); *Music with Max Jaffa* (1958); *Miss MacTaggart Won't Lie Down* (1966); *Talk of the Devil* (1967); *Gold Is Where You Find It* (1968); *The Pale-Faced Girl*; *It All Goes to Show* (1969); *A Hole Lot of Trouble* (1970); *A Couple of Beauties* (1971; rel. 1973).

Features: *A Girl in a Million* (1946); *Things Happen at Night* (1947); *Celia* (1949); *The Man in Black*; *Someone at the Door*; *The Lady Craved Excitement* (1950); *The Rossiter Case*; *Whispering Smith Hits London* (US: *Whispering Smith Versus Scotland Yard*); *Cloudburst*; *A Case for P.C. 49* (1951); *Love's a Luxury* (US: *The Caretaker's Daughter*); *Double Identity*; *Bulldog Drummond* (1952); *Wheel of Fate*; *Murder at 3am* (1953); *Profile*; *One Way Out* (1954); *The Gelignite Gang* (US: *The Dynamiters*, 1956); *Undercover Girl* (1957); *Murder at Site Three* (1959); *Trouble with Eve*; *Ticket to Paradise* (1960); *Freedom to Die* (1961); *Emergency*; *Gaolbreak* (US: *Jailbreak*); *Dead Man's Evidence*; *The Night of the Prowler* (1962); *The Marked One* (1963).

SELLAR, Ian

Ian Sellar was born in Troon, Strathclyde. He began his career working with another highly individual Scottish film-maker Bill Douglas, acting as a runner on *My Childhood* (1972) and then as assistant director on *My Ain Folk* (1973). He was subsequently assistant director to Kevin Brownlow on his English Civil War drama *Winstanley* (1975) and to Joseph Despins on his eccentric musical *Moon over the Alley* (1975). The experience seems to have had a formative influence: the combination of authenticity and lyricism in all these films is also typical of Sellar's best work as a director. In particular Douglas' portrayal of a deprived Scottish childhood finds a direct echo in Sellar's debut feature, *Venus Peter*.

In the late 1970s Sellar wrote and directed three short experimental films on video – *Leicester Square* (1975), *Southwark*

(1976) and *Jubilee Street* (1977) – funded by the BFI's Production Board. In 1981 he enrolled at the National Film and Television School, where he left his studies temporarily to direct his script of *Over Germany/Maikäfer Flieg* . . . (1983) for Channel 4 and the German television company ZDF. His short film *Albert's Memorial*, based on David Cook's novel, marked another important stepping stone.

Both of Sellar's features to date have been mounted with the producer Christopher Young. *Venus Peter* (1989), based on Christopher Rush's *A Twelvemonth and a Day*, a memoir of his childhood in the Fife fishing village of St Monans, was shot on location in the more remote Orkney community of Stromness. Sellar depicts with characteristic sympathy the lonely childhood of Peter (beautifully played by the nine-year-old Gordon Strachan), mixing realism with fantasy as Peter dreams forlornly of his father's return from the sea. As well as evoking childhood longing, the film creates a vivid image of a fast-vanishing way of life in a remote Scottish fishing village; its accomplished cast, including Ray McAnally and Sinead Cusack, is another strength.

Sellar's only other feature film is *Prague*, made for the BBC, but premiered like *Venus* at the Cannes Film Festival, with limited cinema exposure to follow. His story of a young Scot (Alan Cumming) trying to unravel the secrets of his family history shares the earlier film's concern for the past's pervading influence on the present. Sellar conjures up a similarly vivid sense of place, making apt use of Prague's visual splendour to create an atmospheric backdrop for the drama unfolding on its streets.

After *Prague*, Sellar made a fascinating television documentary, *Why East Grinstead*? (1994), about the popularity of cult religions in an otherwise ordinary West Sussex town. Between 1996 and 2000 he was Head of Directing at the National Film and Television School. Since then he has written the script for Robert Bradbrook's acclaimed short film, *Home Road Movie* (2001), a nostalgic evocation of childhood that blurs fantasy and reality in a child's mind through an inventive mix of live action and animation.

(Robert Shail)

BIBLIOGRAPHY: Hopkins, John, 'Video Art: The Work of Ian Sellar', *VFI*, May 1979 pp. 30–1; Kent, Nicolas, '*Venus Peter*', *Sight and Sound*, Spring 1989, pp. 113–16; Rush, Ian, '*Venus Peter*: From Pictures to Pictures', in Eddie Dick (ed.), *From Limelight to Satellite: A Scottish Film Book* (London: BFI, 1990).

FILMOGRAPHY: *Leicester Square* (short, 1975); *Southwark* (short, 1976); *Jubilee Street* (short, 1977); *Albert's Memorial* (short, 1985); *Venus Peter* (1989); *Prague* (UK/Fr, 1992).

SEWELL, Vernon (1903–2001)

Vernon Campbell Sewell was born in London on 4 July 1903 and educated at Marlborough public school. He began his career as camera assistant at Nettlefold Studios, Walton-on-Thames, in 1929 and moved on to become camera operator, sound recordist art director and editor. He also revealed ingenuity in the use of foreground models to achieve special effects and attracted the attention of Michael Powell, who wrote the script of Sewell's first directorial assignment, *The Medium* (1934), which made extensive use of such models. He was production assistant on Powell's *The Edge of the World* (1937) and claimed in 1994 to have directed some sequences of his *The Spy in Black* (1939). Sewell directed several short films in the 1930s, including the VD cautionary tale, *A Test for Love* (1937), but made his name with the still gripping wartime drama *The Silver Fleet* (1943), made for Powell and Pressburger's Archers company. Ralph Richardson plays a Dutch shipbuilder who fakes collaboration with the Germans while organising resistance and sabotage. Sombre self-sacrifice and a tragic denouement more than balance out the derring-do heroics. Gordon Wellesley co-wrote the film and is technically – but not otherwise – its co-director.

Sewell turned down the opportunity to direct *Madonna of the Seven Moons* (Arthur Crabtree, 1944), and went to work with producer Louis Jackson at British National. After *The World Owes Me a Living*, his interesting study of First World War flyers coping badly with peacetime Britain, he had a big financial success with *Latin Quarter*, a gothic remake of *The Medium*, sumptuously and inventively lit by Gunther Krampf. *The Ghosts of Berkeley Square*, with Robert Morley and Felix Aylmer as spirits condemned to haunt a London house until it is visited by a reigning monarch, was less successful despite its jokes and special effects, and most of Sewell's remaining career was confined to B-movies. He made nearly thirty of these, some well above the usual cut-price standards of film-making at this level. A keen yachtsman, he used his own vessel for such films as *Ghost Ship*, starring his wife Joan Carol; *The Floating Dutchman*, with an opening sequence that anticipates Hitchcock's *Frenzy* (1972); and *Dangerous Voyage*, a dim little thriller with minor US star William Lundigan. His best work of this period is in economical and highly effective little thrillers such as *The Man in the Back Seat*, a minimalist tale of a pair of thugs on the run, with a chilling payoff; *The House of Mystery*, which juxtaposes the rational and the supernatural and has a striking finale; and, best of all, *Strongroom*, which again ends unexpectedly after a very tense, absorbing eighty minutes. This is Sewell's most wholly achieved film, though the horror films he made for 'fun' at the end of his career have their admirers. The fact that he had private means allowed him a robust individuality, though it probably meant that he pursued his career less determinedly than he might have done. He died at his home near Durban, South Africa, on 21 June 2001.

(Brian McFarlane)

BIBLIOGRAPHY: BECTU History Project interview, July 1994, tape held in BFI National Library, London; Long, Stanley, Obituary, *Stage, Screen and Radio*, Sept. 2001, p. 22; McFarlane, Brian, *An Autobiography of British Cinema* (London: Methuen, 1997).

FILMOGRAPHY: Shorts: *The Medium* (1934); *Facts and Figures* (doc.); *Men Against the Sea* (doc.) (1935); *A Test for Love*; *Breakers Ahead* (1937); *What Men Live By* (1939).

Features: *The Silver Fleet* (1943); *The World Owes Me a Living* (1945); *Latin Quarter* (1946); *The Ghosts of Berkeley Square* (1947); *Uneasy*

Terms (1948); *Jack of Diamonds* (1949); *A Trek to Mashomba* (doc.); *The Dark Light*; *The Black Widow* (1951); *Ghost Ship* (1952); *The Floating Dutchman*; *Counterspy* (US: *Undercover Agent*) (1953); *Dangerous Voyage* (US: *Terror Ship*); *Radio Cab Murder* (1954); *Johnny, You're Wanted* (1955); *Where There's a Will*; *Soho Incident* (US: *Spin a Dark Web*); *Home and Away* (1956); *Rogue's Yarn* (1957); *The Battle of the V-1* (1958); *Wrong Number* (1959); *The Man in the Back Seat*; *The Winds of Change*; *House of Mystery* (1961); *Strongroom* (1962); *Strictly for the Birds*; *A Matter of Choice* (1963); *Some May Live*; *The Blood Beast Terror* (1967); *Curse of the Crimson Altar* (US: *The Crimson Cult*, 1968); *Burke and Hare* (1971).

SHABAZZ, Menelik (1954–)

Menelik Shabazz was born in Barbados in 1954, but came to Britain when he was six. He became interested in film-making while studying at North London College, and went on to graduate from the London Film School in 1975. His films are characterised by a strong sense of black identity and the struggle against racism and exploitation. *Step Forward Youth* (1977), for example, challenges the racist attitudes encountered by black youths which Horace Ové had explored in his pioneering feature film *Pressure* (1975). *Blood Ah Go Run* (1982) is an account of 1981, the year that Brixton erupted into riots and thirteen black partygoers perished when arsonists struck a house in New Cross.

Shabazz's best-known film is *Burning an Illusion* (1981), the tale of a black secretary who is forced to confront the racist attitudes of the society she has adjusted to when her boyfriend is wrongfully arrested and beaten by the police. The film was suffused with Shabazz's characteristic anger at the injustices faced by ordinary black people. Despite a warm reception from critics and audiences, *Burning an Illusion* opened few doors for Shabazz and it was seven years before he was able to make another feature-length film. *Time and Judgement* (1988), made for the Ceddo Film and Video Workshop, is an allegorical survey of the 1980s from a Rastafarian point of view. Made at a time when the tide was turning against avant-garde cinema, it failed to consolidate Shabazz's career as a director, though *Catch a Fire* (1995), his dramatised documentary about the 1865 Morant Bay rebellion in Jamaica, was widely shown at film festivals. In 1998 he diversified into journalism as founder editor of *Black Filmmaker Magazine*, and organised an annual Black Film Festival, creating useful platforms for a sector of film-makers severely hit by the shift towards genre-based cinema.

(Paul Ward)

BIBLIOGRAPHY: Jaafar, Al, 'Interview', 'Black World', *Sight and Sound* supplement, July 2005, p. 6; Korte, Barbara and Claudia Sternberg, *Bidding for the Mainstream? Black and Asian British Film since the 1990s* (Amsterdam and New York: Rodopi, 2004); Leahy, James, 'Bearing Witness and Burning an Illusion', *Monthly Film Bulletin*, Apr. 1989, pp. 101–2; Pinkerton, Lee, 'A Whole Heritage of Celluloid', *The Voice*, 15 June 1998, p. 48.

FILMOGRAPHY: *Step Forward Youth* (short, 1977); *Burning an Illusion* (1981); *Blood Ah Go Run* (short, 1982); *GLC Bombing* (short, 1985); *Time and Judgement – A Diary of a 400 Year Exile* (1988); *Catch a Fire* (short, 1995).

SHARMAN, Jim (1945–)

Jim Sharman was born in Sydney, New South Wales, on 12 March 1945. He began his career in the theatre, and made his film debut in 1972 with the fantasy *Shirley Thompson versus the Aliens*. Though hardly noticed at the time, this and Sharman's subsequent Australian feature, *The Night, the Prowler* (1978), are now acknowledged as perceptive satires on Australian conservatism. Sharman's best-known film is *The Rocky Horror Picture Show* (1975), based on *The Rocky Horror Show*, a successful fringe musical devised by actor Richard O'Brien and directed by Sharman. On stage, the blend of 1950s' science fiction, 1960s' gothic horror, glam-rock and gender-bending proved a hit with audiences. The production's star turn was Tim Curry, cast as 'sweet transvestite' Dr Frank N. Furter, who gives strait-laced guests Brad and Janet a night to remember. The film version, financed by 20th Century-Fox, acquired American leads Susan Sarandon and Barry Bostwick. Curry reprised his stage role, as did fellow cast members Patricia Quinn, Little Nell

and O'Brien himself. A commercial failure on its initial release, the film went on to achieve a cult following in the United States as one of the first 'Midnight Movies' demanding active audience participation. Sharman and O'Brien reunited in 1981 for *Shock Treatment*, a disappointing spin-off, also backed by 20th Century-Fox; little has been heard of him since.
(Daniel O'Brien)

BIBLIOGRAPHY: Adler, Sue and Robyn Anderson, 'Jim Sharman', *Cinema Papers*, Mar./Apr. 1978, pp. 269–71, 316; Kuipers, Richard, 'Jim Sharman', *IF*, Sept. 1999, p. 60.

FILMOGRAPHY: *Shirley Thompson versus the Aliens* (Austral., 1972); *The Rocky Horror Picture Show* (UK/US, 1975); *Summer of Secrets* (Austral., 1976); *The Night, the Prowler* (Austral., 1978); *Shock Treatment* (UK/US, 1981).

SHARP, Don (1922–)

Donald Sharp was born in Hobart, Tasmania, on 19 April 1922 and acted in amateur productions before joining the Australian Air Force during the Second World War. After being sent home to recover from tuberculosis, Sharp decided to turn professional and in 1948 moved to Britain. In 1950 he wrote, co-produced and co-starred in the boat-racing drama *Ha'penny Breeze* (Frank Worth, 1950). Following another year in hospital, Sharp joined Group 3 where he scripted a number of films, including an adaptation of his novel *Conflict of Wings*, which he directed with John Eldridge in 1954. Sharp went on to direct the children's film *The Stolen Airliner*, and several low-budget features, including *The Golden Disc*, starring pop idol Terry Dene and Sharp's wife Mary Steele, and *It's All Happening*, the Tommy Steele vehicle that marked his transition from rock 'n' roller to popular song-and-dance man. Sharp garnered more praise for *Linda*, a drama that gave Carol White her first starring role as a girl who falls in love with a boy from a street gang (Alan Rothwell).

Sharp came into his own in the 1960s with a series of films made for Hammer Studios and the independent producer Harry Alan Towers, most of them with Christopher Lee in the main role. His first Hammer film, *Kiss of the Vampire*, suffers from an anodyne cast, but has a superbly staged finale featuring an attack by bats. Sharp and Lee first collaborated on the Hammer swashbuckler *The Devil-Ship Pirates*, but made more impact with *The Face of Fu Manchu*, the best of two films that Sharp made for Towers with Lee as Sax Rohmer's super-villain. The film makes good use of Dublin locations to represent 1920s London; it also benefits greatly from Sharp's assured handling and the casting of Nigel Green as Fu Manchu's unflappable nemesis, Nayland Smith. After *The Brides of Fu Manchu*, Sharp returned to Hammer for *Rasputin the Mad Monk*, with Lee in flamboyant form. Sharp's confident handling of action and suspense and his seamless melding of sinuous tracking shots, breathless pacing and carefully composed widescreen framing make it his best film for Hammer.

In the early 1970s Sharp made two undistinguished contemporary horror films – *Psychomania* and *Dark Places* – but he also successfully salvaged the big-budget Alistair Maclean thriller *Puppet on a Chain*. When the fashion for British horror films faded he was able to switch to solidly crafted action thrillers. *Callan* was based on the ITV series of the same name with Edward Woodward as a world-weary British secret agent; while *Hennessy* is notable as one of the few films of the period to deal convincingly with the Irish problem and the threat posed by the IRA. Sharp's version of *The Thirty-Nine Steps* successfully returned to the period setting of Buchan's original novel, with Robert Powell as a plausible, though surprisingly humourless and intransigent Richard Hannay. The $9 million adaptation of Alistair MacLean's *Bear Island*, filmed in British Columbia and at Pinewood, sadly failed to come alive on screen and proved to be his final collaboration with Christopher Lee.

In the 1980s Sharp mainly worked in television, returning to Australia to make the six-part series *Tusitala – The Teller of Tales* (1986). He rounded out his long and varied career with a trio of hugely successful television miniseries derived from best-selling novels by Barbara Taylor Bradford, *A Woman of Substance* (1983), *Hold the Dream* (1986) and *Act of Will* (1989).
(Sergio Angelini)

BIBLIOGRAPHY: Koetting, Christopher, 'Costume Dramas', *Hammer Horror*, June 1995, pp. 8–13; Koetting, Christopher, 'Taste for Excitement: An Interview with Don Sharp', *Filmfax*, Feb./Mar. 1998, pp. 111–14, 122–6; Pirie, David, *A Heritage of Horror* (London: Gordon Fraser, 1973), pp. 114–19.

FILMOGRAPHY: *Conflict of Wings* (US: *Fuss Over Feathers*; assoc. dir., John Eldridge, 1954); *The Stolen Airliner* (1955); *As Old as the Windmill* (short); *Carve Her Name with Pride* (2nd unit dir. Lewis

Gilbert); *Harry Black and the Tiger* (2nd unit dir. Hugo Fregonese) (1957); *The Adventures of Hal 5*; *The Changing Years* (short, co-dir. Hugh Popham); *The Golden Disc* (US: *The Inbetween Age*) (1958); *The Professionals*; *Linda* (1960); *Two Guys Abroad* (unrel.); *The Fast Lady* (2nd unit dir., Ken Annakin) (1962); *Kiss of the Vampire*; *It's All Happening* (US: *The Dream Maker*) (1963); *Witchcraft*; *The Devil-Ship Pirates* (1964); *The Face of Fu Manchu*; *Curse of the Fly*; *Those Magnificent Men in Their Flying Machines* (2nd unit dir. Ken Annakin UK/US) (1965); *Our Man in Marrakesh* (US: *Bang! Bang! You're Dead*); *The Brides of Fu Manchu*; *Rasputin the Mad Monk* (1966); *Rocket to the Moon* (US: *Those Fantastic Flying Fools*, 1967); *The Violent Enemy* (1968); *Taste of Excitement* (1969); *Puppet on a Chain* (2nd unit dir. Geoffrey Reeve, 1970); *Psychomania* (US: *The Death Wheelers*, 1971); *Dark Places* (1973); *Callan* (1974); *Hennessy* (1975); *The Thirty-Nine Steps*; *The Four Feathers* (1978); *Bear Island* (UK/Can, 1979); *What Waits Below* (aka *Secrets of the Phantom Caverns*, 1984).

SHARP, Ian (1946–)

Born in Clitheroe, Lancashire, on 13 November 1946, Ian Sharp pursued a successful career as a television director before making his feature debut in 1979 with *The Music Machine*, a low-budget production exploiting the disco craze. Touted as Britain's answer to *Saturday Night Fever* (John Badham, 1977), the film stars Gerry Sundquist, whose character dreams of escaping the dole queue via a dance contest. Sharp attracted more attention with *Who Dares Wins*, a clunky right-wing action movie with Lewis Collins (who had starred in the television series *The Professionals*) as an SAS officer and Judy Davis as a misguidedly idealistic terrorist leader. Sharp returned to television to direct episodes of *Minder* (1982), *Robin of Sherwood* (1984) and *Yesterday's Dreams* (1987); but also served as second-unit director on *Who Framed Roger Rabbit* and *GoldenEye*. He displayed his ideological flexibility in two interesting television films: *The Secret Weapon* (TVS, 1990), based on the true story of Mordechai Vanunu, the liberal Israeli who was lured from his safe haven in England, drugged, kidnapped and incarcerated for exposing Israel's nuclear weapons programme; and *Pursuit* (HTV/Columbia, 1990), a fictional story about a Nazi officer who disguises himself as a Jew. After a television adaptation of *Tess of the D'Urbervilles* (LWT, 1998), Sharp returned to the big screen with *Mrs Caldicot's Cabbage War*, a modest comedy starring Pauline Collins. It was released, after long delays, in 2003 but attracted dismissive reviews and little interest from audiences.

(Daniel O'Brien)

BIBLIOGRAPHY: Brett, Anwar, 'Making a Last Stand: Wrinklies to the Rescue in *Mrs Caldicot's Cabbage War*', *Exposure*, Spring 2001, pp. 6–7; 'The Music Machine', *Continental Film Review*, Feb. 1979, p. 5.

FILMOGRAPHY: *The Music Machine* (1979); *Who Dares Wins* (US: *The Final Option*, 1982); *Who Framed Roger Rabbit* (2nd unit dir., Robert Zemeckis, US, 1988); *Split Second* (co-dir., uncredited, Tony Maylam, 1991); *GoldenEye* (2nd unit dir., Martin Campbell, US, 1995); *Mrs Caldicot's Cabbage War* (2003).

SHAUGHNESSY, Alfred (1916–)

Alfred Shaughnessy was born in London in 1916, shortly after the death in action of his Canadian father. His American mother subsequently married an equerry to the Prince of Wales. He was educated at Eton, and having briefly sampled the army and the Stock Exchange found his *métier* in the theatre, writing sketches and lyrics for revues. After wartime service he joined the script department of Ealing Studios in 1946.

From script-reading, Shaughnessy moved on to acting as assistant to Henry Cornelius on *Passport to Pimlico* (1949) and Thorold Dickinson on *Secret People* (1951). Seconded in 1951 to Group 3, the state-funded low-budget outfit of which Michael Balcon was Chairman, he turned writer-producer on the comedies *Brandy for the Parson* (John Eldridge, 1952) and *Laxdale Hall* (John Eldridge, 1953). His chance to direct came in 1956 from the trade-union-backed production company ACT Films, for whom he made a lean little thriller, *Suspended Alibi*. His next film, *Cat Girl*, an early entry in the British horror cycle, packed an erotic charge that suggested Shaughnessy might have excelled in this genre. No more horror movies being on offer, Shaughnessy tackled *Six-Five Special*, a film adaptation of the top television pop show of the day. His fourth and last film as director was *The Impersonator*, from his own original story – an intriguingly off-beat thriller about a murderous pantomime dame.

Shaughnessy had been writing for television since the early 1950s, and in 1971 he hit the jackpot with *Upstairs, Downstairs*, the saga of a London townhouse during the first third of the twentieth century, made for London Weekend Television. It ran for sixty-eight episodes (of which Shaughnessy wrote fifteen), and was endlessly screened and re-screened all over the world. He continued to write for television until the mid-1980s.

(Philip Kemp)

BIBLIOGRAPHY: Shaughnessy, Alfred, *Both Ends of the Candle* (London: Peter Owen, 1978); Shaughnessy, Alfred, *A Confession in Writing* (Padstow, Cornwall: Tabb House, 1997).

FILMOGRAPHY: *Suspended Alibi* (1956); *Cat Girl* (1957); *Six-Five Special* (1958); *The Impersonator* (1961).

SHEPHERD, Horace (1892–1960)

Horace Shepherd was born in Richmond, Surrey, on 10 October 1892. A talented musician, he wrote orchestral scores for the British presentations of numerous prestigious silent films including *Way Down East* (D. W. Griffith, 1920), *The Four Horsemen of the Apocalypse* (Rex Ingram, 1921) and *The Sea Beast* (Millard Webb, 1926). In 1926 he became musical director for Fox Films in Britain, scoring *Seventh Heaven* (Frank Borzage, 1927), *Sunrise* (F. W. Murnau, 1927) and others; he also supplied accompaniments to many Universal releases.

With the onset of talkies, Shepherd transferred his attention from live accompaniments to film soundtracks. Industrious and flexible, his musical assignments ranged from Augusto Genina's artistically ambitious *Prix de beauté* (1930) to experimental broadcasts for BBC Television. But increasingly he moved into production. After a cartoon series featuring Bingo the dog failed in 1930, he found a niche in the quota market producing and directing a daunting array of travelogues, musical and interest shorts through his company Inspiration Films. To save on costs, paintings and postcards were sometimes used to generate footage, and in his musical shorts the camera rarely budged an inch. He also ventured into fiction features, initially with *The Music Maker* (1936), a sentimental quickie about an old violinist struggling to complete a symphony before he dies.

Interspersed with the musical medleys and celebrations of picturesque English scenery that Shepherd busied himself with in the 1940s are two more unusual credits. In 1942 he composed, arranged and conducted the music for Lance Comfort's melodrama *Hatter's Castle* (1942), greatly enhancing its brooding atmosphere; and in 1948 he directed *The Flamingo Affair*, a low-budget feature about an ex-army officer who finds it difficult to adjust to his diminished status in post-war Britain and is ensnared by a femme fatale into the black market. Though Shepherd's direction is unremarkable, the subject's topicality and a guest appearance by Stéphane Grappelly keep the film lively. One other film, *A Ray of Sunshine* (1950), a modest revue compered by Ted Ray, reached feature length. Shepherd continued making shorts until his death in Holloway, north London, on 10 March 1960.

(Geoff Brown and Robert Murphy)

BIBLIOGRAPHY: Clay, Andrew, 'Men, Women and Money: Masculinity in Crisis in the British Professional Crime Film 1946–1965', in Steve Chibnall and Robert Murphy (eds), *British Crime Cinema* (London and New York: Routledge, 1999); Low, Rachael, *Films of Comment and Persuasion of the 1930s* (London: George Allen & Unwin, 1979); Shepherd, Phyllis, letter about her husband's career, *BFI News* no. 20, Nov. 1975, p. 2.

SELECTED FILMOGRAPHY: Shorts: *Moments with the Immortals* (series, 1933); *Representations of Famous Pictures* (series); *Voices Immortal* (series) (1934); *The Romance of England* (series, 1935); *Romantic England* (series); *Romance of Industry* (series) (1936); *This England* (series); *Symphonies in Stone* (series); *Famous Painters* (series); *Famous Women of the Past* (series) (1937); *The Immortal Brush* (series); *Old Homesteads of England* (series); *Old English Taverns* (series); *London Past and Present*; *Songs of the Homeland* (series); *Melodies of the Moment* (1938); *Paradise Island*; *Spirit of England* (series); *Moods of a Metropolis*; *Safety Fast*; *Cavalcade of the Navy* (series); *Eddie Carroll and His Boys*; *Radio Nights* (1939); *Lovely Wales*; *Danger Coast of Britain*; *Love on Leave* (1940); *Musical Cocktail*; *Once upon a Time* (1941); *Swingonometry*; *Harry Parry and His Radio Rhythm Club Sextet*; *Valley of the Windrush* (1943); *Cotswold Idyll*; *Winter Scene* (1944); *Westminster Abbey*; *Sport of Princes* (1945); *Mist in the Hollows*; *Rhythm*; *Picking up the Threads*; *Cornish Holiday*; *Candy's Calendar* (1946); *Musical Masquerade* (1946); *What Do You Know?* (series, 1946–51); *Things Great and Small*; *Snowdonia*; *Making the Grade*; *Musical Romance*; *Life Is Nothing without Music* (1947); *Land of Legend*; *On the Roofs of London*; *Movie Memories*; *Stéphane Grappelly and His Quintet*; *Eugene Pini and His Orchestra* (1948); *A Touch of Shamrock*; *Music Parade* (1949); *A Crazy Day with Max Wall* (1950); *Mirth and Melody* (1951); *The Great City* (1952); *The Windrush* (1953); *Winston Lee and His Orchestra* (series, 1954); *Corners of a Capital* (1955); *Beautiful Bedfordshire* (1956).

Feature films: *The Music Maker* (as Hugh Kairs, 1936); *The Flamingo Affair* (aka *Blonde for Danger*, 1948); *A Ray of Sunshine: An Irresponsible Medley of Song and Dance* (1950).

SHERIDAN, Jim (1949–)

Producer, director, writer, actor, Jim Sheridan was a prominent figure of the New Wave of Irish film-making in the 1990s. The characteristics that define the movement define Sheridan's film-making itself – an acceptance of, if not affection for, the forms and contents of mainstream genre film-making, and a simultaneous urge to shatter these norms by a subtextual examination of specifically Irish issues. In short, a balance between mainstream entertainment and social statement, a use of personalised drama to make political critiques.

Born in Dublin on 6 February 1949, Sheridan attended University College, Dublin, in 1972, and went on to study at the Abbey School of Acting before co-founding Dublin's Project Theatre. In 1981 he moved to New York where he became Director of the Irish Arts Centre.

Sheridan returned to Ireland to make his first feature film, *My Left Foot* (1989), based on the autobiographical novel by the disabled Dublin working-class painter and writer Christie Brown. Mixing Hollywood biopic elements with an examination of social contradictions – disability and ability, art and commerce, conflicting class perspectives – it was a huge success; Daniel Day-Lewis and Brenda Fricker both won Academy Awards for their performances.

Sheridan's adaptation of John B. Keane's rural play *The Field* featured an intense Richard Harris as Bull McCabe, an obsessed farmer who has spent his life cultivating a desolate field owned by a local landlady. Brilliant at times, *The Field* was marred by shifting the action of the play back to the 1930s, replacing Keane's socialist critique of Ireland's 1960s' capitalism with a vague exposition on the heritage of the Great Famine in rural Ireland.

In 1993 Sheridan and Arthur Lapin established the company Hell's Kitchen and made *In the Name of the Father*, adapted by Sheridan and the former political prisoner Terry George from Gerry Conlon's autobiography, *Proved Innocent*. The film deals with events surrounding the wrongful imprisonment of Conlon (played by Daniel Day-Lewis) and others for the IRA bombing of a Guildford pub in 1974. Combining powerful drama with a high-voltage flow of factual information, it forcefully exposes corruption within the British legal system and remains Sheridan's most skilful and contentious work.

In 1997 Sheridan produced and co-wrote *Some Mother's Son*, directed by Terry George, a political drama focusing on two mothers whose sons are involved in the 1981 IRA hunger strikes. He went on to direct *The Boxer*, a film that examines changing Republican attitudes in the lead-up to the Belfast Agreement that was finally signed in April 1998. Danny Flynn (Daniel Day-Lewis), ex-boxer, ex-IRA prisoner, attempts to redress his past by running a non-sectarian boxing club in Belfast. Though critically well received, the film's polemics lacked the force of Sheridan's best work.

Sheridan has since co-produced *Agnes Brown* (Angelica Huston, 1999), *On the Edge* (John Carney, 2000) and *Bloody Sunday* (Paul Greengrass, 2002). *In America*, written by Sheridan and his daughters Kirsten and Naomi, is based on his family's experience in New York in the 1980s.

(Eugene Finn)

BIBLIOGRAPHY: Barton, Ruth, *Jim Sheridan* (Dublin: Liffey Press, 2002); McLoone, Martin, 'In the Name of the Father', *Cinéaste* vol. 20 no. 4, 1994, pp. 44–7; Sheridan, Jim, 'Words, Pictures, and Buildings', *Film Base News*, no. 12, Apr./May 1989, pp. 10–12.

FILMOGRAPHY: *My Left Foot* (1989); *The Field* (1990); *In the Name of the Father* (UK/US/Ir, 1993); *The Boxer* (UK/US/Ir, 1997); *In America* (US, 2002); *Get Rich or Die Tryin'* (US, 2005).

SHERIDAN, Kirsten (1976–)

Kirsten Sheridan was born in Dublin on 14 July 1976, the daughter of film director Jim Sheridan. She played small roles in her father's *My Left Foot* (1989) and *The Boxer* (1997) and collaborated with her father and her sister Naomi on the script for *In America* (Jim Sheridan, 2002). After attending Dun Laoghaire film school, she wrote, produced and directed her first short film, *The Bench*, in 1995, and helped out as camera operator and assistant director for other independent film-makers. Subsequent work in shorts included a documentary (*Walking into Mirrors*), a drama (*Patterns*) about autism and, most ambitiously, *The Case of Majella McGinty*, a black comedy about a child's misinterpretation of reality in Derry during the Troubles of the 1970s.

Her debut feature, *Disco Pigs* (2001), was adapted from a play by Enda Walsh about the passionate but increasingly fraught relationship between two seventeen-year-olds, bonded as babies but now troubled by the onset of sexuality. Its artistic pretensions made the project a good candidate for Irish, European and UK government funding, though distribution beyond film festivals proved a problem. Sheridan and Walsh are inventive in transcending the story's stage origins and Cillian Murphy's charismatic presence is an asset, but fairy-tale whimsicality fits ill with his psychopathic charm. At times almost an Irish equivalent of *Badlands* (Terrence Malick, 1973), the film founders on its lurching swings between touching innocence and a degree of extreme violence that drains away sympathy from the decreasingly interesting characters. Nonetheless, Sheridan's boldness and originality bode well for her future.

(Robert Murphy)

BIBLIOGRAPHY: 'Animal Harm: Kirsten Sheridan on *Disco Pigs*', *Film Ireland* no. 83, Oct./Nov. 2001, pp. 12–15; Patrick, John, 'Transformer', *Film Ireland* no. 82, Aug./Sept. 2001, pp. 16–18.

FILMOGRAPHY: *The Bench* (short, Ir, 1995); *Gentleman Caller* (short, Ir, 1996); *Walking into Mirrors* (short, Ir, 1997); *Patterns* (short, Ir, 1998); *The Case of Majella McGinty* (short, Ir, 1999); *Disco Pigs* (UK/Ir, 2001).

SHERMAN, Gary (1945–)

Gary Sherman was born in Chicago in 1945. He began his career making television commercials, most famously for Coca-Cola, where he was responsible for the New Seekers singing 'I'd Like to Buy the World a Coke'. His debut feature, *Death Line* (which he wrote under the pseudonym Ceri Jones), was a modestly budgeted British horror film that stands as a rare instance of an American film-maker examining London as perceptively as John Boorman explores Los Angeles in *Point Blank* (1968) and John Schlesinger New York in *Midnight Cowboy* (1969). Sherman based his script on a Victorian anecdote about navvies entombed after the collapse of a half-built tube tunnel; in *Death Line*, the descendant of these workmen is a cannibal creature who picks off late-night commuters from Russell Square Station and communicates by crying out the only phrase he knows, 'Mind the doors!' Unashamedly gruesome, the film has a streak of black comedy, with a fine lead performance from Donald Pleasence (and a one-scene cameo from Christopher Lee as a nasty civil servant). Pleasence's tea-drinking copper struggles through red tape to solve the mystery, but uncovering the truth does little to alleviate the gloom of this grim little film.

On returning to America, Sherman continued to make horror films, but *Dead & Buried* (1981) suffered from the conflicting demands of its many producers, and *Poltergeist III* (1988) is marred by the weak ending necessitated by the untimely death of its child star, Heather O'Rourke. Latterly Sherman has transferred his talents to American television.

(Kim Newman)

BIBLIOGRAPHY: Andrews, Nigel, '*Death Line*', *Financial Times*, 17 Nov. 1972; Del Toro, Guillermo, 'Notes from the Underground', *Sight and Sound*, Jan. 1995, p. 41; Wood, Robin, '*Death Line*', *Monthly Film Bulletin*, Jan. 1973, p. 6; Wooley, John and Michael Price, '*Deathline*: The Tracks of Your Tears', *Fangoria* no. 221, Apr. 2003, pp. 42–7, 82.

FILMOGRAPHY (UK only): *Death Line* (US: *Raw Meat*, 1972).

SHONTEFF, Lindsay (1935–2006)

Lindsay Shonteff was born in Toronto on 5 November 1935. He left school at sixteen and after making *The Bum* (1957), an amateur film about a Toronto tramp who murders for money but is run down by a truck, was accepted as a low-ranking crew member on Bill Davidson's *Ivy League Killers* (1959). He was encouraged by fellow enthusiast Sidney J. Furie to make his professional debut with *The Hired Gun* (1961), a cut-price Western. Disappointed by the few opportunities opening up for him in Canada, Shonteff followed Furie to England. Prospects initially appeared dim, but Furie was able to pass on to him *Devil Doll*

(1963), a black-and-white thriller. Though Shonteff showed little aptitude for suspense, another thriller followed, *Curse of Simba* (1965), with supposedly African exteriors shot on Hampstead Heath.

Shonteff hit his stride with *Licensed to Kill* (1965), a funny, clever spoof of the James Bond films. It was successful enough to lead to a five-picture deal with Columbia; but, ever the maverick, Shonteff refused to countenance corporate infringements on his creativity and decamped to Hong Kong to make *Sumuru* (1967) for independent producer Harry Alan Towers. With a cast including Shirley Eaton, Klaus Kinski, George Nader, Frankie Avalon and Wilfrid Hyde-White, this ought to have been Shonteff's finest hour, but his vision of the film as a comedy conflicted with Towers' demand for oriental thrills and the result was a messy compromise.

Shonteff's career might have come to a full stop here had he not raised a tiny budget of £11,000 to make *Clegg* (1969), a violent private-eye thriller successful enough to lead to other projects, albeit ones less prestigious than Columbia might have backed. *Night after Night* (1969) was interfered with and stuck in distribution limbo, but *Permissive* (1970) – a remarkably bleak study of the unsavoury underside of the rock music scene, originally titled *Susy Superscrew* – proved a success, as did *The Yes Girls* (1971), a more conventional dose of soft-core pornography.

Shonteff's 1970s' output, mostly produced by his wife Elizabeth Gray, is bewilderingly eclectic. After making a violent thriller, *The Fast Kill* (1972), he directed two exercises in high-camp japery, *Big Zapper* (1973) and *The Swordsman* (1974), and then tried to emulate Furie's success with *The Ipcress File* (1965) by adapting Len Deighton's *Spy Story* (1976). Unfortunately too much talk and not enough action led to disappointing box-office returns. Shonteff bounced back with another passable Bond spoof, *No. 1 of the Secret Service* (1977), but then lost out again with a weak sequel, *Licensed to Love and Kill* (1979). Subsequently he charted new territory with *How Sleep the Brave* (1981), a Vietnam combat film shot on location in Berkshire. He finally returned to North America in the early 1990s, making *The Running Gun*, a Western, and *Ice Cold in Phoenix*, a psychological thriller, in Arizona; both films suffered considerable delays before being released.

Allan Bryce, in a not uncritical assessment of Shonteff's achievements, argues that:

> See enough of Lindsay's films and you'll begin to appreciate the recurring elements that add that unique Shonteff touch: the oddball casting, the bizarre locations (Gerrard's Cross standing in for Vietnam), the sleazy characters . . . the constant bouts of explosive violence that go on far too long to be convincing, his imaginative use of widescreen, and, of course, the completely incomprehensible plots. (Bryce, 1994, p. 22)

This may not constitute much of an addition to the art of cinema, but Shonteff's buccaneering enterprises make a welcome antidote to the sometimes dull predictability of corporate film-making. Lindsay Shonteff died in England on 11 March 2006. (Robert Murphy)

BIBLIOGRAPHY: Bryce, Allan, 'Lindsay Shonteff: Last of the Independents Interviewed', *Dark Side* no. 22, July 1992 pp. 13–22; Bryce, Allan, *Nickels and Dimes and No Time: The Ups and Downs of Lindsay Shonteff*, in Stefan Jaworzyn (ed), *Shock Xpress 2* (London: Titan, 1994), <www.lindsayshonteff.com>; Leader, Raymond, 'Shonteff's Way to Independence', *Screen International*, 28 Aug. 1976, p. 15; Upton, Julian, 'The Last Years of British Exploitation Cinema', *Bright Lights* no. 33, July 2001 <www.brightlightsfilm.com/33/britishexploitation1.html>.

FILMOGRAPHY: *The Bum* (short, Can, 1957); *The Hired Gun* (Can, 1961); *Devil Doll* (1963); *Curse of Simba* (aka *Curse of the Voodoo*); *Licensed to Kill* (US: *The Second Best Secret Agent in the Whole Wide World*) (1965); *Run with the Wind* (1966); *Sumuru* (aka *The Million Eyes of Su-Muru*, 1967); *Clegg*; *Night after Night after Night* (as Lewis J. Force) (1969); *Permissive* (1970); *The Yes Girls* (aka *Take Some Girls*, 1971); *The Fast Kill* (1972); *Big Zapper* (aka *The Sex Life of a Female Private Eye*, 1973); *The Swordsman* (aka *Zapper's Blade of Vengeance*, 1974); *Spy Story* (1976); *No. 1 of the Secret Service* (1977); *Licensed to Love and Kill* (1979) *How Sleep the Brave* (1981); *The Killing Edge*; *Lipstick and Blood* (1984); *Number One Gun* (1990); *The Running Gun* (1992; rel. 1996); *Ice Cold in Phoenix* (1992; rel. 2004).

SHUREY, Dinah (1887–?)

Dinah Shurey was born Dorothy Shurey in London, c. 1887. During the Great War she served with the French Red Cross and contributed to organising Lena Ashwell's frontline concerts. Returning to England, she acted as business manager to the actor-manager H. V. Esmond and for some time was assistant director at Master Films. The company folded in 1922, and in 1923 Shurey founded Britannia Films. Her first production, *Afraid of Love* (Reginald H. West, 1925), prompted controversy and censor cuts by co-starring a socialite involved in a recent court case about non-consummation of marriage. Later, after persuading the Admiralty to lend her several battleships, the energetic Shurey achieved wider success with a series of wartime melodramas. Shurey employed bright young men, just starting out, on her production team, but kept a strong hand over all aspects of film-making. *Second to None* (1926) was produced by Shurey and directed by Jack Raymond. She shared production and direction of *Carry On!* (1927) with Victor Peers, but took sole directorial control of *The Last Post* (1929). Other key team members included the experienced scenarist Lydia Hayward and Moore Marriott, an effective leading man in *Second to None* and *Carry On!*

Against the emphasis on post-war trauma in 1920s' British cinema, crystallised in the figure of the 'wounded man', Shurey's films revert to traditionally popular themes of cross-class male friendships and rivalries forged by patriotic sentiment and noble sacrifice. The convincing pictures of naval activity and glimpses of ordinary sailors' lives – even the interiors of *Second to None* were shot at sea – gave audiences pleasure, but critics registered surprise at the 'unblushing exaltation of warlike fervour' of Britain's only woman director, and the editor of *The Film Weekly* complained of 'patriotic clap-trap'. When the journal's iconoclastic columnist Nerina Shute asserted that 'it is pathetically obvious that women can't produce films', citing Shurey's 'appalling pictures' as evidence, Shurey sued for libel and won. In 1930 she set up a renting company, Showman Films, which distributed a sound version of *The Last Post*. But the sound era had no room for Shurey: in 1932 Britannia Films ceased activity, as did Showman shortly afterwards, and she was left bankrupt.

Shurey's position as a woman active in the industry was recognised in her membership of the Film Group set up by the Federation of British Industries in the mid-1920s. In 1930 the Film Society invited her to present a reel of *The Last Post* at its 'All-Woman Programme'. However, alongside the more sophisticated work of Dorothy Arzner and the experimentalism of Germaine Dulac it could only seem old-fashioned.
(Christine Gledhill)

BIBLIOGRAPHY: *Yorkshire Post*, 30 Nov. 1926; Nerina Shute, 'Can Women Direct Films?' *Film Weekly*, 10 June 1929, p. 12; 'Film Weekly Sued for Libel: Woman Director's Action', *Film Weekly*, 8 Feb. 1930, p. 25.

FILMOGRAPHY: *Carry On!* (co-dir. Victor Peers, 1927); *The Last Post* (silent, 1929; sound, 1930).

SIDNEY, George (1916–2002)

Born into a Long Island showbusiness family on 4 October 1916, George Sidney acted on the stage from an early age. He joined MGM in the early 1930s, working his way up from messenger boy to director of screen tests and shorts before making his feature debut with *Free and Easy* (1941). Sidney quickly established himself with brash entertainments such as *The Harvey Girls* (1946), *Annie Get Your Gun* (1950) and *Show Boat* (1951), and occasional non-musicals like *The Three Musketeers* (1948) and *Scaramouche* (1952).

Sidney's last film as director and producer was *Half a Sixpence*, a Paramount musical made in Britain. Adapted from H. G. Wells' novel *Kipps* (previously filmed by Carol Reed in 1941), it was expressly designed as a vehicle for the all-singing, all-dancing, all-grinning Tommy Steele, who had enjoyed long runs with the stage production in London and New York. Gillian Lynne's choreography is more energetic than imaginative and there is only one memorable number ('Flash, Bang, Wallop!') in David Heneker's score; Geoffrey Unsworth's cinematography is heavy on diffusion, and the star overplays in every key from comedy to pathos. Nonetheless, Sidney did his usual polished, professional job, the film cost one-fifth as much as the year's other British-based roadshow blockbuster, Richard Fleischer's *Doctor Dolittle*, and was a box-office success in the UK if not in the US. Sidney died in Las Vegas, of complications from lymphoma, on 5 May 2002.
(Sheldon Hall)

BIBLIOGRAPHY: Masson, Alain, 'George Sidney: Artificial Brilliance/The Brilliance of Artifice', in Rick Altman (ed.), *Genre: The Musical: A Reader* (London: Routledge & Kegan Paul/BFI, 1981); Monder, Eric, 'George Sidney's Hi-Tech Vaudeville Show', *Film Comment*, July/Aug. 1994, pp. 50–9; Sidney, George, 'The Three Ages of the Musical', *Films and Filming*, June 1968, pp. 4–7.

FILMOGRAPHY (UK only): *Half a Sixpence* (UK/US, 1967).

SIEGEL, Don (1912–1991)

Donald Siegel was born in Chicago, on 26 October 1912, and studied in Britain at Cambridge and RADA. Back in America, he joined Warner Bros. as a film librarian, becoming in turn assistant editor, director of inserts, head of montages and second-unit director. He made two Academy Award-winning short subjects in 1945, and then directed his first feature, *The Verdict* (1946). Siegel established his reputation with a run of distinguished B-movies and low-budget programmers, notably *Riot in Cell Block 11* (1954) and *Invasion of the Body Snatchers* (1956). After spending most of the 1960s working in television, he hit the big time with five Clint Eastwood vehicles, including *Dirty Harry* (1971).

Late in his career Siegel made two films in Britain, neither of which ranks among his best. Both involve a theft of diamonds: in *The Black Windmill*, they are used as ransom by spy Michael Caine to help rescue his kidnapped son. Despite capable action sequences and some characteristic Siegel themes – such as the maverick law enforcer who bucks the system – it is generally flat and pedestrian. *Rough Cut*, an attempt at a 1960s-style caper thriller, coasts on the charm of its star, Burt Reynolds, but has little of the director's usual edge and energy. Siegel ran afoul of its producer David Merrick's constant interference, eventually being fired from the picture; after a similar experience with Bette Midler on *Jinxed!* (1982), he retired. Siegel died of cancer in Nipoma, California, on 20 April 1991.
(Sheldon Hall)

BIBLIOGRAPHY: Pirie, David, 'Siegel's Bluff', *Sight and Sound*, Autumn 1973, p. 204; Rosenthal, Stuart and Judith M. Kass, *The Hollywood Professionals Volume 4: Tod Browning, Don Siegel* (London: Tantivy/New York: A. S. Barnes, 1971); Siegel, Don, *A Siegel Film: An Autobiography* (London: Faber and Faber, 1993).

FILMOGRAPHY (UK only): *The Black Windmill* (UK/US, 1974); *Rough Cut* (co-dir., uncredited, Robert Ellis Miller, US/UK, 1980).

SIMMONS, Anthony (1922–)

Anthony Simmons was born on 16 December 1922 in London, a city he documented with tenderness and honesty in films that earned critical respect but never pushed him forward in the industry as far as his talents deserved. He trained as a barrister, and made his first professional contact with cinema researching the Italian industry for a UNESCO publication. Excited by Ital-

ian neo-realism, in 1947 he made a documentary about life in a Bulgarian village. Success arrived with the Venice Film Festival prize-winner *Sunday by the Sea* (1953), a vivid thirteen-minute impression of Londoners enjoying an outing to Southend, the first of numerous films made through Harlequin Productions, formed by Simmons, Leon Clore and John Arnold in 1951.

In *Sunday by the Sea* and its equally compact successor, *Bow Bells*, a lively depiction of London's East End, Simmons and his cameraman Walter Lassally presented a lyrical, humanist view of working-class life, not far in attitude from Lindsay Anderson's shorts and other manifestations of 'Free Cinema'. As with Anderson, the jump into features proved difficult. For Harlequin, Simmons supported John Arnold's directing debut (*The Passing Stranger*) in 1954, and served as a co-producer of Losey's heated suspense drama *Time Without Pity* (1957); but his own feature debut, *Your Money or Your Wife* (1960), a cheaply made comedy with Donald Sinden and Peggy Cummins, proved a chore for all concerned, especially the audience.

Simmons' next feature emerged five years later. *Four in the Morning*, crisply photographed by Larry Pizer, was originally planned as a documentary on Thameside life in London, but the National Film Finance Corporation encouraged its expansion into a fiction feature. A girl's body is washed ashore in the early hours; a casual affair flares and fades; a fraught young mother (Judi Dench) with a howling baby quarrels with her drunken husband. Each strand forms part of a downbeat, sensitive tapestry of relationships under pressure, where the women, exhausted and bitter, always bear the brunt. Festival prizes at Locarno and Cannes and critical support at home cemented the film's status, but its melancholy realism clashed with the new spirit of 'Swinging' London, and cinema bookings were few.

Simmons' third feature emerged after nine years of modest endeavours, including television commercials. His script for *The Optimists of Nine Elms* (1974) had originally been written with Buster Keaton in mind. In 1964 it appeared as a novel; in 1973, in a final transformation, the property became a vehicle for Peter Sellers, cast as the busker who befriends Battersea slum children. Eccentric caricature dogged Sellers' performance, but the film's general treatment stayed wistful, well observed and only faintly sentimental.

In *Black Joy* (1977), based on a play by Jamal Ali, the focus shifted to another London area, Brixton. The combustible real-life black-and-white mix found scant reflection; instead Simmons offered a bustling, good-humoured outsider's view of the black community, with helter-skelter dialogue, a pounding soundtrack (soul and reggae) and a light spattering of stereotypes. Reviews were kindly; distribution remained poor.

After an unfortunate brush with the mainstream – he was fired after several weeks on ITC's romantic adventure *Green Ice* (Ernest Day, 1980) – television became Simmons' main employer. The high point was *On Giant's Shoulders* (BBC, 1979), an Emmy award-winning drama about a thalidomide boy and his effect on the couple who adopt him. Simmons' halting progress through the industry is scarcely unusual for British documentary talent; but the mordant beauty of *Four in the Morning* makes it especially regrettable. His last completed feature remains *Little Sweetheart* (1988), an unlikely thriller shot in Florida, produced by the BBC for cinema release; it found few takers.

(Geoff Brown)

BIBLIOGRAPHY: Hodgson, Clive, 'Anthony Simmons', *National Film Theatre Programme*, Apr. 1980, pp. 34–5; BECTU History Project interview, tape held in the BFI National Library, London; Murphy, Robert, *Sixties British Cinema* (London: BFI, 1992).

FILMOGRAPHY: Shorts and documentaries: *Bulgarian Village* (1947); *We Who Are Young* (as Andrew Taylor, 1952); *One Great Vision* (as Andrew Taylor); *Sunday by the Sea* (1953); *Bow Bells* (1954); *The Gentle Corsican (*1956); *Blood Is Life* (1957); *From First to Last* (1962); *No Short Cut* (1964); *Greenwich – A People's Heritage* (1976).

Features: *Your Money or Your Wife* (1960); *Four in the Morning* (1965); *The Optimists of Nine Elms* (US: *The Optimists*, 1974); *Black Joy* (1977); *Little Sweetheart* (aka *Poison Candy*, 1988).

SIMPSON, John

John Simpson is an Irish writer and director. His amusing short *Silicone Valerie* was followed by *Freeze Frame*, an intriguing feature with Lee Evans playing a man so paranoid that he insists on recording his whole life on videotape. Unfortunately, the film loses momentum as the implausible plot unfolds.

(Robert Murphy)

FILMOGRAPHY: *Silicone Valerie* (short, 1997); *Freeze Frame* (2004).

SIMPSON, Julian (1972–)

Julian Simpson was born in London on 6 March 1972. He studied film at university, but soon dropped out and used his student loan to make *Any Dream Will Do*, a macabre story of a man who ends up murdering his dinner guests. Simpson worked for a time in advertising, and spent five years raising £3 million to make his debut feature, *The Criminal*, which has most of the virtues and only a few of the vices of the recent spate of low-budget British crime films. Virtuoso camerawork and flashy editing techniques help make palatable an overcomplicated plot, and Simpson maintains a tight grip on the disconnected chronological structure that most post-Tarantino thrillers seem to demand. *The Criminal*'s film noir opening is convincingly Kafkaesque (the protagonist – a musician played by Steven Mackintosh – is known as 'J') and foreshadows its later descent into a paranoid conspiracy reminiscent of Alan J. Pakula's *The Parallax View* (1974). However, the sound design is thin and many of the secondary characters are woefully under-written.

After his adventurous debut Simpson went on to make *Without You* (2003), a half-hour thriller for the BBC about a man who murders his wife, then loses the car in which he has hidden her body, and episodes of *Murder Prevention* (2004) and *The Inspector Lynley Mysteries* (2005).

(Sergio Angelini)

BIBLIOGRAPHY: Tutt, Louise, 'Case Study: *The Criminal*', *Screen International*, 2 Feb. 2001, p. 23.

FILMOGRAPHY: *Any Dream Will Do* (short, 1994); *The Criminal* (1999).

SINYOR, Gary (1962–)

Gary Sinyor has established a modest but distinctive niche within British cinema as a director of comedies ranging from the whimsically romantic to the quirkily satirical. At its best, his work evokes the spirit of Ealing in its eccentric humour and affectionate mockery of aspects of British cultural identity.

Born in Manchester in 1962, Sinyor attended the National Film and Television School and made his feature debut with Vadim Jean as co-director of *Leon the Pig Farmer* (1992), still his most distinctive film. Drawing heavily on Sinyor's own Jewish background, the film paints a gently parodic picture of a confused young Jewish man, played by Mark Frankel, who is shocked to discover that he was actually conceived by artificial insemination and is the biological son of a Yorkshire pig farmer. The film works a familiar vein of Jewish humour, building on themes established in his earlier short film script, *The Unkindest Cut* (Jim Shields, 1990). The jokes are bolstered by fine comic performances from the strong cast, especially Brian Glover as the pig farmer. Despite its low budget, the film became a considerable popular and critical success, winning the Chaplin Award for Best First Feature at the Edinburgh Film Festival.

None of Sinyor's solo features to date have realised the promise of *Leon the Pig Farmer*. His first, *Solitaire for 2*, is an awkwardly playful romantic fantasy about a body-language lecturer (Mark Frankel again) whose courtship of an attractive palaeontologist (Amanda Pays) is complicated by her ability to read minds. The material has possibilities; but the production plainly needed more time on the drawing board. All is not what it might have been either in *Stiff Upper Lips*, a well-timed parody of Merchant Ivory productions, featuring Georgina Cates as the virginal Edwardian heroine who discovers sex. There are occasional funny moments, but a flabby screenplay and overly broad direction squanders the potential of the idea and cast. Sinyor showed more discipline in his Hollywood debut, *The Bachelor*, an updated version of the old chestnut about the man with one day to find a bride, though Chris O'Donnell's pallid comic gifts and the script's crass reworking of Buster Keaton's *Seven Chances* (1925) still left him tethered to poor material. Sinyor's Anglo-Canadian comedy *Bob the Butler* was premiered on American television.

(Robert Shail)

BIBLIOGRAPHY: Hooper, Caroline, 'Art of the Deal', *Screen International*, 7 Aug. 1992, pp. 8–9; Johnson, Lucy (ed.), *Talking Pictures: Interviews with Contemporary British Film-Makers* (London: BFI, 1997); Trower, Marcus, 'Gary Sinyor: Writer-Director', *Empire*, Mar. 1995, pp. 42–3.

FILMOGRAPHY: *Leon the Pig Farmer* (co-dir. Vadim Jean, 1992); *Solitaire for 2* (1995); *Stiff Upper Lips* (1997); *The Bachelor* (US, 1999); *Bob the Butler* (Can/UK, 2005).

SIODMAK, Robert (1900–1973)

Robert Siodmak was born on 8 August 1900 in Dresden, Germany. His first film was the realist social drama *Menschen am Sonntag* (1930), co-scripted by his brother Curt Siodmak and Billy Wilder. Being Jewish, Siodmak's future in the German film industry was threatened when the Nazis came to power: consequently he moved to Paris in the early 1930s and to Hollywood in 1939. In America he directed brilliant psychological thrillers such as *Phantom Lady* (1944), *The Spiral Staircase* (1945) and *The Killers* (1946), films that made creative use of Expressionist lighting to reinforce their darkness of mood.

In 1951 Siodmak came to England (avoiding the McCarthy witch-hunt) to make *The Crimson Pirate*, an enjoyable pirate romp, with Burt Lancaster saving a Caribbean island from a dastardly tyrant. This swashbuckler, while gently spoofing the genre, offered as exciting a finale as any of its predecessors. Eight years later Siodmak returned to Britain to direct *The Rough and the Smooth*, based on Robin Maugham's story about an archaeologist (Tony Britton) infatuated with a psychologically damaged girl (Nadja Tiller). Its flawed hero and sexually perverse femme fatale upset contemporary critics but it can now be seen as an inventive and unusual English variant on Siodmak's American films noirs.

Siodmak made films intermittently in Europe until the late 1960s, but his dark vision of society made him increasingly uncommercial. He died from a heart attack on 10 March 1973 in Locarno, Switzerland. Though still underrated as a director, his technically and thematically complex thrillers provided a perfect medium for his pessimistic explorations of the human condition.

(Linda Wood)

BIBLIOGRAPHY: Dumont, Hervé, *Robert Siodmak: Le maitre du film noir* (Lausanne: Éditions l'âge d'homme, 1981); Lazaroff, Deborah, *Robert Siodmak: A Biography* (London: McFarland, 1998); Nolan, Jack Edmund, 'Robert Siodmak', *Films in Review*, Apr. 1969, pp. 218–40.

FILMOGRAPHY (UK only): *The Crimson Pirate* (1951); *The Rough and the Smooth* (US: *Portrait of a Sinner*, 1959).

SKEET, Brian (1966–)

Brian Skeet was born in the UK in 1966. He worked for BBC Television, eventually directing editions of the history programme *One Foot in the Past* (1993). Documentaries on American writers L. Frank Baum and Larry Kramer enhanced his reputation and, in partnership with producer Ian Benson, he won backing from Granada and Canal+ to make his feature debut, *The Misadventures of Margaret* (1998). Skeet attempts to emulate the wit and charm of tight Hollywood comedies like *The Awful Truth* (Leo McCarey, 1937) and *Bringing up Baby* (Howard Hawks, 1938), but ends up with something more akin to the floppy experimental fantasies of the late 1960s. Parker Posey is so eccentrically charismatic that her amorous skitterings among nuns, dentists and Frenchmen initially seem intriguing; but she's eventually overwhelmed by the shapeless script and Skeet allows the film to become unforgivingly tedious.

Despite a frosty critical reception and poor box-office returns Granada reaffirmed their faith in Skeet by co-financing *The Weekend*, a lugubrious drama about grief and loss set among a formidably bitchy bunch of affluent New Yorkers, dominated by Gena Rowlands and Brooke Shields. Achievement matched ambition more closely here but audience and critical enthusiasm remained muted.

(Robert Murphy)

BIBLIOGRAPHY: Glucksman, Mary, 'Production Update', *Filmmaker* vol. 7 no. 1, Autumn 1998, p. 83.

FILMOGRAPHY: *The Boy Who Fell in Love* (short, 1994); *The Misadventures of Margaret* (aka *Les Mésaventures de Margaret/Les Folies de Margaret*, UK/Fr, 1998); *The Weekend* (UK/US, 2000).

SKOLIMOWSKI, Jerzy (1938–)

Jerzy Skolimowski was born on 5 May 1938 in Lodz, Poland. By the time he graduated from the Lodz Film School in 1963 he had already published poetry, played minor film parts and written scripts and dialogue for the films of two older colleagues, Andrzej Wajda and Roman Polanski. After making various short films he directed his feature debut, *Rysopis/Identification Marks: None*, in 1964. Two films followed featuring the same protagonist, Andrzej Leszczyc, a young man looking for a place in contemporary Poland, played by Skolimowski himself. *Walkower/Walkover* (1965) was well received, but *Rece do góry/Hands Up!* (1967) was shelved because of its critical portrayal of Polish Stalinism precipitating Skolimowski's decision to leave Poland. Since then he has worked in several countries, including the UK. His films often concentrate on outsiders and people literally or metaphorically displaced – reflecting Skolimowski's own position as an émigré artist. *The Adventures of Gerard*, a lightweight treatment of Conan Doyle's stories about a gallant but not particularly bright Napoleonic officer, was shot in Spain in 1968 but not released until 1970, by which time Skolimowski was in Britain making *Deep End*. This sensitive exploration of disturbed adolescent sexuality, set in a seedy and sex-obsessed London, provides a dark antidote to the 'swinging' clichés of the 1960s. His next British film could not have been more different in setting. *The Shout*, adapted from a novella by Robert Graves, opens with a cricket match in an idyllic rural setting – but the match is being played against mental asylum inmates. Once again Skolimowski takes us into an uncertain and uneasy world, in which Alan Bates' intrusive stranger might be a deluded idiot or a man with real supernatural powers, including an ability to kill with his shout. As in *Deep End*, Skolimowski shows his ability to create a tense, claustrophobic atmosphere and convey an evocative sense of place.

In the early 1980s Skolimowski made two films for Channel 4. *Moonlighting* was his quirky response to the introduction of martial law in his native Poland in December 1981. Jeremy Irons plays the leader of a group of Polish builders renovating the house of a rich Londoner. Worried that they will want to go home and not complete the job, he keeps his fellow countrymen in the dark about Poland's political situation. Although *Moonlighting* is ostensibly about Polish problems, it captures the mood of Thatcherite Britain, with its growing division between rich and poor. *Success Is the Best Revenge*, made two years later, is more autobiographical, featuring Michael York as an expatriate theatre producer living in London. Skolimowski's own house (the one being renovated in *Moonlighting*) provides the main setting and his wife (Joanna Szczerbic) and two sons play major roles. Haphazard and discursive, it is held together by Skolimowski's cinematic inventiveness and eye for detail. Of his later films, the most significant is *30 Door Key* (1991), based on a novel by the Polish émigré author Witold Gombrowicz, in which Skolimowski returns to his early fascination with the transition between adolescence and adulthood.

In recent years Skolimowski has occupied himself with painting, which he now regards as a greater passion than cinema.

He also occasionally plays small roles in the films of other directors, including *Mars Attacks!* (Tim Burton, 1996) and *Operacja Samum* (Wladyslaw Pasikowski, 1999).
(Ewa Mazierska)

BIBLIOGRAPHY: Powers, John, 'Under Western Eyes', *American Film*, Dec. 1986, pp. 38–42, 52; Strick, Philip, 'Skolimowski's Cricket Match', *Sight and Sound*, Summer 1978, pp. 146–7; Yakir, Dan, 'Polestar', *Film Comment*, Nov./Dec. 1982, pp. 28–32.

FILMOGRAPHY (UK only): *The Adventures of Gerard* (UK/Switz); *Deep End* (UK/US/Ger) (1970); *The Shout* (1978); *Moonlighting* (1982); *Success Is the Best Revenge* (1984); *30 Door Key/Ferdydurke* (UK/Pol/Fr, 1991).

SLOMAN, Anthony (1945–)

Anthony Barney Sloman was born in Waltham Abbey, Essex, on 6 May 1945. He jned the oiBritish film industry in the mid-1960s, working as assistant editor on Hammer's *One Million Years B.C.* (Don Chaffey, 1966) and Joe Massot's psychedelic comedy *Wonderwall* (1968). His directorial debut, *Sweet and Sexy*, tapped into the prevailing *Zeitgeist* of sleazy disillusion, but his jokey depiction of sex and violence in a low-life milieu was deemed unacceptable by the British Board of Film Censors and the film was banned. It was finally released, cut to fifty-eight minutes, in 1972. By this time Sloman had made a second feature, a suburban housewife sex drama, *Not Tonight, Darling!*

Such films were a flimsy foundation upon which to build a directing career, and by 1974 he was back working as assistant editor on *Can You Keep It Up for a Week?* (Jim Atkinson). But the adaptable Sloman soon found more stimulating challenges. He acted in Kevin Brownlow's *Winstanley* (1975) and Peter Greenaway's *The Falls* (1980), edited Chris Petit's *Radio On* (1979) and was sound editor on a variety of other films. An inveterate fill buff, he became a Governor of the BFI, conducted interviews with directors and other luminaries at the National Film Theatre, and reviewed films for the *Radio Times*. He continues to work as editor, writer and producer, though he shows no inclination to return to directing or sexploitation.
(Robert Murphy)

FILMOGRAPHY: *Sweet and Sexy* (US: *Foursome*, 1970; rel. 1972); *Not Tonight, Darling!* (1971).

SMART, Ralph (1908–2001)

Ralph Smart was born to Australian parents in London in 1908 and his director's career embraces work in both Australia and the UK. He began as an editor for British International Pictures in 1927, and in the 1930s collaborated on scripts, working among others on Michael Powell's *The Night of the Party* (1934) and *The Phantom Light* (1935), and numerous Gainsborough comedies. He also directed interest and documentary shorts for Merton Park, Publicity Films and other companies before going to Australia in 1940 to make films for the Department of Information and the Royal Australian Air Force. Australia's desire to promote greater coverage of the country's war effort brought him back into contact with the British industry: when Harry Watt arrived from Ealing to mount what became the cattle-drive saga *The Overlanders* (1946), Smart served as associate producer. Subsequently he made his feature-directing debut with *Bush Christmas* (1947), a charming all-location adventure about bush children searching for a stolen mare, made for Rank's fledgling Children's Entertainment Films. After a period in Britain Smart returned to direct *Bitter Springs*, Ealing's third and least successful Australian epic, with Tommy Trinder and Gordon Jackson doing their best to mollify disgruntled Aborigines when Chips Rafferty and his family settle on their land. Ealing's treatment of Aboriginal land rights was notably sympathetic, though the film's desire to be even-handed bit into its strengths as an adventure-drama.

No serious intentions underlined Smart's features made in Britain, all unremarkable in technique and material, but also unpretentiously likeable. He directed 'The Facts of Life' episode of *Quartet*, bringing an engaging light touch to a young man's seduction in the South of France. *A Boy, a Girl and a Bike*, capturing something of post-war Britain's egalitarian spirit, benefits from refreshing Yorkshire location-shooting, stalwart character actors and attractive young stars (including Diana Dors, Anthony Newley and Honor Blackman). *Always a Bride* is a low-key but surprisingly witty comedy about confidence tricksters on the Riviera. After 1955 Smart concentrated on the small screen, working as producer and director on many British series including *The Adventures of Robin Hood*, *The Buccaneers* and *Danger Man*, before switching to Australian television in 1970. He retired to Spain, where he died in February 2001.
(Brian McFarlane)

BIBLIOGRAPHY: Pike, Andrew and Ross Cooper, *Australian Film 1900–1977* (Melbourne: Oxford University Press, 1980).

FILMOGRAPHY Shorts: *The Woodpigeon Patrol* (co-dir. F. R. Lucas, 1930); *Trust Peggy* (1935); *Here's Health*; *The Window Dresser's Dream*; *Sweet Success*; *The Gods Look Down*; *Getting into Hot Water*, *The Man Who Knew Too Little* (1936); *Two Frightened Ladies*; *Workaday*; *For Dealers Only*; *The World Rolls On* (1937); *The Green* (1938); *Island Target* (Austral, 1945); *Get off the Hose* (1954).

Features: *Bush Christmas* (1947); *Quartet* ('The Facts of Life' episode, co-dirs. Ken Annakin/Arthur Crabtree/Harold French, 1948); *A Boy, a Girl and a Bike* (1949); *Bitter Springs* (1950); *Never Take No for an Answer* (co-dir. Maurice Cloche, 1951); *Curtain Up* (1952); *Always a Bride* (1953).

SMIGHT, Jack (1926–2003)

Jack Smight, who was born in Minneapolis on 9 March 1926, worked as an actor and disc jockey before moving to California and directing for television. He made his feature debut with *I'd Rather Be Rich* (1964) and scored a box-office hit with *Harper* (UK: *The Moving Target*, 1966), the inaugural film of Jerry Gershwin and Elliott Kastner's company, Winkast.

When Winkast shifted base to Britain, Smight directed its first UK production, *Kaleidoscope*. The film is everything its title, date and London locations promise: a riot of red buses and miniskirts, flashy optical effects and obtrusive scene transitions (usually accompanied by sitar music). Warren Beatty stars as an American playboy criminal involved in a complicated but thoroughly inconsequential plot to rob a chain of casinos using marked playing cards while wooing Susannah York's trendy fashion designer.

Smight's career includes some interestingly offbeat projects, such as the Rod Steiger vehicles *No Way to Treat a Lady* (1968) and *The Illustrated Man* (1969), and a great many more routine ones. He became a contract director at Universal, where he alternated between cinema and television work. *Frankenstein: The True Story* is a hybrid: a two-part, three-hour television movie, filmed at Pinewood and released theatrically in a truncated version in Britain and Europe. Despite its misnamed title, it numbers among the more intelligent screen adaptations of Mary Shelley's novel, with a literate screenplay co-written by Christopher Isherwood and fine performances from an all-star cast, including Michael Sarrazin (as the Creature) and James Mason. Smight retired in 1989 and died of cancer in Valencia, California, on 1 September 2003.

(Sheldon Hall)

BIBLIOGRAPHY: Arneel, Gene, 'Frankenstein: The True Story', *Films Illustrated*, Oct. 1974, p. 50; 'Young Execs Go for Modern Scripts and Smight Hails Shift', *Film Daily*, 12 Sept. 1967, pp. 1, 3.

FILMOGRAPHY (UK only): *Kaleidoscope* (1966); *Frankenstein: The True Story* (UK/US, 1973).

SMITH, Christopher (1970–)

Christopher Smith was born in Bristol in 1970, and studied on Bristol University's postgraduate film production course, where he made the short *10000th Day*. Between leaving film school in 1997 and making his feature debut in 2004, Smith directed *The Day Grandad Went Blind* (1998), a comedy-drama about an old man finding a lottery ticket, for the Welsh television channel HTV, wrote episodes of *EastEnders* and helped produce Barry Norman's film review programme for Sky TV. Determined to make a low-budget feature, he abandoned his gangster film script when the market became glutted by attempts to cash in on the success of *Lock, Stock and Two Smoking Barrels* (Guy Ritchie, 1998) and turned to horror.

Creep (2004), the dire tale of a young woman who misses the last train and finds herself locked in the London Underground system, where she becomes the prey of a flesh-eating monster, bears resemblance to Gary Sherman's *Deathline* (1972), but Smith brings his own refreshingly original perspective to the subject. His heroine, played by the muscular German actress Franka Potente, is a hedonistic party girl who puts herself in dangerous situations, but she is much meaner and tougher than the usual horror film victim, and the monster she confronts, convincingly brought to life by Sean Harris, is both horrifying and sympathetic. Her struggle to survive – which reduces her to the status of the shattered, homeless wrecks who share the Underground network with the monster – is also a saga of discovery into a world of disused stations, secret tunnels and abandoned storage facilities, hidden from the eyes of those who dutifully follow instructions to mind the gap and stand well back from the edge of the platform. Reviews were mixed but audiences in the UK responded positively.

(Robert Murphy)

BIBLIOGRAPHY: Hennigan, Adrian, Interview with Christopher Smith <www.bbc.co.uk/films/2005/01/20/chris_smith_creep_interview.shtml>; Kempster, Grant, 'Sounds of the Underground', *Film Review*, Feb. 2005, p. 78; Sweet, Matthew, 'Nightmare on the Northern Line', *Evening Standard*, 13 Jan. 2005, p. 31.

FILMOGRAPHY: *The 10000th Day* (short, 1997); *The Day Grandad Went Blind* (short, 1998); *Creep* (UK/Ger, 2004); *Severance* (2006).

SMITH, George Albert (1864–1959)

George Albert Smith, the British film pioneer, was born in London on 4 January 1864. He first received public attention as a result of his activities as a popular hypnotist in Brighton in the early 1880s. In 1892 he acquired the lease to St Ann's Well Garden in Hove, and in 1894 staged a public exhibition of a series of dissolving views, using a powerful long-range limelight apparatus. Smith's skilful manipulation of the lantern to produce an effective dissolving view would be very important to his role in the development of film editing from 1898 to 1900. Cutting between lenses – in effect from slide to slide – enabled lantern stories to deal with changes in time, perspective and location. The same technique can be seen in a film like *As Seen through the Telescope* (1900), where Smith guides the viewer from long shot to close-up to long shot.

Smith was interested in the relationship between lantern slides, lantern projection and film, including the integration of still and moving images in performance, and he used the popular stories that had already been converted into lantern slide sets as the narrative basis for much of his exploratory work in the new medium. His 1897 promotional booklet for St Ann's brought together the old and new technologies, advertising 'High Class Lecture Entertainments with Magnificent Lime-Light Scenery and Beautiful Dioramic Effects' and 'Cinematographe. Displays of Animated Photography, Interesting and Sensational Moving Pictures'.

In 1896 Smith had acquired his first film camera from Alfred Darling, the Brighton-based mechanical engineer, and built his 'film factory' (his film processing works) the following year. By the late 1890s, he had developed a successful commercial film production and processing business. Smith's largest customer became the Warwick Trading Company, and through this relationship he started a partnership with its managing director, Charles Urban. Smith's films in the years 1897 to 1903 were largely comedies and adaptations of popular fairy tales and stories. His wife Laura Bayley, an experienced actress who understood visual comedy and the interests of seaside audiences, performed in many of his most important films, including *Let Me Dream Again* (1900) and *Mary Jane's Mishap* (1903).

Smith made only the studio shot of the train carriage in *The Kiss in the Tunnel* (1899), but when he inserted it into Cecil Hepworth's phantom ride, *View from an Engine Front – Train Leaving Tunnel* (1899), he created an edited film that demonstrated a new sense of continuity and simultaneity across three shots. This filmic imagination was radical for the time and Smith used his innovation to develop a series of films in 1900 – *Grandma's Reading Glass*, *As Seen through a Telescope*, *The House That Jack Built* and *Let Me Dream Again* – that established Smith's significance as a major film pioneer. These four films depict a number of short narrative actions and as such are probably best described as narrative fragments. However, they each introduced editing concepts that would be central to the future development of film form such as interpolative close-ups, subjective and objective point-of-view shots, reversal, the creation of dream-time and a dissolve effect. They revealed film's distinctiveness as a new visual medium and demonstrated to his contemporaries how to create a filmed sequence.

Grandma's Reading Glass offered a new way of entering into a fictional world by sharing a vicarious visual pleasure. Renouncing the conventions of a theatrical perspective – the fixed view from the stalls – that had been the dominant model for film production up to 1900, Smith presents a new filmic understanding of space and time. The logic of the narrative is that we can see what the grandson can see through the reading glass. Magically, as if through the action of a spiritualist medium, we enter into his mind in order to share his vision. The sights revealed by this cinematic illusion are of everyday objects but they all possess a degree of charm and beauty, especially the close-ups of the human eye and the cat's head.

After 1900, the two-colour additive process known as Kinemacolor came to dominate the rest of Smith's career in film. It was launched in Paris and London in 1908 and transformed by Urban into a new enterprise, the Natural Color Kinematograph Company. The company had success in the period 1910 to 1913, producing over a hundred short features from its studios in Hove and Nice. However, a patent suit brought against Kinemacolor by William Friese-Greene in 1914 led to its collapse and ended Smith's career in the film business. In the late 1940s Rachael Low and others interested in the early history of British cinema realised Smith's importance. He was made a Fellow of the British Film Academy in 1955, before he died in Brighton on 17 May 1959.

(Frank Gray)

BIBLIOGRAPHY: Barnes, John, *The Beginnings of the Cinema in England 1894–1901, Volumes 2–5* (Exeter: University of Exeter Press, 1996–8); Bottomore, Stephen, 'Smith versus Melbourne Cooper: An End to the Dispute', *Film History* vol. 14 no. 1, 2002, pp. 57–73; Burton, Alan and Laraine Porter (eds), *Pimples Pranks & Pratfalls: British Film Comedy before 1930* (Trowbridge, Wilts: Flicks Books, 2000); Gray, Frank, 'Smith the Showman: The Early Years of George Albert Smith', *Film History* vol. 10 no. 1, 1998, pp. 8–20; Gray, Frank, 'Smith versus Melbourne Cooper: History and Counter-History', *Film History* vol. 11 no. 3, 1999, pp. 246–61; Gray, Frank, 'George Albert Smith's Visions and Transformations: The Films of 1898', in Simon Popple and Vanessa Toulmin (eds), *Visual Delights: Essays on the Popular and Projected Image in the 19th Century* (Trowbridge, Wilts: Flicks Books, 2000); Low, Rachael and Roger Manvell, *The History of the British Film 1896–1906* (London: George Allen & Unwin, 1948); Thomas, D. B., *The First Colour Motion Pictures* (London: HMSO, 1969).

SELECTED FILMOGRAPHY: *Football*; *Queen Victoria's Diamond Jubilee Procession* (series); *The Miller and the Sweep*; *Miss Ellen Terry* (series); *Brighton Sea-Going Electric Car*, *Paddling* (aka *Children Paddling at the Seaside*); *Hanging out the Clothes* (aka *The Maid in the Garden*); *Nursing the Baby*; *Gymnastics* (series); *Comic Shaving* (aka *Comic Barber*); *The Miller and the Sweep* (second version); *Comic Face* (aka *Man Drinking*); *Weary Willie*; *The X-Rays* (aka *The X-Ray Fiend*); *The Sign Writer* (aka *The Awkward Sign Writer*); *Making Sausages* (aka *The End of All Things*); *Tipsy-Topsy-Turvy*; *The Haunted Castle* (1897); *The Runaway Knock*; *A Practical Joke* (aka *A Joke on the Gardener*); *The Grand National*; *Phantom Ride*; *The Policeman, the Cook and the Copper*, *Comic Costume Race*; *Maypole Dance*; *Brighton* (series); *Animated Portrait: Miss Marie Lloyd*; *The Baker and the Sweep*; *The Lady Barber* (aka *Suffragette in the Barber Shop*); *The Corsican Brothers*; *Cinderella and the Fairy Godmother*, *Faust and Mephistopheles*; *Photographing a Ghost*; *Santa Claus* (aka *The Visit of Santa Claus*); *The Mesmerist; or, Body and Soul*; *Aly Sloper*, *Animated Clown Portrait*; *The Dog Show* (1898);

Firemen and Police Obstacle Race (series); *The Legacy*; *A Good Joke*; *A Hilarious Bank Holiday Crowd*; *The Sandwiches* (aka *The Hungry Countryman*); *Good Stories*; *The Haunted Picture Gallery*; *A Game of Chess and Kisses*; *The Gambler's Wife*; *The Inexhaustible Cab*; *Aladdin and the Wonderful Lamp*; *Dick Whittington*; *The Kiss in the Tunnel* (1899); *A Jolly Old Couple*; *The Two Old Sports*; *Two Grinning Yokels*; *The Conjurors*; *An Incident on Brighton Pier*; *A Quick Shave and Brush Up*; *Let Me Dream Again*; *The Dull Razor*; *Snapshotting an Audience*; *Grandma Threading Her Needle*; *Scandal over the Teacups*; *The Old Maid's Valentine* (aka *The Valentine*); *The Two Old Sports' Political Discussion*; *The Two Old Sports' Game of Nap* (aka *The Winning Hand*); *A Bad Cigar*; *The House that Jack Built*; *As Seen through a Telescope*; *Grandma's Reading Glass*; *The Prehistoric Monsters at Crystal Palace*; *Two Jolly Old Fellows*; *The Village Choir*; *Where Did You Get It?* (1900); *Whisky Versus Bullets*; *The Bill Poster's Revenge*; *The Monocle – Me and Joe Chamberlain*; *The Kitten Nursery*; *The Little Doctor and the Sick Kitten* (aka *The Sick Kitten*); *The Last Glass of the Two Old Sports* (aka *The Last Bottle at the Club*); *A Good Story*; *Photograph from an Area Window* (aka *A Study in Feet*); *The Adrian Troupe of Cyclists*; *In the Green Room* (1901); *The Monk in the Monastery Wine Cellars*; *The Two Old Sports at the Music Hall*; *Too Much of a Good Thing*; *Oh That Collar Button!*; *The Comedian and the Flypaper*; *The Cakewalk*; *The Donkey and the Serpentine Dancer*; *Tommy Atkins and His Harriet on a Bank Holiday*; *Tommy and the Mouse in the Art School* (aka *Little Willie and the Mouse*); *Topsy-Turvy Dance by Three Quaker Maidens*; *At Last! That Awful Tooth*; *The Monk's Macaroni Feast*; *The Monk's Ruse for Lunch*; *The Monk in the Studio*; *His First Cigar, Probably His Last*; *Episodes in the Life of a Lodger*; *That Awful Cigar*; *Pa's Comment on the Morning News*; *After Dark; or, The Policeman and His Lantern*; *Mother Goose Nursery Rhymes*; *The Amazons' March and Evolutions* (aka *The March of the Amazons*); *Pantomime Girls Having a Lark*; *Hilarity on Board Ship* (1902); *Mary Jane's Mishap or, Don't Fool with the Paraffin*; *Lettie Limelight in Her Lair*; *John Bull's Hearth* (aka *John Bull's Fireside*); *The Free Trade Bench*; *The Baby and the Ape*; *Dorothy's Dream* (1903); *The Final Cup-Tie Match* (1906); *The Great Football Cup Final* (1907); *A Visit to the Seaside* (1908); *Review of British Navy at Southend and Spithead* (series); *Choosing the Wallpaper*; *Kinemacolor Puzzle* (1909); *State Ceremonies at the Death of King Edward VII* (series, 1910); *The Coronation Procession* (series); *The Royal Progress* (series)(1911).

SMITH, Herbert (1901–1986)

Herbert Smith was born in the Minories in the City of London on 30 June 1901. After a spell with G. B. Samuelson, he joined the British Lion Corporation, set up by his older brother Sam in 1927, and worked there in various capacities throughout the 1930s. As a director, he tended to concentrate on musical revues and low-budget comedies. His first feature was *On the Air* (1934), which used the excuse of a local fund-raising concert to parade a succession of variety artistes including Max Wall, Wilson, Keppel and Betty, and band leader Roy Fox. *In Town Tonight* (1935), *Soft Lights and Sweet Music* (1936), *Calling All Stars* (1937) and *Around the Town* (1938) worked to a similar formula. Later in the 1930s, Smith developed an association with the popular South Yorkshire comedian Sandy Powell, directing five of his films in quick succession. *It's a Grand Old World* (1937) was typical fare, with the ever-optimistic Sandy winning the pools just in time to save the ancestral home of his upper-class girlfriend (Gina Malo).

Throughout the war and post-war period, Smith was an associate producer at Two Cities, working on *Tawny Pipit* (Bernard Miles, 1944), *Odd Man Out* (Carol Reed, 1947) and *Hamlet* (Laurence Olivier, 1948). He became production manager at Denham but when the studios were closed in 1951 he took early retirement and ran a beach café at Westgate-on-Sea in Kent. A well-loved character, he was occasionally tempted back into the industry, producing, for example, *The Tommy Steele Story* (Gerard Bryant, 1957) and *Six-Five Special* (Alfred Shaughnessy, 1958). He died in his sleep at Margate Hospital on 4 February 1986.

(Alan Burton)

BIBLIOGRAPHY: Levi, Peta, 'One of the Early Film Moguls: Herbert Smith', *Classic Images* no. 135, Sept. 1986, pp. 10–11; Low, Rachael, *Film Making in 1930s Britain* (London: George Allen & Unwin, 1985).

FILMOGRAPHY: *Musical Film Revues Nos. 1–10* (1933); *On the Air* (1934); *In Town Tonight*; *Night Mail* (1935); *British Lion Varieties Nos. 1–9*; *Soft Lights and Sweet Music*; *They Didn't Know* (1936); *Calling All Stars*; *It's a Grand Old World*; *Leave It to Me* (1937); *I've Got a Horse*; *Around the Town* (1938); *All at Sea*; *Home from Home* (1939).

SMITH, Mel (1952–)

Mel Smith was born in Chiswick, west London, on 3 December 1952. At Oxford he studied psychology, without completing his degree, and was President of the Oxford University Dramatic Society. After working as an assistant director at the Royal Court Theatre in London and the Crucible in Sheffield, he made his showbusiness mark with Rowan Atkinson, Griff Rhys Jones and Richard Curtis as part of the team on the BBC comedy series *Not the Nine O'Clock News* (1979–82). With Rhys Jones he enjoyed great success with *Alas Smith and Jones* (1984–98); the pair also worked productively on the film *Morons from Outer Space* (Mike Hodges, 1985). Smith's work as a cinema director has proved more uneven.

His first feature film, *The Tall Guy*, emerged in 1989, a strenuous and uneven romantic satire written by Richard Curtis, with Rowan Atkinson, Jeff Goldblum and Emma Thompson. Smith then moved back to television to direct episodes of the American cult comedy *Dream On* (1990–6). This led to an unsuccessful American feature, *Radioland Murders*, based on a story by George Lucas, a frenetic murder farce set in 1939 during a Chicago radio station's first night on the air. Ironically, Smith had chosen the project in preference to the more modest but phenomenally popular *Four Weddings and a Funeral* (Mike Newell, 1994). His own big cinema success came when he returned to Britain to renew his relationship with Curtis and Atkinson as director of the jovially unsubtle *Bean* (1997), in which Atkinson's bumbling, virtually mute hero created in the television series *Mr Bean*

(1989–95) mimes his way through improbable, escapades. The technique and international appeal of the Bean character has prompted comparisons with Jacques Tati's Monsieur Hulot, though Smith's direction scarcely suggests Tati's elegance.

After *Bean*, Smith returned to television as executive producer on the BBC series *Too Much Sun* (2000), an undistinguished comedy about an English actor (Mark Addy) in Hollywood. *High Heels and Low Lifes* (2001) was similarly unambitious, a slight, short and formulaic feature about two women attempting to blackmail a gang of bank robbers. Attractive performances by Minnie Driver and Michael Gambon failed to make up for a B-movie plot and meandering direction. Tim Firth's script for *Blackball* promised a quirky tale of class warfare on the bowling greens of Torquay, but the plot is disappointingly one-dimensional and Smith directs with the subtlety of a pneumatic drill. Unsurprisingly *Blackball* failed to capture the popular audience that flocked to *The Full Monty* (Peter Cattaneo, 1997) and *Calendar Girls* (Nigel Cole, 2003).

(Tom Ryall)

BIBLIOGRAPHY: Kemp, Philip, 'Bean', *Sight and Sound*, Aug. 1997, p. 41; Lowe, Andy, 'Mel Smith', *Total Film*, Aug. 2001, pp. 38–9; Mackenzie, Suzie, 'Brazil Gut', *Time Out* no. 735, 20 Sept. 1984, pp. 11–12.

FILMOGRAPHY: *The Tall Guy* (1989); *Radioland Murders* (US, 1994); *Bean* (1997); *High Heels and Low Lifes* (2001); *Blackball* (2003).

SMITH, Percy (1880–1945)

Frank Percy Smith was born in London in 1880. He was keen to exploit the educational possibilities of film, but employment at the Board of Education offered little opportunity, and he began working for the film entrepreneur Charles Urban, who had been impressed with a photograph Smith had taken of a bluebottle's tongue. During the First World War Smith made a series of films depicting battles through animated maps and also worked as a naval photographer. When the war was over he turned to comedy with *The Bedtime Stories of Archie the Ant*, featuring insect characters in a natural environment; but his real love was the *Secrets of Nature* series made for British Instructional Films. Beginning in 1922, the series continued into the 1930s when it became *Secrets of Life* and thrived until Smith's death in 1945. Technological changes such as the coming of sound were easily absorbed – commentary worked equally well as intertitles or spoken words – and Smith's films fascinated successive generations much as David Attenborough's wildlife documentaries have on television.

Smith was a true pioneer, inventing original and bizarre methods for time-lapse and micro-cinematography involving all kinds of home-made devices (including alarms all over his home to wake him up in the middle of the night if the film in the camera needed changing). With endless patience, he could spend up to two and a half years completing a film. He also had the popular touch, with the happy knack (as he put it himself) of being able to feed his audience 'the powder of instruction in the jam of entertainment'. Modern film technique could hardly better the results achieved by Smith in the first decades of the century and his early masterpiece, *Birth of a Flower* (1910), has never been out of distribution. In the 1930s Smith tended to rely on his colleagues Mary Field and H. R. Hewer to direct, while he concentrated on his painstaking photography. He died at his home in Southgate, north London, on 24 March 1945.

(Bryony Dixon)

BIBLIOGRAPHY: Blakeston, Oswell, 'Personally about Percy Smith', *Close-Up* vol. 8 no. 2, June 1931, pp. 143–6; Low, Rachael, *A History of the British Film 1906–1914* (London: George Allen & Unwin, 1949); 'Percy Smith' (obituary), *Sight and Sound*, Apr. 1945, pp. 6–7; Talbot, Frederick A., *Moving Pictures: How They Are Made and Worked* (London: Heinemann, 1912).

FILMOGRAPHY: *Birth of a Flower* (1910); *Kineto War Map* series: *Fight for the Dardanelles*; *How the Canadians Saved the Day* (1915), *The Russo-Rumanian Advance* (1916); *Kineto Review: Spiders and Their Victims* (1922); *The Bedtime Stories of Archie the Ant* series: *Bertie's Cave*, *Tale of a Tendril*; *The Pit and the Plum* (1925); *Secrets of Nature* series (1922–33): *Insect Artisans* (co-dir. Mary Field, 1923), *The Phantom*, *The Gnat*, *Life of a Plant*, *The Battle of the Plants* (1926), *The Plants of the Pantry* (1927), *The Frog*, *Life in the Balance*, *Mitey Atom* (1929), *The Strangler* (1930), *Down Under*, *Waterfolk* (co-dir. Mary Field) (1931), *The Thistle* (co-dir. Mary Field), *The Filter* (1934); *Secrets of Life* series (1934–50); *Self-Defence by Plants* (1935).

SMITH, Peter (1936–)

Peter Kingsgate Smith was born in London in 1936. He co-directed *Knees up, Mother Brown*, a short film about jolly old East End ladies, before studying at the London School of Film Technique, where he made *Isaiah*, a documentary about the Salvation Army. After leaving, he assisted Kevin Brownlow on *Abel Gance – The Charm of Dynamite* (1968) and made two sympathetic, socially concerned documentaries. *Three for Society* gave a voice to three sufferers from cerebral palsy; *All Things Bright* examined the work of volunteers from the Spastics Society in helping similar victims of the disease. A series of short children's films and a filmed interview with the painter Edward Burra followed.

In 1974 Smith won backing from the BFI Production Board for *A Private Enterprise*, a feature film, co-written with the novelist and journalist Dilip Hiro, about a young Indian's attempt to start his own business making plastic elephants in the unwelcoming environment of Birmingham in the early 1970s. Refreshingly unique in its view of Britain from an immigrant's point of view, the film is judicious in its treatment of the hostile, wary or at best patronising locals, and wittily perceptive about the Indian community. The leading character, an ambitious but penniless engineer (Salmaan Peer), finds himself ill-at-ease with the exploited foundry workers he lodges with, the know-it-all older businessmen he seeks to borrow money from and the pretty but insufferably dim woman he is tempted to marry for her dowry. Shot on a tiny budget of £15,000, the film proved too low key to attract much attention, though its view of Britain in the 1970s finds reflection in later films like *Brothers in Trouble* (Udayan Prasad, 1995) and *East Is East* (Damien O'Donnell, 1999).

Smith went on to a successful career in television, directing episodes of *The Sweeney*, *Shoestring* and *Bergerac* before making *No Surrender* (1985), one of the last feature films to be financed by the National Film Finance Corporation. Alan Bleasdale's script packs in too much, combining parallel stories about a nightclub manager (Michael Angelis) whose predecessor has left him facing a New Year's Eve double-booking of rival Protestant and Catholic pensioners – with a punk rock band and an incompetent comedian to entertain them; and the long night of the soul suffered by the ageing leader of the Protestant Orange Order (Ray McAnally), whose weariness with the bombast of sectarian violence finally leads him to seek reconciliation with his son-in-law. Smith keeps a tight control over the plot convolutions and roots the semi-farcical events in the reality of grimly run-down Liverpool, though with so much going on, peripheral characters such as Elvis Costello's neurotic magician hardly have time to make an impact. *No Surrender* set the template for later bitter-sweet comedies like *Brassed Off* (Mark Herman, 1996) and *The Full Monty* (Peter Cattaneo, 1997), but in the mid-1980s the shock of industrial decline was still raw and the promise that things could only get better less certain.

Smith returned to television rather than seeking a cinema career, and was rewarded with satisfying drama serials such as Peter Ransley's *The Price* (1985) and *Seaforth* (1994), an adaptation of John Le Carré's *A Perfect Spy* (1987), and the Anglo-German television film *Murder East – Murder West* (1990). Latterly he has found a comfortable niche directing episodes of the Home Counties detective series *Midsomer Murders* (2000–5).
(Robert Murphy)

BIBLIOGRAPHY: Ellis, John (ed.), *1951–1976 British Film Institute Productions* (London: BFI, 1977); Korte, Barbara and Claudia Sternberg, *Bidding for the Mainstream? Black and Asian British Film since the 1990s* (Amsterdam and New York: Rodopi, 2004); Petit, Chris, 'Co-production', *Time Out* no. 258, 7 Feb. 1975, p. 15; Petley, Julian, 'In the Worst Possible Taste', *Broadcast*, 10 May 1985, pp. 26–7; Rohrer, 'No Surrender', *Sight and Sound*, Summer 1985, pp. 194–5.

FILMOGRAPHY: *Knees up, Mother Brown* (doc. short, co-dir. Luciana Della Mura, 1964); *Isaiah* (doc. short, 1967); *Three for Society* (doc. short, 1969); *All Things Bright* (doc., 1970); *The Trouble with 2B* (series of six shorts, 1972); *Edward Burra* (doc. short, 1973); *A Private Enterprise* (1975); *No Surrender* (UK/Can, 1985).

SNOWDEN, Alison (1958–) and David Fine (1960–)

Partners in and outside work, animators Alison Snowden and David Fine first joined forces as students at the National Film and Television School in the early 1980s. *Second Class Mail* (1984), directed by Snowden with Fine's assistance, established their special territory: the loves and disappointments of the suburban downtrodden, charted with rueful humour and split-second comic timing.

When they met, Fine was the more experienced; born in Toronto in 1960, he had been a prolific amateur film-maker in his teens, and had also made films in the National Film Board of Canada's student programme. Snowden, born in Nottingham in 1958, enrolled at the NFTS after art courses at Mansfield and Coventry. At first her training centred on live-action filming; but *Second Class Mail*, made in three months at the end of her last year, abundantly revealed a gift for animation, and won her an Academy Award nomination. Dancing coloured circles at the start suggest a tribute to Oskar Fischinger's abstract art. Here lies the first joke: the patterns belong to the middle-aged heroine's headscarf, bobbing along towards a pillar-box. Her post brings a parcel containing an inflatable male lover, as homely in looks as herself; it does not survive the encounter intact. Fine's sound effects contribute much to the wordless film's comic impact; while Snowden's games with space and perspective greatly enliven her minimalist designs.

The film's success led to a work offer from the National Film Board of Canada. The couple jointly directed *George and Rosemary*, a charming and gentle treatment of the erotic fantasies of two senior citizens; another Canadian film, *In and Out*, offered all of life from the womb to the grave in nine minutes. Hopes of moving into live action were unfulfilled, and they returned to animation projects and commercials in Britain. In 1993 they completed the Academy Award-winning *Bob's Birthday* (1993), twelve minutes of a London dentist's mid-life crisis on the night of his fortieth birthday, co-produced by the NFB and Channel 4. It unfolds like a live-action television comedy, with ample dialogue and simple, stylised characters (with the animators' trademark potato-shaped noses and frumpy physiques) flatly displayed against semi-realistic backgrounds. Snowden herself voiced the character of Margaret, the wife whose surprise party does not run to plan. The film is poignantly observant as well as funny, but as visually bleak as a simple comic strip.

There followed a successful television series, *Bob and Margaret*, produced through the Canadian company Nelvana, and screened worldwide. Snowden and Fine took personal charge of the first two series (1998–9), directing the voices, supervising artwork and scripts; for the remaining two, set for funding purposes in Canada, they served as consultants only. Since then, several other television series have been in development; none has so far emerged. The mordant comic-strip manner of *Bob's Birthday* certainly suits the small screen; but we still wait for another Snowden–Fine film with the high visual wit of *Second Class Mail*.
(Geoff Brown)

BIBLIOGRAPHY: Pilling, Jayne (ed.), *Women and Animation: A Compendium* (London: BFI Exhibition & Distribution Division, 1992); Summerfield, Gideon, 'Hot off the Press', *Televisual*, Apr. 1995, pp. 20–2; 'The 50 Hottest Names in Animation', *Creation*, June 1999, pp. 15–16; Waller, Ed, 'Animated Anxiety', *Televisual*, Jan. 1998, pp. 33–4; <www.awn.com/snowden-fine>.

FILMOGRAPHY: *Second Class Mail* (Snowden only, 1984); *George and Rosemary* (Can); *People and Science: A Test of Time* (Can) (1987); *In and Out* (Can, 1989); *Pink Komkommer* ('Test of Time' segment, Can, 1991); *Bob's Birthday* (UK/Can, 1993).

SOFTLEY, Iain (1958–)

Iain Softley was born in West London in 1958. He involved himself in theatrical productions while reading English at Queen's College, Cambridge, and after graduating worked on music videos. He then became a researcher and director of music documentaries for television until he made his first feature film in 1994. *Backbeat*, set in the early 1960s during the Beatles' stint in Hamburg, centres on Stuart Sutcliffe (Stephen Dorff), the 'fifth Beatle'. The film explores Sutcliffe's love affair with German photographer Astrid Kirchherr (Sheryl Lee), John Lennon's jealousy and Sutcliffe's growing detachment from the group before his death from a brain haemorrhage just as the band achieves its breakthrough. It was critically well received and sufficiently successful commercially for Softley to gain American funding for a second feature film.

Hackers depicts the lives of a group of young computer hackers (with names like 'Crash Override', 'Acid Burn', 'Cereal Killer', 'Phantom Phreak' and 'The Plague') led by the then-unknown Angelina Jolie and Jonny Lee Miller. Their exploits in unravelling theft and conspiracy in New York are entertaining, and Softley makes effective use of both images and music. The film was not a big box-office success on its first release but its reputation has subsequently risen. Softley's third feature film was an adaptation of Henry James' *The Wings of the Dove*. Together with scriptwriter Hossein Amini, he attempted to overturn the conventions of the heritage film – using abstract images and a synthesiser soundtrack for the opening credits, and carefully undercutting the sumptuous period settings, dress and decor.

> Because of the complex ambiguities and dark sides to the story, we both seized on the idea of a *film noir* treatment. I wanted the film to have a strong graphic feel, so there are visual themes of grid patterns, silhouettes, and top shots . . . (Nocenti, p. 53)

Softley and Amini's subversion of convention appealed to rather than offended audiences and critics, and the film was nominated for four Academy Awards.

Softley's next film, the genuinely strange *K-Pax* (2001), starring Kevin Spacey and Jeff Bridges, left many critics bemused and bewildered. But its odd story of a psychiatric patient who claims to be an alien proved enticing enough to bring in more than enough to cover its $48 million budget. *The Skeleton Key*, a psychological horror film, was less successful commercially but it confirmed Softley's reputation as a director capable of making original and challenging films within the mainstream international industry.

(Pamela Church Gibson)

BIBLIOGRAPHY: Minns, Adam, 'In the Frame', *Screen International*, 23 Oct. 1998, p. 20; Nocenti, Annie, 'From Script to Film: *The Wings of the Dove*', *Scenario* vol. 3, no. 3, Autumn 1997, pp. 53, 201–2; Pennington, Adrian, 'Director: Iain Softley', *Premiere* (UK), May 1996, p. 36.

FILMOGRAPHY: *Backbeat* (1994); *Hackers* (US, 1995); *The Wings of the Dove* (UK/US, 1997); *K-Pax* (US/Ger, 2001); *The Skeleton Key* (US, 2005).

SPEED, Lancelot (1860–1931)

Though forgotten now, Lancelot Speed played a vital role in the development of British animation during the First World War. Born in London in 1860, Speed initially trained in medicine at Cambridge University, but after furthering his interest in art at the Slade School he developed a flourishing career as a magazine and book illustrator. His drawing style was straightforward, almost prosaic, though his concern for exact detail gave authenticity to historical, mythical or fantastic settings, as in Andrew Lang's *The Red Fairy Book* (1890) and his iconographic illustrations for *Legends of King Arthur and His Knights* (1912).

In 1914 Speed was appointed an artistic adviser to the newly formed Neptune Film Company. He designed the company logo, advised on settings and costumes, and leaped into service as an animator with the start of hostilities, after two years of private experiments. *Bully Boy No. 1*, available in early October 1914, launched a series of 'lightning sketches' mounted in the broad comic style of the war propaganda cartoons popular in Britain's newspapers. The gags' goal was the humiliation of the 'Hun' and the 'bully boy' himself, Kaiser Wilhelm: the first film ended with the disturbingly Freudian imagery of Germany's sausage being devoured by the British bulldog. Captions relied heavily on puns and contemporary slang. Techniques used were primitive but varied, including stop-motion photography of live-action footage featuring Speed drawing, and cut-out jointed models moved and positioned against drawn backgrounds. In 1917, with Neptune's collapse, Speed began producing for his own company, Speed Cartoons: films like *Tank Pranks* and *The U-Tube* continued to amuse wartime audiences.

As the book illustrator of H. Rider Haggard's *She*, Speed was the natural choice to design Will Barker's 1916 film version, but no similar live-action work followed. In peacetime, Speed began a lengthy one-reel series adapted from A. B. Payne and Bertram Lamb's *Daily Mirror* children's comic strip 'Pip, Squeak and Wilfred'. Twenty-six adventures featuring the animal trio (a dog, a penguin and a rabbit) emerged between February and August 1921. Speed stayed faithful to the strip's design, and the characters' popularity ensured keen audiences, though the original's slapstick spirit proved hard to duplicate with a low budget and cut-out models; overall, the series looked slipshod and dated. Despite their limitations, Speed's films remain historically significant for their mixed-media techniques, their indigenous subject matter and their early proof of animation's value for populist and political causes. He died in Deal, Kent, on 31 December 1931.

(Geoff Brown and Paul Wells)

BIBLIOGRAPHY: Gifford, Denis, 'Lancelot Speed', in Maurice Horn (ed.), *The World Encyclopaedia of Cartoons* (New York: Chelsea House, 1980); Gifford, Denis, *British Animated Films, 1895–1985: A Filmography* (Jefferson, NC: McFarland, 1987); Low, Rachael, *The History of the British Film 1914–1918* (London: George Allen & Unwin, 1950); Reed, Bowler, 'An Interview with the Inventor of the "Bully Boy" Cartoons', *The Bioscope*, 5 Nov. 1914, pp. 497, 499.

FILMOGRAPHY: *Bully Boy No. 1; General French's Contemptible Little Army; Sleepless; Sea Dreams* (1914); *A Chip off the Old Block; or, The Half-a-Crown Prince; The Jolly Roger; Turkish Delight; Bully Boy No. 8* (1915); *Tank Pranks; The U-Tube* (1917); *Tommy Atkins; Old Father William; Britain's Effort* (1918); *Britain's Honour* (1919); *The Wonderful Adventures of Pip, Squeak and Wilfred* (series, 1921).

SPENCE, Richard (1957–)

Richard Spence was born in Doncaster on 6 December 1957. After studying Latin and Greek literature and philosophy at Merton College, Oxford, he joined the BBC as a trainee producer in 1982. He worked as a producer/director on the current affairs magazine *Nationwide* and the arts documentary programmes *Omnibus* and *Arena*, before switching to Channel 4. His major break as a director of television drama came in 1989, when (alongside Chris Bernard) he directed half the episodes in Debbie Horsfield's series *Making Out*, a well-liked comedy-drama about a group of women factory workers in Manchester.

Subsequently Spence directed several well-received television films. *You, Me and Marley*, which pitted frustrated Belfast teenage joyriders against the violent civic 'justice' meted out by the local IRA, won awards at the Geneva, Edinburgh and Rennes film festivals. *Skallagrigg*, which interwove the stories of two children from different decades suffering from cerebral palsy to expose and condemn able-bodied society's continuing incarceration and dehumanisation of the disabled, won the 1994 BAFTA for Best Single Television Drama.

Spence's *Different for Girls*, a courageous, category-defying transsexual comedy-romance written by Tony Marchant, won international festival acclaim and modest cinema releases in Hong Kong, the USA and much of continental Europe. Ageing punk motorbike despatch rider Prentice (Rupert Graves) runs into his school best friend Karl (Steven Mackintosh) to discover – first to his perplexity, then to his confused fascination – that following gender reassignment surgery Karl has become the cautious, conformist Kim. Like much of Spence's best work, *Different for Girls* was issue-based and sharply critical in its view of contemporary Britain – where it remained unreleased until 1998 and was pulled from cinemas after just three days.

Spence has also directed two US straight-to-video features: *Blind Justice*, a Western for HBO starring Armand Assante and Elisabeth Shue, and *New World Disorder*, an improbably plotted cyber-crime thriller featuring an obese Rutger Hauer. He continues to direct interesting work for television in the UK: *Promoted to Glory* (2003), featuring Ken Stott, Lesley Manville and Kevin Whately, uses echoes of Dennis Potter and a clever dream flashback structure to explore a street-drinker's unorthodox encounter with the Salvation Army – and to subvert the saccharine clichés one might expect from an ITV Christmas drama.

(Claire Monk)

BIBLIOGRAPHY: Culf, Andrew, 'BBC Moves into Cinema Territory', *Guardian*, 21 May 1995; Gray, Louise, '*Skallagrigg*', *Sight and Sound*, May 1994, p. 64; Medhurst, Andy, '*Different for Girls*', *Sight and Sound*, Apr. 1998, pp. 37–8.

FILMOGRAPHY: *You, Me and Marley* (1992); *Skallagrigg; Blind Justice* (US) (1994); *Different for Girls* (1996); *New World Disorder* (US, 1999).

SPIERS, Bob

Bob Spiers was born in Glasgow. In 1976 he made his debut in television, directing an episode of the BBC comedy *It Ain't Half Hot Mum*. He went on to direct episodes of *Dad's Army, Are You Being Served?* and *The Goodies*, and won a BAFTA for the second series of *Fawlty Towers*. In the 1980s he was equally successful with *The Comic Strip Presents . . .*, notably *Five Go Mad in Dorset*, and in the 1990s with *Absolutely Fabulous*. He finally made a feature film in 1997: a remake of *That Darned Cat* for Disney. However, it was his reputation as Britain's top television comedy director that brought him the assignment to direct a big-budget vehicle for the Spice Girls – *Spiceworld: The Movie*. Spiers attempts to emulate the zany humour of Richard Lester's *A Hard Day's Night* (1964), but the five Spice Girls, feisty and energetic though they are, lack the casual charm of the Beatles. Nonetheless, the film was an international box-office success.

After television work in Britain and Australia, Spiers went on to direct *Kevin of the North*, a comedy set in Alaska that fared badly in competition with Disney's similarly themed *Snow Dogs* (Brian Levant, 2002).

(Stephen Griffiths)

BIBLIOGRAPHY: Lyttle, John, 'Always Look on the Dark Side', *Independent*, 7 Jan. 1993, p. 21.

FILMOGRAPHY: *That Darned Cat* (US); *Spiceworld: The Movie* (1997); *Kevin of the North* (aka *Chilly Dogs/L'Aventurier du grand nord*, UK/Can, 2001).

SPOTTISWOODE, Roger (1945–)

Roger Spottiswoode was born on 5 January 1945 in Ottawa, Ontario, where his father, the noted film theorist Raymond Spottiswoode, worked for the National Film Board of Canada under John Grierson. Brought up in Britain, Spottiswoode began work as a messenger boy at Eyeline Films in 1964 and soon progressed to become an assistant editor. He was hired by Sam Peckinpah to work on *Straw Dogs* (1971), and followed the director back to the US, where he spent the next ten years working as an editor, screenwriter, producer and second-unit director. Thanks to his Canadian passport, Spottiswoode was able to make his directorial debut with *Terror Train* (1980), a horror film he was originally only supposed to edit. He was then asked to rescue the beleaguered *The Pursuit of D. B. Cooper* (1981), much of which had already been shot by Buzz Kulik and John Frankenheimer. Spottiswoode reworked the film in collaboration with writer Ron Shelton and the two went on to make *Under Fire* (1983), a political thriller set in 1979 Nicaragua that is still Spottiswoode's most impressive achievement, and *The Best of Times* (1986), a mixture of wry comedy and sport that looks forward to Shelton's later works as a director.

Spottiswoode next began a collaboration with screenwriter Dan Petrie Jr, which resulted in two popular films for Disney: *Shoot to Kill* (1988), largely shot in Canada and featuring a great performance by Sidney Poitier; and the Tom Hanks comedy -thriller *Turner & Hooch* (1989). Spottiswoode's best films tend to focus on diffident anti-heroes shaped by the counter-culture experiences of the 1960s; though his only film actually set in that period is the disappointing *Air America* (1990), a comic look at CIA activities in 1969 Laos that he inherited from its original writer-director Richard Rush.

Spottiswoode returned to the UK to shoot the biographical drama *Mesmer* (1994), based on Dennis Potter's last screenplay. Despite a fine central performance by Alan Rickman, the film ran into problems with its distributors and was barely released. On the other hand, *Tomorrow Never Dies* (1997), another efficient if uninspired chapter in the Bond series, was a huge commercial success. Once again collaborating with (an uncredited) Dan Petrie, Spottiswoode tried to go for a more realistic and down-to-earth approach, with mixed results. Petrie also worked on *The 6th Day* (2000), an Arnold Schwarzenegger vehicle about cloning that comes in a poor second to Schwarzenegger's similar *Total Recall* (Paul Verhoeven, 1990). More interesting are the films Spottiswoode made for television in America and Canada. These include *And the Band Played On* (US, 1993) about the development of the AIDS crisis in America; *Hiroshima* (Can/Jap, 1995), a three-hour dramatisation about the dropping of the first atomic bomb; *The Matthew Sheppard Story* (US, 2002), a look at a notorious 1998 hate crime in Wyoming; and *Spinning Boris* (2003), a well-imagined fantasy of what might have happened if Boris Yeltsin had brought in American expertise to revive his political career. Spottiswoode is at his best in these fact-based dramas where he is able to give his liberal sensibilities full rein.

(Sergio Angelini)

BIBLIOGRAPHY: French, Philip, 'Master of All Trades', *Observer*, 5 Feb. 1984; Taylor, Paul, 'Out of the Cutting Room into the Fire', *Monthly Film Bulletin*, Jan. 1984, pp. 4–5.

FILMOGRAPHY: *Terror Train* (Can, 1980); *The Pursuit of D. B. Cooper* (US, 1981); *Under Fire* (US, 1983); *The Best of Times* (US, 1986); *Shoot to Kill* (UK: *Deadly Pursuit*, US, 1988); *Turner & Hooch* (US, 1989); *Air America* (US, 1990); *Stop! Or My Mom Will Shoot* (US, 1992); *Mesmer* (UK/Can/Ger/Aus, 1994); *Tomorrow Never Dies* (UK/US, 1997); *The 6th Day* (US, 2000); *Ripley Under Ground* (US/UK, 2005).

SPURRIER, Paul (1967–)

Paul Spurrier was born in Norwich on 23 May 1967 and educated at Norwich Cathedral School. He began acting from the age of seven, appearing in films such as *The Wild Geese* (Andrew V. McLaglen, 1978), and in several television dramas, notably the 1981 version of F. Anstey's role-switching comic novel *Vice Versa* (Ron Francis), where he swapped places with Peter Bowles (playing his father). He went on to study film-making at the University of Southern California and the London International Film School. Alongside barely screened personal films ('I generally lose interest once I've made them'), he wrote computer database programs and made corporate videos for Blockbuster Video, Pizza Hut and the Ministry of Defence, among others. The profits accumulated over five years were used by Spurrier and producer Chris Leeson as the budget (variously quoted as £25,000 and £100,000) for their first feature, *Underground*.

The film covers twenty-four hours in the life of a fifteen-year-old drug-dealer. Spurrier deploys his tiny budget sparingly and effectively, using a virtually unknown cast (apart from brief cameos by Ian Dury and Chrissie Cotterill), and serving as his own cameraman and editor as well as writing and directing. The result is an exemplary lesson in low-budget film-making, with authenticity and originality more than making up for occasionally wooden acting and crudity in plot development. *Underground*'s disturbing vision of a society where drug-taking is all-pervasive attracted favourable reviews, but the film only reached late-night cinema audiences. Spurrier seems unlikely to fit either into the corporate world of Hollywood deal-makers or the cosier confines of British television. Appropriately for such an idiosyncratic film-maker, Spurrier went on to make *P*, a Thai-language horror film about a bar-girl using magic to take blood revenge on those who exploit her.

(Robert Murphy)

BIBLIOGRAPHY: Botsford, David, 'Independent Feature Film "Underground" Sheds Light on London's Drug Culture', 'Underground' official website <skyport.com/cfs/underground/titlepage.html>; Hawkins, Linda, 'The Importance of Being Father', *TV Times*, 24 Sept. 1981, p. 3; Snook, J., 'Beyond Trainspotting', 'Underground' official website: <skyport.com/cfs/undeground/titlepage.html>.

FILMOGRAPHY: *Underground* (1998); *P* (UK/Thailand, 2005).

SQUIRE, Anthony (1914–2000)

Jack Francis Anthony Squire was born in London on 5 May 1914, the son of poet Sir John Squire. He served as a flying-boat pilot in the Second World War, eventually transferring to the RAF Film Unit. After the war he directed sponsored documentaries and branched into fiction with the short stories of *Files from Scotland Yard* (1951). He was more prestigiously employed to direct the aerial sequences in David Lean's *The Sound Barrier* (1952), and his subsequent career alternated between his own very modest directing assignments and work as second-unit director on big-budget action films from *The Blue Max* (John Guillermin, 1966) to *Eye of the Needle* (Richard Marquand, 1981).

In the 1950s Squire also co-wrote and produced *A Hill in Korea* (Julian Amyes, 1956), and directed several episodes of television series *The Adventures of Sir Lancelot* and *William Tell*. In the 1960s he wrote episodes of *The Saint*, but was otherwise kept busy on other people's films; in the 1970s he found time for sponsored documentaries such as *Artistry in Tureens* (1973) and *Facets of Glass* (1975). In the final phase of his career he directed films and television programmes for children, including *Mr Selkie* (1978), featuring an ecologically conscious seal; an adaptation of Enid Blyton's *The Island of Adventure* (1982); and a children's television series *Neptune's Children* (1985). He died on 15 May 2000.

(Robert Murphy)

FILMOGRAPHY: *Increase the Harvest* (doc. short, 1946); *The Gates of Power* (doc. short, aka *Stairway to the Sea*, 1949); *Files from Scotland Yard* (1951); *Power for All* (doc. short); *The Sound Barrier* (aerial unit dir., David Lean) (1952); *The Heart of the Matter* (African location dir., George More O'Ferrall, 1953); *Double Cross* (1956); *Mission in Morocco/Misión en Marruecos* (Sp, 1959); *The Blue Max* (aerial unit dir., John Guillermin); *All in a Day's Flying* (doc. short) (1966); *Casino Royale* (2nd unit dir., Joe McGrath/John Huston/Ken Hughes/Val Guest/ Robert Parrish, 1967); *Flash Bang Wallop!* (doc. short, 1968); *Darling Lili* (aerial unit dir., Blake Edwards); *On Her Majesty's Secret Service* (stock car sequence dir., Peter Hunt) (1969); *Four Men Went to Sea* (doc. short, 1971); *New York* (doc. short, 1972); *The Ukibec Connection* (doc. short); *Artistry in Tureens* (doc. short) (1973); *11 Harrowhouse* (2nd unit dir., Aram Avakian, 1974); *One of Our Dinosaurs Is Missing* (2nd unit dir., Robert Stevenson); *Facets of Glass* (doc. short) (1975); *The New Alchemy* (doc. short, 1976); *Candleshoe* (2nd unit dir., Norman Tokar, 1977); *Revenge of the Pink Panther* (2nd unit dir., Blake Edwards); *Mr Selkie* (1978); *Condorman* (2nd unit dir., Charles Jarrott); *Eye of the Needle* (2nd unit dir., Richard Marquand) (1981); *The Island of Adventure* (aka *Enid Blyton's The Island of Adventure*, 1982); *Sword of the Valiant – The Legend of Gawain and the Green Knight* (action sequence dir., Stephen Weeks, 1983).

STAFFORD, Brendan J. (1915–1991)

Brendan James K. Stafford was born in Dublin on 1 February 1915. In the 1930s he ran a photographic studio in the city. Michael Powell, impressed by the quality of his work, encouraged him to come to England to work as a stills photographer at Denham Studios. During the Second World War Stafford joined the army but was discharged on medical grounds and encouraged to work for Strand Films, one of the units producing government-funded information and propaganda films. Throughout the 1940s he directed several shorts for Strand, Gaumont-British Instructional and other companies (having made his debut, *Foolsmate*, for the Irish Tourist Board). However, his main interest remained cinematography and he always acted as his own cameraman.

In 1950 he ventured into fiction, co-directing the modestly thrilling *Stranger at My Door*, a topical melodrama set in Dublin about an ex-soldier who turns to burglary to fend off a blackmailer. Blackmail also occupies *The Armchair Detective* (1951), a more routine B-film, featuring the BBC radio detective played by Ernest Dudley in his only big-screen outing. Stafford sought out more exotic adventures and settings for *Men Against the Sun*, an Anglo-Kenyan production with John Bentley as an engineer defying lions and female missionaries to extend the Nairobi–Mombasa railway to Uganda.

Subsequently Stafford worked as director of photography, occasionally adding lustre to enterprising low-budget features, particularly Lance Comfort's disturbing *Bang! You're Dead* (1953) and John Lemont's *The Shakedown* (1959). He also found plenty of work on filmed television series, from *The Third Man* to *The Prisoner*. He retired in the early 1970s but was tempted back to light Roy Ward Baker's Sherlock Holmes mystery *The Masks of Death* (1984) and Claude Whatham's bloodthirsty *Murder Elite* (1985), both made for Kevin Francis' Tyburn company. He died in Hampshire on 16 July 1991, well remembered as a prolific and popular cinematographer.

(Robert Murphy)

BIBLIOGRAPHY: Moore, Chris, 'Brendan Stafford' (obituary), *FTT & BETA News*, Sept. 1991, p. 24; Sturgess, Ray, 'Brendan Stafford' (obituary), *FTT & BETA News*, Oct. 1991, p. 19.

FILMOGRAPHY: Documentaries and shorts (selective): *Foolsmate* (Ir, 1940); *Cine-Sport* (magazine series, 1942); *A Nation Once Again* (co-dir. John Desmond Sheridan); *A Car Is Born*; *The Millionth Car* (1946); *The Mediaeval Monastery*; *One in a Million* (1947); *Voyage of the Trade Wind*; *Trade with Africa* (1948); *Hermione's Hamburger Heaven* (1950); *Crystal Clear* (Ir, 1959).

Fiction (complete): *Stranger at My Door* (co-dir. Desmond Leslie, 1950); *The Armchair Detective* (1951); *Men Against the Sun* (Kenya/UK, 1952).

STANLEY, Richard (1966–)

Richard Stanley was born in Fishhook, South Africa, in 1966 and attended the Cape Town Film and Video School, where he made rough drafts of his later feature *Dust Devil* and the still-planned project *A Season of Mists and Rain*. He went on to shoot documentaries and pop videos, including goth-themed clips for Fields of the Nephilim.

While shooting *Voice of the Moon*, a documentary on the Afghan resistance to the Soviet invaders, Stanley was informed that Palace Pictures liked his script for a futuristic lady-and-monster film *Hardware*, and wanted him to direct it. With additional backing from British Screen and Miramax a modest £1 million budget was raised and a young production team assembled to make the film at the Roundhouse, a run-down arts centre in north London. Stanley's astonishing imagery – drawing as much on arcana like the artwork installations of the Survival Research Laboratories as on commercial science-fiction cinema – made up for indifferent acting and a weak plot and *Hardware* was a box-office success on both sides of the Atlantic.

Stanley's follow-up feature, *Dust Devil*, an ambitious Namibian-set horror film dealing with a shape-shifting serial killer, proved to be a troubled production, and relations with Palace were not improved by the publication of Stanley's diary of the shoot, 'I Wake up Screaming'. *Dust Devil*'s box-office returns in the UK were meagre and despite desperate attempts to salvage the film by re-editing, it proved equally unpopular in the United States.

Stanley began directing his own adaptation of H. G. Wells' *The Island of Dr Moreau*, but with a cast that included Val Kilmer and Marlon Brando he had little chance of winning any power struggles, and he was soon replaced by John Frankenheimer. No subsequent feature films have come his way, but he displayed continuing evidence of talent with two feature-length documentaries: *The Secret Glory*, a fascinating study of Nazi mysticism and grail lore; and *The White Darkness*, a perceptive and absorbing account of Haitian voodoo.

(Kim Newman)

BIBLIOGRAPHY: Finney, Angus, *The Egos Have Landed* (London: Heinemann, 1996); Hughes, Dave, 'Island of Lost Opportunities', *Fangoria*, Sept. 1996, pp. 31–6; Kermode, Mark, 'Blow up a Storm: The Making of Dust Devil', *Sight and Sound*, Sept. 1992, pp. 14–17; Short, Sue, 'No Flesh Shall Be Spared: Richard Stanley's *Hardware*', in I. Q. Hunter, *British Science Fiction Cinema* (London and New York: Routledge, 1999); Stanley, Richard, 'I Wake up Screaming: A Diary', in John Boorman and Walter Donohue (eds), *Projections 3* (London: Faber and Faber, 1994).

FILMOGRAPHY: *Rites of Passage* (short, 1983); *Incidents in an Expanding Universe* (1987); *Hardware*; *Voice of the Moon* (aka *Afghan Voices*, doc. short); *Hardware* (1990); *Dust Devil* (1992); *The Brave* (1994); *The Island of Dr Moreau* (replaced by John Frankenheimer, 1996); *The Secret Glory* (doc., 2001); *The White Darkness* (doc., 2002).

STAPLETON, Frank (1962–)

Frank Stapleton was born in Dublin in 1962. After making his first short film, *A Second of June*, in 1984, he studied psychotherapy at the R. D. Laing Philadelphia Association in London. In the 1990s he produced and directed cultural documentaries for Irish television, culminating in the superb series *Irish Dreamtime* (2000), an exploration of the evolving nature of heritage, drawing on the perspectives and experiences of everyday Irish men and women.

Irish heritage and identity were also the subject of his first feature, *The Fifth Province*, a black comic *mélange* of surreal fantasy, irony and cinematic self-reference. Scripted by Stapleton and novelist Nina Fitzpatrick, the film centres on guesthouse-keeper Timmy Sugrue (Brian F. O'Byrne), a persecuted young man living with his overbearing Irish mother, whose inner world emerges through psychoanalytic sessions. The film might have come from the pen of novelist Flann O'Brien, especially in its evocation of the 'fifth province' of Timmy's mind – a place of infinitely absurd possibility, where cows explode, Hungarian archaeologists investigate the Celtic kings and the Irish President is black. But the 'fifth province' is also European Ireland, with its Brussels-sponsored bypasses and European-funded scriptwriting conferences. Stapleton's film is unique in the New Wave of Irish film-making for its playful juggling of social satire on modern Ireland's growing European identity and its criticism of notions of a 'mythic' Ireland.

(Eugene Finn)

BIBLIOGRAPHY: Traynor, Des, 'Frank's Wild Years', *Film Ireland* no. 72, Aug./Sept. 1999, pp. 14–16.

FILMOGRAPHY: *The Fifth Province* (Ir/UK/Ger, 1999).

STEIN, Paul (1892–1951)

Paul Ludwig Stein was born in Vienna on 4 February 1892. As a youth he acted in the Berlin theatre and at eighteen went to New York, where he supplemented his work as a stage manager on Broadway with film script assignments for minor companies. Returning to Europe, he established a reputation playing comic stage roles in Vienna and Berlin and gained further acting experience in films. After mounting two independent productions he joined the Ufa studios in Berlin in 1920 as a director, working on romantic dramas and comedies, several starring the flamboyant actress Pola Negri.

Stein's experience as a director of women led him to *My Official Wife* at Warner Bros. in 1926, the first of three vehicles for the gracious and commanding Irene Rich, all with European settings. Subsequent work for DeMille, Pathé Exchange and United Artists brought further romantic stories from the woman's point of view, with stars including Jetta Goudal, Leatrice Joy and Constance Bennett, though he also chalked up the operetta-style musical *The Lottery Bride* (1930), a disaster of some magnitude. He directed Pola Negri in her Hollywood talkie debut, *A Woman Commands*, and Lillian Gish in hers, *One Romantic Night*. Stein proved as misplaced in Hollywood as either lady, and by February 1932 he was back in Europe, directing the elegant silent star Corinne Griffith in the mawkish tearjerker *Lily Christine* for Paramount British at Elstree; it proved her last film. BIP's *The Song You Gave Me*, a flat musical-comedy starring Bebe Daniels, was little better; still, he settled in at the company and its successor, Associated British, throughout the 1930s, taking charge of dramas and musicals, often with a European flavour. Things improved with *Red Wagon* (1934), a powerful circus drama based on a popular novel by Lady Eleanor Smith, and two bitter-sweet musicals, *Blossom Time* (1934) and *Heart's Desire* (1935), starring the mellifluous Austrian tenor Richard Tauber. Stein found less success with other musical offerings. *Mimi*, based on the same novel as *La Bohème*, proved uninspiring despite its operatic associations and the presence of Douglas Fairbanks Jr and Gertrude Lawrence; while *Café Colette* engineered an unwise marriage between music and spy melodrama.

Ironically, Stein often flourished most outside his perceived specialties. He showed a deft touch with comedy in *Jane Steps Out* and crime drama in *Black Limelight*. An even greater tension and chill was generated in *Poison Pen* (1939), based on Richard Llewellyn's play about a village plunged into internecine strife by an anonymous letter writer. Stein effectively blends scenic views of the English countryside with a suggestion of underlying malevolence, making particularly good use of Flora Robson as the vicar's spinster sister, driven mad by being taken for granted as everybody's kindly aunt.

Stein stayed in Britain during the Second World War, turning out modest comedies and thrillers. Moving to British National in 1944, he was eventually allowed bigger budgets for *Waltz Time*, a return to a nostalgically evoked Vienna, and *Lisbon Story*, another musical espionage drama set during the last stages of the war. Both films are enhanced by Tauber's singing, though both pointedly find other, younger men to take the lead role. Less wisely, *The Laughing Lady* attempts to make stars of the singing duo Ann Ziegler and Webster Booth in a Technicolor musical set during the French Revolution. Stein's last two films were untypical but original: a topical germ-warfare thriller, *Counterblast*, and a clever whodunit and radio spin-off, *The Twenty Questions Murder Mystery*. Paul Stein died in London on 2 May 1951.
(Margaret Butler)

BIBLIOGRAPHY: Cole, Hubert, 'A Mercurial Maker of Stars', *Film Weekly*, 17 Aug. 1934, p. 7; Dent, Arthur, 'To Paul Stein' (obituary), *Today's Cinema*, 9 May 1951, p. 27; Stein, Paul, 'Heading for British Supremacy', *Picturegoer* no. 145, 3 Mar. 1934, p. 10.

FILMOGRAPHY (UK only): *Lily Christine* (1932); *The Song You Gave Me* (1933); *Red Wagon*; *Blossom Time* (US: *April Romance*) (1934); *Mimi*; *Heart's Desire* (1935); *Faithful* (1936); *Café Colette* (US: *Danger in Paris*, 1937); *Jane Steps Out*; *Black Limelight* (1938); *Just Like a Woman*; *Poison Pen*; *The Outsider* (1939); *Gentleman of Venture* (US: *It Happened to One Man*, 1940); *The Saint Meets the Tiger* (1941); *Kiss the Bride Goodbye*; *Twilight Hour* (1944); *Waltz Time* (1945); *Lisbon Story*; *The Laughing Lady* (1946); *Counterblast* (US: *The Devil's Plot*, 1948); *The Twenty Questions Murder Mystery* (US: *Murder on the Air*, 1950).

STELLMAN, Martin (1948–)

Martin Stellman was born in London in 1948. He dropped out from Bristol University to join a fringe theatre group before enrolling at the National Film School in the late 1970s. While there he worked on the scripts of Franc Roddam's *Quadrophenia* (1979) and Franco Rosso's *Babylon* (1980), and directed the short *Cheap Perfume*. His most impressive writing achievement was the taut political conspiracy drama *Defence of the Realm* (David Drury, 1985), though he was unhappy with producer David Puttnam's softening of the film's onslaught on political expediency. With his next script, *For Queen and Country* (1988), Stellman insisted on directing the film himself. This bleak account of a black soldier's return to civilian life after the Falklands War imports American-style action-revenge motifs into British cinema, with not very convincing results. Denzel Washington's ex-paratrooper, cursed with a Dick Van Dyke cockney accent, finds himself adrift among drug-pushers, gun-toting policemen and the detritus of a London sink estate. Too many melodramatic clichés, and Stellman's surprisingly soft-hearted view of British soldiers, jar uneasily with the grim realism of the film's culminating violence – closely modelled on the 1985 Broadwater Farm riot.

Stellman regarded *For Queen and Country* as a turning point: 'My broad political engagement is still there. But I don't want to make another "state of Britain" picture. I feel like it's the end of a phase and I'm now interested in exploring more interior, personal subjects' (Sibley, p. 9). Unfortunately few opportunities presented themselves to this interestingly prickly writer/director, though his career revived in 2000 when he wrote the thriller *Tabloid* (David Blair). Since then he has contributed as a writer to the BBC children's fantasy series *Shoebox Zoo* (2004).
(Robert Murphy)

BIBLIOGRAPHY: Sibley, Adrian, 'Urban Western', *Films and Filming*, Jan. 1989, pp. 8–9; 'Who's in Town', *Films in Review*, Aug./Sept. 1989, pp. 416–17.

FILMOGRAPHY: *Cheap Perfume* (short, 1980); *For Queen and Country* (UK/US, 1988).

STEMBRIDGE, Gerry (1958–)

Gerard Stembridge was born in Limerick on 27 November 1958. *The Truth About Clare*, a pseudo-documentary reconstructing the suicide of a young woman, made for RTÉ television, marked his industry debut in 1990, but he made his name in Ireland as the writer of RTÉ's satirical radio show *Scrap Saturday*, performed by Dermot Morgan (later to find fame in the television sitcom *Father Ted*). Stage plays – *Lovechild* (1992), *Ceausescu's War* (1993) and *The Gay Detective* (1996) – consolidated his reputation and in 1996 Stembridge scripted and directed his first feature film, *Guiltrip*. The account of an abusive relationship in small-town Ireland between an army corporal and his wife, the film was critically well received but too downbeat to attract a large audience. After writing scripts for *Ordinary Decent Criminal* (Thaddeus O'Sullivan, 2000) and *Nora* (Pat Murphy, 2000), Stembridge wrote and directed *About Adam*, which, in contrast to the gloomily repressive atmosphere of *Guiltrip*, depicts an Ireland free of Catholic guilt. As in Kieron J. Walsh's *When Brendan Met Trudy* (2000) Dublin is presented as a chic urban space, a suitable setting for carefree sexual adventure.

Stembridge returned to television in 2001 with the comedy *Black Day at Black Rock*, about an Irish village that learns it is to have a group of refugees billeted on it. A versatile and iconoclastic talent, Stembridge regularly works in theatre and has appeared as an actor on television and in cinema.

(Ruth Barton)

BIBLIOGRAPHY: Bosley, Rachael K., 'Production Slate: An Irish Casanova', *American Cinematographer*, Sept. 2000, pp. 33–7; Clarke, Donald, 'The Film's the Thing', *Film Ireland* no. 79, Feb./Mar. 2001, pp. 35–7; Tierney, Michael, 'Minister for Transport, Gerry Stembridge', *Film West* no. 43, Spring 2001, pp. 14–17.

FILMOGRAPHY: *Guiltrip* (Fr/Ir/It/Sp, 1996); *About Adam* (Ir/UK/US, 2000).

STEPHENSON, John

John Stephenson, a respected member of Jim Henson's Animatronics workshop, acted as second-unit director on *The Adventures of Pinocchio* (1996) and *Lost in Space* (1998) before directing a likeable version of George Orwell's *Animal Farm* (1999) for American television. He made his feature debut with a charming adaptation of E. Nesbit's Edwardian novel *Five Children and It* with a cast ranging from Kenneth Branagh to Norman Wisdom.

(Robert Murphy)

FILMOGRAPHY: *The Adventures of Pinocchio* (2nd unit dir., Steve Barron, US/UK/Fr/Ger/Cz, 1996); *Lost in Space* (2nd unit dir., Stephen Hopkins/Friedrich Karl Praetorius, US/UK, 1998); *Five Children and It* (UK/Fr/US, 2004).

STERLING, William (1926–)

William Sterling was born in Sydney on 14 September 1926. After working in Australian television he came to Britain in 1965, producing BBC Television drama, from the soap opera *Compact* (1965) to the 1968 *Sherlock Holmes* series with Peter Cushing and Nigel Stock. He also directed episodes of the science-fiction serial *Counterstrike* (1969), and *A Memory of Two Loves* (1971), an ATV 'Love Story' play. His cinema debut came in 1972 when he wrote and directed a misguided version of *Alice's Adventures in Wonderland* for Josef Shaftel Productions. With mildly psychedelic settings, weak songs, a timid script and a cast stuffed with British notables (Dudley Moore to Flora Robson) often hidden behind ungainly masks. Sterling's handling, awkward and plain, at least allows the period flavour to float into the air and intrigue. Afterwards he prepared a follow-up musical script for Shaftel, *Cinderella*, but no film, and no further credits, emerged.

(Geoff Brown and Robert Murphy)

BIBLIOGRAPHY: Ross, Del, 'Live Action versus Cartoon Techniques', *Film Making* vol.10 no. 12, Dec. 1972, pp. 22–5.

FILMOGRAPHY: *Alice's Adventures in Wonderland* (1972).

STEVENSON, Robert (1905–1986)

Robert Stevenson was born in Buxton, Derbyshire, on 31 March 1905. After studying mechanical sciences and psychology at Cambridge, where he also edited the journal *Granta*, he began his career in a newsreel agency. In 1930 he entered the film industry as a writer and general assistant for Gainsborough, where his first script assignment was a musical, *Greek Street* (Sinclair Hill, 1930). For the next five years he co-wrote a variety of films, from two musical-comedies with Jack Hulbert, *Sunshine Susie* (Victor Saville, 1931) and *Love on Wheels* (Victor Saville, 1932), to the Edgar Wallace thriller *The Ringer* (Walter Forde, 1931). Together with Hulbert he co-directed *Falling for You* (1933) and *Jack of All Trades* (1936). One of production chief Michael Balcon's favoured protégés, Stevenson also broadened his experience with the foreign ventures of Gaumont-British, working in France as dialogue director on *La Bataille* (Nicolas Farkas and Viktor Tourjansky, 1933), and in Berlin's Ufa studios, where he supervised English-language versions of German films and joined Paul Martin in co-directing *Happy Ever After* (1932), the English edition of Martin's Lillian Harvey musical *Ein blonder Traum*.

From 1936, Stevenson directed nine modestly budgeted but high-quality films in England, the first and best of which was *Tudor Rose*, a sturdy but moving historical drama based on the life of Lady Jane Grey, with Nova Pilbeam fresh and poignant as the young pawn trapped in Tudor political manoeuvrings. Others made for Gaumont-British included the spirited potboiler *The Man Who Changed His Mind* (1936), with Boris Karloff as a mad doctor; a lively account of H. Rider Haggard's African adventure *King Solomon's Mines* (1937), with Cedric Hardwicke, Roland Young and Paul Robeson pausing for song; and *Non-Stop New York* (1937), a droll, sharply characterised thriller largely set on a transatlantic plane. All three films also starred Stevenson's wife of the time, the glamorous Anna Lee.

When Michael Balcon became Head of Production at Ealing he recruited Stevenson to direct *The Ware Case* (1938), a strong courtroom drama adapted from a popular play, starring Clive Brook; and *Young Man's Fancy* (1939), a mordant romantic comedy about a young lord (Griffith Jones) who rejects a society heiress for a human cannonball (Anna Lee). He also made *Return to Yesterday* (1939), a piquant and touching drama about the provincial theatre, for Balcon, but as the war clouds gathered, Stevenson, a pacifist, left Britain to take up a contract with David O. Selznick.

At first, Stevenson's work in Hollywood was just as diverse as in England, ranging between the romantic melodrama of *Back*

Street (1941), a visually ambitious and powerful adaptation of *Jane Eyre* (1944) with Orson Welles, and *To the Ends of the Earth* (1948), a clever thriller with atmospheric photography. In 1956, after a period in television, Stevenson settled at Disney where he remained, busy and productive, until his retirement in 1976. Although he returned to Britain for only two more films – Disney's *Kidnapped* (1960) and *In Search of the Castaways* (1962) – his nostalgia for his home country is discernible in several other Disney entertainments, including the highly successful *Mary Poppins* and *Bedknobs and Broomsticks*. He died in Santa Barbara, California, on 30 April 1986.
(Margaret Butler)

BIBLIOGRAPHY: McFarlane, Brian, *An Autobiography of British Cinema* (London: Methuen, 1997); McFarlane, Brian, 'Jack of All Trades: Robert Stevenson', in Jeffrey Richards (ed.), *The Unknown 30s: An Alternative History of the British Cinema 1929–39* (London: I. B. Tauris, 1998); Nolan, Jack Edmund, 'Films on TV', *Films in Review*, Aug./Sept. 1969, pp. 432–4; Roberts, John, 'Robert Stevenson', *Films of the Golden Age*, Spring 1997, pp. 35–9; Stevenson, Robert (letter), *Films in Review*, Nov. 1969, p. 579.

FILMOGRAPHY: *Happy Ever After* (co-dir. Paul Martin, 1932); *Falling for You* (co-dir. Jack Hulbert 1933); *Tudor Rose* (US: *Nine Days a Queen*); *The Man Who Changed His Mind* (US: *The Man Who Lived Again*); *Jack of All Trades* (US: *The Two of Us*, co-dir. Jack Hulbert) (1936); *King Solomon's Mines*; *Non-Stop New York*; *Owd Bob* (US: *The Victor*) (1937); *The Ware Case* (1938); *Young Man's Fancy*; *Return to Yesterday* (1939); *Tom Brown's School Days* (US, 1940); *Back Street* (US, 1941); *Joan of Paris* (US, 1942); *Forever and a Day* (US, co-dirs. René Clair/Edmund Goulding/Cedric Hardwicke/Frank Lloyd /Victor Saville/Herbert Wilcox, 1943); *Jane Eyre* (US, 1944); *Dishonored Lady* (US, 1947); *To the Ends of the Earth* (US, 1948); *I Married a Communist* (UK: *The Woman on Pier 13*, US); *Walk Softly, Stranger* (US) (1950); *My Forbidden Past* (US, 1951); *The Las Vegas Story* (US, 1952); *Johnny Tremain* (US); *Old Yeller* (US) (1957); *Darby O'Gill and the Little People* (US, 1959); *Kidnapped* (1960); *The Absent Minded Professor* (US, 1961); *In Search of the Castaways* (1962); *Son of Flubber* (US, 1963); *The Misadventures of Merlin Jones* (US); *Mary Poppins* (US) (1964); *The Monkey's Uncle* (US); *That Darn Cat!* (US) (1965); *The Gnome-Mobile* (US, 1967); *Blackbeard's Ghost* (US); *The Love Bug* (US); *The Mickey Mouse Anniversary Show* (co-dir. Ward Kimball, US) (1968); *Bedknobs and Broomsticks* (US, 1971); *Herbie Rides Again* (US); *The Island at the Top of the World* (US) (1974); *One of Our Dinosaurs Is Missing* (US, 1975); *The Shaggy D.A.* (US, 1976).

STEWART, David A. (1952–)

David Stewart was born in Sunderland on 9 September 1952. A successful pop musician, Stewart is best known for his partnership with singer Annie Lennox. As the Eurthymics, Stewart and Lennox contributed to the soundtrack of *Nineteen Eighty-Four* (Michael Radford, 1984), though against the director's wishes. In 1993 Stewart wrote and directed *Taking Liberties with Mr Simpson*, a short film about a probation officer with a dark secret, which was shown at the Edinburgh Film Festival. *Honest*, an attempt at a retro 1960s' caper movie, followed in 2000. Melanie Blatt and Nicole and Natalie Appleton from the girl group All Saints play London East End sisters who turn to crime, carrying out jewel heists disguised as men. Despite the contribution of veteran writers and script doctors Dick Clement and Ian La Frenais, *Honest* proved a messy confection of sentimentality and misplaced nostalgia. With All Saints' pre-teen fans excluded by an 18 certificate, the film struggled to attract an audience and appears unlikely to launch Stewart into a new career as a film director.
(Daniel O'Brien)

BIBLIOGRAPHY: Bright, Spencer, 'All Saints and the Sinner', *Daily Mail* Weekend Section, 27 May 2000, pp. 28–30.

FILMOGRAPHY: *Taking Liberties with Mr Simpson* (short, 1993); *Honest* (2000).

STIRNER, Brian (1949–)

Born the son of a radio and television repairer in Chiswick, west London, in 1949, Brian Walker changed his name to Brian Stirner while studying at RADA. After playing the shy young soldier whose progress to the D-Day landings is charted in Stuart Cooper's *Overlord* (1975), Stirner went on to direct stage plays and write and act for television. His first feature film, *A Kind of Hush* (1999), is a sensitive and intelligent study of six teenage boys who become self-styled vigilantes as they attempt to come to terms with childhood abuse. Stirner worked closely with unknown actors to achieve a subtle naturalism in performance. Set around the then-run-down King's Cross area in London, the film combines the observational strengths of British social realism with lyrical passages that display Stirner's sense of visual composition.

A Kind of Hush was funded by Lottery money and British Screen, but received a frustratingly limited release. Stirner has subsequently directed television drama series such as *The Inspector Lynley Mysteries* (2003–4), but has yet to make another feature film.
(Andrew Spicer)

BIBLIOGRAPHY: Stirner, Brian, 'What Makes a Film Bomb', *Guardian*, 5 May 2000, p. 23; Wigg, David, 'Romeo Lost His Sight – and Learned to See', *Daily Express*, 23 Aug. 1977.

FILMOGRAPHY: *A Kind of Hush* (1999).

STONE, Andrew L. (1902–1999)

Andrew Lysander Stone was born on 16 July 1902 in Oakland, California, and began working in the film industry at the age of sixteen. He graduated from distribution to lab work, the props department and, from 1927, directing two-reelers. In the 1930s and 40s Stone wrote, produced and directed comedies and musicals, most notably the all-black *Stormy Weather* (1943). That year he formed a production company with his wife, Virginia, who served as co-producer and editor on their subsequent projects. From 1950 they specialised in thrillers shot entirely on location for authenticity and economy, including the sinking-ship suspense film *The Last Voyage* (1960).

The Stones came to Britain for three films in the mid-1960s. *The Password Is Courage*, a factually based, tongue-in-cheek wartime prisoner-of-war yarn with Dirk Bogarde as a habitual escaper, contains effective sequences but gives the impression of hasty last-minute cutting, pasted over with occasional voiceover narration (a persistent Stone trait). *Never Put It in Writing* is a poor Irish comedy starring Pat Boone, and *The Secret of My Success* a whimsical, mildly misogynist farce in three episodes, which failed to make a major star of James Booth.

Stone then applied his all-location principle to two vacuous, large-scale musicals filmed in Europe, *Song of Norway* (1970) and *The Great Waltz* (1972), respectively biopics of Grieg and Johann Strauss II. He subsequently retired save for a stint as assistant director on *Rollercoaster* (James Goldstone, 1977). He died, aged 96, on 9 June 1999.

(Sheldon Hall)

BIBLIOGRAPHY: Brownlow, Kevin, Interview, *Film* no. 33, Autumn 1962, p. 18; Brownlow, Kevin, 'Andrew L. Stone' (obituary), *Variety*, 27 Nov. 2000, p. 71; Mason, James, 'The Man Who Wants Men of Steel', *Films and Filming*, Aug. 1958, p. 6; Shivas, Mark, 'The Password Is Cleaning Cloths', *Movie* no. 4, Nov. 1962, p. 30; Stone, Andrew, 'A Method of Making Films', *Movie* no. 4, Nov. 1962, pp. 28–9.

FILMOGRAPHY (UK only): *The Password Is Courage* (1962); *Never Put It in Writing* (1964); *The Secret of My Success* (1965).

STOW, Percy (1876–1919)

Percival Edwin Stow was born in Islington, London, in 1876. He began his career in 1901 working for Cecil Hepworth, who discovered he had an affinity for trick films. In 1903 Stow made *The Unclean World*, a spoof on the *Unseen World* microscopic films of the Warwick Trading Company. The same year he assisted Hepworth in making *Alice in Wonderland*, at 800 feet the longest British film then made. When Hepworth broke with his business partner Henry Lawley, Stow went with Lawley and founded the Clarendon Film Company in Croydon; the first films were ready for distribution by July 1904. Stow became principal director of the company, and took over complete charge when Lawley left in 1908. He specialised in making short comics, but in 1910 Stow began releasing a series of seventeen adventure films about a dashing naval hero, Lieutenant Rose, chiefly portrayed by P. G. Norgate, and popular enough for British and Colonial to concoct a rival naval hero, Lieutenant Daring, by the end of the year. Rose's last adventure emerged in February 1915.

Under Stow's leadership, Clarendon eventually turned to making larger-scale productions, crime or historical dramas, mostly handled by Wilfred Noy. Stow himself was happier with humbler fare, releasing simple trick films and comics until 1916, by which time their appeal and market were waning. He died of tuberculosis in Torquay, Devon, on 10 July 1919.

(Simon Brown)

BIBLIOGRAPHY: Low, Rachael, *The History of the British Film 1906–1914* (London: George Allen & Unwin, 1973); Low, Rachael, *The History of the British Film 1914–1918* (London: George Allen & Unwin, 1950).

FILMOGRAPHY: *How the Burglar Tricked the Bobby*; *The Indian Chief and the Seidlitz Powder*, *Interior of a Railway Carriage – Bank Holiday*; *The Glutton's Nightmare* (1901); *That Eternal Ping-Pong*; *The Quarrelsome Couple*; *The Countryman and the Flute*; *The Coster and the Donkey*; *When Daddy Comes Home*; *The Frustrated Elopement*; *How to Stop a Motor Car*; *Peace with Honour* (co-dir. Cecil Hepworth) (1902); *The Lady Thief and the Baffled Bobbies*; *Getting up Made Easy*; *The Absent-Minded Bootblack*; *Alice in Wonderland* (co-dir. Cecil Hepworth; *Only a Face at the Window*; *The Revolving Table*; *The Neglected Lover and the Stile*; *The Adventures of a Bill-Poster*, *The Knocker and the Naughty Boys*; *Fun at the Barber's*; *The Tragical Tale of a Belated Letter*, *A Free Ride*; *The Unclean World*: *The Suburban-Bunkum Microbe-Guyoscope*; *The Unexpected Bath*; *Saturday Shopping*; *Stop That Bus!* (US: *How the Old Woman Caught the Omnibus*) (1903); *An Up-to-date Studio*; *The Joke That Failed*; *Off for the Holidays*; *Attempted Murder in a Railway Train*; *The Burglar and the Girls*; *The Convict and the Curate* (US: *The Convict's Escape*; *Once Too Often*; *Fighting Washerwomen*; *Father's Hat; or, Guy Fawkes' Day*; *The Adventures of Sandy MacGregor*, *The Mistletoe Bough*; *The Broken Broom* (US: *A Kiss and a Tumble*); *The Stolen Pig* (1904); *The Love Letters*; *The Gamblers* (1905); *Dangerous Golfers*; *Blind Man's Buff*, *Above and below Stairs*; *Saturday's Wages*; *An Unlucky Day*; *Mr Brown's Bathing Tent*; *Willie and Tim in the Motor Car*, *Jimmy and Joe and the Water Spout*; *When Father Laid the Carpet on the Stairs*; *The Sailor's Wedding*; *Father's Birthday Cheese*; *The Village Blacksmith*; *Beauty and the Beast*; *The Stolen Purse* (1905); *When Father Got a Holiday*; *How Baby Caught a Cold*; *The Truant's Capture*; *Saved by a Lie*; *Who Stole the Beer?*; *The Coster's Revenge*; *Beer Twopence a Glass*; *Those Boys Again*; *How Father Killed the Cat*; *Rescued in Mid-Air*, *Caught by the Tide*; *The Stolen Bride*; *A Double Life*; *The Artful Dodger*, *The Horse That Ate the Baby*; *When Mother Fell Ill at Christmas*; *The Runaway Van* (1906); *Disturbing His Rest*; *Paying off Old Scores*; *An Overdose of Love Potion*; *The Sunday-School Treat*; *The Wreck of the Mary Jane*; *Curing the Blind*; *The Story of a Modern Mother*, *Adventures of a Bath Chair*, *The Absent-Minded Professor*, *An Awkward Situation*; *An Anxious Day for Mother*, *That's Not Right – Watch Me!*; *The Water Babies; or, The Little Chimney Sweep*; *The Pied Piper*, *A Wet Day*; *A Soldier's Wedding* (1907); *The Little Waif and the Captain's Daughter*, *The Captain's Wives*; *The Downfall of the Burglars' Trust*; *The Scandalous Boys and the Fire Chute*; *The Memory of His Mother*, *Poor Aunt Matilda*; *Three Maiden Ladies and the Bull* (aka *Beware of the Bull*); *Three Suburban Sportsmen and a Hat*; *Mr Jones Has a Tile Loose*; *If Women Were Policemen*; *Saved by the Telegraph Code*; *Follow Your Leader and the Master Follows Last*; *The Old Composer and the Prima Donna*; *Got a Penny Stamp*; *Robin Hood and His Merry Men*; *John Gilpin*; *The Missionary's Daughter*, *A Wild Goose Chase*; *The Cavalier's Wife*; *Algy's Yachting Party*; *Nancy; or, The Burglar's Daughter*, *A Modern Cinderella*; *The Puritan Maid and the Royalist Refugee*; *The Tempest*; *When the Man in the Moon Seeks a Wife*; *The Martyrdom of Thomas à Becket*; *Ib and Little Christina*; *The Old Favourite and the Ugly*

Golliwog (1908); *His Work or His Wife*; *The Love of a Nautch Girl*; *The Crafty Usurper and the Young King*; *Hard Times*; *The Invaders*; *The Morganatic Marriage*; *A Lesson in Electricity*; *Juggins' Motor Skates*; *An Aerial Elopement*; *Put a Penny in the –*; *Pater's Patent Painter*, *When Father Wears Stays*; *The Dear Old Dog*; *A Glass of Goat's Milk*; *Three Sailormen and a Girl*; *Bobby the Boy Scout; or, The Boy Detective*; *Never Late; or, The Conscientious Clerk*; *The Stolen Favourite*; *Electric Transformation*; *Father's Baby Boy*; *An Ingenious Safe Deposit*; *In Love with a Picture Girl*; *The Professor's Strength Tablets*; *Under the Mistletoe Bough*; *The Jealous Doll; or, The Frustrated Elopement* (1909); *When We Called the Plumber In*; *The Truth Will Out*; *The Magic of Love*; *Lieutenant Rose and the Robbers of Fingall's Creek*; *Cock-a-Doodle-Doo*; *That Skating Carnival*; *Tommy's Locomotive*; *Mary Was a Housemaid*; *The Light that Failed*; *A Hero in Spite of Himself*; *The Man Who Couldn't Laugh*; *Lieutenant Rose and the Foreign Spy*; *Lieutenant Rose and the Gunrunners*; *Off for the Holidays*; *His Little Son Was with Him All the Time*; *His Week's Pay*; *Frightened Freddy the Fearful Policeman*; *Frightened Freddy – How Freddy Won a Hundred Pounds*; *A Window to Let*; *Miss Simpkin's Boarders*; *A Child's Prayer*, *Lieutenant Rose and the Stolen Submarine*; *The Burglar Expected*; *Mr Breakneck's Invention*; *What the Parrot Saw*; *Lieutenant Rose and the Chinese Pirates*; *Wait Till I Catch You*; *What a Pretty Girl Can Do*; *Only One Girl; or, A Boom in Sausages*; *When Father Buys the Beer*, *Mary Had a Lovely Voice*; *The Nervous Curate*; *The Curate's New Year Gifts* (1910); *Lieutenant Rose and the Stolen Code*; *A Ticket for the Theatre*; *I'm So Sleepy*; *The Doll's Revenge*; *Frightened Freddy and the Desperate Alien*; *Lieutenant Rose and the Boxers*; *The Actor's Artifice*; *Our Intrepid Correspondent*; *A Pair of New Boots*; *Great Scot on Wheels*; *Baden-Powell Junior*, *Sarah's Hero*; *Silly Sammy*; *Servants Superseded*; *Little Tom's Letter*, *First Aid Flirtations*; *The Little Boys Next Door*, *Clever Illusions and How to Do Them*; *Frightened Freddy and the Murderous Marauder*, *A Test of Affection*; *Lieutenant Rose and the Royal Visit*; *The Stage-Struck Carpenter*, *Getting Dad's Consent*; *The Doctor's Dilemma* (aka *What Could the Doctor Do?*); *Dolly's Birthday Present*; *Speedy the Telegraph Boy*; *Oh, It's You?* (1911); *A Matrimonial Muddle*; *Lieutenant Rose and the Stolen Ship*; *Lieutenant Rose and the Moorish Raiders*; *He Would Speak*; *The Widow's Might*; *Percy's Persistent Pursuit*; *A Tale of Tails*; *Electrical House-Building*; *Lieutenant Rose and the Hidden Treasure*; *A Pair of Handcuffs* (aka *Links of Love*); *A Tame Cat*; *Mind the Paint*; *Mr Diddlem's Will*; *Sheepskin Trousers; or, Not in These*; *Grandma's Sleeping Draught*; *A Peppery Affair*, *Don't Touch It!*; *Her Relations*; *Which of the Two*; *Molly Learns to Mote*; *The Suit That Didn't Fit*; *Lieutenant Rose and the Train Wreckers*; *The Electric Leg*; *Midnight Marauders*; *When Jack Comes Home*; *Lieutenant Rose and the Patent Aeroplane*; *Where's Baby?*; *All's Fair in Love*; *She Must Have Swallowed It*; *A Breech in Breeches*; *Lieutenant Rose in China Seas*; *A Bald Story*; *Mother's Day Out* (1912); *Business as Usual During Alterations* (aka *Open During Alterations*); *Love Versus Pride*; *Love and the Varsity*; *Maudie's Adventure*; *The Coster's Wedding* (aka *Coster Joe*); *A Modern Dick Whittington*; *Kindly Remove Your Hat; or, She Didn't Mind*; *The Crowd Outside; or, Waiting for You*; *What Could the Poor Man Do?*; *Sweep! Sweep! Sweep!*; *Be Sure and Insure*; *Suffragettes in the Bud*; *A Cunning Canine* (aka *A Little Doggerel*); *Milling the Militants*; *Coming to the Point*; *Bill Bumper's Boy*; *A Present from Father*, *Dad Caught Napping*; *The New Hat*; *It's Best to Be Natural*; *Not Wanted*; *The New Letter Box*; *A Violent Fancy*; *Miss Gladeyeslip's Vacation*; *Hay Ho!*; *A Surprising Encounter* (aka *The Misfits*); *Lieutenant Rose and the Stolen Bullion*; *Incompatibility of Temper*, *There Are Girls Wanted Here*; *The Home Beautiful*; *Unskilled Labour*, *Auntie's Secret Sorrow*, *A Horse! A Horse!*; *Ringing the Changes*; *He Who Takes What Isn't His'n*; *It's Love that Makes the World Go Round*; *The Rent in A-Rear*, *Sold!*; *What Happened to Lizzie*; *Two Flats and a Sharp*; *Mrs Rabbit's Husband Takes the Shilling*; *When Mother is Ill*; *Gigantic Marionettes* (1913); *Lieutenant Rose and the Sealed Orders*; *When Every Man's a Soldier*, *Aunt Susan's Way*; *Grandpa's Will*; *The Kinema Girl*; *George's Joy Ride*; *The Puddleton Police*; *That's Torn It!* (1914); *How Lieutenant Rose R.N. Spiked the Enemy's Guns* (1915); *Only One Pair*, *The Black Triangles*; *Leaves from a Mother's Album*; *A Question of Hairs* (1916).

STRICK, Joseph (1923–)

Joseph Strick was born on 6 July 1923 in Braddock, Pennsylvania, and educated at UCLA. After making the acclaimed documentary short *Muscle Beach* (co-dir. Irving Lerner, 1948) and the little-seen independent feature *The Big Break* (1953), he worked in television and commercial science while taking several years to complete his breakthrough film *The Savage Eye* (co-dirs. Ben Maddow/Sidney Meyers, 1959). Strick acquired the film rights to James Joyce's modernist classic *Ulysses* from director-cinematographer Jack Cardiff, and raised the production costs of under $1 million from British Lion and the American distributor-exhibitor Walter Reade.

Widely regarded as unfilmable because of its stream-of-consciousness narrative and sexually explicit language, the novel was not so much adapted as illustrated by the film. Taking place over a single day in Dublin in a series of fragmentary episodes, with extensive use of fantasy and voiceover monologue, the film's largely interior action culminates in a twenty-five-minute soliloquy by Molly Bloom (Barbara Jefford) on her adulterous sex life. Rich in colourful obscenities never before heard in mainstream cinema, this sequence caused enormous censorship difficulties, but a distribution strategy exploiting the censorship furore brought the film commercial success.

Ten years later, Strick returned to Ireland to film a far more orthodox adaptation of Joyce's earlier, semi-autobiographical novel *A Portrait of the Artist as a Young Man*. It is verbose and flatly shot in the manner of a BBC classic serial, and though well acted by the likes of T. P. McKenna and John Gielgud, the characters are little more than mouthpieces for the book's rhetorical prose. Strick has since directed only the documentary *Criminals* (1996). (Sheldon Hall)

BIBLIOGRAPHY: Canby, Vincent, '"Ulysses" Plans Mass Premieres', *New York Times*, 31 Aug. 1966; Geist, Kenneth, 'Interview with Joseph Strick', *Interview* vol. 1 no. 6, 1970, p. 20; Phelps, Guy, *Film Censorship* (London: Victor Gollancz, 1975); Trevelyan, John, *What the Censor Saw* (London: Michael Joseph, 1973).

FILMOGRAPHY (UK only): *Ulysses* (UK/US, 1967); *A Portrait of the Artist as a Young Man* (1977).

STUDDY, G. E. (1878–1948)

George Ernest Studdy was born in Devonport, near Plymouth, in June 1878. He failed to follow his father's footsteps into a military career thanks to an accident with a pitchfork, which injured his foot. After three years as a stockbroker, he attended evening classes at Heatherley's Art School, London, and studied animal anatomy at Calderon's Animal School. He had drawings accepted by *Boy's Own* and *Comic Cuts* and in 1912 was invited to submit regular weekly full-page illustrations to *Sketch* magazine. In 1915 he made a series of war cartoons for the *Gaumont Graphic* newsreel. During the 1920s and 30s, his 'Studdy dog', soon named Bonzo, enjoyed a reputation as 'the most famous puppy dog in the world', appearing in advertisements, children's comics and as a neon sign in Piccadilly Circus. Bonzo books, including *Lucky Dip* (1923) and *Puppy Tails* (1923), contained colour plates of the dog alongside stories, puzzles and rhymes, and enjoyed translations in French and German. In October 1924 the film producer William A. Ward collaborated with Studdy and ten assistant artists to produce the first of twenty-six films featuring Bonzo for New Era Films. *A Sausage Sensation* (1924) premiered at Marble Arch Pavilion, London, and was attended by King George V and Queen Mary on their debut visit to a public cinema. *Bonzo Broadcasted* (1925) featured Bonzo in romantic mood, but also playing Hollywood characters like 'Bon Chaney'. The films ran for around ten minutes each, and were released throughout 1924 and 1925. In 1926 Studdy published an essay on his method, but he did not continue his involvement in the film industry. He died in July 1948.

(Paul Wells)

BIBLIOGRAPHY: <www.chessy2.freeserve.co.uk>. The George Studdy and Bonzo website.

FILMOGRAPHY: *His Winning Ways: Studdy's War Studies*; *Studdy's War Cartoon: A Sea of Crime*; *Studdy's War Cartoon: Money Talks*; *Studdy's War Cartoon: A Spring Tonic*; *Studdy's War Cartoon: A Fight to the Finish*; *Studdy's War Cartoon: Convalescent*; *Studdy's War Cartoon: The Record Breaker*; *Studdy's War Cartoon: The Little Zeppelin* (1915); *A Sausage Sensation*; *Bonzo*; *Circus Bonzo* (1924); *Bonzo No. 2*; *Bonzo No. 3*; *Bonzo No. 4*; *Bonzo No. 5*; *Cheekee – The Vamp*; *Bonzoby*; *Out on the Tiles after a Cat Burglar*; *Topical Bonzette*; *Detective Bonzo and the Black Hand Gang*; *Playing the 'Dickens' in an Old Curiosity Shop*; *Bonzolino, or Bonzo Broadcasted*; *Polar Bonzo*; *Tally Ho, Bonzo*; *Bonzo in the Nursery*; *Bonzo R.A.*; *Adventures of Fido*; *Scout's Good Turn* (1925).

STURGES, John (1911–1992)

John Sturges was born in Oak Park, Illinois, on 3 January 1911. After directing plays at college in Santa Monica, he rose through the ranks of the film industry. He was successively colour consultant in RKO's art department, production assistant and editor for David O. Selznick, and director of training films for the US Army Air Force. He co-directed the wartime documentary *Thunderbolt* (1945) with William Wyler, and the following year began directing B-movies, first at Columbia and then MGM. As a freelance producer-director he showed a flair for action and pictorial composition in thrillers, Westerns and adventures such as *Bad Day at Black Rock* (1955), *The Magnificent Seven* (1960) and his most popular film, *The Great Escape* (1963).

Sturges' only British project was his last, an adaptation for Lew Grade's ITC of Jack Higgins' best-selling novel *The Eagle Has Landed*. A canny amalgam of elements from *Went the Day Well?* (Alberto Cavalcanti, 1942), *Where Eagles Dare* (Brian G. Hutton, 1968) and *The Day of the Jackal* (Fred Zinnemann, 1973), it involves a team of German paratroopers and fifth columnists – noble warriors and romantic idealists all – who infiltrate a small English village to kidnap or assassinate the visiting Winston Churchill.

According to its star, Michael Caine, the film's quality suffered because Sturges absented himself from post-production in order to go deep-sea fishing. It is indeed top-heavy with flabby exposition and, despite good action sequences, peculiarly lacking in suspense; nonetheless it performed reasonably well at the international box office. Sturges died in California on 18 August 1992 of a heart attack brought on by emphysema.

(Sheldon Hall)

BIBLIOGRAPHY: Caine, Michael, *What's it All About?* (London: Random House, 1992); McAsh, Iain F., 'John Sturges: A Matter of Basic Training', *Films Illustrated*, July 1976, pp. 408-10.

FILMOGRAPHY (UK only): *The Eagle Has Landed* (1977).

STURRIDGE, Charles (1951–)

Charles Sturridge was born in Kensington, London, on 24 June 1951. At sixteen he appeared as one of the schoolboys (Markland) in Lindsay Anderson's *if . . . .* (1968). At Oxford he was President of OUDS, the university's dramatic society, and directed several productions. He then joined Granada Television, where he was plunged into the very different world of *Coronation Street*. His break came in 1979 when he was given the opportunity to take over the direction of their ambitious adaptation of Evelyn Waugh's *Brideshead Revisited* (1981) after the slated director, Michael Lindsay-Hogg, took up a Hollywood assignment.

Given *Brideshead*'s enormous success, Sturridge has since kept a surprisingly low profile. Eschewing Hollywood, he directed *Runners*, a Channel 4 film scripted by Stephen Poliakoff about a father descending into the world of the London homeless in an attempt to retrieve his missing daughter. After a stylish black-and-white contribution to Don Boyd's *Aria*, Sturridge returned to heritage territory with adaptations of Waugh's *A Handful of Dust* and E. M. Forster's *Where Angels Fear to Tread*, both of which were only modestly successful. They were followed by *Fairy Tale: A True Story*, based, like Nick Willing's *Photographing Fairies* (1997), on the Cottingley fairies affair. Sturridge puts more emphasis on the children than the adults and affirms their faith over their elders' scepticism; and the film draws interesting correlations between the magic of the fairies and the 'magic' of industrial progress.

With his tendency to make films that leisurely explore ideas, Sturridge has found a more receptive environment in television than in the cinema. *A Foreign Field* (1993) sensitively depicts the enduring friendship between two war veterans (Alec Guinness and Leo McKern) who return to Normandy fifty years after D-Day. The film asserts the importance of valuing individuals not just for who they are, but who they have been, and notes how both the naivety of youth and the nostalgia of old age can distort our reflections. *Gulliver's Travels* (1996) casts American television star Ted Danson as Gulliver, and restores what is often regarded as an exotic children's fairy tale to its proper status as an allegory of human society. The same intelligence and thought is found in his biographical dramas. *Longitude* (2000) conveys the magnitude of English horologist John Harrison's work and the power of science not just to advance civilisation but to inspire dreams, wonder and beauty, while *Shackleton* (2002) uses the exploits of Polar explorer Edward Shackleton (Kenneth Branagh) to explore the nature of heroism. Heroism of a different sort is explored in *Lassie* (2005), a British remake of the popular American family film *Lassie Come Home* (Fred M. Wilcox, 1943). Sturridge updates the tale, refuses to wallow in sentimentality, and makes Lassie's exploits believable and engaging. It will be interesting to see wheher this venture into the mainstream marks a new direction in his career.

(Sarah Cardwell)

BIBLIOGRAPHY: 'Charles Sturridge', in Joshua Kendek (ed.), *Contemporary Theatre, Film and Television*, vol. 23 (Michigan: Thomson Gale, 1999); Crampton, Robert, 'Heroes of the Hour', *The Times* Magazine, 18 Dec. 1999, pp. 24, 27–8, 30; Summers, Sue, 'The 28-Year-Old Who Won TV's £3 Million Brief', *Evening Standard*, 2 Nov. 1979.

FILMOGRAPHY: *Runners* (1983); *Aria* ('La Vergine degli Angeli' section); *A Handful of Dust* (1987); *Where Angels Fear to Tread* (1991); *Fairy Tale: A True Story* (1997).

STYLES, Eric (1967–)

Eric Styles was born in 1967 in Neath, Wales. After graduating from the National Film and Television School in 1991, he began his career directing documentaries for BBC Cardiff, establishing himself with *The Dream*, a six-part series about the conflicts facing a successful Welsh rugby team, and *Birdbrain*, which won the 1997 British Short Film Festival's Cinematography Award. His first feature, the messy, interesting *Dreaming of Joseph Lees*, is boosted by appropriately intense performances from Samantha Morton and Rupert Graves (as the eponymous, one-legged geologist) and fully exploits the melodramatic proclivities of the screenplay. Although the ending is more enigmatic than satisfying and Styles is too self-consciously lyrical, the film showed him as an idiosyncratically talented director with a tendency towards the perverse.

Styles' next film was *Relative Values*, a version of Noël Coward's play, which must have appeared dated in 1951 and seemed antediluvian fifty years later. Nevertheless, despite its outmoded class sympathies and the simplistic contrast of snooty British and vulgar American values, Styles' orchestration of scenes of conflict and manipulation involving Julie Andrews, Stephen Fry and Colin Firth occasionally brings it to life. Further disappointment followed with *Tempo* a patchy Euro-thriller that failed to gain a theatrical release.

(Brian McFarlane)

BIBLIOGRAPHY: James, Nick, 'Medium Cool' (discussion with contemporary film-makers), *Sight and Sound*, Aug. 1998, pp. 12–15.

FILMOGRAPHY: *Birdbrain* (short, 1996); *Dreaming of Joseph Lees* (1999); *Relative Values* (UK/US, 2000); *Tempo* (UK/Can/Fr/Lux, 2003).

SUGARMAN, Sara (1962–)

Sara J. Sugarman was born in the North Wales seaside resort of Rhyl on 13 October 1962. In 1979 she joined the cast of the BBC's school saga *Grange Hill*, and went on to act in films such as *Those Glory Glory Days* (Philip Saville, 1983) and *Sid and Nancy* (Alex Cox, 1986). Following a brief and unhappy period studying at RADA, she enjoyed a more rewarding experience as a student at film school in Bournemouth, and embarked on a series of quirky, prize-winning shorts. *Valley Girls*, about two Welsh cleaning ladies who win a trip to Hollywood, hinted at an eccentric and darkly surrealistic talent and brought her the opportunity to make her debut feature. *Mad Cows*, adapted from Kathy Lette's comic novel about the trials of a twenty-something mum in London, proved a disappointment and quickly disappeared from British screens. Sugarman's next film, *Very Annie Mary*, based on her own script and shot on location in Pontycymer, was more assured. Australian Rachel Griffiths copes much better playing a Welsh woman than Rochdale-born Anna Friel had in playing the Australian heroine of *Mad Cows*, and Sugarman shows insight and humour in exploring the clash between the fire-and-brimstone traditions of Chapel and the banalities of modern commercial culture. Though the film was much less widely distributed than the witless *Mad Cows*, it allowed Sugarman an eagerly seized second chance to display her talents and led her to Hollywood to make the Disney box-office hit *Confessions of a Teenage Drama Queen*.

(Alan Burton)

BIBLIOGRAPHY: 'A New Direction', *Creation*, Apr. 1999, p. 8; Armour, Nicole, 'Distributor Wanted. *Very Annie Mary*', *Film Comment*, May/June 2001, pp. 18–19; Winstone, Keely, 'Meet the Mad Cows', *Televisual*, Nov. 1998, pp. 18-20.

FILMOGRAPHY: *Up the Valley* (short, 1995); *The Village* (short); *Valley Girls* (short) (1996); *Anthrakitis* (short, 1998); *Mad Cows* (1999); *Very Annie Mary* (aka *Annie-Mary à la folie!*, Fr/UK, 2001); *Confessions of a Teenage Drama Queen* (US/Ger, 2004).

SUGG, Stewart

Stewart Sugg was a student on the postgraduate course in film and television at Bristol University during the early 1990s. His short *The Gingerbread House* won prizes at festivals and led to a career in television. He broke out with *Fast Food* (1998), a feature film made on a budget of £50,000, which explored a seedy London inhabited by bored and generally incompetent petty crooks. Douglas Henshall is effective enough as the leading man but he struggles for direction in an inconsequential plot, and Sugg's constant reference to better films makes his effort look too much like a film school exercise.

Nonetheless, *Fast Food* displayed enough competence and enthusiasm for finance to follow for *Kiss Kiss (Bang Bang)*, a more cleverly scripted crime-comedy, enlivening the clichéd tale of a hitman who wants to retire with the odd comedy of an overgrown baby tentatively coming to terms with a world of whisky, women and guns. Adventurous casting (Chris Penn as the babyish Bubba, Stellan Skarsgård as the hitman Felix) and Sugg's more confident direction ensured a warmer reception than *Fast Food* had received, but the plethora of British crime films made it difficult to stand out in the marketplace.

(Robert Murphy)

FILMOGRAPHY: *The Gingerbread House* (short, 199?); *Fast Food* (1998); *Kiss Kiss (Bang Bang)* (UK/Den, 2001).

SULLIVAN, Tim (1958–)

Tim Sullivan was born in West Germany in 1958, but brought up in England. He helped out on *Chariots of Fire* (Hugh Hudson, 1981) during his final year at Cambridge University, and joined Granada as a researcher in the early 1980s. He soon switched to directing, serving his apprenticeship on *Coronation Street* before moving on to more prestigious Granada assignments, most notably *Thatcher: The Final Days* (1991), a dramatised documentary memorable for Sylvia Syms' cheekily accurate impersonation of Margaret Thatcher. After collaborating with producer Derek Granger and director Charles Sturridge on adaptations of Evelyn Waugh's *A Handful of Dust* (1987) and E. M. Forster's *Where Angels Fear to Tread* (1991), Sullivan made his cinema debut in 1995 with *Jack and Sarah*, a modestly budgeted romantic comedy about a well-heeled lawyer (Richard E. Grant) whose life is shattered when his wife dies in childbirth.

Granada had commissioned the script in 1991, and belatedly put it into production with hopes of duplicating the popularity of *Four Weddings and a Funeral* (Mike Newell, 1994). Friendly reviews brought *Jack & Sarah* success in British cinemas, but stereotyped characters and overly pedestrian dramatic pacing ensured a lukewarm reception in the international market. Nevertheless, the film's pleasing fairy-tale ethos, mirroring the short-lived reaction against Thatcherite money-grubbing (Jack finds salvation by bonding with his baby daughter and chooses his new wife on the basis of her cherishing skills), makes it more interesting than most subsequent British romantic comedies. Afterwards, Sullivan returned to television drama, honing his skills on Granada's long-running thirtysomething drama *Cold Feet*.

(Robert Murphy)

BIBLIOGRAPHY: Summers, Sue, 'The British are Coming', *Independent on Sunday*, 18 June 1995, p. 32; Considine, Pippa, 'Production Close-Up – *Jack & Sarah*', *Televisual*, May 1994, pp. 18–19.

FILMOGRAPHY: *Jack & Sarah* (UK/Fr, 1995).

SUMMERS, Jeremy (1931–)

Jeremy Summers, born in St Albans in 1931, is the son of film director Walter Summers. After working as an assistant director, he made his debut as a director in television with episodes of *Interpol Calling* (1959) and *International Detective* (1960), and in cinema with *Depth Charge* (1960), an unusual B-film about the attempt to defuse a fished-up depth charge. Summers' career falls into several distinct sections. *The Punch and Judy Man*, a Tony Hancock vehicle, and *Crooks in Cloisters*, in which a criminal gang masquerade as monks to evade arrest, are comedies of a relatively downbeat kind, both featuring a sometimes uneasy mixture of humour and more serious drama. In the mid-1960s Summers switched to teenage pop movies with *Ferry Cross the Mersey* (starring Gerry and the Pacemakers) and *Dateline Diamonds* (the Small Faces and Kiki Dee). Subsequently he worked with producer Harry Alan Towers on a series of international co-productions. The first and best of these was *The Vengeance of Fu Manchu*, the third in a series of Fu Manchu stories starring Christopher Lee. It lacked the panache of the previous two films (*The Face of Fu Manchu* and *The Brides of Fu Manchu*, both directed by Don Sharp) but was an energetic rendition of the by-then familiar Fu Manchu formula. The other Summers–Towers films – *House of a Thousand Dolls*, *Five Golden Dragons* and *The Face of Eve* – were less distinctive, although *Five Golden Dragons*, with Christopher Lee, George Raft, Brian Donlevy and Dan Duryea, does boast an impressive cast of villains.

Since the late 1960s Summers has worked mainly for British television, initially on glossy series such as *Randall and Hopkirk (Deceased)*, *Jason King* and *The Protectors*, and more recently on the soap operas *Coronation Street* and *Brookside*. In the 1970s he made two films for the Children's Film Foundation, *One Hour to Zero* and *Sammy's Super T-Shirt*.

(Peter Hutchings)

BIBLIOGRAPHY: BECTU History Project, tape no. 503, held in the BFI National Library, London.

FILMOGRAPHY: *Depth Charge* (1960); *The Punch and Judy Man* (1962); *Crooks in Cloisters* (1963); *Ferry Cross the Mersey* (1964); *Dateline Diamonds*; *San Ferry Ann* (1965); *The Vengeance of Fu Manchu*; *House of a Thousand Dolls*; *Five Golden Dragons* (1967); *The Face of Eve* (1968); *One Hour to Zero* (1977); *Sammy's Super T-Shirt* (1978).

SUMMERS, Walter (1896–1973)

Walter George Thomas Summers was born into a theatrical family in Barnstable, Devon, on 2 September 1896. He gained considerable stage experience before joining the London Films Company in 1912 as an assistant to George Loane Tucker. The First World War temporarily put his film career on hold, but on leaving the army as a captain awarded the Military Cross and the

Distinguished Service Medal, Summers was employed by Cecil Hepworth. Disliking the novelettish type of subjects the company made, he left and, after further service with the Territorial Unit in India in 1920, joined G. B. Samuelson as a scriptwriter. He quickly established a good rapport with the ebullient entrepreneur, scripting *Married Love* (Alexander Butler, 1923), a rather demure rendition of the then-infamous book by Marie Stopes, co-directing two films with Samuelson and making his debut with *A Couple of Down-and-Outs* (1923), a modest tale about a soldier who becomes a tramp.

When Samuelson experienced financial difficulties, Summers moved to British Instructional Films, best known for its reconstructions of historical events, where he made the impressive and widely acclaimed *The Battles of the Coronel and Falkland Islands* (1927). The films that followed, especially *Bolibar* (1928) and *The Lost Patrol* (1929), enhanced his burgeoning reputation, and he showed himself with the new medium of sound films with a lively Betty Balfour musical, *Raise the Roof* (1930).

When BIF was taken over by British International Pictures, Summers was offered a contract. BIP was a major company but one with a reputation of making films on the cheap. A director like Summers, who possessed boundless energy and was totally dedicated to getting the film made, was an invaluable acquisition but he was too eccentric and forthright ever to become a company man. Initially he was given considerable leeway, both in resources and stories – he was allowed to make the anti-war film *Suspense* (1930), for example, and to shoot *Timbuctoo* (1933) on location in Africa – but by the mid-1930s he was being restricted to routine studio assignments.

Reflecting on his early work as a scriptwriter, Walter Summers observed: 'I didn't wait for inspiration. I was a workman, I worked on the story until it was finished. I had a time limit you see. We made picture after picture after picture' (Pedler, p. 35). This ethos applied to his directing assignments too. Churning out product became so ingrained that when given larger resources, with for instance *The Return of Bulldog Drummond* (1934), he seemed to lose his sureness of touch. But by the end of the decade he had found his *métier* with macabre thrillers and fast-moving whodunits. *Premiere* (1938), a backstage murder mystery, and the much-filmed crime melodrama *At the Villa Rose* (1939) are atmospheric and full of odd little cameos and deft directorial touches. *The Dark Eyes of London* (1939) and *Traitor Spy* (1939) were produced at BIP's second-string Welwyn Studios, and look less glossy. Nonetheless, Greta Gynt's frail but intrepid heroine, Bela Lugosi's unctuous villain and Summers' fast-moving direction help make *The Dark Eyes of London* a film richly deserving its 'H' (for horror) certificate. *Traitor Spy*, an eve-of-war spy story, is more realistic, and as well as Summers' characteristic vigour and inventiveness, offers fascinating glimpses into London's low life.

Summers rejoined the army during the Second World War, and though he returned to Associated British in 1946 he never directed another film. Disappearing into undeserved obscurity, he died in April 1973 in Wandsworth, London. His son Jeremy also pursued a career as a director, initially in films, later in television.

(Linda Wood)

BIBLIOGRAPHY: Low, Rachael, *The History of the British Film 1918–1929* (London: George Allen & Unwin, 1971); Low, Rachael, *Film Making in 1930s Britain* (London: George Allen & Unwin, 1985); Pedler, Garth, 'Walter Summers', *The Silent Picture*, Autumn 1972, pp. 31–5.

FILMOGRAPHY: *Stable Companions* (co-dir. uncred, Albert Ward, 1922); *I Pagliacci*; *Afterglow* (co-dir. G. B. Samuelson); *A Couple of Down-and-Outs* (1923); *The Unwanted*; *Who Is the Man?*; *Zeebrugge*; *The Cost of Beauty* (1924); *Ypres* (doc.); *The Perfect Crime* (short) (1925); *Nelson*; *Mons* (doc.) (1926); *The Battles of the Coronel and Falkland Islands* (doc., 1927); *Bolibar* (1928); *The Lost Patrol*; *Chamber of Horrors* (1929); *Raise the Roof*; *Suspense*; *The Man from Chicago* (1930); *The Flying Fool*; *The House Opposite*; *Men Like These* (US: *Trapped in a Submarine*) (1931); *Deeds Men Do: A Synchronised Version of the Famous Battles of the Coronel and Falkland Islands* (doc.); *Across the Sahara: The Record of a Journey to Timbuctoo* (doc.); *Dual Control* (short) (1932); *Timbuctoo* (co-dir. Arthur Woods, 1933); *The Return of Bulldog Drummond*; *The Warren Case*; *What Happened Then?* (1934); *Royal Cavalcade* (co-dirs Herbert Brenon/Norman Lee/Thomas Bentley/Will Kellino/Marcel Varnel); *McGlusky the Sea Rover* (US: *Hell's Cargo*) (1935); *Music Hath Charms* (co-dirs., Alexander Esway/Thomas Bentley/Arthur Woods); *The Limping Man*; *Ourselves Alone* (co-dir. Brian Desmond Hurst) (1936); *Lucky Jade*; *The Price of Folly* (1937); *Premiere* (1938); *At the Villa Rose* (1939); *The Dark Eyes of London* (US: *The Human Monster*); *Traitor Spy* (US: *The Torso Murder Mystery*) (1939).

SYKES, Peter (1939–)

Peter Sykes was born in Melbourne on 17 June 1939. He won a scholarship to study choreography and worked briefly as an opal miner and for Melbourne's Rediffusion Television. In 1966 he came to England, where he worked with fellow Australian Don Levy on his avant-garde feature film *Herostratus* (1968), and went on an eighteen-month training course with BBC Television. As a freelance film-maker he directed a controversial documentary *Walkabout to Cornwall*, about a group of Australian surfers settled in Newquay, Cornwall, and served as Peter Brook's executive producer on *Tell Me Lies* (1967). Sykes then made a fifty-eight-minute experimental film, *The Committee*, starring Manfred Mann singer Paul Jones and with a score from Pink Floyd. The film divided critical opinion but displayed enough of Sykes' talent to get him work directing episodes of the cult television series *The Avengers*. His first mainstream film was *Venom*, a contemporary horror story about sex and spiders, scripted by Derek and Donald Ford and set in the forests of Bavaria. Subsequently he made two horror films for Hammer, *Demons of the Mind* and *To the Devil a Daughter*.

Sykes was one of a number of young directors employed by Hammer in the 1970s – others included Peter Sasdy and Robert Young – who introduced elements of social critique and anti-authoritarianism into the studio's by then overworked gothic horror format. *Demons of the Mind* was a scathing indictment of the monstrous authority of the father over his children, while *To the Devil a Daughter*, which was Hammer's last horror production, was an ambitious and stylish Satanic thriller let down only by an overly abrupt conclusion. In these, as in the comedy-horror *The House in Nightmare Park*, Sykes demonstrated an ability both to conjure up sinister, oppressive atmospheres and to break down some of the established conventions of British horror. Although he was able to follow *To the Devil a Daughter* with *Jesus*, a well-received adaptation of St Luke's Gospel, he has directed little since the collapse of British horror production in the late 1970s.

(Peter Hutchings)

BIBLIOGRAPHY: Gilbert, Basil, 'Peter Sykes', *Cinema Papers* no. 13, July 1977, pp. 34–6, 95; Pirie, David, 'New Blood', *Sight and Sound*, Spring 1971, p. 75; Press book, *Demons of the Mind*, 1972.

FILMOGRAPHY: *The Committee* (1968); *Venom* (aka *Spider's Venom*, 1971); *Demons of the Mind* (aka *Blood Will Have Blood*, 1972); *Steptoe and Son Ride Again*; *The House in Nightmare Park* (aka *Crazy House*) (1973); *To the Devil a Daughter* (aka *Child of Satan*, 1976); *Jesus* (co-dir. John Krish, US, 1979); *The Blues Band* (doc. short, 1981).

SZKOPIAK, Piotr (1966–)

Piotr Szkopiak was born in Camberwell, London, on 14 March 1966. He began a career in television as a production assistant in MTV Europe's news department, later moving to BSkyB, where he co-created the film magazine programmes *Xposure* and *The Movie Show*. In 1995 his short film *Let Sleeping Dogs Lie* attracted attention, and after co-producing and editing *The Killing Zone* (Ian David Diaz, 1999), a dark crime-comedy, he wrote, directed, produced and edited his own feature debut. *Small Time Obsession* (2000) follows the fortunes of a group of young men and women of London's Polish community as they come to terms with parents, romance and their future lives. Szkopiak combines three tenuously linked strands around his spaniel-eyed hero Michael K (Alex King): his dog-like devotion to his best friend's girlfriend, his obsession with his greyhound Bullitt (named after the Steve McQueen film, as he explains to an uncomprehending Geordie gangster) and his attempt to distance himself from the increasingly dangerous involvement of his friends with professional crime. None of the strands work, and despite the occasional interest generated by the London-Polish setting (and Michael's authentically Polish parents), Szkopiak brushes aside the problems he creates for his characters and the film collapses into soggy cliché. Before *Small Time Obsession* was released he told *Total Film* magazine, 'You have to see your film playing at the Empire, Leicester Square . . . and if you can't see it there, you're making a TV movie.' But box-office returns were disappointing and Szkopiak went back into television, directing episodes of the popular soap opera *Emmerdale*.

(Ewa Mazierska)

BIBLIOGRAPHY: Caplan, Nina, 'Small Time Obsession', *Sight and Sound*, July 2000, p. 54; 'Independents' Day: Smalltime Obsession', *Total Film* no. 40, May 2000 p. 138.

FILMOGRAPHY: *Let Sleeping Dogs Lie* (short, 1995); *Small Time Obsession* (2000).

TAIT, Margaret (1918–1999)

Margaret Caroline Tait, a distinctive talent among independent British film-makers, was born in Kirkwall, Orkney, on 11 November 1918. She attended school in Edinburgh where she later studied medicine, qualifying in 1941; during the Second World War she served in India with the Royal Army Medical Corps. After working as a locum doctor in England, Tait studied at the Centro Sperimentale di Cinematografia in Rome between 1950 and 1952. Her first films date from this period – *The Lion, the Griffin and the Kangaroo* (1952) is a short film about foreign students at the University of Perugia – but the work that clearly signposted her future was *A Portrait of Ga* (1952), a four-minute 16mm film about her mother, made on her return to Orkney. Lyrical and personal portraits of people and places in Orkney and the Scottish mainland remained her speciality. Some early films flirted with the documentary form – *The Drift Back* (1956) was sponsored by Orkney Council; but Tait soon settled into her own individual, unsubsidised niche from her small workshop/studio in Edinburgh, documenting inner and outer landscapes with a free-flowing mix of simple, intimate reportage and visual poetry, sometimes punctured by animation. *Happy Bees* (1955), in joyful colour, turned the camera on her own family; *Aerial* (1974), made in the year she returned to Orkney, was constructed from images of the four elements; *Landmakar* (1981) detailed an Orkney crofter's work through the year. As well as making over thirty films Tait also published three books of poetry and two volumes of short stories.

The honesty and integrity of Tait's work won her many admirers, but it was not until the early 1990s that a variety of funding sources, including Channel 4 and the BFI, united to allow her to stretch to a narrative feature. *Blue Black Permanent* (1992), made after Tait had survived cancer and was in her seventies, concerns the struggles of an Edinburgh photographer (Celia Imrie) to come to terms with the death in her childhood of her poet mother (Gerda Stevenson), drowned in the seas off Orkney. The narrative's moves between past and present caused some structural strain, but Tait's powerfully resonant imagery of ordinary surroundings, from domestic clutter to the changing sea, holds the film together. Though the *Blue Black Permanent* was given only a limited release, it confirmed Tait's reputation as an idiosyncratic and gifted film-maker. She died in Firth, Orkney, on 16 April 1999, one year after completing her last short work, the playful and reflective *Garden Pieces*.

(Peter Todd)

BIBLIOGRAPHY: Cook, Benjamin and Peter Todd, *Subjects and Sequences: A Margaret Tait Reader* (London: Lux, 2004); Curtis, David, 'Britain's Oldest Experimentalist: Margaret Tait', *Vertigo*, Summer 1999, pp. 62–3; Leggett, Mike, 'Margaret Tait', in David Curtis (ed.), *A Directory of British Film & Video Artists* (Luton and London: John Libbey Media/Arts Council of England, 1996); Sussex, Elizabeth, 'Margaret Tait', *Guardian*, 13 May 1999; Todd, Peter, 'The Margaret Tait Project', *Media Education Journal* no 33, Spring 2003, pp. 27–30.

FILMOGRAPHY: *One Is One*; *Three Portrait Sketches* (1951); *The Lion, the Griffin and the Kangaroo* (co-dir. Peter Hollander); *A Portrait of Ga*; *Calypso* (1952); *Happy Bees*; *The Leaden Echo and the Golden Echo*; *Orquil Burn* (1955); *The Drift Back*; *Rose Street* (1956); *Hugh MacDiarmid – A Portrait*; *Palindrome*; *Where I Am Is Here* (1964); *The Big Sheep*; *Splashing* (1966); *A Pleasant Place* (1969); *He's Back (The Return)*; *John MacFadyen (The Stripes in the Tartan)*; *Painted Eightsome* (1970); *Aerial*; *Colour Poems*; *On the Mountain*; *These Walls* (1974); *Place of Work*; *Tailpiece* (1976); *Aspects of Kirkwall: Shape of a Town*; *Aspects of Kirkwall: Occasions* (1977); *Aspects of Kirkwall: The Ba Over the Years*; *Aspects of Kirkwall: The Look of the Place*; *Aspects of Kirkwall: Some Changes*; *Landmakar* (1981); *Blue Black Permanent* (1992); *Garden Pieces* (1998).

TAYLOR, Donald (1911–)

Donald Taylor, born in London on 22 February 1911, studied at Oxford University and began his film career in 1931 performing menial tasks at John Grierson's Empire Marketing Board Film Unit. By 1933 he was directing in Lancashire, filming material recycled into several shorts. The following year he married Grierson's sister Marion (1907–1998), herself a film-maker, though professionally he soon moved away from Grierson's coterie. In 1935, together with Ralph Keene, he remodelled the moribund Strand Film Company into Britain's first documentary unit free of government sponsorship or direct commercial ties. For three years Paul Rotha served as its combative Director of Productions; following his departure in 1937, Strand's output began to reflect Taylor's own interest in films worthy of general audiences and wider commercial distribution.

Writing in 1979, Rachael Low used the potent term 'fallen angel' to describe Taylor's standing among solemn-minded documentarians in the late 1930s. Entertainment became as important as instruction: whether as director, producer or Strand's managing director, Taylor now presided over mild travelogues, films in praise of Imperial Airways and Julian Huxley's popular shorts investigating man and the natural world. The need for propaganda material in the Second World War generated product with greater backbone, like Ralph Bond's *Post 23* (1941), a tribute to the wartime community spirit, and Taylor's own *Night Watch* (1942), a particularly effective 'five-minuter' combining a salute to air-raid wardens with a couple's comic hunt for privacy.

Taylor's most elaborate Strand venture as a director was *Battle for Music* (1943), a feature-length portrait of the London Philharmonic Orchestra's successful struggle to overcome bankruptcy, the loss of performing venues and instruments, and other hazards of war. The LPO members make awkward actors, but nothing dents the film's continuing strength as a musical document and a moving witness to co-operative endeavour. Cinema bookings were few. More takers were found for three half-hour films presenting the BBC's popular *Brains Trust* panellists answering questions sent in by the public, though audiences' reactions remained mixed.

In October 1943 Taylor resigned as Strand's managing director. For a while he continued in documentary employment with Gryphon Films and the Crown Film Unit, tucking in religious films for Rank along the way. But with non-fiction opportunities shrinking, Taylor increasingly turned toward the commercial feature industry. His first unsatisfactory brush had been in 1937 when he helped patch up Alexander Korda's aviation history film *The Conquest of the Air* (his version was soon superseded by others). He returned to the fray in 1953–4 with two small thrillers made for his own company, Hedgerley Films. *The Straw Man*, an insurance fraud drama, intermittently simmered with tension; but the secret-service antics of *The Night of the Full of Moon* quickly collapsed into the ridiculous. Neither restored the fallen angel's wings.

Taylor later functioned mostly as a producer, on product ranging from interesting horrors (John Moxey's *The City of the Dead*, 1960) to Joan Littlewood's film of her stage success, *Sparrows Can't Sing* (1963). His last recorded sighting is as the co-director of *Piraparana* (1965), a short documentary study of a tribe living in the Amazon rain forests.

(Geoff Brown)

BIBLIOGRAPHY: Low, Rachael, *Documentary and Educational Films of the 1930s* (London: George Allen & Unwin, 1979); Rotha, Paul, *Documentary Diary* (London: Secker and Warburg, 1973); Taylor, Donald, 'In the Service of the Public: The New Sociological Cinema', *Sight and Sound*, Winter 1993-4, pp. 128–31.

FILMOGRAPHY: Non-fiction: *Lancashire at Work and Play*; *Spring Comes to England* (1934); *Citizens of the Future*; *So This Is Lancashire*; *Lancashire, Home of Industry*; *Taking the Plunge* (aka *Order of the Bath*) (1935); *Give the Kids a Break*; *6d Telegram* (1936); *The Conquest of the Air* (prepared with Alexander Shaw from existing material, 1938, unrel. in this form); *Home Guard* (assoc. dir., Ivan Moffat); *Citizens' Army* (assoc. dir., Ivan Moffat); *Night Watch* (1941); *The Way to His Heart*; *Hogsnorton* (1942); *The BBC Brains Trust* (three films, co-dir. Howard Thomas, 1942–3); *Battle for Music* (1943); *Flax* (1944); *Shaping the Future* (1946); *Ruth* (1948); *Which Will Ye Have?* (US: *Barabbas the Robber*, 1949); *Piraparana* (co-dir. Brian Moser, 1965). Fiction: *Point of No Return* (short); *What a Husband!* (short) (1952); *The Straw Man* (1953); *The Night of the Full Moon* (1954); *Horas de pánico* (Sp/US, 1957); *The Dawn Killer* (serial, 1959).

TAYLOR, John (1914–1992)

John E. Taylor was born in Kentish Town, London, on 5 October 1914. A talented cinematographer, director and producer of documentaries, he was among John Grierson's first recruits at the Empire Marketing Board Film Unit, joining when he left school at fifteen. He soon became associated with some of the period's major documentary films, spending twenty months working with Robert Flaherty on *Man of Aran* (1934) before assisting Basil Wright on *The Song of Ceylon* (1934) for the GPO Film Unit. At Grierson's instigation Taylor spent two years studying art appreciation and English literature at Edinburgh University, working on films during vacations: he served as cameraman on Cavalcanti's *Pett and Pott* (1934) and Edgar Anstey and Arthur Elton's *Housing Problems* (1935). Returning full time to the GPO, he accompanied Cavalcanti on his Switzerland excursion in 1936, generating footage used most extensively in *We Live in Two Worlds* (Albeto Cavalcanti, 1937). Subsequently Taylor worked outside the GPO, making his directing debut at Strand with *Air Outpost* and *Dawn of Iran*, then joining Wright in the newly founded Realist Film Unit, where he directed the pollution warning *The Smoke Menace* (1937) and *The Londoners* (1939) – both part of the sociologically oriented series sponsored by the British Commercial Gas Association, begun with *Housing Problems*. Taylor's films featured elaborate commentaries, reportage, eloquent photography and historical exposition (a particular feature of Realist documentaries). *The Londoners*, the lengthier and more ambitious of the pair, also used verse by W. H. Auden and an impressive reconstruction of past slums and grime in pursuit of its contrast between the city's dishevelled past and the modern city benevolently managed by the London County Council.

Taylor's work on *The Londoners* won him attention and praise, though his responsibilities at Realist became increasingly those of a producer. The company undertook many commissions during the war; alongside routine food and agriculture shorts, Taylor stewarded the feature-length *Soldier, Sailor* (Alexander Shaw, 1944), *Your Children and You* (Brian Smith, 1945) and other films on children's health, and the series *The Technique of Anaesthesia* (1944), made for ICI. In 1947 he became Head of the Crown Film Unit, where despite unfavourable conditions he attempted to foster new talent. The CFU enjoyed considerable success with Terry Bishop's documentary *Daylight in Udi* (1949), but Taylor felt his independence compromised when Grierson became Controller of the Central Office of Information's Films Division; by the time *Udi* won its Academy Award in 1950, he had left to work freelance. His most notable achievement in the 1950s was as co-producer of Countryman Films' *The Conquest of Everest* (Thomas Stobart/George Lowe, 1953). But he continued to direct films up to the 1980s, working through British Transport Films and his own Pilot Productions, specialising in outdoor documentaries exploring and celebrating Britain's natural history and environment. John Taylor was married to the actress Barbara Mullen, and his sister Margaret was married to John Grierson. He died in London on 15 September 1992.

(Geoff Brown and Alan Burton)

BIBLIOGRAPHY: Cole, Sidney, Obituary, *Stage Screen & Radio*, Nov. 1992, p. 12; 'John Taylor', *Film Dope* no. 21, Oct. 1980, pp. 32–3; 'John Taylor Interview', BECTU History Project, tape no. 34, 1988, held in the BFI National Library, London; Sussex, Elizabeth, *The Rise and Fall of British Documentary* (Berkeley: University of California Press, 1975).

FILMOGRAPHY: *Air Outpost* (co-dir. Ralph Keene); *Dawn of Iran* (aka *Dawn in the East*); *The Smoke Menace* (1937); *The Londoners* (1939); *Letter from Aldershot* (co-dir. Philip Leacock, 1940); *Goodbye Yesterday*; *Island People* (co-dir. Philip Leacock); *A Visit from Canada* (1941); *A Seaman's Story* (1942); *Opus 65*; *The Heart Is Highland*; *Farmer Moving South*; *Journey into History* (co-dir. Alexander Shaw) (1952); *Journal of the Outdoors Nos. 7–18* (1953); *The England of Elizabeth*; *Holiday*; *Lancashire Coast* (1957); *The Secret World* (1958); *First Report on Modernisation*; *An Artist Looks at Churches* (1959); *The River of Life* (1960); *Second Report on Modernisation* (1961); *The Living Pattern* (1962); *The Port of Hull*; *South Wales Ports* (1963); *Southampton Docks*; *Fifth Report on Modernisation* (1964); *The Vanishing Coast* (1965); *The Good Way to Travel* (co-dir. Nick Nicholls); *Just Your Cup of Tea* (1966); *People + Leisure =*; *One of Many* (1968); *Changing Britain: Environment in the Balance* (1970); *Living Naturally* (1972); *To Be United and Free* (1975); *Museums of Tehran* (1977); *Waterplay* (1978); *The Sea – Our Future* (1981); *Log Book of the Regina Maris* (Ger, 1985).

TEAGUE, Colin

After studying at the London International Film School in Covent Garden, Colin Teague directed episodes of *London's Burning* and *Holby City* for television, and *North West One*, a short, laddish comedy about a footballer, his wife and his best friend. He made his feature debut, *Shooters*, in collaboration with

Glenn Durfort; a British gangster film unusual for its deglamourised underworld peopled by desperate characters, whose violence stems from bad-tempered irrationality rather than cool professionalism or innate evil. Patchy plotting, a downbeat ethos and the plethora of crime films made in the wake of *Lock, Stock and Two Smoking Barrels* (Guy Ritchie, 1998) conspired to delay its release until 2001, by which time the genre had fallen out of fashion.

In his second film, *Spivs*, Teague and his co-writers, Gary Young and Mike Loveday, tell the familiar tale of a small-time gang who inadvertently tread on the toes of a bigger rival – in this case the Russian Mafia and their people-smuggling racket. Teague relies too much on visual trickery and homages to other films, not enough on firming up his characters and clarifying his plot. But he avoids investing his small fry with heroism: Ken Stott's Jack, lumbered with two refugee children and feckless colleagues, is most impressive when he is least in control. Until the tacked-on happy end, originality just about outweighs predictability, though insufficiently to win over critics and audiences. (Robert Murphy)

FILMOGRAPHY: *North West One* (short, 1999); *Shooters* (co-dir. Glenn Durfort, UK/Neth/US, 1999; rel. 2001); *Spivs* (2004); *The Last Drop* (2006).

TEMPLE, Julien (1953–)

Julien Temple was born in London on 26 November 1953. He had little interest in cinema until he studied at King's College, Cambridge, and discovered Jean Vigo, the director who would become his hero. While attending the National Film and Television School, he encountered another, equally influential manifestation of the anarchist spirit: the Sex Pistols. During their short, turbulent life he became virtually their cinematic amanuensis, a process that culminated in his first feature, *The Great Rock 'n' Roll Swindle* (1979). By this time the band had already split acrimoniously, and without the participation of John Lydon/Johnny Rotten the film turned into something of a vehicle for Malcolm McLaren, the Pistols' former manager. Structured around this Situationist Svengali's ten lessons on fleecing the music business, *Swindle* effectively evokes the punk spirit by juxtaposing wildly assorted footage, tossing counter-cultural heroes Ronnie Biggs and Mary Millington into the bizarre bricolage along with British cinema stalwarts Irene Handl and Liz Fraser.

Along with Temple's short films about punk, particularly the wartime documentary parody *Punk Can Take It*, a theatrically released promo for the UK Subs, *Swindle* clearly heralded the arrival of a distinctive cinematic talent. Opportunity knocked with *Absolute Beginners*, an adaptation of Colin MacInnes' seminal 1950s' novel made for Stephen Woolley's Palace Pictures with backing from Goldcrest Films. Endless production difficulties and too many writers led to an uneven film that disappointed audiences despite the box-office appeal of David Bowie, and attracted hostile reviews; though for Temple to make a kinetic, imaginative, cinematic British musical in the mid-1980s now seems a considerable achievement.

Significantly the film was much liked in America, where Temple directed the enjoyably wacky science-fiction musical *Earth Girls Are Easy* (1988) and a series of music promos, a field in which he had already established a reputation. A second American feature, *Bullet*, a violent crime thriller, went straight to video. Back in Britain, he mounted three films in short succession. The long-planned biography *Vigo: Passion for Life* (1999) proved a strangely missed opportunity to convey his favourite director's artistic worth. Though it never reached enough audiences, *Pandaemonium* (2000), a lyrical, spirited and unconventional account of the Coleridge/Wordsworth relationship, proved much more forceful and entertaining, swinging through visual phantasmagoria and twentieth-century incursions to capture the poets' wild rebellious youths. *The Filth and the Fury* returned to the Sex Pistols saga, replete with coruscating live footage, but this time conveyed from the band's point of view. Many critics, however, remained unforgiving, and this interesting and original director has still to find the recognition he deserves.
(Julian Petley)

BIBLIOGRAPHY: Case, Brian, 'Miracle in Soho', *Stills* no. 24, Feb. 1986, pp 24–8; Flynn, Bob, 'Who Does Julien Temple Think He Is?', *Guardian* G2 Section, 4 June 1999, pp. 8–9; Johnston, Trevor, 'Beginner's Luck', *Film Directions* vol. 8 no. 31, 1986, pp. 14–15; Vermorel, Fred and Judy, *Sex Pistols* (London: W. H. Allen, 1981).

FILMOGRAPHY Shorts and promos (selection): *Where Is Your Love?* (1970); *The Tunnying of Elinour Rummyng*; *Sex Pistols Number 1* (co-dir. John Tiberi) (1976); *Jubilee Riverboat* (co-dir. John Tiberi, 1977); *My Way* (Sid Vicious); *Come on Everybody* (Sid Vicious) (1978); *Punk Can Take It* (UK Subs, 1979); *My Perfect Cousin* (The Undertones, 1980); *Biceps of Steel*; *It's Going to Happen!* (The Undertones) (1981); *Poison Arrow* (ABC); *The Comic Strip*; *Do You Really Want to Hurt Me?* (Culture Club); *Picture Music* (1982); *Come Dancing* (The Kinks); *Come on Eileen* (Dexy's Midnight Runners) (1983); *Venceremos: Working Week* (1984); *Absolute Beginners* (David Bowie, 1985); *The Wind* (2001); *The Ancient Forests* (2002).

Features: *The Great Rock 'n' Roll Swindle* (1979); *The Secret Policeman's Other Ball* (co-dirs. Roger Graef/Thomas Schwalm, 1982); *Jazzin' for Blue Jean* (short, 1984); *Absolute Beginners* (1986); *Aria* ('Rigoletto' segment, 1987); *Earth Girls Are Easy* (US, 1988); *Bullet* (US, 1995); *Vigo: Passion for Life* (1999); *Pandaemonium*; *The Filth and the Fury* (2000), *Glastonbury* (doc., 2006).

TENNYSON, Pen (1912–1941)

Penrose Tennyson was born in Chelsea on 26 August 1912, the eldest great-grandson of the Victorian poet Alfred Lord Tennyson. His father was a senior government official. Tennyson was educated at Eton and Oxford, but left university after only two terms and in 1932 joined the scenario department at the Gaumont-British studios in Shepherd's Bush. He was promoted to third assistant director on *The Good Companions* (Victor Saville, 1933), and then to assistant director to Alfred Hitchcock on *The Man Who Knew Too Much* (1934) and *The 39 Steps* (1935) – where he also doubled for Madeleine Carroll in high heels and a blonde wig. While at Gaumont-British, Tennyson was active in helping establish the Association of Cine-Technicians (ACT) as an effective union.

Michael Balcon, a personal friend of the family, 'looked upon Pen as if he were my own son' (Balcon, p. 196), and took a close interest in his career. Tennyson followed him first to MGM, acting as assistant director on *A Yank at Oxford* (Jack Conway, 1937) and *The Citadel* (King Vidor, 1938), and then in 1938 to Ealing, where he made his directorial debut as the youngest feature director then working in Britain. That same year he married the actress Nova Pilbeam, whom he had met while working on *The Man Who Knew Too Much*. *There Ain't No Justice* (1939), based on a tough novel by James Curtis, set out to be an exposé of corruption in the boxing world but never hit hard enough, anticipating the cycle of earnest, conscientious films that Basil Dearden would make at Ealing in the post-war period. Graham Greene, trenchant as ever, noted that 'the whole picture breathes timidity and refinement' (Greene, p. 323).

Tennyson's second film, *The Proud Valley* (1940), also set out to be an exposé but was hijacked by events. Set in a mining community in South Wales, it was planned to end with the miners defiantly opening a pit closed by the blinkered mine-owners. Overtaken by the outbreak of war, the film was changed in the interests of national solidarity to show the workers winning over the bosses by dint of their patriotic fervour. But in the earlier part of the film Tennyson created a powerful sense of community (always a key Ealing concept), even if he could do little with the stilted acting of Paul Robeson, awkwardly cast as a saintly and self-sacrificing black seaman whose fine singing voice gets him a job in the mine.

Convoy (1940), a naval flag-waver, much praised at the time, now looks old-fashioned and stagy with its unconvincing shipboard sets and its roster of 1930s' actors giving clipped performances as stiff-upper-lip officer types. With the arrival of Cavalcanti and his documentary-trained colleagues Ealing would soon develop a far more downbeat and realistic style of war movie. But Tennyson did not survive to take advantage of it. Refusing exemption, he had joined the navy as a lieutenant and was about to take charge of the Admiralty's Educational Film Unit. On 7 July 1941 he was flying from Shetland to the naval base at Rosyth in a small Fleet Air Arm plane when it crashed, killing all those on board.

(Philip Kemp)

BIBLIOGRAPHY: Balcon, Michael, 'Sub-Lieutenant F. Penrose Tennyson', in Derek Tangye (ed.), *Went the Day Well* (London: Michael Joseph, 1995); C.T. [Charles Tennyson], *Pen Tennyson* (London: A. S. Atkinson, 1943); Greene, Graham, *Mornings in the Dark*, edited by David Parkinson (Manchester: Carcanet, 1993).

FILMOGRAPHY: *There Ain't No Justice* (1939); *The Proud Valley*; *Convoy* (1940).

TENNYSON D'EYNCOURT, Walter (1899–)

Walter Tennyson d'Eyncourt, sometimes credited as Walter Tennyson, was born on 25 April 1899 in Charlwood, Surrey, and brought up at the Tennyson family home, Bayons Manor, in Tealby, Lincolnshire. Along with his twin brother Alfred d'Eyncourt, he worked as a film actor in Britain in the 1920s, and also gained Hollywood experience as an assistant at MGM; later, Alfred often served on his films as producer or co-producer. In 1935 Walter made his debut as director with the modest comedy-thriller *Alibi Inn*, written by Sydney and Muriel Box, and continued with other low-budget productions aimed at circuit audiences, including *Annie Laurie* and *King of Hearts*, both starring Will Fyffe, and *Little Miss Somebody*, a treacly melodrama starring Binkie Stuart, Britain's answer to Shirley Temple. None of them stirred any critical interest.

During the war, Tennyson changed tack and directed various propaganda films and service shorts, mainly for the Army Film and Photographic Unit, which he had joined in 1939. Two films produced in 1941 centred on the strategic importance of Iceland and the North Atlantic routes: *Northern Outpost* and *Guards of the North* (made for the National Film Board of Canada). *Lofôten* gave an eyewitness account of the Lofôten raid of March 1941; *The Army Lays the Rails* demonstrated the Royal Engineers' work in securing rail communication for army forces. The most crisply packaged and effective film was *Troopship* (1942), a brief record of life on board a vessel bound for the Far East.

Tennyson returned to the commercial industry on demobilisation in 1945, but never again directed. He joined Sydney Box as an assistant producer, acting as Box's associate producer on the Scottish melodrama *The Brothers* (David Macdonald, 1947). His final screen credit was as producer of Vernon Sewell's taut adventure tale *Jack of Diamonds* (1949).

(Alan Burton)

FILMOGRAPHY: *Alibi Inn*; *Father O'Flynn* (co-dir. Wilfred Noy); *When the Cat's Away* (short); *The Ghost Walks* (short); *The Strange Case of Mr Todmorden* (short) (1935); *Annie Laurie*; *King of Hearts* (co-dir. Oswald Mitchell) (1936); *Little Miss Somebody* (1937); *Trouble for Two*;

Two Days to Live (1939); *Mistaken Identity*; *The Body Vanished* (1939; rel. 1942); *Northern Outpost* (doc. short); *Loföten* (doc. short, co-dir. Harry Watt); *Guards of the North* (doc. short, Can) (1941); *Troopship* (doc. short, co-dir. Hugh Stewart); *The Army Lays the Rails* (doc. short, co-dir. Gerald Keen) (1942).

THIELE, Wilhelm (1890–1975)

William Thiele was born Wilhelm Thiele-Isersohn in Vienna on 10 May 1890. He trained as an actor at the Vienna Konservatorium, and made his stage debut at nineteen in a production of *The Merchant of Venice*. His first three films – *Carl Michael Ziehrer, der letzte Walzerkönig* (1921), *Carl Michael Ziehrer, Märchen aus Alt-Wien* (1923) and *Franz Lehár* (1923) – established him as a director with a penchant for light musical subjects, particularly operetta. Following a spell as scriptwriter and literary manager at Ufa he took full advantage of the coming of sound, establishing the German film operetta tradition with a series of carefree contemporary musicals, including *Die Drei von der Tankstelle* (1930), a spirited story about three young owners of a petrol station and their love for a wealthy customer (Lillian Harvey), and *Die Privatsekretärin* (1931), featuring Renate Müller singing her way through romantic entanglements with her bank manager boss. The films were popular and influential, and encouraged Michael Balcon to try similar formulas in England.

Thiele's first British film, *Marry Me* (1932), a remake of his frothy *Mädchen zum Heiraten* (1932), maintained much of the zest of his German output. Little attempt was made to Anglicise the material; Renate Müller repeated her role as a Berlin gramophone factory worker, fighting for the heart of the firm's cheery publicity manager (Ian Hunter). More traditional fare followed with *Waltz Time*, a freely adapted version of Johann Strauss' *Die Fledermaus*, made with an eclectic cast including Fritz Schulz, Evelyn Laye and Gina Malo.

In 1935 Thiele left for Hollywood, where he was only modestly successful. His knack for musicals showed in his first American venture, *Lottery Lover*, but there was little need for his specific skills in the routine assignments that followed, including *Bridal Suite* (1939), *The Ghost Comes Home* (1940) and several Tarzan pictures. In the 1950s he worked in television and directed his last films, including the successful comedy *Der letzte Fußgänger* (1960), in Germany. He died in Woodlawn Hills, California, on 7 September 1975.

(Geoff Brown and Kevin Gough Yates)

BIBLIOGRAPHY: 'Filmography', *Kinolehti* no. 6, Dec. 1972, pp. 23–4; 'Homenaie Postumo: Wilhelm Thiele', *Film Guia* no. 11, Dec. 1975/Jan. 1976, p. 48; Horak, Jan-Christopher, 'Wilhelm Thiele', *Cinegraph: Lexicon zum deutschsprachigen Film* (Munich: edition text+kritik, 1984).

FILMOGRAPHY (UK only): *Marry Me* (1932); *Waltz Time* (1933).

THOMAS, Edward

Edward Thomas found success as a playwright in 1988 with *House of America*, a Tennessee Williams-like concoction of fantasy, incest and other pitfalls of family life, set among the derelict minefields of South Wales. He became Artistic Director of Fiction Factory Theatre, writing, directing and touring with several more of his own productions. In 1993 he collaborated with Marc Evans on *Silent Village*, a fascinating documentary about Cwmgiedd, where Humphrey Jennings had shot *The Silent Village* (1943), his homage to the Czech villagers of Lidice, murdered by the Nazis in reprisal for the assassination of Reinhard Heydrich. Thomas went on to adapt *House of America* (1997) for Evans, who imposes a distinct visual style and a consistency of tone that make remarkable sense of the play.

Thomas was less successful in his own directorial debut, an adaptation by James Hawes of his novel *Rancid Aluminium*. A chaotic plot about a businessman seeking redress for his financial troubles by forging links with a murderous Russian entrepreneur is only made explicable by an irritating voiceover from Rhys Ifans. Steven Berkoff's Mr Kant, whose limited grasp of English justifies Berkoff's reliance on mime, is an enjoyable comic-book villain, but the two stooges played by Ifans and Joseph Fiennes, pouring out bad dialogue in unconvincing accents, make it a difficult film to sit through.

Thomas renewed his partnership with Evans in 2003, co-producing *Dal: Yma/Nawr/Still: Here/Now*, an evocation of the Welsh bardic tradition made for his Fiction Factory television company.

(Robert Murphy)

FILMOGRAPHY: *Rancid Aluminium* (2000).

THOMAS, Gerald (1920–1993)

In partnership with producer Peter Rogers, Gerald Thomas made one of the most successful series of comedy films in the history of British cinema, stretching from *Carry On Sergeant* (1958) to *Carry On Columbus* (1992). He was born in Hull on 10 December 1920, and trained to become a doctor. But his studies were interrupted by the Second World War and after four years in the army he decided it was too late to return to medicine. He joined Denham Studios, working his way up to become assistant editor on Olivier's *Hamlet* (1948).

From 1951 Thomas edited several films directed by his older brother Ralph, including *Appointment with Venus* (1951) and *Doctor in the House* (1954); he also acted as second-unit director on *Mad About Men* (1954) and *Above Us the Waves* (1955). His directing debut came the following year with *Circus Friends* (1956), a charming Children's Film Foundation production featuring thirteen-year-old Carol White, along with a clever dog and a performing pony. Adult drama followed in *Time Lock* (1957), a taut and absorbing thriller adapted from an Arthur Hailey play originally broadcast on Canadian television, though the film retained a child protagonist – a six-year-old boy accidentally locked inside a bank vault. Thomas handled the dramatic tension well, and did equally good jobs with the whodunit twists and turns of *The Vicious Circle* and *The Duke Wore Jeans*, a silly but likeable vehicle for pop singer Tommy

Steele. But his versatility abruptly shrank following the unexpected success of *Carry On Sergeant*. The lowbrow vulgarity of this farce about an incompetent National Service platoon, loosely based on a play by R. F. Delderfield, was greeted disdainfully by most film critics, but audiences loved it, and box-office success ensured a swift sequel. More by luck than judgment, Thomas and Rogers had hit upon a winning formula in the tradition of music hall and the saucy picture postcard, satisfying the national liking for lavatorial humour, men in drag and sexual innuendo.

Thirty other *Carry On* comedies followed, regularly featuring the same team of stalwart character actors, including Sid James, Charles Hawtrey, Hattie Jacques, Kenneth Williams, Barbara Windsor and Joan Sims. These low-budgeted films were slickly mounted; Thomas knew his craft as well as his audience. Irreverent pokes at British institutions (the army, hospitals, schools, the police) were followed by spoofs of film genres. Throughout the 1960s the series' success was ensured with entries like *Carry On Spying* (which introduced Barbara Windsor's cheeky charms), the irresistibly ludicrous *Carry On Screaming* and *Carry On Cleo* – uncharacteristically lavish because Thomas was able to use the sets built for *Cleopatra* (Joseph L. Mankiewicz, 1963). During the 1970s imagination began to flag and by the end of the decade *Carry On Emmanuelle* showed the impossibility of combining the innuendo ethos with an increasing cinematic demand for sexual explicitness. *That's Carry On* (1977), a compilation of clips with a new framing story, presaged the continual recycling of vintage *Carry Ons* on British television.

Along the way Thomas did make a variety of other comedy films, ranging between the acerbic *Please Turn Over* (1959) and the gentle *Nurse on Wheels* (1963); the modest wit of *The Big Job* (1965) and the ponderous set-piece charms of *The Iron Maiden* (1962). *The Second Victory* (1986), set in Austria in the aftermath of the Second World War, marked a late return to serious drama. Subsequently Thomas and Rogers were persuaded to revisit the old formula for *Carry On Columbus* (1992), but by this time many of their regular acting team had died; Thomas cast the film with some of the new generation of 'alternative' comedians likes Julian Clary and Rik Mayall, but they proved poor recompense and the film was not a success with audiences. In 1993 Gerald Thomas donated his production files to the BFI National Library; he died later that year on 9 November at his home in Beaconsfield. His nephew is the film producer Jeremy Thomas. (Janet Moat)

BIBLIOGRAPHY: Bilbow, Marjorie, 'Gerald Thomas Carries on in Austria with Second Victory', *Screen International*, 21 Dec. 1985, pp. 28–9; Medhurst, Andy, Obituary, *Sight and Sound*, Feb. 1994, p. 41; Summers, Sue, 'The Rudest Men in the Movies', *Daily Telegraph*, 26 Sept. 1992.

FILMOGRAPHY: *Mad About Men* (2nd unit dir., 1954); *Above Us the Waves* (2nd unit dir., 1955); *Circus Friends* (1956); *Time Lock*; *The Vicious Circle* (US: *The Circle*) (1957); *The Duke Wore Jeans*; *Carry On Sergeant*; *Chain of Events*; *The Solitary Child* (1958); *Carry On Nurse*; *Carry On Teacher*, *Please Turn Over* (1959); *Carry On Constable*; *No Kidding* (US: *Beware of Children*); *Watch Your Stern* (1960); *Raising the Wind*; *Carry On Regardless* (1961); *Carry On Cruising*; *The Iron Maiden*; *Twice round the Daffodils* (1962); *Nurse on Wheels*; *Carry On Cabby* (1963); *Carry On Cleo*; *Carry On Jack*; *Carry On Spying* (1964); *The Big Job*; *Carry On Cowboy* (1965); *Don't Lose Your Head* (aka *Carry On Don't Lose Your Head*); *Carry On Screaming* (1966); *Follow That Camel* (aka *Carry On Follow That Camel*, 1967); *Carry On Doctor*, *Carry On up the Khyber* (1968); *Carry On Again, Doctor*; *Carry On Camping* (1969); *Carry On Loving*; *Carry On up the Jungle*; *Carry On Henry* (1970); *Carry On at Your Convenience*; *Carry On Matron* (1971); *Carry On Abroad* (1972); *Carry On Girls* (1973); *Carry On Dick* (1974); *Carry On Behind* (1975); *Carry On England* (1976); *That's Carry On* (1977); *Carry On Emmanuelle* (1978); *The Second Victory* (1986); *Carry On Columbus* (1992).

THOMAS, Jeremy (1949–)

Jeremy Thomas was born on 26 July 1949 in Ealing, west London, the son of director Ralph Thomas. He joined the film industry as a cutting-room assistant in the late 1960s, rising to edit Philippe Mora's fascinating documentary about America during the Depression years, *Brother Can You Spare a*

Dime? (1975). He had intended to follow his father and his uncle (Gerald Thomas) into directing, but was deflected by the challenge of producing Mora's *Mad Dog Morgan* (1976), an Australian epic starring Dennis Hopper as a legendary nineteenth-century bushranger. On returning to Britain Thomas set up the Recorded Picture Company to produce Jerzy Skolimowski's *The Shout* (1978). Other innovative productions followed, including Nagisa Oshima's *Merry Christmas, Mr Lawrence* (1982) and Stephen Frears' *The Hit* (1984). But his most fruitful collaborations have been with Nicolas Roeg, as producer of *Bad Timing* (1980), *Eureka* (1982) and *Insignificance* (1985); and Bernardo Bertolucci, with whom he made *The Last Emperor* (1987), *The Sheltering Sky* (1990), *Little Buddha* (1993), *Stealing Beauty* (1996) and *The Dreamers* (2003).

In 1998 Thomas made his only venture into directing, an adaptation of Walker Hamilton's novel *All the Little Animals*, a modern fairy tale about how lack of care for animals' lives leads to general callousness and cruelty. A solid script and intelligent casting (Christian Bale as an abused young man healed by contact with nature, Daniel Benzali as his brutal stepfather, John Hurt as a grouchy animal rights activist) help the film avoid whimsy, though uncertainty of tone and lurches into melodrama limited its prospects at the box office. No doubt Thomas could have directed more films had he wished; instead he has helped younger directors push their way into this crowded field, producing Jonathan Glazer's *Sexy Beast* (2000) and David Mackenzie's *Young Adam* (2003).

(Robert Murphy)

BIBLIOGRAPHY: Cody, Sebastian, 'Interview: Jeremy Thomas', *AIP & Co* no. 44, July 1983, pp. 11–14; Falk, Quentin, 'Calling All the Shots', *Exposure*, Winter/Feb. 1998, pp. 14–17; Stanbrook, Alan, 'Framed: Jeremy Thomas', *Sight and Sound*, Summer 1988, pp. 178–9.

FILMOGRAPHY: *All the Little Animals* (1998).

THOMAS, Ralph (1915–2001)

Ralph Thomas modestly referred to himself as a journeyman director, but several of his films rise above this quotidian level. Certainly, few post-war British directors were so prolific, and none is more representative of mainstream film-making of the 1950s and 60s. There are comedies, colonial adventures, war films, thrillers, period pieces, spy capers (serious and spoof): he is perhaps the British genre director *par excellence*.

Ralph Philip Thomas was born in Hull on 10 August 1915 and educated at Tellisford School, Clifton, and Middlesex University College. He entered the film industry in 1932 and gained wide experience in various production departments, especially in the cutting room. He worked at Sound City, first as clapper-boy, then as camera assistant, and from 1935 to 1939 he edited at Elstree, Isleworth and Shepperton. The war years were spent as a regimental officer, 9th Lancers, then, when invalided out in 1944, as an instructor at the Royal Military College, Sandhurst.

Joining Rank's Gainsborough Studios in 1946, Thomas first worked in the trailer department, which he found a useful training in narrative economy. While making the trailer for the mermaid comedy *Miranda*, he met producer Betty Box; the two established a working association lasting twenty-five years. His first three films for Gainsborough, all produced by Antony Darnborough, are long-forgotten comedies, though the idiotic *Helter Skelter* has a few moments of comic inspiration, involving a wobbling desk made from aspic. Thomas hit his stride when the Rank Organisation relocated production to Pinewood, where his first film was the taut chase thriller *The Clouded Yellow*. The film resonates with that post-war malaise (especially visible in Trevor Howard's ex-Secret Service agent), which gives shading to so many British films of the time, and is innovatory in its reliance on use of location filming in London, Newcastle, Liverpool and the Lake District.

Thomas and Box's next film was *Appointment with Venus*, a mild wartime comedy-thriller in which David Niven and Glynis Johns abduct a pedigree cow from the Nazi-occupied Channel Islands. Another noirish thriller, *Venetian Bird*, with Richard Todd an unsympathetic protagonist, but with well-utilised, seedy Venetian settings followed in 1952. After minor entertainments, including *The Dog and the Diamonds* for the Children's Film Foundation, they unexpectedly hit the jackpot with the popular comedy *Doctor in the House*, skilfully adapted by Nicholas Phipps from the novel by Richard Gordon. The film survives well as a paean to youthful high spirits, with its attractive cast working every joke about the medical profession for all – and more – than their worth. The ingredients are lightly tossed with a sure touch, and once or twice the tone deepens touchingly, as in the scenes with Maureen Pryor's young mother. Six sequels followed to inevitably diminishing returns, both aesthetic and commercial, with Michael Craig and Leslie Phillips replacing Dirk Bogarde after the first few.

Bogarde's career was largely tied in with the Thomas–Box team at this stage: Rank's leading star, he was often cast in films to which he was not greatly suited, including Thomas' location-filmed adventures *Campbell's Kingdom* and *The High Bright Sun*, both of which could have benefited from a more conventionally rugged leading man. However, Bogarde is appropriately sensitive as an intelligence officer who falls for his Japanese-language teacher in *The Wind Cannot Read*, and is equally well cast as a romantically dissolute Sydney Carton in *A Tale of Two Cities*. Both films, along with Thomas' decent remake of Hitchcock's *The 39 Steps*, are among the better films to emerge from Pinewood in the late 1950s.

Though Box and Thomas found it irksome being tied to a formula, they used the Rank Organisation's voracious appetite for 'Doctor' films as a bargaining counter to gain financial support for more personal projects. Thomas teamed with the producer William MacQuitty to make *Above Us the Waves*, a fictional but strongly authentic account of the successful attack on the German battleship *Tirpitz* by British midget submarines. Box was able to persuade the Conservative-supporting Rank to back *No Love for Johnnie*, a sympathetic if unflattering portrait of an ambitious Labour Party politician. A strangely neglected film in view of its pertinence to current British politics, this acrid study of political opportunism – Peter Finch plays a Labour MP willing to sell out his left-wing principles for a place in the government – is made with remarkable integrity and insight.

Two other films from the beginning of the 1960s also deserve mentioning. Lilli Palmer headed a good cast in *Conspiracy of Hearts*, a wartime story about nuns hiding Jewish children in their Italian convent. Sympathetic Italian officers (Ronald Lewis), ruthless Nazis (Albert Lieven), a lovable rabbi (David Kossoff) and a beautiful young nun (Sylvia Syms) might constitute the usual Second World War cinema clichés, but Thomas still manages to steer the film from sentimentality to genuine poignancy. With *The Wild and the Willing*, dealing with students at Lincoln University (which would not come into existence until some thirty-five years later), Thomas was on less sure ground. Rebellious youth was not his forte, but the talented young cast, including Ian McShane, Samantha Eggar and John Hurt, all making their cinema debuts, give the film some sparkle.

Thomas' later films are disappointing. The public continued to patronise the 'Doctor' films, though they became increasingly threadbare. There were two final films with Bogarde, the louche spy thriller *Hot Enough for June*, and *The High Bright Sun*, an unsatisfactory melodrama using the Greek Cypriot rebellion against British sovereignty as a background. Better were the outrageous pastiches *Deadlier Than the Male* and its sequel *Some Girls Do*, with Richard Johnson highly effective as an updated Bulldog Drummond doing battle with beautiful but dangerous female adversaries. They were followed by the abysmal penis-transplant comedy *Percy*, a box-office success that led to a worse successor, *Percy's Progress*. Thomas was more ambitious with *Quest for Love*, based on one of John Wyndham's science-fiction stories, which fruitfully pairs Joan Collins with Tom Bell. A modest but well-respected professional to the end, Thomas was able to recruit David Niven and Gloria Grahame for his last film, *The Biggest Bank Robbery* (1980), a caper film with an unduly sentimental view of the English underworld.

His brother Gerald Thomas directed all the *Carry On* films, produced by Peter Rogers, husband of Ralph's producer Betty Box; his son Jeremy Thomas is a noted producer. Ralph Thomas died in London on 17 March 2001.

(Brian McFarlane)

BIBLIOGRAPHY: Dixon, Wheeler Winston, 'Interview with Ralph Thomas: British Film Director, *Classic Images* vol. 249, Mar. 1996, pp. 34, 36, 40, 42–3; Falk, Quentin, 'Don't Knock the Distributor Say Thomas & Medwin', *CinemaTV Today*, 26 Jan. 1974, pp. 10–11; McFarlane, Brian, *An Autobiography of British Cinema* (London: Methuen, 1997); Thomas, Ralph, 'My Way with Screen Humour', *Films and Filming*, Feb. 1956, p. 5.

FILMOGRAPHY: *Once Upon a Dream*; *Helter Skelter*; *Traveller's Joy* (1949); *The Clouded Yellow* (1950); *Appointment with Venus* (US: *Island Rescue*, 1951); *Venetian Bird* (US: *The Assassin*, 1952); *The Dog and the Diamonds*; *A Day to Remember* (1953); *Doctor in the House*; *Mad About Men* (1954); *Doctor at Sea*; *Above Us the Waves* (1955); *The Iron Petticoat*; *Checkpoint* (1956); *Doctor at Large*; *Campbell's Kingdom* (1957); *A Tale of Two Cities*; *The Wind Cannot Read*; *The 39 Steps* (1958); *Upstairs and Downstairs* (1959); *Conspiracy of Hearts*; *Doctor in Love* (1960); *No, My Darling Daughter*; *No Love for Johnnie*; *A Pair of Briefs* (1961); *The Wild and the Willing* (US: *Young and Willing*, 1962); *Doctor in Distress* (1963); *Hot Enough for June* (US: *Agent 8¾*, 1964); *The High Bright Sun* (US: *Maguire Go Home*, 1965); *Doctor in Clover*; *Deadlier Than the Male* (1966); *Nobody Runs Forever* (US: *The High Commissioner*, UK/US, 1968); *Some Girls Do* (1969); *Doctor in Trouble* (1970); *Percy*; *Quest for Love* (1971); *It's a 2′ 6″ Above the Ground World* (US: *The Love Ban*, 1973); *Percy's Progress* (1974); *The Biggest Bank Robbery* (US: *The Mayfair Caper*, 1980).

THOMSON, Margaret (1910–2005)

Margaret Thomson was born in Sydney in 1910, but she was brought up in New Zealand and, after attaining a degree in zoology, emigrated to England in 1934. She was recruited by H. Bruce Woolfe for Gaumont-British Instructional in 1936 and put her scientific expertise to good use by directing a six-film educational series examining different British ecosystems. By 1938 she was editing at the Shell and Strand film units, and she later directed films for the Trade and Industrial Development Association.

After a brief spell away from film-making, Thomson returned to directing in 1941, finding regular work at the Realist Film Unit making instructional films for the wartime home-front propaganda campaign. Making films for both general and specialised audiences, the topics she dealt with ranged from basic gardening skills to specialist agricultural and medical training films. Considering the diversity of subjects, all of the films are characterised by Thomson's visual simplicity, clear instruction and ability to relay complex information to her audience in a non-patronising manner.

After the war Thomson produced two children's films but returned to directing to make recruitment films for the Ministry of Education. In 1948 she went back to New Zealand where she directed documentaries such as *Railway Worker* (1949), but returned to Britain in 1950 to direct for the Crown Film Unit. In 1953 she made a fiction film for children, *Child's Play*, for John Grierson and John Baxter's Group 3; and for several years she worked as a children's acting coach at Pinewood Studios. In the final stage of her career she returned to non-fiction film-making, setting up a documentary company with her husband, Bob Ash, and directing industrial and government-sponsored films and filmstrips, including several for the National Coal Board, until she retired in 1977. Margaret Thomson died on 30 December 2005.
(Sarah Easen)

BIBLIOGRAPHY: BECTU History Project interview, 1990, tape held in the BFI National Library, London; 'First Kiwi Woman Film-Maker Profiled on eTVV', *Onfilm* vol. 12 no. 6, July 1995, p. 5; 'Women at Work', *Kinematograph Weekly* (Studio Review supplement), 2 Oct. 1952, p. 10.

FILMOGRAPHY: *Chalk Downlands; Meadowlands; Moorlands; Woodlands; Heathlands; Downlands* (1937); *Marshlands* (1938); *Cultivation; Storing Vegetables Outdoors* (1941); *Clamping Potatoes; Hedging; Ditching; Making a Compost Heap; Storing Vegetables Indoors; Garden Tools* (1942); *Clean Milk; Making Good Hay; Making Grass Silage; Re-seeding for Better Grass; Saving Your Own Seeds* (1943); *The Technique of Anaesthesia* (series: dir. of four of eleven films, 1944); *Children Learning by Experience; Children Growing up with Other People* (1947); *Railway Worker* (NZ, 1949); *First Two Years at School* (NZ); *A Family Affair* (1950); *Troubled Wind; Child's Play* (1953); *East in the West; Continuous Observation* (1954); *Friend of the Family; Whole Works – Better Ways* (1955); *Yorkshire Imperial on Thames* (1957); *Training for Industry* (1959); *Coronary Angiography; Talking about Epontol; Tuberculosis – the Forgotten Disease* (1960); *A Sense of Belonging; Most Precious Gift* (1962); *Sonic Aid for the Blind* (1965); *Theatre Technique for Nurses* (1966); *Bandage of Today* (1967); *Every Baby a Wanted Baby* (1969); *Margin of Safety* (1970); *First Aid Filmstrips* (1972).

THORPE, Richard (1896–1991)

Rollo Smolt Thorpe was born on 24 February 1896 in Hutchinson, Kansas. After performing in vaudeville he began appearing in films in 1921, and directed two-reel comedies and Westerns from 1923. He had already made over a hundred movies when he joined MGM for *Last of the Pagans* (1935); he remained under contract with the studio for most of the next three decades. The archetypal Hollywood workhorse, Thorpe was noted less for his talent than for his ability to deliver pictures on schedule and within budget. This he apparently achieved by changing set-ups only when an actor blew a line and refusing to shoot more than one acceptable take of each shot ('For a cameraman it was boring as hell', recalled Freddie Young).

Thorpe's most lavish assignment was the trio of medieval swashbucklers he made with Robert Taylor at MGM-British. *Ivanhoe* is the most spectacular of these, *Knights of the Round Table* – the first British CinemaScope production – the most stolid, and *The Adventures of Quentin Durward* the sprightliest. The first two were among MGM's highest grossers of the 1950s and *Ivanhoe*, the biggest British-based production made to that date, represents Thorpe's best work. Director and star returned to Britain for *Killers of Kilimanjaro* and *The House of the Seven Hawks*, with locations in India and Holland respectively. The former is a railway-building adventure, the latter a tepid crime yarn modelled on *The Maltese Falcon* but distinguished only by Taylor's rugged personality.

The Truth About Spring, made for Universal, is a twee nautical comedy that failed to draw convincing American accents from John and Hayley Mills. The last of Thorpe's nearly two hundred films was *The Scorpio Letters*, a spy thriller intended for US television but released theatrically in Britain, where it was shot. Thorpe retired to Palm Springs where he died, aged ninety-five, on 1 May 1991.
(Sheldon Hall)

BIBLIOGRAPHY: Roberts, John, '30 Years of Films Directed by Richard Thorpe', *Classic Images* no. 166, Apr. 1989, pp. c-12–14; Young, Freddie, *Seventy Light Years: A Life in the Movies* (London: Faber and Faber, 1999).

FILMOGRAPHY (UK only): *Ivanhoe* (1952); *Knights of the Round Table* (1953); *The Adventures of Quentin Durward* (US: *Quentin Durward*, 1955); *Killers of Kilimanjaro; The House of the Seven Hawks* (1959); *The Truth About Spring* (1965); *The Scorpio Letters* (1967).

THRAVES, Jamie (1969–)

James Thraves was born in Dagenham, Essex, on 2 July 1969. He studied illustration and animation at Hull Polytechnic, where he made two short films before graduating in 1991: *Small Orange House*, and *Scratch*, a disturbing monochrome account of a young man who compulsively scratches his head. The film won several awards and caught the attention of music video and commercial producer John Stewart. Thraves' next short, *The Take Out*, about a night at the dog-track, was made for Stewart's Oil Factory company with support from the BFI New Directors' scheme. Thraves then enrolled on the Royal College of Art's MA in the Film and Television School though he retained his links with Stewart who co-produced his two RCA films, *The Hackney Downs* and *Down in the City*, and later his début feature, *The Low Down* (1999). Thraves also directed music videos, twice winning the MVPA Video of the Year award, most impressively with Radiohead's *Just* (1996).

Filmed in hand-held Super-16, *The Low Down* is a free-wheeling gem of social observation. The chief character is Frank (Aidan Gillen), an art-school graduate in his late twenties living in Hackney, north-east London, who has hit what should be a crossroads in his life but is paralysed by inarticulate inertia. Built up from vignettes of raffish London life and sometimes painfully inconclusive exchanges, *The Low Down* is interested far more in character, place and atmosphere, gestures and skin textures than narrative events. Like many of the best British films

of its decade, it was poorly distributed and received mixed reviews; while admirers praised its offbeat coverage of twenty-something malaise, others were frustrated by its lack of plot and mistook this for lack of substance.
(Claire Monk)
BIBLIOGRAPHY: Monk, Claire, 'Projecting a "New Britain"', *Cinéaste, Contemporary British Cinema* supplement, Autumn 2001, pp. 34–7, 42; Smith, John, '*The Low Down*', *Sight and Sound*, Feb. 2001, p. 43; Radford, Jasmine, 'Headliners', *Empire*, Mar. 2001, p. 21.
FILMOGRAPHY (not including music videos): *Small Orange House* (short); *Scratch* (short) (1991); *The Take Out* (short, 1993); *The Hackney Downs* (short, 1994); *Down in the City* (short, 1995); *I Just Want to Kiss You* (short, 1997); *The Low Down* (1999).

TICKELL, Paul (1949–)

Paul Tickell was born in Carlisle in 1949. After training to be a Catholic priest, he attended university, moving into the London-based music industry in 1977. Between 1982 and 1988 he worked for London Weekend Television, primarily on arts programmes. He went on to direct a series of high-profile documentaries, including *Punk and the Pistols* with John Lydon, Vivienne Westwood and Malcolm McLaren, for the BBC's *Arena* programme in 1995. In the same year his short film about Russian Afghan war veterans-turned-black marketeers, *Zinky Boys Go Underground*, won a BAFTA award.

Tickell completed his first feature, the Irish-set *Crush Proof*, in 1998. Again dealing with socially marginalised young men whose chief outlet for their energies is crime, the film combines gritty realism with stylised violence and stabs at mythological significance. The film's uneven style meant it fared badly in multiplexes, while its portrayal of lesbianism as a perversion offended critics who might have overlooked its rough edges. Tickell continued this thematic path with his adaptation of B. S. Johnson's novel *Christie Malry's Own Double-Entry*. The film follows the descent into murder of Malry (Nick Moran), a terrorist with accountancy training, who records his activities as debits and credits. Both Tickell's films are marked by a fascination with male violence, and suggest an erratic talent in search of subversive material.
(Ruth Barton)
FILMOGRAPHY: *Zinky Boys Go Underground* (short, 1995); *Crush Proof* (UK/Neth/Ir, 1998); *Christie Malry's Own Double-Entry* (Neth/UK/Lux, 2000).

TILL, Eric (1930–)

Eric Till was born in Worthing, West Sussex, in 1930. After National Service with British Forces Broadcasting in Hamburg, he joined the BBC. But impatient at his lack of progress, he left for Canada in 1954. He worked for the National Ballet Company for eighteen months, but only finally found his feet when he joined the Canadian Broadcasting Company. Here, along with fellow British expatriates David Greene and Charles Jarrott and the Canadian Ted Kotcheff, he was given a remarkably free hand in directing new and classic drama for television. He branched out into features with *A Great-Big Thing*, an original but desultory exploration of a young man's angst, shot on location in Montreal on a shoestring budget. It was eventually released in North America (though not in the UK) in 1968, by which time Till was back in Britain working on *Hot Millions*, an MGM-financed caper film starring Peter Ustinov and Maggie Smith. In contrast to the meandering pace of *A Great-Big Thing*, *Hot Millions* moves along smartly, and might have been a box-office hit had the market not been glutted by similar, if less crisply directed, caper films.

Till followed up in 1970 with *The Walking Stick*, from a novel by Winston Graham about a crippled woman seduced by a conman into helping with a jewel robbery. Till is no Hitchcock (who had filmed Graham's *Marnie* in 1964) and suspense is notably lacking; but he is much kinder to his characters, and we empathise with the flowering of the repressed victim (Samantha Eggar) and her perplexed disillusion as she gradually realises that her wonderful new life is a sham. Again, market conditions made for a disappointingly muted response, and as the British film industry entered its long decline Till went back to Canada to adapt John Hopkins' innovative drama *Talking to a Stranger* for Canadian television and make a Canadian feature, *A Fan's Notes* (1972), which materialised into something darker than the anticipated light comedy and was shunned by its financial backers. He made a final return to Britain to direct *It Shouldn't Happen to a Vet* (1976), an amiable film but with no ambition to outgrow its television spin-off status.

Till resumed his career in Canada, where as well as directing for television he became a mainstay of feature film production, latterly making two prestigious Canadian/German co-productions, *Bonhoeffer: Agent of Grace* and *Luther*.
(Robert Murphy)
BIBLIOGRAPHY: D'Arcy, Susan, 'It Shouldn't Happen to a Vet. Or a Film Director. But it Does. And It Did. To Eric Till', *Films Illustrated*, Mar. 1976, pp. 274–5.
FILMOGRAPHY: *A Great-Big Thing* (Can); *Hot Millions* (1968); *The Walking Stick* (1970); *A Fan's Notes* (Can, 1972); *It Shouldn't Happen to a Vet* (US: *All Things Bright and Beautiful*, 1976); *Wild Horse Hank* (Can); *Improper Channels* (Can) (1979); *If You Could See What I Hear/Au-delà du regard* (Can, 1982); *Bridge to Terabithia* (Can, 1984); *A Nest of Singing Birds* (Can, 1987); *Oh, What a Night* (Can); *Farther West* (Can, 1992); *Bonhoeffer: Agent of Grace/Bonhoeffer – Die letzte Stufe* (Can/Ger, 2000); *Luther* (Can/Ger, 2003).

TOMLINSON, Lionel (1907–?)

Richard Lionel Tomlinson was born in London on 5 December 1907. He worked as an editor in the late 1930s on cheap but effective thrillers, most notably Richard Bird's *The Terror* (1938) and Walter Summers' *Premiere* (1938) and *At the Villa Rose* (1939). After RAF service in the war he directed shorts and documentaries and was then dragooned into service on four diverse B-films. *Death in High Heels*, like Sidney Gilliat's *Green for Danger* (1946) based on a novel by Christianna Brand, was made with an inexperienced cast in the cramped interiors of Marylebone

Dudley Sutton and Samantha Eggar in *The Walking Stick* (Eric Till, 1971)

studios and emerged looking murky and unconvincing. *Who Killed Van Loon?*, made for Hammer, proved a much more diligent affair. Raymond Lovell revels in villainy as a crook who kills one man and frames another's daughter in his attempt to secure a cache of diamonds. A well-constructed script and efficient, no-nonsense direction (shared with producer Gordon Kyle) make for thrilling entertainment. Unfortunately the glimmer of talent was extinguished in Tomlinson's two subsequent films. *My Hands Are Clay* is a dull and unconvincing Irish melodrama about a disturbed sculptor; *Take a Powder*, co-directed with actor and writer Julian Vedey, is a weak comedy that squanders its topical theme of espionage and atomic scientists and is overindulgent to its star Max Bacon. No further features followed, but he kept busy until the 1960s with interest shorts like *London Nights*, and television commercials innumerable. By the end of the decade he was working for Tyne-Tees Television.
(Robert Murphy)

FILMOGRAPHY: *Death in High Heels*; *Who Killed Van Loon?* (Co-dir. Gordon Kyle) (1947); *My Hands Are Clay* (UK/Ir, 1948); *Take a Powder* (co-dir. Julian Vedey, 1953); *London Nights* (doc., 1960).

TOURNEUR, Jacques (1904–1977)

Jacques Tourneur made three films in Britain, the most distinguished of which, *Night of the Demon*, is a work of distinct and poetic power in a field of British cinema increasingly dominated by the more forthright spectacle of Hammer horror films. Born in Paris on 12 November 1904, and naturalised American in 1919, Tourneur maintained a European feeling for subtle visual spectacle and naturalistic acting; qualities also visible in the French and American films of his father, the director Maurice Tourneur.

Jacques Tourneur began directing features in France in 1932. Returning to Hollywood in 1935, he slowly climbed MGM's ladder, directing second units and two-reel productions. In the 1940s he hit his stride working at RKO for producer Val Lewton; films like *Cat People* and *I Walked with a Zombie* used hints and shadows to find new ways of scaring people. His first British production, *Circle of Danger* (1951), made at London Film Studios for David E. Rose's Coronado Productions, featured Ray Milland as an American in Scotland, investigating his brother's mysterious death during a Commando raid in the war. Quietly played and somewhat underpowered as drama, the film was still mounted with visual elegance and used Tourneur's foreign perspective to good advantage.

Tourneur returned in 1957 for *Night of the Demon*, expanded by Hitchcock's former script collaborator Charles Bennett from a tale of the supernatural by M. R. James, and shot at Elstree for Hal E. Chester's Sabre Film Productions. Like Hitchcock, Tourneur delighted in seeking horror in the ordinary surface of British life – a walk through the woods, a children's party suddenly interrupted by a violent storm, a farming family staring frostily at an intruder, a railway station's night-time steam and commotion. With a finger on developing public taste, the producer insisted on toothy close-ups of a demon Tourneur had always planned as a creature of mystery and suggestion. But not even these additions could lessen the film's power. The film's character interplay is intriguing: Niall MacGinnis' insidiously charming devil-worshipper Dr Karswell is a far more sympathetic figure than Dana Andrews' arrogantly sceptical American psychologist. Bennett's original script was further adapted by an uncredited Cy Endfield, who had taken shelter in England from America's HUAC investigations; not for nothing, perhaps, is this a story of fear, self-protection and betrayal.

Tourneur's feeling for the strangeness of ordinary life could find only a limited outlet in his last British film, *City under the Sea* (1965), a hotchpotch of fantasy elements loosely linked to Edgar Allen Poe, co-produced with American International Pictures. Comedy sequences shoe-horned into Charles Bennett's original script by the producer Louis M. Heywood made the result sillier than necessary, though Tourneur managed to conjure up some atmospheric menace for the early scenes. Another Anglo-American fantasy venture, based on H. G. Wells' novel *When the Sleeper Wakes*, was planned, but Tourneur made no further features. He retired to France and died in Bergerac on 22 December 1977.
(Geoff Brown)

BIBLIOGRAPHY: Fujiwara, Chris, *Jacques Tourneur: The Cinema of Nightfall* (Baltimore, MD: Johns Hopkins University Press, 2000); Porter, Vincent, 'Strangers in a Foreign Land', *La Lettre de la Maison Française d'Oxford* no. 11, Autumn 1999, pp. 59–74; Tourneur, Jacques, 'Taste without Clichés', *Films and Filming*, Nov. 1965, pp. 9–11; Tourneur, Jacques, 'Biofilmographie de Jacques Tourneur, commentée par lui-même', *Présence du Cinéma*, Autumn 1966, pp. 56–83.

FILMOGRAPHY (UK only): *Circle of Danger* (1951); *Night of the Demon* (US: *Curse of the Demon*, 1957); *City under the Sea* (US: *War-Gods of the Deep*, 1965).

TOYE, Wendy (1917–)

Wendy Toye was born in London on 1 May 1917, and at the age of three and a half appeared on stage at the Royal Albert Hall as a member of a juvenile dance troupe. Her solo turn brought her considerable publicity, and Toye began to perform in music halls and charity shows with many of the day's top stage stars. By the age of five she was working on a regular basis as 'stooge' for the famous musical-comedy star Hayden Coffin. At the age of nine, she appeared at the Palladium in *Japanese Legend of the Rainbow*, a ballet she had choreographed herself, set to music by Scarlatti. The presentation was an enormous success, and Toye became much in demand, choreographing ballets and dance routines. She was invited to perform with Serge Diaghilev's Ballets Russes, where she met the film-maker/artist Jean Cocteau. Toye later appeared at the Café de Paris as a member of the Markova-Dolin Ballet Company, and gradually took on more commercial work, including choreographing the Crazy Gang's routines at the London Palladium. In 1932 she made her film debut among the Marie Rambert Corps de Ballet in Anthony Asquith's *Dance Pretty Lady*, and in 1935 secured a character part in Paul Merzbach's *Invitation to the Waltz*. But she was more interested in absorbing the technical process of film-making than establishing a career as an actress; by the 1940s she had moved on to film choreography, arranging the dances for *The Young Mr Pitt* (1942) and, a more important assignment, Herbert Wilcox and Anna Neagle's *Piccadilly Incident* (1946).

From the 1930s to the early 1950s, Toye remained a popular and dependable stage choreographer and director, working in both the UK and the US, where her direction of the 1949 Broadway production of *Peter Pan* with Boris Karloff and Jean Arthur brought her additional acclaim. Around this time, she met the actor and producer George K. Arthur, who had purchased the rights to several short stories. Toye expressed interest in directing one of them, *The Stranger Left No Card*, and was allowed to make it as a twenty-three-minute film on a budget of £3,000. Precisely timed to a synchronised musical score, the film proved a delightfully sinister parable, strongly influenced by Cocteau and René Clair. Alexander Korda was sufficiently impressed to offer Toye a contract, though she had little enthusiasm for the routine crime films he initially offered. Her 'In the Picture' episode of *Three Cases of Murder* displayed talent and imagination; and she vigorously steered through the twisting plot of Francis Durbridge's *The Teckman Mystery*. But she felt more affinity with her next assignment, *Raising a Riot*, a lively and inventive comedy about a naval officer (Kenneth More) having to cope with his unruly brood of children.

In January 1956 Korda died of a heart attack, and Toye's contract was shifted to Rank, where she made two more comedies: *All for Mary*, a slim skiing holiday frolic with Kathleen Harrison, Nigel Patrick and David Tomlinson, and *True as a Turtle*, a nautical comedy starring John Gregson, Cecil Parker, June Thorburn and Keith Michell. Both films performed well at the box office, though they are sillier and sloppier than *Raising a Riot*. Toye's last feature, *We Joined the Navy*, made for Associated British, gave her more scope with its large cast of talented character actors and chaotically farcical plot, but it was followed only by a short, *The King's Breakfast*, and television work. In 1981 she remade *The Stranger Left No Card* for Anglia Television as part of their *Tales of the Unexpected* series, with Derek Jacobi in the title role; in 1986 she served as an associate producer on the television movie *Barnum!* starring Michael Crawford.

Although Wendy Toye complained that Rank refused to support her desire to direct projects more ambitious than her comedies, she took pride in the fact that she never went over budget, and that her responsible example paved the way for other women to enter the field. She continued directing stage comedies until the mid-1990s.

(Wheeler Winston Dixon)

BIBLIOGRAPHY: Dixon, Wheeler Winston, 'An Interview with Wendy Toye'; and Merz, Caroline, 'The Tensions of Genre: Wendy Toye and Muriel Box', in Wheeler Winston Dixon (ed.), *Re-viewing British Cinema 1900–1992* (Albany: SUNY Press, 1994); Harper, Sue, *Women in British Cinema: Mad, Bad and Dangerous to Know* (London: Continuum, 2000); Paskin, Sylvia, 'A Picasso for Every Season', *Monthly Film Bulletin*, Aug. 1986, pp. 253–4; Paskin, Sylvia, 'A Delicate but Insistent Trail of Confetti . . .', *Monthly Film Bulletin*, Sept. 1986, pp. 290–1; Paskin, Sylvia and Pam Cook, 'The Director Left No Card – Wendy Toye', *Monthly Film Bulletin*, Oct. 1986, p. 292.

FILMOGRAPHY: *The Stranger Left No Card* (short); *Three Cases of Murder* ('In the Picture' episode) (1953); *The Teckman Mystery* (1954); *On the Twelfth Day* (short); *Raising a Riot*; *All for Mary* (1955); *True as a Turtle* (1957); *We Joined the Navy* (1962); *The King's Breakfast* (short, 1963).

TRAVERS, Alfred (1906–?)

A director with eclectic credentials, Alfred Travers was born in Constantinople in 1906. Educated in Turkey, Switzerland and England, he became proficient enough in German to act in films (*Die Villa im Tiergarten*, Franz Osten, 1926) and serve as assistant to the director Paul Czinner in Germany and France. The Second World War stopped his roving; settled in England, he buckled down to information and propaganda shorts for government agencies, promoting among others Boy Scouts, the electrical industry and the Rijksvoorlichtingsdienst, the Dutch government exiled in London.

Their Invisible Inheritance (for the British Electrical Development Association) prompted the *Monthly Film Bulletin* to muse that the advertised labour-saving devices and electricity-friendly homes would outstretch the grasp of many people in hard-pressed Britain (February 1946, p. 27). Travers' features, when they came, pursued their own line in unreality. In 1945 he joined British National, managing two films before the company was wound up in 1948. The musical *Meet the Navy* (1946), inspired by the Royal Canadian Navy's touring stage revue, reached its minor peak with the show's production numbers, presented in Technicolor. *Dual Alibi*, a circus murder drama, gave clear hints that stripper Phyllis Dixey could not act, but Herbert Lom's roles as twin trapeze artists bent on vengeance carried the film to some kind of victory.

Thereafter Travers freelanced, working on television series, and switching disconcertingly in the cinema between high-art ventures and potboilers. Reunited with Czinner, he helped devise a multi-camera system for the reproduction of staged operas and ballets, first displayed in Czinner's *Don Giovanni* (1955); his technical assistance also benefited later films presenting the Bolshoi and Royal ballets. In between, with brow lowered, he directed a weak Irish comedy in the Ealing mode, *The Strangers Came*, and five other supporting features endangered by silly scripts or slack direction. The inheritance comedy *Girls of the Latin Quarter*, one of a trio for Border Film Productions, failed on both counts; but *The Primitives* (1962), an implausible thriller about jewel thieves who double as club entertainers, remains surprisingly spirited and watchable. With such a motley career, no one one should be surprised by his last traceable film: a version of the 1961Whitehall Theatre farce, *One for the Pot* (1968), derived from a stage production in Johannesburg. Travers' death date is unknown.

(Geoff Brown)

FILMOGRAPHY: *Men of Tomorrow* (doc. short, 1942); *Glorious Colours* (doc. short, 1943); *Beyond the Pylons* (doc. short); *Their Invisible Inheritance* (doc. short) (1945); *Meet the Navy* (1946); *Dual Alibi* (1947); *The Strangers Came* (US: *You Can't Fool an Irishman*, 1949); *Solution by Phone* (1953); *Alive on Saturday* (1957); *Men of Tomorrow* (1958); *Girls of the Latin Quarter* (1960); *The Primitives* (1962); *Raka* (SA); *One for the Pot* (SA) (1968).

TROCHE, Rose (1964–)

Rose Troche was born to Puerto Rican parents in Chicago on 30 May 1964. She studied film and photography at the University of Illinois, and made her name with *Go Fish* (1994), a gritty study of the New York lesbian scene, shot on a tiny budget in black and white. In 1998 she came to England to make *Bedrooms and Hallways*, a disappointingly limp romantic comedy featuring Kevin McKidd as a gay man who reviews his options on his thirtieth birthday, and settles finally for his tomboyish teenage sweetheart (Jennifer Ehle). Dealing with men in London, Troche is able to offer far fewer insights than she was with women in New York, and clichés and stereotypes abound.

Troche pointed out to a journalist that being gay was by no means synonymous with being radical, that for many gays: 'all they want is to have exactly what their parents have but in this different situation' (Moylan, p. 55). Troche explored her own relationship with conservatism in *The Safety of Objects* (2001), a warm, subtle study of American suburbia based on short stories by Amy Michael Homes, financed primarily by the British-based Renaissance Films. Troche ingeniously interweaves the stories of four troubled families linked together by a car crash disaster, extending sympathy not just to the finely characterised mothers, but to unhappy husbands, angst-ridden teenagers and confused children. Disappointingly, the film failed to reach the mainstream American audience, but Troche found an outlet for her talents directing episodes of the offbeat American series *Six Feet Under* (2001), *The L Word* (2004) and *Touching Evil* (2004).

(Robert Murphy)

BIBLIOGRAPHY: Moylan, Katie, 'Rose Troche', *Film West* no. 35, Feb. 1999, pp. 54–5; Jilla, Shireen, 'Women on the Verge', *Premiere* [UK], Dec. 1994, pp. 40–6.

FILMOGRAPHY (UK only): *Bedrooms and Hallways* (1998); *The Safety of Objects* (UK/US, 2001).

TRONSON, Robert (1924–)

Though Robert Tronson's reputation rests on the quiet realism and psychological probings of his film *Ring of Spies*, the bulk of the director's career was spent in television. Born in Chillmark, Massachusetts, in 1924, Robert du Coudre Tronson entered the British film industry in 1950, and from the mid-1950s to the late 1990s directed over three hundred and fifty television plays and series episodes. Prestige adaptations of books and novels featured in the early days (*Women in Love*, *A Doll's House*); later, popular entertainment predominated, from *The Troubleshooters* (1964) to *Hetty Wainthropp Investigates* (1996). His cinema career spanned only the first half of the 1960s.

In 1961 *Man at the Carlton Tower* inaugurated a run of five supporting features in Merton Park's series inspired by the writings of Edgar Wallace – crime thrillers marked at best by a dry humour and tautly unfolding plots. For other companies he directed *The Traitors*, a competent cold war thriller, and *Farewell Performance*, a *mélange* of pop music and murder.

Ring of Spies, based on Britain's Portland spy scandal of 1961, was initiated by Frank Launder, who, along with other film-makers on the board of British Lion, was anxious to improve the quality of the films that accompanied their own features in double bills. Various script details echo the light-hearted comedy of Launder's usual output, but the film's strength lies in its cold war chill and the sober exploration of the behaviour and lives of the two government employees who, for financial reasons rather than politics, pass secret documents to a KGB spy-master, Gordon Lonsdale.

Tronson's unforced approach entirely suited the pursuit of surface realism. Characters kept their real names; apart from the Navy's Underwater Weapons Establishment at Portland shooting took place in many authentic locations – from London rendezvous points where papers were exchanged to the suburban haven where their details were transmitted. But Tronson's achievement stretched beyond wrapping up spies and spy games in the cloak of the mundane. Through the powerful characterisations of Harry Houghton (Bernard Lee) and Elizabeth Gee (Margaret Tyzack) he created a disturbing and critical portrait of the forces trapped inside conventional British society, forces unleashed by drink, sexual passion and frustration into reckless material greed.

Mindful perhaps of a forthcoming exchange of spies between Lonsdale and a British spy, Greville Wynne, jailed in Russia, the Commissioner of Police pressurised British exhibitors into curtailing the film's release. Had *Ring of Spies* been more widely seen, Tronson's cinema career might have advanced further. In the event it only proceeded to a Guinness promotion film, a safety film for steel workers and *Antekdhikissi/An Act of Reprisal*, a 1964 feature made in Greece featuring Jeremy Brett. Thereafter, for forty years, Tronson returned to the embrace and anonymity of television.

(Geoff Brown)

BIBLIOGRAPHY: Durgnat, Raymond, '*Ring of Spies*', *Films and Filming*, May 1964, p. 23; Murphy, Robert, *Sixties British Cinema* (London: BFI, 1992); Shaw, Tony, *British Cinema and the Cold War* (London: I. B. Tauris, 2001).

FILMOGRAPHY: *Man at the Carlton Tower*; *Man Detained*; *Never Back Losers* (1961); *Number Six*; *The Traitors* (1962); *On the Run*; *Farewell Performance*; *Ring of Spies* (US: *Ring of Treason*) (1963); *All in Good Time* (doc.); *Antekdhikissi/An Act of Reprisal* (Gr) (1964); *Against the Tide* (doc., 1965).

TRUFFAUT, François (1932–1984)

François Truffaut's film career was ended prematurely by his death at the age of fifty-two, yet by then he had been consecrated as one of the greatest directors in French cinema. He was born in Paris, on 6 February 1932. After an unhappy childhood he left school at fourteen; gravitating towards cinema, he was taken under the wing of film theorist André Bazin, who employed him as a contributor to the innovatory film journal *Cahiers du cinéma*. Truffaut's first feature film, *Les Quatre Cents Coups* (1959), was the first big success of the French New Wave; *Jules et Jim* (1962) sealed his international fame, gaining the Best Film Award from the British Film Academy.

Truffaut's opinion of British cinema was notoriously dismissive, and his only foray into Anglo-Saxon territory was *Fahrenheit 451*. Based on the novel by Ray Bradbury, the film was a dystopian fantasy set in the future, depicting a totalitarion world where all literature has been banned. A redemptive tale of individuals fighting against the system, *Fahrenheit 451* was conspicuous for its stylised aesthetics and spectral use of colour; it received mixed reviews, despite a fine performance by Oskar Werner, and the presence of British icon Julie Christie in both the leading female roles. The film's eccentric charms, particularly the final sequences with 'the book people' in the snowy woods, have prompted favourable reassessments.

Truffaut's last film was *Vivement Dimanche!* (1983); he died of a brain tumour in Neuilly, France, on 21 October 1984.
(Elisabetta Girelli)

BIBLIOGRAPHY: Nicholls, David, *François Truffaut* (London: Batsford, 1993); Truffaut, François, *Truffaut by Truffaut* (New York: Harry N. Abrams, 1987); Truffaut, François, *La Nuit Américaine: scénario, suivi du journal du tournage de Fahrenheit 451* (Paris: *Cahiers du cinéma*, 2000).

FILMOGRAPHY: *Fahrenheit 451* (1966).

TRUMAN, Michael (1916–1972)

Michael Claude Derek Truman was born on 25 February 1916 in Bristol and worked as an assistant editor at various studios – Stoll, Sound City, Worton Hall and Denham – throughout the 1930s. When war broke out in 1939, he became a production supervisor on army training films until 1944, when he joined Ealing Studios and established a solid reputation as the editor of *It Always Rains on Sunday* (Robert Hamer, 1947), *Saraband for Dead Lovers* (Basil Dearden, 1948) and *Passport to Pimlico* (Henry Cornelius, 1949). In 1951 he moved up to become producer on *The Lavender Hill Mob* (1951) and continued to work with its director Charles Crichton on *The Titfield Thunderbolt* (1953) and *The Divided Heart* (1954).

In 1955 he was finally given the chance to direct. *Touch and Go* concerns a middle-aged furniture designer (Jack Hawkins) who tries unsuccessfully to persuade his boss to introduce more modern designs. Infuriated by what he sees as timid inertia, he decides to emigrate to Australia, but his daughter is reluctant to abandon her boyfriend and the problem of rehousing the family cat becomes a major issue. Eventually, he is offered his job back on better terms and the family stay put. Technicolor failed to enliven a conventional story with few surprises, as well as giving the usually intractable Hawkins an uncharacteristically vacillating role. However, Margaret Johnston who played Hawkins' wife, Helen, remembered Truman as a talented and subtle director who would 'just drop a word or two if he felt certain things should be different' (McFarlane, p. 335).

In common with several of his Ealing colleagues, Truman moved into television, working on two of the most popular series of the time, *Danger Man* and *The Saint*. He returned to the big screen in 1962 with *Go to Blazes*, a refreshingly lively comedy in which a trio of thieves disguise themselves as firemen in order to rob a bank. Its eclectic trio of robbers – Daniel Massey, Norman Rossington and Dave King – gives the film an unusual edge and Truman shows himself entirely free of late Ealing whimsy. Truman's subsequent films, the murder mystery *Girl in the Headlines* (1963) and the thriller *Daylight Robbery* (1964), were more routine, and he spent the remainder of his career in television, directing *Danger Man* between 1964 and 1966. He died on 11 July 1972 in Newbury, Berkshire.
(Margaret Butler)

BIBLIOGRAPHY: Barr, Charles, *Ealing Studios* (London: Studio Vista, 1993); McFarlane, Brian, *An Autobiography of British Cinema* (London: Methuen, 1997).

FILMOGRAPHY: *Touch and Go* (US: *The Light Touch*, 1955); *Go to Blazes* (1962); *Girl in the Headlines* (1963); *Daylight Robbery* (1964).

TUCHNER, Michael (1934–)

Michael Tuchner was born in Berlin on 24 June 1934 but brought up in England. After leaving University College, London, he joined the BBC as an editor and began his career as a director on the BBC magazine programme *Tonight*. He moved on to direct television plays such as Roy Minton's *Sling Your Hook* in 1969, and made his feature debut in 1971 with *Villain*, a brutal crime drama set in London's East End. Scripted by television comedy writers Dick Clement and Ian La Frenais, the film stars Richard Burton as Vic Dakin, a sadistic, homosexual gangster clearly based upon the recently jailed East End gang boss Ronnie Kray. *Villain* did well at the UK box office and Tuchner reunited with the film's producers Alan Ladd Jr and Jay Kanter for the revenge thriller *Fear Is the Key*, an efficient Alistair MacLean adaptation with well-directed action sequences and conscientious performances by Barry Newman, Ben Kingsley and Suzy Kendall.

Tuchner turned to family entertainment with *Mister Quilp*, a musical version of Charles Dickens' *The Old Curiosity Shop* financed by *Reader's Digest*, and *The Likely Lads*, a relatively successful spin-off from Clement and La Frenais' television sitcom. It was a television play, however – Jack Rosenthal's *Bar Mitzvah Boy* (1976) – that attracted American attention and led to the similarly Jewish-themed television film *Summer of My German Soldier* (1977). Other 'movies of the week' followed and a feature film, *Trenchcoat*, starring Margot Kidder. He returned to Britain to make *Wilt*, a big-screen adaptation of Tom Sharpe's comic novel starring Mel Smith and Griff Rhys Jones, and went to New Zealand to make *The Rainbow Warrior*, but Tuchner's main career is as an American television film director.
(Daniel O'Brien)

BIBLIOGRAPHY: Falk, Quentin, '"Go Anywhere" Tuchner Finishes his First Feature for Five Years', *Screen International* no. 15, May 1982, p. 62; Williams, John, 'Michael Tuchner, Likely Lad', *Films Illustrated*, Jan. 1976, p. 183.

FILMOGRAPHY: *Music* (doc., 1969); *Villain* (1971); *Fear Is the Key* (1972); *Mister Quilp* (1975); *The Likely Lads* (1976); *Trenchcoat* (US, 1983); *Wilt* (1989); *The Rainbow Warrior* (NZ/US, 1992).

TUCKER, Anand (1963–)

Anand Tucker was born in Bangkok in 1963 and brought up in Hong Kong. He studied film at the Harrow campus of the University of Westminster and gained a place on the BBC's Production Trainee Scheme in 1990. After making several arts and music items for BBC 2's *The Late Show* he left to join Andy Paterson and Nicholas Kent's Oxford Films and Television Company, where he made the BAFTA-winning documentary *A Vampire's Life* (1993), about the novelist Anne Rice, and his first feature film, *Saint-Ex* (1996), an imaginative biography of the novelist and aviator Antoine de Saint-Exupéry. The film was allowed a brief window at the London Film Festival but the BBC, which had put up much of the money, insisted on screening it on Christmas Day 1996, curtailing any further cinema exposure. However, the good working relationship established with Paterson as producer and Frank Cottrell Boyce as writer continued on *Hilary and Jackie* (1998), a biography of the cellist Jacqueline du Pré, who had been struck down by multiple sclerosis in the midst of a dazzling career in the 1960s. Telling the story in two overlapping versions from the different perspectives of Jackie and her older sister Hilary has its disadvantages, but it pays off with the startlingly powerful performances of Emily Watson and Rachel Griffiths (both were nominated for Academy Awards) and an emotional intensity that enabled the film to reach a wider audience than du Pré aficionados.

The film's success encouraged Tucker, Paterson and Cottrell Boyce to set up their own production company, Archer Street Ltd, which after some tribulation over rights, financial backing, stars and directors produced a handsome, well-received adaptation of Tracy Chevalier's novel *Girl with a Pearl Earring* (Peter Webber, 2003). Tucker returned to directing with *Shopgirl* (2006), starring Steve Martin in an adaptation of his own short novel about a salesgirl and her rich but older admirer.

(Robert Murphy)

BIBLIOGRAPHY: Bruzzi, Stella, 'Butterfly on the Wall', *Sight and Sound*, Jan. 1999, pp. 32–4; 'Emily Watson – Conversation with Hilary du Pré', *Interview*, Jan. 1999, pp. 52–7; Macnab, Geoffrey, 'Tucker Gives Thanks to Dog Day Afternoons', *Screen International*, 21 Oct. 2005, p. 11.

FILMOGRAPHY: *Saint-Ex* (1996); *Hilary and Jackie* (1998); *Shopgirl* (US, 2006).

TUCKER, George Loane (1872–1921)

A dynamic director who also produced, wrote and occasionally acted in his films, George Loane Tucker was born in Chicago on 12 June 1872. He worked as a railway clerk before taking up acting in the theatre; then in 1911 he began directing short films for the Independent Moving Picture Company (Imp). He is best known for his first feature, *Traffic in Souls* (1913), a frequently powerful white slavery drama with vividly used New York locations, and one of the first American films of extended length. Lurid advertising, some public controversy and the film's own strengths helped it become a popular success, spawning several imitations.

Before its release Tucker left America for the UK, where he worked from 1913 to 1917 and became the leading creative light of the London Film Company, newly founded by R. T. Jupp, who ran the largest of the British exhibition circuits, Provincial Cinematograph Theatres. Jupp knew the popularity of American films and deliberately sought American influence, hiring Tucker and another American, Harold Shaw, to run his company. Players and scenario writers were also imported: one of Imp's leading ladies, Jane Gail, the plucky heroine of *Traffic in Souls*, played in twelve Tucker productions between 1914 and 1915. The London Film Company regularly turned to works of literature and stage performers to bring life and legitimacy to their films, and was able to provide sizeable budgets for Tucker's adaptations of Anthony Hope's *The Prisoner of Zenda* and *Rupert of Hentzau* (both 1915). He followed their success with two ambitious films adapted from novels by the popular author Hall Caine, *The Christian* in 1915 and *The Manxman* the next year (filmed again by Hitchcock in 1929). Tucker's version, which cost upwards of £20,000 and was made on location on Caine's home territory, the Isle of Man, was widely praised for its care and subtlety; reviewing the American release, *Variety* considered it 'as nearly perfect a photodrama as it is possible to conceive' (13 April 1917).

Despite the success of individual films, the fortunes of the London Film Company now began to turn. There were problems with finance and also personnel: Harold Shaw left early in 1916, and by the end of the year Tucker had gone to the USA on what was advertised as a business trip; he never returned. He resumed his American career, working initially for Samuel Goldwyn; the crime drama *The Miracle Man* (1919) became a major popular success, but illness and an early death cut short any further development. The London Film Company briefly resumed production after the First World War, though without the old flair.

At the time Tucker was highly regarded by the industry press in Britain, and his respect for the traditions of British theatre and literature meant he was equally well liked by actors and authors. Unfortunately, of his British films only an incomplete print of *The Revenge of Mr Thomas Atkins*, a minor propaganda comedy, survives; and his fame, such as it is, rests upon *Traffic in Souls*, his one surviving American film of importance. Tucker died in Los Angeles on 20 June 1921. He was married to the actress Elizabeth Risdon, his heroine in *The Manxman* and other London Film Company productions.

(Simon Brown)

BIBLIOGRAPHY: Green, R. Judd, 'George Loane Tucker: Author – Actor – Producer', *Pictures and Picturegoer*, 8 July 1916, p. 284; Low, Rachael, *The History of the British Film 1914–1918* (London: George Allen & Unwin, 1950); Low, Rachael, *The History of the British Film 1906–1914* (London: George Allen & Unwin, 1973); Thompson, Frank, 'George Loane Tucker: The First of the Immortals', *Film Comment*, Jan./Feb. 1996, pp. 42–5.

FILMOGRAPHY (UK only): *The Third String* (short); *She Stoops to Conquer*; *The Black Spot* (short); *The Cage* (short); *A Bachelor's Love Story* (short); *The Difficult Way*; *England Expects*; *On His Majesty's Service* (US: *0–18; or, A Message from the Sky*); *Called Back*; *The Fringe of War*; *The Revenge of Mr Thomas Atkins* (1914); *1914*; *The Middleman*; *The Prisoner of Zenda*; *Rupert of Hentzau*; *Sons of Satan*; *The Shulamite*; *Jelfs*; *The Christian*; *His Lordship* (short); *Her Uncle* (short) (1915); *Mixed Relations* (short); *An Odd Freak* (short); *The Game of Liberty* (US: *Under Suspicion*); *The Morals of Weybury*; *Arsene Lupin*; *The Man Without a Soul* (US: *I Believe*); *The Mother of Dartmoor*; *A Mother's Influence*; *The Manxman* (1916).

TUCKER, Joe

Joe Tucker was born in Leicester, and trained as an actor at the Webber Douglas Academy of Dramatic Art in London. He made brief appearances in Angela Pope's *Captives* (1994), Carine Adler's *Under the Skin* (1997) and Mike Leigh's *Career Girls* (1997), along with numerous television performances. In 1993 a pub incident sparked Tucker and his brother Paul into imagining how they would react if one of them was attacked and left brain-damaged by a bullying hard man. Both came up with the idea of enlisting the help of a contract killer who turns out to be a blusterer with no violent credentials. Paul's story became *The Last Yellow*, initially a play, subsequently a screenplay filmed by Julian Farino in July 1998. Joe persevered with his own version, shooting *Lava* on a £1 million budget a year later.

Critics derided *The Last Yellow*'s uncertainty of tone and stagy air, encouraging Tucker to seek a more stylised look and avoid the problem of getting his unlikely avengers from Leicester to London by setting *Lava* entirely in Notting Hill. Unfortunately his characters are pathetically one-dimensional (including a gang of crudely stereotyped black drug-dealers introduced to up the body count and allow cutaways to Carnival-enriched street life), and with murder played for laughs there is little dramatic tension. Rejected for the London Film Festival in 2000, the film finally reached British screens in 2002, attracting indulgent reviews but tiny audiences. Tucker, whose own performance as a character viewing the world through a thick haze of military fantasy almost transcends the film's limitations, then returned to acting, notably in Mike Leigh's *All or Nothing* (2002).

(Robert Murphy)

BIBLIOGRAPHY: Falk, Quentin, 'Go with the Flow', *Exposure*, Spring 2000, pp. 30–1; Gilbey, Ryan, 'Revenge: A Dish Best Served Funny', *Independent* Review Section, 25 Jan. 2002, p. 12.

FILMOGRAPHY: *Lava* (2002).

TULLY, Montgomery (1904–1988)

Born Geoffrey Wycombe Montgomery-Tully in Dublin on 6 May 1904, Montgomery Tully was one of several directors who lent some distinction to the British B-feature, handling formulaic material effectively throughout his career. He was a writer before entering the film industry as a documentary director, and went on to write several screenplays and direct three features for British National. The best, *Murder in Reverse* (1945), is a powerful, astringent crime-thriller; *Spring Song* (1946), a musical, and *Mrs Fitzherbert* (1947), a costume romance, seemed less fitted to his talents. Tully moved on to Gainsborough, where he scripted and directed *Boys in Brown* (1949), a flawed but interesting depiction of Borstal life, based on Reginald Beckwith's play.

In the 1950s Tully worked for various second-feature production companies, most often Merton Park, where he directed a succession of low-budget crime-thrillers designed for the American market. *Thirty-Six Hours* (1954), with Dan Duryea as the falsely accused hero, *Dial 999* (1955) and *Man in the Shadow* (1957) were tense and exciting, and *No Road Back* (1957) had some depth of characterisation. *Escapement* (1958), a cold war fantasy-thriller about brainwashing, also retains its interest, as does the sub-gothic *The House in Marsh Road* (1960). Tully also directed several half-hour episodes for the *Scotland Yard* series, most notably *Wall of Death* (1956); hour-long Edgar Wallace supporting features, including *The Man Who Was Nobody* (1960); and episodes for the television series *Man from Interpol* (1960). After the demise of the low-budget crime thriller, Tully turned to science fiction, but *The Terrornauts* and *Battle Beneath the Earth* had little of the solid distinction of Tully's best crime films. He died in London on 10 October 1988.

(Andrew Spicer)

BIBLIOGRAPHY: 'British Feature Directors: An Index to Their Work', *Sight and Sound*, Autumn 1958, p. 303; Dixon, Wheeler Winston, 'The Doubled Image: Montgomery Tully's *Boys in Brown* and the Independent Frame Process', in Wheeler Winston Dixon (ed.), *Re-viewing British Cinema 1900–1992*, (Albany: SUNY Press, 1994); Dixon, Wheeler Winston, 'The Marginalized Vision of Montgomery Tully', *Classic Images* no. 224, Feb. 1994, pp. c8–10, c12, 56–7; 225; Mar. 1994, pp. 6, 52–6.

FILMOGRAPHY: *From Acorn to Oak* (doc. short, 1938); *Behind the Guns* (doc. short); *Salute to the Farmers* (doc. short) (1940); *Murder in Reverse* (1945); *Each for All* (doc. short); *Spring Song* (US: *Springtime*) (1946); *Mrs Fitzherbert* (1947); *Boys in Brown* (1949); *A Tale of Five Cities/Passaporto per l'oriente* (US: *A Tale of Five Women*, co-dirs. Romolo Marcellini/Emil E. Reinert/Wolfgang Staudte/Géza von Cziffra, UK/It, 1951); *Girdle of Gold* (1952); *Small Town Story* (1953); *The Diamond* (US: *Diamond Wizard*); *Five Days* (US: *Paid to Kill*); *Thirty-Six Hours* (US: *Terror Street*); *Devil's Point* (US: *Devil's Harbor*); *Late Night Final* (short); *The Silent Witness* (short) (1954); *The Glass Cage*; *Dial 999* (US: *The Way Out*) (1955); *Wall of Death* (short); *The Case of the Rue Morgue* (short); *Destination Death* (short) (1956); *The Lonely House* (short); *Inside Information* (short); *The Case of the Smiling Widow* (short); *The White Cliffs Mystery* (short); *Night Crossing* (short); *The Counterfeit Plan*; *The Hypnotist* (US: *Scotland Yard Dragnet*); *The Key Man*; *Man in the Shadow*; *No Road Back*; *Print of Death* (short) (1957); *Crime of Honour* (short); *The Crossroad Gallows* (short); *Escapement* (US: *The Electronic Monster*); *The Strange Awakening*

(US: *Female Fiends*); *The Long Knife*; *Man with a Gun*; *The Diplomatic Corpse*; *I Only Arsked!* (1958); *Man Accused* (1959); *Jackpot*; *The Price of Silence*; *Dead Lucky*; *The House in Marsh Road*; *The Man Who Was Nobody* (1960); *The Middle Course*; *Two Wives at One Wedding*; *The Third Alibi* (1961); *She Knows Y'Know*; *Out of the Fog* (1962); *Clash by Night* (US: *Escape by Night*, 1963); *Master Spy*; *Boy with a Flute* (short) (1964); *Who Killed the Cat?* (1966); *The Terrornauts* (1967; rel. 1971); *Battle Beneath the Earth* (1967).

TURNER, Paul (1945–)

Born in Cornwall in 1945, Paul Turner has spent most of his life in Wales. After working as a film editor at BBC Wales, in 1981 he directed *Trisgel*, a short film based on a Welsh legend, and went on to make several dramas for the Welsh-language television channel S4C, notably *Wil Six* (1984), which amusingly evoked a Welsh rural childhood, and *Tra Bo Dwy/There's Always Two* (1986), a powerful study of a lesbian relationship.

Turner's impressive feature film *Hedd Wyn* (1992), made for S4C, uses extended flashback and stream of consciousness to tell the story of Ellis Evans – posthumous winner of the Welsh Eisteddfod poetry chair, killed on the First World War battlefield near Passchendaele in 1917. The elegiac film presents the farmer-poet's equivocal views of the war, and gained much from a fine script by poet Alun Llwyd. Despite an Academy Award nomination in 1994 for Best Foreign Language Film, the Royal Television Society Best Drama award and six BAFTA Cymru (Wales) prizes, *Hedd Wyn* still failed to find a British distributor.

Turner's next film, *Cwm Hyfryd/Beautiful Valley* (1993), made for S4C and not given a theatrical release, is a slice of contemporary industrial life centred on the increasingly fragile relationship between an unemployed South Wales miner and his common-law wife. He went on to direct the thriller *Dial/Wild Justice* (1994) and several imaginative dramas for SC4 such as *Terfysgwyr Tryweryn/Terrorists of Tryweryn* (2003).

(David Berry)

BIBLIOGRAPHY: Berry David, *Wales and Cinema: The First Hundred Years* (Cardiff: University of Wales Press, 1994); Macnab, Geoffrey, 'Hedd Wyn', *Sight and Sound*, July 1994, p. 43.

FILMOGRAPHY: *Trisgel* (short, 1981); *Hedd Wyn* (1992); *Dial/Wild Justice* (aka *Covert Assassin*, 1994).

TWIST, Derek (1905–1979)

According to his autobiography *A Life in Movies*, Michael Powell had no doubt who he wanted to edit his film *The Edge of the World* (1937): 'We need an editor with the eye of a hawk, the memory of an Indian, and a heart of granite. I want Derek Twist.' Derek Norman Twist, born in London on 26 May 1905, had been on the editing staff of Gaumont-British since 1931, and had edited several earlier Powell films, as well as *The 39 Steps* (Alfred Hitchcock, 1935).

From the late 1930s Twist's experience widened. He wrote scripts for Warner Bros. at Teddington. In the war he served as Commanding Officer of the newly formed RAF Film Production Unit, and in 1944 took charge of a detachment sent to document the Allies' invasion of Europe; footage surfaced in Twist's own *The Air Plan* (1945) and *The True Glory* (Carol Reed/Garson Kanin, 1945).

Demobbed in 1947, Twist needed challenges beyond the editing bench. He certainly found one with his feature debut, *The End of the River*, a dramatically awkward drama about the ebb and flow of an Amazon Indian's life, featuring Sabu, made under Powell and Pressburger's aegis. Though over half the footage was shot on location, the visual benefits proved limited; but the film still remains significant for its exotic and unusual ambition, not the norm in the late 1940s. In subsequent films Twist shrank back to the parochial, with modestly agreeable results. *All Over the Town*, with Norman Wooland, spun light-hearted fun from local politics and corruption, and the need for new post-war housing. The brandy-smuggling comedy *Green Grow the Rushes*, the first feature co-operatively produced by the film-makers' union ACT, threatened to dilute Ealing formulae to the point of undrinkability, but eased digestion with lively character actors and the Kent marshland setting. Richard Burton's role as the smuggler Hammond was his last before Hollywood called.

In 1951 Twist formed Templar Productions with the producer John W. Gossage. The immediate result was the enormously popular RAF drama *Angels One Five* (George More O'Ferrall, 1952); Twist co-produced and wrote the script. This proved his finest hour in feature film-making. Two modest dramas apart, he then concentrated on television, directing episodes of *Douglas Fairbanks Presents . . .* and producing for Granada. His last film credit was in 1967 as production manager on the children's film *Calamity the Cow*. Twist was married to the actress Vida Hope, and died on 15 August 1979 in Chelmsford.

(Geoff Brown)

BIBLIOGRAPHY: Powell, Michael, *A Life in Movies* (London: William Heinemann, 1986).

FILMOGRAPHY: *The Air Plan* (doc., 1945); *The End of the River* (1947); *All Over the Town* (1949); *Green Grow the Rushes* (1951); *Police Dog* (1955); *Family Doctor* (US: *RX Murder*, 1958).

URBAN, Charles (1867–1942)

Charles Urban was not a film director, but as the most important producer of films in Britain in the pre-1914 period he wielded considerable influence on the overall direction of early British film. He was born on 15 April 1867 in Cincinnati of German immigrant parents, and set up a Kinetoscope parlour in Chicago in 1895. The Bioscope projector was developed for him, and with this notable asset he was taken on by Edison conces-

sionaries Maguire & Baucus, who in 1897 sent him to London to be their British manager. The dynamic Urban had an immediate effect on the company's business and British film in general. He renamed the company the Warwick Trading Company, and built up a considerable reputation based upon actuality film (notably of the Anglo-Boer war), high-quality equipment and the distribution of films by Lumière, Méliès, Williamson, the Sheffield Photo Company, G. A. Smith and others.

He formed the Charles Urban Trading Company in 1903 and there developed his personal vision of cinema, based upon actuality, travel, science and natural history. He cultivated scientific film-makers with a populist streak, notably F. Martin Duncan and Percy Smith, and significantly extended the educational use of film. He also produced fiction films of generally meagre quality, many through his French offshoot Eclipse. Urban's greatest triumphs came with the two-colour (red-green) Kinemacolor system, the world's first natural colour film system, invented by G. A. Smith in 1906. Kinemacolor was a worldwide sensation between 1908 and 1914, the highlight being the two-hour epic *With Our King and Queen Through India*, which depicted the 1912 Delhi durbar.

Urban's fortunes turned in 1914, starting with a court case brought by William Friese-Greene (inventor of a rival colour film system), which led to the invalidation of the Kinemacolor patent. Urban produced a wartime documentary feature, *Britain Prepared* (1915), but he had mixed fortunes trying to sell the film, and other British official war films, while in America in 1916. Urban's impulsive approach was ill-suited to the subtleties needed for political propaganda, but he enjoyed greater success once America had entered the war.

After the war, Urban chose to stay in America, where he hoped to revitalise his business through the combination of a new colour system (Kinekrom), a process for showing films on a disk (the Spirograph), and the exploitation of his film library for the burgeoning educational film market. His plans were wildly overambitious, and his business collapsed dramatically in 1925. He returned to Britain, and spent his last years in London and Brighton, where he died on 29 August 1942.

Urban brought American glamour to the early British film industry. Although sometimes an overbearing figure, he was equally an inspirational one, whose belief in the ability of film to educate while it entertained, and always to be reaching for higher things, thrilled many with the possibilities of the medium in cinema's most impressionable years.

(Luke McKernan)

BIBLIOGRAPHY: McKernan, Luke (ed.), *A Yank in Britain: The Lost Memoirs of Charles Urban, Film Pioneer* (Hastings, E. Sussex: The Projection Box, 1999); McKernan, Luke, 'Putting the World before You: The Charles Urban Story', in Andrew Higson (ed.), *Young and Innocent? The Cinema in Britain, 1896–1930* (Exeter: University of Exeter Press, 2002).

URBAN, Stuart (1958–)

Stuart Urban was born on 11 September 1958 in Newport, Isle of Wight. His half-hour 16mm film *The Virus of War*, made with a cast and crew of children when he was thirteen, was shown at Cannes. After studying history at Oxford, Urban went into television and by the late 1980s was directing episodes of the drama series *Bergerac* and *Gentlemen and Players*. In 1993 *An Ungentlemanly Act*, an untidy, authentic, and affectionately patriotic account of the Argentinian invasion of the Falkland Islands, made for the BBC, won the BAFTA Award for Best Single Drama. Urban went on to direct two episodes of *Our Friends in the North*, Peter Flannery's epic drama dealing with the hopes and dreams of a group of bright working-class young people from the 1960s to the 90s, and write the screenplay for John Mackenzie's *Deadly Voyage* (1996), an HBO/BBC co-production based on the true story of a group of African asylum-seekers meeting a grisly fate at the hands of people smugglers.

Urban's feature debut, *Preaching to the Perverted* (1997), was an improbable comedy about a pornography-obsessed MP who details his handsome young researcher to expose the activities of an American dominatrix. Guinevere Turner's Mistress Tanya is as prim and squeaky-clean as a Barbie doll, and the plot plods with grinding predictability, but insights into the world of bondage and sado-masochism and the accumulating spirit of cosy tolerance make the film ultimately enjoyable. Following *Against the War*, a documentary expressing objections to the NATO bombing of Serbia, Urban returned to features with an ambitious venture into the religious conspiracy/mystical quest genre. The premise of *Revelation* – a Templar plot to reconstitute Christ from the DNA of his blood preserved on the nails hammered into him on the cross – is outlandish enough to be interesting, but Urban mires the plot with a wooden cast (headed by mad-eyed Udo Kier and an embarrassingly kittenish Natasha Wightman), implausible action and reams of expository dialogue. It will be interesting to see where his career goes from here.

(Robert Murphy)

BIBLIOGRAPHY: Jones, Alan, 'Stuart Urban's Revelation: A Shivers Interview', *Shivers* no. 87, Feb. 2001, pp. 22–5; Jones, Alan, '*Revelation*', *Cinefantastique* vol. 34 no. 1, Feb. 2002, pp. 48–9; Salisbury, Mark, 'Oh Christ! It's *Revelation*', *Fangoria* no. 221, Apr. 2003, pp. 48–51; Urban, Stuart, 'History as Farce' (letter), *Sight and Sound*, Sept. 1992, p. 71.

FILMOGRAPHY: *The Virus of War* (short, 1972); *Preaching to the Perverted* (1997); *Against the War* (doc., 1999); *Revelation* (2002).

USTINOV, Sir Peter (1921–2004)

Peter Alexander Ustinov, of mainly Russian descent, was born in London on 16 April 1921. During a cosmopolitan and eclectic career he directed eight disparate feature films, besides being famous for his flamboyant acting style, his humanist commitments, his plays and other writings, and skill as a raconteur. By 1940 he was acting in films; three years later he began screenwriting, collaborating on the training short *The New Lot* and its feature expansion, *The Way Ahead* (Carol Reed, 1944). In 1946 he made an auspicious directing debut at Two Cities with *School for Secrets* (1946), skilfully juggling drama and comedy, humanising the remote subject of wartime boffins and their struggle to develop radar. His nose for unusual material was also displayed in the mildly satirical *Vice Versa* (1948), quirky and awkward in about equal measure, based on F. Anstey's Victorian comic novel; and the quietly appealing *Private Angelo* (1949), featuring Ustinov as a reluctant Italian soldier.

He returned to cinema in the 1960s, most forcefully with the Anglo-Allied adaptation of Herman Melville's *Billy Budd*. This period drama, set in the late 18th century, tells the tragic story of a young seaman tormented by his master-at-arms. In a rage, the seaman finally strikes back with fatal results, and the captain, played in an unusually subdued manner by Ustinov himself, is reluctantly forced to carry out the strong arm of navy law. The film, shot by Robert Krasker, features powerful performances from Robert Ryan as the bully and particularly from Terence Stamp as the seaman. *Billy Budd* raises many issues about questions of loyalty, humanism and morality, and remains one of the few great costume dramas of the 1960s. Aside from the muddle of *Memed My Hawk*, comedy dominated Ustinov's other films; the most rewarding and coherent is *Romanoff and Juliet* (1961), an American version of his stage satire about the cold war. Peter Ustinov died at his home in Switzerland on 29 March 2004.

(Erik Hedling)

BIBLIOGRAPHY: Durgnat, Raymond, *A Mirror for England* (London: Faber and Faber, 1970); Friel, J. C., 'Ustinov's Film *Billy Budd*, a Study in the Process of Adaptation', *Literature/Film Quarterly*, Summer 1976, pp. 271–85; Ustinov, Peter, *Dear Me* (Boston, MA: Little, Brown, 1977).

FILMOGRAPHY: *School for Secrets* (US: *Secret Flight*, 1946); *Vice Versa* (1948); *Private Angelo* (co-dir. Michael Anderson, 1949); *Romanoff and Juliet* (US, 1961); *Billy Budd* (1962); *Lady L* (1965); *Hammersmith Is Out* (US, 1972); *Memed My Hawk* (1984).

VAJDA, Ladislao (1906–1965)

Ladislao Vajda (sometimes László or Ladislas Vajda) was born Liszlo Vajda in Budapest on 18 August 1906, the son of screenwriter Ladislaus Vajda. He entered Hungarian cinema as a teenager, working as a cutter, a cameraman and eventually directing throughout Europe. In England, he co-directed *Where Is This Lady?*, an English version of *Es war einmal ein Walzer* (Viktor Janson, 1932), the Franz Lehár musical he had edited in Germany. He returned to Britain in 1936 to direct *Wings over Africa* and *The Wife of General Ling*, both written by the Hungarian screenwriter Akos Tolnay. He continued to direct mainstream comedies and dramas in Hungary and Italy before settling in Spain for *Doce lunas de mile* (1943), *El testamento del virrey* (1944) and a string of others.

After the Second World War, he worked on two British films set in Italy, sharing direction with John Clements on *Call of the Blood* and directing *The Golden Madonna*, Phyllis Calvert's attempt to escape the increasingly formulaic roles she was asked to play by the Rank Organisation. His final British film, *The Woman with No Name*, starred Calvert as an amnesiac who begins a new married life with a Norwegian fighter pilot (Richard Burton) only to discover that she already has a husband, from whom she has run away. It is deftly and ambitiously directed, with atmospheric thunderstorm and nightmare sequences, but is weakened by Allan Gray's maladroit score. Thereafter, Vajda worked in Spain (where he became a citizen in 1954), with excursions to Germany, Switzerland and France, directing films including *Un ángel pasó por Brooklyn* (1957), *María, matrícula de Bilbao* (1960) and *Der Lügner* (1961). He died in Barcelona after a heart attack on 25 March 1965, while shooting *La dama de Beirut* (1965).

(Kevin Gough-Yates)

BIBLIOGRAPHY: 'Das Porträt: Ladislao Vajda', *Filmwoche*, 11 Nov. 1961, p. 11.

FILMOGRAPHY (UK only): *Where Is This Lady?* (co-dir. Victor Hanbury, 1932); *Wings over Africa* (1936); *The Wife of General Ling*

(1937); *Call of the Blood* (co-dir. John Clements, 1948); *The Golden Madonna* (1948); *The Woman with No Name* (US: *Her Panelled Door*, 1950).

VARNEL, Marcel (1892–1947)

Marcel Varnel, born Marcel Hyacinth le Bozec in Paris on 16 October 1892, came to England with experience and gifts that set him apart from most British film directors at work in comedy in the 1930s and 40s. Educated at the Collège Chaptal, Paris, and Charterhouse public school in England, he began in the business as a juvenile actor and graduated to direction in 1920, specialising in operettas and musical comedies. Five years later he moved to America and the Shubert brothers' stage productions; light entertainment again predominated, with occasional excursions elsewhere, including Pirandello's *As You Desire Me*. In 1931 he signed a Hollywood contract with Fox. Devotees of bad fantasy-adventures may be grateful for *Chandu the Magician* (1932), co-directed with William Cameron Menzies, but Varnel found pleasure in neither his assignments nor the Fox factory environment, and after four minor films he relocated to London.

By February 1934 he was at work at British International Pictures, Elstree, shooting a lively comedy-adventure, *Freedom of the Seas*. Comedy dominated Varnel's British output from the beginning, and once he joined Gainsborough in 1936 the studio's chief roster of comic stars all came his way: Will Hay, the Crazy Gang and later Arthur Askey. Their background lay in variety and radio; script material leaned heavily on cross-talk routines, topical references and puns. Varnel conquered the obvious obstacles by giving even the wildest slapstick sequences an organic shape, using a free-ranging directing technique far removed from the rigid alternation of long shots and mid-shots that imprisoned many British directors. His first Hay vehicle was *Good Morning, Boys!* (1937); seven others followed, none better than *Oh, Mr Porter!* (1937) in the balance struck between narrative momentum, comic routines and the interplay between Hay's sniffing incompetents and the capering stooges of Moore Marriott's decrepit old-timers and lazy youth Graham Moffat. A fast worker on the set, Varnel maintained plenty of speed inside the films, supplementing formal scripting with improvisation to catch the spontaneity of stage routines. Memorable set-pieces included Hay's class of schoolboys running amok in a Paris nightclub in *Good Morning, Boys!* and the trio's attempt to manoeuvre a firemen's pole in *Where's That Fire?*. The Crazy Gang – hydra-headed, more anarchic – proved less amenable to film treatment, though in his four films with the team Varnel still had his victories, especially in the Gold Rush fantasy *The Frozen Limits* (1939), famously greeted by Graham Greene as a film to rival Keaton and Lloyd, and 'the funniest English picture yet produced'.

In the summer and autumn of 1939 Varnel turned his attention to George Formby (*Let George Do It!*, the first of nine vehicles) and Arthur Askey (*Band Waggon*, the first of three). At first the war made little difference: the stars' demotic appeal proved a special asset in wartime, and the lampooning of authority figures, a comedy staple, was easily turned into home-front propaganda. Earlier films had parodied teachers, the police, even (in *Oh, Mr Porter!*) the IRA. Now Nazis became the butt of the jokes. Formby personally thumped the Führer in a dream sequence in Ealing's *Let George Do It!* before waking to unmask spies in Norway; in *The Ghost of St Michael's* German infiltrators reached Hay's schoolboys, evacuated to a remote Scottish castle. Later Formby vehicles like *Bell-Bottom George* and *George in Civvy Street*, made for Columbia-British with less experienced collaborators, buckled under the strain of keeping the comedy fresh, and Varnel began to find greater success in the theatre. He staged a series of American comedies in the West End for the producer Firth Shephard; *Arsenic and Old Lace* (1943) ran for over three years. Away from Formby, he directed the film version of a benign stage comedy, *This Man Is Mine*, and was set to produce another theatre adaptation, the whimsical historical drama *The First Gentleman* (Alberto Cavalcanti, 1948), when he was killed after losing control of his car near Rake, Sussex, on 13 July 1947. Colleagues suspected he had been panicked by a wasp or fly; Varnel suffered a severe insect phobia. The loss of his expertise in popular comedy was keenly felt in the British industry; paradoxically, in his native France, where none of his films were distributed, he remains an unknown figure. His son Max Varnel (1925–1996) followed him into the film business and directed numerous B-thrillers in the 1950s and 60s.

(Geoff Brown and Leo Enticknap)

BIBLIOGRAPHY: Obituary, *Cine-Technician*, Sept./Oct. 1947, p. 157; Parkinson, David (ed.), *The Graham Greene Film Reader: Mornings in the Dark* (London: Carcanet, 1993); Richards, Jeffrey, *The Age of the Dream Palace* (London: Routledge & Kegan Paul, 1984); Sutton, David, *A Chorus of Raspberries: British Film Comedy 1929–1939* (Exeter: University of Exeter Press, 2000).

FILMOGRAPHY (UK only): *Freedom of the Seas*; *Girls Will Be Boys* (1934); *Dance Band*; *Royal Cavalcade* (co-dirs. Thomas Bentley/Norman Lee/Walter Summers/W. P. Kellino/Herbert Brenon); *I Give My Heart* (US: *The Loves of Madame Dubarry*; *No Monkey Business* (1935); *Public Nuisance No. 1*; *All In* (1936); *Good Morning, Boys!* (1937); *O-Kay for Sound*; *Oh, Mr Porter!* (1937); *Alf's Button Afloat*; *Convict 99*; *Hey! Hey! USA!*; *Old Bones of the River* (1938); *Ask a Policeman*; *Where's That Fire?*; *The Frozen Limits* (1939); *Band Waggon*; *Let George Do It!*; *Gasbags*; *Neutral Port* (1940); *Hi, Gang!*; *I Thank You*; *The Ghost of St Michael's*; *South American George*; *Turned out Nice Again* (1941); *King Arthur Was a Gentleman*; *Much Too Shy* (1942); *Get Cracking*; *Bell-Bottom George* (1943); *He Snoops to Conquer* (1944); *I Didn't Do It* (1945); *George in Civvy Street*; *This Man Is Mine* (1946).

VARNEL, Max (1925–1996)

Born Max Le Bozec in Paris on 21 March 1925, Max Varnel was the son of Marcel Varnel, the Frenchman who directed some of the funniest and most quintessentially English comedies of the 1930s. He entered the industry in the late 1940s as third assistant director on *Dear Mr Prohack* (Thornton Freeland, 1949). In the 1950s he worked as assistant director on a number of films, including *The Magic Box* (John Boulting, 1951) and *The Cockleshell Heroes* (José Ferrer, 1955), and was second-unit director on *Interpol* (John Gilling, 1957). When he began to direct his own films, they were obdurately second features, mostly made for the Danziger brothers and mostly blandly forgettable. However, once or twice his regular screenwriter Brian Clemens turned out a meatier-than-usual screenplay, giving the actors something to get their teeth into. One such was *A Woman Possessed* (1958), in which Margaretta Scott's fine performance, as a rich, too-dominant mother who interferes with her son's marriage, made the situation seem newer than it was. *Return of a Stranger* (1962), in which a psychopath returns to kill the husband of a girl he once assaulted, had occasional frissons and the benefit of a solidly convincing American lead, John Ireland. However, it would have taken more flair and originality than Varnel or his mostly second-string actors could muster to make silk purses in the Danzigers' bargain-basement studio. Varnel moved into television in the 1960s, continuing his career in Australia until the 1980s when he directed episodes of the long-running soap *Neighbours*. He died from a heart attack in Sydney on 15 January 1996.

(Brian McFarlane)

BIBLIOGRAPHY: Gray, Darren, Obituary, *Stage*, 8 Feb. 1996, p. 31.

FILMOGRAPHY: *Interpol* (US: *Pick-Up Alley*, 2nd unit dir., John Gilling, 1957); *No Safety Ahead*; *Moment of Indiscretion*; *A Woman Possessed*; *Links of Justice* (1958); *The Great Van Robbery*; *Web of Suspicion*; *Top Floor Girl*; *Crash Dive*; *The Child and the Killer*; *Sentenced for Life* (1959); *A Taste of Money* (1960); *A Question of Suspense*; *The Silent Invasion*; *Part-Time Wife*; *Murder in Eden*; *Fate Takes a Hand*; *Enter Inspector Duval* (1961); *Return of a Stranger*; *Mrs Gibbons' Boys* (1962); *The Rivals* (1963).

VARNEY-SERRAO, Arthur (1893–1960)

A man of many pseudonyms, with a ragamuffin career marked by more pipe dreams than solid achievements, Arthur Varney-Serrao was born Amerigo Serrao in Italy in the early 1890s. His upbringing was both privileged and artistic: his father, Teodoro, a lawyer, worked for the British government in Italy; his American mother, Luella Varney, was a sculptor noted for portrait busts. On Teodoro's death, mother and son settled in America, where Serrao became a citizen in 1923, though he clung to his European aristocratic charm and, perhaps fraudulently, claimed himself a baron. Throughout the 1920s he worked in Hollywood, assisting Griffith, Sennett and Monty Banks; in 1927 he directed his first feature, an Argentine rancher story, *Winds of the Pampas*. He billed himself as Arthur Varney or Arthur Varney-Serrao – names also used when he moved to England in 1930 to take advantage of American distributors' need for low-cost British productions.

Within three years he made six quota films, chiefly released by Paramount or Fox, working regularly with scenarist Brock Williams. None apparently survive. The first, *The Road to Fortune*, one of two starring Guy Newall, pursued a talkative blend of comedy and romantic drama. Serrao found a warmer response from trade critics with the out-and-out comedy of *Enter the Queen*, featuring rich idler Richard Cooper and his bibulous butler Herbert Mundin; and especially *Almost a Divorce*, made for British and Dominions, advertised in its publicity as 'Daring. Diverting. Devastating'. Once more alcohol fuelled much of the humour; but better mounting and classier playing from Sydney Howard and Kay Hammond (seen in lingerie) helped give the film a bigger profile. Mundin was also featured in two lowly comedy vehicles of his own, *The Wrong Mr Perkins* and *Immediate Possession*.

Serrao's English connections continued on his return to America. Adopting the pseudonym Grover Lee, in 1933 he mounted a rural drama, *Get That Venus*, at the Metropolitan Studio, Fort Lee, using British backing and a British script (Val Valentine); it was barely distributed. Other equally shadowy directing work followed. From 1934 his artistic fortunes, almost all bad, became interlinked with the actress, writer and director Nell Shipman, pioneer maker of silent outdoor adventures. Mostly loving partners for over twenty years, they laid elaborate plans for films, studio production centres and other enterprises. They often lived in extreme poverty, perfecting what Shipman's screenwriting son Barry termed the 'art of the one-toothbrush move' for fleeing low-rent hotels. In the mid-1940s, as Peter Varney, Serrao found small acting parts at major studios, and continued to hatch production plans. Only one project, made in

Virginia, reached the screen: *The Story of Mr Hobbs* (1947), a raw and naive clam-digging drama with political elements, directed by Lorenzo Alagia (another Serrao pseudonym). Most of this film survives. In low health by the end of the 1950s, Serrao still dreamed of his pot of gold, seeking out the Danziger brothers in London, among others, for a series of European co-productions. He died in his Newark rooming house on 22 November 1960, long forgotten by the British industry he touched thirty years earlier with his charm, modest skill and cheek.
(Geoff Brown)

BIBLIOGRAPHY: Armatage, Kay, *The Girl from God's Country: Nell Shipman and the Silent Cinema* (Toronto: University of Toronto Press, 2003); Trusky, Tom (ed.), *Letters from God's Country. Nell Shipman: Selected Correspondence & Writings, 1912–1970* (Boise, ID: Hemingway Western Studies, 2003).

FILMOGRAPHY (UK only): *The Road to Fortune*; *Enter the Queen* (1930); *The Eternal Feminine*; *The Wrong Mr Perkins*; *Immediate Possession*; *Almost a Divorce* (1931).

VAS, Robert (1931–1978)

The documentary-maker Robert Vas was born in Budapest on 3 March 1931 and came to England after the Hungarian uprising in 1956. His style of film-making was very much in keeping with that of Lindsay Anderson and Karel Reisz, who helped him raise funding for his first film, *Refuge England*, and included it in their final Free Cinema programme at the National Film Theatre.

Refuge England, which centres upon an immigrant arriving in England from Hungary and trying to understand the strange environment and behaviour of its inhabitants, is imbued with a sense of wonder and bewilderment. A similar affectionate observation is apparent in *The Vanishing Street*, which starts with a shot of a Whitechapel street market community through the cross-trees of the surveyor's lens and ends with the wrecking ball smashing through the old buildings to clear the way for new high-rise housing.

Unlike Reisz and Anderson, Vas remained totally committed to documentary and, after a short period working for the National Coal Board, he went on to make a seminal series of films for the BBC. These include *The Golden Years of Alexander Korda* (1968), the first serious study of the Hungarian film-maker who did so much to establish a viable British film industry; and *Heart of Britain* (1970), a tribute to Humphrey Jennings, the documentary-maker most admired by the Free Cinema directors. Vas also made films about Eastern Europe, including *The Issue Should Be Avoided* (1971), about the Katyn Forest massacre of 1940; *My Homeland* (1976), a celebration of Hungarian culture and the 1956 uprising; and a three-hour examination of the life of Stalin (1973). Vas was allowed a remarkable degree of freedom to make what he wanted, though his controversially non-Establishment view of the General Strike, *Nine Days in '26* (1974), was postponed because of an oncoming general election, and requests for repeat showings have fallen on deaf ears. He had planned to make films about the Gulag Archipelago and the wartime bombing of Dresden before his untimely death on 10 April 1978.

In the BBC documentary tribute to Vas directed by Barrie Gavin, Karel Reisz said of him that his aim was to 'inspire thought, to remind and warn'. Though his career was tragically cut short, Robert Vas left an enduring legacy of honest and poetically acute films
(Bryony Dixon)

BIBLIOGRAPHY: Davies, Brenda, Obituary, *BFI News* no. 34, July 1978, p. 3; Gavin, Barrie and Alan Rosenthal, 'Witness: In Memoriam, Robert Vas', *Sight and Sound*, Summer 1978 pp. 186–9; *Robert Vas Film-Maker* (BBC documentary), Barrie Gavin, 3 May 1978.

FILMOGRAPHY: *Refuge England* (1959); *The Vanishing Street*; *Finale* (1962); *Mining Review 17th Year Numbers 7, 8 and 12*; *The Frontier* (1964); *Wish You Were Here*; *Master Singers: Two Choirs and a Valley* (1965); *The Survivors* (1967).

VAUGHN, Matthew (1971–)

Matthew Vaughn was born on 7 March 1971 in Beverly Hills, California, the son of television producer Kathy Ceaton and minor aristocrat George De Vere Drummond (though until 2002 Vaughn thought his father was the actor Robert Vaughn). He was brought up in London, and after dropping out of university produced Scott Michell's *The Innocent Sleep* (1996). It was not a success and it took Vaughn two years to raise the £1.6 million budget for Guy Ritchie's *Lock, Stock and Two Smoking Barrels*

(1998). After they eventually secured PolyGram as distributors the film proved highly popular at the box-office, spawning the even more successful *Snatch* (Guy Ritchie, 2000). Forced labour on two projects he had little enthusiasm for – Barry Skolnick's *Mean Machine* (2001) and Ritchie's *Swept Away* (2002) – and Ritchie's reluctance to direct *Layer Cake*, a project Vaughn had carefully nurtured, finally propelled him towards the director's chair.

In *Layer Cake* Vaughn dispensed with the comic extravagance of Ritchie's crime films and showed a cooler, darker underworld. A strong cast makes the first half seem intriguing, but when Vaughn tries to untangle his over-convoluted plot, character development is abandoned and emotional involvement drains away among the juvenile clichés and contrivances. UK audiences were taken in by the film's spurious glamour, and though *Layer Cake* played less well in America, studio executives were sufficiently impressed by Vaughn's slickness to offer him Hollywood assignments. He is married to the German model Claudia Schiffer.

(Robert Murphy)

BIBLIOGRAPHY: Norman, Neil, 'The IoS Profile: Matthew Vaughn', *Independent on Sunday*, 3 Oct. 2004, p. 23; Vaughn, Matthew, 'This Is a Serious Gangster Movie', *Empire*, Oct. 2004, pp. 102–5.

FILMOGRAPHY: *Layer Cake* (2004).

VESTER, Paul (1941–)

Paul Vester was born in Cambridge in 1941. He studied at the Central School of Art in London, where he made his first animated films, *Repetition* and *Anima* (both 1968). After attending the Royal College of Art's School of Film and Television from 1968 to 1969, he joined the Halas and Batchelor studio as a director of commercials and industrial films. *Football Freaks* (1971), featuring Paul Anka and the Crewcuts on the soundtrack, established Vester's reputation, and in 1972 he established an independent animation studio, Speedy Cartoons. The company was sustained mainly by Vester's animation on the Yorkshire Television puppet series *Mr Trimble* and, between 1975 and 1980, by his commercials for French television.

With support from the Arts Council, Vester was able to make a more personal project, *Sunbeam* (1980), a vividly coloured homage to the Fleischer brothers' cartoons of the 1930s and 40s set to the contemporary popular song 'What's at the Top of a Sunbeam'. The film won widespread distribution when it was released with *Chariots of Fire* (Hugh Hudson) in 1981. This unexpected success allowed Vester the opportunity to travel in North and South America, where he gathered material for *Picnic* (1987), a short sardonic take on the human propensity for violence. He also remained much in demand as a director of commercials – increasingly for American as well as British television.

In 1991 he shot documentary footage for *Abductees*, a project to explore people's experiences of alien abduction. Animated sequences followed in 1993 and the film was finally completed in 1995, when it was shown as part of a documentary on Vester for Channel 4's *Fourmations Secret Passions* series. *Abductees* both celebrates and mocks the narratives of five New Yorkers who recall their experiences under hypnosis. Exploiting animation's capacity to reveal states of mind, Vester uses various graphic design and animation styles to show the potential sources of these unconscious recollections, creating an ambivalent film that both disturbs and amuses. The film later became part of a compilation, *Cartoon Noir* (1999), which also included works by Piotr Dumala, Suzan Pitt and Jirí Bárta.

In 1997 Vester moved to Los Angeles, working on advertising campaigns at the Rhythm and Hues studio and the Klasky Csupo studio. He has taught at the School of Experimental Animation, Cal Arts, and received a Guggenheim Fellowship during 2003–4 while working on a new film, *In the Woods*.

(Paul Wells)

BIBLIOGRAPHY: Felstein, Roma, 'When Bits on the Side Can Help a Career', *Broadcast*, 31 Jan. 1986, p. 15; Wells, Paul (ed.), *Art and Animation* (London: Academy Group/John Wiley, 1997).

FILMOGRAPHY: *Repetition*; *Anima* (1968); *Football Freaks* (1971); *Sunbeam* (1980); *Picnic* (1987); *Voles: The Case of the Missing Sock* (1994); *Abductees* (1995).

VIDOR, King (1894–1982)

King Vidor was born in Galveston, Texas, on 8 February 1894. A former projectionist and freelance news cameraman, he began his Hollywood career in 1915, working as an extra. By 1919 he had turned feature director and established an international reputation with *The Big Parade* (1925) and *The Crowd* (1928). After the mid-1930s, Vidor was accepted into the Hollywood mainstream, though he retained a maverick independence. In 1938 MGM hired him to direct *The Citadel*, one of the studio's British prestige productions. The film was adapted from a novel by A. J. Cronin, and stars Robert Donat as a dedicated young doctor who finds his ideals tested in a Welsh mining village. Abandoning the poverty-stricken community for an affluent Mayfair practice, he slowly becomes corrupted by the easy life until a tragic event restores him to his senses. Donat was paired with Hollywood star Rosalind Russell and the heavyweight supporting cast included Ralph Richardson, Rex Harrison, Francis L. Sullivan and Emlyn Williams (who also worked on the script). While the ending is softened from the original book, *The Citadel* is a solid example of Hollywood craftsmanship, distinguished by Donat's committed performance and Vidor's incisive direction. Back in Hollywood, Vidor continued to work on major projects, notably David O. Selznick's *Duel in the Sun* (1947). He retired from film-making after the troubled production of *Solomon and Sheba* (1959), a dull biblical epic that flopped at the box-office. He died of a heart ailment in Paso Robles, California, on 1 November 1982.

(Daniel O'Brien)

BIBLIOGRAPHY: Durgnat, Raymond and Scott Simmon, *King Vidor, American* (Berkeley and London: University of California Press, 1988); Williams, J. Danvers, 'King Vidor: An Interview', *Film Weekly*, 24 Dec. 1938, pp. 6–8.

FILMOGRAPHY (UK only): *The Citadel* (1938).

VIERTEL, Berthold (1885–1953)

Berthold Viertel was born in Vienna on 28 June 1885. He studied philosophy at the University of Vienna and quickly established himself as a radical poet and critic through contributions to *Die Fackel* and other journals. He enlisted in the Austrian Army in the First World War and then became, variously, an actor, literary manager and director for Austrian and German theatres. Shifting between mediums, he worked for Max Reinhardt, translated dramas, contributed to the cabaret Simplizissimus and in 1922 directed his first film, *Ein Puppenheim*. The following year he directed a major production of Ibsen's *A Doll's House* and founded the avant-garde theatre group Die Truppe, which had an honourable but brief life and died in debt. In 1926, in collaboration with Béla Bálaz and Karl Freund, he directed the influential, but now lost film, *Die Abenteuer eines Zehnmarkscheins* (1926).

In 1929, Viertel left for Hollywood, where his wife, Salka Steurmann, was to have a fruitful career as an MGM scriptwriter (under her married name of Salka Viertel). He collaborated on scripts for Murnau's *Four Devils* (1929) and *City Girl* (1930), and directed films such as *The One Woman Idea* (1929), *Seven Faces* (1929), *Man Trouble* (1930) and two films with Claudette Colbert, *The Wiser Sex* and *The Man from Yesterday* (both 1932). In search of more challenging material, he incautiously returned to Germany, the day after Hitler became Chancellor in January 1933, to co-script and co-direct an adaptation of Hans Fallada's novel *Kleiner Mann was Nunn?*. As a Jew, and a particularly outspoken one, he was soon in trouble with the Nazi authorities and his name was taken off the film (which was credited solely to Fritz Wendhausen). Now floundering for work, he accepted an offer from Gaumont-British to make a film in England.

Little Friend, based on a novel by Ernst Lothar about a child who believes that she is witnessing the breakdown of her parents' marriage, was boldly experimental. (Christopher Isherwood, who worked on the script, used his experiences of working with Viertel as the basis for his novella *Prater Violet*.) Viertel makes good use of Günther Krampf's photography to create a subjective, dream-like quality that emphasises the emotional responses of the young girl (Nova Pilbeam) to her predicament. *Little Friend* was successful enough for Gaumont-British to commission a second film, though Viertel's plans for *The Chained Eagle*, a life of Lord Byron as a champion of liberty, were vetoed and instead he was asked to make *The Passing of the Third Floor Back*, from a play by Jerome K. Jerome. Its allegorical aspects – a Christ-like stranger wields a mysterious influence over the tenants of a cheap boarding house living in terror of poverty and humiliation – again allowed Viertel to use atmospheric lighting (from cinematographer Curt Courant) to guide the audience to a view of the characters.

Berthold Viertel with Peggy Ashcroft

The sort of subtle Expressionism Viertel had pioneered in his first two British films was absent from *Rhodes of Africa*, though he managed to avoid the usual clichés of British Imperialist epics. As he told *The Times*:

> Our ideas about hero-worship have changed. A man is worth as much as the ideas for which he stands . . . I saw Rhodes and his main opponents, Lobengula and Kruger, each representing the land in a different stage of development: the primitive man, the patriarchal farmer, and the representative of progressive capitalism spreading modern civilisation. (13 April 1936)

Changes at Gaumont-British meant that Viertel was not offered further films, and by the late 1930s British film production generally was in crisis. Viertel produced Max Catto's play *They Walk Alone* for the London stage in 1938, but his British residency permit was not renewed and in May 1939 he returned to Hollywood. During the war, his family home became a cultural centre for German-speaking exiles, though he made no more films. After 1945, and a second marriage, to Elisabeth Neumann, he remained in Europe as a guest theatre producer in Berlin and as Director of the Vienna Burgtheater. He died in Vienna on 24 September 1953.

(Kevin Gough-Yates)

BIBLIOGRAPHY: Gough-Yates, Kevin, 'Berthold Viertel at Gaumont-British', in Jeffrey Richards (ed.), *The Unknown 1930s: An Alternative History of the British Cinema 1929–1939* (London: I. B. Tauris, 1998); Isherwood, Christopher, *Prater Violet* (London: Methuen, 1946); Viertel, Berthold in interview with T. T. Fleming, 'The Problems of the "Third Floor Back"', *Film Weekly*, 3 May 1935, pp. 17, 41; Viertel, Berthold, 'Christopher Isherwood and Dr Friedrich Bergmann', *Theatre Arts*, May 1946, pp. 295–8; Viertel, Salka, *The Kindness of Strangers* (New York: Holt, Rinehart and Winston, 1969); Witt, Peter, 'Lothar Mendes and Berthold Viertel Talk about Their Latest Films', *Picturegoer* no. 150, 7 Apr. 1934, pp. 14–15.

FILMOGRAPHY (UK only): *Little Friend* (1934); *The Passing of the Third Floor Back* (1935); *Rhodes of Africa* (US: *Rhodes*, 1936).

VILLA, Colm (1960–)

Colm Villa was born in Derry, Northern Ireland, in 1960. After studying politics at the University of Nottingham he joined the BBC where he worked on drama series such as *Bergerac*. He made his first film, *Open Asylum*, in 1982. A political thriller concerning a young Belfast man blamed by the media for a terrorist bombing, it showed Villa's ability to use a popular genre to examine political realities – in this case the media's influence on the Troubles. Between 1982 and 1986 Villa attended the National Film and Television School where he made two short films: *Cuban Breeze*, an ambitious prison drama about an Irish prisoner's escape from a high-security Florida prison to an idyllic life in Honduras; and *Paradiso*, an intense study of a father–son relationship tarnished by a crime. Villa returned to feature films with the futuristic science-fiction allegory *Sunset Heights* (1998). Set in Derry ten years after the British have withdrawn, it concerns Luke Bradley, an unlikely super-hero who attempts to get to the bottom of his son's murder and is inadvertently drawn into a feud between rival gangs. At times highly dramatic (a shoot-out in which the hero takes cover under a truck full of live-stock is enormously effective) and conjuring an infernal atmosphere derived from Celtic mythology, *Sunset Heights* is an adventurous attempt to deal with the Troubles through action-movie allegory. (Eugene Finn)

BIBLIOGRAPHY: McLoone, Martin, *Irish Film: The Emergence of a Contemporary Cinema* (London: BFI, 2000).

FILMOGRAPHY: *Open Asylum* (1982); *Cuban Breeze* (short, 1985); *Paradiso* (short, 1986); *Sunset Heights* (1998).

VORHAUS, Bernard (1904–2000)

Bernard Vorhaus brought an outsider's eye, an American pace and a distinctive feel for the cinema medium to his work in Britain. Toiling as a director in the 'quota quickie' field in the 1930s, he quickly made his mark in the industry; resurrected fifty years later, his films struck home with another generation, happy to find signs of life in a corner of British cinema often thought a graveyard. Like Michael Powell, another 'quickie' director, Vorhaus showed that with a lively imagination even the most recalcitrant script could be turned into genuine cinema, rather than dialogue with illustrations tacked on.

He was born in New York City on 25 December 1904 into a prosperous immigrant family. Childhood visits to the Fort Lee studios in New Jersey with his elder sister Amy, a scenario writer, sparked his interest in the medium. By the 1920s he was a writer himself, working in Hollywood for Columbia and Fox; among other tasks he ghost-wrote Fox's intensely romantic box-office hit *Seventh Heaven* (Frank Borzage, 1927). He moved into direction with a silent two-reel drama, *Sunlight* (1928), lost from sight in the excitement of talking pictures.

With no work looming, Vorhaus came to England for a holiday in 1929. He stayed for eight years. The talkie bedlam gave him a niche at Wembley as production supervisor for British Sound Film Productions. When the company collapsed, Vorhaus re-edited some of its variety shorts into *Camera Cocktails*, and proceeded to his first feature, *On Thin Ice*, a society thriller, indifferently received, now a lost film. With *Money for Speed*, Vorhaus displayed more individuality, building his romantic triangle around the thrills of speedway racing, energetically shot on location. His editor was another industry newcomer, David Lean.

Subsequently, Vorhaus chiefly worked for producer Julius Hagen at Twickenham Studios, the factory for many quota productions, turned out on lowly budgets on two-week shooting schedules. His first task was *The Ghost Camera* (1933). Much in the story was mundane, though there is some risqué fun in a country guesthouse between hesitant hero Henry Kendall and spirited heroine Ida Lupino. Vorhaus refused to settle for commonplace images, breaking up the courtroom climax with a subjective, lurching camera, intercutting a crescendo of close-ups as the judge lays out the murder evidence. In his next film, *Crime on the Hill* (1933), Vorhaus spiced up a standard country-house murder yarn with irony, lively characterisations and, in the case of actress Sally Blane, intimations of the erotic.

Not every assignment could be saved by Vorhaus' nimble handling. Alongside the pliable West End actors hired for the films – Lewis Casson, John Mills, Henry Kendall, among others – there was John Garrick, an actor-singer of unbending mien, who counteracts Vorhaus' creative efforts in *Street Song* and *The Broken Melody*. Sometimes scripts arrived with their own limitations; another lost film, *Ten Minute Alibi*, suffered especially, in Vorhaus' view, from its stage-play straitjacket. The writers of *The Broken Melody* – in which a composer (the oleaginous Garrick) imprisoned on Devil's Island after a crime of passion escapes and writes an opera about it all – perhaps needed a strait-jacket of their own.

In one film particularly, *The Last Journey* (1935), material and method, style and substance, fused together with exhilarating

Henry Kendall puzzles over the mystery of *The Ghost Camera* (Bernard Vorhaus, 1933)

results. This film had to move fast: it was set on a runaway train hurtling towards destruction at the hands of a driver facing retirement, tormented by jealousy. As in *Money for Speed*, Vorhaus wanted real thrills and spills, not studio mock-ups; the location shooting and fast cutting generated a level of excitement far beyond the British norm. The basic plot was banal, but Vorhaus' presentation kept the train and its passengers jostling happily along. The crazed driver, the bigamist and his new acquisition, two fleeing crooks, the detective in disguise, the doughty stoker on the footplate, the handy brain specialist: Vorhaus stamped them all with humanising quirks and avoided cardboard caricatures. For a low-budget supporting feature, *The Last Journey* made a considerable impact. *Dark World* (1935), a more lurid thriller, made for Fox-British, also received strong reviews; unfortunately this is another lost film.

By this time Hagen's ambitions were rising. A lavish remake of Griffith's *Broken Blossoms* was mounted at Twickenham in 1935, directed by Hans (later John) Brahm; Vorhaus served as technical supervisor. His next venture as director, *Dusty Ermine*, was another beneficiary of Hagen's largesse: a theatre thriller about counterfeiters, it was opened out to embrace extensive location work in the Swiss Alps. Vorhaus gave the play a vigorous shake, adding an eccentric role for newcomer Margaret Rutherford, and filled the screen with striking images whenever the characters took to their skis.

Hagen's financial difficulties deepened in 1936. Vorhaus' last British film, *Cotton Queen*, an uncongenial North Country comedy, was made for the American producer Joe Rock. Out of work, and out of pocket, Vorhaus accepted an offer from Herbert J. Yates, President of Republic Pictures, and returned to America. He joined Hollywood's assembly line, tackling motley medium-budget projects, and sharpening his left-wing sympathies on the Spanish Civil War. Resuming feature film-making after the Second World War, he ventured into independent production, and found some success with *So Young So Bad* (1950), an earnest drama about delinquent girls, before the HUAC and the anti-Communist witch-hunts drove him into exile.

He returned to England in 1951, but unlike fellow exiles Joseph Losey and Cy Endfield chose to retreat from the industry. He developed a flat-conversion business in London, Domar Properties, and lived long enough to relive his past achievements when his career as one of the brightest, least British of British directors was rediscovered in the 1980s. He died in Tooting, south London, on 23 November 2000.

(Geoff Brown)

BIBLIOGRAPHY: Angelini, Sergio, 'The Archive Presents . . . A Tribute to Bernard Vorhaus', National Film Theatre Programme, Mar. 2001, pp. 46–7; Brown, Geoff, 'Vorhaus: A Director Rediscovered', *Sight and Sound*, Winter 1986/7, pp. 40–3; Brown, Geoff, 'Money for Speed: The British Films of Bernard Vorhaus', in Jeffrey Richards (ed.), *The Unknown 1930s: An Alternative History of the British Cinema, 1929–1939* (London: I. B. Tauris, 1998); Eyles, Allen and David Meeker, *Missing Believed Lost: The Great British Film Search* (London: BFI, 1992); Vorhaus, Bernard, *Saved from Oblivion: An Autobiography* (Lanham, MD: Scarecrow Press, 2000).

FILMOGRAPHY (UK only): *London Town* (doc., 1929); *Camera Cocktails* (1932); *On Thin Ice*; *Money for Speed*; *The Ghost Camera*; *Crime on the Hill* (1933); *The Broken Melody*; *Night Club Queen*; *Blind Justice*; *Street Song* (1934); *Ten Minute Alibi*; *The Last Journey*; *Dark World* (1935); *Dusty Ermine* (US: *Hideout in the Alps*, 1936); *Cotton Queen* (1937).

WALKER, Norman (1892–1976)

Norman Walker's directing career spanned forty-five years, from the late silent period to the early 1970s. *Turn of the Tide*, a refreshing tale set in a Yorkshire fishing village, brought him praise and attention in 1935. But for much of his later career he led a subterranean existence outside the circuit cinemas. From 1938 onwards he was a mainstay of J. Arthur Rank's religious film unit GHW Productions, making shorts and features in line with Methodist beliefs.

Walker's evangelistic spirit took time to manifest itself. Born in Bolton on 8 October 1892, he began in the theatre, acting in Manchester with Annie Horniman's repertory company. During the First World War he served with the North Lancashire Regiment, reaching the rank of captain. Cinema finally beckoned in the 1920s. His first production, a 1926 comedy short, *Oxford Bags*, found distribution through Gaumont. But most of his early career took place under the aegis of John Maxwell at Elstree. Initially working as an assistant, he graduated to directing features with *Tommy Atkins* in 1928. Subsequently he captained British International Pictures' multilingual melodrama *The Hate Ship* (1929), took charge of an interesting drawing-room drama, *Loose Ends* (1930) and gave the company a substantial box-office success with the comedy *The Middle Watch* (1930).

Courteous and intelligent, but not always a diplomat, Walker abruptly departed Elstree in 1932 after frictions with the management. He found success again with *Lilies of the Field* (1934), an entertaining romantic comedy, one of several films made for Herbert Wilcox. *Turn of the Tide* then pointed the way forward. Keen to bring wholesomeness and spiritual uplift to film production, Rank had joined forces with Lady Yule to create British National Films; *Turn of the Tide* was their first feature. Franz Planer's location photography brought a realistic tang of the open air and sea to this drama of fishing, rivalry and love; Walker provided attention to detail, dogged sincerity and careful handling of a talented cast that included Geraldine Fitzgerald and Wilfrid Lawson.

After three more conventional studio features, Walker joined forces with Rank, lending his surname's initial to GHW Productions along with Benjamin Gregory, a Methodist canon, and Lieutenant-Colonel R. J. V. Hake. In a 1937 talk Walker pronounced: 'If the message of the Kingdom of God is to succeed in the cinema it must conceal itself under the guise of entertainment' (Macnab, p. 15). Walker duly took charge of all GHW films produced with wide audiences in mind. *The Great Mr Handel* was slow moving, but blessed with a finely tuned Wilfrid Lawson performance, mellow Technicolor and the composer's best-known music; the religious content only emerged in its final stages. *Hard Steel* and *They Knew Mr Knight*, by comparison, spun their moralities with a heavier hand. *Sunday Thoughts*, early entries in his long series of short homilies, also reached the Odeons; they were not always received kindly.

In 1945 Walker was appointed manager of D & P Studios, the hub of Rank's commercial empire. But by 1948 he returned to GHW's base at the small Gate studio, Elstree, generating many short films for church consumption and several features, including *John Wesley* (1953), chiefly aimed at American congregations. In 1959 GHW was acquired by Betty Box and her husband Peter Rogers, a former employee, who used the company to make *Carry On* films; undeterred, Walker and Rank continued under the name of Religious Films. Walker died in 1976, six years after his last substantial film, *The Challenge*, which sought a Christian moral in the construction of a rural power station. (Geoff Brown)

BIBLIOGRAPHY: Aldgate, Tony, 'Loose Ends, Hidden Gems and the Moment of "Melodramatic Emotionality"', in Jeffrey Richards (ed.), *The Unknown 1930s: An Alternative History of the British Cinema 1929–39* (London: I. B. Tauris, 1998); Macnab, Geoffrey, *J. Arthur Rank and the British Film Industry* (London: Routledge, 1993); Murphy, Robert, *Realism and Tinsel: Cinema and Society in Britain 1939–49* (London: Routledge, 1989).

FILMOGRAPHY: Shorts and non-fiction: *Oxford Bags* (1926); *Skipper of the Osprey* (1933); *Faith Triumphant*; *The Way of Salvation*; *The Grace of Forgiveness* (1938); *Beyond Our Horizon*; *The Crown of Righteousness* (1939); *The First Easter* (1940); *Sunday Thoughts* (series, 1942–71); *Methodism and the Miner* (1953); *At Home and Abroad* (1954); *And Now Tomorrow* (co-dirs. Lawrence Barrett/Duncan Spence); *It Could Happen Here* (1956); *Time We Woke Up* (1957); *The Story of Fred James*; *The Singapore Story*; *The George Muller Story* (1959); *Design for Living*; *Veterinary Research and the Farmer* (1960); *God Loves You*; *Becoming a Son* (1962); *A Call to Worship* (co-dir. Duncan Spence); *The Centurion's Servant*; *The Fulfilment* (1963); *Adventurous Journey* (1964); *Marvellous and It's Real!*; *Wonderful and It's True!* (1968); *The Last Supper*; *Remember Me* (1971).

Feature: *Tommy Atkins*; *Widdecombe Fair* (1928); *A Romance of Seville*; *The Hate Ship* (1929); *Loose Ends*; *The Middle Watch* (1930); *Uneasy Virtue*; *The Shadow Between* (1931); *Mr Bill the Conqueror* (US: *The Man Who Won*); *Fires of Fate* (1932); *Forging Ahead*; *The Flaw*; *The Fortunate Fool*; *The House of Trent* (1933); *Dangerous Ground*; *Lilies of the Field*; *The Way of Youth* (1934); *Key to Harmony*; *Turn of the Tide*; *Debt of Honour* (1935); *Our Fighting Navy* (US: *Torpedoed!*); *Sunset in Vienna* (US: *Suicide Legion*) (1937); *The Man at the Gate* (US: *Men of the Sea*, 1941); *Hard Steel* (aka *What Shall It Profit*); *The Great Mr Handel* (1942); *They Knew Mr Knight* (1945); *The Promise* (1952); *John Wesley* (1953); *The Shield of Faith* (1956); *The Supreme Secret* (1958); *First Things First*; *Unless You Become*; *The Family of God* (1964); *Where Is Your Faith* (1965); *The Crowning Gift* (1967); *The Challenge* (1970).

WALKER, Pete (1939–)

Pete Walker, the son of music-hall comedian Syd Walker, was born in January 1939. By the late 1950s he had tried his hand as a stand-up comedian, an actor and a technician at Brighton Film Studios; he then moved to the United States where he worked briefly in the television industry. Returning to England, he specialised in producing short 'nudie' films for the burgeoning 8mm market. Walker's first cinema films reflected this background with their reliance on exploitative scenes of nudity and violence. The 1970 production *Cool It Carol!*, while still containing the nudity required for a low-budget exploitation feature, represented an advance both in terms of ambition and achievement. The story about a young couple seeking fame and fortune in London and becoming drawn into the sex industry might have been hackneyed, but Walker treated the subject in a mature and sensitive way. His next two films, the psychological thriller *Die Screaming, Marianne* and the remarkably silly 3-D sex-comedy *Four Dimensions of Greta*, were unimpressive. However, *The Flesh and Blood Show*, although little appreciated by critics on its initial release, was an audacious combination of an Agatha Christie-like story and grisly horror; it marked the beginning of Walker's association with the horror genre.

Walker's reputation as a genre film-maker is based largely on three horror films from the mid-1970s, *House of Whipcord*, *Frightmare* and *House of Mortal Sin*. Each of these presented a grim suburban world in which unsuspecting young people were subject to violent assaults from representatives of an older, repressive generation. In *House of Whipcord* an elderly judge runs a private prison in which young women are punished for what he considers their sinful behaviour; in *Frightmare* an elderly cannibalistic woman literally consumes members of the younger generation. A relentlessly realistic treatment of the material, coupled with a nihilistic sensibility that rarely allowed the forces of good to triumph, made for unsettling viewing; in certain respects these films are closer to disturbing American horrors such as *The Texas Chainsaw Massacre* (Tobe Hooper, 1974) than to anything in the British horror tradition.

Walker's later films lack the intensity of his best work. After making *House of the Long Shadows*, a throwback to a simpler and more reassuring type of horror story starring horror stalwarts Peter Cushing, Christopher Lee, Vincent Price and John Carradine, he gave up directing and moved into cinema exhibition and property development.

(Peter Hutchings)

BIBLIOGRAPHY: Castell, David, 'The Exploits of Pete Walker', *Films Illustrated*, Mar. 1976, pp. 264–5; Chibnall, Steve, *Making Mischief: The Cult Films of Pete Walker* (Guildford, Surrey: FAB Press, 1998); Hunt, Leon, *British Low Culture: From Safari Suits to Sexploitation* (London: Routledge, 1998); McGillivray, David, *Doing Rude Things: The History of the British Sex Film, 1957–81* (London: Sun Tavern Fields, 1992); 'Pete Walker: Scare Monger . . .', *Empire*, June 1998, p. 56.

FILMOGRAPHY: *I Like Birds* (1967); *Strip Poker* (1968); *School for Sex* (1969); *Man of Violence*; *Cool It Carol!* (1970); *Die Screaming, Marianne* (1971); *Four Dimensions of Greta*; *The Flesh and Blood Show* (1972); *Tiffany Jones* (1973); *House of Whipcord*; *Frightmare* (1974); *House of Mortal Sin* (1975); *Schizo* (1976); *The Comeback* (1978); *Home Before Midnight* (1979); *House of the Long Shadows* (1983).

WALKER, Rob (1943–)

Robert Walker was born in Richmond, Surrey, in 1943. He adapted and directed Dario Fo's satirical farce *Can't Pay, Won't Pay* among other theatrical achievements before moving into television. He made his name with adventurous dramas, including Howard Brenton's *Dead Head* (1986), Martin Flannery's *Blind Justice* (1988) and David Pirie's *Wild Things* (1988). Upmarket drama serials followed: *Rules of Engagement* (1989), a claustrophobic thriller set in Portsmouth during the Second World War; *Die Kinder* (1990), Paula Milne's tale of a mother's attempt to retrieve her children, caught in the murky past of her German activist husband. More routine assignments followed in the 1990s, including a Ruth Rendell mystery, *The Mouse in the Corner* (1992), the mediocre *Little Napoleons* (1994) and episodes of the ill-fated *Harry* (1993), whose Darlington settings drove Michael Elphick to drink.

In 2000 Walker finally directed a feature film, *Circus*, a convoluted film noir set in Brighton. Much was hoped from David Logan's script (the film was bankrolled by Columbia), but Walker fails to make much sense of its twists and turns, and none of the cast look comfortable in their roles. Perhaps the film might have worked if directed with Tarantinoesque panache, but one suspects that Walker faced an impossible task grafting noirish conventions onto the tradition of British seaside humour. Audiences in Britain were lukewarm, and in America totally indifferent.

(Robert Murphy)

BIBLIOGRAPHY: Murrell, Rachel, 'I Wanna Tell You a Story', *Television Today*, 26 May 1994, p. 21.

FILMOGRAPHY: *Circus* (UK/US, 2000).

WALLACE, Edgar (1875–1932)

Richard Horatio Edgar Wallace was born on 1 April 1875 in Greenwich. After working for many years as a journalist, Wallace came to prominence with his first mystery novel, *The Four Just Men* (1905), published with the ending removed as part of an advertising campaign that offered a £500 prize to readers who submitted the right conclusion. As many readers guessed correctly, this nearly bankrupted Wallace. He made up for it subsequently with a prodigious output of over 170 books and two dozen plays, though extravagant tastes and a love of horse-racing always laid siege to his earnings.

In 1915 Wallace wrote his first film script, *Nurse and Martyr* (Percy Moran), a privately financed film on the life of Edith Cavell. Following his success in transferring his stories to the West End stage, in 1927 Wallace joined the board of the newly established British Lion Film Corporation, selling them rights to his works for seven years. Carol Reed, associated with Wallace in the theatre, served as his personal assistant; his son Bryan Wallace, after Hollywood experience, joined the firm as a scenario writer. A. V. Bramble's *Chick* (1928) began the run of Wallace mystery adaptations; eight were produced within the first year, directed by Bramble, Arthur Maude or G. B. Samuelson. Tentatively handled and cramped by modest budgets, they performed poorly at the box office, and Wallace needed little persuading to try his own hand at directing. He cut a colourful figure at Beaconsfield, parading in breeches and boots in the Hollywood manner. 'I shall make my first picture a commercial triumph', he told journalists in 1929 after directing *Red Aces* (Chapman, p. 83). It was not to be: this silent outing for his popular detective character J. G. Reeder was thought stagy and implausible, and generated equally poor takings. The studio's conversion to sound came slowly: by February 1930 Wallace was back directing *The Squeaker*, one of his most popular and typical thrillers, with the true identities of both policeman and villain only revealed at the end. Sound, and the cockney edge of Gordon Harker (featured in several of Wallace's stage hits), made this more plausible than *Red Aces*. But British Lion only made a success with Wallace when they joined with Gainsborough to upgrade the product, beginning with Walter Forde's *The Ringer* (1931).

Though Wallace directed no more films, his fascination with cinema continued: when he died of pneumonia in Hollywood on 10 February 1932 he was working on a draft script for *King Kong* (Merian C. Cooper/Ernest B. Schoedsack, 1933). His novels and plays continued to provide a fertile source for British films across the decades, ranging in mood from the Imperial adventure of *Sanders of the River* (Zoltán Korda, 1935) to the squalid horrors of *The Dark Eyes of London* (Walter Summers, 1939). Between 1960 and 1964 the series of hour-long crime adaptations filmed at Merton Park proved popular supporting features; concurrently, around thirty crime thrillers were made in Germany, where Wallace continues to attract a cult following.

(Sergio Angelini and Geoff Brown)

BIBLIOGRAPHY: Chapman, James, '*Celluloid Shockers*', in Jeffrey Richards (ed.), *The Unknown 1930s: An Alternative History of the British Cinema 1929–1939* (London: I. B. Tauris, 1998); Lane, Margaret, *Edgar Wallace: The Biography of a Phenomenon* (London: Heinemann, 1938); Nolan, Jack Edmund, 'Edgar Wallace', *Films in Review*, Feb. 1967, pp. 71–85; Pauer, Florian, *Die Edgar Wallace-Filme* (Munich: Goldmann, 1982).

FILMOGRAPHY: *Red Aces* (1929); *The Squeaker* (1930).

WALLER, Anthony (1959–)

Anthony Waller was born in Beirut, Lebanon, on 24 October 1959. After graduating from the National Film School in 1981 he won a prize for Best Fiction Short at the Munich Festival of Student Films with *When the Rain Stops* and worked in Germany throughout the 1980s in various capacities (vision-mixer, editor, camera operator, director, producer) on commercials, television shows, trailers and pop videos. He supervised the assembly of the compilation movie *Als die Liebe laufen lernte – 2. Teil*, but his first real feature was *Mute Witness*, shot over many years, with a cameo from Alec Guinness in the can long before the rest of the principal photography was completed. A self-consciously Hitchcockian (more properly, De Palmaesque) thriller about a voiceless girl who chances across the shooting of a snuff movie after hours in a Russian film studio, this effective minor suspense movie won Waller a mid-range assignment, *An American Werewolf in Paris*, the long-delayed sequel to *An American Werewolf in London* (John Landis, 1981). Shot in Luxembourg with typical late-1990s reliance on computer-generated imagery, the film includes an enjoyably witty moment when a xenophobic French werewolf explains why he prefers to dine on Americans, but is otherwise undistinguished. *The Guilty* is an adaptation of a novel by Simon Burke based on his 1992 television series, with lawyer Bill Pullman seduced by calculating Gabrielle Anwar. All Waller's films – even Uli Edel's *The Little Vampire* (2000), which he worked on as executive producer – have international settings and return to the theme of bewildered foreigners imperilled in strange lands, but so far they have tended to be makeshift and conventional.

(Kim Newman)

BIBLIOGRAPHY: Gingold, Michael, 'Mute Witness: Something to Scream About', *Fangoria*, Aug. 1995, pp. 56–9; Vie, Caroline, 'A Director from London, a Werewolf in Paris', *Fangoria*, Nov. 1997, pp. 46–50.

FILMOGRAPHY: *When the Rain Stops* (short, 1981); *Als die Liebe laufen lernte – 2. Teil* (Ger, 1989); *Mute Witness* (UK/Ger/Russ, 1994); *An American Werewolf in Paris* (UK/US/Lux/Fr, 1998); *The Guilty* (US, 2000).

WALLER, Tom (1975–)

Thomas J. Waller was born in Hull, Yorkshire, in 1975. He was educated at Ampleforth College, a Roman Catholic public school, and studied film editing at the Northern Film School in Leeds. On graduating in 1995 he set about raising a budget of £80,000 from private investors to make the feature film *Monk Dawson*, based on a novel by Piers Paul Read. A seminary boy becomes a Benedictine monk in the 1960s, and is sent by his order to Chelsea, where a Sloane Ranger siren introduces him to the permissive society. After sexual betrayals on the night of the Queen's Silver Jubilee and again on that of Margaret Thatcher's election victory, he is happy to renounce the world for placid contemplation on Holy Island. Waller stretches his meagre resources with some skill, drawing adequate performances from his second-string actors, digging out picturesque locations up and down the country, and recreating the sweep of history, particularly the 1970s, with modest authenticity. But this was a saga more suited to television than cinema; predictably *Monk Dawson* failed to reach much of an audience. A career directing television adaptations of Agatha Christie and Catherine Cookson beckoned. Instead, Waller opted for more personal projects, directing *Eviction*, a ten-minute film about oppression in nineteenth-century Ireland, and producing *Butterfly Man* (Kaprice Kea, 2002), a low-budget feature about an English backpacker's travails in Thailand.

(Robert Murphy)

BIBLIOGRAPHY: Alberge, Dalya, 'Novice Earns a Blessing from Author of Wayward Monk's Story', *The Times*, 13 May 1997, p. 5.

FILMOGRAPHY: *Monk Dawson* (1998); *Eviction* (short, 1999).

WALLS, Tom (1883-1949)

Thomas Kirby Walls was born in Kingsthorpe, Northampton, on 16 February 1883. After growing too heavy to pursue his ambition to become a jockey, he served as an apprentice in a Swindon locomotive works, and signed on as a constable with the Metropolitan Police, before turning to acting and making his stage debut in 1905. The following year he toured in America, and went on to build a strong theatrical career as an actor and producer, culminating in the popular farces staged in London at the Aldwych Theatre in the 1920s and early 30s. These carefully constructed plays, written by Ben Travers, featured a shifting kaleidoscope of recognisable English caricatures: Ralph Lynn and Walls' men-about-town of varying intelligence, always getting into vaguely risqué scrapes; Robertson Hare's hen-pecked husbands; Mary Brough's lower-class battle-axes; Winifred Shotter as the pretty girl sucked into the maelstrom.

In 1929 Herbert Wilcox invited Walls to transfer the Aldwych farces to the screen for his British and Dominions company, beginning with *Rookery Nook*, among the earliest British talkies. The cycle progressed throughout the early 1930s; when Wilcox switched distributors from W and F to United Artists in 1933, Michael Balcon reached a deal to shift production to Gaumont-British's Lime Grove studios. It proved a prickly association. In his autobiography, Balcon wrote of coming to regret the licence granted Walls, particularly over casting, 'as Tom's choices were not always made on acting ability' (Balcon, p. 91). He also felt that Walls 'did not understand films in any technical or creative sense' (p. 92). Though later films advanced on the awkward cutting and proscenium stage look of *Rookery Nook*, Walls never saw any reason to rein in his tendency to overplay his crustier roles, and his method of shooting remained unadventurous, even when the subjects progressed from stage farces to screen originals by Travers. However, stilted theatricality did not worry audiences, and the Walls films won massive popularity in Britain. The witty dialogue and intricate plots of the best examples – *Turkey Time*, *A Cuckoo in the Nest* and, in less farcical mode, *Lady in Danger* and *For Valour* – still have the ability to entertain; and the core Aldwych world of upper-middle-class rogues and rascals, sprightly young women and gentle innuendo now seems fascinatingly stylised.

After *Old Iron* (1938), an untypical character drama, produced independently for his T. W. Productions, Walls found no more opportunities to direct. A keen racehorse owner and gambler – his colt April the Fifth had won the Epsom Derby in 1932 – his wealth appears to have dissipated; matters improved in the 1940s when he returned to the screen as a character actor. Working in friendlier circumstances for Balcon, he was surprisingly effective as a brave old Yugoslav patriot in Ealing's *Undercover* (Sergei Nolbandov, 1943) and a Cornish fisherman in *Johnny Frenchman* (Charles Frend, 1945). Elsewhere, he made a convincingly sinister villain in Karel Lamac's *They Met in the Dark* (1943), and managed a Yorkshire accent better than most as the genial patriarch in Walter Forde's trouble at t'mill saga *Master of Bankdam* (1947). He continued acting until shortly before his death in Ewell, Surrey, on 27 November 1949.

(Geoff Brown and Lawrence Napper)

BIBLIOGRAPHY: Adams, Annette, 'Tom Walls Hits Back at His Critics', *Picturegoer*, 25 Nov. 1933, p. 13; Balcon, Michael, *Michael Balcon Presents . . . A Lifetime in Films* (London: Hutchinson, 1969); Gwen, Hollis, 'An Exception to Every Rule', *Picture Show*, 15 Oct. 1949, p. 12; Low, Rachael, *Film Making in 1930s Britain* (London: George Allen & Unwin, 1985).

FILMOGRAPHY: *Rookery Nook*; *On Approval*; *Canaries Sometimes Sing* (1930); *Tons of Money*; *Plunder* (1931); *A Night Like This*; *Thark*; *Leap Year* (1932); *The Blarney Stone*; *Just Smith*; *Turkey Time*; *A Cuckoo in the Nest* (1933); *Dirty Work*; *A Cup of Kindness*; *Lady in Danger* (1934); *Foreign Affaires*; *Fighting Stock* (1935); *Pot Luck*; *Stormy Weather*, *Dishonour Bright* (1936); *For Valour* (1937); *Second Best Bed*; *Old Iron* (1938).

WALSH, Aisling (1958–)

Aisling Walsh was born in Dublin in 1958. She studied fine art at the Dun Laoghaire Institute of Art, Design and Technology and gained a place at the National School of Film and Television, where she served as assistant director on Terence Davies' *Death and Transfiguration* (1983) and directed *Hostage* (1984), a forty-minute drama about a terrorist group hiding out in an isolated Irish farmhouse. *Joyriders*, a low-budget feature set in a still economically backward Ireland, followed in 1988; but it made little impact, and Walsh turned to television, making her mark as the director of Lynda La Plante's crime drama serial *Trial & Retribution* (1997).

While attempting to finance her second cinema feature, Walsh directed three television films, *Forgive and Forget* (2000), *Little Bird* (2000) and, most impressively, *Sinners* (2002), a harrowing study of the treatment of unmarried mothers in Church-run laundries in the 1960s, written by Lizzie Mickery (simultaneously the subject of Peter Mullan's *The Magdalene Sisters*, 2002). *Song for a Raggy Boy*, her feature project, emerged in 2003. Based on Patrick Galvin's autobiography, it shares similarities with *Sinners* in exploring how Ireland's repressive religious culture led to brutality and abuse against young people deemed to have broken the rules. Galvin's experiences as a traumatised veteran of the Spanish Civil War, fighting sadism and obscurantism as a teacher in an Irish reformatory school, is effectively dramatised by Walsh, who exposes the parallels between the Church's cruel discipline in these sealed-off communities and the triumphant march of Fascism in the world outside.

Walsh was one of the twenty-five directors invited to contribute an episode to the compilation film *Visions of Europe* (2004), though she reached a far wider audience as director of the splendidly melodramatic BBC serial *Fingersmith* (2005).

(Robert Murphy)

BIBLIOGRAPHY: Sheehy, Ted, 'Close Up: Aisling Walsh/Case Study: *Song for a Raggy Boy*', *Screen International*, 28 Feb. 2003, p. 34.

FILMOGRAPHY: *Joyriders* (1988); *Song for a Raggy Boy* (Ir/UK/Den/Sp, 2003); *Visions of Europe* ('Invisible State' episode, Den/Ger, 2004).

WALSH, Kieron J (1964–)

Kieron Walsh was born on 24 November 1964. After winning three Fuji Film awards for his graduate piece, *Goodbye Piccadilly* (1988), Walsh moved to the Royal College of Art in London, where he made another award-winning short, *Bossanova Blues* (1991). After a short black comedy, *Out of the Deep Pan* (1995), about a pizza delivery service in Belfast, made for the BBC, he directed three episodes of the series *The Young Person's Guide to Becoming a Rock Star* (1998) for Channel 4.

Walsh made his feature film debut with the romantic comedy *When Brendan Met Trudy*. Scripted by Roddy Doyle, this film, along with Gerry Stembridge's *About Adam* (2000), articulated a new amorality and youthful energy associated with Dublin in the economic boom of the 1990s. A play on Jean-Luc Godard's *À bout de souffle/Breathless* (1959), it stars Flora Montgomery as a cat burglar and Peter McDonald as a repressed, cinephile schoolteacher. Though Walsh overdoes his multiple homages to classic cinema, the film performed well at the Irish box office and was a modest success in Britain.

In 2000, Walsh became one of the contributors to the 'Beckett on Film' project, directing *Rough for Theatre I* with David Kelly and Milo O'Shea. In 2002 he made *Watermelon*, with Anna Friel as an not altogether convincing Irish girl in London, for Granada Television. Walsh often makes cameo appearances in his films and his directorial style is marked by pacy, irreverent visuals.

(Ruth Barton)

BIBLIOGRAPHY: Power, Paul, 'When Kieron Met Roddy', *Film West* no. 42, Winter 2000, pp. 20–3; 'When Roddy Met Kieron', *Film Ireland* no. 79, Feb./Mar. 2001, pp. 12–13.

FILMOGRAPHY: *Goodbye Piccadilly* (short, Ir, 1988); *Bossanova Blues* (short, 1991); *Out of the Deep Pan* (short, Ir, 1995); *When Brendan Met Trudy* (Ir/UK); *Rough for Theatre I* (short, Ir) (2000).

WALSH, Raoul (1887–1980)

Raoul Walsh was born on 11 March 1887 in New York City to Irish and Spanish parents. He led an adventurous early life, including working as a cowboy, and became a stunt rider and actor in films. D. W. Griffith gave Walsh his directing break with *The Life of General Villa* (co-dir. Christy Cabanne, 1914), and he went on to make some of the biggest hits of the silent era, including *The Thief of Bagdad* (1924) and *What Price Glory?* (1926).

During a career trough in the mid-1930s Walsh made two British films, *O.H.M.S.* and *Jump for Glory*, with essentially the same story: an American tough flees the scene of a killing, adopts a new identity in England and redeems himself with a selfless act of sacrifice. These are corny, hackneyed melodramas, lacking the polish and slickness of his Hollywood work. Walsh made his best-remembered pictures, including *The Roaring Twenties* (1939), *High Sierra* (1941) and *White Heat* (1949), while under contract to Warner Bros., and towards the end of this period he returned to Britain to make *Captain Horatio Hornblower R.N.* for the company at Denham, with location-shooting in Spain. It proved to be a splendid historical spectacle with some exhilarating action scenes and a sturdy hero in Gregory Peck (wisely retaining his native accent).

A subsequent British-produced costume adventure, *Sea Devils*, with Rock Hudson involved in smuggling and espionage in the Channel Islands, is on a smaller scale and in a minor key. Walsh's final film in the UK was *The Sheriff of Fractured Jaw*, a comedy-Western with the disastrous star combination of Kenneth More and Jayne Mansfield. It shares plot and personnel with *Carry On Cowboy* (Gerald Thomas, 1965) but has none of that film's wit, style or sophistication. Walsh continued making films until 1964 and died in Simi Valley, California, on New Year's Eve 1980.

(Sheldon Hall)

BIBLIOGRAPHY: Canham, Kingsley, *The Hollywood Professionals, Volume One: Michael Curtiz, Raoul Walsh, Henry Hathaway* (London: Tantivy/New York: A. S. Barnes, 1973); Hardy, Phil (ed.), *Raoul Walsh* (Edinburgh: Edinburgh Film Festival, 1974); Walsh, Raoul, *Each Man in His Time: The Life Story of a Director* (New York: Farrar, Straus and Giroux, 1974).

FILMOGRAPHY (UK only): *O.H.M.S.* (US: *You're in the Army Now*); *Jump for Glory* (US: *When Thief Meets Thief*) (1937); *Captain Horatio Hornblower R.N.* (1951); *Sea Devils* (1953); *The Sheriff of Fractured Jaw* (1958).

WARCHUS, Matthew (1966–)

Matthew Warchus was born the son of a Yorkshire vicar on 24 October 1966. After studying music and drama at Bristol University, he went on to direct musicals, West End productions and Shakespearean and Jacobean plays. He enjoyed particular success with Yasmina Reza's *Art*; and his reputation for dynamic and inventive productions brought him the opportunity to direct a film in America. *Simpatico*, based on a play by Sam Shepard, unravels the back-story of three friends haunted by a horse-race betting scam they carried out in their youth. Nick Nolte, Jeff Bridges and Sharon Stone give convincing performances as the guilt-ridden plotters, but Warchus has to resort to younger actors in fuzzy flashbacks to tell their story, and the current scam around the infertile stallion Simpatico is woefully underdeveloped. They emerge as tiresome rather than tragic figures, making the contrast between them and their victim, Albert Finney's racing commissioner who has turned the catastrophe into an opportunity to build himself a new life, less effective than it might have been. Despite *Simpatico*'s flaws, Warchus deserves some credit for an intelligent, ambitious debut, though he subsequently returned to the stage, directing Yasmina Reza's *Life (x) 3* in London and New York.

(Sarah Cardwell)

BIBLIOGRAPHY: Roberts, Alison, 'The Surprise Outside', *Evening Standard*, 27 Jan. 2000, p. 52; Whitley, John, '"It was Like Jumping from an Aeroplane"', *Daily Telegraph*, 18 Jan. 2000, p. 18.

FILMOGRAPHY: *Simpatico* (UK/Fr/US, 1999).

WARNER, Deborah (1959–)

Deborah Warner was born in Oxford on 12 May 1959 and studied stage management before setting up her own theatre company, where she met long-time collaborator Fiona Shaw. After a series of award-winning productions for the RSC and other companies, she directed Shaw in *Hedda Gabler* (1993), *The Waste Land* (1995) and *Richard II* (1997) for television.

The Last September, Warner's only feature, is adapted from Elizabeth Bowen's novel about an Anglo-Irish family in 1920s' County Cork whose lifestyle is disrupted by the rise of Irish

Nationalism. It has many of the elements of the country-house costume drama: prominent British actors, beautiful photography and a measured tone and pace. Its Irish setting ensures authenticity and the cinematography of Slawomir Idziak (best known for his work with Krzysztof Kieślowski) is stunning, but the bravura acting of the older actors – Fiona Shaw, Maggie Smith, Jane Birkin and Michael Gambon – distracts attention from the romantic dilemmas of the young heroine (Keeley Hawes), torn between a British officer and an Irish Nationalist fugitive.

Warner's English National Opera production of Bach's *St John's Passion* was televised; and her modern dress version of Euripides' *Medea* won prizes in London and Broadway, but it is unlikely that she will follow her male theatrical counterparts Sam Mendes and Stephen Daldry in pursuing a film career.

(John Riley)

BIBLIOGRAPHY: Holben, Jay, 'A Lush but Torn Landscape', *American Cinematographer*, June 2000, pp. 20–6.

FILMOGRAPHY: *The Last September* (UK/Fr/Ir, 1999).

WARREN, Norman J. (1942–)

Norman J. Warren was born in London on 25 June 1942 and entered the film industry in the late 1950s as an assistant to Anatole and Dimitri de Grunewald. He worked as an editor until his short film *Fragment* brought him the opportunity to direct two sex dramas, *Her Private Hell* and *Loving Feeling*. Apparently unhappy at being associated with sexploitation, Warren did not direct again until the mid-1970s when he made three low-budget horror films: *Satan's Slave*, *Prey* and *Terror*. Warren's cult reputation rests on these films.

Like Pete Walker, who also made sex films before switching to horror, Warren's films are characterised by a visceral and realistic type of horror totally different from Hammer's films of the 1950s and 60s. Warren's films lack the intensity of Walker's work but, on very limited resources, they make effective and atmospheric use of locations. This is most notably the case in *Prey*, where Warren transforms a silly story about a cannibalistic alien stalking two lesbians in an isolated country house into something genuinely disturbing.

Since the late 1970s, Warren has worked as a director only sporadically and – with the exception of the science-fiction/horror *Inseminoid* – none of his films has been widely distributed.

(Peter Hutchings)

BIBLIOGRAPHY: Chibnall, Steve, 'Alien Women: The Politics of Sexual Difference in British SF Pulp Cinema', in I. Q. Hunter (ed.), *British Science Fiction Cinema* (London: Routledge, 1999); Fenton, Harvey, Peter Lynch and Jason Slater, 'Legacy of Terror', *Flesh and Blood* no. 5, Sept. 1995, pp. 30–4; McGillivray, David, *Doing Rude Things: The History of the British Sex Film, 1957–81* (London: Sun Tavern Fields, 1992).

FILMOGRAPHY: *Fragment* (short, 1966); *Her Private Hell* (1967); *Loving Feeling* (1968); *Satan's Slave* (US: *Evil Heritage*, 1976); *Prey* (aka *Alien Prey*, 1977); *Terror* (1978); *Outer Touch* (aka *Spaced Out*, 1979); *Inseminoid* (US: *Horror Planet*, 1980); *Warbirds Air Display* (doc. short, 1984); *Gunpowder*; *Bloody New Year* (aka *Time Warp Terror*) (1987).

WATKINS, Peter (1935–)

Peter Watkins was born in Norbiton, Surrey, on 29 October 1935. After education at Cambridge and RADA, he began making amateur films. His shorts *The Diary of an Unknown Soldier* and *The Forgotten Faces* brought him to the attention of the BBC, where with *Culloden* (1964) he established an innovative style combining newsreel techniques (echoing the 1950s' American television series *You Are There*) with drama acted out by 'real people' – here the amateur actors of Canterbury's Playcraft theatre and the people of Inverness. An anachronistic television crew follows the build-up, the fighting of and the brutal aftermath to the 1746 Battle of Culloden. Through bold montage, revealing close-ups and hand-held camera movements, Watkins deconstructs both the historical myth surrounding Bonnie Prince Charlie, the Scottish Jacobite pretender for the crown (shown as an indecisive ditherer), and the cinematic conventions of traditional costume drama.

Culloden aroused extraordinary critical interest and in 1965 the BBC gave Watkins *carte blanche* to employ the same techniques on an exploration of the effects of a nuclear strike on Britain. In *The War Game* realistic depictions of nuclear havoc are mixed with interviews with actors impersonating survivors and Establishment figures (whose rationalisations look increasingly uncomfortable as the horror unfolds). The BBC refused to show the finished product, ostensibly because its content was considered too horrifying for the medium of broadcasting, though its anti-war, anti-government stance was widely seen as the real reason. *The War Game* was allowed a limited theatrical release in 1966 and won several awards including an Academy Award for Best Documentary Feature. It was finally shown on television in 1985.

Watkins' television fame encouraged the American company Universal to back him in his only British feature, *Privilege*, intended as a 'swinging' but bilious snapshot of Britain in the near future. Filtered once again through the device of a television news enquiry, Johnny Speight's original story tells of a teenage idol (Paul Jones, ex-singer with the Manfred Mann band) used by the government to manipulate youth into conformist submission. Limp acting from Jones and his co-star Jean Shrimpton and a slow, meandering narrative led to critical derision and audience indifference. Watkins duly left Britain to live and work abroad. Settling in Sweden, he made *Gladiatorerna* (1969), a more carefully organised vision of the future, exploring a society where deadly sports competitions have taken the place of war. A similar project followed in the USA. In *Punishment Park* (1971) those who have opposed the state are tricked into bidding for their freedom in a heavily rigged game where most of them are hunted down and shot. Most Americans found this a too outspoken attack on their values, though the film pleased more radical European audiences.

Returning to Europe, Watkins found succour in Scandinavia's own solitary, anguished artists, making lengthy, well-received biographical films about Edvard Munch and August Strindberg in the 1970s. Then in France in 1999 he finally realised his most ambitious project, *La Commune (Paris, 1871)*, a massive portrait of the Paris Commune shot with a video camera, using massed amateur forces, much political anger and his trademark technique of looking at historically recreated events through modern media eyes. Different versions last between five and nine hours: though rarely seen, it is likely to remain Watkins' monument.

(Erik Hedling)

BIBLIOGRAPHY: Cook, John R. and Patrick Murphy, 'After the Bomb Dropped: The Cinema Half-Life of *The War Game*', *Journal of Popular British Cinema* no. 3, 2000, pp. 129–32; Gomez, Joseph, *Peter Watkins* (Boston, MA: Twayne, 1979); Walker, Alexander, *Hollywood, England* (London: Harrap, 1986); Welsh, James Michael, *Peter Watkins: A Guide to References and Resources* (Boston, MA: G. K. Hall, 1986).

FILMOGRAPHY: *The Web* (short, 1956); *The Field of Red* (short, 1958); *The Diary of an Unknown Soldier* (short, 1959); *The Forgotten Faces* (short); *Dust Fever* (short, unfinished) (1961); *The Controllers* (doc. short, 1964); *The War Game* (1966); *Privilege* (1967); *Gladiatorerna/Gladiators/The Peace Game* (Swe, 1969); *Punishment Park* (US, 1971); *Edvard Munch* (Swe/Nor, 1976); *Aftenlandet/Evening Land* (Den, 1977); *Resan/The Journey* (doc., Swe/Can, 1987); *Fritänkaren/The Freethinker* (1994); *La Commune (Paris, 1871)* (Fr, 2000).

WATT, Harry (1906–1987)

The son of a Scottish Liberal MP, Raymond Egerton Harry Watt was born in Edinburgh on 18 October 1906. He studied at Edinburgh University, but failed to complete his degree. After a spell in the merchant navy and a number of short-lived industrial jobs, he joined John Grierson at the Empire Marketing Board Film Unit in 1932. While learning the basics of film-making with Grierson in London, Watt also gained valuable experience assisting the director Robert Flaherty with *Man of Aran* (1934), on location in Ireland. In 1936, on Grierson's recommendation, he became a director for the newly established London unit of the American newsreel series *March of Time*; his most notable assignment, *England's Tithe War* (1936), reported on a bitter dispute in Suffolk between tenant farmers and the Church of England over rent collection. For the GPO Film Unit, Watt went on to direct most of *Night Mail*, best remembered of all the 1930s' documentaries, where W. H. Auden's poetry and Benjamin Britten's music helped make the night-time journey from London to Glasgow evocative and exciting.

In 1937 Alberto Cavalcanti succeeded Grierson as the Unit's head. Cavalcanti had directed commercial feature films, and under his tutelage Watt developed a unique form of story documentary. In *The Saving of Bill Blewett* (1936) and *North Sea* (1938), soundtrack commentary was abandoned: necessary points were funnelled instead into simple, realistic stories structured from ordinary events, peopled entirely by non-actors. With *Bill Blewitt*, the story about a fisherman resourceful enough to buy his own boat from his post office savings pales beside fascinating details of life in the mid-1930s in the Cornish fishing village of Mousehole. *North Sea*, reconstructing the rescue of an Aberdeen trawler through the use of ship-to-shore radio, proved much more dramatic, and established a template for the great story documentaries of the Second World War.

Together with Cavalcanti and Humphrey Jennings, Watt was the mainstay of the GPO Film Unit at the outbreak of war. With Jennings and Pat Jackson he was responsible for *The First Days* (1939), important in setting the tone of stoic restraint that was to characterise British propaganda; he also handled interior scenes on *London Can Take It!* (1940), the vivid and influential record of the Blitz, co-directed with Jennings. When Ian Dalrymple succeeded Cavalcanti at what became the Crown Film Unit, Watt was able to persuade his new boss to mount a fifty-minute story documentary about a British bombing raid over Germany. Powerful and gritty, *Target for To-night* (1941) was the first British documentary to reach a wide audience in commercial cinemas. Its success was such that RKO asked Watt to make a similar film about Americans serving with the RAF in the 'Eagle Squadron', but high casualties made such an ambitious project a dangerous proposition. Instead Watt moved to Ealing, where Cavalcanti was attempting to marry fiction with documentary realism. Watt's *Nine Men* (1943), a fictional but highly authentic account of the remnants of a British platoon holding out in a desert fort (actually in Wales), exemplified the new ethos.

After collaborating on the script for Charles Crichton's *For Those in Peril* (1944), a sober dramatic account of the Air-Sea Rescue service, Watt tried to move into a different area, directing and co-writing *Fiddlers Three*, a musical comedy with Tommy Trinder and two mates transported in time back to Nero's Rome. It was not a happy experiment, and he only found his feet again with *The Overlanders* (1946), where he successfully dramatised the story of Australian farmers migrating across the country to escape the threat of Japanese invasion. Ealing sent him back to Australia to make *Eureka Stockade*, the story of a mid-nineteenth-century insurrection in the Australian goldfields, planned by Watt as the first of a series of films, shot in different Commonwealth countries, reflecting the birth of democracy. This tough struggle for social justice was a tale after Watt's own heart, but it exposed his weakness in sustaining narrative tension in a long and complex story.

Though the democracy theme was abandoned, Watt's Commonwealth travels continued with two African sagas, *Where No Vultures Fly* and *West of Zanzibar*: both stronger films, dramatically. Watt's fine eye for realist detail was applied to stirring stories about a well-intentioned white game-warden (the square-jawed Anthony Steel) protecting the great beasts of East Africa's jungle from nefarious poachers. Though now rarely shown, the films were tremendously popular with British and colonial audiences and became two of Ealing's biggest box-office successes. For a brief spell in 1955–6, Watt worked as a producer for Granada Television, presenting a wildlife programme. But he rejoined Ealing and returned to Australia in 1958 for what became the studio's final feature, *The Siege of Pinchgut*, a competent location-shot drama about three escaped convicts making a last stand on a tiny island in Sydney Harbour. Glossier and more assured than *Nine Men*, it still harked back to the same documentary realist ethos. His last cinema films, two minor ventures made in Norway and Denmark, emerged in 1961.

Watt's was a modest talent, but one he deployed knowledgeably and effectively. With his documentaries, it may be difficult to disentangle his contribution to *Night Mail* from Basil Wright's (responsible for bringing in Britten and Auden), or to determine whether he or Jennings deserves most credit for *London Can Take It!*. But the direct impact and urgency of *North Sea* and *Target for To-night* are distinctive; and though not all of his Ealing features found the ideal balance between story and theme, fiction and reality, he still achieved greater lasting success in the feature industry than most other British documentary directors. Harry Watt died in Amersham, Buckinghamshire, on 2 April 1987.

(Leo Enticknap)

BIBLIOGRAPHY: Barr, Charles (ed.), *All Our Yesterdays: 90 Years of British Cinema* (London: BFI, 1986); Barr, Charles, *Ealing Studios*, 2nd edn (London: Studio Vista, 1993); Orbanz, Eva (ed.), *Journey to a Legend and Back: The British Realistic Film* (West Berlin: Verlag Volker Speiss, 1977); Sussex, Elizabeth, *The Rise and Fall of British Documentary* (Berkeley: University of California Press, 1975); Watt, Harry, 'Down Under', *Picturegoer*, 22 June 1946, pp. 8–9; Watt, Harry, *Don't Look at the Camera* (London: Paul Elek, 1974).

FILMOGRAPHY: Documentaries: *Six-Thirty Collection* (1934); *B.B.C. – Droitwich* (1935); *Radio Interference*; *England's Tithe War* (*March of Time*, British series); *Night Mail* (co-dir. Basil Wright); *The Saving of Bill Blewitt* (1936); *Big Money* (1937); *North Sea*; *Distress Call* (1938); *The First Days* (co-dirs. Humphrey Jennings/Pat Jackson, 1939); *Front Line*; *Britain at Bay*; *London Can Take It!* (aka *Britain Can Take It!*, co-dir. Humphrey Jennings); *Squadron 992*; *Britain at Bay* (1940); *Lofoten* (doc. short, co-dir. Walter Tennyson); *Christmas Under Fire*; *Target for To-night* (1941); *Twenty One Miles* (1942); *People Like Maria* (UK/Ukr, 1958); *Vidunderhunden bara* (aka *Messenger of the Mountains*, Nor, 1961).

Fiction: *Jamaica Inn* (2nd unit dir., Alfred Hitchcock, 1939); *Nine Men* (1943); *Fiddlers Three* (1944); *The Overlanders* (1946); *Eureka Stockade* (1949); *Where No Vultures Fly* (US: *Ivory Hunter*, 1951); *West of Zanzibar* (1954); *The Siege of Pinchgut* (1959); *Den hvide hingst* (aka *The Boy Who Loved Horses*, Den, 1961).

WEBBER, Peter

Peter Webber studied art history as an undergraduate and then enrolled on the radio, film and television course at Bristol University. After graduating in 1988 he edited Richard Kwietniowski's *Flames of Passion* (1990) and Cheryl Farthing's *Rosebud* (1991), before moving into television to direct sections of Keith Floyd's cookery programmes and Antoine de Caunes' *Eurotrash*. He broke out of anonymity with the stylish documentary *A to Z of Wagner* (1995), the morbidly atmospheric drama *The Temptation of Franz Schubert* (1997) and a topical drama about tunnel-dwelling road protestors, *Underground* (1999). He consolidated his reputation further with *Men Only* (2001), a controversial drama serial exploring the decline into depravity of a group of seemingly ordinary men; *The Stretford Wives* (2002), a tragi-comedy about the financial and emotional crises of three Manchester sisters; and an episode of the cult American television show *Six Feet Under* (2001).

However, it was his return to editing for Anand Tucker's *Saint-Ex* (1996) that led to his first feature commission. When financing delays forced Mike Newell to relinquish his role as director of *Girl with a Pearl Earring*, Tucker and production partner Andy Paterson called in Webber, whose eclectic record fitted with their desire to make a film that dispensed with the usual conventions of British costume drama. Their faith was rewarded by a sparse, atmospheric drama, which told its fragile story through images rather than dialogue, looks more than action. Though little happens, audiences were drawn in by the intense relationship Webber builds between the artist Vermeer (Colin Firth) and his reluctant model Griet (Scarlett Johansson). The film was internationally successful and won Webber his ticket to Hollywood where he was invited to make a prequel to the Hannibal Lecter films.

(Robert Murphy)

BIBLIOGRAPHY: 'Earring Director Aims at Diversity', *Screen International*, 26 Sept. 2003, p. 9; Magid, Ron, 'Lighting Vermeer', *American Cinematographer*, Jan. 2004, pp. 94–102; Morrow, Fiona, 'Going Dutch' *Time Out*, 30 Dec. 2003, p. 13.

FILMOGRAPHY: *The Zebra Man* (short, 1994); *Girl with a Pearl Earring* (UK/Lux, 2003).

WEEKS, Stephen (1948–)

Stephen Weeks was born in Grimsby, Lincolnshire in 1948 and began directing while still at school with a series of short films on architectural subjects for Southern Television. Subsequently he worked in advertising until 1970 when he made his first film for the cinema, *1917*, a short set in the trenches during the First World War. On the basis of this, Weeks was hired by Amicus Films to direct *I, Monster*, an adaptation of Robert Louis Stevenson's *The Strange Case of Dr Jekyll and Mr Hyde*. Hampered by a ponderous screenplay by producer Milton Subotsky and an experimental 3-D shooting process that was abandoned in mid-production, Weeks nevertheless conjured up an effective period atmosphere. His next film was *Gawain and the Green Knight*, an ambitious attempt to present a mythic rite-of-passage narrative that became a more conventional adventure story after pressure from the production company. In an attempt to escape such interference, Weeks shot his third film in India. *Ghost Story* was another period drama, uneven but with some unsettling moments and a fine performance by Marianne Faithfull. *Sword of the Valiant*, Weeks' last feature to date, was a remake of his own *Gawain and the Green Knight* and did not receive a wide release.

In 1984 Weeks returned to India to shoot *The Bengal Lancers*, a historical drama starring Christopher Lee and Trevor Howard, but the finance for the film collapsed after only a fortnight's shooting and the production was abandoned. Weeks then concentrated on restoring Penhow Castle, reputedly the oldest inhabited castle in Wales. In 2002 he announced that he was selling Penhow and moving to the Czech Republic, where he is now involved in property renovation.

(Peter Hutchings)

BIBLIOGRAPHY: Blackhurst, Chris, 'Legal Lancers Ride into Battle over Epic Film', *Independent on Sunday*, 10 Jan. 1993, p. 7; Pirie, David, 'New Blood', *Sight and Sound*, Spring 1971, p. 74.

FILMOGRAPHY: *1917* (short, 1970); *I, Monster* (1971); *Gawain and the Green Knight* (1973); *Ghost Story* (1974); *Sword of the Valiant – The Legend of Gawain and the Green Knight* (1982).

WEISS, Jirí (1913–2004)

Jirí Weiss was born on 29 March 1913 into a wealthy German-Jewish family in Prague. After abandoning law studies, he worked in journalism and advertising. An amateur experimental film *Lidé na slunci/People in the Sun*, won a prize at the Venice Film Festival in 1935; subsequently he joined the shorts department at Prague's Barrandov Studios, concentrating on documentaries. After the German occupation of Czechoslovakia he came to Britain, where he worked on wartime propaganda shorts and became involved in the activities of the Czech Army in exile. Fiercely patriotic and a committed socialist, Weiss found a congenial first home with the film unit of the Political Committee of the London Co-operative Society. By November 1939 a vivid documentary *The Rape of Czechoslovakia*, compiled from footage Weiss spirited out of the country, was ready for release. Thereafter he moved between companies, widening his experience with fiction elements and the use of non-professional actors. For Pioneer Films he took charge of the fictional *John Smith Wakes Up*, featuring Eliot Makeham as a London bookseller who dreams his son is a Nazi; for the Crown Film Unit he directed *Before the Raid*, a powerful semi-documentary about peaceable Norwegian fishermen stirred to resistance against Nazi occupiers. Working with the Czecho-Slovak Film Unit, he made *Night and Day*, detailing the work of a Czech squadron on operations with RAF Coastal Command. He also edited English-language versions of documentaries put out by the Soviet War News Film Agency.

Writing in *Documentary News Letter* in 1941, Weiss poured generous praise on Britain's emerging war documentaries: 'They have touched every subject with a breath of human feeling; they have introduced on the screen their people as the hero (Weiss, 1941, p. 233).' Among Weiss' own output, *Before the Raid* shows the clear influence of the British model. There is extensive location photography (Portmahomack, on Scotland's north-east coast, standing in respectably for a Norwegian fishing village); and its non-professional cast are eloquently ordinary presences throughout, though sometimes awkward in scenes of physical combat.

As soon as circumstances allowed, Weiss returned to Czechoslovakia, where in 1947 he made his first feature, *Uloupéna hranice* (*The Stolen Frontier*), an impressive study of the corrosive effect of war and fanaticism, set in 1938 in a Czech border village. The documentary-realist tradition remained an influence. Weiss weathered the Stalinist era with more artistic success than many: he became a leading figure in post-war Czech cinema, reaching international audiences with *Vlcí jáma/The Wolf Trap* (1957) and *Romeo, Julie a tma/Sweet Light in the Dark Window* (1961), another war-haunted film about a young Jewish woman hidden from the Gestapo. Ironically, he found less success with *90° in the Shade/Tricet jedna ve stinu* (1965), specifically designed as an international venture with British producer Raymond Stross. Filming took place at the Barrandov Studios with a mostly British cast. Anne Heywood, James Booth, Donald Wolfit and Ann Todd settled well enough into the petty crimes and doomed love in David Mercer's script, but the downbeat air stopped the film travelling widely; it never reached British cinemas at all.

With the Russian occupation of Prague in 1968, Weiss' career was again disrupted. He eventually settled in America, teaching cinema in New York and Santa Barbara, writing plays, fiction and memoirs, but no film project came to fruition. Within Europe he achieved one last success with the German-French co-production *Martha und Ich* (1990), an absorbing semi-autobiographical story of family upsets and war clouds with Michel Piccoli and Marianne Sägebrecht. Jirí Weiss died in Santa Monica, California, on 9 April 2004.

(Geoff Brown and Alan Burton)

BIBLIOGRAPHY: 'Latest Co-operative Film Presents "The Home Front"', *Co-operative News*, 9 Mar. 1940, p. 4; 'New London Film', *Co-operative News*, 14 Oct. 1939, p. 3; Weiss, Jirí 'An Allied Film Unit', *Documentary News Letter* vol. 2 no. 12, Dec. 1941, p. 233; Weiss, Jirí ,'Film in Czechoslovakia', *Sight and Sound*, Spring 1943, p. 92.

FILMOGRAPHY (UK only): *The Rape of Czechoslovakia* (1939); *John Smith Wakes Up*; *Home Front* (1940); *Eternal Prague* (1941); *Who Killed Jack Robins?* (1942); *Before the Raid* (1943); *Night and Day*; *A Letter from Prague* (assoc. dir., Frantisek Sádek) (1945); *90° in the Shade/ Tricet jedna ve stinu* (UK/Cz, 1965).

WEST, Jake (1971–)

After making the short gothic horror film *Club Death*, Jake West raised £20,000 to make *Razor Blade Smile*, a modern vampire film. Crude dialogue and a meandering plot are partly compensated for by Eileen Daly's likeable if amateurish performance as a highly erotic vampire wreaking vengeance on the Masonic order founded by her sinister, odd-looking mentor (Christopher Adamson). West edited Nigel Wingrove's *Sacred Flesh* (1999), worked on the dream sequence for Simon Hunter's *Lighthouse* (2000) and put together the trailer for Rob Green's *The Bunker* (2002), before making his second feature, *Evil Aliens*, a comedy-horror film about a sceptical television crew coming face to face with predatory aliens in a Welsh rural backwater. West's obvious affection for the genre results in a witty script and sequences that make up for the film's tight budget with inventive flair and a bold disregard for good taste. The sort of cinema represented by West and other enthusiastic genre directors like Neil Marshall, Rob Green and Simon Hunter might have few pretensions to art, but it is fuelled by an admirable commitment to ingenious, original, low-budget film-making.

(Robert Murphy)

BIBLIOGRAPHY: <www.jakewest.com>.

FILMOGRAPHY: *Club Death* (short, 1995); *Razor Blade Smile* (1998); *Whacked – the Film* (short, 2002); *Evil Aliens* (2005).

WEST, Walter (1881–?)

Walter West was born in London in 1881. His interest in the film industry led to a partnership with businessman G.T. Broadbridge and the foundation in October 1914 of their company Broadwest. By the following year they had acquired a small studio at Esher where West directed himself and also oversaw the work of contract directors. In 1916 Broadwest moved to a larger and better-equipped studio in Wood Street, Walthamstow, and West sought to combine popularity with quality by introducing Matheson Lang to the screen in his stage production of *The Merchant of Venice* (1916). It was a considerable critical and box-office success and West proceeded to establish a stock company of well-known actors, poaching Gerald Ames, Violet Hopson, Ivy Close, Gregory Scott and, after the war, Stewart Rome, from Cecil Hepworth with offers of higher salaries and good working conditions.

West's wartime service in the Royal Flying Corps restricted the company's output, but he used this experience to study audience preferences at first hand. Broadwest's production policy mixed male-oriented crime adventures with problem dramas adapted from controversial novels featuring women's issues, and propaganda films such as *The Women's Land Army* and *A Munition Girl's Romance* (both 1917), which emphasised the important role women were playing in the war effort. High-quality performance combined with authentic set dressing and location shooting gave Broadwest's films an edge that enabled the studio to survive the war.

In 1920 the company acquired a second studio in Catford, though West's new speciality, 'rattling good turf pictures' based on popular novels by Andrew Soutar and Nat Gould, were often shot on location. In September 1921 Broadwest was dissolved and West and his wife, the American-born actress Violet Hopson, both set up their own companies to continue making racing pictures. *Kissing Cup's Race*, *What Price 'Loving Cup'?* and *The Lady Owner* were particularly successful.

West's films were sometimes criticised for their use of unnecessary subtitles, but praised for their fresh twists on well-worn conventions, crisp storytelling, lively acting and attractive photography. However, the worsening financial climate put an end to Walter West Productions. West directed *A Daughter of Love* for Stoll and *A Trainer and Temptress* for Astra-National, but by 1926 he was bankrupt. Nevertheless, he was able to make a series of shorts for Gainsborough featuring the famous jockey Steve Donoghue, and he set up a new company, Q.T.S., to produce two Victorian melodramas – *Maria Marten* and *Sweeney Todd* – on the back of their successful theatrical revivals. The latter was cleverly 'book-ended' by a contemporary frame and featured a bravura performance from Moore Marriott as the 'demon barber' Sweeney Todd.

West's career in sound was hampered by his weak use of dialogue and faulty grasp of the intricacies of character construction, but he continued to make occasional racing shorts and documentaries in the 1930s and 40s.

(Christine Gledhill)

BIBLIOGRAPHY: Burrows, Jon, *Legitimate Cinema: Theatre Stars in Silent British Films: 1908–1918* (Exeter: University of Exeter Press, 2003); Low, Rachael, *The History of the British Film 1914–1918* (London: George Allen & Unwin, 1950); Low, Rachael, *The History of the British Film 1918–1929* (London: George Allen & Unwin, 1971); West, Walter, 'The Trail of the Stars', *Pictures and Picturegoer*, Feb. 1924, pp. 41–2.

FILMOGRAPHY: *Full Up* (short); *The Thick and Thin of It* (short) (1914); *A Bold Adventuress*; *The Mystery of a London Flat* (aka *A London*

Flat Mystery); *By the Hand of a Brother* (aka *By a Brother's Hand*); *The Woman Who Did* (1915); *Burnt Wings*; *The Hard Way*; *The Merchant of Venice*; *The Answer* (1916); *The Knockout Blow*; *The Women's Land Army*; *The House Opposite*; *A Munition Girl's Romance*; *The Ware Case* (1917); *The Ragged Messenger*, *Missing the Tide*; *A Turf Conspiracy*; *Sisters in Arms*; *A Fortune at Stake*; *Not Negotiable* (1918); *Under Suspicion*; *The Woman Wins*; *A Daughter of Eve*; *The Gentleman Rider* (aka *Hearts and Saddles*); *Snow in the Desert* (1919); *A Dead Certainty*; *Her Son*; *The Case of Lady Camber* (1920); *Kissing Cup's Race*; *The Loudwater Mystery*; *A Sportsman's Wife*; *Vi, of Smith's Alley*; *The Imperfect Lover* (1921); *The Scarlet Lady*; *When Greek Meets Greek*; *Son of Kissing Cup*; *The White Hope*; *Was She Justified?* (1922); *Hornet's Nest*; *The Lady Owner*, *Beautiful Kitty*; *What Price 'Loving Cup'?*; *In the Blood* (1923); *The Stirrup Cup Sensation*; *A Great Turf Mystery* (1924); *A Daughter of Love*; *A Trainer and Temptress* (1925); *Steve Donoghue Series of Racing Dramas* (*Riding for a King*, *Beating the Book*, *Come on, Steve*, *The Golden Spurs*, *The Stolen Favourite*, *Dark Horses*, *A Knight of the Saddle* aka *Knight of the Pigskin*, shorts); *Woodcroft Castle:* episode 7 of *Haunted Houses and Castles of Great Britain*; *The Brotherhood* (short) (1926); *Maria Marten*; *Sweeney Todd* (1928); *Warned Off* (1929); *Aura No. 1* (musical short); *Aura No. 2* (Musical short) (1930); *Hundred to One* (short); *A Day in the Life of Gordon Richards* (doc.) (1933); *Bed and Breakfast* (1937); *We Do Believe in Ghosts* (short, 1947); *Kings of the Turf* (doc.); *Champions in the Making* (doc.) (1949).

WHATHAM, Claude (1935–)

Claude Whatham was born in Manchester on 2 December 1935. He studied art and design at High Wycombe Technical College and theatre design at the Bristol Old Vic School. After working in the theatre and a spell with the design team at the BBC he trained as a director with Granada Television, where his varied output included drama, music and current affairs. In 1966 Whatham returned to the BBC; prestigious drama assignments included John Mortimer's *A Voyage Round My Father* (1969) and an adaptation of Laurie Lee's *Cider with Rosie* (1971).

In 1973 Whatham's first feature film "*That'll be the Day*", tracing the fictional genesis of a British rock star, scored a major public success. David Essex starred as the grammar school hero of Ray Connolly's script, who turns his back on educational opportunity for the thrills of fairgrounds, seaside resorts, an early marriage and, above everything, rock and roll music. Throughout, Whatham's direction remained orthodox and unobtrusive, but his effective use of locations reflected Connolly's keen eye for the tawdrier corners of British life in the 1950s, and he managed one moment of definite magic when Essex dances briefly with a door. Well-played cameo parts from Ringo Starr, Keith Moon and Billy Fury bustled around the boyish Essex; the lively rock and roll soundtrack proved another strong asset.

Despite the film's wide popularity, Whatham's cinema career failed to advance much further. The sequel, *Stardust*, in which Essex's Jim MacLaine overreaches himself in a Beatles-like group, followed in 1974; but this time Michael Apted directed, in a more flamboyant style. Though neither of Whatham's next two films were directly made for television, both *All Creatures Great and Small* and *Swallows and Amazons* suggested the small screen with their modesty, animals, children, insistent close-ups and tidy scenery. More television work duly followed, ranging from the biographical series *Disraeli* (1978) and a respectfully received adaptation of D. H. Lawrence's story *The Captain's Doll* (1982) to several episodes of *Tales of the Unexpected* (1980). Over the next decade occasional and varied cinema features emerged: *Sweet William*, a story of seduction adapted from Beryl Bainbridge's novel, capturing British middle-class manners and feelings with at times exasperating precision; *Hoodwink*, an engaging Australian caper movie; a little-seen serial killer thriller, *Murder Elite*; and the deftly handled but bland *Buddy's Song*, a return to the territory of *That'll be the Day*, with Roger Daltrey as an ageing Teddy Boy. None of the films made much impact, and Whatham has essentially remained what he was at the start, a competent television director.

(Janet Moat)

BIBLIOGRAPHY: 'All Creatures Great and Small', *Films Illustrated*, Mar. 1975, p. 246; Watts, Janet, 'Forceps Saga', *Guardian*, 23 Mar. 1976.

FILMOGRAPHY: "*That'll be the Day*" (1973); *All Creatures Great and Small*; *Swallows and Amazons* (1974); *Sweet William* (1980); *Hoodwink* (Austral, 1981); *Murder Elite* (1986); *Buddy's Song* (1991).

WHELAN, Tim (1893–1957)

Born on 2 November 1893 in Cannelton, Indiana, Tim Whelan acted on stage before entering Hollywood's film industry as an actor and writer in 1920. His career flourished under Harold Lloyd: he contributed, among others, to *Safety Last* (1923), *Girl Shy* (1924) and *The Freshman* (1925), all directed by Fred C. Newmeyer and Sam Taylor. It was the expanding British film industry that gave Whelan his chance to direct, beginning in 1928 with the comedy *Adam's Apple*, the first British vehicle of another American import, the comedian Monty Banks. Returning to America, Whelan busied himself with comedy scripts at RKO, chiefly for Bert Wheeler and Robert Woolsey. Crossing the Atlantic again he then hit his stride with a series of crisply managed entertainments featuring the Gaumont-British stable of comedy stars, notably *Aunt Sally* (1933), with Cicely Courtneidge, and *The Camels Are Coming*, with her husband, Jack Hulbert.

Whelan finally made his American directing debut for MGM in 1935 with *The Murder Man*; less successfully, he directed Courtneidge in her only Hollywood picture, *The Perfect Gentleman*. Returning to England, his portfolio widened. George Eliot's novel *The Mill on the Floss* (1937) offered few opportunities for speed and wit; but *Farewell Again*, produced by Erich Pommer for Korda's London Films, proved a major success with its expert dovetailing of character and sentiment among soldiers returning from India for six hours' home leave. When Pommer formed his own company, Mayflower, with Charles Laughton and Alfred Hitchcock, Whelan directed Laughton and Vivien Leigh in their first production, *St Martin's*

Lane W.C.2. For Korda, Whelan turned out two upper-class society dramas, *Action for Slander* and *The Divorce of Lady X*; but he was less at home with their stiff upper lips than with the sparky fun of the Jack Buchanan/Elsie Randolph comedy *Smash and Grab*, and *Q Planes*, where Ralph Richardson's eccentric Scotland Yard inspector tracks down missing test planes with the aid of umbrella, bowler hat and wickedly delivered lines ('Come and meet Blenkinsop – he's a perfect swine!').

For the action sequences in *The Thief of Bagdad* (1940), Whelan supplied acrobatics and American pep – neither of them trademarks of the director he largely replaced, Ludwig Berger. Pace, sustained atmosphere, good humour, versatility: these were Whelan's best attributes. In 1940, when Korda shifted production of *The Thief of Bagdad* to Hollywood, Whelan moved alongside. There he settled into a lesser and more anonymous career, mostly at RKO, making spy dramas, Westerns and Frank Sinatra's first two starring vehicles (*Higher and Higher, Step Lively*). He returned to England briefly in 1947 to make the involving *This Was a Woman*, the melodramatic tale of a power-crazy wife (Sonia Dresdel) who poisons her husband. Harold Lloyd's world had been left far behind. Whelan died in Beverly Hills on 12 August 1957, two years after his last feature, *Texas Lady.*

(Geoff Brown)

BIBLIOGRAPHY: Kulik, Karol, *Alexander Korda: The Man Who Could Work Miracles* (London: W. H. Allen, 1975).

FILMOGRAPHY (UK only): *Adam's Apple* (US: *Honeymoon Ahead*, 1928); *When Knights Were Bold* (1929); *It's a Boy!*; *Aunt Sally* (US: *Along Came Sally*) (1933); *The Camels Are Coming* (1934); *Two's Company* (1936); *The Mill on the Floss*; *Farewell Again* (US: *Troopship*); *Action for Slander*, *Smash and Grab* (US: *Larceny Street*) (1937); *The Divorce of Lady X*; *St Martin's Lane W.C.2* (US: *Sidewalks of London*) (1938); *Q Planes* (US: *Clouds over Europe*); *Ten Days in Paris* (US: *Missing Ten Days*) (1939); *The Thief of Bagdad* (co-dirs. Ludwig Berger/Michael Powell, 1940); *This Was a Woman* (1948).

WHITEHEAD, Peter (1937–)

In his films *Wholly Communion*, *Tonite Let's All Make Love in London* and *The Fall*, Peter Whitehead flourished briefly as a vivid chronicler of the social, musical and political revolutions sweeping through the Western world. But as the 1970s advanced, the independent scene shrank, Whitehead's films settled into a time capsule and his singular energies found expression in other endeavours, predominantly novel-writing, and the trapping and breeding of falcons.

Peter Lorrimer Whitehead was born to working-class parents in 1937 in Liverpool. His middle name inspired Lorrimer Films, his production company in the 1960s, and Lorrimer Publishing, which launched its notable *Classic and Modern Film Scripts* series in 1966 with three screenplays by Godard. This was not accidental: Godard proved a major influence on Whitehead's fragmented, freewheeling style; though his first film, *The Perception of Life* (1964), a Nuffield Foundation Unit short exploring theories about living matter through the history of microscopes, pointed more toward his science education at Cambridge University. From Cambridge Whitehead moved to the Slade School of Fine Art in London in the early 1960s, where he joined Thorold Dickinson's newly formed film department. From thence he set out as a freelance, working lucratively for a while in the newly burgeoning pop-promo field.

Wholly Communion, a thirty-three-minute portrait of the 1965 'International Poetry Incarnation' at the Royal Albert Hall, established Whitehead's reputation for whirling hand-held camerawork and an instinctive sympathy for shakers of the status quo. Following filming, the Rolling Stones' manager Andrew Oldham invited Whitehead and his camera to document the group's tour of Ireland in September 1965: management troubles meant the resulting film, *Charlie Is My Darling*, was never properly released. Its successor, *Tonite Let's All Make Love in London* (1967), was an impressionistic kaleidoscope of the 'swinging' capital city. 'The total effect', mused the *Monthly Film Bulletin* in February 1968, 'is like flicking over the pages of last week's "colour supplement"': an effect that at least ensures the film's importance as social history.

In *The Fall*, completed in 1969, Whitehead's stance developed significantly beyond that of the hand-held observer. Anger at America's war in Vietnam had already helped fuel *The Benefit of the Doubt*, an exploration of Peter Brook's stage production *US* (the subject also of Brooks' *Tell Me Lies*, 1967). Now an invitation to make a 'Tonite' film about New York took him to America itself. In New York Whitehead became embattled alongside protesting students at Columbia University; and the wayward, two-hour film he ultimately fashioned was as much about himself as the heated events he witnessed. Most critics greeted it warily.

After *The Fall*, Whitehead collaborated with the Franco-American artist Niki De Saint Phalle on *Daddy* (1973), an *outré*, erotically charged family drama. *Fire in the Water* (1977) mixed past Whitehead footage with Nathalie Delon communing with nature; the director subsequently branded the film a mistake. But these films, little seen, were essentially footnotes to his cinema career. Falconry took over, along with mysticism, wild adventures in the Middle East and, from the 1980s, the writing of novels – heady cocktails of social satire, science fiction, conspiracy theories and sex. *Tonite Let's All Make Love in London* (1999) borrowed the film's title for a tale about American manipulation of British counter-culture, centred on the poetry event celebrated in *Wholly Communion*. Whitehead's last brush with film-making was as the willing subject of Chris Petit and Iain Sinclair's television film *The Falconer* (1998), a visually and structurally complex portrait of a fiery but enigmatic figure.

(Geoff Brown)

BIBLIOGRAPHY: Sargeant, Jack, *The Naked Lens: An Illustrated History of Beat Cinema* (London: Creation Cinema Collection, 2001); Whitehead, Peter, 'I Destroy Therefore I Am . . .', *Films and Filming*, Jan. 1969, pp. 14–20; Whitehead, Peter, 'Mind Games', *Films and Filming*, Feb. 1974, pp. 16–21; <www.peter-whitehead.com>.

FILMOGRAPHY: *The Perception of Life* (short, co-dir. June Goodfield, 1964); *Wholly Communion* (short, 1965); *Charlie Is My Darling* (1966); *Tonite Let's All Make Love in London*; *The Benefit of the Doubt* (1967); *The Fall* (1969); *Daddy* (1973); *Fire in the Water* (Switz, 1977).

WICKES, David (1940–)

David Nevil Wickes was born in Leamington Spa in 1940. The bulk of Wickes' work – as a producer/writer/director – has been in British television, where he has tended to specialise in crime and gothic subjects. A production trainee at Granada in the early 1960s, he later took a television director's course with Associated-Rediffusion and went on to handle a variety of documentaries, current affairs programmes and outside broadcasts. From the late 1960s, he worked on detective series: notably *Softly, Softly*, *Van Der Valk*, *The Sweeney* and *The Professionals*.

His first cinema credit is *Sweeney!*, with John Thaw and Dennis Waterman mixed up in assassination plots and political intrigue. Slightly upping the violence, nudity and swearing of the television series, *Sweeney!* is most memorable for its bleak, paranoid end. Hero Regan sets up an 'untouchable' villain for assassination, the shock coming not from the underhand act but from sidekick Carter's angry freeze-frame accusation. Wickes' only purely cinematic venture is the disappointingly dull *Silver Dream Racer*, a motorcycle drama starring a mullet-headed David Essex.

In 1973, Wickes devised the unusual true crime series *Jack the Ripper*, in which Barlow (Stratford Johns) and Watt (Frank Windsor), the detectives from *Softly, Softly*, sift through the evidence in the famous murder case, to which Wickes returned in the 1988 miniseries *Jack the Ripper*, enlisting Michael Caine as his police investigator. Caine reappeared in twin roles for Wickes' television film *Jekyll & Hyde* (1990). *Frankenstein: The Real Story* (1992), a worthy attempt at taking the old classic seriously, followed, but Wickes' television version was soon eclipsed by Kenneth Branagh's more spectacular *Mary Shelley's Frankenstein* (1994). More recently he produced and was one of several veteran directors on Brian Clemens' *CI5: The New Professionals* (1998).

(Kim Newman)

BIBLIOGRAPHY: 'A David Wickes Special', *Screen International*, 5 Nov. 1983, pp. 32–49; Summers, Sue, 'David Wickes', *Screen International*, 24 Apr. 1976, pp. 21–2; 'The Road to Frankenstein', *In Camera*, Summer 1993, pp. 9–10.

FILMOGRAPHY: *Sweeney!* (1977); *Silver Dream Racer* (1980).

WILCOX, Herbert (1890–1977)

Though less well known and appreciated than his contemporaries Michael Balcon and Alexander Korda, Herbert Wilcox was one of the most important and successful British film-makers from the early 1920s to the 50s, producing more than one hundred films, half of which he directed himself. Despite his eventual bankruptcy, his considerable entrepreneurial skills enabled him to sustain a continued presence over a long period in a notoriously unstable industry.

Herbert Sydney Wilcox was born on 19 April 1890, in the London suburb of West Norwood. In his autobiography he proclaims himself Irish, though he was brought up in England, and in films such as *Victoria the Great* he displays a patriotic pride in being British. The two main phases of his career were the formative 1920s when he entered the industry and established a reputation as an enterprising young producer; and the period from 1932 until the late 1950s, when his career became focused almost exclusively on Anna Neagle, the actress, singer and dancer whom he married.

Wilcox began in the film business just after the First World War, selling American films to exhibitors in Yorkshire, after which he moved into production. In 1922 he formed a company, Graham-Wilcox, with the fledgling director Jack Graham Cutts, and by 1925 had established himself as a successful producer/director with a sharp nose for publicity. He produced films in conjunction with German companies, pioneered the use of American stars to improve the saleability of British product in the United States and experimented with colour, using Prizma Color in sequences of *Flames of Passion* (Graham Cutts, 1922). In addition, he was involved with the American entrepreneur J. D. Williams in setting up the British National company (later to be absorbed into British International Pictures) and the Elstree studio complex.

In 1927 Wilcox established the British and Dominions Film Corporation, and found early success (and censorship trouble) with *Dawn* (1928), his own film about Nurse Edith Cavell, executed by the Germans in the First World War for assisting escaped prisoners in Belgium. In a testimonial, George Bernard Shaw extravagantly claimed its director as 'a young film poet' (Low, 1971, p. 66). Wilcox was never that – his visual manner always remained prosaic – but with its sobriety, single-minded focus and majestic central performance by Sybil Thorndike, *Dawn* demonstrated new maturity in a film-maker previously content with showmanship alone. Wilcox was quick to recognise the importance of the sound film and before B & D's own sound studio had been built at Elstree he rented studio space in Hollywood to produce a highly talkative melodrama, *Black Waters* (Marshall Neilan). In London the film was trade-shown in May 1929, a few weeks before Hitchcock's *Blackmail*, usually regarded as the 'first British talkie'. Wilcox was also involved in British cinema's Technicolor developments in the 1930s, incorporating colour sequences in *Victoria the Great* and shooting *Sixty Glorious Years* entirely in colour.

Goodnight Vienna (1932) began Wilcox's long professional and personal relationship with Anna Neagle: of the forty-plus films Wilcox directed thereafter, more than thirty were vehicles for Neagle. In the 1930s many of them were biographies, ranging from the racy remake *Nell Gwyn* (a subject first treated in 1926 with Dorothy Gish) to the hagiographic accounts of Queen Victoria (*Victoria the Great*, *Sixty Glorious Years*). The Cavell story was revisited as *Nurse Edith Cavell*, first of a series of productions made for RKO in America.

Wilcox and Neagle followed *Cavell* in America with *Irene*, *Sunny* and *No, No, Nanette*, adaptations of venerable musical comedies – pleasant escapism at best; he also contributed to Hollywood's pro-British pageant *Forever and a Day*. But his career only took wing again once he returned to England. Another biographical film, the subdued and serious *They Flew Alone*, based on the life of aviator Amy Johnson, was followed by *The Yellow Canary*, an espionage thriller with Neagle daringly cast as a seemingly pro-Nazi society lady, shipped off to Canada as a security risk. Their next films, *I Live in Grosvenor Square* (1945) and *Piccadilly Incident* (1946), proved highly wrought melodramas on the wartime themes of separation and loss. They also celebrated upper-class England and launched a cycle of hugely popular films pairing Neagle with Michael Wilding, known as the 'London series'. Later entries such as *Spring in Park Lane* (1948) and *Maytime in Mayfair* (1949) were unashamedly escapist semi-musicals, with ball gowns, Rolls-Royces, lavish settings and lovably eccentric aristocrats much in evidence: judging by box-office receipts, this was just what a public still suffering from food shortages and bomb damage wanted.

Wilcox's films of the early 1950s adhered closely to past formulae. The seriousness and sobriety of *Dawn* re-emerged in *Odette* (1951), a surprisingly authentic account of the experiences of the SOE agent Odette Sansom in occupied France, featuring scenes of Gestapo torture and cruelty that still seem harrowing today. Neagle as Florence Nightingale in *The Lady with a Lamp*, proved a blander experience; *Lilacs in the Spring* rounded up her past roles as Nell Gwyn and Queen Victoria in an absurd farandole kicked off, like *Piccadilly Incident*, by an air raid in the Second World War. The final stage of Wilcox's career brought various attempts to align his brand of showmanship and entertainment with the popular music of the day in films featuring singer Frankie Vaughan, ending with the dated and sentimental *The Heart of a Man* (1959). It proved to be Wilcox's last film in a career that had survived through all the industry's various crises since the 1920s. He died in London on 15 May 1977. Wilcox's films have long been neglected by critics and historians, but his knack for satisfying public taste served him well for over three decades. In 2004 a BFI survey of cinema ticket sales in Britain revealed the 20.5 million admissions clocked up by *Spring in Park Lane* as the largest ever achieved by a British film.

(Tom Ryall)

BIBLIOGRAPHY: Drazin, Charles, *The Finest Years: British Cinema of the 1940s* (London: André Deutsch, 1998); Low, Rachael, *The History of the British Film 1918–1929* (London: George Allen & Unwin, 1971); Low, Rachael, *The History of the British Film 1929–1939* (London: George Allen & Unwin, 1985); Street, Sarah, *British National Cinema* (London and New York: Routledge, 1997); Wilcox, Herbert, *Twenty-Five Thousand Sunsets: The Autobiography of Herbert Wilcox* (London: Bodley Head, 1967).

FILMOGRAPHY: *Chu Chin Chow* (1923); *Decameron Nights* (Ger: *Dekameron-Nächte*); *Southern Love* (US: *A Woman's Secret*) (1924); *The Only Way* (1925); *Nell Gwyn* (1926); *Mumsie*; *Madame Pompadour*, *Tiptoes* (1927); *Dawn* (1928); *The Bondman*; *The Woman in White* (1929); *The Loves of Robert Burns* (1930); *Money Means Nothing*; *Carnival* (US: *Venetian Nights*); *The Chance of a Night Time* (1931); *Yes, Mr Brown*; *Goodnight Vienna* (US: *Magic Night*); *The Blue Danube* (1932): *The Little Damozel*; *The King's Cup*; *Bitter Sweet* (1933); *The Queen's Affair* (US: *Runaway Queen*); *Nell Gwynn* (1934); *Peg of Old Drury* (1935); *This'll Make You Whistle*; *Limelight* (US: *Backstage*); *The Three Maxims* (US: *The Show Goes On*) (1936); *London Melody* (US: *Girls in the Street*); *Victoria the Great* (1937); *Sixty Glorious Years* (US: *Queen of Destiny*, 1938); *Nurse Edith Cavell* (US, 1939); *Irene* (US); *No, No Nannette* (US) (1940); *Sunny* (US, 1941); *They Flew Alone* (US: *Wings and the Woman*, 1942); *Forever and a Day* (US, co-dirs. René Clair/Edmund Goulding/Cedric Hardwicke/Frank Lloyd/Victor Saville/Robert Stevenson); *The Yellow Canary* (1943); *I Live in Grosvenor Square* (US: *A Yank in London*, 1945); *Piccadilly Incident* (1946); *The Courtneys of Curzon Street* (US: *The Courtney Affair*, 1947); *Spring in Park Lane*; *Elizabeth of Ladymead* (1948); *Maytime in Mayfair* (1949); *Into the Blue* (US: *Man in the Dinghy*, 1950); *Odette*; *The Lady with a Lamp* (1951); *Derby Day* (US: *Four against Fate*); *Trent's Last Case* (1952); *Laughing Anne*; *Trouble in the Glen* (1953); *Lilacs in the Spring* (US: *Let's Make Up*); *King's Rhapsody* (1955); *My Teenage Daughter* (US: *Teenage Bad Girl*, 1956); *These Dangerous Years* (US: *Dangerous Youth*, 1957); *Wonderful Things*; *The Man Who Wouldn't Talk* (1958); *The Lady Is a Square*; *The Heart of a Man* (1959).

WILDER, Billy (1910–2002)

Samuel Wilder was born in Sucha, Austria-Hungary (now Poland), on 22 June 1910. He worked as a scriptwriter in Germany and France, where he also directed *Mauvaise graine* (1934), before moving to the United States in 1933. He pursued a successful career as a scriptwriter until 1942, when he began to direct the screenplays he wrote in partnership with Charles Brackett. His third directorial effort, *Double Indemnity* (1944), effectively defined the film noir genre for generations to come. The partnership with Brackett came to an end with the mordant *Sunset Boulevard* (1950), but Wilder began a new partnership with writer I. A. L. Diamond, starting with the phenomenally successful *Some Like It Hot* (1959) and *The Apartment* (1960).

Wilder and Diamond came to Britain in 1969 to make *The Private Life of Sherlock Holmes*, with Robert Stephens and Colin Blakely as Holmes and Watson. Filmed at Pinewood Studios and in Scotland, with a $10 million budget, it was intended as a three-hour-plus epic comprising a prologue, four adventures and an extended flashback showing Holmes' student days. When plans for a 'roadshow' release of the film were abandoned, it was cut to a standard length, with only two of the intended six segments surviving. By turns melancholy and romantic, it remains one of his finest achievements. Wilder died of pneumonia in Beverly Hills on 27 March 2002.

(Sergio Angelini)

BIBLIOGRAPHY: Gillett, John, 'In Search of Sherlock', *Sight and Sound*, Winter 1969–70, pp. 26–7; 'Watson, John H.', '*The Private Life of Sherlock Holmes* and The Curious Case of the Missing Footage', *Movie Collector* vol.1 no. 7, July/Aug. 1994, pp. 10–17, and vol.1 no. 8, Nov./Dec. 1994, pp. 25–9.

FILMOGRAPHY (UK only): *The Private Life of Sherlock Holmes* (US/UK, 1970).

WILLIAMS, Brock (1894–1964)

Homerville Brock Williams was born in Truro, Cornwall, in 1894. He gained his first film credit adapting Agatha Christie's Hercule Poirot murder mystery *Black Coffee* (Leslie Hiscott, 1931) from stage to screen. Innumerable similar assignments followed throughout the 1930s, initially for Julian Hagen at Twickenham. Later, he moved upriver to Warner Bros. at Teddington, where he was responsible for Michael Powell's *Crown v. Stevens* (1936) Arthur Woods' *Where's Sally?* (1936) and later Thorold Dickinson's *The Prime Minister* (1941), among many others. After the studio was destroyed by a flying bomb in 1944 Williams transferred to Gainsborough, where he wrote the screenplay for the clever ghost story *A Place of Your Own* (Bernard Knowles, 1945). He also acted as scenario editor on the melodramas *Madonna of the Seven Moons* (Arthur Crabtree, 1944) *Love Story* (Leslie Arliss, 1944), and *They Were Sisters* (Arthur Crabtree, 1945).

In a half-hearted attempt to maintain Gainsborough's successful reputation for melodramas after most of the creative personnel had moved on, Williams was required to direct his own screenplay for *Root of All Evil* (1947), the saga of a wronged woman who overcomes poverty and prejudice to achieve riches but surrenders everything for love. Unfortunately a turgid pace, and the lack of affinity between Phyllis Calvert and her leading men Michael Rennie and John McCallum, led to terminal dullness. Williams made a second stab at directing with *I'm a Stranger* (1952), but this was a much less ambitious affair, a throwback to the quickies of the 1930s, with a bunch of ill-matched characters squabbling over a will. Williams returned to what he did best, writing routine but efficient B-films. When paired with an equally workmanlike director, such as John Gilling on *The Gilded Cage* (1955), Charles Saunders on *Naked Fury* (1959) and *The Gentle Trap* (1960), or Lance Comfort on *Rag Doll* (1961) and *The Painted Smile* (1961), the results were satisfactorily entertaining. He died in Richmond, Surrey, on 19 February 1964.
(Robert Murphy)

FILMOGRAPHY: *Root of All Evil* (1947); *I'm a Stranger* (1952).

WILLIAMS, Emlyn (1905–1987)

George Emlyn Williams was born on 26 November 1905 in Mostyn, a Welsh mining village. A scholarship took him to Oxford University, where he began an acting career that lasted until the 1980s, and included performances for stage, cinema, television and radio. As a playwright he had particular success with *Night Must Fall* (1935) and *The Corn Is Green* (1938), both of which were later filmed. In addition to screen acting ranging from *The Man Who Knew Too Much* (Alfred Hitchcock, 1934) to *The Walking Stick* (Eric Till, 1970), he wrote a number of screenplays, among them *Friday the Thirteenth* (Victor Saville, 1933) and *Evergreen* (Victor Saville, 1934). His books include two volumes about his early life, *George* (1961) and *Emlyn* (1973), and *Beyond Belief* (1967), on the Moors murderers.

He was the director of one film, *The Last Days of Dolwyn*, which he also wrote and acted in, as the man who returns to the Welsh village that cast him out as a child, and which is now to be flooded to supply the English with water. It lacked the commercial success and dramatic tension of Williams' best stage work, though it is helped by fine performances from Edith Evans and a young Richard Burton, and the story has an interesting, if ultimately circumvented, nationalist dimension. Set against the nostalgia evoked through Otto Heller's beautiful photography, Williams' role also suggests an intriguingly ambivalent attitude towards his roots. He died in London on 25 September 1987.
(Guy Barefoot)

BIBLIOGRAPHY: Berry, David, *Wales and Cinema: The First 100 Years* (Cardiff: University of Wales Press, 1994); Harding, James, *Emlyn Williams: A Life* (London: Weidenfeld & Nicolson, 1993).

FILMOGRAPHY: *The Last Days of Dolwyn* (1949).

WILLIAMS, Richard (1933–)

Richard Williams was born in Toronto on 19 March 1933, but has spent most of his professional life in the UK. Though best known for his work on *Who Framed Roger Rabbit* (Robert Zemeckis, 1988), Williams has a considerable portfolio of work, and his publication *The Animator's Survival Kit* is essential reading for anyone seriously interested in animation. One only need watch the 'Maroon Cartoon' *Somethin's Cookin'*, supposedly made in 1947 and featured at the beginning of *Who Framed Roger Rabbit*, to see how Williams has lived through, absorbed and perpetuated the finest traditions in cartoon history.

Williams began his career work with *Yellow Submarine* director George Dunning, and then worked in the expanding television commercials industry. His first film, *The Little Island* (1958), a philosophical treatise playing out the obsessive imperatives of 'beauty', 'truth' and 'goodness' as competing monsters, indicated his interest in the compulsive side of the human spirit. Four years later the more commercial success of *Love Me, Love Me, Love Me* (1962) enabled him to establish his own studio, which attracted many animators keen to embrace Williams' perfectionist approach. Later, he was to engage Disney veterans Art Babbitt, who developed 'Goofy' and worked on the 'Mushroom Dance' in *Fantasia* (1940), and Milt Kahl, animator of Shere

Khan in *The Jungle Book* (Wolfgang Reitherman, 1967), to train young animators at his studio.

In the 1960s Williams continued to balance his commercial work – notably a series of advertisements for Truman Bitter – with personal films like *A Lecture on Man* (1962); he was also responsible for the extraordinary animated titles and bridging sequences for Tony Richardson's *The Charge of the Light Brigade* (1968). Drawing upon satirical cartoons from *Punch*, and an older tradition of caricature stretching back to Hogarth, Gilray and Rowlandson, Williams enhanced the tenor of Charles Wood's script, which both celebrates and mocks Victorian achievements and values. Williams' other notable title sequences include *What's New Pussycat* (Clive Donner, 1965), *Casino Royale* (Val Guest/Joseph McGrath/Ken Hughes/John Huston/Robert Parrish, 1967) and, most famously, *Return of the Pink Panther* (Blake Edwards, 1974).

In 1966 Williams illustrated *The Exploits of the Incomparable Mulla Nasruddin* (Jonathan Cape, 1966), a collection of Sufi folk tales about the wise fool Mulla Nasruddin, and he determined to turn the stories into a feature film. Despite his Academy Award-winning success with the television special *A Christmas Carol* (1971), *The Thief and the Cobbler* (as the Nasruddin film became known) suffered several false starts, including an elaborate test sequence funded by Saudi Prince Mohammed Feisal, which was widely admired but considered too costly. Williams won an Emmy for Best Animated Programme with *Ziggy's Gift*, made for American television in 1981, and, along with the work he had done for *The Thief and the Cobbler*, this led Steven Spielberg and Robert Zemeckis to commission him to work on their adaptation of Gary K. Wolf's cult novel *Who Censored Roger Rabbit?*. Williams resolved the problems of blending live action and animation, won an Academy Award, and further extended his reputation as a consummate artist, but the costs and delays in the project did not win him the anticipated support he needed for *The Thief and the Cobbler*. Warner Bros. retreated from a potential deal in the light of Disney's forthcoming release of the similarly themed *Aladdin* (1992), and the version that emerged as *The Princess and the Cobbler* (1994) was completed by television animator and producer Fred Calvert, after Williams lost the rights to the film. Miramax purchased and released another bowdlerised and hugely re-cut version, entitled *Arabian Knight* (1995). Williams' masterpiece remains unseen in the form he wanted, but it endures as one of animation's legends, and a potent influence on the generations of animators who worked to bring it to fruition.

(Paul Wells)

BIBLIOGRAPHY: Canemaker, John, *The Animated Raggedy Ann and Andy – An Intimate Look at the Art of Animation* (Indianapolis and New York: Bobbs-Merrill, 1977); Grant, John, *Encyclopaedia of Walt Disney's Animated Characters* (New York: Hyperion, 1993), pp. 318–25; Grant, John, *Masters of Animation* (London: Batsford, 2001), pp. 197–203; Ohmer, S., '*Who Framed Roger Rabbit?*: The Presence of the Past', in John Canemaker (ed.), *Storytelling in Animation* (Los Angeles, CA: AFI, 1988), pp. 97–104; Williams, Richard, *The Animator's Survival Kit* (London and New York: Faber and Faber, 2001).

FILMOGRAPHY: *The Little Island* (1958); *The Story of the Motor Car Engine* (co-dir. Erwin Broner, 1959); *Love Me, Love Me, Love Me*; *A Lecture on Man* (1962); *The Dermis Probe*; *I. Vor Pittfalks* (unfinished) (1965); *Nasruddin/The Cobbler, the Thief and the Grand Vizier/The Thief and the Cobbler* (begun 1968; cut and re-edited version rel. as *Arabian Knight*, 1995); *A Christmas Carol* (UK/US, 1971); *Raggedy Ann & Andy* (US, 1977); *Who Framed Roger Rabbit* (animation dir., Robert Zemeckis, US, 1998).

WILLIAMSON, James (1855–1933)

James Williamson was born in Pathhead, near Kirkcaldy, in Scotland, on 8 November 1855, and trained in London to become a master chemist. In 1886 he moved to Hove, East Sussex, with his wife and family to establish a pharmacy. For the next decade, Williamson developed a keen interest in photography and optical entertainments, and as a Kodak agent acquired a good understanding of photography's technical and chemical nature. In 1896 he introduced X-Ray photography to Sussex

and in November presented the first programme of films to the Camera Club at Hove town hall.

Williamson began to make films in 1897 and his first catalogue of 1899 listed sixty titles, the majority of which were single shots between sixty and seventy-five feet in length. His first edited multi-shot narrative film was *Attack on a China Mission – Bluejackets to the Rescue*. This four-shot work of 230 feet, his longest film to date, was made in the autumn of 1900 and followed a summer of inspired film-making by G. A. Smith, his Hove friend and counterpart. It is in the context of Smith's development of English film form that Williamson conceived and executed this film, which marks his move from 'non-continuous' to 'continuous' narrative.

Williamson's next significant multi-shot film was *Fire!* (1901), a contribution to the 'fire' drama genre apparent across the media in cinema, theatre, magic lantern lectures and newspaper reports. *Fire!*, like *Attack on a China Mission*, reflected Williamson's understanding of the rescue narrative and his ambition to find the means to develop a more complex and arresting film structure. By designing a carefully constructed and edited five-shot work of fiction made on locations and a set with a real fire brigade's apparatus and staff, Williamson created a film that was simple in form, yet radical for its time. His subsequent social dramas and ingenious trick films, especially *The Big Swallow* (1901), maintained the same spirit of innovation.

In 1902, Williamson's commitment to narrative fiction continued with two 'picture stories', as he referred to them, based on the experiences of soldiers returning home from South Africa. They both express an intelligence and compassion missing from most of the period's war-related films and entertainments. In *The Soldier's Return* (1902), a soldier back from the Boer War collects his mother from the workhouse and re-establishes their home together. This gentle five-shot, three-location, two-minute drama was partly filmed at the Brighton Workhouse. Williamson's second story of a returning soldier, *A Reservist, before the War, and after the War* (1902), provides a more negative portrait of the post-war experience. In the first scene, before the war, we are introduced to a young family at home in pleasant surroundings. Following the intertitle 'After the War' we return to the same interior. But it has now undergone a tragic transformation: it is almost empty of furniture, a sick child is cradled in his mother's arms and there is no fire in the hearth. This transition from comfort to poverty is presented as the direct result of the reservist's war service and his subsequent unemployment.

The lucid and careful narrative organisation Williamson deployed in *A Reservist, before the War, and after the War* is also evident in *The Little Match Seller* (1902), *Remorse: A Tragedy in Five Acts* (1903), *The Old Chorister* (1904), *Two Little Waifs* (1905) and *The £100 Reward* (1908), offering proof that film drama, as opposed to a lantern drama or stage drama, could now be conceived as a distinct and viable entity. Williamson's films also illustrate the shift within film acting from pictorialism to naturalism; in all his films the acting style is restrained and conforms to the new naturalism being developed on the contemporary stage in order to interpret the works of Ibsen, Pinero and Shaw.

In 1902 the Williamson Kinematograph Company opened its first purpose-built film production studio and film processing works in Hove. His family played a distinctive role in the new business by helping to create scenarios and make sets and costumes, and taking acting roles, big and small. Tom Williamson's part as the anarchic boy upsetting the pillars of society in *Our New Errand Boy* (1905) vividly expresses this enthusiasm for film-making and his father's provocative imagination.

Williamson's dramas and comedies were sold and exhibited across Europe and America. In 1907 his son Alan opened the company's New York office and in 1909 James attended the European Convention of Film Producers and Publishers in Paris. But in that same year changes in the world film market led Williamson to withdraw from film production. In 1910 the company moved to London, where it concentrated entirely on manufacturing cameras and printers. The Williamson apparatus acquired an excellent reputation and was used throughout the world. James Williamson died of a heart attack at his home in Richmond, Surrey, on 18 August 1933.

(Frank Gray)

BIBLIOGRAPHY: Barnes, John, *The Beginnings of the Cinema in England 1894–1901, Volumes 2-5* (Exeter: University of Exeter Press, 1996–8); Gray, Frank, 'James Williamson's "Composed Picture": Attack on a China Mission – Bluejackets to the Rescue', in, John Fullerton (ed), *Celebrating 1895* (Sydney: John Libbey & Co., 1998); Sadoul, Georges, *British Creators of Film Technique* (London: BFI, 1948); Sopocy, Martin, *James Williamson: Studies and Documents of a Pioneer of the Film Narrative* (London: Associated University Presses, 1998).

FILMOGRAPHY: *Ring-a-Ring of Roses*; *Fox-and-Geese*; *Hove Coastguards at Cutlass Drill*; *Hove Coastguards at Flag Drill* (1897); *Henley Regatta* (series); *Two Naughty Boys Upsetting the Spoons*; *Two Naughty Boys Sprinkling the Spoons*; *Two Naughty Boys Teasing the Cobbler*; *Washing the Sweep*; *Winning the Gloves*; *The Forbidden Lover*; *Sloper's Visit to Brighton*; *Volunteers* (series); *Trip in Brighton Queen* (series); *Sir Roger de Coverley*; *Sussex County Cricketers*; *Military Ride by a Lady Cyclist*; *Another of the Same/Lady Cyclists*; *Clown Cricketers/Clever Cricket*; *Maypole Dance/Children Plaiting the Maypole*; *Express Train and Level Crossing*; *Fishing Smack Race*; *Procession of Sunday School Children*; *Children Bathing on Hove Beach*; *Minuet*; *The Jealous Painter*; *The Clown Barber*; *The Fraudulent Beggars*; *Norah Mayer The Quick-Change Dancer*; *Blacksmiths at Work*; *Horses Ploughing*; *Oxen Ploughing*; *Sheep Washing*; *Highland Fling*; *Sword Dance*; *Military Sports* (series); *Bank Holiday at the Dyke*; *Switchback Railway*; *Harvesting*; *Threshing Turnip Seed/Seed Threshing*; *A Sussex Ox Wagon*; *Fire Brigade Sports* (series); *Sailing Boats*; *Barnum's Procession* (series); *Lawn Tennis*; *Cycle Parade* (1898); *Tug o' War*; *Tearing*; *The Jovial Monks No. 1*; *The Jovial Monks No. 2*, *Tit for Tat*; *Courtship under Difficulties*; *The Sleeping Lovers* (1899); *Clever and Comic Cycle Act*; *The Disabled Motor*; *Attack on a China Mission – Bluejackets to the Rescue*; *Circular Panorama of Windsor Castle*; *La Marguerite*; *Great Glove Fight*; *Military Tournament* (series); *Panorama* *of Folkestone from the Pier; Panorama of Dover Harbour* (1900); *Scene on the Beach at Brighton; Bicycle Polo; The Elixir of Life; Over the Garden Wall; The Marvellous Hair Restorer; The Puzzled Bather and His Animated Clothes* (US: *The Bather*); *Are You There?* (US: *A Telephone Romance*); *The Big Swallow* (US: *A Photographic Contortion/Eaten Alive*); *Fire!; The Magic Extinguisher* (US: *Magic Cone*); *Stop Thief!; Teasing Grandpa; Tomorrow Will Be Friday; Cyclist Scouts in Action; Harlequinade: What They Found in the Laundry Basket; Queen Victoria's Funeral* (series) (1901); *Ping-Pong; Burlesque of Popular Composers; The Soldier's Return; A Workman's Paradise; An Extra Turn; Those Troublesome Boys; A Lady's First Lesson on the Bicycle; Plumpton Steeplechase; Coronation through London on Wednesday June 25* (series); *Coronation Procession* (series); *Naval Review* (series); *Scotland* (series); *Panorama on the Belfast and North of Ireland Railway; Magnificent Panorama of the Fleet* (series); *Professor Reddish Performs His Celebrated Bicycle Dive; A Day in Camp with the Volunteers; Close Quarters: 'with a Notion of the Motion of the Ocean'; Sambo; The Acrobatic Tramps; The Imperial Troupe of Russian Dancers; Captain Clives and His Clever Dog Tiger; Fighting His Battles over Again; An Amateur Bill Sykes; The Little Match Seller; A Reservist, before the War, and after the War* (1902); *Spring Cleaning; Quarrelsome Neighbours; Remorse: A Tragedy in Five Acts; A Trip to Southend or Blackpool; The Wrong Poison; The Wrong Chimney; No Bathing Allowed; Wait Till Jack Comes Home* (US: *When Our Sailor Son Comes Home*); *The Deserter; An Evil-Doer's Sad End; The Dear Boys Home for the Holidays/Boys Will Be Boys; Juggins' Motor* (1903); *The Great Sea Serpent; Oh! What a Surprise; They Forgot the Gamekeeper; The Clown's Telegram; The Student and the Housemaid; Two Brave Little Japs; The Stowaway; An Interesting Story; All's Well That Ends Well; Gabriel Grub the Surly Sexton; The Old Chorister; The Tramp's Revenge; An Affair of Honour; Brown's Half Holiday; Sausages; Rival Barbers; The Prodigal Son; or, Ruined at the Races; Our New Errand Boy; The Polite Lunatic; In the Good Old Times; Two Little Waifs; An Eclipse of the Moon* (US: *Moonbeams*) (1905); *Her First Cake; The Angler's Dream; The Sham Sword Swallower; Mrs Brown Goes Home to Her Mother; The Miner's Daughter; A Day on His Own; A Wicked Bounder; Where There's a Will There's a Way; Flying the Foam and Some Fancy Diving* (1906); *Cheating the Sweep; The Village Fire Brigade; The Orange Peel; The Brigand's Daughter; After the Fancy Dress Ball; Bobby's Birthday; Pa Takes up Physical Culture* (US: *Poor Pa's Folly*); *Why the Wedding Was Put Off; Just in Time; Moving Day; Getting Rid of His Dog; The Orphans* (1907); *A Day's Holiday; The Rival Cyclists; The £100 Reward; The Professor's Great Discovery; She Would Be a Suffragette; Uncle's Picnic; My Wife's Dog; The Ayah's Revenge; The Little Mother; The Great Bargain Sale; Sunshine after Storm; The Reconciliation; A Countryman's Day in Town; The Rent Collector* (1908); *'Arry and 'Arriet's Evening Out; Saved by a Dream; The Letter Box Thief; The Tower of London* (1909).

WILLING, Nick (1961–)

Nicholas Willing was born in Portugal in 1961, the son of artists Victor Willing and Paula Rego. In 1980 he enrolled at the National Film and Television School in Beaconsfield, where he directed two animated and two live-action shorts, one of which, *Lifeclass*, won the Golden Dragon at the Krakow Film Festival.

After directing an Anglo-Spanish animatronics television series, *Gophers* (1990), Willing served as second-unit director on *The Muppet Christmas Carol* before making his feature debut with *Photographing Fairies* (1997). The story of a sceptical photographer investigating images of mysterious winged creatures taken by two little girls, it was one of two films released in the same year based on the Cottingley fairies hoax (alongside Charles Sturridge's *Fairytale: A True Story*). Willing's film was beautifully shot, but marred by a convoluted, unpersuasive storyline.

Over the next four years Willing directed two American big-budget television films for Hallmark and NBC: the $21 million Emmy award-winning *Alice in Wonderland* (1999) with lavish special effects and an all-star cast including Miranda Richardson as the Queen of Hearts and Whoopi Goldberg as the Cheshire Cat; and the spectacular but less warmly received, *Jason and the Argonauts* (2000). He returned to Britain for *Doctor Sleep*, a scary, psychologically convincing occult thriller, made with backing from BBC Films and the Lottery-backed Film Consortium. Starring Goran Visnjic, Shirley Henderson and a chillingly effective Fiona Shaw, this story of a hypnotherapist caught up in the pursuit of a ritualistic killer was welcomed by critics, but proved too low key to make much impact at the box office. Willing's episode of the BBC series *Sea of Souls* (2004), where a six-year-old boy is convinced he is the reincarnation of a dead Scottish teenager, explored similar occult themes. Willing moved to snowy Nova Scotia to make *The River King*, a sensitive thriller starring Ed Burns, Jamie King and Jennifer Ehle, which confirms his reputation as a talented and unpredictable director.

(Eleanor Burke)

BIBLIOGRAPHY: Bradshaw, Nick, 'Nick Willing', *Time Out*, 3–10 Sept. 1997, p. 24; Tutt, Louise, 'Kismet Wakes up to Willing/Harrald's Sleep', *Screen International*, 28 Feb. 1997, p. 15.

FILMOGRAPHY: *The Golden Grape* (short, 1983); *The Muppet Christmas Carol* (2nd unit dir., Brian Henson, US 1992); *Photographing Fairies* (1997); *Doctor Sleep* (US: *Close Your Eyes*, 2003); *The River King* (UK/Can, 2005).

WILLS, J. Elder (1900–?)

James Ernest Elder Wills was born in London on 26 April 1900. He entered the film industry in the 1920s, establishing himself as an art director at British International Pictures on Arthur Maude's *Poppies of Flanders* in 1927, and working regularly and prolifically in the industry until 1960. His 1930s' achievements included Gracie Fields' *Sing as We Go* (Basil Dean, 1934) and George Formby's *No Limit* (Monty Banks, 1935); in the 1950s Ken Hughes' atmospheric film noir *The House Across the Lake* (1954) and Val Guest's *The Quatermass Experiment* (1955).

His first experience directing came with Associated Sound Film Industries' series *Little People Burlesques* (1930), juvenile Hollywood parodies with music, featuring Ottorino Gorno's marionettes; directing colleagues in the series included John Grierson and the European visitor Henrik Galeen. Another ASFI enterprise, *M' Blimey*, a supposed short comedy about Africans shooting a travel film in Britain, stayed on the shelf. He made more headway with features. *Tiger Bay* (1933) was de-gutted by censorship restrictions but retains vestiges of interest for its depiction of the Chinese community in Cardiff's Tiger Bay and the attractive performances of René Ray and Anna May Wong. *Everything in Life* (1936) is an uncomfortably stilted operatic melodrama; *Sporting Love* (1936) an unambitious but lively vehicle for now unfashionable 1930s' comics Stanley Lupino and Laddie Cliff. More durable are Wills' two films with Paul Robeson. *Song of Freedom* (1936) is a complicated but engrossing drama allowing Robeson to sing apposite and moving songs; its successor, *Big Fella* (1937), is sketchier and more trivial, an indication that Wills was less than comfortable in the director's chair.

In 1936 Wills ventured into production with his own company shortly before the industry entered a disastrous slump. In February 1939 his liabilities stood at £3,690 and he filed for bankruptcy. He redeemed himself with honourable and very useful service in the Second World War, designing novel forms of camouflage and inventing devices to be used by special agents, such as ingeniously concealed booby-traps and radio transmitters. He was able to draw on his experience of working with the Special Operations Executive as art director on the two best films about British Second World War undercover operations, *Against the Wind* (Charles Crichton, 1947) and *Circle of Deception* (Jack Lee, 1960).

(Robert Murphy)

BIBLIOGRAPHY: 'J. Elder Wills' £3,690 Losses', *Kinematograph Weekly*, 9 Mar. 1939, p. 19.

FILMOGRAPHY: *Little People Burlesques* (series of shorts, co-dirs. Henrik Galeen/Jack Harrison/John Grierson, 1930); *M'Blimey* (short, 1931); *Tiger Bay* (1933); *Song of Freedom*; *Everything in Life*; *Sporting Love* (1936); *Big Fella* (1937).

WILSON, Donald B. (1910–2002)

Donald Boyd Wilson was born on 1 September 1910, in Dunblane, Perthshire, the son of a colonel killed at Gallipoli in 1915. He attended the Glasgow School of Art, worked briefly as a newspaper columnist and sketch writer, and was recruited by Walter Mycroft into the British film industry in 1932 after successfully rewriting songs for a BIP musical at Elstree. He wrote scripts, served as art director on the swashbuckling *McGlusky the Sea Rover* (Walter Summers, 1935), but found his niche as a proficient assistant director, working with Paul Stein on *Mimi* (1935), Walter Forde on *Land Without Music* (1936), Thornton Freeland on *Jericho* (1937) and Sam Wood on *Goodbye Mr Chips* (1939). He also worked in shorts as a producer and director.

During the Second World War Wilson's organisational abilities were fully utilised as an adjutant-general whose tasks included making maps and guides for Allied troops in Europe, and dealing with the guards and prisoners at the newly liberated Belsen concentration camp. After the war he helped to set up MGM's Borehamwood studio but left to establish the independent production company Aquila with Frederick Wilson (no relation) and David Rawnsley, the inventor of the Independent Frame system, which was intended to increase efficiency by making extensive use of back projection. He directed *Warning to Wantons* (1948), a gauche but amusing comedy, unusual in its acknowledgment that women might be interested in sex; and produced Michael Barry's *Stop Press Girl* (1949) and Frederick Wilson's *Floodtide* (1949) and *Poet's Pub* (1949).

Aquila failed to survive into the 1950s, but Wilson produced *Prelude to Fame* (Fergus McDonnell, 1950) for Two Cities and *Miss Robin Hood* (John Guillermin, 1952) for Group 3 before being recruited by Michael Barry, Head of BBC Drama since 1952, into television. He enjoyed some success with his adaptation of Hilary St George Saunders' thriller *The Six Proud Walkers* (Brandon Acton-Bond, 1954); in 1955 he became Head of the script department; in 1962 Head of Serials, among other tasks overseeing the launch of *Doctor Who*. In 1967 he resigned in order to adapt and produce a twenty-six-part serial from the John Galsworthy novels comprising *The Forsyte Saga*. International success led to other ambitious drama serials, notably *The First Churchills* (1969) and *Anna Karenina* (1977).

Wilson's decision to produce and write rather than direct, and to work in television rather than the film industry, may have resulted in a lower public profile than many of his contemporaries, but his career was enviably fruitful and creative. He died of natural causes at his home in Gloucestershire on 6 March 2002.

(Robert Murphy)

BIBLIOGRAPHY: BECTU History Project, tape no. 205, held in the BFI National Library, London; Hayes, Paul, Obituary, *Stage*, 28 Mar. 2002, p. 13; Lentz III, Harris, Obituary, *Classic Images* no. 326, Aug. 2002, p. 63; Purser, Philip, Obituary, *Guardian*, 12 Mar. 2002, p. 18.

FILMOGRAPHY: *Warning to Wantons* (1948).

WILSON, Frederick (1912–)

Frederick Charles Wilson was born in London on 13 August 1912, brought up in Elstree, Hertfordshire, and educated at Watford Grammar School. He entered the film industry as a general dogsbody at BIP in 1928 and worked his way up to become an editor, initially of 'quota quickies' like *Ask Beccles* (Redd Davis, 1933) and then of more prestigious pictures such as *A Stolen Life* (Paul Czinner, 1939), *The Lamp Still Burns* (Maurice Elvey, 1943) and *Caesar and Cleopatra* (Gabriel Pascal, 1945). In the later 1940s he directed *Floodtide* and *Poet's Pub* for Aquila, a company he formed with David Rawnsley (whose Independent Frame technique the company used) and Donald Wilson (no relation). *Floodtide* is a mild romantic drama set against a Scottish shipbuilding background, poorly integrated into the film via the IF technique. There is some sense of reality about the shipyard scenes but not much in the studio-set interiors, where romance blossomed (real-life as well as on screen) between Gordon Jackson and Rona Anderson. Anderson also starred in *Poet's Pub*, adapted from Eric Linklater's novel, and filmed in the grounds of Pinewood Studios. It is an amiable tale of romance in a run-down country inn, with jewel thieves, Joyce Grenfell and a pageant thrown in.

After several second-unit director jobs and a spell with the Crown Film Unit, for which he made the novel Technicolor instructional *The Dancing Fleece*, Wilson returned to editing. He helped to found, and was first Chairman of, the Guild of British Film Editors, cut *The Wind Cannot Read* (Ralph Thomas, 1957), *North West Frontier* (J. Lee Thompson, 1959), *Arabesque* (Stanley Donen, 1966), *The Quiller Memorandum* (Michael Anderson, 1966) and other films; and in the late 1960s served as executive editor on Universal's British and European output. His last film as director was the Children's Film Foundation feature *The Camerons* (1974).

(Brian McFarlane)

BIBLIOGRAPHY: Gillett, Philip, *The British Working Class in Postwar Film* (Manchester and New York: Manchester University Press, 2003); Wilson, Freddie, 'A Museum of Recollection', *Guild of British Film Editors Journal* no. 53, Dec. 1979, pp. 8–13.

FILMOGRAPHY: *Floodtide*; *Poet's Pub* (1949); *The Dancing Fleece* (doc. short, 1950); *The Net* (2nd unit dir., Anthony Asquith, 1953); *Checkpoint* (2nd unit dir., Ralph Thomas, 1956); *North West Frontier* (2nd unit dir., J. Lee Thompson, 1959); *The Camerons* (1974).

WILSON, Maurice J. (1892–1978)

Maurice James Wilson was born in London on 10 September 1892. He entered the film industry in 1926, working for the trailer firm Winads. He was sufficiently on the ball to produce three well-cast talkies in 1930: *Comets* (Sasha Geneen), a revue featuring Billy Merson, Charles Laughton and Elsa Lanchester; *Infatuation* (Sasha Geneen), a short play with Godfrey Tearle as a man who falls for an actress (Jean de Casalis) finally revealed as his own mother; and *Sleeping Partners* (Seymour Hicks), a stage farce written by Sacha Guitry. In 1936 he set up the tiny Highbury Studios, and in 1938 founded Grand National Pictures. An ambitious start was made with Carol Reed's *The Stars Look Down* (1939), but finance proved a problem and the company was dormant during the war years.

When the war ended, Grand National began production with *What Do We Do Now?* (1945), a miscellany of variety acts slung together inside a loose plot about a lost brooch, directed by the actor Charles Hawtrey. Wilson himself co-directed *The Voice Within*, a dingy thriller about an IRA gunman (Kieron Moore) who murders a policeman and is eventually shamed into giving himself up in order to clear his brother. He fared better on his own with *The Turners of Prospect Road*, a modestly likeable working-class comedy featuring Wilfrid Lawson as a taxi-driver who trains an unwanted pup left in his cab to become winner of the Greyhound Derby. Wilson returned to production with *A Tale of Five Cities* (Montgomery Tully, 1951), a melodrama starring Bonar Colleano as an amnesiac serviceman who seeks to restore his memory with the help of five European women (including Eva Bartok and Gina Lollobrigida). A dozen more films followed, most of them low-budget comedies and thrillers directed by Montgomery Tully. Though further significant success eluded him, Maurice Wilson kept working until a few months before his death, aged eighty-five, in Westminster on 21 April 1978.

(Robert Murphy)

BIBLIOGRAPHY: Obituary, *Screen International*, 29 Apr. 1978, p. 48; 'Wilson Goes to States on G.N. Tie-Up', *Today's Cinema*, 17 Oct. 1945, pp. 3, 21.

FILMOGRAPHY: *The Voice Within* (co-dir. Isadore G. Goldsmith, 1945); *The Turners of Prospect Road* (1947).

WINGROVE, Nigel (1957–)

Nigel Wingrove was born in 1957. In his mid-twenties he moved to London, where he worked in graphic design and advertising before becoming involved in the film industry. Thus far, he has been more influential as a producer and distributor than as a director. His company, Salvation Films, specialises in sex and horror and runs three video labels (Redemption, Jezebel and Purgatory), as well as the production company Gothica. Wingrove has been a passionate and lucid campaigner against censorship, arguing that UK laws are arbitrary and obscure.

As a director his best-known film, *Visions of Ecstasy*, is also his least seen. An eighteen-minute short, it depicts the documented fantasies of St Teresa of Avila, a sixteenth-century Carmelite nun. An erotic vision depicting her having sex with Christ on the cross proved too much for the British Board of Film Classification, which banned the film on the grounds of blasphemy.

Wingrove remixed his ideas into his feature debut, *Sacred Flesh*, which was shot digitally over eight days. Despite its low budget (the film was originally intended to run only fifty minutes) it provides ample evidence of Wingrove's fascination with religious imagery, sex, horror and his censor-baiting, anti-Establishment stance. This time, the image of a lesbian kiss between a nun and a female Christ proved less controversial, and the film was released theatrically with only minor cuts.

(Sergio Angelini and Simon Brown)

BIBLIOGRAPHY: Hewitt, Charles, 'Stripping Costs', *Creation*, Apr. 2000, pp. 23–5; Reville, N. J., 'Obscenity, Blasphemy and the Law', *Journal of Media Law and Practice*, June 1990, pp. 42–4; Wingrove, Nigel, 'The Distributor's Tale', *Sight and Sound*, May 1998, p. 17.

FILMOGRAPHY: *Axel* (short, 1988); *Visions of Ecstasy* (short, 1989); *Faustine* (short, 1990); *Sacred Flesh* (2000).

WINNER, Michael (1935–)

Michael Winner has been one of the most controversial British directors of recent times, consistently critical of an indigenous cinema culture that he regards as failing to support film-makers who see film as popular entertainment.

Winner was born in London on 30 October 1935 to Jewish expatriate parents, a Polish mother and Russian father. During his conventional middle-class education (boarding school and Cambridge, where he read law), Winner displayed enormous energy and self-belief, bluffing his way into film studios and interviewing stars. He learned his craft as assistant director on television series, shorts and B-features, including a spy thriller, *Shoot to Kill* (1961), which he also wrote, and the nudist picture *Some Like It Cool* (1961). He graduated to first features with *Play it Cool* (1962), a pop musical starring Billy Fury.

Winner's first significant film was *West 11* (1963), a sympathetic study of rootless drifters in the-then seedy Notting Hill area of London. Filmed on location (always Winner's preference), with a script by Willis Hall and Keith Waterhouse, the film remains an interesting contribution to the working-class realism wave of the early 1960s. Following differences with his producer, Daniel Angel, Winner (who had wanted to cast Julie Christie in the main female role) resolved to produce as well as direct his films and set up his own company, Scimitar. *The System* (1964) and the hectic, dystopian *I'll Never Forget What's 'is Name* (1967) were paired pieces starring Oliver Reed that continued Winner's exploration of alienated youth adrift in a rising tide of affluence, dreaming of an alternative life they can never achieve. These films and the exuberant 'Swinging London' comedy *The Jokers* (1966), also starring Reed, were well suited to Winner's restless, intrusive camera style and staccato editing. They were followed by *Hannibal Brooks* (1969), a witty Second World War comedy written by Dick Clement and Ian La Frenais, which attracted attention in America and led to Winner pursuing a Hollywood career in the 1970s.

Winner now developed a new reputation as an efficient maker of violent action thrillers, often starring Charles Bronson. The most successful and controversial was *Death Wish* (1974), with Bronson cast as a liberal architect who embraces vengeance after the murder of his wife and daughter. An intelligent analysis of the deep roots of vigilantism in American society, *Death Wish* is restrained in its depiction of violence. With his obsessive need to work, Winner accepted many inferior projects, including two weak *Death Wish* sequels, though occasionally he tried to make more prestigious films, notably *The Nightcomers* (1972), a prequel to Henry James' *The Turn of the Screw*, made in Britain with Marlon Brando; and *A Chorus of Disapproval* (1989), a satisfying version of Alan Ayckbourn's bittersweet comedy.

By the 1990s Winner had become less prolific, and reaped no benefit from the Lottery-prompted rise in genre film-making, which favoured the young and inexperienced. *Dirty Weekend* (1993), a rape-revenge movie with a female vigilante, aroused considerable controversy, but hardly enhanced Winner's reputation; *Parting Shots* (1998), a comedy-revenge-thriller suffused with allusions to *Death Wish* and restaurant scenes invoking Winner's current incarnation as a food critic, is perhaps his swansong. (Andrew Spicer)

BIBLIOGRAPHY: Gough-Yates, Kevin, *Michael Winner – Director* (London: National Film Theatre, 1970); Harding, Bill, *The Films of Michael Winner* (London: Frederick Muller, 1978); McFarlane, Brian, *An Autobiography of British Cinema* (London: Methuen, 1997); Winner, Michael, *Winner Takes All: A Life of Sorts* (London: Robson, 2004).

FILMOGRAPHY: *The Square* (short); *The Clock Strikes Eight* (short) (1958); *Danger: Women at Work* (short); *Swiss Holiday* (short) (1959); *Climb up the Wall*; *Pony Tale* (short); *Young Entry* (short); *Out of the Shadows* (US: *Murder on the Campus*) (1960); *Shoot to Kill*; *Girls, Girls, Girls* (short); *It's Magic* (short); *Behave Yourself* (short); *Haunted England* (short); *Some Like It Cool* (1961); *Play It Cool*; *The Cool Mikado* (1962); *West 11* (1963); *The System* (US: *The Girl Getters*, 1964); *You Must Be Joking!* (1965); *The Jokers* (1966); *I'll Never Forget What's 'is Name* (1967); *Hannibal Brooks*; *The Games* (1969); *Lawman* (US, 1971); *The Nightcomers*; *Chato's Land* (US); *The Mechanic* (US); *Scorpio* (US) (1972); *The Stone Killer* (US, 1973); *Death Wish* (US, 1974); *Won Ton Ton, the Dog Who Saved Hollywood* (US, 1975); *The Sentinel* (US, 1977); *The Big Sleep* (US, 1978); *Firepower* (US, 1979); *Death Wish II* (US, 1981); *The Wicked Lady* (1983); *Scream for Help* (US, 1984); *Death Wish 2* (US, 1985); *Appointment with Death* (US, 1988); *A Chorus of Disapproval* (US, 1989); *Bullseye!* (US, 1990); *Dirty Weekend* (1993); *Parting Shots* (1998).

WINSOR, Terry (c.1955)

Terry Winsor's *Essex Boys* (2000) was unusual among the deluge of British crime films in not marking the debut of an aspiring young director. It was also unusual for being tightly plotted, grippingly acted and uncomfortably convincing. Winsor had made his debut in the early 1980s with *Party Party*, a feature about a teenage New Year's Eve party, expanded from his National Film School graduation film. Critical opinion generally agreed that the forty-minute original was much better, and Winsor turned his talents to commercials. In 1985 he went to America and attempted another teen film, *Morgan Stewart's Coming Home*, a troubled production on which Winsor and his co-director Paul Aaron sunk their identities in the pseudonym 'Alan Smithee'. After making *Cresta Run*, a barely released satire, he returned to Britain to make television films and commercials.

British film noir: *Essex Boys* (Terry Windsor, 2000)

Fool's Gold (1992), co-written with Jeff Pope, was a well-researched and dramatically effective reconstruction of the Brinks-Matt security vault robbery at Heathrow Airport, where crooks escaped with £26 million in gold bullion. Two less serious films followed: *The Magician* (1993), also scripted by Pope, explored the effects of a conman's encounter with counterfeit IRA money; *The Great Kandinksy* (1995) starred Richard Harris as an ageing but incorrigible escape artist.

Work on the ITV police series *Thief Takers* (1996) prepared the way for *Essex Boys*, another collaboration with Pope (by this time Head of Factual Drama at Granada), inspired by the murder of three gangland drug-dealers found shot dead in a Land Rover on an isolated farm track in Essex. Sean Bean, who had served Winsor well as the ruthlessly efficient gang leader in *Fool's Gold*, plays a psychopathically violent criminal whose release from prison sets in chain events leading to treachery and murder. Winsor keeps a tight grip on the convoluted plot and cleverly shifts the emphasis towards Alex Kingston's Lisa Locke, an Essex girl who has matured into a resourceful femme fatale. Noirish cinematography, a strong cast and well-chosen of Essex locations offered further pleasures, but failed to prevent *Essex Boys* getting lost in the crowd. Winsor returned to television, where he directed *Hot Money* (2001), a Granada drama about three Bank of England cleaning ladies who outwit security guards to make off with a haul of used banknotes, and episodes of the mountain rescue series *Rockface* (2002).
(Robert Murphy)

BIBLIOGRAPHY: Henry, Georgina, 'Profile: Terry Winsor', *Televisual*, Jan. 1985, p. 94; Winstone, Keely, '*Essex Boys*', *Televisual*, June 1999, pp. 45–6.

FILMOGRAPHY: *Party Party* (1983); *Morgan Stewart's Coming Home* (aka *Home Front*, co-dir. Paul Aaron, US, 1985; rel. 1987); *Cresta Run* (US, 1990); *Essex Boys* (2000).

WINTER, Donovan (1933–)

Donovan Winter was born into an Irish family in London in 1933. He played small roles in British films of the 1950s, including *The Galloping Major* (Henry Cornelius, 1951), *Appointment in London* (Philip Leacock, 1953) and *Moulin Rouge* (John Huston, 1953), and appeared as the stalwart provincial detective Sergeant Scott in the 'Scotland Yard' short *Bullet from the Past* (Kenneth Hume, 1957), which he also wrote. His documentary about early morning London, *The Awakening Hour* (1957), was included in one of the Free Cinema programmes at the National Film Theatre, but Winter's eclectic talent remained undefined. In 1960 he tried his hand at melodrama, directing *The Trunk*, a convoluted tale of blackmail and murder; in 1962 he ventured into the nudist market with *World Without Shame*. Subsequently, documentaries about Hyde Park, holidays on the Norfolk Broads and life aboard the *Queen Mary* intermingled with a collection of stories overheard in a ladies loo (*A Penny for Your Thoughts*, 1966) and a medium-length romance set in Brighton (*Promenade*, 1968).

Come Back Peter (1969), an attempt to repeat the success of *Alfie* (Lewis Gilbert, 1966) by borrowing the same formula but adding more sex, foundered on the inability of Christopher Matthews to match Michael Caine's charisma and Winter's crudely functional script. The film was re-released in 1972 with added sex scenes featuring twin sisters Mary and Madeleine Collinson, though not to great acclaim. Two more sexploitation films – *Escort Girls* and *The Deadly Females* – followed in the 1970s, both of them distinguished by a downbeat emphasis on ugliness, unhappiness and sexual dissatisfaction. Winter's attempt to move slightly upmarket with his bank robbery hostage thriller *Give Us Tomorrow* (1978) was scuppered by EMI's decision to make it share a bill with Pete Walker's *Home Before Midnight* (1979).

Winter's abrasive presence – he did much to clear the cinema screens of Rank's tepid *Look at Life* fillers – and fierce independence is to be welcomed in a world too often characterised by self-serving complacency. No one has yet claimed that his films are a treasure trove of subversive creativity, but their unpredictability and occasional flashes of inspiration make them tattered monuments to dogged, unsubsidised enterprise.
(Robert Murphy)

BIBLIOGRAPHY: Sheridan, Simon, *Keeping the British End Up: Four Decades of Saucy Cinema*, 2nd edn (London: Reynolds & Hearn, 2005); Winter, Donovan, 'Do We Need or Deserve a British Film Industry?', *Films and Filming*, Feb. 1977, pp. 22–5; Winter, Donovan, 'Give Us a Chance' (letter), *Screen International*, 29 Sept. 1979, p. 4; Winter, Donovan, 'Film Industry – the No-Hoper!', *Showbiz* no. 11, 30 May 1980, p. 3; Winter, Donovan, 'Directors Crying Wolf Once Too Often' (letter), *Screen International*, 31 Aug. 1985, p. 6.

FILMOGRAPHY: *The Awakening Hour* (doc. short, 1957); *Honeymoon in Broadland* (doc. short); *The Great Expedition* (doc. short) (1959); *The Trunk* (1960); *World Without Shame* (1962); *Harmony Abroad* (doc. short) (1965); *Swing Aboard The Mary* (doc. short, 1965); *Open Forum* (doc. short); *A Penny for Your Thoughts* (aka *Birds, Dolls and Scratch*, short) (1966); *No Parents Allowed!* (short, 1967); *Promenade* (1968); *Come Back Peter* (aka *Some Like It Sexy*; *Sunday in the Park* (doc., 1970); *Escort Girls* (1974); *The Deadly Females* (1976); *Give Us Tomorrow* (1978); *Roller Force* (doc. short, 1980).

WINTERBOTTOM, Michael (1961–)

Michael Winterbottom's films represent the most striking and varied body of work of any British director to emerge from the late twentieth century. Born in Blackburn, Lancashire, on 29 March 1961, he studied English at Oxford; before enrolling on the post-graduate course in film-making at Bristol University. Initially he worked in the cutting rooms at Thames Television, graduating to direction with television drama episodes and two documentaries about Ingmar Bergman. Winterbottom has regularly cited major European figures as influences – including Godard, Wenders, Truffaut and Bergman himself – and the settings and style of his own work displayed a continental slant from the beginning. The energetic comedy romance *Forget about Me* (1990), second in a long line of collaborations with the writer Frank Cottrell Boyce, focused on two Scots soldiers serving in West Germany, entangled with Hungarian girls during an excursion to Budapest. The equally lively *Under the Sun* (1992), shot in Spain in a spirit of improvisation and serendipity, followed the fortunes of a shy backpacking girl, learning to fend for herself. Both television films enjoyed festival exposure.

Other television ventures pursued subjects and settings closer to home, though the hard gaze of Winterbottom's camera still ensured distinctive results, particularly in *Family* (1994), a harrowing four-part series written by the novelist Roddy Doyle. The violent father and damaged children at the centre of the series found echoes in Winterbottom's later films, particularly *Go Now* (1995), an energetic and compassionate television drama about an ordinary working man (Robert Carlyle) fighting multiple sclerosis, and *With or Without You* (1999), a frisky romantic drama disturbed by mounting marital disharmony.

In 1994 Winterbottom formed Revolution Films with Andrew Eaton, his producer on *Family*; his first cinema feature, *Butterfly Kiss*, emerged the following year. Building on his adventurous television work, this spiky lesbian road movie written by Cottrell Boyce made few concessions to the commercial consensus. A sociopathic drifter with chains and chest bruises (Amanda Plummer) seduces a mousy service-station employee (Saskia Reeves) and leads her into her world of random murder and casual violence. Winterbottom gets good visual mileage from the dreary geography of motorway tarmac, car parks and motels: some compensation for the over-episodic structure and fancy words about punishment and hell that ultimately lead nowhere. After this arresting debut, Winterbottom entered the prestige literary adaptation field with *Jude* (1996). Typically, he picked one of the bleakest possible properties, Thomas Hardy's novel of dashed hopes and illicit love. Sombre and stark in every way, it remains a compelling and underrated film, with a mesmerising performance from Kate Winslet as stonecutter Jude's vivacious cousin, made wan by the kicks of fate.

With typical eclectic flair, Winterbottom switched to a very different style, subject and period for *Welcome to Sarajevo* (1997). Shot on location, the emotional drama incorporates authentic news footage within its true story of a television reporter (played by Stephen Dillane) setting professional objectivity aside, determined to rescue an orphan child. The film is not afraid to be tart, though some star-struck casting and a script overladen with irony muffle its final impact. Three offbeat romantic dramas followed: the overstrained *I Want You* (1998), a seaside drama of obsessive love with Rachel Weisz, filmed in Hastings; the Belfast-set *With or Without You*; and, most individual of all, *Wonderland* (1999), a sad family jigsaw puzzle built up from what at first seem scattered scenes about the lives of three sisters (Gina McKee, Shirley Henderson and Molly Parker). With its restless, hand-held photography by Sean Bobbitt, drab settings (London, November, wet) and obsessive Michael Nyman score, the film presents a very different vision of London from the tourist views of its contemporaries, *Sliding Doors* (Peter Howitt, 1998) and *Notting Hill* (Roger Michell, 1999).

Winterbottom collaborated again with Cottrell Boyce on *The Claim*, an adaptation of Hardy's *The Mayor of Casterbridge*, transposed to the Sierra Nevada; *24 Hour Party People*; and the idiosyncratic futuristic drama *Code 46*. *The Claim* (2000) has more in common with Robert Altman's *McCabe and Mrs Miller* (1971) than with even the most unorthodox heritage product. Impressive ice-bound visuals include the astonishing spectacle of a complete wooden house dragged uphill by horses, but characters in the script's games of love, power, revenge and redemption lack body, and the film proved too offbeat for mainstream audiences. *24 Hour Party People* (2002) is a more populist affair, in loud and vivid pursuit of Manchester's punk rock explosion of the late 1970s and beyond, with comedian Steve Coogan well cast as the charismatic music promoter Tony Wilson. Casting proved less of an asset with ill-matched Tim Robbins and Samantha Morton in *Code 46* (2003), though this blend of science fiction and film noir set in an overcrowded future is never less than intriguing.

Among recent films, the Berlin Film Festival prizewinner *In this World* (2002) best demonstrates Winterbottom's distinctive gifts. Shot on digital video by a tiny crew, this involving documentary-style drama about two Afghan refugees travelling overland from Pakistan to seek asylum in England follows no commercial habits in looks, material or technique. One is not even particularly aware one is watching a British film, until the cool emotional temperature and lack of catharsis chill the final stages. His later DV venture, *9 Songs* (2004), could almost have been deliberately mounted to exorcise British restraint: an hour-long diary of a passionate affair, intercut with rock concert footage, the film features an unusual degree of explicit sex, though with few rewards for the viewer. By contrast, *Tristram Shandy: A Cock and Bull Story* (2005) is Winterbottom's most immediately enjoyable film – an exuberant, brilliantly inventive portrait of movie-making madness, spun round the struggles to make a viable film out of Laurence Sterne's unfilmable eighteenth-century comic novel.

Winterbottom's dizzyingly eclectic output can be loosely tied together by two general concerns. Like the French New Wave directors who helped sharpen his style, he is dedicated to 'people and places' films, largely created on location, exploring a wide range of geographical and social settings. Through all the variations in mood and technique, he seeks to combine social realism with stylistic experiments, bold photography and expressive use of the widescreen shape. Though the artistic achievements have varied, and no film has enjoyed wide commercial success, in his determination to make idiosyncratic and innovative British films Winterbottom has established an enviable international reputation.

(Geoff Brown and Pamela Church Gibson)

BIBLIOGRAPHY: Atkinson, Michael, 'Cinema as Heart Attack', *Film Comment*, Jan./Feb. 1998, pp. 44–7; Epstein, Jan, 'Welcome to Sarajevo', *Cinema Papers*, Mar. 1998, pp. 28–30, 45; Fennell, Nicky, 'Winter Wonderland', *Film West*, Feb. 2000, pp. 42–4; Sinyard, Neil and Melanie Williams, '"Living in a World That Did Not Want Them": Michael Winterbottom and the Unpopular British Cinema', *Journal of Popular British Cinema* no. 5, 2002, pp. 114–23.

FILMOGRAPHY: *Butterfly Kiss* (1995); *Jude* (1996); *Welcome to Sarajevo* (1997); *I Want You* (1998); *With or Without You*; *Wonderland* (1999); *The Claim* (UK/Fr/Can, 2000); *24 Hour Party People*; *In this World* (2002); *Code 46* (UK/US, 2003); *9 Songs* (2004); *Tristram Shandy: A Cock and Bull Story* (2005); *The Road to Guantanamo* (co-dir. Mat Whitecross, 2006).

WISE, Robert (1914–)

Robert Wise was born in Winchester, Indiana, on 10 September 1914. He first came to prominence as an editor working on *Citizen Kane* (Orson Welles, 1941) and *The Devil and Daniel Webster* (William Dieterle, 1941), before producer Val Lewton asked him to complete *The Curse of the Cat People* (co-dir. Gunther von Fritsch, 1944). Wise quickly rose through the ranks as a director, tackling a broad range of projects, including crime thrillers, musicals, Westerns, biopics, sporting dramas, war films and fine science-fiction films like *The Day the Earth Stood Still* (1951) and *The Andromeda Strain* (1970).

The Haunting (1963), a ghost story set in New England but actually shot in the UK, ranks among Wise's most accomplished and complex works; he was always at his best in films that portray alienation and claustrophobia. The atmospheric and subtle direction echoes the films he made for Lewton; and Wise's characteristic theme of people trapped in a hermetically sealed environment is superbly realised.

Wise's biggest success came with the atypically sunny and uncomplicated musical *The Sound of Music* (1965). *Star!* (1968), a darker biopic of the British entertainer Gertrude Lawrence that utilises a newsreel opening and flashback structure reminiscent of *Citizen Kane*, was less popular despite the reappearance of Julie Andrews in the starring role. Wise's films of conflict and isolation in enclosed spaces, whether set in boxing rings, New York tenements, submarines, the Hindenburg or the *Starship Enterprise*, remain a rich, distinguished and surprisingly personal body of work in the commercial cinema.

(Sergio Angelini)

BIBLIOGRAPHY: Leeman, Sergio, *Robert Wise on His Films* (Los Angeles, CA: Silman-James Press, 1995).

FILMOGRAPHY (UK only): *The Haunting* (1963).

WOLLEN, Peter (1938–)

Peter Wollen was born in London on 29 June 1938 and studied English at Christchurch College, Oxford. His *Signs and Meaning in the Cinema*, first published in 1969, helped to transform the discipline of film studies by incorporating the methodologies of structuralism and semiotics. Unusually for a British film theorist, Wollen has also been active as a film-maker. He co-wrote Michelangelo Antonioni's *The Passenger* (1975) and made his debut as a director with *Penthesilea: Queen of the Amazons* (1974), the first of six films co-written and co-directed with his then-wife, Laura Mulvey. The low-budget *Penthesilea* portrayed women's language and mythology as silenced by patriarchal structures. Acknowledging the influence of Godard's *Le Gai savoir*, Wollen intended the film to fuse avant-garde and radically political elements. The resulting work is innovative in the context of British cinema, although unsurprisingly its relentlessly didactic approach did not make for mass appeal.

For *Riddles of the Sphinx* (1977), their most remarkable collaborative work, Wollen and Mulvey obtained a BFI Production Board grant that enabled them to work with greater technical resources. Rewriting the Oedipal myth from a female standpoint, they use formal devices – most impressively choreographed circular pans – to create an expressionist effect that complicates and enhances the film's narrative content.

Amy! (1980), commemorating Amy Johnson's solo flight from Britain to Australia, synthesises themes previously covered by Wollen and Mulvey, but it is heavy-handed and deliberately ahistorical. More watchable is *Crystal Gazing* (1982), in which formal experimentation is muted and narrative concerns emphasised. The film was criticised in some quarters for the absence of an explicitly feminist perspective, but it enjoyed generally favourable reviews. *Frida Kahlo & Tina Modotti* (1982), a short film tied to an international art exhibition curated by Wollen, and *The Bad Sister* (1982), a cumbersome drama made for Channel 4 from a novel by Emma Tennant, were the final projects on which Wollen and Mulvey collaborated.

Wollen's only solo feature, *Friendship's Death* (1987), was the bizarre and absorbing story of the relationship between a British war correspondent and a female extraterrestrial robot on a peace mission to Earth, who, missing her intended destination of MIT, lands inadvertently in Amman, Jordan, during the hijacking of 'Black September', 1970. The film's intelligent wit, coupled with outstanding performances from Tilda Swinton and Bill Paterson, makes this Wollen's most compelling film.

Wollen has taught film at a number of universities and is currently Chair of the Department of Film, Television and New Media at the University of California, Los Angeles.

(Eleanor Burke)

BIBLIOGRAPHY: Field, Simon, 'Two Weeks on Another Planet', *Monthly Film Bulletin*, Nov. 1987, pp. 324–6; Friedman, Lester D., 'Interview with Peter Wollen and Laura Mulvey on *Riddles of the Sphinx*', *Millennium Film Journal* nos 4/5, 1979, pp. 14–32; Mulvey, Laura and Peter Wollen, 'Written Discussion', *Afterimage*, July 1976, pp. 31–9; Wollen, Peter, *Signs and Meaning in the Cinema,* 2nd edn (London: Secker and Warburg, 1972).

FILMOGRAPHY: *Penthesilea: Queen of the Amazon* (co-dir. Laura Mulvey, 1974); *Riddles of the Sphinx* (co-dir. Laura Mulvey, 1977); *Amy!* (short, co-dir. Laura Mulvey, 1980); *Crystal Gazing* (co-dir. Laura Mulvey); *Frida Kahlo & Tina Modotti* (short, co-dir. Laura Mulvey); *The Bad Sister* (co-dir. Laura Mulvey) (1982); *Friendship's Death* (1987).

WOOD, Sam (1883–1949)

Samuel Grosvenor Wood was born in Philadelphia on 18 July 1883. Having abandoned the real estate business for acting, he changed profession once more in 1917, becoming an assistant director to Cecil B. DeMille. In 1920 he graduated to fully fledged director, his best-known films including two Marx Brothers comedies, *A Night at the Opera* (1935) and *A Day at the Races* (1937). The brothers disliked his reliance on multiple takes of every scene for the editors to fashion into an acceptable end product; but his reliability was appreciated by the MGM bosses, who assigned him to one of its prestige British productions, *Goodbye, Mr Chips* (1939). Based on a novel by James Hilton, the film relates in flashback the life of a hidebound, introverted schoolmaster (Robert Donat), who, having devoted himself to educating the young, finds his true love (Greer Garson), only for her to die in childbirth.

Well received by critics, *Goodbye Mr Chips* was a huge popular success, with Donat winning an Academy Award for his performance. While the film often verges on the maudlin, it remains a popular favourite. By contrast, the lively musical remake (Herbert Ross, 1969), starring Peter O'Toole and Petula Clark, is barely remembered today. Wood returned to Hollywood, where his later films included *Our Town* (1940) and *King's Row* (1942). He died from heart failure after finishing *Ambush*, on 22 September 1949.

(Daniel O'Brien)

BIBLIOGRAPHY: Lane, Conrad, 'Sam Wood: Politically Incorrect', *Films of the Golden Age*, Winter 1996/7, pp. 72–80; Wood, Sam, 'My Impressions of England', *Picturegoer*, 29 July 1939, p. 11.

FILMOGRAPHY (UK only): *Goodbye, Mr Chips* (1939).

WOODS, Arthur (1904–1944)

Arthur Bickerstaffe Woods, one of Britain's most promising directors of the 1930s, was born in West Derby, Lancashire, on 17 August 1904, the son of a shipping millionaire. In love with cinema and theatre since boyhood, he studied medicine at Cambridge, but left in 1924 without completing his degree and tried his fortune as a stage actor. After further experience designing sets, in 1926 he changed course again and joined the staff of H. Bruce Woolfe's British Instructional Films. The *Secrets of Nature* series of shorts kept him busy as editor and, occasionally, director; he also worked as art director on features, including Anthony Asquith's *A Cottage on Dartmoor* (1930) and *Tell England* (1931). When British Instructional was absorbed into BIP, Woods joined the writing department, helping to keep the factory rolling with scripts for comedians Stanley Lupino and Leslie Fuller, and Allan Dwan's Ruritanian comedy *I Spy* (1933). After performing directorial salvage duties on British Instructional's *Stark Nature* and BIP's *Timbuctoo*, built up from African expedition and location material, Woods finally went on the floor in November 1933 with his own first feature, the First World War drama *On Secret Service*, a sturdy tale of love and espionage based on the German thriller *Spione am Werk* (Gerhard Lamprecht, 1933). A mixed bag of films followed. A superficial script scuppered the historical drama *Drake of England* (1935), but modest sparks flew in the musical *Give Her a Ring*, another German adaptation, and the defiantly British *Radio Parade of 1935*, packed with variety turns, featuring Will Hay as the aloof and crotchety head of a broadcasting corporation whose talent shortage is eventually solved by his own gifted employees. The film explodes into Dufaycolor at the end for a futuristic television outside broadcast.

At the end of 1935, the versatile and efficient Woods was snapped up by Warner Bros. for their Teddington studio, where they produced their quota of British films required for exhibition by the 1927 Cinematograph Films Act. In less than five years, Woods made seventeen films for the company, beginning with the breezy farce *Where's Sally?*; romances, thrillers, musicals and other comedies followed. He displayed panache in *The Nursemaid Who Disappeared*, a whodunit from a Philip MacDonald novel, partly adapted by *Kinematograph Weekly* editor Connery Chappell, and, in a more macabre vein, *The Dark Stairway*. Melodramas like *Mr Satan*, where Franklin Dyall's armaments dealer almost starts a world war, and *The Return of Carol Deane*, a mother-love weepie with Bebe Daniels suffering an unjust murder charge and saving her long-lost son from gamblers, proved too plot-driven to allow much room for subtlety. Woods found more believable and resonant subject matter in his best-known film, the powerful and atmospheric *They Drive by Night* (1939).

In this adaptation of James Curtis' low-life novel, Emlyn Williams' Shorty Matthews, released from prison for a minor offence, is accidentally implicated in a sordid murder. In the course of evading the authorities he flees up the rainswept Great North Road, but an encounter with a dance-hall hostess (Anna Konstam) persuades him to return to London and prove his innocence by unmasking the real culprit, a mincing sex maniac wonderfully played by Ernest Thesiger. This is a remarkable film for its style and technical proficiency alone: made even more remarkable by its evasion of the censors' strict control over British cinema in the 1930s. 'Perhaps they didn't know what some of the words meant', Grahame Greene mused in his enthusiastic review (Parkinson, p. 284).

In between assignments, Woods, an experienced pilot, directed the flying sequences of the comedy-thriller *Q Planes* (Tim Whelan, 1939). Bigger budgets followed with his move to MGM-British at Denham, where in November 1939 he began shooting *Busman's Honeymoon*, a glossy and popular adaptation of a Dorothy L. Sayers mystery, starring Robert Montgomery as Lord Peter Wimsey and Constance Cummings as Harriet Vane. Hollywood appeared to beckon; instead Woods signed up for war service with the RAF. On 8 February 1944 he was killed in an air crash at Emsworth, Hampshire. With eleven of his Warners' films seemingly lost, a proper assessment of his tantalising career may never now be possible; but the achievement of *They Drive by Night* stands unassailed.

(Geoff Brown and Leo Enticknap)

BIBLIOGRAPHY: Eyles, Allen and David Meeker, *Missing Believed Lost* (London: BFI, 1992); Parkinson, David (ed.), *The Graham Greene Film Reader: Mornings in the Dark* (Manchester: Carcanet Press, 1993); 'The Archive Presents . . . Arthur Woods', National Film Theatre Programme, July 2001, p. 22.

FILMOGRAPHY: *Bathtime at the Zoo* (short, 1929); *The Daily Dozen at the Zoo* (short); *Stark Nature* (co-dir. C. Court Treatt) (1930); *Timbuctoo* (co-dir. Walter Summers, 1933); *On Secret Service* (US: *Secret Agent/Spy 77*); *Give Her a Ring* (1934); *Radio Parade of 1935* (US: *Radio Follies*); *Drake of England* (US: *Drake the Pirate*) (1935); *Music Hath Charms* (co-dirs. Thomas Bentley/Alexander Esway/Walter Summers); *Once in a Million* (US: *Weekend Millionaire*); *Where's Sally?* (1936); *Rhythm in the Air*; *Irish for Luck*; *Don't Get Me Wrong*; *Mayfair Melody*; *The Windmill*; *The Compulsory Wife*; *You Live and Learn* (1937); *The Singing Cop*; *The Dark Stairway*; *Mr Satan*; *Thistledown*; *Glamour Girl*; *The Return of Carol Deane*; *Dangerous Medicine* (1938); *The Nursemaid Who Disappeared*; *Q Planes* (US: *Clouds over Europe*, dir. aerial sequences, dir. Tim Whelan); *They Drive by Night*; *Confidential Lady* (1939); *Busman's Honeymoon* (US: *Haunted Honeymoon*, 1940).

WOOLCOCK, Penny (1951–)

Born in Buenos Aires in 1951 and brought up in Montevideo, writer-director Penny Woolcock came to Europe when she was seventeen after her participation in a radical theatre group attracted police attention. It was not until she was in her late thirties that she became involved in film-making, joining the Trade Films co-operative in Gateshead, where she directed episodes of the left-wing *Northern Newsreel* (1987) along with *When the Dog Bites* (1988), a fifty-minute fusion of documentary and drama that takes a controversially critical look at the fading steel town of Consett. She experimented with fiction in *Women in Tropical Places* (1990), written with animator Candy Guard. A surreal drama, made with backing from the BFI and Tyne-Tees Television, the film concerns an Argentinian woman who flies to Newcastle to marry her mysterious fiancé, in the process receiving enlightenment from an ageing comedienne and her skinhead daughter.

After *Macbeth on the Estate* (1997) for the BBC – an ambitious attempt to rework Shakespeare to fit a drug-ridden Birmingham housing estate – Woolcock made her mark with *Tina Goes Shopping* (1999) and *Tina Takes a Break* (2001), two innovative dramas about the life of a poverty-stricken single mother, produced for Channel 4's documentary strand *Cutting Edge*. *The Principles of Lust*, a deliberately shocking tale about a failed writer (Alec Newman) who stumbles into a world of orgiastic sex and bare-knuckle fighting just when he is settling into a romantic relationship with a young mother and her child, employed similar filming techniques – hand-held cameras, real locations, spontaneous rather than rehearsed performances – though it relied on experienced actors for the main parts.

Despite the low budget (less than £1 million – again from Channel 4), the film's sensationalism ensured a multiplex release, though predominantly dismissive reviews and uncertain word of mouth soon killed it off. The revelation of an underside of frenzied hedonism in Sheffield is fascinating, but the protagonist's dilemma over whether to sponge off his girlfriend or hang out with sexually deviant petty criminals strains audience patience. Good performances (particularly from Sienna Guillory as the embodiment of domestic bliss and Marc Warren as the representative of unbridled excess) do not quite make up for a one-dimensional script and too-loosely focused direction.

At this point it is difficult to determine whether Woolcock has opened up a new path in cinematic realism or reached the end of her journey into the lower depths of British society. However, her willingness to tackle controversial subjects – she was also responsible for filming *The Death of Klinghoffer* (2003), John Adams' opera about the Palestinian hijacking of the *Achille Lauro* cruise ship – and her contempt for safe, over-rehearsed methods make her a welcome antidote to conformity and shallowness in British cinema.

(Robert Murphy)

BIBLIOGRAPHY: Romney, Jonathan, 'It's a Hard-Knock Life', *Independent on Sunday*, 29 Feb. 2004, p. 7; Soutar, Ian, 'Excuse Me, I Have to Film an Orgy . . .', *Sheffield Telegraph*, 12 Mar. 2004, p. 24; Woolcock, Penny, 'Telling Fact from Fiction', *Broadcast*, 31 Oct. 2003, p. 16.

FILMOGRAPHY: *The Principles of Lust* (2003); *Mischief Night* (2006).

WOOLFE, H. Bruce (1880–1965)

Devoutly patriotic, over six foot two and 'square of jaw and shoulder' (*Bioscope*, 1927), Harry Bruce Woolfe exerted a commanding presence as a film-maker in the 1920s. Born in Marylebone, London, on 4 June 1880, he entered the film trade as an exhibitor in the East End in 1911. Demobilised in 1919 after war service, he nurtured a strong belief in cinema's educational value and founded British Instructional Films (BIF) in the grounds of Ideal's studios at Elstree. *The Battle of Jutland*, produced slowly with few assistants, emerged in 1921: a novel three-reel reconstruction of Admiral Beatty's furious German engagement in 1916, contrived from archive sources, animated diagrams and models. The film's unexpected success spurred Woolfe to larger Great War endeavours. *Armageddon* (1923), launched with a Royal premiere, spent six reels revisiting Lord Allenby's Palestine campaign, adding to the stylistic mix of actors and staged scenes directed by A. V. Bramble. *Zeebrugge* (1924), one reel longer still, used a similar amalgam to celebrate the raid in 1918 on German U-boats in the Belgian port. Proudly British, stately in pace, unquestioningly following official Allied propaganda, these reconstructions may not seem so viable now, either in aesthetics or politics, and they have long been neglected by film history. But Woolfe's work was pioneering; and in a time of financial turmoil within the industry, achieving success with factual material rather than commercial fripperies was itself a considerable achievement.

Woolfe's other major success in the 1920s was the long-running *Secrets of Nature* series – one-reel shorts constructed from footage supplied by a team of scientists and photographers. Edgar Chance's *The Cuckoo's Secret*, an unblinking study of nest behaviour, launched the series in 1922. Woolfe supervised most of the films until 1925 himself; from 1927, Mary Field assumed overall control, filling them as before with Percy Smith's microscopic photography of plants, insects and water life, the birds and small mammals of Oliver Pike, Walter Higham and others, and her own less scientific topics. As with the war films, *Secrets* found success among brows of all levels. In London the shorts entered the Film Society programmes; even Grierson and Rotha murmured words of praise.

With BIF firmly established, Woolfe increasingly assumed a supervisory role. Though production of interest films continued, much of the company's resources shifted towards fiction. In Woolfe's own *Sons of the Sea* (1925), location coverage of naval training and ships at sea became wedged inside a flimsy adventure story enacted by real naval officers. No one took much notice. Instead, critics' eyes fixed on the work emerging from Woolfe's new university-educated recruits, particularly Anthony Asquith, with *Shooting Stars* (1928), *A Cottage on Dartmoor* (1929) and his other early features. Reconstructions continued for a time under Walter Summers' direction, concluding with *The Battles of the Coronel and Falkland Islands* (1927), most widely successful of the Great War surveys, though trick shots and studio work sat awkwardly at times with the aquatic firings and sinkings staged with thirty-seven 'battleship actors', as they were termed in the credits.

The same year, 1927, BIF was reconstructed successfully as a public company. The coming of sound and the 1930s brought many changes; and after several false moves Woolfe relocated to Gaumont-British in 1933, taking charge of the new subsidiary company Gaumont-British Instructional until 1944, where he continued *Secrets of Nature* under a new title, *Secrets of Life*, and generated mostly modest instructional films. As the Grierson school of film-making gained prestige, Woolfe began to be seen by the new sparks as an Establishment left-over – a view his eminence on committees and his morale-boosting three-reeler *England Awake* (1932) did everything to cement. When Paul Rotha made *Contact* and other films under Woolfe's aegis in the mid-1930s, the pair's resentment appeared mutual. Though Rotha had mentioned Woolfe's early output in *The Film Till Now* (1930) as 'excellent examples of the documentary film', the Grierson brand developed fundamental differences. Politically, Woolfe's productions leaned heavily to the right, Grierson's to the left. Woolfe followed a functional aesthetic; the Griersonians fostered wider, bolder creativity and the poetic interpretation of daily life. Yet for all the hostilities, Woolfe played a vital part in developing factual films, and several future documentarians, like Stuart Legg and J. B. Holmes, found their first work with his company; indeed Legg assisted in directing *England Awake*.

Secrets of Life aside, Woolfe's later output was not designed for the cinema mainstream. Government sponsors who preferred safety to imagination gave Woolfe commissions; some came from the British Social Hygiene Council, which toured public awareness films on venereal diseases in mobile cinemas. The educational market was growing steadily; by 1939 Gaumont-British Instructional had produced over two hundred classroom films, simple in design and execution. The 1940s brought Service training films, children's entertainments and more wildlife shorts. In 1949 Woolfe began working through his newly-formed Science Films, finally withdrawing from active film-making in the early 1950s. H. Bruce Woolfe died in Brighton on 16 December 1965, leaving an output, a character and a career well worth further investigation.

(Geoff Brown and Alan Burton)

BIBLIOGRAPHY: Bryher, 'The War from More Angles', *Close Up*, Oct. 1927, pp. 44–8; Field, Mary, 'H. Bruce Woolfe', *Visual Education*, Jan. 1956, p. 7; 'From Army Hut to World's Largest Educational Film Studio', 1936 press release, microfiche held in the BFI National Library, London; Low, Rachael, *The History of the British Film 1918–1929* (London: George Allen & Unwin, 1971); Low, Rachael, *Documentary and Educational Films of the 1930s* (London: George Allen & Unwin, 1979); 'Pen Portraits of Producers: Facts about Men behind British Films', *The Bioscope*, 18 June 1927, p. 66.

FILMOGRAPHY: *Hampton Court* (doc. short); *Evolution of the Caddis Fly* (doc. short); *A Wanderer in London* (doc. short); *The Moon and Its Phases* (doc. short); *Our Life on the Thames* (doc. short) (1919); *The Battle of Jutland* (doc., 1921); *Secrets of Nature* (doc. series, 1922–5); *Armageddon* (doc., co-dir. A. V. Bramble, 1923); *Zeebrugge* (doc., co-dir. A. V. Bramble, 1924); *Sons of the Sea*; *Palestine* (doc.) (1925); *England Awake* (doc., co-dir. John Buchan, 1932).

WOOLLEY, Richard (1948–)

Richard Woolley was born in Somerset in 1948. He completed a degree in history at King's College, London, and studied film-making at the Royal College of Art between 1970 and 1973 after making a documentary about how the 1967 Sexual Offences Act had changed the lives of homosexuals in Britain. He went on to make experimental films in West Berlin and act, write and direct with a touring theatre company before directing two features. *Telling Tales* (1978), made on 16mm with backing from the Yorkshire Arts Association, takes an occasionally enlightening look at the conventions of depicting working-class and middle-class behaviour. *Brothers and Sisters* (1980), made on 35mm with the support of the BFI, is set in Leeds at a time when the 'Yorkshire Ripper' had murdered several women and had not yet been caught. Woolley's shrewd observations, and a promising plot about two politically opposed brothers with secretive lives both coming under suspicion, is disappointingly nullified by a flat visual style and a trite message that all men are potentially guilty of violence to women.

Woolley encouraged others to make films as Film Officer for Yorkshire Arts Association in the early 1980s. His own film-making continued with a forty-minute comedy, *Waiting for Alan* (1987), for Channel 4, and a children's film, *Girl from the South* (1989), made while he taught on the scriptwriting MA course at Leeds Polytechnic. Subsequently he served as Director of the Dutch Film and Television Academy in Amsterdam, Dean of Film and Television at the Hong Kong Academy of Performing Arts and Professor of Film and Television at the University of York.

(Robert Murphy)

BIBLIOGRAPHY: Hodge, Adrian, 'Brotherly Feelings', *Screen International*, 16 Aug. 1980, p. 11; Woolley, Richard, 'Life after B.F.I. A Personal View', *First Cut* no. 12, 1981, p. 15; Woolley, Richard, 'The Facility to Unite', *Screen* vol. 25 no. 6, Nov./Dec. 1984, pp. 17–22.

FILMOGRAPHY: *In Between Peace* (short, 1972); *Kniephofstrasse* (short, 1974); *Inside and Outside* (short, 1975); *Telling Tales* (1978); *Brothers and Sisters* (1980); *Girl from the South* (1989).

WORTH, Jan (1952–)

Jan Worth was born in Halifax in 1952. She made *Taking a Part*, a forty-six-minute dramatised documentary about two young women working as prostitutes, while studying at the Royal College of Art. Following the film's favourable reception at the Edinburgh Film Festival, she gained backing from the BFI and Channel 4 for *Doll's Eye*, an experimental feature film about the lives of three women from different sectors of society. A very low budget and the deconstructionist quirks of British independent film-making of the period make for an uneven film, but one still fascinating for its insights into the more radical side of London life in the early 1980s.

Worth's refusal to allow her characters to conform to conventional stereotypes diminishes the dramatic intensity of her films but helps create their historically valuable aura of realism – slices of unusual lives travelling along unpredictable trajectories. She went on to teach film-making and scriptwriting, most recently at the Northern Media School in Sheffield.

(Robert Murphy)

BIBLIOGRAPHY: Harvey, Sylvia, '*Doll's Eye*: An Interview with Jan Worth and Annie Brown', *Framework* no. 21, Summer 1983, pp. 50–4; Mackintosh, Helen, 'Warning Signs', *City Limits* no. 88, 10 June 1983, p. 10.

FILMOGRAPHY: *Taking a Part* (1979); *Doll's Eye* (1982).

WREDE, Caspar (1929–1998)

Caspar Wrede was born in Viipuri, Karelia, Finland, on 8 February 1929. One of the first cinema directors to come out of British television, Wrede's small-screen credits include a *Twelfth Night* (1957), with Robert Hardy as Orsino, and the nuclear-themed, debate-heavy *The Poisoned Earth* (1961), an early hint of the mix of whimsy and portentousness that runs through his slender filmography.

Private Potter, a pacifist fable in which ordinary soldier Tom Courtenay mutinies because God appears to him, was the first of several collaborations with playwright Ronald Harwood, with whom Wrede co-wrote the script. *The Barber of Stamford Hill*, Wrede's lesser-known second film, was adapted by Harwood from his own television play. The ambitious *One Day in the Life of Ivan Denisovich*, scripted by Harwood from the novel by Aleksander Solzhenitsyn, was shot in snowy Norway with Courtenay martyred again as the gulag internee. Wrede also produced and plays a small role.

Wrede's final film is his least pretentious and most effective – the siege drama *Ransom* – with Sean Connery as a Scandinavian police chief playing hardball in negotiations with British hijacker Ian McShane in an isolated, snowbound airport. While structured around another ethical debate, it also has workable suspense mechanics and an interesting star performance. After 1975 Wrede devoted himself to the theatre. He was the prime mover in setting up the Royal Exchange Theatre in Manchester and during the next two decades directed more than twenty productions there. He died of cancer in Helsinki, Finland, on 28 September 1998.

(Kim Newman)

BIBLIOGRAPHY: Harwood, Ronald, 'Northern Light for the Theatre', *Guardian*, 30 Sept. 1998, p. 22; Obituary, *Classic Images* no. 281, Nov. 1998, p. 58; Obituary, *The Times*, 8 Oct. 1998, p. 25.

FILMOGRAPHY: *Private Potter* (1962); *The Barber of Stamford Hill* (1963); *One Day in the Life of Ivan Denisovich* (1970); *Ransom* (1975).

WRIGHT, Basil (1907–1987)

The humanitarian poet of the British documentary movement, Basil Charles Wright was born into a wealthy liberal family in Sutton, Surrey, on 12 June 1907. After attending Sherborne School he studied classics and economics at Cambridge University. Intending to become a creative writer, he fell under the spell of Europe's advanced cinema and began to make amateur experimental films with his own camera. In London his interest in the aesthetics of film-making was fed by screenings at the Film Society.

Impressed with one of Wright's efforts, John Grierson hired him in November 1929 as the first recruit at the Empire Marketing Board Film Unit; they remained lifelong associates. Initially Wright edited existing footage to fit EMB purposes, most elaborately in *Conquest* (1930), designed to show industrial technology's role in the development of North America. Russian montage habits influenced the cutting, though better indications of Wright's mature work appeared in films made from his own material: *The Country Comes to Town* (1932), a hymn to food manufacture in the countryside, and *O'er Hill and Dale* (1931), documenting the lambing season on the Cheviot hills. In *The Long View*, his history of cinema, Wright used as an epigraph Grierson's phrase 'All things are beautiful if you have got them in the right order', and these modest films – observant, precise yet lyrical – launched Wright's own search for the most perfect order, the most beautiful things.

Basil Wright (right)

In 1933, the year when the EMB film-makers metamorphosed into the GPO Film Unit, Grierson sent Wright to the West Indies and Ceylon to shoot material for packaging into promotional one-reelers. In *Windmill in Barbados* (1933) especially, evocative photography blended happily with fluid editing and authentic sounds, though the aesthetic triumph masked Wright's struggle, here and elsewhere, to puncture the official line by criticising colonial exploitation. The trip to Ceylon, with John Taylor as assistant, duly generated its own one-reelers, but the principal outcome was *The Song of Ceylon* (1934), Wright's most acclaimed and personal film: a four-reel symphony of images and sounds, forged from the director's newly born passion for the Orient and the Buddhist religion. The four sections evoke Sinhalese life and culture in images photographed and edited with immense finesse, shaped within a montage-driven circular structure inspired by the magic circle of the Buddhist mandala. The film is also notable for its complex soundtrack, recorded in close collaboration with the composer Walter Leigh, brilliantly juggling native and Westernised music, spoken commentary and the shivers of reverberating gongs in unexpected, disjunctive combinations of sound and image.

If Wright had found 'the right order' in *The Song of Ceylon*, the order proved difficult to recapture in films with less exotic subject matter. As his career developed, he became increasingly sucked into producing, never his favourite task, though he made vital contributions to major films, including *Night Mail* (Harry Watt, 1936) and *A Diary for Timothy* (Humphrey Jennings, 1946). In 1937 he formed the independent documentary unit Realist Films. The first year's crop included Wright's *Children at School* (1937), a three-reel report on state-supplied education in Britain, its facts and analysis enlivened by the director's sensitive eye and the camerawork of A. E. Jeakins, henceforth a regular collaborator. *The Face of Scotland* (1938), made for the Films of Scotland scheme, avoided pretty scenery-gazing for a poetic treatment of hardy lives and a challenging environment.

Writing, lecturing and administrative work kept him from directing during the Second World War. He produced official propaganda films through the Grierson-dominated Film Centre and, following earlier experiences with *World Film News*, helped found and edit *Documentary News Letter*, the movement's chief mouthpiece during the 1940s. After briefly serving as supervising producer at the Crown Film Unit, in 1946 Wright founded International Realist – a name in line with his strong conviction in cinema's power to spread understanding. *Waters of Time* (1951), his first major post-war film, made with Bill Launder for the Festival of Britain, looked no further than the Port of London; but its mastery of its topic was typical, along with the balance between lyric poetry and practical fact. *World Without End* (co-dir. Paul Rotha, 1953), a survey of UNESCO's work in Thailand and Mexico, proved less visually appealing but better fitted the International Realist template. In his remaining output, Wright's love of Greek culture inspired *Greece the Immortal Land* (1958) and a shorter survey of Greek sculpture. *The Stained Glass at Fairford* (1956) surveyed a Gloucestershire church's medieval windows, while *A Place for Gold* (1960) celebrated the craft of its sponsors, the Worshipful Company of Goldsmiths. All imparted their material crisply, sometimes poetically, though with little sign of the creative heat that had generated *The Song of Ceylon* – the masterpiece made when Wright the artist had not yet given way to Wright the public servant. In retirement, Wright gathered his experiences and knowledge into his personal history of the cinema, *The Long View*, published in 1974. He died in London on 14 October 1987.

(Geoff Brown and Jamie Sexton)

BIBLIOGRAPHY: Aitken, Ian (ed.), *The Documentary Film Movement: An Anthology* (Edinburgh: Edinburgh University Press, 1998); Beveridge, James, *John Grierson: Film Master* (New York: Macmillan, 1978); Grierson, John, 'Close-Up: Basil Wright', *Documentary News Letter* vol. 7 no. 63, Mar. 1948, pp. 34–5; Low, Rachael, *Documentary and Educational Films of the 1930s* (London: George Allen & Unwin, 1979); Sussex, Elizabeth, *The Rise and Fall of the British Documentary Movement* (Berkeley: University of California Press, 1978); Thomas, Sari, 'Basil Wright on Art, Anthropology and the Documentary', *Quarterly Review of Film Studies* vol. 4 no. 4, Autumn 1979, pp. 465–81; Wright, Basil, 'Filming in Ceylon', *Cinema Quarterly*, Summer 1934, p. 109.

FILMOGRAPHY: *Conquest* (1930); *The Country Comes to Town* (1931); *Lumber* (revised as *King Log*, 1931–2); *O'er Hill and Dale* (aka *The Shepherd*, 1932); *Liner Cruising South*; *Windmill in Barbados*; *Cargo from Jamaica* (1933); *The Song of Ceylon*; *Monsoon Island*; *Negombo Coast*; *Pett and Pott* (assoc. dir. with Stuart Legg, Alberto Cavalcanti) (1934); *Children at School*; *Modern Orphans of the Storm* (co-dir. Ian Dalrymple) (1937); *The Face of Scotland* (1938); *Postal Special* (1939); *This Was Japan* (1945); *The Story of Omolo* (1946); *Bernard Miles on Gun Dogs* (1948); *Waters of Time* (co-dir. Bill Launder, 1951); *World Without End* (co-dir. Paul Rotha, 1953); *The Stained Glass at Fairford* (1956); *Greece the Immortal Land* (1958); *Greek Sculpture 3000 BC to 300 BC* (co-dir. Michael Ayrton, 1959); *A Place for Gold* (1960).

WRIGHT, Edgar (1974–)

Born 18 April 1974 in Poole, Dorset, the precocious Edgar Wright was twenty when he made *A Fistful of Fingers*, a feature-length Western. This affectionate parody of Sergio Leone's histrionic Westerns, shot on location in Somerset for less than £10,000, found few cinema outlets but attracted enough favourable attention to launch his career. He directed episodes of Matt Lucas and David Walliams' *Mash and Peas* (1996) for the Paramount Comedy Channel and with Walliams created a darker comedy series, *Asylum* (1996). Wright was snapped up by the BBC to direct episodes of more mainstream comedy series, before Simon Pegg and Jessica Stevenson, who had acted in *Asylum*, recruited him as a suitably zany and inventive director for their offbeat sitcom *Spaced* (1999).

Edgar Wright with zombie from *Shaun of the Dead* (2004)

Shaun of the Dead is virtually a *Spaced* spin-off, though Wright and Pegg grasp with both hands the opportunity of working on a bigger canvas, paying appropriate homage to George Romero's *Dawn of the Dead* (1978) while revelling in the clichés of their suburban English sitcom milieu. Although not particularly funny or frightening (the zombies are reassuringly easy to dispose of), the film's unpretentious good nature made it a box-office success on both sides of the Atlantic.

(Robert Murphy)

BIBLIOGRAPHY: Jones, Alan, 'Dead Man Walking', *StarBurst* no. 308, Mar. 2004, pp. 34–9; Purves, Libby, 'A Comedy Zombie Movie Shows What Life Is Really Like in Today's Britain', *The Times*, 13 Apr. 2004, p. 18; 'The Wright Stuff' (interview), *Televisual*, Apr. 2000, p. 17.

FILMOGRAPHY: *A Fistful of Fingers* (1995); *Shaun of the Dead* (UK/US/Fr, 2004).

WYLER, William (1902–1981)

William Wyler was born on 1 July 1902, in Mulhouse, France. He came to the United States in the 1920s and began directing in 1925, filming six Westerns in succession at Universal (he was the nephew of the company's founder, Carl Laemmle). In the

1930s he was signed by Samuel Goldwyn and soon came to be regarded as one of the most able of studio directors, renowned for eliciting excellent performances from his actors, and for ordering umpteen takes of a scene. Wyler's best work from this period includes *Jezebel* (1938), *Wuthering Heights* (1939), *The Letter* (1940) and *The Little Foxes* (1941). After winning an Academy Award for the British-set *Mrs Miniver* (1942), he joined the US Air Force as a major.

During the war he made the documentary *The Memphis Belle* (1944) partly in the UK. After his huge success with *The Best Years of Our Lives* (1946), Wyler started making films overseas, including *Roman Holiday* (1953) and *Ben-Hur* (1959) in Italy, and *How to Steal a Million* (1966) in France. The exteriors for *The Collector* (1965) were filmed in London, though the studio scenes were shot in Hollywood. A dark antidote to contemporary films celebrating 'Swinging London', *The Collector*, based on a novel by John Fowles, centres upon a lonely man (Terence Stamp) who, after winning a huge amount of money through the football pools competition, tries to live out his fantasies by kidnapping a beautiful art-school student (Samantha Eggar). The film benefits enormously from the sensitive performances Wyler obtains from his two leads: Stamp, a handsome and charismatic actor, makes himself convincingly dowdy and repulsive; Eggar allows her flamboyant beauty to fade gradually into sickly despair. Wyler made three more films, including the hugely successful musical *Funny Girl* (1968), before retiring in 1970. He died on 27 July 1981, in Beverly Hills, California.

(Sergio Angelini)

BIBLIOGRAPHY: Herman, Jan, *A Talent for Trouble* (New York: Putnam, 1995).

FILMOGRAPHY (UK only): *The Collector* (UK/US, 1965).

WYNNE-SIMMONS, Robert (1947–)

Robert Wynne-Simmons was born in Sutton, Surrey, on 18 August 1947. He began making films while still at school and, after graduating from Cambridge, joined the BBC as a trainee editor in 1970. He was also commissioned by Tigon Films, a specialist in low-budget horror movies, to write a compendium film, initially titled *The Devil's Skin*. Inspired both by the Christian subjugation of pagan cults and by 1960s' child murderer Mary Bell, Wynne-Simmons produced a script that eventually became *Blood on Satan's Claw* (1971). During pre-production, Wynne-Simmons and director Piers Haggard abandoned the compendium format, amalgamating the various plot strands into a single narrative set in seventeenth-century rural England. The end result is offbeat, atmospheric and genuinely eerie.

In 1972 Wynne-Simmons left the BBC to take the directors course at the newly established National Film School, where he made a short film, *Easycar Brenda*, and began work on a feature, *A Journey Out of Hell*, about the poet John Clare's escape from a lunatic asylum. In 1978 he joined Radio Telefís Éireann as a film editor, and in 1980 directed *Double Piquet*, a short film about a thief who is transported back into a dangerous past when he steals an antique snuffbox. He then produced, wrote and directed *The Outcasts*, a location-shot feature financed by the Irish Film Board and Channel 4. Set in rural Ireland, the film centres on a doomed romance between a shy, put-upon village girl and a wandering fiddler. An interesting excursion into myth, magic and superstition, the film won prizes at international festivals but his second feature for Channel 4, about the Irish music industry, was pre-empted by Alan Parker's *The Commitments* (1991) and failed to materialise. Wynne-Simmons has subsequently made interesting short films and a series of dramas under the title *When Reason Sleeps* (1986–7) for Channel 4.

(Daniel O'Brien)

BIBLIOGRAPHY: Mac Cárthaigh, Lir, 'On the Edge of Reality', *Film Ireland* no. 97, Mar./Apr. 2004, pp. 24–7; Wynne-Simmons, Robert, 'Money into Peat', *AIP & Co*, Jan./Feb. 1986, p. 6.

FILMOGRAPHY: *L' eredità del diavolo* (short, 1962); *The Fugitive* (short, 1964); *The Scrolls* (short, 1965); *The Far Cry* (short, 1967); *Easycar Brenda* (aka *London Sketches 1*, short, 1972); *A Journey Out of Hell* (unfinished, 1974); *Double Piquet* (short, 1980); *The Outcasts* (1982); *Scherzo* (short, co-dir. Hannah Kodiceková, 1992).

YATES, David (1963–)

David Yates was born in St Helens, Lancashire, in 1963. After studying at the National School of Film and Television in the late 1980s, he made a number of interesting shorts and began a career in television directing episodes of *The Bill* and a series of documentaries about south coast seaside resorts. In 1997 Yates directed his first feature film, *The Tichborne Claimant* (1998), a likeable and intelligent costume drama based on the Victorian case of an Australian butcher who claimed to be the true heir to a wealthy English earl. Yates effectively plays with our sympathies over the ostensibly bogus, certainly unlikely, but perhaps genuine litigant. Splendid central performances from Robert Pugh as the Claimant, John Kani as the black manservant who masterminds his campaign, and an array of elderly actors (most impressively Charles Gray), failed to compensate for a lack of romance, and the heritage film audience was unmoved.

Television executives, however, were more appreciative of Yates' talent, and, after directing episodes of William Ivory's clever mini-series *The Sins* (2000) for the BBC, he was given charge of their prestige adaptation of Anthony Trollope's *The Way We Live Now* (2001). He showed his versatility by moving on to Paul Abbot's timely political conspiracy-theory thriller *State of Play* (2003); and alternating the genteel whimsy of *The Young Visiters* (2003) with the harrowing realism of *Sex Traffic* (2004), which avoids both sentimentality and sensationalism in mapping the disturbing growth of coercive prostitution in Eastern Europe. Yates is an unassumingly modest director ('writing is a much purer form of artistic expression; directing is more like crisis management', he claimed in 1999), though his current projects may suggest otherwise: after making Richard Curtis' popular political romantic comedy *The Girl in the Café* (2005) for BBC Television and HBO he will return to the big screen as director of *Harry Potter and the Order of the Phoenix* (2007).

(Robert Murphy)

BIBLIOGRAPHY: 'Band of Gold', *Creation*, Apr. 1998, pp. 10–12; Charity, Tom, 'Outrageous Fortune', *Time Out*, 3 Nov. 1999, p. 28; Wood, David, 'Striving for Perfection', *Broadcast*, 'Production Show Supplement', 14 May 2004, p. 13.

FILMOGRAPHY: *When I Was a Girl* (short, 1989); *The Weaver's Wife* (short); *Oranges and Lemons* (short) (1991); *Good Looks* (short, 1992); *Punch* (short, 1995); *The Tichborne Claimant* (1998); *Rank* (short, 2002).

YATES, Peter (1929–)

Peter Yates, the son of an army officer, was born in Aldershot, Hampshire, on 24 July 1929 and educated at Charterhouse and RADA. He entered repertory theatre in the late 1940s as an actor, and then worked as a racing driver and manager for the internationally successful Stirling Moss. He dubbed foreign-language films into English and edited documentaries before becoming an assistant director on such films as *The Inn of the Sixth Happiness* (Mark Robson, 1958), *The Entertainer* (Tony Richardson, 1960) and *The Guns of Navarone* (J. Lee Thompson, 1961). From 1962 he directed episodes of the television series *The Saint* and *Danger Man*.

Yates made his feature debut with the energetically vacuous Cliff Richard musical *Summer Holiday*, the second most popular film at the UK box office in 1963. His next film, an adaptation of the play *One Way Pendulum*, which he had directed at the Royal Court, could not have been more different. Yates resists the temptation to add visual eccentricity to N. F. Simpson's tale of a madly eccentric family, and the film is dryly amusing, but its absurdist comedy had little popular appeal. He returned to the mainstream with *Robbery*, a methodical, mechanically efficient thriller based on the 1963 Great Train Robbery, which carries Yates's only scriptwriting credit and suggests an interest in charting process and procedure that recurs throughout his work. Its opening car chase – as taut as the denouement is limp – won him his first Hollywood assignment, the sleek, glacial Steve McQueen vehicle *Bullitt*, which became a smash hit and one of the seminal films of the 1960s.

Yates moved to New York and continued to make films in America; his few subsequent British films have usually been backed by Hollywood studios. Creatively he peaked between 1968 and 1973, with a number of capably handled thrillers and action films. *Murphy's War* is an exciting adventure with some spectacular stunt flying and an engagingly grungy performance

from Peter O'Toole. *The Hot Rock*, a lightweight caper-comedy, adds visual wit to William Goldman's wry script. *The Friends of Eddie Coyle*, perhaps the director's best film, is a cold, sombre, yet sympathetic study of underworld informers, with Robert Mitchum entirely convincing as the seedy, doomed Coyle.

Yates' career has since embraced clumsy farce (*For Pete's Sake*), coarse black comedy (*Mother, Jugs & Speed*), a pair of clunky blockbusters (*The Deep*, *Krull*) and a turgid period drama (*Eleni*). The tender observation of teenage delusions in *Breaking Away* and the grandiloquent theatrics of *The Dresser* arguably won more praise than they deserved, for all their calculated assurance. More interesting is a loose trilogy of thrillers with a political background: the messy but likeable *Eyewitness*, the mildly Hitchcockian *The House on Carroll Street* and the slick *Suspect* (especially well edited by the director's regular collaborator, Ray Lovejoy).

The Run of the Country, a sensitive Irish melodrama adapted by Shane Connaughton from his own novel, was the only one of Yates' 1990s' pictures to merit British theatrical distribution. The Goldman-scripted *Year of the Comet* is undoubtedly both men's worst film, while *Roommates*, a sentimental comedy-drama starring Peter Falk, and *Curtain Call*, with Michael Caine and Maggie Smith as the ghosts of bickering Broadway stars, sat on the shelf for several years before receiving very limited releases. More recently Yates has directed adaptations of Cervantes' *Don Quixote* (by John Mortimer, 2000), and *A Sep-*

arate Peace (by Wendy Kesselman, 2004), John Knowles' popular novel about American teenage boys growing up in the shadow of the Second World War, for American television.
(Sheldon Hall)

BIBLIOGRAPHY: Day, Barry, 'The Suggestive Experience', *Films and Filming*, Aug. 1969, pp. 4–7; Gow, Gordon, 'Pressure', *Films and Filming*, Apr. 1971, pp. 18–22; Gow, Gordon, 'Breakaway', *Films and Filming*, Feb. 1980, pp. 12–15; Sibley, Adrian, 'Peter Yates – Director with a Difference', *Films and Filming*, June 1988, pp. 6–8; Yates, Peter, 'Dialogue on Film', *American Film*, Apr. 1984, pp. 14–18.

FILMOGRAPHY: *Summer Holiday* (1963); *One Way Pendulum* (1965); *Robbery* (1967); *Bullitt* (US, 1968); *John and Mary* (US, 1969); *Murphy's War* (1971); *The Hot Rock* (UK: *How to Steal a Diamond in Four Uneasy Lessons*, US, 1972); *The Friends of Eddie Coyle* (US, 1973); *For Pete's Sake* (US, 1974); *Mother, Jugs & Speed* (US, 1976); *The Deep* (US/UK, 1977); *Breaking Away* (US, 1979); *Eyewitness* (UK: *The Janitor*, US, 1981); *Krull*; *The Dresser* (1983); *Eleni* (US/UK, 1985); *The House on Carroll Street* (US, 1986; rel. 1988); *Suspect* (US, 1987); *An Innocent Man* (US, 1989); *Year of the Comet* (US/UK, 1992); *Roommates* (US, 1992; rel. 1995); *The Run of the Country* (US/Ir, 1995); *Curtain Call* (US, 1997; rel. 1999).

YOUNG, Emily (1970–)

Emily Young was born in London in 1970, the daughter of journalist Hugo Young. She studied English at the University of Edinburgh before spending a year learning Polish and being admitted to the Polish National Film School in Lodz. Her short *Second Hand* won the Cinefondation Award at Cannes in 1999, facilitating the financing of her first feature, *Kiss of Life* (2003), an ambitious attempt to imbue an English social-realist drama (the original title was *Helen of Peckham*) with the visionary concerns of a director like Krzysztof Kieślowski. The film charts the desperate attempt by aid worker Peter Mullan to get back from the war-torn Balkans to deal with a crisis in his own family life, though its real concern is death and the aura that gathers around those recently deceased. By tragic coincidence Katrin Cartlidge, who was to have played Helen, died suddenly two weeks before shooting began. She was replaced by the Lithuanian actress Ingeborga Dapkunaite, who along with Mullan and the rest of the cast gives an impressively convincing performance. Despite clever cross-cutting, flashbacks, and ghostly encounters, the disparate elements never quite gel. But Young deserves credit for telling her story through images rather than dialogue, and dealing intelligently with death, memory and love.
(Robert Murphy)

BIBLIOGRAPHY: Hunt, Nick, 'Close Up: Emily Young/Case Study: *Kiss of Life*', *Screen International*, 4 Apr. 2003, p. 18; Pulver, Andrew, 'Great British Hope', *Guardian* G2 Section, 23 May 2003, p. 9.

FILMOGRAPHY: *Life Without Daphne* (short, 1994); *Second Hand* (short, UK/Pol, 1998); *Wieza Babel/ The Tower of Babel* (doc. short, UK/Pol, 1999); *Kiss of Life* (UK/Fr, 2003).

YOUNG, Harold (1897–1970)

Of Irish descent, Harold M. Young was born in Portland, Oregon, on 13 November 1897. He began working in films in 1920, in Mack Sennett's cutting rooms, and was editing features by 1925. In 1927 he edited Alexander Korda's second American production, *The Private Life of Helen of Troy*. The association lasted despite the usual arguments and conflicting temperaments – 'Harold being Irish and Korda being Korda', as Young's widow recalled (Kulik, p. 72). In 1931, when Korda set up shop at the Joinville Studios, Paris, Young was brought over as chief editor; he also took charge of Korda's developing programme of British productions, leading to the big splash of *The Private Life of Henry VIII* (1933) and the lesser films in its wake.

In April and June 1934 Young gained his first directing experience with Warner 'quota quickies' at Teddington. Slight and silly comedies, neither *Leave It to Blanche* nor *Too Many Millions* proved films on which to build a career. But then in August a Korda crisis loomed. For *The Scarlet Pimpernel*, his new attempt to recapture the international audiences of *Henry VIII*, Korda had hired as director the American Rowland Brown, already in England writing scripts (one was *Leave It to Blanche*). Brown's tone was wrong, Korda quickly decided – melodramatic when the light touch was required. Young was picked to replace him, though anecdotal evidence places Korda on the set as guide, collaborator and ultimate arbiter. What emerged, whether from Korda or Young, was a film swift in pace, pleasing in visual trappings, eventually weak in plot, but always strong in the jousting of characters, with Raymond Massey's villainous Chauvelin brilliantly partnering Leslie Howard's adventurer in fop's clothing. Young's place as editor was taken by another American import, William Hornbeck, who stayed with Korda until 1940.

Whether irked by Hornbeck or by Korda, or lured by the film's wide box-office success, Young subsequently cut his Korda ties and returned to Hollywood to direct there. It proved a fateful decision. *Without Regret*, a modest Paramount romantic drama, was followed into the 1950s by thirty-one other films, chiefly forgettable supporting features for Universal, with some Poverty Row flotsam thrown in, like PRC's *Machine Gun Mama* (1944). Was Young himself without regret? Who knows. Harold Young died in Beverly Hills, California, on 3 March 1970.

(Geoff Brown)

BIBLIOGRAPHY: Kulik, Karol, *Alexander Korda: The Man Who Could Work Miracles* (London: W. H. Allen, 1975).

FILMOGRAPHY (UK only): *Too Many Millions*; *Leave It to Blanche*; *The Scarlet Pimpernel* (1935).

YOUNG, Robert (1933–)

Robert William Young was born in Cheltenham, Gloucestershire, on 16 March 1933. He began his film career making sponsored films such as *Cow Care* (1970) for the Midland Bank, before making his first feature film, *Vampire Circus* (1972), one of the best of Hammer's later productions. In his creation of an atmosphere of foreboding and tense unease, Young showed a propensity for horror not apparent elsewhere in his career, apart from his contribution to the 1980s television series *Hammer House of Horror*. During the 1970s he also directed *Keep It Up Downstairs*, a sex-comedy, *The World Is Full of Married Men*, an adaptation of a best-selling Jackie Collins novel, and a forty-minute adaptation of a Chekhov story, *Romance with a Double Bass*, with strong performances from John Cleese and Connie Booth.

In the 1980s and early 90s Young worked mainly in television, directing episodes of *Minder*, *Bergerac*, *Robin of Sherwood* and *Jeeves and Wooster*. Directing Michael Palin and Robert Lindsay in Alan Bleasedale's ambitious and incisive drama series about Liverpool politics, *GBH* (1991), revived his film career, and he subsequently made *Splitting Heirs*, with John Cleese and Eric Idle, and *Fierce Creatures*, with Cleese and Michael Palin. Both of these films, with their mix of Python comedians and American actors – Rick Moranis in *Splitting Heirs*, Jamie Lee Curtis and Kevin Kline in *Fierce Creatures* – were designed to have transatlantic appeal, although neither was very successful at the box office. *Fierce Creatures* – an attempted follow-up to *A Fish Called Wanda* (Charles Crichton, 1988) – had a troubled production history. Test screenings went badly, and as Young was not available to do the required reshoots Fred Schepisi was called in to finish the film. Young went on to make an Anglo-American television adaptation of *Jane Eyre* (1997), with Samantha Morton making the heroine far less insipid than usual; and an amiable family comedy, *Captain Jack*, scripted by Jack Rosenthal. He continues to direct successfully for television.

(Peter Hutchings)

FILMOGRAPHY (Fiction only): *Vampire Circus* (1972); *Romance with a Double Bass* (short, 1974); *Keep It Up Downstairs* (1976); *The World is Full of Married Men* (1979); *Hostage* (UK/Arg, 1992); *Splitting Heirs* (1993); *Fierce Creatures* (co-dir. Fred Schepisi, 1997); *Captain Jack* (1999).

YOUNG, Terence (1915–1994)

Shaun Terence Young's long career in British cinema encompassed a variety of genres and international co-productions, but he is best remembered as the director of three of the first four James Bond films.

Born in Shanghai on 20 June 1915, Young began his film career as a scriptwriter in 1939 and wrote screenplays throughout the 1940s, ranging from the wartime melodrama *Dangerous Moonlight* (Brian Desmond Hurst, 1941) to *The Bad Lord Byron* (David Macdonald, 1949). He directed some of the action sequences in *Dangerous Moonlight* and might even have directed *Henry V* had he been able to gain release from his Guards regiment. Finally he made his directorial debut in 1948 with *Corridor of Mirrors*, a psychological drama starring Eric Portman as a rich recluse morbidly obsessed with the past. After two lighter films he drew on his wartime experiences for *They Were Not Divided* (1950), which followed the careers of two Welsh Guardsmen fighting in the Ardennes; and *The Red Beret* (1953), celebrating the achievements of a British paratroop regiment, the first of several made for Irving Allen and Albert Broccoli's fledgling company Warwick Films, which specialised in making routine action-adventures more marketable by importing American players. *The Red Beret* featured Alan Ladd; Victor Mature starred in Young's three other Warwick films – *Safari* (1956), *Zarak* (1956) and the prisoner-of-war story *No Time to Die* (1958).

Young's pre-Bond career spanned diverse popular genres, encompassing the musical comedy *One Night with You* (1948), the cold war thriller *Valley of Eagles* (1951), period melodrama in *That Lady* (1955) and imperial adventure in *Storm Over the Nile* (1955). Among the more striking films from this period are the lurid Soho gangster thriller *Too Hot to Handle* (1959), starring Jayne Mansfield, and *Serious Charge* (1959), which dealt interestingly with issues involving homosexuality and sexual repression.

The Bond films reunited Young with Broccoli, co-partner with Harry Saltzman in a new company, Eon Productions. In *Dr No* Young enthusiastically took to the mix of violent action, easy sex and glamorous locations; though the tone for the series was more decisively set with the second Bond film, *From Russia with Love* (1963), where the action elements were undercut by Sean Connery's deadpan one-liners. After Guy Hamilton's *Goldfinger* (1964), he returned for *Thunderball* (1965), a huge box-office success now chiefly remembered for its impressive underwater sequences.

Young was involved in European co-productions as early as 1960 with the ballet film *Black Tights*, and much of his post-Bond output consists of multilingual films, sometimes featuring American stars such as Charles Bronson. Except for the Hitchcockian *Wait Until Dark* (1967), genuinely frightening at times, his Hollywood assignments proved equally undistinguished genre entries, reaching a nadir with the disastrous Korean War film *Inchon* (1981). There is little of distinction either in his later British-based films, though *The Amorous Adventures of Moll Flanders* (1965) has its moments of bawdy fun; and the frozen spectacle of *Mayerling* (1968) occasionally sparks into life. Young remained a chameleon working without a definable identity within the confines of mainstream commercial production and the uninspired quality of much of his output suggests a director who was not really trying; but after his lucrative encounters with Mr Bond perhaps he did not need to. Terence Young died of a heart attack in Cannes on 7 September 1994.

(Robert Shail)

BIBLIOGRAPHY: Chapman, James, *Licence to Thrill: A Cultural History of the James Bond Films* (London: I. B.Tauris, 1999); Lane, John Frances, 'Young Romantic', *Films and Filming*, Feb. 1967, pp. 58–60; Obituary, *Classic Images* no. 244, Oct. 1995, p. 59; Perry, George, *The Great British Picture Show* (London: Pavilion, 1985); Walker, Alexander, *Hollywood, England* (London: Harrap, 1986).

FILMOGRAPHY: *Corridor of Mirrors*; *One Night with You* (1948); *Woman Hater* (1949); *They Were Not Divided* (1950); *Valley of Eagles* (1951); *The Red Beret* (US: *Paratrooper*); *The Tall Headlines* (1953); *That Lady*; *Storm Over the Nile* (co-dir. Zoltán Korda) (1955); *Safari*; *Zarak* (1956); *Action of the Tiger* (1957); *No Time to Die* (US: *Tank Force*, 1958); *Too Hot to Handle*; *Serious Charge* (1959); *Black Tights* (US/Fr, 1960); *Orazie e curiazi* (co-dir. Ferdinando Baldi, It, 1961); *Dr No* (1962); *From Russia with Love* (1963); *The Dirty Game* (US/Fr/Ger/It); *The Amorous Adventures of Moll Flanders*; *Thunderball* (1965); *The Poppy Is Also a Flower*/ *Poppies Are Also Flowers* (UK: *Danger Grows Wild*, US, 1966); *Triple Cross*; *Wait Until Dark* (US); *The Rover* (US/It) (1967); *Mayerling* (1968); *The Christmas Tree* (US/Fr/It, 1969); *Cold Sweat* (US/Fr/It/Belg, 1970); *Red Sun* (US/Fr/It/Sp, 1971); *The Valachi Papers* (US/Fr/It, 1972); *La guerriere dal seno nudo* (It/Fr/Sp); *The Klansman* (US) (1974); *Foxbat* (co-dir. Po-Chih Leong, HK, 1977); *Bloodline* (UK: *Sidney Sheldon's Bloodline*, US/Ger, 1979); *Inchon* (US, 1981); *The Jigsaw Man* (1983); *Run for Your Life* (US/It, 1988).

YOUNG, Tony (1917–1966)

George Anthony Young was born in Tynemouth, Northumberland, in 1917. After the Second World War he joined the editing department of Gainsborough Pictures and later worked as a cameraman. In 1951 he made his debut as director with *Penny Points to Paradise*, a loosely strung comedy starring Harry Secombe, Spike Milligan and Peter Sellers at the time they were making a name for themselves as 'those crazy people' on what would become *The Goon Show*. Young's career went in a different direction. His subsequent films *My Death Is a Mockery* and *Port of Escape* are gloomy crime melodramas, interesting in the way they play out the problems of post-war adjustment; *Hands of Destiny* and *The Eternal Question* comprise stories woven around the chiromancer Josef Ranald; *Hidden Homicide* is a routine murder mystery enlivened by James Kenney's performance as a malevolent female impersonator; *Them Nice Americans* (1958) a genial comedy countering British prejudice against American GIs.

In the 1960s Young made *The Runaway* and *Delayed Flight* for cut-price producer Bill Luckwell; but they are much less interesting than 'The Choking Horror', 'The Mystery of the Marie Celeste – Solved', 'The Whistling Spy Enigma', 'The Terrible Revenge of Fred Fu Manchu' and several other fifteen-minute episodes of *The Telegoons* (1963–4), a brilliantly conceived puppet series, produced by Young's Grosvenor Films for BBC Television, cheaply but effectively recycling *Goon Show* scripts from the 1950s. He died of cancer in Chatham, Kent, in 1966.

(Robert Murphy)

FILMOGRAPHY: *Penny Points to Paradise* (1951); *My Death Is a Mockery* (1952); *Hands of Destiny* (1954, re-edited with new material for US market as *The Eternal Question*, co-dir. Ron Ormond, 1956); *Port of Escape* (1956); *Them Nice Americans* (1958); *Hidden Homicide* (1959); *The Runaway*; *Delayed Flight* (co-dir. Michael Luckwell) (1964).

Z

ZAMPI, Mario (1903–1963)

Mario Zampi was born in Sora, Italy, on 1 November 1903 and came to England in 1922 after experience in Italy as an actor, editor and associate producer. He did whatever came along in the British film industry, settling with Warner Bros. as an editor at their Teddington Studios in the 1930s, until in 1937 he and Filippo del Giudice set up Two Cities Films (the two cities being Rome and London). Zampi directed *13 Men and a Gun*, a First World War melodrama made in English and Italian versions, and *Spy for a Day*, a Great War comedy starring popular Lancashire comic Duggie Wakefield as a farm hand mistaken for a German spy. He also produced the company's first big success, *French Without Tears* (Anthony Asquith, 1939), but when war broke out both Zampi and Del Giudice were interned on the Isle of Man. Del Giudice was released in late 1940 but the less fortunate Zampi was sent to Canada for the duration.

When the war was over, Zampi returned to film-making in Britain and turned out second features, one of which, *The Fatal Night*, has acquired cult status as a scary haunted-house thriller. His reputation rests, however, on his 1950s' comedies, starting with *Laughter in Paradise*, a multi-story, crackpot-will farce in which four people are required to act out of character in order to inherit. He showed a real flair for handling this very British comedy, featuring Alastair Sim, Joyce Grenfell, George Cole and other popular comic talents. Indeed the rest of his career is marked by his skill in allowing such comedians to flower in films that hold up well because of the lightness of Zampi's orchestrating touch. Cole, for instance, is very funny as the sanitary inspector mistaken for an atomic scientist in *Top Secret*; as the faint-hearted Terence charged with killing the hated landlord in *Happy Ever After*; and as Fingers, an inept crook, in *Too Many Crooks*. All these films have the benefit of witty screenplays by Michael Pertwee, usually in collaboration with Jack Davies, and their contribution to Zampi's success should not be overlooked. Pertwee also wrote what may be Zampi's best film, *The Naked Truth*, a hilariously satirical tilt at scandal sheets – and at their not-wholly-innocent victims – which maintains its black edge until the end. Peter Sellers as nasty television star Sonny MacGregor, Terry-Thomas as a hypocritical peer, Peggy Mount as a children's writer and Dennis Price as the unctuous scandalmonger all excel, the director ensuring that they each have a comic character to get their teeth into. *Now and Forever* is a soppy romance but virtually all the rest of Zampi's oeuvre is worth cherishing.

His son Guilio Zampi worked as editor on several of his father's earlier films and was associate producer on them all from 1954. Mario Zampi died in the Italian Hospital, London, on 2 December 1963.

(Brian McFarlane)

BIBLIOGRAPHY: 'British Feature Directors: An Index to Their Work', *Sight and Sound*, Autumn 1958, p. 304; Obituary, *The Times*, 3 Dec. 1963; Vincent, R. Quilter, 'Interview with George Cole, Nadia Grey and Mario Zampi', *ABC Film Review*, Aug. 1952 p. 4.

FILMOGRAPHY: *13 Men and a Gun* (UK/It, 1938); *Spy for a Day* (1939); *The Phantom Shot* (1947); *The Fatal Night* (1948); *Shadow of the Past*; *Come Dance with Me* (1950); *Laughter in Paradise* (1951); *Top Secret* (US: *Mr Potter Goes to Moscow*, 1952); *Ho scelto l'amore* (It, 1953); *Happy Ever After* (aka *Tonight's the Night*, 1954); *Now and Forever* (1955); *The Naked Truth* (1957); *Too Many Crooks*; *Bottoms Up* (1959); *Five Golden Hours* (UK/It, 1961).

ZEFFIRELLI, Franco (1923–)

Gian Franco Corsi Zeffirelli was born in Florence on 12 February 1923. He was drawn to the theatre while attending university, and worked as an actor and scenographer. After working as assistant director on Visconti's *La terra trema* (1948) and *Senso* (1954), Zeffirelli went on to direct his own films and operatic productions.

Zeffirelli's contribution to British cinema includes three flamboyant Shakespeare adaptations. *The Taming of the Shrew*, starring Richard Burton and Elizabeth Taylor, abandoned the confines of a stage play, transporting the action into a sweeping cinematic space. *Romeo and Juliet* radically broke from tradition, starring teenagers Leonard Whiting and Olivia Hussey in the lead roles; sumptuous costumes and a romantic music score added to the film's appeal, making it one of the most successful Shakespeare adaptations ever. Zeffirelli continued to surprise with *Hamlet*, for which he cast Mel Gibson in the title role; although alterations to the original text displeased many critics, the film was a commercial success. He was also responsible for an adaptation of Charlotte Brontë's much-filmed *Jane Eyre*; Zeffirelli's version, with Charlotte Gainsbourg as Jane and William Hurt as Rochester, was a sombre production favouring a psychological approach over gothic thrills. His last two films, both of which have British connections, have been the semi-autobiographical *Tea with Mussolini*, described in *Sight and Sound* as 'a film for the perfect evening out with your ageing gay uncle' (though it's $14 million US box-office takings suggest wider audience appeal), and an homage to Maria Callas, *Callas Forever.*

(Elisabetta Girelli)

BIBLIOGRAPHY: Hapgood, Robert, 'Popularizing Shakespeare: The Artistry of Franco Zeffirelli', in Lynda E. Boose and Richard Burt (eds), *Shakespeare, the Movie: Popularizing the Plays on Film, TV, and Video* (London: Routledge, 1997); Medhurst, Andy, 'Tea with Mussolini', *Sight and Sound*, Apr. 1999, pp. 60–1; Zeffirelli, Franco, *Zeffirelli: The Autobiography of Franco Zeffirelli* (London: Weidenfeld & Nicolson, 1986).

FILMOGRAPHY (UK only): *The Taming of the Shrew* (It/US, 1967); *Romeo and Juliet* (UK/It, 1968); *Brother Sun, Sister Moon* (UK/It, 1973); *Hamlet* (UK/US/Fr/Sp, 1990); *Jane Eyre* (Fr/It/UK, 1996); *Tea with Mussolini* (UK/It, 1999); *Callas Forever* (It/Sp/Fr/UK/Rom, 2002).

ZEISLER, Alfred (1892–1985)

Alfred Zeisler was born in Chicago on 26 September 1892, the son of German-Jewish emigrants. He worked as an actor and stage producer in Berlin before entering films in 1921 as a scenario writer, and assistant to Fritz Lang on *Der müde Tod* (1921). By 1924 Zeisler was a producer for Ufa, eventually becoming one of its three heads of production, along with Erich Pommer and Günther Stapenhorst. As producer, he was involved in *Viktor und Viktoria* (Reinhold Schünzel, 1933), *Gold* (Karl Hartl, 1934) and other successful films, several duplicated in French versions. He began directing in 1930, making crime thrillers and light entertainments, including the underworld tale *Schuss im Morgengrauen* (1932) and a popular bicycle racing comedy, *Strich durch die Rechnung* (1932). Arriving in London in 1935, he joined other emigrants at the short-lived company Garrett-Klement Pictures, making an unusual and mildly pleasing Capra-like comedy, *The Amazing Quest of Ernest Bliss*. Cary Grant was imported to take on the central role, a playboy who learns that it is better to give than receive during an attempt to live humbly on his wits. Effective camerawork by Otto Heller, another mid-European exile, helped to offset some of Zeisler's variable direction. Though made in studios at Elstree, the Board of Trade deemed the film's personnel too foreign to register it for the British quota.

Zeisler stayed on to make *Crime over London* (1936) for Romanian-born producer Marcel Hellman and Douglas Fairbanks Jr's Criterion company. Basil Sydney plays a convincingly embittered Brit who leads an American gang in a wages snatch at a big London department store. Witty dialogue courtesy of Harold French, a grouchy performance from Joseph Cawthorne as the store-owner and his criminal double, and well-paced action leading to a shoot-out in the toy department all make it surprisingly enjoyable. His final film in Britain, the bilingual *Make-Up*, is an improbable circus drama starring Nils Asther as a surgeon-turned-clown who solves the mystery of the lion-tamer's murder.

In 1937 Zeisler returned to America and an uncertain future. He wrote screen treatments, and up until 1953 found occasional tiny acting roles as sentries, attachés and German officers in the productions of major studios, especially 20th Century-Fox. As a director, however, he was only hired by bottom-budget outfits. With Monogram's *Enemy of Women* (1944), his experiences dealing with Joseph Goebbels at Ufa generated a dull sensation-seeking biographical drama, portraying the Minister of Propaganda as a sexual predator and systematic liar. Among his three remaining films, the best received was *Fear* (1946), a taut little spin on Dostoevsky's *Crime and Punishment*. Zeisler died in humble circumstances on 1 March 1985 in Camano Island, Washington State.

(Geoff Brown and Kevin Gough-Yates)

FILMOGRAPHY (UK only): *The Amazing Quest of Ernest Bliss* (US: *Romance and Riches/The Amazing Adventure*); *Crime over London* (1936); *Make-Up* (1937).

ZELNIK, Fred (1885–1950)

Friedrich Zelnik was born in Czernowitz, Romania, on 17 May 1885. He studied law at the University of Vienna but took to the theatre as an actor and director and started to appear in films in Berlin in 1910, working initially for Oskar Messter. Five years later he moved into production, and in 1917 began directing unpretentious entertainments, some for his own companies, others for the German subsidiaries of Fox and First National. Many featured his wife, the dancer and actress Lya Mara, whom he built into a major star. Critical attention arrived in 1927 with the ambitious social drama *Die Weber* (*The Weavers*), based on Gerhard Hauptmann's play, but he quickly returned to the frivolous with *Das tanzende Wien* and *Meine Herz ist eine Jazzband*. His involvement in Britain's film industry began in 1929 with an Anglo-German Edgar Wallace thriller, *Der rote Kreis,* featuring Mara and Stewart Rome, shot in Berlin but equipped with talkie sequences by Sinclair Hill at British Sound Film Productions, Wembley. The English edition, *The Crimson Circle*, also carried a synchronised score by Edmund Meisel. After an unsuccessful trip to Hollywood, Zelnick returned to escapist fare in Germany, but quickly moved to England when Hitler came to power in 1933. *Happy*, first of two films made for BIP at Elstree, was a speedy remake of *Es war einmal ein Musikus*, his last German production; it has a few well-choreographed sequences but is mainly memorable as a record of the amiable knockabout comedy of Stanley Lupino, Laddie Cliff and Will Fyffe. *Mister Cinders* (1934), adapted from the musical comedy, with Clifford Mollison, music by Vivian Ellis and photography by Otto Kanturek, has a stronger sense of fantasy and is more successful.

Zelnik then teamed up with the Austro-Hungarian producer Max Schach, making two other musicals with larger budgets and a stronger continental flavour. *Southern Roses* benefits from two strong leading ladies (Gina Malo and Chili